D1093610

THE
PULPIT COMMENTARY

Edited by

H. D. M. Spence

and

Joseph S. Exell

Volume 11
JEREMIAH
LAMENTATIONS

MACDONALD PUBLISHING COMPANY
MCLEAN, VIRGINIA 22102

ISBN 0-917006-32-1

LAMENTATIONS

EXPOSITION BY

T. K. CHEYNE

HOMILETICS BY

W. F. ADENEY

HOMILIES BY VARIOUS AUTHORS

J. R. THOMSON   D. YOUNG

THE LAMENTATIONS OF JEREMIAH

INTRODUCTION

THE Book of Lamentations has no author's name attached to it in the Hebrew Bible, which, indeed, places it far away from Jeremiah in the so-called *K'thūbhīm* or Hagiographa, between Ruth and Kohéleth (Ecclesiastes). It is the Septuagint which, in some manuscripts, appends " of Jeremiah " to the descriptive title " Lamentations," at the same time grouping it with the prophecies of Jeremiah and the (apocryphal) Book of Baruch. But before we can form an opinion as to the justice of this view of the authorship, and the romantic tradition connected with it (see below), we must first of all take a general survey of the book and gather up all its internal evidence as to date and origin ; and also we must illuminate this by the results of a critical study of the Old Testament.

One of the most interesting of these results is the discovery of a great lyric movement among the conquered Jews, as well those in Babylon as those who remained in their much-loved home. " If I forget thee, O Jerusalem," was their dominant thought, even when surrounded by the wonders of Babylonian art ; and it naturally expressed itself in lyric verse. Ewald has done much to enable modern students to realize the vast debt which we owe to the Captivity and the subsequent period for much of the most precious part of the Psalms, and, by including his translation of the Lamentations in the same volume with the Psalter (he even inserts the former as a portion of the sacred hymn-book), he has brought vividly before us the essential unity of the great lyric movement referred to. We have spoken of these psalms and lamentations as expressions of a mood ; they are this most truly ; but they are something more. Nursed up on the writings of the prophets, the authors of these lyric poems were in a sense prophets, just as the prophetic writings addressed to the later Jews may to a certain extent be classed with the lyric literature. The truths which the lyric or elegiac poets had imbibed from the prophets gave a colour even to the expressions of grief, and so, monotonous as the Book of Lamentations may be, it has justly been admitted as a sacred Scripture into the Old Testament canon. The authorship of Jeremiah may be doubtful, and yet we cannot fail to recognize in this short elegiac book that peculiar quality which, in all its degrees of manifestation, the Jewish doctors agree with us in describing as inspiration.

The common theme of the Lamentations is the terrible fate which befell Jerusalem when the Chaldeans captured the city (B.C. 588) and carried away its inhabitants (less fortunate in one sense than those of the country districts) to Babylon. That they were all written at the same time is, however, to say the least, improbable; the third, and in a still higher degree the fifth, will be found to present some striking points of dissimilarity to the rest. Let us first of all endeavour to characterize the three which have most in common, and each of which begins with the word ēchāh, how! viz. the first, the second, and the fourth. Even in this narrower group, indeed, some divergences will strike the reader, but they are not sufficient to compel us to assume a diversity of authorship. Each elegy is in the strictest sense alphabetical (which means that every verse or half-verse or every group of verses begins with one of the twenty-two letters of the Hebrew alphabet; comp. Ps. ix., x., xxv., xxxiv., xxxvii., cxix., cxlv.), but with this difference—that whereas in the first the initial letters come in their usual order, in the second and fourth the letter פ (pe) precedes the letter ע (ayin).[1] Another unimportant technical divergence is that the verses of ch. i. and ii. are in the original, as a rule, composed of three lines, and those of ch. iv. of four. It may seem strange, at first sight, that so artificial a form as the alphabetic should have been selected for elegies. But further consideration will show that it was really both natural and appropriate. These elegies were probably not so much intended for private use as for a liturgical purpose, for which the alphabetic form, so convenient for the memory, would be a great recommendation. It has for ages been the custom to read the Lamentations in the synagogues on the ninth day of Ab, the anniversary of the burning of the temple, and, as this is a very ancient fast-day (Zech. vii. 3), it is reasonable to conjecture that the Lamentations, or some of them, were from the first designed for this solemn occasion. The didactic element which now and then appears in the poems gives an additional appropriateness to the alphabetic form, as a reference to the alphabetic psalms will at once show.

The contents of these three elegies, in spite of their monotony, indicate a certain difference in the point of view of the writer or writers. The first directs the attention to the sorrow-laden Mater Dolorosa (if the application suggested by a living poet may be allowed), the widowed city, Zion. The cause of the catastrophe is but lightly touched upon, and the description

---

[1] This is in itself not more surprising than other irregularities of Hebrew poets in the handling of alphabetic versification. What is surprising is that the same violation of order should be found in one of the psalms which there is no ground for assigning to the author (or to any of the authors) of the Lamentations. For there can hardly be a doubt that Hitzig, Delitzsch, and Bickell are right in transposing vers. 15 and 16 (Hebrew, 16, 17) of Ps. xxxiv. Let any one try the two modes of reading these verses together with the following verse, and judge for himself.

cannot be said to maintain itself at the height of the opening verse. The second points out the true author of Zion's calamity; it is Jehovah, who has fulfilled his threats of old, and turned against his people like an angry warrior. The fourth has more touches than the rest which reveal (so far as picturesqueness of detail can be accepted as evidence) the hand of an eye-witness of the tragic events. The sufferings of various classes, due to God's anger at their sins, are affectingly described, and the malignant joy of the Edomites represented, not merely as a recollection (Ps. cxxxvii. 7), but as a present fact. The second and the fourth are generally considered the most striking of the elegies from a poetical point of view.

Before introducing the question of authorship, we have still to examine briefly the two remaining poems—the third and the fifth. The former agrees with the three elegies already considered in the technical respect of its alphabetic structure, and more particularly with the second and fourth (in the order of the chapters), inasmuch as the same two initial letters are transposed. It is, again, connected with the first and second by the sub-division of each of its verses into three lines. It differs, however, from all the other elegies in its peculiar exaggeration of the alphabetic form, since it not merely distinguishes a single verse by one of the Hebrew letters, but a whole triplet of verses. This evidently hampers the poet in the expression of his thoughts;—the third is the least rhythmical and the least poetical of all the Lamentations. In contents, too, it differs to a remarkable degree from the other elegies. Instead of describing the calamities of the nation, the writer points, or seems to point, to himself. "I am the man that hath seen affliction," he begins, and he continues to speak of himself as the great sufferer except in vers. 22—47, where he passes into a description of the circumstances of the nation, and only refers to himself as a member of the community ("Let us search and try our ways," etc.). His account of his own sufferings reminds us, by its highly coloured phraseology, of certain of the psalms which purport to be the utterances of an individual, but which contain many phrases which are hyperbolical in the mouth of an individual Israelite. In the case of this third Lamentation, as well as in that of this important group of psalms, we seem irresistibly driven to the inference that the writer (whether Jeremiah or another) adopts the rôle of a poetical representative of the Israelitish people, or at any rate of the pious believers who formed the kernel of that people.[1] This accounts for the curious alternation in ch. iii. of expressions which point to an individual Israelite with those which distinctly refer to the people, and for the seemingly extravagant character of the former, and also for the fondness which the author betrays for the great poem of Job, the hero of which is, in the intention of the writer (to be carefully distinguished from the intention of the traditional narrative), obviously a type of the righteous man in affliction.[2] Compare, for instance, ch. iii. 4 with Job xvi. 9, 10; ch. iii. 7, 9 with Job

---

[1] 'The Prophecies of Isaiah,' by the present writer, 2nd edit., vol. ii. pp. 188—190.

[2] Ibid., pp. 245—247.

xix. 8 ; ch. iii. 8 with Job xxx. 20 ; ch. iii. 10 with Job x. 16 ; ch. iii. 12, 13 with Job vii. 20 and xvi. 12, 13 ; ch. iii. 14, 63 with Job xxx. 9.

And if the writer of ch. iii. at one point does fall out of his assumed *rôle*, this too has to some extent a parallel in Job, for both Job and his friends now and then "fall into language which implies that Job is not an individual, but plurality of persons." Neither poet was able to keep up the personification, or representative symbol, with entire consistency.

Before passing on to the second of the elegies reserved, we may, it would seem, draw one definite inference from the preceding data, viz. that the third chapter of Lamentations is not by the author of ch. i., ii., iv. A similar result is obtained by an examination of the elegy which forms the fifth chapter. Turning to the Hebrew text, we are at once met by the fact that, unlike the companion elegies, it is not alphabetical, *i.e.* it does not make each of its verses begin with one of the Hebrew letters. Still, there is an approximation to the alphabetic form ; the number of its verses (which are two-lined) is the same as that of the Hebrew letters, viz. twenty-two (comp. Ps. xxxiii., xxxviii., ciii.) It seems as if the close observance of the canons of alphabetic versification were too great a restriction for the writer of this elegy, just as some of the greatest English sonneteers have felt the laws of the Italian sonnet confine their freedom of thought and expression unduly. The treatment of the subject is slightly varied in this elegy, which is little more than an enumeration of the insults heaped upon the Jews by their enemies. The poet speaks near the end of the elegy (ver. 20) as if this sad state of things had already continued a long time, from which it has generally been inferred that the poem was composed rather later than the rest of the collection. We must remember, however, that, as J. H. Newman says—

> " . . . time is not a common property;
> But what is long is short, and swift is slow,
> And near is distant, as received and grasped
> By this mind and by that, and every one
> Is standard of his own chronology."
>
> ('The Dream of Gerontius,' p. 23.)

To extreme grief, a few years might appear an age, and the short, simple sentences of which the poem consists have the ring of such genuine feeling, neither diluted by reflection nor overlaid by rhetoric, that we may well be reluctant to assume a very late date. They may conceivably have been improvised in the midst of persecution by one of the scanty remnant which remained in Judah even after the third deportation of exiles. Some of the writer's friends have sought refuge in Egypt (*i.e.* on the north-east frontier of Egypt, whither Jeremiah himself was carried by force, see Jer. xlii., xliv.) ; others have submitted to Assyria (a conventional term for the great Mesopotamian empire) ; the remainder of them are tyrannized over by upstarts of servile origin, such as many a modern Turkish pasha, placed over the land of Judah by the Babylonian suzerain. Yet so much relaxed are the bands of order, that savage, nomad tribes can venture to plunder them of their crusts of bread. Worse than all, Jerusalem is in ruins and uninhabited, and seems to have been so for an age, by the "pathetic fallacy" explained above.

We have seen that the fifth elegy in the collection can hardly be the work of the Prophet Jeremiah, who was probably already in Egypt when the poem was written. But we have also seen that, both in form and in contents, it differs from the other elegies, and we may now add that, linguistically, there is almost as little to connect it with its companions as with the Book of Jeremiah. The question, however, still remains whether at least some part of the Book of Lamentations (viz. either ch. i., ii., iv., or ch. iii. alone) may not be the composition of that gifted prophet.

Let us first of all consider the internal evidence, and let us test the theory of Jeremiah's authorship by its applicability to the third chapter of the book, as the part which, upon the face of it, can most easily be claimed as Jeremiah's. It will be readily admitted that, if we take the poem literally, it points to Jeremiah more distinctly than to any other known individual. The deep affection which the writer betrays for his people, his sensitive nature, and the bitter sufferings which he (apparently) describes himself to have undergone, correspond to peculiarities which we have already had to notice in the character and life of Jeremiah. Some of the characteristic expressions, thoughts, or images of Jeremiah's have also been pointed out in this chapter; compare, for instance, ch. iii. 47, 48 with Jer. iv. 6, 20, vi. 1, 14 ("breach" equivalent to "destruction"), ix. 1, xiii. 17, xiv. 17 (incessant tears); ch. iii. 64—66 with Jer. xi. 20 (appeal for vengeance). This comparison of expressions and ideas, however, is of very little worth. The parallels are but few in number, and, so far as they are valid (the last-quoted breaks down on examination), are easily accounted for on the theory of the writer's acquaintance with Jeremiah's prophecies, and they are altogether outweighed by the numerous expressions never found in the Book of Jeremiah (such will be found in all but three verses of the third chapter of Lamentations). As to the general suitability of this prolonged monologue to the character and life of the prophet, we need only refer to what has been said already in the Introduction to the Book of Jeremiah. Considering what a large body of literature there is, in which the spirit and even the expressions of Jeremiah may be recognized (e.g., besides Lamentations, Deuteronomy, Kings, Job, Isa. xl.—lxvi., and certain of the psalms), it would be rash in the extreme to refer any part of it to that much-imitated prophet. There is certainly no direct statement in this elegy which compels us to regard either Jeremiah or any other prophet as the author.

The case for ascribing the remaining elegies to Jeremiah is proportionally weaker. There are, no doubt, expressions and ideas familiar to us in Jeremiah. Compare e.g. ch. i. 2, 19 with Jer. xxx. 14; ch. i. 11 with Jer. xv. 19; ch. i. 16 and ii. 11 with Jer. ix. 1, etc.; ch. i. 15 with Jer. xiv. 17 and xlvi. 11; ch. ii. 14 and iv. 13—15 with Jer. v. 30, 31 and xiv. 13, 14; ch. ii. 11, 13, iii. 47, 48, and iv. 10 with Jer. iv. 6, 20 and xiv. 17, etc.

But these, again, are far outweighed by the expressions unknown to Jeremiah, which occur in almost every verse of these elegies (see the lists in Naegelsbach's 'Jeremiah,' Introduction, § 3), and at least three passages militate rather strongly against the authorship of that prophet, viz. ch. ii. 9 (where the writer regards the cessation of prophetic visions as a misfortune, contrast Jeremiah's denunciations in Jer. xxiii.) ; iv. 17 (where the writer speaks of having formerly expected help from Egypt, contrast Jer. ii. 18, 36) ; and iv. 20 (where Zedekiah is spoken of respectfully and hopefully as Jeremiah can hardly be supposed to have done).

The external evidence for the authorship of Jeremiah consists of a tradition, accepted, perhaps, by Josephus ('Antiquities,' x. 5, 1), and certainly by the Talmud ('Baba Bathra,' fol. 15, col. 1) and the later Jewish and Christian scholars. The earliest authority for it is a statement prefixed to the Septuagint (and repeated with a few additional words in the Vulgate) in the following terms :—"And it came to pass, after Israel was taken captive, and Jerusalem made desolate, that Jeremias sat weeping, and lamented with this lamentation over Jerusalem, and said." This cannot, however, have formed part of the Hebrew text of Lamentations, else the Massoretic editors of the text (who beyond reasonable doubt believed Jeremiah to be the author of the book) would certainly have handed it on to us. It has, indeed, been suggested that the compiler of Chronicles attributed the book to Jeremiah, because he reports that "Jeremiah lamented for Josiah," and that his words (apparently) "are written in the Lamentations" (2 Chron. xxxv. 25) If this view is correct, the compiler of Chronicles interpreted the words, " the breath of our nostrils, the anointed of the Lord " (ch. iv. 20), which really refer to Zedekiah, of Josiah. The view is not to be hastily rejected, although it is also possible that the statement in the Septuagint is due to a misinterpretation of the passage in Chronicles. In any case, the tradition cannot be traced up to the time of Jeremiah, and is too evidently fictitious—first, because Jeremiah was not an eye-witness of the sad circumstances described in the Lamentations ; and secondly, because, even if he had been so, such a tender-hearted man (whose prophetic utterance is almost stifled by tears) cannot be imagined as amusing himself, amid the ruins of Jerusalem, with inditing these highly artificial, not to say rhetorical, compositions in a style absolutely new to him. No; poems like these cannot have been produced till the worst misery of conquest had been partly mitigated by time. They are (from a literary point of view) the efforts of highly educated men to relieve their feelings by the help of art. They are more than this, no doubt ; they are an evidence of the working of the Spirit of God on the minds of the more spiritually minded Jews, leading them to contrition and repentance. But we must before all things adopt a purely literary point of view in an inquiry as to date and authorship, and then we cannot but recognize that the first four Lamentations (which are alone now in question) are too elaborately artificial to have been the work of " Jeremiah sitting amid the ruins of Jerusalem." There is genuine feeling in them, however, only it has already been softened by time. To assert, with Dean Plumptre, that the born poet "accepts the discipline of a self-imposed law just *in proportion* to the vehemence of his emotions," is incapable of proof from modern European poetry, and, if possible, still more opposed to the facts of Hebrew literature Some of the examples which the dean adduces are merely the rhetorical exercises of poets learning their craft; others merely concessions to the taste which every now and then prevails for superfine elaboration in every branch of art; others, again (and these few examples are alone in point), the attempts of the artists to help Nature to recover her balance, when the recovery has already begun and emotion has already lost its overwhelming vehemence. Members of the much-suffering Jewish race have many a time, since the Lamentations were written, had recourse for comfort to similar styles of composition, and verified the words of a great French critic, "When the passion is sincere, even the most artificial form assumes something of beauty."

Before we conclude, let us briefly review our position. The first, second, and fourth chapters of Lamentations may conceivably be by the same author; and though that author is certainly not Jeremiah, yet he is probably acquainted, whether by the ear or by the eye, with the prophecies of Jeremiah. He was contemporary with the fall of Jerusalem, and indited these elegies not long after for a liturgical purpose. It is, however, equally possible that they are the work of different authors, belonging to the same circle or school of literary craftsmen. About the same time, or a little later, the fifth and last seems to have been written, and very certainly not by the author of any of the foregoing Lamentations. The date of the third elegy may have been as early as that of the others, or it may have been written at some later time;—the personification of the people is thought by many critics to be a characteristic of those quiet literary men among the Jewish exiles in Babylon, to one of whom they attribute most if not all of the second part of the Book of Isaiah. In any case the author of the third Lamentation must have been acquainted with the other elegies (except the fifth), as there is a general similarity in the diction of the first four chapters of the book.[1] There seems, in fact, to have been a peculiar and fixed vocabulary, traditional in this school of elegiac poets, just as there has been in other schools of writers. Jeremiah was probably the favourite book of these poets (next to the Psalter, so far as this book was in existence); and so, if a title must be given by way of defining the authorship, we might, perhaps, style the entire book, on the analogy of a portion of the Psalter, "The Book of the Lamentations of the sons of Jeremiah."

The elegies on which we have been engaged were the forerunners of a large body of synagogue poetry; many of the *kīnōth* (as one large class of the post-canonical as well as the five canonical elegies were called) were suggested by passages of the Book of Lamentations. Most of them, indeed,

---

[1] See the third section of the Introduction to Naegelsbach's 'Commentary on Lamentations,' appended to the same writer's 'Jeremiah' in Lange's Old Testament series (translated).

were specially written for that very fast-day which we have already con-
jectured to have occasioned the composition of the canonical Lamentations.
The most beautiful of the *kīnōth* is probably that of Yehuda ben Samuel
Halevi (twelfth century A.D.), which may be known even to some general
readers by Heinrich Heine's poem in the 'Romanzero,' and which has been
critically illustrated by A. von Oettingen, 'Die synagogale Elegik des
Volkes Israel u. s. w.' (Dorpat, 1853), with which may be compared
Delitzsch's delightful and instructive work, 'Zur Geschichte der jüdischen
Poesie.' Lastly, for a comprehensive article on the Hebrew elegy (in its
Biblical forms) see a paper by Professor C. Budde, of Bonn, which opens
the second volume (1882) of Stade's *Zeitschrift* for Old Testament studies.

For the exegetical and critical literature on Lamentations, we need only
refer to the list of works on Jeremiah in Vol. I., adding, however, Bickell,
'Carmina Veteris Testamenti Metricè,' Innsbruck, 1882 (a critically revised
text of the chief poetical passages in the Old Testament, more to be trusted
in the Lamentations than in the Psalms); Plumptre, 'Jeremiah and
Lamentations,' in vol. iv. of Bishop Ellicott's 'Commentary,' London, 1884
(a truly popular and interesting work by a many-sided scholar).

THE LAMENTATIONS OF JEREMIAH

EXPOSITION.

CHAPTER I.

Vers. 1—11.—A WAIL OF DISTRESS FOR JERUSALEM.

Vers. 1, 2.—The fate of Jerusalem is described in language which resembles here and there that used in Isaiah of fallen Babylon (Isa. xlvii. 1, 8). It is probably the finest passage in the whole book, and has inspired some grand lines in Mr. Swinburne's picture of the republican *mater dolorosa*—

"Who is she that sits by the way, by the wild wayside,
In a rust-stained garment, the robes of a cast-off bride,
In the dust, in the rainfall, sitting with soiled feet bare,
With the night for a garment upon her, with torn, wet hair," etc. ?

Ver. 1.—**How.** The characteristic introductory word of an elegy (comp. Isa. i. 21 ; xiv. 4, 12), and adopted by the early Jewish divines as the title of the Book of Lamentations. It is repeated at the opening of ch. ii. and ch. iv. **Sit solitary.** Jerusalem is poetically personified and distinguished from the persons who accidentally compose her population. She is "solitary," not as having retired into solitude, but as deserted by her inhabitants (same word as in first clause of Isa. xxvii. 10). How **is she become as a widow** ! etc. Rather, *She is become a widow that was great among the nations ; a princess among the provinces, she is become a vassal.* The alteration greatly conduces to the effect of the verse, which consists of three parallel lines, like almost all the rest of the chapter. We are not to press the phrase, "a widow," as if some earthly or heavenly husband were alluded to ; it is a kind of symbol of desolation and misery (comp. Isa. xlvii. 8). "The provinces" at once suggests the period of the writer, who must have been a subject of the Babylonian empire. The term is also frequently used of the countries under the Persian rule (*e.g.* Esth. i. 1, 22), and in Ezra ii. 1 and Neh. vii. 6 is used of Judah itself. Here, however, the "provinces," like the "nations," must be the countries formerly subject to David and Solomon (comp. Eccles. ii. 8).

Ver. 2.—**In the night.** Not only by day, but even in the season of rest and unconsciousness. **Her lovers . . . her friends** ; *i.e.* the neighbouring peoples, with which Judah had formed alliances, such as Egypt (Jer. ii. 36), Edom, Moab, Ammon, Tyre and Sidon (Jer. xxvii. 3). This is a favourite phrase of Jeremiah's (comp. Jer. iii. 1 ; iv. 30 ; xxii. 20, 22 ; xxx. 14), but also of Hosea (ii. 5, 7, 10, 12, 13 ; viii. 9) and Ezekiel (xvi. 33, 36, 37 ; xxiii. 5, 9, 22). The national God was conceived of as the Husband of the nation ; and the prophets retained this idea and elevated it, just as they did circumcision and many other Eastern traditions.

Ver. 3.—**Is gone into captivity because of affliction** ; rather, *is gone into exile,* etc. The poet is not thinking of the deportation of the captives, but of those Jews who sought refuge for themselves in foreign lands (comp. Jer. xl. 11). An objection has been raised to this view that the number of fugitive Jews would not be large enough to warrant their being called "Judah." But we might almost as well object on a similar ground to the application of the term "Judah" to the Jews who were carried to Babylon. The truth may, perhaps, be that, after the fall of Jerusalem, the Jewish nation became split up into three parts : (1) the Jews who succeeded in escaping into Egypt or elsewhere ; (2) those who were carried captive ; (3) the mass of the common people, who remained on their native soil. Keil, however, retains the view of the Authorized Version, only substituting "out of" for "because of." "Out of" the misery into which the Jews had been brought by the invasions of Necho and Nebuchadnezzar they passed into the new misery of captivity. **Among the heathen;** rather, *among the nations.* **Between the straits.** The phrase is peculiar, and reminds us of Ps. cxviii. 5, "Out of the strait I called unto thee." "A strait," or narrow place, clearly means adversity, just as "a large place" (Ps. cxviii. 5) means prosperity.

Ver. 4.—**The ways of Zion do mourn.** The roads leading to Jerusalem, usually so thronged with pilgrims, are desolate and "mourn" (comp. ch. ii. 8 and Isa. iii. 26; xiv. 31). **All her gates are desolate.** No one goes in or out of Jerusalem, and there is no concourse of citizens in the shady recess of the gates. **The virgins are afflicted.** So Zeph. iii. 18. The sorrow was on account of the cessation of the festival, in the music of which they took a leading part (comp. Ps. lxviii. 25).

Ver. 5.—**Are the chief;** rather, *are become the head.* Comp. Deut. xxviii. 44, where, as a part of the curse of Israel's rebellion, it is foretold that "he [the stranger] shall become the head, and thou shalt become the tail." **Before the enemy.** Like a herd of cattle.

Ver. 6.—**Beauty;** rather, *glory.* **Like harts that find no pasture;** and therefore have no strength left to flee. An allusion to the attempted flight of Zedekiah and his companions (Jer. xxxix. 4, 5).

Ver. 7.—**Remembered;** rather, *remembereth.* **Miseries.** The Hebrew is difficult, and perhaps means *wanderings.* **At her sabbaths;** rather, *at her extinguishment.* The word has nothing to do with the sabbaths; indeed, a reference to these would have been rather misplaced; it was no subject of wonder to the Babylonians that the Jews celebrated a weekly day of rest, as they had one of their own (*sabattu*).

Ver. 8.—**Therefore she is removed;** rather, *she is become an abomination* (literally, *an impurity;* comp. Lev. xv. 19). The poet leaves out the preliminary clause, "therefore she is grievously punished." It was the humiliation of Jerusalem, rather than her sin, which brought upon her the contempt of her neighbours. The destruction of a city is often compared to the ill treatment of a defenceless woman (Isa. xlvii. 3; Nah. iii. 5).

Ver. 9.—**She remembereth not,** etc.; rather, *she thought not upon,* etc. An allusion to Isa. xlvii. 7. **O Lord, behold,** etc. This is the language in which the "sigh" (ver. 8) finds expression.

Ver. 10.—**Her pleasant things;** or, *her precious things;* that is, the treasures of the palaces of Jerusalem (2 Chron. xxxvi. 19), and still more those of the temple (2 Chron. xxxvi. 10); comp. Isa. lxiv. 11). **For she hath seen;** rather, *yea, she hath seen.* **The heathen entered,** etc. In Deut. xxiii. 3 only the Ammonites and Moabites are excluded from religious privileges; but in Ezek. xliv. 9 the prohibition is extended to all foreigners.

Ver. 11.—**All her people sigh,** etc. The sufferings of Jerusalem did not come to an end at the capture of the city. Some think that this verse relates solely to the miserable survivors. This is possible; at any rate, it includes the contemporaries of the writer. "Sigh" and "seek" are participles in the Hebrew. **To relieve the soul;** literally, *to bring back the soul.* The "soul," *i.e.* the principle of life, is conceived of as having for a time deserted the fainting frame. **See, O Lord,** etc. Another piteous cry of Jerusalem, preparing the way for the second half of the elegy.

Vers. 12—22.—The same subject; Jerusalem the speaker.

Ver. 12.—**Is it nothing to you?** The Hebrew is very difficult, and the translation therefore insecure. Keil, however, adopts a rendering very near that of the Authorized Version " (Cometh it) not unto you?" *i.e.* "Do ye not heed it?" Ewald supposes the phrase to be abbreviated from "Do I not call unto you?" (comp. Prov. viii. 4); but this would be a very harsh construction. The Septuagint has Oἱ πρὸς ὑμᾶς; the Targum, "I adjure you;" the Vulgate, *O vos;*—all apparently pronouncing *lu* instead of *lo.* At any rate, the object of the words is to heighten the force of the appeal which follows.

Ver. 13.—Three figures—fire, a net, sickness, for the calamities which have come upon Jerusalem. **From above;** *i.e.* from heaven. **Spread a net for my feet,** as though I were a wild beast (comp. Jer. xviii. 22). **Turned me back.** The consequence of being entangled in the net was that he could go no further, but fell into the hands of his pursuers.

Ver. 14.—**Is bound . . . are wreathed.** The transgressions of Jerusalem are likened to a heavy yoke. So numerous are they that they are said to be "wreathed," or twisted together, like ropes. **Into their hands.** The Hebrew has simply "into hands;" following a suggestion of the Septuagint. Budde would read, "Into the hands of adversaries."

Ver. 15.—**Hath trodden under foot;** rather, *hath rejected;* i.e. hath punished. Comp. Ps. cxix. 118, 119, where "thou rejectest [same verb as here] all them that wander from thy statutes" is followed by "thou puttest away all the ungodly of the earth like dross." **Hath called an assembly;**

rather, *hath proclaimed a festival.* When Jehovah summons the instruments of his vengeance, the prophets describe it as the "proclaiming a festival." The Persians or Chaldeans, as the case may be, obey the summons with a holy glee, and destroy the enemies of the true God (comp. Isa. xiii. 3). **Hath trodden**, etc.; rather, *hath trodden the winepress for* (i.e. to the ruin of) *the virgin daughter of Zion.* The poet carries on the figure of the festival. It is a vintage which is to be celebrated, such a vintage as is described in Isa. lxiii. 3 (comp. Joel iii. 13). The choicest youth of Judah are to be cut off like grapes from the vine. "Virgin daughter" is a frequent figure to express inviolate security (so Jer. xiv. 17).

Ver. 16.—**For these** things, etc. After the reflections of vers. 13—15, the poet gives vent anew to his bitter grief. **Mine eye, mine eye.** A repetition quite in Jeremiah's manner; comp. Jer. iv. 19; vi. 14 (repeated viii. 11); xxii. 29; xxiii. 25. The Septuagint and Vulgate, however, have "mine eye" only once. **Relieve** my soul (see on ver. 11).

Ver. 17.—Again the poet passes into the tone of reflection, thus relieving the strain upon the feelings of the reader. **Spreadeth forth her hands.** The gesture of supplication and entreaty (comp. Ps. xxviii. 2; lxiii. 4; Isa. lxv. 2). That his **adversaries**, etc.; rather, *those who are about him are his adversaries.* The neighbouring peoples, who ought to be sympathetic and friendly, gloat over the spectacle of his calamities. They both hate and (comp. ver. 8) despise the fallen city.

Ver. 18.—**People**; render, *peoples.*

Ver. 19.—**For my lovers**; render, *to my lovers* (see on ver. 2).

Ver. 20.—**My bowels.** The vital parts, especially the heart, as the seat of the affections, like σπλάγχνα. **Are troubled**; literally, *are made to boil.* So Job xxx. 27, "My bowels boil" (a different word, however). **Is turned**; or, *turns itself;* i.e. palpitates violently. **At home** there is **as death.** So Jer. ix. 21, "For death is come up into our windows, and is entered into our palaces." By "death," when distinguished, as here, from "the sword," pestilence is meant; so e.g. in Jer. xv. 2; xliii. 11. But the poet says here, not that "there is death," but merely "*as* death," i.e. a mild form of pestilence, not the famine-typhus itself. Or, perhaps, he means "every form of death" (Virgil's "plurima mortis imago").

Ver. 21.—**Thou wilt bring.** The Hebrew has, "Thou hast brought;" it is the perfect of prophetic certitude, which represents an event certainly foreseen as if it had already taken place. Ewald, however, takes this to be the precative, a variety of the perfect which certainly exists in Arabic, but has not been quite satisfactorily shown to exist in Hebrew (see Driver, 'Hebrew Tenses,' § 20 [13]). **The day** that **thou hast called**; i.e. foretold by the prophets (comp. Jer. xxv. 17—26). But very probably we should read, with the Septuagint, "Thou wilt bring the day; thou wilt call the fit time."

Ver. 22.—**For my sighs** are many. This is not mentioned as the reason why God should punish Jerusalem's enemies; we ought rather to understand, either from ver. 20, "Behold, my distress;" or simply, "Deliver me."

HOMILETICS.

Ver. 1.—*The solitary city.* The first elegy on the desolation of Jerusalem opens with a lament over her solitariness, widowhood, and humiliation.

I. THE SOLITARINESS. 1. *How it is to be measured.* (1) *By the nature of the place.* It is a city that is solitary. A deserted town strikes us as more lonely than the most dreary moor. We do not expect people in a wilderness; we look for them in a city. Streets which never echo to a footfall, windows which never brighten with a face, doors which are never opened, houses, palaces, shops, factories, markets, all silent and empty, —this is indeed a picture of desolation. It is contrary to experience, expectation, and purpose. (2) *By the former condition of the place.* It used to be populous. Jerusalem was no sleepy old provincial town, but a busy capital. Crowds would throng the streets, little children play, and old men stand gossiping at the corners, and hucksters set up their stalls, where now no live creature is to be seen, save, perhaps, a few lean dogs prowling after their unclean food. The contrast of the past thus aggravates the distress of the present. 2. *Why it is most sad.* The loss of men is the great trouble. Fine buildings have been thrown down, marble statues broken, gold and precious stones stolen. But these are not the worst evils. Had all remained untouched, still the trouble would have been heart-rending. The people are gone! Chicago rises out of her ashes in greater splendour because her people remain. Jerusalem is most desolate because her citizens have been carried into captivity. The strength of a city is its population. The power of a nation is in its people. The vigour of a Church is in its membership. A splendid cathedral, with a rich full service, but no congregation, fails in comparison with the homeliest mission, if the latter gathers the people. Doctrine may be sound and "means of grace" abundant, yet we shall not advance except as we hold the people.

II. WIDOWHOOD. Unintentionally and perhaps unconsciously, the inspired poet uses an illustration to describe the desolate condition of Jerusalem, which may serve as a hint of her deeper distress. "She is become as a *widow.*" Who had been her husband? The favoured city used to be regarded as the mystic bride of the Eternal. She had often been accused of unfaithfulness to her marriage vows. Now the faithless wife is punished by becoming the miserable widow. Jerusalem loses the presence and favour of God. It is said that the Shechinah was seen there no more. The greatest loss is to be bereft of God. They who are unfaithful to God will find that he will forsake them. Many would retain the privilege of blessings from God, while renouncing the obligation of fidelity to God. The unfaithful wife is loth to lose the support and position contributed to her by her husband. But this inconsistency cannot be allowed. Christ the Bridegroom remains faithful. But if his bride, the Church, dishonours his Name, she will lose her Lord and become as a widow.

III. HUMILIATION. The city had been the princess among the provinces. She now not only loses her dependencies; she loses her own independence; she becomes a vassal to a strange city. Humiliation will be the peculiar punishment of the great who abuse their rank. The doom of pride will be shame. Few troubles are more galling than to have to come down openly in the sight of those over whom a certain superiority had been maintained. 1. *Loss of position and character results in loss of influence.* When the Church falls, her power over the world will disappear. Christian elevation of character is essential to Christian influence among men. 2. *Loss of power entails loss of liberty.* Jerusalem weakened and conquered becomes a vassal. Only the strong can be free. Spiritual failings lead to the loss of spiritual liberty. 3. *When the Church ceases to influence the world she will become subject to the world.* The fallen suzerain becomes a vassal. The Church can only retain her liberty by maintaining her supremacy. This is the great truth the abuse of which has led to the monstrous pretensions of Rome. The lawful supremacy of the Church must be spiritual, and this may be lost and the Church subject to the spirit of the world, even while she is greedily grasping after temporal power, perhaps just because she does hanker after this lower advantage.

Ver. 2.—*Comfortless.* In her distress Jerusalem looks for comfort to those neighbouring nations which flattered her during her prosperity and behaved then as "lovers;" but she is disappointed in finding that they all desert her in the hour of her need.

I. IT IS NATURAL TO SEEK FOR COMFORT IN ADVERSITY FROM THE FRIENDSHIPS OF PROSPERITY. Jerusalem had her "lovers." This fact throws a significant light on the statement that she had "become as a widow" (ver. 1). What shame that she, the wife of the Eternal, should have to be spoken to of "lovers"! But having them she must find her comfort in them. She dare not look to her husband for comfort. In plainer language, the Jews had adopted the idolatry of neighbouring nations as well as renounced the exclusive and retiring position which had been required of them by their God. It was fitting that they should find their consolation from the Babylonian invasion in these foreign connections and religions. If we let our business, our pleasure, our ambition, or any other earthly thing usurp the place of God in our hearts, the time will come when we shall have to try what help we can get in trouble from our idol.

II. UNWORTHY CONNECTIONS WILL AFFORD NO COMFORT IN TIMES OF TROUBLE. The lovers are for pleasure; adversity dismisses them. How bitter is the disappointment! how mortifying is the revelation! The true husband could have been depended on, but the bad lovers for whom he was forsaken coldly turn from the piteous pleading of the sufferer. Thus must it be with every one who forsakes the one Friend and Comforter. No other balm of Gilead will heal the broken heart. What can the pleasures of society say to one who has failed and disgraced himself? What consolation can a materialistic philosophy whisper in the ears of the mourner by the grave? How will the science of the history of religion smooth the pillow of the dying man?

III. THE LAST DROP OF THE BITTER CUP IS TO BE COMFORTLESS. Mere formal consoling is a weariness when it is not an insult to grief. But the comfort of sympathy, the soothing of love, and the cheering of congenial companionship are Divine remedies for sorrow. They are lights in the gloom, though they do not bring the day; gentle hands to wipe away the tears, the flowing of which they may not be able to stanch. The most desolate picture is that of one like Jerusalem in this elegy, weeping sore in the night, with no friendly ray to break the darkness, and no one to remove the tears that fall upon the cheeks unheeded and neglected, crying for comfort only to the pitiless silence. 1. Let us learn to dwell in faithfulness with God, that we may enjoy his unfailing sympathy. 2. Let us extend hands of brotherly compassion to the sorrowing, that, whatever be the grief, its last anguish may be spared; and then, through human comfort, we may lead up to the Divine consolations.

Ver. 4.—*The abandoned feasts.* Jerusalem was the religious centre of the nation. Thither the tribes came up to present themselves before the Lord. Great assemblies and joyous feasts were held there for the benefit of all the Jews. But after the Babylonian destruction all this was suspended. None now came to the solemn feasts. The high-roads which were wont to be thronged with pilgrims mourn for the lack of travellers; the gates through which they used to press are unused; priests sigh with weariness and distress, having no glad offerings to present; and the virgins who led the song and dance in honour of God are smitten with affliction.

I. IT IS A CALAMITY FOR PUBLIC WORSHIP TO CEASE. Some regard public worship as an onerous duty and others as a superfluous infliction. But they who enter into the privileges of it heartily and spiritually know that it is a boon to the worshipper. As the sabbath is made for man, so also is the institution of worship. To be deprived of it is to suffer loss. 1. The loss of the *joy of worship.* There is a gladness in expressing love to earthly friends which should be found in the outpouring of our devotion to God. To mingle with the song of the angels is to taste the joy of the angels. 2. The loss of *the elevating influence of worship.* The soul rises on the wings of its own prayer. Worship is aspiration, and aspiration elevates. If we never worship we stagnate in worldliness. True worship is spiritual and may be enjoyed most in private. But public worship greatly helps this spiritual worship with most people. 3. The loss of the *social influence of worship.* Public worship affords mutual help in worship. Numbers give warmth and life to it.

II. IT IS A CALAMITY FOR JOYOUS FESTIVALS TO CEASE. The loss is twofold. 1. The loss of *the joy itself.* The gladness of worship is no small part of the brightness of a devout man's life. Rob him of this, and you darken his sky. There are clouds enough; we cannot afford to lose the sunlight which pierces and sometimes illumines them. 2. The loss of *the influence of the joy.* (1) This joy purifies. It keeps out unholy pleasures by satisfying the soul with its own blessedness. (2) This joy strengthens. In gladness we can serve God most earnestly. If, then, the unavoidable loss of joyous exercises of religion is a calamity, how great is the error of those who voluntarily convert religion into a thing of gloom!

III. IT IS A CALAMITY FOR RELIGIOUS INTERCOURSE BETWEEN MEN TO CEASE. The festival was an occasion for the meeting of Jews from all quarters. Townsmen met countrymen. Herdsmen from the south met agriculturists from the north. When this assembly was interrupted, the people suffered in many respects. 1. The loss of *brotherly association.* We are tempted to forget our brethren if we cease to see them. Solitary Christians tend to become selfish Christians. Brotherly sympathy is fostered by brother-fellowship. 2. The loss of *mutual stimulus.* The strong would urge on the weak, and the more spiritual inspire the less spiritual. There were prophets in these assemblies. 3. The loss of the *breadth of variety.* We become narrow by isolation. Intercourse broadens us. Christians should seek opportunities to meet with their fellow-Christians, to gain width and liberality of view.

Ver. 6.—*Her beauty departed from Zion.* I. ZION HAD A BEAUTY OF HER OWN. The dwellings of Zion shone splendid in cedar and gold. A softer beauty was shed over her from old memories and tender associations. The spiritual Zion has her beauty. It is not the magnificence of marble columns and gilded decorations. The beauty of Zion is the beauty of her worship and life. 1. *The beauty of holiness.* Purity is beautiful as impurity is ugly. This high spiritual loveliness is like the glory of God. 2. *The beauty of love.* Zion was the place where the tribes assembled. Here all jealousies were to be laid aside and all quarrels healed. What is more beautiful than concession and forgiveness? This beauty should characterize the Church of Christ. "Behold, how good and how pleasant it is for brethren to dwell together in unity!" etc. (Ps. cxxxiii.). 3. *The beauty of joy.* Zion was the centre of festive gatherings. The sacred hill used to echo with shouts of gladness; it was enlivened with the timbrel and song of happy maidens. The joy of Divine grace imparts a sweetness to the very countenance of the faithful servant of God.

II. ZION LOST HER BEAUTY. The fine city was sacked by ruthless soldiers; the splendid edifices rifled or fired; the pomp and pageantry dissipated by sword and axe. But the higher beauty of Zion was also lost, and lost before she was robbed of her external grandeur. Her holiness was corrupted. Sin destroys the spiritual beauty of the Christian. His white priestly garments are defiled when he descends into the mire of moral degradation. It is not only that sin will be visited with certain definite pains and penalties. Before that happens there is an indescribable loss in the tarnished character and marred beauty of the soul which, to one who is awake to the evil condition into which he has fallen, must be a shame and grief.

III. THE LOSS OF THE BEAUTY OF ZION WAS A MOURNFUL CALAMITY. This beauty is no idle ornament, to be put off and on at the caprice of the wearer and for objects of idle display. It is the pledge of her King's favour, the inspiration of her own best life, and the secret of her influence. 1. *Health is lost.* As when the sunlight which flashes on silvery lakes and mountain snows fades away, the chills and mists of night creep over the valley, so, when the glory of God departs from a soul, coldness, darkness, and death take its place. 2. *Influence is lost.* Christians are to be the light of the world. Losing their brightness, they cease to draw others to Christ. The fair countenance of the bride of Christ wins many guests to the wedding feast. Let her see that it is not marred, lest her Lord be dishonoured.

Ver. 7.—*Pleasant things in the days of old.* I. IN TIMES OF TROUBLE WE CALL TO MIND THE PLEASANT THINGS IN THE DAYS OF OLD. 1. *There have been pleasant things in the days of old.* Few lives, if any, are wholly joyless from cradle to grave. There are rifts in the clouds of the darkest lot. Indeed, for most of us, the pleasant things far outnumber the painful. 2. *These pleasant things are too often undervalued when in our possession.* The fact that they may become subjects of fond and sad regret should lead us to take more account of them while they are with us. Let us not add to the lamentations of the loss of them remorse for an ungrateful and depreciatory treatment of them. 3. *Trouble calls up the recollection of these pleasant things.* (1) It does this because it leads to reflection. We may observe a great contrast between the intellectual effects of joy and sorrow. Joy is usually thoughtless, sorrow meditative. When joy does stimulate the intellect, it urges it to look forward and inspires hope; but sorrow turns its gaze backward and contemplates the past. 2. It does this by the force of contrast. One experience suggests the thought of its opposite. Darkness makes us dream of light, silence of music, pain of joy. 4. *Such recollections are likely to exaggerate the pleasantness of the past.* Memory is not an even mirror. It is warped by prejudice and emotion. When we regret the loss of past happiness, we exalt that happiness in memory above what it ever was in experience. Unconsciously we drop the vexations out of notice. We remember the fine view, and forget the weary climb that preceded the enjoyment of it. The roses of a regretful memory have no thorns. The soft evening lights spread a glamour over the past which gilds its plain features and softens its rugged form and hides its ugly defects in a delicious haze of dreamy melancholy.

II. RECOLLECTIONS OF PLEASANT THINGS IN THE DAYS OF OLD EXAGGERATE THE DISTRESS OF TIMES OF TROUBLE. On the whole, it may be, life is prosperous. The balance is in favour of the pleasant things. But we cannot take life in the lump. We consume it piecemeal; and that portion which is with us at each moment is for us the life itself—the whole life. Our real living is in the present. It is true that "we look before and after," and hope may greatly lighten the burden of the present, but only by coming into the present as the twilight of dawn enters the world before sunrise—a real light. 1. This fact helps us *to see a more even equalizing of lots than is obvious at first.* If man is born to trouble, he who seems at one time to have an unfair advantage will have to pay for it by the keener suffering of his adversity when that comes. 2. This fact should *warn us against the folly of enjoying the present without preparing for the future.* The more heartily we enjoy earthly treasures the worse will be our distress if we have no treasure in heaven to inherit. 3. *It is foolish to yield to fond regrets of the pleasant things in the days of old.* The past cannot be recalled. Let it die. The future is ours. The west will not brighten again with a return of the fading glow of sunset, but a new day will break in the east. 4. We may call to mind the happy things in days of old, not to increase our present distress, *but to encourage hope.* The sun did shine, then it may shine again. God is the same now as ever. If he blessed in the past he can bless in the future. Former mercies encourage us to hope for better things still to come.

Ver. 12.—*Sorrow unequalled, yet unheeded.* Jerusalem sits alone in her unparalleled grief, and the bitterness of it is intensified by the pitiless disregard of spectators. Bedouins of the desert pitch their tents in sight of her ruined towers, and merchants passing north and south see her deserted streets, and yet all gaze unmoved at the heart-rending picture.

I. THE SORROW WAS UNEQUALLED. 1. *Never was city more favoured than Jerusalem.* She was the chosen seat of Divine grace. In her temple stood God's mercy-seat. High privileges of revelation and spiritual blessings descended on her sons and daughters. The loss of these privileges brought a distress that men who had never enjoyed them could not feel. They who have tasted of the heavenly gift will find the outer darkness more terrible than those who have had no anticipation of the joys of the wedding feast. Apostate Christians will suffer agonies which the heathen and godless will not have to endure. 2. *Never was city more loved than Jerusalem.* This city of sacred memories and tender associations was dear to the hearts of her inhabitants. Her overthrow brought a grief that was proportionate to this love. The most fatal wound is one aimed at the heart. We are pained most cruelly when we are wounded in affection. What grief can be greater than that of parents for ruined children, and especially when the parents' sin has been the children's temptation? 3. *Never was city more visited by Divine wrath than Jerusalem.* Here is the secret of her deepest trouble. She is afflicted in the day of God's fierce anger. God is most angry with her because she has sinned against most light, most ungratefully, and most rebelliously.

II. THE SORROW WAS UNHEEDED. It would be thought that such unequalled grief would arrest the attention of the most hasty and strike pity into the hardest. But no; it seems that all will pass by with cold and stony indifference. 1. *Note the causes of this indifference.* (1) *Callousness.* Men look with the eye who do not feel with the heart. The very sight of misery often encountered hardens men's sensibilities. (2) *Selfishness.* People are self-absorbed. Sympathy requires effort, attention, self-renunciation. It costs more than the selfish will give. (3) *Contempt.* The worst trouble of Jerusalem was her humiliation. But humiliation leads to contempt. Now, it is hard to pity those who are despised. 2. *Consider the exceptions to this indifference.* (1) *Good Samaritans.* Thank God, such exist, though no synagogue honours them. One such is worth scores of priests and Levites who "pass by on the other side." (2) *The Divine compassion.* The sufferer looks down and looks around him and sees no pity. If he will look up, he will see that the very Being who smote in righteous wrath is waiting to heal in merciful forgiveness (Hosea vi. 1).

In conclusion, a parallel may be drawn between the sorrow of Christ and that of Jerusalem. The text cannot be understood to be written of our Lord. But it may illustrate that sorrow which far surpassed all other human grief. To how many is it as nothing! They pass the cross as Arabs and Phœnicians passed Jerusalem in her ruin. Yet, is it nothing to them? (1) Their sins caused Christ's sorrow. (2) Christ's sorrow can save their souls. (3) Christ's sorrow calls, not for pity, but for gratitude and faith.

Vers. 13, 14.—*Fourfold trouble from God.* I. THE TROUBLE IS FROM GOD. This is the characteristic of it that the writer dwells upon with most concern. 1. *We should recognize the Divine origin of trouble.* We miss the meaning and purpose of it if we do not see the hand that sends it. Earthly means may be used, as the King of Babylon was the agent for the destruction of Jerusalem. But all punishment for sin is inflicted by the Judge of sin. 2. *We should remember that trouble from God is most terrible trouble.* It springs from that most fierce anger, the anger of outraged love. It is directed by almighty power and cannot be evaded or resisted. It stops the alleviation of the best consolations by flowing from the same source from which those consolations would come. 3. *We should observe the purpose of trouble from God.* He doth not willingly afflict. If he sends distress it is for an object. What is that object? It may be to punish sin; then let us search out the sin and repent of it. It may be to wean us from earth; then let us cease from the idolatry of carnal things. It may be to teach us our weakness; then let us learn humility in our trouble. It may be to train us in patience and faith and spirituality; then let these graces have their perfect work.

II. The trouble is fourfold. It is various in form, touching one in one way and another most in a different way. But for each it is complex. 1. *It burns as fire.* At once it is felt to be fierce, poignant, and consuming. Thus does God seek to burn the chaff out of us. 2. *It catches our feet like a net.* God arrests the headlong career of folly with the net of trouble. It flings the heedless man to the ground, entangles his feet, and vexes his feelings. But it saves him from rushing on to his ruin. We may thank God for the distresses which stop our course when that runs in a wrong direction. 3. *It gives us pain and faintness like a sickness.* Thus are we humbled and subdued. The faintness of heart that sorrow brings is the best remedy for headstrong self-will and pride. 4. *It burdens like a yoke.* The transgressions bound and wreathed by the hand of God press upon the neck of the guilty. Several points in the image of a yoke may be observed. (1) It is a weight oppressing and wearying; (2) it is a constraint, hindering free action and imposing irksome conditions of motion; (3) it is connected with other impediments; (4) it presses very close upon our person; (5) it is carried about with us wherever we go, burdening us in all scenes and all circumstances; and (6) it is so "bound" and "wreathed" that it cannot be shaken off. Nevertheless, this trouble is sent for our good. It will be removed in due time if we repent and seek the grace of God in Christ. After it has gone, the relief from the distress of it will heighten the enjoyment of forgiveness.

Ver. 18.—*The righteousness of God confessed.* I. The righteousness of God as a fact. 1. *What it is.* In its fulness and breadth it is the goodness of God, his sinlessness, his pure and holy character. But it has characteristics of more special importance. Righteousness in God is conformity with truth, justice, and honour. It means that God has no subtle double-dealing, but acts in perfect integrity. He moves in straight lines. Further, it means that God is fair to all, doing, if not the same thing to each, which would often be unjust, that which is fitting for every one. It also includes God's regard for the standard of right in his government, his care to make his creatures righteous, and his determination to check all unrighteousness. 2. *Why we are to believe in it.* It is declared most forcibly by those who know God best. Sceptical strangers may doubt it; but they who have entered into the presence of God, whether in holiness or in inspiration, alike agree in testifying to the righteousness of God. The deeper our Christian experience the more shall we be brought to admit this great truth. II. The righteousness of God hidden under a cloud. There are times when it is hard to say from our hearts, "The Lord is righteous." Doubts and difficulties should be boldly faced, for God cares for no lip-service of unbelieving flatterers. 1. *Trouble darkens our vision of the righteousness of God.* We fail to see the object of the storm while the darkness of it lowers over us. It seems to be greater than it is, and more than just, because we cannot take a fair view of it. 2. *Our own trouble seems to be out of proportion to that of other people.* We feel the full weight of our own burden; our neighbour's burden is seen at a distance, and then only seen, not felt. In her grief Jerusalem feels that she is visited with a strange pre-eminence of sorrow. Never was sorrow equal to hers (see ver. 12). This appears to be unjust. 3. *Our trouble looks more than we deserve.* So we think till we see our sin. To the impenitent God must often seem unjust. 4. *God has many purposes in sorrow that are unknown to us.* Therefore we fail to see the justice of the blow. But part of the discipline of trouble depends on our ignorance of its end. If we knew whither it was leading us we should not be led. Darkness is necessary for the training of faith.

III. THE RIGHTEOUSNESS OF GOD CONFESSED. This is grand! In the midst of wailing and weeping Jerusalem confesses that the hand that dealt the blow was right. 1. *Faith is requisite for this confession.* The righteousness cannot be seen; it is still shrouded in darkness. But faith holds to it. Thus we must use in the darkness the knowledge which we have won in the light. 2. *Penitence is also necessary for this confession.* When we confess our guilt we are ready to confess God's righteousness, but not till then. Even Job had to abhor himself and repent in dust and ashes in order to see the righteousness of God (Job xlii. 6).

HOMILIES BY VARIOUS AUTHORS.

Vers. 1, 2.—*The contrasts of adversity.* The key-note of this strain of sorrow, this poetical and pathetic dirge, is struck in the opening words of the composition. The heart of the prophet laments over the captured and ruined city. How natural that the present should recall the past! Jerusalem, now in the hands of the Chaldeans, was once, in the days of David and of Solomon, the scene of glory and the seat of empire, the joy of the whole earth. So much the sadder is the contrast, the deeper the fall, the bitterer the cup of woe.

I. THE ONCE POPULOUS CITY IS SOLITARY. Not the walls, the streets, the palaces, the temples, but the inhabitants, are the true strength and glory of a city. Formerly Jerusalem was thronged with citizens who took pride in her majesty, of sojourners who came to gaze with wonder and admiration upon her splendours. Now her population has been reduced by famine, by exile, by war; and silence is in her streets.

II. THE CITY ONCE A PRINCESS IS TRIBUTARY. The time was when other cities acknowledged her sway, paid her their tribute, sent her of their produce and of the labour of their sons. Now she is reduced to subjection, yields her treasure to the foe, and the toil of her children is for the profit of the alien.

III. THE CITY THAT ONCE WAS JOYFUL WEEPS. Mirth and music have given place to mourning, lamentation, and woe. No longer are the sound of the viol and the harp, the voice of the bridegroom and the bride, heard in her dwellings. They resound with the cries of grief and anguish. She weepeth in the night, and her tears are on her cheek.

IV. THE CITY ONCE THE SPOUSE OF THE LORD IS WIDOWED. To Jerusalem it had been said, "Thy Maker is thy Husband!" But because of her unfaithfulness and apostasy the Lord has forsaken her; she is become as a widow, unprotected, deserted, solitary, and comfortless.

V. THE CITY ONCE RICH IN ALLIES AND HELPERS IS UNFRIENDED. Not only is she feeble within, she is friendless without. In prosperous days neighbouring nations sought her good will and alliance, and were forward with their offers of friendship and of help. All this is of the past; those who vowed faithfulness have proved treacherous, and have became the enemies of Judæa in the extremity of her desolation, forsaking, and woe.—T.

Ver. 4.—*The decline of national religion.* Nowhere has the great truth of the close dependence of national prosperity upon national religion been more plainly and emphatically taught than in the writings of the Hebrew prophets. Their spiritual insight detected the true cause of national degradation. Whoever looks below the surface may see that the decline and fall of nations may usually be traced to spiritual causes, to the loss of any hold upon eternal principles of righteousness and piety.

I. THE OPEN SYMPTOMS OF THE DECLINE OF A NATION'S RELIGION. Those here mentioned are in circumstances and colour local and temporary; they were determined, as a matter of course, by what was peculiar to the religion of the country and of the day. 1. *The roads of Zion are forsaken.* There is no concourse upon the roads leading up to the metropolis, as was the case in the days of Judah's prosperity. 2. *The gates are deserted and unentered.* There was a time when the busy population passed to and fro, when the people gathered together at the gates to discuss the news of the day, the affairs of the city, when the royal processions passed in splendour through the gates leading to the country. It is now so no longer. 3. *The festivals are unfrequented.* Formerly, when the great and sacred national feasts were being held, multitudes of Israelites attended these holy and welcome assemblies to share in the pious mirth, the cheering reminiscences, the fraternal fellowship, distinctive of such solemn and joyous occasions. But now there are none to celebrate the mercies of Jehovah, none to fulfil the sacred rites. To the religious heart the change is not only afflicting, it is crushing. 4. *The ministers of religion are left to mourn.* The priests who are left, if permitted to fulfil their office, do so under the most depressing influences; and no longer are there virgins to rejoice in the dance. The picture is painted in the darkest, saddest colours. We feel, as we enter into the prophet's lamentations, how dreary and hopeless is the state of that nation which God gives over to its foes.

II. THE CAUSE OF THE DECLINE OF A NATION'S RELIGION. This ever begins in spiritual unfaithfulness and defections. The external observances of religion may be kept up for a season, but this may be only from custom and tradition. The body does not at once decay when the spirit has forsaken it. To forget God, to deny his Word, to break his laws, to forsake his mercy-seat,—such are the steps by which a nation's decline is most surely commenced, by which a nation's ruin is most surely anticipated.

III. THE REMEDY FOR THE DECLINE OF A NATION'S RELIGION. 1. Confession. 2. Repentance. 3. Prayer for pardon and acceptance. 4. Resolution to obey the Lord, and again to reverence what is holy and to do what is right. 5. The union of all classes, rulers and subjects, priests and people, old and young, in a national reformation.—T.

Ver. 7.—*Mournful memories.* The recollection of the past may be the occasion of the highest joy or of the profoundest sorrow. To remember former happiness is one of the great pleasures of human life, if that happiness did but lead on to its own continuance and increase. The first beginnings of a delightful friendship, the first steps of a distinguished career, are remembered by the prosperous and happy with satisfaction and joy. It is otherwise with the memory of a morning of brightness which soon clouded, and which was followed by storms and darkness. In the text the anguish of Jerusalem is pictured as intensified by the recollection of bygone felicity.

I. THE PRESENT CALAMITY EXCITES BY CONTRAST THE RECOLLECTION OF PROSPEROUS TIMES. 1. *Affliction, homelessness, and misery* are the present lot of Jerusalem. The city is in the hands of the enemy. The people have no longer a home which they can cling to, but face the prospect of exile, destitution, and vagrancy. 2. *Helplessness.* In times of prosperity neighbours were eager to offer aid which was not needed; in these times of adversity no friendly proffer of help is heard. 3. *Mockery.* The Jews are a people from the first separated from surrounding nations by their laws, their customs, their religious observances. As an intensely religious people, they have ever set their hearts upon their revelation, upon the God of their fathers and his ordinances. Consequently they are most easily and most deeply wounded in their religious susceptibilities. Strange that a nation condemned to defeat and capture for its unfaithfulness to Jehovah should yet observe the appointed sabbaths, and keenly feel the ridicule and the contempt incurred by such observance! Her adversaries mocked her sabbaths.

II. THE RECOLLECTION OF PROSPEROUS TIMES ENHANCES THE ANGUISH OF PRESENT ADVERSITY. Time has been when Jerusalem, her monarch, citizens, and surrounding population have enjoyed peace, plenty, respect from other nations, liberty of worship, and joyful solemnities. The force of contrast makes the memory of such time bitter and distressing. Their "crown of sorrow is remembering happier things."

APPLICATION. Let present privileges and prosperity be so used that the memory of them may never occasion bitter regret and misery.—T.

Ver. 10.—*Spoliation and profanation.* The presence of a foreign foe in its capital has always been regarded, and is still regarded, as among the heaviest calamities that can befall a nation. In our own times, a neighbouring nation has been required to endure this humiliation and indignity, shocking its patriotism and its pride. We can understand how bitter must have been the anguish of the Jews when the Chaldean hosts patrolled their city, quartered themselves upon its inhabitants, appropriated its wealth, and violated the sanctity of its temple.

I. THE POSSESSIONS OF THE JEWS WERE FORCIBLY APPROPRIATED BY THEIR ADVERSARIES. The greed of the conqueror has ever been the theme of satire and reproach. *Væ victis!* "Woe to the conquered!" is an old proverb, founded upon an older propensity of human nature in its military condition. The pleasant and desirable things of a city are the spoil of the conqueror. It was so when the Chaldeans entered Jerusalem, sacked the city, and laid their hands upon whatever pleased their fancy.

II. THE HOLY HOUSE OF JERUSALEM WAS SACRILEGIOUSLY ABUSED BY THE HEATHEN CONQUERORS. The temples of their gods are always the object of a nation's reverence and sometimes of affection. But the Jews had especial reason for venerating their sanctuary; it was the scene of their sacrifices and offerings, the depository of their oracles, the spot where the Shechinah-glory was displayed. The more sacred portion of the edifice was reserved for the priests; even the devout Jews were not suffered to enter these consecrated precincts. What, then, must have been the disgust, the horror, with which the pious contemporaries of Jeremiah, and especially the prophet himself, witnessed the profanation of the sanctuary, as the Chaldean soldiers polluted it with their heathen presence and speech! Their feelings were injured in the most susceptible part of their nature.

APPLICATION. Retribution is not an accident; neither is it the mere outworking of natural laws. There is Divine providence superintending it; it has a meaning, for it witnesses to human responsibility and sin; it has a purpose, for it summons to repentance and newness of life.—T.

Ver. 12.—*Unparalleled woe.* The prophecy here rises into poetry. The captured and afflicted city is personified. Like a woman bereaved and desolate and lonely, bewailing her misfortunes, and pouring out the anguish of her heart, Jerusalem sits in her solitary desolation and contempt, and calls upon bystanders to remark her sad condition, and to offer their sympathy to unequalled anguish.

I. THE CONSCIOUSNESS OF SORROW, DESOLATION, AND SHAME. How extreme is the distress and humiliation here depicted is apparent from the fact that this language has been attributed to our Divine Saviour when hanging upon the cross of Calvary. If a city never endured sorrow like that of Jerusalem, certainly no human being ever experienced agonies so piercing as those which the Captain of our salvation willingly bore for our sake when he gave his life a ransom for many.

> "All ye that pass by,
> To the Saviour draw nigh;
> To you is it nothing that Jesus should die?
> For sins not his own
> He died to atone;
> Was pain or was sorrow like his ever known?"

II. THE ADMISSION THAT AFFLICTION IS OF DIVINE APPOINTMENT, THAT IT IS CHASTISEMENT. When Jerusalem came to herself she could not fail to recognize a Divine hand in the miseries which befell her. The scourge was the army of the Chaldeans, but the hand was the righteous and retributive hand of the Eternal. It is too common for those who are in trouble to murmur against Providence, to exclaim against the injustice of providential appointments. Yet true wisdom points out that the path of submission and resignation is the right path. When once the mind is brought to acknowledge, "It is the Lord!" there is a prospect of spiritual improvement.

III. THE CRY FOR SYMPATHY. By a striking figure of speech, Jerusalem is represented as calling upon surrounding nations for interest and compassion. "Is it nothing to you? . . . Behold, and see!" Human sympathy is welcome in seasons of sorrow. Yet true help and deliverance must be from God, and from God alone. It is better to call upon the Lord than to call upon man; for he is both ready to sympathize and mighty to save.—T.

Ver. 18.—"*The Lord is righteous.*" In nothing is the distinction more marked between religions of human origin and device and the religion which is the revelation of infinite Wisdom and Truth, than in the views they respectively afford of the moral character and attributes of Deity. Whilst the heathen freely attribute to their gods qualities

which are detestable in man, the Scriptures represent the Supreme as perfectly right-eous. The acknowledgment here made by Jeremiah was made by Moses, by Nehemiah, by Daniel, and indeed is virtually, if not verbally, made by the writer of every book of the Old Testament. And the new covenant is based upon the revelation of a righteous Ruler and Father.

I. GOD IS RIGHTEOUS IN HIS CHARACTER. It is certainly no progress, but a retro-gression towards ignorance and barbarism, to represent the supreme Intelligence as destitute of moral attributes, exercised in the fulfilment of wise and benevolent pur-poses. Affliction and anguish sometimes obscure men's judgment of the character and the dealings of God. It was not so with Jeremiah, who, in lamenting the troubles of his nation and of himself, did not distort the representation he gave to his countrymen of the attributes of the Most High.

II. GOD IS RIGHTEOUS IN HIS LAW. The theocratic government of the Hebrews was based upon the just character and the holy Law of the eternal King. To some minds the reflection might have seemed inappropriate and unwelcome in the depth of disaster. But a true prophet, a true religious teacher, feels bound to set forth the fact that the rule under which men live as individuals and as communities is a righteous rule; the justice of the Law abides although that Law be broken, and although its penalties be incurred and endured.

III. GOD IS RIGHTEOUS IN HIS RETRIBUTION. This is probably the thought most prominent in the text. The fate of Jerusalem was a hard fate, a lamentable fate, but it was not an unjust fate. The people reaped as they had sown. An onlooker might readily have acknowledged this, but it was a merit in a sufferer so to do. For the chastened to confess the justice of their chastisement is a proof that already the chas-tening is not in vain.—T.

Ver. 20.—*The cry of the contrite.* Trouble, when it leads to an inquiry into its cause, when it prompts to submission and to repentance, proves a means of grace. The cry of suffering and distress may have no moral significance; the cry of contrition and of supplication is a sign of spiritual impression, and is a step towards spiritual recovery.

I. THE OCCASION OF AFFLICTION AND CONTRITION. This is here specified, and the reality and severity are manifest. Within, *i.e.* in the homes and streets of the city, there is dearth; without, *i.e.* in the field, there is destruction by the sword. Thus in two strokes national calamity and disaster are depicted.

II. THE TOKENS OF AFFLICTION AND CONTRITION. Man's bodily nature is expres-sive of his spiritual state. Severe suffering and distress display themselves in organic, physical disturbance. The prophet feels in his bodily frame the disturbing effects of the trials he has undergone, the lively sympathy he has experienced.

III. THE CONFESSION TO WHICH AFFLICTION AND CONTRITION LEAD. Identifying the nation with himself, the prophet exclaims, "I have grievously rebelled." There is candour and justice, there is submissiveness, there is spiritual discernment, in this outspoken acknowledgment. No excuse, no extenuation, no complaint, is here, but a plain confession of ill desert. Rebels against a rightful authority, against a just, for-bearing Sovereign, what could the Jews expect but such humiliation as they actually experienced? "If we *confess* our sins, he is faithful and just to forgive."

IV. THE CRY OF AFFLICTION AND OF CONTRITION. 1. It is a cry *unto the Lord.* Judah had looked for earthly friends and helpers, and had learned by bitter experience the vanity of such expectations. And now Judah sought the Lord whom by sin and rebellion she had offended. 2. It is an entreaty *for Divine regard* and consideration. What had happened was indeed by permission of Heaven. But the regard implored was one of sympathy, commiseration, and kindness. 3. It is a cry *for deliverance.* It is dictated by the assurance that he and only he who wounded can heal and comfort and restore.—T.

Ver. 1.—*Widowhood—the emblem of loneliness.* I. THE FORCE OF THE EMBLEM. Another emblem might have been used. Or the statement as to loneliness might have been left in its simplicity without any comparison at all. Why, then, this particular emblem? Because it sets forth the separation between two parties to a peculiar con-nection—a connection intended to have all the permanence which anything in this

earth can have. Of the husband and wife it is to be said that " they twain have become one flesh," and when the wife becomes a widow she is left in a peculiar and irremediable loneliness, even though she be in the midst of kindred, neighbours, and friends. So also we may say that the inhabitants of Jerusalem, together with the place itself, its site, its houses, its streets, had become one great whole. The children of Israel wandered through the wilderness for forty years, but when at last they left it, it would not have been suitable to say that the wilderness had become as a widow.

II. A VIEW THUS SUGGESTED AS TO THE CAUSE OF SEPARATION. One kind of loneliness had come as a terrible visitation because another kind of loneliness had not been sought as an imperative condition of security. Had not Balaam said, " The people shall dwell alone, and shall not be reckoned among the nations " (Numb. xxiii. 9)? Israel was to dwell in safety *alone.* What could be expected if the people mixed again so recklessly with those from whom they had been separated by a course of Divine marvels? It may also be noticed that Jerusalem would not have been left as a widow if the people of Jerusalem and the country altogether had had in them the spirit which prompted to deal wisely and compassionately with every widow. The widow had been carefully provided for by Mosaic enactments, *e.g.* in the solemn feasts and in the time of harvest. Yet in the first chapter of Isaiah's prophecies we find him denouncing the princes of the once faithful city because the cause of the widow did not come unto them.

III. A GROUND OF HOPE. Widowhood is evidently a state on which the loving God looks down with infinite tenderness and desire to help. Jerusalem became as a widow, yet the separation was not for ever. Her exiled inhabitants returned. Yet this was a small matter compared with the greater truths taught alike by the separation and the restoration. Things nearest and dearest to us may have to be taken away for a time, but all that belongs to our real welfare and to our complete relation to even the whole universe will come back in due time. We must not mistake eclipse for destruction.—Y.

Ver. 2.—*Nights of weeping explained.* Nights of weeping and constant tears upon the cheeks. Thus the metaphor is kept up with which this first song of lamentation begins. The sensitiveness of the woman-nature helps to bring out the prostration of Jerusalem. It is not only that her *condition* is lamentable, but she herself, in all the feelings of her heart, is a prey to the keenest anguish. People do not always see their own sad state as others see it. There is either a shallowness of nature or something has happened to deaden the sensibilities. But in this verse we have both the mention of tears and of most sufficient causes for tears.

I. FIRST CAUSE: WANT OF SYMPATHY AND SOLACE. Jerusalem has no *comforters.* Not even Job's comforters. For, though Job's comforters were sufficiently irritating and mistook blisters for salves, yet comfort was their errand. Bad as Job's state was, it would have been worse still if in his time of sore trouble he had been left quite alone, especially if professed friends had not come near him. But here the widowed Jerusalem has no comforter; and yet she had had many lovers, many who had been drawn irresistibly by the charm of her attractions. Jerusalem was proud of these attractions, and yet they did not belong to the essence of her existence. The attractions perished, and with the perishing of them the lovers whom they drew became cold. The attractions perished, but Jerusalem herself remained with all her needs, and yet with none to minister. Where do we mean to look for comforters when our hour of deepest trouble comes? Many to whom we may look will be able to do nothing for us; some to whom we may look will not try to do anything: happy then shall we be if we have reason to say, " In the multitude of my thoughts within me, *thy* comforts delight my soul " (Ps. xciv. 19).

II. SECOND CAUSE: FRIENDS HAVE BECOME ENEMIES. When the attractions of Jerusalem faded away, not only did the lovers depart, but they had to seek new satisfactions elsewhere, and for many selfish reasons they would act in sympathy with the conquerors of Jerusalem. When she was a strong city, it suited surrounding peoples to be friendly; but when she became desolate and the whole land was lost, then it seemed the interest of these peoples to be hostile to Jerusalem. Indeed, their connection with Jerusalem was really hostile even when they meant friendship. Their open and strenuous hostility from the first would have been a better thing. Professed friends, without meaning it, may so mislead as to do more harm than the bitterest enemy could ever do. The real friend is he who, for the sake of truth and of the highest interests, is not afraid to be reckoned for the time an enemy.—Y.

Ver. 4.—*Zion forsaken as a religious centre.* I. THE PECULIAR GLORY OF ZION IN THE PAST. The ways of Zion mourned now, but the very fact that such a thing should be said showed that they had once been filled with rejoicing. The gates had been crowded with worshippers from every district of the land. Zion was glorified as the site of the temple, and the temple was glorified as holding within its imposing walls the ark of the covenant. Zion was the city of solemnities. Things were done there not according to will-worship or mere immemorial tradition, but according to Jehovah's definite instructions given in the wilderness through Moses centuries before. Praise continually waited for God in Zion. Jehovah loved the gates of Zion more than all the dwellings of Jacob. There was no day without its morning and evening sacrifice, and every sabbath and new moon brought their peculiar additions. Nor must we forget the Feast of the Passover, of the firstfruits, of the Pentecost, and the great feast of the seventh month. If as nothing more than times of mirth and relaxation, these would play a large part in the life of the people, and true prophets and whosoever among the priests had deep reverence for God would get much strength out of these services, finding in them, according to the measure of their faith, zeal, and diligence, constant means of grace.

II. THE PECULIAR HUMILIATION OF ZION IN THE PRESENT. The thought of Zion probably carried to the Israelite more associations than did the thought of any other place. The great periodic assemblies at Zion manifested the history, the privileges, the strength, the unity, of the nation. There may have been intervals of comparative neglect, but we know that in the time of Hezekiah there was a great keeping of the Passover. Thus, so far as outward observances were concerned, the machinery of Divine service must have been in good working order. But it is also very evident that the nation at large got no real good out of the numerous and elaborate rites which Jehovah had commanded. We may quote words of Hosea which, while they show the prominent position occupied by Zion in the national life, also explain the reason why God brought such desolation to Zion. " I will also cause all her mirth to cease, her feast-days, her new moons, and her sabbaths, and all her solemn feasts " (Hos. ii. 11). Religion had been turned into mere merry-making. The house of prayer became a house of revelling. Jehovah had declared emphatically by his prophets that offerings had no value detached from righteousness and mercy. What wonder, then, that from condemning words he should advance to condemning deeds ? Forsaken Zion itself spoke as if with a prophetic voice. It was when they remembered *Zion* that the exiles in Babylon wept, and when their masters wanted from them a song of Zion they could only reply that it was not possible to sing Jehovah's song in a strange land. There is warning in all this desolation of Zion as to how great discernment is needed to make sure that the elements of our worship are acceptable to God, edifying to ourselves, and not merely for self-pleasure.

III. We must not forget that BRIGHTER DAYS ARE PROPHESIED FOR ZION. The same old Zion was again crowded, but of this we must not make too much. Jesus himself had to say that the rebuilt house of his Father had become a house of merchandise and even a den of thieves. There is the ideal Zion, part of the heavenly Jerusalem, where the holiest service will be the highest joy, where our religion will no longer be imperilled by formality, superstition, or superficiality.—Y.

Ver. 11.—*The real need of the soul made manifest.* I. REAL NEED CAN ONLY BE MADE MANIFEST BY PRACTICAL EXPERIENCE. The greatest need of the natural life is bread, taking the word " bread " as representative of all food. Clothing and shelter, while they may indeed be reckoned as needs, are not needs after the same imperative fashion as food ; and every one, however easily his daily bread comes to him, will assent to this same general truth that food is the great need of natural life. But he will only really feel this in such circumstances as are indicated in this verse. For a long while these people of Jerusalem had found bread lying to their hands when they were hungry. They could buy it and have abundance of pleasant things beside. The feeling of their hearts was that they could not do without these pleasant things, and when at last they gave them up to keep body and soul together, it must have been with terrible pain they made the surrender. And what is true of bread for the natural life is also true of the Bread coming down from heaven for the spiritual life. Christians, living in the midst of all manner of pleasant things of this world, with no lack of money to buy them and faculty to enjoy them, try to feel at the same time that more than all pleasant things are the grace, the life, the wisdom, the everflowing fulness of the Spirit, which come from Christ. But all the testimony of believers proves that the pleasant things need to be withdrawn before it can be apprehended that Christ is emphatically the Bread. It is when we lose relish of nature's best contributions to our happiness that Christ comes forward, confident as ever in his power to satisfy us.

II. THE VALUE OF TREASURES CAN ONLY BE KNOWN BY WHAT THE OWNER IS WILLING TO DO TO RETAIN THEM. All the pleasant things belonging to the *community* were already gone. The sanctuary had been desecrated and pillaged. Much private property had doubtless gone. But some the owners would be able to hide—jewels and such-like wealth as went into small compass. Among these pleasant things would be family heir-looms, loving gifts, possessions with respect to which the receiver had said to the giver, "I will keep this thing till I die." But now the great pressure comes, and one pleasant thing after another goes for a few handfuls of corn. The soul is threatening to depart from the body and it must be turned back; "for what shall it profit a man, if he gain the whole world and lose his own soul?" And now notice that there are treasures of the heart, such treasures as come from faith in Christ and fidelity to him, which are not given up even to preserve natural life. Multitudes have gone willingly to death that thereby they might testify to the truth as it is in Jesus. They have laid firm hold of his own word, "Whosoever will lose his life for my sake shall find it" (Matt. xvi. 25).—Y.

Ver. 12.—*The observation of suffering.* I. A SEEMINGLY UNREASONABLE COMPLAINT. "Is it nothing to you, all ye that pass by?" So speaks Jerusalem, personified under the guise of the weeping widow, with the tears on her cheeks and the beauty faded, deprived of all her pleasant things, and left in solitude so far as her familiar supports and consolations are concerned. She sits, as it were, by the highway, and the crowd passes on, taking no notice. Why, indeed, should it take notice? The spectacle of a conquered nation and a pillaged capital was not a rare thing. The nations asked to sympathize had been through the same experience themselves. We are all prompted to say, "Surely no trouble has been like our trouble;" and yet, as our observation of human affairs enlarges, we see how human nature, in every individual instance, is made to know its extraordinary capacity for suffering. Nevertheless, the piteous appeal here is not a baseless one. The trouble of the children of Israel had not come upon them after the manner of a common nation. They were peculiar in constitution, privileges, and history. If only there had been eyes to see it, there was something very signifi-cant to demand attention. But the thing to be seen did not lie on the surface, nor was it to be discovered save by faculties specially illuminated. The downfall and the sufferings of Israel, as they are to be seen both in the Scriptures and subsequent history, belong to the things that are to be spiritually discerned. Therefore this complaint, while superficially it may be called unreasonable, is yet reasonable enough, if we only consider the position and mission of Israel, and the work which, even in her degrada-tion, she has done for the world.

II. THE NEED THERE IS TO MARK JEHOVAH'S SURE VISITATIONS ON THE DISOBEDIENT. This is the critical element in the appeal that widow-like Jerusalem makes to the passers-by: "Look at me as the greatest illustration of the certainty with which Jehovah punishes those who rebel against him." We must, of course, beware of the conclusion that suffering always means punishment; but where we can see that it is punishment we must mark it as such, so that we ourselves may be admonished and may also more effectually admonish others. Here was a nation that in obedience might have rested confidently and happily in Jehovah's promise. The power behind that promise was more than all the armies of the great empires round about. But when the power was withdrawn it meant not merely suffering; the withdrawing had in it the nature of a judicial, solemn sentence from Jehovah himself.—Y.

Ver. 18.—*The acknowledgment that suffering is deserved.* I. THE CLEAR RECOGNITION ON THE PART OF THOSE VISITED THAT THE SUFFERING WAS OF JEHOVAH'S BRINGING. Secondary causes were prominent, but behind them was a Divine cause most important to be perceived in all the intensity of its working. Those who desolated Jerusalem did so from the worst of motives, motives always to be condemned; and these motives, keenly inspiring as they were, would have ended in nothing save for the weakness in which Israel had been left by its apostasy from God. When we are suffering for our sin and folly it is good if we can recognize that the suffering is of God's producing. Because that which God produces God can remove in the hour of repentance. Whereas what man produces he may not be able to put right again, even when he is so disposed. II. A REASON IS GIVEN FOR DECLARING JEHOVAH RIGHTEOUS. He has done righteously to those who have rebelled against his commandments. God has made us so that we can distinguish between the right and the wrong. We need ever to be on our guard against saying that a thing is right because God does it. What is admitted here is that it is a right thing for God to inflict chastisement on the disobedient. The greater the disobedience the severer must be the chastisement. The commandment of God was always a right thing in itself; and the prophets had again and again illustrated the righteousness of particular commandments and the evident miseries that flowed from neglecting them. Recollect that this great blow upon Israel came after many lesser ones. It was not as if Israel could plead that the commandments were dubious or the warnings scanty. III. It must not be forgotten that JEHOVAH'S RIGHTEOUSNESS IS EQUALLY SHOWN IN HIS TREATMENT OF THE OBEDIENT. It is of the greatest importance to recollect this, because unfortunately the disobedient are more noticeable than the obedient, and the treatment of the disobedient, by consequence, more noticeable than the treatment of the obedient. The spirit of our life determines, by a most fixed law, the way in which God will treat us. It is perfectly impossible for the disobedient to escape suffering. But it is equally impossible for the obedient to lose their reward. Joy and blessedness, the exquisite peace and rapture of holiness, must come to them by the very nature of things.—Y.

Ver. 21.—*A wicked gladness.* I. THE WRONG FEELING WITH REGARD TO SUFFERING FOR SIN. People are here represented as rejoicing over the sufferings of others. Not that they take delight in suffering as suffering, but those who suffered were their enemies. Those now suffering had once inflicted suffering on others. They had been a source of danger, provoking jealousy, and producing humiliation. Hence, when Israel fell into all this solitude and misery, other peoples not only failed to pity, but even positively rejoiced. This was just what might be expected, and even if some of the heathen nations said, "This serves Israel right for neglecting Jehovah," it was certainly nothing more than the simple truth. The wrong thing was the exultant feeling, the gladness of heart over all this suffering. There is no fear but what we shall sympathize with the suffering of the innocent, the pain coming from some accident or disease; but when it is an *evil-doer* who suffers, then we are only too easily betrayed into language expressing gladness of heart. And we should never be *glad* with respect to any suffering whatever. Let it be remembered, too, that gladness is only one out of several possible wrong attitudes with respect to suffering. If while others are suffering for their sins we allow ourselves to get into any of these wrong attitudes with respect to them, then our unchristian state of mind may prove a very serious obstacle in the way of their repentance and amendment. The censuring, lecturing spirit must be guarded against, and also the spirit that looks down as from a position of superior goodness. We must restore others in a spirit of meekness, considering ourselves, lest we also be tempted. II. THE RIGHT FEELING WITH REGARD TO SUFFERING FOR SIN. The absence of the wrong feeling can only be secured by the presence of the right one. If selfish gladness, the gladness springing from envy and jealousy, is to be kept out, it must be by constantly cultivating pity for all suffering. Pity is to be the very first feeling with which all suffering is contemplated. Pity must, indeed, be well under control, and never allowed to open the way for a greater suffering by taking away a lesser one, but it must always be the prevailing feeling. Then also we must take care to rejoice with the rejoicing. It increases the happiness of others to know that we are glad because of their happiness

Our work as Christians is only part done in removing the evil; our thoughts are to be chiefly fixed on producing and establishing the good with all its fruits so pleasant to the spiritual eye, so pleasant to the taste of the inner man. The enemies of Israel saw Israel fallen, and rejoiced that Jehovah had done this. When we see the fallen lifted up and walking along in the strength of Christ, let us rejoice exceedingly because of what the Father of our Lord Jesus Christ has done. It is worth all our efforts to keep out of our hearts mean satisfaction because of the disappointments and confusion of others.—Y.

EXPOSITION.

CHAPTER II.

ZION'S JUDGMENT IS OF GOD. LAMENTATIONS AND SUPPLICATIONS.

Ver. 1.—**Hath the Lord covered**; rather, *doth . . . cover*. **The daughter of Zion**; *i.e.* Jerusalem. **Cast down from heaven.** Here and in Matt. xi. 23 we have a parallel to Isa. xiv. 12, where the King of Babylon is compared to a bright star. "Cast down" whither? Into the "pit" or dungeon of Hades (Isa. xiv. 15). **The beauty of Israel**; *i.e.* Jerusalem, exactly as Babylon is called "the proud beauty [or, 'ornament'] of Chaldea" (Isa. xiii. 19). **His footstool**; *i.e.* the ark (Ps. cxxxii. 7), or perhaps the temple as containing the ark (1 Chron. xxviii. 2; Ps. xcix. 5).

Ver. 2.—**Habitations**; rather, *pastures.* The word properly means the settlements of shepherds in green, grassy spots, but here designates the country parts in general, distinguished from the "strongholds" of Judah. **Hath polluted.** So Ps. lxxxix. 39, "Thou hast profaned [same word as here] his crown [by casting it] to the ground." The wearer of a crown was regarded in the East as nearer to divinity than ordinary mortals; in some countries, indeed, *e.g.* in Egypt, almost as an incarnation of the deity. To discrown him was to "pollute" or "profane" him.

Ver. 3.—**All the horn**; rather, *every horn;* i.e. all the means of defence, especially the fortresses. **He hath drawn back his right hand**; *i.e.* he hath withdrawn his assistance in war. **He burned against**; rather, *he burned up.*

Ver. 4.—The beginning of the verse seems slightly out of order (see the Septuagint). **And slew all that were pleasant,** etc. The correct rendering is, *And slew all that was pleasant to the eye: in the tent of the daughter of Zion he poured out his fury like fire.* The Authorized Version (following the Targum) seems to have thought that the youth of the population alone was intended. But, though Ewald also adopts this view, it seems to limit unduly the meaning of the poet. By "tent" we should probably understand "dwelling," as Jer. iv.

5, and often; Isa. xvi. 5, "the tent of David;" Ps. lxxviii. 67, "the tent of Joseph."

Ver. 5.—**Was as an enemy: he hath swallowed**, etc. The threefold division of the verse is, unfortunately, concealed in the Authorized Version, owing to the arbitrary stopping. The grouping suggested by the Massoretic text is—

"The Lord is become an enemy, he hath swallowed up Israel;
He hath swallowed up all her palaces, he hath destroyed all his strongholds;
And hath increased in the daughter of Judah moaning and bemoaning."

The change of gender in the second line is easily explicable. In the first case the poet is thinking of the city; in the second, of the people of Israel. The rendering "moaning and bemoaning" is designed to reproduce, to some extent, the Hebrew phrase, in which two words, derived from the same root, and almost exactly the same, are placed side by side, to give a more intense expression to the idea.

Ver. 6.—**Violently taken away**; rather, *violently treated;* i.e. broken up. **His tabernacle**; rather, *his booth.* "Tent" and "dwelling" are interchangeable expressions (see ver. 4); and in the Psalms "booth" is used as a special poetic synonym for "tent" when God's earthly dwelling-place, the sanctuary of the temple, is spoken of (so Ps. xxvii. 5; xxxi. 20; lxxvi. 2). The Authorized Version, indeed, presumes an allusion to the proper meaning of the Hebrew word, as if the poet compared the sanctuary of Jehovah to a pleasure-booth in a garden. It is, however, more natural to continue, *as a garden*, the sense of which will be clear from Ps. lxxx. 12, 13. The Septuagint has, instead, "as a vine"—a reading which differs from the Massoretic by having one letter more (*kaggéfen* instead of *kaggan*). This ancient reading is adopted by Ewald, and harmonizes well with Isa. v. 1, etc.; Jer. ii. 21 (comp. Ps. lxxx. 8); but the received text gives a very good sense. "Garden" in the Bible means, of course, a plantation of trees rather than a flower-garden. **His places of the assembly;** rather, *his place of meeting (with God).* The word occurs in the same sense in Ps. lxxiv. 3. It is the temple which is meant, and the term is borrowed from the famous phrase, *ōhel mō'ēdh* (Exod. xxvii. 21; comp. xxv. 22).

Ver. 7.—**Her palaces**; *i.e.* those of the daughter of Zion, especially "high buildings" (this is the true meaning of *'armōn*) of the temple. **They have made a noise**, etc. Comp. Ps. lxxiv. 3, "Thine enemies roar in the midst of thy place of meeting." The passages are parallel, though, whether the calamities referred to are the same in both, cannot *à priori* be determined. The shouts of triumph of the foe are likened to the festal shouts of the temple-worshippers (comp. Isa. xxx. 29; Amos v. 24).

Ver. 8.—**He hath stretched out a line.** It is the "line of desolation" mentioned in Isaiah (xxxiv. 11; comp. Amos vii. 7; 2 Kings xxi. 13). Such is the unsparing rigour of Jehovah's judgments.

Ver. 9.—**Are sunk into the ground**; *i.e.* are broken down and buried in the dust. **The Law is no more.** The observance of the Law being rendered impossible by the destruction of the temple. Comp. this and the next clause with Ezek. vii. 26.

Ver. 10.—**They have cast up dust**, etc. A sign of mourning (Josh. vii. 6; 2 Sam. xiii. 19; Job ii. 12).

Ver. 11.—**My bowels are troubled** (see on ch. i. 20). **My liver is poured upon the earth.** A violent emotion being supposed to occasion a copious discharge of bile. **The daughter of my people.** A poetic expression for Zion or Judah.

Ver. 12.—**Corn.** Either in the sense of parched corn (comp. Lev. xxiii. 14; 1 Sam. xvii. 17; Prov. xxvii. 22) or a poetic expression for "bread" (comp. Exod. xvi. 4; Ps. cv. 40).

Ver. 13.—**What thing shall I take to witness for thee?** rather, *What shall I testify unto thee?* The nature of the testifying may be gathered from the following words. It would be a comfort to Zion to know that her misfortune was not unparalleled: *solamen miseris socios habuisse malorum.* The expression is odd, however, and, comparing Isa. xl. 18, A. Krochmal has suggested, *What shall I compare?* The correction is easy. **Equal**; *i.e.* compare (comp. Isa. xlvi. 5).

Ver. 14.—**Thy prophets.** Jeremiah constantly inveighs against the fallacious, immoral preaching of the great mass of his prophetic contemporaries (comp. Jer. vi. 13, 14; xiv. 13—15; xxiii. 14—40). **Have seen vain and foolish things**; *i.e.* have announced "visions" (prophecies) of an unreal and irrational tenor. Comp. Jer. xxiii. 13, where the same word here paraphrased as "irrational" (literally, *insipid*) occurs. **Dis-**

covered; *i.e.* disclosed. **To turn away thy captivity.** The Captivity, then, might have been "turned away," if the other prophets had, like Jeremiah, disclosed the true spiritual state of the people, and moved them to repentance. **False burdens.** Suggestive references to these false prophecies occur in Jer. xiv. 13, 14; xxiii. 31, 32 (see the Exposition on these passages). **Causes of banishment.** So Jeremiah (xxvii. 10; comp. 15), "They prophesy a lie unto you, to remove you far from your land."

Ver. 15.—**Clap . . . hiss . . . wag their heads.** Gestures of malicious joy (Job xxvii. 23) or contempt (Jer. xix. 8; Ps. xxii. 7). **The perfection of beauty**; literally, the *perfect in beauty.* The same phrase is used in Ezekiel (xxvii. 3; xxviii. 12) of Tyre, and a similar one in Ps. l. 2 of Zion.

Vers. 16, 17.—On the transposition of the initial letters in these verses, see Introduction.

Ver. 16.—**Have opened their mouth against thee.** As against the innocent sufferer of Ps. xxii. (ver. 13). **Gnash the teeth.** In token of rage, as Ps. xxxv. 16; xxxvii. 12. **We have seen** it (comp. Ps. xxxv. 21).

Ver. 17.—**His word that he had commanded**, etc. "Commanded," *i.e.* given in charge to. Comp. Zech. i. 6, "My words and my statutes, which I *commanded* my servants the prophets." Zechariah continues, in language which illustrates the foregoing words of this verse, "Did they not take hold of [overtake] your fathers;" where the persons spoken of as " your fathers" are the same as those who are represented by the speaker of the elegy. "In the days of old;" alluding, perhaps, to such passages as Deut. xxviii. 52, etc. **The horn of thine adversaries.** "Horn" has a twofold meaning—"strength" or "defence" (comp. ver. 3), and " honour" or " dignity " (comp. 1 Sam. ii. 1). The figure is too natural to need explanation.

Ver. 18.—**Their heart cried unto the Lord**, etc. "Their heart" can only mean "the heart of the people of Jerusalem." For the expression, comp. Ps. lxxxiv. 2, "My heart and my flesh cry aloud to the living God." To avoid the rather startling prosopopœia in the next clause, Thenius supposes a corruption in the group of letters rendered " wall," and attaches the corrected word to the first clause, rendering thus: "Their heart crieth unto the Lord in vain; O daughter of Zion, let tears run down," etc. Another resource, which also involves an emendation, is that of Ewald, " Cry with all thy heart, O wall of the daughter of Zion." **O wall**, etc. The prosopopœia is surprising, but is only a degree more striking than that of ver. 8 and ch. i. 4. In Isa. xiv. 31 we find an equally strong one, " Howl, O gate." Most probably, however, there is something wrong in the text; the following verses seem to refer to the daughter of Zion. Bickell reads thus: " Cry aloud unto the Lord, O virgin daughter of Zion." **Like a river**; rather, *like a torrent.* **Give thyself no rest.** The word rendered " rest " means properly the stiffness produced by cold.

Ver. 19.—**In the beginning of the watches.** This would seem to be most naturally explained as referring to the first watch of the night. When most are wrapped in their first and sweetest sleep, the daughter of Zion is to " arise and cry." Others explain, " at the beginning of each of the night watches; " *i.e.* all the night through. Previously to the Roman times, the Jews had divided the night into three watches (comp. Judg. iii. 19). **Pour out thine heart like water**; *i.e.* give free course to thy complaint, shedding tears meanwhile. The expression is parallel partly to phrases like "I am poured out like water" (Ps. xxii. 14), partly to "Pour out your heart before him" (Ps. lxii. 8).

In the top of every street; rather, *at every street corner* (and so ch. iv. 1).

Ver. 20.—**To whom thou hast done this**; viz. to Israel, the chosen people. And **children**; rather, (*even*) *children.* The children are the " fruit " referred to. Comp. the warnings in Lev. xxvi. 26; Deut. xxviii. 56; and especially Jer. 'xix. 9; also the historical incident in 2 Kings vi. 28, 29. **Of a span long**; rather, *borne in the hands.* The word is derived from the verb rendered " to swaddle" in ver. 22 (see note).

Ver. 22.—**Thou hast called as in a solemn day.** The passage is illustrated by ch. i. 15, according to which the instruments of Jehovah's vengeance are "summoned" by him to a festival when starting for the holy war. **My terrors round about.** Almost identical with one of the characteristic phrases of Jeremiah's prophecies, " fear [or rather, ' terror'] on every side " (see on Jer. vi. 25). **Have swaddled**; rather, *have borne upon the hands.*

HOMILETICS.

Ver. 1.—*God not remembering his footstool.* The ark was regarded as God's footstool; and the temple in which the ark was kept was also sometimes called the footstool of God. When the temple was destroyed and the ark stolen, or broken, or lost, it looked as though God had forgotten his footstool. The symbolism of the ark and the ritual connected with it give a peculiar significance to this fact.

I. GOD NO LONGER REMEMBERS THE PLACE WHERE HIS PRESENCE WAS MOST FULLY MANIFESTED. The Holy Land, Jerusalem, the temple, the holy of holies, the ark,—these are the sacred places, of increasing sanctity as the circle narrows, till the very footstool where God touches earth is reached. 1. The presence of God in our midst is *no guarantee against the natural consequences of our misdeeds.* On the contrary, if he is with us to protect in times of simple distress, he is with us as Judge to condemn when we fall and contract guilt. 2. The presence of God at one time is *no guarantee of its permanence.* The footstool may be God's no longer if it prove unworthy of him. The Church which was once the temple of the Holy Spirit may become deserted by its heavenly Guest. That we enjoy the communion of God now is no reason for being confident that we shall not lose that privilege through unbelief or other sin. 3. *We cannot assume that God will never reject us because he has once made use of us.* The footstool may be supposed to have been used by God as of some service to him. Nevertheless it was discarded. If the servant of God proved unfaithful, his Master's livery will not save him. He will be discharged and disgraced.

II. GOD NO LONGER REMEMBERS HIS MERCY-SEAT. The footstool of God's peculiarly manifested presence was also his mercy-seat. There the assurance of atonement was confirmed when the high priest entered with sacrificial blood and intercession. Yet even the mercy-seat can be forgotten in the day of God's anger. We trust that in wrath he will remember mercy. But there are clouds of anger too black for us to see the mercy that shines behind them. 1. *The mercy which is in the heart of God is not to be regarded as nullifying his wrath.* It is so represented by some who take one-sided views of the Divine character. But the All-merciful can be a consuming fire. 2. *If God has once been merciful to us we may not conclude that he can never be angry with us.* On the contrary, if we sin against light and love we provoke the greater wrath. The very fact that the footstool was privileged to be a mercy-seat will aggravate the wrath which must be poured upon it when it is disgraced.

III. GOD NO LONGER REMEMBERS THE PLACE OF PRAYER. At the footstool of God the suppliant kneels pleading for deliverance. But his prayer is unheard. God may refuse to hearken to prayer. Where he is wont to stoop and listen to cry and sigh of burdened souls he may be regardless. 1. *Impenitence* will lead to God's disregarding our prayer. 2. When wrath is necessary, the *mere cry for escape must be unheard.* 3. When chastisement is for our good, *mercy itself will refuse to listen to the prayer for deliverance.* The surgeon must disregard the cries of his patient. He must harden himself to save the sufferer.

Vers. 4, 5.—*The Lord as an enemy.* I. THE LORD MAY BECOME TO US AS AN ENEMY. We must not suppose the relations of God to those who forsake him to be purely negative. He cannot simply leave them to their own devices. He is a King who must needs maintain order and restrain and punish rebellion, a Judge who cannot permit law to be trampled underfoot with impunity, a Father who cannot abandon his children, but must chastise them in their wrong-doing just because he is so closely related to them. Let it be well understood, then, that, in opposing ourselves to God, we run counter to a power, a will, an active authority. We provoke the anger of God. We do not simply strike ourselves against the stone, we cause the stone to fall upon us and grind us to powder.

II. NOTHING CAN BE MORE TERRIBLE THAN FOR THE LORD TO BECOME TO US AS AN ENEMY. The very thought of God as an enemy should strike terror into one who finds it is a fact. 1. *God is almighty.* It is at once apparent that the war must end in defeat for the rebel. 2. *God is just.* Then he must be in the right with the great controversy. We must be fighting on the wrong side when we are fighting against God. 3. *God is gracious.* How fearful must be the wrong-doing that provokes so kind a God to enmity! 4. *God is our Father.* Our Father become as our enemy! The unnatural situation proclaims its own horror. The nearness of God and his love to us make the fire of his wrath the more fierce. The wrath of the "Lamb" is more awful than the raging of him who goes about as a roaring lion seeking whom he may devour.

III. GOD DOES NOT BECOME TO US AS AN ENEMY UNTIL WE HAVE PROVED OURSELVES TO BE ENEMIES TO HIM. He has no wish to quarrel with us. He is changeless in his constancy of righteousness and love. It is we who break the peace. The declaration of war between heaven and earth is always issued by the lower world. It is not necessary, however, that our enmity should be overt in order that God may be seen as an enemy. Secret alienation of heart, quiet neglect of God's will, self-willed indifference to God, will constitute enmity. The fact that the enmity begins on our side will take away all excuse suggested by our feebleness in comparison with the greatness of God.

IV. THOUGH GOD MAY BECOME TO US AS AN ENEMY, HE WILL NOT REALLY BE AN ENEMY. He may act like an enemy, but he will not act in enmity. He will never hate the creature that he has made. His apparent enmity is very fearful because it results in actions of anger and punishment. Still behind all is the pitying heart of Divine love. God pities most when he strikes hardest.

V. THROUGH THE ATONEMENT OF CHRIST GOD CEASES TO BE TO US AS AN ENEMY. Christ is our Propitiation. By the sacrifice of himself he makes peace. And he does not simply influence our hearts in reconciling us to God. There is a Godward aspect of the atonement. This is not to induce God to love us, since the love of God precedes and originates the very mission of Christ. But in the mysterious counsels of Divine wisdom the atonement of Christ is rendered necessary for the cessation of God's inimical action (1 John ii. 1, 2).

Vers. 6, 7.—*The rejected altar.* In the first elegy we read how the feasts are neglected by the people (ch. i. 4). Now we see that God himself has broken them up and cast off his altar. Thus we advance a stage in understanding the deplorable condition of Jerusalem. At first the human side only is seen and the visible facts are lamented over. Then the Divine side is discerned and the terrible cause of the cessation of the solemn festivals revealed. It is not simply that the people cease to present themselves before the altar. God has abandoned and rejected all the temple services.

I. HOW GOD REJECTS THE ALTAR. We must bear in mind that the altar belongs to

God and that all the ordinances of worship are his. Religion is not merely human and subjective. It relates to God and it goes out of the human world reaching up to the Divine. There is scope, therefore, for God's action in it. He may refuse his action. He may not hear the prayers, nor accept the offerings, nor employ the services, nor succour the needs of the worshipper. Then he rejects the altar. This is represented as being done with violence, destruction, and a Divine abhorrence. The desolation wrought by Babylon is traced up to the hand of God. So when our religious privileges are broken up by earthly means we should inquire whether God's displeasure is behind the calamity. It is not necessarily. But it may be.

II. Why God rejects the altar. 1. Because *the worship is insincere.* If we practise the forms of devotion without the heart of it our hypocrisy will only insult God. 2. Because *the worshipper is corrupt.* Thus was it with the Jews in Isaiah's time. God says, " Your new moons and your appointed feasts my soul hateth . . . when ye make many prayers, I will not hear : your hands are full of blood " (Isa. i. 14, 15). So David says, " If I regard iniquity in my heart, the Lord will not hear me " (Ps. lxvi. 18). 3. Because *the offering is unworthy.* The Israelite was to bring his best to God. No blemished sacrifice would be accepted. If we give less than the best in our power we make an unworthy offering. If only spare time and superfluous money are offered to God, how can we expect him to receive such mean and niggardly service? He will have our brightest hours, our richest devotion, our hearts and lives and all, or he will take nothing.

III. With what results God rejects the altar. When once the altar is rejected by God all sacrifice and service are vain. It matters little that the enemy throw down the stones of it. If it remains intact it is worthless. We may have full assemblies of people and rich and elaborate services and all the pomp and ceremony of worship ; and it will be for nothing if God reject the worship. We think too little of this Divine side of religion. We are too much inclined to rest in the decorum and grace of becoming human forms of worship. Let it be known that the one end of worship is to reach God. If he is met by the soul, it matters little what means be used in worship. If he refuses to accept us, the form of worship is a mockery and a delusion.

Ver. 9 (last clause).—*" No vision."* I. The teaching and vision of prophetic truth constitute an important element in religious life. The writer laments the loss of teaching and vision as abnormal and disastrous. The vision of the prophets was not simply nor chiefly concerned with the distant future and recondite counsels of providence. It dealt with present facts and unveiled their true character. It guided in the present and with regard to the uncertainties of the very near future. The humbler office of teaching was associated with it. The prophet, a seer of visions in private and on special occasions, was a teacher among his fellow-men and under ordinary circumstances. It is important to see how essential the knowledge of truth is to a healthy spiritual life. Without it devotion becomes superstition. Religion is based on revelation. The school precedes the workshop. Teaching must prepare the way for service.

II. There are times when teaching and vision cease. The two may not fail exactly at the same time. But the stream will not flow long after the fountain is dried. The teaching that is continued after all inspiration has died out will be arid, formal, lifeless, unreal. Ideas will take place of facts, and words of ideas. Now, the vision, which is the starting-point of all knowledge of truth, is intermittent. There have been ages fertile in prophecy and there have been barren ages. In the days preceding the ministry of Samuel " the Word of the Lord was rare, and there was no vision scattered abroad " (1 Sam. iii. 1). After the roll of the Old Testament was complete, prophecy ceased. It revived in the apostolic age. Spiritual insight and Divine knowledge have been intermittent since then, sleeping in the dark ages, flashing out in the days of St. Bernard, dried up by the dreariness of scholasticism, swelling out in fresh energy with the Reformation, withering again at the end of the seventeenth century, and brightening once more from the close of the eighteenth. What shall be the next turn ?

III. The abuse of prophetic vision and teaching leads to the cessation of them. The prophets prophesied falsely (ver. 14). They preached peace when there was no peace (Jer. xxiii. 17). As a penalty for their treason to their sacred trust of truth they lost the gift of spiritual vision. Disloyalty to truth warps our perceptions of truth. False living hinders true thinking. There is nothing which so deadens and blinds the spiritual faculties as indifference to truth. Beginning with telling a conscious lie, a man comes at last to accept falsehood without knowing it.

IV. THE REJECTION OF PROPHETIC VISION AND TEACHING ALSO LEADS TO THE CESSATION OF THEM. The people were as guilty as their teachers. They refused to hear truth and asked for pleasant words. They declined to obey the truth which they had heard. The penalty of disobedience to Divine truth will be the loss of that truth. If we refuse to go as the vision of God in our souls directs, that vision will fade out, leaving us no light of heaven, but only gloom or false lights of earth.

Ver. 14.—*The vision of falsehood and folly.* Visions from the Lord have ceased (ver. 9). But the prophets continue to see visions of earthly limitation or even of diabolical delusion. These visions are false and foolish. Better have none than such.

I. PROPHECY IN ITS CORRUPTION SEES THE FALSE AND FOOLISH IN PLACE OF THE TRUE AND WORTHY. 1. *The mission of prophecy is to see and declare wisdom and reality.* The attractiveness of the teaching is a snare if the matter of it is vain. People naturally favour the pleasant utterance of pleasant things. Doctrines are sometimes chosen because they are liked rather than because they are known to be sound, or the style and language of the preacher are more heeded than the substance of his message. But, if we were in earnest, ugly truths would always be accepted in preference to specious falsehoods. 2. *The corruption of prophecy substitutes falsehood and folly for truth and wisdom.* This may be experienced unconsciously. The teacher may not know that he has fallen. It is not only that his tongue utters lies, his eye sees no truth. His vision is distorted and he knows it not. He is not aware that he sees men as trees walking. Nor does he know that his folly is not wisdom. The failing of spiritual vision and decay of wisdom are the more calamitous because they are unconscious. They are a sort of spiritual insanity. 3. *The evil of the corruption of prophecy is in the widespread delusion and degradation that it produces.* "Thy prophets have seen vain and foolish things for thee." The prophet is a teacher as well as a seer. When the teacher errs the scholars are misled.

II. THE FAILURE TO DISCOVER INIQUITY IS A PROOF THAT A PROPHET'S VISION IS FALSE AND FOOLISH. 1. *A prophet is required to see human as well as Divine truth.* It needs inspiration to read the secrets of the heart as much as to discover the mysteries of the unseen heavens or of the distant future. A prophet should be a discerner of spirits. If he cannot read the signs of the times he is a failure. 2. *The failure to see iniquity is one especial evidence of perverted prophetic vision.* The physician is first of all called upon to discover his patient's disease. If he cannot detect this the rest of his work is of little use. Prophets may dream of the millennium and discourse of the celestial spheres; but so long as they are blind to the sins that men around them are perishing in, their primary mission must fail. Now, it needs a Divine inspiration rightly to see iniquity. Conventionality of thought leads to a complacent satisfaction with the normal state of the world. We must be out of it and above it to observe how it has fallen. The preacher who cannot see the sins of his age is worse than useless. He is a deluding flatterer. The individual man who is blind to his own sin has not the first ray of spiritual light which may guide him aright.

III. THE FALSE AND FOOLISH VISION OF PROPHECY DOES NOT RESTORE PROSPERITY, BUT ON THE CONTRARY IT DIRECTLY LEADS TO RUIN. By vainly promising pleasant things it brings disastrous ones. The false prophets opposed Jeremiah and said the Captivity would not come. By that very falsehood they helped to hasten it. Had they preached repentance and warned of wrath, the doom might have been averted. None prepare souls for ruin more certainly than smooth-speaking flattering optimists. When danger is near, the warning prophet may be the deliverer of his hearers. If the preacher fail to produce conviction of sin he cannot lead to salvation in Christ. So long as men do not see their lost condition they are in danger of their soul's ruin. To them a pleasant religion is a fatal religion. A Jeremiah, a John the Baptist, and a John Knox are the best friends of their generation.

Ver. 16.—*The triumph of the foe.* I. THE TRIUMPH OF THE FOE OVER JERUSALEM. Strangers mock with scorn and derision, enemies vent their rage with hissing, gnashing of teeth, and a spiteful satisfaction that the day they have looked for has come. Why should these cruel feelings be roused against the prostrate city? Her previous condition must have provoked them. 1. *Great prosperity.* This excites envy in the less prosperous, and envy soon sours into hatred. Jealous and selfish natures have a positive pleasure in seeing the loss of special privileges in the more favoured, although that loss may bring no advantage to themselves. 2. *High pretensions.* Jerusalem claimed to be especially favoured and blessed by God. She looked down with scorn on her neighbours. Such an attitude was galling to them and led to an outburst of delight when the proud city lay grovelling in the dust. Contempt provokes enmity. No calamity receives less pity than the downfall of pride. 3. *Reserved isolation.* Jerusalem kept herself apart from other cities. She felt that she had a peculiar vocation. Such exclusiveness would excite dislike. The unsocial are unpitied. It may be that the separation is inevitable or conscientious. Still, it incurs not the least aversion.

II. THE TRIUMPH OF THE FOE OVER THE CHURCH. The fall of Jerusalem was the fall of the Church. The enemies of the Eternal rejoiced in the destruction of his temple and the scattering of his people. There are always adversaries on the look out for disaster in the Church of Christ. The evil spirit of the world is vexed and shamed by the standing rebuke of a pure Church. Corrupt men see in her an example contrasting with their own conduct and thereby condemning it. Thus there arise dislike and enmity. The shame of the Church is a relief to this worldly opposition. There have been times when the Name of God has been insulted through this evil pleasure of the wicked in the shame that the sin and failure of his people have brought upon his cause. Here is a motive for preserving the sanctity of the Christian Church. The loss of it will not merely involve suffering to the Church herself; it will encourage the foes of Christ by giving them the elation of victory, and it will dishonour his Name by making his work appear to fail.

III. THE TRIUMPH OF THE FOE OVER A SOUL. There are spiritual enemies watching for every slip that a soul may make, enemies that are confounded by its growing purity and faithfulness, but rendered insolent and jubilant by its fall. Whenever we sin we afford a triumph to the evil one. We think that we are pleasing ourselves. But there must be some mistake or our sin would not give so much satisfaction to our enemy. The laugh of Mephistopheles should have been a warning to Faust. Perhaps the most stinging smart of future retribution will be the devilish glee with which the miserable lost soul will be welcomed into the place of darkness.

Ver. 17.—*Ruin from God.* In the fifteenth and sixteenth verses we find strangers and enemies indulging in unseemly jubilation over the fall of Jerusalem. Now, we see —what they do not see—that the cause of that fall was the direct action of God. This fact aggravates the dismay and wretchedness of the suffering city, for it signifies that her own King and Friend has brought about her ruin—not outsiders and antagonists. God himself has handed her over to the contempt and derision of the world. At the same time, the sight of God's hand in the calamity reveals the folly of the world's triumph. How shallow and ignorant that appears to be directly the veil which covers the awful action of God is lifted! Man's spite and malice sink into insignificance before the awful wrath of God, as the growling of beasts of the forest is drowned in the dread roar of thunder. The triumph of man is also shown to be misplaced. Man has not done the deed. He is but a spectator. This is a dread work of God. Let human passion be hushed before the solemn sight.

I. GOD BRINGS RUIN. This is a terrible statement. Looking at the particulars of the action itself, we see only the more of its horrors as we observe: 1. God does it *deliberately.* He devises it—plans, considers, and calmly executes the ruin. 2. God does it *in fulfilment of his Word.* "In the days of old" the ruin is threatened. The storm is long in brewing. An ancient promise makes the coming of it certain. 3. God does it *by authority.* He "had commanded" it. With all the authority and power of divinity over innumerable agents bending in perfect compliance to his will, God executes his solemn threat. 4. He does it *destructively.* He throws down. This shows violence and hurt. 5. He does it, to all human appearance, *pitilessly.* There is nothing visible that might mitigate the blow. No acts of mercy are seen to alleviate the misery. 6. He does it *to the satisfaction of enemies.* "He hath caused thine enemy to rejoice over thee," etc. This is the most sure sign that the ruin is complete.

II. THE FACT THAT GOD BRINGS RUIN IS NOT INCONSISTENT WITH HIS CHARACTER. It appears to be so, for it represents the Creator as a destroyer, and the God of love as a God of enmity. The difficulty should be examined. Then some light may break upon it. 1. *The goodness of God makes him the enemy of all evil.* He would cease to be good if he became universally complacent. As a righteous Judge he must condemn sin; even the Son of man, the Saviour of the world, had a mission of destruction. He came with fan to winnow out the chaff, and fire to burn it; he came to destroy the works of the devil. 2. *God makes external ruin that he may produce internal salvation.* He destroys the city that he may save the citizens. Jerusalem is overthrown in order that the Jews, through this chastisement, may be delivered from the ruin of their souls. So God breaks up a man's home and wrecks his hopes and flings him on the ash-heap of misery, in a merciful design to urge him to repentance and so to save the man himself. 3. *God is more concerned with the goodness than with the pleasure of his creature.* He certainly does not show the mild benevolence that characterizes some sanguine philanthropists. A safe house and abundance of bread are not the greatest things to be preserved, because pleasure and comfort are not the first requisites of the soul. Pain and loss may be blessings if they lead to purity and obedience. It is well for this life's pleasure to be ruined if thereby the soul is saved for life eternal.

Ver. 19.—*A cry to God in the night watches.* A fearful picture! Jerusalem is besieged. Famine is becoming fatal. Young children are seen fainting for hunger at the top of every street. The hearts of their parents are rent with anguish, as the little ones beg piteously of their mothers for food and drink (ver. 12), and none can be had, so that they swoon for very weakness. Suddenly a new turn is taken. The citizens have sunk down in sullen despair. Night has come like a cloak to cover the scenes of misery and death. Then a voice rings through the darkness, " Arise, cry out." This voice bids all hearers pour out their hearts in prayer to God.

I. THE CRY IS TO GOD. Hitherto we have had nothing but doleful lamentations. The language has been that of hopeless grief and bitter regret. No relief has been found or even sought. But there is one refuge in the direst trouble, and now that refuge is remembered. When we can do nothing else we can cry to God, for he is near though hidden from view, and merciful though striking in wrath, and able to save though no way of escape seems possible. It needs some rousing of the soul thus to seek God. We must " Arise." Spiritual lethargy is the worst consequence of sorrow. Let us beware lest our troubles paralyze our prayers. Prayer implies spiritual wakefulness.

II. THE CRY IS IN THE NIGHT. 1. *The time when trouble seems most hopeless.* It is in the night that the mourner weeps his most bitter tears. 2. *The time of reflection.* In lonely night watches the troubled soul has time for thought, and thought is then pain. 3. *The time of earthly darkness.* Then, perhaps, the spirit may feel most closely the nearness of the Father of spirits. The cry is to be in the beginning of the watches— either at the first watch or at the opening of each of the three watches. Let prayer come first. Let us not waste time in lamenting before we seek relief from God.

III. THE CRY IS HEARTFELT AND CONFIDENTIAL. " Pour out thine heart like water before the face of the Lord." 1. It comes from the *heart.* All real prayer must be the outcome of true and deep feelings. 2. It is a *full and free confidence in God.* The heart is poured out like water. This is in itself a relief. God expects our complete confidence and will hear prayer only when we give it to him. 3. It is no more than *the pouring out of the heart before God.* There is no definite request. Perhaps it is difficult to know how to ask for relief. Perhaps the grief is too overwhelming for any such thoughts of aid to be entertained. But it is enough that the whole trouble is poured out before God and left with him. Prayer is too often a dictating to God. It should be more of a simple confidence in God. It would be better if there were more confession and confidence, and less exact petition and definition of what God is to do in order to please us. We are to pour out our hearts and leave all with him. Then he will do the best for us. 4. *In deep trouble heartfelt prayer is wrung out of the sufferer.* Then he must be real. Sorrow melts the stony heart which has held itself in proud reserve, and thus it pours out itself like water. We have the example of Christ, whose agony passed into prayer, to urge us to find the relief of confiding fully in God.

HOMILIES BY VARIOUS AUTHORS.

Ver. 1.—*The anger of the Lord.* Men have fallen into two opposite extremes of opinion and of feeling with regard to the anger of the Lord. There have been times when they have been wont to attribute to the Eternal the passions of imperfect men, when they have represented the holy God as moved by the storms of indignation, as subject to the impulses of caprice and the instigations of cruelty. But in our own days the tendency is the contrary to this; men picture God as all amiability and forbearance, as regarding the sinful and guilty with indifference, or at all events without any emotion of displeasure. Scripture warrants neither of these extremes.

I. THERE ARE OCCASIONS WHEN GOD IS ANGRY WITH EVEN THE OBJECTS OF HIS SPECIAL FAVOUR. Jerusalem was the "daughter of Zion;" the temple was "the beauty of Israel;" the ark was God's "footstool." But as even human love is not necessarily or justly blind to the faults of those beloved, so the Lord is displeased with those whom he has endowed with peculiar privileges and blessings, when they are unmindful of his mercies and disobedient to his laws. "As many as I love," says the Divine Head of the Church, "I rebuke and chasten."

I. FROM THE HEARTS OF THE DISOBEDIENT GOD HIDES HIMSELF AS IN A CLOUD. When the sun is concealed behind a cloud, nature is chill, dull, and gloomy. The Lord is the Sun in whose light his people find joy and peace; when he hides his face they are troubled, for no longer is it the case that "they look unto him and are lightened." The heart and conscience of those who have offended God are overcast with spiritual gloom and unhappiness. So Israel found it; and there are none who have known the blessedness of God's fellowship and favour who can bear without distress the withdrawal of the heavenly light.

III. UPON THE HEADS OF THE REBELLIOUS GOD HURLS THE BOLT OF HIS DISPLEASURE. The tempest long lowered over the doomed city; at last it broke in fury, and Jerusalem became a prey to the spoiler and was cast down to the ground. The prophet clearly saw, what in an age of ease and luxury men are prone to forget, that there is a righteous Ruler from whose authority and retributive power no state and no soul can escape. "God is angry with the wicked every day." Yet in the midst of wrath he remembers mercy, and the penalties he inflicts answer their purpose if they lead to submission and to sincere repentance.—T.

Vers. 6, 7.—*Retribution in Church and state.* There are occasions when it is well to ponder seriously the calamities which befall a nation, to lay them to heart, to inquire into their causes, and to seek earnestly and prayerfully the way of deliverance, the means of remedy. "They that lack time to mourn lack time to mend."

I. IT IS WELL TO LOOK THROUGH NATIONAL DISASTERS TO THE PROVIDENTIAL RULE WHICH ALONE FULLY EXPLAINS THEM. The ruin which overtook Jerusalem and Judah was wrought by the armies of the Chaldeans. But the inspired prophet saw in the Assyrian hosts the ministers of Divine justice. The sufferings of the Jews were not accidental; they were a chastening, a discipline, appointed by the Lord of hosts, the King of kings. The Eternal had a controversy with his people. They had not listened to his Word, and therefore he spoke to them in thunder.

II. THE POLITICAL AND ECCLESIASTICAL AUTHORITIES OF A NATION ARE ALIKE RESPONSIBLE FOR NATIONAL SINS. The kings and chiefs had sought their own honour and ease and prosperity. The priests and prophets had discharged their offices in a manner perfunctory and formal. Under their natural and appointed leaders the nation had erred, had lapsed into idolatry, into sensuality, into practical unbelief. Rulers had not ruled in equity; teachers had not taught with faithfulness and fearlessness. Like king, like subjects; like priest, like people. All were to blame, but those were most culpable whose responsibility was greatest.

III. CHURCH AND STATE ALIKE ENDURE THE PENALTIES OF TRANSGRESSION AND DISOBEDIENCE. 1. The picture of desolation, as regards the religious life of the people, is a very dark and dreary picture. The religious celebrations and festivals fall into neglect; the very sabbath is all but forgotten; the sacrifices cease to be offered upon the altar; the sanctuary is no longer the scene of sacred solemnities; the priests are despised. 2. The case is equally distressing as regards the political situation. The walls of the palaces are either broken down, or, instead of housing the princes of the land, afford quarters to the troops of the enemy. The royal family are consigned to humiliation and to scorn. And the temple and the city resound no longer with the praises of Jehovah, but with the brutal shouts of the Chaldean soldiery.—T.

Ver. 9.—*Law and prophecy suspended.* Judah was professedly and actually a theocracy. The form of government was a monarchy, but the true Ruler was Jehovah. Spiritual disobedience and rebellion were Judah's offences; and it was the natural outcome of perseverance in these that the Lord should withdraw his favour, and leave his people to eat of the bitter fruit of their own misguided planting. And it was one consequence of the Divine displeasure that the highest privileges Jehovah had bestowed, the most sacred and precious tokens of his presence, should be for a season withdrawn. It is the climax, as Jeremiah conceives it, of Judah's misfortunes, that " the Law is no more; her prophets also find no vision from the Lord."

I. THIS TEMPORARY PRIVATION WAS OF LOCAL AND NATIONAL PRIVILEGES. It was so far as the Law was Jewish, that it ceased to be observed in Jerusalem. When the city was in the possession of heathen troops, when the temple was in ruins, when the priesthood was in disgrace, there was no possibility of observing the ordinances which the Law prescribed. The sacrifices and festivals came to an end. There were none to observe them and none to minister. And it was so far as the prophet was a functionary of the time and place, that he ceased to utter the mind of the Eternal. There were prophets of the Captivity; but Jerusalem, the true home of this noble class of religious teachers, knew their voice no more. For them was no vision which they might see in the ecstasy of inspiration, and depict in glowing colours before the imagination of the attentive multitude.

II. THE ETERNAL LAW OF RIGHTEOUSNESS, THE EVER-LIVING WITNESS OF SPIRITUAL PROPHECY, CAN NEVER CEASE. The words, the commandments and prohibitions, the outward ordinances, might pass away for a season of Divine displeasure, might be absorbed in the fuller revelation of the gospel. But the principles of the moral law, the obligations of unchanging righteousness, can never cease; for they are the expression of the mind and will of him whose kingdom is an everlasting kingdom. The vision may no longer be granted to the seer of Jerusalem; the city may stone her prophets or the Lord himself remove them. But every purified eye shall through all time behold God's glory, and the ear that is open to truth and love shall not cease to recognize the still, small voice of Heaven.—T.

Ver. 13.—*Commiseration.* The spirit of the prophet deserves our warm admiration. Jerusalem, its king and its citizens, had treated him with injustice and indignities. But in the day when his predictions were fulfilled and the city was overwhelmed by disaster and humiliation, so far from boasting over her, Jeremiah regarded her state with profoundest pity. Observe in this verse—

I. THE AFFECTIONATE AND ADMIRING LANGUAGE BY WHICH THE PROPHET DESIGNATES THE AFFLICTED CITY. Not a word of insult or of contempt, but, on the contrary, language evincing the deepest, the fondest interest. The population that had so despised his prophecy and had treated him so ill is here personified in language apparently more appropriate to times of prosperity. Jeremiah bewails the state of the daughter of Jerusalem, the virgin daughter of Zion.

II. THE TENDER COMMISERATION OF THE PROPHET WITH THE CITY'S WOES. 1. He pronounces the sorrows of Jerusalem *unequalled.* It is a common mode of expressing sympathy to assure the afflicted that others have the same griefs and trials to endure. No such consolation is offered here; the prophet looks around in vain for a case so distressing. The breach is "great like the sea." This is either a figure drawn from the vastness of the ocean, with which the great woe of Judah is compared; or it depicts the enemy as rushing in upon Jerusalem, as the sea in its fury makes a breach in the wall of a low-lying territory, and, sweeping the defences away by irresistible force, creates a desolation, so that a waste of waters is beheld where villages and fruitful fields once smiled in peace and plenty. 2. He pronounces the sorrows of Jerusalem *irremediable*. A mortal wound has been inflicted, which no leechcraft can heal. If Jerusalem is again to flourish it must be by a revival from the dead. For nothing now can save her.

APPLICATION. 1. The captive city is a picture of the desolation and misery to which (sooner or later) sin will surely bring all those who submit themselves to it. 2. The commiseration shown by the prophet is an example of the state of mind with which the pious should contemplate the ravages of sin and the wretchedness of sinful men. 3. The gospel forbids despondency over even the most utter debasement and humiliation of man. "There is balm in Gilead ; there is a Physician there."—T.

Ver. 15.—*The glory and the shame of Jerusalem.* Contrast with misery escaped heightens the joy of the rescued and the happy ; and, on the other hand, contrast with bygone prosperity adds to the wretchedness of those who are fallen from high estate.

I. THE BEAUTY AND RENOWN OF JERUSALEM IN ITS PROSPERITY. Into these many elements entered. 1. Its *situation* was superb. Nature pointed out the heights of Zion for a metropolis. Especially when beheld from the brow of Olivet the city impresses every traveller with admiration. 2. Its *history* and memorable associations. Won by the valour of David, adorned by the magnificence of Solomon, the home of heroes and of saints, this city possessed a fascination with which few cities of the earth could compare. 3. Its *sacred edifice* ranked alone, far above all the temples of the ancient world. Not that its architecture was commanding or beautiful in the highest degree ; but that its erection, its dedication, the presence of the Eternal, all lent an interest and a sacredness to the peerless building. 4. Its *sacrifices* and *festivals*, which were attended by hundreds of thousands of worshippers, were altogether unique.

II. THE DISGRACE OF JERUSALEM. This appears : 1. From its ruinous and almost uninhabitable condition. 2. From the slaughter or dispersion of its citizens. 3. From its degradation from its proud position as the metropolis of a nation. 4. From the hatred, scorn, and insults of its triumphant enemies.

APPLICATION. There is a day of visitation which it behoves every child of privilege and mercy to use aright. To neglect that day is surely to entail a bitter overtaking by the night of calamity and destruction.—T.

Vers. 18, 19.—*The entreaty of anguish.* This surely is one of those passages which justify the title of this book ; these utterances are "lamentations" indeed ; never did human sorrow make of language anything more resembling a wail than this.

I. THE SOULS FROM WHICH TEARFUL ENTREATIES ARISE. The true language of passion —this utterance is lacking in coherence. The heart of the people cries aloud ; the very walls of the city are invoked in their desolation to call upon the Lord. Clearly the distress is that of the inhabitants of the wretched city, of those survivors whose fate is sadder than that of those who fell by the sword.

II. THE CIRCUMSTANCES THAT OCCASION THE ENTREATY. 1. Personal want, suffering, and distress. 2. The spectacle of the woes of others, especially of children. Literature has no more agonizing picture than this of the young children fainting and dying of hunger in every street.

III. THE BEING TO WHOM THE SUPPLICATIONS OF THE ANGUISHED ARE ADDRESSED. In such circumstances vain is the help of man. Upon whom shall Jerusalem call but upon the Lord, the King of the city, the great Patron and Protector of the chosen nation, who has forsaken even his own people because they have forgotten him, and in whose favour alone is hope of salvation ?

IV. THE CHARACTER OF THE ENTREATY URGED. 1. It is *sorrowful,* accompanied by many tears, flowing like a river and pausing not. 2. *Earnest,* as appears from the description—heart, eyes, and hands all uniting in the appeal with imploring prayer. 3. *Continuous ;* for not only by day, but through the night watches, supplications ascend unto heaven, invoking compassion and aid.—T.

Ver. 20.—*Consideration besought.* How truly human is this language ! How real was the eternal Lord to him who could shape his entreaty thus! As if to urge a plea for pity, the prophet implores him who has been offended by the nation's sins, who has suffered the nation's misery and apparent ruin, to consider; to remember who Judah is, and to have mercy.

I. THE CIRCUMSTANCES THAT CALL FOR CONSIDERATION. 1. Famine and the inhuman conduct to which famine sometimes leads. 2. Death by the sword. 3. The privation of those religious offices which are the centre and inspiration of the nation's life. 4. The common suffering of all classes; prophet and priest, children and old men, virgins and youth, are alike overtaken by want, by wounds, by death.

II. THE GROUNDS UPON WHICH CONSIDERATION IS BEGGED FOR. 1. The main appeal is to Divine pity and benevolence. 2. The former mercies shown to Judah seem to be brought implicitly forward in this language. Israel has been chosen by God himself, favoured with privileges, delivered, protected, and blessed in a thousand ways. Will God cast off those in whom he has taken an interest so deep, for whom he has done so great things?

III. THE HOPE WITH WHICH CONSIDERATION IS ASKED. Hitherto the regard of God in recent events has been a regard of displeasure and of censure. But if the attitude of the stricken be no longer one of defiance, but of submission, it may be that the Lord will turn him again, will be favourable unto his afflicted people, will restore them to former prosperity, enriched with the precious lessons of their adverse experience.—T.

Ver. 1.—*The manifestation of Jehovah's wrath with Israel.* It will be noticed that the words "anger" and "wrath" occur again and again in these first three verses. Figure is heaped upon figure in order to bring out the practical effects of this anger. We need not pursue these figures into detail; each of them speaks for itself. Let us rather notice—

I. HOW THEY INDICATE THE EXTENT OF PAST FAVOUR. The very fact that, in order to show the character of Jehovah's anger, such strong figurative expressions are possible proves that in former days there had been many indications of his complacency with Israel. Not that Israel had been really better in the past than in the present, but she had to be dealt with in a long-suffering way, and the long-suffering of Jehovah is a quality which shows itself by abundance of most positive favours. God looked upon Israel according to the bright possibilities of excellence that lie in human nature. Israel did sink very low, but that was because she had the capacity of rising very high. Thus God heaped upon Israel favours, as if to show that he would not entertain any doubt as to her willingness to respond to his requests. And so the black anger-cloud resting on Israel's present looks blacker still when contrasted with the Divine brightness and clearness of Israel's past. God has cast down the beauty of Israel, and that casting is as from heaven to earth. That which God has not remembered in the day of his anger is something which he had reckoned useful to himself, even as the footstool is useful to the king seated on his throne. Thus the extent of present anger measures the extent of past favour.

II. HOW THESE FIGURES INDICATE THE REALITY OF JEHOVAH'S WRATH. The very heaping up of these strong figures should make us feel very deeply that God's wrath is not itself a figure. God's anger is not to be reduced to a mere anthropomorphism. We are misled in this matter, because human anger is never seen without selfish and degrading elements. An angry man, in all his excitement and violence, is a pitiable sight, but nevertheless it is possible for a man to be angry and sin not. The man who cannot understand the reality of God's anger will never comprehend the ideal of humanity. The sensitive musician would laugh to scorn any one who told him that, while he was pleased with harmony, he should not be disturbed by discord. Again and again Jesus was really and righteously angry, showing in this, not least, how he was partaker of the Divine nature. When we are in wrong ways and God is consequently against us, his opposition and displeasure must be shown in ways that cannot be mistaken.—Y.

Ver. 5.—*Jehovah reckoned as an enemy.* I. HOW FAR WAS THERE REALITY UNDER THIS APPEARANCE OF ENMITY? God might look like an enemy, but it did not therefore follow that he was one. But even if Jehovah behaved himself like an enemy, it must also be asked whether there was not a necessity that he should do so. If Israel had to say, "Jehovah acts as an enemy towards us," Jehovah had to say, "My people act as an enemy towards me." These people had now for a long time been travelling in the wrong way, and it was in the very nature of things that the more they advanced the more opposition should multiply and become intensified. God not only appeared to be an enemy, but in certain respects he really was an enemy. He hated the evil that had risen to such a height among those whom he had taken for his own. Our love for evil is ever the measure of his hate of it; and the more determined we are to cling to it, the more his hostility will appear. God himself always keeps in the same path of law and righteousness and order. When we, according to our measure, follow in his footsteps, then real opposition there cannot be; but the moment we think fit to become a law to ourselves and do what is right in our own eyes, then inevitably he must oppose us.

II. THIS ENMITY WAS LARGELY IN APPEARANCE ONLY. When Israel said that Jehovah was as an enemy, they got their idea of enmity from the hostile proceedings of individuals and communities. But God cannot be the enemy of any man as men are enemies one to another. His motives are different and so are the results of all his opposition. One man forming hostile plans against another acts from malicious motives, or at all events from selfish ones. There is no basis of reason in what he does. He is not hostile to the lower in order that he may show himself friendly to the higher. Besides, we must not look merely at outward manifestations of enmity. There may be the deepest enmity and greatest power of inflicting injury where outwardly all looks harmless. Those who profess to be our friends and whom we reckon to be our friends may yet inflict worse injuries than all avowed enemies taken together. God is the true Friend of every man, however he may be thought at times to put on the appearance of an enemy.—Y.

Ver. 9.—*The prophetic office suspended.* There is something of a climax about this statement that the prophets find no vision from Jehovah. Jeremiah has already spoken of God destroying the outward resources and defences of Jerusalem. Next, he mentions the exile of the king and the chief men, and then, as if to hint that it was a still greater calamity, he tells us how the prophet had no longer anything to see or to say. He did well to magnify his own office; for no office could be more important than that of the man whom God chose to communicate needed messages to his fellow-men. Observe—

I. THE NATURE OF THE PROPHETIC OFFICE AS HERE INDICATED. A prophet was one who had a vision from the Lord. He was no prophet unless he could truly preface his address with "Thus saith the Lord." And must there not be something of this kind still? With respect to Divine things, what can any of us say that shall have power and blessing in it unless as we speak of what God has made us see? The prophetic office has ceased, but who can doubt that there must be some permanent reality corresponding with it? and therefore we should ever be on the look out for men who have had visions from the Lord. All advances in the interpretation of Scripture truth must come by revelation from on high. Otherwise the most diligent searching ends in nothing but pedantry and verbosity.

II. NOTICE THE DEPRIVATION HERE SPOKEN OF. What does it mean? How is it to be looked upon as part of Jerusalem's punitive visitation? The reply to this is that the institution of prophecy was part of the honour which Jehovah had put upon his people. The people could say that God was constantly raising up amongst them those whom he chose for a medium of communication. However unwilling they might be to listen to the real prophets, and however they persecuted them, still the fact remained that men like Jeremiah were rising again and again. For all we can tell, those whose written prophecies remain may have been a most minute portion numerically of the total company of the prophets. Now, if all at once the prophetic voice ceased or came at long intervals and with few words, this must have been most significant to those who had power to notice. It meant that God had little or nothing to say to the people. That he had communications with every individual willing to put himself in a right attitude there can be no doubt. Prophets who received nothing to give as a message would at the same time receive all they needed for their own edification and comfort, and now there is an abiding vision for all. God's communications to us are not after the "sundry times and divers manners" mode referred to at the beginning of the Epistle to the Hebrews. The Spirit of God revealing the uplifted Christ makes every one of us a prophet to himself.—Y.

Ver. 10.—*The silence of the elders.* I. THEIR FORMER SPEECH. They are said to keep silence now; this, of course, suggests that silence had not been their former habit. Old men have a peculiar right to speak, are often expected to speak, and can always plead that years have given them experience and many opportunities of observation, and with respect to these particular elders here it is not difficult to imagine what the *topics* and the *manner* of their former speech might be. For instance, imagine younger men going to them and asking what their opinion was as to the predictions of Jeremiah. They would not all have the same opinion, but many, it is to be feared, would make very light of what he said. Nor is it likely that they spoke of him in a very considerate way. The elders of Israel were, according to a national custom, largely the teachers of history. It was their business to tell their sons and their son's sons the great things that had been done in the days of old. And we know how easy it is to remember only success and forget disaster. Jeremiah coming in with his denunciations and threatenings would exasperate the elders not least. The chances are that again and again they had given advice at the foundation of which lay their unbelief in Jeremiah. Besides this, they would be advisers in general, and in particular matters would often be right enough. Thus when they cast discredit on a prophet of Jehovah others would take up their words as words of authority and soberness.
II. THEIR PRESENT SILENCE. They neither speak of their own accord nor do they answer when addressed. They keep silence. It is the silence of grief, humiliation, wounded pride, and shame. The only thing they could say, if they did speak, would be to confess in the amplest manner their sins, their blunders, their egregious self-confidence. But in truth their very silence spoke as if with loudest voice. It was as if they said, "We abdicate any right we have had to advise and lead. We admit to the full our responsibility in having done so much to bring disaster on the people." Old age is not necessary to bring wisdom and insight into the problems of life. Jeremiah, who had gone out to prophesy when little better than a lad, was right, and old men with an egotistical and absorbed confidence in their own opinions were wrong. If we would avoid being stricken with a shameful silence in our old age, it must be by listening obediently in earlier years to far other voices than those which come from the promptings of the natural man.—Y.

Ver. 12.—*The suffering of the children.* It must be noticed how the mention of the children follows on the mention of the elders. There is suffering at each extreme of life, and hence we are to infer that there is suffering all between. The elders suffer in their way and the children and the sucklings suffer in theirs. The elders are bowed down with confusion, shame, and disappointment. The children know nothing of this, but they are tormented with the pangs of hunger; and what a pathetic touch is that which represents them as breathing out their little lives into the bosom of their mothers! The sins of the parents are being visited upon the children. It has often been represented as a monstrous iniquity that things should be put in such a light, but is it not an undeniable fact that the little ones suffer what they would not suffer if progenitors always did what was right? These children were not clamouring for dainties and luxuries. Corn and wine, the common food, the pleasant grape-juice, what they had been used to and what all at once they began to miss. What is here said is a strong admonition to us to consider how the innocent and unsuspecting may be affected by our unrighteousness. All our conduct *must* affect others, and it *may* affect those who cannot lift a hand to avert ill consequences. The sufferings of children and infants, the immense mortality among them,—these are things awful to contemplate; and yet nothing can be more certain than that the clearing away of prejudice and ignorance and hurtful habits founded on bare tradition would bring into child-life that abundance of joy which a loving Creator of human nature meant children to attain. But even with all the suffering there are compensations. These hunger-stricken children cried for bread, and getting none they poured out their lives into their mothers' bosoms; but they had no self-reproach. Remorse did not add another degree of agony to starvation. The suffering which touches the conscience is the worst, and the little ones escape it altogether.—Y.

Ver. 14.—*The share of the prophets in ruining Jerusalem.* I. WHAT THE PROPHET OUGHT TO BE. The prophet of those times was a man bound to say things having depth and substance in them. And though the prophet has ceased, so far as formal office is concerned, yet there are still Divine things to be seen, and, when seen, spoken about by those qualified to speak. There are the deep things of God to be penetrated and explored by those willing to receive the insight. The Holy Spirit of God, offered so abundantly through Christ, is a Spirit of prophecy to all who have it. They need no formal prophet, inasmuch as they have a word, living and piercing, to all who take a right relation towards it. God means us to be occupied with serious, substantial matters, so large and deep and fruitful that we shall never outgrow our interest in them. The heart of man in its meditating power was made for great themes. The heart can never be *filled* with mere trifles. That is good advice given to preachers of the gospel to speak most on the greatest themes, such as are set forth again and again in the Scriptures, and, whether these things be preached about or not, every individual Christian should think about them. For while we cannot secure the topics of preachers, the topics of our own thoughts depend upon ourselves. It is just those who concern themselves a great deal about dogmas who are also most interested in the details of life and conduct. II. WHAT THE PROPHET MAY SINK TO BE. These prophets felt bound to magnify their office and say something. They ought to have spoken the truth; but for this they lacked inclination and perhaps courage. The next best thing would have been to remain silent; but then where would the prophet-reputation have been? and, more serious question still with some, what would have become of the prophet-emoluments? Hence we have here the double iniquity that the false was spoken and the true concealed. The prophets could only get credit for their falsehoods by a careful concealment of the truth. They had, as it were, to paste on truth a conspicuous label, proclaiming far and wide, "This is a lie." This verse suggests how they had the common experience of one lie leading on to another. The true prophet said that the burden Israel had to bear and the exile into which it had to go arose from its iniquities. Whereas the false, or rather the unfaithful prophet, having set iniquity as the cause of trouble altogether on one side, could only go on inventing explanations which explained nothing. Ezek. xiii. is a chapter which may very profitably be read in connection with this verse. The great lesson is to search for truth no matter with what toil, and keep it no matter at what cost.—Y.

Ver. 22.—*The completeness of Jehovah's visitation.* I. THE COMPARISON BY WHICH THIS IS SET FORTH. "Thou hast called as in a solemn day." At certain periods there were vast commanded gatherings of the people to Jerusalem. They came from far and wide and from all parts of the compass, and so, as they converged upon Jerusalem, they might be justly said to encircle it. And encircling it, they did so with a definite purpose. They were as far as possible from being a mere promiscuous crowd, in which each one could come and go at his own sweet will. At the centre of the circle stood Jehovah, giving the commandment to each which brought them all together. And we may infer from the use of the comparison here that the commandment must have been generally complied with. It was, indeed, a commandment not very hard to obey, requiring as it did mere outwardness of obedience. People living in quiet country places would be glad of the reason for occasional visits to Jerusalem. Well would it have been if the people had tried to carry their obedience a little further! if, when the solemn assemblies had gathered together, there had been in them the right spirit! A gathering of bodies is not so hard, but a gathering of hearts in complete union and sympathy, perfectly responsive to the will of God, who shall secure that? II. THE ASSEMBLY OF TERRORS AT GOD'S COMMAND. God called together the people, and they came; but when they came, instead of attending to God's will, they pursued their own. But now God is represented as calling together all the agents that can inflict pain upon man and cause him terror; and they come with one consent, folding Israel round with an environment which cannot be escaped. There is no ultimate escape for the selfish, sinful man. He may get the evil day put off; he may find gate after gate opening, as he thinks, to let him away from trouble and pain; but in truth he is only going deeper and deeper into the corner where he will be completely shut up. God can surround us with providences and protections if we are willing to trust him. No other power can *surround* us with causes of terror. Our own hearts may imagine a menacing circle, but it only exists in imagination. If we seek the Lord he will hear us and deliver us from all our fears (Ps. xxxiv. 4). But no one can deliver us from God's just wrath with all who are unrighteous. That God who breaks the circle with which his enemies seek to enclose his friends, also makes a circle in which those enemies must themselves be effectually enclosed.—Y.

EXPOSITION.

CHAPTER III.

Vers. 1—21.—MONOLOGUE SPOKEN BY AN INDIVIDUAL BELIEVER WHOSE FATE IS BOUND UP WITH THAT OF THE NATION; OR PERHAPS BY THE NATION PERSONIFIED (see Introduction).

Ver. 1.—**Seen.** "To see" in Hebrew often means " to experience;" *e.g.* Jer. v. 12; Ps. xvi. 10; Eccles. viii. 16. **By the rod of his wrath.** The idea is, not that Babylon has humbled Israel as Jehovah's instrument, but that God himself has brought these troubles upon his people. "He hath led me, hath hedged me about," etc.

Ver. 3.—**Is he turned; he turneth**; rather, *he turneth again and again.*

Ver. 4.—**Made old**; more ¦literally, *worn away*, as a garment (comp. Isa. l. 9; li. 6). **Broken my bones.** So Job complains, " His wrath teareth and persecuteth me " (Job xvi. 9); and, a still closer parallel, Hezekiah, " As a lion, so will he break all my bones " (Isa. xxxviii. 13). Comp. Ps. li. 8, " The bones which thou hast broken."

Ver. 5.—**He hath builded against me, and compassed** me. A figure from the siege of a town. **Gall.** For the true meaning of the word, see on Jer. viii. 14. We need not trouble ourselves about it here, for the word is evidently used as a kind of " ideograph" for bitterness. **Travel**; literally, *weariness.*

Ver. 6.—This verse is verbally reproduced in Ps. cxliii. 3. **In dark places**; *i.e.* in Hades (comp. Ps. lxxxviii. 7). **As they that be dead of old.** A strange comparison; for what difference can it make whether the dead are men of the ancient or the modern world? The rendering, however, though perfectly admissible, is less suitable to the context than *as they that are for ever dead;* who have entered " the land from which there is no return " (an Assyrian title of Hades). Comp. " the everlasting house," *i.e.* the grave (Eccles. xii. 5), " the everlasting sleep" (Jer. li. 39, 57).

Vers. 7—9.—Three figures, interrupted by a literal statement of the ill success of prayer. A traveller who finds himself suddenly caged up by a high thorn hedge

(comp. Job iii. 23; Hos. ii. 6). **A prisoner** with a heavy chain. Again, a traveller suddenly shut up by solid stone walls (comp. Hos. ii. 8).

Ver. 7.—**My chain**; literally, *my brass* (comp. Judg. xvi. 21; 2 Kings xxv. 7).

Ver. 8.—**He shutteth out my prayer.** There is a kind of barrier through which these futile prayers cannot penetrate (comp. on ver. 44).

Ver. 9.—**Inclosed**; or, *walled ¯up ;* the participle of this verb is rendered " masons " in the Authorized Version of 2 Kings xii. 12. **Made my paths crooked**; *i.e.* hath compelled me to walk in byways (comp. margin of the Authorized Version, Judg. v. 6). But this hardly seems appropriate to the context. The *semitas meas subvertit* of the Vulgate is preferable. Render, therefore, *turned my path upside down* (comp. Isa. xxiv. 1). An analogous expression in Job xxx. 13 is rendered in the Authorized Version, " they mar my path." Thenius thinks that the destruction of a raised causeway is the figure intended; but the word is quite correctly rendered " paths;" see the note of Delitzsch on Isa. lix. 8.

Ver. 10.—**Was**; rather, *is.* **As a bear . . . as a lion.** The comparison of the enemy to a lion is not uncommon; see *e.g.* Jer. iv. 7; v. 6 (see note); xlix. 19; l. 44; Ps. x. 9; xvii. 12; Job x. 16. The bear is only once mentioned in such a context (Hos. xiii. 8). The two latter passages may possibly have been in the mind of the writer, as Jehovah is in both the subject of the comparison.

Ver. 11.—**Hath turned aside my ways;** *i.e.* hath caused me to go astray. Comp. Ps. cxlvi. 9, " The way of the ungodly he maketh crooked," *i.e.* he leadeth them to destruction. **Made me desolate**; or, *made me stunned* (" astonied," Ezra ix. 3 in our Bible). So ch. i. 13, 16.

Ver. 12.—**Set me as a mark.** Precisely as Job complains of Jehovah, " He hath set me up for his mark " (Job xvi. 13).

Ver. 13.—This verse seems strangely short—it consists of only four words in the Hebrew. Probably something like " his weapons," or "the weapons of death" (Ps. vii. 13), has fallen out. Restore them, and the verse becomes a two-membered one, like its companions. **To enter into my reins.** So Job (xvi. 12), "He cleaveth my reins asunder." "Reins," equivalent to "inward parts," like "heart," with which it is often combined; *e.g.* Jer. xi. 20; xvii. 10; xx. 12.

Ver. 14.—**A derision to all my people.** If the text-reading is correct, these are the words of Jeremiah (or one like Jeremiah), describing the ill return accorded to his friendly admonitions. But the Massora mention Ps. cxliv. 2; 2 Sam. xxii. 44; ch. iii. 14, as passages in which "my people" is used, whereas we should expect "peoples." The Syriac Version of our passage actually translates "to all peoples," and the prefixed "all" certainly favours the plural, and so, in a far higher degree, does the view we have been led to adopt of the speaker of this Lamentation (see Introduction). The correction ('*ammim* for '*ammi*) has been received by Archbishop Secker, by Ewald, and by J. Olshausen. **Their song.** A reminiscence of Job xxx. 9.

Ver. 15.—**With bitterness**; literally, *with bitternesses;* i.e. bitter troubles. A reminiscence of Job ix. 18. **With wormwood;** *i.e.* with a drink of wormwood (comp. Jer. ix. 15; xxiii. 15). We are slightly reminded of Ps. lxix. 21, "They gave me gall for my meat."

Ver. 16.—**He hath also broken my teeth with gravel stones;** *i.e.* he hath (unnatural as it may seem in Israel's Father) given me stones instead of bread (comp. Matt. vii. 9). The Jewish rabbi commonly called Rashi thinks that a historical fact is preserved in these words, and that the Jewish exiles were really obliged to eat bread mixed with grit, because they had to bake in pits dug in the ground. So too many later commentators, *e.g.* Grotius, who compares a passage of Seneca ('De Benefic.,' ii. 7), "Beneficium superbè datum simile est pani lapidoso." **He hath covered me with ashes;** rather, *he hath pressed me down into ashes.* A figurative expression for great humiliation. So in the Talmud the Jewish nation is described as "pressed down into ashes" ('Bereshith Rabba,' 75).

Ver. 17.—**Thou hast removed my soul;** rather, *thou hast rejected my soul.* The words look like a quotation from Ps. lxxxviii. 14 (Hebrew, 15), where they are undoubtedly an address to Jehovah. But there is another rendering, which grammatically is equally tenable, and which avoids the strangely abrupt address to God, viz. *My soul is rejected (from peace).*

Vers. 19—21.—These verses prepare the way for a brief interval of calmness and resignation.

Ver. 19. — **Remembering;** rather, *remember.* It is the language of prayer.

Ver. 20.—**My soul,** etc. This rendering is difficult. In the next verse we read, "This I recall to my mind, therefore I have hope," which seems inconsistent with ver. 20 as given in the Authorized Version. An equally grammatical and still more obvious translation is, *Thou (O God!) wilt surely remember, for my soul is bowed down within me.* The latter part of the line is a reminiscence of Ps. xlii. 5, at least, if the text be correct, for the closing words do not cohere well with the opening ones. The Peshito (Syriac) has, "Remember, and revive [literally, 'cause to return'] my soul within me," which involves a slightly different reading of one word. But more tempting than any other view of the meaning is that of Bickell, though it involves a correction and an insertion, "My soul remembereth well and meditateth on thy faithfulness."

Ver. 21.—**This I recall to my mind,** etc.; viz. that thou wilt remember me, or, thy faithfulness (ver. 20). Here again there appears to be a reminiscence of a passage in Ps. xlii. (ver. 4). Others suppose that "this" refers to the following verses; but in this case a new section would begin in the middle of a triad (the triad of verses beginning with *zayin*), which is certainly improbable.

Vers. 22—36.—RESIGNATION AND HOPEFULNESS.

Ver. 22.—**It is of the Lord's mercies,** etc.; literally, *The Lord's mercies that we are not consumed.* But the "we" is difficult, especially considering that in ver. 23 (which is clearly parallel) the subject of the sentence is, not "we," but "the Lord's mercies." Hence it is probable that the reading of the Targum and the Peshito (adopted by Thenius, Ewald, and Bickell) is correct, "The Lord's mercies, verily they cease not" (*tammū* for *tamnū*).

Ver. 24.—**The Lord is my Portion.** A reminiscence of Ps. xvi. 5 (comp. Ps. lxxiii. 26; cxix. 57; cxlii. 5).

Ver. 26.—**Should both hope and quietly wait;** rather, *should wait in silence.* "Silence" is an expression of the psalmist's (the Lamentations are psalms) for resignation to the will of God; comp. Ps. lxii. 1 (Hebrew, 2); lxv. 1 (Hebrew, 2), and see Authorized Version, margin. The thought of the verse is that of Ps. xxxvii. 7.

Ver. 27.—**In his youth.** The thought of this verse reminds us of Ps. cxix. 71. Youth is mentioned as the time when it is easier to adapt one's self to circumstances, and when discipline is most readily accepted. The words do not prove that the writer is young, any more than vers. 9 and

100 of Ps. cxix. prove that the psalmist was an aged man (against this view, see vers. 84—87). There is no occasion, therefore, for the textual alteration (for as such I cannot help regarding it), "from his youth," found in some Hebrew manuscripts in Theodotion, in the Aldine edition of the Septuagint, and in the Vulgate. The reading was probably dictated by the unconscious endeavour to prop up the theory of Jeremiah's authorship. The scribes and translators remembered, inopportunely, that the trials of Jeremiah began in early manhood.

Vers. 28—30.—**He sitteth alone**, etc.; rather, *Let him sit alone . . . let him keep silence* (ver. 28) . . . *let him put* (ver. 29) . . . *let him give . . . let him be filled* (ver. 30). The connection is—since it is good for a man to be afflicted, let him sit still, when trouble is sent, and resign himself to bear it.

Ver. 28.—**Because he hath borne** it; rather, *when he* (viz. God) *hath laid it*.

Ver. 29.—**He putteth his mouth**, etc. An Oriental manner of expressing submission (comp. Micah vii. 17; Ps. lxxii. 9).

Ver. 30.—**He giveth** his **cheek**. Notice the striking affinity (which is hardly accidental) to Job xvi. 10; Isa. l. 6. The ideal of the righteous man, according to these kindred books, contains, as one of its most prominent features, the patient endurance of affliction; and so too does the same ideal, received and amplified by the greatest "Servant of Jehovah" (Matt. v. 39).

Vers. 31—33.—Two grounds of comfort: (1) the trouble is only for a time, and God will have compassion again (vers. 31, 32); and (2) God does not afflict in a malicious spirit (ver. 33).

Ver. 33.—**Willingly**; literally, *from his heart*.

Vers. 34—39.—These two triads form a transition to the renewed complaints and appeals for help in the following verses. The first triad is probably an amplification of the statement that "the Lord doth not afflict willingly." This being the case, the injustice which darkens human life cannot be approved by him.

Ver. 34.—**To crush**, etc. With manifest reference to the cruelties of the Babylonian conquerors of the Jews.

Ver. 35.—**Before the face of the Most High**. In ancient phraseology, to bring a case before the judges was to bring it "unto the deity" (*'el hā-'elōhīm*), Exod. xxi. 6; comp. xxii. 8; or (as the Septuagint in one passage paraphrases it, "unto God's judgment-place," *i.e.* to a sacred spot where judges held their session.

Ver. 36.—**Approveth not**. The sense is an excellent one, but it is very doubtful whether it can be obtained without altering one of the letters of the word in the text

(reading *rāçāh* for *rā'āh*). The text-reading is, "the Lord seeth not." This may be explained either as "the Lord regardeth not (such things)," or as a question, "Doth not the Lord regard (this)?"

Vers. 37—54.—EXHORTATION TO REPENTANCE; RENDERED, LAMENTATION.

Vers. 37, 38.—True, God does not desire our misfortunes. But equally true is it that they do not happen without his express permission (comp. Isa. xlv. 7; Amos iii. 6).

Ver. 37.—That **saith, and it cometh to pass** (comp. Ps. xxxiii. 9; Gen. i. 3, etc.).

Ver. 39.—**Wherefore doth a living man complain**, etc.? The God of whom the poet speaks is the Searcher of hearts. Why, then, should a man complain when he knows that he deserves his punishment? The close of the verse should run, (*Let*) a man (rather *sigh*) over his sins.

Vers. 40—51.—Confession of sin, followed by sighs and groans.

Ver. 40.—**Let us search**. Our troubles being caused by our sins, let us search them out and correct them.

Ver. 41.—**Our heart with our hands**. It is to be sincere prayer; "spreading out the hands" is not enough by itself (Isa. i. 25).

Ver. 42.—**We . . . thou**. The pronouns are expressed in the Hebrew, and are meant to be spoken with emphasis.

Ver. 43.—**Thou hast covered with anger**. The clause seems imperfect; perhaps "thyself" has fallen out of the text (see next verse).

Ver. 44.—**That our prayer should not pass through**. So Isa. lviii. 4, "Ye do not so fast at this time as to make your voice to be heard on high;" Ps. lv. 1, "Hide not thyself from my supplication."

Vers. 46—48.—Here occurs a break in the alphabetic order, as these three verses begin, not, as they should, with *ayin*, but with *pe* (see Introduction).

Ver. 46.—This verse is almost a verbal repetition of the first line of ch. ii. 16.

Ver. 47.—**Fear and a snare**. An alliteration in the Hebrew, borrowed from Jer. xlviii. 43 (comp. Isa. xxiv. 17).

Ver. 48.—**Runneth down**, etc. (comp. ch. i. 16).

Ver. 49.—**Trickleth down**; rather, *poureth down*. **Ceaseth** not; literally, *is not silent* (comp. Jer. xiv. 17).

Ver. 51.—**Affecteth mine heart**; rather, *paineth me;* literally, *paineth my soul*, the soul being mentioned as the centre of the feelings and emotions. **The daughters of my city**. The sad fate of the virgins of Jerusalem oppressed the spirit of the writer (comp. ch. i. 4, 18; ii. 10, 21).

Vers. 52—66.—THE SPEAKER'S SUFFERINGS; AN EARNESTLY BELIEVING PRAYER FOR DELIVERANCE. He speaks as a representative of the nation; if we should not rather say that the nation itself, personified, is the speaker. In the first triad some have supposed a reference to the persecution suffered by Jeremiah at the hands of his countrymen. The "dungeon," or rather "pit," will in this case be the "dungeon" ("pit") mentioned in Jer. xxxviii. 6. But a "pit" is a figure in the psalms for destruction (Ps. xl. 2; lxix. 15), and there is nothing recorded in Jeremiah as to the "princes" having cast stones at Jeremiah, or rolled a stone on to the top of the "pit." Besides, the "pit" into which the prophet was cast had "no water, but mire."

Ver. 52. — **Mine enemies . . . without cause.** These words ought to be connected, as in the Hebrew.

Ver. 54.—**I am cut off.** Some words have to be supplied, and Ps. xxxi. 22 suggests which these are :—" I am cut off from before thine eyes," *i.e.* from the region on which the eyes of God rest.

Ver. 55.—**I called.** Bunsen renders, "Then I called." But there is no connection indicated in the Hebrew between this and the preceding triad. **Out of the low dungeon;** literally, *out of the pit of the lower parts (of the earth)*—a phrase borrowed from Ps. lxxxviii. 6 (Hebrew, 7). Sheol, or Hades, is signified.

Ver. 56.—**At my breathing**; rather, *at my sighing;* literally, *at my relieving myself.*

Ver. 57.—**Thou drewest near,** etc. The sacred poet reminds Jehovah of his former gracious interpositions.

Ver. 58.—**Thou hast pleaded,** etc. The reference is still to a former state of things which came to an end. It would make this plainer if we were to alter the rendering, *Thou didst plead . . . thou didst redeem.* The speaker likens his case to that of a poor man who is opposed at law by a rich oppressor, and who, for want of an advocate, will, to all appearance, become his victim. Suddenly Jehovah appeared and supplied this want. Such are God's "wonders of old time."

Ver. 59.—**Thou hast seen my wrong.** Here the speaker returns to the present. This is clear from the following words : **Judge thou my cause.**

Ver. 62.—**The lips** stand here for "the fruit of the lips;" and the verb which governs the nouns is "thou hast heard," in the preceding verse.

Ver. 63.—**Their sitting down, and their rising up.** Elsewhere the phrase is a comprehensive expression for all a man's occupations (comp. Ps. cxxxix. 2; Isa. xxxvii. 28). **I am their music**; rather, *their song;* i.e. the subject of their taunting songs, p. in the parallel passage, Job xxx. 9; comas Ps. lxix. 12 (Hebrew, 13).

Ver. 64.—**Render unto them,** etc. The sacred poet is familiar with the psalms; here we have a condensation of Ps. xxviii. 4. The tone of vers. 64—66 reminds us of passages in the Book of Jeremiah (see Jer. xviii. 23; xx. 12).

Ver. 65.—**Sorrow of heart**; rather, *a covering of the heart;* spiritual blindness, like the "veil upon the heart" in 2 Cor. iii. 15. **Thy curse unto them.** This should rather form a separate interjectional clause, "Thy curse upon them!"

HOMILETICS.

Ver. 1.—" *The man that has seen affliction.*" In the first and second chapters of Lamentations the desolation of the city of Jerusalem is described and deplored. The third chapter brings the picture to a focus by giving us the plaint of a single individual —either one typical or exceptionally distressed citizen, or the city regarded imaginatively as an afflicted man. Our sympathy is most moved by individual appeals. We are horrified by disasters that affect thousands ; but we are more touched by the details of the suffering of one person. Nearness is requisite for sympathy, a nearness of view, at least, that enables us to see the humanity of the sufferer. Statistics of public distress do not so affect us as the sight of a few severe cases that are brought under our own eyes. We cannot pity "the masses;" we pity this man and that woman. Therefore we should bring ourselves into contact with the sufferers of our own neighbourhood, and not be content to follow only such promptings of benevolence as may arise from a distant survey of large fields of distress afforded by the formal reports of charitable institutions.

I. THE MAN THAT HAS SEEN AFFLICTION HAS CLAIMS UPON THE CONSIDERATION OF HIS FELLOW-MEN. The sufferer of Jerusalem arrests our attention. He has a right to do so. Great distress is by itself sufficiently important to demand our notice. Moral merit will add to the force of the appeal of suffering. But even where the merit is lacking the suffering itself still has claims upon us. We must not roughly shake off the obligations of sympathy by the observation that the client is ill deserving. If the ill desert mean that the complaint is false and the distress a sham, of course it is to be visited with contempt or punishment. But suppose, with evil character, there is also real distress. In such a case we should take the distress into consideration. We may not help in the same way in which we would assist a deserving case, for perhaps similar assistance would be wasted, or abused, or in some way harmful. But we must remember that charity is not limited by merit. Like the mercy of God to sinners, it should flow out to those whose only claim upon it is their want and woe. Great sorrow does not atone for sin, especially where it leaves the sufferer impenitent. But it does call for pity. Whether she were innocent or guilty, we feel deep compassion for such a victim of torture as Beatrice Cenci, and even imagine a certain sacredness about her solitary pre-eminence of distress that hushes all harsh judgments.

II. The man that has seen affliction is in danger of regarding his sufferings as without parallel. He feels his own trouble more acutely than that of his neighbour. Thus he comes to regard himself as exceptionally distressed. Pain is a good school in which to learn sympathy with others in similar trouble. But the sympathy is commonly attained after one's own agony is lulled. It comes with the recollection of it called up by the sight of the present distress outside us. But while pain is being endured, especially if it is very acute, it tends to make the sufferer selfish for the time being. At least it wraps him up in himself and makes him magnify the severity of his own lot in comparison with that of other people. Let us be on our guard against this illusion, and the unkindness to others and murmuring and despair of ourselves which may come out of it.

III. The man that has seen affliction has gained knowledge of some of the deepest facts of life. We do not know life till we have felt pain. Buddha, while kept from all suffering in his palace, was ignorant of the world and of man. Suffering opens the eyes to the facts of life and breaks up many idle dreams. Mere show and pretence are then felt to be vain and mocking. True friends are discriminated from idle acquaintances. The value of inward things is discovered.

IV. The man that has seen affliction has experienced a valuable discipline. This is a useful "means of grace." It may be sent to punish sin and check the thoughtless sinner on his road to ruin. Or it may be to remind the careless Christian of his declension. Or it may be like the pruning of the fruitful branch, a stimulus to make the fruitful Christian more fruitful. Various ends may be served. But in all cases the suffering is meant for our good. Nevertheless, the enjoyment of the advantage aimed at in the providential arrangement depends on the use we make of our trouble. We may receive this grace in vain. If we harden our heart under it it will be useless to us. Such a result is doubly disappointing, for we do not escape the pain, yet we come out of the ordeal worse instead of better.

V. The man that has seen affliction is a type of Christ. Like " the Servant of the Eternal," in the latter part of "Isaiah," this unnamed sufferer of the Lamentations seems to foreshadow the unique distress of the Man of sorrows. Christ claims our attention by his suffering, and the more that he suffered for us. He did not simply imagine his distresses to be great. He never posed for pity. But never was sorrow like unto his sorrow. He entered deeply into human experience by his sufferings, and became a High Priest touched with the feeling of our infirmities. Made perfect by suffering, he gives to us the fruits of his cross and passion as more than a "means of grace"—as bread of life and blood of redemption.

Ver. 6.—" Dark places." The sufferer feels as though he were in the dark places of the dead, in the everlasting house which no tenant ever quits.

I. God sometimes sets his people in dark places. He permits the light of gladness to fade and the vision of truth to be dimmed and the conscious brightness of his presence to be lost, so that the soul is plunged in black depths of sorrow, doubt, and loneliness. Then the dismayed sufferer feels himself lost, well-nigh dead. But he is not dead, nor even deserted by God. The very fact that he admits that God has set him in the dark place is a confession that the hand of God has been with him. Real death and utter desolation come from the desertion of the soul by God; the chastisement that he directly imposes evidences his presence and energy, and it therefore promises life.

II. WHILE IN THE LIGHT WE SHOULD BE PREPARED FOR THE DARK PLACES. We stumble in the dark, and are terrified and confounded by it because we do not know it and are not in readiness for it. Like Adam in ' Paradise Lost,' we are surprised at the first coming on of light. Because we expect the night and know that a new day will follow, we can contemplate the deepening gloom of evening without apprehension. The miner, prepared for the darkness of his subterranean work, takes his lamp with him. Every soul should be warned that it is likely some day to be plunged into spiritual darkness. If ready with the quiet inward light of faith, it need fear nothing. While we know that God's rod and staff are with us to comfort us, we shall not be dismayed, though we shall be saddened, at being called to walk through the valley of the shadow of death.

III. SOULS LEARN LESSONS OF LIGHT IN DARK PLACES. In a deep well the stars above are visible at noon. In deep humiliation heavenly light is seen that is lost in the garish show of earthly commonplace life as well as on the heights of pride and presumption. Tears of sorrow purge the vision of the soul. It is well sometimes to be alone in the dark with God.

IV. THERE ARE DARK PLACES OF SPIRITUAL DEATH THAT ARE MORE AWFUL THAN THE ABODE OF DEPARTED SPIRITS. To the old-world view Hades was a realm of sinless gloom. But worse than the darkness of this Hades is the darkness of those who are dead in trespasses and sin. Such men carry hell within their own breasts. The blackness of death broods over their spiritual natures so that they feel no qualms of conscience, and are awake to no voices from heaven. These darkest places are never assigned by God to his creatures. If they are found in them it is because they have plunged into them of their own will.

Ver. 7.—*Hedged about.* I. EVERY LIFE IS SURROUNDED BY DIVINE LIMITATIONS. God hedges all of us about. Some have a narrow field of freedom and others a wider field. But every man's field is fenced in. Within certain limits we have scope for choice and will. Yet even there choice is fettered. For there is not only the hedge that bounds our area of action, there is the chain on our own person that hampers our movements. Free-will is far from being unlimited. Or, if the will is not fettered, the execution of it is. Note some of the things that make up the hedge which God plants about us. 1. *Physical limitations,* laws of nature, circumstances of our habitat, the measure of our bodily powers, special hindrances in external events that go contrary to us, and, with some, disease, maiming, or other bodily impediment beyond our control. 2. *Mental limitations.* There is a limit to what we can think of, imagine, or desire. Our knowledge is limited—both knowledge of ends and knowledge of means. As one who finds himself a stranger in a mountainous country is shut in on all sides because he does not know the passes, our ignorance fetters us and hinders us. 3. *Moral limitations.* God fences our way with his Law. There are forbidden fields which no material barrier shuts off, yet from which the mysterious, invisible bands of righteousness keep us back. Thus the man whose conscience is awake is often aware of being hedged in and chained down where one of duller spirituality feels free to roam at pleasure.

II. THESE DIVINE LIMITATIONS ARE FELT TO BE IRKSOME TO US WHEN OUR WILL IS IN CONFLICT WITH GOD'S WILL. All finite beings must be hedged about by their natural limits. Angels must be within the fence of their powers and rights. Pure spirits are under the law of God. But to these beings the barriers cannot be irksome. They must be submitted to with meek and happy complacency. No wistful gaze is cast beyond into forbidden pasture, no covetous greed vexes with longings for the unattainable or the unlawful. But we men on earth live in frequent conflict with our heavenly Father's will. We find the walls to be hard because we fling ourselves upon them. Our chain galls us because we chafe and fret ourselves against it. The wandering sheep is torn by the hedge, while the quiet obedient sheep knows nothing of the briars. When we rebel against God we murmur at his restraints. But, it is said, is not the bondage the same while unfelt? and is it not ignominious to be oblivious of it? and is there not something noble even in the hopeless blow that is struck for freedom? The most subtle spiritual temptation of the devil takes this form, and it tempts to the most wicked sin—rebellion against God for its own sake. And it is a delusion. For the highest obedience is not the restraint of our will before God's will, but the assimilation of the two. We learn to will what God wills. Then we keep within the Divine limitations, and yet they cease to be limitations to us. They never touch us because we never attempt nor wish to cross them. Here lies the secret of peace as well as of holiness. So lofty an attainment can only be reached through that oneness with Christ of which he speaks when he prays that his disciples may be one with him and the Father, as he is one with the Father (John xvii. 21).

Ver. 18.—*Strength and hope perished.* The sufferer feels as though his strength, or rather in the expressive word of the Hebrew, his "sap" were destroyed, and with it his hope also; and he attributes this desperate condition to the action of God. It is a condition of spiritual affliction the pathology of which demands careful investigation, for it is symptomatic of a great progress of inward trouble.

I. IT INDICATES THAT EXTERNAL CALAMITIES HAVE PRODUCED INTERNAL DISTRESS. Every calamity assails the soul. But for a while the citadel holds out. Without the storm beats furiously. Within there is security and comparative quiet. At length, after a certain force of trouble is attained, in the addition of wave upon wave as in Job's case, or in the access of some one overwhelming disaster as in the destruction of Jerusalem, the defence fails, the enemy enters the breach and pours in a flood over the whole fortress. Sorrow of heart follows the loss of wealth, sickness, or other trouble of outer life.

II. IT INDICATES THAT DISTRESS OF SOUL HAS UNDERMINED THE POWERS OF ENDURANCE. The "sap" perishes. For a time a man holds on bravely, though with bleeding heart. But as the grief grows upon him he "breaks down," he can stand it no more, he says he cannot bear it. In one sense he can bear any amount of trouble that does not extinguish his being. He can pass through it and come out of it alive. But to bear trouble in the sense of keeping self-possessed and calm under it may be no longer possible. Wild and reckless anguish takes the place of sober, patient grief. The strength of soul is gone. The spirit that bore up against the blast is broken. Crushed and helpless, the sufferer no longer contends with the storm, but permits himself to be tossed and dashed about at the sport of the cruel waves.

III. IT INDICATES THAT THE LOSS OF STRENGTH HAS ENDED IN DESPAIR. Hope also perishes. A broad line must be drawn between sorrow that is lightened by hope and sorrow without hope. So long as the faintest ray still glimmers on the horizon the prospect is not utterly dark. When hope goes the soul is indeed abandoned to its distresses. The most acute pain may be borne with comparative equanimity so long as there is prospect of relief. Directly that prospect is destroyed a much smaller trouble becomes unendurable. Now and again we meet with a soul that has lost hope; we see it drifting on the wild sea of life without rudder or compass, a mere wreck of its former self.

IV. IT IS AN INTERNAL CONDITION THAT SHOULD NOT BE TAKEN AS INDICATIVE OF CORRESPONDING EXTERNAL FACTS. We need not assume that there will be no bright future, for the desponding despair is not its own justification. It is often irrational, almost insane. It springs from grief that is big enough to hide all prospect of better things, but not to destroy the possibility of their ultimate arrival. The very fact that the trouble is traced to God—this trouble is "from the Eternal"—should help us to distrust the doleful prophecy of despair. If God our Father sends trouble, it is well. He will surely bring good out of it. For one who has faith in Christ no distress should be allowed to end in despair.

Vers. 19—21.—*God taking notice of man's affliction.* In his distress the sufferer cries to God, calling upon his great Helper to note his condition and remember it. Then he is calmed by prayer, and rests in the assurance that God does not forget his trouble. Recalling this thought to mind, he recovers hope.

I. THE CRY FOR GOD'S NOTICE. 1. *It is to God.* At first it seems as though God had forgotten his afflicted child. The vision of the Divine countenance is clouded; no voice speaks out of the darkness. Desolate and despairing, in misery that is bitter as wormwood and gall, the troubled soul seems to be deserted of God in the hour of greatest need. Then the sufferer cries out to God. Here is instinctive wisdom. We may or we may not be observed by our fellow-men, and though human sympathy is a consolation, and indifference an additional bitterness, still in the heaviest trouble man can do little. It is not his notice that we should be most anxious to attract. The clamour of the afflicted for pity is an indication of weakness. But we do need God's sympathy; this is true healing balm. To him let the cry of trouble ascend. 2. *It is for God's notice.* It is not for relief, but for remembrance by God. There is good reason to trust that the remembrance will result in the relief. Nevertheless, the first and chief necessity is that God would take notice of us in trouble. If he do so we can leave the rest to him. It would be well if our prayers implied more simple reliance on the goodness of God, without perfect definitions of what we desire him to do for us.

II. THE ASSURANCE OF GOD'S NOTICE. No sooner is the cry out of his lips than the sufferer comforts himself with the assurance that God does remember his affliction. Thus speedily is the prayer answered, even in the very act of uttering it. Nevertheless, it is not to be thought that God did not remember the affliction till he had been implored to do so. We should rather understand that it was always under the pitying eye of God, only the Divine compassionate recognition of it was not discovered until prayed for. Thus we often pray to God to do for us what he is already doing, and receive an answer to our prayers in the opening of our eyes to see the Divine action that has been hitherto unobserved. We pray that God *will* be merciful to us. He answers our prayer, not by becoming merciful, but by showing us that he is and has been merciful all along. This revelation comes to us in two ways. 1. *We are able to believe more in the character of God, in his love and mercy.* Then we can apply this faith to our present circumstances, and infer with confidence that such a God must be remembering us even when we see no proof of his notice, as a child when lost at first despairs, but, after reflecting on the love of his father and mother, comforts himself with the assurance that they will surely never desert him. 2. *We are able to see indications of God's notice.* Sometimes we can see how God is working for our deliverance when we shift our standpoint and regard our life from the footstool of prayer.

III. THE HOPE THAT SPRINGS FROM GOD'S NOTICE. This is enough. God observes us. Still the trouble is great and bitter. But we know that he will not permit us to perish. As the shipwrecked crew wave garments and make frantic efforts to attract the attention of a passing vessel, and recover hope directly they see indications that they are discovered, so troubled souls should lose all despair as soon as they learn that they are seen by God. It may still be impossible to see how God will save. But we can trust that to him. Now, that we may enjoy this hope, it is necessary for us to call to mind the fact that God is remembering our affliction. Much depends on the aspect of affairs on which we dwell. If we turn to the wormwood and gall our lot will seem to be bitter without mitigation. We must voluntarily direct our thoughts away to the unseen remembrance of God, that we may receive the comfort of hope.

Vers. 22, 23.—*The unceasing mercies of God.* It would seem, according to the best authorities, that we ought to read the first of these two verses thus: " The Lord's mercies, verily they cease not, surely his compassions fail not." Thus we are assured of the enduring character of God's mercies. How striking is this assurance, coming where it does after monstrous dirges of despair! In the Lamentations we meet with one of the richest confessions of faith in the goodness of God. The black clouds are not universal; even here there is a break, and the brightest sunlight streams through, all the more cheering for the darkness that precedes it. This is a remarkable testimony to the breadth and force of Divine grace. No scene is so terrible as absolutely to exclude all vision of it. Its penetrating rays find their way through chinks and crannies of the deepest dungeon. Were our eyes but open to see it, every one of us would have to confess to indications of its presence. Surely it is a great consolation for the desponding that even the exceptional sufferer of the Lamentations sees the unceasing mercies of God!

I. GOD'S MERCIES NEVER CEASE. 1. *We have no claim upon their continuance.* Mercies are to the undeserving. It is much that such as we receive any. We could have no right to complain if they all ceased. The least of them is beyond our merit. 2. *We have done much to provoke the cessation of them.* (1) By ungratefully accepting them; (2) by complainingly ignoring them; (3) by sinfully abusing them. 3. *They sometimes appear to cease.* They are not always equally visible. But as the moon which seems to wax and wane never changes in itself, the grace which appears to us to fluctuate, and even at times to be extinguished, is never lessened, much less is it destroyed. 4. *They change their form.* The morning light varies from the evening light. Yet both come from the same sun. God's mercy is sometimes cheery, at other times it seems to frown upon us. But the wrath is mercy in disguise; and not only so, but under the circumstances that make it necessary it is more merciful than gentleness would be. There may be more mercy in the surgeon's knife than in the bed of down.

II. God's MERCIES ARE CONSTANTLY RENEWED. The same mercies will not last for ever. They are gifts and acts for a definite time. What suits one age does not agree with another. God adapts his grace to the immediate needs of the hour. His mercies are not statuesque and immobile. They are living and suitable to need. They are never anachronous. They are never stale. God gives to each of us new mercies. He is living and acting in our midst every day and at each immediate moment. We read of God's mercies in writings of David and St. John. But we have not to exhume the antique mercies that were bestowed on these men of the olden times. Our own mercies are fresh to-day. As God keeps the old world green by renewing it every spring, so he refreshes and invigorates his people by spring-times of grace. Moreover, it is well to see how he does this daily, and to wake in the morning with a joyous thankfulness in prospect of the entirely new mercies of the new day.

III. THE CEASELESSNESS OF GOD'S MERCY IS A PROOF OF HIS FAITHFULNESS. 1. *It is the fulfilment of his promise that he will never leave nor forsake his people.* 2. *It is also a sign that he is still acting according to his ancient word.* For the mercy, being not only continued, but also renewed, shows us that God is fulfilling his promise in the immediate present. The friend who builds us a house may be considered to be faithful to his promise to shelter us as long as the house stands. But he who promises daily bread gives an additional proof of faithfulness by visiting us every day. The manna showed that God was daily present to fulfil his purposes of grace. Daily mercies are recurrent reminders of the faithfulness of God.

Ver. 24.—*The secret of hope.* The reader of the psalms is familiar with the utterance, "The Lord is my Portion." The characteristic peculiarity of the adoption of this confession of faith by the sufferer of the Lamentations is his taking it as a ground of hope. The present is so dark that he can have little joy even in God. Earthly things are so unpropitious that he can hope little from them. But with God for his Portion he can look forward from the troubles of the present and the threatenings of earthly calamities to an unearthly joy in the future. Let us endeavour to see how to have God for our Portion is the secret of hope.

I. GOD IS THE BEST OBJECT OF HOPE. 1. *Consider how God can be an Object of hope.* We hope in God when we hope to enjoy his presence, to bask in the sunshine of his love, to enter into the life of communion with him. To know God is satisfaction to the intellect. To have fellowship with God through love is to have rest and joy in the heart. To be reconciled to God is to have the trouble of conscience allayed. All the deepest longings of the soul find their end and satisfaction in God. 2. *Consider how God is the one perfect Object of hope.* The greatest disappointment of an earthly hope is when the thing anticipated is given to us and yet the joy expected from it is not forthcoming. We clasp our treasure and find it to be dross, or we see it to be gold and we find that it will not stay the hunger of our souls. We are larger than the biggest earthly hope. Our aspirations soar above the highest of them. But God is higher and deeper and greater than the largest desire of any soul. He is just what we all need for rest and gladness. He cannot disappoint us. If money is our portion it may be lost, or it may not buy ease of heart. If power, pleasure, success, or any other common end be our portion, we may be most wearied when we have gained most. God is the Portion to satisfy hope, and he only.

II. GOD IS THE BEST GROUND OF HOPE. We have most assurance that our hope will not fail us when we trust in him. Why? 1. Because he is *good.* Malignant beings take pleasure in frustrating hope; cruel people do it with indifference; and selfish and thoughtless men unwittingly. But God, who is love itself and who ever regards the needs of his children with merciful consideration, is too gracious to disappoint the hope we have in him. 2. Because he is *faithful*. He has invited our confidence and promised his inheritance to his obedient and trustful children. Thus he has pledged his word. His honour is involved. He will never prove false to his promise. 3. Because he is *almighty*. With the best intentions a man may be compelled to disappoint the confidence reposed upon him through simple inability to meet it. The bankrupt cannot pay his debts, however honest he may be. But as there is no limit to the power of God, so there will be no failure of hope in him. 4. Because hope in God is *lawful and right*. We need not fear that the strictest judgment will condemn it. It is a holy hope, and it is therefore likely more and more to be satisfied, as the judgment of God condemns and destroys unworthy objects of ambition.

Vers. 25, 26.—*Quiet waiting*. We are here first reminded that God does not disregard those who seek him. Though his grace may be delayed, it will come in due time. Then we are told that this waiting for God's response to our prayers is for our good, provided it be patient.

I. GOD VISITS WITH GRACE THOSE WHO SEEK HIM, THOUGH THEY MAY HAVE TO WAIT FOR HIM. 1. *He expects to be sought after*. To wait for God implies attention and watchfulness. But direct effort to find grace in God is involved in seeking him. There are who say that this is a sign of distrust; that we should wait without seeking God; that to go after him implies impatience at his tarrying; and, in short, that all prayer which is positive petition, shows self-will, impatience, and distrust. But this hypercritical view of prayer is a delusion. For the act of seeking may develop a trustfulness and bring about a preparedness which would not be found without it. We have the invitation of Christ to " seek that we may find." 2. *He may delay his response to our appeal*. He may make us wait. The reason for this cannot be any reluctance or indifference on God's part. But it may be that the time is not ripe for our receiving the response, or that we shall be disciplined into preparedness by waiting, or that, other interests beyond our own being concerned, the answer must tarry on account of them. Be the reason what it may, we must be warned to expect this delay, or we shall be grievously disappointed, perplexed, and even thrown into doubt and despondency. 3. *He will surely respond in due time*. God is good to all who truly wait for and seek him. He is not a capricious, partial, respecter of persons. Nor does he require a certain amount of merit in the petitioner. Our want is our sole claim, and the most unworthy are the most needy. But observe: (1) we must truly seek God himself, and not merely pleasant things from God; and (2) though God is good to all who thus seek him, his goodness does not take the same form to each. To some it is healing balm, to others purging hyssop.

II. WAITING FOR GOD'S GRACE IS GOOD FOR THOSE WHO SEEK HIM, PROVIDED THAT THEY WAIT QUIETLY. 1. *God permits them to wait for their own profit*. Whatever other ends may be served by the delay, the good of the petitioner is aimed at in the providential arrangement. How? (1) By testing *faith*. Thus it is seen whether faith be real, enduring, and constant. (2) By requiring *submission*. One of the most essential conditions of profiting by Divine grace is willingness to submit to the will of God. (3) By exercising our own *spiritual powers*. If the timid swimmer were succoured the moment he cried for help, he would never gain confidence and strength. (4) By affording us opportunity for *consideration*. While we wait we can think. We may then measure our need and see what will supply it. Looking at the approaching salvation in the light of hope and imagination, we are better prepared to enjoy it. 2. *In order that this waiting may be profitable it must be quiet*. Impatience wrecks faith and submissiveness and obedience, and all the graces that are necessary for a right reception of Divine salvation. It is difficult to be quiet while waiting. We grow restless and fret ourselves as the weary hours drag past. It is harder to wait than to work, because work occupies us as waiting does not. Yet we lose much for lack of patience. We are not quiet enough to hear the still small voice that would bring salvation. In our patience we must possess our souls if we are to receive into them the richest gifts of the goodness of God.

Ver. 27.—*Youth*. I. THE YOKE BELONGS TO YOUTH. It is common to hear youth spoken of as a time of pleasure. Older people do their best to damp the joyousness of the young by telling them that these are their happy days, soon will come the dark days of trouble, let them enjoy the bright time while it lasts. Even if such a view of life were correct, the wisdom of thrusting it forward is not easy to discover. Why spoil the feast by pointing to the sword of Damocles? Why direct the walk on a fair spring day to the graveyard? Surely it were wiser to say, "Sufficient unto the day is the evil thereof." But this view is false. It arises from the disturbed imagination of later years. Grown morose with care, men look back on the earlier days of their life and imagine them to have been far brighter than those they now enjoy; but they only do so by that common trick of memory that selects the pleasant pictures and drops the unpleasant ones. 1. Youth is a time of *restraint.* With all their lightness of heart, children feel the bonds of authority and long for the time when they shall be their own masters. It is difficult for grown men who have the free command of their own actions to understand the irksomeness of the necessary bonds of childhood. Restrained in the nursery and in the schoolroom under law and supervision, liable to ignominious rebuke, many children feel themselves in slavery. Wiser treatment gives more liberty; but still it necessarily continues many restraints. And in full-grown life, when the bondage is more galling, young men commonly have to obey and submit to direction more than older men. 2. Youth is a time of *toil.* Men generally have to work hard in their younger years. The hours of labour are longest; the tasks imposed are the most disagreeable; the wages paid are the lowest. Most men as they advance in years work for shorter hours at more agreeable tasks and for greater rewards.

II. THE YOKE IS GOOD FOR YOUTH. We have seen that it is incorrect to regard youth as a time of exceptional pleasantness. For a normal life the day brightens as it lengthens, at least till the meridian is attained, and even later the soft light of evening is to many a source of deep, calm joy unknown in the feverish excitement of youth (see Wordsworth's poem on the superiority of the quiet September songs of the birds to their wild, restless spring songs). Nevertheless, the very yoke of youth is good. 1. If it must be borne at all, *the yoke can be best borne in youth.* The mind is then most supple to shape itself to the unwonted burden and pressure of it. Then a man can yield to authority with most pliancy and face hard labour most confidently. 2. *The yoke is necessary for youth.* It is a good thing to bear it in youth. (1) *Restraint* is then necessary. Liberty would be abused. Until an independent conscience has been developed, instructed, and strengthened, the external conscience of authority is needed. (2) *Work* is also good for youth. Even the discipline of unpleasant tasks is wholesome. It conquers self-will and the idle love of pleasure, and trains in self-denial. 3. *Later years are benefited by the yoke of youth.* Even if the years during which it is borne are not so happy as they might be, the man himself is better in the whole of his life. He profits by the discipline. He learns habits of self-restraint and industry. He is able better to appreciate the privileges of advancing stages of life.

Vers. 31—33.—*Chastisement only for a season.* I. THE FACT THAT CHASTISEMENT IS ONLY FOR A SEASON. God does "cast off" and "cause grief." His love does not nullify his wrath. When grieved and disowned by God the soul feels utterly desolate. But the terrible judgment is only for a season. It will end in reconciliation and compassion. This great truth gives an entirely new complexion to our views of life and providence. We see at times the severe side. But we misjudge if we take that as a sample of the whole. Indeed the very severity prepares the way for mercy; for God can show compassion after chastisement to a degree that would not be good before the wholesome discipline. The sunshine, which would wither the plants before the storm, coming after it helps them to grow and flourish on the water it has brought to their roots. 1. *This fact is no ground for reckless indifference.* For (1) the wrath is terrible enough while it lasts; (2) it must endure as long as impenitent guilt is persisted in; and (3) sin that presumes on mercy is the most gross and culpable ingratitude. 2. *This fact should be a consolation in trouble.* Hope may buoy up the sufferer. And resort may be had to prayer. It seems as though the soul were abandoned. But if God has not cast it off for ever, he must still feel interest in it, and may therefore be appealed to for mercy. 3. *This fact is an encouragement to repentance.* Endless punishment discourages repentance. It acts in the opposite way from that of all useful punishment.

It tends to confirm sin. It is the prospect of mercy that softens the heart and prompts feelings of penitence.

II. THE REASON WHY CHASTISEMENT IS ONLY FOR A SEASON. This reason is to be found in the character of God. " He doth not afflict willingly," or rather, " from his heart." There is an essential difference between chastisement and mercy. Chastisement is necessary and sent reluctantly, but mercy springs from the heart of God and is given willingly. That is a false and libellous representation of God, according to which the theologian describes the outpouring of Divine wrath as though there were a real satisfaction to God in the process of causing pain to his creatures. The description of everlasting perdition as given to lost souls with a flood of wrath is more like the action of a malignant demon than that of a merciful God. It is sometimes so spoken of as though every attribute in God but mercy were eternal. Truth, justice, holiness, wrath, vengeance, are to endure for ever. Only mercy has its day. Only this one grace is short-lived and soon to be exhausted. The calumny is a direct contradiction to Scripture, which teaches over and over again that the mercy of the Lord endureth for ever. This attribute at least is eternal. This one springs most directly from the heart of God; for it is the fruit of love. While we say God is angry at times, we do not say God is anger, because anger is not of the essential nature of God. But we do say, not only God loves, but God is love. But it may be said, if God does not afflict " from his heart," why does he afflict at all? It must be because the circumstances of his children make it necessary. He does it not for his own sake. Then he must do it for their sakes. Seeing, however, that the chastisement is not agreeable to them, there must be some object in it, some result of it by which they are to profit. It must, therefore, cease in due time, that it may give place to that happy result.

Ver. 38.—*How evil and good both proceed from God.* The Hebrew prophets show no inclination towards Persian dualism. They never attempt to solve the mystery of evil by the doctrine of two principles in nature, a good and an evil principle, in any respect co-ordinate one with another. On the contrary, they emphasize the monism of their creed by ascribing sole supremacy and originating power to " the Eternal." Nevertheless, they do not teach that moral evil is caused by God. This they regard as springing from the heart of man. In the verse before us we have no question of this darkest kind of evil. It is not sin, but suffering, that is referred to, as the context clearly shows. We have just been told that God will not cast off for ever because he does not afflict from his heart. We are now reminded that it is not the less true that God sends adverse as well as pleasant things.

I. THE WHOLE OF OUR LIFE-EXPERIENCE IS UNDER THE DIRECTION OF GOD. Our conduct is in our own hands; but what is not thus immediately dependent on our own will is directed by God. Other men influence us, but they are overruled by the Most High. Chance and accident seem to strike us, but chance and accident only exist to our ignorance. They are not really, for Providence excludes them. We sometimes speak of visitations of God, as though he came and went. But that only means that we perceive his action at one time more than at another. God is ever working in us. " In him we live, and move, and have our being." Things great and small, pleasant and painful, spiritual and physical, eternal and temporal, are under the hand of God and regulated by his will.

II. GOD TREATS US IN VARIOUS WAYS. He sends both evil and good. He has not one unchanging method of action. He varies his treatment according to requirement. To one he sends more evil, to another more good. Yet to none does he send experience of one kind only. The hard lot has many mitigations. The pleasant places have their shadows. As we pass through life we see how God deals with us in wise suitableness, now sending most good, now most evil.

III. WE MUST NOT INFER THAT IF GOD IS WITH US NO TROUBLE CAN BEFALL. If evil as well as good proceeds from the mouth of the Most High, no assurance of the presence of the Author of both will justify us in disbelieving in the coming of either experience. We must be on our guard or we shall be disappointed. We must be prepared to expect evil things even while we are under the care of God.

IV. WE MUST NOT INFER THAT IF EVIL BEFALL US GOD CANNOT BE WITH US. This inference of unbelief is the natural consequence of disappointment in the presumption that, if God is with us, we cannot suffer trouble. There is real comfort in the thought that evil is sent by God, if only by the removal of the common assumption that it indicates desertion by him.

V. WE MAY INFER THAT IF EVIL PROCEEDS FROM GOD IT IS PERMITTED FOR THE SAKE OF ULTIMATE GOOD. For God does not delight in sending evil. His heart is not in it. But his heart is in mercy. He may seem to send the two indifferently; but he does not bestow them with equal pleasure nor with similar results, for the good is sent for its own sake, and the evil only that it may lead to higher good in the future.

Ver. 40.—*Self-examination.* It is interesting to watch the progress of the thoughts and feelings of the writer who addresses us as a sufferer in the overthrow of Jerusalem. At first he bewails his lot, then he calls to God for assistance. After doing so he regains faith, and calls to mind the merciful kindness of God. This helps him to the assurance that the trouble is but temporary. He feels that since it comes from God it must not be complained of. It is rather a call to reflection and self-examination.

I. CHASTISEMENT SHOULD LEAD TO SELF-EXAMINATION. It does us little good until it makes us thoughtful. We must sit still under it and think. Then we should turn our thoughts in upon ourselves. We are inclined to look anywhere else, to discuss the justice of God, to complain of the conduct of men, to criticize the course of events. But the one thing necessary is to look within. This is difficult, as any one who has honestly tried it knows quite well. It is not necessary habitually. Too much introspection develops a morbid subjectivity. But there are special occasions for self-examination, and trouble is one of them.

II. SELF-EXAMINATION SHOULD INVESTIGATE CONDUCT. It is "our ways" that we are to inquire into. 1. The important question is as to *what we do and how we live.* People examine their feelings. The examination is delusive and unwholesome. They examine their opinions. But opinions should not be matters of moral trial so much as questions for calm intellectual testing. The chief point is as to our behaviour. 2. The most important questions of conduct are those which concern our *habitual actions.* "Our ways" are not isolated deeds, but courses of action. We may be surprised into a fall or spurred into a good deed. More significant is our normal, everyday conduct. This is what we should investigate most closely.

III. THE INVESTIGATON OF CONDUCT SHOULD BE SEARCHING AND JUDICIAL. 1. It should be *searching.* Evil is subtle. Plausible excuses cover bad deeds. We must not be content with condemning conscious and confessed wickedness. The hidden evil of our heart must be searched out. The detective must do his part before the magistrate does his. 2. It should be *periodical.* We must "try" our ways. It is unprofitable and demoralizing to conscience to confess guilt which we do not feel and see. Until we are convinced of it we are dishonest in attempting to blame ourselves for it. Conviction must precede the sentence. We should also be just to ourselves. Wholesale self-accusation is often dishonest and rarely profitable. We want point and specific charges in our judgment of ourselves—the Law of God, the voice of conscience, the example of Christian standards by which to try ourselves. If we find the process difficult, we may pray that God will carry it on for us (Ps. cxxxix. 23, 24).

IV. THE CONVICTION WHICH FOLLOWS THE TRIAL OF OUR OWN CONDUCT SHOULD LEAD US TO REPENTANCE. It is of no use unless it does this. The mere sense of guilt is depressing and, left to itself, may lead us to ruin through despair. Repentance should follow. We are to know that we are in the wrong way only in order that we may turn from it to the right way. We all sin, and therefore self-examination should lead all of us through conviction of sin to repentance. Then we can return to God. He waits only for our confession of guilt. When we own to it he will pardon it.

Ver. 44.—*God covering himself with a cloud.* There are dark hours when God not only seems to be hidden from view, but to be so wrapped in thick clouds that even our prayers cannot penetrate to him. Let us consider when and how far this is really the case.

I. SOMETIMES IT IS ONLY APPARENT. We lose heart and confidence. Discouraged and saddened, we cease to believe that God is listening to our cry. We can never see God nor hear any audible response to our cry and must always pray in faith;

and therefore when faith fails we are ready to say that God does not hear us. We should remember that God's attention is not confined to the evidences of it that he may afford to us. He may hear us without telling us that he does, or he may simply delay the response for good and wise reasons. Let us, therefore, beware of the folly of judging of God's actions by our own passing moods.

II. SOMETIMES IT IS REAL, BUT MERCIFUL. God does not always accept our prayers even when he is regarding us favourably. 1. He may be *trying our faith.* It may be better for us that our faith should be tested and strengthened than that we should have the particular thing we desire. 2. We may be asking *unwisely.* Perhaps the greatest unkindness would be to answer our foolish prayer according to our wish. The mother must turn a deaf ear to the cry of her child for a poisonous fruit. It is hard thus to refuse. Nothing tries love more severely. It is a proof of the great love of God that he is firm in thus apparently treating us with indifference when all the while his heart yearns to comfort us.

III. SOMETIMES IT IS BOTH REAL AND WRATHFUL. God will not always hearken to prayer. There are circumstances that raise great banks of clouds between our souls and Heaven such as the most vehement petition cannot pierce. 1. *Unrepented sin.* If we have sinned ever so heavily and confess our iniquity, heaven is open to hear the faintest sigh of penitence. But against impenitence it is firm as brass. 2. *Self-will.* So long as we are praying, rebelliously demanding our own way and not submitting to God's will, no prayer of ours can reach his throne in heaven. We may dare to lay our wish before God in humility, but yet in frank expression of it. Nevertheless, it can only be entertained by God when we add in spirit, if not in words, " Not my will, but thine, be done." Thus may we cry to the void and have back only the mocking echo of our foolish prayer. We may send urgent requests towards heaven, and they will only lose themselves in the thick, black clouds of Divine disfavour which come between us and God. It is hopeful, however, for a soul to know this. When we see the cloud we are half-way towards the removal of it.

IV. IT IS THE WORK OF CHRIST TO DISSIPATE THE CLOUD THAT SHUTS OUR PRAYER OUT FROM GOD. 1. He permits us to pray *in his Name,* with his authority, and pleading his merit. 2. He teaches us to pray *in the right spirit* of penitence, submission, and faith.

Vers. 49, 50.—*Tears which only God can wipe away.* I. THERE ARE TEARS WHICH ONLY GOD CAN WIPE AWAY. Jerusalem is so desolate that one who mourns her sad estate weeps such tears. But in all ages there have been sufferers in similar grief. 1. When sorrow is *acute.* The lighter troubles may be patiently endured, or resisted, or mitigated, or driven away by sympathy and brotherly aid. There are troubles which no man can touch, sores which no balm of Gilead can ease, a secret bitterness known only to the heart of the sufferer. In such agonies of distress comfort is a mockery, to attempt to console is only to intrude into the sanctuary of sorrow and to harrow the wounds we cannot heal. 2. When sorrow is *chronic.* The sudden flood of tears may be quickly stanched. There are people of mercurial temperament who seem to be in the depths of despair one moment and elated with pleasure the next. It is not difficult to stay the tears of these shallow natures. But when the tears flow on through the bright day as in the long night, this weeping without intermission passes the bounds of human aid. The broken heart, the ruined life, hopes shattered, and joys buried in the grave, open a fountain of grief that only God can stay. Now, it is important to recognize this fact. If we are only driven to see it by hard experience, we may lose ourselves in despair before we can find any consolation in God. It is well to know when we are in smooth water that storms are coming which our vessel cannot weather. Then we may be prepared to look for a haven.

II. THERE ARE NO TEARS WHICH GOD CANNOT WIPE AWAY. The sufferer weeps "till the Lord look down, and behold from heaven." But when God looks the tears will be dried. Relief comes from God. It comes in a look from God. It comes when heaven is open to the troubled soul. One look from heaven is enough. How is this? 1. When God looks from heaven *he manifests himself.* He is always regarding us. But at times it seems to us that we are forgotten and deserted by him. Then again we see that he is observing us. The newly manifested nearness of God is a consolation.

2. When God looks *he shows compassion.* We express compassion by the eye more than by the voice. The look of pity is its surest, gentlest, most touching expression. This is the look of God when he beholds distress. 3. When God looks at the sufferer *he sends help to him.* God is not one who can contemplate suffering and then " pass by on the other side." With him to see want is to aid it. It is therefore enough that God regards us. The rest must follow. 4. When God looks from heaven *he draws the sufferer up to himself.* He attracts by his wonderful look of loving-kindness. The revelation of heaven lifts the troubled spirit up to heaven. By communion with heaven earthly tears are wiped away.

Ver. 57.—*" Fear not ! "* The recollection of how God has forbidden one not to fear in the past is a plea in praying that he will remove the ground of fear in the present.
I. WE MUCH NEED DIVINE ENCOURAGEMENTS TO OVERCOME FEAR. 1. *In real danger.* It is not only the coward who fears. Indifference often gets the credit of courage. Many fear not simply because they are blind. To see would be to tremble. For the great powers of the universe, " the terror by night and the arrow that flieth by day," and the spiritual temptations that threaten our souls, are too strong for us. 2. *In the threatening aspect of the future.* Heavy clouds will gather to windward. Storms are plainly brewing out at sea. Whether they will burst over our heads or not we cannot say. But the very uncertainty adds to the terror ; for fear feeds on vague alarms and may be conquered when the worst is known. 3. *In the mystery of life.* Even when we see no threatening danger the awful unknown is peopled to our imagination with strange horrors. 4. *In the fears of others.* Nothing is so contagious as fear. Hence the madness of panics. It is hard to be brave among the timorous. 5. *In hours of weakness.* When we are weary courage flags. We can be brave at noon, but midnight awakens fear. Guilt is full of alarm.
II. WE HAVE MANY DIVINE ENCOURAGEMENTS TO OVERCOME FEAR. 1. *In directly urging us not to fear.* He has said, " Fear not!" He will not mock with empty words. 2. *In promises of help.* The Scriptures teem with words of grace for troubled souls, as when they are bidden to cast their burden upon God because he will sustain them, to call upon him in the day of trouble and he will hear them, etc. By the veracity and honour of God we have enough assurance in any one of these promises to dispel fear. 3. *In the fatherly character of God.* If we had no instruction not to fear and no promise of help, we might still know enough of God to rest confident that all must be well when we are in his hands. The child fears nothing when nestling on its mother's bosom. Who shall fear that leans upon the bosom of God ? 4. *In our personal relations with God.* Let it be noted that everybody under all circumstances is not to be urged to cast fears to the wind. The guilty should fear. The impenitent have no excuse for abandoning fear. They who are at enmity with God should dwell in great trembling. It is when reconciled through Christ, forgiven and restored to our home, that as redeemed souls we can shake off fear.
III. DIVINE ASSURANCES AGAINST FEAR SHOULD INSPIRE OUR PRAYERS FOR HELP IN DANGER. We are to remember how God has bidden us not to fear. Here is a grand source of confidence when we cry for help. For it is the very Word of God that has led us to stand facing the storm. His action must be true to his Word. Nevertheless, we do need to pray for help in danger. God's promises are conditional. When he dissuades us from fear it is on the understanding that we seek refuge beneath the covert of his wings. To the storm-tossed soul he says, " Fear not ! " but he expects that soul to welcome him as its Pilot. Then the storm will be weathered. God's assurance of safety is for those who turn to his protection. It is those who are " in Christ Jesus " for whom there is no condemnation, and who therefore need fear nothing.

Vers. 59—66.—*The great appeal.* We can see the advantage to justice of appealing from a lower to a higher court. Sometimes the process has to be repeated and the case tried again and again until the best attainable verdict is got from the very highest tribunal. In the East, where justice was commonly neglected by indolence, outraged by violence, or prostituted by bribery, men felt strongly the value of an appeal. To the believer in the supreme Judge it was a great satisfaction that he could turn from the corrupt and venal courts of human judicature to the high court of Heaven. It may often be a relief to make this appeal. For absolute justice between man and man is rarely obtained. Three things are wanted to make the result satisfactory—clear evidence, a just verdict, and a firm execution of the sentence.

I. CLEAR EVIDENCE. It is difficult to make one's condition rightly apprehended by men. Frequently there are facts that cannot be explained, or the whole transaction stands on a different ground from what people imagine, or its features are warped by the atmosphere of prejudice through which it is regarded. But God sees clearly and knows all. "Thou God seest me" is the comforting reflection of the vexed soul. "Thou hast seen my wrong," "Thou hast seen all," is the first consolation. But for this assurance to give comfort it is necessary that our cause should be just. God sees truly both the merit and the fault. It is useless to appeal to God with a bad case. There is no deceiving him. Let us see that our cause is always one which we can refer to the thorough investigation of the all-seeing God.

II. A JUST VERDICT. The evidence may be clear, yet the decision may be unjust if the judge is partial or corrupt. It is the comfort of one who makes the highest appeal that God not only knows all, but will decide righteously. "Judge thou my cause," says the troubled soul. God will judge all causes at the great tribunal of the judgment-day. Injustice can only live till then. Should not the oppressed bear his brief wrongs with calmness when he knows that they will soon be righted? It is interesting to see that "the day of the Eternal," which the Jews anticipated as the great judgment-day, was not regarded by them with terror, as it is often regarded by Christians. This fact may be, perhaps, partially due to a duller sense of personal sin. But surely it is chiefly owing to the grand Hebrew love of righteousness. We see strange mysteries of inequality and injustice that are at times perfectly bewildering. The judgment of Heaven will set all right. And even now God may do much for his children by his providence.

III. A FIRM EXECUTION. The sufferer prays that God will "render unto them a recompense." A Christian spirit should deliver us from the thirst for vengeance that was too pronounced even in the most devout Hebrew. But we must beware of a weak quasi-humanitarianism that would sacrifice justice and wholesome retribution to a one-sided gentleness. 1. It is necessary that justice should be done in action as well as that a just sentence should be pronounced in word. 2. It is for the good of all concerned—the victim, the public, and even the wrong-doer, that guilt should be chastised. 3. It is well to transfer vengeful feelings which we cannot utterly destroy into a passive resignation of our case to God. We are not to avenge ourselves, if only because God has said, "Vengeance is mine; I will repay."

HOMILIES BY VARIOUS AUTHORS.

Ver. 1.—*Afflicted by God.* Every child of God, nay, every son of man, has endured affliction. Jeremiah and the city which he here personifies and represents may be said to have experienced affliction in an extraordinary degree. A fact so universal cannot be without special significance in human life. But not all the afflicted discern this underlying and profitable meaning.

I. AFFLICTION LEADS SOME TO DOUBT THE EXISTENCE OF GOD. It is not uncommon for people to say in their hearts, what some even venture to say with their lips, "If there were a God, I should not be suffered to pass through misfortunes and sorrows so distressing and so undeserved."

II. AFFLICTION LEADS SOME TO DOUBT GOD'S BENEVOLENCE AND KINDLY INTEREST IN HUMAN BEINGS. Not denying the existence of Deity, these afflicted ones question his moral attributes. They ask, "If God were a Being of boundless benevolence, would he suffer us to go through waters so deep, flames so fierce? His kindness and compassion—were such attributes part of his nature—would interpose on our behalf and deliver us."

III. SOME WHO BELIEVE THAT GOD PERMITS AFFLICTION MISINTERPRET IT AS A SIGN OF HIS WRATH. This it may be; this it *was* in the case of Jerusalem. Yet God in the midst of wrath remembers mercy; he doth not keep his anger for ever. And there are instances in which no greater misinterpretation could be possible than the view that suffering is mere penalty, that those who suffer most are necessarily sinners above all their neighbours.

IV. AFFLICTION SHOULD BE REGARDED BY THE PIOUS AND SUBMISSIVE AS A PROOF OF DIVINE MERCY AND AS MEANT FOR THEIR GOOD. Scripture represents suffering as the chastening of a Father's hand. The experience of many a Christian is summed up in the language of the psalmist: "It was good for me that I was afflicted."

V. AFFLICTION MAY THUS BECOME, IN THE EXPERIENCE OF THE PIOUS, THE OCCASION FOR DEVOUT THANKSGIVING. How often have mature and holy Christians been heard to say, "I would not, upon looking back, have been without the ruggedness of the road, the bitterness of the cup"!—T.

Vers. 7—9.—*The way of life hedged and built up.* The man who enjoys prosperity seems also to enjoy liberty; his way lies straight and level and open before him. But it often happens in human life that liberty is changed into restraint, that every path that is smooth and peaceful is closed, that, in the figurative language of this passage, a hedge is planted, a fence is staked out, a wall is built across the traveller's way.

I. MAN'S DELIGHT IS NATURALLY IN LIBERTY AND PROSPERITY.

II. PROVIDENTIAL CIRCUMSTANCES SOMETIMES COMPLETELY DEPRIVE HIM OF SUCH LIBERTY AND PROSPERITY. 1. One may miss the object of his heart's earthly desire. He may have set his affection upon some object, he may have directed his aspiration towards some aim, he may have purposed some course in life; and all these expectations and hopes may come to nothing; circumstances may conspire against the fulfilment of such desires and intentions. 2. Another may find great delight in the service of God; and suddenly health may fail and such service may consequently be forbidden, or powers of mind may be enfeebled, or means may be reduced, or fellow-labourers, apparently necessary, may be removed by death.

III. THERE IS DANGER LEST IN SUCH A POSITION EVEN GOOD PEOPLE SHOULD BECOME IMPATIENT AND REBELLIOUS. Believing that the Almighty has power to remove every obstacle, and to make plain the roughest path, they are tempted to question the interest, the care, the benevolence of the Supreme, and to give way to fretfulness and murmuring, and to ask "Why should not God make light my heavy chain, pluck up the cruel hedge, break down the impenetrable wall?"

IV. YET IN SUCH CIRCUMSTANCES THE PATH WHICH GOD HAS APPOINTED SHOULD BE RECOGNIZED AS THE RIGHT PATH. Resignation to his will, waiting for his time of deliverance, confidence in his goodness,—such is the attitude of heart in which true consolation and ultimate prosperity will be found.—T.

Ver. 8.—*Unheard prayer.* There were seasons when it seemed to the prophet that God not only refused to interpose in his behalf, but refused even to listen to his prayer. In such faithless and yet not unnatural imaginations and fears many truly pious natures have participated. Complaints are made by the afflicted that they have prayed, but have prayed in vain; that God has "shut out" their prayer.

I. THERE IS PRAYER WHICH GOD DOES SHUT OUT, *i.e.* THE PRAYER OF SELFISHNESS AND SIN. Men ask and receive not, because they ask amiss. They ask for gifts which God has never promised to bestow and which he has never encouraged them unreservedly to desire. There are bad things which men ask God for and which it would harm the suppliants to receive. There are things not bad in themselves, the bestowal of which, however, upon certain persons and in certain circumstances would be spiritually harmful. Such gifts are withheld, not in malevolence, but in mercy.

II. THERE IS PRAYER WHICH IS NOT UNHEARD, BUT THE ANSWER TO WHICH IS NOT IMMEDIATE AND IS NOT JUST WHAT IS EXPECTED. Denial is one thing, delay is another. Perhaps it may be said that every true prayer is both heard and answered. For every acceptable petition takes the tone of our Saviour's ever-memorable and incomparable prayer, "Not my will, O my Father, but thine, be done." Misinterpretation is to be avoided. The reason of delay, of seeming denial, is to be sought in ourselves. God often withholds for a season, in order to awaken our faith and submission, what he intends eventually to confer.—T.

Ver. 17.—*Prosperity forgotten.* What a touching picture of extreme adversity and distress do these words present: "I forgat prosperity"! Days of happiness are so distant that they have faded into oblivion; their memory is obliterated by recurring sorrows, by continuous misfortunes.

I. ADVERSITY DOES NOT FULFIL ITS INTENDED PURPOSE IF IT LEADS TO DESPAIR. There are natures in which a reverse of circumstances induces depression, which gradually deepens into despondency. Where this is the case there is ground for fearing that the affections and desires have been too much centred upon things earthly and perishable, that the gifts of a kind Providence have been regarded as possessions to which those who enjoy them have a right, that the higher purposes of this earthly discipline called life have been neglected.

II. ADVERSITY SHOULD BE REGARDED BY THE CHRISTIAN AS TEMPORARY, AND AS AN APPOINTMENT OF DIVINE WISDOM AND LOVE. To forget prosperity in the past is to forget that, for the devout, obedient, and submissive, there is prosperity in reserve in the future. The cloud comes over the sky, but the sunshine of the morning will be followed in due time by the brightness which shall close in glorious sunset. The disciple of Christ cannot lose sight of the fact that his Master was "a Man of sorrows and acquainted with grief," and that he assured his followers that "in the world they should have tribulation." But the voice that foretold conflict promised victory. To the faithful favour shall be restored and prosperity shall be renewed. "Weeping may endure for a night, but joy cometh in the morning."—T.

Vers. 19, 20.—*Remembering affliction.* As the prophet entreats the Lord to remember the afflictions he and his countrymen have passed through, he records his own vivid recollection of bygone misery and humiliation. Now, the counsel of the world would be—Forget your troubles; they are past; why allow them to disturb and to distress the mind? There are, however, good reasons why this advice should be rejected, why the afflictions we have passed through should sometimes be recalled to mind.

I. THIS EXERCISE SERVES TO REMIND US OF THE UNCERTAINTY AND VICISSITUDES OF THIS LIFE. It is well that in days of prosperity men should not forget how soon the sky may be clouded, that in times of health liability to sickness and disease should be borne in mind, that the living and the active should hear a voice gently counselling them *Memento mori!*

II. THIS EXERCISE SERVES TO PRESERVE US FROM A DISPOSITION TOWARDS WORLD-LINESS. In prosperity it is very common for men to cling to this world, to over-estimate its wealth, its pleasures, its honours. Let them remember days of adversity; let them consider how possible it is that such days may recur; and thus preserve themselves from the threatened sin of worldly mindedness.

III. THIS EXERCISE MAY LEAD US TO GLORIFY THE DIVINE DELIVERER. Affliction is to many a thing of the past; they have left the tempestuous seas and are in the quiet haven. Let such consider by whose great mercy such deliverance has been effected, to whom their gratitude is due. Who interposed upon their behalf and brought them into safety? Do they forget to sing, "This poor man cried, and the Lord heard him, and delivered him out of all his troubles"?

IV. THIS EXERCISE MAY SUGGEST THE EXPECTATION OF HEAVEN, AND MAY LEND ATTRACTIVENESS TO THE PROSPECT. The past naturally suggests the future. In remembering the afflictions of earth we are reminded of that state where "the wicked cease from troubling, and the weary are at rest."—T.

Ver. 21.—*Hope reviving.* At length the unmitigated anguish and desolation expressed in the previous parts of this book seem relieved. A ray of light breaks through the dense mass of clouds. Despondency gives place to hope.

I. FROM WHAT STATE THIS LANGUAGE BETOKENS A REVULSION, A REACTION. Jeremiah has, not unnaturally, been plunged into distress, dismay, despondency. The terrible calamities which have befallen his nation are sufficient to account for this. Yet, as a child of God and a believer in Divine providence, he could not remain in desolation, he could not abandon himself to despair.

II. THE ORIGIN OF HOPE. How was the prophet lifted out of the discouragement and despondency into which he had fallen? It seems that here, as so often, hope sprang out of humility. When his heart was bowed and humbled within him, then he began to lift up his eyes unto the hills from whence alone his help could come.

III. THE GREAT OBJECT OF HOPE. The prophet saw nothing in existing circumstances which could afford a ground for anticipating better things and brighter days. But his hope was in the Lord, who listens to the lowly, the penitent, the contrite, and, in answer to their cry, delivers and exalts them in due time.

IV. THE EXPECTATIONS OF HOPE. When within the prophet's heart the star of hope arose, to what did it point, with its enlivening, cheering rays? To consolation, to deliverance, to revival of natural life, to renewal of Divine favour. No hope, based upon God's faithfulness and compassion, is too bright for him to fulfil and realize.—T.

Ver. 22.—*Sparing compassion.* At this point the meditations of the prophet take a turn. He looks away from his own and his fellow-countrymen's afflictions and directs his gaze heavenwards. The scene of his vision changes. No longer the calamities of Jerusalem, but the character and the purposes of the Most High, absorb his attention. There is a rainbow which spans even the stormiest sky. Earth may be dark, but there is brightness above. Man may be cruel or miserable, but God has not forgotten to be gracious.

I. THE LORD'S GRACIOUS ATTRIBUTES. These are described as (1) his mercies and (2) his compassions. It is the glory of revelation that it makes known a personal God, invested with the noblest moral attributes. The heathen saw in the calamities of cities and nations, either the caprice of angry deities or the working of inexorable fate. The Hebrews saw the presence, interest, and superintending providence of a God of righteousness, holiness, and grace.

II. THE UNFAILING EXERCISE OF THESE ATTRIBUTES FOR THE RELIEF AND SALVATION OF MEN. If "we are not consumed," it is not through any excellence or merit of ours, but because of the forbearance and pity of him who does not willingly afflict the children of men. We tempt the Lord by our ingratitude and rebellion to lay aside his compassion, but he is greater and better than our highest and purest thoughts of him: "His compassions fail not."

III. THE ADVANTAGES MEN ENJOY THROUGH THE EXERCISE OF THESE ATTRIBUTES. There is (1) a negative advantage—we are not consumed; and (2) a positive advantage—we are saved and blessed. The language of the prophet receives its highest illustration in the dispensation of the gospel. It is in Christ Jesus that the attributes here celebrated appear in their greatest glory, and secure the largest and most lasting results of good for men. Hence the privilege of listening to the glad tidings. And hence the obligation under which all Christians are laid to extol the mercies and compassions of God, revealed in his Son, and practically securing for all who believe the blessings of forgiveness, acceptance, and eternal life.—T.

Ver. 23.—"*New every morning.*" Human life abounds in novelties. It is made up of experiences which combine novelty and repetition. But the mercies of the Eternal are ever new; no day breaks which does not open up some new prospect of Divine faithfulness and loving-kindness towards the children of men.

I. THE SAME MERCIES ARE REPEATED AFRESH. Because a gift of God resembles a previous gift, it does not, therefore, fail in being a new proof of Divine beneficence and favour. The most necessary blessings are those which are most frequently bestowed, and are those which we are most likely to receive without attention and to undervalue.

II. NEW MERCIES ARE CONSTANTLY BESTOWED. The successive stages of our earthly pilgrimage reveal fresh wants, call for fresh supplies from the bounty and benevolence of our God and Father. With new needs come new favours. Varying duties, fresh relationships, and changing circumstances are the occasion of ever-renewed manifestations of Divine goodness. And our repeated errors and infirmities are the occasion of new manifestations of Divine forbearance and forgiveness.

III. NEW CLAIMS ARE THUS ESTABLISHED UPON HUMAN CONSECRATION AND OBEDIENCE. If a human benefactor who has upon some one important occasion come to our assistance deserves lifelong gratitude, how can the claims of God be justly conceived and practically acknowledged, seeing that the hours of every day are laden with his favours? If a motive is needed to a new life, a life of devotion and holy service, where can a more powerful motive be found than here? Often as we have partaken of Divine goodness, often as we have enjoyed the assurance of Divine forgiveness, we are called upon by the favours which are new every morning to renewed devotion of ourselves to the God of all grace and forgiveness.

IV. NEW OCCASIONS ARE THUS AFFORDED FOR RENEWED PRAISES AND THANKSGIVINGS. With every new morning nature offers a new tribute of praise to Heaven. Shall man alone be silent and ungrateful? Shall the Christian, who is the chosen recipient of Divine favours, be slow to acknowledge their heavenly source, to praise the heavenly Giver?

"New mercies each returning day," etc.

T.

Ver. 24.—*The Portion of the godly.* When the land of promise was divided among the tribes of Israel, no inheritance was assigned to one of the number, viz. the tribe of Levi. It appeared good to Divine wisdom that the consecrated and sacerdotal tribe should be distributed among the population, and that a regular provision should be made for their maintenance. To reconcile the Levites to their lot, it was declared to them by Jehovah himself that *he* was their Portion. The language here appropriated by the prophet, as his faith and hope revive, is language which every true servant of God may take to himself.

I. THE LORD IS AN INCOMPARABLE AND UNRIVALLED PORTION. Without the Divine favour, the greatest, the wealthiest, the most prosperous, are poor; with this favour, the lowliest and the penniless are rich. For that which pertains to the soul exceeds in value that which is external; circumstances are not unimportant, but to the just and reflective mind they are inferior to what is spiritual.

II. THE LORD IS A SUFFICIENT AND SATISFYING PORTION. With what jubilant, triumphant exultation did the psalmist exclaim, "The Lord is the Portion of mine inheritance, and my cup"! He who made and redeemed the soul can alone fully satisfy and supply it. Well might the apostle assure his Christian readers, "All things are yours;" and well might he reason for their encouragement, "Shall not God with Christ also freely give you all things?"

III. THE LORD IS AN ETERNAL PORTION. Whilst "riches take to themselves wings and fly away," whilst "the bubble reputation" bursts, whilst death levels the kings of the earth with the beggars,—the spiritual possessions of the pious remain undiminished in preciousness. In fact, the true value of the Portion of the godly can only be known in eternity. Here the estate is in reversion; there it is fully possessed and everlastingly enjoyed.—T.

Vers. 25, 26.—*Waiting for salvation.* It is to most persons easier to work than to wait. Yet there are possessions, dignities, influence, which even here and now can only be attained by waiting. And religion, which is the highest discipline of the spirit, encourages this attitude and, indeed, in many instances demands it.

I. THE ATTITUDE OF THE PIOUS SOUL. He who is graphically described in these verses: 1. *Seeks God.* For we are not called upon to be utterly passive; we are not led to expect that blessings will come to us without any exertion upon our part. To seek God in our daily life, in the order of his providence, in the pages of his Word, is a reasonable and profitable exercise. 2. *Hopes for his salvation.* And why not? Has not the Most High revealed himself as a Saviour? And is not salvation the blessing we most urgently need? 3. *Quietly waits for it.* This beautiful expression implies that the word of promise is believed, and that without doubting the soul expects its fulfilment. A rebuke to those who think that seeking God is accompanied with noise and excitement.

II. THE REWARD OF THE PIOUS SOUL. 1. There is what may be called the reflex influence of waiting. The expectant seeker and suppliant finds the very posture he is led to assume good and profitable. "In quietness and in confidence shall be your strength." 2. The Lord is actually good unto such as wait for him. He is pledged to this. His servants have ever found this to be the case. For the expectation honours him from whom the blessing is expected. The patient are delivered from their troubles, and to those who seek the Lord his glory is unveiled.—T.

Ver. 27.—*The yoke in youth.* This is not a welcome lesson. It is natural to all, and especially the young, to resist authority, to defy restraint, to resent punishment. As the young ox has to be brought under the yoke, as the young horse has to be accustomed to the bit and the bridle, the harness and the saddle, so the young must learn the practical and valuable lesson of endurance and submission.

I. IN HUMAN LIFE A YOKE IS IMPOSED UPON ALL. In some cases it is easier and in others more galling ; but there is no escape, no exception. Labour must be undergone, the daily burden must be borne, restraints must be endured for the sake of the general good, sacrifices must be made, patience must be called forth and cultivated.

II. WHEN FIRST FELT IN LATER LIFE, THE YOKE IS ESPECIALLY HARD TO BEAR. It sometimes happens that youth is sheltered from the storm of adversity, which beats fiercely upon the inexperienced and the undisciplined only in later years. It is well known how severely trouble is felt in such cases ; for the back is not fitted to the burden, the neck is not bent to the yoke.

III. THE DISCIPLINE EXPERIENCED IN YOUTH FITS FOR THE TOIL AND SUFFERING OF AFTER LIFE. This is why it is "good" then to endure it. Many of the noblest characters have known trouble in early life, and have thus learned the wholesome lessons of adversity which have stood them in good stead in after years. They who are afflicted in their youth learn the limitation of their own powers, learn the inexorable necessities of human life, and become apt scholars in the great school of Divine providence.

IV. RESISTANCE TO THE YOKE IS WRONG AND FOOLISH, SUBMISSION IS RIGHT AND WISE. It is hard to kick against the goads ; it is useless to resent the appointments of Divine wisdom. There are cases in which a rebellious spirit lasts all through life, and it is unquestionable that misery accompanies it. On the other hand, if the yoke be borne early and borne patiently, it becomes easier with custom. And those who are strong to suffer are also strong to serve.—T.

Ver. 30.—*The cheek to the smiter.* Probably these verses should be translated by imperatives. The prophet, profiting by his own experience and by that of his countrymen, admonishes all to meekness and submission. In resistance is neither peace nor deliverance ; in patient subjection and waiting is true wisdom, for such is the way to contentment and to final salvation.

I. SUCH MEEKNESS IS CONTRARY TO NATURAL INCLINATION, AND IS INDICATIVE OF A CHASTENED SPIRIT. He who is smitten naturally smites again. But to act upon this principle is to perpetuate a state of war and strife. Revenge is indeed often honoured in the world, yet the world's records are records of the wretchedness which this habit produces. On the other hand, the Christian principle, commended by our Lord in language which seems borrowed from this passage, is a principle of forgiveness and meek submission, the prevalence of which does much to mitigate asperity and to check wanton injuries.

II. SUCH MEEKNESS IS INCULCATED BY THE LORD JESUS BOTH BY PRECEPT AND EXAMPLE. He was reviled, yet he reviled not again. And in taking without resentment or complaint the unjust stripes and blows and many indignities he endured, our Saviour has given the world the most glorious example of victory over self, of superhuman meekness.

III. SUCH MEEKNESS IS CONTRIBUTIVE TO THE HAPPINESS OF THOSE WHO EXHIBIT IT AND TO THE EDIFICATION OF THOSE WHO WITNESS IT. The meek and lowly in heart find rest unto their soul. And society is profited by every illustration of the power and beauty of self-government and self-control, of conciliation and patience.—T.

Vers. 31—33.—*Divine benignity.* It required great faith on the part of Jeremiah and his countrymen to think and to speak thus of God. It was easy for them to believe in the justice and in the power of God ; their own affliction witnessed to these attributes. But it was a triumph of faith for those so afflicted to acknowledge the kindness and compassion of the supreme Ruler.

I. IT IS NOT INCOMPATIBLE WITH GOD'S GOODNESS TO AFFLICT MEN. He "causes grief." His providence appoints that human life should be largely a discipline of affliction, that human transgressions should be followed by chastisement. The Scriptures teach us that we may look all the stern and terrible facts of human life full in the face, and yet retain our confidence in the infinite kindness of the Divine Ruler.

II. GOD OBSERVES A LIMIT IN AFFLICTING HIS PEOPLE. His chastening is for a time. He will not always chide. He will not cast off for ever. For it is not implacable revenge, it is fatherly discipline, which accounts for human griefs.

III. COMPASSION AND MERCY ARE DISCERNIBLE BENEATH DIVINE CHASTENING. It is benignity which delivers the children of men from the waters, so that they are not overwhelmed; from the flames, so that they are not consumed. But it is benignity also (although this is a hard lesson for the afflicted, and a hard lesson for the philosopher of this world) which appoints affliction and chastening. God does not allow our sufferings willingly, i.e. from his heart, as delighting in them. It is not for his pleasure, but for our profit, that we may be partakers of his holiness. And herein we see, not only the highest wisdom, but the purest love.—T.

Ver. 38.—*The source of evil and of good.* This passage may easily be misunderstood. Some have attributed moral evil as well as moral good to the great Ruler of the universe, and by making God the author of sin have introduced confusion into the moral realm. The presence of sin in the world is by the permission of the Most High; but, whilst we cannot understand the reasons for this permission, we are not at liberty to represent him as sanctioning evil. The good and evil of this passage are natural, not moral.

I. THERE IS HERE AN ASSERTION OF UNIVERSAL AND PARTICULAR PROVIDENCE. The inequality of the human lot has ever been the theme of meditation, inquiry, and study. It has been attributed to chance, to men themselves, to the operation of law. But the enlightened and religious mind recognizes the voice and the hand of the Most High in human society, even when the immediate causes of what takes place are apparent. Nothing is so vast as to be above, and nothing is so minute as to be beneath, Providence. The afflictions and sufferings of life, as well as its joys and prosperity, are all allowed and all overruled for good to God's people. And all may become means of grace and blessing to such as receive them in a teachable and submissive spirit. Accordingly—

II. THERE IS HERE AN IMPLICIT SUGGESTION OF THE MANNER IN WHICH GOOD AND EVIL SHOULD BE RECEIVED BY MEN. This is not to be regarded as a speculative question merely, though it is a subject upon which thinking men must needs exercise their thoughts. But inasmuch as we all receive both good and evil in the course of our life, it cannot be other than a matter of supreme concern to us to decide in what spirit all that happens to us shall be accepted. 1. It will be well to remember that there is nothing purposeless; that there is intention, meaning, in all providential arrangements. 2. The devout mind will recognize benevolence in the "dispensations" of providence, will see the movements of a Father's hand and hear the tones of a Father's voice. 3. The Christian cannot overlook the obvious fact that the real good can only be acquired by those who receive the happiness of life with gratitude and bear the afflictions of life with submission and cheerfulness.—T.

Ver. 39.—*Why murmur?* The world is full of complaints and murmuring. It sometimes is observable that those whose lot is peculiarly fortunate, whose circumstances are peculiarly favourable, are foremost in complaint when anything occurs to them which does not fall in with their expectations, which does not correspond with their desires. On the other hand, we now and again meet with the poor, the suffering, the friendless, who display a cheerful, uncomplaining disposition.

I. ALL PUNISHMENT IS DESERVED BY THOSE UPON WHOM IT IS INFLICTED. Conscience testifies to this. God hath not "rewarded us according to our iniquities." No afflicted one can plead innocence, can justly affirm that he has been treated with undue severity. For this reason affliction should be endured in silence and with submission.

II. WHEN GOD CHASTISES HE DOES SO IN EQUITY, AND NOT IN INJUSTICE OR CAPRICE. The heathen attribute to arbitrary and fickle deities, even to malevolent deities, many of their misfortunes. But to us God is "righteous in all his works." To rebel against him is to question the wisdom of the only Wise, the justice of the supremely Righteous. The afflicted should look through the chastisement to the hand which inflicts it.

III. TO REBEL AGAINST GOD IS TO RESIST HIS PURPOSES OF COMPASSION WHICH INTEND

OUR GOOD. Observe that murmuring is not only wrong, it is most inexpedient. A complaining spirit is inconsistent with the disposition which alone can receive the wholesome lessons and discipline of sorrow and can turn them to highest and lasting profit.—T.

Ver. 40.—*Repentance.* Sin and suffering are the topic of much thought and inquiry and speculation. But it is of supreme concern to the sinner and the sufferer to *act* aright. He may or may not be able to explain the mysteries of the human heart, of the Divine government. But it is most important that he should repent and turn unto the Lord.

I. THE CONDITION OF REPENTANCE. The unreflecting and careless will not repent. There are two conditions necessary to such an attitude of mind. 1. Those afflicted because of sin should search themselves. To take a favourable view of self is natural; but truth and justice require that every man should look below the surface, should explore his inmost nature. Thus the springs of action, its hidden motives, will be brought to light. 2. They should consider against whom they have sinned. It was a profoundly just exclamation of David, "Against thee, thee only, have I sinned!" We may indeed wrong our fellow-men, but we sin against our Creator and Lord. Conduct must be looked at in this light, in order that it may lead to repentance.

II. THE NATURE OF REPENTANCE. This exercise of the heart is accompanied with sorrow for sin, but it consists mainly (1) in turning away from sin, and (2) in turning unto the Lord. This involves the seeking of pardon and acceptance, and the acceptance by faith of the Divine terms of mercy.

III. THE PROOF OF REPENTANCE. This may be said to consist in: 1. The hatred and loathing of the evil in which the sinner in his impenitence took pleasure. 2. The love and pursuit of holiness as pleasing unto God.—T.

Ver. 41.—"*Sursum corda!*" Religion takes possession of the whole of our nature. A service professedly of the heart, and of the heart alone, is a hypocritical service, which because of its insincerity God cannot accept, inasmuch as it is contradicted by the life. On the other hand, how can the Searcher of all hearts be pleased with a service which is of the hands, the outward posture and actions only, in which the heart has no share? The true worship and homage consists in the combination of the spirit and the body.

I. HEART AND HANDS ARE LIFTED IN PENITENCE AND CONFESSION. It seems to this exercise that the prophet here admonishes and invites. The heart has been engrossed by earthly pursuits and pleasures; and these it now quits, directing its contrite sighs to heaven, and lifting with it the clasped hands of penitence.

II. HEART AND HANDS ARE LIFTED IN EARNEST ENTREATY. In its anguish, in its conscious helplessness, the heart seeks mercy and acceptance with God; the hands are raised as in supplication, to give expression to the imploring petitions.

III. HEART AND HANDS ARE LIFTED IN BELIEVING CONFIDENCE. There is encouragement to trust in the Lord. The repenting and confiding Church of the Redeemer is ever lifting holy hands to heaven, in expression of that sentiment which is the condition of all blessing. It is the attitude of hope. "I will lift up mine eyes unto the hills whence cometh my help." And as the eyes of faith behold the God of grace upon the throne of power, they draw the heart upwards; the hands follow, and the posture of the spiritual nature is becoming to man and honouring to God.—T.

Vers. 48—51.—*Sympathetic sorrow.* This passage is sufficient to justify the title prefixed to this collection of sacred lyrics. It is indeed a "lamentation." And, what is deserving of special notice, the lament is not for personal affliction, it is occasioned by the distress and woe of the fellow-countrymen of the prophet.

I. THE OCCASION OF THIS SYMPATHETIC SORROW. 1. The affliction of "the daughters of the city." Whether by this expression we are to understand dependent towns or literally the maidens of Jerusalem, in any case it is the calamities of his countrymen that awaken compassion. 2. This affliction is of the extremest kind, even "destruction." Some of those whose woes call forth the prophet's commiseration are homeless, some are wounded, and some are slain. A hard heart can witness the distresses of fellow-creatures unmoved; but a sensitive nature views them with poignant sorrow. Our Lord wept over the same city when, at a later period, he foresaw a fate impending over Jerusalem even worse than that which occasioned the lamentation of Jeremiah.

II. THE CHARACTERISTICS OF THIS SYMPATHETIC SORROW. 1. It is cordial; not the sympathy of words merely, but of the heart. Politeness may dissimulate; sincere pity will feel. The sorrows of the soul because of human sin and woe are prompted by sympathy and consecrated by religion. 2. It is manifested. In the East and among simple nations grief displays itself in a more demonstrative way than amongst ourselves. There was nothing extravagant or unmanly in the pouring down of tears, in the running down of rivers of waters from the eyes, described in these verses. The manner in which sympathy is exhibited may vary, but this passage may suggest to us that the expression of compassion ought not to be withheld. 3. It is unintermitted; it ceases not. Such sympathy is not a mere paroxysm of grief; it is constant, enduring whilst the occasion of it endures.

III. THE PURPOSE AND HOPE ACCOMPANYING THIS SYMPATHETIC SORROW. Men sometimes speak of the uselessness of tears, the vanity of grief, etc. The godly sorrow exhibited by the prophet was not of this order; it had an aim, and that aim was the relief of those who were commiserated. Penitence and supplication were regarded as means to procure the regard, the interposition, the delivering mercy of Jehovah. Help, and help from above,—this is the practical design which blends with the anguish and the tears of the Christian.—T.

Vers. 55, 56.—*The cry from the dungeon.* There seems every reason for believing that, in these words, the prophet is recording his own actual experience. Under the reign of Zedekiah, when the doom of Jerusalem was near at hand, the faithful Jeremiah prophesied to the people, and by his warnings and predictions so offended the princes who were in authority in the city that they cast him into the pit of the prison. By Divine goodness he was delivered from this misery by the agency of the eunuch Ebed-Melech. Like a truly godly man, he witnesses to that God who is ever the Hearer of his people's prayers.

I. THE CRY FROM THE DEPTH. It was indeed *de profundis* that Jeremiah raised his voice and called upon the Lord. From sorrow, suffering, destitution, desertion, misery, helplessness, let men cry unto the Lord. The evil condition that impels them to such a cry is not all evil; there is "the soul of goodness" in it. The dungeon of oppression, of persecution, thus becomes a church indeed.

II. THE WITNESS OF THE RESCUED. The prophet testifies that his cry had not been unheeded. Even when immured in a pit so deep that his voice could not reach his fellow-men, his entreaty had reached the ear and roused the pity of the eternal Lord. And he who had heard had answered too, and had sent his messenger to deliver his servant. Where is there a child of God who has not experienced the compassionate interposition of the Most High? The Church should be as one of those temples whose walls are covered with tablets and brasses testifying to mercies received at the hand of the All-gracious.

III. THE CONFIDENT PRAYER. All former troubles were as nothing compared to this disaster which now overtakes the city, the nation. Renewed calamity prompts to renewed entreaty, and the memory of compassionate interposition incites to faith and hope. "The Lord *hath* been mindful of us; he *will* help us."—T.

Vers. 57, 58.—*Prayer heard and answered.* How natural that the mind of a pious man should, in seasons of distress and calamity, revert to the bygone days, remember the clouds by which they were overcast, and take encouragement at the vivid recollection of gracious interposition and help!

I. THE DAY OF DELIVERANCE. 1. This was a day of need and of distress, of sore need and of bitter distress. 2. It was a day of prayer, a day in which Divine aid had been zealously and urgently implored.

II. THE VOICE OF THE DELIVERER. "Thou saidst, Fear not!" How often are these words represented by the prophets to have been spoken by Jehovah! How often by the evangelists to have been spoken by Christ! They seem to constitute a "note" of Divine utterance.   They are as reassuring and consolatory to man as they are appropriate and becoming to God.

III. THE FACT OF DELIVERANCE.   Comforting words are welcome ; how much more the exercise of mighty power !   This passage depicts (1) the approach of the mighty One, and (2) the redemption of the captive's life.   What was literally true of Jeremiah's bodily condition is true of the spiritual state of sinful man ; and all temporal interpositions are an emblem of the delivering, the redemptive grace of God in Jesus Christ.

IV. THE ACKNOWLEDGMENT OF DELIVERANCE.   The testimony of the prophet is an example to all who have experienced the blessedness of Divine love and grace.   Such acknowledgment should be grateful, cordial, public, and everlasting.—T.

Vers. 59—63.—*The Lord's knowledge of his people's sufferings and wrongs.*   The first thought which occurs to people when oppressed and afflicted is—The Lord takes no heed ; he has no compassion ; he will not help ; my judgment is passed over from my God.   But it is afterwards felt that such language is language of impatience and injustice.   And the pious soul comes to rest almost satisfied beneath the blows and contempt of men, because a conviction springs up—It is all known to the omniscient and sympathizing Lord.

I. GOD, IN HIS PROVIDENCE, PERMITS HIS PEOPLE TO SUFFER AND ENDURE CALUMNIES, REPROACHES, AND WRONGS.   Their endurance of such, now and again, is an unquestionable fact.   And if there be a God, and such a God as revelation declares, it is certain that he suffers his people to pass through much that is painful to flesh and blood.

II. GOD DOES NOT ALWAYS AND AT ONCE REMEDY THE ILLS WHICH BEFALL HIS PEOPLE.   The thought occurs to the oppressed and wronged—Can it be that he sees and hears all that is said and done to us, unmerited as it is on our part ?   If he does, how mysterious that he withholds his hands from avenging us, from discomfiting our cruel foes !

III. DIVINE DELAY IS NO PROOF OF DIVINE INDIFFERENCE.   Christ stood upon the mountain-top, and by the misty moonlight watched his disciples tossed upon the lake, toiling in rowing, and sorely harassed.   But he loved them, and if he did not come forthwith to their relief there was a good reason for his delay.   So oftentimes men think God careless because their probation is prolonged ; but in truth wisdom and love are the motives of all his acts and of even his apparent tardiness.

IV. GOD THUS TRIES HIS PEOPLE'S FAITH AND STEADFASTNESS AND PREPARES THEM FOR HIS SALVATION.   After the stormy tempest how grateful is the rainbow !   After the black night how welcome is the dawn !   The mere contrast, however it might heighten joy, would not account for God's action in testing his servants.   But there are moral ends to be secured.   And the furnace alone can separate the dross from the gold.   The storm alone can try, can elicit, can perfect, the faith of the mariner and his confidence in the Lord who seems to sleep.—T.

Vers. 64—66.—*Righteous recompense.*   Our conscience requires and approves of justice.   Our weakness is too often in danger of cherishing resentment and malevolence. It is not safe, on most men's part, to hope for retribution upon their personal enemies. Perhaps the record of Jeremiah's feelings is not intended to be taken for an inculcation, or even a permission, of such imprecations upon our foes.

I. THE GROUND UPON WHICH DIVINE JUDGMENT IS INVOKED.   1. It was not personal offence given which suggested such a cry for vengeance.   2. It was the overt, deliberate conduct of men who acted in disobedience and defiance towards God, and with inhumanity and barbarity towards their fellow-men.

II. THE TRIBUNAL TO WHICH THE CONDUCT OF THE WICKED IS REFERRED.   1. Not the fallible court of human justice or human requital.   2. But the court of Divine equity, in which none receives good for evil, in which every plea for mitigation of sentence is heard, and from which none can depart with a complaint upon the lips.

III. THE PURPOSE FOR WHICH RETRIBUTION IS IMPLORED.   1. Not for the gratification of vindictive feelings.   2. Not for the exaltation of the oppressed at the expense of the oppressor.   3. But for the speedy deliverance of God's wronged and harassed people.   4. For the advancement of God's cause upon earth.   For the honour of God's glorious Name.   "Shall not the Judge of all the earth do right ?"—T.

Ver. 18.—*The sum of a terrible experience.* This chapter must doubtless be taken as the utterance of Jeremiah's own feelings—feelings induced by the continual stress and difficulty of his life. Through the first seventeen verses he alludes to some opponent and tormentor continually thwarting his every purpose, not for a single moment leaving him free. Are we to suppose, then, that the prophet really believed all these untoward experiences to come from some one agent who had special designs against him? or was he thus only trying to make more forcible the story of his sufferings? However this is to be settled, some of our difficulty is taken away when we find, on coming to ver. 18, this clear reference to Jehovah: " My strength and my hope is perished from the Lord." These words we may take to mark about the lowest point in reckless and unadvised speaking. They give a sort of confession as to what a deadly member the tongue may become in hours of suffering. What we *only feel* to be the reality is taken to be the reality, whereas the reality may be immensely better. The prophet came to speak in a worthier way, and lived to admit that, in the very depths, he discovered what God's disposition to him really was. Note how the prophet made a double mistake.

I. HE SAID HIS STRENGTH AND HOPE WERE PERISHED. Yet these things, even when composed of purely natural elements, are not so easily destroyed. Even with all the weakness that belongs to human nature, there is immense strength in it. After a long life men wonder to look back and see what they have actually achieved, and the strain they have undergone. While we may be alarmed in the midst of our troubles and vicissitudes, God looks on very differently, knowing how much strength there is to get over them. The resources of our own natures have to be developed, and the resources of grace connected with them. Then, when the strength is brought out, the hope naturally springs forth at the same time. There is hardly a greater peril in life than to act from the conclusions coming to us in gloomy moods.

II. HE SAID HIS STRENGTH AND HOPE WERE PERISHED FROM GOD. *From God.* How came he to say such a thing, or even to think it for a moment? Probably because he had not sufficiently recollected wherein it is that God's favour really appears. To that God who has all power nothing would have been easier than to have made the prophet's path outwardly pleasant and straightforward. But where would have been the gain in that? The thing really wanted was that, when Jeremiah was left alone, bereft of earthly comfort and stays, he should be led into a state of mind where he could say, " Though I seem alone, and in my solitude weak and hopeless, yet I am not alone ; for the God who made me a prophet is with me in ways which cannot be comprehended by my innumerable enemies."—Y.

Ver. 21.—*How hope rises from the depths of despair.* This utterance needs to be contrasted with that in ver. 18. There the prophet says that hope is perished. Here he has hope, grounded on a " therefore " and strengthened by a resolved attitude of mind. Thus we are helped to get an explanation of his past depression, or, as we might even call it, despair. We are helped to distinguish between abiding Divine realities and the way in which they are coloured or concealed by our moods. How is it, then, the prophet is here able to come to such an inspiring resolution? Two things are to be noticed.

I. THIS HOPE COMES BY CONSIDERING THE RIGHT THINGS. The prophet says, " This will I recall to my mind," or " take to heart." *This*, that is to say, such things as he goes on to mention later in the chapter. He said that he had been led into darkness and confinement. That he had been *led* was only his own way of putting the thing ; the important point to note is that he got into such confusion of mind, such preoccupation with mighty evils, as to be unable to see life in the whole. Darkness had covered gracious truth, or clouds had risen between it and his spiritual vision. We can easily come to the most melancholy conclusions if only we determine to shut certain considerations from the mind. Let it also be noted that, as satisfying hope comes from considering the right things, so delusive hope comes from letting the mind dwell exclusively on the wrong ones. And what is true of the production of satisfying hope is true of other satisfying states of mind. So men may pass from unbelief to the firmest and most fruitful faith, and from selfishness to love.

II. THIS HOPE COMES FROM CONSIDERING THE RIGHT THINGS IN THE RIGHT SPIRIT.

As the expression may be rendered, there must be "a taking to heart." Loss of hope comes from taking to heart the sad side of human life. The same things are, of course, before us all. There is enough mysterious misery in the world to oppress any human heart that thinks of nothing else, but then along with this we should ever have before us, as things to be searched into with all earnestness, the great facts of the loving revelation of God in Christ Jesus. The resurrection of Jesus, rightly considered, will give a hope rooted deep below the most discomposing powers of this world. It is not enough to place the great facts before us; they must be dealt with as being very dear and necessary to the heart.—Y.

Vers. 22, 23.—*The unfailing compassions of Jehovah.* Here indeed is a full retractation of the reckless falsehood recorded in ver. 18. He who had hinted that God was a Destroyer, that he delighted, as it were, in reducing his children to despair, is now found glorying in the same God as the great Preserver, the one effectual Guardian of man's existence and peace.

I. NOTE THE DESTROYING POWERS THAT BESET HUMAN LIFE. God's mercies are the only guarantee against our being consumed. How great, then, must be the perils of life! Jeremiah had nothing to do but look back on his own experience, and then he would be filled with wonder to think he had got so far. Think of the vivid way in which Paul summed up the perils of his life. It is indeed true that we do well not to think too much of such perils. All the comfort would be taken out of life if we thought of them too much. But there they are, and times do come when it is useful to pass them before the mind. And especially we should note those perils which are perils because they have temptation in them. One of the greatest perils of life is to make an inadequate estimate of perils. The greatest of all perils is to be false to truth and goodness for the sake of life or even of temporal prosperity. Our passions, our fears, and our pride are all ready to league with the great enemy of God and of mankind.

II. NOTE THE ONLY ADEQUATE DEFENCE AGAINST THESE DESTROYING POWERS. 1. *That defence is to be found in Jehovah.* With him alone is the might and the power requisite to make due provision. Man is ignorant and prejudiced, continually going into the way of death, under a firm conviction that it is the way of life. If Jeremiah had been left to himself, to his own prudence and his own notions of safety, the chances are he would have been a dead man in no long time after he had begun prophesying. The true wisdom is to put ourselves into the hands of God. Then the way of duty becomes the way of safety. We are no longer misled by appearances. We suffer from the lesser danger and escape the greater. We discover how true it is that a man may lose his life, and yet in the very losing find it. 2. *The compassion and faithfulness of Jehovah are specially insisted on.* We ask constantly why men do things, and what motives are at the bottom of their doings. And we must ask the same things with respect to God. From the thing done we may rise to understand the heart of the doer. And then, knowing what his character is, we may confidently calculate what sort of things he will do in the future. God's mercies are new every morning—light after darkness, strength after sleep, conscious life with all its large endowments after hours of unconsciousness. And great is his faithfulness. The irregularities and forgettings of human procedure are not to be found in the dealings of God. And this is just the responsibility that comes to us from all the attainments of science, that the deeper we search into the constitution of the universe, the more we should be impressed with the greatness of God's faithfulness.—Y.

Ver. 24.—*Those who have Jehovah for their Portion.* I. EVERY MAN HAS HIS PORTION. That which is his capital, which constitutes his resources, and out of which he has to build up the results of his life. It was only natural that an Israelite should make a great deal of *portions.* Israel had a portion, divinely secured and wonderfully packed with the raw materials of wealth. Each tribe had its portion, given by lot, so that there was no ground of complaint, and so to each household in due time there came a portion. In Israel, as in every other nation, there were the rich and the poor—those with great possessions and those with none at all. Thus there are inequalities, and not the least of them are those which inhere in the constitution of the individual. Our portion depends, not on what we legally possess, but on what we have the energy and the skill to use. The greatest of a man's natural resources are in himself. Otherwise he may sit among large possessions which are of no more use to him than are his hoards to a miser.

II. EVERY MAN HAS IT IN HIS OWN POWER TO REMOVE THE INEQUALITIES OF HIS PORTION. Jeremiah shows us how. Whatever his natural portion may have been, it had well-nigh vanished through the hatred of his people and even of his own acquaintance. Nor must we forget that he was speaking in the midst of a desolate land. Many portions had gone and left their owners not knowing which way to turn. But now Jeremiah both assures us of his own resources and advises us where to seek ourselves, by saying, "Jehovah is my Portion." Thus he turns away the mind from mere external property. It is the dreadful character of all mere external wealth that there is only so much of it, and therefore, just in proportion as some grow rich, others must become poor. Besides which there is to be considered that moment when riches will take to themselves wings and flee away, and that still more serious moment when flesh and heart will fail. Thus we see that the complaint about the inequalities of life has more plausibility than force. All purely natural portions are reduced to the same vanity at last, and the man who trusts in them has but wasted his time and procured for himself the deepest disappointments. Whatever we may lack, we need not lack that portion which consists in the promises of God made to them who truly trust in him.

III. THE CONSEQUENCE OF HAVING GOD FOR A PORTION. The life is filled with hope. A man can only hope according to his portion. If his portion is in this world, his hope will have a corresponding character; whereas if his portion is really in God, his hope will partake of the necessary elevation and fulness of his portion. God takes care that those who are really his should have a feeling in their hearts which makes them look forward to a future always better than the present. We are saved by hope. The process is yet far from complete, but it is our right to rejoice that we are in the hands of One who will make salvation complete in his own time.—Y.

Vers. 25, 26.—*God's goodness to the hopeful and the patient.* God's goodness is one thing; that it should be made manifest to men so that they may get comfort out of it is quite another. Bad men will never see God to be good. Not being good themselves, not having kindly, generous, and unselfish feelings towards others, they can never come to look upon God from the point of view necessary to get a manifestation of his goodness. Hence we notice—

I. How GOD'S GOODNESS APPEARS TO THOSE BEHAVING THEMSELVES IN A RIGHT WAY. About the first thing that is required is to believe that God is good, however much his goodness is concealed, and however trying the experiences of life may be. We must not be contented to say, "Peradventure something good will come somehow." But rather let us say, "The manifestation of the goodness will depend on our making ready for it." We must wait. So to speak, we have to take our turn. When the seed is sown, the harvest must be waited for. God could give us certain good things immediately, but not the best things. The child cannot receive the things of the man. The servant can only get his reward when his service is completed, and that in a worthy manner. Then besides waiting there is seeking. There is no proper attitude towards God without a combination of the passive and the active. God has made excellence in true knowledge the result of strenuous, long-continued effort.

II. THE GREAT ATTAINMENT IN ALL TIME OF TROUBLE IS TO HAVE A DUE MINGLING OF HOPE AND PATIENCE. Jehovah can save, if only we have what may be called spiritual presence of mind. If we say, "I must get rid of my troubles *now*, or I shall straightway give up the struggle," then, indeed, the prospect of salvation retires to an immense distance. What is wanted is that we should put all our highest interests in the hand of God, and then go quietly about our daily opportunities of serving him. When the passenger goes on board ship at the beginning of a long voyage he puts complete confidence in the captain, and thus he hopes and quietly waits for the voyage to come to an end. Through all perils of the sea he can only hope and quietly wait, knowing that the master of the vessel is the only one who can guard against the perils. And so in the voyage of life; we cannot shorten it, we cannot determine what its circumstances will be; but we can put ourselves in the hands of the great Guide. He will look after our safety, if we only take heed to our part in the doing of his work. Let silent waiting be our rule. We are very likely to say foolish things in our criticism of the Divine ways, and therefore it is well to keep silent. But while we are silent we may think a great deal. That is good advice of the psalmist, "Commune with your own heart . . . and be *still*." It is through inward questionings and discontent with received traditions that we are to get at the comfortable truth at last. But if we go on talking we are very likely to discompose and mislead others. The moods in which we are doubting, fearful, and weary, we should do our very best to keep to ourselves.—Y.

Ver. 27.—*The discipline of youth.* Remember how early Jeremiah was called to prophesy. He says at the beginning, "Ah, Lord God! behold, I cannot speak : for I am a child" (Jer. i. 6). He had to bear the yoke in his youth, and doubtless this did much to fit him for a useful and well-controlled life afterwards. The comparison, of course, is plain. An ox might be put under the yoke when quite young, and then, though the restraint would be irksome for a while, at last the sense of restraint would pass away, and the yoke become second nature ; whereas if an ox had never been tried with the yoke until full-grown, the chances were it would not accept it in a docile and serviceable way. There is this difference between the youthful ox and the youthful human being, that the youthful ox is entirely in the hands of his master, while the youthful human being has his own choice. For we do not take the yoke here to mean chiefly the external circumstances of life. The yoke is that which we take upon ourselves, seeing that it is the right and manly thing to do. Self-denial is a yoke. The effort needful in forming right habits is a yoke. The subordination of the present to the future, the lower to the higher, the human to the Divine, is a yoke. Not that we are to leave external circumstances altogether out of the question. Men who had hard times when young have come to be thankful, in after years, for those very hard times. It is better to be an orphan than to be the child of parents who have both the means and the disposition which make them lavishly indulgent. Only bear in mind that external circumstances have not in themselves any disciplining power. The materials of a yoke might be used to make something else. The decision rests with us. One may make a yoke out of prosperity and favourable circumstances, while another so chafes and sulks under adversity as to become worse every day.—Y.

Vers. 31—33.—*God's good purposes in causing pain.* All this is the language of hope and continues naturally what is said in vers. 21 and 24. The existence of present trouble presses upon the heart, but along with it there is the confident assurance of future deliverance. Observe, then, certain admissions, along with the cheering qualifications which accompany them.

I. THE LORD CASTS OFF. There is a discontinuance of the signs of his presence. Enemies get their own way, and, worst of all, the prophets find no vision from the Lord. He is not towards Israel as he used to be. But then, what a qualification comes in! *Not for ever.* Indeed, the casting off only emphasizes the bringing back. The casting off must not be taken too literally. God does not cast off as men do. They cast off and do not wish to bring back, or, if they so wish, they find they are not able. When God casts off, though there is a feeling of separation, and something is lost that is not to be gained by any effort, still the truth remains that in God even the castaway lives and moves and has his being. God casts men off, as it were, that they may realize their weakness and true state, and then, when they make the full discovery, God's hand is stretched out to restore.

II. THE LORD CAUSES GRIEF. Great grief, pain of body and pain of heart, must have come from the casting off. And it is of no use to make nice distinctions between God causing pain and permitting pain. Really we do not know much about the causes of pain, and it may be that we attribute to God much that we ourselves produce. The one clear thing is that God shows forth a multitude of mercies. To most of us a multitude of mercies came before there were any pains at all, and the mercies remain through the pains, even though at times they be greatly eclipsed. We may be wrong in attributing the infliction of pain to God, hampered as we too often are by the conceptions of earlier ages. But we can never be wrong in glorifying God for the multitude of his mercies. We may spoil and misuse the mercies and thus make pain, but the mercies we could not get for ourselves. Our very wrong-doing makes fresh mercies to arise in view. They are many, and each one of them is a great deep of love and wisdom.

III. THE LORD AFFLICTS THE CHILDREN OF MEN. This is but saying what is already said. The new thing is the qualification. He does not do it *willingly.* The distinction is plain between injury inflicted with malice and injury inflicted with reluctance. There have been, and, alas! there still are, too many who put all their heart into the hurting of others. Their very end is to cause pain; whereas the end God has in view is to remove the causes of pain. The surgeon does not inflict pain willingly—he inflicts it because he cannot help it; and thus he welcomes and utilizes to the full the agent which brings unconsciousness while he performs his operation.—Y.

Vers. 40—42.—*Approaching God in sincerity.* I. THE ASCERTAINING OF OUR TRUE STATE. Such is the exhortation of ver. 40. The talk of complaining people is generally the hasty outbreak of superficial thought—if, indeed, such loose operations of the mind are worthy to be called thought at all. Searching is above all things needful. Beneath the surface with which we are only too easily contented there are deep possibilities of good and evil. Note the figure here employed. We are in a way—further advanced to-day than we were yesterday. There is no standing still. This way we are urged to search and try—asking whither it goes, who are our predecessors, our leaders, our companions. Then note the result of all our searching and testing. The way is one in which God is not. He walks in quite another way, and therefore we must turn to him. Only one result of a real searching is deemed possible. The man without God who yet concludes that all is right, has in truth left the most important matters unexplored.

II. THE RETURN TO GOD MUST BE A REAL RETURN. There had, perhaps, been abundant lifting up of the hands on the part of many, with no lifting of the heart. But many more had not even lifted up the hands. We must not say that posture and gesture are mere trifles. To God, of course, the mere gesture in itself can matter nothing, but from its associations it may matter a great deal. Prayer to the unseen and spiritual One is such a difficult thing that we may welcome every aid. Still, the great matter is to lift up the heart. Lift it up—filled with gratitude, humility, repentance, submissiveness.

III. A SUGGESTION OF THE GREAT DIFFICULTY YET TO BE OVERCOME. God has not pardoned. On one side there is transgression and rebellion; on the other side, God angry with all this. And what is wanted is that Israel should see transgression as transgression, rebellion as rebellion. Here we are amid the confusion of life, and we do not see that for all the worst way in which that confusion affects us we are ourselves responsible. With a humble and repentant heart, taking continual cognizance of God's righteous will, we could ride as in an ark over that deluge which overwhelms others. But with pride and selfishness in our hearts we are strong against all ameliorating forces. We will not come to God that in him we may have first pardon and then safety, peace, and blessing.—Y.

Ver. 51.—*The eye and the life.* "Mine eye affecteth mine heart." More correctly, "Mine eye paineth my soul, or my life;" that is, what I see, so melancholy is it, that it preys on my mind and undermines my health. Note—
I. THE EFFECT OF THE SENSES ON THE LIFE. The eye is more than an optical instrument. The effect produced by the image on the retina depends upon who it is that sees and what it is that he sees. Age, education, peculiarities of experience, will make all the difference. The very exercising of the senses was evidently intended to give pleasure. There is correspondence between the eye and the beautiful and sublime in nature; between the ear and melodious and harmonious sounds; and yet some peculiar experience may interpose, so that there shall no longer be beauty in the beautiful, melody in the melodious. What we *get* from the exercise of our senses will depend upon what we *bring.* The prophet saw desolation all around him where once there had been crowded and prosperous life. What could he do but feel as if a broken heart would be the end of his thoughts? But the spoilers would look at the scene differently, for to them it was the place of enrichment and triumph.

II. COMPENSATIONS FOR THE LOSS OF SENSE. Loss of vision is a serious matter to one whose intellect is full of life and activity. So Milton seems to have felt, judging from his touching references to his blindness in his poetry. But this makes it all the more needful to recollect the other side. The blind have exemptions from some pains. They do not see the painful sights of the streets: the drunkard, the ragged beggars, the weary faces—weary with incessant struggling for a position or a livelihood. They can guess much of the trouble of the world, but many of the manifestations of that trouble they only know when they are told. We do well to keep in mind and rightly estimate the compensations for natural losses.

III. RESPONSIBILITY FOR THE RIGHT USE OF OUR NATURAL POWERS. The expression of the prophet here indicates that he was in the right way. To have looked on such a scene with indifference or only mild regret would have argued a very wrong state of mind indeed. Surely in the judgment the question to many will be, "What use did you make of your eyesight? Did you gather up impressions which made you feel how deep is the spiritual sickness of the world, how certain it is that only Christ can make the world better? And further, did you lend practical help to bring men within reach of the saving power of Christ?" To this extent it will be better in the day of judgment for many blind than for those who have gone through the smitten world with both eyes open and yet as if they did not see.—Y.

Ver. 55.—*Jeremiah calling out of the dungeon.* This is no mere figure for a great extremity, as we are made to feel when we read ch. xxxviii. of the prophecies. It was not from amid mere restraint that the prophet cried, but from miry depths, most perilous, painful, and disgusting. Note—

I. THE PUTTING INTO THE DUNGEON. God does not stretch forth his hand to prevent his servants from being put into such dreadful circumstances. He looks on while they are haled to prison and even to death. For a lesson has to be taught with regard to the limitations of human power. Jeremiah's enemies might say to him, while down in the miry pit, "Where is now thy God?" but this was because they estimated God's favour to men according to the presence or absence of certain outward things. God's favour is not shown by preserving us in certain external possessions. Even life may have to be yielded for his sake. God does not interfere miraculously, even with the conduct of wicked men, unless there is some very special reason. What he says is, "You shall really be safe whatever men may do." He who allowed his Son to be put to death, did then open wide, so that no man can shut it, the gate that leads to eternal life.

II. THE TAKING OUT OF THE DUNGEON. This was in answer to prayer. And the prayer came from a spirit of trust that no gloom and discomfort of the pit could destroy. If Jeremiah had allowed himself to say that his conjunction with Jehovah had been a mere delusion, then he might have been left in the pit. And even with all his faith he might have been left in the pit. But then there would have been a clear assurance that death was better than life. And, indeed, it is probable that, if God had allowed his servant to go out of the world at the hands of his enemies, he might have been spared a great deal of pain and sorrow. What is to be looked to in these matters is, not the present ease of the individual, but the best way in which his life can be used for the good of men and the glory of God. Prisons are no prisons, pits are no pits, if God chooses to give to his servants liberty and continue to them their natural life. In one way or another he brings his servants out of the horrible pit and out of the miry clay.—Y.

Vers. 60—66.—*Jeremiah and his enemies.* I. THE PROCEEDINGS OF THESE ENEMIES. The spirit of vengeance is in their hearts. Jeremiah has spoken steadily against them what Jehovah had laid on him to say. They know the language in which they have been described. It was, of course, just the thing to be expected that bad men should cherish vengeful purposes. And Jeremiah had to bear the consciousness of this—the very painful consciousness that he was the cause, however innocent, of showing up the worst passions in the hearts of others. This spirit of vengeance manifested itself in two ways. 1. *Reproach.* He was called all sorts of names, held up to derision and execration. He indeed had to reproach, but then there was a measure and dignity in the words he employed. His reproaches were meant to call the reproached ones to repentance. But the reproaches from his enemies meant immediate danger to him— danger from the populace on the one hand, and the authorities on the other.   2. *Plotting.* Society was just in the state when plots could be carried out with success. Jeremiah did not make one enemy or a few enemies, but many. They were wicked men, and doubtless had subordinates ready to hand for any knavery that was going on.

II. JEREMIAH'S BELIEF THAT GOD'S EYE WAS UPON THESE ENEMIES. "Thou hast seen." It is a great matter to feel that God has his eye upon all human wickedness. We may suffer greatly from it, and yet see only a very small part of what he sees. We are for ever running into extremes, exaggerating or palliating, magnifying the reality or else diminishing it. We look at things too much in reference to our individual selves, and as they concern us. But God sees things as they truly are, in all their relations and possibilities. Some things are worse than we think them, others better. And so we are enabled to feel that all wickedness is kept within comparatively innocuous limits. The mischief only reaches the outside of what is attacked, for the same God who watches the wicked watches the good at the same time.

III. THE PRAYER OF JEREMIAH.   (Vers. 64—66.) The vehemence, the almost savageness of these words staggers us. But then, we are not to expect the gentleness of a Christian from an old Jewish prophet. We are not required to justify every petition of God's servants. We have to distinguish between the prophet taken out of himself by inspiration and the man of like passions with ourselves, who has to pass through a long discipline before he can pray as he ought to pray. We may feel here that a silent waiting upon God would have been better than any imprecations of vengeance, and yet, at the same time, we must acquit Jeremiah of anything like personal malice. He wished that the wicked might be recompensed *according* to the work of their hands. The wicked wished Jeremiah to be treated according to the ferocity of their own hearts.—Y.

Ver. 63.—*The music of the wicked.* I. THE PLEASURES OF BAD MEN. Musical tastes are, of course, irrespective of moral character. There are certain original qualities both in eye and ear which remain and demand satisfaction, whatever the moral character may become. If a person of musical tastes becomes a Christian, than his Christianity may be the better for his music, or possibly, if he is not careful, it may become worse. On the other hand, if a person of musical tastes becomes an utterly selfish and self-indulgent man, then music will become the instrument of all that is bad. And so we find that great excellence in arts has been found intermingled with the grossest profligacy. Men are not necessarily better because intellect and tastes have been cultivated. The only power which, allowed to work, must make men better is the Holy Spirit of God, and where he is working, such things as music and pictures may be welcomed to give additional beauty.

II. A MALIGNANT TENDENCY IN THE PLEASURES OF BAD MEN. Bad men must ever be hindered and thwarted by the good, and when the bad get any sort of temporary triumph over the good, they will make it a cause of exultation. To some degraded and embittered hearts great is the pleasure of giving pain. This is the peril of satirists. Great intellectual gifts and powers of literary expression are concentrated on a few polished verses, which pain the subject of them all his life. There is no diviner instrument than pain as a means to an end, but surely that heart is set on fire of hell that can make pain an end in itself.—Y.

Ver. 64.—*The principle of retribution.* Whatever the feelings in the prophet's heart may have been, at all events he lays down something like a principle on which he expects God will act in dealing with the wicked. It is not because he hates them, or because they have hurt *him,* that he wants them to suffer, but because they have done wrong. Further, he wants to see them dealt with according to the wrong they have done. Perhaps we ought to look at this question of recompense apart from its being made a matter of prayer. One would not like to think of it as a desirable petition in any prayer, that the wicked might be dealt with according to their wickedness. God's law will secure all that is necessary, and we may trust the working of that law. Men will be recompensed according to the work of their hand, only this expression, "the work of their hand," must be taken with a very liberal meaning. What the heart of the wicked purposes, his hand generally carries out to some extent, and yet many qualifications must be made. To go literally according to the work of the hand would be to deal too severely in some instances, too leniently in others. We have to infer the heart from the hand, and our calculation of motives is a very rough-and-ready one. Human law, trying to be just and adequate, is not unfrequently unjust and cruel. We are so under the influence of things seen and temporal that a punishment only looks real when we can see it in operation, manifest to all. Our confidence should rather be that God has so made things by their very nature that a wicked heart becomes a miserable one. Whatsoever a man sows, he reaps. But then there is also another thing to be considered, and that is that God makes room for repentance. He who sows repentance will reap forgiveness and renewal of heart. We cannot undo the works of our hands, but God can bring good out of evil.—Y.

EXPOSITION.

CHAPTER IV.

THE SUFFERINGS OF JERUSALEM; NO CLASS IS EXEMPT. EDOM'S TRIUMPHING.

Ver. 1.—**How is the gold become dim!** . . . **the stones of the sanctuary,** etc. "Alas for the sad sights of the capture of Jerusalem! The most fine gold has lost its brilliance now that the fire of Nebuzar-adan (2 Kings xxv. 9) has passed over it, and the precious stones, consecrated to Jehovah, have been cast out into the open street!" Not that the latter part of this description can have corresponded to literal fact. None of the hallowed jewels would have been treated with such indifference. The expression must be as figurative as the parallel one, "to cast pearls before swine," in Matt. vii. 6. The precious stones are the "sons of Zion," who are compared to "fine gold" in ver. 2, precisely as they are in Zech. ix. 16 (comp. ver. 13, "Thy sons, O Zion ") to "the stones of a crown." They are called "stones of the sanctuary," in allusion, perhaps, to the precious stones employed in the decoration of the temple according to 1 Chron. xxix. 2 and 2 Chron. iii. 6. But we may also translate *hallowed stones,* which better suits the figurative use of the phrase. Those, however, who adopt the literal interpretation, explain "the stones of the sanctuary" of the hewn stones of the fabric of the temple, which are described as "costly" in 1 Kings v. 17. But how can even a poet have represented the enemy as carrying these stones out and throwing them down in the street? On the other hand, in an earlier lamentation we are expressly told that the young children "fainted for hunger in the top of every street" (ch. ii. 19).

Ver. 2.—**The precious sons of Zion;** *i.e.* not merely the nobility, but the people of Judah in general. It is needless (as the literal interpreters of ver. 1 are compelled to do) to alter *b'nê* (sons) into *bāttê* (houses)

or *'abnê* (stones). The comparison of men to potters' vessels is familiar to the Hebrew writers (comp. Isa xxii. 24; xlv. 9).

Ver. 3.—**The sea-monsters;** rather, *the jackals (tannîn,* the Aramaic form of the plural for *tannîm).* **Cruel, like the ostriches in the wilderness.** So in Job (xxxix. 14—16) it is said of the ostrich that she " leaveth her eggs in the earth, and warmeth them in dust, and forgetteth that the foot may crush them, or that the wild beast may break them. She is hardened against her young ones, as though they were not hers." The description is literally true, if we add a detail not mentioned by the sacred poet. The eggs destined for hatching are deposited in a nest-hole scratched in the sand, but there are other eggs laid, not in the sand, but near it, to all appearance forsaken. These eggs, however, are not exposed in simple stupidity, though they do often fall victims to violence. "They are intended for the nourishment of the newly hatched young ones, which in barren districts would at first find difficulty in procuring food" (Houghton, 'Natural History of the Ancients,' p. 198).

Ver. 4.—**Breaketh it unto them.** The Jewish bread, consisting of round or oval cakes (comp. 1 Kings xix. 6).

Ver. 5.—**They that did feed delicately,** etc. *i.e.* luxuriously. The rendering has been disputed, but without sufficient ground. "They that did eat at dainties," *i.e.* pick at their dainty food, is forced. The Aramaic mark of the accusative need not surprise us in Lamentations (comp. Jer. xl. 2). **Brought up in scarlet;** rather, *borne upon scarlet; i.e.* resting upon scarlet-covered couches. The poet speaks of adults, not of children.

Ver. 6.—**The punishment of the iniquity** . . . **the punishment of the sin.** This is a possible rendering (see Gen. iv. 13; Zech. xiv. 19), but the renderings, "the iniquity," "the sin," are preferable, and yield a finer meaning, viz. that the punishment having been so severe, the guilt must have been in proportion. **And no hands stayed on her.** To make the picture of sudden destruction more vivid, the poet alludes to the ordinary circumstances of the capture of a city, the "hands" of a fierce soldiery ever "whirling" a destroying sword. Comp. "the swinging of the hand of Jehovah Sabáoth, which he swingeth against it" (Isa. xix. 16).

Ver. 7.—**Her Nazarites**; rather, *her eminent ones* (just as Joseph is called *n'zir ekháv*, "eminent among his brethren"). The rendering of the Authorized Version is lexically possible, but is intrinsically improbable. The Nazarites constituted too small a portion of the Jewish people to receive so prominent a place in the elegy. **Rubies**; rather, *corals*. **Their polishing** was **of sapphire**; literally, *their shape was (like) a sapphire.* But the point in which the sapphire is compared to the bodies of the princes is evidently not the outline of its form, but its gleaming brilliant appearance; so that the Authorized Version is substantially correct.

Ver. 8.—**Their visage is blacker than a coal**; rather, *their appearance is darker than blackness*—one of the hyperboles which seem to indicate that the poem was not written at the very moment of the calamity described (comp. Job xxx. 30). **Not known in the streets.** Another point of contact with the Book of Job (ii. 12). **Their skin**, etc. Again we must compare the lamentations of Job (xix. 20; xxx. 30). Ps. cii. 5 may also be quoted; for the second half of the verse is too short unless we insert "to my skin" before "to my flesh."

Ver. 9.—The miserable condition just now described maintains a sad pre-eminence even when compared with the fate of the slain in battle. And why? **For these pine away** (literally, *melt away*), **stricken through** (with the pangs of hunger). The Authorized Version takes the subject of the second half of the verse to be the famished. But it is, perhaps, more natural to take it to be those wounded in a battle, to whom the expression, "stricken through," is actually applied in ch. xxxvii. 10; li. 4. In this case the line had better be rendered thus: *For those pine away, stricken through, leaving the fruits of the field* (which they no longer need). The word rendered "pine away" would be particularly applicable to those who perished from loss of blood.

Ver. 10.—**The pitiful women.** Strange contrast between the compassionate nature of woman (comp. Isa. xlix. 15) and the dread horrors of this moral as well as physical catastrophe (comp. note on ch. ii. 20).

Ver. 11.—**Hath accomplished** means here, not "hath finished," but "hath poured out in full measure," as in the song of Moses Jehovah declares that he will "spend his arrows upon them"—the Hebrew verb is the same as here (Deut. xxxii. 23). To show the completeness of Zion's ruin it is compared to a fire which **hath devoured the** (very) **foundations thereof.**

Ver. 12.—**The kings of the earth**, etc. And yet Jerusalem had been taken twice before its capture by Nebuchadnezzar (see 1 Kings xiv. 26; 2 Kings xiv. 13). How is the language of the second part to be accounted for? It will help us to an answer if we observe that the later Jews seem to have acquired an exorbitant confidence in their national future ever since the Book of Deuteronomy had become as it were canonical in the reign of Josiah. "The temple of Jehovah" was ever in their mouths (Jer. vii. 9), and the strong outward regard paid to the directions of the Law seemed to them to justify their believing in the fulfilment of its promises. And, in fact, the grand deliverance of Jerusalem in the reign of Hezekiah might, even without this misunderstanding of Deuteronomy, have inspired a firm faith in the security of Jerusalem. A sacred poet had already, on the occasion of that deliverance, declared of the holy city that "God upholdeth the same for ever" (Ps. xlviii. 8), and also (in vers. 4, 5) used the same hyperbole as the author of this lamentation to express the wide-reaching interest felt in the fortunes of Jerusalem.

Ver. 13.—**For the sins of her prophets**, etc. Instead of connecting this verse by a comma with the following, we should rather view it as a unit in itself, and understand at the beginning, "All this hath happened." The sins of the prophets and priests are mentioned together by Jeremiah (vi. 13; xxiii. 11), as well as by Isaiah (xxviii. 7). But we are nowhere else told that the spiritual leaders of the people, in these closing years of the Jewish state, were guilty of shedding innocent blood, unless this is to be inferred from the incident related in Jer. xxvi. 7, etc.

Ver. 14.—**They**; *i.e.* the prophets and priests. **Wandered as blind** men. The leaders of the people are blinded by ignorance, for they know not the only true way of averting calamity, and by passion, for they have not that "eye" of the soul (Matt. vi. 22, 23) which alone enables a man to see the good and the right course for himself individually, The "wandering," or, rather, "staggering" (comp. Ps. cvii. 27, Authorized Version), however, may also refer to the panic-stricken condition of those self-deceived deceivers when overtaken by God's punishment; comp. "wine of reeling" (Authorized Version, "astonishment"), Ps. lx. 3; also the prophecies in Deut. xxviii. 28, 29; Jer. xxiii. 12. The doubt is whether "have wandered" refers to some period before the final catastrophe, or to the consternation produced by that awful surprise. The latter view seems the more probable. **They have polluted themselves,** etc. Their acts of violence have been continued to the very end of their term of power. Their garments are still stained with blood when the summons to depart into exile reaches them.

Ver. 15.—**They cried unto them,** etc. As they leave the city they are pursued by the maledictions of those whom they have oppressed. **It is unclean.** The cry with which the leper was directed to warn off passengers, lest they should become infected (Lev. xiii. 45). There may be an allusion to this, but, though commonly accepted, the view is not certain, as the "leper" in the present case is not the person who raises the cry, but those who meet him. **When they fled away and wandered.** The clause is difficult. If the text is correct, Keil's explanation may perhaps pass, "When they fled away, (there) also they wandered," alluding to the "wandering" ascribed to them with a somewhat different shade of meaning in the preceding verse. In any case there ought to be a fuller stop than a comma after "touch not," which words close the first of the two parallel lines of which the verse consists. But very probably "when" (Hebrew, *ki*) is an intrusion, and we should begin the second line thus: "They fled, they also wandered about." **They said among the heathen,** etc. Even in their place of exile they found no rest (comp. Deut. xxviii. 65). This is better than understanding "the heathen" (literally, *the nations*) to mean "the Chaldean army," and the place of sojourn prohibited to be Jerusalem.

Ver. 16.—**Hath divided them;** *i.e.* hath scattered them, like "I will divide them in Jacob" (Gen. xlix. 7).

Ver. 17.—**As for us, our eyes,** etc.; rather (correcting the reading of the first word), *Our eyes were still wasting away (as we looked) for our help in vain.* To the very last the Jews leaned on "that broken reed," Egypt (Isa. xxxvi. 6); how vain that hope would be Jeremiah had already told them (Jer. xxxvii. 7, 8). **In our watching;** *i.e.* earnestly and continually; or, *on our watch-tower.*

Ver. 18.—**They hunt our steps,** etc. Realistic attempts to explain this line have not been wanting, but seem unsuccessful. The Chaldeans were either within the city or without. If within, they would not need literally to "hunt the steps" of the Jews; if without, they had not war-engines adequate to shooting the inhabitants at some distance. Probably the expressions are metaphorical; they are similar to those used in ch. iii. 52, immediately after which we meet with such a purely poetical phrase as, "They have cut off my life in the pit [Authorized Version, 'dungeon'], and cast a stone upon me," (see note on ch. iii. 52—56).

Ver. 19.—**Swifter than the eagles of the heaven.** Jeremiah, or his imitator, repeats the figure which occurs in Jer. iv. 13. There is probably no special reference to the circumstances of the capture of Zedekiah (Jer. xxxix. 4, 5); the escape of many fugitives would be similarly cut off.

Ver. 20.—**The breath of our nostrils.** The theocratic king was the direct representative of the people with Jehovah, and to him the promises of 2 Sam. vii. were conveyed. He was also, in a sense, the representative of Jehovah with the people. His throne was "the throne of Jehovah" (1 Chron. xxix. 23). A similar conception of the king was generally prevalent in antiquity. Most of all among the Egyptians; but, even in imperial Rome, we find Seneca ('De Clementiâ,' i. 4, quoted by Archbishop Secker, in Blayney) declaring, "Ille (Princeps) est spiritus vitalis, quem hæc tot millia (civium) trahunt." For the Jewish, or Old Testament, conception, see Ps. xxviii. 8, where (as the Septuagint shows) "his people" and "his anointed" are used almost synonymously. **Was taken in their pits.** A figure from hunting (comp. ch. i. 13; Ps. vii. 15). The fate of Zedekiah is referred to. **Among the heathen;** better, *among the nations.* The rendering of the Authorized Version suggests that the Jews hoped to preserve at least a qualified independence under their own king, even after their captivity.

Ver. 21.—**Rejoice and be glad.** An ironical address to Edom, who is bidden to enjoy her malicious triumph, but warned that it will be but short-lived. How ungenerously the Edomites behaved at the fall of Jerusalem we are repeatedly told (see on Jer. xlix. 7). **In the land of Uz.** As to the situation of Uz, see on Jer. xxv. 20. **The cup;** one of Jeremiah's images (see Jer. xxv. 15).

Ver. 22.—**The punishment of thine iniquity** or, *thy guilt* (see on ver. 6). The prophet speaks with the confidence of faith, and sees the guilt wiped away, and the danger of a future captivity removed by the purification which the Jewish national character has undergone. **He will discover thy sins.** God is said to "cover over" sins when he remits their punishment, and to "discover" them when he punishes them (comp. Job xx. 27, 28).

HOMILETICS.

Vers. 1, 2.—*Fine gold dimmed.* Gold is a precious metal, partly because it is less liable to corrode than other metals. It will not rust like iron nor even tarnish like silver. For fine gold to be dimmed is for it to undergo exceptionally severe treatment. Such was the treatment of the gold of the temple after the Chaldean siege of Jerusalem. Josephus describes how the gold glittered on the temple walls in his day; and doubtless the effect of the earlier temple's splendour must have been similarly dazzling. But when covered with the dust of a ruined city, smoked with its fires, neglected and defiled, this fine gold would lose its brilliancy. In the dimming of the brightness of the temple mourning patriots saw an illustration of the shame that had come over the nation, and especially of the degradation of the noblest of the citizens of Jerusalem. But whenever rich gifts and graces of God are corrupted we may echo the same lament, " How is the gold become dim ! "

I. FINE GOLD IS DIMMED WHEN NOBLE GIFTS OF NATURE ARE PUT TO BASE USES. Nature is wealthy with precious things that in themselves and in the eye of God are purely good. The beauty of earth and sea, the wonder of natural forces, the delicate organizations of plant and animal, all things created by the hand of God, are fine and fair and worthy. And these things are given us as our heritage. Science opens to our use many a secret treasure-house. Art and manufactures result from the appropriation of natural resources. But how often are they degraded by being turned to the service of evil, in constructing instruments of war, in ministering to luxurious self-indulgence, in pampering intemperate appetites, etc. !

II. FINE GOLD IS DIMMED WHEN RARE TALENTS ARE WASTED OR ABUSED. Intellectual ability, artistic taste, gifts for music, philosophy or science, stored knowledge, refined culture, natural genius, and educational acquisitions are like fine gold. Yet this gold may be dimmed : 1. *When the gifts and acquirements are idly neglected.* Noble promises disappoint the beholder with a miserable failure. Even so coarse a sin as drunkenness has its victims among the sons of genius. When sensuality, sordid love of money, self-satisfied conventionality, feverish worldly ambition, or any other low pursuit draws the soul away from the high vocation marked out for it by its own peculiar gifts, the fine gold is dimmed. 2. *When the talents are prostituted to low ends.* The gold may be used, but, instead of adorning a temple, it decorates a voluptuary's banquet-hall. The evil use of it degrades the precious metal. Great endowments are too often similarly degraded. They are used for ill. The painter, unlike Fra Angelico, who, working on his knees and for God, made the exercise of his art an act of worship, forsakes his ideal to please the low tastes of his patrons. The writer neglects truth to flatter the popular cries of the day. The philosophic genius absorbs his mental gifts in mercenary calculations. Thus the fine gold is dimmed.

III. FINE GOLD IS DIMMED WHEN YOUTH IS ILL SPENT. For youth is the golden age of life. If not in liberty and ease, for the yoke must then be fitted to the shoulders, still, in freshness, vigour, and opportunity, it is like the morning going forth in its strength, bright as gold. But when the promise of childhood is belied by the performance of manhood, how is the fine gold become dim ! Young men who have not yet lost the bloom of first innocence should beware of the fatal temptations which threaten to cast the beauty and purity of their souls into the mire. We all have an opportunity to begin life well. Some fine gold is then bestowed upon every soul. Let us see to it in these early years that the treasure of a good conscience before God and man is not lost.

IV. FINE GOLD IS DIMMED WHEN A CHRISTIAN FALLS INTO SIN. The graces of the spiritual life are as finest gold. God counts his people as his jewels (Mal. iii. 17). Rare, and bright, and beautiful, glorious and golden in the sunlight of God's love, is the character of true saintliness. There is no beauty comparable to the beauty of holiness. But alas ! when the saint trails his white robe in the foul ways of sin and casts the pearls that adorn him to the swine, how is all the glory and beauty degraded ! Nothing looks more repulsive than a fine garment besmirched with filth ; it is far worse than the beggar's rags, to which dirt seems natural. The fallen Christian defiles himself and dims his gold and brings shame on the Name of Christ by his sin.

V. FINE GOLD IS DIMMED WHEN THE CHURCH IS CORRUPTED. Like Jerusalem of old, the bride of the Lamb should be all-glorious with grace and goodness. The golden perfection of humanity should characterize this society and make it a worthy kingdom of heaven upon earth. But how often has the fine gold been dimmed, in pagan additions to primitive Christianity, in superstitions of the dark ages, in cruelties and immoralities of the Middle Ages, in Catholic prejudice and Protestant bitterness, in the arid rationalism of Germany and the worldly conventionalism of England!

Vers. 3, 4.—*The violation of maternal instincts.* I. MATERNAL INSTINCTS ARE AMONG THE MOST WIDESPREAD AND DEEP-SEATED ORDINANCES OF PROVIDENCE. 1. *Widespread.* They are shared by the lower animals as well as by human beings. The fiercest monsters are careful of their cubs. The most stupid know how to tend and rear their offspring. Roaming jackals of the desert have their lairs where they give suck to their little ones. The varied fields of animal life all bear evidence to this wonderful instinct. It is seen among all races of men. Brutal degraded classes, untrained savages, fierce warlike people, all possess it. 2. *Deep-seated.* These instincts are far deeper than any merely social tendency. They are strong and vital as appetites. The mother feels for her child as for part of herself. Many desires and habits will be abandoned before these instincts will fail. They outlive virtue and principle and dwell still in the vicious.

II. THE VIOLATION OF MATERNAL INSTINCTS IS ONE OF THE MOST HORRIBLE EVENTS. 1. In proportion to the profound and almost universal character of these instincts is *the outrage on nature* itself that the violation of them involves. We judge of an influence by the forces it has to overcome. It must be very strong if it can conquer great resistance. To conquer such resistance as that offered by the maternal instincts the evil influence must be powerful indeed. Therefore the violation of these instincts must be a proof of a most exceptionally energetic force of evil. Lady Macbeth must have sold herself to a very demon of ambition before she could unsex herself enough to say—

> " I have given suck, and know
> How tender 'tis to love the babe that milks me :
> I would, while it was smiling in my face,
> Have pluck'd my nipple from his boneless gums,
> And dash'd the brains out, had I so sworn, etc."

2. Moreover, the *fatal effect* of the violation of maternal instincts is another proof of the terrible evils of the corruption that can make it possible. These instincts are essential to the very continuance of life on our globe. Creatures that come into the world with so much feebleness as is the case with human beings would perish were they not protected in infancy by the wonderful passionate care of maternity.

III. THAT MUST BE A FRIGHTFUL CALAMITY WHICH CAN LEAD TO THE VIOLATION OF MATERNAL INSTINCTS. Such was the calamity of the siege of Jerusalem. Then hunger and despair led parents to neglect their children. The worst mad violation of maternal instincts had been anticipated in a siege of Samaria, when a mother devoured her own child (2 Kings vi. 24—29). Such things have been done since. They force us to realize the barbarous cruelty of war which some would hide beneath its foolish pomp and pageantry. They also make us see the evil of extreme misery. There is a point beyond which suffering ceases to be beneficial. It then becomes a positive curse. It tears up the very roots of the most precious growths of nature. It drives to worse moral degradation than luxury tempts to, though in the eyes of a merciful God the guilt cannot be regarded with so much wrath where the misery that urges to it is so pitiable. Therefore it should be the work of the Christian philanthropist to remove physical wretchedness, not only for its own sake, but also as one of the first means for preventing crime and vice.

Ver. 5.—*Reverses of fortune.* I. REVERSES OF FORTUNE ARE NOT UNCOMMON. It is not only in the rare case of a protracted siege, when at last rich and poor both suffer from the severities of famine, that we may see some who once fed delicately wandering desolate in the street. All who have gone down into the haunts of the very poor and have investigated the severest cases of wretchedness know how many of the most abject paupers have enjoyed wealth and luxury in former years. Even in an orderly society such as our own the number of these violent reverses of fortune is appalling. Let no one boast of his assured comfort.

II. REVERSES OF FORTUNE ARE MOST PAINFUL. We rarely miss what we have never known. There is, therefore, much mitigation to the hardness of the lot of those who are born in the most miserable circumstances, arising from the fact that they have never experienced anything better. But the greatest distress is in coming down from affluence, comfort, and honour to poverty, distress, and shame.

III. REVERSES OF FORTUNE ARE FREQUENTLY MERITED. We must beware of the error of Job's friends. The innocent may and often do suffer from a most grievous succession of calamities. Still, those three men had much to say for their view. Their mistake was in making it universal in its application. It is rarely that the seed of the righteous man has to beg for bread. Good men may have a humble lot and sometimes may have to suffer considerable loss. But usually the greatest degradation and misery follows the folly or sin of the sufferer. Probably the one vice of intemperance is the cause of more than half the cases of the very worst reverses of fortune.

IV. REVERSES OF FORTUNE SHOULD EXCITE PECULIAR COMMISERATION. The happy and prosperous should look out for such cases. The most sad among them are often the hardest to find. They hide in shame and misery. Especially when the degradation is moral it becomes a Christian work to seek to restore the fallen. The Son of man came, not so much to preserve the prosperous nor to raise those who had never known better things, as to seek and to save the lost sheep of the house of Israel, i.e. those who had once been privileged and had fallen from their first estate.

V. REVERSES OF FORTUNE DO NOT JUSTIFY LOSS OF FAITH IN GOD. They tempt men that way. " Curse God, and die," a voice whispers into the ear of the despairing man. But it is the voice of folly as well as of sin. For: 1. *We must expect to be governed in many mysteries by the great and all-wise God.* It may be rational to disbelieve in the existence of God ; but it cannot be rational to believe that he is, and yet to doubt his wisdom or goodness. 2. *The reverse is often due to the fault of the sufferer.* 3. *It may be overruled for his good.*

VI. REVERSES OF FORTUNE MAY BE REVERSED. So was it in Job's case ; the end of the patriarch's life was even brighter than the beginning of it. 1. This may happen *on earth.* In suffering we are too ready to lose heart. We paint the future in dark shades manufactured solely from present experiences. But there are more resources in the world than we dream of. 2. It will surely come *in the next world* to all who trust in God. Then the second reverse will be as joyous as the first was miserable. For the same principle will apply in both cases, and the great change will heighten the sense of the new condition. Happy are they who, in Christ, though suffering and despised, are looking forward to this glorious reverse of their present dark fortunes.

Ver. 12.—*Incredible calamities.* Not only had Jerusalem believed herself invincible, but she had been so long preserved in safety and so signally delivered in extreme danger, as in the Assyrian invasion when Hezekiah was king, that neighbouring nations had come to look upon her as secure from harm, and to regard such calamities as those which came in the wake of the Chaldean invasion as incredible. There are men whose condition in the eyes of the world is as safe as that of Jerusalem was to the kings of the earth, and who nevertheless may fall into a greater ruin than the overthrow of Jerusalem.

I. THE CAUSES OF POPULAR DISBELIEF IN APPROACHING CALAMITIES. 1. *Self-confidence.* Jerusalem believed herself to be safe. Proud in the favour of Heaven, she scorned to fear danger. This attitude of assurance impressed her neighbours. They thought there must be good ground for such loud bravado, or they did not think but simply acquiesced in the opinion of herself which the boastful city published abroad. Thus does the world often take men at their own estimates of themselves, not troubling to test these partial verdicts. 2. *Previous security.* Jerusalem seemed to bear a charmed life. She had braved many a fierce storm. The enemy had swept up to her very gates. But there they had been flung back by mysterious interventions of Providence. So the world believes in the prosperity of the prosperous. She indolently takes for granted that what has been will be.

II. THE FOLLY OF POPULAR DISBELIEF IN APPROACHING CALAMITIES. 1. *Insufficient evidence.* The grounds of this notion are irrational. It is foolish to take people at their self-valuation; but it is more foolish for the people thus accepted to take the popular voice, which is only the echo of their own vanity, as a justification for it. And when the past security engenders confidence, they who do not know what subsequent changes of circumstances have taken place cannot reasonably give security for its continuance. 2. *Ignorance of the real sources of prosperity and danger.* The heathen kings knew not the God of Israel. They knew nothing of the secret of Jerusalem's safety in the days of her prosperity, nor did they see the sure presages of her ruin. Worldly men, who do not understand wherein the safety of a soul consists, are poor judges of that soul's prospects.

III. THE DANGER OF POPULAR DISBELIEF IN APPROACHING CALAMITY. Though it is foolish it is influential, because it is readily accepted as an agreeable solace to fear. Thus Jerusalem was deluded by the flattery of her neighbours. When there is a general opinion that all is well it is hard for individual souls to see and feel their danger. In a condition of worldly ease the prophet of repentance is opposed by the mocking indifference of popular opinion, and souls are lulled to sleep with a hollow security that says, "Peace, peace," when there is no peace. The antidote to this dangerous anodyne of conscience must be sought in the Word of God, which speaks of judgment, and warns us to flee from the wrath to come for refuge where only safety can be found, not in the flattery of our neighbours, but at the cross of Christ.

Ver. 14.—*Blindness.* The prophets and priests are so dismayed that they wander through the streets of Jerusalem like blind men. No doubt the confused movement of these men as they run to and fro, not knowing whither to turn, is the chief idea in the mind of the poet. But the image of blindness by which he illustrates it is suggestive of the secret of their confusion. They were, indeed, as blind men because spiritual blindness had seized on them.

I. THE MEN WHO WERE BLINDED. Priests and prophets. 1. Blindness would be *least excusable* in these men. They were not like the illiterate, nor even like the mass of the laity. Priests were trained in traditional lore, and prophets had access to new fountains of truth. 2. Blindness would be *most dangerous* in these men. They assumed the position of "men of light and leading." The world was made to believe that whoever else might be in darkness these teachers were fully illuminated. Their blindness was most fatal because they were "blind leaders of the blind."

II. THE CHARACTER OF THEIR BLINDNESS. It was spiritual. These teachers had all their senses and faculties. They could see the standards and chariots and hosts of the invader. They could measure his forces and calculate his movements. They had intellectual as well as physical eyesight. But they could not see the hand of God in the whole transaction. They failed to discern that moral condition of the nation which had called the judgment of Heaven down upon its head. They were quite at sea as to the future. They did not understand the Divine purpose of the chastisement; and they were helpless when called upon to guide their followers in the great emergency. When the wolf broke into the fold the shepherds were hopelessly confounded. So must it be with all unworthy guides. The moment of need will discover their worthlessness.

III. THE CAUSE OF THIS BLINDNESS. Sin (see ver. 13). Priests and prophets had shed the blood of the just. Gross abuse of power and tyrannous violence were iniquities enough to blunt the spiritual vision of the most gifted. This is one of the most terrible fruits of sin. It always tends to deaden conscience and darken the eye of the soul. We must do right if we would see truth. It is not only sensuality, passion, and gross worldliness that debase the soul beyond the power of perceiving higher things, but more spiritual sins—pride, bigotry, self-will, etc.—also blind it. Purity of heart is essential to clearness of vision.

IV. THE EFFECT OF THIS BLINDNESS. "They wandered as blind men in the streets." Darkness of vision leads to confusion in action. We must see clearly that we may walk straightly. A confused conscience will make an uncertain will. Practical truth is not merely a subject for discussion in the seclusion of the study. It is a necessary chart to guide our course by. When the seeing and teaching of this is at fault all life is thrown into helpless disorder.

V. THE CURE FOR THIS BLINDNESS. This is not suggested here. It is not the function of Lamentations to console and heal. But there is a remedy. For Christ came to "open the blind eyes" (Isa. xlii. 7). He is "the Light of the world," and all who follow him "shall not walk in darkness, but shall have the light of life" (John viii. 12).

Ver. 15.—*Contamination.* So horrible is the condition of Jerusalem after the siege that men regard the holy city as an unclean place, like a haunt of lepers or an abode of the dead. They cry, "Go aside! Unclean! Go aside! go aside!" as they would to one who incautiously approached too near to one of these banned spots. The dread of contamination is a natural testimony to the instinct for purity; but it is often sadly perverted, for while no feeling should be more related to truth and fact, it happens that no feeling is more subject to artificial, conventional regulations. We need to inquire what are the true causes of contamination and how real contamination may be avoided.

I. WHAT ARE THE TRUE CAUSES OF CONTAMINATION? It is uncleanness that defiles. The primitive notion of uncleanness is connected with material things—the dirt that soils a garment, etc. Then disease which is loathsome and offensive, and death with its attendant corruption, are felt to be defiling. But to the soul true defilement can only come from what is morally impure. As Christ teaches, it is internal not external (Luke xi. 38—40). Jerusalem, when in her prosperity she abandoned herself to idolatry and immorality, was more unclean than when she lay in ashes a charnel-house of slaughtered citizens. Yet no man cried, "Unclean!" in the prosperous times. The degradation was thought to be defiling, while the sin which led to it was connived at. This mistake is common in various forms. The criminal with the brand of punishment upon him is shunned, while the far more vicious man who has contrived to keep himself safe is courted. Parents fear the corruption of manners which their children may contract by mingling with social inferiors, and yet permit them to mix with far more corrupt society if only the rank of it be higher than their own. Many people look with contempt on certain kinds of honest business, who will engage in pursuits of very questionable morality without compunction. Thus some regard trade as degrading and betting as gentlemanly. They would be ashamed to be connected with a shop; they have no shame in their connection with the turf. We want a healthier conscience, that will declare no honest pursuit to be dishonourable and no immoral one to be respectable simply because patronized by rank and fashion.

II. HOW IS REAL CONTAMINATION TO BE AVOIDED? Granted that we know what things are defiling and can distinguish them from the objects of conventional ostracism; how are we to behave ourselves in regard to the unclean things? We are to avoid contact with them. But here a difficult question arises. As Christians we are to be the salt of the earth. It is our mission to purify the impure. But if we shun it, how can we change it? If we neglect politics because we see politicians to be acting dishonourably, and business because we wish to avoid tricks of trade, and society because we must escape the corrupting influences of unwholesome amusements and scandalous conversation, shall we not be handing over politics, business, and society to the unchecked influence of evil? The answer to this question seems to be that the departure must be in spirit and from the spirit of those things that are degrading. We are not to flee bodily. We may do so in vain. For the corruption of the world may pursue the hermit to his cell and torment his mind with evil imaginations in the desert. But if we forsake all sympathy with the unclean our soul cannot be touched by it. Thus Christ ate and drank with publicans and sinners and passed through their foul atmosphere without defilement. Especially if the object is to do good we may be sure that the consciousness of a mission and the cleansing influence of Christian charity will prevent contamination. Thus a pure-minded Christian woman is able to go into the haunts of vice on an errand of mercy and return scatheless as the snowdrop that lifts its head from the impure soil.

Ver. 22.—*The end of punishment.* Here is a gleam of prophetic hope. From doleful lamentations the poet is able to look forward and see the end of the sad desolation of Jerusalem.

I. PUNISHMENT HAS AN END. Nothing is everlasting but God, and the life which God gives and the goodness of that life. Evil, darkness, pain, and death are temporal phases of being. This may seem to many an unjustifiably dogmatic statement. Text for text we may find passages of Scripture to support it and to contradict it. It is when we take into account the drift of the whole Word of God, the character of God therein revealed and the purposes of punishment and of all dark facts of providence as far as these purposes are made known to us, that we are led more and more to believe in the victory and duration of the blessed and the overthrow and cessation of the evil phases of experience.

II. THE END OF PUNISHMENT IS DETERMINED BY ITS OBJECT. What is the object of punishment? This may be manifold. 1. *It is not the satisfaction of vengeance in One who is wronged.* For (1) such a satisfaction could only be required by sinful human passion, never by the good will of God; and (2) if such a satisfaction were required, it would not be punishment, which is quite another thing. 2. *It is partly the deterring of possible offenders.* In so far as law must be vindicated for the sake of its future observance the punishment must be severe, but not beyond that point. 3. *It is chiefly for the restoration of the offender.* This was the reason given for the terrible calamities that overwhelmed the guilty city of Jerusalem. Human punishment under criminal laws is so far a failure that the primary end of it is rarely achieved. But with God's all-wise government it is held in view and mainly aimed at. Therefore the punishment is called "chastisement." What is required of chastisement is that it should be sufficient. For it to be endless would be to defeat its object. Moreover, it does not require to be measured by the offence alone. Even if it were so measured it need not be everlasting, since no finite being can commit an infinite sin. But it is measured by the change required to be wrought in the guilty person.

III. THE PROSPECT OF THE END OF PUNISHMENT SHOULD HELP US TO BEAR IT. God sends chastisement on earth. And he does not except any from it—at all events he does not except Christians, for "whom the Lord loveth he chasteneth." If there were no hope to the chastised, and punishment were a sign of being cast off for ever by God, we might well sit down in sullen despair. But there is encouragement in the thought that it is temporary, is working our good, and may be lightened and shortened by prompt repentance and patient submission.

IV. THE GUILTY AGENTS OF PUNISHMENT WILL BE PUNISHED. Edom had triumphed over Jerusalem. Edom was to have her sin discovered and punished when Jerusalem was restored. So Babylon's doom was promised (Isa. xiii.). Satan, the great enemy of souls, may be used as an instrument for our chastisement. But his day of doom is drawing near. Then he can torment us no more.

V. CHRIST PUTS AN END TO PUNISHMENT. It is not necessary that we should endure our punishment to the end. If we had to do so where would the end be? The awful prospect would shut out all view of any end, whatever we might reason about its far-off certainty. But Christ has accomplished for us by his suffering and sacrifice a work of redemption which will save with full, free, and immediate pardon all who repent and trust in him.

HOMILIES BY VARIOUS AUTHORS.

Ver. 1.—*The gold dimmed.* Present adversity brings to mind, by force of contrast, the prosperity of bygone days. The Hebrew prophet of sorrow might well recall the golden days of old.

"A poet's crown of sorrow is remembering happier things."

His touching and poetic language affords—

I. A LESSON OF HUMAN MUTABILITY. The exclamation reminds us of those oft-quoted words, *Ilium fuit!* Troy was, but is no more! The proudest cities have crumbled into ruins, the most splendid palaces have mouldered into dust.

II. A LESSON THAT PRECIOUS THINGS MAY TURN TO VILE. The homes of kings, priests, and prophets, were possessed by the brutal soldiery; the city of David and Solomon resounded with the ferocious cry of the Chaldeans. Sin can bring the brightest and the most glorious of human societies and institutions into decay and contempt.

III. A LESSON THAT SACRED THINGS MAY BE PROFANED. "The stones of the sanctuary" were flung about. The very temple of Jehovah became a ruin, the sacred solemnities came to an end, and the voice of the priests and the Levites ceased in the precincts. Sin can rust even the fine gold.

IV. A LESSON OF THE UNSPARING ENMITY OF MAN. The Chaldeans were not deterred by any consideration from carrying out their wrath to the bitterest extremity. The tender mercies of the wicked are cruel. *Væ victis!* is an old cry.

V. A LESSON AS TO THE EXACTING NATURE OF DIVINE RETRIBUTION. The hand was the hand of the Chaldean, but the judgment was the judgment of God. When men rebel against him, no human power or splendour can preserve them from his righteous indignation and just retribution.—T.

Ver. 2.—"*Precious sons . . . fine gold,*" . . . become "*earthen pitchers.*" The prophet's appreciation of the proper dignity and value of his nation was naturally very exalted; in proportion were his sorrows and humiliation when his country rebelled against the Lord, and became, in consequence, a prey to the despised and hated foreigner. The reflections are applicable, not to Judah only, but to all the sinful and rebellious among men; for there is no escape from the action of the moral law, from the chastisement of the righteous Judge.

I. THE TRUE VALUE AND PROPER DIGNITY OF MAN. Comparable to "fine gold" in beauty, preciousness, and use, is our humanity when in the state designed by the Creator, free from the corroding rust of sin, and minted and stamped with the image and superscription of the Most High.

II. SIN INVOLVES CHASTISEMENT, AND CHASTISEMENT BRINGS DISGRACE. The striking contrast between gold, fine and solid, on the one hand, and "earthen pitchers" on the other hand, is a pictorial and effective representation of the change which took place in Judah. A holy nation, a kingdom of priests, the chosen of the Eternal, was reduced to the level of the poorest, meanest tribe vanquished and despoiled by an unsparing enemy. Here, as so often, the chosen nation was an emblem of humanity. For though man be by nature the sublimest of God's creatures, when he is abandoned to sin and all its consequences he sinks below the level of the brutes.

APPLICATION. Only Divine grace and power can restore the beauty and dignity of which sin has robbed humanity. The gospel of Christ transforms the earthen pitcher into the fine gold of the sanctuary.—T.

Vers. 3—5.—*The horrors of famine.* A more graphic, a more terrible picture than this of the misery of a captured, starved, and desolated city, no pencil could paint. If the circumstances of the famine-stricken population of Jerusalem are portrayed with too literal a skill and with too sickening an effect, it must be borne in mind that the description is not that of an artist, but of a prophet, and that the aim is not merely to horrify, but to instruct, and especially to represent the frightful consequences involved in a nation's sin and apostasy.

I. PHYSICAL SUFFERINGS ARE DESCRIBED. If the condition of the wretched citizens be examined, they are seen to be afflicted with all physical evils, *e.g.* with hunger and want, with emaciation and feebleness of body, with homelessness, squalor, and filth, with pestilence and death.

II. MORAL DEGRADATION IS DENOUNCED. A siege, the sack of a city, have sometimes called out exalted self-sacrifice and heroism; but they have sometimes been the occasion of the bursting forth into flame of the vilest passions—of avarice, cruelty, selfishness, and lust. In this passage we observe an atrocious exhibition of selfish indifference to the pains and necessities of others, and especially a display of cruelty towards children which contrasts with the parental instincts and tenderness of the brutes. To so low a level does sin bring human nature.

PRACTICAL LESSONS. 1. In plenty and peace let men cherish gratitude. 2. Let those who are prosperous commiserate the famine-stricken and the victims of war. 3. Let generous provision be made for the wants of the destitute.—T.

Ver. 12.—*The impregnable taken.* The natural position of Jerusalem was such as to mark it out for a stronghold, as to invite its possessors to fortify it and to deem themselves invincible. When David conquered it by daring and valour, he made it the metropolis of the nation. Succeeding kings strengthened the walls and completed the fortifications, so that Jerusalem became one of the strongest fortresses of the ancient world. And at this time Nebuchadnezzar had only taken the city after a siege extending through a year and a half.

I. THE IMPRESSIVE CONTRAST. 1. One such contrast was upon the surface and obvious to every eye. The mighty and apparently invincible was vanquished and desolated. 2. Another contrast was apparent to the mind of the observing and reflecting : the city favoured by God himself was abandoned, spoiled, and desolated. If Jehovah had not gone out of the gates, the Chaldeans could not have entered in. 3. The contrast was one universally amazing and astounding. "The kings of the earth, and all the inhabitants of the world, would not have believed it."

II. THE INSPIRED EXPLANATION OF THIS CONTRAST. It was not chance, it was not "the fortune of war," it was not the consequence of some political machinations, some military strategy, that the proud city of Zion fell into the hands of the foreign conqueror. Unfaithfulness and rebellion against God were the true explanation. The Lord only forsakes those who forsake him. All men, all nations, endure chastisement for sin. Blessed be God ! in the midst of wrath he remembers mercy.—T.

Vers. 13, 14.—*The degradation of the prophets and the priests.* There is a somewhat obscure reference in this passage to some incidents which took place during and after the siege of Jerusalem. The book of Jeremiah's prophecies casts some light upon the language of his lamentations. It is evident that the offices of priest and prophet were vilely abused at this period of Judah's degradation, that the prophets prophesied in false and flattering words, that the priests burned incense to idols, that both professions were debased to selfish ends, and that both were accountable to a very large extent for the calamities of the nation. No wonder that prophets and priests became the objects of national detestation, that Jew and alien alike shunned and hated them.

I. THE NOBLEST OFFICES, WHEN MISUSED, BECOME THE GREATEST CURSE. The priests were "holy unto Jehovah ;" the prophets were the commissioned ministers of the All-wise, and they spake his words to men. But when they retained their name, but lost the spirit and the moral authority attaching to their position, they misled and oppressed their countrymen. Alas for the nation whose leaders in Church and state are selfish and corrupt ! they who should be an honour and a blessing become then a disgrace and a curse. Let the great and the consecrated take warning, and watch and pray.

II. WHEN SPIRITUAL AND INTELLECTUAL LEADERS ARE DEBASED THEIR INFLUENCE UPON A NATION IS MOST DELETERIOUS AND DISASTROUS. "Like priest, like people," says the old proverb. In modern communities it is observable that the journalists and the clergy have amazing power in giving a tone to public life. Where these are corrupt the very springs of a nation's life are poisoned ; all classes are affected by the influences which are potent for harm as they had otherwise been for highest good.

III. THE UNFAITHFULNESS OF THE LEADERS BRINGS PENALTIES AND CALAMITIES UPON THE PEOPLE. The constitution of human society is such that one must needs suffer for another. As the sins of the prophets and the iniquities of the priests had no small share in bringing about the ruin of Jerusalem, so a corrupt literature and a selfish clergy will bring any nation, however powerful, into misery and contempt.—T.

Ver. 17.—*Vain help and hope.* When Jerusalem was besieged by the Chaldeans its inhabitants seem to have looked for assistance from their Egyptian neighbours. This was a policy and an expectation displeasing to Jehovah, who ever taught his people to rely, not upon an arm of flesh, but upon the eternal King of righteousness. In verse the prophet pictures the attitude of the Jews as day after day they strained their weary eyes to catch some glimpse of an approaching deliverer. How striking a picture of the folly and vanity of those hopes which man fixes upon his fellow-man !

I. THE DISTRESSED AND HARASSED NATURALLY HAVE RECOURSE TO HUMAN AID. As the Jews looked now to Assyria and again to Egypt for allies and helpers, so the children of men have recourse to human counsellors, philosophers, and saviours to deliver them from the perplexities and sorrows and fears to which human nature is always subject.

II. IT IS PROVIDENTIALLY APPOINTED THAT EXPERIENCE SHOULD CONVINCE MEN OF THE VANITY OF ALL HUMAN HELP. When application after application fails to bring relief, when hope after hope is disappointed, then, and perhaps not until then, men learn how vain is the help of man, and perceive the wisdom of the advice, " Put not your trust in man, or in the son of man, in whom is no help."

III. GOD INTENDS BY SUCH DISCIPLINARY EXPERIENCE TO DRAW HIS PEOPLE TO HIM-SELF. When the eyes are dim and weary with looking earthward for deliverance, then they may be lifted heavenward. And when the help of man is sincerely acknowledged to be vain, then the help of God is at hand.—T.

Ver. 18.—*The end is come!* The progress of the enemy's works, the approach of the enemy's forces, the frequency of the enemy's assaults, all tended to dishearten the citizens of the besieged Jerusalem. The prophet represents the discouraged and dis-mayed citizens as gazing with terror upon the assailants and their strategy, and exclaim-ing in despair, " Our end is come!" The dealing and the discipline of God with the souls of the disobedient and rebellious may well awaken the same conviction and elicit the same cry.

I. THE END OF OUR OWN RESOURCES. It is sometimes only when men have tried what is in their power, have done their best to solve their spiritual difficulties and to make their way secure, that, convinced of their own insufficiency, they admit themselves to be altogether in the wrong.

II. THE END OF OUR RESISTANCE TO OUR FOES. Men strive to carry on the conflict in their own strength, and they strive in vain. " Wearied in the greatness of their way," convinced that they are no match for the spiritual enemy, they may confess that, left to themselves, they cannot conquer, they cannot withstand.

III. THE END OF ALL OUR HOPES OF DELIVERANCE. Those hopes may have buoyed up for days and years; but when they have issued only in disappointment how can the discouraged do other than at last for ever abandon them?

IV. THE END OF OUR REBELLION AGAINST GOD. If this be the effect produced by long experience of the wretchedness and the futility of such hostility, there will be reason for gratitude. They who lay down the weapons of rebellion shall receive mercy and experience deliverance.—T.

Vers. 1, 2.—*Fallen reputation.* I. THE WEIGHT OF THIS REPUTATION. The position of the people was comparable to gold in its glitter and attraction. Gold has its use and iron has its use, and we may be glad we have both; but if one of these two had to be given up, it would certainly be the gold. Iron means immensely more in modern civilization than gold. But if frequency of mention is to count for anything, gold was much more valued among the Israelites than iron, and being so, it had a large place in the symbolisms of the tabernacle service and in the splendours of Solomon's temple. Hence any one with a high reputation might very well be compared to gold. People run after such a one even as they do after gold. There is a time when the crowd are not contented to speak well of a man; they must praise him extravagantly, using the language of superlatives, and showing that their standard, if standard it can truly be called, is far from an ideal one.

II. THE CHARACTER OF THE REPUTATION. Had Israel ever been worthy of this com-parison with fine gold? On what was the comparison based? It is to be feared that it rested very much on mere appearance. Remember the saying, " All that glitters is not gold." Jehovah had made Israel to glitter by taking it out from among the nations and making it the object of great demonstrations of his power. But, so to speak, this was only gilding over the impure and incoherent mass of common humanity with a coating of pure gold for a certain purpose. The men and women who made up Israel were at heart like men and women elsewhere. But by giving them a certain outward splen-dour God furnished a symbol of that true golden nation which is made up from individual believers in him.

III. THE DESTRUCTION OF THE REPUTATION. The gold becomes dim. The com-parison was once to gold out of which vessels for honour are made, beautifully shaped and decorated. But now the comparison is to the common clay out of which the potter makes his cheap and fragile ware. And yet, after all, if gold be a standard of preciousness, these sons of Zion were indeed comparable to it; only the gold is in the unpurified state, mixed very intimately with baser elements that take away the use and glory of the gold. Man in his *best* natural state may have his reputation lifted too high; in his *worst* natural state that reputation may sink too low; but when God takes the natural man in hand and renews, purifies, and disciplines him, then it will be seen that the most splendid and pleasing of visible objects is only a feeble hint of that glory wherewith God has chosen to glorify his own children.—Y.

Vers. 3, 4.—*Natural affection gone.* I. NOTE AN UNFAVOURABLE CONTRAST WITH THE LOWER CREATION. Everything is to be estimated according to its nature. It matters little what the sea-monster here stands for. It is sufficient to know that some fierce destructive creature is thought of. Truly there is a vast difference between the brutes whose very nature it is to destroy in order that they may live, and man who never looks more worthy of his position in the scale of being than when he is doing his very best to preserve life, risking even his own life for this end. And yet even in the most savage brutes there is natural affection. To stoop to a very common sight, what is more suggestive of some of the deep mysteries of existence than to see a cat one moment patiently suckling its own young, and the next moment stealthily and silently making its way to spring on some defenceless bird? If, then, it is put into the nature of these fierce creatures thus to care for their young, what care is it not right to expect from man, the highest creature whom we know? There is hardly any limit to what he can do for his offspring in the way of guarding its weakness and developing its power; and yet how negligent he can become! The lower creation puts him to shame. Jeremiah here speaks of cruelty, but we do well to remember that there is a thoughtlessness, an indolence, and a selfishness which are productive of as bad effects as any cruelty can produce. More evil, it has been truly said, is wrought from want of thought than from want of heart.

II. WHAT IT IS THAT PRODUCES THIS CONTRADICTION TO NATURE? Generally stated, it is the stress of circumstances that does it. "The daughter of my people" would not have become cruel if her life had gone on in its ordinary way. But all at once the supplies that have been so regular become uncertain, and at last virtually stop. The cruelty, if in such circumstances it may be truly called so, is an involuntary one. And yet it is not involuntary in this sense, that the state of things was altogether unpreventable. The famine came from disobedience to God. We are not left to make a superstitious inference as to this connection. It is stated on authority. It were presuming far too much to trace a connection between particular suffering and particular wrong-doing, but where the connection between particular wrong-doing and particular suffering is made perfectly plain, we shall be very foolish if we do not take heed to it. Whatever wrong thing we do will have some evil consequences, and we know not how soon they may come, how widely they may spread, and how much suffering and difficulty they may bring to the innocent.—Y.

Ver. 5.—*Social revolution.* I. AN ILLUSTRATION OF THE INSTABILITY OF HUMAN SOCIETY. We may consider it either as the instability of wealth or the instability of rank. It shows how no class of the community is able to say that, whatever happens in the way of stress or destitution, it will keep right. Men build up societies in which rank comes from the accumulation of wealth or the exercise of power that is in a man by nature. But these human societies thus built up cannot reckon on permanence. Greed is excited on the part of others, and the higher a man has risen the lower he may fall.

II. THE ILLUSTRATION HERE SHOULD MAKE US CONSIDERATE OF THOSE IN HIGH POSITION. The high are of necessity the few. Their position is seen from the outside and from a distance. What we do see is very likely to mislead us, for our eye lights on outward splendour and the appearance of much leisure and the ability to do very much what one likes. But the many journals and memoirs that have been published revealing the inner life of courts and titled circles show that human beings may be none the less miserable because the misery is gilded over. Our pity may be needed at any moment for the man of rank and privilege. Whatever the outward differences may be, the inward heart is the same, and that must have its sorrows, its disappointments, and its perils.

III. WE ARE TAUGHT THE NEED OF CAUTION IN GLORIFYING HUMAN CIVILIZATION. What many people reckon to be the highest civilization needs material wealth in great profusion to keep it up. There must be classes to paint pictures, carve statuary, and give long periods of time to the elaboration of artistic conceptions, whatever they may be. And what a satire on all this it is to recollect how fragile and fading some of these art treasures have proved! The ignorant and narrow-minded under-value these things, but then it is also possible to over-value them, to get so occupied with them as to forget the deepest things of humanity, the things that endure. The civilized, refined, natural man may be good, but how much better is the spiritual man, even though he be rude in speech and full of error in his tastes! Truly we may say, he that is least among spiritual men is greater than the highest of attainments among natural men.—Y.

Ver. 6.—*The sin of Sodom.* God was doing nothing new or indefensible in allowing Jerusalem thus to be wasted and humiliated. The Israelites had in their possession illustrations more than one of how great sin had been followed by great suffering. Jeremiah quotes Sodom, and he might have said something about Egypt when God visited it with the plagues. We must not, of course, press too literally the statement that the sin of Jerusalem was greater than that of Sodom. The prophet's aim is simply to insist that no sin could have been greater than that of Jerusalem. If it was a right and a necessary thing that Sodom should be so suddenly visited, so completely overwhelmed, then assuredly no complaint could be made against the severe treatment experienced by Jerusalem. Indeed, relatively, Jerusalem might think itself very well off. If the height on which Jerusalem stood had sunk in another Dead Sea, there would have been no ground for complaint. No impartial Israelite, looking at the privileges of Israel, considering how much it had been instructed and warned, and how patiently it had been dealt with, could do anything but confess that on the whole it had been mildly visited. We must, however, be careful here not to attribute anything arbitrary to God. We shall naturally be very much perplexed if we allow ourselves to think that, though Sodom's sin was less than Jerusalem's, yet it received a greater punishment. It is only by a figure that we talk of communities being punished. Punishment is strictly an individual thing. Communities may suffer, and the suffering will be according to the needs of God's government at the time. The cities of the plain were utterly swept away, that the rest of the world might not become as bad as they were. These visitations have to be looked on somewhat in the light of surgical operations. One patient in the hospital needs to have a limb amputated that the whole body may be saved. Another can have his body saved without the loss of a part of it.—Y.

Ver. 9.—*Sword and hunger.* I. WORSE THINGS THAN WAR. Better, says the prophet, to be swiftly slain in battle than have the slow and gnawing death of hunger. None worthy the name of Christian can but appreciate and admire the zeal, devotion, and self-abnegation of those who toil incessantly in the things that make for peace. War is so dreadful an evil that hardly too strong things can be said against it. And one of the strong things said is with respect to the immense suffering produced by war. Yet after all there is a great deal that deceives imagination here. Suffering is crowded into a small space, and puts on a horrible aspect, and thus it looks huger than it is, and so when we are appalled at the continuance in the world of great wars full of carnage, we shall do well to recollect that war is by no means the worst of things so far as power of inflicting suffering is concerned. Evidently the prophet saw starvation as a more horrible thing than war. It may, of course, be said the war was the cause of the famine, and very likely it was, but then, what was the cause of the war? Good men in their enthusiasm come in with all sorts of ready remedies for great evils, not sufficiently considering how one evil is connected with another, and how the stopping up of one channel may only fill other channels all the more. Who can dry up the fountain of all evil?—that is the question.

II. THE DREADFUL ACCOMPANIMENTS OF FAMINE. Is there anything worse than the carnage of a battle-field? Yes; the pangs of a multitude slowly dying of starvation.

There is death from disease, death from decay, death of the strong man in full health from violence ; but worse than any surely is this slow torment of hunger. What an instance of the rigid way in which law binds us down, unless there be some Divine reason for interfering with the operations perceptible to us ! He who intervened to feed the five thousand and the four thousand could have intervened to keep these wretched women from laying their hands on their own children for food. What necessity was there in the one case which there was not in the other? Some there must have been, though we may fail to grasp it as a whole. Doubtless if we could only see clearly it would then become manifest that there is no lack in the giving of food, but that it is we who lack wisdom in developing and distributing what is given.—Y.

Ver. 12.—*A seeming impossibility achieved.* I. THE VALUE OF A REPUTATION. Jerusalem had a far-spread reputation for security. It was a reputation, too, which prevailed among those with whom it was desirable it should prevail, namely, the kings of the earth. A reputation for security is to a certain extent an element in security, and what we have to do is to let it have its just value. For instance, in a world where solicitations to evil abound it is well if those who have all the inclination to tempt us nevertheless say in their hearts that we are beyond such temptations, and therefore it would be mere waste of time to attack us. Jerusalem had probably escaped many sieges through this far-spread feeling.

II. THE CAUSES OF THIS REPUTATION. Here is the value of history. A tradition springs up that Jerusalem is impregnable. Failures in attacking it are contrasted with successes in attacking other places. It is not that any particular invader fails, but different nations and different commanders. Furthermore, the people of Jerusalem come to accept what seems an unquestionable privilege. If it has come to be a foregone conclusion among their enemies that their city is impregnable, how much more may they themselves rest in such a conclusion ! But what had made this conclusion possible ? Was it the position of Jerusalem ? No doubt this counted for something, for other walled places beside Jerusalem have had the reputation of being able to defy all attack. The great thing, however, was the purpose of God that Jerusalem should stand against its enemies. To him must be laid the origin of this wide and deep feeling. He who had been as a shield to the individual warrior became as a high and fenced wall to the city. Jerusalem is the contrast to Jericho. Well-defended Jericho can be made to fall without any visible force, and Jerusalem can be made to stand against the most furious accumulations of the heathen.

III. THE WORTHLESSNESS OF MERE REPUTATION. Reputation by itself is always to be looked upon with caution. If we would have reputation to be a valuable element in judgment, it must be by asking in whose voice the reputation lies. The voice of the multitude, the voice that takes up a cry and as it were transmits an echo, what is it worth? The people of Jerusalem had come to rest in the comfortable feeling that their city was reckoned impregnable. Do not let our safety rest in what other people think about us. If our safety is not of God, if it does not rest in trusting him and obeying him, then sooner or later that will happen to us in our life which happened to Jerusalem. The walls of our life will be broken down, our most precious treasures taken away, our hearts made desolate.—Y.

Ver. 13.—*Shedding the blood of the just.* Consider—
I. THE THING THAT IS DONE. It is not merely that life is taken away ; nor is it even that murder is committed. It would be bad enough if even the most wicked of men were maliciously slain—slain, not because of his wickedness, but because of some evil motive on the part of the slayer. But here those who are slain are just men, and slain because they are just. All they needed in order to live on was to fall in with prevailing and popular iniquities. Instead of this, they set their faces against the multitude that are doing evil. They must, as a matter of necessity to their own consciences, say and do things which are a continual exasperation to the wicked. They do not mean to exasperate, they may be in the spirit of their life most meek, gentle, and unaffected; but all this will avail nothing— the wicked are bound to pick a quarrel with them, even as the wolf in the fable picked a quarrel with the lamb. And let it be observed that shedding the blood of the just is only the climax of the persecuting treatment which the just must be ready to experience.

The wicked are often quite willing to stop short of the climax if they can gain their ends by something less. Not all at once do they proceed to the shedding of blood. It is well for those who, if they be indeed Christians, are assuredly to be reckoned among the just to remember what they have to number among the possibilities of their endeavour to live a truly righteous life. No mere human civilization will ever secure the just man from the risk of having to lose his life for his righteousness.

II. THOSE WHO DO IT. Once again, as so often, the prophet and priest stand forth in a shameful revelation. Their life is so contrary to their office. The prophet whose force should have come from the strong righteousness of his heart within and be directed straight against all evil-doers, is found ranging himself with the wicked and making evil put on the semblance of good. And as for the priest, he does holy things with his hands and offers sacrifices for sin, while those whose lives are a continual protest against sin he hates and strives to slay. Not that we must reduce the prophet and the priest here spoken of to the level of vulgar murderers. Doubtless, in many instances, they persuaded themselves they were right and doing God service. Fanaticism and class feeling, where each one blows the flame of his neighbour's zeal, will urge men on to the greatest atrocities. There may be no danger, most likely there will be no opportunity, that we should go as far as these prophets and priests, but we need to guard against having their narrow spirits in our hearts. We may not shed the blood of the just, but nevertheless we may do much to hinder and trouble them.—Y.

Ver. 20.—*A disappointed confidence and a desecrated sanctity.* There seems to be indicated in these words a great attachment to the kingly office and a great confidence in it. It is the same spirit continuing and probably intensified which caused the people ages before to demand a king. And is it not thus suggested to us what a deep feeling there is in the human heart to have some one individual to look up to as having rule over us? " The right Divine of kings " is a principle which more than once in history has been seen pushing itself to disastrous issues, but that is no reason for asserting that " the right Divine of kings " is an absurdity. It is only an absurdity when a weak fallible mortal holds himself, by virtue of his ancestry and kinship, to have little less than absolute control over multitudes of his fellow-men. The question is not whether kingship is right, but who shall be the king. And especially does this need to be recollected among the changing forms of government so perceptible in modern times. Now that despotisms are tending to limited monarchies, and limited monarchies becoming more limited, and extensions being made of republican territory, it is more than ever important to insist on the kingdom of God, the kingdom of heaven. Not without deep reason does the proper government for man stand before us in the New Testament as a kingdom. The collective wisdom of mankind can only be at best a puzzling mixture of knowledge and ignorance, prudence and rashness. Blessed is he who feels that the real Anointed of the Lord is the proper Being to guide. Under his shadow we can live the true life in that safety of the spirit which is of far more moment than that mere external safety from the Gentiles, which counted for so much in the esteem of the Israelite of old. In no pits has the Lord Jesus Christ ever been taken.—Y.

EXPOSITION.

CHAPTER V.

Vers. 1—18.—INSULT UPON INSULT HAS BEEN HEAPED UPON JERUSALEM.

Ver. 2.—**Our inheritance.** The land had been "given" to Abraham (Gen. xiii. 25; xvii. 8), and was consequently inherited by Abraham's posterity. **Our houses.** Not as if the Chaldeans had actually taken up their abode in some of the houses of Jerusalem. The expressions are forcible, but inexact. The land was seized; the houses were destroyed (Jer. lii. 13).

Ver. 3.—**We are orphans and fatherless;** *i.e.* "We are like the most desolate of beings," as the Targum already explains it. Hence in the next clause the mothers of Israel are likened to widows.

Ver. 4.—**We have drunken our water,** etc. The Jews were not yet carried away to Babylonia when this was written, but had to pay a dear price to the new lords of the soil for the commonest necessaries of life.

Ver. 5.—**Our necks are under persecution.** Persecution is here compared to a yoke. But this rendering and explanation hardly suit the phrase, which rather means, " *We are pursued close upon our necks.*" The harassing conduct of the Babylonian conquerors is compared to the pursuit of a foe fast gaining upon a fugitive.

Ver. 6.—**We have given the hand**, etc. Starvation awaits the Jews unless they submit to one or the other of their hereditary foes. Some escape to Egypt and "give the hand" (*i.e.* surrender, Jer. l. 15) to the lords of the fertile Nile valley; others acquiesce in the fate of the majority, and sue for the alms of the Babylonians.

Ver. 7.—**We have borne their iniquities.** The fathers died before the iniquity was fully ripe for punishment, and their descendants have the feeling that the accumulated sins of the nation are visited upon them. This view of national troubles is very clearly endorsed by one important class of passages (Exod. xx. 5; xxxiv. 7; Numb. xiv. 18; Jer. xxxii. 18). The objection to it is forcibly expressed by Job (xxi. 19), " God [it is said] layeth up his iniquity for his children : [but] let him requite it to himself, that he may feel it ! " Hence Jeremiah (xxxi. 30) and Ezekiel (xviii. 1, etc.) insist on the truth that every man is punished for his own sins. Of course the two views of punishment are reconcilable. The Jews were not only punished, according to Jer. xvi. 11, 12, for their fathers' sins, but for their own still more flagrant offences.

Ver. 8.—**Servants have ruled**; rather, *slaves.* The Babylonians in general might be called slaves, by comparison with the "kingdom of priests" (Exod. xix. 6), and the "sons" of Jehovah (Isa. xlv. 11; Hos. i. 10). Or the expression may mean that even baseborn hangers-on of the conquering host assumed the right to command the defenceless captives.

Ver. 9.—**We gat our bread**; rather, *we get our bread.* The allusion in the following words is perhaps to murderous attacks of Bedawins (as we should call the Ishmaelites) on the Jews who attempted to gather in the scanty harvest.

Ver. 10.—**Was black like an oven.** The translation is misleading ; there is no real parallel to ch. iv. 8. Render, *gloweth.* It is the feverish glow produced by gnawing hunger which is meant. **The terrible famine** ; rather, *the burning heat of hunger.* Hariri, the humoristic author of the cycle of stories in rhymed Arabic prose and verse, called 'Makāmāt,' puts into the mouth of his ne'er-do-well Abu Seid very similar words to describe a famished man—

" Dess Eingeweide brennend nach Erquickung schrein,
Der nichts gegessen seit zwei Tagen oder drein."

(Rückert's adaptation, third Makāma.)

Ver. 12.—**Princes are hanged up by their hand** ; *i.e.* by the hand of the enemy. Impalement after death was a common punishment with the Assyrians and Babylonians. Thus Sennacherib says that, after capturing rebellious Ekron, he hung the bodies of the chief men on stakes all round the city (' Records of the Past,' i. 38). Bonomi gives a picture of such an impalement from one of the plates in Botta's great work (' Nineveh and its Palaces,' p. 192).

Ver. 13.—**They took the young men to grind** ; rather, *the young men have borne the mill.* The lower millstone seems to have been specially hard, and therefore heavy (see Job xli. 24), and to carry it about must have required a more severe exertion even than the constant turning of the millhandle. Dr. Thomson "cannot recall an instance in which men were grinding at the mill" (' The Land and the Book,' edit. 1881, p. 108), and both Exod. xi. 5 and Matt. xxiv. 41 presuppose that it was women's work. The conquered Jewish youths, however, share the fate of Samson—

"Eyeless, in Gaza, at the mill with slaves."
(' Samson Agonistes,' 41.)

"Eyeless," indeed, they may some of them have been, as putting out the eyes was a common Oriental punishment (comp. Jer. xxxix. 7). **The children.** This is, perhaps, too strong. The Hebrew *na'ar* is applicable, not only to children, but to *youths* at the age for marriage (Gen. xxxiv. 19) or war (1 Kings xx. 15). **The wood**; not the wooden handle of the mill, but the wood required for fuel.

Ver. 14.—**From the gate.** The place where the elders, technically so called, assembled for legal proceedings, and where the citizens in general met together for social concourse (comp. Gen. xix. 1; Ruth iv. 11; Ps. lxix. 12; Amos v. 12, 15; Dan. ii. 49). **From their music** (comp. Jer. vii. 34; xvi. 9).

Ver. 16.—**The crown is fallen**, etc. ; rather, *the crown of our head is fallen.* The Jewish people is compared to a rich man at a banquet, crowned with a diadem (comp. Isa. xxviii. 1). Jeremiah has a similar phrase in his prophecies (xiii. 18). It evidently expresses figuratively the prosperity and honour formerly enjoyed by the now vanquished people.

Vers. 17, 18.—These verses form a transition to the final appeal. The thought of the desolation of Zion overwhelms the spirit of the poet. But he will soon be able to lift himself up again when he recalls the sublime truth of the inviolable security of Israel's God. **Foxes** ; rather, *jackals.*

Vers. 19—22.—FINAL APPEAL TO GOD FOR THE REVERSAL OF THE JUDGMENT.

Ver. 19.—**Remainest**; better, *art enthroned.*

Ver. 20.—**Wherefore dost thou forget us,** etc.? The poet does not say, " Wherefore hast thou forgotten us?" One of the psalmists, indeed, does go so far (Ps. lxxiv. 1); but the poet of this lamentation, with a more tender and trustful reserve, adopts the tense of feeling (the imperfect) in preference to that of fact (the perfect), and asks, "Wherefore dost thou [to my feeling] forget us? Wherefore, if Jehovah's power is still unbroken, does he allow Israel to feel herself forsaken?" The fact is certain, viz. that the land of Israel is desolate, and (the poet seems to imply) desolate for some time already. The interpretation is hypothetical, and, as the last verse will show, the poet cannot bring himself to believe that it can be accurate.

Ver. 21.—**Turn thou us**, etc. Not "bring us back to thee," *i.e.* to the sacred land (as Thenius), for it is not a speech of the exiles, but of the Jews left behind, at least for the present, in Judæa. "Turn thou us" means "Bring us into a state of reconciliation with thee." The next petition, **Renew our days as of old,** means, "Restore the old happy mode of life, each man with his own vine and his own fig tree, undisturbed by the fear of invasion, and rejoicing in the sense of the favour of Jehovah." The first petition has the priority because only on repentance and recovered purity of heart and life can Jerusalem rise from her ashes. Isaiah had said this long ago (i. 26, 27), and the elegiac poet repeats it (comp. Jer. xxxi. 18).

Ver. 22.—**But**; rather, *unless.* The poet wishes to suggest that the idea seems to him inconsistent with the covenant relationship of Jehovah towards Israel. May we not compare a striking passage in Isaiah which should probably be rendered thus : "A wife of one's youth, can she be rejected? saith thy God" (Isa. liv. 6)? Both passages express, in a most delicate way, the incredulity of the writers with regard to the absolute rejection of Israel. And thus this melancholy Book of Lamentations concludes with a hope, "faint, yet pursuing," of the final realization of the promises to Israel. The interpretation adopted admits of no reasonable doubt, in spite of the fact that ancient doctors of the synagogue thought otherwise when they established the custom of repeating ver. 21 after ver. 22 had been read, in order to soften the supposed gloomy impression of ver. 22.

HOMILETICS.

Ver. 1.—*A prayer of distress.* I. IT IS OFFERED TO GOD. The whole of this last elegy is in the form of a prayer. Other laments are interspersed with cries to Heaven. This poem is one continuous address to God. We see here true wisdom ; for mere complaining is useless. To wail to the winds is foolish and vain. To make our troubles known to our fellow-men often avails little, for we may only weary them instead of eliciting their pity, or, if we do succeed in gaining commiseration, that may be of little real use to us. But God is the great Comforter. His ear is ever open to the cry of his distressed children. His heart is always tender to feel compassion for their woes. His hand is strong and willing to work substantial deeds of helpfulness.

II. IT DESCRIBES THE MOURNFUL CONDITION OF THE SUPPLIANT. The poet refers to "what has come upon us" and "our reproach." Subsequent verses describe the miserable condition of the Jews in more detail. It is much that we can unbosom our souls before God. The mere relief of confiding in him is a comfort. Moreover, if we desire his help we must make this confidence. Reserve on our part necessitates apparent indifference on his part. We need not fear of wearying him with our plaints. Indeed, if we were more open-hearted in confiding our troubles to God we should come to have fewer troubles to concern ourselves with.

III. IT ASKS FOR DIVINE NOTICE. 1. "*Remember.*" It seems as though God must have forgotten and deserted his children when he has permitted them to fall into grievous distresses. 2. "*Consider.*" We need God's thought for us. Our case is such that the wisdom of God as well as his grace is necessary for our salvation. The great work of Christ is a proof of Divine thought, study, consideration. 3. "*Behold.*" Here is a nearer attention. God is not only asked to remember and think of our case, but to inspect it himself. And when he looks he heals. When once we are assured that God remembers, considers, and beholds our trouble, we can leave it with him, well knowing that he will not mock our cries by listening without answering.

Ver. 2.—*The lost inheritance.* I. THE EARTHLY INHERITANCE OF ISRAEL WAS TURNED TO STRANGERS. Canaan, the land promised to Abraham and his seed, was always regarded as more than a mere possession. It was considered to be received from God as an inheritance, and held by a Divine right. Yet even this sacred soil was taken away from the people. Strange races from the East settled down upon it, and the rightful owners were driven into captivity or compelled to pay for water from the wells their fathers had dug, and for fuel from their own woods (ver. 4). A second time the people have been driven from their inheritance, and Turkish mosques now desecrate the city of the Jews.

II. The spiritual inheritance of Israel was turned to strangers. The Jews were more than possessors of one little favoured land. To them were entrusted the oracles of God. Prophets and priests gave them peculiar privileges in spiritual things. They were a people of God's own possession. The blessings of the Jews were to culminate in the advent of the Messiah. The Messiah came. He came to his own inheritance, and his own people received him not; for Christ first offered himself to Jews, and Christ was first refused by Jews. In rejecting Christ the house of Israel rejected its true inheritance. Gentiles took up the privileges which Jews despised. We and other nations of Gentile Christendom are the strangers to whom their inheritance is turned over.

III. The Christian inheritance may be turned to strangers. There have been Christian lands, such as North Africa and Asia Minor, which have lost their Christianity and have passed into the possession of the bitterest foes of the Crucified. Within the pale of Christendom the inheritance may be lost. If we permit unbelief to lay hold of people who once enjoyed full faith in Christ, this result will take place. When men who are unbelievers at heart get possession of Christian pulpits and undermine the very faith they are supposed to be preaching, is not this a terrible instance of the inheritance passing to strangers?

IV. The inheritance is turned to strangers because the conditions on which it is held are violated. This truth applies to all three cases just described—to Israel's earthly inheritance and her spiritual inheritance and to the Christian inheritance. The land was not given to strangers till after strange gods had been admitted into the land. It was always designed by God that the privileges of the gospel should be given to Gentiles as well as to Jews (e.g. Isa. lx. 3). But it was owing to their refusal of these privileges that the Jews lost their own share in them. The inheritance was to have been widened to admit new citizens; the old citizens cast themselves out of it, and so gave place to the new. In like manner Christ never takes the candlestick from any portion of his Church till his people have faithlessly cast him out of their hearts.

V. The lost inheritance is to be restored. Whether Israel will return to Palestine is only a question for the curious, and of no great practical interest. For so long as the people are restored to God and truly prosperous it cannot much matter on what spot of the globe they reside. In their palmy days many of them were in the habit of wandering far from their native land. But the true restoration, restoration to the spiritual inheritance in God, is promised to all who will return to him (Isa. lxi. 1—3).

Ver. 3.—*Orphanage and widowhood.* In the desolation of Jerusalem the inhabitants felt like orphans and widows, bereaved of the stay and comfort of life, uncared for and homeless. Many would be literally orphaned and widowed after the great slaughter of the siege. The sad condition of these greatest sufferers brings before our notice the similar trouble of those who are similarly situated in our own day.

I. Orphanage and widowhood involve overwhelming sorrow. The mournful condition of the sufferers is the first thing to strike us. Their sorrow is keen because it concerns a nearest and dearest relative, and it is the more dreadful because it strikes a whole family. Moreover, the trouble is not simply one of affection. The breadwinner is lost. The prop and strength of the household is cut down. The protector of the helpless is removed. The guide and counsellor of the young is no more.

II. Orphanage and widowhood show us the broken character of human life. There is a oneness in a true family. All the members together constitute a unit. But when death claims the head the family is broken and its completeness destroyed. Then part is on earth and part in the other world. The widow and her children thus bear testimony to the imperfection of earth, to the transitoriness of what once seemed perfect, and to the need of a future life wherein the severed threads may be reunited and the Divine idea of the family realized.

III. ORPHANAGE AND WIDOWHOOD ARE UNDER THE ESPECIAL CARE OF GOD. He is the "Father of the fatherless and the Judge of the widow" (Ps. lxviii. 5). If God sends exceptional trouble, he also feels exceptional compassion and gives exceptional aid. Helplessness is the greatest claim on the Divine pity. The heavier the need of any sufferers the more likely is it that God will come to their deliverance. It is true that he may not restore lost comforts. A shadow, long and dark, may long lie across the path of orphans and widows. But unseen hands will be tending them, if not for their wealth and pleasure, yet for their peace and blessedness. God sometimes helps by raising up friends. He may also aid by rousing the faculties of the sufferers. Under the pressure of necessity a widow, left with the care of a family, may develop capacities that slumbered in neglect so long as they were not called for.

IV. ORPHANAGE AND WIDOWHOOD HAVE A FIRST CLAIM ON CHRISTIAN CHARITY. Where God's compassion is strongest ours should be also. If the trouble is great and the sufferers have not brought it upon themselves by their own folly or fault, the sympathy should be particularly large and active. The care of widows and orphans was one of the first characteristics of the Church, distinguishing it from the selfish indifference of paganism. With all our desire for the spiritual welfare of men, and all our zeal in preaching the gospel, this elementary duty of Christianity must have a first place in our energies if we would not be justly accounted hypocrites.

Ver. 7.—*Children suffering for the sins of their parents.* I. IT IS A FACT THAT CHILDREN DO SUFFER FOR THE SINS OF THEIR PARENTS. It was apparent in the times of the Captivity; for owing to Josiah's reformation the moral condition of the nation then was better than it had been a generation or so before; yet the blow, which was caused by the greater guilt of the fathers, fell upon the children. It may often be observed in history that the greatest catastrophes do not fall on the most guilty, but on their successors, who are often better men. Thus James II. was a better man than Charles II., though the Stuart dynasty ended in the younger brother; and Louis XVI. was comparatively innocent, and yet he had to suffer for the vices of Louis XIV. and Louis XV. In private life, poverty, disease, and disgrace are inherited by children from their parents. Now, it is a sign of the robust truthfulness of the Bible that this dark fact is distinctly recognized. There is no attempt to shun it because it is mysterious. We have in the Bible an honest, brave confronting of the evils of life, and not a system which is only beautiful to contemplate in idea and which cannot be squared with facts.

II. THIS FACT IS A WARNING TO PARENTS. The selfishness that incurs disastrous consequences on a man's family is too often ignored if those consequences are not immediately apparent. But it should be exposed and reprobated. Thus the intemperate man is sometimes regarded as a kind and good-natured man because he displays no malice of temper. Surely his cruelty in impoverishing his household and risking the health of his children should be considered a gross sin. If a man will not hold his hand for his own soul's sake, let him consider how he will wreck his family and ruin innocent sons and daughters before he yields to temptation.

III. THIS FACT SHOULD NOT SHAKE OUR FAITH IN GOD. 1. Men in all ages have faced it clearly and yet have retained their trust in Providence, *e.g.* the writers of the Bible. 2. The very idea of faith implies that we must confide and wait in the darkness where we cannot understand. 3. The necessary greatness of the scheme of the government of a world should lead us to expect mysteries in it.

IV. THIS FACT SHOULD HELP US TO UNDERSTAND PART OF THE DIVINE IDEA OF LIFE. It is a sorrowful sight—innocent little children plunged into poverty and distress through no fault of their own, solely on account of the sins of those who should be their greatest benefactors! But it shows us that God does not treat us as isolated units. He takes notice of families as such. There is a "solidarity" of mankind. Everywhere we see the innocent suffering with the guilty. Social and domestic life are under providential care. And it may be best for the world as a whole that the several societies and collective bodies of which it consists should be governed with blessing and discipline than that each individual should receive only his own private grace and judgment. Moreover, if this is the case, inasmuch as the individuals profit by the corporate life and prosperity, this treatment by families and cities and nations may turn out in the long run to be the best for the separate persons.

Ver. 19.—*Consolation in the supremacy of God.* The Divine supremacy is often regarded as a topic of dread rather than as one of comfort. The awful throne towers above poor humanity, sublime and majestic, and men turn from it to seek refuge at the humbler footstool of mercy. But the writer of this elegy finds deep satisfaction in contemplating the supreme and eternal government of God.

I. THERE IS CONSOLATION IN THE FACT THAT GOD IS ENTHRONED. Above the tumult, above the darkness, stands the throne of God. God is King over all, not only reigning in majesty, but also ruling in might. 1. *Evil is not supreme.* It rears its head in boasts and threats. It dwells in high places. But it does not reach to the highest. 2. *Evil is under government.* Not only is it not supreme, but in the lower domain where it seems to rove at will it is not really free. It is chained, checked, and overruled. The kingdom of God extends over the rebellious haunts of iniquity. 3. *Justice is above all.* Wrong must give place to righteousness. Law must triumph over disorder. The fair order that is the image of God's equitable and righteous will is ultimately to supersede the hideous confusion of man's lawlessness. Even now God is reigning and working through the chaos to the development of life and beauty. 4. *Goodness controls everything.* He who is enthroned supreme is our Father, the kind and merciful God. His rule must reflect his character. For such a Lord to be supreme is for all the law and government of his kingdom to be inspired with love.

II. THERE IS CONSOLATION IN THE FACT THAT GOD'S THRONE IS ETERNAL. The eternal is always of first moment. Whatever be the force, or size, or character of any temporal thing, its transitoriness makes it as an unsubstantial dream compared with the solid endurance of what is eternal. God's eternal throne renders the petty thrones of evil, so hastily set up and so swiftly cast down, like mere passing shadows. 1. *Nothing can overthrow the throne of God.* We see good causes frustrated, good men crushed and bad powers apparently victorious; but they cannot take the citadel. The throne above looks down upon their petty victories with scorn. 2. *Goodness will outlive evil.* The temporary phase of darkness cannot endure like the everlasting kingdom of light. Generation after generation comes and goes; still the grand old throne stands above all, immovable. In one age, wild dreams of new religions possess the minds of men. In another, lethargy and degeneration of character are prevalent. But all these shadows pass, and the throne still abides. Like the rock about which the surf fumes and frets, the throne of God dwells firm and calm in the midst of all earthly changes. 3. *Evil will be made to work for good.* The everlasting throne will draw all transitory things into subjection to itself. We can endure our passing troubles if we are children of God and citizens of the kingdom of heaven, because these very troubles must do the will of our gracious Lord.

Ver. 20.—*Questioning God.* I. IT IS NATURAL THAT WE SHOULD WISH TO KNOW THE PURPOSE OF GOD'S DEALINGS WITH US. There is no subject for inquiry that touches us more nearly or that affects us in such important matters. God's treatment of us concerns our highest welfare for time and eternity. It is in all the experience of life—our many blessings, our varied trials, our greatest prosperity, and our heaviest trouble. Surely it is natural that we should ask whither are all these waves driving us, and why do they sometimes beat so strangely and severely.

II. THERE IS MUCH IN GOD'S DEALINGS WITH US THAT WE CANNOT UNDERSTAND. It seems that he has forgotten us when we are permitted to fall into great and lasting trouble. Short, sharp affliction may be faced. But long-enduring distress wears out hope and faith, and makes it appear more and more as though the lonely sufferer had been deserted by God. The purpose of this is not easy to discover. The whole dispensation is just inexplicable.

III. THE RIGHT WAY TO DISCOVER THE PURPOSE OF GOD'S DEALINGS WITH US IS TO ASK HIM. We often discuss vainly when we have no data to start with. But speculation is sure to fail if it goes beyond all evidence and clear reason. Prayer is the one safe resource. It would be well if we had enough faith in God to confide our doubts to him. For it is too often only unbelief that makes us silence doubt. If we truly trusted God we should more bravely confess to him all that troubled and perplexed our minds. In response to such confidence God may reveal to us a new way of looking at our experience that shall help us to understand something of its object ; or he may simply reconcile our minds to the mystery—perhaps an equally beneficial result.

IV. WE MAY REST ASSURED THAT GOD HAS A PURPOSE IN HIS DEALINGS WITH US. It is there, though we cannot see it. We may say, " Wherefore dost thou forget us ? " and we may not be able to receive an answer to our question. Yet we should not doubt that there is a " wherefore." God does nothing aimlessly. He certainly cannot be putting his children to pain without an object, nor without one that is adequate to the cost. The knowledge of this fact should quiet fear and restless doubt, even if the object itself remains hidden in mystery.

V. WE MUST BEWARE OF QUESTIONING GOD QUERULOUSLY. We have no right to demand an explanation from God. To couch complaints in the form of inquiries is insulting to God. Let the questioning be humble and submissive, and the answers are sure to come in peace, if not always in light.

Ver. 21.—*Renewal*. When they do not lead to improvement lamentations are profitless, though they may be unavoidable. It is vain to mourn the past if our grief does not help us to make the future better. Sorrow for sin is good only when it leads to an active repentance. It is therefore necessary that a true consideration of the miserable condition into which evil living has brought us should rouse an earnest desire for a new and better life.

I. RENEWAL MUST BE THE WORK OF GOD. The writer does not simply resolve to do better, nor hope that a happier state of affairs will come about of its own accord. He prays. And the object of his prayer is to plead with God to produce the great change which is so much needed. 1. *We cannot accomplish the renewal.* (1) We cannot change our own hearts ; they are too corrupt and too hard. (2) We cannot bring back the old days. The past is lost for ever. If it is to be equalled or surpassed by the future, a Divine providence alone can accomplish the great work. 2. *God does bring about renewal.* He renews the face of the earth. He sends spring-time into wintry lives. No soul is so corrupt that God cannot renew it ; no life is so desolate that God cannot brighten it. We try vainly to turn ourselves. But God is strong as well as gracious. If only he turn us we shall be surely turned.

II. RENEWAL MUST BE IN OUR EXPERIENCE. The mistake is to suppose that God must change to us. But there is no need for him to turn. He is always good and always willing to be favourable to his children as soon as they submit and obey. Till then nothing can induce him to do so unrighteous an act as to turn from wrath to pleasant treatment. The necessary change lies all on our side. Men used to think that night was the desertion of the earth by the sun, and day the enjoyment of his return. They were wrong. They now know that the sun is not thus fickle. So it is with the soul's night and day. A primitive and narrow theology says that God changes—now going, now returning. Larger knowledge shows that he abides the same, and that as our distress is in turning from him, so our redemption must be in returning to him.

III. RENEWAL MUST BEGIN WITH OUR INNER LIFE. The writer wisely prays to be turned back to God before he prays for the renewal of the old days. It is a common mistake to seek for the external fruits of forgiveness before the internal. The first thing is to bring the soul back to God. Other happy consequences will follow. It is vain to pray for the brightness of noon before our part of the earth has revolved towards the sun. It is to be noted that the great change in the soul is a turning to God. God draws us to himself. Redemption is reconciliation to God. To be near him, to trust and love and obey him, to seek more and more of his light and life,—this is the renewed health and blessedness of the soul that is restored from the wretchedness and ruin of sin.

IV. RENEWAL WILL AFFECT OUR WHOLE EXPERIENCE. After the interior life is renewed the exterior also undergoes a happy transformation. The Jew yearned for the old happy days of peace and prosperity. We inevitably clothe the joyous past with a glamour of affection. Many a lost joy seems inconceivably bright now it has gone. Yet God may bring it back, if not in the old form, for the exact past is irretrievable, yet in even richer sweetness. The penitent muses sadly over the innocent days of old in the dear home now long since broken up. He would give worlds to bring back that peaceful time before all his sin and shame. It cannot return. But far off, at last, there may be reunions in the better world and rejoicings that will outdo the brightness even of those happy days.

HOMILIES BY VARIOUS AUTHORS.

Ver. 1.—*The Lord's remembrance besought.* The inhabitants of Judah and Jerusalem had looked, now to Egypt and now to Assyria, for help and deliverance. Events had shown upon how broken a reed they had leaned. Their experience was now leading the best among them to another and a surer, higher, Refuge. As the spokesman of his repenting fellow-countrymen, Jeremiah entreats the remembrance and the regard of Jehovah.

I. ADVERSITY SOMETIMES LEADS MEN TO SEEK THE REGARD AND FAVOUR OF THE GOD WHOM IN PROSPERITY THEY HAVE FORGOTTEN. That trouble may foster self-control and patience is a commonplace of moral teaching. But it only answers its highest end when it leads the afflicted to seek and call upon their God. In the noon-day of happiness, the healthy, busy, and joyous too often forget him to whom they are indebted for all. Providence is forgotten when the sun shines; clouds and darkness seem to have a natural tendency to remind the soul of God.

II. THE LORD'S REMEMBRANCE AND CONSIDERATION ARE AN ASSURANCE OF HELP AND DELIVERANCE. That the Omniscient is not perfectly aware of all that happens to man is not for a moment to be supposed. The language of the prophet is human language, adapted to our ignorance and infirmity. The Lord will be entreated; he summons his children to think of him; and he promises to draw near to those who draw near to him. The sinner may well dread the all-including gaze of the righteous Judge; but the lowly and believing penitent may well take courage when he learns that the Lord has not forgotten to be gracious.—T.

Ver. 7.—*The moral continuity of nations.* Man is naturally not merely gregarious, but social. The powers that be, an apostle teaches us, are ordained by God—from which we learn that political and social life have a Divine sanction. Accordingly, the Judge of all deals with men, not only as individuals, but as communities. This fact was present to the mind of the prophet when he wrote these words.

I. THE FACT OF NATIONAL ACCOUNTABILITY TO THE MORAL GOVERNOR. The history of the Jews is the history of a theocracy; but it embodied lessons which are adapted to all mankind. Nations have national privileges, national responsibilities, national proba-tions, national rewards and punishments.

II. NATIONAL RETRIBUTION IS SOMETIMES DEFERRED FOR A SEASON. The prophets appear to have had a clear view of this law. Wrong-doing in one generation was seen to be followed by punishment in a succeeding age. Jeremiah is the author of the well-known proverb, "The fathers have eaten sour grapes, and the children's teeth are set on edge." The seed (to change the figure) is sown by one generation; a following generation reaps the harvest.

III. THE CERTAINTY THAT PENALTIES WILL BE INFLICTED UPON THE IMPENITENT. There is indeed a sense in which even the repenting and reformed suffer for the sins of those who have gone before them. But for the impenitent and unreformed there is no exception, no escape. We, says the prophet, speaking of himself and of his rebellious and ungodly contemporaries—"we have borne the iniquities of our fathers." The apostasy and rebellion of the former generations were visited upon those who endured the horrors of the siege and the degradation of the Captivity. There is mystery in the providential appointment that, not only shall every man bear his own burden, but that some shall bear the burden of those also who have gone before them. But the fact remains, and it gives solemnity to the life of families and of nations.

IV. THE LESSON IS THUS IMPRESSED UPON ALL MEN—HOW SERIOUS AND REAL A THING IS NATIONAL PROBATION! The teaching which was profitable for Israel is equally adapted to England, and indeed to all the nations of mankind. The Lord is King, and from his government and authority none of the earth's inhabitants is free.—T.

Ver. 8.—*None to deliver.* Bitterness was added to the misery of the Jews when Chaldean slaves—advanced to eminence and power on account of their ability—were placed in authority over them. But there was no choice; resistance was impossible and deliverer there was none. In this respect the condition of the inhabitants of Jerusalem may represent that of sinful, helpless men.

I. A CRUEL BONDAGE. Sinners have yielded themselves up to obey the enemy of their souls, the foe of God. This is (1) *a usurper*, who has no right to rule over men; (2) *a tyrant*, who with unjust and unreasonable exercise of authority oppresses those beneath his power; (3) *a cruel master*, whose service is slavery, whose stripes are many, whose wages are death and destruction.

II. A SEEMINGLY INEVITABLE FATE. The conquered Judæans had looked hither and thither, in the crisis of their fate, for some friend and helper, but they had looked in vain. Similarly the captive of sin can find no earthly deliverer; his fellow-men are his fellow-sinners and fellow-captives; there is no eye to pity and no hand to save.

III. A SOLITARY BUT SUFFICIENT CONSOLATION AND REFUGE. The restless waves answer their purpose when they toss the imperilled mariner towards the haven of refuge. Affliction and adversity, chains and dungeons, oppressors and torturers, may make the one only Deliverer welcome. The Lord God has revealed himself to us as the Saviour of all men. There is no prison from which he cannot set the captive free; there are no gyves and fetters he cannot strike off; there are no foes from whose hands he cannot rescue and deliver.—T.

Ver. 15.—*The cessation of joy.* This fate had been foretold. "Then will I cause to cease from the cities of Judah, and from the streets of Jerusalem, the voice of mirth, and the voice of gladness, the voice of the bridegroom, and the voice of the bride: for the land shall be desolate." Well is it for those who take the warning which is given beforehand, and do not wait, as Jerusalem waited, for the stern lessons of a retributive Providence.

I. THERE IS CESSATION OF JOY WHICH IS NOT PUNITIVE. The health, the elasticity of spirits, the pleasures of youth, cannot be protracted to old age. "Earth's joys grow dim, its glories fade away." Days of sickness, of poverty, of bereavement, of sorrow, are appointed by the Lord of the human lot, to follow days of brightness. The wail of sorrow will replace the song of gladsome joy. Yet all this experience may be spiritually disciplinary and helpful; there may be in it nothing of punishment, nothing of Divine displeasure.

II. THERE IS CESSATION OF JOY WHICH IS THE SIGN OF DIVINE ANGER AND THE FULFILMENT OF DIVINE THREATENING. Such was the case with Judah, upon whom the siege and the Captivity came, not without warning, not without space for repentance. In fact, sin puts an end to the joy which it promises to increase and perpetuate, and brings about the mourning and distress against which it pretends to ensure us. The retrospect of those whose joy has ceased becomes in such cases a retrospect of human rebellion and Divine forbearance. Conscience awakes and admits that sorrow is merited.

APPLICATION. Yet there is a way of repentance. God will renew the days of his people as of old. This is the cry and the hope of the penitent: "Restore unto me the joy of thy salvation."—T.

Vers. 16, 17.—*The degradation of sin.* The promise of sin is something very different from this; no flattery is untried, no prospect withheld, which may induce men to rebel against God. But, as with our first parents, as with the dwellers in Jerusalem, so is it in the experience of all men; the promises which sin makes are unfulfilled; the wages of sin are death.

I. THE PICTURE OF DEGRADATION. It is highly figurative language which the prophet here employs; but it is not exaggerated, it is not unjust. 1. The *head* is uncrowned. Judah's independence and freedom was as a crown to the head; but the Chaldeans tore it off and flung it away. They who defy God must lose in so doing all that is most honourable, most sacred, most precious. 2. The *heart* is faint. Judah's joy was turned into mourning, her hopes were dashed to the ground; how could the heart be other than faint? The ways of sin are ways of disappointment, weariness, and distress. The heart of the transgressor sinks within him when he sees the fruit of his doings. 3. The *eyes* are dim with watching for deliverance, with tears of woe.

II. THE CAUSE OF DEGRADATION. Judah may have been unwilling to admit the truth, and may have been disposed to attribute calamities to second causes. But the prophet was just, and laid his hand upon the true explanation when he confessed on behalf of his countrymen, " We have sinned! " Trace up human misery and national disaster to the source, and this is to be reached only when we come to defection and departure from the righteous Lord.

III. THE CONSCIOUSNESS OF DEGRADATION. "Woe unto us! " is the cry of the prophet. When men sin and suffer but fail to acknowledge their own ill desert, the intentions of Providence are as yet unfulfilled. The sin must be taken home; the punishment must be acknowledged just; the confession must be penitent, sincere, and frank.

IV. THE LESSONS OF DEGRADATION. 1. Let the virtuous and obedient abjure self-confidence and cherish trust in God. 2. Let the tempted beware of the foe, and watch and pray lest they sin and come into this torment. 3. Let the smitten sinner repent and turn unto the Lord and seek pardon and renewal.—T.

Ver. 19.—*The eternal throne.* The believer in God has this great advantage over the atheist and the agnostic—he has a firm conviction that all things are under the control and rule of a wise, righteous, and benevolent King, who reigns both in heaven and on earth. Afflictions, personal and relative, may distress his mind; calamities may overwhelm his imagination and baffle his reason; but he has this consolation—he knows that the Lord remains for ever on his throne.

I. GOD'S ETERNAL THRONE CONTRASTS WITH THE PERISHING THRONES OF EARTH. The King of Judah, defeated and carried captive, was torn by a foreign hand from the throne of his power and glory. All earthly monarchies are transitory and all earthly monarchs are mortal. They perish, but God endureth.

II. THE STABILITY OF GOD'S THRONE RESTS UPON THE RIGHTEOUSNESS OF HIS DOMINION. " A sceptre of righteousness is the sceptre of thy kingdom." Injustice and oppression may prevail for a season, but only right is indestructible and immortal. Even in his mercy the Supreme has regard to the claims of justice and to the maintenance of rightful authority.

III. THE DEFEAT OF GOD'S ENEMIES IS ASSURED. They may rage and they may take counsel together, but the Lord has them in derision. All their assaults upon his kingdom must fail, and those who lead those assaults must come to shame and misery. No weapon that is formed against God and his people shall prosper.

IV. THE VICTORY OF GOD'S CAUSE IS CERTAIN. Kingdoms rise and fall, princes are elevated and dethroned; but the King of kings goes conquering and to conquer. All his foes are put beneath his feet, and on his head are many crowns.—T.

Ver. 21.—*" Turn us again! "* The Scriptures are the volume of hope; they lend no countenance to despondency; they rebuke despair. Deep as was the degradation of the Jews, far as they had wandered from God's ways, inexcusable as they had defied his authority, there was for them a place of repentance. And Jeremiah closes this Book of Lamentations with language of confident supplication and well-grounded hope of better times.

I. THE NEED OF TURNING. The whole of the book thus closed witnesses to this necessity. Judah had gone wrong, had wilfully taken the path of rebellion and defiance. In this respect her case represents that of every culpable transgressor. The end of the way of sin is death, is destruction without remedy. It is a stern truth, but it is a truth, and a truth which mercy reveals.

II. TO WHOM THE TURNING MUST BE. " Turn us unto *thee!* " Away from the sin which has misled, away from the human counsellors and helpers in whom is no wise counsel and no sufficient help, away from self, to God against whom the sinner has transgressed and to whom he needs to be reconciled. The old phrase, " conversion unto God," is one full of truth, meaning, and appropriateness.

III. By whom the turning must be effected. The prayer is unto the Lord; for he alone can turn the wanderer unto himself. By the authority of his Law, by the winning, melting power of his gospel, by the sweet constraint of his Spirit, he alone can transform the heart, reverse the steps, and renew the olden days of those who have transgressed but have now at length sought his favour and forgiveness.—T.

Ver. 2.—*The fate of inheritance and houses.* The Israelite reckoned a great deal on his inheritance, that which came to him as an Israelite; and in this he did quite right, seeing how he was bound to dwell on the promises made to Abraham. There was the national territory, sanctified and made a peculiarly valuable thing by the manner in which it first came into Israel's hand. Then there were the tribal inheritances and the family inheritances. So that altogether inheritance was continually before the Israelite mind; inheritance became almost a part of self. Doubtless many tracts of land had run down in the same families for generations. And now the foreigner comes in to reap the riches of these lands and dwell in the houses built on them. What the Israelites failed to recollect was that the inheritance they esteemed so much was not the real inheritance in the eyes of God. The visible land, out of which comes the corn, the wine, the oil, is only the type of that deeper, that truly exhaustless spiritual land, where we are to sow plentifully, assured that a harvest cannot fail. There is the inheritance, corruptible, defiled, that doth fade away. There is the house made with hands, temporal, on the earth. And then, all unconscious of the pains we are preparing for ourselves, we let our heart's best affections get round these things. The loss of the inheritance, the loss of the houses, was the way to gain, if only the loser could see it. Doubtless what we may fail to possess of temporal things some one else gets hold of; but his getting is not with a firm, abiding grasp. These lamenting Israelites would reckon that the loss of inheritance and houses, which made them so miserable, would make the new possessors correspondingly happy; and such would be the case for a time, but only so long as the brightness of the first delusion lasted. God does not mean that we should ever say of any really good thing that our inheritance is turned to strangers, our houses to aliens. Of the really good things there is enough and to spare for all. Christ sends out his apostles to urge every one towards the inheritance of the saints in light; and in the house of him who is Father of Jesus and of all that believe in Jesus there are many mansions, many abiding-places, a place for every one wishing to dismiss the restless, craving spirit, and abide in such a place.—Y.

Ver. 7.—*The sin of the fathers and the suffering of the children.* This chapter is the complaint of those who suffer. "We," "us," "our,"—these are the prominent words. The complainers are those who have lost inheritance and houses, become fatherless, and entered into a galling servitude. And now what do they give as the reason of all this terrible experience? This—that "our fathers have sinned."

I. The measure of truth in this. The fathers had sinned. That was an historical fact. The utterances of former prophets, recorded, perhaps, in far greater abundance than we have any idea of, attested the iniquities of past generations. No generation of which there was any record had been without its disobedience. And had it not also been said that the sins of the fathers should be visited on the children? Hence there is plain logic in these words, "Our fathers have sinned, . . . and *we* have borne their iniquities." Great is the suffering in bodily pain, in privation, and in emotion, of every generation; and each generation has a right to say that some, at all events, of this suffering would have been escaped if only preceding generations had lived according to the full law of righteousness. Hence the appeal to us, when self-indulgence presses with all its energies, to consider others. Indulging self, we have to make ready for after-pains; but those pains cannot be kept within the limit of our own lives.

II. True as this statement is, there is a measure of defect in it. Note exactly how the point is put: "Our fathers have sinned, and are not;" that is, "they cannot suffer any more, and now the suffering comes on to us." In such an aspect of the situation there is great pathos, but we need to travel round to the other aspects also. There is a difference between retribution and suffering. Some kinds of pain and injury may be inherited to the third and fourth generation, but a guilty conscience belongs to the individual. The worst pains, the worst consequences, and those on which the Saviour looks with the most pity, are surely those coming out of our own wrong-doing; and searching into the connection between the sins of past generations and the suffering of the present one will do harm rather than good, if such a searching tends to obscure our own lawlessness, our own want of attention to the requirements of God. There is, indeed, a great difference in kind between the suffering coming on us from the wickedness of others and that which comes from our own.—Y.

Ver. 14.—*The occupation of the elders gone.* I. THE PLACE OF OLD MEN IN A COMMUNITY. As men grow old they may get past certain kinds of work, but they need not cease to be useful, nor need age become, unless from bodily frailty, a burden and a weariness. There is much for an old man to tell from the stores of his experience and observation. He may show what ought to be avoided, even if he cannot always tell what ought to be done. The elders sat in the gate, where the throng passed in and out, and where they could see more people probably than anywhere else. An old man should endeavour to be useful and to mingle with the life of the world as long as he can. It is right that he should be in the way of all the respect and veneration he can receive, not because these things are necessary to his happiness, but because those who give them are the better for their giving. A society without its troops of children at one end, full of life and eagerness, and its sprinkling of hoary heads crowned with glory at the other, would soon feel that very important elements were lacking. Elders sitting in the gate bore testimony to a certain stability and continuity in the social life of Jerusalem.
II. THE PECULIAR ASPECT OF THE CALAMITY FURNISHED BY THE FACT THAT THE OLD MEN HAVE FORSAKEN THE GATE. There is no longer anything to take them to the gate. Where of old they had many pleasures, now they will have nothing but pain. The place of honour would only become a place of insult, and in all likelihood only too many of these elders had been advisers of the wrong sort, men with a serene and firmly rooted confidence in their own opinion. To the warnings of a prophet old men can often reply that such things have been said over and over again without coming true; and then, when all at once the threatening takes effect, what can they do but retire into as much obscurity as possible? These same old men, many of them, must have had much to do with the state of affairs that made all these calamities a Divine necessity.—Y.

Ver. 16.—*Discrowned Jerusalem.* I. THE PAST HONOUR OF JERUSALEM. The crown has fallen from the head; a crown, therefore, has been upon the head. The lament is not over something striven for and not attained, but over something, as it seems, securely possessed and now irretrievably lost. Notice how Ezekiel is instructed to put the matter (xvi. 12). In making Jerusalem to know her abominations there is a contrast with former privileges. Jehovah says, "I put a beautiful crown upon thine head . . . and thy renown went forth among the heathen for thy beauty." Unquestionably Jerusalem and the land of which she was the radiant centre shone forth gloriously among the Gentiles. The great example of this is that queen of the south who came from the uttermost parts of the earth to hear the wisdom of Solomon. God for his own purposes, inscrutable, and yet, as we must believe, beneficent, constituted it so that Jerusalem was like a fair woman crowned with a crown of pure gold. Other cities had their strength, glory, peculiarities, but Jerusalem was uniquely glorious. And so human individuals may have most attractive natural endowments. There may be physical beauty, or genius, or some ineffable charm of character, or great intellectual capacity, something that lifts man or woman above the common crowd, and thus puts upon them a bright and manifest natural crown. The same great secret power that glorified Israel glorifies men still, not for what they do, nor for any claim they have, but that in their glory they may stimulate and inspire others, and multiply the happiness of every life coming within their sway. It was for the sake of the nations that Jehovah glorified Jerusalem and made her beautiful.
II. HER PRESENT HUMILIATION. The crown has fallen from the head, but the mark of past and lost regality remains. It cannot be obliterated. The higher a nation climbs, the further it can fall and the more terrible becomes the spectacle of its fall. It needed all the slow and majestic ascent of Rome to greatness to make Gibbon's great book possible. Thus, looking from such a height, he had pathetic struggles and contrasts to depict, which would else have been impossible. So, also, we contemplate

the aberrations and miseries, the cynicism and misanthropy coming out in the lives of geniuses who have missed their way, men of richest endowments who, from the depths of self-indulgence and debauchery, might well cry, " The crown is fallen from my head." And so we see that the great crown to be desired is, not that which comes through natural differences or differences in social position, but that which comes through the divinely inspired quality of one's living. " The hoary head is a crown of glory, if it be found in the way of righteousness" (Phil. iv. 1 ; 2 Tim. iv. 8 ; Jas. i. 12 ; 1 Pet. v. 4).—Y.

Ver. 17.—*The faint heart and the dim eyes.* I. THE PENETRATING EFFECT OF THE DIVINE CHASTISEMENTS. Jerusalem had been satisfied with outward things. Wherever it turned, there had been enough to satisfy its pride and its pleasure. And now Jehovah, by efficient agents, had taken these outward things away. The difference that had been made in Jerusalem was perceptible to any eye. But another difference could only be known when it was confessed, namely, the difference made in the hearts of the people when their outward circumstances were so completely changed. Proud, resolute men, full of joy in their selfish purposes, found the interest of life completely gone. It would have availed nothing if all these chastisements had ended in leaving the people real Stoics, able to say that it was all the same whether they kept their temporal possessions or lost them. God did not desolate Jerusalem for any delight that he took in this ; it was to find a way to humble hearts that were unsubdued after every prophetic appeal. When men are delightedly occupied with the things of sense, then it is a great end gained if, through losses and changes, their hearts become faint and their eyes dim. For then they may accept the ministry of Christ to put into their hearts an energy which will tend for righteousness and direct their eyes to look on the world in the right way. II. THE CAUSE HERE SPECIALLY MENTIONED. The hill of Zion has become a desolation ; it has become again a mere height in the wilderness, such as doubtless it had been at some time before in the immemorial past. That Zion is here specified seems to point to the sorrow and despair caused by the overthrow of religious ordinances. The very fact that Jehovah had allowed the place devoted to him to become thus desolated made his displeasure with the people to become a much more vivid thing. It seemed as if he needed no more a habitation in their midst.—Y.

Vers. 19—22.—*The only resource acknowledged to be in God.* It will be felt that this prayer is a fitting conclusion to the book. What could be more proper than that these people, having looked all *around* with an ever-deepening sense of loss and humiliation, should now look *above* ? Upon earth, in strength or skill of man, there is nothing to be looked for ; if anything is to be got, it is by looking to heaven. I. AMID ALL THESE CHANGES THE CONTINUANCE OF JEHOVAH IS PERCEIVED. Zion has become desolate, but the true throne of God is not there. That God lives, unchangeable, unaffected by our lapses and losses, is the last safeguard of hope, and it is an impregnable one. Much is it to be desired that, amid all the vicissitudes of life, we should have this sense of something unchanging. II. THE SENSE OF SEPARATION FROM GOD. This was the crown of troubles to some of the people, that God seemed to have forgotten them and forsaken them. But when God remembered them and manifested his presence, all that the people in general did was to take his gifts and think nothing of the Giver's will and purpose. God, of course, had neither forgotten nor forsaken. What the people called forgetting was only a different kind of remembering. What they called forsaking was only a closer presence. III. THE UNQUENCHABLE HOPE OF THOSE WHO TAKE THE RIGHT VIEW OF GOD. This chapter has had in it the tones of penitence and contrition. It is admitted that the cause of all this desolation is the people's turning away from God. And now there is the petition which results from a full self-discovery. Inward weakness is discovered. The last cry of the book indicates that the turning of men to God is the great thing to be desired. Not a restoration to external possessions and comforts, but a turning to God consequent on his turning to us. The results that come from our being turned to God by his power will one day be seen to justify all the loss and pain needed to bring them about.—Y.

HOMILETICAL INDEX

TO

THE LAMENTATIONS OF JEREMIAH

JEREMIAH

EXPOSITION BY

T. K. CHEYNE

HOMILETICS BY

W. F. ADENEY

HOMILIES BY VARIOUS AUTHORS

D. YOUNG   S. CONWAY

J. WAITE   A. F. MUIR

THE
BOOK OF THE PROPHET JEREMIAH

VOL. I

INTRODUCTION

§ 1. The Life, Times, and Characteristics of Jeremiah.

1. THE name of Jeremiah at once suggests the ideas of trouble and lamentation ; and not without too much historical ground. Jeremiah was, in fact, not only " the evening star of the declining day of prophecy," but the herald of the dissolution of the Jewish commonwealth. The outward show of things, however, seemed to promise a calm and peaceful ministry to the youthful prophet. The last great political misfortune mentioned (in 2 Chron. xxxiii. 11, not in Kings) before his time is the carrying captive of King Manasseh to Babylon, and this is also the last occasion on which a king of Assyria is recorded to have interfered in the affairs of Judah. Manasseh, however, we are told, was restored to his kingdom, and, apostate and persecutor as he was, found mercy from the Lord God of his fathers. Before he closed his eyes for ever a great and terrible event occurred— the sister kingdom of the ten tribes was finally destroyed, and one great burden of prophecy found its fulfilment. Judah was spared a little longer. Manasseh acquiesced in his dependent position, and continued to pay tribute to the " great King " of Nineveh. In B.C. 642 Manasseh died, and, after a brief interval of two years (it is the reign of Amon, a prince with an ill-omened Egyptian name), Josiah, the grandson of Manasseh, ascended the throne. This king was a man of a more spiritual religion than any of his predecessors except Hezekiah, of which he gave a solid proof by putting down the shrines and chapels in which the people delighted to worship the true God, Jehovah, and other supposed gods under idolatrous forms. This extremely popular form of religion could never be entirely eradicated ; competent travellers agree that traces of it are still visible in the religious usages of the professedly Mohammedan peasantry of Palestine. " Not only have the fellahs preserved (Robinson had already a presentiment of this), by the erection of their Mussulman *kubbes*, and through their fetish-worship of certain great isolated trees, the situation and the memory of those sanctuaries which Deuteronomy gives up to the execration of the Israelites entering the promised land, and which it points out to them crowning the lofty summits, surmounting the hills, and sheltering themselves under the

green trees; but they pay them almost the same worship as the ancient devotees of the Elohim, those Canaanitish *kuffars* of whom they are the descendants. These *makoms*—so Deuteronomy calls them—which Manasseh went on constructing, and against which the prophets in vain exhaust their grandiose invectives, are word for word, thing for thing, the Arab *makams* of our modern *goyim*, covered by those little cupolas which dot with such picturesque white spots the mountainous horizons of the arid Judæa."

Such is the language of an accomplished explorer, M. Clermont-Gannman,[1] and it helps us to understand the difficulties with which Hezekiah and Josiah had to contend. The former king had the support of Isaiah, and the latter had at his right hand the equally devoted prophet, Jeremiah, the year of whose call was apparently the one immediately following the commencement of the reformation (see ch. 1. 2; 2 Chron. xxxiv. 3). Jeremiah, however, had a more difficult task than Isaiah. The latter prophet must have had on his side nearly all the zealous worshippers of Jehovah. The state was more than once in great danger, and it was the burden of Isaiah's prophecies that, by simply trusting in Jehovah and obeying his commandments, the state would infallibly be delivered. But in Jeremiah's time there seems to have been a great revival of purely external religion. Men went to the temple and performed all the ceremonial laws which concerned them, but neglected those practical duties which make up so large a portion of true religion. There was a party of this kind in Isaiah's time, but it was not so powerful, because the misfortunes of the country seemed to show clearly that Jehovah was displeased with the state of the national religion. In Jeremiah's time, on the other hand, the continued peace and prosperity which at first prevailed was equally regarded as a proof that God looked favourably upon his people, in accordance with those repeated promises in the Book of Deuteronomy, that, if the people obeyed the Law of Jehovah, Jehovah would bless their basket and their store, and would keep them in peace and safety. And here it must be remarked (apart from the higher criticism, so much is as clear as the day) that the Book of Deuteronomy was a favourite reading-book of religious people at this time. Jeremiah, himself (surely a representative of the most religious class) is full of allusions to it; its characteristic phrases recur continually in his pages. The discovery of the book in the temple [2] (2 Kings xxii.) was, we may venture to surmise, providentially permitted with a view to the religious needs of those times. No one can deny that Deuteronomy was peculiarly adapted to the age of Josiah and Jeremiah, partly because of the stress which it lays on the importance of religious centralization as opposed to the liberty of worshipping at local shrines, and partly because of its emphasis on the simple moral duties which the men of that age were in serious danger of forgetting. No wonder, then, that

---

[1] 'La Palestine Inconnue ' (Paris, 1876), pp. 49, 50.

[2] The question, on which Old Testament critics are so much divided, as to the Mosaic or post-Mosaic origin of the Book of Deuteronomy receives a special treatment elsewhere.

Jeremiah himself should take up the study of the book with special earnestness, and that its phraseology should impress itself on his own style of writing. There is yet another circumstance which may help us to understand our prophet's strong interest in the Book of Deuteronomy. It is that his father was not improbably the high priest who found the Book of the Law in the temple. We know, at any rate, that Jeremiah was a member of a priestly family, and that his father was named Hilkiah (ch. i. 1); and that he had high connections is probable from the respect shown to him by successive rulers of Judah—by Jehoiakim and Zedekiah, no less than by Ahikam and Gedaliah, the viceroys of the King of Babylon. We may safely assume, then, that both Jeremiah and a large section of the Jewish people were deeply interested in the Book of Deuteronomy, and, though there was no Bible at that time in our sense of the word, that this impressive book to some extent supplied its place. There was, however, as has been indicated above, a danger connected with reading the Book of Deuteronomy, the exhortations of which so repeatedly connect the national prosperity with obedience to the commandments of God. Now, these commandments are obviously of two kinds—moral and ceremonial; not that any hard and fast line can be drawn between them, but, roughly speaking, the contents of some of the laws are more distinctly moral, and those of others more distinctly ceremonial. Some of the Jews had little or no conception of the moral or spiritual side of religion, and thought it enough to perform with the strictest punctuality the ceremonial part of God's Law. Having done this, they cried, "Peace, peace;" and applied the delightful promises of Deuteronomy to themselves. And it *seemed* as if Providence justified them, for, as was noticed just now, the kingdom of Judah was freer from external danger than it had been for a long time. Another consideration may be added. The prophet Nahum, as is well known, predicted the complete destruction of the tyrannical power of Assyria. In B.C. 626, *i.e.* in the fourteenth year of Josiah, a great step was taken towards the fulfilment of that prediction; a powerful rival kingdom to Assyria (though in nominal subordination to it) was established at Babylon, and the Medes, now a powerful and united kingdom, advanced upon Assyria from the east. This was just at the time when Josiah was beginning his reformation, and Jeremiah beginning to prophesy. Could there be a more manifest token (so many professedly religious people might urge) of the favour of God to his long humiliated people? Jeremiah, however, thought otherwise. Cassandra-like, he began his dirge when all were lulled in a deep sense of security. The spiritual state of his country seemed to him utterly rotten. He agreed, it is true, with those would-be religious persons that the local shrines and chapels ought to be abolished, and he could not object to their strict observance of the appointed rites and ceremonies; but he did from the bottom of his heart abhor and detest the supposition that a mere ceremonial worship could be pleasing to God (see those remarkable, though at the same time obscure, passages, ch. vii. 8—15, 21—23; xi. 15).

2. Jeremiah did not cease preaching, but with very little result. We need not wonder at this. The visible success of a faithful preacher is no test of his acceptableness before God. There are times when the Holy Spirit himself seems to work in vain, and the world seems given up to the powers of evil. True, even then there is a "silver lining" to the cloud, if we have only faith to see it. There is always a "remnant according to the election of grace;" and there is often a late harvest which the sower does not live to see. It was so with the labours of Jeremiah, who, like the hero Samson, slew more in his death than in his life; but on this interesting point we must not at present linger. Jeremiah went on preaching, but with small apparent success; when all at once a little cloud arose, no bigger than a man's hand, and soon the fair prospects of Judah were cruelly blighted. Josiah, the favourite, as it seemed, of God and man, was defeated and slain on the field of Megiddo, in B.C. 609. The immediate result was a tightening of the political yoke under which the kingdom of Judah laboured. The old Assyrian empire had long been declining; and just at the beginning of Jeremiah's ministry there occurred, as we have seen, one of those great events which change the face of the world—the rise of the great Babylonian power. It need hardly be said that Babylon and the Chaldeans occupy a large place in the prophecies of Jeremiah; Babylon was to him what Nineveh had been to Isaiah.

But, before entering upon this subject of the relations of Jeremiah to the Babylonians, we have first to consider a question of some importance for the study of his writings, viz. whether his references to foreign invaders are covered entirely by the Babylonian aggression. Is it not possible that an earlier danger may have left its impress on his pages (and also on those of Zephaniah)? Herodotus tells us that the Scythians were masters of Asia for twenty-eight years (?), that they advanced to the borders of Egypt, and that, on their return, some of them plundered the temple of Ascalon (i. 106). The date of the Scythian invasion of Palestine can, it is true, only be fixed approximately. The Canons of Eusebius place it in Olympiad 36.2, equivalent to B.C. 635 (St. Jerome's Latin version), or Olympiad 37.1, equivalent to B.C. 632 (Armenian version). At any rate, it ranges between about B.C. 634 and 618, *i.e.* between the accession of Cyaxares and the death of Psamnutichus (see Herod., i. 103—105), or more precisely, perhaps, between B.C. 634 and 625 (accepting Abydenus's account of the fall of Nineveh). True, one could wish for better evidence than that of Herodotus (*loc. cit.*) and Justin (ii. 3). But the statements of these writers have not yet been disproved, and they suit the chronological conditions of the prophecies before us. A reference to the Babylonian invasion seems to be excluded in the case of Zephaniah, by the facts that in B.C. 635—625 Babylonia was still under the supremacy of Assyria, and that from neither country could any danger to Palestine then be apprehended. The case of Jeremiah is, no doubt, more complicated. It cannot be maintained that any discourses, in the form in which we now have them, relate to the Scythians; but it is possible that passages originally spoken of the Scythians have been inter-mixed with later prophecies respecting the Chaldeans.   The descriptions in ch. iv., v., viii., of the wild, northern nation, sweeping along and spreading devastation as it goes, seems more strikingly appropriate to the Scythians (see Professor Rawlinson's description, 'Ancient Monarchies,' ii. 122) than to the Babylonians.   The difficulty felt by many in admitting this view is doubtless caused by the silence of Herodotus as to any mischief wrought by these nomad hordes in Judah ; of course, by keeping the coast-road, the latter might have left Judah unharmed.   But (1) we cannot be sure that they did keep entirely to the coast-road.   If Scythopolis is equi-valent to Beth-shan, and if " Scytho-" is correctly explained as " Scythian," they did not ; and (2) the pictures of devastation may have been principally called forth by the later invasion.   According to ch. xxxvi. 1—4, Jeremiah dictated all his former prophecies to Baruch, either from memory or from rough notes, as late as B.C. 606.   Is it not possible that he may have heightened the colouring of warnings suggested by the Scythian invasion to adapt them to the later and more awful crisis?   Nay, more, is not this expressly suggested by the statement (ch. xxxvi. 32) that " there were added besides unto them many like words " ?   When you once grant that prophecies were written down subsequently to their delivery, and after-wards combined with others in the form of a summary (a theory which does not admit of a doubt either in Isaiah or in Jeremiah), you therewith admit that features of different periods have in some cases most probably been combined by an unconscious anachronism.[1]

We may now return to that more pressing danger which has so deeply coloured the discourses of the prophet.   One striking feature about the rise of the Babylonian power is its rapidity ; this is vigorously expressed by a prophet contemporary with Jeremiah—

> " Behold ye among the nations, and look,
> Astonish yourselves, and be astonished ;
> For, he doeth a deed in your days,
> Which ye will not believe, when related.
> For, behold, I raise up the Chaldeans,
> The passionate and impetuous nation,
> Who goeth through the breadth of the earth,
> To possess himself of dwelling-places which are not his."

(Hab. i. 5, 6.)

In B.C. 609 Babylon had still two seemingly vigorous rivals—Assyria and Egypt ; in B.C. 604 it had the undisputed mastery of the East.   Between these two dates lie—to mention the events in Palestine first—the conquest of Syria by Egypt, and the reattachment of Judah, after the lapse of five centuries, to the empire of the Pharaohs.   Another still more surprising

---

[1] On the whole Scythian question, see further Ewald, 'History of Israel,' iv. 255, 256 ; Duncker, 'History of Antiquity,' iii. 271—274 ; Payne Smith (whose expressions seem to the present writer too hasty and dogmatic), 'Speaker's Commentary,' v. 314.

event remains—the fall of Nineveh, which, so very short a time previously, had made such a show of warlike power under the brilliant Assurbanipal (B.C. 648—626). In vol. xi. of the 'Records of the Past,' Mr. Sayce has translated some striking though fragmentary texts relative to the collapse of this mighty colossus. "When Cyaxares the Mede, with the Cimmerians, the people of Minni, or Van, and the tribe of Saparda, or Sepharad (cf. Obad. 20), on the Black Sea, was threatening Nineveh, Esarhaddon II., the Saracos of the Greek writers, had proclaimed a solemn assembly to the gods, in the hope of warding off the danger. But the bad writing of the tablets shows that they are merely the first rough text of the royal proclamation, and we may perhaps infer that the capture of Nineveh and the overthrow of the empire prevented a fair copy from being taken " (p. 79).

Thus was the prediction of Nahum, uttered in the height of Assyrian power, fulfilled; the sword devoured her young lions, her prey was cut off from the earth, and the voice of her insolent messenger (like the Rabshakeh in Isa. xxxvi.) was no more heard (Nah. ii. 13). And now began a series of calamities only to be paralleled by the still more awful catastrophe in the Roman War. The Chaldeans became the waking thought and the nightly dream of king, prophets, and people. A reference was made just now to Habakkuk, who gives vent to the bitterness of his reflections in complaint to Jehovah. Jeremiah, however, fond as he is supposed to be of lamentation, does not give way to the language of complaint; his feelings were, perhaps, too deep for words. He records, however, the unfortunate moral effect produced by the danger of the state on his fellow-countrymen. It took the form of a religious reaction. The promises of Jehovah in the Book of Deuteronomy appeared to have been falsified, and Israel's God to be incapable of protecting his worshippers. Many Jews fell away into idolatry. Even those who did not become renegades kept aloof from prophets like Jeremiah, who boldly declared that God had hidden his face for the sins of the people. Those who have read the life of Savonarola will be struck by the parallel between the preaching of the great Italian and that of Jeremiah. Without venturing to claim for Savonarola an equality with Jeremiah, he can hardly be denied a kind of reflection of Old Testament prophecy. God's Spirit is not tied to countries or to centuries; and there is nothing wonderful if mountain-moving faith were blessed in Florence as it was in Jerusalem.

The prospects held out by Jeremiah were gloomy indeed. The Captivity was to be no brief interlude in Israel's history, but a full generation; in round numbers, seventy years. Such a message was, from its very nature, doomed to an unfavourable reception. The renegades (probably not a few) were, of course, disbelievers in "the word of Jehovah," and many even of the faithful still hoped against hope that the promises of Deuteronomy, according to their faulty interpretation of them, would somehow be fulfilled.

It cost Jeremiah much to be a prophet of ill; to be always threatening "sword, famine, pestilence," and the destruction of that temple which was "the throne of Jehovah's glory" (ch. xvii. 12). But, as our own Milton says, "when God commands to take the trumpet and blow a dolorous or a jarring blast, it lies not in man's will what he shall say."[1] There are several passages which show how nearly intolerable Jeremiah's position became to him, and how terribly bitter his feelings (sometimes at least) towards his own enemies and those of his country. Take, for instance, that thrilling passage in ch. xx. 7—13, beginning (if one may correct the version)—

> "Thou didst entice me, O Jehovah! and I let myself be enticed;
> Thou didst take hold on me, and didst prevail;
> I have become a derision all the day long,
> They all mock me."

The contrast between what he hoped for as a prophet of Jehovah, and what he actually experienced, takes form in his mind as the result of an enticement on the part of Jehovah. The passage draws to its end with the solemnly jubilant words—

> "But Jehovah is with me as a fierce warrior;
> Therefore shall mine enemies stumble and not prevail,
> They shall be greatly ashamed, because they have not prospered,
> With an everlasting reproach that shall never be forgotten.
> And thou, O Jehovah of hosts, that triest the righteous,
> That seest the reins and the heart,
> Let me see thy revenge upon them,
> For unto thee have I committed my cause.
> Sing ye unto Jehovah; praise ye Jehovah:
> For he hath delivered the soul of the poor from the hand of evil-doers."

But immediately after this chant of faith, the prophet relapses into melancholy with those terrible words, which recur almost word for word in the first discourse of the afflicted Job—

> "Cursed be the day wherein I was born:
> Let not the day wherein my mother bare me be blessed," etc.[2]

And even this is not the most bitter thing which Jeremiah has said. On one occasion, when his enemies had plotted against him, he utters the following solemn imprecation:—"Give heed to me, O Jehovah, and hearken to the voice of them that contend with me. Should evil be recompensed for good? for they have digged a pit for my soul. Remember how I stood before thee to speak good for them—to turn away thy wrath from them. Therefore deliver up their children to the famine, and spill them into the hands of the sword; and let their wives become childless, and widows; and let their men be slain by the plague, their young men smitten of the sword in battle. Let a cry be heard from their houses, when thou bringest suddenly troops upon them: for they have digged a pit to take me, and hid

---

[1] 'Reason of Church Government,' bk. ii.
[2] Compare similar passages in ch. xiv., xv., xvii. 15—18.

snares for my feet.   But thou, O Jehovah, knowest all their counsel against
me to slay me: forgive not their iniquity, neither blot out their sin from
thy sight, but let them be (counted as) fallen ones before thee; deal with
them (accordingly) in the time of thine anger " (ch. xviii. 19—23).   And
now, how are we to account for this?   Shall we ascribe it to a sudden
ebullition of natural anger?   Some will reply that this is inconceivable in
one consecrated from his youth to the service of God.   Let us remember,
however, that even the perfect Exemplar of consecrated manhood gave
utterance to feelings somewhat akin to those of Jeremiah.[1]   When our
Lord found (from the point of view of his humiliation, we may say
" found ") that all his preaching and all his wonderful works were thrown
away on the scribes and Pharisees, he did not hesitate to pour out the
full vials of his wrath on those " hypocrites."   Doubtless " he felt pity as
well as anger, but he thought the anger had a better right to be expressed.
The impostors must be first unmasked; they might be forgiven afterwards, if they should abandon their conventionalties.   The lover of men is
angry to see harm done to men."[2]   Jeremiah, too, like our Lord, felt pity as
well as anger—pity for the nation misguided by its natural " shepherds,"
and was willing to extend forgiveness, in the name of his Lord, to those
who were willing to return; the addresses in ch. vii., xxii. 2—9 are
manifestly intended for those very " shepherds of the people " whom he
afterwards so solemnly curses.   Natural feeling, no doubt, there was in his
communications, but a natural feeling purified and exalted by the inspiring
Spirit.   He feels himself charged with the thunders of an angry God; he
is conscious that he is the representative of that Messiah-people of whom
a still greater prophet speaks in the name of Jehovah—

> " Thou art my servant, O Israel, in whom I will get myself glory."
>
> (Isa. xlix. 3.)

This latter point is well worthy of consideration, as it suggests the most
probable explanation of the imprecatory passages in the Psalms as well as in
the Book of Jeremiah.   Both psalmists and prophet felt themselves representatives of that " Son of God " (Hos. xi. 1), that Messiah-people, which
existed to some slight extent in reality, but in its full dimensions in the
Divine counsels.   Jeremiah, in particular, was a type of the true Israelite,
an Abdiel (a " servant of God ") among the faithless, an adumbration of
the perfect Israel and the perfect Israelite reserved by God for future ages.
Feeling himself, however indistinctly, to be such a type and such a repre-
sentative, and being at the same time " one of like affections ($\delta\mu\omega\iota\sigma\pi\alpha\theta\eta\varsigma$)
with ourselves," he could not but use language which, however justified,
bears a superficial resemblance to vindictive enmity.

---

[1] It is best to speak guardedly.   There was, doubtless, some human dross left in Jeremiah; and only the perfect " Servant of Jehovah " could appropriate the description in
Isa. xlii. 2, 3.

[2] 'Ecce Homo,' p. 270 (ch. xxi.).

3. Jeremiah's warnings became more and more definite.　He foresaw, at any rate in its main outlines, the course which events would shortly afterwards take, and refers expressly to the dishonoured burial of Jehoiakim, and the captivity of the youthful Jehoiachin.[1]　In the presence of such misfortunes he becomes tender-hearted, and gives vent to his sympathetic emotion precisely as our Lord does in similar circumstances.　How touching are the words !—

> "Weep not over one that is dead, neither lament for him ;
> Weep (rather) for one that is gone away ;
> For he will return no more,
> Nor see his native country."

　　　　　　　　　　　　　　　　　　　　　　(Ch. xxii. 10.)

And in another passage (ch. xxiv.) he speaks both kindly and hopefully of those who have been carried away into exile, while those who are left at home are described, most expressively, as "bad figs, very bad, that cannot be eaten."　"All that we hear of the later history helps us," Mr. Maurice remarks, "to understand the force and truth of this sign.　The reign of Zedekiah presents us with the most vivid picture of a king and people sinking deeper and deeper into an abyss, ever and anon making wild and frantic efforts to rise out of it, imputing their evil to every one but themselves,—their struggles for a nominal freedom always proving them to be both slaves and tyrants at heart."[2]

The evil, however, was perhaps by nothing so much intensified as by the hearing which the people, and especially the rulers, accorded to the flattering prophets who announced a too speedy termination to the clearly impending captivity.　One of these, named Hananiah, declared that in two years the yoke of the King of Babylon should be broken, and the Jewish exiles be restored, together with the vessels of the sanctuary (ch. xxviii.).　"Not in two but in seventy years," was virtually Jeremiah's reply.　If the Jews who remained did not submit quietly, they would be utterly destroyed.　If, on the other hand, they were obedient, and "brought their necks under the yoke of the King of Babylon," they would be left undisturbed in their own land.

This seems to be the place to answer a question which has more than once been asked —Was Jeremiah a true patriot in so continually expressing his conviction of the futility of resistance to Babylon ?　It must be remembered, first of all, that the religious idea with which Jeremiah was inspired is higher and broader than the idea of patriotism.　Israel had a divinely appropriated work ; if it fell below its mission, what further right had it of existence ?　Perhaps it may be allowable to admit that such conduct as Jeremiah's would not in our day be regarded as patriotic.　If the Govern-

---

[1] There is nothing inconceivable in this, even if we should grant that the prophecy, ch. xxi. 1—xxiii. 40, was modified in expression—in a word, edited—in the reign of Zedekiah, the uncle and successor of Jehoiachin.

[2] Maurice, 'Prophets and Kings,' p. 420.

ment had fully committed itself to a definite and irrevocable policy, it is probable that all parties would agree to enforce at any rate silent acquiescence. One eminent man may, however, be appealed to in favour of Jeremiah's patriotism. Niebuhr, quoted by Sir Edward Strachey, writes thus at the period of Germany's deepest humiliation under Napoleon: "I told you, as I told every one, how indignant I felt at the senseless prating of those who talked of desperate resolves as of a tragedy. . . . To bear our fate with dignity and wisdom, that the yoke might be lightened, was my doctrine, and I supported it with the advice of the prophet Jeremiah, who spoke and acted very wisely, living as he did under King Zedekiah, in the times of Nebuchadnezzar, though he would have given different counsel had he lived under Judas Maccabæus, in the times of Antiochus Epiphanes."[1]

This time, too, Jeremiah's warning voice was in vain. Zedekiah was mad enough to court an alliance with Pharaoh-Hophra (the Egyptians called him Uah-ab-ra, the Greeks Apries), who, by a naval victory, had "revived the prestige of the Egyptian arms which had received so severe a shock under Necho II."[2] The Babylonians would not pardon this insubordination, and a second siege of Jerusalem was the consequence. Undaunted by the hostility of the popular magnates ("princes"), Jeremiah urgently counsels immediate surrender. (At this point, it is expedient to be brief; Jeremiah himself is his best biographer. There is, perhaps, nothing in all literature which rivals the narrative chapters in his book for dispassionate truthfulness.) He is rewarded by close imprisonment, but his policy is justified by the event. Famine raged among the besieged inhabitants (ch. lii. 6 ; Lam. i. 19, 20, etc.), till at length a breach was effected in the walls ; a vain attempt at flight was made by the king, who was captured, and with most of his people carried to Babylon, B.C. 588. Thus fell Jerusalem, nineteen years after the battle of Carchemish, and, with Jerusalem, the last bold opponent of Babylonian power in Syria. A few poor inhabitants, indeed, were left, but only to prevent the land from becoming utterly desolate (2 Kings xxv. 12). Their only consolation was that they were allowed a native governor, Gedaliah, who was also a hereditary friend of Jeremiah. But it was a short-lived consolation ! Gedaliah fell by an assassin's hand, and the principal Jews, fearing the vengeance of their new lords, took refuge in Egypt, dragging the prophet with them (ch. xlii. 7—22 ; xliii. 7 ; xliv. 1). But Jeremiah had not come to the end of his message of woe. Did the Jews, he asked, expect to be secure from the Babylonians in Egpyt? Soon would their foes be after them ; Egypt would be chastised, and the Jews would suffer for their treason. And now the unhappy consequences of the misreading of the Deuteronomic Scripture became fully visible. It was from their infidelity, not to Jehovah, but to the queen of heaven, that their calamities proceeded, said the Jewish exiles in Egypt

[1] Strachey, 'Jewish History and Politics in the Times of Sargon and Sennacherib,' p. 222, note.
[2] Dr. Birch, 'Egypt,' p. 180.

(ch. xliv. 17—19). What answer could Jeremiah make? His mission to that generation was closed. He could only console himself with that heroic faith which was one of his most striking qualities. During the siege of Jerusalem he had, with a Roman belief in his country's destinies, purchased a piece of ground at no great distance from the capital (ch. xxxii. 6—15); and it was after the fate of the city was sealed that he rose to the highest pitch of religious enthusiasm, when he uttered that memorable promise of a new and spiritual covenant in which the external helps of prophecy and a written Law should be dispensed with (ch. xxxi. 31—34). And in this heaven-born assurance of the immortality and spiritual regeneration of his people he persisted to the end.

4. It was impossible to avoid giving a brief abstract of Jeremiah's prophetic career, because his book is to such a large extent autobiographical. He cannot limit himself to reproducing " the word of the Lord ; " his individual nature is too strong for him, and asserts its right of expression. His life was a constant alternation between the action of the " burning fire " of revelation (ch. xx. 9), and the reaction of human sensibilities. Truly has it been observed that " Jeremiah has a kind of feminine tenderness and susceptibility; strength was to be educed out of a spirit which was inclined to be timid and shrinking; " and again that " he was a loving, *priestly* spirit, who felt the unbelief and sin of his nation as a heavy, overwhelming burden." Who does not remember those touching words ?—

" Is there no balm in Gilead ? is there no physician there ?
Why then hath not healing appeared for the daughter of my people ?
Oh that my head were water, and mine eye a fountain of tears,
That I might weep day and night for the slain of the daughter of my people !"

(Ch. viii. 22 ; ix. 1.)

And again—

" Let mine eyes run down with tears day and night,[1]
And let them not cease :
For the virgin daughter of my people is broken with a great breach,
With a very grievous blow."

(Ch. xiv. 17.)

In this respect Jeremiah marks an epoch in the history of prophecy. Isaiah and the prophets of his generation are fully absorbed in their message, and allow no space to the exhibition of personal feeling. In Jeremiah, on the other hand, the element of human feeling is constantly overpowering the prophetic. But let not Jeremiah be disparaged, and let not those triumph over him who are gifted with greater power of self-repression. Self-repression does not always imply the absence of selfishness, whereas Jeremiah's demonstrativeness is not called forth by purely personal troubles, but by those of God's people. The words of Jesus, " Ye would

---

[1] This has been well brought out in Keble's verses on Jeremiah ('Lyra Apostolica').

not," and "But now they are hid from thine eyes," might, as Delitzsch remarks, be placed as mottoes to the Book of Jeremiah.

Jeremiah's rich individual consciousness extends its influence over his conception of religion, which, without being less practical, has become more inward and spiritual than Isaiah's. The main object of his preaching is to communicate this deeper conception (expressed, above all, in his doctrine of the covenant, see on ch. xxxi. 31—34) to his countrymen. And if they will not receive it in the peace and comfort of their Judæan home, then —welcome ruin, welcome captivity! By uttering this solemn truth (ch. xxxi.)—that a period of enforced seclusion was necessary before Israel could rise to the height of his grand mission—Jeremiah preserved the spiritual independence of his people, and prepared the way for a still higher and more spiritual and evangelical religion. The next generation instinctively recognized this. Not a few of those psalms which belong most probably to the Captivity (especially Ps. xxii., xxxi., xl., lv., lxix., lxxi.) are so pervaded with the spirit of Jeremiah that several writers have ascribed them to the pen of this prophet. The question is a complicated one, and the solution can hardly be so simple as these writers appear to suppose. We have to deal with the fact that there is a large body of Biblical literature impregnated with the spirit, and consequently filled with many of the expressions, of Jeremiah. The Books of Kings, the Book of Job, the second part of Isaiah, the Lamentations,[1] are, with the psalms mentioned above, the chief items of this literature; and while, on the one hand, no one would dream of assigning all these to Jeremiah, there seems, on the other, to be no sufficient reason for giving one of them to the great prophet rather than the other. With regard to the circumstantial parallels in the above-named psalms to passages in the life of Jeremiah, it may be observed (1) that other pious Israelites had a similar lot of persecution to Jeremiah (cf. Micah vii. 2; Isa. lvii. 1); (2) that figurative expressions like "sinking in the mire and in the deep water" (Ps. lxix. 2, 14) require no groundwork of literal biographical fact (not to remind realistic critics that there was no water in Jeremiah's prison, ch. xxxviii. 6); and (3) that none of the psalms ascribed to Jeremiah allude to his prophetic office, or to the conflict with the "false prophets," which must have occupied so much of his thoughts.

Still, the fact that some diligent students of the Scriptures have ascribed this group of psalms to Jeremiah is an index of the close affinities existing on either side. So, too, the Book of Job may be more than plausibly referred to as influenced by Jeremiah. The tendency of careful criticism is to hold that the author of Job selects a passionate utterance of Jeremiah's for the theme of his afflicted hero's first discourse (Job iii. 3; comp. ch. xx. 14); and it is difficult to evade the impression that a feature in the deepest prophecy of the second part of Isaiah is suggested by Jeremiah's pathetic comparison of himself to a lamb led to the slaughter (Isa. lii. 7; comp. ch. xi. 19). Later

---

[1] On the question whether Jeremiah really wrote the Lamentations, Old Testament scholars are divided.

on, an intensified interest in the details of the future contributed to heighten the estimation of Jeremiah's works (Dan. ix. 2; comp. 2 Chron. xxvi. 21); and several traces of the extraordinary respect in which this prophet was held appear in the Apocrypha (2 Macc. ii. 1—7; xv. 14; Epist. Jer.) and in the Gospel narrative (Matt. xvi. 14; John i. 21).

Another point in which Jeremiah marks an epoch in prophecy is his peculiar fondness for symbolic acts (e.g. ch. xiii. 1; xvi. 1; xviii. 1; xix. 1; xxiv. 1; xxv. 15; xxxv. 1). This is a subject fraught with difficulty, and the question may reasonably be asked whether his accounts of such transactions are to be taken literally, or whether they are simply visions translated into ordinary narrative, or even altogether imaginary—recognized rhetorical fictions. We must remember that the flourishing age of prophecy is over, the age when the public work of a prophet was still the chief part of his ministry, and the age of decline is come, in which the quiet work of laying up a store of testimony for the next generation has acquired greater importance. The chapter with Jeremiah's going to the Euphrates and hiding a girdle "in a hole of the rock" till it became good for nothing, and then taking another journey thither to fetch it again, is no doubt rendered more intelligible by reading "Ephrath" instead of *P'rāth*, i.e. "the Euphrates" (ch. xiii. 4—7); but the difficulty is, perhaps, not entirely removed. May not this narrative (and that in ch. xxxv.) be regarded as fictitious with fully as much ground as the equally positive statement in ch. xxv. 17, "Then took I the cup at Jehovah's hand, and made all the nations to drink"?

There is yet another important feature for the student to notice in Jeremiah—the diminishing emphasis on the advent of the Messiah, i.e. of the great ideal victorious King, through whom the whole world was to be brought into subjection to Jehovah. Though still found—at the end of a passage on the bad kings Jehoiakim and Jehoiachin (ch. xxiii. 5), and in the promises given shortly before the fall of Jerusalem (ch. xxx. 9, 21; xxxiii. 15)—the personal Messiah is no longer the centre of prophecy as in Isaiah and Micah. In Zephaniah he is not mentioned at all. It seems as if, in the decline of the state, royalty had ceased to be an adequate symbol for the great Personage to whom all prophecy points. Every one remembers that, in the last twenty-seven chapters of Isaiah, the great Deliverer is spoken of, not as a King, but as a persuasive Teacher, reviled by his own countrymen, and exposed to suffering and death, but in and through his sufferings atoning for and justifying all those who believed in him. Jeremiah does not allude to this great Servant of Jehovah in words, but his revelation of a new and spiritual covenant requires the prophecy of the Servant for its explanation. How is the Law of the Lord to be written in the hearts of a rebellious and depraved humanity? How, except by the atoning death of the humble, but after his death royally exalted, Saviour? Jeremiah prepared the way for the coming of Christ, partly by his putting out of sight the too dazzling regal conception which prevented men from realizing the deeper evangelical truths summed up in the prophecy of the "Servant of the Lord." It ought to be added (and this is another respect in which Jeremiah is a remarkable waymark in the Old Testament dispensation) that he prepared the way of Christ by his own typical life. He stood alone, with few friends and no family joys to console him (ch. xvi. 2). His country was hastening to its ruin, at a crisis which strikingly reminds us of the times of the Saviour. He lifted up a warning voice, but the natural guides of the people drowned it by their blind opposition. In his utter self-abnegation, too, he reminds us of the Lord, in whose human nature a strong feminine element cannot be mistaken. Doubtless he had a less balanced mind; how should this not be the case, for we are speaking of him in relation to the unique, incomparable One? But there are moments in the life of Jesus when the lyrical note is as clearly marked as in the utterances of Jeremiah. The prophet weeping over Zion (ch. ix. 1; xiii. 17; xiv. 17) is an adumbration of the sacred tears in Luke xix. 41; and the suggestions of the life of Jeremiah in the great prophetic life of Christ (Isa. liii.) are so distinct as to have induced Saadyab the Jew (tenth century A.D.) and Bunsen the Christian to suppose that the original reference was simply and solely to the prophet.[1] It is strange that the most esteemed Christian writers should have dwelt so little on this typical character of Jeremiah; but it is one proof of the richness of the Old Testament that so striking a type should have been reserved for later and less conventional students.

5. The literary merits of Jeremiah have been frequently contested. He is accused of Aramaizing diction, of diffuseness, monotony, imitativeness,[2] proneness to repetition,[3] and to the use of stereotyped formulæ;[4] nor can these charges be denied. Jeremiah was not an artist in words, as to some extent was Isaiah. His poetic flights were restrained by his presentiments; his utterance was choked by tears. How could he exercise his imagination on depicting woes which he already so fully realized? or vary a theme of such unchanging importance? Even from a literary point of view, however, his unpretending simplicity is not to be despised; as Ewald has already remarked, it forms a pleasing contrast (be it said with all reverence to the Spirit common to all the prophets) to the artificial style of Habakkuk. But

---

[1] Grotius, with a true instinct, remarks, "Hæ notæ in Jeremiam quidem congruunt priùs, sed potius sublimiusque, sæpe et magis κατὰ λέξιν, in Christum."

[2] See the Commentary, *passim*.

[3] Kuenen ('Historisch-kritisch Onderzoek,' vol. ii. 248) gives a long list of almost identical passages, from which I take the commencement: ch. i. 18, 19 (xv. 20); ii. 15 (iv. 7); ii. 28 (xi. 13); iv. 5 (viii. 14); iv. 6 (vi. 1); v. 9 (29; ix. 8); vi. 13—15 (viii. 10—12); vi. 22—24 (l. 41—43); vii. 16 (xi. 14; xiv. 11); vii. 31—33 (xix. 5—7; xxxii. 35); vii. 33 (xix. 7; xvi. 4; xxxiv. 20).

[4] Such are—"sword, famine, and pestilence," or "sword and famine" (ch. xiv. 12—16; xv. 2; xvi. 4; xxi. 7, 9; xxiv. 16; xxvii. 8, 13; and twelve other passages); "the voice of mirth and the voice of gladness" (ch. vii. 34; xvi. 9; xxv. 10); "terror on every side" (ch. vi. 25; xx. 3, 10; xlvi. 5; xlix. 29); "feed with wormwood, and give water of gall to drink" (ch. viii. 14; ix. 15; xxiii. 15).

above and apart from his literary merits or demerits, Jeremiah deserves the highest honour for his almost unparalleled conscientiousness. Under the most trying circumstances, he never swerved from his fidelity to the truth, nor gave way to the " grief that saps the mind." In a quieter age he might (for his talent is chiefly lyrical) have developed into a great lyric poet. Even as it is, he may fairly claim to have written some of the most sympathetic pages of the Old Testament; and yet—his greatest poem is his life.

§ 2. Growth of the Book of Jeremiah.

The question naturally suggests itself—Do we possess the prophecies of Jeremiah in the form in which they were delivered by him from the thirteenth year of the reign of Josiah onwards? In reply, let us first of all look to the analogy of the occasional prophecies of Isaiah. These, it can be reasonably well proved, have not come down to us in the form in which they were delivered, but have grown together out of several smaller books or prophetic collections. Analogy is in favour of a somewhat similar origin of the Book of Jeremiah, which was, at any rate once, much smaller. The collection which formed the nucleus of the present book may be conjectured to have been as follows:—Ch. i. 1, 2; i. 4—ix. 22; x. 17—xii. 6; xxv.; xlvi. 1—xlix. 33; xxvi.; xxxvi.; xlv. These were, perhaps, the contents of the roll referred to in ch. xxxvi.—if at least, with the great majority of commentators, we give a strict interpretation to ver. 2 of that chapter, in which the command is given to write in the roll " all the words that I have spoken unto thee . . . from the days of Josiah, even unto this day." On this view of the case, it was not till twenty-three years after Jeremiah's entrance upon his ministry that he caused his prophecies to be committed to writing by Baruch. This obviously excludes the possibility of an exact reproduction of the early discourses, even if the main outlines were, by God's blessing upon a tenacious memory, faithfully reported. But even if we adopt the alternative view mentioned in the introduction to ch. xxxvi., the analogy of other prophetic collections (especially of those embodied in the first part of Isaiah) forbids us to assume that we have Jeremiah's original utterances, unmodified by later thoughts and experiences.

That the Book of Jeremiah has been gradually enlarged can, indeed, be shown (1) by a simple inspection of the heading of the book, which, as we shall see, originally ran thus : " The word of Jehovah which came to Jeremiah in the days of Josiah, etc., in the thirteenth year of his reign." It is clear that this was not intended to refer to more than ch. i., or, more precisely, to ch. i. 4—ii. 37, which appears to represent the earliest discourse of our prophet. Two further chronological specifications, one relative to Jehoiakim, the other to Zedekiah, appear to have been successively added, and even the later of these will not cover ch. xl.—xliv. (2) The same result follows from the remark at the close of ch. li., " Thus far are the words of Jeremiah." This evidently proceeds from an editor, in whose time the book terminated at li. 64. Ch. lii. is, in fact, not an independent narrative, but the conclu-

sion of a history of the kings of Judah—the same historical work which was
followed by the editor of our " Books of the Kings," except that vers. 28—30
(a notice of the number of the Jewish captives) appears from the chronology
to be from another source ; it is wanting, moreover, in the Septuagint Version.

Granting (1) that the Book of Jeremiah was edited and brought into its
present form subsequently to the time of the prophet himself, and (2) that
an important addition in the narrative style has been made to it by one of
its editors, it is not à priori inconceivable that it should also contain passages
in the prophetic style not by Jeremiah himself. The passages respecting
which the greatest doubt exists are ch. x. 1—16 and ch. l., li. (the longest
and one of the least original of all the prophecies). It is unnecessary
to enter upon the question of their origin here; it is enough to refer the
reader to the special introductions in the course of this work. The case,
however, is sufficiently strong for the negative critics to make it desirable
to caution the reader not to suppose that a negative position is necessarily
inconsistent with the doctrine of inspiration. In words which the author
asks permission to quote from a recent work of his own, " The editors of
the Scriptures were inspired ; there is no maintaining the authority of the
Bible without this postulate. True, we must allow a distinction in degrees
of inspiration, as the Jewish doctors themselves saw, though it was some
time before they clearly formulated their view. I am glad to notice that
one so free from the suspicion of rationalism or Romanism as Rudolf Stier
adopts the Jewish distinction, remarking that even the lowest grade of
inspiration (b'rūakh hakkōdesh) remains one of faith's mysteries " (' The
Prophecies of Isaiah,' ii. 205).

§ 3. Relation of the Received Hebrew Text to that represented by the Septuagint.

The differences between the two recensions relate (1) to the arrangement
of the prophecies, (2) to the reading of the text.

1. Variation in arrangement is only found in one instance, but that a
very remarkable one. In the Hebrew, the prophecies concerning foreign
nations occupy ch. xlvi.—li. ; in the Septuagint they are inserted immediately after ch. xxv. 13. The following table will show the differences :—

Hebrew text.				Text of Septuagint.
Ch. xlix. 34—39	...	...	...	ch. xxv. 14—18.
Ch. xlvi. 2—12	...	...	...	ch. xxvi. 1—11.
Ch. xlvi. 13—28	...	...	...	ch. xxvi. 12—26.
Ch. xlvi. 40—51	...	...	...	ch. xxvi. 27, 28.
Ch. xlvii. 1—7	...	...	...	ch. xxix. 1—7.
Ch. xlix. 7—22	...	...	...	ch. xxix. 7—22.
Ch. xlix. 1—6	...	...	...	ch. xxx. 1—5.
Ch. xlix. 28—33	...	...	...	ch. xxx. 6—11.
Ch. xlix. 23—27	...	...	...	ch. xxx. 12—16.
Ch. xlviii.	...	...	...	ch. xxxi.
Ch. xxv. 15—38	...	...	...	ch. xxxii.

Thus not only is this group of prophecies differently placed as a whole, but the members of the group are differently arranged. In particular, Elam, which comes last but one (or even last, if the prophecy on Babylon be excluded from the group) in the Hebrew, opens the series of prophecies in the Septuagint.

Which of these arrangements has the stronger claims on our acceptance? No one, after reading ch. xxv., would expect to find the prophecies on foreign nations separated from it by so long an interval as in the received Hebrew text; and thus (the latter being notoriously of comparatively recent origin, and far from infallible) it would seem at first sight reasonable to follow the Septuagint. But there must be some error in the arrangement adopted by the latter. It is incredible that the passage, ch. xxv. 15—26 (in our Bibles), is rightly placed, as in the Septuagint, at the very end of the foreign prophecies (as part of ch. xxxii.); it seems, indeed, absolutely required as the introduction of the group. The error of the Septuagint appears to have arisen out of a previous error on the part of a transcriber. When this version was made, a gloss (viz. ch. xxv. 13) destructive of the connection had already made its way into the text, and the Greek translator seems to have been led by it to the striking dislocation which we now find in his version. On this subject the reader may be referred to an important essay by Professor Budde, of Bonn, in the 'Jahrbücher für deutsche Theologie,' 1879 (see p. 533). That the whole of the verse (ch. xxv. 13) is a gloss had already been recognized by the old Dutch commentator Venema (1765), who will hardly be accused of rationalistic tendencies.

2. Variations of reading were of common occurrence in the Hebrew text employed by the Septuagint. It may be admitted (for it is self-evident) that the Greek translator was but ill prepared for his work. He not only often attaches wrong vowels to the consonants, but is sometimes so completely at a loss for the meaning that he introduces Hebrew words untranslated into the Greek text. It would also appear that the Hebrew manuscript which he employed was badly written, and disfigured by frequent confusions of similar letters. It may further be granted that the Greek translator is sometimes guilty of deliberately tampering with the text of his manuscript (striking instances of this may be found in ch. xxv. 25 and xliii. 13, and less conspicuous ones in ch. ii. 18, 25, 30; iv. 6; viii. 6; xviii. 2, 22; xxii. 14, 30; xxx. 5); that he sometimes abridges where Jeremiah (as often) repeats himself; and that either he or his transcribers have made various unauthorized additions to the original text (as, for instance, ch. i. 17; ii. 28; iii. 19; v. 2; xi. 16; xiii. 20; xxii. 18; xxvii. 3; xxx. 6). But a candid examination reveals the fact that both the consonants and the vocalization of them employed in the Septuagint are sometimes better than those of the received Hebrew text. Instances of this will be found in ch. iv. 28; xi. 15; xvi. 7; xxiii. 33; xli. 9; xlvi. 17. True, there are interpolations in the text of the Septuagint; but such are by no means wanting in the received Hebrew text. The Septuagint is sometimes nearer to the original simplicity than the

Hebrew (see, for instance, ch. x.; xxvii. 7, 8 *b*, 16, 17, 19—22; xxviii. 1, 14, 16; xxix. 1, 2, 16—20, 32).[1]   And if the Greek translator takes offence at some of the repetitions of his original, so in all probability have the transcribers who have, without any evil intention, modified the received Hebrew text.   On the whole, it is a favourable circumstance that we have, virtually, two recensions of the text of Jeremiah.   If no prophet was more unpopular during his life, none was more popular after his death.   A book which is known " by heart " is much less likely to be transcribed correctly, and much more exposed to glosses and interpolations, than one in whom no such special interest is felt.

§ 4. Exegetical and Critical Literature.

The Latin Commentary of St. Jerome only extends to the thirty-second chapter of Jeremiah.   Aben Ezra, the most talented of the rabbis, did not write on our prophet; but the works of Rashi and David Kimchi are easily accessible.   Modern philological exegesis begins with the Reformation.   The following commentaries may be mentioned:— Calvin, ' Prælectiones in Jeremiam,' Geneva, 1563 ; Venema, ' Commentarius ad Librum Prophetiarum Jeremiæ,' Leuwarden, 1765; Blayney, 'Jeremiah and Lamentations, a New Translation with Notes,' etc., Oxford, 1784 ; Dahler, ' Jérémie traduit sur le Texte Original, accompagné de Notes,' Strasbourg, 1825 ; Ewald, ' The Prophets of the Old Testament,' English translation, vol. iii., London, 1878 ; Hitzig, ' Der Prophet Jeremia,' 2nd edit., Leipzig, 1866 ; Graf, ' Der Prophet Jeremia erklärt,' Leipzig, 1862 ; Naegelsbach, ' Jeremiah,' in Lange's Commentary, part xv. ; Payne Smith, ' Jeremiah,' in the ' Speaker's Commentary,' vol. v. ; König, ' Das Deuteronomium und der Prophet Jeremia,' Berlin, 1839 ; Wichelhaus, ' De Jeremiæ Versione Alexandrinâ,' Halle, 1847 ; Movers, ' De utriusque Recensionis Vaticiniorum Jeremiæ Indole et Origine,' Hamburg, 1837 ; Hengstenberg, ' The Christology of the Old Testament ' (Clark's edit.).

§ 5. Chronology.

Any chronological arrangement of the reigns of the Jewish kings must be largely conjectural and open to criticism, and it is not perfectly clear that the writers of the narrative books in the Old Testament, or those who edited their works, intended to give a critically accurate chronology adequate for historical purposes.   The most tedious problems relate to the times previous to Jeremiah.   One difficulty, however, may be pointed out in the chronology of the concluding reigns (see Robertson Smith, ' The Prophets of Israel,' p. 415).   According to 2 Kings xxiii. 36, Jehoiakim reigned eleven years.   This agrees with ch. xxv. 1, which makes the fourth year of Jehoiakim synchronize with the first of Nebuchadnezzar (comp. ch. xxxii. 1).   But, according to ch. xlvi. 2, the battle of Carchemish took place in the fourth year of Jehoiakim, which was the last year of Nabopolassar, the father of Nebuchadnezzar.   This would make the first year of Nebuchadnezzar synchronize with the fifth year of Jehoiakim, and we

---

[1] Nearly all the references in this paragraph are from vol. ii. of Kuenen's ' Historisch-kritisch Onderzoek:' Leyden, 1861–65,—a book unsurpassed among introductions to the Old Testament for completeness, accuracy, and sobriety of judgment, and written on an entirely different plan from the author's equally able but (in the judgment of orthodox theologians) biassed work on ' The Religion of Israel.'

should have to conclude that the latter king reigned not eleven but twelve years.

The following table, which is at any rate based on a critical use of the sometimes discordant data, is taken from Professor H. Brandes' ' The Royal Successions of Judah and Israel according to the Biblical Narratives and the Cuneiform Inscriptions' :—

B.C. 641 (spring)	First year of Josiah.
B.C. 611 (spring)	Thirty-first year of Josiah.
B.C. 610 (autumn)	Jehoahaz.
B.C. 609 (spring)	First year of Jehoiakim.
B.C. 599 (spring	Eleventh year of Jehoiakim.
B.C. 598-7 (winter)	Jehoiachin. Beginning of the Captivity.
B.C. 597 (summer)	Zedekiah appointed king.
B.C. 596 (spring)	First year of Zedekiah.
B.C. 586 (spring)	Eleventh year of Zedekiah. Fall of the kingdom of Judah.

THE

BOOK OF THE PROPHET JEREMIAH

——◆◆——

EXPOSITION.

CHAPTER I.

AN ACCOUNT OF THE CALL AND CONSECRA-
TION OF JEREMIAH TO THE PROPHETIC
OFFICE, FOLLOWED BY TWO EXPRESSIVE
SYMBOLS OF THE MATTERS WHICH HE HAS
T ANNOUNCE.

Vers. 1—3.—There are some indications
that the original form of the heading has
been somewhat modified. Notice (1) that
the words with which ver. 2 opens are identical with one of Jeremiah's characteristic
formulæ for introducing a prophecy (comp.
ch. xiv. 1; xlvi. 1; xlvii. 1; xlix. 34); and
notice (2) the awkward connection of vers.
1 and 2, and 2 and 3 respectively. (The Septuagint has endeavoured to efface this awkwardness in part, and is so far unfaithful to
the original record, but probably preserves
an earlier form of the opening words, τὸ
ῥῆμα τοῦ Θεοῦ). It is a reasonable conjecture that the passage originally ran thus:
"The word of the LORD which came to Jeremiah in the days of Josiah," etc.; vers. 1
and 3 being added later, which involved
a change in the construction.

Ver. 1.—**The words of Jeremiah.** This
introductory formula only occurs here and
in Amos i. 1. The editor of Jeremiah and of
Amos deserts the usual phrase ("burden" or
"utterance," "vision," "the word of the LORD
which came," etc.) in order to give fuller
information concerning the origin of the
prophetic writers (but see on ver. 2). On the
name Jeremiah, and on the position occupied by Hilkiah, see Introduction. **That were**
in Anathoth. So Vulgate; Septuagint, however (followed by Payne Smith), makes the
relative refer to Jeremiah (ὃς κατῴκει). But
in this case would not the phrase have been
"Jeremiah the priest," etc. (comp. Ezek.
i. 1)? Anathoth was one of the priestly
cities (Josh. xxi. 18); it lay on or near the
great northern road (Isa. x. 30), and has
been identified by Dr. Robinson (so also by
Lieutenant Conder) with 'Anâta, situated
on a ridge, an hour and a quarter north-
north-east from Jerusalem.

Ver. 3.—**Unto the end of the eleventh
year,** etc. The limit is accurate with regard
to ch. i.–xxxix. The later prophecies have
a superscription of their own (see ch. xl. 1).
In the fifth month (comp. ch. lii. 12, 27).

Vers. 4—19.— *The call of Jeremiah.*

Ver. 4.—**Unto me.** For the change of
person, comp. Ezek. i. 4.

Ver. 5.—**Knew thee;** *i.e.* took notice of
thee; virtually equivalent to selected thee
(comp. Gen. xxxix. 6; Amos iii. 2; Isa.
lviii. 3; Ps. cxliv. 3). Observe, the predestination of individuals is a familiar idea
in the Old Testament (comp. Isa. xlv. 4;
xlix. 1; Ps. cxxxix. 16). It was also
familiar to the Assyrians: King Assurbanipal declares at the opening of his 'Annals'
that the gods "in the body of his mother
have made (him) to rule Assyria." Familiar,
too, to the great family of religious reformers.
For, as Dean Milman has truly observed,
"No Pelagian ever has or ever will work a
religious revolution. He who is destined
for such a work must have a full conviction
that God is acting directly, immediately,
consciously, and therefore with irresistible
power, upon him and through him. . . . He
who is not predestined, who does not declare, who does not believe himself predes-

tined as the author of a great religious movement, he in whom God is not manifestly, sensibly, avowedly working out his pre-established designs, will never be saint or reformer" ('Latin Christianity,' i. 111, 112). **Sanctified thee**; *i.e.* set thee apart for holy uses. **Ordained**; rather, *appointed*. **Unto the nations.** Jeremiah's prophecies, in fact, have reference not only to Israel, but to the peoples in relation to Israel (ver. 10; ch. xxv. 15, 16; xlvi.—xlix.; l. and li.?).

Ver. 6.—**Ah, Lord God!** rather, *Alas, O Lord Jehovah!* It is a cry of alarm and pain, and recurs in ch. iv. 10; xiv. 13; xxxii. 17. **I am a child.** I am too young to support such an office. The word rendered "child" is used elsewhere of youths nearly grown up (comp. Gen. xxxiv. 19; xli. 12; 1 Kings iii. 7).

Ver. 7.—**Thou shalt go**, etc. Thoughts of self are altogether out of place in one who has received a Divine commission. Jeremiah's duty is simple obedience. In pursuing this path he cannot but be safe (ver. 8).

Ver. 9.—**Touched my mouth**; literally, *caused (his hand) to touch my mouth.* Jeremiah had said that he was unskilled in oratory; the Divine answer is that the words which he has to speak are not his own, but those of Jehovah. Two things are obvious : 1. The touching of the lips is not purely metaphorical, as in Ps. li. 15 (comp. Ps. xl. 6); it represents a real experience. 2. This experience, however, can only have been a visionary one, analogous to that vouchsafed to Isaiah at the opening of his prophetic ministry. In the grand account given by Isaiah of his inaugural vision (which has evidently influenced the form of the vision of Jeremiah), we read of the same significant act on the part of one of the seraphim. It is the same act, certainly, but it symbolizes, not as here the communication of a prophetic message (comp. Matt. x. 19), but the purification of the lips. Does it not seem as if Isaiah had attained a deeper insight into the spiritual regeneration needed by the prophet than had been granted to Jeremiah? Another point in which Jeremiah's account seems inferior to that of Isaiah is plastic power. Notice how Jeremiah dwells upon the meaning of the words; this is a reflective element which diminishes the poetic power of the narrative. A word may be added to explain that "visionary" is not here used in opposition to "based on fact." That the two epithets are susceptible of combination is well shown in the vision described by Père Gratry, in his 'Souvenirs de ma Jeunesse' (pp. 102—105), the reality of which is not in the least impaired in the writer's mind by its thoroughly inward character: "Dans toutes ces scènes intérieures, je n'imaginais rien . . . c'étaient de saisissantes et très-énergiques réalités auxquelles je ne m'attendais nullement."

Ver. 10.—**I have set thee**; literally, *I have made thee an overseer, or vicegerent* (comp. Gen. xli. 34; Judg. ix. 28, where the Authorized Version renders the cognate noun "officer"). **To root out . . . to plant**, viz. by pronouncing that Divine judgment which fulfils itself (comp. ch. v. 14; Numb. xxiii. 25; Isa. ix. 8, 9; lv. 11). As there is so much more threatening than promise in Jeremiah's writings, the destructive side of his activity is expressed by four verbs, the constructive only by two.

Vers. 11—16.—Two trials or probations of Jeremiah's inner sight (2 Kings vi. 17). Two visions are granted him, which he is required to describe. The first expresses the certainty of his prophetic revelation; the second indicates its contents.

Ver. 11.—**A rod of an almond tree.** The name here adopted for the almond tree is peculiarly suitable in this connection. It means "wakeful;" the almond, blossoming in January, is the first to "wake" from the sleep of winter.

Ver. 12.—**I will hasten my word**; literally, *I am wakeful over my word*; alluding to the meaning of the Hebrew word for almond.

Ver. 13.—**A seething pot.** There is a variety of Hebrew words for "pot." The word here used suggests a vessel of large size, since pottage for a whole company of prophets could be cooked in such a pot or caldron (2 Kings iv. 38). From Ezek. xxiv. 11 we may infer that it was of metal. A "seething pot" in ancient Arabic poetry is a figure for war. The same symbol occurs in Ezek. xxiv. 3—12, but with a different application. **The face thereof** is **toward the north**; rather, *toward the south*; literally, *from the face of the north.* The "face" of the pot is the side turned to the prophet. We may suppose the contents to be on the point of boiling over.

Ver. 14.—**Out of the north.** Previously to the battle of Carchemish, the Babylonians are only mentioned vaguely as a northern people (see ch. iv. 6; vi. 1, 22; x. 22). Strictly speaking, they were an eastern people from the point of view of Palestine; but the caravan-road which the Chaldæan armies had to take entered Palestine at Dan (comp. ch. iv. 15; viii. 16), and then proceeded southward. (On the question whether a Scythian invasion is referred to, at least conjointly with the Babylonian, see Introduction.) **An evil**; rather, *the evil*; viz. the calamity which in deepening gloom forms the burden of the prophet's discourses. **Shall break forth**; literally, *shall open ;* i.e. let loose by opening (comp. the use of the same verb in Isa. xiv. 17, literally, "looseth not his prisoners homewards;" and Amos viii. 5, literally, "that we may open," *i.e.* "bring forth wheat"). There is, however, some difficulty in explaining the choice of this expression. We might indeed suppose that the caldron had a lid, and that the removal or falling off of this lid is the "opening" referred to by the phrase.

Ver. 15.—**I will call**; literally, *I am calling ;* i.e. I am about to call. **The kingdoms of the north**; alluding possibly to the varied origin of the population of Assyria and Babylonia. But more probably it is simply a suggestive phrase for the wide extent of the hostile empire referred to (comp. ch. xxv. 9). **They shall set every one his throne**, etc. The kings or the generals, representing "all the families," etc., shall set up the high seat of power and judicial authority at the broad space within the gate of the city, which constituted the Oriental forum (comp. Gen. xxiii. 10; Josh. xx. 4; Job xxix. 7; xxxi. 21). Thither the besieged would have to come to surrender themselves (2 Kings xxiv. 12) and to hear their fate. A similar prediction is made with regard to Nebuchadnezzar (ch. xliii. 9, 10). It is true the seat of authority is there said to be placed at the entrance of the palace, but this was in fact another place where justice was wont to be administered (ch. xxii. 2, 3). Jerome's view, adopted by Rosenmüller and Nagelsbach, that "to set one's seat" means "to besiege" is against usage, and does not accord with the opening words of ver. 16. There is, however, an element of truth in it. The judgment executed ministerially by the northern kings or generals began with the siege of Jerusalem and the other cities, and hence the words with which the prophet contiiues. **And against all the walls**, etc. We should have expected something like "and shall set themselves in array against," etc. (comp. Isa. xxii. 7 *b*); see, however, last note.

Ver. 16.—**I will utter my judgments**; or, *I will hold a court of justice upon them ;* literally, *I will speak judgments with them.* The expression is peculiar to Jeremiah (comp. ch. iv. 12; xii. 1; xxxix. 6; lii. 9), and includes both the examination of the accused, and the judicial sentence (see ch. xxxix. 5; lii. 9). **All their wickedness**, etc. Their "wickedness," *i.e.* their infidelity to Jehovah,

showed itself in burning incense to "other gods," and bowing down to their images. "Burned incense" is, however, too narrow a sense. The root-meaning of the verb is to be fragrant, and the causative conjugations will strictly mean only "to make a sweet odour," whether by the offering of incense or by burnt offerings (comp. ch. xi. 12; 2 Kings xxiii. 8, where a causative conjugation is used in the same wide sense here postulated; also Ps. lxvi. 15 and Isa. i. 13, where the word usually rendered "incense" seems rather to mean "a sweet smoke"). The prophet says, "of other gods" (not "of false gods"), out of consideration for the ignorance of his hearers, to whom Baal and Moloch really were as gods; in fact, that expressive word (*elîl*) which Isaiah uses ten times to express the unreality of the other so-called gods, occurs only once, and then not in quite the same sense (see ch. xiv. 14) in Jeremiah. But the prophet's own strict monotheism is proved by such passages as ch. ii. 27 *a* ; viii. 19 *b* ; xvi. 20.

Ver. 17.—**Gird up thy loins**, as an Oriental does before making any kind of physical exertion, whether walking (Exod. xii. 11; 2 Kings iv. 29), running (1 Kings xviii. 46), or fighting (Job xii. 21). **Be not dismayed.** A want of confidence on Jeremiah's part will issue in his utter discomfiture by his enemies. "Dismay" in Hebrew has a twofold reference, subjective ("dismay") and objective ("ruin," "discomfiture"). Both references can be illustrated from this verse. (Comp. the command and—ver. 18—promise to Jeremiah with the command and promise to Ezekiel—iii. 8, 9.)

Ver. 18.—**Brasen walls.** The plural is used instead of a collective term for the whole circle of fortifications. In the parallel passage (ch. xv. 20) the singular occurs; the same alternation of plural and singular as in 2 Kings xxv. 10; 1 Kings iii. 1. The combination of figures strikingly expresses the invincibility of one whose strength is in his God. **The kings of Judah.** Why the plural? Most reply, because Jeremiah would have to do with successive sovereigns. But this meaning would have been just as well conveyed by the singular: "the king of Judah," without any name being added—would mean the king who from time to time happened to be reigning. "Kings of Judah" in Jeremiah seems to have a special meaning, and to include all the members of the royal family, who formed a numerous and powerful class (see on ch. xvii. 20).

HOMILETICS.

Vers. 1—3.—*On the external surroundings of the life of Jeremiah.* These words, which constitute the preface to the Book of Jeremiah, are evidently intended to furnish a historical setting for the writings of the prophet. But they also throw light on his character and work. For, though the true life of every man is his inner spiritual life, we cannot estimate the worth of this until we have taken account of the circumstances in which it is placed, the aids and the hindrances it receives from without. Let us consider, therefore, the spiritual significance of the main historical surroundings of the work of Jeremiah.

I. THE OFFICIAL RELATIONSHIP OF JEREMIAH. 1. Jeremiah *had the advantage of being the son of a priest.* He had probably received a religious education from his childhood. The religion of his fathers must have been familiar to him. Its solemn rites and suggestive symbols were often before his eyes. Possibly, like St. Paul, who was trained in Jewish theology before he became a Christian (Gal. i. 14), he may have found the Law a schoolmaster to bring him to a higher religion. The children of Christian ministers have peculiar privileges in the early knowledge of Scripture, Church life, etc., which they have opportunities of acquiring. 2. Yet *this official relationship of Jeremiah's had its disadvantages.* It was quite exceptional. Not more than three of the prophets were of sacerdotal origin. For the most part the priestly class regarded the prophetic with jealousy, if not with envy. (1) Officialism is *conservative,* and opposed to the free and revolutionary spirit of prophecy. (2) It is also *formal,* and tends to repress the inward and spiritual experiences of which prophecy is the highest outcome. It speaks well for Jeremiah that the spirit of prophecy was not crushed out of him by the dry traditionalism and the rigid ritualism of his priestly connections. 3. It is noteworthy that *the official relationship of Jeremiah was entirely overshadowed by his prophetic mission.* He is known to history not as the priest, but as the prophet. Official religious services are quite secondary to spiritual work.

II. THE CHARACTER OF THE AGE OF JEREMIAH. 1. Jeremiah *entered on his mission in the midst of the reformation of Josiah.* Yet the prophet's work was entirely disconnected from that of the king. Political religious activity is very different from personal spiritual work. Ecclesiastical reforms will not effect spiritual regeneration. The king's overthrow of the idols does not dispense with the need of the prophet's call to repentance. 2. Jeremiah *continued his mission after the failure of Josiah's reformation and during an age of national decay.* The character of the age changed, but the prophet remained unchanged. Weak men may be content to echo the popular cries of the day. It is too often the mission of the servant of God to contradict these familiar voices. The true prophet is not the creature of his age, the mouthpiece of the *Zeit-geist;* he is called to resist this influence. 3. Jeremiah *closed his mission amidst scenes of national ruin.* It was given him to see the fulfilment of his warnings of doom, but not that of his promises of restoration. Hence he is the prophet of tears. Jesus also wept over Jerusalem, but he brought redemption. We should be thankful that we live in these latter times when we can see the realization of the promises of " the Book of consolation."

III. THE DURATION OF THE MISSION OF JEREMIAH. It lasted for at least forty years; how many more after the overthrow of Jerusalem we do not know. 1. This fact speaks much for the *prophetic power* of Jeremiah. Many men can only rouse themselves to one supreme effort. True greatness is as much seen in the continuance of powers as in supreme exhibitions of them. 2. This fact is a grand proof of the *faithfulness* of the prophet. Almost the whole of his work was done "in opposition." We admire the young martyr who summons up a momentary heroic courage to seal his testimony with his blood; but greater honour is due to the aged confessor who has persevered through a lifelong martyrdom, and, though spared to old age, is also " faithful unto death." 3. This fact sheds light on *God's ways with man.* Jeremiah commenced his stern prophetic denunciations forty years before the destruction of Jerusalem. This suggests to us (1) that God mercifully delays the execution of his threats to give man time for repentance; and (2) that the forbearance of God, which postpones the evil day, does not frustrate the justice which must ultimately bring it upon the impenitent.

Ver. 5.—*Predestination.*   I. CONSIDER THE CHARACTERISTICS OF A DIVINE PRE-DESTINATION.   1. This implies (1) *foreknowledge*—God has his idea about a man and his mission before he forms the initial germ of his life ; (2) a *sanctifying,* or *setting apart,* by which the man is considered by God in relation to his destined mission, and treated accordingly ; and (3) a *preordination,* a Divine action in accordance with the Divine idea and purpose which tends to carry these into effect.   Every life is prophesied in the mind of God by God's thought of it, and comes into the world girded with Divine purposes, wrapped up and drawn onwards by the unseen threads of the designs of God. 2. This predestination does not involve *fatalism ;* it is consistent with human freedom of action and personal responsibility.   On the one hand we must conclude, from its existence, that there are certain possibilities with which God endows a man, and certain limits with which God has hedged him about.   But on the other hand, we must recognize that it depends on the man's own will and effort whether he use those possi-bilities, and attain to the end enclosed within those limits.   He has a Divine vocation, but he may neglect it ; he may fail in realizing God's idea of his life.   There rests on him the responsibility of accomplishing his destiny.

II. CONSIDER THE GROUNDS FOR BELIEF IN A DIVINE PREDESTINATION.   1. It is re-vealed in *Scripture* (*e.g.* Acts ii. 23 ; Rom. viii. 29 ; 1 Pet. i. 2).   2. It is involved in the *idea of the providence* of a supreme God.   God foresees all the future ; in every act of his all other events and their relation to this must be present to the mind of God.   With such knowledge a universal control of events, such as is implied by a providence not interfering from without now and again at critical moments, but immanent in the whole course of the world, must imply a Divine preordination.   3. It is proved to us by *experience.*   (1) We are born with certain peculiarities, faculties, powers, tendencies.   The prophet, like the poet, *nascitur, non fit.*   (2) The external circumstances of life are largely beyond our control.   The child cannot determine the sphere of life into which it is to enter at birth.   All the opportunities and duties which result from these circum-stances are made for us, not by us.   They bring a mission and open up a career, by chance if there be no providence, but by preordination if there be a providence.

III. CONSIDER THE PURPOSE OF A DIVINE PREDESTINATION.   1. It must often be *mysterious.*   Until we review life as a whole we shall not be able to interpret the meaning of its several parts.   We cannot judge of the architect's design by examining the separate stones which lie scattered in the builder's yard.   But : 2. It is not *arbitrary.* The very idea of destiny as determined by a Being of infinite thought implies purpose based on reason.   God would not determine events simply to manifest his unfettered rights of sovereignty.   Such aimless caprice could only emanate from a senseless despot. 3. It is turned to a *good purpose.*   This must be so, for if God is good his designs must be good.   The predestination is (1) for the good of the agent, who is blessed by being selected for Divine service ; and (2) for the good of the world.   The elect are chosen instruments for benefiting the whole world.   Thus Jeremiah was destined to be " a prophet unto the nations."   The Jew was an elect people that he might be the channel of blessing to all mankind (Gen. xii. 3 ; Rom. iii. 2).   The Christian is a chosen vessel that he may carry grace to others, and serve as the salt of the earth, as the light of the world.

IV. CONSIDER THE PRACTICAL EFFECT OF THE DOCTRINE OF PREDESTINATION.   It con-tains no excuse for indolence and no reason for despair, for God fits all of us for some service, the accomplishment of which depends on our own faithfulness.   1. It should lead us to *inquire what is God's will,* rather than to carve out a career for ourselves. 2. It should make us *humble, submissive, obedient,* and *diligent* in service, since there is a Divine idea of our life which God expects us to realize.   3. It should inspire *courage* in the midst of difficulties.   Jeremiah was brave in the thought that he was fulfilling a Divine destiny.   Such a thought inspires energy in face of enmity, contempt, isolation, and apparent failure.

Vers. 6—9.—*Diffidence overcome.*   I. DIFFIDENCE IS A DIFFICULTY TO BE OVERCOME. 1. Jeremiah shrank from his mission, not through the cowardice that fears danger, nor through the indolence that dislikes effort, nor through the selfishness that declines respon-sibility, but through the *diffidence* of youth, sensitiveness, and humility.   (1) Youth is naturally diffident.   The world is all unknown ; powers are not yet proved by experience.

(2) Sensitiveness inclines to diffidence. There is a confidence which depends simply on denseness and callousness. Acute feeling is a great hindrance to bold action. Jeremiah felt the miseries of his nation deeply, and it was peculiarly difficult for such a man to assume the position of a stern censor. (3) Humility leads to diffidence. If we think little of ourselves we are not likely to be forward in accepting posts of responsibility. 2. Now, this diffidence is an *evil thing*. It may not be sinful in its origin, but perfectly innocent, and even a mark of amiable characteristics. But it is injurious in its effects, and becomes positively guilty if indulged in when God has provided us means for overcoming it. The most gifted are often the most diffident. Hence if they yielded to their reluctance to fulfil their vocation, the greatest and best work of the world would be left undone. There is also a danger lest diffidence should become an excuse for indolence, selfishness, and cowardice. If unrestrained it will lead to these vices. People are often greatly to blame for shrinking from posts of responsibility, although they may even imagine they are earning the honours of modesty and humility.

II. GOD PROVIDES MEANS FOR OVERCOMING DIFFIDENCE. God never calls a man to any work without securing to him the means for performing it. Thus having called Jeremiah to his service, God sends help for overcoming the young man's diffidence. 1. *The consciousness of a Divine mission.* "Thou shalt go to all that I shall send thee." It is well to feel that we are not doing our own work but God's. If we fail, what does that matter to us so long as we are doing his will? The thought of duty is itself an inspiration. We are not simply to attempt what we imagine to be a good thing; we are called for a purpose, sent on a mission, and the thought that we are about our Father's business should allay the hesitation of natural diffidence. The ambassador is armed with the authority of his master and backed by his master's power. The prophet is sent by God with God's authority. All who are working God's will are similarly supported by God's authority. 2. *The realization of the presence of God.* "I am with thee." We may be diffident while we look to self; but when we look away to God we see the Source of strength and victory. Indeed, our very diffidence may be a means of securing our true strength by making us seek the help of God. Self-distrust may lead to trust in God. Thus when weak in ourselves we may become strong in him (2 Cor. xii. 10). If we go in God's strength we have no more occasion to fear, since success no longer depends on our ability but on his assistance. 3. *The direct inspiration of the Spirit of God.* "Behold I have put my words in thy mouth." God is not only present by our side to assist and deliver us, but he is within the soul, infusing light and power. The prophet fears he cannot speak the needed words. The words he is to speak are not his own but God's. He is the messenger, God is the real speaker. If then he can but discern the voice of God within him, and interpret this to the people, all diffidence arising from his own imcompetence should vanish. Every work which is done for God can only proceed from God, and when it does thus come from God we need not fear its failure. God can accomplish his own will in us as well as by his immediate actions in the world.

Ver. 10.—*The power of prophecy.* I. THERE IS A POWER IN PROPHECY. Prophecy is not simply a light, a revelation of truth; it is also a voice of authority, a means of active influence, a power. The Divine word in the prophet is like the Divine word in nature—an energizing word. God speaks, and it is done. The New Testament references to prophecy are made in obedience to this thought. The fulfilment of prophecy is there quoted not so much, as in modern evidential literature, as a proof of supernatural foresight, but rather as the effect of a Divine power which has realized the purpose of the ancient Word of God. This or that is said to be done "*that* it might be fulfilled which was spoken by the prophet." God's Word is always a power (Heb. iv. 12). The Bible is not simply a revelation; it is a means of influence. The preacher should see that he is clothed with power. His mission is to influence as well as to teach.

II. THE SOURCES OF THE POWER OF PROPHECY ARE SPIRITUAL. The authority conferred on Jeremiah is not that of the secular arm. He is to exert his influence by no material force. His power is different in kind from that of a political government. The claim of the papal authority founded on this verse is unwarranted, since this does not confer the power of the sword but direct spiritual influence. Neither is the power of prophecy in the least allied to magic or sorcery. It is not a miraculous material force. 1. It is the *power of truth*. Truth is strong; knowledge is power. The prophet sees the deep principles of God's government, and in the discernment of them lies the force of his utterances. 2. It is the *power of right*. The prophet takes his stand on the side of justice, purity, goodness. In the end the might must go with the right. 3. It is the *power of God*. The prophet is nothing in himself; he is God's servant; the authority he wields is God's. So the power of the preacher is not to be sought in reason, in eloquence, nor in official authority, but in the truth of his message, in the righteousness of his cause, and in his fidelity to the will of God.

III. THE RANGE OF THE POWER OF PROPHECY IS WORLDWIDE. Jeremiah was a Jew. Yet he was "set over the nations and over the kingdoms." 1. God is the King of kings and his authority concerns *kingdoms* as well as individuals. Political questions are amenable to the influence of Divine truth and righteousness. 2. God's truth does not only concern the Church. It is for the *world*—if the world will obey, for its blessedness; if it will not heed, for a judgment upon it.

IV. THE EFFECTS OF THE POWER OF PROPHECY ARE REVOLUTIONARY. It is no wild and transient influence, but a great stirring energy. Translated into modern language, this means that truth, right, and the will of God are powerful factors in history, disarranging human schemes and bringing higher designs into effect. 1. This power is *destructive*. Jeremiah is to "root out," etc. Evil is not a mere negation—simple darkness. It must be fought and cast out. Christ sent "a sword" (Matt. x. 34). The era of the Reformation was a destructive age. It is the duty of the preacher to protest against evil, to denounce it, to seek its overthrow, and not to shrink for fear of consequent disturbances. Warfare is better than guilty peace. 2. This power is ultimately *constructive*. Jeremiah is "to build and to plant." The destructive agencies of God are simply intended to clear off obstructions, and make the way for a new and better order. The disintegrating power of criticism should be regarded as only preparatory to the creative influence of living truth. The gospel is chiefly a constructive power, making men new creatures, building up the kingdom of God in our midst, bringing about a new heaven and a new earth.

Vers. 11, 12.—*The almond rod.* The early budding almond rod is symbolical of the wakeful attitude of God at a crisis in human events. God's manner of acting at this period of Jewish history may be regarded as typical of what we may expect again under similar circumstances.

I. THERE ARE OCCASIONS WHEN GOD'S WATCHFULNESS AND ENERGY ARE ESPECIALLY MANIFEST. God never sleeps (Ps. cxxi. 4). While we sleep he keeps watch. Though we do not mark his presence nor even think of it, he is still looking upon us and never ceasing from his activity. Yet he is said to awake as though from sleep (Ps. xliv. 23), because to us he appears to be more wakeful at one season than at another. 1. There are times when God watches unseen, and times when he makes his watchfulness manifest to us by his acts; then he is said to awake. 2. God generally acts in quiet ways unnoticed and not directly interfering with us; but now and again his ceaseless activity is more pronounced, and is specially felt by opposing our course; then God seems to have aroused himself. Such times are awful crises of existence. We should be prepared to expect them, and not presume on the present obscurity of the Divine actions. Some day it will be as though God awoke with the voice of a trumpet and the might of a host suddenly revealed.

II. GOD NEVER DELAYS HIS ACTION BEYOND ITS DUE TIME. When it is time for God to "awake," he does "awake." It seems as though he tarried; but he has a reason for waiting. 1. He does not come to deliverance at the moment we expect him (1) because it is well we should be tried by distresses, or (2) because high purposes beyond our own lives are to be attained through the things which are occasioning us trouble, or (3) because we have not sought his aid with true faith and submission, or (4) for causes beyond our comprehension. 2. He does not come to judgment (1) because he waits for sin to ripen, or (2) because he is long-suffering and gives time for repentance, or (3) because larger issues than those which touch us are involved in the act of judgment. Still, in both cases he comes at the right time. He is not a slothful God. He is wakeful, and his actions may be typified by the almond branch.

III. GOD'S JUDGMENTS SOMETIMES FALL SUDDENLY AND SWIFTLY. We may have but short warning of their approach. The execution of them may be rapid. The storm which has long been brewing may burst quickly. The harvest which has ripened slowly may be gathered in with haste. The impending judgment may not be discerned till it is too late for escape. When the rain began to fall it was too late for man to seek refuge in the ark. When the Jews saw the hosts of Nebuchadnezzar approaching there were no means for saving their country from ruin. It is foolish and wrong to neglect the salvation of God until we discern his judgment looming over us. "To-day if ye will hear his voice, harden not your hearts."

Vers. 13, 14.—*The seething pot.* I. THE VISION OF THE SEETHING POT FORESHADOWS APPROACHING DOOM. God is about to "hold his session" upon Jerusalem and the cities of Judah. 1. They who are *most favoured* by God must expect the severest judgment if they prove unfaithful to him. The Jews were a favoured people. Their privileges were great; if they abused these their guilt and consequent punishment must be proportionately great. Therefore, instead of considering the past mercies of God as a ground for expecting to escape the penalties of our offences, we should see in them the measure of his future severities upon us if we sin in face of the special inducements to devotion afforded by those mercies. 2. The revelation of impending judgment is a great *motive for faithful preaching.* This vision of the seething pot is given to Jeremiah to rouse him to undertake his prophetic duties. A large part of his work consisted in gloomy predictions of coming doom. This was peculiar to the age. There are ages when similar preaching is especially appropriate. But as sin always makes for death the preacher is always called to raise a voice of warning.

II. THE VISION OF THE SEETHING POT ILLUSTRATES THE CHARACTER OF THE APPROACHING DOOM. 1. It is *gradually prepared.* The vessel is slowly heated to the boiling point. The guilt of sin accumulates and the evil consequences gather in force until they burst upon the victim with the energy of long pent-up wrath. 2. It breaks forth *suddenly.* Suddenly the vessel boils over. Judgment may be delayed and gradual in the preparation, and yet suddenly surprise us when at length it falls upon us. 3. It is *violent and overwhelming,* as the seething pot suggests fury, tumult, and, in its boiling over, a rushing forth of its scalding contents.

III. THE VISION OF THE SEETHING POT SUGGESTS THE SOURCE OF THE APPROACHING DOOM. The pot was turned towards the south and heated by fires in the north. 1. Punishment may come from the *most unlikely quarter.* The Jews had turned to Babylon for friendship, and from Babylon came their ruin. Our most trusted friends may become the instruments of our keenest suffering. 2. *Lawless violence may be overruled by providence* to work the ends of God's righteous laws. The doom is not to come from within the range of the theocracy and through the influence of those who consciously executed the Divine decree, but from far-off regions, wholly beyond the light of Israel's religion. Thus God makes the wrath of man to praise him. So storms and earthquakes, revolutions and invasions, tumults in nature and tumults in the human world, work ultimate good results in clearing and purifying the air, sweeping away pestilent corruption, and preparing for a new and wholesome order. 3. The more luxurious Southern races have frequently been visited by terrible invasions of hardier races from the North. The Scythians in the East, the Goths in the West, were scourges of God, and wholesome scourges, helping to reform the corrupt and indolent peoples who lived in dread of their invasions. We should see wise and good purposes of providence in these terrible events of general history, as we see them in the special history of Israel.

Vers. 17—19.—*Encouragements to fidelity.* It was no easy matter for Jeremiah, young, modest, and sensitive, to come boldly forward and threaten the judgment of God against his country. But if God calls a man to any task, he will help him through with it, and Jeremiah receives encouragements proportionate to his duty.

I. THE DUTY. Consider what the duty of faithful service laid upon the prophet included. 1. *Energy.* He is to gird up his loins, and arise. God is not satisfied with passive submission to his will. God cannot be faithfully served by the indolent. All our powers are required for his service, and they must be employed without distraction. 2. *Obedience.* Jeremiah is to speak just what God commands him. Fidelity is not simply devotion to God, it is devotion according to his will—the devotion of servants, not that of patrons. 3. *Thoroughness.* The prophet is to speak "all" that God commands him. It is treason for the ambassador to suppress those elements of his commission which are displeasing to himself. The servant of God must not select from the revelation of Divine truth the words which suit his purpose and neglect the rest. He is not to shun to declare "the whole counsel of God"—threats as well as promises, difficult sayings and mysteries as well as plainly acceptable doctrines. 4. *Fearlessness.* "Be not dismayed." Fear is not only painful; it is injurious by paralyzing effort. Cowardice is sin.

II. THE ENCOURAGEMENTS. It is our duty to be faithful, though fidelity should bring our ruin; but such a result will not follow it. Consider the various inducements Jeremiah receives to a faithful discharge of his difficult task. 1. *A revelation of momentous truths.* God says, "Thou *therefore* gird up thy loins," etc. The word "therefore" carries us back to the visions of the almond rod and the seething pot. The truths revealed in these visions themselves furnish a motive for the prophet to declare them. The seer should become a prophet. Truth is not the private property of the few; it is the rightful heritage of all. It is the duty of him who knows to enlighten the ignorant. More especially is this the case in regard to spiritual truths, practical truths, and truths which concern the highest welfare of mankind. 2. *A warning of Divine displeasure.* "Be not dismayed at them, lest I make thee indeed dismayed." The fear of God is a safeguard against the fear of man. Cowardice provokes danger. The Christian has no armour provided for his back. 3. *An assurance of Divine protection.* This is given in a succession of strong images, that it may be felt in all its certainty and importance. For we need not only to know that God will protect us, but to realize this if we are to be brave and strong. Thus Jeremiah is made to feel that, in spite of his youth and sensitiveness, he will be strong as a fortress and firm as brazen walls. None are so independent before men as they who are wholly dependent on God. 4. *A promise of victory over opposition.* The young prophet is taught to expect opposition. (1) It is foolish to ignore the approach of trouble. A surprise sometimes leads to a defeat from very inferior foes. Danger foreseen is danger half overcome. The Bible never makes light of the difficulties and hardships of life (Luke x. 3). (2) No ground of confidence is more inspiring than the knowledge that the danger clearly, fully apprehended will yet be certainly overcome. This was the assurance given to Jeremiah. The same assurance is offered to every faithful servant of God (Isa. xliii. 1).

HOMILIES BY VARIOUS AUTHORS.

On Jeremiah's ministry in general. "It is sufficient," said our Saviour, "that the disciple be as his Lord." Now, of all his servants few answered more closely to this description than did the prophet Jeremiah. In a very deep and real sense his life was a type of our Lord's. It is in the spiritual world as in the natural, a close resemblance exists between the separate parts and the entire organism to which they belong. The root, stem, bud, flower, fruit, and seed are each constructed on the same type as the tree itself. However widely diversified they may seem in form or function, their essential nature is the same. Hence every leaf is a miniature of the tree on which it grows; trunk, branches, foliage, are each patterned in it. And likewise every branch is but a reproduction on a smaller scale of the whole tree.[1] But this is only what we find constantly exemplified in the spiritual world. What miniature lives of Christ are those of men like Joseph, Moses, David, and many more! And amongst such as are illustrious in this respect stands Jeremiah. Like him, the consciousness of the Divine call was with him from childhood (cf. Luke ii. 49 and ch. i. 6). He too was persecuted with murderous hate by his own townsmen. As Christ was driven from Nazareth, so was Jeremiah from his native Anathoth (ch. xii. 6). His vehement denunciations of the corrupt priests and prophets of his day remind us of the reiterated woes pronounced by our Lord on the "scribes and pharisees, hypocrites," of his day. Like our Lord, Jeremiah also was the prophet who stood nearest to and told most plainly of the dread catastrophe which overwhelmed Jerusalem and her people.

[1] Macmillan.

Jeremiah was the prophet of Jerusalem's destruction by the Babylonian Nebuchadnezzar; our Lord of the like destruction by the Roman Titus. Both beheld the glories of the temple, and both told of the swiftly coming days when there should "not be left one stone upon another, which should not be thrown down." The footsteps of him who, beyond all others, was "despised and rejected of men," Jeremiah, in so far as it was possible to him, anticipated. The bitter tears shed by our Saviour over impenitent Jerusalem are shadowed forth in the prophet's prolonged and profound lament over his own idolatrous and disobedient countrymen. His well-known words, "Is it nothing to you all ye that pass by?" uttered concerning the sorrows of Jerusalem and her people, have come to be so universally appropriated to our Lord, that the prophet's own deep distress which they tell of, and the occasion of that distress, are alike almost if not entirely forgotten. "His sufferings come nearest of those of the whole army of martyrs to those of the Teacher against whom princes, and priests, and elders, and people were gathered together." To him, as to the great apostle, was it given to know "the fellowship of Christ's sufferings, and to be made conformable unto his death." And we may venture to prolong the parallel, and to apply to Jeremiah the august words which, in their supreme meaning, can belong to but One alone. "Wherefore God also hath highly exalted him, and given him a name which is above every name." In that high recompense Jeremiah, so far as any servant of God may, shares. For the honour in which his name came to be held was very great. As time rolled on he was regarded as the chief representative of the whole prophetic order. By some he was placed at the head of all the prophets. At the time of the Christian era his return was daily expected. He was emphatically thought to be "the Prophet —'the Prophet like unto Moses,' who should close the whole dispensation." No wonder, then, that one devout student after another has been struck by the closeness of the resemblance here briefly pointed out, and has delighted to trace in the prophet's history foreshadowings of the "Man of Sorrows," who, more than any other, was acquainted with grief.—C.

Vers. 1—3.—*Introductory statements concerning Jeremiah's parentage and period of his ministry.* I. HIS PARENTAGE. He was the son of Hilkiah, not that Hilkiah who was high priest during the reign of Josiah, but of some similarly named priest. Even amid the terrible corruptions of that period, there appear to have been a few faithful souls who held fast to the fear of the Lord. We have their names, Huldah, Shallum, Baruch, etc. From amidst these Jeremiah sprang. The Lord can call and convert and consecrate to his work whom he will; but his more common way is to come to the habitations of his people, when he would find some whom he destines for special and honoured service. The homes of the godly are the hope of the Church. Amidst the children of the believing are to be found those whom God will generally employ to carry on his work. This is one way in which the promise is fulfilled, "Them that honour me I will honour."

II. HIS PROFESSION. He belonged to the priesthood. Terrible are the charges which are brought against the priests and prophets of that day. They had reached the limit of utmost degradation. They are said to "deal falsely," to be "profane;" and their conduct is described as "a wonderful and horrible thing." Yet Jeremiah belonged to this deeply fallen class. How difficult must have been his position! how constant his resistance to the contagion of their example and influence! When from amongst those who are of the same order, who have common interests, common duties, and who are thrown together in so many and close relationships, one stands aloof and turns upon his companions in severe and solemn rebuke as Jeremiah did, such a one needs to be strong as "a defenced city, and an iron pillar, and brazen walls" (ver. 18) Jeremiah stands before us as a noble proof that the tide of evil, however strongly it may run, may yet be resisted; none are of necessity borne down by it but, by the same grace which was given to Jeremiah, they may stem the fierce current and defy its power. Ten thousand of the saints of God have done this; why should not we?

III. THE REASON OF ALL MEN COUNTING HIM AS A PROPHET. "The word of the Lord came unto him." He did not *say*, "I am a prophet;" but all men felt he was. For his words had power; they were mighty to the pulling down of the strong holds of sin. It was not simply that he announced that there should be a "rooting out and pulling down" (cf. ver. 10), but the words which he spoke so wrought in men's minds that these results followed. Hence men, conscious of the power of his words, confessed that it was "the word of the Lord" which had come to him. This is the old prophetic word which, whenever spoken, constrains men to confess the presence of God (cf. 1 Cor. xiv. 25). And St. Peter (2 Epist. i. 19) says concerning it, "We have, surer still, the prophetic word." "More sure," he meant, than even the wondrous voice and vision of "the holy mount," for that was but a transient testimony given once and to the three favoured apostles of the Lord alone; but the prophetic word, that which woke up the response in men's hearts, and by which the secrets of each soul were disclosed—that was a more constant, more universal, more powerful, and therefore a more sure testimony than aught beside. And *the occasions* when this "word of the Lord" comes to any of his servants are well known. See how particular and definite the dates are here. "In the thirteenth year of the reign of King Josiah. It came also in the days of Jehoiakim," etc. The coming of the word of the Lord to any soul is a marked and memorable period. He through whom that word is spoken is conscious of an unusual power, he realizes the Divine presence in an altogether unusual manner. He is more passive than active. It is said of the holy men of old, that they "spake as they were moved [borne along] of the Holy Ghost," and this, St. Peter declares (2 Epist. i. 21), is ever a characteristic of the prophetic word. And those who hear the word know that the Lord is speaking through his servant. Listlessness and unconcern give way to serious concern. Some can tell the very day and hour when they first heard the "word of the Lord." They had listened to sermons and read the Scriptures again and again, but one day they felt that the Lord himself was speaking to them, and they could not but give heed. Like as the people of Judah and Jerusalem knew when the voice of God, though they despised it to their ruin, was speaking to them, so do men now. And if we have heard it for our salvation, the time, the place, the speaker, will often be vividly remembered in connection with it, like as those who heard Jeremiah knew the very year when the "word of the Lord came" to him. It is ill for both hearers and speakers alike if they be unable to point to periods when they were conscious that "the word of the Lord" came to them. For a preacher never to realize the sacred glow and the uplifting of soul which accompany the utterance of the prophetic word; or for a hearer to have so dulled his conscience, so destroyed his spiritual ear, that though the word of the Lord be spoken his heart never responds, his soul never realizes the presence of God;—from the sin and sorrow of either may God mercifully save us.

IV. The date and duration of Jeremiah's ministry. We are told when it began, and how long it lasted. It began when the evil days for Judah and Jerusalem were drawing very near. It was in vain that the devout King Josiah endeavoured to turn back the hearts of the people to the Lord God of their fathers. But though the long-suffering of God had been so tried and was now almost ceasing, yet, ere they were given up to the punishment which was their due, God raises up his servant Jeremiah and the band of faithful men who stood by him (cf. 2 Chron. xxxvi. 15—21). For forty years—for that is the period covered by the reigns of the several kings spoken of—Jeremiah exhorted, warned, entreated, threatened, prayed, wept; but all in vain. Therefore God's wrath at length rose against them, and there was no remedy. "Behold the goodness and the severity of God!" How reluctantly will he abandon any to the results of their own ways! how slow is he to let come upon them that which they have long deserved! Yea, he is the long-suffering God. But whilst we fail not to remember and to rejoice in this, let us not fail either to remember and to dread the other equally sure fact, that "God is a consuming fire" to those who set at nought all his counsel, and will have none of his reproof (Prov. i. 24—33). Those to whom Jeremiah prophesied found it so, and so will all who sin in like manner now.—C.

Vers. 4—19.—*The dread commission.* I. What was it? (Cf. ver. 10.) It was to denounce the judgments of God against his people. At the end of the commission there is mention made of "building and planting;" but the chief charge is of an altogether opposite character. Jeremiah was set over the nations "to root out, and to pull down, to destroy, and to throw down." It was a terrible undertaking. He was to spare no class, no rank, no order. Kings, princes, priests, and people were all to be alike solemnly warned of the sure judgments that were coming upon them. And the like work has to be done now. How prone we all are to speak with bated breath of the retribution of God! how ready, to ourselves and to others, to explain away or to soften down the awful words of God against sin and the doers thereof! Preachers and teachers of God's truth, beware lest the blood of those who perished because you warned them not be required at your hands (Ezek. xxxiii. 6)!

II. BUT IT IS A DREAD COMMISSION. The shrinking of Jeremiah from it is manifest all through this chapter. Before the heavy burden which he was to bear was fully disclosed to him, he exclaims (ver. 6), "Ah, Lord God! behold I cannot speak: for I am a child." And the assurances, aids, and encouragements which are given him all show how much needed to be done ere his reluctance and trembling fear could be overcome. The whole chapter tells of God's gracious preparation of his servant for the arduous work he had to do. And whosoever now undertakes like work, if he have no realization of its solemnity and burden, it is plain that God has not called him to speak in his Name. To hear a man tell of the awful doom of the impenitent in a manner that, if it be not flippant, yet seems to relish his task, and to hail it as an opportunity for rhetorical display, is horrible in the extreme, and will do more to harden men in sin than almost anything beside. The subject is so sad, so serious, so terrible, that he who believes in it at all will be sure to sympathize with the prophet's sensitive shrinking from the work to which he was ordained. If when sentencing criminals who have broken the laws of man to their due punishment, humane judges often break down in tears, though their punishment touch not the soul,—how can any contemplate the death that is eternal unmoved or without the most solemn compassion and tenderest pity? And to increase the fear and shrinking with which Jeremiah regarded the work before him, there was the *seeming presumption* of one so young—little more than "a child" in years, experience, or knowledge—undertaking such a work. *The hopelessness* of it also. As well might a sparrow think to fly full in the face of a hurricane, as for the young prophet to think to stay the torrent of sin which was now flooding and raging over the whole life of his people. Sin and transgression of the grossest kind had become their habit, their settled custom, their ordinary way. All that he had to tell them they had heard again and again, and had despised and forgotten it. What hope of success was there, then, for him? And *the fierceness of the opposition* he would arouse would also deter him from the work. It was not alone that the faces (ver. 17) of kings, princes, priests, and people would darken upon him, but they would (ver. 19) "fight against" him, as we know they did. Well, therefore, might he say, "Ah, Lord! I cannot." And to-day, how many are the plausible reasons which our reluctant hearts urge against that fidelity in such work as Jeremiah's which God requires at our hands! But God will not allow them. See—

III. HOW HE CONSTRAINED JEREMIAH TO UNDERTAKE THIS WORK. 1. Ver. 5: he gave him certainty as to his being called to the prophetic work. To know that we are indeed called of God to any work is an unfailing source of strength therein. 2. Ver. 7: he made him feel that necessity was laid upon him; "thou *shalt* go;" "thou *shalt* speak." (Cf. Paul's "Yea, woe is me," etc.) So Jeremiah himself afterwards says (ch. xx. 9) God's word was like "a burning fire shut up in my bones, and I was weary with forbearing, and I could not stay." What a help to the preacher of God's truth is such a conviction as this! 3. Ver. 8: he promised his presence and delivering grace. Consciousness of security and safety in God will give a dauntless courage in the face of any and of all opposition. 4. He gave him special qualifications for his work. Words and power of speech (ver. 9). Immovable and unflinching strength of will, a determination and resolve that would not waver (ver. 18). 5. He showed him that the rooting up and the destruction were not ends in themselves, but to lead on to planting and to building afresh (ver. 10). To know that we are working on to a good and blessed end is no small encouragement to us in working through all manner of difficulty to reach that end. 6. He made him vividly realize the nature and nearness of the judgments he foretold. This was the purpose of the visions of the rod of the almond tree and the seething pot (vers. 11—15; for explanation, see exegesis). The first vision told of God's judgment close at hand. The second, of the quarter whence these judgments come, and of the fierce, furious character of the foes who should come upon them.

Jeremiah was enabled to "see well" the visions, that is, to realize very forcibly what they meant. Oh, if we could but more vividly realize what the anger of God is against sin; if we could have a vision of the wrath of God; with how much more power and urgency should we plead with men to flee from the wrath to come! 7. Ver. 16: he reminds Jeremiah of the sins that called for these judgments. A deep sense of sin 'is indispensable to those who would earnestly warn of the doom of sin. 8. And (ver. 19) God again gives his servant the blessed assurance, "They shall not prevail against thee; for I am with thee to deliver thee." Thus did God equip the prophet and prepare him for his work. His God supplied all his need. It was a stern warfare on which he was to go, but he went not at his own charges. If we be summoned to difficult duty, we shall be supplied with all-sufficient strength. Only let us be careful to avail ourselves of the help assured, lest (ver. 17) we be dismayed and God confound us before our enemies. Dread, therefore, no commission that God entrusts thee with, for along with it will ever be found the grace, all the grace, needed for its successful discharge.—C.

Ver. 10.—*The ministry for a corrupt age.* I. MUST BE RAISED UP BY GOD. Such an age will have its ministers, but they will be prophets who will prophesy only smooth things. But a true ministry for such an age will not be produced by it, but be given to it from God. "See, *I* have set thee," etc.

II. WILL BE ENDUED WITH DIVINE POWER. "I have set thee *over* the nations . . . to root out," etc. None who contemplate the marvellous effects of such a ministry and compare them with the natural powers of him who exercises it, but must see that the ascendancy he has gained and the spiritual power he wields are of God and not of man.

III. WILL MAKE NO COMPROMISE WITH SIN. See the number and force of the words used to indicate the ruthless antagonism which the prophet would manifest toward the wickedness of his day. Nothing less than its complete overthrow would fulfil the ministry entrusted to him.

IV. WILL DEMAND ON THE PART OF THE PROPHET, AND WILL GAIN FROM THE GRACE OF GOD, A FEARLESS AND AN UNCONQUERABLE COURAGE. (Vers. 17, 18.)

V. ITS END AND RESULT BLESSED. "To build and to plant" (ver. 10). The encumbered ground had first to be cleared and cleansed, but that done, the fabric of a true life should be upreared, and principles pure, holy, and blessed should have root in the hearts of all.—C.

Vers. 11—16.—*Jeremiah's visions.* I. WHAT WERE THEY? (Cf. vers. 12—14.)

II. WHEREFORE WERE THEY? In all probability, for the sake of vividly impressing the mind of the prophet with the message he was to deliver, and so ensuring that that message should be delivered with greater power. Hence the question, "What seest thou?" (ver. 11) was designed to arouse and arrest his attention, and for the same reason, when that attention had been awakened, the Divine commendation, "Thou hast well seen," is given. Cf. for similar questions and similar visions, ver. 13; ch. xxiv. 3; Amos vii. 8; viii. 2; Zech. iv. 2; v. 2, and in each case the motive seems to have been the same.

III. THEIR SUGGESTIONS FOR OURSELVES. 1. *Concerning God's punishment of sin.* (1) Its not being apparent to us is no reason for denying it. Certainly the vision of the stem, or branch, of the almond tree would not to an ordinary observer have suggested it. Nor either the second vision, that of the "seething pot," although that did undoubtedly present somewhat more of a troubled aspect. Yet both alike needed that their meaning and interpretation should be given. Their significance did not lie on the surface. Only a divinely illumined eye could see that the early-budding almond tree which, because of its outstripping other trees, being in advance of them all in yielding its fruit, was called the "wakeful" or "watchful" tree, meant that the Lord was "watchful over his word to perform it." Nor was the interpretation of the second vision much more evident than that of the first. And so continually, in connection with ungodly men, there are events occurring and signs of varied kind are given, which to those who are taught of God tell plainly how God is "watchful over his word to perform it;" but to others thay tell nothing of the kind. They are like the prophet's almond tree and seething pot, which had no meaning until that meaning was pointed out. The people of Judah and Jerusalem saw nothing in these circumstances, any more than in the prophet's visions, to alarm them very much. And so, still, ungodly men are at ease in the presence of facts and indications which fill those who believe God's Word with unspeakable alarm. How foolish, then, is it to take the unconcern, the powerlessness to understand God's signs, which characterize ungodly men, as any evidence of the unreality of that which God has declared! "As it was in the days of Noah, so shall it be," etc. Lot was as "one that mocked unto his sons-in-law." The Jews crucified our Lord because he saw so clearly and declared so plainly the character of their trusted leaders and the destruction that was coming—one even more terrible than that which Jeremiah foretold. But the Jews neither saw nor believed anything of the kind. (2) Its being by means of natural laws does not make it the less God's punishment of sin. The rapid growth and yield of the almond tree was a perfectly natural thing: there was no interference with the orderly course which such forms of plant life assume. And the war between the empires of Egypt and Babylon, in the vortex and whirlpool of which Jerusalem was dragged in and dragged down; all this which the prophet's second vision told of, was it not the inevitable though sad misfortune of any such diminutive power as was that of Judah and Jerusalem when placed in like circumstances? Her lot was cast just in the place where the two raging seas of Egypt and Babylon met. What wonder if her poor little barque went to pieces beneath the violence of those waves? It was sad enough, but yet perfectly natural; indeed, one may say, inevitable. And so it would be quite possible to explain all God's punishment away, and to regard it like the early blossoming of the almond tree, and like the seething troubles which must come upon little kingdoms placed as Judah was, when great empires on either side of her go to war, as only what was to be expected, what was in keeping with the natural order of things. Let any one read Gibbon, and from his account of the decline and fall of the Roman empire, you would gather no idea of a Divine righteousness arising to inflict merited punishment on an awfully corrupt and degraded people. Believers in God can and do see this, but the great historian has not felt himself bound to point out any such cause of the long series of disasters which he so eloquently relates. The inspired prophet and seer of Patmos has, however, done this; and in the Book of the Revelation, the woes coming upon that blood-stained empire are told of in symbolic but terrible form, and in connection with that God-defying wickedness which was the source and cause of them all. And so to-day, under cover of the fact that God works according to the natural order of things, men evade the teaching of the events that befall them. Because God punishes sin by the action of his natural laws, men deny that he punishes sin at all. His hand is not recognized in it, and therefore no repentance is awakened. They deem themselves unfortunate, and that is all. If we would be more faithful with ourselves, we should "hear the rod and who hath appointed it." No calamities or disasters come without meaning and intent; they are sent for moral and spiritual purposes, however much they may appear to be but natural and necessary events. Each of them will own, if interrogated, "I have a message from God unto thee." (3) It will increase in severity if there be need. The first vision is simply that of the almond tree; an emblem of gentleness rather than of severity. But the second vision, that of the boiling caldron, suggested a far other and more terrible visitation (cf. the plagues in Egypt, which increased in terribleness as they went on). And it is ever so even unto the "consuming fire" (Heb. xii. 29). (4) *It often comes from unexpected quarters.* The "seething pot" that the prophet saw had its face northward. Now, the reader of the history of the times of which our prophet tells—the times of King Josiah—will know that it was from the south, from Egypt, they expected that troubles would arise. And in the next chapter (ver. 16) mention is made of trouble that did arise from that quarter, though what particular event is referred to it is not easy to say. But the great trouble was to come from the north, from the last quarter from which they anticipated it. King Josiah lost his life in doing good service to that northern power, the great Assyrian kingdom, by fighting against Egypt. It was not, therefore, to be expected that *thence* calamity would come. But nevertheless it *was* thence that their great overthrow and destruction came. And little do the transgressors against God ever know or even dream whence his judgments against them will arise. It is not only "in such an hour," but from such a quarter "as they think not, that the Divine displeasure breaks upon them.   A transgressor against God is safe nowhere : nothing may be visible to his eye, everything may be going on in orderly course, and he may have full confidence that all is well.   But notwithstanding this, events soon to happen may prove that he has wrongly read the whole of God's providence, and that his security is least where he thought it was greatest and most certain.   Happy, and happy alone, is he who hath made the Lord God his trust, and whose hope the Lord is.   2. *Concerning the Divine love.*   We have seen wherefore these visions were given.   They reveal to us that Divine love which would warn men from ways which bring upon them such sore judgments.   The desire of God to save guilty men, to leave nothing undone by which they may be turned and kept back from evil, is manifest in all this.   He would not have his message miss its mark by reason of any lack of deep impression and vivid realization of the truth on the part of the messenger.—C.

Vers. 4—9.—*Jehovah calls Jeremiah and gives him ample encouragements.*   I. THE PURPOSE FOR WHICH JEREMIAH WAS BROUGHT INTO EXISTENCE.   This is stated in a very solemn and impressive way in ver. 5.   Jehovah presents himself to Jeremiah as he who formed him in the belly, and even before then recognized him as one who was to do a special work.   So with regard to Moses, Isaac, Samuel.   The circumstances of their birth direct our thoughts to the special ends to be worked out by their earthly life.   To each of them the same words might have been spoken as to Jeremiah.   Moreover, if true of them, this word is true of all.   Jehovah is the Fashioner of all mankind, and since he does nothing without some purpose, it follows that for every one of us, equally with Jeremiah, there is a recognition, a consecrating, an ordaining.   In a few instances there may be a special publication of the purpose, but the purpose itself is real in every instance.   Therefore our business clearly is to find out what God would have us be, our eyes open to his presence, our ears to his voice.   Then if we have discovered what God would have us be, if there is a deepening impression on our minds that we are in the right way, this very thought, that God saw the proper work of our life or ever we entered upon it, will assure us that the work cannot fail.   We shall feel that requisite strength in the doing of it, and full success at the end of it, are made certain.   The failings of life come—and it is easy to see that they must come—from putting our own purposes athwart the settled purpose of God.   We may rebel against the work which he calls upon us to undertake, but it is very certain that any work put in its place must end in disappointment and disaster.   To Jonah as to Jeremiah, God might have said somewhat the same as is here recorded.   It is an awful thought for sinners, in the collapse of their own plans, that they might have been successful and rejoicing, if only they had been from the heart obedient to the plans of God.

II. THE ANSWERING PLEA OF JEREMIAH.   An *opposing* plea it can hardly be called, but it is the not astonishing statement of a difficulty that from the human point of view looks very great.   When God makes his first approaches to men, asking them to do something special, what is more natural than that they should see huge difficulties in the way of obedience?   How fertile was the self-distrusting Moses in suggesting difficulties when God came to him in Horeb (Exod. iii. 4)?   Take special notice that the difficulties of such men as Moses and Jeremiah are not meant to be mere excuses, but are felt to be real reasons.   Such is emphatically the position here.   Jeremiah was but a lad ; it is possible that he had not yet attained to what we should call a young man (Gen. xli. 12 ; 1 Kings iii. 7).   At such an age one is valued for listening and learning rather than for talking.   That the prophet made such an initial reply to Jehovah was a good sign rather than a bad one.   Deep humility and a keen consciousness of natural weakness are welcome features in the man whom God would make his servant.   It is tolerably certain that among the elders of Anathoth Jeremiah would have the reputation of being a quiet, unpretending lad.   If a young man of another reputation had stood forward as a prophet, there would have been fair ground to charge him with presumption.   But when one stands forward who ever looks doubtfully on his own abilities, is no self-asserter, and forms by preference a member in the background of every scene, such a standing forward at once suggests that there is some superhuman motive behind it.   Jeremiah's plea is therefore a recommendation.   Unconsciously he gives a valid certificate of fitness for his work.   At the same time, this plea suggests all the difference which there is between the youthful Jeremiah and the youthful Jesus.

Jesus in the temple seems in his natural element, not too young even at twelve years of age to show an ardent interest in all that concerned Divine worship and service.

III. THE AMPLE ENCOURAGEMENT WHICH JEHOVAH GIVES TO JEREMIAH. In a few words, God puts before his servant all that is needed and all that can be supplied. 1. *There will be clear commands from God, and from the prophet there must be corresponding obedience.* Not with Jeremiah rests the deciding of whether he shall go here or there, or to what place first and to what last. He is always a sent man, and when he comes into the presence of his appointed audience, his message is a provided message. Thus it is ensured that he never finds himself in the wrong place or speaking at the wrong time. Well does God know how little we are able, of ourselves, to decide when to speak and when to be silent, what to say and what to leave unsaid. 2. One consequence of God's message faithfully delivered will be hostility and menace from the hearers, and therefore *there is an exhortation to courage, and an indication of the ground which makes that courage possible.* When Jeremiah gets into a certain presence and speaks a certain word he will be threatened. The threatening must be expected; it shows that the arrow of God's truth has found its home. All the powers of the human face will be called into malignant exercise against the prophet. The eye, the tongue, the muscles of the face will all be joined in strong combination to express the contempt and hatred filling the brain that lies behind. In no way can Jeremiah escape this experience; he must face the enemies, but in doing so he has the assurance that his Commander is near to deliver. 3. *God makes now an actual communication to the prophet.* The path is not yet taken, the audience is not yet in view, but by way of earnest inspiration the words of the Master are put into the servant's mouth. This of course was an indescribable experience. What it is to have the words of God in one's mouth can only be known by an actual enjoyment of the privilege. The only way in which we can discern how real and fruitful this experience was, is by observing its effect. There is no more hesitating, no turning from one answered plea to find another more cogent. Henceforth the prophet goes on steadily and faithfully in his mission, and his perfect service is best proved by this, that in due time he meets with the indicated opposition, and receives from God his promised protection.—Y.

Ver. 10.—*The vast compass of the prophet's work.* I. THE WIDE EXTENT THE PROPHECIES COVER. Primarily they had to do with Jerusalem and Judah and all the families of the house of Israel. But this was only the beginning. They went on to affect in the most intimate way all the nations and the kingdoms. The principles of righteousness and truth and Divine authority concern all. They can no more be kept within certain geographical bounds than can the clouds and rains of heaven. On this day, when the Great I AM came to the youthful Jeremiah, *he* set him over the nations and over the kingdoms, and here is the reason why these prophecies, with their grand ethical deliverances, have still such a firm hold upon Christendom, upon the Gentile just as much as the Jew. Wherever there still remains the worshipper of stocks and stones, wherever the oppressor is found, and the man who confides in the arm of flesh, and the man who is utterly indifferent to the glory of God,—then in that same place there is occasion to insist most strenuously upon the continued application of Jeremiah's words. The prophets were more than indignant patriots; they were and are still witnesses to an ideal of humanity, nowhere regarded as it ought to be, and only too often neglected, if not contemptuously denied. He who came forth to condemn his own people for lapsing into idolatry did thereby equally condemn other nations for not departing from it. The gospel for every creature is preceded by a body of prophecy, which is shown also to concern every creature, not by laborious inference, but by such explicit words as we find in this verse.

II. THE DEPTH OF THE WORK TO WHICH THESE PROPHECIES POINT. The work is not only wide; it is deep as it is wide. The ultimate aim is set forth in two figures: 1. Building. 2. Planting. On these two figures Paul dwells very suggestively in writing to the Corinthians. The constructive work of God in the human soul needs more than one figure sufficiently to illustrate it. But all true building must be on a sufficient foundation; all Divine planting, if it is to come to anything, must be in a suitable soil. Hence there goes beforehand an unsparing work, to destroy things already in existence. Buildings already erected must be pulled down; plants already growing must be uprooted and put beyond the chance of further growth. We have done things which ought to have been left undone; and the word to Jeremiah is that they must be undone, in order that the things which ought to be done may be fully done. The terms indicating destruction are multiplied to emphasize the need, and prevent escape into ruinous compromise. There must be no tacking on of a new building to certain humanly cherished parts of the old. Constructions after the will of God must not be liable to a description such as that of the image which Nebuchadnezzar saw in his dream; all must be strong, pure, and beautiful from basement to summit. In the garden of the Lord there can be no mixing of heavenly and earthly plants. A clean sweep—such is necessitated for the glory of God and the blessedness of man. Thus at the very first is given a hint of the hostility which Jeremiah would provoke. Pulling down means the expulsion of self from its fortress, and its bereavement of all that it valued. Every brick detached, every plant uprooted, intensified the enmity one degree more. "Destroy," "overthrow," are the only words that can be spoken as long as anything remains in which human pride and selfishness take delight. But at the same time, the prophet goes forth to build and to plant. He takes nothing away but what he leaves something infinitely better behind. When God sends a messenger to us, his great first word is "thorough;" and even though he has to make his way through human pains, tears, murmurings, and semi-rebellions, he keeps to the word. Remember, then, that he who pulls down also builds; he who uproots also plants; and he builds and plants for eternity.—Y.

Vers. 11—14.—*The almond tree and the seething pot.* He who put his word into the prophet's mouth also put a new power of vision into his eyes, and gave him to see signs such as tended to fix permanently in his mind deep convictions with regard to the power and purposes of God. Thus the prophet was assured of his ability to see more than others could see. Both through eye and ear he was fortified in the consciousness that his prophetic office was no empty boast.

I. THE ROD OF THE ALMOND TREE. Probably much such a rod as those which were laid up in the tabernacle overnight in order to certify beyond all question the divinely appointed office of Aaron (Numb. xvii.). This narrative, we may be pretty sure, would be transmitted with special care from generation to generation of the priesthood, and to it the mind of Jeremiah may at once have turned. That rod which once helped the priest is now found helping the prophet. It was the sign of how much living and fructifying energy might break forth where there was only the appearance of death. The auditors of Jeremiah's prophecies might say they saw no sign of impending calamities. In all self-confidence they might say, "Peace and prosperity will last out our time." And so Jeremiah goes forth with the remembrance of the almond rod, well assured that by God's power the most unexpected things may happen with the utmost suddenness. The words of prophecy may long lie dormant, and some may treat them as dead and obsolete; but none can tell at what moment the long quiescent may start into the most vigorous activity. Was it not all at once, after a long period of quietude, that Jesus came forth with a sudden outburst of miraculous energy and teaching wisdom? It is precisely those who have been long *dead* in trespasses and sins who sometimes startle the world by a sudden exuberance of the Divine life within them.

II. THE SEETHING POT. Here again is the exhibition of energy, and a sudden and irresistible change from quiet into furious and threatening movement. A pot boiling over with the vehemence of the fire under it, is an excellent emblem of how God can stir up his destroying wrath against the rebellious. What can be quieter than the water as it lies in the pot? what quieter than the fuel before it is kindled? and yet the light touch of a very small flame sends fuel and water into activity, and that activity soon rises into fury. The water that only a few minutes ago was still and cold is now turbulent and scalding. Just in the same way, God can take these "families of the kingdoms of the north," and make them the instruments of his wrath and chastisement, little conscious as they are of all the use to which they are being put. Everywhere in close proximity to us there are *latent* forces of destruction, and these with startling rapidity may become *patent*. Consider how soon the beautiful and cheering heavens may be filled with the elements of deadly storm.—Y.

Ver. 17.—*The consequence of unreasonable fear.* God has already exhorted Jeremiah to courage, and given him the strongest assurances of his own unfailing presence. But now he adds *warning.* Fear of the enemies of God will bring not only suffering but shame. The man who goes out to fight for his country, and turns in cowardice on the day of battle, only escapes the enemy to die a disgraceful death at the hands of his own people. To meet the threatenings of men, we must have in our hearts not only the strength of God but the *fear* of God. Those who turn from the weapons of God's enemies, whom in God's strength they should meet and conquer, find God himself in arms against them. He himself visibly and signally confounds the unfaithful, and thus even in the unfaithfulness of the messenger he who sends him is all the more honoured. As yet, of course, Jeremiah had not been tried, and all through his prophecies there is no sign that personal fear ever entered his mind. He had a very sensitive nature; he was often, almost continually one may say, the subject of depressing emotion, but the fear of no man, however dignified and powerful that man might be, deterred him from a plain exposure of his misdoings. And yet, although the prophet did not fall into unfaithfulness, it was well to warn him beforehand. Warning never comes unsuitably to any servant of God. He who stands should never take it amiss if he be exhorted to take heed lest he fall. And all the securing words with which God follows up the warning here do not make that warning one whit less needful. The prophet was to become like a fortress, as far as God could surround him with protection; but all the protection would avail him nothing, if he became careless as to his own believing connection with God. When faith fails, the whole spiritual man becomes vulnerable, and to become vulnerable soon leads to being actually wounded.—Y.

Vers. 1—3.—*A protracted ministry.* The ministry of Jeremiah attracts attention because of its length, the varied scenes amidst which it was carried on, and the external aspect of failure worn by it from first to last. May there not be in these and other respects a moral attaching to it for those who in distant ages can regard it as a whole, and in connection with the subsequent Divine evolution of events of which it spoke? Contrast it with that of John the Baptist.

I. ITS BACKGROUND OF CIRCUMSTANCE. Five reigns: for the most part brief; two of them ridiculously or tragically so. Beginning in a fitful flush of religious enthusiasm, and ending in a long and shameful captivity. Foreign politics were unusually interesting. The Medo-Babylonian overthrow of Syria was about to take place when he began; in the twenty-third year of his ministry Nebuchadnezzar laid the foundation of Babylonian empire in the victory of Carchemish, in which Israel was subdued, and universal rule passed into his hands; the invasion of Judæa followed in four years, and in the eleventh year of Zedekiah Jerusalem was taken. Personally his had been a chequered career. For twenty-two years comparatively obscure; for the most part probably at Anathoth. But towards the end of this period he came to Jerusalem. We find him in the temple (ch. vii. 2); in the gates of the city (ch. xvii. 19); in prison (ch. xxxii. 2); in the king's house (ch. xxii. 1; xxxvii. 17); and then at times in Egypt. There are two traditions as to his death—one that he was stoned by the Jews in their settlement at Tahapanes, in Egypt; the other that Nebuchadnezzar, having in the twenty-seventh year of his reign conquered Egypt, took him and Baruch with him to Babylon. In any case, he probably lived to an extreme age.

II. ITS MESSAGE. To warn against idolatry, by exposing its real nature and declaring its consequences. But through all and beyond all, to declare the indestructibleness of the kingdom of God, the certain advent of "The Lord our Righteousness," and the ultimate glory and happiness of a redeemed and purified people. Of scarce any other prophet can it be said that his predictions were so absolutely, and to present perception hopelessly future. Yet is his tone on this account none the less believing and confident.

III. ITS DIVINE SIGNIFICANCE. The "burden" of Jeremiah is identical from reign to reign, although the illustrative and occasioning circumstances vary. May we not say that: 1. *The personality of the prophet had a place in the Divine intention?* Certain we are that its influence was second only to that of his words, if even to that. His astonishment, sorrow, hope, etc., are all instructive and remarkable. 2. *The word of God has to deal with the continuity and development of error, and will outlast it.* The best antidote to error is the healthful development of truth. There is no phase of depravity, transgression, or unbelief for which the Word of God has not, in its historic evolution, some doctrine, reproof, correction, or instruction in righteousness. Revealed through human lips and lives by the operation of the Holy Spirit, it is a living, manifold growth, intimately associated with the vicissitudes of that human life it has to correct and redeem. There can never be a time when the gospel will have no word for the inquiring, wondering, suffering, sinning, unbelieving spirit of man. 3. *The ministry of the prophet was a visible sign of the Divine long-suffering.* "But to Israel he saith, All day long I have stretched forth my hands unto a disobedient and gainsaying people" (Rom. x. 21; Isa. lxv. 2). "O faithless and perverse generation, how long shall I be with you? how long shall I suffer you?" (Matt. xvii. 17).—M.

Vers. 4—10.—*The call of the prophet.* As these are elements both ordinary and extraordinary in the prophetic office, so preparation, etc., for it must be of both kinds. Much that may be said of it will be applicable to all other service in God's Church; and there will be some conditions and circumstances that must necessarily be peculiar and abnormal. The behaviour, too, of one called to such a high office must ever be interesting to observers.

I. THE SPIRIT IN WHICH SUCH AN OFFICE SHOULD BE ASSUMED. Like Moses and others of whom we read, Jeremiah was of a backward and retiring disposition. It required insistance and remonstrance on the part of Jehovah to persuade him to undertake the task. His low thoughts of himself as contrasted with the mighty office to which he was called, held him back. There are some things that come most gracefully when they are spontaneous. The general duty, love, and service, owing by the creature to the Creator, etc., are of this kind. But for special work and appointment, requiring great qualifications and especial help of God, modesty and hesitation are a recommendation rather than otherwise. Our question, pointed first of all homewards, should be, "Who is sufficient for these things?" A feeling like this is helpful and preparative, as leading to the perception of the true strength and fitness that come from God, and to a constant dependence upon him. Many long idly for "some great thing to do," others hesitate because the thing is too great.

II. THE MANNER IN WHICH GOD PREPARES MEN FOR EXTRAORDINARY SERVICE IN HIS CHURCH. Where direction and impulse are needed revelation is made. The spirit of the prophet is not left in doubt. A hesitating, vacillating prophet were a worthless messenger to the faithless. Revelation is therefore made to him of: 1. *His anticipative choice in the counsels of God.* This predestinating grace of God is a frequent assertion of the Old Testament. It is a mystery we cannot fathom; but is consistent with the free choice of the subject addressed. It has its effect in the voluntary acceptance of the appointment through persuasion and appeal. A discovery of this nature can only be for the few, who are called to especial responsibilities, etc., and has no reference to the general demands of duty, affection, zeal, which address themselves to all. 2. *Future Divine evidence, protection, and inspiration.* God will be with him, and will fit him for all he has to do. So Christ to his disciples, "Lo, I am with you alway, even unto the end of the world" (Matt. xxviii. 20). This is to meet the exigencies of Divine service, and is not intended for personal aims and ends. Many a lowly worker in the Master's service is thereby endued with irresistible power. It is a conviction for which we are encouraged to seek grounds and assurances. 3. *Authority amongst the nations to destroy and to restore.* This is a moral investment. Just as God enforces truth and righteousness with accompanying mysterious sanctions, so he clothes his messenger with an authority the consciences of men will recognize even when their perversity of will inclines them to disobey.

How much of this spirit of certitude and conviction is needed for the ordinary life of the Christian? Have we the measure of it we require? or are we inefficient and useless because of our lack of it? There can be no question that such a spirit is inculcated by Christianity, and that reasonable grounds are afforded us all upon which to be thoroughly persuaded in our own mind. Let us act upon our deepest convictions and most unalterable certainties. This is the only way to attain to a sound apprehension of Divine things, and an efficient condition of service.—M.

Ver. 11.—"*What seest thou?*" (cf. Amos vii. 8; viii. 2; Zech. iv. 2; v. 2). The seer is encouraged and impelled to the exercise of his gifts. His first duty is plain, viz. to test his own powers of vision; and next, to ponder the significance of what he sees. So the spiritually endowed are summoned to the performance of the special work to which they have been called; and the newly discovered gift lifts them into a new sphere of responsibility and action.

I. GOD-GIVEN GIFTS ARE A STEWARDSHIP TO BE EXERCISED WITH THE UTMOST CAREFULNESS AND ENDEAVOUR.

II. WE CANNOT TELL HOW HIGHLY WE ARE ENDOWED UNTIL WE TRY OURSELVES TO THE UTMOST; AND THE BEST GIFTS MAY BE IMPROVED BY CULTIVATION.

III. THE WELFARE OF MULTITUDES MAY DEPEND UPON THE FAITHFULNESS OF ONE. Of many it might be asked, "Do they see at all?" Vision is a Divine gift to those who are to be leaders of men; and in lesser measure is given to all for their salvation if they will but open their eyes.—M.

Vers. 12—16.—*Hastening ills.* (For the first fig, cf. Matt. xxiv. 32.) The vision of the prophet is twofold, viz. a wakeful almond rod, and a boiling pot. They are symbols of quick accomplishment and violent invasion. As the almond rod is wakeful or ready to sprout when planted, and "first to wake from the sleep of winter," so the evils prepared by God will be quickly brought to pass. The boiling pot would seem to be the Chaldeans, who invaded Israel from the north. As swiftly and violently as the pot boils over, so will God make the wrath of men to praise him. The ills are swiftly approaching, but they are self-produced by Israel. When we compare this statement with the forgiving character of God, we must feel how great the sin and the provocation that could so move him. Yet on the very edge of his destroying vengeance he remembers mercy, and will have his people repent. Notice—

I. SINNERS MUST NOT CONCLUDE THAT THEY ARE SAFE BECAUSE OF PRESENT IMMUNITY. Jeremiah was as the eye of Israel just opened to the impending dangers. Many would even now reject his message; but the warning is given: 1. Through an intensely sensitive mind, that it may produce a vivid impression upon the imagination and heart of those who hear the prophet. 2. Seasonably, that although but a short time remains, there may be opportunity of repentance and reform.

II. GOD BEGINS THE CHASTISEMENT OF HIS PEOPLE GENTLY, BUT IF THEY REPENT NOT HE WILL INCREASE AND HASTEN HIS JUDGMENTS UNTIL THE EVIL IS WHOLLY AT AN END. The first emblem is one of rapid yet natural development; it is otherwise indefinite. The second is more suggestive of punishment and destruction. The first speaks only of such punishment as may be needed from time to time, and of the unceasing vigilance of the offended God; the second is sudden, overwhelming, and beyond all reckoning or measurement.

III. IDOLATRY IS THE SIN OF WHICH GOD IS MOST INTOLERANT. It is the transfer of affection and trust to an unworthy object, and an insult to God and degrading to themselves. They who indulge in it are warned that their punishment will be constant and rapidly successive; and that they are on the brink of signal, terrible manifestation of Divine wrath.—M.

Vers. 4—10.—*The prophet's call.* We see in the case of Jeremiah a striking instance of a man constrained by force of circumstance and by a Divine call to occupy a position and to do a kind of work for which he was not naturally either qualified or disposed. Of a highly sensitive and timid nature, a tender heart, a desponding spirit, he was inclined to mourn in secret over the abounding evils of the time rather than publicly to rebuke them. But as soon as the Divine summons comes to him, he "confers not with flesh and blood," he forgets his fears and infirmities, and for forty long years patiently withstands the tide of iniquity and adversity—a noble example of blended tenderness and strength. In this account of the prophet's call, note—

I. GOD'S SOVEREIGNTY IN THE RAISING UP OF MEN TO DO HIS WORK. Jeremiah was "known" and "sanctified"—dedicated by God to his sacred office—before his birth. His "ordination," appointment, now is but the fulfilling of an antecedent Divine purpose and choice. Most of the illustrious men of old bear some conspicuous mark of such Divine election upon them, *e.g.* Moses, Gideon, Samson, Cyrus. St. Paul devoutly recognized it in himself, in spite of all his blind hostility to the name of Christ in former years (Gal. i. 15). We fail too often to take sufficient note of this mystery of God's foreknowledge and predetermination underlying the progress of the kingdom of truth and righteousness in the world. And yet we understand its history, we get at the heart and core of its meaning, only so far as we look through all surface appearances and, holding fast to the equally sure principles of human freedom and responsibility, discern the will that works out steadily, through chosen instruments, its own eternal purpose.

II. THE SHRINKING OF A LOWLY SPIRIT FROM A POSITION OF EXTRAORDINARY DIFFICULTY AND DANGER. "Ah, Lord God! behold, I cannot speak, for I am a child." This was the honest expression of conscious personal unfitness. 1. *The feeling was very honourable to him.* Who that knows himself would not tremble on being summoned to such a work? To take up a solemn responsibility with a light heart and easy self-confidence is the mark of a vain spirit that courts rebuke. He who has any true sense of the greatness of his mission from God will often

" Lie contemplating his own unworthiness."

2. *It was a sign of his real fitness for the work.* Humility is the basis of all that is great and good in human character and deed. "God resisteth the proud, but giveth grace unto the humble." The cry, "Who is sufficient for these things?" is a symptom of inherent nobleness and slumbering power. Jeremiah's feeling that he was "but a child," prepared him the better to become the representative of the Divine majesty and the vehicle of Divine strength.

III. THE SPIRITUAL CONSTRAINT OF WHICH ALL TRUE SERVANTS OF GOD ARE CONSCIOUS. The prophetic inspiration came upon him and compelled him to deliver his message. "The word of the Lord was in his heart as a burning fire shut up in his bones, ... and he could not stay " (ch. xx. 9). A Divine commission thus asserting itself in the inward consciousness of him who received it, might well be called the " burden of the Lord." Great reformers, preachers, missionaries, martyrs, have ever been moved by some such Divine afflatus. So felt Peter and John before the Jewish Council : " We cannot but speak the things which we have seen and heard " (Acts iv. 20). So felt St. Paul : " Necessity is laid upon me ; yea, woe is unto me, if I preach not the gospel " (1 Cor. ix. 16). " Say not, I am a child : for thou shalt go to all that I shall send thee, and whatsoever I command thee thou shalt speak." He must " speak " who is thus commanded ; he must " go " who is thus sent.

IV. THE COURAGE AND STRENGTH WITH WHICH GOD ENDOWS ALL WHO THUS OBEY HIS BIDDING. The ministry of Jeremiah is a signal example of the way in which the grace of God may clothe [the most timid spirit with dauntless energy and victorious power. He will never be " afraid of the faces of men," who knows that the Lord is with him. The fear of God casts out all other fear. Many a " little child " has thus become preternaturally brave ; " out of weakness made strong." The history of the kingdom of God among men abounds with illustrations of the way in which he " chooses the weak things of the world to confound the mighty." And every patient, heroic Christian life bears witness to the sufficiency of his grace. You can glory even in infirmities, reproaches, necessities, and distresses, if the " power of Christ " does but rest upon you (2 Cor. xii. 9, 10).

V. THE MASTERY OF TRUTH OVER ALL THE HOSTILE POWERS OF THE WORLD. Jeremiah was " set over the nations and over the kingdoms," not as a prince, but as a prophet ; not as wielding any form of mere brute force, but as the instrument of that silent energy of truth that casts down the strongholds of Satan in every land. His word was " like a fire and like a hammer that breaketh the rock in pieces " (ch. xxiii. 29). Divine truth is the mightiest of all forces alike to " root out and to pull down, ... to build and to plant." The sovereignty of the world is his of whom it is written, " He shall smite the earth with the rod of his mouth, and with the breath of his lips shall he slay the wicked " (Isa. xi. 4). The " many crowns " are on the head of him whose " Name is called The Word of God."—W.

EXPOSITION.

CHAPTER II.

The second chapter forms the introduction of a group of discourses (ch. ii.—vi.), which should be read together. It is called by Ewald (and the position of the prophecy favours this view) the first oracle which Jeremiah delivered in public ("oracle" is, in fact, the nearest English equivalent to those two remarkable Hebrew synonyms, *massā* and *nĕŭm*—especially for the latter). This would bring it into the thirteenth year of the reign of Josiah (see ch. i. 3), though of course we cannot be sure that references to a later period may not have been inserted afterwards. It is, obviously, only a summary of the prophet's spoken words which we have in this most impressive discourse. In order to appreciate it, we must bear in mind the external political relations and the internal religious condition of the kingdom of Judah. These have been already touched upon in the general introduction. Suffice it to remind the reader that Josiah's reformation—in the strict sense of the word—did not begin till the eighteenth year of that king's reign; and that the state of things was at this time complicated by a dangerous alliance with that power against whose religion the teaching of the prophets of Jehovah was a continual protest (on the Egyptian alliance, comp. Ewald, 'History of Israel,' iv. 218). The first section of the prophecy is a general introduction, already full of serious charges against the people (vers. 1—9); in the second, the special occasion of the discourse is declared in the form of a question, and the sin referred to is rebuked (vers. 10—19); in the third, Judah's inveterate idolatry is denounced, and the disappointment and ruin to which it led candidly pointed out (vers. 20—28); and in the fourth, "half in earnest and half in ironical satire" (Ewald), the prophet points the moral of this foolish Egyptian fever which has seized upon rulers and people (vers. 29—37).

It is always interesting to notice how later inspired writers hasten to do honour to their predecessors. Originality is not an object with the prophets, but rather the developing and adapting the truths long ago "delivered." The whole group of prophecies to which ch. ii. belongs contains numerous points of contact, in ideas or phraseology, with the song of Moses (Deut. xxxii.). The following have been indicated :—Cf. ver. 5 with Deut. xxxii. 4; vers. 11, 12 with Deut. xxxii. 1, 21; ver. 20 with Deut. xxxii. 15; vers. 26—28 with Deut. xxxii. 6, 18, 37, 38; ver. 31 with Deut. xxxii. 5; ch. iii. 19 with Deut. xxxii. 6; ch. iv. 22 and v. 21 with Deut. xxxii. 6; ch. v. 7 with Deut. xxxii. 15; ch. v. 14 with Deut. xxxii. 22; ch. v. 28 with Deut. xxxii. 15; ch. vi. 11 with Deut. xxxii. 25; ch. vi. 15 with Deut. xxxii. 35; ch. vi. 19, 30 with Deut. xxxii. 18, 19.

Ver. 1.—**Moreover**; literally, *and*. The introductory formula agrees with ch. i. 4. We have as it were two parallel prophecies (ch. i. 4, etc., and ch. ii. 1, etc.); both branching out of the original chronological statement in ch. i. 2 (see Introduction).

Ver. 2.—**In the ears of Jerusalem.** Presumably Jeremiah had received his call at Anathoth (comp. ch. i. 1). **I remember thee**, etc.; rather, *I remember for thy good the kindness of thy youth.* It is an open question whether the "kindness" spoken of is that of God towards the people, or of the people towards God. The usage of the Hebrew (*khésed*) admits of either acceptation; comp. for the first, Ps. v. 7, xxxvi. 5, and many other passages; for the second, Hos. vi. 4, 6 (in ver. 6 rendering for "mercy," "goodness") and Isa. lvii. 1 (rendering "men of piety"). But the context, which dwells so strongly on the oblivion into which the Divine benefits had been allowed to pass, is decidedly in favour of the first view. How beautiful is this condescending language! Jehovah's past feelings come back to him; at least, so it appears to the believer, when God lets the light of his countenance shine forth again (comp. ch. xxxi. 20; Hos. ix. 10). He even condescends to overlook the weakness and inconsistency of the Israel of antiquity. He idealizes it (*i.e.* Jeremiah is permitted to do so). This is in harmony with other prophetic passages (see Isa. i. 26 ("as at the first"); Hos. xi. 1, 3, 4; Ezek. xvi. 6—14). The figure of the bride recurs constantly (see Hos. ii. 19, 20; Isa. liv. 4, 5; Ezek. xvi. 8). **Thine espousals**; rather, *thy bridal state.* **When thou wentest after me** (comp. Deut. viii. 2, "all the way which Jehovah thy

God led thee these forty years in the wilderness").

Ver. 3.—**Israel was holiness,** etc. Israel was a consecrated people (comp. Exod. xix. 5, 6; Deut. vii. 6; xiv. 2; xxvi. 19). Isaiah, fond as he is of the phrase "Israel's Holy One," does not expressly enforce the correlative truth, as Jeremiah does here. **The firstfruits of his increase;** rather, *his firstfruits of increase.* Israel is compared to the firstfruits (*rēshīth*) of the land, which were devoted to the house of the Lord (Exod. xxiii. 19; Numb. xviii. 12, 13). So in Amos vi. 1, the title given him is "the chief [margin, 'firstfruits'] of the nations" (in ch. xxxi. 7, a synonymous and cognate word, *rōsh*, takes the place of *reshīth* for "chief"). **All that devour him shall offend;** rather, *all that ate him incurred guilt,* or became guilty of a trespass. Foreigners were forbidden to eat of consecrated things; by breaking this law they became guilty of a "trespass," having invaded the rights of Jehovah (Lev. xxii. 10, 15, 16). The word for "trespass" is the same as that rendered "guilt."

Ver. 5.—**What iniquity,** etc.; rather, *what unrighteousness,* etc. (comp. Deut. xxxii. 4, "a God of faithfulness and without unrighteousness," alluding to the "covenant" between Jehovah and Israel). God's condescending grace (his *'anāvāh,* Ps. xviii. 36). As if he were under an obligation to Israel (comp. Micah vi. 3, etc.; Isa. v. 3). **Vanity;** *i.e.* the idols; literally, *a breath* (so ch. x. 15; xiv. 22; xvi. 19). **Are become vain.** The whole being of man is affected by the want of solid basis to his religion (comp. ch. xxiii. 16; Ps. cxv. 8); and the evident allusion to our passage in Rom. i. 21 (St. Paul has ἐματαιώθησαν, as Septuagint here). The clause is verbally repeated in 2 Kings xvii. 15, with reference to the ten tribes.

Ver. 6.—**Neither said they,** etc.; as their children's children were forced by stress of trouble to say (Isa. lxiii. 11; see note). **A land of deserts and of pits.** The first phrase applied to the region through which the Israelites passed ("a wilderness") was vague, and might mean merely pastureland. The remainder of the description, however, shows that "wilderness" is here meant, as often (*e.g.* Isa. xxxv. 1; l. 2), in the sense of "desert." Though recent travellers have shown that the Sinaitic peninsula is not by any means universally a "desert," and that in ancient times it was still less so, it is not unnatural that an agricultural people should regard it as a most inhospitable region, and should even idealize its terrors (comp. Deut. viii. 15). "Pits," *i.e.* rents and fissures in the soil, in which the unwary traveller might lose his life (ch. xviii. 20, 22).

Ver. 7.—**A plentiful country.** "A Carmel land," as it were (so Payne Smith). "Carmel" is strictly an appellative noun, meaning "garden-land," *i.e.* land planted with vines and other choice plants. So ch. iv. 26; Isa. xxix. 17; xxxvii. 24.

Ver. 8.—**The priests,** etc. The blame principally falls on the three leading classes (as in ver. 26; Micah iii. 11). First on the priests who "handle the Law," *i.e.* who have a traditional knowledge of the details of the Law, and teach the people accordingly (Deut. xvii. 9—11; xxxiii. 10; ch. xviii. 18; see also on ch. viii. 8); next on the "pastors," or "shepherds" (in the Homeric sense), the civil and not the spiritual authorities; so generally in the Old Testament (see ch. iii. 15; x. 21; xxii. 22; xxv. 34; Zech. x. 3; xi. 5, 8, 16; Isa. xliv. 28); and lastly on the prophets, who sought their inspiration, not from Jehovah (comp. note on ver. 30), but from Baal. **To prophesy by** (by means of) **Baal,** or rather, *the Baal,* implies that prophecy is due to an impulse from the supernatural world; that it is not an objectifying of the imaginations of the prophet himself. Even the Baal prophets yielded to an impulse from without, but how that impulse was produced the prophet does not tell us. We are told in 1 Kings xxii. 19—23, that even prophets of Jehovah could be led astray by a "lying spirit;" much more presumably could prophets of the Baal. *The Baal* is here used as a representative of the idol-gods, in antithesis to Jehovah; sometimes "Baalim," or the Baals, is used instead (*e.g.* ver. 23; ch. ix. 13), each town or city having its own Baal ("lord"). Things that **do not profit.** A synonym for idols (comp. ch. xvi. 19; Isa. xliv. 9; 1 Sam. xii. 21). An enlightened regard for self-interest is encouraged by the religion of the Bible, at any rate educationally. Contrast Comtism.

Ver. 9.—**I will yet plead,** etc. Repeated acts of rebellion call forth repeated objurgations and punishments. **With your children's children.** For God "visits the iniquity of the fathers upon the children" (Exod. xx. 5).

Ver. 10.—Justification of Jehovah's judicial action towards Judah. Consider the heinousness of the offence. **Pass over**— rather, *pass over to*—**the isles of Chittim;** *i.e.* the islands and maritime countries of the West, represented by Cyprus (see on Gen. x. 4). For the wide use of Chittim, comp. Numb. xxiv. 24; Dan. xi. 30). **Kedar,** in the narrower sense, is a large tribe of Arabian origin, whose haunts were between Arabia Petræa and Babylonia. Here, however, it is used in a wider sense for the Arab tribes in general (so ch. xlix. 28; Isa. xxi. 16, 17).

Ver. 11.—**Hath a nation changed their gods?** *Has any heathen nation ever changed its idol-god for another?* The prophet clearly implies a negative answer; and yet it must be admitted that the adoption of a new religion, under the pressure of conquest or a higher foreign civilization is not an unknown phenomenon in the ancient world. **Glory;** *i.e.* source of all outward prosperity (comp. Ps. iii. 3, "my Glory, and the Lifter up of my head"). Religion was, in fact, the root of national life in antiquity; contrast our own division between the sacred and the secular! Jehovah elsewhere receives the title "the Pride of Israel"—Authorized Version, rather weakly, "the Excellency of Israel"—(Amos viii. 7; Hos. v. 5. Comp. the parallel passages, Ps. cvi. 20; Rom. i. 23).

Ver. 12.—**Be astonished.** "Be appalled" would more nearly express the force of the Hebrew (so ch. xviii. 16; xix. 8). **Be ye very desolate;** literally, *become dry;* i.e. not so much "shrivel and roll up" (on the analogy of Isa. xxxiv. 4), as "become stiff with horror."

Ver. 13.—**Two evils.** Israel has not merely offended, like the heathen, by idolatry, but by deserting the only God who can satisfy the needs of human nature. **The fountain of living waters.** So ch. xvii. 13 (comp. Ps. xxxvi. 9). *Fountain;* literally, *tank* or *reservoir.* Such reservoirs were "dug in the ground (see on ch. vi. 7), and chiefly intended for storing living waters, *i.e.* those of springs and rivulets" (Payne Smith). **Cisterns, broken cisterns.** A cistern, by its very nature, will only hold a limited amount, and the water "collected from clay roofs or from marly soil, has the colour of weak soapsuds, the taste of the earth or the stable." Who would prefer such an impure supply to the sweet, wholesome water of a fountain? But these cisterns cannot even be depended upon for this poor, turbid drink. They are "broken," like so many even of the best rock-hewn cisterns (Thomson, 'The Land and the Book,' p. 287). How fine a description of the combined attractiveness and disappointingness of heathen religions, qualities the more striking in proportion to the scale on which the religious problem is realized (*e.g.* in Hinduism)!

Vers. 14—19.—*Israel's punishment and its cause.*

Ver. 14.—**Is Israel a servant?** The speaker is evidently the prophet, who exclaims in surprise at the view which his prophetic insight opens to him: "quasi de re novâ et absurdâ sciscitatur" (Calvin). For Israel is a member of Jehovah's family; he is not a servant (except in the same high sense as in Isa. xl.—liii., where "servant" is virtually equivalent to "representative"), but rather in the highest degree a free man, for he is Jehovah's "firstborn son" (Exod. iv. 22). How is it, then, that he is dragged away into captivity like a slave who has never known

freedom? The view of some, that "servant" means "servant of Jehovah" (comp. ch. xxx. 10), and that the question therefore is to be answered in the affirmative, is less natural. "Servant," by itself, never has this turning; and there is a precisely similar term in the discourse at ver. 31, where the negative answer of the question does not admit of a doubt.

Ver. 15.—**The young lions,** etc. A fresh figure, and a most natural one in Judæa (comp. 1 Sam. xvii. 34); already applied to the Assyrians by Isaiah (v. 29, 30). **Burned;** rather, *made ruinous* (comp. "ruinous heaps," 2 Kings xix. 25).

Ver. 16.—**Also the children of Noph,** etc. This is the climax of the calamity. *Noph,* called Moph in the Hebrew text of Hos. ix. 6, is generally identified with Memphis (after the Septuagint), which was called in the inscriptions Mennufr, or "the good abode," but may possibly be Napata, the Nap of the inscriptions, the residency of the Ethiopian dynasty (De Rougé). **Tahapanes.** The Hebrew form is *Takhpanes* or *Tahkpankhes.* This was a fortified frontier town on the Pelusiot arm of the Nile, called in Greek Daphnæ (Herod., ii. 20), or Taphnæ (Septuagint here). **Have broken,** etc.; rather, *shall break,* or (for the pointing in the Hebrew Bible requires this change) *shall feed off* (or *depasture*). From this verse onwards, Judah is personified as a woman, as appears from the suffixes in the Hebrew. Baldness was a great mark of disgrace (2 Kings ii. 23; ch. xlviii. 45). There is a striking parallel to this passage in Isa. vii. 18—20, where, in punishment of the negotiations of Ahaz with Assyria, the prophet threatens an invasion of Judah both by Assyria and by Egypt, and employs the very same figure (see ver. 20). So here, the devastation threatened by Jeremiah is the punishment of the unhallowed coquetting with the Egyptian power of which the Jewish rulers had been recently guilty. The fact which corresponds to this prediction is the defeat of Josiah at Megiddo, and the consequent subjugation of Judah (2 Kings xxiii. 29). The abruptness with which ver. 16 follows upon ver. 15 suggests that some words have fallen out of the text.

Ver. 17.—**Hast not thou procured this?** rather, *Is it not this that doth procure it unto thee (namely) that thou hast forsaken,* etc.? or, *Is it not thy forsaking Jehovah that procureth thee this?* **When he led thee by the way.** The prophet thinks, perhaps, of the rebellion of the forefathers of Israel, who too soon ceased to "go after" Jehovah (comp. ver. 2), and whose fickleness was imitated but too well by their descendants. This view is favoured by the phraseology of Deut. i. 33; viii. 2, 15. But we may, if we prefer it, explain "by (or, rather, *in*) the way," on the analogy of the promise in ch. xxxi. 9, "I will lead them . . . in a straight way," *i.e.* I will grant them an uninterrupted course of prosperity. The omission of the adjective in the present passage may be paralleled by Ps. xxv. 8, "Therefore will he instruct sinners in the (right) way."

Ver. 18.—**What hast thou to do in the way of Egypt?** rather, *with the way to Egypt.* Isaiah (xxx. 2—5; xxxi. 1) and Hosea (vii. 11, 16) had already inveighed against an Egyptian alliance. The name given by Manasseh to his son and successor (Amon) suggests that at one period in his reign an Egyptian policy was in the ascendant, which coincides with the tradition preserved in 2 Chron. xxxiii. 11, of an Assyrian captivity of Manasseh. Jehoiakim at a later period was a vassal of Egypt (2 Kings xxiii. 31, 35). **To drink the waters;** taking up the idea of the second clause of ver. 13. **Sihor,** or Shihor, occurs again in Isa. xxiii. 3, as a name of the Nile. It properly means, not so much "the black" as "the dark grey" (connected with *shakhar*, the morning grey), from the colour of the water. Rosenmüller's contrast between the muddy waters of foreign streams and the "fountain of living waters" is uncalled for; besides, the Nile water has always been held in high esteem. The Septuagint has Γηών, *i.e.* Gihon, also a name of the Nile according to Ecclus. xxiv. 27. **The way of**—rather, *to*—**Assyria.** It is true that Assyria was, to say the least, powerless to interfere for good or for evil, when these words were written. But in ver. 5 the prophet has already warned us that his complaints are partly retrospective. It would seem that the Assyrian party from time to time gained the upper hand over the Egyptian in the councils of the State. Or perhaps the prophet may refer to the Quixotic fidelity to Assyria of Josiah (see below on ver. 36). **The river;** *i.e.* the Euphrates, "the great river" (Gen. xv. 18). Babylonia it should be remembered, was in nominal subjection to Assyria; the Euphrates was the boundary between Syria and Palestine on the one hand, and Assyria—here the Assyrio-Babylonian region—on the other.

Ver. 19.—**Shall correct . . . shall reprove;** rather, *chastise . . . punish.* It is a constantly renewed punishment which follows the ever-repeated offence.

Ver. 20.—Here a new section begins. **I have broken . . . burst.** This is, grammatically, a possible rendering, but inconsistent with the second person in **thou saidst,** unless indeed (with Ewald) we suppose that something has fallen out of the text between the first and the second clauses of the verse. The best critics, except Ewald and Dr. Payne Smith, are agreed that we should follow the

Septuagint and Vulgate in rendering "thou hast broken . . . (and) burst." This does not, strictly speaking, imply a new reading of the text, for *ti* was the old form of the suffix of the 2nd pers. fem. sing.; there is a precisely similar case in Micah iv. 13. It is a true description of the history of Israel before the exile. It would almost seem as if there was a fusion of two races among the Israelites, and that the smaller but nobler stock supplied all the great men in the sphere of religion; just as in Florence, most of the men who have illustrated her annals bear names of Teutonic origin. So we might argue, if we wished to explain the Biblical history from purely natural causes. But God (to apply the Caliph Omar's words) "knoweth his own." **Bands** (see on ch. v. 5). **I will not transgress.** This is the translation of the marginal reading in the Hebrew Bible, which, though implied also in the Targum, is probably a conjecture of the Jewish critics. The text reading (also that of the Septuagint and the Syriac) is, "I will not serve," (equivalent to "I will not be a slave any longer"). Obviously this does not harmonize with the rendering "I have broken," etc., in the first clause (unless, with Dr. Payne Smith, we explain "I will not serve" as virtually equivalent to "I will still serve my idol-gods"); hence the Jewish critics, by just adding a κέραια (Matt. v. 18), changed "serve" into "transgress." They did not venture to alter the next clause, which, quite as much as the first, presupposes the reading "serve" (see next note). **When**—rather, *for*—**upon every high hill,** etc. Bare, treeless heights were favourite spots for sacrifices, especially for Baal; groves, and leafy trees in general, for the lascivious rites of Asherah and Ashtoreth. The apparently extreme statement of the prophet is not to be minimized. Travellers still tell us of vestiges of ancient and doubtless pre-Christian idolatrous worship still visible on almost every attractive spot in the open country in Palestine. **Under every green tree.** We have no single word to convey the "fluid" meaning of this expressive word. It combines, in fact, the senses of pliant, sappy, leafy (comp. note on ch. xi. 16). **Thou wanderest;** rather, *thou wast stretching thyself out.*

Ver. 21.—**A noble vine.** Jeremiah means the choicest kind of Oriental vine, called *sorek* (from the dark-red colour of its grapes), and mentioned again in Isa. v. 2. The figure of the vine is one endeared to us by its association especially with our Lord; it was endeared to the Jews by the annual festivities of the vintage. The sacred writers are never afraid of its palling on the ear by repetition (comp. ch. v. 10; vi. 9; xii. 10; Isa. v. 1—7; xxvii. 2, 3; Ezek. xvii. 6; Ps. lxxx. 8—16). **A right seed;** *i.e.* a vine-shoot of the genuine sort. "Seed" for "shoot," as in Isa. xvii. 11 (comp. ver. 10). **The degenerate plant**; rather, *degenerate shoots* (if at least the text is right).

Ver. 22.—**Nitre** does not mean the substance which now bears that name, but "natron," a mineral alkali, deposited on the shores and on the bed of certain lakes in Egypt, especially those in the Wâdy Natrun (the ancient Nitria, whence came so large a store of precious Syriac manuscripts). In ancient times, this natron was collected to make lye from for washing purposes (comp. Prov. xxv. 20). **Sope**; rather, *potash;* the corresponding vegetable alkali (comp. Isa. i. 25). **Thine iniquity is marked.** So Kimchi and Gesenius (through a doubtful etymology); but the Aramaic use of the word favours the rendering *stained*, i.e. filthy. The word is in the participle, to indicate the permanence of the state (comp. "Will all great Neptune's ocean wash this blood," etc.? 'Macbeth').

Ver. 23.—**How canst thou say**, etc.? This is not a mere rhetorical fiction equivalent to "or if thou shouldst perhaps say," but probably represents an objection really made by the inhabitants of the kingdom of Judah. Their fault was not in neglecting the public worship of Jehovah in his appointed temple, but in superadding to this, idolatrous rites inconsistent with the spiritual religion taught by Jeremiah. The people did not, it seems, regard this as tantamount to "following Baalim," just as some converts to Christianity in our own foreign missions might exclaim against being accused of apostacy, because they secretly carry on certain heathen practices. The prophet, however, applies a more rigorous test to their conduct. **Baalim**; the plural of Baal, used for "other gods" (ch. i. 16; comp. on ver. 8). **Thy way in the valley.** *The valley* in this context can only be that of Hinnom (see on ch. vii. 31), which from the time of Ahaz had been defiled with the rites of "Moloch, horrid king" (see 'Paradise Lost,' i. 392—396). Thou art a **swift dromedary.** Ewald would attach this half of the verse to ver. 24; and there is something to be said for this plan. *Swift dromedary* is, properly speaking, in the vocative. The ardour of the people for idolatry is expressed by the comparison of it to the uncontrollable instinct of brute beasts. The word rendered "dromedary" is in the feminine gender; it means strictly the young she-camel which has not yet had a foal. **Traversing her ways**; rather, *interlacing her ways;* i.e. running backwards and forwards at the impulse of passion.

Ver. 24.—**A wild ass**, etc. The type of wildness and independence (comp. Gen. xvi. 12; Job xxxix. 5—8). That **snuffeth up the wind**; to cool the heat of her passion. In

her occasion . . . in her month; *i.e.* at the pairing-time.

Ver. 25.—**Withhold thy foot**, etc. Hitzig, with unnecessary ingenuity, explains this with reference to the fatiguing practices of the heathen cultus, comparing 1 Kings xviii. 26, where "vain repetitions" of "Baal, Baal," and (as he thinks) barefoot religious dances, are mentioned as parts of the worship of Baal. Umbreit's view, however, is far more natural. "God the true husband exhorts Israel not to run barefoot, and with parched throat, like a shameless adulteress, after strangers" (Payne Smith). **There is no hope**; *i.e.* the exhortation is in vain (so ch. xviii. 12).

Ver. 26.—**Is . . . ashamed.** It is the perfect of prophetic certitude.

Ver. 27.—**And to a stone**, etc. *Stone* ('*ebhen*) is feminine in Hebrew, and therefore addressed as the mother.

Ver. 28.—According to **the number of thy cities**, etc. A remarkable statement, and one that well illustrates the superficial character of Hezekiah's reformation. True, Manasseh's reactionary reign had intervened, but his counter-movement would not have been so successful had it not been attended by the good wishes of the people; and besides, the last years of Manasseh, according to the tradition in 2 Chron. xxxiii. 12—16 were devoted to undoing the mischief of his former life. The force of the prophet's words is strikingly brought out by M. Renan (he led an expedition to Phœnicia), who has shown that every district and every town had a cultus of its own, which often only differed from the neighbouring cultus by words and titles (*nomina, numina*); comp. Baal-Hamon, Baal-Hazor, etc. Dr. Payne Smith well expresses the argument of Jeremiah: "When every city has its special deity, surely among so many there might be found one able to help his worshippers."

Ver. 29.—**Wherefore will ye plead with me?** How can ye be so brazen-faced as to attempt to justify yourselves?

Ver. 30.—**Have I smitten your children.** The cities and towns of Judah are represented as so many mothers, and the populations as their children. It would, no doubt, be more natural to take "children" literally; but then we must read the verb in the next clause, "*Ye* have received," as the Septuagint actually renders. In the former case the "smiting" will refer to all God's "sore judgments"—sword, drought, famine, pestilence; in the latter, to the loss of life in battle. **Your own sword hath devoured your prophets** (comp. 2 Chron. xxiv. 21; 2 Kings xxi. 16). Manasseh's persecution (which extended, according to Josephus, especially to the prophets) may account for the preponderance of "false prophets" referred to in ver. 8 (cf. Matt. xxiii. 29).

Ver. 31.—**0 generation, see ye.** It is doubtful whether *generation* here means "contemporaries" (equivalent to "men of this generation"), or, like γενεά sometimes in the New Testament, a class of men united by moral affinity (comp. Ps. xiv. 5; lxxviii. 8). In the latter case we should rather attach the pronoun in "see ye" to "O generation," and render "O (evil) generation that ye are!" So Hitzig, Keil, and Payne Smith; Ewald and Delitzsch adopt the first rendering. **Have I been a wilderness, etc.?** "Have I not been the source of light and happiness to my people, and of all temporal blessings?" (comp. ch. ii. 6). So the Divine speaker in Isa. xlv. 19, "I said not unto the seed of Jacob, Seek ye me in vain," or more literally, "in chaos" (same word as in Gen. i. 2); "chaos" and "the wilderness" are both images of that which is utterly unremunerative. **A land of darkness.** This is, of course, not literally accurate as a description of the Arabian desert. "Darkness" is here used as a synonym for "misery." Cloud and rain occupy precisely opposite places in the estimation of nomadic and agricultural peoples respectively. "The Bedouins," says an Arabic scholast, "always follow the rain and the places where rain-drops fall;" whereas a townsman of Mecca calls himself "child of the sun." So Indra and Varuna, originally belonging to the cloudy and rainy sky, are in the Vedic hymns endowed with solar traits. It should be added here that it is an old problem, and too difficult a one for us to investigate, whether we should render "the darkness of Jah" (Jehovah) or (as Authorized Version) simply "darkness." The former rendering will mean very great darkness, such as Jehovah sends in judgment (*e.g.* to the Egyptians, Exod. x. 21—23). On this question, see Dr. Ginsburg on Cant. viii. 6 (where a similar doubt exists), Geiger's 'Urschrift und Uebersetzungen der Bibel,' p. 276; Ewald, 'Lehrbuch der Hebräischen Sprache,' § 270 c. **We are lords;** rather, *we have broken loose.* It is, however, a difficult word, which only occurs elsewhere in Gen. xxvi. 40; Hos. xii. 1; Ps. lv. 3.

Ver. 32.—**Or a bride her attire.** The prophet perhaps means the magnificently adorned girdle which the bride wore on her wedding day (comp. Isa. xlix. 18). But the word only occurs again in Isa. iii. 20, and its precise signification is uncertain.

Ver. 33.—**Why trimmest thou thy way?** rather, *How well thou contrivest thy way,* etc.? **Therefore hast thou also taught, etc.** The meaning which floated before our translators seems to be this: "so utterly immoral is thy course of life, that even the worst of

women ['wicked ones' is in the feminine] have been able to learn something from thee" (so the great Dutch scholar, De Dieu, in 1548). But a more natural rendering is, "Therefore [*i.e.* to gain thine ends] thou hast accustomed thy ways to those evil things." *Nemo repente fuit turpissimus.* It required a deliberate "accustoming," or "training" (such is the literal meaning of *limmad*), to produce such a habit (ἕξις) as is here rebuked.

Ver. 34.—**Also in thy skirts, etc.;** or, *there is even found in thy skirts* (or, perhaps, *in thy sleeves*—the wide sleeves of an Eastern mantle). The fact which follows is adduced as the crowning evidence of wickedness. **Blood of the souls** is explained by the statement in Lev. xvii. 11, "The soul of the flesh [*i.e.* of the body] is in the blood;" hence the importance of the blood in the Mosaic sacrifices. The historical reference of this passage of Jeremiah may well be to the persecution of Manasseh, who is said to have "shed innocent blood very much" (2 Kings xxi. 16). It is Judah, no doubt, who is addressed, but the prophets mostly assume the "solidarity" of king and people (analogous to that of a forefather and his posterity); Manasseh, moreover, probably had the support of a large section of the population, at any rate in so far as he favoured the inveterate cultus of the high places or local sanctuaries. **I have not found it by secret search;** rather, *thou hast not found them breaking through* (*houses*). The phraseology agrees with that of Exod. xxii. 2, the law against "breaking through;" it suggests that the houses of all but the highest class in ancient as well as often in modern Palestine, were made of mere sun-dried brick, which could be easily "dug into" (comp. Ezek. xii. 5; Matt. vi. 19, 20, in the Greek). [Lieut. Conder states, it is true, that in hilly districts of Palestine the houses of the villages are built of stone, but he adds that the stone is simply taken from the ruins of the ancient towns.] Burglars caught in the act might be killed (Exod. xxii. 2), but the innocent victims of persecution could not be brought under this category, and hence those who slew them were really guilty of murder. **But upon all these;** rather, *but because of all these things;* i.e. not for any crime, but because of thine apostasy and zeal for the false gods ("these things," as in ch. iii. 7); so Hitzig, Keil, Payne Smith; less naturally De Dieu, "because of those false gods."

Ver. 35.—**Because.** This "because" is misleading; there is no argument, but the statement of a supposed fact. The particle so rendered merely serves to introduce the speech of the Jews (like ὅτι). **Shall turn;** rather, *hath turned.* Judah had so long been undisturbed by any foreign power, that the people fancied the promises of Deuteronomy were being fulfilled, and that they, on their part, had pleased God by their formal obedience (comp. 2 Kings xxii. 17). **I will plead with thee.** Here, as in some other passages (*e.g.* Isa. lxvi. 16; Ezek. xxxviii. 22), the word includes the sense of punishing.

Ver. 36.—**Why gaddest thou about so much**—many render, *Why runnest thou so quickly;* but the verb simply means to "go," and it is enough to refer to foreign embassies, such as are alluded to in this very chapter (ver. 18)—**to change thy way?** The "way" or policy of Judah was "changed," according as the party in power favoured an Egyptian or an Assyrian alliance. **Thou also shalt be ashamed of;** rather, *thou shalt also be brought to shame through.* **As thou art ashamed of Assyria** (correct rendering as before). This is certainly difficult, for in the reign of Josiah it would appear that the political connection with Assyria still continued. Is it possible that Jeremiah, in these words, has in view rather the circumstances of Jehoiakim than those of Josiah? Does he not appear to look back upon Judah's final "putting to shame through Assyria" as a thing of the past? And to what event can this expression refer but to the overthrow of Josiah at Megiddo (so Graf)?

Ver. 37.—**From him;** *i.e.* from Egypt, personified as a man (so whenever a people is referred to; a land is represented as a woman). Egypt was, in fact, the only great power capable of assisting Judah at this time (see Introduction); yet even Egypt, the prophet says, shall disappoint her Jewish allies, for Jehovah has **rejected thy confidences** (*i.e.* the objects of thy confidence). As a matter of fact, "the King of Egypt came not again any more out of his land" after Necho's crushing defeat at Carchemish (2 Kings xxiv. 7; comp. ch. xxxvii. 5).

HOMILETICS.

Vers. 1—3.—*Recollections of the happy past.* It is pleasing to see how the prophet of judgment opens his first oracle with touching reminiscences of the early happy relations between God and his people. Thus the young man connects his new utterances with ancient experience and the old well-tried principles of spiritual religion. Thus, too, he leads the way from thoughts of God's goodness and memories of early devotion to a right condition of reflectiveness and tenderness of heart, in which the revelation of dark truths of the future will be less likely to harden his hearers in rebellion than if they had been spoken abruptly and harshly.

I. MANY OF US, LIKE THE JEWS, MAY BE REMINDED OF A HAPPY PAST. In years of deepening disappointment the sunny days of youth rise up to memory and rebuke the cynical mood which sorrow is too ready to engender. In years of lessening spirituality the holy seasons of early devotion may be recalled to mind to startle us out of our self-complacency. It is well to reflect upon such a past history as that of the Jews. 1. This was marked by *peculiar blessings on God's side.* (1) It was a time when God's love and kindness were felt with all the fresh receptiveness of youth; and (2) it was memorable for remarkable Divine protection and blessing. 2. This was characterized by *great fidelity on the side of Israel.* In spite of frequent murmurings and rebellions, the age of the Exodus had been the heroic age of Israel's national and religious history. (1) The people then followed God with affectionate devotion; they "went after him." (2) They consecrated themselves in purity and in service; "Israel was consecrated unto the Lord." (3) They were the earliest true servants of God— God's "firstfruits." Yet the first may become last (Matt. xx. 16). (4) This devotion was witnessed under trying circumstances. It was "in the wilderness, in a land that was not sown." God's love is sometimes most manifest when outward circumstances are most distressing, and men are often more faithful to God in the wilderness than in the land flowing with milk and honey. What a strange irony of history is this, that though, while passing through the wilderness, the people looked forward to their happiness in the possession of the promised land, after they have had long possession of it they are led to look back on those early homeless wanderings as containing the most blessed age of their existence! But true happiness is ever found, not in external comfort, but in spiritual blessedness. Can we recollect early days when the battle of life was hard, and we longed for the ease which came with success, and now see that there, in that hard battle, our best days were lived, our true blessedness was realized? Such a memory must be full of pathetic suggestions.

II. THE RECOLLECTION OF A HAPPY PAST IS PROFITABLE. 1. *God remembers the past.* Not like the sour censor who remembers only our past faults, but rather like the kind parent who delights to call to mind the goodness of his children's early days, God makes no mention of the sins of the wilderness life, but dwells graciously on its happy features. God remembers our past for our good: (1) as a link of affection after subsequent sin has driven us from him; (2) as an ideal to which he would bring us back; and (3)—still for our good—as a standard by which to measure our present condition, and a just ground for wholesome chastisement. 2. *We are to recollect our happy past.* Israel is reminded of his early days. If we have "lost our first love," it is well that we should know this: (1) that we may see how far we have fallen, and repent (Rev. ii. 4, 5); (2) that the recollection of the blessedness of early devotion may revive the longing for its return; (3) that the consciousness that this was once attained may encourage us to believe that it is a possibility, and therefore may be attained again. *In conclusion,* note: 1. It is foolish simply to regret the happy past. The use of memory is not to give to us profitless melancholy, but to lead us actively to do better for the future. 2. It is a mistake for us to seek *simply* to regain the lost past, because (1) this is gone irrevocably, (2) the new age requires new forms of life, and (3) we should seek better things in the future. The second Adam is better than the first Adam before the fall. The kingdom of heaven is more glorious than the garden of Eden. The ripe Christian is higher in the spiritual life, though he may have fallen in the past, than the innocent child who has never known evil but has not experienced the discipline of life.

Vers. 5—7.—*The ingratitude of sin.* Of the many aspects under which sin may be viewed none is more sad than that of ingratitude to God. Every act of sin is a distinct act of ingratitude; for every such act is an offence against him who has shown to us nothing but love, and from whom we are taking innumerable favours in the very moment of our transgression.

I. THE INGRATITUDE OF SIN IS SEEN IN THE FORGETFULNESS OF GOD'S SAVING MERCY. So the Israelites forget the glorious deliverance from Egypt, and preservation amidst the horrors of the wilderness (ver. 6). God is resorted to in distress only to be ignored, forsaken, insulted, directly rebelled against, when he has effected a deliverance.

II. THE INGRATITUDE OF SIN IS SEEN IN THE IGNORING OF THE PRESENT GOODNESS OF GOD. (Ver. 7.) The Israelites were eating the fruit of the good land which God had given to them while they were rebelling against him. This is even worse than ingratitude for past blessings. Such ingratitude might attempt to plead the excuse of failure of memory; ˌbut ingratitude for present mercies can only arise from gross spiritual blindness or wilful disregard of all claims of justice and affection.

III. THE INGRATITUDE OF SIN IS SEEN IN THE FALSE CHARACTER WHICH IS ASCRIBED TO GOD. God asks, "What unrighteousness have your fathers found in me?" The conduct of the Jews was a direct indictment of the character of God. They deliberately insulted him, and rejected him for heathen deities. Such conduct could only be justified by the discovery that he was not what he claimed to be. After God has revealed himself to men in myriadfold evidences of goodness, there are some who hold, if they do not confess to, such evil conceptions of his character as amount to the basest calumnies of heartless ingratitude.

IV. THE INGRATITUDE OF SIN IS SEEN IN THE CHARACTER OF THE GODS WHO ARE PREFERRED TO JEHOVAH. These are "false" gods. Jews who knew that converted religious worship into an unreality, and thus became themselves hollow and unreal. For this miserable result did they forsake the God of heaven and earth, their Saviour and constant Benefactor! If they had found a rival with some pretensions to worth the insult would have been less. Herein is the grossness of the insult to God seen in all sin. What do men prefer to him? Transient pleasures, earthly dross. The pearl of great price is flung away, not for a smaller pearl, but for dust and ashes.

V. THE INGRATITUDE OF SIN IS SEEN IN THE ABUSE AND CORRUPTION OF GOD'S GIFTS. God gave the Israelites "garden-land," and they defiled it; they made *God's heritage* an abomination. When we sin we do so by employing the very powers which God has bestowed upon us. We insult him by turning his own gifts into weapons of rebellion. We blaspheme him with the tongue which he has made.

Ver. 8.—*Wickedness in leading men.* The great indictment of Israel reaches its climax in the accusation of the leaders of the people. Even they who should have been the guardians of truth and the vindicators of right have turned aside to evil ways. After this the defection of the whole nation appears utter and hopeless. We have here an instance of the terrible condition into which a country has fallen when its leaders, its teachers, its responsible civil and religious authorities, are unfaithful to their mission and set examples of wickedness.

I. CONSIDER THE SIGNS OF WICKEDNESS IN LEADING MEN. 1. These are often unrecognized until the evil has wrought disastrous effects. For there are circumstances which make them difficult to detect, viz: (1) *External propriety.* The priests still minister at the altar, the Law is still slavishly observed in ceremonial details, rulers still exercise authority, prophets still write and preach in orthodox language, and on the outside all things go on respectably, while there is rottenness hidden within. This was specially the case after the reformation of Josiah, when an outward respect for religious observances was established without any purification of heart or revival of spiritual life. (2) *Respect for authority.* Many people are too subservient to question the character of their leaders. They would rather unite with their rulers in crucifying Christ than recognize his claims against the authority of these men. They do not judge of the character of their leaders by any standard of morals, but found their standard of morals on that character. 2. The signs of wickedness in leading men may be detected in its bearing on the *special functions* of their respective offices. The priests are the temple servants of Jehovah, yet they never seek their Master. They who are familiar with the precepts of the Law know nothing of the person and will of the Lawmaker. The civil rulers who are ruling under a theocracy directly transgress the Law of God. The prophets lend themselves to a corrupt source of inspiration. So now again we may see men abusing the powers of office, and sinning in the very exercise of the responsibilities which are entrusted to them for the sake of the maintenance of right and truth. Therefore we must be on our guard, and not simply follow those who claim to lead because of their rank or office. Men of leading are not always men of light. We must "try the spirits" (1 John iv. 1), and judge of the character of those who claim to lead us by their actions, "Ye shall know them by their fruits" (Matt. vii. 16).

II. CONSIDER THE PECULIAR GUILT OF WICKEDNESS IN LEADING MEN. 1. It is *contrary to knowledge.* The priests handle the Law. Men of influence are usually in a position to learn what is wise and good. Teachers of religion may be presumed to know more than the average of men. How great, then, is their guilt when their conduct is corrupt (Rom. ii. 21—23)! 2. It is *contrary to profession.* These leaders set themselves up as examples to others, and then even they go wrong. They who assume a high position should justify that position by manifesting a high character. More is expected of the professed Christian than of the confessed man of the world. 3. It is an *abuse of great responsibility.* If men wilfully employ positions of trust as means of violating the very objects of those trusts, their guilt is proportionate to the privileges they have received and the honours they have accepted. He who uses a Christian pulpit to propagate doctrines subversive of Christianity is guilty of base treason.

III. CONSIDER THE INJURIOUS EFFECTS OF WICKEDNESS IN LEADING MEN. These will be great in proportion to the influence of the men, and will partake of the special characteristics of that influence, viz.: 1. *Breadth.* Leading men have a wide influence, and the seeds of evil which they sow will be widespread. 2. *Depth.* Leading men have power at their disposal. Their example is weighty. 3. *Subtlety.* Dignity, prestige, authority, disguise the evil which would be recognized if it were stripped of the pomp of office. Therefore: (1) see that good men are chosen for posts of influence, and let the selection and education of civil and religious leaders be a matter of more prayer and thought on the part of the Church; and (2) be not too ready to follow with blind obedience those who may be in high positions. Be independent and watchful. Follow the one infallible Leader, "the Good Shepherd," Christ.

Ver. 13.—*Broken cisterns.* I. ALL MEN NEED SPIRITUAL REFRESHMENT. The soul has its thirst (Ps. lxiii. 1). 1. This is *natural.* We are born with instincts which reach out to the unseen, and the worldly habits which deaden these instincts cannot utterly eradicate them. If they could, we should cease to be men and become merely rational brutes, for "man is a religious animal." 2. This is intensified by the *experience of life.* Thirst is increased by a heated atmosphere, hard work, disease, and special agents, *e.g.* salt water; so spiritual thirst is deepened by the heat and burden of life, by its toil and battle, by the fever of passion and the weariness of sorrow, by the poison of sin and the disappointment of delusive promises of satisfaction. How pathetic is this picture! If the living water is forsaken, cisterns—even poor, broken cisterns, with scant supply of foul water, are resorted to, for in some way the burning thirst of the soul must be quenched.

II. THEY WHO FORSAKE GOD INJURE THEIR OWN SOULS. Hitherto the prophet has spoken of the guilt of unfaithfulness. He now speaks of the loss this entails. It is right that *we* should first think of the simple sinfulness of our sin, for this is its most important feature. But it is profitable to consider also the folly of it, and the misery that it must bring upon us. This is not to be all relegated to the world of future punishments. It is to be felt now, and would be felt keenly if men were not blind to their own condition. As godliness has the promise of the life which now is as well as of that which is to come, so ungodliness brings present loss. This must not be looked for in the direction of material profit and loss, of bodily pain and pleasure, towards which the Jew was too much inclined to turn his attention. It is inward and spiritual, yet it is not the less real. For the spirit is the self. When the noise of the world is stilled, in silent watches of the night, in lonely hours of reflection, does not the poor homeless soul feel some sense of unrest, some vague thirst which no pleasure or possession has yet satisfied?

III. THE INJURY ARISING FROM FORSAKING GOD IS FOUND FIRST IN THE VERY LOSS OF GOD. God is more to us than all his gifts. The greatest loss of the prodigal son is not the food which he craves for in the land of famine, but the father whom he has forsaken. God is the chief source of the soul's refreshment. Men talk of the duty of religion. They should consider its blessings, and learn to seek God as they seek their bread and water—the first necessaries of life. God is a Fountain of living water. 1. His refreshing grace is *ever flowing,* and in great abundance, not limited in quantity as that of the largest cistern may be so that there is enough for all, and it may be had at all times. 2. It is *fresh,* like the mountain stream bubbling forth cool from the rock, not like the stale waters of the cistern. "He giveth more grace" (Jas. iv. 6), and "grace for grace" (John i. 16). The Christian does not have to go back to the grace of God in past ages. There is a fresh stream now flowing, and prayer opens to us fresh supplies of the love and help of God. 3. It is *wholesome and invigorating,* unlike the earthy waters of the cistern. How foolish, then, to turn aside from such a supply for anything! We need no better.

IV. THE INJURY ARISING FROM FORSAKING GOD IS INTENSIFIED BY THE UNSATISFACTORY NATURE OF THE SUBSTITUTES MEN TURN TO. 1. These are *self-made.* God makes the fresh spring, man makes the cistern. Can our work equal God's? 2. They are *limited in supply*—reservoirs, not flowing streams. 3. They are often *impure*; the cistern soon gets impregnated with unwholesome matter. 4. They are *imperfect of their kind.* The cisterns are broken; what little unwholesome water they have leaks away. All these characteristics apply to the waters men turn to in preference to God —*e.g.* human religion, philosophy, public occupation, social distraction, pleasure; these all fail to slake the soul's thirst. "Cor nostrum inquietum est donec requiescat in te."

Ver. 19.—*Sin self-corrected.* I. SIN BRINGS ITS OWN CHASTISEMENT. 1. Sin reveals its evil character as it comes into existence, and is no sooner completed than it is regarded by its parent with disgust. The wicked action which looks attractive in desire is repulsive to reflect upon. The very sight and thought and memory of sin are bitter. The burden of guilt, the shame of an evil memory, the sin itself is thus its own chastisement. 2. Sin naturally produces its punishment. The penalty of sin is not arbitrarily adjudicated nor is it inflicted *ab extrâ.* It is the natural fruit of sin. It is reaping what we have sown (Gal. vi. 7, 8). This fruit the guilty man must eat as his bread of sorrows (Prov. i. 31). Thus intemperance naturally breeds disease, mental degradation, poverty, and dishonour. Greedy selfishness brings upon a man dislike and provokes retaliation. Unfaithfulness to God deprives us of the communion of his

Spirit and the protection of his providence. We have to wait for no formal sentence, no executioner. The law within us carries its own sentence, and is its own executioner, and even as we do wrong we begin to bring upon ourselves the penalty of our conduct. II. THE CHASTISEMENT OF SIN IS TO REPROVE AND CORRECT. The headache of the morning is a warning to the drunkard not to repeat the debauch of the night. 1. Chastisement corrects by bringing us to our right mind. It sobers a man, and thus helps him to look at his life in a true light. 2. Chastisement corrects by revealing the true character of sin. Its charms are all torn off, and the hideous monster is revealed in its naturally hateful shape. Then we see that all sin involves our forsaking God, and is due to the loss of respect for his will—the loss of the "fear of God" according to the Old Testament view, the loss of love to God according to the Christian view. III. IT IS NOT WELL TO WAIT FOR THE CORRECTIVE INFLUENCE OF CHASTISEMENT BEFORE REPENTING OF SIN. 1. The chastisement may be a terrible experience from which we would fain shrink if we knew the nature of it. 2. Sin is evil in itself, and the sooner we stay our hand from it the better for ourselves, for the world, and for the honour of God. It is better not to fall than to fall and be restored. 3. God has provided a higher means than chastisement for delivering us from sin. This is an exercise of his goodness to lead us to repentance (Rom. ii. 4). The gospel shows us how Christ can save us from our sins by drawing us to himself and constraining us by his love to walk in his footsteps of holiness.

Ver. 22.—*The stains of sin.* I. SIN STAINS THE CHARACTER AND LIFE OF MEN. 1. Sin leaves *stains* behind it. No man can have clean hands after touching it. These stains are of two classes : (1) internal—the soiled imagination, the corrupted will, the vitiated habit which a single act of sin tends to produce; and (2) external, in the form of guilt before God, and lowered reputation in the sight of men. 2. The stains of sin are *not natural*. They are no part of the true colour of a man's character. They are all contracted by experience. 3. These stains are all *evil things*. They are not like marks of immature development or of the necessary imperfection of humanity. They are products of corruption. II. NO MAN CAN WASH THE GUILT OF SIN FROM HIS CHARACTER. (Ch. xiii. 23.) The Jews were attempting this by denying the offences charged against them or excusing them. They would not admit their apostacy; but in vain. 1. Sin cannot be *undone*. We cannot recall the past. History is unchangeable. What we have done we have done. 2. Sin cannot be *hidden*. We can never hide it from God, who searches the heart (1 John iii. 20). We cannot long or perfectly hide it from man. It will colour our lives and reveal itself in action, in conversation, in countenance. 3. Sin cannot be *excused*. We may point to our training, our temptations, our natural weakness, our ignorance; and no doubt these facts are important as determining the degree of our guilt (Luke xxiii. 34). But the sin itself, greater or less as it may be, cannot be explained away. Our sins are our own or they would not be sins. 4. Sin cannot be *expiated* by us. Sacrifice is of no real avail. That was only acceptable as a symbol and type of God's method of cleansing sin. Penance could only act as discipline for the future; for the past it is no better than a fruitless sacrifice. Future goodness cannot atone for the past; for that is required on its own account, and if it were perfect it would be no more than it ought to be—we should still be "unprofitable servants." III. NO MAN CAN WASH THE STAIN OF INDWELLING SIN FROM HIS LIFE. Men have tried all methods; but in vain. 1. *Simple determination* to conquer it. But he who commits sin is the slave of sin (John viii. 34), and a slave who cannot emancipate himself. The worst effect of sin is seen in the corruption of the will. Hence we have not the power to reform until our will is renewed, *i.e.* until, in New Testament language, we are "born again." 2. *Change of external circumstances.* This is a helpful accessory of more effectual means, but it is not sufficient in itself, because sin is internal, and no change of scene will effect a change of heart. A man may cross the Atlantic, but he will be the same being in America that he was in England. He may be lifted from the dunghill to a throne, but if he had a vicious nature in his low condition he will carry that with him to his new sphere. Base metal does not become gold by receiving the guinea's stamp. Sanitary arrangements, education, reforming influences, etc., are all helpful, but none are fundamental enough to effect the complete change. The stains are too ingrained for any such washing to remove them.

IV. IN THE GOSPEL OF CHRIST WE MAY SEE THE MEANS FOR CLEANSING BOTH THE GUILT OF CHARACTER AND THE STAIN OF INDWELLING SIN. 1. *Guilt* is shown to be removed by the free forgiveness of God in Christ, for no merits of our own, but for the sake of his work and sacrifice; by no effort of ours, but on condition of repentance and the faith which trusts him as our Saviour, and submits to him as our Lord (Acts x. 43). 2. The *stain of indwelling sin* is shown to be removed by the renewal of our nature, so that we are born "from above" and "of the Spirit" (John iii. 3—8), and become new creatures in Christ by means of the same faith of trust and submission (2 Cor. v. 17).

Vers. 35—37.—*False confidence.* I. THE GROUNDS OF FALSE CONFIDENCE. 1. *Assumed innocence.* Israel says, "I am innocent;" "I have not sinned." This assumption may result from (1) self-deception, or (2) hypocrisy. 2. *A claim to be favoured by God.* Israel says again, "His anger has turned from me." Present peace is taken as a warrant for expecting continued security, so that the very forbearance of God is converted into an excuse for presumption and indifference. Perhaps, too, pride comes in and aids the assumption that the guilty people are special favourites of Heaven and will be protected, whatever wrong they do. This was the mistake of the contemporaries of our Lord when they relied on the mere fact that they were Abraham's children (John viii. 39). 3. *Trust in human aid.* Judah turned first to Assyria, and then to Egypt. So men look to worldly associations for security in trouble. 4. *Reliance on diplomatic skill.* Israel turned from Assyria to Egypt when the former power failed and the latter was in the ascendancy. Men think to protect themselves by their own ingenuity.

II. THE FAILURE OF FALSE CONFIDENCE. The reasons of this may be noted: 1. *The reality of sin.* This is not the less real because it is denied. God still sees it. It still bears its necessary fruits. 2. *The rejection of God.* Israel turned from God to man. How then could he expect God's continued protection? 3. *Lack of principle.* Israel turned about from Egypt to Assyria. There was no settled policy. When expediency is the sole guide of conduct we are sure to be landed in ultimate failure. 4. *The character and fate of the human objects of confidence.* These were rejected by God. They who trust them must share their doom. It is always vain to "put confidence in princes" (Ps. cxviii. 9). But when these are bad men, godless men, rejected by God, the consequences of trust in them will be fatal. We are always involved in the fate of what we trust ourselves to. If we trust to the world, to human aid, to errors and falsehoods, to evil things, the certain overthrow of these must involve us in its ruin.

HOMILIES BY VARIOUS AUTHORS.

Vers. 1—14.—*A sweet remembrance embittered;* or Divine delight turned by his people's ingratitude into Divine distress.

I. GOD GREATLY DELIGHTS IN HIS PEOPLE'S LOVE. See the similitude he employs: "the love of thine espousals." It is difficult for us to recall any period in the history of Israel when such high praise as this was merited by them. For it is of their love to God rather than of his to them—though there was never any doubt about that— that the prophet is here speaking. But when was Israel's love at all of such devoted and intense order as to deserve to be thus spoken of? It is difficult to say. And he that knows his own heart will be slow to credit himself with any such ardent affection as is spoken of here. The explanation of such language is found in that joyous appreciation by God of all movements of our hearts towards him which leads him to speak of our poor offerings as if they were altogether worthy and good. Cf. "Lord, when saw we thee an hungred, or athirst," etc.? (Matt. xxv. 44); also our Lord's estimate of the widow's two mites; the cup of cold water given in his Name, etc. Still, whilst the believer is compelled to confess that his Lord's loving estimate of his poor service and affection is an exaggerated one, it is one which is nevertheless founded upon a very blessed fact. There is such a thing as the child of God's "first love," when our delight in God was intense, real, abiding; when prayer and service were prompt and frequent and delightful. Then we were content to leave the world, and to go out into the dreary wilderness if but our God led the way. Then there was not, as now there too often is, a wide separation between our religious and our common life; but, as ver. 3 tells, we ourselves and all we had were counted as holy unto the Lord. We sought that in whatsoever we did we might do all unto the glory of God. Now, such service is a delight to the heart of God. We are shown, therefore, that we can add to or diminish the joy of God. Such power have we. And the Divine appreciation of such service is shown by his anger towards those that in anywise hurt his servants. "All that devour him," etc. (ver. 3). The Book of the Revelation is one long and awful declaration of how the Lord God will avenge his saints.

II. BUT THIS DIVINE DELIGHT HAS BECOME DIVINE DISTRESS. The remembrance has become bitter. The cause of this change is by reason of his people having forsaken him. As is the joy of God at men's hearts yielding to him, so is his grief at their unfaithfulness. The heart of God is no figure of speech, but a reality. It rejoices in our love, it mourns over our sin. And this all the more because of the aggravation attending such forsaking him. For: 1. *It is in violation of solemn vows and pledges of fidelity which we have given him.* The yielding of the soul up to God is likened unto the espousal of the soul to God. At the time we made our surrender we joyfully confessed, "Thy vows are upon me, O God: O my soul, thou hast said unto the Lord, Thou art my Lord." Now, to go back from God is to violate all these sacred vows. 2. And whatever departures from God have taken place, *they have been without any provocation whatsoever.* Ver. 5, "What iniquity have your fathers found in me?" etc. Has he been hard with us, or impatient, or unready to answer prayer, or faithless to his promise? Can any who have forsaken God charge him so? 3. And such forsaking of God *has been an act of base and shameful ingratitude* (cf. ver. 6). God had brought Israel up out of the land of Egypt, etc. And he had brought them into a plentiful country, but they had polluted it, etc. (ver. 7). All men are under a vast debt of gratitude to God, even the heathen—so St. Paul teaches us—who never heard his Name. But how much more vast is the debt of those who have "tasted that the Lord is gracious," and known his redeeming love, and who yet "turn back and walk no more with him"! 4. Such departures from God are characterized by *most unheard-of and monstrous foolishness.* The prophet in contemplating it (ver. 12) calls on the heavens to be astonished, etc. For such conduct *was unheard of* (cf. vers. 10, 11). Idolatrous nations remained true to their gods, though they were no gods; but Israel, etc. Too often is it that the professed people of God are put to shame by those who make no such profession at all. And it was as monstrous as it was unheard of (cf. ver. 13). It was as if any should abandon the waters of some bright, pure running fountain for the muddy mixture of a tank or cistern, which at the best is almost repulsive to one accustomed to the fountains of living water. And the folly of such exchange is even exceeded, for not only was it this foul cistern for which the living fountains had been forsaken, but even these very cisterns were flawed and fractured so that they could "hold no water." The force of folly could no further go. And men do the like of this still. As, *e.g.,* when they forsake the faith of the Father in heaven for the creed of the materialist, the agnostic, the atheist; when they choose rather the peace of mind which contemplation of their own correctness of conduct can afford instead of the joyful assurance of sin forgiven and acceptance with God, gained through Jesus Christ our Lord; when, in the controversy that is ever going on between God and the world, they decide for the world; when, reliance is placed on a religion of sacraments, professions and forms of worship, instead of that sincere surrender of the heart to God, that spiritual religion which alone is of worth in his sight; when the lot of the people of God is rejected in order that the pleasures of sin may be enjoyed for a season, and in many other such ways. 5. *And the sin is of such desperate character.* For see (ver. 8) how it has mounted up and overwhelmed those who from their profession and calling we should have thought would have been above it. The ministers of religion, the priests, pastors, teachers, have all been swept away by the torrent of sin. When those whose lives are given to prayer, to the study of God's holy Word, and to that sacred ministry which should be a bulwark and defence, not only for those for whom, but also for those by whom, it is exercised; when these are seen to be involved in the common corruption, then the case of such a Church, community, or nation is hopeless indeed. See, too, *the insensibility* that such sin causes. In ver. 2 Jeremiah is bidden " *Go and cry in the ears* of Jerusalem." As you would bend down your face to the ear of one in whom the sense of hearing was all but dead, and would place your lips close to his ear, and by loud, clear utterance strive to make him hear, so had it become necessary by reason of the insensibility which their sin had caused, to deal with those to whom the prophet wrote. It is one of the awful judgments that overtake the hardened and impenitent, that whereas once they would not hear the voice of God, they at length find they cannot. Oh, then, let the prayer of us all be "From hardness of heart, and contempt of thy Word and commandment, good Lord, deliver us."—C.

Vers. 14—19.—*The Divine ideal, how lost and regained.* The prophet has in his mind what was God's original thought for Israel, the Divine ideal concerning him ; and along with that the mournful and utter contrast of his actual condition. An indignant "No" is the answer which rises to the prophet's lips as the questions, "Is Israel a slave ? Is he a homeborn slave?" are asked. He thinks of God's words (Exod. iv. 22). But then there stares him in the face the most distressing but yet most unanswerable fact that Israel has become altogether such an one. "He *is* spoiled ; the young lions roar over him," etc. (ver. 15). Applying the story of Israel to ourselves, we learn—

I. THE DIGNITY AND GLORY WHICH GOD DESIGNED FOR HIS REDEEMED. They were to be as *his sons* (cf. John i. 12, and parallels). Think of the ideas which we associate with the relationship of sons. Take the story of Abraham and Isaac as setting forth in human form what these relationships are. What affection, what confidence, what sympathy, what affluence, what honour, were Isaac's because he was Abraham's son ! All that appertained to him no doubt manifested his happy consciousness of the place he held in his father's love. His looks, his tones, his dress, his demeanour, the respect paid to him, the freedom of his intercourse with Abraham, the influence he had with him,—all made manifest his honoured and his happy position. Now, all that which was Isaac's because he was Abraham's son, God purposes should be ours because we are his. Were the Divine ideal fulfilled, all that appertains to us would reveal the terms on which we stand towards God. Our look, our voice, our demeanour, our freedom from care, the general brightness of our life,—all would show our happy consciousness that we were the "sons" of our Father in heaven. The delight that Isaac had in Abraham, the delight that children have in their parents (Prov. xvii. 6), above all, as the supreme example of true sonship, the delight that Jesus had in God, we should increasingly realize. Such is God's ideal for his redeemed.

II. THE SAD CONTRAST WHICH ACTUAL FACTS TOO OFTEN PRESENT TO THIS IDEAL. This contrast Jeremiah presents in a series of vivid similitudes. 1. *Israel is "spoiled."* That is, he who had been a beloved son, happy, honoured, and free in his father's affluent home, is made a prey of, bound, beaten, abused, carried off as a slave. 2. Next he is likened to some unhappy traveller who, passing by a lion's lair, has fallen a victim. The beast's talons are fastened in his quivering flesh as he lies prostrate on the ground, and its fierce, exultant yells over him make the forest ring again. 3. The next is that of a wasted land, the desolated homesteads, the stripped fields, the torn-down vineyards, the flocks and herds all driven away. 4. The next, that of once goodly cities, their buildings now a heap of smouldering ruins. 5. And last, that of mocked and insulted captives in Egypt. Their captors have inflicted on them the indignity, so terrible in the eyes of a Hebrew, of shaving off their hair ; the words "broken the crown of thy head" rather meaning "shorn the crown of thy head." Now, all these pictures which would call up vivid ideas of humiliation and suffering before the minds of Israel, the prophet suggests in these several sentences, in order to show the contrast between what God proposed for Israel at the first, and that to which he had now fallen. But that which was true of Israel is true now, once and again, of those who should have continued as God's sons. Does not that verse " Where is the happiness I knew?" etc., and the whole tone of that well-known hymn, describe a spiritual condition all too common? Our very familiarity with it shows how often there has been the sad experience of which it tells. One reason why we love the Psalms so much is that they clothe our own thoughts in the very words we need ;

they say what our hearts have often said, and not least do they thus speak for us when, as they so often do, they confess the smart, the shame, the pain, and the manifold distress which our sin has brought upon us.

III. THE CAUSE OF THIS CONTRAST. (Ver. 17.) Did not thy forsaking of Jehovah thy God procure thee this? Let conscience confess if this be not the true explanation of ver. 19. Let us beware of explaining away the true cause, and sheltering our sin beneath some convenient excuse.

IV. THE REMEDY FOR THIS CONDITION OF THINGS. 1. There must be the clear perception of its true cause. Ver. 19, "*Know* therefore and *see* that," etc. To further this most salutary knowledge was the reason of so many distresses coming upon Israel, and for the same reason God will not suffer sin to be only pleasant, nor the cup of iniquity to be free from bitterness. To the riot and gaiety of the prodigal in the "far country," God added on the poverty, the swine-feeding, the rags and wretchedness, the husks for food, and the desertion by all his so-called friends,—all that misery that he might "come to himself," which whilst his riches and riot lasted he never would. And this is God's way still. He would have us know and see that it is an evil thing and bitter to forsake the Lord. 2. And when this has been thus known and seen, would we regain what we have lost, we must have done "with the way of Egypt and the waters of Sihor," that is, we must resolutely abandon those forbidden ways in which we have hitherto been walking. Ver. 18 is an earnest expostulation with such as have wandered from God. It seems to say to such, "What hast thou to do to be going after the world's sinful ways, or to be looking for help from her Sihor-like, her foul dark, waters? Oh, have not her ways harmed thee sufficiently already? will not the burnt child dread the fire? Wilt thou again belie thy name, and live rather as the devil's slave than as God's child? Was the one sorrow and shame which thy sin heaped upon thy Saviour not sufficient, that thou must crucify the Son of God afresh, and put him anew to open shame? Shall the dove vie with the vulture in greed for foul food, or the lamb find satisfaction in the trough of the swine? As soon shouldest thou, child of God, love sin and its evil ways." Let us remember for our great comfort, when well-nigh despairing of deliverance from the dread power of sin, that Christ has as certainly promised to deliver us from this, the power of sin, as he has from its guilt. The earnest look of trust to him, pleading his promise herein,—this repeated day by day, and especially when we know that "sin is nigh," will break its mastery, and win for us the freedom we need.—C.

Vers. 20—37.—*Jehovah's indictment against Israel.* Note—

I. ITS MANY COUNTS. 1. Their *sin of outrageous character*. It is spoken of as in ver. 20, because it so commonly involved the grossest fleshly sins, and because it involved shameful denial of God. Cf. ver. 27, "Saying to a stock, Thou art my father," etc. And it was chargeable with numerous and shameful murders (ver. 30). Killing the prophets of God; ver. 34, "In thy skirts is found the blood of the souls of the poor innocents," etc. 2. *Of long standing.* Ver. 20, "Of old time thou hast broken thy yoke" (see exegesis for true translation), "and saidst, I will not serve." 3. In *no wise chargeable to God.* Ver. 21, "Yet I had planted thee a noble vine," etc. 4. Was *ingrained into their very nature* (ver. 22). All manner of endeavour had been made to cleanse away the defilement, but its stain remained in them still. 5. Was *fiercely and determinately pursued after* (vers. 23, 24, 33; see exegesis). They "worked all uncleanness with greediness." 6. And this in spite of all that might have taught them better. (1) Warnings (ver. 25, where they are entreated to have done with such wickedness). (2) Miserable results of their idolatry in the past (vers. 26—28). (3) Divine chastisements (ver. 30). (4) God's great mercy in the past (ver. 31). God had not been to them as a wilderness. (5) The honour and glory God was ready to place upon them (ver. 32), like as a husband would adorn his bride with jewels. 7. And their sin is aggravated by (1) their shameless assertion of innocence (vers. 23, 35); (2) their persistence in sin (ver. 36), "gadding about to change their way," going from one idolatry to another, one heathen alliance to another.

II. THE MISERABLE DEFENCE OFFERED. It consisted simply in denial (vers. 23, 35). It augmented their guilt and condemnation (ver. 37).

III. THE INSTRUCTION FROM ALL THIS FOR OUR OWN DAY AND FOR OUR OWN LIVES.

1. It shows us the terrible nature of sin. (1) The lengths it will go. (2) The gracious barriers it will break through. (3) The condemnation it will surely meet. 2. It bids us not trust to any early advantages. Israel was planted "a noble vine, wholly a right seed." 3. The folly and guilt of denying our sin (cf. 1 John i. 8, "If we say that we have no sin," etc.). 4. The needs be there is for us all of the pardoning and preserving grace of our Lord Jesus Christ.—C.

Ver. 22.—*The sinner's attempt to wash away his sin.* I. WHEREFORE HE MAKES THE ATTEMPT. Sometimes it is that (1) conscience is aroused; or (2) the Word of God is too plainly against him; or (3) Divine providence threatens ominously; or (4) like Felix, he trembles as some Paul preaches.

II. THE MANNER IN WHICH HE PROCEEDS. 1. He partially abandons known sin, as Pharaoh, Nineveh, Israel at time of Josiah's reformation, Herod. 2. Multiplies religious services. 3. Is ready with good resolves. 4. There is some stir of religious feeling. Tears are shed, the emotional nature is excited, and there is some temporary tenderness of conscience. Added to all this there may be : 5. Self-inflicted punishments, bodily mortifications. Such is the washing with nitre and the taking of much soap which the prophet describes.

III. ITS USELESSNESS. The stain of the iniquity is there still (ver. 22). How powerfully is this confessed in the great tragedy of 'Macbeth'! After his dread crime, the conscience-stricken wretch thus speaks—

> "How is't with me, when every noise appals me?
> What hands are here? Ha! they pluck out mine eyes!
> Will all great Neptune's ocean wash this blood
> Clean from my hand? No; this my hand will rather
> The multitudinous seas incarnadine,
> Making the green—one red."

IV. THE TRUE CLEANSING WHICH IT SUGGESTS AND INVITES US TO. Isa. i. 18, "Come now, and let us reason together," etc.—C.

Ver. 25.—*A dread snare of the devil.* I. IN WHAT IT CONSISTS. The persuading the sinner that "there is no hope."

II. ITS TERRIBLE CHARACTER. It leads the sinner to excuse himself in his sin by the false belief that he is delivered to do all his abominations. It encourages him to go on in his sin (cf. ver. 25), instead of resolutely breaking away from it.

III. HOW MEN FALL INTO IT. By letting sin become the habit of their lives; the constant repetition of separate sinful acts forges the chain of habit, which it is hard indeed for any to break through.

IV. HOW MEN MAY GET OUT OF IT. 1. By prayerful pondering of the many proofs which show that this suggestion of Satan, that "there is no hope," is one of his own lies. These proofs are to be found in the plain statements, and in the many examples of the Word of God, which tell of God's grace to the very chief of sinners. They are to be found also in the recorded biographies and observed lives of many of the people of God. And also in our own experience of God in the past. 2. By then and there committing our souls into the hands of the Lord Jesus Christ for pardon, for restoration, and for safe keeping for the future. 3. By renewing this self-surrender day by day, and especially when we are conscious that danger is near. So shall we be able to say, "My soul is escaped as a bird out of the snare of the fowler."—C.

Vers. 36, 37.—*The restlessness of sin.* "Why gaddest thou about so much to change thy way?" etc.

I. THIS IS A COMMON COURSE OF CONDUCT IN SINFUL MEN.

II. THE REASONS FOR ADOPTING IT ARE OF VARIOUS KINDS. 1. Hope of larger gain. 2. Prospects of increased pleasure. 3. Disappointment with the way that has hitherto been tried. 4. Conscience will not be quiet in continuing the present way, etc.

III. BUT IT IS ALL OF NO AVAIL. The same wretched result is reached whichever way is taken (vers. 36, 37).

IV. God in all this is saying, "Let the wicked forsake his way, and the unrighteous," etc. (Isa. lv.).—C.

Ver. 2.—*God's estimation of his people's love.* A remarkable passage : to be taken in its evident meaning, and not to be explained away. What a loving use to make of the past faithfulness and attachment of his people ! He would remind them of them, that they may repent and return.

I. It is full of interest to him. To those who feel intense love for others, it is exceedingly grateful to find their love reciprocated. High, pure, disinterested love, like that of God for men, never receives equal return ; but what it does elicit it prizes beyond all its intrinsic value. The parent thinks more of the child's love for him than the child of the parent's. 1. *It spoke of trust.* There is no fear or selfishness in love Divine love awakens. The wilderness could not daunt the simple hearts of faithful Israel. They were willing to take God at his word, and to look for the land of promise. So with respect to Christ. 2. *It spoke of gratitude.* He had saved them from Egypt's bondage, and made them his own freemen. No service was too arduous; no trial too severe. Jesus has saved us from sin and its consequences ; we owe to him a deeper gratitude. 3. *It spoke of an affection that was its own reward.* There was delight in the presence and communion of God. Worship was rapture. The chief interest of life was spiritual and Divine. The life of Israel was separated and sanctified to God. Love that could manifest itself thus was a sign and guarantee that the love of God had not been in vain.

II. Its failings are condoned by its genuineness. No mention is made of their murmurings, their disobedience, and unbelief. Where the true spirit of Divine love is exhibited God can forgive defects, etc. To him it is enough for the present that we do our best, and are true and earnest. So at the first signs of repentance he is willing to forget all our offences. What is good and real in men, is of infinitely more value to him than we can imagine, and for the sake of that he is willing to cover the guilty past. This is all the more precious a trait in the Divine character that it *does not spring from ignorance* of us. He knows us altogether, our secret thoughts, our down-sitting and our uprising. The readiness of God so to forgive and to overvalue past love and trust on the part of his people, ought to fill us with compunction and shame. We ought to ask, " Was *this* our love ? " " Lord, when saw we thee an hungred," etc. ?

III. Though transient, it elicits an eternal attachment and leaves an undying memory. " I remember." It ought to be a strong motive to the Christian to think that his little works of faith and labours of love are so highly prized, and so long remembered. " For thy works' sake." Who would not rather charge the memory of God with such gracious memories, that " heap up wrath against the day of wrath " ?—M.

Vers. 2, 3.—*First love to God.* We have here a picture of the idyllic days of the soul's first love for God. The emphasis is on the sentiment—its depth, reality, and attractiveness. It is spoken of as something in which God delights ; as in the odour of a rose, the beauty of a landscape, or the pleasant melody of a song.

I. It is attractive. For its spontaneity ; its spirit of self-sacrifice ; and its absoluteness.

II. It is immediate in its influence upon character and life. Generous sacrifice. Dominance of spiritual aims and interests. Personal holiness.

III. It is full of promise. Not only what it is, but what it may become. In one sense the bud is more valuable than the leaf, or flower, or fruit. It has the interest of growth and the future about it. Israel's best gifts, then, were to God but "firstfruits." God only knows what capacity of spiritual progress and enlargement is ours ; and he alone can tell the influence and importance of his people's faithfulness.—M.

Ver. 3.—*Guilty instruments of Divine judgment.* A great problem in morals. Pharaoh's " heart is hardened," and yet his guilt remains. Nations are raised up to punish Israel for unfaithfulness, yet they " offend " in doing this very thing.

I. Wherein the guilt of instruments of Divine vengeance may consist. At least two explanations of this are to be found : 1. *In the distinction between the formal and the material character of actions.* The essential evil or good of an action is in the intention, the subjective conditions that originate and give character to it. It is subjective, not actualized; or its actualization in one of several forms or directions is indifferent. Towards any of these the Divine power may direct the impulse and tendency; or they may be shut up to them through the unconscious influence of providence, working in wider cycles. 2. *In the overdoing or aggravation of the appointed task.*

II. WHAT IT IS THAT AGGRAVATES THE GUILT OF THE WICKED INSTRUMENT OF DIVINE WRATH. It is the character of God's people, and the relation they bear to him. They have been " holiness unto the Lord." In so far as this character is interfered with or injured by the instruments of vengeance, the latter shall be the more guilty. In so far, too, as hatred for this character, either as past or present, in God's people has actuated the vengeance inflicted, the avengers " shall offend." (Cf. for a similar sentiment, Matt. xviii. 6.) The Divine Being declares his personal attachment to those he has chosen, and his identification with them. To injure them is to injure him. They also represent, even in their apostasy, the stock from which salvation is to come, and the world's spiritual future.—M.

Vers. 4—9.—*The indictment of Israel.* The chosen nation is arraigned in all its generations and in all its orders. It is a universal and continuous crime; and it ran parallel with a succession of unheard-of mercies, deliverances, and favours. In these respects it corresponds to the sin of God's people in every age—forgetfulness of past mercy, abuse of present blessings, the corruption and perverseness of those who were entrusted with Divine mysteries and sacred offices.

I. JEHOVAH APPEALS TO HIS CHARACTER AND DEALINGS IN THE PAST IN DISPROOF OF THERE BEING ANY EXCUSE IN THEM FOR THE SIN OF HIS PEOPLE. Inquiry is challenged. History is rehearsed. So it always has been. The reason for the sins, etc., of God's people is in themselves and not in God. God is just, and all the allegations and murmurs of unbelieving and disobedient Israel are lies. So the excuses Christians often give for their faults and offences are already answered in advance. We have received from him nothing but good. His help and protection were at our disposal; but we forsook him, and sinned against both him and ourselves.

II. THE ENORMITY OF THE OFFENCE IS THEN SET FORTH. The recital is marked by simplicity, symmetry, force, and point. It contains the undeniable commonplaces of history and experience, but the artist's power is shown in the grouping and perspective. 1. *It is ancient and hereditary.* The fathers, the children, and the children's children. Just as they could not go back to a time when God had not cared for them and blessed them, so they could not discover a time when they or their forefathers had not shown unbelief and ingratitude. It is pertinent to ask in such a case, "Must there not be some hereditary and original taint in the sinners themselves?" What will men do with the actual existence of depravity? How will they explain its miserable entail? Human history in every age is marked by persistent wickedness; Christianity suggests an explanation of this. It is for objectors to substitute a better. 2. *It consists in ingratitude, unbelief, and the service of false gods.* The Exodus with all its marvels and mercies, the blessings that surrounded them in the present, go for nought. They are forgotten or ignored. And idols, which are but vanity, are sought after to such an extent that their worshippers "are like unto them." This is the history of religious defection in every age. Forgetfulness of God, ingratitude, and the overwhelming influence of worldly interests and concerns, and the lusts of our own sinful nature, work the same ruin in us. How many idols does the modern world, the modern Church not set up? 3. *It is marked by the abuse of blessings and the breach of sacred trusts.* When men are rendered worthless by their sinful practices, they cannot appreciate the good things of God. Divine bounty is wasted, and blessings are abused. Sacred things are desecrated. Those who ought to be leaders and examples are worse than others. The priest who, if any one, ought to know the " secret place," " the holy of holies," of the Most High, is asking where he is. The lawyers are the greatest law-breakers. The pastors, who ought to guide and feed, are become "blind mouths." And the prophets are false. *Corruptio optimi pessima.* How hard is the heart that has once known God! "If the light that is in you be darkness, how great is that darkness!" The backslider, the child of holy parents, etc., who shall estimate their wickedness?

III. FOR ALL THESE THINGS MEN WILL BE BROUGHT INTO JUDGMENT. The assurance is very terrible: "I will yet plead with" (*i.e.* reckon with or plead against) "you, . . . and with your children's children will I plead." This is the same Jehovah who "keepeth mercy for thousands," but "visiteth the iniquity of the fathers upon the children." There is a solidarity in Israel, Christendom, and the race, which will be brought to light in that day. "It is a fearful thing to fall into the hands of the living God," and to bear our offences in the company of transgressors and the universal connection of the world's sin. "But as in Adam all have died, so in Christ shall all be made alive." Jesus is set forth as the Head and Representative of the humanity he redeems. Let us seek oneness with him through faith.—M.

Vers. 10—13.—*The marvel of unbelief.* A magnificent apostrophe. Yet this is no mere rhetoric. There is a terrible reality in the phenomenon to which attention is directed. Chittim, the general name of the islands and coast of the eastern Mediterranean, stands for the extreme west; and Kedar, the general name of the Arabs of the desert for the extreme east of the "world," with which the prophet and his hearers were familiar. Our "from China to Peru" would represent its meaning to us.
I. THE CONSIDERATIONS THAT MAKE IT MARVELLOUS. The people themselves were but dimly conscious of the strangeness of their apostasy. The prophet seeks to rouse their better nature by the most striking comparisons and illustrations. 1. *He compares it with the general fixedness of heathen systems.* A tendency to subdivide and stereotype life in the family, society, and the state is shown by idolatry. Idolatries reflect and pamper human desires and ideas, and enter into the whole constitution of the people. They undermine the moral life and spiritual strength, and flourish upon the decay they have made. Their victims are helpless because they are moribund or dead. The words of Isaiah are justified in such a case; "from the sole of the foot even unto the head there is no soundness in it," etc. This is the reason of the perpetuation of error and superstition; but the fact is there all the same, and it is in striking contrast to the vacillation and apostasy of God's people. That which only appears to be good is clung to with reverence and tenacity from age to age. That which is acknowledged to be best, and in part realized to be so, is cast aside repeatedly. 2. *Look too at the character of him who is forsaken.* He has already told them a little of God's doings (vers. 5—7). Now it is sufficient to describe him as the "Glory" of Israel. The heavens, which look at everything all the world over, are to wonder and to be horror-struck at this unheard-of ingratitude and folly. 3. *Disadvantage and dissatisfaction must evidently result.* The action of the apostate is twofold—negative and positive. Describe the figure. How great the labour of worldliness; and its disappointment!
II. HOW SUCH CONDUCT CAN BE ACCOUNTED FOR. If it were the result of genuine and honest experience, it might be fatal to the claims of Jehovah. But it is explained by: 1. *The influence of the near and sensible.* The physical side of our nature is more developed than the spiritual. Our need appeals to us first and most strongly on that side. Abraham, who pleaded for Sodom, lied for Sarah. Jacob, the dreamer of Bethel, is the craven at Penuel. How unaccountable the yielding of the man of God to the false prophet (1 Kings xiii.)! After David's signal escapes and deliverances, he yet said in his heart, "I shall now perish one day by the hand of Saul. There is nothing better for me than that I should speedily escape into the land of the Philistines." Elijah, after all his miracles and testimonies, sighs out, "Let me die." Peter, upon whose witness Christ was to found his Church, is addressed as he is ready to sink at the vessel's side, "O thou of little faith, wherefore didst thou doubt?" Paul, who had withstood them "that seemed to be pillars," quails beneath the "thorn in the flesh." 2. *The demands made by true religion.* Self has to be denied. The whole carnal life is condemned. *Diligence* is insisted upon. We have to "pray without ceasing," to labour and not faint. We have to "press toward the mark for the prize." *Patience* is demanded, and the Christian profession commits us to *indefinite sacrifice.*—M.

Ver. 18.—*The unreasonableness of appealing to worldly assistance in spiritual enterprises.* This was the tendency of Israel when her faith grew weak. It is shown even now by those who trust to the arm of flesh, and who seek worldly alliances for the Church. We ought to be deterred from this when we consider—

I. The opposition of the character and aims of the world to those of spiritual religion.

II. The unreliableness of the worldly.

III. The dishonour and spiritual peril of such alliances.—M.

Ver. 19.—*God's method of punishing apostasy.* I. Its own sin is to find it out. II. That the true character of its actions and the bitter fruits of its sin may appear.—M.

Vers. 26—28.—*The shameless shame of idolatry.* I. Its degrading influence. It violates all morality. Is repeatedly affronted by the discoveries which are made of its wickedness and folly. It affects the whole nation from the highest and the best. The reason is debased and set at nought.

II. Calamity is the test of its pretensions. Whilst things go well with the idolater he forgets God or consciously dishonours him. But when he is overtaken with the consequences of his evil deeds he is not ashamed to call upon God. The unreasonableness and inconsistency of this conduct are no barrier to it. Beneath the unbelief and worldliness of men there is a tacit belief in the goodness and power of God. In prosperity they are idolaters, in adversity they find their way back to the God they had despised. This is the universal and permanent inconsistency of the world life.—M.

Ver. 28.—*" Lords many and gods many."* The multiplicity of idols contrasts with the unity of the true God. It involves inconsistency, spiritual confusion, etc. But here the argument is—

I. That idolatry is a local, exclusive, and separative principle.

II. It is thus the creature and the occasion of ignorance, prejudice, and discord.

III. It is therefore bound to disappear before the light and progress of humanity.—M.

Ver. 30.—*Rejecting the chastisements of God.* The spiritual benefits of pain, calamity, etc., are contingent for the most part upon their being received in a right way—as from God, and not by accident. They are intended to discover our sins to us, and to lead us to the love and righteousness of God. Where this result is not effected, " chastisement is not accepted."

I. The possibility of refusing chastisement.

II. Misery and pain are not of themselves ministers of grace.

III. Rightly received, our greatest griefs may become our greatest mercies. —M.

Ver. 35.—*The plea of innocence a culminating sin.* We do not know to which particular charge this reply is given. Perhaps the key is contained in 2 Kings xxiii. 26. An external reformation was considered enough in the reign of Josiah, and it was assumed that the anger of God was thereby turned away. The prophet assures them that this was a mistake, and more than this, a sin in itself.

I. Deadly sin may exist in the mind which is not specially conscious of it.

II. Such unconsciousness exhibits perverted moral nature and callousness of heart.

III. It provokes the more severe judgment from God.—M.

Vers. 1—8.—*Israel's desertion of Jehovah viewed in the light of the past.* Desertion rather than apostasy is the word by which to describe the offence charged against Israel in this chapter. Apostasy from principle is too abstract and unemotional a way of putting the thing. The spectacle presented to us is that of one person deserting another in the basest and most ungrateful way. It is a desertion without excuse, aggravated by every circumstance which can aggravate it. And now Jehovah sends his servant to bring the reality of this desertion distinctly before the nation. And suitably enough he sends him to " cry in the ears of Jerusalem." Whatever is sounded forth in the capital by a man who has had the words of God put in his mouth may be expected to go to the ends of the land.

I. The whole nation is spoken to. God has the power to look at human life in the light of a unity which the individual man is scarcely able to conceive. Here he looks not only at the living generation of those who had sprung from Jacob, but all backward through the past; each generation is, as it were, a year in the life of one who still lives, and is able to look back on things that happened centuries ago as events of his own youth. Thus not only is it true that one generation goes and another comes, while *God* abides for ever, but it is also true that while one generation goes and another comes, Israel abides for ever. Israel is spoken to as a full-grown man might be spoken to, exhorted in the midst of backsliding and unworthy habits to look back on the far different promise of his youth.

II. The nation is spoken to as sustaining a most endearing relation to God. Even as a husband loves and cherishes his wife, so God has loved and cherished Israel. He looks back into the past, and he sees a great fall. The youth of Israel, according to his present view of it, was a time of love and devotion. No doubt there were murmurings and rebellions; and indeed, when we think of some of the things that Israel did during the leadership of Moses, the words of God seem exaggerated in speaking of the kindness of Israel's youth and the love of its espousals. But then we must bear in mind that we know only in a very imperfect way what is recorded, whereas God saw all, and to him the enthusiasm of the people on certain memorable occasions was very significant. He remembered all those events in which Israel rose to the height of its better self, and indicated the possibilities that might be expected from it. Such events now stand forth like sunny heights in memory. They are reasons why God should not allow his people quietly to depart, further and further, into the alienations of idolatry. This is what makes the present attempt at restoration so full of interest, that it is an attempt to bring back the erring spouse to her first love.

III. The nation is viewed in the light of a past in which Jehovah had made great promises and entertained great expectations with regard to Israel's future. They were reckoned a holy nation. They were as firstfruits of the whole earth, to which he attached an especial value. Levi he brought in sacred nearness to himself in lieu of the firstborn of Israel. It is one of Christ's distinctions that he has become the firstfruits of them that slept; and so here there was a nation which was the first to step out from long-accustomed idolatry. The glory of Abraham's faith in the unseen was still, as it were, resting on Israel in the wilderness. Jehovah told the people where to go; he gave them bread, water, and defence against enemies, in a land of peculiar desolation and danger. Promises for the future were given in the most effective way by distinguished services rendered in the present. When at last the Israelites settled down in Canaan, it might have been said to them, "May you not be sure that he who has freely, amply, and just at the right time, supplied your every need, will also, in all the generations to come, whatever their peculiar experiences, do the same thing?" God had taken his people into the deepest darkness, and put out every earth-enkindled light, just that he might manifest in greater glory and attractiveness that light which is the portion of all unwavering believers in himself. Thus the past of Israel glorified the God of Israel; and at the same time, it not only disgraced Israel itself, but had in it such elements of God's favour and assiduity as made the national desertion of him a great mystery.

IV. Observe how completely it is brought out that the desertion is a national act. The *priests* appointed mediators in offering and atonement between Jehovah and his people; the *expounders of the Law*, whose business it was to keep ever manifest the difference between right and wrong; the *shepherds*, such, for instance, as every father at the head of his household, providing and guiding; the *prophets*, who should have been the messengers of Jehovah;—all these, far away from their right place, are found in the very forefront of iniquity. Jehovah is not only ignored; he is almost treated as if he were unknown. The people carelessly let their superiors think for them. When the priest in the parable went by on the other side, the inferior Levite would have thought it presumption to have acted differently.—Y.

Vers. 10, 11.—*Heathendom gives an unconscious rebuke to apostate Israel.* From a humiliating contrast of the present conduct of Israel with what might have been reasonably expected from the peculiar experiences of the past, God now turns to make a contrast more humiliating still with heathen nations. The request to look *back* is succeeded by a request to look *round*. Search through every nation, inquire in every idol temple, watch the religious life of idolaters, and everywhere you will see a fidelity which puts the apostate children of Israel to shame. The heathen gods themselves Jehovah has indeed put to shame, notably the gods of Egypt and Philistia; but in spite of all, the heathen are still clinging to the falsehoods in which they have been taught to believe. Their fanatical devotion is, indeed, a pitiable thing, but even in the midst of all that is pitiable, God can find something to be used for good. This very fidelity to what is so false and degrading may be used to point a keen reproach to those who owe but do not pay allegiance to Jehovah.

There is thus suggested as a topic the UNCONSCIOUS REBUKES WHICH THE WORLD GIVES TO THE CHURCH. The heathendom on which Jehovah bade his people look has long passed away. In spite of the fidelity here indicated, the temples have fallen into ruin and the idols are utterly vanished. Nay, more; increasing signs come in from year to year, that all heathendom is gradually dissolving, so that, in one sense, Jehovah's words may be said no longer to apply. But we know that, in the spirit of the words, they continue to apply only too forcibly. It is but the *form* of the idol that passes away; the reality is the same. Thus he who calls himself and wishes to be thought a believer in Christ, does well to look out and see what he can gather by way of spiritual instruction and rebuke from the world. The world has much to teach us if we would only learn. Jesus himself gave the New Testament parallel when he spoke of the children of the world being wiser in their generation than the children of light. And though we should be very foolish to pay any attention to the world, when it puts on the air of a wiseacre and talks with the utmost self-conceit of things it does not understand, there is all the more reason why we should learn all we can by our own divinely directed observation. How the world rebukes us, for instance, every time we see *men of science searching after truth!* Think of the patient attention given day after day with the telescope, the microscope, and all the apparatus of the experimentalist in physics. Think of the perils and privations of the traveller in tropic and in arctic zones. Think of the unwearied hunting of facts, for possibly a whole lifetime, in order to turn some hypothesis into an established truth. And we also have truth to attain. Jesus and his apostles often spoke of truth which we have to make our own; understanding it, believing it, and making it part of our experience. But that truth assuredly is not to be won without effort. The question may well be asked if such differences would continue to exist among Christians as do exist, provided they only set themselves in reality and humility to discover all that may be known on the subject-matter of their convictions. A man of science, for instance, would not grudge the labour needed to learn another language, if he felt that an increase of knowledge would prove the result to be worth the labour. But how many Christians can be found who have any notion that it might be worth their while to learn the Greek Testament for themselves instead of depending upon even the best of translations? Again, the world rebukes us as we consider *the enthusiasm of terrestrial citizenship.* There is much for the Christian to learn as he contemplates the spirit breaking forth in many men at the thought of the land that gave them birth. How the feelings of such men glow to fever heat with the exhibition of a national flag, the singing of a national anthem, or the mention of great military and naval triumphs, with the names of the captains who achieved them! Then think of what is better still, the unwearied labours of social reformers, simply from love to their country, to lessen crime, vice, disease, and ignorance. In view of all this deep attachment to the land where the natural man has sprung into existence and is sustained, may not Christ well ask his people, if the heavenly πολιτεία into which they have been introduced by the second birth, is as dear to them? Then, what a rebuke comes to us as we look at *the efforts of commercial enterprise.* What toil there is here! what daring investments of capital! what quick combinations of the many to attain what cannot be done by the one! what formation of business habits so as to make easy and regular what would otherwise be difficult, perhaps impossible! And yet it is all done to get that wealth on which the Scriptures have so many warning words to speak. As these gods of the nations were no gods, so the wealth men think so much of is really no wealth at all. We are not to look towards the goal of their desires, nor follow in their steps. But as earnestly as they look towards the goal of an earthly fortune, we should look towards that of a heavenly one. As we stand among men clinging to riches which they cannot keep, and clinging none the less firmly because the riches are hollow, let us bear in mind how easy it is for us who are but sinful mortals also to be deluded away into neglect of the true riches.—Y.

Ver. 13.—*Forsaking the fountain of living waters.* I. THERE IS SUGGESTED HERE AN INCONCEIVABLE ACT OF FOLLY. It is a thing which could be believed of no one in his sound senses that he would leave a fountain of living water, knowing it to be such, and enjoying the use of it; and be contented with a cistern such as is here described. A fountain is that from which he benefits without any trouble; it is a pure gift of grace, and all he has to do is to take up his habitation by it. Why, then, should he leave a fountain for a cistern, even if the cistern were ready-made? Still less credible is it that he should take the trouble to make a cistern. And the incredibility reaches its height when we are asked to suppose him doing all this with the end of possessing a broken cistern that can hold no water. Such broken cisterns the people of Israel seem to have known only too well. Dr. Thomson says there are thousands such in Upper Galilee, which, though dug in hard rock and apparently sound, are all dry in winter; at best they are an uncertain source of supply, and the water, when collected, is bad in colour and taste, and full of worms. The whole action, then, of the character here indicated is scarcely conceivable, unless as the expression of fear in a diseased mind. In somewhat of this way we have heard of men acting, who, after having made great fortunes, have become victims to the horrid delusion that they are paupers, and must make some sort of provision against utter destitution. So we might imagine the victim of delusion, with fountains all round him, still insisting upon having some sort of cistern provided. Note, moreover, that the aspect of folly becomes more decided when we consider that it is *water* which is treated in this way. The water which is offered so freely and continuously in the fountain is a thing which man *needs*, and yet it is for the supply of that which is a great and may be a painful need that he is represented as depending on broken cisterns which with great toil he has constructed for himself.

II. THERE IS MENTIONED AN INDISPUTABLE ACT OF DESERTION. Israelites, stung to wrath by a charge of folly, might reply that they had not left a living fountain for broken cisterns. This, however, was but denying the application of a figure; the historical fact which the prophet had connected with the figure they could not possibly deny. Assuredly they had forsaken God. Not simply that at this time they were without him, but, having once been with him, they had now left him. Had he not taken them up when they were in the weakness, dependence, and waywardness of national infancy? Had they not received all their supplies from him, and gathered strength and prestige under the shelter of his providence? They owed the land in which they lived, and the wealth they had heaped up, to the fulfilment of his promises, and yet they were now worshipping idols. Their worship was not a momentary outbreak like the worship of the golden calf, soon after leaving Egypt, and when they had so long been living in the midst of idolaters. It was a steady settling down into the worst excesses of an obscene and cruel worship, after long centuries during which the Mosaic institutions had been in a place of acknowledged authority. What extenuations there may have been for this apostasy are not to be considered here. The thing insisted upon is the simple undeniable fact of the apostasy itself.

III. THIS DESERTION OF JEHOVAH IS DIVINELY ASSERTED TO BE AN ACT OF THE GROSSEST FOLLY. We have noticed the figure under which this act is set forth; and if Israel meant to get clear of a humiliating charge, it was only by denying that God was indeed a fountain of living water. The figure, therefore, resolves itself into a sort of logical dilemma; and the fact is clearly shown that in spiritual affairs men are capable of a folly which, in natural affairs, they are as far from as possible. Man holds within him a strange duality of contradictions. In some directions he may show the greatest powers of comprehension, insight, foresight; may advance with all the resources of nature well in hand. But in other directions he may stumble like a blind man, while around him on every hand are piled up the gracious gifts of a loving and forgiving God. There is no special disgrace to any individual in admitting what a fool he may be in spiritual things. In this respect, at all events, he is not a fool above other fools. He may see many of the wise, noble, and mighty of earth who have lived and died in apparent neglect as to the concerns of eternity and the relation of Christ to them. Men toil to make securities and satisfactions for themselves, but if they only clearly *saw* that they are doing no better than making broken cisterns, their toils would be relinquished the next moment. It is but too sadly plain how many neglect the revelations, offers, and promises of God; but who can doubt that if they could only really see him to be the true Fountain of living waters, the neglect would come to an end at once?—Y.

Ver. 26.—*A shame to be ashamed of.* There is, as Paul tells us (2 Cor. vii.), a godly sorrow and a sorrow of the world; a godly sorrow working out a repentance never to be regretted, and a sorrow of the world which works out death. So there is a shame and humiliation which is profitable in the right way and to the highest degree, when a man comes into all the horrors of self-discovery, and is ready to declare himself, feeling it no exaggeration, as the chief of sinners. Such a shame is indeed the highest of blessings, since it gives something like a complete understanding of what human nature owes to the cleansing blood of Christ, and to the renewing power of the Spirit. But there is also shame and humiliation such as the gaoler at Philippi felt when he suspected his prisoners were gone, and degradation was impending over him at the hand of his masters. It is to such a shame that our attention is directed here. The shame of a thief, not for the wrong he has done, but because he is detected in the doing of it. Israel, we see, is being dealt with in very plain language. Already the nation which God had so favoured, and from which he had expected so much, has been spoken of as lower than an idolater. And now it is likened to the thief in the moment when his knavery is discovered. Consider, then, as here suggested—

I. WHY THE SINNER SHOULD BE ASHAMED. The thief, of course, ought to be ashamed, and ashamed whether he is caught or not. He ought to come into such a state of mind as to acknowledge his offence and make restitution, even when otherwise his offence might remain undiscovered. He should be ashamed because he has done wrong; because he has broken a commandment of God; because he lives on what has been won by the industry and toil of his neighbours; because, in addition, he is robbing his neighbours of what benefit should have come to them from his own industry and toil. Some have enough to make them bow their heads in despair of ever being able to make restitution; and it is just when we thus begin to estimate the sense of shame that should fill the thoughts of the thief that we also come to have a clear idea of what a universal feeling amongst mankind shame should be. "The thief should be thoroughly ashamed of himself," you say, "in all possible ways." True, he ought. But now take to mind the home-pressing words of the apostle, "Wherein thou judgest another, thou condemnest thyself; for thou that judgest doest the same things" (Rom. ii. 1). Nay, there may be more to be said for the thief than for thee. Only too often he has a bad start, and no real chance of getting out of bad associations. He may get so hemmed in with temptations as to find it very difficult to resist. And in any case, the thief has no more cause to be ashamed of his theft than any other sinner for his own particular mode of self-indulgence. God does not draw the distinctions which we are compelled to do, between wrongs that are crimes and wrongs that are not crimes. His distinctions are made on altogether different principles—principles which abide. If the thief has wronged his neighbour in one way, be sure of this, that you have wronged him in another. If the thief has sinned against God in one way, you have sinned against him in another. You may go through the world without the slightest fear of anything leaping to the light such as will bring the detective's tap upon your shoulder, and nevertheless you have yet to be bowed in unspeakable bitterness of shame because you have been defrauding God and missing the great end of life. What is wanted is that all of us should come to ourselves—being guided by that unerring Spirit which guides into all truth, and self being revealed by the light of the cross and of eternity.

II. WHY THE SINNER ACTUALLY IS ASHAMED. Discovery is what he dreads; discovery puts him in utter confusion. Discovery is disgrace and ruin, so far as his future relation to men is concerned. Henceforth he passes into a suspected and avoided class; he has lost the mark of respectability and confidence. The sad thing is that, in the eyes of a large part of mankind, discovery seems to make all the difference. One may do a great deal of wrong with social impunity, if only there is cleverness enough to keep on the hither boundary of what is reckoned criminal. Those who are most serenely indifferent to the Law of God will fall into all sorts of sins, real and far-reaching evils, rather than transgress a certain social code. It is not so long ago since the duel ceased to be a part of the social code of England; and what a curious standard of honour was involved in such a practice! There are countries still where a man is disgraced if he refuses to fight ; if he fights and kills his man it is reckoned no shame at all. The most immoral and debauched of men are yet curiously sensitive to what they choose to consider points of honour. People will plunge over head and ears into debt, and run into the wildest extravagance, that they may flourish a little longer in the social splendour which they know they have not the honest means to maintain. They feel it is a greater disgrace to sink in the world than to be unable to pay their debts. How needful it is for the Christian to take up all positions which he feels to be right—right according to the Divine will, no matter how much he may be exposed to the reproach of folly, Quixotism, and fanaticism ! Let us pray that we may ever have a godly shame when the light of heaven is thrown on us, and we are contrasted with God in his holiness and Jesus in his perfect manhood. Let us equally pray that we may never be ashamed of Jesus. It is a harder thing than many seem to think, even though they are constantly acknowledging in hymn and prayer what they owe to Jesus in the way of gratitude and service.—Y.

Ver. 37.—*Why the confidences of men do not prosper.* The people of Israel are set forth, even within the limits of this one chapter, as having multiplied and extended their confidences; and yet it could not be said that they were prospering. Men with the religious element in their nature strongly clamouring for satisfaction, had turned to the gods of neighbouring nations, and multiplied these objects of worship until it could be said, "According to the number of thy cities are thy gods, O Judah." God compares them to thirsty people who, with a copious fountain in their midst, work and toil to make cisterns, only to find that the end of their labour is in broken cisterns which can hold no water. And then, when their broken cisterns had proved quite unavailing, they fly to drink of Nile and of Euphrates. Evidently their confidence had not prospered, and a continuance and increase of adversity was threatened, the cause of it all being that their confidences were such as God, in his righteousness and majesty, must inevitably reject. Consider—

I. WHY THIS QUESTION AS TO THE SUFFICIENCY OF HUMAN CONFIDENCES IS SO IMPORTANT. The answer is that men cannot do without confidences. The events of a single day of life might be registered in such an aspect as to show what a confiding creature man is. Faith has become so much a habit with him as to be almost a second nature. Hence, even in the great concerns of life, we find many reposing trust with very little inquiry. Looking at others, we find their lives proving the need of confidence by the very frequency of doubt and irresolution in them. They are ever asking the question, yet never quite able to answer it, "What is the best thing for me to do?" And then, as so often happens, the end of hesitation and perplexity is, that they seem to have no choice at all, and go submissively towards the confidence that happens to be most inviting at the moment. Seeing, therefore, that we are compelled to have confidences, it is of the first importance to discover in what sort of confidences prosperity will alone be found.

II. MANY ACTUAL CONFIDENCES OF MEN PROVE FAILURES IN THE END. They approach men invitingly, they seem to stand well in the judgment of past generations, they may be the objects of very general approval, and yet, when they are searched into, when the truth concerning them is got from the bottom of the proverbial well, that truth is seen to be well expressed in the words which say men have not prospered in them. There is, for instance, a very plausible appearance of prosperity in worldly wealth. Many fail to acquire it, and when they acquire it, fail to keep it; but this is held to come in the majority of cases from some fault in the man, and not in the stability of his possessions. To say that a possession is as safe as the Bank of England is to utter the strongest conviction as to its stability and security ; and yet such confidences fail because they are not enough for *the whole man.* It is just one of the perils of wealth that man should let his whole heart rest upon it; should come to let the comforts, occupations, and hopes of life depend upon external possessions. There is failure also when men put confidence in self, confidence in present views of life, present feelings, present vigour of body and mind, in natural qualities, such as shrewdness, self-control, presence of mind, and in habits of attention, industry, and promptitude, that have been cultivated. What manifest failure also often comes from too much confidence in the judgment of man! The counsels of the wisest, most experienced, most successful of men, must be listened to with discretion.

III. THE REASON WHY SUCH CONFIDENCES DO NOT BRING PROSPERITY IS MADE PLAIN. They are not confidences after God's own heart. They are an ungodly waste of affections and energies given for higher purposes and more durable occupations. The practical lesson is that we should reject all confidences if we are not made quite certain that God approves them. Blessed is that man who has found his way, it may be through many losses and agonizing pains, to the truth that the unseen is more trustworthy than the seen, the eternal than the temporal. One who has thus risen into the sphere of Divine realities may have his confidences rejected and despised of men. What do these rejections matter? He who has firm hold of God himself need not to care for contemptuous words. The hard words of worldly men cannot destroy spiritual prosperity.—Y.

Ver. 13.—*The people's sin.* This is the sum and substance of the charge the prophet was called to bring against Israel. Idolatry was their destroying sin, the root of all their discords and miseries. It involved the renunciation of their allegiance to the God of their fathers, and in this their conduct was without a parallel. No instance of such apostasy could be found elsewhere. Those whom God had chosen to be witnesses for him before all the world were put to shame in this respect by the very heathen whom it was their mission to enlighten and bless. But we may regard this as the condemnation of the whole human race. "They have forsaken," etc. Note the view we get here—

I. OF THE BEING OF GOD AND THE RELATION HE SUSTAINS TOWARDS US. "The Fountain of living waters" (see also ch. xvii. 13; Ps. xxxvi. 9). 1. *He is emphatically the Living One.* The grand distinction of the Bible is that it reveals "the living God." The Name Jehovah, the mysterious and incommunicable Name, was expressive of this. "And God said to Moses, I AM THAT I AM," etc. (Exod. iii. 14). Absolute existence—essential, independent, necessary being—is the idea it conveys. The knowledge of such a spiritual Being, of a personality kindred with our own but absolutely exempt from its limitations, is our supreme need. David did but utter forth the insatiable longing of our nature for its true home, its only possible resting-place, when he cried, "My soul thirsteth for God, yea, for the living God." We want, not mere vague impressions of infinitude and eternity, but an Infinite and Eternal One in whom we may trust. Not mere abstract ideas of truth, and beauty, and righteousness, and love, but One of whom these are the unchanging attributes, and to whom, in the frailty of our nature, we can fly for refuge. "Our heart and our flesh cry out for the living God." 2. *He is the Giver and Sustainer of all other forms of spirit-life.* The "Fountain" of life; all other existences are dependent upon him. "The Father of spirits;" "we also are his offspring;" "in him we live and move and have our being." Whether our spirit-life once given can ever become extinct again may be a matter of doubt and controversy, but certainly it cannot be regarded as absolute and necessary existence. Though God may have endowed our nature with his own immortality, we do not possess immortality in the sense in which he does. "He only hath immortality." Ours is not self-existent being; it is dependent on him from whom it came—an outflow of the "Fountain" of life. 3. *He is the Source of all that nourishes, enriches, and gladdens this dependent creature-life*—"the Fountain of living waters." "Living waters" are the Divine satisfactions of the human soul. The Scriptures abound with similar figurative representations (Gen. ii. 10; Zech. xiv. 8; John iv. 14; Rev. xxii. 1, 17). Every age has had its witness to the truth that man's real satisfactions are only to be found in God. In Christ that witness is perfected, that truth verified. "This is the record," etc. (1 John v. 11, 12). Here are the conditions of infinite blessedness for every one of us. To be separated from God in Christ, to turn away from him, is to perish, to doom yourself to the pangs of an insatiable hunger and a quenchless thirst. "This is life eternal, that they might know thee," etc. (John xvii. 3). This is death eternal—*not* to know him, to refuse the knowledge of him, to dream that you can live without him.

II. THE FOLLY AND EXCEEDING SINFULNESS OF SIN. The "two evils" here spoken of are but two forms, two sides, of one and the same thing. There is the self-willed departure from God, and there is the endeavour in that to lead a self-determined and self-sufficient life. 1. *They have forsaken me.* All sin is a forsaking of God. Adam turned his back on God when he listened to the voice of the tempter. The prophet rebukes here the shameful idolatries of the people. Think what idolatry means. It has, no doubt, its fairer side, in which it is seen to be the ignorant but still honest expression of the religious sentiment in men—the blind "feeling after God if haply they may find him." But think how it arose, and what its issues have been. St. Paul tells us how it was born of the corruption of man's nature, and has ever since been the Satanic means of deepening that corruption (see Rom. i. 20, *et seq.*). So is it with every sinful life. It begins with a more or less intentional and deliberate renunciation of God. The exact point of departure may not be very definitely marked; but as the life unfolds itself, the fact that this is its true meaning becomes more manifest. How marvellous a picture of this dread reality of moral life does our Lord's parable of the prodigal supply! Such is the history of prodigal souls. Happy are they who "come to themselves" before it is too late to return to the forsaken home of the Father. 2. *The dream of a self-determined and self-contained life.* "They have hewed them out cisterns" of their own, which shall render them, as they think, independent of the "Fountain of living waters." Here is the idea of a proud endeavour to find in one's self and one's own self-willed way all necessary good. But it is altogether vain. The cisterns are miserably shallow, and they are "broken." It is true of every man, indeed, that his satisfactions must spring from what he finds within rather than from his earthly surroundings; but then he is "satisfied from himself" only because he has learnt to link himself with the Divine Source of all blessedness—the living God.

> "Here would we end our quest;
> Alone are found in thee
> The life of perfect love, the rest
> Of immortality."

W.

EXPOSITION.

CHAPTER· III.

That this chapter (to which the first four verses of ch. iv. ought to have been attached) belongs to the time of Josiah seems to be proved by ver. 6, and the years immediately following the reformation are not obscurely referred to in vers. 4, 10. Naegelsbach gives a striking distribution of its contents. The general subject is a call to "return." First, the prophet shows that, in spite of Deut. xxiv. 1, etc., a return is possible (vers. 1—5). Then he describes successively an invitation already uttered in the past, and its sad results (vers. 6—10), and the call which will, with a happier issue, be sounded in the future (vers. 11—25); this is followed by an earnest exhortation, addressed first to Israel and then to Judah (ch. iv. 1—4).

Ver. 1.—**They say,** etc.; as the margin of Authorized Version correctly states, the Hebrew simply has "saying." Various ingenious attempts have been made to explain this. Hitzig, for instance, followed by Dr. Payne Smith, thinks that "saying" may be an unusual equivalent for "that is to say," "for example," or the like; while the Vulgate and Rashi, followed by De Wette and Rosenmüller, assume an ellipsis, and render, "It is commonly said," or "I might say." But far the most natural way is to suppose that "saying" is a fragment of the superscription of the prophecy, the remainder of which has been accidentally placed in ver. 6, and that we should read, "And the word of the Lord came unto me in the days of Josiah the king, saying." So J. D. Michaelis, Ewald, Graf, Naegelsbach. **If a man put away his wife.** The argument is founded on the law of Deut. xxiv. 1—4, which forbade an Israelite who had divorced his wife to take her again, if in the interval she had been married to another. The Jews had broken a still more sacred tie, not once only, but repeatedly; they worshipped "gods many and lords many;" so that they had no longer any claim on Jehovah in virtue of his "covenant" with his people. **Shall he return,** etc.? rather, *Ought he to return?* The force of the term is potential (comp. Authorized Version of Gen. xxxiv. 7, "which thing ought not to be done "). **Shall not** in the next clause is rather *would not.* **Yet return again to me.** So Peshito, Targum, Vulgate, and the view may seem to be confirmed by the invitations in vers. 12, 14, 22. But as it is obviously inconsistent with the argument of the verse, and as the verb may equally well be the infinitive or the imperative, most recent commentators render, "And thinkest thou to return to me?" (literally, *and returning to me!* implying that the very idea is inconceivable). Probably Jeremiah was aware that many of the Jews were dissatisfied with the religious condition of the nation (comp. ver. 4).

Ver. 2.—**Lift up thine eyes,** etc. No superficial reformation can be called "returning to Jehovah." The prophet, therefore, holds up the mirror to the sinful practices which a sincere repentance must extinguish. **The high places;** rather, *the bare hills* (comp. on ch. ii. 20). **In the ways hast thou sat** for them. By the roadside (comp. Gen. xxxviii. 14; Prov. vii. 12). **As the Arabian in the wilderness.** So early was the reputation of the Bedouin already won (comp. Judg. vi.). Jerome *ad loc.* remarks, "Quæ gens latrociniis dedita usque hodie incursat terminos Palæstinæ."

Ver. 4.—**Wilt thou not,** etc.? rather, *Truly from this time thou callest unto me* (literally, *Dost thou not,* etc.? a common way of giving an energetic assurance). The prophet admits the apparent revival of faith in Jehovah which attended the compulsory reformation under Josiah, but denies that it was more than apparent (comp. ver. 10). **The guide of my youth;** rather, *the companion* (the familiar associate); so in Prov. ii. 17. Comp. ch. ii. 2, and especially Isa. liv. 6, "and a wife of youth" (*i.e.* married in youth, "that she should be rejected [how incredible a thing!]"

Ver. 5.—**Will he reserve?** rather, *Will he retain,* etc.? It is a continuation of the supposed address of Judah. **To the end?** rather, *everlastingly?* **Behold, thou hast spoken,** etc.; rather, *Behold, thou hast spoken it, but hast done these evil things, and hast prevailed* (i.e. *succeeded*). The substance of the two verses (4 and 5) is well given by Ewald: "Unhappily her power truly to return has been exhausted, as not long ago after fresh signs of the Divine displeasure she prayed in beautiful

language to [Jehovah] for new favour and abatement of the old sufferings, [but] she immediately fell again into her sin, and carried it out with cool determination."

Ver. 6.—**The Lord said also unto me,** etc. It has been suggested (see on ver. 1) that this introductory clause belongs rather to ver. 1. Some sort of introduction, however, seems called for; Ewald supposes a shorter form, such as "And the Lord said further unto me." The view is not improbable, for although there is evidently a break between ver. 5 and ver. 6, there are points of contact enough between vers. 1—5 and the following discourse to prove that they represent the same prophetic period· (comp. ver. 10 with ver. 3, vers. 8, 9 with ver. 1, ver. 12 with ver. 5, ver. 19 with ver. 4). **Backsliding Israel;** literally, *apostacy Israel.* Usually a change or modification of a name is a sign of honour; here, however, it marks the disgrace of the bearer. Israel is apostacy personified (comp. vers. 14, 22). **She is gone up;** rather, *her wont hath been to go up.*

Ver. 7.—**And I said after she had done,** etc.; rather, *and I said, After she hath done all these things, she will return unto me.* **And her treacherous sister.** Observe the distinction between the two sisters. Israel had openly broken the political and religious connection with Jehovah (Hos. viii. 4); Judah nominally retained both, but her heart was towards the false gods (comp. the allegory in Ezek. xxiii., which is evidently founded upon our passage).

Ver. 8.—**And I saw, when for all the causes,** etc.; rather, *and I saw that even because apostate Israel had,* etc. But this is exceedingly strange in this connection. The preceding words seem to compel us either (with the Vulgate) to omit "and I saw" altogether, or (with Ewald) to read the first letter of the verb differently, and render "and she saw," taking up the statement of ver. 7 ("saw; yea, she saw," etc.). The latter view is favoured by a phrase in ver. 10 (see note below). The same corruption of the text (which is palæographically an easy one) occurs probably in Ezek. xxiii. 13. The error must, however, be a' very ancient one, for the Septuagint already has καὶ εἶδον.

Ver. 9.—**Through the lightness of her whoredom;** *i.e.* through the slight importance which she attached to her whoredom. So apparently the ancient versions. The only sense, however, which the word *kōl* ever has in Hebrew is not "lightness," but "sound," "voice," and perhaps "rumour" (Gen. xlv. 16). Hence it is more strictly accurate to render "through the cry," etc. (comp. Gen. iv. 10; xix. 13), or "through the fame," etc. (as Authorized Version, margin). But neither of these seems quite suitable to the context, and if, as King James's translators seem to have felt it necessary to do, we desert the faithful translation, and enter on the path of conjecture, why not emend *kōl* into *k'lōn* (there is no *vav*, and such fragments of true readings are not altogether uncommon in the Hebrew text), which at once yields a good meaning —"through the disgrace of her whoredom"? Ewald thinks that *kōl* may be taken in the sense of *k'lōn;* but this is really more arbitrary than emending the text. **With stones,** etc. (see ch. ii. 27).

Ver. 10.—**For all this;** *i.e.* though Judah had seen the punishment of apostate Israel (ch. iii. 7, 8). So Rashi, Naegelsbach, Payne Smith. Most commentators suppose the phrase to refer to Judah's obstinate wickedness (ver. 9), but this gives a weak sense. "Judah defiled the land, etc., and yet notwithstanding her repentance was insincere" —this is by no means a natural sequence of ideas. The right exposition increases the probability of the correction proposed at the beginning of ver. 8.

Ver. 11.—It is very noteworthy that Jeremiah should have still so warm a feeling for the exiles of the northern kingdom (more than a hundred years after the great catastrophe). **Hath justified herself.** "To justify" can mean "to show one's self righteous," as well as "to make one's self righteous," just as "to sanctify" can mean "to show one's self holy" (Isa. viii. 13), as well as "to make one's self holy." In spite of Israel's apostacy, she has shown herself less worthy of punishment than Judah, who has had before her the warning lesson of Israel's example, and who has been guilty of the most hateful of all sins, hypocrisy (comp. ver. 7).

Ver. 12.—Israel, therefore, shall be recalled from exile. Her sins are less than those of Judah, and how long and bitterly has she suffered for them! **Toward the north.** For Israel had been carried captive into the regions to the north of the Assyrian empire (2 Kings xvii. 6; xviii. 11). Comp. the promise in ch. xxxi. 8. **I will not cause mine anger to fall upon you;** rather, *my face to fall towards you* (i.e. upon your return).

Ver. 13.—*The condition of restoration to favour.* Israel is to acknowledge, or perceive, notice, recognize, her guilt. **And hast scattered thy ways;** alluding to that "gadding about" in quest of foreign alliances, reproved in the preceding chapter (ii. 36). Comp. "interlacing her ways," ch. ii. 23.

Ver. 14.—**Turn, O backsliding children.** There is a play upon words, or rather upon senses, in the original, "Turn, ye turned away ones" (comp. ver. 12). To whom is this addressed? To the Israelites in the narrower sense, for there is nothing to indicate a transition. Long as they have

been removed from the paternal hearth, they are still "sons." **For I am married unto you.** The same Hebrew phrase occurs in ch. xxxi. 32. Its signification has been a subject of dispute. From the supposed necessities of exegesis in ch. xxxi. 32, some (*e.g.* Pococke and Gesenius) have translated, "for I have rejected you," but the connection requires not "for" but "though," which, however, is an inadmissible rendering; besides, the Hebrew verb in question nowhere has the sense of "reject" elsewhere (yet the Septuagint already has it, virtually at least, in ch. xxxi. 32, *q.v.*). The literal meaning is *for I have been a lord over you,* i.e. a husband. Israel is despondent, and fears to return. Jehovah repeats his invitation, assuring Israel that he does not regard the marriage bond as broken. He is still (in spite of ver. 8) the husband, and Israel the bride (comp. Hos. ii.; Isa. l. 1; liv. 6, etc.). **One of a city, and two of a family.** The promises of God are primarily to communities, but this does not prevent him from devoting the most special care to individuals. "One of a city, and two of a family," even though there should be but one faithful Lot in a city, and two such in a family (larger than a city, a single tribe containing only a few *mishpākhōth*, or clans), yet I will admit these few to the promised blessings." Calvin's remark is worth noticing: "Hic locus dignus est observatu, quia ostendit Deus non esse, cur alii alios expectent; deinde etiam si corpus ipsum populi putrescat in suis peccatis, tamen si pauci ad ipsum redeant, se illis etiam fore placabilem." The historical facts to which the prophecy corresponds are variously regarded. Theodoret, Grotius, etc., suppose it to have been fulfilled exclusively in the return from Babylon; St. Jerome and others think rather of the Messianic period. Hengstenberg finds a continuous fulfilment, beginning at the time of Cyrus, when many belonging to the ten tribes joined themselves to the returning Judahites. He finds a further continuation in the times of the Maccabees, and in fact a continually growing fulfilment in preparation for that complete one brought in by Christ, when the promised blessings were poured out upon the whole δωδεκάφυλον (Luke ii. 36). "Zion and the holy land were at that time the seat of the kingdom of God, so that the return to the latter was inseparable from the return to the former." Dr. Guthe, however, the latest critical commentator on Jeremiah, thinks that the passage can be explained otherwise, viz. " from each city one by one, and from each family two by two." This gives a more obvious explanation; but the ordinary rendering is more natural, and the explanation based upon it is in the highest degree worthy of the Divine subject. The doubt, of course, is whether in the Old Testament a special providence is extended elsewhere so distinctly to the individual. But Jeremiah is pre-eminently an individualizing prophet; he feels the depth and reality of individual as opposed to corporate life as no one else among the prophets. (At any rate, one point is clear, that the prophet foresees that the number of the exiles who return will be but small compared with the increase to be divinely vouchsafed to them; see ver. 16.)

Ver. 15.—**Pastors.** In ch. xxiii. 4, the same word is rendered in the Authorized Version "shepherds," which would be less open to misunderstanding here than "pastors," civil and not spiritual authorities being intended (see on ch. ii. 8). The prophecy is, of course, not inconsistent with passages like ch. xxiii. 5, but as the national continuance of Israel was guaranteed, it was natural to refer to the subordinate civil authorities. **According to mine heart;** better, *according to my mind;* for here, as also in 1 Sam. xiii. 14, it is something very far from perfection which is ascribed to the chosen rulers. "Heart" is sometimes equivalent to "understanding."

Ver. 16.—**When ye be multiplied;** a common feature in pictures of the latter days (ch. xxiii. 3; Ezek. xxxvi. 11; Hos. ii. 1). **They shall say no more, The ark of the covenant of the Lord.** A definition of the Messianic period on its negative side—the ark shall be no longer the centre of religious worship. We must remember that the ark is represented in the Law as the throne of Jehovah, who was "enthroned upon the cherubim" on the lid of the ark. It is in virtue of this sacramental presence that the temple is called the "dwelling-places" of Jehovah (*e.g.* Ps. xlvi. 4; lxxxiv. 1, where Authorized Version has wrongly "tabernacles"). Now, in the Messianic period the consciousness of Jehovah's presence was to be so widely spread, at any rate in the centre of God's kingdom, the holy city, that the ark would no longer be thought of; it would be, if not destroyed (we know, as a matter of fact, that the ark was destroyed in some unrecorded way), yet at least become utterly unimportant. Jerusalem would then naturally succeed to the title "Jehovah's throne" (applied to the temple in ch. xiv. 12). **Neither shall it come to mind.** The same phrase is used of the old heaven and earth as compared with the new (Isa. lxv. 17). In the concluding clauses, "visit" should rather be "miss," and "that be done" should be "it [viz. the ark] be made." On the whole subject of the prophetic descriptions of the worship of the Messianic period—descriptions which often wear at any rate a superficial appearance of inconsistency, see the luminous remarks of Professor Riehm, 'Messianic Prophecy,' pp. 161—163. At the same time, we must be extremely cautious how far we admit that Old Testament prophecies of the latter days have received a complete fulfilment in the Christian Church, considering how far the latter is from the realizable ideal, and also the importance attached in the New Testament as well as in the Old to the continuance of Israel as a nation.

Ver. 17.—*Jerusalem's spiritual glory.* With Jeremiah's description, comp. that of Ezekiel, "The name of the city from that day shall be, The Lord is there" (xlviii. 35). This gives us the positive aspect of the Messianic period (comp. on ver. 16). Jerusalem shall be the spiritual centre of the universe, because it is pervaded by the presence of the Most High (comp. Isa. iv. 5). May we explain with Dr. Payne Smith, "Jerusalem, *i.e.* the Christian Church"? Only if the provisional character of the existing Church be kept well in view. **All the nations;** *i.e.* all except the chosen people. The word for "nations" (*goyim*) is that often rendered "heathen." **To the name;** or, *because of the name*, i.e. because Jehovah has revealed his name at Jerusalem. The phrase occurs again with a commentary in Josh. ix. 9, "Thy servants are come because of the name of Jehovah thy God, for we have heard the fame of him, and all that he did in Egypt." But we must not suppose that "name" is equivalent to "revelation;" rather, there is here an ellipsis—"because of the name" is equivalent to "because of the revelation of the name," or better still, ". . . of the Name." The "Name of Jehovah" is in fact a distinct hypostasis in the Divine Being; no mere personification of the Divine attributes (as the commentators are fond of saying), but (in the theological sense) a Person. The term, "Name of such and such a God," is common to Hebrew with Phœnician religion. In the famous inscription of Eshmunazar, King of Zidon, Ashtoreth is called "Name of Baal;" and to whichever proper name the religious term Name may be attached, it means a personal existence in the Divine nature, specially related to the world of humanity; or, to use the language of Hengstenberg, the bridge between the latter and the transcendent heights of God as he is in himself. In short, the Name of Jehovah is virtually identical with the Logos of St. John, or the second Person in the blessed Trinity. Hence the personal language now and again used of this Name in the Old Testament, *e.g.* Isa. xxx. 27, "The Name of Jehovah *cometh* from far . . . *his lips* are full of indignation;" Isa. xxvi. 8, "The desire of our soul was to thy Name;" Isa. lix. 19, "So shall they fear the Name of Jehovah from the west, and his glory from the rising of the sun." Comp. also Prov. xviii. 10; men do not run for safety to an abstract idea. Nor will all nations in the latter days resort either to a localized or to a spiritually diffused Jerusalem in the future, to gratify a refined intellectual curiosity. **Neither shall they walk,** etc.; *i.e.* the Israelites of the latter days; not the "nations" before mentioned (as Hengstenberg). The phrase occurs eight times in Jeremiah, and is always used of the Israelites. The word rendered "imagination" is peculiar (*shĕrī-rūth*). As Hengstenberg has pointed out, it occurs *independently* only in a single passage (Deut. xxix. 18); for in Ps. lxxxi. 13, it is plainly derived, not from the living language, from which it had disappeared, but from the written. (The close phraseological affinity between the Books of Deuteronomy and Jeremiah has been already indicated.) The rendering of the Authorized Version, which is supported by the Septuagint, Peshito, Targum, is certainly wrong; the Vulgate has *pravitatum;* the etymological meaning is "stubbornness." The error of the versions may perhaps have arisen out of a faulty inference from Ps. lxxxi. 13, where it stands in parallelism to "their counsels."

Ver. 18.—The reunion of the separated portions of the nation (comp. Ezek. xxxvii. 16, 17; Hos. i. 11; Isa. xi. 12, 13). Observe, Israel is converted first, then Judah. This detail in the prophecy is not to be pressed. Not that the force of any prophecy is to be evaded, but that in this case the form of the statement is so clearly conditioned by the abounding sympathy of the prophet for the ten tribes. These had been so long languishing in captivity that they needed a special promise. The form of the promise is imaginative; this seems clearly to follow from the fact that in no other passage (except, indeed, ch. xxxi. 9) is there a reference to the spiritual primacy of Ephraim in the restored nation. **Out of the land of the north**; *i.e.* Assyria and (ch. i. 14) Babylonia. The Septuagint inserts, "and from all the countries," agreeably to ch. xvi. 15; xxiii. 3; xxxii. 37. Of course, it would not be an accurate statement that the exiles from Judah were confined to "the land of the north." This is a fair specimen of the supplementing tendency of the Septuagint, though it is possible, and even probable, that the Hebrew text has suffered in a less degree from the same tendency on the part of later copyists.

Ver. 19.—The concluding words of the last verse have turned the current of the prophet's thoughts. "Unto your fathers." Yes; how bright the prospect when that ideal of Israel was framed in the Divine counsels! Condescending accommodation to human modes of thought; **But I said** fails to represent the relation of this verse to the preceding. Render, *I indeed had said,* and continue, *How will I,* etc. **Put thee among the children.** This is a very common rendering, but of doubtful correctness. It assumes that, from the point of view adopted (under Divine guidance) in the prophecies of Jeremiah, the various heathen nations were in the relation of sons to Jehovah. This is most improbable; indeed, even Exod. iv. 22 does not really favour the doctrine of the universal fatherhood of God in the fullest sense of the word. Moreover, the pronoun rendered "thee" is in the feminine, indicating that the prophet has still in his mind the picture of Israel as Jehovah's bride. It would surely be an absurd statement that Jehovah would put his bride among the children! Render, therefore, *How will I found thee with sons!* comparing, for the use of the Hebrew verb, 1 Sam. ii. 8, and for that of the preposition, Isa. liv. 11. It is, in fact, the familiar figure by which a family or a nation is likened to a building ("house of Abraham," "of Israel"). Jehovah's purpose had been to make Abraham's seed as the dust of the earth (Gen. xiii. 16). Instead of that, the restored exiles would be few, and weak in proportion, so that the Jewish Church of the early restoration period is represented as complaining, "We made not the land salvation, neither were inhabitants of the world produced" (Isa. xxvi. 18). A special Divine promise was needed to surmount this grave difficulty. **A goodly . . . nations;** rather, *a heritage the most glorious among the nations.* So in Ezekiel (xx. 6, 15) Palestine is described as "the glory of all lands." The want of irrigation, and the denudation of the land, have no doubt much diminished the natural beauty and fertility of Palestine; but wherever moderate care is bestowed on the soil, how well it rewards it! **Thou shalt call me . . . shalt not turn;** rather, *thou wilt call me . . . wilt not turn.* It is the continuation of Jehovah's ideal for Israel. In response to his loving gifts, Israel would surely recognize him as her Father, and devote to him all her energies in willing obedience. **Father** is here used, not in the spiritual and individualizing sense of the New Testament, but in such a sense as a member of a primitive Israelitish family, in which the *patria potestas* was fully carried out, could realize. The first instance of the individualizing use of the term is in Ecclus. xxiii. 1—4. (For the Old Testament use, comp. Isa. i. 2; lxiii. 16; Exod. iv. 22; Hos. xi. 1.)

Ver. 20.—**Surely.** The word acquires an adversative sense from the context, as in Isa. liii. 4, and is virtually equivalent to "but surely." **From her husband**; literally, *from her friend* or *companion*. The choice of the word seems to indicate the inner hollowness of the married life. The woman only sees in her husband the companion, behind whose back she can follow her own inclinations.

Ver. 21.—Another of those rapid transitions so common in emotional writing like Jeremiah's. The prophet cannot bear to dwell upon the backsliding of his people. He knows the elements of good which still survive, and by faith sees them developed, through the teaching of God's good providence, into a fruitful repentance. How graphic is the description! On the very **high places** (or rather, *bare, treeless heights* or *downs*, as ver. 2) where a licentious idolatry used to be practised, **a sound is heard** (render so, not *was heard*)—the sound of the loud and audible weeping of an impulsive Eastern people (comp. ch. vii. 29). **For they have;** this evidently gives the reason of the bitter lamentation; render, *because they have.*

Ver. 22.—**Return, ye backsliding children,** etc.; more literally, *Turn, ye turned-away sons; I will heal your turnings* (as Hos. xiv. 4). It seems strange at first sight that this verse does not stand before ver. 21. But the truth is that ver. 21 describes not so much the "conversion" of the Jews as their willingness to "convert" (an archaism of King James's Bible, which we may well regret), or "turn" to God. Christ must touch, or at least make his presence felt, in order that the sick man may be healed; a special call of God must be heard, in order that the sinner may truly repent. **Behold, we come unto thee.** Efficacious, and not "irresistible" grace, is the doctrine of the Old Testament.

Ver. 23.—**Truly in vain,** etc. An obscure and (if corruption exists anywhere) corrupt passage, which, however, it is hopeless to attempt to emend, as the corruption consists partly in wrong letters, partly in omitted letters or words (or both); and, moreover, the text employed by the Septuagint appears to have presented the same difficulty. The latter point is especially noteworthy. It is far from proving that the traditional text is correct; what it does suggest is that the writings of the prophets were at first written down in a very insecure manner. The rendering of the Authorized Version is substantially that of Hitzig, who explains "the multitude of [the] mountains," as meaning "the multitude of gods worshipped on the mountains"—too forced an expression for so simple a context. It seems most natural to suppose (with Ewald, Graf, and Keil), a contrast between the wild, noisy cultus of idolatrous religions, and the quiet spiritual worship inculcated by the prophets. Compare by way of illustration, the loud and ostentatious demonstrations of Baal's ritual in 1 Kings xviii., with the sober, serious attitude of Elijah in the same chapter. The word rendered in the Authorized Version "multitude" has a still more obvious and original meaning, viz. "tumult;" and probably the Targum is not far from the true sense in rendering, "In vain have we worshipped upon the hills, and not for profit have we raised a tumult on the mountains."

Ver. 24.—**For shame;** rather, *and the Shame* (i.e. the Baal). The words *Bosheth* ("Shame") and *Baal* are frequently interchanged; so again in ch. xi. 13 (comp. Hos. ix. 10). So, too, Jerubbesheth stands for Jerubbaal (2 Sam. xi. 21; comp. Judg. vi. 32); Ishbosheth for Eshbaal (2 Sam. ii. 8; comp. 1 Chron. viii. 33). **Hath devoured the labour of our fathers,** etc.; a condensed way of saying that Baal-worship has brought the judgments of God upon us, our flocks and herds, and all the other "labour" (or rather "wealth," *i.e.* fruit of labour) of our fathers, being destroyed as the punishment of our sins (comp. Deut. xxviii. 30—32). Another view is that the "devouring" had to do with the sacrifices, but it is improbable that the sacrificial worship of Baal had developed to such a portentous extent, and the former explanation is in itself more suitable to the context.

Ver. 25.—**We lie down;** rather, *Let us lie down;* said in despair, just as Hezekiah says, "Let us enter the gates of Sheol" (Isa. xxxviii. 10). A prostrate position is the natural expression of deep sorrow (2 Sam. xii. 16; xiii. 31; 1 Kings xxi. 4). **Our confusion covereth us;** rather, *Let our confusion* (or *reproach*) *cover us* (*like a veil*) (comp. ch. li. 51; Ps. lxix. 7).

HOMILETICS.

Ver. 4.—*Filial reminiscences of God.* We are here brought from the view of God as a Husband to that of him as a Father, for only when we consider his various relations with us can we measure the depth of our sin or the motives we have for returning to him.

I. GOD'S PEOPLE CAN CALL TO MIND OLD MEMORIES OF HIS FATHERLY GOODNESS. 1. In our own experience of his grace he has revealed himself as a *Father*. He is the Source and Origin of life. In him we continue to exist (Acts xvii. 28). He is constantly protecting us and enriching us with his gifts. 2. God may be discerned as the *Companion of his people's early days*. (1) He was with his people—a Companion—not merely blessing them from a distance. (2) He was with his people as a *Friend*, holding kindly intercourse, condescending to intimate communion, accompanying them as a Stay and Solace through their pilgrimage. (3) He was with his people in their *youth*. None are too young to be honoured with the friendship of God. Happy are they who have been in communion with God from their youth up, instead of only coming to him at the eleventh hour! They enjoy the most of him, have longest time for his service, have most advantages for growing and ripening in religious experience. As we look back on our early days, we may often discern how God has been with us in dark scenes where his presence was unrecognized at the time, and has been sustaining and cheering us when we have not recognized the hand from which the comfort was coming.

II. OLD MEMORIES OF GOD'S FATHERLY GOODNESS MAY BE ABUSED. It would seem that the Jews often fell into this mistake. 1. *We may assume that the past blessing of God is all that we need*. Because we once enjoyed his presence we may be too ready to rest satisfied as though all must be well with us henceforth for ever. But we cannot live in the past. It is vain to waste our time in idle self-congratulations on our early devotion if later years have found us wandering far from God. We must not say that all is done that our souls need if we can point to an early time when we were introduced to filial relations with God. It is nothing to us that God was the Friend of our youth if he has been rejected in our later days. Indeed, this early memory will be our accuser for subsequent unfaithfulness. 2. *We may assume that if God was once our Father and Friend he will always stand in those relations to us*. But if we lose our first love we lose the blessings which are connected with it. The past is no security for the present. The momentous questions is, Do we now stand in a true filial relation with God? Is he still our Friend? If he was valued as a Companion in the freshness of youth, is he not wanted in the toils and battles of manhood? will he not be needed in the weariness of age? in the darkness and mystery of the lonely passage of death?

III. OLD MEMORIES OF GOD'S FATHERLY GOODNESS MAY BE CONSIDERED WITH PROFIT. 1. They may *reveal our subsequent unfaithfulness*. We compare ourselves with ourselves and see how we have fallen. 2. They may lead us to *see the blessedness of an earlier estate*, to be awakened to the loss we have suffered, and to be roused to the desire for a return to it. 3. They may *help us to trust God*. He was our Father and our Friend in early days. He is changeless. If, then, we repent and return to him, will he not permit us still to cry, "My Father;" and again to enter into the blessed influences of friendly fellowship with him? So the prodigal remembers his early days, and is induced by old memories to say, "I will arise and go to my father" (Luke xv. 18).

Ver. 10.—*Insincere repentance.* I. REPENTANCE IS INSINCERE WHEN IT DOES NOT POSSESS THE WHOLE HEART. Judah is accused of being "false," and of turning to Jehovah "feignedly," because she did not turn "with her whole heart." 1. True repentance must be found in the *heart*. Mere confession with the lip without a change of feeling is a mockery (Isa. xxix. 13). Simple amendment of external conduct is no repentance unless it is prompted by a sincere desire to do better, by a return to the love of goodness. 2. True repentance must possess the *whole* heart. It is not consistent with a lingering affection for sin. The penitent must not look back regretfully, like Lot's wife, on the pleasant things he is renouncing. Repentance must be for *sin*, not for certain sins selected from the rest for condemnation; it means the desire to abandon all wickedness. People sometimes repent insincerely by confessing and abandoning trifling faults, while they cling to greater evils. A right repentance searches the dark depths of the soul and brings forth old buried sins, forgotten but not yet forgiven, darling bosom sins which have grown into the very life and can only be torn out from a bleeding heart, common sins which are classed among a man's habits and which he excuses to himself as being "his ways." Such repentance is no superficial emotion, no sentiment of the hour stirred in the church only to be forgotten as soon as a man re-enters his worldly associations. It must be thorough, profound, overwhelming. Yet it is not to be measured by the number of tears shed, but by its practical fruits, the solid proofs of a desire for a better life (Luke iii. 8—14).

II. INSINCERE REPENTANCE CANNOT BE ACCEPTED BY GOD. 1. Such repentance is *inexcusable.* Judah had failed to profit by the solemn lessons of her sister's sin and ruin. In face of such terrible warnings, how foolish to cling still to the old life even while pretending to turn from it! 2. Such repentance is only *self-deceiving.* The hypocrite would deceive God, but failing to do this he deceives himself. He is the dupe of his own design. For he imagines that his fraud will serve him some good purpose, whereas it is detected by God and frustrated from the first. 3. Such repentance is *useless.* Judah gains no deliverance by her feigned repentance. God is Spirit, and can only be approached in spirit (John iv. 24). Any other pretended return to him is no return. We do not come to God by simply entering a church, nor please him by the mechanical observance of an external service (Isa. i. 11—15). The insincere repentance is a double mistake, its trouble is all wasted, its tears all shed to no purpose, and the falsehood of it is a new offence increasing guilt before God. To turn to God only with the lip is thus not merely not to turn to him at all, it is to wander still further from him. Let us beware, therefore, of using the familiar language of confession if we are not really desiring to renounce sin and be reconciled to God. Let repentance, of all things, be true and whole-hearted.

Vers. 12, 13.—*God inviting the return of his sinful children.* This invitation is offered to "backsliding Israel" in preference to "false Judah" (ver. 11). There seemed to be more hope of the former. Openly wicked men are more easily led to repentance than hypocritical pretenders to goodness. Christ came not to call the righteous, but sinners (Matt. ix. 12, 13), and his invitations were more readily accepted by publicans and reprobates than by Pharisees.

I. THE INVITATION IS FROM GOD. Before men return to God he seeks them. The Father calls to his children while they are yet in rebellion against him. In the quarrel between man and God all the wrong is on man's side, yet God is the first to bring about a reconciliation. 1. We have *not to reconcile God to us*, but to be reconciled to him (2 Cor. v. 20). Any difficulty on God's side has been removed by his own act in the sacrifice of his Son. Now it only remains for us to return. 2. We have *not to wait for God's willingness to receive us*, nor to persuade him. Already he has invited us, and he now waits to be gracious.

II. THE MOTIVE FOR THE INVITATION IS THE GOODNESS OF GOD. We must not imagine that there is in us any inherent attractiveness, any merit which in the eye of God outweighs our sin, any valuable qualities which make us necessary to him. The reason for God's anxiety to have his children return is simply his love for them, and this love is not derived from their worthiness, but from his nature. 1. It is because *God is "merciful,"* i.e. this is his peculiar characteristic; and mercy is exercised not according to desert, but according to need. Therefore the less man's desert is the greater will be the outgoing of God's mercy, because the deeper will be man's wretchedness. 2. It is because *God's anger is temporary*, while his mercy "endureth for ever." God says, "I will not keep mine anger for ever;" but he does keep his love for ever. We say "God is love," but we do not say "God is anger." He exercises anger when this is required, but to serve an end—to establish justice, to punish sin, etc., whereas he exercises love for its own sake. This latter is more fundamental, in the very heart of God, and outlives the wrath. Hence behind the passing anger that denounces and punishes, there is the eternal love that invites to reconciliation.

III. THE ONE CONDITION FOR ACCEPTING THE INVITATION IS THE ACKNOWLEDGMENT OF GUILT. "Acknowledge thine iniquity." 1. This acknowledgment is *necessary.* We can only return to God by forsaking our sin, for it is just our sin which keeps us from him, and as long as this is retained must still keep us from him. Indeed, separation from God and sin are but two aspects of the same spiritual condition. We can only be forgiven when we admit our guilt, and only be welcomed by God when we humble ourselves before him. 2. This acknowledgment must be *complete.* It must include a recognition of (1) positive disobedience—"thou hast transgressed," etc.; (2) the multitudinous variety of sins—"and hast scattered thy ways;" (3) the disregard of God's voice even when he has spoken in love and urged us to return. 3. This acknowledgment is *sufficient*. "*Only* acknowledge thine iniquity. No sacrifice, penance, or partial reformation is first required on our part. The new and better life must *begin* with our return to God.

Ver. 14 (second clause, "and I will take you," etc.).—*Religious individualism.* I. BY NATURE MEN LIVE SEPARATE, INDIVIDUAL LIVES. Man is social, yet he is personal. 1. Each soul has its own personality, separate from that of every other soul by immeasurable oceans. Sympathy unites souls, but does not destroy this individuality of being. Each soul has its own secret life, and the deeper the spiritual experience is the more lonely, hidden, and incommunicable will it be. There are dark recesses of consciousness in the shallowest heart which no stranger can fathom (Prov. xiv. 10). 2. Each soul has its own separate course to live, its peculiar privileges and privations, blessings and trials, its duties which no other soul can fulfil, its reserved heritage, its vast destiny. Starting from near points, our lives may branch out in all directions till they are utterly isolated in the lonely solitudes of the infinite possibilities of being. 3. Each soul has its own necessary variety of nature. No two are alike. The unity of mankind is a oneness, not of unison, but of harmony.

II. GOD DEALS WITH MEN SEPARATELY AND INDIVIDUALLY. 1. His love is towards men as individuals. The size of the human family is no impediment to this with an Infinite Being who possesses infinite capacities of thought and affection. Even among men the parent of a large family has as individual a love for each of his children as the parent of a small family. 2. God approaches man individually. The outward voice of invitation is general: "whosoever will" is invited. But the inward voice, in conscience and spiritual communion, is private. Yet this fact is not a restriction on our enjoyment of God's favours, for he speaks thus inwardly to all who will listen to him.

III. MEN MUST RETURN TO GOD SEPARATELY AND INDIVIDUALLY. Each must repent, trust, pray for himself. A nation can only return as the units return, "one of a city, and two of a family." We must enter the "wicket-gate" in single file. No association with Christendom, a Christian nation, a Church, a Christian family, will secure our personal redemption. Even families are divided here. Each must say for himself in the singular, "*I* will arise;" "*My* Father;" "*My* God." Still: (1) We may help one another, and owing to the influence of sympathy there may be "two of a family," while perhaps there is only "one of a city;" (2) after we return to God we may naturally unite in his service as his family, his Church, the one body of which Christ is the Head; and (3) though a few may return at first, it is to be the work of these few to increase their number till the whole apostate family is reconciled to God.

Vers. 16—18.—*The blessings of redemption.* The blessings which are here described as following the restoration of Israel are partly national and material in form, but they contain, in the heart of them, those deep spiritual elements of the Messianic ideas which constitute the blessings of redemption. Note the chief characteristics of these—

I. THE NEGATIVE CHARACTERISTICS OF THE BLESSINGS OF REDEMPTION. 1. *Freedom from the old life of sin.* "Neither shall they walk any more after the stubbornness of their evil hearts." This implies (1) that the conquest of sin is itself a good to God's people, and not merely a painful and self-denying means for securing some other good; and (2) that this conquest is to be complete and final. Bad as were the subsequent failings of the Jews after the Captivity, they were cured for ever of their old sins of idolatry and of participation in the immoral and cruel rites of their neighbours' religions. Many as are the defects and falls of the Christian, these do not equal the evil of his old life. 2. *A change from the old habits of religion.* The Jews will no longer have the ark, the seat of a localized Divine presence, and they will not want this. We can never exactly recover the past. Paradise cannot be regained. The new Jerusalem will not be like the old garden of Eden. The restored Christian cannot return to the primitive innocence of childhood. But he need not altogether regret this impossibility. With the innocence of childhood there were associated its ignorance, its weakness, its restraints. With redemption there comes a new and larger life. The ark is lost; but this need not be regretted since with it the limitations and material conditions of the Divine visitations are gone also.

II. THE POSITIVE CHARACTERISTICS OF THE BLESSINGS OF REDEMPTION. 1. *The enjoyment of God's full presence.* God's throne is to be no longer the mercy-seat at the ark: (1) confined to one small sanctuary; (2) separating the religious from the secular; (3) hidden from the common gaze of men. All Jerusalem will be God's throne. God will dwell in the midst of his people, revealed to all, consecrating the affairs of daily life (Zech. xiv. 20). 2. *The glorifying of God in the earth through the instrumentality of his people.* "All the nations shall be gathered," etc. God's people are honoured by being the means of attracting others to him. Thus they are "a city set on a hill" (Matt. v. 14). The blessings of the gospel in Christ are offered to the world. The glory of the Saviour and the joy of his people will be completed by the acceptance of them by all nations. 3. *Brotherly love.* The old enmity of Israel and Judah will cease (Isa. xi. 12, 13). Christ is the Prince of peace. His advent prepared the way for peace on earth. As his kingdom spreads, peace must also extend over the troubled world. Even now the individual Christian must find his joy in exercising the peaceful spirit and practising brotherly love (Heb. xiii. 1).

III. THE CONDITIONS FOR RECEIVING THE BLESSINGS OF REDEMPTION. 1. *Return to God in repentance.* This is implied in the previous verses. Repentance precedes restoration. 2. *Multiplication of numbers.* These blessings were to come after the people were "multiplied and increased." We cannot expect the full Christian blessings till the Church has grown largely in numbers. God has special blessings for his *Church.* The Holy Spirit came at Pentecost, when the whole Church was gathered together (Acts ii. 1). These privileges of Christianity are of such a nature that they are not lessened by distribution, but the more they are scattered abroad, the more valuable do they become to every individual who enjoys them. 3. *A fitting time.* These blessings were not enjoyed at once. For some we still wait. "The kingdom of heaven is like a grain of mustard seed." Its growth is gradual; so is also the enjoyment of its blessings.

Ver. 22.—*Invitation and response.* I. THE INVITATION. 1. The *object* of the invitation. God calls on his people to return to him. Not simple reformation of morals, but the restoration of personal relations with God as the Father of his people is desired. 2. The *condition* of the invited. They are apostate children; *i.e.* (1) they are far from God, though (2) they were once near to him, and (3) they are still his children. As sinners, men have all lost a first estate of innocence, but have not lost, and can never lose, their filial relationship to God. Hence (1) the greatness of their guilt and (2) the hope of their restoration. 3. The accompanying *promise.* God invites and does not drive; he here exchanges threats for promises. God will heal, not simply receive his children. God alone can heal their apostacies. Man repents of sin, but God cures it. It is our part to turn from the evil, God's to destroy that evil. Sin is washed out, not by the tears of penitence, but by the blood of Christ. The healing is of the apostacies themselves, not simply of their painful effects. Christ saves from *sin.* This is what God most requires in us, and what we most need for our own blessedness (John i. 29).

II. THE RESPONSE. 1. An expression of *willing obedience.* "Behold, we come unto thee." This response must be *voluntary.* God waits for man's return, does not force it; since what he desires is not the abject submission of vanquished enemies, but the loving reconciliation of children. This response must also be *active.* "We come." The penitent does not simply "accept" the grace of God in a passive faith. He must "arise and go" (Luke xv. 18). This implies exertion of will, active obedience. 2. An indication of the *grounds* of that obedience. "For thou art the Lord our God." God invites by a promise of blessing to his people; they respond by turning from the thought of their own profit to that of the character and claim of God. The great motive to return is found in what God is rather than in what he does, because the return is to him and not merely to his blessings. Men will return to God when they see what there is in him to attract them to his feet. Hence the importance of knowing God (Job xxii. 21). Christ invites us by revealing the Father (John xiv. 6, 7). (1) We should think of the revealed *character* of God as a ground for returning to him. Israel returns by remembering the ancient Name "Jehovah," with its glorious significance and its sacred memories. (2) We should think of God's peculiar *relations* with us. Israel thinks of "Jehovah *our* God." This relationship points to God's claim upon us, rising out of his recognized authority as "ours," and the special covenant bonds of those who have once yielded themselves to him, and also to the peculiar grace God bestows on his people, which both increases the obligation and facilitates the effort to return.

Ver. 23.—*From false to true salvation.* I. THE NEED OF SALVATION. This seems to be confessed before as much as after repentance. In both conditions Israel must turn somewhere for deliverance. 1. The need is *universal.* Israel was in national danger ; but socially and privately men felt a vague sense of unrest and helplessness, and their heathen rites were a proof of this. The mystery of existence, the weariness of toil, the sorrow and disappointments of common experience, the terror of death, make men feel their helplessness. All religions witness to this fact. 2. The need is felt to be such that *only religion can meet it.* Men instinctively cry to their gods in the storm (Jonah i. 5). This element of religion is retained when every other vestige of it has vanished. This element is common to the most diverse forms of religion, the most degraded equally with the most elevated. Is not such a fundamental fact of human nature a ground for hope? Can we believe that such a deep, instinctive cry will meet with no response?
II. THE FALSE HOPE OF SALVATION. Israel had turned to the pagan worship on the hills for deliverance ; but in vain. 1. Superficially regarded, there was *much to recommend this.* (1) It was conspicuous and imposing—on the hill-tops. (2) It was noisy ; there was tumult on the mountains. The more noise and bustle there is in a thing the more important does it seem to those who forget that the real power is with "the still small voice" and the "gentleness" that makes great. (3) It was popular ; in religious matters, as in all else, unthinking people go with the multitude. (4) It was multiform ; not one temple service, but sacrifices on every hill. Unspiritual people put faith in the number of prayers, the amount of gifts, etc., rather than in the motive and spirit which prompt them. (5) It was easy to follow ; it required no purity of life, no spiritual effort of faith. Men like a cheap religion. 2. *Experience proved the hope to be false.* The salvation was hoped for in vain. Heathen gods neither protected from external foes nor cured the internal wretchedness of Israel. This must have been the case, because (1) they were not gods at all, the ground of the hope did not exist ; (2) the corruption which was permitted and encouraged in the rites with which these gods were served was the very source of the nation's ruin. The hope of salvation was the cause of destruction. So is it whenever men turn from God to lower grounds of confidence. The very apostacy thus committed is the source of the ruin which it is expected to avert. It is a great thing to have made the discovery of this fact. To see the mistake of the false hope is the first step towards deliverance.
III. THE TRUE HOPE OF SALVATION. "Truly in Jehovah our God is the salvation of Israel." 1. God only *can* deliver, since he only can control nations and subdue the hearts of individual men. 2. God *does* deliver by his providence in outward events and his spiritual help in the internal battle with sin. 3. God is *known* as the Deliverer by his actions in the past. Israel turns to "Jehovah *our* God," the God who had often shown himself as a Saviour. He who rightly reads the story of his own past life will see in it reasons for trusting God for the future. 4. God is *sought* as the Deliverer when all other refuges fail. After making the painful discovery mentioned in the earlier part of the verse, Israel comes to recognize the true salvation, but not till then. Trouble is good if it reveals the rottenness of our mistaken hope in time to set us free to seek the true hope. Yet how sad that men should need to have the veil thus forcibly torn from their eyes !

Vers. 24, 25.—*Shame.* I. SHAME IS THE NATURAL ACCOMPANIMENT OF GUILT. 1. *Distinguish shame from modesty.* Modesty is the fear of shame. Modesty shrinks from doing the thing which when done will result, or ought to result, in shame. Thus modesty pertains to innocence, shame to guilt. 2. *Distinguish natural shame from guilty shame.* Natural shame results from the exposure of what should be kept private but is pure in itself—this applies to spiritual as well as bodily delicacy ; guilty shame is associated with that which, whether revealed or not, is morally bad. 3. *Distinguish false from true shame.* The blush of innocence when falsely accused, the shrinking from the disapproval by others of conduct which we feel conscientiously bound to pursue, and similar feelings, are instances of the former. They simply result from weakness. Such shame is a needless pain, but it is only culpable when it leads to weak subserviency to what we know is not right—the fear of man which bringeth a snare. True shame is not simply the distressing consciousness of the disapproval of others, but the consciousness that this is well deserved.

II. REPENTANCE LEADS US TO REGARD SIN WITH SHAME. Israel then names Baal, the god of her former worship, "Shame." To the penitent "all things are new." The sins in which he gloried are now objects of the deepest shame. 1. Men must *see sin in a true light* to regard it with shame. The Israelites are here represented as confessing sin; they feel it is their own act: "We have sinned;" they feel that their fathers' sin does not extenuate the guilt of the new sin of the children, but, on the contrary, adds to the cumulative guilt of the nation. 2. When sin is thus regarded, the *shame is overpowering and overwhelming*: overpowering, for Israel says, "Let us lie down in our shame," there is no resisting the influence of it, it crushes to the dust in humiliation; and it is overwhelming, "let our confusion cover us;" such shame is no superficial and transient emotion. It is all-absorbing.

III. THE SHAME FOR SIN IS A WHOLESOME CORRECTIVE. Nothing is more painful. Self-love, self-conceit, and self-respect are all cruelly wounded. Yet the bitter medicine is a true antidote to the sweet poison of sin. 1. It opens our eyes to the *fatal consequences* of wickedness. In regarding Baal as "shame," the people seem to discover for the first time that he had "devoured the labour of their fathers from their youth." The passion of sin throws a false glamour about it and its effects which shame dissolves. 2. It serves as a *strong deterrent from future sin*. It makes our old ways look horrible, disgusting, contemptible. We wonder how we could have loved them, and so long as the shame lasts nothing could induce us to return to them. Unfortunately, shame soon dies away, and if disregarded leaves men harder than before. Therefore it should not be trusted in by itself, but used as a means to lead us to the enduring security against sin in Christ (Rom. viii. 1—5).

HOMILIES BY VARIOUS AUTHORS.

Ver. 4.—*A call to the young.* We need not hesitate so far to turn these words aside from their original meaning as to regard them as a Divine appeal to the young; especially if we understand that the prophet is here calling on Judah to return to the freshness of her "youth;" that "at this time," this hopeful reign of the good King Josiah, she should renew her covenant with Jehovah and the "love of her espousals" (ch. ii. 2). In the days of youth the heart is most freely open to Divine influences, and it may be expected to respond readily to such an appeal as this. Note—

I. THE DEEPEST TRUTH OF RELIGION IS THE FATHERHOOD OF GOD. That he is the Father of our spirits is the basis of his claims upon us. The quality of our religious thought, the drift of our religious opinions, the tone of our religious life, depend very greatly on our faith in this truth. Fatherhood is our highest conception of God, and includes within it all aspects of his being, and all the relations he sustains towards us. This crowns them all, embraces all. We cannot rise above and beyond it. Our ideas are essentially defective if we fall short of it. Not that the actual human fatherhood worthily represents it; that, at its best, is but a marred and broken copy—a feeble, distant reflection—of the Divine. And yet the essential elements remain in spite of accidental faults. Power, wisdom, love, judicial authority, kingly rule, protective tenderness,—these are the attributes of its ideal. And from the human, with all its imperfections and perversions, we rise to the Divine.

II. THE APPREHENSION OF THIS SACRED RELATIONSHIP IS SPECIALLY BEFITTING THE SEASON OF YOUTH. What more natural than that young people should think of God as their Father; that this idea of him should give shape and colouring to all their other religious ideas, and blend with all their views of life, and all their impressions of personal duty? Those who have grown old—old in the habit of frivolous thought, in the carnalizing ways of the world, in the debasing service of sin, are often dead to the impression of it. Their hearts are too much estranged to feel its charm. But shall not they who still have the dew of their youth upon them, the bloom of its quick sensibility and pure affection, love to hear a *Father's* voice?

III. Nevertheless, THE FULL DISCOVERY OF THIS RELATION MARKS A CRISIS IN THE HISTORY OF ANY SOUL. It is generally connected with the painful discovery of sin and need. "I write unto you, little children, because your sins are forgiven you for his Name's sake, ... because ye have known the Father" (1 John ii. 12, 13). How suggestive is this of the hidden causes, the secret springs, the earliest realizations of Divine life in the soul! One of its first evidences is the recognition of the Father. The cry, "Abba, Father!" is the first that it breathes forth. But this comes with and through the recognition of Christ, the Son, the Saviour. "No man knoweth the Father save the Son, and he to whomsoever the Son shall reveal him" (Matt. xi. 27). And it is a revelation that brings the assurance of "forgiveness for his Name's sake." The sense of dreary distance from God—guilt, shame, hunger, degradation,—this is the prelude to the sweet satisfactions of the life of sonship. It is the prodigal "coming to himself." When we are thus painfully feeling our way back to him, God comes forth in Christ to meet us, embracing us in the arms of his great love, breathing, weeping out upon us the infinite tenderness of his fatherly heart. Then we feel that we can dare to take that sacred name "Father" on our lips. It has a deep and blessed meaning in it never known before. And fear and shame and sorrow give place to the joy of eternal reconciliation.

IV. THE NATURAL RESULT OF THIS DISCOVERY WILL BE FULL PERSONAL SURRENDER TO THE FATHER'S GUIDANCE AND CONTROL. "Guide," literally, *Husband;* and the word "husband" is suggestive of all thoughtful and kindly guardianship, the wisdom that directs, and the strength that sustains. Youth needs such guardianship: 1. *Because of its special moral dangers*, worldly fascinations, Satanic temptations, acting on quick natural susceptibility. 2. *Because of its inexperience.* Experience is the growth of years. It is not of itself always the parent of the highest practical wisdom, but the want of it calls for the help of a superior power. 3. *Because of its weakness of moral principle.* There may be excellent natural dispositions, germs of Christian virtue in the soul, but they are not yet developed. They are but latent possibilities of good. When put to the test, they may be found wanting. God's grace alone can ripen them into mature and steadfast principles. 4. *Because beneath its fairest promise there may be hidden seeds of evil*, which only need the outward incentive to bring forth deadly fruit. 5. *Because the after-destiny depends so much on how the steps of youth are guided.* Let the young give heed to the Father's voice, and yield themselves to his loving control, if they would tread the path of honour and safety and blessedness.—W.

Ver. 22.—"*Backsliding Israel.*" "Backsliding" was the characteristic vice of the Jewish people throughout the whole course of their history. Their career was one of perpetual sinning and repenting, until the great apostacy, the final "falling away." And in this we see what is too often a truthful reflection of the individual life of men. The Jews were emphatically a representative people. Not merely does their recorded history represent the method of God's ways, but it illustrates the folly and treachery, the moral weakness and waywardness of our human nature. Dwell on the individual application of this passage. Consider—

I. THE EVIL INDICATED. "Backsliding" is suggestive of a turning away from God, a departure from the path of truth and righteousness, a fall from some higher state of spiritual consciousness or moral life. This evil may assume different forms. It may consist: 1. *In the loss of the simplicity and integrity of religious faith.* In an age of mental restlessness like the present, men too easily lose their hold of truth, which is the very hope and life of their souls. We may look with perfect composure upon the conflict between truth and error as regards its general and ultimate issues, but dare not forget how disastrous its bearings upon the individual life may be. There are revolutions in the history of religious thought, as in the history of nations, which it is as vain to think of arresting as it would be to attempt to turn back the ocean tide; but it is a mournful thing when, under such conditions, the mind that once had a firm grasp of the vital elements of Christian truth has slipped from its moorings and drifted out into the wild sea of doubt and uncertainty. To a really earnest spirit the recovery of a lost faith is generally a painful process. How many have travelled back, as with wounded, bleeding feet, to positions of clearer vision and firmer standing which they once occupied, but in an evil hour had forsaken! As sometimes after a bright morning, which has been followed by a day of cloud and storm, there is again at sunset a glorious outbursting gleam of the radiance that had been obscured; so is it with their souls. They return to rest calmly in the truth that they had for a while lost sight of, and "at eventide," as in the morning, "it is light." 2. *In the decline of religious feeling*, the decay of those affections in which religious life consists. This is that secret spiritual "backsliding" that directly affects the soul's personal relation to God, and the consciousness of which sometimes extorts the bitter cry, "Oh that I were as in months past!" etc. (Job xxix. 2—4). It may arise from no change in religious belief. While a departure from the simplicity of the faith is generally connected with a lowering of the tone of religious feeling, the converse of this is not always true. But the faith has lost its life-giving force. The light it sheds has no warm, kindling glow. It is the light of the moon rather than the sun—clear and cold, having no power to quicken the frame of nature, to develop its beauty and fruitfulness, to awaken its music, and fill it with exulting joy. The carnalizing influences of the world, the wear and tear of daily life, inevitably lead to this internal spiritual decay, unless there is a perpetual renewal of the life "whose springs are hidden and Divine." 3. *In practical departure from the standard of religious duty.* The backsliding of the heart cannot long be concealed. It betrays itself in many ways—in a forsaking of the paths of Christian service, in some manifest lack of moral integrity, in a relapse into some form of vicious habit, perhaps in a complete loosening of the bonds of religious restraint, and utter abandonment to the pursuits of an ungodly life. It is of such a case that our Lord says, "If the salt have lost his savour," etc. (Matt. v. 13); and again, "No man, having put his hand to the plough," etc. (Luke ix. 62); and St. Peter afterwards affirms, "It had been better for them not to have known the way of righteousness," etc. (2 Pet. ii. 21).

II. GOD'S METHOD OF HEALING. "I will heal your backslidings." This is the gracious persuasion by which he seeks to reclaim his children from their guilty wanderings. How may we expect him to fulfil the promise? 1. *By awakening in us a vivid sense and penitent acknowledgment of the wrong.* We can scarcely be delivered from it till we have seen all the sin and shame of it—its real meaning, the source from whence it springs, the end to which it leads. Until all this is deeply felt and freely confessed before God, the first step in the process of recovery has not been taken (see Ps. li. 3, 4; xxxii. 5; 2 Cor. vii. 10, 11). 2. *By moving us to trust simply in his forgiving and renewing mercy.* Our only refuge is in the Divine mercy, and there is no other way of mercy than that which the gospel reveals. The guilt of our backslidings can alone be cancelled by the blood of Christ, and the secret cause of them removed by the grace of his Spirit (1 John ii. 1, 2; iii. 5—9). "There is no prescription for the sickness of the heart but that which is written in the Redeemer's blood," for in this alone have we both the pledge and the channel of the saving love of God. 3. *By creating in us the energy of a nobler life.* "Return," etc. It is a question, after all, of moral resolution and self-determining spiritual power.

> "Full seldom does a man repent, or use
> Both grace and will to pick the vicious quitch
> Of blood and custom wholly out of him,
> And make all clean, and plant himself afresh."

But God gives this gracious energy to those who seek it, and such "repentance unto life" is the true "healing."—W.

Ver. 1.—*The offer of a great forgiveness.* I. CONSIDER THE ILLUSTRATION BY WHICH IS SHOWN THE EXTENT OF JEHOVAH'S MERCY TO THE LOST. By an illustration drawn from the power allowed to the Israelite husband, Jehovah shows how great is his spirit of mercy and his desire that the deserting wife, so terribly described in the preceding chapter, should return. The reference is evidently to Deut. xxiv. 1—4. There the husband is invested with an authority which almost seems arbitrary, although from Numb. v. it also appears that an accused wife had a right of appeal to ordeal, which ordeal would infallibly certify either innocence or guilt. The essential point here, however, lies in this, that there was an *ordained inability* for the wife to return to her first husband. The marriage tie, in spite of all the apparent facility of divorce, was not a thing to play fast and loose with. The way of departure might seem comparatively easy, but the way of return was altogether hedged up. We behold a curious mixture of indulgence and severity—*indulgence* for a time because of the hardness of the people's hearts; *severity*, in order that society might be kept together at all. For a husband to take back such a wife was ordained a ceremonial pollution, which needed to be cleansed away. But if such a return was impossible, still more evidently impossible was the return of one who had lived as a harlot. Yet thus did Israel, once the loving, devoted spouse (ch. ii. 1), now appear to Jehovah. Her life of desertion from Jehovah is described as one continuous, shameless exhibition of the harlot's lust. And it is just in the light of all this terrible impurity that the word comes to her, "Return again to me, saith the Lord."

II. CONSIDER HOW IT COMES THAT GOD CAN ADDRESS SUCH AN INVITATION. It is the old story of God's power to do things which man, however loving and merciful he may be in disposition, finds to be quite beyond his reach. Man, with the best intentions, with the most sympathetic heart, is limited in his resources to the outcast by the necessities of human society. To put one who has been an habitual thief in a position of serious trust, is a thing so hard as to be practically impossible. The victims of vicious inclinations may be deeply pitied, and yet the moment one tries to give them any large measure of help, the claims of others somehow come in to forbid. But God, as he rises far above man in his love and mercy and insight into the sinning human heart, so he rises—if one may thus put it—higher still in his power to give an amply sufficient help. God can bring back into the privileges and possibilities belonging to his Church, he can bring under all the penetrating potencies of his grace, the very worst apostate. What creature can be thought of more defiled than the harlot? Human reclaiming agencies can do nothing to serve her or save her, except as they put in their forefront the loving-kindness of God in Christ Jesus. It is well for us when we have to consider the impure, the degraded, the despairing slaves of vice, to consider also these encouraging words of God, "Return to me." Think much of him who spoke them, and then of the sort of people to whom they were spoken. Those who are most of all suffering in social outlawry may read all the horrible descriptions of abandonment to impurity found not only in this prophet but in others, and then say with the most joyful hope, "If Israel, being such, was *pressed* to return, I also may return." Hosea gives the appropriate words for such, "I will go and return to my first husband ; for then was it better with me than now" (Hos. ii. 7). And to keep up the figure, what will the end of such a Divine invitation and such a human resolution be? It is found in Rev. xxi., where we read the following request, "Come hither, I will show thee the bride, the Lamb's wife." The first Israel sank into an indescribable shame ; the second Israel will rise into an indescribable glory.—Y.

Ver. 4.—*Israel's cry to the Father and the Friend.* I. OBSERVE THE SUDDEN CHANGE OF RELATION WHICH IS THUS BROUGHT BEFORE US. Hitherto we have had before us Jehovah's description of Israel under the guise of a wife departing from her husband into the most degrading and shameless conduct. And now our thoughts are suddenly turned, with nothing to prepare for the transition, to a new relation—that of father and child. Note that it is not God who directly presents himself in this relation. "Father" is a term put into the mouths of the people in the preceding chapter and also in this. In ch. ii. 27 they are represented as saying to a *stock*, "*Thou* art my father ;" and now they say to *Jehovah*, "*Thou* art my Father, the Friend, the Companion of my youth." It may be that there was no depth of real sincerity in the cry, even though it is described as a cry, and not a mere perfunctory recognition—at all events, it sets forth a fact. Jehovah was a Father to the nation of Israel in this sense, that it was by his peculiar and necessary power that Israel was separated in all sorts of profoundly significant ways from the great mass of mankind. When Abram started forth, not knowing whither he went, this was to him a sort of being born again ; an entirely new life lay before him, with expectations that he never could have cherished but that God planted them deep in his heart. And thus the name is a right and needful name to use. Israel is doing what it ought to do when it says, "Abba, Father!" The idea evidently is that Israel has learned to speak to God much in the same way that an English child learns to say "papa" or "father" (Isa. viii. 4).

II. OBSERVE THE CONDUCT BY WHICH WHAT IS GOOD IN THIS RECOGNIZED RELATION OF FATHER IS MANIFESTED. It was true that Jehovah had been Father to Israel; it was moreover true that he had been Guide, Friend, and Companion to Israel's youth. It is not always the case that fatherhood means a loving and cherishing companionship. But here it is emphatically the case. Jehovah was a very close Companion to Israel in its youth; not really nearer, of course, than he had been since, but near in such a way that the people were compelled to note his proximity to them, and constant watchfulness over them. This, therefore, as Israel looked back upon its youth, was the right way for it to speak of Jehovah. Being Father, he had also been a true Companion and Support. "Guide of my youth" does very well for a rendering, if we bear in mind all that the guiding implies. There is a guiding which is a mere trade, a mere selling of the guide's knowledge. He takes up any stranger, shows him the way, gets his pay, and then the relation is at an end. But the practical guiding here comes from a deep love and solicitude. Further, it must be remembered that Jehovah's friendship and companionship were the friendship and companionship of one competent to guide. Friendship by itself is, of course, not sufficient to constitute guiding capacity. We see, then, that the expression of this verse is a very suggestive one by which to address God. *All fathers may learn from it the spirit of a right relation towards their children.* It is the name which they should desire their children to associate with their childhood. It should be a remembrance having a binding power when the child has become a man, and the father an old man. It should be possible to look back on a childhood where the father was a true companion, one whose companionship was full of true befriending and guiding. There is also indicated *the spirit in which youth should look beyond earthly dependencies to God himself.* He who was so much to a youthful nation of old will be of inestimable service to the ignorance, weakness, and abounding need of all youth. Especially should this consideration have force when one thinks of the significance in the doctrine of being born again. He who is born again has then a second youth, even though he be in the full strength of natural manhood. And what is wanted is that the man in his strength and his wide outlook on the possibilities of life should choose a truly humble position before God. The expression is also one that *may point back to a submissive, hopeful youth, wherein many Divine impressions were made,* and from which there has been a great backsliding. Then how beautifully would such an expression come from the lips of the returning prodigal, "My Father, thou wast the Guide of my youth, and now after a bitter experience of trying to make my own way, which has ended in a mere drifting before the strong currents of passion and self-indulgence, I come back to thee"! It is sad to have the friendship of father and child broken, sad at any time, but saddest of all when it is not through some meddling whisperer or repeater of a matter (Prov. xvi. 28; xvii. 9), but through the voluntary and obstinate departure of one of the friends.—Y.

Ver. 5.—*Actions speak louder than words.* Israel, we see, is represented as speaking with a very pathetic remembrance of God's great favours in the remote past. At present, indeed, there is a withholding of the rain that means fruitfulness and prosperity, but that Father who has been the Guide of Israel's youth, surely he will soon bring the rain, with all that follows it, in spite of any appearances to the contrary, such as his anger with Israel suggests. Such is the way that Israel *speaks;* but how does it *act?* Is there to be alteration in God without alteration in man? It is of no use for the sinning nation simply to wait as if God's righteous chastisements would be exhausted by lapse of time. There *might* have to be waiting, but assuredly there *would* have to be *repenting,* and the bringing forth of fruits meet for repentance. But instead of this God is confronted with persistent transgression. He who had been Friend, Companion, and Guide in youth could not have been so without a *docile acceptance* of the companionship. The guidance in youth meant that Jehovah had a right to expect a manhood of holy service. But so far from the people giving this, the expectation in their heart is that God will still provide for them and let them do as they like. They do not seem to understand that it is they who by their transgressions provide for the sustenance and continuance of the anger of Jehovah. That anger is not like a storm which

rises one knows not how, and presently subsides without man being able to do anything for its removal.   God's anger was as a fire, and the wickedness of the people was
like dry and highly combustible fuel before the flame.   The one thing needful was to
stop the fuel, and the fire would then very speedily burn out.   To say with the lips,
"My Father, thou wast the Guide of my youth," will only be of use when there is
something like correspondence between what is spoken and what is done.—Y.

Ver. 15.—*God will provide pastors according to his own heart.*   I. THE NEED SO
EMPHATICALLY IMPLIED THAT SUCH PASTORS SHOULD BE GIVEN.   The shepherd's occupation, it need hardly be said, is one that comes up again and again in the Scriptures, both
in the literal sense of the word and the figurative one.   And even in the literal occupation there was, doubtless, often need of men who could be described as shepherds after
God's own heart.   Every shepherd who was faithful, observant, courageous, and altogether superior to the hireling spirit, was to that extent a shepherd after God's own
heart.   Such a one might possibly not be after God's own heart in other respects.
Many are very watchful over the brutes committed to their charge, and utterly thoughtless about the shepherding of their own souls and of the various human beings
dependent on them and influenced by them.   Then passing to the figurative flocks and
shepherds, there are very pathetic representations in the Scriptures of the mischief consequent on the unfaithfulness of those rulers and providers who had been set over God's
people.   Take such a man as King Ahab.   He was not a man after God's own heart,
and what is the result?   Going out against the King of Syria, Ahab, not very hopeful
of a favouring word, consults Micaiah, the faithful prophet of God : "I saw all Israel
scattered upon the hills, as sheep that have not a shepherd;" which was not only a
warning of utter defeat, but a bitter charge against Ahab that he had been utterly
faithless to his trust (1 Kings xxii. 17).   There is so much of the sheep-nature in the
human breast.   How many have been troubled because there is no shepherd (Zech. x.
2)!   Every time the confession is uttered, "All we like sheep have gone astray," there
is a hint of pastoral unfaithfulness somewhere or other.   The sheep-nature in the
human breast has never been better set forth than in the anxiety of the departing
Moses with respect to a competent successor (Numb. xxvii. 17).   Food needs to be provided.   There must be a guarding against self-willed wandering away from the supplies
and comforts belonging to a constant member of the flock.   There are the perils from
wild beasts (1 Sam. xvii. 34).   There is the work needed to bring back that which is
lost.   Look at Zech. xi. 16, where there is a hint of what the shepherd has to do—
visiting those that are cut off, seeking the young ones, healing the broken, bearing that
which standeth still (see also ch. l. 6; Ezek. xxxiv.; John x.).
II. THE FACT THAT SUCH PASTORS WILL ASSUREDLY BE PROVIDED.   Great is the requirement, and there has often been a grievous disappointment in getting it met, but
assuredly it can be met.   The rulers in Israel had not all been as Ahab.   That same
Moses, who was so anxious concerning his successor, had been himself taken from
faithful oversight of another man's sheep in order to deliver Israel from Pharaoh's
clutch, and lead him towards the green pastures and still waters of the promised land
(Exod. iii.).   David, who had followed the ewes great with young, no doubt gently
leading them when needful, gathering the lambs in his arm and carrying them in
his bosom, who also had smitten the lion and the bear, was now taken to feed Jacob
the people of God, and Israel his inheritance (Ps. lxxviii. 71; Isa. xl. 11).   Not only
had he been faithful as a shepherd, but he had also grown ever more conscious of the
sheep-nature in himself, and the sheeplike requirements of his own life, and so,
looking away from his flock upwards, he beautifully says, "Jehovah is my Shepherd."
He had lions following his own soul (Ps. vii. 2; x. 9; xvii. 12; xxii. 13).   Those are
fitted to be shepherds after God's own heart who, feeling their own needs, make
Jehovah *their* Shepherd.   It is important to remember how David is declared as the
man after God's own heart (1 Sam. xiii. 14; Acts vii. 46; xiii. 22).   So God is here
speaking through Jeremiah, with that confidence which comes from actual experience of
the true and the brave among his own chosen.   Then there is the great work of Jesus
to be considered.   It is very significant that in ch. xxiii., after a reference to the unfaithful shepherds, there is a promise of faithful ones, their work being set forth more
explicitly even than here; and then God goes on to speak of the righteous Branch

which shall be raised to David, the King who shall reign and prosper and execute judgment and justice in the earth: he is the Governor who shall feed the Lord's people Israel (Matt. ii. 6); he is the Great Shepherd of the sheep brought again from the dead (Heb. xiii. 20); he who is also the Lamb in the midst of the throne, shall meet those who are gathered out of the great tribulation, and feed them, and lead them "unto living fountains of waters" (Rev. vii. 17); and thus being himself the Great Shepherd, he is competent to convey to all under-shepherds the resources whereby in all wisdom they may feed the hungry with knowledge and understanding. If Jesus makes us truly righteous, then with the lips of the righteous we shall be able to feed many. The duties of a pastor after God's own heart will appear in all their magnitude to one who is considering the pastoral work of Jesus himself. Such a one will take heed to himself, and to all the flock over which the Holy Ghost hath made him overseer, feeding the Church of God which he hath purchased with his own blood. He will have his eye on the grievous wolves that enter in, not sparing the flock. He will carry out the spirit of the commandment which God gave to Moses at Sinai: "Neither let the flocks nor herds feed before the mount" (Exod. xxxiv. 3); by doing his best to keep all within his charge from thoughtless trifling with holy things. It is a great matter to be put in a position of spiritual pastoral responsibility; and all in such positions may joyfully remember that God will give them all needed strength. It is a sad thought for the careless pastor that it should so often be needful for the strangers to stand and feed the flocks he should feed—men that to a certain extent may be reckoned unauthorized. And yet what can be done? Flocks must not die of hunger; and as the real physician is he who cures the disease, whatever his professional standing may be, so the real shepherd is he who feeds the flock, and the brand of interloper is affixed to him in vain. And so God would invite all his people to do what they can to be true shepherds. In one sense the shepherds are as many as the sheep. It is better to be ministering to the deep, undying wants of men, than just to their passing pleasures. He who strives to make himself acceptable to men by an incessant watching of their whims and prejudices is very much like the prodigal who found nothing better to do than feed the *swine*. It is God's will that we should feed *sheep*.—Y.

Ver. 16.—*The superseding of the ark.* Along with the denunciations and painful descriptions which Jehovah has put into the mouth of the prophet, there now begins to be mingled a gracious, evangelical element. God's severest condemnations are meant to pave the way for return, repentance, reconciliation, and a reception of still more abundant gifts than before. Far and wide Israel has been scattered, but scattered only to be brought together again. Though there be but one in a city and two in a nation, God will find out the isolated ones and draw them back to him. Then, with pastors after God's own heart, what can there be but increase and multiplication of the flock of God? And then comes what is evidently meant to be considered as a great blessing, though at first it seems to point to another sad apostasy, and to forgetfulness of one of the holiest and most precious treasures of the past. The ark of the covenant, with the tables of the Law deposited within, was the very centre of religious associations to the nation. But now it is to be no more spoken of. God, indeed, trusts that the memory of it was to pass away. Reading such a verse as this, how one is made to feel the importance of time as an element necessary to the proper understanding of things! Such words as these spoken by Israel at an earlier date would have been a very bad sign, but spoken at the time when all was ripe for them, they become just as much a sign for good. The ark of the covenant—the literal ark with the literal tables of stone—could not be a permanent institution. For centuries it had been holy—holy not in word only, but also in deed. Consider how God honoured it, when for a time it was lodged in Philistia; consider the calamities that came upon the men of Bethshemesh and upon Uzzah, for their thoughtless handling of the ark. Much thus happened to make the Israelite very careful how he dealt with it. David and Solomon in particular were very solicitous to honour the ark to the utmost of their power. This is seen not only in the bringing of the ark up into the city of David, and the putting of it into the temple by Solomon, but perhaps even more in the conduct of Solomon to Abiathar, when Abiathar was implicated in the offence of Adonijah. Solomon spared the man he would otherwise have slain, because he had borne the ark of the Lord God before David (1 Kings ii. 26). But there can be no doubt that as generation succeeded generation, the general feeling would become so mixed with superstition as to do more harm than good. The people had said, "The ark of the covenant of the Lord," but their saying had not amounted to much. The ark had been remembered, but the writing on the stones within had been forgotten. The longer it stood as the central object of a unique ritual, the more it became a symbol of separation from other nations. That which had been given so that one set of thoughts should be associated with it, thoughts to help in making pure, reverent, and watchful, had ended in having quite another set of thoughts associated with it. And so both the object itself seems to have vanished, and at the same time its dominion to have ceased. It is surely a very remarkable thing that all through the Books of Ezra and Nehemiah there is no reference to the ark. The vessels of God's house are mentioned, an altar was set up and offerings made, and in due time a temple built; but there is no word of the ark. Its work was done, and we are not so much as told what became of it. We know that the brazen serpent was declared Nehushtan, but the withdrawal of the ark God manages in complete silence. So true it is that—

> "God fulfils himself in many ways,
> Lest one good custom should corrupt the world."

Y.

Ver. 17.—*The gathering of the nations to Jehovah's throne.* I. THE NEW CHARACTER IN WHICH JERUSALEM APPEARS. It is no longer to be considered simply as the centre of Israelite affection and devotion, the city where was the palace of a human king, and the temple of Jehovah as the peculiar deity of Israel. It is no longer to be the place of a peculiar worship. Its character henceforth is to be far more glorious, one in which Israel shall lose nothing, yea, rather gain, in remembering what it has been able to contribute in attaining such an end. Jerusalem, that had been associated with all sorts of idolatrous abominations, is first of all to be desolated and humbled, whatever human pride and glory there was in it extinguished; and then the true glory will come. The city shall be Jehovah's throne, the throne of him who is God above all gods and King above all kings. And when men would recognize the authority of a king, his throne is the place they must come to. Hence to Jehovah, seated on his throne, all the nations are to be gathered; forsaking national idols and national ideals, all that is local and narrow and self-originated will vanish. The ark of the covenant passes away, and the tables of stone become unnecessary, for from his throne Jehovah will take means whereby he may write on the fleshy tables of every human heart the two great principles, " Love God and love thy fellow-man."

II. HOW THE GATHERING IS TO BE BROUGHT ABOUT. How clear it is that, the ark of the covenant passing away, mere local, terrestrial Jerusalem must also cease to have any peculiar value! The taking away of the ark of the covenant is really the taking away of all in the way of dependence that is merely visible and material. It is plain that the gathering together to Jerusalem cannot mean an actual travelling there from all parts of the earth's surface. Not that the mere local Jerusalem can become as a common spot of earth. After these northern desolators, of whom Jeremiah so often spoke, had done with it, it was rebuilt, and in due time became the scene of great spiritual redeeming acts profoundly affecting every child of man. The thought of the local scenes where Christ died, rose again, and ascended into glory, may well help every sinner in his believing approaches to his Saviour. Those who gather at Jerusalem gather there by virtue of the power which there is in every believing heart. Innumerable pilgrims, on piety intent, have gone on pilgrimage to Jerusalem, doing laborious penances by the way, only to discover in the end that they have been walking after the imaginations of their evil hearts. There may be great value in a journey to the Holy Land, if only those who go there have first of all had their minds opened to apprehend the work which he who died at Jerusalem did for them; otherwise their travels, whatever the human joy and interest of them, may only add to their subsequent condemnation. To go to Jerusalem spiritually is the great thing. The Jerusalem of our journey is situated in the pages of the New Testament rather than in Palestine. It is as we read the Gospels that we feel how Jerusalem is indeed the throne of Jehovah in this sense, that there, through his Son Jesus, he manifested righteousness, power, and love, all the glorious attributes of his eternal reign. The transactions at Jerusalem are incomparable. No transactions in any one nation, however much they may affect the career of that nation, can rival the transactions at Jerusalem. The Englishman as an Englishman may feel his deep concern in Magna Charta and the Bill of Rights. The American as an American thinks of Philadelphia and the Declaration of Independence. The negro as a negro remembers Lincoln and the proclamation which gave freedom to the slaves. But underneath the natural, the peculiar, the merely terrestrial, there is another man, the man who has to think of sin within him, and death and eternity before him. Such a man, if he thinks rightly, will feel that it is towards Jerusalem that his most earnest considerations should gather. All who truly ponder the great questions of life must gather there, and thence in faith their thoughts will ascend to the true, the heavenly, the everlasting Jerusalem.—Y.

Ver. 21.—*A sincere repentance in an appropriate place.* How came this voice to be heard on the high places—this weeping and this supplication? The answer seems to lie in ver. 20, where there is interposed a suggestion that Israel, because of its past defections, would fail to prove capable and worthy of that glorious future which has been just depicted. How then can Israel reply except by an abundant outflow of the signs of penitence? There is weeping; there is deprecation of any such withdrawal of Jehovah's contemplated goodness; there is a most emphatic declaration that they had indeed been utterly perverse and had forgotten Jehovah. The submission to him, the acknowledgment of him, shall now be complete. The words put into the lips of the repentant people (vers. 22—25) are not extorted and grudging words, with a counter-resolution underneath to back out if any chance should offer. The eyes of the apostates have been opened; Israel has come to itself. What has been sought in vain on hills and mountains in the cruel service of heathen deities is to be got in full and abiding power from God. Observe now how—

THESE HIGH PLACES WERE MOST APPROPRIATE FOR THESE TEARFUL ACKNOWLEDG-MENTS AND THESE ENTREATING APPROACHES TO GOD. 1. *The thing done had been a great public wrong.* Where men have sinned is the place for them to confess their sin. Now, this was not a sin in some secret place; it was not a sin confined to the thoughts of the heart, and known only to God; it was not some private, domestic wrong-doing. The whole nation shared in the sin of the high places. Even if some were not actually idolatrous, yet by their silence and inaction they condoned the idolatry. All surrounding nations must be cognizant of it. Sins in public cannot be got rid of without an equally public repentance and suffering. Who can tell what audacious and mocking words may have been spoken concerning Jehovah by the heathen around?—" Why, this Jehovah, whose temple and service are in Jerusalem, and who has no image, has really no power over the people! He has a name to live, but surely he is dead!" Elijah mocked the priests of Baal, and he had cause, for, unhappy men that they were, *they had believed in a lie.* But priests of Baal might also many times have mocked the people of Israel, for in one sense they had the truth, but *they did not believe in it.* Of course, in the end, such people were bound to make a very public acknowledgment of their folly and unbelief. 2. *By this weeping, etc., on the high places, there was a particularly impressive condemnation of idolatry.* He who forsakes a course of action necessarily condemns that action, and reproaches all who still continue in it, reproaches them none the less because reproach may not be at all intended. Such a return to Jehovah as is indicated in the concluding verses of this chapter is also, by the very act, a downright blow against idolatry. Let men who will persist in wrong courses know that they must be prepared for painful experiences when their companions, every now and then, desert them. There will always be some one discovering that the course is wrong, and going over to the other side. Take a very important instance of such exposure as we find it in the New Testament. Pharisaism and Jewish pride are there condemned from two great sources of judgment. One of these we find in Jesus, who spoke, we know how severely, against the Pharisees and their doings. From his words we feel how bad their spirit must have been and their inner life. But perhaps it is not too much to say that Saul's condemnation of them is still more striking; shown not in words so much, but oh, how clearly in deed! when he came out from them, showing he was no more of them. 3. There is thus a great warning *to all who are acting doubtfully in the blaze of public life.* If such have occasion to turn, they must turn in public. Any one who stands well out before his fellows had need take care what he says and does, for he knows not what may be the force of circumstances, what revolutions there may be in his convictions. How much nations have had to suffer—perhaps will have to suffer to the end of time—just because they are not careful of the beginnings of evil in their midst! Look at what it cost America to get rid of negro slavery when once it had grown into a far-spreading and lucrative custom.—Y.

Vers. 1—5.—*Sin, Law, Grace.* We have here represented to us—

I. SIN IN ITS MOST AWFUL FORM. It was the sin of *idolatry.* This was especially grievous in the sight of God, since Israel was designed to give light to all other nations. They were raised up for the very purpose that through them the knowledge of God might flow forth to the whole world. The destinies of humanity depended on them. Hence if the light that was in *them* were darkness, "how great," etc.! Their corruption was the poisoning of the fountain, which would render deadly all its streams. Hence it is that this sin is so commonly represented in the prophetic writings under the images of harlotry and adultery—crimes which, when found in any belonging to him, the Israelite would most fiercely resent. By the nature and measure of their own hatred for such outrages on the purity of their home life, would God have them understand somewhat of the nature and measure of his hatred of that idolatry into which as a nation they had fallen, and against which God's prophets were for ever uttering their earnest protest. And to aggravate their wickedness, they had been guilty thereof again *and again* (ver. 1). They had become lost to all sense of shame in regard to it (vers. 2, 3). They had not waited to be tempted and persuaded, but had gone after their sin, greedily, seeking it rather than it them (ver. 2). They had persisted until the land was polluted by their sin (ver. 3). They had become so hardened that God's corrections failed to produce any result save to make them more brazen-faced in their wickedness than before (ver. 3). And they had gone on to this degree of criminality that they dared to mock God with mere lip service (vers. 4, 5). " Ay, and from this time forward thou criest to me, My Father, the Friend of my youth art thou. Will he always bear a grudge and keep it up for ever ? Behold thou speakest thus and doest wickedness and carriest it out " (Keil's translation). *Corruptio optimi pessima est.* The sin of such as Israel—and *we* are such, raised up, qualified, designed to be the means of vast blessing to others, as is God's purpose with his Church,—is more aggravated and assumes forms more terrible than is possible to others.

II. LAW IN ITS MOST RIGHTEOUS UTTERANCE. (Ver. 1; cf. Deut. xxiv. 4.) " *They say;*" it was a well-known fact that the Law would not hear of the forgiveness and restoration of those who had sinned in the manner Israel had. Such leniency would open the door wide to the most glaring iniquity. " Plato, Plato," said Socrates, " I do not see how God can forgive sin." Sin once committed becomes a fact. Facts have their necessary, immutable and eternal consequences, which only by a miracle can be set aside or escaped. (See sermon by Rev. T. Binney, on ' The Law our Schoolmaster,' etc.; also J. Cook, of Boston, Monday Lectures : ' The Atonement.') There is no gospel for the sinner anywhere outside *the* gospel. The Law, as here, binds the wrong-doer to the inevitable issues of his own wrong-doing. Forgiveness and restoration are simply impossible. But note—

III. GRACE IN ITS MOST MARVELLOUS MANIFESTATION. Ver. 1, "Yet return again to me, saith the Lord." There is doubt as to the meaning of this; some read it (see exegesis) as a question to which a negative answer is required. But the whole tone and intent of the chapter (ver. 12) uphold the gracious meaning which belongs to the words as they stand and which we therefore accept. But if righteous Law forbids the sinner's return, how can grace invite such return ? The elder son in the parable was much scandalized at the father's welcome of his prodigal younger brother. It did seem to be an improper thing to do. The practical reply to all such objections—and they have never ceased to be urged in all ages of the Church—is to point to actual facts. What has been the result of the belief of God's wondrous grace ? Has a scriptural faith been proved to foster a sinful life ? Are they who humbly rest on God's grace in Christ the licentious, the ungodly, the profane ? The Evangelical Church can fearlessly press questions like these. And if it be asked what is the philosophy of this ? how is it that what seems likely to produce such ill, in fact does not? the answer is, that when the sinner comes in contrition and faith to the cross of the Lord Jesus Christ, the new life, the gift of regeneration, which is ever in connection with the cross, is given to him. He is started on a new career, on which he is certain to make progress, slow it may be, but sure nevertheless. And as day by day he repairs again to that same Saviour, the powers of the new life are replenished and renewed, and so, instead of the full free forgiveness which, when he returned to God, was bestowed upon him, causing him to take encouragement to live on in sin, it has wrought in him a holy hatred of it, and led him to turn from it more and more. No, the wondrous grace of God, which is told of in this word, "Yet return again to me," does not make void the Law, but it establishes the Law (cf. Rom. viii. 1).—C.

Vers. 6—10.—*An old and sad but very true story.* I. GOD LOOKING FOR FRUIT BUT NONE FORTHCOMING. 1. The fruit God looked for was Judah's repentance (cf. the history of the times to which Jeremiah refers). Idolatry was rampant in the northern kingdom. The southern also had been very far from free from it. But at this time God looked for a true repentance on Judah's part. 2. And such fruit was reasonably expected. There was the personal example and influence of King Josiah and the band of faithful men who were endeavouring to promote a true religious reformation. They had seen the degradation which followed Israel's sin (ver. 9); how Israel had fallen so low as to worship stocks and stones, the "most scoundrel idols," as Matthew Henry calls them. They had heard the gracious appeal of God to Israel (ver. 7). They had seen the judgments of God which had followed when his grace was rejected. How severe and terrible these had been! God "had put Israel away" (ver. 8). For nearly a century Israel had been in dread captivity by reason of their sins. And the sin which had brought down their judgments was the sin which Judah herself was guilty of. And the judgment had not happened to an alien nation or in a remote land. No, but to Judah's own sister, to members of the same family, of one blood and lineage; and close to her own door, hence under her own eye. What more arousing and alarming call to the unconverted could there have been than all this? And to lend further force to this call, there was in Judah the presence of the temple, the possession of all manner of religious privilege. How reasonable, then, was the expectation that Judah should turn away from her idolatry and unfeignedly repent! But the like of all such reasons for the expectation of a true turning to God exists in the case of many to-day. Every influence and argument for such turning to God as bore upon Judah then, bears upon many still. 3. But that which God desired was not forthcoming. It is the burden of the prophet's complaint that what Israel had done, and worse, was chargeable against Judah. And as now, all too often, those from whom real religion may reasonably be expected are found not only as evil, but outstripping others in ungodly ways. This is part of the story told us by these verses.

II. Another is that of MEN SEEKING TO PALM OFF ON GOD FICTITIOUS FRUIT INSTEAD OF GENUINE. (Ver. 10.) Cf. the history of the reformation in Josiah's day—how justly it is described in this verse! It was sudden, partial, external, shortlived. And such feigned reformations are common enough still. Cf. Luke xi. 21—26; and sermon No. 613 by Spurgeon : "And as the devil looks round and finds the place swept, he finds it garnished too. The man has bought some pictures: he has not real faith, but he has a fine picture of it over the fireplace. He has no love to the cross of Christ, but he has a very handsome crucifix hanging on the wall. He has no graces of the Spirit, but he has a fine vase of flowers on the table of other peoples' experiences and other peoples' graces, and they smell tolerably sweet. There is a fireplace without fire, but there is one of the handsomest ornaments for the fireplace that was ever bought for money. It is swept and garnished. Oh, the garnished people I have met with! garnished sometimes with almsgiving, at other times with long-winded prayers; garnished with the profession of zeal and the pretence of reverence. You will find a zealous Protestant— oh, so zealous!—who would go into fits at the sign of a cross, and yet will be guilty of nameless vice. You find persons shocked because another boiled a tea-kettle on a Sunday, or insured his life, or assisted at a bazaar, who will cheat and draw the eye-teeth out of an orphan child if they could get sixpence by it. They are swept and garnished. Walk in, ladies and gentlemen! Did you ever see a house so delightfully furnished as this? How elegant! how tasteful! Just so: but men may be damned tastefully, and go to hell respectably, just as well as they can in a vulgar and debauched fashion." *Wherefore do men thus act?* Because conscience has been aroused by God's dealings with them, and it will not let them rest without doing something. The question now comes, how little can they do which will be sufficient to still the inconvenient and uncomfortable clamour of conscience? and such turning to God "feignedly," such reformations as that of Judah under King Josiah, such sweeping and garnishing of the house empty of any true love to God, is the device they resolve upon. Then next, in this sad story, we see—

III. GREATER CONDEMNATION THAN EVER COMING UPON MEN IN CONSEQUENCE. 1. They are branded with a worse name than others (cf. "treacherous Judah," vers. 7, 10). Under pretence of being faithful to God, guardians of the temple, the priesthood, the Law, making loud profession, they were idolatrous even as Israel. Hence the name of infamy, "treacherous." And Christ's most terrible words were for the "hypocrites" of his day. 2. A place less tolerable in the day of judgment will be assigned them, than that of those who sinned in like manner but without any such religious profession (ver. 11). Oh, then, what need for the prayer—

> " Search me, O God, and try my heart,
>   For thou that heart canst see;
>   And turn each cursed idol out
>   That dares to rival thee."

                                                                    C.

Ver. 11.—*The comparative advantages of Judah and Israel; professors and non-professors.* I. LET JUDAH AND ISRAEL BE TAKEN AS REPRESENTING RESPECTIVELY PROFESSORS OF RELIGION AND THOSE WHO MAKE NO SUCH PROFESSION. Judah did make such profession, but Israel stood aloof, neither worshipping at the temple nor joining in the appointed feasts.

II. OBSERVE THAT ISRAEL IS SAID TO HAVE " JUSTIFIED HERSELF MORE," ETC. (Ver. 11.) 1. This was true, for a sterner sentence went out against Judah than against Israel. (1) A more infamous name is given to her than to Israel; she is called "Treacherous." (2) And her punishment was more severe. Israel had long been prepared to mingle more or less readily with other nations. An assimilating process had been going on for many generations, religiously, socially, and politically. Hence they were looked upon much as the Pharisees of our Lord's day looked upon the publicans and sinners whom he so graciously welcomed. And we find that, as a fact, they soon became merged into the nations whither they had been carried away captive. They had no such memories, no such antipathies as the people of Judah, and hence their exile must have been more tolerable. The piteous psalms which bewail the hard lot of the captive came not from them, but from the exiles of Judah. It was they who " by the rivers of Babylon sat down and wept as they remembered Zion." The iron entered into their soul as it could hardly have done in the case of Israel. And the like facts—(1) and (2)—are seen in the case of unworthy professors of religion. See our Lord's holy hate, hear his scathing words of scorn and doom, in regard to the hypocrites of his day. And the world, too, looks on them with a contempt it keeps for none other. *And they suffer as none other can.* If the grace of God be still in them, who can describe the remorse, the self-abasement, the shame, with which they view the punishment that has come upon them? 2. And the *reasons* wherefore it was less tolerable for Judah than for Israel were: (1) Judah's privileges were so much greater. (2) Her warnings had been more numerous, more plain, more arousing, more prolonged (cf. the history and previous verses). (3) Her inducements to loyal obedience were stronger. Hence her sin brought the greater doom, " And the Lord said," etc. (ver. 11). And these are the reasons—greater privileges, louder warnings, more powerful inducements to obedience—which, when they are all disregarded and set at nought, compel, yea, create a scourge for the fallen Church, such as they who have never made any such profession can never feel. Therefore—

III. INQUIRE WHAT IS THE JUST CONCLUSION THAT SHOULD BE DRAWN FROM THE FACT NOW OBSERVED. 1. Is it this: that it is better to be Israel than Judah; to stand aloof from all profession of religion than to make such profession? (1) No; for it was *better* to be Judah than Israel. There were possibilities, and these generally realized, of greater blessedness in Judah than could be attained in Israel. Compare the histories of the kingdoms of Judah and Israel, and see if the brightest and most numerous examples of sanctity, as well as the greatest displays of God's favour, to say naught of the joy of his appointed worship, were not in Judah rather than in Israel. And so in like manner we affirm that it is better to be the avowed disciple of Christ, notwithstanding the possibility of a more terrible fall, than to be numbered with the crowd of those who neither possess nor profess any regard for God. For larger blessing, in the form of increased moral resemblance to God, of joy in God, and of greater security from the power of sin, —these certainly belong to those who are as Judah rather than to those who are as Israel. All God's favour is open to them as it is not to those in whom God's fear does not dwell. (2) And again, No; for we do not reason in such manner in regard to other things. True, "He that is down need fear no fall;" but we do not, on the strength of that dismal proverb, begin immediately to prefer the lot of the fallen one to that of him who, by God's providence, is set on high and stands upright. The rich man does not hasten to make himself poor that he may be free from the fear of becoming so. Nor does the man who is blessed with vigorous health desire the condition of the invalid because in that condition there can be no fear of loss of health. Then why should the far less blessed lot of Israel, and of those outside the professed Church of God whom Israel represents, be preferred to the better and brighter lot of Judah and of God's Church, though a fall terrible and sad is possible here which could not be there? (3) And it would be right still to prefer the lot of Judah, even if Israel had been simply let alone by God. If God had sent no punishment to Israel, it would have been better to be Judah, with the possession of God's favour, although the possession involved the possibility of its loss, than to have been without that favour at all. But when we see that the judgment of God came upon Israel as well as upon Judah, then much more, notwithstanding the sad fact declared in this ver. 11, was it better to have been Judah than Israel. And so, were there no judgment on the world, and God's anger came only on a fallen Church, better even then to be of the Church than of the world. But when we know that there is a judgment of the world as well as of the Church, that sin has no immunity anywhere, then, though sin in the Church be worse than sin in the world, still let me be there where the favour, the joy, and the grace of God are, and not where they can never come. 2. But the true lesson of what we have been considering is, "Let him that thinketh he standeth take heed lest he fall." Judah, and the Church of God whom Judah represents, need to remember that, notwithstanding their high position of privilege, corruption and sin *may* lay hold upon them, and should that happen, their sin and their doom will be the most terrible of all (cf. Epistle to Church at Laodicea). Therefore hearken to our Lord's words, "Watch and pray."—C.

Vers. 12—19.—*Confession of sin the indispensable prerequisite for its pardon.* That this is so is shown by the evident fact that if it could have been dispensed with it would have been. For the desire of God to pardon his guilty people is, as this section shows, intense. He will not cease to seek after them even when the punishment of their sin has actually come upon them. Hence (ver. 12) he addresses them in the lands of their exile, Mesopotamia, Assyria, and Media (2 Kings xvii. 6), and three times (vers. 12, 14, 22) implores them to "return." He "fills his mouth with arguments," and endeavours by every kind of assurance and promise to induce them to return. Ver. 12: they shall be completely forgiven. Ver. 14: they ought to return, for they are his by right, as the wife is the rightful possession of the husband. Ver. 14: they are the object of his constant regard, so that they cannot be concealed from his eye or hindered from his help. No, though in a whole city, or tribe, or nation, there should be but "two" or even "one," still his hand would reach them there, and bring them out and restore them to Zion. Ver. 15: and those who in days gone by had so grievously led them astray, should do so no more, for now, "pastors," *i.e.* rulers and guides, whether in the State or in religion, should be such as were "according to God's own heart," and these should feed them with knowledge. Ver. 16: and under this happy rule they should greatly multiply in the land. And, better still, they should so realize and rejoice in the spiritual presence of God that they should no longer need the

aid of the ancient symbols of that presence, such as the ark of the covenant of the
old dispensation.   Ver. 17: and Jerusalem should be so filled with the Lord's presence
that they should call the city "the throne of the Lord."   And the "nations" should
be converted, and their wickedness be forsaken.   Ver. 18: and Judah and Israel should
be one, and in unity and affection possess the land.   Such were the glorious hopes
with which God sought to win back his people's hearts to himself, and they conclusively show how intensely the heart of God was set upon his people's return.   But
eagerly desirous as God was for this restoration of his lost children to his heart and
home again, he is evidently held back from indulging such affectionate promptings
by considerations that could not be overlooked.   What they were, the demand that he
makes for *confession of sin* plainly shows.   They are—

I. The Law of righteousness.   Sin is the violation of that Law, and until due atonement and acknowledgment have been made, sin ought not to be forgiven.   I may, in
accordance with our Saviour's commands, refrain from inflicting punishment on one who
has wronged me, even though he have not repented of his wrong; and that refraining from
inflicting punishment, or from demanding what is my right, is forgiveness in the sense
our Lord meant; but he did not mean, for it would be a command impossible to obey—
that I should receive such a one into the same confidence and love which I bear towards
a dear friend who has never deserved anything else.   Therefore my forgiveness of such
an unrepentant offender, though granted in accordance with our Lord's command, and
well-pleasing in his sight, and the best I am capable of, is nevertheless not complete,
not perfect; for perfect forgiveness, that which God would bestow upon sinful men,
means far more than the remission of penalty: it means restoration to the love, the
fellowship, and the confidence of God.   But this cannot be apart from due atonement
made on the part of the wrong-doer.   The Law of righteousness, the Law written upon
our hearts as well as inherent in the nature of things, forbids such forgiveness apart
from the essential condition of such forgiveness.

II. And the well-being of his household is that other consideration which restrains
the prompting of affection to forgive sin unconditionally and from mere pity.   Man is
not the whole of God's household.   He may be only the one sheep who has gone
astray.   The rest, the ninety and nine blessed ones who need no repentance.   But to
pardon sin without atonement would be to confound all moral distinctions, to discourage the good, and to teach the wrong-doer to regard his wrong as a very slight
matter; it would be to carry the discords of earth into the presence of God, and to
reproduce there the sins and sorrows of this world.   Therefore let the love of God
towards sinful man be inconceivably great, and it is so, still it is held back in its
exercise by these considerations now named.   But where sin is confessed as God
demands it should be, then, as is promised here and in many other Scriptures beside,
God's pardoning love can go forth and the sinner be restored to the favour, which he
had lost.   And the reason of this is not because the sinner's poor and inadequate confession of his sin is a sufficient atonement for the wrong he has done, but because, when
he sincerely makes that confession, he is *invested with the acceptableness of Christ.*
For Christ has made that atonement perfectly which man can only offer in the most
imperfect way; "man's repentance needing too often to be repented of, and his very
tears to be washed in the blood of Christ."   But Christ looked upon sin as God looks
upon it, hated it as God hates it, consented to God's judgment concerning it by
bearing the penalty of it; "he bore our sins in his own body on the tree," and so made
that true, that perfect confession and atonement which we can never make.   And he
did this in our nature, and as our Representative.   So now, when we come in his Name,
sincerely repenting of sin, though that repentance be inadequate in itself, yet because
it is "the mind of Christ," and looks upon sin sorrowing over it as he did, our imperfect
atonement is accepted in his perfect one, we have the fellowship of his sufferings, his
atonement is in our measure reproduced in us, and we are made conformable to his
death.   Pardon thus bestowed neither violates the Law of righteousness nor is inconsistent with the well-being of the whole family of God.   Hence it is that, as in ver. 13,
the demand is made for confession of sin, and then of their iniquity in all its aggravated
forms.   Without such confession pardon cannot be bestowed.   Not till the prodigal
"came to himself," went to his father and said, "I have sinned," was he forgiven, notwithstanding all the yearning of the father's heart after his lost child.   Now, to bring

men to this looking upon their sin as God looks upon it, as the Lord Jesus looks upon it, is the object of God's disciplines, of the pain and smart which so often accompany sin, and of so much of the teaching of the Bible and of God's providential government. And those who have trusted in Christ are continually to be "looking unto Jesus," for in that trustful look is the sure guarantee of the preservation of the "mind of Christ" in them in regard to sin, and so of their for ever abiding in the favour and love of God. This mind of holy hatred and sorrow on account of sin it is the especial work of God's Holy Spirit to produce in men; that Spirit who is given to them that ask his aid, more readily than even parents give to their children what those children they so much love need and ask for.—C.

Ver. 14.—*Married to God.* "Turn, O backsliding children, saith the Lord; for I am married unto you."

I. THIS SEEMS AN INCREDIBLE STATEMENT. Had it been spoken of angels, or of unfallen man, or of eminent saints, it would have been more easy of belief. But it is of men desperately wicked, and to such, that God says, "I am married unto *you.*" What infinite condescension and love!

II. BUT NEVERTHELESS IT IS TRUE. For: 1. We have the marriage lines, the record of the transaction, the very words of the covenant deed (cf. Ps. lxxxix. 3, 28; Heb. viii.; ch. xxxii. 38—40). In all these God declares that he has taken us to be his for ever: "They shall be my people, and I will be their God." 2. Our children are his. He bids them all call him by the blessed name of Father. 3. He repeatedly declares that we were the objects of his choice. Cf. Eph. i., "He took not on him the nature of angels, but he took on him the seed of Abraham." And this because we "were partakers of flesh and blood, he himself also took part in the same;" "God *so* loved the world;" "He came to seek and to save that which was lost" (cf. also Eph. v. 25—27). 4. He has given us the sign and token of our being his in the sacrament of our baptism. That which the wedding ring is to the wife, baptism is to us: it declares the blessed fact that we are God's, and separates us for *his* Name, the Name of the Father, the Son, and the Holy Ghost. 5. He has endowed us with his goods: "All things are yours, . . . the world, or life, or death, or things present, or things to come; all are yours" (1 Cor. iii. 22). 6. He is always with us: "In him we live and move," etc. He is not far from any one of us: "I will never leave thee nor forsake thee." 7. He is jealous of our love: "I the Lord thy God am a jealous God." What is the Bible but one long record of the disquiet of the heart of God when the love of those to whom he is "married" is turned from him? Hence the eternal law, "Thou shalt have no other gods before me;" "Thou shalt love the Lord thy God with all thy heart." A man has a right to claim that she whom he has married should love him. He has no such claim on any other. And so because the Lord God condescends to hold this relationship towards us, he too claims our love: "Thou *shalt* love the Lord thy God." 8. We are on the way to dwell with him in his eternal home. We are not there yet, but we are on the way. "We are coming up from the wilderness," and if we faithfully recognize our relationship to God, we shall be "leaning upon our beloved" (Cant. viii. 5). 9. He has done for us, and does for us still, what only such a near and dear relationship can account for. Even the compassionate friend will not feel himself bound, though he will minister relief, to go and share the very same lot as that of those whom he compassionates. And the father of the prodigal did not make himself poor as that prodigal was. He lifted him up, but he did not himself stoop down. No; that which the Lord God has done is more than the love of friend, brother, father; it is the love of the husband alone. For the husband, if he be worthy of the name, will share the lot of the wife. And if she must suffer hardship, he will share it with her. If she dwell in mean abode, he will not be happy to dwell elsewhere. But does not all this describe what the Lord God hath done? "He, though he was rich, yet for our sakes became poor." The word "married" is not a mere metaphor, it is the alone explanation of the Incarnation and of the Atonement. The general benevolence of God, not even the fatherhood of God, will adequately tell wherefore he so humbled himself and lived here "as a poor meek man upon earth," and then died for us; but the *husbandhood* of God, the fact that he declares when he says, "I am married unto you," will account for it and explain all. We have to live here in this wilderness world, to be tried, tempted, troubled, and at length to die, and we have also to resist even unto blood, striving against sin; and therefore he himself also took part in the same. Then if this statement of the text be true—

III. VAST CONSEQUENCES FOLLOW. 1. Forgetfulness or disregard of this relationship in which we stand to God must be utter misery. Perhaps hell is never so nearly brought up and made known in all its hideous wretchedness here on earth as by means of a marriage in which one side has lost all love for the other. Oh, the drag of the marriage bond then! What an iron chain; what a fetter it is! How it frets! How it galls! How simply horrible it has become! Penal servitude for life is but a mild description of it. From ever knowing it by experience, may God deliver us all! But such things, alas, are, and between men and women who have vowed to love and cherish each other "until death do them part." But we do not recognize so readily that well-nigh all the sorrow of this life of ours is because we have forgotten or disregarded our relationship to God. *That* marriage also is a bond which can never be severed. And if we have no love to God, no delight in him, no trust or confidence, oh, how that bond will gall, will irritate, will fret, and so become the very "strength of sin"! The unrest, the distress, the wild attempts to win happiness in lawless ways, the sting of conscience, the inward remorse, are all accounted for by the consciousness that men have of their obligation to God whilst that obligation is being grievously disregarded. On the other hand: 2. Due response rendered to the love of God towards us must be our deep, our indestructible, our ever-advancing joy. See the proofs of this in the return of the prodigal: "They began to be merry." Listen to David: "O God, thou art my God," etc. "I will go unto the altar of God, unto God my exceeding joy." Behold the martyrs. Rather than be severed from God by denial of him, let what shame, agony, loss, death, that might come upon them. Ask those who know what the love of God is, if it be not as we say. That pure joy which a true wife has in the husband she loves and reveres, that is the type of the joy in God which we may have and should have, and to which even the worst of us, the miserable backsliders, are by God himself entreated to return. How happy in his protection! How certain that he will be prompt to help in all peril and emergency! How free the outpouring of the heart in loving confidence! How sure of his love always! —no doubt ever clouding that certainty. And how sure, too, of his sympathy, his wise counsel, his constant support! And to all this God invites us, yea, he by this word of his bids us claim it as our right—a right he will at once recognize. It is wonderful; the condescension and the love of it are so marvellous that we are slow to comprehend, slower still to believe it, and slowest of all to realize and rejoice in it. But yet it is most assuredly true. Therefore, Lord, increase our faith; we believe, but help thou our unbelief.—C.

Ver. 19.—*The great difficulty overcome.* "How shall I," etc.? A different rendering has been proposed for this verse, but inasmuch as the general meaning and spirit of the prophecy are maintained in our common translation, we prefer to abide thereby. So read, the verse brings before us—

I. GOD'S GRACIOUS PURPOSE OF LOVE TOWARDS SINFUL MEN. He would put them "among the children," etc. Think what this involves. Picture to ourselves the lot of the children in the home of an affluent, affectionate, wise, and godly father. What condition fairer, more enviable, can be conceived? What freedom from all care! What unrestrained, confiding, loving intercourse between the children and their father! What healthful development and direction of character and disposition! How sheltered; how secure; how happy in the abiding consciousness of their father's love! How full of all good their position cannot but be! But the brightest, fairest lot that ever fell to any children in an earthly home fails fully to set forth what it must be to be set amongst God's children, and to be numbered amongst his sons and daughters. Blessed indeed are such; how blessed none but they who are thus "set among the children" can fully know. But such was the gracious purpose of God towards man, nothing less than this. He created us for this very purpose, with this very intent. And it is the reason and motive of the creation of every newly born child. For this every human soul is endowed with faculties which can find their complete exercise and enjoyment only amongst God's children: "God hath made us for himself, and our hearts have no rest until they find rest in him." But the verse, by its very form, indicates—

II. The terrible thwarting and hindering of that gracious purpose which has taken place. "*How* shall I put thee," etc.? plainly denoting that there is some giant obstacle in the way. In the case of Israel the previous portions of this prophecy show clearly what this was. But it is equally true of us all. And this dread hindrance to God's carrying out his purposes of grace towards us consists not so much in what we have done as in what we are. The *heart* of man is not right in the sight of God, and whilst that is so, God cannot set us amongst his children. Transgressions and offences are but the symptoms of the deadlier evil that lurks within, not the evil itself. That consists in the state of heart Godwards which, alas! characterizes us all, until the new heart and the right spirit be given. What should we say if towards ourselves as parents our children were to order themselves as we do towards God?—rarely thinking of us, placing no confidence in us; though we would delight to have them speak to us, yet maintaining a sullen silence always; in their hearts disliking us and resenting the expression of our will; disobeying us on the slightest pretext, and choosing for their friends those they well know to be our foes. If any parent was so unhappy as to have such a son or daughter, how could he set such a one amongst his other children who love him as children should? And that this is the case between the unrenewed man and God, let conscience and men's works, words, and ways witness. This being so, how can we "marvel" that our Lord hath said, "Ye *must* be born again"? But we are shown also—

III. This difficulty, vast as it is, triumphantly overcome. In the latter part of the verse and in the confessions of the twenty-second and following verses it is clear that a great change has taken place. The rebel heart has gone, the child's heart has come in its place. The erewhile sinful godless soul is heard calling upon God as "My Father," and in daily conduct is found *not* turning away from him. What a change! No wonder that the Scripture emblems of it are all drawn from contrasts the most vivid and intense that experience furnishes or the mind can conceive: life and death, darkness and light, crimson red and snow whiteness, leprous and pure; as one possessed of the devil, and as one calm, sober, and in his right mind;—such are some of them. But the beholding of so great a change leads of necessity to the inquiry how it was brought about. Hence note—

IV. The means whereby this was accomplished. These were as they ever are, the manifestation of the love of God. In Christ God came to seek and to save his self-lost children. But they, instead of welcoming the Christ of God, crucified and slew him. That rebel alienated heart which is common to us all wrought this awful crime. But it is when by the Holy Spirit men are led to see what they have done to him who so loved them as to come from heaven to save them, there is produced that conviction of sin, that deep and genuine repentance, that sense of his infinite love, and that consequent entire trust in him,—all which are the very elements of that heart of a dear child which calls God "My Father," and which will not turn away from him. I have read of one who was for ever reclaimed from the deadly sin of drunkenness by the deep anguish of heart which he experienced when he found that one day, when brutalized by drink, he had smitten to the ground his own dear child, and wounded her with a wound the scar of which she would never lose; and that he had done this whilst she was lovingly seeking to lead him away from the place and the people who were tempting him to his ruin. When he came to himself and knew what he had done, his horror and remorse had no bounds. "The drink! ay, it was all the drink!" he exclaimed when, years after, telling the story. "Could I ever touch it again? I kept my finger lightly on the little maid's forehead, and lifted my face to heaven, and vowed that I would never touch the murderous thing again as long as I lived, and with a broken heart I prayed the Lord to help me." That well-known story serves to illustrate how, in this great matter of man's restoration to God, he who once was a godless rebel becomes filled with another heart, and God can, as he desires to, place him amongst the children. For when I clearly see the wounds which I in my mad sin have inflicted on him who sought to save me, and who tenderly loves me still notwithstanding all I have done, the sight of his cross and of those wounds will fill my soul with such a hatred of sin and love of God that I am no longer what I was; I am born again, I have passed from death unto life. Yes, it is the sight of the love of God in Christ which turns the sinner into the child of God, and wins for him a place amongst the children of God. With what fervour, then, may we pray the blessed Spirit to fulfil his work in and for us and for all men!—C.

Ver. 20—ch. iv. 2.—*God's way of restoration; or, the experiences of a young convert.* In ver. 19 we have given us the expression of the Divine perplexity in regard to lost Israel: "How shall I place thee among the children," etc.? But ere the verse closes we behold the problem solved, the seeming impossibility accomplished, for the lost is found, and he that was dead is alive again. The rebel Israel has become the loving obedient child. And now in these verses (20—ch. iv. 2) we seem to have a telling of the experience of the restored one, a setting forth of how God had dealt with him. It is given in the form of a dialogue between God and Israel, and is an accurate description of the Divine process of restoration.

I. THERE IS THE BRINGING HOME OF SIN TO THE CONSCIENCE. (Ver. 20.) God charges upon lost Israel great and grievous sin. He likens the wrong he has suffered at the hands of Israel to the most grievous wrong it is possible for a man to suffer, and which of all others a man resents the most. The accusation is terrible. Thus sharply and sternly does God deal with the soul he would save. He does not gloss over, or palliate, or in any way make little of our sin, as we are apt to do; but he shows it to us so clearly that the sight of it is almost more than the heart can bear.

II. THIS CONVICTION OF SIN IS FOLLOWED BY A DEEP REPENTANCE. (Ver. 21.) Israel is represented as seeing her sin, and then from the very high places which had witnessed her guilt is heard her weeping and supplication. The soul that has never known the smart and pain of the conviction of sin will never earnestly turn to the Great Physician for the healing that is needed.

III. THE PROCLAMATION OF MERCY FOLLOWS. Ver. 22, "Return, ye apostate children, I will heal your apostasies." Just as to the enraptured ears of the penitent who was weeping over the Saviour's feet there came the blessed sound of his pardoning word, assuring her her sins were forgiven and that she might go in peace, so here God is represented as declaring his mercy to the weeping, supplicating Israel. And the heart the Lord hath dealt with knows that thus it is. A voice not audible, but real, is heard in the soul, assuring the contrite one of the forgiveness he needs and craves.

IV. IN SUCH A HEART PROMPT BELIEF, INSTANT ACCEPTANCE OF THE OFFERED MERCY, FOLLOWS. Ver. 22, "Behold, we come unto thee; for," etc. As well might the steel filings refuse to be moved by the magnet that lies by them as the sin-convinced and contrite heart fail to lay hold on the promise set before it in the gospel. No sooner has God said, "Return, I will heal," than the answer is heard, "Behold, we come."

V. Then follows THE CONFESSION AND REPENTANCE OF FAITH. (Vers. 23—25.) There had been confession and repentance before the soul had heard and accepted the offer of pardon; but that which follows is more full, more deep than that which went before. We repent more deeply of sin after we have known God has pardoned us than before we had that blessed knowledge. See here: 1. Their confession of the utter vanity of all their idols (ver. 23). 2. Their confident assurance that God alone can be their salvation (ver. 23). 3. Their confession of the disgrace and infatuated folly which had characterized them as a people for so long a time (ver. 24). They call their idolatry "shame," and own how it has destroyed both their substance and themselves. 4. They acknowledge the complete righteousness of God's judgment against their sin, and their own just exposure to his wrath (ver. 25). "Let us lie in our shame and our disgrace cover us, that we have sinned," etc. (Lange's translation). And thus it ever is: the more we realize God's pardoning love, the more intense will be our perception of the baseness and utter evil of the sin that has been forgiven.

VI. This CONFESSION IS FOLLOWED BY FURTHER ASSURANCES OF GRACE. (Ch. iv. 1, 2.) Return to God shall be followed by return to their own land. "If thou returnest to me, thou shalt return (unto thy land), and if thou puttest away, etc., thou shalt not remove," *i.e.* into exile again. "And if thou shalt swear by Jehovah with sincere, righteous, and true heart," *i.e.* "if thou wilt truly give thyself up to God, then the heathen nations outside, seeing how thy God shall bless thee and shall heap his favours upon thee, shall come and bless themselves in him, and shall glory in him," *i.e.* they shall have done with their idolatries and be converted unto God. With such gracious promises would God encourage Israel in the new and better way in which they are represented as walking; with such gentleness would he make them, as he in like manner makes all who truly turn to him, great.—C.

Ver. 16.—*Supercession of external religious ordinances and institutions.* This is because of the necessarily temporary nature of these, and the spirituality to which they are intended to minister, and which subsequently they may hinder.

I. THE TRUE WORSHIP OF GOD IS SPIRITUAL. It is not to bow before an altar or an ark that God calls us to his temple, but to see himself face to face, to discover our need of him, and to delight in his presence. Nor is this communion to be occasional or intermittent. The whole life is to be affected by spiritual influences. A true life may thereby become worship, and "daily toil temple service." This arises from the nature of God. "God is a Spirit: and they that worship him must worship him in spirit and in truth."

II. THE MOST SACRED SYMBOLS ARE ONLY USEFUL AS THEY HELP TO THIS, AND WHEN IT IS ATTAINED ARE NO LONGER REQUIRED. This may be said not only of external church furniture, rites of worship, etc., but even of words and doctrines themselves, which are but imperfect representations of the Divine glory. When the building is finished the scaffolding is removed. The final end of education is not to load the mind with dead knowledge, but to culture and strengthen it. Ceremonial and doctrinal teaching are intended to lead men into personal experience of God and communion with him. When that is attained they fall into the background.

III. THAT RITUAL WORSHIP SHALL GIVE PLACE TO SPIRITUAL IS DISTINCTLY PROMISED. 1. *An incentive to the spiritual use of rites.* 2. *An assurance of Divine favour and love.* 3. *A promise of Christ and communion through him.*—M.

Ver. 19.—*"Put among the children."* A promise deeply and tenderly evangelical. Israel and Judah had forfeited this position because they had broken the covenant. But the forgiving love of God is shown in his declaring that they should be reinstated. The force of the phrase is well explained as that of "bestowing a rich paternal benediction," or of restoring to the rights and privileges of inheritance.

I. THE SINNER HAS FORFEITED HIS POSITION IN THE FAMILY OF GOD. All through Scripture this relation is shown as depending upon mutual agreement and obligation. The covenant is the title-deed to the inheritance of God's children. The breaking of this on the part of the sinner destroys his claim and position. In the parable of the prodigal son we have the consciousness of this on the part of the transgressor beautifully described—"I am no more worthy to be called thy son." Moral harmony between the soul of man and God is of the essence of the filial relation. A lost position; a possibility that we have destroyed by our own act. Henceforth the sinner is a spiritual orphan, or a "child of Satan." There is no claim upon God save on condition of renewed obedience. He is subject to the wrath of God's wounded love and outraged honour.

II. READOPTION IS THE GUARANTEE OF ALL HIGHEST BLESSINGS. It is only children of God who are heirs of God; if, then, we would enjoy the privileges and blessings of his house, we must be reinstated in that which we have lost. But this is only possible on repentance and belief. We are assured here and elsewhere that the sinner can regain this title and relation without lessening of the dignity, privilege, and affection. When once this has taken place there is no bar to the bestowal of God's richest benediction. As his children, as those who are actuated by his love and governed by his Spirit, there is ample security that his blessings shall not be abused. A holy confidence and communion are established, and the true end of being is once more secured.

III. THIS IS AN ACT OF GOD'S FREE GRACE. The initiative is not the sinner's. Overtures of mercy come from him he has offended. There is nothing to compel God to do this. He is perfectly free, and any obligation into which he enters is sealed only by his voluntary promises. There is abundant evidence, too, of a Divine satisfaction and joy in the exercise of pardoning love. It is spoken of as a long hoped for and gladsome consummation. The "Abba, Father!" of the restored one is music in the heart of God. This is the only true joy—the joy of reconciliation. Who can doubt his welcome with such assurances as this? God wills not that any should perish, but that all should come to him and live.—M.

Vers. 21—25.—*Typical penitence.* It is difficult if not impossible to fix any historic date for the fulfilment of this prophecy. Not a few competent scholars maintain that it is yet unfulfilled. But in any case it is a picture of the future, and may be accepted as a description of the penitence that is well-pleasing in the sight of God. All through it is spiritual, and the national circumstances involved are put thoroughly into the background.

I. The upspringing of godly sorrow for sin. (Ver. 21.) It is not the expression of annoyance and pain at the consequences of sin. A deeper sentiment inspires the host of weeping supplicants. Sin itself is the grief. The cry is from men who feel they have lost their way, that there is no satisfaction in the foul and inconsequent rites of idolatry. The religion and the life that flows from it are felt to be profoundly and utterly false. Memories of past spiritual privileges and endearing ties overpower their hearts. They do not wait, but pour forth their sorrow on the very scene of transgression. Their sin is before them. God is the Being they have offended, and to him therefore do they cry, in heartfelt and unrestrainable sorrow.

II. The Divine response. (Ver. 22.) The fatherly heart of God cannot resist the "voice heard upon the high places." He waits not, but forthwith addressing them already as "children," encourages their approach. Their offence is declared, but equally is the promise given, "I will heal your backslidings [apostasies]." This expresses the objective and subjective influence of Divine forgiveness. It not only removes the sin so that forthwith and henceforth it is as if it had never been, but it destroys the causes and tendencies of the evil. The source is cleansed, the disposition changed, and the way cleared for thorough reconciliation with God.

III. The acceptance of the Divine invitation. (Ver. 22.) God is taken at his word. No delay takes place. As the way of return has been shown, so they hasten to avail themselves of it. His authority and relation to them are acknowledged. They obey him.

IV. The accepted sinner's confession. (Vers. 23, 24.) The "vanity," waste, and ruin attendant upon idolatry are declared. God is recognized as the only Saviour. Testimony like this has often proved more powerful in converting sinners than many sermons. It is due to God, and may be profitable to others.

V. The accompanying emotions. (Ver. 25.) Shame predominates. But it is not accompanied by despair. There is a false shame which prevents the sinner coming to God; there is a true shame which coexists with acceptance of proffered mercy, and earnest effort to retrieve the past. We ought not too readily to forget "the wormwood and the gall."—M.

EXPOSITION.

CHAPTER IV.

Vers. 1, 2.—The form and structure of the translation require a change. Render, *If thou wilt return, O Israel, saith Jehovah, wilt return unto me; and if thou wilt put away,* etc., *and not wander; and wilt swear, As Jehovah liveth, with good faith, with justice, and with righteousness; then shall the nations bless themselves by him, and in him shall they glory.* The clause, "and not wander," seems too short; the Septuagint had a choicer reading, "and put away, etc., from his [thy] mouth, and not wander from before me." It is the close of the prophecy which we have here. The prophet subjoins a promise which he has heard from Jehovah. True, it does not appeal to Israel's self-love (as Isa. xlviii. 18, 19; Ps. lxxxi. 13—16), but to a nobler feeling of responsibility for the world's welfare. Israel has been entrusted with a mission, and on the due

performance of this mission hangs the weal or woe of humanity. Hence Jehovah's longing for Israel's repentance. If Israel will but "return," and obey God's commandments, all nations will be attracted to the true religion. The form of expression used for the latter statement is borrowed probably from Gen. xxii. 18; xxvi. 4 (it is less closely parallel with Gen. xii. 3; xviii. 18). To "bless by" any one is to use his name in the benediction formula. Seeing Israel so blessed through his allegiance to Jehovah, all nations shall wish themselves a similar blessing (the reverse of the process in ch. xxix. 22; comp. Isa. lxv. 16). To "swear, As Jehovah liveth," means to call Jehovah to witness to the truth of a statement. This is to be done "with good faith," etc., *i.e.* the object of the oath must be consistent with honesty and probity. **Abominations;** *i.e.* idols, as often (see 2 Kings xxiii. 24).

Ver. 3.—There is no occasion to separate vers. 3, 4, from the preceding prophecy. We have other instances of as sudden a transition from the Israelites (in the narrower sense) to the men of Judah (see Isa. viii. 6—14; x. 1—4; xxviii. 1—6; in the writer's commentary). "For" is here not causal, but explanatory: "I say this not only to the men of Israel, but to you, O men of Judah, who need the admonition to repentance, how deeply!" (see ch. v. 2). **Break up your fallow ground;** the same figure as in Hos. x. 12. To understand it, we must read the clause in connection with the following one. **Sow not among thorns.** The prophet means, though he does not say so, the roots which will spring up into thorns. "Do not plant your good resolutions in a heart filled up with the roots of thorns,' but first rake up the soil, and clear it of noxious germs, and then sow the seed which will grow up in a holy life" (comp. Matt. xiii. 7).

Ver. 4.—**Circumcise yourselves to the Lord.** A significant passage. All the Jews were circumcised, but not all were "circumcised to the Lord." There were but too many who were "circumcised in uncircumcision" (ch. ix. 25), and the prophet sternly reduces such circumcision to the level of the heathenish rite of cutting off the hair (ch. ix. 26; comp. Herod. iii. 8). Jeremiah seems to have been specially anxious to counteract a merely formal, ritualistic notion of circumcision, sharing in this, as in other points, the influence of the Book of Deuteronomy, so lately found in the temple (comp. Deut. x. 16). To him the venerable rite of circumcision (older, certainly, than Abraham) is a symbol of the devotion of the heart to its rightful Lord (comp. St. Paul in Rom. ii. 28, 29; Col. ii. 11; Phil. iii. 3).

Vers. 5—31.—A revelation of grievous purport has suddenly reached the prophet. See how the foe draws nearer and nearer, and how alarm drives the scattered population to seek for refuge in the fortified cities. Can such be the issue of the promises of peace with which Jehovah has encouraged his people? Such are the contents of the first paragraph (vers. 5—10). Next, in short, detached figures the prophet sets forth the sin of the people and its punishment. Like a scorching simoom is the former; like swift clouds, and like a whirlwind, is the onward march of the instruments of the latter. Swift, indeed, must repentance be, if it is to outrun punishment. For the northern peoples are already here (vers. 11—18). The impression is so strong on the mind of the prophet

that he vents himself in language such as the last man might employ on the morrow of the final judgment day (vers. 19—26). And now, "lest what precedes might seem only poetry" (Payne Smith), the Divine decree is solemnly announced. The judgment is irrevocable; but there is a gleam of hope: "I will not make a full end." On the question whether the Scythians or the Babylonians are mainly alluded to, see Introduction.)

Ver. 5.—**Cry, gather together;** rather, *cry aloud.*

Ver. 6.—**Set up the standard.** The "standard" was a tall pole with a flag, pointing in the direction of Zion, for the guidance of fugitives. **Retire, stay not;** rather, *save your goods by flight; linger not.* The former verb occurs again in the same sense in Exod. ix. 19; Isa. x. 31. **From the north.** The expression suits either the Scythians or the Chaldeans (see on ch. i. 14).

Ver. 7.—**The lion;** the symbol of irresistible might and royalty (Gen. xlix. 7; Rev. v. 5). **Of the Gentiles;** rather, *of the nations.* There is no reference to the distinction between Jews and Gentiles; the Jews themselves are not allowed to escape. An ordinary lion attacks individual men; this lion destroys nations. **Is on his way;** literally, *has broken up his encampment*—a phrase perhaps suggested by the nomad Scythians.

Ver. 8.—**Is not turned back from us.** As we in our folly believed (ch. ii. 35).

Ver. 9.—**The heart . . . shall perish;** *i.e.* they shall lose their reason. The same verb in Ethiopic means "to be mad." The "heart" in Old Testament language is the centre of the intellectual as well as of the moral life (comp. Hos. iv. 11; Job xii. 24; Prov. xv. 28). So St. Ephrem the Syrian says ('Works,' in Syriac, ii. 316, quoted by Delitzsch), "The reason expatiates in the heart as in a palace."

Ver. 10.—**Ah, Lord God!** rather, *Alas! O Lord Jehovah* (see on ch. i. 6). **Thou hast greatly deceived this people,** etc. Much difficulty has been felt in interpreting this verse, partly because it seems directly to charge Jehovah with "deceit," and partly because the prophecy, **Ye shall have peace,** on which this charge is founded, accords exactly with the strain of the "false prophets" (see ch. vi. 14; xiv. 13; xxiii. 17). Hence some (*e.g.* Ewald) have altered the points of the verb at the beginning of the verse, so as to enable them to render, "And one shall say," the subject understood being either a "false prophet" or one of the people. This view is not in itself impossible (Keil's objection will not bear examination), but is not absolutely necessary, for the present is not the only passage in which Jeremiah, under the influence of strong emotion, charges Jehovah with "deceit" (see ch. xx. 7, a synonymous word is used; and comp. 1 Kings xxii. 23), and the words, "Ye shall have peace," may be meant to summarize the cheering promises in ch. iii. 14—18. Jeremiah may (it is not incorrect to conjecture) have supposed the fulfilment of his prophecy to be nearer than it really was (comp. 1 Pet. i. 11); hence his disappointment, and hence his strong language. So St. Jerome, "Quia supra dixerat, In illo tempore vocabunt Jerusalem solium Dei, etc., et nunc dicit, Peribit cor regis, turbatur propheta et in se Deum putat esse mentitum; nec intelligit, illud multa post tempora repromissum, hoc autem vicino futurum tempore." To suppose, with Keil, that Jeremiah refers the prophecies of the "false prophets" to God as their ultimate Author, seems inconsistent with Jeremiah's own statements in ch. xiv. 14 (comp. ch. v. 13). Moreover, we have parallels elsewhere in the prophets, as well as in the Book of Job, for the use of language with regard to Providence which a calmer judgment would condemn. A notable instance is Isa. lxiii. 17, where the Jewish Church, through its mouthpiece the prophet, throws the responsibility of its errors upon Jehovah. Depressed by melancholy, they give way for the moment to those human "thoughts" which are not as "My thoughts." They felt the "burden of the mystery." **Unto the soul;** *i.e.* unto the life.

Ver. 11.—**Shall it be said to this people;** *i.e.* words like these may be used *with reference to* this people. **A dry wind,** etc.; literally, *a clear wind* (but the notions of dryness and heat are closely connected with that of heat; comp. Isa. xviii. 4). The prophet doubtless means the east wind, which is very violent in Palestine, and, of course, quite unsuitable for the winnowing process. **High places** should rather be *bare hills*. **Toward;** or (is) *the way of*. So Hitzig, supposing the conduct of the Jews to be likened to a wind which brings no blessing, but only drought and desolation.

Ver. 12.—**Even a full wind from those** places. The passage is obscure, but this is a very possible rendering. "Full," equivalent to "violent;" "those (places)," equivalent to the bare hills spoken of in ver. 11. Keil and Payne Smith, however, render, "a fuller wind than those," *i.e.* a more violent wind than those which serve for winnowing the corn; while Hitzig (see on ver. 11) supposes "from those" to mean the persons described in ver. 11 as "the daughter of my people." **Unto me;** or perhaps *for me*, at my beck and call. **Now also will I,** etc. We

must supply the other term of the antithesis from the context: "As they have sinned against me, so will I also now hold a court of justice upon them" (see on ch. i. 16).

Ver. 13.—**He shall come up as clouds,** etc. It is needless to name the subject; who can it be but the host of Jehovah's warlike instruments? (For the first figure, comp. Ezek. xxxviii. 16; for the second, Isa. v. 28; lxvi. 15; and for the third, Hab. i. 8; Deut. xxviii. 49.) **Woe unto us!** etc. The cry of lamentation of the Jews (comp. ver. 20; ch. ix. 18).

Ver. 14.—**Thy vain thoughts.** The phrase specially belongs to sins against one's neighbour—such sins as are described in ch. vii. 5—9 (Keil). "Vain" should rather be "wicked" (immoral); the root-meaning of the noun is "a breath" (the symbol of material or moral emptiness).

Ver. 15.—**For a voice declareth,** etc. There is no time to lose, for already news of the foe has arrived. He is now at Dan, the northern frontier-town, and is heard of almost as soon in the hill-country of Ephraim.

Ver. 16.—**Make ye mention,** etc. This verse contains a call to the neighbouring nations to take notice of an event which nearly concerns them all. True, it is only the investment of Jerusalem which can as yet be reported, but there can hardly be a doubt of the issue, and the capture of the principal fortress will at once be followed by that of the other fortified "cities of Judah." **Against** in the second clause should rather be *concerning*. (For the use of "behold" before an imperative, comp. Ps. cxxxiv. 1.) **Watchers;** *i.e.* besiegers (comp. ver. 17), who like the panther lie in wait for every one who comes out of the city, to kill him (ch. v. 6; comp. ch. vi. 25).

Ver. 17.—**As keepers of a field.** The prophet compares the tents, or perhaps the booths (1 Kings xx. 12, 16), of the besieging army to the booths of the guardians of the crops (Isa. i. 8; Job xxvii. 18).

Ver. 18.—**This is thy wickedness;** *i.e.* the effect of thy wickedness. (For the following words, comp. ch. ii. 19; iv. 10.) **Because;** rather, *truly*.

Ver. 19.—**My bowels.** It is doubted whether the speaker in vers. 19—21 is the prophet or the whole nation. Ver. 19 reminds us of Isa. xv. 5; xvi. 11 and xxi. 3, 4, and would be quite in harmony with the elegiac tone of our prophet elsewhere; the Targum too already regards the passage as an exclamation of the prophet. On the other hand, the phrase "my tents" (ver. 20) certainly implies that the people, or the pious section of the people, is the speaker. Both views may perhaps be united. The prophet may be the speaker in ver. 19, but simply (as is the case with so many of the psalmists) as the representative of his fellow-believers, whom in ver. 20 he brings on the stage more directly. Ver. 19 is best rendered as a series of exclamations—

"My bowels! my bowels! I must writhe in pain!
The walls of my heart! My heart moaneth unto me!
I cannot hold my peace!
For thou hast heard, O my soul, the sound of the trumpet,
The alarm of war!"

Observe, the "soul" hears; the "heart" is pained. So generally the one is more active, the other more passive. The Hebrew margin gives, for "I must writhe," "I must wait" (comp. Micah vii. 7); but this rendering does not suit the context. **The walls of my heart.** A poetical way of saying, "My heart beats."

Ver. 20.—**My tents.** Jeremiah uses a similar phrase in ch. xxx. 18 (comp. also 2 Sam. xx. 1; 1 Kings viii. 66; xii. 16; Ps. cxxxii. 3; also Isa. xxix. 1, "city where David encamped, i.e. dwelt"). The expression is evidently a "survival" of the nomadic, tent-dwelling age. (Comp. the parallel phrase, "my curtains," i.e. my tent-curtains; comp. ch. x. 20; Isa. liv. 2; Cant. i. 5.)

Ver. 21.—**Shall I see the standard.** (See on ver. 6.)

Ver. 22.—**For my people is foolish.** The Lord gives no direct answer to the complaining question in ver. 21. He simply states the moral ground for Judah's calamity, and implies that this will last so long as the people continue to be "foolish," i.e. virtual deniers of the true God.

Ver. 23.—**I beheld.** The prophet is again the speaker, but in a calmer mood. God's judgment has been pronounced, and it is not for him to rebel. He has now simply to record the vision of woe which has been granted him. He foresees the utter desolation into which not only the land of Judah, but the earth in general, will be brought, and which reminds him of nothing so much as the "waste and wild" condition of the earth previous to the first creative word. But why is "the earth" mentioned in this connection? Because the judgment upon Judah is but one act in the great general judgment which, when completed, will issue in a fresh order of things (comp. Isa. iii. 14, 15, where side by side are mentioned Jehovah's judgment of "the peoples" and of "his people," and Isa. xxiv., where the judgment upon the enemies of Israel is interwoven with the judgment upon "the earth"). **Without form, and void;** rather, waste and wild (to represent in some

degree the characteristic assonance of the original—*tōhū va-bōhū*) ; more literally, *immovable and lifeless.* It is the phrase used in Gen. i. 2 for primeval chaos. *Tōhū* and *bōhū* occur in parallel lines in Isa. xxxiv. 11, to express utter desolation ; *tōhū* alone five times in the Book of Isaiah, and once in Job. **They had no light.** The heavens were in the same condition as on the third day, subsequently to the creation of the heavens, but prior to that of the luminaries.

Ver. 24.—**Moved lightly** ; rather, *moved to and fro.*

Ver. 26.—**The fruitful place;** rather, *the garden-land* (see on ch. ii. 7). Not "the Carmel" (Keil, Payne Smith) for the context refers to the whole of the country, not to any single tract. The article before the two appellatives is the generic. **At the presence of;** rather, *by reason of.*

Ver. 27.—The vision breaks off, and the prophet emphasizes its truthfulness by the announcement of the Divine decree. "Desolation, and yet not a full end," is its burden. This is the same doctrine of the "remnant" which formed so important a part of the prophetic message of Isaiah and his contemporaries. However severe the punishment of Judah may be, there will be a "remnant" which shall escape, and become the seed of a holier nation (Amos ix. 8; Isa. iv. 2; vi. 13; x. 20; xi. 11; Hos. vi. 1, 2).

Ver. 28.—**For this** ; i.e. because of the impending judgment. **Be black.** "To be black" is equivalent to "to put on mourning" (comp. ch. viii. 21; xiv. 2).

Ver. 29.—**The whole city.** The reading of which this is a version can hardly be the right one; for "the whole city" can only be Jerusalem, and in ver. 6 the people outside are bidden to take refuge in the capital. Hence Ewald, Hitzig, and Payne Smith (after Septuagint, Targum) would slightly amend the word rendered "city," so as to translate "the whole land" (of Judah). **Shall flee;** literally, *fleeth.* So afterwards render, "have gone," "is forsaken," "dwelleth." It is a vivid dramatic representation of the effects of the invasion. **Bowmen.** It is singular that Herodotus should say nothing about the use of the bow by the Chaldeans. But the monuments give ample evidence that they were a people of archers. So of course were the Scythians, as Herodotus testifies. **The rocks;** i.e. the limestone caverns which abound in Palestine, and which were frequently used as strongholds and hiding-places (see Judg. vi. 2; xv. 8; 1 Sam. xiii. 6; xiv. 11; xxiv. 3 (especially); 1 Kings xviii. 13).

Ver. 30.—**And when thou art spoiled,** etc. It is Jerusalem who is addressed—Jerusalem, personified as a woman, who decks herself out finely to please her admirers.

All these arts are in vain, for a violent repulsion has converted her lovers into her deadly enemies. And when Jerusalem is "spoiled," or taken by storm, what device will there be left to attempt? The "lovers" are the foreign powers to whom the Jews paid court (ch. ii. 18, 36, 37). **Though thou rentest thy face**, etc; alluding to the custom of Eastern women, who try to make their eyes seem larger by putting powdered antimony (the Arabic *kohl*) upon their eyelids. So, for instance, did Jezebel (see 2 Kings xi. 30); and one of Job's daughters received the name Keren-happuch, "box of antimony," *i.e.* one who sets off the company in which she is, as antimony does the eye. An old author, Dr. Shaw, writes thus : "None of these ladies take themselves to be completely dressed till they have tinged the hair and edges of their eyelids with the powder of lead ore. And as this operation is performed by dipping first into this powder a small wooden bodkin of the thickness of a quill, and then drawing it afterwards through the eyelids over the ball of the eye, we have a lively image of what the prophet (Jer. iv. 30) may be supposed to mean" (Shaw, 'Travels in Barbary and the Levant,' 2nd edit., p. 229).

Ver. 31.—**For I have heard a voice**, etc. This explains the preceding statement, "They will seek thy life." It is this murderous plot which calls forth the "cry as of a woman in pangs." **Bewaileth herself;** rather, *sigheth deeply*. **Her hands**; literally, *her palms*. **Is wearied because of murderers;** rather, *fainteth into the hands of* (literally, *is weary unto*) *the murderers*.

HOMILETICS.

Ver. 3.—*Fallow ground.* Fallow ground is land that has fallen out of cultivation, or that has never been cultivated, and this has its counterpart in the broad fields of humanity, in the nations or individual men who are not under the influence of spiritual cultivation.

I. FALLOW GROUND IS COMPARATIVELY FRUITLESS. It may not be utterly fruitless. Even the bramble bears its wholesome fruit, and good thoughts and good deeds spring up in the midst of heathen nations and irreligious people. God's Spirit has not wholly deserted any. But such fruit is poor compared with the fruit of cultivation, and the crop of it is thin. The good which still pertains to a neglected soul is imperfect, and small in the extreme compared with the good which would spring up in that soul under proper spiritual influences. The highest thought, the purest morality, the noblest effort, the largest charity, are only to be found where the spiritual life is cultivated by worship, instruction, and discipline.

II. FALLOW GROUND BEARS WEEDS. If there are no flowers in a neglected garden, the soil will not be unoccupied. Dropped by birds in their flight, borne on the wings of the wind, in some way, myriads of seeds will find entrance into that garden and spring up in luxuriant growth. The neglected garden is not a barren desert ; it is a wilderness. The neglected soul will not be merely deficient of good ; it will bear a crop of evil. The heart cannot endure a void. If it is not filled with pure thoughts, it will indulge in unholy imaginations ; if it has no object of worthy love, its affections will descend and twine about some debased object ; if it is not active in doing good, it will be diligent in doing harm. In proportion to the gifts and powers of the soul will be the evil that will come out of it when neglected ; the more fertile the soil, the more abundant the crop of weeds.

III. FALLOW GROUND IS SUSCEPTIBLE OF CULTIVATION. It is not rock, but good soil. The most brutalized man is not yet a brute. Conscience slumbers, is not killed. The Divine image in the soul is worn in the traffic of worldliness and fouled in the mire of sin, but it is not effaced. The disobedient son is still a son. Hence there is hope for the most neglected heathen, the worst sinner, the oldest enemy of Christ.

IV. FALLOW GROUND MUST BE BROKEN UP. Throw bushels of wheat among the thorns, and the thorns will only "choke" it (Matt. xiii. 7). Till the old evil is torn from the heart, the new truth cannot grow and bear fruit there. Men must repent of sin before they can receive the seed of eternal life to profit. John the Baptist must precede Christ. So long as we are cherishing any sin we are preventing the growth of fruitful graces. The mere hearing of the truth is not enough. If the heart is hard, it will not receive it (Isa. vi. 10). If the heart is preoccupied, the truth will be soon forgotten, or at best will be crushed out of all living energy. Hence the heart must not only be cleared of weeds, it must be softened. The plough must break up the fallow ground.

V. IT IS OUR DUTY TO BREAK UP THE FALLOW GROUND. Men must be prepared for receiving the gospel of Christ. We are too eager to sow the seed. Hence the slight returns we have for so much effort and expenditure. People are called to "accept Christ" who do not know Christ, and would have no room in their hearts to receive him if they did know him. Much so-called "gospel preaching" thus meets with ridicule, or indifference, or bewildered surprise. If we were less hasty in seeking brilliant results we should see more true, fruitful returns for our work. Christ was not always and only crying, "Come unto me!" "Follow me!" Less pleasing, and in some eyes less important, words were often seen by him to be necessary. Men need instructing as well as inviting, rebuking as well as exhorting.

VI. THE DUTY OF BREAKING UP THE FALLOW GROUND IS GREAT AND PRESSING. How much fallow ground there is (1) in the *world!*—think of India, China, Africa, the godless of Europe; (2) in the *Church!*—how many enjoy its privileges! how few maintain its work! and (3) in *our own hearts!*—what faculties are wasted! what opportunities for good neglected!

Ver. 10.—*Divine illusions.* I. GOOD MEN MAY MISJUDGE GOD'S ACTIONS. The words of the text are not spoken with Divine authority; on the contrary, they are given in historical narrative as a record of the personal utterance of the prophet. He does not preface them with the august claim of authority, "Thus saith the Lord;" he distinctly says, "Then said I." Without needing to look for any other rendering of the text, we may consider it as throwing light on the condition of the prophet's mind, rather than as a difficult scriptural declaration of God's character and mode of acting. Thus we may see in it an expression of hasty judgment, misunderstanding, irritable impatience, complaint. If so, it warns us to beware of the prejudiced or impassioned utterances of the best and wisest men (Ps. cxvi. 11), and to be more cautious in forming judgments on difficult aspects of providence and religion, since even prophets err.

II. IT IS DIFFICULT TO JUDGE RIGHTLY OF GOD'S ACTIONS WHILE WE ARE IN THE MIDST OF THEM. We are too near to have the right perspective. The character of an action cannot be judged till its ultimate design is revealed. Many things look wrong because they are parts of a whole the remainder of which is unseen. Pride, passion, self-interest, and prejudice pervert our judgment. We must wait for time to clear up many dark passages in earthly providence (John xiii. 7). The inconsistency which seemed palpable to Jeremiah is less felt by us.

III. GOD'S ACTIONS ARE SOMETIMES ILLUSORY TO US. There was a measure of truth in the rash cry of the prophet. God never deceives. Yet his utterance may be misunderstood by us. God is said to harden the heart when his action results in this evil condition through the misconduct of men, and not at all through his wish to bring that evil about. So God might almost be said to deceive (though the expression is misleading) when his Word is such that we fall into a misconception in hearing it.

IV. THE ILLUSORY CHARACTER OF SOME OF GOD'S ACTIONS IS DETERMINED BY COMMON LIMITATIONS AND IMPERFECTIONS. Some truths are revealed, while qualifying truths are necessarily hidden because we could not understand them. No mention is made of the time of the fulfilment of a promise; hence we think it will be immediate, and are disappointed when we see delay and find unexpected troubles coming first. One part of God's Word may seem to contradict another when they refer to different conditions, but conditions not yet revealed to us.

V. TRUTH AND HUMAN WELFARE ARE BETTER SERVED BY THESE ILLUSIONS THAN BY REVELATIONS WHICH ADMIT OF NO MISCONSTRUCTION. If the child were never allowed to stumble, he would never learn to walk. We are educated by temporary illusions for higher truths than could be attained by plainer paths. Thus we know more of God and of heaven through the anthropomorphic and materialistic language of much of Scripture, which has resulted in gross misconceptions at times, than we should have learnt from language made bare enough to be unmistakable.

Ver. 14.—*The cleansing of the heart a necessary condition of salvation.* I. SALVATION IS PROMISED ON THE SIMPLEST POSSIBLE CONDITIONS. The very mention of conditions suggests difficulties, delays, barriers. But the only conditions required are in our own power, are simply such as are necessary to make the reception of the salvation of God possible to us, and do not refer to the source of it. We are not to save ourselves, not to purchase nor to merit salvation, but only to be in a right condition to receive it.

II. SALVATION IS ONLY POSSIBLE WHERE THERE IS A CLEANSING FROM WICKEDNESS. The soul that clings to sin cannot also grasp the Saviour. If it would be right to deliver men from the painful consequences of wickedness while they remained under the power of it, it must have been wrong ever to have permitted those consequences. If it is not unjust to forgive the impenitent, it is unjust to punish them, which is absurd.

III. THE CLEANSING FROM WICKEDNESS MUST BE IN THE HEART. There all sin has its origin. Clean hands are vain without a pure heart. Reformation must not simply be moral, it must be spiritual—not a change of habits, but a purification of thought, affection, and desire.

IV. THE DUTY OF CLEANSING OUR HEARTS FROM WICKEDNESS RESTS UPON OURSELVES. The text is not a promise, but an exhortation. True, no one can purify himself by his own efforts alone (ch. ii. 22). God has provided the fountain for uncleanness, and only they who wash in this are clean. But men must plunge into the purifying flood, must make the effort of repentance, must seek the cleansing which is promised through Christ, must submit to the baptism of the Holy Ghost, must actively apply themselves to the execution of good deeds in the power given by God. Compare the words of Isaiah (i. 16).

V. THERE IS NO REASON TO DELAY THE CLEANSING OF OUR HEARTS. "How long shall thoughts of wickedness lodge within thee?" The longer repentance is postponed, the more difficult does it become; the more numerous are the stains of sin, the nearer is the approach of doom. Since it is for men to seek the cleansing of their souls, any delay must be attributed to their negligence, not to God's unwillingness to help them.

Ver. 22.—*The folly of misdirected wisdom.* I. WICKEDNESS IS FOLLY. The "fool," according to Scripture, is both morally corrupt and intellectually imbecile (*e g.* Ps. cvii. 17). There is a truth underlying the saying of Socrates, that "Virtue is knowledge, and vice is ignorance." It is apparent, indeed, that men may have an intellectual conception of the right while they do wrong, as also that good men may fall into error. But, on the other hand: 1. We cannot progress in goodness till we *discern the way*; we must know God to love him, recognize the good to choose it. 2. Immorality *deadens the faculty of spiritual intuition*; purity purges the vision of the soul. 3. Wisdom is not mere intelligence, but *applied intelligence*, practical intelligence. It is not perfected till it is practised. He who knows the good is not wise until he does it; and he who does right from instinct, habit, or mere inclination is not really performing a moral action. An action is moral when it is performed with an intelligent regard to principle, *i.e.* when it is under the direction of spiritual wisdom.

II. THE FOLLY OF WICKEDNESS MAY BE ASSOCIATED WITH MISDIRECTED WISDOM. The "fool" in spiritual things may be a worldly wise man and clever in the execution of wickedness. Ironical as is the language of the text, it may often find a literal application. Shrewd business men may be spiritually blind. Men who are wakeful and eager in material concerns become dull and listless when they touch higher interests. This may be explained by two considerations. 1. *We develop most wisdom in regard to those things which interest us most.* Interest rouses attention, quickens perception, excites inquiry, stimulates intellectual activity; while lack of interest leaves the mind in a slumberous condition, working at half-power. If we feel no interest in goodness, we shall be dull and foolish in regard to it. 2. *Spiritual wisdom depends upon a spiritual tone of mind.* The greatest intelligence is not capable of detecting subtle harmonies and discords if it is not accompanied by "an ear for music." The cold intellect, which is but a huge calculating-machine, has not the fitting powers of perception for discerning spiritual truth. This requires a spiritual sympathy (1 Cor. ii. 14). Therefore (1) let the man of conscious intellectual power beware of the danger of assuming to judge spiritual questions before he has acquired the requisite spiritual qualification; and (2) let us all beware of attaching too much weight to the religious motives of people who may be able business men, clever literary critics, and even profound students of science, and yet in moral regions " blind leaders of the blind."

III. MISDIRECTED WISDOM IS THE HEIGHT OF FOLLY. The very ability, misapplied, witnesses for the foolishness which permitted so gross a mistake. These people who are " wise to do evil " are on the whole " foolish," " sottish," and " have *no* understanding." The man who is prudent enough to exercise forethought for this life only enhances his folly in having none for the future life (Luke xii. 16—21). He who knows much of worldly things is convicted of grossest darkness in not knowing God. The born fool is excused by his misfortune of nature. But how foolish for the man who shows himself capable of wisdom to neglect the highest wisdom! Note, in conclusion, (1) the common mistake of honouring men for their intellectual ability rather than for their moral character; (2) the error of those who pride themselves in "knowing the world," while they are ignorant of God (Rom. xvi. 19); and (3) the need to turn from intellectual pride to childlike trust for the source of true wisdom (Matt. xi. 25).

Vers. 23—26.—*Chaos the result of sin.* I. SIN HAS A RETROGRESSIVE MOVEMENT. In his vision of the earth desolated by a Divine judgment on sin, Jeremiah sees a relapse to the primeval condition before the dawn of creation, and in his graphic description uses the very words of the narrative in Genesis. He describes the earth as " waste and wild." Every step in sin is a step downward, backward. It is backsliding. How rapid this is! One generation sees the fall back to the condition from which it had taken ages to build up the order of the world. One day's sin may undo the work of years in a soul's progress. One age of misrule may throw a nation back for centuries.

II. SIN HAS A DISINTEGRATING INFLUENCE. It breaks up the fair order of the world and tends to reduce it to chaos. Religion and morality are the chief securities for order, the strongest bands of social unity. Vice is a social solvent, destroying ties of trust and affection, undermining the foundations of industrial co-operation. It is corruption, and corruption means decomposition. This may be applied (1) politically, (2) socially, (3) personally.

III. SIN HAS A DESOLATING EFFECT. The earth is seen as not only wild; it is " waste," *i.e.* fruitless, solitary, desolate. The fruitful place becomes a wilderness, and the whole land desolate. The result of the retrogressive and disintegrating influences of sin is not to reduce the world to a state of elementary simplicity. It introduces confusion, turmoil, disaster, death. The loss of goodness involves the admission of evil passions, and the advent of these is followed by the irruption of misery with no prospect of peace but in death and destruction (Jas. i. 15).

Ver. 30.—*The abject helplessness which resorts to false pretensions and its failure.* I. ABJECT HELPLESSNESS. This follows the discovery or punishment of sin. It is when Israel " is spoiled." Israel is boastful and self-confident before the disaster comes; the prophet advises him to consider what he will do after it has fallen on him. What can be done in such a case? The sin cannot be undone; once revealed it cannot be hidden again; punishment from God cannot be successfully resisted by man. It is vain, then, to call on the mountains to fall and cover us (Luke xxiii. 30). How dreadful to be thus confounded! left without excuse, without refuge, without remedy! How much better to anticipate this conclusion and prevent it!

II. FALSE PRETENSIONS. There are the refuges now resorted to and trusted in for the future, but in vain. 1. Outward glory is a mockery when once internal wretchedness is discovered. What use are purple and fine linen to the leper? 2. When character is revealed, profession counts for nothing. 3. When true worth is destroyed, the most frantic attempts to recover it at the last moment will prove fruitless. The character once lost is hard to retrieve. Consider, then, the common mistake of living for appearances, making the outside of life respectable while the heart is corrupt, and, in the event of discovery, not repenting and amending, but simply excusing one's self, " making the best of the matter," trying still to put on a fair show. This is common at all times. So many people are more anxious to seem good than to be good. All the petty contrivances and miserable deceptions of such lives will be one day disclosed.

III. ULTIMATE FAILURE. "Thy lovers will despise thee, they will seek thy life."
1. Once discovered, the attempt to win favour by false appearances will not only defeat
its own object; it will aggravate the evil it is intended to avoid. It aims at securing
honour; but when detected it is the butt of ridicule, the deserved occasion of contempt. 2. The friends of sinful days become foes in the time of trouble. The *lovers* of
the daughter of Zion are the first to despise her and seek her life. The ties of friendship in wickedness are brittle. This is based on selfishness. No high constancy can be
expected from people of bad character. The only friend who will be a refuge in the
shame and ruin which follow sin, is not the partner in guilt, but the very God against
whom the sin is committed.

HOMILIES BY VARIOUS AUTHORS.

Vers. 1—4.—*The duty of reality in religious profession.* The reformations of Jehu
and Josiah were superficial and short-lived. Something more thorough was required.
A real, immediate return to Jehovah was demanded.
I. THE SIGNS OF UNREALITY. 1. *Retention of the memorials and symbols of the
guilty past.* They may not be used, but they are there. There has not been strength
of will to remove them, or the fear of man has produced vacillation. Externally the
heathen temple stands side by side with the house of God, and may claim equal respect
with it. 2. *An uncertain and wavering attitude.* Blowing hot and blowing cold.
Compromising with existent evils. Postponing needed reforms. 3. *Unrighteousness of
life.* This is one of the gravest evils. A creed which does not affect conduct must be
either untrue or not heartily believed. An enigma of the anti-slavery times was the
fact that amongst the pro-slavery advocates were many of the most orthodox clergy,
whereas the leaders of the agitation for freedom were secularists, Unitarians, and men
of vague or heterodox religious opinions.
II. EVILS ATTENDANT UPON UNREALITY. 1. *Confusion is created between the true
and the false religions.* 2. *A constant temptation exists in the relics and practices of
evil that are retained.* 3. *Moral influence upon unbelievers is lost, and unrighteousness
encouraged.* 4. *Spiritual growth is seriously impeded.* It is a "sowing among
thorns," or upon the exhausted and unfruitful soil of superficial emotion and fancy.
As wild land can be cleansed from weeds only by deep and repeated ploughing, so the
spiritual nature must be thoroughly moved by penitence and steadfast resolution.
III. GOD'S FEELING TOWARDS UNREAL WORSHIPPERS. He cannot accept their penitence. Their services are an abomination to him. His anger is represented as a
smouldering fire ready to break forth in destruction.—M.

Ver. 10.—*Human uncertainty coexisting with Divine illumination.* The prophecy
now uttered does not harmonize with that of ch. iii. 12—25. The *times* of fulfilment
are unknown to the prophet. This element of uncertainty in all prophecies, even those
of Christ ("for of the times and the seasons knoweth no man," etc.) is noteworthy.
This outburst of annoyance and misconception illustrates—
I. THE TEMPTATION LATENT IN SUPERIOR DIVINE KNOWLEDGE. The moral balance
and perspective are threatened with disturbance. Hence the impulse to expostulate
with God—to speak as if from a superior standpoint of morality. Seeming contradictions are encountered which would have no existence to a simpler or less
illuminated spirit. It is as if the moral nature of man were only practically sufficient
for what is revealed to him by the ordinary faculties and means of knowledge.
II. THE SORROW ACCOMPANYING EXCEPTIONAL GIFTS. The prophet, no more than the
poet or man of genius, is to be envied. How hard to be the custodian of a truth men
will not receive! to be conscious of evils impending which one cannot avert! The *exceptional sensitiveness* of the prophetic temperament, and the *keener vision* of the seer, are
the occasions of an incommunicable sadness, and even, at times, of overwhelming concern.
Especially is this the case where patriotic feeling identifies the prophet on the one side
with his people, and devout spirituality leads him nevertheless to acknowledge the
righteousness of God. There was no more human or loving heart in Israel than

Jeremiah's, and if they would not heed his counsels, he was helpless. To be "before the age" in such a sense is not so enviable as we might imagine.

III. THE RESERVE THAT MARKS THE COMMUNICATION OF TRUTH. Partly necessitated by limitation of human nature; partly due to the subordination of the prophet, teacher, etc., to the special task before him. We should lose more than we should gain if, constituted as we were, we were to receive unlimited revelations of the future. The practical and immediate import of Divine revelation is therefore our first concern. To-day is a little space cleared for duty. Opportunities of well-doing occur in constant succession. "What is that to thee?" might well be asked of many a one that concerns himself with things beyond his ken: "follow thou me."—M.

Ver. 22.—*The wisdom of this world.* That there is such a thing we may well believe, for Christ himself noticed and commended it: "The children of this world are wiser in their generation than the children of light." Within a certain range it is often seen to the disadvantage of the "wisdom that is from above."

I. IT IS GREAT IN QUESTIONS OF MEANS, METHODS, AND POLICY. Attention is directed to these continually. A certain pride is exhibited in skill and power of manipulation. There is something very attractive to a certain order of mind in the opportunities the world affords for manœuvre, dexterity, intrigue. The world prizes and encourages cleverness in practical, external matters. It can even appreciate the business qualities and the reliable character of Christians, when their inspiring principle is utterly ignored or intensely disliked. How much has the Church of to-day to learn of the world in merely practical concerns, knowledge of human nature, and adaptation of herself to her surroundings!

II. IT IS MARRED BY: 1. *Dislike to what is worthy and good.* Disillusion from worldly dreams may coexist with this. But men without lofty ideals cannot be happy or satisfied. 2. *Heedlessness as to the impending judgments of God and the eternal future.* 3. *Consciousness of worthlessness and uselessness of its own efforts.*—M.

Ver. 3.—*Fallow ground.* Such an analogy as this reminds us that the materials of the highest wisdom are always lying close within our reach, sometimes in very unlikely places. The world without is a mirror in which we see our own moral life and the laws that govern it reflected. Air, earth, and sea are full of teachers whom God has sent to rebuke in us all that is false and evil, and lead us into all that is true and good. The prophet, in the text, does but give an articulate voice to the silent eloquence of one of these. Apply personally some of the lessons taught.

I. THE LIFE OF EVERY MAN IS A PROCESS OF SPIRITUAL HUSBANDRY. There is a true analogy between the soul of a man and the field in which a farmer sows his seed. In each case there are latent productive elements, that may be turned either to good or evil according to the conditions of their development—capacities of indefinite improvement or of indefinite deterioration, of boundless fruitfulness or of boundless waste. The prolific virtue of the soil will nourish alike the germs of precious corn or of noisome weeds; and, whichever it be, the heavens above, by all the influences they shed down upon it, will promote the process. Thus will the faculties of our spiritual nature foster either the seeds of Divine excellence or of satanic corruption, and then all the laws to which our nature is subject, and all the associations of our life, will help to elaborate the issue, until we reap either a glad harvest of fruits that will endure for ever, or one of shame and sorrow—thorns and weeds and briars fit only for the flames. "He that soweth to his flesh," etc. (Gal. vi. 8). Hence the solemn necessity for some Divine power so to control and govern the secret dispositions and tendencies of our nature as that in our case the law shall be fulfilled in the nobler and better way. "Make the tree good," etc. (Matt. xii. 33).

II. In this husbandry of the soul, NEGLECT LEADS TO LOSS AND WASTE AND RUIN. "Fallow ground" is land untilled, uncultivated, which no plough turns up and into which no seed is cast. It may be purposely left to rest, that it may not exhaust itself, and that its internal resources may be all the richer afterwards. But the point of the analogy is this—that it naturally becomes encumbered with "thorns." In the spiritual husbandry, while fruitfulness is the result only of diligent labour, ruin follows from simple neglect. The land of the slothful husbandman will soon present the picture of weedy, thorny desolation. To be ruined, to sink into a state of utter poverty and barrenness and destitution of all satisfying good, the souls of men only need to be left alone. " While men sleep the enemy sows tares." " What shall it profit a man," etc. ? (Mark viii. 36). Our Lord speaks of the soul as being "lost" simply through being forgotten in the eager pursuit of a kind of good which can never of itself enrich and satisfy it. This implies that its native propensities are for the most part of a downward tendency. It bears within it the seeds of moral decay. The "fallow ground" spontaneously produces " thorns."

III. IT IS VAIN TO SOW SEEDS OF TRUTH AND GOODNESS IN HEARTS PREOCCUPIED WITH OTHER AND INCONGRUOUS THINGS. How many there are whose religious career may well be described as a "sowing among thorns"! They have religious susceptibilities; they are familiar with religious influences; but their secret hearts are the home of mean ambitions, tainted with the "lust of the eye and the pride of life," or they are entangled with a network of worldly associations or bound by the chains of some bad habit, from which they have not the courage or the strength to set themselves free. And so their spiritual condition is a strange medley of good and evil. Every better affection and impulse within them has some form of moral weakness by its side that nullifies it. Strong as their heavenward aspirations may sometimes be, there is nothing like whole-heartedness in their pursuit of the nobler good. No wonder they are "barren and unfruitful in the knowledge of Christ." The ground must be cleared before a better result can be expected. How many a sower, going forth in the name of the Great Husbandman, is oppressed in spirit with the thought that much of the seed that he scatters falls "among thorns"! He has to contend with a thousand obstructive forces in men's hearts, and knows well that, unless some mightier force goes with his message to overbear all these, they will "choke the Word." Let the young especially watch and pray against the encroachment upon them of influences fatal to their higher life. It is a comparatively easy thing to overmaster the sins and follies of youth. Far otherwise when they have become the confirmed and cherished habits of the man. "Break up your fallow ground!" It is hard to do this. It involves much self-crucifixion. We all like to live at ease—to yield to the strongest influences of the passing hour, as the sluggard does, who allows himself to be overcome by the spell of sleep, and to dream away the hours and moments that ought to be spent in the wakeful activities of life. But this is not the way to reach the heights of heavenly glory and blessedness. It is the certain road to poverty and ruin, to despair and death. Not on grounds of self-interest alone is the appeal of the text to be urged. Consider what a loss to the world is involved in every barren, undeveloped human soul and life. It is a great calamity to a country to have large tracts of its territory lying waste and desolate, while many of its people, perhaps, are perishing for lack of bread, or compelled to flee to other lands to find a field and reward for their labour. How sad that, in a world of such overwhelming spiritual need and destitution as this, the powers of any human soul, that might exercise a redeeming influence upon it, should be left idle or allowed to run to waste!—W.

Ver. 14.—*Vain thoughts.* I. THE LIFE OF EVERY MAN IS GOVERNED BY HIS THOUGHTS. "As a man thinketh in his heart, so is he" (Prov. xxiii. 7). True as it is that the essential moral quality of the man will always determine the order of his thinking, the converse also is equally true. Thought is the formative principle of all personal life— kindles feeling, touches the springs of purpose, guides the course of moral action. What are character and conduct but the definite expression of secret thought?

> " That subtle husbandman,
> That sows its little seed of good or ill
> In the moist, unsunned surface of the heart.
> And what it there in secrecy doth plant,
> Stands with its ripe fruit at the judgment day."

II. EVERY MAN IS RESPONSIBLE FOR THE TENOR OF HIS THOUGHTS. If not, there could be no room in this matter for remonstrance or appeal. The law of the association of ideas may be such that it is as impossible to prevent some particular thought from recurring to the mind as to stay the tide of the ocean; but it is certainly possible for us to regulate our *habitual mental conditions*. It is given to us by watchful, prayerful self-discipline, especially by occupying the mind with higher and nobler things, to secure that the main drift of our thinking shall be in the right direction. We can choose our own fields of daily contemplation. Those thoughts will "lodge" in us which we most encourage and cherish, and for this we are accountable.

III. THE CHERISHING OF VAIN THOUGHTS IS NECESSARILY DEGRADING IN ITS EFFECT. "Vain thoughts" are iniquitous thoughts, sinful thoughts. "The thought of foolishness is sin" (Prov. xxiv. 9). It is impossible to measure the corrupting power of such thoughts. No evil imagination or purpose can enter the mind, and be allowed for a moment to dwell there, without leaving some moral stain behind it. Accustom yourself to any extent to the play of such influences, your whole being becomes contaminated by them, and—

> "The baseness of their nature
> Shall have power to drag you down."

Our minds cannot be in frequent contact with mean or grovelling objects of contemplation without finding that they poison all the streams of moral life within us. "To be carnally minded is death" (Rom. viii. 6).

IV. THE ONLY CURE FOR THIS EVIL TENDENCY IS THE DIVINE RENEWAL OF OUR SPIRITUAL NATURE. "Out of the heart proceed evil thoughts" (Matt. xv. 19). Let that be sanctified, and their power over us shall cease. Superficial expedients, mere external restraints and corrections, are of little use. We need something that shall go to the root of the disease. The fountain of life within must be cleansed if the streams that flow from it are to be pure. The temple at Jerusalem was externally beautiful, its roof so bright with burnished gold that nothing less pure than the glorious sunbeams could rest upon it; but that did not prevent it from being internally the haunt of many a form of hollow hypocrisy, and the scene of a base, worldly traffic—"a den of thieves." Let the Spirit of God make our souls his temple, and that holy Presence shall effectually scatter all vain and corrupt imaginations. They cannot "lodge" where the heavenly glory dwells. Every thought of our hearts shall then be "brought into captivity to Christ."—W.

Vers. 3, 4.—*The peril of profession without possession of real religion.* This will be shown if we consider—

I. THE SCENE HERE PRESENTED TO US. 1. The fallow ground; that is, ground unoccupied, free. Not hardened, as the wayside (cf. Matt. xiii.); not shallow-soiled, as the stony ground; not poor and barren, but capable of yielding rich return. 2. Sowers about to cast in seed—good seed. 3. A stern prohibition of their work. They are commanded to "sow not." A reason is given—the fallow ground that looks so fair is full of thorns. They are bidden "break up," *i.e.* purge, cleanse, this ground. And all this on penalty of God's sore displeasure (ver. 4, etc.).

II. ITS SIGNIFICANCE. 1. *For those to whom Jeremiah wrote.* (1) *They* were as the fallow ground, at this time free from open visible idolatry which had been their disgrace and ruin. All *that* King Josiah had put a stop to. So now they were free to begin afresh, to take a new departure, to turn over a new leaf, as fallow ground is ready for a new sowing (cf. the history of the times). (2) And they were about to sow the seed, *i.e.* they were about to adopt the outward forms of the divinely appointed Jewish worship. Externally they would conform to the ancient faith, and in large measure they did so. (3) But now there comes the strange, stern prohibition of the text, and in so much that follows. They are bidden to refrain from this external religion, these outward rites. And the reason is given—their hearts were yet unchanged, full of the seeds of all their former wickedness, and until these "thorns" were purged out no good, but only evil, could come of any mere external conformity. It had no value in the eyes of God, it only aroused his sore wrath. But let them "*break up the fallow ground*" (cf. vers. 4, 14). Let there be a true inward repentance before they approach God with the visible signs and forms of his worship. Let them not think that by any such mere formal service they could turn aside the anger of God. Such the significance of this scene in regard to Judah and Jerusalem in the days of Jeremiah. But note: 2. *Its significance for ourselves.* (1) There are many whose character corresponds to the "fallow ground."

Free from gross external fault, morally fair, decent, and reputable. Not thoughtless and trifling, as the wayside hearers (cf. Matt. xiii.). Not obstinately self-willed, as the stony-ground hearers, who are represented by the emblem of a superficial soil having stretched beneath it a hard, pavement-like rock, through which the rootlets of the sown seed cannot thrust themselves to reach the nourishment of the soil beneath. Nor are they incapable of yielding good service to God; on the contrary, they have, like the fallow ground, all capacities for yielding a rich return. (2) And such persons often sow the seed of religious profession and observance, and assume the varied external signs of true religion. It is not necessary to inquire their motives, but they do this. And when we see them we are all well pleased. We hope very much from them, as no doubt Josiah hoped much from the external religiousness of the people with whom he had to do. But God sees not as man seeth. His eye penetrates beneath the surface. And the fallow ground may be full of thorns; that is, the heart of him who makes all this external profession—comes to the Lord's table, teaches in a Sunday school, leads in prayer, perhaps enters the ministry of the Church,—his heart may all the while be unrenewed, impure, filled with the seeds of thorns, which wait only their opportunity to bear their baneful harvest. (3) Hence God forbids such sowing amongst thorns. How stern his denunciations, how awful his threatenings, to those who are guilty of this sin! Do any inquire, Wherefore this severity? The reply is : (*a*) Hypocrisy is hateful to him. See our Saviour's denunciations of hypocrisy (cf. Matt. xxiii.). He who was gentle and full of grace to all others, had no words too scathing for this sin. No doubt his stern words were designed also to open the eyes of the people who were deceived by the false professions of those to whom our Lord spoke so severely. And we can hardly doubt, either, that there was a gracious purpose in regard to the men themselves, to awaken and alarm them, if by any means it might be possible. But still, he who to us is the Manifestation of God, makes evident how hateful in his sight is all religious profession that rests on no reality within. (*b*) A further reason for the severity which is so marked here is the extreme peril of such sowing amongst thorns to the sowers themselves. Few things are more deceiving to a man's soul than to be professing religion, and to be accounted by others as truly religious, when he is not so. It is bad to be an unregenerate man ; it is worse to be such and not to know it ; but the worst condition of all is to be such, and to be believing all the while that you are the reverse, and that for you salvation is sure. But this dread self-deception is fearfully fostered by this sin, which God here so severely condemns. (*c*) And yet another reason for this Divine condemnation is that by this sin the Name of God is blasphemed. The world is keen-eyed, and soon detects the mere outside religion of those whom this word contemplates. And because of the base coin the genuine is suspected, and the way of godliness despised. Therefore note—

III. THE SOLEMN SUGGESTIONS OF THIS SUBJECT TO OURSELVES. 1. To those who have been guilty of this sin. You have been, you are now, it may be, making loud religious profession, and yet your heart is not right in the sight of God. We do not say, "Throw up your profession, abandon all religious ways ; " but we do say, " Have done with insincerity." Resolve that the fallow ground *shall* be broken up, the heart truly yielded to God. Implore him to give you the *reality*, that your profession may be a lie no more. 2. Let all remember that this purging of our hearts, this cleansing of our souls, needs to be *continually* done. The thorn seeds float continually over the fallow ground, and, if it be not continually cleansed, they will take root, and the good seed will be choked. 3. The Divine condemnation of sowing amongst thorns is not designed to deter our sowing where the grace of God has cleansed us from such thorns. Many read these terrible threatenings, and fear to take upon them a religious profession, lest they should be found unworthy and untrue. But if God has given you to repent of sin, to long after holiness, to look daily to your Lord for grace and help, then he *has* washed your heart from wickedness (ver. 14), and you may, you ought, openly to avow his name, observe his appointed ordinances, and engage in any way his providence may invite you in his direct and recognized service. 4. And let not those who neither possess nor profess religion deem themselves better off because those who profess without possessing are so severely dealt with. Let them remember that if the righteous— and to the outward eye these *are* righteous—scarcely be saved, where shall the ungodly and the sinner appear ?—C.

Vers. 5—31.—*The proclamation of woe.* Such is the character of this entire section, and we observe upon this proclamation—

I. THAT, LIKE ALL SUCH, IT IS PROMPTED BY DIVINE LOVE. The most fearful judgments contained in the whole Bible are those denounced by our Lord Jesus Christ. The most awful words ever spoken are those which proceeded out of the mouth of him at whose graciousness all-men wondered. It is evident, therefore, that they were the utterances, as is this one here, of Divine love. They are beacon-lights set up as a warning, that men may not suffer their vessels to run on those rocks against which they warn, and of whose peril they are the evidence and sign. There was time for those to whom Jeremiah spoke to turn unto the Lord and find salvation, though indeed it was the eleventh hour. And that they might be driven to this, morally compelled to come in to the mercy of God, is the object of these terrible threatenings, these blasts of the alarm-trumpet of God's love. And in keeping with this intent, this proclamation—

II. SETS FORTH IN A VIVID, STRIKING FORM THE JUDGMENTS THAT IT DENOUNCES. 1. Under the emblem of a lion bursting forth from its thicket upon its defenceless prey (vers. 7, 8). 2. Under that of a terrible tempest (vers. 11—13). 3. Under that of a cordon of "watchers," who guard every corner and the entire circumference of a field in which the game they are hunting for has taken refuge. So should Judah and Jerusalem be beleaguered and hemmed in until captured and destroyed (vers. 16, 17). They who would lead men away from sin to God must not shun to set forth in the most impressive way possible to them the dread evil of that which they would have them forsake. Hence the lurid pictures of the unquenchable flame and the undying worm which our Saviour presents to us, and hence these vivid representations of the prophet Jeremiah.

III. IS INTERMINGLED, AS IT HAS BEEN PRECEDED, WITH EXHORTATIONS TO THAT REPENTANCE BY WHICH THE THREATENED JUDGMENTS WOULD BE TURNED ASIDE. (Vers. 8, 14.) So in declaring the judgments of God against sin, we should never let it be forgotten how God hath said, "As I live, saith the Lord God, I have no pleasure in the death of the wicked; but rather," etc. This section is a model of the method in which the more awful portions of our message to men should be declared. Hence note how it—

IV. IS A BURDEN OF THE LORD ON THOSE WHO ARE CHARGED WITH IT. (Vers. 19—31.) Jeremiah could not refrain from delivering his message, and could not but know that to many it would be delivered in vain; but it was with grief and pain of heart he foretold what he knew must come. See our Saviour's tears over Jerusalem. Listen to St. Paul, "Of whom I tell you even weeping." Would that we all knew how to combine this faithfulness and this yearning tenderness in the delivery of this message! Then would men be aroused, as too often they are not now, to "flee from the wrath to come."

V. IS CERTAIN TO BE FULFILLED IF THE SIN WHICH IS THE CAUSE OF IT BE NOT FORSAKEN. Few things are more solemnizing to the careless soul than to have plainly brought before him the sure fact that God has never gone from his word, awful though that word might have been. He did not here. All that Jeremiah foretold came to pass. The anguish of his heart was not caused, any more than were the Redeemer's tears, by a merely fancied calamity. We are not able to tell what will be all the characteristics and elements of the Divine retribution on sin, but of its *reality* none who read the book of God's written records, or the book of his providence as seen in historic facts, can for one moment doubt. Oh for a far deeper conviction of these soul-subduing truths on the part of all who preach and all who hear God's holy Word!—C.

Ver. 10.—"Ah, Lord God! surely thou," etc. *Inflicted infatuation, or the deceived of God.* I. THERE ARE SUCH. How else can they be described who, in spite of the plainest declarations of God against their wickedness, persist therein, persuading themselves that they have no cause to fear? Such was the way of these to whom Jeremiah spoke. They and their false prophets were continually saying, "We shall have peace" (cf. ch. v. 12, 31). And there have been other instances (cf. Pharaoh, hardening his heart against God). And there are many now. The Bible speaks, providence speaks, conscience speaks, Christ's ministers speak, the Holy Spirit speaks pleading with them; but they heed not, they turn a deaf ear to every voice. What can this be called but infatuation? And it can only be explained as Jeremiah here explains it, as a Divine judgment. "Ah, Lord God! surely *thou* hast deceived them." The evidence that their course was one that must bring punishment was so glaring, so strong, so irresistible, that none but the infatuated could possibly disregard it.   Now, it is the testimony of the Word of God that such blindness is judicial, is from God.   God hardened Pharaoh's heart.   Our Lord refers more often than to any other Old Testament Scripture, to that word of Isaiah's which tells of the Divine will, that "seeing, they [his enemies] may see and *not* perceive, and hearing, they may hear and *not* understand."   Men who will not hear come at length to find they cannot.   So with Judah and Jerusalem; they were at this time "given up to a strong delusion, that they should believe the lie"—that peace could be their lot in spite of what they were.   We speak of gospel-hardened men, and, alas! we too often see such.   And this is in keeping with God's law of habit —a law most beneficent to those who obey him, but terrible in its effects on the dis- obedient.   For separate actions crystallize into habits, whereby such actions, no matter what their character, become easy to us, and at last can be performed without any effort of our will.   So that separate acts of obedience to God will at length become a blessed and holy habit of obedience, and separate acts of sin repeated again and again will become a direful habit of sin, from which we cannot break away.   And because all this is in accordance with a Divine law, therefore God is said to harden men's hearts, to hinder their understanding of his Word, to give them over to strong delusions and, as here, to "deceive the people."

II. THE CAUSE IS CLEAR.   Ver. 18, "Thy way and thy doings have procured these things unto thee."   It is from no decree of reprobation, from no predestination to sin, but from the inevitable action of the law of God which ordains that "ways" and "doings" such as Judah's were shall at length so utterly deceive those who are guilty of them that the most glaring falsehood is not too glaring for them to believe.

III. ITS DOOM IS JUST.   Is it unjust that a man shall be filled with the fruit of his own ways? that what a man soweth that he shall also reap?   Holiness must become impossible if its opposite be not possible too.   The same law necessitates both.   It is no arbitrary infliction, but the natural outcome of what a man has been and of what he has persistently done.   It is as natural as that the harvest should follow the sowing of its own seed.   The most dreadful element in the sinner's doom—the worm that dieth not—will be the ever-present reflection that he has brought it all upon himself.   He himself made the bed on which he has to lie.   And if still the doom of these wicked men be objected to, as it is, we reply, remembering how it is ever the necessity of any moral condition to be seeking to assimilate its surroundings to itself, so that goodness seeks to make others good, and evil seeks to make others evil—remembering this we say, with the late Dr. Arnold, "It is better that the wicked should be destroyed a hundred times over than that they should tempt those who are yet innocent to join their company."   And this is what they would be sure, from the very necessity which arises from what they are, to be ever seeking to accomplish.   Therefore we say their doom is just.

IV. THE AWAKENING AWFUL.   (Ver. 9.)   See the picture of dismay and despair which the prophet draws (cf. Rev. vi. 17).   Self-deception, however hardened into habit by long years' use, cannot endure for ever.   There will be an awakening.

V. THE LESSON PLAIN.   Break away at once from sin lest it coil round thee like a serpent, lest repeated transgression become links, and the links a chain which will bind thee so fast that thou canst not escape.   Therefore break away now, turn to the Lord Jesus, invoke his aid, day by day look to him, and thou art saved.—C.

Ver. 14.—"O Jerusalem, wash thine heart from wickedness, that thou mayest be saved."   *The loving charge of the Great Searcher of hearts.*   The text shows us—

I. GOD INTENSELY DESIRING MAN'S SALVATION.   This is evident from the pleading tone of the text.   It is like the pathetic cry of the Saviour over the same Jerusalem, when her people rejected him.   And this Divine distress over the sinner's rejection of salvation, or in any wise missing of it, is attested not by any one Scripture alone, but by many, and by a multitude of other witnesses beside.   How many Divine utterances there are which breathe the like loving concern to that well-known one which says, "As I live, saith the Lord God, I have no pleasure in the death of the wicked; but that the wicked turn from his way and live" (Ezek. xxxiii. 11)!   And the Divine words of love are confirmed by the supreme deed of love.   "God so loved the world."   Surely the remem- brance of this Divine yearning for our eternal salvation should touch and subdue our hearts. If we knew of one who, when we were prostrate with disease, out of love came to us, despising all risk of contagion, and watched over us night and day, on the alert at every turn and stage of the dread foe that was threatening our life, who in every way showed himself heedless of his own comfort or safety, so only as he might win us back to health; how in after years should we regard such a one? Would not even the most selfish cherish a warm regard, a grateful recollection? And most men would take care to let it be known what was their estimate of such self-sacrificing love. "But," saith God, "Israel doth not know; my people doth not consider."

II. God declaring that man must do his part if that salvation is to be won. If the whole matter rested with God, such language as our text, in which man is charged, importuned to bestir *himself*, would have no meaning, would be what we will not even suggest. And our text but embodies the same truth as to the need of man's co-operation with God which lies upon the surface of every "Come unto me" uttered by our Lord or by his apostles and ministers in his Name. Our salvation is not a case in which God but speaks and all is done, and commands and all stands fast. The work of grace is not accomplished as one tree is made an oak, the other an elm. We look with delight and wonder at the manifold triumphs of mind over matter which the varied discoveries of science have in this century achieved. But the salvation of a soul has the higher glory of the triumph of mind over *mind*—that in strict harmony with the laws and liberties of mind, and in spite of inherent and inveterate opposition, the love of God shall conquer and subdue, and the "unruly wills of sinful men" shall cheerfully own and yield to the Divine sway. But in such a salvation man must do his part; he is not left out in the scheme, and here, as in so many other Scriptures, he is called upon to be a worker together with God that he "may be saved." How this truth shatters the delusion and the fatal self-deception of those who comfort themselves in their disregard of God by a wresting of the doctrine of the Holy Spirit's work, as if it were one which absolved them from all endeavour, instead of prompting them thereto and aiding them therein. And some Christian workers need also to be reminded of this same truth; for they are tempted at times to excuse and account for their want of success on the ground of the sovereignty of the Divine working—the Spirit, like the wind, blowing where it listeth—rather than on the ground of their own laggard following of the Divine leading and their failure to co-operate with God. *Man must do his part*—this is the law writ large over all God's Word and works and ways.

III. God showing to man what his part is. "Wash thine heart," etc. Then: 1. Wickedness is a *defiling* thing. It is to the soul what the mud and mire of the street, what all material foulness, are to the body. Sometimes this is made manifest even now. On a man's face may be read the moral defilement of his soul. But generally men are too cautious for that, and in this world men take care not to let the inward defilement appear. We are formed to love what is fair-looking and pure and wholesome, and we turn away from its opposite. And wicked men know this, and are careful to maintain appearances. But if *hereafter*, as now, God "gives to every seed its own body," he shall then, as is plainly taught, give to every soul its own body—a body that will take its nature, shape, and form from the moral characteristics of the soul. Oh, what transformations there may be then! The character of the soul determining what the body shall be. Some then, who here have had no form nor comeliness, shall be seen then as the angels of God; and others who here have lacked no natural beauty, shall be shunned as were those who in our Lord's days on earth were possessed with an unclean spirit. Oh for the purged vision, that we might see our souls as God always sees them! Then surely we, seeing how wickedness ever pollutes and defiles, should turn from it with loathing, as now we too seldom do. 2. And the defilement is such as *cleaves* to the soul. "*Wash* thine heart," etc. The abode from which the evil spirit went forth for a while, but then in his lordly manner declared he would return to it, as he did—that abode was only "swept," not washed; that defilement which lay loose and light about the house could be thus got rid of, but that which cleaved to it continued there still. He who would be saved must deal thoroughly with his soul. No light, easy, partial amendment will do. This God teaches us by this earnest word, "*Wash* thine heart," etc. 3. And this cleansing must be of the heart. The whole chapter is a protest against the mere external purifying which the sinful people were seeking to palm off upon God instead of the true inward cleansing which he demanded, and with which alone he would or ever will be content. 4. And this *we* must do. Had we been told that the blood of our Lord Jesus Christ can alone do this, or had we been bidden pray like David, " Purge me with hyssop, and I shall be clean: wash me, and I shall be whiter than snow." " Wash me throughly from mine iniquity, and cleanse me from my sin; "—such declarations and counsels we could readily have understood, but for us to be told to do ourselves what so many Scriptures repeatedly declare God alone can do—how is this? Well, let the story of the blind man whom our Lord bade go and wash in the pool of Siloam, and who because he obeyed won back his sight,—let his story answer the question. It was the grace of the Lord Jesus restored him, but yet this much that he could do he had to do. But never, never on the ground of that washing in Siloam would the restored man claim for himself the credit of his own restoration, and so, although we be bidden wash our hearts from wicked-ness, yet who does not know that there lies behind these words the promise of the cleansing fountain, in which alone we can wash and be clean? And every one who seeks to obey this word will soon find his own utter powerlessness to rid himself of the clinging, cleaving wickedness of his heart, and the necessity he is under to answer back to this word of the Lord's, " Lead me, then, Lord, to that cleansing stream, where only it is of any avail that I seek to wash my heart from wickedness."

IV. GOD ENCOURAGING MAN TO DO HIS PART BY THE PROMISE OF SALVATION. " Wash thine heart, . . . *that thou mayest be saved.*" The promise is contained in the command. We can appeal to experience to verify this implied promise. In the hour when sin would assert its mastery, let the soul turn in instant trust and prayer to the Lord Jesus Christ, and he shall find that he is saved. Sin will slink away, like Satan did at the word of the Lord, and in such experience of Christ's saving power we have the pledge and earnest of the full salvation which shall be ours when he who has begun the work in us has perfected it according to his word.—C.

Ver. 14.—*Vain thoughts.* " How long shall," etc.?

I. THEY ARE THE PROLIFIC SOURCE AND CAUSE OF ALL WICKEDNESS. " As a man thinketh in his heart, so is he." St. Paul, desiring all things lovely and of good report, all that has praise and virtue, to abound in the disciples of Christ, bids them " *think* on these things " (Phil. iv.). Therefore vain thoughts must lead to and produce wickedness. " They are the spawn of the evil heart, from which all other wickedness is produced." They are not to be here understood as merely trifling, foolish, empty thoughts, but thoughts that are evil, impious, sinful, wicked. They are the thoughts which bring forth sin, which in its turn brings forth death. " Keep thy heart with all diligence, for out of it," etc.

II. THEY RENDER SALVATION IMPOSSIBLE. The cleansing of the heart from them, their dislodgement therefrom, is set forth as indispensable to Jerusalem being saved— a condition that must be fulfilled. " Blessed are the pure in heart : for they shall see God." The converse of this is true also and equally, " Without holiness," that is, without this pureness of heart, " no man shall see the Lord." How manifestly true this is! What would a man whose heart is full of these thoughts do in the " Father's house"? It would be hell to him. He would be anywhere rather than there.

III. THEY ARE VOLUNTARILY ENTERTAINED. They have come to the door and have sought and obtained entrance. They have been bidden " come in," and the heart has consented to " lodge " them. The protest that the prophet utters against them, were they not voluntarily admitted and retained, would be unmeaning. There would be occasion for profound pity, but none for blame. But conscience owns the truth that the prophet's word implies.

IV. THEY CAN BE GOT RID OF. Men are called upon to " wash their hearts " from them and to expel them. It is, therefore, plainly within men's power to do this. The words of these exhortations suggest the method. 1. Turn to Christ, in trust and prayer, especially to him as your crucified Lord. Behold the fountain of his blood. Such turning to Christ for pardon and for purity will " wash thine heart from wicked-ness." 2. By a vigorous act of the will, like as when our blessed Lord found the evil one lodging wrong thoughts in his mind, he gave him no place, but sternly bade him and this begone. And this was ever his way. It must be ours. 3. But leave not the heart empty. Bring in at once other thoughts, holy, Christ-like, that demand prompt, vigorous, and continuous work for Christ; so shall vain thoughts quit their hold and home in thy heart, and lodge there no more.

V. THEY ARE GRIEVOUS IN THE SIGHT OF GOD. Note the pathos and pleading of the appeal. " O Jerusalem, . . . How long? " Men take cognizance only of words and deeds, and are content if these be in keeping with the laws society has laid down. But God notes the thoughts of the heart, and grieves when they are " vain." What fervour this fact should lend to our prayers for purity of heart, that its thoughts may be cleansed by the inspiration of God's Holy Spirit!

VI. THEY ARE RUINOUS IN THEIR EFFECTS. (Cf. vers. 15—17.) They lead to sin and that to death. Are we conscious that such thoughts have lodged or are lodging within us? Listen to the Divine appeal, and implore his grace that you may respond thereto as he would desire.—C.

Ver. 27.—" Yet will I not make a *full* end." *God's reserve of mercy.* This Divine resolve regarding the reserved remnant of the people of Judah and Jerusalem, who should be excepted from the desolation that was coming, is declared several times. Here in the text, then again in ch. v. 10; xxx. 11, and once again in ch. xlvi. 28. And these are but the echo of what God said to Israel long ages before in the desert of Sinai, as we read in Lev. xxvi. 44. And in other parts of Jeremiah's prophecies, and in the writings of all the prophets, this Divine resolve to mercifully reserve from destruction a portion of Israel is more or less plainly declared. Thus, then, God does not conceal that the end he makes will not be a full end. And there were many reasons why this fact should be declared. 1. It would show that God was mindful of his covenant with their fathers; that their " unfaithfulness could not make the faithfulness of God of none effect." The scoff of the unbeliever, the dismay of the true-hearted, would be alike prevented, for, by God's not making a full end, the way was yet plain for the accomplishment of all that he had spoken. 2. Moreover, such declaration would sustain the faith of the faithful. They would see how they were not forgotten, that God's watchful care was over them, and that amid the coming desolations he would find means to deliver those who put their trust in him. 3. And the keeping open of this door of hope was calculated to persuade some to enter through that door and so be saved. This is why, even when a man has sinned away well-nigh all his life, when he has made an end of nearly every opportunity of return to God, we go and stand by his bedside, dying sinner as he is, and tell him that " a full end " is not yet made; even now Christ waits to be gracious, and will in no wise cast out. We tell of this hope in the trust that now, even at the last, the guilty one may turn to Christ and live. But we know that an " end " was indeed made to the national life of Israel. The terrific judgments which came upon them, and which the prophet in this chapter so vividly describes and so bitterly bewails, did make an end to all their national glory. Their land became desolate, their cities were destroyed, the holy and beautiful house of God was burnt with fire, their kings were slain, the throne overturned, the whole people carried into captivity; their cup of national sorrow was full to overflowing. But God did not suffer the agents of his righteous judgment to make a *full* end. Accordingly, in the days of Cyrus and his successors there came a restoration, although partial, poor, and incomplete, and under Ezra and Nehemiah Jerusalem and the house of the Lord were raised from their ruins and rebuilt. A remnant of the people was saved, the full end was not allowed to come, has never been allowed to come, though Israel's national glory, yea, their very existence as a nation, has long since passed away. But whilst the oft-repeated words of the text refer mainly to Judah and Jerusalem, they really declare *a principle of the Divine procedure,* a continual law of his government and rule. God's way is, when making an end, not to make a full end. He has ever a reserve of mercy. Now, concerning this principle, we observe—

I. IT IS IN PERPETUAL OPERATION. 1. It finds illustration, yea, may be said to be ever ruthlessly at work, *in the kingdom of nature.* Look at the story of *creation.* Whatever may have been the material condition of our globe prior to the period told of in the sacred record, we cannot conceive of it as having been eternally " without form and void." The researches of science seem to give a very different account from that. But whatever may have been its condition, and we can hardly doubt that it had an order and beauty of its own, an end was made to all that ere the last creation era dawned. But yet not a full end. The material for the new creation was there, and it took new form and order according to the creative word. All had become desolate, but out of that God brought forth a new condition of things, which he himself declared to be " very good." And what is this *doctrine of evolution*, concerning which in these days we hear so much—what is it but a further illustration in the kingdom of nature of the law of the text? " The survival of the fittest "—what does that imply but that there has been an end made of all the unfit and the less fit. But the whole order has not perished ; there has been an end, but not a full end, and the fittest have been reserved. 2. And how frequent in the pages of *history* are the illustrations and examples of this principle of the Divine procedure ! The destruction of the world by the Flood,—that was an end, but not a full end, for Noah and his house were saved. Earlier still, when God drove out from Eden the parents of our race,—what an end was then made of all that was bright and blessed in their lives ! but still not a full end. For, as St. Paul tells us, " the creature was made subject to vanity, *in hope*." Hope, *the* hope, of redemption and restoration through the promised Seed of the woman, was God's illustration of this law then. The destruction of the generation of Israel that came up out of Egypt with Moses, and whose carcases fell in the wilderness ; but their children were God's reserve of mercy in their case. And outside the pages of the Bible, thoughtful students of history, who love to trace the hand of God therein, are able to point to many an illustration of this law. Take the story of one man— Alfred the Great : he and the little Saxon band that clave to him were God's reserve of mercy for our land in those dark days, and saved us from coming to a full end, though we had come so near to it. And there are many, many more to which we cannot now allude. And in the history of *the Church* also how often has this been seen ! Take the call of Abraham, for example. The religion of the ancient patriarchs had all but died out, an end had nearly come. But by the Divine call of Abraham it was prevented from being a full end ; a new era was introduced when he became " the father of the faithful and the friend of God." And to pass over all intermediate illustrations of this same law, though they be many, and some of them most notable, we may refer to the revival of evangelical religion in the last century. An end had come to well-nigh all earnest religion ; the land was desolate with more than a material desolation. There was " a famine, not of bread, but of the hearing of the Word of the Lord." But God suffered it not to be a full end. Wesley and his trusty band, Whitefield and those who laboured with him, became, under God, the means of a new departure, the introducers of a better order of things which has continued to this day. And it has been the same *in families*. Take the prophetic family in the days of Samuel. But for him it would have come to a full end. Take the most illustrious instance of all,—the house and lineage of David. To what nearness to extinction it had come when the Saviour, the predicted Stem who should grow out of the root of Jesse, was born at Bethlehem, and that course of events began which have made the name of David, great before, yet infinitely and eternally great now by means of him of whom it was foretold by the angel to his mother, that he should " sit upon the throne of his father David," and of whose kingdom David himself sang that it " should have no end." 3. And what are many of God's *providential dealings* with men, his afflictive dispensations especially, but further illustrations of this same law ? " Ye have heard of the patience of Job." The lives of Joseph, of David, of Elijah, of Daniel, of Paul, and, above all, of our Lord,—what are they but instances in which " it pleased the Lord to bruise them, and to put them to grief " ? He saw fit to make an end to much of that which naturally they loved, and for a weary while to cloud over and conceal well-nigh all the brightness of their lives. But in no case was there a full end made, nor ever will there be. To many of us the Lord God comes and makes an end of what we would so much like to guard and keep—health, wealth, friends, prosperity, our inward joys, our outward gladness ; God sends his angel of discipline and bids him make an end—though not a full end—of these things. Yes, it is oftentimes God's way. 4. And what are *his spiritual disciplines* but the carrying out of the same principle ? Do we not read, " Then Manasseh knew that the Lord he was God " ? of the prodigal, that " he came to himself," and said, " I will arise and go to my father, and say unto him, Father, I have sinned ? " of Peter, that " he went out and wept bitterly " ? Yes, often does he bring down our hearts so that we cry out, " Why art thou cast down, O my soul ? "

But he never makes a full end. False hope and trust have to go, but trust that is true, hope that is of God, come under the law of his reserve of mercy—they are the spared remnant, and whilst an end is made of all the rest, these survive.   5. And what will *death itself* be but our last experience of this law ? Heart and flesh shall fail, the outward man shall perish, there shall be an end made of all that belongs to this world so far as we are concerned, and the place that has known us here shall know us no more for ever. But whilst it will be an end, so much so that our bodies shall return, " earth to earth, dust to dust, ashes to ashes," still it will not be " a full end." We—the true self—shall still remain ; though the body go back to its earth, " the spirit shall return unto God who gave it." Yes, the law of the text is seen everywhere. It is a principle of the Divine procedure that is in perpetual operation ; it was brought to bear upon Judah and Jerusalem in the days of Jeremiah, and it bears upon nations, Churches, families, individuals, men, whenever God sees that the time has come for its application. But—

II. It is a principle that prompts inquiry as to its reason and intent. This making an end, even though it be not a full end, has much about it that may well, if not perplex, yet give rise to earnest, thoughtful inquiry on the part of him who observes it. Without question, it is often a severe law, a principle prolific in pain. It was so in the case of those to whom Jeremiah wrote. " The righteous scarcely were saved," but " the ungodly and the sinners," who formed the vast majority, were not saved at all. Yes, though God made not a full end, the end he did make was terrible indeed.   Now, we know it is not possible for us so to understand all the ways of God that we may fully rise to—

> " The height of this high argument,
> And justify the ways of God to men."

But this much we may say : the surgeon's knife that cuts away the poisoned flesh in order to save life is a severe operation, yet one that even he who writhes beneath it will consent to and be thankful for. The burning houses that cannot be saved are allowed to burn on, and men's efforts are all turned towards the saving of those that are yet untouched. If Israel was to be preserved faithful as the keeper of the oracles of God—and, humanly speaking, the welfare of the whole world depended upon her fidelity in this matter—then the cankered portion of her people must be cut off, that the rest, yet in health, might continue so. " Our God is a consuming fire." His judgments will, must, burn on until all that is rotten and unsound has perished from the way. The dread doom of the world to come is described by a word that tells of the action of the surgeon's knife, or of the vine-dresser's pruning implements, which are used to cut away that which is evil or worthless, that that which is healthful may be preserved, strengthened, and developed according to the will of God. Yes, it is dreadful when God comes forth to make an end of wickedness and the wicked ; but it would be more dreadful still—the whole history of mankind attests it—if he did not. But it is a work from which he shrinks. " As I live, saith the Lord "—and can we dare, or would we wish, to disbelieve him ?—" I have *no* pleasure in the death of the wicked ; but rather that he should turn from his wickedness and live." " Why will ye die, O ye house of Israel ? " And we may say more than this. In the repetition of our text, which we have in the tenth verse of the next chapter, we see another purpose designed by these terrible dealings of God with his people. They were getting behind " battlements," trusting in defences and safeguards which were of no avail ; withdraw-ing their confidence from God, who had never failed them, to place it in those professed protectors who would always fail them, even as they had ever done. Hence one pur-pose of the stern process through which Judah and Jerusalem had to pass was the taking away of those " battlements " which were " not the Lord's." Their looking to the rulers of other nations, the gods of other nations, or to such poor material resources as they could themselves supply, was fatal to that reliance on the Lord God which had been their distinguishing feature in their happiest and most glorious days. But it was essential to the fulfilment of God's purposes in regard to them that this reliance upon God should by any means be restored. Therefore it was necessary that God should make an end of and destroy these " battlements," taking them utterly away. And in pursuance of this same main design, God would set the faithful amongst them free to live a new, a happier, holier, and every way better life. For they were hampered, entangled, ensnared, thwarted, and hindered at every turn by the hideous mass of moral wreckage by which they were surrounded. They could hardly move for it. There must, therefore, be a clearance made if God's people were to enter upon, as he was determined that they should, that new, that better life, to which he recommended them, and after which they yearned. "Now, all these things happened unto them for an ensample," and we may see in them, if we will, the motive and intent of the like dealings of God with men in our day. Thou troubled child of God, afflicted very much, of whose earthly comforts, enjoyments, and possessions God has been pleased to make so large an end, thou seest the reason why. And thou whose soul he has brought very low, taking from thee all thy trust and confidence, so that now he has made "thy very spirit poor," canst thou not understand wherefore he hath so dealt with thee? And our death, which makes an end of all that in this world we have called our own, it too finds its explanation in what was the evident purpose of God's dealing with his ancient people. It was and it is, either for the putting away—if even by a terrible process—of the evil and wrong that are yet in men; or for the destruction of every false confidence, or for the setting the soul free— as his disciplines do, and as at last his messenger, Death, will do—to serve him in newness of life to his honour and glory, and to our own eternal joy. But in what has now been advanced we have only spoken of the reason wherefore God makes an end of so much, why he comes in these often terrible ways. We have yet to ask, "*Why are we spared? Why is there this reserve of mercy?* Why is not a full end made?" And looking at the history of God's ancient people, answers to these questions also may readily be found. To have made a full end would have given occasion to the enemies of God to blaspheme. We remember how Moses pleaded this argument when sore wrath had gone out against Israel, and it seemed as if a full end was to be made. And the promise of God to Abraham would have been set aside, the covenant which he made with their fathers in the days of old. And the language which we find in the Scriptures, the language of intense tenderness and love towards his people, proves that to have made a full end would have broken the heart of God. "How shall I give thee up?" "I have written thee on the palms of my hands." "Can a mother forget her sucking child, that she should not have compassion on the son of her womb? Yea, she may forget; yet will not I forget thee." In view of such love, how could there be a full end? And the Lord Jesus Christ has rendered such condemnation needless. For they who are spared when God judges the world, are spared not for any inherent intrinsic excellency in themselves, but they are they who have believed on the Name of God's dear Son. Hence they have the righteousness of faith, the germ, the guarantee, the generator of all righteousness; and they have the indwelling of the Holy Ghost by whom they shall be strengthened to live in newness of life. All the possibilities to secure which God makes an end of so much in those who have not come to faith, they already have, and hence God is able, even as he is willing, to except them from the destruction that comes on all beside. And to mention but one other reason for this reserve of mercy—for God not making a full end; he sees in these spared ones those by whom his "way shall be made known upon earth, and his saving health among all nations." They are to be the instruments of his grace, his channel of untold blessing to all mankind. Therefore doth God care for and guard them, and amid all destruction no evil is suffered to befall them, nor any plague to come nigh their dwelling.

III. And now, lastly, we note that this principle of the Divine procedure which we have been considering IS ONE WHICH WE MUST ALL OF US BE PREPARED TO HAVE APPLIED TO OURSELVES. Yes, God will look down upon us all, as Churches, families, individuals, and will mark what in us and who of us will be found worthy to stand in the great day when he separates the chaff from the wheat. Ah! this is the great question which concerns us. "Where, then, shall I myself be? Shall it be amongst those whom God must put away, or amongst those whom he shall delightedly spare?" What question can compare with this? But the material for its answer may be found by asking— *Where are we now?* The destroying powers of the world, the flesh, and the devil are abroad; they are slaying their thousands and their tens of thousands. But are they destroying us? Or are we—as God grant it may be—amongst his "reserve of mercy"? Are we living unto God? Can we look up to our Lord and Saviour and appeal to him who knoweth all things, to attest the love and trust towards him that abide in our heart?   Oh, if it be so, and the life of prayer, of obedience, of self-surrender, be ours now, then we can, with humble but strong confidence, predict that when the last destroyer comes, even Death, whilst he will be permitted to make an end of much that here we rejoice in, yet he shall by no means make " a full end " of us.   No, his coming, which is so terrible to the unbeliever, shall for us be but a setting us free, a delivering us from the bondage of corruption " into the glorious liberty of the children of God," so that our soul shall escape as a bird from out the snare of the fowler, and we hence-forth shall " live unto God."

> " Then shall the day, dear Lord, appear
> That we shall mount and dwell above,
> And stand and bow amongst them there,
> And see thy face and sing thy love."

An end, a full end, will have been made of all that is corruptible, all that distresses, all that defiles, all that death can in any way touch; but it shall not be a full end of *us*, rather shall it be the beginning of a life so holy, so blessed, that all the past shall seem to have been no life at all.   Look, then, at the two companies which have been brought before us.   There are those whom God's judgments are making an end of, and there are those whom those judgments cannot touch—God's reserve of mercy.   Look at these latter again; they are clothed in white robes, and they have palms in their hands.   For they have come " out of great tribulation, and have washed their robes, and made them white in the blood of the Lamb.   Therefore are they before the throne of God, and serve him day and night in his temple. . . . They hunger no more, neither thirst any more; neither doth the sun light on them, nor any heat.   For the Lamb which is in the midst of the throne shall feed them, and shall lead them unto living fountains of waters : and, God shall wipe away all tears from their eyes."   Therefore, O Lord, make *us* to be numbered with thy saints now and in glory everlasting.—C.

Vers. 20, 30.—" Suddenly are my tents spoiled."   " When thou art spoiled, what wilt thou do ? "   *A surely coming confession compelling a present serious question.* Note the historic reference of the words to the people to whom the prophet spoke. Applying them in more general sense, let us observe—
I. THE CONFESSION.   " Suddenly," etc.   This confession.   1. *Not that of the child of God*, for his tents cannot be spoiled.   (1) The peace of mind which he enjoys.   That rests on the sure basis of what Christ has done for him.   The varied disturbing powers of this world cannot touch that.   Nothing can separate him from the love of God (Rom. viii. at end).   (2) The righteousness which God has given him.   That springs from a source, and is sustained by a power, that is supernatural and therefore beyond the power of this world to give or take away.   (3) His most cherished possessions. True, the child of God is subject, like other men, and at times it seems more than other men, to sudden reverses of fortune, to loss, bereavement, and the other manifold sorrows of this life.   But though he cannot but lose his earthly treasures, and deeply feel their loss, yet all the while his true treasure remains intact, for it is not here, but yonder. And even when with one hand God takes away his earthly treasures, with the other he so graciously ministers support and consolation that, in the might of a Divine faith and love, he is able to say, " The Lord gave, and the Lord hath taken away; blessed be the Name of the Lord."   (4) His life.   That is not capable of being spoiled. If he is called upon suddenly to lay it down, or to give it up amid much pain and dis-tress, he is able to say, as dear old Richard Baxter did when he lay a-dying, and when asked by a friend how he was, " Almost well."   Yes, the nearer death, the nearer life to the child of God.   It is a blessed exchange for him, come how, come when, come where it will.   Therefore this confession cannot be his.   But, as it was in the days of Jere-miah, it is : 2. *The confession of the worldling and all those who are living without God.* For their tents *are* suddenly spoiled.   (1) The peace of mind in which they often seem so established.   To our eyes they appear not to be troubled, neither to be plagued as other men are (cf. Ps. xxxvii.).   How easy and unconcerned they are ! but the text comes true to them.   *Remorse* may suddenly spoil their tents.   Like " Esau, who found no place of repentance, though," etc.   *The events of God's providence* may be the spoiler; carrying off their riches, striking down their wealth, turning away their friends.   Every-

thing may seem to be slipping away from them. And then, oh how true our text is of them then! And the approach of death, with the "fearful looking for of judgment." And should none of these have succeeded in this life to shatter their false trust, how will the *dread solemnities of God's judgment day* certainly do this! See the consternation of those on the left-hand side of the Judge, who asked, " When saw we thee," etc. ? (2) The moral rectitude, the credit for righteous character, on which they have stayed their souls. This too may be, will be, suddenly spoiled. Sometimes sudden temptation will do this. Unguarded by any Divine power, the man's weak resolves give way under unusual pressure, and character is blasted and the good name gone, as in a moment. Transient visions of the Divine holiness, the claims and requirements of God's Law flashing upon him as did the lightnings from Mount Sinai,—such manifestations will reveal the man to himself, and " spoil" his self-complacency for ever. The light of eternity *must* do this. Tried by the standard God has given, self-righteousness must give way. (3) His external prosperity on which his heart was fixed. To have nothing but what this world can give, and to have *that* suddenly taken away, as it often is, as at death it all must be,—whose should this confession be if not his of whom we are speaking? (4) His life itself, to which he clung so tenaciously, oh, what a wrench that will be when the man to whom this life was all is by the hand of death ruthlessly torn away from it! And oftentimes this is sudden, unlooked for, at such an hour as he thinks not, as he has made up his mind that it will not come. Like him to whom God said, " Thou fool!" These, then, are they from whom this confession—bitter lamentation and wail of woe rather should it be called—is heard. What agony of heart can be conceived more awful than that of the worldling and the godless, when "suddenly their tents are spoiled"? God grant it may not be ours. Note—

II. THE QUESTION, "What wilt thou do," etc. ? Who can tell what the delirium of dismay and despair will drive a man to under such circumstances? See Judas the traitor. Suddenly his tent—the hope of his gains—was "spoiled," and we know what, in the remorse and despair which fastened upon him, he did. But some will harden themselves still more. Others will plunge into business, pleasure, sin, and there seek to drown the tortures of the mind. It is impossible to forecast what one and another will do, and least of all can they tell themselves. But it is *God* who asks this question, and that with the gracious intent that we should turn to him for the answer. Let us do so. Perhaps your tents *are* spoiled already. Before, therefore, you say what you will do, ask of God what thou shouldest do. 1. Is it thy inward peace, the calm and unconcern of thy life, that is spoiled? Then "acquaint thyself with God, and be at peace." 2. Is it thine estimate of thine own righteousness? Do not seek to mend or patch it up in any way (cf. Phil. iii.). Seek from Christ the righteousness that is of faith. 3. Is it thine earthly prosperity that is shattered? "Set your affections on things above, and not on things on the earth." Have your treasure for the future in heaven. There, "where neither moth nor rust," etc. 4. Is it thy very life that is being taken from thee ? Oh, wait not until this tent is actually spoiled.

> "To Jesus do thou fly,
> Swift as the morning light,
> Lest life's young golden beams should die,
> In sudden endless night."

III. THE ORDER IN WHICH THIS CONFESSION AND QUESTION ARE PLACED. The question is asked *before* the spoiling takes place. Like as it is asked, "How shall we escape if we [neglect so great salvation?" The intent is that we should, by turning to God and coming within his sure defence, escape that spoiling of our tents which must come on all not within that defence. And so in the other question, which is like unto it, the intent manifestly is that we should *not* neglect so great salvation. Then let this good will of the Lord be done. Come over amongst those whose tents cannot be spoiled, and away from those upon whom the spoilers shall fall certainly, suddenly, and soon.—C.

Vers. 19—30.—" *The fellowship of Christ's sufferings.*" The extreme anguish of the prophet which is revealed in these verses justifies the affirmation that, like St. Paul, Jeremiah also knew " the fellowship of Christ's sufferings." Consider—

I. THEIR NATURE. 1. The sight of the constant dishonour done to God. This was part of our Lord's suffering. Living amongst men at all involved it. It has been said truly that, if the Son of God became incarnate, he must be a "man of sorrows." But if it be a pain and outrage to an affectionate son to hear his father, whom he knows to be worthy of all honour, yet nevertheless insulted, and to see him daily dishonoured, what must have been the sufferings of our Lord at what he daily had to see and hear! And to Jeremiah this was one chief part of his sorrow. To him the Name of God was dear; his honour and glory precious; but let these chapters tell what scenes continually came before him. "Rivers of water run down mine eyes because men keep not thy Law." Dishonour done to God has ever been distress and pain to his servants. 2. The endurance of the scorn and hate of men. To some men this is nothing. They answer scorn by scorn and hate by hate. They choose war rather than peace. But in proportion as a man is of a loving disposition, and has lavished his love upon any, he will desire, yea, yearn for, a response. Do not parents desire it in their children? Would they not be distressed indeed if they did not receive it? And so with our Lord. He had no armour of indifference, or contempt, or hate against men. But he opened his heart to them. There was no stint in the love he lavished upon them. Hence he could not but long to receive a response to that love. The cross itself was wreathed with attractiveness for him, because it, though nothing else would, would draw all men unto him. And in the fellowship of this suffering Jeremiah shared. He, though deeply loving his people and faithfully serving them, yet was denied the response of trust and love which he would fain have gained. He, too, "was despised and rejected of men." 3. The realizing, by the power of affectionate sympathy, the awful consequences of his countrymen's sin. It is the effect of such sympathy to cause the sufferings of those we love to come before us in such terrible vividness that they fill the soul with an anguish that is almost intolerable. Hence our Lord's deep distress (cf. "O Jerusalem, Jerusalem!" etc. and his lament over the doomed city and people). But in this suffering of our Lord Jeremiah had indeed fellowship (cf. vers. 23—30.) He saw the destruction that was coming on Judah and Jerusalem in its *entireness.* "The whole land is spoiled;" "The whole land shall be desolate." In its *suddenness.* "Suddenly are," etc. (ver. 20). In its *duration.* Ver. 21, "How long shall I see the standard?" etc. It could not be a passing storm, but an abiding wrath. And more still, he sees *how deserved* it all was (vers. 18, 22). And then how *awful!* It was as if original chaos had come again (ver. 23; cf. Gen. i.). It was as the dread and never-to-be-forgotten manifestation of God at Sinai, when the mountains trembled and all who beheld were stricken with fear (ver. 24). For the devastation caused by the "spoilers" had been so thorough, they had done their work in such fearful fashion, that districts heretofore teeming with population were now solitary and lone as the desert; and so stripped were they of all that could minister to life, that the very birds had fled away (vers. 25, 26). The awful spectacle was clearly visible to the prophet's eye, and, as he looked upon it all and knew how certain was its advent, he cries out as in the agony of dread bodily pain (ver. 19). 4. The witnessing day by day the decay of all goodness and the firmer hold of sin. Our blessed Lord's tears over Jerusalem, his oft "sighing," his agony, his long lament over the guilty people, were not caused only, nor chiefly, by the mere fact of their sufferings, but it was because of the increasing alienation from God, the ever-hardening heart, the mighty power of sin upon them, that his bitterest tears were shed and his deepest agony endured. And so with Jeremiah. Pain and distress were evils undoubtedly, but they were as nought compared with the moral degradation, the spiritual wickedness, which he saw around him and increasing every day. 5. The being compelled to utter the "amen" of his soul to the judgment of God as "true and righteous altogether." With what agony would a father witness the accumulation of proof upon proof that his son whom he loved had been guilty of crime that deserved and must receive condign punishment! To be obliged to own to himself that his beloved son is righteously condemned—what sorrow that! And this confession our Lord made. His death meant this—his assent to the judgment of God against sin that that judgment was just. Death was the penalty, and he submitted to it. And never has death been, nor can it be to any child of God, what it was to our Lord. The realization of sin, the consciousness that on him was the iniquity of us all, and how awful but how just was the wrath of God against it,—this explains that exceeding bitter cry from out the darkness, " My God, my God, why hast thou forsaken me ? " And, in his measure and degree, Jeremiah had the fellowship of this suffering also. It is the sorrow of sorrows to him that there was no alternative; God *must* punish sin like that of his countrymen. How glad would he have been could he have seen any—however little—light in the darkness! But it was all dark ; there was not a solitary redeeming ray. The condemnation was awful, but God was just who judged so.

II. THE UNIVERSALITY OF THIS FELLOWSHIP. Like as in every leaf of the tree the whole fabric of the tree is pourtrayed, root and trunk, branch and foliage, so in the experience of every member of Christ's mystical body, however humble that member may be, there is shown the resemblance of Christ himself. See Abraham interceding for Sodom, Moses for Israel, Samuel mourning for Saul; Elijah's ministry and that of all the prophets, Paul's and that of all the apostles, and where there are any who have " the mind that was in Christ Jesus," who are filled with love to God and love to man, to whom sin is hateful and holiness dear. It will be a measure and a test of our own possession of the mind of Christ if those sad facts, which were the source to him and to all his true-hearted servants of such great sorrow, are likewise sources of sorrow to us and make us know the fellowship of his sufferings.

III. ITS EXCEEDING BLESSEDNESS. It may seem an anomaly and contradiction to speak of " blessedness " as appertaining to " suffering," but it is nevertheless true that exceeding blessedness does belong to the fellowship of Christ's sufferings. For : 1. It wins for us the ministries that sustained our Lord. These were such as the full enjoyment of the love of God, uninterrupted communion and intercourse with him, the open vision of the " joy set before him " in the winning back of the world to God,— such were the supports of Christ's ministry, and the like has been given to all who have entered into his sufferings. See the bright onlook of Jeremiah (cf. ch. iii. 15—18 and 11) and of all the prophets; of St. Paul and all the apostles. And see, too, their joy in God, the rest of their hearts in his love. Such have been and such will be the supports of such souls. 2. It fortifies us impregnably against all the power of the wicked one. Satan will not waste his time and energy on those who are within the sure defence of this holy fellowship. His darts cannot reach where they stand, or, if they reach and strike, they cannot penetrate the " armour of God " in which they are clad. Sin has no charm, but repels : holiness attracts with a magnetic might. " They are born of God, and the wicked one toucheth them not." 3. It gives tremendous power over the hearts of men. What is the great need of our day but this, a ministry that has entered into this fellowship ? one penetrated with the love of God and the love of men, to whom the favour of God is life, and the judgments of God the ununspeakable woe of the soul ? How would such men speak and pray and plead ? It was the secret of St. Paul's power, and of the great ministers for Christ in all ages. It won all the triumphs of the early Church, it was manifest in Bernard, Francis, Wesley, Whitefield, and many more. Men cannot resist the power with which such speak. It constitutes those who have entered into it God's true priests. They have power when they plead with God for men, and when they plead with men for God. Such is another element of the exceeding blessedness of this fellowship of Christ's sufferings.

IV. ITS ALONE ENTRANCE. This entrance is by fellowship with Christ in our daily life. Let us look much upon him as he is shown to us in his gospel and in the Scriptures generally, and as we see his likeness reproduced in the lives of the truest of his people. Let there be much looking to him in the exercise of daily trust, committing and commending our whole interests to his care. Let there be much converse with him in devout meditation, worship, and prayer. Let there be much service done for him in all such ways as he points out for us, and the result will be that we shall come so to see, hear, touch him, so to realize his living presence, and then so to love him, that all that affects him will affect us. We shall have fellowship in it all, and, therefore, in this fellowship of his sufferings in which all his chosen have shared.—C.

Vers. 30, 31.—*Broken reeds*, concerning which note—
I. WHAT THEY ARE. They are the friends that are kept simply by either: 1

Wealth. " Though thou clothest thyself with crimson " (ver. 30). The garb of the rich, telling how Jerusalem had won some of her professed friends. 2. *Splendour.* " Deckest thee with ornaments of gold." Jerusalem could make a grand show, put on much pomp by which the eyes of men were dazzled and deceived. And outward show will deceive many men. But those thus attracted know how, when the splendour pales and the outward show can no more be kept up, to fall away and show what " broken reeds " they are. 3. *External beauty.* The " painting " spoken of was an Oriental device to increase the beauty of the countenance. But weak indeed is the hold which mere outward beauty can have on any who have been attracted by it. It fades, and they along with it.

II. THEIR APPARENT TRUSTWORTHINESS. Had there never been anything at all like helpfulness in them, no reliance could have been placed upon them. But the lures which drew them had power enough to make them profess much and then to practise somewhat. Hence they seemed to be *real* friends.

III. THEIR TRUE CHARACTER. When they can no longer gain aught by her who believed in them, they turn round upon her and " seek her life " (ver. 30). It was so with Jerusalem, it will be so with such as are like her. And yet men go on seeking after these outward things which can win for them only friends of this wretched sort, whilst those inward qualities which have no charm for such, but have all charm for the worthy and the good, are little valued and therefore little cultivated.

IV. THE DREAD INCREASE OF SORROW THEY ARE THE CAUSE OF. A more appalling picture of utter agony and distress of soul cannot be imagined than that given in ver. 31. It is said that when Cæsar saw Brutus amid his assassins, he covered his face with his mantle and let his murderers do their worst. No stab could be so deadly as the discovery that his trusted friend had become his murderer. " Et tu, Brute ! " And part of the deep sorrow of our Lord was that Judas, " his own familiar friend," should betray him. If, then, to the stainless soul the discovery of such treachery can cause such sorrow, how must the sorrow of those who, in addition to this, have the memory of their own sin, be deeper and more dreadful still ?

V. THE WAY OF WISDOM, WHICH KNOWLEDGE OF THEM POINTS TO. Surely it is this—to turn from all such " broken reeds " to " the rod and the staff " which Christ furnishes for all his pilgrims.

> " One there is above all others,
> Well deserves the name of Friend," etc.

C.

Ver. 31.—" *There shall be weeping.*" The text is a solemn and awful declaration of the retribution of God upon impenitent men.

I. NO TRUTH MORE DOUBTED OR DENIED THAN THIS. Lot was " to his sons in law as one that mocked." And so it is still ; this truth scarce gains any hearing and yet less belief. Reasons of this are : the prevalent scepticism as to all religious belief ; the special dislike to such a subject as this ; false views as to the love of God ; the busy energy of the evil one, who will not suffer men to consider and ponder this truth.

II. BUT IT IS NEVERTHELESS THE TRUTH OF GOD. Scripture is full, plain, and earnest in the matter. The premonitions of conscience endorse the Word of God. The course of observed events lends its strong testimony. The common consent of the wisest and best of men confirms it. The analogy of all human government supports it.

III. AND DEMANDS THEREFORE TO BE MADE KNOWN. Compassion would prompt to its proclamation. The severe displeasure of God against the watchman who neglects to warn the people urges this. The example of our Lord, who ever insisted on it. Its manifest fitness to arouse and arrest the sinner. Beware, therefore, of yielding to the temptation to be silent on this theme.

IV. BUT TO BE PREACHED ONLY BY SUCH AS BELIEVE AND FEEL ITS TRUTH. Unbelieving or unfeeling setting forth of these awful verities will but steel the heart of the ungodly against them. But in the spirit of Jeremiah, and yet more in the spirit of our Lord, let men be warned that for the impenitent there remaineth the dread retribution of God.

Ver. 1.—*The kind of return which Jehovah requires.* In ch. iii. there has been much spoken concerning return. There is the impossibility pointed out of a divorced wife returning to her husband; yet Jehovah's own people, whose conduct has been even worse, he presses to return. The fact is mentioned that Israel had been told to turn, yet had not turned. There is also the fact that Judah had made a feigned turning. A true return is seen to be the prime condition of all the glorious future which God had shadowed forth, first for Israel, and then for all nations. And then the chapter concludes with a touching outburst of penitential emotion. From all which it will be clearly seen how timely and needful is the exhortation which introduces ch. iv. Return of *a certain kind* is, after all, not so difficult, if only there be certain conspiring circumstances. The most undemonstrative and unlikely man may have his feelings roused up, and then comes decided utterance. Right words are spoken, right purposes declared. But what of the carrying of them out? What about the difficulties in the future—the fightings without and the fears within? The return which God desires is a permanent return, just as when, after a long frost, there comes a complete thaw, and, with genial warmth following, renewed life, growth, and fruitfulness.

I. Observe how God recognizes the instability of the apostate people. It is not simply that he apprehends instability in their resolutions towards himself. Their very apostasy is itself an unstable thing. With all the hold which idolatry seems to have upon them, they are not thoroughly fixed in it. Evidently there are ways of appealing to them which draw forth a resolve to make some sort of turning. Never should we forget that sinners, even the most persistent of them, are unstable in their ways. Instability there of course is from the common fluctuations of life; but, more than that, the very purposes of the sinner are more unstable than he thinks. A thick-skinned conscience is often more in appearance than in reality; the penetrable point has not been discovered—that is all. Even when to all outward appearance a man seems quite contented with the life which others condemn, he may have very trying διαλογισμοί within him. Hence the strange anomaly sometimes presented of wicked men doing deeds of helpfulness to others. Gamblers, out of their unrighteous gains, are known to indulge in most eccentric acts of beneficence. After all, the powers of evil have a most uncertain tenure over those who may seem most their slaves.

II. The only turning from evil which can be complete and profitable is the turning towards God. Not only from sin, but towards God. That is the only way of keeping clear both of Scylla and Charybdis. To turn from a life that is self-condemned, by trying to make another path of one's own, may seem to be successful for a while, but in truth it is only travelling in a circle. The man whose springs of knowledge and strength are in himself, or in the counsels of men, will come back to where he started. Think, for instance, of those drunkards who have taken pledges of total abstinence, and set their feet towards a manlier and purer life, only to find very soon that appetite and habit are not so easily mastered. At last, after many failures, a permanent keeping comes. There is a struggle, crowned with victory, because the soul, having lost all its self-confidence, has really turned to God. The departure into sin is *from God*, and to him must be the only satisfactory return.

III. The forsaking of sin must be a complete forsaking. Into this demand for completeness there must be put the utmost significance of the word. God's people might visit all the high places in turn, and laboriously erase every outward vestige of idolatry. On everything like an approach to idolatry the most rigorous penalties might be imposed. There might be a domiciliary visitation, and a ransacking of every house from garret to basement, lest there should be anything hidden away, such as Laban's seraphim which Rachel stole. But what of all such exertions? They could only end in the taking of abominations out of *the sight of man.* The essential thing was to take them out of *the sight of God.* The high places and groves in every *heart* must be purged of their idolatries. Here the edicts of a king and the vigilance of reforming enthusiasts were of no avail. By the very necessity of the case, the putting away must be an individual act. Forth from the heart proceed the outward visible abominations, and the only way of stopping the procession was by a thorough cleansing of the source whence it came. Such prayers are wanted as for the creating of a clean heart, and the setting of one's secret sins in the light of God's countenance. The heart, deceitful and desperately wicked, only God can know, and only God can cleanse. He himself must be besought to direct affections, purposes, imaginations, towards things pure, holy, and Divine. Remember, then, that a thing may be out of man's sight and yet right over against the eyes of God. Even that which may not at present disturb your conscience may yet be very offensive to him. Thus it will be seen that a real turning to God is very difficult, and needs much submission and humility. One has to walk very circumspectly. Wavering is one of the greatest perils, and may very soon be fatal. He who wavers, vacillates, and turns to look round to the things that are left, loses the direction; and that direction, once lost, who knows how much else may be lost before it can be recovered?—Y.

Ver. 2.—*Jehovah's requirement with respect to the oath.* Jehovah has just told his people that, with unwavering resolve, they must put their abominations out of his sight. This exhortation, general as it is, is very emphatic; but it chiefly serves to lead on to something more explicit. Jehovah singles out one peculiar abomination, and fixes the attention of his people on that. The truth is, if they sweep this abomination away, all is done that needs to be done. These abominations, so odious to the pure eyes of Jehovah, were bound together in a kind of organic unity. The infliction of a fatal blow on any one of them inevitably brought death and withering on the others. Just as he who stops the action of one of the vital organs of the body stops the action of them all. Look, then—

I. AT WHAT JEHOVAH REQUIRES WITH REGARD TO THE OATH. There were many solemn appeals that had in them the nature of an oath. God at once directs attention to the most solemn of all, the appeal to himself by his own peculiar Name and his own enduring existence. The passages are too numerous to mention in which there is record of people saying, "As Jehovah liveth." Now and then, no doubt, the words were spoken with solemnity and sincerity, and also with a steady remembrance afterwards of the holy Name which had thus come to the lips. But in the great bulk of instances it was only an idle word. A man gets excited, and then the most solemn words rush from his mouth, with no thought of the meaning they express. Or, worse still, there may be the deliberate attempt to consecrate a falsity, and get it received for undoubted truth, so that others may act from it and rest upon it with the utmost confidence. Now, to the removal of all this false swearing, God would have his people earnestly to apply themselves. Note that God does not say here what Jesus afterwards said, "Swear not at all." The time was not ripe for such an exhortation. The words of Jesus aim directly at that ideal state when every man shall speak truth as naturally as he breathes pure air; when it shall be as impossible for him to speak or even think the false as to live amid carbonic acid gas. One may say that even here, in this word through Jeremiah, there is nothing to bind the hearer to an oath. The injunction has a permissive element. A man needs not to say, "Jehovah liveth;" but if he does say so, let him bear in mind all that the expression involves. It is the most solemn way of securing that all speaking and acting shall be true and sincere; that all judgments shall be according to proven facts and Jehovah's declared principles of justice; and that all life, in short, should be pervaded and filled with energy by a spirit of righteousness. To begin with, what an abomination it was to say, "As Jehovah liveth," when the practice showed that whatever true recognition of Deity obtained among these people was on the high places and towards the heathen idols! Then from this it was only too easy to bring forward Jehovah's Name in connection with all sorts of falsehood, cruelty, and oppression. The change is to come by bringing truth into the oath. There must ever live in the mind of the oath-taker a distinct apprehension and conviction as to Jehovah's real, enduring existence. It must be remembered how he said to Moses, "I am that I am." And, following the history of Israel onward, there must be an ever clearer perception of his character, of his power, of his constant observation of individual life, and his fiery, consuming anger against all iniquity. Then, if all this truth, justice, and righteousness appear where before there was such a loathsome sink of deception and corruption, what will be the result?

II. THE NATIONS WILL ENTER INTO AN INEXPRESSIBLY SATISFACTORY RELATION TOWARDS JEHOVAH. His aspect, in their eyes, altogether alters. A step is taken—a great step, and one that makes all others easy—towards that gathering of the nations to Jehovah's throne which is mentioned in ch. iii. 17. There is now something to awe and to attract the hitherto worshippers of idols. They say that a man is known by his friends. If the man be one not yet seen, living at a distance, he can only be judged of by those professing to be his friends, with whom we come into actual intercourse. If those whom we see be upright, generous, magnanimous, loving, we shall have no difficulty in crediting that the unseen one is the same. Israel having been what it had been, it was little wonder if the heathen came to have a very poor opinion of Jehovah. But Israel is now called to a very different life, and, in particular, to make such a use of the oath as that the nations shall not merely have their opinion of Jehovah altered, but shall find in him a source of blessing to themselves and one in whom, without risk of shame and confusion, they can continually glory. Jehovah, God of Israel, whom Israel at last has truly honoured, obtains then more than a bare acknowledgment. He is exulted in as Lord and Benefactor to all the nations of the earth. "And I heard as it were the voice of a great multitude, and as the voice of many waters, and as the voice of mighty thunderings, saying, Alleluia: for the Lord God omnipotent reigneth" (Rev. xix. 6). This is the consummation of creation's choral song, and it comes from practising truth, justice, and righteousness in such a way as will fully please Jehovah.—Y.

Ver. 3.—*Thoroughness in spiritual culture.* There is put before us here an agricultural figure, which our observation of fallow ground in England, at present, fails to give us the power of understanding. When we look at an English ploughman turning a piece of meadow-land into arable, there does not seem anything very difficult about his work. Why, then, should breaking up the fallow ground be so hard? Why should this be reckoned an appropriate figure for something evidently difficult, something, it would seem, habitually shirked and the necessity of attending to which the men of Judah and Jerusalem did not sufficiently recognize? The answer is to be found in a state of things which, after all our efforts, will probably present itself imperfectly to the mind. By many of the Hebrew husbandmen the cultivation of their land seems to have been managed in a very imperfect, careless, happy-go-lucky sort of way. In the moveless East, what things are to-day tell us pretty well what they were two thousand years ago. Dr. Thomson, speaking of the plain of Gennesaret—a district which Josephus describes as extremely fruitful—says, "Gennesaret is now pre-eminently fruitful in thorns. They grow up among the grain, or the grain among them." And again on the same page, "These farmers all need the exhortation of Jeremiah, 'Break up your fallow ground, and sow not among thorns.' *They are too apt to neglect this;* and the thorns, springing up, choke the seed, so that it cannot come to maturity" ('Land and the Book,' p. 348). The truth, then, was that the land was but half reclaimed from the wilderness. To have properly reclaimed it, and then kept it in a satisfactory state, would have required a great deal of trouble. And since from such fertile land the husbandman, with but little effort, could get enough to serve the passing day, he did not concern himself *to make the land do its best.*

Hence we see that this admonition, whatever its first aspect of obscurity, is really a most important one for all of us. The exhortation is to nothing less than *thoroughness in spiritual culture.* Thoroughness in the cultivation of the heart, as a soil wherein the seeds of Divine truth are sown, pays in the highest sense of the word. Look at what science, skill, and the bold investment of capital for the enrichment of the soil and for machinery to save labour, have done for modern farming. The full productiveness of God's earth seems to be apprehended by comparatively few. And if this is so in things natural, there is no wonder at all that we should be so little conscious of the thoroughness required in cultivating our spiritual nature. There are many human hearts where subsoil ploughing is as yet unknown. There is a soil that grows an abundant crop from plants of human origin, but the seed that God sows either falls dead or dies after a brief struggle to find hold and sustenance in the heart. The word through Jeremiah here is but the germ from which our Lord expounded his parable of the four kinds of soil. There is laid on each one of us a heavy burden—the stewardship of a human heart. And yet it is a precious and honourable burden. Far beyond the ripest, sweetest, and most copious fruits of the soil beneath our feet, is the fruit that may come from within us. But the culture must be thorough. True, that means toil, patience, watchfulness, discrimination; but what great work was ever done without them?—Y.

Ver. 9.—*Despair among the leaders in Israel.* Let us consider how Jehovah leads the prophet up to the emphatic, and what we may call consummating, announcement of this verse. One severe sentence comes on another, until at last the prophet himself, crushed and overwhelmed, gives utterance to the sense he feels of contradiction to former gracious words. This cheerless outlook to Israel, he says, is as a sword piercing to the soul. Looking back, then, through the previous eight verses, we find a spirit of *thoroughness* running through the whole. Jehovah has asked for thoroughness, and seems to intimate that the demand will be practically neglected. Thoroughness in turning to him; thoroughness in the putting away of all abominations; thoroughness in observing the sanctity and obligation of the oath; thoroughness in the culture of spiritual life; thoroughness in circumcision of heart; thoroughness everywhere, is the order of the day. Then on the other hand—because, in spite of all remonstrances, there is a clinging to the superficial modes in which all merely human reformations are managed—we are confronted with the thoroughness of God's work. *If men will not be thorough, at all events God will be so.* His fury will come forth like the unquenchable flame; his agents, in the shape of invincible armies, will bear down resistlessly on his unfaithful people; and, as a sort of climax, the very heads and guides will acknowledge themselves utterly overcome. Such is the scene presented in ver. 9. Consider—

I. HOW THE CONSTERNATION AND HUMILIATION OF THESE MEN NOW IS IN CONTRAST TO THEIR PREVIOUS CONDUCT. We do not stay here to make discriminations among the four classes of prominent men here indicated. The general truth underlying the conduct of all of them is that the leading persons in the State would assuredly lose their self-confidence. Brazen and complacent as that self-confidence is, Jehovah is undermining it in secret, and it will come down with a crash. These men were associated in deception; each one deceived, first of all, himself; and then by a continuous mutual action and reaction, the power both of deceiving and of being deceived became very great indeed. The king, upon giving the slightest encouragement, would become a centre for all sorts of flatteries and arrogant assurances; and indeed, as long as it was a matter of keeping their own people in subjection, these leaders might have comparatively little difficulty. They knew what they were dealing with, and could keep it in bounds by virtue of long practice and cleverly transmitted tricks of management. There was a certain ground of experience which they went upon in all their contemptuous refusals to listen to God's prophet. But now there comes up, all at once, a danger outside their experience, and not only defying their resources, but coming down on those resources like a deluge, and utterly sweeping them away. When the downtrodden and aggrieved in their own borders begin to mutter sedition and meditate conspiracy, they may, perhaps, stop this peril in its beginning; but when the majestic destroyer of the Gentiles is on his way, how shall he be met? The lion out of the thicket is manageable enough if the man against whom he advances happens to have a loaded rifle in his hand, and the power of using it with unerring aim; but what if he has nothing more than a cudgel? Kings and princes, priests and prophets, might successfully join in counsel to mislead and keep down their own people; but a strong and proud army, that has come forth like a mighty wild beast intent on prey, is not to be turned back by mere counsels. In the last resort *strength* must be opposed to strength. The sole virtue of skill lies in this, that it can make the most of strength. But where the strength is lacking, *skill can do nothing.* No amount of skill can make a walking-stick do the work of a rifle, and the great peril of most human lives lies just in this, that they go on in the contented use of ordinary resources for ordinary needs. Practically speaking, extraordinary needs are not thought of till they come. There are voices to us, even as to these kings, princes, priests, and prophets of old; but we do not heed them, and meanwhile the lion out of the thicket, all unsuspected, is coming nearer and nearer to us.

II. NOTE THE FORCIBLE EXPRESSION WITH REGARD TO THE KINGS AND PRINCES Their hearts are to perish. Not but what priests and prophets may have the same experience. Hebrew parallelism is to be borne in mind. The description of king and princes applies also to priest and prophet, and *vice versâ*. They were overwhelmed in a common catastrophe. It is the heart-perishing itself we would call attention to, whoever the subject of it might be. One is reminded of the similar expression, tolerably frequent in the Old Testament, of the heart *melting*. With regard to the king, there

would be an utter collapse of all kingly dignity and pretension. It is not the mere conquest of territory and the desolation of it that can turn the supreme master into a
complete slave. Complete subjection is only achieved when body and mind are alike
in bondage. Many a captive has shown himself nobler than his captor; his heart
being swelled out with even an increase of vitality, courage, and resource in the very
hour when the ungodly seem to have triumphed. Discrowned kings have sometimes
been more regal than on the coronation-day itself. The thing to be marked here is that
these leaders being *cast down outwardly* were equally cast down *inwardly*. The
whole nature crashes down in ruins. The dispossessed leader becomes as dejected
in soul as he is in station. What a warning *for us*, then, is this melancholy prediction!
It is very certain that to us the outward casting down, at all events, must come.
Natural resources, limited and temporary at the best, are always showing weak points,
always needing patching up, and the most that can be done is to postpone the evil
day. And then what is the end to be? Are our hearts also to perish? Is there
to come on us utter despair and brokenness of spirit? It need not be so. Look on
the courage of genuine Christians in captivity, in martyrdom, in poverty, amid the
attacks of slander, in the midst of spiritual non-success. If the heart perish, it will
be for want of believing resort to the succours which come down from the heavenly
places. God can so unite, inspire, instruct, and gladden the heart of every believer, as
effectually to deliver it from perishing. And remember, we are every one called to be,
if not kings, at all events viceroys in our own life. There must be no yielding to presumptuous and audacious dictation of men. He who leans upon the mere assertions of
others, because he is himself indisposed to make the necessary effort for finding out
truth, must be prepared at last to get into that state which is described as one in
which the heart perishes.—Y.

Vers. 11—13.—*The uses of the wind.* Not all the uses of the wind are set forth here,
but enough is mentioned to remind us how God can turn a *beneficial* agent into a
destructive one very rapidly and decisively. The force of the unquenchable fire has
already been spoken of (ver. 4); and it is a sufficiently dreadful thought that fire, so
genial, so useful, with such a place in the house, and—so far as Israel was concerned—
such a place in the service of God, should thus have become, in the thoughts to be
associated with it, dreadful as sword, famine, or pestilence. The man who has had his
house burned down, to the utter loss of all his goods, will henceforth be apt to make
grim comments in his own heart when he hears men extolling the benefactor fire. And
now God comes to another great force in the material world, and shows how it can be
the symbol of the workings out of his holy wrath. 1. *Observe how he calls attention to the beneficial working of the wind.* Frequently the force of the wind is of such
a moderated, yet effectual kind, that it is used to fan and to cleanse. These invading
hosts, it was to be remembered, were not essentially destructive. They were made up
of human individuals, each of whom had measureless capabilities of benefiting his
fellow-men. Possibly from these very northern lands there had come buyers and
sellers, bringing commercial prosperity to Israel. Is it not plain that we should always
consider, when one approaches us in a hostile and threatening way, that it may be
possible by a certain course of conduct to have him come in a very different way?
Many enemies have been friends, and after their enmity has come to a head and done
much damage, it is possible for them to become friends again. This destroying wind,
fierce and dreadful as it was for a time, would yet subside, and fanning and cleansing
work be done again. 2. *It is worth noticing that the Spirit of God which has such
large power to bless has also power to destroy.* The Spirit of God is, on the highest
authority, compared to the wind. Indeed, that is what the name signifies—the breath
or wind from God. Working through Peter in the glorious apostolic days, we see that
Spirit healing the lame man; we hear him speaking mighty, convincing, renewing
words to thousands hitherto indifferent; bringing men into correct and firm apprehensions of truth that had been misunderstood or not understood at all; and filling their
minds with such a light of promise as gave reality and indescribable charm to the
future. But that same Spirit struck down Ananias and Sapphira with an appalling
and fatal blow, and made Elymas the sorcerer suddenly blind. Only a turn is needed,
and the open hand which God extends, the hollow of it filled with the gifts of his

grace, can be closed so as to smite in wrath. God does not need to go far afield for the instruments of his chastisement. The energy of his Holy Spirit can destroy as well as make alive; and Jesus, who is Saviour, is also appointed to judge and condemn.—Y.

Ver. 14.—*The unwashed heart and the vain purposes cherished in it.* There are here an *exhortation* and a *question* which, taken together, pierce very deep, and suggest once more the true cause of all the terrible calamities which are to befall Israel; for though Jerusalem is addressed, the repentance and remedy for all the evils in question must come from the action of a united people. Jeremiah's words in ver. 10 are in a measure representative words; they indicate the way in which the nation would conclude that Jehovah had *promised* one thing; whereas quite another thing had *happened,* and that evidently by his disposition. And so Jehovah meets Jeremiah with this word, so that he shall not persist in a mistaken attempt to harmonize Jehovah's predictions. Further, he is to declare the same thing to Jerusalem, that being the great centre where kings and princes, priests and prophets are gathered together. Instead of looking outward and ignorantly complaining of God, let them look inward, with practical intent, and see what they can do by way of heart-reformation. These stupendous perils can all be removed, but Jehovah by himself cannot remove them. In one sense, of course, he could do so. The wind might be made to subside, the lion be driven back to his thicket, the destroyer of the Gentiles annihilated. But there would be no permanent putting right in this if Israel remained the same. Israel indeed might think that, if only the enemies vanished, then the sword would indeed be withdrawn from the soul. The hearts of the king and princes did not perish simply because of the hosts that were gathered against them. This was a reason so far; but in another sense no reason at all, seeing it did not go to the root of the matter. But now Jehovah does go to the root of the matter; his Word is indeed a sword reaching deeper than the superficial thoughts of the people.

I. THE EXHORTATION. 1. *The heart is to be cleansed.* The heart. Persistently does God drag these people to look within. Either they were not willing to do so, or not able to do so, or, what is perhaps a more correct way of putting it, they lacked both willingness and ability. They would look anywhere but to the true cause of all their ills and to the true sphere where redemption and security were to be worked out. If they would only attend to their hearts and see in their hearts what God saw in them, all the seeds of peril, corruption, and everlasting shame, then they would get on to the right way, and being delivered from fundamental errors in their thoughts, they would come to the apprehension and practice of fundamental truths. They had already been told of the mockery of a mere outward circumcision, and enjoined to *circumcise* their hearts. Now the figure is varied, and they are told to cleanse their hearts. It is because the heart of the king and the prince is so polluted that it perishes. If it were a clean heart it would be a strong heart, invincible against panic and despair. 2. *The filth that is to be taken out of the heart is wickedness.* It takes a long time to work the conviction into the minds of many people that wickedness is as filth. These very people loathe the waifs and strays who think nothing of being constantly begrimed with dirt. To such the impurity of the great unwashed is a loathsome thing; it nauseates them to come within sight or scent of it. But let such recollect that even if, as far as their bodies are concerned, they have daily changes of fine linen, white and clean, that is a mere trifle if the consciousness within be habitually defiled by inhuman and degrading thoughts. There is, of course, a very practical truth in the common saying that "Cleanliness is next to godliness;" but cleanliness of the conscience, removal of every slimy stain of self, is but one of the aspects of perfect godliness. If only we are labouring to cleanse our hearts from wickedness, all other cleanliness will assuredly follow. In proportion as wickedness is cleansed out, there will follow all outward decencies, courtesy of manner and refinement of tastes. The right inwardly grows to the comely outwardly; but if that inward right be lacked, then all apparent comeliness is but the whited sepulchre. 3. *The mode of cleansing.* The word chosen to indicate this is a very significant one. The mere general term for cleansing is not sufficient; nor even the more restricted but still general term for cleansing with water. The washing to be done is that sort which in the literal instance is to be done by a vigorous trampling of the feet. The Hebrew word is the same one in which the profoundly penitent David prays that God would wash him from his iniquity, and again to wash him so that he should be whiter than snow (Ps. li.). And so here we have another instance of the unremitting thoroughness which marks this chapter. It is *the heart* that is to be cleansed, and that by the most vigorous kind of washing. The accumulated filth of years has entered into the very texture of the fabric. The truth is that the only way of carrying out the exhortation is to submit the heart to him in exactly the same spirit as David did. God is *the Cleanser*, and only when our nature has passed through all his purifying agencies shall we *really* know what perfect human nature is. We do indeed see that perfection in Jesus, but with such distorted vision that the seeing cannot be called seeing as we ought to see.

II. The QUESTION. The thoughts with respect to which the question is asked are really purposes. This will come out more clearly on considering some of the expressions in which the same Hebrew word is used; *e.g.* when the woman of Tekoah spoke to David of God *devising means* to bring back his banished (2 Sam. xiv. 14); so Eliphaz tells Job that God disappoints the *devices* of the crafty (Job v. 12). Several of the Proverbs contain the word. The *thoughts*, i.e. *counsels*, of the righteous are just (Prov. xii. 5). Where there is no deliberation, *purposes* are disappointed (Prov. xv. 22). There are many *devices* in a man's heart, but the counsel of God shall stand (Prov. xix. 21). Purposes are established by counsel, *i.e.* there must be wisdom in forming them, and prudence in carrying them out. A comparison of these selected passages will amply suffice to show what God means by vain thoughts, and what sort of practical thoughts he would wish us to put in their place. Man is meant to live with definite ends in view, on which he may expend his strength and faculties. But when these ends are his own—self-originated and self-gratifying—then they are emphatically vain. They can only continue by deceiving the mind that proposes them and holds to them. The question therefore is as to when our eyes shall be opened to perceive the right purposes of life, the solid and attainable ones, the purposes that are not vain, because they are God's purposes and because he provides all resources needed for carrying them out. Jerusalem wished these terrible troubles from outside to be at an end, just that it might resume its own projects. On the other hand, God wished it from the very heart to adopt his projects in order that then he might take all obstacles and enemies completely out of the way.—Y.

Ver. 22.—*Those who are wise to do evil.* This description of "my people" has a curious resemblance to the exhortation of our Lord when he told his friends to be wise as serpents and harmless as doves. These people, according to Jeremiah's observation, had all the wisdom of the serpent, but it was for serpentine purposes. And the worst of it was that they hurt themselves the most. Note—

I. The REFERENCE TO MAN'S GREAT POWERS. Even in his headlong, infatuated descent to ruin, the great powers are manifest. It is the very perversion and ruin of what is so noble in its original constitution that helps to give one an insight, deep even though melancholy, into all that makes up the nobility. A *temple* in ruins fills one with thoughts which could never be excited by looking at a dilapidated shed. Jeremiah looks upon Jerusalem and the men who are leaders there (ver. 9), and their great human faculties cannot be concealed from him. When man sinks into sin, this does not destroy the great human powers; it simply distorts their operation. We look at men as they are, and whatever the sad reflections coming into our minds, we still see the supremacy in terrestrial creation, the power to adapt means to ends, and all that strength and suppleness of intellect which are so much more than the greatest strength of a brute.

II. These GREAT POWERS MUST BE USED. The human intellect cannot be left to lie like a dead sword in the scabbard. In one sense the intellect is but an instrument. having in itself no character either for good or evil, any more than a piece of machinery. Everything depends on the disposition and intents of the man using it. But then the intellect, instrumental as it is, is not a mere instrument, but has a living connection with the rest of human nature. It must act, with more or less energy, according to the individuality of its possessor. These faculties must be used, if not for good, then for evil. History abounds in instances of wicked and selfish men who have achieved their mischievous ends by that very intellectual force which was given for something very different. Hence the importance of early training and direction, so far as one will can alter the course of another. Every individual whose faculties are diverted from good purposes is so much gain to the powers of evil. There is no neutral ground to which to retire. To go out of the one path is to go into the other. This was the sad thought that, even while Jerusalem was going down, lower, lower, towards the hour of its capture and desolation, there were yet in it many men who had the power, if only their hearts had been right, to do much towards saving and blessing their country. But all their thoughts, their utmost acuteness of mind, were given to build and enrich self.—Y.

Vers. 23—27.—*A threatened return from cosmos to chaos.* It is impossible to read this passage without having the first chapter of Genesis brought to mind. Moreover, it was intended that it should be brought to mind. In Gen. i. we have the brief, sublime description, impossible to forget, of the advance from *chaos* to *cosmos.* Here in Jeremiah we have a very sad and suggestive indication of possible return from *cosmos* to *chaos.* These two words, it will be admitted, are often used very loosely. Particularly is this true of the latter. We talk of things having got into a chaotic condition, when if such really were so, it would be a very terrible condition indeed. *For what is chaos?* It is the state indicated at the very beginning of the Scriptures, the state out of which God fashioned what we call the *cosmos* or the world. Bear in mind that the creation described in Genesis is not the making of something out of nothing, but the fashioning of formless, empty matter into an orderly collection of appropriate parts and beyond that an innumerable array of living, active organisms. "The earth was without form and void." Strictly speaking, the earth spoken of in Genesis was as yet an ideal thing. "And darkness was on the face of the abyss." As the writer of the narrative conceived it, there stretched out from the formless, empty earth an impenetrable, rayless depth of space. *This is chaos,* where there is no ray of light, not even the slightest beginning of order, not even the smallest seed of life. But with the moving of God's breath upon the face of the water *cosmos begins.* Light comes; and then day and night are defined, and heaven and earth, and so on through the familiar procession of God's wonderful works, till cosmos gets its terrestrial crown in the fashioning of man. It is worth while for all who would rejoice in the works and ways of God to get a clear notion of the difference *between chaos and cosmos.*

Then bearing this difference in mind, WHAT A TERRIBLE PROSPECT JEREMIAH HINTS AT IN THIS PASSAGE! Just by the profit and glory of the *ascent* from chaos to cosmos in Genesis do we measure the loss and shame of the *descent* from cosmos to chaos in Jeremiah. It is earth we see, with the men and women, the domestic and social bonds, city and country, all occupations of mankind, all that is highest in human attainments; and this aggregation, which comes from man's toiling development of the cosmical elements presented to him, is seen sliding back to chaos again. There can be no mistake about it. Mark, it is not what the prophet *hears,* but what he *sees.* "I beheld" is repeated. And looking out he sees not the accustomed scene of life and activity, but the earth without form and void. He looks for the heavens where dwell the sun by day and moon and stars by night, but there is no light of any sort. The mountains and hills, which always were so significant of strength and grandeur to the Hebrew imagination, show signs of being moved away. No man could be seen. There are several words in Hebrew all rendered by the English word "man," but Jeremiah's word here is the same with that in Gen. i. 26. Then, moreover, all the birds of the heaven fly away. Other inhabited and cultivated places have become as the wilderness, but not as an uninhabited wilderness. Note Isa. xiv. 23: Babylon is there described as being made a possession for the bittern. Thus it is indeed desolated, but evidently the birds do not fly away from it. Here, however, even the birds, which so easily flit from place to place, disappear as if they had no hope of making in this place their nests and finding in it their sustenance. Thus every detail points to the chance, the possibility, of Chaos resuming his ancient reign. But now observe—

THERE IS AN ARREST BEFORE SUCH A DEPLORABLE CONSUMMATION. "I will not make a full end." Man the individual and men the social community may slide a long way towards destruction, may be as it were on the brink, without a remedy; and yet God can so act as to arrest, restore, and consolidate anew, with such internal purity and coherency as will defy further lapse. Note the full significance of the use of the word κόσμος in the Greek Testament.   It was into the κόσμος that the true Light came. John's great directing word to his disciples as he saw Jesus coming to him was, "Behold the Lamb of God, which taketh away the sin of the κόσμος."   Where all should be perfect order, vigorous life, and exuberant fruitfulness, there is discord, contradiction; everything jars, and there is a never-intermitting groan of pain.   All this Jesus can take away, and must take away.   It is through him that whatever promises and hopes lie in ver. 27 are to be carried into effect.   This whole passage, therefore, suggests an aspect in which the need of Christ's work and the reality of it may be very profitably considered.—Y.

Ver. 30.—*Departed charms that cannot be restored.*   The figure here is of a woman, once beautiful and attractive.   There is thus a return to the theme of ch. ii., where the idolatrous land is set forth as a wife departing from her husband.   In the days of her beauty she has fascinated many lovers; but now the beauty is gone, and she makes desperate attempts to compensate for vanished charms by external adornments; only to find her efforts cause for deeper humiliation.   Consider—

I. The CHARM OF NATURAL ATTRACTIONS.   There is a time when youth and beauty are comparatively independent of external aids.   So there was a time in Israel when no special devices were needed to keep the admiration and envy of the world.   David and Solomon made the kingdom great, not by a dexterous concealment of poverty and hollowness under external magnificence, but by a simple and scarcely avoidable exhibition of the greatness of *real* resources.   The kingdom was one of strong men, valiant warriors, and overflowing material wealth.   So it is with individuals still.   They attract and influence, not by vain pretensions, but by what they really are.   The attractive element in them may be overvalued, but at all events it is not a mere appearance. Nothing is gained by refusing to admit the success and charm of natural resources. Confidence in them is justified by the way in which the world receives and encourages those who possess them.

II. The FOLLY OF FORGETTING THAT NATURAL ATTRACTIONS MUST FADE AND DISAPPEAR.   Probably they are but comparatively few—those vain men and women who use dyes, cosmetics, and paints, under the notion that thereby they conceal the ravages of time.   Nevertheless, ludicrous as such devices are, there are only too many who do the same thing, so *far as the essential principle is concerned.*   They cannot be got to admit the failure of power and faculty.   Habit is too strong to enable them rightly to apprehend their diminished resources.   Hosea said of Ephraim, "Gray hairs are here and there upon him, yet he knoweth not" (vii. 9).   There may even be a nobler side to such a spirit, viz. the resolution not to give way before difficulties.   But we must take care that an admirable element in conduct does not blind us to what may be disadvantageous or even perilous in it; *e.g.* one hears sometimes of judges afflicted with deafness—a most dangerous infirmity in the administration of justice, and at least a most discommoding one to all who have to address the judge.   What is needed is that, even in the days of youth and strength, of unimpaired faculties of sense and intellect, one should remember that far other days are coming.   Consider in connection with this the last eighteen verses of Ecclesiastes.   The spectacles and the speaking-trumpet are all very well in their way, so far as they make an easier, smoother slope to the grave; but what folly it is to be assiduous about these things, and utterly careless about that new, Divine, and eternal life which shows itself in all the grandeur of its peculiar principle and strength, precisely amid the decays of the natural man!   What sadder sight can there be than an old man, clinging to the worn, torn, weather-beaten, age-marked sides of his earthly tabernacle, and doing his best to resist every incursion from the forerunners of death; simply because he knows of no better mansion, because he is utterly ignorant of the "house of God not made with hands, eternal in the heavens"!—Y.

EXPOSITION.

CHAPTER V.

Is the punishment thought too severe? Then let the moral condition of Jerusalem be inquired into. Must not such transgressions precipitate its people into ruin? There are four well-marked sections or strophes.

Vers. 1—9. — Gladly would Jehovah pardon, if his people showed but a gleam of sound morality. But they are all deaf to the warning voice—the Law of God is flagrantly violated. In particular the marriage tie, as well the typical one between man and woman as the anti-typical between the people and its God, is openly disregarded (comp. Hos. iv. 1; Micah vii. 2; Isa. lxiv. 6, 7; Ps. xiv. 3).

Ver. 1.—**If ye can find a man.** "A man" is explained by the following clauses. It is a man whose practice and whose aims are right, of whom Jeremiah, like Diogenes with his lantern, is in search. (It is evident that the prophet speaks rhetorically, for himself and his disciples, however few, were doubtless "men" in the prophetic sense of the word.) **Judgment . . . the truth**; rather, *justice . . . good faith*, the primary virtues of civil society.

Ver. 2.—**And though they say, The Lord liveth.** Though they asseverate by the most solemn of all oaths (contrast ch. iv. 1, 2). **Surely.** So the Syriac. This rendering, however, involves an emendation of one letter in the text. The ordinary reading is literally *therefore*, but may etymologically be taken to mean "for all this," "nevertheless."

Ver. 3.—**Are not thine eyes upon the truth?** rather, *surely thine eyes are upon* (equivalent to *thou lookest for and demandest*) *good faith*, alluding to ver. 1.

Ver. 4.—**Therefore I said**; rather, *and as for me, I said*. **They are foolish**; rather, *they act foolishly* (as Numb. xii. 11). **For**; rather, *because*. Their want of religious instruction is the cause of their faulty conduct. In fact, it was only after the return from Babylon that any popular schools were founded in Judæa, and not till shortly before the destruction of the temple that the elementary instruction attained the regularity of a system (Edersheim, 'Sketches of Jewish Social Life in the Time of Christ,' pp. 134, 135). **The judgment of their God.** A similar phrase occurs in ch. viii. 7. "Judgment (*mishpat*) here (as in some other passages) has acquired a technical sense. This may be illustrated by the corresponding word in Arabic (*din*),

which means (1) obedience, (2) a religion, (3) a statute or ordinance, (4) a system of usages, rites, and ceremonies" (Lane's 'Lexicon,' *s.v.*). "Judgment" is, therefore, here equivalent to "religious law," and "law" is a preferable rendering.

Ver. 5.—**The bonds** are the thongs by which the yoke was secured to the neck (comp. Isa. lviii. 6). In ch. ii. 20 the word is rendered "bands."

Ver. 6.—This verse reminds us of a famous passage in the first canto of Dante's 'Commedia,' in which Dante the pilgrim is successively opposed by three wild beasts—a panther, a lion, and a she-wolf. That the poet had Jeremiah in his mind cannot be doubted. The deep knowledge of the Scriptures possessed by mediæval theologians (and such was Dante) may put many Protestants to shame. Curiously enough, whereas the early commentators on Dante interpret these wild beasts of vices, the moderns find historical references to nations. On the other hand, while modern expositors explain Jeremiah's wild beasts as symbols of calamities, Rashi and St. Jerome understand them of the Chaldeans, Persians, and Greeks. **A lion out of the forest.** The first of a series of figures for the cruel invaders of Judah (comp. ch. iv. 7). The frequent references (see also ch. xii. 8; xxv. 38; xlix. 19; l. 4) show how common the lion was in the hills and valleys of the land of Israel. **A wolf of the evenings**; *i.e.* a wolf which goes out to seek for prey in the evening. So the Peshito, Targum, Vulgate (comp. "wolves of the evening," Hab. i. 8; Zeph. iii. 3). But there is no evidence that *'erebh*, evening, has for its plural *'arābhōth*, which is, in fact, the regular plural of *'arābah*, desert. Render, therefore, *a wolf of the deserts*, i.e. one which has its den in the deserts, and falls upon the cultivated parts when it is hungry. Luther, "the wolf out of the desert." **A leopard**; rather, *a panther*. The Chaldeans are compared to this animal, on account of its swiftness, in Hab. i. 8.

Ver. 7.—**How . . . for this?** rather, *Why should I pardon thee?* **Thy children**; *i.e.* (since "the daughter of Zion" is equivalent to Zion regarded as an ideal entity) the members of the Jewish people (comp. Lev. xix. 18, "the children of thy people"). **When I had fed them to the full.** So Ewald, following the versions and many manuscripts (there is no marginal reading in the Hebrew Bible). This gives a good sense, and may be supported by ver. 28; Deut. xxxii. 15; Hos. xiii. 6. But the reading of the received

Hebrew text, though somewhat more difficult, is yet perfectly capable of explanation; and, slight as the difference is in the reading adopted by Ewald (it involves a mere shade of pronunciation), it is not to be preferred to the received reading. Read, therefore, *though I made them to swear (allegiance), yet they committed adultery.* The oath may be that of Sinai (Exod. xxiv.), or such an oath as had been recently taken by Josiah and the people (1 Kings xxiii. 3; 2 Chron. xxxiv. 31, 32). The "adultery" may be taken both in a literal and in a figurative sense, and so also the "harlots' houses" in the next clause. It is also well worthy of consideration whether the prophet may not be referring to certain matrimonial customs handed down from remote antiquity and arising from the ancient system of kinship through women (comp. Ezek. xxii. 11).

Ver. 8.—**As fed horses in the morning.** The rendering *fed horses* has considerable authority. "Lustful horses" is also possible; this represents the reading of the Hebrew margin. The following word in the Hebrew is extremely difficult. "In the morning" cannot be right, as it is against grammar; but it is not easy to furnish a substitute. Most moderns render "roving about;" Fürst prefers "stallions."

Vers. 10—18.—Provoked by the open unbelief of the men of Judah, Jehovah repeats his warning of a sore judgment.

Ver. 10.—**Her walls.** There is a doubt about "walls," which should, as some think, rather be *vine-rows* (a change of points is involved; also of *shin* into *sin*—the slightest of all changes), or *shoots*, or *branches* (comparing the Syriac). The figure would thus gain somewhat in symmetry. However, all the ancient interpreters (whose authority, overrated by some, still counts for something) explain the word as in the Authorized Version, and, as Graf remarks, in order to destroy the vines, it would be necessary to climb up upon the walls of the vineyard. (For the figure of the vine or the vineyard, comp. on ch. ii. 21.) **Take away . . . not the Lord's.** The Septuagint and Peshito read differently, translating "leave her foundations, for they are the Lord's" (supposing the figure be taken from a building). As the text stands, it is better to change **battlements** into *tendrils.* Judah's degenerate members are to be removed, but the vine-stock, *i.e.,* the believing kernel of the nation, is to be left. It is the key-note of the "remnant" which Jeremiah again strikes (see ch. iv. 27).

Ver. 12.—**It is not he.** Understand "who speaks by the prophets" (Payne Smith). It is hardly conceivable that any of the Jews absolutely denied the existence of Jehovah. They were practical, not specu-lative unbelievers, like men of the world in general.

Ver. 13.—**And the prophets,** etc. A continuation of the speech of the unbelieving Jews. **The word is not in them.** The Authorized Version gives a good meaning, but it involves an interference with the points. The pointed text must be rendered, *he who speaketh (through the prophets, viz.* Jehovah) *is not in them.* Thus the Jews hurl against prophets like Jeremiah the very charge which Jeremiah himself brings against the "false prophets" in ch. xxiii. 25—32. **Thus shall it be done;** rather, *so be it done;* i.e. may the sword and famine, with which they threaten us, fall upon them.

Ver. 14.—**My words in thy mouth fire.** (See on ch. i. 9, 10.)

Ver. 15.—**O house of Israel.** After the captivity of the ten tribes, Judah became the sole representative of the people of Israel (comp. ch. ii. 26). **A mighty nation.** The Authorized Version certainly gives a part of the meaning. The Hebrew word rendered "mighty" (*'ēthān*), rather, "perennial," is the epithet of rocks and mountains (Numb. xxiv. 21; Micah vi. 2); of a pasture (ch. xlix. 19); of rivers (Deut. xxi. 4; Ps. lxxiv. 15). As applied in the present instance, it seems to describe the inexhaustible resources of a young nation. Render here, *ever replenished;* i.e. ever drawing anew from its central fountain of strength. Does not this aptly convey the impression which a long-civilized nation (and the Jews, who have been called "rude," were only so by comparison with the Egyptians and Assyrians) must derive from the tumultuous incursions of nomad hosts? The description will therefore fit the Scythians; but it is not inappropriate to the Chaldeans, if we take into account the composite nature of their armies. **An ancient nation;** *i.e.* one which still occupies its primeval seat in the north (ch. vi. 22), undisturbed by invaders. **Whose language thou knowest not.** So Isaiah of the Assyrians, "(a people) of a stammering tongue, that thou canst not understand." The Jews were no philologists, and were as unlikely to notice the fundamental affinity of Hebrew and Assyrian as an ancient Greek to observe the connection between his own language and the Persian. When the combatants were to each other βάρβαροι, mercy could hardly be expected. The sequence of vers. 49 *b* and 50 in Deut. xxviii. speaks volumes.

Ver. 16.—**Their quiver.** (See on ch. iv. 29.) **As an open sepulchre**; *i.e.* furnished with deadly arrows, "fiery darts." So the psalmist, of the "throat" of deceitful persecutors (Ps. v. 9).

Ver. 17.—**Which thy sons and thy daughters,** etc.; rather, *they shall eat thy sons and* *thy daughters*. In the other clauses of the verse the verb is in the singular, the subject being the hostile nation. **They shall impoverish**, etc.; rather, *it shall batter . . . with weapons of war* (so rightly Payne Smith); *khérebh*, commonly rendered "sword," is applied to any cutting instrument, such as a razor (Ezek. v. 1), a mason's tool (Exod. xx. 25), and, as here and Ezek. xxvi. 9, weapons of war in general.

Vers. 19—29.—Judah's own obstinacy and flagrant disobedience are the causes of this sore judgment.

Ver. 19.—**Like as ye have forsaken me**, etc. The law of correspondence between sin and punishment pervades Old Testament prophecy (comp. Isa. v.). As the Jews served foreign gods in Jehovah's land, they shall become the slaves of foreigners in a land which is not theirs.

Ver. 21.—**Without understanding**; literally, *without heart*. This seems at first sight inconsistent with ver. 23, where the people is described as having indeed a "heart," but one hostile to Jehovah. The explanation is that a course of deliberate sin perverts a man's moral perceptions. The prophet first of all states the result, and then the cause. So in Ezek. xii. 2, "Which have eyes and see not," etc.; "for they are a rebellious house."

Ver. 22.—**Fear ye not me?** The Hebrew places "me" emphatically at the beginning of the sentence. **By a perpetual decree.** This is one of the evidences, few but sufficient, of the recognition of natural laws by the Biblical writers; of laws, however, which are but the description of the Divine mode of working, "covenants" (ch. xxxiii. 20; comp. Gen. ix. 18) made for man's good, but capable of being annulled (Isa. liv. 10). Comp. Prov. viii. 29; Job xxxviii. 8—12.

Ver. 23.—**A revolting and a rebellious heart.** The heart is the centre of the moral life virtually equivalent to "the will;" it is "revolting" when it "turns back" (so literally here) from God's Law and service, and "rebellious" when it actively defies and opposes him.

Ver. 24.—**That giveth rain**, etc. The second appeal is to the regularity of the rains. Dr. Robinson remarks that there are not at the present day in Palestine "any particular periods of rain, or succession of showers, which might be regarded as distinct rainy seasons," and that, unless there has been some change in the climate of Palestine, the former and the latter rains seem to correspond to "the first showers of autumn, which revived the parched and thirsty earth and prepared it for the seed, and the later showers of spring, which continued to refresh and forward both the ripening crops and the vernal products of

the fields" ('Biblical Researches,' iii. 98). **He reserveth unto us**, etc.; literally, *he keepeth for us the weeks—the statutes of harvest*; i.e. the weeks which are the appointed conditions of harvest. The prophet means the seven weeks which elapsed from the second day of the Passover to the "Feast of Harvest," or "Feast of Weeks" (Pentecost) (Exod. xxiii. 16; xxxiv. 22; Deut. xvi. 9, 10).

Ver. 25.—**Have turned away these** things. "These things" are the benefits mentioned in the preceding verse (comp. ch. iii. 3; xii. 4). Thus the judgment is not entirely future; a foretaste of it has already been given (comp. 1 Kings xvii.; Amos iv.).

Ver. 26.—**They lay wait**, etc.; rather, *they spy* (literally, *one spieth*), *as fowlers lie in wait*. **A trap**; literally, *a destroyer*; i.e. an instrument of destruction (comp. Isa. liv. 16, where "the waster" (or destroyer) probably means the weapon referred to previously).

Ver. 27.—**A cage.** The Hebrew word *k'lûb* is used in Amos viii. 1 for a basket such as was used for fruit; it seems to be the parent of the Greek word κλωβός, used in the 'Anthology' for a bird-cage. The root means to plait or braid; hence some sort of basket-work seems to be meant. Connecting this with the preceding verse, Hitzig seems right in inferring that the "cage" was at the same time a trap (comp. Ecclus. xi. 30, "Like as a partridge *taken in a cage* [ἐν καρτάλλῳ, a peculiar kind of basket], so is the heart of the proud"). Canon Tristram suggests that there is an allusion to decoy-birds, which are still much employed in Syria, and are carefully trained for their office ('Natural History of the Bible,' p. 163). But this seems to go beyond the text. **Deceit**; *i.e.* the goods obtained by deceit.

Ver. 28.—**They overpass the deeds of the wicked**; rather, *they overpass the common measure of wickedness* (literally, *the cases of wickedness*); or, as others, *they exceed in deeds of wickedness*. **Yet they prosper**; rather, *so that they (the fatherless) might prosper*; or, *that they (the rich) might make it to prosper*.

Ver. 29.—A repetition of ver. 9 in the manner of a refrain.

Vers. 30, 31.—The result of the prophet's examination of the moral condition of the people.

Ver. 30.—**A wonderful and horrible thing**, etc.; rather, *an appalling and horrrible thing hath happened in the land*. The word rendered "appalling" (or stupefying) has a peculiar force. It only occurs again in ch. xxiii. 14, though a cognate adjective is found in ch. xviii. 13 (comp. on ch. ii. 11).

Ver. 31.—**The prophets . . . the priests.**

(See on ch. ii. 26.) **Bear rule by their means**; rather, *rule at their beck* (literally, *at their hands*, comp. ch. xxxiii. 13; 1 Chron. xxv. 2, 3; 2 Chron. xxiii. 18). An example of this inteference of the false prophets with the priestly office is given by Jeremiah himself (ch. xxix. 24–26). **My people love** to have it **so**. Sometimes the prophets speak as if the governing classes alone were responsible for the sins and consequent calamities of their country. But Jeremiah here expressly declares that the governed were as much to blame as their governors.

HOMILETICS.

Ver. 1.—*Forgiveness for many through the righteousness of one.* I. GOD IS GREATLY DESIROUS TO PARDON HIS CHILDREN. The command is given to "run to and fro" and search for the one righteous man. God thus expresses his anxiety to forgive. "He *waiteth* to be gracious." The first movement towards exercising pardon comes from God even before men desire it. He will lay hold of the smallest ground for forgiveness. If the one righteous man can but be found, God will forgive the city.

II. SOME RIGHTEOUSNESS IS NECESSARY AS A GROUND FOR FORGIVENESS. If the righteous man cannot be found, the condition of the city is hopeless. There is a propitiatory power in righteousness. Good men are priests, and their lives sacrifices of value for the advantage of others. The righteousness of Christ is an essential element in the atonement (Heb. x. 9, 10). It was not possible for the sin of man to be forgiven except on condition of this. Pardon is offered to men only through this (Acts xiii. 38).

III. THE RIGHTEOUSNESS WHICH AVAILS WITH GOD MUST BE SOLID AND PRACTICAL. A vain, religious boast counts for nothing (ver. 2). 1. The goodness to be sought for is not devoutness of demeanour, but the exercise of justice and the effort to keep good faith. 2. This is to be looked for, not in the temple, but in the streets and lanes and places of public concourse, *i.e.* in daily life. The best evidences of character are to be seen in home life and conduct in business. When the domestic and commercial morality of a city is corrupt, the condition of that city is ruinous, whatever may be the assiduity and decorum with which religious observances are maintained.

IV. THE RIGHTEOUSNESS OF ONE MAY BE EFFICACIOUS FOR THE SECURITY OF MANY. Sodom and Gomorrah would have been spared for the sake of ten righteous men (Gen. xviii. 32). Lot was the providential means of saving Zoar (Gen. xix. 21). The one man Christ secures salvation for the whole world (Heb. vii. 24, 25). There is much that is mysterious in the principle of Divine grace which is here revealed—much that we cannot explain. Still, there are truths entering into it which may be discerned, *e.g.* injustice cannot be done by God in the smallest respect; the righteous are " the salt of the earth," they preserve by preventing complete corruption; there is hope for the city in which but one righteous man lives, since he may be the means of leading others back to righteousness—this principle is one on which God acts in forgiving, not in distributing bare rights; all that he requires is a safe and justifiable ground on which to exercise pardon, not a fund of merit such as could constitute a claim on his grace.

Ver. 3.—*Fruitless chastisement.* I. THE PURPOSE OF CHASTISEMENT IS CORRECTION. 1. It is to lead men by outward suffering to *inward grief* ("they have not grieved"). No more hopeless condition can be found than pleasure or indifference in sin. The tears of penitence are the first preparations for reformation. 2. It is to lead men, through outward suffering and inward grief, to a genuine conversion of character (God looks for a restoration of " good faith"), and to bring them *back to God* ("they have refused to return"). It is no end in itself, no good except as leading to a further good. It is not given in vindictive rage nor to satisfy the claims of abstract justice. Though it springs directly from the wrath of God, that wrath is based on his eternal love. Because God loves his children he must be angry when they sin. Because he desires their good he must not spare his rod (Prov. iii. 11, 12). The purpose of chastisement is not so mysterious as is commonly supposed. People often exclaim vaguely, "These troubles must be sent for *some* good purpose." The purpose is not all hidden. It is mainly that we may be brought nearer to God.

II. THE CORRECTION AIMED AT IN CHASTISEMENT IS NOT ALWAYS ATTAINED. A terrible delusion possesses multitudes of suffering people. They have faith enough to believe that trouble is sent for their good, but not spirituality enough to see how to use it for that end. Such people assume that it must benefit them, however they behave under it. Some suppose that if they suffer in this world they will certainly receive compensation in the next. Such ideas imply that chastisement cannot be deserved, or that the mere endurance of it is meritorious, or that, if not exactly punishment for sin, it must be a necessity to be borne now or hereafter for its own sake or to satisfy some strange will of God. But chastisement is a "means of grace," and, like other "means of grace," may be frustrated. We may receive this grace in vain (2 Cor. vi. 1). Consider the causes of the fruitlessness of chastisement. 1. *Stoical hardness.* We may be stricken, but not grieve. 2. *Thoughtlessness.* We may feel inward grief, but not reflect on our condition and need. 3. *Pride*, which suffers pangs of grief but no contrition for sin. 4. *Impenitence.* We may "refuse to receive correction," harden our wills against submission, and rebel in impatience and complaining against God, instead of returning to him.

III. FRUITLESS CHASTISEMENT IS WHOLLY AN EVIL THING. Like every other grace, if abused it works injury. Sent to bless, it is converted into a curse. 1. It is *wasted suffering.* As such it must be reckoned as an evil. Pain in itself is not a good thing. If it works no good, natural instinct is right in regarding it as bad. 2. It leads to an *aggravation of wickedness.* The very abuse of it is a sin. The wrong temper in which it is received is so much more wickedness added to the long catalogue of unrepented sin. One more call from the Father is spurned by his children. 3. It *leaves the heart harder* than it finds it. Sorrow, if it does not soften the sufferer, will harden him, as friction, which abrades the tender skin, renders the tough skin more thick and horny.

Vers. 12, 13.—*Culpable unbelief.* The Jews are accused of unbelief as a sin. It is therefore sometimes to be regarded in this light (*e.g.* Heb. iv.). Let us consider the characteristics of a culpable unbelief and its origin.

I. UNBELIEF IS MORALLY CULPABLE WHEN IT ARISES FROM AN EVIL HEART. 1. This unbelief must be distinguished (1) from that of *ignorance*; (2) from that of *prejudice*, bad education, etc.; (3) from that of *honest doubt.* 2. It is recognized (1) as residing in the *will* rather than in the intellect—a result of wishing a thing not to be true; and (2) as coloured by *custom*, worldly proclivities, base passions, ill feeling against all that the highest truth is concerned with. It is practically equivalent to the wilful rejection of truth. He who is blamed for this is not blamed for his opinions, but for the moral determining causes of them. We are not responsible for our beliefs, in so far as they are purely intellectual, but we are responsible for them in so far as they are formed under moral influences.

II. THE EVIL TENDENCIES TOWARDS A CULPABLE UNBELIEF ARE ABUNDANT AND POWERFUL. These are not to be found in a simple proneness to err, a natural weakness of faith, nor in the dangers accompanying daring speculation. They are to be traced in conduct and practical affairs. 1. *Untruthful habits.* Israel had dealt treacherously with God (ver. 11). We must be true to discern truth. If the eye is evil, the whole body is full of darkness. There is a close connection between those two evil things which go under the name of infidelity—treachery and unbelief, lack of faithfulness and lack of faith. 2. *Resistance to the will of God.* The language of the people betrays an animus, a spirit of enmity to God. "They have belied the Lord." Nothing blinds like hatred. 3. *Love of ease.* The words of Jeremiah were not pleasant; he threatened terrible things. Therefore his hearers refused to accept his message. Their conduct was most illogical, since truth is not affected by our liking for it—are there not many unpleasant truths?—and most injurious to themselves, since it was for their own interest to give heed to the warning of approaching calamity, that foresight might mitigate the force, if it could not now prevent the falling, of the blow. Yet this conduct was most natural. It is constantly to be observed that people listen to the teachers whom they like rather than to those whom they believe to be speaking the most important truths, and accept the opinions which suit their inclinations rather than those possibly less agreeable ideas which stand on the surest foundation of fact. 4. *Spiritual deadness.* The Jews deny the inspiration of the prophets. To them weighty words such as those of Jeremiah are mere "wind." So there were those who derided him who spake with the weightiest authority and "as never man spake." Sin deadens the soul to the perception of God's voice in nature, in the Bible, in Christ, in conscience.

Ver. 19.—*Suitable retribution.* In anticipation of their astonishment at the character of the retribution that is to fall upon them the Jews are to be shown that this is fitting and rightly corresponds to their conduct.

I. THEY WHO FORSAKE GOD IN PROSPERITY WILL FEEL THE LOSS OF GOD IN ADVERSITY. According to the religious conduct in sunny days will be the condition of rest or ruin in dark days.

II. THE FALSE GODS OF PROSPERITY PROVE WORTHLESS IN ADVERSITY. Israel served heathen gods in their own land. In their captivity they are to be slaves to strange men. The gods are then nowhere. Men make gods of wealth, pleasure, fame, etc., and find that, though these may be worshipped, they can do nothing to deliver their devotees.

III. THEY WHO THROW OFF THE SERVICE OF GOD MUST SUBMIT TO HARDER SERVICE. They think to be free, but they really are the slaves of sin (John viii. 34). They reject the easy yoke and light burden of Christ only to find themselves bound in the galling fetters of Satan.

IV. THE ABUSE OF BLESSINGS IS NATURALLY PUNISHED BY THE LOSS OF THEM. In their own land the Jews had proved unfaithful to the God who had given it them. They are rightly punished by exile to a strange land, where they must miss his gracious government.

Vers. 22—24.—*Man rebuked by nature.* Man considers himself to be "the lord of creation." He alone of all creatures is made in the image of God. Yet there are things in nature which should put him to shame. Jeremiah indicates two of these.

I. THE DIVINE ORDER OF NATURE REBUKES THE WILFUL DISOBEDIENCE OF MAN. 1. *Nature is ever obedient to the law of God.* (1) The greatest powers of nature submit to Divine ordinances. The sea, vast and mighty, is bound by his decree (Job xxxviii. 8—11). (2) The wildest convulsions of nature do not transgress these ordinances. The waves may toss and roar, but they cannot pass the bounds that God has set them. Hurricanes, thunder-storms, earthquakes, are as subservient to law as the silent sunshine and the peaceful growth of spring. (3) The simplest means in accordance with Divine laws are sufficient to restrain the fiercest forces of nature. God has placed the *sand* as a bound of the sea, and the storms are driven back from the sandy beach as surely as from the coast of iron crags. (4) The obedience of nature to these Divine ordinances is everlasting and without exception. The sea is bound by perpetual decrees. 2. *Man alone is disobedient to the Law of God.* He is the great exception to the order of the universe. The wild sea never transgresses God's decrees; man is the sole transgressor. The possibility of this strange, solitary rebellion among all the orders of God's kingdoms of nature is explained by the constitution of man and the character of the obedience which is required by this. Nature is under necessity; man is free. Nature's obedience is unconscious, material; man's is deliberate, moral. He is to fear, to tremble, *i.e.* to obey under the influence of thoughts and feelings of reverence. Lacking these, he can be bound to the throne of God by no chains of compulsion. But how terrible to use the high endowment of liberty only to set at defiance the august decrees before which all other creatures bow unceasingly!

II. THE DIVINE BENEFICENCE OF NATURE REBUKES THE UNGRATEFUL REBELLION OF MAN. 1. *The order of nature is beneficent.* God gives the rain "in its season." He keeps for men "the appointed weeks of the harvest." The regularity and harmony of the physical world are beneficial to men. The sun never fails to rise. If it once failed, what disasters would follow! If the motion of the earth were irregular no life could continue to exist. The order of the seasons is a distinct blessing (Gen. viii. 22). Instead of shrinking from "the reign of law" as from a cruel tyranny, we should welcome it when we remember that the laws of nature are but the material expression of the will of God, and that will the outcome of his goodness. 2. *This beneficence of nature shows all sin to be a mark of ingratitude.* God smiles on us in nature (Matt. v. 45). How then can we, while blessed by the very sunshine of that smile, rise up in revolt against him? If the grandeur and splendid harmony of nature do not awe us, shall not its gentleness and kindliness attract us to loyal obedience to him who is at once the Fountain of law and the Father of mercies?

Vers. 30, 31.—*The most appalling condition to which a nation can sink.* After enumerating the sins of his people in ever-darkening series, the prophet at length reaches a form of evil worse than all others, at the sight of which he starts back with an exclamation of horror; this is corruption at the very fountain of instruction and worship, and the willing acquiescence in it by the nation.

I. CONSIDER THE FEARFUL NATURE OF THIS EVIL.   1 *False prophecy.* The prophet should be the highest oracle of truth.   If *he* utters lies, knowledge is corrupted at its source.   The guilt of such conduct is exceptionally great, because (1) it is a sin against light; (2) it is a prostitution of the highest powers to the basest ends; and (3) it is a cause of widespread ruin to those who follow these "blind leaders of the blind." 2. *Subservient priesthood.* The priests were at the beck of the false prophets.   These men had not the excuse of the prophets.   The prophets represented a progressive religion—a religion of inward lights, a religion in which new departures were expected, and therefore one in which the excuse of honest though mistaken enthusiasm might be urged in defence of a lapse into error.   But the priests were the custodians of a rigid ritual defined by a written Law.   They were put in trust, and their apostasy was a deliberate act of unfaithfulness.   The Christian teacher, though free from the letter of the Law, and gifted with the spiritual freedom of prophecy, is put in trust with the gospel (1 Tim. i. 11).   If he, while retaining the influence and emoluments of his office, consciously forsakes the guidance of the New Testament for the fascinations of ground- less speculation, he too is guilty of unfaithfulness; and if he knows the speculation to be false, but accepts it out of deference to its popularity, he is guilty of base treason like that of the commander of a fortress who surrenders to the enemy from sheer cowardice.   3. *Popular acquiescence* in these evils.   "My people love to have it so." This is pleasing, since (1) the false prophets flatter and prophesy smooth things, while the true prophets like Jeremiah must often rebuke and denounce judgments; and (2) the priests are satisfied with an unspiritual religion, ritual without morality, perhaps even immorality in religion.   But this fact completes the terrible depravity of the nation.   The people cannot plead ignorance nor compulsory obedience.   The willing followers of corrupt religious leaders must share their guilt; nay, they are responsible for the aggravation of it by fostering with applause that which would die out if neglected.

II. CONSIDER THE FINAL RESULT OF THIS EVIL.   "And what will ye do in the end thereof?"   It was characteristic of the false prophets that they aimed only at imme- diate popularity, and thought only of the present, while the true prophets were con- cerned with the future.   But the future will some day be the present.   Is it not best to inquire what this is becoming while yet there is time to modify it?   1. Consider the *moral* results of this depravity, the corruption of conscience, the falsifying of the nature of those who live in falsehood, the destruction of all spiritual life in those who lower spiritual functions before the claims of worldly convenience.   2. Consider the *penal* results of this depravity.   Can *this* of all evils go unpunished?   (See ver. 29.)

HOMILIES BY VARIOUS AUTHORS.

Ver. 1.—*A wicked city spared for the sake of one saint.* The challenge is very bold and striking.   It proves how thoroughly the prophet, as taught by the Spirit, had read the national corruption.   At the same time it furnishes a gauge of the long-suffering mercy of God, and the influence for good of one true man.   Jerusalem, the chief city, is chosen as representing what is best and most influential in the nation; and its streets and lanes as the haunts of the multitude, the merchants, the artisans, and common people, who would represent the general public morality.   It is as if he had said, "In practical life, amid the miscellaneous throng, seek for the just and honourable man." What light this throws upon—

I. THE EXTENT OF CORRUPTION POSSIBLE IN HUMAN NATURE!   The Jewish metropolis had been highly favoured.   The priesthood had its head-quarters there.   The chief messages of the prophets had been delivered in its precincts. It was the centre of influence, national spirit, and intelligence. Yet the effect of all this was morally and spiritually *nil*. Worse even than Sodom and Gomorrah in actual spiritual condition, as certainly it would be far less tolerable for it than for them in the day of judgment. *Ideally* it was the city of the saints and of heavenly peace and order; *actually* its temple was a den of thieves, and its streets the scenes of universal dishonesty, godlessness, and corruption. As has been said of a certain metropolis of Christendom, it would appear to have been the case that "the more churches the less religion." Allowing it to be a rhetorical exaggeration, it was nevertheless a terrible statement to be able to make. But the great cities of the modern world have filled with a like despair the minds of the wisest thinkers. The measure of man's possible degeneration and depravity who can fix?

II. THE IMPORTANCE OF INDIVIDUAL INFLUENCE IN SPIRITUAL THINGS! The spectacle of Abraham praying for the cities of the plain is most impressive. But may it not be paralleled by the unconscious influence of good men? Even accepting the statement as a challenge, was it not a great thing to say that one man by his holiness could have saved the city? Suppose there had been such a man. One can imagine what would have been his sorrow at the universal evil, and his feeling of helplessness and uselessness amid the prevalent irreligion. Yet would his presence there be no light matter, no vain thing. Though he knew it not, he would have been the saviour of the people—immediately from the judgment of God, possibly in the future from the sin that was destroying it. The value, therefore, of individual influence in spiritual matters is incalculable; and no Christian can say that he is of no use. *Godward* the prayer of the faithful may soar in constant intercession and mediation; *manward* his character and works are a constant testimony to the unbeliever.

III. THE INFINITENESS OF GOD'S LONG-SUFFERING LOVE. The presence of one good man in the wicked city would have been *an appeal to God's justice* that could not be despised. He could not "destroy the righteous with the wicked." But far more would it have been *an appeal to his love*. The hope of the future would have been wrapped up in that solitary saint. In him grace would find a secret sanctuary, and the forces of salvation a vantage-point from which to sally forth to the rescue of perishing souls and the work of national, yea, of world-wide, regeneration. The judgments of God are not inflicted arbitrarily or in haste. He has "no pleasure in the death of the wicked." Any reasonable excuse for merciful intervention or delay is welcome. Countless acts of mercy and forgiveness, countless opportunities for repentance, have occurred ere the uplifted axe has dealt its terrible stroke. Learn, then, from this that: 1. *The life as the prayer of a righteous man availeth much with God.* 2. *That God will save us if we will only let him*; and 3. *He will begin his work of salvation from the least, and carry it on even to the greatest.*

IV. THE REASONABLENESS AND RIGHTEOUSNESS OF VICARIOUS SUFFERING THROUGH CHRIST.—M.

Ver. 3.—*What God requires of man.* "O Lord, are not thine eyes upon the truth?" This is better rendered, "O Lord, look not thine eyes for fidelity?" *Faith* is the grand requirement. It is the condition of communion between man and God, and man and man. Scripture lays stress on this. Faith cannot be a mere logical abstraction or a condition beyond the reach of man. It must be practical—within the power of the will, and such as may be reasonably looked for in all. "Fidelity," the Old Testament equivalent for the New Testament "faith," has its expression in reality, honesty, thoroughness. These are the marks of the man God delights to honour, and they are the obligation of all (cf. Micah vi. 8).

I. THE SIMPLICITY, REASONABLENESS, AND NECESSITY OF IT. God could not ask for less than man demands of his fellow, and society requires for its stability and advancement. It is obviously independent of the accidents of culture, fortune, or position; and for any solid understanding between God and man, absolutely indispensable. We are God's stewards, servants, representatives, etc. Having this, we have all; wanting this, all our other acquirements are vain.

II. THE SCARCITY OF IT. A little while ago we read that not a just man could be found in all Jerusalem. Here it is said that even in the most sacred oath there is false swearing. The want of this quality, rather than its presence, strikes the inquirer. This it is that gives rise to wars, jealousies, selfishness, sin in all its forms.

III. THE REASON FOR ITS ABSENCE IN MOST MEN. Because men are sinners, alienated from the life of God and unconscious of his claims. The carnal nature is unable of itself even to be real, to be truly honest, or to discharge faithfully and completely the most ordinary duties. A supernatural aid is required. A Saviour must die. Through him the soul must be united with God in a true love and holy understanding. The better nature thus awakened, the trust and confidence and love thus created must be reinforced by the Spirit. How terrible the thoughts, "Thou God seest me"! "Be not deceived: God is not mocked"! "His eyes are as a flame of fire"! "The Word of God is sharper than any two-edged sword," etc.! Who shall deceive that all-seeing One? The eyes of Jehovah, reading the secrets of the soul, look for *fidelity*, for *faith*.—M.

Ver. 18.—*Sparing mercy.* The judgments described as about to be inflicted are very fearful, but they were amply deserved. The wickedness of the people was such as to justify their complete destruction. Yet they were spared ere they were totally extinct! Why this unlooked-for restraint?

I. IT HAS CHARACTERIZED ALL GOD'S JUDGMENTS OF MANKIND ON EARTH. The Fall, the Flood, the Exodus, etc., the sparing of the remnant of Benjamin, etc.

II. THERE IS BUT ONE EXPLANATION FOR IT. It is the possibility of *some* turning to him truly in the first instance; and, secondly, through them, of the race being saved in the future. God has never utterly cut off even the most sinful. *Love*, and not mere vengeance, behaves in this way. 1. *Has he not spared us?* 2. *He has never abandoned his purpose of saving " the whole world."*—M.

Ver. 22.—*God's power in restraining the forces of nature.* An old, yet ever new, illustration of his power. The tiny grains of sand, the "Portland Beach" of shingle or pebbles, is enough to hold back the mighty ocean. It is but one of many impressive illustrations of his restraining power and goodness.

I. IT IS CALCULATED TO INSPIRE REVERENCE AND LOVE.

II. OUR HELPLESS DEPENDENCE UPON HIM IS THUS SHOWN.

III. THE POWER OF GOD IN THE SPHERE OF MORAL INFLUENCE AND SAVING GRACE as thereby suggested.

> "'Thus far and no further,' when addressed
> To the wild waves, or wilder human breast,
> Implies authority that never can
> And never ought to be the lot of man."

It is God's prerogative. Let us not defy him or arrogate to ourselves that which is his. Let us rather yield ourselves to his gracious dealings and fatherly purpose.—M.

Ver. 1.—*Can a righteous man be found in Jerusalem?* God's warnings still go on concerning the same thing—the deeply seated, the deeply destructive wickedness of the people. But though the same subject has to be spoken of, there is no monotony in the treatment of it. It can be looked at from fresh points of view, and put into fresh lights. A careful reading of ch. iv. will show how many different things can be said concerning wickedness; and now, with ch. v. 1, the reproaches and appeals still continue. Note—

I. THE INDIVIDUALIZING ASPECT OF THE APPEAL. The nation and Jerusalem and the leaders in it have all been referred to; but as long as there are generalities and nothing more individuals will think they can get away from blame under cover of them. Here, then, is a bold challenge which fastens up in a corner every dweller in Jerusalem. The challenge, of course, is not to be taken literally. The true state of things may be known, and known very distinctly, without any running to and fro at all. Let every one take a glance at those whom he knows, and then come home to a candid inquiry concerning the life within his own breast. It is an easy thing to blame others, to throw the fault of disaster upon those who occupy prominent positions. Followers are to blame as well as leaders. The iniquity of Jerusalem, deep, turbid, incessant as the stream of it is, is made of many contributions which, individually considered, may seem very slight. A few men in every age are called to toil for the removal of evils of which, personally, they are not guilty; but every one has the opportunity of improving the world, by doing his best to keep his own heart right. Others are to blame, and there are times when they must be faced, blamed, and resisted; but there is given a *daily* need, duty, and opportunity to do in our own hearts what no one else can do for us.

II. How COMPREHENSIVE AND CONFIDENT THE CHALLENGE IS. It amounts to this, that there cannot be found in all Jerusalem one man who is just in all his dealings, and a seeker after truth. *Not one.* Must we, then, take this literally? The answer is, *No,* and *Yes.* It would have been strange if Jerusalem had become so utterly bad a place that every soul within it was perverted from the ways of right and truth. There must have been some men desiring and striving to live a right life. We bear in mind what God said to Elijah when Elijah said, in the despair and bitterness of his heart, that only *he* was left to serve God. Not so by any means; the searching God, who counts hearts where fallible men can only count heads, told his prophet there were still seven thousand with knees unbowed to Baal. And did not Jeremiah discover from his own experience that there were some on Jehovah's side (ch. xxvi. 24; xxxix. 15—18)? But they were not enough to exert a leavening and recovering influence. And yet the very men whom we may call good and just and true, seeing something of the right, and trying to do it as far as they saw, would have drawn back in confusion and self-distrust if they had been asked, in a direct way and so that the question could not be evaded, "Do you answer this description?" "Are you doers of justice and seekers after truth?" In trying to answer such a question, would not the moments of unfaithfulness and hesitation come to mind—the occasions when they were tempted to escape from loss and pain by some convenient compromise? It will never do for us to congratulate ourselves on being a great deal better than others so long as we come short of what God wants us to be.

III. The thing to be specially considered is, how THIS ACCUSATION APPLIES TO THE GREAT MASS OF THE PEOPLE. Many would have said, cynically enough, "Justice and truth are no concern of ours." These are words that sound very well in general statements; but directly the attempt is made to bring them close to the individual, it is alleged that they do not apply, or else there is the name and not the thing. Things are called just which are not just, and true which are utterly false. Let men of noble minds talk of justice and truth, and only too many are found to allege that such speaking is but cant and hypocrisy. When Jesus said to Pilate that he came into the world to bear witness to the truth, Pilate answered him with the question, "What has truth got to do with the matter?" Men want to get on, to get rich, to get known, to live easily, to satisfy the lust of the flesh and the lust of the eye and the pride of life; and the claims of justice and truth would make sad havoc with such purposes. Those who have learned from Christ that justice and truth are great necessities of life, necessities in a far higher sense than food and clothing, have often to notice, with great pain and concern, the number of those who do not seem to have any conception of what it is really to do justice and seek after truth. They do not comprehend the objects which God and Christ set before them any more than a blind man comprehends colours. Why, then, blame them? it may be asked. The blame is that they will not come to Christ that they may have sight. To Christians the power and disposition are given to do justice. The spirit is put in them to seek for truth as those who seek for hid treasures, and those who seek with such a zeal and impulse can never seek in vain.—Y.

Vers. 3—6.—*Chastisement thwarted by universal stubbornness.* I. THE FACT THAT GOD'S CHASTISEMENTS ARE THWARTED. The chastisements are evidently indicated as severe, and the reason of the severity is hinted in the [preliminary question. God is looking for truth, looking for it in the midst of oaths broken and despised. He looks for faithfulness in all the ways in which it can be shown. There must be correspondence between promises and performances; there must be stability of character; the character must be such that men will be the same out of sight as in sight, working as ever in the Great Taskmaster's eye. Moreover, God cannot be put off by the most plausible appearance of fidelity; he knows always whether the heart is steadfast in its affection and zeal. And thus seeing all this insincerity among his people, this carelessness about truth, he chastises them to make them feel *their wrong*, attend to *his will*, and alter *their deceiving ways* so as to correspond with it. They are told beforehand what is coming, and the very instrument of chastisement is displayed before them. They had no ground for saying, "Suffering came upon us, and we knew not why it came." We know that Jeremiah's words must have been very pungent and irritating, and the irritating element was just this, that he persistently spoke of conquest, desolation, and exile as lying in the immediate future for his fellow-countrymen. And here Jeremiah, with the prophet's melancholy privilege, sets forth the future as present. The stroke has fallen; the suffering, the loss, the humiliation, are keen; but there is no understanding in the mind, and no sign of repentance and return. Their faces are harder than the rock. If some sculptor could put into a marble face all that outwardly marks the stubborn mind, that would be the expression of Israel now towards Jehovah. No subdued look in the eye; no irrepressible quivering of the lips preliminary to saying, "Father, I have sinned . . . and am no more worthy to be called thy son" (ch. iii. 4).

II. THE REASON WHICH THE PROPHET ADVANCES FOR THIS STUBBORNNESS. Remember what we have said already—and let it be said again, for it is essential to a right understanding of the passage—that the purpose of the chastisement was distinctly set forth beforehand. The people had not to grope in the dark as to the reason of their suffering. There was no room for disputing, if only Jeremiah were accepted as indeed a prophet of Jehovah. And to Jeremiah himself the intention of the chastisement was, of course, plain by the very clearest light. And, since it is natural for us to suspect that what is plain to us should be plain to others, Jeremiah could see only one reason for this distressing want of recipiency. Those who are so stubborn he thinks can be but a part of Israel, the poor and foolish, the degraded, brutalized residuum of the nation. Thus Jeremiah illustrates, by this interposed conjecture of his, a very common and perilous tendency among *thinking* men. We may not be unwilling—indeed, we may only be too eager—to admit the degradation of a large part of mankind, and their stolid indifference to all that is noble, refined, and truly humane. But then, on the other hand, there is an excessive exaltation of the natural man. Genius, intellect, success in research and discovery, such as that of a Newton and a Faraday—these are glorified beyond their due. It is forgotten that while men have natural powers whereby they can *climb* very high, they must come to God in humility and ask for wings of faith if they are to discover the highest kind of truth, the truth to which man must *soar* rather than *climb*. Jeremiah reckons that what he certainly cannot find in some he will assuredly find in others. He will turn away from the ignorant rabble, and go to the men of substance, the men with responsibility, such, doubtless, as the king and the princes, the priests and the prophets. But he goes only to fail, only to discover that the wise men of this world are as little disposed to attend to the preaching of the *prophet* as Paul afterwards discovered them to be to the preaching of the *apostle*.

III. And so we come to THE REAL REASON OF THE STUBBORNNESS. It is something which lies in universal sinful human nature, apart from any special defects or special excellences. The stubbornness may sometimes suddenly vanish where we should expect it to continue, and where we should expect it to vanish it may not only continue but become to all appearance invincible. The heart of unbelief is found in every rank. The experience of Jesus would seem to have been that the poor and the foolish, as Jeremiah would have classified them, were more ready to turn to him than the great. An excellent commentary on the passage we have been considering is to be found in the first and second chapters of Paul's First Epistle to the Corinthians.—Y.

Ver. 10.—*The vineyard spoiled because of the degenerate branches.* I. LOOK AT THE FIGURE WHICH UNDERLIES THIS EXHORTATION. We find in other parts of Scripture passages curiously rich in illustration of the emphatic exhortation here. Turn to Isa. v. 1—7: here is presented to us the picture of a vineyard protected by a fence against marauders and wild beasts, planted with the choicest vine, and tilled in the most complete and careful manner. But when the vineyard, in spite of all care, only yields wild grapes, then the hedge and the wall are taken away and the cultivated land lapses into wilderness. Ps. lxxx. contains a very similar passage, save that it is the language of appeal from a suffering people instead of a warning from a disappointed God. God is described as having cast out the heathen to make room for the vine which he had brought from Egypt. And in the land where he planted it it grew downwards and upwards and outwards, spreading far and wide. "Why then," say the people, "hast thou broken down her hedges, so that all which pass by the way do pluck her? The boar out of the wood doth waste it, and the wild beast of the field doth devour it." Once again, there is a very striking passage in Prov. xxiv. 30, 31. The wise man passes the vineyard of the man void of understanding, and finds it full of thorns and nettles, and *the stone wall thereof broken down.* Hence the vineyard, with its need of a strong wall kept in good repair, comes before us almost as distinctly as if it were a familiar sight.

II. CONSIDER NOW THE EXHORTATION ITSELF. *The wall* round this vineyard of God, even this vineyard which he so plainly set apart and has cared for so much, is to be broken down. We have not far to seek for the reason. The branches of the vine are not Jehovah's. "I had planted thee a noble vine, wholly a right seed: how then art thou turned into the degenerate plant of a strange vine unto me?" (ch. ii. 21). The wall is not yet in such case as that round the vineyard of the man void of understanding. It has not dropped to pieces through sloth. Its fate, it may be said, is even worse, for it has to come down by an act of judgment. Protection is a mockery and reproach when the thing protected fails to reward the care that has been lavished upon it. God breaks down the fence that he may make a clear way for the removing of the branches. The branches, one may say, are fixed in a true vine and draw nourishment from good soil; yet wild, sour, deluding, discreditable grapes are all the result. The branches, therefore, are to go, but only the branches. A full end is not to be made. The trunk, the roots, still stay. For indeed a word has, by-and-by, to be spoken by Jesus, concerning the vine and the branches, and the branches which are to *abide* in the vine that they may bring forth fruit. God will destroy all profitless connection with himself. If men avail themselves of the strength and opportunity which he gives to bring forth fruit, not such as will glorify him, but such as suits the perverted taste of men, then all the branches on which such fruit comes must be unsparingly cut away. And what a thought that fruit which men so much value is after all in God's sight, which gives the true estimation, a sour and worthless thing!—Y.

Ver. 14.—*Those who call the word of Jehovah a lie.* It has been a common folly, in connection with all the revelations which God has made at sundry times and in divers manners, to despise the authority of the messengers. Noah, Moses, David, and many others up to Jesus himself, could tell, along with Jeremiah, the same essential experience of contempt, rejection, and persecution. It is not for God to use those outward pomps and recommendations on which men count so much. A message unwelcome in itself is easily made of no repute when the messenger is devoid of outward state. Outward show, as every age can tell, counts for a great deal. Perhaps the visit of the Queen of Sheba would have been made far less of if she had not been a queen, or had come without the barbaric treasures which she spread forth in such great abundance. Simple lovers of truth, when their station happens to be obscure, are not much remarked. Here then was Jeremiah, asserting that he had come with a message from the Lord of the utmost moment, and he is rejected with the brusque intimation that his message is a lie and he himself an impostor. And this rejection is all the more noticeable because *the words of the prophet must surely have had a strange impressiveness.* None of the prophets could have spoken in the routine fashion of a herald announcing the proclamation which many times, perhaps, he has announced before. They must all, at least in the judgment of a few, have spoken with authority and not as the scribes. And Jeremiah at all events must have stood before the people, having every channel of outward expression filled from the sad experiences and emotions of his own inward life. The sorrows of which he spoke were as sorrows that he saw rising before his mind's eye in all the horrors of their reality. The words, as he says in ch. xx. 9, were often words that he tried to keep back, but that which was as a burning fire shut up in his bones must break out at last. And therefore, when the words did come, they were charged with a force of personal conviction and brotherly entreaty which in itself ought to have been enough to arrest attention. Moreover, sword and famine, future calamities with all their aggravations, were not the only things of which the prophet spoke. He had to deal *with an actual present* as well as a foreshadowed future. The present in which he and his audience lived teemed with idolatry, perjury, fraud, and oppression. These things were not lies. It was no lie to point to the manifest seed that Israel was sowing, and surely there was nothing more really reasonable than that there should be a reaping according to the sowing. At this height of rejection, then, God steps in *to vindicate and honour his faithful servant.* It is a melancholy kind of distinction, but a distinction nevertheless. His words were not only true words, but most terribly near to their fulfilment. It was not that Jeremiah himself was an agent in destroying, but his words became so immediately true, there was such a rapid production and concentration of the agents of destruction, as to make it quite proper to say that these words of the prophet were as consuming fire. But a few years, and many of these despisers found that the alleged lies were only too painfully true. It is not over lapsing centuries that we have to look for the fulfilment of Jeremiah's gloomy prediction. Isaiah long before had sounded the note of warning, and now the peril is close at hand. It was inevitable that Jeremiah should speak with an urgency and excitement absent from the messages of his great predecessor. As the time of chastisement drew nearer, the warnings had to be louder, more disturbing, possibly more continuous. The mariner setting out on his voyage may be warned of some special danger lying in his track; but the adviser, while he may speak very earnestly, will not speak as does the man who, when the helmsman is close upon the danger, shouts to him, with utmost excitement and agitation, at once to change his course. God gave to Jeremiah this melancholy satisfaction, that while he had been, to his heart's deepest sorrow, a messenger of woe, he had yet been approved, on the surest evidence, as a messenger of truth.—Y.

Ver. 22.—*A lesson from the raging sea.* I. WE OBSERVE GOD FIXING LIMITS WITHIN WHICH HIS CREATURES EXERCISE THEIR POWER. Jehovah speaks here of the sea in particular, but just because it happens to be an excellent representative, for the purpose in view, of the rest of his creation. We may notice God's boundaries in many places and at different seasons, and surely it must often strike thoughtful minds, as they walk by the mighty deep, that there is, in the arrangement of sea and land, an exquisite illustration of the unfailing wisdom of God. Here is this vast mass of water, covering the surface of the globe, ever in motion and yet ever keeping its place. The true state of the case is even more wonderful than that which was presented to Jeremiah. To him the earth was a flat expanse, and the beach would have the aspect of an embankment which really kept the water back. We, aided by the discoveries of science, know that the real limiting forces of the sea work in a much more mysterious manner. But, of course, the fundamental truth is the same. There must be a great and loving intelligence at work, keeping the waters within their appointed bounds.

II. OBSERVE THE COMPARISON WHICH IS MADE BETWEEN DISOBEDIENT MAN AND THE SEA IN A STATE OF STORM. The sea easily gets a kind of personality, and the sea in a storm is very like a proud man chafing against the barriers which confine him, and trying to break them down. More than that, when God looks down into human society, underneath the (to us) often calm surface, he must see little else than stormy agitation, one human billow dashing against another, each individual in his self-assertion contributing to make a general disturbance, and a disturbance which apparently will not soon have an end. And yet the sea, with all its fury and roar and threatening, with all the destruction it may work out in its own sphere, is powerless to overwhelm the solid land. In the strength of their confidence, men would build large cities close to the ocean-brink and inhabit them without fear. They will go down and look at the tempest in its utmost fury, sure that they are safe. A few yards make all the difference between the agony of deadly peril and perfect ease of mind. The more furious the storm is, the grander it makes the sight without in any wise diminishing the feeling of safety.

III. HENCE THERE IS INDICATED THE FOLLY OF ALL HUMAN OPPOSITION TO GOD. The storm rises; it may destroy many ships and lives; but in due time the calm returns and the great features of the scene appear the same. The land is still there. And so men may chafe against the commandments and purposes of God, and may go on without intervals of calm, even exceeding the sea in the continuity of their violence.

But what does all the strife avail? The boundaries are fixed. If in that which is natural God has taken so much care in the line between sea and land, is it not certain that he will take equal care in that which is spiritual? God's work continues on the solid land, away from all disturbance of his foes. Nay, more, looking at the figure here from the Christian point of view, we see that even within what seems its own sphere, the raging of the sea can soon be stopped. Let us think of Jesus quelling the waves, and we shall feel that the greatest storms of opposition and persecution are entirely in the hands of God. How long these storms may rage and what they may do entirely depend on the purpose which he wishes them to subserve.—Y.

Vers. 26—29.—*The worst kind of wickedness found among the people of Jehovah.* God's people are well acquainted with the voice of those scorners who speak as if hypocrisy was the invariable accompaniment of a religious profession. They do discover, it must be admitted, far more frequently than they ought to discover, that religious profession is a mere pretence; and thereupon they never forget the few well-established instances which are a ground, in season and out of season, for a sweeping charge of hypocrisy. But such people, unfortunately for themselves, are not readers of the Scriptures; else they would discover that God does not wait for outside malevolent critics to make the most of the hypocrisies to be found amongst his people. God not only sees and laments this peculiarly odious form of wickedness, but is exceedingly plain in his description and terribly severe in his denunciation. In this matter outsiders cannot tell God's people anything they do not know already. Note—

I. THAT WHICH OUGHT TO BE FOUND AMONGST GOD'S PEOPLE. This is just the thing which makes the whole discovery so inexpressibly sad—that this wickedness is found where there should have been found a character diametrically opposite. It is the scene of the wickedness that indescribably aggravates the wickedness itself. That a good man, a really good man, should be found in a den of thieves is impossible. Vain would it be for him to continue there and yet plead his uprightness. A den of thieves does actually give character to every one who willingly inhabits it, and so, passing from the bad to the good, a certain high reputation must attach to every one who openly ranks himself among the people of God. It was not because these Israelites dwelt in a certain territory or were descendants from certain ancestors that they were reckoned the people of God. There was a covenant, the terms of which were to be taught to every generation and diligently observed by it. And this covenant emphatically required that these people should live among themselves an upright, brotherly, loving life. Without this, worship was vain; indeed, without this, worship, in the true sense, was impossible. In the home, union was to be preserved by subordination and purity; and in society, by the safety of life and property to the individual. God's people are "the people of his pasture and the sheep of his hand," and it is manifest that, in the right order of things, a sheep's clothing should cover a sheep and not a wolf.

II. THAT WHICH ACTUALLY IS FOUND. Wicked men are found where none but the devout, the upright, and the gentle ought to be. Further, this wickedness is so marked off by bold and indignant expressions that every one guilty of it may know Jehovah's eye to be upon him. For such a man there lies no way of escape among vague generalities. He cannot get off by alleging, with apparent seriousness, that, while there are undoubtedly deceivers among the people of God, he at all events is not to be numbered amongst them. If a man is behaving himself after the fashion here described, he certainly must know it. With regard to certain actions, the nature of them may come out so openly that it is easy to effect the consequent exclusion and separation of the offender from the people of God. But there yet remain many wickednesses, the worst of wickednesses, which a man may go on committing and yet keep his name written in the human record of those who profess service to God. He may even make his very position a vantage-ground for the laying of his snares and the perfecting of his wiles. He may be able so to conceal his hand and his purpose as to deceive even his victims, who, instead of arguing that because there is great wickedness the doer of it must be a bad man, begin at the other end and say that a maker of long prayers cannot possibly be bad; he may be driven to the infliction of a painful blow, but, that must be reckoned his calamity rather than his fault. Now, the descriptions in this passage make it evident that God sees into all the doings of such men. And at this particular time these men had become very successful, and we must infer very influential. Wherever money is heaped up it makes influence. And even though such oppressors were not numerous, their very position gave them power. But over against them, with all their power, all their wealth, all their pretensions, there is that God who marks every tear and groan and writhing of the oppressed. This passage is but one out of many in which God shows his hatred to all injustice. Some of the so-called friends of humanity, who are never tired of asserting their friendship and pressing their claims, make one of their great claims to be in this, that they oppose all acknowledgment of God. Depend upon it, God is the true Friend of humanity; he first, and afterwards are those whom he inspires with his own indignation against wrong, and endows with the strength, patience, resolution, and all Divine resources needed to destroy it. What wonder is it that God should speak of vengeance against such a nation as permits and extenuates the monstrous evils denounced in this passage?—Y.

Vers. 30, 31.—*Mutual helpers in wrong-doing.* I. THE TEMPTATIONS HERE SET FORTH. Three classes are mentioned—the prophet, the priest, and the people in general. Each class plays only too well its iniquitous and deplorable part, just because of the strong assistance which it gains from the attitude of the others. Each class acts as tempter in its turn, and that none the less effectually because it may do it unconsciously. Each one also tempts because he is tempted, and one hardly knows where the malign influence begins save by remembering the words of James, "Every man is tempted when he is drawn away of his own lust and enticed." The prophet, however, is here put first, and this can hardly be without reason. On him there did indeed lie a peculiar burden of responsibility. The prophets here mentioned, we may take it, were not false prophets, although they spoke falsely. The false prophet was he who pretended to be a prophet, although God never sent him; and of such there were doubtless some in the land at this very time. But the horrible thing here was that men whom God had set apart to speak the truth used the prophetic office to tell convenient lies, such as seemed to afford security and profit. Jonah, in his cowardice fleeing from duty, is an illustration of what many other prophets must have done, only they went further and never came back to truth and peace. We know how men in all ages have sold the heritage of faculty which God has given them to the service of lying and darkness. Instead of fighting where their hearts ought to have been, among the soldiers for truth and liberty, they have become mercenaries under despots. These prophets on whom Jehovah had put his hand had allowed themselves to be filled with fear and greed and schemes for worldly success, instead of with the Spirit of Jehovah. They went not with what was true, but with what was acceptable. How much higher the faithful prophets should stand in our esteem when we consider the temptations they resisted, the pains they suffered, the pious heroism which marked their sometimes long career! Imagine what the consequences would have been if the apostles had altered and trimmed the gospel. Then there were *the priests.* "The priests bear rule by their means." The allusion may be to the hands of the prophets, but perhaps a better meaning is to take it that the prophet sinned in *his* way, and the priest again in *his* way. The prophet's great instrument of service was his *mouth*, and with this he *prophesied falsely*. The priest's great instrument of service was *his hand*, and this he used to get *superstitious deference to his privileges*, instead of for the purpose of presenting, with his whole heart, offering and atonement for the people. In addition to this, there may have been, and very likely was, a corrupt understanding between priest and prophet. Then both priest and prophet had in their eyes *the great* mass of the people. God himself looked down on this unfaithfulness of the great officials with a warmth of indignation that would soon burst into flame, but the people regarded it all with a very different feeling. They "loved to have it so." When a true prophet came, speaking truth, his message was so hateful and humiliating that they denied his office. "Surely the man who speaks such things cannot be a prophet; a madman he may be, or a fanatic, or a disloyal man whose Israelite form hides a foreign heart; anything you like, but *not a prophet*." But when the prophet comes speaking lies, looking into the faces of his audience for all that he has to put into their ears, then his office will be approved. And so with the priest. If he makes it clear that burnt offerings and all sacrifices are nothing without repentance and reform, he will be thought very little of. He must let the people sin and sin as much as they like. They will cram the temple area with multitudes of flocks and herds to take the effect of sin away, if only they may go on sinning. What God had given to teach the dreadful malignity of sin, these priests had turned into an agency for making it seem a mere trifle.

II. THERE WAS ALSO AN OPPORTUNITY OF REBUKE AND REMONSTRANCE. The people were not obliged to accept these priests and prophets on their own *ipse dixit*. It was not because a man came forth with his "Thus saith the Lord" that he was to be followed. Anybody can say, "Thus saith the Lord." The devil attempted persuasions of this sort when he came to Jesus in the wilderness. There must be a strict searching into what is said. One purpose for which God used prophets and priests was as a test of those whom they had to do with. God wishes to know the extent of our regard for the truth, and he has not left us helpless in discovering that truth with the almost certainty. There is always something to appeal to. Every true prophet with his "Thus saith the Lord" had behind him a Law and testimony, already written and indisputably valid, to which he could point. Each prophet as he came along was more firmly tied to the truth, because he had behind him so many who had already spoken, and whom he must not contradict. So the apostles could be checked in speaking lies or inventions, because an appeal was possible to what Jesus had said in the flesh. There were twelve men with one message, and only as long as the message was one were people bound to receive it. And happily, if a difference had arisen, there was always the means of testing which speaker was right. "No man speaking by the Spirit of God calleth Jesus accursed." As things stand to-day, it is perfectly clear that we can test every one professing to be a messenger of Divine truth; we can test him effectually. We are not left unprovided amid modern imposture, knavery, and delusion.—Y.

Ver. 1.—*True manhood*. Without any introduction, let us plunge at once into our subject, which is *True manhood*. It opens broadly before us in the suggestions which both this verse and the chapter from which it is taken contain. And first of all we will note—

I. THE DIVINE DEFINITION AND DESCRIPTION OF IT. It consists in executing judgment and seeking the truth. The Lord asks importunately that "*a man*" may be found, and then he defines and describes what he means by "a man," in the words, "one that executeth judgment, that seeketh the truth." Such is his description of true manhood. So, then, the true man is he to whom truth—that which is right, that which is in accordance with the will of God—is the all-important thing. The habit of his mind, the purpose of his life, is to discover this truth—to know what is right. And when what professes to be truth comes before him, he weighs it in the balance of conscience, tests how it tallies with the mind and will of God; and according to its agreement thereto he approves or disapproves, he gives his judgment. And then, when his judgment is formed, his mind made up, as we say, he does not linger in the outer courts of mere approbation, but he presses on into the very sanctuary, the holy of holies, of corresponding action—he "*executeth* judgment." Having sought, seen, approved the right, he does it; not once now and then, but habitually. Such is the *man* after God's own heart, such the Divine description of what manhood really is. And now observe: 1. How *complete* a definition this is! For what form of goodness or excellence is there that this does not include? Whatever is right for a man to do or be comes under this description. Our well-known word, "virtue," will help us here; for what is virtue but simply that which becomes, which properly belongs to the idea of, the *vir*, the grand old Roman name for man regarded in his higher nature, as contrasted with the lower idea of man in regard to those qualities which he possesses in common with the brutes around him? Man spoken of as merely the human creature was designated by another word; but man as intelligent and moral, man in his nobler being, they designated by that word *vir*, from which our word "virtue" comes. Therefore "this word 'virtue' corresponds as closely as possible with our word 'manliness.' They are equivalent terms. Then, if we know what virtue is, we know what true manhood is. It includes all moral excellence whatsoever. It is the fruit, the certain fruit, of a man's seeking the truth, and then, when he has found it and conscience tells him that he has found it, of his straightway practically putting it into action, embodying it in word and deed. It is the product of the three highest faculties God has given to man—intellect, conscience, will. It there-fore must embrace all that belongs and is becoming to the *vir*, the man, and must exclude all that is contrary thereto." 2. And how *catholic* a description it is! In it "there is neither Greek nor Jew, circumcision nor uncircumcision, barbarian, Scythian, male nor female, bond nor free ; " there is neither—that is, neither exclusively—Buddhist, Mahommedan, Christian, Jew ; neither Romanist, Eastern, Anglican, Lutheran, Pres-byterian, Congregationalist, nor any other sect nor creed whatsoever. For " God is no respecter of persons," but, as St. Peter said to Cornelius, " In every nation he that feareth God and worketh righteousness is accepted of him." Thus catholic, thus all-embracing, is this Divine description of a true man. God's chosen ones consist of all the good. 3. But how *condemnatory* of the world's standards! Before what tinsel imitations of the true manhood does the world bow down! How many glorify physical strength—the Samsonian type of man! And indeed the possession of a physical frame capable of much toil, much endurance, that shrinks not from hardships, and laughs at bold and daring enterprises before which other men quail ; a body well organized, its varied functions all working powerfully and smoothly like the several parts of a perfectly adjusted machine ;—that *is* a great gift of God. But to make a man's physical qualities the measure of his manhood, that cannot be worthily thought of for one moment. And so, too, if we take *intellectual* distinction—that, though far nobler than the physical, will fall before the high claim of the Divine ideal. And as for *secular* distinction—that greatness which consists in what a man has, wealth, rank, power, rather than what he is,—that claim will not stand for one moment. The world may, does, fall down before these things, and before the last it absolutely grovels ; but in the high courts of God's judgment they go for nothing at all. And at that bar not a little that has the world's free licence as consistent with manhood is frowned upon and utterly condemned. No ; right, truth, virtue, all that is in harmony with God's will,—this is what the man after God's mind seeks, finds, and habitually does. 4. And how *commendatory* to the conscience is this Divine definition of manhood! Put it before any thoughtful man, and at once he confesses it worthy of God to set forth and blessed for man to seek after. Here the excellent of the earth in all ages and in all lands have found a common meeting-place, and, when unbiassed conscience has spoken, have come to a cordial embrace. 5. But how *Christ-compelling* is this Divine description of true manhood! For he who sets himself to embody it, and really enters on the glorious endeavour, will speedily find that he wants a model, a motive, and a might which assuredly he cannot find in the world around him. A *model ;* for mere abstract descriptions help but little. What can the most brilliant word-painting do to enable you to realize what a lovely landscape is like ? It can do something, but not very much. But let the gifted artist draw the scene, let him in beautiful picture portray it, and how much more vividly we realize it then! The mechanician must have his model to work from if he is to do successful work. And so, would we realize the description God has given us of a true man, we also must have our model. But there is only One who is flawless and altogether perfect—the Lord Jesus Christ. Patriarchs, prophets, psalmists, apostles, saints, even the most worthy, are none of them perfect ; for we have to modify here, correct there, and absolutely reject elsewhere. It is, therefore, to the life of our blessed Lord and Master that this Divine description of manhood forces me would I find the one example I may safely, always, and everywhere copy. But I want a *motive* also ; for when I begin my great endeavour I find it no holiday task. It brings no worldly gain, it wins no human applause. My natural bent and bias are utterly against it. Ease and comfort are ever crying, " Spare thy-self." Companions on the road are few, and not all of them to my liking, and the way is narrow and rough and steep. What, then, can alone spur me on and constrain me by a compulsion I cannot resist ? What but a sense of Christ's great love, and the supreme solicitude to " be accepted of him," which flows therefrom ? There is abso-lutely no other motive which will serve for the *whole* way. Some will take me a part of the way, and others a further part, but all will fail long ere the true end is reached. Therefore am I again driven to Christ, that, as he is my Model, so he may be my Motive too. But he must also be my *Might*. The power to endure, the strength to toil, the daily grace for daily need,—whence can it come but from him who has said, "Because I live, ye shall live also?" True manhood, real virtue, is therefore an impossible thing apart from Christ. More or less stunted and distorted forms of it there may be, but the Divine ideal, never. May he help us to remember this. Thus, then, complete, catholic, condemnatory of the world's standards, commendatory to the conscience, compelling resort to Christ, is this Divine manhood of which our text tells. But note—

II. THE DIVINE DISAPPOINTMENT AND DISMAY AT NOT FINDING IT WHERE IT MAY SO JUSTLY HAVE BEEN EXPECTED. Observe the words of our text, how they challenge the most thorough search everywhere, implying that the Lord himself had made such search—he whose eyes (ver. 3) "are upon the truth," who is keen-visioned to discover his own in the densest crowd or in the most obscure abode. But now he challenges any to make a like search. Let them run to and fro in the by-streets, in the broad ways, in market-places, in all parts where men congregate; let them in every such place see, know, seek, if they can find even one true man. And the challenge is made not in scorn nor in anger, but in disappointment and dismay. For where, if not amongst God's own professed people, and in the centre of their worship, Jerusalem; where, if not there, could such as God sought be found? But not even there were they; there were "none righteous; no, not one." But what was found this whole chapter plainly declares. There was horrible wickedness—wickedness which only such appalling images as the seventh and eighth verses of this chapter could fitly describe. And this not amongst the ignorant poor only, but amongst the great, the well instructed also (vers. 4, 5). And where there was a form of religion the power was wanting, as the second verse tells. They might use devout words, but the Lord, whose eyes were on the truth (ver. 3), knew how hollow that profession was. So that there was not one man such as God desired. And, though willing to spare, God was forced to punish (ver. 9). This and much more of a like sort prevails all through the chapter. But the contemplation of it fills the Divine mind with disappointment and dismay. It is deep distress to him that he cannot find what he so much desires to find. Are we quite sure that the like question might not be asked in our day? Is the Divine ideal of manhood so constantly realized? Is there not very much to make a devout heart fear lest a like search might lead to a too much like result? Let us remember what it is God looks for in us. Not that which the world thinks so much of, but this manhood; and he mourns when he finds it not. And let it be our prayer that more and more *we* may be men according to his mind. Note next—

III. THE DIVINE DEMONSTRATION OF THE DELIGHT AND JOY HE HAS IN IT. He says if there be but one such man, he will spare Jerusalem for his sake. Such is the meaning of the last clause of this verse. What higher proof (save one which we will note anon) could he give of his estimate of this manhood? He gave large proof when he told Abraham that if there were ten righteous in Sodom he would spare the city for their sakes. And he is continually doing the like of what he here said he would do. He is continually blessing the bad for the sake of the good. "Ye are the salt of the earth," said our Lord to his disciples, implying thereby that, but for his people, the world would go to corruption. "For the elect's sake those days shall be shortened"— the days, he meant, of Jerusalem's destruction, which were then, as in Jeremiah's time, swiftly drawing on. And how often we read of bad and wicked descendants and successors on the throne of David, who for his sake were dealt with far other than they deserved! And to-day, how many godless children of pious parents are for like reason dealt with in like manner! The Church might well, did she choose, challenge the world to say where it would be without the Church. The impious sneer at, persecute, and despise the godly; but were it not for those they so shamefully use, theirs would be a short shrift and a quick going down into hell. And let all who are living godly in Christ Jesus be cheered by knowing that, though persecuted by the world, they are yet most precious in the Lord's sight. Now finally note—

IV. THE SUPREME DEMONSTRATION GOD HAS GIVEN OF HIS DELIGHT AND JOY IN IT. We turn to the gospel for this, and it enables us to reply to the Divine challenge to "find a man;" for we have found *him* "of whom Moses and the prophets did write"—the man Christ Jesus. He has answered to the Divine description, and for his sake not a city alone, but a world, is to be pardoned. "For he is the Propitiation for our sins, and not for ours only, but," etc. And our pardon will be not as Sodom's or Jerusalem's would have been—leaving the people still the slaves of sin; but the beginning of a new life, in which we shall grow more and more into the fulness of the stature of the perfect man, the Divine ideal embodied in Christ Jesus. But such is the Divine delight in this Man that, for his sake, he pardons *whosoever* believeth on him. God hath laid help for us "on One who is mighty" to save. Let us, then, go and put in our claim, confessing our deep need of pardon, but pleading God's own promise, that for the sake of this Man—his own "beloved Son in whom he is well pleased"—he should pardon us. And the answer will come back, "Go in peace; be of good cheer: thy sins be forgiven thee."—C.

Ver. 3.—*An unfailing appeal.* "O Lord, are not thine eyes upon the truth?" Text uttered in protest against the pretence and hypocrisy everywhere prevailing in the prophet's day. But the appeal is vindicated whatever we understand by "the truth." Consider it in regard—

I. To THE TRUTH AS SPOKEN BY GOD, IN HIS WORKS AND IN HIS WORD. See this in the constancy and invariability of the order of nature. The reign of law is because "the eyes of the Lord are ever," etc. See it in the fulfilment of ancient prophecies, especially those which concern our Lord Jesus Christ; and we are to believe it in regard to those many promises of God, the fulfilment of which yet waits.

II. To THE TRUTH WRITTEN—to try and test thereby all our teachings and beliefs. See our Lord, in the temptation, how *his* eyes were ever on the truth. Hence his "It is written" foiled the tempter again and again. "To the Law and to the testimony," etc. The Bereans—and their example is held up as noble—searched the Scriptures daily, to see if the teachings they heard "were so;" so, that is, as the apostles affirmed.

III. To THE TRUTH IMPLANTED—to encourage and avenge it. His grace implants truth in the character, and leads to its being acted out in the life. Now, the eyes of the Lord are ever upon such men. As he *hates* the hypocrites, so he loves the sincere, the "Israelites indeed, in whom there is no guile." His eyes rest on them ever with delight. His Spirit cheers and encourages them amid all outward distress and persecution. His hand will verily avenge them as "his own elect," in his own good time.

IV. To THE TRUTH INCARNATE—to behold and bless all those who are in him. "I am the Truth," said the Lord Jesus. How we love to attract the attention and to enjoy the smile of recognition and approval on the part of those who are greater than ourselves in this world! Would we come under the notice and smile of the Lord God, we must come to him upon whom his eyes are ever resting with delight, even to his well-beloved Son, the Truth incarnate. Until we are "in him" we are in the cold shade, and without hope or help. In him the eyes of the Lord are on us as they are on him, and "he makes his face to shine upon us."—C.

Ver. 3.—*The sorrow of sorrows.* "Thou hast stricken them, but they have not grieved," etc.

I. To BE STRICKEN OF GOD AND AFFLICTED IS IN ITSELF VERY PAINFUL TO CONTEMPLATE. When such sorrow comes it is: 1. To teach the servant of God how to sympathize with and succour other troubled ones. 2. To loosen them from the clinging bands of this world. 3. Because such sorrow is the inevitable pain and distress attendant upon that glorious contest for "the prize of our high calling," for which contest our Father, out of love to us and because of his joy in us, and knowing that we shall win it, has entered us. Still, notwithstanding these facts and others like them, the afflictions of the righteous are painful indeed.

II. BUT SORROW IS YET MORE SORROWFUL WHEN IT IS SELF-CAUSED. Such was the sorrow of many of those whose tears and lamentations we read of in Scripture—David, Peter, Esau. "It was my own fault:" this is the reflection which calls into dread life and activity "the worm that dieth not." But still, when, as with the contrite hearts, Manasseh, David, Peter, etc., of whom Scripture tells, their sorrow is of a godly sort, then, sad as it is, its result makes it blessed.

III. BUT THERE IS A SORROW OF SORROWS, AND IT IS TOLD OF HERE. It is when, as this verse tells, God sends his corrections and sore afflictions upon men, and yet they are none the better for them, but even worse. Pharaoh is the great illustration of this deepest sorrow. It is not all who can say, "Before I was afflicted I went astray: but now have I kept thy Word." But of too many that word is true which says, "Though thou shouldest bray a fool in a mortar . . . yet will not his foolishness depart from him" (cf. Rev. xvi. 10; Acts xxvi. 14). 1. *But what is the cause of these failures on the part of God's chastisements?* They are such as these: (1) Sentence against an evil work is not executed *speedily.* (2) The fearful force of the desire after the evil object overwhelms and bears down all thought of the punishment that must follow. (3) The assigning of the affliction that comes to other causes than the true one. To this day the Jews do not see that their rejection of the Lord Jesus was the reason of God's rejection of them, nor that it is *his* blood which is upon them and their children. 2. But without question *such sorrows are the most lamentable of all;* for: (1) they reveal the virulence, the deep-seated character, and the dread hold which sin has gained; (2) they necessitate and foretell yet more severe judgments from God; (3) they cast most sad doubt on the question whether such persons will ever be saved at all.

CONCLUSION. Is sorrow resting upon us? Then: 1. Rest not until you have found out its cause. "Show me wherefore thou contendest with me" should be our appeal. 2. Let the possibility that your sorrows may leave you unblessed, that God's purpose and intent may be lost upon you, send you to the throne of grace with importunate prayer that so it may not be with you.—C.

Vers. 3—5.—*The rich and the poor meet together.* They do so—
I. IN MOST MOURNFUL WAYS. 1. *In their common exposure to sorrow and death.* 2. *In their yet more mournful subjection to the bondage of moral evil,* both alike leagued together in rebellion against God (cf. text). From which learn: (1) No circumstances alone will shut out sin. (2) If one condition of life has its moral disadvantages, so has another. (3) That this does not affirm that all are on one level in this respect. They are not so; they who have knowledge and have been taught God's truth may and will justly be expected to compare favourably in conduct and character with those not so privileged. (4) That the terribleness of the might of sin is seen in the fact that it leaps over the fences and safeguards of happy circumstances and abundant knowledge, as easily as it finds entrance where there are no such fences at all. But the mournfulness of this meeting of the rich and poor leads us to look out for and rejoice in other and more happy ones. And there are such. Note, therefore—
II. THE BLESSED MEETINGS OF THE RICH AND THE POOR. 1. *In their common possession of a moral and spiritual nature.* Those great capacities whereby " a man is so much better than a sheep" are the property of rich and poor alike—to love and be loved; to search out knowledge, to worship, trust, and delight in God. Man is God's jewel, whether it be set in all fit and beautiful surroundings or whether by some malign cause it have fallen into the mud. By its nature, not its surroundings, are we to judge of it. 2. *In Christ.* "He was rich, . . . he for our sakes became poor"—thus for ever uniting the two together. He was, whilst on earth, at the same time both rich and poor, having at his command more than the vastest resources of the rich, and yet day by day sharing the lot of the poor. He was the Son of man, the Head and Representative of all men—of humanity at large. 3. *At the cross.* The common malady craves and finds the common medicine. The sorrows of the contrite heart are those of no class at all, but are the experience of rich and poor alike; and the cross alone can soothe them, and thither therefore they alike come. These all are clothed in the robe made white in the blood of the Lamb. 4. *In the everlasting kingdom of our God.* There the barriers of caste and class, which here seem so fixed that they can never be moved, will be broken down, and character alone will determine whether we shall stand high up or low down on the steps of the eternal throne. The love of God in Christ will be the great uniting bond, and, as that rules and governs us, so will our companionship and our condition be ordered. There the rich shall be rid of the many hindrances of their lot which make it so "hard for a rich man to enter into the kingdom of God;" and there the poor shall have said farewell for ever to all the privation and painful toil of earth. The tears of all shall flow no more. *Then let us learn:* (1) To

cherish sympathy with all our brethren. The poor with the rich, and they with the poor. It is equally difficult but equally obligatory on each. (2) To be eager in telling to the poor of this gospel of the meeting of the rich and the poor. (3) To come to Christ and to his cross, and to abide there, that the Spirit of him who was the Friend and Saviour of all may dwell in us more and more.—C.

Ver. 4.—*The moral disadvantages of the poor.* Jeremiah recognizes and refers to these disadvantages as a well-known fact, and he tells how he expected to find in them an explanation of the deplorable wickedness with which Jerusalem was filled. "Therefore I said, Surely these are poor," etc. We note—

I. THAT THESE ARE THE REAL EVILS OF THE LOT OF THE POOR. At once all manner of other distresses which attend poverty arise to our minds, and therefore we would observe: 1. *That we do not deny that their physical and social disadvantages are also evils.* To be ill fed, ill housed, ill clothed, as so many of the poor are,—who can make light of a lot like theirs? Therefore: 2. *Still less do we deny our duty to relieve their physical evils to the utmost of our power.* 3. *But we do deny that these are their chief evils.* For: (1) Many of these are more than counterbalanced by what is so commonly found amongst the rich. Dr. Channing says, "When I compare together different classes as existing at this moment in the civilized world, I cannot think the difference between the rich and the poor in regard to mere physical suffering so great as is sometimes imagined. That some of the indigent among us die of scanty food is undoubtedly true, but vastly more in this community die from eating too much than from eating too little, vastly more from excess than starvation. So as to clothing: many shiver from want of defences against the cold; but there is vastly more suffering among the rich from absurd and criminal modes of dress, which fashion has sanctioned, than among the poor from deficiency of raiment. Our daughters are oftener brought to their grave by their rich attire than our beggars by their nakedness. So the poor are often overworked; but they suffer less than many among the rich, who have no work to do, no interesting object to fill up life, to satisfy the infinite cravings of man for action. According to our present modes of education, how many of our daughters are victims of *ennui*—a misery unknown to the poor, and more intolerable than the weariness of excessive toil! The idle young man, spending the day in exhibiting his person in the street, ought not to excite the envy of the overtasked poor; and this cumberer of the ground is found exclusively among the rich." (2) And their intellectual disadvantages are nearly as great an evil as those that belong to their outward lot. "Knowledge is power," but to be without knowledge is to lack the power to lighten, to elevate, to refine, to cheer, and in ways manifold to ameliorate our lot in life. Therefore to lack knowledge and education deserves to be looked upon with even more compassion than the lack of physical comforts. But still, the chief evil of poverty is its moral disadvantage. Now—

II. THESE MORAL DISADVANTAGES OF THE POOR ARE SUCH AS ARISE FROM: 1. *The difficulty of maintaining self-respect.* All the world seems agreed to regard the poor as the "lower orders," and to confine the term "respectable" to those who have enough and to spare. And when poverty necessitates the receiving, and yet more the asking, of charity, how hard it is then to maintain that erect moral bearing, that spirit of independence, which is so essential to the formation of all true, worthy moral character! 2. *The almost impossibility of mental culture.* How can the man who has to continue at prolonged and laborious bodily toil from morn to night, day after day all his life long, and only then can earn scarce sufficient to provide for his actual bodily necessities, be expected to be other than rough, rude, illiterate, and contented to be so? What mockery it seems to talk of mental cultivation to a man like that! But shut off from such cultivation, how utterly is the door closed upon him which leads to so much that would cheer and brighten his whole life, and would lift him up in the scale of moral being! 3. *The risk to all moral delicacy and refinement which their crowded and wretched habitations involve.* If men are obliged to herd like cattle, only less comfortably than they, how can "a man be better than a sheep" in such case? 4. *The temptation to envy and sullen discontent at their beholding what seems to them the so much brighter lot of the well-to-do.* The patience of the poor beneath the awful injustices and hardships which arise from the unequal distribution of wealth is a marvel. Especially, too, when they have daily to endure the supercilious and half-scornful treatment which the possesssion of wealth almost invariably begets towards those who have it not. 5. *The hard struggle which faith in God and his goodness cannot but have amid the hardships of poverty.* It is true that men would be far happier if they were better men, but it is also true that vast numbers of men would be better if they were only happier. When our children are happy they are good; it is unhappiness makes them cross and wrong. There is no more heartbreaking fact to a thoughtful and compassionate mind than this, that the blessing of faith in God and the love of God, which the poor most of all need, is for them the hardest of all to win and keep. 6. *The dread temptation to sensual indulgence which the hardships of their lot expose them to.* Can we wonder that these men rush to the gin-shop, the tavern, and there in strong drink forget for a while the miseries of their common life? It is a piteous fact that it is the most wretched of the poor who drink most desperately. (Let the reader turn to Dr. Channing's sermon on ' Ministry for the Poor,' to see many of these points worked out.) Such are the real evils of the lot of the poor, beside which their outward hardships are small in comparison.

III. FROM ALL THIS WE LEARN WHY WE SHOULD COMPASSIONATE THEIR LOT, AND WHAT IN IT WE SHOULD CHIEFLY ENDEAVOUR TO RELIEVE. When their moral disadvantages move our compassion, as they should and as they did our Lord's, we shall strive most of all to counteract and remove them. How shall we do this? We reply, *After the manner of our Lord.* Chiefly by ministering to their souls. He went about everywhere *preaching and teaching.* The very greatest kindness that can be done to a poor man is to bring him to Christ, to get him by God's grace thoroughly converted. That will lift him up and bless him every way. It will not despise secondary means. Our Lord fed the poor, healed them, ministered to their temporal relief frequently. But he did not do this indiscriminately. They were by no means his chief works. That chief work was a ministry to their souls. And so those who copy his example will not despise secondary means—charity, wise sanitary laws, education. But all these will be put in the second place, not in point of time and attention, but in esteem and worth. They will be counted only as *aids* to what is far better than themselves. It may be that the Church has not availed herself of these aids as she should, but has left them to the care of the State more than she should. Still, it is ever those who are most intent on the moral well-being of the poor who are found to the front in all schemes for their physical and social well-being. So that the excellence of our Lord's method is that, whilst it aims at the highest good, it more than any other seeks to promote and indeed secures as a help to that highest, the lower and temporal good of those to whom it ministers. *And it has a rich reward.* "Blessed are ye poor," said our Lord, "rich in faith and heirs," etc. Not a few of the greatest saints, the martyrs, the heroes of the faith, have been drawn from the ranks of the poor. The grace of the Lord Jesus Christ has come to them, and straightway they have been as it were transformed. They have risen up above the low levels of their old life—so mean, sordid, foul, godless oftentimes—and have come to be like the Lord himself. And to-day, how perpetually may we see amid the godly poor all the disadvantages of their lot which we have enumerated above, completely overcome! They reverence conscience; they envy not the rich; they cultivate and rejoice in the purest and tenderest home affections; though ignorant of most of human learning, they have the fear of God and the knowledge of his Word, and so are wise with a wisdom before which mere human wisdom dwindles into insignificance. They keep themselves from all vice, they love and trust God with a simplicity of utter trust and calm confidence, beautiful and blessed even to contemplate—how much more to possess! "Blessed are ye poor!" Thus, then, after the manner of our Lord, would we strive to meet and overcome the moral disadvantages of the poor.—C.

Ver. 7.—*How men curse their blessings.* "When I had fed them to the full," etc.
I. GOD DOES THIS AT TIMES. Cf. Gen. III. 17, "Cursed is the ground for thy sake," etc.; Hag. i. 11, etc. And whenever he makes our good and pleasant things the means of our punishment. Hezekiah's riches and prosperity were the lure which drew upon him the oppressing Assyrians. And so the body which, when possessed of all its faculties and in health, ministers so much good to man, God, in judgment upon the

man's sin, may for the sake of the sinful soul cause that disease, pain, impotence, may curse it. And the mind also—that may become a den of malignant, impure, profane thoughts.

II. BUT MEN DO THIS FAR MORE FREQUENTLY. The noblest physical gifts may be shattered, wrecked, by sins against the body. The mind—capable of such high service and a channel of such vast blessing—men may, do, pollute, corrupt, and pervert and so curse their blessings. The moral nature—this a great gift of God, the power to judge, choose, resolve; but see how soon man cursed that and turned his blessing into a curse. The gifts of providence are also abused in the same way (cf. text). The home. Oh, what joy comes to men through the blessings that were designed to be for ever associated with that word! But how often men, by self-indulgence, neglect, evil example, utter failure in parental duty, turn the blessing of home into a curse! And even the gospel of Christ itself—God's unspeakable gift—men may make the knowledge of it to be "a savour of death unto death" for themselves. "This Child is set for the *fall* of many in Israel," said Simeon of our Lord.

III. BUT IT IS A CRIME WHICH GOD CANNOT AWAY WITH. "How shall I pardon thee for this?" etc. "Shall I not visit," etc.? (ver. 9). Cf. parable of fruitless fig tree— "Cut it down," etc.; the talents—"Take from him the talent," etc. And the human conscience everywhere assents to this judgment of God. We judge in like manner ourselves. We feel that such are without excuse. Let us, then, consider our blessings, and ask ourselves, "What are we doing with them? how are we using them?" Let it be our daily prayer and endeavour that we fall not into this great sin.

IV. GOD'S WAY IS TO TURN OUR CURSES INTO BLESSINGS. (Cf. Neh. xiii. 2.) 1. *He has done so even with sin.* What curse could be greater? Yet, by the redemption there is in Christ, even that is so made subject that now

> "We may rise on stepping-stones
> Of our dead selves to higher things."

2. *And he has done so with sorrow.* Grief had been for ages going about the world, a sad-robed, sombre, and ever-tearful guest in whatever house she took up her temporary abode: and there was no house she did not visit. But since the Lord Jesus became the "Man of sorrows, and acquainted with grief," she, in virtue of that acquaintance, has changed her very nature, and the curse is turned into a blessing. She ministers help to the soul, in releasing it from the bonds of this evil world and in uplifting it towards its true Father and home in heaven. 3. *And so with death.* Its sting is taken away. To them who are in Christ he is rather a friend than a foe, for he it is who opens the door of our prison-house and lets the soul go free and rise to that place—

> "Where loyal hearts and true
> Stand ever in the light,
> All rapture through and through,
> In God's most holy sight."

C.

Ver. 10.—*Battlements not the Lord's.* Jeremiah is telling of the defences of Judah and Jerusalem. In the approaching invasion they should fall and prove utterly worthless; for, by reason of the people's sin, that blessing of the Lord which had made their battlements impregnable hitherto was withdrawn, and so, the people being no longer the Lord's, their defences were not either, and so were no defences at all. But often those who are not under the Divine displeasure—nations, Churches, individuals— are found relying on defences that are not Divine, thinking to find shelter and safety within battlements that are not the Lord's; and when such is the case the Lord would ever have such battlements taken away. The course of his providence not seldom makes plain his displeasure in these things; for they get torn down and destroyed hopelessly if they who trust in them are not wise in time, and themselves take them away. There are many references in Scripture to such battlements. They are spoken of either as "walls daubed with untempered mortar," or as "broken cisterns which hold no water," or, more plainly, as "refuges of lies," or as "a house built upon the sand," or as the building upon the foundation of "wood, hay, stubble." Such are some of the parallels to the truth taught in the text. But take some illustrations of this erecting of and trusting in battlements *not* the Lord's.

I. IT HAS BEEN SEEN IN THE DEFENCE OF THE CHURCH OF CHRIST. Nothing in the world is so precious, so essential to the world, as the Church of Christ, and he has promised to preserve it unto the end. But men have often tried to plant, maintain, and spread it in anything but Divine ways; *e.g.* when: 1. *They have relied on the secular arm.* They have done so, and with what consequences let the present state of Christendom tell. When will men trust the glorious inherent power of the faith of Christ, and throw to the winds those carnal weapons which she wields only to her own wounding? When will she hear the voice of God saying, concerning such battlements, "Take them away; they are not the Lord's"? 2. *Organization* is another of these very questionable defences. That it has its use, and is capable of much and valued service, he would be a fool who should deny. But the peril is lest the artificial and merely human supports which organization supplies should be allowed to serve instead of that Divine *life* which alone is the true defence of any Church. Church arrangements which necessitate that when that life is wanting everything shall collapse about such a Church, that it shall cease to be and not present the mere *simulacrum* of what it is not,—it is a question if this be not a better order than one which, by means of its elaborate organization, keeps up the show of Church life when the reality is not there. 3. And the same may be said of *all those adventitious aids to the Church of Christ upon which men are apt so much to rely.* Wealth, social position, learning, eloquence, numbers, gifts, and other such advantages,—let a Church place her trust in any of these, and the command of the text will go forth at once. But the true defence of a Church is the life that is in her, the manifest godliness of her members; *that* is a battlement which is the Lord's, and which none can take away.

II. IT HAS BEEN SEEN IN THE DEFENCE OF THE FAITH OF THE CHURCH. The faith of the Church is, without doubt, most precious; and it is our duty to contend earnestly for it. But men have sought to guard and defend it in wrong ways. 1. *Persecution* has been tried. 2. *Demanding subscription* to fixed creeds. There may be and are good reasons for demanding such subscription, but it cannot be said that such subscription has kept the faith one and entire in all the members of the Church. Probably there is more unity of belief in those Churches which demand no such subscription than in those who do. 3. *Relying mostly on the intellectual defences of the faith.* There are such, many, varied, cogent, clear, invaluable, but they may be all read and mastered, and the citadel of the heart be not won. But the true battlement of the faith is in the fact that it commends itself to every man's conscience in the sight of God. Let conscience be awakened and then the faith presented, and the fitness of the faith to the needs and teachings of conscience are visible at once.

III. IT IS CONTINUALLY SEEN IN MEN'S CONDUCT IN REGARD TO THEIR OWN PERSONAL SALVATION. What else is: 1. *Trust in sacraments?* They are, without doubt, means of grace to the believer in Christ—the experience of myriads of saints attests that; but he who looks to them as a *viaticum* that will open a way to heaven for the vilest, surely that is a refuge of lies. 2. *Reliance on human priests?* This reliance is by no means confined to the Church of Rome. Deep seated in men's mind is the idea that ministers of religion can really help the soul in its great needs. Much of sending for ministers in cases where death is anticipated is based on this false belief. 3. *Trust in such poor righteousness* as we can offer to God; what can it do? 4. *Resting on an imagined leniency* in God, which will prevent his carrying out the threatenings of his holy Law as he has said he would? How many soothe and still all disquiet of conscience by such false confidence as this!—a confidence which the facts of life, apart from the Word of God, utterly shatter and show to be false. But the true defence of the soul is Christ; *that* battlement is the Lord's, yea, is the Lord himself, and he will keep that which is committed to him even unto the great day.—C.

Ver. 24.—*The silken fetter.* In ver. 22 the prophet has spoken of the soft, unstable sand holding in and beating back the mighty surgings of the sea; but here he tells of what would seem a still more unlikely thing, that the goodness of God should lead men to fear him. He selects that prominent proof of God's goodness, the giving of the rains and the harvest, as a type of all, and he takes for granted that men *ought* to have found in this goodness of God an argument for his fear.   Now we remark—

I. THAT THIS IS AN UNUSUAL ARGUMENT. We could understand other attributes of God being appealed to as grounds for fearing him—his majesty, his power, his justice, his wrath—but his *goodness* seems to call for almost every other feeling than that of fear.   Joy, gratitude, benevolence, praise, but not fear.   We delight ourselves in his goodness, we bask in it as in the blessed warmth of the sun, but we never *fear* it, or see in it a reason for such regard of God.   And it is certain that this expectation of the prophet, that God's goodness should lead us to his fear, was not based on any supposition or belief that there was aught of fearfulness about the goodness of God.   Of the devil's goodness when he turns himself into an angel of light, when he quotes Scripture, as he did at our Lord's temptation, and when he pours honey into our cup,—of his goodness we may be afraid.   It is but a mask.   And of some *men's* goodness we may be afraid—men who are "false as the smooth, deceitful sea," "adders' poison under their lips;" they betray with a kiss.   And men were wont to fear the goodness of the gods they worshipped.   They imagined they would be jealous if they saw a man prospering overmuch.   Hence to appease them men would inflict loss and injury on themselves.   See the story of Polycrates.   Nor either because there is aught of fatality attached to the goodness of God.   It is not as the beautiful flush on the countenance, which, lovely as it may appear, is a mark of doom clearly discernible to the experienced eye.   For no such reasons as these are we to *fear* God and his goodness.   Nevertheless—

II. GOD'S GOODNESS IS A PROPER REASON FOR A HOLY FEAR. 1. For it reveals a Being so far removed above all our conceptions of human goodness, One who stands on so infinitely higher a level of moral excellency, that a sacred awe fills our soul as we contemplate what God is and what his love is, especially his love to us in Christ. "There is forgiveness with thee, that thou mayest be feared."

> "Oh, how I fear thee, living God,
>   With deepest, tenderest fears,
> And worship thee with humble hope
>   And penitential tears!"

2. And because God's goodness reveals the intensity and depth of his love, and therefore reveals a corresponding wrath against all who outrage that love.   The gentlest mother yearning with affection for her children,—let those little ones be wronged, what a fury will she become towards the wrong-doer, and all because her love is so great!   And so, "according to God's love, so is his wrath."   There is no wrath like that "of the Lamb." 3. And because God's goodness in its temporal manifestations is but granted for a while.   He reserves his right to recall it when he will.   Hence if riches, or any other form of earthly good and present earthly joy,—if these increase, set not your heart upon them.   It is terrible to have all our peace of heart and mind, all the joy of our life, identified with and dependent upon what one day God may recall.   Every channel of God's goodness thus becomes a possible channel of deep suffering and distress.   If, then, your delight in the gift have not led you to the love and trust of the Giver, what comfort will you have when the gift is withdrawn?   What an argument this for the comment of our text! 4. Remember, again, the depraved nature which we carry about with us, which ever seeks to pervert to evil what God gives us for our good. "Jeshurun waxed fat, and kicked."   Prosperity is a sore temptation, before which many a man falls.   God's gifts are the material out of which many build a screen, a wall which shuts them off from God. 5. And because God's goodness heightens our responsibility.   How stern the word, "*Cut* it down; why cumbereth?" etc.!   Goodness and love and care had been thrown away upon it.   If God, then, have pleaded with us by his love, as we know he has, what if our hearts be still estranged from him?   "He that from God's mercy gathers no argument for his fear, may conclude thus much—that there is indeed forgiveness with God, but no forgiveness for him" (South).   Then let us ask—

> "Lord, let thy fear within us dwell,
>   Thy love our footsteps guide;
> That love shall all vain love expel,
>   That fear all fear beside."

C.

Ver. 24.—*God's gifts of the rains and the harvest.* "The Lord our God, that giveth rain, both the former and the latter, in his season: he reserveth unto us," etc. To a country so liable to drought as Palestine, the regular, periodic rainfall was of the utmost importance. If they had not the former rain—that which came first after seed-time—the seed would not germinate in the soil; and if, when near the harvest, the rain did not come again, there would be no full corn in the ear: it would not swell out and mature in any way to the husbandman's content. "Hence the people of those lands speak of the weather and the crops with a more immediate reference to God than is usual with us. It is said that the common expressions of the peasantry are such as much impress travellers with their apparently devout recognition of the Almighty's agency." A lady and her party were one day traversing, under the conduct of their Arab guide, the fertile plains west of the Carmel range. "Rain began to fall in torrents. Mohammed, our groom," so the lady tells, "threw a large Arab cloak over me, saying, 'May Allah preserve you, O lady, while he is blessing the fields!'" "Blessing the fields,"—what a beautiful synonym for the rain! But it indicates the constant dependence of those lands on these rains, and the people's sense of the high value of this gift of God. The husbandman relies entirely upon the early and the latter rain, and if these do not fall copiously in their season famine will ensue. Therefore, when wishing to point out some signal mark of the Lord's favour to his people, the prophet selects this, that he "giveth rain, both the former and the latter, in his season," etc. The prophet knew that every heart would assent and own the goodness of the Lord herein. Probably he was more sure of it there and then than he would be here and now. We have got so mystified with the modern doctrines of "the order of nature" and "the uniformity of natural law," that we have come to regard the universe almost as a great machine, the regular working of which excites no surprise, and demands and obtains still less gratitude. But all this is very sad. Happy they who, in the coming round of the seasons, the fall of the rain and the blessed harvest, are both able and glad to confess, "It is the Lord, who giveth food to all flesh: for his mercy endureth for ever." But let this verse not so much suggest the literal facts here commemorated by the prophet, as those other and higher spiritual facts which they resemble and suggest. The three blessed gifts of God in the natural world spoken of, tell of gifts like to them in the spiritual world. And first they remind us of—

I. THOSE PERSONS WHO ARE SO HAPPY AS TO REALIZE ALL THE THREE: the two rains—both the former and the latter—and the harvest. Now, there are many such, God be praised for them! In their own religious life they know what God's blessing of the former rain is. There was such vivid realization of the love of Christ, such hatred of sin, such sweet sensitiveness of conscience, such free intercourse with God in prayer, such bright onlooks into the glory to be revealed, such ready delight in worship and in work, such prompt siding with the will of God—in a word, such enjoyment of him, that it is still, and will ever be, a delightful retrospect.

> "What peaceful hours we then enjoyed!
> How sweet their memory still!"

"That was the early rain. The seed had just been sown, and the Master, to make it take deeper root, and to make it spring up faster into the green blade, gave them the sacred shower of his loving presence." And then there came afterwards *the latter rain.* For such is needed even in the holiest Christian's life. The early excitement, the power of novelty, which is a power in the religious life as in all other, wore off, as it is its nature to do. Many weary leagues of life's pilgrimage had to be traversed, many disappointments to be met with, many trials to be endured, many temptations—subtle, strange, strong—had to be met and overcome, and they left the soul weary and exhausted. And, but for the blessed latter rain, the strength and vigour of the Divine life in the soul would have died down. But then there came, brought about in one way and another, the second baptism of the Holy Ghost. And, by means of that, separate acts of obedience crystallized into blessed habits, which made their discharge prompt, easy, and effective. The power of prayer became more marked, the knowledge and experience of the truth of God's Word deepened. The unseen and eternal came out of the mist and vagueness of former years into clear, well-defined reality, so that the seeing him who is invisible came to be a daily vision; and the walk with God grew to be constant, delightful, and more intimate each day. And so the harvest of peace with God, of holy calm, of settled obedience, and of loyal, happy service, was daily reaped. And in the case of those who have passed into the skies, the harvest of glory has been reaped also, or rather is being reaped, the joy of which is ever-during with the eternal life of the soul. So again and again has it been in the experience of the Christian life. And likewise has it been also in *the work and service* rendered to Christ. That, too, in many an instance, has had its former rain of blessing. It was begun in Christ and for Christ. Tokens of the Lord's presence were not wanting even at the very outset. Sinners were converted, believers were edified, souls were saved, as the result of the early toil in the Master's vineyard. The sermons may have been juvenile, unskilled in mere sermonic art, but they had the Divine power with them. The teaching given to the scholars in the class may have been sadly unscientific, and wanting in symmetry and system; but Jesus was commended to the children, and his love so spoken of that they listened, were touched, were persuaded, were saved. And then years after *the latter rain came.* For a long while the work went on in a quiet, almost monotonous way. There appeared no stir, no great impression made. But he who gave the early rain now sent the latter also. And a new outpouring of the Spirit's influence was given. And again and increasingly the Word was spoken with power; the influence of Christ's servant told with all the added strength that life-long consecration to that work gave to it, and many a soul confessed the might of that ministry which Christ enabled him to discharge. And a blessed harvest was reaped, day after day, week by week; the sickle of the Word seemed never so keen, the hand that wielded it never so vigorous, the sheaves never so large, until the reaper was called away to join in the glad festivities of the eternal harvest-home. Yes, so it has been again and again. And, would we have it so with ourselves,—and would we not?— let it not be forgotten that the realization of these blessings—the early and the latter rain, and the harvest—*in our work* depends upon our personal realization of them in *our own souls.* The soul not alive in and for God can never accomplish much in his work and service. We must " take heed to ourselves " would we successfully take heed to our work, and be the means of salvation to others. Yes, let us remember this. But be encouraged by remembering also that *it is God's way and wont to send this threefold blessing.* This verse speaks of his giving these great gifts as his customary habit. It is not an exceptional or strange thing with him, but that which we may, and even should, look for. May he help us so to do, and then give us our heart's desire! But next consider—

II. THOSE LESS HAPPY ONES WHO REALIZE ONLY TWO OUT OF THESE THREE GIFTS OF GOD. They have had the early and the latter rains, but the harvest they have not yet rejoiced in. There are such experiences, both in the Christian life and in Christian work. The men were truly converted to God at the first, and they have in after years felt the power of his Spirit again and again; but that harvest of settled peace and joy, that power habitually to walk with God in the comfort of his love, and in prompt, joyful obedience to his will, has not come to them. And they grieve over it much. And yet more is this delay of the harvest often known in the *sphere of Christian work.* The *whole Christian Church* mourns to-day over this delay of harvest. The early rain of the Pentecostal day fell refreshingly upon them; and since then there have been spring-tides of Divine influence, copious outpourings of the Spirit of God, latter rains in deed and in truth. But the harvest—where is that? Where is the world, or even one entire nation, won for God? The boundaries of the kingdom of Satan do not seem much diminished, nor those of the kingdom of God much enlarged. And so, too, *individual Churches* have, in like manner, been blessed with early and latter rains, but the harvest of their work has not come. They can tell you of times in their history when there seemed a general movement Godwards; when the people met for prayer in unwonted numbers and with unwonted fervour. Their early history may have been one of difficulty and struggle, but these were overborne by a glorious awakening, a girding of them with power, by the Spirit of the Lord manifestly setting up his standard in their midst. "And the Lord added to them daily such as should be saved." And in more recent years they have had like and even larger experiences of his glorious presence. But yet the harvest is not reaped. Not only is the neighbourhood around hem still for the most part as it was, untouched, unimpressed by the power of the gospel, but many who gather with them Sunday by Sunday, and in their week-day assemblies, are yet unconverted and unsaved. Where is the harvest? Why does it not come? "How long, O Lord, how long?" these servants of God continually cry to him. And so, too, with the *individual worker* for Christ. He, too, can look back on a time when he began his holy labour, whether in more prominent or more obscure place it matters not; but there was given to him the early, and since then there has been the latter, rain. But he looks round his class, his family, his school, his congregation, and oh, what a scant portion of the field is as yet even begun to be garnered for Christ! How powerless his words seem to fall on many of them! How unanswered his prayers on their behalf still seem to be! *Now, what are we to say to all this?* Well, these three things we may surely say: First, that God *reserves* the weeks of harvest. He has appointed them, but the day of their coming he has reserved in his own power. The husbandman must have long patience; the growth and development of the holy seed is an orderly, and is generally a slow, process. All God's greatest works are slow. Science is ever teaching us this. What ages upon ages do the geologist and the astronomer demand for the processes of which they tell! How our little chronologies dwindle into insignificance besides those vast periods which they have conclusively shown to have been occupied by the Creator in perfecting those phenomena of which their several sciences take account! And, in the far greater and more difficult work of the moral and spiritual regeneration of human souls, shall we be impatient if God do not begin, continue, and end it all in the short space of *our* little lives? Surely this is to be unreasonable, is improper, is wrong. But remember, too, that the harvest itself *is a long process.* They are "*weeks* of harvest." The ingathering has begun when only one sheaf in a field has been reaped. The Lord Jesus said, "The fields are white already unto harvest," when he held in his hand only one solitary ripe ear of corn, the conversion of the woman of Samaria. Hence we may possibly be mourning that the harvest has not come, when in fact it has actually begun. Why, my brother, it began in you from the first hour that you were converted to God. He was cutting the bonds that bound you to this world when he first called you to himself; and all the varied means by which he is separating you from the world is but the reaping continually going on; and when the sickle of death comes and cuts down this bodily life of yours, it will be but the last stroke of the reaper that tells that the harvest for you is finished at last. And so with *your work.* The harvest is begun. That child's heart you won for Christ here, that soul that was brought to Jesus through the Word preached by you there, those others gathered to the Redeemer's feet elsewhere,—what were these blessed facts but the beginning of the harvest, a beginning that is to go on? You are not strong enough to reap all the Lord's field; be content that he lets you reap a part. Other workmen are to enter in where you may not, and to their arm shall fall the sheaves that you may not gather. So say not any more, "The harvest is delayed." Why, you are actually engaged in it now. You are not a mere sower, but you are a reaper too. And remember the full harvest shall be reaped. He is the Lord of it, and will not let it waste; by one means or another it shall all be gathered in. This is what we have to say to you who mourn at the harvest's delay.

III. But there are others less happy still. THOSE WHO CAN CLAIM TO HAVE REALIZED ONLY ONE OF THESE THREE GIFTS OF GOD. The harvest is not theirs, nor both the former and the latter rains, but only one of them. Now, this one may be only the former rain. In their religious life they were blessed with this; the wonted happy results followed; but since then there has been a standstill, and those observing them are, as St. Paul was in reference to the Galatians, "in doubt" about them, and sorrowfully ask the question, "Ye did run well; who did hinder you?" Their goodness has been "like the morning cloud and the early dew"—it has gone away. And so also in *much of religious work.* At the beginning there was a zeal and fervour and force which promised great things, but it all soon died down. They had no staying power, and because all was not accomplished in one vigorous rush and charge, and because the difficulties that had to be overcome presented a more stubborn and obstinate front than was anticipated, those who went forth to do battle with them became discouraged and soon turned back. In these cases, both in the life and the work, though there was the former rain, the latter has not as yet fallen. Now where, as is often the case, this has

been owing to neglect of those Divine aids which God has placed within our power—
the blessed aids of prayer, watchfulness, and the diligent use of grace already given—
then not pity but censure must be awarded to those of whom we speak. "They have
not because they asked not;" or if they asked they "asked amiss." Ah, what a sad
amount of such asking amiss there ever is!—asking as a substitute for working, instead
of as an aid and encouragement thereto; asking, but with motives marred by selfishness, strife, and many forms of that "regarding iniquity in the heart," which ever bars
the coming of the needed answer. And so there have been decline and decay, and a
fresh fall of the heavenly rain is indeed wanted. Oh, do these words apply to any of
us, either in regard to our stunted life or our ineffectual work? It may be so. But,
thank God, such sad facts are not always the cause. God may be pleased, notwithstanding that his servants wait upon him for the outpouring of his Spirit they so much
desire, to delay his answer. The rains of God have their season, and he best knows
what and when that season is. His purpose is to stir you up to yet more earnest
prayer, to greater energy of spiritual endeavour. All the night through did Jacob
wrestle with the angel, ere he won the glorious name of Israel. Not till after so long
and so arduous a struggle that his physical strength gave way, the sinew of his thigh
shrank, and he seemed reduced to utter powerlessness;—not till then was the victory
won. If, therefore, any of us, in our own religious life or work, are still waiting in
prayer and watching thereunto, but yet the desired answer has not come, regard it not
as denial, but only as a delay sent to test and try your faith—that faith more precious
in the sight of God than gold and silver, and which when tested shall come forth
triumphant, to the praise and glory of his grace. But there are those who have the *latter*
rain only. Is it not so with all those instances of late repentance, of eleventh-hour
turning to God? Such coming to God at the last does now and then occur, and the
promise of our Lord, "Whosoever cometh unto me I will," etc., is made good. Such
have the latter rain, but they can hardly be said ever to have known the former. And
so, too, with those who all their lifetime have been subject to bondage, have walked in
darkness and have seen no light,—to these tried children of God light often comes at
eventide; they have the latter rain, but not the former. And it is so also in many departments of Christian work. Take the long and painful history of many of our missions.
For how many years, amid how many discouragements, from deaths, desertions, disease,
and the like, have the pioneers of those missions toiled on as the missionaries in Central
Africa, so repeatedly deprived by death of one and another of their little band, are
yet doing! The early rain has never come, but the latter we are sure they and all
such shall have. Oh, how they deserve and demand our sympathy and our earnest
prayers! Shame will it be on the Church at home if these be withheld. But we
believe they are not and will not be. These are, however, a third class less blessed
than those who have both the former and latter rain, and still less than those who have
added on the crown and consummation of all their toil—the joyous harvest. But far,
far more blessed are they than that other and last class of whom also we are reminded—

IV. THOSE WHO HAVE NEITHER OF THESE BLESSINGS—NEITHER FORMER NOR LATTER
RAIN, NOR HARVEST. The profession of the Christian life may be made, and one or
other form of Christian work may be undertaken, but all manner of motives, all manner
of reasons, save the alone right and true one, may account for such facts. The religion
and the work may alike be hollow, formal, insincere; a life and a work on which
neither the former nor the latter rains of God's Spirit will ever come, and the only
harvest which shall be reaped will be one of "shame and everlasting contempt." There
is no *Divine* life in the man's soul, and therefore none in his work either. No more
pitiful spectacle can any contemplate than this, and from being examples of it may God
in his mercy deliver us all. But there is no need of this. The Lord our God is wont
to give "rain, both the former and the latter, in his season," and to reserve unto us the
appointed weeks of harvest. This is his declared will. Why, then, should we be without his blessing? Oh, let every one resolve that if importunity of prayer can for
Christ's sake win it, we will know the joy of both the former and the latter rain, and
will anticipate and look out for the appointed weeks of harvest! You who have had both
the former and the latter rain, be ready for the reaper's work. You who have had but
the former rain, plead mightily for the latter too; and you who have had neither,
whether in your own life or in your work, remember the fault is your own, but resolve

in the strength of God's grace that it shall be so no more.   Turn to him your Lord and Saviour, who came that you might have life, and might have it more abundantly, and beseech him to give you what you must have or die.   And so for you and for us all we would pray—

> "Diffuse, O God, those copious showers,
>   That earth its fruit may yield,
>   And change this barren wilderness
>   To Carmel's flowery field."

C.

Vers. 27, 28.—*The devil's lure.*   "Their houses are full of deceit, *therefore* they are become great," etc.

I. SEVERAL OF THESE LURES ARE NAMED HERE. 1. *Wealth :* "They are waxen rich." 2. *Luxury :* "They are waxen fat, they shine." 3. *Impunity :* "They overpass, . . . they judge not, . . . yet they prosper." 4. *Success :* "They prosper."

II. AND THE LIKE LURES ARE HELD OUT STILL.   Satan is ever seeking, and with sad success, to seduce men by such and similar snares.

III. IT IS WHAT WE MIGHT EXPECT.   For that Satan should in this manner tempt men is in keeping with his constant method of parodying and travestying all the good works of God.   What virtue, what Christian grace, is there that he does not caricature—modesty by servility, prudence by meanness, generosity by careless waste, etc. ? And so here, "The blessing of the Lord, it maketh rich," and hence Satan sets to work to devise a blessing of his which also shall make rich—and this is his great lure.

IV. AND THIS LURE IS MADE THE MORE ATTRACTIVE BY THE FACT THAT GOD OFTEN SUFFERS HIS SERVANTS TO FALL INTO GREAT DISTRESS.   "Many are the afflictions of the righteous ;" "In the world ye shall have tribulation."   For God desires that we shall love him for himself, yea, when our earthly interests even plead against him.   Such trial of our faith is exceeding precious in his sight.

V. OUR DUTY AND DEFENCE, THEREFORE, IS : 1. To look right on beyond the present reward, even to "the end." 2. To expose to others the treachery of these apparent rewards. 3. To pray for and cherish the spirit of Nehemiah, who said, "So did not I, because of the fear of God." 4. To yield our heart and soul up to the better attraction of Christ and his cross, until we come to say of him, "*Thou* art 'mine exceeding joy.'"—C.

Ver. 31.—*A wonderful and horrible thing indeed.*   Consider—

I. IN WHAT IT CONSISTED. 1. "The *prophets prophesy falsely*."   The prophets were not mere predicters of future events, but the utterers of God's will—those who *spoke forth*, as the very word "prophet" denotes, the hitherto undeclared mind of God.   For this purpose they were specially selected, trained, privileged, commissioned.   Hence every inducement that could possibly bear on them to lead them to be faithful to their high charge and trust was theirs : love of their country ; approval of their own conscience ; the fear of God ; the sure, if not present, reward of their fidelity which they would receive from God.   But yet they prophesied falsely.   We could have understood : (1) *Their hesitation* in the discharge of their duty.   See how Jeremiah himself shrank from it, so stern and arduous was it.   It was no light matter to be a prophet in those days. (2) *Their silence even.*   Fear may have rendered them dumb, or hopelessness of doing any good may have silenced them.   But that they should prophesy falsely—they from whom fidelity at all costs might have been looked for—that was "a wonderful and horrible," etc.   The fountains of truth were poisoned, the helm of the ship was in the hands of those who would steer her on to the rocks.   The light that was in Israel was darkened, therefore how great was their darkness !   What force such a fact as this lends to the urgency with which : (*a*) *God's prophets*—his ministers to-day are such—should take heed to themselves and to their doctrine ; and (*b*) *God's people* should remember in fervent prayer those on whom so high and solemn a charge is laid. 2. "*The priests bear rule by their means.*"   The priests were the more familiar ministers of religion.   They were a permanent order, not raised up for special occasions, and they came into contact with men continually.   They were supposed "to keep knowledge." They had all the traditions of their order, all the memories of their history and of God's favour to them. They were independent of the prophets, but were much bound to the people for their sympathy and support. But whilst independent of the prophets, they were greatly assisted by them in furthering the service of God. And they also had means of knowing the truth. They were able to try the spirits, whether they were of God. Hence they might have known the falsity of the false prophets. And they ought to have exposed it. But instead they combined with them, accepted the aid of their falsehood, and bore rule by their means. For, corrupt as the people were, they would speedily have discovered the wickedness of the priests had not the prophets sided with them. Now the poison spreads. The priests, coming into contact with all the people, propagate the falsehood of the prophets, shelter themselves behind their authority, and deceive those who trusted in them. Yes, it is "a wonderful and horrible," etc. It is in the power of some to originate falsehood: this the prophets did. It is in the power of others to spread that falsehood abroad: this the priests did. Leagued together, the people who trusted them were in evil case indeed. But there was a further element of sorrow to be yet added. 3. *The people loved to have it so.* (1) This showed that: (*a*) conscience was dead or drugged; (*b*) all perception of their true wisdom was gone; (*c*) there was no remedy but the fire of the judgment of God. (2) It is explained by probable facts that: (*a*) the poison was disguised; (*b*) large licence was allowed. (3) It reveals the awfully contagious nature of moral evil. The dread possibilities of national corruption, against which we are bound to watch and pray.

II. THE QUESTION IT GIVES RISE TO: "What will ye do in the end thereof?" That is, to what lengths will they go when their wickedness has full hold upon them? to what depths of degradation will they fall? to what resources will they turn when God's judgments come? The sadness of the question lies in the impossibility of satisfactorily answering it. It leads us to the brink of an abyss, at which we can only shudder and pray that none of us may fall therein.

CONCLUSION. 1. Thank God that such prophets and priests are the exception to the rule. 2. That when such exceptions are met with, God has provided a remedy against them—in his infallible Word; in his Spirit, leading us into all truth. 3. Try all that human ministers say by these tests. 4. Seeing how much depends upon them, and what power for good or ill they cannot but have, pray with all importunity that God send only faithful men into his ministry, and preserve in their fidelity those who are there already.—C.

Vers. 20—24.—*Nature's witness against blind eyes and rebellious hearts.* Three forms of evil are rebuked here.

I. THE DULNESS OF SPIRITUAL SENSIBILITY THAT FAILS TO DISCERN THE DIVINE MEANING OF NATURE. Israel and Judah are addressed as a "foolish people, without understanding," etc. Their crimes and sorrows sprang in great part out of their blindness and thoughtlessness (Isa. i. 3; v. 12, 13). They would not use even the powers of spiritual discernment they possessed. They perceived not the Divine presence in natural things—the sounding shore, the revolving seasons—so as to bow with adoring reverence before it. Few things are stranger or sadder than the insensibility of the spirits of men to the Divine in nature. "They have eyes, but do not see" the "invisible things" of the Great Creator "through the things that are made, even his eternal power and Godhead." They must be startled into the recognition of the present God. When some event out of the ordinary course occurs, they stand in awe before it, but in the familiar round of nature they find nothing Divine. We are all more or less open to this charge. The earthquake, the lightning flash, the hurricane, set us thinking of the majesty of him who wields such mighty forces at his will; but we forget the still more marvellous exercise of power that maintains the silent harmony of the spheres, holds the due balance of earth and sea, chases away the darkness of the night by the gently spreading dawn of every new morning, brings the grass blades and the flowers up out of the cold sod, ripens the fruit upon the trees, and changes the green carpet of the springing corn into the golden glory of the harvest. Of course it cannot be expected that any incident in the familiar daily round of nature should produce precisely the same effect on us as some new and startling phenomenon. The glory of the setting sun, that we have gazed upon a thousand times before, must needs be less to us in this respect than that of some flaming meteor that bursts suddenly upon the darkness and is gone. But it is deeply significant of the dulness of our spiritual sensibility that we can gaze so often on the world of wonders around us without being solemnly impressed with the presence of the living God.

II. THE SELF-WILL THAT SPURNS THE DIVINE CONTROL. A contrast is here drawn between the subjection of the great sea to the laws God's will has imposed on it, and the bounds his hand has drawn around it, and the insubordination of the rebellious spirit of man. It is a grand expression of Divine power in the material realm that the sea-shore presents. We are impressed with the majestic force of the rolling tide, but, after all, there is something still more wonderful in the solid strength of the belt of sand that resists and restrains it. (Even as the moral strength of a man is seen not so much in the ungoverned fury of his passions, as in the calm resolution that controls them.) The sea is subject to restraint; not so the wayward spirit of man. The sea, in its wildest raging, obeys the laws that are imposed on it, and "its own appointed limits keeps;" but the rebellious heart of man defies all authority other than its own impulses. How deep the mystery of this difference between material and spiritual forces! How awful the prerogative of a being on whom God has conferred a moral freedom like his own! He will never violate that freedom in any of his dealings with us; that were to destroy the very nature he has given. But in proportion to the dignity of the self-determining power, so dreadful must be the penalty of abusing it.

III. THE INGRATITUDE THAT YIELDS NO RETURN OF LOVE FOR THE DIVINE BENEFICENCE. It was an aggravation of the guilt of Israel that they were as unmoved by the perpetual manifestation of the goodness of God as they were by the revelations of his power. Even that did not lead them to repentance or teach them to fear him. Few evidences of the thoughtful goodness of God have been more conspicuous through all the ages than the beneficent round of the seasons. In spite of all the wickedness of man's ways, "he left not himself without witness, in that he did good," etc. (Acts xiv. 17). The appeal this great fact makes to the consciences and hearts of men is specially forcible as bearing on those whose calling is to be fellow-workers with God in developing the harvests of the earth. "Labour is a sublime necessity," not as a mere "necessity," but because of its moral meaning and moral uses. And of all physical labour, the husbandry of the earth is most rich in moral associations, as educating men to lowly dependence on God, and grateful devotion to him in response to his fatherly providence and long-suffering grace.

Learn—As all Divine manifestations speak to us alike of infinite power and infinite beneficence, so the result in us should be the blended affections of fear and love.—W.

EXPOSITION.

CHAPTER VI.

A prophecy, in five stanzas or strophes, vividly describing the judgment and its causes, and enforcing the necessity of repentance.

Vers. 1—8.—Arrival of a hostile army from the north, and summons to flee from the doomed city.

Ver. 1.—O ye children of Benjamin. The political rank of Jerusalem, as the capital of the kingdom of Judah, makes it difficult to realize that Jerusalem was not locally a city of Judah at all. It belonged, strictly speaking, to the tribe of Benjamin, a tribe whose insignificance, in comparison with Judah, seems to have led to the adoption of a form of expression not literally accurate (see Ps. lxxviii. 68). The true state of the case is evident from an examination of the two parallel passages, Josh. xv. 7, 8, and xviii. 16, 17. As

Mr. Fergusson points out, "The boundary between Judah and Benjamin . . . ran at the foot of the hill on which the city stands, so that the city itself was actually in Benjamin, while, by crossing the narrow ravine of Hinnom, you set foot on the territory of Judah" (Smith's 'Dictionary of the Bible,' i. 983). It is merely a specimen of the unnatural method of early harmonists when Jewish writers tell us that the altars and the sanctuary were in Benjamin, and the courts of the temple in Judah. The words of "the blessing of Moses" are clear (Deut. xxxiii. 12): "The beloved of the Lord! he shall dwell in safety by him, sheltering him continually, and between his shoulders he dwelleth;" i.e. Benjamin is specially protected, the sanctuary being on Benjamite soil. And yet these highly favoured "children of Benjamin" are divinely warned to flee from their sacred homes (see ch. vii. 4—7). Gather yourselves to flee; more strictly, *save your goods by flight.* In ch. iv. 6 the same advice was given to the inhabitants of the country districts. There, Jerusalem was represented as the only safe refuge; here, the capital being no longer tenable, the wild pasture-land to the south (the foe being expected from the north) becomes the goal of the fugitives of Jerusalem. **In Tekoa.** Tekoa was a town in the wild hill-country to the south of Judah, the birthplace of the prophet Amos. It is partly mentioned because its name seems to connect it with the verb rendered **blow the trumpet.** Such paronomasiæ are favourite oratorical instruments of the prophets, and especially in connections like the present (comp. Isa. x. 30; Micah i. 10—15). **A sign of fire in Beth-haccerem;** rather, *a signal on Beth-hakkérem.* The rendering of Authorized Version was suggested by Judg. xx. 38, 40; but there is nothing in the present context (as there is in that passage) to favour the view that a fiery beacon is intended. Beth-hakkérem lay, according to St. Jerome, on an eminence between Jerusalem and Tekoa ; *i.e.* probably the hill known as the Frank Mountain, the Arabic name of which (*Djebel el-Furaidis,* Little Paradise Mountain) is a not unsuitable equivalent for the Hebrew (Vineyard-house). The "district of Beth-hakkérem" is mentioned in Neh. iii. 14. The choice of the locality for the signal was a perfect one. "There is no other tell," remarks Dr. Thomson, "of equal height and size in Palestine." **Appeareth**; rather, *bendeth forward,* as if it were ready to fall.

Ver. 2.—**I have likened . . . a comely and delicate** woman. This passage is one of the most difficult in the book, and if there is corruption of the text anywhere, it is here. The most generally adopted rendering is, "The comely and delicate one will I destroy, even the daughter of Zion," giving the verb the same sense as in Hos. iv. 5 (literally it is, *I have brought to silence,* or perfect of prophetic certitude). The context, however, seems to favour the rendering "pasturage" (including the idea of a nomad settlement), instead of "comely;" but how to make this fit in with the remainder of the existing text is far from clear. The true and original reading probably only survives in fragments.

Ver. 3.—**The shepherds with their flocks,** etc.; rather, *To her came shepherds with their flocks ; they have pitched their tents round about her; they have pastured each at his side.* The best commentary on the last clause is furnished by Numb. xxii. 4, " Now shall this company lick up all that are round about us, as the ox licketh up the grass of the field."

Ver. 4.—**Prepare ye war;** literally, *sanctify* (or, *consecrate*) *war.* The foes are dramatically described as urging each other on at the different stages of the campaign. The

war is to be opened with sacrifices (comp. Isa. xiii. 3 with 1 Sam. xiii. 9); next there is a forced march, so as to take the city by storm, when the vigilance of its defenders is relaxed in the fierce noontide heat (comp. ch. xv. 8); evening surprises the foe still on the way, but they press steadily on, to do their work of destruction by night. The rapidity of the marches of the Chaldeans impressed another prophet of the reign of Josiah —Habakkuk (see Hab. i. 6, 8). **Woe unto us! for the day goeth away**; rather, *Alas for us! for the day hath turned.*

Ver. 5.—**Let us go**; rather, *let us go up.* "To go up" is the technical term for the movements of armies, whether advancing (as here and Isa. vii. 1) or retreating (as ch. xxi. 2; xxxiv. 21; xxxvii. 5, 11).

Ver. 6.—**Hew ye down trees**; rather, *her trees.* Hewing down trees was an ordinary feature of Assyrian and Babylonian expeditions. Thus, Assurnaçirpal "caused the forests of all (his enemies) to fall " (' Records of the Past,' iii. 40, 77), and Shalmaneser calls himself "the trampler on the heads of mountains and all forests "(Ibid., p. 83; comp. p. 90). The timber was partly required for their palaces and fleets, but also, as the context here suggests, for warlike operations. "Trees," as Professor Rawlinson remarks, " were sometimes cut down and built into the mound " (see next note); they would also be used for the " bulwarks " or siege instruments spoken of in Deut. xx. 20. **Cast a mount**; literally, *pour a mount* (or " bank," as it is elsewhere rendered), with reference to the emptying of the baskets of earth required for building up the "mount" (mound). Habakkuk (i. 10) says of the Chaldeans, "He laugheth at every stronghold, and *heapeth up earth,* and taketh it " (comp. also 2 Sam. xx. 15; Isa. xxxvii. 33). The intention of the mound was not so much to bring the besiegers on a level with the top of the walls as to enable them to work the battering-rams to better advantage (Rawlinson, ' Ancient Monarchies,' i. 472). **She is wholly oppression**, etc.; rather, *she is the city that is punished; wholly oppression is in the midst of her.*

Ver. 7.—**As a fountain casteth out**; rather, *as a cistern keepeth fresh* (literally, *cool*). The wickedness of Jerusalem is so thoroughly ingrained that it seems to pass into act by a law of nature, just as a cistern cannot help always yielding a supply of cool, fresh water. **Violence and spoil**; rather, *injustice and violence* (so ch. xx. 8; Amos iii. 10; Hab. i. 3). **Before me,** etc.; rather, *before my face continually is sickness and wounding.* The ear is constantly dinned with the sounds of oppression, and the eye pained with the sight of the bodily sufferings of the victims. The word for " sickness " is applicable to any kind of infirmity (see Isa. liii. 3, 4), but the context clearly limits it here to bodily trouble.

Ver. 8.—**Be thou instructed**; rather, *Let thyself be corrected* (Authorized Version misses the sense, a very important one, of the conjugation, which is *Nifal tolerativum* (comp. Ps. ii. 10; Isa. liii. 12). The phrase is equivalent to " receive correction " (ch. ii. 30; v. 3), and means to accept the warning conveyed in the Divine chastisement. **Lest my soul**, etc.; rather, *lest my soul be rent from thee* (Authorized Version renders the same verb in Ezek. xxiii. 17, " be alienated ").

Vers. 9—15.—It is an all but complete judgment which Jehovah foreshows. Unwilling as the people are to hear it, the disclosure must be made.

Ver. 9.—**They shall throughly glean**, etc. " Israel " has already been reduced to a " remnant; " the ten tribes have lost their independence, and Judah alone remains (ch. v. 15). Even Judah shall undergo a severe sifting process, which is likened to a gleaning (comp. Isa. xxiv. 13; Obad. 5; ch. xlix. 9). The prospect is dark, but believers in God's promises would remember that a few grapes were always left after the gathering (comp. Isa. xvii. 6). **Turn back thine hand.** If the text is correct, the speaker here addresses the leader of the gleaners. Keil thinks this change of construction is to emphasize the certainty of the predicted destruction. But it is much more natural (and in perfect harmony with many other similar phenomena of the received text) to suppose, with Hitzig, that the letter represented in the Authorized Version by " thine " has arisen by a mistaken repetition of the first letter of the following word, and (the verbal form being the same for the infinitive and the imperative) to render *turning again the hand.* In this case the clause will be dependent on the preceding statement as to the " gleaning ".of Judah. **Into the baskets**; rather, *unto the shoots.* The gleaners will do their work with a stern thoroughness, laying the hand of destruction again and again upon the vine-shoots.

Ver. 10.—**Their ear is uncircumcised**; covered as it were with a foreskin, which prevents the prophetic message from finding admittance. Elsewhere it is the heart (Lev. xxvi. 41; Ezek. xliv. 7), or the lips (Exod. vi. 12) which are said to be " circumcised; " a passage in Stephen's speech applies the epithet both to the heart and to the ears (Acts vii. 51).

Ver. 11.—**Therefore I am full**; rather, *But I am full.* **I will pour it out.** The text has " pour it out." The sudden transition to the imperative is certainly harsh, and excuses the *conjectural emendation* which underlies the rendering of the Authorized Version. If we retain the imperative, we must explain

it with reference to Jeremiah's inner experience. There are, we must remember, two selves in the prophet (comp. Isa. xxi. 6), and the higher prophetic self here addresses the lower or human self, and calls upon it no longer to withhold the divinely communicated burden. All classes, as the sequel announces, are to share in the dread calamity. **Upon the children abroad**; literally, *upon the child in the street* (comp. Zech. viii. 5). **The assembly of young men.** It is a social assembly which is meant (comp. ch. xv. 17, " the assembly of the laughers ").

Ver. 12.—**Shall be turned**; *i.e.* transferred. **Their fields and wives.** Wives are regarded as a property, as in Exod. xx. 17 (comp. Deut. v. 21).

Ver. 13.—**Given to covetousness**; literally, *gaineth gain;* but the word here rendered " gain " implies that it is unrighteous gain (the root means " to tear "). Unjust gain and murder are repeatedly singled out in the Old Testament as representative sins (comp. Ezek. xxxiii. 31; Ps. cxix. 36; Isa. i. 15; ch. ii. 34; and see my note on Isa. lvii. 17). There is a special reason for the selection of " covetousness " here. Land was the object of a high-born Jew's ambition, and expulsion from his land was his appropriate punishment (comp. Isa. v. 8, 9).

Ver. 14.—**They have healed**, etc. The full force of the verb is, " they have busied themselves about healing " (so ch. viii. 11; li. 9). *Of the daughter.* Our translators evidently had before them a text which omitted these words, in accordance with many Hebrew manuscripts and the Septuagint; Van der Hooght's text, however, contains them, as also does the parallel passage (ch. viii. 11). **Slightly**; or, *lightly;* Septuagint, ἐξουθενοῦντες. **Saying, Peace, peace.** Always the burden of the mere professional prophets, who, as one of a higher order—the bold, uncompromising Micah—fittingly characterizes them, " bite with their teeth, and cry, Peace; " *i.e.* draw flattering pictures of the state and prospects of their country, in order to " line their own pockets " (Micah iii. 5).

Ver. 15.—**Were they ashamed?** The Authorized Version certainly meets the requirements of the context; there seems to be an implied interrogation. Most, however, render, " They are brought to shame; " in which case it seems best to take the verb as a perfect of prophetic certitude, equivalent to " they shall surely be brought to shame." **When**; rather, *because.* **Nay, they were not at all ashamed**; rather, *nevertheless they feel no shame* (i.e. at present). **They shall be cast down**; rather, *they shall stumble.*

Vers. 16—21.—Without hearty repentance, there is no hope of escape. But hitherto Judah has rejected all admonitions. What availeth mere ceremonial punctuality?

Ver. 16.—**Stand ye in the ways**; literally, *station yourselves on* (or, *by*) *roads*, i.e. at the meeting-point of different roads. There (as the following words state) the Jews are to make inquiry as to **the old paths.** Antiquity gives a presumption of rightness; the ancients were nearer to the days when God spoke with man; they had the guidance of God's two mighty "shepherds" (Isa. lxiii. 11); they knew, far better than we, who "are but of yesterday, and know nothing" (Job viii. 9), the way of happiness. For though there are many pretended "ways," there is but "one way" (ch. xxxii. 39) which has Jehovah's blessing (Ps. xxv. 8, 9).

Ver. 17.—**Also I set**; rather, *and I kept raising up* (the frequentative perfect). **Watchmen**; *i.e.* prophets (Ezek. iii. 17, and part of Isa. lii. 8; lvi. 10). **Hearken**, etc. Probably the words of Jehovah. Standing on their high watch-tower (Hab. ii. 1), the prophets scrutinize the horizon for the first appearance of danger, and give warning of it by (metaphorically) blowing a trumpet (so Amos iii. 6).

Ver. 18.—**Therefore hear**, etc. Remonstrance being useless, the sentence upon Israel can no longer be delayed, and Jehovah summons the nations of the earth as witnesses (comp. Micah i. 2; Isa. xviii. 3; Ps. xlix. 1). **O congregation, what is among them.** The passage is obscure. "Congregation" can only refer to the foreign nations mentioned in the first clause; for Israel could not be called upon to hear the judgment "upon this people" (ver. 19). There is, however, no other passage in which the word has this reference. The words rendered "what is among them," or "what (shall happen) in them," seem unnaturally laconic, and not as weighty as one would expect after the solemn introduction. If correct, they must of course refer to the Israelites. But Graf's conjecture that the text is corrupt lies near at hand. The least alteration which will remove the difficulties of the passage is that presupposed by the rendering of Aquila (not Symmachus, as St. Jerome says; see Field's 'Hexapla') and J. D. Michaelis, "the testimony which is against them."

Ver. 19.—**The fruit of their thoughts.** That punishment is the ripe fruit of sin, is the doctrine of the Old (Isa. iii. 10; Ps. lviii. 11, margin) as well as of the New Testament (Jas. i. 15).

Ver. 20.—**To what purpose . . . incense from Sheba?** This is the answer to an implied objection on the part of the Jews, that they have faithfully fulfilled their ceremonial obligations. "To obey is better than sacrifice" (1 Sam. xv. 22); "And what doth the Lord require of thee, but to do justly, and to love mercy, and to walk humbly with thy God?" (Micah vi. 8; comp. Isa. i. 11; Amos v. 21—24; Hos. vi. 6; Micah vi. 6—8). All these passages must be read in the light of the prophets' circumstances. A purely formal, petrified religion compelled them to attack the existing priesthood, and a holy indignation cannot stop to measure its language. *Incense from Sheba;* frankincense from south-west Arabia. This was required for the holy incense (Exod. xxx. 34), and as an addition to the *minkhah,* or "meal offering." **Sweet cane.** The "sweet calamus" of Exod. xxx. 23, which was imported from India. It was an ingredient in the holy anointing oil (Exod., *loc. cit.*). Not to be confounded with the sugar-cane.

Ver. 21.—**I will lay stumbling-blocks, etc.** Of the regenerate Israel of the future it is prophesied (Isa. liv. 15) that his enemies shall "fall upon him [or, 'by reason of him']." Of the unregenerate Israel of the present, that he shall "fall" (*i.e.* come to ruin) upon the "stumbling-blocks" presented, not without God's appointment, by the terrible northern invader.

Vers. 22—30.—The enemy described; the terror consequent on his arrival; a rumoured declaration of the moral cause of the judgment.

Ver. 22.—**From the north country** (so ch. i. 14 (see note); iv. 6). **Shall be raised;** rather, *shall be aroused.* **The sides of the earth;** rather, "the recesses (*i.e.* furthest parts) of the earth" (so ch. xxxv. 32; Isa. xiv. 13).

Ver. 23.—**Spear;** rather, *javelin* (or, *lance*). **They** are cruel. The cruelty of the Assyrians and Babylonians seems to have spread general dismay. Nahum calls Nineveh "the city of bloodshed" (iii. 1); Habakkuk styles the Chaldeans "bitter and vehement, terrible and dreadful" (i. 6, 7). The customs brought out into view in the monuments justify this most amply, though Professor Rawlinson thinks we cannot call the Assyrians (with whom the Babylonians may of course be coupled) naturally hardhearted. "The Assyrian listens to the enemy who asks for quarter; he prefers making prisoners to slaying; he is very terrible in the battle and the assault, but afterwards he forgives and spares" ('Ancient Monarchies,' i. 243). **Their voice roareth.** The horrid roar of the advancing hosts seems to have greatly struck the Jews (comp. Isa. v. 30; xvii. 12, 13).

Ver. 24.—**We have heard the fame thereof.** The prophet identifies himself (comp., for the same phenomenon, ch. iv. 19—21; x. 19, 20) with his people, and expresses the general feeling of anxiety and pain. The phraseology of the closing lines reminds us of Isa. xiii. 7, 8.

Ver. 25.—**Go not forth into the field.** The "daughter of Zion" (*i.e.* the personific population of Jerusalem) is cautioned against venturing outside the walls. **The sword of the enemy**; rather, *the enemy hath a sword.* **Fear is on every side**; Hebrew, *māgōr missā-bīb;* one of Jeremiah's favourite expressions (see ch. xx. 3, 10; xlvi. 5; xlix. 29; and comp. Ps. xxxi. 13 [14].). Naturally of a timid, retiring character, the prophet cannot help feeling the anxious and alarming situation into which at the Divine command he has ventured.

Ver. 26.—**Wallow thyself in ashes**; rather, *sprinkle thyself with ashes*, a sign of mourning (2 Sam. xiii. 19; so Micah i. 10). **Mourning, as for an only son.** The Septuagint renders πένθος ἀγαπητοῦ (comp. Gen. xxii. 2, where in like manner the Septuagint renders, not "thine only son," but "thy beloved son"). Possibly this was to avoid a supposition which might have occurred to some readers (it has, in fact, occurred to several modern critics) that the "only son" was Adonis, who was certainly "mourned for" by some of the Israelites under the name of Thammuz (Ezek. viii. 14), and whose Phœnician name is given by Philo of Byblus as 'Ιεούδ (*i.e.* probably *Yakhidh*, only begotten, the word used by Jeremiah; comp. Βηρούθ, equivalent to Berith). M. Renan found a vestige of the ancient festival of Adonis at Djebeil (the Phœnician Gebal) even at the present day. There would be nothing singular in the adoption of a common popular phrase by the prophet, in spite of its reference to a heathen custom (comp. Job iii. 8), and the view in question gives additional force to the passage. But the ordinary explanation is perfectly tenable and more obvious. The phrase, "mourning [or, 'lamentation'] for an only begotten one," occurs again in Amos viii. 10; Zech. xii. 10. In the last-mentioned passage it is parallel with "bitter weeping for a firstborn."

Ver. 27.—**I have set thee**, etc.; literally, *as an assayer have I set thee among my people, a fortress.* Various attempts have been made to avoid giving the last word its natural rendering, "a fortress." Ewald, for instance, would alter the points, and render "a separater [of metals]," thus making the word synonymous with that translated "an assayer;" but this is against Hebrew usage. Hitzig, assuming a doubtful interpretation of Job xxii. 24, renders ". . . among my people without gold," *i.e.* "without there being any gold there for thee to assay" (a very awkward form of expression). These are the two most plausible views, and yet neither of them is satisfactory. Nothing remains but the very simple conjecture,

supported by not a few similar phenomena, that *mibhçar*, a fortress, has been inserted by mistake from the margin, where an early glossator had written the word, to remind of the parallel passage (ch. i. 18, "I have made thee this day a fortress-city," '*ir mibhçar*). In this and the following verses metallurgic phraseology is employed with a moral application (comp. Isa. i. 22, 25).

Ver. 28.—**Grievous revolters**; literally, *rebels of rebels.* **Walking**; rather, *going about*, as a pedlar with his wares (so Prov. xi. 13; xx. 19; Lev. xix. 16). Jeremiah had good reason to specify this characteristic of his enemies (see ch. xviii. 18). **Brass and Iron**; rather, *copper and iron*, in short, base metal.

Ver. 29.—**The bellows are burned.** The objection to this rendering is that the burning of the bellows would involve the interruption of the process of assaying. We might, indeed, translate "are scorched" (on the authority of Ezek. xv. 4), and attach the word rendered "of the fire" to the first clause; the half-verse would then run: "The bellows are scorched through the fire; the lead is consumed," *i.e.* the bellows are even scorched through the heat of the furnace, and the lead has become entirely oxydized. But this requires us to alter the verb from the masculine to the feminine form of third sing. perf. (reading *tammāh*). It is better, therefore, to give the verb (which will be Kal, if the *nūn* be radical) the sense of "snorting," which it has in Aramaic and in Arabic, and which the corresponding noun has in Hebrew (ch. viii. 16; Job xxxix. 20; xli. 12). The masculine form of the verb rendered "is consumed" is still a difficulty; but we have a better right to suppose that the first letter of *tittōm* was dropped, owing to its identity with the second letter, than to append (as the first view would require us) an entirely different letter at the end. This being done, the whole passage becomes clear: "The bellows puff, (that) the lead may be consumed of the fire." In any case, the general meaning is obvious. The assayer has spared no trouble, all the rules of his art have been obeyed, but no silver appears as the result of the process. Lead is mentioned, because, before quicksilver was known, it was employed as a flux in the operation of smelting. **Plucked away**; rather, *separated*, like the dross from the silver.

Ver. 30.—**Reprobate silver . . . rejected them**; rather, *refuse silver* (as the margin) *. . . refused them.* The verbal root is the same.

HOMILETICS.

Ver. 7.—*Wells of wickedness.* I. If wickedness is abundant and persistent, it must come from a deep source. The wickedness of Israel is constantly renewed— ever fresh and abundant, like water in a well. Such water must flow out of deep fountains. The continuity of a course of sin proves that its origin is deep-seated. The sin of hasty temper is less than that of deliberate calculation, the fall before sudden temptation more excusable than the wilful choice of evil, the occasional slip less culpable than the continuous habit of wickedness. This habitual sin must be rooted in a man's nature. Springing out under all circumstances, it is seen to be, not an outside defect, but a fruit of his own inner life. Constantly flowing in spite of all restraints of law, social influence, and conscience, it shows how thoroughly corrupt the heart must be (Matt. xv. 18).

II. If wickedness is deep-seated in the heart, it must flow out in frequent acts. The spring cannot restrain its waters; the heart cannot repress its imaginations. These must come forth and express themselves in deeds. Men may aim at living two lives—an inner life of sin and an outer life of propriety; but the attempt must ulti- mately fail. The greater the evil of the heart, the more completely must this colour the life.

III. Deep-seated and ever-flowing wickedness provokes the severest judg- ment from God. Jeremiah points to this as the terrible justification for the approach- ing desolation of the land. 1. In itself it is most heinous, and carries the greatest guilt. 2. It is so radically evil that it impregnates the whole nature of the people in whom it dwells, so that they cannot be regarded as doers of wickedness only, but as wicked; not as those who have committed acts of dishonesty, untruth, violence, etc., but as thieves, liars, murderers, etc. 3. Ever-flowing, it promises no better things for the future. If left to itself, it will but repeat the sickening tale of the past with aggravated depravity. 4. It is the source of evil to others. The sin flows out. It must be checked for the protection of all who come under its influence.

Vers. 10, 11.—*The indifference of men and the burden of truth.* We have here revealed to us a conflict in the mind of the prophet. At first it seems vain for him to speak, for none heed his warnings (ver. 10); but then he feels the awful burden of his message compelling utterance. While he looks at his audience he loses heart and sees little good in attempting to influence them; but when he looks within at his trust he finds that this has claims and powers before which he must bow obediently. Thus the teacher of high truth is often discouraged when he considers the unfitness of men to receive it, until he realizes more fully the majesty of the truth itself which possesses him and is not simply a treasure to be regarded as his property, but a Lord demanding his faithful service.

I. The indifference of men. Here was the source of Jeremiah's discouragement, and we can sympathize with him. What is the use of uttering truths that men are not fit to receive—only to waste our powers, create misunderstandings, and provoke opposition? 1. *The reception of truth depends on the condition of the receiving mind.* Language requires ears as well as tongues. Outward ears are useless without the inward ears of an understanding mind. An ass has no lack of ears, but what are a prophet's words to him? There are people to whom the solemn utterance of the most awful truths is but so much noise. Therefore (1) it behoves men to beware of mocking at the supposed folly of any teaching till they have ascertained whether the fault lies with the teacher or with the taught. And (2) it is not enough to utter truth; we should seek for men the right preparation for receiving it—the ploughing of the hard soil in readiness for the sowing of the seed. 2. *When the mind is in a wrong con- dition for the reception of truth this may meet with ridicule and dislike.* Truth may meet with ridicule. The word of Jehovah was "a mockery to the Jews." Ridicule may be both a result of misunderstanding the truth and a cause of further mistakes. Truth may also meet with dislike. The Jews had "no delight" in the Divine Word. This was a proof of their not understanding it; for to know it is to love it (Ps. cxix.

16). It was also a cause of their not rightly receiving it; for dislike to truth blinds the eye to the nature of it.

II. The burden of truth. In spite of all these grounds for discouragement, Jeremiah feels that he must utter his message when once he considers its origin and character. 1. *Truth is a trust from God.* It is "the fury of the Lord" that possesses the prophet, not the mere passion of his own thoughts. He who holds a Divine truth is a steward of an oracle of God. Woe to him if he consult his own convenience and rely only on his own judgment when, as a steward, he is called to be faithful to his Master's will. His duty is to speak; the consequences may be left to God. 2. *Truth is an inspiration from God.* Jeremiah is "full of the fury of Jehovah." The Spirit of God has possessed him; he is brought into sympathy with the thought and feeling of God: he must needs utter this. If men feel the inspiration of truth they will be carried away by it and poor considerations of worldly expediency will be swept on one side by the flood of a Divine passion. 3. *Truth is a burden on the soul which cries for utterance.* Jeremiah exclaims, "I am weary with holding in!" "Woe is me!" cries St. Paul, as he thinks of the suggestion to restrain his preaching the gospel. Under great passions men do not speak measured words, chosen in strict consideration for their hearers; they speak to give vent to their own souls. The grandest utterances of humanity, in prophecy and in poetry, are free from all calculations as to the reception of them by an audience. They are unrestrainable expressions of the soul; like the songs of birds flowing from the very fulness of the heart. 4. *Truth is for the good of mankind.* Jeremiah must speak, for what he utters concerns others than himself. No one has a right to the monopoly of any great truth. It is common property, and he who hides it steals it. If his excuse is that men cannot understand it, let him remember (1) that he is not an infallible judge of the capacities of other men; and (2) that his duty is to bear his testimony, whether men will hear or no, and to leave all further responsibility with them.

Ver. 14.—*False peace.* I. The craving for peace is natural. These false prophets gained their influence by professing to satisfy a natural instinct. The Jews dreaded war with their great neighbours. 1. All wicked men are at heart in a *state of unrest.* The soul that sins is at war with God, with the law and order of the universe, with its own nature. 2. This condition is *distressing.* The outward warfare begets inward unrest. Then, above all things, peace is the great want of the soul. Wealth, success, happiness, can be spared if but this jewel is still preserved. All great philosophies and all earnest religions set themselves to the task of discovering or creating it.

II. The pretensions of false peace are plausible. The prophets dissuaded their hearers from attending to the warning words of Jeremiah, and endeavoured to make them believe that they were in no danger. There is much that is very popular in arguments such as theirs. 1. They agree with the *wishes* of the hearers. Men are always inclined to believe what they wish. 2. They flatter the *pride* of the populace. The people are told that they are too great and too favoured of Heaven to suffer any serious calamity, and they are only too ready to believe it. 3. They claim the merits of *charity.* They promise pleasant things. This looks more charitable than the threatening language of stern censors. Hence the prophets win favour for their apparent geniality and liberal sentiments. 4. They require *no sacrifices* from those who accept them. The doctrine is popular because the practice flowing from it is easy. The flattering prophets called to no reformation of character. 5. They have *appearances* in their favour. At present all looks fair. Is not this a presumption that the future will be happy? The sun is rising in gold and crimson; why, then, prophesy the approach of a storm?

III. The pretensions of false peace are ruinous. 1. These pretensions do *nothing to secure* the peace. They simply lead men to believe that they are to enjoy it. Such a belief cannot alter facts. If there is no peace we do not make peace by crying, "Peace, peace!" This is the language of folly and indolence. 2. These delusions only *aggravate the danger.* They prevent men from preparing for the calamity by blinding them to the near advent of it.

IV. There is a way by which the natural craving for peace may be satisfied.

The deceiving prophets do not make peace; they only talk of it. But in the teaching of true prophets and apostles the way to secure solid peace is revealed. 1. This is shown to be *not immediate*. Jeremiah was right in saying that the people must suffer before they enjoyed peace. Christ, the Prince of peace, came to "send a sword" (Matt. x. 34). The gospel does not preach "peace at any price," but peace after victory in warfare, rest after patient endurance of tribulation. 2. This is shown to be through *repentance and renewal of life*. The deceiving prophets promise peace to the people as they are. While we are in sin we cannot have true peace (Isa. xlviii. 22). Peace follows the advent of the Spirit of Christ (John xiv. 26, 27).

Ver. 16.—*The old paths.* I. CONSIDER THE RECOMMENDATION TO FOLLOW THE OLD PATHS. 1. The course of life should be determined after *thoughtful deliberation.* Jeremiah is to "stand in the ways and see." It is foolish to go with the multitude without individual convictions of what is right, or to follow our own private impulses blindly and aimlessly. 2. The choice should fall on a *good way.* Other ways may be smooth, pleasant, flowery at the starting, only to lose themselves in the pathless wilderness, while this may look more rugged and steep at first; but it should not be the present attractiveness, but the direction, the whole course and the end of a way, which should determine our choice of it. 3. There are *old paths* of right. Religion has not to be made anew. It is not left for the latest saint to discover the way of holiness. 4. Having found the right way, we should forthwith "*walk therein.*" Knowledge is useless without practice; nay, guilt is aggravated if, knowing the right, we follow the wrong. 5. In the right way is *rest* for the soul. Even while on the earthly pilgrimage many quiet resting-places may be found (Ps. xxiii. 2), through all the course an inward peace may be enjoyed (Prov. iii. 17), and at the end will be found the perfect rest of the home of God (Heb. iv. 9).
II. CONSIDER THE GROUNDS ON WHICH THIS RECOMMENDATION IS BASED. 1. Old ways have been *tested by experience.* We choose for a guide one who has already traversed the country. In an unknown land we naturally turn to beaten tracks in preference to following stray footprints across the wild, or striking out for ourselves a pathless way. If others have done rough pioneer work, why should not we avail ourselves of it? If they have reached the goal, they have proved that it is attainable by their way. This is fact; that a new way will be easier or shorter is conjecture. There is, therefore, a presumption in favour of the old. 2. Old ways in religion are *nearer to the original fountains of inspiration.* Israel was referred back to the old ways marked out by Moses, the great founder of the Jewish faith. Christians are referred back to primitive Christianity, to the teaching of the apostles, to the life and example of Christ. Christianity is not a speculation, a creation of the spirit of the age. It is a tradition, a following of those Divine counsels which are indicated in the New Testament.
III. CONSIDER THE LIMITATIONS TO THE APPLICATION OF THIS RECOMMENDATION. 1. The old ways are to be followed only in so far as they are *good.* Still we must judge by our own conscience. Antiquity must not be taken as a despotic master. There are bad old ways. The first-born man struck out an evil way; it was left to Abel, the second-born, to show the better course. 2. In considering the character of an old way, we must take note of the *character and light* of those who founded it. There have been dark ages in the past. Corruption soon crept in. Things are not good just in proportion to their age. Christians must look, not to the Puritans, the Reformers, the mediæval Church, the Fathers, but, passing numerous errors and corruptions, reach back to Christ himself for the true old way. He is the Way (John xiv. 6). 3. We must ever *progress* beyond the attainments of the past. We are to follow those old ways that are good; we are to build on the one foundation. But we are not to be content with having the foundation. The fabric must rise higher and higher (1 Cor. iii. 11—15). Christianity is a religion of progress. It is not to be subject to revolutions. Progress must follow the lines laid down by Christ and his apostles. Christianity is not strengthened nor adorned, but only burdened and hidden, by a mere accretion of human ideas and institutions; yet it is a seed which grows, developing larger, fuller life out of its own essential principles (Matt. xiii. 31). Jeremiah himself took a great stride forward beyond the limits attained by antiquity, though in the direction of the

old path, *i.e.* in the spirit of the religion of his fathers (ch. xxxi. 31—34). "These times are the ancient times, when the world is ancient, and not those which we count ancient, *ordine retrogrado,* by a computation backwards from ourselves" (Francis Bacon).

Ver. 17.—*Watchmen.* I. THE MISSION OF THE WATCHMEN. 1. They are *appointed by God.* God raises up prophets, preachers, teachers of righteousness. Unless they have a Divine call they are usurping a position to which they have no right (Gal. i. 1, 15). Hence see (1) the authority of the watchmen; (2) the merciful kindness of God in providing warning and instruction. 2. They are to *observe what goes on around them.* The prophets are seers of spiritual truths, observers of events of history in the light of those truths, and thus, as watchmen, able to discern approaching dangers. The Christian teachers must not be wrapt up in abstract truth. They must see the application of this, note the condition and needs of men, discern the "signs of the times." The prophets were political leaders. They discoursed on subjects which in our day would be discussed in the newspaper. 3. They are to *blow the trumpet.* The seer is to be a prophet. He who knows truth must make it known to others. The watchman must not simply "*let* his light shine;" he must blow a trumpet, demand attention, compel men to hear. The enemy is at the gate. This is no time for mild disquisitions on military tactics; it is a moment when men must be awaked from their sleep and summoned to arms. The Christian preacher speaks to men who are asleep and in great danger. His duty is not simply to let the truth be known. He must arouse, urge, "compel" men to hear his message.

II. THE RECEPTION OF THE MISSION OF THE WATCHMEN. The watchman has done his duty in sounding the trumpet. If none will hear, he is free. 1. Men must *hearken* to the Divine message before they can profit by it. To be warned is not to be saved. If men refuse to accept the truths of Christianity these can do them no good, and they are left free to follow or to neglect them. 2. Men must *obey* the Divine message before they can profit by it. It is nothing to tremble at the warning of judgment unless we are moved to actions of precaution. Felix trembled, and was none the better for this proof of the powerful effect of the preaching of St. Paul (Acts xxiv. 25). 3. If the Divine message is heard and disregarded, the folly, guilt, and ruin will only be aggravated. The plea of ignorance is gone. Indifference is converted into obstinate rebellion (ver. 19).

Ver. 20.—*Worthless sacrifices.* I. SACRIFICES ARE WORTHLESS WHEN THEY ARE NOT OFFERED IN THE RIGHT SPIRIT. The mere gifts are of no use to God (Ps. l. 8—13). They are only valuable as expressing the thoughts and feelings of the giver. Religious services are simply good as the outward expression of worship. 1. Sacrifices are worthless when they are not prompted by *spiritual devotion;* religious services are unacceptable when they are only external performances. The true sacrifice must be of the *will, i.e.* self-dedication. 2. Sacrifices are worthless when they are accompanied by *immorality of conduct.* Worship at church is a mockery if daily conduct in the world is corrupt (Isa. i. 15).

II. WORTHLESS SACRIFICES MAY HAVE ALL THE EXTERNAL CHARACTERISTICS OF ACCEPTABLE SACRIFICES. 1. They may be offered *to God.* There may be a real intention to approach God, yet this is vain if the heart is wrong. 2. They may be according to *prescribed order.* The formally obedient Jews were rigidly subservient to the ordinance of the authorized ritual. 3. They may be *costly*—incense from Sheba, sweet cane from India. But men cannot buy acceptance with God by signing heavy cheques.

III. THE OFFERING OF WORTHLESS SACRIFICES IS A SERIOUS FAULT. 1. It is an *insult to God.* Better offer nothing than the worthless gift when all he really asks for, the heart, is withheld. 2. It is a source of *self-delusion.* The offering being given, the conscience feels relieved, false pride is stimulated, and the real spiritual condition is hidden. People have a vague feeling that they have done a good thing in attending church, in sitting out a service, in mechanically following the forms of worship. Yet, as this is really utterly worthless, the impression of self-complacency it produces is highly injurious.

Vers. 27—30.—*Testing fires.* Under the image of an assayer and his fire, Jeremiah is led to regard his mission, and the troubles of Israel, with which this is so much concerned, as means for testing the character of the Jews.

I. THE STANDARD OF MEASUREMENT IS DIVINE TRUTH. The prophet is to be an assayer. Men are to be judged by the truths of righteousness which he is inspired to see and to declare. God has revealed standards of judgment. We are not free to shape our lives according to fancy, taste, or unaided private judgment. The truths of Scripture constitute the standard by which we shall be measured. This will be applied according as it is known. Jeremiah was the watchman before he was the assayer. He blew the trumpet, preached the truth he saw. They who have not received the fuller revelation will be judged by what light they possess (Rom. i. 18—20; ii. 12).

II. THE TEST IS APPLIED IN THE FIRES OF AFFLICTION. Trouble is not only sent for discipline and chastisement; it is a test, a revealer of character. It reveals a man to himself and to others. If he has any true spiritual life, any precious metal, it must come out when, one after another, the worthless ideas and feelings fail before the searching flames of the baptism of fire. Trouble shows: 1. Whether religion is real and heartfelt, or formal and superficial. 2. How far faith is a practical trust, and how far it is a barren conviction. 3. Whether love and devotion to God are deep enough to stand against the temptation to rebel or despair.

III. THEY ARE UTTERLY WORTHLESS WHO DISPLAY NO GOOD QUALITIES AFTER THE SEARCHING TRIAL OF AFFLICTION. This follows from the preceding statements. It was terribly applicable to Israel. We should ask how far it applies to ourselves, and beware of two delusions, viz.: 1. The delusion that merit may be still hidden after God has applied his most thorough test. A religion which is completely secret, never discoverable, must be a poor and worthless thing. The heart cannot be right if it never gives proof of good qualities when tested in all ways. 2. The delusion that trial can destroy spiritual worth. The silver is not burnt if it is not forthcoming. True religion will survive the hardest test that may be applied to it. It is only the superficial, unreal sentiment of religion that is scorched up by persecution and affliction; the growth on the barren rock, not that in the good soil (Matt. xiii. 5, 20, 21).

IV. GOD WILL REJECT NONE WITHOUT FULL TRIAL. Character is to be assayed. God judges before he condemns. The reprobate silver has been well tried. No soul is reprobated by God till every means has been used to search for some good in it. See, then, the merciful intention of trial. The fires are fierce because the intention is to discover some small good thing hidden from every milder test, if only this exists. God is not anxious to find the evil, but to find the good, in men, as the assayer is searching for silver. He will gladly welcome the faintest indication of the least good. No genuine silver can miss the Assayer after his most searching tests. God will abandon no soul till he has sought for all that can be brought in its favour. He is loth to give his children up (Hos. xi. 8).

HOMILIES BY VARIOUS AUTHORS.

Vers. 4—8.—*The apostate city that cannot be let alone.* Godlessness is condemned by its impracticableness as a universal and thorough-going principle of human life. It is also an evil that defies ordinary restraints, and constantly becomes worse. "This is the strongest and most dangerous mining-powder of cities and fortresses when sin, shame, vice, and wantonness get the upper hand" (Cramer). The city that has forsaken God is—

I. A SOURCE OF MISCHIEF AND UNCLEANNESS. It is likened to a fountain casting forth wickedness. It is an originative agent of evil. Its private, social, and public life multiplies occasions and causes of sin. There is no power within itself sufficient to restrain or purify. Its very laws and regulations tend to foster vice. As of the natural heart our Saviour said that out of it "proceed evil thoughts, murders, adulteries, etc.," so, where there are multitudes of such, there will be an exaggeration of the individual tendency and influence. As the leader of fashion, and dominant authority in new customs and ideas, there is an *éclat* transferred from it to what is evil. Its existence becomes, therefore—

II. AN OCCASION OF INJURY AND DANGER TO ALL WHO HAVE TO DO WITH IT. It is as a fire that has broken out amidst combustible material. By-and-by "the wicked city" is felt to be an intolerable evil. It is a menace to the peace and good government of its neighbours. They cannot afford to ignore it. No time must be lost in bringing it to reason. Its excitements and dissipations wax madder and more widespread. No time can be lost. Hence the avengers come from all quarters in haste and eagerly. "Sanctify war against her! Arise, let us go up at noon!"—the heat being no barrier to their setting out; "Arise, and let us go up in the night!"—the darkness and weariness being forgotten in their hatred and vengeance. For the same reason no terms can be made with it. The Mosaic regulations in warfare are set aside (Deut. xx. 19, 20). There is no chivalrous respect inspired by it, and as it shows no mercy, none is accorded to it.

III. IT IS A CONTINUAL OFFENCE TO GOD. God's love for it had been great, and he had purposed to make it a centre of redeeming love. This aim had been thwarted. So it has been with the city life of man everywhere. As a natural development, and a providential result in human history, the city is intended to enlarge the powers of doing good and to bless the world. But how seldom has this been the case! The centralization of life has but intensified its corruption. Is there any place where the salvation of society seems more hopeless than in our great cities? And God's patience threatens to give out. He cannot bear the noisomeness of its evil. He is about to turn from it in utter loathing and final abandonment. But not yet. Warning is given; a prophet is sent. Nay, the Son himself, if haply they will hear him, in whom alone a sufficient antidote is found. In him is salvation, for of the holy city, the New Jerusalem, the scene of regenerated society, he is Centre and Lord. He is the "Fountain opened for sin and for all uncleanness."—M.

Ver. 13.—*The ministry of deceit.* The extent to which corruption prevailed is suggested when even the prophets and priests share the general apostasy: "Every one dealeth falsely."

I. THE DUTY IT HAD TO FULFIL. The priest dealt with ritual, the prophet with moral and doctrinal questions in religion. They had to act as the spiritual guides and overseers of the people of God. Here they are represented as behaving like quack doctors in cases of grave injury or disease. They were appointed for the spiritual health and well-being of men. Circumstances in the condition of their flocks would determine the manner in which they should exercise their functions, and the special direction in which their attention should be directed. Israel had fallen into serious wickedness. It was no isolated acts of transgression of which she was guilty; her whole spiritual state was one of alienation from God. In such a case the utmost faithfulness and severity were required; as the surgeon has to probe the wound, and use sharp instruments for excising the part that is diseased; or the physician has to make a thorough diagnosis of a patient, and in desperate sickness to use desperate remedies. Here an opposite course had been pursued. The gravity of the "hurt" was overlooked or ignored, and merely outward signs of amendment were regarded as complete reconciliation with God. 1. *That which separates men from God is no slight matter.* It is a deadly thing. If it continues, it must inevitably destroy. The observances of religion will be nullified until it is put right. Men must be told of their sin, not merely in a round and general manner, but judiciously, and according to the specialities of individual or class peculiarities. The unbelief of the natural man is the parent of his misdeeds and sin, and keeps him from any real communion with God. 2. *The minister of religion is bound to be discerning and faithful.* 3. *It is only through a real and spiritual repentance that reconciliation can be effected.* At such a juncture spiritual religion ought to have been insisted on, and the enormity of the offence exposed. Preliminary acts of contrition; experiences and discoveries of the heart such as conviction of sin, etc.; the necessity of love, obedience, and faith ought not to be slurred over.

II. FAILURE IN THIS DUTY AND ITS CAUSES. The root-cause is undoubtedly the share which the religious teachers had in the general depravity. There was also a consequent lack of spiritual discernment. The greatness of the fall from the former position occupied by Israel was not appreciated, and the nature of true religion was not understood. A ministry under court patronage and a merely popular ministry are alike subject to the temptations to please rather than to deal honestly with the evils of individuals, society, and the state, and to rectify them. "They who live to please must please to live." There is such a thing always as a making of religion too easy either in its moral conditions or its doctrinal realizations. It is fearfully wrong to say a man is a Christian when he is not a Christian; or so to deal with him in pastoral relations that he fancies himself in possession of salvation and spiritually secure when he is in heart and life far from God. Flattery has a thousand forms, and there is no falsehood to which it contributes that is more insidious or wide-reaching than this.

III. THE RESULTS. These are terrible in the extreme. From the authority of office they are credited in their declarations, and national and individual offences are condoned and perpetuated. Possible for a man to be deceived on this most vital question; to think himself a child of God when he is in reality a child of Satan. Death-bed repentances. 1. *The divorce of morality from religion.* 2. *The intensified wrath of God at hypocrisy and sham religion.* 3. *Eternal death and irretrievable loss.*—M.

Ver. 16.— *The old paths.* Men are surrounded from their earliest years with various religious systems, the claims of which conflict. To a conscientious mind, intellectual disquietude is the first result of this; in those less in earnest it produces and justifies indifference. All religions tend, under these circumstances, to assume the aspect of speculative questions, and the moral life is increasingly detached from religious sanctions. Morality must thereby be impaired, if it do not ultimately disappear. The prophet, therefore, recalls the people to the consideration of religion as a practical question. It is with him a question not of pure theory, but of conduct and experience. He urges the settlement of the conflict upon these grounds, and furnishes certain criteria by which to determine it.

I. ANTIQUITY IS A TEST OF TRUE RELIGION. Man is a religious being by nature, and God has never left himself without a witness in the world. There has been no generation in which some have not sought and found him. From the very first, therefore, there must have been religious conditions observed, which from their nature must be, as they were intended to be, permanent. The argument for the existence of God, for instance, is greatly strengthened by the evidence of the recognition of him by primitive and ancient peoples. Even in their errors and mistakes, when their views and observances are collated and compared, witness is given to fundamental truths. But the argument is stronger still when the people appealed to are those who, like Israel, have an historical faith. Ages of faith were behind them, illustrated by mighty heroes and saintly men of God. For ages a certain communion had been observed between the nation and its theocratic Head. What was the secular character of those ages? Were they marked by political strength, social order and purity, and commercial prosperity? Were the leaders of the people men whose ideal of life and actual behaviour commended themselves to the general conscience of the world? Was it to be supposed that any essential truth for the spiritual guidance of men had to be discovered thus late in the day? Were men to be always on tiptoe to learn what the last finding of research might be? There were paths that had been tried by holy men. When the nation was at its best, it acknowledged God in these ways. The vast majority of those who were holiest and best had tried them and found them satisfactory.

II. BUT DISCRIMINATION IS REQUIRED. The children of Israel were to "stand in the ways," *i.e.* to examine the different systems of religion and morals that laid claim to their attention. Critical and historical judgment had to be exercised. It is *not simply the oldest religion that is to be retained and followed,* but that in the religious history of the past which has most evidently conduced to noble action, spiritual health, and well-being. The heathenisms of the world are self-condemned; immorality has ever tended to destruction. The Englishman, therefore, is not to look to the Druids for infallible teaching; nor Christians to the saints of the Old Testament times. The dictum of Ignatius is sound: *Nobis vera antiquitas est Jesus Christus.* But the teaching and personality of Jesus were commended by their essential agreement with Mosaicism in its most ancient form; as that in turn was but a confirmation and elaboration of patriarchal convictions, experiences, and revelations. The truth that has been held in all ages is retained in each new development of revelation and history, but it is spiritualized and grounded upon deeper and wider sanctions.

III. THE NATURAL HUMAN DESIRE FOR MERE NOVELTY HAS TO BE OVERCOME. True religion is not to be despised because it is old. The truth, when carefully studied and spiritually realized, is ever new and fresh. And the "new truths" to which advancing time introduces us are justified only as we can organically and spiritually evolve them from their archaic predecessors. Obligations which are merely relative will change or disappear with the relations upon which they are founded, but the cardinal truths of heart and life must ever retain their authority, and new experience will but tend to deepen and strengthen their hold upon the religious nature. If, on the other hand, the teachings of experience and the warnings of prophets are despised, new heinousness will be added to the wickedness of the wicked. It will be wilful disobedience, and as such will be more severely punished.

IV. OBEDIENCE TO THESE DOCTRINES OF EXPERIENCE WILL CONFIRM AND SATISFY THE SOUL. If, in spite of these corroborations, the doctrines were productive of misery and spiritual unrest, then they would go for nothing. But this is the final and absolute criterion—Do they tend to the welfare and increase of spiritual life, and to the satisfaction of the deepest longings of the soul?—M.

Vers. 18—20.—*The reasonableness of the Divine judgments.* The language employed suggests publicity. The world is called into solemn council—a "congregation" for judgment. 1. *Not that upon questions of this nature the carnal mind is any authority of and by itself.* "Who art thou that judgest?" might well be asked of any who assumed such an office. It is only as confirming and justifying the action taken by God. Thus understood, the testimony of the world is most valuable, being different from what might be expected. It is a great mystery, this judgment of God's apostate people by the heathen nations. 2. *And yet we must not understand it as a mere figure of speech.* There is a real endorsement of the righteous judgments of God in the mind of the world—one of those revealing circumstances which show "the Law of God written upon their heart." When the question is a broad, simple, and evident one, even the most perverted soul will affirm the sentence of Heaven. Unbelief is only superficial. Beneath the crust of hardened consciences there still remains a primitive sense of justice; and to this will the final sentence of condemnation appeal, when we shall give account of the deeds done in the body. The sinner will not only hear the decision from the great white throne, but he will stand self-condemned; and the universal assembly will confirm the verdict. 3. *How fearful, too, must have been the guilt of God's people that on this occasion such umpires could have been so confidently appealed to!* The features of their criminality that are emphasized are these: *obstinacy* and *hypocrisy.* The latter is but the abettor of the former. The unreality of Israel's repentance was especially abhorrent to Jehovah. It vitiates all the costly articles and enhancements of their worship, and is but the cloak of a real continuance in sin. If, then, they do in heart refuse to obey God, what more reasonable than that he should suffer the laws of his universe to deal with them, and punish them with "the fruit of their thoughts"? The angels of vengeance that wait upon sin, licentiousness, luxury, and waste, will be suffered to do their work; and they shall learn by experience that "the way of transgressors is hard." But the instant that the spirit of reality and sincerity revisits their hearts, his ear will be open to their cry, and his mercy will redeem.—M.

Vers. 27—30.—*The prophet a spiritual assayer.* Of interest as a description of process of refining precious metals among ancient peoples. The grinding and washing of the ore to discover and separate the precious metals, the fusing of the silver with lead in order to its further purification, and the repetition of this under severer heat, are processes which are used to illustrate the influence of the words of revelation upon the human heart. These words—

I. REVEAL CHARACTER. "Some believed, and some believed not," is the consequence always following upon the faithful preaching of the truth. "It is a hard saying; who can hear it?" How instantaneous were the results in this way attendant on the proclamations of Biblical prophets and preachers! They addressed the conscience, the affection, and the will, and pressed for a verdict and practical following up of opinion in action. Much more is this the case with the gospel, because of its deeper and more spiritual force. It is by hearing the Word, and looking into the mirror it affords, that a man is discovered to himself.

II. DETERMINE DESTINY. Sometimes in a good, sometimes in a bad sense. In the case before us it is wholly the latter. As there was no reality or earnestness in Israel, so there was no point at which a commencement could be made towards reformation. They are all concluded guilty and worthless. It was a severe judgment, but was meant in mercy to the people themselves. They were thereby warned of the need of radical change, and the supernatural, saving grace of God. It is by the determinations and effects produced by the hearing of the Word that the future is influenced. There is a distinct moral responsibility incurred each time the truth is proclaimed in our hearing. Nothing else so searches into and potently affects the moral nature, because the conscience is most vividly aroused and reality in all its naked force bursts upon the soul. The furthest developments of personal character, interest, and occupation may be thus conditioned: " See, then, how ye hear ! "

III. ARE CAREFULLY ADAPTED, BY INCREASINGLY SEVERE PROCESSES, TO EFFECT THEIR END. They result in rejection, and this is rendered inevitable by the utter worthlessness of character and work exhibited. If there is any good in a man, the truth will discover it, and sympathetically develop and reinforce it ; if not, it will only the more utterly and unquestionably condemn him. The ear does not try words more delicately or decisively than words of God try the heart. According to their spiritual state will men be condemned, approved ; received or rejected by the hearing of the gospel. Some men have been tried and condemned by it already; to others it opens more and more widely the door of hope.—M.

Vers. 1—8.—*A dreadful onlook.* Such was the vision of Jeremiah which he saw concerning the coming wrath upon Judah and Jerusalem. It was the sad sight which the sinners in Jerusalem never, but the seer ever, saw clearly, vividly, heart-brokenly. The vision of Jeremiah for Jerusalem was the forerunner of our Lord's in substance, spirit, and result. Now, with regard to this awful onlook of the prophet which is here related, note—

I. How SOLITARY IT WAS. The people of Judah and Jerusalem were in no fear, and for forty years and more this vision was not realized. Other eyes saw nothing to be troubled about, and men generally were at ease in Zion. It was only the purged vision of the prophet that pierced the future and portrayed the dread realities of that fast-coming day. *He* saw clearly what others saw not at all. And so it is always. But why is this ? Why do sinners *not* see ? Take an answer from those senseless exhibitions in which the performers place themselves in positions of frightful peril, so that a moment's unsteadiness of nerve, the slightest slipping of hand or foot, would lead to their immediate inevitable and dreadful death ; running all this risk to amuse the gaping, shameless crowds, who stare, stamp, and shout their applause at what never ought to be done. But let these performers provide us a reply to the question we have asked. They will tell you that at first they approached those dangerous places with great fear ; how it was long ere they could walk with ease along that slender cord, or stand fearless on that dizzy height. But they got at length so used to these things that now they go through their perilous performances without the slightest fear. And so is it with grievous sinners against God. They have got so used to the threatening of his anger that they think nothing of it after a while, and go on unconcernedly until almost the moment of his vengeance bursts upon them. " Because sentence against an evil work is not executed speedily, therefore," etc. Their heart wishes that there may be nought to fear. The long-suffering and forbearance of God are perverted, by the deceitfulness of sin, to foster that belief, and so they at length persuade themselves that what God's servants see so clearly and warn them of so faithfully has no real existence, and " as it was in the days of Noah, so is it also in the days when the Son of man cometh." Oh, what need for the prayer, " From all the *deceits* of the world, the flesh, and the devil, good Lord, deliver us " !

II. How VIVIDLY SEEN. Jeremiah sees the hurried flocking of the Benjamites (see Exposition), the terrified inhabitants of Jerusalem, to some common centre in the city, and then their hasting away out of the southern gates towards Tekoa, one of the southernmost cities of the land, and furthest off from the dread invaders, who were speeding from the north. The alarm-trumpet sounding its shrill notes amid the quiet streets of Tekoa; he sees the signal-fires blazing from the height of Beth-haccerem, and answered by other like fires, all telling of distress; and then, from hill-summits yet further away, he sees the never-ending train of fierce and victory-flushed soldiers marching ruthlessly on in all the pride and pomp of war, streaming along the great northern roads, the open highway whereby they entered the holy land. He sees the various encampments, the spoliation of the whole district round, the eager haste of the foe to attack the great fortress of Jerusalem, the goal of all their hopes and the prize of their arduous campaign; he sees the varied preparations for war, the building of the engines of attack, the burning of her palaces; in short, the whole dread details of a city doomed to destruction at the hands of a besieging army. Thus vivid was the vision. And such clearness of onlook is given to God's seers that they may thereby more deeply impress and more surely move the minds of those they are sent to. It is well to muse over things unseen and eternal until they become real to us, until our faith becomes the evidence of the things not seen, and gives substance, shape, and body to the things hoped for. Then as those who have tasted and handled and felt the powers of the world to come, we shall speak with unwonted power, and men through us will also see what they have never seen before. But—

III. How WELL FOUNDED THIS VISION WAS. For the prophet came to the conviction of the coming wrath upon his country, not on any light grounds, but on such as in all ages may lead to a like conviction. 1. *There was the extreme importance of Jerusalem*, as an almost impregnable mountain fortress. In the frequent wars between Egypt and Assyria this fortress was the object of much solicitude to either side. And besides her strength there was her wealth and her fame, so that Jerusalem became a coveted possession to one great monarchy after another. Jeremiah (ver. 2) compares her to a beautiful and luxuriant pasturage (cf. Exposition). And as shepherds would covet such pasturage for their flocks, so the enemies of Jerusalem would covet her. So attractive, so desirable was she in their esteem. This fact, then, of the worth of Jerusalem to Assyria was one reason wherefore Jeremiah knew that that lawless and rapacious nation would certainly attack her. 2. *The "delight in war" which characterized Assyria.* Vers. 4, 5 represent the language of their soldiers, their eagerness to be led to the attack, their impatience at every hindrance, their disregard both of the heat of noon or darkness of night. They were a people ever on the look out for plunder and aggrandizement, and seized on the very first pretext that offered for invasion and capture. 3. *The prophet's clear perception that God was on the side of Israel's foes.* Ver. 6, "Thus hath the Lord of hosts said." It was, therefore, his will. It had been borne in upon his mind that God's wrath was ready to be poured out. He had been told so by the Spirit of God; he "spiritually discerned" the dark facts of the future, so that they stood out vivid and clear before the eye of his soul. 4. *And his conviction that such was God's will could not but be deepened by the constant presence before him of the atrocious wickedness of the doomed city.* Ver. 7, "As a fountain," perpetually, copiously freely, irresistibly, "casts out her waters, so did Jerusalem cast out," etc. The moral corruption of the people made him certain that the holy God of Israel would not suffer it to go on unpunished. And it is ever so. Let a nation, a family, a Church, an individual, give themselves up to wickedness and gross violation of the commands of God, it is certain that sentence of death is on them. Execution may be deferred, but unless there be repentance it will certainly be carried out. There were special features about the vision that was given to Jeremiah, but every believer in God sees in substance the very same. The deep-felt conviction of the godly is the expression of the will of God. What such a one binds on earth is bound in heaven, and whose sins such retain they are retained. It is a terrible fact, then, when any come under the grave moral condemnation of the people of God, for their condemnation is but the echo of those thunders they have heard reverberating around the throne of God.

IV. How MERCIFULLY SENT. Their purpose was obvious. Many years God would yet wait. Thus he gave this call to repentance, and waited long to see if it would be needed. The most loving words of Jesus are those which make our hearts tremble and our spirits quake with fear; those which tell of the everlasting fire and the never-dying worm. For these awful declarations are the expedients of love to drive, to terrify, to force away from the edge of the precipice of ruin those whom no other means will withdraw therefrom. And that this is the intent of these awful representations of God's wrath is seen in ver. 8, where God pathetically pleads with Jerusalem to be "instructed" by his words, "lest his soul depart from" her. Remember, then: 1. *It is only the eye, purged by the Spirit of truth, that can see the truth as to ourselves or others.* Until thus cleansed, we may be going down to our graves with a lie in our right hand. 2. *Praise and bless God for his loving warnings to the wicked.* Pray that they may be heeded, and be careful not to disguise or diminish them by prophesyings of peace when there is no peace. 3. *Hasten to be yourself and to bring others to be safe within the shelter of the love of God, where no evil can befall and no plague ever come nigh.*—C.

Ver. 1.—*Signal-fires.* "Set up a sign of fire in Beth-haccerem." Introduction—Illustrate from Homer's description of such signal-fires, or from Macaulay's poem, 'Defeat of the Spanish Armada.' Take them as illustrative of the warnings of God against sin.
I. REVIEW SOME OF THESE SIGNAL-FIRES. 1. The Bible. 2. The ministers of God's truth. 3. Conscience. 4. Present judgments upon men's sin.
II. NOTE WHEREFORE THEY SHOULD BE SET UP. 1. Men are living in grievous sin. 2. God's judgments are near at hand. 3. Men are in a state of false security. 4. They will rally the good to increased exertion. 5. They will arouse and arrest the wicked. 6. That like fires may be enkindled by the faithful, who have seen them and taken the warning, and will therefore send it on. 7. God's sore judgment will come upon those who do not set them up.
III. HOW THIS MAY BE DONE. 1. By faithful preaching. 2. By living in the fear of God. 3. By separation from the ungodly. 4. By seeking to save all over whom you have influence from the wrath to come.
IV. WHEN DONE, LET THESE WARNINGS BE AS SIGNAL-FIRES. 1. Such as all must observe. 2. Such as all will understand. 3. Set up from sense of the reality both of the threatened danger and the people's need. 4. Kept burning steadily in spite of all that would quench them.
V. THE SIGNAL-FIRES THAT GOD SETS UP HAVE THESE CHARACTERISTICS. 1. The Bible. 2. Conscience. 3. Present judgments.
VI. LET OURS HAVE THE SAME.—C.

Vers. 2, 3.—*The Lord's pasture.* Patterns of things spiritual and eternal are scattered broadcast over God's universe. Nothing is more pleasant than to trace these resemblances out. Our Lord was ever "likening" things in the kingdom of heaven to things he saw around him in the world. His own word, "parables," tells of things "placed by the side" of others for comparison of their likenesses or contrasts. The prophet in these verses "likens" Jerusalem—the daughter of Zion—to a beautiful and luxuriant pasturage (cf. Exposition). He was speaking of the material city. But *that* daughter of Zion leads our thoughts to the heavenly Jerusalem, the city of God, the Church, "which he has purchased with his own blood." Now, that may be fitly likened to such a pasture; it is the Lord's pasture. For—
I. THERE THE SHEEP OF THE GOOD SHEPHERD FIND REST AND REFRESHMENT AFTER THE OFTEN WEARY JOURNEY OVER THE WAYS OF THE WORLD. (Cf. Ps. xxiii., lxxxiv.) See the many testimonies to the spiritually refreshing and restful influence of the worship of the Church. "He maketh me to lie down in green pastures," etc.
II. THERE HIS SHEEP FIND PASTURE. "I will abundantly bless her provision: I will feed her poor with bread." By the ministry of God's truth, by the application, through the Holy Spirit's grace, of the things of Christ. Christ's people are fed as with the Bread of life.
III. THE COMELINESS AND BEAUTY OF THE CHURCH OF CHRIST JUSTIFY THIS COMPARISON. True, the Church has not yet put on her "beautiful garments." The prophetic visions of her glory and majesty still wait to be realized. "The bride" has not yet "made herself ready." But even as she is, in her garments of humiliation, treading her painful way as a weary pilgrim, who is like unto her? Where are moral beauty and grace to be found such as she possesses, and has shown—yea, is showing still—in spite of all imperfections? Even now—oh, how much more by-and-by!—the Church of Christ,

the Lord's pasture, is the fairest, loveliest scene this poor sin and sorrow stricken earth presents. Even now she is Christ's bride, and all spiritual beauty and comeliness are summed up in that.

IV. For attractiveness. Cf. ver. 3, which tells how other shepherds were irresistibly drawn to this pasturage, and how eagerly they led their flocks there. As concerned the earthly Jerusalem this had no happy meaning, but as concerns Christ's Church its meaning is happy and blessed indeed. It is good that the fowls of the air should lodge in the branches of the great tree, which has sprung from the tiny seed planted by the Lord. And it is good that "nations, and peoples, and tribes, and tongues" should, as many already have been, and as all others will be, drawn by the attractiveness of the rich and luxuriant pasturage which the Lord's pasture offers. It is a weary world; self and sin are cruel taskmasters; they have no green pastures into which they lead their sheep. The opened ear of those whose hearts are touched with Christ's sympathy perpetually hears the cry for help, the longing to be led into the pasture of the Lord. It is a reproach to every professed disciple of Christ if he do not, by what he is and by the spirit of his life, attract others to the Lord's pasture, and lead them to say, " We will go with you, for we see that the Lord is with you."

V. It is there where the Lord leads his sheep. Many think they can be Christ's without uniting themselves to his people, keeping amid the world's ways and standing aloof from the Lord's pasture. But this is wrong. There is a sense in which the old saying, " Nulla salus extra ecclesiam," is true, and nothing casts graver doubt on the reality of our discipleship than absence of sympathy with other disciples, and no liking for their companionship. Love for "the brethren" is given as one note of having "passed from death unto life." It is the Lord's will that his people should be banded together in their several folds, and the instinct of the renewed heart almost certainly leads it to desire this pasturage. Hence, as a fact, there are scarce any, if any, of the disciples of Christ who are not found in one or other of the folds into which the one flock of the Good Shepherd is divided.

Conclusion. Ask two questions: 1. *Of those who are not Christ's.* Do you find that the ways of the world are really better than the Lord's pasture? is it better to serve sin and self than Christ? We are sure that there can be but one answer. Why, then, do you not hear the voice of the Good Shepherd and "follow" him? 2. *Of those who are his.* Are you careful not to blotch and blur that likeness? Many do this, so that the likeness cannot be traced, and the world turns away from it, not drawn by what it sees. Strive to let men see in you somewhat—much—of that spiritual grace and beauty which will lead men greatly to desire to enter the Lord's pasture for themselves.—C.

Ver. 4.—*Sorrow because of eventide.* "Woe unto us! for the day goeth away, for the shadows of the evening are stretched out." It is not thus that we are wont to welcome the going away of the day, the quiet peaceful hours of eventide. How *beautiful*, even in its outward aspect, is oftentimes the evening hour, the gradual subsidence of the varied sounds of the busy day, the glorious sunsets, the rich radiance of the evening sky, the exquisite tints and colourings of the hills as the mellow light of evening falls upon them, the ruby glow which adorns, glorifies, and almost transfigures the sun-clad peaks of mountainous lands! Yes, eventide is an hour of beauty, in which Nature puts on her almost loveliest garb now that the "garish day" has gone. It is a scene on which the eye delightedly rests. And it is the hour of *reunion* also. From the scattered districts where one and another have pursued their daily toil, the members of the family, the household, the village, come home, and in pleasant converse talk over the events of the day, and forecast the events of to-morrow. The hearts of the children turn to the fathers, and the heart of the fathers to the children, in the happy intercourse which is only possible on the blessed Sunday or at the evening hour. And it is the hour of *rest.* The plough stands still in the furrow, for the ploughman has gone home; the toil-worn horse roams in his pasture or feeds peacefully in his stable. The man of business has shut up his ledger, and left the city and the office, and rests quietly amid his family at home. The night has come, in which no man can work. And if we take the symbolic meaning of the day and regard it as telling of *the day of life,* even then the ideas of calm, rest, and serene quiet gather around it. What a beautiful old age is that described in the seventy-first psalm—beautiful for its confidence in God, for its humility and meekness, for the vigour of its desire for God's glory, and for its bright onlook into the future! And such beauty often belongs to old age, so that "at eventide there is light." We probably all of us know of some on whom the shadows of evening are falling fast, because the day of their life "goeth away;" but how calm, how serene, how peaceful, how bright, is their old age! They do not say, nor do others say concerning them, "Woe unto us! for the day," etc. But in the text we have a precisely *opposite feeling*, one of dismay and sore grief because of the day's departure. And this lamentation is one uttered, not alone by those of whom the prophet wrote, but by many others also. Therefore let us—

I. LISTEN TO THOSE WHO MAKE THIS LAMENTATION. And: 1. There were *those of whom Jeremiah wrote*. The Chaldeans, who were about to invade Judæa and Jerusalem. The text occurs in a vivid description of the troubles they would bring upon his people. He is representing their eagerness, their furious haste to assail and capture the doomed city. Hence the interruption of nightfall is fiercely resented by them. They would lengthen out the day if but they could. Like as Joshua bade the sun stand still (Josh. x.), that he might complete the overthrow of his enemies, so would these Chaldeans like that the sun should stand still, that they might complete the overthrow of theirs. And because that cannot be, therefore they exclaim, "Woe unto us!" etc. What a lesson these Chaldean soldiers give to the professed soldiers of Christ! Would that we had the like zeal in our endeavour to win the kingdom of heaven! But it is only the violent, those who are in real earnest and put forth all their "force," who shall take it. 2. But if we take the day as referring to the day of life, we shall often hear *in Holy Scripture* the like lamentation. The saints of the Old Testament, how they shrank from death: "Oh, spare me, that I may recover strength, before I go hence, and be no more;" "The dead praise not thee, neither any that go down into silence;" "The living, the living, shall praise thee, as I do this day." The overflowing gratitude of the hundred and sixteenth psalm is because of deliverance from the dreaded death. How Hezekiah (Isa. xxxviii.) piteously wept and prayed that he might not die! They knew not that to depart was far better; death was to them only gloomy, silent, dark, and where fellowship with God was not. Hence this "Woe unto us!" etc., expresses the common feeling of Old Testament times at the going away of the day of life. 3. But there are *those who still make like lamentation*. Let us listen to them. (1) Those from whom *the day of opportunity* is going away. We none of us like to miss opportunities. Even to miss a train vexes us. How much more when we see slipping fast from us the power of gaining and doing great good! The scholar who has let slip the opportunities of winning the knowledge which would fit him for his life's work, but now must go forth all ill equipped, and so must with shame take a lower place. The youth or man who has failed to win the confidence of those about him, and now has to leave them without the great advantage which their confidence would have given him. The professed disciple of Christ who has some child, some companion, some one over whom he had influence, leaving him for a distance, or, more grievous still, by death, and he has never used his opportunity of speaking to him on behalf of Christ. This is a woe indeed, a reflection bitter to have resting upon one's conscience. The brother or sister, the husband or wife, the companion or friend, who have let go opportunities of showing kindness, of comforting and helping those who looked to them for such comfort and help, and now it is too late. Ah! that is a dreadful thought, to think of what you might have done for them and ought to have done but did not, and now can never do. All these are instances in which those from whom the day of opportunity is going away will often lament, "Woe unto us!" It is with a bitter pang that we see "the shadows" of that "evening stretched out." (2) Those from whom *the day of prosperity* is going away. Listen to the patriarch Job (xxix. 3): "Oh that I were as in months past, as in the days when God preserved me!" And all through the chapter he continues his sad lament over happy days gone by. And so now to see the like befall ourselves—health, wealth, friends, dear children, or those even dearer still, all going from us, what wonder that such say, "Woe is us!" etc.? But sometimes it is on account of the going away of the day of *spiritual* prosperity. The mournful retrospect of days of purity, peace, strength, enjoyment of God, delight in his worship, usefulness in his service; but these now all gone or fast disappearing. Ah! the backslider, the man who suffers himself to lose his religion, has many bitter moments of regret and remorse. How he curses the sinful folly which led him to lend an ear to the deceitful suggestions of the wicked one, and which have brought him to this wretched pass! Yes, it is a terrible thing to see the day of spiritual prosperity going away and the shadows of its evening stretched out. (3) Those from whom *the day of a life lived without God* is going away. This must be dreadful indeed. They have drunk up all that the cup of this world has to give them; there is not a drop left, and there is no provision made for the eternity to which they are hastening. With what intensity of bitterness will the "Woe unto us!" of such be uttered! For though such perceive that eternity is near, and God's awful judgment bar, yet how difficult, how all but impossible do they find it to hurry on their preparations as they would fain do! The lips unused to pray cannot pray. The habits of unbelief and worldliness won't be broken. Faith will not come. They have so long turned away from Christ that now they cannot turn to him. Pride holds back the confession which their repentance would make, that all their past life has been one melancholy mistake. Such are some of the great difficulties which stand in the way of him who, at the close of a long life lived without God, would then turn to God. And as he sees that now this world is lost to him, and the next not won and all but impossible to be won, how inevitable the exceeding bitter cry, "Woe unto us!" etc.! But now—

II. LET US ENDEAVOUR TO LIGHTEN THIS LAMENTATION, AND TO COMFORT THOSE WHO SAY, "WOE UNTO US!" 1. Those who lament the going away of *the day of opportunity.* Remember that *all* opportunity is not gone. "Why should a living man complain?" "A live dog is better than a dead lion." (Illustrate from Foster's essay on 'Decision of Character.' Story of a spendthrift who had lost a vast estate suddenly resolving that he would regain it, and at once setting about to earn money, though ever so little, and at length, by dint of prolonged, hard, and often degrading toil and of rigid economy, accomplishing his resolve. Such victories have been won in spite of temporal loss.) Remember *all* is not gone. And where spiritual opportunities have been let go, sad as such loss is, others yet remain. "Sleep on now, and take your rest;" that was our Saviour's way of telling his unwatchful disciples that they had lost the opportunity of ministering to him as he had asked them. But in the next breath he says, "Rise, let us be going: behold, he that betrayeth," etc.; that was his way of telling them that there were opportunities for other service yet awaiting them. Peter, when he went out after his denial of his Lord, and wept bitterly, thought that nevermore would he have opportunity of doing aught for that dear, dear Lord whom he had so shamefully denied. But 'twas after that the Lord said to him, "Feed my lambs," "Feed my sheep." Therefore waste no time in mere brooding over lost opportunities. Confess your faithlessness, and seek forgiveness, and then ask the Lord to show you what yet remains that you may do for him. And be sure that he will graciously deal with you as he did with his apostle of old. 2. Those who lament the going away of *the day of prosperity.* If you are not a believer in Christ—one born again of the Holy Ghost unto him, then I know not how to comfort you or how to lighten your lamentation. I can only counsel you to kneel and pray that this loss of temporal good may lead you to him who waits to give you eternal good, in the gain of which all earthly loss will be forgotten. God grant you may follow this counsel. But if you are a child of God, then remember *Christ will be with you in your trial.* Was there not another with the three Hebrew youths in the furnace of fire, so that its fierce flames burned them not, and they walked up and down as if beneath the cool shade of the trees of Paradise? Manifold and great good to you and through you is undoubtedly designed by letting such trial come to you. To give you holy skill and blessed tenderness in ministering to other troubled souls; to impart to you deeper knowledge of yourself; to make you the means of making known to others what Divine grace can do. This was why God suffered Job to be so tried, and why the Lord put the faith of the Syrophœnician woman to so severe a strain. Did not our Lord himself become the "Man of sorrows and acquainted with grief"? What do we not all owe to that? And so through his people becoming more or less men of sorrows and acquainted with grief, large blessing shall flow down to others. Then do not think it all "woe" if the day of your earthly prosperity does seem to be "going away," and the shadows of its evening be stretched out. 3. Those who lament the going away of the day of a life lived without God. To such we would say that it is a rare mercy that they are distressed at all. For many die as they have lived, indifferent and unconcerned about God and things eternal. But if alarm and fear have been awakened, that is a token of mercy. The dying robber on the cross beside our Lord, at that last hour turned to him, and was *not* refused the mercy he craved. Christ " saves to *the uttermost* all that come unto God by him." Give glory to him by even now turning to him, as he bids you do. But let none presume on the possibilities of such repentance at the very last. " The Gospels tell of one such, that none may despair ; but of only one, that none may presume." " Remember now thy Creator in the days of thy youth."

> " To Jesus may we fly
> Swift as the morning light,
> Lest life's young golden beams should die
> In sudden endless night."

If we be found in *him*, then the exceeding bitter cry of our text will never be heard from us. The day of opportunity will not leave us. If the day of earthly prosperity do leave us, then it will be because the Lord hath provided some better thing for us. And when the day of life goeth away and we with it, it will be but " to depart and be with Christ, which is far better."—C.

Vers. 4, 5.—*How the kingdom of heaven is to be taken.* " Prepare ye war," etc. It is lawful to learn from the children of this generation, who are wiser in their affairs than the children of light. Therefore, from the way in which the enemies of Judah should assail her, we may learn how the kingdom of heaven is to be won. There is—

I. The recognition of the reality of the struggle. " Prepare ye war," etc.

II. Casting aside of all suggestions of ease. " Let us go up at noon ; " the burning heat did not matter.

III. Impatience of hindrances. " Woe unto us ! for the day," etc.

IV. Resolve to encounter any and every peril rather than be put back from their enterprise. " Let us go up by night."

V. Determination not to rest till the power of the foe be utterly destroyed. " Let us destroy her palaces," etc.—C.

Ver. 6.—*The real director of human affairs.* " For thus hath the Lord of hosts said, Hew ye down trees," etc. Nothing could seem a more purely human affair than the invasion of Judah and Jerusalem by the armies of Babylon. Its motives, methods, means, results, were all just such as were perfectly comprehensible and according to the manners of that age and the peoples concerned. One event followed another in natural sequence, and was fully explained, so men would say, by what went before. And so in reference to a still more notable event—the crucifixion of our Lord Jesus Christ. To the eye of an ordinary historian, that supreme event was brought about in altogether a common and ordinary way. But as concerning that event, so concerning this of which Jeremiah tells, it is distinctly declared that *God* was overruling and directing all that took place. Not that God was the author of the wickedness which seemed triumphant in these events—especially in the " wicked hands " by which our Lord was " crucified and slain." No, but just as, when a fire has broken forth and is threatening to devour and destroy on all hands, wise and skilful firemen, when they cannot quench it, will contrive to lead it in a given direction, will order the path it shall take as seems to them best, *so* God, when he sees the raging fire of wickedness has broken forth, guides and orders the path it shall take, the work it shall do. Wickedness is never attributable to God, but the development and form it shall assume are so. Hence in the text, the Lord of hosts is represented as the real Commander of the armies that were to invade Judah and Jerusalem ; it was *his* orders they were in fact obeying, though nothing was further from their thoughts than this. And so we are taught that *God* is behind all human affairs, ordering and directing them according to his will.

> " There's a divinity that shapes our ends,
> Rough-hew them how we will."

And now we ask—

I. WHY SHOULD NOT THIS BE SO? Many reply that if you find an adequate cause for any given effect, there is no need to look for any other. But, in answer, see, I let this book fall; what causes it to fall? The law of gravity will adequately explain it. But was that the real cause? Was not *my will to let it fall* that real cause? And so in human affairs, we may see the immediate antecedent, but we have a right to ask, "What lies behind that?" You say, "Sufficiently plain motives led to such and such conduct;" but we ask, "Who brought these motives into action? who or what set them at work so that these results have come about?" Further—

II. GOD IS A PERFECTLY HOLY BEING, AND THEREFORE MUST DESIRE TO HAVE ALL MORAL NATURES MADE LIKE UNTO HIMSELF. "Good and upright is the Lord, *therefore* will he teach sinners in the way." "The righteous Lord loveth righteousness;" hence we are bidden, "Give thanks at the remembrance of his holiness." Hence it is certain that he will employ all means consistent with the nature he has given us to bring our wills into harmony with his own. Therefore when we see a whole system of things, an entire course of events, tending to and actually producing this result—for the Captivity did cure Israel of their idolatry, they went no more after false gods, nor have they done so ever since—we at once put it down to him whose nature and whose will we know.

III. AND OUR INDIVIDUAL CONSTITUTION SUPPORTS THIS VIEW. There are Divine laws for the body, the mind, the affections. And to bring us into harmony with his laws, which are the expression of his will, he has "begirt us round" with safeguards and guides which, if we heed, happy are we, but if we neglect, we suffer. It is certain that the health of our whole nature follows obedience to these laws; and, on the other hand, the misery which results from disobedience declares plainly his will, and shows that he is behind all those facts which we call the causes of these results, and is himself *the* Cause of them all. Now, this is true in the case of each single person. May it not, therefore, be true in the case of the world at large, and in regard to what we call "causes and effects"? Then note further—

IV. THE UNITY OF PURPOSE WHICH IS SEEN THROUGHOUT THE ORDERING OF THE UNIVERSE, SO FAR AS WE CAN TRACE, SEEMS TO INDICATE ONE MIND GOVERNING ALL. Read history, or such a book as Creasy's 'Decisive Battles of the World,' and note how each great struggle has helped forward the advance of humanity, has bettered the condition of mankind, so that it is terrible to think what, in many instances, would have been the consequences had the events fallen out in an opposite way. The hand of God in history is clearly discernible by all who believe heartily in the living, all-holy, all-loving God.

V. And, of course, THE WHOLE AUTHORITY OF SCRIPTURE SUPPORTS THIS DOCTRINE. (Cf. the story of Joseph, and his answer to his brethren, "It was not you that sent me hither, but God.")

VI. Learn in CONCLUSION: 1. To cast out from your minds every idea or thought of chance, fate, or any mere haphazard coming about of events. 2. How seriously we ought to look at the events of our own lives, and inquire God's meaning in regard to his dealings with us. We are not to be drawn off from this by the imagination that our little lives are far too insignificant for God to care for or direct. Does not God paint the roadside flower, the wing of the moth? Is there anything minute or insignificant in his esteem? 3. Rejoice and be exceeding glad. "Our Father's at the helm." "What we know not now we shall know hereafter." Therefore "rest in the Lord, and wait patiently for him."—C.

Ver. 7.—*Sin compared to a "fountain."* I. THE COMPARISON JUST. For: 1. *Naturalness.* A fountain or spring bursting out on the hillside excites no surprise as if it were an unheard-of, an extraordinary thing. Nor does the outflow of sin from the human heart. 2. *Continuance.* The streams of each may sing—

> "But men may come and men may go,
> But we flow on for ever."

3. *Having their source "from within."* Out of the depths both alike come. 4. *Unchangeableness in character.* What they were once they are always. 5. *Spon-*

taneousness. No force is needed to draw forth their streams. 6. *Copiousness.*
7. *Effectiveness.* The course of a stream is ever discernible by its effects. It tells on
all that it touches, it leaves nothing as it was before it came. 8. *Force.* The fountain
will have way given to it. It will break all barriers that block its way.

II. THE LESSON IS OBVIOUS. Shall we *divert* its streams, and compel them to run
only in quiet safe places where they will cause us no worldly harm? This is what
most men try to do, and very often succeed in doing. But this is not God's plan. His
charge is, " *Make the fountain good.*" And this he can do; he can create a clean heart
and renew a right spirit within us. "He that believeth in me," said our Saviour,
"from within him shall flow rivers of living water;" not, as now, rivers of death.
O Christ—

> "Thou of life the Fountain art,
> Freely let me take of thee:
> Spring thou up within my heart,
> Rise to all eternity."

C.

Ver. 8.—*The worst woe of the wicked.* "Be thou instructed, O Jerusalem, lest my
soul depart from thee."

I. THERE ARE MANY WOES WHICH ACCOMPANY SIN. "Many sorrows shall be to the
wicked." All observation attests the truth of this word.

II. BUT THERE IS ONE WHICH MAY FITLY BE SPOKEN OF AS THE WORST OF ALL. It is
this—God's soul departing from the sinner. This indeed is terrible. It is so amongst
men. We hear at times of those who have worn out the love even of those who loved
them most tenderly. They have made the soul of those who loved them to depart
from them. Sons have done this for fathers and mothers, friends for friends,
husbands for wives and wives for husbands; and to have thus driven away a deep and
earnest love is a depth of ruin than which none in this world can be more terrible.
But to have worn out the love of God—to have made *his* soul to depart from us, what
woe can compare to that? His providential favour may depart from us, and that is
sad. Our realization of his love in our hearts may depart from us, and that is sadder
still. But for his love itself to depart, that is the worst of all.

III. WHAT, THEN, CAN CAUSE SO GREAT A CALAMITY TO COME UPON A MAN? It is his
refusing instruction (cf. Prov. i., "Seeing thou hatest knowledge," etc.). This Judah
and Jerusalem were doing; this all too many are doing now.

IV. BUT THIS GOD DEPRECATES GREATLY, AND IMPLORES US NOT TO BE GUILTY OF.
" Be thou instructed, O Jerusalem," (cf. our Saviour's tears over Jerusalem). Appeal.—C.

Ver. 9.—"*Turn back thine hand.*" The text, no doubt, tells of the utter and
complete desolation which would result from the Chaldean invasion of Judah and
Jerusalem. In vivid dramatic form Jehovah is represented as bidding the invading
armies go over their ruthless work again, and make the desolation yet more awful.
Like as the grape-gatherer, after he had to all appearances stripped the vine of its
clusters, would " turn back his hand " amongst the tendrils, and search once more over
the whole branch to see that no solitary cluster had escaped him (" tendrils," rather
than " baskets," are what is meant; see Exposition); so, if there were a solitary village
or homestead which had escaped the fury of the foe, they are bidden go back on their
work, that none whatever might escape. Such the meaning, and it was ruthlessly
fulfilled. But the form of expression may be applied, not merely to the ministers of
God's vengeance, as in the text, but to those who serve him in ways far more acceptable and ordinary. We, therefore, take the charge, "Turn back thine hand as a
grape-gatherer," and address it—

I. TO THOSE WHO ARE AT WORK FOR GOD. The *self-satisfied*, who look at their work
with too much content, as if it could not be bettered,—these need this charge. And the
discouraged, who are for throwing up their work, abandoning it in sorrow and despair,
believing they can do nothing more,—to them God would say, "Turn back thine hand."
To *those who desire to do their work thoroughly.* Go over it again. See how Paul was
constantly in the habit of "turning back his hand," *i.e.* going over the Churches that
he had established, revisiting them, in order that he might "confirm" them in the

faith (cf. Acts, *passim*). "Line upon line, line upon line," is God's counsel to us in this matter.

II. To THE STUDENTS OF HIS WORD. To none more than to these is this charge necessary, if they are to keep a living interest in God's Word. We come to be so familiar with the main themes, and the forms in which they are expressed, that reading of the Bible comes to be a work in which no thought is aroused, or attention arrested, and ,we weary of it terribly. Now, it is to the diligent searcher, who will "turn back his hand," go over his work again, and not be content with the truths which lie only on the surface and which every eye can see,—to him shall there be revealed clusters of precious truths which he had never seen before, and the Word of God shall yield to him what it yields only to searchers like himself.

III. To THOSE ANXIOUS FOR THE FRUITS OF GOD'S GRACE IN THEMSELVES. To true-hearted believers it is often a cause of regret that their fruits seem so few and so poor. How often the confession is made of this spiritual fruitlessness! But we need not, ought not, to stay in complaints and confessions. "Turn back thine hand," and search if there may not be more fruit found, and of a better kind. "In *me* is thy fruit found," says God, and it may be we have been looking in the wrong places and to wrong sources for that which we so earnestly desire to see. We may "go on unto perfection," for so bids us the Word of God. Our "whole body, soul, and spirit may be preserved blameless," and we may be "the sons of God without rebuke;" for Christ "is able [has power] to save to the uttermost," and therefore we may be "filled with all the fulness of God." So, Christian brother, "turn back thine hand as a grape-gatherer," and think not thou hast gathered all the fruits of the Spirit that may be borne by thee. Thou hast not.

In conclusion, note how the subject tells of : 1. The *worth* of those objects which we search after. The action of the grape-gatherer, in carefully going over the branch again, testifies to his sense of the value of that for which he searches. And so here in I., II., III. 2. And what is yet left to be gathered *will be more readily found* because of the others that have been gathered. The solitary remaining clusters are seen more easily now that the others which hid them are cleared away. And he who desires to do more work for God, to know more of the truth of God, to bear more fruit unto God, shall find that his former work has been for his help, and on account thereof he is more sure of success. "Herein is my Father glorified, that ye bear much fruit;" therefore "turn back thine hand."—C.

Vers. 9—17.—*The preacher's bitter cry.* Profound distress marks the prophet's utterances in this section. The lament over the incorrigible wickedness of men and his own baffled work is loud and long and bitter exceedingly (cf. Christ's tears over Jerusalem ; Paul's sorrow over his countrymen).

I. WHAT CAUSED THIS BITTER CRY? His perception of the judgment of God drawing nigh (vers. 9, 12, 15). The obstinacy of the people (vers. 10, 16, 17). The hopelessness of reformation (ver. 13). *All* were corrupt, and the prophets and priests were even leaders in sin (ver. 14). Even the Lord's voice had been despised (ver. 16). Now, when facts like these occur, the judgment of God threatening but those exposed to them obstinately refusing warning; and when those who should have warned them and been their guides in the ways of God are themselves godless, and the voice of God has been heard and deliberately despised, then, as the faithful servant of God sees this awful guilt and its sure, inevitable, and swift-approaching judgment,—then it is that a sense of despair, a deep grief fills the soul, as well it may.

II. WHAT IS A PREACHER TO DO UNDER SUCH CIRCUMSTANCES? The first thought is to turn away from the doomed people and to speak no more to them in God's Name. But it is better to take example from the prophet, who was verily as one of those servants who, when those called to the prepared feast would not come, but "made light" of the gracious invitation, each saying, "I pray thee have me excused," went out, at his lord's bidding, into the highways and the hedges and compelled them to come in. So did Jeremiah now (ver. 11). It grieved him to the heart that God's Word should be despised, and he became "full of the fury of the Lord" (cf. ch. xx. 9). Hence he poured out his full heart upon young and old, men, women, and children, wherever he found opportunity of unburdening his soul on this great theme. He was inspired by God to do this, and the fact teaches us that preaching, which may seem to be of no use for the accomplishment of one result, may yet be of much use in regard to another. Jeremiah's testimony, though it did not save the people from captivity, was of great service to them there, and to the whole Jewish people ever after. His words, which seemed as idle tales when he spoke them, became mighty through God in after days. The neglect, therefore, of our message now should not lead us to cease delivering it, but should rouse us to more zeal, and make us " weary with holding in" (ver. 11). We may be sure that whenever God moves us to speak earnestly his Word, he intends to make our message a means of blessing *some*when and *some*where.

III. WHAT THE PREACHER'S GRIEF REVEALS. It tells much: 1. *Of God.* (1) Of *his love;* for it is ever he who inspires his servants with deep solicitude for men's salvation: it is he who through them is saying, "How can I give thee up?" (2) Of *his righteousness;* for the vivid realization of the coming judgment which his servants have is given them that they may impress upon the impenitent and the ungodly the sure issue of their sins. The prophets who see and declare God's love are they who declare his righteousness also. 2. *Of the preacher himself.* How truly he is sent of God! It is the Spirit of God speaks through him, the love of God leading him to deep love for his fellow-men. If our hearts are greatly filled with a yearning for men's souls, if "rivers of water run down our eyes because men keep not God's law,"—such solicitude is a sure sign of the presence of God with us, and a pledge of his help in delivering our message. 3. *Of men.* How desperately set they are against God! how absolute their need of the renewing power of the Holy Ghost! See what the prophet says (ver. 10): "Their ear is uncircumcised, and they cannot hearken." The habit of sin has caused their ear to be overgrown, and its power of hearing stopped, "so that," etc. How should the preacher ever remember this, and supplicate the mighty aid of the Divine Spirit if his message is to do any good!

IV. QUESTIONS IT SUGGESTS. 1. *For preachers and teachers.* Do we know anything of the prophet's grief? Facts all too plentiful and too closely resembling those which filled Jeremiah with the fury of the Lord (ver. 11) abound in our day. Do they excite any similar feeling in ourselves? What need we have to pray and watch against becoming used to sin! and for sympathy with the prophets of God and yet more with Christ, their Lord and ours! 2. *For those who hear the Word of God.* Are you becoming the cause of such grief to any of God's servants? Remember theirs is but the foreshadowing of your own, which will be far greater if you heed not their word. Rather heed that Word, and so become not their bitter grief but their joy now, and their cause of rejoicing in the day of the Lord.—C.

Ver. 10.—*The uncircumcised ear.* I. WHAT IS THIS? Not a *physical* defect, although the figure employed seems to tell of some fleshly growth which has formed over the cavity of the ear, and so destroyed the power of hearing. Nor a *mental* defect. They were acute enough ; they readily understood the prophet's meaning when he spoke to them. Their minds were at that very time busy about all sorts of plots and schemes, which they hoped to carry out. Nor was it a *moral* defect. They knew the right, the true, the good. Conscience was still at work and goading them with her reproaches. Hence they devise means (ver. 14) to lull and quiet it. And they had the power of choice, and deliberately chose ways of their own rather than those of God. True, it is said in the text, " And they cannot hearken." But that tells only of what is the perpetual result of refusing continuously to hear God's Word. Let a man tie his arm to his side for six months, and see what power of using it he has left after that. It will have become *atrophied.* And so in like manner do the functions of the soul, the limbs of our spiritual nature. The "will not" in regard to their use darkens down into the dreadful " cannot " of the judgment of God. There is no more awful fact for the faithless servant of God, nor more blessed one for the faithful, than this law of habit. The utterance of it concerning the wicked is, as here, "They cannot hearken ;" but concerning the good, " My heart is fixed, O God, my heart is fixed: I will sing and give praise." But it is a *spiritual defect.* It is the result of " the alienated *will,*" that which the Bible calls " the unrenewed heart," " the carnal mind," " the unregenerate nature." All such expressions tell of the *will* of man turned away from God, and having no higher motive than to please and gratify self. *That* is the radical defect of us all, and it is that which the prophet here terms " the uncircumcised ear." It by no means always involves the outrageous wickedness which is told of in their prophecies; it can exist and yet never " commit abomination," as did these to whom Jeremiah spoke.   It is found in company with much outward religiousness, much moral propriety, much amiability of character; but wherever it is, Christ's word concerning all such is, " Ye *must* be born again." It is in its nature fierce, savage, unsubdued still.   It often seems to be tamed, and moves about soft-footed and gently as if it never could do harm; but let some lure be held out to it, some provocation be given, and then its ferocity and all its hideous evil will reveal itself at once.   Accustomed as we are to see this evil nature held in check by the usages of society, the habits of civilized life and a refined selfishness, we are often blind to its true character, and " marvel " much at our Saviour's reiterated word, " Ye must be born again."

II. ITS EFFECTS. 1. Disregard of and dislike to the Word of God. " To whom shall I speak?" said the prophet. He could get no one to listen to him. And this is the too frequent experience of our own day.   How deserted the churches are, and where they are better attended, what kind of listening is it that prevails?   Granted the intolerable dulness of many preachers, but the evil is not probed when this is said.   The true cause is " the uncircumcised ear " that Jeremiah tells of.   But not only have men "no delight in " the Word of God, they count it " a reproach."   They come to be ashamed of its being thought that they should regard it with interest or have any real care for it. The tone adopted regarding those who do delight in God's Word is one of scorn and contempt. 2. Men go on unchecked in sin (cf. vers. 13, 15, and *passim*).   Surely it is a question not merely for the Church, but for thoughtful men of the world, whether it be well for any community or people to be throwing aside all the restraints of God's Word, as so many are doing.   The history of Israel of old is a beacon-light, warning the people of our day of what comes from despising the Word of the Lord. 3. God's judgments come upon such people (ver. 12). 4. Men become shameless and hardened (ver. 15). 5. The heart of God's faithful servants is sorely troubled (cf. ver. 10).   Here the prophet mourns over their " uncircumcised ears."

III. ABETTORS AND MINISTERS TO THIS EVIL. 1. Unfaithful priests and prophets (ver. 13). 2. The hardening effects of the people's own sin.

IV. THE REMEDY. Yet more impassioned and earnest ministry of the Word.   There must be no giving up of work or abandoning it in despair.   But—as ver. 11—more intense devotedness in the endeavour, futile as it may appear, to save men from death. 2. The fiery disciplines of God.   He is " a consuming fire; " and the fire of his love will burn fiercely on until the evil on which it fastens is burnt out of the soul, the Church, the nation, he loves.   Oh, the awfulness of the love of God!   If God were *not* love, there might be a possibility of a soul being allowed to perish in its sins and to go its own way to death unchecked; but as the fondest mother will subject her child to terrible suffering for the saving of its life, so, too, will God.

CONCLUSION. What a summons comes to us from these truths: (1) to seek the renewing grace of the Spirit of God; (2) to take heed how we hear!—C.

Ver. 14.—*The vampires of the soul.*   There is a hideous creature called the vampire bat, that is said to destroy its victims by sucking their life-blood.   Whilst thus destroying them, it gently fans them with its wings, and so keeps them in a profound slumber, from which the probabilities are that they will never wake.   And what other are they who lull the souls of sinful men to the sleep of death by " saying, Peace, peace; when there is no peace "?   No greater crime can be imagined than this of which our text tells.   The physician who should pamper a man in his disease, who should feed his cancer or inject continual poison into the system, whilst at the same time he promised sound health and a long life,—such a physician would not be one-half so criminal as the professed religious teacher who should knowingly bid those entrusted to his charge to be at ease and to take comfort, when he ought to be crying, " Woe unto them that are at ease in Zion!"   The pilot who should pretend to steer a ship toward its proper haven, but all the while was of intent driving her upon unseen rocks, would not be a worse traitor than the man into whose hands the helm of human souls is entrusted, and whose professed duty it is to steer them towards Christ, but who, instead of so doing, was guiding them to utter ruin, by flattering them that all was well when all was ill.   In the great day, when all shall render up their account to God, what awfulness of doom will not be reserved for him who has been chargeable with blood-guiltiness like this? We observe—

I. THAT IT IS AN ALL TOO FREQUENT SIN. 1. The prophets of Judah and Jerusalem were guilty of it, notwithstanding that (1) they knew the truth; (2) they professed the truth; (3) they were ordained to teach the truth. Still, out of all manner of evil motive they were guilty of this sin. Oh, let all who teach, whether in the pulpit, the home circle, or in the school, remember that their sacred charge and duty may not merely be imperfectly fulfilled—that it ever is; nor even neglected merely, sad as that is; but it may be utterly perverted, and that which was designed to be for our own and others' great good may become the means of our and their more terrible condemnation. From this may God save teachers and taught alike! 2. And there are now those who are bidding men be at peace when there is no peace. (1) They who bid men be at peace on the ground of their moral integrity, their respectability of character, and of the righteousness with which they are credited amongst their fellow-men. God forbid that we should decry or depreciate the value of character, reputation, and integrity amongst men. No, indeed; but all the same we feel that it is a plea all too feeble, and one that cannot avail such as we are before the bar of the all-holy God. (2) They who teach men to trust in sacraments or Church ordinances of any kind. These, too, are precious in their proper place, but regarded as a valid claim to eternal life, apart from the disposition of the heart Godwards, they will save no man, and he who trusts them or teaches others to trust them, is guilty of saying, "Peace, peace," etc. (3) They who rely on a faith which is fruitless in love to God and man. This is the characteristic of all forms of Antinomianism, and though that be "a way which seemeth right unto many men, the end thereof is death." 3. But let us remember that *we* may practically be preaching this fatal peace. Christian men and women, who do nothing for the salvation of those around you; who are eager about amusements, business, worldly position, and all such things, but who are unmoved or but very little moved at the ungodliness in the midst of which you live; what is the conclusion that others draw from this unconcern? Why, that you don't believe what you profess, and that therefore they need not either. And so you encourage them to say, "Peace, peace," etc. Whose conscience is there that does not smite him here? and who of us is there that has no need of the prayer, "Deliver me from blood-guiltiness, O God, thou God of my salvation"? And all who are unconcerned about their own eternal welfare. Fathers and mothers who have not sought the Lord, you will die in your sins if you repent not; but you will die not to yourselves merely; you will drag your children down with you, for you are teaching them to be unconcerned and indifferent, when neither you nor they possess any true peace at all. 4. But after all, those who are the most guilty of saying, "Peace, peace," etc., are *sinful men to themselves.* The devil taught men the way very early in the history of our race. "Ye shall not surely die;" so he lyingly declared to our first mother, and she, all too willing to believe that there would be peace though she did disobey God, ruined herself, her husband, and all her children by that one deed. And ever since men who love to disobey have encouraged themselves in their sin by this fatal flattery of their souls of which our text tells. They did so in the days of Noah, "until the flood came and took them all away." See also Belshazzar's feast at the height of merriment, when the handwriting appeared on the wall, and that night Babylon was taken and her king slain. So has it been with the Jewish people—in Jeremiah's time, and so in our Lord's. The Captivity shattered that first false peace, and the utter destruction of Jerusalem the second. And we are told it will be so at the last, in that "day when the Son of man cometh." Observe, then, some of the deceits whereby men beguile themselves into saying, "Peace, peace," etc. They are such as these: (1) The infinite mercy of God. (2) "I am no worse than those who make a religious profession. If they are saved, I shall be too." (3) "Yes, I am going to repent and turn to God; I certainly mean to one day." (4) Religious profession: "I am baptized and take the sacrament." (5) Denying the truth of the Bible: "I have no proof that there is a God, a heaven, or indeed that I have a soul. It is all a 'perhaps;'" so men say. And there are many other such deceits. But now—

II. NOTE HOW THE LIE THAT IS IN ALL SUCH SAYING OF "PEACE, PEACE," ETC., MAY BE DETECTED. A man may hold up a phial of liquid that is colourless, clear, sparkling, that seems in all respects like pure, wholesome water. But the skilled chemist drops into it the fitting test, and at once the poisonous substance is precipitated, and thus is made evident to all. Now, with all these deceits of which we have been telling, their true nature may be made manifest if we apply those tests which only the true peace of God will endure. For, if the peace in which we are trusting be a true one and not a deception, it will: 1. Always tend to the making of us holier, purer, more Christ-like. God's peace always does this. It "keeps our hearts and minds in Christ Jesus," it "rules" in our hearts. 2. Stand under the hardest blows of misfortune and earthly sorrow. Listen to its voice: "Though he slay me, yet will I trust in him;" "The Lord gave, and the Lord hath taken away; blessed be the Name of the Lord." Now, will peace such as springs from such sources as those told of help a man in straits like those of Job? 3. Be with him in death. 4. Have Christ at the heart of it as its Alpha and its Omega, its beginning and its end.

III. But our surest safeguard is not in our being able to detect the false peace, but in possessing the true. That is ours when we surrender our souls to Christ. Then we shall have peace indeed. (1) Peace from fear of God's condemnation; (2) peace from dread of guilt; (3) peace from the tyranny and oppression of "the evil one;" (4) peace from the crushing power of earthly sorrow; (5) peace from the terror of the grave and the judgment day; (6) peace in the conscious possession of the love of God. Such is the true "peace of God." Oh, how foolish, then, to barter *that* for the false and fatal pretences of peace which are for ever beguiling the hearts of sinful men! May he who is "our Peace," even Christ, cause us to give heed to his own loving call, "Come unto me all ye that labour and are heavy laden, and I will give you rest"!—C.

Ver. 15.—*The sin against the Holy Ghost.* I. This sin is set forth here. For the sin is no one definite act, but a condition of mind which renders repentance hopeless and persistence in sin certain (cf. Revised Version, Mark iii. 29, where the true reading is as there given, "is guilty of an eternal *sin*"). But is not this the condition described in the text, described vividly, accurately? They had hardened themselves till repentance, yea, even shame, on account of "abomination" was utterly absent from them. "'They were not at all ashamed,' no tinge of it, not the least 'blush' was visible. Was it not certain that such people who would go on, as they did, in sin, were in danger of eternal sin?" Hence they had never forgiveness, and the prophet was forbidden (see ch. vii. 16) even to pray for them (cf. 1 John v. 16).

II. Other instances of it or approximations to it. 1. Those who with unblushing effrontery ascribed Christ's holy ministry and his deeds of merciful might to Satanic power. They cried out, "Show us a sign from *heaven*," implying that thus far he had only shown them signs from hell. 2. Those who were responsible for the cry, "His blood be on us, and on our children!" And there are instances now. The condition of shamelessness in sin and of helplessness as to repentance may be, and we fear at times is, reached. Therefore note—

III. The steps by which men reach this condition. 1. By disregard of the rebukes of conscience, stifling them, instead of going, as they would prompt, to the mercy-seat, and there confessing the sin. 2. By persistence in sin. 3. By the commission of great sins. 4. By loss of self-respect. 5. By forfeiture of character and the esteem of men.

IV. Its doom. "It hath never forgiveness." "They shall fall among them that fall; they shall be cast down, saith the Lord." Wherefore this? 1. Because sin and sorrow are linked together by a chain that cannot be broken. Therefore where there is eternal sin there must be eternal punishment. The latter keeps pace with the former, and dogs its footsteps for ever. It cannot but be so. 2. Because such men are murderers of other men's souls. They are centres of rebellion against God, of deadly spiritual contagion. Blood-guiltiness is upon them, yea, they are steeped therein. 3. Because God could not be God and not abhor such condition of soul as this sin betrays.

V. Its solemn lessons. 1. Cherish a holy hatred of sin, for its tendency is ever to reproduce itself, and so to become eternal. 2. Beware of disregarding the monitor within—conscience, God's voice in our souls. To do so is to drive away the trusty sentinel who guards the approaches of the soul against its deadly foes; to pierce and undermine those blessed walls which keep back the inrush of the ocean upon the whole land. Let us not do aught like this. But pray—

> " Quick as the apple of the eye,
> O God, my conscience make,
> Swift to discern when sin is nigh,
> And keep it still awake."

3. Is sin upon your conscience now? At once confess it, and so find from your Lord forgiveness for it, and more—deliverance from it and from all possibility of that dread sin which the text describes and which hath never forgiveness.—C.

Ver. 16.—*The good old paths.* It is noticeable in the order of nature how God has secured the true adjustment and hence the highest well-being of his universe by means of *the action of contrasted and opposite forces.* By means of that power which the mighty mass of the sun has to draw everything to itself—if this were left alone to operate, the whole of those innumerable orbs that now circle round the sun as their centre would be drawn in upon it and perish. But this is prevented by the action of an opposite force, called the centrifugal, as the first-mentioned is called the centripetal. This opposite force tends, by the velocity with which the planets revolve around the sun, to drive them off and away from it: thus, by the effect of these opposite forces, that perfect harmony and unerring order of the whole stellar universe, which has been the admiration of all observers in all ages, are preserved. *Chemistry* also can furnish illustrations not a few of the beneficent action of opposite forces, where either left alone would work only harm. In the *great law of sex*, the constitution of all life, plant life as well as animal, as male and female, this in all its aspects is another marked instance of the same Divine method. In *political life*, the two great tendencies, monarchial and democratic, or the rule of the one *versus* the rule of the many—the mutual strugglings of these two—keep the world in such equilibrium as we see. In *religion*, the Catholic principle which makes self nothing, and the Protestant principle which makes self all-important, each man having to give an account of himself to God,—these are both designed to contend the one against the other, and whilst Catholicism is to check the selfish individualism into which Protestantism is apt to lapse, Protestantism is in its turn to struggle against that servility of mind into which the principle of self-abnegation, the essential principle of Catholicism, is prone to degenerate. It is in the resultant of these two forces that the purest form of religious life is found. And in regard to *the life of obedience to God*, the life which he would have us live here on earth, that, too, is governed by the action of opposed laws. There is the law which works through our bodily nature, and which if left alone would make us, not in body only but in soul, of the earth earthy, for ever " grovelling here below." But there is the opposed law which works through our spiritual nature; but, blessed as it is, it needs to be disciplined and made perfectly healthful to us by means of the salutary necessity of giving heed in due measure to the lesser law just spoken of. The first preserves us from being mere enthusiasts, the second from the far greater peril of enslavement to the world, the flesh, and the devil acting through them. And in those two tendencies, one of which is plainly referred to in this sixteenth verse and the other implied, the love of the old is contrasted with the love of the new. Here, again, we have set before us two great forces in humanity, which by their mutual contentions preserve it in tolerable health and comfort, and ensure its steady, onward progress. Conservatism and liberalism are not the products of any one national revolution, like our own in 1688, but they are two God-implanted tendencies of the human mind, each of which has its appropriate and most useful function, and neither of which can be dispensed with without harm to the whole body politic in every nation under the sun. To lie like a log on the ocean of human life, useless and despised amid the nationalities of the world, is the doom of those who will blindly close their eyes to the fresh light and truth which are for ever breaking forth upon the world; to run upon the rocks and make shipwreck of everything is the doom of those who despise the teachings of experience, and care only to be for ever finding out some new way and to follow some new guide. But let these two act and react each on the other—the love of the old upon the love of the new, the tendency to be always looking back upon the tendency to be always looking forward, and then the result is that men will come generally to practically act upon that prudent, though to many minds most prosaic, maxim which counsels—

> " Be not the first by whom the new is tried,
> Nor yet the last to lay the old aside."

But in regard to the way in which God would have us go, our text teaches—

I. THAT THERE ARE NO NEW WAYS. From the beginning that which the Lord God hath required of man has been, even as it yet is, that we should "do justice, love mercy, and walk humbly with our God." The gospel of the Lord Jesus is not to supersede or make void this eternal law, but to establish it as it never had been or could have been before. " What the Law could not do in that it was weak through the flesh, God sending his own Son in the likeness of sinful flesh," did, " that the righteousness of the Law might be fulfilled in us." For this end, by the grace of our Lord Jesus Christ, the burden of guilt is taken off from us, and a new heart and a right spirit given. But the law of life is ever the same. It is the old and good way.

II. NEVERTHELESS, MEN ARE CONTINUALLY DEVISING NEW WAYS. It was so in Jeremiah's time; it is so in our own. By denials of truths most surely believed amongst us for many generations, or by additions thereto, or by substitutions of other forms of faith, men have done to-day as in the days of old. Every magazine and newspaper, besides innumerable volumes ever issuing from the press,—all alike are popular as they throw over old ideas and propound "some new thing." Science and secularism and superstition between them would, long ere this, have destroyed the good old way, had it not been so firmly constructed that all these powers combined are not adequate for such a task.

III. IN THESE NEW WAYS WHAT IS TRUE WILL BE FOUND TO BE OLD, AND WHAT IS NOT OLD WILL BE FOUND TO BE NOT TRUE. For there are *tests* by which new teachings may be tried, and ought to be tried, and by which the prophets of God tried the new teachings of their day. 1. *The test of conscience.* The human conscience confesses God. It is borne in upon the human heart that God is. Nothing can permanently stifle or destroy that confession, which Conscience, left to herself, would ever make. The very word "conscience" implies the recognition of some other being as with us, in us, around and about us. It confesses God. All teachings, therefore, that deny God, or explain him away as a blind force or law, or identify him with his universe, the pantheist's God,—these teachings by this sure test are tried, and found wanting. 2. *The test of result.* Note what is the result of any professed truth upon *personal happiness.* God, who has given us so many things richly to enjoy, must from his very nature purpose the blessedness of his children. But if a system is offered us, the inevitable result of which is to blot out hope, to shut us up to this often most miserable life, as all they would do who would take from us the Christian hope—then its drear and dread effect upon the heart of man proclaims it false. See, too, how any teaching tells upon *character.* Here is a surer test still. Whatever else is dark and obscure, goodness and truth must ever be right. But if any new doctrines tend to deteriorate character, as many of them do, to make sin easier and virtue more difficult; if they throw the reins upon our lower nature; if they take away the great motives to nobleness of life;—then again they are demonstrated false. And note their effect upon *society generally.* Can the denial of God's existence, of the religious basis of morality, as Mr. Herbert Spencer denies it, of the authority of Holy Scripture, of the sanctity of the sabbath, of the Divine mission of the Son of God, of the resurrection of the dead, the judgment and future blessedness or woe depending upon our lives here;—can the denial of any of these things, which, alas! is common enough now, tend to the good of society? Must not the general well-being of mankind be greatly threatened if such doctrines be generally accepted? But doctrines that would thus destroy good are *ipso facto* declared to have no part nor lot in the kingdom of truth. By these tests of conscience and result let the new ways be tried, and it will be seen that what in them is true is old, and what is not old is not true.

IV. WHEREFORE, THEN, DO MEN DEVISE THESE NEW WAYS? The causes are sometimes: 1. *Intellectual.* Mental restlessness on the part of some will lead men, even in the most perilous matters, to be doubting the old and devising what is new. And God often suffers them to wander in the far and drear country of mental unrest, and to feed upon its husks, and so come to themselves, and arise and go back to their Father's heart and home, from whence it had been better had they never strayed. 2. Sometimes, and more often, *moral*. Religion is that which binds. It is a ligature, a restraining cord upon the evil propensities of our nature. If, therefore, doctrines be offered which will relax that little-loved bond, they will be eagerly welcomed. A faith that will give not true liberty, but "licence," men will ever love. 3. And always *spiritual*. Where the heart is surrendered to Christ the mind will not be ensnared by these subtleties of the evil one. If the Holy Spirit of God have wrought in us the great regenerating change, we shall have liberty and deliverance from all these. Safety from the wanderings of the intellect, as well as from the worse wanderings of our sinful nature, are alike ensured to him who has given himself up unreservedly to God.

V. But those who would walk in the way God would have them go may know the way by its being "old" and good. All old ways are not good, but the way of God is both. It is old, therefore familiar to many; has been often described, is well marked out; its different stages are well known. "The wayfaring man, though a fool, need not err therein." And it is good. It leads to him who is the supreme Good—God. It has been the chosen way of all the good. It makes those good who walk therein. He who alone on this earth of ours was perfectly good—our Lord Jesus—walked in it, and lives to enable us to walk therein also. It is the will of God that we should walk therein. "Its ways are all ways of pleasantness, and all its paths are peace." "Ye shall find rest to your souls." For all these reasons it is the good way as well as the old; therefore let us "stand," "see," and "ask" for this way, and this way alone.—C.

Ver. 16.—*At the meeting of the ways.* "Stand ye in the ways," etc.

I. This is where very many are. The young especially. Paths stretch out on either hand, some of them inviting, some repelling. But for the young, and for many others beside who have not yet fully chosen their path, the present is a time when a decided choice must be made. If the matter were to be settled according to the inviting or other aspect of the *beginning* of the ways, the one we should choose would soon be fixed upon. But we have to take into consideration the progress of the way, and, above all, the end of the way. Here the text gives—

II. Good counsels for all who have come to this meeting of the ways. We are bidden: 1. *Pause a while.* "*Stand* ye in the ways." Oh, if we could but secure this thoughtful pause! if we could but induce those we are now contemplating to "ponder" a while the paths before them! if it were but realized that the way we take is a matter for consideration, and that only a fool would rush heedlessly on! 2. *Investigate.* As one at the meeting of the ways, but not certain which was the right one for him, would look along each way in turn, and "see" which appeared to be the most likely to bring him to his desired destination. Therefore we are bidden, not only "stand," but "see." 3. *Inquire.* Other travellers come along—men who are familiar with the district, who have traversed one or other of these roads themselves. Then let us avail ourselves of their knowledge and experience, and "ask" as to these ways. 4. *And let your mind be made up as to the character of the way you desire to walk in.* Let there be no mere vague, listless looking over all the paths without much concern which of them you take; but we are bidden, "Ask for the *old* paths . . . the *good* way."

> "The way the holy prophets went,
> The way that leads from banishment,
> The King's highway of holiness."

All the "old" paths are not also "good ways;" far from it. But there is an old, and therefore well-known, well-trodden, and hence unmistakable way, which also is the good way. One purpose of the lives of God's faithful people is that, by the observation in the record of them, men may be led to ask for the paths in which these walked, feeling sure the way they took must be a good, *the* good way. Happy they who have been led to resolve they will find out the secret of such men's lives and make it their own. These will ask, not for any way, but for the old paths, the good way.

III. GREAT ENCOURAGEMENTS TO FOLLOW THIS COUNSEL. 1. It is implied that if such guidance be asked it will be given. For, if that guidance were not given, how could any walk in these paths? That it is open to them to do so proves that the guidance asked has been given. And so it ever will be. 2. It is promised that, if we walk in the old and good way, we shall find "rest" to our souls. After all, this is everything. If a man has inward rest and peace, heaven for him has begun below. What matters it what we have if this rest be not? What matters what we have not if this rest be ours? And it is a *true* rest—not a mere lethargy of the soul or sleep of conscience, but that "rest which remaineth for the people of God," the rest of faith, the rest promised by the Lord Jesus when he said, "Come unto me, . . . and I will," etc.

IV. CHRIST HIMSELF IS THAT WAY—THE OLD, THE GOOD WAY. Let the will be utterly surrendered to him; let our faith daily look to him; then "he shall be made to us of God, wisdom, and righteousness, and sanctification, and redemption." This is what he meant when he said, "*I* am the Way."

> "This is the way I long had sought,
> And mourned because I found it not;
> Till late I heard my Saviour say,
> 'Come hither, soul, *I* am the Way.'"

And *so* we shall find rest to our souls.—C.

Vers. 18—30.—*God's appeal for vindication of his vengeance.* Note—
I. THE CHALLENGE. (Ver. 18.) God summons the nations, the congregations, the earth, to serve as on a grand jury, and to vindicate by their verdict the righteousness of his procedure. Now, from this challenge we learn : 1. *The universality of conscience.* There is a moral sense, a knowledge of right and wrong, implanted in all men by God. It is "the light that lighteth every man that cometh into the world." 2. That God desires to have this universal conscience approving what he has done. (1) He takes for granted that his procedure will be scanned and judged by men. (2) But this he desires and approves. (3) He asks only for a true deliverance upon the case before them. 3. God desires us to regard his actions, not as right because they are his, but as his because they are right. It is a perilous thing to defend the rectitude of Divine actions—as they have been defended, *e.g.* the massacres of the Canaanites—on the ground that his will makes them right. *That* is not the method whereby we are to "vindicate the ways of God to man." Abraham did not so, but asked, "Shall not the Judge of all the earth do right?" Not *make* right, but *do* it. But what condescension on the part of God, thus to submit himself to our judgment! But he does this because he so yearns for our love, and because love cannot be apart from moral approval.
II. THE STATEMENT OF THE MATTER ON THE PART OF GOD. 1. God declares what he will do (vers. 19—21). 2. How he will accomplish his purpose (vers. 22, 23). 3. How terrible its accomplishment will be (vers. 24—26). And then he gives : 4. The grounds of his procedure (vers. 19, 28, 29).
III. THE CALLING OF THE WITNESS. (Ver. 27; cf. Exposition.) Jeremiah was to observe and declare the guilt of those whom God condemned.
IV. THE VERDICT ANTICIPATED. (Ver. 30.) Men shall call them "reprobate silver."
CONCLUSION. Let us tremble at that righteousness of God which the whole earth will confess when he condemns the sinner. Let us lay hold on that righteousness of God which is for us in Christ.—C.

Ver. 19.—*The fruit of thought.* I. THOUGHT HAS FRUIT. In all departments of life its fruit is seen—scientific, political, social, moral, religious. Thoughts are *born* in some one mind. *Sown* by words spoken or written, and by the influence of the lives of those in whom they are born; they *germinate* by contact with other minds; they *appear above ground* in the tendencies of any given age; they *bear fruit* in the achievements of the age.
II. THOUGHT BEARS GOOD FRUIT OR EVIL, ACCORDING AS THE LAW OF GOD IS HEEDED OR REJECTED. "Wherewithal shall a young man cleanse his way? By taking heed thereto *according to thy Word.*"

III. THE CHIEF PARTAKER OF THE FRUIT OF THOUGHT WILL BE THE THINKER. (Cf. text.) And it is true both of good thoughts and ill. As a man thinketh so is he.

CONCLUSION. Let it be our prayer that we may come into full sympathy with him who said, " How precious are *thy* thoughts unto me, O God ! " So shall the fruit of our thoughts be precious likewise.—C.

Ver. 20.—*Abhorred sacrifices.* I. THERE ARE SUCH. (Cf. text; Ps. l.; etc.)

II. THEY MAY HAVE MANY OF THE CHARACTERISTICS OF ACCEPTABLE SACRIFICES. 1. Costly: " Incense from Sheba." 2. Regular. 3. Correct.

III. BUT YET THEY ARE ABHORRED OF GOD. " To what purpose," etc.? (Cf. our Lord's denunciations of hypocrites.) This because: 1. They lack sincerity. 2. They yield no fruit in holy obedience. 3. They cause the Name and worship of God to be hated of men. 4. They render more hopeless the true repentance of the offerer.

IV. WHEREFORE ARE THEY OFFERED ? 1. Conscience will not allow men to throw off all regard for religion. 2. Custom demands it. 3. Worldly interests are served by it. 4. There is a secret reliance upon them as furthering their good before God.

V. WHAT DO SUCH FACTS TEACH US ? Not to throw aside outward forms of worship : many do this on the ground of insincerity often associated with them. But to see that whilst we worship outwardly we worship also in spirit and in truth. To measure the worth of our worship by its power over our conduct. To join on all our poor, marred offerings, which is all that at the best they are, with the perfect sacrifice which Christ has offered for us all.—C.

Ver. 29.—" *The bellows are burned.*" The text is a homely and unusual one, but its graphic force may help all the more to impress the truth taught by it. ".The prophet likens the people of Israel to a mass of metal. This mass of metal claimed to be precious ore, such as gold or silver. It was put into the furnace, the object being to fuse it, so that the pure metal should be extracted from the dross. Lead was put in with the ore to act as a flux (that being relied upon by the ancient smelters as quicksilver now is in these more instructed days). A fire was kindled, and then the bellows were used to create an intense heat, the bellows being the prophet himself. He complains that he spoke with much pathos, much energy, much force of heart, that he exhausted himself, without being able to melt the people's hearts; so hard was the ore that the bellows were burned before the metal was melted—the prophet was exhausted before the people were impressed ; he had worn out his lungs, his powers of utterance; he had exhausted his mind, his powers of thought ; he had broken his heart, his powers of emotion ; but he could not divide his people from their sins, and separate the precious from the vile " (C. H. Spurgeon). Now, from the text learn—

I. IT IS THE PURPOSE OF GOD SO TO MELT AND SUBDUE THE HEART OF MAN THAT HE MAY MOULD IT AFRESH, AND ACCORDING TO HIS OWN GRACIOUS WILL. Now to this end there are needed : 1. *A Divine fire* which shall bear upon the heart of man. But the Holy Spirit is such a fire, which, if it be quenched, woe is unto us ! 2. That that fire *shall glow with fervent heat.*

II. TO SECURE THIS HE MAKES USE OF MANY AND VARIED APPLIANCES WHICH THE PROPHET HERE LIKENS TO " BELLOWS." 1. *The prophets own ministry* in the case of Judah and Jerusalem at that time. 2. The faithful ministry of his truth *by his prophets now.* 3. *His Law, his Word, the varied means of grace.* 4. *His mercies, especially the mercy of God in Christ.* 5. *His chastisements and judgments.* These more especially referred to here. Such are some of these appliances.

III. Now, IT IS POSSIBLE FOR ALL THESE TO BECOME UTTERLY INEFFECTUAL. This is what is here meant. God's *messengers, Law, mercies, chastisements,*—all in vain. And such things *happen now.* There are those whom nought can move. *What is the cause ?* Not that the Divine heat did not bear upon the heart that was to be melted. Not that those appliances were left unused whereby the understanding, the conscience, the affections, and the will might be rendered more susceptible of the Divine influences. But *the obduracy of the heart.* The perversity and evil of that baffled all the earnest endeavours of God's grace in regard to that heart.

IV. Now, WHEN " THE BELLOWS ARE BURNED," WHEN ALL MEANS HAVE BEEN

TRIED AND FAILED TO WIN THE HEART FOR GOD, NO CONDITION CAN BE MORE AWFUL OR DEPLORABLE. 1. It is sad *for God's ministers.* Jeremiah, Paul, Christ, and thousands of his ministers since have prayed and wept over obdurate hearts. 2. *But it is far more sad for these hard-hearted ones themselves.* (1) They are without excuse. (2) There is no hope of their repentance. (3) They are in danger of eternal sin.

CONCLUSION. 1. Christ's ministers must expect that, *so far as they can see,* they will, at times, labour in vain in regard to the salvation of souls. The bellows will be burned, and the ore remain unmelted still. 2. They are to be sustained by the thought that God will deal with them, not according to the results of their work, but according to its fidelity. 3. Let the impenitent be warned.—C.

Ver. 16.—*The good way.* The prophet here employs the memory of the past as a motive to repentance. He would fain persuade the people to return to the better ways in which their fathers walked. The calamities that were falling so heavily upon them were the result of their having forsaken those good old ways. Let them consider how they have fallen, search out the real causes of the trouble and sorrow they endure, retrace their wandering steps, and the old prosperity shall come back to them again. Note here—

I. THE DIVERSE WAYS MEN TAKE, diverse as regards their moral quality and issues. "Stand ye in the ways." Think of the various kinds of moral life that men are leading. Amid the social conditions and relations of this world we are as travellers with many paths branching out in different directions before them, who must choose their own. We may know little of the internal experiences of our associates in the pilgrimage of life, but the broad types of character, the general tendencies of moral habit, are open enough to our view. The "ways" are many, but there is only one path of eternal rectitude and blessedness. There is the way of reckless transgression, of thoughtless indifference, of base avarice, of exclusive devotion to earthly ambitions, of mere virtuous respectability, of religious indecision, etc.; and there is the way of faith and piety, "the path of the just which is as the shining light, that shineth more and more unto the perfect day." Men cannot help to some extent revealing outwardly the tenor of the life within them. Every one of us bears more or less clearly upon him the stamp of a certain distinctive character. Whatever the bent of his spirit may be, it will always betray itself, in look, manner, speech, conduct, by the books he reads, the friendships he forms, the places he frequents, the gratifications in which he delights, through a thousand channels of self-revelation. We are all "living epistles" of something—some type of character, some order of moral life—"known and read of men."

II. THE THOUGHTFUL OBSERVATION THESE CONDITIONS DEMAND. "Stand in the ways, and see." It is a great thing to know how to "see." There are those who "seeing, see not." One of the first lessons in the moral science of life, as in physical science, is observation—to know how to note facts and trace laws and draw conclusions, to know how to learn and to turn what is learnt to good account. The characters and lives of others are not to be to us mere matters of amusement or philosophic specula- tion, much less ill-natured criticism; but sources of instruction, teachers of practical truth. They all have their admonitory and exemplary use. The higher advantages of social life have never been reaped, the very rudiments of our duty as social beings have not been mastered, till we thoroughly apprehend this. Let the young specially lay the lesson to heart. Their position is favourable—the plain of life before them, not yet entangled in a network of circumstantial difficulties, nothing to undo that ought never to have been done, no false steps to retrace that were rashly taken. But how soon may they be drawn into forbidden and dangerous paths if they do not consider! As the ship glides imperceptibly from the open sea into the broad mouth of the river, whose distant banks are hidden, so easily are they led captive to the power of evil if they allow themselves to drift with the tide of outward influence and inward impulse, and will not *think.* At the same time, enlarged experience of life may be expected to give added force to its moral lessons. Beset as a man may be with associa- tions that seem to determine his course for him in spite of himself, it is always possible for him to pause and consider his way. The darkness and confusion of the storm may be too great to allow the sailor to take his observations and find out his real place on the pathless ocean ; not so with any man as concerns his relation to the heavenly powers and the eternal realities. He has always light enough to "discern between the righteous and the wicked, between him that serveth God and him that serveth him not" (Mal. iii. 18). The true way of life is clearly revealed to those who are willing to " see." "The wayfaring man, though a fool, shall not err therein " (Isa. xxxv. 8).

III. The practical result to which such observation must lead. "Ask for the old paths, where is the good way, and walk therein." Asking and acting, inquiry after the right way, and a resolute determination to follow it ; when these conditions are supplied there can be little doubt as to the issue. A life of practical godliness, based on faith in revealed truth, springing from the inspiration of the spirit of truth and purity in the secret soul,—this is the way. It is the "old way." New as regards the light Christianity has shed upon it, new as regards the revelation of him in whose redeeming work its deep foundations have been laid, it is "old" as regards its essential principles of faith and righteousness. The martyrs, prophets, and holy men of every age have left their glowing footprints upon it. Elijah ascended from it in his chariot of fire. David made the statutes of the Lord his delight as he pursued his pilgrimage along it. Abraham trod the same path, led on by the star of promise. Upon it Enoch walked in lowly fellowship with God. It is stained with the blood of righteous Abel.

> "Our glorious Leader claims our praise
> For his own pattern given ;
> While the long cloud of witnesses
> Show the same path to heaven."

The way is as plain as Divine teaching and human experience can make it ; let us gird up the loins of our minds to " walk in it."

IV. The reward of practical obedience. "Ye shall find rest unto your souls." " Rest," for beings such as we are, is the repose of the mind in discovered truth, the pacification of the conscience in the assurance of Divine forgiveness, the satisfaction of the heart in the embrace of real good, the balance of all our powers in a holy service. In the life of faith and godliness, the life Christ gives to all who come to him, can such rest alone be found. "Take my yoke upon you, and learn of me, . . . and ye shall find rest unto your souls " (Matt. xi. 29).—W.

Ver. 7.—*Jerusalem like a fountain casting forth evil.* A fountain, as mentioned in Scripture, is generally suggestive of a most gracious and abundant supply of the highest good ; even as in ch. ii. 13 and John iv. 14. How very noteworthy, then, to find that the fountain, which naturally suggests all that is bright, beautiful, and refreshing, should be so turned away from its common place in poetic use as to become the most impressive illustration of Jerusalem's polluted heart! Indeed, an imaginative writer would probably get severely criticized if he used the figure of a fountain for such a purpose ; and yet, when one thinks it over, this very unexpectedness makes the figure more instructive. The poetry of a prophet must, above all things, have arresting power in it. Think, then, of the fountain. Think of it, first of all, in its usual aspect, pouring forth a bright, pleasant-sounding stream, as inspiring to the mind as it is refreshing to the thirsty mouth. But all this view must be instantly and decidedly put away. Instead of the clear, sparkling water there must come into the mind the thought of a feculent, poisonous flood, and of the force that lies behind it, some deep inward energy hidden in the secret places of the earth. A continuity of most pestiferous evil comes from these secret places, and even by such an image as this is the actual wickedness of Jerusalem set forth. The hearts of its people are gathering-places for a destructive stream, always flowing forth and always replenished. They never get tired of their wickedness and never repent of it. Then one remembers that the hearts of men were destined for a very different purpose. Just as the devout heart perceives that God meant these crevices and great caverns in the earth to gather and pour forth the refreshing streams of water, so he meant the hearts of the children of men to gather and pour forth all manner of loving, hopeful, patiently pursued projects for the good of others and for the glory of God. The woman of Samaria evidently came to Jesus with a heart that was indeed a fountain casting out wickedness, but she heard the delightful news that Jesus could give her water which should be in her "a well of water springing up into eternal life." There is another Jerusalem besides this earthly and polluted one. Jeremiah was not the only one who told people to fly out of it because of impending destruction. Jesus, in his prophetic words, spoke with even greater emphasis—a thing to be expected. The earthly Jerusalem, great and glorious as it once was, is now called spiritually Sodom and Egypt, for it is the place *where our Lord was crucified* (Rev. xi. 8). The Jerusalem to be thought of henceforth is the holy Jerusalem, descending out of heaven from God. It has many glories, many beauties, many surpassing gifts of grace for needy men, and not the least is this, that there is " a pure river of water of life, clear as crystal, proceeding out of the throne of God and of the Lamb." And may we not say that this river is constituted by the numberless fountains that flow out of every renewed heart ? The glory of the river is God's, but the service and dedication which bring that river into existence are the privilege of God's people. We are to let our thoughts dwell on the deplorable fountain Jeremiah speaks of here, only that we may see more clearly and gratefully the spring of true and abiding goodness which he can put in its place.—Y.

Ver. 13.—*Covetousness a universal sin.* It is not so much of covetousness in itself that the prophet is here speaking, as of the universality of it. From the least even to the greatest the spirit of the spoiler is in the hearts of the people. The words, of course, are not to be taken literally as to individuals; but there is this universality about them, that they apply to every class. That a man is rich, and increased with goods, and that he has, indeed, a great deal more than he can ever enjoy in his own person, is far from being a general ground for supposing that he will be contented with his possessions. The more he has and the higher he stands, the more he may want to have and the higher he may want to get. And so all the way up the ladder from the lowest round, men are continually struggling with one another. It is a ladder, the lowest round of which will hold a great multitude, but it ever narrows as it ascends ; and the covetous who happen to be also strong and consequently victorious over their feebler competitors, go clambering on as long as one's eye rests upon them. No one ever seems to reach the top of the ladder ; and it may be said moreover that, though there seem many who are free from the spoiling spirit, it simply arises from this, that there has been nothing to bring the dormant germ into life and activity. No one can tell what possibilities of evil lie within him. And may not the essential element in covetousness be a strong motive force even when it is hidden away under the appearance of something else ? One thing is very certain, that covetousness prevailed from the least even to the greatest in Jerusalem ; it will also do so in every other human society. It is in human nature to have strong desires of the heart, strong and imperative even as hunger and thirst; and these desires will go out after things that can be seen and felt, enjoyed with the senses. To whom these things may of right belong is, alas ! a secondary consideration with many men. They simply do not reflect upon it at all. Life resolves itself into a struggle between him who wants and him who has, and, if the truth must be spoken, the victor in such a struggle is practically a robber. There may be no physical violence, no shedding of blood ; but if there is the enriching of one's self at the expense of another, then the essential wrong is present. Let us allow the covetous man whatever credit there may be in this, that he does not form his covetous designs for any pleasure that he has in rapacity, but rather that he is rapacious in order to carry out his covetous designs. He wants to be rich and strong, and the only way he can do it is by crushing others into poverty. Hence this is reckoned an unavoidable accompaniment. It never strikes men of this sort that there is a more excellent way to satisfy and exhilarate the heart. *God's eye is upon this universal desire for large possessions,* and he can make a Divine and truly wise use of the desire. He turns our thoughts to the heavenly, the unseen, the eternal. Man does well in having the largest views as to possessions; he does well in looking to an immense increase of goods. It is a grand thing when he can pull down his barns and build greater, if it is only spiritual wealth that he is heaping up. In this gathering of goods there is no spoiling of the brethren, leaving them hungry, naked, and unsheltered. The spiritual wealth of the godly man makes poverty to none. Nay, rather—beautiful contrast—the richer he becomes, the richer he makes all with whom he comes in *living* contact.—Y.

Ver. 14.—*Healing the hurt slightly.* There is here an illustration of the false dealing referred to in the previous verse—an illustration from the prophets in particular, and, as might be expected, the specimen given shows how seriously this false dealing affected the prospects of the nation. There is, it will be observed, a plain statement of the matter wherein the prophets were deceivers; and there is also a figure setting forth the practical result of the deception.

I. CONSIDER THE PLAIN STATEMENT OF THAT WHEREIN THE PROPHETS ARE FOUND LIARS. They say, " Peace, peace; when there is no peace." The plain statement comes later than the figure, but it is needful to consider it first. War, invasion, humiliating conquest,—these had been threatened by the true prophet, but the false prophets come in and declare that there shall be peace. The word " peace " was probably one of the ordinary mutual salutations of the people; and these prophets, going out into the public places when war had been threatened, may have thrown into the salutation a special emphasis, as much as to say, " This Jeremiah speaks a lie when he prophesies war." And this word of the prophets showed that they did not comprehend where the hostility really lay. The hostile relations between the invading human hosts and Israel amounted to the merest trifle compared with the hostility between Jehovah and those who had been named as *his people.* The essence of the struggle lay, not in its being a struggle between invader and invaded, but between rightful Master and rebellious servants. The invader indeed may not have been conscious of any particular enmity against Israel. The chief passion in his heart may have been nothing more than savage lust for the exercise of force and the acquirement of spoil. But between God and his people there was a deep breach in all right relations. God wars against them, and therefore they were not to suppose that peace was secured, even if they kept on amicable terms with foreign nations. But, in truth, no amount of finessing, parading, and boasting could keep them permanently right with foreign nations. To suppose this was to suppose that they could pluck the weapons of God's chastening anger from his firm grasp. When God takes the wicked to become his sword, his sword they are, to be wielded with no uncertain efficacy. Men make the blunder of thinking there is peace, when they have only conciliated what enemies they can see and hear into invisibility and silence.

II. CONSIDER THE FIGURE WHICH ADDS TO THE FORCE OF THE PLAIN STATEMENT. It is a figure which does much to bring to the individual Israelite the serious consequences of this false dealing on the part of the prophets. War, while always a national disaster and anxiety, may leave individuals unscathed; nay, there are always a few who manage to build up some sort of prosperity and renown by successful war. But here is a figure which speaks of healing and of hurt, and of those who have to heal the hurt. The prophet is set forth as the surgeon, whose business it is to enter the home and put right again the malady that may be afflicting some member of it. This figure, too, it will be observed, tells us something of the feeling of the people, and thereby goes beyond the plain statement as to the false dealing of the prophets. 1. *There is a consciousness that all is not right.* There is a hurt. There is something to be healed. There is a sense of uneasiness, a sense which somehow must be taken away. The words of Jeremiah inflict superficial wounds and bruises at the least. There is a pain in the inward consciousness which is like the slashing of a whip upon the tender skin. Such messages as those which God put into the prophet's mouth were sure to hurt the pride of a nation, and rouse its patriotism into egotistic fury. Then we may be sure that some of the people would feel that the prophet might be speaking the truth. Some things he said were undeniable. The idol-worship was plain; so were the trickery and oppression which abounded in the common life of the people. And all this sense of uneasiness, which is really the sign that conscience is not utterly dead, only needs to be treated rightly in order to be roused into a vigorous life. 2. *The nature of the hurt is misunderstood.* This is the least that can be said. It may have been understood by some of the prophets, and yet, for their own base purposes, misrepresented. Jeremiah describes the hurt by its true name. The word in the Hebrew is a very strong word, meaning something very serious, something which demands great skill and effort, if it is to be put right. Who can exaggerate the seriousness of the crisis, when some malady going to the very heart of a man seems to awaken no corresponding alarm, either in his own mind or in the mind of his physician? And what a serious charge to bring against a physician if he seeks to lull alarm by making out the trouble to be a mere trifle! Yet this is just what many do. When the sense of unrest gets into the life, it is counted but as a physical illness. Change of air and scene are prescribed for symptoms which can only be permanently removed by change of heart. The more worldly and unspiritual a man is, the more dogmatism, reckless-ness, and overbearing arrogance he will show in lecturing those who have become disturbed in their consciences. 3. There is thus declared to be healing, when *there is not the slightest possibility of it.* Assurances are given which have no real foundation in anything the assurer knows or has done. He has been giving great attention to the visible cuts and bruises, and the deep, internal, organic injury is more firmly fixed than ever. Men will thus play the physician, try to get credit for their skill, and do untold harm, when they ought rather, in all humility and modesty, to confess their ignorance.—Y.

Ver. 16.—*The ancient paths to be sought and walked in.* I. THE ADDRESS IS TO THOSE WHO ARE ALREADY WALKING IN A CERTAIN WAY. There is activity of the whole life, a conscious and chosen activity. We are sometimes spoken of as being asleep and needing to be awakened out of sleep, and even as being dead and needing to be renewed to life; but here there is rather an approach to the other extreme in the aspect of sinful man that is presented. One kind of movement in human life lies beyond choice. Man must move on, from birth, through time, into eternity. This is a move-ment which, as he does not produce it, so neither can he in the least retard it. But now we are called to notice another kind of movement, that which man chooses— emphatically chooses—and into which he throws oftentimes his whole energy. Thus there is no man but what is in a path which he has chosen. However much he may seem to be the sport of circumstances, yet it will be found, in the complete inspection of his heart, that he loves to have circumstances moving him rather than that he should do what he can towards controlling circumstances. Moreover, the address is to those who are walking in a *wrong* way. Evidently they are *persisting* in it. And it is not only wrong, but *seriously*, even *fatally*, wrong. Yet, though the address is to those in the wrong way, there is every reason why those who happily are *in the right way* should also consider the appeal. If it is very difficult to turn from the wrong way into the right, it is very easy to make some divergence, at first imperceptible, from the right way, and so become most dangerously entangled in the wrong one.

II. THERE IS AN APPEAL TO THOSE ADDRESSED, TO GIVE THE MATTER IN QUESTION MOST EARNEST CONSIDERATION. There is surely a great deal in these two words, *see* and *ask.* The difference between right and wrong is also the difference between the soul's highest bliss and deepest misery; but it is a difference only to be comprehended when the soul is thoroughly in earnest to get to the bottom of all that is involved in the difference. Hence we are told to look; and we must be sure that we see as we ought to see. It is quite possible to have eyes and to look towards a thing, and yet to be practically blind, not discerning the real nature of it. A man's ways may be right in his own eyes; he may think the warnings of others, or the differing course that they take, to be mere scrupulosity, ending in nothing. Wherefore a man is to distrust his eyes, and add to what they may tell him the information to be gotten by the hearing of the ear. It is interesting to notice how sometimes the eye confirms the ear, and sometimes the ear the eye. Here the man is to make the tongue follow the eye, asking to follow upon seeing; so that he may get information on a matter of the utmost moment from authorities on whom he may depend with the utmost confidence. We must not dare to blame any one but ourselves if we make some gross error in the conduct of our life. God knows how easily the children of men wander; and so he expects them to do all they can by way of making sure that they are in the right road. Consider how alert some people are, in travelling by rail, lest perchance an omitted inquiry may send them in a wrong direction. A prudent man will never miss his way for want of asking. Yet these very people, who are reckoned prudent in such a small matter as finding their way from one place to another on the surface of the earth, are indifferent to an event which it is awful to contemplate, when they are told to see and ask if they be in the right way for eternity.

III. OBSERVE THE DEFINITENESS WHICH IS GIVEN TO THE LOOKING AND THE ASKING.

Man is not sent out on a vague quest, with nothing to guide and to limit him.   If he will look where God points, and ask the questions which God puts into his mouth, his quest will soon be at an end.   The right path is indicated by infallible signs.   It is *the ancient one*; the way which began to be trodden, not one or two generations back, but as far back as the record of human relations extends.   The right way is older than the wrong.   The way appointed for the first progenitors of mankind, when they stepped out where none had been before them, is the way for us.   As to *essentials*, Christ points out no different way from that which Adam was set to travel.   Adam's path was to be the path of strict *attention*, so that he might understand God's will; of strict *obedience* in doing the will when understood; and of perfect *trust* in God, feeling that his commandments for his dependent and finite creatures were the best, even though reasons for them might not be given.   The most ancient of all paths prescribed for men is that of a willing handing over of one's life to the will of that wise, loving, and holy One who is supreme.   All that Christ has told us, all he has done for us, is for the purpose of leading us into an effectual compliance with the requirement. Does not the experience of Enoch show that the right path is an ancient one?   What more can be said of the most devoted Christian, rich in all the resources of grace, than that he has walked with God?   What else can there be but true good and rest undisturbed when one is under the immediate influence of that God whose own peace knows not the slightest invasion amid all the commotion of the universe?   Real rest, a rest to the heart, was wanted by these people of Israel, and all that was so much wanted would surely come if only the ancient paths were found and once more frequented.—Y.

Ver. 20.—*Sweet and fragrant things made abominable to God.*   I. OBSERVE THE TROUBLE WHICH MEN WHO ARE REALLY UNGODLY MAY TAKE IN CONNECTION WITH RELIGION.   *Real religion* means, of course, a great deal of trouble and self-denial, watchfulness and prayer.   But when there is *only the appearance* of religion, there may also be much trouble, considerable time may be appropriated, and there may be considerable expenditure of money.   So it was here.   Materials for holy service were brought from a far country, and, being probably expensive in themselves, they would become more expensive still by the distance they had to be brought.   The expense would also look greater because it was on articles which were not manifestly a necessity of life.   Men must spend money for food and raiment and a roof to shelter them, and out of the money so spent they plainly get something; but here, in return for all the trouble and cost of getting the incense, etc., to Jerusalem, there is a very plain intimation that the offering of it does not effect the slightest good, does not in the least improve the position of those who offer.   And this very rejection by Jehovah makes us see more clearly the trouble these people took.   For we may be sure that the word through Jeremiah would not stop them in their offerings, useless as they were.   The less there is of intelligent and pure devotion in religion, the more there is of superstitious, terrified clinging to habitual outward forms; and the same kind of action continues still, in many ways and in all communions.   People without any real love to God in their hearts, or real submission to him, go through a great deal in the way of forms and ceremonies, and delude themselves with the notion that somehow they will be the better for it all.

II. OBSERVE THE CERTAINTY THAT THIS TROUBLE IS ALL IN VAIN.   Those who bring the offerings are not left in even the slightest doubt.   They have not the excuse of being able to say that in some way or other, which they do not understand, there will come a benefit out of their offerings.   There is a refusal in the most decided and solemn way.   Although these gifts may find their way into the house of God, and the altar itself be used in connection with them, they are not therefore accepted. They are just as much refused as a gift would be if the bringer of it had the door of the house where he brought it slammed in his face.

III. THE REASON OF THE REFUSAL.   Though not here expressed, the reason, from what is said elsewhere, is perfectly plain.   These gifts, sweet and fragrant as they are in themselves, become an insult because of the men who bring them.   Growing in their natural place, they play their part in adding to the beauty and perfume of God's world ; but now the fragrant has become as it were stinking, because of the defiled hands through which it has passed.   What men bring to God they must bring with clean hands and a pure heart. The great use of these gifts with their pleasant qualities was to signify what was sweet and fragrant and devoted in the hearts of the people. But when God knew that the gifts were bestowed through superstition or formality, or through the fear lest neglect might bring disaster on some cherished scheme, how could he accept these gifts? Consider further how, in many instances at least, the money was got that procured these gifts. They were the fruits of robbery, fraud, and oppression. When we read how some of the spoils of conquest in ancient times not unfrequently went to enrich an idol temple, how thankful we should be that in God's Word there is such plain dealing with those who think that some great gift to religious uses can condone their wickedness. Then, of course, in such cases the greater the expense of a man's religion the greater also was the amount that had to be gotten in wrongful ways. The Pharisee extortioner had to give several extra turns to the screw in order that he might get just that special sum which was needed to keep up his reputation as a religious man.—Y.

Ver. 30.—"*Reprobate silver.*" Two important things are to be remembered with regard to the meaning of the words in this verse. 1. That Jeremiah uses the same Hebrew verb where we have the two different words, "reprobate" and "rejected." What Jeremiah really says is that the silver bears the name "rejected silver," because Jehovah has rejected it. 2. The verb employed is commonly used to signify the action which is opposed to choosing; *e.g.* in Isa. vii. 15 the time is spoken of when a child becomes able to *reject* the evil and to *choose* the good, and in Isa. xli. 8, 9 there is a still more striking instance, because of its bearing on the words now under consideration. These are the words: "Thou, *Israel,* art my servant, *Jacob,* whom I have chosen, the seed of *Abraham my friend.* Thou whom I have taken from the ends of the earth, and called thee from the chief men thereof, and said unto thee, *Thou art my servant;* I have *chosen* thee, and not *rejected* thee." Thus it will be seen that we are not simply to think of *rejection* over against *approval.* Silver ore, being put through the most searching test possible, may respond to the test by coming out approved silver. But he who is thus *able to approve* is not necessarily in the position which *requires him to choose.* He may only have the duty of an assay agent, which stops with reporting the result of his test; he who has employed is the man to make the choice. Now, God tries in order that he may decide for himself whether to choose or reject; *e.g.* he rejected Saul from reigning over Israel, which of course means that, from the hour of rejection, Saul's throne was considered vacant. We can now proceed to point out the truths implied in this verse. 1. *There can be no adequate discernment of the merit or demerit of any man unless by God himself.* Only when God rejects can the stamp "rejected" be put on any one. Men may set up their canons of approval; they may apply their tests, philosophical, or political, or literary, or even theological. They may reject and excommunicate, pursuing with fiercest hatred all who are not approved according to their tests. Thus there will be a partial and temporary rejection, but since it comes from no adequate inquiry, the rejection itself will be rejected by a higher authority. Of this we have a conspicuous, we may even say the supreme, instance in Ps. cxviii. 22, "The stone which the builders *rejected* [the same Hebrew word as Jeremiah uses, be it observed] is become the head of the corner." It may be, indeed, that he whom some men reject may in the end be rejected by God also, but it will be for very different reasons. 2. *The reasons for rejection we must try to discover.* The Lord rejects those who claim to be accepted. He will reject the claim when it is that of mere national descent, as when Jesus said to the proud Jews who opposed him, that out of the stones he could make children to Abraham. God rejects all mere formal acknowledgment of him; it is not enough to say, "Lord, Lord." He rejects all that is the mere exercise and effort of intellectual faculties. In short, he rejects all that does not begin with a complete acceptance of Christ, and hence go on in the spirit of entire submission to him. Illustrations of what prompts to rejection are furnished both before and after this verse, *e.g.* in ver. 20, where the incense, etc., is rejected, *i.e.* of course, the men who offer the incense, and in ch. vii. 14, where the admired temple is threatened with overthrow. A mere building is shown to be nothing in God's sight unless it is frequented by such as are themselves acceptable to him. Observe also, in ascertaining the reason for rejection, how the word "silver" is kept. The thing tested is rejected, not because it is counterfeit, but because it is persistently impure. It will not yield up those baser elements which are so intimately blended with it, and effectually destroy the value and hide the lustre of the pure silver. And yet remember how high rejected man rises above rejected silver. Man in his freedom may relent from his stubbornness and submit to those renewing and purifying processes which will result in the silver being approved and chosen. 3. *There is no chance of establishing and commending what the Lord rejects.* Saul did his best to struggle against the Divine decision, but there is no more pitiable sight in all the records of kingship than that which he presents in the struggle. We also must reject those whom God rejects; and there can be no mistake about it that we must reject those who reject God—such as are spoken of in 2 Kings xvii. 15, those who rejected the statutes of God and the covenant that he had made with their fathers, and the testimonies which he testified against them.—Y.

EXPOSITION.

CHAPTER VII.

Ch. vii.—x.—Severe rebukes of idolatry alternating with announcements of the impending judgment. The circumstances connected with this discourse, or part thereof, appear to be detailed in ch. xxvi. Among the parallelisms between the two sections, notice especially the reference to the fate of the temple of Shiloh (comp. ver. 14 with ch. xxvi. 6). The date of the original utterance of the prophecy is thus fixed for one of the early years of the reign of Jehoiakim. Ch. x. 1—16, however, requires separate consideration.

Vers. 1—7.—The Divine requirements and the corresponding promise.

Ver. 2.—**Stand in the gate**; *i.e.* not an outer gate (for the outer court would be filled with the people whom Jeremiah was to address), but one of the three gates which led from the inner court to the outer. Probably it was the gate where Baruch recited the prophecies of Jeremiah at a later period, and which is designated "the new gate of the Lord's house," and said to have been situated in the "upper" *i.e.* inner court (ch. xxxvi. 10; comp. ch. xxvi. 10). We may conjecture that either one of the three great festivals or some extraordinary fast had brought a large number of people together at the temple.

Ver. 4.—**The temple of the Lord.** Notice the iteration of the phrase, as if its very sound were a charm against evil. It reminds us of the performances of the howling dervishes at Cairo, who "sometimes remain for hours, incessantly shouting the Muslim confession of faith (*lá iláha*, etc.)" (Dr. Ebers, in Bädeker's 'Egypt,' p. 150). The phrase is repeated three times to express the earnestness of the speakers (comp. ch. xxii. 29, "O earth, earth, earth"). These

false prophets evidently retained a large amount of the old materialistic faith of the Semitic nations (to whom the Israelites belonged by race), which localized the presence and the power of the divinity. The temple was, in fact, their palladium, and as long as it stood, the national independence appeared to them to be secured. They faithfully handed on the teaching of those prophets of the last generation, who, as Micah tells us (iii. 11), were wont to "lean upon the Lord, and say, Is not the Lord among us? none evil can come upon us." How Isaiah met this error we may collect from Isa. xxviii. 16 (see my Commentary). Are **these**; *i.e.* these buildings (comp. 2 Chron. viii. 11, where for "the places" the Hebrew has "these").

Ver. 5.—**If ye throughly amend, etc.**; a development of the idea of ver. 3. The true palladium of Judah would be the faithful performance of Jehovah's moral laws, especially those referring to the conduct of the rulers. Observe the stress which all the prophets lay on the virtues of civil life.

Ver. 6.—**The stranger, the fatherless, and the widow**; specially commended to the care of the Israelites (Exod. xxii. 21, 22—a passage belonging to one of the most evidently primitive portions of the Pentateuch; Deut. xxiv. 17, 19, 21; xxvii. 19; comp. Isa. i. 17, 23; x. 2; Ezek. xxii. 7). **In this place**; *i.e.* specially in Jerusalem, but not altogether excluding the rest of the kingdom (see vers. 3, 7).

Ver. 7.—**For ever and ever.** It is doubtful, both here and in ch. xxv. 5, whether these words should be joined to "gave" or "cause you to dwell." Still, the latter connection is both in itself the more probable one, and that suggested first of all by the accentuation (this, however, is not here decisive). It was not the extent of the original promise, but that of the enjoyment of the gift, which was in question. A more exact rendering of the prophet's formula is that of the Septuagint, ἐξ αἰῶνος καὶ ἕως αἰῶνος : i.e. from the most remote antiquity to the most distant future.

Vers. 8—15.—The formalism of Jewish religion exposed. The lesson of Shiloh.

Ver. 8.—**Lying words**; such as those quoted in ver. 4.

Ver. 9.—**Will ye steal**, etc.? rather, *What! stealing, murdering*, etc.? The construction is formed by a series of infinitives, preceded by an interrogative expressing extreme surprise, equivalent to "Is this your way of life—a course of theft, and so forth?"

Ver. 10.—**And come**, etc.; rather, *and then ye come*, etc. **We are delivered to do**, etc.; rather, *we have escaped, in order to do*, etc. To make the concluding words of the verse a part of the speech seems hardly fair to the Jews, who would certainly not proclaim that they had made their escape from the threatened judgment with the object of prosecuting abominable acts. Such a view, moreover, greatly weakens the force of the emphatic "We have escaped." "In order to do," etc., are the words of the prophet, who thus lays bare the secret intentions of these formal worshippers.

Ver. 11.—**Even I have seen it**; understand, "and I will therefore destroy the house which gives shelter to evil-doers."

Ver. 12.—**But go ye unto my place which** was in Shiloh. Jeremiah attacks this false confidence in the temple of Jerusalem, by pointing to the destruction of an earlier sanctuary, of which very little is known, indeed only so much as to give an edge to our desire for more. It is certain, from Josh. xviii. 1 and 1 Sam. iv. 3, that the tabernacle and the ark found a resting-place at Shiloh (an Ephraimitish town to the north of Bethel), nearly the whole of the period of the judges, or more exactly between the latter days of Joshua (Josh. xviii. 1) and the death of Eli (1 Sam. iv. 3). Manifestly, then, there must have been some sort of "house," i.e. temple, at Shiloh; a mere tent would not have been sufficient for so long a period. This presumption is confirmed by the language of Jeremiah, and by the expressions of the narrative books. The fate which the prophet is bidden to announce for the existing temple is analogous to that which fell upon "Jehovah's place in Shiloh." The latter was, therefore, not merely a deportation of the ark, such as is referred to in 1 Sam. v. And when the narrator of the times of Samuel speaks of Eli as "sitting by the door-post of the temple of Jehovah" (1 Sam. i. 9), is it more natural to suppose that the word "temple" is here applied to the tabernacle, or that there was really a house, however rude, as sacred in the eyes of the faithful as was afterwards the splendid

temple at Jerusalem? The latter view is strongly confirmed by Judg. xviii. 31, "All the time that the house of God in Shiloh existed" (Authorized Version is misleading), and Judg. xix. 18, where the Levite travelling to Mount Ephraim says, "I am going to the house of Jehovah." It is no doubt strange at first sight that so little information is given us as to this central sanctuary of the true religion; but are there not other omissions (especially in the history of the judges), which are equally strange as long as we look upon the Old Testament as primarily an historical document? We do know something, however, and more than is generally suspected; for when the right translation is restored in Judg. xviii. 31, it follows, from a comparison of this and the preceding verse, that the temple of Shiloh was destroyed simultaneously with the captivity of the northern tribes. The impression produced by this emphatic announcement of Jeremiah is revealed to us by a later passage in his book (see ch. xxvi.).

Ver. 13.—**Rising up early and speaking**; i.e. speaking zealously and continually (so ver. 25 ; ch. xxv. 4 ; xxvi. 5 ; xxix. 19). It is an expression peculiar to Jeremiah.

Ver. 14.—**To Shiloh.** Shiloh and the temple of Shiloh are interchanged, precisely as Jerusalem and the temple of Jerusalem (ch. xxvi. 9 ; Micah iii. 12).

Ver. 15.—**I will cast you out of my sight**; viz. into a foreign land (see Deut. xxix. 28). The land of Israel was in a special sense "Jehovah's land" (Hos. ix. 3 ; Lev. xxv. 23). **Ephraim**; here used for the northern tribes collectively, as Isa. vii. 2 ; Hos. iv. 17 ; v. 9 ; xii. 1.

Vers. 16—20.—The hypocrisy of the worship of Jehovah proved; its punishment.

Ver. 16.—**Pray not thou for this people.** Abraham prayed for Sodom (Gen. xviii. 23—32); Moses and Samuel for Israel (Exod. xxxii. 11—14 ; xvii. 11 ; Numb. xiv. 13—20 ; Ps. cvi. 23 ; 1 Sam. vii. 9, 10 ; xii. 17, 18, 23); and Jeremiah would fain perform the same pious duty to his people. We have a specimen of his intercession in ch. xiv. 19—22 (comp. ch. xviii. 20), followed immediately by a rejection of his prayer, parallel in thought to the present passage. Verbal parallels are ch. xi. 14 ; xiv. 11. **Cry**; i.e. cry for help (see on ch. xiv. 12); parallel with "prayer," as ch. xi. 14 ; Ps. xvii. 1 ; lxi. 1.

Ver. 17.—**In the streets.** A climax. There is no sense of shame left.

Ver. 18.—**The children . . . the fathers . . . the women.** All ages were represented in this idolatrous act, thus justifying the sweeping character of the judgment as described in ch. vi. 11. **Cakes** (comp. ch. xliv. 19). The word is peculiar (*kavvânîm*), and perhaps entered Palestine together with the foreign rite to which the cakes belonged. Various conjectures have been offered as to their nature, but without any demonstrable ground. Sacrificial cakes were not uncommon. Hosea refers to the luscious raisin-cakes used by idolaters (Hos. iii. 1). **To the queen of heaven.** This title of a divinity only occurs in Jeremiah (here and in ch. xliv. 17—19, 25). It reminds us, first, of titles (such as "queen of the gods") of the Babylonio-Assyrian goddesses, Bilat (Beltis) and Istar, who, though divided in later times, were "originally but two forms of the same goddess" (Sayce, *Transactions of Society of Biblical Archæology*, iii. 169). It is, however, perhaps an objection to the view that Bilat or Istar is intended, that neither here nor in ch. xliv. is there any allusion to that characteristic lascivious custom which was connected in Babylonia with the worship of Istar (Herod., i. 199). The phrase has, however, another association. It reminds us, in the second place, of the Egyptian goddess Neith, "the mother of the gods." The first mention of "the queen of heaven" in Jeremiah occurs in the reign of Jehoiakim, who was placed on the throne by Pharaoh-Necho, one of the Saïte dynasty (Saïs was the seat of the worship of Neith). If the "queen of heaven" were a Babylonio-Assyrian goddess, we should have looked for the introduction of her cultus at an earlier period (*e.g.* under Ahaz). But it was in accordance with the principles of polytheism (and the mass of the Jews had an irresistible tendency to polytheism) to adopt the patron-deity of the suzerain. Subsequently Judah became the subject of Nebuchadnezzar; thus it was equally natural to give up the worship of an Egyptian deity. Jewish colonists in Migdol would as naturally revert to the cultus of the Egyptian "mother of the gods" (see Grätz, 'Monatsschrift,' Breslau, 1874, pp. 349—351). The form of the word rendered "queen" being very uncommon, another reading, pronounced in the same way, obtained currency. This should be rendered, not "frame," or "workmanship" (as Authorized Version, margin), but "service." The context, however, evidently requires a person.

Ver. 19.—**Do they provoke me,** etc.? literally, *Is it me that they provoke* (or, *vex*)? *Is it not themselves?*

Ver. 20.—**Upon man, and upon beast.** That all creation shares in the curse of man is repeatedly affirmed in the Old Testament as well as the New. Inferentially, this doctrine appears from the narrative of the Fall, and still more clearly from Isaiah's description of Paradise regained (xi.). Hosea speaks of sufferings of the animals arising out of the guilt of Israel (iv. 3), and a consciousness of the "solidarity" of all living creatures is ascribed to a Ninevite king in the Book of Jonah (iii. 7, 8). In general, the origin of this community of suffering is left mysterious, but in Gen. vi. 12 it is expressly stated as the cause of the Deluge, that "all flesh [*i.e.* both man and beast] had corrupted its way upon the earth;" *i.e.* apparently, that contact with man had led to a corruption of the original innocence of the lower animals. It is a common experience that intercourse between Christianized (not to say civilized) man and the domestic animals produces a sometimes pathetic change in the psychic phenomena of the latter. Is the reverse process utterly inconceivable?

Vers. 21—28.—Jeremiah dispels the illusion that God's claims are satisfied by a merely formal service.

Ver. 21.—**Put your burnt offerings,** etc. Throw all your sacrifices into a mass, and eat them at your pleasure. Ye have my perfect permission, for they are of no religious value. According to the Law, the burnt offerings were to be entirely consumed by fire, while the other sacrifices were mostly eaten by the offerers and by their friends. There is a touch of contempt in the phrase, **eat flesh;** they are merely pieces of flesh, and ye may eat them.

Ver. 22.—**I spake not unto your fathers,** etc. An important and much-disputed passage, from which Graf, Colenso, and Kuenen derive one of their chief subsidiary arguments for the post-Exile date of the Levitical legislation. The prophet here appears to deny *in toto* that Jehovah at Mount Sinai had given any injunctions on the subject of sacrifice. But the prophet must at any rate be consistent with himself; he cannot utter anything by Divine command which is fundamentally at variance with other equally authoritative declarations. Do the statements of Jeremiah elsewhere justify us in accepting the words in their literal, superficial meaning? There are three other passages which have a claim to be considered. In ch. xvii. 26 the prophet draws a picture of the happy condition in which the Jews might be, were they only obedient. One of the features of this picture is that the Jews would still bring all the various kinds of sacrifices to the house of Jehovah. In ch. xxxi. 14 a similar description is closed with the promise to "satiate the soul of the priests with fatness," implying that there would be a great abundance of thank offerings in regenerate Israel. In ch. xxxiii. 11, among other blessings of the future, the prophet mentions the praiseful exclamations of those who would bring the sacrifice of thanksgiving. These passages do not contain any statement respecting the origin of the sacrificial system; but they do expressly assert that Jehovah contemplates that system with pleasure, and apparently that he designs it to be permanent among his people Israel. Let us now turn to ch. xxxiii. 17—24. Here the prophet, in the Name of Jehovah, declares that there is a Divine covenant "with the Levites, the priests," who shall never "want a man before me . . . to do sacrifice continually." A covenant with the priests implies a covenant with the people, the priests being the representatives of the people. This passage, therefore, is more distinct than those previously quoted; it does appear to maintain that the range of the Sinaitic covenant included the duties of the priesthood, *i.e.* sacrifices. On the other hand, it should be observed that the genuineness of this latter passage is not beyond dispute, the whole section in which it occurs (ch. xxxiii. 14—26) being omitted in the Septuagint. We have now to inquire, Is there a real discrepancy between the words of Jeremiah (strictly speaking, of Jehovah) in the verse now before us, interpreted literally, and the passages adduced above? Are they more inconsistent than such an utterance as ch. vi. 20 (first half of verse), which appears to deny the utility of sacrifices altogether? If the latter may be explained as a forcible oratorical exaggeration, why not also the present passage? Jeremiah sees the people attaching a pernicious importance to the *opus operatum* of sacrifice. On one occasion he tells them that Jehovah cares not for sacrifices; he means, as the context shows, the sacrifices of men without spiritual sensibilities. On another, that Jehovah never commanded their fathers to sacrifice; he means (may we not presume?) the mere outward forms of the ritual, divorced from the sentiment and practice of piety, which, as Hosea tells us (vi. 6), Jehovah "delights in and not [equivalent to 'more than'] sacrifice." There is, therefore, no fundamental inconsistency between the passage before us and the three passages first quoted, and if so there can be no real discrepancy with the last-mentioned passage, for the priests (as was remarked) perform their functions on behalf of the people, and the permanence of Jehovah's covenant with the priests depended on the spiritual life of the people they represented (read ch. xxxiii. as a whole). This view seems less arbitrary than that of Ewald, who thinks that the sacrifices spoken of in our passage are merely the free-will offerings of the rich; and than that of Dahler, who interprets,

"My chief care was not to prescribe rules for holocausts and sacrifices, but this is what I commanded thee above all," viz. moral obedience. According to it, the prophet's denial is not absolute, but relative—relative, that is, to the notion of sacrifices entertained by the Jews whom he addresses. Of course, Graf's view, that the denial is absolute, will equally well suit the context. The people were surprised at Jeremiah's objurgations, because they thought they had fulfilled the claims of the covenant. Jeremiah's purpose is equally well fulfilled whether his denial is qualified or unqualified, absolute or relative. Our object has been to separate the exegesis of our passage from a still doubtful controversy, and to offer a tenable view of it, based upon grounds purely internal to Jeremiah. It may be suggested, however, to the student of Leviticus, that even if the Levitical legislation in its present form were proved to be of a post-Exile date, it would still be doubtful whether any believing temple-worshipper could help assuming that Jehovah had, from the first existence of the nation, given his direct sanction to the offering of sacrifices. If so, it is comparatively unimportant (except with regard to the progressive revelation of the strictness of the law of truth) whether the Levitical code was given to Moses at Mount Sinai in its present form or not.

Ver. 23.—**But this thing . . . Obey my voice,** etc. Comp. Deut. vi. 3, "Hear [the verb rendered here 'obey'] therefore, O Israel, and observe to do it; that it may be well with thee," etc. The words, **I will be your God;** rather, *to you a God,* etc., occur in Lev. xxvi. 12 (comp. Exod. vi. 7; Deut. xxix. 13). **Walk ye in all the ways,** etc., is not a citation, but reminds us of passages like Deut. ix. 12, 16; xi. 28; xxxi. 29. **That it may be well unto you is a** characteristic phrase of Jeremiah (ch. xlii. 6; xxxviii. 20; xl. 9); but is also frequent in Deuteronomy (comp., besides the passage quoted above, Deut. iv. 40; v. 16; vi. 18; xii. 25).

Ver. 24.—**Imagination;** rather, *stubbornness* (see on ch. iii. 17). **Went backward, and not forward;** rather, *turned their back, and not their face* (literally, *became backwards, and not forwards*).

Ver. 27.—**Therefore thou shalt speak,** etc. rather, *and though thou speak . . . yet will they not,* etc.; *and though thou call unto them, yet will they not answer thee.*

Ver. 28.—**But thou shalt say;** rather, *thou shalt therefore say.* **A nation;** rather, *the nation.* "What one nation in the earth is like thy people, even like Israel, whom God went to redeem for a people to himself?" (2 Sam. vii. 23). And yet "this is the nation that have not hearkened," etc. **Truth**; rather, *good faith* (as ch. v. 1). **Is cut off from their mouth**; *i.e.* their oaths to Jehovah are false oaths (ch. v. 2).

Vers. 29—34.—Tophet, the greatest of all abominations; the beginning of the Divine retribution.

Ver. 29. — **Cut off thine hair.** The "daughter of Zion," *i.e.* the community of Jerusalem, is addressed; this appears from the verb being in the feminine. It is a choice expression which the prophet employs—literally, *shear off thy crown* (*i.e.* thy chief ornament). The act was to be a sign of mourning (see Job i. 20; Micah i. 16). Some think there is also a reference to the vow of the Nazarite (the word for "crown" being here *nézer*, which is also the word rendered in Authorized Version, "separation," *i.e.* "consecration," in the law of the Nazarite (Numb. vi.). But neither in this context nor anywhere else have we any support for the application of the term "Nazarite" to the people of Israel. **On high places**; rather, *on (the) bare hills* (see on ch. iii. 21). **The generation of his wrath**; *i.e.* on which his wrath is to be poured out (comp. Isa. x. 6).

Ver. 30.—**They have set their abominations**, etc.; alluding, doubtless, to the altars which Manasseh built "for all the host of heaven in the two courts of the house of Jehovah," and especially to the image of the Canaanitish goddess Ashérah, which he set up in the temple itself (2 Kings xxi. 5, 7).

Ver. 31.—**The high places of Tophet**; rather, *the high places of the Topheth*—(on the "high places" (Hebrew *bamoth*)—here probably artificial mounds to erect the altars upon, and on "the Topheth," see Commentary on 1 Kings). **In the valley of the son of Hinnom.** Hitzig and others would take Hinnom as a noun meaning "groaning" (Rashi, the great Jewish commentator, had already proposed this view), which is at first sight very plausible. But this name of the valley is already found in the description of the boundaries of Judah and Benjamin in Josh. xv. 8; xviii. 16. **To burn their sons**, etc. (On the worship of Moloch (Saturn), see on Lev. xviii. 21, and comp. Ezek. xvi. 20, 21, from which it appears that the children were first slain before being "caused to pass through the fire.")

Ver. 32.—**The valley of slaughter**; with reference to the great slaughter reserved for the unbelieving Jews. The scene of their sin shall be that of their punishment. **Till there be no place**; rather, *for want of room* (elsewhere).

Ver. 33.—**And the carcases**, etc.; almost verbally identical with Deut. xxviii. 26.

Ver. 34.—**The land shall be desolate**; rather, *shall become a waste*. The curse denounced upon the disobedient people in Lev. xxvi. 31, 33 (for another parallel between this chapter and Lev. xxvi., see ver. 23). In both passages the word for "waste" is *khorbah*, which, as Dr. Payne Smith remarks, is "used only of places which, having once been inhabited, have then fallen into ruin." Hebrew is rich in synonyms for the idea of "desolation."

HOMILETICS.

Vers. 1—7.—*Preaching repentance.* I. THE OCCASION. It was in the gate of the temple, where the crowd of worshippers would pass, and at the time of their going up to worship. 1. In a *public place*, (1) that men might not have to seek the preacher, but rather be sought by him; and (2) that all might hear, for truth, warnings of judgment, and gospels of deliverance are for all. 2. At the *entrance to the place of worship*, because (1) worship should be associated with instruction; (2) many people who observe religious ordinances need to be convinced of their sin and urged to repentance as much as the "publicans and sinners;" and (3) we must repent of sin before we can be accepted by God; so Jeremiah was to preach to the people as they went in to the temple, not as they came out.

II. THE ACCUSATION. The Jews are not accused of *Church* sins, neglecting religious ordinances, etc. Their sins were against common morality. 1. Though men may be very observant of *religious ordinances* they may yet be guilty of the *grossest wickedness* (ver. 6). 2. God is most concerned with our *conduct in daily life*. Here is the true life, the life which occupies the larger part of our time, engages most of our energies, gives freest scope for good or evil.

III. THE EXHORTATION. Practical amendment is sought. 1. There must be an *amending*. Repentance is not merely sorrow for the past; it is a change of desire and effort for the future. 2. This must be *practical*. The Jews are to amend their "ways." True repentance is more a matter of conduct than of emotion. It must bring forth fruits (Matt. iii. 8). 3. This must be *definite*. Particular sins are specified as to be abandoned (ver. 6). Men must repent of their own sins, their characteristic sins, their habitual sins. We are too ready to renounce the sins which do not belong to us, and to pass over our most familiar sins unnoticed. 4. This must be *thorough*. The Jews are to "throughly amend" their ways. A half-hearted repentance is a mockery. As well not flee from the City of Destruction at all as linger regretfully about its vicinity like Lot's wife, only to suffer a similar fate to hers.

IV. THE ADMONITION. The Jews are warned of the danger of a false ground of confidence (ver. 4), and threatened with approaching judgment. 1. If we believe that men are in danger, that is a *false charity which hides the danger* out of consideration for feelings of mere temporary comfort. 2. There is an *advantage in using the minatory* language of Scripture, though (1) with deep solemnity, (2) with sadness and kindliness of purpose, (3) without the amplification of imaginative sensationalism, (4) accompanied by clear indications of the way of escape and encouragements for hope in following it.

V. THE PROMISE. (Ver. 7.) Repentance is to be followed by forgiveness and the restoration of favour. God charges us with our sins, and threatens judgments, all in love that he may thus lead us to safety and blessedness. The most wicked men may find forgiveness and ultimate salvation if they will but repent and turn to God (ver. 6).

Ver. 4.—*The confidence of superstition.* I. CONFIDENT LANGUAGE IS NO GUARANTEE FOR A SECURE FOUNDATION OF TRUST. The Jews are vehement in exclamation; but their words are boastful without ground. Frequent repetition is no evidence of the truth of a saying. Yet, though against all reason, and by mere force of urgency, how many convictions have been thus forced on the belief of mankind! Trite sayings are commonly accepted for true sayings. We do not think to test the genuineness of the old worn coin so much as that of the new coin. We naturally believe that with which we are familiar. Indeed, we may persuade ourselves to believe almost anything by simply dwelling upon the idea of it till this becomes inseparable from our consciousness. And all this without the slightest reason!

II. THE SUPERSTITION OF RELIGION MAY BE FOUND IN MEN WHO HAVE LOST THE SPIRITUALITY OF IT. The Jews neglected the spiritual worship, which was all that was really valuable in the temple service, but they clung to the idea that there must be a sanctity about the very walls of the temple which would make it a place of safety for those who took shelter within them. Superstition is the disease of religion. When spiritual holiness is gone, a sanctity is ascribed to material things. They who have no faith in God may have strange faith in charms and spells, like the Jews who, perhaps, thought to work a charm by the threefold iteration of their cry, "The temple of the Lord," etc.

III. NO REAL SECURITY CAN BE FOUND IN EXTERNAL THINGS. The temple building was no palladium to the bad men who sought refuge in it. It is vain to be near the Church if we are far from God. Religious ordinances, membership in a Church, official association with religion as priest, prophet, or minister, and the like outside affairs, contain no promise whatever of protection, and the man who shelters himself beneath the whole of them and does not seek spiritual shelter is as much exposed to the tempest of judgment as if he stood out in the open plain of bare infidelity.

IV. THE TRUE TEMPLE OF THE LORD IS THE HEART OF A GOOD MAN. God does not dwell in temples made with hands. Earthly temples of stone may represent his dwelling, but they cannot bring him nearer to men nor confine his presence within limits. But the soul of a good man is a real temple wherein God's Spirit truly abides and effectively operates (1 Cor. vi. 19). Such a temple is safe from all harm. Thus we must seek safety, not by entering a temple, but by becoming a temple—not by securing the external protection of holy things while the heart and life are unholy, but by receiving God within the heart and sanctifying the life to him.

Ver. 13.—*The voice unheeded.* I. GOD IS EVER SPEAKING TO HIS CHILDREN. There is a Divine voice speaking, not to favoured prophets in rare moments of spiritual elevation, but to all men, that all who will may hear. This voice comes to us in many forms. 1. The voice of *nature*—the proclamation of the power and wisdom of God in the awful, silent speech of the stars (Ps. xix. 3), and the gentler language which tells of his tenderness and beneficence in the cheery songs of spring and the glad shout of the harvest. 2. The voice of *history*. God is in history, and speaks to us through the events of the past, warning by judgments (ver. 12), inviting by acts of deliverance and gifts of mercy (see Ps. cv.). 3. The voice of *providence* in daily life. Has not God been speaking to us through our own experience—using various prophetic agencies—the advent of a new joy, the cloud of a great sorrow, a visitation of the angel of death to the home? has he not repeatedly roused, invited, pleaded, and consoled us with voices from out eternity? 4. The voice of *prophecy*. God had often so spoken to the Jews before the days of Jeremiah, and reference is plainly made to this fact in the text. That voice still lives, because truth is eternal. Thus God speaks to us through the inspired thoughts of the Bible. 5. The voice of *Christ*. He is the "Word" of God made articulate in the dialect of men (John i. 1—14). He who sees Christ hears the voice of God. 6. The voice of *conscience*. This is God speaking within the soul. Every time we feel compunction at doing wrong, or an inward urging to do the right, God is pleading in our heart by direct communion, spirit with spirit.

II. THE VOICE OF GOD IS URGENT. God speaks with urgency—"rising up early and speaking." 1. The urgency of God's voice is a proof of his *great love to his children*. He speaks with frequency, repeating the same unheeded lesson, and even when none attend to his voice. God speaks to his children before they pray to him. The first impulse to spiritual communion comes from God, not from us (Ps. xxvii. 8). Christ stands at the door and knocks (Rev. iii. 20). We may see in this an evidence of the long-suffering mercy of God—a mercy which "endureth for ever," and we may see an encouragement to listen and turn to him. Still he "waiteth to be gracious." 2. The urgency of God's voice is a proof of *the great importance* of what he says. God is urgent. What tremendous destinies must turn on a question which even he must rouse and bestir himself about! We might expect that any voice from the awful majesty of God would be full of deep and vast meaning. What must be the significance of his words when even he speaks with earnest insistance, with pressing urgency? How can such an utterance be passed unheeded?

III. GOD'S VOICE IS OFTEN NOT HEEDED. He speaks with the authority of the majesty of heaven, with the yearning love of a Father, with the urgency which betokens matters of profound interest, and with a direct reference to the most fearful woe and the most glorious blessedness of his children. Yet men turn aside with indifference. What are the causes of this appalling wonder? 1. *Spiritual deafness.* There are men who have no ears for the voice of God. Yet God can open our ears if we are willing to hear. 2. *Hatred to the highest truth.* Men stop their ears against the sound of honest words which are hateful to sinful hearts. 3. *Consciousness of guilt.* Fearing words of doom, men refuse to hear any words from God; but (1) the doom will not be the less because the warning is unheeded, and (2) God warns to save. 4. *Unbelief.* Doubt as to whether a voice is Divine is often natural, and if the doubt grows into widespread scepticism the cause may be intellectual rather than moral. But when once a voice is recognized as Divine, unbelief is distrust in God; it is "making him a liar."

IV. THE REFUSAL TO GIVE HEED TO GOD'S VOICE IS A FATAL EVIL. 1. It aggravates guilt by adding to it (1) fresh rebellion against our great King, (2) ingratitude to the pleading love of our merciful Father, (3) wilful sin against light. 2. It leaves the purpose of God's voice uneffected. He urges and pleads with his children, but he does not force them to return to him. If they will not heed his voice that voice is lost upon them, and the ruin from which it would call them unaverted.

Ver. 16.—*Forbidden prayers.* Certain prayers must be regarded as unlawful.

I. PRAYERS OF POSITIVE DEMAND. Many men pray as though they were dictating to God. Prayer is petition, not command. The suppliant should assume the attitude of a mendicant.

II. PRAYERS WHICH AIM AT TURNING THE WILL OF GOD. We may believe that God will do in answer to prayer what he would not do apart from prayer, because the very prayer may be the one essential condition which makes that fitting which would not be fitting without it. But this must be in accordance with God's will, which is always perfect, while ours is often evil.

III. PRAYERS FOR WHAT IS WRONG IN ITSELF. God cannot grant such prayers. We may pray for all men, but we may not pray for every imaginable favour to be given to all men. Thus it is wrong to pray that the impenitent wicked should not be punished. The purpose of the text seems to be just to forbid this prayer. Jeremiah is not to pray that the calamities he sees approaching may not fall on the guilty people. It would be bad for them and an outrage on justice that, while they refused to hear the Divine voice warning them of their danger and inviting them to the way of safety, God should hear the voice of any intercessor pleading that the threat should not be accomplished, and that the wicked people should be saved from just punishment.

Vers. 21—28.—*Declension.* Jeremiah endeavours to rouse a sense of guilt in his hearers by pointing to the sad downward course of their history when this is regarded in the light of Divine requirements and inducements to follow them.

I. THE DIVINE REQUIREMENTS. These were not for the offering of mere formal sacrifices, but for obedience to God in heart and conduct (1 Sam. xv. 22). Men need to be repeatedly reminded of this fact, because there is a common tendency to separate religion from morality, to believe that God is pleased with the performance of Church services by those whose lives are spent in sin and selfishness, and that the devotions of the sanctuary atone for the wickedness of daily life. Jeremiah and the prophets generally teach (1) that religious services are worthless except as expressions of inward devotion, and (2) that no religious service is acceptable while obedience in common life is neglected.

II. THE INDUCEMENTS TO FULFIL THESE REQUIREMENTS. 1. *A clear statement* of them. Jeremiah was not the first to reveal them. They were well known and easily understood. 2. *Rewards promised for obedience.* It would be "well with" the people if they walked in all the ways that God commanded them. Disobedience led to the Captivity. Obedience is the only condition on which we can enjoy liberty. 3. *Repeated warnings.* (Ver. 25.) By all forms in which the Divine voice reaches us God is continually reminding us of his will and urging us to obedience.

III. THE CAUSES OF DECLENSION. 1. *Inattention.* "They hearkened not." People are too preoccupied by worldly concerns to give the requisite thought to higher interests. 2. *Self-will.* "They walked in the counsels and stubbornness of their evil heart." Men disobey through the conceit of superior knowledge and through the obstinacy of selfish aims.

IV. THE CHARACTER OF DECLENSION. 1. *Departure from God.* Israel turned "the back and not the face" to God. In disobeying the will of God we necessarily cease to walk with God, lose the light of his presence, become godless. 2. *A constant deterioration of morals.* The contemporaries of Jeremiah "did worse than their fathers." Progress is the natural order. But, left to itself, the leaven of wickedness will spread as surely as the seed of goodness would grow if that were allowed free development.

V. THE CONSEQUENCES OF DECLENSION. 1. *Hardening against the reception of truth.* (Ver. 27.) The people have reduced themselves to such a condition that they cannot receive the prophet's message. 2. *Inability to profit by correction.* "This is a nation that . . . receiveth not correction" (ver. 28). 3. *Destruction of the value of religious services.* The burnt offering should express the dedication of the worshipper. But as it does nothing of the kind, it is worthless, and may as well serve as flesh for a common meal (ver. 21). Religion, which should be the inspiration of morality, is dead and powerless in the hands of people of corrupt lives. The noblest exercise of humanity is thus reduced to a nullity.

Ver. 32—ch. viii. 3.—*Horrors of retribution.* I. THERE IS REASON TO BELIEVE THAT HORRORS OF SIN WILL BE FOLLOWED BY HORRORS OF RETRIBUTION. 1. *Justice* requires a proportionate relation of punishment to sin. The Jews had sinned greatly. It was right that they should be punished with severity. Mild views of the requirements of punishment may be the result of a dulness of conscience which does not recognize the depth of guilt. When men are most deeply convinced of sin, they are also most apprehensive of the merited wrath of God. 2. Punishment, to be *effective*, must be proportionate to guilt. In its three functions as deterrent when threatened, chastisement for correction when received, and warning to others when witnessed, it can only be effectual if a due proportion be observed. 3. The *nature of God* leads us to suppose that he may exact horrible retribution for horrible sin. He is almighty, and if his anger, which is slow to rise, is at length roused, this must be terrible indeed. God is long-suffering, merciful, ready to forgive; but he is not weak and indifferent to the great evils of sin. It is not reasonable to suppose that the Divine anger will be the less in its outpouring because it is long withheld.

II. THERE ARE INDICATIONS OF THE HORRORS OF RETRIBUTION IN THE SCRIPTURAL REVELATIONS CONCERNING IT. Jeremiah is speaking chiefly of physical horrors which are to accompany the overthrow of Jerusalem. But he suggests that these contain certain necessary elements of retribution. 1. *Death.* Tophet shall be a valley of slaughter. The great and ultimate punishment is always regarded, not as pain, but as death (Rom. vi. 23). 2. *Shame.* The corpses are to be unburied and exposed to the ravages of unclean animals—for the Jew a fearful degradation. Sin exposed, confounded, defeated, will reflect burning shame on the sinner. 3. *Anguish.* "The voice of mirth," etc., will cease; men will prefer death to life (ch. viii. 3). 4. *A peculiar relation of penalty to offence.* Tophet, the scene of horrible wickedness, shall be the spot for retributive slaughter. Where wretched men immolated their children their own dead bodies shall be cast. The sun and moon and stars which they worshipped shall look down on their bones bleaching out in the open.

III. THERE ARE TIMES WHEN IT IS NECESSARY TO MAKE MEN THINK OF THE HORRORS OF RETRIBUTION. The language of Jeremiah is explicit and graphic. 1. Details of future retribution should not take the chief place in instruction. They lose their effect by too frequent repetition. By themselves they are not able to produce a better life, but may result in hardness, unbelief, and disgust. The love of God in Christ is *the* great power to lead to holiness. 2. Nevertheless we must not shun to declare "the whole counsel of God." Thoughts of retribution may be powerful means for rousing convictions of sin, if they are accompanied by appeals to conscience which make men feel the due proportion of guilt to punishment.

HOMILIES BY VARIOUS AUTHORS.

Vers. 1—3.—*Keeping the temple gate.* It was probably not the outer gate, but one of the gates which led from the outer to the inner or upper court (cf. ch. xix. 14; xxvi. 10; xxxvi. 10). "From this point the prophet could view the whole assembly of the people in the outer court, as well as the gates leading from without into it" (Lange). Christ seems to have stood thus at times.

I. THE PREACHER OF TRUTH DOES WELL TO CHOOSE THE MOST IMPRESSIVE POSITIONS, OCCASIONS, AND CIRCUMSTANCES FOR THE DELIVERY OF HIS MESSAGE. The great aim of the preacher is to get a hearing for what he has to say. Tact (to a certain degree), artistic juxtaposition and arrangement, sympathy with the spirit of the times, etc., are indispensable qualities to him who would give the Word of God bold and effective expression. Public occasions may, therefore, frequently be utilized for special services, etc. Passing movement and contemporary events may give fresh interest to permanent truth. A curious ingenuity is sometimes exhibited in making the preacher inconspicuous and reducing his office to a matter of routine. He ought always to feel that his message is an extraordinary one, requiring all the earnestness and effort of which he is capable to convey it with due effect. And even then it must have suffered at his hands, and in much he will be an unprofitable servant.

II. RELIGIOUS OBSERVANCE MAY BE VERY FASHIONABLE, AND ALL BUT UNIVERSAL, WHERE THERE IS LITTLE REAL RELIGION. One has to distinguish between the outward and the inward, the religion of rite and ceremony and that of the heart. Here apparently the representatives of "all Judah" were assembled, and yet it was no sign of national piety, but rather the contrary. Instead of the carnal nature being checked and corrected, it was directly fostered by such worship. *Public worship* is a phrase which often includes elements that have nothing to do with the worship of God. That the services of God's house should be chaste and attractive will be generally admitted. But architectural adornments, musical accessories of an ornate or merely artistic nature, displays of rhetoric, and similar additions to the essential character of the worship, may prove popular and entertaining, and yet be spiritually pernicious. In the case of Judah the whole worship was on a low intellectual and spiritual key. The gods of heathenism and Jehovah were worshipped alike, and the licentious rites of idolatry mingled with the sacrifices of the Law. This had resulted in the temple being polluted and becoming a "den of thieves." Our aims in worship, the purity and concentration of our hearts, the moral relation between our every-day life and our temple service, have all very intimately to do with the question of the value of public religious observances.

III. RIGHTEOUSNESS OUGHT TO BE PRELIMINARY TO WORSHIP. "Amend your ways and your doings" is the demand the prophet makes in proof of the genuineness of their worship. Religion is a matter of life, and not of showy observances and empty protestations. The best proof that we intend serving God is that we have already begun to do so in business and morals. This duty, although difficult, is the best preparation for exalted spiritual experiences and sincere adoration. Men are not fit to appear before God when their misdeeds are still being repeated and their moral habits are not under the influence of his Spirit.

IV. UNREAL WORSHIP OF GOD IS CERTAIN TO BE DETECTED AND EXPOSED. We can imagine the shame of the nobility and people whom the prophet from his unlooked-for vantage-point so sharply rebuked.—M.

Vers. 4—7.—*Who shall dwell in the house of the Lord?* I. AN UNWARRANTABLE ASSUMPTION. They arrogate to themselves, not only the exclusive possession of a meeting-place between God and man, but they speak of themselves as in a special and peculiar sense the temple of God. 1. There is an argument latent here. The temple is looked upon as a permanent and immovable building—a place of intercourse between Jehovah and his people. It is the only place of the kind, and it will stand for aye. But the Jews are so related to the temple, so bound up with its existence and maintenance, that they esteem themselves identified with it, and therefore partaking of its attributes. By an easy transition, to which language affords many parallels, they come to say, "The temple of the Lord is this [*i.e.* are we]." 2. And yet this very pretension, when spiritually interpreted, expresses a gracious and mysterious truth. That is the intention and aim of man's creation. Every man, as man, is made to be a temple of the Holy Ghost. This is his purpose and obligation; but, instead of this, how opposite is the actual condition of most men! Not, therefore, as a matter of course, independently of moral resolve and Divine inspiration, but as something to be striven after and earnestly realized in holiness of life, is man the "temple of the Lord." 3. And as is often the case, the illegitimate narrowing and monopoly of this Divine indwelling is the very sign of its absence. They who rest upon other than moral grounds for the claim to the presence of God within them are usurpers. It is the universal privilege of those who serve God acceptably in spirit and in life. That which has a moral condition cannot be confined to local or sectarian limits.

II. A COMMANDMENT WITH PROMISE. A rehearsal of common duties enjoined by the Law of Moses. It is terse, prosaic, detailed, and altogether opposed to the absurd pretension it is meant to correct. Just those duties, too, are mentioned which the prophet was well aware had been neglected by Judah. There is nothing brilliant or magnificent about the catalogue of deeds. They are just such actions as are obligatory upon all men. It was not even necessary for a man to be a Jew to do them; for when the Gentiles do these things it shows that there must be a law written upon their hearts by nature or grace. And yet the greatest in Jerusalem could not, any more than the heathen, do the least of them perfectly. How gracious that to them, therefore, is attached this promise of temple consecration! So the grand human duties and merciful dispositions, without which life would be so hard, are recommended and enforced by that comprehensive promise, to be immediately realized in personal blessing and consecration, to be completely fulfilled when "the tabernacle of God shall be with men."—M.

Vers. 13, 25.—"*Rising up early.*" A striking expression concerning Jehovah. In ver. 25 it is strengthened: "Daily rising up early." It speaks to us—

I. OF THE ANXIETY OF JEHOVAH FOR HIS PEOPLE. He who has important business on hand, or dear ones in trying circumstances, or great results dependent upon immediate and strenuous exertion, will show diligence in some such way. He will be unable to rest. So it is with God and his Church. Not that he can be said to *fear* or be uncertain as to the issues. But the interest he has in the fortunes and spiritual state of his people is of this description. It is no impassive God who is presented to us in Scripture. A profound concern for the interests of our race ever fills the mind of God. His deepest affections are engaged. He mourns the sin and rejoices in the salvation of men.

II. OF HIS DILIGENCE IN PROVIDING FOR THE WANTS OF HIS PEOPLE. It is no aimless, helpless anxiety that fills his breast. The most practical measures of help and direction are devised and carried into execution. Prophets, the plenipotentiaries of Divine grace, are sent in immediate response to the needs and demands of men. No age of the world or the Church but has its thick succession. Heaven is in continual activity on behalf of sinners. The choicest spiritual gifts are ceaselessly rained upon the earth. The most devoted servants of God are raised up and sent. Truth in quick evolution anticipates the spiritual necessities of those who would seek God. There is no flagging, no cessation, from Adam's fall to the uplifting of the second Adam. And onward from that Divine spectacle, in which was displayed the "fulness of the Godhead bodily," events hurry to the culminating glories of Pentecost and the marriage supper of the Lamb.

III. IF THIS BE THE CASE, HOW OUGHT WE TO STUDY AND LAY HOLD OF THE MESSAGE OF SALVATION? Is there not a contrast between the affectionate concern and sacrifice of God and the languid indifference or stubborn refusals of men? How shall we escape if we neglect this infinite mercy? How shall we excuse the manner in which we listen to the Word of God?—M.

Vers. 17—20.—*Idolatry a detailed insult to Jehovah.* This is frequently stated in the Bible. It must be the case from the very nature of the worship of false gods. It is a denial and robbery of the true God. But the description here given helps us to realize more completely the intense sinfulness of the worship of idols, because of the circumstances attending it.

I. AGGRAVATING CIRCUMSTANCES. 1. *It was done publicly in the streets of Jerusalem and the cities of Judah.* God was displaced from the land he had given. The place that was consecrated by the faith and worship of the saints and the ceaseless mercies of Jehovah is desecrated by the orgies and profanities of heathenism. The worship of the "queen of heaven" (the female representative—Astarte—of the nature principle, of which Baal is the male principle) could not but be public. As the Baal worshippers poured forth their libations to the sun-god in broad day, so the worshippers of the moon made no secret of their devotions. It was done literally and perforce "in the face of heaven." And celebrations of the most obscene description mingled with their sacrifices. Yet was there no shame. 2. *It absorbed the attention and energies of the people.* Here is a picture of a whole family, from the eldest to the least, occupied in tasks connected with the worship of Astarte. How different from the perfunctory or imperfect service rendered to Jehovah! No time was left for the true worship. And is it not just so to-day under new forms and conditions? The idolatry of pleasure, gain, ambition, personal and social ideals,—does it not absorb the minds and bodies of its devotees? How little time is left for Christian duty and sacrifice! How weary and useless are those faculties which are professedly placed at the service of God! Our life-work is too often in the market-place, in the forum of personal display and self-seeking, etc., instead of the service of Jesus and the house of God. 3. *It involved the waste of the natural products of the land.*

II. THE DELIBERATE INTENTION. There was not wanting this expressed defiance. The idea is that they would annoy and exasperate Jehovah with impunity to themselves, as mean natures delight in awakening the jealousy, etc., of others. In this way they showed how completely they misunderstood the relations of Jehovah with his world and his people, his command over the forces of nature, and his power of retaliation through the ordinary laws of nature.

III. ITS RECOMPENSE. 1. *According to natural laws.* Affecting, therefore, the objects they required for their sacrifices to Astarte, and cutting off the supplies requisite for man and beast. 2. *To their own confusion.* God will be unaffected; they them-

selves will be put to shame. The idolater and atheist are their own worst enemies.
3. *Not to be escaped or ended.* They are playing with fire. It will soon find its proper
objects in themselves and their profaned offerings. Nor will they be able to quench
that which they have kindled. So helpless will transgressors ever be. In the least of
the calamities that they provoke upon themselves there is a beginning of penal fires
and eternal miseries.—M.

Vers. 31—33.—*The desecration of Tophet.* This valley was the scene of Solomon's
Moloch-worship, of the child-sacrifices of Ahaz and Manasseh, and of the varying
idolatrous rites of succeeding times. If the temple still maintained externally its
consecration to Jehovah and its position as the centre of the theocracy, the valley of
Ben-Hinnom was the acknowledged centre and high place of Moloch. Its vicinity to
Jerusalem brought it into prominent opposition to the temple. Some signal exhibition
of the Divine wrath is, therefore, called for. This is furnished by the iconoclastic zeal
of Josiah, the great slaughter of Israel in war, and the gradual use of it as a receptacle
for filth, sewage, unburied dead, etc. The prophecy, repeated in ch. xix. 11, is
speedily translated into history. We have here an instance of the Divine laws—
    I. THAT THAT WHICH IS MORALLY CORRUPT SHALL ENTAIL DESTRUCTION. Where
there is filth in God's universe there will be fire. Corruption *is* the beginning of
death, in this world and that which is to come.
    II. THE INWARD, MORAL CHARACTER OF THINGS AND PERSONS SHALL HAVE EXTERNAL
PHYSICAL EXPRESSION. It will not always be concealed. That which is whispered in
the ear shall be spoken from the house-top. The trap will be labelled and the pitfall
plainly shown. The externalizing processes of history and development in nations,
individuals, etc., tend to declare by outward and unmistakable signs the real character.
Of this Tophet is an illustration. The judgment its revolting practices bring upon its
votaries is the occasion of its permanent defilement. It gradually is transformed into
a scene of physical abomination, and, to the spiritual imagination, the type and symbol
of eternal perdition. Gehenna fires—how different their first and last senses, and yet
how related! The same law will operate in holy and spiritual men. The inward
nature will cast the slough of corruption, and shall be clothed upon with a "body,"
which shall express, further, and fulfil it. When that which is really and spiritually
filthy is sentenced to be "filthy still," the saints shall find embodiment and circumstances corresponding to their inward condition, and constituting the elements of their
reward.—M.

Vers. 1—34.—*The relations of righteousness and religion.* This chapter, as indeed
so much other of Jeremiah's prophecies, teaches not a little concerning this great theme.
In this chapter we note how it shows—
    I. THAT RIGHTEOUSNESS IS THE PRINCIPAL THING. 1. It is God's *solemn* demand
(ver. 2). (1) Jeremiah is charged to proclaim it in the Name of the Lord and as *his* word.
(2) He is to go where there will be a vast congregation of the people: "In the gate of
the Lord's house." (3) Probably at a time of national gathering, at one of the feasts,
so as to secure a yet larger audience. (4) At a moment when the word of the Lord
might be expected to win most attention from them—as they were "entering in at the
gates to worship the Lord." 2. It is God's *perpetual* demand. See the whole chapter,
the whole prophecy. "Amend your ways and your doings" (ver. 3) is its constant
appeal. 3. At first it was *his only* command, and it is ever *his first* command (ver. 22).
Our first parents were commanded to obey before sacrifice or any rites of religion were
appointed. And so with Israel (ver. 22). The moral Law was given before the ceremonial. And it was given in a far more imperative form. The moral Law begins
"Thou *shalt;*" the Levitical (Lev. i. 2—ii. 1), "If any man will." Hence from all
the foregoing it is evident that righteousness stands before all else in the Divine esteem.
    II. RELIGION WAS GIVEN FOR THE SAKE OF AND AS AN AID TO RIGHTEOUSNESS.
Righteousness is not for the sake of religion, but *vice versâ.* No doubt they render mutual
help, but the proper relation of the two is as aforesaid. And religion can be a help to
righteousness and ought ever to be, even as it has often been and is. 1. *By supplying
fresh motives.* Apart from religion, righteous conduct becomes simply morality, and
bases itself upon laws of expediency, or at best draws its force from motives that rise no

higher than earth and man and the present life. But religion gives *the love of God in Christ* as its all-constraining force. Under the influence of this, what have not men done and borne; and what will they not do and bear? 2. *By lending intensity to those already in action.* How puny the power of *hope*, when it has none other recompense than that which this life and this world can furnish, contrasted with its invincible force when the recompenses of eternity, made known to us by religion, are set before it and held out to it! And so with the motive of *fear.* What an immense addition is made to the deterrent force of fear when the idea of God and *his* awful displeasure are present before the mind!

> "His love will all vain love expel,
> His fear all fear beside."

3. *By furnishing a perfect example.* In our blessed Lord's life, short as it was in duration, and far removed from us as it is in time, place, and circumstance, neverthe-less in it there is to be found a standard and model of righteous conduct for all ages and all lands, such as can be found nowhere else. His life has been the compass by which many a saint has steered across the difficult ocean of life, and by its aid arrived safely at the desired haven. 4. *By winning for us, in response to our fervent prayers, the ever-present and potent help of the Divine and transforming Spirit.* By his aid the very "body of sin" within us is crucified, and we become new creatures in Christ. 5. *By its ordinances of worship :* its continual teaching, its Church fellowship, and its varied sacred observances, keeping alive within us those beliefs and sentiments which are ever the most powerful prompters to all righteousness of life. Thus the Israelite of old found the Law of God (cf. Ps. cxix.) his perpetual aid, and the worship of God's house a constant solace and strength. And it is so still. By the truths and the ordi-nances of religion, the weak, wavering will is steadied, the feet are kept from falling, and the soul is preserved from death. Such ought ever to be the case, ever is so, where religion is the worship of God in spirit and in truth ; and this was the Divine design and intent in giving it to us.

III. BUT THEY ARE AT TIMES FOUND ASUNDER. Religion may flourish, but righteous-ness be only conspicuous by its absence. It was so in the time of the prophet. We see a whole apparatus of religion—temple, altar, priests, sacrifices, services ; nothing omitted in external observances. And there was a national profession of it ; large sums of money were lavished on it, and there was a universal outward regard for it. But, on the other hand, all this went on whilst the most gross unrighteousness characterized the very people who outwardly were so religious (cf. vers. 5, 6, 9, 18). This was an appalling fact. Nor, alas! is it one that now has no existence; the same sad separation of religion from righteousness may be too often seen in our days as of old. The murderous banditti of Southern Europe are diligent at Mass, and pay all honour to the Virgin and saints. The midnight assassins of Ireland are all good Catholics. And many a chapel and church in our own land has amongst its seemingly most religious worshippers, men who are cruel, hard, fraudulent, impure—" saints at the prayer-meeting and sacrament, but very devils at home."

IV. THEY MAY BE EVEN OPPOSED TO ONE ANOTHER. Not merely separate, but antagonistic. Yes, religion, which was designed to minister to righteousness, may not only be severed from it, but be actually found undermining it, sapping its very life and strength. Thus: 1. *By begetting false confidence.* (Cf. ver. 4.) The Jews thought that all this religion must guarantee them immunity from the Divine displeasure, must ensure them his safeguard and protection. He, so they thought, could never suffer harm to come to his own temple—" the temple of the Lord." And still it is hard to persuade our hearts that all our religion goes for nothing, and worse than nothing, when it brings forth no fruit of righteousness. So many prayers, such liberal gifts, such good desires, such correctness of creed and of outward demeanour, such devotional fervour,—surely these things must propitiate Heaven, must ward off the Divine displeasure ! (Cf. G. Eliot's character, Bulstrode, the fraudulent but very religious banker, in ' Middlemarch.') 2. *By teaching men truths which they can readily wrest to evil.* (Cf. ver. 10.) The meaning (see Exposition) is not " We cannot help ourselves ; God has given us over to sin ; " but " We are delivered by our religious observances—sacrifices and the like; the score is cleared off ; we are secured against harm ; we may go and live as we list." Thus they " turned the grace of God into lasciviousness," and " continued in sin that," etc. And is not this done still? It is to be feared that not a few suck a poisonous pleasure from the blessed doctrine of the forgiving love of God. Thus the gospel itself may become a " savour of death unto death " to those who thus "make Christ the Minister of sin." And because religion has been seen so often severed from righteousness, and sometimes even ministering to unrighteousness, many have been and are eager to sweep it away altogether as a hindrance rather than a help to moral well-being. A highly educated German gentleman, whom the writer met abroad, expressed it as his strong and deliberate conviction that the religiousness and the decay of a people stand related as cause and effect. He argued that England must sink because her leading statesman was an eminently religious man. And were religion necessarily or generally severed from righteousness, still more if it were necessarily or generally *opposed* to righteousness, then it would deserve the denunciation of all right-minded men, and the sooner it were swept utterly out of the way the better. But all we can say is that if righteousness be not found in company with religion, it is to be found nowhere else ; and if the Church of God, the great company of those who profess to be actuated by religious motives and aims, do not furnish and nurture God-like and righteous souls, then there is no other company on the face of the earth that does so. Bad as the Church may be, the world is far worse.

V. WHAT, THEN, IS OUR DUTY? Not to inveigh against religion, still less to seek its destruction, but to do all we can to restore the original and God-designed relationship between it and righteousness. "What God hath joined together, let," etc. And it is on this restoration of right relationship between the two that God so strenuously and sternly insists here and throughout his Word. If (ver. 3) they *will* amend their ways, then his blessing ; but if not, he will have no mercy. He cites the instance of Shiloh as a solemn warning to them (ver. 14). He forbids Jeremiah even to pray for them whilst they continue as they are (ver. 16). He pours his contempt upon all their religion, their burnt offerings, and sacrifices (ver. 21), whilst severed from righteousness. He tells them that all along in their history, from the first until now, he had asked for, though he had never received it from them, not religion merely, but *righteousness*— obedience to his Word (vers. 21—28). Instead of that they had committed all abomination, and therefore they should miserably perish (vers. 29—34). How dreadful, then, must be the separation, and yet more the antagonism, between these whom God united ! As he gave Eve to be a help-meet to Adam, so did he give religion to be the help-meet of righteousness. Let us tremble with a holy fear if we find ourselves able to go on contentedly in religious observances, whilst conscience becomes less and less sensitive, and our love and loyalty to righteousness grow feebler day by day. Our subject shows us that such a disastrous condition is possible. But that we may escape it, let us resolve that, inasmuch as God has given us religion for our help—a help which our blessed Lord himself ever made use of—

> " Cold mountains and the midnight air
> Witnessed the fervour of his prayer ; "

—we will know the possibilities of help towards holiness which undoubtedly it contains. Let us set ourselves to seek the " baptism of the Holy Ghost " and " the enduements of power " which come therefrom. If we do thus set ourselves to seek these, they shall be ours, for they are most certainly promised ; so shall religion and righteousness abide in that most intimate and hallowed union which God from the first designed for them, and our righteousness, ministered to by its God-given help-meet religion, shall far exceed that of the scribes and Pharisees, yea, shall advance ever nearer to that most glorious attainment, in which we shall be as our Saviour bid us be—" perfect, as our Father in heaven is perfect."—C.

Ver. 3.—*The indispensable condition of all grace.* " Amend your ways," etc. See how this demand for amendment is reiterated in this chapter and throughout this prophecy. And we observe—

I. IT IS EVER SO. 1. *See the Word of God.* The prodigal had to come away from the far country first. John the Baptist, our Lord, and his apostles all preached repentance before pardon. The Law comes before the gospel. 2. *Conscience confirms the justice of this demand.* We feel it to be a monstrous thing that, without any turning from sin even in purpose, there should be an expectation of God's grace. 3. Men make this same demand of those who rebel against their laws. 4. God's providence upholds this demand. The constitution of things is for the obedient and against the transgressor (cf. Butler's 'Analogy').

II. AND THE REASONS ARE BECAUSE SIN: 1. *Outrages God.* What order or happiness can there be in that household where the authority of the head is openly set at naught? 2. *Is dogged by sorrow and death.* The avenging deities were said to be shod with wool, so that their footsteps, ever following the transgressor, were not heard. It was the vision of sin and its awful issues that caused Jesus to sigh, to be troubled in spirit, and to weep; it was his agony. Now, God would save us, but cannot until we have done with wickedness. 3. *Binds the soul to enmity against God.* Deeds of wrong are the devil's sacraments, whereby he seals on the soul his own impress and pledges the soul to serve him. Every solitary act of sin deepens that impress and makes that pledge more irrevocable. Therefore, if the soul is to be saved, that bond *must* be broken. 4. *Amendment in conduct is the first step towards the restoration of the soul.* A man may break off ill-doing, and yet his heart be very far from right with God. Still, because every victory over sin strengthens the conscience and weakens the power of sin, its hold is thus loosened upon the soul, and the work of restoration is so far advanced.

III. BUT COMPLIANCE WITH THIS MOST RIGHTEOUS DEMAND IS: 1. *Often very difficult.* Ask the drunkard, the impure, the worldling, the gambler, if they find it easy to break away from their besetting sins. How like a set of fiends they clamour for their wonted indulgence! "Hoc opus hic labor est." 2. *But never impossible.* No; for along with every Divine command goes forth the strength needed for obedience. How absurd, on mere human principles, for our Lord to bid the man with the withered hand to stretch it forth; the palsied to rise, take up his bed, and walk; and Lazarus to come forth from his tomb! But all these facts are recorded to encourage those who would turn to the Lord, but yet "are sore let and hindered." We often ask—

> "Oh, how shall feeble flesh and blood
> Burst through the bonds of sin?
> The holy kingdom of our God,
> What soul shall enter in?"

And there could be but one sad answer were it not that he who gives the command gives also the needed help. Yes—

> "There is a way for man to rise
> To that sublime abode;
> An offering and a sacrifice,
> A Holy Spirit's energies,
> An Advocate with God."

3. *And ever blessed.* (Cf. vers. 3, 7.) All those precious sentences with which the sermon on the mount opens, and which we call the Beatitudes, were addressed to those who had resolved, by God's grace, to amend their ways. Christ has no other word for them than that they are blessed, and what his Word affirms all they who have followed his leading do with grateful heart confirm. Yes, "blessed are they that do his commandments, that they may have right to the tree of life, and may enter in through the gates into the city." 4. *But if refused, is awfully avenged.* Too often it is refused. It was so here. All manner of excuse attempted, and though these "lying words" (ver. 4) were and are exposed again, the refusal is persisted in, and then "the wrath of God arises, and there is no remedy." "From all such hardness of heart and contempt of thy holy Word and commandment, good Lord, deliver us."—C.

Ver. 4.—*How men deceive themselves.* "The temple of the Lord, the temple of the Lord," etc. The people of Jerusalem were flattering themselves that no harm would come to them because of the presence in their midst of the temple of the Lord. And men flatter themselves in like manner still. Now let us—

I. CONSIDER THEIR ARGUMENT. God had said, "In this house will I dwell." They knew that, and hence it seemed impossible that it should be devastated by the heathen. It was the place of which he had said, "There 'mine honour dwelleth.'" The cloud of glory had filled it, the Shechinah brightness rested on the mercy-seat. Was it to be imagined that he who of old had smitten with death those who presumed even to look into or to touch the ark of God, who had smitten monarchs with leprosy for lack of due respect to it, would now suffer the bands of the idolaters to lay waste his sanctuary, in which it was enshrined? Moreover, once and again salvation for Israel had gone forth from the temple of God, deliverance and victory had there been won. The prophetic prayer of Solomon who had built it told of mercy and help that should surely come to Israel through that temple. Thus ancient teachings, glorious events, the manifested presence of God, many promises in connection with the temple of the Lord, all combined to lead men to look upon it with an undue trust, and to believe that, so long as it reared its sacred front in their midst, it would prove as a palladium, a shield and defence for them all. Therefore they met all Jeremiah's warnings, and all misgivings of their own consciences, by the oft-repeated cry, " The temple of the Lord, the temple of the Lord, the temple of the Lord, are these!" And that which answers in our day to the Jewish trust in these "lying words," as Jeremiah terms them, is the confidence that is placed in the Church, her sacraments and ministers; or in past religious experiences, or in present moods of feeling; and yet more in the endorsement of our religious profession by our acceptance into the Church's fellowship and our admission to her ordinances. Such answer now to the "lying words" Jeremiah denounced then. But note—

II. WHAT OF WORTH THERE IS IN THIS ARGUMENT. There can be no doubt that the tares owe a great deal, owe everything in fact, to the wheat amongst which they have been sown. But for the wheat, they would have been plucked up long ago. And God's dealings with men had so often confirmed what our Lord's parable teaches, that the tares had come to congratulate themselves that they had no cause for fear. For ten righteous men Sodom would have been spared. For Moses' sake all Israel had been borne with, when but for his intercession God's righteous anger would have swept them away. The descendants of David had cause many times to bless themselves that, though so unlike their great ancestor in obedience to God, they were yet of his house and lineage. " For the elect's sake," said our Lord, " those days "—days of Jerusalem's final doom—" shall be shortened." And so here in the text, the people of Jerusalem could not but know that they were wicked in the extreme; but because they, though tares, were blessed with the presence of what they thought God counted as wheat—the temple and all its hallowed associations—they laughed at the idea of any great calamity coming upon them. And in the present-day parallels to that old trust in "lying words," what of worth there was in those words then, there is in the like of them now. The Church, with all its hallowed associations, *is* God's wheat, or rather, does assuredly contain all there is of it. For what manner of definition of the Church of God will any one presume to lay down other than this, that it consists of *all* the good? Broader it is not; but *so* broad it is. The presence, therefore, of the godly in any community is a guarantee of good to that community. " Ye are the salt of the earth," said our Lord. But for his Church the world would rot. Let any who sneer and persecute Christ's servants, whether in school, work-room, office, shop, or where else—and such persecution is common enough—let them remember that, but for such as those on whom they are pleased to pour their contempt, their own career would be cut very short indeed. If, then, the temple of the Lord, to which the Jews were trusting, was as the wheat, then the wicked people who were looking to it for safety were in the right, and their words were not lying words.

III. ITS WORTHLESSNESS NOTWITHSTANDING. In all those instances in which the tares had been spared for the sake of the wheat, there had been two conditions fulfilled. It had been really wheat which sheltered the tares, and there had been sufficiency of it. There was not enough of it when the Deluge came, nor when Sodom was destroyed; and so, in like manner, should ever the wheat fall short, it will go ill with the tares then. But did the temple and its ritual and its associations fulfil either of these conditions? No doubt the mere structure, her very stones, had worth in God's sight. Just as, for the sake of the dearly beloved soul that once has dwelt within that now lifeless corpse, we hang over it with tenderest fondness, and would not put it away from us were we not compelled; so, because of the true worship that had gone up from that temple, and because of the many saintly men who there had drawn near to God, that material shrine had a certain value and would not lightly be allowed to perish. But if there were preciousness in the temple, there was not sufficiency of it to outweigh or to cover over the iniquities which surged around it, yea, invaded its very courts, and of which it was made the unwilling occasion. Instead of being a palladium, or any sort of guarantee of safety to that godless nation, its towers and courts, its altars and ever-ascending sacrifices, were ever calling down vengeance upon those who so shamefully used them. And, indeed, it could hardly be said to be as God's wheat at all. The temple had often been the vehicle of that " worship in spirit and in truth " which alone God desires, and for the sake of such worship it had a relative preciousness. But let that worship cease—as it had long ceased—then the temple became as a mere corpse, beautiful, tenderly loved indeed, but still corruptible, corrupting and spreading corruption, and therefore demanding to be put out of the way. Now apply all this to the false truths of our own day. Will the Church, her sacraments, her ordinances, your membership with her, your frequent moods of religious feeling, your current creed, your loud profession of attachment to her, your manifold religious privileges,—will any or all of these things, precious though they every one of them be, compensate for that surrender of your true self to God which is his perpetual desire and demand? Will they not rather, as did the presence of the temple and their innumerable privileges for the Jews, heighten your guilt, and make more glaring your sin, because they show that you have been amongst those "to whom much has been given," and of whom, therefore, " much will be required "? No worship, however magnificent, costly, constant ; however hallowed by association, or authorized by venerable usage, or sanctioned by the holiest of the Church of God, or even owned by God as the means of uplifting many hearts heavenward and Godward ; if such worship be wanting, as, alas ! it may be, in the all-essential element, the "worship in spirit and in truth ; " if there be no outgoings of the *heart* in it all, as too often there is not,— then it will prove no shield from but a provocative to that holy wrath of God which sooner or later awaits every godless soul.

IV. THE VERY SERIOUS SUGGESTIONS IT OFFERS. 1. *The utter hatefulness of sin.* (1) It turned the very temple of the Lord and its sacrifices, which had been designed to be "a savour of life unto life" to those who by means of them drew nigh to God, into "a savour of death unto death." And so still, even Christ the Rock, the sure Foundation, becomes by this wresting power of sin a crushing stone which, falling on the head of the sinner, grinds him to powder. (2) It drags down the innocent with the guilty. That temple of the Lord, the holy and beautiful house, what had that done? Had it not deserved all honour and love from those amid whom it stood? And now the sin of the people was to overwhelm her in utter and irretrievable ruin. The man whose wickedness pulls down innocent and loving wife and children, and drags *them* in the mire which he has chosen to wallow in, as we see their misery, how odious his sin appears! And this is ever one of sin's works. It drags in and down the innocent, the pure, the beloved. Behold those blackened ruins, those polluted altars, those blood-stained courts, and see a parable of sin. 2. *The testimony that these refuges of lies, such as that in which the Jews trusted, do surely give of our need of a real refuge, a true defence.* Men who deny *the* Saviour most are yet ever confessing that they and all men do need *a* Saviour. They who would not trust in God trusted in the mere material temple. 3. To what are *we* trusting? In "lying words"—which God forbid !—or—which may God grant !—in those words of the Lord Jesus, which are able to make us wise unto salvation?—C.

Vers. 5—16.—*Strange church-goers.* I. LOOK AT THEM AS JEREMIAH SAW THEM. Thieves (vers. 6, 9), most cruel oppressors, murderers, adulterers, etc. Yet they were all going into the temple to worship the Lord. Strange church-goers indeed.

II. ASK IF THERE BE ANY SUCH NOW? What if some angel of God, unseen by us, were to mark on the foreheads of all who enter our churches now their true characters in the sight of God : would there be no fraudulent, no oppressors of the poor, none whose hearts, though not their hands, are chargeable with having shed innocent blood? Let us each one ask, " What name would be put upon *me*? "

III. INQUIRE WHAT POSSIBLE MOTIVES CAN ACTUATE THEM. 1. With some, no doubt, it is a cloke to cover up their real character. 2. Or a tribute paid to the demands of fashion, custom, society. What would be thought of them if they did not go to church? 3. Or a method of quieting conscience. They come away and think they have wiped off the score that was against them. They say (ver. 10), "We are delivered [see Exposition] to do," etc. 4. Or to set an example to those they are pleased to call "the lower orders;" like the philosophers of old, who, whilst they held all religions to be equally false, yet regarded them all as indispensably useful. 5. Or as a means —for so many regarded such things—of propitiating the Divine favour and securing a title to heaven by-and-by. But there is no end to the motives which lead such men to do that which, to more honest-hearted people, appears a mockery, an absurdity, and yet worse.

IV. LISTEN TO THE LORD'S WORD TO SUCH. He tells them: 1. They were getting no good whatsoever from such worship (ver. 3). 2. They were completely deceiving themselves (ver. 4). 3. They were neglecting that amendment of their ways which would save them (ver. 5). 4. They were grossly insulting God (vers. 10, 11). 5. They were blind to notorious facts: e.g. Shiloh (ver. 12); Ephraim (ver. 15). 6. Thorough reformation was alone the way of life for them (vers. 3, 7). "Be not deceived; God is not mocked: for whatsoever a man soweth, that shall he also reap. For he that soweth to his flesh shall of the flesh reap corruption; but he that soweth to the Spirit shall of the Spirit reap life everlasting."—C.

Vers. 9—11.—*Sacrilege.* I. WHAT DO WE GENERALLY UNDERSTAND BY THIS WORD? 1. Some use it of disregard of ritual. 2. Others of secular employment of sacred places or things. 3. Others of those persons whom they regard as unauthorized presuming to minister in holy things. 4. Others of robbing churches, etc. But without discussing these, let us note—

II. WHAT GOD COUNTS AS SACRILEGE. It is declared here (ver. 11). It is when men turn the Church of God into a den of robbers. Our Lord charged this upon the religionists of his day. Jeremiah charges it, in God's Name, upon those to whom he was sent. Costly, splendid, correct, continual worship was duly carried on. Irreverence—and how much less sacrilege!—would seem to be a charge utterly unfit for those who worshipped in such manner. And yet, though the word be not here used, the thing itself is emphatically told of as the very crime which these people were flagrantly guilty of. Turning God's house, which was called by his Name, into a den of robbers,—if that be not sacrilege, what else is? They robbed one another (vers. 5, 6). They robbed God. And the temple was their haunt, as their den is the robbers' haunt; and there they found rest, and prepared themselves for further crime (ver. 10), as does the robber in his den. It is an awful indictment. But under one or other of the counts of such indictment they are assuredly chargeable who frequent the house of God, not for the high and holy purposes for which the worship of God was designed, but that, as in ver. 10, they may get peace of mind in regard to their past sins and so be free to go and sin again. "With such usage the temple is not a place of salvation, but a refuge for robbers, where they purify themselves from the blood of their evil deeds, so as to be the readier for new ones." Therefore all they who "make Christ a Minister of sin," who, instead of deliverance from sin, get comfort in it by their religious observances, who shelter themselves from all fear of God's anger and silence the warnings of conscience by "coming and standing before God in his house which is called by his Name," though their object be only "to be delivered to do all these abominations," and not at all to be saved from them,—these are the sacrilegious, and their profanation of holy things is the worst of all.

III. THINK OF THE RESULTS OF SUCH SACRILEGE. 1. How God is dishonoured! 2. How his service is made hateful in the eyes of men! What a stumbling-block it is to those who would turn to God! 3. How it hardens the man's own soul! 4. How it necessitates the judgment of God!

IV. WHAT SHOULD SUCH A SUBJECT TEACH US? Surely, when in the house of God, to pray that if any have come there in sacrilegious manner, God's Spirit, the Lord of the temple, may meet with them and turn them from their evil way. Should we not also search and see if there be *any* such evil way in ourselves? And let our prayer be unto him who when on earth drove forth with scourges the "robbers" whom he found in the temple, that he would be pleased, by the scourge of his Spirit and his Word, to drive forth from all in his house now all in them that would rob him of his glory and their souls of eternal life.—C.

Vers. 12—16.—*Warning voices.* I. SUCH VOICES ARE PERPETUALLY HEARD. The prophet speaks of three such here. 1. Shiloh (ver. 12). 2. The Lord himself (ver. 13). 3. Ephraim (ver. 15).
II. And THEY TELL EVER THE SAME TRUTHS. 1. The Divine anger against sin (ver. 12). 2. The utter uselessness of their "trust in lying words" to escape that anger (ver. 14). 3. The absolute need of repentance.
III. And MEET, ALL TOO OFTEN, WITH THE SAME RECEPTION. They were rejected. " Ye heard not; and I called you," etc. (ver. 13).
IV. But are VINDICATED IN LIKE AWFUL MANNER. 1. By their sin becoming ineradicable, so that they are given over to a reprobate mind, and are "guilty of an eternal sin" (cf. Mark iii. 29). Hence (ver. 16) the prophet is forbidden to pray for them (cf. 1 John v. 16). 2. By the judgment of God falling upon them (ver. 15).
CONCLUSION. 1. Watch and pray against unbelief in these warnings. 2. Take heed to them yourselves. 3. Hold them up to others. 4. Bless God for them.—C.

Vers. 12—14.—*Shiloh, or the God-forsaken shrine.* It is to many minds impossible to avoid a feeling of deep sadness when we look upon the ruins, noble even in their desolation, of some former beautiful and august sanctuary of God. There are many such scattered over this and other lands : Tintern, Furness, Melrose, etc. Our imagination pictures them when in the zenith of their glory, with their many stately towers and tapering spires, their long-drawn aisles and lofty roofs, the glorious vista of high-arched nave and choir and glittering sanctuaries stretching away further still in the dim distance, the gleaming altars, the magnificent service, the vast throng of kneeling worshippers, the soul-enchanting music, and the murmur of myriad prayers. The memories of saintly men and women who have worshipped and are buried there crowd upon the mind, and we wistfully wonder where and why that consecrated genius has flown which had power to rear for God shrines so glorious as those whose ruins we are beholding must once have been. It is sad to think of such glory and beauty as these forsaken shrines once had gone for ever. The Jews who came back from the Captivity wept when they thought of the glory of the ancient temple, which they never more might see. But if the departure of *material* glory may cause sadness to the mind, how much more the departure of that which is *spiritual!* If we mourn that we shall no more have the presence of some fair temple of the Lord, how much more when we lose the Lord of the temple! And it is such sadder loss that Shiloh, the God-forsaken shrine, has to tell of. And we observe upon it that—
I. THERE ARE FEW MORE MOURNFUL HISTORIES THAN THAT OF SHILOH. Shiloh was one of the earliest and most sacred of the Hebrew sanctuaries. There for full three hundred years the ark of God remained and the priests of the Lord ministered. As soon as the promised land was mainly subdued, Joshua brought the ark of God from Gilgal, near the Jordan, to Shiloh. The place was probably chosen for its seclusion and hence its safety, it being off the great highways of the land. Bethel, which otherwise might have been chosen as especially sacred, was yet in the hands of the Canaanites. Hence Shiloh, in the territory of the powerful tribe of Ephraim, and of their great ancestor Joseph, a tribe which more and more had been coming to the front amongst their brethren, was chosen for the sanctuary of the ark of God. There, as afterwards at Jerusalem, " the tribes went up, the tribes of the Lord, unto the testimony of Israel, to give thanks unto the Name of the Lord." What glad festivals; what gracious deliverances; what Divine responses to their inquiring of the Lord; what holy memories of thronging worshippers, of accepted sacrifices, of saintly priests and prophets who had dwelt there, were all associated with that shrine at Shiloh! There Eli ministered, and Hannah came to present her offerings, to pour out her prayers and to pay her vows. There she brought Samuel, and there the Lord called him to his high service as he ministered before him. All their truest and noblest life drew its inspiration from the God who had placed his Name there, and whom there they went to worship. But at length, under the rule of Eli, that well-meaning but weak-willed high priest, priesthood and people alike sank down into a state of moral and religious degra-

dation from which Eli was powerless to deliver them. His own sons led the way in abominable wickedness, and became sons of Belial even beyond others. So low had they fallen, that they had come to regard the ark of God as a kind of fetish, and hence they carried it down to battle against the Philistines, thinking thereby to certainly win the day. But the ark of God was taken, its besotted priests slain, and Eli, hearing the dreadful tidings suddenly, died, a worn-out and broken-hearted old man. From that hour, as the seventy-eighth psalm tells, God "forsook Shiloh, the tent which he placed among men ; . . . he refused the tabernacle of Joseph, and chose not the tribe of Ephraim." And it was all because, as the same psalm tells, Israel "tempted and provoked the most high God, and kept not his testimonies : but turned back, and dealt deceitfully like their fathers : they were turned aside like a deceitful bow. For they provoked him to anger with their high places, and moved him to jealousy with their graven images." Wherefore "he was wroth, and greatly abhorred Israel." And now, ages after, Jeremiah bids the people of his day go to Shiloh, and see what God did to it for the wickedness of the people. They might trace out, perhaps, the foundations of her ancient walls, and discover the vestiges of the former sanctuary ; but now no altar bore the sacred fire, the smoke of no sacrifice ascended, no priest ministered, no God gave answer, no song of the Lord went up ; the whole place was probably ravaged and overthrown by the enemies of Israel, who had carried off their great treasure, the ark of God. Well might the wife of Phinehas, in the hour of her agony, call her new-born, but now fatherless, and soon to be altogether her orphan, child, I-chabod, for indeed the glory had departed, the ark of God was taken, and the Lord had forsaken Shiloh. Oh, the sorrow, the shame, the unavailing remorse which would over-whelm the faithless priesthood and the godless people, when they beheld that God-abandoned shrine, and remembered wherefore this calamity had come upon them ! Yes, this story is a sad one ; but it is most salutary also, and therefore we may well heed the word of the Lord which says to us, "Go ye now unto my place which was in Shiloh, where I set my Name at the first, and see what I did to it for the wickedness of my people Israel." But we observe—

II. THAT SHILOH HAS MANY PARALLELS. Shiloh is not the only God-forsaken shrine of which the Bible tells or of which we have had knowledge. No ; there are all too many like it. There was the temple of the Lord in Jeremiah's time. All its splendour, its solemn ritual, its lavish sacrifices, its ever-burning altar fire, could not save it. The stern sentence went forth against it, and it was burnt with fire and laid in ashes on the ground. There was the temple which was afterwards built on the return from Captivity, and which was so beautiful and adorned in the time of our Lord ; concerning that, too, Jesus said, "Behold, your house is left unto you desolate !" And it was the same with many Churches, those "spiritual houses" which, after our Lord's time and in his Name, were reared "for a habitation of God through the Spirit." The Christian Church at Jerusalem. The honour of being the mother Church of Christendom was taken from her and transferred to Antioch, and ultimately it was overwhelmed altogether in the destruction that came on the city in which it was gathered. And there were the Churches of Asia ; their "candlestick was removed out of its place," as the Lord warned them would be the case, and now secular historians bear their testi-mony to the truth of that warning word. Gibbon tells how "in the loss of Ephesus the Christians deplored the fall of the first angel, the extinction of the first candlestick of the Revelation ; the desolation is complete ; and the Temple of Diana or the Church of Mary will equally elude the search of the curious traveller. The circus and the three stately theatres of Laodicea are now peopled with wolves and foxes. Sardis is reduced to a miserable village ; the god of Mahomet, without a rival or a son, is invoked in the mosques of Thyatira and Pergamos ; and the populousness of Smyrna is supported by the foreign trade of Franks and Armenians. Philadelphia alone has been saved by prophecy or courage. At a distance from the sea, encompassed on all sides by the Turks, her valiant citizens defended their religion and freedom above four score years ; and at length capitulated with the proudest of the Ottomans. Among the Greek colonies and Churches of Asia, Philadelphia is still erect ; a column in a scene of ruins." They have thus all disappeared, as Christian Churches almost utterly ; they are as Shiloh and Jerusalem—their houses in which they worshipped God left unto them desolate. And there have been many other Churches since, and some nearer our own time and in our own land. And many still, perhaps, need sorely the admonitory counsel to go to Shiloh, and see what the Lord has done there. But not in material edifices alone, nor even in those gathered communities to which more properly the name of Churches belongs, need we go to find instances of God-forsaken shrines. For inasmuch as we all are "temples of the Holy Ghost," so St. Paul tells us, and our own experience confirms his word, it is possible to find only too many illustrations of this same mournful fact. Take the ever-memorable example and warning of the fallen apostle Judas. What a shrine of the Holy Ghost he once was! How richly gifted! how gloriously endowed! He came with the rest, saying, "Lord, even the devils are subject to us through thy Name." He with the rest "ate and drank in Christ's presence, and in his Name did many wonderful works." He enjoyed the fellowship of Christ, and by him was sent forth in his Name. But behold him giving place to the devil, yielding his soul up to the demon of covetousness and worldly ambition, and then acting as the guide to them who arrested the Lord, betraying the Son of man with a kiss, and then, when too late he awoke to see the madness and horror of what he had done, rushing forth to seek and find a suicide's grave in the Aceldama, "the field of blood," purchased by the price of his traitorous gain. And Ananias and Sapphira and Demas and yet others, what are they all but deplorable instances and names of these God-forsaken shrines? And have we not known such? Men who prayed, and worshipped, and taught, and preached, and then, having denied the Lord who bought them, fell away, and found henceforth nothing but "a fearful looking for of judgment" and of the "fiery indignation" of God destined to be poured out on all such as they. Ah! it is a sight which might well make angels weep, and which drew forth the bitter tears of the Son of God himself.

III. AND IN EVERY CASE THE CAUSE OF THIS FORSAKING OF THEM BY GOD WAS ONE AND THE SAME. It was always "wickedness." Not any outward circumstance, not any of those secondary causes which we are so apt to regard as the real cause. But this which these verses so plainly declare. It was so even in those ruined edifices to which we referred at the beginning of this homily. History will tell you how gross immorality and horrible corruption found a too-ready home in those fair fabrics which had been reared for far other purposes and with far other design. But "wickedness" having made them its haunt and home, the people, roused to fierce wrath, rose up and tore them down, and their grey, ivy-clad stones utter forth to this day such message as that in our text. And in all those other instances to which we have pointed, whether temples made with hands, whether Churches or individual men, it has ever been sin, sin, which has wrought all this evil. And in that every-day fact of bodily death we have the standing type of this terrible truth, "The wages of sin is death." That body once so bright, so full of energy, so lit up with intelligence and love, so possessed too, it may have been, with the Spirit of God, so fair, so lovely to look upon when life dwelt in it, now in death,—what is it but a God-forsaken shrine, and hence doomed to return, "earth to earth, dust to dust, and ashes to ashes"? We are so accustomed to death that this its solemn lesson we are ever forgetting or putting out of sight.

IV. BUT ALL THESE SHILOHS HAVE A MESSAGE FROM GOD UNTO US, ACCORDING TO WHAT WE ARE. We every one of us are either examples of these forsaken ones, or becoming so, or, blessed be God, still habitations for him through the Spirit. Now, if we be already forsaken of God, then if this fact be—as surely it should be, and as we trust it is—a matter of sore distress to us, then there is a gracious word to us if we be willing to hear it. All of us were once "temples of God." We can look back to the time when none of the unclean spirits that now haunt and harm us so terribly had any home in our souls; when thoughts were pure, hands undefiled, and our lips unpolluted with evil. Our fathers and mothers brought us to be baptized, or in other ways recognized the blessed truth that we belonged to the Father, the Son, and the *Spirit*. And in our childhood days we, as all children are, were members of the kingdom of heaven. But what are we now? O God, it is dreadful to think of what some are now! The desolate ruins of once glorious Churches; the lifeless bodies that we carry to the grave are but faint types of what some of these God-forsaken ones have become. And can it be that any are willing to continue so, and thus make it inevitable that God should sweep you away into the hell of all corruption? Oh no; you cannot be willing that that should be. Well, then, if you tremble at such doom, as well you may, listen: *God will re-enter his shrine, and make you once again his temples.* Yes, he will do that. He will "restore your souls and lead you in," etc. But first, as when Hezekiah cleansed the temple, you must cast out the manifold uncleanness that is there. There must be a thorough purging, a real repentance. God will not come back to a sin-inhabited and evil-loving soul. You must "throughly amend your ways." This is indispensable. See how in this chapter and throughout his Word God insists upon this. And then, as the high priest was wont to do, come bearing the blood of atonement into the presence of God; come, that is, pleading the Name of Jesus for acceptance and pardon and restoration,—and you shall behold, in the shrine of your soul, the cloud of glory once again shining there and the presence of God again manifested there. Thus come day by day, and you shall find how Christ saves "to the uttermost all that," etc. But are you of those whom God is now forsaking? Is the dread process of crowding out God by the bringing into the shrine of your heart those many things God hates and with which he will not abide, going on in you? Ah! that may be so. As others, so you were once the temple of the Holy Ghost, and perhaps there came a day when more than ever you welcomed him as your Ruler, because he had taken of the things of Christ and had shown them unto you. You made your open confession and avowal of your desire to be ruled and governed by him; you pledged yourself by his help to be Christ's faithful servant always. And for a time you were so: you were careful, conscientious; you remembered your Lord's word, "Watch and pray;" you readily abandoned all that stood between you and the doing of his will; you walked with God. But a change has come over you. One by one you received into your heart likings, and desires, and beliefs, and dispositions which were contrary to the Spirit of Christ. These suggestions you listened to, their counsels you obeyed. And so the love of the world fastened on you, propensities and habits which war against the soul took hold of you, and now you, whose heart was once a shrine of God, will, if the sad process I have spoken of goes on much longer, be forsaken of him altogether. Oh that the consideration of the doom of Shiloh may fill us with a holy fear, and lead us to such prayer as that which the well-known verse expresses!—

> " Search me, O Lord, and try my heart,
> For thou that heart canst see,
> And turn each cursed idol out
> That dares to rival thee."

But some of you are to be congratulated that you are still temples of God, still shrines of the Holy Ghost. Well, then, cherish his presence as the greatest joy of your life. For "he is your life." You would not invite to meet and abide with a dear and honoured earthly friend those with whom you well knew he had no sympathy nor they with him, who were distasteful and hostile to him. You would not treat an earthly friend so. Be careful, then, not so to treat the Spirit of God, who now dwells within you. Be full of solicitude not to grieve him, yet more to do nought that would drive him from you. "Walk not after the flesh, but after the Spirit." So shall God dwell in you and you in God, and that more and more to your ever-increasing strength and purity and joy. Thus though, as we have now done, you may go in devout thought to Shiloh, and behold what God has done there, yet you shall be able with thankful joy to know that never, never shall you be as that God-forsaken shrine.—C.

Vers. 13—16.—*The Divine long-suffering worn out.* The above section brings before us, as do many other Scriptures, this very certain and very serious truth of God's patience being not only exhaustible, but exhausted. We observe—

I. THE DIVINE LONG-SUFFERING IS A VERY PRECIOUS FACT. Nations, Churches, individuals—have not we ourselves?—have been examples of it. What have not all of us owed to the fact that the Lord is long-suffering, and "willeth not the death of a sinner, but rather that he should turn," etc.? But—

II. THIS TRUTH HAS VERY OFTEN BEEN MUCH ABUSED. 1. In men's *thoughts*; for they have allowed themselves to pervert the truth of the "eternal hope," and to think that in no way can the finite will of man exhaust the infinitude of mercy which there is in God. 2. And in their *words* also they have so set forth the long-suffering of God as to leave on men's minds the impression that it was practically infinite. We love to sing such verses as those which tell how

> " None can measure out thy patience
> By the span of human thought,
> None can bound the tender mercies
> Which thy holy Son hath wrought."

And there is a sense in which these words are most blessedly true, but it is undeniable that such words are often pressed to a meaning which practically encourages the sinner to go on in sin. 3. And yet more is this truth abused in *deed*. Those to whom the prophet was writing had abused the long-suffering of God (cf. the closing verses of the Second Book of Chronicles). And how fearfully frequent is this abuse in the present day! How many reckon securely on making their peace with God, and having all the great affairs of their souls fully settled for eternity, although they go on, day by day and year by year, living in total disregard both of God and of his will. Therefore it is necessary to insist with all urgency—

III. THAT THE LONG-SUFFERING OF GOD CAN BE WORN OUT. The above section of this prophecy plainly declares this fact. And the fate of Jerusalem stands not alone in evidence of this (cf. the story of the Deluge, and how long then the long-suffering of God waited). Those who perished in the wilderness—how often were they warned! And, indeed, it may be said that God never brings ruin upon nation, Church, or individual soul without warning, repeated, plain, and urgent. But the fact that he does send such ruin proves that men may tempt God too far.

IV. AND THAT WHICH WILL EXHAUST THE LONG-SUFFERING OF GOD IS CLEARLY SHOWN US. It is not the fact of sin, great sin, repeated sin, but it is when, as in the case before us, *sin has been persisted in in spite of every kind and degree of plainest warning*. "He that being often reproved hardeneth his neck," etc. (Prov. xxix. 1). Now, such was the conduct of those told of here. God had not merely let them know of the peril of their conduct, but his loving solicitude for them had shown itself in the most marked ways. Note expressions in ver. 13: God not only spoke to them, but like as "those who watch for the morning" rise up early, so God himself awoke early, *i.e.* he chose the most favourable hours, the most probable means for gaining attention to the truths which he, by his prophets, spoke to them. But it was all of no avail. "Ye heard not; . . . ye answered not" (cf. ch. vi. 16, 17). Now, it is sin persisted in, in spite of all such Divine solicitude so repeatedly manifested, that God will not pardon (vers. 14, 15). It is an unpardonable sin, and like such sin its forgiveness is not even to be prayed for (ver. 16, and cf. 1 John iv. 16).

V. CONSIDER THE REASON OF THIS REFUSAL TO FORGIVE. It is not because there is not love sufficient in God to pardon, but because his love is so great, because he *is* love. For God's love is not as that of too many earthly parents—a partial and unjust thing, loving one child at the expense of the others—but his love is for *the children*. His *whole* family are the subjects of his incessant and tenderest solicitude. Now, if a rebellious child come away from its rebellion, and have done with it, coming and confessing, "Father, I have sinned," with what joy the Father welcomes such returning one back! And so do the angels of God. No harm, but only good, results. But if there be no repentance, and the spirit of rebellion burns on in the heart of the child, how, consistently with true regard for the welfare of the other and obedient children, can the Father deal with that one as he does with these? It would turn heaven into hell, and make the Father's house, now the home of blessedness and the blessed, a scene of eternal discord. It could not be. Now, it is because such despising of the long-suffering of God destroys the hope of repentance, renders impossible the sighing of the contrite heart, and renders certain the going on in rebellion, that therefore this sin wears out the long-suffering of God and hath never forgiveness. The very love of God necessitates that he who is separate and alien in heart from the children of his love should be separate and alien from them in every other respect as well. And therefore, because it would be praying against the well-being of God's children, the prophet is forbidden to pray for the forgiveness of this sin. It is the unpardonable sin, the sin unto death, the sin against the Holy Ghost.

CONCLUSION. *We learn what alone bars the mercy of God.* Not this or that sin, however great. Still less the circumstance of death. But this "despising the forbearance of God." What need, then, for us all to pray, "Keep back thy servant also from presumptuous sins; let them not have dominion over me: . . . I shall be innocent from the *great* transgression "!—C.

Ver. 16.—*Prohibited prayers.* The text a distinct instance. We remark—

I. SUCH PROHIBITION OF PRAYER SEEMS VERY STRANGE. Are we not bidden " pray without ceasing," " in all things by prayer and supplication . . . make our requests known unto God " ? Are we not promised, " Ask, and ye shall receive " ? Did not the Lord say, " Men ought always to pray, and not to faint " ? And, in a case more nearly resembling the one before us in the text, did not Samuel say to the rebellious people of his day, " But God forbid that I should sin against the Lord in ceasing to pray for you " ?

II. IT IS NEVERTHELESS A FACT. And this prohibition is repeated (ch. xi. 14; xiv. 11; cf. also Exod. xxxii. 10).

III. AND WE HAVE WHAT IS SIMILAR NOW. There is no express command not to pray for the reversal of the laws of nature. But yet we never do pray for such things. David's servants wondered that when his child was dead he should altogether cease from fasting and prayer; but he answered, " Wherefore should I fast? can I bring him back again ? " (2 Sam. xii. 23). And even before death has actually taken place, when there is no hope of life, we find it all but impossible to pray for such life. And so in regard to what we know would be derogatory to the honour of God and his righteousness; we should never think of praying for aught like that. Or for what cannot be in the nature of things. Now, in all these things it is as if we had been prohibited to pray for them, seeing that we never do so pray. As children give over praying their parents to do this or that when they see by the expression of their countenance that it cannot be, and, on the contrary, when they see the faintest look of " yes," they urge their request with a renewed importunity of clamour; so is it in our prayers before God. We must see the look of " yes " on the face of God in more or less degree, or our prayers die down. But if it *be* seen, then they rise up, press on and forward with a vigour unknown before. This is a law of all prayer. And in regard to prayer for such as are told of in the text, it may be that Jeremiah was not expressly told in so many words that he was not to pray for them, but it was borne in upon his mind that he could not. And it is sadly possible that such conviction may be borne in upon the minds of God's people now concerning some reprobate ones. There comes over the soul the deep feeling that such and such a one " is joined to his idols," and that you can only " let him alone." The disciples of the Lord were bidden, when their message was spurned, to cast off the dust of their feet as a testimony against them. Paul did so with the hardened Jews. And such solemn conviction as to the utter godlessness of any on the part of a company of God's people is that " binding on earth " which will be ratified by, because it is but the result of, the " binding in heaven." They of whom the Church feels deeply that " their sins are retained," those sins are retained. And so through this solemn conviction, this despair of the soul's turning to God, prayer for such soul may become impossible. God has practically said concerning such to his people, " Pray not thou for this people, neither," etc.

IV. THIS IS A FACT OF MOST MOMENTOUS IMPORT TO THOSE WHOM IT CONCERNS. To be given up by God's servants may be the token that you are given up by God. Their feeling about you may be—we do not say necessarily is, but may be—but the reflection of God's. Happy are they who put joy and gladness into the hearts of God's servants, and for whom they with earnestness and strong faith can pray. But sad is the outlook of those for whom those same servants of God feel they cannot pray. Oh, pray that prayers for you may never be counted by God or by his people as amongst prohibited prayers !—C.

Ver. 18.—*Idolatrous worship both a warning and a model.* The text vividly portrays the worship rendered to the heathen goddess, whose sumptuous and licentious worship had so fascinated those to whom the prophet wrote.

I. IT IS A WARNING. For it shows the deadly contagion of sin. Now, when the head of the household goes after evil, he speedily draws in and down wife and children, until the whole family is corrupted, and they become a household of wickedness. The text reveals whole families engaged in the worship of idolatry, each member taking an active and eager part. They become so many societies for the propagation of ungodliness. In the sanctity or the sin of the parent the children are sure to share. In the first, by the grace of God; in the second, by the fatal force of a father's example. A father can lift his children up to heaven or he can drag them down to hell, and some do. See the text.

II. BUT IT IS A MODEL ALSO. In what we are here told, the heathen shame the Church. Idolatrous worship may well put to the blush much of the worship of God. For in the worship told of in the text, false and horrible as it was, nevertheless we see much that we might well copy. 1. *It was a worship that made all work.* What a busy hive of workers each household is seen to be! But where is the counterpart of this in the Church of Christ? A whole family eager and active for Christ—the father, the mother, and all the children—would be a unique fact. How lazy, how indolent, is the greater part of our religion! 2. *The children were interested in it.* We are heartbroken that the great masses of our countrymen stand aloof from the worship of God. Did we interest them in it when they were children? We had them all in our hands, as we have their children now. Are our modes of worship, our representations of God's truth, our methods of instruction, such as shall make them love God's worship when they grow up? What would we not give to see our children so eager in God's worship as were the children told of in the text in idol-worship? 3. *Both sides of the house were agreed on this great question.* Husband and wife were of one mind, and each did what they could to further it. It was the general rule. Is it so now in regard to God and his service? Does the husband never hinder the wife? does the wife always help the husband on the heavenward road? 4. *There was fit work for each, and each did it.* The children could gather sticks, the men kindle the fires, and the women, etc. When will there arise in the Church some who will point out some fresh and wise methods of enlisting *all* in her work? We have now two or three regular plans in operation; but if any be unfit or unwilling for them, as many are, there is nothing else for them. What we need is what these idolaters in their sad worship seem to have found—a work for *every* one, and every one at his work. But meanwhile let each one who is standing in the vineyard idle, not because unwilling to work, but because no one has hired him, no one has pointed him to the work for which he is really fit—and there are many such—let him take his case to the Lord, and ask, "Lord, what wilt thou have me to do?" and he may rest assured, no matter whether he be little child or grown-up man, an answer will come to him soon.—C.

Ver. 19.—*The recoil of sin.* I. THE RESULTS OF SIN ON OTHERS ARE TERRIBLE. 1. What may not be their deadly influence *upon those with whom the sinner comes in contact?* How hereditary, how contagious, how virulent, the poison of sin! As no man liveth unto himself, so also "no man dieth unto himself." If he die by reason of his sin, he ever drags down others into the same doom. 2. *And their results Godward.* It is said they "provoke him to anger;" "God is angry with the wicked every day;" "God is slow to anger, and of great mercy." But still sin is "the abominable thing that he hates." He will not tolerate it in his children, and hence, however severe the measures necessary to separate it and them, those measures will be taken. "Our God is a consuming fire." But—

II. THE RECOIL OF SIN ON THE SINNER HIMSELF IS TERRIBLE ALSO. It is described in the text. 1. *It provokes him to anger.* It is not alone the Lord whose anger is aroused, but the sinner's anger also is provoked. As he looks back on the folly, the utter madness, of what he has done, how completely he has been deceived, what rage of remorse fills his soul! How he flogs himself with the lashings of his own self-upbraiding! What epithets of anger and contempt does he heap upon his own head! He is filled with the fruit of his own ways. And another of these bitter fruits is: 2. *Confusion of face.* He is ashamed, abashed, confounded, because of his sin. He is so (1) *before his own conscience.* He cannot bear to think of himself. From the companionship of his own thoughts he flees as from a haunting ghost. Like a sheeted spectre conscience seems to be pointing at him with its dread finger, its stony eyes ever glaring upon him, so that, turn which way he will, he cannot escape their gaze. He is ashamed of himself, covered with confusion of face before his own conscience. Oh, miserable, miserable wretch that he is! (2) *Before God.* He cannot pray. He shuns the throne of grace. His iniquities have so " taken hold of him" that he cannot "look up." All joy, all confidence, all hope in God, have fled. He feels himself an outcast from the Divine presence; he would feel the eye of God upon him if he knelt down to pray, and that he cannot bear. (3) *Before man.* He cannot for ever conceal his sin and folly, and even when it is as yet undiscovered, he is conscious of this "confusion of face" in the presence of others. And when at length the sin is discovered, oh, what agony of shame and remorse then! Death is chosen rather than life, and men rush to the suicide's grave as to a positive relief. "Anywhere, anywhere out of the world," which has become aware of their sin! Oh, this awful recoil of sin! "I believe that if the mental sufferings of such backsliders could be written and faithfully published, they would astound you, and be a more horrible story to read than all the torments of the Inquisition. What racks a man is stretched upon who has been unfaithful to his covenant with God! What fires have burned within the souls of those men who have been untrue to Christ and his cause! What dungeons, what grim and dark prisons underground, have saints of God lain in who have gone aside into by-path meadows instead of keeping to the King's highway! He who sins must smart, especially if he be a child of God, for the Lord hath said of his people, ' You only have I known of all the people of the earth, therefore I will punish you for your iniquities.' Whoever may go unchastised, a child of God never shall" (Spurgeon).

III. THE ALONE CURE FOR THIS CONFUSION OF FACE IS THE CONTRITE CONFESSION OF THAT WHICH HAS CAUSED IT. God's word is passed that such confession shall avail; but let not him who has gone back from God think that the return will be as easy as the departure. It will not. David was never the same after his sin as he was before. Oh, it is dreadful to think of this recoil of sin, and how it staggers and wounds and weakens the soul for the whole life long. We *slide* back, gliding easily as over smooth ice. Not so do we return. Still, let the return be ever so difficult, the Lord bids us return, and he will heal all our backslidings. Oh, let us all go straight away to the cross of our Lord Jesus Christ, for fear we should be backsliders; for there is the surest standing-ground, there our footsteps never slip! And if we have thus sinned, and sin's recoil is now terribly felt by us, then still go to the same cross; for our only hope of healing is there, and there alone.

> "Come, let us to the Lord our God
> With contrite hearts return ;
> Our God is gracious, nor will leave
> The penitent to mourn."

C.

Ver. 20.—*The innocent victims of sin.* I. THERE ARE MANY SUCH. All forms of life are mentioned here—human, animal, plant from the stateliest trees down to the lowliest herb—and all shall suffer because of the sin of but a portion of them. How many, even of men, were innocent! and the young children—what had they done? Yet none were to escape, though it was but a portion of the men of the day who had done such wrong.

II. HENCE SOME SAY, "THE WAY OF THE LORD IS NOT EQUAL." But: 1. The summing up of all life in one head, constituting it a corporate unity, giving a *solidarité* to all life, especially to all human life, is the Divine order. 2. And though sin and sorrow come by means of it, yet a far larger balance of good is produced by it. What do we not owe to our all being members one of another? True, evil comes, but good yet more. Were we all isolated, separated, independent, there would be no guarantee for our good even then, but there would be certainty of infinite loss. If the sins of the fathers are visited on the children unto the third and fourth generation, the mercy of the Lord is unto *thousands* of generations "of them that love him and keep his commandments" (Exod. xx. 6). 3. And though because of it "in Adam all died," yet because of it also "in Christ shall all be made alive." This interlinking of one with all and all with one is, therefore, a matter for great thankfulness, and, though attended with present evils, not at all of complaint.

III. AND THE THOUGHT OF THESE INNOCENT VICTIMS OF SIN IS MOST SALUTARY. 1. *It often holds back from sin.* This is one way in which God "out of the mouth of babes and sucklings has ordained strength." How often fathers and mothers will, for the sake of their children, that they might not be harmed, keep back from sin, to which but for such motive they might have yielded! 2. *It deepens repentance for sin.* (Cf. 2 Sam. xxiv. 17.) 3. *It makes sin more hateful to us.* What must that be which destroys not us only, but our children, innocent of all sin? And it may be that the thus furnishing of additional safeguards against sin, and of additional motives to obedience, was one reason in the Divine mind for constituting us all "members one of another."

IV. And the thought of the innocent Victim of sin, our Lord Jesus, is the most salutary of all. For he transforms us from victims into victors—victors over the condemning, the attractive, the defiling, the enslaving power of sin. And it is as we "look unto" him, as our souls habitually trust him to do all this for us, that we cease to be victims of sin, and become victors over it. Let us give glory to him by accepting his offered grace.—C.

Vers. 21—28.—*The indispensable condition of well-being.* This is laid down in ver. 23—obedience to God. It is the teaching of the entire Bible, of our Lord, the prophets, his apostles. The gospel is for this—to secure it more perfectly; and the sacrifices of the ancient Law were for the same reason. But men have ever rebelled against this. They were doing so in Jeremiah's time. They sought to make their sacrifices and burnt offerings a substitute for the obedience God commanded. Hence, as Hezekiah was compelled to destroy the venerable relic, the brazen serpent, which, intended as an aid to faith, had become the object of faith, so now Jeremiah was compelled to speak slightingly of the appointed sacrifices and worship of the temple for the very same reason. Ver. 21: he mocks at their repeated sacrifices, and (ver. 22) declares that at first God never desired or commanded any such things—only that they should obey his voice. He implies that they were afterwards given but as safeguards and helps to their obedience, which, without them, could not be secured. That obedience (ver. 23) he emphasizes as the one thing needful—the only thing for which God cared, but which they had persistently and, what was worse (ver. 26), increasingly refused. So that now (ver. 27) they were fixed in their disobedience, and no words, however divinely authorized, however earnestly urged, would have effect, and there was nothing left but to declare (ver. 28) their utterly abandoned character and condition. And the like conduct is seen still. Men still are ever attempting to evade the Divine rule of life. By reliance on sacraments, profession of religion, adherence to orthodox creeds, resting in feelings and periods of religious excitement when their emotional nature has been deeply stirred,—in almost anything rather than in that God faith in whom is shown only by obedience to his will. And the habit of this grows, and its results, as of old, become worse and worse, and all exhortation and warning fall on deaf ears and hardened hearts, and men still become as those who "obey not the voice," etc. (ver. 28). Let us remember that this is the subtle temptation of all ages, all Churches, and all people; and let us pray that God would write upon our hearts the sure truth that the one only evidence of our having so "named the name of Christ" as to be "in him" is our "departing from iniquity."—C.

Ver. 29—ch. viii. 3.—*The harvest of sin.* I. We read in other Scriptures of "the joy of harvest." Such shall be the joy of God's redeemed people when his purposes of grace are fulfilled in and for them. It will be a joy unspeakably glorious.

II. But here we have portrayed another harvest—that of sin. Here there is no joy, but bitter lamentation and weeping and woe (ver. 29). We are shown: 1. The *seed* from which this harvest springs (ver. 30)—the doing evil in the sight of the Lord; setting their abominations in his house (ver. 30). 2. We see its *growth*—in open and unblushing idolatry; in the debasement of their nature. They had come to sacrifice their own children to their idol-god, to such horrible cruelty had they sunk down. 3. We see its *harvest,* (1) in death, widespread and terrible (vers. 32, 33); (2) in the flight of all joy and gladness (ver. 34); (3) in public and deep degradation (ch. viii. 1, 2); (4) in utter despair (ch. viii. 3).

III. And though differing in outward circumstance, yet in substance and reality the same harvest will ever spring from the same seed. 1. *All evil-doing is such seed.* And sheltering this under the cloak of religion,—this is the same seed. 2. And its *growth* will be in like manner. Progressive daring in sin; the debasement of our nature. 3. And its *harvest* will be seen, (1) in widespread spiritual death, and often in terrible death-beds; (2) in the loss of all joy and gladness; (3) in degradation before men; (4) in awful despair.

CONCLUSION. Remember, "God is not mocked: whatsoever a man soweth," etc.—C.

Ver. 4.—"*Lying words.*" These were "lying words," as being used by false men for a false purpose. Literally true, for it *was* "the temple of the Lord" that stood in the midst of the land, and in the gate of which this message was delivered,—they were false in spirit, for the deceitful prophets thought thus to make the sanctity of the material structure a cover for the iniquities of the people—a charm to ward off their threatened punishment. The cry was indicative of a hollow and rotten condition of things throughout the entire system of social life. "The prophets prophesied falsely, and the priests bore rule by their means, and the people loved to have it so" (ch. v. 31). We may take these words in three different lights, as reflecting—

I. THE SPIRITUAL PRIDE THAT LEADS MEN TO THINK THEMSELVES THE SPECIAL OBJECTS OF THE DIVINE FAVOUR. This was the characteristic vice of the Jewish people. The distinctions God conferred on them—that they were separate among the nations as "Abraham's seed" and the chosen covenant people, that they had the temple of the Lord among them—were made occasions for national vain-glory, instead of incentives to holy character and noble deed. The same principle is illustrated whenever superior enlightenment, knowledge of truth, spiritual gifts, personal sanctity, ecclesiastical advantage, etc., lead in any way to self-exaltation. Nothing more unseemly than this. If in any such sense "the temple of the Lord" is with us, it may be expected that the shadow of it will produce in us a solemn sense of responsibility. Special privilege brings with it corresponding obligations. Whatever tokens of his favour God bestows on us, their due effect is to lead us to walk with the greater self-forgetfulness and reverential fear before him.

II. THE HYPOCRISY THAT MAKES THE "FORM OF GODLINESS" A SUBSTITUTE FOR ITS "POWER." What availed it that the temple of the Lord stood among them, if the spirit of devotion had departed? The sacred shrine in which they boasted was but a mockery of their internal falseness. The essence of Pharisaism lies in this resting in the outward and apparent, to the neglect of the inward, the spiritual, the real. None so far from God as they who imagine that a mere round of external observances will please him apart from the sincere homage of the soul. "This people draweth nigh unto me with their mouth, and honoureth me with their lips," etc. (Matt. xv. 8).

III. THE SELF-DECEPTION THAT PUTS ON THE GARB OF A RELIGIOUS PROFESSION AS A CLOKE FOR SIN AND A SHIELD FROM ITS PENALTY. The people did wickedly, and then went and stood before the Lord in the house called by his Name, and said, "We are delivered" (ver. 10)—a striking illustration of the folly of those who dream that, so long as they pay public homage to the sovereignty of God's claims, they may violate his laws with impunity. It is a delusive dream that must have, sooner or later, a dread awakening. The mere material temple, glorious as it may be, is no sanctuary for a guilty conscience and a corrupt life. Simply to "lay hold on the horns of the altar" will not save us from the Divine retributions, the Nemesis that tracks the footsteps of the transgressor. Merely to cry, "Lord, Lord!" will never avert from men the sentence, "Depart from me, ye workers of iniquity" (Luke xiii. 25—27).—W.

Vers. 1—14.—*The doom of the temple.* I. THE MESSAGE TO THOSE CONCERNED CANNOT BE ESCAPED. The message is to men who make their boast and confidence in the temple. To be within temple reach seems to place them in a kind of fortress. Such must evidently be met on their own ground. And thus the prophet is sent to the temple gate. There, assuredly, all who took any deep interest in the temple would be found. Jeremiah himself belonged to the priests, and there is no saying but what, prophet as he was, he had to take an allotted share in the temple service. Possibly the message may have been repeated on several occasions, and likeliest of all on those occasions when the temple precincts were crowded with visitors. And when the temple was destroyed, would there not be many to remember that the threatening of destruction was uttered in the very gates of it? Thus we see that there is no want of directness and closeness in dealing with the unfaithful; and no want of courage and candour on the part of the man who was chosen to warn.

II. THE MESSAGE IS TO MISTAKEN WORSHIPPERS. To look round with pride and say these buildings are the temple of God, was as the utterance of some first principle. These worshippers, precise enough in outward forms, had a superstitious feeling that whatever vicissitudes might come elsewhere, Jehovah would keep the place of worship secure. The mistake lay in thinking that God valued the temple for itself. Yet it had not been *made* by his command, in the same sense as the tabernacle had been; rather, it was accepted as a sign of David's deep religious feeling and Solomon's pious regard for his father's wishes. There is nothing to show that out of his own will God would ever have commanded the erection of a temple. It was unseemly in the eyes of David that he should be dwelling in a house of cedar, when the ark of God was behind curtains. But this feeling had in it a certain barbaric element, a fondness for outward pomp and display. It was the best that was in the king's heart, and so it was accepted. He did what he could. But there was no inherent sacredness in the temple, that it should be kept inviolate amid the wreck and defilement of everything else. The people needed to be taught this truth in very plain language. The feeling towards the building is made manifest in such a passage as Ezra iii. 11—13. In fact, the more the people became alienated in heart from the God of the temple, the more enthusiastic, fanatical even, they seem to have become with regard to the mere building.

III. THE WAY IN WHICH THE MISTAKE IS SOUGHT TO BE REMOVED. There is no heaping of scorn on the feeling of the people. Their feeling is rather made the occasion of strengthening the hold of God's truth upon them. If they *really* value the temple, they are shown the way by which they may keep it and dwell within it. Jehovah shows very distinctly that in his eyes the true glory of Jerusalem is not the temple, but the sort of people who dwell in the city. It is better to have a community of the pious, the upright, the truly brotherly, dwelling in cottages, than to have whole streets of splendid palaces, inhabited by luxurious, self-indulgent oppressors. *Men* hold in high esteem buildings, pictures, books, statues, great fruits of human intellect. *God* looks at good actions; little but significant kindnesses—the giving of the cup of cold water, the visiting of the sick, and the feeding of the hungry. A community of men, selfish to the core, will not be preserved for the sake of a splendid building; but that building may be preserved if a community of good men will be really pleased by its preservation. The truth, however, is that a community, living such a life as God here indicates should be chosen, would care very little about the pomps of a building. They would prefer to spend their substance in satisfying pressing needs of men. Many of the ecclesiastical buildings of to-day are inexcusably sumptuous. They are put up to gratify the lust of the eye, and meanwhile the spiritual glories of the upper room at Jerusalem and the Pentecostal miracle are quite forgotten. The publican, the penitent after God's own heart; went up to the temple; but what were its material splendours to him, as he stood, smiting his breast, and saying, " God be merciful to me a sinner "?

IV. THE MESSAGE IS CLINCHED BY A CLOSELY FITTING EXAMPLE FROM HISTORY. One instance is enough to prove a negative. The feeling in the hearts of the people is that God will fence the temple site around, for the sake of the temple. But Shiloh is at once brought forward as a capital instance to the contrary. Evidently it still remained in a ruined, neglected state, for any one to go and see it. Israel knew what Shiloh had been at the first, and they could see how different it was now. In reading history, we are bound to profit by all of Divine warning that may appear in what we read.—Y.

Ver. 18.—*The family joined in idolatry.* I. REMEMBER GOD'S IDEAL OF AN ISRAELITE FAMILY. This is not set before us in any particular passage, but we can gather it from different institutions and commandments. Religion not only concerned the individual in his relation to the priest, the altar, and the holy of holies, and in his general relations to his fellow-men; but there was a very special mention of institutions and regulations which made the individual remember his position in the family. These institutions and regulations were as vital bonds, making the family into a true organic unity. There were the dedication of the firstborn, and the institution concerning the meaning of the Passover feast (Exod. xiii.). There was the command to honour father and mother. So connected with the passage now under consideration, there was the setting apart of the dough (Numb. xv.). A continual instruction and training in Divine things was to be provided for. A mother could have no greater honour than that her children should rise up and call her blessed. Thus gathering together many passages that might be cited, we see that God meant the family to be a great agent for the advancement of his people in all that was good; and the same family ideal comes out with equal prominence and beauty in the New Testament. The natural family may, so far as Christ is concerned, count for much, if only each individual in the family will live up to his opportunities. Still, Christ insists upon the natural family being subordinate to the spiritual family. It is one of the illustrations of the great disintegrating and reconstituting power of the gospel of Christ, that it breaks up the family which is held by nothing stronger than natural bonds. The ideal family of the children of God, those who are the spiritual and abiding Israel, must be gained at any cost. The notion of a family gives one of the aspects in which Christians may be perfectly associated together.

II. LOOK AT THE DEGRADED POSITION IN WHICH THE ISRAELITE FAMILY ACTUALLY WAS. The parents are confirmed idolaters, and are dragging down their children to their own level. The children are sent out to gather fuel towards an idolatrous offering, when they should be learning of the nature, the will, and the promises of Jehovah. A desecrated temple has been spoken of, turned into a den of robbers; but what is that compared with a desecrated family? How insidiously, how gradually, how irresistibly, these children are drawn into idolatry! Gathering wood might be an interesting, amusing occupation, more like play than work. What idea could the children have of the awful insult to which this gathering would contribute? They would grow up, as by a second nature, to kindle fires and knead dough themselves. And it was so easy to treat the child in its way, to tell it to go out and gather wood; far easier than to bear patiently with its waywardness and inattention, and thus lead it on to some understanding of Israel's glorious past. For such treatment meant that the parent should be a learner also, he and his children moving onward together into an enjoyment of the fulness of the Divine promises. And yet God had done much for these parents to make the teaching of his truth as easy as it could be made. He had given things to be set before the children's eyes at periodic intervals. But here, in this deep and pleasing infection of idolatry, is an influence which seems to work successfully against all that God can do. What could be hoped from rising up early and sending the prophets, when there was all this counter-working in the Israelite home?

III. CONSIDER THE POSSIBILITY OF STILL ACHIEVING THE IDEAL. Much may be done towards making even the natural family a holier and more edifying institution than in most cases it is. The humiliating description here shows how much depends upon the parents. How much there is still, even among families nominally Christian, which is just as horrible in this way as this family idolatry among the Israelites of old? Children are sedulously schooled into the worship of Mammon. Selfish and heedless parents are eager to send them to work, when as yet they should know only the home, the school, and the playground. Too often is the maxim reversed that the parents should provide for the children. Christian parents, at all events, should hold themselves bound by the most solemn obligations to do all they can for the training of their children in godliness. There is an ideal of parental duty, and that ideal is seen in action when we look towards the great Father in heaven. Assuredly there would be more God-fearing children if there were more really God-fearing parents. But what cannot be gained by looking up to human guidance and example, can be gained by looking to God. He gathers his children out of many human households, and gives them his own Word to be an impulse and a guide. He puts into their hearts a love of the spiritual brotherhood, which is a deeper feeling than any that nature knows. And the end of it all will be that his children will be perfectly joined together in one mind, in the praise and service of him who alone is worthy to be praised and served by all.—Y.

Ver. 28.—*The inveterate disobedience of Israel.* All along, from ver. 21, this is the theme, viz. the *disobedience* of Israel. Now, to give full force to a charge of disobedience there must be the means of furnishing ample proofs that *directions* have first been given—plain, earnest, and authoritative. And this is just what we find here. God refers his people back over the long years in which, by divers agencies, he had laid before them his righteous and beneficent will. What he commended was for his glory; for his glory because for his people's good; for his people's good because for his glory. The present state and prospects of the people are very humiliating, but assuredly no part of their humiliation can be laid to the charge of their God. The cloudy and the fiery pillar was but a symbol of most distinct guidance for the whole heart. The people were not suffered to wander for lack of expostulation and warning. When a lad turns out badly, criticizing speech **is** often directed against the parents, as if somehow *they must* be at fault. They *may* be at fault indeed, but there is no *must* in the matter. Hasty criticism at such a time, from the very injustice of it, adds a cruel intensity to the pain and disappointment already existing. But hasty criticism cannot be silenced by merely deprecating it, and parents at such moments would do well to remember that they stand in relations to their disobedient children not unlike those in which, as is represented here, Jehovah stood towards Israel of old. The most loving and watchful and patient of parents never did for his children near so much as Jehovah did for Israel. There was the instruction of their wonderful career, in which God had moved so sublimely among them. There were the ten commandments, formulated so distinctly, and set in such a grand historical frame. There were all the rites and ceremonies filled with instructing power to those who would seek to understand them. And there was also, accumulating generation after generation, the great mass of prophetic truth. Man is what he is, not for want of light, but for want of disposition to use and obey the light when it appears. There is an indisposition to attend to truth and to fidelity in all duty, until at last the very feeling of what faithfulness and righteousness are vanishes from the breast. But still the excuse is attempted, and persisted in with shameless impudence, that the word which professes to come from God must have in it something defective, something that effectually prevents it from being received. But it is only from the unrenewed mind that talk of this kind comes. Those who have had their eyes opened to the truth of God soon begin to discern that in that truth there is no lack of guidance, or inspiration, or comfort, or any good thing which can uplift and satisfy the heart. And we may be sure that God, who has given this immense and fruitful body of truth, has brought it nearer to the individual conscience than the individual in his perversity will always acknowledge. Men are indulged too much in the complaint that nobody has spoken to them about their souls. A miserable egotism often lies at the bottom of such complaining. If they know by any means whatever—and it matters not how slight the hint may be—that there is something written for the obedience of all mankind and for their consequent advantage, then these complainers are bound to attend to it. Men are not so foolish in the quest of worldly gains. Then they will go upon the slightest hint, and follow it up discreetly and warily. Why, then, should they be so foolish in the matter of spiritual gain? Because " truth is perished, and is cut off from their mouth."—Y.

EXPOSITION.

CHAPTER VIII.

Vers. 1—3.—Punishment will even overtake the sinners who have long since been deceased.

Ver. 1.—They shall bring out the bones. Not only shall many of the dead bodies remain unburied, but the sepulchres of those who have till now "lain in honour, each one in his house" (Isa. xiv. 18), shall be violated. The **inhabitants of Jerusalem** meant are evidently those of the upper class, for the others were buried, with but little regard to the security of the corpses,

in the valley of Kedron (2 Kings xxiii. 6). According to some, the motive of this invasion of the chambers of the dead is avarice (comp. Herod., i. 187, Darius at the tomb of Nitocris); but the context, without excluding this view, rather suggests malice and contempt. Thus "the wrath of man" was to " praise" Jehovah (Ps. lxxvi. 10).

Ver. 2.—And they shall spread them, etc. Not as an act of solemn mockery, for the agents are idolaters themselves, but God so overrules the passions of his unconscious instruments that no more effective ceremonial could have been devised. **Whom**

they have loved, etc. The prophet is designedly diffuse in his description. With all their misspent zeal, these unhappy idolaters cannot even find tombs.

Ver. 3.—**Which remain.** The words are certainly to be omitted in the second place where they occur. In the Hebrew they stand after **in all the places,** and the word for " places" is feminine, whereas the participle, " the remaining," is masculine. The Septuagint and Peshito have nothing corresponding. There is a clerical error in the Hebrew.

Ver. 4—ch. ix. 1.—The incorrigible wickedness of the people, and the awfulness of the judgment.

Ver. 4.—**Moreover thou shalt say,** etc.; literally, *and thou shalt say.* The section is introduced by a formula which connects it with ch. vii. 2, 28. **Shall they fall,** etc.? rather, *Do men fall . . . doth a man turn away?* One of those appeals to common sense in which the prophets delight. Who ever sees a fallen man stay quietly on the ground without attempting to rise? or a man who has wandered out of the path persist in going in the wrong direction?

Ver. 5.—**Slidden back . . . backsliding.** The verb is the same verb (in another conjugation) as in ver. 4, and the noun is a derivative from it. The Authorized Version, therefore, has slightly weakened the force of the argument. **They hold fast deceit.** They cling to a false view of their relation to their God (comp. ch. iv. 2; v. 2).

Ver. 6.—**I hearkened and heard.** The Divine Judge condescends to speak after the manner of men. He will be his own witness; for it is his own people, Jeshurun, which is on its trial. **Not aright.** It is a compound expression, equivalent to " insincerely," " untruly " (comp. Isa. xvi. 6). **Repented . . . turned;** rather, *repenteth . . . turneth* (or, *returneth*). **To his course.** The Hebrew text, sometimes represented as having a different reading (" courses," in the plural) from the margin, really gives the same reading with one letter misplaced. The singular stands in the parallel passage, ch. xxiii. 19, and offers no difficulty. **As the horse rusheth;** literally, *overfloweth.* Both the Authorized Version and the Vulgate (*impetu vadens*) efface the second metaphor. The uncontrollable passion of both people and war-horse is compared to the all-subduing course of a winter stream or torrent.

Ver. 7.—The appeal to the regularity of animal instincts reminds us of Isa. i. 3. **Yea, the stork,** etc. The migratory birds obey their instinct with the most unfailing regularity. Those referred to are: (1) the stork, whose " regular and sudden return is one of the most interesting natural sights of

Palestine. The expression ' stork in the heavens' refers to the immense height at which they fly during migration" (Tristram); (2) the turtle, or turtle-dove, whose return is the sure sign of spring (Cant. ii. 11); (3 and 4) the crane and the swallow, or rather, " the swift and the crane." These birds are again mentioned together in Isa. xxxviii. 14 (the psalm of Hezekiah), where special reference is made to the penetrating quality of their note. " The whooping or trumpeting of the crane rings through the night air in spring, and the vast flocks which we noticed passing north near Beersheba were a wonderful sight." The introduction of the swallow in the Authorized Version is misleading, as that bird is not a regular migrant in Palestine. The note of the swift is a shrill scream. "No bird is more conspicuous by the suddenness of its return than the swift," is the remark of Canon Tristram, who saw large flocks passing northwards over Jerusalem, on the 12th of February ('Nat. Hist. of Bible,' p. 208). It is an interesting fact that the swift bears the same name (*sûs*) in the vernacular Arabic as in the Hebrew of Jeremiah. **The judgment;** better, *the law* (see on ch. v. 4).

Ver. 8.—**How do ye say, We are wise?** Jeremiah is evidently addressing the priests and the prophets, whom he so constantly described as among the chief causes of Judah's ruin (comp. ver. 10; ch. ii. 8, 26; iv. 9; v. 31), and who, in Isaiah's day, regarded it as an unwarrantable assumption on the part of that prophet to pretend to instruct them in their duty (Isa. xxviii. 9). **The law of the Lord is with us.** " With us;" *i.e.* in our hands and mouths (comp. Ps. l. 16). The word *tōrāh,* commonly rendered " Law," is ambiguous, and a difference of opinion as to the meaning of this verse is inevitable. Some think these self-styled " wise " men reject Jeremiah's counsels on the ground that they already have the divinely given Law in a written form (comp. Rom. ii. 17—20), and that the Divine revelation is complete. Others that *tōrāh* here, as often elsewhere in the prophets (*e.g.* Isa. i. 10; viii. 16; xlii. 4), simply means " instruction," or " direction," and describes the authoritative counsel given orally by the priests (Deut. xvii. 11) and prophets to those who consulted them on points of ritual and practice respectively. The usage of Jeremiah himself favours the latter view (see ch. ii. 8; xviii. 18; and especially xxvi. 4, 5, where " to walk in my *Tōrāh* " is parallel to " to hearken to the words of my servants the prophets." The context equally points in this direction. The most natural interpretation, then, is this: The opponents of Jeremiah bade him keep his exhortations to himself, seeing that they themselves were wise and the divinely appointed teachers of the people. To this Jeremiah replies, not (as the Authorized Version renders) **Lo, certainly in vain made he it**, etc.; but, *Yea, behold! for a lie hath it wrought—the lying pen of the scribes* (so Authorized Version, margin). *Sŏfĕrîm* (scribes) is the term proper to all those who practised the art of writing (*sêfer*); it included, therefore, presumably at least, most, if not all, of the priests and prophets of whom Jeremiah speaks. There are indications enough that the Hebrew literature was not entirely confined to those whom we look up to as the inspired writers, and it is perfectly credible that the formalist priests and false prophets should have availed themselves of the pen as a means of giving greater currency to their teaching. Jeremiah warns his hearers to distrust a literature which is in the service of false religious principles—a warning which prophets in the wider sense of the term ('The Liberty of Prophesyings') still have but too much occasion to repeat. [It is right, however, to mention another grammatically possible rendering, which is adopted by those who suppose *tōrāh* in the preceding clause to mean the Mosaic Law: "Yea, behold, the lying pen of the scribes hath made (it) into a lie;" *i.e.* the professional interpreters of the Scriptures called scribes have, by their groundless comments and inferences, made the Scriptures (especially the noblest part, the Law) into a lie, so that it has ceased to represent the Divine will and teaching. The objections to this are: (1) the necessity of supplying an object to the verb—the object would hardly have been omitted where its omission renders the meaning of the clause so doubtful; (2) that this view attributes to the word *sŏfĕrîm* a meaning which only became prevalent in the time of Ezra (comp. Ezra vii. 6, 11).]

Ver. 9.—**The wise men are ashamed.** It is the perfect of prophetic certitude, equivalent to "the wise men shall certainly be ashamed." And why? Evidently because they have not foreseen the calamities impending over their nation. They have preached, "Peace, peace; when there was no peace" (ver. 11); and hence they find themselves "taken" in the grip of a relentless power from which there is no escape. **What wisdom**; literally, *wisdom of what?* i.e. in respect of what?

Vers. 10—12.—These verses are almost the same as ch. vi. 12—15; the differences are in ver. 10. They are omitted in the Septuagint, and Hitzig regards them as an interpolation, at any rate from the point where the present passage coincides verbally with its parallel. His grounds are: (1) that ver. 13 follows more naturally on ver. 10 *a*

(". . . them that shall inherit them") than on ver. 12; (2) that ver. 10 is deficient in symmetry; and (3) that the deviations from ch. vi. 13—15 sometimes loosen the connection of the clauses, sometimes sink into the colloquial style. The arguments seem to be inconclusive. Jeremiah is apt to repeat himself (Graf refers to ver. 14 = ch. iv. 5; ver. 15 = ch. xiv. 19; ch. v. 9 = v. 29, ix. 8; ch. vii. 16 = xi. 14; ch. l. 41—43 = vi. 22—24; ch. l. 44—46 = xlix. 19—21); and the element which is common to this paragraph and to ch. vi. 12—15 seems equally appropriate in both connections. It should be added, however, that the cautious and reverent Bleek has come to the same conclusion as Hitzig. **To them that shall inherit them**; rather, *to them that shall take possession of them*, i.e. by violence.

Ver. 13—ch. ix. 1.—Further description of the judgment; grief of Jeremiah.

Ver. 13.—**There shall be no grapes**, etc.; rather, *there are no grapes . . . and the leaf is faded.* It is the actual condition of things which the prophet describes. Elsewhere Judah is compared to a vine with bad grapes (ch. ii. 21); here the vine does not even pretend to bear fruit. Another figure is that of a barren fig tree (comp. Matt. xxi. 19). **And the things that I have given them**, etc.; rather, *and I gave them that which they transgress* (viz. laws). The construction, however, which this rendering implies is not perfectly natural, though supported by most of the ancient versions (except the Septuagint, which omits the words), and it is better to alter a single vowel-point, and render, "And I will give them to those who shall pass over them." The phrase **to pass away** is constantly used of an invading host; *e.g.* Isa. viii. 7; Dan. xi. 10, 40.

Ver. 14.—**Why do we sit still?** The prophet transports us by a stroke of his pen into the midst of the fulfilment of his prophecy. The people of the country districts are represented as urging each other to flight. True, it is the resource of despair. No defenced cities can defend them against the judgment of Jehovah. **Let us be silent**; rather, *let us perish;* literally, *let us be put to silence.* **Hath put us to silence**; rather, *hath caused us to perish;* i.e. hath decreed our destruction. **Water of gall**; a phrase characteristic of our prophet (see ch. ix. 14; xxiii. 15). It is a little difficult to find a rendering which shall suit all the passages in which *rosh* (gall) is mentioned. In Deut. xxxii. 33 (and so Job xx. 16) it is clearly used for "venom" in general; and yet in ver. 32 of the same chapter it obviously means a plant. Another general application of the term seems to have been to bitterness in general, the ideas of bitterness and poisonousness being taken as interchangeable. The Authorized Version may therefore stand.

Ver. 15.—**Health**; rather, *healing*. Another rendering is *tranquillity* (same sense as in Eccles. x. 4). **Trouble**; rather, *terror*.

Ver. 16.—The invader is introduced with the same mysterious indefiniteness as in ch. iv. 13. **From Dan**; *i.e.* from the northern frontier (see on ch. iv. 15). **Trembled**; rather, *quaked* (so ch. xlix. 21). **His strong ones**. The phrase "strong ones" generally denotes oxen, but here (as in ch. xlvii. 3; l. 11) horses.

Ver. 17.—A new image to intensify the impression of dreadfulness. **Serpents, cockatrices**; rather, *serpents (even) basilisks*. The second noun is in apposition to the more general "serpents." "Basilisks" (*Serpentes regulos*) are the renderings of Aquila and the Vulgate. Some species of highly venomous serpent is clearly intended; more than this we cannot say. The root probably means "to hiss." Canon Tristram thinks of "a very beautifully marked yellow serpent, and the largest of the vipers found in the Holy Land," called the *Daboia xantheina*. He adds that it is one of the most dangerous ('Nat. Hist. of Palestine,' p. 275).

Ver. 18—ch. ix. 1.—The captivity of Judah and the deep sorrow of Jeremiah.

Ver. 18.—**When I would comfort myself**, etc. The text is here extremely difficult, and if there is corruption anywhere it is in the opening of this verse. Ewald and Graf suppose an ellipsis, and render, "(Oh for) my enlivening [*i.e.* an enlivening for me] in trouble!" Hitzig more naturally renders in the vocative, "My enlivener in trouble," which he supposes to be in apposition to **my heart**. De Dieu (1648) wavers between this and the view that it is an address to his wife, "Quæ marito solatio est." (See, however, ch. xvi. 2.)

Ver. 19.—**Because of them that dwell in**, etc. The Hebrew simply has "from them," etc. The prophet is transported in imagination to the time of the fulfilment of his prophecies. He hears the lamentation of his countrymen, who are languishing in captivity. **Is not the Lord in Zion**, etc.? is the burden of their sad complaints; "king" is a familiar synonym for "God" (comp. Isa. viii. 21; xxxiii. 22; but *not* Ps. lxxxix. 18, which is certainly mistranslated in Authorized Version). But why "in Zion"? "Zion" was properly the name of the eastward hill at Jerusalem, where lay the oldest part of the city (called "the city of David"), and the highest portion of which was crowned by the temple. **Why have they provoked me to anger**, etc.? is the reply

of Jehovah, pointing out that their sufferings were but an exact retribution for their infidelity (comp. ch. v. 19).

Ver. 20.—**The harvest is past**, etc. For "summer," read *fruit-gathering* (the vintage began in September). The people again becomes the speaker. The form of the speech reminds one of a proverb. When the harvest was over and the fruit-gathering ended, the husbandmen looked for a quiet time of refreshment. Judah had had its "harvest-time" and then its "fruit-gathering;" its needs had been gradually increasing, and, on the analogy of previous deliverances (comp. Isa. xviii. 4; xxxiii. 10), it might have been expected that God would have interposed, his help being only delayed in order to be the more signally supernatural. But **we are not saved** (or rather, *delivered*).

Ver. 21.—**For the hurt**, etc.; literally, *because of the breaking*, etc., *I am broken*; comp. ch. xxiii. 9, and the phrase "broken in heart" (Isa. lxi. 1, etc.). The prophet feels crushed by the sense of the utter ruin of his people. **I am black**; rather, *I go in mourning* (so Ps. xxxviii. 6; xlii. 9). The root means rather "foulness" or "squalor" than "blackness" (comp. Job vi. 16, where "blackish," an epithet of streams, should rather be "turbid").

Ver. 22.—No hope or remedy is left; again a proverbial expression. **No balm in Gilead**. Gilead appears to have been celebrated in early times for its balsam, which was exported by Ishmaelites to Egypt (Gen. xxxvii. 25) and by Jewish merchants to Tyre (Ezek. xxvii. 17). It was one of the most costly products of Palestine (Gen. xliii. 11), and was prized for its medicinal properties in cases of wounds (comp. ch. xlvi. 11; li. 8). Josephus mentions this balsam several times, but states that it only grew at Jericho ('Antiq.,' xv. 4, 2). Tristram searched for balsam in its ancient haunts, but in vain; he thinks Jeremiah means the *Balsamodendron gileadense* or *opobalsamum*, which in Arabia is used as a medicine both internally and externally. But if Pliny ('Hist. Nat.,' xxiv. 22) may be followed in his wide use of the term "balsam" so as to include the exudations of the "lentiscus" or mastick tree, then "balm of Gilead" is still to be found; for the mastick tree "grows commonly all over the country, excepting in the plains and the Jordan valley" ('Nat. Hist. of Bible,' p. 336). **Is there no physician there?** We hear but little of physicians in the Old Testament. They are only mentioned again in Gen. l. 2 (but with reference to Egypt, where medicine was much cultivated), and in 2 Chron. xvi. 12; Job xiii. 4. From the two latter passages we may, perhaps, infer that physicians were rarely successful; and this is certainly the impression produced by Ecclus. xxxviii. 15, " He that sinneth before his Maker, let him fall into the hand of the physician." The remedies employed in the Talmudic period quite bear out this strong saying (see Lightfoot, 'Horæ Hebraicæ,' on Mark v. 26). The physicians of Gilead, however, probably confined themselves to their one famous simple, the balsam. **Is not the health . . . recovered?** Gesenius renders, less probably, "hath no bandage been applied to the daughter of my people?"

HOMILETICS.

Vers. 4—6.—*Persistent depravity.* I. Persistent depravity must be distinguished from a casual lapse into sin. 1. This is marked by a *constant habit* of sin, a falling without rising again. The best man is often guilty of mistakes, but he soon seeks to recover himself (Ps. xxxvii. 24). His habit is upright, the direction he follows on the whole, though now and then he may lose ground for a short time, is right. But the man who is persistently depraved makes the wrong way his main course, and if he ever deviates from it does so accidentally or only under some temporary impulse, soon returning as by instinct to wallow in the mire, where only he feels at home (2 Pet. ii. 22). 2. This is characterized by *absence of repentance* after sinning. No man is heard to repent (ver. 6). After a good man has fallen into sin he is overwhelmed with shame, plunged into dark depths of grief, tortured with bitter pangs of contrition, like Peter when he " went out and wept bitterly." But the persistently depraved man feels no such distresses. The sun shines as brightly after he has contracted a new crime as before. His serene self-complacency is not ruffled by one spasm of inward revulsion. 3. This is characterized by an *impetuous impulse* to sin. A good man may fall into sin. One who is persistently depraved rushes into it. To the former sin comes as defeat after a battle in which his better nature has fought and failed; to the latter it comes unresisted, welcomed: he " returneth to his course " with eagerness, " as the horse rusheth into the battle."

II. Persistent depravity is far more culpable than a casual lapse into sin. All sin is culpable. Sin cannot be entirely accidental in any case, or it would cease to be sin. But persistent sin is by far the most evil form of sin. 1. A casual fall may be induced by powerful external temptation; persistent depravity must rise from an *internal appetite.* 2. A casual fall may come as a sudden surprise when a man is off his guard; persistent depravity must be *clearly perceived and consciously cherished.* 3. A casual fall may be the result of a sudden outburst of passion which results in something approaching temporary insanity; persistent depravity must be *calm and cold-blooded*, standing the test of reflection. This is altogether beyond what could be anticipated. You are not surprised that a man should stumble occasionally in the darkness of this world, amidst the snares and pitfalls of temptation, with the natural weakness of humanity, or that he should sometimes miss his way or be lured aside from the right road to pleasanter paths; but that he should not care to rise after falling, not think of returning when he sees the error of his way, but should keep to it with a consistency which would be heroic in a better course,—such depravity is unnatural and monstrous.

Ver. 7.—*A lesson from the birds.* It is interesting to observe that the Scripture references to natural history are not directed so much to theological arguments as to moral lessons. While questions concerning the being and nature of God absorb almost the exclusive attention of the natural theologian, the prophet, who assumes the belief of his hearers in the immanence of God in Nature, is more concerned to show how she rebukes man for his own shortcomings and incites to goodness by her mute example. The scriptural treatment is, therefore, more nearly followed by the regard for the human and moral aspects of nature in the spirit of Wordsworth and Ruskin, which is characteristic of the better thought of our own age, than by the cold, prosaic examination of the physical world, as simply affording one section of the evidences of religion, which was pursued in the days of Paley.

I. The birds remind us that we are surrounded by Divine ordinances. Migratory birds have their appointed times. Every creature has its special vocation.

To the lower animals this comes as a necessary law, as a course determined by unconscious instinct. To man it comes as a mandate of duty, an impulse in the conscience, a way to be clearly perceived and freely chosen. But, though the same method for exacting the performance of the Divine ordinances which obtains in nature is not enforced on man, those ordinances extend to him; to him also they come with Divine sanction. Though man is physically free to rebel, morally he is no more his own master than are the birds who are bound by the laws of their instincts. Freedom from compulsion is not freedom from obligation.

II. THE BIRDS REMIND US THAT IT IS AS WELL TO OBEY THE DIVINE ORDINANCES. In their migrations they find their welfare secured. Driven by the inward impulse of Divine law written on their instincts, they speed them over vast tracts of unknown lands, and at length find themselves in the clime and at the season which is best suited for them. What an image of implicit faith! We are called to go forth, like Abraham, we know not whither, but like him to find a possession in the unknown land (Heb. xi. 8). The future is unseen, the way is wild and pathless, dark clouds as of brooding storms gather on the horizon; but if we take as our compass the known will of God, we too shall find sunny climes beyond the seas of trouble, a home at the end of our pilgrimage.

III. THE BIRDS, BY THEIR EXAMPLE, REBUKE OUR DISOBEDIENCE TO THE DIVINE ORDINANCES. Free to roam through illimitable regions of air, the high-flying stork, the turtle-dove, the swift, and the crane all keep to their true course, not dropping down, tempted by the attractions of leafy vales or fruitful gardens, not turned aside terrified by the horrors of high mountains, lonely deserts, or stormy seas, till they reach their destination in punctual obedience to the mysterious law of their nature. These migratory birds are representative of external liberty restrained by inward law. We are not under any outward compulsion nor any inward law of instinct like that of the birds. But we are capable of following a higher law. We have light which is denied to them, and high motives of fear and love to prompt to obedience. If we disobey, the obedience of the birds is an ever-recurring rebuke.

Vers. 8, 9.—*Untrustworthy literature.* I. LITERATURE MAY HAVE MANY ATTRACTIONS AND YET BE UNTRUSTWORTHY. 1. *Authority.* They were official prophets and teachers whom Jeremiah opposed. Errors gain power when they are pronounced *ex cathedrâ.* The belief in papal infallibility is but one instance of a common human weakness. 2. *Pretentiousness.* The self-styled wise men of Jeremiah's age were confident and boastful. The world is too ready to take a man at his own estimate of himself. Vehement assertion is often accepted instead of solid proof. 3. *Numerical force.* Jeremiah stood as one against many. No mistake is greater than the assumption of so-called common sense, that truth may be presumed to reside with the majority. How often from the days of Noah downwards has it been found with the few! 4. *Popular style.* These "wise" men knew how to suit the taste of the multitude; they could prophesy smooth things. There is a fearful fascination in literary style. The great danger to the cultivated is that they should select for their guides those writers whose language is most pleasing in place of those whose arguments are most sound. Lies may be commended by brilliant epigrams, and unwholesome passions fostered by splendid poetry. The ease and fluency of Hume and the wit of Voltaire were effective with many persons who would not have been moved by bare arguments.

II. IF LITERATURE IS UNTRUE IT SHOULD BE TREATED AS WORTHLESS. 1. Style is but the vesture of thought, and thought is but idle fancy if it *does not correspond to fact.* The first question to be asked about a writer is not, "Are his ideas novel, original, striking? are they beautiful, grand, imposing? are they pleasing, popular, acceptable?" but simply, "Are they true?" If this question in answered in the negative, all other recommendations may be considered as worse than worthless. The sweeter the bait, the more dangerous the trap. 2. The test of truth in religious literature is *conformity to the Word of God.* The Scripture is a guide and authority to the Christian. God's word in nature, providence, and conscience must be heard and interpreted if men would speak truly on these subjects. The profession to be speaking Divine words founded either on a pretended revelation or a boast of superior intelligence, is vain unless the private words of the individual harmonize with the general truth of God's world-wide revelations. 3. *Experience* will test the truth of literature. If literature concerns itself with serious subjects, it cannot be regarded as a trifle of idle hours. It will be brought into judgment. Experience will try it. No lie can be eternal. The self-styled "wise" men will "have to be ashamed," "dismayed and taken," when events contradict their untrue language.

Ver. 11.—(See on ch. vi. 14.)

Vers. 14, 15.—*Despair*. I. DESPAIR WILL ARISE ON THE PERCEPTION THAT THERE IS NO WAY OF ESCAPE FROM RUIN. The miserable Jews are pictured as first sitting still helplessly, and then rousing themselves to enter the fenced cities, only to find that death awaits them there as surely as in the open plain. People are too ready to believe that "something will turn up," and so hold on, in confidence and indifference, till their eyes are suddenly opened, and they see room for nothing but despair.

II. DESPAIR WILL ARISE ON THE RECOGNITION OF THE WRATH OF GOD. The Jews are to see that their God has put them to silence. Philistines, Egyptians, Assyrians, Chaldeans, might all be resisted; but who shall resist God? Men can only fight against God with confidence until they perceive him fighting against them. Then hope is madness.

III. DESPAIR WILL BE HEIGHTENED BY THE SENSE OF GUILT. The Jews are to see that their calamity is the punishment of sin. It is deserved. It is justly given. Men hope on while they refuse to admit their sin; but conviction of sin is fatal to hope.

IV. DESPAIR MAY FOLLOW A CONFIDENT HOPE. The Jews had looked for peace and for a time of health. Yet none came. Hope may be very bright and yet very delusive. The splendour of the sunrise contains little promise that the day will close without storms. Subjective confidence is no guarantee of objective truth. Things are not the more true because we believe them very firmly. We may feel safe and be in danger. A peaceful death is no security for a joyful resurrection. It is little that a man has overcome the fear of death; the important question is whether he has removed the ground for that fear. The faith that saves is not confidence in our own security, but submissive and obedient trust in Christ.

V. THE POSSIBILITY OF DESPAIR IS REVEALED, NOT TO PRODUCE IT, BUT TO WARN US FROM IT. If it were inevitable, or, being experienced, invincible, it would be cruel to prepare any for it. Why not let the poor doomed wretch enjoy his brief hour of sunshine before he is sent "to dwell in solemn shades of endless night"? But the revelations of a possibly dark future are given in mercy to warn us from sowing the seeds of despair and to point to the way of escape. No soul need despair since there is One who "is able to save them to the uttermost that come unto God by him" (Heb. vii. 25).

Ver. 20.—*Harvest contrasts*. The seasons have their lessons for all of us, teaching both by analogy and by contrast; for the warnings suggested by the opposition of our own condition to that of the natural world may be as instructive as the encouragements arising out of the harmony between the two. To Jeremiah the harvest came in its brightness only to show the condition of the Jews in the deeper shadow. A similar experience may occur to those of us who have no harvest-song in the soul to respond to the harvest-gladness of the world without.

I. THE MOST HOPEFUL EXTERNAL EVENT IS NO SECURITY FOR DELIVERANCE FROM THE GREATEST TROUBLES OF LIFE. Even harvest did not bring deliverance. People are too ready to rest their confidence on various indications of God in the outside world. 1. *Time*. The harvest is a new waymark in the course of time. Many trust blindly to time to bring them some help, while they do not stir a finger to secure it. 2. *Change*. The harvest indicates a new season. The sanguine are too ready to believe that any change must be for the better. 3. *Material prosperity*. The harvest brings bread for the body. Must it not, therefore, lay the foundation of perfect and lasting good? To those men whose "god is their belly" the harvest would seem to promise complete satisfaction. 4. Indications of the *merciful kindness of God*. He sends the harvest. Then, it is reasoned, he wishes to bless, and therefore will permit no harm. But experience proves the error of these anticipations, and reflection should soon detect the fallacy which underlies them. Outward events do not always correspond to inward experiences; the latter have their own separate conditions. God may deal mercifully with us now and in earthly things, but his present forbearance is no proof that we shall never suffer from his righteous wrath in the season of judgment.

II. The most hopeful external event deepens the sense of the internal distress with which it is contrasted. The harvest past, and yet undelivered! 1. *A new stage of time* has gone, and the deliverance is still delayed. 2. *Outside events* change, but the essential condition remains unchanged. 3. *Material good* is enjoyed while real good is still unattained, and this makes the minor blessing seem but a mockery. 4. *God is merciful,* and yet we are not delivered! Some fearful evil must be at the foundation of such a strange condition. 5. *A time of rest* is looked for but comes not. After harvest should come rest. Distress is heightened by the disappointment of expected deliverance. 6. *Approaching troubles* increase the gloom of present distress. The harvest is *past.* Now we look forward to chill autumn, to stormy winter. Not saved in harvest! What are we to expect in less propitious times?

Ver. 22.—*"Balm in Gilead."* I. The world needs remedies for moral and social healing. Jeremiah regarded the Jews as wounded by the cruel calamities which were to overwhelm them; but beneath the wounds he detected an unhealthy national condition which equally needed healing. Men suffer thus from the external wounds of adversity and from the internal disease of sin. How small a part of mankind can be considered in a thoroughly healthy condition! Men are not only imperfectly developed; they are suffering from positive disorders. The world needs medicine as well as food—the physician as well as the farmer. Nations need healing for political disorganization within and wrongs of subjection to a foreign yoke without. Society sadly requires to be purified, even regenerated. Individual men suffer from the smart of sorrow and the disease of sin—both signs of an imperfect, disorganized condition, needing cure. The one disease which is at the root of all the chief maladies of mankind is moral evil. The forgiveness of sins must come as a healing of sickness (Mark ii. 9).

II. Many professed remedies are forthcoming. Gilead has her balm. Every new physician has his patent nostrum. The world does not suffer from the small number of remedies which have been proposed to cure all the ills that flesh is heir to. It is rather in danger of being poisoned by a superabundance of most incongruous drugs. Every religion brings its own remedy. Philosophy, in its highest ambition, aims at a practical cure of society. Political innovations, social reforms, education, sanitary improvements,—all seek this result.

III. No earthly remedies suffice for the needed cure. The balm of Gilead is found in abundance, but, alas! it will not heal the smart of Israel. Physicians advise, but their advice is futile. Nothing could effect the deliverance of the Jews in the days of Jeremiah, though lying prophets and astute politicians did their best. No earthly remedy can heal the widespread evil of the world (Isa. i. 6). 1. Earthly remedies are *external.* They may change the social order; they cannot cure the false ideas, irregulated passions, and vitiated conscience of which the habits of society are but symptoms. Spiritual disease must be treated with spiritual medicine. The physician for the body can do little in ministering to "the mind diseased." You cannot make men moral by the strictest puritanical legislation. (1) The disease of *sin* is in the heart, and the remedy must reach the heart. (2) So the deepest *distress* of mankind cannot be cured by the amelioration of physical comforts. A princely legacy is no consolation to a mother for the loss of her child. 2. Earthly remedies *partake of the character of the disease.* Human religions bear on their faces the marks of that very moral corruption which they aim at destroying. Sin can only be cured by something outside the sinful world; sorrow, by something above the scene of human distresses. We must go further than Gilead for the true balm, for Gilead will share with Israel the trouble for which we seek a remedy.

IV. God has provided his own remedy for the moral and social healing of the world. Christ is "the good Physician." The miracles of healing which he wrought on the bodies of men were signs of the work he came to effect for their souls.

1. *Christ's remedy comes from higher than human sources.* The healing of the sinless One is not tainted with the corruption which marks all simply human attempts at cure. 2. *Christ's remedy goes to the root of the evil* of mankind. His great work is not to effect an external revolution of society, but to cleanse the conscience (Heb. ix. 14) and heal the heart. 3. Individually, healing is brought to *all*, and the worst cases are just those for which Christ chiefly came (Matt. ix. 12). When all other remedies fail, his is most effectual, because it is (1) most needed, and (2) most glorified by the result. 4. *Society* must be healed by the application of Christian principles to politics, to commerce, to literature, to recreation, to domestic life.

HOMILIES BY VARIOUS AUTHORS.

Vers. 4—7.—*Apostasy an anomalous and incalculable thing.* I. THE ANALOGIES OF COMMON SENSE AND INSTINCT ARE FALSIFIED. (Vers. 4—6.) If a man fall, he will rise again to his feet; if he has made a mistake or gone in a wrong direction, and discovers it, he will turn again, unless he be absolutely bereft of his senses. One might expect similar behaviour in spiritual matters. But in the wickedness and defection of Israel it was not so; their apostasy seemed perpetual. The migratory birds are taught by instinct when to return. The season of their coming again is almost as calculable as that of their going. But the departure of the sinner is incomprehensible, and his return cannot with certainty be expected. Nay, the likelihood is he will continue in his sin, and pursue his own destruction to the bitter end. In this, as in many other instances, the career of the sinner can only be explained on the score of infatuation. His moral sense is perverted or destroyed. In place of that quick response which conscience ought to make to the voice of duty, there comes over his spirit an insensibility to moral considerations, and a growing ignorance of things Divine gradually deepening into outer darkness.

II. IT IS UNMOVED BY THE CONSIDERATIONS THAT OUGHT TO AFFECT IT. (Ver. 5.) The growing misery and unhappiness which it occasions are not strong enough to check the tendency to sin, if indeed their connection with it is clearly perceived or acknowledged. The cravings of the spiritual nature have to give place to "the lust of the flesh, the lust of the eye, and the pride of life." By-and-by they are stilled, not by being satisfied, but by being stifled; and a curious heedlessness, which is deaf to all the voices of prophetic warning and entreaty, increasingly characterizes it. Under such circumstances it is difficult to discover any common point of contact or argument that shall be valid to both parties. When reason is left behind, it is not to higher, but to lower, susceptibilities that appeal has to be made.

III. THE CONCERN, THE CLAIMS, AND THE GRACIOUS PROVISION OF GOD ARE AS NOTHING. (Ver. 6.) The saint in the times of his calamity calls upon God to incline his ear. In the fearful condition and moral insensibility of his people to their wickedness and danger God is represented as of himself inclining his ear and listening attentively for the lightest sigh of repentance. He calls, but no notice is taken. The means of salvation he has provided are neglected or abused. The form of godliness is cultivated when the spirit has fled and the exercises of religion are the chief foes to its reality. What can be the conclusion to all this? They are spiritually dead. There is neither power nor inclination to seek for better things. Nothing but supernatural grace and long-suffering love can avail to save them.—M.

Vers. 8—12.—"*Peace, peace; when there is no peace.*" The present condition of the country, the evils that lowered upon the horizon,—these alike bore their message even to the natural conscience. If Israel was in the right way, and really understood the will of the Lord to do it, why these scandals, miseries, and impending evils? Again, the better to reach the perception of those who were thus unable to draw the inference for themselves, the condemnation was to be in kind—a sort of elementary lesson in the "correspondences" that marked the Divine government of the world was to be read to them. The scribe who had prophesied "smooth things" would be confronted with his own writings and compelled to eat his own words.

I. DIVINE ILLUMINATION ALONE CAN GIVE TRUE UNDERSTANDING OF GOD'S WORD.

The priests and scribes, because of familiarity with holy things, claimed to be wise. They were satisfied with the spiritual state of Israel. Had they been wise, they would have anticipated what took place. The Holy Spirit alone bestows Divine insight and foresight.

II. THE DESPISERS OF DIVINE TRUTH, AND THOSE WHO FALSELY PRETEND TO ITS CUSTODY, WILL BE PUT TO SHAME. "Refuges of lies" will be swept away. The judgment, when it comes, will find them wholly unprepared and helpless. "Take heed that the light that is in thee be not darkness." "Blind leaders of the blind," the *sorrowing* comes to them in vain for comfort, or is deceived to his own hurt; at last the victim of a misplaced confidence, to find himself "of all men most miserable." The *sinner* meets with no true correction or instruction; and in his desperation he receives from them no help. Their judgment is that they will share the fate of their victims and dupes.—M.

Vers. 13—15.—*False hopes ministering despair.* The lessons of life are not readily learned by most men. They require to be frequently repeated ere they produce an impression. God, therefore, deals severely with his people, whose delusion is the more unpardonable because of the piety of their fathers and the light of revelation which had been given. He will, therefore, make to "pass away from them" one by one the things that he had given: the fruits of the earth shall be cut off; the comforts of life shall be at an end; trouble and sorrow shall seize upon them.

I. HOW HARD IT IS FOR MEN TO REALIZE THAT THE OUTWARD BLESSINGS OF LIFE DO NOT OF THEMSELVES SATISFY, AND CANNOT BE RELIED UPON! Each of us can remember how, one by one, the things of life had to be taken from him ere he learnt their real littleness and insufficiency. This is often the way God seeks to bless us. He takes away the object whose possession is misunderstood and whose properties are abused, that he may remove the temptation from the heart and leave it free for heavenly affections. "We can do without happiness, and instead thereof find blessedness." But to only a few is it given to know this. The multitude are as foolish scholars, "ever learning, and never able to come to a knowledge of the truth."

II. HOPE WHICH HAS BEEN SO MISPLACED AND BETRAYED TOO FREQUENTLY INTRODUCES TO DESPAIR. As the lesson has not been learned, there is no perception of the real mistake. The old blunders are repeated until, in the sweeping away of all that we had held dear, we feel that life itself is not worth living, because we can see no real good within our reach. "Who will show us any good?" We are convicted, too, of unpardonable folly. The dissatisfaction with the things of life is gradually equalled, if not surpassed, by dissatisfaction with ourselves. We are conscious of needs that are not met and yearnings that refuse to be stilled. And beneath all these is the miserable consciousness that, in pursuits so trifling and tastes so mean, our true nature is being degraded. We grieve over our shattered idols and our vanished comforts, and yet more, are angry with ourselves that we should so grieve. The question will at last come, "If these things be our chief good, what security is left of ultimate happiness? If the real end of life has not been sought, we are not only unfortunate—we must be culpable." For to seek the truth, etc., of life is not only a possible enjoyment we have missed, but a duty we have neglected. And yet of our own selves we feel unable to retrace our steps. Having the desires we have, which have been strengthened by years of indulgence, we cannot all at once or of our own motion replace them with better ones. A feeling of helplessness, convicted folly and sin, and indefinite degradation gradually dawns upon our affrighted conscience. How shall we escape from the consequences of our own actions? Whither shall we flee who, in seeking our good always in material things, have been living in practical atheism? We can do nothing else but, like the smitten Israelites, betake ourselves to our closets and sit still.

III. BUT THE JUDGMENTS OF HEAVEN UPON THE SINNER, HOWEVER TERRIBLE IN THEMSELVES, ARE NOT MEANT TO PRODUCE THIS DESPAIR. The false trust is removed, that we may find the true one. The worst calamities of life, and its grievous disappointments, will be more than compensated for if they lead us to the Saviour. The prophet, speaking representatively for Israel, says, "Let us submit to God's judgment, and confess our sin as its cause." "Silence before the Lord" is the sure way to his restored favour and help.—M.

Ver. 20.—*Occasions of hoped-for salvation that have not availed.* Probably a proverbial expression. It is not admissible for us to understand the words of help expected from Egypt, which would be to make them an anachronism. They well describe the result of hoping against hope, and in this sense might be spoken by those who have been reduced to extremity by worldliness of spirit and unholiness of life. "It is plain that a great part of Israel imagined, like their heathen neighbours, that Jehovah had need of them as much as they had need of him ; that their worship and service could not be indifferent to him ; that he must, by a natural necessity, exert his power against their enemies, and save his sanctuaries from profanation. This, indeed, was the constant contention of the prophets who opposed Micah and Jeremiah (Micah iii. 11 ; ch. vii. 4, *seq.* ; xxvii. 1, *seq.*); and from their point of view the captivity of Judah was the final and hopeless collapse of the religion of Jehovah" (W. Robertson Smith).

I. How MANY OCCASIONS HAVE THERE BEEN ON WHICH WE HAD EXPECTED AN IMAGINARY GOOD, OR LOOKED FOR A DELIVERANCE WHICH NEVER CAME! The man who has sought for wealth becomes rich only to find that his possessions fail to yield him the satisfaction he expected. False expectations have been entertained by the victims of misfortune that God would deliver them. True, they have no claim upon him, and they know that, if they were to be requited as they deserved, they would be left alone. The victim of unhallowed desires, hurried and driven as by an inward demon, fancies that, in his own nature or the course of life, he will come to a turning-point. He will "sow his wild oats" now ; by-and-by he will settle down and marry and be respectable and virtuous. The events of life to which he looks forward take place, but there is no deliverance wrought by them. So many seek the Divine favour in formal religious observances, and do not find it. When many around us are being awakened from their indifference and converted to God, we are alarmed at our own spiritual deadness. The time of grace has slipped past unimproved. God has been gathering in his children, and we are left out.

II. To WHAT CONCLUSION OUGHT THIS TO LEAD US? That we ought to be anxious and in earnest there can be no question. Our chances appear desperate. Our power of moral recovery is greatly lessened as compared with the freshness of childhood's days. But whilst there is life there is hope. We have reason to congratulate ourselves that we have not been cut off in the midst of our sins. The door is still open. Let us, as those "born out of due time," awake to righteousness, and seek with tears an offended but loving Father. "Now is the accepted time; . . . now is the day of salvation."—M.

Ver. 22.—"*Physician, heal thyself.*" Gilead, an outlying district of Palestine, was celebrated for its aromatic balsam, of great virtue for wounds, sores, etc. The natives of the place doubtless became expert in the application of their famous herb. By virtue of its possession, Israel might be said to be the healer of the surrounding nations. Even more so in a spiritual sense it was the physician of men's souls, holding for others and for all time the saving truth of God. But the evils which came upon itself—social, political, spiritual—had now increased to such a degree that it might well be asked, were the sources of saving health exhausted, or were the possessors of spiritual wisdom wholly extinct?

I. WHAT FOUNDATION WAS THERE FOR THE PRETENSION OF ISRAEL TO BE THE SAVIOUR OF THE NATIONS? Its own internal condition was deplorable. Materially and spiritually it was more in need of healing than those it regarded as barbarians and heathen. So of the Church which has become corrupt a similar question may be asked. If those who profess the faith of Christ do not exhibit its fruits or possess its peace, they belie their profession and discredit the cause of their Master. When professed believers are as troubled with earthly cares and as downcast amid earthly trials as others, men of the world will doubt the efficacy of their religion, belief, and life. This is the burning question of Christendom through all time. Has it any means of curing the evils of humanity, the miseries of life, the wickedness inherent in human nature?

II. HAD THE UTMOST USE BEEN MADE OF THE RESOURCES AT COMMAND? Was there any one who knew the nature of the evil, and how to cure it? Why did they not seek Jehovah? Christians are frequently at a loss, not so much for lack of an orthodox creed as of a realizing faith. They have not been in the habit of going to Christ with their cares and sorrows. Earthly things have been allowed to divert their attention from truth and righteousness as the principles of life. But sometimes great mischief is done by wrong expectations of what Christ will do for his people. Men sow to the flesh and expect to reap a spiritual harvest, or their faith in Christ is but another avenue to an earthly end. Under such circumstances they cannot fail to be disappointed. We must look to religion for its proper functions; to Christ for what he has promised to give. Have we any grief which we do not, cannot take to Christ? Are we consciously resting on him for moral guidance and support and spiritual fellowship? They who always and in all things rest their souls upon a living Saviour will know that there is " balm in Gilead," etc.—M.

Ver. 2.—*Befooled indeed.* This is what we say when we see men giving heed to the plausible statements of gross impostors, and, in consequence, lavishing their time, energy, and wealth in the hope of large recompense; but who, when the time comes that the hoped-for gain should be theirs, find themselves deceived, defrauded, helpless, and utterly ruined men. These are they who are the prey of bubble companies, lying advertisements, and the other ten thousand frauds into which unwary persons are beguiled. But is not this what we may say when we read of those told of in our text? Was there ever more flagrant, piteous, and awful instance of men being made fools of indeed? For—

I. LOOK AT THESE UTTERLY DECEIVED ONES. 1. *They were worshippers of the gods of the heathen.* The sun, the moon, and all the host of heaven: these were the objects of their worship. Reference is continually made to them and to their worship (2 Kings xxiii. 5; xxi. 3, etc.). 2. *And they were most earnest worshippers.* Note the piling up of expressions to indicate this. (1) They "*have loved*" them. Here is the root of all real worship. The object must be loved, and these people were drawn to and attracted by these false gods. (2) They "*served*" them. This follows as a sure consequence. It is not said they believed in them; but that matters not: if there be that in the object of our worship which makes us like it—love is almost too sacred a word as applied to false gods—we shall serve it readily enough. (3) And then they "*walked after*" them. That which lured them at the first drew them more and more, and so it became the habit of their lives. (4) And they "*sought*" them. When they found the worship of some of these gods was pleasant, they sought out more of them; or it may mean that they got at last to have a real faith in them, and hence "consulted them as oracles, appealed to them as judges, implored their favour, and prayed to them as benefactors." (5) And they "*worshipped*" them. See them at their worship on Mount Carmel, on the day when Elijah challenged their priests to put to the test his God and theirs. None could doubt the sincerity of their worship or the earnestness with which they cried all that morning long, " O Baal, hear us! " And those to whom Jeremiah wrote were such thorough worshippers of these gods. They withheld no proof of their devotedness. 3. *But yet they were utterly deceived and disappointed.* See in text and in immediate context how these gods dealt with them. Ardent votaries as they had been, those whom they worshipped let all the hideous woes come upon them which are told of here: death, desolation, degradation, and despair. That was what their gods did for them. They had spent their all on these pretended physicians, and were nothing bettered, but made worse indeed.

II. ENDEAVOUR TO EXPLAIN BOTH THEIR INFATUATION AND THEIR DISAPPOINTMENT. 1. *As to their infatuation.* It can hardly be possible for any reader of the history of these people to avoid asking the question, "Wherefore was it that they were so given to idolatry?" Their whole national history showed that nothing but sorrow and shame had come from idolatry, and yet here they were for ever, not merely falling into it, but deliberately and persistently going after it. What could be the reason? (1) Partly, no doubt, the example of the great and mighty nations around them. We must remember what an infinitesimally small kingdom that of Judah was—about the size of an ordinary English county, and how insignificant they were; how the influence, therefore, of the great empires which pressed them on either side could not but be felt. And this was all on the side of idolatry. Idolatry had done *them* no harm; the gods they worshipped had, so it would seem, lifted them up to greatness and power surpassed by none. All seemed to say to the poor, weak, little kingdom of Judah, "You had far better do as we do and trust our gods rather than your own." (2) The spirituality of the worship God required, and the absence of all such demand on the part of idolatry, was another argument for idolatry and against the worship of God. No graven image, no representation of God, nothing that would help the senses to conceive of God as like to themselves, was granted to the Jews; God was a Spirit, and he was to be worshipped in spirit and in truth. No statue, no image, no painting, no symbol even, was to represent him. It was not allowed that the Jew should be able to place in his house or carry about with him, as other nations did, any material emblem of his God (cf. Deut. iv. 15; Isa. xl. 18). But spiritual worship of this kind has ever been found far more difficult to maintain: it demands a condition of heart and mind so purified that to the gross and sensual such worship is impossible, and to the ordinary mind it is far from easy. The anthropomorphisms of the Old Testament, and the Incarnation itself, are condescensions of God to the confessed feebleness and incapacity of man for such pure worship. But, on the other hand, idolatry, abounding with "chambers of imagery," lending itself to all the clamour of the senses,—what wonder that it was preferred? (3) Add on to this the fact that strict obedience to the Levitical Law involved such isolation from all other people, such scrupulous care, such heavy sacrifices of time, wealth, ease, and the good will of men; in short, was altogether, as St. Peter afterwards said (Acts xv. 10), "a yoke which neither our fathers nor we were able to bear;" whilst idolatry wooed them with its sensuous, brilliant, luxurious, and easy rites; and again we ask, what wonder that idolatry was preferred? (4) And present earthly good seemed to be associated with it, and absent from the worship of God (cf. ch. xliv. 15—19, "For then had we plenty of victuals, and were well, and saw no evil. But since we left off, . . . we have wanted all things"). And (5) lastly, the licence allowed by the lax moral code of idolatry, and its positive sanction of gross licentiousness; this, contrasted with the stern frown of the true Jewish faith upon all such sin, was more than sufficient to attract in crowds a people so debased as the Jews had now become. Then, as still, the most powerful and the most depraved passions of human nature were not only permitted free indulgence by idolatry, but actually patronized, protected, and prescribed. All ancient history attests this, and the result on the heathen world, not only history but God's providence and his Word alike (Rom. i.) have plainly declared. 2. *As to their disappointment.* Idolatry, however for the moment it may seem to have brought good along with it (cf. *supra*), resulted at last in such unparalleled woe as the prophets, one and all, continually declared must come from it. But whilst no idolatrous nation has ever stood permanently in its greatness—let the decayed and perished empires of antiquity witness—there can be little question that sentence against the evil work was executed more speedily, more sternly, and more notoriously against the Jews than against any other idolatrous nation whatsoever. It cost them more than any other people, and they have not paid "the uttermost farthing" even yet. The rabbis say that in every one of the innumerable cups of affliction which Israel in the course of the long ages has had to drink, there has been mingled some of the dust of that golden idol-calf which Moses ground to powder beneath Mount Sinai. We are told how, when he had done this, he cast the powder into the stream from whence the camp drew its water, and made all the people drink of it. Now, wherefore was sorer judgment meted out to Israel than to others because of their idolatry? (1) Because they were the beloved of the Lord. A man may see a strange child doing a disgraceful action and may take comparatively little notice; but if it be his own son, whom he loves, will he not feel and resent it then as otherwise he never would? (2) And "chiefly because to them were committed the oracles of God." They were to be the channel along which the truth of revelation was to flow to mankind at large, and if that channel were not kept free from pollution, neither could the living waters which flowed along it. Hence the prompt and stern measures which were ever taken to preserve Israel in the faith of God, or to restore them if they had wandered. It could not be, therefore, that Israel should permanently and entirely lapse into idolatry. The well-being of the world hinged on their handing down pure and uncorrupt the oracles of God and the faith of their forefathers, and because "God so loved the world," the cup of idolatry was ever made bitter and nauseous to his people, so that they might hate to drink of it.

III. TRY TO TURN THIS WHOLE SUBJECT TO GOOD ACCOUNT. 1. *The votaries of the world may in these verses behold their own portraiture and read their sure reward.*

For (1) they do after this manner give themselves to the world. They "love," "serve," "walk after," "seek," and "worship" it. (2) And their infatuation is explained by like reasons. (3) And their reward will be to be utterly deceived and disappointed. God will say to each one of them, "Thou fool!" (Luke xii. 20). 2. *The worshippers of God may profitably contemplate a model which too many of them too seldom follow, of earnest devotedness in their worship.* "The children of this world are wiser in their generation than the children of light." Would that the devotedness of the world to its god were equalled by the devotedness of the Church to theirs! 3. Every one may behold, in the tremendous and deadly attraction of the world, fresh, urgent, and constant need of being "kept by the power of God" in the love of God. Well may each day begin with this prayer—

> "Lord, I my vows to thee renew;
> Scatter my sins like morning dew,
> Guard my first springs of thought and will,
> And with *thyself* my spirit fill."

C.

Vers. 4—11.—*Backsliding in its worst forms.* All departures from God are evil, but some are only temporary, and are quickly followed by repentance, return, and restoration. There are others, however, of a far more serious kind, and we have in these verses a great deal told us concerning them. We are told of some of—
I. THEIR CHARACTERISTICS. 1. *So contrary to men's wonted ways.* For when men find that they have brought evil on themselves, they will at once seek to undo such evil (ver. 4). If a man fall, he will not lie still in the mire or in the road, but will get up again as speedily as may be. If he have mistaken his path and got on a wrong track, will he not, as soon as he discovers his mistake, quickly retrace his steps that he may get into the right way? That is how men act in the common affairs of life. But, though Judah and Jerusalem knew well that they had fallen, yet they showed no desire to rise, and though they could not but know they were altogether out of the right way, they showed no willingness to return. 2. *Resists the strivings of God's Spirit* and all his drawings of them to himself. Ver. 7 implies such God-implanted instincts in men's souls, but declares that, unlike the ever-obedient birds, man resists and refuses the call of God. 3. *Becomes shameless.* (Vers. 6, 12.) This feature we have had noticed before (cf. ch. vi. 15); it arrested the prophet's attention as being evil exceedingly. 4. *Determined and defiant.* (Ver. 6.) 5. *Is at last perpetual.* (Ver. 5.) They have gone into an evil way, and they abide in that way, no power of Divine grace being able to draw them therefrom. So terrible is this worst form of backsliding, it is perpetual.
II. THEIR CONSEQUENCES. The evil fruit such sin bears is shown here. 1. *Deep sorrow to the heart of God.* How pathetic is this lament! How it echoes the anguish of those words, "How shall I give thee up!" "How often would I have gathered thee!" etc.! Such is the tone of these (vers. 4—8). The Divine grief is audible through every part. 2. *Shame to the backsliders themselves.* (Ver. 9.) It is ever so. These chapters have been giving illustration upon illustration of this result. And our own observation and the experience of all who have turned from God to sin—all alike confirm what God's Word has said. 3. *Utter and absolute ruin.* (Ver. 10.) The dreadful sorrows of the vanquished in beholding their most beloved ones torn from them to a fate worse than death, and their lands which they had inherited from their fathers taken possession of by their conquerors,—these common incidents of war are cited as illustrative of the utter ruin which would come upon these ungodly ones. And evermore will men find it an exceeding bitter thing to depart from the living God. We are also shown some of—
III. THEIR CAUSES. 1. *Deception.* Ver. 5, "They hold fast deceit." How many are the falsities by which men are deceived, and to which they hold fast as if they were sure facts on which their souls might rest (cf. vers. 8, 11; vii. 4, 8)! 2. *Dislike of God's ways.* "They refuse to return." They had no desire to detect the falsity of their trust; they were glad to have any excuse for refusal. 3. *Strong preference for the world's ways.* Ver. 10, "Every one . . . given to covetousness." The ways of God suffered not such worldliness, but the ways they had chosen gave free permission. Here is ever the secret of departure from God. But can nothing be done? "Is there no balm in Gilead?" (ver. 22). Note, then—

IV. THEIR CURE. How shall this evil spirit be cast out and the right spirit be restored? In ver. 6 the process is shown to us. There is: 1. *Realization of the results of our sin.* The backslider is represented as contemplating with dismay the awful consequences of his sin, and asking, " What have I done?" It is "the conviction of sin" which is the beginning work of God's Spirit in the sinner's heart. See the prodigal contemplating the ruin he had brought upon himself. This was the first step in his "coming to himself." 2. *Repentance of our wickedness.* (Ver. 6.) Not general repentance, but each man seeing *his own* wickedness and repenting of that. The man has come to look on it as God looks on it. Formerly he loved his sin, now he hates it. One element of our Saviour's atonement was this, that he in our nature and as our representative, looked upon our sin as God looked on it, and so offered to God for us a true repentance. We, however contrite in heart, could offer none such, for as it has been truly said, " Our very repentance needs to be repented of, and our tears washed in the blood of Christ." But this element of all true atonement—that he who makes such atonement looks on the wrong done as he who has been wronged looks on it—was present in Christ's atonement, and is one reason wherefore " the blood of Christ cleanseth from all sin." 3. *Confession.* This is the " speaking aright" which is told of in ver. 6. They had been denying, excusing, maintaining their sin heretofore, anything but speaking aright about it; but now there is heard the right language of confession: " I have sinned." 4. *Practical turning from the evil way.* As before each had turned determinedly to his own self-chosen course (ver. 6), now they would turn from it. Such is the way of the backslider's return and restoration, a way up which there is no smooth easy sliding as there was down, but in which every step has to be firmly made and resolutely kept to—a way difficult indeed, but, blessed be God, not impossible.

V. THEIR COUNSEL. Let each wanderer from God ask himself the question, " What have I done?" 1. Such inquiry can do no harm; and: 2. Is likely to be of great advantage. 3. The time for such inquiry is lessening day by day. 4. " It is a fearful thing " for an unforgiven man " to fall into the hands of the living God."—C.

Ver. 6.—*The way home.* The text suggests much concerning this way from the far country of sin to the home of our Father and God. The Lord is here lamenting that none of the people of Jerusalem were walking in it. Note—

I. THE STAGES OF THE WAY. 1. *Realization of the ruin wrought by our sin.* The soul is represented as contemplating this ruin, and asking, " What have I done?" This is the first stage. 2. *Repentance.* Each one is to repent of " his wickedness." We are not to lose ourselves in a general confession of sin, as too many do, but to think of our own sin apart from that of other people, and to think of what is especially *our* sin. Thus personal and particular, our repentance is the more likely to be genuine and godly. 3. *Confession.* " These that have sinned, these and these only speak aright when they speak of repenting, and it is sad when they who have so much work for repentance do not say a word of repenting." But confession is this " speaking aright " which God desires to hear from us. Now, this confession is so acceptable to God because it glorifies his holiness and his love. His *holiness;* for the sinner has come to see sin as God sees it, and hence to hate and abhor it. He is of one mind with God about it as he never was before. And his *love;* for confession casts itself in faith upon a love that is deeper than its sin. Deep as is God's abhorrence of sin, the sinner in confession appeals to and lays hold on a love that is deeper still. Hence, when the sinner makes his sincere confession before God, he is at once right out of " the far country," and home in the heart of God. The robe, the ring, the shoes, are put upon him; the feast is prepared, and the merry-making, the joy in the presence of the angels of God, at once begins.

II. THE ATTENTIVE OBSERVER OF THOSE WHO TRAVEL BY THIS WAY. It is God who is represented as bending down his ear, hearkening to what is said, listening for any words of confession, and ready to hear them if spoken. The text is the language of gracious expectation and desire on the part of God. It calls to mind the father's waiting for the prodigal's return. How often had he looked with longing, loving gaze down the road along which his returning son must come, if ever indeed he would come! He had looked so often that a speck in the far distance would at once be discerned by him. Hence, " when a great way off," the father saw him. And so here God is represented as thus waiting for his guilty people's return. And how much there is to confirm our faith in this Divine solicitude for the sinner's salvation! Look at the very *constitution of our nature.* That, as Bishop Butler has shown, is evidently on the side of virtue, that is, of obedience to God, and against the disobedient. "Who will harm you, if ye be doers of that which is good?"—thus the apostle appeals to the universally recognized fact, that the constitution of man's nature is such as to favour the good. And, on the other hand, the declaration that "the way of transgressors is hard," is based on another like fact of universal experience. Such is one evidence of "the care" with which, as George Herbert sings, "Lord, with what care thou hast begirt us round!" Then *the revelation of his truth* is yet further in evidence. That truth, as ministered to us by the written Word or by the lips of prophets, apostles, pastors, teachers—it matters not—is a perpetual proof of the Divine solicitude for our eternal good. And *his providence,* making it to be well with the righteous and ill with the unrighteous. Well and ill with each respectively in mind, body, and estate. And *his Spirit.* That Spirit speaking to us in conscience and in the powerful pleadings of his grace in our hearts, of which we are all so often conscious. And, last of all, God has shown us this loving care of his for us in *his Son.* He has shown himself in a manner adapted to touch and move all hearts, and to draw all men unto him. Now, all this mass of evidence is in keeping with that solicitude which this verse and so many other portions of God's Word reveal as felt by him towards sinful men. And if it be asked "What moves this solicitude?" the character of God furnishes the answer. The *holiness* of God. "Good and upright is the Lord, therefore will he teach sinners in the way." And we are bidden "Give thanks at the remembrance of his holiness." It is the nature of holiness to be distressed at all that contradicts it and is unlike itself. It rests not until it has assimilated all around it to itself. Here, then, is one reason of God's perpetual appeals to sinful men. His *wisdom* also. It is the characteristic of God's wisdom to adjust means to ends. How wonderfully and beautifully this is seen in all departments of nature! But for the fulfilling of the high purposes of his grace, what instrument can he find more fit than the regenerated, redeemed soul? Even now and here we see this. A soul aglow with love and faith towards God, what will not that soul do for God? Hence to the principalities and powers in heaven shall be made known by the one Church—the company of the redeemed shall evidence it—the manifold wisdom of God. His *love* also. If the beholding of scenes of distress touch our hearts and make us eager to render help, can we imagine that he who made us is less willing than ourselves to show pity and render help? Our Lord's argument is, "If ye, evil though ye be, know how"—and we do know how—"to give good gifts to your children, how much more will your heavenly Father give," etc.? Humanity, as it has been well said, is the heavenly Father's sick child. Will not the Father's love, therefore, be all the more called forth to that child? And his *compassion* also. For this life is the critical period of that child's malady. It is the time when the great question of its life or death is being determined. Terrible forces are against it, and the struggle is now at its most momentous hour. This fact would cause the Father's love to go forth, as it has gone and is going forth, in active compassion, in open manifestation of its solicitude. Such are some of the considerations which lead to our Father's attentive observance of all those who travel by this homeward way.

III. THE END OF THE WAY. They who come there will find restoration to the Father's love, the implantation of a new nature, the complete pardon of the past, power to live as God's dear child for the future, and ultimately the everlasting dwelling in the very presence and home of God.

IV. BROOKS BY THE WAY. It is said, "He shall drink of the brook by the way, therefore shall he lift up the head." We may apply these words to the travellers in the way we are speaking of; for they need, in the weary and often most difficult journey, the refreshments which God alone can supply. Such aids are given in the promises of God, the fellowship of God, the communion of fellow-travellers on the way, and in the service and worship of God.

V. THE SOLITARINESS OF THE WAY. It is but "here and there a traveller" that is found. The way is not thronged. This verse is God's lament that scarce any are found willing to go along this road; for it is not the way of worldly advantage. They who "are given to covetousness" (ver. 10) will never choose this way. They have persuaded themselves that they are as well off and better where they are. They are deceived, and, what is worse, are willing to be deceived : "They hold fast deceit, and so refuse to return." We should have thought that surely it would be otherwise. 1. *Reason* bids them return (ver. 4). If a man have fallen, he will not lie content on the earth, but will arise. If in an ordinary journey he have missed his way, he will at once retrace his steps. Reason rules in such cases, but not here. 2. *Conscience* bids them return. They could not but know that their sin had done them sore harm ; but none of them asked, " What have I done?" however loudly conscience might summon them to such repentance. 3. *God's Word* bade then return (ver. 8), but lo! certainly in vain he made it. 4. *Providence* bade them. The events that had taken place were all admonitions of God; but though the birds of the air marked and obeyed the providence of God, sinful man " knew not the judgment of the Lord " (ver. 7). Hence the way is solitary.

CONCLUSION. But the question for us is, "Are *we* in this way?" Let us bless God if we are, and press on therein. Let us note how short the day is in which we can travel, how its few fleeting hours are lessening, lest when we would start on the way we have to exclaim (ch. vi. 4), " Woe unto us! for the day goeth away, for the shadows of the evening are stretched out."—C.

Ver. 18—ch. ix. 1.—*The prophet's grievous lament.* I. ITS GRIEVOUSNESS. (Vers. 18, 21, ch. ix. 1.) Ver. 18, " When I would comfort myself," etc. All hope dies down, is crushed beneath the overwhelming evidence of the hopelessness of his people's condition. Ver. 21 : he is as if wounded, his heart is clad in the garb of deepest woe, the black raiment of the mourner. Ch. ix. 1 : he has exhausted his power of telling forth his deep grief, his eyes refuse to weep more, though his heart be sore pierced, and the troubles of his people are unrelieved. Therefore he desires that he might weep continually.

II. ITS GROUNDS. 1. *They were still trusting in lying words* (ver. 19), reckoning that, because the temple of Jehovah and the throne of David belonged to them, therefore they should have been secure. Though in distant lands, in actual captivity—for there the prophet contemplates them—they were still imagining that the possession of the temple and David's throne should have been their sure safeguard. It is terrible to see God's judgments coming upon guilty men, but when these judgments themselves seem to fail in teaching the needed lesson, that is a greater sorrow still. 2. *The time of redemption was over.* (Ver. 20.) The long harvest days, the bright summer weather— symbols of all days of opportunity—these were gone. The days when they might have turned to God and found deliverance, " the wrath of God had arisen against them, and there was no remedy." But what a retrospect is his who has to say as did lost Israel, " The harvest is past," etc.! For: (1) Such seasons remind us of our privileges and obligations. (*a*) It is a time of fruitfulness, of great privilege, grace, and goodness. God makes man's cup to overflow. Youth and days of gospel privilege. Sundays, sacred services, etc. (*b*) It should be a time of great activity. The natural harvest and summer-time is so. For: (*c*) It is a season of such limited duration. (2) But men often let these times pass away unimproved. (*a*) The world hinders them. (*b*) Perversion of Scripture truths. (*c*) Belief that they are well enough as they are. (*d*) Procrastination. (3) But once gone, the fruits of that summer and that harvest can never be saved. Such facts as these open the floodgates of grief in hearts like that of Jeremiah. 3. He could see no means of restoration or recovery whatsoever (ver. 22), no balm and no physician anywhere.

III. ITS WORD TO ALL WHO SHOULD KNOW OR ARE THE CAUSES OF SUCH GRIEF NOW. 1. Christ's servants should be in sympathy with the prophet's lament. It is because *we* are so indifferent the world is so. " Si vis me flere flendum est," it is ever saying, but in vain, to the professing Church. Oh for the compassion of Jeremiah and yet more of Christ! If we sowed in tears we should reap in joy. If so we went forth " bearing precious seed, we shall doubtless come again rejoicing, bringing," etc. 2. But you who cause such grief, think you not that if such be the result of anticipating God's judgments upon sin, the enduring of them must be far worse? And that is your part in them. Christ himself assured the weeping women who followed him to Calvary that the woes of them who crucified him would be worse than his own. " If they do these things in a green tree, what shall be done in the dry ? "

CONCLUSION. Then, instead of causing sorrow to the faithful servants of God by resisting their appeals, yield to them, and so gladden these servants, and the angels of God, and the heart of God, and the Son of God. So you yourself shall "enter into the joy of your Lord."—C.

Ver. 22.—*Christ and the Holy Ghost realities after all.* "Is there no balm in Gilead?" etc. One of the commonest taunts of ungodly men—and it has been so in all ages—against the believer in God and in his redeeming grace, has been their apparent utter absence amongst such vast multitudes of people for so many centuries, and this though the conditions were such as needed, and that in most distressing manner, both their presence and their power. And one of the subtlest and saddest temptations to which the human mind is subject is that of doubting the grace of God. "My tears have been my meat day and night, while they continually say unto me, Where is now thy God?" The taunt of the psalmist's enemies had roused up the demon of doubt concerning God and his love, and no wonder, then, that the psalmist's tears flowed fast both day and night. Now, the text is one of those sad questionings to which the force of distressing facts will now and again give rise. It contains three questions, and we will note concerning them these three things—their meaning, their occasions, their answers.

I. THEIR MEANING. And take: 1. The *literal meaning* of the balm and the physician about which the prophet so mournfully inquires. Balm was a resinous gum which flowed from the side of a tree or shrub found on the sunny slopes of Mount Gilead, and counted very precious. When Jacob would counsel his sons how they might propitiate Joseph, who held their brother in captivity, he told them to take him a present of "a little balm" (Gen. xliii. 11). It was an article of merchandise (Gen. xxxvii. 25), regarded as of invaluable efficacy in medicine (cf. ch. xlvi. 11; li. 8). Its name was derived from a word which told of the manner in which it was procured from the tree that bore it. The side of the tree was pierced, and the precious balm then flowed forth. The physicians of the day constantly made use of it, and had studied the best means of applying it. But it is evident that the prophet is speaking under a figure. Note, then: 2. The *metaphorical meaning.* He speaks of the lost "health of the daughter of my people," and means by that the national ruin which was so fast coming on Judah and Jerusalem—ruin of all kinds, spiritual, moral, temporal. By the "balm" he means some method of recovery for his people, and by the "physician" some skilled, sagacious, powerful deliverer, who should be able to employ these methods and so save the land. The prophet was in despair about this; he saw no hope nor help anywhere, and hence the piteous cry, the mournful question of our text. To every one who professed to have found the balm and the physician the ruined land so needed, he addressed the unanswerable question, "Why then is not the health," etc.? 3. *Their evangelic import.* It has all along been seen that the terms used here were capable of such application. The "balm" is a beautiful symbol of Christ. The Mount Gilead, the tree, the pierced side, the stream thence issuing, and its mighty healing power,—these severally send our thoughts to Mount Calvary, the cross, the pierced side of the Saviour, the precious blood, and the unquestionable spiritual healing might there is therein. And Scripture is ever speaking of sin as a disease; of man as one whose health needs recovery. The analogies are obvious. And the "physician," who is he but that Divine Spirit whose office it is to take of the things of Christ and show them unto men? He so shows to us the meaning and intent of our Saviour's sacrificial death, that "by his stripes we are healed." Yes; whilst we all are the stricken with mortal disease, Christ is the Balm that surely heals, and the blessed Spirit is he who reveals Christ to the soul. "For no man can say that Jesus is Lord"—that is, in all the full meaning of those words, and with sincere intent—"but by the Holy Ghost."

II. THEIR OCCASIONS. What led to these questions being asked by the prophet? and what tends to their being asked still? 1. By *the prophet.* The ruin of his land and people. The awful calamities that were at that moment overhanging the doomed nation. But: 2. By *men still.* It is the contemplation of the threefold fact of sin, sorrow, and death. (1) *Of sin.* Think of the myriads of mankind who have lived and died on this earth of ours, and all of them unblessed by the light of the gospel. Think of the rampant wickedness, the hideous vice, the festering corruption, the indescribable moral pollution that characterizes vast masses of mankind, indeed *the* mass of mankind. And think of the corruption of Christianity: what a veneer of religion! what a counterfeit of godliness! what a hollow mockery so great part of it is! And coming closer home, the saddened contemplator of the ravages of sin may turn his gaze inward into his own heart, and as he reflects on the slender hold which Divine and holy principles have upon him—

> "What scanty triumphs grace has won,
> The broken vow, the frequent fall;"

and as he cries out at times almost in despair at seeing the strength of the chains by which his soul is bound, "O wretched man that I am!" etc.,—the words of our text fit in with his mournful mood. It seemed to him as if there were "no balm in Gilead, no," etc. (2) *Of sorrow.* To St. Paul, as he penned the eighth chapter of the Epistle to the Romans, the whole creation seemed to "groan and travail together in pain." What is the progress of mankind but one long procession of mourners! Oh, the tears and sorrows of the broken-hearted, the helpless, the desolate and afflicted of all ages and of all lands! What a catalogue do they fill! The mind reels as it contemplates the dark mass of human woe. Its faith in the Divine Fatherhood staggers as if smitten with a deadly blow, and is half forced to the conclusion, which to a sad and an increasing number seems self-evident, that there is *no* balm in Gilead, *no* physician there. (3) And the *reign of death* produces similar feelings. As men see how the king of terrors stalks triumphantly through the land, how ruthless is his tyranny, how crushing his power, how dark the grave into which we so soon descend, and how helpless we all are against his might, it does seem at times as if there were no deliverer and no deliverance. But note—

III. THE ANSWERS TO THESE QUESTIONS. 1. *To those which inquire, " Is there no balm . . . physician there?"* some answer "No." Sin, they say, is a mistake which education will rectify, and the operations of the great law of evolution will gradually eliminate. In fact, there is no such thing as "sin" in the sense religious people think. Therefore, whilst for the race there is hope, for the present and past generations there is none. Sorrow, also, they teach, is the result of ignorance of natural laws or of disregard of them. The progress of knowledge will gradually lessen it; that is all that can be said. And as to death, that, of course, is the inevitable, and ends all. The only immortality is in the influence which a man exerts in those who come after him. As to "the Resurrection and the life"—*credat Judæus.* Such is the dismal gospel of this nineteenth century. But the Christian reply to these questions is unhesitatingly, "Yes; there is a Balm and a Physician for the sin-stricken soul, whether of the individual or of the whole human race. And for the heart riven with sorrow, broken with grief. And for all those, too, over whom Death has reigned with such cruel power. Because we believe in Christ and in the Holy Ghost, we believe in the 'Balm' and in the 'Physician' humanity needs." But then comes: 2. *The last and seemingly unanswerable question.* "Why then is not," etc.? What are we to reply to this? (1) For one large part of those whom it concerns, the sin, sorrow, and death ridden multitudes, *we deny* that which the question assumes. For the Balm and the Physician have done or are doing their blessed work on them. We appeal to the throng of the redeemed, the blessed dead, myriads of whom are now with God.

> "White-robed saints in glory,
> Cleansed from every stain."

With the eye of faith we behold them, and we believe in their existence as we believe in our own, and the yearning of our hearts is to be with them. And *they* are a great cloud of witnesses to the Balm and to the Physician both. But—as unbelievers will demand clamorously that we should do—we come down to this world and this life that now is. Well, then, we appeal to the fact that there *are* regenerated, renewed, saintly souls living here on earth to-day, walking in purity, integrity, and in the light and love of God. *They* are God's witnesses to what the unbeliever denies. Furthermore, there are a vast number in whom this process of healing *is going on.* Slowly, it may be, and with sad retrogressions at times, but really, notwithstanding. The tide is

a long, long time coming in, but it does come in. Healing is always a gradual work.
" Nemo repente fuit ' sanctissimus,'" any more than " turpissimus." A man cannot
leap into heaven, as, thank God, he cannot leap into hell. But because healing is only
gradual, do we deny its existence? But we know there are vast multitudes more to be
accounted for than those we have as yet told of. (2) Therefore for this part we say
concerning them, *wait.* St. Paul had evidently pondered this problem, and he has
taught us that there are due times and seasons appointed in the wisdom of God for
the manifestation of Christ to men (cf. 1 Tim. ii. 6; Eph. i. 8—10; Phil. ii. 9;
Col. i. 20), but that in the " dispensation of the fulness of times " it is God's " good
pleasure " to " gather together all things in Christ," all the living and all the dead.
And it is impossible not to see how the heart of the holy apostle exults in the beatific
vision, the " breadth, and length, and depth, and height " of the glorious completed
living temple of the Lord God. Therefore, in view of revelations like these, we say
that before the reality of the work of Christ and the Holy Ghost are denied, we are
bound to *wait.* And if it be objected that the waiting has been and may be for so
long, we reply that it is because men *will* not come unto Christ that they might have
life. The remedy of redemption is not forced upon any soul. A man's soul is not
saved by his will being crushed, by his ceasing to be a man and becoming a machine.
We cannot but believe and know—the individual conversion of every true child of
God demonstrates it—that God has ways and means to bring " the unruly wills of
sinful men " into accord with his own, and this in perfect harmony with the moral
freedom he has given man. How long and how dreadfully far the human will may
go in resisting God we cannot tell, but we may not believe that it is greater than God
himself and can exhaust all the Divine resources. The hunger and misery of the
prodigal brought him " to himself," the consuming fire of the dread captivity which
Jeremiah is foretelling burnt out for ever the love of idolatry amongst Israel; and there
are other like fires of God's holy love which may have like results. Therefore, we
say, that until—if we may so speak—God has thrown up the case of sin and sorrow
stricken humanity, we have no right to affirm that there is " no balm in Gilead," etc.
In regard to *sorrow,* that has a ministry of spiritual healing of its own, which has
gone on ever since " the Man of sorrows " became " acquainted with grief." As his
messenger, Grief has gone about from house to house, from heart to heart, a veritable
sister of mercy, though clad in coarse and unlovely garb. Up and down the streets of
this weary world, and in and out every one of its homes, she perpetually goes; but no
one ever meets her in the new Jerusalem, in the city of our God, for her ministry is
not needed there. Then as to *death,* we say that in all the drear, dark, hopeless power
of it " Christ *has* abolished death." We can, and by every graveside we do—challenge
death as to its sting, and the grave as to its victory. Therefore we say, and with glad
hearts, that the health of the daughter of the people is recovered, or is recovering, for
that there is both Balm in Gilead and a Physician there.

CONCLUSION. But whilst we bid the unbeliever wait ere he pronounce with certainty
that there is neither Balm nor Physician, we would earnestly and affectionately beseech
him not to wait ere he has recourse to them. Disease does not become easier to cure
by being allowed to go on unchecked. It only gives the physician far more trouble,
and the patient far more pain. And the analogy holds good in regard to the disease of
sin. Come, then, to Christ now.—C.

Ver. 22.—*The balm of Gilead.* There were those who treated the crimes and
miseries of the nation as a trifling matter; they sought to " heal the hurt slightly, saying,
Peace, peace; when there was no peace " (ver. 11). Not so the prophet. He is
keenly alive to the dreadful evils of the time. He takes the sins and sorrows of the
people on himself, makes them his own. Tender human sympathy, as well as Divine
compassion, breathes in the words, " For the hurt of the daughter of my people am I
hurt." And it is not sorrow alone but " astonishment " of which he is conscious.
" Why is not her health recovered ? " Can it be that there is no remedy ? The "balm
of Gilead " is taken as the symbol of a healing moral power. Is it so, then, that the
very nation that was called to diffuse a redeeming influence over all the world is
unable to cure herself—has no medicine for her own diseases, or none to apply it ?
Such is the wonder with which a thoughtful, earnest spirit will often contemplate the

moral condition of the world, in view of the fact that God's "saving health" in the gospel has so long been made known to it. Consider—

I. THE DIVINE REMEDY FOR THE MORAL MALADIES OF THE HUMAN RACE. This remedy is the spontaneous fruit of the love of God. On the ground of that love we may justly expect such a remedy. It is not likely that a God of infinite benevolence would leave the human race to perish. Though redemption is "of grace," yet there is everything to make it antecedently probable. Though nature contains no revelation of it, yet to the eye on which the light of the gospel has once fallen, the whole constitution of the universe is full of dim prophecies and promises of some such triumphant grace. The spirit of boundless beneficence that pervades and governs it—the fact that for every want there is a supply, for every appetite that which gratifies it, for every danger a safeguard, for every poison its antidote; above all, the silent witness in favour of mercy that is graven more or less deep on every human heart;—all this is so much in harmony with the great redemption as in a sense to anticipate it. But it is facts, not probabilities, with which we have to deal. The gospel is God's actual answer to our human necessities, the sovereign remedy his love has provided for the sins and sorrows of the world. He heals them by *taking them upon himself* in the person of Jesus Christ his Son. "He was wounded for our transgressions," etc. (Isa. liii. 5); "Who his own self bare our sins," etc. (1 Pet. ii. 24); "Where sin abounded, grace did much more abound," etc. (Rom. v. 20, 21). Note respecting this Divine remedy: 1. *It goes to the root of the disease.* It does not effect a mere superficial reformation, as human methods for the most part do; does not flatter with the appearance of health while leaving the malady to strike its roots down deeper and deeper into the soul. It reaches at once the secret springs of all mischief, destroys the germs of evil in human nature, changes the outward aspects of the world's life by giving it a "new heart." 2. *It is universal in its application.* All national diversities, all varieties of social condition, of age, of culture, of intellectual development and moral life, etc., are alike open to its application, and it is the same for all. 3. *It is complete in its efficacy.* Every element of human nature, every department and phase of human life, bears witness to its healing power. A perfect manhood and a perfect social order are the issue it works out. 4. *It stands alone,* not one among many, but absolutely the only remedy. It enters into no kind of competition with other methods of healing. It has the solitary and supreme authority of that which is Divine. "Neither is there salvation in any other: for there is none other name," etc. (Acts iv. 12).

II. THE HINDRANCES TO ITS UNIVERSAL EFFICIENCY. "Why then is not," etc.? The reason lies, not in any want of fitness in the remedy, or in any lack of power or willingness in him who provides it, but in certain human conditions that nullify its action and thwart his purpose. 1. *In the self-delusion that leads men to think that they have no need of cure.* "They that are whole need not a physician," etc. (Matt. ix. 12). The sense of moral sickness is the first step to healing. 2. *In the vain self-trust by virtue of which men dream that they can cure themselves.* How many and how plausible are the expedients by which the world seeks to rid itself of its own maladies! How slow is human nature to confess its helplessness! 3. *In the obstinacy of spirit that refuses the Divine method.* "Are not Abana and Pharpar, rivers of Damascus, better than all the waters of Israel?" etc. (2 Kings v. 12). Anything rather than God's way of healing by the blood of atonement and the regenerating grace of the Spirit! 4. *In the lethargy and neglect of those whom God has called to minister the healing power.* Who shall say how much of the continued sin and misery of the world lies at the Church's door? If all who have themselves known the virtue of this sovereign balm were but more thoroughly in earnest in their efforts to commend it and to persuade men to apply it, how much more rapidly would the health of human society everywhere be recovered!—W.

Vers. 1, 2.—*The bones of the dead idolaters cast out before their cities.* I. ASK HOW THIS SPOLIATION COMES TO PASS. One cannot suppose that it came by the *intention* of Jehovah. Rather would it arise as a necessary part of wholesale pillage. Considerable treasures might be lying in the tombs of these grandees of Israel, and much might also have been hidden in them for purposes of safety, and therefore, seeing that this hideous devastation had to happen, it was fitting to call attention to it beforehand. It was another indication of how completely, for its sins, Jerusalem had been handed over to the foreign destroyer. It makes all the difference to mention such a terrible circumstance beforehand, as an illustration of the severity of God's dealings. Thus it is seen that the spoliation cannot be laid to his charge. And though it must be taken as a sign how barbarous the ancient civilization was at bottom, this is but a consideration by the way. The real cause of this hideous spectacle was in the idolatry of those who had covenanted to love and serve Jehovah, to walk after him and seek him and worship him. These dead ones had forsaken God and taught their posterity to forsake him also; and now there was none among the living able to protect the bones of the dead from such horrible insult.

II. OBSERVE THAT THE HUMILIATION HAS A PECULIAR CONNECTION WITH THE IDOLATRY OF THE PEOPLE. Not only are the tombs emptied, but the bones are scattered before the host of heaven. The enemy was not thinking of this exhibition, but it happened so very opportunely. Sun, moon, and stars looked down upon the scene thus strewn with the bones of the illustrious, as if in rebuke for the use which Israel had tried to make of them. They had worshipped and served the creature in opposition to the Creator, and this was what had come of it. These bones had strengthened the living body to worship the sun, and now the sun shone steadily down on them, as if in public rejection of what was not only a mistaken honour to the creature but a shameful insult to the Creator. The very things we misuse become the instruments of our humiliation.

III. THE GENERAL QUESTION OF THE TREATMENT OF DEAD BODIES IS SUGGESTED FOR CONSIDERATION. Various are the customs of men with respect to the treatment of the dead, but many of them have one common element, in that they try to preserve the visible, tangible relics of life as long as possible. There is something very touching in the hopes and beliefs which are represented by an Egyptian mummy, as if the survivors felt that life had receded into some deep, inscrutable chamber, again to come forth in due time and reanimate its old tenement. We think of how Joseph must have been under the influence of a feeling of this kind, when he gave such strict commandment concerning his bones. Still, it is part of the salvation wherewith Christ saves his people, that we are lifted above these haunting considerations as to the corporeal frame. It is according to the Spirit of Christ that we should labour, by exercise and self-denial, to make the living body an efficient agent of his will; but when the life has gone, no sentimental treatment of ours can alter the fact that the body is mere matter, fast under the chemical laws which will soon resolve it into its constituent elements. Have not the bodies of God's saints been shamefully maltreated, both during life and after death? Think out of what a mangled and bleeding form the spirit of Stephen took its flight to everlasting bliss. If there be force in the injunction of Jesus not to fear what men can do to the sentient body, how much more may it be urged not to fear what they can do to the senseless corpse. The enemies of the noble and fearless witnesses of truth have shown more than once their contemptible spirit by the way in which they have treated the dead. They could not get at them when living, and they thought it was something of a triumph to insult their remains when gone; e.g. Wycliffe and Cromwell. The scattering of these bones before sun, moon, and stars would have been a thing to glory in, if the men to whom they belonged had been soldiers in the noble army of martyrs.—Y.

Ver. 3.—*A pitiable condition: death preferable to life.* I. REMEMBER MAN'S NATURAL DREAD OF DEATH. The very force of the prophet's expression here lies in this, that it contradicts the habitual feelings of the human breast. The natural preference is to choose life rather than death; nay, it can hardly be called preference at all. There is an instinctive prompting to ward off everything that may be fatal. Whatever the drawbacks and pains of life may be, life is chosen rather than death. In most instances the suicide is held not responsible for the state of his mind at the time. We must all die indeed; yet death is so alien to every predominating feeling of the mind when in health and prosperous circumstances, that even when death comes near others, it is viewed as if it had little or nothing to do with us. And so when Jeremiah's word came to these people in Jerusalem, they, at least the young and the strong among them, would receive it very incredulously. That things should ever become so bad as to make death desirable would seem to them to show that the threatener of such a doom was overdoing his warnings.

II. LIFE MAY BECOME SO FULL OF PAIN AND MISERY THAT THIS NATURAL DREAD MAY BE REVERSED. When the blow was struck and Jerusalem fell into the hands of the hosts from Babylon, thousands would be thankful that, amid so much destruction, their lives were spared. To lose possessions and go into exile would seem a light price to pay for the preservation of life. But with the increased experience of exile itself its dreadfulness became manifest. How could it be otherwise? The captivity and exile were not of an ordinary nation, but of one whose God was Jehovah. These people had been in the enjoyment of peculiar privileges and satisfactions, which they had come to accept as a matter of course; and when they lost them, they would then discern, if never before, something of their true value. It was out of a land of promise, a land reserved for the people of God, that they had been cast, and no lapse of time could content them to be as other nations. It is just because man has within him such capabilities for enjoying life that he can be driven to the other extreme of desiring death. Life could not be so blessed as Christ holds out the hope of its being, unless there were also the possibility of its being correspondingly wretched.

III. It is thus suggested that we should aim at reaching a state of mind such that EITHER LIFE OR DEATH SHOULD BE EQUALLY ACCEPTABLE. To *prefer* life to death is a natural feeling, but certainly not the feeling which a believer in God and Jesus should have. And to prefer death to life is the feeling which comes after a time of struggling, weariness, pain, and disappointment; but what darkness of the mind does this not prove! what inability to profit by the light which shines in Christ! The Christian medium lies between the two extremes. Not to wish to live, nor to wish to die, but to be in Christ's hands, so that as long as we are living there may be an availing of every opportunity of service, and when we die a fresh proof that faith in the Saviour who also died, but rose again, is no deluding vanity. It is one of the glorious aspects of Christ's salvation that he can save men from crying out for death rather than life, just because he can lift them into an experience of joy and peace which overbear the sense of temporal pain and loss.—Y.

Vers. 4—7.—*The unnatural conduct of Jerusalem.* Still more humiliation for the proud, self-satisfied city. The prophet comes with a heavenly light, revealing the very foundations of her glory, and showing how unsubstantial they are, how easily exposed as contradicting truth and the highest propriety. What is aimed at here is to set before man, by the force of contrast, what he ought to be, in the sum of all his faculties made one by a will which acts according to the commandment of God. And so we see—

I. A LESSON FROM THE SUBORDINATE PART OF MAN'S NATURE. If a man falls, he instantly attempts to rise again. Even if there is some serious injury, it is commonly discovered by the failure of the man's attempt to rise; and so from the subordinate part of our nature there is a rebuke to the higher and governing part. A very striking instance of such a rebuke would be given in the falling of a drunken man to the ground. He staggers to his feet again if he can. If he remains on the ground it is a sign, to use the common expression, that " he is very far gone indeed; " and in such an instance may we not truly say that the body is rebuking the will for its imbecility and its base slavery to appetite? So if a man is going anywhere, and turns unwittingly from the straight path; such a turning may be made very easily, and the wrong path be kept in for a while, but presently there will be some sign to show the error, and with more or less delay there will be a return to the right path. Here, then, are two instances, level with the experience of everybody, of what is natural for man to do, viz. come back from a wrong state as soon as ever he can; and if the position be only looked at truly, it will be seen that it is as unnatural for a man to remain in spiritual degradation as to continue lying on the ground.

II. A LESSON FROM THAT PART OF THE CREATION WHICH IS SUBJECTED TO MAN. There is the horse. He can be so trained as to become a potent force in the battle-field, and if he becomes uncontrollable and rushes hither and thither, as dangerous to friend as to foe, it is not because of any rebellious purpose, but a brief madness has seized on him. Let a few hours pass, and he may be submissive and serviceable as before. " We put bits in the horses' mouths, that they may obey us; and we turn about their whole body."

" The ox knoweth his owner, and the ass his master's crib : but Israel doth not know, my people doth not consider." The very birds of the air, seemingly so free from all restraint, come and go according to certain laws. If the beasts which man has tamed to his use, and on which he daily depends, were to treat *him* as *he* treats *God*, what an awkward, nay more, what a perilous scene this world would become! The whole visible universe, ground beneath, air around, and far away into the immensities of space, are crowded with admonitions to perversely disobedient man. These birds mentioned here, by certain wondrous intimations to which they are ever heedful—exceptions only going to prove the rule—help to carry on the government of God. They are faithful to their nature, and their faithfulness is again but a sign of God's own faithfulness in the orderliness of the seasons. Then go beyond the ordinary subjection of God's creation to his will. Look at what we call " miracles." Think of the passage of the Red Sea, the speaking of Balaam's ass, the obedience of the fish in the Sea of Galilee to the will of Jesus, the storm becoming a calm, the venomous serpent dropping innocuous from the hand of Paul. What rebukes these are to man, who persists in walking in his own way! Man himself proceeds with all confidence in the training of brute beasts. He takes the colt and the puppy, and makes them abundantly useful. He is pretty sure how they will turn out. The trouble he takes with them is rewarded in the end. But with regard to his own child, though he has watched over it far more carefully than any of his beasts, he may be bitterly disappointed. His training may be mocked, as it were, and put to shame—and so, rising from the human parent to the thought of God in heaven, we see Israel similarly perverse, negligent of all that has been done to make right ways for it and keep it in them.—Y.

Vers. 8—12.—*The exposure of pseudo-wisdom.* I. THE CLAIM MADE. Those on whom Jeremiah presses his appeals for a change of purpose reply, if not by plain words, at all events by equally plain actions, that they are so wise in their own conceits as to need no guidance from an outsider. A profound belief in one's own insight and skill may of course be justified by results ; such a belief has been a very important factor in many great achievements. But it is also to be noticed that to have this belief without any corresponding reality is an evil which may afflict a man at every age of his life. It belongs to the young in their ignorance, and the old, with all their experience, may not be free from it. That experience, even though long, may have been a narrow one, and yet, with all its narrowness, full of blunders. But the recollection of all that should make such old men humble avails nothing to diminish the dogmatism of their advice to others. A certain official and social position is also a grand vantage-ground to air a reputation for wisdom. Nothing is then needed but an abundance of self-assertion to gain acknowledgment from the weak and the ignorant. These great men of Jerusalem would point scornfully at Jeremiah, the lonely prophet. Their city polish would perhaps be in strong contrast to the rustic airs of the man from Anathoth, and, as if to make their claim of wisdom more definite, they fell back on what seemed an unanswerable challenge. " Is not the Law of Jehovah with us ? " The meaning of this seemed to be that they could boast of a certain outward conformity with Mosaic institutions. They certainly did attend to the incense and the sweet cane, the burnt offerings and the sacrifices (ch. vi. 20). Moreover, what they asserted for themselves implied a correspondingly humiliating opinion of Jeremiah. They were wise, and of course he was a fool. They had the Law of Jehovah, and Jeremiah, in pretending to utter Jehovah's words, was of course nothing better than an impostor.

II. THE DIVINE WAY OF EXPOSING THIS CLAIM. These self-constituted wise men meet the prophet with a declaration as to what they think themselves to be. " We are wise men," they say, nor does the prophet throw back the shortest, directest answer that was possible. It would have been of no use to say, " You are fools." But it was of use to project himself into the future, and indicate what would happen to these boasters. When the homes of these pseudo-wise are broken up, and their wives and fields become the spoil of the conqueror, then it will be clear beyond a doubt where the wisdom is and where the folly. Folly will be condemned of her children, even as wisdom is justified of hers. Where now are the writings of these wise men ? Jeremiah said at the time that they were full of lies, and we may be sure that, like all reflections of popular fashion and prejudice, they passed very quickly out of vogue. " The Law of

Jehovah is with us," said these wise men; but it was a valueless connection, whereas the prophet had that Law written in his heart. Being in full sympathy with all that was right, and loving, and generous, and pure, he was a fit subject for the solemn impulses that came to him from on high, and thus he went forth to speak on themes immeasurably deeper than the passing phenomena of an age. And so it is that his words, despised and rejected at the time, nevertheless abide, and are felt to be very precious by all who lack wisdom. As we notice the arrogance of spurious wisdom here and also in such passages as John vii. 48 and 1 Cor. i. 22, we turn away to welcome that heavenly light which in the very shining of it proclaims its source to be entirely different from any earth-enkindled light. Our true wisdom in presence of the Law and the prophets, the Christ and the apostles, is to feel very deeply how ignorant, benighted, and astray we are without them. And there is true wisdom also in that power of the heart which enables us to discern between the false prophet and the true, the false Christ and the true. Such wisdom may be found in the heart of a little child or of a man on the common level of humanity, when it is utterly lacking among many who lead the world in temporal affairs. Full of darkness and duplicity must the minds of these leaders in Jerusalem have been when they lacked the power of seeing that Jeremiah, unpromising as his outward appearance might be, was indeed a prophet of God.—Y.

Ver. 17.—*The serpents which cannot be charmed.* I. THERE ARE SERPENTS WHICH CAN BE CHARMED. Serpent-charming must have been a not unfamiliar sight to the Israelites (see 'The Land and the Book,' pp. 154, 155). This means, taking the figure away, that there were many great and pressing evils which lay within human resources to mitigate, perhaps to remove. Thus when sore famine fell upon Canaan, Jacob found corn, though he had to send as far as Egypt. The resources thus employed are, no doubt, exceptional, and need peculiar skill and aptitude to discover and use them; but still—and this is the thing of importance here to remember—they are within the reach of the natural man. To say that necessity is the mother of invention is only another way of saying that there are serpents which can be charmed. Man stands upon the known and the achieved, that he may reach forward and win something more from the unknown. Not everybody can charm a serpent, but some can. So there are a few physicians, one here and another there, who have wonderful skill in the cure of special diseases. Part of the ills of human life can be swept away by wise and timely legislation. Epidemics may be restrained and made comparatively mild by cleanliness and attention to sanitary rules. Ills which in one age have been thought beyond remedy, in the next age are perfectly understood as to their causes and their cure.

II. THERE ARE SERPENTS WHICH CANNOT BE CHARMED. We may assume that it was so literally; that there were certain serpents which proved obdurate against every wile. And the danger of the serpent's bite would in such an instance become most dreadful, just from this very insensibility to everything in the shape of a charm. An enemy was to be brought on Israel whom no bribe, no promise, no art of persuasion whatever, could turn back. If he was to be turned back, it must be by main force or by Divine interposition. So we have to consider that, whatever ills we may succeed in neutralizing, there are others still left behind, unabated in their deadly efficiency by any resources we have in ourselves. It matters little that we can charm some serpents, if we cannot charm all. If there be left only one superior to our skill, that one is enough to ruin all. The most successful charmer among us will discover his match at last. He may charm poverty away, only to find, in a little while, *ennui* and possession without enjoyment. He may have the experience indicated in Prov. xxiii. 32: he may charm away, as he thinks, the peril of the wine-cup, and exult in assured mastery, only to discover at last that the foe with whom he has been trifling "bites like a serpent, and stings like an adder." So a man may achieve most of his purposes, charming away, as it were, obstacles on every side, only to find in the end that he cannot charm his conscience, that it will not be silent and sleep before the memory of much wrong-doing.

III. THERE ARE SERPENTS WHICH CAN BE MORE THAN CHARMED. There is much in the conjecture that the reference to the serpent here is suggested by the mention of Dan in the previous verse. Jacob's word for his son Dan was, "Dan shall be a serpent by the way, an adder in the path, that biteth the horse heels, so that his rider shall fall backwards" (Gen. xlix. 17). But we shall do wisely in considering the reference as having a deeper connection with the work of him who is the serpent from the beginning (Rev. xx. 2). All the painful serpent-bites of life, all the deadly ills, proceed from the brood which in some way or other originate with him. And thus thinking of him, the great dragon, the devil, the adversary, we must needs think of the correspondingly profound work of Jesus over against his work. *Jesus was a serpent-charmer;* and his efficacy as a charmer is most graciously manifested in the miracles which he wrought to remove physical defect, disease, and death. These miracles had in them something of the nature of a charm. They did not destroy the maleficent power, but they curbed it, made it for the time dormant and inoperative. But after having done all these miracles, Jesus is seen proceeding to a work which is more than that of the charmer. He who was lifted up to draw all men to him makes the victim of the serpent-bite impervious, for all future existence, to any further danger. The bite may come, in the sense of inflicting pain, but the peril is past. The serpent-poison becomes neutralized by the vigour and purity of that eternal life which is in Christ Jesus the Lord.—Y.

Ver. 20.—" *The life is more than the meat.*" After the subsidence of the Deluge, there was a promise given to Noah that, " while the earth remaineth, seed-time and harvest, . . . summer and winter, . . . shall not cease." Scanning the surface of the Scripture narrative, it appears as if this promise had not been kept, seeing there is a record of several notable and protracted famines; and moreover, we have only too good reason to suppose that millions in the successive ages of the world have perished from famine. We must hold, however, to God's promise having been kept in the spirit of it; its non-fulfilment, so far as human experience is concerned, must arise from some other cause than the unfaithfulness of God. An inquiry into these painful experiences is suggested by the utterance of this verse. The meaning seems to be that harvest and summer, the annual gathering of the corn and the wine and the oil, have nevertheless, in some way or other, left the people who should have profited by them, unprovided for. The words may be applied in two ways. 1. *When there is an actual gathering of harvest.* There may be an abundance, even a superabundance, of the fruits of the earth, and yet those who sowed and planted, watched and watered, may not get the slightest benefit. Now, not to get the expected benefit from these things means, if not destruction of life, at least a considerable impairment of it; for natural life depends upon them. And ch. v. 15—24 casts no small light on this state of things. There the mighty men from the north are spoken of, and Israel is addressed as follows :—" They shall eat up thine harvest, and thy bread, which thy sons and thy daughters should eat : . . . they shall eat up thy vines and thy fig trees." Strangers pluck the rich fruit of the husbandman's toil, and he himself is trampled into privation, reduced to the bare subsistence of a slave taken in war. Thus we see how God may lay before a man that which through the sin and folly of the recipient he may not be able to use. Think of the prosperous man in the parable, who had such abundant crops that he must needs build bigger barns, and yet in the very day of his pride was taken away. What is wealth unless God, in the prosecution of his own wise purposes, chooses to give security in the possession of that wealth ? 2. *When the harvest itself fails.* The harvest season may pass and the summer close, only to leave men with empty garners, in hunger and despair. Whither shall they turn, when drought, blasting, and mildew, palmerworm and locust, cankerworm and caterpillar, have done their work? Then it is that " those who are slain with the sword are better than those who are slain with hunger, for these pine away, stricken through for want of the fruits of the field " (Lam. iv. 9). Thus, whether the harvest be given or withheld, the practical result is the same. The people are not saved. God may bring the harvest to a complete and beautiful maturity, may, so to speak, save the harvest—and " save the harvest " is not an unfamiliar expression to those who are engaged in the vicissitudes of agriculture—only to teach thereby a more impressive lesson to the people who live so that they cannot be kept safe. What force there is in the expression of this verse if we take it to mean, " The corn is saved; the vintage is saved; the olives are saved ; all the pleasant fruits of the land are saved; but *we are not saved* "! The life is more than the bodily nourishment, and when men will not take heed to *the higher things* which belong to *the life,* it is just what might be expected that they should have disappointments in *the lower things* which belong to *the nourish-*

ment. The true material wealth of every land, when we get at the substance of it, lies in what its soil produces ; and when men boast, as they are apt to do, that their own land has gotten them their wealth, it is needful that Jehovah should show them how completely he controls the roots and fruits of everything that he has made to grow for human food. No wonder evil comes to those who do not say in their hearts, " Let us now fear Jehovah our God, that giveth rain, both the former and the latter, in his season : he reserveth unto us the appointed weeks of the harvest " (ch. v. 24). Malachi puts into striking words the fundamental reason for the sore complaint we have been considering, and the way in which it may be brought to cease (ch. iii. 9—11).—Y.

Vers. 21, 22.—*Why the hurt of Israel is not healed.* I. IT IS NOT FOR WANT OF EARNESTLY CALLING ATTENTION TO THE HURT. Jeremiah had wearied and vexed his fellow-countrymen by his persistent warnings. In ver. 21 he insists on how the hurt of Israel had become his hurt. In one sense he was not hurt, for he had kept clear of all idolatrous and unjust ways ; he was in a different service and different kind of occupation. But though separated thus, he was also united even as a member to the rest of the body, and had to suffer where he had not sinned. His fellow-countrymen, perhaps, said to him, in substance if not in so many words, " Leave us to go our way, and go you yours ; if we sin, we sin, and if we suffer, we suffer, and it is no concern to any but ourselves." The sinner in his suffering and his heart-corruption must be a cause of great trouble to those who are trying to serve God. They cannot go by on the other side and leave him. No matter how self-occupied one may have been before he came under the control of the Divine will, afterwards he must occupy himself with such things as concern the spiritual health and blessedness of all mankind. Jeremiah sets us a great example in thus speaking of himself as being individually wounded. If sinners continue careless, impenitent, incredulous as to the wrath of God and their pitiable state of alienation from him, there is all the more need that God's people should feel instead of them. These Israelites could not say they were left without warning and urgent remonstrance, for the man upon whom the business of warning had been laid cried and mourned over the troubles of others, because in a very deep sense they were his own. Vain, therefore, was it for the people, in after years, amid the gloom of exile and bereavement, to say they had not been properly warned.

II. IT WAS NOT FOR WANT OF A MEDICAMENT. In wounds of the body, Israel knew where to go. They found balm in Gilead, and Gilead was not far off, even supposing they had always to go there to get the balm. Balm of Gilead might be made to grow nearer than Gilead. Thus we see the medicament *was easily procured*—a very important consideration. The incense for the altar they brought all the way from Sheba, but the balm for healing grew much nearer. Easiness of procurement, however, would have been little without efficiency. A *certain* remedy brought from the ends of the earth is better than a *doubtful* one near to home ; only, of course, there must be foresight to lay in a stock, so that it will be at hand when wanted. Evidently this balm of Gilead which grew within Israelite territory was a famous and trusted balm. Only some popular and widely known agent of healing would have served the purpose of the prophet for quoting here. And is it not plain that the God who thus provided for bodily wounds a balm so easily obtained and so efficient in its action, might also be trusted to provide an available and thorough cure for the worst of spiritual ills? Assuredly the prophet means that an affirmative and encouraging answer is to be given to his question. There is balm in Gilead. There is peace for the guilty conscience, purity for the turbid and defiled imagination, strength for the weakened will. The springs of all our pollution and pain can be dried up, and their place know them no more for ever.

III. IT WAS NOT FOR WANT OF A PHYSICIAN. The medicament is good, but it may require to be applied by a skilful and experienced hand. The physician can do nothing without his medicaments, and the medicaments are oftentimes nothing without the physician. A physician is needed to prepare the way for saving truth, to apply it in its most efficacious order, and to press it home in close and vigorous contact with that which has to be healed. The balm of Gilead is not given that it may be trifled with, that it may film over deep evils with a deceptive appearance of removal. In applying that balm there may have to be pain, intense pain for a time, in order that a worse pain may be for ever taken away. The pain coming from self-indulgence must be succeeded by the pain coming from self-denial. Men have to discover that the pains of sin are the smitings of God, and when they have made this discovery they will be in a fair way to learn that only he who smites can also heal. Do not let us unjustly complain of incurable ills; let us rather confess that we are much in the condition of the poor woman who, after spending much on many physicians, found, by a simple faith touching the true Source of healing, what she had long vainly sought.

IV. THE REASON PLAINLY LAY WITH THE PEOPLE THEMSELVES. They would listen to no warning. Balm was offered, and the physician's skill to apply it, but they would not come to be healed. They preferred the pleasures of sin along with its risks and pains. That their state was bad they knew, but they believed it was not near so bad as the prophet made it out to be. Only physicians can tell how many cases of bodily disease might be cured if the sick were willing to go to the root of the matter, and mend their habits as to eating and drinking, working and playing. Ignorance, indifference, prejudice, and unblushing lust of the flesh lie at the bottom of much bodily disease, explaining both how it originates and how it continues. And similar causes operate with regard to such ills as afflict the consciousness of the entire man. Sinners must have a will to go to Jesus if they expect healing and life, and then life more abundantly.—Y.

EXPOSITION.

CHAPTER IX.

Ver. 1.—The Hebrew more correctly attaches this verse to ch. viii. **Oh that my head were waters,** etc. A quaint conceit, it may be said. But "if we have been going on pace for pace with the passion before, this sudden conversion of a strong-felt metaphor into something to be actually realized in nature, is strictly and strikingly natural." So Bishop Doane, quoting, by way of illustration, Shakespeare's 'Richard II.,' "meditating on his own utter annihilation as to royalty:"

"Oh that I were a mockery king of snow,
   To melt before the sun of Bolingbroke!"

The tone of complaint continues in the following verse, though the subject is different.

Vers. 2—22.—Complaint of the treachery and folly of the people; lamentation over their consequences.

Ver. 2.—**A lodging place of wayfaring men;** a "khan" or "caravanserai," to use the terms now so familiar from Eastern travel, where "wayfaring men" could at least find shelter, and the means of preparing their provisions. Comp., besides the parallel passage in Ps. lv. 6, 7, our own Cowper's fine reminiscence of Jeremiah: "Oh for a lodge in some vast wilderness!" etc. **Adulterers, ... treacherous men** (see ch. ii. 20; iii. 8, 9; iii. 20; v. 11).

Ver. 3.—**And they bend their tongues,** etc.; rather, *and they bend their tongue as their bow of falsehood, and they use not their valour in* (literally, *according to*) *good faith*. There is a sad, stern irony in these words, which remind us of Isaiah's (v. 22) "valiant men— for drinking wine," and of our own prophet's

repetition of himself in ch. xxiii. 10, "Their valour is—untruth." A less pointed form of the same figurative statement is that of the psalmist in Ps. lxiv. 3. **Upon the earth;** rather, *in the land*. The Authorized Version pays very little regard to the context in its rendering of the ambiguous word *ereç*.

Ver. 4.—**Take ye heed every one of his neighbour.** Such was the result of clinging to an unprogressive religion—one which refused to be spiritualized by the prophets. Certainly, if the established religion was so inefficacious, it was self-condemned. Here we find the prophet depicting a state of society in which the elementary bonds are already dissolved, and suspicion becomes the natural attitude even of a good man. We find a very similar picture in the last chapter of Micah—a chapter, it is true, which stands apart from the rest of the book, as it implies a greater development of wickedness than the rest of Micah and the contemporary prophecies of Isaiah would lead us to expect. Are these prophetic descriptions just and accurate? We may allow something, no doubt, for the warmth of feeling natural to every human preacher, even under the influence of inspiration; but we must not allow ourselves to explain away the obvious meaning of the prophets. The latter and their disciples were "the salt" of their country; and in proportion as their influence declined, the natural effects of a non-moral, purely ritualistic religion showed themselves on a larger scale. **Every brother;** *i.e.* every fellow-tribesman or fellow-citizen. **Will utterly supplant.** There is nothing in the context to suggest an allusion to Gen. xxvii. 36 (Jacob). The verb has its common sense of deceiving. The tense should be the present, not the future, both here and in the next verse. **Will walk;** rather, *goeth about* (see ch. vi. 28).

Ver. 5.—**They have taught their tongue,** etc.; again an intimation of the unnaturalness (in the higher sense) of vice (comp. on ch. ii. 33).

Ver. 6.—**Thine habitation,** etc. According to St. Jerome, this is addressed to the prophet; but it is better to follow the Targum, which makes the clause refer to the Jewish people. The connection is (as Dr. Payne Smith points out), "Trust no one; for thou dwellest surrounded by deceit on every side."

Ver. 7.—**I will melt them.** It is the same word as that used in Mal. iii. 3 of the "refiner and purifier of silver." Purification, not destruction, is the object of the judgment which is threatened! Strange that mercy should find place, after the offence of the criminal has been found so grievous! But, lest we should expect too favourable an issue, the prophet adds, in the name of Jehovah, **For how shall I do?** or rather, *How should I act? How otherwise should I act?* The continuation is a little doubtful. The Hebrew has, "by reason of the daughter of my people;" but this can hardly be right. We naturally expect something to justify the preceding statement. The reading of the Septuagint answers to our anticipations by rendering ἀπὸ προσώπου πονηρίας θυγατρὸς λαοῦ μου, and this is confirmed by the parallel passage ch. vii. 12 (comp. ch. xi. 17; xxxii. 32).

Ver. 8.—(Comp. Ps. lv. 21.) **As an arrow shot out;** rather, *as a sharpened arrow;* but this is based on the marginal reading, and is itself a slightly forced rendering. The Hebrew text (*i.e.* the consonants), and also the Septuagint and Vulgate, have "as a murderous arrow."

Ver. 10.—This and the next six verses contain a description of the sad fate of the sinful land and people. At first the prophet speaks as if he saw it all spread out before him. Then, in the character of a surprised spectator, he inquires how this came to pass, and receives the Divine answer, that it is the doom of self-willed rebellion. **The habitations** should rather be *pastures.* The country, once covered with grazing flocks and herds, is now so utterly waste that even the birds cannot find subsistence.

Ver. 11.—**I will make,** etc. Notice how the utterances of the prophets stand side by side with those of Jehovah. A true prophet has no personal views; so that whether his revelations are expressed in the one form or the other makes no difference. **Dragons;** rather, *jackals.*

Ver. 12.—**For what the land perisheth.** A closer rendering would be more forcible:

Wherefore hath the land perished, is it burned up like the wilderness with none that passeth through?

Ver. 13.—There is no answer, for the wise men are ashamed (ch. viii. 9); so Jehovah himself takes up his speech. **My law which I set before them;** not in reference to the publication of the Law on Sinai, but, as Keil rightly points out, to the oral exhibition of the *Tŏrāh* by the prophets. **Neither walked therein;** viz. in the Law. (On the precise contents of the term here rendered "Law," see note on ch. viii. 8.)

Ver. 14.—**Imagination;** rather, *stubbornness* (see on ch. iii. 17). **Baalim.** The Hebrew has "the Baalim;" practically equivalent to "the idol-gods" (see on ch. ii. 8). **Which their fathers taught them.** "Which" refers to both clauses, *i.e.* to the obstinacy and the Baal-worship.

Ver. 15.—**I will feed them, . . . with wormwood.** A figure for the bitter privations of captivity (comp. Lam. iii. 15, "He hath filled me with bitterness, he hath made me drunken with wormwood"). Wormwood and gall—*i.e.* the poppy (Tristram)—are combined again in Deut. xxix. 17.

Ver. 16.—**I will scatter them also,** etc. (comp. Deut. xxviii. 64; Lev. xxvi. 33). **I will send a [the] sword after them.** Even in the land of their captivity they shall have no rest. A special prophecy to the same effect was addressed to the Jewish fugitives in Egypt (ch. xliv. 27). In both cases it is the unbelievers who are referred to; the nation as such was, through its Divine calling, indestructible.

Vers. 17—22.—A new scene is introduced. To give an idea of the greatness of the impending blow, all the skilled mourners are sent for to raise the cry of lamentation. But no, this is not enough. So large will be the number of the dead that all the women must take their part in the doleful office. The description of the mourning women is as true to modern as to ancient life in the East. "And, indeed," says Dr. Shaw, a thoughtful traveller and an ornament of Oxford in the dark eighteenth century, "they perform their parts with such proper sounds, gestures, and commotions, that they rarely fail to work up the assembly into some extraordinary pitch of thoughtfulness and sorrow" ('Travels in Barbary and the Levant,' 2nd edit., p. 242; comp. Amos v. 16; Eccles. xii. 5).

Ver. 18.—**That our eyes may run down,** etc.; a justification of this artificial system. The piercing notes of the hired mourners are to relieve the sorrow of the afflicted by forcing for it a vent.

Ver. 19.—**Forsaken;** rather, *left.* **Our dwellings have cast us out;** rather, *they have cast down our dwellings.*

Ver. 20.—**Yet hear**; rather, *for hear.*

Ver. 21.—**Death is come up**, etc. "Death," equivalent to "pestilence" (as ch. xv. 2), the most dreaded foe of a besieged population. (For the figure, comp. Joel ii. 9.) **The children from without.** The ideal of Zechariah is that " the streets of the city should be full of boys and girls playing in the streets thereof" (viii. 5). But the pitiless reaper, Death, shall cut off even "the playful child from the street" (so we might render more literally). **Streets**, in the parallel clause, means the "broad places" where men congregate to tell the news.

Ver. 22.—**Speak, Thus saith the Lord.** These words are in three important respects contrary to the style of Jeremiah : (1) such a prefix as "speak" is unique; (2) such a phrase as כה נאם ” is also unique in Jeremiah; (3) when our prophet does use the formula נאם ” it is not at the beginning of a verse. They are omitted by the Septuagint translator, who presumably did not find them in his copy of the Hebrew, and the text gains greatly by their removal. The following words are mistranslated in the Authorized Version, and should run, not **even**, but *and*, **the carcases of men shall fall**, etc. It is most improbable, however, that a fresh Divine revelation should begin with "and." With other points, the word rendered "speak" would mean "pestilence." Possibly the word fell out of ver. 21, where it would find an excellent place in the second clause (as an explanatory parallel to "death," as in Ps. lxxviii. 50), which would thus obtain greater roundness and symmetry. **As the handful**; *i.e.* as thickly as one heap of corn succeeds another under the deft hand of the reaper.

Vers. 23, 24.—These two verses were hardly composed for their present position, though a connection may, of course, be thought out for them. Perhaps a comparison of Hab. iii. 17, 18, may help us. There the prophet looks forward to a complete desolation resulting from the Chaldean invasion, and yet declares that he can even exult in his God. So here. All subjects of boasting have been proved untrustworthy ; but one remains—not wisdom, not valour, not riches, but the knowledge of the revealed God.

Ver. 24.—The knowledge of God relates to three leading attributes, the combination of which is very instructive. First, **loving-kindness.** This is not to be understood in a vague and general sense of the love of God to all mankind ; the term has a special connotation with regard to the Israelitish people. God shows loving-kindness to those with whom he is in covenant ; hence the combination "loving-kindness and faithfulness"

(Ps. lxxxv. 10, corrected version), and as here (comp. Ps. v. 7, 8 ; xxxvi. 5, 6), "mercy and righteousness." Israel is weak and erring, and needs mercies of all sorts, which Jehovah, in his "loving-kindness," vouchsafes. Next, **judgment**, or justice. Jehovah is a King, helps the poor and weak to their right, and punishes the wrong-doer (comp. ch. xxi. 12). Then, **righteousness**—a similar but wider term. This is the quality which leads its subject to adhere to a fixed rule of conduct. God's rule is his covenant ; hence "righteousness" shows itself in all such acts as tend to the full realizing of the covenant with Israel, including the "plan of salvation." It is by no means to be confined to exacting penalties and conferring rewards.

Vers. 25, 26.—A further enforcement of the doctrine that no outward privileges, if dissociated from inward moral vitality, will avail.

Ver. 25.—**All them which are circumcised with the uncircumcised**; rather, *all the circumcised in uncircumcision,* or, as Ewald turns it, "all the uncircumcised-circumcised." But what does this enigmatical expression signify? Hitzig, Graf, and apparently Dr. Payne Smith, think that it has a twofold meaning : that, as applied to the Jews, it means circumcised in the flesh, but not in heart, and, as applied to the heathen, simply uncircumcised (the one-half of the phrase neutralizing the other, like "a knife without the blade," "angels with horns and hoofs," etc.). The latter meaning, however, is surely very improbable, and it would only become necessary if it were proved that circumcision was practised by none of the nations mentioned but the Jews. This is not the case. There is no doubt that the Egyptians were circumcised in very early times (see the drawing of a bas-relief in the Temple of Chunsu at Karnak, given by Dr. Ebers in his 'Egypten und die Bücher Mosis'). The assertion that only the priests underwent the operation has no older evidence than that of Origen (edit. Lommatzsch, iv. 138), "in whose time it is quite possible that the Egyptians, like the later Jews, sought to evade a peculiarity which exposed them to ridicule and contempt." As to the Ammonites and Moabites, we have, unfortunately, no information. With regard to the Edomites, it is true that, according to Josephus ('Antiq.,' xiii. 9, 1), they were compelled to accept circumcision by John Hyrcanus. But it is still quite possible that, at an earlier period, the rite was practised, just as it was among the ancient Arabs, the evidence for which is beyond question (see the writer's article, "Circumcision," in 'Encyclopædia Britannica,' 9th edit.). (On the statement that "all these [the] nations are uncircumcised," see below.)

Ver. 26.—**All that are in the utmost corners**; rather, *all that are corner-clipped*; i.e. that have the hair cut off about the ears and temples. Herodotus tells us, speaking of the Arabs, "Their practice is to cut the hair in a ring, away from the temples" (iii. 8); and among the representatives of various nations, coloured figures of whom are given in the tomb of Rameses III., we find some with a square place shaved just above the temples. The hair below this shaven place was allowed to grow long, and then plaited into a lock. It is to such customs that Jeremiah alludes here and in

ch. xxv. 23; xlix. 32. A prohibition is directed against them in the Levitical Law (Lev. xix. 27; xxi. 5). **For all these nations are uncircumcised**; rather, *all the nations*, etc. Another obscure expression. Does it mean (taken together with the following clause), "The Gentile peoples are uncircumcised in the flesh, and the people of Israel is equally so in heart"? But this does not agree with facts (see above, on ver. 25). It is safer, therefore, to assume that "uncircumcised" is equivalent to "circumcised in uncircumcision" (ver. 25). The next clause will then simply give the most conspicuous instance of this unspiritual obedience to a mere form.

HOMILETICS.

Ver. 1.—*Grief for others.* I. THE RIGHT SPIRIT IN WHICH TO REGARD THE MISERIES OF OTHER MEN IS ONE OF GRIEF. A less worthy spirit is too common. 1. *Self-congratulation.* The evil condition of others is simply used as a dark background on which to throw out in relief our own superiority. 2. *Indifference*—the spirit of Cain, which cries, "Am I my brother's keeper?" 3. *Vindictiveness.* Jeremiah denounced the sins of Israel, and threatened punishment. Yet he regarded these sins with no Pharisaical sternness, and he could not contemplate the punishment of them with indignant satisfaction. Even if men are deserving punishment, that punishment is still pitiable. Sin inclines a good man to sorrow as much as to anger. II. GRIEF FOR THE MISERIES OF OTHERS WILL BE INDUCED BY A TRUE APPRECIATION OF THOSE MISERIES IN A SPIRIT OF SYMPATHY. 1. *A spirit of sympathy.* Jeremiah felt the distresses of his nation as private sorrows. He was a true patriot. We must feel one with men before we can rightly regard their troubles. 2. *A true appreciation* of the miseries of men. Sympathy implies knowledge. We do not feel aright because we do not take the trouble to inquire into the condition of others. Much apparent hard-heartedness arises simply from ignorance—but culpable ignorance. True sympathy will feel distress for the real evil of others, not only for their transient moods. It may need to weep over those who foolishly rejoice, and rejoice for those who weep wholesome tears of penitence. III. GRIEF FOR THE MISERIES OF OTHERS MAY BE OUR BEST MEANS FOR HELPING THEM. Barren pity is a mockery when active aid is called for. 1. But genuine sympathy is the strongest *motive* to help. 2. We can *intercede* in prayer most effectually when we make the sorrows of others our own. Christ's sorrow for men was an important element in his intercession. 3. *Sorrow* for others may move them to view their condition in a true light. Tears may avail where warnings are lost. We have no greater motive to repentance than can be furnished by a right feeling of what Christ has suffered through our sin. IV. GRIEF FOR THE MISERIES OF OTHERS IS NOT ALONE SUFFICIENT FOR THEIR DELIVERANCE. Jeremiah wept over his nation, yet the threatened desolation was not averted. Christ wept over Jerusalem, but Jerusalem was destroyed. Though God is "grieved" at our sin, we may fall into ruin. His grief is a strong inducement to repentance, but every man must repent and seek deliverance for himself.

Vers. 4—8.—*Falsehood.* I. SIN CULMINATES IN UNIVERSAL FALSEHOOD. The intellectual aspect of sin is untruth. Every sin is a lie. The triumph of sin is the overthrow of all truth and trust. II. FALSE RELATIONS WITH GOD LEAD TO FALSE RELATIONS WITH MEN. Religion and morality mutually influence each other. The worship of a god known to be false develops a life of falseness. The hypocritical service of God is likely to be accompanied by dishonest dealings with men.

III. HABITS OF FALSEHOOD ARE FATAL TO HUMAN WELFARE. Society reposes on trust. Commerce is impossible without good faith. Universal distrust must involve social disintegration. The state, the family, all mutual organization, must then fall to pieces. Falsehood only succeeds by abusing trust; but by so doing it tends to destroy trust; and when it has accomplished this end it will be ineffectual. Universal lying would be useless to everybody.

IV. FALSEHOOD IS REGARDED BY GOD AS A PECULIARLY WICKED SIN. For this especially the people must be punished (ver. 9). Deceit amongst men is a sin against God, who is the Truth eternal. It is a spiritual sin, a sin most near to the diabolical (John viii. 34). It is a sin which is peculiarly injurious to the spiritual nature of the sinner, tending to destroy conscience (Matt. vi. 23). It involves both injustice and cruelty towards men.

Ver. 9.—*A visitation of God.* I. CHASTISEMENT IS A VISITATION OF GOD. The phrase "a visitation of God" has been too much confined to calamitous events. God visits us every hour in gentleness and mercy. Still, it is important to recognize that he also comes in chastisement. He *comes,* does not simply order, but himself executes chastisement. 1. We should *recognize* the Divine visitation. Outwardly the trouble may have a human origin. The calamities of the Jews arose out of a Chaldean invasion, but the prophets saw above and behind that invasion a Divine purpose. God was in those armies from Babylon. God is in our troubles. 2. This fact should make us *dread to incur* chastisement. We cannot resist it, for if God is in it, all his might and majesty are there. 3. This fact should make us submit to the chastisement when it comes as *just and good.* Its origin is not Satanic, but Divine. If God is in it he must ever be true to his character; his fiercest anger can never break the bounds of what is just and fair; he must always be ready to show mercy when this is possible (Hab. iii. 2).

II. CHASTISEMENT IS DETERMINED BY THE PERSONAL RELATIONS BETWEEN GOD AND MEN. It is God's soul being avenged. God's vengeance is quite unlike ours; it is never cruel or intemperate; it is always governed by justice and consistent with unchanging love. It is, however, more than judicial punishment. It is an action arising out of personal feeling and determined by our personal offences against God. Sin is more than transgression of Law,—it is ungrateful rebellion against God; and punishment is more than the cold vindication of Law,—it is the result of the provoked anger of God. Such anger is right, for it is not kindness but weakness that allows a father to receive insult from a child unmoved. The greater the love, the greater will be the righteous anger when this is wronged.

III. CHASTISEMENT IS NECESSITATED BY THE CONDUCT OF MEN. It is "for *such* things" and "on *such* a nation." God does not love vengeance. He does not send punishment as an arbitrary exercise of sovereignty. Therefore our chastisement is virtually in our own hands. Even after meriting it, we alone are to blame if the full force of the blow falls upon us. For God has provided a way of escape, and offers forgiveness to all who repent and submit. Therefore it is foolish for men to complain of their hard lot in falling under the storm of a visitation of God in wrath.

IV. THE NECESSITY FOR CHASTISEMENT MAY BE RECOGNIZED BY OUR COMMON INTELLIGENCE. The text is an appeal to reason, a question which unbiassed minds could answer only in one way. If chastisement is not seen to be reasonable, it must be either (1) because the depth of guilt is not felt, or (2) distorted views of chastisement have been entertained. This will be such as befits the offence.

V. THE PERSONAL CHARACTERISTICS OF CHASTISEMENT INVOLVE PERSONAL ELEMENTS IN REDEMPTION. Hence the necessity for a "propitiation." Thus Christ redeems us by becoming a Propitiation for our sins (1 John ii. 2).

Vers. 12—16.—*The causes of national disaster.* I. IT IS PROFITABLE TO INQUIRE INTO THE CAUSES OF NATIONAL DISASTER. 1. *Intellectually,* this is a subject of profound interest, dealing with fundamental principles and the vast issues to which they lead when working on the largest scale. 2. *Morally,* it is of great practical importance for the warning it supplies to all nations. The sight of terrible ruin rushing down upon a people is appalling, but the awe with which it strikes us will not have much wholesome effect till we have an intelligent appreciation of the sources from which it comes, and are thus enabled to watch them and guard against them.

II. SPIRITUAL WISDOM IS REQUISITE FOR THE DISCERNMENT OF THE CAUSES OF NATIONAL DISASTER. They do not lie on the surface. No study is more difficult than that of the philosophy of history. Unless the mind is awake to spiritual facts, the inquiry will not go beyond secondary causes, or attempting more will commit injustice. The prophets needed inspiration for this as much as for the prediction of future events. No mere literary historian is fit for the work. Only a prophet can be fully equal to it, and other men can only pursue it with safety when they walk in his footsteps. Hence the immense value of the historical elements of the Old Testament to the statesman.

III. THE CHIEF CAUSES OF NATIONAL DISASTER ARE MORAL. Material causes are visible on the surface, such as famine, plague, invasion, revolution. Political causes lying deeper may be easily discerned, such as diplomatic complications, class divisions, violent changes in popular sentiment. But beneath all such influences there are great moral causes. 1. These act through *providence*. God takes note of the conduct of nations, judges, ministers. 2. They also act *directly*. Luxury is enervating; injustice destroys the confidence of a people in its government, etc.

IV. ONCE REVEALED, THE MORAL CAUSES OF NATIONAL DISASTER ARE SIMPLE AND INTELLIGIBLE. The prophets make these clear to us in the case of their own nation. 1. Negatively, the causes were traced to *disobedience* to the will of God, culpable because this was well understood—" set before them." 2. Positively, they were found in *wilful stubbornness and demoralizing idolatry*. God was the shield of his people. When he was forsaken they were defenceless. Nations are only secure while they are governed by the will of God, by justice and humanity. Godlessness, bearing fruit in falsehood, cruelty, and vicious lawlessness of passion, is a sure source of national ruin. The state of the public conscience is more important to a nation than that of its army.

Vers. 23, 24.—*False boasting and true confidence.* I. FALSE BOASTING. 1. We are inclined to overvalue our *own possessions.* The wise man thinks wisdom the one source of security, the strong man strength, the rich man riches. That bulks most largely which lies most near to us. 2. The very *good* that is in a thing may deceive us by tempting us to overvalue it. Wisdom, strength, and riches are all good in their way. Trust in them is very different from trust in fraud and violence. Not regarding them as enemies, we are in danger of confiding in them as saviours instead of simply employing them as servants. 3. The *number* of earthly resources leads us to assume that security must be found in some of them at least; for when one fails we can fall back on another. But if the best do not protect in the extremity of danger, will inferior aids suffice? Wisdom is greater than strength, and strength than riches. If wisdom fails, what can the rest do for us? 4. The *variety* of advantages contained in earthly resources deceives us as to their value. Wisdom promises to outwit the enemy or devise some means of evading ruin. Yet the wisdom of the wisest Jews was defeated by those who came from the land of "the wise;" and how can it avail against the supreme wisdom? Strength as physical prowess and national power may be imposing and yet not almighty. Samson was weak under a woman's wiles. Goliath fell before the sling of the stripling David. Riches may buy much. They could not prevent the Chaldean invasion. They cannot buy off sickness, disappointment, death, the punishment of sin. Nebuchadnezzar found the possession of the world no security against the most humiliating affliction (Dan. iv. 28—33). The rich fool was mocked by his own prudence (Luke xii. 16—21).

II. TRUE CONFIDENCE. 1. This is to be sought in the *knowledge of God.* Wisdom, the best of earthly resources, is not sufficient for protection, but it is the type of a higher wisdom, wherein is the secret of safety. This is a wisdom which concerns itself, not with petty devices, subtle schemes, cunning, and cleverness, but with the highest knowledge, bearing fruit in "the fear of God" (Ps. cxi. 10). We must know God to trust him. 2. The knowledge of God will reveal to us the *special grounds* for confidence in him, viz. (1) loving-kindness, disposing him to help the needy; (2) justice, making it apparent that he will concern himself in human affairs as the King ruling all into order; and (3) righteousness, showing that in the broadest way he will maintain the right. Hence it will be apparent that God can and will help us only in accordance with these principles of his character; and we must know them, not only to learn thereby to confide in him, but also to bring ourselves into that spirit which will justify us in expecting his mercy, *i.e.* reconciliation to his love, submission to his government, and obedience to his righteous will.

Vers. 25, 26.—*Impartial justice.* I. SPECIAL PRIVILEGES DO NOT INTERFERE WITH THE IMPARTIAL EXERCISE OF DIVINE JUSTICE. Judah is specially privileged, and prizes circumcision as a seal of the peculiar favour of Heaven (Gen. xvii. 9—14). Yet Judah must take its place in the indiscriminate catalogue of corrupt nations. If privileges are noted in God's exercise of justice, this can only be as an aggravation of guilt. The citizens of favoured nations, the heirs of rank and wealth, persons whose lives have been peculiarly successful and unvisited with the usual amount of trouble, all stand in this position. Their present happy condition is no guarantee for favour in the day of Divine judgment, but, on the contrary, a reason for regarding the ingratitude of sin as, in their case, the more culpable.

II. THE OBSERVANCE OF EXTERNAL ORDINANCES HAS NO INFLUENCE ON THE IMPARTIAL EXERCISE OF DIVINE JUSTICE. Their utility is solely as regards their effect on men. They are profitable only in so far as they assist the corresponding spiritual acts, which are all that God takes note of (Col. ii. 11). The circumcised in body who are not circumcised in heart will suffer just as if they had never been circumcised at all. The ordinance without the spirituality is an offence rather than a pleasing thing. It shows knowledge; it is a mockery to God. This must be so, (1) because God is spirit, and can only be served spiritually; and (2) because the highest justice is concerned with thoughts, motives, deeds of the soul, rather than with the ambiguous actions of the outer life.

III. NO EXCEPTIONS WILL BE MADE TO THE IMPARTIAL EXERCISE OF DIVINE JUSTICE. All kinds of nations are classed together. Cultivated Egyptians and wild Arabs, scrupulous Jews and idolatrous Ammonites, all come before the same judgment-bar, all have the same fair trial and righteous sentence. 1. The *heathen* are not excluded from God's judgment; for (1) he is the God of all the earth, and of those who ignore him as well as of those who recognize him; (2) the heathen have a light of nature and a conscience by which to guide their conduct; (3) God's judgment is reasonable, and can adapt requirement to opportunity, so that the heathen will have as just treatment as those who are more privileged. 2. The *Jews and professedly religious* are not excluded. Many people make an utterly unwarrantable assumption that their respectability, position in the Church, etc., are such that the stern ordeal of the judgment is not for them. In his vision of judgment Christ made no such exceptions (Matt. xxv. 31—46).

HOMILIES BY VARIOUS AUTHORS.

Ver. 1.—*Vicarious grief.* It is a common occurrence in the history of God's Church that when general indifference to religious truth, to impending judgments, or depraved spiritual condition, etc., is exhibited by the multitude, one or at most a few are sensible of the nature and extent of the evil. Knowledge in such a case is nearly always sorrow. This is intensified when remonstrances are unheeded, and efforts of reform are defeated. It is the righteous man, the reformer, who is most affected by the situation, and who feels most keenly the disgrace and danger.

I. IN THE HIGHEST THINGS IT IS THE FEW THAT MUST FEEL FOR THE MANY. This has been the law from the beginning. It is a necessity of nature. It is a Divine appointment. Pure feeling, even when painful, appears as a stewardship in one or two hearts, perhaps in one alone. Joseph is moved to tears at the heartlessness of his brethren. Jonathan is ashamed for his father Saul. Elijah laments in loneliness and despair the apostasy of Israel. Jesus weeps over Jerusalem; painfully wonders at the slowness of heart to believe exhibited by his own disciples; is " sore amazed" at the cup of iniquity he has to drink. Jeremiah is here evidently in the same succession of vicarious suffering. We see the same principle working in our own circle of acquaintance. Men, women, sorrowing and suffering for others, who are themselves unconscious or are partially so.

II. WHAT ARE THE COUNTERVAILING ADVANTAGES WHICH LIGHT UP THIS MYSTERY? It cannot be wholly to the detriment of those in whom it is illustrated. The justice of God is involved in the question. 1. *The keenest joys spring from or coincide with the deepest, purest sorrows.* 2. *By-and-by the sorrow will transfer itself to its objects, in the grace of repentance.* 3. *In at least one illustrious instance, it exerts an atoning, mediatorial influence for sinners with God.*—M.

Vers. 2, 3.—*The man of God's longing for seclusion.* I. IT IS THE NATURAL RECOIL OF A PURE HEART FROM WICKEDNESS. When the knowledge and love of God are in the heart, sin appears more loathsome. The love of goodness will show itself in a hatred of evil, and a desire to be separated from its workers. In some this love of God and goodness overpowers even the natural attachments and ties of life. And it may be carried to such an excess as to become a spiritual disease, in its way as sinful as the causes that give rise to it. Monasticism has its root in a good and proper feeling carried to excess, and without the restraining and modifying considerations that ought to accompany it. In the instance before us (and like instances)—
II. IT SPRINGS FROM NO SELFISH MOTIVE. Jeremiah did not seek for the "luxury" of grief; sufficient the wanderer's tent, or the comfortless caravanserai of the desert. Nor has he any desire to attitudinize. It is a loneliness that shall not be conspicuous; a losing of himself amongst strangers who care not for him and notice him not. Nor did he seek to evade the duties of life. If he separated himself, it was not to escape from the impending dangers he had announced; nor to intermit his spiritual activities. "He wished there to *weep* for them" (Zinzendorf); to study the problem in fresh and more hopeful aspects; to recover his mental and spiritual calm; to recruit his spiritual energies for a new and more successful effort. So in our own day, the underlying motive must ever determine the lawfulness, the character, and the continuance of our spiritual retirements.
III. GOD DID NOT REBUKE IT, BUT HE DID NOT SEE FIT TO GRATIFY IT. Here the longing, if it ever grew into a prayer, was not answered, at least at once, or in the way conceived of. Whilst the day of grace lasted, and God's people were open to repent and to be influenced by his words, he is detained amongst them. When all possibilities were exhausted, then the dungeon of the king's prison or the shame of the Egyptian exile might serve the purpose. *But even then the essential craving was satisfied.* There is a longing that is its own answer. To some it is given to experience solitude and spiritual detachment in the midst of the busy throng of transgressors for whom they yet ceaselessly work. This centrifugal tendency may be productive of greater concentration, real compassion, and capacity for usefulness, when it is controlled and overcome by a sense of overmastering responsibility, and a "heart's desire and prayer to God for Israel, that they may be saved."—M.

Vers. 2—6.—*The self-opposition and futility of the sinner's life.* A strong argument against the practice of a thing may often be found in the supposition that it should become universal. This is valid in the case of the practices and desires of wicked men. The idea of Hobbes concerning the original state of human society is ingenious and conceivable from this very reason, were it not contradicted by the world's history.
I. ONE SIN ENTAILS ANOTHER, AND CRIME LEADS TO CRIME. (Ver. 3.)
II. UNIVERSAL WICKEDNESS PRODUCES UNIVERSAL DISTRUST AND MISERY. (Ver. 5.)
III. EVIL-DOING IS A WEARY AND FRUITLESS TOIL.
IV. ITS FUTILITY CULMINATES WHEN IT ROBS A MAN OF THE KNOWLEDGE AND FELLOWSHIP OF GOD, AND EVEN OF THE DESIRE FOR THEM. (Ver. 6.)—M.

Vers. 12—16.—*The affliction of God's professed people an enigma to be explained.*
I. THE MYSTERY. This consists partly in the particular subjects of it, and partly in the degree to which it has gone. It is spoken of here prophetically as a future thing that has already taken place; and the problem is stated accordingly as a realization, and not a thing only conceived of. From time to time the history of Israel and Judah presents such scenes. It is by no means one of uninterrupted progress. There are backward movements, standings still, interruptions, sharp and humiliating national disasters, and long epochs of civil war, political nonentity, or foreign captivity. 1. *Yet*

have there not been many gracious promises to the contrary? 2. *On the whole, the past reverses of Israel have been retrieved, and a measure of continuous progress attained.* 3. *The special affliction referred to is unprecedented, and its result would almost appear to be final.* The history of the Christian Church and of individual believers presents features analogous to this. The slow progress of the world's evangelization. The comparative absence of spiritual blessing in the midst of God's children. Their divisions, scientific scepticism, or unscientific superstition, like parasites, strangling the tree of the Church and draining away its life. Or the mystery appears in the individual Christian. His creed is orthodox, his behaviour outwardly presenting little that is blameworthy; and yet worldly business is a constant series of reverses and dishonourable compromises; his influence is lost; afflictions come upon him, and he cannot bear up under them; the peace of Christ is not his; etc.

II. THE POINT OF VIEW FROM WHICH IT IS TO BE REGARDED. This very important to be determined. *The apostate people* of God fail to realize the extent to which they have fallen, and confound the formal rites of religion with its spirit and reality. They at first attribute it to natural causes, or treat it as a temporary thing that will right itself, etc. *The heathen,* looking on *ab extrâ,* imagine that the Jehovah of Israel is no longer able to deliver, or that he has ceased to care for her. *Here* it is declared to be a judgment upon apostasy—utter departure from truth and righteousness, and the sterner because of that fact. And when we look at all the circumstances of the case, this interpretation seems more probable—to carry, as it were, its evidence with it. *The key, therefore, is for the most part an inward one;* at first, at any rate, wholly so. This it is which constitutes the main element of difficulty in the troubles of God's people. Hence the room there must be for mistakes, and the ease with which a wholly erroneous view may be taken with superficial probability. And this suggests *how large a part of the Church's function is fulfilled in merely being a problem and a mystery to the carnal mind.* When judgment begins at the house of God, it is time for all attentively to look on and inquire why it is so. Greater perils lie on the side of unfaithfulness than of mere unbelief. And in the last resort conscience must be appealed to in explanation of mysteries of reverse and trouble. Thereby God is knocking at the door of the heart both of the world and the Church. It is of the utmost importance that we settle the question between us and him.

III. AN INTERPRETER WANTED. (Ver. 12.) When men are at a loss, or there is radical difference of opinion, it is evident that some authority is required to decide the question. The world and its canons are by the nature of the problem ruled out of court. And the apostate is too blinded with his own sin and too callous through repeated acts and prolonged habits of wrong-doing to be trusted in the matter. At this juncture the advantage of revelation and of the prophetic office appears. So far as God is concerned, the seer speaks with the authority of direct inspiration; so far as the culprit is concerned, he occupies a representative position, and as one of those implicated, yet himself innocent, acts as general conscience. This is God's way—to raise a testimony and extract a confession from the heart of the transgressor himself, or from the midst of those upon whom his judgments fall. And the same end is accomplished now through the Spirit and the Word. The saint becomes the mouth-piece of the Saviour, and the world is convinced of "sin, of righteousness, and of judgment."—M.

Ver. 21.—*The death of the wicked contrary to nature.* Various respects in which this is so: it is sudden; it defies all the resources of comfort and protection; it is untimely, and cuts off the young in their bloom—the children for the fathers' sin, the hope of the nation and the family. "Death will not, as an enemy lurking without, attack those only who venture out to him, but will assault the people, penetrating into all their houses, to fetch his sacrifices" (Naegelsbach, in Lange). Why so?

I. IT IS BECAUSE THE LAWS OF GOD AND OF NATURE HAVE BEEN SHAMEFULLY VIOLATED.

II. THE TRIAL AND PUNISHMENT OF THE CONFIRMED SINNER ARE SWIFTLY REMOVED TO ANOTHER JUDGMENT-SEAT.

III. IT IS INTENDED AS A DEMONSTRATION AGAINST EVIL AND A TERROR TO EVIL-DOERS.—M.

Vers. 22—24.—*The knowledge of God the only real "glory" of man.* Comparison of the earthly acquisitions and properties of the natural man with those which are spiritual and Divine frequent in Scripture. In history and in life they are seen in competition. It is not that the one class of gifts is to be wholly despised and the other alone sought. A correct perspective must be established. It is *the* "glory" of a man that requires in the first place to be determined. After that is settled, all other things will take their due place and precedency.

I. THE "GLORY" OF MAN MUST DEPEND UPON THE END FOR WHICH HE HAS BEEN BROUGHT INTO EXISTENCE. This is written in his nature, confirmed by providence, and made clear by revelation. In the words of the Westminster Catechism, "*The chief end of man is to glorify God, and to enjoy him for ever.*" Everything else must be subordinated to this; but if pursued in its place, will show itself to be a perversion of his nature, and will end in calamity and misery. How very few care to satisfy themselves upon this momentous question! Hence the necessity for the teachings and warnings of experience. 1. *The "glory" of man will be declared by the manner in which the circumstances of his earthly lot affect it in the working out of that end.* Each of the qualities and properties upon which men usually pride themselves has been tried in this way and found deficient. The *wisdom* of the world has a thousand times been shown to be foolishness before God. There are a myriad problems for which it has no key. "Might" has been reduced to nothingness by the least of the duties and experiences of the spiritual life. Disease and death can bring down the mighty from their seats, and stay the greatest worker at his task. Many a time has the cherished object after which one has laboured with apparent success been snatched away just when about to be attained. And "wealth" is similarly discredited. The moth and the rust can corrupt the treasures of earth, and the thief breaks through and steals them from their most guarded security. The accident of fortune may give or take away the greatest fortune. And when death comes, all these earthly possessions have to be left behind. They cannot avail for what lies beyond. How seldom are these gifts used for the highest end! And how unavailing of themselves would they be to secure it! 2. *The "glory" of man must depend upon the success with which it contributes to secure that end.*

II. THE KNOWLEDGE OF GOD IS INDICATED UNMISTAKABLY BY THESE TESTS AS THE ONLY TRUE "GLORY" OF MAN. God is identified with the ultimate aim of our being. He made us, and it is for him we live. Consequently, the better we know him, the better shall we be able to serve him. 1. *Imitation of God will spring from the knowledge of him.* The more we know of him the more we must love him, and admiration will lead to resemblance in spirit and in life. "We love him, because he first loved us." 2. *Knowledge depends on and leads to obedience.* (John vii. 17.) The knowledge of God sheds light upon the universe and life, and directs the soul and body into the channels of health, happiness, and usefulness. 3. *It is connected with and culminates in Divine fellowship.* In this way the character and presence of God are brought into closest contact with the spirit of man, his character is moulded into the image of the Divine original, and the joys of communion deepen and enlarge into the blessedness of heaven. "This is life eternal, [even now] to know thee the only true God, and Jesus Christ, whom thou hast sent."—M.

Ver. 1.—*The testimony of tears.* Tears are an unusual, a strange sad sight in a strong man. But here Jeremiah appears utterly broken down. He abandons himself to a very agony of sorrow. His tears remind us of those of our Lord and of St. Paul. But they are also a relief to the overburdened heart. Like the cry of the sufferer in sore pain. We are glad when we behold one enduring some crushing sorrow enabled to pour forth his grief in tears. The heart-broken prophet has evidently felt them to be such a relief. His thoughts of his country's sorrows, when they lie too deep for tears, are greater than he can bear. He would, therefore, that he might be able continually to weep. But tears are admonitory. They bear a very powerful testimony, which we shall do well to give heed to. For they bear witness—

I. To HIS PROFOUND CONVICTIONS. 1. *In regard to the truth of the message he has delivered.* When we behold God's servants, such as Jeremiah and St. Paul and others, labouring with all energy of soul, with infinite self-sacrifice, exposed to every form of ill, and "with many tears," we are constrained to inquire the motive of such a life. But only one of three suppositions is possible. (1) Either he who labours is a deceiver. He is consciously acting a part. But this supposition in regard to prophets and apostles of God's Word has long been given up. "The world has renounced almost to a man this hypothesis. It refuses to believe in the possibility of a hypocrite whose writings inculcate and whose conduct exemplifies the highest order of moral excellence; it refuses to believe in a benevolent, modest, self-denying, high-minded, humble, magnanimous liar, in whom falsehood speaks with the very tongue, looks through the very eyes, and personates the very gestures and tones of truth; it refuses to believe that a man with no earthly motive for it, and every earthly motive against it, should spend the best part of a lifetime in cheating men into truth and virtue which he had himself utterly renounced" (H. Rogers). But if this hypothesis be rejected, then there is another. (2) He has deceived himself. He is the victim of enthusiasm, the unconscious agent of a bewildered and disordered brain. But this hypothesis also will not bear investigation. For such enthusiasms are generally short-lived, they are soon detected, and the common sense of mankind refuses to participate in them. No instance can be found of a mere enthusiast persuading whole nations and convincing the purest, the most sober, and the most thoughtful of whole communities, and in such manner that the falsehood thus originated shall live on and acquire power over men's minds increasingly. And there are other tests whereby enthusiasm may be discriminated from the deliberate convictions of the sober mind, and every one of such tests, when applied to the history of faithful witnesses for God's truth, fail to show that these witnesses were, though not dishonest, yet merely mistaken enthusiasts. There remains, therefore, (3) only the other alternative, that the message which they delivered with so much earnestness was true. And the tears of the prophet and apostle do alike bear this testimony, and its force men have everywhere felt. And would we convince an unbelieving world of the truths we profess to hold, we must manifest more of a like conviction. If some wan, worn, emaciated preacher, bearing on him evidently the marks of the Lord Jesus, whose whole life had been, like that of Jeremiah or St. Paul, one long sacrifice for the truth,—if such a one could appear amongst us, then would the world believe, as it now altogether refuses to whilst those who profess belief show such few tokens of the reality of their belief. 2. *In regard to the dread peril of those who disobey God.* We know with what impassioned earnestness Jeremiah had pleaded with his infatuated countrymen; how he had exhorted, implored, and wept in his endeavour to win them from their wicked ways. And now, when it seemed all in vain, we behold him sunk in sorrow, dissolved in tears. Wherefore this? Were the theory of the universalist true, that there is no "fearful looking for of judgment," that all will be made blessed in the coming hereafter, irrespective of what they have been or what their conduct in this life,—then such tears as we are contemplating now would be unmeaning. Had the prophet held such views, had our Lord, had St. Paul, their deep distress would have been inexplicable, because altogether uncalled for. Or even if the theory of those who hold that "death ends all" been that of God's servants, still such distress would be far more than could be accounted for. Or even if it were that only the blessedness of the righteous were missed, and all others would simply perish, then too the future of the ungodly would call for no such sorrow. Or that by such devices as those of the Romish Church—Masses, indulgences, and the like—the guilty soul, though indeed its doom were terrible, yet it might by these devices be rescued from such doom,—then too there could have been no tears such as these. But contemplating the overwhelming sorrow of men like Jeremiah when beholding the judgment of the ungodly, we are shut up to the conviction, which evidently possessed him so profoundly, that it is a fearful thing for an unforgiven man to fall into the hands of the living God. 3. *In regard to the exhaustion of all present resources of help.* Could Jeremiah have *done* anything to turn aside that judgment which he so vividly and with such distress anticipated, he would not have given himself up to tears. They are the evidence that all resources are exhausted, that nothing more can be done, that as he says (ch. vi. 29), "The bellows are burned." The language of such tears is the voice of God saying, concerning the hardened and impenitent, "He is joined to his idols: let him alone." God save us all from having to shed, and still more from causing, such tears as these. But they bear witness also—

II. To PROFOUND COMPASSION. He who has known the compassion of God for his own soul will, in proportion to the depth of that knowledge, feel compassion for the souls of others. Indifference and unconcern are no longer possible to him who knows the love of God when he sees men perishing in sin. "The love of Christ constraineth" him. And the same compassion, thus begotten, leads him to mourn when the offer of God's mercy is refused. Such tears, being interpreted, tell of his passionate but useless desire that the sinner's doom *had been averted.* Cf. David's exceeding bitter cry, "O Absalom, my son, my son!" etc. And they are made to flow the more freely by the remembrance that that lost condition *might have been* so altogether different. There was no necessity for it. That which could not have been avoided, which we feel to have been inevitable, we bear with more calmness. But when there is the consciousness, such as David had concerning Absalom, that he might have come to an end so different, to an end as honourable and blessed as this was disgraceful and miserable, that reflection made his tears flow faster than before. And when it is not mere folly *but grievous sin* which has brought God's judgment upon men, then the compassionate heart grieves yet more; a further drop of bitterness is infused into the cup, and such tears as we are contemplating have this sorrow in them as well as the others we have spoken of. And that now there *is no hope, no remedy,*—this is the last and worst reflection which wrings the compassionate heart with uttermost grief. Jeremiah beholds the house of Judah "left unto them desolate;" the daughter of his people not merely "hurt," but slain. How is it that, with like reasons for such compassion as that of Jeremiah, we know so little of it? "Rivers of waters run down mine eyes, because they keep not thy Law"—so spoke God's servant in the hundred and nineteenth psalm. But who can say that now? Compassionate Saviour, give us of *thy* mind.

III. To THE BEHOLDERS OF SUCH GRIEF. 1. *Are you workers for God?* Then remember that disappointment and present failure have been the lot of many of the noblest of the servants of God. There is a goodly fellowship of such. 2. *Are you believers in God?* Then remember his sure promise as to what shall follow this "sowing in tears," this "going forth weeping, bearing precious seed." We are not to think that we have seen the last result of our toil because that which we do see is so distressing. 3. *Are you rejecters of God?* Then remember that God puts such tears "in his bottle," and they are treasured by him; and their testimony, whilst it will be for the salvation of those who have shed them, will be far more terrible judgment against those who have caused them. "Weep not for me," said our Lord on his way to the cross, "but weep for yourselves, and for your children. . . . If they do these things in a green tree, what shall be done in the dry?" Yes, these tears tell of the sorrows of God's people, but they predict a worse sorrow still for his hardened foes. Look, then, O thou who hardenest thyself against God, and ask thyself, "If this be the sorrow I have caused, what shall that be which I shall have to bear?" Remember that it is not only here that there are tears, but in the future abode of the impenitent it is distinctly declared, "*There* shall be weeping." Then cease to cause such tears here, that you may never have to shed tears far more bitter there.—C.

Ver. 1.—*The moral degradation of women.* The expression, "the slain of the daughter of my people," suggests this subject. Therefore we may thus apply the prophet's words. Note—

I. THE MORAL DEGRADATION OF THE DAUGHTERS OF A PEOPLE IS A JUST CAUSE FOR THE DEEPEST SORROW. For think of what and how much is slain in these slain ones. The ruin of health, and the early and often dreadful death, are the least that is slain. Happiness is slain—that of the victim, and of those to whom she was once precious. The joyous hopes once cherished. The influence which might have been so pure and purifying, now corrupt and corrupting. The character once honoured, now dragged in the mire. The *soul*, in all its moral worth and spiritual energies and desires, that too is slain. Therefore, when contemplating such cruelly slain ones, the prophet's piteous cry of anguish is no more than such utter woe constrains.

II. BUT SUCH SORROW SHOULD TURN INTO SCORN AND WRATH FOR THE SLAYERS OF THESE SLAIN. Beware of the hideous complacency with which the world regards such murderers. Pray to be kept from the paths of such "bloody men."

III. BUT SUCH SORROW SHOULD NOT FORGET THAT THERE IS A DIVINE SPIRIT THAT

CAN " BREATHE UPON THESE SLAIN, THAT THEY MAY LIVE." The Spirit of Christ did so breathe upon one such, and she lived. He said to her, " Thy sins are forgiven. . . . Thy faith hath saved thee; go in peace" (Luke vii. 36—50).—C.

Ver. 2.—*Sighings after the wilderness.* The text reminds us of Ps. lv. 5, "Oh that I had wings," etc.! of Elijah's longing that he might die; of the similar dejection of Moses. Even our Lord said, "O faithless generation, how long shall I be with you? how long shall I suffer you?" But such desire as that of the text is in itself—

I. UNNATURAL. We are formed to mingle with our fellow-men, to live with them, not away from them. 1. It is in intercourse with them *life becomes interesting to us.* We are taken out of ourselves, fresh sources of pleasure and advantage are continually opened up to us. 2. *Sympathy* also is in fellowship. Our joys are more than doubled and our sorrows more than halved by the power of that sympathy which solitude can never know. 3. *Opportunities of doing good* are not to be had "in the wilderness," and when we "leave" our people. 4. Nor are the *benefits they can confer on us* to be found there. Heart and mind and soul are blessed by companionship and injured by solitude and isolation. Hence such wish as that of the text is, apart from the motive given, unnatural.

II. AND IT MAY BE WRONG. 1. It is so when it is the child of *impatience.* Doubtless there is much often to try our patience, and to make us wish that we could have done with it all. But we should not think much of the labourer who, because the toil was arduous, threw up his work ere the day was done; or of the soldier who left in the midst of the campaign. 2. Yet more culpable is it when it springs from *indolence.* There are many who dislike real work in any form. Exertion and effort are shrunk from everywhere. And in their religious life it is the same. And from such poor motive such wish as that of the text sometimes springs. 3. Still worse is it when it comes of *unbelief.* When all faith is gone, and the dark, dread falsehood begins to get hold of a man, that rest is only to be gained by breaking out of this life altogether.

III. BUT IT MAY PROCEED FROM CAUSES WHICH CAN ONLY EXCITE OUR COMPASSION. 1. Extremity of suffering: Job, Paul. 2. Experience of human infidelity, as in Ps. lv. 3. When all the purposes for which God ordained us to live in fellowship with one another are unattainable. Such was the case with Jeremiah. Pleasurable interest in such fellowship as was his could not be for him, but only daily vexation of his righteous soul (cf. Lot). Sympathy he could neither give nor find. Ever so desirous of doing them good, they spurned and despised all his efforts. And as to gaining good from them, it was but a continual contact with pollution. What wonder, then, that Jeremiah longed to be away from such a scene? "The hermits of the East, the anchorites of the desert, are more closely linked with ourselves in feeling than some at first may think. Our impulses are often identical with theirs; and if our actions vary it is because our standard of right, not our nature, is changed. In the life of each man there are hours when he sighs for the desert; hours when, bowed down by the sense of sin in himself and the sight of it in others, wearied out by striving to teach a stiff-necked generation, disheartened at seeing the 'good cause' advance so slowly, he can scarcely refrain from following, in his small way, the example of that emperor who exchanged the palace for the cloister, and the crown for the cowl." These are moments such as came to Jeremiah now. "The Emperor Charles uttered in deeds what we have all breathed in sighs. We do and we must long to flee away and be at rest; but then it must remain a longing, and nothing more" (G. Dawson).

IV. AND GOD HAS MADE PROVISION FOR ITS SATISFACTION. Not by giving us permission to retire to desert solitudes, except, as with Elijah and Paul, it may be for a while to prepare for future and higher service. But in the manner that the psalmist suggests where he says, "Oh that I had wings like a dove! for then," etc. Yes, *wings like a dove will bear us into the present rest of God.* The dove is the emblem of *meekness.* Like the lamb amongst the beasts, so the dove amongst the birds is the symbol of lowly meekness and gentleness. But lowly meekness is the way to rest, the rest God gives, the peace of God. Listen to our Saviour: " Come unto me, all ye that labour . . . Take my yoke. . . . For I am meek and lowly in heart: and ye shall find rest unto your souls" (Matt. xi.). The dove is the emblem of *purity*. It was not only amongst those birds that were counted clean, but was especially selected for presentation to God in sacrifice, as that which was pure alone could be. The doves were allowed to fly about the temple and to rest on its roofs and pillars (see H. Hunt's picture of the 'Finding in the Temple'). But purity opens the door of heaven, and enraptures the beholder with the beatific vision there. "Blessed are the pure in heart: for they shall see God." Wings are these, therefore, well likened to those of a dove, "covered with silver, and her feathers with yellow gold." Yes, "keep thyself unspotted from the world," and God shall so manifest himself to thee that thy soul shall be at rest, let the wicked rage around thee as they may. And the dove was the selected symbol *of the Holy Spirit.* "I saw the Holy Spirit descending like a dove," said John the Baptist. But his wings will bear thee where thou mayest see the fatherly love of God, his wisdom guiding all, and his gracious purpose being more and more accomplished. "He will take of the things of Christ and show them unto thee." And in them thou *shalt* have peace. The psalmist's passionate longing may then be fulfilled for us. We may have "wings like a dove." These, of meekness, purity, and the blessed Spirit of God. And so, without quitting the station assigned us or departing to any wilderness, we may have even now the rest of God.—C.

Ver. 7.—*The doings and doom of deceit.* The verses from ver. 2 to the text set forth its doings, and the text and remainder of the chapter foretell its doom. Note—
I. DECEIT. It is a terrible indictment that the prophet brings. He affirms that deceit is: 1. *Universal.* Ver. 2, "They be *all*," etc. Ver. 6, "Thine habitation is in the midst of deceit;" *i.e.* it is everywhere, all around you. That: 2. It has broken up the most sacred relationships: "They be all adulterers" (ver. 2). 3. It has turned their solemn assemblies into a conclave of liars (ver. 2). 4. It is practised deliberately. Ver. 3: as a man deliberately bends and takes aim with his bow. 5. It has mounted the judge's seat (ver. 3; cf. true translation of phrase, "They are not valiant for the truth"). 6. It has smoothed the way for all evil. "They proceed from evil to evil" (ver. 3). 7. It has destroyed all confidence (1) between neighbours, (2) between brethren (ver. 4). 8. It is diligently studied. Ver. 5, "They have taught," etc. "They take the utmost pains to go crookedly." 9. It is cruel and deadly in its aims (ver. 8). In view of a condition of things so horrible, how unanswerable is the demand of ver. 9, "Shall I not visit them for these things?" etc. ! It will be found in all the judgments of God upon nations that those judgments have never come until there was no other way of dealing with such nations, if the moral life of the world was to be maintained.
II. ITS DOINGS. 1. *It had made dwelling amongst them intolerable to the righteous.* (Cf. ver. 2.) Jeremiah longs to get away from them. The most desolate solitude would be preferable to living amid such a people as this. It is an ominous sign for a community when the godly, however compassionate, however long-suffering, can no longer endure to dwell in their midst. 2. *It had made the thought of God intolerable to themselves.* Vers. 3, 6, "They know not me, saith the Lord." Just as a man may meet one whom he desires to have nothing to do with, but when he meets him will pass him as if he did not know him; so deceit had made these people, as it makes all such, desirous of having nothing to do with God. Therefore they will not recognize or acknowledge him in any way. 3. *And at last it had made them intolerable to God.* Ver. 7: God asks, "What else can I do for the daughter of my people?" (cf. Exposition). There was nothing now but for the judgment of God to go forth against them. Therefore note—
III. ITS DOOM. Ver. 7, "Therefore thus saith," etc. And down to ver. 22 these awful judgments of God are set forth. Inquire, therefore, what there is about deceit which renders it so hateful in the sight of God. 1. *There can be no doubt that it is so.* "Lying lips are an abomination unto the Lord" (cf. Ps. xv.; Acts v.). "All liars shall have their part in the lake that burneth," etc. 2. And some of the reasons are: (1) Deceit cometh from Satan, who was "a liar from the beginning," and "the father of lies." It was by his lies that our first parents were deceived and sin was brought into the world. (2) It is the source of infinite misery and distress. It is "the deceits of the world, the flesh, and the devil" which still work well-nigh all our sorrow and our shame. (3) It tends to the destruction of human society. All our well-being and comfort depend upon good faith being maintained between man and man. "But now,

where fraud and falsehood, like a plague or cancer, comes over to invade society, the band which held together the parts compounding it presently breaks, and men are thereby put to a loss where to league and to fasten their dependencies, and so are forced to scatter and shift every one for himself. Upon which account every notoriously false person ought to be looked upon and detested as a public enemy, and to be pursued as a wolf or a mad dog, and a disturber of the common peace and welfare of mankind; there being no particular person whatsoever but has his private interest concerned and endangered in the mischief that such a wretch does to the public" (South). A sin, therefore, so destructive of the well-being of his children cannot but be abominable in the eyes of the Father of us all. 3. It shuts God out of the heart altogether. God has made us for himself, but deceit bars fast the door of man's heart against him. God can only be worshipped in spirit and in truth; but deceit renders this primary condition of such worship unattainable. 4. But God in his anger remembers mercy. Ver. 7, "Behold, I will melt them, and try them," that is to say, he will, as the smelter casts the metal into the fire not to destroy but to refine it, to purge away its dross, and then, that being done, tests and tries it to see that the process has been effectual; so God will send his judgments upon his people, not to destroy, but to purify them, and he will afterwards test them again, give them another opportunity of serving him. He might have destroyed, but this he will not do. He "will melt them, and try them." But less than this he cannot do. "What else," etc.? he asks. It is a dread process; Judah and Jerusalem found it so, and all who compel God to cast them into such a crucible find it to be a dread process. Our blessed Saviour wept over Jerusalem, although he told them that when next they saw him they should say, "Blessed is he that cometh in the Name of the Lord." It was the thought of that furnace for fire through which they must be passed ere they would come to this better mind that drew forth those tears. Let none, therefore, deem the judgment of God a subject for trifling with, because, as here, God says its purpose is to "melt and try," rather than to destroy.

Conclusion. Let this consideration of the doings and doom of deceit lead us to listen to the Lord's appeal, "Oh, do not this thing that I hate!"—C.

Vers. 10—22.—*The terrible threatenings of love.* There are few more awful passages of Scripture than this. The doom denounced on the guilty people is indeed dreadful. Nevertheless that doom had not yet descended. There was a merciful pause, during which space was given for repentance. Meanwhile the prophet was bidden to utter these threatenings. Notice—

I. How TERRIBLE THEY ARE. 1. *In themselves.* The fertile hills and pastures of their country shall be laid waste, so that no living creature can find food (ver. 10). Jerusalem is to be utterly destroyed and desolate (ver. 11). The deep anguish of the people—their very meat to be as "wormwood," and their drink as "water of gall" (ver. 15). They shall be carried captive and scattered among the heathen, and even then shall not escape the sword (ver. 16). They shall be overwhelmed with sorrow, their eyes shall gush out with tears (vers. 17—19). Death shall reign everywhere (ver. 21); and shall be accompanied with deepest degradation (ver. 22). It is not possible to conceive of more hopeless misery than is portrayed in these vivid descriptions of the wrath that was to come. 2. *Because of their righteousness.* Unrighteous suffering can be borne, and those who bear it are bidden by the Lord to count themselves as "blessed" because of it (Matt. v. 11, 12). And sorrows that come to us in the course of God's providence, and the reason of which we do not know, these we can bear sustained by the faith of the Father's love. But when sore suffering is sent to us as the direct punishment of sin, and the righteous because so deserved anger of God is evident, then those consolations which are open to us under other sufferings are closed to us under these. The bitter reflection, "It was all our own fault; it might, it ought to have been avoided," makes the pain we endure, and the calamities that overtake us, more terrible than otherwise they could possibly be. We take refuge from man's anger and from ordinary sorrows in God's love, but sin that has brought down God's righteous judgment has also closed against us that most blessed shelter and every shelter, and we are left without defence. And another element in their terribleness is: 3. *The certainty of their fulfilment.* "God is not mocked: whatsoever a man soweth, that *shall* he also reap." The threatenings of God are not, as are many of the threatenings of men, mere empty vapourings, great swelling words, never designed to be fulfilled. Let the records of all human history, of all human lives, whether told of within or without the pages of the Bible, attest the absolute certainty of fulfilment which evermore characterizes the threatenings of God. When and where has he ever threatened and failed to fulfil his threat? Let the Fall, the Flood, the destruction of Sodom, the plagues on Egypt, the deaths of the generation of unbelievers in the wilderness, and ten thousand instances more, all prove the steadfastness of God to his word. And it is this fact of the absolute certainty of his threatenings being fulfilled that adds to them a yet further terribleness. There is no chance of escape, no hope of God's relenting; as certain as the fixed laws of nature are these awful denunciations of God to him who persists in bringing them upon himself.

II. BUT THEY ARE THE THREATENINGS OF LOVE. 1. He who utters them is the God who in his very nature and essence is love. How manifold are the proofs of this in creation, in providence, in grace! He, therefore, has no pleasure in the death of the wicked; judgment is his "strange work." 2. Those against whom they are uttered are the objects of his love. His love for them is deeper than his anger against them. Hence it is that the contrite sinner never fails to gain the pardon he seeks. "Fathers of our flesh" may "chasten after their own pleasure, but he for our profit" (cf. ver. 7). 3. His purpose in these threatenings is a loving purpose. He would compel by the scourge of fear his rebellious children to abandon their evil ways. 4. And if at length he is compelled to execute his threatenings, it is out of love that he does so. For the love of God is towards his *children*, not to any one particular child, and the welfare of the family is the chief consideration. *Salus populi suprema lex.* If consistently with that the transgressor can be restored, he will be, but not else. Hence, as an earthly father would not permit one of his children, ill with terrible and contagious disease, to mingle with the other children; or, as in the far more sad case of utter moral wickedness, intercourse with the rest would be forbidden; so, for the sake of the rest of his children, God will separate them from the wicked and the wicked from them. But it is love which constrains to this, and hence it is that the seeming contradiction is true, that he who is the God of love is also "a consuming fire." The very fatherhood of God is the most fearful fact of all others against the persistently rebellious and ungodly soul. Hence—

III. SUCH THREATENINGS ARE EVER THE MOST TERRIBLE OF ALL. Cf. the threatenings of our Saviour. The most awful utterances to be found in the whole Bible proceeded from his lips—the lips whose words were wont to be so "gracious" that the people "wondered" at them. It is his sayings which have lit up the lurid glare of the fires unquenchable of hell, and it is he who has made our souls shudder at the sight of "the worm that dieth not," and of the "outer darkness" where there is "weeping and wailing and gnashing of teeth." See, too, the Revelation of St. John. That apostle, whose great theme is the love of God, whose soul was more attuned to the music of love than that of any other, wrote that awful book, which is full throughout of "mourning, lamentation, and woe," and which almost reeks with the blood and fire and smoke of torments of which it tells. These facts can only be accounted for— and there are more like them—on the ground that the threatenings of love are ever the most terrible of all. And they are so, for such reasons as these: 1. Love so hates what tends to the harm of those it loves. Hence it brands with its deepest curse that sin which harms God's children most of all. One chief argument with many minds for the retention of capital punishments is that only so can a government or nation mark its sense of the supreme wickedness of the crime it so punishes. Punish it as other crimes are punished, and it will come to be regarded as no worse than they. And in like manner God would inspire us with a holy abhorrence of sin by the awful condemnation that he has pronounced against it. 2. Love so yearns to rescue those it loves. The rope may cut and wound the hands of the drowning sailor to whom we have thrown it, but we do not mind that if thereby he be drawn safe to shore. The knife of the surgeon may cut deep and cause fearful pain, but if it saves the imperilled life we are thankful notwithstanding. So God sends forth these stern, rough, and terrible threatenings, that souls under the spell of sin may be awakened, alarmed, made to tremble, and to "seek the Lord while he may be found." No gentler means will avail; therefore these, so love resolves, shall not be left untried. It will shrink from nothing to accomplish its compassionate purpose of rescuing from the murderous sin the soul it loves. 3. And there is no wickedness so deep as that of outraging love. Men will never see sin in all its hatefulness until they see it as outrage done to love. Whilst they are taught only that it is disobedience to sovereign rule rather than despite and shameful wrong done to a Father's heart, they will not look upon it as they should, nor repent of it as they must. Even in human esteem, outrage done to a loving heart adds intensity to the condemnation with which we view and sentence disobedience done to law. We all recognize that such wickedness is the worst of all. We cannot wonder, then, that the threatenings against wrong persistently done to the love of God are terrible as they are, and the most terrible of all.

CONCLUSION. 1. Beware of bringing upon yourselves such threatenings as these. Those which are fulminated forth by hatred, or by pride, or by sovereignty, or by law,— these, though they may be terrible, are not to be compared with those that we have been considering. "The wrath of the Lamb" is the most awful of all. 2. Beware of despising them. So far from believing what has now been shown, men argue in directly opposite way, and, because the threatenings are those of love, they conclude that they may safely be disregarded, they will never be carried out. But what has now been shown proves that this is the very last thing we can venture to do. 3. Beware of concealing them. It is to be feared that, in these soft, easy days on which we have fallen, the Lord's watchmen do very often fail to "blow the trumpet and give warning." From blood-guiltiness such as that let us pray to be delivered. For are there not many now whom nothing but the startling peal of the trumpet of God's threatened judgments will ever arouse or alarm? Assuredly there are. Therefore, in view of the doom of the ungodly, as well as by the love of Christ, let us "*beseech* men to be reconciled to God."—C.

Vers. 12—15.—*The inquest on the slain of Judah and Jerusalem.* I. GOD DEMANDS IT. 1. For his righteousness is impugned. Men had not failed, could not fail, to notice the terrible judgments which God had sent upon Judah and Jerusalem, and, as is implied by his own declaration of their causes (ver. 12), they had either not seen or had denied the righteousness of what had been done. This questioning of the Divine righteousness and equity is a procedure all too common still. 2. And thus the Divine hold on the loyalty of men's hearts is threatened. For unless men regard God as righteous, just, and good, no power in the universe can make them yield him the homage of their hearts. How much of the alienation of heart in the present day may be attributed to the representations of God which a false theology has set forth! Men will not, for they cannot, love such a being as too many preachers represent God to be. They may be threatened with everlasting perdition, but it will make no difference. For God himself has given us a nature which renders impossible our yielding our hearts' homage to any one—be he whom he may—that our hearts do not regard as worthy of that homage. 3. But God's supreme solicitude is for this homage of our hearts. Hence what threatens it must be intolerable to him. Therefore he seeks for vindication before the hearts of men, and demands this inquiry.

II. AN UNIMPEACHABLE JURY IS IMPANELLED. It is not just any one who can be trusted to make this inquiry. The frivolous, the unthoughtful, would fail to grasp the problem involved, and the ungodly who suffered these judgments would be sure to assign them to any and every cause rather than the true one. Therefore those who are summoned to this inquest are (1) the wise—those who will intelligently consider all the facts of the case; and (2) those "to whom the Lord hath spoken"—those, that is, who have been divinely enlightened, who are in sympathy with truth and righteousness. God summons such, and fearlessly demands, now as of old, the most thorough investigation into the righteousness of all his ways.

III. THEY ARE BIDDEN WELL AND TRULY TRY THE CASE BEFORE THEM. He would have them so consider it that they may "understand" it in all its bearings, reasons, and ends. He tells them what he has done and what he yet will do, and what are his reasons for his conduct. He does not conceal that his judgments are tremendous, notorious, certain to excite inquiry, to be challenged, and by many to be condemned. But he appeals to the "wise," and to those "to whom the Lord hath spoken," to consider and understand what he has done. God calls not for mere credulity from any of us; he asks for no mere blind faith; but it is to a "reasonable service" he summons us, and this reasonableness he would have us consider and "understand." "I speak as to wise men; judge ye what I say:" such is his appeal.

IV. And when they have "understood" the righteousness of God they are to "declare" it. There is no greater service that can be rendered than "to vindicate the ways of God to man;" to "commend the truth to every man's conscience in the sight of God." The believer is established, the waverer brought to decision, the sinner —like as Felix, when Paul "reasoned of righteousness and judgment"—is made to tremble, the scorner and the atheist are silenced.

V. The effects of that verdict will be varied. 1. It will strike terror to the hearts of the enemies of God; for it will rob them of the comfort they had in regarding God's judgments as unjust. Even this "drop of cold water" they may not have. 2. It will give great peace of mind to all beholders of God's strong rule; for it will show that his rule is not strong and supreme alone, but absolutely righteous. 3. It will make God's people "sing unto the Lord a new song," because "he cometh to judge the earth" (Ps. xcvi.). It will assure them of the triumph of righteousness, and the utter impotency and impermanency of wrong. But let each one ask himself, "How will that verdict affect *me*?"—C.

Ver. 14.—*Hereditary sin real sin.* God here declares that he will punish those who have walked "after Baalim, which their fathers taught them." Therefore the fact of their having been trained in this sin by their fathers is not held to acquit them of guilt in what they do. Their sin, though hereditary, is real.

I. This seems unjust. It has often been objected to that because the fathers ate sour grapes the children's teeth should be set on edge (Ezek. xviii. 2). Why should I be punished for another's man's sin?

II. But it is the Divine Law. The sins of the fathers *are* visited on the children. "By the offence of one all men were made sinners" (Rom. v.). And in daily life how perpetually we see this law in ruthless operation!—children punished in health, fortune, character, reputation, in mind, body, and soul, all through their fathers' sin. They walk in the ways of Baalim because their fathers taught them. And yet, unjust though their punishment *may* appear—

III. Conscience endorses it. Who knows how much of that strong passionate nature which led David into such dreadful sin may have been inherited? Indeed, he says, "Behold, I was shapen in iniquity," etc. (Ps. li.). But this does not hinder him from taking all the blame of his sin upon himself. All the way through we hear his confession—"my sin," "my transgression," "mine iniquity." And never does the conscience awakened to a sense of sin think of palliating such sin by the plea of its being the result of inheritance. Thus conscience witnesses to the righteousness of the Divine Law.

IV. And so does human law. What judge ever pardoned a criminal because he had a bad father? We execrate "bloody Queen Mary" notwithstanding she had a bloodthirsty father.

V. The explanation is: 1. That hereditary sin does not destroy *conscience*. That speaks in all; it is "the light that lighteth every man that cometh into the world," the inward monitor which ever condemns crime and approves righteousness (cf. Rom. ii. 14, 15). 2. Nor does it destroy *understanding*. Teachers of righteousness are on every hand, from whom all may learn. 3. Nor does it destroy the *power of will*. It may weaken, but it does not destroy. Therefore, in spite of hereditary sin, every man knows, and can choose if he will, that which is right; and therefore he is held accountable before every tribunal—that of God, of conscience, and of man. 4. But there is yet another reason given by St. Paul: "*God hath concluded all in unbelief, that he may have mercy upon all*" (Rom. xi. 32; Gal. iii. 22). A cruel Roman emperor wished that all Rome had but one neck, that he might kill it with one blow. God hath in his infinite grace gathered up all our humanity into one, even in Christ, so that, as sin had destroyed all by one stroke (Rom. v.), the grace of God in Christ might save all by the one righteousness of the One; so that "where sin did abound, grace," etc. That gathering up of humanity into one in Adam, which seems at first sight to have worked such injustice, is altogether met, and far more than met, by the again gathering up of all in One, even in Christ, which works such grace. But that ultimate redemption which is in Christ does not hinder, but that meanwhile, and for a weary while, hereditary sin may work woeful sorrow and harm. Therefore—

VI. THIS FACT APPEALS: 1. *To all parents.* Seek to cut off the entail. We may have received such sad inheritance, but let us, as we may, reject it for ourselves, and in so doing refuse to hand it on to others. Again and again has God given grace to some one member of a godless house—as to Josiah, son of that Amon of whom it is said, " But Amon sinned more and more "—who has for himself and those who come after him broken the bad succession and begun a new and blessed departure. When we have done our best, our children will have a sufficiently heavy burden to bear; let us not make that burden heavier, life more terrible, and holiness and heaven far less attainable for them, by handing down to them a legacy of evil example and of unhallowed habits and propensities inherited from ourselves. Do not let us sin so against our children. Yet many do. 2. *To all children.* Your fathers' sin will not excuse yours. God has turned judgment away from many an evil son because he had a godly father, but never because he had an ungodly one. Therefore if yours be the sad and too frequent lot of those who inherit evil from their parents, reject that inheritance, and seek and gain from your heavenly Father, though you may not be helped herein by your earthly one, the better, the most blessed inheritance of the children of God.—C.

Vers. 21, 22.—*Death's doings.* Behold—

I. DEATH'S CARNIVAL. In many an ancient continental city you may see portrayed in still vivid colours, on the roofs of their covered bridges,—as on that of the old bridge at Lucerne,—on the walls of their churches, and elsewhere, the grim ' Dance of Death.' These verses remind of those paintings, and tell in yet more fearful form of Death's dread carnival. With what diabolic zest he is represented at his work here! He is shown to us, not as coming in in ordinary manner to the sick-chamber, where his coming has long been expected and may even be welcomed; but as breaking in roughly, unexpectedly, cruelly, like a thief coming in at the windows. Nor as drawing near to the poor, the defenceless, the miserable; but entering into our palaces, the abode of the great, the rich, the strong. Nor as calling home those whose day's work is done, who have lived their life, and to whom eventide has long ago arrived; but as cutting ruthlessly down the dear young children in the very blossom of their days. Nor as ridding the earth of the cruel and vile; but tearing from us the innocent, the children. Nor are vigour, strength, and promise any more a defence against him than decrepit old age; for "the young men" are his victims even as others. And no multitude of slain will satiate him. Ver. 22 represents the numbers of the dead as so great that they have to be left unburied and uncared for to rot upon the open field. It is true that this frightful picture is taken from the awful experiences of a besieged city, but with slight modifications it is true everywhere and always. This life is the carnival of Death. What are men but a long succession of mourners? As the poet says—

> " Our hearts like muffled drums are beating
> Funeral marches to the grave."

And when we contemplate the cruel consequences of this carnival of Death, which is going on still, the mind and heart reel, and faith in the fatherhood of God would fade utterly out of men's souls were it not that in brighter colours still the Word of God portrays—

II. DEATH'S CONQUEROR. *Christ* has abolished death. The broken pillar, the turned-down torch, the "Vale, vale, in æternum vale," of the old pagan world, have now no appropriateness because no truth. Death is sorrow still, even to those who believe in him who is "the Resurrection and the Life; " but it is not and cannot be that hopeless, unutterable, unfathomable woe which it was till he came who hath abolished death. No doubt this terrible verse (ver. 21), which tells of Death's dread doings, is yet far more true than we would like it to be, and often and often, in the blank desolation and shattered hopes which earth's bereavements bring to us, we fail to derive all the consolation and help which Death's glorious Conqueror has given to us. But, nevertheless, he has given them, and it is true that " Blessed are the dead which die in the Lord." Let us see to it that we are, by a living abiding trust, " in the Lord," and then, though we sorrow, and sorrow bitterly still, yet it will not be, it is not, " as those that have no hope."—C.

Vers. 23—26.—" *Whereof to glory.*" Introduction. Cannot understand these prophecies without a knowledge of the history of the times. This is true of all prophecies, and especially of these. Therefore we will glance at such history as we proceed. Note— I. THE GLORYING THAT IS CONDEMNED. 1. That of the wise man in his *wisdom.* The statesmen of Jeremiah's days had been thus glorying. They had prided themselves in their political sagacity. For many years they had formed alliances, now with one power and now with another. And they seemed to have managed well, for, for nearly a whole century, Judah had been, though so weak a power and so valuable a prize, left unattacked. Therefore no wonder that the wise men gloried in their wisdom. But now political trouble was beginning again. Egypt had become a great power, and was warring against Assyria. In this war the king Josiah sided with Assyria, and was slain in the battle of Megiddo. Thus they were without their king, and compelled to ally themselves with Egypt and to share in her fortunes, which to the eye of the prophet were the reverse of bright. Great troubles were drawing near, and it is in view of them that Jeremiah says, " Let not the wise man," etc. 2. The strong in their *strength.* The army of Judah was large, their fortress of Jerusalem was all but impregnable, but Jeremiah saw that all this would not avail. Their utter overthrow was fast hastening on. The great Babylonian power which had absorbed the Assyrian should accomplish this. Hence the word, " Let not the strong man," etc. 3. The rich in their *riches.* The long continuance of peace had enabled the nation to accumulate vast wealth. But this only made them yet more an object of desire to their approaching invaders. Their wealth was their woe. 4. The children of Abraham *in the covenant, of which circumcision was the sign* (vers. 25, 26). From the time of Hezekiah's reformation until the time when Jeremiah wrote, Judah and Jerusalem had professed the ancient faith. The temple service had gone on, the sacrifices offered, etc. There had been a short, sad interval during Manasseh's reign. But so far as profession went they had been worshippers of God. And of late years Josiah's reformation had led to still louder profession. And in this profession we know they trusted very implicitly (cf. ch. vii.). But it had not preserved them from the Divine displeasure in days gone by, nor in the present, nor would it in days to come. For beneath all this profession the moral and spiritual condition of the nation was most evil. Even in Hezekiah's day Isaiah had told the people that, in spite of all their profession, " the whole head was sick," etc. (cf. Isa. i.). And that this was so was shown by the readiness with which they followed Manasseh in his idolatries, and joined in the persecution of the faithful servants of God. And when Manasseh repented, and there was again an external profession, it was scarcely any better. But the monstrous conduct of Amon, who " sinned more and more," made the people desire the old ways. Hence, when Josiah came to the throne, they were prepared for his reforms. But again it was only a change of custom, not of character; outward, but not inward. Jeremiah sought to help forward a true reformation, for it was indeed needed (see his description of the moral condition of the people, vers. 2—8 in this chapter). Hence it was that he told them their circumcision was no better than uncircumcision. *Apply all this* to ourselves: (1) *As a nation.* We have all these several advantages above named: wise statesmen, great strength, vast wealth, universal religious profession; but all these, apart from moral and spiritual worth, will go for nothing. It is " righteousness," and that alone, that " exalteth a nation." (2) *As individuals.* We are not to despise any of these things. They are God's good gifts; but they will not save us. We may not glory in them as a sure safeguard. II. WHEREOF WE MAY AND SHOULD GLORY. (Cf. ver. 24.) This means that there should be: 1. *Intellectual apprehension* of the truth in regard to God. His character is shown: (1) In his exercise of loving-kindness. It is well to be open-eyed to the many and varied proofs of this—in creation, providence, redemption, grace. And it is well to be able to trace these proofs and to show that God is good. (2) In his exercising judgment. He has given proofs of this also, and that is but a partial and therefore most misleading theology that shuts out of view the sterner aspects of the Divine Father. As in Christ we see most of all how God exercises loving-kindness, so too in him we may see the sure warnings of his judgment. "If they do these things in a green tree, what shall be done in the dry?" "If the righteous scarcely be saved, where," etc.? (3) In his exercise of righteousness. How full the proofs of this also! How manifest in Christ, his teachings, life, death, his Spirit's work now, etc.! Now, it is most desirable to understand all this, for the mind to grasp these sure truths. Too much of the religiousness of the day is weak, flaccid, unstable, because there is wanting knowledge and understanding in the truth. We are apt to be satisfied with an emotional religion, with the play of feeling and the outgoing of the affections. But for all this to be reliable we must *understand* as well as feel. 2. In that he "knoweth" as well as understandeth. This is more than to understand. For "to know" continually means, in Bible language, to approve, to be in sympathy with, to delight in, etc. (cf. "I will not know a wicked person;" "The Lord knoweth the way of the righteous;" "This is life eternal, to know thee the only," etc.). And so here to know God is to have moral sympathy, personal experience, inward approval and delight in regard to God. Now, he who thus understandeth and knoweth God hath "whereof to glory." The prophet desired that his people might have this glorying, for this would save them, whilst all the other things in which they gloried but left them to perish. Appeal to all who profess religion and who instruct others. Can you thus glory? Do you understand? Better still, Do you *know* God in his loving-kindness, judgment, righteousness?—C.

Vers. 23, 24.—*The chief good.* The people had little reason to glory in their wisdom, or power, or wealth. These natural resources had utterly failed them as a safeguard against the avenger and destroyer. The prophet directs them to an infinitely surer ground of trust, a higher cause of rejoicing. These words are a striking appeal to faith, all the more remarkable because of the desperate circumstances of the time. In spite of all the desolation of the land, the wreck and ruin of all their pride as a nation, let them hold fast to their faith in the living God, and especially in those attributes of his being and principles of his government—loving-kindness, judgment, righteousness —which such circumstances tend to obscure and seem even to disprove. We fix our minds now simply on this thought—*the knowledge of God and personal fellowship with him are immeasurably more worth our seeking and rejoicing in than all those endowments which to the carnal eye are so full of charm.* There is a natural tendency in men to rejoice unduly in the good that they derive by birth, or education, or the favour of providence, forgetting that the *chief good* is something of a different kind, something that must come to them in a different way. Nothing that tends to enrich and adorn and gladden our life in this world is to be despised; but if we measure things by a true standard, and esteem them according to their real and relative value, we shall place everything else that men call good or great beneath that which connects us directly with God and heaven and immortality. Note respecting this higher good—
I. IT IS MORE TRULY OUR OWN THAN ANYTHING ELSE CAN EVER BE. This is seen if we consider: 1. *The way in which it becomes ours.* The surface acquirements and adornments of life—wealth, social position, favourable circumstances, etc., cannot be called "ours" in the sense in which that which is an inherent element of our individuality is ours. And even as regards personal qualities, there are important differences. Whatever natural gifts belong to us, our own will has had nothing to do with our possession of them. Their development may be dependent on it, but in their origin they are not so. Whereas the affections that connect us with God tell how the deepest depths of our being were stirred at their birth within us. Nothing so truly ours as that which has thus become ours. 2. *The absolute satisfaction it brings.* All the "springs of our being" are in God. He is the true Home and blissful Centre of rest for every human spirit. "The good man is satisfied from himself" (Prov. xiv. 14), not because of anything in the resources of his own finite being, but because he has learnt by the utter renunciation of all trust in these to find his true "self" in God. 3. *Its perpetuity.* We may soon be bereft of all other endowments; this we can never lose. There is no possession over which a man can rejoice in this world which is not precarious and uncertain. And though the sense of this need not check our free use

and hearty enjoyment of it, it will always cast some slight shadow over the sunshine of our delight. But there is no shadow here, no sense of insecurity, no fear of disappointment. Have your soul in conscious fellowship with God, and you may rest in the thought that "nothing shall ever be able to separate you from his love" (Rom. viii. 38, 39). "This is life eternal," etc. (John xvii. 3). "The water that I shall give him shall be in him," etc. (John iv. 14).

II. UNLIKE OTHER FORMS OF GOOD, IT IS INCAPABLE OF ABUSE. What natural gift is there that men may not turn, and have not actually turned, to some purpose contrary to that for which it was given? The false use grows, not so much out of any quality or tendency in the thing itself, as out of the innate perversity of our human nature. And there is nothing in the thing itself, or in the fact of our possessing it, that necessarily acts as a cure for that perversity. Intellectual capacity, genius, literary culture, rank, wealth, etc.,—how often have these been allied with moral corruption, and given their possessors the ability to inflict incalculable mischief on the human race? The graces of holy character which spring from fellowship with God cannot, in the nature of things, be thus abused. You cannot conceive of their being prostituted to evil ends. They bear within them the pledge of their Divine use and issue.

III. IT ENABLES US, AS NOTHING ELSE CAN, TO APPRECIATE ALL THAT IS TRUE AND GOOD IN THIS PRESENT WORLD. You must know God before you can rightly understand and realize the highest profit of the world in which he has placed you. There are two popular errors in this direction—one is the error of supposing that the apprehension of the truth of nature depends solely on mental capacity and scientific investigation. Does not the inability of some of the most illustrious thinkers of every age to find out the Divine in nature, rather show that it is more a question of spiritual sympathy than of intellectual power? The other error is that of supposing that the power to procure the good of this life is the same thing as the power to enjoy it. And yet how many pampered children of wealth and fashion are there who bear upon their faces the marks of weariness and discontent! Their souls are withered by excessive physical indulgence and artificial culture. They have lost the capacity of pure and simple enjoyment, and childlike wonder and delight are things to them unknown. Let your spirit be in fellowship with God, let your "heart be set to hallow all you find," and the deepest treasures of truth and the sweetest satisfactions of life are within your reach. God has made purity of heart the condition, not only of knowing himself, but of knowing the best of his gifts. It both creates and verifies—

> "The cheerful faith that all which we behold
> Is full of blessing."

"Godliness with contentment is great gain" (1 Tim. vi. 6). "Blessed are the meek," etc. (Matt. v. 5). "All things are yours," etc. (1 Cor. iii. 21—23).

IV. IT GIVES US THE POWER TO CONFER HIGHEST BENEFIT ON OUR FELLOW-CREATURES. We are disposed sometimes to envy the talents, the range of influence, the means of usefulness, that others possess. It seems a grand thing to us to be in certain commanding positions, and have resources that may be used at pleasure for the working out of certain desired ends. Remember, however, that what can alone give worth to these things are precisely those personal, moral qualities that are within the reach of all. The influence of godly character is deeper, more radical, more productive of enduring fruits of blessedness than any other kind of influence. Who would not rejoice in the power to confer this highest good upon the world?—W.

Ver. 1.—*Incessant weeping over the calamities of Israel.* We have here *still another measure* of how great, in the estimation of the prophet, the calamity was which had fallen upon his people. Other measures have already been given, in the despoiling of the tombs (ch. viii. 1, 2), in the exile worse than death (ch. viii. 3), in the visitation of serpents which were beyond the charmer's power (ch. viii. 17), and in the suffering through the sin of his people, which even a true servant of God could not escape (ch. viii. 21). And now this extraordinary desire of the prophet comes in to make plain from yet another direction how great he reckoned the impending calamity to be. We may well imagine that as he set before Jerusalem these gloomy prospects, the people in their light-heartedness replied, "Why make all this ado? Why try thus to alarm us by these threatenings and cries and tears?" The exclamation of ver. 1 guides us to what the prophet's answer would be. "My tears, which you count so causeless, rather fall short—short beyond all expressing—of the occasion for them." The fact is that the deepest, tenderest human pity and sorrow, when compared with the actual needs of fallen man, are but as a slight thaw that vainly struggles with the penetrating frost of the heart. Not that human beings lack the power of deep emotion. Whole peoples will be responsive enough to certain touches. But who is to bring before the hearts of all men a sufficient perception of what it is that underlies and perpetuates the misery of the whole world? The thing wanted is an abiding pity for men lying in the suffering of sin. It is perfectly true that there is not pity enough for men because of their poverty, their bodily defects and infirmities, and all miseries that are visible to the natural man. But the real reason why even this pity falls so lamentably short is that there is no searching consideration of what lies deeper than any visible miseries. *Nothing effectual* can be done with the *seen* unless the *unseen* is put right. Then we may be sure of it that the seen will come right with wonderful quickness and stability. We must make our hearts to dwell with the utmost pity on those who are not yet born again, not yet living the life of faith, not yet in living union with the great Source of eternal life, not yet rejoicing with the joy of the Holy Ghost. If we ourselves are really in process of salvation, and with our increased knowledge of truth comprehending more and more what salvation will bring with it for ourselves, then it will not appear to us extravagant and rhapsodical rhetoric that a prophet should wish his head to be waters, and his eyes a fountain of tears. It is unmanly and utterly despicable to weep for trifles, to weep over some spoiled gratification of self; but what sort of a heart must that man have who can watch, free from the deepest agitation, his brethren going on heedlessly into perdition? Jeremiah would have been unworthy of his call and his visions as a prophet if he had fallen short of his exclamation here. Not, of course, that we are to make too much of *the mere shedding of tears.* In the case of the prophet copious tears were the index of a heart within right in its thoughts, steady in its purposes. But there are many instances where copious tears have no such value. They come and go like a thunder-shower, lasting us briefly and leaving as little trace behind. Men of few tears may be men of a large, wise, far-seeing kindness. He who never gives to beggars in the street may yet be doing much to make beggary cease altogether. Jeremiah's wish, then, was the wish of a man who saw deeply into the confusions of his time; and yet he did not see as deep as Jesus. Those few tears that Jesus dropped amid the bereaving agonies of Bethany, had in them more of a pure and profound pity over men than all the tears that sinners themselves have shed. No sinful man can imagine that ideal of human life which was ever before the eyes of the Son of God. He alone knows how far man has fallen; he alone knows how high fallen man can be raised. He sees what men miss who do not repent and believe in him. He sees what possibilities of remorse and shame and self-condemnation may be opening up in eternity to the negligent and the impenitent. What wonder, then, that he spoke of the worm that dieth not, and the fire that is not quenched! What tears must not be shed over those who choose to sow the wind, seemingly forgetting that they must reap the whirlwind!—Y.

Ver. 2.—*The lodging-place in the wilderness.* I. WHAT IT IS THE PROPHET WISHES FOR. The occurrence of the word "wilderness" may easily mislead us into thinking that the prophet's wish was for solitude, and thus we may be disposed to reproach him, as if, Timon-like, he wanted to get away from his fellow-men altogether. But it is not on the word "wilderness" that we must fix our attention to discover the prophet's feeling. The reference to a traveller's lodging-place is the main thing to be considered. It is not between some hermit's humble, solitary shelter and the well-built house, which is but one out of many making up the stately city, that the contrast is made, but rather between the inn of the traveller and the abode of the man who, day after day, has to mingle busily in the society of which he forms a part. If you are staying at an inn for the night, it matters very little, so far as acquaintance is concerned, who your fellow-guests may be. You scarcely meet them; you are in their company for a few hours, and on the morrow each takes his several way. Jeremiah prefers to live in an inn, where he would see a succession of strange faces, to living even amongst his own people.

Then that the inn should be in a wilderness was a sort of necessity, to round his wish off and make it perfectly express the state of his mind. Travellers had often wide stretches of wilderness-land to cross, where, just because it was wilderness, some sort of shelter needed to be provided for the night. But it might not be an inn in anything like our understanding of the word—perhaps nothing more than a rough enclosure, where only that was provided which the bare necessities of the moment demanded.

II. WHY THE PROPHET WISHES FOR THIS. The settled society in which the prophet has been living has become rotten in all its important relations. Jeremiah has a people whom he must describe as "my people." He is connected with them by a tie of nature which no repugnance of his can destroy. But, though they are his people, that cannot make him to overlook, excuse, or tolerate their iniquities. Nay, the very fact that they are his people helps to make the iniquity more burdensome to him; for with one's own people one has so much to do. A righteous son of Sodom, if such a character were imaginable, sickened with all the abominations around him, might well have left his kinsfolk, if they would not listen to his warning or profit by his refusal to join in their wrong-doing. And Jeremiah may be looked on here pretty much as if he had been a dweller in Sodom, for Jerusalem was spiritually Sodom. Adultery, knavery, habitual lying and wrong-doing,—these were sad elements to be charged as going to the substance of the social life of the people. And the prophet wished to be free from all entanglement with such. Of course we are not to take his wish literally. It is but an emphatic way of indicating how separated he was in the spirit of his mind from such considerations as ruled in only too many hearts of Israel. Though among his people, he was not of them. United according to the flesh, there was a great gulf between them according to the spirit. His people though they were, he yet was compelled to look upon them as travellers whom he casually met just for a little time. And so must God's people ever learn to look upon many of those whom they are continually meeting on earth. *For enduring society* there must be something more than natural ties, frequent intercourse, or community of intellectual tastes and pursuits. It is a small thing to be brought together in the concerns of time if we are not also brought together in the concerns of eternity. Sad it is to think that there may be a closer bond between those who have never met on earth than between those who, on earth, have lived for years together! Those who are travelling to the same place may never meet by the way, but when they do meet it is not in the traveller's mere lodging-place, but where there are many *mansions*, and whence they "go out no more for ever." A mansion is itself a place that *abides*, and those who dwell in it are meant to *abide* also.—Y.

Ver. 3.—*Wickedness prevailing, and why it prevails.* "These wicked people," says the prophet, "prevail, but their prevailing does not come by truth and good faith."

I. WE HAVE HERE AN ADMISSION THAT WICKEDNESS PREVAILS. It is, indeed, one great consideration in the prophet's unutterable grief that wickedness is so strong and successful. Man, weak and puny as he is in some respects, is in others strong to achieve very impressive results. In mere physical strength there are many brutes that far excel him, but he has faculties which so multiply his strength as to put the rest of creation under his feet. That man, with his peculiar nature, should be strong to do good, means that if his choice so falls he may also be strong to do evil. The prophet looks out, then, upon wicked men who prevail in their plots and schemes. He has no wish to minimize their success. He uses a strong word to indicate it. The word used to indicate the prevailing of the waters at the Deluge is the word also used to indicate the prevailing of the wicked here. The wickedness is not only extensively present, but manifestly successful. There must be no shirking of this fact. It is another matter, indeed, what the success may be worth, and how long it may last; but there it is, such as it is. The wicked prevail by putting the good into prison, and even to the taking away of their lives. They prevail by seducing the weak and self-indulgent into temptation. They prevail by deceiving the simple. They go upon the maxim that everything is fair, and has in it the highest necessity if it helps toward the attainment of their ends. And their ends they do attain, making a boast of their success, and sneering at the scrupulosity of those who will not follow in their steps.

II. THE INSTABILITY OF THIS PREVAILING IS HINTED AT. Integrity, truth, good faith, are thrown to the winds. The prophet does not need to have extorted from him an admission that the wicked prevail; but along with the admission he makes an assertion which, even in the midst of his melancholy, gives him confidence and a measure of satisfaction. This prevailing, great and proud as it is, cannot last, for it lacks the essential constituents of endurance. The man who gains his ends by deceit and perfidy must of necessity deceive himself as much as he does others. He persuades himself that he will never grow weary of what he so much enjoys. He forgets, too, that every one whom he deceives may be thereby learning a lesson which some day may come back in unexpected and terrible treachery to himself. There is not a single instance of wicked prosperity that need alarm or perplex us. The more wickedness raises its head in boasting, the more sudden may be the final overthrow.

III. THOSE WHO CLEAVE TO TRUTH ALWAYS PREVAIL IN THE END. They do it by the best kind of prevailing—that of vanquishing the evil in their own hearts; and, so far as their overcoming is also an overcoming of others, they do it in such a way as provokes no retaliation. He who has a settled regard for what is real and true and abiding, keeps out of his future those very things which bring confusion to the wicked. The prevailing of the righteous may not, indeed, be exhibited so as to impress the eyes of the world; but that is a small matter. He who overcometh looks forward to God's rewards, which are such that the world cannot appreciate them. The great thing is to be calmly conscious in our own breasts that we are winning the victory God would have us win.—Y.

Vers. 4—8.—*The social bond a rope of sand.* This is very strong language for a man to use concerning the society in which he lives, but it harmonizes with the strength of the language which the prophet has been using with respect to himself in vers. 1, 2. A very bad state of things cannot be described by mild words. Such descriptions as that in this passage make plain how just and necessary the impending desolation of Jerusalem was. He who has just expressed such wishes for himself must speak with words that startle when he comes to counsel all who, in the midst of many perils, would wish to act prudently.

I. THERE IS AN IMPLICATION HERE AS TO WHAT SOCIETY IN ISRAEL MIGHT HAVE BEEN. Without looking for perfection, it was reasonable to expect something a great deal better than what the prophet saw. *There is the strength and help coming from real friendship.* The more men are brought together the more chances they have of making most precious friendships. Modern facilities of intercourse have probably done much to enlarge such relations. Men meet oftener and communicate more easily than they were once able to do. But it ought to be especially true of those living near one another that neighbourhood and acquaintance, other things being equal, should lead on to friendship. The claim of friendship is recognized as something special—beyond the claim of kindred, humanity, and common country. In time of trouble we look to friends as those to whom we have a right to look, and we must be ready for similar claims upon ourselves. The prophet indicates also *the claim of brotherhood.* Brother should help brother. Not, of course, that mere natural nearness can compensate for deeper differences of disposition and temperament; but the remembrance of a common parentage should have at least the negative effect of destroying all temptation to injure. Then there is *general integrity in all dealings between man and man.* It is one of the most reasonable of all expectations that we shall so live and act that our word shall be as good as our bond. That which is fair and just towards every one should be wished and provided for. The good name of each should be the care of all.

II. THERE IS A VERY BOLD STATEMENT AS TO WHAT THE SOCIETY IN ISRAEL ACTUALLY WAS. The man who could speak thus must have been a man of great courage—a man into whom God had put a spirit of resolution agreeing with the words he had to speak. Stern, unsparing words are only belied and made to look ridiculous when uttered by a faltering lip. If the prophet's words here were true, this was a society only in name. Some may say that such words could not be true—that things could not possibly be so bad. But, remember, these are the words of a prophet of God, and God is he who searches the heart and can tell exactly how far advanced in corruption a society is at any particular time. Note how a skilled physician will assert the existence of mortal mischief in a patient when as yet there is no sign of it to others, and also predict with tolerable correctness how long it will take the mischief to run its course. And shall not God be much more discerning? All doleful statements as to the rottenness of society have come to be called jeremiads, as if they were really in the same class as the statement of Jeremiah here. But very often such doleful statements are only the result of ignorance and partial views, coming from a defect in him who sees and not in the thing seen. Jeremiah stated the simple truth here. If there had been hopeful signs they would have been mentioned, for God never lacks in an encouraging recognition of the preservative elements in society. To one who notes the warnings of Isaiah it will be nothing wonderful that the evils perceptible in his time should have strengthened into the deplorable universality indicated here. And even now, in places where the outward signs of Christianity abound, there are proofs that society might, in no very long time, approach the description of Jeremiah. The same evils are continually present, though kept in check. No one trusts a stranger. He must first of all take the lowest place, and do such things as need the least amount of trust, and so gradually work himself into the highest place of esteem. No one complains that he cannot win confidence at the first. Family jars and disputings are proverbial. Jesus, we know, divides brother against brother; but it is nothing new that he thus brings into society, for Jacob is the supplanter of Esau, and brother complains against brother to this very Jesus, because he thinks himself defrauded of his rights in the inheritance. There were two couples of natural brethren in the company of the apostles, and in their carnal days they were found hotly embroiled in the dispute as to who should stand greatest in the kingdom. There are abundant seeds of evil in society which are mercifully prevented from having free scope, else the result might soon show us that Jeremiah was in no wise going beyond the essential truth in what is said here.—Y.

Vers. 23, 24.—*Exultation of heart and life according to the will of God.* I. MAN IS SET BEFORE US HERE AS BEING IN A STATE OF VERY LIVELY EMOTION. He is spoken of as glorying; and the Hebrew word used is such as suggests the idea of a man, not only intensely pleased within his own breast, but whose pleasure, like heat bursting into flame, finds vent in words and songs of exultation. The glory and exultation felt by the mind within may appear in many ways—in the face, in the gestures, in the speech; but the prophet indicates here the highest kind of expression, that of poetic and musical utterance. Genius comes in to render permanent certain experiences of exultation, the record of which would otherwise speedily pass away. There is thus set before us a certain state of mind and a certain expression of it. And be it observed that this state of mind is not condemned in itself; nay, it is rather invited and encouraged. It is only condemned when it is produced by a wrong consideration of the objects exciting it, and there is a plain direction how to produce it in the right way. Hence we see how God intends man to be raised into great activity of emotion. It is a wicked thing to repress and starve the feelings. Some there are who act as if the expression of emotion were a thing to be ashamed of; they seem to think they are doing a good work in trying to kill everything like living feeling within them. Now, it is perfectly certain that God would encourage everything which gives the emotions a large part to play in human life, and particularly the joyful emotions. Notice, for it is an interesting thing to notice, how it is Jeremiah, the weeping prophet as he is called, who here points out to his erring brethren the way to the best sort of exultation. The truth is that Jeremiah was a rejoicing believer as well as a weeping prophet. He wept over Jerusalem, as did the greater One who came long after; but it is plain that he must also have had deep joys in his own soul, even as Jesus had. God wishes us to cultivate the singing, exultant heart; for that we all may have, even when we lack the singing lip. We are to have much grief and pity, continual sorrow of heart, because of the world's sins, but it argues a great lack and a great loss if we have not much joy because of God's salvation. The exultation which comes from a selfish use of the world and a selfish success must be put away, but only that another and purer kind of exultation may take its place.

II. THE WARNING LEST THIS EXULTATION, WITH THE CONSEQUENT EXPRESSION OF IT, SHOULD BE PRODUCED IN A WRONG WAY. Three classes are spoken of—the wise, the strong, the rich. Wise and strong by natural endowments; rich by the acquirement of visible, tangible possessions. And wise, strong, and rich men may rejoice and boast and sing when, perhaps, their feelings should rather tend to the other extreme, of mourning and humiliation. A word on the warning to each of these classes. 1. *The wise.* The existence of the wise man is recognized. A wise man is not of necessity to be always contrasted with the foolish. He has a right to the name of wise if his practical faculties of mind rise above the common level. When such a one has shown himself foreseeing and cautious, patient to wait when action would be hurtful, yet prompt to decide when decision is necessary—when, in short, he has obtained a general reputation for wisdom—it is then only mock-modesty for him to pretend that his gifts are not beyond those of common men. Wisdom is the strength of the mind, and the man who has it cannot be unconscious of it, any more than the man strong in body can be unconscious of his strength. But this wisdom, while it is to be used, disciplined, made the most of, is not a thing to glory in. The more it is looked at, the more its limits will be seen. See how easily it can be misused. It was said of Burke that he gave up to party what was meant for mankind, although he would strenuously have maintained that, through party, he got his best means for serving mankind. But of many it is only too true that their great faculties of intellect, meant for the good of men and the glory of God, have been deliberately given up to that which hurts men. Wisdom, as wisdom, is not to be gloried in. It must be an instrument in a higher hand before it can work out such a result as will fill the contemplating mind with exultation and praise. 2. *The strong.* How much men admire strength—strength of body, or strength to maintain and carry out some settled purpose! The young men who contended in the Grecian games gloried in their strength, and so did their kinsfolk and all the people who took pride in the land that produced such. And yet glorying of this sort would not bear reflection. Assuredly it could not endure in a renewed mind to think that the prize of victory had been gotten by the defeat and humiliation of a brother man. Glorying in strength means looking back on victories of brute violence, such victories as Goliath was wont to rejoice in. Glorying in strength means sitting down at the banquet with the blood-stained conqueror, and singing of his achievements amid the flush and insolence of wine. And it means also the encouragement and the formation of similar hopes and purposes for the future. Such feelings of glorying in mere strength the beast of prey may have as he goes up and down in the forest, but they are not the feelings of a man considering the possible range of his thoughts and aspirations. A strong man must employ his strength usefully, recollecting that it was given so that, with a devout and obedient mind in a strong body, he might serve God in his day and generation. 3. *The rich.* Rich men glory in their wealth, and not without plausibility. They find that it stands excellently well in the place of wisdom and strength. They can buy the wisdom and the strength of others; and the more freely they expend, the more also, in certain ways, they obtain. He who professes to despise wealth never gets credit for sincerity; and yet it is perfectly certain that those who profess to glory in this same wealth are preparing for themselves, in one way or another, a terrible humiliation. Let them lose their wealth, and they will waken to the discovery that they have also lost their attractions. There is more to be said for glorying in one's wisdom and strength than in one's external possessions; for the wisdom and strength, whatever their shortcomings, are really a part of the man, while the external possessions are little better than an accident.

III. Man is directed to a cause of exultation which, with the utmost confidence, he may allow to operate freely on his mind. There is a song for man to sing worthy of his highest powers—a song in which he may glory with respect to himself, because he has become somewhat of that which he ought to be. We are not allowed to sing exultingly and proudly of our own natural powers, even if they were the powers of a Plato, a Shakespeare, or a Newton; but there is a sure standing-place for us to exult lawfully in *what we have become.* The least in the kingdom of heaven is greater than the greatest born of women. We may always magnify humanity when we see one of ourselves coming to a true knowledge of God. The peculiar possibility of glory to man is that he is able to know his Maker. *Understand* and *know.* Surely these words mean a great deal; one can hardly put too much of meaning and encouragement into them. Through Isaiah, Jehovah said, "The *ox* knoweth his owner, and the *ass* his master's crib: but *Israel* doth not know, my people doth not consider." And yet, if Israel will only consider and turn, it is capable of knowing God as no brute, however docile, attentive, and faithful it be, can ever come to know its master. The brute gives to its master a brute's recognition; it does the utmost its faculties enable it to do; but in coming to man we come to one who can be so altered as to know God even as a child knows its father. The true glory of the worst of men is that *he can be regenerated.* The glory of the best of men is that *he has been regenerated.* The great end to be aimed at is that every man should exult in his having been made *a partaker of the Divine nature.* The more he thinks of his Saviour, the more he will glory in this—that he, in spite of all his spiritual ignorance and blindness, has had in him a power to be so renewed and uplifted; that he has become one of the exceeding great multitude, who owe eternal blessedness to the work of Christ. To speak of the possibility of such glorying as comes from the knowledge of God was a great matter in relation to these children of Israel. They had fallen into the most appalling errors as to the character and disposition of deity. They had come to have gods many—gods who were the patrons of cruelty, rapacity, tyranny, injustice, lust, and covetousness. They had to practise, as a matter of religion, things opposed to those very things in which Jehovah here represents himself as delighting. What was required from them, therefore, was to listen humbly and attentively to those prophetic expostulations which pointed towards light, truth, redemption, and a new song to be put in their mouths by Jehovah himself. And a similar way is to be ours if we would be sure of glorying in the Lord. The way of God in this matter is by the truth as it is in Jesus, and into that way God's Spirit must lead us, and keep us in it even to the end, amid all the difficulties arising from the natural pride of human hearts.—Y.

EXPOSITION.

CHAPTER X.

Whoever wrote the prophecy in vers. 1—16 of this chapter, it was not Jeremiah; but of course, as the passage forms part of a canonical book, its claims to the character of a Scripture remain the same as if it were the work of our prophet. It is obvious at the very outset that it interrupts the connection; vers. 17—25 stand in no relation to vers. 1—16, but attach themselves most naturally (see below) to the concluding verses of ch. ix. The author tells us himself, as clearly as he can, that the people whom he addresses are free as yet (or at any rate have freed themselves) from the guilt of idolatry, and consequently cannot be the same as those who are so severely chastised for their polytheism in ch. vii. 17, 18, 30, 31. The style too is, on the whole, very different from that of the writer of the preceding chapters (see the details in the introduction to this passage in the Commentary of Naegelsbach). But how can we account for such an insertion? Only by the view already mentioned (supported by a large number of facts throughout the prophetic literature), that the prophecies were edited, and here and there supplemented by the "sons of the prophets" (if the term may be ap-

plied in a new sense), *i.e.* by persons providentially raised up for this purpose, and endowed with at least a younger son's portion of the prophetic Spirit. In the times of the editor of Jeremiah, to whom we owe the first sixteen verses of this chapter, the Jews must have been in danger of falling into idolatry, and our prophet, guided by the Divine Spirit, took up the pen to counteract this danger. His name has not come down to us; indeed, self-abnegation is the characteristic of inspired writers. How uncertain is the authorship of at any rate not a few of the psalms, and of all the historical books! And have we a right to be surprised that the prophets too, absorbed in their glorious mission, have sometimes forgotten to hand on their names to posterity? It is of course possible, in the abstract, that some fragments of the passage are really due to Jeremiah; but how are we to distinguish them from the rest? Hitzig thinks that vers. 6—8 and ver. 10 are the great prophet's work; but these are the very verses the origin of which is the most doubtful, since they are entirely omitted in the Septuagint. One thing is certain—that the passage vers. 1—16 stands in close relation to the latter part of the Book of Isaiah. The prophetic writer, whoever he was, had his mind saturated with the ideas and phraseology of that magnificent work. The similarity, however, is hardly so close as to justify the view that Isa. xl.—lxvi. and ch. x. 1—16 are productions of the same inspired writer. [It is no objection to the theory here advocated that the passage is found in the Septuagint; for no one has ever supposed that the process of editing the Scriptures was not already long since finished when the Alexandrine Version, or rather collection of versions, was made.] It is a singular fact that ver. 11 is written in Chaldee (see note below).

Ver. 2.—**The way of the heathen.** "Way" equivalent to "religion" (comp. ὁδὸς, Acts ix. 2, etc.). **Be not dismayed at the signs of heaven**; alluding to the astrological calculations based upon extraordinary appearances in the sky. Diodorus Siculus remarks (ii. 30)—and his statement is fully confirmed by the Babylonian cuneiform tablets—that "the appearance of comets, eclipses of the sun and moon, earthquakes, and in fact every kind of change occasioned by the atmosphere, whether good or bad, both to nations and to kings and private individuals [were omens of future events]." A catalogue of the seventy standard astrological tablets is to be found in the third volume of the British Museum collection of inscriptions. Among the items we read, "A collection of twenty-five tablets of the signs of heaven and earth, according to their good presage and their bad;" and again, "Tablets [regarding] the signs of the heaven, along with the star (comet) which has a corona in front and a tail behind; the appearance of the sky," etc. There can hardly be a doubt that the prophetic writer had such pseudo-science as this in his eye (see Professor Sayce, 'The Astronomy and Astrology of the Babylonians, with translations of the tablets,' etc, in the *Transactions of the Society of Biblical Archæology*, iii. 145—339).

Ver. 3.—**The customs of the people.** "People" should, as usual, be corrected into *peoples*—the heathen nations are referred to. The Hebrew has "the statutes;" but the Authorized Version is substantially right, customs having a force as of iron in Eastern countries. It seems to be implied that the "customs" are of religious origin (comp. 2 Kings xvii. 8, where "the statutes of the heathen" are obviously the rites and customs of polytheism. **For one cutteth a tree**, etc. This is intended to prove the foregoing statement of the "vanity," or groundlessness, of idolatry. The order of the Hebrew, however, is more forcible, *for as wood out of the forest one cutteth it*, viz. the idol.

Ver. 4.—**They deck it . . . that it move not.** The close resemblance of this verse to Isa. xl. 19, 20; xli. 7, will strike every reader. "Move" should rather be *totter*.

Ver. 5.—**They are upright as the palm tree**; rather, *they are like a pillar* (i.e. *a scarecrow) in a field of cucumbers*. This is the interpretation given to our passage in ver. 70 of the apocryphal Epistle of Jeremiah (written in the Maccabean period, evidently with reference to our prophecy), and is much more striking than the rival translation, "like a palm tree of turned work," *i.e.* stiff, immovable (comp. Virgil, 'Georg.,' iv. 110, 111; Horace, 'Sat.,' i. 8, 1—4). **They must needs be borne . . . they cannot do evil**; a reminiscence, apparently, of Isa. xlvi. 7; xli. 23.

Ver. 6.—**Forasmuch as there is none**; rather, *so that*, etc. But practically it is merely a strengthened negative. There is **none like unto thee**; none, that is, among those who claim to have Divine power (comp. the phrase, "God of gods," Deut. x. 17; Ps. cxxxvi. 2). It would appear from some passages, however, as if the heathen did not worship mere nonentities (though idols are sometimes called "things of nought," *e.g.* ten times by Isaiah) by comparison with Jehovah, but that there was a dark background of awful personal or quasi-personal reality (*e.g.* Deut. iv. 7; 2 Chron. xxviii. 23).

Ver. 7.—**O King of nations.** As time went on, the sacred writers became more and more distinct in their assertions of the truth that Jehovah, the Self-revealing God, is not Israel's King only, but also of the world (comp. Ps. xxii. 28; xlvii. 7, 8; xcvi. 10). **To thee doth it appertain**; viz. that men should fear thee. **Forasmuch as**, etc. (see above, on ver. 6). **Among all the wise men.** "Men" is supplied, but doubtless rightly. It is a contest—how unequal a one!—between Jehovah and the sages of the heathen (comp. "Yet he also is wise," Isa. xxxi. 2).

Ver. 8.—**Brutish and foolish.** In fact, the original meaning of the idolatrous religions had begun, probably, to fade, and the worship of Bel and Nebo had become (as the worship of the Egyptian gods became at a later period) increasingly formal and ritualistic. **The stock is a doctrine of vanities**; rather, *an instruction of vanities*; i.e. all that the idols can teach is vanities. Against this is the plural ("vanities," not "vanity"); it is more natural (and also more in accordance with usage; comp. Gen. xli. 26, Hebrew) to render, *the instruction of the vanities is wooden* ("vanities" has the constant technical sense of "idols;" see ch. viii. 19; xiv. 22; Deut. xxxii. 21; Ps. xxxi. 6). The clause then furnishes a reason for the folly of the heathen; how should they attain to more than a "wooden" knowledge, when the idols themselves are but wood? A bitter truth in an ironical form.

Ver. 9.—This verse apparently once followed ver. 5. Like vers. 7 and 8, it is omitted in the Septuagint. **Silver spread into plates,** etc. The silver and gold were meant for the coating of the wooden image (comp. Isa. xxx. 22; xl. 19). **Tarshish;** *i.e.* Tartessus, in south-west Spain, between the two mouths of the Bætis, or Guadalquivir. **Gold from Uphaz.** A place bearing this name, or anything like it, is not known from other sources than the Old Testament writings; and hence a corruption of the text has naturally been suspected (Ophir into Uphaz). As, however, *r* and *z* are not easily confounded, either in the earlier or the later Hebrew characters, this view must be abandoned, though it has the authority of several ancient versions of this passage (including the Peshito and the Targum). The name occurs again in Dan. x. 5. The Peshito, moreover, curiously enough, translates *zāhāb mūfāz* in 1 Kings x. 18 (Authorized Version, "the best gold") by "gold from Ophir." **Blue and purple.** The Hebrew has no word, strictly speaking, for either "blue" or "purple." Both these words here used probably express colouring matter rather than colours (this is certain of the latter word, which properly designates a kind of mussel, the shell of which yielded dye). The first produced a violet purple, the second a reddish purple.

Ver. 10.—**The true God;** literally, *a God in truth,* the accusative of apposition being chosen instead of the usual genitive construction, to emphasize the idea of "truth."

Ver. 11.—**Thus shall ye say,** etc. This verse is, unlike the rest of the chapter, written in Chaldee, and greatly interrupts the connection. Whether it is a fragment of a Targum (or Chaldee paraphrase) representing a Hebrew verse really written by Jeremiah, or whether it is a marginal note by some scribe or reader which has found its way by accident into the text, cannot be positively determined. What is certain is that it is not in its right place, though it already stood here when the Septuagint Version of Jeremiah was made. To argue, with the 'Speaker's Commentary,' that the latter circumstance is decisive of the correctness of the passage in its present position, implies a view of the unchangeableness of the text in the early centuries which few leading scholars will admit.

Vers. 12—16.—Repeated with a slight variation in ch. li. 15—19.

Ver. 12.—**He hath made the earth,** etc. (comp. the frequent references to the Divine creatorship in the latter part of Isaiah (xl.

22; xlii. 5; xliv. 24; xlv. 12, 18; li. 13). **By his discretion;** rather, *by his understanding.*

Ver. 13.—**When he uttereth his voice,** etc. The phrase is difficult, but the Authorized Version probably gives the right sense. God's "voice" is the thunder (Ps. xxix. 3), which is accompanied by the gathering of heavy clouds ("His pavilion round about him," Ps. xviii. 11). **He causeth the vapours to ascend,** etc.; the storm-clouds coming up more and more thickly from the horizon. From this point the verse agrees with Ps. cxxxv. 7 (the psalm is full of such reminiscences, and is obviously very late). **Lightnings with rain;** rather, *for the rain.* The lightnings are, as it were, the heralds or attendants of the rain. **The wind out of his treasures;** a noble figure, used elsewhere of the snow and hail (Job xxxviii. 22), and of the waters of the sea (Ps. xxxiii. 7).

Ver. 14.—Before these natural miracles, all men, except those who have been enlightened by revelation, are *without knowledge* (so, and not in his knowledge, we ought to render); *i.e.* without insight into their origin and meaning (compare the overwhelming series of questions in the sublime theophany in Job, ch. xxxviii., xxxix.). **Every founder is confounded by,** etc.; rather, *every goldsmith is brought to shame by the graven image;* for how can the work which has needed all the resources of his skill deliver him?

Ver. 15.—The very essence of idols is **vanity;** they are unreal as "a breath;" they are, not so much **the work of errors** as a *work of mockery, i.e.* not *opus risu dignum,* but a work which rewards the efforts bestowed upon its production by disappointment.

Ver. 16.—**The portion of Jacob;** *i.e.* Jehovah. The phrase appears to have been coined at a lower level of religion, when every nation was supposed to have its own patron deity; just as the prophet says, ironically, to the fetish-worshippers of Israel, "Among the smooth stones of the stream is thy portion" (Isa. lvii. 5), and Moses, in Deuteronomy (iv. 19), speaks of the host of heaven as having been "divided [*i.e.* assigned] unto all nations under the whole heaven." But, of course, the phrase is susceptible of a high, spiritual application (comp. Ps. xvi. 5; cxlii. 5). God's people are, by their very conception, an ἐκλογή, chosen out by God, and choosing him, and not the world, for their portion. "Making the best of both worlds" is an object implicitly condemned by this consecrated phrase. **The former of all** things. How much more forcible is the original phrase: "... of the whole," *i.e.* the universe! "To form" is a phrase constantly used of God in the second part of Isaiah. **The rod of his** inheritance. "Rod" should rather be *tribe*. The twelve tribes had an inner unity, as contrasted with other peoples; comp. Ps. lxxiv. 2 and Isa. lxiii. 17 ("tribes").

Vers. 17—22.—This passage connects itself immediately with ch. ix., where the invasion of Judah and the dispersion of its inhabitants have been foretold. Here, after describing dramatically the departure of the latter into exile, the prophet reports a distinct revelation of the same fact, so that this can no longer be assumed to be mere imaginative rhetoric. The Jewish people is then introduced, lamenting her sad fate, but expressing resignation.

Ver. 17.—**Gather up thy wares.** "Wares" should rather be *bundle*. There is no allusion to trafficking. **O inhabitant of the fortress**; rather, *thou that dwellest besieged*.

Ver. 18.—**I will sling out**; a forcible image, to express the violence of the expulsion; comp. Isa. xxii. 17, 18 (ver. 17 needs correcting). **At this once**; rather, *at this time* (comp. ch. xvi. 21). Invasion was no novelty to the Jews, but had hitherto merely produced loss of goods rather than of personal liberty. **That they may find** it so; better, *that they may feel it*. Others supply as the subject "Jehovah," comparing Ps. xxxii. 6, "In a time of finding" (Authorized Version, "When thou mayest be found"). Jeremiah himself says, "Ye shall seek me, and shall find, when ye shall search for me with all your heart" (ch. xxix. 13 = Deut. iv. 29). Still, these passages are hardly quite parallel, as the object of the verb can be easily supplied from the connection. The Vulgate apparently reads the text with different vowels, for it renders *ut inveniantur;* the Septuagint has "that thy stroke may be found."

Ver. 19.—It is rather doubtful (as in the parallel passage, ch. iv. 19—21) whether the speaker here is the prophet, or "the daughter of my people," who, in ch. vi. 26, is called upon to "make most bitter lamentation." Of course, the prophet cannot dissociate himself from his people; and we may therefore, perhaps, consider both references united. **Hurt**; literally, *breach ;* a term so used for political calamities. **A grief**; rather, *my grief;* but "grief" is meant to include both physical and mental sufferings (literally, *my sickness*).

Ver. 20.—**My tabernacle**; rather, *my tent*. It is very striking how present to the minds of the Israelites was the consciousness of their pastoral origin. Hence the cry, "To your tents, O Israel" (1 Kings xii. 16);

comp. also, "And the children of Israel dwelt in their tents, as aforetime" (2 Kings xiii. 5). **My cords . . . my curtains.** The "cords" are those which, by being fastened to poles and stakes, keep the tent steady; the "curtains," of course, are the covering of the tent (comp. Isa. liv. 2).

Ver. 21.—**The pastors**; *i.e.* the civil authorities (see on ch. ii. 8). **They shall not prosper**; rather, *they have not prospered;* or, better still, *they have not acted wisely*, the notion of prospering being rather suggested than expressed (the same word is used in Isa. lii. 13).

Ver. 22.—**Behold, . . . is come**; rather, *Hark! tidings! Behold, it cometh!* The tidings are that the foe is at hand, advancing with a great commotion, with clashing spears, prancing horses, and all the hubbub of a great army. **A den of dragons**; rather, *of jackals* (as ch. ix. 11).

Vers. 23—25.—These verses confirm the view taken above, of the speaker of this whole section. Jeremiah and the people, each is, in a sense, the speaker; but here the prophetic faith seems to run rather in advance of that of his fellow-countrymen. They form, however, a fitting sequel to the charges brought against the people in ch. ix. The speaker admits that he (either the people of Judah personified, or Jeremiah as a representative of its best portion) fully deserves chastisement for having attempted to go his own way (comp. Isa. lvii. 17). He has now attained an insight into the truth that man's duty is simply to walk in the path which God has marked out for him. He only asks that Jehovah would chastise him **with judgment**, or, more clearly, *according to what is just*. "The contrast is between punishment inflicted in anger, the object of which is to cause pain to the criminal, and that inflicted as a duty of justice, and of which the object is the criminal's reformation" (Payne Smith). The fear expressed, however, is not exactly **lest thou bring me to nothing**, which is too strong for the Hebrew, but *lest thou make me small*. Israel was secured against annihilation by the promise of Jehovah, but feared he might possibly survive only as the shadow of his former self.

Ver. 25.—This verse is repeated, with slight differences, in Ps. lxxix. 6, 7. The fault of the heathen is that they exceeded their commission (Isa. x. 6, 7; xlvii. 6; Zech. i. 15), and aimed at destroying, instead of merely punishing, Jehovah's erring people. **His habitation**; rather, *his pasture* (comp. ch. xii. 10).

HOMILETICS.

Vers. 1—5.—*The folly of paganism.* I. THE FOLLY OF PAGANISM PROVES THE WEAKNESS OF SUPERSTITIOUS FEARS. The Jews were tempted to fear astrological portents (ver. 2) and idol-powers (ver. 5). Yet a little reflection was enough to show that these things were impotent for harm. The lowest religion is a product of fear. Superstition finds converts where rational faith fails. The trouble thus resulting from the weakness of men can only be dissipated by boldly confronting the source of terror and thoroughly examining it.

II. THE FOLLY OF PAGANISM REVEALS THE MISTAKE OF YIELDING TO ITS FASCINATIONS. For this miserable inanity the Jews were abandoning the God of heaven and earth! Religion should be accepted, not for its attractiveness, but for its truth. It must be a reality or it will be a snare. Yet how many are led to adopt systems of religion without any regard to the truth of the ideas they contain, but simply out of liking for their ritual, emotional sympathy for their poetry, or even mere love of the musical accompaniments of the worship connected with them!

III. THE FOLLY OF PAGANISM IS AN EVIDENCE IN FAVOUR OF THE TRUTH OF THE RELIGION OF THE BIBLE. The reason and imagination of men in all ages, in all climes, in all degrees of civilization, have been set to the task of inventing religions (consciously sometimes, but for the most part unconsciously and therefore the more genuinely), and the result in all cases is far inferior to Christianity. A mere comparison of religions should lead us to prefer this, and a simple conclusion from such a comparison is that this must be of Divine origin.

Vers. 6, 7.—*The incomparable greatness of God.* I. GOD IS GREAT. This simple item of the Mohammedan's creed must be accepted with equal reverence by the Christian, though it forms but one part of his conception of the Divine nature. There is danger lest we should regard the goodness of God in such a way as to detract from his majesty. Truly considered, it enhances the supreme glory of God's greatness. God is great in power, in wisdom, in resources, in essential being. God is also great in character, in purpose, in the just and good principles of his actions. The worship of a God of mere power is the cringing of a slave, and has no spiritual value, but rather degrades the devotee by destroying independence of conscience and moral courage. It would be our duty to resist a being of infinite power if that power were not used righteously, for such a being would not be God, but an infinite demon; and though resistance were hopeless, it would be better to be a martyr to conscience than the degraded minion of an unrighteous despotism. But God is worthy of all worship because his greatness of power reposes on greatness of character.

II. THE GREATNESS OF GOD IS INCOMPARABLE. The Jews were led to see that their God was not one among many deities, not even the supreme God, the Zeus of a pantheon of lesser divinities, but the only God, and out of all comparison with all other beings. God is infinite. You cannot compare the infinite with anything finite. The greatest existence which has any limit is as far from the infinite as the smallest. This is as much larger than a world as it is larger than a grain of sand. The being of God is entirely distinct from all other orders of being—vastly greater than the universe of them—in its fulness incomparable to any. Yet: 1. God, being infinite, contains in himself all possibilities of being, and therefore all may see their ideal perfection in him though he transcends all (Heb. ii. 10). 2. God has made man in his own image, and in his power of thought, freedom of will, and moral conscience, man has characteristics like the Divine in kind, though incomparable with that in degree (Gen. i. 26). Christ is the "express Image of his substance" (Heb. i. 3), "but only so because in him dwelleth all the fulness of the Godhead bodily" (Col. ii. 9).

III. THE INCOMPARABLE GREATNESS OF GOD SHOULD MOVE ALL MEN TO FEAR BEFORE HIM. All should fear because: 1. He is too great to be concerned with a few; all nations, all mankind, are equally under his sway. 2. He is infinitely above the greatest, so that kings and wise men, persons of the highest rank and of the most profound genius, are as much below him as if they were beggars and fools. 3. He is so vast in being, power, and character, that it is no mark of noble independence to resist him, but only a sign of foolish pride which will certainly be humiliated. The fear of God thus engendered is an awe, a reverence, not mere terror. The gospel tempers this with the confident love of children, but does not destroy it, since perfect love, while casting out terror, infuses feelings of reverence.

Vers. 10, 12, 13.—*The nature of God.* The true nature of God is seen in contrast with the objects of heathen worship. Error is sometimes serviceable in furnishing an occasion for a clearer definition of truth. Christian theology has grown up through controversies with heresy and unbelief.

I. THE NATURE OF GOD. 1. God is *real.* Jehovah is the true God. He is not only superior to heathen deities. They are non-existent. He alone is. Religion is based on facts. Its first affirmation is this—" God is." It is not a growth of the poetic imagination, a fabric of baseless speculation, nor merely " morality touched with emotion," without any object for that emotion to rest upon. It is the worship of a God who exists. Otherwise no poetic charm nor practical expediency can make it anything but a delusion, which all who venerate truth should abjure. 2. God is *living.* The word "God " is not a name for the totality of being, for the unconscious forces of the universe, for a blind " Not ourselves that makes for righteousness." All faith affirms more. No worship is justified without the belief that God is spirit, thinking, willing, living. God is, indeed, the one self-existent life, the life in which all other life is contained (Acts xvii. 28). 3. God is an *everlasting King.* He is eternal and changeless—not a God of the past alone, but equally active in the present. He is not only the Creator who formed the world ages ago, but the King who now rules it. Our worship is not merely veneration for what he has done, but a constant appreciation of what he is doing, and prayer touching his future action—a real and effectual communion with a living and acting God. 4. These thoughts of the nature of God should induce *submission and reverence.* None can compare with him. All are in his power. His eternal presence demands constant attention, and his ceaseless activity requires a correspondence in all our activity.

II. THE MANIFESTATION OF THE NATURE OF GOD. 1. It is seen in *creation.* Power is revealed in the original formation of all things, wisdom in their orderly establishment (ver. 12). A real world can only come from a real God. A living world must derive its vitality from an original source of life. The less cannot produce the greater. All that we see in the universe must have been originally in the thought and power of God. 2. It is seen in the *present activities* of the world. The tumult of waters flows in obedience to God's voice. Clouds, and wind, and lightning, and rain, follow his directions (ver. 13). The great energy of the physical world testifies to an energizing power behind it. The universe is not a beautiful crystal, nor a fossil relic of past life. It is replete with force, undergoing perpetual change, and constantly developing fresh forms of vitality. Such a condition of things implies that the real and living Creator must be also an ever-present Ruler, " an everlasting King."

Ver. 16.—*God the Portion of Israel.* I. GOD IS PECULIARLY RELATED TO HIS OWN PEOPLE. The previous verses describe the universal supremacy of God and the claims he has over all his creatures. He is not one among many gods, but the only God; he is the Creator of all things, in him all things consist, all men live only through him. He is gracious to all his human family, he is willing to give his richest blessings to all mankind. Still, there are other and special relations which God holds only with those who trust and love and obey him. They who seek God will find him as the negligent will never do. They who choose God for their Portion will be chosen by him for peculiar favours. This is quite consistent with the universality of the being and activity of God.

II. GOD'S PECULIAR RELATION WITH HIS PEOPLE ADMITS OF NO RIVALRY. God must be *the* Portion of his people or in no sense peculiarly theirs. Israel cannot retain the special privileges of the covenant with Jehovah while breaking the conditions of that covenant which require unwavering fidelity (Deut. xxviii. 14). He who would find his portion in God must not also seek it in the world. He may have many worldly advantages while pursuing higher aims, because these may be " added unto him;" but he must "seek *first* the kingdom of God " (Matt. vi. 33).

III. GOD'S PECULIAR RELATION WITH HIS PEOPLE IS AN UNSPEAKABLE BLESSING TO THEM. 1. He makes them *his inheritance,* i.e. prizes them as property, values them "as the apple of his eye" (Deut. xxxii. 10), as his "peculiar treasure" (Mal. iii. 17). If God showers down upon all his creatures mercies countless as the stars of heaven, what must be the wonder and the glory of their state whom God thus prizes and marks for special favour! 2. They find in him *their Portion.* (1) The Portion is God, not the gifts of God, for the Giver is better than his gifts. God is more to his people than all he bestows upon them. (2) This portion is independent of all earthly circumstances; it may be enjoyed in sickness, in poverty, in human contempt. (3) It is the highest blessedness of the soul—enjoying God, living in the light of his love, receiving the essential blessedness of Heaven.

IV. THE BLESSING OF THIS PECULIAR RELATIONSHIP WITH GOD IS OPEN TO ALL MEN. The Jews too often rested their claim on inherent national rights—their birthrights. But the New Testament declares the spiritual Israel to be the true Israel (Gal. vi. 15, 16), and this Israel is composed of all who walk "according to the rule" of faith in Christ. Therefore the broad invitation for all to follow Christ opens the door for all to the closest relationship with God. If all are invited to Christ who is the Way, all may become God's peculiar inheritance, and find their Portion in him (1 Pet. ii. 9).

Vers. 23, 24.—*Confession and correction.* I. GENUINE CONFESSION INVOLVES A CLEAR RECOGNITION OF DUTY AND A WILLINGNESS TO RECEIVE NECESSARY CORRECTION. 1. There must be a *recognition of duty.* We cannot confess the wrong till we know the right. Conscience awakes only when a standard of right outside ourselves is perceived. 2. There must be a *willingness to receive necessary correction.* If we make honest confession of sin, we imply that we desire to be free from it. But a right understanding of our own condition in the light of God's requirements makes the necessity of correction apparent.

II. A CLEAR RECOGNITION OF DUTY WILL SHOW THAT THIS CONSISTS IN SELF-ABNEGATION TO A HIGHER WILL. The essence of sin is self-will. The first sin was an act of disobedience. All wickedness is a rebellion against a supreme authority. Man is not free to live to himself, swayed only by his own lawless caprice. He has a vocation to fulfil. 1. He has no *right* to go his own way. He is a servant. He is lawfully subject to a righteous Lord, before whom duty requires him to say, "Not my will, but thine, be done." 2. He has not *light* enough to direct his own steps. Future accidents cannot be anticipated. The ultimate effects of the simplest action are not to be traced beforehand. Hence the need of a higher direction. 3. He has not *power* to succeed in his own way. If he starts by himself, making the awful experiment of a self-sustained pilgrimage through the toils and storms of life, he will assuredly make shipwreck. Our duty is not to live for self, nor even for God in our own way or by our own unaided strength, but to do his will, in his way, by his aid. Thus the Christian, looking for authority, guidance, and strength in Christ, is taught to say, "To me to live is Christ."

III. A WILLINGNESS TO RECEIVE CORRECTION ARISES FROM A PERCEPTION OF ITS JUSTICE AND UTILITY WHEN VIEWED IN THE LIGHT OF THE REQUIREMENTS OF DUTY. 1. It must be recognized as *just,* not only merited, but coming in a fair degree. We could not willingly accept a correcting chastisement which was disproportionate to guilt. 2. It must be recognized as given on *principles of righteousness,* not out of vindictive wrath. 3. It must be recognized as sent for a *merciful purpose.* It is correction, not simply retribution. This is wholesome, and given, not in anger, which would be fatal (Ps. ii. 12), but in love (Prov. iii. 12). Such correction we should not murmur under, but welcome, accept as a blessing, and even pray for. But we shall only do this when we are impressed with a right sense of duty, which makes us acknowledge that we are not to live for ourselves, and must be subdued and trained by all necessary means to submission and obedience and a true feeling of our own helplessness, requiring the help of Divine discipline. *Because* man's way is not in himself he may naturally ask for wholesome correction.

HOMILIES BY VARIOUS AUTHORS.

Vers. 2—5.—*The helplessness of heathen gods a conclusive argument against them.*
How is the superstitious worship of nature and inanimate objects to be corrected? It
is obvious that the attributes attached by the worshippers to the idols they worship
are wholly foreign to them. It is ignorance, association, and the tendency to transfer
subjective ideas to objects of sense, that have largely to do with this. The correction,
therefore, must be furnished by a real analysis of the idol—a taking of it to pieces, and
examining how it came into existence. But—

I. Let us inquire what worship involves. It is evident that an impression must
exist of the power of the object worshipped to help or to hurt. In some way men have
associated it with the production of evil or good in human destiny. A sense of
dependence is generated. Fear arises, to degenerate into vulgar terror or to refine itself
into the sentiments of reverence and respect. A being greater than ourselves is needed
to constitute a veritable God to the human heart.

II. Tested by this, idols and celestial signs cannot be gods. 1. *Careful obser-*
vation will show that, whilst there may be agreement between certain changes of the
heavenly bodies and the changes of weather, physical condition, etc., these are not
producible as by a responsible will but according to the fixed laws of nature. 2. *The*
stars of heaven and the idols of earth are alike constituted of inanimate matter. 3. *In*
addition to this, the latter are wholly the creatures of man. 4. *Neither the heavenly*
bodies nor the idols can help themselves.—M.

Vers. 6, 7.—*The uniqueness of Jehovah.* When other gods have been proved to be
false, it is very important that this unlikeness of God to anything else should be
established. His claim to attention and reverence is thereby held in judgment.

I. In what respects Jehovah is unique. 1. *In idea.* It is a wondrous conception
—a being so great, infinite, eternal, and unchangeable in his being, wisdom, power,
holiness, justice, goodness, and truth. As a conception it stands alone, commands
respect, and invites reverent investigation. Such goodness with such power and
wisdom! 2. *In pretensions.* (1) He claims our sole worship; (2) our highest and
holiest service is his by right, and is unworthy of him; (3) our welfare and destiny
are in his hands. 3. *In works.* There is nothing he has claimed to be which he has
not made good in his works—creation, providence, grace.

II. This conception of God as unique harmonizes with the instincts of the
human spirit, and the teachings of history and nature. It has cast its spell over
the mightiest intellects, and commanded the homage of the purest and best of men.
In the worship of him whom it represents the highest longings are satisfied, and the
most characteristically human sympathies and principles encouraged. The unity of
nature; the mental principle that traces everything to a great First Cause; the manner
in which the system of religion of which he is centre and dominating principle explains
this, and harmonizes the life of man with his surroundings;—are all indications that
point to the same conclusion.—M.

Ver. 19.—*Grief borne that cannot be cured.* I. An instance of the power of
true religion. His sorrow was intense. No one could understand or sympathize
with it. Yet he is able to put it under and, although not removing it wholly, to bear
it. This is alike removed from self-indulgence and stoicism.

II. The considerations that affected him in this way. He had to finish his
task. It was practical, and could admit of no interruption. The sense of duty is,
therefore, supreme—patience, submission. His grief is recognized as a personal
stewardship. He is responsible for its expression and repression. It has a special
relation to his own character and life. He regards it, therefore, as sent from God, and
not, therefore, to be hastily dismissed. How it enriched his nature, increased his personal usefulness, and enhanced the value of his writings to generations then unborn!

III. Christianity is tested by the manner in which it enables men to bear
affliction. The relation of our sorrows to our personal and spiritual salvation. The
ministry of sorrow. The hopes of the future alleviating and directing into profitable

reflection and effort. "Our light affliction, which is but for a moment, worketh," etc.—M.

Vers. 1—17.—*Idolatry.* This section of Jeremiah's prophecy is one of the notable passages in the Scriptures concerning idolatry. It is like that in Ps. cxv., and in Isa. xl., xliv. It states or suggests much of great interest on this subject, and which deserves to be well considered by us. There is—

I. THE TREMENDOUS FACT OF IDOLATRY. See: 1. The *multitudes* of mankind who have avowed such worship. 2. The *wide extent* of the world's inhabited countries over which it prevails. 3. Its *permanence.* It has lasted on from age to age, and has been handed down unchanged from generation to generation, so that the prophet could challenge his countrymen to tell of any nation which had ever changed their gods (cf. ch. ii. 11). And though vast portions of mankind have professedly thrown aside their idols, yet there are still more who have not even at the present day. Idolatry is the dominant religion of the world to-day, if numbers are considered, even as it was in the days of Jeremiah, and this notwithstanding—

II. ITS MANIFEST ABSURDITY. How scathing is the ridicule which the prophet pours out upon such monstrous worship! With what sarcasm he dwells upon the fact of their being mere wooden dolls, hideous as a scarecrow in a garden of cucumbers (cf. Exposition, ver. 5), chipped into such shape as they have by the hands of the men who worship them, decked with tawdry finery, must be nailed up lest they should tumble down, and "must needs be borne because they cannot go" (ver. 5), and are, of course, powerless either for evil or for good. And the prophet points out (ver. 8) that the absurdity is none lessened when the idols are of a more costly sort. They may be plated with silver and adorned with gold (ver. 9), and the workmanship may be of a much more elaborate and artistic kind. But it is all the same; the idol is nothing but a piece of wood, and that which is taught about them is "a doctrine of vanities," *i.e.* utterly false and absurd. But though idolatry be thus manifestly absurd, yet we are forced to admit the fact of—

III. ITS NEVERTHELESS STRANGE BUT STRONG ATTRACTIVENESS. How else can not only the multitude of its votaries be accounted for, and their fidelity to it, but also *the high rank and leading position of those nations who adhered to it?* They were not mere barbarous savages who worshipped idols, but the foremost peoples of the world. The empires of Egypt, Babylon, Assyria, Greece, Rome, were all sworn upholders of idolatry (cf. Acts xvii.). And to-day it is not the mere fetish-worshippers of the South Seas and Africa who are idolaters, but people such as the Chinese and Hindoos—to say nothing of those who in Christian Churches bow down before tinsel-decked images or pictures of virgins, apostles, and saints, and, if they do not worship them, render them homage which can hardly be distinguished from worship. And a yet further proof of this attraction is that *the well-instructed people of God*, the seed of Israel, the possessors of the oracles of God, were for ever falling into this sin. This entire chapter is one appeal and protest against their so doing. And we know how often in the past they had bowed down to idols. The command which stands at the head of the Decalogue, by its position there, by its fulness of expression, and by the severity of its sanctions, shows that the attraction of the idolatry which it denounced was indeed terrible, and therefore needed to be thus solemnly forbidden. And age after age the same command had to be repeated, and its violation sternly punished, notwithstanding that (ver. 16) "the Portion of Jacob" was "not like" these wretched idols—no indeed, but was the alone true God, the living God, the everlasting King (ver. 10). And yet there were needed this command and appeal; yes, and the consuming fire of God's wrath which fell upon Israel in their captivity, before the taint of idolatry could be burnt out of them. Now, how was this? Note, therefore—

IV. ITS PROBABLE REASON AND CAUSE. We cannot observe the tremendous fact of idolatry without being led to inquire into its origin. It is not sufficient to refer to the licence it gave to the sensual nature of man; if such licence were all that was desired, why couple it with some form of worship? The explanation must lie deeper than this. And that missionary would get on very poorly with any tolerably educated heathen if he were to assume that the idolater worshipped the hideous idol before which he bows himself down. He would tell you that he did nothing of the kind, but that which he worshipped was the unseen powers of which that idol was the symbol. No doubt idolatry degenerates into actual idol-worship. That with which something Divine has been so long associated comes to be regarded as itself Divine, and worshipped accordingly. And then idolatry has sunk down into fetishism. And it may be often seen where you would least expect it. But originally idolatry was not the worship of images. That worship may probably be thus explained. 1. Man cannot do without a deity of whom, in some form or other, he must be conscious, and whose presence he can realize so as to be able to look to him in time of need. Man cannot be a thorough atheist. His instinctive religiousness and tendency to worship cannot be ever kept under. For a while it may, but let heavy sorrow come, or let fear and dread fill his mind, and he will, he must, then call upon God. 2. But God will not reveal himself to us except to our spirits. He can be only spiritually discerned. Not through any of our senses, or through our intellect, but through the Spirit alone. "They that worship him must worship him in spirit and in truth." 3. But such coming to God involves purity of heart and life. "If I regard iniquity in my heart, the Lord will not hear me." And not only purity, but great spiritual effort. How difficult we find it to realize the presence of God, to hold down our minds, and to summon the energies of the will when we pray! "We know not how to pray as we ought." And permitted sin, defiling the conscience and destroying our confidence, will ever hinder spiritual worship. 4. But these imperative conditions of worship —that it should be in spirit, and that it should be pure—men like not. Still, they must worship. What, then, is to be done? The idol is the solution. To avoid the strain and effort of the spirit, men have taken as a symbol some material thing—as the Israelites at Sinai took the golden calf—and so have sought to represent God to their minds. The idolater persuades himself he cannot know the Deity directly, and therefore will avail himself of the aid some sensuous object will afford. And such symbol he can carry about with him, and there is no need of purity of heart for such worship—it can be done without. What wonder, then, that man, averse to spiritual exercises and sensual-hearted, should have everywhere fled to idolatry, as in fact he has done? It is an endeavour to have the favour of God on cheaper terms than he demands; on conditions easier and more agreeable to our fallen nature. But in regard to the idolatries into which Judah and Jerusalem so often fell, there must be remembered not only the force of those universal causes of idolatry now considered, but *the further force of powerful example all around them.* Who were the mighty nations with whom they had most to do? Egypt, Assyria, Babylon. Tyre also, in her wealth and might, stood on their northern border, and yet others, whose fame reached them from afar, flourished and grew strong. But all these worshipped idols. Happiness, success, strength, and power seemed to be with these nations and not with the worshippers of Jehovah. And all this Judah saw and deeply observed, and at length came to believe that it was better for them to serve idols than to serve God (cf. for proof of this, ch. xliv. 17—19). For Israel to keep from idolatry was to swim against wind and tide, and to do so when wind and tide promised to bear them on to a condition of prosperity greater than they had ever known. And Jeremiah knew that in Babylon, where they were going, they would be exposed to the full force of this temptation. The devil of idolatry would come to them, and, pointing to the glory of Babylon, would say, "All these things will I give thee, if," etc. And to fortify them against this temptation was the object of the prophet's earnest appeal. The tempter would suggest to them, "You have lost everything by worshipping God. Your conquerors, who hold you now in their power, and have destroyed your city, your temple, your land, have gained all their glory by worshipping their gods. Do you the same; learn their ways."

V. ITS CONSEQUENCES. These have been very terrible. With Israel God dealt very sternly. His *direct vengeance* came upon them again and again. It was hanging over them at this time as a dark thunder-cloud. But besides this, there were *the natural results* of such worship—results which were conspicuous in Judah and Jerusalem, and have ever been so in all idolatrous nations (cf. ver. 8). They became "brutish," "given over to vile affections" (cf. Rom. i. 20—32).

VI. ITS SURE BUT ONLY ANTIDOTE. *Living faith in the living God*—this alone, but this surely, would enable them to resist, not only the clamour and cravings of their lower nature, but also the seductive force of the seeming success which idolatry had won and they had lost. Only such faith would serve them, and hence, in vers. 6, 7, 10—13, 16, the prophet bids them remember the incomparable glory, majesty, and power of the Lord, the true God, the living God (ver. 10), and the terribleness of his wrath. He reminds them that God is Creator (ver. 12) and Preserver (ver. 13). He who formed the earth governs it still, and he is *their* God, and they are his people. He is their "Portion," and "Israel is the rod of his inheritance" (ver. 16). And this which would be Israel's safeguard must be ours still. Let that living faith in the living God be lost, and at once resort will be had to symbols and substitutes for God, which, though in form they may be far different from the idols of the heathen, yet in substance and effect are the same.

VII. Its present-day lessons. There are such, for the peril of Israel is our own. 1. For we also may—and many do—substitute reverence for those things which are associated with the worship of God for that worship in spirit and in truth which he alone cares for. Symbols, sacraments, creeds, Churches, religious observances,—any one of these may become an idol, that is, a substitute for God. They demand no strain and energy of our spiritual nature; the senses or the intellect can grasp them; and they make no such strenuous demand upon the surrender of the will, the yielding of the heart to God; they will let us do as we like, if not entirely yet far more than true spiritual worship ever will. And thus, though we be called Christians, we may be idolaters after all. 2. And let us guard against being deceived by the sanction which worldly success and present good so often lend to ways which God forbids. There was very much around Israel whose desirableness said to them, "Come with us, and we will do you good." Idolatry did seem to answer, whilst their religion did not. And the way of the wicked will often seem to prosper, whilst "waters of a full cup" of sorrow "are wrung out" to the people of God. The mighty bribe which Satan pressed upon our blessed Lord, if he would but renounce the way of the cross appointed for him by his Father, and take "all the kingdoms of this world and the glory of them"—that same bribe is pressed upon myriad souls still. 3. By constant and earnest worship of God let us cherish and keep alive in our hearts that living faith in the living God made known to us in the Lord Jesus Christ, which alone can, but surely will, meet and overcome all those temptations to idolatry, which now, as of old, beset every human soul.—C.

Ver. 16.—" *The Portion of Jacob.*" By this expression, "the Portion of Jacob," is meant the Lord God. Once again it is met with in Jeremiah's prophecy (ch. li.), where several of the verses of this chapter, our text amongst the rest, are repeated word for word. It is interesting to inquire the probable reason for this beautiful but unusual name being given to God. That God is the Portion of his people is a precious truth often declared. But this form of that precious truth is unusual, and may well lead us to ask why God is so called. And there can be little doubt, I think, that the motive of the prophet was to touch the hearts of those whom he addressed, and, if so it might be, to waken up again a longing after this "Portion of Jacob," which they were so fast letting go. There was an appealing power in this name, and for that reason it was probably chosen. The devout Jew loved to think and tell of God as the God of Jacob. You meet with the two names thus linked together perpetually in the psalms and often elsewhere. "The God of Jacob is our Refuge," "The Name of the God of Jacob defend thee," etc. Sometimes we read of God as the God of Abraham, and as the God of Isaac, but more commonly as the God of Jacob. Now, why is this? Is it not because that Jacob was more thoroughly the representative and father of the Jewish people than any other patriarch? Abraham was a great hero of the faith; Isaac's career was too still and serene to be at all a pattern of their own; but Jacob, he was the typical Jew, both in the mingled good and evil of his character, and in the manifold trials and vicissitudes of his life. A sorrowful, struggling, and often sinful man was he, sore chastened of the Lord again and again, but never given over unto death; like the bush burning in the fire but never burnt, and coming out of God's disciplines the better for having passed through them. In him the Jews saw their own character and career vividly portrayed, and they loved to feel that God was the God of Jacob; the God, therefore, whom they needed, and in whom he who was the truest representative of all their race found strength and solace and salvation. Thus this appellation here given to God, "the Portion of Jacob," was calculated to waken up many very tender and holy memories, and might lead, as was sorely needed, to a better mind towards God amongst those to whom the prophet spoke, and to a turning away from those idolatries by which now and for so long they had been sinning against God and destroying themselves. And the Portion of Jacob waits to be ours as well as his. Jacob was not only a representative Jew, but also *a representative man.* For men are but rarely cast in the heroic mould of Abraham, nor is their career quiet and uncheckered like that of Isaac. But in the sins and sorrows, the struggles and falls, the temptations and trials of Jacob they behold themselves. God by this name declares himself to be the God of, the Portion of, all sinful, sorrowing, struggling, and much-tried men everywhere and at all times; the God, therefore, that *we* need, the Helper *we* want. He is the God who is revealed to us in our Lord Jesus Christ, in whom there is neither Greek nor Jew, no distinction of any kind, but who is "the Saviour of all men, specially of them that believe." If, then, this Portion of Jacob may be our Portion too, we shall consider with more interest what that Portion consists of, what it was that Jacob possessed in God. And to see this let us recall to our minds the records that are given of the patriarch's career. As we study them we shall readily see what portion Jacob had in God, and how precious a possession it was. And—

I. IN GOD HE FOUND UNSPEAKABLE GRACE. Was there ever a more wretched, guilty sinner than Jacob, when he fled away from his home in just fear of his outraged brother's wrath? He had entrapped him once and again, inflicting on him grievous wrong; he had deceived his aged father; he had lied again and again in the basest and most hypocritical way. Altogether the man was odious in the sight of all; all our sympathies go over in a rush towards the frank if foolish Esau. Jacob's character was at this time nothing less than repulsive. His mother was probably the only living soul who had either faith in or affection for him. He had deserved the reprobation of all. And we cannot but believe that he must have felt very much of this, and that it was with a sense of deepest sin and shame he fled away to Padan-aram, from his father's and mother's home. Man had cast him off; would not God do the like? For his sin had not been that of one who had never known God. God had been about him all his days; he had learnt to know, to fear, and desire God. He had been, as all knew, an avowedly religious man. His sin was therefore all the more unpardonable, as his guilt was all the greater. He is shown to us out on the wide stony track over the mountains which form the backbone of Palestine. The day has ended, the sun gone down; he is all alone, the night is gathering round him. The ground is strewn with huge fragments of the bare, barren rock of which the mass of those mountains is composed. On the cold hard ground he lays himself down to rest, helpless, hopeless, forsaken, he might well think, both of God and man. But it was not so, for God came to him there. "In the visions of the night the rough stones formed themselves into a vast staircase reaching into the depth of the wide and open sky, which without any interruption of tent or tree was stretched over the sleeper's head. On the steps of that staircase were seen ascending and descending the messengers of God; and from above there came the Divine voice, which told the houseless wanderer that, little as he thought it, he had a Protector there and everywhere; that even in this bare and open thoroughfare, in no consecrated grove or cave, 'the Lord was in this place, though he knew it not.' This was Bethel, the house of God, the gate of heaven." What the effect of this glorious vision must have been upon him we can hardly ever estimate. The nearest Scripture parallel probably would be the effect of the father's gracious reception upon the returning prodigal. Somewhat akin to his feelings must have been those of Jacob at this time. For what he had seen and heard had shown him beyond doubt that God had not cast him off, had not dealt with him after his sins nor rewarded him according to his iniquities. It was like the kiss of the Divine forgiveness, the joy of conscious realization of God's redeeming love. Yes; Jacob found *this* Portion in God, the fulness of forgiving love. But is not this the Portion we want, the God we need to know? Not one who will cast us away from his presence and throw us over when we have done wrong. If God were strict to mark iniquities, who of us could stand? But the God, the Portion of Jacob, meets our need; for as Jacob was sinful and often falling into sin, so are we.

II. Another element of this portion which Jacob possessed in God was the CONTINUAL AND MOST COMFORTING MANIFESTATIONS OF GOD which he was privileged to enjoy. How continually in his career are we met with instances of God's appearing to him! And besides the distinctly recorded instances, the impression is left upon the mind that it was the constant privilege of Jacob to hold intercourse with God, to talk with him as a man talketh with his friend. Yes; the God of Jacob was One who was graciously willing to come near to his servant, and to be known by him as his God—a God near at hand, and not afar off. But who can estimate what these Divine communications did for Jacob?—how unspeakably valuable an element in his portion this was? What courage, what confidence, what bright hope, what strength of faith, it must have imparted to the patriarch's mind! And such blessedness is assured to all believers. "I will come unto them, and will manifest myself unto them," said our Saviour. "I have set the Lord alway before me; because *he is at my right hand,* I shall not be moved." "God is our Refuge and Strength, a *very present* Help in trouble." It is because we cannot realize God's presence, can in no way feel him near to us, that therefore our hearts fail us for fear and our souls are cast down within us. But he to whom God reveals himself as he did to Jacob has in that fact a safeguard and protection from fear such as nought else can afford.

III. But another element in the portion which Jacob had in God was that of PURIFYING DISCIPLINE. Assuredly he was not left without chastisement; yea, it was a very scourging that was dealt out to him on account of his sins. Men are apt, both in reading the Bible and in observing the too frequent failures of godly men now, to look steadily at the sins of men like Jacob and David and others, and to wonder how such men can be regarded as God's people at all; but they do not look on and observe how sorely they are punished for their faults, and how they in this world find, beyond well-nigh all others, that "the way of transgressors is hard." Whoever else may seem to sin with impunity, the children of God may not and do not. No doubt Rebekah and Jacob thought they had done a very wise and clever thing when, by deceiving Isaac, they fraudulently obtained the blessing which belonged to Esau as the firstborn. But Rebekah, in the long years of melancholy bereavement of her favourite son—for she never saw him again after that day he fled from his home—had abundant leisure to see and repent of her folly and her sin. And Jacob, as he ate the bread of servitude and dwelt a stranger in a strange land, haunted with dread of Esau, was made to know that his trickery and fraud had borne him but a wretched harvest. The consuming fire of God's holy love burnt fiercely on until this dross which was so mingled with the pure ore of Jacob's faith was purged out of him. And this is ever an indispensable and a never-absent part of the portion of Jacob. The purging, purifying disciplines of God's holy love we shall all have to submit to according to our need of them. And this should render the Portion of Jacob not less but more precious in our esteem. If we willingly submit to much pain and distress in order that the health of the body, which at best can last only for a few short years, may be secured, may we not much rather submit ourselves to whatever of painful discipline God may appoint in order to secure the health of our souls, which shall live for ever? How dreadful would it be if God were not thus to purge and cleanse us; if he were to allow the cancerous growth of our sins to spread and grow until it had obtained such hold on us that death, eternal death, must follow! But this, out of fatherly love to us, he will never allow; and therefore Jacob was, and so we must be, held down to the suffering which his disciplines cause until their perfect work is done, and we are presented faultless before the presence of his glory with exceeding joy. Oh, let us be more anxious that God's will should be done in us than that his hand should be taken off from us. Never, never may he say concerning any one of us as he did concerning Ephraim, "He is joined to his idols: let him alone."

IV. GOD'S PROVIDENTIAL GUARDIANSHIP AND CARE was a further element in the portion of Jacob. How God watched over him! how truly Jacob could say, "He knoweth the way that I take"! Never was there any man to whom these words were more appropriate than they were to him. With what constant interest did God appear to mark all the way by which Jacob had to go! His eye was never off him, his hand never withdrawn, his help never wanting when needed. Even when Jacob did not dream that God was near him, he was so in fact. So that he had to confess as at

Bethel, "Surely God is in this place, though I knew it not." Hearken how he speaks of God when blessing the sons of Joseph. He tells of him as "the God which fed me all my life long unto this day, the Angel which redeemed me from all evil." Such was his confession of that never-failing care, that incessant interest with which the Lord God had watched over every stage of his life's journey. How all his very steps had been ordered by the Lord! This is another characteristic of the portion which Jacob had in God. And must not that man be blessed who consciously realizes that he has this God for his Help? To have our lives made God's care, our interests his concern, to have his angels evermore keeping watch and ward over us, encamping round about us to deliver us,—this is another blessed element in the portion of Jacob and of all like him.

V. MEETNESS FOR "THE INHERITANCE OF THE SAINTS IN LIGHT." Gradually, step by step, sometimes with seeming retrogression, but ever advancing on the whole, Jacob was lifted up from the low level of his former spiritual life, and ceased to be any longer Jacob, and became Israel. Such elevation, such meetness for "the inheritance of the saints," was and ever is part of the portion of Jacob, and a most blessed part it is.

And now, IN CONCLUSION, let us ask, *Is there such a Portion anywhere else?* Our text affirms, "The Portion of Jacob is not like them." The prophet is speaking of the wretched idols before whom his countrymen were so prone to bow down. It seems wonderful that any should have ever thought that the God of Jacob was like them. Like them! when even to think of them was to despise them with utter contempt. What a contrast to him, whom mind, and heart, and will, body, soul, and spirit could never sufficiently adore! It seemed monstrous that any should substitute for him those wretched idols, upon whom the prophet, in the preceding part of this chapter, pours forth his bitter scorn. But he means by the assertion we have been considering to declare that the Portion of Jacob is *an incomparable Portion.* None can be put beside, still less put in the place of him. And this is a truth for to-day. We ask again the question, "Is there such a Portion anywhere else?" Oh that they whom the psalmist calls "men of the world," and of whom he says, "they have their portion in this life," would compare the two—Jacob's and their own! Ah! you who have not the Portion of Jacob, we allow that you may have very much that is bright and fair. God may fill your veins with health, your coffers with gold, your houses with all luxury, your gardens with flowers, your fields with fruits, and your life with comfort and outward peace; but you are like those trees which in the winter-time are called Christmas-trees. "One feels a kind of pang at the first sight of such trees. No doubt it is beautiful in its way, with the little lights twinkling among the branches, and the sweet gifts of affection hanging from every twig. But the tree itself, are you not sorry for it?—rooted no longer, growing no more, no more circulation of the living sap, no sweet discoursing by its means between air and soil, between soil and air. The last waves of its life are sinking, and the more you hang upon it and the more you gather round it the faster it will die" (Dr. Raleigh). And if we have not the Portion of Jacob, we are like one of these trees. Loaded it may be with all manner of pleasant things, and surrounded with affection, but dying all the while. But "the Portion of Jacob is not like them"—one that will abandon you at the close of your life, or maybe long before, and leave you helpless and forlorn. Oh no; but then, when "heart and flesh fail," God will be "the Strength of your heart," and your "Portion for evermore." *That* is the portion of Jacob, and oh may God grant that it may be yours and mine, and that of all we love! Amen.—C.

Vers. 17, 18.—*Wherefore God doth judge the world.* It is not of the world at large, but of Judah and Jerusalem, that the prophet is here speaking. But nevertheless the judgments of God and the design wherewith they were sent, though having reference only to one people, are true examples of all like judgments, whenever, wherever, and however they come. Therefore note—

I. THE JUDGMENTS FORETOLD. The people are to be driven forth into exile and captivity. The whole book tells of their sorrows. Jeremiah's prophecy is one long denunciation of the wrath of God about to come on the guilty land. He was sent to declare this in the hope that those to whom he spoke might yet turn to the Lord and live; like Noah, that "preacher of righteousness" who warned the godless of his day of the judgment that was coming upon them. More particularly in these verses Jeremiah declares (ver. 17) *that not even the meanest and poorest will escape.* The "wares" spoken of tell rather of the few mean possessions, the small trifling properties, of a poor man, which in his haste he would gather together in a bundle and so endeavour to save (cf. Exposition). In former judgments it was mainly the high and lofty, those of wealth and station, who had suffered; but now all, from the highest to the lowest, should be included in the overwhelming desolations about to be poured forth. And so the prophet represents the poor and wretched hastily gathering up their little effects, and making off with them as best they may. And ver. 18 adds yet other terrible features to this delineation of the judgment that is coming: "Behold, I will sling out," etc. This, therefore, shows how ready they must have been for such treatment. David selected smooth stones from the brook, such as were fit and apt for his sling, and with them he went forth to meet Goliath. Not any missile, not any stone, would serve. And so if it were possible, as it was, for a people to be "slung out" of a land, they must have made themselves fit for such judgment, or else they would not have been subjected to it. And this they had been doing for many a long year. "When the husbandman seeth that the harvest is come, he putteth in the sickle." This is true of the visitation of judgment as well as of grace. *The violence* of the people's expulsion from their land is also indicated: as a stone is hurled forth from the sling. And the *completeness* of the judgment: "at this once," *i.e.* completely, thoroughly, at one blow. Former judgments had been partial, temporary, long drawn out. This was to be complete, perpetual, and "at once," as a stone is in a moment driven forth from the sling. And their *far-distant destination* is suggested. God intended that they should be carried far off into the land of their exile (cf. Isa. xxii. 18). But note—

II. THE FACT THAT THESE JUDGMENTS ARE DECLARED TO HAVE A PURPOSE BEYOND THEMSELVES. All was to be done "*that they may find.*" It is plain, therefore, however we supply what must come after the word "find," that there was a definite Divine purpose in all these calamities. They were not to be an end in themselves, but to lead on to one beyond. And surely this must be the purpose of all God's judgments; he can have no satisfaction in them simply as punishment. His heart is set on what is to come forth out of them, and the result has regard to them. "That *they* may find;" they who have sinned so terribly, they shall learn by these judgments that he sends.

III. WHAT THAT PURPOSE IS. What is it that they may find? Our translators have simply added the words "it so," thus leaving undetermined what the finding is to be. But surely that which God would have them find is all that which hitherto they could not be persuaded to believe in, *e.g.* the bitterness of disobedience, the vanity of idols, the sure truth of God's word, the uselessness of all religion that is not from the heart, etc. But all this to the intent that they may find, as at last many of them did, the way of repentance and return to God. God had made them for himself, as he has made us all for himself. It is blasphemy to think of him as creating human souls, endued as they all are with such vast capacities, with any other design. And hence it is that the heart of man is unquiet, has no rest, until it find rest in God. God will not suffer it to be otherwise, blessed be his Name. And since for Judah and Jerusalem nothing else would do, they should go into bitter exile, and suffer as in the very fire, "that they might find" God; that they might come to themselves, and say, "I will arise and go to my father," etc. "God *will* have all men to be saved, and to come to the knowledge of the truth;" and for the persistently impenitent a most awful will it is. As the late Duke of Wellington was wont to say, "There is only one thing worse than a great victory, and that is a great defeat;" so we may say there is only one thing worse for the ungodly than this set will of God for their salvation, and that is that his will should not be as it is.

IV. WHAT, THEREFORE, WE ARE TO LEARN FROM THIS. 1. Give thanks and praise to the Lord God for his most gracious purpose concerning men, that they should find him (cf. Ps. c., "Oh be joyful in the Lord, all ye lands, . . . for it is *he* that hath made us, and not we ourselves; we are *his* people, and the sheep of his pasture"). 2. Compel him not, as Judah did, to resort to sore judgments ere we will seek and "find" him. 3. At once take Christ's yoke and learn of him, and so find rest in our souls by finding him.—C.

Ver. 19.—*Submission.* I. THE GRIEF CONTEMPLATED. It is told of in ver. 17, etc. And it was indeed great; the "wound was grievous;" for: 1. It was so *universal.* It affected all classes and in all ways, in mind, body, and estate. 2. So *severe.* It was not a "light affliction," but "the iron entered into their souls." 3. And it was *self-caused.* The fangs of remorse were fastened in them by the consciousness they could not escape, that they had brought all their sorrows upon themselves. 4. And they *drew down so many others,* and innocent ones, in their own doom. This is ever one of the most fearful torments to the soul of the guilty. "I have ruined, not myself only, but my wife, children, parents, friends." The dart, if it be plunged first into the heart of those we love, will rankle in our own all the more terribly when it pierces us. 5. And the *light of God's countenance was gone.* With that we can bear anything. Paul and Silas sang praises in the dungeon at Philippi. But withdrawn, driven away by our sin, then is the soul sad indeed. 6. And it was *irreparable.* The wrath of God had arisen, and there "was no remedy" (cf. ver. 20). But note—

II. THE SPIRIT IN WHICH IT WAS BORNE. "But I said, Truly this is a grief, and I must bear it." Now, these words might be used to express a spirit of sullen hardihood. Some have so understood them. But we rather regard them as the language of pious submission. It is the true Israelite who speaks; not the godless, idol-loving multitude, but the chosen of God who were mingled among them. And that this is so is shown : 1. By the check the speaker puts upon his lament. He was about seemingly to launch out in great complainings when he arrests his speech by recollections of a different kind : "But I said," etc. He would not allow himself in any more complaint; he replies to all such thoughts by the considerations he now brings forward. 2. He recognizes the cause of all these sorrows (ver. 21). It was their failure to "seek the Lord," the pastors becoming "brutish"—their grievous sin. Mere sullenness would never make such a confession as this. 3. And the spirit of vers. 23—25, so lowly, devout, and filled with sacred desire,—all these show that we are to understand ver. 19 as the utterance, not of defiant hardihood or any other evil spirit, but as that of submission. Parallels, therefore, are to be found in the submission of Aaron at the death of his sons (cf. also Lam. iii. 18—21, 39, 40; Micah vii. 9; Ps. lxxvii. 10; xxxix. 9, etc.).

III. THIS SPIRIT GREATLY TO BE COMMENDED. 1. *For its nature.* It is not the spirit of *a stoic,* of one who sets his teeth firm, and resolves to endure, come what may ; but it is tender, gentle, and keenly susceptible of pain. Nor is it *silent.* Its voice is heard in prayers, confessions, praises, and it is ever desiring more of God's presence and grace. Nor is it *slothful.* It will be open-eyed to see and alert to act if aught can be done to minister relief or gain deliverance. Thus it does not violate any good instinct or dictate either of nature or conscience, as it would do were it characterized by either of the undesirable qualities named. They each have some sort of semblance of submission, but are far away removed from being identical with it or necessary to it. But submission consists in that calm composure of our whole nature, that meek acquiescence in the will of God, however painful that will may be. And therefore this spirit is commendable : 2. *For its comeliness.* How morally beautiful and lovely it is ! We never tire of it, never do anything but in our hearts admire and praise it, and long to make it our own. How our hearts go out towards those that have eminently manifested it ! As Aaron (cf. *supra*); Job saying, "The Lord gave, and the Lord hath taken away," etc. ; Moses ; and above all, our Saviour. Notwithstanding all his present and most deserved glory as our risen Lord, it is to him on the cross, crowned with thorns, in all the glory of his meek submission—to him the heart of humanity ever turns with adoring love and trust. 3. *For its self-conquest.* Under the smart and distress of great loss and disaster, how ready the understanding is to think hard thoughts and to utterly resent what God has done ! And the will, how sullenly it frowns upon God, and with lowering brow refuses to submit ! And the passions, how they rage in torrents of tears and wild wailing cries of angry agony ! And the lips, what hard speeches they are prompt to utter (cf. "I said in my haste, All men are liars")! And the hands, how eager to take revenge upon any who have been the means and instruments of our affliction ! But the spirit of submission holds all these hot, eager forces in, as with bit and bridle, and bids them all be still. They are, as were the lions before Daniel, awed and subdued by his calm, hallowed presence. Blessed is he who can thus conquer himself. None else shall conquer him, and least of all any of the mere circumstances of life (cf. Prov. xvi. 32). 4. *For its wisdom.* "There are few things in the world so totally and entirely bad but some advantage may be made of them by a dexterous management; and it is certainly a man's wisdom to make the best of a bad condition, there being a certain kind of pious and prudential husbandry by which a man may so improve a calamity as to make the endurance of it the performance of a duty, and by his behaviour under it to procure a release from it. We should, with Isaac, take the wood upon our shoulders, though we ourselves are designed for the sacrifice; and who knows but, as in his case, so in ours also, a patient resignation of ourselves to the knife may be the sure and direct way to rescue us from it?" (South).

" He always wins who sides with thee;
To him no chance is lost;
Thy will is sweetest to him when
It triumphs at his cost.

" Ill that thou blessest turns to good,
And unblest good to ill;
And all is right that seems most wrong,
If it be thy sweet will."

5. *For its acceptableness to God.* The Lord Jesus Christ was the " my beloved Son, in whom I am well pleased," because of it; because his meat and his drink was ever to do the will of the Father who sent him. " Blessed are the meek." " Humble yourselves therefore under the mighty hand of God, that," etc.

IV. NOT EASY, BUT NEVERTHELESS FULLY POSSIBLE, OF ATTAINMENT. Not easy, because all our instincts under the smart of pain and loss (cf. *supra*) protest against it. Because also the maxims of the world are directly contrary to it. But attainable by *practice.* " Let him train himself whilst young to lesser self-denials and mortifications; let him learn to put up with and pass by a slight undervaluing word, and in time he shall find himself strong enough to conquer and digest an injurious action; let him learn to overlook his neighbour's incivility, and in time he shall be able with patience and firmness of mind to endure his insolence and cruelty, and that without being discomposed by any instigations to revenge; and let him accustom himself to do this often, and at length he shall be able to do it always" (South). And yet more by *communion and intercourse with the Lord Jesus Christ.* We catch the tones and habits and thoughts of those with whom we most associate. Live in close companionship with Christ, and the spirit of him who " when he was reviled, reviled not again," shall be formed in us, and more and more shall we know how " blessed are the meek," and how surely God " will exalt us in due time " (cf. Phil. ii. 5—11).—C.

Vers. 20, 21.—*The ruin wrought by the prayerless pastor.* I. CONSIDER THE SCENE PORTRAYED BY THE PROPHET. Consider it both before and after that dread invasion of which he was ever warning his countrymen. 1. *Before that invasion,* whilst Judah was at peace, there might often have been witnessed over the wide downs and pasture-lands of Palestine the shepherds' encampment; for Palestine was an eminently pastoral country, as the psalms of David and the teachings of our Lord plainly show. And hence up and down the land might have been seen the shepherds' tents, whole camps of them, dotting the plains or valleys with their slender poles, their broad curtains and strong cords holding them erect and securing them firmly to the ground on which they stood. The swarthy children would be running in and out, and at even-time the greater portion of the whole inhabitants of these tabernacles would be gathered around or within them. And in the immediate neighbourhood, carefully watched by their shepherds, would be the flocks quietly grazing, in which consisted their whole wealth. It was a pastoral scene the peacefulness and beauty of which were as manifest as the commonness of it in the happier days of Palestine and her people. 2. *But after the invasion,* in the unhappy days which, when Jeremiah spoke, were drawing so terribly near, when the land should be overrun by the armies of Babylon, there would be as often seen the actual circumstances portrayed in our text. The tent thrown down, its cords cut, its curtains a shapeless heap upon the ground, left to decay and rot by those who had wrought its ruin. And all would be silent and still; no merry prattle of children heard, or the coming and going of the men and women who once had made that tent their home. A few blackened ashes alone telling where the camp-fire had been. The flocks all scattered; those that the foe had not destroyed driven off and wandering in the wilderness, none knew where. It is a picture of utter and most mournful desolation.

II. ITS MEANING. Its intent is to represent what was about to happen in regard to the Church and people of Judah. The temple should be overthrown and burnt with fire; her holy places profaned, her altars broken down, her sacred services all brought to an end, the solemn feast-day no more observed. Her children—they who ministered at her altars and sang the high praises of the Lord—should have gone forth from her and be as though they were not, and all the congregation of the people, the flock of the Lord, should be scattered. And all this came to pass, as we well know, violently and as in a moment, like as a stone is suddenly hurled forth from the sling (ver. 18). But the prophet's picture has a yet wider application; for it tells of the terrible desolation which may come upon any Church, whether in a nation, or a community, or in any given district. Under the vivid imagery which Jeremiah employs we may see represented the deplorable disaster of a Church's desolation, and whence and how it comes. Therefore let us look at: 1. *The overthrown tent.* By it we may see represented the destruction of the whole organization of the Church. How beautiful is the spectacle presented to the outward eye by a Church that enjoys the blessing of God! Behold her *sanctuaries.* Look upon them, from the stately cathedral down to the humblest house of God in the land. Here, with dome and towers and spires piercing the sky, pointing upwards, heavenwards, and breaking the dull level of men's common habitations, and of the buildings which they have reared for their dwellings, their labour, their trade. And out in the country, on the hillside, scattered over the wide plains and along many a quiet valley, in hamlet, village, and town, we behold the sanctuaries built for God, and the stream, larger or smaller, of worshippers that continually go up to them to worship. Each one of these sanctuaries a centre of light and warmth, of energy and holy toil, blessing and being blessed. And think of *the sabbaths* of the Church—those blessed days of rest, when the weary round of toil is made to hush its noise, and for the time to cease. The plough stands still in the furrow, the horses roam in the meadow or gladly rest in the stall; but the ploughman is gone home, that he may, if he will, give heed to the husbandry of the soul and to the preparation for the harvest of heaven. Nor, in this survey, may we pass by *the Church's worship.* What myriads of jubilant anthems and glad psalms and triumphant hymns go up heavenwards, with a merry noise! What help for all who desire it is won by those who give heed to the holy truth that is at such times proclaimed! Ah! if spiritual thought and feeling could, by some Divine chemistry, be made visible, what a glorious scene would be witnessed! Like unto the rainbow which was round about the throne, beautiful to behold, would the worship of the Church be seen, even as it is seen by him to whom and for whom and by whom it is all rendered. Think, too, of *the work of the Church.* The ships that bear her messengers, charged to proclaim the glad tidings of the gospel to all mankind, speed their way through all seas, across all oceans, and enter every harbour. Ah! yes; Christ's Church on earth, faulty, imperfect, unfaithful, as she so often and so largely is,—where would the world be without her? and where would the wretched and the lost find their truest friends, if not in her? But all this outward organization, this visible tabernacle of the Church, is contemplated, *not* as in her happy ideal, but in the very reverse. The prophet's picture portrays the tabernacle thrown down, and desolation everywhere. Hence her sanctuaries forsaken, profaned, or left to decay and ruin; her services abandoned or turned into mere performances of worn-out ceremonies; her sabbaths no longer days of guarded rest, but like all other days; her work paralyzed and dropped more and more, and all her external framework and organization overthrown. Try and realize what that would be. And this is not all. 2. *Her children are represented as having gone forth from her.* When all is well with a Church, it is our joy to see the children taking the fathers' place, coming forward to uphold the standard which the aged hands of the seniors are compelled to let go. How delightful such a scene is we need hardly say. But there is nothing of this kind contemplated here, but, on the contrary, those to whom the Church would naturally look to carry on her work are seen borne away captive by the foes of the Church, and as slaves to the world. 3. And the last feature in this sad picture is *the scattering of the flock.* The people at large, for whose interests the Church was bidden to care, turning from her with disgust, scouting her claims, running riot in sin, unchecked, unhindered, unwarned; sinking down into awful depths of wickedness and spiritual ignorance, living "without God and without hope in the world." Such is the scattering of the flock, the alienation of her children, and the spoiling of her tabernacle, from all which may God evermore keep and defend us. But that we may be thus defended, let us—

III. INQUIRE THE CAUSE OF SUCH DISASTER. It is clearly stated in ver. 21, "The pastors have become brutish, and have not sought the Lord." 1. Who are these pastors? It would be a mistake to suppose that only ministers are meant. Jeremiah did not mean these only, but all to whom the flock of God were entrusted—kings, rulers, judges, parents, and teachers, heads of families, and all to whom, by virtue of their position, the charge and responsibility of watching over the souls of others was given. 2. Now, these pastors had "become brutish." By which is meant, first of all, unintelligent, stupid, blind to the meaning of facts, and incapable of perceiving what needed to be done; with no quick apprehension, if any at all, of their responsibility, their duty, or the peril that threatened both their flock and themselves; settled down into the stolid apathy and indifference of ignorance, of dulled perception, and of blindness of heart. Brutish, too, because unspiritual, materialized, worldly, earth-bound; having little or no regard for anything beyond what this life can give or take away; caring more for the fleece of the flock than for its faith and fidelity. And brutish, it may be, in a yet lower sense, because sensual; like those of whom Paul tells with bitter tears. "Whose god," he says, "is their belly, who glory in their shame, who mind earthly things." 3. "The pastors have become brutish." What an awful association of ideas! Can any condition be conceived of more horrible than this? No wonder such disastrous results followed. Think how dreadful such a fact must be for *the honour of Christ*. How his Name must be blasphemed! How such must crucify the Son of God afresh, and once more put him to open shame! How again the Lord Jesus, pointing to the wounds in his sacred hands and feet and side, must declare, "These are the wounds with which I was wounded in the house of my friends"! Blessed Saviour, keep us from such sin as this. And how dreadful for *the Church of Christ*, which he has purchased with his own blood! How such men discourage the Church! how they chill its ardour! how they stagger its faith! how they weaken its strength! how they imperil its very life! And how dreadful for *the world!* "Woe unto the world," said our Saviour, "because of offences!" This he said in pity for the world, hindered, made to stumble and fall by those who should only have helped it on its way to God. How many will be hardened in wickedness, encouraged to despise all religion, furnished with fresh subject for impious mockery and new arguments for sin; by such as they of whom our text tells! And how dreadful for *these brutish ones themselves!* "But woe," said Jesus, "unto them by whom that offence cometh!" "Who shall abide the day of the Lord's coming" to execute his wrath on them? Who, indeed! God, in his infinite mercy, save us from ever knowing what that wrath is. 4. *But how came this awful fall?* What brought down these pastors to this dreadful condition? And the answer to this question is plainly given. *They did not seek the Lord; they were prayerless pastors*: and that explains all. Now, this did not mean that there was no worship, no praise, no prayer, ever offered. We know there was. The temple service went on and the sacrifices were presented as usual. But there was no true, heartfelt prayer. They did not really *seek* the Lord. And so with ourselves, there may be, and there probably will be, the keeping up of pious customs, the daily prayers, the ordinary worship; but for such seeking of the Lord as is here told of, and the neglect of which worked such ruin, there must be far more than this. There must be that full application of the heart and mind, that lifting up of the soul to God, that drawing out of the affections after him, that cleaving of the desires to him, that ardour and yet that patience, that humility and yet that boldness which time cannot measure, which make long prayers seem short to him who offers them, and short prayers, if of necessity they must be short, count as long prayers with him who, for Christ's sake, mercifully receives the soul who follows hard after him. This is the kind of prayer which can alone be our safeguard from the abyss into which the pastors here told of fell. Would we escape it, we must seek the Lord *so;* all else is as seeking him not at all. It is no holiday task, but one demanding all the energies of the soul. How many, how mighty, how manifold, how subtle, are the difficulties in the way! There is the earth-bound heart, that ever clogs our souls with its clinging·clay; that makes them like the bird with the lime of the bird-snarer on its feathers, unable either to fly or go: when it would soar aloft it is powerless to spread its wings, and so is as if chained to the ground. And incessant occupations clamour for attention, and are ever telling us we have no time. And indolence and sloth keep suggesting thoughts of ease and self-sparing. And want of practice in this, as in everything else, makes real prayer very difficult. And Satan, when he sees the soul threatening to escape him by means of such prayer—as by such means it ever will escape him—bends all his energies to thwart and hinder, to baffle and beat down, such prayer. All this is so, but yet we *must* thus pray. And let us not be disheartened. All these difficulties have been overcome by ten thousand of the saints of God, and shall be by us. And, for our help, remember our Lord's intercession. Join all our prayers—poor, weak things as at their best they are—on to his almighty, all-prevailing intercession, and in this also we shall come off "more than conquerors through Christ who hath loved us." So shall we be kept from being one of those wretched pastors who have become brutish, and have, therefore, only scattered the Lord's flock; yea, we shall be made and be confessed, now and hereafter in our Lord's presence, as one of the pastors after his own heart.—C.

Vers. 23—25.—*Fruits of a chastened spirit.* From what foul soil do the fairest flowers spring! Beautiful as they are, they are rooted in that which is altogether unbeautiful. The sweet perfume of many woods, seeds, flowers, will not be given forth until they are gashed with the axe, or bruised, or crushed, or otherwise seemingly maltreated. We could not have the many-hued arch of the exquisitely tinted rainbow were it not for the drear, dark clouds and the descending rain. The most precious of the psalms were wrung out of the heart of David when that heart was well-nigh borne down with grief. And here, in these verses, it is the chastened spirit of Judah, personified in the prophet who speaks, that utters itself in the lowly confession of the twenty-third verse, the holy submission of the prayer of the twenty-fourth verse, and the settled hatred of them who hate God which burns in the twenty-fifth. Consider, then, these fruits, and may God make them to abound in ourselves.

I. THE CONFESSION. Ver. 23, "O Lord, I know," etc. Now, this is a confession: 1. *Of humble dependence upon God.* It is an acknowledgment that, however much man may propose, God will dispose; that man's goings are of the Lord. The life of each is, as God told Cyrus (Isa. xliv.), guided, governed by him. Illustrations are everywhere: the cruelty of Joseph's brethren; the oppression of Israel in Egypt; the crucifixion of our Lord (cf. Acts ii. 23); the persecution of the Church (Acts viii. 3); Paul's early life; etc. All these are instances in which, whilst men did exactly as they liked, acting with choice as unfettered as it was evil, they were nevertheless made to subserve the Divine plans, and their evil was compelled to work out good. Man may have power to "walk," but whither his steps will lead he cannot "direct." "The way of man is not in himself." He is free to choose his way, and for his choice he is responsible; but he is not allowed to determine all that shall come of that choice or what its issues and results shall be. Every time that men find their plans turn out altogether differently from what they expected or designed, proves the truth of the prophet's word. God has planned the life of each one of us. He intends certain results to be secured by our lives.

> "There's a divinity that shapes our ends,
>   Rough-hew them how we will."

And our wisdom is to see and confess and conform ourselves to the Divine plan—happy they who do so!—and not to thwart or hinder it, as so many are bent upon doing, and hence, in the manifold sorrows of their lives, find it "hard to kick against the pricks." Our wisdom is daily to pray, "Cause me to know the way wherein I should walk; make plain my path before my face." 2. *Of their own folly and sin.* There are many teachers who will instruct us in this truth of our own incompetence to order our ways; all that is needed is that we be willing to learn. Such teachers are: (1) *Reason.* It is reasonable that, as we are the creatures of God, he should have the control of our lives. (2) *Scripture.* We have cited some instances already. (3) *Observation.* The world is strewn with the wrecks of men who have disregarded the chart given them of God, and have run upon the rocks in consequence. (4) But the most strenuous and resistless teacher of all is *Experience.* He will make a man learn, almost whether the man will or no. And it was this teacher who had been instructing, in his emphatic manner, Judah and her people. By the miserable mess they had made of their lives, and the frightful calamities which now were close at their doors (ver. 22), they had at length come to see and confess their own wretched ordering of their way. Hence now the confession, "O Lord, I know that," etc. It is a blessed fruit for folly and fault to bear. It is not the natural fruit, but one of God's gracious grafts. Peter's folly of boasting bore such fruit when "he went out and wept bitterly." Let our prayer be that the faults and follies, the sins and sorrows, with which our lives are scattered over may make us see and own, "O Lord, I *know* that," etc. 3. *Of their trust, nevertheless, in God's infinite love.* For not improbably this confession has not only an upward look to God as the Director of men's ways, and an inward look upon their own sin, but also an outward look upon those dread foes who were hastening to destroy them. And this was their comfort that, after all, these enemies of theirs were in God's hands. No doubt they designed fearful things against God's people (cf. ver. 25). But then, "the way of man is not," etc. Hence even these fierce, relentless foes might be held in and turned about by the bit and bridle of God. Had not God, in the days of the good King Hezekiah, proved this in regard to the King of Assyria and his army? Had he not, as Isaiah said, "put a hook in his nose ... and turned him back by the way by which he came"? And this confession breathes this hope and trust that God would do the like by their enemies now about to fall upon them. It is a real comfort to know that all our enemies, whether human or spiritual, are under the control of God. Even the apparently omnipotent prince of evil has but a limited power. *He,* too, cannot direct his own way. "The Lord, he is the true God, the living God, the everlasting King" (ver. 10).

II. THE PRAYER. Ver. 24, "O Lord, correct me, but," etc. 1. *This is a model prayer.* For: (1) It confesses wrong. It owns the need of correction. The man is no longer right in his own eyes. He is seen, like the publican, "standing afar off," etc. (2) It desires to be put right (cf. Ps. li.). As there, so here, there is the longing for renewal, the clean heart, the right spirit. (3) It deprecates, not the correction, but the wrath of God. The man has a clear view of that wrath—its crushing, destroying power. It is good to have this. Without it there is the danger of our looking lightly upon our sin. 2. *It is a most instructive prayer.* It teaches us: (1) That all the corrections we have received have been fatherly ones—"in judgment," not "in anger." For had they been in anger we had not been here at all. (2) That we are alive and in God's presence proves that the love of God, and not his anger, is ours still. For his anger would have "brought us to nothing." (3) That there are corrections in anger. There have been such. Where are Egypt, Nineveh, Babylon, Rome? God brought them "to nothing." And there will be for all who harden themselves against God. (4) That, seeing all need correction and will therefore receive it, either "in judgment" or "in anger," our wisdom is to make this prayer our own. One or other of these corrections we must have. Which shall it be? This prayer was answered for Israel. They have *not* been brought to nothing, and they *were* corrected. That sin of idolatry which brought on them God's correction they have, ever since that correction, utterly abandoned. Then let us make this prayer our own.

III. HOLY ANGER AGAINST THE ENEMIES OF GOD. We can readily see that vers. 23 and 24 are the fruits of a chastened spirit, but this fierce utterance of ver. 25 seems of another kind. But it is not. No doubt it has somewhat of the fierceness which belonged to that stern age, but it is none the less a real fruit of a right spirit. We ought to be very doubtful of our own spirit, however meek and contrite it is, if it be not accompanied with an intense detestation of evil. "Do not I hate them, O Lord, that hate thee? and am not I grieved with those that rise up against thee?" Such sentiment is a true note of the Spirit of God, and a religious life that lacks it is sure to be lacking in vigour, strength, and reliability. It is not personal hatred that finds utterance here, so much as a deep sense of the wrong done to God and the hindrance that is placed in the way of his will. The seventy-ninth psalm is an expression of this petition. Our

age, and the temperament that so soft an age induces, are apt to make us be too easy
with sin and sinners. We are so bred up in the idea of the "Gentle Jesus, meek and
mild," that we forget how anything but gentle and mild he was to the hopelessly bad
who were, in regard to the spiritual well-being of his people, doing as is here said,
"eating up Jacob, devouring him," etc. What awful words poured forth from the
Saviour's lips towards such! Let us suspect a meekness that makes us mild towards
such. A man may make the confession of ver. 23, and offer the prayer of ver. 24, and
fall and fall again; but if he have the stern spirit of ver. 25, that deep, intense hatred
of evil, sin is far less likely to have dominion over him for the future; he will be
"strong in the Lord, and in the power of his might." Therefore, whilst we crave that
fruit of the Spirit which is seen in vers. 23, 24, let us crave that also which we have
here in ver. 25. It is the result of our being "strengthened with might by the Spirit
of God in the inner man," and leads on, in blessed, successive steps, to our being "filled
with all the fulness of God."—C.

Ver. 23.—"*The way of man.*" The prophet probably speaks here not merely for
himself, but in the name of the whole nation. He gives articulate utterance to the
better elements of thought and feeling existing among them, their conscious short-
sightedness as regards the meaning and issue of their own national experiences, their
helpless dependence on the unseen Divine power that is working out through the
terrible events of the time its own all-wise purposes. An important view of human
life is here presented before us. Consider (1) *the fact asserted;* (2) *the influence it
may be expected to have over us.*
I. THE FACT ASSERTED. "The way of man is not in himself," etc. All human life
is a "way," a journey, a pilgrimage, through various scenes and circumstances, to the
"bourn from whence no traveller returns." And, free as we may be and accountable
for our own actions, there is a sense in which it is equally true that it is given to none
of us to determine what that way shall be. We are called on to recognize a governing
power external to ourselves, above and beyond ourselves. Look at this fact in two
lights as indicative of: 1. *Moral inability.* A man's own judgment and impulse are
not in themselves a safe rule for the conduct of his life. He cannot always trace the
mutual relation of interests and events, is liable to be deceived by appearances, blinded
by the glamour of his own feelings, misled by the force of his own self-will. The very
complexity of the circumstances among which he "walks" is often a source of danger.
He is as one surrounded by the diverse interlacing paths of a forest; he needs both
external guidance and internal influence to direct his choice. The right way is not "in
himself." 2. *Practical restraint.* No man has the actual power to determine altogether
the course of his own life. Free as he may think himself to be to take what "steps"
he pleases, he is, after all, often ruled by circumstances over which he has no control.
He is not always master of his own movements, cannot do the thing that he would,
constrained perhaps to do something totally different from what he intended. Who has
not found himself to have been drifted, by the silent, unobserved current of events, into
a position entirely other than he would have chosen for himself? Who has not had to
accept, as the issue of his own doings, something strangely unlike what he looked for?
"Man proposes; God disposes."

> "There's a divinity that shapes our ends,
> Rough-hew them how we will."

Human history—national, social, individual—is full of illustrations of the governing and
restraining effect of some mysterious force that underlies all the phenomena of life.
Faith penetrates the heart of this mystery, and discerns in it a personal Divine providence, the energy of a will that is "holy and just and good."
II. THE INFLUENCE THIS FACT MAY BE EXPECTED TO HAVE OVER US. Such a truth,
even in the purely negative form in which this passage presents it, may well have a
marked effect on the whole habit of our daily thought and action. It teaches several
important lessons. 1. *Distrust of self.* If our judgment is thus fallible, our impulse
misleading, our power limited, shall we think to make our own will the sole rule of
life? "Trust in the Lord with all thine heart; and lean not unto thine own understanding," etc. (Prov. iii. 5, 6); "Go to now, ye that say, To-day or to-morrow we will

go into such a city," etc. (Jas. iv. 13—16).   2. *Thoughtful observation of the course of events*, with a view to trace the path of the providence that is over us.   Hidden as the power that governs our life may be, the teachable mind discerns ever more and more clearly the method of its working.   "The secret of the Lord is with them that fear him," etc. (Ps. xxv. 14); "The meek will he guide in judgment," etc. (Ps. xxv. 9). 3. *Practical obedience to the call of present duty.*   Dark as our way may be, we cannot go far wrong if we follow the dictates of conscience.   Be true in everything to your own sense of right and to the clear lines of Divine Law, and you may safely leave all issues with God.   4. *The calm repose of faith.*   In the confused conflict of adverse circumstances, in the deep night of our sorrow and our fear, we hear a voice that whispers to us, "All is well."   It must be so if we believe that almighty Love is Lord of all.—W.

Vers. 1—12.—*What men fear and what they ought to fear.*   I. WHAT MEN FEAR. *They fear mere images of their own manufacture.*   Note the connection between vers. 2 and 3.   In ver. 2 the heathen are spoken of as being dismayed at the signs of heaven.   Probably these signs, considered in their more particular and direct connection with the dismay, were really images on earth, representing the supposed Divine dignity of the bodies in the heavens.   The heavenly bodies were signs to the believer in Jehovah— signs of the power and wisdom of Jehovah.   But what signs could they be to the heathen ? In their eyes they were themselves Divine realities, and the signs on earth in the shape of images.   If this view be correct, it makes dismay at the signs of heaven look more than ever absurd; for these signs were of man's own making.   He goes out to the wood and cuts down one tree, and it supplies material for common use, beams and flooring and furniture for his dwelling-place.   He takes another tree, neighbour and of the very same kind, and of this he makes an image, to be an object of dread, to be approached with trembling solicitude and doubt.   The very chips and shavings that come off as it is being shaped may be burnt, but it itself is sacred, decked with silver and gold, perfected by the most cunning art of the time, surrounded probably with the choicest treasures of the land where it is worshipped.   And yet in itself it is nothing. When it grew in the wood it bore leaves and fruit, and had vital movement in it.   By its life it spoke to those who had ears to understand.   Other trees cut down, even when they become dead wood, are useful; but here is dead wood not only useless but so treated that it becomes full of the worst peril to all associated with it, a centre of abominations, delusions, and cruelties.   And *it must be felt as a very extraordinary thing* that what men thus make with their own hands should be regarded with such perpetual dread and circumspection.   Partly it may be accounted for by the force of education.   Those who had been brought up having their minds sedulously filled with certain associations in respect to these images, would either fail to see any absurdity in fearing them or, in spite of the absurdity, would be unable to get over the fear.   It is very absurd to be afraid of walking through some secluded churchyard at midnight, but many people could only do so with the utmost trepidation—even those who show plenty of good sense in their ordinary affairs.   The mystery lies not so much in the continuance of image-worship as in the origin of it; and this is a mystery we have no power to penetrate. A more practical thing is to take heed to the counsel here given.   *These* works of your own hands cannot hurt you.   Neglect them, they cannot resent the negligence.   Pile up before them all you can in the way of gift and honour, and yet you get not the least good in return.   You may be hurt by other works of your hands, but assuredly not by them; and if you are hurt—as it seems by the instrumentality of these images—yet be sure of this, that the hurt comes from Jehovah's anger because you are honouring and worshipping the creature in opposition to the Creator.   And if it be said, "How does all this dissuasion against *image-worship* concern *us?*" the answer is plain that, although we do not make images of wood, we may have conceptions in our own minds which are as truly the cause of empty terror as any visible image that man ever made.   The ultimate meaning of the counsel here is that it is vain to fear anything or any one save the omnipotent God.

II. WHAT MEN OUGHT TO FEAR.   Images are presented in this passage, first, in themselves, in all their emptiness, as pure fabrications of human superstitions; and then they are brought into the presence of the exceeding glory of Jehovah, and thus the exhibition of their nothingness is completed.   Moreover, the glory of Jehovah shines more brightly still by contrast with the darkness and shame that are over against it. He is the great and strong One, the living One, and the everlasting King. The ever-living God over against dead and degraded matter!—can there be a greater contrast? And to bring out God's strength, his strength to make his wrath felt as real suffering in the lives of those who displease him, the contrast is made, not between the living God and dead idols, but between the omnipotent Ruler and the kings of the nations. Take the kings of the nations; take him who rules the widest territory, controls the largest resources, shows in himself the greatest resolution and force of character, achieves the most splendid reign that history can record—take such a one, and yet what is he over against Jehovah? Jehovah is the King of the nations. It is his power that moulds them and gives them their destiny, their place in his economy of the ages. And as Jeremiah contemplates all this, he says, "Who would not fear thee?" Certainly there are none but what would fear, and with a properly befitting fear, if only they could properly regard the object presented to them. But while men are fearing that which need not be feared, they depart further and further from a sense of him who holds in his self-sufficing being complete power over all their best interests. When they suffer, being deceived by lying lips, they attribute their suffer-ing to the wrath of a God whom they themselves imagine; and so, fixing their minds by a kind of fascination on the wrong cause, they fail to have even the least suspicion of the right one. If, when a blow falls upon us, we could trace that blow back, and see how much of it comes from God, and with what purpose it comes, then how much useless suffering would be spared! But blows come on men in the dark, and they prefer to remain in the dark with their evil deeds rather than be freed from their misconceptions by coming to the light.—Y.

Ver. 2.—*The dismay of the heathen at the signs of heaven.* By the signs of heaven here are doubtless meant those heavenly bodies given for signs and seasons, days and years (Gen. i. 14); this view still further helping to explain the reference in ch. viii. 2 to sun and moon and all the host of heaven. Why *these* should terrify it is not very easy for us to comprehend, surrounded as we are by quite different associations. Often, indeed, there is cause of terror in the heavens above us, as when the depths of the celestial spaces are hidden from us by the thunder-cloud, and when the stormy blasts go forth on their errand of destruction over land and sea. But such terrors, we know, come from things nearer the earth. Sun and moon and all the host of heaven have quite a different effect on our minds. And we know, too, from the refer-ences to them in the Scriptures, that they did not terrify those who knew God. The Book of Psalms shows nothing of dismay at the signs of heaven; rather it sets them forth as helping to produce cheerfulness, enjoyment, and elevating adoration towards him who made them. Such feelings have never been absent from the minds of those who have really comprehended whose handiwork the heavenly bodies are, and why he brought them into existence. How is it, then, *that by such a strong expression they are here represented as being objects of terror?* The answer is, that the maker of them being unknown, and the purpose of them being undiscernible, to those whose minds were darkened by wicked works, they had to make their own conjectures. And thus they filled the darkness of their ignorance with horrid, stupefying errors. To sun and moon and all the host of heaven they came to attribute a kind of personality. And then to the personality thus conceived there would be attached the two contrasted states of mind of complacency and wrath. *Complacency* appeared in the warmth, brightness, and clearness of day, and the cloudless skies of night, when moon and stars were revealed in all their milder splendour. *Wrath*, on the other hand, would seem to be shown by the eclipse, the waning of the moon, by rolling clouds, destructive storms, thunder and lightning, long droughts, meteors, comets, etc. And once having got into their heads that sun, moon, and stars had Divine dignity about them, it was nothing very wonderful that these heathen should be thus terrified by everything in the way of celestial commotion. In every such commotion the frowning faces of the celestial gods would be visible, and every injury thus coming would be reckoned as a blow from them. The words of the messenger to Job, telling him how the light-ning had destroyed his flocks, may be adduced as a very striking illustration of dismay at the signs of heaven. What does the messenger tell Job? That *the fire of*

God had fallen from heaven. But the messenger did not know that; all he knew was that some extraordinary flame had destroyed the sheep. He went beyond the actual fact of his experience, and from it made such an inference as his superstitious mind naturally led him to make. Thus, then, we may take it this dismay at the signs of heaven was produced; and once it became thoroughly fixed in the mind that every eclipse, comet, storm, death by lightning, was an expression of Divine wrath, the next thing would be an instant attempt to make propitiation and avert further mischief. And it is easy to see that, as priestcraft grew in power, all would be done that could be done to make the people believe that the signs of heaven needed constant remembrance in order to keep them acting favourably towards the inhabitants of earth. Such, then, was the way of the heathen; but the way of Jehovah's people was to be quite different. These signs of heaven were no sufficient cause of terror, and indeed were to be quite differently regarded. God says to his people, "Be not dismayed;" but the command cannot directly produce obedience. There must be a showing, a clear showing, that there is no cause for terror. Terror because of the signs of heaven can only come from ignorance. The moment the mind takes in the great general drift of Gen. i., that same moment dismay will yield to an intelligent veneration towards God. A savage, seeing the express train rush past him, with its thunder and mystery, at the rate of fifty miles an hour, is as a matter of course utterly terrified and bewildered. But there would be no terror and bewilderment if he only really knew all the wisdom, patience, and controlling power which have made that express what it is. Furthermore, who would think of denying the immense utility of railways to the world because every now and then there is some hideous disaster to a train? And, similarly, through all the mysterious destructions which from time to time come in the natural world, we must look at something beyond and above them. Jesus Christ, who came into the world to make manifest and explicit the love of God as a great reality, is higher than any of these causes of temporal pain and loss. We are not permitted to get any satisfactory view of suffering as a whole, and we do well to refrain from putting any speculation of our own in the place of such a view. Our wisdom is to get more and more of a practical knowledge of God. Only so can it become possible for us to say that "we shall not fear, though the earth be removed, and though the mountains be carried into the midst of the sea."—Y.

Ver. 23.—*The way of man not in himself.* I. MAN IS NOT TO BE THE CHOOSER OF HIS WAY. "I know that the way of man is not in himself." It is surely not without significance that אָדָם is here used for "man." To the Hebrew there must always have been the opportunity of peculiar suggestions upon the occurrence of this word. Adam would rise to mind, the first man, with God's purposes for him, and his speedy calamitous departure from those purposes. God made Adam that he might go in God's way. When the two accounts of the creation of man are taken together, it will be seen how abundant is the evidence that the way of Adam was not in himself. His only condition of safety, peace, and happiness was in strict compliance with the Divine injunctions. And with regard to the descendant of Adam, he who can read the account of Adam and see the essential correspondence between ancestor and posterity, is there not everything to teach him that his way also is not in himself? Why, he is some little distance advanced in the way before he is conscious that it is a way at all. The preservation of his life and the direction of it have been at the disposition of others. And when life—as far as individual responsibility is concerned—really begins, how wise he proves to be who looks for the pointing of God's finger, and feels that he must follow it! The man who insists that he can make his own way only finds it perish at last. Because no way can be considered just as a way; whether it is pleasant or painful, easy or difficult, is not the great matter, but whither it leads, what lies at the end of it. As it would be foolish for a man to take charge of a ship, ignorant of his destination and how to reach it, so it is equally foolish for a man to suppose that any way will do so long as it is as comfortable and easy as he can make it. Man's right way must be according to God's clear will; and it is the way of trust in Jesus who is the Son and Christ of God. Note, further, the strong expression of individual assurance here given. "I know," says Jeremiah. He knew it indeed from his own experience. The way in which he now was, of prophet and witness for Jehovah, was not of his choosing. He did not think himself fit for it. And yet so far was he from being right in his own impressions as a young man, that it appears God had chosen him for a special purpose or ever his existence had begun. It is a great blessing to a man when, either from experience of his own wanderings or prudent observation of the wanderings of others, he can say in this matter, "I know." He spares himself much anxiety and shame who is humble enough to put himself under Divine guidance.

II. God must establish man when he is in the right way. "It is not in man that walketh to make sure of his steps." In other words, though he may have begun the journey rightly, that is no proof that he will go on without hindrance or disaster to the end. In days when the journeys of most people, even long journeys, would have to be undertaken on foot, this expression with regard to the walking man would be very significant. The perils of such a journey were well known—perils from robbers, perils of losing one's way in the dark and sometimes probably in the daylight, perils through trusting to strangers who may deceive or insufficiently inform him, perils through sickness far from home and friends. And so in the great spiritual way there is needed humility all through. The way is made up of little steps, and a false step may not be possible to retrieve. Divine knowledge and Divine intimations must stand in the place of our experience. Faith in God's wisdom which cannot fail, and in God's Word which cannot lie, must be our resource in all perplexity. There are times when common sense and right feeling are enough to guide our conduct, yet even these are more the gift of God than may at first appear. We cannot, then, be too minutely observant as to our need of Divine light and truth and assurance. Thus, being found in the right way and enduring to the end, we shall be safe.—Y.

Ver. 24.—*God's correction of his people.* A preliminary difficulty is felt here, in that this earnest deprecation seems to apply to the position of an individual. Ver. 23 is easily taken as being the utterance of Jeremiah himself, but ver. 24 can only apply with propriety to the nation. Such an utterance as that of this chapter must evidently be taken as a combination made up by several speakers. Jehovah speaks; Jeremiah speaks; the nation speaks; and in such an outburst as that of ver. 24 the nation speaks fitly, not as a multitude, but as with the voice of one man. It will be noticed that there is a correspondence with ch. iii. 4, where Israel is represented as possibly addressing Jehovah, and saying, "My Father, thou art the Guide of my youth." And here is an ample confession that the filial, dependent, submissive spirit is needed still.

I. Observe the admission of wrong-doing. "Correct me," uttered at all, is an admission that correction is deserved. The whole of the supplication of course implies a reference to the relation of father and child, as if Israel said, "My Father, I have done wrong, and I know that all wrong-doing children, when the wrong is discovered, must expect to be corrected." The correction of children by their parents must have been very familiar to all Israelites; the Book of Proverbs, in many of its pithy sentences, being in part a consequence of this familiarity and in part a cause of it. A most important part in the benefit of correction came from its very certainty, from the child's knowledge that the correction could not be escaped. Though the *extent* of it might be an open question, the certainty was to be no question at all. The position might be put thus: If an earthly father, being evil, yet has firmness enough not to overlook the least departure from his commandments, then the pure Jehovah above, who is regarded as the Father of Israel, cannot be less strict to mark iniquity. Israel has done wrong, and to make an ample admission of the wrong, to welcome the needful chastisement, is nothing more than what is right. There is no merit in such an admission; the suppliant who makes it is only doing what he ought to do. To continue insensible of the wrong adds to the wrong, and makes correction as correction altogether in vain.

II. A fear lest the correction may become excessive and injurious. Israel has before its mind, the conception of a father in his relations, powers, and duties. But since the measurements are made from the earthly father with all his imperfections, it follows that not only are the encouraging aspects of the relation seen, but also dreadful possibilities as to how far the chastising force may go. Israel argues too closely from the father on earth to the Father in heaven. The earthly father is seen boiling over with rage, beating his child in the wildness of his fury, not because it has done wrong, but because it has thwarted him. It is important to notice this very partial way of conceiving the fatherhood of God; this exaggeration of mere might. There is thus given an index to the insufficiency of the knowledge which the Israelites had of God, and a proof how much Jesus was needed to come in and *reveal* the Father, bringing the serenity and composed action of his attributes into full view. God, of course, never acts with fury and frenzy as we apply these words to man. God produces results through man, and there may be fury in the human agents, but in the God behind them there is none. The narrow notion of Jehovah expressed in vers. 24 and 25 itself needed to be corrected. His favour towards Israel was not an arbitrary thing, nor could it be right that his imagined wild fury might justly expend itself on heathens. If Israel was to be corrected with judgment, the same judgment was surely needed to correct the heathen. If there is fury with them, there can be no true dealing in judgment with Israel. Severity with the heathen as typical enemies of the typical people of God is another matter; but severity must never be confounded with fury.

III. THE KIND OF CORRECTION DESIRED. "Correct me, but with judgment." Correction, to have any proper effect, must be deliberate, and proportioned to the offence that has been committed. While it comes from a fatherly purpose, it must come also with the calmness and impartiality of a judicial procedure. A charge is made; evidence is adduced and examined; defence, denial, extenuation, are listened to; everything must be weighed; and so he who is corrected will feel in his conscience that the correction is just. The severity is not blind and measureless force. If it cannot fall short of a certain standard of pain, neither will it exceed it. Any other sort of dealing has no right to the name of correction at all. Foolish Rehoboam, threatening to chastise the people with scorpions, is an illustration of what must ever be avoided by those who are in power. Be it a child or be it a man who is smitten, no good can be done unless there is the sense that the smiting is just.—Y.

EXPOSITION.

CHAPTER XI.

The superscription in ver. 1 evidently belongs to the three chapters xi.—xiii., though ch. xi. and xii. are more closely connected with each other than with ch. xiii. To which period the group of prophecies belongs— whether to the reign of Josiah, or of Jehoiakim, or of Jehoiachin, or to various periods, is a matter of dispute. It contains at any rate one passage (ch. xii. 7—17) which was almost certainly put in by a later editor. It is doubtless Jeremiah's work, but seems out of place here (see below, on this passage). Naegelsbach's analysis of ch. xi., xii., is striking. The fundamental idea of the entire discourse he assumes to be the antithesis of covenant and conspiracy, and proceeds thus: 1. A reminder of the renewal of the covenant between Jehovah and the people lately made under Josiah (ch. xi. 1—8). 2. First stage of the conspiracy; all Israel, instead of keeping the covenant with Jehovah, conspires against him (ch. xi. 9— 13). 3. The punishment of the conspiracy is an irreversible, severe judgment (ch. xi. 14—

17). 4. Second stage of the conspiracy; the plot of the men of Anathoth (ch. xi. 18—23). 5. Third stage; the plot in the prophet's own family (ch. xi. 1—6). Naegelsbach, however, with violence to exegesis, continues thus (assuming the homogeneousness of ch. xii. 1—6 and 7—17): 6. Israel's conspiracy punished by a conspiracy of the neighbouring peoples against Israel (ch. xii. 7—13). 7. Removal of all antitheses by the final union of all in the Lord (ch. xii. 14—17).

The opening verses of this chapter give us (as we have seen already in the general Introduction) a most vivid idea of the activity of Jeremiah in propagating a knowledge of the Deuteronomic *Tōrāh* (*i.e.* the Divine "directions" with regard to the regulation of life). It may even be inferred from ver. 6 that he made a missionary circuit in Judah, with the view of influencing the masses. It was, in fact, only the "elders" of the different towns who had taken part in the solemn ceremony described in 2 Kings xxiii. "The words of this covenant" had been ratified by the national representatives; but it required a prophetic enthusiasm to carry them home to the hearts of the people. Hence it was that "the word came to Jeremiah from Jehovah, saying, Hear ye the words of this covenant, and speak unto the men of Judah," etc.

Ver. 2.—**Hear ye . . . and speak.** To whom is this addressed? To Jeremiah and his disciples. The Septuagint, indeed, followed by Hitzig and Graf, read (instead of "speak ye"), "Thou shalt speak unto them," adopting one different vowel-point. But this involves an inconsistency with the first verb, and is not at all necessary, for why should we suppose Jeremiah to have been completely isolated? If the prophet had well-wishers even among the princes, it stands to reason that he must have had more pronounced adherents in the classes less influenced by the prejudices of society.

Ver. 3.—Here begins a series of direct references to Deuteronomy, determining the date of the discourse. **Cursed be the man,** etc.; alluding to Deut. xxvii. 26 (which has, however, not "obeyeth," but "confirmeth," *i.e.* ratifieth as his own personal rule of conduct. **The words of this covenant;** rather, *the words of this ordinance.* The rendering "covenant," however, is not so much erroneous as unsuitable in this context; it is a secondary meaning of the Hebrew *b'rîth,* the original sense being rather "authoritative appointment" (from *bārāh,* to cut, hence to decide). Nothing, perhaps, is so injurious to a correct understanding of the Scriptures as persistently rendering a Hebrew or Greek word by the same supposed equivalent. "Covenant" is no doubt appropriate in some passages (*e.g.* Josh. ix. 6; 1 Sam. xviii. 3), because an "appointment" between men, if equals, involves "giving and taking;" but is inadequate when the parties are not equals, and most of all when the superior party is the Divine Being. In these cases we must clearly recur to the original meaning of "appointment" or "ordinance;" and we have one such case here (see also Hos. vi. 7; 2 Kings xi. 4; Job xxxi. i.; Ps. cv. 10; but *not* Gen. xvii. 9). Διαθήκη (1, an arrangement; 2, a will or testament; 3, a covenant) is to some extent parallel (see Cremer's 'Biblico-Theological Lexicon of New Testament Greek,' *s.v.*).

Ver. 4.—**From the iron furnace;** rather, *out of the iron furnace.* It is Egypt which is thus described (comp. Deut. iv. 20; 1 Kings viii. 51). The oppression in Egypt was like the furnace in which iron is rendered malleable by heat (so Isa. xlviii. 10, "I have tested thee in the furnace of affliction").

Ver. 5.—**The oath which I have sworn** (so Deut. vii. 8; comp. viii. 18). **As it is this day;** a Deuteronomic formula (see *e.g.* Deut. ii. 30; iv. 20), appealing to the test of experience. **So be it, O Lord.** The Hebrew has "Amen, Jehovah." "Amen" equivalent to "true, faithful, trustworthy;" or used in this way as a formula of asseveration, "may it be verified by facts" (the Septuagint has γένοιτο); comp. ch. xxviii. 6.

Ver. 6.—**Proclaim all these words,** etc. This command probably points to a missionary circuit of Jeremiah, as suggested above. Others render, "read aloud" (comp. 2 Kings xxii. 8, Hebrew); but Jeremiah receives the direction to "proclaim" or "cry" elsewhere (ch. ii. 2; iii. 12, etc.). So Gabriel, in the Koran, directs Mohammed to "cry," *i.e.* to proclaim or preach (Sura xcvi. 1).

Vers. 7, 8.—A condensation of ch. vii. 23—26. **Imagination;** rather, *stubbornness* (see on ch. iii. 17). **I will bring;** rather, *I brought.* **All the words.** "Word" sometimes means "thing spoken of;" here, for instance, the curses specified in Deut. xxviii.

Ver. 9.—**A conspiracy.** The language is figurative. Jehovah is the King of Israel; to commit sin is "to rebel against" him (Authorized Version sometimes weakens this into "transgress"); and to encourage one another in wickedness is "to conspire against" God. We need not suppose any open combination against spiritual religion; it is enough if "the spirit of the time" was directly contrary to it.

Ver. 10.—**Their forefathers.** The Hebrew has "their fathers, the former ones." The allusion is to the sins of the Israelites in the wilderness, and in Canaan under the judges. The prophets are constantly pointing their hearers back to those early times, either for warning (as here) or for encouragement (ch. ii. 1; Hos. ii. 15; Isa. i. 26; lxiii. 11, 13). **And they went after;** rather *and they (themselves) have gone after.* The pronoun is expressed in the Hebrew, to indicate that the prophet's contemporaries are now the subject.

Vers. 11—13.—A summary of Jeremiah's usual prophecies (comp. ch. iv. 6; vi. 19; xix. 3; and especially ii. 28; vii. 17).

Ver. 13.—**That shameful thing;** rather, *the shame.* The name Baal is changed, to mark the abhorrence of the speaker, into Bosheth (see ch. iii. 24). Manasseh, we are told, "raised up altars for Baal" (2 Kings xxi. 3).

Ver. 14.—**Therefore pray not thou,** etc. First Jehovah declares that even the intercession of the prophet will be of no avail (see on ch. vii. 16), and then that the belated supplications of the people themselves will be ineffectual to avert the calamity. **For their trouble.** The four most ancient versions, and some of the extant Hebrew manuscripts, read "in the time of their trouble" (as in ver. 12). The confusion between the two readings is easy, and the reading of the versions is to be preferred.

Ver. 15.—**What hath my beloved to do in mine house?** "My beloved" is evidently the Jewish people, who in ch. xii. 7 is called "the dearly beloved of my soul." The Divine Speaker expresses surprise that one who has now so poor a claim to the title of "my beloved" should appear in his holy house. It is spoken in the spirit of that earlier revelation of Isaiah, "When ye come to appear before me, who hath required this at your hand, to trample my courts?" (Isa. i. 12). The Jews, it would seem, came to the temple to pray, but their prayer is not accepted, because it is associated with unholy practices. They thought by formal prayers and sacrifices to pay off their debt to the Deity, and so be free to go on with their old devices (as in ch. vii. 15). This seems the best view of the difficult words which follow, but it implies a correction of the certainly ungrammatical rendering of the Authorized Version—seeing **she hath wrought lewdness** —into *to work the wicked device*. But here begins the most obscure part of the verse. **With many** cannot be right; for "with" has nothing corresponding to it in the Hebrew; the word in the original simply means "the many," and as it is immediately followed by a noun in the singular with "and," and a verb in the plural, it is plain that it must (if correctly read) be part of the subject of the latter. The Septuagint, however, has a different reading, which may very well be correct, and out of which the received Hebrew reading may easily have grown—" Can vows and holy [*i.e.* hallowed] flesh remove from thee thy wickedness [or perhaps, ' thy calamity ']?" The connection thus becomes easy. " Vows and holy flesh " (*i.e.* the flesh of sacrifices, Hag. ii. 12), naturally go together ; the only other possible way of taking the passage (assuming the correctness of the received text)—" the great ones and the holy flesh shall pass away from thee " — is obviously inadmissible. "Vows and sacrifices," however, precisely express the true association of ideas. A man made a vow, and he generally paid it in the form of a sacrifice. But, inquires Jehovah, " Can such vows and such victims please God, and expiate thy wickedness [or, ' avert thy calamity ']? *Then thou mightest rejoice.*" The latter words are not, indeed, more exact than those of the Authorized Version, but are in accordance with grammar, and suit the preceding question. It is not certain, however, that the text is right here ; the Septuagint has ἢ τούτοις διαφεύξῃ. (Notice that Keil, conservative to a fault in matters affecting the received text, agrees with the above correction, which is also adopted by Ewald, Hitzig, and Graf.)

Ver. 16.—**A green olive tree.** The olive tree is "one of the most thriving, hardy, and productive trees in the East" (it was the first tree elected king in the parable, Judg. ix. 8), and with its "foliage of a deep, perennial green," furnishes a striking symbol of healthful beauty. A psalmist, speaking in the character of the typical righteous man, compares himself to a "green olive tree in the house of God" (Ps. lii. 8). The word rendered "green" is one of those which are the despair of translators (see on ch. ii. 20). It gives a picture in itself. We seem to see a flourishing, sappy tree, with abundance of pliant, gracefully moving, perennially green branches. **With the noise of a great tumult.** Either the tumult of the *mêlée* of battle is meant (the same uncommon word is used with such a reference in Ezek. i. 24) or the crashing of thunder. "With a rushing mighty sound " would be a more forcible rendering. (For the concluding figure, comp. Ezek. xxxi. 12.) **He hath kindled fire,** etc. There is no occasion to explain this as merely the perfect of prophetic certitude. It was literally true that the fire of war had already devastated the fairest portion of the Holy Land. Israel (expressly referred to in ver. 17) had already been carried into captivity, and Judah was, to the prophetic eye, as good as destroyed. Here, no doubt, that wonderful perfect of faith does come in.

Ver. 17.—**The Lord of hosts, that planted thee.** He who "planted" Israel (comp. ch. ii. 21) could also uproot it ; and though, for the sake of his covenant with Abraham, he would not destroy it utterly, yet he could not but interpose as Judge to punish its manifold transgressions. Israel and Judah are mentioned together; for the prophets, so far as we know them from their works, did not recognize the separation of the two kingdoms. **Against themselves** ; rather, *for themselves* ; i.e. to please themselves.

Ver. 18.—Here, as Naegelsbach puts it, begins the second stage of the "conspiracy." **Hath given me knowledge,** etc. ; rather, *gave me knowledge, and I knew it.* **Then** ; *i.e.* when I was in utter unconsciousness. Jeremiah had no presentiment of the murderous purpose of his townsmen, till by some "special providence" it came to his knowledge.

Ver. 19.—**Like a lamb or an ox** ; rather, *as a mild lamb* (as one of the old translations has it), equivalent to *quasi agnus mansuetus* (Vulgate). Jeremiah says that he was as unsuspicious as a tame lamb which has grown up with its master's family (2 Sam. xii. 3). The Arabs use the very same adjective in a slightly different form as an epithet of such tame lambs (Bochart, ' Hierozoïcon,' i. 520—522, edit. 1663). It is impossible to help thinking of that "Servant of Jehovah," of whom Jeremiah was a type, who is said, in prophetic vision, to have been "brought as a lamb to the slaughter," and "not to have opened his mouth" (Isa. liii. 7). **The tree with the fruit thereof**; apparently a proverbial expression. Giving the words their ordinary meaning, the rendering would be, *the tree with its bread* (*b'lakhmō*). Our translators appear to have thought that the transition from "bread" to "fruit" was as justifiable in Hebrew as it is in Arabic (in which *'uklu* means properly "food" in general, but also "date fruit"). Fruit, however, was not such an important article of food with the Israelites as with the Arabs; and we must either, with Hitzig, suppose a letter to have intruded into the text, and render (from a corrected reading *b'lēkhō*), *with its sap* (comp. Deut. xxxiv. 7, Hebrew), or else appeal to the etymology of *lekhem* (commonly "bread"), which is "firm, consistent," and render, *the tree with its pith* (Hence *laḥmu* in Arabic means "flesh," and *luḥmatu*, "a woof"). It is no credit to St. Jerome that he followed the absurd version of the Septuagint, "Let us put wood into his bread."

Ver. 20.—(Parallel passage, ch. xx. 12.) **Unto thee have I revealed my cause.** This is the literal rendering, but a comparison of Ps. xxii. 8 and Prov. xvi. 3, suggests that the meaning is "Upon thee have I rolled my cause." This expression is certainly not only more forcible, but more appropriate than the other. Jeremiah's cause was not a secret which needed to be "revealed" to Jehovah, but a burden too heavy for so finely strung a nature to bear alone. Grammatically, the preferred meaning is quite justifiable, though less obvious, as there are other instances of an interchange of meanings between two classes of verbs (see on ch. xxxiii. 6).

Ver. 21.—**Prophesy not,** etc. The men of Anathoth tried first of all to effect their object by threatening. **In the name of the Lord** should be rather, *by the name,* etc. The phrase is exactly parallel to Ps. lv. 1, "Save me, O God, by thy Name, and judge me by thy strength." The Name of God is equivalent to his revealed presence or personality. Baal's prophets prophesied "by Baal" (ch. ii. 8), *i.e.* by an impulse thought to proceed from Baal; Jehovah's by the consciousness of his revealed presence.

Ver. 22.—**Their sons and their daughters,** etc. The lot of the weaker sex and of the male children under the military age is contrasted with that of the young warriors.

Ver. 23.—Even **the year,** etc.; better, *in the year of their visitation* (or, *punishment*), taking the accusative as that of time.

HOMILETICS.

Vers. 1—8.—*The ancient covenant.* I. THE OBJECT OF THE COVENANT. This was to secure obedience. No covenant was required on God's side, since he is ever willing to bless and changeless in his beneficence. But for the sake of men's faith and to secure their allegiance God graciously condescended to enter into covenant bonds. It is therefore foolish to claim the fulfilment of God's promises irrespective of our conduct. They are "covenant" promises—*i.e.* conditional and assured on certain terms. If we break the terms we can no longer expect the fulfilment of the promises.

II. THE SANCTIONS OF THE COVENANT. 1. *The obligations of gratitude.* The past mercies of God are recited; *e.g.* deliverance from Egypt. 2. *Promises of future good.* If faithful, Israel was to take possession of the "land flowing with milk and honey." 3. *Threats in case of disobedience.* If they proved unfaithful, the people were to find the land of promise full of troubles, and ultimately to be expelled from it (Deut. xxviii. 15). 4. *Constant Divine pleading.* The covenant could not lapse through forgetfulness. Prophets were sent again and again to urge its claims on the people (ver. 7).

III. THE OBLIGATION OF THE COVENANT. This was an ancient covenant; yet it was still binding. God was still fulfilling his part in blessing his people. The obligation was not such as time could affect. What is inherently right once is right eternally. Truth does not lose force with age. The Bible contains covenants which age has made venerable, but not feeble. Its commands and promises are eternally fresh and living, and when the merely local and personal exterior is laid aside, the essence of them applies as much to us as to the Jews. The appetite for mere novelty which characterizes much intellectual inquiry in the present day, as it did that of the Athenians of St. Paul's age (Acts xvii. 21), ignores the fact that the most important question is "What is true?" not "What is new?" Old familiar truths must be noticed that they may be remembered and practised, though of course not to the exclusion of new truths. The New Testament does not abolish but perfects the spiritual truth of the old. It contains that and more.

IV. THE BREACH OF THE COVENANT. The people are accused of disobeying the precepts of the covenant (ver. 8). Disobedience involved both the loss of the promised blessings and the execution of the threatened curses. They who accept special privileges incur special obligations. They who enter into a Divine covenant will be judged by the terms of that covenant. Christians will be judged, not simply by the common law of righteousness in conscience and nature, but by the special requirements of the New *Testament*, i.e. of the *covenant* of Christianity.

Vers. 11—13.—*Idolatry confounded.* I. TROUBLE IS A TOUCHSTONE FOR RELIGIOUS TRUTH. The idolatry that is played with in prosperity is found to be useless in adversity. The Jews had regarded mere stocks and stones as their gods. But in the season of real distress they turn from these and cry to the true God to arise and save them. 1. *The ground of confidence which gives way in the hour of need is worse than useless;* it is treacherous and ruinous, and the discovery of its true character confounds those who have relied on it. A religion which will not stand the test of trouble is a mockery. 2. *Trouble reveals the vanity of an insincere faith.* In trouble we need the true, the real; all false religiousness, all playing at devotion, breaks down then. If our religion has been vain and ill founded, we are then discovered and made to be ashamed, "like a thief when he is found" (ch. ii. 26). · 3. *There is a deep instinct which cries out for the true God in the hour of distress.* Old memories then revive, scouted faiths reassert themselves, the first cry of the child to his Parent breaks out again involuntarily, and the godless man in his agony groans, "O my God!"

II. IF WE HAVE FORSAKEN GOD IN PROSPERITY WE HAVE NO RIGHT TO EXPECT HIM TO SAVE US IN ADVERSITY. The religion which we accept in our general life is that to which we should justly look in our hours of need. Here is the natural irony of religion. A man is punished by being left to the protection of the creed of his own choice. It must always be remembered, indeed, that whenever we truly repent and seek God spiritually he will receive and save us (Hos. vi. 1). But the mere cry for God's help in distress is not repentance, nor is it a spiritual return to God. It is a selfish utterance, and may be made while the heart is still far from God, and the sins which drove us from him still unrepented of. It would be neither just nor good for us that God should respond to so degraded and unspiritual a prayer.

III. ALL GROUNDS OF RELIGIOUS CONFIDENCE EXCEPT FAITH IN THE TRUE GOD PROVE FALSE AT THE TEST OF TROUBLE. This is the result of applying the touchstone of trouble; this is the lesson of bitter experience when men are left to cry to their false gods in the hour of need. 1. If there were any worth in these grounds of confidence it *would* be seen then. (1) They should answer to men's requirements, for men have made them to suit their own wishes. (2) They should be sufficient in number for help. "According to the number of thy cities are thy gods, O Judah." How many religious refuges have men made for themselves! Shall *all* these human inventions fail? (3) They should be sufficiently various to afford the required help. Every city had its peculiar cult. The human notions of religion are infinitely various. Cannot a man find one to meet his need out of the whole catalogue of creeds? 2. Experience furnishes the answer to these questions, and shows the certain failure of all the creeds of human invention. They must fail: (1) Because they are human. How can the god whom a man has made save him? (2) Because they are commonly materialistic—the stock and stone of the Hebrew idolatry find their counterparts in the materialistic philosophy and schemes of merely physical amelioration of modern men. (3) Because they are numerous, and therefore none of infinite value, but all limited in range. (4) Because they are reflections of our own thought, not higher influences to lead that thought. Every city had its god embodying the ideas of the city. Men have their separate creeds corresponding to their inclinations and prejudices. Such creeds afford no refuge when deeper questions open up in the dark night of distress.

Vers. 16, 17.—*The olive struck by lightning.* Under the image of an olive tree consumed by lightning fires the prophet portrays the devastation which will come upon

Israel in spite of former prosperity. This is a type of the similar doom which may overtake the happy and prosperous.

I. THE HAPPY PROSPERITY. 1. The olive tree was *green*—perennially green. Prosperity may be constant and unbroken before the descent of judgment. 2. It was *fair*. Prosperity may come with much honour and gladness. 3. It was *fruitful*. The life may abound in good to others. 4. It was *planted by God*. (Ver. 17.) All good comes from him, and it is a great good to be established in our way of life by God's will and help. Yet none of these good things sufficed to avert a terrible doom. Present prosperity is no security against future adversity. The goodness of the past will be no safeguard against the punishment of sins of later years. The long-tried, honoured, useful man who falls into sin at the end of his life must not delude himself into supposing that his earlier career will shield him from all troublesome consequences.

II. THE FEARFUL DEVASTATION. The green and fair and fruitful tree was struck in the thunderstorm, and its branches consumed with fire. 1. The devastation was *from above*—by fire from heaven. God who planted also destroyed. Punishment is sent by God. 2. It was *sudden*. The lightning flash is instantaneous. The terrible ruin of sin may fall in a moment. 3. It was *irresistible*. The tree is passive and helpless in the storm. Its very magnitude only invites the blow which will destroy it. 4. It was *destructive*. Fire consumed the branches. The fires of judgment are consuming fires— they burn to destroy (Matt. iii. 12).

Vers. 18—23.—*The conspiracy of Anathoth.* This incident may afford us some lessons on the subject of persecution, in its occasion and character, the behaviour of the persecuted and the righteous action of God in dealing with it.

I. THE OCCASION OF THE CONSPIRACY ILLUSTRATES A COMMON CAUSE OF PERSECUTION. Jeremiah had been proclaiming unwelcome truths. He had exposed sin and threatened judgment. Such preaching was unpopular, and the men of Anathoth sought to stay it by force (ver. 21). 1. *The faithful preacher must expect to meet with opposition.* Unpopularity is no proof of incompetence (*i.e.* if it arises from the subject-matter of the teaching, not from the style of the teacher). Christ, who began his mission with public favour, ended it amidst universal contumely. 2. *The most needful truth is the most unwelcome.* The smooth words of false prophets of "peace" are acceptable. But they are narcotics given to men who should be roused to flee for their lives. The only hope for those who are spending wicked lives is in their being awakened to a sense of guilt and danger. The effort to awaken them, however, stirs their resentment.

II. THE CONDUCT OF THE CONSPIRATORS REVEALS THE TRUE CHARACTER OF PERSE- CUTORS. 1. It is *foolish*. Truth cannot be destroyed by suppressing the voice that utters it. Some day it will declare itself in spite of all hindrance. 2. It is *unfair*. Words are met by force. To silence a voice is not to reply to it. Violent opposition to the spread of ideas is a tacit confession of inability to meet them on their own ground of reason, a virtual confession of their force of truth. 3. It is *destructive of social order*. Jeremiah's fellow-townsmen conspire against him. The persecuting spirit divides nearest neighbours. It is the greatest enemy to brotherly charity (Matt. x. 36). 4. It is *treacherous*. While Jeremiah was ignorant of their enmity—led like a lamb to the slaughter—the men of Anathoth were plotting against his life. 5. It is *murderous*. The tree is to be destroyed with its fruit. Professing a good purpose, persecution is invariably possessed by a cruel spirit. 6. It covers *enmity to God* in opposition to his servants. Jeremiah was bidden no longer to prophesy in the Name of Jehovah. It could not be denied that he spoke with Divine authority. Therefore to silence him was to refuse to receive the message of God.

III. THE BEHAVIOUR OF THE VICTIM EXEMPLIFIES THE RIGHT COURSE TO BE PURSUED UNDER PERSECUTION. 1. Not to *desist* from the duty which provoked the persecution. Jeremiah met with little but opposition throughout his long life; yet he remained faithful to the last. 2. Not to *rashly embrace danger*. Jeremiah sought deliverance. It is childish to court persecution. 3. To *seek help from God*. Jeremiah at once committed his cause to God. God alone (1) can help; (2) has the authority to execute vengeance (Rom. xii. 19); (3) judges righteously, impartially, without the bias of passion; and (4) discerns the motive of men and the degrees of guilt trying "the reins and the heart."

IV. THE ACTION OF GOD TYPIFIES THE ULTIMATE EXECUTION OF DIVINE JUDGMENT.
1. *Punishment* must follow such wickedness. Though it is delayed, the vengeance must
come. 2. This punishment will be *severe.* " The young men shall die by the sword,"
the children by famine. Fearful sin must bring fearful penalties. 3. This punishment
will be *without exception.* No remnant of the men of Anathoth will be spared. All
are guilty; all must suffer. There is a popular impression to the effect that the
number of sinful persons lessens the blame attaching to each individual. It is a
mistake. If all sin, each will be punished individually as much as if one only were
guilty. No conspiracy of men, however widespread, however subtle in schemes, however violent in action, can defeat the ends of Divine justice (Prov. xi. 21).

HOMILIES BY VARIOUS AUTHORS.

Ver. 5.—*The response of the spiritual conscience to the words of God.* " And I said,
Amen, Jehovah." This expression, uttered by Jeremiah with apparent originality, is
really an echo of Deut. xxvii. 15. There it expresses the agreement of the whole
congregation of Israel: here it is the word of one mouth. The adoption by the prophet,
at this juncture, of words so solemnly significant is very impressive. One stands sponsor
for many; a righteous and earnest man for a nation of callous transgressors. And is
it not often so? What, indeed, would our poor, erring, depraved humanity do with
itself were it not for these individual, mediatorial spirits, whom God raises up from
time to time through the ages to interpret his will and to keep it in reverent obedience
and spiritual trust for them who as yet are ignorant and alienated from his life? The
service such men render is of vast importance and but imperfectly understood.

I. ONLY THOSE WHO ARE IN COMMUNION WITH GOD CAN TRULY UNDERSTAND AND
APPROVE HIS JUDGMENTS. The commandment is intelligently alluded to, and its
penalty stated. The correspondence of Judah's condition with that anticipated in the
original passage is pregnantly suggested. All the more so that the transgressors did not
feel or admit the correspondence. The prophet alone could say, " Amen; " but he said
it emphatically and representatively. How many of God's people find a similar
difficulty in acquiescing in his dispensations? They do not examine themselves, or
their conscience is not sufficiently awakened, and consequently they fail to recognize
his judgments and to profit by them as was intended.

II. GOD RAISES UP THOSE WHO SHALL RESPOND TO HIS VOICE AND MAINTAIN
PROVISIONALLY HIS COVENANT RELATIONS WITH THE WORLD. The prophets were not
only mouthpieces of Divine truth; they were saints whose consecration was essential
to their spiritual discernment and the due exercise of their functions. The people
were for the most part spiritually asleep or dead. In their spiritual and moral
constitution a medium was provided sensitive enough for the perception and transmission of Divine communications. It was no exaggeration to speak of these
messengers as "prepared, ordained, and sent." They were specially raised up for this
duty of sustaining the conscious relations of God with his people. This was a dim
foreshadowing of the Messiah-consciousness. In a certain sense the prophet repented,
believed, obeyed, for the whole people, even as the high priest made solemn offering
once a year for the sins of the whole people. Not that this spiritual condition of the
inspired seer and saint could be effectual for individual salvation of others; but that it
exercised a certain representative and general influence. The prophet held the truth
as it were in trust for others, continually and energetically sought to mediate between
Jehovah and Israel, and urged the people to acts of repentance and obedience. With
each prophet it might be said that a new opportunity was given, a new day of grace
afforded, for the return of the apostate nation to its primitive covenant relations with
God. And in the succession of the prophets a guarantee was given of the enduring
character of those relations, even when the covenant itself was flagrantly broken and
practically set aside by those whom it chiefly concerned. The essential point was that
there should be no age without some person or persons who should sustain a conscious
spiritual connection with Jehovah for themselves and their race.

III. THAT WHICH THE FEW HAVE UNDERSTOOD AND ACCEPTED SHALL BECOME THE
COMMON INHERITANCE OF ALL. The prophet was for the most part a solitary and

a lonely man. This isolation of his lot was his grief, but the persistence of the succession of the prophets proved the unswerving purpose of God ultimately to save, not only Israel, but the world. There might be from time to time but one or two who could say "Amen" to his judgments, but some day the people as a whole would themselves endorse and approve them. And soon in the "fulness of the time" Christ would come, who is the faithful and true Witness, the "Amen" of all the Divine Law and promise. In his world-wide reign as our Representative, Prophet, Priest, and King, through faith in him, the race will be constituted into a new Israel, to keep the word of God. In this transfer of influence the law is that the communication shall proceed from the higher consciousness and consecration to the lower; the travail for souls, etc., being but a detailed sponsorship, one day to be done away with, when "all should know him, from the least even to the greatest."—M.

Ver. 10.—*Spiritual atavism; or, the sins of the fathers.* There are punishments and consequences of ancestral sin which reach even to descendants of remote generations. This seems to imply a descent of responsibility—a subject full of difficulty and mystery. The unity of the race in its sin and misery is, with St. Paul, an argument for the probability and even certainty of its unity in the grace of salvation. The doctrine of original sin is treated in Scripture as antecedent to the doctrine of salvation by faith in Christ. In connection with this subject, notice—

I. THE INFLUENCE OF HEREDITY. In modern times the laws of heredity have been scientifically investigated, and startling results brought to light. Tendency can be traced from parent to child in gradually deepening lines and more confirmed manifestations. Spirit as well as body acknowledges this law, and, whether in health or disease, its operation is now placed beyond all dispute. But another law or modification of this law is perceived working alongside of it, namely, the law of atavism, in which not the general tendency towards improvement or degeneration is observed, but an apparently arbitrary and capricious recurrence of ancestral peculiarities that had long disappeared from the race. Of this nature seems to have been the present sin of Israel. It was not in the line of continuous succession, but a recurrent phase after intervals of normal and religious life. Thus it showed that the power of evil had only been "scotched," not killed; and that it was ready on the slightest provocation to assert itself in the rankest forms. How much that is mysterious in the conduct of individuals can be traced to the influence of such a principle! The two selves of every man represent influences that have been at work in his progenitors from remotest time.

II. HOW SOLEMN THE RESPONSIBILITY OF PARENTS. No care can be too great in relation to those we bring into the world. Our own nature and character should be diligently cultivated, and the utmost attention paid to parental example, family influence, and educative circumstance in their upbringing. It will not do to ignore the fact that, from generation to generation, there are transmitted both physical and spiritual tendencies which have largely to do with the formation of character and the determining of destiny. For good or for evil, the parent exercises a despotic influence upon all whom he brings into the world.

III. YET THE ACCOUNTABILITY OF THE CHILDREN REMAINS. In the sad entail of evil there are many bright instances of bold and pronounced departure from ancestral sin. The individual is not wholly subject to predetermining influences. If so, moral freedom would be but an illusion. A power is required to break the tyranny of inherited sin, and this is provided in the grace of God. The gospel is the development of this grace as an effectual and adequate means of salvation.—M.

Ver. 14.—*The staying of intercession.* The desperate condition of Israel is shown in this prohibition. How great must have been the sin of God's people, ere prayer on their behalf could have been forbidden! What could have been the reason of this?

I. WHILST SIN IS PERSISTED IN THERE CAN BE NO REMOVAL OF DIVINE JUDGMENTS. The righteousness of God has, after long-suffering mercy, brought these upon his people. The wisdom of their imposition is infallible; and they spring from the depths of an inscrutable, infinite love. Whilst, therefore, the condition which involved their imposition is unchanged, it would be presumption to suggest their removal. It is rather for the righteous conscience of saints sorrowfully to approve the action of the Supreme

Magistrate, as he draws his cordon round the transgressor and compels him to capitulate. The real calamity in connection with these judgments is the spiritual wrongness which necessitates them, and not the physical conditions through which they are executed. Most men suppose that if the pain or inconvenience is removed the evil is at an end, and the question between them and God settled. They still go on to sin. Impunity confirms and hardens them in their transgression. We have not learned the real lesson of calamity until we have detected its moral sources or occasions, and sought to rectify them before God.

II. DIVINE JUDGMENTS MAY IN CERTAIN INSTANCES BE GREATER MERCIES THAN THE REMOVAL OF THEM WOULD BE. When judgment continues to rest upon the transgressor, it is not mere vengeance which is represented, but mercy working on the lines of severity. It is God's emphasis upon his commandment which must be heeded. The blessing that is latent in it waits the appearance of a repentance not to be repented of. Like pent-up waters, it will flow in an overwhelming stream when once the barriers of law have been removed by the sinner's return to God.—M.

Vers. 18—23.—*Perils of prophesying.* The conspiracy of which these verses speak seems to have been sudden as it was secret. It affected the mind of the prophet in a peculiarly painful way, as it was the men of his own district who were concerned in it— his friends, probably even kinsfolk, who looked upon him as their worst enemy. The crime was all the more heinous that the means taken to execute it were underhand. It is possible that they greeted him with expressions of kindness and hospitality, and that everything was done to prevent his suspecting his real danger. Upon his discovering the plot, it is possible that they ceased to conceal their intentions, and, thinking him in their power, urged him " prophesy not in the Name of the Lord."

I. THE PERILS OF THE PROPHET arose from : 1. *A hatred of the truth in his hearers.* There was something unpalatable in the continual denunciations of their wickedness. Their spiritual and patriotic pride was wounded. The demands made upon them by the righteousness of Jehovah they did not care to yield to; and the dislike of the prophet arose from his association with his message. No vengeance, therefore, could be too great. It is not imprisonment they seek to inflict, but death itself, and death in such an obscure and ignominious way that " his name may be no more remembered." 2. *Their fear of the consequences of his prophecies.* The future which he described as inevitable was not pleasant to contemplate. The words he spoke threatened to overturn their most cherished designs and to rob them of their precious things. 3. *Ignorance as to how these might be averted.* By an easy process of association they came to look upon Jeremiah as not simply declaring, but in a sense causing, the evils of which he prophesied. They reasoned, therefore, to the foolish conclusion that if they could destroy him they would free themselves from the dangers which he threatened. The preacher has often to incur dislike of this sort from his hearers. It is of the nature of the carnal mind so to misapprehend the things of God and the things that make for peace. At certain times stern denunciation and declaring of the true consequences of evil action are not to be regarded as enmity, but friendship. The word spoken by an inspired mind is to be distinguished from the expression of mere bitterness and dislike. Paul had to entreat his converts not to count him their enemy when he sharply reproved them.

II. THESE PERILS ARE WARDED OFF by: 1. *Direct revelation.* This is an advantage which the ordinary servants of God may not count upon. It was vouchsafed occasionally to prophets and apostles, but there is something in the spiritual mind which enables it to detect more quickly than others the symptoms of hatred to the truth. Promptings and suggestions to certain action in the midst of circumstances to ordinarily human eyes unsuspicious, have been too frequent in the history of the Church to be doubted. And even where no direct information may be given as to the reason of certain courses of action, which God's saints may be moved to observe, the results clearly prove the presence of a careful and ever-watchful Providence. 2. *Faith in God.* Jeremiah said, " Unto thee have I revealed my cause " (better, " Upon thee have I devolved my cause "). He evidently felt that his duty was to commit the whole matter into the hands of God. And this is ever the safest way. The judgment, the prevision of man, are to be distrusted. The soul should cast itself by faith upon God, who is able to save.

3. *Greater boldness in the course of action assumed.* This was a distinct moral advantage. The men whose action was inspired by fear were certain to be influenced by it. Superstitious dread of the effects of his words would produce a reaction from their cowardly plans. And they would feel themselves more and more helpless as they saw how they aggravated their own punishment. So the preachers of the gospel and the servants of Christ generally must not consult with flesh and blood, but be bold in proclaiming the whole will of God, in preaching the Word, being "instant in season and out of season." There are allies and reinforcements latent in the constitution even of the worst enemies of the cross of Christ.—M.

Ver. 3.—*The doom of disobedience.* This new discourse, which begins with ch. xi., is a continuation of the same sad monotone of denunciation and doom which goes on throughout well-nigh the whole of Jeremiah's prophecies. The curse pronounced here on the disobedient—

I. IS VERY TERRIBLE. The words, "Cursed," etc., are fearful words to come from the lips of the God of grace and mercy. And that which they threatened was terrible also. What a catalogue of woes, which were denounced against the guilty people, might be compiled from these chapters! And how exactly the event answered to the prediction! Read the history of the destruction of Jerusalem and of the sufferings of the people, which is given in the records of the times, for proof of this. It is a dismal story, heart-sickening, and one from which we should at once turn away were it possible for us to do so. But all this, which was written aforetime, was written for our learning, and therefore we cannot but give heed. For not only is the curse terrible—

II. IT IS ALTOGETHER JUST. What makes a sentence, such as is pronounced here, just? Is it not such considerations as these?—1. *That the Law which has been violated should have been altogether righteous.* None can read over the moral Law given by God to his people without confessing its righteousness. "The Law was holy, just, and good." Those who disobeyed it and were punished by it could not dispute its righteousness. 2. *That it should have been fully known.* If ignorance could have been pleaded the equity of the sentence might have been questioned. But amid all possible publicity and solemnity the Law was given at the first; and at a time (ver. 4) when their hearts, by reason of God's exceeding goodness to them, were peculiarly susceptible to impression. And ever since then, by repeated, prolonged, and earnest appeal (ver. 7) that obedience should be rendered. 3. *When conscience consents to the Law that it is good.* (Ver. 5.) They said "Amen" to it. The prophet is not giving his personal account only, but referring to the fact that all the people said "Amen" when the curse upon disobedience was pronounced from Mount Ebal; cf. also a more recent "standing to the covenant" to which probably Jeremiah alludes (2 Kings xxiii. 3). 4. *When the transgression has been notorious.* (Ver. 8.) It was not simply that they would not obey, but they would not even listen, and they went on in their own way, utterly disregarding the covenant to which they had promised obedience (cf. also vers. 9, 10). 5. *When ingratitude has been added to disobedience.* (Ver. 4.) What had not God done for them? How deep was the obligation to obey! 6. *When forbearance has been exercised.* For a thousand years and more they had been suffered to occupy the land of promise (ver. 5, "As it is this day"). Wherever, then, was there or could there be a righteous doom if this were not?

III. AND AS NECESSARY AS RIGHTEOUS. Remember the purpose for which God had chosen Israel—that they might be the channels of his truth and righteousness to all other people. God was merciful to them and blessed them, "that his way," etc. (Ps. lxvii.). "In thee and in thy seed," said God to Abraham, "shall all the nations," etc. But if the men of the nation had rendered themselves incapable of this service, it was essential for the well-being of the world that they should make room for more faithful men. And this they had to do.

IV. AND CERTAIN OF ACCOMPLISHMENT IF THE DISOBEDIENCE BE NOT FORSAKEN. The judgment that came upon Judah and Jerusalem was not at all a solitary isolated fact. The like of it had happened before, has since, happens now, and will again whenever like provocation is given, as it all too often is. God's way of dealing with Israel is God's way of dealing with *man* everywhere and in all ages; therefore his way of dealing with *us.* God's Law, his demand for obedience, man's disobedience, and the consequent doom, are all facts with which we are familiar. The history of Israel is but an example of what is ever taking place. Even the gospel of the Lord Jesus, however much it may avert the eternal results of our transgressions, will not save us from the present temporal consequences in this world. " These all died in faith," so we read in the Epistle to the Hebrews, of those " whose carcases," nevertheless, " fell in the wilderness." " The way of transgressors is," has been, must, and ever will be, " hard."—C.

Ver. 4.—*The precious recompenses of obedience.* " Obey my voice, . . . according to all which I command you: so shall ye be," etc. The earlier verses of this chapter form part of that earnest reminder which Jeremiah was commanded by God to address to the men of Judah and Jerusalem concerning a transaction with which they had all had very much to do. That transaction was their solemnly pledging themselves, as they had done during King Josiah's recent reign, to observe the ancient covenant which the Lord God had made with their fathers. The sixty or seventy years before King Josiah's time had been years dreary and degraded in the national life of the people. Even Hezekiah, the last pious King of Judah before Josiah, had secured only a very partial reformation, and in the days of his godless son Manasseh, and in those of his even worse grandson Amon, who " sinned more and more," the religious life of the people all but died out. The sacred Scriptures in which this covenant was contained had, during these miserable years, been neglected and put out of sight as writings for which they had no longer love nor use; as a book which we do not want is either got rid of or put away on some high shelf, to make room for others which we more highly prize. " The nation did not want to hear the Law which testified against their multiplied transgressions, nor to listen to a condemnation of the idols they had chosen." But in King Josiah's reign, in some out-of-the-way corner, buried beneath no one knows what worthless rubbish, a copy of the despised Word of God was discovered. It produced on the pious monarch a profound impression. He was overwhelmed with shame and dismay when he compared the commands of the covenant of God with the actual conduct of the people. He shuddered to think of the judgments which must come upon them—and which had already come upon the neighbouring nation of Israel—unless they repented and turned to God. But he did not waste time in unavailing regrets. He at once took practical measures to bring about that religious reformation which he saw to be so much needed. He therefore summoned all the people of Judah to Jerusalem, and caused the book of the Law to be publicly read to them; then he made all the people renew the covenant which they had so long forgotten. For a time it seemed as if the reformation and repentance were real; but the old idolatries began to make their appearance again after a while, and when Jeremiah was sent from God to remind them of their violated vows they had fallen back into a condition as evil as, if not worse than, that of former days. Therefore the prophet opens his commission by the awful denunciation of Jehovah's curse upon the disobedient. He would startle and arouse them, if it might but be possible, so that they might awake to righteousness and to God ere wrath arose against them and there should be no remedy. And here he tells of the precious recompenses of obedience, " So shall ye . . . God." Consider, then—

I. THESE PROMISES. 1. " *Ye shall be my people.*" Now, by this is meant, amongst other blessings, that they shall be *the object of his care.* How many are the proofs that this is a constituent part of the heritage of his people! Were not Israel so? Did he not watch over them continuously? " He suffered no man to do them harm; yea, he reproved kings for their sakes." " He gave his angels charge over them to keep them in all their ways." The rage of Pharaoh, the cruel thirst of the hot, waterless sands, the threatened famine of the breadless desert, the marauding Amalekite, the pestilence that walked in darkness, and the destruction that wasted at noonday,—not one of these was suffered to harm them. How full are the Law, the prophets, and the psalms with sweet assurances of the tender care of God over his people! Nor does the New Testament come behind the Old in like gracious declarations. And the experience of all God's people swells the volume of testimony to his loving solicitude and watchfulness over us. " And such honour have all his saints." And to be of his people means also *to be the abode of his Spirit.* That Spirit should dwell in them, rule and mould them after the Divine will. True, God's ancient people do once and again seem to have been utterly abandoned of that Holy Spirit. But there was ever a faithful remnant, ever a godly few, of whom the Lord was wont to say, "They shall be mine in that day when I make up my jewels." And we must remember that there were long periods in Israel's history when, as a nation, they lived under the blessed guidance of that Spirit. These more happy periods are passed over in silence, as all such in the records of nations are, so that the saying has passed into a proverb, "Happy the nation that has no history." It is of the sad, troubled times that history tells, not of the long, eventless, peaceful times. When at rest, they walk in the fear of the Lord, and possess the comfort of the Holy Ghost, and are multiplied. Oh the joy of this possession of his Spirit! The thought of losing it made the contrite psalmist cry out in his agony, "Cast me not away from thy presence, and take not thy Holy Spirit from me." "I will put my Spirit within you" was ever one of the choicest promises of God to his people, and one of the surest tokens that they were his people. And it is so still. To be his is to be guided and governed of that good Spirit, to have our understandings purified, our affections wisely controlled, our hearts, our wills, under his direction always, so that we turn away from what is evil and cleave to that which is good. And it includes, furthermore, the *being made the channels of his grace.* Others shall be blessed through us, as it was said to Abraham, "In thee and in thy seed shall all the nations of the earth be blessed." God's people are the salt of the earth, the light of the world. How unspeakably great and blessed is the influence of the true people of God! In their presence impurity, profanity, selfishness, sin in all its forms, hide their shameful heads and slink away, whilst all things lovely and of good report flock around them and attend upon them continually. And finally they become *the inmates of the home of God.* The heavenly inheritance, of which the earthly Canaan, the land promised to the fathers of Israel, was the type and symbol, becomes theirs. They enter it through the gates of death, and these gates once passed, they are in his presence, where "there is fulness of joy, and at his right hand there is," etc. Such are some of the elements of this great joy of God taking us for his people, a joy which, of his infinite mercy, may he make us all to know. 2. "*I will be your God.*" This cannot mean less than that *he will be known to them as their God.* They shall be able to realize his existence, his presence, his constant nearness to them. True, the God of Israel, whose promise this is, was not known by any organ of sense; he was no material God that their hands could handle; he spake with no human voice that their ears could hear; he appeared to them in no visible form that their eyes could see; he was manifested then, as now, only to their spirits. But when they worshipped him in spirit they felt that he was at their right hand, so that they could not be moved. Hence they went about their daily work and engaged in all the occupations of their lives, consciously realizing the presence of God; so that they constantly spoke of him as "their God," "our God," "my God,"—so near, so real, so present was he to them. They could not if they would, and they would not if they could, escape from his presence or withdraw from the observation of his eye, or from the guidance and guardianship of his hand. In such manifestation of himself to them did he fulfil his word, "I will be your God." Nor was this all. Not only was he realized by them but *rejoiced* in. "I will go unto the altar of God, unto God my exceeding joy," was the delighted declaration of the saints of old and is so of the saints to-day. Such joy had they in him that, when all earthly affairs were disastrous for them, when the fig tree did not blossom, and when there was no fruit in the vine, and the labour of the olive failed, and the fields yielded no meat, when the flock was cut off from the fold and there were no herds in the stall,—when, that is, ruin stared them in the face and met them on every side, nevertheless they could rejoice in the Lord, and joy in the God of their salvation. "My soul shall make her boast in the Lord," was their perpetual song; and it is the song still of all those to whom God has said, "I will be your God." And his word came true yet further by *their coming to resemble him.* It is ever the result of worship to conform the worshipper to the deity he worships. Hence it was said of the worshippers of idols, "They that make them are like unto them, so is every one that trusteth in them." Accordingly it has ever been found that they who bowed down to gods impure, cruel, and treacherous, became themselves impure, cruel, and treacherous. But, on the other hand, they who have worshipped the God of Israel have become like him—righteous, just, and true, merciful, and pure, and good. "I will be your God" meant, therefore, "I will make you like myself," and this promise God ever fulfils. And it means also, "*I will be your rest.*" The soul whose God the Lord is, reposes on him. The storms of life may rage, its tempests beat, but "firm and unmoved are they who rest their souls on God." Everything may appear to be slipping away from a man, and he may seem to be like one gliding down a steep, smooth slope, ever faster and faster to the precipice over which he will be hurled into destruction, unable to grasp any friendly rock or branch, or to find foothold anywhere—and men's circumstances are like that sometimes; but they to whom this word, "I will be your God," is fulfilled, do find foothold in God and can stay themselves upon him. Hence, when heart and flesh fail, God is the Strength of their heart and their Portion for evermore.

II. THE CONDITION OF THEIR FULFILMENT. They were faithfully to do the commandments which he had made known to them: "Obey my voice, so," etc. And this condition is not abrogated; it is in as full force to-day as it was in the days of old. But when it is complied with, then, not merely by the gracious appointment of God, but also in the way of natural result, there follows the enjoyment of the promised blessings. For: 1. Obedience tends to such enjoyment of God, inasmuch as *it prevents the rising of those mists whereby the sight of God is shut out from the soul.* Travellers along the Rhine or over the mountains of Switzerland know to their cost how often the most glorious scenery the world contains is completely hidden from their view by the uprising of some wretched mist, wrapping in cold, dark, impenetrable fog all that upon which their eyes would have so delightedly rested. They want to gaze upon all that loveliness; they have come for that very purpose; but they cannot for those thick clouds. And oh, what a beautiful vision is the face of God! How good it is to gaze upon him, and to behold the shining of his countenance! And this we should do were it not for those mists with which disobedience to God's will ever blots out all that otherwise we should so delightedly see. "If our hearts condemn us not, then have we confidence toward God;" but when they do condemn us, confidence vanishes, and, as by a veil of impenetrable cloud, the face of God is hidden from our view. We have lost him; we cannot realize him; he is as if he were not, and the soul is forlorn and wretched and exposed to all manner of ill. Now, this sad experience, which is as common as it is sad, shows how the obeying of the voice of God must tend to the enjoyment of him, inasmuch as it prevents all that which hides God from our souls. 2. And before obedience that *wall of the rebellious will,* which more than aught else displeases and dishonours God and keeps him out from the soul, "falls down flat," as did the walls of Jericho before the obedient tribes of Israel. That will must be subdued, that stronghold of evil must be pulled down, and obedience is the strong hand that accomplishes this much-needed work. That strong fortress cast down, the soul becomes the possession of God, and the hitherto rebellious forces of the soul own him as their God. Or, to take another similitude, obedience unbars that fastened door before which the Lord Jesus has stood so long and knocked, but in vain, for admission. He desires to enter and to make us the glad partakers of his grace. But till that door be unbarred all this cannot be. 3. Obedience, furthermore, *keeps us in those paths along which alone God is to be met.* Full well we know that there are paths innumerable along which men go, along which we have gone ourselves; but God is never to be met with in them. But along the path by which obedience leads us, there we do meet with him, and are blessed by him. 4. And without this obedience God *cannot carry out* his purposes of grace. This is what we are told in the verse that follows our text. God asks for obedience, "that I may perform the oath which I have sworn unto," etc. Therefore without this he is held back from what he earnestly desires, and he cannot do the things that he would. God cannot admit the ungodly and the disobedient into the blessed land of promise. To do that would be to perpetuate for ever the sins and sorrows of time. Therefore—

> "Those holy gates for ever bar
> Pollution, sin, and shame."

But "blessed are they that do his commandments, that they," etc. (Rev. xxii. 14). Now, the first step of this obedience—that which introduces to all these recompenses—is to surrender to the Lord Jesus Christ (John vi. 28, 29).—C.

Vers. 16, 17.—*The first last.* Many, indeed, are the instances in which those who were placed first in opportunity have been found last in attainment. Privilege, favour, education, help of all kinds, have been at their disposal, and yet the results which had been designed for them, and which so surely should have been theirs, they have missed (cf. Matt. xi., "Woe unto thee, Bethsaida!" etc.). And in ordinary life, as well as in the records of the Bible, may we learn how frequently, not the strong and mighty, but "the lame take the prey." The first are last and the last first. Now, of such sad and shameful failures these verses supply a notable instance. Under the imagery of a green olive tree, fair and of goodly fruit, the prophet pictures the condition and prospects of the people of God when he first planted them. No similitude could more strikingly convey to the mind of the inhabitant of Judah and Jerusalem the idea of happy and sure prosperity. But, next, the prophet portrays a far different scene—that same tree, but black and charred, its trunk riven, its fruit and foliage all gone, and its branches broken down; for the thunderbolt and the scathing lightning, the wild tempest and the fierce wind, have all done their deadly work upon it, and now it stands a mere blackened stump, instead of the beauteous and fruitful tree it once was. From that height of favour to that depth of disaster were Judah and Jerusalem to fall. They who had been first should be last.

I. THEY WERE FIRST. The imagery employed by the prophet tells in what respects. 1. *In the favour of God.* The olive was a favourite tree, held in highest esteem by the people of the lands where it grew; hence it is used here and elsewhere as an emblem of those whom God favours and has pleasure in (cf. "I am like a green olive tree in the house of my God," Ps. lii. 8). The Bible seems to love the tree. It is the first named of any known tree (Gen. viii. 11), and is the subject of the first parable (Judg. ix. 8). It is everywhere spoken of as precious; hence, when Judah and Jerusalem are thus named, we regard it as a name of endearment, telling how precious they were in God's sight. This is borne out by direct statements and by the recorded deeds of God, which show the esteem in which he held them. 2. *In beauty.* No doubt the beauty of the olive tree exists partly in the eyes of the beholder, who looks upon it with affection for all the service it renders him. But to others also there is unquestionable beauty in the olive which, with its "noble groves, covered with foliage the whole year round, spreading like a silver sea along the base of the hills and climbing their ascending terraces, speaks loudly of peace and plenty, food and gladness" (see Ruskin, 'Stones of Venice,' vol. iii. pp. 175—177). And without doubt it was beautiful in the eyes of those to whom the prophet wrote. But there is a moral beauty as well as that which is material, and of which the material is a fit symbol. And, compared with the disorder, the violence, the foulness, the wickedness of all kinds, in which the rest of the world was sunk, Israel was as a garden of the Lord—a green olive tree, "fair" and comely to look upon. In them that which was lovely and of good report, that which had virtue and praise, were found as nowhere else. Love to God and love to man, justice, truth, and piety were held in esteem amongst them as amongst none others. 3. *In usefulness.* The olive tree was not merely fair, but "of goodly fruit." From that fruit came one of the commonest and most essential articles of the Eastern's food. Its oil was employed in connection with almost everything that they ate. Its berries gave flavour to the peasant's bread. The evening lamp was kindled with the oil pressed from it. And that same oil was used to anoint their priests and kings, for the lamp in the holy place, and to mingle with many of their sacrifices. To "anoint the head with oil" was deemed most delightful and refreshing (Ps. xxiii.). Wounds were dressed with it (Luke x. 34), and the sick were anointed with it (Mark vi. 13; Jas. v. 4). The wood of the tree was employed in the sacred furniture of the temple, and there seemed to be no part of the tree which did not in some way render service to man. Now, such was the purpose of God in regard to his people, that in them "should all the nations of the earth be blest." They were to be the channel of blessing to all people. Through them God's "saving health" should be known "amongst all nations." 4. And *in permanence.* Their blessedness was to abide. The "greenness" of the tree spoken of here refers to its perpetuity and strength. The olive is known to live to a great age. It is not improbable (see Kitto) that some of the olive trees now on the Mount of Olives are contemporaneous with our Lord. The tax paid on them is that which was assigned to such trees when first the Turks became masters of Palestine. All trees planted since are taxed far more heavily. But of the great age to which the olive tree attains there can be no doubt. It brings forth fruit in old age, and its leaf doth not wither (Ps. i.). It was, therefore, a fit emblem of permanent prosperity and strength. Such was the Divine intent in regard to his people. Their blessedness was to abide. Thus in all these and yet other ways were they first. But—

II. THEY BECAME LAST. See the terrible similitude employed—the charred and shattered tree. But not more terrible than true. The smouldering ruins, the devastated city, the desolate land, which a few years afterwards the prophet looked upon, showed how true his word had been. They had become last indeed. Exalted to heaven, they had been thrust down to hell. None can avoid inquiring—

III. THE CAUSE OF ALL THIS. It is declared to be threefold. 1. *The evil of the people themselves.* (Ver. 17.) Their persistence in idolatry in spite of all remonstrance, warning, and every inducement which should have withdrawn them from their sin. "Do not the abominable thing which I hate" had in every variety of manner been said to them by God, but in vain. He hated it because it was the root of so many other sins, and the destroyer of all the good he had purposed both for and through them. 2. *Their evil returning upon themselves.* Ver. 17, "The evil . . . which they have done against themselves." This is ever the way of sin (Prov. viii. 36). It wrongs our entire nature. What a man sows he reaps. The reason is debased, conscience trampled on, the power of will prostrated, the soul imprisoned, the affections perverted, the imagination defiled, the body often diseased, character ruined, substance wasted, all the true springs of happiness poisoned or stopped. He has sown to the flesh, and of the flesh he has reaped corruption. Yes, sin is ever done *against ourselves.* 3. *The woe which comes from the provoked anger of God.* Besides these natural results of sin—the reaping which is according to the sowing, and which are terrible enough in themselves—there come the punitive inflictions of the wrath of God. History as well as the Bible is full of proofs of this on a large scale, and so are the experiences of individual transgressors, though in more limited form. And wherever sin, the primary cause, is found, there sooner or later will come these other causes which together work so dread a doom.

CONCLUSION. What effect should the contemplation of facts like these—and they are written and wrought for our learning—have upon us? Should they not cause us to reject at once and for ever all those suggestions which Satan is ever plying us with—that sin will not be punished, and the transgressor may, after all, go free? In view of facts like these, how can that be believed? And should they not lead us to offer as our daily prayer the petition, "Give us a heart to love and dread thee, and diligently to live after thy commandments"? And not only to dread and deprecate the wrath which sin provokes, but to desire and seek after that preoccupation of the heart with the love of God which will bar out sin.

> "Guard my first springs of thought and will,
> And with *thyself* my spirit fill."

C.

Ver. 17.—*The limits of long-suffering love.* I. GOD'S DEALINGS WITH HIS ANCIENT PEOPLE WERE THOSE OF LOVE. That he should have chosen them and brought them into covenant with himself; that he should have taken such precautions to preserve them in that covenant. See the time selected for its establishment (cf. ver. 4)—when their hearts were susceptible and softened by his great goodness to them, and therefore the more ready to receive and keep the impression of his will. And how forbearing he had been! For more than a thousand years they had been in possession of the land, though they had so often sinned. See, too, the mighty motives to which he appeals—fear of the curse pronounced on the disobedient, hope of the precious recompenses promised to such as should obey. And he enlists conscience on his side. They all said "Amen" to the covenant of God (ver. 5). And perpetually he had been reminding them of his covenant (ver. 7). All this—and it is paralleled by God's dealings with men now—proves the loving solicitude with which God regarded his people.

II. AND THAT LOVE WAS LONG-SUFFERING. It was not alone that he had allowed them so long possession of the land promised to their fathers, though they had often forfeited it; but now, not till his forbearance had (vers. 8—10) manifestly failed in its purpose and was being even perverted into an occasion for fresh sin, did he "change his way" toward them. And even then, many years' respite was given in which repentance and so forgiveness and restoration were possible. And to further this end Jeremiah was sent to them. And all this is like God's dealings still. Take the history of ancient and of all nations that have fallen, and the several steps of Israel's career will be found 'to have been trodden by them also: a time of great favour; disobedience; warning, repeated, earnest, continued; respite even at the last; sin persisted in notwithstanding all; then the long-threatened destruction. And it is true of families, Churches, individuals, to-day as of old.

III. BUT THAT LOVE HAD ITS LIMITS. The ruin that came upon Israel, upon Judah, and has so often come upon those like them, proves this.

IV. WHEN THESE LIMITS WERE REACHED, NOTHING COULD THEN AVERT THE THREATENED PUNISHMENT. (Cf. vers. 11—17.) Not: 1. *The piteous "cry"* of distress (ver. 11). 2. Still less (ver. 12) any *appeal to their idol-gods.* "They shall not save them *at all,*" no, although (ver. 13) throughout the whole land, "in every city," and in every street of every city these idol-gods had their altars, their incense, and their worship. 3. Nor even the *acceptable prayer of the righteous.* (Ver. 14 and ch. vii. 16.) How dreadful this! 4. *Multiplied sacrifices.* (Ver. 15; cf. Exposition.) The prophet's meaning, which is quite obscured in our translation, seems to be to protest against their flocking to the house of God, seeing how guilty they had been—it could do them no good; and also against their thinking that "the holy flesh" of sacrifices would turn away wrath from a people who "rejoiced when they did evil." 5. Nor the fact of *past privilege and favour.* (Ver. 16.) No, although God had made them as a green olive tree (ver. 16). Himself "planted thee," yet he will himself kindle the fire that shall rage and devour it.

V. FROM ALL WHICH MEN EVERYWHERE ARE TO LEARN: 1. *To dread every sin.* For we cannot tell when and where those limits of God's long-suffering are reached. That sin to which a man is tempted may be the overstepping of them so far as he is concerned. If he do that, the word may go forth, "Let him alone" (cf. Rev. xxii. 11). We are apt to think that any time will do to turn to God. It will not. It is not universally nor commonly true

> "That while the lamp holds out to burn,
> The vilest sinner may return."

It is untrue; for the probability of a man then, at the very last, turning his heart to God, when up till then he has ever turned his heart away from God, is small indeed. The limit was passed when the Spirit of God left him, and that may be long before death comes. Probably death has nothing whatever to do with it either way. We should then say to ourselves, when drawn to any sin against which God's Holy Spirit is protesting and pleading, "If I disobey him now he may leave me altogether." 2. *To desire God.* The clearing of the heart of sin is not sufficient, the heart must be occupied. The house to which the evil spirit came back bringing others worse than himself, was swept and garnished, but it was "empty." So if men's hearts be "swept" from ill deeds, yet if they be not occupied, evil will come back. It is when the love of God possesses our heart that there is no fear of our even approaching, still less of overstepping, the limits of his long-suffering love. This is our sure, our only safe-guard.—C.

Vers. 18—23.—*The baffled plot.* These verses are an episode. Like as the miracle of the healing of her who touched the hem of our Lord's garment was an episode in connection with the healing of the daughter of Jairus (Mark v. 21, etc.), so this account of the plot against Jeremiah's life comes in here, breaking the thread of his discourse, which is not renewed again till ch. xii. 7. Scripture has many instances of similar plots contrived against the servants of the Lord; they are found in the histories of Joseph, David, Nehemiah, Elisha, Paul, of our Lord, and of others. In this one, note—

I. ITS CIRCUMSTANCES. Jeremiah had given dire offence to the men of Anathoth, his own city, men who, like himself probably, were associated with the priestly office.

"Between the priesthood and the prophets there had hitherto been more or less of conflict, but now that conflict was exchanged for a fatal union. 'A wonderful and horrible thing was committed in the land; the prophets prophesied falsely, and the priests bore rule by their means;' and he who by each of his callings was naturally led to sympathize with both, was the doomed antagonist of both—victim of one of the strongest passions, the hatred of priests against a priest who attacks his own order, the hatred of prophets against a prophet who ventures to have a voice and will of his own. His own village, occupied by members of the sacred tribe, was for him a nest of conspirators against his life. Of him first in the sacred history was the saying literally fulfilled, 'A prophet hath no honour in his own birthplace' (Ἐν τῇ πατρίδι αὐτοῦ, Luke iv. 24)" (Stanley). They objected not so much to his prophesying, for there were plenty of them who did this, but to his strenuous assertion—an assertion that their own consciences assented to, that he spoke in the Name of the Lord (ver. 21). Warnings so faithful but yet so terrible were little liked, as they ever are by those who so much needed them. And since they could not silence him in any other way, they determined to take away his life. Secretly and craftily they laid their plot. Jeremiah had not the least suspicion of it. "I was," says he (ver. 19), "like a lamb," that is, a pet or house lamb, such as the Orientals often keep (see Exposition). He went in and out amongst his brethren, trusting them, and thinking no ill, whilst all the time this dark and deadly plot was being devised against him. And it would have been successful, we can hardly doubt, had he not been "warned of the Lord" (ver. 18). The shock, the dread revulsion of feeling, which the tidings caused him is evident in the almost unmeasured grief and indignation which the following verses express. His first utterance is a cry for vengeance (ver. 20) on them, an appeal to the righteous God to uphold his cause. Then comes a denunciation of the Divine doom upon them, then an aggrieved remonstrance (ch. xii. 1) and complaint addressed to God himself in view of the prosperity of these ungodly and wicked men, followed by a fierce demand for revenge (ch. xii. 3); all which is replied to (ch. xii. 5) by a sharp but loving rebuke, a revelation of yet further treachery, and that on the part, not of mere acquaintances and neighbours, but of his own brethren, the inmates of the same home, children of the same father; and finally (ch. xii. 6) God, who had already baffled their first plottings against him, now puts him on his guard against all that they should afterwards devise, bidding him "believe them not, though," etc. (ch. xii. 6). Of the manner in which they purposed to carry out their deadly scheme, or how God revealed to his servant what was going on, we are not told; only the above noted facts are stated. But these are full of interest and instruction. Note, therefore, some of—

II. THE SUGGESTED LESSONS. They are such as these. 1. "Having the form of godliness but denying the power thereof, means subjection to the power of all ungodliness though denying the form thereof." See these would-be murderers of the prophet; they were consecrated priests. 2. "He that keepeth Israel shall neither slumber nor sleep." The plotters against the prophet's life were discovered and declared by him to whom "the darkness and the light are both alike," and so his servant was forewarned and saved. Therefore, "They that trust in the Lord shall be," etc. 3. "The servant will often have to be as his Master, and the disciple as his Lord." Like the Lord Jesus, Jeremiah was hated of his countrymen and brethren (cf. Homily on ch. i. 1—3, p. 10, for more of these resemblances). Several of them are recorded in these verses. The hatred felt towards him by his countrymen and in his father's house. The cause of that hatred. The deadly plots which were devised against him. The innocence and gentleness—"like a lamb," etc.—which characterized the hated one. And such fellowship with Christ is the law of his service. 4. "Resemblance between the Master and his servant may be often close but is never complete." However natural Jeremiah's outburst of rage and indignation, we cannot help noticing how far short in moral elevation he falls of him who prayed, "Father, forgive them," etc., and of the first Christian martyr, who was taught of Christ to pray, "Lord, lay not this sin," etc. The perfect Example is Christ; we can "call none good but One," that is, him. 5. "Wrongs that God will suffer against himself he will not suffer against his people." Jeremiah was avenged within a very little time and in ample manner, but the wrongs God had suffered from the same people he had borne for centuries, and even then there was a reserve of mercy—he made not "a full end." 6. "Let our eyes be ever toward the Lord, for he will pluck our feet out of *every* net"—Satan's, Sin's, Sorrow's, Doubt's, Death's.—C.

Vers. 1—12.—*The covenant with the fathers binding on the children.* Here it is necessary to go back over all the history of Israel, and consider the great covenant transactions between God and his people. Such transactions we find to have been filled with great solemnity, so that they might make a deep mark in history. We trace the beginnings of the great covenant in God's dealings with Abraham. Indeed, the covenant with Israel as a nation was the necessary consequence of the covenant with Abraham as an individual. Then, as Jeremiah says here, there was a definite interchange of promise in the day when Jehovah brought Israel out of Egypt. He could then ask them for an undertaking of obedience and separation from the idolatrous and impure heathens. While they were in servitude to Egypt and manifestly crushed in spirit, it was not possible to ask anything from them. But when Jehovah had abundantly proved his power, his grace, and his nearness, when he took his stand amid the freshness of glorious Divine achievements, then the covenant appeared, to the generation to which he proposed it, in all its fitness, as an instrument for the attainment of further ends. The gracious purposes of this covenant are made strikingly apparent in the continuance of it even after the people had lapsed into their riotous gathering around the golden calf (Exod. xxxiv. 10). But this covenant in all its amplitude, and with all the difficulties surrounding the observance of it, is nowhere set forth with greater solemnity and particularity than in Deut. xxvii.—xxx. There we find the curses and the blessings detailed and illustrated, and the provision made that between Ebal and Gerizim, in the very midst as it were of the land of promise, the covenant should receive a great national acceptance. "*But,*" an Israelite might have said to Jeremiah, "*these things happened so long ago.*" Men think they can easily set aside claims that rise out of the distant past. In the case of this particular claim, however, no such rejoinder was possible. In 2 Kings xxii. we read of the discovery of the Book of the Law in the reign of Josiah, and in ch. xxiii. we read of the decisive and comprehensive action which Josiah took upon making the discovery. The description in ver. 2 of how he gathered in the house of the Lord all the men of Judah and the inhabitants of Jerusalem, priests and prophets, and small and great, reminds us of the gathering long before, between Ebal and Gerizim (Josh. viii. 35). All the people, we are further told, "stood to the covenant." Josiah was enabled to make a general overthrow of all the external visible instruments of idolatry, and what is of particular moment to be observed is the keeping of the Passover as arising out of this renewed covenant (2 Chron. xxxv. 1—19). It was like coming face to face with that great event in the early history of the people, their deliverance from the iron furnace. Thus when we bring into one view all these great transactions in relation to the covenant, we see how weighty and urgent is the message Jehovah here sends Jeremiah to deliver. His covenant was with a nation in the whole duration of its existence. Each generation as it died handed on its *land*, its possessions, its national customs, but in the midst of all it had to hand on this covenant. The land was Israel's only upon a certain condition. The owner of a piece of land may covenant with some one that he and his heirs and assigns shall have the use of the land in perpetuity, on the observance of certain conditions. If these conditions are willingly, perhaps eagerly, accepted, there is no just right to complain of forfeiture if the conditions are completely and carelessly set at nought. God's works, we are made to observe, go on to their completion through the service of many generations of his creatures. How many generations of insects have died in making the beautiful coral islands! We amid our spiritual light and advantages are the inheritors of many privileges. We have the use of an estate, which has been enriched by the toils and sufferings, the prayers and tears, of many ancestors. But we can inherit no privilege, no joy, no promise, no hope, without inheriting the responsibilities of a covenant. We may, indeed, neglect the covenant, but surely it requires great audacity to assert that we have even the faintest pretence of right to do it.—Y.

Ver. 14.—*Intercession unavailing.* God here forbids Jeremiah to intercede for the people in their sore trouble. Similar expressions are found in ch. vii. 16; xiv. 11;

xv. 1. It was evidently meant that the prophet should feel how unavailing all intercession was.

I. WE HAVE HERE A VERY PAINFUL EXCEPTION TO A VERY IMPORTANT RULE. The rule is to pray, to pray continually, and to pray with not the least fervency and devotion when our prayers are intercessions. God delights in the dependent and confiding approaches of his people; and intercession must be specially a joy to him because it looks away from individual good, and exemplifies most effectively the loving of one's neighbour as one's self. Moses, Job, Samuel, Daniel, are all found interceding for transgressors. Hence the very forbidding here makes continual remembrance of the needs of others all the more a duty. We have to pray for those who lack the faith or the disposition to pray for themselves. And especially we have to bear in mind him "who ever liveth to make intercession" for the spiritually needy. It is worth noting that, while God here forbids Jeremiah to intercede for the people, he is represented in Rom. xi. 2—4 as reproving and enlightening Elijah when he interceded *against* the people. We must give special pains to say for sinners all that we can. And in order to do this, we must be observant and pitiful; for as a general rule we have a quick eye for faults, and become censorious by a kind of second nature. It wonderfully suits the inclinations of fallen man to be an accuser of his brethren.

II. WHY THE EXCEPTION IS HERE MADE. There are two considerations here. 1. *The petition, as to its literal aim, could not be granted.* It was evidently a petition for the delivery of Judah and Jerusalem from the special calamity now so near. That calamity had become necessary. There was no choice for the people but to drink the waters of the full cup now wrung out for them. God, in refusing to hear Jeremiah, had really the same end in view as the prophet himself; but the prophet, in his keen sensitiveness, wished the end to come by some less painful way than through desolated Jerusalem. But God knew that this was the right way—just because it was the way of humiliation and loss, and thus, in refusing *the special supplication* of the prophet, God was really taking *the best way of answering it*—paradox though it may seem to say so. 2. *Jeremiah's own position had to be considered.* We may conclude that it was reckoned one of the distinctions of a prophet that he could act as intercessor. Jeremiah, we know, was asked to pray to God for the people (ch. xxxvii. 3; xlii. 2); and just at the times when the refusal was most emphatic, the appeal for intercession may have been most urgent. Well, then, was it that Jehovah should, as it were, stop the mouth of his servant in his supplication, so that no one could take up a reproach and say, "If thou wert indeed a prophet, thy petition for us would immediately avail." The honour of Jeremiah as a faithful servant was dear to his Divine Master. This is brought out very clearly by the reference to Moses and Samuel in ch. xv. 1. It was no shame to him to fail where Moses and Samuel could not have succeeded.

III. OBSERVE WHAT LAY BEYOND THE PRESENT REFUSAL. Though all is so stern and forbidding here, we look further on in the book, and there is brightness again. Ch. xxix. 1—14 is a beautiful contrast to the word we have been considering. Desolation and exile were a cheap price to pay for such a restoration into favour as God there provides. He has shut the gates of mercy for a while; but only for a little while—seventy years, two generations of men! The permanent command, only to be set aside by a special interference, is that which says, "Pray for the peace of Jerusalem: they shall prosper that love thee" (Ps. cxxii. 6).—Y.

Vers. 16, 17.—*The fated olive tree.* I. GOD'S COMPARISON OF HIS PEOPLE TO THE OLIVE TREE. There would have been force in the comparison if applied to any flourishing and fruitful tree, but there was peculiar propriety in directing the thoughts of the people to the olive. The olive was already associated in sacred history with the return of hope after the Flood, and doubtless, in the times of Jeremiah, it was one of the most valuable of trees, as it still is, for the richness of its produce, and the variety of ways in which that produce meets the common wants of men. The extensive olive groves, composed of trees that reach no great height, and unattractive to a mere casual glance, were yet more to the people than all the cedars of Lebanon. And as the people were led to consider these olive trees, full of vigour, abounding in blossoms, many of which never came to fruit, and yet, after all, left abundance of fruit behind, as they recollected all the use of the olive, for food, for light, for anointing, for soap-making;—the thoughtful among them would feel that God could have employed no better figure to suggest how full Israel was of productivity of the most practical sort. Mention is made in Hosea (xiv. 6), as well as here, of the beauty of the olive tree. In one sense the olive was not beautiful. As far as the picturesque was concerned, many trees excelled it. But, after all, the deepest beauty, the only beauty that will bear inspection, is that which comes from pleasant experiences and associations; and those who were rich in profits from the labour of the olive would see in it a beauty absent from many trees otherwise more attractive. The olive, to one seeing it for the first time, might seem a tree of small practical use. But experience proved that its performance was great, and so it became more and more a name of honour. And this tree, having in it such capabilities, *God had planted*. The olive tree needs a special soil to bring out all its capabilities. Dr. Thomson says, speaking of a certain plain full of olive-orchards, "The substratum of these plains is chalky marl, abounding in flint. . . . In such soil the tree flourishes best, both in the plains and upon the mountains. It delights to insinuate its roots into the clefts of the rocks and crevices of this flinty marl; and from thence it draws its richest stores of oil. If the overlying mould is so deep that its roots cannot reach the rock beneath, I am told that the tree languishes, and its berries are small and sapless." And so God planted his people, being such as they were in his eye, in a land promised and duly prepared. Nay, in a certain sense, they were planted even before they reached the land of promise. They were planted and became fruitful as soon as ever God took them in hand, fruitful even amid the pains of Egypt and the desolations of the wilderness.

II. THE DESTRUCTION OF THIS OLIVE TREE. All the wealth that came from this olive tree was being used for bad purposes. The fatness of the soil went into the olive, but the fatness of the olive did not come back to God in grateful and proportionate service. Nay, rather, it was used against him; and the harm it did was to some extent measurable by the good it might have done. The axe is laid, not only at the root of the tree that brings forth no fruit, but also at the root of the tree that brings forth its fruit to be used in hostility against him who planted the tree. Israel might say, "Is it not plain that God favours us, for are we not as the green, fair, fruitful olive? Why, then, should we believe threatenings that seem contradicted by these signs of favour?" These were signs of favour indeed, but they were also grounds of expectation. And when the expectation was utterly disappointed, and when the fruit of Jehovah's gracious dealings was used to prop up the abominations of idolatry, it was time for him to work in all the severity of righteous judgment.—Y.

Vers. 18—23.—*The prophet in his own country.* This passage describes a peculiar peril to Jeremiah, and a peculiar peril to those who conspired against him.

I. A PECULIAR PERIL TO JEREMIAH. His life was full of perils—"perils from his own countrymen" in many ways, perils from the palace with its great men, from priests and false prophets, from every devotee of idolatry, from every one, in short, whose vices and iniquities he lashed with the scourge of his Heaven-inspired tongue. He would expect to make enemies in these directions. But here is peril from *an unexpected source.* He was not at all prepared for it, and when the knowledge of it in all its hideous reality came upon him, he was correspondingly excited. Yet, though the peril was unexpected, it was by no means *to be marvelled at.* As soon as we look at the position of Jeremiah and the consequent feeling of his kindred, we cease to wonder. Much may be said, and justly, of the strength of natural affection; but the selfishness so deeply settled in every human breast, and so potent, is stronger than any tie of nature. Perhaps a mother's love may be trusted to stand out against it, but Scripture shows, in more than one instance, to what lengths a brother's jealousy will go. Think of Cain and Abel, Joseph and his brethren, Moses and Miriam, and David and his elder brethren. Christ said that "a man's foes should be they of his own household;" but this was not a new thing. It was but the continuing of an old and sad difficulty in the way of regenerating the world. If things had gone as they ought to have gone, it was in the comparative retirement of Anathoth that Jeremiah should have found some slight opportunities of rest in the midst of his arduous public labours. That he had some quiet place of rest and of converse with like-minded spirits is very probable, but he would find it as Jesus did. Jesus, we know, found his nearest approaches to home life in Capernaum and Bethany, and not at all in Nazareth. We may surmise that he never had as much as one quiet day there after his public ministry began. The relatives of Jesus said that he was beside himself, and probably they feared that the strange things he did and the ever-increasing hostility he provoked would bring suspicion on themselves. And so it was very awkward for these kinsfolk of Jeremiah in Anathoth. Every one ran the risk of being pointed at as brother, or uncle, or cousin of that madman the prophet. Further, this peril, being from an unsuspected source, *went on to its height without suspicion.* The prophet puts his position very touchingly and forcibly by the figure of the tame lamb. As the lamb goes along with those to whose company it has been accustomed, all unconscious of their slaughtering designs, so the prophet meets his brethren, those with whom he played as a child, those whose faces were among the first he could remember. Why should he suspect them? True, he knows that far too often brother has been the sworn and relentless enemy of brother; but let this be the experience of others. He cannot believe it till by actual taste he finds the bitterness in his own cup. Jeremiah's experience stands here to teach us, not to be suspicious, not to let caution and wariness degenerate into a cynical putting on of armour against everybody, but to let both our safety and our peace of mind lie in our nearness to God. The nearest of brother men is too weak, too uncertain, to be made an object of trust.

II. THERE WAS A PECULIAR PERIL TO THE CONSPIRATORS. Though there was a danger where Jeremiah never thought of looking, it was precisely upon that danger that Jehovah had his observant eye (ch. xvii. 9, 10). What the conspirators would reckon one of their greatest helps, namely, that the proposed victim did not in the least suspect their designs, doubtless proved in the end a very material help to the faith and endurance of the prophet. Had not God made a sure provision for him where he did not even suspect that there was anything needing to be provided? Let the wicked know this, that whatever they reckon to be their peculiar advantage will assuredly turn out to be their peculiar weakness, difficulty, and, indeed, weapon of decisive overthrow. The prophet's kinsfolk made the not uncommon blunder of thinking that they would get rid of difficulties in getting rid of one peculiarly awkward and irritating difficulty that lay close to them. There is one great difficulty we never can get rid of, and that is the omniscience of God. Let there be a warning, then, to all those who belong to the πατρίδ of a prophet. Let them be careful how they set themselves against anything strange and peculiar in any one belonging to them. Self-delusion, of course, is possible, and a man may mistake some "Will-o'-the-wisp" for the steady prophetic illumination. But he is not likely to be converted by threatening and repression. It is only by Gamaliel's policy that either impostors or victims of delusion can be truly exposed. The men of Anathoth, kinsfolk and neighbours alike, were not required to believe in Jeremiah on his first appearance, but they were required to wait and see whereto this thing might grow. What a pity they had not some shrewd and commanding Gamaliel to keep them in the path of prudence!—Y.

EXPOSITION.

CHAPTER XII.

Ver. 1.—Painfully exercised by the mysteries of the Divine government, the prophet opens his grief to Jehovah. **Righteous art thou,** etc.; rather, *Righteous wouldest thou be, O Jehovah, if I should plead with thee;* i.e. if I were to bring a charge against thee, I should be unable to convict thee of injustice (comp. Ps. li. 4; Job ix. 2). The prophet, however, cannot refrain from laying before Jehovah a point which seems to him irreconcilable with the Divine righteousness. The rendering, indeed, must be modified. **Yet let me talk with thee of thy judgments**

should rather be, *yet will I debate questions of right with thee.* The questions remind us of those of Job in Job xxi., xxiv. Thus to have been the recipient of special Divine revelations, and to be in close communion with God, gives no security against the occasional ingress of doubting thoughts and spiritual distress. Wherefore **are all they happy,** etc.? rather, *secure.* The statement must be qualified by what follows. In the general calamity the wicked still fare the best.

Ver. 2.—**Far from their reins;** *i.e.* from their heart (the seat of strong impulses and desires); comp. Ps. xvi. 7; xxvi. 2.

Ver. 3.—**Hast seen me, and tried**; rather, *seest me, and triest*. **Pull them out.** Perhaps this is correct, and there is an allusion to the figure of the plant in ver. 2. But the verb need mean no more than "separate" (comp. ch. vi. 29). **Prepare them**; literally, *consecrate them*, as victims for the sacrifice.

Ver. 4.—**How long,** etc.? The verse is decided rather differently by the Hebrew accents. The question should end at **wither**, and the following words run on. **Every field** should be *the whole field* (i.e. open country). The connection has caused some difficulty. But drought is constantly described as a judgment (ch. iii. 3; v. 24, 25; xiv. 2—7; xxiii. 10), and it is a prophetic doctrine that the lower animals suffer for the fault of man. **Because they said**; rather, *because they say*. The speakers are the ungodly. The subject of the following verb is uncertain. Some think it is God; but when God is said to "see" (*i.e.* take notice of) anything, it is always something actually existing. The subject must, therefore, be the prophet, of whom the ungodly scoffingly declare, **He shall not see our last end**, because his predictions are mere delusions.

Ver. 5.—Jeremiah's impatience corrected. The expressions are evidently proverbial. The opposition to the prophet will reach a still higher pitch; and if he is so soon discouraged, how will he bear his impending trials? **And if in the land of peace,** etc.? a second figure, the translation of which needs amending. *If (only) in a land of peace thou art confident, how wilt thou do in the pride of Jordan?* The "pride of Jordan" means the thickets on its banks, which were notorious as the haunts of lions (ch. xlix. 19; l. 44; Zech. xi. 3). "Lions' bones have been found by Dr. Roth in the gravel of the Jordan. Lions are seldom or never found now west of the Euphrates, although they occasionally cross the river" (Rev. W. Houghton, 'Bible Educator,' i. 22).

Ver. 6.—An example of the "treachery" referred to in ver. 1; a conspiracy against Jeremiah in his own family. **Have called a multitude after thee**; rather, *have called aloud after thee*, as one raises a hue and cry after a thief.

Vers. 7—17.—A separate prophecy. The key to it is in 2 Kings xxiv. 1, 2, where it is related that, after Jehoiakim's rebellion against Nebuchadnezzar, "Jehovah sent against him bands of the Chaldees, and bands of the Syrians, and bands of the Moabites, and bands of the children of Ammon, and sent them against Judah to destroy it." The prophecy falls into two strophes or sections, vers. 7—13 and vers. 14—17. In the first we have a complaint of the desolation produced by the guerilla warfare; in the second, a prediction of the captivity of the hostile

peoples, not, however, without a prospect of their return home and conversion to Jehovah. It is evident enough that this passage stands in no connection with what precedes. The whole tone is that of a description of present scenes and not of the future. Sometimes, no doubt, a prophet, in the confidence of faith, represents the future as though it were already past; but there is always something in the context to determine the reference and prevent ambiguity. Here, however, there is nothing to indicate that the description relates to the future; and it is followed by a prediction which presupposes that the preceding passage refers to the literal past.

Ver. 7.—**I have forsaken mine house.** The "house" is here not the temple, but the people of Israel, as the parallel clause shows (see Hos. viii. 1, and comp. Heb. iii. 6; 1 Tim. iii. 15). Jehovah, not the prophet, is evidently the speaker. **I have left**; rather, *I have cast away*. **Into the hand of her enemies.** The Hebrew is more expressive: "Into the palm of the hand." Bonomi ('Nineveh and her Palaces,' p. 191) has an engraving from the monuments of guests at a banquet, holding their drinking-vessels in the deeply hollowed palm of their hand. So here the people of Israel, in her weak, fainting state, needs only to be held in the quiet pressure of the palm of the hand. The remark and the illustration are due to Dr. Payne Smith.

Ver. 8.—The reason why Jehovah has given up his people. Israel (or, more strictly, Judah) has proceeded to open hostility against his God. **He is unto me**—or rather, *has become unto me*—as a lion in the forest; a familiar circumstance (comp. on ver. 5 and ch. iv. 7). **Therefore have I hated it.** "To hate" is a strong expression for the withdrawal of love, shown by the giving up of Israel into the power of his enemies, as Mal. i. 3 (Keil).

Ver. 9.—The first part of this verse is mistranslated. Instead of **Mine heritage is unto me**, etc., it should be, *Is mine heritage unto me* (i.e. to my sorrow, a *dativus ethicus*) *a coloured bird of prey? Are birds of prey round about her?* The passage is difficult, but the following seems the most plausible explanation:—Jehovah is represented as surprised to see his chosen people a prey to the heathen (a strongly anthropomorphic description, as if Jehovah had not anticipated that his "giving up" his people would have such sad results). It seems to him (adopting human modes of speech) as if Israel were "a coloured bird of prey," the bright plumage of which excites the animosity of its less brilliant comrades, who gather round it and pull it to pieces. It is an allusion to the phenomenon, well-known to the ancients (Tacit., 'Ann.,' vi. 28; Suet., 'Cæs.,' 81; Plin., 'Hist. Nat.,' x. 19), of birds gathering round and attacking a strange-looking bird appearing in their midst. The prophet might have simply said "a bird;" why does he say "a bird of prey (*'ayit*)"? Probably because he has just described the hostile attitude of Israel towards Jehovah under the figure of a lion. Some particular, rare kind of vulture seems to be intended. Sennacherib apparently uses a cognate word (*'it*) for the vulture ('Taylor Cylinder,' iii. 68). Bochart and Gesenius, following the Septuagint, think "hyena," and not "bird of prey," is the right rendering in the first clause; but Gesenius does not offer any other passage for the meaning *bestia rapax*. **Come ye, assemble all the beasts of the field.** There is a parallel passage in Isa. lvi. 9, where, as here, the "beasts of the field" (*i.e.* the wild beasts of the open country) are the heathen powers employed as God's instruments for chastising Israel (comp. also Ezek. xxxiv. 5, where the same figure occurs). "The prophet adopts the strongest way of expressing that Israel, utterly bereft of his natural defenders, lies at the mercy of the great heathen empire" (note on Isa. lvi. 9). **Come to devour;** rather, *bring them to devour.*

Ver. 10.—Another simpler and more natural image, expressing the same idea, as those in ver. 9. The favourite way of representing Jehovah's relation to his people is that of a vine-proprietor to his vineyard (see on ch. ii. 21). How would a vineyard be ruined if a band of shepherds were to drive their flocks among the tender vine-shoots! The **many pastors** (or, *shepherds*) are clearly Nebuchadnezzar and his generals (comp. ch. vi. 3). **My pleasant portion.** Jehovah is the "portion" of his people; his people and its land are the "portion" of Jehovah (see on ch. x. 16). The epithet "pleasant" expresses the emotion of the surprised speaker.

Ver. 11.—**Layeth it to heart;** rather, *laid it to heart.* Inconsiderateness is repeatedly spoken of as an aggravation of the moral sickness of Israel (Isa. xlii. 25; lvii. 1, 11).

Ver. 12.—**Upon all high places through the wilderness;** rather, *upon all bare heights in the wilderness* (see on ch. iii. 2). Hardly with a reference to their pollution by idolatry; the mention of "the wilderness" (or pasture-country) suggests that it is merely a feature in the impoverishment of the country (a

contrast to Isa. xlix. 9). **The sword of the Lord shall devour;** rather, *the Lord hath a sword which devoureth.* It is the heavenly sword (Isa. xxxiv. 5), the symbol of Divine vengeance (see below on ch. xlvi. 5).

Ver. 13.—A description in proverbial language of the absence of "peace" (literally, *soundness*, i.e. prosperity, security), from which "all flesh" in Judah at this time shall suffer. The trouble of sowing has been in vain, for *they have reaped thorns* (so we must render grammatically, and not **shall reap,** and in the next clause **shall not profit** ought to be *have not profited*). **And they shall be ashamed of your revenues;** rather, *be ashamed then of your produce;* but it is more natural to emend the pronominal suffix, and render, *and are ashamed of their produce* (the Authorized Version seems to have very nearly taken this easy step). It is, of course, the produce of husbandry which is referred to.

Ver. 14.—Here occurs a transition. The prophet comes forward with a denunciation in the name of Jehovah. **All mine evil neighbours;** the hostile peoples mentioned in 2 Kings xxiv. "My neighbours," because Jehovah "dwelleth in Zion." **Pluck them out of their land;** viz. by deportation into a foreign land. Judah and the neighbouring nations shall share the same fate. This is indicated by the use of the same verb "to pluck out" in the next clause with reference to Judah (comp. 1 Kings xiv. 15, Hebrew). In the case of Judah, however, to be "plucked out" is a mercy as well as a judgment, considering who they are "out of" whose "midst" the Jews are "plucked."

Ver. 15.—**I will return, and have compassion.** The rendering is too Hebraistic; the sense is simply, *I will again have compassion.* The prophets offer no partial or "nationalistic" view; of the mercy of God (comp. on ch. xlviii. 47).

Ver. 16.—Israel has been converted and restored, and if the other nations follow his example and **swear by my name,** *i.e.* adopt the religion of Jehovah (comp. Isa. xix. 18), they shall be rewarded by being suffered to dwell safely in Israel's midst. Observe the contrast with ver. 14. Before, Israel had dwelt amidst them to his own detriment; now they shall dwell amidst Israel to their profit.

HOMILETICS.

Vers. 1, 2.—*The prosperity of the wicked.* I. THE DIFFICULTY. The prosperity of the wicked was a difficulty of peculiar force to the Jews, since it seemed to contradict an item of their peculiar faith—the doctrine of temporal rewards and punishments. The difficulty is less to us Christians; but it is idle to deny its existence. It is threefold. 1. *The success of wickedness.* The treacherous plans of the wicked often succeed.

Their violent actions are often unchecked and produce fatal results. How is it that these evil things are not frustrated before they ripen to perfection? That wicked men should plot evil, should attempt evil, we can imagine; but that they should be allowed to carry it out—often only because many accidents are favourable—this is hard to understand. "Wherefore doth the way of the wicked prosper?" 2. *The security of the wicked.* After they had succeeded we should expect that they would discover the vanity of their most prosperous efforts. But they not only attain their objects. They find these to be satisfactory, and are able to enjoy them with calm self-complacency. Here is the greater mystery: after completing their bad deeds the wicked are left in undisturbed enjoyment of the fruits of them. "Wherefore are all they secure that deal very treacherously?" 3. *The Divine blessing apparently enjoyed by the wicked.* Not only does their own work succeed, but Providence bestows favours upon them. Outside events of life over which they have no control minister to their prosperity. Here is the greatest element of the difficulty. God has planted them, and they enjoy fruitfulness through his help.

II. THE WAY TO TREAT THE DIFFICULTY. 1. *Face it.* Jeremiah boldly confronted his troublesome thoughts. People often try to hush up their doubts. The result is that a subtle spirit of scepticism spreads unconsciously through all their ideas, and its disintegrating influence undermines all solid faith. Suppressed doubt is fatal to sincerity. It begets indifference to truth. We cannot hold firmly the truths we know till we distinctly separate these from those we doubt. The suppression of doubt is cowardly. Doubt can only be conquered by being boldly confronted. 2. *Do not charge God foolishly.* Jeremiah did not accuse the justice of God. We are dim-sighted and weak in our judgment. Much of this great world must be a mystery to us. We must not assume that, because we cannot justify the ways of God, they admit of no justification. It is foolish as well as rebellious to presume to be the judge of God. 3. *Bring the difficulty to God.* Doubt should drive us to prayer. God only can enlighten our darkness. God graciously permits his children to plead and debate with him (Isa. i. 18). Doubt is not necessarily a result of any misconduct. But, however it arises, it is best to confess it to God.

III. THE DIRECTIONS IN WHICH TO LOOK FOR A SOLUTION OF THE DIFFICULTY. 1. *The righteousness of God.* Jeremiah sees the difficulty, but it does not drive him from faith in the justice of God. Religion makes constant demands on faith—the personal faith of trust in the character of God where appearances are against what we believe that character to be. Confidence in the unwavering righteousness of God will help us to look for certain indications of a solution of the difficulty occasioned by the prosperity of the wicked. Right must and will be done, and if it is not yet accomplished it will be ultimately. From the character of God we may thus reason to his certain action (Gen. xviii. 25). 2. Hence we have an argument in favour of *future rectification.* Jeremiah expects it to come even in this life, though it is long deferred (ver. 3). The Christian looks for it in the great judgment, and the fruits of this in the life to come. 3. The difficulty may be lessened even for the present by the reflection that *material prosperity is not real prosperity.* It may be well for a good man to suffer. Prosperity may be an evil. True welfare consists not in success, not in security from calamity, but in inward peace, in progress in the Divine life.

Ver. 2 (last clause).—*God near to the mouth but far from the life.* I. IT IS POSSIBLE TO HAVE THE NAME OF GOD ON OUR LIPS WHILE THE THOUGHT OF GOD IS ABSENT FROM OUR MINDS. This is the case with mere formal worshippers, who use the language of devotion without realizing to themselves its meaning. The danger of it besets us all. Words come to be handled like coins, without any distinct recognition of what they represent. This applies especially to words which refer to God, since it requires a high act of abstraction to keep constantly before us the ideas of the unseen Object of such language. Understand that these empty words are worse than wasted breath; they are a mockery to God, a deception to men, and a source of self-delusion to the speaker of them.

II. IT IS POSSIBLE TO HAVE THE NAME OF GOD ON OUR LIPS WHILE THE LOVE OF GOD IS ABSENT FROM OUR HEARTS. We may not fall into the first mistake. The language may not be empty words. The thought of God may be present. Yet this may be a mere thought—a cold and barren idea, having no influence on our affections. This religion of words and notions is a vain thing. Indeed, it is not a religion at all; it is only a theology. Religion does not begin till the heart opens to receive God. It consists not in the intellectual recognition of God, but in the love of God (Deut. x. 12).

III. IT IS POSSIBLE TO HAVE THE NAME OF GOD ON OUR LIPS WHILE THE POWER OF GOD IS ABSENT FROM OUR CONSCIENCES. God may be spoken of, thought of, approached with a certain affection, though not the true love of our hearts, and yet be practically disregarded. His will may still be of no account to us. We may still not make our lives subservient to his Law. There is then no evidence of God in our conduct. Though our thought may be religious, our life is godless.

IV. IT IS POSSIBLE TO HAVE THE NAME OF GOD ON OUR LIPS WHILE THE SPIRIT OF GOD IS ABSENT FROM OUR SPIRITS. The deepest fact of religion is the indwelling of the Spirit of God—the real presence of God. God inhabits the soul as a temple. We may have much religiousness without this. The Name of God may be inscribed on the portals of the temple while the shrine is empty of his presence.

V. IT IS POSSIBLE TO HAVE THE NAME OF GOD UPON OUR LIPS AND TO BE VERY WICKED. If the Name be only on our lips, this is no sign of moral and spiritual goodness. The wicked contemporaries of Jeremiah were many of them religious precisionists; yet their moral guilt was none the less for all their language of devotion.

VI. IT IS POSSIBLE TO HAVE THE NAME OF GOD ON OUR LIPS AND TO SUFFER ULTIMATE RUIN. Formalism and hypocrisy may prosper for a time. Those men who had the Name of God on their lips were the wicked who *prospered* (ver. 1). Yet they were doomed to ultimate punishment. It is important to remember this constantly, since we are too ready to be deceived by professions and appearances.

Ver. 5.—*A dark prospect.* If Jeremiah was ready to despair when he discovered the conspiracy of the men of Anathoth, how would he bear the news of the treachery of his own brethren? His condition under the lesser trouble made the prospect of greater trouble most alarming. The Divine admonition which such a situation showed him to need may be of value to others who may be repeating the experience of the prophet.

I. DESPAIR UNDER LESSER TROUBLE MAKES THE ANTICIPATION OF GREATER TROUBLE A DARK PROSPECT. 1. Greater trouble may *reasonably be expected.* God usually prepares us for the endurance of trials by sending them by degrees, and reserving the more severe till we have been trained to the endurance of milder ones. Few men can say that they have drunk the cup of sorrow to the dregs, and none can know what bitter drops may yet be in store for them. 2. The advent of greater trouble is *not itself an alarming fact.* Trouble is fearful only in proportion as it strikes fear into us. If we are prepared to meet it we need have no terror. God can give strength equal to our requirement, and for the sterner trial the more abundant support. The man's trouble is greater than the child's, but so is the man's strength. 3. The one cause of alarm is in *our weakness.* If this is revealed before slight tests, it must be much worse when the strain is harder. The important point is not that after enduring the foot-race we shall fail in contending with the chariots, but that, failing in the one trial, we may expect only failure in the other.

II. THE PROSPECT OF GREATER TROUBLE SHOULD HELP US TO BEAR THE LESSER. Some of us are too ready to "give way" at once. But there is more power of endurance in all of us than we are ready to acknowledge to ourselves. After the latest wrench of the rack we cry out that we can bear no more; yet another and still another turn is given, and we do bear it. The prospect of this possibility should make us husband our strength. The very sight of danger may be a stimulus to courage by inspiring a heroic spirit. Life is generally pitched in too low a key, and thus men whine under slight smarts and shrink before mean difficulties. If the same men saw more imperative calls to energy and endurance, they would rouse themselves and call up latent powers which as yet lie slumbering unheeded.

III. FAILURE BEFORE LESSER TROUBLE SHOULD LEAD US TO SEEK BETTER MEANS FOR THE ENDURANCE OF THE GREATER. 1. It is *more important* that we should be able to bear the greater trouble. This is a more serious matter, and defeat under it involves a more overwhelming disaster. Therefore it is exceedingly needful to learn the lesson of our weakness before this has brought us into a more terrible condition of distress.

2. It is also *more difficult to endure* the severer strain.   The strength which is barely sufficient for the cares and toils of a quiet home life will fail utterly if a man has to contend with lions in the wild thickets of the lonely Jordan valley. If health breaks down before the soft breezes of summer, how will it stand before the frost and fog of winter? If the young man falls into vicious habits while under the protection of his father's home, what will become of him when he goes out into the world? If the prospect of sickness and earthly sorrow fill one with hopeless distress, how will he pass through the valley of the shadow of death? how will he endure death itself? 3. These questions should not make us despondent, but should drive us through self-diffidence to *seek the help of God*. Failure in small things will be good for us if it teaches us a wholesome lesson on our own weakness, and so inclines us to turn to a higher source of safety. Then we shall find that God's strength is made perfect in our weakness (2 Cor. xii. 9).

Ver. 7.—*The forsaken heritage.* I. GOD REGARDS HIS PEOPLE AS HIS HERITAGE. The temple was God's house, the Jews were God's heritage. The Church is now the habitation of the Spirit of God, and her members are God's possession. This fact implies: 1. That God dwells with his people. 2. That he takes delight in them. 3. That he may be expected to protect them from harm. 4. That he has rights over them and claims their submission to himself. 5. That his honour is concerned with his people's conduct, so that their wickedness is not a matter of indifference to him, but is an insult to his Name.

II. GOD MAY FORSAKE HIS HERITAGE. God's people have no such "vested interests" that nothing can destroy their claims upon him. The present enjoyment of God's favour is no guarantee that this will be perpetual. 1. History shows that God *has* forsaken his heritage in the past; *e.g.* the Jews, ancient Christian Churches of Asia and Africa, individual Christians who have fallen from the faith. 2. It is reasonable to expect that he *will* do this when honour and righteousness require it. Let us, therefore, not presume on the favour of God.

III. GOD ONLY FORSAKES HIS HERITAGE WHEN THAT HAS BECOME CORRUPT. God never leaves his people till they leave him. He is not changeable, capricious, arbitrary in his favours. His love never wanes, his grace never fails, his help and blessings are never limited. The change begins on man's side. It is found in rebellion against God. 1. In *self-will*. The heritage becomes like a lion of the forest—*i.e.* no longer tame, but swayed by its own wild passions. 2. In *evil-doing*. The lion is fierce and destructive —a beast of prey. 3. In *direct opposition to God*. The lion "cries out against" God.

IV. GOD'S HERITAGE IS IN A TERRIBLE CONDITION WHEN IT IS FORSAKEN BY HIM. Birds and beasts of prey come up to devour the heritage. 1. It needs *no positive act of God's* to bring desolation on his sinful people. If he but withdraw his protection, the natural evils of the world and the special evils which they have provoked will be enough to bring ruin on their heads. 2. God's people will *suffer in an especial way* by the withdrawal of the Divine presence. The heritage is "like a speckled bird." It is strange, and so it draws upon itself opposition. The Jews were a mark for the enmity of the heathen through the singularity of their national customs. Christians are often singled out for opposition from the world for similar reasons. If they have lost their peculiar protection, their peculiar position and nature will invoke a peculiar ruin.

Ver. 13.—*Profitless labour.* I. PUNISHMENT WILL CONSIST IN PART IN THE PROFIT-LESSNESS OF LABOUR. This will perhaps be the special punishment of industrious bad people. To them it will be peculiarly painful, for in proportion to the zest and earnest-ness with which any work is carried on will be the bitterness of disappointment when this is seen to fail. Thus the victorious general is punished by being robbed of his conquests, the statesman by having his political schemes frustrated, the inventor by finding his invention superseded or rendered futile, the literary man by seeing his pro-ductions treated with neglect.

II. LABOUR MAY BE GOOD IN ITSELF AND YET PROFITLESS. It need not be mis-taken in direction nor incompetent in execution. 1. It may be *real sowing*. "They have sown"—have not simply run uncertainly nor beaten the air with indefinite energy. 2. It may be the sowing of *good seed.* "They have sown wheat." 3. It may be *assiduous and arduous.* "They have put themselves to pain."

III. LABOUR WILL BE PROFITLESS IF IT BE CURSED BY GOD. "They are ashamed of their increase because of the fierce anger of Jehovah." 1. *We cannot succeed in our work without the blessing of God.* This is necessary, not only for those things in which we can do nothing and are wholly dependent on him, but also in regard to our own efforts. Man sows, but God must give the increase. We cannot order the seasons, command the weather, determine the germinating power of nature. The farmer is but the attendant of nature. The real work of the farm is done by nature, and nature is a name we give to the action of God. If, therefore, God did not follow with his work, the farmer might as well scatter sand of the desert over his fields as sow good wheat. So also all our labour depends on God's blessing for its fruitfulness. 2. *The curse of God will destroy the fruits of labour.* Tremendous destructive agencies are in his hands. He can send frost to nip the tender buds, drought to wither the growing plant, blight to destroy the filling ears, storms to beat down the ripe corn. Sickness, commercial disaster, wars, etc., may frustrate the wisest, ablest, most industrious efforts of men. Therefore let us learn (1) to live so that we dare ask for God's favour; (2) to labour at such work as God will approve; and (3) to seek the blessing of God upon our efforts (Ps. xc. 17).

Vers. 14—17.—*General punishment and general restoration.* I. PUNISHMENT IS GENERAL. It is not selective, it is impartially administered. 1. *The people of God do not escape.* If the Christian falls into sin, the Law of God must be vindicated on him at least as rigorously as on the worldly man. Judah had shared the sins of her neighbours; she must also share their punishment. If sin is general, so must be its penalties. No religious position which does not secure us against wickedness will protect us against its consequences. 2. *The godless do not escape.* The heathen nations are to suffer with Judah. Though they were sometimes the instruments in the hands of God for the chastisement of Judah, they were not on that account exonerated from blame for the bad motives of their conduct. The sin of others is no excuse for us in wronging them. The executioner of the law is himself subject to the law. They who do not admit the authority of God are not the less subject to his authority. Men who refuse to submit to the Law of God will be judged by that Law as certainly as those who have freely gone under its yoke. It is not for us to choose our government in spiritual things, but to submit to the one righteous government which God has set over all men. In the execution of this it will be found that all men have sufficient light to render them accountable for their actions, though the degree of their responsibility will vary with the degree of their knowledge.

II. RESTORATION IS GENERAL. This is offered to the heathen nations as well as to Judah. As general punishment must follow general sin, so general restoration will follow general repentance. Here, too, God is impartial. 1. This restoration is not the less perfect for each individual by being general. "Every man" is to come and each to his "own land" and his "own heritage." There are men who seem to fear the broadening of the mercies of God, lest they should become less valuable to each recipient, and so they would jealously narrow them to protect their full privileges for a few. Such ideas are not only basely selfish—since the holders of them quietly assume that they are among the few—they are dishonouring to the grace of God, which is exceeding abundant, with enough for all who need it. 2. The general character of the restoration is its most happy feature. It will mean the abolition of war, rivalry, jealousy, separation, and the enjoyment of peace and brotherhood, the realization of the glory of the unity of the race through harmony in the unity of faith. "Then shall they be built in the midst of my people." Thus through the great restoration, *i.e.* through the perfected redemption in Christ, we may look for the fulfilment of the great ideal human brotherhood. 3. The conditions of this restoration are the same for all, viz. (1) the compassion of God, and (2) repentance and amendment. They who taught Judah to serve Baal must learn with Judah to follow the true religion. But if this condition is not fulfilled, the restoration can never be enjoyed.

HOMILIES BY VARIOUS AUTHORS.

Vers. 1—4.—*Moral difficulties with the providence of God.* The tone of this address to Jehovah is strikingly contrasted with that to the men of Anathoth. To them he is as a lion or a brazen wall. To Jehovah he is as a fretful child, ignorant, wilful, perverse, and requiring to be corrected.

I. THE PROSPERITY OF THE WICKED A STUMBLING-BLOCK TO FAITH. (Vers. 1, 2.) David even is envious over this, and many a saint has felt its bitterness in his soul. That there are instances enough to make the idea plausible that wickedness is the best policy, we all know. The difficulties that beset the honest trader or the conscientious courtier and statesman are proverbial. And often just those measures which are most clearly condemned by Scripture and conscience appear to be the means most justified by the circumstances of the case. This view, however, is corrected by larger experience. It does not take all the facts within its scope, or it does not rightly interpret them. It is impossible for a mere outsider to judge of any one's actual happiness, or the private conditions which most powerfully affect the possession and enjoyment of wealth or high position. The teachings of history and of individual experience will in the end lead to the conclusion, " Better is little with the fear of the Lord than great treasure and trouble therewith " (Prov. xv. 16).

II. THE IMPULSE TO FORCE JEHOVAH'S HAND. (Ver. 3). This is the meaning of Jeremiah's imprecation. To one who sees by supernatural aid the tendencies of things, it must be very hard to refrain from this. Judgments that are justified to the moral nature sometimes appear to be mysteriously delayed. What would be well done had better be done quickly. But this is the presumption of the creature, the promptings of ignorance and not of faith. God can afford to wait. It is his character to have long patience, and the results more than justify this in the end. He will work out his purposes in his own way and in his own time, notwithstanding the impatience of his servants inquiring, " What or what manner of time ? " There is a species of tempting Providence closely connected with this in many spiritual men. They have the clearest conviction that certain things are right and proper for them to do, and, without consulting as to seasonableness or the best means for their accomplishment, they hasten to do them, and then expect that God will recoup them for the loss they incur or extricate them from the difficulties in which they have entangled themselves. This certainly is not waiting upon the Lord, but an arrogant assumption of his prerogatives. It was the principle that lay at the root of Moses' great transgression; and even the disciples had to be rebuked because they knew not what spirit they were of.

III. THE TONE OF THE PROPHET'S PRAYER. Superficially it appears reasonable, considering the character and position of those to whom he refers. And there is at any rate a formal recognition of the righteousness of God to begin with. It is evident, too, that the conscience of the prophet is without offence in the sight of God, and yet there can be no doubt that the language he adopts is not to be justified. He is carried away by excess of zeal, but it is zeal without knowledge, and he himself will be the first bitterly to regret his presumption. It is a perilous thing for any man to attempt to judge his fellows by infallible standards. One thing in the behaviour of the prophet was to be commended. He did not conceal these thoughts within himself. He says, " Let me talk with thee," conscious that in this openness of soul lay his moral safety. A few minutes' honest communion with God will tap many a festering sore and correct many a subtle error of spirit and life. The last lesson of Divine revelation is not severity but love.—M.

Vers. 5, 6.—*A prophet's foes they of his own household.* These two verses are related, and must be read together in order to get at their proper sense. The prophet had complained of the treachery and prosperous circumstances of the enemies of Jehovah; whereupon he was told that worse things were in store for him—that his own family would be his fiercest opponents. This was in a degree the lot of Christ; it is experienced by many of the true servants of God.

I. THE WORD OF GOD IS NOT ACCORDING TO THE WILL OF THE FLESH, AND THERE-

FORE MAY BE EXPECTED TO EXCITE HATRED AND OPPOSITION WHERE THAT ASSERTS ITSELF.

II. THE SERVANT OF GOD WILL OFTEN BE TRIED BY THE FAILURE AND DEFECTION OF HIS MOST CHERISHED FRIENDS.

III. IT BEHOVES ALL WHO ARE ENTRUSTED WITH DIVINE TRUTH TO ASK THEMSELVES WHAT IS THE GROUND OF THEIR CONFIDENCE.—M.

Vers. 7, 8.—*Leaving all for God.* (Naegelsbach is of opinion that the words of vers. 7—13 "are to be understood as having a double reference," *i.e.* both to the prophet's own feelings and to Jehovah's judgment. Zwingli and Bugenhagen consider that Jehovah begins to speak at "Go" or "Come," in ver. 9. There is evidently an intimate blending of the prophetic with the Divine consciousness throughout the whole passage.) A hard duty, but one often devolving upon faithful servants of Jehovah. Indeed, spiritually, it is the first condition of discipleship imposed by Christ. Only thus can the soul preserve its equipoise and integrity in what may be required of it. The Master will brook no rival.

I. THE REASONS FOR SUCH A SACRIFICE. It is possible that for one with the keen, affectionate nature of Jeremiah, much intercourse with his family and friends would have interfered with the performance of his duty. He was appointed to discharge an anomalous function, for which the greatest concentration of energy and spirit was required. Even though he had to weep as he spoke the words that God had commanded him, he must speak. His duty to the nation overshadowed or pushed into the background the claims of friends. So the follower of Christ may be subjected to discipline in providence, or to voluntary self-deprivation of a like kind by the demands of spiritual work. And it behoves all who labour in the cause of truth to hold themselves spiritually detached from those things and relations which might impede true usefulness.

II. KEEN PERSONAL SORROW IS FREQUENTLY OCCASIONED BY IT. That it was a real trial to Jeremiah there can be no doubt; and probably the special discovery made to him (ch. xi. 18 *seq.*,) was intended to facilitate the transfer of attachment to Jehovah. The endearing terms—"mine house," "mine heritage," "the dearly beloved of my soul," and the manner in which he repeats the history of his estrangement, prove how deeply the trial had affected him.

III. THEREBY IS TESTED THE LOYALTY OF THE SAINT TO GOD. In a question between one's friends and Jehovah, the settlement ought not to be doubtful to the mind of the saint. The reasons for withdrawal from entangling relations may not immediately appear, but the believer can with confidence leave them in the hands of God, by whom they will in due time be revealed. There is a danger in the midst of ordinary human relations that Jehovah shall be considered simply as an addition to our obligations, instead of being the supreme and all-modifying influence of our life. In proportion to the severity of the experience will be the consolations to be received.—M.

Vers. 14—17.—*Mercy and judgment.* In these verses we have one of the "larger words" which make the whole world's testament of salvation and life. The threatenings are stern and will be executed to the letter; but the promises seem to transcend the immediate occasion. A gate of hope and redemption was herein opened to multitudes who at that date were not included in the covenant of Israel. The conditions upon which their possible comprehension within the future Israel is based are moral and spiritual, and therefore truly universal.

I. THE GREATEST JUDGMENTS OF GOD UPON THE NEIGHBOURS OF ISRAEL BUT CORRESPONDED WITH THEIR CRIMES. That grave evils were inflicted upon the enemies of Israel cannot be denied. Multitudes were put to a painful death. Nations were uprooted, and human life appeared to be looked upon as an insignificant thing. In judging of this, however, it must be remembered that they had done and were ready to do similar things to Israel and Judah. The moral platform, too, upon which they lived has to be considered. Ages of depravity and barbarism, upon which higher appeals would have been utterly lost, had to be imaginatively impressed and overawed. And there were not wanting testimonies of conscience amongst the enemies of Israel themselves to justify this course. But—

II. EVEN IN BEING PUNISHED FOR THE SAKE OF ISRAEL, THEIR DESTINY WAS LINKED WITH HERS. If at first their lot would appear to be hard and inconceivably hopeless, yet in the end there can be no question that they were gainers by the association. In common life, with those whom they subdued they received manifold advantages, especially of a spiritual kind, and the choice was set before them of good as well as evil. On the principle, therefore, that it is better for one to suffer even severely at first if afterwards he may retrieve his position and attain to a higher and more desirable one through the initial discipline, it was better for these nations to be brought to book in this way for Israel's sake. Enemies to begin with, they might, and in many cases did, become friends and fellow-heirs of the promise.

III. APPARENT LENIENCY TOWARDS ISRAEL IS JUSTIFIED BY ULTERIOR PURPOSES OF UNIVERSAL BLESSING. As compared with her neighbours, it might appear as if one measure were meted out to her and another to them. But this is only contemporary and relative. The punishment inflicted has to be estimated by the spiritual deprivations which accompanied it. The deferring of Israel's hope must have been a keener sorrow than any mere temporal reverse. It must be remembered that through Israel, the seed of Abraham, all nations were to be blessed. To avert from her utter extinction was indirectly to ensure the greater benefit to the future. But that to be made to cease as a nation from the face of the earth would have been relatively less painful than many of the dispensations through which she had to pass, cannot but be allowed.

IV. IN THE MIDST OF DESERVED JUDGMENT THE FREE MERCY OF GOD IS THE MORE CONSPICUOUS. How unlooked for this promise concerning the future of Israel's enemies! The silver thread of hope traverses the dark labyrinth of judgment. It is only the wisdom of infinite Love that could so disentangle spiritual possibilities from such stupendous and widespread ruin. How glorious the mercy which can so assert itself! The only phrase that can describe the phenomenon is "grace has reigned." The individual sinner, in the midst of his deserved miseries, may take comfort from this. However great the wretchedness and ruin which he has brought upon himself, and however long continued his alienation from God, if he but turn now from his wickedness, a way of escape will be opened up for him through the sacrifice of Christ.—M.

Ver. 1.—Perplexing questions. "Wherefore doth the way of the wicked prosper?" etc. Unquestionably they very often do. Some of the reasons are—

I. THEY ARE MORE SHREWD. "The children of this generation are wiser than the children of light." They give more heed to the laws of success, are more alert to seize opportunities and to guard against those men and things which would work them harm. No amount of piety will compensate for inattention to the laws of success.

II. THEY ARE LESS SCRUPULOUS. Where success is thus won by some seemingly short cut which a godly man hesitates to take, it will not seldom be found, after a while, that the apparently long way round of the righteous was yet the nearest because the truest road. But meanwhile the ungodly appear to have the best of it.

III. THEIR ATTENTION IS MORE CONCENTRATED AND UNDIVIDED. The godly man cannot say in regard to the pursuit of this world's goods, "This one thing I do;" but the ungodly can. Whilst "not slothful in business," the Christian has also to "serve the Lord." Whilst a citizen of this world, he is also a citizen of another country, even a heavenly one, and by his faith he has avowed that he seeks that country. His attention must therefore be divided, as his who sows only to the flesh is not.

IV. THE LONG-SUFFERING OF GOD. The ungodly are his children, though ungrateful ones, and the heavenly Father would woo and win them back. Therefore in all gentleness he deals with them, making his sun to shine and his rain to descend on them as on his faithful children. The long-suffering of God is to lead to repentance.

V. TO TEST, IMPROVE, AND DECLARE THE FAITH OF THE GODLY. If righteousness were a royal road to riches, and faith infallibly led to fortune, where would be the room for trust in God? how would such trust be tested and deepened, and how would it ever be made manifest? The devil would have had reason for his taunt concerning Job, "Doth Job serve God for nought?" But that there may be such men as Job, heroes of the faith, pure, noble, God-fearing souls, saints indeed, God does at times let such men serve him for nought so far as this world is concerned, and hands over this world's wages to the devil, that he may with them bribe, as he in vain sought to bribe our

Lord, those who will " fall down and worship him." But that these questions may not perplex us, let us live day by day in view of the unseen and eternal, walking with God, holding communion with him; so shall our estimates of this world's prosperity be corrected, and we shall be able to behold with calmness the allotment of that prosperity to the ungodly rather than to ourselves.—C.

Ver. 3.—*Imprecatory prayers.* " Pull them out like sheep," etc. There are many of these. Some of them, like this one, are very terrible (cf. Ps. cix.; cxxxvii. 9, etc.). How are they to be understood? how justified? Of what use are they to us now? Questions like these cannot but be started in reading such prayers. The difficulty of them has been felt by almost every Christian and even humane reader. To get rid of such difficulty—

I. SOME HAVE SPIRITUALIZED THEM. The slaughter work which they call for is to be done, not on human bodies, but on human wickednesses, those inward and deadly foes which are so many and which hate us with cruel hatred. But whilst it is quite lawful to so make use of these petitions, it cannot be said that this is what they who first prayed them meant.

II. OTHERS HAVE TRIED TO TURN THEM SIMPLY INTO PROPHETIC PREDICTIONS—mere announcements of what God would do. But such alteration would never have been thought of but for the moral difficulty of letting them stand as they are. And the alteration is not permissible.

III. OTHERS, VERY MANY, HAVE EXPLAINED THEM ON THE GROUND OF THE IMPERFECT SPIRITUAL CONDITION OF GOD'S ANCIENT PEOPLE. " They knew," it is said, " no better. True, their prayers are wrong, unchristian, cruel, but they are to be excused because of the dim light, the very partial knowledge, of those days." But, in reply, it is clear that they were *not* ignorant; they had plain laws against revenge (cf. Lev. xix. 8; Exod. xxiii. 4, 5). And hence St. Paul, when arguing against revenge, cites the Old Testament, as in Rom. xii. 19, 20, quoting from Deut. xxxii. 35 and Prov. xxv. 21 (cf. also Prov. xx. 22; xxiv. 17). And Job (xxxi.) emphatically disavows both the act and thought of revenge; and so David (Ps. vii. 4, 5). And see David's conduct in regard to Saul twice. See, too, his gratitude to Abigail for holding him back from revenge (1 Sam. xxv.). And they had numerous laws enjoining mercy (cf. also Balaam's speech, given in Micah, " What doth the Lord require of thee, but to do justly, and to *love mercy*," etc. ?).

IV Others have said that such revengeful utterances are but the human element in the Old Testament writers—that they were not inspired when they thus speak. But David claims inspiration (2 Sam. xxiii. 1, 2). And the apostles claim it for him; and with especial reference to the hundred and ninth psalm, one of the most notable of these utterances (Acts i. 16). And they were composed for the temple service as acts of worship. Hengstenberg says of them, " They were from the first destined for use in the sanctuary. The sacred authors come forth under the full consciousness of being interpreters of the spiritual feelings of the community, organs of God for the ennobling of their feelings. They give back what in the holiest and purest hours of their life had been given to them." Hence we are compelled to regard these utterances as being only—

V. THAT WHICH IT WOULD BE RIGHT FOR A GOOD MAN, PLACED IN THE LIKE CIRCUMSTANCES, BOTH TO FEEL AND UTTER. Let it be remembered: 1. They knew nothing or but little of the great day of future judgment as we do. 2. The judgments implicated are all *temporal.* It can never be right to pray for the eternal damnation of any soul, and this they never do. 3. Many of the expressions are poetical. 4. These desires for the overthrow of their enemies were: (1) *Natural.* Resentment against wrong, anger on account of it, and desire that it may be punished, are implanted in us. Let us but place ourselves in their position. How did we feel in the time, *e.g.,* of the Indian Mutiny? (2) *Necessary.* In those fierce days a stern and fierce spirit was needed if any people were to hold their own at all (cf. Isaac Taylor, on ' Spirit of the Hebrew Poetry'). (3) *Based on the eternal truth of God's retributive justice.* God had declared by word and deed this attribute of his. Could it, then, be wrong that they should call on him to show himself what he had declared himself to be? (4) *Left to God to carry out.* " Unto God," says Jeremiah, " have I revealed [or, ' committed '] my cause. (5) *And in the New Testament we have some similar utterances.* (Cf. Matt. xxiii. 11.) (6) *And we ourselves in war*—which we all allow to be at times lawful—*act on these very principles,* and do for ourselves what the Old Testament saints only besought God to do. Hence conclude that, in like circumstances and for similar reasons, such prayers as these are not evil. What the New Testament condemns is revenge for private personal injuries, for persecution when suffered for the gospel's sake; but not war for defensive purposes, and therefore not the stern spirit which is essential to war. And one practical lesson from all such utterances is that they reflect what exists in God—a determined and fierce hatred against wickedness—and therefore they awaken a salutary fear of that vengeance and an earnest desire to "flee from the wrath to come."—C.

Ver. 5.—*Failure in little things.* "If thou hast run with the footmen," etc.? The prophet of God was weary hearted. Like Job, like the writer of the thirty-seventh psalm, like John the Baptist, he was sore perplexed at God's dealings. The wicked prospered, the righteous were cast down. Hence he sadly asks, "Wherefore doth," etc.? (ver. 1). Now, God answers such questionings as these in different ways. Sometimes by showing his servant the true state of the ungodly, making him "to understand their end." Sometimes by revealing to the righteous the vast superiority of their portion over that of the ungodly. Sometimes by gently soothing the ruffled spirit. At other times, as here, by rousing rebuke and sharp remonstrance, bidding him bethink himself, if he broke down under these comparatively small trials, how would he bear up when much more terrible ones had to be endured? If running with "footmen" was too much for him, then how would he "contend" with the swift "horses"? If he could feel secure only in a quiet land (see Exposition), how would he do in a region full of peril like that of the jungle-land, the lair of the lion and other fierce beasts of prey, which stretched along the banks of the Jordan? Greater trials were to come to him than he had as yet known; how would he meet them if he failed in the presence of these lesser ones? Now, in applying the principle here laid down, note—

I. GOD PUTS UPON US FIRST THAT WHICH IS LESS, AND AFTERWARDS THAT WHICH IS GREATER. In all departments of life. 1. Our *physical powers* are taxed first lightly, afterwards more heavily. 2. So our *mental powers;* the easy lessons first, then those that are more difficult. 3. So with our *moral life;* temptation comes "as we are able to bear it." 4. So in *business life;* the lesser responsibilities and duties first. 5. And so in the *spiritual life;* God does not expect from the young beginner that which the veteran in his service can alone render.

II. AND THE LESS IS TO PREPARE US FOR THE GREATER. Childhood is to prepare for youth, that for manhood, and all our life here for our everlasting life yonder. But—

III. FAILURE IN THAT WHICH IS LESS CARRIES WITH IT FAILURE IN THAT WHICH IS GREATER ALSO. This is the law implied by the question of ver. 5. And it is a universal law. Therefore we may ask this question, "If thou hast run," etc.? 1. Of such as are *unable to bear the lesser trials of life.* What unmanly complaining we often hear, though in the presence of sorrows compared with which their own are as nothing! If they fail here and now, what will they do there and then? 2. *Of such as find a little prosperity do them harm.* This is the reason why many are kept poor. God sees that they would be puffed up, spiritually injured in many ways, if worldly prosperity were granted them; and hence he keeps it away. A little was given, as if to test them, but they could not bear it; and hence in God's love they were not tried again. 3. *Of such as fall before slight temptation.* If conscience is set aside and trampled on in lesser matters, it will be served no better in such as are greater. 4. *Of such as are looking for a more convenient season than now to yield themselves to God.* Will the opposition of your own heart, of the world around you, of the power which habit has over you, become less? But if you yield thereto now, how will it be when all these have become, as they will, more powerful still?

IV. BUT THE REVERSE OF THIS LAW IS TRUE ALSO. Victory over the less will lead to victory over the greater. By the successful running with the footmen we shall be prepared for the severer contest with horses. Hence little trials borne well prophesy our bearing well such as may be greater, should God please to send them. And if, when entrusted with but a few things, we are found faithful in them, the Lord whom we serve is likely to make us "ruler over many things." The lesser temptation resolutely withstood prepares for withstanding the greater when it comes; and the overleaping of the frail barriers that now may oppose our self-surrender to Christ ensures that nothing at any future time shall be able to keep us back from him, nothing shall "separate us from the love of Christ."—C.

Vers. 7—13.—*The hiding of God's face.* Here is a most terrible condition of things set forth. It may be taken as telling of the calamities which ensue when God hides his face from his people. It is terrible every way. Because—

I. OF HIM BY WHOM HIS FACE IS HIDDEN. It is God. We feel such conduct from our fellow-men according to our estimate of the person who manifests it. Now, all these facts which make the hiding of his face grievous to us meet in God—righteousness, goodness, wisdom, power. Were he devoid of these, could we question the existence of any of them in him, we could bear with more equanimity his hiding his face from us.

II. OF THOSE FROM WHOM HIS FACE IS HIDDEN. Had they been enemies all along, it would have been taken as a matter of course; that he should have regarded them with favour would never have been expected. Or had they been strangers and aliens to him, then, too, his favour would not have been looked for. Or had that favour never been known or enjoyed, then its absence would not have been felt, nothing that they had been accustomed to would have been missed. But the reverse of all this is the truth. They had been counted by him as friends, as dear children, as precious in his sight; and he had been wont to cause his face to shine upon them. See the endearing epithets by which he describes them. He had counted them as "the dearly beloved of his soul" (ver. 7), "his portion," "his pleasant portion," etc. (vers. 8—10). How dark, therefore, must be the frown of God to such! how intolerable to them his displeasure!

III. OF THAT WHICH ACCOMPANIED THE HIDING OF HIS FACE. There is withdrawal: 1. *From the sanctuary.* "I have forsaken mine house." The customary services went on, but the glow, the unction, the power of them had departed. The place where his honour dwelt, the dearly beloved of his soul, was forsaken by him. 2. *From the people.* His heritage was no longer pleasant to him; he delighted not to dwell amongst them. All that joy, strength, prosperity, which belonged to them when God was amongst them had departed. 3. *From the land.* "The whole land is made desolate." In the outward circumstances and surroundings of the people the effect of God's hiding his face from them became terribly manifest. And there has come a terrible revulsion of feeling on the part of God towards them (see vers. 8, 9). And not only his mind, but his hand, his providence, is awfully changed towards them. He calls on their enemies to come (ver. 9). And they come (ver. 12). And the ruin is complete: "The sword of the Lord shall devour from the one end of the land even to the other" (ver. 12). All their own plans—their sowing of wheat (ver. 13)—for their own good are miserably defeated, they "reap thorns." Thus the inward displeasure of God manifests itself oftentimes in the outward circumstances of a man or nation.

IV. OF THAT ON ACCOUNT OF WHICH GOD'S FACE IS HIDDEN. It was "because no man layeth it to heart" (ver. 11). The lesser judgments of God, his repeated warnings, had been disregarded—hearing they heard not, seeing they saw not; and hence all this. Had the cause of their woe been their misfortune, the result of mistake, or ignorance, or lack of timely counsel, then there would have been some element of consolation amid all they had to suffer. But to add to their distress was the ever-present reflection, "It was all our own fault; we brought it all on ourselves." With what intense hatred, therefore, should we look upon all that grieves the Spirit of God! and with what earnest haste should we endeavour to return unto God, if we have wandered from him! These miseries which beset those from whom God hides his face are his loving scourgings whereby we may be led to say, "I will arise and go to my Father, and will say unto him, Father, I have sinned," etc.—C.

Ver. 9.—*The speckled bird.* A great preacher relates the following incident:—He says, "I had during my early ministry to preach one evening at a neighbouring village, to which I had to walk. After reading and meditating all day, I could not meet with the right text. Do what I would, no response came from the sacred oracle, no light flashed from the Urim and Thummim. I prayed, I meditated, I turned from one verse to another; but the mind would not take hold, or I was, as John Bunyan would say, 'much tumbled up and down in my thoughts.' Just then I walked to the window and looked out. On the other side of the narrow street in which I lived I saw a poor, solitary canary bird upon the slates, surrounded by a crowd of sparrows, who were all pecking at it as if they would tear it to pieces. At that moment the verse came into my mind, 'Mine heritage is unto me as a speckled bird; the birds round about are against her.' I walked off with the greatest possible composure, considered the passage during my long and lonely walk, and preached upon the peculiar people and the persecutions of their enemies, with freedom and ease to myself, and I believe with comfort to my rustic audience. The text was sent to me, and if the ravens did not bring it, certainly the sparrows did." But while the use here made of the text is a legitimate one, it certainly is not its meaning. That, therefore, as in all cases, has the priority of claim to be considered, and we note how it tells—

I. OF WHAT MAY BE THE RELATION OF GOD'S HERITAGE TO HIMSELF. He who had once so loved them as to call them by all endearing names, "the dearly beloved of my soul" (ver. 7), "mine heritage" (ver. 8), "my portion," "my pleasant portion" (ver. 10), and whose hand had been wont to follow the dictates of his heart, had now completely changed towards them. His love had departed, and in place thereof had come aversion and anger (cf. Homily on vers. 7—13). Sad as it is, this similitude shows what may come to be the relation between God and his people. "Therefore have I hated it" (ver. 8), saith God. We cannot but inquire the cause of so terrible a change. It was because "no man layeth it to heart" (ver. 11); no man, i.e. would give heed to God's words and signs of warning, but went on in sin just the same. They would not repent, but persisted in their evil ways. But we may take the words also as suggesting—

II. WHAT WILL BE THE RELATION OF GOD'S PEOPLE TO THE WORLD. The world will hate the Church. "The birds around" will come "against her." Sometimes it seems as if it were not so. For unquestionably there are many portions of God's heritage that the world does not persecute. The age of martyrdom is over. God has shut the lions' mouths. He puts his fear upon the world; they see that God is with his people; or they are partly in sympathy with them. But at other times it is true as it was with that poor bird amongst the sparrows. "Well may we pity a godly wife bound to an ungodly husband; alas! full often a drunkard, whose opposition amounts to brutality. A tender, loving spirit, that ought to have been cherished like a tender flower, is bruised and trodden underfoot, and made to suffer till the heart cries out in grief. We little know what lifelong martyrdoms many pious women endure. Children also have to bear the same when they are singled out by Divine grace from depraved and wicked families. Only the other day there came under my notice one who loves the Lord. I thought if she had been a daughter of mine I should have rejoiced beyond all things in her sweet and gentle piety; but the parent said, 'You must leave our house if you attend such and such a place of worship. We do not believe in such things, and we cannot have you about us if you do.' And nobody knows what godly working men often have to put up with from those among whom they labour. Frequently the working men are great tyrants in matters of religion. If a man will drink with them and swear with them, they will make him their companion; but when a man comes out to fear God, they make it very hard for him." Yes; God's heritage is in the eyes of the world "as a speckled bird," etc. But let God's servants remember, when they are thus tried, that they have fellowship with Christ. They were forewarned of it; Christ did not conceal the cross from them. "Behold," he said, "I send you forth as sheep amongst wolves." But they cannot do you much harm (cf. Matt. 10). The day is soon coming when their power will be for ever destroyed. Meanwhile, keep away from them as much as you lawfully may. Do not needlessly provoke them; whilst harmless as doves, be wise as serpents also. Do not be like them, and do not be afraid of them. Go not alone with them; have the Lord Jesus ever with you, and you will be able to meet them in all holy and courageous wisdom and meekness. If the persecution be very great, ask the Lord to place you somewhere else, if so it may be. And till he does, and always, pray for them—Sauls may become Pauls.

III. IT IS A RELATION IN WHICH GOD'S HERITAGE MUST STAND EITHER TO GOD OR TO THE WORLD. There cannot be compromise. "No man can serve two masters." "If any man love the world, the love of the Father is not in him." "The friendship of the world is enmity against God." "Ye *cannot* serve God and mammon." Whose aversion, then, will you have, since that of God or of the world you must have? Your peril is not that you should deliberately choose to have the aversion of God rather than that of the world, but that you should seek to compromise. But that also is impossible. In coming to a decision be sure you take eternity into view, and may God who compels you to make this great choice help you—as he will if you seek his grace—to choose, like Moses, "rather to suffer affliction with," etc.—C.

Vers. 14—17.—*The tide that has no ebb, but ever flows.* Such is the grace of God.

I. IT HAS NO EBB. It seemed to be going back in regard to those to whom the prophet wrote. What terrible calamities were threatened and also came! How dark the face of God seemed towards them! But they were to be restored Ver. 14, "I will pluck out the house of Judah from among them." And even yet God's mercies to his ancient people are not done. Another restoration is to be theirs. "The gifts and calling of God are without repentance" (cf. Rom. xi.). And Israel is but a type of humanity at large. God has not created all men in vain. Man, as such, is precious in his sight; "the dearly beloved of his soul." And notwithstanding the dark records of human history—man's sins and sorrows—God's love is upon him still. He "so loved the world," and that love has not ceased. The tide of his grace has not ceased to flow. But there may be barriers in the way of its onward progress. Human sin is such. It is so in nations and in individuals, and not only do men by their sin bar for themselves the inflow of God's grace, but for those who come after them. And to break through and break down these barriers is a work of time. Ages and generations may elapse. In mountainous regions you may often see a river flowing through what was manifestly once the bed of a vast lake. But after the lapse of long ages the waters rose and burst through the barriers that held them back from the valleys and plains beneath, and from that moment the river has flowed on in the channel in which we now see it. So will it be with God's grace to mankind at large. Its waters shall rise, and by-and-by the rocky barriers of man's sins, and all that man's sin has built up, shall be broken through and broken down, and then "the knowledge of the Lord shall cover the earth as the waters cover the seas." The tide has never gone back ; it has been but delayed. Wise and holy fatherly love is at the root of all things, and is the key which unlocks, as none else will, all the problems of life. That love held his people down to the sufferings they had to endure until the evil mind departed from them, and so it holds humanity down and individual souls down to what they have to endure until they be changed in the spirit of their minds. But all this while the tide of his gracious purpose is rising, and soon that which hinders shall be taken out of the way. Judah was to go into captivity, but Judah was to be "plucked out" from thence, and that is but a pattern of God's dealings with us all.

II. But not only has this tide no ebb, IT FLOWS ON EVERMORE. Not only was Judah to be restored, but forgiveness and salvation are offered to her "evil neighbours" (ver. 14), who had done her harm. God's purpose in the election of some is not the reprobation of the rest, but the salvation of all. "In thee and in thy seed shall all the nations of the earth be blessed." The "evil neighbours" had corrupted Judah (ver. 16), and they had persecuted her (ver. 14); but now the set time to favour them also had come, and salvation is offered to them (ver. 16). Thus the tide of God's grace flows on evermore, and where it seemed as if it would never come. From all which we may learn : The redemption of the world is the purpose of God. But every nation and people in their own order. The elect are the firstfruits; those nearest to them come next. If any refuse, their national life is lost (ver. 17). But the unfaithfulness of man shall not make the faith of God of none effect. Let us take this tide at its flood ; it will lead us on to life eternal. It is *the* "tide in the affairs of men" which calls us to launch forth upon it, that it may bear us to never-ending bliss.—C.

Vers. 1—5.—*The prophet's complaint.* The writings of the prophets are often as much historic as they are prophetic; historic of personal as well as national experiences, of inward thoughts and emotions as of outward incidents. In tracing the current of events, the writers disclose the workings of their own spirits, and in expounding and vindicating God's ways with Israel or with other nations, they indicate the method of his dealings with themselves. This was singularly true of Jeremiah, and we have here a striking illustration of it. This passage probably marks the time when the people of his own native city of Anathoth, and even his kindred, his "brethren of the house of his father," could no longer bear his faithful rebukes, and he was compelled to take refuge in Jerusalem (ch. xi. 21; xii. 6). Consider (1) *the prophet's state of mind* as here made manifest; (2) the meaning and force of *God's remonstrance.*

I. THE PROPHET'S STATE OF MIND. It contains a singular mixture of good and evil, thoughts and emotions both noble and base. So conflicting and even contradictory sometimes are the voices of the truest human heart. This outburst of hostility from the men of Anathoth has plunged his spirit in confusion. Like a ship checked in its course, with its sails taken aback by a sudden squall, its guiding principles and powers are for a while disturbed, and its balance lost. Note different elements of feeling. 1. *Deep perplexity.* He cannot reconcile the events that are taking place and the seeming prosperity of the wicked with the known rectitude of the Divine character. "Righteous art thou, O Lord; . . . yet let me talk with thee of thy judgments," etc. Why this "yet"? If he is thus convinced of God's righteousness, why this wish to reason with him? There is a conflict between unbelief and faith, between the disposition to judge by sensible appearances and the desire to judge by eternal principles. And the difficulty is aggravated by the fact that the designs of the wicked seem to succeed because God smiles on them. "Thou hast planted them," etc. This fact of successful wickedness under the wing of a Divine Providence is the deep and awful mystery that has been a source of perplexity and trouble to thoughtful men in every age. David felt the full force of it (Ps. lxxiii.). His "feet had well-nigh slipped" because of it, "until he went into the sanctuary of God," and then the problem was solved. It is when we get away from our carnal reasonings into the sanctuary of spiritual contemplation and the realm of faith that we can alone hope to understand these things. When God's ways most perplex and confound us we must keep fast hold of right thoughts about himself. His judgments are a mighty deep. But as beneath the heaving, storm-tossed ocean there lie great mountains of the solid world, so does God's righteousness underlie all the agitations and conflicting phases of human history. Faith in that will give us rest and peace. 2. *The sense of his own rectitude.* "But thou, O Lord, knowest me," etc. This is not the utterance of vain self-righteousness. A "conscience void of offence," the persuasion that our purpose is pure and our hearts right with God, is never to be confounded with spiritual pride. Without a shadow of vain-glory you may know well that you are better than many around you, and could not do as they do. There are times in a man's history when nothing but the sense of personal rectitude can sustain him. When calamity comes upon him, when he falls, perhaps, from some high position and is cast forth upon the world homeless and friendless, what a bitter ingredient in his cup is an accusing conscience! On the other hand, he may defy everything to rob him of his peace, and, like Job, may preserve his soul in serenity in spite of blighted hopes and withered joys, a taunting world and scornful friends, if he can say, "My witness is in heaven, and my record is on high" (Job xvi. 19). 3. *The spirit of revenge.* "Pull them out," etc. He would fain antedate the day of slaughter. This may have been an unguarded, momentary outburst of impatient resentment. But it was none the less evil and irreligious. Why was he rebuked for it if it were not wrong? (Similar examples in Moses, Elijah, Jonah, the disciples James and John.) Let us beware how we take God's judgments into our own hands. "Vengeance belongeth unto me; I will recompense, saith the Lord" (Rom. xii. 19). Never let us speak as if the punishment of the wicked, which is the Lord's "strange work," were regarded by us with complacency. 4. *Human sympathy.* "How long shall the land mourn," etc.? The prophet is true to himself here. He grieves for the misery inflicted on the innocent by the wrong-doing of others. The humane heart groans with the "groaning creation," and sighs for the time when all shall be renewed. He who "endured the contradiction of sinners against himself" teaches us to take upon ourselves, as he did, the sins and sorrows of the world.

II. THE DIVINE REMONSTRANCE. "If thou hast run with the footmen," etc. (For explanation of these references, see Exposition.) There is extreme gentleness in this rebuke. It is interesting to note how uniformly gentle the reproofs God administered to the prophets were. Two things are noticeable in this remonstrance. 1. *It refers to Jeremiah's want of courage*, and says nothing about his mental perplexity. We are reminded that the best cure for our morbid conditions of thought and feeling is that we should brace up the energies of our soul to bear whatever Providence may see fit to lay upon us, and valiantly to contend for the cause of truth and goodness in the face of all opposition. 2. *It speaks of severer trials that are in store for him in the future.* Life is for us all a course of Divine discipline, in which all lesser tests of faith and fortitude are intended to prepare us for sterner conflicts and nobler victories.—W.

Vers. 1—4.—*The prophet puzzled by the prosperity of the wicked.* I. HOW THIS PUZZLE ARISES. It arises from the presence of a number of facts together, the coexistence of which the prophet finds it impossible to explain. 1. *There is his assurance as to the character of Jehovah.* He speaks confidently as to the Divine righteousness. Observe how it is the thing that he starts with. All our doubts will get cleared up in the end, however long the process may be, if only we start with the sure practical conviction that Jehovah is, and that he is righteous. "Thy righteousness is like the great mountains." And as one would not doubt the existence of them, so neither must one doubt the righteousness of God. Jeremiah could not, but become acquainted with the character of one who was so constantly manifesting himself to him. Besides, there was the history of Jehovah's consistent and glorious dealings in the past to fall back upon, and it was presumed that Jeremiah was well acquainted with that history. If it had not been so, there would have been little use in referring him to Moses and Samuel (ch. xv. 1). It was no earthly governor swayed about by all sorts of motives with whom Jeremiah had to deal. 2. *From the manifest wickedness of the wicked and their equally manifest prosperity.* Jeremiah has no more doubt about the character and deserts of his enemies than he has about the character of his God. He speaks as if there were some close connection between the wickedness and the prosperity, and as if the unscrupulous man could boast himself without contradiction being possible as to the results of his audacity. It seems to the prophet as if there should be an instant and complete stoppage of all this pride and deceit. 3. *From some special advantages they have had not of their own procuring.* "Thou hast planted them." This is a way of indicating that all outward circumstances favoured men when they started on their knavery. They were well placed for the attainment of prosperity, and the same kind of outward circumstances had continued. They had grown and brought forth fruit. It seemed that if they had been planted at random, planted anywhere else, these wicked purposes would have been comparatively fruitless. Probably Jeremiah's notion was that *God* located every man in his starting-place, and if so, it is easy to see how such a consideration would increase his perplexity. 4. *From the hypocrisy of the wicked.* While Jeremiah sees only too plainly their wickedness, they pretend to be righteous and devout and God-honouring. The name of Jehovah is, perhaps, oftener on their lips than on the lips of the prophet himself. They may be full of zeal for the temple, for incense, for offering; they may even make capital by reproaching Jeremiah for his utterances on these subjects (ch. vi. 20; vii.). 5. *From the suffering they inflict on the land.* The wicked may prosper, and yet in their very prosperity suck away the life-blood of a nation. That is no true prosperity where the rich get richer and the poor get poorer. The words of the prophet suggest that there was grinding and rapacity, and thus no encouragement to the tiller of the soil to do his best. Truly have the fruits of the earth been called " kindly," for they are kindly to one who will diligently cultivate. But no one will diligently cultivate if the fruits of his toil are to come to one who reaps where he has not sown, and gathers where he has not strawed. 6. *From the scorn these wicked heap on the prophet himself.* " They said, He shall not see our last end." Of course we are not to suppose that the prophet was influenced here by considerations of personal resentment. Doubtless what chiefly moved him was to maintain his sacred work. These wicked men were like the scoffers of whom Peter speaks, walking after their own lusts, and saying, " Where is the promise of his coming ? "

II. HOW THE PUZZLE WAS TO BE DIMINISHED. By the time we reach the end of the Book of Jeremiah, God's judgments on all the prosperous wicked are amply manifested. When Jeremiah came to close the roll of his prophecies, and reflect on all that God had said in them and done even in Jeremiah's own time and under his own eyes, and when further he recollected his own hasty complaints, he would surely feel that a trustful and patient waiting for the full event would have been much wiser. Perhaps no prophet ever saw more of the accomplishment of his own prophecies than Jeremiah did. He did see the end of those who, in their pride and fatness, had reviled him. Let us be true and faithful to what the Spirit of truth has made known to us as the will of God, and everything in the way of vindication will come if we only wait. We must not mistake precipitation and impetuosity for zeal. God's people have to wait for their own perfection and their own reward; they have also to wait for the execution of God's judgment against his enemies. Through all the centuries that have passed since Jeremiah's complaint here, oppression and robbery have continued, and they continue still. And as we think of such things, it will be well for us if we can end our thoughts where Jeremiah began : "Righteous art thou, O Lord."—Y.

Vers. 7—11.—*The inheritance that has lost its charms.* I. WE HAVE HERE REGRETFUL THOUGHTS OF THE PAST. We can see what the prophet once hoped and desired. Not only what he had hoped and desired in those dreams of youth before God had touched his heart and claimed the service of his lips, but also what he had hoped and desired since becoming a prophet. Dear as Anathoth with its inhabitants may have been before, it would become dearer still when he thought of impending calamities to the whole land. There are cherished objects indicated by the words "house," "inheritance," and "desire of the soul." What is precisely indicated by these words it is of course impossible for us to say ; but any of us, thinking for a little of the objects that lie nearest to our hearts, will comprehend that the prophet is here speaking of separations he had found it very hard to achieve. He did not pretend that alienation from house and heritage and kindred was an easy thing. Then we must bear in mind that the references here have a deeper meaning than to Jeremiah's purely human relations. It is pretty well agreed that the full truth of these words is only reached when we think of Jeremiah as representative of Jehovah. God's separation from his people was the thing of most serious moment. God had a house ; God had an inheritance ; God had a beloved object, an object of desire (Deut. xxxii. 9). God had been with these people now for many centuries, and there was much to make them precious in his sight. They were the seed of Abraham, the descendants of those whom he had delivered from Egypt and guided through the wilderness into the land where they now dwelt. Things might have been so different, if only the people had been of a different spirit. There was no necessity in the nature of things that Israel should have become so idolatrous, so hostile to Jehovah, any more than there was necessity that Anathoth should become a place of mortal snares and perils to the prophet. What a fall there was from the triumphal march across Jordan, under Joshua, to the march at the heels of a conqueror all the way from Jerusalem to Babylon! Again we say things might have been so different. That which God had cherished might have become a rich earthly manifestation of his glory. The vineyard on a fruitful hill might have become what it was intended to be—a fruitful vineyard.

II. PRUDENT AND DECISIVE ACTION IN PRESENT NECESSITIES. Natural affection must yield to spiritual duty. Jeremiah might doubtless have kept the good will of his kinsfolk, such as it was worth, if only he had been able and disposed to remain silent as a prophet. Happily there is no hesitation, there is no sign of its even being possible. Let us seize on every record that illustrates how strong, how immovable, those become who put their trust in God. The path that Jeremiah had to tread was trodden afterwards by Jesus himself. His kinsfolk would have interfered with main force to stop what they reckoned the vagaries of one who was beside himself; and so as far as Jesus could be said to have had any abiding-places, they were in Capernaum and Bethany, not in Nazareth. So with Jeremiah. He had to give up all that on earth he had any natural claim to, and throw himself on God, and those who perchance might help him for the sake of God. Nor was he disappointed. There is certainly no indication here of the compensations that came to the prophet for his fidelity and self-denial. It is hardly the place to mention them. But we do see this clearly, that when once the lower is relinquished, decisively relinquished, and a higher station taken up, the lower is seen to be lower. Temporal and natural relations, that count for so much when one is in the midst of them, are seen then in their comparative unimportance. Let it not be supposed that, after cutting off the right hand, one must of necessity wait for the fulness of life eternal to get anything like compensation. The compensation begins in the very act of self-sacrifice. Does not the prophet here say that what had once been so loved had come to put on such a threatening, maleficent aspect that he also had come to hate it? What has had to be relinquished for Christ only leaves so much the more of opportunity to grasp and to use the spiritual wealth which is in him.—Y.

Ver. 10.—*Shepherds where they ought not to be.* The words of this verse suggest a degradation of the vineyard, which may have been accomplished in one of two ways. The prophet may have been indicating the miseries of his country by a scene from real life, a literal spoiling of a vineyard by the literal flocks of careless or unscrupulous shepherds. Either a vineyard becomes neglected by its owner, and so lays itself open to the inroads of a roaming flock, or the shepherd comes, and, regardless of all right, breaks his way in by sheer force. In a land where there were both vineyards and flocks, nothing was more likely than that the oppression of the weak by the strong should be illustrated in some such way. And when we pass to the figure, recollecting that Israel was reckoned as a flock and its rulers as shepherds, then we begin to discern how these rulers are once more to be blamed. Neglect is the least thing to be laid at their door; they are chargeable with even more than neglect, even with high-handedness and utter lack of regard for neighbourly rights. These rulers are charged in other places for their want of fidelity in making due provision for the flock; here, while they make a sort of provision, they do it in a way which indicates how little they think of the real interests of their sheep. 1. *There is presented to us here a picture of two occupations, two possessions, both right in themselves.* It is not the robber who desolates this vineyard, the man to whom violence is an ordinary element. It is the shepherd, the man whose work is every whit as useful and commendable in its way as that of the vinedresser. God made the surface of his earth for his creatures, animate and inanimate, and there is an appointed and sufficient place for all. There are pasture-grounds where the sheep may grow and by its wool provide clothing for men, and there are the tillage-grounds whence come the corn, the oil, the wine, which are equally for the sustenance and pleasure of men. 2. *The mischief which may be done by a selfish occupation with one's own interests.* In one sense the shepherd could not be too careful about his own interest. He had food to search for, his flock to keep together, wanderers to restore, wild beasts to drive away. This was all very difficult, but the difficulty should have taught him to look sympathetically at the interests of others. The vinedresser would have in his own way as hard and anxious a life as the shepherd. There are difficulties enough in human existence from things which cannot be helped. Why should they be added to by the thoughtlessness of those who can be thoughtful if only they care to be, unselfish if only they care to be? A shepherd with the heart of a brother in him would be doubly careful when he came near a vineyard. It was easy for his heedless sheep to do a damage which, once done, no amount of regret could undo. 3. *Heedlessness of the interests of others works to our own serious damage in the end.* The position of these kings of Israel and Judah had to be set forth by more than one image. Their people had to be looked at in the aspect of a flock and of a vineyard, and so indeed each one of us has to look at his own life in more aspects than one. A narrow, one-sided view is ruinous; it may have temporary advantages, but they are soon gone, and then the full folly of short-sightedness will appear. These kings lived a self-indulgent life, and gathered round them a favoured few, whom they enriched and pampered in like manner. Meanwhile the land was suffering from oppression and injustice, and these great ones advancing to an overthrow, the completeness of which would be intensified by the remembrance of past follies. That is the truly prudent man who is always looking beneath the surface and beyond the present. To find an easy, ready-to-hand way out of present difficulties may be the surest way of making future difficulties altogether unmanageable.—Y.

Ver. 13.—*Sowing wheat and reaping thorns.* It is true that "whatsoever a man soweth, that shall he also reap." It is also true that "men cannot gather grapes of thorns, or figs of thistles." And at the same time it is emphatically true that men may sow wheat and yet reap thorns. The contradiction is only on the surface; it suggests inquiry, and the further the inquiry is continued, the more it is seen what serious truth is contained in the prophet's statement. Consider, then, the statement in two aspects.

I. AS SHOWING THAT MEN DO NOT REAP WHAT THEY HAVE SOWN. They sow wheat. It is surely not to a *mere semblance* of wheat-sowing that the prophet here refers. It is true that men sow unconsciously the seeds of misery, of a bitter and shameful harvest, the gathering of which they cannot escape. It is true that the men who consult present pleasure and the present appearances of things are every day sowing evil seed, without having the least suspicion that they are sowing at all. It is even true that men may be so led away by errors of education, or habits received by mere tradition, as to go on all life through in what they suppose to be right, but which nevertheless is utterly wrong. All this, however, is rather to be classed under the sowing of tares which are like wheat. The prophet is here dealing with the sowing of something really good, and something capable of truly satisfactory results. The truth he would indicate is more fully set forth in our Lord's parable of the four different kinds of seed. The seed which the sower went forth to sow was *all good seed*. The seed which fell in the good ground was not one whit better than what fell by the wayside. We see, therefore, that a large part of good seed is not reaped. Just according to the area comprised by the terms "trodden ground," "stony ground," and "thorny ground," is there force in the statement that wheat has been sown, and yet wheat not reaped. The prophet's reference is to the great, unquestionable, and peculiar privileges of Israel. The Lord had not dealt with any nation as he had dealt with Israel. Other nations had found rising up amongst them men of genius and worldly wisdom and originating power; but no other nation of antiquity shows in its history any man like a Moses, a Samuel, or a David, or even the very least of the prophets. We look upon Israel, therefore, as representative of all who have enjoyed abundance of religious privileges, of those whose early days have been in the midst of religious instructions and associations. Yet out of this very class the worldliest of the worldly have come. For all the truth that has been bountifully sown not one stalk of result is to be seen. Mark that what is to be first noticed is the negation of good results. Is it not a sad thing that one should have to read first of all of so much Divine truth coming down from heaven, so many glorious revelations, so many angelic visits, so many inspired prophets and witnesses, and then, on the other hand of so little manifest result in regenerated and purified human lives?

II. AS SHOWING THAT MEN REAP WHAT THEY HAVE NOT SOWN. Thorns, of course, could not be reaped unless thorns were planted, but no one would deliberately plant thorns. That would be to say, at the very beginning of one's possibilities of choice, "Evil, be thou my good." But the heart of man, rich, deep, inexhaustible ground as it is, has come under a curse of which Gen. iii. 18 is but a shadowy suggestion. The vicious willingness of the ground to bring forth thorns and thistles every husbandman knows full well. Ch. iv. 3 needs to be borne in mind: "Sow not among thorns." Men shrink from the toil and suffering needful to uproot the false and the injurious, and still more difficult do they find the watchfulness and determination which would prevent thorns from getting hold at all; and yet it is perfectly certain that thorns, allowed to continue, will in time destroy anything like abiding fruit from the good seed. Note the important difference between the tares and the thorns. The wheat and the tares grow together till the harvest; then the tares are easily separated and burnt. The *perfected* wheat is as easily separated and *garnered*. But the thorns choke the wheat, and there is never any real gathering at all. Wheat that does not reach maturity is worth nothing *as wheat*. It cannot be put into the garner. Hence the *keeping down* of the thorns is every whit as important as the *pushing forward* of the wheat. If the negative conditions are neglected, the positive conditions are nullified. Israel was now, as we see, sunk in the filthiest abominations of idolatry. But it had come to this through a long neglect of the most earnest warnings. Note in particular Numb. xxxiii. 55, "If ye will not drive out the inhabitants of the land from before you; then it shall come to pass, that those which ye let remain of them shall be pricks in your eyes, and thorns in your sides." The idolatry of Israel was a far worse thing than the idolatry of the heathen; just as a neglected garden overrun with weeds and briars is worse than a weedy and briery corner of the wilderness (Lev. xxvi. 16; Deut. xxviii. 38—40; Micah vi. 15; Hag. i. 6).—Y.

EXPOSITION.

CHAPTER XIII.

The chapter falls into two parts—the one describing a divinely commanded action of the prophet, symbolical of the approaching rejection of the Jewish people, the other announcing in literal language the ruin especially of the king and the queen-mother, and emphasizing the inveterate corruption which rendered such a blow necessary. The mention of the queen-mother (see ver. 18) renders it probable that Jehoiachin is the king under whom the prophecy was composed. It is true that other kings besides Jehoiachin ascended the throne in the lifetime of their mother; but the express and repeated mention of the queen-mother in the account of Jehoiachin (2 Kings xxiv. 12, 15; comp. ch. xxix. 2; xxii. 26) warrants the inference that Nehushta, Jehoiachin's mother, was a more powerful personage than other queen-mothers. This will be confirmed if, with Hitzig and Bertheau, we accept the statement of the text of the Chronicles (2 Chron. xxxvi. 9), that Jehoiachin was eight (not eighteen) years old on his accession (see on ch. xxii. 28).

Vers. 1—11.—The entire people of the Jews is like a good-for-nothing apron.

Ver. 1.—A linen girdle; rather, a linen apron. "Girdle" is one of the meanings of the Hebrew ('ēzōr), but is here unsuitable. As ver. 11 shows, it is an inner garment that is meant, one that "cleaveth to the loins of a man" (in fact, the περίζωμα of the Septuagint, the lumbare of the Vulgate). The corresponding Arabic word, 'izār, has, according to Lane, the meaning of "waist-wrapper." Israel was to Jehovah in as close a relation spiritually as that in which the inner garment referred to is to him who wears it materially. There is an Arabic proverb which well illustrates this: "He is to me in place of an 'izār" (Freytag, 'Studium der Arab. Sprache,' p. 298). "A linen apron" may perhaps be specified, because linen was the material of the priestly dress (Lev. xvi. 4), and Israel was to be spiritually "a kingdom of priests." But this is not absolutely necessary. The common man used linen in his dress as well as the priest; the only difference between them was that the priest was confined to linen garments. But an "apron" would in any case naturally be made of linen. Linen; literally, flax (a

product of Judah, Hos. ii. 5). Put it not in water. The object of the prohibition is well stated by St. Jerome. It was at once to symbolize the character of the people of Israel, stiff and impure, like unwashed linen, and to suggest the fate in store for it (ver. 9).

Vers. 4—6.—After Jeremiah has worn the apron for some time, he is directed to take it to P'rath, and hide it there in a cleft (not "hole") of the rock. A long interval elapses, and he is commanded to make a second journey to the same place, and fetch away the apron. What does this P'rath mean? It is by no means easy to decide. Hardly "the Euphrates," (1) because the common prefix, "the river," is wanting, though in so extraordinary a narrative it was peculiarly needed; (2) because of the length of the journey to Babylonia, which has ex hyp. to be made twice; and (3) because the Euphrates is not a rocky river. Ewald suggested that "some wet place near Jerusalem" probably had the name of P'rath, and indicates a valley and spring called Forah, about six English miles north-east of Jerusalem. Mr. Birch appears to have hit independently on the same spot, which he identifies with the Parah of Josh. xviii. 23, about three miles north-east of Anathoth, and describes as a picturesque gorge between savage rocks, with a copious stream (Quarterly Statement of the Palestine Exploration Fund, October, 1880, p. 236). This combination, however, involves an emendation of the text (P'rath into Pārāh)—logically it involves this, as Mr. Birch has seen; Ewald's comparison of the Arabic furât, sweet water, seems inconsistent with his reference to Parah—for which there does not seem to be sufficient necessity; and it is better to adopt the view of the great old French Protestant scholar, Bochart, that P'rath is a shortened form of Ephrath, i.e. at once Bethlehem and the district in which Bethlehem lay (see 1 Chron. ii. 50; iv. 4; and perhaps Ps. cxxxii. 6). It need hardly be said that the limestone hills of this region afforded abundance of secluded rocks. There may, of course, be at the same time an allusion to the ordinary meaning of P'rath, viz. Euphrates, on the analogy of the allusion in Isa. xxvii. 12. Those who hold the view here rejected, that P'rath is equivalent to the Euphrates, sometimes suppose that the narrative is a parable or symbolical fiction, such as Luther, Calvin, and others find in Hos. i., iii., the thing signified being in this case the carrying captive of the people to Babylon; and this seems the best way of making this interpretation plausible.

Ver. 6.—**After many days.** To allow time for the apron to become rotten.

Ver. 7.—**I went . . . and digged.** The apron, then, had been covered with a thick layer of earth.

Vers. 8—11.—Explanation of the symbol. Could there be a greater humiliation for Judah and Jerusalem than to be compared to a rotting linen apron? The hard things said of this evil people in ver. 10 must of course be understood with the limitations indicated in the note on ch. ix. 15, 16. **Imagination** should (as usual) be *stubbornness*. The explanation in ver. 11 is a strong argument for the rendering "apron" (see above, on ver. 1).

Vers. 12—14.—Here another symbol is introduced—a symbolic phrase rather than a symbolic action. The first symbol referred to the people as a whole; the second represents the fate of the individual members of the people. The words, **Thus saith the Lord God of Israel,** are omitted in the Septuagint, and certainly the form of the following phrase seems hardly worthy of so solemn an introduction. **Every bottle.** It is an earthenware bottle, or pitcher, which seems from ver. 13 to be meant (comp. Isa. xxx. 14), though the Septuagint renders here ἀσκός. **The kings that sit upon David's throne;** rather, *that sit for David upon his throne;* i.e. as David's heirs and successors. The plural "kings" is to include all the kings who reigned during the final period of impending ruin. **With drunkenness.** The effect of the "wine-cup of [the Divine] fury" (ch. xxv. 15). **Dash them one against another.** This is merely the development of the figure of the pitchers; not a prediction of civil war. The pitchers, when cast down, must of course fall together into pieces.

Vers. 15—19.—An admonition to seize upon the only means of escape.

Ver. 16.—**Give glory,** etc. Let your tribute to your King be that of humble submission to his will. The precise application of the phrase must be derived from the context (comp. Josh. vii. 19; Mal. ii. 2). **Upon the dark mountains;** rather, *upon mountains of twilight.* A "mountain" is an image of a great obstacle (Zech. iv. 7; Matt. xxi. 21). As Judah is walking along, the hitherto even tenor of his way gives place to huge mountains wrapt in an impenetrable dusk, over which he will stumble and fall if he does not repent in time.

Ver. 17.—Should all admonitions be in vain, Jeremiah will return (like Samuel, 1 Sam. xv. 35) and give vent to his sorrowful emotion. **The Lord's flock.** Jehovah is likened to a shepherd (comp. Zech. x. 3).

Ver. 18.—The extent of the calamity shown in individual instances. For the fulfilment, see 2 Kings xxiv. 15. After a reign of three months, the young prince and his mother were carried to Babylon. **And to the queen;** rather, *and to the queen-mother* (literally, *the mistress*). It will be noticed that, except in two cases, the names of the mothers of the reigning kings of Judah are scrupulously mentioned in the Books of Kings. This and the title of "mistress" are indications of the high rank they enjoyed in the social system. In the case of Asa, we are told that he removed his mother, Maachah, from her position as "mistress," or queen-mother, on account of her idolatry (1 Kings xv. 13). The political value of the station is strikingly shown by the ease with which Athaliah, as queen-mother, usurped the supreme authority (2 Kings xi.). From an historical point of view, the "queen-mother" of the Jews is a most interesting personage; she is a relic of the primitive age in which relationship was reckoned with regard to the mother (so with the Accadians, Etruscans, Finns, etc.). It should be added, however, that once (viz. 1 Kings xi. 19) the same title, "mistress," is applied to the queen-consort. **Humble yourselves, sit down;** rather, *sit down in abasement;* i.e. take the station suitable for your abased circumstances (comp. Isa. xlvii. 1). **Your principalities;** rather, *your head-ornaments.*

Ver. 19.—The rendering of the Authorized Version is substantially right, as the events referred to are obviously future. The tense, however, in the Hebrew, is the perfect—viz. that of prophetic certitude. Jeremiah sees it all in prophetic vision, as if it were actually taking place. **The cities of the south.;** *i.e.* of the dry, southern country of Judah, called the Negeb—**shall be [are] shut up**—*i.e.* blocked up with ruins (as Isa. xxiv. 10)—**and none shall open** them (openeth them), because all Judah will have been carried captive. (For fulfilment, see ch. xxxiv. 7.)

Vers. 20, 21.—The captivity being still (in spite of the perfect tense) a thing of the future, the prophet can seek to awaken the conscience of the careless under-shepherd by showing how self-caused is his (or rather her) punishment.

Ver. 20.—**Lift up your eyes.** The verb is fem. sing., the pronoun (in suffix form) masc. plu.,—a clear indication that the person addressed is a collective. Probably the "daughter of Zion" is intended, which, in a certain sense, might be called the "shepherd" or leader of the rest of the nation. **From the north.** Again this horror of the north as the source of calamity (see on ch. i. 14).

Ver. 21.—**What wilt thou say,** etc.? The rendering of the verse is uncertain, though the Authorized Version undoubtedly requires correction. The alternatives are, *What wilt thou say when he shall appoint over thee (but thou thyself hast trained them against thee) familiar friends as thy head?* and, *What wilt thou say when he shall appoint over thee those whom thou hast taught to be thy familiar friends as thy head?* The rendering "familiar friends" is justified by Ps. lv. 13; Prov. xvi. 28; xvii. 9; Micah vii. 5. The "captains" of Authorized Version, or rather "tribal chiefs," is unsuitable.

Ver. 22.—**Thy heels made bare**; rather, *treated with violence.* The fate held out to the daughter of Zion (trained to walk along with "tinkling ornaments," Isa. ii. 18) is to plod wearily along with bare feet (comp. Isa. xlvii. 1).

Ver. 24.—**As the stubble.** "The word means not what we call stubble, but the broken straw which had to be separated from the wheat after the corn had been trampled out by the oxen. Sometimes it was burnt as useless; at other times left to be blown away by the wind coming from the desert, on which see ch. iv. 11; Job i. 19" (Payne Smith).

Ver. 25.—**The portion of thy measures**; *i.e.* thy measured portion. But it is probably safer to render, *the portion of thy garment,* the upper garment being used instead of a bag to hold anything (comp. Ruth iii. 15; 2 Kings iv. 39). **In falsehood**; *i.e.* in false gods (ch. xvi. 19).

Ver. 26.—**Therefore will I,** etc. But the Hebrew is much more forcible, "And I also," etc., implying, as Calvin remarks (comp. Prov. i. 26), a certain retaliation. **Upon thy face**; an allusion to Nah. iii. 5.

Ver. 27.—**I have seen,** etc. The Hebrew is again more forcible than the English. It runs, "Thine adulteries and thy neighings," etc.! (this is an exclamation as it were; then more reflectively), "I have seen thine abominations." **Neighings;** *i.e.* passionate craving for illegitimate objects of worship (comp. ch. ii. 24, 25; v. 8). **In the fields.** The Hebrew has the singular. The "field," as usual, means the open country. **Wilt thou not,** etc.? rather, *How long yet ere thou be made clean?* In ver. 23 the prophet had vehemently declared his people to be incorrigible. But, like the tender Hosea, he cannot continue to hold such gloomy thoughts; surely Israel, God's people, must eventually be "made clean"! But this can only be as the result of judicial affliction, and these afflictions will be no slight or transient ones.

HOMILETICS.

Vers. 1—11.—*The spoiled girdle.* I. GOD'S PEOPLE ARE LIKE A GIRDLE TO GOD. 1. They are his *peculiar property.* The girdle is a private personal possession. It belongs solely to the wearer. When all ordinary property is taken from him he retains the clothes on his body. Even the bankrupt has a right to these. 2. They are *near to God.* This girdle—really an under-garment—is close to the person of the wearer. God does not simply hold his people as an absentee landlord holds his property. He draws them near to himself. He cherishes them with affection, sustains the burden of them, carries them with him in his glorious out-going to works of wonder and mercy and in his blessed in-coming to Divine peace and sabbatic repose. 3. They are *a glory to God.* (Ver. 11.) Garments are worn, not only for clothing, but to add grace and beauty. God's people are more than safe with him; they are glorious. It is true that they have no inherent grace which they can add to the splendour of God, but they can adorn that splendour by reflecting it, as the clouds which gird about the rising sun seem to increase its beauty by reflecting its own rich rays. 4. They are *required to cleave to God.* God graciously takes his people near to himself; yet they must voluntarily bind themselves to him in love, in devotion, in submission, in obedience.

II. GOD'S PEOPLE, IN THEIR SIN, ARE LIKE A GIRDLE DEFILED AND UNWASHED. 1. Jeremiah was forbidden to put the girdle in water (ver. 1). Whilst living in this world the best men daily contract stains of sin; but God has provided a fountain for cleansing, and by daily penitence and faith in his purifying grace the soul may be made and preserved pure (Zech. xiii. 1). As all have sinned and do sin, all need this constant cleansing. To neglect it is to become increasingly foul and unfit for the honour that God bestows upon his people. 2. This corruption is manifest (1) in *neglect* of the will of God—"they refuse to hear my words;" (2) in wilful *obstinacy*— they "walk in the stubbornness of their heart;" (3) in positive *disobedience and impurity*—they "they walk after other gods, and serve them, and worship them;" (4) in inveterate *impenitence*—they "would not hear."

III. THE PUNISHMENT OF GOD'S SINFUL PEOPLE IS LIKE THE SPOILING OF THE GIRDLE.

1. They are *cast off.* The unwashed girdle can be worn no longer. In their holiness God's people were his glory; in their defilement they are his dishonour. God can endure the presence of nothing impure (Heb. xii. 14). 2. They are left to their own *increasing defilement.* The unwashed garment is buried, and becomes only worse. The most terrible punishment of sin is to be left to sin unchecked. Vice then becomes ingrained—a second nature. 3. They are *dishonoured.* The girdle is visibly marred with the earth in which it is buried. Internal impurity is punished with external shame. Punishment is appropriate to guilt. Pride is chastised by humiliation. 4. Though their sin may be hidden for a time, it will be *revealed at last.* The girdle is buried only to be exhumed. The longer it was buried the worse must have been its condition when it was again exposed to view. The corruption of the heart cannot be ultimately concealed; it must reveal itself in the life. In the resurrection-life, wherein the body is spiritual and fits truly and expresses clearly the soul that inhabits it, the foul soul will be compelled to inhabit a foul body. 5. They are rendered *worthless.* The girdle is utterly spoiled—profitable for nothing. Sin not only dishonours, it destroys. The girdle becomes rotten. As dirt rots a garment, so sin rots a soul. It not only makes it foul and hideous, but it destroys its faculties and energies, degrades its essential nature, and introduces the corruption of death (Jas. i. 15).

Vers. 12—14.—*The parable of the wine-flagons.* I. THE PROUD ARE LIKE WINE-FLAGONS. Jeremiah is thinking chiefly of the aristocracy of his nation (ver. 13) and their pride (ver. 17). The metaphor, therefore, specially designates the proud. These are swelled-out and pretentious, but not solid, and do not contain anything good of their own. They are brittle. Pride is itself a source of danger (Prov. xvi. 18). II. THE WRATH OF GOD IS LIKE FERMENTING WINE. It is a disturbing influence, breaking in upon the quiet of self-complacency. The more its natural tendency to reduce us to repentance is suppressed by pride, the more terribly will its presence agitate us. The larger the flagon, the more wine will it contain; the greater the rank, the greater the trouble when universal retribution comes. The more empty the flagon, the more wine will it contain; so the less of real solid worth there is in a man's life, the more room will there be for the exercise of Divine wrath against his wretched condition. III. THE EFFECT OF THE WRATH OF GOD ON THE PROUD IS LIKE THE ROLLING OF WINE-FLAGONS FILLED WITH FERMENTING WINE. The flagons are imagined to be drunken, and to behave as drunken men would behave. In this condition they exemplify the state of those into whom God has poured the vials of his wrath. This does not simply work in them, leaving their exterior undisturbed. Spiritual though it is, it affects the whole life. We cannot escape the effect of God's anger by ignoring spiritual facts and living in the outside, worldly life alone. This and all our experience will be disturbed. The flagons strike one another. Companions in the pleasures of sin become mutual enemies in the punishment of it. Moral corruption leads to social discord. Civil war is one of the greatest calamities which can overtake a nation, and when this arises, not from any contention for right or liberty, but from the outburst of wild passions, selfish greed, etc., it is doubly destructive. In such an event wickedness becomes its own executioner.

Ver. 16.—*Darkness.* I. SIN PLUNGES THE SOUL INTO DARKNESS. "Light is sown for the *righteous*" (Ps. xcvii. 11). The darkness of evil thoughts and an evil will throws its shadow out on the world, and ultimately brings gloom over the whole of life. 1. This darkness is *distressing.* The benighted feel a horror of great darkness falling upon them amid the wild and lonely mountains. When God withdraws the sunshine of his grace this mournful condition must be the experience of the godless. 2. It is *confusing.* They "stumble upon the twilight mountains." Without God we have no true guide in life. There are mountains of difficulty to be overcome in our earthly pilgrimage, steep and toilsome and dangerous. How dreadful to venture unenlightened and unguided through such pathless wilds! If the life were to be spent in a paradise, it would be sad to dwell amidst its beauties in perpetual gloom; but, seeing that it is a pilgrimage over the mountains, it is fearful to be left in darkness. 3. It will *grow into deeper darkness.* At first it is a twilight. Some hope that this is the herald of the dawn; but they are mistaken—it is the portend of the night. The mingled lights and shadows will melt into the blackness of midnight. The mixed joys and sorrows, hopes and fears, of this life, which some sanguine souls suppose to be the worst condition they will be in, and likely to give place to rest and joy hereafter, will end to the sinner in the terrible darkness of a much worse future retribution. 4. The *present light* is no guarantee that the darkness is not approaching. The brightest day may be followed by the blackest night.

II. THE PROSPECT OF THIS DARKNESS SHOULD WARN MEN TO AVERT IT. 1. It is *not inevitable.* It has not yet come. There is still time to escape. If there were no remedy, all warnings would be useless. The very utterance of warnings implies that the terrors to which they refer may be avoided. 2. The contemplation of its approaching advent should urge men to *seek an escape.* The prospect is gloomy, and many will not face a gloomy prospect. They dislike allusions to unpleasant subjects. But it is necessary to contemplate such sad truths, that men may be roused by selfish fear when they will not be moved by the love of God. 3. The *way of escape* is to be found in "giving glory to God." It is returning from rebellion to the service of God, humbling ourselves, rejecting the pride which clings to the old sin, and regarding God alone as worthy of honour, and so submitting to his will and obeying his commands as to glorify him by our acts. To the Christian all this is implied in faith in Christ which involves the humbling of ourselves before him, and our trust in his grace which glorifies his love, and loyalty to his will which honours his rights of royalty.

Ver. 18.—*Royalty humbled.* I. GOD IS THE JUDGE OF KINGS. They are as far beneath God as are the meanest beggars. Their rank is no protection against the execution of Divine justice; their power no security against the consequences of the wrath of God. No earthly honour or power will serve men when they stand before the great throne of judgment.

II. WICKED KINGS WILL MEET WITH SEVERE PUNISHMENT. The greater the privileges they have had, the more have they been able to abuse them, and therefore the greater their guilt. The larger their influence has been, the more harm have they done in using that influence for evil purposes. All who are entrusted with exceptional power should remember that this incurs exceptional responsibility.

III. THE PRIDE OF KINGS WILL BE PUNISHED WITH HUMILIATION. Every sin will have its appropriate retribution. "Whatsoever a man soweth, that shall he also reap," not only in the main characteristics, but in particular features. Pride thus naturally sows the seed of shame (Prov. xxix. 23).

IV. THE GREATNESS OF THE PRESENT PROSPERITY OF WICKED KINGS WILL ENHANCE THE SUFFERING OF THEIR FUTURE RETRIBUTION. They who stand highest can fall lowest. Poverty is felt more keenly by people who were once in affluence than by the children of the poor. The memory of his former luxuries must have added keenness to the sufferings of Dives in Hades. We are not to infer from this that future retribution is only a compensation for the inequality of the joys and sorrows of this life, that kings will suffer for their very greatness (for the wicked poor will be wretched hereafter, while the good and great will be blessed in the future with heavenly treasures), but that if we are *unfaithful,* the measure of future distress will necessarily be partly determined by that of present enjoyment. We need not, therefore, be envious of the prosperity of the wicked. Rather it should fill us with horror, grief, and pity as we consider what a fool's paradise they live in—what anguish will grow out of the contrast of it with the certain retribution of all sin!

Ver. 23.—*The Ethiopian's skin and the leopard's spots.* I. SIN BECOMES INHERENT IN THE NATURE OF MEN. The black of the Ethiopian's skin and the spots of the leopard are natural. Sin is, of course, originally unnatural. Yet it is so ingrafted into the very life of men that it becomes part of their nature. 1. Men *inherit* tendencies to evil; *e.g.* the child of the drunkard is likely to feel strong temptation to intemperance, etc. We are not to blame for what we inherit; but we do suffer through it. The degraded moral nature is a fact, and one for which the possessor of it suffers, although he will not be responsible for it, nor punished simply for having it, but only for the way in which, with his free-will, he yields to it, and, on his own account, makes it still more corrupt. 2. Men *habituate* themselves to sin. Habit is second nature. The sin which is wilfully chosen becomes a tyrannous habit. We are colouring our very being by the tone of our thoughts and actions. What we do to-day, that we will be to-morrow. We are the result of our own past deeds. He who speaks or acts a lie becomes a liar; he who indulges in impurity becomes an unclean being; he who follows selfish impulses becomes a creature of selfishness. Thus every man is building up a habitation for his soul by his own deeds. What shall this house be? A temple of divinity? a palace of pure delights? a charnel-house of corruption? or a prison of gloom?

II. THIS INHERENT CONDITION OF SIN MAKES IT IMPOSSIBLE FOR ANY MAN TO IRRADI-CATE IT. 1. *Self-reformation is impossible.* Sin is not a mere defilement to be washed off. It is ingrained. It is in the blood, in the life, in the nature. Action is according to character. If the character is corrupt, so must be the action. It is true we are free to do as we will, but so long as our nature is corrupt we shall will to do evil, because the will is part of the nature. But apart from the vexed question of the freedom of the will, every man is conscious of the difficulty of overcoming opposing habits, even when his will is roused against them. When he would do good evil is present with him, and this evil is so strong that it can only be regarded as a law of (corrupted) nature (Rom. vii. 21—23). 2. *Perfect reformation must be sought from God.* This must be regeneration (John iii. 3). Man can do much with himself, but only God can "create" in him "a clean heart" and make him "a new creature." Therefore, to be born again, we must be born "from above." Regeneration must be the work of the Spirit, which is the brooding source of all life. But this is possible for all (Matt. xix. 26). The impossibility for self-reformation should not leave us in sullen indifference, but should rouse us to seek the one sure means of renewal in crucifixion of the old life and spiritual resurrection to a new life, through yielding ourselves up to the influence of the grace of God in Christ Jesus.

HOMILIES BY VARIOUS AUTHORS.

Vers. 1—11.—*The marred girdle.* This and the following emblem are intended to symbolize the characters and punishment of pride in spiritual and carnal men respectively. The "girdle" of linen cloth worn by the priest represents the close relation of Judah and Jerusalem to Jehovah. He had chosen them, and taken them into closest fellowship. They were as his cincture to declare his character and glory to men. But they had abused his confidence. For them, therefore, the fate was reserved which is described in connection with the girdle. Where the cleft of the rock was, in Ephrath or Euphrates, is not quite plain; but the probability is that the last-mentioned is really meant, and that a journey to it was indeed made by the prophet.

I. THE DIGNITY AND IDEAL CHARACTER OF GOD'S PEOPLE THUS SET FORTH. The linen girdle worn by the priests was a portion of their appointed and consecrated garments. It represented, therefore, the idea of consecration arising from nearness and closeness. They were highly favoured amongst the nations as being brought into immediate relation with Jehovah. "As the girdle cleaveth to the loins of a man, so have I caused to cleave unto me the whole house of Israel, and the whole house of Judah, saith the Lord" (ver. 11). And as the girdle, by bracing the body, becomes a means of strength, so Israel was to be the power of God amongst the nations of the world. They were to be as kings and priests before God, to show forth his righteousness and to execute his will.

II. THE CONDITION UPON WHICH THESE HAVE TO BE MAINTAINED. Simply because they had been so designed in the eternal purpose. They had no security for this position being retained. It would not do for them to rely upon prestige. With spiritual strength relaxed and moral purity lost, they were no longer fit for the honourable service to which they had been called. It was only as their spiritual life rose to the height of their calling, and maintained itself from age to age by means of Divine truth and continual exercise of faith, that they could expect to retain their privileges. But this Israel was far from seeing. She required, therefore, to be taught the truth of it by experience, and nothing would do this better than that which the symbol suggested. Their outward circumstances and position would be made to correspond with their inward character, so that all men, and even they themselves, would cease to be deceived. This is ever the order of the Divine government. He will set our secret sins in the light of his countenance.

III. The messenger of God should spare no effort to embody and enforce the truth he has to declare. Whether Ephrath in Israel or Euphrates was meant, a journey of considerable length had to be taken, and much trouble was involved. But the prophet did not grudge this if thereby he might appeal through the imagination the more forcibly to the heart of his people. So sometimes ancient prophets had to submit to themselves being made signs that were spoken against. There can be no question that the manner adopted by the prophet of illustrating his message was most effective and striking. And it was clear even to the simplest understanding. An illustrative style of discourse is carefully to be distinguished from a florid one; and anything which conveys more vivid impressions to one's self is more likely to add impressiveness and vivid force to what one has to say to others. This going to Euphrates on the part of the prophet was quite an important business, but it was justified by its result. And so preachers should spare no pains to link the truth of God with the actions, the experiences, and the interests of men.—M.

Vers. 12, 15.—*Broken pitchers; or, worldly sufficiency and its punishment.* I. The signs of this disposition. The threatenings of God are interpreted as if they had been truisms of blessing justified by the unbelievers' own experience. The prophet is therefore despised, and his message wrested from its original meaning. The people were so oblivious to their own guilt that they looked forward without fear to the future, or they professed to do so. They had clothed themselves in triple armour of self-sufficiency against Divine warnings. So the worldly mind continually prophecies good for itself instead of evil, and inverts the messages of Divine grace. The sharpest experiences and most signal reverses are not enough to rid it of this folly, and thereby it condemns itself.

II. How it is dealt with by God. That this is provoking to the Divine mind is evident. It is a fresh element added to the guilt already denounced. The insult to the messenger of God must be avenged, and this is accomplished: 1. *By removing all ambiguity from his words.* Their real meaning is explained so that no one can mistake it. In this pointed disillusion there is the greater emphasis imparted to the original message. God will not suffer any one to remain in ignorance of his final destiny, whether it be good or evil. 2. *The doom already predicted is repeated with expressions of Divine determination and anger.* Civil discord and national destruction are plainly set forth, and whilst these take place the ear of an offended God is turned away. He will " not pity, nor spare, nor have mercy, but destroy them."

III. It is well, therefore, for men to give reverent heed to Divine warnings and instructions. Sometimes in the history of the Church omens, dreams, and visions have been given whose meaning was not clear, but on prayerful solicitation it has been revealed. Wilful blindness cannot escape punishment, because it provokes the just anger of God. But to those who ask in humble inquiry what the will of the Lord may be, he will return a gracious answer, and declare how the evil may be averted.—M.

Ver. 16.—*Days of grace and how they should be spent.* The mind of the prophet was full of the doom which he had predicted, and he was apprehensive of the spiritual results of exile and confusion with heathen nations. The people themselves, however, did not exhibit any such anxiety. They treated his words as idle tales, or as the expression of ill nature and enmity. The relation of these two is a typical one. From age to age the preacher of righteousness urges his pleas and presses for immediate attention to reformation of life. As constantly those addressed put off the needed repentance and waste the time which is afforded them for working out their salvation.

I. The present is to be regarded as a gracious opportunity for repentance and spiritual service. The element of time in these, as in other prophecies, is left for the most part indefinite. Exact dates would defeat the purpose the message of the prophet has in view. It was sufficient for him to impress upon them that there would be but a short time between the present and the fate he had described. It was a sign of God's grace that he had been sent to warn them. They were to listen to his voice as to the voice of Jehovah. And in the event of repentance, that which was near at hand might be indefinitely postponed or altogether averted. But in any case the really essential work of repentance ought to be done whilst they had clear views of the nature of their sin and the requirements of God's Law. From Josh. vii. 19 it is evident that the phrase, "Give glory to the Lord," meant nothing else than to repent. It suggests the honour of God, which is acknowledged and felt by the humbled sinner as he bows before the footstool of grace and tells out the dark history of his sin. The lower he is in his own estimation the higher is that throne of glory before which he lies prostrate. And at such a time the grandest conceptions are given of the greatness, the power, and the love of God. His forgiveness shines forth in new, unspeakable splendour. And the restored sinner is eager to declare to others the grace which he himself has received. But all this is necessarily a work of time, and demands for its adequate fulfilment the full possession of our faculties and the clearest perceptions of truth.

II. THE RISKS INCURRED BY DELAY IN THESE DUTIES ARE THEN DESCRIBED. The figure is that of a traveller in a mountainous region who loses his way amongst the dark rocks until eventually the deepening gloom leaves him in despair and death. The picture is very vivid, and appeals to the deepest human feeling. It suggested the mental and spiritual confusion which were likely to arise from unlooked-for reverses, from captivity in a heathen land, and from forgetfulness of the traditions of Israel. But it is even more truly correspondent with the condition of those who have delayed making their peace with God until they have suffered mental eclipse, or been overtaken by the terror, the weakness, etc., of a death-bed. The worth of "a death-bed repentance" has been rightly discounted by every preacher and writer of the Church. There is but one instance of such a thing in Scripture. It is but seldom that resolutions formed under such circumstances, in the event of restoration to health, avail against the temptations and lifelong habits of the sinner.—M.

Ver. 17.—(See on ch. x. 19.)—M.

Ver. 23.—*Moral helplessness: how induced.* I. THE EXTENT TO WHICH IT MAY GO. The metaphors employed are intended to illustrate the difficulty of getting rid of that which has become a part of one's self, or which has become natural to one. It is evident that superficial means would never produce the effect supposed, because that which seems to be superficial has really its root in the nature, and would be reproduced similarly in place of that which was removed. The doctrine is that there are certain evils into which men fall which may appear to be external, matters of custom and observance, but which have really their origin in the depravity of the heart. Any merely external reform, like that of Josiah, would fail to effect a permanent change, because the source of the errors and transgressions which were corrected was deeper than the remedy could reach. And this is the case with the sins of men. To cease to do evil we have not only to stay the hand but to purify the heart. To cease to do evil we must cease to think it, to feel it, and to conceive it. So helpless is the sinner when he stands face to face with the problem of reformation. Effort after effort is made and fails. It is bound to fail because the source of the wrong-doing has not been rectified. *To change himself*—who is capable of this feat?

II. CAUSES OF IT, REAL AND UNREAL. Excuses readily suggest themselves to the sinner who would avoid the humiliation of repentance. He may ask the question, as if it were a mystery, "Wherefore come these things upon me?" Or, ignoring the witness of conscience, he may attribute his weakness to circumstances and external influences. This is the error which the prophet refutes. With great skill he shows the terrible power of habit: how men continue to do that which they have been doing simply because they have been doing it. The feet acquire a fatal facility in transgression, and the hands a skill in working evil. They almost act automatically when things forbidden are suggested. But when the commandments of God are concerned they are unfamiliar with the duties enjoined, and the will is not resolute enough to persevere in them.

III. Its GREAT REMEDY. Seeing that in himself the sinner is without strength, it would appear at first as if he could only despair. But this is not the teaching of the prophet. He has already counselled vigorous effort, and implied that a commencement and continuance in well-doing were possible. But the change could only begin at a spiritual point, viz. repentance. And this, as Scripture abundantly shows, though within the power of every one, is a supernatural grace. A true sorrow for sin may be induced in answer to prayer, by the study of Scripture, and the contemplation of Christ; but it is always the work of the Holy Spirit. When that grace, however, has once been attained, it is open to the sinner to reverse the process by which he has been enslaved. After conversion evil habit will assert itself, and can only be met by constant dependence upon Divine grace and constant effort after holiness. The good habit formed by repeated and regular actions according to the Law of God is the best antidote to the evil one.—M.

Vers. 1—12.—*The ruined girdle; or, it may be too late to mend.* The much-needed lesson of this section was taught by means of one of those acted parables of which we have so many instances both in the Old Testament and in the New : *e.g.* Zedekiah's horns of iron (1 Kings xxii. 11); the strange marriages of Isa. viii. 1, Hos. i. 2; the two yokes (ch. xxvii. 2); and in the New Testament, our Lord's standing the little child in the midst of the disciples; the washing the disciples' feet; the withering of the fig tree; the taking of Paul's girdle (Acts xxi. 11), etc. The present instance seems very strange, and to us it would have appeared unmeaning, uncouth, and simply grotesque. But to Orientals, and especially to Jews, the dramatic action of the prophet—for we regard what is here said as having been literally done—would be very impressive. It was a strange garb for the prophet to be arrayed in. It would attract attention, be the subject of much comment, and, when the prophet continued to wear it, though soiled and in much need of washing, this would cause more comment still, and would indicate to the people that the strange garb and conduct of the prophet had meaning and intent which it would be well for them to give heed to. Then the taking of the girdle to Euphrates—whatever place be meant—burying it there, leaving it; and then finding it and fetching it back, and no doubt exhibiting it, ruined, worthless, good for nothing;—all this would rivet the people's attention, and deeply impress their minds. Now, one evident, if not the chief, lesson designed to be taught by this to us curious procedure, was the irreparable ruin that would come upon the people through the exile and captivity which they were by their sin bringing upon themselves. Many, no doubt, had comforted themselves with the idea—as is the manner of all transgressors—that if trouble did come to them it would not be so bad as the prophet made out. They would get over it, and be but little the worse. This dramatic parable was designed to shatter all such notions, and to show that Judah, like the much-marred girdle, would be, after and in consequence of their exile, "good for nothing." Note, then—

I. THE FIRST PART OF THE PARABLE—THE GIRDLE WORN. This would encourage their delusion. For the likening of them to a girdle, especially to a linen girdle—a priestly and therefore a sacred vestment—and to a chosen and purchased girdle, would vividly declare to them how precious they were in God's sight. 1. For as the girdle (ver. 11) was worn close to the person of the wearer, it denoted how *very near to the heart of God they were* who by this similitude were set forth. The known favour of God led them, as it had led others, to presume that they could never try God too much. He would be sure to bear with them and forgive them, do what they might. 2. Then the girdle was a portion of the dress most necessary to the wearer, and so denoted how *necessary his people were to God.* Had not God said, over and over again, in every variety of way, " How can I give thee up? how can I make thee as Sodom ? " (Hos. xi. 8; ch. ix. 7)? As the girdle was indispensable to the comfort, the decorousness, the strength of the wearer, so God taught by this figure that he could not do without his people. 3. Moreover, as the girdle was adorned and ornamented, and thus was a most valuable portion of the dress, so it showed that his people were to God a *cherished ornament and praise.* They were to be to him "for a name, and for a praise, and for a glory " (ver. 11). And as such God had worn this girdle and put it on him. And his people knew all this, and *presumed upon it.*

II. THE SECOND PART—THE GIRDLE UNCLEANSED. This would show wherefore their ideas must be a delusion. "Put it not in water" (ver. 1). The prophet was bidden to wear it in this soiled and foul condition, and no doubt he did so. It would provoke the contempt, which adornments associated with uncleanliness ever excite. But its intent in thus being worn unwashed was to depict the moral state of those to whom the prophet was sent. As they would put away from them a soiled and unclean girdle, so they were to learn that God, though he might bear long with a morally unclean people, would not always do so. And—

III. THE THIRD PART OF THE PARABLE—THE GIRDLE PUT AWAY. This would show that their presumptuous ideas were actually a delusion. The girdle was so spoiled by its burial by the Euphrates that it was henceforth "good for nothing." And all this came true. It was but a miserable remnant of the people that came back from Babylon, and as an independent nation they have never since regained the position that they then lost. All their national glory came to an end; the lesson of the marred girdle was literally fulfilled.

IV. THE WHOLE A PARABLE THAT HAS MANY APPLICATIONS. To Churches, to individuals, to all the gifted of God's grace in time, talents, opportunities, and, above all, in the presence and help of the Holy Spirit. They will be tempted to presume, to think they can never forfeit these things, that God will be ever gracious to them as he has been in the past. This parable is a word for all such, and should prompt the earnest and constant putting up of the psalmist's prayer, "Keep back thy servant . . . from presumptuous sins," etc.—C.

Vers. 12—14.—*Vessels of wrath.* This is another similitude having the same general purpose as the former one. "Every earthen flagon (cf. ch. xlviii. 12)—the inhabitants of Jerusalem, her king, her priests, and prophets—will be filled with the wine of the intoxicating beverage of God's wrath (cf. ch. xxv. 15; Isa. xxviii. 7; li. 17; Ezek. xxiii. 31; Ps. lx. 3; lxxv. 8) given them as a punishment for the pride and cruelty and impiety which they drank greedily as wine; cf. Rev. xiv. 8; xviii. 3, where the harlot drinks the wine of her own fornication and gives it to others, and intoxicates herself and them with it (Rev. xvii. 2; xviii. 6), and therefore God gives her the cup of his wrath, and she reels under it" (Wordsworth). The awful threatenings of these verses teach us much concerning the characteristics of those whom the Lord "will not pity, nor spare, nor have mercy, but destroy" (ver. 14).

I. THEY GRADUALLY BECOME VESSELS OF WRATH. Not till they are filled with their intoxicating sin are they certainly to be so called. But this goes on day by day.

II. THEY COME TO JEER AND MOCK AT BOTH THE MESSAGE AND THE MESSENGERS GOD SENDS TO WARN THEM. Ver. 12, "Do we not certainly know," etc., as if they would say, "Tell us something we do not know." It is an utterance of unbelieving and mocking contempt.

III. THEY ARE AS DRUNKEN MEN: bereft of reason, unable to help themselves or their brethren, the sport of fools, and at the mercy of the most contemptible foe. Either torpid and insensible to all that concerns them, or else filled with fury and lost to all natural affection, hurting and destroying those nearest and dearest to them (ver. 14).

IV. ALL VESSELS, LARGE AND SMALL, ARE FILLED ALIKE. (Ver. 13.) Not alone the common people were to be thus filled, but the magnates of the land—king, priests, etc.

V. THEY ARE MUTUALLY DESTRUCTIVE. (Ver. 14.) Such is the doom of sin.

CONCLUSION. We all are vessels. We all shall be filled. But what with? Pray that it may not be with the wine of the wrath of God, but "with the fulness of God" (Eph. iii.).—C.

Vers. 12—14.—*The last results of sin.* I. GOD AND HIS MESSAGE MOCKED.
II. OUR ENTIRE NATURE UNDER ITS CONTROL.
III. ALL RANKS AND ORDERS POSSESSED BY IT.
IV. EVERY MAN'S HAND AGAINST HIS FELLOW.
V. GOD KNOWN ONLY AS THE GOD OF WRATH.—C.

Ver. 15.—"*Be not proud.*" It is difficult to see what those whom the prophet was addressing had to proud of; but it is certain that they were proud, and that thereby they were, more than by aught else, hindered from receiving the word of God. The inflated shape, the mean material, and the easily destroyed nature of those " bottles " to which he had likened them, as well as the arrogant boastful talk of the drunkard, whose doings theirs he predicted should resemble; both these comparisons show how vividly the prophet discerned in them this besetting sin of pride, and the ruin it would be sure to work them. Let us, therefore, note—

I. SOME OF THE REASONS FOR THIS EXHORTATION, " Be not proud." 1. The main reason which the prophet here urges is *its antagonism to the Word of God*. Now, such antagonism cannot but be, for: (1) *The Word of God despises what men most esteem*. (*a*) Their own moral worth. How high men's estimate of this! how low that of the Word of God! (*b*) Their own capacities. Man deems himself capable of self-support, self-deliverance, and self-salvation. The Word of God tells him he is utterly dependent on God for all things, be he who he may. (*c*) The world—its maxims, honours, wealth, etc. (2) *It esteems what men most despise*. (*a*) Such qualities of mind as meekness, forgiveness of injuries, humility, indifference to the world, great regard to the unseen and the spiritual. (*b*) Persons who have nothing but moral excellence to recommend them, be they poor, obscure, and despicable in the world's esteem. (*c*) Courses of life which may involve " the loss of all things," so only as we " may be accepted of him." 2. Its other terrible fruits. Some of these are given in the verses following. It will not suffer men to give glory to God; it leads men into deadly peril (ver. 16). It causes deep distress to those who care for their souls; it will end in their utter ruin (ver. 17).

II. HOW OBEDIENCE MAY BE RENDERED TO IT. Probably there is nothing but that threefold work of the Holy Spirit of which our Lord speaks which will ensure such obedience. Pride is too deeply rooted in the hearts of men to yield to any lesser force but: 1. *The conviction of sin*—destroying all man's self-complacency. 2. *Of righteousness*—filling him at the same time with admiration of the righteousness of Christ, with despair of attainment of it, but with joy that, though he cannot have it in himself, he yet has it by virtue of his faith in Christ. 3. *Of judgment*—destroying the supremacy of the world over his mind, and so delivering him from the temptation to its pride. This work of the Holy Spirit lays the axe at the root of the tree, and ere long hews it down. Let, then, this Holy Spirit be sought in all sincerity, and let his guidance be ever followed; so shall " the mind of Christ " be increasingly formed in us, and we shall learn of him who was " meek and lowly in heart," and so find rest in our souls.—C.

Vers. 16, 17.—*Lost upon the dark mountains*. " Give glory to the Lord," etc.

I. THE SCENE PORTRAYED. It is that of unhappy travellers overtaken by night, when crossing some of the perilous mountain tracks of Palestine. A traveller overtaken as these seem to have been by a night storm, is in imminent danger of falling over precipices and perishing miserably. Even by day the way is perilous: the paths are easily lost, or are strewn with rocks, or they lead along steep and slippery slopes, or by overhanging cliffs, where a single footslip may plunge the heedless passenger headlong to a frightful death in the far depths below. But how much more dangerous such journey must be when night overtakes the travellers, is evident. The fading light has gone, but the journey has still to be pursued. And now comes that stumbling upon the dark mountains, which is so terrible and inevitable. There is the anxious looking for the fitful light of moon or stars, and occasionally hope arises that the clouds will break and some glimmer appear. But this hope has been speedily quenched by the clouds gathering over again, and with the added darkness of the rain-storm, so that the darkness is " gross," like unto that of the shadow of death. Every step, therefore, is fraught with frightful peril, and not a few thus benighted amid such mountain passes perish miserably ere the morning dawn. Such is the scene portrayed.

II. THAT WHICH IT REPRESENTS. 1. *The temporal calamities which God sends—as to the Jews—in punishment for their sins*. All earthly distress has the sad tendency to unhinge the mind, to fill with foreboding fear, and greatly to perplex and overwhelm; but when to the natural effects of such earthly distress there is added the consciousness of guilt and of having deserved what God has sent, then the dismay, distress, and despair which are suggested by the prophetic picture are miserably increased. 2. *The hardened sinner's despair of God's mercy*. The vision of judgment and wrath has come upon him, but the remembrance of his sins crushes hope of mercy (cf. Judas "going out and hanging himself"). 3. *The entanglements of sin.* It is a great mistake to imagine that those who are enslaved by any sin are happy in it. Not a few of them endure a very hell in their frantic but futile endeavours to break the chain which long indulgence has forged and fastened around them. The bitter repentance, the unavailing remorse, every gleam of hope of deliverance so soon quenched, the reck-lessness of despair, the groaning as of the prisoner appointed to death,—all these are realities known to the slaves of sin, and should make every soul shudder lest the like should come upon him. 4. *The procrastinator's death-bed.* He who has been convinced over and over again that he ought to seek the Lord, but has ever put it off,—his feet are likely to "stumble upon the dark mountains" when the night of the shadow of death draws upon him.

III. How such misery may be avoided. It was very near: the prophet's words imply that the oft-threatened doom was at their very doors. And so the like doom may be near to many now. *But yet it may be avoided.* Giving heed to God's Word (ver. 15). We have much hope when we see an earnest heeding of that Word, a really serious attention paid to it. But that by itself is not enough. There must be the actual "giving glory to God;" by confession of sin, acknowledging the wrong done; by casting the soul on God for forgiveness in lowly trust; by forsaking the evil that has roused the just anger of God. "Let the wicked forsake his way, and the unrighteous man," etc.

IV. The great reason for fear that this misery will not be avoided after all. It was and it ever is the accursed *pride* (vers. 15, 17) that will not allow of such giving heed to the Divine Word and such giving glory to him. All the instincts of the unrenewed heart are up in arms against such self-abasement. Any sacrifice will be brought rather than that of the broken and contrite heart.

V. The utterly hopeless condition of those thus lost. (Ver. 17.) See the prophet's piteous tears. He can do nothing—every resource has been tried and failed, and he can but "weep sore in secret places" for the "pride" that has ruined those he would fain have saved. Oh then, sinful heart, down, down before thy God, and "give glory to him," as he would have thee do, as it is so right and reasonable and good for thee to do, as the ministers of God entreat thee to do.—C.

Ver. 20.—*The neglected trust demanded.* "Where is the flock that was given thee," etc.? This word is addressed to the rulers of Judah and Jerusalem. Their people, the nation over whom they ruled, were God's flock, his "beautiful flock." That flock had been entrusted to the rulers' care. The influence of those in power was very great. As were the leaders of the people—especially the king—so were the people themselves. They could be led like a flock, and were so. Tremendous, therefore, was the responsi-bility of those in power, to whom was entrusted this flock of the Lord. But they had used their great authority and power badly. Ruin had come or was about to come upon the flock (cf. vers. 18, 19); they were to be scattered, scattered wholly, and the greater portion of them lost. To these careless and guilty shepherds the Lord now comes, and asks for the flock he had placed in their hands. "Give an account of thy stewardship," was said to those who were to be no longer stewards because of their faithlessness. Now, this question, "Where is the flock," etc.? is one which should be often heard sounding in the ears of many others besides those to whom it was first addressed, e.g.—

I. To the pastors of the Church. The Church of God is his flock, his "beautiful flock." Its members are very dear to him, "purchased with his own blood." The Church is given, entrusted, to pastors. When Christ ascended up on high he gave some "pastors." This method of ordering his Church is the one he has willed. His blessing has evidently rested on it. What does not the Church of God owe to her faithful pastors? But whatever their character they cannot but have great influence. They are trusted by the people. They have received special gifts for their work in the form of mental and moral endowments. They are much prayed for. They are specially set apart for the charge of the Church of God. They have every induce-ment to fidelity. Faithful, the love of their charge will gather round them; the fear of God will dwell within them; the crown of life awaits them. And these mighty motives, acting upon hearts already prepared by God's grace and devoted to this high office, have for the most part secured a great degree of fidelity in it. Hence a character and reputation have become associated with the office, which cannot but invest with much influence, as it does with much responsibility, all those who occupy it. But in spite of all this there may be, as there has been at times, great unfaithfulness. Hence the flock has been scattered. The Church has suffered in numbers, in purity of doctrine, in consistency of life, in spirituality of character. Its enjoyment in all holy service goes; its power for good in the neighbourhood where it dwells goes; its regard for all that marks vigorous life in a Church all goes; and ere long its "candlestick is removed out of its place." Perhaps its numbers may not greatly diminish. There shall be the observance of the sabbath, its services, its sermons, its sacraments—orderly, regular, frequent. Many things may conduce to this. Its name may live, but it is dead. Oh, the awfulness of this! And if it have been through the negligence and unfaithfulness of the pastor, who shall deliver him from the charge of blood-guiltiness which will lie at his door? What will he answer when the question is addressed to him, as one day it surely will be, "Where is the flock that was given thee, thy beautiful flock?" Let every pastor of Christ's Church consider this and pray—

> "Chief Shepherd of thy chosen sheep,
> From death and sin set free,
> Let every under-shepherd keep
> His eye intent on thee."

II. To ALL PARENTS. Our children are the Lord's flock, his "beautiful flock." They are very dear to him. He puts his arm round every one of them; he takes them all up in his arms and blesses them. He declares by his Word and by their baptism that they are of his kingdom, and he both promises vast reward to those that receive them in his Name, and threatens with dreadful doom all those who "offend" them. But parents have unspeakable influence over them. They mould and fashion them, not in outward form and habits alone, but in inward character. For a long time they are as God to their children, who know no higher authority, no higher help. Hence they trust their parents utterly. And to guard against the abuse of this tremendous trust, God has implanted the instincts of parental love, and given every motive to parents to guard and keep well those he has entrusted to their care. Now, if through parental unfaithfulness those children become renegades from God, he will surely ask this question, "Where is the flock," etc.? Let remembrance of this lead to earnest prayer and diligent heed, so that each parent at last may have the unspeakable joy—as he may have—of standing at last before God, and saying, with glad thankfulness, "Behold, here am I, and the children, thou hast given me."

III. To EVERY INDIVIDUAL SOUL. For the sum of all the faculties, opportunities, talents, the whole of the varied gifts and capacities which together form our spiritual nature—judgment, affection, conscience, intellect, will,—all these are the flock of God which is entrusted to every individual man; and by due care and cultivation of them he can preserve and develop them into an offering of worship and consecration which God will ever accept and bless. Every man has the making of his own life by the help of God. There is scarce any degree of honour and joy which he may not win by faithfulness in the use of that which God has entrusted to him. Concerning them all God says, "Occupy till I come." And how vast and varied is the help God gives to us in this great work! What means of grace are provided! What recompense even here and now is given! Victory over self; a mind at peace; blessed influence over others; the love and esteem of the good; free communion and intercourse with God himself; the consciousness of the Divine love; the bright and blessed hope of the eternal life hereafter. So that even now "in keeping of God's commandments there is great reward." But if we be unfaithful here and "waste" all our "goods"—these high gifts, faculties, and opportunities—sowing to the flesh when we should be sowing to the Spirit, then this question will be heard concerning all these things, "Where is the flock," etc.? And then we search in vain for any answer to the next question (ver. 21), "What wilt thou say when he shall punish thee?" Therefore let us each keep continually before our minds such truths as those that are taught in the well-known hymn—

"A charge to keep I have,
A God to glorify,
A never-dying soul to save
And fit it for the sky.

"Help me to watch and pray,
And on thyself rely;
Assured if I my trust betray
I shall for ever die."

C.

Vers. 21, 22.—*Sin its own scourge.* I. THERE ARE OTHER SCOURGES FOR SIN. The direct and positive inflictions of the Divine wrath. Not alone the Bible but the great books of history and experience must all be denied if we deny such positive punishment of sin. Never has there been yet any system of laws for moral beings which has been left to be simply self-acting, and which therefore have had no positive sanctions of penalty for transgression added. And God's Law is not such. As the Jews and other nations and individuals have found, and as the unrepentant will find hereafter, if not now, God's Word upon this matter is most assuredly true.

II. BUT SIN IS ITS OWN SCOURGE. That scourge is woven and knotted with many cords. 1. *Conscience,* ever passing sentence of judgment. 2. *Habits of wrong-doing,* hateful but fast clinging to the soul, and by which it is "tied and bound." 3. *The manifold difficulty of repentance.* The man would heartily turn from his evil way, but he has got into the current just above the falls, and it is bearing him on and down, resist as he will. 4. *The sight of children, companions, etc., corrupted and perhaps ruined by our evil example.* Oh, what a horror is this: seeing those whom, for every reason human and Divine we were bound to cherish and guard from evil, cursed by *our* sin! 5. *The moral disapprobation of the good around us.* Their sentence of condemnation is felt to have a binding power. What they "bind on earth is bound in heaven." 6. *The "fearful looking for of judgment."* Such are some of the cords which, woven together, make up the dreadful scourge wherewith sin scourges itself.

III. AND THIS SELF-MADE SCOURGE IS THE MOST TERRIBLE OF ANY. Deep and unfathomable as were the sufferings of our Lord, he distinctly declared that those coming on his enemies were worse. "Weep not for me," he said, "but weep for yourselves, and for your children. . . . If they do these things in a green tree," etc. It is evident, therefore, that suffering in which the consciousness of sin enters must be worst of all. Those "stripes by which we are healed," though they "ploughed deep furrows" on the body of our blessed Lord, yea, upon his inmost soul, still there are stripes more terrible even than they. The quenchless fire of God's positive inflictions would be more tolerable were it not for the gnawing of that undying worm—the sinner's own remorse. Are not they, then, "fools" indeed who "make a mock at sin"?—C.

Ver. 23.—*An awful condition indeed.* "Can the Ethiopian change his skin," etc.? This verse tells of one who has brought himself to such a pass that he cannot cease from sin. It is an awful condition indeed. Note—

I. SOME OF THE ELEMENTS WHICH MAKE IT SO. They are: 1. *The memories of a better past.* There was a time when his soul was unsullied, his hands clean, his heart pure, his life unstained; when he could hold up his head in conscious integrity by the grace of God. But that is all gone. 2. *The prostration of his will.* He is continually making resolves, but they are frail as cobwebs, they are broken through by the slightest temptation now. The power to firmly and steadfastly resolve seems gone from him. He has resolved so often, but in vain, that his will now refuses to rise to the endeavour. 3. *The powerlessness of all means of deliverance.* He attend's God's house, he reads the Scriptures, he kneels in prayer, he goes to the Lord's table still it may be, but they have lost their power to hold him back from his sin. They seem to be of no use at all. 4. *The fearful onlook to God's judgment.* He sees it coming swiftly upon him. He is ever terrified at the near approach of the day when he will be utterly lost. "Lost! lost!" he is ever saying to himself. He fears exposure, he fears the final doom, and knows not how to escape. 5. *Shame in the presence of the good.* He is haunted by the feeling, "If they but knew me as I am!" and he knows the day is coming when they will know, and he will be cast out as vile. 6. *The thought of the misery and shame he will bring upon others.* Perhaps he has wife, children, father, mother, a number of friends and relations, whom he knows he will drag down with him in his own ruin. 7. *The temptation to recklessness born of despair.* Satan is ever suggesting to him that, as he cannot regain what he has lost, he had better take his fill of such pleasure as he has. And too often he yields. 8. *The perversion of his understanding.* It is his interest to believe there is no God, and hence his intellect is busy in gathering together materials for this belief and for doubting and denying all religious truth. And so he sinks down into atheism and all ungodliness. Yes; his is an awful condition indeed. But consider—

II. SOME COUNSELS TO THOSE WHOM THESE TERRIBLE TRUTHS CONCERN. 1. Remember you cannot be certain that you have come to this condition. Satan will endeavour to persuade you that there is no hope. But believe him not. You are lost if you believe him. Steadfastly refuse to believe. 2. If the thought that such should be your condition distresses you, take it as a token for good that God has not given you up. 3. Remember that others have been saved who were as near being lost as you. 4. Rouse yourself to use all means of help which God has given you. (1) Let there be special seasons of prayer. (2) Avoid the occasions of your sin. (3) Put every hindrance you can in the way of your sin ; such as altering your manner of life, avoiding being alone, reading such Scriptures and such books as will tend to deepen your sense of the sin and show you how to escape from it. (4) Avail yourself of the counsels of some wise and godly friend. (5) Fill up your time, hands, and thoughts with useful and absorbing work. (6) Do not despise small victories ; they lead on to greater ones. (7) "Pray without ceasing." Remember that God is able and has promised to "save to the *uttermost* all that come unto God by Christ." Thus doing, even *thou* shalt be saved.—C.

Ver. 27.—*The one thing needful.* "Wilt thou not be made clean? When," etc. ?

I. MEN ARE SPIRITUALLY UNCLEAN. Like as the Lord looked down upon the occupants of the porches at Bethesda, and saw but a multitude of impotent folk (John v.); so now, as "his eyes behold the children of men," he sees a similar though a far more terrible sight—the mass of mankind spiritually diseased. This is manifestly true of the heathen world. The abominations and the cruelties that are practised there show the virulence of the soul's malady amongst them. And if we look at the mass of those who profess and call themselves Christians, in how many of these is the profession profession only, a veneer of religious customs covering a corrupt and sin-loving heart. And if it be so with the professing Church, what must it be with those who reject all the means of grace which the Christian Church enjoys?

II. BUT GOD GREATLY DESIRES THAT MEN SHOULD BE DELIVERED FROM THIS UNCLEANNESS. "He will have all men to be saved and to come to the knowledge of the truth." He desires this: 1. *From his very nature.* He himself is the most holy God. But all moral qualities ever strive to reproduce themselves in those around them. Let a man be characterized by orderliness, truthfulness, sobriety, purity, and in proportion as he is so the contact of those of opposite character will be painful to him, and he will endeavour to make them like himself. And so, because "good and upright is the Lord, *therefore* will he teach sinners in the way." 2. *His righteousness* also. The sense of outrage and wrong which sin must produce in the heart of God makes him angry with the wicked every day. 3. *His compassion.* Sin is sorrow. We wonder at the priests of Baal persisting in cutting and wounding themselves. But is not every sinner just such a one? And with this added sorrow—that their wounds are for eternity, and not for the short life here alone. On the other hand, to be "made whole" spiritually is to be made blessed for ever.

III. YET MEN WILL NOT. The tone of the question, the woe which precedes it, the comparison of the sinner with the Ethiopian and the leopard, etc. (ver. 23), the half-despairing cry, "When shall it once be?" (ver. 27),—all this shows the prophet's conviction of man's persistent clinging to his sin. Were the question concerning bodily disease, it would be unnecessary. Who would not be delivered from that? But when it is spiritual healing, men will not. From the *consequences* of their sin they are willing to be delivered—the punishment, the remorse, the shame, etc.—but not from the sin itself. True, at times, in the first keen pangs of remorse, and under the vivid sense of shame, they would be willing *then* to be rid of the sin itself. But their return to their sin shows how momentary and superficial this feeling was. And men would be willing, perhaps, *if by some one act* the whole cure could be effected ; if the being made whole was not so slow, so difficult, so self-denying a process. And, in fact, they do hope that by some one act—a death-bed repentance—the whole process will be accomplished.

IV. But without man's own consent he cannot be made whole. God does not by a mere act of power make a man spiritually whole, as he makes one tree an oak, another an elm. The will must consent. We have this awful power of compelling Christ to " stand at the door and knock ; " for the door of our hearts is opened from the inside. *We* must undo the bolts and remove the bars. No view of the Holy Spirit's influence which contradicts this can be a true view. We can, and alas! do, say " No " to God. But also we can, and he is ever pleading with us to, say " Yes " to his call.

V. But one day it shall be given. " My people shall be willing in the day of my power." Christ wept over Jerusalem, but yet he told them that when next he came they should say, " Blessed be he that cometh in the Name of the Lord ; cf. also the predicted repentance of the Jews, " They also which pierced him," etc. (Zech. xiv.). But oh, what "everlasting burnings," what awful scourgings, has Jerusalem had to go through before, like the prodigal, she came to herself! Let none abuse this doctrine. If we will say " Yes " to God now, and come to Christ in loving self-surrender, we shall find his yoke easy and his burden light ; but if we will say " No," then we shall have to come to ourselves ; and what may not that involve? Truly, " now is the accepted time," etc.—C.

Ver. 16.—*A solemn warning.* This is an appeal to the fears of the people ; one of the many instances in which the prophet seeks to win them to the way of righteousness by the presage of impending woe. Utter destruction is before them (ver. 14), the twilight is fast deepening into " gross darkness." But even now it is not too late for them to avert the calamity by their repentance. It is not mainly through their fears that Christianity exerts its influence over men. But, as many of the discourses of Christ show, men may sometimes sink into conditions of moral insensibility from which only an alarming voice will awaken them. And the gospel has its side of terror. Even the gracious Saviour and his apostles spoke of "wrath to come." Consider (1) *the duty,* (2) *the motive.*

I. The duty. " Give glory to your God." Several distinct elements of thought and life are involved in this. 1. *A recognition of the sacred and indissoluble relation in which we stand towards God.* However we may have forsaken him, he is still " the Lord our God." We are still his dependent creatures, his needy children. To please him, to serve his purposes, to show forth his glory, must, in the very nature of things, be the end of our existence. All religious life begins with the devout acknowledgment of this supreme personal relationship. 2. *A due sense of the claims God has, on the ground of what he is in himself, on our regard.* The true glory of the Divine Being is his infinite moral perfections. When Moses said, " I beseech thee show me thy glory," God answered, " I will make all my goodness pass before thee, and I will proclaim the Name of the Lord before thee." We " give glory to God " when, gazing upon the beauty and majesty of his intrinsic moral excellences, we yield back to him a due response of reverence, and admiration, and trust, and love. 3. *Practical surrender to his service.* "Glorify God in your body and in your spirit, which are God's " (1 Cor. vi. 20). The actual homage of a godly life is indicated here—the consecration of all the powers of our nature as a " living sacrifice " upon the altar of the Lord. If the Name of the Lord our God is hallowed in our hearts, we shall thus give ourselves and our all to him. Practical goodness akin to his own is the best and most acceptable tribute we can pay. We honour him most when we most strive to be like him in all holy character and Godlike deed.

II. The motive. " Before he cause darkness," etc. Here is a prospect that may well awaken fear. Something more than mere external calamity is suggested. There is internal distress, mental perplexity and bewilderment ; a condition in which the spirits of the people become a prey to all kinds of misleading and deluding influences, wildly groping after a good that is lost and gone from them for ever. Few pictures of imagination could be sadder than that of men looking and longing for the light, only to find the darkness growing more and more deep and dense around them. It is often something like this when men are unfaithful to their real convictions and negligent of the acknowledged claims of God. Trifle with truth and conscience, and you cannot wonder that truth should become to you a mere mocking shadow, and conscience a perpetual foe to your peace. Despise the sacred privileges and obligations of life, and you make them to be sources of heavy condemnation. Let the light be scorned or abused, and it turns into "the shadow of death." "Walk while ye have the light, lest darkness come upon you: for he that walketh in darkness knoweth not whither he goeth" (John xii. 35).—W.

Ver. 23.—*A moral impossibility.* This passage expresses the hopelessness of the prophet as regards the success of any human effort to persuade the people to forsake their evil ways, or by any efforts of their own to save themselves. It suggests—
I. THE INVETERACY OF SIN. 1. Arising from *the depravity of nature.* The dark spots and the ebon skin have a hidden cause. Sins are the natural outcome of sin. All forms of wrong-doing are but symptoms on the surface of a secret moral disease. "Out of the heart proceed evil thoughts," etc. (Matt. xv. 19). 2. *The force of habit.* "Use is second nature." Custom has a power over men that rivals that of native propensity. As good habit is a most effective educator of every form of virtue, so, on the other hand, when habit has been allowed to foster the evil tendencies of a man's nature, he becomes hopelessly "tied and bound with the chain of his sins."
II. THE MORAL IMPOTENCE IT ENGENDERS. Sin not only corrupts the springs of a man's moral life, but paralyzes all his nobler powers, robs him of the ability to act out the better instincts of his nature. The voice of natural conscience may not be wholly silenced, the natural heart may not be utterly destitute of good impulses; but there is no redeeming power in these. As well expect the darkness to give birth to light, and life to spring spontaneously out of death, as suppose that a sin-loving, sin-hardened man will of himself forsake his evil ways. He will never be able by his own hand "to pluck the vicious quitch of blood and custom wholly out of him." The complete moral helplessness of humanity was made abundantly evident before the full revelation of gospel grace. It was when we were "without strength" that Christ "died for the ungodly."
III. THE WONDROUS EFFICACY OF THE REGENERATING POWER OF GOD. The most defiled and degraded nature may be transformed by the touch of him who made it. Even the skin of the Ethiopian and the leopard's spots must yield to the sovereignty of the Divine energy. Deep-rooted and habitual as the evil in a man's heart and life may be, the blood of Jesus Christ cleanseth him from it, and when the Spirit of Christ moulds the substance of his being he becomes "a new creature: old things are passed away; behold, all things are become new" (2 Cor. v. 17).—W.

Vers. 1—11.—*The marred girdle.* I. THE SIGNIFICANCE OF THE GIRDLE. This is set before us clearly in ver. 11. God chose something which should illustrate the close connection between Israel and himself, and yet which should illustrate at the same time how easily that connection could be severed. The girdle was, of course, a familiar part of an Israelite's apparel. Not exactly a necessity, for a man could perhaps do without it; and yet a necessity in this sense, that habit had made it so. The very function of the girdle was to bind; otherwise it was, as a girdle, of no use. Thus, by likening the people to a girdle, God indicated that, in a certain sense, he had made them necessary to himself. He had placed them in a conspicuous position, where the service they could render was very important. He meant that he and his people should be viewed together; he always in relation to them, they always in relation to him. Hence the variety of terms in which he indicates his purpose in making the children of Israel to be as his girdle. "That they might be unto me for *a people.*" Jehovah was to look on them with a feeling of ownership and mastery which he was not able to feel with regard to other nations; and they, in turn, were to look up to Jehovah, feeling that all their purposes and actions were to be determined by his will. Jehovah meant that one of the most suggestive and comforting names by which he could be known should be that of the God of his people Israel, and that in turn Israel should be known as the people of Jehovah. In them Jehovah was to be praised; in them he was to be glorified.

Other nations might play the part of girdle to their deities, but there was really nothing of substance to gird. But when Jehovah drew Israel to himself, there was the opportunity of a real, glorious, and ever-extending service before them. Other nations chose and fabricated their gods; Jehovah chose and separated Israel, and in doing so intended the connection to be a very close one, and provided all the means by which it might become such.

II. THE INSTABILITY OF THE GIRDLE. The very Israelite who was to be taught lessons by this girdle, when he chose a girdle for himself, was generally able to make it serve his purpose. He would get it of some durable substance, to wear long. Elijah and John the Baptist were girt with leathern girdles. The Israelite, in the girdle with which he was familiar, dealt with that which was altogether under his control. The longer he wore it, the easier he found it, and the more amenable to his touch. If it began to tear and slip, and to slacken and hinder just when it should have been tightest and most helpful, its owner would very soon get rid of it as a deceiving girdle. But while Jehovah could bring his people very close, and compel them in a certain sense to remain with him, he could not make them cleave to him. Cleaving could only be done with purpose of heart, and must be a voluntary action. These people were not as a piece of linen or leather, to be folded exactly as the wearer might choose. If they had been they could not have rendered the service Jehovah wished from them, and in the result they showed that they did not wish to cleave to God. He could not trust them. Again and again he tried them, only to find that they cared nothing for their relation to him, nothing for the golden opportunity of setting forth his praise and glory.

III. THE HUMILIATION OF THE GIRDLE. Jeremiah was told to take this linen girdle and bind it round his loins. Linen was the material of the priests' garments; and was not Israel a consecrated people? Jeremiah, belonging to a priestly family, would easily be able to get hold of a linen girdle; although the directions given to him here would seem to show that this particular girdle was, in some way, to excite special attention. Notice how the instructions were given to the prophet bit by bit. At first he is simply told to put on the girdle. It was there to teach its own lesson to all who had eyes to observe and a disposition towards timely repentance. Then with his girdle he was to take a journey to Euphrates. That such a journey was long, difficult, and dangerous, is true as men count length, difficulty, and danger, but to a prophet the greatest difficulties and dangers come from refusing to take the way of God, however long it may be. Jonah had to go to Nineveh; what is there unreasonable in supposing that Jeremiah had to go to the neighbourhood of Babylon? It may have been just as profitable a use of time to take long journeys there as to go on giving testimony against those who resolutely closed their ears. Besides, it was by Euphrates that the girdle Israel was to be marred. It was to be shown to them that, if they would not act as a girdle, they could easily be made useless for any other purpose. If they would not be God's people, they should achieve no position for themselves. If they would not honour the name which he had given them, there was no other name by which they could get distinction. If they would not be to his praise and glory, as the girdle cleaving firmly and serviceably to him, then they should be to his praise and glory as the marred girdle. If we will not do what God wishes us to do, then he takes care that we shall not do what we ourselves wish to do. The girdle brought back from Euphrates was found profitable for nothing. That which is meant for salt of the earth and loses its savour, is thenceforth good for nothing but to be cast out and to be trodden underfoot of men.—Y.

Vers. 15, 16.—*A demand for the timely giving of what is due to Jehovah.* It will be observed that the previous verses of this chapter set forth the doom of Jehovah's apostate people by two very expressive figures. There is the figure of the girdle, marred and become good for nothing by lying so long in the damp recess of the rock. There is also the figure of the inhabitants of Jerusalem, from those high in station down to the common people, every one of them become as it were a living wine-skin, filled with drunken fury, destroying one another and being destroyed. This figure, bordering on the grotesque, presents as impending a very terrible scene. But with the verses now to be considered there returns what we may call an evangelical interval. Though in these prophecies of Jeremiah gloom of necessity predominates, yet there are equally necessary intervals of light, intervals where the mercy of Jehovah is clearly revealed, and his never-failing desire that his people should return to him.   There is, of course, practically, no hope for these people so far as their present social state is concerned.   They will go on their own way; but to the last God will also make his appeal.   Notice now the things which God asks for here.

I. ATTENTION.   " Hear ye, and give ear."   These people have never really attended to the import of the prophetic messages.   Either they have been totally indifferent or they have been irritated by some word they did not like, and so the complete message has fallen uncomprehended upon their ears.   For instance, the why and wherefore of the prophet's extraordinary journey to the Euphrates, they did not trouble themselves to consider.   And it is plain from ver. 12 how entirely they missed the meaning of the prophet's saying respecting the bottles being filled with wine.   The parabolic sentence was to them nothing more than mere commonplace.   And of course, so long as attention was lacking, truth was of no use.   There is an analogy between the receiving of truth and the receiving of bodily food.   As food must be properly introduced into the physical system, so truth must be properly introduced into the mind, brought before the understanding of the individual, firmly grasped by him in its reality, so that it may become a real and beneficial element in the life.

II. HUMILITY.   There must be submission to the prophet as a proved messenger from God.   Pride is going to be the ruin of these people.   The prophet himself was humbly obedient to all commandments of God; why, then, should his audience be proud?   The grandees of Jerusalem do not like to be talked to by the comparative rustic from Anathoth.   The elders resent remonstrances from a man comparatively young.   Those whose boast it perhaps was that they had never been in bondage to any man, do not like to hear of conquest and captivity.   There is no getting at truth and right without humility.   Because truth means, not only the reception of that which is true, but the casting out of the old and the loved and the often boasted of.   It is very hard for a man to cut himself off from the past and show by a very different future how he feels the errors and follies of which he has been guilty.   It is hard for the διδάσκαλος like Nicodemus to go down from his chair and become a μαθητής, stumbling among the rudimentary principles of the kingdom of heaven.

III. THE GIVING OF GLORY TO JEHOVAH.   " Give glory to Jehovah your God."   These people had been giving elsewhere what *they reckoned* to be glory, but which, so far from being glory, was indeed their own deepest shame.   Glory of a certain sort they had plenty of, but they came short of the glory of God.   They did not, in the conduct of their life, show a proper response to the wisdom by which God had created them as men and separated them as a people.   By their present doings they were exposing the Name of Jehovah to insult and scorn from all round about.   This asking for glory to be given was a request reasonable in itself.   If a master is a good master, it is not right that his servant should act so as to make the master's reputation suffer.   If a father is a good father, it is not right for his child to act as if he had been deprived of all beneficial influences in the way of teaching and training.   What is thought of a man who basely forgets his nationality and laughs at the feelings that gather around the idea of fatherland?   And hence the Name of Jehovah was a name to be magnified in word and deed and every outcome of life on the part of his people.   We ourselves must labour to praise God with our whole hearts.   And more than that, we must live as those who show the power of *God*, saving us and lifting us into an altogether higher life.

IV. THE GIVING OF THIS GLORY PROMPTLY ON ACCOUNT OF PERIL TO THOSE WHO REFUSE TO GIVE.   The figure employed is that of a traveller on a journey.   He gets into the wrong road, gets indeed altogether out of any proper road; but he persists in mere wandering, refuses to be warned, will not accept guidance back to the proper path.   He sees dangers, many dangers, but because it is daylight he manages to escape them.   And now, as the darkness momentarily increases, the warnings also increase in urgency.   When the darkness is fully come, where will he be?   On the mountains, not able to take one confident step in any direction, lest it be over the precipice.   Furthermore, in the case of a traveller, he has always this resort, that if darkness comes amid such dangers he can stand still till the return of the dawn.   But here is the contrast in that the expected dawn will never come.   This rebellious, God-dishonouring generation is virtually walking into captivity of its own accord.   As far as it is concerned, it will look in vain for restoration. The restoration will belong, not to it, nor even to its children, but rather to its children's children. Those who wander from God wander into a state where they are self-destroyed, because the resources of which they boasted themselves have come to nothing. Glorify God, willingly, in the light, or you will end by glorifying him unwillingly, in the darkness. Think of what came to Herod because he did not give the glory to God.—Y.

Ver. 20.—*A searching question to the shepherd.* The position of a king towards his people was illustrated by the position of a shepherd towards his flock. Hence the question here was doubtless meant for the special attention of the king. The nation was largely in the hands of the king for the time being. Formal authority belonged to him, and it was generally joined with corresponding power; hence the responsibility by which he was justly held for the exercise of his authority, and yet it is plain that such a question as this could only have a partial application to the responsibilities of any particular king. Whoever the king may have been at the time this prophecy was uttered, it was no "beautiful flock" that had been handed to him. He had received it after the neglect and abuse of many predecessors. The nation itself, considered in its collective capacity and through all its past growth, is here impersonated and addressed. Consider—

I. To WHAT CLASSES OF PERSONS SUCH A QUESTION AS THIS MAY BE CONSIDERED AS STILL ADDRESSED. Evidently it bears on all who have to do with the *government* of any people. Just, firm government has much to do—though how much cannot be exactly expressed—with the welfare of every community. The personal conduct and example of governors is also a very important matter. Better kings in Israel might have helped to make a better people, and this influence of government becomes ever a more important thing to recollect, because the people are becoming more and more their own governors. Each individual has only an infinitesimal part, but it is a real part, and therefore the conduct of each most surely affects the aggregate. It is plain how this question bears on the *parental relation.* It did so bear on Israel of old, and it bears equally on all who have offspring put in their charge, to train as far as they can, for the service of Christ, in their day and generation. *Teachers* may be said to have a "beautiful flock" in their charge. The deep influence of Dr. Arnold on his pupils shows how a teacher may bring out all the beauty of his flock. The application to spiritual teachers and pastors under Christ, the great Teacher and Pastor, is obvious. And, generally, every one must consider those around him, on whom, by daily companionship or any way of sufficient contact, he exercises influence. Every one is responsible, not only for that which is formally handed to him, but just as much for all that he can in any way keep. Let no one suppose that he himself has nothing to do but be cared for. Just as we are every one of us sheep in one sense, so we are shepherds in another.

II. WHAT IS REQUIRED IN ORDER TO GIVE THE RIGHT ANSWER TO THIS QUESTION. Nothing but this, that we can truthfully assert ourselves to have been *faithful.* It cannot be required that we should lose none of the sheep. Not even the most faithful shepherd that trod the pastures of Palestine could manage that. He could only do his best to be provident, watchful, and courageous, so as to be himself free from blame if a sheep was lost or fell a prey to the wild beast. And not one of the kings of Israel or Judah could have said quite so much as this. Some of them, indeed, showed not the slightest notion that sheep had been put into their hands at all. Depend upon it, if there were more of this faithfulness there would be more success in gathering and preserving a flock for God. Faithfulness is the least that can be shown in our relations to others. Of course, meddlesomeness, censoriousness, bigotry, must not be mistaken for it. No good can be done if individual liberty is not respected, but nothing must prevail on us to deviate in the slightest from the line Christ has marked out. Those of Christ's sheep who, being most conscious of their own incapacity to make a way, keep their eyes fixed on the way their Master makes for them, are really doing something of the shepherd's work. Every one living and acting by the rule Christ has given is more of a shepherd than he thinks. Then, for comfort, let it be kept in mind that no faithfulness of ours will prevent the waywardness and wilfulness of others. Jesus warned Judas, but Judas went obstinately off into his own way. Paul, faithful as none of us can ever hope to be, had to bewail many who, professing faith, yet walked contrary to the will of Christ. The great thing to be aimed at is that we should be clear from the blood of all men (Acts xx. 26—30).

III. It will be seen that this was a question FOR FLOCKS AS WELL AS FOR SHEPHERDS. Rulers are responsible for right leading, but subjects and followers are not altogether as sheep, that they should blindly follow those in formal authority. Truth has not been put within the formal shepherd's exclusive protection. We must take care whom we follow. It is a delusion to suppose that we can hand ourselves over spiritually to the guidance of any one less than Christ. Others may help and suggest; only he can command. Paul came to his hearers with arguments and persuasions, laying before them the truth, which they were able to receive because it was the truth, not because the authority of the speaker made it true. All New Testament preaching goes on the assumption that every one can be fully persuaded in his own mind. The same Scriptures are open to reader as to preacher. None can have their eternal interests perilled except by their own negligence.—Y.

Ver. 23.—*A natural impossibility.* I. THE NATURAL IMPOSSIBILITY HERE PRESENTED. It is a profound and momentous truth, God himself being the witness—the heart-searching God—that man who is accustomed to do evil cannot turn to good. This truth is not baldly stated here, but is illustrated in such a way that there can be no possible doubt as to God's meaning. Observe that the impossibility referred to is a *natural* one. It is not said that under no circumstances whatever can a man accustomed to do evil be enabled to do good. The thing affirmed is that the power of habit and custom is so strong that he cannot turn himself. If we are inclined to doubt this, and indulge in that glorification of human nature which is at once so easy and so perilous, we have only to think of the illustrations here employed. It is vain to discuss with a man who is determined to magnify the power of the natural man towards that which is right and good. The better plan is to assure one's own heart of the truth which God would make plain by these illustrations of his own giving. If any one asserted that an Ethiopian could change his skin or a leopard his spots, he would be reckoned a fool past arguing with. But there are multitudes who think it is very good advice to tell the poor slave of worldliness and passion to be a man and exert the strength of his will and turn away from evil. Now, what God says here by his prophet is that every such attempt must end in disappointment. No doubt there are certain times and stages in life when it is hard to accept such a view. It is a humbling and limiting view, one which exhibits in such an uncompromising way our weakness. But the sooner we come to take such a view—to take it practically and not in a mere speculative manner—to feel that the way of self-recovery and self-perfecting is closed against us, the better it will be for us.

II. THE CONSEQUENT NEED OF A GRACIOUS INTERVENTION. This is not stated here, but we know that it is meant to be remembered. In all such emphatic assertions of human inability there lies the suggestion that we may look confidently and ought to look promptly for abundance of Divine help. God puts his hand on our mouths to stop all proud words, but at the same time he would lead us to lay hold of his promises and be filled with his strength. A clear vision of our own inability means a clear vision of the need of Divine intervention, and a clear vision of the *need* of Divine intervention may be expected to prepare for an equally clear vision of the *reality* of that intervention. That which measures the impossibilities in the corrupted natural man helps to measure the reasonable purposes and expectations of the man who is renewed by the Spirit of God. When we have got the life that is hid with Christ in God, we have something within us which defies the corruptions so powerful before. The Christian, full of the Divine Spirit, is found able to utter all sorts of paradoxes. Though he cannot, of himself, make one hair white or black, he can be "suffering, yet alway rejoicing; poor, yet making many rich." There is a way, then, by which those accustomed to do evil can be brought to do good. There are resources which more than make up for the greatest lack of natural strength. If we only seek for those resources in the right place, we cannot fail to find them.

III. THE TEACHING TO BE DERIVED FROM THE EMPLOYMENT OF THESE PECULIAR ILLUSTRATIONS. Thousands of images were available to show natural impossibilities, but *these two* are employed. It will be observed that they relate to the alteration of external appearance. God could change the skin of the Ethiopian, could change the spots of the leopard; but he leaves them as they are, because no good purpose could be served by the alteration. Where an alteration is really wanted, he can make it, with results that are profitable now and promise a far greater profit in eternity. So far as the merely agreeable is concerned, it would certainly have been pleasanter for the negro if those features which make him an object of ridicule to the ignorant, the proud, and the fastidious, were taken away. But it is God's principle to interfere with nature only where sin has made the interference necessary. Many negroes—God be thanked —have found the better part, the one thing needful; and, compared with this, what is the most disturbing of surface discomforts? Continual comfort at the heart, a comfort which cannot be taken from him, makes him forget all these. There would be no object in changing the spots of the leopard; let us rather rejoice that God takes away from men the leopard-ferocity which makes them as dangerous as any beast of prey. How often we seek vain and useless things, making ourselves miserable over physical defects and peculiarities, and continuing quite indifferent to the washing of the heart from wickedness. Instead of being anxious after things we cannot change and need not change, let us pray and strive after that possible, fundamental, radical change which will bring in due time perfection of the whole man. God, working from the heart, will cause that in due time we shall be perfect and entire, lacking nothing.—Y.

EXPOSITION.

CHAPTER XIV.

This chapter must be read in connection with the following one. They describe chiefly Jeremiah's twofold attempt at intercession (see vers. 7—9 and 19—22)—a tender and appealing attempt indeed. The terrible sufferings of the people during a drought went to the prophet's heart. He even ventured, when repelled the first time, to intercede anew, on the ground of the covenant, but in vain. On receiving (ch. xv. 2—9) a revelation of the bitter fate in store for his people, he bursts out into a heart-rending complaint that his own destiny should throw him into such a whirlpool of strife. His Lord at once corrects and consoles him (ch. xv. 10—21). There are doubts, however, about the connection of these latter verses.—The date of the drought is not stated; but as the punishment of Judah is described as future, and no reference is made to the captivity of Jehoiachin, we shall probably be right in setting it during the reign of Jehoiakim.

Ver. 1.—**The dearth**; rather, *the drought*, or, more literally, *the droughts*, the plural being used to indicate the length of time the drought lasted.

Ver. 2.—The tenses in the following description should be perfects and presents; the Authorized Version, by its inconsistency, destroys the unity of the picture. **The gates thereof**; *i.e.* the people assembled

there. **They are black unto the** ground. "To be black," in Hebrew, is "to be dressed in mourning" (so *e.g.* Ps. xxxv. 14, "I bowed down in black"). Here we must understand the same verb which is expressed in the psalm, "They bowed down in mourning attire to the ground." "Black," however, is not to be taken literally; it means rather "squalid, unwashed" (of garments).

Ver. 3.—**Their nobles**—*i.e.* the upper classes of Judah and Jerusalem—**have sent their little ones**; rather, *their mean ones*; i.e. their servants, or perhaps (as Naegelsbach and Payne Smith) simply, "the common people;" it was not a matter concerning the rich alone. **To the pits**; *i.e.* to the cisterns. **Covered their heads**; a sign of the deepest mourning (2 Sam. xv. 30; xix. 4; Esth. vi. 12).

Ver. 4.—**The ground is chapt.** Perhaps; but it is more obvious to render, *is dismayed*, according to the usual meaning of the word. Words which properly belong to human beings are often, by a "poetic fallacy," applied to inanimate objects (as in ver. 2). **In the earth**; rather, *in the land*.

Ver. 5.—**Even the animals starve. Yea, the hind also.** The hind, contrary to that intense natural affection for which she was famous among the ancients, abandons her young.

Ver. 6.—**The wild asses . . . in the high places**; rather, *on the bare heights*. "The wild asses," says a traveller cited by Rosenmüller, "are especially fond of treeless mountains." **Like dragons**; render rather, *like jackals* (as ch. ix. 11; x. 22). The allusion is to the way jackals hold their head as they howl. We are told that even the keen eyes of the wild asses fail, **because** there was [is] **no grass**; rather, *herbage*. They grow dim first with seeking it so long in vain, and then from lack of nourishment.

Ver. 7.—The intercession of Jeremiah begins. **Do thou it**; a pregnant expression, equivalent to "act gloriously" (as Ps. xxii. 31; Isa. xlv. 23). **For thy name's sake.** Jehovah's "Name" pledges him to be merciful to his people, and not to make a full end of them, even when they have offended (comp. "Our Redeemer was thy name from of old" Isa. lxiii. 16).

Ver. 8.—How pathetic a supplication! Jehovah will surely not be **as a stranger in the land**—the strangers, or "sojourners," like the μέτοικοι, enjoyed no civic rights, and consequently had no interest in the highest concerns of the state—**and as a wayfaring man** that turneth aside—or perhaps, *pitcheth his tent;* for the traveller in Palestine doubtless carried his tent with him then as now—**to tarry for a night.** With the latter figure compare the beautiful comparison of the hope of the ungodly to "the remembrance of a guest that tarrieth but a day" (Wisd. v. 14).

Ver. 9.—**As a man astonied**; rather (comparing the Arabic *dahama*), *as one struck dumb*. But Dr. Payne Smith, with much reason, is more than half inclined to follow the Septuagint reading, equivalent to "as one in a deep sleep." **Leave us not**; literally, *lay us not down;* as if a burden of which the bearer is tired.

Vers. 10—16.—The answer of Jehovah.

Ver. 10.—**Thus have they loved to wander, . . . therefore the Lord doth not accept them**; *i.e.* with such pertinacity have they been set upon "wandering" (roving lawlessly about), that the Lord hath no more pleasure in them. "Therefore," is, literally, *and.* "Thus," or "so," is used in the same sense as in 1 Kings x. 12, which runs literally, ". . . there came not so [abundantly] almug timber." The particle of comparison has given much occupation to the commentators (see Payne Smith's note), but the above view is at once simple and suitable to the context; for Jeremiah has already admitted that "our backslidings are multiplied" (ver. 7). *The Lord doth not*, etc. (to the end of the verse), is quoted *verbatim* from Hos. viii. 13. Jeremiah puts conspicuous honour on the older inspired writers; he has no craving for originality. Nearly all has been said already; what he has to do is chiefly to adapt and to apply, **He will now remember**, etc. The emphasis is on "now." Nothing is more remarkable in the prophets than the stress laid on the unerring justness of the time chosen for Divine interpositions. When the iniquity is fully ripe, it as it were attracts the punish-

ment, which till then is laid up in store (comp. Gen. xv. 16; Isa. xviii. 5; xxxiii. 10).

Ver. 11.—**Pray not for this people.** So in ch. vii. 16 (on which see note); ch. xi. 14.

Ver. 12.—**Their cry.** The word is very forcible; it is the shriek in which an unsophisticated man gives vent to his pain and grief. **An oblation.** It is the vegetable offering (Authorized Version, "meat offering;" Luther, "speisopfer") which is referred to in the so-called *minkhah* (literally, *gift*). Though sometimes offered separately, it regularly accompanied a burnt offering. **I will not accept them.** Dr. Payne Smith tries to soften the rejection of these worshippers by the remark that "there is a time when the most genuine repentance avails nothing to avert the temporal consequences of sin." But the analogy of other similar passages (*e.g.* Isa. i. 15) warrants the view of Keil that the ground of the rejection of the worship is its heartless formalism and insincerity, which was equally a bar to Jehovah's favour and the prophet's intercession.

Ver. 13.—"Pleading with Providence, the good prophet lays the blame on ill teaching, but the stern answer (ver. 14), admitting the plea as true, rejects it as inadequate (ver. 14), and denounces sorrows which (vers. 17—22) the prophet passionately deprecates" (Rowland Williams). **Ah, Lord God!** rather, *Alas! O Lord Jehovah* (see on ch. i. 6). **The prophets say unto them.** The greater part of the prophetic order had not kept pace with its more spiritual members (Isaiah, Jeremiah, etc.). They still traded on those natural gifts of divination (Micah iii. 6) which were, no doubt, where genuine, of Divine origin, but which, even then, needed to be supplemented and controlled by a special impulse from the Spirit of holiness. Jeremiah, however, declares, on the authority of a revelation, that these prophets did not divine by any God-given faculty, but "the deceit of their own heart" (ver. 14). The Deuteronomic *Tōrāh*, discovered after a period of concealment at the outset of Jeremiah's ministry, energetically forbids the practice of the art of divination (Deut. xviii. 10).

Ver. 14.—**A thing of nought.** The word, however, is collective, and means all the various futile means adopted for prying into the future.

Ver. 16.—**I will pour their wickedness**; *i.e.* the fruits of their wickedness (comp. ch. ii. 19, "Thine own wickedness shall correct thee").

Vers. 17—21.—The prophet's grief, and second intercession.

Ver. 17.—**Therefore thou shalt say**, etc. There is something strange and contrary to verisimilitude in the prefixing of this formula, not to a Divine revelation, but to a mere expression of the pained human feelings of the prophet. It is possible that the editor of Jeremiah's prophecies thought the paragraph which begins here needed something to link it with the preceding passage, and selected his formula rather unsuitably. **Let mine eyes run down**, etc. (comp. ch. xiii. 27). Jeremiah's tender compassion shows itself in his choice of the expression, **the virgin daughter of my people**, just as we feel an added bitterness in the premature death of a cherished maiden.

Ver. 18.—A picture of the state of things after the capture of Jerusalem : the slain without, the famine-stricken within. The latter are described allusively as "sicknesses of famine" (so literally). As a peculiarly striking evidence of the downfall of greatness, it is added that even prophet and priest have **to go about into a land that they know not**. The verb used here can obviously not have its ordinary sense of going about for purposes of traffic. Aramaic usage suggests, however, a suitable meaning; what the prophet sketches before us is a company of these ex-grandees "begging their way" into an unknown land.

Ver. 19.—**We looked for peace**, etc.; a repetition of ch. viii. 15.

Ver. 20.—**Our wickedness, and the iniquity of our fathers**. There is a mysterious connection between the sin of the past and of the present. So in another prophet we read, "Your iniquities and the iniquities of your fathers together [will I requite]."

Ver 21.—**The throne of thy glory;** *i.e.* the temple (ch. xvii. 12; Ezek. xliii. 7), or Jerusalem (ch. iii. 17). It is the same conception where Jehovah is said to "dwell between" [or, 'sit upon'] "the cherubim" (Isa. xxxvii. 16; Ps. lxxx. 1; xcix. 1).

Ver. 22.—None of the **vanities**, or false gods (ch. iii. 17), of the heathen can deliver us in this our strait (want of rain). "Rainmakers" is still a common name of soothsayers among savage nations. *Thou alone art God, and our God;* or, in Jeremiah's phrase (not, Art **not thou he**, etc.? but) *Art thou not Jehovah our God?* and the ground of the appeal follows, Jehovah is the Maker of **all these** things; *i.e.* all the heavenly phenomena, especially the clouds and the rain.

HOMILETICS.

Vers. 1—6.—*A plague of drought.* I. A PLAGUE OF DROUGHT IS AN INSTANCE OF A NATURAL CALAMITY OCCASIONING GREAT DISTRESS. Jeremiah gives a vivid picture of the trouble such a plague causes. Men of all classes, from the noble to the ploughman, suffer under it ; the animal world is driven from its natural instincts; universal desolation and agony prevail. Yet this is all *natural*. It is not the result of war nor of any human interference; it is a natural calamity. Nature is not always placid and pleasing. She has her frowns, her storms, her droughts. The world is not a waste, howling wilderness; but neither is it a garden of Eden. Thorns spring up among the wheat. Even away from the perpetual deserts fertile fields are occasionally parched and withered. We must expect a mixed experience in human life, as we meet with it in nature. Showers of blessing are not always falling. There come also periods of dearth, seasons of natural distress.

II. A PLAGUE OF DROUGHT IS AN EXAMPLE OF ONE FORM OF THE PUNISHMENT OF SIN. Though the drought is natural, it is not, therefore, to be separated from all relation to human and moral affairs. God rules Nature through her laws when he does not supersede them. In his government of men God may overrule natural events to the execution of his decrees. When such a calamity as a plague of drought falls upon a land, it is well to ask whether there are no national sins for which it is sent as chastisement. Sometimes the calamities of nature are the direct result of human conduct. Thus Palestine now suffers from lack of water, partly because the felling of trees has diminished the rainfall, and partly because what rain there is is quickly drained off for want of proper irrigation arrangements. Still, we must not assume that every natural calamity is sent for the punishment of sin. This is but one among many Divine purposes. Wholesome discipline, ulterior advantages, the avoiding of worse though unseen calamities, etc., may enter into the Divine reasons for permitting the trouble. Such calamities should make us *examine* ourselves, not humiliate ourselves without thought and clear conviction of conscience.

III. A PLAGUE OF DROUGHT IN NATURE SHOULD SUGGEST THE POSSIBILITY OF SPIRITUAL DROUGHT. Outward things are symbolical of inward experiences. There is a drought of the soul—when the soul is not partaking of the "water of life," and it is the most fearful kind of drought. Yet, while the physical calamity excites all attention and occasions universal distress, this calamity is often unheeded. But the effects of it are not the less destructive. The soil becomes barren, unfruitful; the heavenly graces within, the instincts of Christian charity, are lost; the spiritual vision fails. It is unnatural not to feel thirst in a season of drought. The soul that is in this condition will first come to itself with a feeling of deep distress, a pain of inward longing, a panting and thirsting after God (Ps. lxiii. 1).

IV. A PLAGUE OF DROUGHT SHOULD MAKE US MORE THANKFUL FOR THE COMMON BLESSINGS OF DAILY LIFE. The commonest blessings are the most valuable. The first necessary of life is air, and air is the most abundant thing in nature. The next most important requirement is water, and water is usually exceedingly plentiful. Gold and diamonds are rare, but these can easily be spared. This very fact, which is a result of God's providential care, induces an ungrateful neglect. We take without thought that which we are always receiving. We must lose it to appreciate it. In sickness we prize health; in thirst we value water. It would be more wise and grateful to acknowledge God's blessings while we have them, instead of requiring him to take them from us to teach us their worth.

Ver. 7.—*A plea for mercy in spite of guilt.* I. WE CAN ONLY PLEAD FOR GOD'S MERCY AFTER A FRANK ADMISSION OF OUR OWN GUILT. The common habit of people is to take the opposite course—to excuse themselves, extenuate their faults, or ignore, or even deny them. But this is vain before God, and while persisted in it shuts the door against forgiveness. God can only forgive sin that is confessed, can only have mercy on the humble and penitent. This confession must be frank and full. Such a confession is contained in the prayer of Jeremiah. 1. *Personal* guilt is admitted—"our iniquities." 2. The shame of *increasing* guilt is admitted—"our backslidings." If we feel we are better than we once were, we excuse our present imperfection on the ground that it is at least an improvement on the past. It requires a genuine penitence to admit that we have been growing worse. 3. Sin is seen to be an offence *against God*—"We have sinned against thee." It is not a mere fault in ourselves; it is a direct act of warfare with Heaven. David said this (Ps. li. 4); so did the prodigal son (Luke xv. 18). 4. Sin is recognized as *abundant*—"Our backslidings are many." It is vain to confess some sins whilst denying others, or to attempt to represent them as less numerous than they really are. This keeping back of part of the confession mars the whole of it. 5. Guilt is acknowledged to be *open* before God—"Our sins *testify*." 6. It is seen to be a bar to our claim of simple right—they testify "against us." Condemnation, therefore, may justly follow the plain evidence of guilt. Our own sins are witnesses to oppose any plea we may found on our personal deserts.

II. OUR OWN GUILT, WHEN FRANKLY ADMITTED, IS NO HINDRANCE TO THE MERCY OF GOD. The only hindrance is impenitence. The ground of God's mercy is not our desert, but his goodness. If there is anything in us which predisposes him to be gracious, this is not our worth, but our want. The more wretched the condition to which our sin has brought us, the more urgent the call to his pity. The one plea is "for his Name's sake." 1. For the sake of God's *character*. His Name expresses what he is. His highest name is "Love." By this name we plead for mercy. Because of what he is, because of his inherent goodness, love, and pity, we implore his help. 2. For the sake of God's *honour*. He has promised to have mercy on the penitent (*e.g.* Deut. xxx. 1—10). Thus he has pledged his Name, bound himself by his own certain faithfulness. 3. For the sake of God's *glory*. His highest glory is his goodness. When he delivers his children his own Name is glorified. Redemption honours God more than creation. The song of the redeemed at the end of the world will be more sweet and more noble than the song of the sons of the morning at the dawn of creation. As Christians we see these truths more clearly revealed in Christ. He is the "Word" incarnate, the "Name," the highest manifestation of the character of God, the fulfilment of his greatest promises, the expression of his brightest glory. For us to pray "for Christ's sake" is the same as praying "for God's Name's sake."

Vers. 8, 9.—*The Hope of Israel a stranger in the land.* I. GOD IS THE HOPE AND SAVIOUR OF HIS PEOPLE. 1. God is the *Hope*. (1) He inspires hope; (2) in him is the ground for the realization of hope; (3) our highest hope is for the possession and enjoyment of God himself; (4) this hope is justifiable in the people of God. He is the Hope of Israel, truly the Hope of the spiritual Israel. 2. God is the *Saviour* in trouble. He is remembered in trouble if he is forgotten in prosperity. In our greatest need he is found nearest to us. Though he does not always prevent us from falling into trouble, he is always ready to help us when we are in. There is to us no more important character of God than that of the Saviour, since, as " man is born to trouble," we all need a Saviour, and he alone can deliver from the great sorrows and sins of life.

II. GOD MAY BE WITH US AS A STRANGER. 1. He may be with us and *unknown*— like the stranger who passes through a country unrecognized. He was received by Abraham as a stranger (Gen. xviii. 2). Hagar and Jacob failed at first to discern his presence. Christ was treated as an unknown stranger by the two disciples journeying to Emmaus. 2. He may be with us but for a *season*—like the traveller who sojourns for a night and is gone the next morning. We may receive temporary visitations of God without enjoying his abiding presence, casual glimpses of the Divine instead of a constant walking with God, the light of Heaven falling now and again on our path while earthly clouds fling long stretches of dreary shadow over the most of it. 3. He may be with us without having *communion* with us—as a stranger, not as a companion —as the traveller who pitches his tent in our land, not as the guest whom we welcome to our hearth. Thus God may be near to us without our receiving him into our hearts as our great Friend. 4. He- may be with us without *acting* for our good —like a mighty man slumbering. So he may see our need and yet we may not be saved.

III. IT IS MOST SAD THAT GOD SHOULD BE WITH US AS A STRANGER. 1. It is sad because the *blessings of his presence are then not received.* (1) He must be known if we are to benefit by his aid. (2) We need his constant presence for constant distresses. (3) God helps by inward grace, which must come through close personal communion. (4) We need the active aid of God, not the mere fact of his presence. 2. It is sad because it is a *violation of our natural relations with God.* God is our Father. Shall our Father be but as a stranger passing through our midst? He is changeless in his eternal love to us. We are bound to him by close and perpetual obligations, and we are in great and constant need of him. How, then, do we ever find ourselves in this unnatural condition? The cause is in us (ver. 10). Great sin cherished in impenitence severs us from God, and makes it necessary that he should depart from us. God is a stranger when with us, (1) because we are too earthly minded to discern his presence, and too occupied with worldly things to think of it; (2) because we do not open our hearts to receive him in inward companionship; and (3) because we do not seek and trust his help in our need (Rom. x. 21).

Vers. 13—16.—*False prophets.* I. OFFICIAL TEACHERS MAY BE FALSE TEACHERS. The false prophets belonged to the recognized order of prophets. No rank in the Church confers infallibility. Popes have been heretics. The authority of a teacher must be sought in his message, not in his office. It is our duty to try the spirits by their correspondence with *known revelation* (1 John iv. 2), by the *fruits* of their lives and doctrines (Matt. vii. 16), and by the standard of our own *conscience* (2 Cor. iv. 2).

II. PREACHING WHICH IS NOT INSPIRED BY THE DIVINE SPIRIT OF HOLINESS IS LIKELY TO BE FALSE. The prophet may have a piercing intellect and a towering imagination. Yet he will err if he be blinded by unholiness and excluded from the revelations of spiritual communion. He speaks only out of his own heart; but the heart is " deceitful above all things." Attempts are constantly made to evolve religious truth out of the inner consciousness of the thinker. No idle dreams are more delusive, since (1) men have not the *materials* out of which to build a theology of their own; (2) they have not the *faculties* capable of using those materials—sin perverts the spiritual vision, prejudice and self-interest distort views of truth.

III. CONSCIOUSLY TEACHING FALSE IDEAS OF RELIGION IS A HEINOUS CRIME. It is using the Name of God in vain (ver. 14). It is abusing the trust of a high office for low purposes. It is likely to involve many in the toils of a fatal deception. It is easy to prophesy smooth things—easy thus to gain a vulgar popularity. But if this is done at the expense of truth, it is an awful sin. All Christian teachers should beware of the temptation to degrade their mission by aiming at pleasing their hearers instead of faithfully proclaiming the will of God.

IV. FALSE TEACHING IN RELIGION WILL BE PUNISHED BY FATAL RESULTS. It ought to be clear to everybody that the first question concerning any teaching is whether it is true. Yet this question is often ignored. The prophet is eloquent; the doctrine is pleasing; the prediction is inviting. But what of all that if it is false? The prophecy will be punished when truth is revealed by facts. Then the false prophet will suffer by the fulfilment in himself of the prophecy he denied, and the people by the coming of the evil day they were too ready to hear discredited.

Ver. 20—ch. xv. 1.—*Prayer for mercy rejected.* I. THE PRAYER IS BASED ON URGENT PLEAS. 1. *A complete confession of sin.* (Ver. 20.) It is acknowledged as hereditary, but as also personal. Therefore all claims must rest on Divine considerations, since no ground for prayer can be found in anything human. 2. *The plea of the Name of God.* This is a plea all men can urge. The character, the honour, and the glory of God are suggested by his Name. For the sake of what he is, and the glory that his mercy will reflect, we may plead for pardon. By his love we beg for his forgiveness. 3. *The plea of disgrace to the throne of God's glory.* This is a more special plea. The temple was the house of God, wherein his glory was manifested. To destroy it was to put an end to the manifestation of Divine glory associated with it. God's glory is reflected on his Church. If the Church is humiliated, disgrace falls on the throne of God's glory. Yet, note, it is only the throne that is directly disgraced, not the glory itself. The tarnished mirror can no longer reflect the radiance of the sun; this is a discredit to the mirror, but not directly to the sun, since there is no diminution of the sun's brightness. Still, indirectly, dishonour is done to the original source of glory. The sun is less admired if its light is less reflected. God is less honoured if his glory is less manifested. 4. *The plea of the Divine covenant.* This is the most special plea. God has made promises. To the fulfilment of these his faithfulness is bound. He has made a covenant with his own people. They who have accepted the covenant plead its special claims. The Christian has not only the universal mercy of God to trust in; he has the special promises of the gospel, the assurance of the privileges of God's restored children.

II. NEVERTHELESS THE PRAYER IS REJECTED. 1. *Intercession is useless for those who will not repent and seek mercy for themselves.* The prayer was that of the prophet on behalf of his impenitent countrymen. The intercession of good men is recognized as powerful. Their character adds weight to their intercession (Jas. v. 16). But not only must Jeremiah's prayer be rejected, even Moses the founder of the nation and Samuel the father of the prophets could not prevail in the present case. The intercession of one greater than Moses, of Christ himself, will not save those who are obstinately hardened against returning to God. 2. *The Name of God includes reference to his justice as well as his mercy.* For his Name's sake he must vindicate the right. The one-sided view of God which excludes all reference to his wrath is dishonouring. Even a man who can never feel righteous indignation is weak and imperfect. For a judge to acquit all criminals would be fatal to justice. 3. *The throne of God's glory is more dishonoured by sin than by external disaster.* The Jews feared discredit to the temple in its desecration by the heathen. It was more desecrated by their corrupt practices in it. To make the temple a den of thieves is more dishonouring than to overthrow it so as not to leave one stone upon another. The sins of Christ's Church are more dishonouring to his Name than her sufferings, her willing subservience to the spirit of the world more humiliating than her apparent lowly condition when trampled under the feet of persecutors. The pure martyred Church is a glory to Christ, the corrupt prosperous Church a shame to his Name. 4. *God's covenant has human conditions.* He condescends to bind himself to bless us so long as we fulfil our obligations to submit to him. Disobedience breaks the covenant. The faithless Christian cannot urge the pleas of the privileges of the gospel.

Ver. 22.—*Prayer for rain.* I. OBJECTIONS TO PRAYER FOR RAIN. 1. *The universality of law.* It seems to have been vaguely imagined till recently that the weather was not subject to laws of nature in the same strict form in which most material things are thus bound. But this surmise was simply based on ignorance. Recently more indications of law have been discovered, and we see the dawn of a meteorological science. How, then, can we expect God to change the weather in response to our prayers? 2. *The limitations of knowledge.* We really do not know what weather is best. What is good for one place is bad for another. The effects of rain and of drought are so far-reaching that it seems vain for us to judge what is best regarding them. But God knows all and is infinitely wise. Why should we not trust to his unerring discretion? 3. *The goodness of God.* If God is well disposed to his creatures, will he not give them what is for their good? Why, then, even if it were possible for the weather to be affected by our prayer, and if we were wise enough to know what was best for the world, should it be necessary for us to pray about the weather, as if God needed to be urged to govern the world for our benefit?

II. REASONS IN FAVOUR OF PRAYER FOR RAIN. 1. *The control of God over the laws of nature.* God is not the slave of his own legislation. Without changing his laws, he can act through them, as men who cannot alter the laws of nature can still alter the facts of nature by their use of those laws. Moreover, are there no spiritual laws? Yet, without violating the principles of the constitution of the spiritual universe, we believe that God can answer prayer for spiritual blessings. 2. *The conditional character of prayer.* The limitation to our knowledge makes it necessary for us to pray on the condition that God will only answer our requests so far as they agree with his wise and righteous will. Prayer for rain, of all prayers, must not be an absolute demand, but a submissive and humble request, accompanied by the desire that not our will but God's be done. We have no right to dictate to God in prayer, and wisdom would not desire such a right. But there need be no limit to the greatness of the objects of prayer when the right condition of trust in God's higher will is observed. 3. *The fact that prayer alters our condition before God.* It may be wise and right for God to do after our prayer what it would not be well for him to do without it. The very prayer may be a link in a chain of causation. Drought may be sent to us, as it was to Judah, with a Divine purpose concerning our conduct. A change in our conduct will then modify the action of that purpose. Prayer may be the best indication of such a change. We have distinct promises that we may receive, when we seek them in prayer, blessings which are withheld so long as we abstain from asking for them (Matt. vii. 7, 8).

HOMILIES BY VARIOUS AUTHORS.

Vers. 7, 9.—*A prayer for God's people in time of his judgments.* The prophet's words, as he intuitively places himself in the position of those who are about to be afflicted. Not, therefore, to be regarded as an ideal prayer, but a true representation of the spiritual state of those who are conscious of their sin and their need of salvation. They explain the lack of apparent answer to prayer, and truthfully interpret the spiritual condition of the awakened sinner.

I. PRAYER IS AN INDEX OF THE SPIRITUAL STATE. Here we have the oscillation between fear and hope, doubt and faith, vividly portrayed. There is a flitting to and fro of the soul between the extremes of dejection and of confidence. All real prayer ought thus faithfully to represent the mind of the petitioner. It is a laying bare of secret thoughts and moral convictions; an unconscious as well as a conscious confession. Whilst it may be said that a man's inner being is revealed in his prayer, he is not to be judged by it by his fellow-men. It is only God who can truly understand the indications which it affords, and only he who has a right to interpret them. There is a rising, a falling, and a rising again in the course of the prayer. It is the Name of God which serves as a reminder and spiritual confirmation.

II. PRAYER IS A SPIRITUAL EXERCISE AND A MEANS OF GRACE. There is evident in this utterance a wrestling with unbelief. Memories of evil crowd upon the soul and seem to darken the horizon. The sinful nation confesses that in itself there is no hope, but as that conviction is arrived at, another asserts itself, namely, that God is the Hope of Israel, and that in his name or character there is the promise and potency of restoration. It is in spiritual transitions like these that the soul is lost and found again. Temptation is anticipated and overcome, sin is cast away, and God is throned in the heart. It is better to make such honest discovery of ourselves to God, even in our weakness and lack of faith, than that we should carry these into the conduct of life. It is in these transitions of despair and hope reaching to and resting in restored faith and settled purpose of righteousness, that the overcoming of the world is already accomplished.

III. THE PRAYER THAT SEEMS TO BE REJECTED NOW MAY YET PROVE A CONDITION OF ACCEPTANCE. Had Israel herself really adopted the words of this her representative mediator, she would have escaped the awful abyss that yawned before her, but she knew not the day of her opportunity. By slow stages of recovery, marked by many relapses, was she to climb to the great truth from which she had fallen, that the Name of God was her salvation and hope. So it is that many a prayer uttered without apparent answer supplies in itself a spiritual condition of ultimate blessing. Its answer is really begun in the change of attitude assumed, and the spiritual truth laid hold of. By-and-by irresolution and uncertainty will give place to faith, and the windows of heaven will be opened.—M.

Vers. 19, 22.—*Prayer a fruit of chastisement.* There is a deeper and more spiritual tone in this utterance. The heart of Israel is conceived of as having been searched and revealed. Repentance is felt, and confession made. The true source of peace and help is sought after ; and the false ones which have been tested are rejected.

I. IN THE DISCIPLINE AND JUDGMENTS OF LIFE GOD TEACHES MEN HOW TO PRAY. Thereby they learn in a stern school their own sinfulness; the misery and desolation of the soul that is alienated from the life of God and exposed to his wrath and curse ; the incapacity of earthly things to deliver or console, and the power of God to forgive and to save. It is in this estimate of themselves and their resources that the foundation is laid for real spiritual desire. When sin has been felt and acknowledged, a relation is established between the soul and God which is immediately recognized in its claims.

II. THE SPIRIT WHICH IS THUS PRODUCED IS ALONE ACCEPTABLE TO GOD. There are many prayers which evidently ought not to be, and with due regard to the needs of the sinner and the honour of his heavenly Father could not be, answered. The chief end of prayer is not gained in the obtaining of the objects that are asked for, but in the gradual assumption of a right relation to God and acknowledgment of his character and authority. Thus it is that some prayers sound like wails of despair, whilst others are full of the breathings of resignation, obedience, faith, and love. It is with this filial tone that true prayer begins. And it is only when we have learned that " whom he loveth he chasteneth, and scourgeth every son whom he receiveth," that we are able to adopt it. " Thy will be done " is the burden of every Christ-taught prayer, as it is the outcome of all true spiritual discipline.—M.

Ver. 21.—*Invoking the honour of God.* Not along ago this phrase, " Do not disgrace the throne of thy glory," was employed in prayer by a convert in a certain religious meeting. Shortly after a letter was sent to the papers, inveighing against the " profanity" of the idea ; in apparently complete ignorance of its scriptural origin and warrant. Often the language of humility may conceal a conception of real arrogance, and so, on the other hand, the most daring appeals to the promises, the character, and the honour of God may have their root in the profoundest reverence and faith. It is high ground to take, simply because no other ground is available.

I. AS SINNERS HAVE NO REASON FOR MERCY IN THEMSELVES, THEY MUST APPEAL TO GOD. Mere pity would be inadmissible as a motive to which to appeal. There is no ground of acceptance in the sinner himself, and consequently there remains only that course of action which will illustrate and glorify the character of God. That God had chosen Israel as his servant, and Jerusalem as the seat and centre of the theocracy, are the only reasons that are valid in approaching him for mercy. Any course of action which would fail to give due respect to the attributes of his character or the purposes of his grace in the world is already forbidden when it is stated. God has been at pains to pledge himself to the ultimate salvation of men. His Name is itself a promise that no compromise shall be entered into or ineffectual means of salvation adopted. Therefore the necessity of Christ's sacrifice and resurrection. In him the justice of God is honoured, and his Name revealed in the hearts of men. It is only as the gospel is perceived as the offspring of the purest, highest motives on the part of God that it can call into existence corresponding motives in the sinner himself.

II. TO THE SAINT THE HONOUR OF GOD SHOULD EVER BE OF MORE ACCOUNT THAN HIS OWN WELFARE. "For Christ's sake" is a formula in which much of this feeling is implicitly expressed. The exigencies of God's kingdom, the furtherance of his purposes of love and grace, the recognition of the principles of righteousness, are essential to a true Christian life as to true prayer. And the keenest susceptibility should be felt to any conduct on the part of God's servants which would seem to injure his cause in the world or to misrepresent his character.

III. GOD'S NAME IS PLEDGED TO AND BOUND UP WITH THE SALVATION OF MEN. It seems a daring and wondrous plea to urge in the presence of him with whom we have to do; but it is the only one which we can truly offer, and it is of infinite avail. If we accept Christ as representing the honour and righteousness of God, are we not assured that every prayer truly offered in his name shall be answered? The welfare and usefulness of God's servants are guaranteed by such a consideration, and we cannot offer it too often or insist upon it with too great earnestness.—M.

Vers. 1—9.—*Thankfulness through contrast : a harvest sermon.* These verses are a terrible picture of drought and famine. Our thankfulness for what God has done for us in the bounteous harvest he has given may be called forth the more by considering the contrast with our happy lot which these verses present. Contrast is a great teacher. It is the black board on which the teacher's white markings are more clearly seen, the dark background of the sky on the face of which the stars shine out the more. Now, this chapter is all concerning, not a bountiful harvest, but a dread famine. We cannot determine the date of this famine, but it appears to have been one of those premonitory judgments of God sent to teach his sinful people wisdom, so that the more terrible judgments of the future years might not be needed. "A terrible drought had fallen upon the land, and the prophet's picture of it is like some of Dante's in its realism, its pathos, and in its terror. In the presence of a common calamity all distinctions of class have vanished, and the nobles send their little ones to the wells, and they come back with empty vessels and drooping heads, instead of with the gladness that used to be heard in the places of drawing water. Far afield the ploughmen are standing among the cracked furrows, gazing with despair at the brown chapped earth, and out in the field the very dumb creatures are sharing in the common sorrow. And the imperious law of self-preservation overpowers and crushes the maternal instincts. 'Yea, the hind also calved in the field, and forsook it, because there was no grass.' And on every hill-top, where cooler air might be found, the once untameable wild asses are standing with open nostrils, panting for air, their filmy eyes failing them, gazing for the rain that will not come. It is a true description—so they say who know what drought in Eastern lands is and does. How it distressed the earth, the beasts, and man, is all vividly portrayed." The pits, some of them natural hollows in the hard rock and in caves, where evaporation was less speedy ; others of them dykes and cisterns, the works of man ;— but all alike were empty. The ground was split by reason of the long drought into wide and deep fissures ; earth's wounds for man's sin, mute mouths crying to Heaven for pity, the lips of earth suffering, waiting for a drop of water to relieve the torment of its awful thirst. And not the land only, but the dumb brutes were involved in the common woe. The hind, driven down from her high places into the fields in search of the grass that has disappeared from the lofty heights, meets with disappointment here also, and in her agony of hunger and thirst forgot and forsook her young, whom she, above most other of the beasts of the field, was wont to care for and cherish tenderly ; and the hardy wild asses (ver. 6) found their hunger even greater than they could bear, and panted in terror and distress. And man—all ranks and ages were smitten, the people generally were languishing. The gates of the cities and other chief places of concourse were "black unto the ground," with the sad, coloured garments of the mourners who bent prostrate there; and one long, loud, bitter cry went up from the whole city of God. *But what a contrast is our condition to theirs!* See it in the aspects of the fields ere harvest was gathered in. In the gifts of all nurturing powers from heaven—rain, dew, and fountains of water. In the abundance provided for man and beast, and in the contentment and peace of the herds of the field. In the glad congratulations of all classes in the land, from the labourer to the noble, because of what God has given. The whole nation rejoices, a cry not of sorrow but of gladness goes up from the homes of the rich and poor, high and low alike. And this contrast is seen also in the thoughts of God prompted by the two events. "The dearth" made the people think that God was as a stranger in the land, one who knew nothing of them or their need. If we felt concerning our distresses that God was as a stranger to us, they would be much harder to bear. But so Judah and Jerusalem thought. Nor was this the worst thought; for if God knew how they were suffering, and yet no help came, did not a yet darker surmise seem warranted? Was it not as if he were "as a wayfaring man that but turned aside to tarry for the night," and who therefore, having no interest in the place or the people, would care but little for them? This was a terrible thought indeed. If our mind be haunted with the dread thought that God looks on unmoved at our affliction, and cares not for our distress—what, then, can we do? But so they thought. The sun rose and set, the stars looked down upon them just as they had done at other times; but there was no heart of love in their calm, unmoved gaze; and so it seemed there was no heart in God, and that he, unmoved by their appeal, left them to perish. Or could it be that, after all their boasting in him as mighty to save, One mightier than he had arisen and overpowered him; that he was "as one astonied, as a mighty man that cannot save"? Was there some cruel fate which, after all, was ruling over their destinies, and so preventing the mighty One, of whom their fathers told, from coming to their help as in the days of old? Such dark and terrible thoughts float about the minds of men in the hour of dire distress such as this dearth had brought upon them. And so all hope was quenched, the voice of prayer was stifled, their hearts died down in complete despair. The dearth in itself was bad enough, causing bodily agony beyond all description, but its horrors were heightened and awfully intensified by the dark thoughts about God to which their distress gave rise. But in all this, what a contrast does our happier lot present? The thoughts of God which the harvest he has given prompt are the very opposite of those which, as we have seen, haunted the minds of those who suffered under the dearth. Not as a stranger ignorant of us and our wants does God appear, but as One who "knoweth that we have need of all these things," and who openeth his hand and filleth us with good. And still less as a wayfaring man, and who therefore has no concern nor care for land or people. Every golden ear of corn has been a tongue as well, and has told eloquently though silently of our Father's care. The wide-stretching fields of corn have been filled with these myriad witnesses to his love, and have stood up in their serried ranks, to give the lie to the unbelieving heart, that would harbour hard thoughts of God. As all with one consent yield to the summer breeze, so with like oneness of consent, do they attest his unfailing goodness and his never-ceasing care. And they proclaim him, too, as the Hope of his people, and their Saviour indeed. He is no "mighty man that cannot save." For all the treasures of the field, created, preserved, and ripened for our use, in spite of all adverse influences which threatened them, all show that he is mighty to save. His hand held in check every hostile power, every destructive storm, every killing frost, every blighting mildew, every creeping caterpillar, and all else that would have robbed us of the corn he has given. Oh, what a gospel do the fields preach! And how differently God might have dealt with us! For whilst there is so vast a contrast between our harvest and that dearth of which these verses tell, there has been no such contrast between our conduct and that which brought upon Judah the calamity from which they suffered. Have we not reason to make the same confession which was made concerning them?—"O Lord, . . . our iniquities testify against us," etc. (ver. 7). What, gratitude then, does such long-suffering love call for from us! Let, then, our harvest lead us to do that which Judah's dearth led the prophet to do—to turn to God, and confess him as our Hope and our Saviour in time of trouble. In this way he is again standing at our doors and knocking for admission. The "miracle of the loaves" is done over again for our comfort and help. We have "the joy of harvest," let him have it also in gathering us into the garner of his faithful souls for time and for eternity.—C.

Vers. 7—9.—*An absent God deplored.* The dearth told of in foregoing verses and the misery caused thereby led to the conviction that God had abandoned his people. In these verses and throughout this section down to ch. xv. 9 we find the prophet pleading with God to return. In these verses we are shown—

I. THE CAUSES WHICH HAD BROUGHT ABOUT THE DIVINE WITHDRAWAL FROM THEM. Their " iniquities," " backslidings," " sins" (ver. 7). Nothing else has such power; sin only can shut out God, but it always will and does.

II. THE HAPPY MEMORIES WHICH MADE IT SO BITTER. God had revealed himself to them in such endearing manner. He had been ever *the Hope of Israel.* He had inspired, maintained, and justified that hope again and again. And he had become the Hope of Israel through having shown himself so perpetually " the Saviour thereof in the time of trouble." The memory of God's servants was stored with recollections of such deliverances, national and individual, from troubles temporal and spiritual; vouchsafed, too, not because of Israel's deserving, but out of God's pure bounty. Now, it was these happy memories which made God's present dealings with them so terrible to bear.

III. THE SAD CONTRAST BETWEEN THE DIVINE MANIFESTATIONS NOW AND OF OLD. We have seen what he had been to Israel, but now, the prophet complains, he is to them very far from what he was then. He is " as a stranger," " a wayfaring man," as one " taken by surprise," as one strong but yet unable to help. Their enemies would taunt them with the reproach that either God was as a stranger, and therefore did not care for them; or, if they denied that, then it must be that there was a stronger than he, who had taken him by surprise and prevented his rendering help to his afflicted people. Either he would not or he could not—on one of the horns of this dilemma they by the force of their present circumstances were thrown. And there can be no doubt that the great mystery of life, its sins and sorrows, do often force perplexed and troubled minds perilously near to one or other of these conclusions, which nevertheless faith affirms to be alike false, and will never admit for one moment.

IV. THE SOURCES OF HOPE UNDER CIRCUMSTANCES LIKE THESE. They are: 1. *The Name of God.* This the prophet pleads (ver. 7). He confesses that all their own conduct is altogether against them. They can have no hope in themselves. But the Name of God remains to be urged in his pleading, and therefore it is this Name that he does urge. " Do thou it for thy Name's sake." Here is a fact which cannot change. When driven out of all hope in ourselves by reason of our sins, we may yet hope in God, and plead the grace and goodness that are evermore in him. 2. *The presence of his appointed ordinances and his chosen dwelling-place in their midst.* This is the meaning of ver. 9, " Yet thou art in the midst of us." The temple, the altar, the sacrifice, the priests, the ark, were all there; the appointed channels of communication between God and his people. And so long as we may go unto his footstool, and the throne of grace is open to us, there is hope in that. God will come to us again in the way of his holy and appointed ordinances, if we will go along that way to seek him. 3. *They were the objects of his love.* " We are called by thy Name." Israel was so. God had chosen them at the first. " When Israel was a child, then I loved him." And it is because of that undying love of God, they who for their sins have lost his presence may yet win it back again.

V. THE PRESENT DUTY. Prayer. The prophet betook himself hereto. " Leave us not," he cries (ver. 9). And nothing barred the success of this prayer but that the people for whom he prayed had no heart in it. God stood ready to forgive and restore. The prophet's prayer was fully answered on the part of God. But those for whom he prayed were not ready, and so their judgment went on. But for ourselves, if we deplore an absent God, let us betake ourselves to these potent arms of all-prevailing prayer, and God shall ere long be again known to us as of old as our Hope and our Saviour in time of trouble.—C.

Vers. 13—16.—*False teachers no adequate excuse for evil conduct.* No doubt the people to whom Jeremiah was sent had been encouraged in their ungodliness by the faithlessness and sin of their prophets. Blind guides were leading the blind, and with the inevitable result. And here Jeremiah pleads, as an excuse for his people's sin, that they had been thus misled. But God refuses to admit the plea. Now, on this, note—

I. FALSE TEACHING IS SOME EXCUSE FOR EVIL CONDUCT. The deepest instincts of our hearts affirm this. Our Lord himself does so, when he says, " He that knew not his Lord's will and did it not, shall be beaten with few stripes." But this word of his, whilst it allows that lack of teaching is some excuse, denies that it is sufficient (cf.

John xix. 11). St. Paul also says, concerning the heathen nations, "The time of this ignorance God winked at."

II. BUT IT IS NOT AN ADEQUATE EXCUSE. For: 1. *The taught are the creators almost as much as the creatures of their teachers.* The people who clamour for smooth things to be prophesied to them will find such prophets forthcoming. Ahab's prophets—all of them but Micaiah—were such. It is true, "like priest, like people;" but it is also true, "like people, like priest." The demand creates the supply. The pastors of the Church are the product of the Church, almost as much as the Church is the product of the pastors. What a worldly Church wants it will have, for the woe both of itself and its pastors alike. 2. *They have a sure test by which to try all their teachers.* " To the Law and to the testimony," etc. Conscience also is ever on the side of God, and is prompt to condemn all teaching that leads to sin. The Holy Spirit likewise pleads in men's hearts for God. And the faithful words of those in whom God's Spirit dwells. None, therefore, are shut up to any human teachers. 3. And where evil teachers have been followed, *it has been in spite of the protest which these other higher and surer guides have uttered,* or would have uttered had they been suffered so to do.

III. BUT IF IT BE ILL FOR THE TAUGHT, IT IS YET MORE ILL FOR THE TEACHERS. " His blood will I require at the watchman's hands." The most awful of our Lord's denunciations were addressed to such evil teachers (cf. the oft-repeated, " Woe unto you, scribes and Pharisees, hypocrites ! " cf. ver. 14, etc.).

CONCLUSION. 1. Let those who are taught by any human teachers test what they receive by the Word of God. Be as the Bereans (Acts xvii. 11). 2. Let those who teach watch anxiously and prayerfully against the temptation to conform their teachings to the likings of their hearers rather than to their needs. Let them remember that the causes of error and false teaching are much more moral than they are intellectual. 3. Let teachers and taught alike sit daily at his feet who said, " I am the Way, the Truth, and the Life."—C.

Vers. 17—22.—*The distracting power of great distress.* The prophet seems blinded by his tears. The distress portrayed here is terrible indeed, and the prophet so realized it that his mind appears to have reeled beneath his apprehensions of the coming calamities. Hence he falls into utterances which can only be regarded, however pardonable and comprehensible under his piteous circumstances (cf. ver. 18), as exaggerated, and in many respects, as all such utterances are, incorrect. Every sentence in ver. 19, etc., is open to grave question. It would be dreadful if they were not. Note—

I. THE PROPHET'S EXPOSTULATIONS. (Ver. 19.) Now, God did not "utterly reject Judah," nor did "his soul loathe Zion." It was his love for his people that determined him at all costs to purge them from their evil.

II. HIS COMPLAINTS. (Ver. 19.) He complains that they had been disappointed and implies that God was the cause why their expectations had failed. They had no right to look for peace, being what they were.

III. HIS CONFESSIONS. Nothing could be more appropriate or more sure to gain the mercy of God than such confession as this, if it were indeed sincere and general on the part of those who had sinned. But this it was not; it was because they would not repent, would not return unto the Lord, that therefore his wrath arose against them until there was no remedy.

IV. HIS ENTREATIES. (Ver. 21.) God never "abhorred" his people, but only their sins; and that God should be thought to " disgrace" the throne of his glory can only be explained on the grounds we have stated. Nor either is it God's way to " break his covenant."

V. HIS PLEAS. (Ver. 22.) Here the prophet pleads truly. There was no hope in any heathen deity, but in God alone. And had the people indeed " waited" upon God, matters had gone more happily with them. But this was just what they did not do. Now, concerning all such utterances as these : 1. *Bear with them.* God did so. He rebuked not his servant, though that servant had spoken unadvisedly concerning him. 2. *Be very slow to believe them.* Cf. Naomi, and her false forebodings of fear. How ill she thought God would deal with her ! How gracious, in fact, that dealing was ! And St.

Paul assures us that "God hath not cast off his people." "All Israel shall be saved." Let us wait on and wait for God. 3. *Be ashamed if by our sin we have caused such distress.* Jeremiah had not sinned, but he mourns as if the sin were his own. Beholding the sorrow our sin causes to those who love us will, if we be not utterly hardened, arouse shame, sorrow, and contrition in our own hearts. 4. If those who know most of the mind of God tremble for us, have we not reason to tremble for ourselves?—C.

Ver. 21.—*A dreadful apprehension.* That God should "abhor" us. Such apprehension filled the prophet's mind, as it has other minds.

I. BUT THIS GOD NEVER DOES. He is our Father; he *so* loved us as to give Christ for us. It is impossible, therefore, let our apprehensions be what they may, that he can abhor us.

II. BUT HE MAY SEEM TO. 1. No one will think thus of God by reason only of *temporal calamities.* These have again and again come and do come to God's servants, but produce no such distressing thought as this (cf. Ps. xxii., "He hath not despised nor abhorred," etc.). 2. Nor will *spiritual distress* alone cause it. There may be loss of comfort in God; no enjoyment in prayer or worship. Sin may again reassert its mastery, and fill the soul with sorrow. Doubts may insinuate themselves into the soul. But none of these will of themselves lead to the thought that God abhors us. 3. They may do so, however, if *the presence of sorrow, temporal or spiritual, be so severe as to throw the mind off its balance.* (Cf. former homily.) Despair has for a while under such circumstances wrought this harm, and that in the holiest minds. Even our blessed Lord knew somewhat of this awful experience (cf. the agony in the garden, and the cry on the cross, "My God, my God," etc.). Elijah, John the Baptist, Jeremiah here, and others have had instances. Cowper the poet also, and the not unfrequent cases of religious melancholy leading either to settled gloom or even suicide. The tenderest pity and compassion are to be felt for such. 4. *Persistent disobedience and repeated backsliding* are the chief causes of this apprehension. When the world, the flesh, and the devil fill the heart, especially the heart which has once been cleansed, then "the last state of that man is worse than the first" (cf. Saul, Judas, Ahithophel). Yes; such sin has power to turn the sun into darkness and the moon into blood, and to make the very stars fall from heaven. God becomes the horror of the soul, and men will "make their bed in hell" if but they may flee from his dreadful presence.

III. THE GREAT DESTROYER OF THIS DREAD. It is suggested by the prophet's own words : "Abhor us not, *for thy Name's sake.*" This is the antidote of all such fearful dread. The Name of God, *i.e.* that by which he has made himself known. And what has been the verdict of all the witness concerning God, which his words and works and ways have borne, but this, that he is plenteous in mercy to all that call upon him—to all that call upon him in truth? He is the "God of all grace." And if Israel of old had proof of this, how much more have we in Christ! Behold God in him; he is the Name of God to us men. Then, where this dread apprehension exists, let Christ be preached, meditated upon, sought in prayer, confessed with the lip, served and followed in the life, waited on continually, and soon this dread shall pass away.—C.

Ver. 14.—*Lying prophets.* Every divinely inspired prophet of the olden times was emphatically a "seer," gifted with the power of looking, as other men could not, into the inmost heart of things—passing events, natural laws, Divine providences—so as to discern their deeper meaning. The past, the present, and the future all came under his survey, inasmuch as he had to do mainly with those absolute and universal truths which are in no way subject to the conditions of time. As the prophet is called a seer, so the subject of his prophecy is often called a "vision." It is remarkable how large a proportion of the prophetic revelations of the Old Testament were of a pictorial, symbolic character (see Numb. xxiv. 4; 1 Kings xxii. 17; Isa. vi. 1; Ezek. xxxvii. i. 10; Hab. ii. 1), and even when they were otherwise, similar phraseology is often used to indicate the prophet's extraordinary power of moral and spiritual insight. But this passage speaks of *false* prophets—men who assumed the prophetic function when not divinely called to it, mere pretenders to the prophetic gift. Ezekiel calls them the "foolish prophets, that follow their own spirit, and have seen nothing" (Ezek xiii. 3). Every age has had some such misleading witnesses. Christ warned the people against them in his day (Matt. vii. 15 ; xxiv. 24). St. John spoke of their uprising as a characteristic of the "last time" (1 John ii. 18; iv. 1). Our own age is certainly no exception. Men may not claim Divine inspiration in the old prophetic sense, but never were there bolder claims to deep spiritual insight, never such adventurous flights into the realms of mystery, never so many dogmatic remedies for the intellectual restlessness or the moral diseases of human nature. Note, here—

I. THAT FREEDOM OF THOUGHT AND OF SPEECH WHICH WOULD SEEM TO BE A FIXED PRINCIPLE OF DIVINE GOVERNMENT. There was nothing to prevent the false prophets from speaking; the people were only forbidden to listen to them. Though it be nothing but a vision of their own diseased fancy, a conceit of their own distempered brain, that men have to deliver, they are allowed to deliver it. Better so, that the false should come out to the light of day, confronting the truth, rather than that it should be suppressed by an external force that may at another time be enlisted on its side. The truth has nothing to fear from public conflict with error and all its forces. A marvellous change, as regards the openness of the conflict, has taken place since the days when Milton wrote his ' Areopagitica ' and Jeremy Taylor his ' Liberty of Prophesying.' No doubt it is full of danger to the weak and wavering, to those whose mental eagerness is not tempered by humility and whose hearts are not "established with grace." But this is God's way of leading the world on to fuller, clearer light. And is it not in harmony with his whole moral administration of human affairs ? He puts awful, destructive powers into men's hands, and he holds each one responsible for the way in which he wields them. There are boundless possibilities of evil around us all, moral as well as physical, and our case would be sad indeed if there were not equal and still greater possibilities of good. It is well that the false prophets should tell out their "dreams," if only that the light of God may expose their emptiness and the breath of God may scatter them.

II. THE NEED OF A SURE CRITERION OF JUDGMENT. How shall we discern between the false and the true? These supposed prophetic utterances of old were subjected to certain tests. 1. *Their verity.* If they were falsified by the facts of history or the inner consciousness of the people, they could not be of God. 2. *Harmony with Divine Law.* They must be favourable to the cause of virtue and morality ; could not promise prosperity apart from repentance, or cry, " Peace, peace," when there was " no peace." 3. *The personal character of the teacher.* The messengers of a holy God must needs be themselves holy. The quality of their message would be reflected in their own life. The same principles hold good now. Such an essential connection exists between truth in thought and truth of feeling, character, life, that every form of doctrine must be judged by its moral influence, both on the teacher and the taught. " By their fruits ye shall know them." Moreover, Christianity refers us to a testing principle of still higher quality and completer efficacy—*the presence of the Spirit of truth and grace in our own souls.* " He that is spiritual," etc. (1 Cor. ii. 15). " Ye have an unction from the Holy One," etc. (1 John ii. 20, 21). There is no safeguard against error but this Divine faculty. As regards an external standard, the Scriptures of eternal truth are the touchstone. " To the Law and to the testimony," etc. (Isa. viii. 20). The voice, the Law, the life of God in your own soul, is a touchstone of still more delicate quality and ready application. If what you read or hear will not bear this test, it is but the " dream " of a false prophet, " the deceit of his own heart," and no true " burden of the Lord."

III. GOD'S SURE VINDICATION OF THE CAUSE OF HIS OWN TRUTH, WHATEVER FORCES MAY ASSAIL IT. (See vers. 15, 16.) The ministry of the true prophets was a marvellous revelation of the Divine power that sustained them and verified their words. They were seldom called to do battle with the false prophets on their own ground, directly to assail their errors by argument and disproof. They were simply called to proclaim the truth, leaving it with God to make it victorious. The apostles of Christ dealt with the abounding theoretical and practical evils of their day on very much the same principle. The thing that is false gains its influence over men's minds by reason of its resemblance to the true. The counterfeit circulates because it seems like the real coin. There is no way in which we can so effectually rebuke it as by setting forth the glory of that of which it is the perversion or the mocking shadow. In the full, clear light and the spreading power of the truth error must, sooner or later, wither and die.

Let us have faith in the triumphant force of God's own Word. "What is the chaff to the wheat? saith the Lord," etc. (ch. xxiii. 28, 29). We may well trust in the ultimate victory of that which is the product of infinite wisdom, and is backed by all the resources of omnipotence.—W.

Vers. 1—6.—*The miseries produced by lack of water.* I. THE BITTER CONSCIOUSNESS THAT AN IMPERATIVE NEED CANNOT BE SATISFIED. Well might there be mourning, languishing, and crying. When we are speaking of need, one of the first questions to be asked is whether the need is natural or artificial. An artificial need, by continued self-indulgence, may come to be very keenly felt; and yet, when circumstances arise which prevent the satisfying of the need, the artificiality of it is clearly seen. But a natural need, when the supplies are stopped, soon shows how clamorous it can become, how productive of unendurable pain. These Israelites had been multiplying artificial needs. They thought they needed visible images, to be richly adorned and constantly worshipped. They thought they needed large external possessions, and so the land became full of covetousness. Rich men tried to increase their riches, and poor men wanted, *above all things*, to get out of their poverty. But all the while the difference between natural and artificial need was forgotten. The natural needs went on being satisfied, because God, who gives rain from heaven, was long-suffering; and the supply came so habitually that the people did not reckon how there was a hand upon the fountain of the waters which could seal them up in a moment. But now, no sooner is the supply stopped than there is deep and inconceivable misery. The idolater will go on living, even if you take his images away; a rich man need not die because he is stripped of his possessions; but what shall one do who cannot get water to drink? The unendurable pain of Dives in Hades came not from the lost wealth and splendour of earth, but because he could not get the least drop of water to cool his tongue.

II. THE VANITY OF HUMAN RESOURCES. Jerusalem now abounds in pools and cisterns, and the probability is that in the time of Jeremiah there was a similar abundance, both within and without the city. Great cities have always had to see to the providing of water, according to their judgment of what was necessary. A due supply of water is one of the most important charges that can be entrusted to any municipality. The authorities of Jerusalem may have done their best according to their lights; but they had forgotten that the most they could do was to provide receptacles for the Divine bounty. They had hewn cisterns without considering that a time might come when there would be no water to put into the cisterns. That time has come, and where is now the wisdom of the wise and the strength of the mighty? Men may flatter themselves that they rule on earth; but it is very plain that the spaces above, where the clouds gather and whence the rains descend, are beyond their control

III. THE NULLIFYING OF HUMAN INDUSTRY. The work of the ploughman is in vain. God requires man to work and study in order to get the fruits of the earth; but it is only too easy for him in all his work and study to forget God. He who expects a harvest will not omit ploughing, sowing, irrigating—without these works expectation would be idiotic—but he may very easily omit faith in God. He may neglect the bestowment of the firstfruits, and all that service of God which the fruits of the earth give us strength to render. Well may such a one be ashamed when the ground is chapped and there is no rain in the earth. This is the sign of his own folly in attending to certain secondary requisites and forgetting the one requisite most important of all. When it is so required, God can feed thousands without any sowing and reaping at all; but no man is allowed to reckon that his sowing will assuredly be followed by reaping. He may sow wheat bountifully, only to reap thorns bountifully, because he has forgotten God (ch. xii. 13). If the sowing is in prayer and humility, in gratitude for the past and reasonable expectation for the future, then the sower will have no need to be ashamed. Whatever other things God's servants may lack, God will put the true, abiding glory upon them.

IV. THE LINKING OF MAN WITH THE BRUTE CREATION IN A COMMON SUFFERING. The hinds and the wild asses suffer, and doubtless they were prominent representatives of many other classes of the brute creation ('The Land and the Book,' p. 172). A common thirst not only brings down the noble to the level of the mean man, but man in general to the level of the brute. It is well that we should have plain reminders, such as cannot be escaped, of the links that bind us to the lower creation. We cannot, at present at all events, get above some of the wants of the brute, although certainly it cannot rise to some of ours; but it is just the wants of the brute that seem to be the only wants many feel. They have enough if they can eat, drink, and be merry.—Y.

Vers. 7—9.—*An appeal out of the depths of separation from God.* I. THE APPEAL OF THOSE WHO ADMIT THAT IN THEMSELVES THEY HAVE NO CLAIM UPON GOD. They have no record of faithful service to present; no array of good deeds goes before them to plead for acceptance and approval. It is all the other way. Their iniquities testify against them; they have backslidden; they have sinned against Jehovah; *at least, so they say.* There is the appearance of having come to themselves. It might seem as if the prodigal nation, so long spending its substance in riotous living, had been brought to a full stop and a place for repentance amid the privations of a waterless land. Why, indeed, should there be any suspicion as to a genuine confession of great iniquities, a genuine and swift submission to Jehovah? Notice that the confession is correct enough as far as the mere words are concerned. But after all, these words were not unlike the statements extorted by the pains of the Inquisition. Confessions and professions have been made by tortured men in their agonies which had no value as genuine utterances of the heart. It is needless to say that, as far as *purpose* is concerned, no resemblance is to be found between Jehovah depriving Judah of its water and Rome torturing heretics to make them recant. There may be *different purposes* where there are *similar results.* This cry of the people showed the *severity* with which they had been smitten; it did not of necessity show the state of their hearts. All that they said was true; their iniquities did testify against them; they were apostates; they had sinned against Jehovah. Only when we look at past confessions of the like sort, we see how little they meant (Numb. xiv. 40; xxi. 7; Judg. x. 10; 1 Sam. vii. 6). It was the parched tongue and not the broken heart that made them speak. And therefore it is that their appeal has to be met with a refusal. Earnestly as they cried, the cessation of chastisement would not have been followed by the renewal of a true obedience.

II. THE APPEAL OF THOSE WHO HAVE BECOME CONSCIOUS OF THEIR OWN HELPLESSNESS APART FROM JEHOVAH. They want water, and there is no way of getting it apart from the mercy of an all-powerful God. The very way in which they speak shows how vain they feel all resources to be save one. But if other resources had been possible, assuredly they would have tried them. They come to God's door, not because it is the right one, but because it is the only one left to try. So passengers begin to think of God and eternity when the captain says the tempest-beaten ship cannot be saved. So sick people send for a minister of religion when the doctor says the disease is mortal. So the doomed criminal makes a fashion of giving all his attention to the chaplain when the plea for mitigation is rejected. What a humiliating position men take in making an appearance of coming to God only when they can get nowhere else! What wonder is it that, under such circumstances, they fail to get a right relation established between God and themselves! Prayers in such circumstances, whatever the language employed, may prove no more than the incoherent shriek of despair, a cry without any real turning to God, without any real trust in him.

III. THE APPEAL OF THOSE WHO CAN CALL TO MIND GOD'S CHARACTER AS ALREADY REVEALED. The description of God in his deeds and disposition had ample warrant from the history of his past dealings. He had been in the midst of his people, "the Hope of Israel, the Saviour thereof in time of trouble," as a mighty man showing himself able to save in the greatest danger. He who now fastened up the clouds and the springs had given waters in the wilderness. He who now made the earth fruitless had given manna which needed neither sowing nor reaping. Jehovah had been behind all the visible agents towards deliverance, victory, and possession of the promised inheritance. His tabernacle had been in the midst of his people, and his glory in the midst of his tabernacle. How easy it is to remember, when necessary, that which, when convenient, it seems just as easy to forget! The clouds of heaven and the mountains in whose secret depths he had wrought at the water-springs had been suffered to hide God; but now that his gracious works are vanished for a while, men suddenly and painfully miss the worker. They can flatter him whom they have not even despised, but rather simply ignored. When the cisterns are empty, when the land is chapped, when there is no water anywhere for man and beast, then they can talk effusively concerning "the Hope of Israel, and the Saviour thereof in time of trouble." What self-accusation is implied in this appeal! It was not in ignorance of Jehovah's claims that they had sinned against him. His past dealings were known and could be recollected under stress of need. If God could speak to Jeremiah as one familiar with the deeds of Moses and Samuel (ch. xv. 1), then we may be sure the God connected with those deeds was also known in his historical manifestations—known to some extent at least to the great bulk of the people.

IV. THE APPEAL OF THOSE WHO HAVE BECOME KEENLY SENSITIVE TO GOD'S SEPARATION FROM THEM. This is set forth by two figures. He has become as a stranger in the land, as a wayfarer pitching his tent for the night. The people profess to wonder why it is so, and yet they need not wonder. He who has been in their midst because, first of all, he has gathered them around him as the recipients of measureless privileges, finds rivals raised on every high place and in every grove. His special commands are shut out from influence on the conduct of daily life. His messenger is scorned by rulers and conspired against by his own kinsfolk. What is all this but to become even worse than a stranger? A stranger may advance through successive grades of acquaintanceship into bosom affection and trust; but if he who is and ought to remain the centre gets pushed out little by little, even beyond the circumference, what force is there potent and exact enough to bring the former relation back? God had told these people how to treat the stranger, but instead of attending to his commands they had ended by making God himself a stranger. Needless, then, was it to ask the question, "Why shouldest thou be as a stranger in the land?" As well might the ebbing sea ask the rock round which it rolled at flood, why it had forsaken it. Jehovah had remained the same in truth, in love, and in purpose. It was the people who had failed, and flowed further and further away from him. They talked of him as a mere wanderer among them, whereas they were the real wanderers, wandering in heart, drifting about from one temporary satisfaction to another (Exod. xxii. 21; Lev. xix. 9, 10, 33; Matt. xxv. 35; Heb. xiii. 2).—Y.

Vers. 10—12.—*The severities of Jehovah—sword, famine, and pestilence.* I. THE OCCASION OF THESE SEVERITIES. This occasion is stated in ver. 10. The people have spoken of Jehovah as a stranger and traveller, which way of speaking gives opportunity for asserting that it is they who are the real wanderers, straying from Jehovah's highway of righteousness and appointed service; and not only have they strayed, but they have loved to stray. The making of a straight path for Jehovah has been very hard and exacting, and the first voice of temptation to turn into an easier road has been listened to. And even now, out of the midst of their agonies, their cry has no repentance in it. They wish God to come into their midst and protect and comfort them, forgetting that if he is to be really in their midst they must turn from their iniquities. They must show clear signs of forsaking their sins before he can relax his severities. Dreadful as this experience of a waterless land is, they must look for the exciting cause of it in themselves. A disobedient child, suffering punishment at the hands of his parent, while he knows that one cause of his pain is the chastising instrument, knows also that it is a cause which only operates because of the wrong that he himself has done. If we would only give due attention, it is within our own power to keep the worst pains out of life.

II. VAIN DEFENCES AGAINST THE SEVERITIES. 1. *The intercession of good men.* Jehovah says once again to his prophet, "Pray not for this people for their good." Jeremiah himself, naturally and commendably enough, is prompted to cry on their behalf. But doubtless they themselves also urge the prophet's intercession. 2. *Fasting.* Outward and visible humiliation; such attire and such attitudes assumed as were congruous with the cry of vers. 7—9. All this was easy enough without any humbling or chastening of the heart. Fasting is too often followed by feasting. For a little while the fleshly comforts of life are superstitiously put aside; but there is the full purpose of resuming them, and making up for lost time. 3. *Burnt offerings and oblations.* The people insulted Jehovah by heaping before him the carcases of slain beasts. An idol was best served, according to the teaching of its priests, by those who made the largest offerings at its shrine. All these doings only emphasized the disobedience of the people. They were very diligent in giving what Jehovah did not want, vainly thinking it might stand in place of what he imperatively required. When God asks us for repentance and obedience, it is the merest trifling both with his expectations and our interests to bring some unusual demonstration of will-worship. Let quality, not quantity, be the first thing. A little of the right is better than the utmost profession of the wrong. A little of the right, firmly rooted, will increase and strengthen with wonderful rapidity.

III. THE SHAPE OF THE SEVERITIES. Sword, famine, and pestilence are coming; coming, plainly set forth as the consuming agents of Jehovah. When Jehovah makes men his *sword*, it is vain to contend against them. The history of God's people had often shown how a few could be victorious and a multitude vanquished. It is he who can put strength into the arm that wields the sword or take that strength away. These invading armies were, of course, not conscious that Jehovah was wielding them in this way. They had their own selfish aims, which God could subordinate and mould toward his own ends. It is the worst of blasphemy for the leader of an army to talk as if he were going on God's errands. Attila was not the scourge of God because he said so, though God may have used him in ways beyond Attila's power to conceive. *Famine.* Here was a destroyer which there was no guarding against. The sword could at least be drawn against the sword, however vain the result. But who could stop a general famine? And even supposing a few rich men could store up grain for a while, there was a third foe in reserve—the *pestilence.* David had his choice as to which of the three dread agents he would prefer; but here they all come together. God has a variety of weapons, and his enemies cannot evade them all. How wise men would be if, instead of vainly trying to shut out alike Divine Law and penalty, they would at once and for ever take up the attitude of entire submission to God! Then they would be defended indeed. By sword, famine, and pestilence, these rich men of Judah and Jerusalem were for ever separated from their ill-gotten gains. But " who shall separate us from the love of Christ? Assuredly not famine or sword," says the apostle; nor pestilence either, he would have added, if he had thought of it. We may be persuaded that nothing has power to separate us from the love of God which is in Christ Jesus our Lord. The mischief is that we reject the protections of that love and all other benefits flowing from it.—Y.

Vers. 13—16.—*The peculiar doom of the false prophets.* I. THE SIN OF THE PROPHETS. That they are found liars is, comparatively speaking, a small part of their offence. Their lie is productive of so much that adds to the peril of the position—so much that is peculiarly insulting to Jehovah. Their sin and the punishment of it were not unlike the sin and punishment of Ananias and Sapphira. Ananias and Sapphira were smitten, not because they had lied, but because they had lied against the Holy Ghost. So with these false prophets here; they prophesied falsely; but that in itself might not have brought a peculiar doom upon them. The offence lay in this, that the false prophecy came at a time when it was peculiarly obnoxious to Jehovah. It was not a distant danger that these false prophets made light of, but one close to the door. The prophet's difficulties, arising from the natural disposition of his auditors, were already great enough. No false prophet was needed to come in with his contradiction. It must also be remembered that there was a peculiarly insulting sin in that these men told their lies *as prophets.* What a dreadful thing for a man to go forth with " Thus saith Jehovah " in his mouth, when the words are the deceit of his own heart ! This expression, " the deceit of their heart," seems to suggest the possibility that in some instances these false prophets were not deliberate liars, but were themselves deluded by a fanatical exaggeration of patriotism. Nevertheless, even so, the sin was none the less, for the spirits of the prophets were subject to the prophets. We had need be very sure that we are duly commissioned when we undertake to speak in the Name of God, else we may land ourselves in most humiliating exposures, and come to a most admonitory end. Thus we come to notice—

II. How THE SIN OF THESE PROPHETS WAS MADE CLEAR. Jeremiah said one thing, the false prophets said the direct contrary, and at the time there seemed no means of vindicating the true prophet beyond all chance of cavil. Doubtless those who were rightly disposed did listen and believe. Their very disposition was in itself a touchstone by which to discriminate between the false and the true; while those disposed to reject could make anything serve for an excuse. The important thing to notice is that the occasion of this great sin was seized upon to predict in due time a terrible, an indisputable, revelation of the sin. Thus an opportunity came for adding detail and emphasis to the prophecy already given. What could not be made plain at the moment would be made abundantly plain hereafter. Sword and famine were not only *certain*, they were *near;* coming within the lives of these living men, who would see these very false prophets die by the sword and famine which they had sneered at as impossible. Those who during *life* had told so many inexpressibly mischievous *falsehoods* with their lips, were made the instruments, their own will not being at all consulted, of uttering most impressive truth in their death. God and his truth and his true prophets and faithful witnesses can wait. Time is increasingly on the side of all truth, while false prophets are condemned out of their own mouths.

III. THE DECEIVED AUDITORS SUFFER JUST AS MUCH AS THE DECEIVING SPEAKERS. The people were not at liberty to plead contradictions in the messages as a ground for continued inaction in the matter of repentance. Such a plea was certain to be seized on, but, while it might help to drug the conscience, it availed nothing to lighten the judgments which Jehovah was bringing on his unfaithful people. That God who is to be reckoned true, though such reckoning makes every man a liar, has assuredly not left himself without ample witness. False prophets can be tested at once by the heart of each individual to whom they appeal, although their exposure before the whole universe may not come for many ages. God gives us for our own sakes the present means of guarding against them. As to his Name and glory, we may be sure he will vindicate them in his own time and way.—Y.

EXPOSITION.

CHAPTER XV.

Vers. 1—9.—Second rejection of Jeremiah's intercession; awfulness of the impending judgment.

Ver. 1.—Though Moses and Samuel, etc. It is a mere supposition which is here made; there is no allusion to any popular view of the intercession of saints (see my note on Isa. lxiii. 16). If even a Moses or a Samuel would intercede in vain, the case of the Judahites must indeed be desperate. For these were the nearest of all the prophets to Jehovah, and repeatedly prayed their people out of grievous calamity (comp. Ps. xcix. 6). Jeremiah had already sought to intercede for his people (see on ch. vii. 16). Cast them out of my sight; rather, *Dismiss them from my presence.* The people are represented as praying or sacrificing in the fore courts of the temple.

Ver. 2.—Such as are for death, etc.; a sternly ironical answer. Death, sword, famine, captivity, lie in wait for them in every possible road. "Death" here means "pestilence" (comp. "the black *death*" in the Middle Ages), as in ch. xviii. 21; Job xxvii. 15. Similar combinations of evils occur in ch. xliii. 11; Ezek. xiv. 21; xxxiii. 27.

Ver. 3.—Appoint; *i.e.* give full power to them as my vicegerents (ch. i. 10). Four

kinds; literally, *families;* i.e. kinds of things. The first-mentioned has reference to the living; the remaining ones to the unburied corpses (ch. xiv. 16; xix. 7; xxxiv. 20). To tear; rather, *to drag along.*

Ver. 4.—Cause them to be removed into; rather, *make them a shuddering unto.* So in the Deuteronomic curses for disobedience (Deut. xxviii. 25).

Ver. 5.—For who shall have pity? or, *for who can have pity,* etc.? (the imperfect in its *potential* sense). The horror which will seize upon the spectators will effectually preclude pity. Who shall go aside? As one turns aside to call at a house. So Gen. xix. 2 (literally, *turn aside,* not "turn in").

Ver. 6.—Will I stretch; literally, *I stretched*—the perfect of prophetic certitude (so in next verse). I am weary with repenting; *i.e.* with recalling my (conditional) sentence of punishment (see on ch. xviii. 1—10).

Ver. 7.—The gates of the land. The phrase might mean either the cities in general (comp. Micah v. 5; Isa. iii. 26) or the fortresses commanding the entrance into the land (comp. Nah. iii. 13). The context decides in favour of the latter view. Ewald's explanation, "borders of the earth" (*i.e.* the most distant countries), seems less natural. I will bereave them, etc. The proper object of the verb is my people (personified as a mother). The population are to fall in war (comp. the same figure in Ezek. v. 17). The tense is the perfect of prophetic certitude ; literally, *I have bereaved*, etc.

Ver. 8.—**To me ;** *i.e.* at my bidding. It is the dative of cause. **Against the mother of the young men ;** rather, *upon . . . young man.* The widow has lost her husband, the mother her son, so that no human power can repel the barbarous foe. The word rendered "young man" is specially used for "young warriors," *e.g.* ch. xviii. 21 ; xlix. 26 ; li. 3. Others, following Rashi, take "mother" in the sense of "metropolis," or "chief city" (see Authorized Version, margin), in which case "young man" must be connected with the participle rendered "a spoiler ;" but though the word has this sense in 2 Sam. xx. 19, it is there coupled with "city," so that no doubt can exist. Here the prophet would certainly not have used the word in so unusual a sense without giving some guide to his meaning. The rendering adopted above has the support of Ewald, Hitzig, and Dr. Payne Smith. **At noonday ;** at the most unlooked-for moment (see on ch. vi. 4). **I have caused** him, etc. ; rather, *I have caused pangs and terrors to fall upon her suddenly.*

Ver. 9.—**That hath borne seven ;** a proverbial expression (comp. 1 Sam. ii. 5 ; Ruth iv. 15). **Her sun is gone down,** etc. The figure is that of an eclipse (comp. Amos ix. 9). **She hath been ashamed,** etc. ; rather, *she is ashamed,* etc. Ewald supposes the sun, which is sometimes feminine in Hebrew, to be the subject (comp. Isa. xxiv. 23) ; but the view of the Authorized Version is more probable. The shame of childlessness is repeatedly referred to (comp. ch. l. 12 ; Isa. liv. 4 ; Gen. xvi. 4 ; xxx. 1, 23).

Vers. 10—21.—These verses come in very unexpectedly, and are certainly not to be regarded as a continuation of the preceding discourse. They describe some deeply pathetic moment of the prophet's inner life, and in all probability belong to a later period of the history of Judah. At any rate, the appreciation of the next chapter will be facilitated by reading it in close connection with ver. 9 of the present chapter. But the section before us is too impressive to be cast adrift without an attempt to find a place for it in the life of the prophet. The attempt has been made with some plausibility by a Jewish scholar, Dr. Grätz, who considers the background of these verses to be the sojourn of Jeremiah at Ramah, referred to in ch. xl. 1, and groups them, therefore, with another prophecy (ch. xxxi. 15—17), in which Ramah is mentioned by name as the temporary abode of the Jewish captives. We are told in ch. xl. 4, 5, that Jeremiah had the choice given him

of either going to Babylon with the exiles, or dwelling with the Jews who were allowed to remain under Gedaliah the governor. He chose, as the narrative in ch. xl. tells us, to stay with Gedaliah ; but the narrative could not, in accordance with the reserve which characterizes the inspired writers, reveal the state of mind in which this difficult choice was made. This omission is supplied in the paragraph before us. Jeremiah, with that lyric tendency peculiar to him among the prophets, gives a vent to his emotion in these impassioned verses. He tells his friends that the resolution to go to Gedaliah may cost him a severe struggle. He longs for rest, and in Babylon he would have more chance of a quiet life than among the turbulent Jews at home. But he has looked up to God for guidance, and, however painful to the flesh, God's will must be obeyed. He gives us the substance of the revelation which he received. The Divine counsellor points out that he has already interposed in the most striking manner for Jeremiah, and declares that if he will devote himself to the Jews under Gedaliah, a new and fruitful field will be open to him, in which, moreover, by Divine appointment, no harm can happen to him. Whether this is really the background of the paragraph must remain uncertain. In a case of this kind, we are obliged to call in the help of the imagination, if the words of the prophet are to be realized with any degree of vividness. There are some great difficulties in the text, and apparently one interpolation (vers. 13, 14 being in all probability an incorrect copy of ch. xvii. 3, 4).

Ver. 10.—**Woe is me, my mother !** This is one of those passages (comp. Introduction) which illustrate the sensitive and shrinking character of our prophet.

" If his meek spirit erred, opprest
    That God denied repose,
What sin is ours, to whom Heaven's rest
    Is pledged to heal earth's woes ? "
        (Cardinal Newman, in ' Lyra Apostolica,' lxxxviii.).

I have neither lent on usury, etc. ; a speaking figure to men of the ancient world, to whom, as Dr. Payne Smith remarks, "the relations between the money-lender and the debtor were the most fruitful source of lawsuits and quarrellings."

Ver. 11.—**The Lord said.** The prophets are usually so tenacious of the same formulæ that even their slight deviations are noteworthy. "The Lord said," for "Thus saith the Lord," occurs only here and in ch. xlvi. 25 (where, however, the phrase has possibly been detached by mistake from the preceding verse). **It shall be well with thy remnant ;** rather, *I have loosed thee for (thy) good,* or, *thy loosing (shall be) for (thy good)*, according as we adopt the reading of the Hebrew text or that of the margin, which differs in form as slightly as it is possible to do. If we accept the historical setting proposed by Grätz for this paragraph, the reference will be to the "loosing" of Jeremiah from his chains mentioned in ch. xl. 4. The rendering given here is, however, only a probable one; it is in conformity with the Aramaic usage of the verb (the Targum uses it in this sense in ch. xl. 4), and is supported by its suitability to the context and, philologically, by the fact of the growing influence of Aramaic upon Hebrew. Gesenius, in his anxiety to keep close to the native use of the root, produces a rendering (of the Hebrew marginal reading) which does not suit the context, viz. "I afflict thee for (thy) good." Jeremiah does not complain of being afflicted by God, but that all the world is against him; Ewald, comparing a different Aramaic verb to that appealed to above, renders, "I strengthen thee," etc., which is adopted by Keil, but does not accord with the second half of the verse so well as the rendering adopted. The Authorized Version follows the Targum, the Vulgate, Aquila, Symmachus, Rashi, and Kimchi, assuming that *shērīth* is contracted from *sh'ērīth* (as in 1 Chron. xii. 38), and that "remnant" is equivalent to "remnant of life." But, though the sense is not unacceptable (comp. vers. 20, 21), the form of expression is unnatural; we should have expected *akhărīth'ka*, "thy latter end" (comp. Job viii. 7). **I will cause the enemy to entreat thee** well. This expression is as difficult as the preceding, and our rendering of it will depend entirely on our view of the context. If "the enemy" means the Chaldeans, the Authorized Version will be substantially correct. Rashi has already mentioned the view that the phrase alludes to Nebuzaradan's respectful inquiry as to the wishes of Jeremiah in ch. xl. 2—5. In this case, the literal rendering is, *I will cause the enemy to meet thee (as a friend)*; comp. Isa. xlvii. 3; lxiv. 4. But if "the enemy" means the Jews, then we must render, *I will cause the enemy to supplicate thee*, and illustrate the phrase by the repeated applications of Zedekiah to the prophet (ch. xxi. 1, 2; xxxvii. 3; xxxviii. 14), and the similar appeal of the "captains of the forces," in ch. xlii. 1—3.

Ver. 12.—**Shall iron break, etc.?** Again an enigmatical saying. The rendering of the Authorized Version assumes that by the **northern iron** Jeremiah means the Babylonian empire. But the "breaking" of the Babylonian empire was not a subject which lay within the thoughts of the prophet. It was not the fate of Babylon, but his own troubled existence, and the possibility that his foes would ultimately succeed in crushing him, which disquieted this conscientious but timid spokesman of Jehovah. The Divine interlocutor has reminded him in the preceding verse of the mercy which has been already extended to him, and now recalls to his recollection the encouraging assurances given him in his inaugural vision (ch. i. 18, 19). Render, therefore, *Can one break iron, northern iron, and bronze?* The **steel** of the Authorized Version is evidently a slip. The Hebrew word is *n'khōsheth*, which means sometimes (*e.g.* ch. vi. 28; Deut. viii. 9; xxxiii. 25; Job xxviii. 2) copper, but more commonly bronze, since "copper unalloyed seems to have been but rarely used after its alloys with tin became known" (Professor Maskelyne). "Steel" would have been more fitly introduced as the second of the three names of metals. "Northern iron" at once suggests the Chalybes, famous in antiquity for their skill in hardening iron, and, according to classical authors (*e.g.* Stephanus the geographer), the neighbours of the Tibareni, in the country adjoining the Euxine Sea, the Tibareni being, of course, the people of Tubal, whom Ezekiel mentions (xxvii. 13) as trafficking in vessels of bronze. Any Jew, familiar with the wares of the bazaar, would at once appreciate the force of such a question as this. Even if iron could be broken, yet surely not steel nor bronze. Thus the verse simply reaffirms the original promises to Jeremiah, and prepares the way for vers. 20, 21.

Vers. 13, 14.—**Thy substance**, etc. These verses form an unlooked-for digression. The prophet has been in a state of profound melancholy, and the object of Jehovah is to rouse him from it. In vers. 11, 12, the most encouraging assurances have been given him. Suddenly comes the overwhelming declaration contained in vers. 13, 14. And when we look closely at these verses, two points strike us, which make it difficult to conceive that Jeremiah intended them to stand here. First, their contents are not at all adapted to Jeremiah, and clearly belong to the people of Judah; and next, they are repeated, with some variations, in ch. xvii. 3, 4. It should also be observed that the Septuagint (which omits ch. xvii. 1—4) only gives them here, which seems to indicate an early opinion that the passage only ought to occur once in the Book of Jeremiah, though the Septuagint translator failed to choose the right position for it. **Without price**; literally, *not for a price*. In the parallel passage there is another reading, "thy high places," which forms part of the next clause. Hitzig and Graf suppose this to be the original reading, the Hebrew letters having been partly effaced and then misread, after which "not" was prefixed to make sense. However this may be, the present reading is unintelligible, if we compare Isa. lii. 3, where Jehovah declares that his people were sold for nothing, *i.e.* were given up entirely to the enemy, without any compensating advantage to Jehovah. **And that for all thy sins, even,** etc.; literally, *and in all thy sins and in all thy borders.* The text is certainly difficult. Externally a parallelism exists between the two halves of the clause, and one is therefore tempted to render literally. As this will not make sense, however, we are forced either to render as the Authorized Version, or to suppose that the text is not accurately preserved. The parallel passage has a different but not a more intelligible reading. Ewald omits "and" in both halves of the clause, which slightly diminishes the awkwardness. **And I will make thee to pass,** etc. The natural rendering of the Hebrew is, "And I will make thine enemies to pass," etc., which clearly cannot be the prophet's meaning. The parallel passage (ch. xvii. 4) has, "And I will make thee to serve thine enemies," etc.; and so the Septuagint, the Syriac, the Targum, and many manuscripts here. **For a fire is kindled in mine anger;** a reminiscence of Deut. xxxii. 22, suggesting that the judgment described in the Song of Moses is about to fall upon Judah.

Ver. 15.—**O Lord, thou knowest,** etc. The prophet renews his complaints. God's omniscience is the thought which comforts him (comp. ch. xvii. 6; xviii. 23; Ps. lxix. 19). But he desires some visible proof of God's continued care for his servant. **Visit me,** equivalent to "be attentive to my wants"—an anthropomorphic expression for the operation of Providence. **Take me not away in thy long-suffering;** *i.e.* "suffer not my persecutors to destroy me through the long-suffering which thou displayest towards them." "Take away," viz. my life (comp. Ezek. xxxiii. 4, "If the sword come and take him away"). **Rebuke;** rather, *reproach;* comp. Ps. lxix. 7 (Ps. lxix. is in the style of Jeremiah, and, as Delitzsch remarks, suits his circumstances better than those of David).

Ver. 16.—**Thy words were found.** Jeremiah here describes his first reception of a Divine revelation. Truth is like "treasure hid in a field; " he alone who seeks it with an unprejudiced mind can "find" it. But there are some things which no "searching" of the intellect can "find" (Job xi. 7; xxxvii. 23; Eccles. iii. 11; viii. 17); yet by a special revelation they may be "found" by God's "spokesmen," or prophets. This is the train of thought which underlies

Jeremiah's expression here. The "words," or revelations, of Jehovah are regarded as having an objective existence in the ideal world of which God is the light, and as "descending" from thence (comp. Isa. ix. 8) into the consciousness of the prophet. So Ezek. iii. 1, "Eat that thou findest." **I did eat them;** I assimilated them, as it were (comp. Ezek. ii. 8; iii. 3). **I am called by thy name;** literally, *thy name hath been* (or, *had been*) *called upon me;* i.e. I have (or, had) been specially dedicated to thy service. The phrase is often used of Israel (see on ch. xiv. 9), and, as here applied, intimates that a faithful prophet was, as it were, the embodied ideal of an Israelite.

Ver. 17.—**In the assembly of the mockers;** rather, *of the laughers.* The serious thoughts arising out of his sacred office restrained him from taking part in the festive meetings to which his youth would naturally incline him (comp. on ch. xvi. 2). **Because of thy hand.** The Hand of Jehovah is a figurative expression for the self-revealing and irresistible power of Jehovah; it is, therefore, equivalent to the Arm of Jehovah (Isa. liii. 1), but is used in preference with regard to the divinely ordained actions and words of the prophets. Thus we are told, in the accounts of Elijah and Elisha, that "the hand of the Lord came upon" them (1 Kings xviii. 46; 2 Kings iii. 15). Such a phrase was probably at first descriptive of a completely passive ecstatic state, and was retained when ecstasies had become rare, with a somewhat laxer meaning. Isaiah uses a similar expression but once (viii. 11); Ezekiel, however, who appears to have been unusually filled with the overpowering thought of the supernatural world, is constantly mentioning "the hand of Jehovah" (see Ezek. i. 3; iii. 22; xxxvii. 1; and especially iii. 14; viii. 3). We may infer from this variation in the practice of inspired writers that, though symbolical, anthropomorphic language is not always equally necessary in speaking of Divine things, yet it cannot be entirely dispensed with, even by the most gifted and spiritual teachers. **Thou hast filled me with indignation;** rather, *thou hadst filled me.* Jeremiah was too full of his Divine message to indulge in impracticable sentimentalities. There was no thought of self when Jeremiah received his mission, nor any bitterness towards those who opposed him. His "indignation" was that of Jehovah, whose simple instrument he was (comp. ch. vi. 11, "I am full of the fury of the Lord").

Ver. 18.—**Why is my pain perpetual?** One who could honestly speak of himself in terms such as those of vers. 16, 17, seemed to have a special claim on the Divine protection. But Jeremiah's hopes have been disappointed. His vexation is perpetual, and his wounded spirit finds no comfort. **As a liar**; rather, *as a deceitful stream*. The word "stream" has to be understood as in Micah i. 14. Many of the water-courses of Palestine are filled with a rushing torrent in the winter, but dry in summer. Hence the pathetic complaint of Job (vi. 15). The opposite phrase to that used by Jeremiah is "a perennial stream" (Amos v. 24). The force of the passage is increased if we read it in the light of Dr. Grätz's hypothesis.

Ver. 19.—If thou return, etc. Most commentators regard these words as containing a gentle rebuke to Jeremiah for his doubts respecting God's care of him. It may be questioned, however, whether such passing doubts could be described as a turning away from Jehovah. If the word "return" is to be interpreted in a spiritual sense, we must surely conclude that the people is addressed (comp. ch. iii. 12; iv. 1). But this does not agree with the context. Hence Grätz's view seems very plausible, that the reference is to the proposal that Jeremiah should place himself under the protection of Gedaliah (comp. ch. xl. 5, "Go back also to Gedaliah," etc.). **Then will I bring thee again**; viz. into the right relation to me, so as to be my minister (Keil). But by altering one of the vowel-points (which form no part of the text), on the authority of the Septuagint, we get a more satisfactory sense, *I will give thee a settled place*. The verb must in any case be coupled with the following one. Jeremiah longs for a quiet home, only as supplying the conditions of prophetic activity. **Thou shalt stand before me.** The phrase is taken from the wont of slaves to stand in their masters' presence, waiting for commands. It is also applied to courtiers (Prov. xxii. 29) and royal councillors (1 Kings xii. 6), to angels (Luke i. 19) and to prophets (1 Kings xvii. 1; 2 Kings iii. 14). Jeremiah was by God's will to find a new and important mission to the Jews with Gedaliah. **If thou take forth the precious from the vile,** etc. The metaphor is derived from metallurgy

(comp. ch. vi. 27—30). The prophet is compared to a smelter. By the fervour of his inspired exhortations, he seeks to draw away from the mass of unbelievers all those who are spiritually capable of better things. The "vine-dressers and husbandmen," whom Nebuzar-adan had left after the capture of Jerusalem, though outwardly "the poor of the land," might yet be ennobled by the word and example of Jeremiah. [Some explain "the precious" and "the vile" differently, taking the former to be the pure Word of God (comp. Ps. xii. 6; Prov. xxx. 5), the latter the base, human elements which are apt to be mixed with the Divine message (comp. ch. xxiii. 28). But was it not the very fidelity of Jeremiah which exposed him to the persecutions of which he has been complaining? Others suppose an inward purification of Jeremiah himself to be intended, "the vile" being those human infirmities of which he had just given evidence, as opposed to "the precious," *i.e.* the spiritual impulses which come from above. But is not such an explanation too evangelical, too Pauline, for this context?] **Thou shalt be as my mouth.** For devoting himself to this possible "mustard seed" of a better and holier people, the prophet should be rewarded (1) by close prophetic intercourse with his God, and (2), as the next clause states, by a moral victory over his opponents. "Mouth" for "prophet," as Exod. iv. 16 (comp. Exod. vii. 1). **Let them return unto thee,** etc.; rather, *they shall return unto thee, but thou shalt not return unto them.* They shall come over to thy side, and thou shalt not need to make humiliating advances to them.

Ver. 20.—And I will make thee, etc.; a solemn confirmation of the promises in ch. i. 18, 19.

Ver. 21.—Out of the hand of the wicked, etc. The "wicked" (literally, *evil*) and the "terrible" may be the banditti, composed of desperate patriots, who ultimately assassinated Gedaliah (ch. xli. 1—3).

HOMILETICS.

Ver. 2.—*Various destinies of punishment.* I. PUNISHMENT WILL BE ASSIGNED AS A DEFINITE DESTINY. It is not casual. It cannot be evaded. It is decidedly appointed and inflexibly executed. The destiny it involves, though not original but a consequence of voluntary actions, is as certain as if it were in accordance with a primary law of nature (Gal. vi. 7, 8).

II. PUNISHMENT WILL BE ASSIGNED IN A VARIETY OF DESTINIES. All the wicked will not suffer alike. There will be various forms of penalty and various degrees of suffering. Some are appointed to the painful death of the plague, some to the sudden death of the sword, some not to death at all but to exile. Punishment will be various, (1) because men's constitutions, capacities, and susceptibilities are various, so that the form of suffering which is suitable for one may not be suitable for another; and (2) because guilt varies in degree (Luke xii. 47, 48).

III. PUNISHMENT WILL BE ASSIGNED TO ALL THE GUILTY WITHOUT EXCEPTION. They may be numerous, yet some penalty will be found for all. The variety of destinies might suggest that among them some would find a way of escape, but, alas! they are all penal. This variety will ever secure the punishment of all. They who escape one form of punishment will only fall into another. Some hope to elude justice because their case is very exceptional. But exceptional punishment is found for exceptional crime.

IV. PUNISHMENT WILL BE SEVERE IN ALL CASES. There is a choice of destinies, but the list is given with somewhat of irony. How terrible is the mildest fate! All future punishment must be inexpressibly awful (Heb. x. 31). Therefore let us not delude ourselves with hoping that ours will be of the milder kind, but seek deliverance from the certain fearful doom of sin in the forgiving mercy of God in Christ.

Ver. 6.—*God weary of repenting.* I. GOD OFTEN APPEARS TO REPENT. He seems to repent of his merciful intentions when the conduct of men has called forth his righteous indignation—even repenting that he had ever made men (Gen. vi. 6), and to repent of his wrathful intentions when his children repent of their sins (*e.g.* Exod. xxxii. 14). Absolutely it cannot be said that God repents (1 Sam. xv. 29). He never does wrong, never errs, is never moved from reason by passion, knows the end from the beginning, and therefore never sees a new thing to modify his thoughts. Yet he acts as if he repented, *i.e.* he grieves for the sorrow he has righteously brought, and desires that it may cease as soon as possible; and he changes his action towards his children as they change their conduct towards him. This fact is not inconsistent with the essential Divine immutability. The sun does not vary in itself because, after developing a flower in moist weather, it withers it in drought. A government does not change its policy if it enters into amicable arrangements with a loyal dependency, though it was carrying out warlike measures so long as the province was in revolt. So God does not change in his own nature because his action is varied according to the varied requirements of his people. Such variation is rather a result of his essential changelessness. Righteousness, which requires the punishment of the guilty, approves of the forgiveness of the penitent; so that if the action of God did not change from wrath to mercy with the change of the guilty person to penitence, it would seem as though the nature of God had been turned aside from its essential righteousness. *Because* the sun is stationary it appears to rise and set as the earth revolves; if it did not so appear it must be moving too; and *because* God is eternally good it must seem to us, who are constantly giving occasion for differences of treatment from the hand of God, that he repents. We can only speak of God after the manner of men; therefore we say he repents.

II. GOD MAY BE WEARY OF REPENTING. Here is a second anthropomorphic expression, which corresponds to a great and terrible fact. 1. We may cease to repent of our sin; then God will cease to repent of his wrath. 2. We may sin so deeply and so persistently that he may no longer find it possible to withhold his threatened punishment. God is long-suffering; he waits for the return of his children. Though the recompense of evil-doing is due, it is deferred; God spares the guilty for the sake of the intercession of the righteous. But this cannot be for ever. We may sin away the grace of God. Though God's mercy endureth for ever the enjoyment of it by the impenitent cannot be perpetual. Eternal mercy may have to give place to eternal justice.

CONCLUSION. Consider (1) the wonderful love of God in repeatedly "repenting" of his wrathful intentions, showing that he does not desire the woe of his children, but does all that is possible to avert it; (2) the great sin of persisting in impenitence after God has shown so wonderful a love; and (3) the danger that God may be weary with repenting, and therefore the folly and presumption of relying upon our present immunity for future safety.

Ver. 9.—*Sunset at noon.* A premature ending of any human affairs may be compared to sunset at noon.

I. THIS IS A COMMON OCCURRENCE. A nation suddenly collapses; a sovereign is overthrown in the height of his power; a life is cut off in middle age. How often do we see these things!

II. THIS IS AN UNNATURAL OCCURRENCE. No such event could occur in the physical world. Therefore it proves that the human world is deranged.

III. THIS IS A CALAMITOUS OCCURRENCE. National modifications may be both peaceful and profitable. Empires are slowly welded together, colonies gradually assume powers and rights of independence, internal reforms are quietly effacing the old order. To the individual natural death in old age is painless. It is the violent and premature end that causes disaster.

IV. THIS IS AN OCCURRENCE RESULTING FROM ERROR OR WRONG-DOING. We cannot say that the cause is always to be traced immediately to the sufferers. With nations it may be generally so, but not with individuals. But still a law of morality, of social order of nature, has been broken, if not by the sufferers still by some agent.

V. THIS IS AN OCCURRENCE THAT MAY COME AS AN ACT OF DIVINE JUDGMENT. It is not universally so, particularly in regard to individuals. But it often is the case. Thus it was with the Jews, with Rome, in the dark ages, etc. Therefore let us beware of presuming on the apparent distance of the day of judgment.

Ver. 15.—*The prayer of the persecuted.* I. THE GROUNDS OF HIS PLEA. 1. *A confessor's fidelity.* Jeremiah was suffering for God's sake. This plea implies (1) innocence; (2) a special claim for God's help. He who can urge such a plea is the heir of one of the great beatitudes (Matt. v. 10). It is important to note that the promise of Christ rests, not on the mere fact of persecution, nor even on unjust persecution, but on persecution for righteousness' sake. The martyr is honoured, not for his suffering, but for his fidelity. 2. *The knowledge of God.* "O Lord, thou knowest." When men misjudge, God knows all. They who are cruelly maligned by men may take refuge in the fact that God knows their innocence. It is better to have his approval in face of a world's scorn and hate, than the flattery of the world for false merits together with the anger of the all-seeing God. How happy to be in such a case that we can fearlessly appeal to God's knowledge of our fidelity in suffering! Too often trouble is consciously deserved. 3. *The long-suffering of God.* The best man can but ask for God's mercy. Often has that been sought in the past. Yet God is not weary of hearing his helpless children's repeated cries. "His mercy endureth for ever."

II. THE OBJECTS OF HIS PRAYER. 1. *To be remembered by God.* It is something to know that God thinks of us. His sympathy is a great consolation. The traveller in the desert is not utterly alone when he calls to mind those dear ones at home, in whose memory he is constantly cherished, and who are therefore with him in spirit, while the unfortunate man who is buried in a crowded city, neglected and forgotten by his old friends, is essentially lonely and desolate. God's remembrance of us is the prelude to his active help. He remembers "for good." If Christ remembered the dying malefactor when he came into his kingdom, that fact carried with it the assurance that the poor man should be with Christ in paradise (Luke xxiii. 42, 43). 2. *To be visited by God.* Our consolation is not in a pitying though absent God, but in an abiding presence and a close communion. If God visits he will come in power to save. 3. *To be avenged of his enemies.* This was a natural desire, considering that (1) the prophet was in the midst of his distresses,—it is easy to judge coolly from the outside when we are not feeling the oppression of cruel persecution; (2) he lived in Old Testament times; and (3) he did not desire to execute vengeance himself but appealed only to the great Judge. For us Christians the right prayer is, not for harm to come upon our enemies, but for their forgiveness, as Christ and Stephen prayed. Still, we may rightly seek for the overthrow of wicked powers, the frustration of iniquitous schemes, and the just and necessary punishment of persistent evil-doers. 4. *For life to be spared.* Jeremiah does not ask for triumph, for comfort and ease, for liberation from his arduous lifelong task, but simply for life. The love of life is natural. Men have work to do, a mission to fulfil, and it is right to desire to have time to complete this. Others were benefited by the life of Jeremiah. He was the prophet of his age, and a voice speaking for all ages. It is our duty to seek to escape persecution if we can do so honourably, that we may continue to serve God and work for the good of mankind (Matt. x. 23). Courting a martyr's death is practically equivalent to committing suicide out of personal vanity, and much the same thing as falling under the second of Christ's temptations. Yet if martyrdom is unavoidable without unfaithfulness, we may honour God and benefit men more by our death than by our life.

Ver. 16.—*The words of God found and eaten.* I. THE WORDS OF GOD REQUIRE TO BE FOUND. They are not emblazoned on the face of the world that the most careless may not miss them. They are hidden treasures to be dug for, pearls of great price to be sought after. Divine truth in nature is only discoverable after thoughtful observation and reflection. The prophets were especially commissioned to toil in deep mines of spiritual thought. Revelation was born in them with labour, fasting, watching, praying. But the words of God are not so hidden that they cannot be discovered by the earnest and prayerful seeker after truth. He that seeks *shall* find (Matt. vii. 8). Many honest, earnest men pass through a season of doubt, but few such remain hopeless sceptics all their lives. Of those who never find the light probably some are suffering from some moral or intellectual perversity which distorts their vision, and others are not content to trust to the measure of light that has been given to them, and remain restless and questioning because they desire satisfaction in a direction wherein it cannot yet be afforded. But so long as all such men do not convert doubt into settled unbelief, and are not satisfied with doubt, we may be assured that ultimately the Father of lights will dispel the darkness that now troubles their souls.

II. THE WORDS OF GOD ARE FOOD. Truth is food for the soul. Christ, the "Word made flesh," is the "Bread of life." Truth is not simply revealed to amuse our curiosity; it is intended to feed our starving souls. The object of relevation is practical. The result of rightly using revelation is seen in an increase of spiritual vitality, in refreshment, heightened energy and growth in the inner life. If the words of God have not attained this end, they have failed of their object. They are food because they are not empty breath but the vehicles of vital truths—of spirit and life (John vi. 63). God is in his own words. They are inspired words. With the spoken words we receive the life-giving Spirit.

III. THE WORDS OF GOD MUST BE EATEN TO PROFIT US. It is not enough that they are spoken, heard, understood, believed, remembered, admired; they must be eaten. 1. We must *apply* them to ourselves. The starving man gains nothing by looking at food through a shop-window. The external intellectual study of truth is profitless to the soul. We must bring it to bear upon our own circumstances—hear the voice of God speaking directly to us and in regard to our immediate conduct. 2. We must *meditate* over the words of God. Food must be masticated and digested. Truth must be analyzed, ideas separated and compared, "inwardly digested," hidden in the soul and quietly thought over. Our common habit is to treat it too superficially and hastily. 3. We must *abstract the vital ideas* from the dry husk of words. Words are not profitable so long as they are regarded from the outside as mere language. We must break the shell and get at the kernel, casting aside the flesh that profiteth nothing and assimilating the spirit that quickeneth.

IV. THE WORDS OF GOD BRING JOY WHEN THEY ARE FOUND AND EATEN. To some they appear to be dull sayings, to some stern utterances of law, to some harsh messages of judgment. This is because they are not properly applied. They must first be truly found and eaten—applied, meditated on, spiritually assimilated. Then they lead to joy, for: 1. All truth is essentially noble, beautiful, and glorious. 2. Even the darker truth is wholesome as a warning, like nauseous medicine that cures pain and restores the serenity of health. 3. The highest truth is a revelation of the love of God —a gospel of good will to men.

V. THE SECRET OF THE JOY AND PROFIT OF GOD'S WORDS IS IN THE RELATION OF THE SOUL TO GOD. Jeremiah is called by the Name of Jehovah, the God of hosts. If we are strangers to God, his words will seem distant and of little interest. We prize the words of those we love. God speaks helpful and comforting words to his own reconciled children.

Ver. 17.—*The sadness and solitude of a prophet.* I. A PROPHET'S COMMUNION WITH GOD DOES NOT PRECLUDE EARTHLY SADNESS AND SOLITUDE. Jeremiah was not plunged into grief through any unfaithfulness; he was under no shadow in regard to heavenly communications; yet he was sad and solitary. 1. Consider the *sadness*. While we are in this world we suffer with it and from its action upon us, even though we may be living very near to God. Christ was a man of sorrows; he sighed and wept and groaned in spirit. It is not sinful to grieve. It is not a proof of unbelief. Faith should engender patience, resignation, peace, and hope; but it cannot destroy natural sorrow. It would not be pious but simply unnatural for the Christian mother not to be wrung with grief at the death of her child. 2. Consider the *solitude*. A good man will not be wrapped up in himself, for out of the love of God springs naturally the love of man. Godliness rouses human sympathy, and this inclines to sociability. So Christ was remarkable for his social habits. Yet there may be an inevitable solitude, and a solitude which is good both for self and for others. The more a good man sympathizes for his brother men the less can he sympathize with them when their conduct is wicked.

II. A PROPHET'S COMMUNION WITH GOD MAY LEAD TO EARTHLY SADNESS AND SOLITUDE. Jeremiah was sad and solitary because he was filled with Divine indignation. His was no atrabiliar moroseness, no theatrical Byronic self-pity. The prophet's sorrow and solitude were reflections of the grief of God for his people's sin and the aloofness of God produced by their wanderings from fidelity. 1. A prophet's communion with God will induce *sorrow for the world's sin and wretchedness*. Jeremiah was a young man. The scenes of mirth which he shunned may have been pure, innocent, and naturally attractive; but his vision of the thought and heart of God made him look behind this superficial joy to the wretchedness it sought to cover, and then it seemed but a mockery to him. 2. This will lead to a *separation from the world*. It will cause a perpetual separation from the spirit of the world as far as that is earthly and sensual, and at times a complete withdrawal to solitude. The Christian is to live in the world as its salt, its light, its leaven of righteousness, and not to flee to the wilderness, selfishly cultivating his own soul for heaven, while he leaves his task undone and his fellow-men in hopeless sin and ruin. But he will meet with occasions for solitude and scenes from which he must withdraw himself, and sometimes feel an inner sense of loneliness as he moves among the gay crowds, since he is a pilgrim and stranger, a citizen of another country, possessed by thoughts and swayed by motives quite outside those of worldly life. Thus Christ, in character and outward habit the most social of men, was in inner life and in secret thought the most lonely. The Christian has a life which is "hid with Christ in God" (Col. iii. 3).

Ver. 19.—*A wide recognition of the good without compromise with the evil.* Jeremiah is bidden to return from his solitude to his mission among his people, when he will be owned and encouraged by God if he will see the goodness that still lingers among them, and yet not enter into any unrighteous compromise with the wicked ways of the multitude of them.

I. WE SHOULD EXERCISE A WIDE RECOGNITION OF THE GOOD IN ALL THINGS—take out the precious from the vile. The gold-washer may find but a grain of gold in a ton of gravel; yet he will search diligently for it, and treasure it when he finds it. Carelessness and uncharitableness lead to an unjust, wholesale repudiation of what is no doubt largely corrupt. But it is not right to judge of things thus "in the lump." 1. Apply the principle to *persons*. Because ninety-nine men out of a company of a hundred are guilty, it is grossly iniquitous to condemn the whole hundred—the one innocent man with the rest. Jeremiah was directed to look out for the pious remnant among the mass of the unfaithful people. We are too ready to ignore the existence of the seven thousand who have not bowed the knee to Baal. Goodness should be recognized in bad society, in heathen nations, in corrupt Christian communities, in questionable avocations. We should beware of sweeping condemnations of a whole class; *e.g.* of actors, of publicans, etc. 2. Apply the principle to *religious systems*. Few are wholly good; but few are wholly bad. The dross and precious metal are mixed, though in varying degrees, in all of them. The various Church systems of Christendom partake of this mixed character. Most Churches have some peculiarly precious ideas to which it seems to be their mission each severally to testify. It is well if we have the insight to seize on these, and the charity to begrudge none of their value because of the error, the superstition, or the perversion with which they may be associated. Thus, not by an amorphous eclecticism which can minister to no deep, organic unity of life, but by a genuine assimilating power, we should learn to gather from all sources the good of spiritual thought. The same process should be observed in dealing with non-Christian religions. Beneath a vast heap of the vile a few glittering gems of precious merit may be found in the Talmud, and also in the Zend-Avesta, in the Koran, in the religious writings of Greece, India, China, etc. 3. Apply the principle to *life generally*. Take the precious from the vile in literature, in conversation, in social usage, in recreation, in politics. Discriminate in all these things. Do not reject the whole of any of them, even if the larger part may be bad, but select the pure and good and reject the evil.

II. WE SHOULD MAINTAIN A STOUT REFUSAL TO COMPROMISE WITH THE EVIL IN ANY-THING. Jeremiah is not to sacrifice principle for the sake of any advantage. He is not to embrace the vile for the sake of the precious, but to separate the two. He is not to yield his position of truth and right for the sake of winning the friendship of his neighbours, but patiently to expect them to come over to him. It is the very love of truth that should make us welcome it in the most unlikely quarters; but if we go on to receive the error that is closely associated with it, we at once become unfaithful to the very motive of our search. The silver is useless so long as the dross is preserved with it. The largest charity cannot sanction any compromise with evil. Compromise belongs to the region of expediency, not to that of truth and righteousness. It is a mistake to conciliate our enemies by yielding up our fortress. If we abandon the essential mysteries of Christianity for the sake of winning over our opponents, we are really only giving them the victory. Should we come to terms, this is at best on their grounds, and the peace we ratify is no record of a victory for Christ. In the end the policy of compromise fails. It indicates weakness and leaves no decided position about which to rally. We must dare to be firm to our principles, and wait patiently till the world comes round to them. This was how Christ acted. If we eagerly recognize the good in everything and earnestly desire to take forth the precious from the vile, we shall find our uncompromising fidelity to principle resting on a firmer and safer basis than if we are narrowly jealous of all good outside our own little circle of notions and habits.

HOMILIES BY VARIOUS AUTHORS.

Ver. 1.—*Sins for which saintly intercession cannot avail.* Moses is spoken of as an intercessor in Exod. xvii. 11; xxxii. 11; Numb. xiv. 13; Ps. cvi. 23: Samuel in 1 Sam. vii. 8; viii. 6; xii. 16—23; xv. 11; Ps. xcix. 6. Noah, Daniel, and Job are mentioned similarly (Ezek. xiv. 14). It is, then, in their special intercessory character that these fathers are referred to. At the time when their intercessions took place they were the leaders and representatives of Israel, and because of their saintliness they had favour with God. But the sins for which Judah and Jerusalem are now to be punished are by this reference declared of a more heinous description than any that took place in those days. It is a mere supposition which is made, evidently no description of the normal relation of glorified saints to Jehovah, but simply a hypothetical statement as to what they, in their earthly capacity, would have failed to do.

I. THE INTERCESSIONS OF RIGHTEOUS MEN AVAIL MUCH. Many a time in the wilder-ness had Moses stayed the impending wrath of God because of murmuring and disobe-dience; and this not simply because he was the civil leader of the people, but through his own saintly, high-priestly character. This is a principle of God's dealings with men. "The effectual fervent prayer of a righteous man availeth much;" and one of the chief occupations of the Church is represented as praying for the salvation of the world and the coming of the kingdom of God. It is because such men represent the future hope of the race, being a kind of firstfruits of them that shall be saved, that they have this power. In themselves too, because of what they are, they are pleasing to God, who delights in their prayers and praises. There is something very striking and touching in this spectacle of one standing for many, and we have to think of how great has been the blessing which has been thus secured to the world through its saints. But they all appear trifling compared with that which Christ has secured through the intercession of his prayers, obedience, and sacrifice. In his case (what could scarcely be said of any saint) his intercession has a solid objective worth because of what it is in itself, and avails as a consideration with God for the cleansing of all who identify themselves with him through faith.

II. BUT THERE ARE CONDITIONS WHICH DESTROY THE EFFICACY OF SUCH INTERCESSION. Their influence is but partial and imperfect, depending as it does upon their own inadequate fulfilment of the Law and will of God. If it were a question of strict account, they themselves would not be able to stand in his presence. It is of his grace that, even for a moment, they may be said to have influence for others. And it may be said that their intercession is but provisional, and, if not followed up by the obedience of those for whom they pray, it will be followed with the more condign punishment upon the transgressors. It is a great tribute to the vicarious power possible to saints that even the most eminent of them should be quoted in such a connection. But it shows how inadequate such a mediatorship would be for the general sin of man. We may do much, each of us, to avert just judgments, to secure opportunities of salvation, and to bring the grace of God to bear upon the hearts of others; but we cannot save them by any communication of our own acceptance with God to them. They must stand or fall according to their own relation to the will of God and the person of his Son. And there are degrees of guilt which far surpass any intercession of this kind. The sin of unbelief especially, if it be unrepented of, will prevent any benefit being received. The permanent position of our souls with respect to Divine grace will depend, therefore, upon their own action or belief. Even Christ cannot save if we do not believe in his Name and obey him.—M.

Ver. 10.—*The offence of faithful preaching.* That the preaching of the gospel should stir up the evil passions of men would at first appear strange. It is the declaration of good news to them that are perishing, and an effort to restore men to happiness and peace. But that it has been accompanied with such manifestations of ill will from the beginning is sufficiently well known. The preaching of the cross has in every age been resisted and resented by the world. It is "to the Jews a stumbling-block, and to the Greeks foolishness; but to them which are called, both Jews and Greeks, Christ the power of God, and the wisdom of God" (1 Cor. i. 23).
I. WITH WHAT THE FAITHFUL PREACHER COMPARES HIMSELF. Jeremiah says that he might have been a brawler, a dishonest debtor, or a usurer to have stirred up the strife and hatred which he experienced. As has been said, lending and borrowing cause most lawsuits. "'I have not lent nor borrowed.' My dear Jeremiah! Thou mightest have done that; that is according to the custom of the country; there would be no such noise about that" (Zinzendorf). Elijah was reproached by Ahab, "Art thou he that troubleth Israel?" (1 Kings xix. 17). St. Paul was persecuted. Even Christ himself was accused of stirring up sedition, and the preaching of the Word has often been accompanied by demonstrations of violence.
II. TO WHAT THIS MAY BE ATTRIBUTED. It is due chiefly to the dislike of men to the truth itself, in whatever shape presented. The natural heart is enmity against God and his Word. Care must be taken to distinguish between accidental and essential provocations of this spirit. The manner of the preacher should never be such as of itself to dispose men unfavourably towards his message. The greatest care ought to be taken to conciliate and to win. But the original hatred of men to truth must not be ignored. It exists, and will have to be reckoned with in one form or another. One man will object to it *in toto;* another to the degree of obedience which it exacts. With some the idea will be pleasing but the practice irksome. If men hated Christ, we need not suppose that they will be more amiable towards us if we are faithful.
III. CONSOLATIONS. These troubles need not afflict us if we remember, with respect to our hearers, that it is not theirs but them we desire. The worst enemies have been reconciled and the fiercest natures subdued by the power of the Word. It is well too in the midst of suffering to have the testimony of a good conscience. To him also who is faithful in the midst of opposition and hatred is that beatitude, Matt. v. 11. But perhaps the strongest consolation of all is in the fellowship of him for whose sake the opposition is experienced.—M.

Ver. 15.—"*Thou knowest it.*" There is One to whom the true prophet and saint must stand or fall. He is anxious, therefore, for his approval. He labours ever as in the great Taskmaster's eye. "Thou God seest me," which is the terror of the sinner, is the chief reward and comfort of the saint. The prophet here consoles himself—

I. By AN APPEAL TO THE JUDGMENT OF GOD. In this connection it is as if conscience itself had been invoked. And yet, better still, if conscience should vacillate God would remain the same. In this way it is well for the best of men to test their motives by continual reference to God. There is no better way of self-examination.

II. By A REFERENCE TO THE SYMPATHY OF GOD. The mere fact that the all-knowing One was constantly regarding his sufferings for his sake, that he had put his tears in his bottle, and that he was able to appreciate his motives, was a comfort to the prophet. If possible, this source of consolation is deepened and enlarged by the greater nearness of God in Christ. The fellow-feeling of our great High Priest and Elder Brother is real and can be depended upon from moment to moment. It is a well of salvation from which we can draw inexhaustible supplies.

III. By COMMITTING IT TO THE DIVINE RESPONSIBILITY. It was in God's hands because it was in God's knowledge. It was not for the prophet to trouble himself as to means of retaliation. He could commit his cause to his Father. The wider issues of it, nay, even its mightiest results, were beyond his own power. What he had to do was to be faithful and trusting and diligent.—M.

Ver. 16.—*God's words a heartfelt joy.* In the midst of the prophet's sorrow this passage occurs as a relieving feature—a memory of spiritual joy. At the same time it is recalled as a consideration that will weigh with him to whom he addresses himself. It defines his entire relation to God and to Israel, and describes his claim.

I. THE WORDS OF GOD TEST AND EXHIBIT THE INWARD LOYALTY OF THE SAINT. It is not merely that a certain feeling has been excited in the mind, but that a welcome has been given to God's revelation. A profound difference is thereby instituted between the prophet and those who were opposed to him. As the psalmist cries, "Thy word have I hid in my heart," in proof of his earnestness and his love of truth, so the prophet would commend himself to God by the attitude he had assumed to the message when it was revealed to him. It is as if he had said, " I have never resisted thy Word, but ever held myself ready to utter and obey it." The test which they apply to the spiritual nature is full of dread to the unworthy ; but to those whose hearts are right with God it is a satisfaction and a source of confidence. " The thoughts and intents of the heart" thereby disclosed are seen to be right and good.

II. THEY REFRESH AND STRENGTHEN HIM FOR SUFFERING AND DUTY. It is as if the prophet were drawing comfort from recollection because his present circumstances are so troublous. But many a time the Word of God comes in a time of perplexity and darkness, bringing with it comforting light. It is greedily welcomed at such seasons and is devoured as by one who has long fasted. It penetrates thereby more deeply into the spiritual nature and more radically influences the springs and motives of conduct. It comes as a distinctly supernatural aid and makes men masters of what had previously overpowered them.

III. THEY BIND HIM MORE CLOSELY TO THEIR AUTHOR. The nature which has been so affected by the words of God cannot be nor regard itself as in the same position with others. Its whole character and destiny are altered. The life is leavened by that which supports and nourishes it. The indwelling Word is a consecrating influence and withdraws men from the pursuits and fellowship of the world. In this way the saint becomes identified with his Lord; a child of grace; a worker in the same great cause ; a subject of like hatred and opposition, and an heir of the same kingdom. By producing the character of holiness they inscribe the Divine Name upon the heart, and link the life and destiny of the saint with the cause of God.—M.

Vers. 19—21.—*The preacher's weakness and strength.* I. HUMAN MOTIVES OFTEN LEAD HIM ASIDE FROM THE PATH OF DUTY, ETC. The prophet is a man like other men and subject to the same passions. It is difficult for him to maintain the attitude of continual spiritual loyalty. Flesh and blood will fail and he will fall into temptations peculiar to his office. Of these he must be especially jealous, and a stricter standard of holiness should govern his conduct. Unfaithfulness in such a position will produce an exaggerated effect upon those whom he influences. His influence itself will cease to be purely spiritual, his love less certain, and his conduct less irreproachable. Deflection like this should be at once corrected, and he who " tries the reins " is especially watchful over those who have to deliver his message and represent his cause. "If thou return." How instant and yet how gentle the reproof!

II. REPENTANT FIDELITY WILL BE REWARDED WITH USEFULNESS AND STRENGTH. 1. *Mediatorship*—to "stand before me." 2. *Infallibility*—"As my mouth." 3. *Irresistible power*—a "brazen wall;" "but not prevail over thee." 4. *The presence and protection of God.*—M.

Vers. 1—9.—*Fearful aspects of the Divine character.* These verses and this whole discourse reveal to us an implacable God. He will not turn away from his wrath nor be moved: 1. By the spectacle of misery presented (ch. xiv.). 2. By the remembrance of former love (ch. xiv. 8). 3. By the earnest prayers of his faithful servant (ver. 1). 4. By the prospect of more terrible miseries yet to come (ch. xiv. 17—xv. 9). Therefore—

I. INQUIRE. Why is God thus? The answer is, he will not change, because the sinner will not. "To the froward he will ever show himself froward."

II. LEARN. That while God's mercy is infinite to those who turn to him, for those who refuse there is no mercy at all.—C.

Ver. 1.—*The limits of intercessory prayer.* "Though Moses and Samuel," etc. 1. This verse seems at first sight to be in contradiction to the many Scriptures which assure us that the "effectual fervent prayers of righteous men avail much." The Bible teems with promises that God will hear when we call upon him. But here is a decided declaration that, let even the holiest and the most eminent for their intercessions stand before God in prayer, they should not avail to secure what was denied. 2. And were there only this verse, the difficulty would not be so great. But experience is continually supplying us with fresh instances in which blessings earnestly sought have yet been denied. 3. And this also in regard to spiritual things. Were it only temporal blessings God refused to give although we asked him for them, we could readily understand that, though they seemed so good in our eyes, in his they might be seen to be hurtful. We know that in such things we do *not* know what is best. But the refusal of prayer is found in regard to things that we know are good and well pleasing to God—in regard to things spiritual and eternal, *e.g.* in the prayers of parents for the conversion of their children, of teachers and pastors for those committed to their charge. 4. Hence from this verse and from such experience of rejected prayer, the sad conclusion has been drawn that, in spite of the most earnest intercession, the souls we pray for may be lost, our intercession be of no avail. For does it not say even to Jeremiah, who himself was an eminent intercessor with God, that there were yet greater than he —such as Moses and Samuel—but that if even they, etc. (cf. references for instances of their intercession). 5. And some have tried to escape the difficulty by drawing a sharp contrast between the intercession of our Lord Jesus Christ and that of these men of God. They have said, had Jesus interceded, it would have been otherwise. But this is not true, for our Lord would not have interceded as Jeremiah did. He also foretold great calamities as overhanging Jerusalem and her people, but we have no record of his ever having prayed that they might not come. He sought unceasingly their eternal salvation, but he did not pray against the destruction of Jerusalem. It is not permissible, therefore, to account for the failure of such intercession as that of Jeremiah, on the ground that it is only human intercession and not that of the Son of God. 6. But before we certainly conclude that intercession for the eternal spiritual well-being of others may after all be in vain, though the intercession have been such as that of the great servants of God here spoken of, who touched the utmost limits of intercessory prayer, let us note (1) *That it was not for spiritual blessings that Jeremiah was interceding.* His piteous entreaties were "concerning the dearth" (ch. xiv. 1), that that might be removed. It was strictly a prayer for temporal mercies and deliverances. It is, therefore, unjust to conclude that intercession for things spiritual and eternal may fail because, as we well know, it may fail for things material and temporal. Note also (2) *That the utmost limits of intercession had been reached.* The prophet himself had offered no scant or insincere petition, and the intercession of these great saints of God spoken of was, we know, of the mightiest order. Before, then, we conclude that such intercession in regard to spiritual things can be of no avail, let us be sure that such intercession has been tried. Is our own such? There may be customary and too often formal prayers offered by parents, pastors, teachers, for the spiritual good of those about them. But can we say that such prayers are mighty intercessions, like those of Moses and Samuel? If we know they have not been such, let us pause before we conclude that such intercession avails not. But in order to ascertain if our intercession has been real, let us note if we are in earnest about our own soul's salvation. If we care not for our own acceptance before God, how can we be solicitous for that of others? And are our prayers followed up by practical effort in the direction of our prayers? Do they lead us to see what can be done to secure the ends for which we pray? Or are they substitutes for such endeavour? Hence it may very often be that we ask and have not, because we ask amiss. We do not intercede in that real, believing, earnest way which alone has a right to expect the blessing it seeks. It is by no means intercession such as that of Moses and Samuel. 7. But if intercession have been such as theirs, then, though answer may be delayed, we are to believe that it will yet come. Delay is not denial. 8. Neither this verse nor experience sets aside the many promises which encourage such intercession. 9. And experience proves its worth. The Church of to-day is in the main the product of the intercession of the Church that has passed into the heavens. Instead of the fathers have risen up the children. 10. Learn, therefore, (1) if God refuse us temporal blessings, it is because he knows better than we do what is best; (2) how best to deal with transgressors God alone knows, and what his wisdom determines none may set aside; (3) that intercession for souls is well pleasing to God and full of hope, since the beloved of God have been ever distinguished for such intercession, and, above all, God's well-beloved Son.—C,

Ver. 1.—*Great intercessors.* I. SUCH ARE MENTIONED HERE. Moses, Samuel, etc. (cf. Exod. xvii. 11; xxxii. 11; Numb. xiv. 13; Ps. cvi. 23; 1 Sam. vii. 8; viii. 6; xii. 16—23; xv. 11; Ps. xc. 6; Ecclus. xlvi. 6). Noah, Daniel, and Job are mentioned in similar way (Ezek. xiv. 14), and Jeremiah himself (2 Macc. xv. 14). And there have been such oftentimes granted to nations, Churches, families (cf. Mary Queen of Scots saying that she feared John Knox's prayers more than all her enemies). And who has not known such intercessors in connection with Christian Churches—men and women whose prayers were amongst the main supports of the life, joy, and strength of those for whom they were offered?
II. THEIR VALUE IS UNSPEAKABLE. Cf. Abraham praying for Sodom. Though the cities of the plain were destroyed, yet what an amount of sin God was ready to pardon in answer to his prayer, if but the conditions which should have been so easy to fulfil had been forthcoming! And "the few names even in Sardis" (Rev. ii.), who can doubt that they, as all such do, warded off for long periods those visitations of God's anger which otherwise would have come upon that Church? And it is not only the evils from which they defend a Church, but the positive good they confer. Such power with God is ever accompanied by a consistency and sanctity of character which is blessedly attractive, inspiring, contagious; and as a magnet they gather round them a band of kindred souls, like as our Lord gathered his disciples round himself. And thus a hallowed influence is sent throughout a whole community.
III. THEIR QUALIFICATIONS. 1. *Sympathy with God.* They must see sin as God sees it—as utterly hateful and wrong. There must be no weak condoning of it or any failure to behold it in its true character. If we ask God to forgive sin, indeed, if we seek forgiveness for wrong done from a fellow-man, are we likely to be acceptable in our request if we regard him who has been wronged as not having much to complain of after all? No; he who would wish God to forgive sin must see it as God sees it, and consent to his judgment concerning it. 2. *Deep love for those for whom he intercedes.* And this cannot be created in a moment. It must be the result of much thought, labour, and pains spent upon them. When we have thus given ourselves to them, we are sure to love them. Places, persons, things, most unattractive to others are deeply loved by those who have devoted themselves to them. And all great intercessors have been such, and must be such as become so, not on the spur of the moment or from any mere movement of pity, but as the result of long and loving labour lavished for their good. 3. *Freedom from the guilt of the transgression, the pardon of which is sought.* Under the Old Testament the priest first offered atonement for himself and

then for the sins of the people. Not until he was purged from sin himself could he intercede for others. The intercessor must be one untainted with the guilt he prays to be removed. The prayer of the wicked can never aid. 4. *Experimental knowledge both of the blessings which he craves and of the sorrows and sufferings which he inter-cedes against.* Of our Saviour, the great Intercessor, it is said, "He himself took our infirmities, and bare our diseases." He was made "in all points like unto his brethren." The joy of God's love and also, by holy sympathy, the bitterness of the dregs of that cup of which the wicked have to drink—were alike known to him. Thus, though he knew no sin, he was *made sin* for us. It was to him as if all the sin of those he so loved were his own, so intensely did its shame, its misery, its guilt, fill up his soul. And with human intercessors there must be like experience. 5. *Faith in God, which firmly holds to the belief that his love for the sinner is deeper than his hatred of the sin.* Unless we believe this we can have no hope in interceding either for ourselves or for others. Faith in the infinitude of the love of God is essential.

IV. THEIR GREAT EXEMPLAR—the Lord Jesus Christ. See how all the qualifications above named combine in him.

CONCLUSION. 1. To the sorrowful and sinful. You need a great intercessor. You have one in Christ. "Give him, my soul, thy cause to plead." 2. To the believer in Christ. Seek to become as Moses and Samuel, and, above all, as our Lord—mighty in intercession.—C.

Ver. 4.—*The sins of the fathers visited upon the children.* This verse contains an explicit declaration that such is God's rule. The calamities about to fall on Judah and Jerusalem were "because of Manasseh the son of," etc. No doubt the sins of Manasseh were flagrant in the extreme, and they were the more aggravated because he was the son of the godly Hezekiah. No doubt his reign was one of dark disgrace and disaster. The sacred writers dismiss it with a few short statements, hurrying over its long stretch of years—it was the longest reign of all the kings of Judah—as if they were (as they were) a period too melancholy and shameful to be dwelt upon. But why should we find that his guilt and sin were to fall upon those who were unborn at the time, and who therefore could have had no share therein?

I. SUCH VISITATION IS AN UNDOUBTED FACT. It is plainly declared to be a Divine rule, and that once and again (cf. Exod. xx., etc.). And apart from the Bible—in the manifest law of heredity—there is the dread fact patent to all. Workhouses, prisons, hospitals, asylums, all attest the visitation of God for the fathers' sins.

II. IT IS A GREAT MYSTERY. It is one branch of that all-pervading mystery into which all other mysteries sooner or later run up—the mystery of evil. There is nothing to be done, so far as its present solution is concerned, but to "trust," and so "not be afraid."

III. BUT NOT WITHOUT ALLEVIATIONS ; *e.g.* 1. *If the sins of the fathers are visited on their descendants, yet more are God's mercies.* The sins descend to "the third and fourth generation," but the mercies to "thousands" of generations—for this is meant. 2. *The descent is not entire.* The sins come down, it is true, upon the descendants, but in their fruits rather than in their roots. A father cannot force on his child his wicked-ness, though he may his diseases and tendencies. 3. *The entail may be cut off* in its worst part at any moment, and very often is. Coming to Christ may not deliver me from physical suffering, but it will from sin. Grafted into Christ a new life will begin, the whole tendency of which in me and in mine is to counteract and undo the results of the former evil life. 4. *And the visitation of the fathers' sins is but rarely because of the fathers' sins only.* The descendants of the age of Manasseh did their works, and what wonder that they should inherit their woes? 5. *And it is a salutary law.* Children are a means of grace to tens of thousands of parents. "Out of the mouth of babes," etc. For, for their children's sakes, parents will exercise a watchfulness and self-restraint, will seek after God and goodness as otherwise they would never have done. The remembrance of what they will inflict on their children by virtue of this law fills them with a holy fear, as God designed it should.

CONCLUSION. 1. *Parents.* What legacy are you leaving for your children? Shall they have to curse or bless you? O father, mother, "do not sin against" your "child." 2. *Children.* What have you received? Is it a legacy of evil example, evil tendency, evil habit? God's grace will help you to break the succession. Refuse it for yourselves, determine you will not hand it on to others. But is it a legacy of holy example, tendencies, and habits? Blessed be God if it be so. What responsibility this involves! What blessing it renders possible for you and those who come after you!—C.

Ver. 9.—*The darkened home.* "She that hath borne . . . was yet day." Perhaps in all the range of human sorrows there is none greater than that which befalls a home when the dearly beloved mother of many children, yet needing sorely her care, is early cut off. Such a piteous case is described here. The prophet, bewailing the coming calamities of his country, adopts the heartbroken language of a husband bitterly mourning the death of his wife and the mother of his many children. He seems to think of her who is gone, and all her sweetness and grace and goodness rise up before him. He thinks of their children and how they will need their mother's care, terribly need it, though never more can they have it, and his heart dies down within him. He thinks of himself and how utterly lonely his lot must be. At such times heart and mind almost give way, and faith and love Godward receive a blow beneath which they reel and sometimes never recover themselves. But this verse is as a holy angel of God, and enters that darkened home; and—

I. IT CALLS TO MEMORY WHAT THE LOST ONE WAS. Her life was as the shining of the sun—bright, cheerful, generous, inspiriting, attracting, healthful, and joy-giving to all.

II. IT DENIES NOT THE FACT WHICH IS SO BITTERLY MOURNED. Her premature death, her sun went down, etc. Nothing can alter that fact. And perhaps, as the very words indicate, circumstances of peculiar sorrow may have surrounded her death. Like her told of in this verse, "she may have breathed out her life as if in laboured sighs, expiring in heavy heart-breaths of grief." Not a calm, gradual, bright sunset, but the very reverse, the sun going down in dark clouds. The power to utter those blessed parting words of counsel and comfort taken from her, and in darkness and silence she had to wend her way to the unseen. But amid all this depth of gloom this verse—

III. SUGGESTS MOST BLESSED TRUTH. The sun of her life has not perished but shines elsewhere. We know that when the sun sinks below our horizon it has gone to gladden and bless other shores. And so with the life of the blessed dead. They all live unto God. All that in them which was so pure, so sweet, so full of the grace of God, has not perished; it is shining elsewhere, it has risen on another shore, the eternal and the blessed. And on us it shall rise again, as the sunrise follows in due time the sunset. That life is not lost but is hidden with Christ in God, and so "when he who is our life shall appear" then shall that now hidden life "appear with him in glory."—C.

Ver. 12.—*A vain contest.* "Shall iron break the northern iron and the steel?" So asks the Lord God of his, at this time not simply lamenting prophet, he was rarely anything but that, but also his complaining prophet. And as we read these verses with which the striking inquiry contained in this verse is connected, we cannot help feeling that his lamentations become him far more than his complaints. Still, who are we, to criticize a great hero of the faith such as Jeremiah undoubtedly was? These verses, from the tenth onwards, are no doubt on a lower, a less spiritual and less self-forgetful level than that which the common strain of his prophecies and prayers maintain. It will be seen that these verses come at the close of a long and most earnest appeal addressed by him to God on behalf of his countrymen. They were suffering fearfully from the dearth of which the opening of the fourteenth chapter tells. Now, all this was then present before the prophet's mind, and these chapters record the expostulations, the pathetic appeals, and the almost agonized prayers which he pours forth on behalf of his suffering land and people. He makes full confession of their sins, but pleads the all-merciful Name of the Lord, and when that did not suffice, he urges the evil teaching that they had received from their prophets and that therefore they may be held guiltless or far less guilty, and when that plea also was rejected he returns to his confessions and earnest entreaties; but it is all of no avail. At the opening of this chapter God says, "Though Moses and Samuel"—men who had once and again proved themselves mighty intercessors for the people, yet even if they—"stood before me, my mind could not be toward this people." The crimes of Manasseh, King of Judah, that king who reigned so long, so disgracefully, and with such disastrous results over Judah, had never been repented of, and never really forsaken. They were rampant still, and therefore the Lord declares this judgment which he had sent upon them must go on—no prayers of his faithful servant could avail to stay its execution. Upon this the prophet pours out a piteous lamentation over the woes of his people, and then, turning to his own position, he complains bitterly of the hatred which was felt towards him by those whom he had sought to bless. "Woe is me, my mother, that thou hast borne me a man of strife and a man of contention to the whole earth!" He had been no usurer nor fraudulent debtor, "yet every one," he cries, "curses me." Then to him the Lord replies, promising him deliverance in the time of evil, and asks the question, "Shall iron break . . . steel?" The ancients knew comparatively little of the manufactures of iron and steel. Amongst the Israelites it was very coarsely wrought, but the best iron was from the north. So bad was their own that an admixture of brass, which among us would be rather thought to lessen its value, was regarded as an improvement. But the iron and steel procured from the people who lived in the far north, on the shores of the Black Sea, was the most celebrated for its tenacity and hardness. Against it the common iron of every-day use could offer but little resistance, and when opposed to it could make little or no impression; it could not "break the northern iron and the steel." And the question of this verse is a proverb denoting the impossibility of any force, though great in itself, overcoming one which by its very nature and by its effects had been proved to be greater still. Our Lord teaches the same truth when he speaks of the folly of that king who thought, with his army of ten thousand, to encounter and overcome another king who came against him with twenty thousand. But whilst the meaning of this verse is plain enough, its application is not so clear. If we connect it with the verses that immediately precede, as many do, then it is a question whose tone is bright, cheerful, and reassuring. But if we connect it with those that immediately follow, its tone is altered and is full of solemn admonition and serious warning. In the first case it refers to Jeremiah himself, and is for his comfort and confidence. It tells him that the enemies who are against him, however ironlike they might be—cold, hard, fierce, strong—and however much they may oppress and afflict him, yet assuredly they shall not prevail against him; for God will make him as the northern iron and the steel, against which all their might shall be in vain. God had promised at the very outset of the prophet's ministry that he would thus strengthen him. Behold, he says, in the first chapter, "I have made thee this day a defenced city, and an iron pillar, and brazen walls against the whole land, . . . and they shall fight against thee, but they shall not prevail against thee; for I am with thee, saith the Lord, to deliver thee." And in the twentieth verse of this chapter the like promise is given over again. So that they have much reason on their side who regard these words as a heart-cheering assurance conveyed to the prophet under the form of a question, and assuring him that, let the power of those who hated him be what it might—as ironlike as it would—the grace of God which would be given him would make him stronger still, would make him as the northern iron and the steel. Let us, then, view these words—

I. AS A REASSURING PROMISE, and make two or three applications of them. 1. And first, to such as Jeremiah himself was at this time—a faithful servant of God, *but much troubled and tried*. What right have we to expect that all things will go smoothly with us in this world, or to be surprised when sore troubles come? Did not our Lord say, "Behold, I send you forth as sheep amongst wolves"? Well, it would be strange if the sheep were to find all things just as they wished amid such surroundings as that. But, as one has said, the sheep have beaten the wolves after all. There are to-day tens of thousands of sheep for every wolf prowling on the face of the earth. It did seem very likely, when the sheep were so few, that the wolves would most certainly have quickly made a clearance of them. But, though here and there one like Saul "made havoc of the Church," the flock, the Lord's fold, went on increasing and multiplying in a marvellous way. Spiritually as well as literally the sheep outnumber the wolves who would destroy them. And what is the explanation but this, that to those who have no might the Lord has increased strength? He has let the wolves be indeed like iron, but his sheep he has strengthened as the northern iron, etc. And this he will ever do. God can temper our souls to such degree of hardness and tenacity that they shall blunt and beat back every weapon that is formed against them. The arrows hurled against us shall fall pointless to the ground, and the armour of God wherein we stand engirt shall more than defend us from the adversary's power. The shield of faith is made, not of our enemies' untempered iron, but of the northern iron and steel told of here. Oh, then, child of God, how is it with thee? Is the world frowning upon thee? are circumstances adverse and involved, and thy way hedged with difficulties? Has death invaded thy home or is it about to do so, and is thy heart saddened thereby? Does disappointment dog thy steps and baffle all thy best-meant endeavours? Is anxiety creeping over thee and filling thee with foreboding fear? Hearken to this word of God, "Can iron," etc.? Can these things, hard and terrible as they are, break down thy defence or break through thy shield? Oh, bring thy soul to Christ, tell him how weak, how defenceless, in thyself, thou art; come to him for the armour of proof thou needest; ask him to give thee good courage and to strengthen thine heart; and then, as thou comest off more than conqueror over all these things, thou shalt triumphantly ask this question for thyself. 2. And we may ask it again in reference *to the opposition of the world against the Church of God.* For that Church is girt with invincible power, and stands like a rock amid the raging of the sea. In vain the tempests hurl the mighty waves against it, in vain do they fiercely smite it as with force sufficient to make it stagger and fall; but whilst you look expecting to see it overthrown, lo, the huge seas that smote it are shivered into clouds of spray, and multitudes of foaming cataracts are seen rushing down its sides but leaving it unharmed and immovable still. And—to return to the metaphor of this verse—the iron of its adversary's weapon has broken against the steel of its impenetrable shield, and the Church of God is unconquered still. Heresy has sought with insidious power to turn it from the truth. Persecution with its fires and all manner of deadly cruelties has threatened every member of its communion, and slain thousands upon thousands of them. Superstition has come with' its priestcraft and pretended super- natural powers and taught men to worship idols in the name of God. Infidelity, the sure offspring of Superstition, disgusted with the miserable shams and the mass of wretched fables which Superstition has taught men for truth, has thrown off all belief, and denied the very existence of God and the whole of the precious faith that the Church has received. The world, a more deadly foe still, with her soft blandishments and her mighty bribes, has done more to pervert the right ways of the Lord than perhaps all the other enemies of the Church altogether; just as on the mass of iron used in the construction of the great railway bridges which span so many of the valleys, straits, and rivers of our land, it is found that a warm morning's sunshine does more to deflect them from their true horizontal line than is accomplished by the ponderous weight of the heaviest engines and trains rushing over them at their highest speed. The soft warmth does more than the heaviest weight. And again and again in the history of the Church of God it has been found that when the world is most smiling then is it most deadly to the best interests of the Church. And in our day, fresh forms of unbelief or disbelief are gathering round the Church, and like a mist enwrapping the minds and hearts of not a few, so that the blessed firmness of faith which once was the common characteristic of the Church is giving way to a general doubt, vagueness, and uncertainty, upon which no firm foothold can be had. But what is our confidence in view of all this? Is it not in the truth, made sure to us by the experience of all the ages, that the Church of God is his especial care, and that therefore his omnipotence is around it, and all the powers of hell shall not prevail against it. Here the Church of God is to-day, in numbers, zeal, faith, charity, not one whit behind the former days. Here in this direction and that there may be loss, but if so, then in other directions we find gain. And the witness of all the history of the Church is this, that the forces that oppose her are but as untempered iron, whilst the power that defends her is as the northern, etc. And should there be any anxious heart who is in much doubt and fear as to his own personal salvation because of the multitude and magnitude of his sins, we would bid such a one take home to him the truth of our text. For although his sins be all he thinks them, and even more—of strength like iron—yet the Saviour's

will to save is as the northern iron and the steel. True, the retrospect over the past may
be grievous, and since that was forgiven it may have been too often reproduced again.
"Thy backslidings," as God told Israel, "have been many;" but art thou hoping in
God? dost thou grieve and mourn over sin and truly desire to be made whole? Then
it *shall* be so with thee; thy salvation shall be accomplished, for thine accusers' power
is but as the iron, whilst thy Saviour's is as the northern, etc. Therefore yield not to
doubt, still less to despair, but go to him who is mighty to save, and ask him to give
thee of his strength that thou mayst now conquer thy sin; so shalt thou no more
doubt of his grace or of thine interest therein. Such are some of the applications of
this question which, taking it as an implied promise, we are justified in making. But
as we said at the outset, if we connect our text with the verses that follow, it will
rather supply lessons of serious warning and admonition. For thus understood, the
iron tells of the power of Israel and "the northern . . . steel" of the invincible power
of the Chaldean armies that were so soon to come against them, and therefore this
question is a declaration of the sure overthrow of Israel when the time of conflict came.
The power of God was against Israel, and then what hope could there be? Their poor
defence would be soon broken, and they would lie at the mercy of their foe. It is,
therefore—

II. A SAMPLE OF THE FATE THAT ATTENDS ALL RANGING OF MERE HUMAN POWERS
AGAINST THE WILL OF GOD. Whenever any such unequal contest is contemplated or
being carried on, this question may be fitly asked. And therefore we ask it: 1. *Of
all these, and they are very many, who think that they can, unarmed of God, successfully wage the war with sin.* We would be unfeignedly thankful that there is felt the
desire to wage this war at all, that there is no fatal apathy or content with sin, but
that there is a real purpose to subdue it and keep it under and to live in all righteousness. Yes, wherever that purpose is, let thanks be given to God. But what all
such need to remember, yet what they very often do not remember, is that the evil of
their own hearts is as "the northern . . . steel," whilst all the strength of their own
resolves is but as common "iron," and when these two come in collision we know the
result. Remember that first of all there is the *guilt* of sin to be provided for, and even
supposing you were to contract no further sin, what is to be said of all the past? How
can your own right resolves and correct future conduct—if it be indeed correct—atone
for that? But supposing it were true that in an amended life there is atonement for
the past, as we overlook the sins of youth, if the mature life be what it should be—
supposing that were true, which it is not, even amongst men, if the past crimes have
been of a serious kind—but supposing it were, and that if a man really turned over a
new leaf all the records of the foregoing leaves should be destroyed, no matter what
those records were—have you any guarantee that the future leaves will be altogether
different from those that went before? The Word of God, and experience also, teach
us that we have not. No doubt some sins may be given up, some evil actions forsaken,
especially if they be such as bring upon us the reproach of man, but the true nature of
the man remains unchanged—he is in himself what he was. "Can the Ethiopian change
his skin," etc.? "then may ye also do good, that are accustomed to do evil." So speaks
the prophet of God; so, too, speaks the experience of life. Of course we do not affirm
all this in regard to the coming up to the standard of society, or of maintaining an
external decency of life, but we do affirm it in regard to the attainment of that
renewed and alone morally excellent character to which God calls us and of which our
Lord Jesus Christ set us the example. You cannot bore through rock with wooden
tools; you cannot with soft iron cut or pierce the hardened steel. And so you cannot,
by the power of your own resolves, break that heart of evil, hardened like very steel,
which every man carries about in him until it is regenerated by the Spirit of God.
The grace of God alone can help you. It is at the cross of Christ, where you gain
forgiveness from all the guilt of the past, that you gain also strength for the better life
of the future; and it is in daily coming to that cross, daily looking unto Jesus, that
blessed Lord who is both your Redeemer and your perfect Pattern, that you become
changed into the same image and made like him. Iron is striving to "break the . . .
steel," whilst you are endeavouring of yourself to save yourself from the past results and
the present power of sin. You cannot do it, and in view of the gracious help the Lord
Jesus Christ offers you it is a sin and an insult to him to persist in the attempt.

2. Finally, I think of another hopeless contest in which also many are still engaged, in which the iron is thinking to "break . . . steel." *It is the contest with God, the combat with the Most High.* God has made us all for himself. Now, he himself so obeys the law of truth and righteousness and goodness that we say he *is* righteousness. "The Lord is righteous in all his ways and holy in all his works." "God is love." Therefore he bids us surrender our hearts, our wills, to him, to obey, love, and serve him. It is not simply right, but most blessed for us as for all his creatures to do this, and the vast majority of them do, and are blessed in consequence. But man has the power of saying "Nay" to God's "Yea," and "Yea" to God's "Nay," and that power he has chosen to exercise. In other words, he has set up his will against the Divine will, and refuses obedience where the will of God and his own are opposed. This is the contest that is ever going on—God seeking to win man's will, his heart to himself, and man persistently refusing. Man wants to have his own way, believing and insisting that it is the good way for him, whilst God knows well that it is a way of evil and of evil only. Therefore by all means God is seeking to draw us from that way to his own. By the voice of conscience and of his Spirit pleading within us, by his providences, his Word, his ordinances, and in other ways still, mostly gentle and gracious, others of them of a sterner kind, but by them all he is aiming at but one result—this, of inducing us to yield to him, to acknowledge his authority, and confess him Lord. And remember this will of his is no passing wish, one which, when he finds he cannot have it, he will cease to care for. Oh no, but it is his steadfast purpose, that upon which his heart is set. "As I live, saith the Lord, all the earth shall be filled with my glory." "To Jesus every knee *shall* bow, and . . . Father." Can we think, then, that instead of this, God will be content with simply destroying man? That would be to confess failure on his part, and so would also the mere infliction of vengeance. Therefore we feel sure that the rebel will have to yield, and the stoutest heart to bow. The iron cannot "break . . . steel." Shall the will of man for ever defy God, and hold out against him? But ah! what of agony and woe will not the rebel will have to go through ere it will own itself wrong! All the awful words of Christ about the quenchless fire and the undying worm—those dreadful sayings of his at which the soul shudders—still are his setting forth thereof. Oh, you whose hearts are still unsurrendered to him, will you provoke him to this? will you force him to hold you down to the consequences of your own doings until you come to see them as he sees them? Then not alone because of the sorrow that must attend the refusal to yield to him, but because such yielding is so right, so blessed, let us cease from the vain and sinful conflict; let the iron no more foolishly think to "break the northern iron and steel," but "let us come and worship and bow down"—not with the knee alone, but in heart—"before the Lord our Maker" and our Redeemer.—C.

Ver. 16.—*How to study the Scriptures.* This verse declares—
I. HOW WE SHOULD DEAL WITH GOD'S WORDS. 1. *We are to "find" them.* We are not to be content with mere surface reading, but to "search the Scriptures." It is certain that without this searching they will never be found. Now, it is this conviction which has led to the recent revision of the Scriptures. They who undertook that work were not ignorant of nor indifferent to the many objections which would be brought against their enterprise. They knew it would be said that such revision would disturb the faith of simple men and women, that it would provoke discord, that it would encourage restless spirits to be ever seeking change, that it would destroy old and sacred associations, that it was unnecessary because by means of commentaries and sermons the true meaning of any passage could be given; but they felt it to be their duty to set forth, as clearly as possible, the very words of Scripture, so that men may "find" them as before they could not do. They knew such work was needed, and they were encouraged by the history of former revisions, that of Jerome and that of our present Authorized Version, against which all the present objections were brought but were soon seen to be futile. Faith has not been disturbed; union and not discord has followed, the meaning of Scripture has been made more manifest, and what is and what is not of real authority—as the Apocrypha—has been declared. And they were encouraged by the fact that the present was an especially favourable time for their work : the existence of so many capable scholars, not only to do the work, but

to test it after it was done; the increased knowledge of the Greek language and literature—a knowledge that, in view of the growing disregard for the languages of antiquity, was not likely to be ever greater than at present; the deepfelt love for the
English of our Bible, thus ensuring the preservation to a great extent of its present tone
and style; the spirit of concord which the proposal has elicited between this country
and America, and between all sections of the Christian Church. Hence for all these
reasons it was felt to be a favourable time to set out afresh on the search for the very
words of God, in order that men might be enabled to " find " them the more readily. And
we may gratefully believe that to a large extent the ends proposed have been secured,
and that by the labours of the revisionists God's words in the New Testament Scriptures
have been " found " as they have not been heretofore. 2. But this which others have
done for us we must do for ourselves. We must " find " God's Word. We must study
it, diligently read it, exercise ourselves in the Scriptures by careful, frequent, continuous
reading, resolved that we will not merely read over the words, but know their meaning.
For the Word of God needs finding. It is hidden away beneath the sound of familiar
words and phrases which, from frequent hearing or repetition, have lost their power
either to arrest or arouse our thought. And prejudice, formality, indolence, indifference,
and other besetments of the soul beside, all do their part to hide from us the true sense
of God's Word. 3. And, when found, God's Word should be spiritually " eaten," i.e.
we must take his words so into our soul's life that, as our daily food ministers to our
bodily life, these words of God shall minister to our soul's life. By the strength
derived from our daily food all the organs of our body, all its functions and forces, are
sustained in health and in working power—brain, heart, limbs, etc. And so, when
God's words are " eaten," they sustain and strengthen the functions and forces of the
soul—its faith, courage, hope, joy, etc. Abraham so believed God's word that he was
able to offer up his son Isaac in obedience to what he believed was God's command.
Job, by the same means, bore in glorious patience his heavy trials. Our blessed Lord
baffled and vanquished the tempter by his threefold thrust of the sword of the Spirit—
" It is written." And all the heroes of the faith have become heroes by reason of this
same " eating " of God's Word. Now, God's Word is thus taken into and made the life
of our souls, not by memory alone. Mere learning page after page by heart, as we say,
will not feed the soul. Let Sunday school teachers remember this. Nor will meditation and reflection upon it be sufficient. There must be added fervent prayer that, by
the Divine Spirit, God's Word may be so inwrought in us that it shall be for us as a
sacrament, a veritable eating of the flesh of Christ. Now, if the Word of God be
thus found and eaten, see—

II. How God's Word will deal with us. It will become " the joy and rejoicing of
our hearts." True religion is ever a joyful thing. " Her ways are ways of pleasantness, and," etc. What is that entire hundred and nineteenth psalm but one continuous affirmation of joy in God's Word? We shall see in the histories which the Bible
records the evidence of a Divine overruling, in its prophecies the proof that the future
as well as the past is under the same control; in its precepts and its holy Law the
righteousness of the Divine rule; and in the Gospels the love that is beneath, around,
amidst, and above all. And to the man of God, what can all this be but " the joy and
rejoicing of his heart "? God's words have done much for us when they have brought
us to repentance, more when we are led to trust in God, yet more when they enable us
to live the life of obedience; but they have not done all they were designed and are
able and willing to do, until they have become " the joy," etc. But we cannot have
the joy first; repentance, trust, obedience, must precede and accompany; let these
be lacking, and joy cannot be.

III. The ground of this joy and rejoicing. " For I am called by thy Name," etc.
The prophet was known as the " man of God." He was so identified with God, so
notoriously consecrated to him, as to be called by his Name. It was the prophet's joy
and delight to be so called, and yet more to be so in reality. Therefore everything
that was the Lord's had interest for him, as an affectionate child rejoices in the letters
of his parents, reads them over and over again, treasures them, obeys them. And he
would joy in these words also because by them he had been led to the joy of his
present favour with God, and by them he was sustained therein. Hence, he being so
unreservedly and joyfully the Lord's, all the Lord's words could not but be what they

were to him. And it is ever so, in proportion as we are the Lord's by a living, loving consecration, will his words be "the joy and," etc.—C.

Ver. 1.—*Fruitless intercession.* These words are addressed to the prophet in his character of intercessor for the people. He had already been told to plead no longer for them (ch. xiv. 11), seeing that their case was hopeless, and the Divine sentence that had gone out against them was irrevocable. Observe—

I. THE POWER THAT HUMAN INTERCESSION MAY HAVE WITH GOD. The fact that such intercession is declared in this case to be vain implies that, under other conditions, it might be effectual. Moses and Samuel often stood before the Lord as mediators on behalf of the people whom they represented (Numb. xiv. 13—20; 1 Sam. vii. 9; Ps. xcix. 6). Not that they had officially any priestly function. They were not priests; their power with God lay in the elevation of their character and the intimacy of their fellowship with him. Every age has borne witness to the reality and efficacy of this power. "The effectual fervent prayer of a righteous man availeth much" on behalf of his fellow-men. Who can tell how much it is owing to such intercession that a guilty world has been saved from hopeless abandonment?

II. THE LIMIT MAN'S OBDURACY PUTS TO THAT POWER. There are times when no human intervention is of any avail. Even the pleading of Moses and Samuel could not have averted the threatened judgments. "My mind could not be towards this people." Why? Simply because of the obstinacy of their unbelief and irreligion. It is not that God is not merciful and gracious and ready to forgive, or that the pleadings of good and holy men have no power with him. It is that the inveterate obduracy of men nullifies all the persuasive influence alike of Divine and human love. God's mind cannot be towards those who with obstinate impenitence refuse his grace. There is a limit beyond which even Divine patience cannot go. The very pleading love of the great Intercessor is defeated in the case of those who will not forsake their false and evil ways. It is not so much an irrevocable Divine decree, it is their own self-willed perversity that dooms them and leaves the stern, retributive laws of God to take their course.—W.

Ver. 16.—*The living Word.* The prophet, remonstrating with God on account of the hardness of his lot, here looks back regretfully to the time of his first call to the prophetic office. It is the language of one disappointed and disheartened by the apparent issue of his life, and the bitterness of whose grief is intensified by the remembrance of hopes unfulfilled, and a joy that has for ever passed away. It is as if God were "altogether unto him as a liar, and as waters that fail." Apart, however, from the peculiar experiences that called it forth, this passage is full of instruction. Note—

I. THE METHOD OF GOD'S REVELATION OF HIMSELF TO MEN. "Thy words were found." The term "found," in a case like this, is suggestive of that which comes to the soul, not so much as the result of its own seeking, but of a spontaneous Divine purpose. All those on whom the quickening light of Divine truth has shone feel more or less distinctly the reality of this. The inspiration has come to them in mysterious and unexpected ways. It has "pleased God to reveal his Son in them." It is not so much that they "know God" as that they are "known of God" (Gal. i. 15, 16; iii. 9). The initiatory step in this gracious process is his, not ours. "Ye have not chosen me, but I have chosen you," etc. (John xv. 16).

II. THE VITAL RELATION TRUTH BEARS TO THE DIVINELY ENLIGHTENED SOUL. "I did eat it." No physical image could be more suggestive of the intimacy of this spiritual relationship. It indicates: 1. *The soul's preparation to welcome the truth.* There is a divinely awakened appetite. 2. *The active participation of the powers of the soul in the process.* It is more than a mere passive reception. 3. *The assimilation of the truth into the very being of the man.* As food is transformed into the living fibre of the body, so that truth becomes a part of the very substance of his spiritual nature, the stay of his strength, the inspiration of his life. The word is translated into the form of holy character and Godlike deed.

III. THE GLADDENING EFFECT OF DISCOVERED TRUTH. "Thy Word was unto me the joy and rejoicing of mine heart." There can be no purer, nobler joy than that which springs from conscious communion with the mind of God. His Word admits us to the realities of a world undarkened by the shadows and undisturbed by the storms that trouble this. Rising through it to the heights of Divine contemplation, the glory of the unseen and eternal surrounds us, and we drink of "the river of the pleasures of God."

IV. THE SELF-CONSECRATION THAT IS THE RESULT OF THE REALIZED POWER OF DIVINE TRUTH OVER THE SOUL. "I am called by thy Name," literally, "Thy Name is called over me." This was the seal and symbol of his personal dedication to his prophetic work. The Word of the Lord dwelling richly in the soul is the unfailing spring of a consecrated and holy life. "Sanctify them in thy truth: thy Word is truth," etc. (John xvii. 17, 19).—W.

Ver. 1.—*The uselessness of intercession once more emphatically stated.* I. A REMINDER OF GOD'S LONG-SUFFERING IN THE PAST. Moses and Samuel had stood interceding before him, and again and again he had glorified himself in mercy and pardon. The mention of these two great historic names suggests to Jeremiah that God can appeal to all the past, confident that no man can complain of him as wanting in long-suffering with the waywardness of his people. They had wandered far and often, and often needed mercy and restoration; but when God forgave them, they soon forgot the mercy and renewed favour. Thus we are enabled to feel how very bad their condition must have become in the time of the prophet. To have listened to the plea of any intercessor would have been to show a mercy which yet was no mercy—a mercy which, while doing no real good to Israel, would have done evil in confusing the boundaries of truth and falsehood. God's mercy must ever be shown as part of his wisdom, and the time comes when severity to one or two generations may be the truest mercy to the whole world.

II. THE HONOUR DONE TO THE MEMORY OF THE GOOD. As servants of Jehovah, Moses and Samuel were great in many ways, but in none greater than as urgent prevailing intercessors. With regard to Moses, see Exod. xxxii. 11—14, 31, 32; Numb. xiv. 13—19. With regard to Samuel, see 1 Sam. vii. 9; xii. 23. The listenings of God to these men showed that his general will was that supplications should ever be made on behalf of all sinners. God delights in seeing his servants pitiful towards all the needs of men, especially those needs which arise from their forgetfulness of God himself. This reference was surely meant to teach Jeremiah, for one thing, that God not only permitted intercession but expected it. Further, the intercessions here referred to were those of righteous men. Moses and Samuel fully appreciated the evil-doings of those for whom they interceded. Doubtless they quite apprehended that evil-doing might on certain occasions reach such a height that intercession could not be expected to prove successful. Those who had had the opportunity of pondering God's dealings in the Deluge and the destruction of Sodom would well understand that intercession had its limits.

III. JEREMIAH WAS THUS REMINDED OF THE DIFFICULTIES OF GOD'S SERVANTS IN FORMER DAYS. Moses and Samuel were not only intercessors, they were intercessors for those who had made life largely a burden and a grief to them. It was not upon a scene where they were comparative strangers that they came in, did their interceding work, and then passed out to return no more. The success of their intercession meant the renewal of their struggles with a wayward and careless nation. If only Jeremiah considered the whole history of Moses and the whole history of Samuel, he would be led to say, "Who am I that I should complain?" These conspiracies, this bitter opposition, this feeling of solitude, were nothing new. We can only serve God in our own day and generation, and we must accept that generation with all its difficulties, only let this be remembered, that there is no servant of God, in any generation, but will need all his faith and meekness and endurance to encounter and vanquish these difficulties in a right spirit.

IV. HONOUR WAS PUT UPON JEREMIAH HIMSELF. His influence with God as a faithful servant was shown every whit as clearly as if he had been successful in his intercession. That influence, indeed, the people might fail to recognize; but this was a small matter if only the prophet himself was made to feel that his God respected the spirit of his prayer. God's way of honouring us is not by making us stand well with the fickle crowd, but by his own smile shining into our hearts and making gladness there. The mention of these two great historic names lifts Jeremiah in the esteem of God to something like a level with them.—Y.

Ver. 10.—*The man who felt he had been born to strife and contention.* These words of the prophet are not, of course, to be taken too literally. They are the language of excited feeling and of poetry, and would not be permissible as a prosaic statement to which the man who makes it may be expected deliberately to adhere. The proper way of regarding the words is to take them as vividly indicating a position which no words could sufficiently describe. Jeremiah sometimes felt himself so hated and so isolated that there seemed but one way of accounting for his experience, and that was that he had been born to it. We know, indeed, that the truth was far otherwise (see ch. i. 5). There we see how Jehovah himself reckoned Jeremiah to have come into this earthly existence, not for suffering, but for a career of noble and useful action, which, rightly considered, was a high privilege. But a man who is constantly suffering from the sin of his fellow-men in all its shapes and all its degrees, cannot be always looking at the bright side and speaking in harmony with such a view.

I. A SERVANT OF GOD MAY HAVE TO LIVE A LIFE OF INCESSANT CONFLICT. Jeremiah's case appears to have been an extreme one, and yet the history of the Church shows that a company by no means few might be reckoned as companions in his peculiar tribulation. It is not for us to say how far our lives shall be marked by external conflict. We must not seek conflict; but we must be ready for it if it comes. God gives to every one who is willing to be his servant a way in which to walk, a way which does not infringe on a single real right of a single human being. From beginning to end that way may be trodden, not only without injury to others, but with positive benefit to them. At the same time, nothing is more possible than that treading in such a way may expose him who strives to walk in it to all the various forms which, according to circumstances or opportunity, opposition may take. And therefore, when we are beginning to feel our way to the carrying out of God's will, we must lay our account with opposition. How much of it may come, how far it may go, how long it may last, we cannot tell; and as we must not provoke it through mere exuberance of energy, so neither must we avoid it for the sake of a temporary peace which is really no peace. If opposition comes—even intense opposition—to the truth faithfully proclaimed, this only shows that the truth has proved itself an arrow, striking home and making its wound, whatever the ultimate consequence of that wound may be.

II. THE MESSAGE OF GOD IS NOT THE ONLY CAUSE OF STRIFE AND CONTENTION. Jeremiah was reckoned as a troubler of Israel, and so in one sense he was; but Israel could only have been troubled by him because, first of all, it was in a condition which admitted of commotion. The wind troubles the waters and raises the waves into destructive fury; but this is just because they are in a condition easily acted on. The prophet, however, has another answer, an answer which served to show how much he marvelled at the universality and intensity of the opposition with which he was met. He is far from being the only troubler of Israel. Suppose he becomes silent; strife and contention would not therefore cease. When he comes in with his reproofs, warnings, and threatenings, it is not upon a scene hitherto tranquil and harmonious that he enters. He finds abundance of quarrelling already, and one fertile source of the quarrelling lies in the relations between borrower and lender. They may cease their strife, and join their forces for a little while against the prophet who is their common enemy; but their mutual exasperation is not forgotten, their quarrel is by no means composed. They will return to it with as much bitterness as ever. The prophet, it will be noticed, speaks as if the hostility to him was a marvel. God has sent him to these men for their good; he has come to turn their steps from the way leading to destruction; and yet, because he tells them the truth, he has become their enemy. We see that his faith in human nature, as easily knowing its own best interests, is hard to shake. He does not at all wonder that the borrower should hate the rapacious lender and the lender hate the defaulting borrower; but there is a deep mystery when the man who comes to warn of danger is hated for his message, and hated all the more just as he becomes more earnest and persistent in the utterance of it.

III. WE SEE THE PROPHET'S CONSCIOUSNESS OF THE PURITY OF HIS OWN MOTIVES. He is sure that *in him* there is no reason for hostility. He had defrauded none; he had

oppressed none.   With all his complainings here, it was well that he had no cause for
self-reproach.   Difficulties we must ever expect from that action of others which we
cannot control; but let them not be increased needlessly by our own selfishness, obstinacy, and arrogance.—Y.

Vers. 15—17.—*The prophet's claim upon Jehovah, and the grounds of the claim.*
That which urged the prophet thus to cry to God for succour is stated with great
emphasis in ver. 18. He is suffering as from a perpetual pain and an incurable wound. It
is by such a cry as this that we are able to estimate something of the continuous reproach
which he must have had to endure. We know how, in later days, the Jews dogged
the steps of Christ and afterwards of Paul; and these persecutors of Jeremiah were
their ancestors. Against them Jeremiah could do nothing himself. So far as human
sympathy was concerned, he was alone or nearly alone, not able to command even the
forbearance of his own kindred, and therefore he had to turn all the more to God. It
was well, indeed, that he was thus shut up to the one resort. In his approach to God,
we find him stating three claims for God's immediate attention to his position.
  I. SUFFERING FOR JEHOVAH'S SAKE. Every suffering man has a claim upon God,
even when his suffering comes by his own transgression. God is very pitiful to the
tortured conscience of the man who has been wakened up out of a selfish and disobedient life. It can be no pleasure to him to see a being of such sensibility as man
suffering from any cause whatever; and when a man is suffering for truth, for
righteousness, for the gospel and the kingdom of God, then we may be sure that there
is a peculiar movement of the Divine nature to help and strengthen such a sufferer.
God would help his servant in this very instance, by enabling him to look at his suffering in the right way. The suffering was an evidence of successful work; successful
because it had been faithfully and courageously done. If only the prophet had softened
some words the Lord had put into his mouth and omitted others, he might have escaped
reproach. But reproach smiting on a good conscience is better than contempt falling
deservedly on the coward who trims to stand well with everybody. Then the prophet
would also be made to feel that it was a good thing to bear what God was bearing himself. His long-suffering towards his enemies requires that his friends should also be
patient. It is better to be abused in bearing testimony for God than to share in the
rancorous conflicts of selfish men. Prophet and apostle alike had this for their
experience, that they were compelled to suffer for the Lord's sake; and he who bore the
clearest, purest testimony of all, viz. Jesus himself, was the one who suffered the most.
That good and true men, trying to serve God, should often become impatient under
biting, bitter words is not wonderful. The true thing to be desired in such a state of
mind is not to escape the reproaches, but to have the inward joy increased, so that it
may be an effectual counterbalance to all that comes from outside. "If ye be reproached
for the Name of Christ, happy are ye" (1 Pet. iv. 14).
  II. THE COMPLETE ASSOCIATION OF THE PROPHET WITH THE PROPHETIC WORD. He did
not receive it into his mind reluctantly and listlessly, but as one who hungered and
thirsted after righteousness. As the word fell on his inner ear it was devoured. It
came to him as from the excellent glory; he recognized it as Divine. He was not as
many, who will pamper and cram themselves with delicacies that are pleasant to the
taste, and turn away with unconcealed aversion from food full of nutrition and health.
Hence they became to him the joy and rejoicing of his inward life. All words of God,
apprehended in their real meaning, give strength, peace, satisfaction, harmony in the
nobler parts of human nature. Jeremiah is thinking of the parallel which may be
drawn between food for the body and food for the spirit. The food which we take,
just because it is pleasant for the taste, may be anything but a joy and rejoicing to the
heart. We must eat what is really good for food, evidently intended for food, if we
would be kept from ill consequences. It was because these words were readily
accepted and fully received that they became a joy and rejoicing to the heart, and then
in the strength, fortitude, zeal, thus communicated, the prophet went forth to his
arduous work. Here surely is the secret of his steadfastness. God had put his words
in his servant's mouth (ch. i. 9); but that was all he could do. It was for the prophet
himself so to treat the words that he should give them with all the added force of his
own sanctified personality. Other men might have uttered the same words, yet so as

to rob them of all force and sting. Notice in particular that if these words of God to the prophet—words mostly so stern, spoken nearly all from the judgment-seat—were nevertheless the joy and rejoicing of his heart, how much more may such an experience be expected from receiving the evident gospel words of the Lord Jesus! "The words that I speak unto you, they are spirit and they are life" (John vi. 63).

III. THE PROPHET'S LIFE WAS CONSISTENT WITH HIS MESSAGE. According to his message, which was soon proved to be a word of truth, the whole land was advancing ever more swiftly into a season of the greatest suffering and sorrow. Yet the people would not believe the message, but went on, just as usual, assembling for their merry-makings. If now the prophet had joined in these merry-makings, the people would have had some plea for their neglect. As it was, they could find no excuse in any inconsistent conduct of his; as he spoke, so he acted. Probably some of them tried to draw him in, to get him away from what, in their shallowness and haste, they would reckon mere morbid fancies. Others would accuse him as being one who cared for no pleasure of life himself, unless it was the pleasure of souring the pleasure of others. And yet we see the prophet could be as thankful for joy and rejoicing of heart as any one. It is the greatest possible mistake to suppose that those who keep away from the world's pleasures are filled with gloom. A service of God, filled with joy, may soon become a real experience. But if talking about it stands instead of the reality, then the pretence will soon be shown by the avidity of our turning towards worldly pleasures.—Y.

EXPOSITION.

CHAPTER XVI.

With this chapter should be taken the first eighteen verses of ch. xvii. The heading of the Authorized Version well expresses the contents of vers. 1—9, provided that "the types" are understood to be typical actions of the prophet himself. "The prophet, under the types of abstaining from marriage, from houses of mourning and feasting, foreshoweth the utter ruin of the Jews." To the inquiry, why these calamities should come upon them, the old and well-known answer is to be given (vers. 10—12), accompanied by a definite prediction of captivity (ver. 13). Then, to relieve the picture, a glimpse of a happier future is introduced (vers. 14, 15); but only a glimpse, for already the Chaldeans, like so many fishermen and hunters, are on the track of the Jews, for a "double" retribution must precede the Messianic promise (vers. 16—18). Strange contrast—the heathen coming to the truth and the Jews (those of the present, not of the future time) deserting it (vers. 19—21)! We will take up the thread of thought again at the opening of the next chapter.—The date of this prophecy would appear to be nearly the same as that of the preceding one, the circumstances of which are similar. The latter part of it will enable us to fix it more precisely (see on ch. xvii. 1—18).

Ver. 2.—**Thou shalt not take thee a wife.** So St. Paul, "I think therefore that this is good by reason of the present distress, namely, that it is good for a man to be as he is" (1 Cor. vii. 26, Revised Version); and Hosea has already drawn an awful picture of "Ephraim bringing forth his children to the murderer" (ix. 9). In ordinary times it was a kind of unwritten law among the Israelites to marry and beget children. Most of the prophets (e.g. Isaiah) appear to have been married. **In this place;** i.e. in the land of Judah. A Jeremianic phrase (comp. ch. vii. 3).

Ver. 4.—**Grievous deaths;** literally, deaths of sicknesses; i.e. all kinds of painful deaths, including (as ch. xiv. 18 shows) death by starvation. **They shall not be lamented.** The absence of sepulture has already been pointed to several times as a feature of the horror of the times (ch. viii. 2; xiv. 16; comp. ch. vii. 33), but this is a new and affecting touch. Dr. Payne Smith aptly refers to the plagues of Athens and London, in which the gentler elements of human nature were for the time almost extinguished.

Ver. 5.—Compare this prohibition with that given to Ezekiel (xxiv. 15—27). **The house of mourning;** literally, of screaming (an uncommon word, only occurring again—of banquetters—in Amos vi. 7). It is, no doubt, the wail of mourning relatives which is meant.

Ver. 6.—Nor cut themselves, nor make themselves bald. Both practices are forbidden in the Law (Deut. xiv. 1; Lev. xix. 28; xxi. 5), but the prohibition was at any rate unknown to the masses (see, for the former, ch. xli. 5; xlvii. 5; and for the latter, ch. xlvii. 5; Isa. xxii. 12, "The Lord Jehovah called . . . to baldness;" Amos viii. 10; Micah i. 16; Ezek. vii. 18). St. Jerome remarks, and incidentally gives a valuable evidence of the tenacity of primitive customs, "Mos hic fuit apud veteres, et usque hodie in quibusdam permanet Judæorum, ut in luctibus incidant lacertos," etc.

Ver. 7.—Tear themselves for them. The verb is used in Isa. lviii. 7 of breaking bread (the accusative is there expressed), and there is no doubt that this is the meaning here. The only question is whether *lāhem*, for them, should not rather be *lĕkhem*, bread (this was read by the Septuagint, Peshito, Vulgate, Targum). St. Jerome sees here an allusion to the funeral feasts (comp. the *parentalia*), and surely he is right. The Jews had a conception of the nature of the life of the other world only less distinct than that of their Egyptian neighbours. The funeral feast was not merely for the living, but for the dead. Indeed, it was primarily intended for the spiritual nourishment of those who had gone before to the unseen world (comp. Bonwick, 'Egyptian Belief and Modern Thought,' p. 48). Chardin, the old traveller, asserts that "the Oriental Christians still make banquets of this kind by a custom derived from the Jews." **The cup of consolation.** It would seem as if the funeral feasts had dwindled among the Jews into little more than a refection for the benefit of the mourners.

Ver. 9.—The voice of mirth, etc.; a striking description, repeated from ch. vii. 34.

Ver. 12.—Imagination; rather, *stubbornness* (ch. iii. 17).

Ver. 13.—A grim irony. In the foreign land ye shall serve your idols to your hearts' content, **day and night** if ye will, "*because,* [not, **where**] *I will not have mercy upon you*" (by delivering you, and so calling you back from your idols).

Vers. 14, 15.—The text of these verses occurs in a more characteristic form and in a better connection in ch. xxiii. 7, 8. The connection here would be improved by inserting the passage before ver. 18; and as displacements are not unfamiliar phenomena in manuscripts, this would not be a violent act. The difficulty is not in the **therefore** introducing the promise, which frequently

occurs in prophecies immediately after threatenings (*e.g.* Isa. x. 23, 24), as if to say, "Things being in such a miserable plight, your God will interpose to help you;" but in the position of ver. 18. How can the prophet say, "And *first* I will recompense their iniquity double," when vers. 16, 17 contain a description of this very double recompense?

Vers. 16, 17.—I will send for should rather be, *I will send.* **Fishers** and **hunters,** by a divinely given impulse, shall "fish" and "hunt" the unhappy fugitives from their lurking-places. There may, perhaps, be an allusion to the cruel ancient practice of "sweeping the country with a drag-net" (Herod., iii. 149), and then destroying the male population: Samos, *e.g.* was thus "netted" and depopulated by the Persians. Habakkuk may also refer to this when he says (i. 15), "They catch them in their net, and gather them in their drag."

Ver. 18.—First—*i.e.* before "I bring them back again into their land"—**I will recompense . . . double;** *i.e.* amply, in full measure (comp. ch. xvii. 18; Isa. xl. 2; Rev. xviii. 6). **With the carcases,** etc. The idols, which "defile the consciences" of those who worship them, are compared to the most unclean and loathsome objects.

Ver. 19.—O Lord, my strength, and my fortress, etc. Jeremiah falls into the tone of the psalmists (Ps. xviii. 2; xxviii. 8; lix. 17). All that is choicest and most permanent in Old Testament religion finds its adequate lyric expression in the Book of Psalms. **The Gentiles shall come unto thee.** The article, however, is not expressed. "Nations," *i.e.* a crowd of peoples, hitherto ignorant of the true God, shall hasten to the scene of Jehovah's great interposition; they have been convinced by Israel's unlooked-for restoration of the unique divinity of Jehovah.

Ver. 20.—But the Jews of this generation, in spite of the manifold proofs of the true religion which have been vouchsafed to them, are deserting the real divinity for the unreal. In a tone of surprise the prophet exclaims, **Shall a man make gods unto himself,** etc.?

Ver. 21.—The final answer of Jehovah. There will be no further grace-time. **I will this once cause them to know;** rather, *I will this time* (comp. on ch. x. 18) *cause them to acknowledge.* The judgment which Jeremiah has had the sad duty of announcing will prove to the blinded Jews that Jehovah alone is true God, alone can strike and heal.

HOMILETICS.

Ver. 2.—*"Forbidding to marry."* I. CELIBACY IS NOT A SCRIPTURAL VIRTUE. Marriage is a Divine institution. It is natural, and God is the Author of nature; it is recognized and regulated by inspired teaching and blessed by Christ; it is a means of human welfare.
II. CELIBACY MAY BE WISELY OBSERVED IN CIRCUMSTANCES OF PECULIAR TROUBLE. Such were the circumstances of Judah in the days of Jeremiah; such, in the opinion of St. Paul, were the circumstances of his own time (1 Cor. vii. 26). Those were not times for wedding festivities; the married would be encumbered and hindered from doing their best for the public weal, and children born then would be born only to a heritage of misery. Similar circumstances may recur.
III. CELIBACY MAY BE WISELY OBSERVED BY MEN WHO ARE CONTEMPLATING TASKS OF PECULIAR LONELINESS, DANGER, OR DIFFICULTY. There are risks that a man may encounter for himself which he should avoid if others would be seriously involved in his fate. There is work which precludes the enjoyment of domestic life. It is not right to undertake obligations to another that cannot be fulfilled. The pioneer of dangerous travel, the John the Baptist of wilderness missions, is better unmarried.
IV. CELIBACY IS A DUTY FOR ALL UNTIL THEY ARE ABLE TO PROVIDE A SUITABLE MAINTENANCE FOR A FAMILY. It is not heroic but selfish to bring a family into a life of certain hardship and misery. The principle which applied to the public circumstances of distress in Jeremiah's age applies to the private circumstances of distress which are met with in every age.

Ver. 12.—*"Worse than your fathers."* I. EACH GENERATION SHOULD BE BETTER THAN THAT WHICH PRECEDES IT. The natural movement of all mankind should be onward and upward. We have the lessons of past history to warn and to inspire us; the continued, increasing, long-suffering mercy of God to urge us to serve him more faithfully; and the growing light of slowly accumulating knowledge to guide us into better paths. Later generations have more aids of Divine revelation than were vouchsafed to the earlier. The Jews under the prophets had more light, more Divine inducements to fidelity, than the Jews under Moses; and Christians have a much clearer light and much more powerful motives in the revelations of God's will and of God's love in Christ. To go back when we ought to go forward is doubly inexcusable. Christians are bad indeed if they fall lower than the men of Old Testament ages, and Protestants of modern times if they do not live up to the attainments of the Mediæval Church.
II. EVIL INCLINES TO GROW WORSE FROM GENERATION TO GENERATION. Men ought to improve; but if they begin a course of evil they deteriorate in it. Nothing in the world is stationary. Nations are either progressing or retrograding. Each generation is either better or worse than its predecessor. Evil has a contagious property, and if it is unchecked it is certain to spread like an epidemic. It is a leaven that, left to itself, will surely leaven the whole mass. We should, therefore, seek to stamp out a sin in its earlier stages. We must not trust to any necessary law of progress, any idea of the inherent goodness of human nature, any thought of the temporary character of evil, but seek at once to resist and overthrow the sin. Here is a warning to parents. Evil tendencies are hereditary. The vice, which seems to do little harm in our own day, taking root and spreading, will break out into worse fruits in our children's time. How sad to leave only a bad example for our children to be referred to!
III. IF EVIL IS TO BE CONQUERED IT MUST BE BY SOME SUPERHUMAN METHOD. The natural laws of progress fail here. Depravity unchecked grows more depraved. Innumerable practical reforms, new systems of morality, draconian codes, etc., have been tried, and all in vain. Josiah made the experiment with his violent reformation, but it failed of anything but superficial good. Some are now trusting to sanitary improvements, to industrial progress, to popular education; but these too will not touch the root of the sore. The history of sin furnishes the greatest proof of the need of a Divine redemption if the world is ever to be saved. For this Christ came, and now the highest progress of the world is to be traced to that new influence of life which he introduced to turn the current of history from deepening depravity to growing truth and righteousness.

Vers. 14, 15.—*The greatest gratitude for the latest blessings.* The circumstances of the Jews are illustrative of those of all of us in the fact that we all have occasion to feel most thankful for the most recent gifts of God's goodness. The reasons for this are manifold, viz.—

I. THE LATEST BLESSINGS ARE MOST THOROUGHLY APPRECIATED. A present impression is stronger than a memory. Even if the good things we are now enjoying are not equal to those we formerly possessed, the immediate good we derive from them is greater than that which we derive from a mere recollection of better times. Thanksgiving tends to become formal and conventional—the empty repetition of phrases which had a deep signification when they were the spontaneous response of the soul to fresh tokens of God's love, but which have become almost meaningless after the occasion for them has fallen into the past. To be real, gratitude must refer to the real mercies which we are now enjoying.

II. THE LATEST BLESSINGS ARE ADDITIONAL PROOFS OF THE GOODNESS OF GOD. We should " sing a new song " as we see new manifestations of Divine love. We have more to be thankful for when we have received two gifts than we had when we were only possessors of one of them. God is constantly adding to the vast pile of his favours to us. The latest stands highest, is, so to speak, mounted on all that precede ; and therefore this calls for the strongest expression of gratitude. Inasmuch as the longer we live the more we have to be thankful for, so also the more deeply should our hearts be stirred with gratitude. The restoration of the Jews is an additional mercy following that of the Exodus. One such stupendous deliverance should call forth never-failing songs of praise, but a second should intensify the volume of those songs.

III. THE LATEST BLESSINGS ARE ALSO THE GREATEST. The restoration is referred to as containing grander blessings than those of the Exodus. Gratitude should be proportionate to favours. This is often not the case, because the best things are least appreciated. Their merits are not superficial nor discernible at first. The spiritual blessings are the highest ; yet to unspiritual men they are the least valued. Thus the chief elements of the Messianic promises of restoration were spiritual, and therefore not so acceptable to the mass of the people as the material blessings promised to the Jews in the first possession of the "land flowing with milk and honey." We are too ready to complain of the present and regret the lost past, ungratefully selecting the troubles of our own time for notice and ignoring its bright features, while we forget the hardships of the past and remember only its last pleasant features, like the Jews, who forgot the rigours of the slavery from which they had escaped, but remembered with regret the flesh-pots of Egypt (Exod. xvi. 3). The Bible favours no sentimental regrets for " the good old times ; " it teaches us that God's goodness is increasingly manifest. The latter times are better than the former, the Gospel age than the Old Testament era, the later years of Christendom than the earlier. The best is not yet revealed. The songs of the future should be sweeter than those of the past, since God has greater mercies in store for us than any we have yet enjoyed. Already God has favoured us more highly than our fathers. We need not search the musty annals of antiquity for proofs of the goodness of God. This is a present goodness, and the richest fruits of it are the latest.

IV. THE LATEST BLESSINGS ARE GIVEN IN SPITE OF OUR GREATEST ILL DESERT. We have added to the tale of our sins while God has been adding to the tale of his mercies. As his goodness has increased with many, their sin has also increased. The Egyptian bondage overtook the innocent ; the Babylonian captivity was a punishment to the guilty. Deliverance from the latter was an act of forgiving mercy. It was a proof of God's forbearance that he continued to be gracious, and of his pardoning love that he forgave the sinful people. Our greatest reason for praise is in God's latest mercy of redemption, restoring us after our falls into sin.

Vers. 16—18.—*Fishers and hunters.* I. THE CHASE. The guilty will be sought after for punishment. If they do not seek God in penitence he will seek them in judgment. However far we may flee from obedience we cannot flee from responsibility. Jonah fled " from the presence of the Lord " (Jonah i. 3), but he was overtaken by a Divine judgment. If God's present long-suffering makes him appear indifferent, the day will come when his wrath will be swift, searching, and far-reaching. Then none of the impenitent can escape. None can *hide* from the approaching doom ; hunters " shall hunt them from every mountain, and from every hill, and out of the holes of the rocks." It will be useless then to " call on the hills to cover us," etc. None will be *over-looked*. Fishers will come with their drag-net, gathering all classes as fish of all kinds and of all sizes are collected in the sea. Rank counts for nothing when kings are hunted like foxes ; intellectual ingenuity can then find no covert of sophistry beneath which to elude the keen scent of the bloodhounds of justice ; exceptional originality can secure no position beyond the reach of the broad sweeping net of a general judgment.

II. THE REASON FOR EXPECTING A FATAL RESULT TO THE CHASE. God undertakes the direction of it (ver. 17). He knows all ; he is ever watching every one of his children, for their joy if they are obedient and submissive, for their shame if they are rebellious and impenitent. 1. God's *eyes* are upon their ways. He does not depend upon hearsay evidence, upon the testimony of his emissaries. Hence (1) none can elude his searching gaze, and (2) we shall not be convicted on false evidence. 2. God's eyes are upon their *ways*. He notes conduct, action, behaviour. 3. God's eyes are upon *all* their ways. The most secret do not escape his notice. Little faults are observed; hidden sins are known ; all is fairly weighed and compared. God does not select conduct for judgment; he observes both the good and the bad, and judges of the whole. 4. *Iniquity* is not hidden. God looks beneath the *ways* to the iniquities which prompt them ; he reads the heart, and judges of conduct by motive. Who can escape such a searching ordeal ?

III. THE FATAL END TO THE CHASE. (Ver. 18.) After conviction follows the sentence. 1. This is a *recompense*. It is earned and it is fairly proportionate to guilt. None of us dare ask for the simple reward of our conduct.

> " Consider this—
> That in the course of justice, none of us
> Should see salvation : we do pray for mercy."

2. It *increases* in severity with the increase of sin. The successive sieges of Jerusalem were successively more terrible ; so were the repeated raids upon Rome. The longer we treasure up wrath for the day of wrath the greater must be the weight of it that will ultimately burst on our heads. 3. It is justly required by *great* sin. This was (1) great moral and religious corruption ; (2) practised in " the holy land "—in God's inheritance, and therefore a sacrilegious defilement of Divine things ; and (3) an abuse of God's blessings in the land God had given the people. The sin of those who enjoy Divine privileges and hold positions in the Church by means of which they can glorify or dishonour the Name of God is, on these accounts, especially culpable.

Vers. 19—21.—*God revealed to the heathen by his judgment on his people.* I. GOD IS REVEALED IN JUDGMENT. Blessings reveal God's love; judgments, his righteous power. They who ignore the perennial tokens of God's loving-kindness may be roused by startling manifestations of his justice. The judgments which fall on the professed people of God are the most striking proofs of his unflinching and impartial justice.

II. THE HEATHEN MAY LEARN THE LESSONS WHICH ARE LOST TO THE PEOPLE OF GOD. The heathen seem to be here described as returning to God before the Jews. Nothing is so blinding as sin against light. The publican repents before the Pharisee. Worldly men are more ready to receive religious impressions than people who were once religious and have fallen away.

III. THE REVELATION OF GOD VOUCHSAFED TO THE SPIRITUAL-MINDED IS HIGHER THAN THE REVELATION MADE TO THE HEATHEN IN JUDGMENT. The latter is grand and striking, but it does not open up the choicer stores of the knowledge of God. Jeremiah prizes these. To him God is a Strength, Fortress, and Refuge. God is not a mere Judge. He is a gracious Father, and this is his chief character. He is a *Strength*— actively saving and inspiring energy ; a *Fortress*—protecting us when attacked in the hard battle of life ; and a *Refuge* in the day of affliction, affording solace to his sorrowing children. God's people enjoy personal relations with him very different from those of men who simply recognize the terrible presence of God in judgment. Thus Jeremiah says, "*My* Strength," etc.

HOMILIES BY VARIOUS AUTHORS.

Vers. 1—4.—*Celibacy as an obligation of the minister of God.* This passage has been quoted in support of the Romish doctrine of the celibacy of the clergy. Like other favourite references of the advocates of this regulation, however, it only requires to be examined to show that its bearing is quite of an opposite character. Its terms are not by any means absolute or universal. Not even the whole lifetime of the prophet nor his entire ministry are within the scope of the prohibition. It was a special revelation for exceptional circumstances, and must not be converted into a general rule.

I. THE LIMITATIONS IMPOSED UPON THE PROPHET, AND THEIR REASONS. 1. *The command related to :* (1) *The prophet himself.* It was in the second person singular. A matter affecting himself alone. (2) *The holy land—" in this place."* Should circumstances lead him elsewhere, the inference is that the restriction would be withdrawn. (3) *The period of time elapsing between the delivery of the special " word of Jehovah " and its fulfilment.* 2. *That Jeremiah himself was alone required to observe this restriction might at first appear strange were it not for his exceptional position.* (1) *As a symbol of the Divine attitude and intention towards Judah.* Not only special actions, such as the hiding of the girdle, were to be of this character, but the whole personality of the prophet. He was representative both of God and the ideal Israel. Therefore he represents the mind of God towards those who usurped the place of the latter. The conditions of the then present relations of God and Judah were not such as warranted an assumption of responsibilities implying for their happy fulfilment the Divine acceptance and favour. In the midst of a luxurious people his celibacy would be impressive. (2) *As an example to others.* The inhabitants of Jerusalem and Judah, whatever they might experience in the future, would not be able to say they had been entrapped or deceived into a false security. The self-restraint and serious, sad aspect he presented were intended to influence the action of the people at that juncture. The calamities foretold would not come upon those who had been unwarned.

II. THE BEARING OF THESE UPON THE QUESTION OF THE " CELIBACY OF THE CLERGY." It is obvious that, as there were many other ministers of God in Judah and Jerusalem at that time to whom the command was not given, it was intended for one occupying an exceptional position. Further, there is no necessary permanent obligation attaching to it. A certain contingency is regarded—a time of distress and bloodshed—and the conduct of the prophet is directed with regard to that. But the celibacy of the clergy is a permanent institution with those who uphold it. No regard is paid to special circumstances or times. And the office of the Christian minister is not to be considered as occupied for a season of short-lived, delusive peace, but instituted and maintained in a world which is being reconciled to God; in which the Holy Spirit is given to them that ask it for direction and comfort; and whose institutions are more and more influenced by the laws of the kingdom of God. So in St. Paul's day it was the " present distress " which gave rise to the injunction. The world was conceived of as approaching a grand climateric; a sudden and overwhelming calamity was to inaugurate Christ's reign amongst men. Much will depend upon this, viz. Is the minister of the gospel a prophet of evil or a preacher of peace and glad tidings? If the latter, it can hardly be necessary that he should assume the bearing of Jeremiah. And the influence of a celibate clergy upon the general institutions of marriage has been found to be pernicious, lowering its relative sacredness and violating the law of nature, which is its greatest safeguard.

III. PRINCIPLES OF GENERAL OBLIGATION INVOLVED. The duties and restraints here imposed upon the prophet are not rightly apprehended when supposed *entirely* peculiar to office and position. They are not wholly those of a class or a special individual, but rather the generally obligatory principles of the spiritual life intensified and specialized. Every Christian ought to hold himself ready to sacrifice and to adapt himself as the duties imposed upon him under given circumstances may require. 1. *The responsibilities of marriage.* One's own happiness merely is not to be consulted in marrying, but the probabilities of comfort and right upbringing of children that may be born. A season of calamity such as that now foretold was a sufficient reason against contracting marriage, as by that means its effects would only be the more widely extended. 2. *Consciousness of God's displeasure ought to exert a restraining influence upon men.* The marriage feast and the usual rejoicings that take place on such occasions show that they are regarded as of a joyous nature, and not amongst the sterner duties. It was but fitting, therefore, that it should be refrained from in view of what was about to take place. It would have shown a heedlessness of God's anger provoking the more signal punishment. The "marrying and giving in marriage" of the antediluvians was a sign of their godlessness and unbelief. 3. *The responsibility of example is here presented in an extreme form.* What would have applied to the case of a private person thus forewarned was of greater force in that of one occupying an exceptional position and necessarily of great public influence. If the declarer of the Divine message had himself exhibited no sign of restraint or chastened severity of life, how could others be expected to believe him? The life of the preacher is the best illustration of his doctrine, and it naturally is regarded by others with special and critical attention.—M.

Vers. 10—13.—*The destiny of sinners a self-created one.* I. As it is in itself. It is a fearful prospect which is here held out to the unbelieving Jews. They are to experience a complete change of condition. The land of promise, national independence and honour, family purity and happiness, and the institution and ordinances of true religion are to be forfeited. The land to which they are to be exiled is unfamiliar to them—full of strange scenes and customs; a scene of bondage and tyranny. This is but an illustration of the eternal destiny of sinners. Much must necessarily be vague in their conceptions of it, but it will be a greater change from their present circumstances and experiences than can be imagined. The parable of the rich man and Lazarus teaches that there will be a complete reversal of relations and conditions. How impossible for the lost to reconcile themselves to circumstances so different from those to which they have been accustomed! Their nature will be wholly enslaved, and the best service they can render will be exacted for objects unworthy of it and known to be so. Hell, so far as Scripture allusion to it can be understood, is represented as abnormal, unnatural, a state in which the soul shall be filled with fruitless regret, and sink into lower and still lower deeps of degradation and misery. It is depicted as a strange and sunless land, irradiated by no celestial smile and no sunrise of hope.

II. As the sinner regards it. The picture drawn by Jeremiah is vague and yet terribly suggestive. It is so foreign to the experience and expectation of his hearers that they look upon it with incredulity and astonishment. Instead of evoking from them expressions of repentance and fear concerning the way in which they are walking, it provokes questions that exhibit the callous indifference and self-deception of hardened hearts. They cannot conceive of such a fate awaiting them. What have they done? Is it just that their conduct should be so dealt with? If any offence had been committed, surely it was out of all proportion to such a judgment, and so on. Is not this the attitude of the sinner to-day? The more awful the future predicted for him the more secure he feels in himself now. He fails to trace the definite line of connection between the germ and the fruit of his sin. It is a part of his infatuation to misapprehend the law of the Divine reward and punishment, and even the real outlines and proportions of the Divine character. 1. *A destiny in his view so disproportionate to his offence becomes incredible.* And just as the Jew could not conceive of the features and characteristics of the life upon which he was to enter when this prophecy should be fulfilled, the transgressor now fails to realize the position he must occupy when circumstance will depend only upon character. Passing consequences may be seen and partly estimated, but the final outcome of it all is, because of its very nature and extent, unreal to him. 2. *The future of the sinner is strange and unreal to him, and therefore fails to impress him as it ought.*

III. As explained by God. This is one of the main purposes of revelation, viz. to connect the present with the future and to interpret their relations. Whilst it is true that every sinner already contains within himself the elements of his future punishment, it is also true that of himself he could not forecast the actual extent or nature of the destiny he is working out. It is necessary, therefore, both for emphasis and enlightenment, to supplement experience with revelation. 1. *Their punishment was but the natural development of their sin.* The latter was of old date. Their fathers forsook Jehovah, did not keep his Law, and went after other gods. The tendency was inherited by themselves, and in aggravated degree: "Ye have done worse than your fathers." They now paid more attention and honour to idols than to Jehovah, and when this is the case it cannot last long. The veil of decency will be cast aside, the real character will betray itself, and shame will cease. They became more and more "sold under sin." The vices of a false religion weakened their character and made them a ready prey to the ambition and rapacity of their neighbours. The same law is apparent in spiritual destiny. Let the sinner be warned. He may be sure his sin will find him out. 2. *It was but right that they should be so punished, as they had added to their ancestral offence an intolerable personal aggravation.* The terms of the covenant were flagrantly violated, and they had forfeited the land by their moral unfitness to occupy it. If an earthly country could be so hallowed as not to admit of being occupied by unclean idolaters, how much less possible must it be for confirmed sinners to stand in the presence of God amidst the multitudes of redeemed! Heaven would be hell to such persons. 3. *The spiritual condition that was so dealt with presented no ground for consideration.* God said, "I will show you no favour." It was a deliberate sin, and there were no signs of repentance. The day of grace, however, was with them whilst the prophet spoke. So is it represented to be with the preaching of the gospel. Whilst God calls to us his mercy still continues. "Now is the accepted time; . . . now is the day of salvation." But in that day present obstinacy will be the worst condemnation. "I called, and ye refused," etc.—M.

Ver. 13.—*Sin a tyrannous and exhaustive service.* I. THAT WHICH WAS AT FIRST A FREE CHOICE WILL IN TIME BECOME A COMPULSORY SERVICE. The waywardness and capricious eclecticism of the idolatrous Jews was to be sternly visited upon them. They had toyed and compromised with idols; soon it would be discovered that that dalliance could not be prolonged. 1. *Jehovah will not continue to accept a half-hearted service.* It was only his forbearance that had suffered it so long. Whilst it might appear possible that Judah would repent, the imperfection of its service was overlooked; but when that imperfection seemed likely to be stereotyped, or when it was increasing with the growth of idolatrous practices, it was no longer to be endured. A mixed worship is dishonouring to God. He refuses to accept half a heart. It is impossible to serve him aright with divided attention and interest. Permission to worship and know him even in part is a privilege which may be withdrawn. The "idolater" would not always be able to walk on the heights of critical spiritual eclecticism. The time would come when what he thought so irksome would be taken away. God would send upon him "strong delusion to believe a lie." And this is rather to be looked upon as a repudiation of Judah by God than as a departure from Jehovah permitted by him to his own hurt. Spiritual power and hallowed circumstance would alike be forfeited, and God would cast off the idolaters. For: 2. *Sinful tendency, when let alone, confirms and strengthens itself.* Daily contact with the obligations and influence of the Law and the temple was a real benefit to the Israelites. It kept them from settling down utterly into idolatrous habits. That religious observance which is so wearisome to the sinner is his safeguard; it keeps him from complete abandonment to the inner depravity of his nature. He is alarmed, warned, disturbed, whenever he is inclined to more than ordinary licence; and even his ordinary lax and sinful life is constantly judged and corrected by the truth which he hears. The Spirit of God continues to plead and wrestle with him, and although he does not wholly yield himself to its influence, he is prevented from wandering quite beyond recall. But let this restraining influence of grace once be withdrawn, the natural impulse to evil, all unchecked, will begin to develop and gradually overmaster the entire nature. This is the explanation of many a life that seems to linger long upon the debatable line between duty and sinful inclination—it is the Spirit of God that has not ceased to strive with it, and not the mere power of the man over his own desires and habits. 3. *The circumstances and opportunities of Divine worship, if persistently neglected and abused, will be withdrawn.* Palestine under the theocracy was a breathing-space for the spiritual aspirations of man. It was a school of purest affection and the most exalted righteousness. Divine power outside of, and also working within, Israel had defended it against the most tremendous invading forces. Let that power be withdrawn, the possibility of every man worshipping God under his own vine and fig tree would be taken away. The Jews would be overpowered by the laws and customs of the idolatrous nations amongst whom they would be dispersed. How much do we owe to the political, social, and personal influences that make for righteousness around us! How slowly and at what infinite cost have they been acquired! And they depend upon unceasing effort for their support and advancement. Civilization is the product of long, manifold, and harmonious effort and growth. It is a gossamer fabric which a day might destroy. Yet is it but an outwork and coarse expression of religion. The latter is the breath and inspiration of the Holy Ghost. Let that breath be withdrawn, and it ceases to live; and its most characteristic and essential institutions gradually become obsolete and sink into a mockery and a snare. We shall probably never know how much we owe to the mere circumstance of religion that surrounds us. Freedom to worship God, encouragement to obey him, and sustaining power to give effect to our spiritual desires, all result from the favourable position in which we are placed. Let us, therefore, seek to foster the institutions and increase the social and political influence of Christianity in the world. Without its presence amongst men, and the hallowed institutions, customs, and observances that embody its spirit, we should find it infinitely more difficult to serve God with conscientious and honest service.

II. THIS SERVICE WILL AFFORD NO REAL SATISFACTION OR PEACE. The exhaustive and absorbing devotion which idolatry entails is not the sign of spontaneous enthusiasm. It arises from the nature of the idols, as senseless, helpless blocks. They, indeed, must cry loudly who would be heard by such gods. In proportion as ritual is more laborious than righteousness, so is idolatry more exacting than true religion. But "the idol is nothing," only the representative of the lusts and ignorance of its worshippers. It is in reality the latter that receive and demand the service. All sin is idolatry in some form or other, and will prove as exacting of the attention and labour of the sinner. Who is not willing to admit that sin is a hard taskmaster? And yet, what are its rewards? The poor soul, hurried and driven by its own overmastering lusts and passions, has no rest, and no solid residuum of comfort is secured; nay, rather a sense of deepening gloom, indefinite, unquenchable craving, and a foreboding of the final wrath of him whom it has insulted and disobeyed. To the victims of wicked habit, etc., as to the devotees of a false religion, the words of Christ are addressed, "Come unto me, all ye that labour and are heavy laden," etc.—M.

Vers. 14, 15.—*The old deliverance forgotten in the new.* I. THE GREATER AND MORE INVETERATE THE TRANSGRESSION, THE GREATER WILL BE THE PUNISHMENT. It was not to be supposed that the past judgments of God, however great, were all that he could or would do. He has many ways of bringing transgressors to their senses; and it is impossible to conceive a limit to his power of imposing penalty. His stern, uncompromising attitude to sin has been witnessed to by many an awful judgment and destruction, even where previous calamities might seem to have exhausted his anger or his invention.

II. THE PROMISE OF GOD APPEARS SIDE BY SIDE WITH THE FIRST ANNOUNCEMENTS OF HIS JUDGMENTS. Even in the way in which it is threatened there is encouragement and hope. It will be an awful experience, but God will redeem his people. So in the beginning of the curse our first parents received an anticipatory evangel. The failures of God's people in social and political experiment were the occasion of the most glorious predictions of Messianic times. This shows the real purpose of God's threatenings. They are intended to produce repentance, and yet there is reality enough in them if that repentance be not forthcoming. Fear is appealed to, but freedom of choice is preserved, and spiritual power called into responsible action.

III. THE MERCIFUL POWER OF GOD WILL BE MORE GLORIOUSLY MANIFESTED IN EVERY NEW CALAMITY WHICH HIS PEOPLE BRING UPON THEMSELVES. The captivity of which the prophet speaks will but give occasion for a grand deliverance, in comparison with which the Exodus from Egypt will sink into insignificance. The judgments of God, however great they may appear, are limited with the strictest exactness, and are within his control. There is reason, therefore, to expect his interference whenever the folly or unbelief of his people imperils his cause. He will preserve a people to praise him, and raise up a generation to call him blessed. So with the backslider from gospel privileges and obligations. He whom Christ has washed in his blood will not be suffered wholly to pass into spiritual death. Grander exhibitions of the Divine grace and power will be afforded. The good Shepherd will go over the dark mountains to recover the wanderer. Those who have been entangled again in the yoke of bondage will be redelivered if they but turn with new obedience and faith to their Saviour. They will be saved, if "as by fire."—M.

Vers. 19—21.—*The heathen turning to the true God.* The prophet, disappointed and broken-hearted, is driven to Jehovah for his own comfort and support. We see here how much it cost him to speak the words he had to utter. Every true minister of Christ must feel in the same manner when he has to deal with hardened sinners, and to become the mouthpiece of Divine warnings and threats. The soul that stands up for righteousness will often find itself without sympathy and alone amongst unbelieving men. Prayer is the refuge that is ever open in such hours. An extremity like this is of all others God's opportunity. Like Elijah in the wilderness, he will receive unexpected succour. He will live, not on bread, but on words and revelations of God. To Jeremiah was given this vision.

I. Whilst Jehovah is deserted by his own people the heathen will seek him. There is a law of displacement visible in God's dealings with his Church from age to age. Like the man in the parable, who prepared the feast and bade many, he is determined that his house shall be filled. 1. *In this way God shows his people that he does not specially need them.* His favour depends upon their faithfulness; if they fail he has others to supply their place. His election is no blind favouritism or arbitrary distinction, but proceeds upon spiritual conditions. 2. *Apostasy from God is due to imperfectly understanding him; but the heathen who turn to him do so with full experience of the effects of their idolatry.* The vanity and nothingness of idols drives them in despair to the true God. Henceforth for them idolatry can have no power. It has been, as the Law was to Saul, a schoolmaster to bring them to Christ. Lessons acquired in so stern a school are not soon forgotten; and the half-hearted disciple, led away of his own lusts and enticed, is supplanted by a steadfast and faithful convert. So every day is the Church of Christ being recruited from the ranks of those who have been the "chief of sinners." We cannot tell in what depths of degradation those may now be sunk who are to shine as stars in the eternal firmament. Let the individual Christian strive, therefore, to make his calling and his election sure. Let the Church see that its candlestick be not removed.

II. Idolatry is a system which refutes itself. 1. *It disappoints the expectations which it has awakened.* 2. *The conscience at last revolts against the excesses to which it leads.* 3. *By-and-by the evident truism, that what man makes cannot be his god, is realized and acted upon.* This process is going on to-day in the great seats of idolatrous worship, and the fiercest iconoclasts are to be found amongst those who have been brought up in heathenism. A similar process to this goes on in the lives of good men as they are gradually freed from the illusions of life and the ensnaring influences of worldly ideas and aims. The disappointments of life are so many waves casting us upon the shore of a heavenly life, and the general drift of earthly experience is in many and many an instance bringing men surely to God.

III. Failing a better revelation, the judgments of Jehovah upon his own people will show the heathen that he is the only real God. This is not the way in which God would prefer to show men his glory and his power. It is by his saving grace he would commend himself to them. And the saints are the appointed teachers of the world. They could tell of his power and his grace, of their own deliverance. They could exhibit the blessings of a people whose trust is Jehovah. But, failing this, they would be made examples. The justice of God will take the place of his mercy which has been abused. In its exceptional severity, its evident connection with and suggestion of supernatural agency, etc., it will attract attention and arouse curiosity. Israel, therefore, even in its calamity and suffering, will serve God. A vicarious virtue will lurk in its captivity, its desolation, and its persecution. God is dealing thus with the unfaithful branches of his Church to-day. The perplexities, entanglements, and griefs that are due to worldly alliance and secular ambitions and desires are well enough understood even by worldly men. Not from Eden, but from the wilderness to which she has banished herself, will the bride, the Lamb's wife, be brought for her new espousals, and with her shall come, as virgins in her train, many who have been taught by her judgments and disciplines.—M.

Vers. 1—9.—*Commands countermanded.* There are three such in this section.

I. THE COMMAND TO MARRY. 1. In every way whereby the will of God can be expressed—by his Word, his providence, his laws, written, moral, social, physical, God has commanded that "a man shall leave his father and mother," etc. "A good wife is from the Lord," her companionship is the most blessed in the world. All artificial hindrances to marriage are, therefore, to be condemned. The same enemy that destroys such myriads of souls for eternity, ruins their happiness, oftentimes, in this life also. For it is the world which frowns upon marriages, unexceptionable in other respects, in which a certain style cannot be maintained or a certain amount of income be secured; and all superstitious teachings that inculcate celibacy as a state more pleasing to God, are equally guilty both in regard to God and man. Disobedience to this command involves such frightful consequences as in themselves to clearly manifest the Divine will, that "it is not good for man to be alone." 2. But here in these verses *the prophet is distinctly forbidden to marry.* (Ver. 1, etc.) And the reasons were probably that, by his abstaining from marriage, he might more powerfully confirm his words as to the coming calamities. It would show his own belief in what he had foretold when it was seen that he would not make for himself a home under such circumstances. It would leave him more free for the arduous duty which he had to discharge. It would save him great sorrow when the evil days should come. And so now there are special cases in which God's will seems to be that a man should not marry. The poverty-stricken ministers of religion, of whom there are so many; the missionary exposed to daily peril of climate, pestilence, savage heathendom; or any to whom it is evident that by their marriage more evil than good will result;—then, just as we may be called upon to do without many other great earthly advantages, so we may be called upon to deny ourselves this. And there may be physical conditions forbidding marriage. No man has a right to transmit to others hereditary disease, whether of body or mind. And there are spiritual hindrances. A man ought to marry only "in the Lord." But all these exceptions are rare; God's general rule is that men should marry.

II. THE COMMAND TO "WEEP WITH THEM THAT WEEP." That there would be no stint of sorrow, no lack of mourners, the awful declarations of this section plainly show. And generally God's will, shown in a thousand ways, is that we should, by sympathy and condolence, "bear one another's burdens, and so fulfil the Law of Christ." But here such sympathy and "weeping with them that weep" is prohibited (ver. 5). This does seem a stern command, and no doubt it is so. But we do not feel called on to condole with criminals on account of the penalties they have to bear; were any to do so, we should regard it as misplaced and mischievous sympathy, calculated only to do harm. And whilst those to whom the prophet was sent were hardened in their sin, sympathy with them on account of their punishment would be also mischievous and wrong. We have continually to be on our guard—for many never are—lest our sympathy for the sinner's suffering should make us forget or think lightly of the sinner's sin. No matter how glaring the crime, there are always some who are ready to agitate for a mitigation of the penalty. Now, it is this hurtful sympathy which God here forbids the prophet to show.

III. THE COMMAND TO "REJOICE WITH THEM THAT DO REJOICE." This also is a constant injunction of the Divine Word, as it is an instinct of the benevolent and Christian heart. Jesus was as ready to go to the marriage festival as to the grave-side. And so should we be. But here again the command is countermanded (ver. 8). And the reason is manifest. God would not suffer his prophet to be in any wise a solace to sinful men. Too many professed Christians are. Nothing is a greater "comfort to Sodom" than the sight of the serenity and joviality of men who profess to believe that sinners are on their way to everlasting woe. The sinner argues—and it is an argument very difficult to refute—that Christians do not believe this, no matter what they say, and hence they, the ungodly, are in no such awful peril after all. The prophet of God was commanded to abstain from all festivity and all outward joy, and no doubt the reason was, lest by any sharing therein, he should throw doubt on the awful message he was charged to deliver. Are the ministers of God bound to do the like now? Our Lord did not. His apostles did not. Nowhere are we bidden to abstain from all earthly joy. Rather are we assured that God has "given us all things richly to enjoy." And the unbeliever's objection on the ground of the inconsistency of our calmness, and yet more of our gladness, notwithstanding the awful peril of ungodly souls, may be met by the reply that we cannot say of those whom yet we would fain see drawn much nearer to God than they to our eyes are, that they are, as those whom Jeremiah addressed, absolutely doomed. We are not forbidden to pray for them, as Jeremiah was; nor to hope that even yet they may turn to God and find mercy. The prophet had no hope; we have much, and it is on the ground of that hope which we cherish that our calmer, brighter moods are justified. Still, one shrinks from saying aught that would seem to sanction the terrible indifference we all too much manifest in regard to the spiritual condition of the world around us. But yet we may say that that condition is not such as to demand—even were it possible, which it is not, to comply with the demand—that we should all cease from joy, and clothe ourselves unceasingly in sackcloth and ashes. We cannot do that; we are not bidden to do that, nor would it be of use were we to do so. We have a gospel to proclaim, a living Saviour to hope in, and a Holy Spirit's energies to second all our prayers and endeavours to win men to God. But at the same time, the believer in God and in his righteous Law cannot and ought not to find pleasure in the rejoicings of the ungodly, or to give any countenance to their defiance of God. No; we are not to go "in the way of sinners," not to sit "in the seat of scorners," though it may be a scene of festivity and mirth. From all such we must turn away. We cannot rejoice with them when they rejoice; in their gladness we cannot share, but only mourn that they do not mourn. Let them turn to God, and we will dwell among them, and in their joy and in their sorrow we will gladly share. But until they do, for us as for God's prophet, his ordinary commands as to sympathy with them are countermanded, and we must stand aside. Light cannot have fellowship with darkness, nor the children of God with the children of the wicked one.—C.

Vers. 10—13.—*Conscience dead.* Conscience is given us of God, to serve as a faithful sentry, warning of the approach of sin and summoning the energies of our souls to resist and reject the intruder. Or as a just judge to unhesitatingly condemn sin, let it be wrapped up in what specious disguise it may. It is the Ithuriel's spear which, the moment it touches any moral action, compels such action to reveal itself of what sort it is. Oh, the unspeakable blessing of an enlightened, healthful conscience that will not suffer sin, any sin, even the least, without prompt and powerful protest! God help us all diligently to guard, profoundly to reverence and faithfully to obey this inward monitor, this true bearer of "the light which lighteth every man that cometh into the world." But these verses reveal a condition of things in which conscience is dead. It has lost all power of perception, its voice is hushed, or rather, what is worse, it sees and speaks falsely. It is a mockery of life, which would be grotesque were it not so profoundly sad. A caricature and parody of what it once was, its powers utterly perverted, bent, warped, so that they "call evil good, and good evil." Note—
I. THE FACT. How else can such a question as this of ver. 10 be accounted for? Was not their sin clear as the sun at noonday? Had it not been for years crying aloud to God for vengeance? Had it not been condemned by all the servants of God, by the written Law of God, by all the voices of God in long succession? And yet these people are asking, "Wherefore hath the Lord pronounced all this great evil against us." It is as if the convicts in our prisons were to begin to ask why they were so treated, and to profess ignorance of their having done aught amiss. But in such case we should say they were playing the hypocrite, pretending an innocence to which they well knew they had no claim. In this case, however, there is no hypocrisy. The question, monstrous as it seems to us, is asked in all good faith. The prophet of God is bidden to give it a serious answer, not to denounce those who ask it as a set of conscious hypocrites. Just as in Matt. xxv. 44, which is a portentous parallel indeed, the condemned there are heard asking when they had been guilty of the sins laid to their charge. It is evident in that case and in this, not that they were consciously liars, but that conscience was simply dead within them. The writer knew also of one who had cruelly defrauded a large number of people, who, believing him to be an eminently religious man, had

entrusted to him their hard-earned savings, with all of which he had made away; but, when brought to justice, condemned, and imprisoned, he could not be got to confess that he had done wrong, but would keep quoting, in regard to himself, texts which tell of the afflictions of the righteous, and how " whom the Lord loveth he chasteneth."

II. THE CAUSE. Conscience is starved by neglect of that seeking of God's grace which is its nutriment and strength. And it is stunned by repeated acts of sin. Men can and do nibble, if we may so speak, at conscience, and gradually rid themselves of it. The clamour of sin drowns the still, small voice, and its protests, perpetually unheeded, are at last withdrawn. So that at length men find themselves able to do evil and think nothing of it; the little rift that sin first made has widened and widened until the whole torrent of waters bursts through, for the faithful dyke that held them back has been gradually destroyed, and so now the whole nature of the man is over- whelmed, submerged beneath the deluge of sin. And, what is most sad, the man feels, no more than do the sunken cities and towns that lie at the bottom of the Zuyder Zee, the rush of the waves that for centuries have rolled over them.

III. THE CURE. Thank God there is one. The sharp surgery of God's judgments arouse the deadened conscience. The rags, the hunger, the degradation of the prodigal woke up his conscience and brought him " to himself." And so it was with the Jewish people. God's judgments made them hate and abhor, as they have done ever since, the idolatries which brought those judgments upon them. It would be dreadful to think that God had no resources whereby, in full harmony with its freedom, he could bring into due subjection and order " the unruly wills of sinful men." Can we conceive of God having created a force greater than himself, which can for ever defy him, and ever maintain, as Milton's Satan in hell, a rebellious though wretched rule? God knew how to convert Israel, Saul, the penitent thief, ourselves, and we may trust him to find means whereby at length to Jesus every knee shall be made to bow. Vers. 14 and 15 contemplate a converted Israel (cf. also Isa. xxx. 18; Matt. xxvii. 33—39). But let a man tremble at the thought of compelling God to deal with him thus. Let him beware how he wastes his conscience, lest it turn against him and suffer him to sin unrestrained.—C.

Vers. 14, 15.—*Great mercies the forerunners of greater still.* At first reading of these verses their truth is hardly apparent to the ordinary reader of the Bible. The deliverance from Egypt was so magnificent an event, accompanied by such manifestations of the Divine glory, that the quiet return of but a comparatively few of the exiles from Babylon pales into insignificance. Hence it is the latter event that seems not worthy to be spoken of in comparison with the former, and not the former in comparison with the latter. The second temple was so greatly inferior to the first that old men who had seen the first wept when they thought of those glories which to the second were quite unattainable; and so the return from Babylon seems to fall far short in glory of the redemption from Egypt. But these verses affirm that the glory of the return from Babylon was to be far the greater. Now, how could this be? It may be said: 1. That in this return there was a display of the *moral power of God rather than his physical might.* That which was needed to bring this about was the exercise of the Divine power on men's hearts rather than any material force. It was by mighty miracles that Israel was brought out of Egypt; it was by the action of God's Spirit on his people's hearts that those who returned from Babylon were induced so to do. For their lot was happy, prosperous, peaceful, so far as this world was concerned. The Books of Esther, Nehemiah, and Daniel show this. Hence it was a strong religious yearning that led to the return of those who returned. The mass of the nation were content to remain, and did remain, and formed "those of the Dispersion," of whom in so many ways we hear in after ages. Hence, as Zechariah says (iv. 6), it was " not by might, nor by power, but," etc. 2. Then, also, in this return there was a *display of God's pardoning love.* Israel was a forgiven people. They had received at the Lord's hand double for all their sins. But God is ever more glorified in the display of pardoning love than in any manifestations of mere power. 3. And there was in it *such a fulfilment of prophecy,* such a demonstration of the overruling power of God in and through all the movements of different nations and ages, as proclaimed God's glory more than power alone could ever do. For these reasons the return of the exiles was a more glorious event than the deliverance from Egypt. 4. And this will be seen yet more if we take the verses as pointing on to *the ultimate restoration of Israel.* Zechariah (xiii. and xiv.) speaks of this, as do many other Scriptures. It was the "hope of Israel" of which Paul told, and he places it in connection with the second advent and the resurrection. 5. And still more if we understand by Israel the spiritual Israel, and regard all these promises as predicting the triumph of the Church. Thus regarded, the deliverance from Egypt was by comparison a very little thing. But when that great triumph comes, where shall *we* be ? God grant that it be amongst those whom on that day he will confess before his Father and the holy angels. But this notable instance in which past mercies promise greater ones to come is only one out of many more. Apply the principle declared—

I. To THE CHURCH AT LARGE. What mercies in the past, what deliverances, the Church has enjoyed : from persecutors, "grievous wolves," superstition, infidelity, etc. ! But all these are to be regarded as pledges of yet greater ones when they shall be needed.

II. To INDIVIDUAL MEMBERS OF THAT CHURCH. Who of us cannot recount, in the course of our lives, *temporal* deliverances : from sickness, poverty, perplexity, sorrow, death, etc. ? We are to take them all as reasons to anticipate greater things still, more to follow. And especially *spiritual* deliverances : from living on in disregard of God, from the power of the world, temptation, sorrow. But there are greater ones still. The Church in its full redemption shall prove the truth of this, and so shall separate members of the Church. All shall confess that the Lord hath "kept the good wine until now."

CONCLUSION. 1. Be not dismayed at the troubles of the present ; do not think God's grace is exhausted. 2. See to it that you share in the first deliverance—that from guilt and sin. Unless we have known the first, we cannot know the second and greater— that final deliverance from all guilt, all sin, all sorrow, all death, in the presence of God for ever.—C.

Vers. 16—21.—*Sin found out.* The striking imagery of these verses teaches us that there shall be no hiding-place, whether by sea or land, where God will not find those whom his vengeance pursues. The sinner may be sure that his sin will find him out.

I. MEN DOUBT THIS. Reasons are : 1. Long impunity has made them bold. 2. Such findings of them out as have taken place, in defilement of conscience, hardening of the heart, loss of peace with God, etc., they do not care for. They only care for public exposure and punishment. 3. They see others go on in sin unpunished. 4. The power which we all have to believe what we wish to believe. 5. The direct agency of the devil in fostering such false belief.

II. BUT THE DECLARATION OF GOD ON THIS MATTER IS NEVERTHELESS TRUE. 1. The Scriptures affirm it (cf. all those which teach the omniscience and omnipresence of God). 2. Conscience attests it. 3. There is nothing in sin to show wherefore it should not be. 4. The revelation of the future life distinctly provides for it. 5. And even now it is continually being proved true. A man's sin finds him out in many ways—in body, mind, estate, reputation, etc. And in one or more of these sin does ever find a man out, even now. 6. The apparent exceptions are accounted for on the ground of (1) God's long-suffering to the sinful ; (2) God's purpose to test and exercise the faith of his own people.

III. A DEEP AND ABIDING CONVICTION OF THIS TO BE GREATLY DESIRED. 1. What restraint it would exercise on the will ! (cf. " How can I do this great wickedness, and sin against God ?"). 2. How exceeding sinful it would make sin appear ! 3. What force it would lend to all endeavours after the reclamation and reformation of the sinful !

IV. AND SUCH CONVICTION MAY BE HAD. It is the sacred and salutary power of prayer thus to make God real to us. In prayer we look to him and we see him looking upon us ; we speak to him and he speaks to us ; by aid of it we walk with him and he walks with us. He who thus lives in daily fellowship with God can never be without the conviction spoken of.

V. BECAUSE SIN IS SURE TO FIND US, LET US AT ONCE SEEK AND FIND CHRIST.—C.

Ver. 19—ch. xvii. 3.— *The accusers of the ungodly.* The prophet appeals to—

I. THE ANTICIPATED CONVERSION OF THE HEATHEN. Ver. 19, "The Gentiles shall come," etc. These heathen peoples will declare the vanity of those idols in which Judah is now trusting (cf. Matt. xi. 20—24).

II. CONSCIENCE. Their sin was "written as with," etc., "on the table of their heart" (ch. xvii. 1). Nothing could erase the memories they all had of their own grievous sin. It was written as if in rock, and as with a pen of iron and a point of diamond (allusion, probably, to the inscriptions on rocks, so frequent in the East). What a witness is conscience! It cannot be silenced nor sophisticated. It keeps a man's sins "ever before" him. "My sin is ever before me," said David. The writing of our sin on the heart's tablets is so deep, so incisive, so clear, that nothing can destroy it. No storms will wash them out; no lapse of time obliterate and decay; no rush of business and occupation will fill up and conceal those deep engravings; no rough contact with the events of life will break them. There they stand, clearly legible, written on the tablets of our hearts—our conscience—as letters written by an iron or diamond pen on rock. To this evidence the prophet appeals (cf. our Saviour's appeal to conscience in the case of the accusers of the woman taken in adultery, John viii.).

III. THEIR WORSHIP. Not alone their conscience, but the horns of their altars, testified against them. These horns, smeared with the blood of their idolatrous sacrifices, blackened with the smoke of their altar fires, reeking continually with the fumes and smoke of their offered victims,—these also were witnesses whose testimony could not be set aside. And what a witness against a man will the worship he offers—the horns of *his* altar—often be: its coldness, its carelessness, its infrequency, its insincerity, its formality, and sometimes its hypocrisy! Yes; the horns of the altar will prove swift witnesses against all who worship God otherwise than "in spirit and in truth."

IV. THEIR CHILDREN. (Ver. 2.) "They would never lose the impression of that horrible idolatry which had snatched so many from their midst. So deep was this impression that the mere sight of green trees and high hills was sufficient to refresh the hideous memory continually." Or it may mean that their children, retaining and practising the idolatry of their fathers, are witnesses against those fathers such as none can set aside. Children may become the means of their fathers' condemnation. They cannot help testifying against them. In their memories, their habits, their very bodies, their sins, they will declare what their fathers were. Thank God, they can and do testify *for* the godly and righteous parents, as Timothy did of his mother and hers. But how awful to think of having one's own children brought forward as witnesses against us! Let ungodly parents ponder this.

CONCLUSION. With such weight of evidence against Judah, what wonder that her punishment was so severe! The sin of Judah, however, too much resembles, in its aggravation and in the evidence brought against it, sin of which *we* may be all too conscious. What can we do but turn to him who has said, "The sacrifices of God are a broken spirit," etc.; and whose blood "cleanseth from all sin"? Blessed be God that we may do this; but "how shall we escape if we neglect," etc.? —C.

Vers. 1—4.—*Domestic relations become a curse.* It is evidently implied that, even in the present deplorable state of Israel, there was much that appeared attractive and profitable in domestic relations. Jesus reminded his servants that, in the days before the Flood, there was "marrying and giving in marriage, until the day that Noah entered into the ark;" and so we may conclude that in the time of Jeremiah there was also marrying and giving in marriage, down to the very coming of the invader on the land. Individuals would go on, following out the promptings of their affections, unable to discern the signs of the times, and the approach of a calamity such as would overwhelm every family existing when it came. When society is in its ordinary state, marriages ending in misery are believed to be exceptional. But here there is a trouble which is to come upon every household. Every family is to be smitten, and Jeremiah, in his loneliness, is called to notice how, though deprived of domestic relations, he is to gain a compensation in other ways. Perhaps at times he was inclined to murmur that he—a man of strife and contention to the whole land—had no home where he might turn and find some refuge and relief, if only for a short interval. Even in those apostate days there must surely have been a few homes at least where there was fidelity to Jehovah; where the parents taught his truth to the children, and the children reverenced the parents according to his commandment. But Jeremiah's way was closed up, so that he had no opportunity of forming such a household for himself. His celibate life did not come by his own selfish resolution, but by the will of God, clearly expressed, and based on certain necessities of Jeremiah's prophetic mission. The prophet, therefore, while he lost some things, was spared some great sorrows when the long-predicted blow at last came on the nation. The external circumstances of life are wonderfully equalized, when the sum of them is able to be calculated. We can only be robbed of the best possessions by our own fault. Jeremiah, however lonely his path may have been, however like to that of him who had "not where to lay his head," was advancing to the state where "they neither marry nor are given in marriage."—Y.

Vers. 5—9.—*The house of mourning and the house of feasting alike forbidden.* It is made plain upon the surface of this command that the house of mourning and the house of feasting are not forbidden in themselves. The man on whom the injunction is laid is a special man, and he is spoken to in special circumstances. All others may cross the threshold of such houses; the prophet alone must remain outside. This peculiar conduct was meant to emphasize his predictions. Every time there is a funeral or a marriage-feast, the terrible judgments shortly coming on the land are once more set forth. The worst sorrows of the present are but as a child's shallow grief compared with the universal and dreadful experiences that are yet to come; and in the joys of the present it would be unseemly for the man to share whose breast is filled with the sense of how soon these joys must pass away. A man who had to live as Jeremiah lived, in such an age, with such a message, seeing visions of so much woe, how could he receive pleasure from any festive gathering, or bring pleasure to it? The more he advances in his mission as prophet the more he has to walk alone. This commanded attitude towards the house of mourning and the house of feasting indicates to us the spirit in which those who may have to make such visits should pay their visits. We must not go to fall in with the wishes of those who are visited, but rather to do the will of God, at whatever cost, and with whatever difficulty. Consider this—

I. WITH REGARD TO THE HOUSE OF MOURNING. One feels that the prophet must have been exposed to much misapprehension in carrying out this command with the symbolic prophecy involved in it. It would be said that he was not only an unpatriotic man but an unfeeling one. Happily we have abundant proof that, whatever the imperfections of Jeremiah, a cold indifference to the griefs of others was not one of them. He may often have had to do violence to his own impulses in keeping away from the homes where the dead were lying; and yet he only did by command what we should sometimes like to do by preference, if it were only possible to do it without wounding the feelings of others. Think of the houses of mourning where little or nothing can be said that is comforting. What could have been done to comfort stricken parents that night when there was one dead in every Egyptian household? There is a way of offering sympathy which, well intended as it is, only exacerbates instead of mollifying. What false consolations, what hackneyed commonplaces, are made use of in the house of mourning! There is a falling back on what is called the good moral character of the dead. Death-bed repentances may be made too much of. The chamber of mourning is the stronghold of an immense amount of very dangerous error in the attitude of man towards God. The temporary pain of the freshly wounded heart of man is more considered than the abiding truth of God. Then what censurable regrets there are! what utter and unconcealed selfishness on the part of survivors! It is not a feeling of pain for what the departed may have lost, but rebellious wrath for what the survivor may have lost. And so we may say that, to enter into a house of mourning where there is the right and Christian spirit, is a matter for joy and not for grief, because indeed the peace and the loving-kindness and mercies of God are there. Let us aim so to live, in such unworldliness and heavenliness of life, that survivors shall not be tempted into vain consolations when we are gone.

II. WITH REGARD TO THE HOUSE OF FEASTING. The absence of Jeremiah from festive gatherings would be as a most significant presence; seeing that he was absent, not by accident, not from any personal feeling, not from any ascetic dislike to such gatherings, but by the special command of God. Not only was he forbidden to become himself a bridegroom, he could not even congratulate any other. It will be noticed that the marriage-feast in particular is referred to. The wedding was a time for a special gathering, and invited guests would make special efforts to be present. Jesus, for instance, at the wedding-feast at Cana. Mere rioting and revelling, and the laughter of fools and such merry-making as cost the Baptist his life, were at all times forbidden. There is much of rebuke to us in this command of the prophet here. He did not take part even in an innocent festive gathering. It jarred on him as he thought of the future, so different and yet so near. And possibly, if we thought more as we ought to think on what has yet to come in the way of judgment and destruction, we should walk through the world feeling that we had no heart even for what is reckoned innocent merriment. We can never be sufficiently serious when the burden of human life, with all its vast and varied trials, comes to lie upon our thoughts.—Y.

Vers. 14, 15.—*Two great recollections.* Here once again we come upon the evangelical element in Jeremiah's prophecies; and once again we have to notice that, when this element does appear, it makes up for its infrequency by the brilliance and emphasis of the prediction. The prophet has just been compelled to speak of domestic suffering, national exile, and the withdrawal for a season of Divine favour. These necessary judgments must be magnified and stated in all their severity; not one of them can be omitted; the cup poured out by Jehovah must be drunk to its last drop. But when all these experiences are over, terrible and yet full of discipline, a glorious future remains. The manner of the prophecy is full of encouragement, and not least in this, that there is such a sudden turning from the deepest darkness to the brightness of noon. We have to consider—

I. THE INDICATION OF WHAT HAD BEEN ONE OF THE MOST CUSTOMARY FORMS OF OATH HITHERTO. On important occasions, when a promise had to be made or an assertion verified, it was the Israelite's habit to make a solemn appeal to the living Jehovah. "As Jehovah liveth" was the general formula, to be combined with more particular references, agreeing with the occasion, as to what this living Jehovah had done in the past. The reference might be to something that had happened in the experience of the individual, and probably still more frequently to greater events in the larger experience of the nation. To give such an appeal all possible solemnity it was needful to think of Jehovah in the most magnifying way; and what could magnify him more than a recollection of the great deliverance from Egypt, which he had wrought out for Israel? That deliverance gave Israel its great chance of service and glory as the people of God. Up to that time a nation of helpless slaves and sufferers—helpless, that is, for anything they could do—they nevertheless became in a very few days a nation of free men, travelling towards a land of their own. And all this was by direct Divine intervention; and not only was it a great deliverance in itself, but all the circumstances made it doubly memorable. The narrative of what had been done needed no embellishments to grave it indelibly on the memory of each generation. Moreover, Jehovah himself had made provision for the continued recollection of the deliverance by the institution of the Passover. He wished it to be remembered. We may well conclude that such a form of oath as appealed to him in his character as the Deliverer of Israel from Egyptian bondage, was peculiarly agreeable; it being always presumed, of course, that the oath was uttered sincerely.

II. THE INDICATION OF HOW THIS VENERATED OATH WAS TO BE SUPERSEDED. Probably at the time of the deliverance from Egypt many Israelites may have said to themselves, "Nothing can ever happen in the history of our nation more memorable than this. Whatever our vicissitudes, whatever our perils, we cannot be more in need of Jehovah's intervention than we have lately been." But when either nations or individuals speak thus, it is in utter ignorance of how deep and terrible human need may become. There was a worse bondage than that of Egypt; it came with no external inconveniences, it was invisible to the outward eye, and, worst of all, it was heedlessly accepted by the bondman himself. The Israelites had fallen into the bodily slavery of Egypt by no fault of their own; there was no point at which it was possible for them to stop the process. But the spiritual enslavement to idols and to every sort of consequent evil came by their own act. They had stooped to the yoke. It is a greater thing that has to be done now, *so far as the result to the Israelite is concerned,* than was done when he was taken out of Egypt. Then he was delivered from *Pharaoh and his host*—a simple matter *comparatively,* for the destruction of Pharaoh and his host in the Red Sea did all that needed to be done.   But now the Israelite has to be delivered from *himself*.   There has to be some sort of change within him, and this we may well believe was brought about by the exile in Babylon.   It is not enough to say that, after a time of exile, God brought them back to Jerusalem.   The mere transport from one place to another would have been no whit more memorable than the deliverance from Egypt.   Surely there must have been a state of heart in the returning generation which made them very different from the generation going away into captivity seventy years before.   That they came back to a true, spiritual, steadfast service of Jehovah is not to be supposed; but neither would they come back to the old idolatry.   The sin into which they were hereafter to fall was a formal service of the true God, mere ceremonialism and Pharisaism, not apostasy to idols.   The great effect of the exile in Babylon was deliverance from formal idolatry, evidently a matter to be more celebrated than the deliverance, centuries before, from bondage in Egypt.   But in the future beyond there was something greater still to be looked for.   There was a possibility of yet another form of oath, if Jesus had not recommended his disciples to dispense with all additions to the simple, veracious "Yes" and "No."   Israel needed to be delivered, not only from formal connection with false gods, but from a *mere formal* connection with the true God.   The Lord lives, who brought Israel out of Egypt.   The Lord lives, who further delivered Israel from temptation to fabricate idols and grovel before them in licentiousness and cruelty.   And we may also add that the Lord lives, who makes individuals of every nation his children by the accepted indwelling of his Spirit; makes them partakers of the Divine nature, with all the glorious consequences thereof.   Further, we may say that Jesus lives, who made the blind to see and who raised the dead.   But it is a still greater thing to say, Jesus lives, who died to restore men to his Father, and rose again to bring life and immortality to light.—Y.

Vers. 19—21.—*The confession of the idolatrous Gentiles.*   I. THE PROPHET'S DESCRIPTION OF JEHOVAH.   God, he says, is his Strength, his Fortress, and his Refuge.   1. *The way in which the describer individualizes himself.*   To the prophet individually Jehovah has a satisfactory relation.   So far as external sufferings and losses are concerned, the prophet cannot escape some share; but so far as concerns his most important interests, he is effectually separated from his fellow-countrymen.   When the invader comes they lose everything; but just then the prophet will be able to say more than ever that Jehovah is his Strength, Fortress, and Refuge.   What he has learned to value most cannot be spoiled by any human hand whatever, and so it is seen that each one of us may be in the midst of a perishing multitude and yet not of them.   These people had long boasted of their resources, their securities, and their satisfaction in life.   They had virtually said to the prophet, "What better are you than us?   Though you speak differently and live differently, your end will be the same."   But the end was not the same.   The invaders took from the people all that was precious to *them*, and then it was made evident that what was most precious to the prophet remained secure and uninjured with him.   2. *The necessity that the prophet should be able to say this.*   Strength, defence, and security for the individual—even in the midst of a nation having none of these things—was not only possible but necessary.   In the last resort, no amount of strength in the community in which we live will do us any good.   There may be strength of a certain kind all around, but that may only emphasize our own weakness.   Suppose the position of Jeremiah reversed.   Actually he was living almost a solitary believer amid a nation of unbelievers; and yet this was far better than to have been an unbeliever amid a nation of believers.   There is no way to make God our Strength, Fortress, and Refuge, save by personal trust and obedience.   3. *The sufficiency of that in which the prophet here expresses his confidence.*   It is when we really address Jehovah, thinking of what we need and of what he is, that the feeling of an inexhaustible sufficiency will come to us.   And this is the way one may come to speak who knows history, who has had somewhat in personal experience both of need and supply, and, above all, who looks heavenward, assured by a feeling of the heart which rises above all reasoning, that he is connected with One able to do exceeding abundantly beyond any conceivable need of man.

II. THE ANTICIPATED CONFESSION OF THE GENTILES.   The words here are words of strong contrast.   The Gentile is openly mentioned, but the children of Israel are thought of at the same time. 1. *The Gentiles are represented as coming to Jehovah.* They have groped their way out of darkness and disentangled themselves from superstitions, while the very people whom Jehovah had brought to himself with so much power and patience, making their way clear and safe, would not inwardly come, even though they were outwardly brought. Their hearts were not changed with their changed circumstances. And it is a thing which cannot be too much remarked, that the Gentiles have long had an understanding, not only of the New Testament, but equally of the Old, which the children of Israel have been utterly unable to reach. And not only are these Gentiles to come; they are to come from the ends of the earth. God's drawing power is felt everywhere. Jerusalem is the centre from which light and truth in their great historical manifestations have gone out. But God can make his centre of spiritual light anywhere, according to the necessities of the individual and of the time. 2. When these Gentiles come they have *a confession to make.* They have to confess the utter emptiness and falsehood of their idolatries. They have, indeed, been taught all these things; sucked them in with their mothers' milk; but this makes their own turning from them all the more remarkable, for what a man is taught he too often clings to, just because he has been taught. It is to be further noticed that these idolatries have always had the same character. The conception is not of gods who once were strong and true, but who have at last come into dotage and are unable to help their worshippers. The lies that tend to deceive and ruin the present generation have actually deceived and ruined many generations before. And yet those things which the Gentiles show signs of forsaking Israel clings to with a mad persistency. Israel has chosen lying, vanity, and loss, and forsaken that great Jehovah whom their fathers inherited. The lesson is, not to value tradition for its own sake, seeing it may only hand down lies. A tradition is nothing unless it is something more than a tradition. There must be the personal experience of God, the personal reception of truth. Every man must come out of Egypt, cross the flood, and come to Sinai for himself. To every such one tradition will become invaluable; for of the things handed down he will know which to receive and transmit, and which to reject. Each of us who comes to reject—intelligently and decidedly, courageously and openly—a lying and empty tradition, at the same time weakens the force of that tradition just as far as our individual influence may extend.—Y.

EXPOSITION.

CHAPTER XVII.

Vers. 1—18 are closely connected with the preceding chapter. We have just been pointed to the striking contrast between the conduct of the heathen and that of the backsliding men of Judah. The inspired orator's indignation swells as he thinks of the inveterateness and indelibleness of Judah's sin (vers. 1—4 are, however, omitted in the Septuagint). Then he passes to a subject immediately suggested by the policy of the court, viz. the true source of safety in dangerous times. Trust in man brings a curse; trust in Jehovah a blessing (vers. 5—13). From this portion of the prophecy we can venture to fix the date of the whole. Ver. 11 is, in fact, a shorter form of the denunciation in ch. xxii. 13—19, which is directly addressed to Jehoiakim; and the most natural view of vers. 5—10 is to regard them as a warning against the negotiations

with Egypt entered into by Jehoiakim after his revolt from Nebuchadnezzar (see Ewald, 'History of Israel,' iv. 261). The emphasis on the deceitfulness of the heart, in ver. 9, is readily intelligible in this connection; it reminds us of the woe pronounced by Isaiah against those who " seek deep to hide their counsel from Jehovah " (xxix. 15), and which undoubtedly refers to a projected Egyptian alliance.

Ver. 1.—**The sin of Judah**, etc. " Judah's sin " is not merely their tendency to sin, but their sinful practices—their idolatry. This is said to be **graven upon the table of their heart**, for it is no mere form, but carried on with passionate earnestness, and as indelible as if engraved **with an iron pen.** How unlike, however, is this record to that of which the same expression is used in Job xix. 24! **With the point of a diamond**; or, *with a point of adamant* (harder than flint, as Ezek. iii. 9 says). Fragments of adamant, says Pliny ('Hist. Nat.,' xxxvii. 15), are sought out by engravers and enclosed in iron; they easily overcome every hardness. **Upon the horns of your altars.** First of all, what altars are referred to ? Those erected for the worship of idols or the two in the temple of Jehovah, which had been defiled by idolatry ? And why is the sin of Judah said to be engraved upon the horns of the altars? Probably because the "horns," *i.e.* the projections at the four upper corners (Exod. xxviii. 2) were smeared with the blood of the victims. The direction in Exod. xxix. 12 and Lev. iv. 7 was doubtless not peculiar to the ritual of the Law.

Ver. 2.—**Whilst their children remember,** etc. The connection of this with the preceding verse is rather obscure. Probably it is intended as an exemplification of the "sin of Judah," the inveterateness of which is shown by their thoughts spontaneously turning to the altars and symbols of the false gods whenever they are near a leafy tree or a high hill (probably "*under* the green trees" is the right reading; comp. 1 Kings xiv. 23; so Targum). To make "their sons" the accusative (with Hitzig and Keil), rendering, "As they remember their children, [even so they remember their altars]," seems unnatural; why should "children" and "altars" be associated in idea? **Groves;** rather, *idols of Ashérah,* the Canaanitish goddess.

Ver. 3.—**O my mountain in the field;** a still more obscure passage. The question is whether "my mountain in the field" is a vocative or an accusative dependent on "I will give." If the former, then the phrase will mean Jerusalem (comp. "rock of the plain," ch. xxi. 13). This, however, does not suit with the second half of the verse ("thy high places," etc.), and still less with ver. 4, which evidently refers to the people of Judah. Added to this, if Jerusalem were here addressed we should certainly expect feminine suffixes. It remains to take "my mountain," etc., as an accusative. It describes, not Jerusalem, but Mount Zion as the site of the temple, the mountain of the house of Jehovah (Isa. ii. 3; Zech. viii. 3; Ps. xxiv. 3). Render, therefore, *my mountain in the field will I give.* The prophet magnifies Zion into a mountain with a widely extended prospect (comp. ver. 12 and ch. xxi. 13). **Thy substance** and **all thy treasures;** *i.e.* those of the people. The part of the verse which begins here is almost the same as ch. xv. 13 (see note). And **thy high places for sin.** Keil explains, Jehovah declares that he will, on account of the sinful practices upon them, deliver up the high places throughout the land. Gesenius, "He will deliver up the high places *with* the sin attaching to them;" Hitzig, " . . . *as* a sin offering." There is a question, however, whether there is not a corruption in the

text, and whether we should not read, with Ewald, "without price for thy sins" (as in the parallel passage, ch. xv. 13).

Ver. 4.—(Comp. ch. xv. 14.) **Even thyself;** literally, *even with thyself,* i.e. with thy bare life (if the text, which is here evidently rather out of order, is correct). **Shalt discontinue.** The word involves an allusion to the Law in Exod. xxiii. 11 and (especially) Deut. xv. 2 (see the Hebrew). The latter passage suggests a correction of the difficult "even with thyself," just preceding, into "thy hand." Thus we get for the opening of this verse, "And thou shalt let loose thy hand" (*i.e.* as Authorized Version, "shalt discontinue").

Vers. 5—11.—In the higher gnomic or proverbial style. God and man, flesh and spirit, are natural antitheses (comp. Isa. xxxi. 3; Ps. lvi. 4). The prayer of the believer is, "Be thou (O Jehovah) their arm every morning;" not Egypt, not Assyria, not any "arm of flesh."

Ver. 6.—**Like the heath in the desert;** as forlorn as some well-known desert plant. But which plant? St. Jerome explains, "Et erit quasi myrice [' tamarisk'], quæ Hebraicè dicitur Aroer (?) sive, at interpretatus est Syrus, lignum infructuosum." The versions agree in supposing the comparison to be to a plant; and a very similar word in Arabic (*ghargar*) means the mountain juniper; Tristram, the dwarf juniper. Most, however, take the word to be an adjective equivalent to "destitute." Dr. Thomson tells a story of a poor destitute woman he found in the desert (comp. ch. xlviii. 6—the form there is *Aroer,* here it is '*ar‘ār;* Ps. cii. 18). **Shall not see;** *i.e.* shall not perceive, or feel any evil consequences (comp. Isa. xliv. 16, "I have seen the fire," equivalent to "I feel the flame"). **A salt land;** *i.e.* one entirely barren (comp. Deut. xxix. 23).

Ver. 8.—**Shall not see;** rather, *shall not fear*—this is the reading of the Hebrew text, and of the Septuagint, Peshito, and Vulgate. The Authorized Version represents that of the margin, which is conformed to ver. 6, but is against the parallelisms.

Vers. 9, 10.—The crooked devices of the human heart, which is characterized as **deceitful above all things** (or, as Delitzsch, 'Biblical Psychology,' English translation, p. 340, "proud;" literally, *uneven* or *rugged;* comp. Isa. xl. 4; Hab. ii. 4, Hebrew; Ps. cxxxi. 2, Hebrew), **and desperately wicked,** or rather, *desperately sick* (see ch. xv. 18, where it is explained by the words, "which refuseth to be healed"). The Septuagint reads this verse differently, "The heart is deep above all things, and it is a man."

Ver. 11.—**As the partridge . . . hatcheth them not;** rather, *as the partridge sitteth on eggs which it hath not laid;* a proverbial illustration of the Divine retributive justice. The prophet assumes the truth of a popular belief respecting the partridge (still a common bird in Judæa), that it brooded upon eggs which it had not laid. As the young birds soon leave the false mother, so unjustly acquired riches soon forsake their possessors. [Canon Tristram rejects this explanation, on the ground that the statement is not true to natural history; the partridge neither steals the broods of others nor needs to do so, as it lays a very large number of eggs. But grammar requires us to translate as suggested above, and consequently excludes any other explanation. May not the unusually large number of the eggs laid by the partridge have led to the fancy that they could not be all its own?]

Vers. 12, 13.—An address to Jehovah in two parts, the first specially referring to the temple regarded as the sacramental symbol of the Divine presence (comp. Ps. v. 7), the second to Jehovah himself. It seems to us, no doubt, singular thus practically to identify Jehovah and his temple; but the prophet's meaning is that God can only be addressed in so far as he has revealed himself. The temple was not, strictly speaking, the "Name" or revelation of God, but it was "the place of the Name of Jehovah," and in the language of strong feeling might be addressed as if it were really the Divine Name. The disciples of the incarnate Name were familiar with the idea that their Master was in some sense the antitype of the temple (Matt. xii. 6; John ii. 19). In proposing this explanation, it has been tacitly assumed that the Authorized Version, **A glorious high throne . . . is the place of our sanctuary**, is wrong. Grammatically, indeed, it is not indefensible; but it is a weak rendering in such a context. Render, therefore, *Thou throne of glory, a height from the beginning, thou place of our sanctuary, thou hope of Israel, Jehovah*. The temple is called "the throne of thy glory" in ch. xiv. 21; "height" is a common synonym for heaven (Ps. vii. 8, Hebrew; Isa. lvii. 15, Hebrew), but is also applied to Mount Zion (Ezek. xvii. 23; xx. 40, quoted by Keil), which is also in Isa. lx. 13 called, "the place of my sanctuary." By adding the concluding words of the address (at the opening of ver. 13), the prophet prevents the suspicion that he attached importance to the mere outward buildings of the temple, like those formalist Jews, whose words are quoted in ch. vii. 4.

Ver. 13.—**They that depart from me.** The abrupt change of person is extremely harsh; the Vulgate, followed by Ewald and Olshausen, supposes that a final *caph* has dropped out, rendering, "they that depart from thee." **Shall be written in the earth**; a contrast to that which is recorded for all time "with a pen of iron" (ver. 1). **The fountain**, etc.; a favourite phrase of our prophet (see ch. ii. 13).

Vers. 14—18.—A prayer of the prophet in this his hour of need. He who makes his boast of Jehovah may reckon upon his help. This is Jeremiah's principle. He prays for healing, **Heal me, ... and I shall be**—rather, *that I may be*—**healed**. He is one of those "broken in heart," whom Jehovah alone can "heal" (Ps. cxlvii. 3).

Ver. 15.—The occasion of this prayer is the hostility of his neighbours, and their mocking question, **Where is the word of the Lord?** The prophecy seems to be floating as it were in mid-air, unable to alight (Isa. ix. 8) and fulfil itself, so that Jeremiah could be plausibly treated as a false prophet (Deut. xviii. 22). Hence, as Keil remarks, the discourse of which this forms the conclusion must have been spoken before the first Babylonian invasion of Judah.

Ver. 16.—**I have not hastened from** being **a pastor to follow thee**; *i.e.* I have not eagerly withdrawn from following thee as a shepherd (or prophet). The prophet does not follow his own vague inclinations; he is but an under-shepherd, and waits on the will of his superior. He is, as Hosea calls him (ix. 7, Hebrew), "the man of the Spirit." If God leads any one, whether people or individuals, it is through the agency of the Spirit (Isa. lxiii. 11, 12); and it is the characteristic of the typical prophet that his ear is "wakened morning by morning" to receive his daily lesson. Only by thus "following" the Divine Leader, can a prophet act as pastor to his people. [The construction is, however, rather simplified by the rendering—a perfectly legitimate one, *... from following thee as a companion.*] **The woeful day.** The word for "woeful" is the same rendered "desperately wicked" (ver. 9); the "day" of Judah's calamity is metaphorically "sick," like the heart of man. So, other words being used, Isa. xvii. 11 (end). **Was right before thee**; rather (since some adjective must be supplied), *was manifest before thee*. He appeals to the all-seeing Eye as a witness to his fidelity to his mission.

Ver. 17.—Jeremiah reckons on Jehovah's protection; he therefore entreats that his God will not bring him to shame by leaving his prophecies unfulfilled. **A terror** is a weak rendering; *a consternation* would be better.

Ver. 18.—(On this terrible execration, with reference to Jeremiah's character, see the general Introduction.) **Destroy them with double destruction.** "Double" here means "amply sufficient" (comp. Rev. xviii. 6, and see on ch. xvi. 18).

Vers. 19—27.—An exhortation to a more

strict observance of the sabbath. The
reward held out is Jerusalem's continuance
in· all its old pomp, both temporal and
spiritual, and the penalty the destruction
of the city by fire. This passage stands in
absolutely no connection with the preceding
and the following prophecies; and we have
just the same sense of suspicion in meeting
with it here, in the midst of perfectly general
exhortations, as in reading the parallel
exhortations to sabbath-keeping in Isa. lvi.
and lviii., surrounded as they are by the
moving and almost evangelical rhetoric of
the second part of Isaiah. Geiger and Dr.
Rowland Williams have hence been led to
conjecture that this section (or part of it)
was introduced into the roll of Jeremiah's
prophecies to assist the reforming movement
of Ezra and Nehemiah. Certainly the regard for the sabbath, so conspicuous in the
later Judaism, dates, so far as we can see,
from the time of Ezra and Nehemiah (see
Neh. xiii.), though it is credible enough
that the perception of the high importance
of this holy day (comp. Heine's 'Princessin
Sabbath') began to acquire greater distinctness as the other parts of the social and
religious organization were seen to be fading
away (comp. art. "Sabbath" in Smith's
'Bible Dictionary').

Ver. 19.—**In the gate of the children of
the people.** It is uncertain which of the
gates of Jerusalem is meant, and not perfectly clear what is the meaning of the title.
Does it mean Israelites as opposed to foreigners, or laymen as distinguished from priests ?
Whereby the kings of Judah come in. Jeremiah appears to use the phrase "kings of
Judah" in a particular sense (see on ver.
20). He may, no doubt, simply mean to
say that those who are from time to time
sovereigns of Judah enter by this gate.
But once grant that the prophet does sometimes use the phrase in a sense of his own,
and that in the very next verse, and it is
very difficult to avoid interpreting it so in
this passage.

Ver. 20.—Jeremiah addresses himself first
of all to the **kings of Judah.** As it would
be very unnatural for a public orator to
appeal to the yet unborn members of the
reigning dynasty, and as there are several
indications that the "house of David" was
able at this period, as also in that of Isaiah,
to exercise a decisive political and civil
influence, even, as appears from ch. xxi. 11,
12, monopolizing the judicial functions, it
is natural to suppose that "kings of Judah"
is here used in a very special sense, viz. of the
members of the various branches of the royal
family ("The sons of the king," Zeph. i. 8;
comp. ch. xxxvi. 26, "Jerahmeel, a king's
son"), and their descendants, who received
the royal title by courtesy (parallels for this

will be found in Gesenius's ' Hebrew Thesau-
rus,' *s.v. mélek*). The queen-mother was probably the leader of this clan; "the mistress,"
as she was called (see on ch. xiii. 18), and the
royal princes (among whom the "house of
Nathan," Zech. xii. 12, would doubtless be
reckoned), constituted in fact a body almost
as numerous as they did (according to
Brugsch Bey) in Egypt, and politically
much more influential; so much so indeed
that only a king of unusual force of character,
like Hezekiah or Josiah, could venture, and
that timidly, to oppose them. The weak-
principled Zedekiah seems to have been
entirely dominated by this powerful caste,
and to have been little more than a *maire du
palais* (the same sense of the phrase is
required in ch. xix. 3, and probably in ch.
xxv. 18).

Ver. 21.—**Take heed to yourselves**; rather,
*Take heed heartily, conscientiously; literally,
in your souls.* So in Malachi (ii. 15, 16),
"Take heed in your spirit" (not, "to your
spirit," as Authorized Version).

Ver. 22.—**Neither do ye any work**; according to the fourth commandment (Exod.
xx. 10; Deut. v. 14).

Ver. 23.—This verse is modelled on ch.
vii. 26, 28.

Ver. 25.—Parallel passage, ch. xxii. 4,
where, however, we simply meet with "*kings*
sitting upon the throne of David," not, as here,
"kings and princes." Has the latter word
come in by accident, owing to the frequent
combination of **kings and princes** in Jeremiah
(i. 18; ii. 26; xxv. 18; xxxii. 32; xliv. 17,
21)? **Shall remain for ever**; rather, *shall be
inhabited for ever.*

Ver. 26.—Parallel passage for the catalogue of the districts of Judah, ch. xxxii. 44.
Three divisions are mentioned. (1) The
neighbourhood of Jerusalem (including the
"cities of Judah"); (2) the land of Benjamin, *i.e.* the northern part of the kingdom;
and (3) the tribe of Judah, with its three
subdivisions—the Sheféla or lowland country
by the Mediterranean Sea, the hill country, and the Negeb or "dry" south country
(comp. Josh. xv. 21—62). The sacrifices
are described with equal explicitness; they
fall into two classes, the bloody (burnt offerings and other sacrifices) and the unbloody
(the vegetable offering or *minkhah*, and the
incense which was strewed upon the *minkhah*, Lev. ii. 1). **And bringing sacrifices of
praise.** This was, no doubt, the title of a
particular variety of sacrifices (Lev. vii. 12;
xxii. 29); here, however, it seems as if all
the preceding sacrifices were summed up
under this designation. St. Paul says, "In
everything give thanks;" and this seems to
have been the prophet's ideal of the sacrifices of the future.

HOMILETICS.

Ver. 1.—*Engraved sin.* I. SIN LEAVES A RECORD OF ITSELF. It is not an isolated act. It begets consequences, plants memories, creates guilt. The record remains even if we do not read it. God still notes it, and will some day confront us with it. Hence it is not enough to amend our ways for the future. We need to have past transgressions blotted out if we are to be restored to peace with God.

II. THE RECORD OF SIN IS ENGRAVED ON THE HEART OF THE SINNER. 1. It is written on the *memory.* Men who have forsaken the scenes of their evil deeds cannot shake off the clinging burden of the memory of them. The criminal is haunted by his crimes. They people his dreams with horrors; they overshadow his waking hours with gloom. Even when sin is put out of mind it is probably buried in the secret chamber of memory, to be ultimately brought to the light of consciousness. The experience of those who have been recovered from drowning and from delirium suggests the idea that forgotten memories can be revived, and that probably the whole of the soul's experience is indelibly written upon the memory. No other recording-angel may be wanted. The soul carries its own indictment in the record it bears of its own conduct. 2. This is also written on the *affections.* Sin begets the passion for sin. Vice springs from the heart, and it corrupts the heart. That which is first committed under the stress of temptation comes at length to be sought with the hunger of a natural appetite.

III. THE RECORD OF SIN IS ENGRAVED ON THE ALTAR OF SACRIFICE. Judah desecrated the altar of Jehovah with idolatrous rites. We desecrate Divine things by sinful conduct. 1. *We cannot leave our guilt* behind us when we enter the temple of worship. If it is not repented of it will vitiate the worship. The sin of the week-day renders worthless the offerings of the Sunday. 2. *Sin directly connected with religion* is peculiarly wicked. The altar is defiled. Thus the offering of gifts from base motives, deceit, and unholiness in worship, stamps our sins with peculiar guilt on the altar of God.

IV. THIS RECORD OF SIN IS NATURALLY INDELIBLE. It is graven with an adamant. 1. It is, therefore, useless to *ignore it.* 2. It is vain to try to *wash it away* by any effort of our own. 3. It is foolish to expect *peace with God till this terrible hindrance has been removed* out of the way. 4. We have every motive to seek in penitence and in faith that God should blot out our sin, not only from his book of remembrance, but also from our hearts, even though it is so deeply written there that nothing short of the creation of a new heart will remove it (Ps. li. 10).

Vers. 5—8.—*The desert shrub and the flourishing tree.* I. THE DESERT SHRUB EXEMPLIFIES THE CURSE OF WORLDLY CONFIDENCE. 1. Note the *character* of worldly confidence. (1) Trust in *man.* There is a trust in man that is natural and right. The foolish and wrong confidence is when man takes the place of God, when the highest trust is in man, when the power of the prince, the skill of the physician, or the astuteness of the lawyer are thought to be sufficient to secure us against the greatest dangers. (2) Reliance on the *arm of flesh.* This illustrates the ultimate ground of such confidence as trust in man. It turns to the flesh rather than to the spirit, *i.e.* to worldly influences rather than to principles of truth, to the mortal rather than to the Divine, to the man who will perish rather than to the God who is eternal. (3) The *departure of the heart from God.* We cannot have a true confidence in God together with a supreme worldly confidence. The one excludes the other. The tree cannot be growing both in the desert and by the water-course. This departure is of the heart. In the heart we trust. Outwardly we may still seem near to God, but if faith has gone the heart has forsaken God. 2. Consider the *curse* of this worldly confidence. It makes one like a desert shrub. (1) *Dwarfed* and stunted in growth—a shrub, not a tree—a miserable shrub of the desert. Though departure from God does not involve sudden destruction, it lowers the spiritual energies, dwarfs the whole life. (2) *Not even benefited by blessings received.* The shrub " shall not see when good cometh." The breath of spring, which brings fresh bloom and growth to other plants, passes over it with no more fruitful effects than the chill blasts of autumn produce. He who has departed from God and lives only in worldly confidence derives no real benefit from the blessings that God still sends him. (3) Suffering from *lack of the chief good.* The shrub is in a parched land, is withered for lack of water (see ch. ii. 13). (4) *Lonely.* "In a salt land, and not inhabited." The soul that is separated from God is essentially solitary, deserted, destitute though immersed in the tumult of worldly society.

II. THE FLOURISHING TREE EXEMPLIFIES THE BLESSEDNESS OF TRUST IN GOD. 1 Note the *character* of trust in God. (1) It is *intelligent.* It is trust in God revealed as Jehovah, as supreme, self-existent, eternal, known in the past for merciful helpfulness. (2) It is *whole-hearted.* It is a simple trust in God, not divided by partial worldly confidence. (3) It is *hopeful.* "Whose *hope* the Lord is." The strongest faith rises into hope. 2. Consider the *blessedness* of this trust in God. (1) *Full and flourishing life*—a tree, not a shrub. He who trusts in God is not only endowed with external blessings, he is enlarged and developed in his own life. (2) *Nourished and refreshed.* The tree is planted by the waters, etc. Trust in God brings and plants us near to the "river of life." (3) *Secured against trouble.* "And shall not see when heat cometh," etc. While the shrub derives no benefit from the most favourable weather, the tree planted by the water does not suffer from the most trying. Trust in God does not prevent the approach of trouble, but it fortifies us against suffering real harm from it. Hidden sources supply the Christian with spiritual nourishment when outwardly the heavens are as brass and the earth as iron. (4) *Perpetual fruitfulness.* "Neither shall cease from yielding fruit." Fruitfulness is a sign of health, perpetual fruitfulness of unbroken health. Fruitfulness is a blessing. The Christian is most blessed in being able to work for good, and to distribute blessings to others as the chief glory of the tree is its fruit-bearing.

Vers. 9, 10.—*The evil heart searched and judged.* I. THE EVIL OF THE HEART. 1. The most important question concerning a man is as to the *state of his heart*—his thoughts, affections, intentions. In the heart we find the true man. The outer life is but the clothing and may be the mask of the man. From the heart spring all the actions of life. The character of the fountain determines that of the stream (Matt. xv. 18, 19). 2. The root of the evil of the heart is *self-will.* It is *rugged* above all things, proud, not compliant with God's will, wrapped up in self. 3. The character of the evil of the heart is *desperate sickness.* (1) *Sickness,* for sin is a disease of the soul, though one for which we are responsible, and it results in suffering, general derangement of life, and finally death; (2) *desperate* sickness, for sin is no simple scratch on the skin of life, no mere temporary functional disorder, but heart-disease, an organic constitutional disease, terrible in its present condition, alarming in its future prospects. 4. The evil of the heart is *inscrutable* to man. "Who can know it?" This is the case, (1) because we cannot read the hearts of our fellow-men, but only judge from external conduct, which is often deceptive; (2) because we are blinded to our own sin by pride, prejudice, and self-admiration; (3) because there is an intricacy and subtlety about all wickedness which makes it difficult to trace it out, a shamefacedness that seeks concealment, and an essential falseness that belies its own nature; and (4) because the disease has made so great progress, has penetrated so deeply, ramified so far, and infected every function of the soul so completely, that it is beyond all measure.

II. THE DIVINE SEARCH AND JUDGMENT. The heart is difficult to understand, but God thoroughly searches it. "Who can know it?" "I the Lord." 1. God *searches and tries,* (1) by his own silent, all-penetrating gaze that detects the darkest secrets; and (2) by the outward action of providence in events which test a man's nature and reveal it to the world, for the judgment of God is ultimately open and with a fair trial, that all may see and acquiesce in the righteousness of the sentence. 2. God *knows* the heart. The search is effectual. The trial is fruitful. God knows us, while the world is deceived. How foolish, then, to play the hypocrite! for it matters little what men think of us, but God's thoughts concerning us are of infinite moment. God will judge justly and reasonably, for he knows all. 3. God will *administer judgment* according to the character of men's actions revealed by his searching and trying. God's knowledge is followed by his action. He is not simply a great contemplative Being. He has an arm to make bare for action as well as eyes to see the evil and the good. Judgment will be for our actions, but according as these are read in the light of the state of our heart. God searches and gives to men according to their ways. This judgment is universal—"to every man," discriminating—to each "according to his ways," and natural—" according to the *fruit* of his doings, according to their natural products, each in its own kind, so that men shall reap what they sow as by a law of nature.

Ver. 11.—*Partridge-nests.* I. ILL-GOTTEN RICHES BETOKEN AN UNNATURAL CONDITION OF SOCIETY. It is not natural that strange eggs should be found in a partridge-nest. Violence and fraud and more subtle sharp-practice are proofs of a disorganized state of society.

II. ILL-GOTTEN RICHES MAY BE MINGLED WITH JUST GAINS. It may not be that all the eggs are strange. The business man who is dishonest in some transactions may be honest in others; but his very correctness may be only a cloak for his fraud.

III. ILL-GOTTEN RICHES MAY PROSPER FOR A TIME. The eggs are hatched. Schemes of fraud succeed. The wicked prosper.

IV. ILL-GOTTEN RICHES WILL ULTIMATELY BE LOST. How often does the ablest device of dishonesty fail of ultimate success ! The swindler is taken at the height of his prosperity. If he is not discovered he cannot take his wealth with him when he dies.

V. ILL-GOTTEN RICHES LEAVE THE POSSESSOR OF THEM CONVICTED OF FOLLY. He thinks himself supremely clever, and smiles with contempt on his credulous victims. But he is really the greatest dupe of his own devices, since in the end all his labour is wasted and his ultimate condition ruinous (Luke xii. 20, 21). " Honesty is the best policy " in the long run, though, as has been shrewdly observed, no man is truly honest who only acts on this maxim.

Vers. 12—14.—*The Hope of Israel.* I. THE REVELATION OF THE HOPE OF ISRAEL. 1. God is revealed as the *Hope* of his people; *i.e.* as the source (1) of their highest good —a " fear " at first (Gen. xxxi. 42), but when better known a " hope ; " (2) of a good not yet attained—a hope, not a full fruition ; but (3) of a good assured for the future—a true hope resting on good promises, not a vain dream. 2. God is thus revealed in connection with the *sanctuary*, (1) because the worship of God enlarges the knowledge of God ; (2) because the sanctuary is the centre of religious instruction, either by symbolic service as that of the temple, or by direct teaching as that of the Christian Churches. God must be known to be loved and trusted. They who neglect the duty of public worship lose the privilege of receiving light on Divine truth which would be a comfort and help to them. 3. *Experience* confirms this revelation of God. The glorious character of God has been true of him " from the beginning." The antiquity of the temple was the proof of this to the Jew, the history of Christendom should be more so to the Christian.

II. THE FOLLY OF FORSAKING THE HOPE OF ISRAEL. 1. It is *foolish* to forsake God. We know that it is wrong ; we have to learn that it is also injurious to ourselves. The character of God should make this apparent. Such a character as has been above ascribed to him shows that he is " the Fountain of living waters," *i.e.* the one Source of pure, life-giving energy. Though no true religion can be founded on low motives of self-interest, self-interest should at least show us the mistake of irreligion. 2. The results of forsaking God are *shame and destruction :* (1) *shame,* because the stay of confidence which was chosen in preference to God is seen at last to be a rotten reed, while God is manifested as worthy of all trust; and (2) *destruction,* for "they shall be written in the earth ; " sin is graven as with a pen of iron upon a rock, but the life of the sinner is written in dust, to be dissipated and forgotten, a wasted career, with nothing solid and lasting about it.

III. THE PRAYER OF CONFIDENCE IN THE HOPE OF ISRAEL. (Ver. 14.) 1. A prayer for *healing.* Though we hope in God we may suffer at present. We need not so much improved circumstances as a bettering of the condition of our own souls—not so much wealth as health. 2. A prayer for *salvation.* The prophet feels himself in danger. Dangers of various kinds wait on all of us. Salvation is a large word, meaning deliverance from all real harm. It is a large thing to ask for, but not too much for faith. 3. A prayer of *assurance*—" I shall be healed." What God does he does effectually. 4. A prayer of humble *thankfulness*—" For thou art my Praise." True faith rests, not on our merits, but on God's mercy, and therefore all prayer should confess his goodness and all supplication be mingled with thanksgiving (Phil. iv. 6).

Vers. 19—27.—*The sabbath.* As Gentiles we were never under the special regulations of the Jewish Law, and as Christians we are free from all formal laws of "ordinances," and called to free spiritual obedience.   Like St. Paul, we may be able to see that no one day is more sacred than other days (Rom. xiv. 5); and if we are unable to go so far as this, we must admit that there is, in the New Testament, no direct command to Christians to observe the first day of the week just as the Jews observed the seventh. Still, to him who is in sympathy with the thoughts of God and desires to do the will of God rather than to seize excuses for liberty only to exercise his own self-will, there is much in the Old Testament sabbath requirements which must command the reverence of his conscience as springing out of Eternal Divine counsels, and representing what is inherently good and profitable.

I. CONSIDER IN WHAT THE OBSERVANCE OF THE SABBATH CONSISTED.   1. *Rest.* "Bear no burden."   Work is holy, but so also is rest, and if work usurp the place of rest it becomes unholy, as anything does which is in the wrong place.   Men bear burdens on their minds.   If the shop is shut but the mind of the tradesman continues devoted to business cares on the Sunday, he is making no more sabbath of the day than if he were openly buying and selling.   The rest needed for refreshment is rest from the toils and anxieties of the mind, quite as much as a cessation of manual labour.   2. *Hallowing the day.*   The Jew treated the sabbath day as essentially holy.   We may have freer notions.   But we, too, can hallow the day if we devote it to sacred uses.   We should remember that it is not the day that hallows the conduct, but the conduct that hallows the day.   Sacred days, like sacred places, are not endowed with a mystical consecration, which transfers its grace to whatever is done in them, but they are simply made sacred by the acts of goodness to which they are devoted.   3. *Personal care* to observe the rest and sanctity of the day.   "Take heed in your souls;" "diligently hearken."   The observance of the sabbath was to the Jew a duty to be personally regarded and conscientiously executed.   If we feel any corresponding duty, the example of the more lax conduct of others should not affect us, nor should we be content with the outward decorum which satisfies the world.

II. CONSIDER THE OBLIGATION TO KEEP THE SABBATH.   1. The sabbath was instituted by the *command of God.*   It was required by one of the ten commandments, and thus exalted to a position of peculiar sanctity.   To the Jew who felt that this law of God was binding on him, the duty of implicit obedience was imperative.   When once we know God's will no valid excuse can be found for neglecting it.   Though the letter of the Mosaic Law was limited and temporal, the spirit of its obligations is eternal, since they spring from the changeless character of God.   It is for us to discover the eternal Divine principle which led to the institution of the sabbath, and see that this is obeyed.   2. It corresponded to the *constitution of nature.*   Changes in nature are recurrent.   Rest and labour alternate in the physical world.   3. It was designed to *benefit men.*   (Mark ii. 27.)   The wealthy might not have felt the requirement, but the burden-bearers and hand-labourers did, and must have enjoyed the repose it afforded them.   Do we need this ?   If in quieter times such a rest was necessary, is it needless in the rush and roar of our wearing modern life ?   If seasons set apart for religious observances were ever profitable, are they useless amid the pressing claims and innumerable distractions of the age we live in ?

III. CONSIDER THE BLESSEDNESS OF OBSERVING THE SABBATH.   The Jews had promises of blessings to the court, the city, the country, and the Church (see Matthew Henry, *in loc.*).   1. This might be expected as the *reward of obedience.*   It is always blessed to do the will of God, though the first doing of it is often painful.   2. This might also be expected, because the sabbath was *made for man.*   It was a beneficent institution.   It is found by experience that the observance of a weekly day of rest is conducive to the prosperity of a people.   3. Accordingly, the *neglect* of the sabbath might be expected to bring disaster (ver. 27).   This was the case with the Jew, not because of the inherent sanctity of the day or of the essential immorality of working on it, but because the breach of the sabbath was a breach of the Law, an act of overt rebellion against God.   If we disobey what we believe to be the will of God, this must be to our own hurt.   4. The blessedness of the observance of the Jewish sabbath teaches us all to avoid treating the day of rest as a *gloomy day,* and making children and dependants dislike it on account of the formalism or harshness of our behaviour.   The day of rest should be the brightest day of the week. To the Christian, Sunday is "the Lord's day," the day of Easter gladness, commemorating the joy of the Resurrection.

HOMILIES BY VARIOUS AUTHORS.

Vers. 1, 2.—*Sin's record.* I. THE RECORD IS INEFFACEABLE. This is contrary to the notions of very many. Sin, when it is committed, wears the aspect of insignificance and triflingness. It is the gratification of a momentary impulse, of a personal and individual character; and it is not supposed that any one else, or at any rate any large number of persons, can be affected by it. The sinner supposes that he himself will be able to condone it, and that, when the active prompting of which he is conscious retires into the background, he will be as he was before. All sins, *e.g.* idolatry, which deeply engage the affections and the highest capacities of men, have a lasting influence upon their character. And when they are systematized into a religion they exert a daily influence which at last fixes itself. But the same is true, in a very serious degree, with all sins. They are contradictions of conscience and the Law of God, and can only be repeated without scruple by inverting and hardening the moral nature. In this sense we are all guilty before God. Our every sin has had its influence upon us, and has left its indelible impress. Conscience stores the guilty memory in its archives; habit perpetuates the evil impulse in conduct; and our relations and associations are involved in the wicked practices which ensue.

II. HOW USELESS, THEREFORE, ATTEMPTING TO EXCULPATE OURSELVES! This arrangement, by which sin leaves its impress upon the character and life, is of God. It is a law of nature, and cannot be set aside by private understanding. Even where it appears to be inoperative, its effects are only accumulating themselves in a more hidden manner, and some day they will be the more overwhelming in their manifestation. It is the common question of the sinner, when addressed by the ministers of God, "Wherein have we sinned?" But this only shows a dulness of spiritual self-knowledge and a general lowering of the moral standard. Others are not so oblivious to the fact. They have witnessed the excesses and been involved in the complications of their immorality. In this case the children whose companions had been sacrificed to Moloch looked on the horns of the altars with aversion and loathing. It was a memory of horrid cruelty never to be effaced. There is every reason to believe that the sin we commit does not cease its work when its immediate outward effects take place. An ever deepening and widening circle of influence results. And, just as now it is impossible for us to plead innocence with so many proofs of our guilt staring us in the face, in the great day of judgment the secret sins will be set in the light of God's countenance, and the thoughts and intents of the heart revealed. Our character will be our condemnation, and many witnesses will rise on every side to swell its testimony.

III. HOW NECESSARY, TOO, THAT THE PRINCIPLE OF SALVATION SHOULD BE RADICAL AND THOROUGH! The sinner needs a saving power that can penetrate to his inmost nature, cleansing the conscience, rectifying the character, and making the weaknesses and defects created by sin a means of grace. And this is supplied by the gospel, which furnishes a new motive and principle to the character and a new law to the conduct. So profound is its effect that it may be said by the saved sinner, "Old things are passed away; behold, all things are become new." It is as a character-power that the "cross" asserts its pre-eminence over every other principle of reformation. There is nothing superficial, partial, or one-sided about it.—M.

Vers. 9, 10.—*Heart mysteries and their Interpreter.* The repudiation of his charges by Judah and Jerusalem leads the prophet to advert to the causes of this behaviour. They not only declare their innocence when guilty, but pursue after unholy aims on the plea of serving God. How are such ignorance and infatuation produced? The reply is that the natural heart is deceitful and corrupt above everything else.

I. THE MYSTERY OF THE HEART. 1. *It is a "mystery of iniquity."* The heart is affected by what it contains. It is itself the greatest dupe and sufferer. And, being so inextricably bound up with evil, it is involved in its danger and judgment.

2. *Exceeding human diagnosis.* No one is so ignorant of his own depravity as the sinner himself; and no earthly eye can read the true significance of the symptoms. 3. *Pre-eminent in this respect.* It is the source of it all. The master is greater than his work. The centre contains all the threads of connection.

II. Its INTERPRETER. 1. *Jehovah.* Because (1) he made it; (2) he is related to it in its constitution and conscience; (3) "All things are naked and laid open before the eyes of him with whom we have to do." 2. *This qualifies and authorizes him to judge.* It is not his only qualification, nor is that the sole reason for his knowledge. But it is obvious that, as knowing man so intimately, he also is able to judge of his state. And he alone has the standard of perfect righteousness.—M.

Vers. 12, 13.—*The saint's Refuge.* The construction of the clauses of the twelfth verse is very difficult, and it is not easy to determine their exact relations. It may be better to take them as simple and independent exclamations, united in their being addressed to a common object rather than by any grammatical nexus: "O throne of glory, height from the beginning, place of our sanctuary!" But, taken by itself, this would have no particular sense. It is only as a preface to ver. 13 that we can thoroughly understand its bearing. Jeremiah, full of anxiety and distress at the general depravity, looks instinctively upon Jerusalem, and reflects that only through that which it represents can the future of Israel be secured. There is a gradually ascending climax of spiritual reference, culminating in the words, "Hope of Israel, Jehovah."

I. THE SAVING POWER OF THE HOLY CITY IS DERIVED FROM HIM OF WHOM IT IS THE SHRINE. It is obvious that the descriptions of Jerusalem are all relative to this, which gathers up and concentrates everything in a person. The series of epithets of vers. 12 and 13 are cumulative, and express a gradually deepening spiritual insight. Through the material the prophet looks until his eye rests upon the spiritual. *God is the centre of attraction and the Saviour of the worshipping soul.* Everything in the ritual and teaching of the temple pointed to him. The glory of the temple was his. It was only as he condescended to use it that men could find therein the spiritual rest and safety they needed. And the same is true of the Church of Christ. It is not the institution which saves, but Christ working in and through it. There is danger of this being overlooked by non-spiritual men. Association connects the grace of salvation with the means or instrumentality, and ignores the original source. It is the virtue of the prophet's insight that it penetrates the veil of rites and ordinances, and fastens itself upon God as the only saving power. 1. *Spiritual men should examine themselves and see whether they rest upon this true spiritual foundation.* The process of the prophet's mind is one through which all true saints have to go. In many instances there will not be the eagle-like directness and happy immediacy of his discovery. There may be clouds and difficulties. But no true satisfaction can be attained until he be discovered and rested in. We are all prone to stay ourselves upon prescription, antiquity, authority, that are merely human. The doctrine, the rite, the priesthood, may inter-vene, not to unite, but to separate. 2. *It behoves those who call themselves by God's name to exalt and honour him.* If there is danger of his being ignored or pushed into the background, the more need is there of a bold and frequent assertion of his power and grace. 3. *It is only by a living, experimental, practical faith that this connection with God can be sustained.* The sorrow and trouble of Jeremiah drive him inwards for comfort. His meditation was like a voyage of the soul through the straits and shallows of ceremonialism into the great ocean of the personal presence and love of God.

II. THE THREEFOLD CLAIM OF GOD'S CITY TO THE REGARD OF MEN. Jerusalem, as the seat of the theocracy, was: 1. *The seat of authority and splendour.* The power of Israel amongst and against the nations consisted in the spiritual influence emanating from Jerusalem and its temple. The house of God, as the centre of all rule and influence, is a *throne.* It is its own protection, and its authority is self-sustained and self-commended. It is a refuge for the oppressed and a place of justice for the wronged. "Go round about her: tell the towers thereof. Mark ye well her bulwarks;" for this city is our city, and "this God is our God for ever and ever." "Because thou hast made the Almighty . . . thy habitation; there shall no evil befall thee, neither shall any plague come nigh thy dwelling." And this power to enforce its mandates and its authority brought with it the glory of security, honour, and respect. Its whole history had been one of growing lustre and renown, and its influence had ever "made for righteousness." The saved sinner breathed freely within its precincts, and the victories of Divine love were celebrated within its courts. Those who believe in Christ constitute a Church which is his abode and " the praise of his glory." The distinction and eternal glory of God is that he is "just, and yet the Justifier of the ungodly." 2. *It is chosen from eternity.* Although only for a few centuries the actual centre of Divine rule in the earth, it was not by accident it had become so. From the beginning it was foreseen in God's thought : "It was set up from everlasting, from the beginning, or ever the world was." This was a conviction deeply fixed in the hearts of all true Israelites. The eternal purpose of God had not only determined upon Jerusalem as his dwelling-place, but, through Jerusalem, that purpose was being carried out in the redemption of mankind. And the Church of Christ must be regarded in like manner as the abode of God's Spirit, chosen from eternity. It is a new dignity for the saints that they had been set apart for this long ere sin had desolated the world. It links the Church with celestial and eternal institutions, and precludes the possibility of its ever having originated in accident or human contrivance.—M.

Vers. 14—18.—*Divine prophecy and human impatience.* I. THE CREDIT OF THE PROPHET IS BOUND UP WITH HIS MESSAGE. He is conscious that this is the case. It is the test laid down by the Law (Deut. xviii. 21, 22), and that it should be so is beneficial. This is the universal law for all who declare the will of God. It is tried by human experience, by spiritual results. The prophet is expected to " heal."

II. MEN TRY HIM BY CHALLENGING A SPEEDY FULFILMENT. Just as in nature men, as Bacon says, would *anticipate,* so in grace. There is a lack of patience, or impatience is made a mask for unbelief. In either sign it is a lack of faith. So men manufacture tests for prayer, for reality of conscience.

III. HE FINDS REFUGE AND COMFORT : 1. *In the answer of a good conscience toward God.* It was not idleness, love of filthy lucre, or eagerness for pre-eminence that led him to the work, but a consciousness that he was speaking God's own word, no man's fancy or device. 2. *In earnest prayer that God will make good his word.* There are elements in this prayer from which we shrink. But should we ? The fulfilling of evil prophecy may sometimes be a national benefit. 3. *In the unshaken faith that what God willeth will be.* He appears to be sore distressed. Perhaps personal perplexity enters into his grief. But there is no sign of lack of faith in its ultimate fulfilment. What a support is that to him who foretells or does the will of God ! " In due season we shall reap if we faint not." "Heaven and earth shall pass away, but my word shall not pass away."—M.

Vers. 19—27.—*The sabbath and its obligation.* I. IT WAS OF UNIVERSAL OBLIGATION. The prophet was to stand in " the gate of the children of the people " and "all the gates " to proclaim its sanctity. The laity and the priests, the princes and the people, were all bound to observe it, as one of the patriarchal and Mosaic institutions. It is expressly enjoined in one of the " ten words," and without reservation of any class.

II. HOW IT SHOULD BE OBSERVED. 1. *By rest.* Labour was to cease as far as practicable. The body was to be set at liberty from its burden. Traffic was to cease. The constant stream which flowed out and in the gates of the temple might still go on, but for a different purpose. Care and worry were to be laid aside. The mind was to abstain from business. 2. *By religious exercises.* (Ver. 26.) It is worthy of remark that this portion of the command is not spoken of as a binding duty like the other, or a merely negative one. It is referred to as part of the blessing that would ensue on thorough sabbath observances ; that they should have sacrifices to give, and be willing and eager to offer them. With the cessation of secular traffic the religious instincts of the people would recover themselves, and their natural channel would be filled. The true rest of man consists, not in mere abstinence from labour, but in the free play of his higher faculties—a change of occupation and interest. And the real wealth and success of man will show itself in his religious gifts. They are poor who have nothing to spare for God. Their conception of life is such that the true riches exist not for them, however they may have succeeded in accumulating material resources. The chief end of man is thus to be secured in the increase of Divine service and the hearty dedication of himself and his substance to Jehovah.

III. THE BLESSINGS THAT WOULD ATTEND UPON SABBATH OBSERVANCE. 1. *National perpetuity*. Jerusalem, the centre of the theocracy, should remain for ever. This indicates the essential and fundamental position occupied by the sabbath amongst Mosaic institutions. It was in this way that the idea and authority of Jehovah were to be impressed upon the heart of Israel. But to the preservation of this primitive revelation was due the strength of Israel within herself and against the heathen. 2. *National prosperity*. It is a goodly spectacle that is presented in this promise. There is no lack of gifts nor of willingness to give. Only a time of profound peace and of abounding harvests could furnish such a demonstration. 3. *National unity*. Jerusalem is the convergent point of many pilgrim trains : " from the places about, . . . from the land of Benjamin, and from the plain, and from the mountains, and from the south." In this way the brotherhood and the solidarity of the people would be sealed. 4. *National piety*. This is the natural outcome even of rudimental religious observances. It is the tendency of true religion to increase upon itself. It cannot remain stationary. Therefore this outburst of enthusiasm and Divine service.

IV. HOW IT IS REPRESENTED IN EVANGELICAL TIMES. So far as it was a physical requirement for the health and efficiency of man, it must still be observed. This is a question for comparative physiology. But the essence of the sabbath is rather in its religious observance. What becomes of that ? The spirit of it is still preserved in the Lord's day, although under new associations and under other obligations.—M.

Ver. 1.—" *The sin of Judah*." That which the prophet has to say concerning it in this part of his prophecy is in answer to the question of ch. xvi. 10, 11, where Judah inquires what their sin is. In reply, the prophet—
I. RECITES THEIR INIQUITIES. (Vers. 11, 12.)
II. DENOUNCES GOD'S JUDGMENTS. (Vers. 13—18.)
III. CITES WITNESSES AGAINST THEM.—C.

Ver. 12.—" *The place of our sanctuary*." Some four hundred years had passed between the date of these words and the marriage of Solomon with the daughter of the Egyptian king. But that remote event, fruitful of consequences as it was at the time, was fruitful also in results for generation after generation in the centuries to come. And it is to one of those results that this verse has reference, or rather was occasioned by it. For ever since that marriage there had been an Egyptian party in the court of Judah, which sought to sway the affairs of Judah in harmony with those of Egypt. On the other hand, there were the representatives of another near and mighty monarchy which sought to render Judah subservient to their interests. This was the Assyrian power. There was consequently a perpetual tendency on the part of Judah, when trouble came, to make alliance with one party or another. Now the Egyptian alliance was preferred, and now the Assyrian—Isa. xxx. and the history of the reign of Josiah and his death are instances in proof. But the prophets of God were ever against these alliances, and lifted up their voices, though in vain, in protest. These verses, 5—12, are one of those despised utterances, denouncing the false trust and exhorting to the true. This twelfth verse—
I. SPEAKS OF THE TEMPLE AT JERUSALEM. 1. For that temple has *a throne*. It was the earthly throne of God. There was the mercy-seat and the cherubim bowing in profound homage over it, and between them was the visible presence of the glory of God, that Shechinah, that wondrous appearance so bright and awful that but one out of all Israel, and he only once a year, could look thereupon and live. " In Salem was his tabernacle, and his dwelling-place in Zion." 2. And it was *a glorious throne*. By reason of its external magnificence; but more especially of the glorious manifestations of God which had been seen in connection with it. 3. And *a high as well as a glorious throne*. Not only because Jerusalem was a mountain-city, " the loftiest in the world, so high and lifted up was the " mountain of the Lord's house," but also because of the spiritual glory—so far excelling all other—which belonged to it. The ancient psalmists and prophets were never tired of declaring and demonstrating how the Lord

was " King above all gods." 4. *Venerable also :* "from the beginning," from the first days of their national life, God had chosen a place for his Name—beneath the rugged cliffs of Sinai then, and now in the magnificent temple, the place of their sanctuary. But—

II. IS DESIGNED TO SUMMON GOD'S PEOPLE TO TRUST IN HIM. 1. For to assert that the place of their sanctuary was a " throne," was to assert that Jehovah was *a King.* Kings occupy thrones. The sovereignty of God is declared by the prophet's words. And what a King! How *glorious,* let all the records of their race declare. How *pre-eminent* over all the gods of the nations, let the gods of Egypt, of Philistia, of Tyre, and others confess. And he was the *eternal God.* " From the beginning " his rule and majesty had been confessed. But the prophet reminds his countrymen of all this that they might see and own the folly of trusting in gods of the heathen as they were so prone to do. 2. And he reminds them *of the nearness of God.* For the place of their sanctuary was his court, his throne, his abode. Therefore to forsake such a God, and one so near, for idol-gods, and they afar off,—what folly, what ingratitude, what sin that! But the same memory cherished concerning God, his glorious sovereignty, his all-superintending power and his nearness to us,—how would this strengthen and cheer our hearts oftentimes! Our sins and sorrows, our faint-heartedness, our fears and dismay, are all largely owing to our forgetfulness of that glorious and precious truth which the prophet here declares. And—

III. MAY BE TAKEN AS A SETTING FORTH OF WHAT OUR SANCTUARIES SHOULD BE. 1. *For God should rule in them.* A Christian Church, whether we speak of the fabric or the people, should be a throne of God. His Law supreme, his will the rule confessed of all. Human governance in any shape or form which will infringe on the Divine authority, is forbidden. Christ is the Head of the Church, and the " crown rights of the Redeemer " should be jealously maintained.

> " Let Cæsar's dues be ever paid
> To Cæsar and his throne,
> But consciences and souls were made
> To be the Lord's alone."

2. And if our churches be the Lord's throne, he will make it *" a glorious high throne."* We should try to make our church buildings glorious outwardly, so far as we may, coveting what is splendid, majestic, beautiful, in architecture, music, adornment, to lay as a tribute at our Sovereign's feet. Where, consistently with other claims, this may be done, it should be. But he himself will make our Churches his " glorious high throne," by coming into their midst. On how many a Sunday his people have known that he has been with them!

> " The King himself comes near
> And feasts his saints to-day."

And by asserting his power over men's hearts. This is his most glorious power—to sway the spirit, to lead the will, to bend the heart. And this, by his Spirit in connection with the proclamation of the Word of his grace, he will do, and so the Church will become " a glorious high throne " of the Lord. 3. And because of " the communion of saints," and the consequent union of the Church of to-day with the Church of all the ages past, therefore the Church is God's throne which has been *"from the beginning."* The Church of to-day is in the honoured succession of the Church of the first days, through its long line of patriarchs, prophets, martyrs, saints, and thus may claim to have been the " glorious high throne " of the Lord " from the beginning." Let us cherish and seek to hand on this succession, and thus justify our claim to the august title contained in these words. But most of all these words—

IV. REMIND US OF CHRIST AND HIS CROSS, THE TRUE SANCTUARY OF SOULS. The cross of the Lord Jesus Christ—type of all ignominy and shame, though it was—has become the Lord's " glorious high throne." From it and by it he has wielded a sovereignty so glorious, so wide, so holy, so enduring, that, far more than the mercy-seat, its ancient symbol, it deserves thus to be described. Whether we consider the number of his subjects, their character, the means by which his rule over them has been won and is sustained, or the nature of his rule,—all justify the ascription to his cross and to him the supreme reference of these words. Let each one ask in *conclusion*—Is the cross of Christ the place of *our* sanctuary, the place where we worship, the beloved retreat of our souls? God grant it may be!—C.

Ver. 17.—"*Be not a terror unto me.*" It is a common observation how all things are affected by the medium through which we view them. This is true in regard to the natural vision, but yet more true in regard to that which is mental and spiritual. Thus God, whom the prophet speaks of (ver. 13) as "the Hope of Israel," the "Fountain of living waters," and as the alone true Healer, he now prays not to be "a terror" unto him.

I. GOD IS SO TO THE UNGODLY. All his attributes are terrible to them. His *holiness*, for it condemns their sin. His *justice*, for it demands their punishment. His *power*, for it reveals the means whereby he can requite them. His *love*, for it makes their sin without excuse. His *wisdom*, for it renders them unable to deceive him. Hence it is that of the wicked it is said, "God is not in all his thoughts." They like not to retain God in their knowledge. To think steadily of them must be a terror to their souls. But—

II. HE SEEMS SO AT TIMES EVEN TO THE GODLY. God *is* to them what in their happier moments' they delight to call him—their Father, their Redeemer, their Strength, their Refuge (cf. ch. xvi. 19). But at times he seems to be "a terror" unto them. *The causes* of this are sometimes : 1. Morbid state of health. 2. Lack of submission to the Divine will. 3. Backsliding. 4. False theological teaching. 5. Dwelling too much on the darker and more mysterious aspects of the Divine providence. 6. Depression of spirits. 7. Prolonged affliction.

III. BUT TRUER AND BRIGHTER THOUGHTS OF GOD MAY BE REGAINED. Various means may be suggested. 1. *Dwelling resolutely on the mercies and loving-kindnesses of God.* This is why St. Paul bids the "careful," those weighed down with care, to make known their requests to God, not only "by prayer and supplication," but "with thanksgiving" also. And elsewhere he bids us "in everything give thanks." For this compels us to go over in our minds the happier circumstances of our lot, and when we do this we shall find—

> " Our cheerful cry will oftener be,
> ' See what the Lord hath done for me.' "

2. And, as the words of St. Paul teach, "*prayer*" will help us. We

> "Kneel and cast our load,
> E'en while we pray, upon our God,
> Then rise with lightened cheer."

The public worship of God in his sanctuary, in union with his people,—how often, like Hannah, the soul has come to God's house burdened but gone away "lightened"! 3. And "*supplication.*" This tells of the more private, personal outpourings of the soul before God. Like the supplication in Gethsemane compared with the prayer—the Lord's Prayer—given for the common united use of his people. Here, too, vast relief is found, and the cloud clears away between us and God, and his face shines upon us once more. 4. Careful conscientious *obedience* and perseverance therein. 5. *Seeking to comfort others.* We learn in teaching, and this is true of the love of God as well as of other truths. 6. *Coming again to the cross of Christ* as having nothing, but looking for all in him.—C.

Vers. 19—27.—*Sabbath sanctification.* I. IN WHAT IT CONSISTS. Not in the mere Judaic strictness of the Old Testament Law, or of that set forth in these verses. All that might be, and yet in its true sense the sabbath be flagrantly violated and its purpose destroyed. But in : 1. *Rest.* This to be both of body and mind. The student may no more pursue his studies than the labourer his toil. Rest both of body and mind from their ordinary pursuits ; rest, not mere slothfulness, but such as will recreate the exhausted limbs or brain. 2. *Worship.* Not that it is to absolve other days from worship or to sanction their unhallowed use, but to lead to the more religious regard of all our days, the one day in seven is specially set apart. 3. *Charity.* In works of mercy and love to our fellow-men. Proclaiming the gospel, teaching the young, visiting the sick, relieving the poor.

II. IT IS OF DIVINE COMMAND. It is coeval with the creation of man (Gen. i. 31; ii. 1—3; Exod. xx. 8—11). And its embodiment in the moral Law seems to denote its permanence and abiding obligation.

III. ITS TRANSFER TO THE FIRST DAY OF THE WEEK DOES NOT ALTER ITS OBLIGATION. Our Lord taught us " the sabbath was made for man," and therefore, though for various reasons its observance was in substance transferred from the seventh day to the first, yet, because the need is permanent, the obligation is likewise.

IV. ALL GOD'S LAWS—AS WELL AS HIS WRITTEN LAW—SANCTION IT. Those that are: 1. *Physical.* The body requires it, is blessed by it, harmed if deprived of it. 2. *Religious* Religion demands set times and observances. Without these it will die out. The sabbath, therefore, is imperatively needed if religion is to be maintained amongst any people. 3. *Moral.* Secular pursuits tend to absorb all the energies of the soul. Worldliness is dominant enough as it is in every man; but the break of the sabbath does much to hold these mighty but malevolent forces in check, and gives opportunity for the exercise of other and counteracting ones. 4. *Social.* The indebtedness of happy family life, of prosperous national life, of friendship between man and man, to the weekly day of rest is unspeakable (cf. prize essay, ' Workman's Testimony to the Sabbath '). 5. *Spiritual.* What records have the sabbaths of spiritual blessing gained on and through the holy observances of that day? Sinners won to God, burdened consciences blessed with peace, tempted souls strengthened, sad and troubled ones made joyful in God, believers helped forward in the heavenly road, etc. All these facts attest the graciousness and the obligation of the command to hallow God's sabbath. And, on the other hand, its disregard has ever been followed by moral and spiritual and often secular deterioration. It has been ill with those who have set at nought this sure law of God. Therefore let us each one do what we may to preserve to our land the unspeakable blessing of the weekly sabbath. Better to err on the side of strictness in its observance than on the side of laxity. But let us not think that we have hallowed the sabbath unless the ends for which it was designed have been secured by us. It is but a means, not the end, and, unless it have furthered in us love to God and man, each sabbath as it returns is but a lost day.—C.

Vers. 5—8.—*Trust: human and Divine.* The prophet here presents before us a vivid contrast between two types of human character. He does this by the use of suggestive images drawn from the realm of nature, as one accustomed to see the great lessons of man's moral life and destiny reflected in visible forms in the sandy desert and sterile places of the wilderness, and in the fertile valleys and woody banks of the flowing river. The imagery is peculiarly Oriental. We can all appreciate it in some measure, but those who have seen the scanty, stunted vegetable growths of the desert side by side with the rich foliage that clothes the moist ravines and the borders of the water-courses, can best understand the exquisite truth and fitness of the analogies. Consider these two opposite kinds of trust—(1) *trust in man,* (2) *trust in the Lord.*

I. TRUST IN MAN. To " make flesh one's arm " is suggestive of personal reliance on merely human and earthly resources, in neglect of the spiritual and Divine. It takes the form of undue self-confidence—confidence in one's own wisdom and strength, or confidence in our fellow-creatures, who are as ignorant and weak and fallible as ourselves, or confidence in that which is outward and circumstantial—worldly riches, sensible gratifications, material guarantees. The features of such a trust are: 1. *Vanity.* Its hope is false and delusive. It has no sure foundation. It seeks life in the region of death. As the plant finds nothing to nourish it in the barren sand, so man can never draw the nutriment his being needs from mere human and earthly resources.

> " Unless above himself he can erect himself,
> How mean a thing is man ! "

And how can that which is fleshly, and therefore perishable, ever satisfy the necessities of an immortal spirit? 2. *Loss:* " He shall not see when good cometh." As the influences that come down upon it from the heaven above are lost upon the plant that is rooted in the desert ground, so this earthly trust robs a man of the power to use aright even the opportunities of higher good that are within his reach. Heavenly influences appeal to him in vain. He knows not the richer possibility of good that surrounds him, fails to apprehend it, cannot see when it cometh. 3. *Fruitlessness.* The "parched places in the wilderness" yield no solid food. Labour bestowed on them is profitless. Such is the "curse" that rests upon the man who makes the "arm of flesh" his trust—a vain hope, destitution of the good that might be his, a withered, wasted life.

II. TRUST IN THE LORD. Blessed is the man whose whole being is rooted and grounded in God. His is a life fed at the unseen and eternal fountains. "Your hearts shall live that seek God" (Ps. lxix. 32). The image of the "tree planted by the waters" is suggestive of certain important aspects of that life. 1. *Growth.* As the tree, by the mysterious prolific energy with which it is endowed, strikes its roots deeper, and spreads forth its branches over a wider space, so the freshness and force of Divine life in the soul manifests itself in ever-deepening, enlarging, heightening forms of moral and practical goodness. This is a matter both of Divine purpose and of natural organic tendency. Spirit-life, like plant-life, knows no stagnation. Where there is no growth there is decay. 2. *Beauty.* Of all the fair objects of nature, a well-grown tree is one of the fairest. The symmetry of its proportions, the blending in harmonious negligence of its forms and colours, the play of light and shade among its leaves and branches, all combine to make it the fitting type of moral dignity and loveliness. We cannot wonder at the graceful imagery of Hebrew poets and prophets when we remember how they dwelt in a land of olives and palm trees, of cedars and lign aloes and pomegranates. Godly character is supremely beautiful. The actual forms of religious life that one sometimes meets with are intensely displeasing. But these are caricatures, not just representations. Only as our piety is pleasing and attractive to men is it divinely true. "Whatsoever things are true, . . . honest," etc. (Phil. iv. 8). 3. *Strength.* Here is the idea of a resistive force. The tree, in the vigour of its life, is able to resist the pressure of unfriendly climatic influences. It fears not the scorching heat, or the driving blast, or the rushing torrent. It is as though it "saw" them not. All religious life is a conflict with difficulties. It flourishes just so far as it is able at once to appropriate the good and repel the evil that environs it. Christ gives "the spirit of power" to them that believe in him—power to overcome the most oppressive and the most seductive influences of a hostile world.

"Where is true faith, all change comes graciously."

And neither providential trials nor the assaults of evil can shake the steadfastness of him whose heart is thoroughly "established with grace." 4. *Productiveness.* "Neither shall cease from yielding fruit" (see also Ps. i. 3 ; xcii. 14). The fruit of the producing tree is the final development, the end and aim of its life. All religious thought and feeling, and all Divine methods of spiritual culture, point to this as their ultimate issue —the production of enduring forms of practical goodness. "Herein is my Father glorified, that ye bear much fruit" (John xv. 8). If Christ is our living root, there can be no limit to this process. The new-born soul knows no decay of its vital energies, but rather an eternal enlargement. "It gives, but still increases." The more it gives the more it increases. "As the outward man perisheth, the inward man is renewed day by day." And when death comes and cuts the body down and lays it in the dust, it only sets the spirit free to put forth the powers of its sanctified life in new forms of service in a nobler sphere, to bear fruit for ever in the paradise of God.—W.

Vers. 1—4.—*The profound impression of Judah's sin.* I. THERE IS IMPLIED JUDAH'S OWN INDIFFERENCE TO ITS SIN. With supernatural clearness of vision, the prophet saw the sin of Judah ; and he spoke concerning that sin with words which Jehovah had put into his mouth. And yet it is evident the people would not admit his representations as being correct and as needing urgent attention. The great bulk of them thought that he was inventing or at least exaggerating. They had lived so long amongst evils as to have become quite used to them ; nay, more, they made a pleasure and a profit of them. And this is just one of the great difficulties in preaching the gospel and trying to persuade men to repentance. They cannot be brought to see that there is anything to repent of; that, as far as the east is from the west, so far are they from being in a right state.

II. Over against this evident indifference there must be set the prophet's EMPHATIC STATEMENT OF THE HOLD WHICH SIN HAS UPON THE PEOPLE. That we do not see the evil of our life proves one of two things—either that there is no evil to see or that we are spiritually blind and cannot see the evil which there is. Now, spiritual blindness has for its usual concomitant spiritual pride; and the man spiritually blind is the very last who will admit that he is so. If we are left to ourselves we shall never discover the original cause and fountain of all our troubles; something outside of ourselves must come in and lead to an altered view of the purposes and possibilities of life. This is not the place to speak of all that is required to produce that alteration of view; but it is very plain that statements such as that of the prophet here must be helpful to produce it. Is it not a great matter for preachers to be able to fall back upon the thorough-going, uncompromising statements of the Word of God? For, though these may find no present practical response in the consciousness of the hearer, yet this very failure is a reason for repeating them over and over again, until in some critical hour the faculty is given of seeing ourselves as God sees us, which is a faculty much more to be desired than the one so often commended of seeing ourselves as others see us. Two things are here referred to—the inscribing instrument and the substance on which the inscription is made. There is a necessity for both in order to make a deep, abiding, noticeable impression. A pencil may make upon a stone a mark of some sort, but it is a mark very easily rubbed out; a pen of iron may write some great truth upon the sand of the seashore, but one wash of the rising wave sweeps it all away. But when you have the materials for a deep inscription, then something is produced which can only be destroyed by destroying that on which it is written. Little wonder was it that these people of Judah would not face the task of inspecting their hearts. Sin is so intimately mixed with the heart that you cannot get it away save by a process tantamount to the removal of the old inward life and the substitution of a new one. Hence the fitness of the petition, "Create in me a *clean* heart, O God, and renew a *right* spirit within me." But there is something more to show the hold which sin has on these people, and that is *the terrible effect upon their children.* A great many details might have been heaped up to show the reality of Judah's idolatry, but one crowning illustration was better still. Not even the most hostile to the prophet could well deny that the force which compelled them to inflict such cruelties on their children in the name of religion was a hideous force. Every evil, in default of ability immediately to see its real nature, must be measured by its worst visible effects. And this is just what the prophet does here, when he puts in the front of his accusation the sufferings of the little ones of Judah. As if these little ones had not enough of unavoidable pain to suffer, without suffering being sought out for them.

III. THE EFFECT OF ALL THIS DEEPLY ROOTED EVIL AS SEEN IN JEHOVAH'S CONSEQUENT INFLICTIONS. (Vers. 3, 4.) The people may cry, in professed amazement, "Why all these sufferings? What have we done that we should be treated in this way?" The answer is that all this spoiling, all this turning of the promised inheritance into a place not worth having, all this bitterness of exile, were not produced in some arbitrary, incomprehensible way. The prophet was not astonished at these judgments coming; he saw them approaching, and knew why they came. Great effects always have great and appropriate causes; and great causes, left to operate freely, will produce great and proper effects. Every human heart holds within it enough to make indescribable misery; and unless that greater cause which God offers to put in certain operation comes in with its counteracting force, we may be sure that indescribable misery will be produced. Wherefore let us pray that more and more we may have eyes to see and perceive, ears to hear and understand.—Y.

Ver. 6.—*The curse upon the man who trusts in man.* In considering this passage it is important to bear in mind that two different Hebrew words (גֶּבֶר and אָדָם) are rendered by the one word "man." A recollection of this difference will bring much more meaning out of the passage.

I. There is suggested for consideration MAN IN HIS OWN OPINION OF HIMSELF. He reckons himself as גֶּבֶר, the strong one. He likes to estimate his great resources and use

them for his own aggrandizement. He is filled with the ambition of achieving greatness in many ways. It is by his strength that he builds Babel and the Pyramids and
all the great structures of both ancient and modern times. He gathers great armies and
makes extensive conquests. He leans to his own understanding and is wise in his own
conceits. And it must be admitted that it is hard for a man in the full strength of
body and mind to take in, as a practical check upon all his castle-building, the necessary
weakness of human nature. The discovery of our weakness will always be a humiliating thing, at least in the first aspect of it. We do not like to relinquish the glory
which comes from physical strength, intellectual skill, in short, from the employment
of all those faculties enabling a man to achieve what is called a successful career.
Genius is semi-deified, while the Spirit of God working through some common man,
who would be nothing without that Spirit, is despised or neglected. Successful military and naval commanders are made into nobles with the general approval. Every
fresh application of natural forces is hailed as a tribute to the glory of mankind. Even
those who are not deceived by the coarser forms of human power are deceived readily
enough by the finer ones.

II. MAN IN GOD'S ESTIMATE OF HIM. This is set forth by a threefold indication of
man's folly and wickedness. 1. *He trusts in man ;* man as set forth by the word אָדָם.
The strong man is assuredly no stronger than that upon which he leans. A building
may be of substantial materials, but all its strength will avail nothing if the foundation
be weak. Mark that it is not a question of trusting in sinful and fallen men. God
does not find fault with us for trusting in bad men rather than good ones. He is speaking of all that essential defectibility, that susceptibility to temptation, which belonged
to man even before he fell. We might put the matter thus : Cursed is the man who
trusts in Adam, who forgets that he himself is beset with temptations, and that in a
moment of heedlessness and vain self-confidence he may fall into shame, confusion, and
perhaps despair. 2. *He makes flesh his arm.* All strength must act through an arm
of some sort. A great deal of human power makes itself felt in a very literal way
through the arm. Sheer strength in wielding the sword or the hammer ; skill, as in
holding the painter's brush, the sculptor's chisel, the musical instrument, and the
innumerable tools of all sorts of handicraftsmen. Thus the arm becomes a great representative, showing all the varieties of human strength in action. Now, where man
shows his folly is in this—that wishing to get his own way, to work out his own
pleasure and glory, he has no better instrument than flesh. What a poor, uncertain
creature man is, if he has nothing better to depend upon than his natural faculties !
The eye may lose its vision, the arm its strength, the hand its skill, and then where are
the schemes and projects of the ingenious brain ? The thing intended by God is that
man should be as an arm to carry out into action the wise and loving projects of the
Divine will. Then there is no failure, no disappointment. What cannot be done in
one way will assuredly be done in another, if only the will and counsel of God stand
supreme in our regard. 3. *His heart departs from Jehovah.* The great privilege given
to Israel was that they had been brought near to Jehovah. Fallen Adam had been cast
out of Eden, but believing Abraham had been drawn near to God. And his descendants in particular, the chosen nation in the wilderness, had been made to approach to
Jehovah, the great I Am, the Source of whatsoever strength and energy are to be found
in his universe. Thus, then, we see the peculiar folly of the children of Israel. All men
are fools because they trust in man and make flesh their arm ; but the Israelite is a fool
more than others because his heart departs from Jehovah. He cannot depart altogether ; he cannot get away from the constraints of the Omnipotent ; he must go
through all the sufferings that are coming upon the guilty land ; and even when he
departs to Babylon he will not leave Jehovah behind. What folly, then, that he does
not make an instantaneous clearance of his miseries by cleaving with purpose of heart
to Jehovah as Jehovah desires to cleave with fulness of blessing to him ! And let us
recollect that, however far from Jehovah our hearts may depart, from his judgments and
penal visitations it is impossible for us to depart.

III. THE CURSE WHICH RESTS ON ALL THIS MISTAKEN SELF-CONFIDENCE. Though
there seems some uncertainty as to the meaning of ver. 6, it is best for practical purposes to take it in contrast with ver. 8. If we plant ourselves down confidently among
our own resources, deceived by the smiles and attractions of first appearances, we must

not be astonished if in due time the appearances vanish and leave the cheerless realities of the wilderness. Where man by his natural vision sees the garden with all manner of rich possibilities, God teaches the believer to discern the desolation and barrenness that lie underneath. Gardens very soon become wildernesses if the heart of the cultivator departs from Jehovah. Men who in the days of their prosperity draw around them crowds of flatterers and dependents no sooner fall into adversity than they fall also into comparative solitude. The time is coming when, if we have nothing better than the help of man to trust to, we shall really have no help at all.—Y.

Vers. 7, 8.—*The blessing on the man who trusts in Jehovah.* I. MAN'S CLAIM TO BE RECKONED AS STRONG NEED NOT BE AN EMPTY ONE. He deserves the appellation of גֶּבֶר if only he will set the right way to obtain it. Weak as he appears from the point of view given, when his natural resources are fully opened up and tested, he may nevertheless become strong by the favour of Jehovah to perform the most extraordinary achievements. From one extreme where the strength of the godless is found to be but a mockery, we are taken all the way to another extreme, illustrated by the confident assertion of the apostle that he could do all things through Christ who gave him inward strength. We are every one of us meant to be strong with a strength which can meet the severest tests; and those who are the weakest in other respects often prove the strongest in spiritual life with what it requires both of activity and endurance. And it is of particular importance to be observed that the man weak of will, easily yielding to temptation, bound these many years by the chain of some dehumanizing habit, can be made strong enough to overcome his enemies and trample them under his feet. There is that in him which can be so renewed, so vivified, that he will become steadfast and energetic in attaining the Divine purpose of existence. Recollect the instance of the man who was above forty years old when his feet and ankle-bones received strength. Jesus of Nazareth did not bring this about merely for this man's physical benefit; but chiefly that those who were inwardly lame should be stimulated to seek him, and have the feet and ankle-bones of the inward man strengthened for a holy and a truly manly service. God must needs pour contempt upon the boastings of the natural man, in order that, when he has effectually humbled him, he may then exalt him into the possession of true strength.

II. THE REQUISITE FOR THE ATTAINMENT OF TRUE STRENGTH IS POINTED OUT. Pointed out clearly and simply. He is the strong man who trusts in Jehovah, and he is strong just as far as he does trust. Notice how the requirement of trust is expressed twice over, first by a verb and then by a noun, both of which have the same root-letters. It is as if we first saw the man in the active exercise of trust, and then the habitual confidence of his nature. We see the man trusting and we also see the trusting man. "All things are possible to him that believeth." When God speaks, the trustful hearer readily acts upon the strength of God meaning what he says. The statements of the gospel transcend human powers of discovery, and they can only be believed because God makes them—he whose regular and beneficent ways in nature prove him to be so true. Man by faith puts himself in the hands of God, his Maker, and then he can do things far beyond what he has hitherto imagined to be practicable. Look at the sublimest illustration of this ever given upon earth; when the man Christ Jesus believingly said, "Father, into thy hands I commend my spirit." Then, in a very few hours, the strength imparted even to the dead was revealed by the resurrection of Christ.

III. THE ILLUSTRATION OF HOW THE BLESSING COMES. Possibly there is here a reference to some regular practice of the foreseeing planter of trees. The necessity of planting trees near water-courses is not obvious to us, seeing that in our moist climate we often see noble umbrageous trees far enough from anything of the kind. The children of this world are wise in their generation. They bear in mind—they have to bear in mind—the scorching heat, the rainless, cloudless heavens, or, if clouds there be, too often waterless clouds, mocking, tantalizing beauties of the sky; and so they plant their trees where they may stretch out their thirsty roots to the passing stream. And yet these same children of this world, prudent for their trees, may yet be foolish for themselves, taking up a position in life admirable for the gaining of temporal ends, but leaving at a great distance the river that flows from "the throne of God and of the Lamb." Thus there is here a lesson from the tree which cannot choose to the man who can choose. We all have our choice of the *essentials* of position. There are two sets of circumstances—those we cannot choose and those we are bound to choose. It is in the power of us all to be planted by the waters. God's gifts of grace flow through fixed and well-defined channels, and to these we must go. We are not allowed to make compromises. A very little seeming difference may, in reality, make all the difference between wisdom and folly in this matter. It did not need that the tree should be planted very far away from the water, a few yards more or less might determine the result. There is also in this illustration the notion of a hidden means of supply. To outward appearance there is no connection between the tree and the river; the connection is underneath, and it is real, increasing, and constant.—Y.

Vers. 9, 10.—*The searching and knowing of the heart.* One is reminded here of the oft-quoted piece of advice, "Know thyself." The prophet's assertion places man before us as the victim of self-ignorance, self-confidence, and self-deception. He talks of truth when his mind is full of error, and thus he is prevented from taking the only real way by which he can attain to the knowledge of truth. In the prophet's assertion and question, and the Divine answer given to the question, there is much which upon the first aspect may humiliate. But the humiliation will itself prove a cause for rejoicing if only it leads us to profit by God's certain knowledge in matters when we are profoundly ignorant.

I. THINK OF THE VAST AND INCREASING EXTENT OF HUMAN KNOWLEDGE. If a man be ignorant of his own heart it surely cannot be because he himself is unfitted for the knowledge. He may have become unfit, and the unfitness may, by neglect, become more pronounced, but he cannot be unfit by reason of his original constitution. One may say that God must have intended him to have sufficient knowledge to keep his inward life right. Otherwise we have this curious contradiction—that man has achieved an immense amount of knowledge with respect to his physical constitution, but is doomed to remain in uncertainty and bewilderment as to the laws of a healthy and a happy inward life. "Who can know the heart?" says the prophet. And yet even with the limited knowledge of his age there were many men, doubtless, who knew many things. We all have the powers of observation, comparison, and experiment, and it is the largest pleasure of some minds to exercise these powers. And yet it is just to minds that are most trained, most confident in the principles of science, and most stored with the results of it, that this question might be put. It is not a question for the child just beginning to learn or for the savage unaccustomed to think; let it be put to man in his highest civilization, and then the fact will be seen that the question is no vain and inappropriate one.

II. Thus we are led to notice THE DREADFUL IGNORANCE WHICH MAY PREVAIL IN THE MIDST OF ALL THIS KNOWLEDGE. The progress of the world does not make the prophet's question one whit less pressing. Nay, it becomes more pressing than ever. Other objects of knowledge have an ever-increasing light cast upon them, and by the very force of the contrast man's inward life appears in still deeper darkness. Whatever the cause of the continued ignorance may be, that ignorance does continue, so far as man's unaided effort to remove it is concerned. In one single mind we too often see exemplified vast intellectual knowledge and complete spiritual ignorance. He who seems to know everything does not know his own heart, and apparently does not care to know it; reminding one of the man who had travelled over the whole world and yet had never beheld a scene as wonderful as any which was visible from a point on his own estate. The time is coming when knowledge will vanish away. But the neglected heart will still remain to force itself, in a way which cannot be resisted, upon the thoughts of its long indifferent possessor.

III. THE CAUSE OF THIS IGNORANCE IS MADE PLAIN. It all lies in the deceitfulness and utter corruption of the human heart. And notice in particular that it is by the heart that the heart is to be known. Heart-knowledge is not like other kinds of knowledge; it depends on the character of him who knows. There is no *essential* contradiction between high intellectual acquirements and a hard, selfish, and perhaps even, in some instances, a profligate life. Men of refined tastes and great intellectual sensibilities may be thoroughly selfish, careless about the toil and suffering of the world, so long as these plant no thorn in their pillows, infuse no bitterness into their cup. But one who would know the heart must be very sure of his own motives, otherwise he may make human nature to appear better in some respects and worse in others than it really is. The description here may, therefore, be taken as applying even more forcibly to the heart that knows than to the heart that is to be known. Here the great difficulty and danger lie. For the deceitful and corrupt heart can be known, if not by any one else, at all events by Jehovah himself. But the deceitful and corrupt heart cannot know; it does not, in the fullest sense of the word, know anything at all. With hearts put right, what a wonderful increase of knowledge and of the profit and pleasure of knowledge will there be! But till then we are not unlike those who suffer from diseased intellects. They come into great contrast with sane people from the way in which their minds get filled with hallucinations and incongruities. And so, if we try to compare ourselves in our notions of things with Christ's teaching, we shall see the difference between the view taken by a sincere sound heart, such as was that of our Lord, and the view taken by corrupt, deceitful hearts, which ours are and must be till we discover the need of a new and pure life to be put into them.

IV. GOD'S PERFECT KNOWLEDGE STANDS IN THE PLACE OF OUR IGNORANCE AND ERROR. God knows us in all our motives, through all our concealments, and can set our secret sins—the operation of destroying causes that lie even below our consciousness—in the light of his countenance. When once we discover how competent God is to search and try, we shall then see that it is vain for us to deny what he affirms, to excuse what he condemns, and to make out that we are not responsible when he lays evil at our doors. Jeremiah's scornful audiences may have said to him, "How come you to know *these* things about us? How come you to be so uncharitable as to bring these dreadful charges?" But then we know that they were not the prophet's own charges, but came from God himself. It was part of Jeremiah's grief that, on Jehovah's authority, he should have to believe things so bad of his nation. What God did to Israel was just; and more and more, as time went on, it was seen to be just. In all great exhibitions of Divine wrath we must be silent, recollecting that God knows what we cannot know, and perceives necessities where we can perceive none.—Y.

Ver. 11.—*Riches wrongly gotten, and the consequence.* Here is an instance of an illustration which, so far as our knowledge is concerned, is more obscure than the thing to be illustrated. But there was, no doubt, with regard to some bird a popular opinion which made the prophet's reference very suggestive to his hearers. The fact supposed is that some bird gathers the young of other birds, despoiling the nests of the real parents, only to find, when the young ones get sufficiently strong, that they can no longer be kept to its nurture and control. Whether there was a real fact corresponding matters very little. If we want a familiar and sufficiently corresponding instance, we may find it in the not unfrequent one of a hen hatching a brood of ducklings, only to find how soon their alien nature is manifested when a pool of water comes within reach. Note—

I. THERE IS A RIGHTFUL GETTING OF WEALTH. External property occupies a position of approval in the Old Testament which is denied to it in the New. All the way through the New Testament the perils and deceptions attaching to mere external wealth are strongly insisted on. If not condemned *per se*, which of course is not possible, it is yet put forward as a heavy burden and perpetual stumbling-block to the Christian who has it. But in the Old Testament that very wealth is magnified, doubtless as a symbol of those better riches which would appear in something of their proper glory and satisfying power through the energetic ministrations of Christ's Spirit. God saw fit for a time to recognize ability, industry, and integrity in a way which would be plain to the most carnal of men. Take Job, for instance. And even in the New Testament a sharp line is drawn between wealth gotten honestly and that which came by extortion and cheating. There is a standard of integrity recognized by the natural man; and God also recognizes this standard, so far as it goes. Miserably short does it fall of his appointed height of perfection, but it is better than nothing. Those who fall short of even the moderate requirements of their fellow-men God will condemn. On them he will set an unmistakable mark. But in order to do this there must be some sort of modified approval of those who, in seeking wealth, strive to keep their integrity and refrain from doing that which may degrade and impoverish their fellow-men.

II. The peculiar uncertainty of ill-gotten wealth. All external wealth is uncertain. "Riches take to themselves wings and flee away." They furnish one of the most impressive testimonies to the instability of terrestrial society. But ill-gotten gains are peculiarly unstable. Every rich man is envied, and few such escape slander. But he who becomes rich by unscrupulous methods has to lay his account with hostility on the part of all whom he has spoiled. Methods of unjust gain cannot but provoke the resolute, persevering, and ultimately successful opposition of all who hate injustice. Recollect the sudden and complete loss which came to the slave-holders of America, when their slaves were freed as a matter of military necessity. It is true that unjust gains seem to be often as stable as just ones; but still the peculiar uncertainty remains. A Christian possessing external wealth bears in mind the uncertainty of it, just as he bears in mind the uncertainty of his own natural life; but the heaper-up of *filthy* lucre has to reckon, not only with the perils of all human life, but also with those inseparable from his own evil courses. In some great storm, fatally threatening the ship of state, such a one may have to be thrown overboard, Jonah-fashion, in order to secure the safety of the rest.—Y.

Vers. 12, 13.—*An inspiring invocation.* We must take ver. 12 as invocatory rather than indicative. The prophet speaks suitably in the language of apostrophe as he refers to the throne of Jehovah and the holy heights where he dwells. "O throne of glory, height of beginning, place of our sanctuary!" It will be felt that this apostrophe is well fitted to make the Hope of Israel a source of real hope in the hearts of Israel.

I. The throne of glory. This may be taken as having, by contrast, a double reference. He who sits on this throne is the Deity, Jehovah; hence all the seats of the Gentile gods may in like manner be considered as thrones. And because he who sits on a throne is reckoned as a king, there is also a contrast with human kings. This reference to the throne of glory amounts, therefore, to a condemnation of all idol shrines and human thrones as places to be ashamed of. The shrines were richly decorated and regarded with the utmost veneration, but this did not make them glorious. The practices of those connected with the shrines and the character of the worshippers showed that instead of glory there was shame. It has been the mark of all who have turned from formal idolatry or from the equally real idolatry of a worldly spirit to the living God, the God of Sinai and the tabernacle, of Calvary and of Pentecost, that they have become more and more ashamed of their ungodly past. Its defilement and unworthiness have been seen in a new light and with new eyes. When the slave becomes a freeman, servitude is more and more seen to be inexpressibly degrading. And so with regard to the thrones of human kings: these are just the places where human selfishness and pride are most conspicuous. To see how base and fiendish a man can become, we have only to select from the occupants of thrones. It is not meant that kings have been worse than common men; but their elevated position has both enlarged their opportunities for mischief, and also exposed them to the gaze of all succeeding generations. A Tiberius or a Nero gets an immortality of infamy, whereas an obscure villain of the same age passes swiftly into oblivion. Those kings who have really glorified thrones did so only as far as they were viceroys to him who is the King of kings. Human thrones may or may not be thrones of glory so far as glory can belong to the creature. Jehovah's throne must be glorious seeing that it is for ever transfigured with the effulgence of him who sits thereon.

II. The height of beginning. "In the beginning God made the heaven and the earth." It is man coming in afterwards who has misemployed and degraded what God fashioned with certain Divine and supremely beneficial ends in view. Out of that which God has made for *his* glory man raises up things to glorify *himself.* The proudest system of idolatry, the system most deeply rooted in the hearts of millions, is but of yesterday when compared with those heavens which are God's throne and that earth which is his footstool. Measured against this height of beginning, the most ancient of human families is only an upstart. It is like the mushroom of a night when set over against some immemorial tree. The abode where and whence the glory of Jehovah is manifested is not a Babel edifice, which, however *high it may rise,* is humiliatingly conditioned by the unstable foundation on which it rests. Human power, at the summit of its splendour, has traversed and conquered large tracts of the earth; and so kings get the name of great; but the greatness is only a momentary, unsubstantial swelling. Their power, like that of the sudden torrent, swiftly passes away. One can imagine how the prophet, while he talked of this height of beginning, looked to the heavens, so unaffected by all the strife and pride of the generations which succeed one another in this lower world. Jehovah has not climbed through long struggles to his height of glory. There may be evolution and graduation among the creatures of his hand, but such conceptions of progress are nothing less than blasphemous when we try to apply them to him.

III. THE PLACE OF OUR SANCTUARY. The place which God had condescended to make holy in his special connection with Israel—the place where the ark of the covenant rested—had become also a place (the history of Israel being witness) where the people of Israel might have every confidence in God. The temples of idols had not an invariable connection with the triumphs of their worshippers; but just in proportion as Israel honoured the ark of the covenant and the God of the ark, in the same proportion they were made to see the effect of their conduct in triumph over their enemies and success in their own affairs. It was because they forsook the ark that they themselves were forsaken in humiliation, adversity, and shame. Not, of course, that the prophet is thinking of the ark only here. The true place of sanctuary is also in his mind—the invisible abode of the invisible Jehovah.—Y.

Ver. 13.—" *Written in the earth.*" I. AN INDICATION OF WHY MEN DEPART FROM GOD. "Those who depart from Jehovah," says the prophet, "shall be written in the earth." Therefore we conclude that their aim is to be written in some more durable and trustworthy substance. When they are spoken of as departing from God, the description is one accommodated to our thoughts rather than exactly correspondent with reality. The connection has been *real* so far as mere opportunity and privilege were concerned, but *nominal* also, because the opportunity and privilege were never seized. God has drawn near to the man; the man has not been inclined to draw near to God. It has seemed to him that in drawing near there would be such a subordination of self as would amount to self-effacement. The lusts of the natural man are everywhere checked and contradicted by the commandments of God. Hence man strives to get away from God and into such relations with his fellow-men as will, he thinks, cause his name to be counted for more. It may be that it is self-glory he is seeking for; to have his name deeply graven on the world's memorial tablets as one who has achieved much and stood out like a Hercules from the common crowd. It may be that he hopes for great power; to have his name written on the hearts of thousands whose interests will be bound up with his so that they cannot succeed if he fails. It is very gratifying to the pride of man to feel that others cannot do without him.

II. THE SURE RESULT OF DEPARTURE FROM GOD. Men go away from God expecting to have their names written in the marble, and a very short experience shows that they are written, as it were, on the most shifty of all materials. From a certain point of view, nothing seems more irregular than the preservation of what was written in ancient ages. Deep letters on hard stones are long faded away, while characters written on parchment or even paper survive to this day, and are now watched with an attention which bids fair to preserve them for many a year to come. But every one can see that what is written in the earth must, in the very nature of things, be quickly obliterated. Such writing may be the amusement of a child; it could never be the serious occupation of a man. And yet it is just by this figure that the folly of apostates from God is set forth. They write their names on a spot exposed to the trampling crowd of their fellow-men; and in their own selfishness they forget of how little account they are to others as selfish as themselves. And yet, in spite of such a warning to those who depart from God, they go on complaining because men forget them. It is just the way in which they must expect to be treated. It is the way of the world. After all, we are but weak creatures, with very limited powers, and we may well be excused if we cannot keep constantly in our minds those who have some claim on our sympathy and help. It is no fault of earth that it is earth instead of adamant. The fault lies with those who allow their names to be written there instead of in the enduring place which God has provided for them.

III. THE EQUALLY SURE RESULT FROM CLEAVING TO GOD. Though not stated in so many words, it is cheeringly implied that those cleaving to God have their names written whence they can never be erased. For their names are indeed written, as it were, on the heart of God himself. He cannot either forget or forsake them. They are ever remembered in the wisdom of his thoughts and the resistless movements of his ways. The best thing that can happen to us in purely human relations is to be written in the hearts of those who love us; when they remember us, not because it is their interest to do so, but out of an unselfish fulness of desire for our welfare and happiness. But how much better is it to be thus remembered by God, seeing that with him there abides a love inexpressibly deeper than any human affection, and, along with this love, a wisdom and power with which even the highest human wisdom and power are not for a moment to be mentioned!—Y.

Ver. 14.—*He whom God heals is really healed.* I. THE CONSCIOUSNESS OF INDIVIDUAL NEED. The prayer is "heal me;" "deliver me." The prophet shows how deep and pressing is his own need by the use of two figures. He feels the need of something being done internally and externally. Internally he is sick at heart, wounded and bruised in spirit. He needs healing from the state of mind produced through being despised and rejected by his fellow-countrymen. Still worse is the gnawing pain produced as he views the wickedness of the land and takes knowledge of the steadily advancing calamities. But we cannot doubt that beyond all this there was the consciousness of his own heart's pollution and unworthiness. So far as natural constitution and natural tendencies were concerned, he who spoke was no better than those to whom he spoke. Thus, in trying to waken others from their lethargy, he became more thoroughly wakened to his own state. The word which God had put into his mouth was spoken, not only to the outside audience, but down to his own sinning and ignorant heart. God cannot take for prophets and apostles those who care little about their own spiritual need. Paul became a better apostle because he reckoned himself, in such sincerity, the chief of sinners. It ought to be no marvel that those to whom we speak are indifferent to their state, if we who speak to them are largely indifferent to our own.

II. THE VANITY OF SEEKING ELSEWHERE THAN TO GOD. The very confidence which Jeremiah expresses that, if only God heals him, he will be truly healed, seems to indicate that he had some experience of other modes of healing, such as had looked very promising at first, but proved utterly vain in the end. As a general rule, we have to be disappointed in human agencies of healing before we can be satisfied with the Divine one. It cannot be said that the nature and depth of the disease are adequately discovered, until we discover, from experience, how vain human resources are against it. We may be able to mitigate symptoms, to deaden pain, to rouse into a temporary cheerfulness; but in the end the relapse is certain and more confirmed than ever. It was a great thing for the prophet to be brought to feel, as he evidently was, that anywhere else he went would be with the probability of failure. With God there is not only the certainty of success, that success is *with him alone.*

III. THE PROPHET'S CONFIDENCE IN GOD AS A HEALER. The way in which he expresses this confidence is most worthy of notice. His confidence is, not that God will do something for him, but that whatever God does will be adequate for the end in view. It is much to feel that one may count upon Divine sympathy and effort; it is still more to feel that whatever help God gives will rise to the intensity of the need. He who gives the spirit of conviction, working deep in the natural heart and showing its diseased state and defiling, polluting activity, gives also the spirit of a real healing. The great ground of apprehension arises, not from the magnitude of the spiritual disease, but from the indifference of the sufferer and his indisposition to submit his heart to God's searching, healing power. The moment we are willing to submit ourselves to the great Physician, that moment the worst disease becomes a manageable and a virtually conquered thing. The course of the healing process may be long, tedious, and painful; but what matter these, if the end be perfect healing and everlasting health?—Y.

Ver. 15.—"*Where is the word of the Lord?*" I. THE PRETEXT AND AIM OF THIS QUESTION. The prophet's subsequent comment on the question shows with what bitter hatred to him it was asked. Sad, indeed, it is to reflect that these very words might be asked in a far different spirit; that they might come from the depths of an ignorant seeking heart, wandering long amid idolatries and human systems of philosophy, without hearing anything to serve as bread of heaven for the deep hunger within. There are people upon whom God's Word has been pressed in every variety of appeal and representation. The Word has sought them out again and again; and yet in the end all they can do is to cast a scornful doubt on whether it is the Word of God at all. It may, indeed, be allowed that they did not mean to insult Jehovah; all they had in view was to express, in the most stinging way, their bitter hatred of this pertinacious, plain-spoken prophet—this man who had come as a comparative youth from little Anathoth, rebuking those who were high in rank, old in years, and looked up to by the bulk of the people. No fallacy infecting the regions of practical life is more pernicious than that which, professing to admit the authority of him who sends, yet discredits the status of his professed messenger. It is thus very easy to evade unpleasant, humiliating messages. So the Jews of our Lord's time were fanatically solicitous to honour their conception of Jehovah, and, as part of this devotion, they ended by crucifying Jesus as a blasphemer. The very people who asked, "Where is the word of Jehovah?" may have been the first to frame plausible repudiations of any wish to blaspheme him. Their great aim and purpose was to put this upstart Jeremiah in his proper place. They probably thought that these scornful speeches might become at last as a gag in his mouth. The lesson is plain: do not reject truth, or in any wise try to evade it because it comes through some one you do not like. What Jeremiah said here, respecting the character and work of these men, was true; and they do not deny the truth. They simply ignore the charges, and by one scornful question hint that the threatenings connected with the charges are but as empty words.

II. THE WAYS IN WHICH THIS QUESTION MAY BE ANSWERED. Jeremiah, we perceive, has his own answer appropriate to his individual circumstances. He falls back on his integrity. God knows the fidelity and obedience of his heart. God had put into his mouth the words he had spoken. They did not rise out of his personal feeling; they were not the breathings of an egotist, a fanatic, a madman, an enemy of his country. But inasmuch as this question is ever being asked by a certain class who will not believe in a Divine plan of the world—partly revealed in Scripture and the partial execution of which is shown in history—it is well to remember how Jehovah has honoured his servants who have had in any way to fill the office of prophets. He who has gone forth to threaten the persistently impenitent has never been without some achieved judgment of God which he might adduce as an illustration. The shadows cast forward into the future have their correspondences in the substances belonging to the past. If we could only summon out of the invisible world the generation which perished in the Flood, the dwellers in the cities of the plain, Pharaoh and his army, those who were destroyed in the gainsaying of Korah, and many others, they would be able to give no uncertain answer to the question, "Where is the word of Jehovah?" The kingdom of God is not in word only; it has in it a power which can be manifested in all needful abundance, with all needful rapidity, and in whatever aspect may be proper to the occasion. God's Word becomes a complete and plainly perceptible deed exactly when the time is ripe. Shall man be able to arrange a time-piece so that when the hour hand and minute hand together point to twelve there shall be the striking which signifies noon has arrived; and shall not God be able to order the mysteries and complexities of the world so as to bring out the intended results just when he wants them? It is not for us to know times and seasons; but most emphatically it is for us to believe that every word of God is true. These very scorners of Jeremiah were about to add, in the course of a few short years at most, an illustration as forcible as any that what God has spoken may be taken as already done. God's calm advancing of his kingdom should do much to make his people calm. It is our fault if the sarcasms of the unbelieving become anything more than words; and mere words are best met by a silent, patient, and believing continuance in well-doing.—Y.

Vers. 16—18.—*The prophet's consciousness of integrity.* We may take it that this one question, "Where is the word of Jehovah?" stands for a great deal in the way of taunt. The appeal to God, with which the prophet follows up the mention of this question, shows how much he felt the attacks made upon him. It would be too much to say that he did not expostulate with his enemies upon their injustice; but evidently his great resort was to the God who had sent him. If men perversely attributed to him daring imposture and bitter malignity, he could do nothing but fall back on God's knowledge of his course and motives. Four points are noticeable.

I. HIS OFFICE AS A PROPHET WAS NOT THE RESULT OF DISCONTENT WITH A PREVIOUS OCCUPATION. He had not hastened from being a shepherd. He was perfectly willing to have continued as a shepherd at Anathoth. It was not he who, looking out on the larger world, had wished to become conspicuous on a busier scene. He left his sheep because God had called him, as he called Moses, David, and Amos. It is true that, if a prophet would do his work *ex animo*, he must choose it; but first of all he must be chosen. It must be made perfectly plain to him, in a sober, wakeful moment, when all the faculties of life are collected, that *he, and not some other person*, was called to this work; to *this work*, and not to some other work. The office of a prophet, with all its toils, sufferings, perils, and temptations, was assuredly not an office to be grasped at. It needed that one should count the cost. We are not told much of the earlier history of the prophets, but some of them, at least, must have known long periods of discipline. For Jeremiah to say that he had not hastened to be a prophet really means that he had gone into the work with great deliberation, slowly and steadily following where God slowly and steadily walked before him. There is no haste in God's dealings, though in crises there may be suddenness and rapidity of action; and therefore there can be no haste with those who are the instruments and messengers of God's dealings.

II. THE REPUDIATION OF EVERYTHING LIKE PERSONAL MALIGNITY. He was *compelled* to speak of a calamitous day, but he spoke as one whose inexpressibly painful duty it is to break bad news. Moreover, it was bad news which concerned him as much as every other member of the nation. He was not a mere outsider, looking on with pity at events which did not concern him individually. The calamities of his native land, although he might be free from their worst effects, could not leave him altogether unsmitten. Doubtless there were moments when he, like Paul, could have wished himself accursed for his brethren's sake. His feelings when he had to speak of impending calamities would be of the same kind (not, of course, so pure and intense) as those which Jesus had when he apostrophized Jerusalem, rushing to its fall, and careless about the things which made for its peace. Terrible truth may be spoken very tenderly and beseechingly. Juries find verdicts condemning to death, and judges pass the corresponding sentences, which they would all of them gladly escape if fidelity to truth and duty left an open way. That tenderness which shirks duty because of present pain and difficulty, often proves in the end to be the worst of cruelty.

III. THE WORDS OF THE PROPHECIES ARE EXPRESSLY ATTRIBUTED TO GOD. It is a natural course to hold a man responsible for all that comes from his lips. The prophet could not escape this responsibility. It was not his to complain that his auditors challenged him as the constructor of these unpalatable speeches. If they looked to him, he in turn did the wise thing, the only thing that could be done—he looked to God. He was able to do this because he had been faithful. He had not garbled or mutilated his message to make it more tolerable. He understood perfectly well what, nevertheless, many fail to understand, that truth depends, not on what men are able to understand, but on what God clearly reveals. The prophet was in no manner of doubt as to the authority by which he spoke. Looking back and reviewing his utterances, he was perfectly sure that he had not confused his own thoughts with the commanded words of Jehovah. If what God reveals for us to speak, we speak; and if what he reveals for us to believe and act upon, we do believe and act upon; then with the utmost confidence we can go to him for support and defence. What could Jeremiah have done in his extremity if he had not been conscious of his fidelity as a prophet of God?

IV. GOD KNEW THE TRUTH OF ALL THAT THE PROPHET WAS ASSERTING. "Thou knowest." God knew his servant's heart; knew the sincerity and simplicity of his service. It was of no use arguing with men. Either they were unable to discern how true and apposite were his words, or, discerning, they were not willing to make a corresponding acknowledgment. But where men were ignorant God had perfect knowledge; where men were indifferent God showed the deepest interest. Hence the prophet could look to him confidently for continued support and ample vindication. Rightly considered, there is nothing revengeful or merely personal in ver. 18. We may well believe that the prophet's great anxiety was that the truth of Jehovah should be honoured, even though it might be by terrible judgments upon despisers and unbelievers.—Y.

Vers. 19—27.—*The hallowing of the sabbath day.*   I. THE PLACE FOR ANNOUNCING THE MESSAGE. 1. *It was a place where the king, as much as the people, would hear.* Whatever else may be signified by "the gate of the children of the people," it seems clear that it was a gate in which, at certain times, the king would be found. In his own house it might be impossible to gain access to him; but the gate was open to all; and there he could not choose but listen to a man who would speak earnestly and commandingly; because the word of Jehovah lodged in him, came from the depths of his concurring heart. The kings, doubtless, by their own individual leadership and encouragement, were responsible for much of the evil of sabbath-breaking. The state of Jerusalem in particular would be largely influenced by them. A corrupt court makes a corrupt capital, and a corrupt capital is not without effect towards the making of a corrupt nation. 2. *It was the place for the greatest general publicity.* One gate is specified, but not one of the gates was to be omitted. The king, with his peculiar responsibilities, was warned in a peculiar way; but there was no one in such a private and irresponsible position as to be without concern in the message. The ten commandments were commandments for every individual among the people; hence the need of a warning which, in the mode of giving it, should be likely to arrest the attention of all. It was Jehovah's message delivered at least as many times as there were gates in Jerusalem. We may well believe that it was delivered over and over again. No note of time is given, but of course the prophet would choose the time when there were most passengers; nor would he omit to deliver the message upon the sabbath day itself. 3. *The message was given upon one of the most conspicuous scenes of transgression.* If the prophet went to one of the most frequented gates on a sabbath, there he found transgressors, crowds of them, in the very act of transgression. They could not deny the act, and all he needed to do was to adduce the commandment against it. God can always make it clear that he does not send forth his prophets without occasion.

II. THE MESSAGE ITSELF. This command with respect to the sabbath day seems to come in very abruptly here. And yet no one who considers the prominence of Jehovah's injunction to "remember the sabbath day to keep it holy" will wonder at the definiteness and emphasis of the prophet's message. The details of his message make it only too sadly evident how far the people had departed from the original commandment. Here we have one of two extremes of disobedience in which the practical attitude of Israel towards this commandment appears. The sacred day which God had hallowed both in word and deed was recklessly and shamelessly made into a common day. If a stranger went into the streets of Jerusalem on a sabbath, he might have great difficulty in discerning by any external sign that it was a sabbath. The people would be going into the city and coming out of it much as on any other day. The other extreme is seen in the reasonless and fanatical formalism of the Jews, who so often attacked our Lord. There is certainly a great difference *externally* between these two extremes. It is very wonderful to consider that such a transition should be possible from the careless crowding of the gates with burdens on the sabbath, to the savage bigotry which attacked Jesus for healing sick folk on the same day. Yet underneath external differences there was the same unabated, worldly, ungodly spirit. Those whom Jesus had to denounce for their shameless trafficking in the holy precincts were the children of those whom Jeremiah had to denounce for doing their own selfish will and needless acts on God's sabbath. And so we see that this passage from the prophet needs to be considered along with those passages in the Gospels where Jesus deals with the sabbatarianism of his time. His painful experiences of such professed honourers of God, and his searching exposures of them, need to be complemented by this message of Jeremiah. We shall always find in Scripture something to check us from "the falsehood of extremes." Sabbatarians twist a commandment; sabbath-breakers trample it underfoot. The evil which Jeremiah deals with here is dealt with even more solemnly by Ezekiel (xxii. 1—12, where in ver. 8 sabbath-breaking is particularly referred to as one of many terrible transgressions. See also Neh. ix. 14; xiii. 15—22; Isa. lvi. 2; Ezek. xx. 12—24; xlvi. 1—5).—Y.

EXPOSITION.

CHAPTER XVIII.

This chapter is the introduction of a group of prophecies (extending to ch. xxv.) of various dates; their sequence has evidently not been determined by chronological considerations. The prophet's first object is, perhaps, to refute the scoffing inquiry (ch. xvii. 15), "What has become of the [threatening] word of Jehovah?" and to justify the glorious promise given at the conclusion of the last chapter. The fulfilment of threatenings and promises alike is conditioned by the moral attitude of the people (comp. Ezek. xxxiii. 11). God, as it were, holds them in either hand, and there is still time (contrast ch. xvi. 21) to choose the sweet and reject the bitter by sincerely turning to their true Friend. Unhappily the people misuses its day of grace, and, instead of listening to God's messenger, seeks to rid itself of him by persecution. Upon this, Jeremiah falls again into the tone of bitter complaint, and, so far from interceding for his people, does the very opposite; on which painful and mysterious phenomenon, see remarks in general Introduction.

Vers. 1—6.—The simple and familiar craft of the potter becomes a parable of religious truth (comp. Isa. xxix. 16; xlv. 9; lxiv. 8; Ecclus xxxiii. 13; Rom. ix. 20; and the account of man's creation in Gen. ii. 7, which has doubtless given rise to the figure). God has the sovereign right to do as he wills with his own handiwork; thus much can be expressed by the figure. But the moral element in Jeremiah's teaching stands outside this, viz. that the Divine action is governed, not by mere caprice, but a regard for character. "The thought is not so much the arbitrariness as the patience of God, who will bring men to be what he would have them be in the end, as the potter eventually twists the clay to the shape he originally intended, stubborn as the clay may be." But whether Jeremiah meant the lesson which Mr. Maurice deduces from his words may be gravely doubted. It is not of individuals that the prophet is thinking, but of the nation, and not of the nation as destined to be all but certainly saved, but as placed before a serious and awful decision. (For different lessons derived from the same figure, see the 'Rabbi Ben Ezra' of Browning.) Egypt and Palestine were, as it seems, at one in the extreme simplicity of the potter's art. Dr. Birch has given us an account of the Egyptian potter at his work, as he appears in the pictorial representations at Beni Hassan ('Ancient Pottery,' pp. 33—35), and Dr. Thomson has described the procedure of a potter in modern Palestine ('The Land and the Book,' p. 520). The chief difference between them seems to be that in Egypt the wheel was turned with the left hand, and the vase shaped with the right, while in modern Palestine the wheel is turned with the foot. "Taking a lump in his hand," says Dr. Thomson, "he placed it on the top of the wheel (which revolves horizontally), and smoothed it into a low cone, like the upper end of a sugar-loaf; then thrusting his thumb into the top of it, he opened a hole down through the centre, and this he constantly widened by pressing the edges of the revolving cone between his hands. As it enlarged and became thinner, he gave it whatever shape he pleased with the utmost ease and expedition." It should be observed that in ver. 3 the "wheels," or rather "two wheels," spoken of are simply the two round plates which formed the horizontal lathe of the potter.

Ver. 4.—**And the vessel that he made,** etc.; rather, *And whensoever the vessel . . . was marred in the hand of the potter, he made it again another vessel.*

Vers. 7, 8.—At what **instant,** etc.; rather, *One instant I may speak . . . but if that nation, against which I have spoken, turn from their evil, I repent of the evil that I thought to do unto them.* A similar rendering for the next verse.

Ver. 12.—**And they said;** rather, *But they go on saying* (comp. Ezek. xxxiii. 17, 20). **There is no hope.** The rendering may be easily misunderstood. The speakers are not, as we might suppose, despondent about their state and prospects, but they seek to check the troublesome preacher by the warning that he has no chance of success (so ch. ii. 25). **Imagination;** rather, *stubbornness* (as constantly).

Ver. 14.—**Will a man leave the snow of Lebanon,** etc.? This passage is unusually obscure. Literally we must, it would seem, render, *Doth the snow of Lebanon fail from the rock of the field* (or possibly, *cease to flow from the rock unto the field*)? This is explained as pointing a contrast to the infidelity of God's people. "The snow never leaves the summit of Lebanon; the waters which take their rise therein never dry up; but my people have forgotten the law of their being, the source of their prosperity." The rendering of the first clause is, however, grammatically dubious (there is no example of this construction of *'āzabh*), and all the old versions point to (or at least favour) a reading, *Shaddai* (the Almighty) instead of *sādai* (the field). If we keep the text, we must explain "the rock of the field" on the analogy of "my mountain in the field" (ch. xvii. 3), as meaning "the rock which commands a wide prospect over the open lowland country," *i.e.* Mount Lebanon. **The cold flowing waters;** *i.e.* the numerous "streams from Lebanon," referred to in Cant. iv. 15. **That come from another place;** *i.e.* whose sources are foreign. But as this does not suit the connection, it is better to take the Hebrew word (*zārim*), usually rendered "foreign," in the sense of "pressing or hurrying along," with Ewald, Graf, and virtually Henderson. It thus becomes descriptive of these streams "as contracted within narrow channels while descending through the gorges and defiles of the rocks." Comp. "like an onpressing stream," Isa. lix. 19 (a cognate verb). **Be forsaken.** The Hebrew text has "be plucked up" (*i.e.* destroyed?); but as this is unsuitable, we must transpose two letters (as in not a few other cases), and render, *dry up.* So Gesenius, Graf, Keil, Delitzsch, and Payne Smith.

Ver. 15.—Because my people hath forgotten me; rather, *Surely,* etc.; or better still, *Yet surely.* It is not uncommon for a particle of asseveration to acquire a contrasting force from the context; see *e.g.* ch. iii. 20; Isa. liii. 4; and, still more completely parallel, Isa. ii. 6; ch. ix. 1, where Authorized Version, with substantial correctness, has "nevertheless." Israel "forgot" Jehovah (as ch. ii. 32); no doubt he was responsible for so doing, but still it was not "of malice prepense." **To vanity;** *i.e.* to the unreal idol-gods. **And they have caused them to stumble;** viz. the idol-gods; these are responsible (for they have a real existence in the consciousness of their worshippers) for this interruption of Israel's spiritual progress (comp. 2 Chron. xxviii. 23). **In their ways** from the ancient paths. "From," however, is interpolated by the Authorized Version; the Hebrew places "the ancient paths" in apposition to "their ways."

"Stand ye in the ways," Jeremiah cried at an earlier period, "and see, and ask for the old paths, which is the good way" (ch. vi. 16). These "old" or "ancient" paths were ideally "their ways," the ways appointed for the Jews to walk in. **To walk in paths;** rather, *in tracks,* footpaths leading up and down and often ending in nothing; or, in other terms, in a way not cast up (Isa. xl. 3, 4, gives a graphic picture of the operation of "casting up a way").

Ver. 16.—The effect of this is to make the land of the transgressors an object of horror and *astonishment* (so render rather than **desolate**).

Ver. 17.—As with an east wind. The east was a stormy wind (Ps. xlviii. 7; Job xxvii. 21). **I will show them the back; as** they have done to Jehovah (ch. ii. 27; xxxii. 33).

Vers. 18—23.—A fresh conspiracy (comp. ch. xi. 18), called forth by the preceding discourse; Jeremiah's prayer.

Ver. 18.—The law—or rather, *direction, instruction,* which was a special function of the priests (Deut. xxxiii. 10; xvii. 9—11) **—shall not perish from the priest.** The Jews were but obeying the Deuteronomic Law (on which Jeremiah, as we have seen, laid so much stress) in alluding to the priests. Unhappily, the priests in Jeremiah's time (ch. ii. 26), as in Isaiah's (Isa. xxviii. 7), were forgetful of their high mission. **Nor counsel from the wise.** The wise men formed an important order in Jewish society, the importance of which in the Divine education of Israel has not been sufficiently recognized. It was their custom to sit in public places, generally in the chambered recess in the city gate, and give advice on questions of moral practice to those who applied for it. But there were wise men and wise men. Some appear to have "mocked" at the earnest preaching of the prophets (hence the solemn rebukes in the Book of Proverbs), others to have as it were prepared the way for the latter by a more or less distinct recognition of the religious foundation of morality, and of these we have ample monuments in the canonical Proverbs. There may also have been other shades and varieties of wise men, for their characteristic was not a faculty of intuition, but rather of reflectively applying fundamental moral principles. One highly esteemed branch of "wisdom" would, of course, be political, and this would be the most liable to perversion. It is of such that Isaiah, like Jeremiah, says that "the wisdom of their wise men shall perish" (xxix. 14). **Nor the word from the prophet.** "The word" is a general term for prophesying. Of course, the speakers take no account of the advance in prophecy from the time, at any rate, of Amos. They are satisfied with the lower order of prophets ("false prophets," as the Septuagint calls them); but still they are afraid of Jeremiah, much as Balak was afraid of Balaam, when that soothsayer was blessing Israel (Numb. xxiii. 25). **Smite him with the tongue**; *i.e.* by slanderous accusations. The same figure as in ch. ix. 3, 8.

Vers. 19, 20.—**Them that contend with me. Shall evil,** etc.? Compare the phraseology of Ps. xxxv. 1—12 (either Jeremiah imitated this psalm or *vice versâ*); and for another point of contact with this psalm, see on ch. xxiii. 12. **They have digged a pit,** etc. Comp. Ps. lvii. 6. **To speak good for them.** See Jeremiah's intercessions in ch. xiv. 7—9, 19—22.

Ver. 21.—**Pour out their blood by the force,** etc.; rather, *spill them into the hands of,* etc. (see Ps. lxiii. 10); a phrase akin to that in Isa. liii. 12. The sword is personified. **Let their men be put to death;** another personification, for the Hebrew has "slain of Death"—pestilence is referred to, as ch. xv. 2.

Ver. 23.—**Let them be overthrown before thee;** *i.e.* count them as those who have been brought to ruin. This explanation seems required by the parallelism, the companion clause meaning "do not regard their sin as cancelled." The ruin may be either spiritual or temporal; the parallelism favours the former (comp. ver. 14; Hos. xiv. 10, where "fall" should be "stumble"). **Deal thus with them.** "Thus" is interpolated by the Authorized Version; "deal" should rather be *deal terribly* ("deal" is constantly used in a pregnant sense; see on ch. xiv. 7).

HOMILETICS.

Vers. 1—6.—*The potter and the clay.* The relations of the potter to his clay afford a familiar and apt illustration of the relations between God and his human family. At first sight this illustration suggests a harsh view of providence and a hopeless prospect for human endeavour. But on closer consideration, while it teaches lessons of humility and reverent submission on our part, it also throws light on the merciful goodness of God, and encourages us both to hope and to act for that which will lead to our highest blessedness.

I. MEN ARE UNDER THE ABSOLUTE POWER OF GOD, LIKE CLAY IN THE HANDS OF THE POTTER. The potter has power to leave the clay untouched or to make out of it either a vessel of honour or a vessel of dishonour, a beautiful vase or an ugly piece of crockery, a dainty cup for a prince's banquet or a coarse culinary utensil. God has absolute *power* over us. He is the Almighty. No man can eventually succeed in resisting the will of God. No Divine purpose can be eternally frustrated. God has also absolute *authority* over us. He has the ultimate right of supreme sovereignty to do as he will with his subjects. Yet there is nothing alarming in this fact, but rather an infinite consolation. For God is not a heartless, conscienceless despot, displaying arbitrary power by mere caprice; he is holy, and exercises his sovereignty according to principles of strict justice, truth, and right. He is gracious, and rules with purposes of love for the good of his creatures. Our dependence on God is, like that of the infant on its mother, the security of our own welfare. Those horrible applications of the doctrine of Divine sovereignty which attribute to it designs that would be accounted cruel in any responsible being are blasphemous insults to the impartial justice and love of God's character. If God's actions are not limited by any physical compulsion or constitutional law, they are governed by his regard to eternal righteousness and by the beneficence of his nature.

II. MEN CAN NO MORE ATTAIN A WORTHY END IN LIFE WITHOUT GOD THAN THE CLAY CAN BECOME A SHAPELY VESSEL WITHOUT THE POTTER. There lies the clay—a dead, heavy, amorphous mass, with no possibility of spontaneously generating forms of beauty, with no secret principle of evolution to work it into something orderly. We are as clay. Except God wrought in us and upon us, we could simply lie helpless, only to waste away with the flux of circumstances. If we are more than clay, it is because God breathes his life into us and sustains us every moment by his indwelling Spirit. If we seem to effect anything actively, it is because he first works in us both to will and to do.

III. GOD HAS A PURPOSE IN EVERY LIFE AS THE POTTER HAS WITH THE CLAY. There is a meaning for the strange discipline of providence. God is shaping us into that form which he deems most fitting. Every life has not the same purpose. The potter makes vessels of innumerable shapes. Yet each life is successful as its own particular purpose is fulfilled. The homely jug may be perfect, though it is very different from the graceful vase. A life is no failure because it is lowly and put only to lowly uses so long as it attains the end for which God designed it. It is important to note that God's first work with us is in forming our own souls aright. The first question is not as to what we do, but as to what we are. The potter is making vessels ; God is making characters, souls, lives. After *this* we may be put to some further end —used for good after we have been made right, as the vessel is of service after the potter has done his work with it.

IV. GOD SHAPES OUR LIVES BY THE DISCIPLINE OF PROVIDENCE AS THE POTTER THE CLAY UPON HIS WHEELS. The wheel of time spins fast, but not carrying us away, changing but not destroying each separate individuality. In providence there are wheels within wheels. We do not understand their meaning. The clay is pressed now below into a solid base, now above into a dainty rim, but it is difficult to see what the final outcome will be till all is finished. So our lives are pressed on one side and on another—something which in our eyes is indispensable is taken away, something which to us seems needless is added. But out of the dizzy whirl, the rush and confusion of life, God is steadily working out his purpose.

V. GOD WILL ULTIMATELY ACCOMPLISH HIS PURPOSE IN US, THOUGH AT FIRST IT SEEMS TO FAIL. (Ver. 4.) The clay is refractory. It must be broken up and remodelled. Man is more than clay. He has free-will, mysterious as may be the connection of this with the almighty sovereignty of God. In a much more terrible way he too is refractory, wilfully and stubbornly. For this he must be broken. His life must be disturbed and shaken up, but only that God may begin again to fashion him for his destined end. Great disappointments, destructive events, the failure of a man's work, the disruption of a Church, the revolution of a nation, may seem simply disastrous. But we see how that by means of these things God, in his infinite patience and gracious perseverance, will finally effect his own great purposes, and so secure the true blessedness of his creatures.

Vers. 7—10.—*God's action determined by man's conduct.* These verses may be read as balancing those that precede. The illustration of the potter at his work shows us simply the Divine side of life. The following verses take us round to the human side, and the human conditions in accordance with which God exercises the rights and power of his absolute sovereignty.

I. GOD DETERMINES HIS ACTION ACCORDING TO THE CONDUCT OF MAN. He does not act blindly, inconsiderately, on general principles alone, without regard to individual cases, nor with one changeless course irrespective of the changes in the behaviour of his creatures. He takes note of these changes and modifies his treatment of men by their varying requirements. 1. This fact is not derogatory to the *absolute sovereignty* of God. A just sovereign considers his people. God acts according to his own will; but his will, though inflexible in moral principles, varies in the choice of particular actions according as the application of those principles varies with the circumstances of the world. 2. This fact is not inconsistent with the *definiteness of the purposes* of God. The potter has his definite design, yet he proceeds with his work to the conclusion or breaks up the clay and begins again, according as he finds it plastic or brittle.

II. A CHANGE ON MAN'S PART FROM REBELLION TO PENITENCE WILL BE MET BY A CHANGE ON GOD'S PART FROM WRATH TO MERCY. God's threats are conditional. Forgiveness is the result of no after-thought, of no change in the " temper " of God. It is contemplated by God from the first, and promised on condition of repentance whenever repentance is genuinely experienced. Therefore there is every encouragement to repentance and hope. The darkest denunciations of judgment refer only to the impenitent. It is not too late to expect the forgiving mercy of God, so long as it is not too late for us to repent. This is reasonable, since the end of punishment is not vindictive but remedial. The mere paying of a penalty is of no good in itself. It might please a vain and vengeful despot, but not a merciful father. If the restoration of his child is effected without it the father will gladly acknowledge that it is needless.

III. A CHANGE ON MAN'S PART FROM FIDELITY TO APOSTASY WILL BE MET BY A CHANGE ON GOD'S PART FROM MERCY TO WRATH. This is a necessary consequence of the preceding principles. God's promises are as conditional as his threats. It would be neither just nor merciful to us for God to continue his favours unabated after we had departed from him. The removal of them is a wholesome warning to us. It springs naturally from the personal relation of God to his people, one which depends on reciprocal sympathy. Therefore it is vain to presume on our past experience of God's goodness·for immunity from the consequences of our later sins, or to suppose that a happy condition of peace with God once attained can never be lost. We may lose it and be in a worse condition than if we had never had it (Heb. vi. 4—6).

Ver. 12.—*Rejected preaching.* I. THE BEST PREACHING MAY BE REJECTED. Jeremiah was a true messenger of God and an able preacher, yet he was unpopular. Christ, who "spake as never man spake," was "despised and rejected of men." No greater mistake can be made than to judge of the value of any preaching by the popularity of it.

II. IT IS THE DUTY OF THE FAITHFUL PREACHER TO BEAR HIS TESTIMONY EVEN IF IT BE REJECTED. He must not be unfaithful to his mission in order to catch the ears of his audience, nor must he silence his voice because it is unheeded. His duty is to speak, whether men will hear or whether they will forbear. If he loyally discharges this duty his conscience is clear.

III. THE REJECTION OF THE PREACHING OF TRUTH IS OFTEN TO BE ATTRIBUTED TO THE PRIDE OF INTELLECT. People have their "own devices." Divine truth does not require the contradiction of intellect nor the suppression of it, but it requires the submission of intellect to well-grounded faith in a God who is worthy of trust, even when he requires our acceptance of dark and painful doctrines.

IV. THE REJECTION OF THE PREACHING OF TRUTH IS OFTEN TO BE ATTRIBUTED TO STUBBORNNESS OF WILL. The Jews are represented as saying, " We will every one practise the stubbornness of his evil heart." The excuse of intellectual doubt may be sought as a cloak for moral aversion to Divine truth. Many who have no doubt of the truth of the message of the servant of God refuse to accept it from sheer opposition to its spiritual requirements.

V. THE TRUTH PREACHED IS NOT AFFECTED BY THE REJECTION OF IT. If the word would be true when accepted it would remain true when rejected. We cannot alter facts by closing our eyes. If we refuse to hear the words of faithful admonition, we shall not escape the doom against which they warn us, but only the more surely run into it. We shall then simply rush blindfolded to meet our fate.

VI. THE REJECTION OF THE PREACHING OF DIVINE TRUTH IS ITSELF A GREAT SIN. If the truth is recognized as Divine, rejection of this is rejection of the voice of God. It is an act of direct resistance to the will of God. It is sinning against light. It is refusing to accept offers of mercy, and returning insult for favours.

Ver. 14.—*Mountain snow.* Any one who has found himself in the valley of Chamounix on a sultry summer afternoon must have felt the striking contrast between the eternal winter of the vast snow-fields of Mont Blanc, spread out in blazing sunlight high above his head, and the dust and heat of the parched land around. The permanence of this mountain snow is suggestive of spiritual lessons.

I. MOUNTAIN SNOW IS AN EMBLEM OF SPIRITUAL LIFE MAINTAINED IN THE MIDST OF WORLDLY SCENES. Mountain snow is found in the hottest countries. You need not travel to arctic regions for perpetual snow, it may be found in the tropics. Christians need not be transported to heaven in order to live a pure Divine life. The duty of the Christian is to preserve this fresh and holy in the midst of the world, not to flee from the world. By remaining in the world the Christian is a means of blessing it as the mountain snow descending in glaciers and streams refreshes and fertilizes the valley. But the Christian's mission to the world is dependent on the preservation of his unworldly spirituality, as the refreshing streams that flow down the gorges of the mountain are dependent on the snows high above them. If the snow fails the stream is dried up. If the spirituality fails the Christian work becomes barren.

II. MOUNTAIN SNOW IS AN EMBLEM OF SPIRITUAL LIFE MAINTAINED IN THE MOST

TRYING TIMES.   The remarkable fact about the mountain snow is that it is perpetual. It is nothing that there is snow on the hills in winter; are not the plains then equally snow-clad?   The Christian who only remains faithful under favourable circumstances is but superficially religious.   The difficulty is to be true when all things are adverse, in the heat and burden of work, under the fierce onslaught of temptation, while the spirit of the age is against us, when Christianity is out of fashion, out of season.   Yet we are to be instant out of season as well as in season (2 Tim. iv. 2), to be independent of the weather, of the social atmosphere, in the changeless purity of a spiritual life.

III. THE CAUSES OF THE PERSISTENCE OF MOUNTAIN SNOW ARE SUGGESTIVE OF THE CAUSES OF THE PRESERVATION OF THE FRESHNESS AND PURITY OF THE SPIRITUAL LIFE.   How is it that we find snow in the tropics, snow in summer?   1. *Great elevation.* A few thousand feet in height will produce climatic changes equal to those caused by a distance of many degrees of latitude.   The Christian must find his fidelity preserved by elevation of life.   He must live on high, a risen life, with affections above the earth, with a treasure in heaven, and his heart there also.   By constant communion with heaven constant purity on earth may be maintained, as the silent solitudes of snow remain through the summer in the cool regions of their great elevation.   2. *Constantly renewed supplies.*   The snows melt under the sun and send roaring torrents down the hillsides, and in course of time they would disappear unless they were renewed. But clouds gather round the mountain summits and descend in fresh snows, and winter on its return makes up for the partial loss of snow in summer.   So the Christian must maintain his spiritual life, not only by the elevation of his own thoughts, but by receiving repeated supplies of heavenly grace.   He may be thankful that he is favoured by " times of refreshing " when the fierce heat of trial is abated, and strength is accumulated for the time of need.

Ver. 18.—*The opposition of officials.*   I. IT IS COMMON TO SEE OFFICIAL PERSONS RESISTING THE WORK OF GOOD AND GREAT MEN.   The prophets usually met with this opposition, and it forced them to become nonconformists.   Christ received the most bitter enmity from the official classes.   This opposition may be traced (1) to *pedantry* —the official only believes in what comes in the regular way of officialism; (2) to *jealousy*—the official is jealous of the greater influence of the unauthorized teacher; (3) to *conviction of unfaithfulness*—the true prophet exposes the faults of his official contemporaries.   The inevitable result is discredit and shame to them, rousing a spirit of revenge.

II. THE OPPOSITION OF OFFICIALS FINDS EXCUSE IN OFFICIALISM.   Have they not their appointed office?   Are they not discharging their regular functions?   They have been so accustomed to the unbroken routine that this seems to them part of the eternal order of things.   They can believe in nothing better.   They cannot conceive the possibility of any alteration in it.   True, the spirit of the Law has evaporated from the service, but the droning of the letter of it shall not depart from the priest.   The wisdom of spiritual insight is no longer enjoyed by the wise man, but there is no end to his casuistical pleading with old worn maxims.   Prophecy in its higher flights is denied to the professional prophet, but there seems to be no abatement of the power to echo the cries of the day and win the popular favour by flattery and hollow rhetoric.   Why, then, listen to the disturbing words of the new teacher?   Thus officialism is always excusing its opposition to new good movements on the plea of its own self-sufficiency.

III. THE OPPOSITION OF OFFICIALISM IS POWERFUL FOR HARM.   For how many scenes of martyrdom is it responsible!   It was this that crucified Christ.   It has peculiar weapons of its own.   It carries the weight of prestige.   It is very effectual with the thoughtless, who are ready to submit to the voice of the recognized authorities, partly out of indolence, partly out of fear, partly out of ignorance.   It needs independence of thought and courage to recognize that this may be all wrong, and truth and right with the irregular minority—the peasant apostles rather than the haughty Sanhedrim, the plain German monk rather than the cardinals of Rome, the simple teachers of truth rather than the recognized masters of the world.

HOMILIES BY VARIOUS AUTHORS.

Vers. 1—10.—*The potter and the clay.* The revelations of God are often given in unlikely places, and common circumstances and scenes may symbolize the divinest mysteries. The profoundest things in God's universe are side by side with the simplest. If the mind be open and the spirit susceptible we shall see God in everything. Is there not a fitness in this ancient handicraft of the potter becoming the symbol of the eternal action of God? The potter's clay suggests —

I. THE INFLUENCE OF GOD UPON HUMAN DESTINY. Some of the forms into which human life builds itself impress the imagination with the presence of a power greater than human, which conditions and determines them. The race, the nation, the Church, represent relations and affinities which are not of merely human origin. But even the individual life, if properly studied, will be found to be associated with the same mystery and full of the same suggestion of a Divine influence. In the case before us it is the Jewish nation which is suggested to the mind of the prophet. The hand of God is apparent in its formation and history. God's influence upon these is felt to be (1) *omnipotent*, (2) *sudden*, (3) *irresponsible*, (4) *to create or to destroy.*

II. CIRCUMSTANCES IN HUMAN NATURE THAT AFFECT DESTINY. The clay in the hand of the potter was marred and had to be remoulded. The allusion here was to the idolatrous practices of the Jews in Jeremiah's own time. The causes at work, therefore, in the marring of the vessel are not mechanical or constitutional in their nature, but moral. The history of the same people has shown that external circumstances are of little account in this question. The chief hindrances to God's purposes with man in nations, institutions, and individuals arise from (1) *original depravity* and (2) *wilful disobedience.* The free-will of man may thwart even the grace of God.

III. THE PURPOSE OF GOD WITH REGARD TO MAN. This is essentially and persistently a creative one. The first effort of the potter is formative; and when, through the marring of the vessel, he has to reduce the clay into the lump again, there still remains an intention to form anew. The effects of sin are shown to be profound from the fact that the potter is obliged to remake what has been marred. The effort of restoring love succeeds upon another, and "where sin abounded grace did much more abound" (Rom. v. 20). There is no nation which has not had many opportunities of recovering its position and influence forfeited by unfaithfulness and unbelief, and there is no sinner hardened in his sins who has not repeatedly rejected a heavenly voice. Each proclamation of God's Word is a fresh opportunity which may avail for salvation to every one who will embrace it.—M.

Vers. 11, 12.—*The fatalism of the wicked.* The conception of God's judicial omnipotence furnished in the parable of the potter is misinterpreted by the wicked. It is made a reason for continuing in their sin, they arguing that it is their fate, or needs be, to follow in the path they have chosen.

I. IN THIS WE HAVE AN ILLUSTRATION OF THE POWER OF EVIL HABIT. Sin has acquired such influence over the nature that it becomes its ruler. A recklessness born of desperation takes the place of prudent and hopeful counsels. The inward indisposition colours the view that is taken of the possibilities of the situation. Instead of the sinner seeing that his condition is due to a continual withdrawal from God, he declares that he is "past feeling," that God's grace cannot save him, and that it is "no use." But—

II. IT IS NOT JUSTIFIED BY: 1. *The condition of God's opposition.* It is the perverseness and unreality of man. He refuses to suffer. False religion God will not accept. 2. *The circumstances of the sinner.* So long as life continues there is hope. The repetition of the gospel's appeal has the same significance. Are there any signs of relenting in his mind now? any stirrings of heavenly aspiration? any shame and sorrow for past sin? God's Spirit has not ceased to strive with him, and he may yet be saved. 3. *The means of salvation that offer themselves.* Christ is both able and willing to save. His sacrifice on the cross is a finished work and a complete atonement for our sin. "The Spirit helpeth our infirmities." He is able to save "unto the uttermost," etc.

III. IT IS A SUPREME EXPRESSION OF WICKEDNESS AND WILL BE PUNISHED AS SUCH. —M.

Vers. 14, 15.—*Jehovah an unfailing Help to his people; or, the " snow of Lebanon."* One of the most striking scenes visible from a great distance is Hermon, with its snow and vapours. It is covered with white snow all the year round, and from its summits flow down cold, pent-up streams to the valley beneath. God asks why Israel has forsaken him; whether there was any failure of his grace and power. Has he not been constant and ever ready to help? How is it, then, that he is forsaken? The snow of Lebanon is, like the dew of Hermon, a symbol of the grace of God abiding upon Zion, from which the streams of grace flow forth in inexhaustible supply.

I. THOSE WHO FORSAKE GOD DO SO BECAUSE OF THEIR OWN PERVERSITY AND NOT BECAUSE OF GOD'S NEGLECT. " Is his arm shortened that it cannot save?" is a question we ought to ask ere we make up our minds to leave God. The secret of spiritual disaffection and apostasy is in ourselves and not in God.

II. APOSTASY FROM GOD IS A TRANSCENDENT INSTANCE OF INGRATITUDE. 1. The providences of God have been unceasing, manifold, and overflowing. They have come without effort of man. Yet the sinner has gone away and obstinately continues in his sin. 2. But in the grace of God there are elements that appeal to our deepest affection and trust. It is so rich, undeserved, and free. Why should he have chosen any one? How often has he healed the backslidings of his people! The cross of Christ is the grandest expression of love of which we know. It " passeth knowledge."

III. WHEN SINNERS FORSAKE GOD IT IS TO THEIR OWN INJURY. 1. *By their pursuit after sinful gratifications they forfeit the enjoyment of Divine mercy.* Providential mercies may not always be withdrawn, but their beneficial effect is destroyed. The fellowship and presence of God are lost. His favour and help cannot be expected. 2. *The sources of pleasure they apply themselves to are disappointing and fatal.* Sinful pleasures soon pall. There is no enduring rapture in the gratification of sense, but an enduring sting remains. The constitution of the sinner is sapped and undermined by his excesses, and the general, social, and political life of the nation corrupted. There is no sorrow so profound and incurable as that which results from the abuse of religious privileges and the loss of the heavenly birthright; it " worketh death." But, in addition to all this, the anger of God is kindled, and who shall extinguish it? He himself can. With him is forgiveness that he may be feared, and plenteous redemption that he may be sought unto. " His mercy endureth for ever." It is only needed that we change in heart and life to recover our lost estate and experience again more than our lost joy.—M.

Ver. 18.—*Ecclesiastical succession versus individual ministry.* The spirit of these words is not hard to divine. " We have a succession of priests, teachers, and prophets assured to us by our traditional institutions; so there is no great loss if Jeremiah be discounted; and we need not fear the cessation of the Divine revelation,—is it not provided against by a sacred succession?"

I. THERE ARE MANY WHO BELIEVE IN THE OFFICE OF THE MINISTRY AS AN INDEPENDENT SOURCE OF INSPIRATION AND TRUTH.

II. THIS IS ALLEGED IN EXCUSE FOR: 1. *Refusing support to special religious effort.* 2. *Contempt and opposition of individual ministers.*

III. IN CORRECTION OF THIS ERROR MAY BE NOTED: 1. *That it is not countenanced by God.* 2. *History has frequently shown its falsehood.* 3. *It is really a reliance upon the human and not the Divine.* 4. *God does his special work nearly always through individuals.* 5. *The dishonour done to the servant is done to his Master.*—M.

Vers. 18, 19.—*The preacher's foes; or, false tongues and deaf ears.* I. THESE OPPOSE MORE OR LESS EVERY TRUE MINISTRY. The persecutors of Stephen " stopped their ears and ran upon him."

II. THEY ARE AN INDIRECT TESTIMONY TO THE TRUTH AND FAITHFULNESS OF THE MESSAGE DELIVERED.

III. THEY MAY RETARD, BUT THEY CANNOT STIFLE, THE DIVINE MESSAGE. The slander can be lived down.   The voice of just men done to death will speak when they are dead.   *Magna est veritas et prevalebit.*

IV. THERE IS A SILENT WITNESS WHO SHALL TAKE ACCOUNT OF ALL.   1. *It is of less consequence to us that men approve and attend than that God should do so.*   The preacher addresses not only a visible, but an invisible, audience.   Of every word that proceeds from his servants' lips God takes note.   2. *He will protect his servant until his work has been accomplished.*   3. *The slanders and indifference of those to whom the Word is spoken will be punished.*   (Matt. xii. 36, 37.)—M.

Vers. 1—10.—*The blessed parable of the potter and the clay.*   Few passages of Scripture have been more misread or with sadder results than this one.   From St. Paul's reference to it in Rom. ix. it has been thought that it taught the absolute sovereignty of God, his right to dispose of men as he pleases; that, in the exercise of that sovereignty, he makes some vessels unto destruction, and that the vessels so made have no ground of complaint whatsoever.   Now, we affirm that, whilst there is much truth in these representations, they are not "the whole truth," still less are they "nothing but the truth."   God is Sovereign, we cheerfully confess, and has right to dispose of us as he will.   But that he exercises these rights in any arbitrary, or capricious, or cruel way, as is taught by this misreading, or that if he did the vessels made for destruction would have no ground of complaint, we altogether deny.   Such teaching has clouded the face of God to many souls and made God our Father "a terror" to them.   But blessed be his Name, this misreading is not the truth.   Let us try to see what that truth is.   In passing, we may note how the command to the prophet to go down to the potter's workshop teaches us how workshops and our common work may have precious lessons about God to teach us if we be like as was the prophet, willing to learn them. The star-studying Magi were led by a star to Jesus.   The centurion by his soldier-life gained true comprehension of Christ.   The fishermen-apostles of how they were to be "fishers of men."   Manifold are the ministers and ministries of God to attentive souls.

> "There is a book, who runs may read,
>   Which heavenly truth imparts;
> And all the lore its scholars need,
>   Pure eyes and Christian hearts."

That is said of the book of nature, so it may be of the book of our lawful work.   Now let us go down to the workshop told of here and learn what we may.   And we are taught—

I. THAT "IT DOTH NOT YET APPEAR WHAT WE SHALL BE."   *We* are the clay.   But who can tell what is to be fashioned out of that mere mass of material?   Every human soul is but as clay in process of formation into some designed result.

II. GOD HAS WISE AND GRACIOUS INTENT IN REGARD TO ALL.   The meanest vessel that the potter makes is an advance in worth and excellence on the clay ere it was fashioned by him.   How much more, then, in the case of the "vessels of honour"!

III. BUT THE CLAY CAN FOR A WHILE MAR AND FRUSTRATE THE POTTER'S PURPOSE. The vessel the prophet saw was marred in the making.   What innumerable instances there have been and are of this!   Not Israel and Judah alone, but other nations, other churches, innumerable separate souls.   And they have had to be broken up and set down from the place of honour for which they were at first intended.   They have with shame to take a lower place.   But—

IV. EVENTUALLY THE MAKER'S WILL WILL BE DONE IN REGARD TO THEM.   "So he made it again another vessel, as seemed good to the potter to make it."   It is never "all the same" to a man if he sins against God.   He may not be destroyed, but his will be "another" position and a worse one.

V. AND ALL THIS IN HARMONY WITH THE NATURE OF THE MATERIAL WROUGHT UPON.   As the potter's work was in harmony with the clay out of which he fashioned his varied vessels, so God's work will be in harmony with the mental and moral nature which he has given to us.   It is to us an inexplicable problem—the harmony of the Divine sovereignty and human freedom.   We cannot tell *how* it will be done, only that it *will* be done.

VI. THE LESSONS OF THE WHOLE ARE: 1. *Of inquiry.* Are we, by obedience to the Divine will, furthering the work designed in us or by disobedience hindering? Ver. 9 teaches that, however good and gracious a purpose God may cherish concerning us, if we " do evil" then God's work will be marred. 2. *Of admonition.* Seeing how terrible a process is the " making again" of the marred vessel—what was it not to Judah and Israel? and the process is not finished yet—let us repent of sin and turn to God now, and so be delivered from so great a woe. It has been said that the most terrible part of the road to heaven is that which the sinner goes over three times— once in his first following of Christ, next when he by sin goes back that way, and the third time when in bitter repentance he travels over it again. 3. *Of praise* to God, that he has revealed so gracious a purpose concerning man, and that his will shall be done. 4. *Of prayer,* that we may be found not resisting but ever obedient to that will.—C.

Vers. 8—12.—*A never-to-be-forgotten principle of interpretation.* These verses plainly teach that all God's threatenings, even the most terrible, and all God's promises, even the most blessed, are *conditional on the continuance of the moral character to which they were addressed.* Now, this is—

I. A CORDIAL AGAINST DESPAIR. When the convicted sinner—as the men of Nineveh—hear the awful denunciations of God's judgment, all hope seems to be forbidden. The Ninevites, to encourage themselves in a forlorn hope, could only say, " Who can tell whether God will be gracious?" But this and the like Scriptures, confirmed by so many facts of experience, forbid all such despair.

II. A CHECK TO PRESUMPTION. How many prate concerning final perseverance who are not persevering at all except in sin and worldliness? But they need to be reminded of this sure condition, one which the great adversary of souls is ever striving to make us forget.

III. AN EXPLANATION OF THE STERN WORDS OF SCRIPTURE. When one would give the alarm of fire he does not whisper the word. So when God would warn sinners he does not soften his words, but in most vivid manner sets before men the awful doom of the ungodly. Thus would God, by his terrors, scare men—if naught else will do— to " flee from the wrath to come," so that " he may repent of the evil he thought to do unto them." Such words are not the utterance of absolute decrees against any soul to whom they are addressed, but loving warnings to such soul to turn to God and live.

IV. A REASON FOR ITS WORDS OF WARNING. These are found in varied form, addressed to disciples of Christ, to those to whom the most glorious promise had been made. See the sermon on the mount; how full of warnings! Therefore this conditionalness of God's words speaks: 1. *To the believer,* and bids him " Be not high-minded, but fear." " If God spared not the natural branches, take heed lest he also spare not thee." 2. *To the ungodly.* See the sure end of thy way: how awful! But see, too, God's earnest desire that thou shouldest forsake that way.—C.

Ver. 12.—*Despair, its causes, consequences, and cure.* " And they said, There is no hope," etc. There is a show of humility about this word. The man has evidently no hope in himself, nor in any Church, nor in any human help whatsoever. Now, this so far so good. To get men away from trusting in an arm of flesh is ever one of God's purposes. And when a man is thus weaned from self and all human reliance it is a good sign. But such distrust at times goes beyond this, to belief that there is no hope anywhere, which is despair. Now, this a sore evil (cf. homily on ch. ii. 25, " A dread snare of the devil "). And to help in overcoming it we would speak—

I. OF ITS CAUSES. They are of varied kinds, but a man is near to despair when he sees: 1. *That his sin is inveterate.* When year after year goes by and still there the sin is. 2. That it is *continually successful* in reducing his will to consent to it. 3. That his defences are only those derived from considerations of the consequences and punishment of his sin. Motives of love to God and Christ, hatred of the sin itself, have ceased to rule him; it is only the fear of what may happen that holds him back, though, indeed, such defence is weak enough. 4. That his sin has rendered ineffectual many special dealings of God with him in regard to it. He has broken through all these gracious barriers one after another. All these are dreadful facts to contemplate, and tend to fill a man with the belief that " there is *no* hope." The good Lord forbid that we should ever have such facts to contemplate concerning ourselves.

II. ITS CONSEQUENCES. They are dreadful in the extreme. They produce *sullen obstinacy* in evil. "They said . . . but we *will* walk after our own devices." Also *unrestrained licence.* The thought comes, " We can but be lost; we will have what enjoyment we may." This is a frightful fruit of despair. If, then, any considering these dread consequences of despair tremble lest they should yield to it, but yet by reason of such facts as those above named are sore tempted thereto, let them remember there *is* deliverance for them. Consider, therefore—

III. ITS CURE. It can only be, it ought only to be, by good hope of deliverance from that which is the cause of thy despair—thy sin. But whence can come this deliverance? Wise and godly men have counselled after this manner. 1. Seek to gain and keep before the mind a deep sense : (1) Of *the guilt* of thy sin. You who have received such light and grace are involved in far deeper guilt and your sin is far more heinous than that of others. (2) Of *the danger* of it. The danger of being hardened by its deceitfulness. Of bringing down on thyself some great temporal judgment as God's punishment of thy sin. Of losing thy peace with God and strength to serve him. Of eternal destruction. (3) Of *the evils* of it. It grieves the Holy Spirit of God. The Lord Jesus Christ is wounded afresh by it. All thy usefulness will be destroyed. God will neither bless thee nor make thee a blessing. 2. Wrestle in prayer. 3. Watch against occasions and advantages of sin. 4. Go again to the Lord Jesus Christ, especially to him as your dying, crucified Lord. Live near his cross, for " his blood cleanseth from all sin." Cleave to him and let thy faith fasten upon him. So—his Word assures and experience proves, for there is no instance to the contrary, but innumerable ones in proof—the chain of thy sin shall be broken, and the sight of this shall so cheer thy heart that the demon of despair shall spread its dark wings and depart and leave thy soul unclouded. (See on all this, Owen on the Mortification of Sin.)—C.

Vers. 18—23.—*Persecution.* The cruel sufferings of God's prophet which here and in other parts of his prophecy are recorded throw not a little light on all like persecution. For, though its rough and brutal forms have for the most part disappeared, still in others it yet lingers, and is the source of much distress. Note, then—

I. ITS CAUSES. They are ever the same—hatred to the faithful Word which the persecuted one persists in preaching. Persecution, therefore, is inevitable where a faithful messenger of God comes into collision with those who hate and will not submit to his message.

II. ITS PRETEXTS. Zeal for the Church and for sacred institutions imperilled by the prophet's preaching. We see them standing up for the priests and the Law and the prophetic order, all which, of Divine appointing, were wronged and injured by the prophet. Persecutors never will own, even to themselves, their own true motives. Those who sought to kill our Lord ever insisted on the highest motives for their conduct. Persecution is such an odious thing that, unless some fair disguise be thrown over it, no one would have anything to do with it. And no doubt some persecutors—like Saul of Tarsus—have been deceived by this disguise, and have sincerely thought they were doing God service. There is never any need for persecution, though our forefathers thought there was ; for if any doctrine be of man only it will come to naught. The facts of life, the Word of God, reason and conscience, are all against falsehoods, and will expose and so extinguish them without persecution. For the nature of man is made for truth, and hence what is contrary to truth cannot long live.

III. ITS INTENT. Revenge and the forcible silencing of an adversary.

IV. ITS METHODS. 1. *Defamation.* "Let us smite him with the tongue." 2. *Ostentatious disregard of his teaching.* "Let us not give heed," etc. (ver. 18). 3. *Whatever " devices" will most of all tell against him.* Sometimes open hostility is not safe. It was not against John the Baptist, nor our Lord, nor here (cf. ch. xxvi. 16). And then other devices have to be sought out, and the finding, when sought by the persecuting spirit, does not take long.

V. ITS RELIEF. Not compromise. To give way where conscience commands steadfastness is to incur such spiritual shame and distress, such hiding of the face of God, as to be more intolerable than the fiercest persecution (cf. the history of Cranmer and his piteous misery). But—as with Jeremiah—turning to the Lord in *prayer*. We cannot commend the spirit of his prayer, it is all unlike our Lord's in regard to his enemies, and therefore not a pattern for us to follow; but it was right, and ever is so, when persecuted by man to turn to him "who endured such contradiction of sinners against himself." His grace will keep us from being wearied and faint in our minds. *Patience*, too, will greatly help. Persecutors soon tire when they find that their methods are of no avail. *Prudence*, likewise, should not be forgotten. Sometimes we may get out of its way, and at no time is there need to provoke persecution by imprudent, ill-timed, and ill-toned obtrusion of the distasteful theme. There are times when at all costs a man must stand to his post and speak out, but there are other times, and more of them, when the quiet, consistent life will do more for God and his truth than the longest and loudest speech. But in such difficult circumstances it is well to keep near to God in constant prayer for counsel and direction how to bear one's self wisely as he would have us. Relief also is found in contemplation of—

VI. ITS SURE RESULTS if faithfully endured. It makes us have real fellowship with Christ. It wins for us a glorious recompense at his coming. Even now the soul is cheered by the communications of his approval and the clear vision of the shining of his countenance upon his faithful servant. And not seldom likewise by beholding the lion turned into the lamb, the persecutor becoming an apostle and preacher of the faith he once destroyed. These are consolations indeed. And confirmation in the truth for which we have suffered is gained by seeing the manifest displeasure of God against the persecutors. How it hardens them in their sin! How it fills up the cup of their iniquity! How sore the vengeance that befalls them! These considerations are derived from the contemplation of the persecution of the Lord's servant Jeremiah. They will be all of them strengthened if we mark the sufferings of the Lord himself. Here, but there most vividly, are seen warnings most solemn against this great sin, and consolations most precious to all the "blessed" who endure.—C.

Vers. 19—23.—*The prophet's prayer for vengeance on his enemies.* (Cf. homily on "Imprecatory prayers," ch. xi. 20.)—C.

Ver. 6.—*The potter and the clay.* The analogy here instituted enshrines truths that are of universal application. They have their individual quite as much as their national bearings. Nowhere does the representative character of the house of Israel appear more clearly than in this passage; nowhere do we get a more striking view of the general method of the Divine dealings with the human race. It suggests—

I. GOD'S ABSOLUTE SOVEREIGNTY OVER THE BEING AND LIFE OF EVERY MAN. The figure of the potter and the clay is one of frequent occurrence in Holy Scripture (*vide* Job x. 9; Isa. lxiv. 8; Rom. ix. 10). It vividly represents the subjection of our nature and our personal history to the Divine control. The fact of our moral freedom, the mysterious prerogative that belongs to us of choosing and following our own way, must needs make the comparison defective. There is some point at which all such physical analogies fail duly to set forth the realities of moral and spiritual life. But it is deeply true as suggestive of the power God has over us to mould us as he pleases. Free as our will may be, is not our whole nature as plastic material in the hands of him who made us? Free as we may be to pursue our own chosen course of life, can we ever escape the "Divinity that shapes our ends"? There is a hidden power, whether we acknowledge it or not, the mastery of which over thought, feeling, purpose, and action is the deepest reality of our existence.

II. HIS FORMATIVE PURPOSE. Distinguish between a sovereign power and one that is arbitrary and capricious. Complete as the Divine mastery over us may be, it is not lawless or purposeless. It has always a definite end in view, and that end is wise and holy and good. As the potter seeks to fashion the clay into some beautiful or useful form that his own brain has first conceived, so God, by his providential and spiritual control, seeks to work out a Divine idea in our being and life, to body forth in us some archetype of moral beauty that exists in his own eternal mind. He would fain fashion us into a noble form and fit us for some noble use. In God's "great house" there are

many utilities. And even the vessel "unto dishonour" has its place and its purpose.
Our faith in the infinitely wise and holy love that governs all leads us to rest in the
thought—

> "That nothing walks with aimless feet;
> That not one life shall be destroyed
> Or cast as rubbish to the void,
> When God hath made the pile complete."

But he who formed us for himself would not have any of us to be content with an
inferior position and a lower aim. He would so mould and fashion us that we shall be
"vessels unto honour, sanctified, and meet for the Master's use" (2 Tim. ii. 21).

III. HIS LONG-SUFFERING PATIENCE. When the potter's work is marred, he presses
the clay into a shapeless mass and casts it upon the wheel again. We are reminded of
the various methods God employs in moulding us to his will, and how if one fails he
will often subject us to another. There are events that sometimes break up the whole
form of a man's life; old ties are severed, old associations pass away; he begins an
altogether new career, with new responsibilities, new moral tests, new possibilities of
good. There are afflictions that change the whole tenor of a man's inward life; his
spirit is crushed, wounded, softened, that it may the better receive Divine impressions.
"God maketh my heart soft," etc. (Job xxiii. 16). "My heart is like wax" (Ps. xxii.
14). Thus does God "humble us to prove us, to know what is in our heart, whether
we will keep his commandments or not" (Deut. viii. 2). There may come a time when
all these Divine methods fail and the soul is found to be reprobate. In ch. xix.
1—11 we have a figurative prophecy of the ultimate abandonment of the Jewish
people to their fate. In this case the vessel has been baked in the fire; it is incapable
of taking a new shape, and is broken so "that it cannot be made whole again." Such
is the doom of the finally impenitent and intractable. But God's patience is very
wonderful. In this world at least the door of mercy is always open. There is always
the possibility of a new and nobler life. He "is long-suffering to usward, not willing
that any should perish, but that all should come to repentance" (2 Pet. iii. 9).—W.

Vers. 1—10.—*The clay in the potter's hand.* I. THE PURPOSE OF THIS PRACTICAL
ILLUSTRATION. It is a practical illustration in the most suggestive sense of the word
"practical." Jeremiah had not to go out of his way to produce a sufficiently impressive
figure of what God was about to do. He had to go through a very peculiar and protracted experience to bring out the lesson of the marred girdle. But here he has only
to go down to the potter at his wheel, a thing he could do at any time; and there is a
lesson particularly plain and forcible, as coming out of the daily life, the simple and
common life, of the people. Notice, then, that Jeremiah was not sent down to learn
just what his own unaided observation might tell him concerning the potter and the
clay. He might, indeed, have drawn out many important lessons, yet overlooked the
one that was most important of all. God wished the prophet clearly to understand and
then distinctly to impress upon the people this truth, that as the potter is to the clay,
in respect of the control which he has over it as clay and in its plastic condition, so
Jehovah is to Israel in respect of his control over its temporal destiny as a nation.
Hence we have to look at the potter's action upon the clay, positively and negatively.
We have to recollect both what he can do and what he cannot do. Within certain
limits his power is resistless; outside those limits he has no power at all. Give the
potter a piece of moist plastic clay; he takes it up, designing to make from it a vessel
of a certain shape and for a certain use. Suddenly he finds it desirable to change the
shape, and because the clay is still moist and plastic he can do this with the rapidity,
expertness, and success which come from long practice. It is this particular power of
the potter which God would have us to understand is his power over us. What the
potter does is limited by the nature of that with which he works. He cannot turn clay
into something else than clay. Clay it is when he first touches it : clay it remains when
its shape is finally decided. Let the vessel be baked in the furnace and come out hard,
its shape cannot then be altered. If it is thrown to the ground it will be broken, it
may even be shivered "so that there shall not be found in the bursting of it a sherd to
take fire from the hearth, or to take water withal out of the pit" (Isa. xxx. 14). No

volition or power of the potter will give to the clay vessel the qualities of a wooden vessel or one of metal. He may fashion it for a vessel of honour or dishonour, just as he pleases; but whatever its use its material is still of clay. And similarly we must recollect that, whatever God does with us, he does in harmony with our nature. He finds us, as to the affections and purposes of our hearts, free agents, and, however great the changes he may affect in our circumstances and our future, all must be done without touching this freedom. The Divine potter here was changing the circumstances of the human clay, just because that clay was so stubborn in submitting to his will so clearly, so lovingly, so often expressed. If we refuse to be moulded into the shape that means for us true peace, glory, and blessedness, then we must be moulded into the shape which will secure at the least peace and blessedness in God's kingdom, and manifest glory to his great Name.

II. THE GREAT RESULT WHICH SHOULD BE PRODUCED BY OUR CONSIDERATION OF THIS ILLUSTRATION. Too readily is it said by many, "If we are as clay in the hands of the potter, then we need not trouble ourselves. God will shape our destiny, whatever we do." But if we look honestly and humbly at this illustration, we shall see that what God would have us above all things to learn from it is that the shaping of our destiny lies practically with *ourselves*. In selfish and ignorant obstinacy we wish our life to take a certain mould. Strenuously, and heedless of all Divine counsel and warning, we try what self can do toward the shaping. Then at last *our purpose* comes to be broken off. All that we have been and all that we have done prove useless so far as our aims are concerned. But for all that we cannot be useless to God. God wishes to work in us a change which would make all our circumstances those of liberty. He wishes to renew our hearts and establish in them a holy love as the central principle. If we refuse this Divine appeal, then we must come under ever-narrowing constraints. We are asked to walk in the liberty of God's children; if we refuse and confess ourselves the enemies of God, then we must be loaded with chains and put in the innermost dungeon. Our wisdom is to turn from our hardness and impenitent hearts, and allow God to lead us into the full μετάνοια (Rom. ii. 4). Then with understanding shall we address God, "We are the clay, and thou our potter" (Isa. lxiv. 8). If we by repentance come back to God and make ourselves clay, such as will have in it a peculiar responsiveness to the touch of God, then we may leave ourselves to his loving-kindness. He will fashion us into just that shape whereby we shall be meet for the Master's service. And if men say in their ignorance that we are turning out but vessels of dishonour, let us recollect that of honour and dishonour God alone is judge. If we only stoop from our pride to do the will of God, God will take care of our position. For is not God he who exalts the humble and abases the proud?—Y.

Vers. 18—23.—*Jeremiah's enemies and his prayer against them.* I. THE CAUSE OF HIS SUPPLICATION. His enemies have entered into a plot against him, and he has heard of the plot. He has to do, we may imagine, not only with the open threats of passionate men, face to face, but also with secret wiles. The language of intense provocation in which he speaks must be remembered in trying to estimate the extent, depth, and bitterness of the hostility against him. *Who were they that thus proposed to join together in ruining the prophet?* Doubtless the three classes embraced by the reference that is made, namely, priest, wise man, and prophet. The priest would go to the wise man and prophet, saying, "See how this fellow speaks against us all." A common hatred and a common peril swallow up for a time all jealousies amongst bad men, and constitute a strong bond of union, a strong incitement to all the ingenuity and designing powers of the mind. We are not left without means of judging as to the motives of these three classes of men and their methods of proceeding when we consider the similar conspiracies against Jesus himself. Men belonging to conspicuous classes of the community attacked him, and they are constantly mentioned as being joined together. This attack gives the strongest evidence, both of the appropriateness of Jeremiah's message and his fidelity in delivering it. Such truth as a prophet has to speak must be met either with penitent friendliness or with bitter and active enmity. It must be reckoned no strange thing if the faithful proclaimer of truth is exposed, not only to reproaches, misrepresentations, and loss of old associates, but even to deep-laid conspiracies. These men, while they were bent on ruining Jeremiah, wished also to do it in a safe and plausible way. It was to be done by a plan. They were going to smite him with the tongue. Very likely they hoped to get him put to death under judicial forms. *Again, one asks—How came the prophet to hear of these plans?* The wise men must have shown a very imperfect kind of wisdom in not being able to keep their designs secret. Indeed, they may have thought that they were secret. The Jews who swore not to eat or drink till they had killed Paul did not reckon that Paul's own nephew had discovered their designs.

II. THE SUPPLICATION ITSELF. In reading this supplication, we vainly try to escape from feeling what a ferocious, savage tone the words have. The dreadful meaning of the words, taken in their natural signification, is only too plain. We must by no means try to defend the prayer; we can only do something to extenuate the language by remembering the provocation the prophet had received, and the spirit of the age in which he lived. It is at least important to remember that he is distinctly conscious of having had good motives towards these enemies. He knew that God meant their good, and he, in speaking, had meant the same. It must be noticed also that, whatever his feelings, he expresses them as a prayer to God. He does not take retaliation into his own hands. His rights and interests, whatever they are, he leaves in the hands of Jehovah. He has, indeed, his own estimate as to what his enemies deserve, but he seeks that they may get their deserts in the way of manifestly Divine judgments. Then he evidently spoke in great excitement. The wrath even of a good man may boil over into language which he would not wish to be held by in cooler moments. We may be perfectly sure that if, in after years, Jeremiah had been reminded of this prayer, and asked if he really, seriously meant that the innocent connections of his enemies should be ruthlessly slaughtered, he would have been quick to plead that his words were those of excitement. Shall it be thought wonderful that *he* should utter such a wish when the disciples of the meek and lowly Jesus had drunk in so little of the spirit of their Master as to wish fire from heaven to come down upon the inhospitable Samaritans? The passage under consideration is just one of those which strongly shows the difference which has been made by the sermon on the mount. If Jeremiah had been a Christian apostle instead of a Jewish prophet, his prayer would have been a very lamentable utterance indeed.—Y.

EXPOSITION.

CHAPTER XIX.

With this chapter, vers. 1—6 of the next ought undoubtedly to be connected to complete the narrative. Jeremiah here comes before us performing another symbolical action. By breaking a potter's vessel he foreshows the ruin impending over Jerusalem for the idolatry practised in the valley of Hinnom. Not (remarks Graf) as if the worship of Moloch had been restored after the death of Josiah; ver. 13, in fact, sufficiently shows that the Tophet had, ever since Josiah's time, continued to be an unclean place, and the sins which are here rebuked are the unexpiated abominations of Manasseh's reign (described in ch. xv. 4, as the immediate causes of the Captivity). Jeremiah's prophecy on the Tophet is followed by one on the fate of a certain Pashur, a high officer in the temple.

The principal prophecy presents striking points of contact with ch. vii. (comp. vers. 4—6 with ch. vii. 30—32; and ver. 13 with ch. vii. 18; viii. 2), and we may presume that the events here related belong to the time to which we have already referred ch. vii., viz. the early part of the reign of Jehoiakim. The same date is confirmed for the narrative of Pashur by the office which is therein given him; for according to ch. xxix. 25, 26, the office was not held by him, but by Zephaniah.

Ver. 1.—**A potter's earthen bottle.** Dr. Thomson speaks of the extreme cheapness and brittleness of the common pottery of Palestine (comp. Isa. xxx. 14). **The ancients of the people.** The natural popular representatives (comp. Exod. iii. 16; 2 Sam. xix. 11; 1 Kings viii. 1 ; xx. 7). It was an announcement concerning the whole people that Jeremiah was about to make. **The ancients of the priests** (comp. 2 Kings xix. 2).

Ver. 2.—**The valley of the son of Hinnom** (see on ch. vii. 31). **The east gate;** rather *the potsherd gate*, i.e. the gate where potsherds were wont to be thrown. Another possible rendering is "sun gate," of which "east gate" is but a paraphrase. But there is evidently a connection between the name of the gate and the action performed by Jeremiah. The Authorized Version seems to have misled Captain Warren into identifying the valley of Hinnom with that of Kedron. He confirms his view, it is true, by the Arabic nomenclature, which speaks of the Kedron as the Wâdy Jehinnam—a nomenclature, however, which is by no means uniform (see Robinson, 'Biblical Researches,' ii. 396, 403). The situation of the "potsherd gate" must remain uncertain.

Ver. 3.—**0 kings of Judah**; *i.e.* the numerous clan of royal princes, kings by courtesy (see on ch. xvii. 20). **His ears shall tingle** (so 2 Kings xxi. 12; comp. 1 Sam. iii. 11).

Ver. 4.—**Have estranged this place**; rather, *have treated this place as strange;* i.e. as one that did not belong to their God, that was unholy (comp. ch. xvi. 18, "They have defiled my land"). **With the blood of innocents**; comp. "Innocent blood, even the blood of their sons and of their daughters" (Ps. cvi. 38)—the children sacrificed in Hinnom to Moloch.

Ver. 5.—**Baal.** This seems to be used loosely for Moloch (comp. on ch. ii. 8).

Ver. 6.—(Comp. ch. vii. 32.) **Tophet**; rather, *the Tophet* (see on ch. vii. 31).

Ver. 7.—**I will make void**; literally, *I will pour out,* alluding to the etymology of the word rendered "bottle" in ver. 1.

Ver. 8.—(Comp. ch. xviii. 16.)

Ver. 9.—The same description, almost verbatim, is given in Deut. xxviii. 53; (comp. Lev. xxvi. 29; Ezek. v. 10). For the fulfilment, see Lam. iv. 10.

Ver. 11.—**As one breaketh a potter's vessel** (comp. Isa. xxx. 14). Dr. Thomson speaks of the utter indifference with which the common pottery of Palestine is handled. It is not only brittle, but so cheap that no one is distressed at breaking it. **And they shall bury them in Tophet**, etc. These words form the conclusion of ch. vii. 32 (see note), the greater part of which is repeated in ver. 6. They are certainly out of place here, and are wanting in the Septuagint.

Ver. 12.—**As Tophet**; *i.e.* an unclean spot, avoided by mankind.

Ver. 13.—**The houses of the kings of Judah**; *i.e.* the palaces and other buildings which together made up "the king's house" (ch. xxii. 6). **Shall be defiled as the place of Tophet.** This is one of the few places in which the Authorized Version has allowed itself to interfere with the received text; for the Hebrew has "which are defiled," etc. The common reading, in fact, seems untranslatable. **Because of all the houses**; rather, *even all the houses.*

Vers. 14, 15.—Here begins a fresh section of the narrative. Jeremiah has executed his commission, and now proceeds to the temple, where he repeats before the assembled people his announcement of the awful judgment.

Ver. 15.—**Upon all her towns.** The cities of Judah are regarded as in a manner subject to the capital.

HOMILETICS.

Vers. 1—13.—*The broken bottle.* That was a strange scene—the royal family, the nobles, the chief priests, together with the populace of Jerusalem, gathered, at the summons of a prophet whose power could not be ignored though his teaching was opposed, in the valley of Hinnom, now reeking with the odours of foul crime; and the prophet facing them, alone and fearless, with a common potter's vessel in his hand, while he draws a most awful picture of impending calamity, and sternly charges his audience with the terrible wickedness which is bringing it upon their heads, and brings his discourse to a dramatic climax by breaking the vessel to pieces.

I. CONSIDER THE CIRCUMSTANCES OF THE DISCOURSE. 1. It was addressed especially to the *leaders* of the people (ver. 1). "To the poor the gospel is preached," but to the great sterner messages must often be declared. Nothing in the history of the prophets is more exemplary than the directness of their accusations of guilt in high places. They were no flattering court preachers. Yet they were court preachers. They did not reserve their harsh words for the poorest and lowest of the people, as modern popular preachers are too apt to do. The leaders were first in crime; they should be first in responsibility. 2. It was spoken on the *site of the greatest wickedness.* The guilty people had the memorials of their crimes before their eyes while judgment was being pronounced for them. Men naturally shun these valleys of Hinnom, these scenes of old sins, the sight of which stings the conscience. But they must revisit them. It is sometimes the duty of the preacher to take his hearers back in memory to the circumstances of the past which they would gladly forget. 3. It was *clearly and boldly expressed*. The language was precise, detailed, and graphic, the description of the approaching ruin vivid and appalling. Jeremiah used no euphemisms. His words are enough to make our blood curdle as we read them, more than a score of centuries after they were spoken. How must they have sounded in the ears of the criminals who heard them as the sentence of their own doom? Lurid pictures of future punishment frequently strike one as unreal, as though only drawn for effect; they rouse unbelief in some, despair in others, or a hardening in sin. Yet a clear and uncompromising statement of the scriptural revelation of the horrors of the future is not to be set aside for more pleasing doctrines, especially in preaching to the great and the self-satisfied. 4. It was accompanied by a *significant action*. Jeremiah broke the bottle in the presence of his audience. This would strike the eye and impress the imagination. It is not enough that we convince the reason of a truth; we must rouse the imagination to realize it before it will be effectual. The Eastern imagery of the Bible is useful to us in this way. The preacher finds the value of illustrations in making truth vivid and interesting. Ideas may be received through the eye as well as through the ear.

II. CONSIDER THE SUBJECT OF THE DISCOURSE. 1. It *accused of sin*, (1) in forsaking God and (2) in practising vice and cruelty. We must feel the intensity of guilt to realize the justice of punishment. 2. It denounced a most *terrible doom*. This was to correspond to the crimes committed. The Tophet of sin was to be the Tophet of punishment. They who had sacrificed children to Moloch would eat the flesh of their sons, etc. 3. It exposed the rottenness of *false confidence*. "I will pour out the counsel of Judah." People imagine that somehow, without repentance, by ingenuity or by daring, they may escape the consequences of their sins. They will find that all such devices must end in ignominious failure. 4. It was accompanied by a symbol of *hopeless destruction*. The bottle was broken. (1) This potter's vessel was a comparatively worthless thing: wickedness robs men's lives of all value. (2) It was very brittle: nothing is so unstable as the security of the wicked before their sins have wrought out their natural consequences. (3) It was broken to pieces: the punishment of sin is destruction—the destruction of a nation for national sin as seen in the breaking up of the Jewish people, the destruction of a soul in the killing out of it of spiritual activities and all the higher capacities of its being.

Vers. 14, 15.—*The warning confirmed*. The warning of the discourse in the valley of Hinnom is confirmed by a repetition of it under more ordinary circumstances.

I. THE CIRCUMSTANCES OF THE CONFIRMATION OF THE WARNING. 1. It was *repeated*. The scribe must bring from his treasury things old as well as things new. Men need "line upon line." Unpopular truths must not only be revealed once for all, they must be impressed upon people until they are accepted. 2. It was repeated in the *temple*. The horrible associations of Tophet were wanting there. All was decorum, order, propriety. Yet the message was not the less true there than in a more congenial place. Terrible truths must be uttered in face of the religious respectability of our Church worship. Such outward correctness should not make us forget the true condition of men's hearts, which is apparent enough in the darker scenes of life, in the Tophets of iniquity. We are tempted to be deceived by the appearance of religious assemblies into a blindness to the greatness of sin which is visible enough in common life. 3. It was repeated in *the ears of all the people*. The leaders were first selected to hear the warning (ver. 1). But it was not confined to them. The people generally were guilty. They had quietly acquiesced in the wickedness of their great men. Nay, they had furthered them in it (ch. v. 31), had followed their example, and become guilty of similar crimes. They, too, must not expect to escape in the hour of judgment.

II. THE FORM IN WHICH THE WARNING WAS CONFIRMED. 1. It was *epitomized*. Truth needs to be broken up into detail that it may be clearly understood and vividly conceived by the imagination. But it is possible to lose ourselves in details and miss the drift of the sum of them. Hence the advantage of broad, sweeping enunciations of principle. 2. It was repeated as a *prediction of real facts*. The warning was not to be regarded as an empty threat, nor as the indication of a danger that might be evaded. "I will *bring* . . . the evil that I have pronounced," etc. It is both weak and cruel to threaten without the intention of executing the threat—*weak*, for the hollowness of the alarm is soon discovered by experience, and then it is impotent; *cruel*, for why create distress about a mere " bogey " danger ? God is merciful, but firm. His threats are conditional, but, while the conditions subsist, the execution is as certain as any event that depends on the uniform laws of nature. 3. It was repeated *without dimi-nution*. *All* the evil pronounced will fall on *all* the towns. The effect of stern warn-ings fades with the lapse of time. We are tempted to think that things will not be so very bad as at first seemed likely, and to take comfort from such reflections. But danger is not lessened by our growing indifference to it. 4. It was strengthened by an appeal to the *increasing necessity* for it. " Because they have hardened their necks, that they might not hear my words." A deep consciousness of guilt makes the just punishment of it seem inevitable. Wilful persistence in wickedness after warning can only increase the guilt and make the punishment the more certain and the more severe.

HOMILIES BY VARIOUS AUTHORS.

Vers. 1, 2, 10, 11.—*The breaking of the potter's vessel.* Another symbolic action, but in this case the revelation to the mind of the prophet was not dependent upon its being performed. It is because of the public significance of it he is enjoined to perform it. The " elders of the priests " and the " elders of the people " are invited to the scene.

I. THE SYMBOL. This was a " potter's earthen bottle [or 'vessel']," and thus had to be carefully distinguished from the " clay " spoken of in ch. xviii. The latter is soft and unshaped, and may be moulded as the potter wishes; but the vessel is already formed and hardened into a certain definite shape, which it is impossible materially to alter. As that represented the *stuff* or *material* of which nations and institutions could be made, this must stand for the *Jewish nation, with its character historically matured and fixed.* Jehovah had already given it the form he intended it to assume, and placed it in certain relations with himself as a theocracy. *The historic institutions and nations of the world are the creation of God.* He has raised them up and con-trolled the forces that moulded and determined their specific character and work. " The powers that be are ordained of God." *The position, character, and life of individual men are also his work.* No man is " self-made " in any fundamental sense of the word. A gracious providence has nurtured and cared for him; and, it may be, saving grace has redeemed and sanctified him. He " is the noblest work of God."

II. THE ACTION. This was threefold, viz: 1. *The vessel was bought.* " Get ; " literally, " buy." Jehovah had redeemed Israel to be a people for himself. The outlays of Divine love and mercy are suggested. The providence and grace of God are now being expended. The blood of Christ was shed for all nations, " the Jew first, and afterwards the Gentile ; " and for every man born into the world. " Ye are not your own : ye are bought with a price." A deeper obligation is thereby incurred to him, and a grander authority on his part justified. We are all made and saved, or, as it may be expressed, made and remade by him. 2. *It was probably poured out.* Ver. 7, " I will make void [literally, 'pour out']." This action would be natural under the circumstances, and highly impressive. And if it be objected that the vessel was empty, that very fact might still render the action the more emphatically significant. Their counsels were also vain and empty. God suffers wicked nations and men to devise evil, but only as it works out his own ends is it allowed to be executed. He will bring to naught the counsel of the ungodly. That which is devised without his blessing will come to no successful issue. 3. *It was broken.* (Ver. 10.) This was intended to depict the extreme and final character of the impending judgment—" As one breaketh a potter's vessel, that cannot be made whole again " (ver. 11). The nationality of the Jews was to be destroyed. The Babylonion captivity, although only obscurely pre-dicted, is apparently alluded to; but some hold that, as this was but an incomplete fulfilment, the Roman conquest must have been meant. *All nations and individuals are on their trial,* and may be subjected to this extreme penalty. God holds the sovereign power in his own hand. There is no remedy; the past is irrevocable. And there is no appeal from his sentence, when the limit of his forbearance has been passed. 4. *It was disgraced* by being cast into Tophet. A double purpose was thereby expressed. The scene of idolatrous rites was to be disgraced by being made the burial-place of the slaughtered thousands of Jerusalem, as, on the other hand, such a burial and the necessity for it would be humiliating to the metropolis of the faith.

III. THE ATTENDANT CIRCUMSTANCES. 1. *It was done in presence of the representatives of the nation.* "Take of the ancients [elders] of the people, and of the ancients of the priests." They were probably responsible for the national guilt, and by their personal and official influence might be able to avert the catastrophe. Those who influence a nation's life—kings, princes, statesmen, ministers of religion, authors, etc.—should be specially appealed to in cases of national sin. So the parent for the child. It is both respectful and just that such persons should be addressed in the first instance. But every man is responsible for his own sin. His intelligence and moral nature must, therefore, be addressed. 2. *The language used was such as to recall the general penalties to be incurred by breaking the Law.* (Deut. xxviii.) The fact was thus suggested that the judgment was wilfully and knowingly incurred. There is nothing new about the evils that come upon transgressing nations and individuals, or about their history. It is not for man to judge. God knows the reasons for his procedure, and the sinner himself is not ignorant. 3. *The meaning of the breaking of the vessel is fully explained beforehand.* This is ever the Divine order. There is "space for repentance" given even to the worst sinners. No man will go wholly unwarned into perdition. Nay, even the historic and so-called secular character of nations, institutions, and individuals is precious in God's eyes, and effort is constantly made to convert it into an influence of blessing. The sinner is offered the "means of grace" that he may become a saint and a servant of the Most High. And it is only as he obstinately continues in his sin that the irrevocable judgment falls.—M.

Vers. 1—15.—*Denunciations of doom.* This chapter is filled with these awful warnings of the prophet. And they are made the more awful by the reflection that, fitted as they were to rouse the most careless and hardened, yet they failed with those to whom they were addressed. And so this sad chapter teaches us such lessons as these: 1. *The earnest purpose of God to save man from his sin.* Hence these warnings. 2. *The awfully hardening power of the sin which could despise them.* 3. *What wise methods are to be employed in the endeavour to arouse and alarm the ungodly.* On this we will dwell awhile. This chapter shows—

I. THAT THOSE MOST LIKELY TO INFLUENCE THEM SHOULD BE SPECIALLY APPEALED TO. Cf. ver. 1, "Take of the ancients," etc. No doubt this was because of their influence over the people generally. If they could be won the rest would follow.

II. WE SHOULD AVAIL OURSELVES OF ANY LOCALITIES LIKELY TO LEND FORCE TO WHAT IS SAID. The prophet led forth his audience to "the valley of the son of Hinnom." It was the Tophet, the Gehenna, the place haunted with memories of Divine wrath against idolatry, and whose ever-burning fire and gnawing worm symbolized the quenchless anger of God against it. With what added power, then, would the prophet's message come when spoken in such a place!

III. SUCH MODES OF ADDRESS SHOULD BE ADOPTED AS WOULD BE MOST LIKELY TO IMPRESS. The prophet was bidden take an earthen bottle, and, after he had solemnly denounced the doom of God against the idolatrous city, he was to dash the bottle on the ground and shatter it utterly, past all possibility of mending. By this dramatic action he was to declare the coming destruction of Judah and Jerusalem. Thus vividly and powerfully to the minds of such as witnessed him would the awful truth he had to tell be impressed on their minds. But also in clear words and in full copious detail he set forth what was to come. Now, such symbolic action as that of the prophet might be of very little service to such as we speak to, however impressive to the Oriental mind, but it teaches us that whatever is likely to deepen the effect of our words upon men's minds we are to use, and fearlessly, as did the prophet, set forth the coming judgments of God. And most of all—

IV. OUR MESSAGE MUST BE GOD'S MESSAGE. *God* put into the prophet's mouth the words he was to speak and taught him how to speak them, and he obeyed. Here is the great essential. If denunciations of judgment be spoken simply as part of an orthodox sermon, or for any other reason than that God has borne in upon our souls the conviction that we must speak such words, we are likely to do but little good—indeed, harm rather than good. And let such servant of God who speaks as God bids him remember that, even when speaking thus, his words may fail in the effect designed and desired. "Lord, who hath believed our report," etc.? They did so here. But they will never entirely fail. God's promise is against that. Some will receive them. Some did even in Jeremiah's day. There was a faithful remnant. And the preacher will have delivered his own soul, and God's righteousness in the doom of the impenitent will be vindicated before all. May we be delivered from the necessity of declaring such doom as that which Jeremiah had to speak of; but if we have to, may we be taught of God, as he was, and have better success.—C.

Ver. 14—ch. xx. 6.—*The sin and punishment of Pashur.* This man is to be distinguished from him of the same name mentioned in ch. xxi. 1. The Pashur mentioned here was a priest, and one holding high office in the temple. After Jeremiah had delivered his discourse at Tophet, he seems to have returned to the city and temple, and then to have spoken in substance the same predictions of woe. Whereupon Pashur, with less patience than those who heard the prophet and had seen his symbolic declaration of the coming ruin when he broke the earthen bottle at Tophet, falls upon him and smites him, and tortured him by putting him in what is called the stocks (see Exposition). Thus—

I. HE CRUELLY PERSECUTED THE PROPHET OF GOD. It was sad that any one should do this. But yet more that it should be the act of a priest of God, and holding high position amongst the priests. What hope can there be of the people when their appointed leaders and those to whom they are wont to look up for instruction and example in what is good thus prostitute their office? Thus the "wicked husbandmen beat" the servants who were sent to them (Matt. xx. 35). And it was the same order that ever opposed, and yet more fiercely, our Lord himself. The sanctity and authority attaching to the priest's office have ever been fatal to the integrity of unworthy holders of the office, and have caused that amongst the most infamous of mankind not a few priests should be found. But—

II. HE FAILED TO SECURE THE END HE HAD IN VIEW. Jeremiah was not silenced, but goaded, as it were, to declare yet more terrible judgments in which Pashur himself should be awfully involved (cf. Paul, "God shall smite thee," etc., Acts xxiii. 3). The stout heart of a true servant of God is an anvil on which many hammers may fiercely smite, but it will wear them out long before they wear it out. Saul of Tarsus found that the persecution he had done so much to further in connection with Stephen only made matters worse. The blood of the martyrs is the seed of the Church. And the reason is that a faith for which men are willing to die convinces all beholders that it must be exceedingly precious and well founded, and inspires them with an irresistible desire to know and possess it for themselves, or at least to know what it is.

III. HE BROUGHT DOWN ON HIMSELF SORE JUDGMENT. Jeremiah declares to him that the Lord "has changed his name to Magor-Missabib, for he will be given up a prey to the torments of mortal anguish, his friends shall be slain before his eyes, Judah carried away to Babylon, all its treasures plundered; he himself shall witness all this and die and be buried in Babylon, "There thou, and all thy friends, to whom thou hast prophesied lies." Thus, look where he would, he should see nothing but terror. Above —the anger of God; beneath—a dishonoured grave; around—calamity and woe on all near and dear to him, and of which he had been largely the procuring cause; within—a conscience tormenting him day and night. It was an awful doom. "Let persecutors read it and tremble; tremble to repentance before they be made to tremble to their ruin."—C.

Vers. 1—13.—*The breaking of the potter's vessel.* I. THE PRELIMINARIES OF THE BREAKING. Spectators of the proper sort needed to be deliberately gathered together in the proper place. We may suppose that the elders of the people and of the priests were peculiarly responsible for all that concerned the safety of the city. This symbolic action was best performed before the select responsible few. As they went forth with the prophet they had time to ask themselves what the meaning of this unusual summons might be. It is, perhaps, a little to be wondered at that they should have gone with the prophet at all. And yet, although none might have quite the right motive for going, each would have his own motive, and so an acquiescent assembly be formed. God knows how to subdue and blend the motives of men for his own purposes. In some minds there would be a superstitious regard for the prophetic office; in others, curiosity would operate; and in a few there might be somewhat of the hearing ear and understanding mind. We are, then, to imagine this company going forth; and they do not go forth at random. It is not for mere seclusion they go out of the city. They are led to the very place which, because of the abominations practised in it, is to be one of the principal causes of future woe. Thus we see how carefully God arranges the circumstances in which his truth is to be proclaimed.

II. THIS BREAKING HAD A REASON. The thing was not done in mere wantonness and thoughtlessness, nor in passion, nor in carelessness. The prophet did not draw his lesson from a jar which some one else had happened to break. He got the vessel with the deliberate purpose, divinely put into his mind, of breaking it. This was far enough away from the purpose with which it was made, and the vessel, once shattered, could be of no further use for this first purpose; but in its destruction it served a far nobler end than if it had been carefully kept to carry water for many long years. Rightly considered, indeed, the vessel was not destroyed, but only its service divinely and wisely changed. So, looking from the symbol to the reality behind it, we must bear in mind that the capture of Jerusalem and the conquest of the land of Israel served certain purposes of God. He did not separate this people and give them this land that at last they might be scattered, even beyond the usual scattering of a conquered people. But when the scattering did come, he sought to make it evident that it was from his hand. It was not a mere chance of war, but something prepared for and prophesied— something to teach and warn the thoughtful among all nations.

III. THE REASONS WHY THIS VESSEL WAS THUS SHATTERED BEFORE THESE SPECTATORS. 1. *To show the ease with which God can shatter any construction of man.* One lesson had already been drawn from the potter's vessel (ch. xviii. 1—10). That lesson was drawn from the plasticity of the raw material. Now another lesson has to be drawn from the fragility of the finished article. This fragility was part of the nature of the article. The potter could not be blamed because the result of his work was so fragile. Fragility, indeed, is a relative quality. An insect could no more have broken this vessel than men by a single blow could level a forest tree. Men talk of their power to do and their power to resist; but this is only in ignorance of the immense, exhaustless power which God in mercy hides from the eyes of man. A potter's vessel may be preserved for millenniums if it is sufficiently guarded; *but it has no strength in itself.* These people of Jerusalem were reckoning on the natural position and artificial securities of their city. Yet these very things would only heighten their calamities and miseries. For they would persist in defence, ever hoping against hope, until, in their extremity, they were forced to devour their very children. We need to bear in mind that, however great our natural advantages, our prudence and foresight, we, as far as our natural life is concerned, are but as this fragile vessel in the prophet's hand. 2. *To show the impossibility of man retrieving the disaster.* " That cannot be made whole again " (ver. 11). This vessel was not merely cracked. It was more than simply broken. It not only fell, but was dashed to the ground with special force and determination. These people of Israel, once scattered, could not gather themselves together again. God could do it, but only God. And God would not do it; because that would only have been to reconstitute the fragile. The breaking of this vessel is only one of many lessons by which God would teach man his natural weakness. He destroys the old and the fragile, that he may put in its place the new and the indestructible. Our wisdom is not to waste time in trying to strengthen what is inherently weak; but to accept with glad thankfulness that real mercy of God which, in destroying the old Jerusalem, makes way for the new and heavenly Jerusalem, that city of God based on the truly everlasting hills.—Y.

EXPOSITION.

CHAPTER XX.

Ver. 1.—The continuation of the preceding narrative. **Pashur the son of Immer.** This man belonged to the sixteenth of the sacerdotal families or classes (1 Chron. xxiv. 14). Another of the same name is referred to in ch. xxi. 1 (see note). The one here mentioned was "chief overseer" (there were several inferior overseers, 2 Chron. xxxi. 13); the eminence of the position appears from the fact that Zephaniah, Pashur's successor (ch. xxix. 26), is second only to the high priest (ch. lii. 24). **Heard that Jeremiah prophesied**; rather, *heard Jeremiah prophesying.*

Ver. 2.—Pashur, being charged with the police of the temple, smites Jeremiah, *i.e.* causes stripes to be given him (a legal punishment, Deut. xxv. 3; comp. 2 Cor. xi. 24), and then orders him to be put into **the stocks**; literally, *that which distorts*—some instrument of punishment which held the body in a bent or crooked position (comp. ch. xxix. 26). The "stocks" were sometimes kept in a special house (2 Chron. xvi. 10); these mentioned here, however, apparently stood in public, at the **high**—or rather, *upper*—**gate of Benjamin, which was by**—or, *at*—**the house of the Lord.** The gate, then, was one of the temple gates, and is called "the upper" to distinguish it from one of the city gates which bore the same name (ch. xxxvii. 13; xxxviii. 7). It is presumably the same which is called "the new gate of the Lord's house" (ch. xxvi. 10; xxxvi. 10), as having been comparatively lately built (2 Kings xv. 35).

Ver. 3.—Symbolic change of name. **Not . . . Pashur, but Magor-missabib**; *i.e.* terror on every side. There is probably no allusion to the (by no means obvious) etymology of Pashur. Jeremiah simply means to say that Pashur would one day become an object of general horror (see on ver. 10).

Ver. 5.—**The strength**; rather, *the stores.* **The labours**; rather, *the fruits of labour;* i.e. the profits.

Ver. 6.—Comp. the prophecy against Shebna (Isa. xxii. 18). Since we find, in ch. xxix. 26, Pashur's office occupied by another, it is probable that the prediction was fulfilled by the captivity of Pashur with Jehoiachin. **To whom thou hast prophesied lies** (comp. ch. xiv. 13). Pashur, then, claimed to be a prophet.

Vers. 7—13.—**A lyric passage**, expressing the conflict in the prophet's mind owing to the mockery and the slander which his preaching has brought upon him, and at the same time his confidence of victory through the protection of Jehovah; a suitable sequel to the narrative which goes before, even if not originally written to occupy this position (see general Introduction).

Ver. 7.—**Thou hast deceived me**, etc.; rather, *thou didst entice me, and I let myself be enticed.* Jeremiah refers to the hesitation he originally felt to accepting the prophetic office (ch. i.). The verb does not mean "to deceive," but "to entice" (so rendered in ver. 10, Authorized Version), or "allure." The same word is used in that remarkable narrative of "the spirit" who offered to "entice" (Authorized Version, to "persuade") Ahab to "go up and fall at Ramoth-Gilead" (1 Kings xxii. 21). In Ezekiel, too, the same case is supposed as possible of Jehovah's "enticing" a prophet (Ezek. xv. 9). The expression implies that all events are, in some sense, caused by God, even those which are, or appear to be, injurious to the individual. Was Goethe thinking of this passage when he wrote the words, "Wen Gott betrügt, ist wohl betrogen"? Applying the words in a Christian sense, we may say (with F. W. Robertson) that God teaches us by our illusions. **Thou art stronger than I, and hast prevailed**; rather, *thou didst take hold on me, and didst prevail.* The expression is like "Jehovah spake thus to me with a grasp of the hand" (Isa. viii. 11).

Ver. 8.—**For since I spake, I cried out**, etc.; rather, *For as often as I speak, I must shout; I must cry, Violence and spoil;* I can take up no other tone but that of indignant denunciation, no other theme but that of the acts of injustice constantly committed (not merely, nor indeed chiefly, against the prophet himself). **Was made**; rather, *is made.*

Ver. 9.—**Then I said**, etc.; rather, *And when I say, I will not make mention of him,* etc., *then it becometh* (i.e. I am conscious of a feeling) *in my heart as a burning fire shut up in my bones; and I weary myself to hold it in, but cannot.* The prophet has repeatedly been tempted to withdraw from the painful duty, but his other and higher self (comp. 'Old Self and New Self' in the 'Lyra Apostolica') overpowers these lower cravings for peace and quiet. The fire of the Divine wrath against sin burns so fiercely within him that he cannot help resuming his work.

Ver. 10.—**For I heard**, etc.; rather, *For I have heard the whispering of many; there is terror on every side. Inform* (say they), *and let us inform against him.* This gives us the reason for his momentary inclinations to silence. He was surrounded by bitter enemies, who were no longer content with malicious words, but urged each other on to lay an information against him with the authorities as a public criminal. The first clause agrees verbatim with part of Ps. xxxi. 13 (this is one of the psalms attributed, by a too bold conjecture, to Jeremiah). "There is terror on every side" (see above, ver. 3, and also note on ch. vi. 25) means "everything about me inspires me with terror." **All my familiars** is, literally, *all the men of my peace;* i.e. all those with whom I have been on terms of friendship (same phrase, ch. xxxviii. 22). **Watched for my halting**; *i.e.* either laid traps for me or waited for me to commit some error for them to take advantage of. The phrase, "my halting," is borrowed (?) from Ps. xxxv. 15; xxxviii. 18 (Hebrew). **He will be enticed;** viz. to say something on which a charge of treason can be based.

Ver. 11.—**As a mighty terrible one;** rather, *as a formidable warrior.* **They shall not prevail.** This was, in fact, the Divine promise to Jeremiah at the outset of his ministry (ch. i. 19). **For they shall not prosper;** rather, *because they have not prospered.*

Ver. 12.—Repeated, with slight variations, from ch. xi. 20.

Ver. 13.—In the confidence of faith Jeremiah sees himself already delivered. He writes in the style of the psalmists, who constantly pass from the language of prayer to that of fruition.

Vers. 14—18.—Jeremiah curses the day of his birth. The passage is a further development of the complaint in ch. xv. 10, and stands in no connection with the consolatory close of the preceding passage. There is a very striking parallel in Job iii. 3—12, and the question cannot be evaded, Which is the original? It is difficult to believe that Jeremiah copied from an earlier poem. Deep emotion expresses itself in language suggested by the moment; and, even after retouching his discourses, Jeremiah would leave much of the original expression. But impressions of this sort cannot be unreservedly trusted. The argument from parallel passages is only a subsidiary one in the determination of the date of books.

Ver. 16.—**As the cities which the Lord overthrew.** It is, so to speak, the "technical term" for the destruction of Sodom and Gomorrah which Jeremiah employs. So deeply imprinted was the tradition on the Hebrew mind, that a special word was appropriated to it, which at once called up thoughts of the awful justice of God (see Gen. xix. 25; Isa. i. 7 (?); xiii. 19; Amos iv. 11; Deut. xxix. 23 [22]; ch. xlix. 18; l. 40). **The cry . . . the shouting.** The cry of the besieged for help; the shouting of the suddenly appearing assailants (comp. ch. xv. 8).

HOMILETICS.

Vers. 1—6.—*Pashur.* At length the smouldering opposition to Jeremiah breaks out into open persecution. Hitherto, though he has been answered by words (ch. xviii. 18) and threatened with violence, no overt act has been committed. Secret enemies have elaborated dark designs, which are alarming enough but come to no serious issue. But now violent hands are laid upon the prophet; and it is not an obscure band of illegal conspirators who contrive evil against him, but the official head of the temple guards formally arrests him and executes upon him the recognized punishment of a criminal. This action bears testimony to the excitement produced by the burning words of the discourse in the valley of Hinnom. So overawing were the utterances of the prophet that no one dared to touch him then; but when he confirmed them in the temple courts the circumstances were altered, and, either from alarm or from rage, Pashur, the chief of the temple police, laid hold of the prophet and brought him to severe punishment. The conduct of Pashur and the fate that is threatened him deserve our careful examination.

I. THE CONDUCT OF PASHUR. 1. Pashur was a *priest* and of high rank in the service of the temple of Jehovah. Such a man should have been able to recognize a true prophet of Jehovah as his fellow-servant. Yet he was first in persecuting him. Official religious positions are no guarantees for spiritual wisdom. But it is scandalous when the professed leaders of the Church are foremost in resisting the declaration of Divine truth and the execution of the will of God. 2. Pashur was a responsible *officer of justice.* Such a man should not have allowed himself to be carried away by a flood of popular indignation, influences of class jealousy, or impulses of personal spite. Judicial crimes are always the most atrocious crimes. They poison justice at its very fountain, they abuse high trusts, they disorganize society, and all this in addition to the inherent wickedness of the acts, which is the same in all who commit them with similar motives. 3. Pashur replied to the words of prophecy with the *arm of force.* He could not answer Jeremiah, so he attempted to repress him. Unable to refute the arguments of the prophet, he endeavoured to restrain the utterance of them. Here we recognize the folly, the injustice, and the cruelty of such persecution: the *folly,* for to silence a voice is not to destroy the unpleasant truth it declares; *injustice,* for nothing can be more unfair than to do violence to a man for uttering words which we cannot deny to be true; and *cruelty,* for it is a man's duty to make known what he believes to be important truths.

II. THE THREATENED FATE OF PASHUR. Jeremiah stood alone, unpopular and unprotected. Pashur was strong in the powers of office and supported by the sentiment of the country. Yet the prophet was more than a match for the officer. Sensitive and naturally retiring, Jeremiah was bold in the conviction of truth, the sense of duty, and the consciousness of the Divine presence. Pashur's policy proved a failure. Jeremiah was not silenced by scourge and stocks. Either Pashur had too much sense of justice left to retain the prophet in prison, or he feared that such an action would be recognized as illegal and damage his position, or he thought the severe but brief corporal punishment of the prophet sufficient. Jeremiah was set at liberty on the day after he was arrested, and then, instead of cautiously measuring his language, he boldly threatened Pashur with a share of suffering in the coming calamity. This was peculiar. Pashur was not to experience the worst, but to witness it. 1. He was to be punished by *fear.* Tyrants are cowards. A long-enduring, harassing fear is more painful to bear than a short, sharp, visible trouble. Many evils are worse in prospect than in experience. Courage and active resistance may make the facing of danger easy, but to be haunted with vague terrors, powerless to do anything to avert them, lashed and stung by innumerable ideal and therefore intangible torments,—this is torture. You can fight a foe of flesh and blood, but a fear is like a ghost. The blow aimed at it passes through it, and it remains still glaring at its victim till his blood freezes with horror. May God deliver us from the awful punishment of an eternal fear! 2. He was to see the words of the prophet *verified by experience.* He tried to silence the warning voice; he could not stay the approaching evil. They who have rejected warnings will be dismayed and confounded when they see them realized in facts. 3. He was to witness the *calamity of his nation.* Probably there was a genuine love of his country in this man. His attack on Jeremiah may have been influenced by a sincere desire for the national welfare. But if so he had put his country before his God. His punishment would come in the humiliation of his nation. Patriotism is no excuse for resisting the will of God. The godless patriot may be punished by seeing the troubles that are brought on his country through its irreligion.

Ver. 7.—*Enticed and overpowered by God.* I. GOD ENTICES HIS SERVANTS. Jeremiah had been led to undertake the prophetic mission with assurances of success and victory (ch. i. 17—19), and he was surprised when he met only with contempt and apparent failure. So others have entered God's service with much confidence in the joy and but little anticipation of the trouble it would bring. There is really nothing either false or unkind in this. 1. *Nothing false;* for (1) though all the future trouble is not predicted, its approach is not denied; we are simply left in the dark in regard to it; and (2) ultimately the servants of God will triumph, and the trouble will be all forgotten and swallowed up in victory. But if the darker experience were clearly revealed at first, it would throw such a shadow over the future that the ultimate triumph would be scarcely thought of, and thus a more false idea of the whole course of life would be produced than that which comes from hiding from us some of its darker scenes. 2. *Nothing unkind.* If the trouble must be faced it need not be anticipated (Matt. vi. 34). If God hides approaching trouble from us he does not forget to provide against it. He takes the burden of it upon himself, so that when the trouble is revealed the grace to endure it is also revealed. Moreover, on the whole, the blessedness of the service of God vastly outweighs its distresses. If the alarm of the latter drove us from the service, the result would be loss to ourselves. It is, therefore, merciful in God to condescend to our weakness and thus lead us on through partial views of truth until we are strong enough to grasp the whole. Still, when the prospect of trouble is revealed it should be faced. Something of this must be considered by us or we may make an ignominious failure. Jeremiah was warned of opposition. Christ discouraged rash, heedless enthusiasm (Luke ix. 57, 58), and bade men count the cost of his service.

II. GOD OVERPOWERS HIS SERVANTS. Jeremiah complained that he was not only enticed but prevailed upon by God by force. "Thou art stronger than I." God never forces a man's will. But still he hedges a man in and uses such influences upon him that many of the experiences of his life may be ascribed to God's supreme power rather than to the man's spontaneous action. If these result in shame and apparent failure, as they often may, at first sight it seems as though God had been dealing harshly with his servant. 1. But we should remember that it is a *blessed thing to suffer for God*. It is an honour to be a true martyr to God's will (Matt. v. 10, 11). 2. We should understand that *good purposes* are being effected through such suffering. It is not without its end. God is honouring us as he glorifies his Son, by making us the sacrifices for the accomplishment of a blessing to mankind. 3. We should believe that a *great reward* in heaven will compensate for the patient endurance of these brief earthly troubles. Without this the problem would be inexplicable. With it all wrongs will be righted.

Ver. 9.—*The burning fire of inspiration.* I. THESE WORDS ARE A PROOF OF THE GENUINE INSPIRATION OF THE PROPHET. He is not thinking of convincing others of the fact of his inspiration, but simply pouring out the trouble of soul that it occasions. The ingenuousness of the utterance and the indirect allusion to the inspiration make them the more valuable. Then, the words of prophecy gained the prophet no power nor popularity, but only contempt and persecution. It is impossible to study the language of Jeremiah without feeling that he was overwhelmed with the consciousness of a Divine spiritual influence, while the dignity, vigour, and moral sublimity of his prophecies make it unreasonable to suppose that he was a self-deceived fanatic.

II. THESE WORDS ARE AN ILLUSTRATION OF THE POWERFUL INFLUENCE OF INSPIRATION. This was not a mere illumination; it was a power. The inspired prophet was not simply gifted with insight into truth; he was swayed by the might of it. He did not feel at liberty to deal with it as he pleased, to mediate on it by himself, to suppress it, to utter it only as his convenience was suited; it was his master, a hand laid heavily upon him, a fire burning in his bosom, that must come out. The same experience is felt by all men who have spiritual relations with truth. They do not hold truth; they find that truth holds them. That inspiration influences the will as well as the intellect is strikingly proved in the case of Balaam (Numb. xxiv.). The reason of this is found in the real presence of the Spirit of God. Revelation is by inspiration, and inspiration is the breathing of God's Spirit into a man's spirit, so that he becomes possessed by it. The tremendous importance of the truth revealed increases this compulsion of utterance. Jeremiah had revealed to him no barren, abstract dogmas, no trivial religious notions, no empty answers to curious prying questions of little practical moment, but terrible truths concerning his people and their highest interests. How could he hide such truths as we have seen he had been entrusted with? If God speaks it must be to utter important words. The burden of them urges their custodian to declare them.

III. THESE WORDS ARE AN EVIDENCE OF THE PAINFUL EFFECTS OF INSPIRATION. No man need desire to be a prophet from motives of worldly ambition or selfish pleasure. The high privilege of inspiration carries with it danger, toil, anguish, terror. Prophecy has its Gethsemanes and its Golgothas. If its mission is faithfully carried out it leads to the cross. If this is faithlessly abandoned the prophet is consumed with inward fires. Inspiration is no substitute for mental labour, no excuse for intellectual indolence. On the contrary, it rouses the whole soul, quickens its energies, and works them to weariness. In so far as any of us are possessed in varying degrees by spiritual influences we shall find the Word of God a fire within us, which burns till we have discharged the mission it brings.

Vers. 10, 11.—*A prophet persecuted by spies.* I. THE PERSECUTION BY SPIES. 1, Consider the *persons* persecuting. (1) They were *mean and weak*. Their names are not given; we know little of their characters and actions; yet the despicable conduct here ascribed to them proclaims them to have been of low and shallow natures. Only such can play the part of a spy. Yet these men could trouble Jeremiah. A spy can persecute a prophet. A gnat can sting a lion. Mean and despicable creatures that can do little good have considerable power of doing harm. This fact is humiliating to our common human nature, and it shows the great need of a Providence to restrain the outrages of wickedness which are so easily executed. (2) They were *numerous*. The prophet stood alone beset on every side with malicious spies. How difficult to be faithful in that dreadful solitude of a crowd of unsympathizing persons! (3) They were Jeremiah's *familiar acquaintances*. Religious and political differences separate the best of friends. When a man's own near acquaintances turn against him the very ground he stands upon seems to be breaking away from beneath his feet. Such men have peculiar power for harm, because (*a*) they have been trusted and (*b*) they know the weak places in a man's armour. 2. Consider the *character* of the persecution. The persecution of spies must have been peculiarly harassing. (1) It was *not open*. It is so much easier to meet a frank foe in the field than to cope with the secret devices of spies. (2) It must have been *tainted with untruth*. The spy would hear enough to misunderstand, and would unconsciously misrepresent in the effort to make his report consistent and telling. The "whispering" would heighten the colour of every tale as it passed from one to another. (3) It was *perpetual*. The spies were always on the watch, ready to take advantage of the first unguarded moment. (4) It was *malicious*. The spies were eager for Jeremiah's halting, hoping to entice him to some mistake.

II. THE REFUGE FROM THIS PERSECUTION. Jeremiah found his refuge in God. 1. He could do so because he was *innocent* and because he was suffering in the *service of God*. How happy to be able thus fearlessly to challenge the arbitration of God between ourselves and our detractors! 2. The help of God is sought because he *knows all*. He sees "the reins and the heart." If the spy is watchful, with his prying looks capable of seeing only the surface of things and with only partial views, and listening only to catch up broken fragments of speech to distort and misrepresent, God is righteously watchful of *all* that his creatures say and do. 3. The help of God is trusted in because he is "a mighty terrible one." "The God is a man of war." The might and majesty of God—so terrible to the godless—are the refuge of his people. It should be remembered by all of us that God is actively concerned with human affairs, and in his providence, without requiring what we call "miracle," can frustrate the devices of the wise and defeat the efforts of the strong.

Ver. 13.—*Thanksgiving for future blessings*. I. WE MAY BE THANKFUL FOR BLESSINGS NOT YET RECEIVED. Jeremiah closes his prayer with praise. No sooner has he asked for God's help than he feels so assured of receiving it that he anticipates it in imagination, and breaks forth into grateful song as though he were already enjoying it. This is a proof of genuine faith. Faith makes the absent seem near and the future appear present (Heb. xi. 1). It influences our whole being—the imagination among other faculties—so that it enables us to conceive the good thing trusted for so vividly and so confidently that the thought of it affects the mind just as strongly as if we saw the object with our eyes and grasped it in our hands. Such an effect is a test of the earnestness and faith of prayer. Some people could not be more surprised than by receiving the exact answer to their prayers.

II. THE FULL DELIVERANCE FROM ALL HARM IS A FUTURE BLESSING FOR WHICH WE MAY BE GRATEFUL. 1. It is a *future blessing*. Jeremiah was not delivered immediately. His life was beset with danger to the end. After the time to which our text refers, he met with worse troubles than any that had hitherto befallen him. The Christian must not expect a sudden and perfect escape from all distress and temptation the moment he prays to God for help. Perfect deliverance can only come with the conquest of the last enemy, death. "Now is our salvation"—our perfect deliverance—"*nearer* than when we first believed" (Rom. xiii. 11), but it is not yet enjoyed. 2. It is, nevertheless, a blessing for which we may be truly *thankful at once*. For it is positively assured to the Christian. The heir of a great inheritance may rejoice in his prospects, though for the present he is in want. But earthly pleasures of hope are checked by fears of possible disappointment. The buds may be nipped by frost; the promising young man may break down before achieving any great work. Nevertheless God is too powerful, as well as too faithful, to fail in fulfilling his promises. Therefore we should anticipate the praises of heaven on earth, sing the songs of Zion in the strange land, and enjoy the vision of the celestial city from Beulah heights though valleys of humiliation and waters of death may lie between.

III. IT IS A GOOD THING TO EXPRESS OUR GRATITUDE FOR FUTURE BLESSINGS. 1. *All gratitude should find utterance in praise.* The grateful heart should rouse the singing voice. Of all feelings thankfulness should be the last to be mute. We may pray for mercy in secret communion with God; we should utter praise as a public testimony to others and as an uncontrollable gladness that must relieve itself in song. 2. The utterance of praise for future blessings is an *assurance of our faith.* It will react upon us and strengthen faith. It will be a solace for the dark hours that may yet intervene before the enjoyment of the anticipated good.

Vers. 14—18.—*Jeremiah cursing the day of his birth.* I. TROUBLE MAY LEAD A GOOD MAN TO THE VERGE OF DESPAIR. Jeremiah was a prophet, a good man, a man of faith, a man of prayer. Yet he cursed the day of his birth. Jeremiah was not without precedents for his conduct. Not to mention Jonah, whose character is by no means exemplary (though, poor man, he may have been good at heart), the patient Job and the courageous Elijah had both regarded existence as a curse, and cried passionately for death. Jeremiah had great provocations to despair. His mission seemed to be a failure; his old friends had become spies in league with his inveterate foes; he stood alone, watched, maligned, hated, cruelly misjudged. We cannot be surprised that his patience broke down. Though impatience and a yielding to despair are proofs of weakness, they are far less culpable than unfaithfulness. Many would have quietly declined the tasks which Jeremiah manfully performed, though they led him to the verge of despair. It must be noted that, though the prophet cursed the day of his birth, he did not flee from the mission of his life; though he longed for death, he did not commit suicide. From his experience, (1) the sorrowful may learn that deeper depths of sorrow have been traversed than any they are in, and yet the light has been reached on the further side; (2) the desponding may see how good men have been near despair before them, and so be encouraged by knowing that their despondency is not a sin of fatal unbelief.

II. IT IS FOOLISH AND WRONG FOR A MAN TO CURSE THE DAY OF HIS BIRTH. He may be a good man who falls into despair, still his despair is a failing. This condition of Jeremiah must be distinguished from that of Simeon. Simeon was ready to depart when his life's work was finished and at God's time. His prayer was one of placid submission to the will of God (Luke ii. 29). But Jeremiah had not finished his life's work; life itself was regarded by him as an evil; his despair was contrary to a spirit of resignation to the Divine will. Jeremiah's language should also be distinguished from that of St. Paul when he expressed his longing to " depart and be with Christ " (Phil. i. 23). The apostle was inspired with a hope of heaven, the prophet moved only by a loathing of life; the apostle was willing patiently to remain and do his work, the prophet felt impatient of life. 1. Such conduct is *foolish,* for the whole value of life is thus judged by one hasty thought in a mood of gloom and distress. Life is too large and multifarious to be estimated in this way. There are recuperative energies in all of us beyond what we can imagine in our moments of weakness. Besides, if the present is dark, who knows what the future will produce? 2. Such conduct is *wrong.* We are not the judges of our own lives. To despair is to complain of the justice of God. The mistake of Jeremiah's hasty impatience is apparent when we consider the value of his life. Jeremiah's life worthless! Why, it was the most valuable life of the age. There may be persons of whom it can be said that it were better for those men if they had never been born. But these are not the men who are usually most ready to despair of their lives. The despondent may take courage from the mistake of Jeremiah, and know that when they think their lives most worthless they may really be of most service.

III. THE CHRISTIAN HAS STRONG INDUCEMENTS NOT TO CURSE THE DAY OF HIS BIRTH. Jeremiah lived before the light and grace of Christianity had been bestowed. We should be without excuse if, while enjoying higher advantages, we imitated his despair. 1. Christianity sheds *light on the purpose of sorrow.* This was a profound mystery to the Jew. Christ has shown us the blessedness of sorrow, the glory of the cross, the utility of sacrifice.   2. Christianity brings *new grace* to help in the endurance of sorrow. Christians have the example of the suffering Christ, the sympathy and healing of the great Physician and the new baptism of the Spirit, to help them to endure the baptism of sorrow.   3. Christianity reveals fresh ground for *confidence in God* in the darkness of trouble.   God is seen as our Father.   His will must be wise and good.   All life must be wisely ordered by him.   Thus we are taught to bend submissively to the higher will that we cannot understand.   4. Christianity inspires *hope* in the final triumph over trouble.   It lifts the veil from eternal things and makes known the "far more exceeding and eternal weight of glory."   It assures us that no true life can ultimately fail, that no true man lives in vain, that, though evil may vaunt itself in the present, ultimately truth and right shall triumph.

HOMILIES BY VARIOUS AUTHORS.

Vers. 1—3.—*The behaviour of the wicked towards the truth.*   I. THEY REGARD THE TRUTH AND ITS MINISTERS AS THEIR GREATEST ENEMIES.   If Pashur had known better he would have refrained from such exhibitions of temper.   The prophet would then have been accounted the greatest benefactor of his country.   Not the soldier on the battle-field nor the statesman in the councils of empire could have rendered so signal a service as Jeremiah did in simply but persistently telling the truth.   Much of what he said was patent to every honest observer.   By saying what he did the prophet did not bring into existence that which did not exist before; and, if it really existed, it was better that it should be recognized and reckoned with.   The evils he denounced were the real enemies of the country, and not those who pointed them out and suggested their reform.   It is, however, unpleasant to the carnal mind to have its faults and sins exposed.   With many the calamity is not that evil should be done, but that it should be found out.   II. THEY ARE NOT SCRUPULOUS AS TO THE MEANS THEY EMPLOY TO SILENCE THEM. He "smote Jeremiah the prophet, and put him in the stocks."   These means of punishment were at hand, and he used them at once.   It was legal power used illegally, or law employed to the detriment of righteousness.   Passionate hatred is shown by the whole course of action.   Could anything else be expected of those who tried to subvert righteousness?   They must needs do it unrighteously.   Even the condemnation of Christ was legal only in appearance.   III. THE BEHAVIOUR OF THE OPPONENTS OF THE TRUTH IS FREQUENTLY CONDEMNED BY ITS OWN INCONSISTENCY AND VACILLATION.   "It came to pass on the morrow, that Pashur brought forth Jeremiah out of the stocks."   1. *The course dictated by passion is seen to be impolitic and foolish.*   2. *The guilty intention is weakened by the outcries of conscience.*   It is this conscience which makes cowards of us all—or heroes.   Here it led to vacillation, which discredited the policy to which Pashur was already committed, and made its author ridiculous.   This is one of the reasons why men can do nothing against the truth.   It shines by its own light and confounds the machinations that have been wrought in darkness.   3. *Truth has a powerful ally in the bosoms of its worst enemies.*   IV. OPPOSITION TO THE TRUTH IS CERTAIN TO FAIL.   "Then said Jeremiah unto him," etc. (ver. 3).   The prophet is only the more vehement and enthusiastic.   Ill-timed antagonism to his message has provoked him to coin a nickname for Pashur, which linked the impending judgment inseparably with his memory.   It was a bad eminence richly deserved.   He was to be the refutation of himself, to see all his predictions falsified, and to reap the curses of those he had deceived as they perished in their sins. How often in his disgraceful exile he must have wished he had let the messenger of God alone (Acts v. 38, 39)!—M.

Vers. 3—6.—*Magor-Missabib; or, the fate of a false prophet.*   The person here mentioned cannot with certainty be identified.   He will the better serve as a type and representative of his kind.   There is no age or country that has not had its Pashur.   I. THE INFLUENCE HE EXERCISED.   1. *Its character.*   Absolute and despotic.   At the suggestion of his own evil heart. Capable of destroying civil rights and character itself. The whole civil and sacred machinery of the land was at his disposal. The public trusted him. The state of things condemned by Jeremiah it was his immediate interest to support, and in turn he could rely upon official support. He identifies himself with the ruling party and becomes its representative and mouthpiece. Vested rights, traditional religion, etc., are his watchwords, because he owes everything to them. 2. *How it was acquired.* Family connection—"the son of Immer the priest." Not by striving to reform abuses, but by fostering and upholding the *status quo.* He who was so oblivious to the wrongs of which the prophet spoke could not have been scrupulous as to the means by which he rose to position and influence. Oriental corruption and intrigue had doubtless had their part in securing his elevation. ("Pashur" probably means "extension," "pride," "eminence.") 3. *How it was employed.* Hastily, on the passionate impulse of the moment. Without regard to the essential justice of the case. And when the error is discovered no true repentance or effort at amends is visible. Cf. the time-serving policy of Agrippa (Acts. xxvi. 32).

II. THE CHARACTER AND DESTINY HE EARNED. By making himself the champion of apostate Judah, and insulting the prophet of God, he is sentenced to the same fate, but in a peculiar and aggravated degree. 1. *It would be his fortune to be looked upon as the representative and embodiment of the system of falsehood which had ruined his country.* He who prophesied falsely will be justly punished by such an association. Instead of saying, "It was Moloch or Astarte that deceived us," the victims of the common disaster will say, "It was the prophet of these false gods who led us astray." How readily does personal influence acquire such a representative character! There are many evil forces and influences at work in society, the state, the Church, etc., which would cease to exist were it not for their accidental connection with some personage who becomes their advocate or their bulwark. 2. *His character and influence would be exposed.* The assurances he had given would one by one be falsified by the fulfilments of Jeremiah's predictions. Instead of being honoured and looked up to, he would become a loathing and a byword. He would outlive his credit, his self-esteem, and his happiness. Shunned by others, he would be unable to trust himself. Each fresh catastrophe would deepen his disgrace and remorse. A "terror round about" would be the name he would earn. 3. *His exemption from immediate destruction would but enhance his punishment.* Like the criminal obliged to stand in the dock and hear all the counts of his indictment made good by the evidence of witnesses, he should outlive the first effects of the national ruin, see all his statements falsified, bear the reproach of his own wicked lies, and yet linger on when life had ceased to be desirable. There is a grotesqueness about this punishment that would make it ludicrous were it not so sad and awful. A more severe punishment could hardly be conceived. And yet it is not more than Pashur deserved. Would that our modern "prophets of lies" could be compelled to witness the consequences of their advice and example! A modified degree of this experience has, indeed, been the sentence inflicted upon many a good man. But Christ takes up the entail of sin and breaks it. We may do better than to stand by and see the evil consequences of former folly; it is for us to strive to rectify them. So the past may be retrieved and the evil days redeemed by those who have been servants of sin "turning many to righteousness."—M.

Vers. 7—18.—*The sorrow and joy of God's servant.* There are many such photographs of the inner heart-life of God's people. It is the touch of nature which brings them near to us. The words and work of Jeremiah become more living and influential when we witness his spiritual struggles.

I. THE SPIRITUAL NECESSITY OF HIS POSITION IS ALTERNATELY COMPLAINED OF AND ACQUIESCED IN. The saint cannot always continue amidst his highest experiences. There are ups and downs, not only of our actual outward circumstances, but of our inward spiritual states. Do not condemn Jeremiah until you are able to acquit yourself. The heavenly mind is not formed easily or at once. There is an inward cross in every true heart, upon which it must needs "die daily." But "the powers of the world to come" ever tend to increase their hold upon the believer. This alternation of mood and feeling is a necessary accompaniment of spiritual growth. Some day the heart will be fixed. "The reproach of Christ" will then be esteemed "greater riches than the treasures of Egypt." This is what we should strive after—inward oneness of heart and purpose with our Master.

II. His experience is transitional. 1. *From doubt to faith.* (Vers. 11, 12.) 2. *From sorrow to joy.* (Ver. 13.) 3. *One day the struggle will end in triumph.*—M.

Ver. 9.—*Why God's servants labour on.* "Then I said, I will not make mention," etc. It was under no small provocation that Jeremiah uttered these words. It was in no fit of mere indolence or infidelity that he cried, "I will not make mention of God, nor speak any more in his Name." He had stretched out his hand, but the people to whom he was sent refused; he had called, but they would not answer. And this had been their wont persistently, until he was weary, utterly weary, and out of heart, and then it was he spoke as we read here and declared he would try no more. If any one be inclined to judge him harshly, let us but read the story of his life—a story most sad, yet glorious too, so far as the grace of God and the true honour of his servant are concerned; but yet a sad story, and one which, when we have read it, will most assuredly check all disposition to censure, with anything like severity, the deeply tried servant of God who in his utter weariness said he would speak no more in the Name of God. Now, all of us who are familiar with our Bibles or who know anything of the way in which those who labour for God often fail, will know that Jeremiah by no means stands alone in his sense of hopelessness and weariness in his work. We remember Moses (Exod. v. 22; Numb. xi. 11); and how Elijah faltered beneath his burden (1 Kings xix. 4); and John the Baptist (Matt. xi. 3); and even the holy Saviour himself (John xii. 29; Luke xxii. 42). Such is the stress which doing the will of God amongst wicked men puts upon the human spirit; no wonder that it well-nigh gives way. From the experience, then, of our Saviour and of so many of his servants we must all of us who are his servants lay our account with manifold and often great discouragements, and yet more with being tried by the temptation on account of these discouragements to abandon our work altogether and to speak no more in the Name of the Lord. Now, *where is the spirit that will resist this temptation,* that will prevent the half-formed resolve to cease endeavour from being wholly formed and carried out? There is such a spirit. This strong temptation may be and has been resisted again and again. What is the secret of Christian constancy and steadfastness in the work of the Lord? We have the answer in this verse. However much any of God's servants may be tempted, as Jeremiah was, to give up his work, he still will not do so if, as was the case with Jeremiah, "the Word of the Lord is in his heart as a burning fire shut up in his bones;" then he will be "weary with forbearing," and he will find that he cannot stay. Even as Elihu (Job xxvii. 18), who said, "I am full of matter," etc.; and as Peter (Acts iv. 20), and Paul (Acts xvii. 6; xviii. 5; 1 Cor. ix. 16); and our Saviour (Luke ii. 49; xii. 50). In all these utterances we have the expression of that spirit which alone can, but surely will, bear up the servant of God amid all his difficulties and hold him steadfast to his duty in spite of every discouragement. But dropping all metaphor, let us inquire into this excellent spirit which renders such service to the tried and desponding soul. *It does exist.* The records of *the mission work* of the Church at home and abroad will furnish not a few instances of men and women whose hearts the Lord hath touched, and who, moved by this Divine impulse, have felt themselves constrained to be up and doing, to penetrate the spiritual darkness around them, and to resist the power of the devil everywhere present. Under the influence of this holy zeal, such servants of God have looked upon the heathen, the degraded, the vile, not with the natural eye alone. That revealed to them only a foul mass of vice and cruelty, sensuality and all human degradation. From such scenes and people nature turns away and would let them alone. But amid and beneath all this moral, spiritual, and physical repulsiveness, the ardent soul of God's servant sees jewels which may be won for Christ, spirits which may be regenerated and restored. His eye looks right on to what, through the grace of the gospel, these degraded ones may become; and absorbed, swallowed up by a holy Christ-like love, he determines to spend and be spent in bringing to bear on that mass of sin and evil the power of that gospel which has done so much already and which is "the power of God unto salvation unto *every one* that believeth." "The Word of God has been in their heart as," etc. *There have been times in our history* when *we* have known somewhat of this sacred impulse which fired the soul of the prophet Jeremiah.

Have we not known seasons when the impulse was strong on us to say something for God? It has come when we have been preaching or teaching, and we have broken away from the calm, not to say cold, tone in which we have been going on, and have spoken to those before us words which have come up from the very depths of our soul, and we have seen in the countenances of our children or our congregation that they, too, were conscious that they were being spoken to in a manner other than usual, and that portion of the day's lesson or the sermon has been remembered when all the rest has been forgotten. And sometimes this impossibility of keeping silence for God has come to us on the railway journey, in the quiet walk with a friend or child, or in social converse, or in the casual talk with a stranger into whose society we may have been for a while thrown; and then we have felt we must say something for God, and it has been said feebly, weakly perhaps, but nevertheless the testimony has been borne, the endeavour has been made. God would not let us be silent; we could not stay from speaking; necessity was laid upon us. These are in their measure instances of the same Spirit as that which moved the prophets and apostles of old, though in a far less degree. But it is evident how well it would be for us all who bear Christ's name to possess in far larger measure than we do this holy and irresistible impulse. The spur is what we too often need; how rarely the bridle! not the holding back, but the urging on. *Whence, then, comes* this sacred and mighty Spirit, under whose influence so many of the saints of God, even as the Son of God, have laboured on in spite of all discouragement and suffering and wrong? It is evident, from the history of Jeremiah and of all other faithful servants of God, that the method by which God impelled them to their work was by bestowing on them such gifts as these—

I. THE KNOWLEDGE OF SIN. For he who has this knows how appalling is the evil under which men live. To him this present world and its inhabitants present but one aspect, that of being under a yoke which no man can bear. He has seen the vision of sin, and it was a sight so terrible that he can never forget it. It haunts him, for he knew it was no dream of the night, but a dreadful reality of the day and of every day. It was no chimera, no fiction of his own imagination, but a real and awful power that has ruled men and still is ruling over men. What scenes of beauty it has destroyed! What fearful misery it evermore produces. There was the *garden of Eden* in all its loveliness, with every fair flower and noble tree, with luscious fruit and every herb fit for the food of man or beast; it was all beautiful, so beautiful that even God pronounced it "very good." And as chief over this fair inheritance there were the first created of our race, in form and mind and soul harmonizing with the beauty and goodness that was all around them. How blest their condition! But the scene changes. We see no longer the garden of Eden, but a weary land bearing thorns and briars; we see, too, haggard and careworn people bending in sore agony over the murdered corpse of their child, murdered by his own brother, their eldest born. What hath wrought this change? An enemy, without doubt, but what enemy? It is sin—the heart of man in rebellion against God. The Bible is full of scenes like these—misery, shame, ruin, death, all, all the work of sin. And sin reigns yet, as he to whom God has given to see the vision of sin knows full well. Who can recount its doings? Who can describe the woes it causes? What ocean would be vast enough to receive the tears it has made to flow? What colours dark enough to depict the moral and spiritual evil it has engendered? And then the sorrows of the souls that are lost, the doom of the accursed of God—the antitype of that which Jesus describes as the "fire that is never quenched, and the worm that never dies." It is the vision of this,—the appalling evil, past, present, and most of all to come,—that has risen up before the soul of him who, beholding those around him under its dominion, finds himself utterly unable to forbear telling them of the Word of the Lord to the end that they may be saved. No wonder that, in view of these dread calamities, "the Word of the Lord was in his heart," etc.

II. But a further knowledge has been given to him to contribute to this same result. Were the vision of sin all, utter and dreadful despair would be alone left to him; but it is not all. Along with the knowledge of sin there is given to him THE KNOWLEDGE OF THE GOSPEL in the Word of the Lord. It is brought home to his soul, by evidence he cannot question, that the gospel of the Lord Jesus Christ is the sure remedy for all human ill. He has a deep conviction that trust in the Redeemer, reliance on his atoning death and sacrifice, will bring peace to the conscience, purity to the mind, strength to the will, hope to the heart, and final and eternal acceptance in the presence of God. Very much of what it can do for the soul in this life he knows it has done for him, and he has seen it do yet more for others. He sees, not only the need of such great salvation as God has provided in Christ Jesus for guilty and miserable man, but also the fitness and adaptation and the actual power of this grace of God. Such is his conviction concerning the Word of the Lord, the gospel of the grace of God; and, thus persuaded of its power to bless and save mankind, he hears on all sides, and coming up from all depths of sorrow and sin, the imperative summons to him to tell of this Saviour and this salvation, and by no means to keep silence. From every hospital and asylum where the victims of vice and sin are reaping what they have sown; from every prison cell; from every place where the ruined in health, in fortune, in character, and in soul are dragging out the remainder of their wretched life; from every gallows-tree; from every impenitent's grave; and from the sinner's hell;—there comes the solemn adjuration which the apostle so keenly felt, "Woe is unto me if I preach not the gospel!" And not the sins alone, though they most, but the *sorrows* of mankind also, utter forth the same appeal. For the gospel of the Saviour is a healing balm to the sick at heart, oil and wine to the wounded spirit; it is the gospel of consolation, of hope, and of peace to the sorrowing myriads of mankind. Feeling all this, how can it be otherwise that "the Word of the Lord is in his heart as," etc.?

III. But there is one other gift needed to the full possession of that Divine Spirit which finds expression in our text. It is THE KNOWLEDGE OF CHRIST. By this is meant, not merely an acquaintance with and belief in the truths concerning our Lord's nature and work, nor even simply such belief in him as will save the soul, but such knowledge of him as is involved in deep love to him and sympathy with those objects on which his heart is set. To know Christ as your own loving Saviour, who has died for *you*, redeemed and pardoned and accepted *you*, and given *you* an inheritance amongst his own; to know him by oft and earnest communion with him, by toil and suffering for him;—this is that knowledge of Christ which, when added on to that other knowledge of sin and of the gospel of which we have already spoken, will lead to that irresistible desire to serve him which his true servants have so often felt and shown. The love of Christ must be the constraining motive, and then there will come love and labour for the souls for whom Christ died. I do not know that it is possible for us to have a deep regard and concern for those whom we have never seen or known unless we see in each individual member of mankind one of the brethren or sisters of Christ, part of Christ's body, one of his members, he being the Head of all. If this be believed, then we see that the soul of each of these men and women, though they may be of different clime and colour, and be altogether strange and perhaps repulsive to us, still, the soul of each of them is as precious to Christ as our own, and as capable of honouring and as ready to honour him as was our own. This love of Christ will lead to the love of Christ in all men, for indeed he is in all men, and this will beget a Divine charity which will be ever a mighty motive to seek their good. Then shall we possess the mind which was in him who wept over Jerusalem and prayed for his very murderers. Then shall we willingly bear disappointment, reproach, loss, or aught other ill which may come to us as we toil on in our Master's service. Here, then, in this deep knowledge of sin, of the gospel, and of Christ, have we the secret of that burning zeal which consumed the heart of Jeremiah and of others like minded to him. May God, of his mercy, give to all who labour in his cause this holy and quenchless zeal! Labouring under such impulse, let come what will to us in this world as the result of our toil, we will still labour on. Blessed Lord Jesus Christ, let thy Word be in our hearts as a burning fire, so that when tempted to forbear making mention of thee and speaking any more in thy Name, we may be weary of such forbearing and feel we cannot stay.—C.

Vers. 14—18.—"*Is life worth living?*" Here is one who evidently thought it was not. How bitterly he grieves over the fact that he was ever brought into existence! It is an illustration, as has been pointed out, of the maddening force of suffering. It drives a man to the use of wild language. For great sufferings generate great passions in the soul. They rouse the whole man into action. And these great passions thus roused often become irrepressible.   Many men of no ordinary meekness and self-control are overborne at such times—Jeremiah, Job, Moses, Elijah; and then they express themselves in unmeasured terms.   It is as a flood broken loose.   Its rushing, foaming waters pour along, and over all that lies in their path.   Hence it is that the prophet here, not content with cursing the day of his birth, utters wild execrations on the messenger that announced it to his father.   Thus passionately does he protest against the misery and misfortune of his life.   Nor has he been alone in such dark thoughts concerning life.   Cf. Job iii., where the patriarch, in almost identical language, deplores the fact of his birth.   And Moses prayed that God would kill him out of hand (Numb. xi. 15); and Elijah (1 Kings xix. 4).   And there have been a whole host of men who have in the most emphatic way affirmed their belief that life is not worth living by refusing to live it any longer—Saul, Ahithophel, Judas, and the suicides of all ages declare this.   And many more who have not given this dread proof of their sincerity have yet maintained the same.   Sophocles said, "Not to be born is best in every way. Once born, by far the better lot is then at once to go back whence we came."   Goethe, as he drew near his end, notwithstanding that all men regarded his career as one which had been highly favoured and very enviable, is reported to have said, "They have called me a child of fortune, nor have I any wish to complain of the course of my life.   Yet it has been nothing but sorrow and labour; and I may truly say that in seventy-five years I have not had four weeks of true comfort.   It was the constant rolling of a stone that was always to be lifted anew.   When I look back upon my earlier and middle life and consider how few are those left who were young with me, I am reminded of a summer visit to a watering-place.   On arriving one makes the acquaintance of those who have already been some time there and leave the week following.   This loss is painful.   Now one becomes attached to the second generation, with which one lives for a time and becomes intimately connected.   But this also passes away and leaves us solitary with the third, which arrives shortly before our own departure, and with which we have no desire to have much intercourse."   And the gloomy musings of Hamlet, "To be or not to be, that is the question," is another example, which has been followed by the whole tribe of those who are called pessimists, of representing life as a curse rather than a blessing.   And we cannot deny that there are many now whose lot in life is so sad, that, if we looked only at the present, we could not vindicate the justice and still less the goodness of God in regard to them.   And the terrible lottery that life is, a lottery in which the blanks far outnumber the prizes, goes far to account for the apathetic indifference with which the deaths of such myriads of children are regarded.   If all parents knew for certain that the lot of their children would be bright or mainly so, how much more jealously would their lives be guarded and avenged!   And there are many men who, whilst they stammer out some kind of thanksgiving for their "preservation and all the blessings of this life," fail utterly to feel thankful for their "creation." They would much rather not have been.   So that there can be no doubt that there is a larger and it is to be feared an increasing number of people who are desperately or despairingly asking the question which stands at the head of this homily, and which this passionate protest of the prophet against his birth has suggested.   But how is all this?   Let us therefore inquire—

I. WHAT ARE THE CAUSES OF SUCH CHEERLESS THINKING AND SPEAKING?   We reply: 1. *Temperament* has a great deal to do with it.   Some are born with a sunny, bright, cheerful disposition; let them go down on their knees and give God thanks for it, for it is a better gift to them, more surely secures their happiness, than thousands of gold and silver.   But others are born with a temperament the very reverse—pessimists from their mothers' womb, always seeing the dark side of things, melancholy, foreboding, complaining.   It is a positive disease, and calls for mingled pity and careful discipline.   2. But more often still it is, *the continued and sore pressure of sorrow.* So was it with Job and here with Jeremiah.   And it is still the bitter disappointments, the miserable failures, "the slings and arrows of outrageous fortune," trouble upon trouble,—these are prolific sources of the sad views of life of which we speak.   3. But most of all, *sin*—moral evil—is the real cause.   The "philosophy of melancholy" finds its true parentage there.   It is this which causes that unrest and torment of soul, that hiding of the face of God and uplifting of the scourge of conscience, which throws all life into shadow and blots out the sun from the heavens.   It is this which leads it to be said of and felt by a man, that it had been better for him that he had never been born.

II. WHAT IS THE TRUTH ON THE MATTER? *Such conclusion as that of the pessimist never can be right*, for our deepest moral instincts teach us that, if life were more of a curse than a blessing, he who is the God of mercy and righteousness would never have given it; and that if it were better for a man that he had not been born, he would not have been born. Life *must* be a blessing or it would not be given. 1. Universal instinct says so. See how men cling to life. The law of self-preservation is the first law of nature. 2. The summing up of the hours in which we have enjoyed peace and satisfaction, and of those which have been darkened by pain and distress, would probably in *all* lives show a vast balance on the side of the former. Let any one honestly make the calculation for themselves. 3. The laws of life all tend to produce happiness; "In keeping of God's commandments there *is* great reward." 4. Good men who may have held dark views of life have done so "in haste," as Ps. xxxi. 22 and cxvi. 11; or through looking at one point of their lives only (cf. the joyous praise of ver. 13; what a contrast and contradiction to the verses that follow!); or in ignorance of the truths and consolations which the gospel has introduced. Thus was it with Job and the Old Testament saints generally, and, of course, with all pagan nations. 5. Evil men are not to be credited. They have themselves poisoned life's springs, and whilst they speak truly enough concerning their own life, they are not competent witnesses as to what all life is. 6. Then "it is the Lord that hath made us, and not we ourselves," and because of this all lands are bidden "be joyful in the Lord" (Ps. c.). Now, how could this be if life were not worth living? 7. The future which Christ has prepared. Let that be taken into view and *quæstio cœdit*. Life is but the porchway to that which is life indeed—the eternal life. Our afflictions, therefore, which here we suffer are light, and "but for a moment," and so, "not worthy to be compared with the glory that shall be revealed." (1) Then, "Sursum corda," "Lift up your hearts;" "*Be* joyful in the Lord," because he hath made us. (2) Be reticent of such thoughts and words as these of Jeremiah. How far short he falls of the apostles of our Lord! They *rejoiced* in tribulations. Jeremiah had better not have so spoken; better have copied him who said, "If I speak thus I shall offend against the generation of thy children." (3) Pray to be kept from temptation so to speak or even think, for such temptation is hard to overcome.—C.

Ver. 9.—*A burning fire within.* The mental condition of the prophet here recalls the beginning of his ministry. Just as he then shrank from taking its responsibility upon him, so now he is ready to throw it up in despair. His life seems to him altogether a failure. He is a disappointed and defeated man. He will "make mention of the Lord no more, nor speak any longer in his Name." Many an earnest ministering spirit has felt like this, overborne by the force of the world's evil, impatient of the slow progress of the kingdom of truth and righteousness. But the prophet cannot so easily throw up his work. God, as at the beginning, is "stronger than he," and holds him firmly in his grasp; holds him to his office and ministry by the force, not so much of outward circumstance as of a spiritual persuasion, by the strong necessity of an inward law. "His Word was in my heart as a burning fire," etc. Note here—

I. THE INHERENT PROPERTY OF THE WORD OF GOD AS A LIVING POWER IN THE SOULS OF MEN. "A burning fire" (see also ch. xxiii. 29). All Divine truth possesses a quality that may justly be thus represented. The Law that came by Moses was a "fiery Law," of which the thunders and lightnings of Sinai were the appropriate associations (Deut. xxxii. 2). And even the inspiration of gospel truth was fitly symbolized by "cloven tongues of fire" (Acts ii. 3). There is not only light but heat, not only a flame but fire. The moral effects are manifest. 1. *Melting.* Icy coldness, hard indifference, stubborn self-will, impenitence, etc.,—all these are softened by the fire of God when it really enters into the soul. A tender sensibility is thus created that prepares it to receive all Divine impressions. 2. *Kindling.* Heaven-tending affections are awakened by it that did not exist before. Latent germs of nobler and better feeling are quickened into new life. There is no limit to the holy energies that may be developed in our nature by the inspiration of the truth of God. In this good sense we may say, "Behold, how great a matter a little fire kindleth!" 3. *Consuming.* It destroys everything in us that is destructible. All that is false, selfish, sensual—all that is "of the earth, earthy"—has in it the elements of dissolution and decay, and cannot resist the purging, purifying force of Divine truth. The dross is consumed that the precious gold may come forth in all its beauty and purity. The solid grain is quickened into fruitful life, the chaff is burnt up as with unquenchable fire.

II. THE OBLIGATION IT IMPOSES. "I was weary with forbearing," etc. (see ch. vi. 11). The soul of the prophet was acted upon by a force that overcame, not only the weakness of his fears, but the strength of his self-will and of every motive that would induce him to relinquish his work. Every earnest, heroic servant of truth is sensible of this inward constraint. It is the constraint (1) of a Divine call, (2) of a masterful conscience, (3) of conscious power to benefit others, (4) of an instinctive impulse to communicate the good one's own soul possesses. St. Paul stands before us as a conspicuous example of this when he says, "For if I preach the gospel, I have nothing to glory of: for necessity is laid upon me," etc. (1 Cor. ix. 16). There is no clearer mark of a noble, Christ-like nature than submission to such a constraint as this.—W.

Vers. 1—6.—*A changed name and a dreadful doom.* The change here, from Pashur to Magor-Missabib, reminds us of other divinely indicated changes of name in Scripture; *e.g.* from Abram to Abraham, from Jacob to Israel, from Simon to Peter, from Zacharias to John. These changes, however, were indicative of advancement and honour; were suggestive of the rise out of nature into grace. But here is a name which becomes at once the memorial of great wickedness and of the sure judgment following upon it.

I. THE NAME BEFORE THE CHANGE. Whatever doubt there may be as to the precise signification of the name Pashur, it seems quite clear that the very meaning of the word had in it something peculiarly honourable. The man himself belonged to a privileged order and held an office of influence and honour; and the name must have been given to him because of something auspicious in the circumstances of his birth. An honourable name is an advantage to its bearer, and to a certain extent also a challenge. He who bears it may so live that in the end there will be the greatest contrast between the name and the character. A less suggestive name, one less provocative of contrasts, might have saved Pashur from the new and portentous name which, once given, would never be forgotten. We are bound to consider well the associations which will gradually gather around the name we happen to bear. Now, at least, the particular name has very little signification in itself; but the longer *we* bear it the more significant it becomes to all who know us. Every time it is mentioned it brings to mind, more or less, our character. Even on prudential considerations one must ever become increasingly careful of what he does, for a single act may obliterate all the associations of respect and confidence which belong to his name. Instead of becoming, what every one may become, the object of respect and confidence to at least a few, he may end in being an object of execration far and wide.

II. WHAT BROUGHT THE CHANGE. His treatment of Jeremiah. His treatment of him, bear in mind, as a prophet. We feel that Jeremiah was not put in prison on even a plausible allegation that he was an evil-doer. That he was a false prophet was the only possible charge to lay against him. Now, Pashur must have known that *he himself* was a false prophet, speaking as God's truth what was only the fabrication of his own self-willed and deceitful heart. If Jeremiah was speaking falsehood, Pashur's duty was to convince him of error, and show the people that he was either a fanatic or a mere impostor. We are not allowed to suppose that what Pashur did he did from some excusable outbreak of zeal on behalf of the building of which he was custodian. A great punishment from the hand of God always argues a correspondingly great offence. It is not so amongst men; there may be a great punishment and a very small offence; sometimes, indeed, no offence at all, measured by the highest law. But when God punishes severely it lets in light upon the character of him whom he punishes. We know that Pashur must have been a bad man; we know it as well as if all his iniquity had been detailed in the most forcible language.

III. THE SIGNIFICANCE OF THE CHANGE. We have not information enough to give us the exact meaning of Pashur; and one might almost think this was meant to heighten the certainty as to the meaning of Magor-Missabib. At present Pashur was in a position of comparative security. If security can be claimed for anything in this world, it seems sometimes to belong to such as hold official positions. But with regard to Pashur all depended on the continuance of Jerusalem. The Lord's house where he was governor was to be destroyed, and then where would he be? Hitherto Pashur has been a nameless unit, involved, but not peculiarly involved, in the general doom. But now he has a prediction all to himself. Henceforth he will be known, must be known, as the man whom Jeremiah threatened with this new and dreadful name. Evidently the name stuck. Some speakers and writers have had this power of giving names that stick. It is not an enviable one, and has often been cruelly used. But God, on whose lips it will always be rightly used, can make it to serve good purposes. The best proof that the name stuck is seen in this, that the prophet's enemies tried straightway to fix the name on him (ver. 10). But everything depends on who gives a name. Jeremiah's enemies might speak of terror, but they could not terrify. God both spoke of terror and in due time brought the terrifying realities around the doomed man. There was nothing at present, and might not be for some time, to show what was coming. But God can wait. We have no doubt that in due time Pashur was forced to the confession that the name was fully justified.—Y.

Vers. 7—9.—*A conflict not to be avoided.* The heart of the prophet is here revealed to us as the scene of a bitter conflict between two sets of motives; one set originating with the vehement will of God, the other in the utterly unsympathizing dispositions of men. The prophet makes us feel that it is utterly insufficient to describe his work simply as difficult. It is done amid a continuity of reproaches, some of which a less sensitive man might not have felt, but which were peculiarly irritating to a man of Jeremiah's sensibilities. Generally it may be observed that God did not send thick-skinned men to be his prophets.

I. THE DIVINELY PRODUCED CONVICTION UNDER THE FORCE OF WHICH HE BEGAN THIS WORK. The people might say, "You speak irritating words to us, and you must not complain if we speak irritating words to you. Those who live in glass houses must not throw stones." Thus it is well for the prophet to assert most emphatically, as he does in ver. 7, that he spoke from *a divinely produced conviction of duty.* God impressed—as God alone can impress—certain irresistible considerations on his mind. Not only was he persuaded, but it was *God* who had persuaded him. The reasons for his prophetic action were not such as he had sought out and discovered for himself. God put them before him in their proper aspect, order, and totality.

II. THE FIRST PAINFUL RESULT OF FIDELITY TO GOD. Perhaps in the youthful confidence with which he began his prophecies he would anticipate that since God had so clearly sent him, the people would as trustfully and obediently receive him. But not all the *genuineness* of a Divine message can commend it any more to the selfish man who naturally hates to be disturbed and threatened. The prophet intimates that the reception he met with was daily, universal, invariable. He seemed to be ordained to stir up the nests and dens and hiding-places of every noxious being amongst men. He who goes among hornets and scorpions must not complain if he has to suffer great agonies from their venomous sting. We are sure, indeed, that the prophet must have had some sympathizers, but the treatment which caused him such agony would also have the effect of making friends keep silent, lest they might be the next to suffer. It is no strange thing that men should become resentful and savage under the home-thrusts of spiritual truth. Men who *love* evil resent even the gentlest approaches of God in trying to take that evil away.

III. THE EARLIER RESULT PRODUCED BY THIS INTOLERABLE TREATMENT IN JEREMIAH'S OWN MIND. It is easy to criticize the prophet, and say that he should not have been so much affected by all these hard words. But it was just the multitude of them that made them intolerable. A man would be cowardly to complain of being stung now and then; but if he is to be exposed to stinging insects every hour of the day, that is an altogether different matter. God made one of the terrible plagues of Egypt out of multitudes of tiny creatures, such as, individually, counted for almost nothing. Let us not, then, talk condemningly of this proposed repression of the prophetic message. He had reached a crisis in which, we may well believe, Jehovah, who sent him, was peculiarly near to him.   May we not reverently say that even as Jesus reached the inexpressible culmination of his mental agony in Gethsemane, so the prophets, in their lesser measure, may have had crises, not unlike that of Gethsemane, when the forces arrayed against them seemed more than they could possibly resist? Profound should our feeling be that it may become a very hard thing to bear faithful testimony for God in an ungodly world.

IV. THE FINAL RESULT. The risk of unfaithfulness is put beyond Jeremiah's control.   He is put between two great "cannots."   He cannot bear the reproaches of the people.   That on the one hand.   But, on the other hand, he finds that he cannot keep unexpressed the message of Jehovah.   God takes his Word into his own keeping. The pain of prophesying, great as it was, was less than the pain of withholding the prophecy.   It is not till we come to deal with God that we learn the real meaning of the word " intolerable."   It is ever a mark of God's true servants, that in times when there is great need of testimony they cannot keep silent.   Better to burn at the stake than to have one's true, inner life burnt up in resisting God.   Paul is a grand example of a man who was forced to speak by the fire within.   He could not be silent ; he could not temporize, compromise, or postpone.   Luther is another instance.   Those destitute of the fire in their hearts cannot understand those who have it ; and therefore it is the very height of ignorant audacity to censure it.   Nothing is more to be desired, whatever pain it may bring with it, than that we should have God's truth as a living and growing fire in our hearts ; and in order to do this, we must be careful not to quench it in the beginnings of its risings within us.—Y.

Vers. 10—13.—*The name Magor-Missabib wrongly applied.*   I. THE HOPES OF JEREMIAH'S ENEMIES.   We have seen in the preceding passage (vers. 7—9) how the prophet was incessantly exposed to exceedingly irritating taunts from his enemies ; and how the pain of these taunts in a measure tempted him to try if he could not escape the pain by ceasing to prophesy.   Jehovah perfectly preserved him from this danger.   The prophetic fire within him, divinely kindled and sustained, was too strong to be thus extinguished.   It grew more and more, and the very taunts of the ungodly became as fuel to make it burn more fiercely.   But this very faithfulness of the prophet only increased his danger as an object of persecution.   His enemies will themselves begin to feel in danger from this continual reference to their evil doings.   Mere mockery has itself a tendency to go further.   Bengel, referring to the development of the persecuting spirit, as illustrated in the apostolic days, says, " The world begins with *ridicule* ; then afterwards it proceeds to *questioning* ; to *threats* ; to *imprisoning* ; to inflicting *stripes* ; to *murder*" (see 'Gnomon' on Acts ii. 13).   Jeremiah has already been for a night in prison, and he knows not how soon a longer and worse imprisonment may come.   He hears threatenings on every hand.   The name Magor-Missabib that, by Divine direction, he has applied to Pashur, is retorted on him, as being, in the opinion of his enemies, a name eminently appropriate to his present circumstances.   So far as the human elements were concerned, his chances of safety appeared very poor indeed. His enemies are numerous and crafty ; and, sharpened by self-interest, they needed no exhortation to be watchful.   Those who compare these confessions of the prophet at different times with the experiences of Jesus at the hands of his enemies, will notice a remarkable parallelism.   What Jesus said with respect to the scribes and Pharisees is peculiarly forcible when considered in the light of Jeremiah's trials : "Ye are the children of them which killed the prophets " (Matt. xxiii. 31).

II. THE SUFFICIENCY OF JEREMIAH'S PROTECTION.   Here is the man of strong faith, and of a speech full of confidence and calmness.   He may well be depressed ; beset as he is with so much malice, brought into close contact with the worst wickedness of the human heart.   But, on the other hand, he has this for his comfort, that, the closer wicked men come to him, the closer he finds himself to God.   This is the service the wicked render to the witnesses of God, that, the more they persecute them, the more they press them towards the great Helper.   The ungodly little dream of the service they render in this respect.   So far as abiding results are concerned, the spirit of intolerance has done the direct contrary of what it was intended to do.   The purposes of evil might have been better served if the Church of Christ had had an easier time of it in the beginning.   He who is potentially the mighty, terrible One in the midst of his people, needs the opposition of the wicked in order that all his power to defend his people may be known. This, indeed, is one of the lessons taught by the sufferings of Jesus even to death. Darkness was to get its hour and its power, that so the Light of the world might be more fully glorified. Never was it more emphatically true than when Jesus was laid in the grave, that Jehovah was with him as a mighty, terrible One. We look with the natural eye, and we see a cold corpse apparently gone the way of all flesh; we look with the eye of faith, and we discern One standing by who at the appointed hour will raise that corpse, and make it the channel of manifestations of life such as were not possible before.—Y.

Vers. 14—18.—*The prophet cursing the day of his birth.* It is very perplexing to find these words following so closely upon the confidences expressed in vers. 11—13. And yet the perplexity is to some extent removed when we recollect how largely man is the creature of his moods. That he is bright and confident to-day may not hinder him from being in the depths of despair to-morrow. It is well for us to see how low a real and faithful prophet of God can sink. One is reminded at once of the similar words put into the mouth of Job. We have advantages, however, in considering this expression of Jeremiah which we lack in considering the similar expression of Job. Of Job we know nothing except as the subject of one of the sublimest poems in the world. What substance of fact may have suggested the poem it is beyond our powers to determine. But Jeremiah stands before us unquestionably a real man, a prominent character in the highway of history.

I. THE FEELING THAT UNDERLIES THIS TERRIBLE IMPRECATION. The *form* of the imprecation is not to be too much regarded. The same feeling will be very differently expressed in different languages and among different races. What Jeremiah means is made clear in ver. 18. Just at this particular time it seems to him that life has been nothing but one huge failure. He has no heart to accept suggestions such as might mitigate his gloom. He will not even allow that life has had any other possibilities than those of failure and shame, and therefore the congratulations attending his birth were misplaced. The more we look into his language here, the more we see that it was very wild and foolish. The important matter is that, in approaching the consideration of these words, we should have a distinct impression of how recklessly even a good man may talk. A recollection of Jeremiah's utterance here will keep us from wondering that there should be so much of foolish and impious talk in the world.

II. THE FACT WAS AS FAR AS POSSIBLE FROM CORRESPONDING TO THE FEELING. We look at Jeremiah's career as a whole, and at the permanent value of his prophecies, and then we see how little moods and feelings count for just by themselves. We gain nothing by saying of any man that it might have been better for him if he had never been born. It is true that Jesus spoke thus of Judas, but we are not at liberty to say what he says; and besides, he was speaking in the language of necessary hyperbole, in order to emphasize the dreadful wickedness of the traitor. The safe ground for us to take is that entrance upon human life in this world is a good thing. Even with all the trials of life, the position of a human being in this world is a noble one, and his possibilities for the future are beyond imagination. While it is right that we should have the deepest compassion for the deformed, the defective, the infirm, we must also recollect that it is better to be the most deformed of human beings than the shapeliest and healthiest of brutes. In face of all the present afflictions of human nature, one thought should be sufficient to brighten them all, namely, the thought of how perfectly comprehensive is the renewing power of God. Within its grasp it comprehends the most imperfect and distorted of human organizations. Jeremiah was making the huge blunder of looking at things entirely from the point of view of his own feelings, and his present feelings. His actions were better than his words. Speaking out of his own feelings, he talked great folly and falsehood; speaking as the prophet of God, his utterances were those of wisdom and truth. The fact was that of no one belonging to his generation could it be more truly said than of him that his birth was a good thing; good for the nation, good for himself, good for the glory and service of Jehovah. We must not bemoan existence because there is *suffering* in it. Suffering may be very protracted and intense, and yet life be full of blessing. Jesus had to suffer more than any man. He shrank from the approach of death with a sensitiveness which we cannot conceive, who have in us the mortal taint by reason of indwelling sin. Nothing reconciled him to the thought of all he had thus to endure save that it was the clear will of God. What was Jeremiah's mental suffering compared with that of Jesus? And yet, though the *life* of Jesus was to be one of peculiar and unparalleled sufferings, his *birth* had angels to announce and celebrate it.—Y.

EXPOSITION.

CHAPTER XXI.

The chapter falls into three parts, two of which seem to be in some sort of connection, while the third is isolated. First comes a warning to the messengers of Zedekiah of the unfortunate issue of the rebellion against Babylon; this is followed by a counsel to the people to give up their futile resistance, and "fall away" to the Chaldeans. The last four verses contain an exhortation to the "house of David" to fulfil their high duties with greater conscientiousness, for fear of the judgment which had already begun to take effect when the former part of this chapter was written. Compare Zedekiah's embassy to Jeremiah with that of Hezekiah to Isaiah on a similar emergency (Isa. xxxvii. 2).

Ver. 1.—**Pashur.** A different Pashur from the one mentioned in ch. xx. 1. This one reappears in ch. xxxviii. 1; he belonged to the fifteenth of the sacerdotal families, named after Melchiah (comp. 1 Chron. ix. 12). **Zephaniah**; mentioned again in ch. xxix. 25; xxxvii. 3. He was of the priestly family or class of Maaseiah (comp. 1 Chron. xxiv. 18), and was next in rank to the high priest (ch. lii. 24).

Ver. 2.—**Nebuchadrezzar.** This form predominates in Jeremiah and Daniel, and is the only form found in Ezekiel. It is, in fact, the correct way of spelling the name, which is in Babylonian *Nabu-kudura-uçur,* i.e. "Nebo, protect [or perhaps, 'has made'] the crown." **According to all his wondrous works**; e.g. the destruction of Sennacherib, which must have occurred in the first instance to the minds of devout Jews.

Ver. 4.—**I will assemble them into the midst of this city;** i.e. I will compel the warriors to give up resistance, and shut themselves up within the walls.

Ver. 7.—**And such as are**; rather, left *which are left.* (There has been an obvious error in the repetition of "and.")

Ver. 9.—**He that abideth in this city,** etc. No doubt Jeremiah often gave this counsel to his fellow-citizens (comp. ch. xxxviii. 1, 17), and it appears from ch. xxxviii. 19; xxxix. 9; lii. 15, that many of the Jews acted in accordance with it. **Falleth**; more distinctly, *falleth away* (as ch. xxxvii. 14, Authorized Version); i.e. goeth over to.

Ver. 11.—**And touching the house,** etc. The formula with which this section is introduced shows that it was attached to vers. 1—7 at the same time as vers. 8—10, although obviously written at a much earlier period.

Ver. 12.—**O house of David.** The "house of David" here, as in Isa. vii. 13, means the various branches of the royal family, the same, in fact, which are called by courtesy "kings of Judah" in ch. xvii. 20 (see note). They appear from the present passage to have monopolized the judicial function. **Deliver him that is spoiled,** etc. The poor man would have no advocate to plead for him; in this case the judge was to see that he suffered no injustice in consequence.

Ver. 13.—Jehovah, standing, as it were, on the Mount of Olives, addresses the proud city beneath him. **O inhabitant of the valley, and rock of the plain**; rather, *O inhabitress;* Jerusalem is personified as a virgin. The poetical description of the capital as a "valley" (the word, however, signifies a valley as wide as a plain) reminds us of "the valley [or rather, 'ravine'] of vision" (Isa. xxii. 1, 5); while "the rock of the plain" recalls "my mountain in the field" (ch. xvii. 3). So, as Graf points out, Babylon is called "a mountain" in metaphorical language (ch. li. 25). It is, however, singular that the prophet should call Jerusalem a "valley" and a "rock" in the same passage. In the former, perhaps, Jeremiah is thinking specially of the lower city, and in the latter of Mount Zion. **Who shall come down against us?** viz. from the "hills round about Jerusalem."

Ver. 14.—**In the forest thereof**; i.e. in the forest of houses (comp. ch. xxii. 6, 7).

HOMILETICS.

Vers. 1, 2.—*God consulted in vain.* I. IT IS VAIN TO SEEK GOD'S HELP WITHOUT REPENTING OF OUR SIN. Zedekiah sends to Jeremiah in his alarm. But he gives no sign of repentance. The dread of coming trouble and the desire to escape it are not penitence ; the fear of hell is not penitence. All men naturally desire to be safe from suffering. But God will only deliver those who also desire to be free from sin, who regret the evil they have done, not merely that which they endure.

II. IT IS VAIN TO SEEK GOD'S HELP WITHOUT SUBMITTING TO HIS WILL. Zedekiah consults God as an oracle ; he wants information. But he gives no indication of a willingness to obey the command of God. He would be glad of Divine aid for his own plans, but he has no thought of yielding himself up to the execution of God's will. Many men would have God for their servant ; their prayer is that God would do their will. Such presumptuous conduct must be rebuked by failure.

III. IT IS VAIN TO SEEK GOD'S HELP FOR DELIVERANCE FROM THAT WHICH IS MORALLY NECESSARY. There is a moral necessity as well as a physical. No sane man would pray that two and two might make five. There are moral impossibilities equally impregnable. A just God cannot forgive the impenitent. All that God does must be for the best, and nothing can induce him to turn from what he knows is best. If men need chastisement God will give it them, though they may most earnestly desire to be delivered from it. It was good for the Jews as a discipline, as well as just as a punishment, that they should be carried captive to Babylon. Therefore, even if all thoughts of inflicting the penalties of justice were in abeyance, God's merciful intentions to his people would make their prayers for escape vain.

Vers. 8—10.—*The choice between life and death.* I. THE CHOICE WAS FREE. It was left to the Jews to choose which course they would take. God has endowed every man with freedom of will, opening up to him a vast range of possibilities. All of us have opportunities for choosing life and blessedness if only we will seek them. A Divine vocation marks out for us a course which we *ought* to follow in preference to the fancies of our own inclination, and a Divine destiny sets us down in a certain sphere bounded by definite limitations beyond which we cannot go; but within these limits we are free from compulsion, and even in regard to the vocation no force is exerted to make us follow it. We are under moral obligation to do so, but we are left to freely acknowledge or reject the claims of that obligation.

II. THE CHOICE WAS MOMENTOUS. It was between life and death. These were the great alternatives of the Deuteronomic covenant (Deut. xxx. 19). The same alternatives are set before us spiritually (Rom. vi. 23). Life is not to be played with; tremendous issues depend on the manner in which it is conducted. Religion is no mere topic of abstract speculation for learned leisure, no empty toy for idle sentiment; it is of vast practical moment, for it deals with the choice of the greatest possible alternatives—life and death.

III. THE CHOICE WAS LIMITED. The choice which was set before the Jews by Jeremiah was gloomy enough. The best prospect offered to them was escape from massacre indeed, but escape to exile and captivity. We may come to such a condition that no effort will restore the lost possessions and gladness of the past. Even though there is no ground for despair, though the worst may be avoided, our conduct may bear such inevitable fruits in poverty, loss of position, alienation of friends, sickness, etc., that our best prospects may be far from satisfactory. This is necessary, for moral choice cannot undo past facts nor overleap the barriers of physical law. It is wise, for the disagreeable fruits of sin may be useful medicines in the form of chastisement. Yet the New Testament offers us a freer choice for the ultimate future; as the alternative of death not captivity and a life of sorrow, but eternal life and liberty, the full restoration to the blessings of God's favour (1 John v. 11, 12).

IV. THE CHOICE OF LIFE INVOLVED SAFETY WITH SUBMISSION. Jeremiah said that death would await those who stayed in Jerusalem to resist the invader from behind the city walls, while they who went out to the field to yield themselves up without fighting would be spared. For this advice the prophet was regarded as a traitor. It was justified, because (1) resistance was utterly hopeless, (2) submission was required by God to a divinely appointed chastisement, (3) the Divine aid with which the Jews had won their victories in the past would not be forthcoming in this case. It is never dishonourable to submit to the will of God. True patriotism will seek the good of the nation rather than its transient glory. The method of escape offered to the Jews illustrates the Christian method of salvation. The Jews were to escape by leaving their ramparts and meeting their foes defenceless in the open field. We are to save our life by losing it. The Jews found safety in submission. The Christian salvation is secured, not by fighting and grasping at our rights, but by yielding to the will of God in Christ, and submitting to this even when it brings chastisement.

Ver. 13.—*God against Jerusalem.* In the fact that God was against her, Jerusalem was to see that all resistance to the Chaldeans must fail. This terrible secret of hopeless ruin may be found in others besides the Jews.

I. IT IS POSSIBLE FOR GOD TO BE AGAINST THOSE WHO WERE ONCE HIS MOST FAVOURED PEOPLE. It is Jerusalem, of all cities, that finds God to be her opponent. Therefore they who have enjoyed the friendship of God in the past have no right to presume that nothing can break that friendship. Moreover, God may be *actively* opposed to us. The opposition may not be all on our side. Though God is love, he can be angry, since even love itself will rouse anger when it is abused; and though he desires ultimately nothing but good, he may first send partial and temporary evil as a means for effecting this.

II. THEY WHO OPPOSE THEMSELVES TO GOD WILL ULTIMATELY FIND GOD OPPOSED TO THEM. The original enmity is on our side, so is the offence, the wrong-doing, the evil passion which stirs up contention. God would ever be at peace with his children, and it is they alone who have imported strife into his family. But after they have done so it is impossible for God to be indifferent to their conduct to him. His honour, insulted, must needs be vindicated—not, indeed, in the selfish way of personal pride, but in the righteous regard for the just and orderly government of his kingdom.

III. NO MORE TERRIBLE FATE CAN BEFALL MEN THAN FOR GOD TO BE AGAINST THEM. The horrors of the sieges of Jerusalem are amongst the darkest scenes of history. Yet the moral effects of God's wrath are far more serious than the material. 1. If God is against us, we *lose all the help* of his favour. It is impossible to measure the grace which, in multiform influences, streams into us and sustains and strengthens us for duty and trial. If all were removed we should perish. If God were wholly against any soul, that soul must at once be driven to outer darkness—be crushed and destroyed, and by negative causes alone; simply through the loss of God's light and life. But no man in this world has been so cursed. Yet even while God withdraws his special favours the loss is so great as to entail certain failure in life. The fruit may not be dashed from the trees, but the summer sun will never come to ripen it. 2. If God is against us, *terrible evils* will befall us. God is ever active in his presence. If we are not blessed by it, we suffer from it. How fearful to have God for our enemy ! All the laws and forces of the universe are then against us. Nature and providence, earth and heaven fulfilling his will, must direct their vast resources against the wretched outlaw. Our opposition to God will be to our own injury, but what much more fearful results must follow his opposition to us ! This dreadful fate is illustrated by our Lord's words, in which he compares those who shall fall on the stone with those on whom the stone shall fall (Matt. xxi. 44).

IV. IF GOD IS AGAINST US, REDEMPTION MUST INVOLVE A CHANGE OF GOD'S RELATION TO US. The atonement must have an aspect towards God as well as one towards man. While man is reconciled to God, God must be propitiated to man. It is true that this language is only possible because we speak of God after the manner of man, and that the atonement does not originate in us or in an independent third party who seeks to reconcile man and God, but in God himself, who sent his Son to redeem the world to himself. Yet, though desiring to be only gracious to men, God must have recognized the necessity of that intercession and sacrifice of Christ which won the favour of the Father to his beloved Son, and so to mankind, of whom Christ was the representative Priest. In Christ, therefore, we need not fear that God is against us (Rom. iii. 25).

HOMILIES BY VARIOUS AUTHORS.

Vers. 1, 2.—*Zedekiah's message; or, the prayer of the ungodly.* I. AN EXAMPLE TO BE IMITATED. Whatever might be said of the general behaviour of the king, his conduct on this occasion appears at first highly sagacious and commendable. 1. *For its acknowledgment of Jehovah as the only Deliverer.* A tremendous danger threatened the state. Zedekiah " counted the cost " and sent to the representative of Jehovah. He did not waste his resources in useless expedients, but frankly accepted the calamity as sent from God, appealing through God's prophet for deliverance. Most men in similar circumstances lose themselves in secondary causes. " It is this unfortunate accident or that. In time circumstances will be better, and we shall right ourselves." 2. *Its respect for God.* Great officers of state sent to a poor prophet. Religion after all may be the chief concern; at least a very important matter, and worthy the attention of the highest in the land.

II. AN EXAMPLE TO BE AVOIDED. 1. *It was tardy.* The warning of the prophet had been given long before, but it was not believed. Not until the visible proof of his veracity appeared before the city was Zedekiah eager to come to terms with the God he had offended. However great the alacrity of men to betake themselves to the offices of religion in times of calamity, their earnestness has not the spontaneous character to which it pretends. They are spurred on by fear. 2. *The power instead of the grace of God was appealed to.* A compliment to Jehovah's past achievements is delicately suggested. No petty business would bring him to ask a favour of God, but this trouble is great and urgent, and beyond human means of dealing with it; therefore God is called in. " It is worthy of his interference who always 'doeth wondrously.' " Now, there is no real humiliation here. Recognition of God's claims is grudgingly and of necessity made, but no word is mentioned of sin or repentance from it; no appeal is made to the forgiving love of God. Human nature is proud even in its necessities and prayers. " Help me now, at this juncture, and—afterwards I shall be able to help myself." God will not accept us unless we come humbly as well as prayerfully. Sin must be confessed. 3. *It contained no promise of amendment.* Jehovah is summoned as a *Deus ex machinâ* for the solution of a humanly impossible problem; but there is no indication that the "desperate resort" will grow into a course of constant waiting upon God. 4. *The duty which ought to have been personal was delegated to others.* Under the garb of respect religion is often really evaded. The Bible teaches the great doctrine of mediation, but it does not tell us how to perform our religious duties by proxy. 5. *Certainty, the note of Divine faith, is conspicuous by its absence.* " If so be that." The case is stated as a distant possibility. The language sounds respectful; it is so diffident, so unpresuming; but it really veils a profound scepticism. There ought to be, there is, no " perhaps " in believing prayer. The king was told that if he and his people repented, God would instantly avert the calamity or convert it into blessing. Perhapses like this are profanities. Besides, the suggestion is dishonouring to God, viz. that he should stay his judgments and the sinner nevertheless continue impenitent. 6. *The whole tone of the message is false and unsatisfactory.* It is that of one driven up into a corner by an unexpected exigency, but resolved that what he is obliged to do shall be barely done, and in such a manner as to give it quite another aspect to those who look on. A moral distance is observed, as of one who is unwilling to allow that religious duties are of personal as well as official and conventional obligation. It is the courtly language of diplomacy, and does not come hot-burning from a heart full of sorrow, faith, and love. What wonder it should not be answered save in scorn and added severity? The sarcasm is sublime.—M.

Vers. 13, 14.—*God's answer to earthly presumption.* The indifference and callousness of Judah and her king would appear to have reached a climax. Ignorance could not be alleged in excuse of it. It had become ingrained systematic unrighteousness; and had added this to itself, that it had rejected the warning counsels of God's prophet. How was it to be dealt with?

I. IT COULD NOT BE LET ALONE. 1. *The long-suffering mercy that had already been shown had been misunderstood.* To delay longer was therefore impossible. 2. *For all sin is a contradiction of the Divine Spirit and rule in the earth.* It is a direct challenge to Heaven. Especially is this the case when a positive law has been revealed, and a direct intimation of God's will made by a living representative. God's honour is therefore involved in the issue. 3. *The interests of truth and the kingdom of God on earth would suffer.* The transgression of one child of God is a stumbling-block to many, and those who enjoy Divine privileges should be especially careful as to how they behave. The world of heathenism witnessing the behaviour of Judah would be confirmed in its unbelief, or would misinterpret the genius of the religion of Jehovah. It might suppose that Jehovah was but a likeness of one of its own gods, full of partiality. This impression must be dissipated, and it could only be so by firm and prompt dealing with the offence.

II. A FINAL PEREMPTORY SUMMONS TO REFORMATION IS GIVEN. It might be supposed enough to have dealt silent and summary punishments upon the guilty land and its king. But this would not consist with : 1. *God's revelation of righteousness.* In blessings as well as in punishments a rational connection had to be shown with the behaviour and deserts of their subjects. The sinner's own conscience had to be addressed ere he was cast off for ever ; and the indictment was of world-wide concern. A warning and an example were required for the general guidance of men, and for their apprehension of the justice of Heaven in punishing those upon whom the calamity came. 2. *God's mercy.* The scheme of redemption does not exclude the possibility of the sinner himself being saved. On the contrary, this is its chief aim. Just as it would not be consistent with God's character to suffer unrighteous practices to continue unrebuked, so "God would not be God" were the penalty to be unannounced and without alternative of salvation. With many sinners of to-day he deals in like fashion. The warning is given with gentle, repeated, and terrible emphasis, and the way of escape is pointed out so plainly that "the wayfaring man, though a fool, may not err therein."

III. HE HIMSELF WILL BE THE ANTAGONIST. "I am against thee" (cf. ver. 5). 1. *This was a reversal of his normal relation to Israel.* It would be hard for people of their habits of thought to realize; and it is stated boldly in order to emphasis. Not mere neutrality. He is to be a belligerent—the belligerent with whom they have to do. They must have felt foredoomed to failure. They knew his power and resources, for had they not been employed on their own behoof in the past? Is not this the present consciousness of many? They know that God is against them. Are they prepared to carry the war on to the end? 2. *It represented the utter wrongness and hopelessness of their cause.* The "rock of the plain" would be of little avail against him. The forces of the world were at his command; and their own hearts would fail them for fear against this ghostly combatant. Against the righteous one the sense of an evil cause would be the parent of discomfiture.

IV. YET THE PUNISHMENT WAS TO COME FROM WITHIN THEMSELVES. "I will punish you according to the fruit of your doings;" "I will kindle a fire in the forest thereof." It is not easy to gather from these vague statements the precise form the punishment would assume. But the description agrees best with the circumstances of Jehoiakim's reign, who built palaces of cedar, and ruled with despotic violence. A literal rendering of the terms of the judgment is scarcely permissible. Is civil war meant? Or court intrigues, that may issue even more disastrously? In any case it would be the result of a reaction against the tyranny and wrong-doing of the court. 1. *The elements of destruction are within the sinner himself.* Many already know something of what hell is in themselves. 2. *The results of sin will be its punishment.*—M.

Vers. 1—14.—*Saved so as by fire.* This chapter has been by some means put out of its proper place; for it treats of King Zedekiah, whilst in later chapters circumstances connected with the reigns of the kings who preceded him are given. But being placed here it serves to show how God's servants, despised at first, come to be honoured at last. The stocks had been good enough for Jeremiah—so the last chapter tells—and his enemies had smitten him as if he were a common felon. Here we find the king and high officers of the court coming and beseeching his intercession and help to avert the calamity which was so fast coming upon them and the nation at large. "Give us of your oil," said the foolish virgins to the wise. And again and again has it been and will it be that the ungodly shall come to covet earnestly the place in God's favour which his servants only enjoy, but which, together with them who sought it when they did not, they have heretofore despised. Those who honour God he will honour, and will cause their enemies to come and confess that God is with them of a truth. Thus did the enemies of Jeremiah at this time acknowledge him as the true servant of God. But it was too late to secure what they desired. "The door was shut." But as the foolish virgins were bidden go to them that sell and buy for themselves, so the prophet of God has one counsel to give them whereby they might be "saved, yet so as by fire." "Behold, I set before you the way of life, and the way of death" (ver. 8). But when we come to see what that way of life was, we see how far different it was from what the king and his people would have chosen for themselves. Note, therefore—

I. WHAT THIS WAY OF LIFE WAS. 1. *It was bare life—*life only. They were to suffer defeat; their weapons to be of no avail, their strong fortress to be taken, their city and their temple in which they gloried to be burnt with fire, and they themselves led into captivity. That now was all that was possible for them. It was too late to avert their calamities, much less to gain victory, or honour, or glory in the war which they were waging. A glorious deliverance such as Hezekiah had known was out of the question. 2. *And even this bare life on hard conditions.* They must surrender themselves to their enemies when the summons came, and meanwhile they must reform their ways (ver. 12). On these terms they should be allowed to live. Refuse them, as many did, and they perished miserably. It was indeed a salvation "so as by fire."

II. ITS MOURNFULNESS. How full of this it was is seen by the plaintive psalms of the Captivity: "By the rivers of Babylon we sat down and wept," etc. And that which made it so mournful was the remembrance of how different their lot might have been. Had they but hearkened to the pleadings of those prophets of God, whose prayers when it was too late they importunately sought, how happy had it been with them then! Salvation in fulness, as their fathers had experienced and rejoiced in again and again, they too might have known. But now—

III. ITS PLAIN TEACHING FOR OURSELVES. Life may be retained, but made so wretched that only one thing could be worse—to have lost it altogether. This certainly true of the present life, it is probably true of the life after this. Beware of that false doctrine which encourages men to believe, that if only they can get within what they are pleased to call "the door of heaven," they need desire no more. This is not humility, but the evil desire to escape that faithful following of Christ which alone will win "the *prize* of our high calling." And since salvation in fulness is offered to us and God desires it to be ours, let us be content with nothing less, lest we be "ashamed before him at his coming," and have "with shame to take a lower place." To any now suffering under judgment of God this history says, "'Humble yourselves under the mighty hand of God.' Accept his terms, see in them your only hope."—C.

Ver. 8.—*A sad but common necessity.* The surrender of a part to save the whole. This was the "way of life" the prophet put before the people. The way of death would be their refusal. "If they would submit to the irresistible pressure of the Babylonian power, then whatever blessings were bound up in the preservation of the house of David and of the holy city would remain intact" (cf. Stanley, 'Lectures on the Jewish Church,' Lect. xi. vol. ii. p. 533). But to resist would not merely be useless, but mischievous in the extreme. It would rouse the rage of their conquerors and involve the destruction of all they held most precious. It would be "a way of death." At the final siege of Jerusalem the Christians retired, but the Zealots drew down upon themselves the rage of the armies of Vespasian and Titus, and so hurried on the ruin of the whole Jewish state. Stanley says of Jeremiah, "It was not indifference to his country, but attachment to its permanent interests, with the yet larger consequences wrapt up in them, which induced him to counsel submission. It was his sense of the inestimable importance of that sacred spot, with its sacred institutions, which caused him to advise every sacrifice for the sake of retaining it. He had the courage, so rare in political leaders, to surrender a part for the sake of preserving the whole—to embrace in his view the complete relations of the great scheme of the world, rather than fix his attention exclusively on the one pressing question of the moment. As there are times when the constitution must be broken to save the commonwealth, when the interests of particular nations or doctrines must give way to the preponderating claims of mankind or of truth at large, so Jeremiah staked the eternal value of the truths which Jerusalem represented against the temporary evils of the Chaldean dominion. It was a bitter pang, but the result seemed to him worth the cost."

> " To steel his melting heart,
> To act the martyr's sternest part;
> To watch with firm, unshrinking eye
> His darling visions as they die;
> Too happy if, that dreadful day,
> His life be given him for a prey."
>
> (Keble).

Now—

I. THIS DREAD NECESSITY IS ONE WHICH MAY BE SEEN CONTINUALLY PRESSING ON MEN. Illustrations are numerous: the throwing over the cargo in storm at sea; the abandonment of outposts to concentrate strength on the key of the position; the cutting off a limb to save the life; the giving up a less important branch of trade to safeguard one more so. And in the religious life we are perpetually summoned to such sacrifice. "Whoso loveth his life shall lose it, but he that loveth his life for my sake shall find it;" "Except a corn of wheat fall into the ground and die," etc. All ventures of faith. And death—"for corruption cannot inherit incorruption," and therefore that the true life may be ours, the fleshly life must die. And our Lord represents the awful doom of the wicked to be a "cutting off of a diseased part," a κολλασις, that—so it should seem—entire destruction may not be needed. It is an awful process, but sternly necessary. God save us from it! And what is the submission of our will to God, the self-surrender for which he ever asks, but the prudent conduct of that king who feels that with his puny force of ten thousand he cannot meet the king who comes against him with twenty thousand, and therefore straightway sends an embassage desiring conditions of peace? But—

II. MEN SHRINK FROM IT. Those before whom Jeremiah placed this "way of life" shrank from it. They would not listen to him. They cruelly persecuted their far-seeing and God-inspired prophet. And it is so still. In common life the proverbial saying, "Nothing venture, nothing have," implies that men are loth to venture. Many a craft hugs the shore, thinking to find safety there, and is driven on the rocks and wrecked, when by putting boldly out to sea the storm might have been safely weathered. The historian of the Crimean War finds fault, once and again, with our generals for their timid policy, which he maintains brought so great sufferings and losses on our army, whilst had a more daring strategy been adopted—as in our recent Egyptian campaign at Tel-el-Kebir—the war might have been speedily and gloriously ended. And in the religious life, how men shrink from this self-surrender! What frantic but futile efforts there are to serve God and mammon, notwithstanding our Saviour has said, "There is no man that hath left house, or lands," etc. (Mark x. 29)! But men cannot be persuaded to believe this. The young ruler who had great possessions (Matt. xix.) went away sorrowful, because he could not make the great venture. And the feeble religious life of so many, the absence of all joy in God's service, is owing to this same cause. Men are ever trying to find a *via media* between the "way of life" and "way of death." The husbandman does not refuse to cast into the earth all he has left of last year's corn, in the trust that it will yield him a bounteous harvest. But we are slow to believe in the wisdom of such sowing in spiritual things.

III. BUT THE REFUSAL TO SUBMIT IS FATAL. It was so in case of those to whom Jeremiah preached, and it has been so a thousand times since. A ship was sinking. A man leaped from her deck into the sea. He was a good swimmer, but he had fastened round him a belt containing gold, which he could not bring himself to abandon, and its weight sank him ere he could reach the boat for which he was making. Our Lord bade him who should be on the house-tops when Jerusalem was besieged "not go down to fetch his clothes." Such carefulness might cost him his life. Our Lord tells of many of the Pharisees who believed on him, but were afraid to confess him, lest they should be put out of the synagogue. And perhaps there are few of the worldly and irreligious amongst us who have not sunk down to where they are now, and will sink down to lower depths still, through this same refusal to give up all for Christ. It may be humiliating and involve present loss, and therefore men let go the eternal gain. To refuse such sacrifice is the way of death. But—

IV. TO CONSENT TO IT IS LIFE. Take our Lord as the supreme example, who, not for himself but for us, threw away that infinite glory, that equality with God, which, being in "the form of God," was ever his; but St. Paul tells us (Phil. ii. 6) he counted it not a thing to be grasped at, a prize which he should cling to with eagerness and retain with tenacity, but "emptied himself of it, and made himself of no reputation." Thus for the time of his incarnation submitting himself to the cruel might of sin and Satan, he gained thereby that infinite exaltation, that salvation of mankind upon which his loving heart was set. " Let this mind," therefore, " be in us which was also in Christ Jesus." And whenever it is found, God rewards it. Self-sacrifice, the cross, is the way to supreme reward. The shepherds were told, at the Nativity, that there was born to them " a Saviour, Christ the Lord." And when they came to Bethlehem they found a Babe wrapped in swaddling clothes, and lying in a manger. What correspondence was there between that saying of the angels and that sight of the infant Jesus? To the outward eye none, but to the eye instructed by God's Word and God's providence, there is every correspondence. For those outward signs of poverty and humiliation which were the characteristic of his life, have formed his title-deeds, his royal right, to the homage of every human heart. " Blessed are the meek," etc.; " He that humbleth himself shall," etc. It is ever so; and especially when we humble ourselves before God, giving up self and sin, giving up and losing, as the world would say, our very life, —then it is we find it, as God grant we may.—C.

Vers. 1—7.—*A king appealing for a prophet's intercession.* I. A KING'S ACKNOWLEDGMENT THAT HUMAN RESOURCES ARE UNAVAILING. The hour and the danger so long and often predicted, referred to all the more earnestly as the hour draws nigh, has come at last. No time is here taken up in narrating the attempts Zedekiah may have made himself to repel the invader. The Scriptures were not meant to give us details of sieges. The likelihood is, however, that it was long before Zedekiah reached anything like an extremity that he made this appeal to the prophet. When an unusual danger comes close at hand it is easy to exaggerate. The man who has been indifferent, imprudent, heedless of all hints that have been given him to make provision for the future, is the very man who, when peril comes, rushes into panic and becomes unable to use the resources he has.

II. A KING'S PRESUMPTUOUS ATTEMPT TO AVAIL HIMSELF OF DIVINE RESOURCES. Nothing is more beautiful than to see one who has found out the vanity of human help turning to God. Only he must come in a right spirit, having made a clear discovery of why it is that man could not help him. Anything of this sort was utterly lacking in Zedekiah's approach. There is no sign of repentance, no word of confession, no resolution of amendment. The only thing in the shape of acknowledgment is that Jehovah is the God who does wondrous works. This is an acknowledgment which we find often in the Old Testament, but it is acceptable to God only when accompanied with a sense of why it is that God does his wondrous works. The more we consider Zedekiah's request, the more will the blindness and audacity of it appear. Here is the king in Jerusalem, bound, if any man ever was, to know the significance of the history of Israel as a whole; and yet he can only see certain great manifestations of power which encourage him to hope that a similar manifestation may now come for his own deliverance. There is no real coming to God, unless we come for things that are according to his will. His power cannot wait upon our selfish needs. There is no telling what might have happened, even at this more than eleventh hour, if Zedekiah had only come with something of true penitence. God knew beforehand that this could not be expected; and thus there is no clearer evidence of the righteousness of Jerusalem's doom and of Israel's expatriation than is furnished from Zedekiah's own lips. He shows that he has lost all sense of the meaning and the necessity of God's great covenant with his people. If only they had been obedient they would never have lacked the benefit of many wondrous works.

III. THE PLAIN AND NECESSARY ANSWER OF JEHOVAH. We see through all that God here says a purpose to make plain that he is now full of activity against his apostate people. The object was not to be attained simply by leaving them, in their natural resources, to the natural resources of the Chaldeans. The contest is not of man against man, but of the man who has forsaken God against the man whom God has taken to be the instrument of his righteous indignation. God must specially intervene and make his presence manifest, to show that all this visitation of suffering is from him. If God has, for a time, to forsake his people, he must needs oppose them. If God be

not for us, he is against us; and so here the defenders of Jerusalem are represented
as having difficulties to deal with such as have arisen through God's own operation.
Their weapons of war do not produce the usual effect. God turns them back upon
those who wield them. This may be more than a mere general figure of speech. It is
quite possible that either the arm wielding the heavy, sharp sword becomes as the arm
of the little child, or else, that remaining strong, the weapon becomes but as the child's
toy. Thus the Chaldeans themselves would learn that some mysterious power was at
work, and that the glory of the victory was not theirs. Furthermore, God was to fight
against these apostates with a weapon of his own. He can make the wicked and the
ambitious his sword, but pestilence is of his own sending. Not all the might of the
Chaldeans could bring a pestilence, nor take it away once it had come. Thus we see
how all this dread combination of events was intended to impress on all, alike amongst
besiegers and besieged, who had minds to understand that God himself was terribly at
work. He was indeed dealing with the people according to his wondrous works; works
necessitated in order to prevent his holy and reasonable wrath from being nothing more
than empty wind.—Y.

Vers. 8—10.—*Escape for the individual among the calamities of the nation.* Even
amid all the thick, impending horrors indicated in the previous passage, a clear and
immediate way of escape is indicated for the individual. Every one going over promptly
and resolutely to the Chaldeans would be at least safe. What might be reserved for
him in the future it was not proper to say. Enough for him to know that he had
security for the present. He who is made safe may expect further communications of
positive blessing in due time. We are not, indeed, to suppose that every one who remained
in the city, exposed to sword, famine, and pestilence, would assuredly perish. That
can hardly have been the case. But this certainly is meant, that every one so remaining would have to take a tremendous risk. Whereas every one who took the suggestion
as to what is here called the way of life, found that the great Preserver of life had thereby
entered into a special covenant with him.

I. THE PLACE LEFT FOR INDIVIDUAL RESPONSIBILITY. God is dealing with a whole
nation. His representative and the representative of this nation's king have just been
in conference. His dreadful, necessary decision as to the nation's fate is communicated.
But now each individual is impressively informed that God is thinking also of him. The
individual must, to some extent, share in the suffering of his people. How far he shall
share depends, however, on his own choice. We cannot be dragged into the worst
experiences of human life merely as sufferers from the wrong-doing of others. The
worst pains, the gloomiest hours of life, can only come from our own wrong-doing.
Whatever faithful remnant there might now be in Jerusalem had a great chance given
to them. Complete exemption from suffering was not possible; but they were offered
a kind of shelter, where the great storm of God's wrath would leave them untouched,
however much it might affect their temporal belongings.

II. ALL THAT THE BEST OF MEN MUST EXPECT FOR THE PRESENT IS A MITIGATION OF
SUFFERING. Whatever advantages come from our connection with the temporal body
politic must be accepted with the risk of corresponding disadvantages. Even while
Israel was in this doomed degenerated state it was the medium of benefits to those who
could use it aright. No Israelite needed to regret that he had belonged to Israel; if
only he had the wisdom to accept all uncomfortable experiences as part of a discipline
that would work out unmixed and abiding good in the end. Those here addressed had
much reason to be thankful that at such a terrible crisis God did so much to make
their position safe. He who has got safe to land from the sinking ship would be
reckoned a monster of ingratitude if he did nothing but grumble because all his
property was lost. He may still have the opportunity of a prosperity as great as he
had in the past, or even greater.

III. THIS REQUIREMENT GAVE A SEARCHING TRIAL TO THE FAITH OF THE BELIEVING.
If any good was to come out of the proposition it must be by acting on it at once. And
such action could not but have some appearance of cowardice and desertion. Indeed,
under certain circumstances, it would have been cowardice and desertion. If Israel
could have been looked on as a human state and nothing more, if the Chaldeans had
been a human enemy and nothing more, then such a departure, *self-prompted*, would

have been nothing less than apostasy from national duty. The sentiment is a noble one: better to die a freeman than to live a slave. This aspect of things vanishes, how·ever, when we recollect that Jerusalem was divinely doomed. This Chaldean army was nothing less than the sword of God, and a timely surrender to the Chaldean was really a timely surrender to him. To go over to them might look questionable enough on a mere hasty, superficial glance; but time would show that it was the right, trustful, obedient course. The real bravery is to withstand the taunts and misrepresentations of unbelieving men; enduring "as seeing him who is invisible." Some, indeed, who escaped to the Chaldeans did so, we doubt not, in a really cowardly spirit. But the Lord knows who are his; and their motives would be revealed in the end. A brave heart cannot be for ever misrepresented; and a mere outward appearance of obedience will have to pass through that fire which tries every man's work, of what sort it is.—Y.

EXPOSITION.

CHAPTER XXII.

Ch. xxii. and xxiii. are connected together by similarity of subject. The temporal and spiritual leaders of the people, who are mainly responsible for the national catastrophe, receive their merited castigation. Vers. 1—8 of ch. xxiii., properly speaking, belong to ch. xxii.; thus we get a well-rounded discourse on the conduct of the kings, with four symmetrical parts or strophes—vers. 1—12, 13—19, 20—30, and ch. xxiii. 1—8. Each begins with a general exhortation or meditation, and continues with a poetical description of the fates, successively, of Jehoahaz, Jehoiakim, and Jehoiachin. The prophecy is concluded, according to the good old rule of Isaiah, by a Messianic promise.

Ver. 1.—**Go down.** Not literally, for the royal palace was probably the highest building in the city (comp. ver. 6); but because of the spiritual eminence of the temple (comp. ch. xxvi. 10, "They came up from the king's house unto the house of the Lord").

Ver. 2.—**And thy people.** The Septuagint reads, "And thy house and thy people;" thus the passage will agree with ch. xxi. 11, 12.

Ver. 4.—Parallel passage, ch. xvii. 25.

Ver. 5.—**I swear by myself.** "Because he could swear by no greater, he sware by himself" (Heb. vi. 13). A synonymous expression is, "As I live, saith Jehovah" (ver. 24).

Ver. 6.—**Unto the king's house of Judah;** rather, *concerning the house of the King of Judah;* i.e. the royal palace, which, on account of its height and its being constructed so largely out of cedar-wood (comp. vers. 14, 23), is called "Gilead, and the summit of Lebanon," just as Solomon's palace was called "the house of the forest of Lebanon"

(1 Kings vii. 2). Of Gilead in general, Canon Tristram writes, "No one can fairly judge of Israel's heritage who has not seen the luxuriant exuberance of Gilead, as well as the hard rocks of Judæa." And again, "Lovely knolls and dells open out at every turn, gently rising to the wooded plateau above. Then we rise to higher ground and ride through noble forests of oak. Then for a mile or two through luxuriant green corn, or perhaps through a rich forest of scattered olive trees, left untended and uncared for, with perhaps patches of corn in the open glades" ('Bible Places,' p. 322). The cedars of Lebanon, however diminished, still bear witness to the ancient fame of this splendid mountain district. **A wilderness, and cities which are not inhabited.** The comparison has a terrible significance when read in the light of De Vogüé's and Freshfield's discoveries. For Gilead itself is full of ruined cities of massive stone architecture. "It is no uncommon thing," says Mr. F. A. Eaton, "to see these houses in a complete state of preservation, built of huge blocks of black basalt, with slabs of the same for the roof, twelve feet long, a foot and a half wide, and half a foot thick, and entrance doors also of basalt . . . great solid stones of the same material being used as lintels at the top and bottom" (Speech at the meeting for setting on foot the survey of Eastern Palestine, November 30, 1880: *Statement of Palestine Exploration Fund,* January, 1880, p. 11). *Cities which are not inhabited;* not, indeed, the cities of Gilead of the time of Jeremiah, but constructed of materials which may reasonably be presumed to have been chiselled in a far more remote antiquity. (The date of the cities in their present state is subsequent to the Christian era.)

Ver. 7.—**I will prepare;** literally, *I will consecrate;* the Babylonians being instruments of the Divine vengeance (see on ch. vi. 4).

Vers. 10—12.—There is a fate worse than

that of the dead Josiah. **Weep not, in com-** parison, for him, but **weep sore for him that goeth away** (or rather, *that is gone away*). The king referred to is probably Jehoahaz, who, though two years younger than Jehoia-kim (2 Kings xxiii. 31; comp. 36), was preferred to him by the people on the death of Josiah. The counsel to " weep sore " for this royal exile was carried out, as Mr. Samuel Cox observes (and we have, perhaps, a specimen of the popular elegies upon him in Ezek. xix. 1—4): "A young lion of royal strain, caught untimely, and chained and carried away captive,—this was how the people of Israel conceived of Shallum" (' Biblical Expositions,' p. 120). The conjecture is incapable of proof; and Ezekiel, we know, was fond of imaginative elegies. But probably enough he was in harmony with popular feeling on this occasion. The identification of Shallum with Jehoahaz is confirmed by 1 Chron. iii. 15 (Shallum, the youngest son of Josiah); the name appears to have been changed on his accession to the throne, just as Eliakim was changed to Jehoiakim (2 Chron. xxxvi. 4). There is, therefore, no occasion to suppose an ironical allusion to the short reign of Jehoahaz, which might be compared to that of the Israelitish king Shallum (somewhat as Jezebel addresses Jehu as " O Zimri, murderer of his lord," 2 Kings ix. 31). This view has the support of F. Junius (professor at Leyden, 1592), of Graf, and Rowland Williams; but why should not the Chronicler, though writing in the Persian period, have drawn here, as well as elsewhere in the genealogies, from ancient traditional sources? There is nothing in ver. 11 to suggest an allusion to the fate of the earlier Shallum.

Ver. 13.—**Shallum,** or Jehoahaz, in his short reign of three months, had no opportunity of distinguishing himself for good or for evil. It was otherwise with Jehoiakim, whose eleven years were marked by the worst characteristics of idolatry and despotism. He "had, besides, a passion for building splendid and costly houses; and as he esteemed his own position secure under the protection of a superior power, he did not scruple severely to oppress his helpless subjects, and wring from them as much money as possible" (Ewald, 'History of Israel,' iv. 252; see 2 Kings xxiii. 33—35). The building mania, to which Oriental sovereigns have always been prone, had seized upon Jehoiakim. The architecture of the original palace no longer, perhaps, suited the higher degree of civilization; the space was as confined as that of a Saxon mansion would have appeared to a Norman. **That buildeth his house by unrighteousness;** *i.e.*, as the second half-verse explains, by not paying the workmen (comp. Hab. ii. 12).

Ver. 14.—**A wide house;** literally, *a house of extensions.* **Large chambers.** The Hebrew specifies " upper chambers "—the principal rooms in ancient houses. **Cutteth him out windows; and it is cieled with cedar;** rather, *. . . his windows, roofing it with cedar.* (This involves no change of letters, but a very slight rearrangement, and the alteration of one point; grammar gains greatly by the change.) " Cutteth out " is, literally, *rendeth;* it is the word used in ch. iv. 30 of the apparent enlargement of the eyes by putting powdered antimony upon the eyelids. Windows are, as it were, the eyes of a building (Graf compares Eccles. xii. 3). Beams of cedar wood were used for the roof of the palace, as being the most costly and durable (comp. Isa. ix. 10). **And painted**—rather, *and painting it*—**with vermilion;** a taste derived from the Egyptians rather than the Babylonians, who seem to have had a difficulty in procuring red.

Ver. 15.—**Shalt thou reign**—rather, *dost thou reign;* i.e. dost thou prove thy royal qualities)—**because thou closest thyself in cedar?** The second part of the clause must at any rate be altered. Some render, " because thou viest (with thy forefathers) in cedar" (*i.e.* in building cedar palaces). Hitzig would strike out "in cedar," as having intruded from the preceding line (such a phenomenon meets us occasionally in the received Hebrew text), but this does not help us to a connected translation of the passage. Graf's rendering is grammatical, and not against usage; it is, "Dost thou reign because thou art eager about cedarwood?" and yet the impression left on the mind is that there is some error in the text. The Septuagint finds a reference to one of Jehoiakim's predecessors, "because thou viest with Ahaz" (so the Vatican Codex), or, ". . . with Ahab" (so the Alexandrine and the Sinaitic or Friderico-Augustan). The latter king is celebrated in the Old Testament on account of his buildings, especially his ivory palace (2 Kings xxii. 39). The former was at any rate addicted to the imitation of foreign ways (2 Kings xvi. 11; xx. 11). **Did not thy father eat and drink?** There was no call upon Jehoiakim to live the life of a Nazarite. " Eating and drinking," *i.e.* enjoying the good things within his reach, was perfectly admissible (Eccles. ii. 24); indeed, the Old Testament view of life is remarkable for its healthy naturalness. There was, however, one peremptory condition, itself as much in accordance with nature as with the Law of God, that the rights of other men should be studiously regarded. Josiah "ate and drank," but he also " did judgment and justice," and so " it was well with him."

Ver. 17.—**But thou, O Jehoiakim, art the**

opposite of thy father. *For* (not, **But**) **thine eyes and thine heart are not but for thy covetousness.** "Covetousness" includes the ideas of injustice and violence (comp. ch. vi. 13 ; viii. 10); hence the second half of the verse emphasizes the cruel tyranny which marked the internal policy of Jehoiakim.

Ver. 18.—Josiah had been bitterly missed and universally lamented (2 Chron. xxxv. 25); and so, only perhaps with less heartiness in most cases, Jehoiakim's other predecessors (ch. xxxiv. 5). The Babylonian kings, too, received the honours of public mourning, *e.g.* even the last of his race, who surrendered to Cyrus, according to the British Museum inscription translated by Mr. Pinches. **Ah my brother! or, Ah sister!** The Septuagint omits the latter part of this phrase, apparently because it seemed inappropriate to the death of Jehoiakim; but the parallelism requires a two-membered clause. According to Movers, the funeral procession is to be conceived of as formed of two parts, condoling with each other on having to share the same fate ('Die Phönizier,' ii. 248). Or perhaps mythology may supply a reason; it is possible that the formulæ of public mourning were derived from the ceremonies of the Adonia; Adonis was an androgynous deity (Lenormant, 'Lettres assyriologiques,' ii. 209), and might be lamented by his devotees as at once "brother" and "sister." (For another view, see Sayce's edition of G. Smith's 'Chaldean Genesis,' p. 267). Ezekiel (viii. 13) testifies to the worship of Tammuz, or Adonis, and the highest compliment a king could receive might be to be lamented in the same terms as the sun-god. Jeremiah does not approve this; he merely describes the popular custom. The recognition of the deeply rooted heathenism of the Jews before the Exile involves no disparagement to Old Testament religion; rather it increases the cogency of the argument for its supernatural origin. For how great was the contrast between Jeremiah and his semi-heathen countrymen! And yet Jeremiah's religion is the seed of the faith which overcame the world. **Ah lord! or, Ah his glory!** *Lord* is in the Hebrew *ādōn* (comp. Adonis and see above). *His glory* is against the parallelism; we should expect "lady" or "queen."

Ver. 19.—Jehoiakim's miserable death, without even the honour of burial. The prediction is repeated in ch. xxxvi. 30, where the statement is made in plain language. At first sight it appears to conflict with 2 Kings xxiv. 6, "So Jehoiakim slept with his fathers: and Jehoiachin his son reigned in his stead;" but it is only appearance, and when we remember that the complete formula for describing the natural death of a king of Judah is, "slept with his fathers, and was buried with his fathers in the city of David" (1 Kings xiv. 31; xv. 24; xxii. 50; 2 Kings viii. 24; xv. 7, 38; xvi. 20), and that the phrase, "slept with his fathers," is used of Ahab, who fell on the field of battle (1 Kings xxii. 40), we are naturally led to the conjecture that Jehoiakim did not die a natural death, but fell in battle in some sally made by the besieged. **Buried with the burial of an ass;** *i.e.* cast out unburied. **Beyond the gates;** rather, *far from the gates.*

Ver. 20.—A new strophe begins here, relative to Jehoiachin, the son and successor of Jehoiakim. **Go up to Lebanon, and cry.** The people of Judah is addressed, personified as a woman (comp. ch. vii. 29). The penetrating character of the long-toned cry of an Arab has been mentioned by Dr. Thomson. In Isa. xl. 9 a similar command is given to Zion; but in what different circumstances! **From the passages;** rather, *from Abarim.* The range of Abarim—Nebo, from which Moses surveyed the land of Israel, belonged to it (Deut. xxxii. 49)—completes the circle of mountain stations; Lebanon was in the north, Bashan in the north-east, Abarim in the south-east. **All thy lovers;** viz. the nations whom self-interest had combined against Nebuchadrezzar, and between whom and Judah negotiations had from time to time been entered into (ch. ii. 36; xxvii. 3). "Lovers" (comp. ch. iv. 30; 30; Ezek. xvi. 33, 37).

Ver. 21.—**From thy youth;** *i.e.* from the time that thou didst become a nation (comp. ch. ii. 2; Hos. ii. 15). It is the Exodus which is referred to.

Ver. 22.—**Shall eat up all thy pastors.** The verb is that connected with the participle rendered "pastors;" strictly, therefore, *shall pasture upon all thy pastors.* The "wind" referred to is doubtless the parching east wind, the symbol of calamity, which is actually called a "sharp" wind in ch. iv. 11.

Ver. 23.—**O inhabitant**—rather, *O inhabitress*—**of Lebanon.** It is the people of Jerusalem which is meant; the "Lebanon" are the palaces of cedar-wood which together are called "the house of the King of Judah" (ver. 6). **How gracious shalt thou be!** rather, *How wilt thou sigh!*

Ver. 24.—**Coniah.** A shorter form of Jeconiah (1 Chron. iii. 1), found again in ch. xxxvii. 1. Perhaps this was the name this king bore prior to his accession, after which it was certainly Jehoiachin; Jeremiah has already spoken of one king by his earlier name in ver. 11. The Divine speaker solemnly announces that though, as the representative of Israel's invisible King, Coniah **were**—or rather, *be*—**the signet upon** his **right hand** (a most valued jewel), **yet would**—or rather, *will*—he **pluck** him **thence**; *i.e.* depose him from his high dignity. The same figure is used in Hag. ii. 23, "I will take thee, O Zerubbabel, and make thee as a signet;" and Ezek. xxviii. 12, where there is a well-attested reading, "Thou (O King of Tyre) art a deftly made signet-ring." (For the fulfilment of the prediction in this verse, see 2 Kings xxiv. 12, 15; ch. xxiv. 1; xxix. 2.)

Ver. 26.—**Cast thee out.** The Hebrew is stronger—"hurl thee" (comp. Isa. xxii. 17, Hebrew). **And thy mother;** *i.e.* the queen-mother Nehushta (comp. ch. xxix. 2; 2 Kings xxiv. 8). She seems to have been particularly influential (see introduction to ch. xiii.)

Ver. 28.—**Is this man Coniah,** etc.? The prophet's human feelings are stirred; he cannot withhold his sympathy from the sad fate of his king. What! he exclaims; is it possible that this Coniah is treated as a piece of ill-wrought pottery ware (comp. ch. xviii. 4), and "hurled" into a strange land? **He and his seed.** These words have caused some difficulty, owing to the youth of Jehoiachin. According to 2 Kings xxiv. 8 he was only eighteen when he was carried captive, while 2 Chron. xxxvi. 9 makes him still younger, only eight (Josiah's age on his accession). Hitzig thinks the latter number is to be preferred; his chief reasons are the prominence given to the queen-mother, and the fact that the length of

Jehoiachin's reign is given with more precise accuracy in 2 Chronicles than in 2 Kings. It is true that the king's wives are mentioned in 2 Kings xxiv. 15. But that he had wives may, according to Hitzig, have been inferred by the late compiler of Kings from the passage before us; or the "wives" may have been those of Jehoiachin's predecessor (comp. 2 Sam. xvi. 21). Graf's conjecture is, perhaps, the safest view of the case, whether we accept the number eighteen or the number eight; it is that the "seed" spoken of was born to Jehoiachin in his captivity, and is reckoned to him by anticipation. It should be mentioned, however, that the Septuagint omits "he and his seed" altogether.

Ver. 29.—**O earth, earth, earth.** The repetition is for solemnity's sake (comp. ch. vii. 4).

Ver. 30.—**Write ye this man childless;** *i.e.* enter him in the register of the citizens (comp. Isa. iv. 3) as one who has no heirs. He may have children, but none of them shall succeed to his place in the community. This is all that the passage means; there is no discrepancy with history: how should there be, when Jeremiah himself has mentioned the posterity of Jehoiachin (ver. 28 and the latter part of this verse)? Yet the Septuagint thought it necessary to avoid the appearance of such a discrepancy by rendering, not "childless," but "one proscribed" (ἐκκήρυκτον).

HOMILETICS.

Vers. 1—5.—*Court preaching.* Jeremiah has been preaching in the valley of Hinnom, in the temple courts and in the streets of Jerusalem; now he is called to enter the king's palace with a message from God. The preacher must not wait for his audience to run after him, but he must create it. He must make his work public, not hiding it in modesty, but bringing it to bear on the widest possible field. He must not be content to maintain his unopposed ministry in the Church, but must boldly carry out his mission in the world. Religion is not a concern for religious people alone; people who will not come to church may be supposed to need it more than those who manifest their interest in it by attendance at regular services. If the court is irreligious there is the more need for the prophet to go into its midst.

I. THE HIGHEST RANK SHOULD NOT BE EXEMPT FROM THE MOST FAITHFUL PREACHING. The Hebrew prophets were remarkable for their clear and bold utterances before kings —often at the peril of their lives (*e.g.* Amos vii. 10—13). Christ expects his servants to be equally faithful and fearless (Acts ix. 15). When court preachers descend to become court flatterers they are doing their utmost to ruin their patrons. Kings may not often need to be addressed in the style of John Knox, in his sermons before Mary Queen of Scots; but they certainly should not be treated only to the drawing-room delicacies of Atterbury. The fastidiousness which makes strong words about unpleasant subjects seem in "bad form" in fashionable congregations is really a sign of sacrificing truth and right to mean pleasantness. Kings are men, and have human failings and sins. Rank confers power for evil as well as for good. The privileges and talents of a high position involve such great responsibilities, that the neglect or abuse of them is a crime of first magnitude in the sight of God. To ignore these truths is to act cruelly to the persons whom the preacher deceives by his smooth words.

II. THE CHARACTER OF THE COURT IS OF GREAT INTEREST TO THE NATION. As men, the king and his courtiers have a right to be dealt faithfully with by the preacher. But as persons in authority, their influence makes their condition of importance to all. The people are largely responsible for the condition of the court, since popular applause and popular censure always carry great weight there. Thus Jeremiah associates the people with the king in the address which is intended chiefly for the king. Even under a constitutional government such as that of our own country, the court has immense influence especially in social circles, and it is of vital interest to us all that this influence should be pure and true and righteous.

III. THE PROSPERITY OF A COUNTRY LARGELY DEPENDS UPON THE MORAL CHARACTER OF ITS GOVERNMENT. This great truth is one of the chief lessons to be derived from the Bible accounts of the history of Israel. We commonly rely too much on physical resources, wealth, commerce, military power, etc.; on political resources, legislative schemes, diplomatic complications, etc. We in England have yet to learn how much of our prosperity depends on honesty in trade, fairness in dealing with foreign nations and a high tone of political morality. To judge by some of our newspapers, it would seem that religion has no business with politics; that a county is glorified when her leaders stoop to underhand work that would disgrace the name of the most unscrupulous lawyer. The doom of Israel should warn us against this political atheism. Three duties are specially to be noted in the discourse of Jeremiah. 1. To *execute* judgment and righteousness; not only to pronounce just verdicts, but to carry out an active policy of justice. 2. To deliver the oppressed; non-intervention may be cowardly and selfish when the weak claim our help. 3. Not to oppress the weak; this applies to nationalities as well as to individuals, and is a warning for our conduct with dependencies, and the native races with which we come in contact in the colonies. For righteousness in these respects the promised reward is, not a mere deliverance from approaching calamities, but glory, riches, triumph.

Vers. 8, 9.—*On visiting the ruins of a city.* What a picture we have here! Many nations passing by on the high-road between Egypt and the East struck with amazement at the ruins of Jerusalem. Is not the sight of a city in ruins always a source of pathetic interest? As we wander about the silent streets of Pompeii the stillness of death is appalling by contrast with the tumult of pleasure and commerce which formerly thronged those once busy thoroughfares. Such a melancholy spectacle rouses thought and inquiry. Gibbon tells us that it was while seated among the ruins of the Capitol that he first thought of writing the history of the decline and fall of the city of Rome. The magnificent ruins of Carnac and of Persepolis naturally lead us to ask how prosperity and power came to pass away from Persia and Egypt. So must it have been in ancient times with the ruins of Jerusalem. Jeremiah warns the citizens that their city, now brilliant in splendour and prosperity, will soon astonish all beholders with its overthrow. We have in the words of the prophet a question and an answer.

I. THE QUESTION. (Ver. 8.) It is put by the heathen nations. These people who cannot understand the religion of Jerusalem can see clearly enough her ruin. The world has eyes for the shame of the Church in her overthrow, though none for her highest glory, that of the beauty of holiness. The question is asked by many nations. The spectacle is open to all, and so startling that many are arrested by it. How true is this even in the case of individual men ! If a Christian falls into sin and shame the scandal rings through the world. 1. This question bears witness to the *horrible* doom of sin. The ruins are so extensive and so completely wrecked, that all who pass by are fascinated and appalled by the sight of them. If strangers are so struck, how must the children of the city feel? Well may they hang their harps on the willows, and sit them down in despair by the waters of Babylon. Yet the temporal ruin of a city is slight compared with the spiritual ruin of a soul. 2. The question bears witness to the *surprise* that this calamity excited. (1) It was in contrast to former *prosperity*. We are too ready to see in prosperity the promise of its continuance. But no delusion can be greater. (2) It was in opposition to the *boasts* of the Jews. They had regarded their city as sacred and invulnerable. So the French under the empire were taught to consider Paris. And this self-confidence carries weight with others; for the world is indolent and thoughtless enough to take people very much at their own estimate of themselves. Nevertheless it is vain. (3) It was in spite of the *supposed protection of God.* The Jews were the elect nation. Hence the expectation of their immunity; but a vain expectation. No Divine favouritism will save us from the consequences of our sins. 3. The question suggests *no possibility of help* from the nations. They may pity, but they can do nothing. The stare of the crowd only aggravates the calamity. Well may such a prospect strike grief into the people interested.

II. THE ANSWER. (Ver. 9.) 1. The cause of this calamity *may be known.* Even the heathen nations may know it. Providence is not so mysterious as we suppose. No study is more lofty or more useful than the study of the moral philosophy of history. Treated only on secular grounds, it may be perplexing and unsatisfactory. But regarded in the light of the principles of the Bible, it may be fruitful in sound results. 2. The cause is *moral.* The hosts of Nebuchadnezzar conquered Jerusalem. Swarms of northern races and Asiatic hordes swept away the power of imperial Rome. Paris fell before the guns and discipline of the German army. Yet in each of these cases moral corruption was behind the physical cause of ruin, sapping the strength of the doomed city and provoking the onslaught of its foes. 3. The special cause was *unfaithfulness to God*: (1) forsaking God—for God never withdraws his protection from his people till they have abandoned their fidelity to him; (2) breaking the covenant—for this had two sides, and God's promised grace is conditioned by the conduct of his people; and (3) positive idolatry—for the unfaithful servant of God never rests with the abandonment of his God. He must serve some master. Such moral and religious corruption justifies punishment and requires chastisement. We may believe that a right understanding of the guilt and necessities of men will ultimately convince us of the righteousness and wisdom of God's sterner dealings, which at first naturally excite our wonder and dismay.

Ver. 10.—*Misspent tears.* I. WHY NOT WEEP FOR THE DEAD? It is natural to do so. The religion of the Bible is not stoicism. Christ wept by the grave of Lazarus. Yet there are times and circumstances which make it fitting not to weep for the dead, and there are always grounds for the mitigation of such grief. 1. The dead are *taken from the evil to come.* This is the idea of Jeremiah. If death was a calamity, the fate of the living at the overthrow of Jerusalem would have been a worse one. If an evil, death is still the less of two evils. Even if we only think of the dead as leaving the sunlight of this upper world and passing to the dim land of shades, still they go to the place "where the wicked cease from troubling, and the weary are at rest." In less calamitous times we should feel that, as God knows all, he may have taken our loved ones to save them from some fearful evil which he, though he alone, saw in their path. 2. The dead are removed according to *the will of God.* David wept for his child while it lived; after it was dead he dried his tears, for then he knew God's will and resigned himself to it (2 Sam. xii. 22, 23). This resignation is more than a sensible recognition of the inevitable; it is a calm and trustful acquiescence in the will of God as righteously supreme—for if the Lord gave, may he not take away?—wise, and good. 3. The dead have *fallen into the hands of God.* In what better hands can they be? How much better to fall into the hands of God than into the hands of man! We dare not dogmatize concerning the deep mysteries of futurity. But one thing we know—"The mercy of the Lord endureth for ever." He is just, he may seem stern; the impenitent must suffer punishment, which can be nothing else but fearful, though fair. Yet may not this be the very best thing for them, even during their sufferings? For it is better for us to suffer for sin than to sin without suffering. And who knows what ultimate designs God may have? 4. The *dead in Christ never need our tears.* We may weep for our own loss, but this is their gain. Weep that the battle is over and victory won? Weep that the pilgrimage is finished and the pilgrim safe at home? Weep that the toil and sorrow, the temptation and sin, of this world are left behind, and the joys of heaven inherited? that the night has ended, the shadows flown away? that the light of the celestial city is beaming on the weary wanderer? Such tears are tears of unbelief.

II. WHY WEEP FOR THE LIVING? This may be required by special causes. Life is a blessing. God gives many joys to his children in this world. The continuance of life is a privilege carrying with it the extension of advantages for faithful service. The brave and loyal servant of God will not selfishly crave a premature release from the duties of his life. Still there is a pathos about all life. "Our sincerest laughter with some pain is fraught." Special circumstances may make it fitting to weep for the living. There are calamities that are worse than death. Such seem to have been realized in the horrors of the sieges of Jerusalem. It is worse to live in sin than to die. The lost and ruined life claims our pity far more than that which is cut off by an early death. What curse could be greater than that of the "Wandering Jew"? Matthew Henry says, "Dying saints may be justly envied, while living sinners are justly pitied. And so dismal perhaps the prospects of the times may be, that tears even for a Josiah, even for a Jesus, must be restrained, that they may be reserved for ourselves and our children (Luke xxiii. 28)." Why should not this situation justify suicide? Because (1) we are not the masters of our own lives; (2) no man can tell what may follow the gloomiest prospects in the boundless possibilities of life, even in this world; (3) the man who lays violent hands on himself in rash, cowardly, and wilful rebellion against God, may expect a worse condition in the future life than that of the man who is called away by Providence, and possibly far worse than any he is attempting to escape.

Ver. 13.—*Dishonest builders.* In no age could these words of Jeremiah be more appropriate than in our own. Whilst we must be most careful to discriminate and not to vent wholesale censure, there can be no doubt that the building trade of our day furnishes numerous instances of an unrighteousness in business transactions which is a scandal to the commercial character of our nation, and which, if it becomes general, must be a sure presage of ruin. I. THE WICKEDNESS OF THE DISHONEST BUILDERS. 1. It is seen in *bad work.* Attempts are made to palm off wretched work with external decorations. There is a double crime here—lying and stealing; the work pretends to be what it is not, and undue payment is wrung out of the purchaser. Is not this commercial immorality to be witnessed in many branches of trade? In how many instances is it impossible to draw the line between the trader and the swindler? We find people accepting it as a maxim that every advantage should be taken of the ignorance, weakness, and trustfulness of others. It is forgotten that work should be done well for its own sake and in justice to others. Remember, God judges us more by the character of our work in the week than by the appearance of our worship on Sunday. 2. This wickedness is seen in the *treatment of workmen.* Those who live in rapidly growing neighbourhoods know how common it is for poor tradesmen to be ruined by the speculative builders to whom they have supplied materials, and for the artisans to have the utmost difficulty in obtaining their wages. This is especially bad, because it is the oppression of the poor and the abuse of confidence. We have no right so to speculate as to risk the property of other people. The cruelties of slavery which accompanied the gigantic building operations of antiquity (*e.g.* in the building of the Pyramids) may be equalled in wickedness by the crime of those who steal the work of the poor to increase the chance of their own aggrandizement. II. THE RUIN OF THE DISHONEST BUILDERS. "*Woe* unto him," etc.! Undue anxiety to get rich overreaches itself and ends in bankruptcy. Dishonesty in trade is poison to successful business in the ultimate issue, for it cuts at the root of the mainspring of all business—trust. The abuse of confidence must finally destroy confidence. No doubt commercial depression is largely due to this cause. If the abuse were general, there could be no commerce in the form that this must assume if it is to be carried on largely with the complicated civilization of modern life. We may be assured, too, that God will not overlook this wickedness. Success may be attained at first. The rich man may have built his palace and may be enjoying its luxuries. The commercial man may have brought his dishonest transactions to a successful termination. Yet the fraud and the cruelty are noted in heaven; and if there is a Judge above, the palace of the great will be no citadel to protect the guilty man from the thunders of Divine judgment.

Ver. 21.—*The voice of God disregarded in prosperity.* I. GOD SPEAKS TO US IN OUR PROSPERITY. 1. There are *important words* which need to be spoken to us at such a time. We can never have all the *wants* of our souls supplied by the richest abundance of material good things, and we need heavenly words for our soul's sustenance then as much as in the conscious helplessness of trouble.   We have special *duties* belonging to the time of prosperity.   Prosperity brings talents, opens up opportunities for enlarged service, calls for renewed devotion of love and gratitude.   There are also peculiar *dangers* attending prosperity, and it is well that we should hear a Divine voice warn us against them, and heed a Divine counsel which will direct us how to conquer them. 2. There are *means* by which God speaks to us in prosperity.   He is ever speaking to us, even when we do not hear his voice—by the Bible we should be reading, by the ordinances of the Church and the institution of preaching, by the course of providence, by the life of nature, by the still small voice of conscience.   But there are special voices of prosperity.   Prosperity speaks to us of the goodness of God exercised towards us in spite of our ill-desert and in a degree beyond all reckoning.

II. THERE IS DANGER LEST WE SHOULD DISREGARD THE VOICE OF GOD IN PROSPERITY. God does not thrust his messages upon unwilling ears.   We may refuse to hear.   Yet he speaks so that we may always hear, so that if we do not heed his voice it must be because we will not hearken to it.   1. Prosperity may disincline us to do this because it *seems to satisfy* us without God.   Really satisfy us it cannot.   But temporarily it acts as an opiate, and when we do not feel the need of God we are tempted selfishly to disregard his voice.   2. Then prosperity is *distracting.*   Sorrow is lonely and silent, and leaves us in the dark night to listen to heavenly voices and gaze on the wonders of the world above.   The garish day of prosperity, with its noisy and dazzling distractions, withdraws our attention from such things.   3. Further, prosperity *begets pride.*   It leads us to think much of self, to yield to self-will, and to rebel against the requirement to act as God's servants and stoop beneath the yoke of his will.   Hence it inclines us to a rebellious disregard for his voice.   4. If men have been hardened against God from their *youth*, it is not likely that they will heed his voice in the time of prosperity.   The longer we neglect this voice the more deaf do we become to it.   It is terrible to think of the folly and wickedness of persistent disregard to God's truth while he is patient and long-suffering and persevering in seeking access to our hearts.   Some great shock seems to be required to disturb this habit of hardened indifference.   An earthquake of adversity may be required to break up such fallow ground.   If trouble comes with this end it is a great blessing.   The adversity of the Captivity was such a blessing to the Jews; it led them to regard the voice that was unheeded in their prosperity.   So our sorrows are often blessings if they make us to hear the voice of our Father in heaven.

HOMILIES BY VARIOUS AUTHORS.

Vers. 1—23.—*Truth-speaking under difficulties.*   The prophet is commanded to go down to the king's palace and deliver his prophecies in the royal audience.   His mission did not admit of time-serving or evasive utterance.   Like that prophet who said to David, "Thou art the man," he had to speak to the king face to face and with great plainness.

I. GOD'S CHILDREN ARE OFTEN CALLED UPON TO WITNESS TO HIM IN DIFFICULT PLACES. In king's courts ; in society ; in unbelieving homes ; in the office, workshop, etc.

II. THEIR WITNESS IS OFTEN IN SHEER CONTRADICTION TO THE ACTIONS AND HABITS THAT PREVAIL THERE.   The sin of Judah was flagrant and open, affecting the most elementary laws of righteousness.   The Law of Moses guarded the widow and the orphan.   The Law of God, in its righteousness, purity, and love, is still strange to the world's life, and is constantly violated in it.   But the duty of witnessing is only rendered the more imperative.

III. THEY ARE SUSTAINED BY : 1. *The consciousness of inner rectitude and duty.*   2. *The witness of conscience in the transgressors.*   3. *The presence and promises of him who sends them.*—M.

Vers. 5, 7, 13, 14.—*Building in unrighteousness.*   The building of a house, be it small or great, is always an interesting and suggestive process.   It is a lengthened operation, expensive, and representing a great part of a man's aims and efforts.   Various purposes may be sought in it according to the character, circumstances, etc.. of the builder—mere shelter, comfort, splendour, protection. As these come into view the object in which they are to be realized becomes representative of the living personality and character with which it is associated. Jehoiakim was a despot, bent upon aggrandizement, and so he sought to build a magnificent palace with forced, unpaid labour. The ambitions of unspiritual men, the exclusive and absorbing projects of earthly life, resemble the palace-building of this Hebrew tyrant in—

I. THE UNION OF EXTRAVAGANT DESIRES AND DISHONEST, UNLAWFUL METHODS. Easy for Jehoiakim to "go in" for a splendid palace, as he is not in the habit of paying his *employés*. Are there not many in modern life who act on the same principle? The desire for self-advancement and aggrandizement overtops every other consideration. 1. *Unlawful methods of securing these are employed.* Speculation; getting on in business in order to get out of it; adulteration; insufficient wages; prices that do not admit of honest manufacture; clap-trap advertisements, etc. 2. *Imagining that others exist for the sake of one's self.* This reverses the golden rule and the spirit of Christ's life.

II. ITS FUNDAMENTAL SIN. This is selfishness—self-glorification, neglect of God and of human claims. The great principles of the Divine kingdom are contradicted;—justice, mercy, brotherly sympathy, etc.

III. ITS RESULTS. 1. *The ruin of the building;* i.e. the life-project—the unhallowed aim. 2. *The ruin of the builder*—for time, perhaps for eternity.—M.

Vers. 8, 9.—*Monumental judgments.* I. EXCEPTIONAL PENALTIES WILL ATTEND THE ABUSE OF EXCEPTIONAL PRIVILEGES. 1. *As a measure of justice.* The position attained by Jerusalem was due not so much to its site as to its being the centre of a theocracy. The foundation of its prosperity was a spiritual one. It was God's elective favour which had lifted it up above the cities of the earth. Presuming upon this, the first laws of righteousness had been violated and the whole conditions of the covenant relation ignored. This assumption of the inalienability of Divine blessings is at the root of every great apostasy. It is doubly unrighteous. (1) As a robbing of God. (2) As a misuse of a falsely acquired advantage and reputation. The robbery of such things is of infinitely greater heinousness in so far as they transcend in their value merely earthly treasures, and differ from them in the terms of their acquisition. It is free grace and unrequited love that are trampled on, and the punishment must therefore be the more exemplary. 2. *As a necessary precaution.* Pretensions so great are apt to mislead others. People who say, "The temple of the Lord, the temple of the Lord are we," may be taken at their own estimation if no marked change takes place in their external condition. God, therefore, uses his judgment in its external signs as an index of his reprobation. Other nations than Israel have illustrated this principle in their decline and fall. The great peoples of Christendom are on *their* trial. There is nothing more hateful in the sight of God than a people that has outlived its religion and yet retains the profession of it. Although the chief penalties of unfaithfulness in spiritual things must be inward, external evidences will not ·be wanting of what has taken place. How colossal the ruin of a power that has once been Christian, and has been exalted through Divine grace for the fulfilment of pledges which have never been redeemed (Matt. xxiii. 37; xi. 23)!

II. THE JUDGMENT OF GOD WILL BE ENDORSED BY THE VERDICT OF THE WORLD. Even the ruins of Jerusalem would be a thing to gaze at. Its desolation would be unlike any other. The epitaph of a forfeited spiritual supremacy would seem to be graven on the very stones. There is ever something unmistakable and peculiar in the condition of those who are rejected by God. Their misery is not as other misery, their ruin not as other ruin. 1. *The spectacle will be self-explanatory.* Not that every sin and failing of God's people would be written in earthly chronicles, but the causes of their decay would be broadly apparent. So is it with the Church from which God removes his candlestick, and the soul in whom the light has become darkness. 2. *It will be morally impressive.* Even in its misery the people of God will instruct the nations; and the Church of Christ will be a spectacle to angels and to men in its failures as in its successes.—M.

Vers. 10—12.—*Fates worse than death.* Josiah's death was still fresh in the memory of the people. But their hopes were reviving at the accession of the young Jehoahaz, his son. For three months he reigned in Jerusalem, following the evil and not the good of his predecessor, and "Pharaoh-Nechoh put him in bands at Riblah in the land of Hamath, that he might not reign in Jerusalem." After appointing Eliakim, another son of Josiah, to reign in his stead, he took the captive prince to Egypt, where he died (2 Kings xxiii. 31—35). The exile of "Shallum" was quite recent at the time of this prophecy, and the nation was naturally more concerned over the tragic fate of Josiah than the evil fortune of his son. Jeremiah hastens to correct this mistake by assuring them of the miserable death of Shallum in Egypt. From this we learn that—

I. DEATH IS NOT THE GREATEST CALAMITY THAT CAN BEFALL MEN. Shallum living, but in shameful exile, was really more to be pitied in himself and to be deplored for the sake of his country, than Josiah dead. The latter was free from the degradations to which his descendants were exposed, and saved the pain of seeing his country rendered tributary; he had also children to occupy his place. But Shallum experienced all his nation's shame, as it were, vicariously, and was helpless to rescue it from the foreign yoke under which the intrigues of his brother had brought it. The hopes of Israel had in a special but easily understood way centred upon Shallum, in whom it trusted to see the restoration of ancient glory. All these are cut off by a decree more than human. He became, therefore, the type: 1. *Of forfeited possibilities of usefulness.* 2. *Of national ignominy.* 3. *Of an irremovable curse.* The apostate professor of religion, the impenitent sinner, etc., are worse than dead. It were better for the offender of the little ones that he had never been born (cf. Heb. x. 26; 2 Pet. ii. 20, 21).

II. THE COMPASSION OF MEN SHOULD BE CALLED FORTH FOR THE MISERY OF THOSE WHOSE WRONG-DOING THEY HAVE SHARED. 1. *Because of its vicarious character.* 2. *Because of the Divine displeasure which it represents.* This extends to themselves, even although they are not personally punished. Shallum, in this respect, is a type of him who was "made sin for us." 3. *In order to practical measures being taken for its relief.* There are many in our own day who, like Shallum, are the victims of national crimes and social sins. It is for those who have escaped the penalty to seek, by practical measures and the earnest presentation of the gospel, to redeem them to a happier life. The outcast and the fallen will be the brightest gems in the crown of the Church which gives itself to their redemption.—M.

Vers. 15, 16.—*True royalty.* The contrast between Josiah and his son has had many a parallel. The family emerges from honest homespun into splendid dishonour, dropping its virtues and its religion as it goes. In all periods of external development and material civilization it is well to remember that true greatness must be in the man and not in his circumstances, and that the richest amongst us cannot afford to do without the graces and benevolence that dignify and adorn even the humblest life.

I. SHAM ROYALTY. "Shalt thou reign, because thou closest thyself in cedar?" With such persons the pomp of circumstance is everything. Autocratic imperiousness is mistaken for empire. The whole superstructure is unsafe because the foundation is false. The ground is undermined. In proportion as men lose the reality of power they grasp at its shadow.

II. TRUE ROYALTY. Essentially a spiritual thing. 1. *In what it consists.* In moral authority and real influence over men. This is never impaired by mere loss of external circumstance. The true king does not require his crown. 2. *How it is secured.* By (1) dependence on God, (2) simplicity of personal wants, (3) singleness of patriotic purpose, (4) sympathy with the ruled. "It was well with him." This repetition is intended to impress. "*Then* it was well with him."—an emphasis of time that was to be noted. Josiah himself had gone away from this ideal life and God cast him off.—M.

Vers. 1—10.—*The mighty pleadings of God.* These verses contain record of what we may fitly term a Divine wrestling with his sinful people to induce them to abandon their wickedness and live, so intense and urgent are the motives which he brings to bear upon them. Note—

I. FOR WHAT GOD PLEADS. "That they should execute *righteousness and judgment.*" It is the King Jehoiakim who is addressed specially, a monarch one of the worst who filled the throne of David. "He remained fixed in the recollections of his countrymen as the last example of those cruel, selfish, luxurious princes, the natural products of Oriental monarchies, the disgrace of the monarchy of David." For the estimate formed of him, cf. ver. 13, etc. To him, therefore, God thus appeals. Now, this appeal is one God is ever making. Righteousness is his supreme solicitude (cf. homily on ch. vii. 1—34, on "Relation of religion and righteousness"). False or corrupted religions are ever characterized by indifference to righteousness. So long as outward adhesion to the creeds and customs they enjoin is given, a wide margin is allowed for the indulgence of the natural and evil propensities of humanity. But a constant characteristic of the religion taught us in God's Word is its demand for righteousness. The gospel is no less stringent than the Law, yea, is more and justly more so, as it has brought to our aid a Divine force by which the demands of righteousness may be more readily met. It does not make void the Law. So far from that, it establishes the Law. If we understand by "belief" that which a man "lives by," which some say is the etymology of the word, and at any rate its meaning, then the scornful lines of the sceptic may be admitted to be true—

> " For creeds and sects let senseless bigots fight;
> His can't be wrong whose life is in the right."

For if those principles of conduct, those governing motives of a man's life, lead him to right, then, though encrusted with what amount of error and superstition soever they may be, they nevertheless, because bearing such fruit, cannot be wrong at the root. And, on the other hand, however orthodox and scriptural the professed creed, if it do not tend to right conduct then that fact proves that the professed belief is not the real one, but one far other. "Be ye holy as I am holy," is ever God's demand. Note—

II. How HE PLEADS. See what forcible arguments he employs. 1. *The mighty attraction of hope.* Thus he would *draw* men off from sin. If those to whom he appeals would but hearken, he would work what would be virtually a miracle for them. He would stay the progress of ruin and decay which were now threatening the state; he would turn back the tide of events which was now rushing on in such vast volume and force to overwhelm the throne and people, and he would re-establish the ancient monarchy of David in all its pristine glory (cf. ver. 4). To do this now that matters had gone so far would be as great a moral miracle as the cleaving of the waters of the Red Sea, and the Jordan, and the destruction of Sennacherib's army, were physical ones. But God would do that if but the wicked king would turn from his wickedness and execute righteousness and judgment. 2. *The mighty compulsion of fear.* Thus he would *drive* them off from their present evil ways. See the terrible threatenings of ver. 5, etc. What a picture the prophet draws of calamity and of shame, which would be theirs if they did " not hear these words "! And to prevent the force of this threat being diminished, he distinctly warns them that his affection for them and the joy he ever had in them will not hold him back from doing what he said. They had been as Gilead and as Lebanon for beauty, fertility, majesty—his choice possession, his precious heritage; nevertheless his wrath would go forth against them if they refused his words. And this appeal to the King of Judah is like the Divine appeal addressed to sinful men now. What promises to draw men to himself, what threatenings to drive them from their sins, the Bible is filled with! So intent is the Divine mind upon righteousness. In face of this earnestness of God in this matter, what fools they must be who make a " mock at sin "!

III. WHY HE THUS PLEADS. Because of: 1. *His love of righteousness.* It is the element in which God lives and moves and has his being. He cannot live in an atmosphere of unrighteousness. It is hateful to him. Righteous men feel thus; how much more, therefore, the righteous God! 2. *His love of men.* How would a father feel towards any one who was ever causing distress and ruin to his children? How he would detest such a person! And, on the other hand, how would he desire that which ever furthers his children's good! Thus God must, out of love for us his children, hate that which ever hurts and harms us, and desire that for us which ever ministers to our good. 3. *His love for the sinner.* God separates between the sinner and the sin, and whilst his love yearns over the sinner, his wrath burns against the sin. All his dealings with us are designed to effect a severance between the two. Death is the last and most effective separater; its keen sickle cuts the last bond that binds God's children to the dominion of sin. "He that is dead hath ceased from sin." Blessed be God that it is so! His providence, his Word, conscience, the strivings of his Spirit, are all designed to the same end, and our Lord was called Jesus because he should "save his people from their sins."

IV. WITH WHAT RESULT HE PLEADS. In this case it was of no use (cf. 2 Chron. xxxvi. 16, etc.). And—alas that it should be so!—it is often the same. When sin has got a certain hold on the will, no considerations will stay its course. No promises, no threats. How solemn a fact this! How it calls us to resist the beginnings of sin, to dread lest it should become such a habit of the soul as that God should say, "He is joined to his idols: let him alone"! But what is the result of God's pleading *on ourselves*? That is the question. God grant we may be able to answer it as he would desire!—C.

Ver. 10.—*Misplaced sorrow.* "Weep ye not for the dead," etc. Reference is to Josiah, the pious and patriotic King of Judah, who died deeply lamented (2 Chron. xxxv. 24, 25), being spared the pain of seeing and sharing the disgrace and suffering of his country (2 Kings xxii. 20). And by "him that goeth away" Shallum is probably meant. He was a younger son of Josiah, and was raised by the people to the throne under the name of Jehoahaz, but was soon carried captive into Egypt, never to return (2 Kings xxiii. 31—35). Taking the words of this verse generally, we note—

I. WE DO WEEP FOR THE DEAD. Not, however, in the same hopeless way in which the dead were mourned ere Christ brought life and immortality to light by the gospel. Still, though in a very real sense Christ has abolished death, we yet weep for the dead. 1. For the *beloved* dead. We can hardly comprehend how, if they be conscious, they can be happy without those they have loved here on earth. We know how much her children were to the fond mother of whom they have been bereaved, how she delighted in them and they in her, and hence we cannot see how she can be happy and blessed apart from them. And the fearful vacancy which the removal of the beloved dead causes in the circle of those who mourn them, the constant and dreary sense of irreparable loss,—all this is sufficient to make us weep for the dead. 2. And for the *holy* dead, as we think of the influence they exerted, the power for good they were to the family, the Church, the neighbourhood. 3. And *for all* who die we mourn. For life itself is a blessing: "All that a man hath will he give for his life." If, therefore, they have been cut off in the prime of their existence, their "sun gone down while it was yet day," we grieve over the possibilities of honour, happiness, and usefulness which are thus lost to them. And if they have been unbelieving and godless, we weep yet more. So far as we can see, the door of heaven is shut on them ere ever they have sought entrance there. It is a fearful thing for a man to die unforgiven, impenitent, and unbelieving. But it is not of such that mention is made in this verse. How can the thoughtful soul do aught but weep for them? But—

II. WE SHOULD AT TIMES WEEP MORE FOR THE LIVING. Great blessing as life is generally, there are times when death is less a reason for tears than life is. It is so when life is a prolonged sorrow, or shame, or suffering, or, especially, sin. Our Lord himself bade the women of Jerusalem weep not for him, but, etc. (Luke xxiii. 28). He thus declared that death—even such as his was to be—was preferable to life such as theirs would soon be. And death is a relief in cases not a few. Has not many a mother, heart-broken by the wild, wicked ways of a godless son, felt often that had he been taken from her when a little child, that sorrow had been less than his life now causes her? And our Lord said of Judas, "It had been better for that man if he had never been born." If sore sorrow can make life to be more pitiable than death—and it can—how much more grievous sin? Such a one is making the worst of both worlds. What is *our* life?

III. BUT IS NOT DEATH, FOR THE GODLY, ALWAYS PREFERABLE TO LIFE? Is it not always the living who are to be pitied? St. Paul says, "To depart and be with Christ . . . is *far better*." And the author of Ecclesiastes declares, "Better is the day of one's death than the day of one's birth." And without doubt the condition of the blessed dead is better than any earthly lot whatsoever. An old divine represents one such as saying to those who mourned him, "Weep not for me. For," he says, "consider the evils I am freed from. I had a sickly, crazy body, especially toward my latter end; wearisome days and nights were appointed me. What would I have given many times for an hour's rest? But now all this is at an end. I shall be no more sick, no more pained; my head shall now ache no more. And are you sorry for this? I had my share also of worldly losses and crosses in my worldly affairs. I had one house burned over my head, and almost all that was in it, in a few minutes, and have had other cares and troubles besides; but now farewell all such cares. And are you sorry for this? You know that as long as I was able I was laborious in my particular calling. I never ate the bread of idleness, but of honest diligence; but now all that toil is over. I am got to bed, where I rest from my labours—from all my labours of that kind—never to return to them again. And will you grieve for this? A great deal of pains I have taken in travelling and attending upon holy ordinances, on sabbath days and on week-days, sometimes above and beyond my strength; but I am now where I have communion with God at the spring-head, without the conduit-pipes of ordinances. And will you grieve for this? You all of you have, and I doubt not some of you feel, a body of death. I am sure I did; and many a time it made me cry out, 'O wretched man that I am!' You know what I mean—the corrupt nature in the carnal mind, the sin that dwells in us, a proneness to evil, a backwardness to good; but death has eased me of that burden. When the health went out of the body that indwelling sin went out of the soul. There was an end of the leprosy that was in the walls. What all the praying and hearing, the sabbaths and sacraments, the care and watchfulness, of forty years would not do, death has done at one blow. Weep not for me, then. I had daily grief in my heart for my own sins, for the sins of others, and for the afflictions of my friends, and for the troubles of the Church of God; but now all tears, even those of godly sorrow, are wiped away from mine eyes. Therefore let none be in yours upon my account. And, lastly, the bitterness of death is past with me. I have shot the gulf; that last enemy, that son of Anak, is vanquished, and I am triumphing. 'O Death, where is thy sting?' And, therefore, weep not for me. But this is not all. If you consider the happiness I am entered into, that fair palace in which death was but a dark entry, you would not weep for me, but rejoice rather. Would you know where I am? I am at home in my Father's house, in the mansion prepared for me there. I am where I would be, where I have long and often desired to be; no longer on a stormy sea, but in a safe and quiet harbour. Would you know how it is with me? I am made perfect in holiness. Would you know what I am doing? I see God. I see him as he is; not as through a glass darkly, but face to face. I am in the sweet enjoyment of my blessed Redeemer, whom my soul loved and for whose sake I was willing to part with all. Would you know what company I keep? Blessed company, better than the best on earth. Here are holy angels and the spirits of the just made perfect. I am set down 'with Abraham and Isaac and Jacob in the kingdom of God,' with blessed Paul, and Peter, and James, and John, and all the saints. And here I meet with many of my old acquaintance that I fasted and prayed with, who got before me hither. And, lastly, will you consider that this is to continue? It is a garland that never withers, a crown that fadeth not away."

IV. STILL WE ARE TO CHOOSE LIFE, IF IT BE GOD'S WILL. St. Paul did so; and we all, notwithstanding the blessed revelation of the gospel, desire life. And it is a natural and lawful desire. God has placed us here; he has visited us here; he has given us something to enjoy and something to do here. He expects us to value what he has bestowed. Christ did not desire that his disciples should be taken out of the world, but only kept from its evil. Paul desired to abide in the flesh, even when he was ripe for glory, and they are the healthiest Christians who in this matter tread in his track.

V. How, THEN, SHOULD THE TWO CONDITIONS OF LIFE AND DEATH BE REGARDED BY US? Are we, as this verse implies, and as is the common way, to count death a great misfortune? Certainly not. The world does, but the believer in Christ should not. Then, on the other hand, should we count life a misfortune, and weep and moan over it? As certainly not. In morbid, unhealthy, and therefore unhappy moods (cf. ch. xx. 14—18), a man may long to die and to have done with the weary woefulness of his life. And at such times—and they do occur—he has felt some sort of sympathy with the ancient stoic, who said that "the best gift the gods had given us in this life was the power of putting an end to it." But the universal instinct of man condemns this, and life is valued even for its own sake, and so it ought to be. " All the days of my appointed time will I wait till my change come"—such should be the soul's language, even under the heaviest trial. But the right regard of life and death is that of St. Paul. He was " willing to wait, but ready to go " (Phil. i. 23, 24). To be in his " strait " is the best position for us. To be evenly balanced between the two desires for life and for death—that is the happiest mood in which a man can be. For the desire of life greatly to preponderate is to come under that fear of death which makes some " all their lifetime subject to bondage." And a preponderating desire for death is certainly not good. The strait of St. Paul is the place. God bring and keep us there! His desire for the " far better " lot of companionship with Christ was met and counteracted by his desire to glorify Christ in life through being helpful to his brethren, for whom it was " more needful " that he should abide in the flesh. And so he was kept in equilibrium, as it were, by these opposed forces, and the result was, as it ever will be, a saintly and devoted life. Paul's " strait " is the only easy position on the earth. Oh, to be in it! If you are held by both of these bonds you will not fear a fall on either side. " Although your life, instead of being in your Father's hands, were at the disposal of your worst enemy, in his utmost effort to do you harm he would be shut up between these two— either to keep you a while longer in Christ's work or send you sooner to Christ's presence. That were indeed a charmed life that should tremble evenly in the blessed balance. This way, we shall do good to men; that way, we shall be with the Lord." Weep not, then, either for the blessed dead or for the holy living; bemoan neither, but bless God for both. But we may weep sore for him that goeth away an exile from God, never in this life, so far as we can see, to return. That sorrow is just; all other is misplaced.—C.

Ver. 13.—*The Nemesis of oppression.* " Woe unto him that buildeth his house by unrighteousness!" It is one of the many precious characteristics of the Bible that it ever represents God as the Avenger of the poor and oppressed. It tells over and over again how God " plentifully rewardeth the proud doer." And it is interesting and most instructive to note the manner in which God does this. Not so much by direct punitive inflictions of his wrath as by the results of those laws according to which his universe is ordered. That law of his universe is against the oppressor, and sooner or later overtakes and overwhelms him.

> " Though the mills of God grind slowly,
>   Yet they grind exceeding small."

Now, here, in these verses, we have a Divine denunciation of oppression: " Woe unto him," etc.! And we note—

I. THERE HAS BEEN, AND YET IS, OPPRESSION. We trust that there is far less of it than once there was, but that it has disappeared we cannot affirm. Here, in our own land of liberty, we may know but little of it, but in the lands of the East, its original home, it prevails still to terrible extent. And the ancient kings of Israel were sorely tempted to allow themselves in it, and often did so, and would have more largely had it not been for the perpetual protest maintained against it by the prophets of God. But if we feel, as we do, that a tyrant and an oppressor would meet but with short shrift in such a liberty-loving land as our own, how was it that oppression became so easy and so common in other lands? Therefore note—

II. THE CAUSES OF OPPRESSION. These will be most readily seen by noticing the lands wherein it has most prevailed. It has ever been where the earth has brought forth fruit of itself abundantly and without demanding much labour from the cultivator. And these lands, with scarce an exception, lie along that belt of the earth's surface which reaches from the East Indies and on westward to Mexico and Peru. It includes the Euphrates valley, Egypt, and then, crossing the Atlantic, it comprises the extinct civilizations of Equatorial America. It may be remarked in passing that Judah and Jerusalem were, at the time of Jeremiah's prophecy, in alliance with Egypt, one of these lands of oppression, and whence the evil lesson would be easily learnt. But it will be asked, Wherefore was oppression more rife in these lands than in others? It has never been so in Northern countries as in these more favoured lands. The explanation lies in such facts as these: 1. All these lands have abundance of heat and moisture. The tropical sun furnishes the one and their magnificent rivers the other. And sometimes, in addition to these rivers, if not in place of them, as in the Gulf of Mexico, a large extent of coast-line ensures that vapours shall arise plentifully from the sea, which, descending on the already heated soil, provides the moisture it needs. 2. In consequence of all this the soil becomes very fruitful, and yields such abundance, and that with so little cost of labour, that it permits the formation of a leisure class, who subsist on its superfluous wealth. 3. These have become the intelligent and learned, and so the powerful, classes. 4. Meanwhile the wage-receiving population has multiplied greatly, and the wage fund having to be spread over so much larger surface, the share of each labourer has become less and less. 5. Here, then, on the one hand is a vast swarm of impoverished people, and as ignorant as they are poor, and on the other a rich, intelligent, and therefore powerful minority. And as the rich grew richer and richer the poor grew poorer and poorer, and gradually sank down, as in these countries they have ever done, into a mass of slaves, the ready victims of the oppressors' power. No doubt other forces were at work at the same time to favour the growth of this oppression—the superstition of the people and the enervating influence of the climate. But thus oppression grew, and its fruits are still visible in the huge Pyramids, temples, palaces, and the like, which remain to show the abundance of labour and the prodigality with which it was used. 6. But in the colder climes of the North the more niggard soil demands continuous, careful, and laborious cultivation, and thus the growth of population was checked and the distribution of wealth became more equal; and at the same time the rugged soil seemed to impart its character to those who cultivated it, and rendered it impossible that such men should ever become the passive victims of oppression. And so, whilst the soft, luxurious climes such as those referred to have never been favourable to the development of the people inhabiting them, those more stern and inhospitable regions, where toil, severe and continued, is necessary would men live, have nurtured races of men who, more than any others, have approached the true ideal of manhood. But whilst the facts now noted became the occasion, opportunity, and temptation to oppression, other laws have been at work, securing that, where this temptation has been yielded to, as it has been so often, there the oppressed shall ere long be avenged. Note—

III. THE NEMESIS OF OPPRESSION. There is such an avenger. For oppression ever kills patriotism and loyalty. What can a horde of wretched slaves care for a country or a rule which has never been other than horribly cruel to them and theirs? Patriotism and loyalty are the offspring of freedom and righteous rule, but never of the oppressor's rule. And thus, sooner or later, "woe" ever cometh "to him who buildeth his house by unrighteousness." For when such a land is invaded, or insurrection arises, or in any way the authority of the rulers is threatened, they have no support in the people who are altogether indifferent as to who their rulers may be, and feel that almost any change must be for the better. See this illustrated in the revolt under Jeroboam, whereby Israel was for ever separated from Judah; in the fall of Nineveh and of Babylon, and in the oft-recurring revolutions and invasions amid the dynasties and thrones of the East (cf. also Buckle's 'History of Civilization' for further illustration). Thus in nature and in providence, as well as in his written Word, God has pronounced "woe" on oppression and the oppressor. Learn from all this: 1. To accept gratefully the sterner conditions of life which may be appointed for us. Sunny skies, warm climates, and prolific soils nurture slaves rather than men. No cross, no crown, is a universal law. 2. Adore and trust in that God who has said so emphatically that he will judge the poor and needy, and hurl the oppressors from their seats. 3. Remember that the woe against unrighteousness falls on *every* house that is built thereby.—C.

Vers. 13—19.—*Son and father : a sad contrast.* A wicked son. Jehoiakim is not only reproached with his wickedness, but reminded of the very different conduct of his honoured father. The contrast is very striking, varied, and instructive. It is seen—

I. IN THE PARENTAGE OF THE TWO PRINCES. Jehoiakim had the great advantage of being the son of an eminently good father. All the impulse and help that could come from such a fact was his. Josiah, on the other hand, was the son of a pre-eminently bad man—of King Amon, of whom it was said, "Amon sinned more and more." Yet, in spite of his godly parentage, Jehoiakim became so evil, whilst Josiah, notwithstanding his evil parentage, became so good. T. Fuller, noting in connection with the genealogies of our Lord a similar fact, quaintly remarks, "I find a good father had a bad son; that is ill news for me: but I find also that a bad father had a good son; that is good news for my son." For further consideration of facts like these, see homily (*infra*) on "Exceptional facts in the law of transmission of character."

II. In their conduct. Jehoiakim lived in splendour amid the misery of the nation, and amused himself with building palaces when the whole land was ground down by heavy taxation (cf. 2 Chron. xxxvi. 3; 2 Kings xxiii. 25). He also took the people's forced labour without pay for these buildings, in violation of Lev. xix. 13; Deut. xxiv. 14, 15 (cf. also vers. 13—15). But Josiah his father did "judgment and justice;" "he judged the cause of the poor and needy" (ver. 15).

III. In character. Jehoiakim's is summed up in the short, stern sentence, "He did evil in the sight of the Lord his God" (2 Chron. xxxvi. 5). And the facts above noted show his rapacity, cruelty, and oppression. But what a contrast to what his father Josiah was (cf. 2 Chron. xxxiv.)!

IV. In happiness. With all his tyranny Jehoiakim could not command happiness for himself. The mutterings of the thunder of the Divine judgments were continually being heard, and the rebukes of the prophets of God, together with those of his conscience, which could not have been silent, and the sullen discontent of his people, all combined to haunt his palace with omens of wretchedness and to fill his heart with fear. On the other hand, it is said of King Josiah that he "did eat and drink, and it was well with him;" the meaning of which is, that he was no ascetic, that he enjoyed life and lived prosperously and joyously. It is ever so. "In keeping of God's commandments there is great reward"—in the sunshine of the soul which comes from the consciousness of the Divine approval, and the testimony of a clear conscience, and the love and esteem of those over whom rule is exercised.

V. In their death. The actual circumstances of Jehoiakim's death are not declared. But sufficient hints are given to show that his sun went down in clouds and darkness, that his end was miserable. "According to one account," says Stanley, "his memory was held in detestation; there were no funeral dirges over him, as there had been over his father and brother, but his corpse was thrown out, like that of a dead ass (cf. ver. 18), outside the walls of Jerusalem, exposed to the burning sun by day and the biting frost by night. And this prophetic curse was darkened with a yet deeper hue by the legend which described how, on the skin of the dead corpse, as it thus lay exposed, there appeared in distinct Hebrew characters the name of the demon Codonazer, to whom he had sold himself. He remained fixed in the recollections of his countrymen as the last example of those cruel, selfish, luxurious princes, the natural product of Oriental monarchies, the disgrace of the monarchy of David." But of King Josiah the record is far otherwise. "So mournful a death had never occurred in the Jewish annals. All the population of the city and the kingdom attended the funeral. There was an elegy over the departed king, probably as pathetic as that which David had sung over Saul and Jonathan. It was by Jeremiah, the most plaintive of the prophets, who then first appears on the scene of public acts. Long afterwards was that sad day remembered, both as it was celebrated on the field of battle and at Jerusalem. The lamentation of Jeremiah was preserved in the memory of the male and female minstrels as a national institution, even till long after the return from the Captivity. Every family shut itself up and mourned apart. In the prospect of the heaviest calamity that could befall the nation, this was the mourning which recurred to them, mourning as one mourneth for his only son, in bitterness as one is in bitterness for his firstborn. The childless mother laid herself down to die; the sun of her life went down as at midday, as in the total eclipse of that fatal year. Josiah was the last royal hero of Israel." Such are some of the contrasts presented by these two careers of the son and father. They teach us: 1. That whilst we should be thankful for the blessings of a pious parentage, we are not to presume upon it as if it were a sure safeguard or a certain prophecy of what our end shall be. 2. That should it be our lot to be the child of ungodly parents, the same grace that made Josiah what he was can surmount all early disadvantages, and make us far other and better than what our start in life may have led men to expect. He who, as did Josiah, will set himself whilst he is yet young to seek the Lord shall surely find him, and also that he who honours God, God will honour.—C.

Ver. 18.—*Exceptional facts in the law of transmission of character.* "Concerning Jehoiakim the son of Josiah King of Judah." The law is that like begets like. It is so physically and mentally to large extent, and morally and spiritually as well. Generally, blessed be God, the children of his servants become his servants too. And, on the other hand, the habit of sin in the parent is reproduced in the child, so that we have criminal *classes*, hereditary drunkards, profligates, and much else of a similar sad sort. But the law has frequent exceptions on both sides. The two names in this verse are both of them instances of such exception. Now, how are we to account for them? We have frequent instances in the Old Testament. The sons of "Aaron the saint of the Lord;" of Eli, the devout high priest; of Samuel, the upright judge. What a set David's children were! And here we have Josiah the good, father of the infamous Jehoiakim. But we have nothing of this in the New Testament. It does not seem to be recognized there that the children of the godly can be otherwise than godly themselves. Even when one of the parents was an unbeliever, a heathen, the faith of the other was held to have such virtue that of their children St. Paul says, "Now are your children holy." We have very many instances of whole households being believers, but none of the children of believers being other than what their parents were. Would to God it were always so now! And, on the other hand, we have, as in the cases of the pious Hezekiah, son of the wicked Ahaz, and Josiah, son of Amon, who "sinned more and more," instances of ungodly parents having godly children. Now, how are these to be accounted for? Consider the sad case—

I. THAT GODLY PARENTS SHOULD HAVE UNGODLY CHILDREN. We are accustomed to assent to the possibility and frequency of this as an unquestionable truth. But is it so? We would ask two questions with a view to a better understanding of the matter. 1. Is it meant that godly parents who have been both able and anxious to train their children for God may yet have ungodly children? (1) *Some godly parents are not thus able.* Probably Josiah was not. The might of evil, the fearful sweep and rush of its tide, was probably in those days, and in that court and city, too great for even the godly king to withstand, and it bore away his son before his eyes. For a prince in that age to be godly was almost a miracle. And that which we have suggested as perhaps and probably accounting for the ungodliness of Josiah's son may explain some similar cases now. (2) *But more are not really anxious about it.* If parents were as anxious about the godliness of their children as they are about their health, education, and start in life, and took as much pains to secure it, such cases as we are considering would be more rare than they are. (3) *The children of believers ought not to need conversion.* They should grow up in the kingdom of God in which their baptism declared them to be already members. But there is a deadly doctrine all too influential in thousands of Christian homes, that children must go into the far country first, and there live more or less prodigal-like, and then afterwards come to themselves, be converted, and return. And of course what is expected of such children happens, as far as the going away is concerned: not always the return. But why should they ever go into that far country? The elder son, though, like Jonah and many a devout Jew (cf. Paul's "I bear them witness that they have a zeal for God," etc.), he was perplexed at the Father's gracious way of dealing with repentant sinners, was the elder son still who had been ever obedient, and to whom the father said, "Son, *thou* art ever with me, and all that I have is thine;" as much as to say, "Why do you complain of my treatment of your poor wretched brother? Yours is far the better lot; you are so much the happier that *you* assuredly ought not to complain." *So* did the father "entreat him," and, no doubt, successfully. But from most mournful forgetfulness of the fact that there is no need that our children should go away, and that they ought not to go away, many parents let them go, or at least acquiesce in their going as something that is inevitable. Hence, as it is of no use to be anxious and guard against the inevitable, they take no such pains about their children's godliness as they do about those other more temporal matters which concern their welfare, and which they know do very largely depend upon the endeavours they, their parents, put forth. They cannot avoid desiring their children's highest good, and in family prayers and private ones it is remembered before God. But the energies of the will are never roused up to seek it as other and lesser things are sought. Would to God they were! Now, we say that if you have a case of real ungodliness in the children of the godly, it is to be accounted for by the fact that either the parents were not able or else not really anxious to train them for God. More often the latter is the sad truth. 2. But we ask, also— What is meant by ungodly? Do you mean those who for a while go astray, but afterwards come back? Of course, if the sin be like Manasseh's, very flagrant and long-continued, then, even though there may be the after coming back, as there was in his case, it must be allowed that such are ungodly. But that stern word should generally be reserved for a life wholly without God, and not be cast carelessly on those who, like so many of God's saints have done, may fall yet rise again; still less on children because of their natural thoughtlessness and incapacity of thinking seriously for a long time about anything. God forbid they should! But if the word "ungodly" be confined, as it should be, to those whose lives are wholly or for the most part without God, then we affirm that such children do not spring from parents both able and really anxious to train them for God. To affirm that they are would be to contradict: (1) *God's word*; *e.g.* "Train up a child . . . and when he is old he *shall not* depart from it;" "Ask, and ye shall receive;" and the many promises to answer prayer. Now, we know that the godliness of our children must be in accordance with the Divine will, therefore all these promises must be set aside if, etc. And St. Paul bids parents train their children "in the nurture and admonition of the Lord;" and he never hints that such training may after all be thrown away. What was the constant baptism of households but an indication of the apostolic and primitive belief that, *as a matter of course*, in the faith of the father the children would share? The promise was to them *and their children*. (2) *Analogies*. If there be real pains to train children in a given manner educationally, socially, morally—as there is on the part of parents—success is gained nearly always. And so it would be in things spiritual. There is no slight done to the truth of the Holy Spirit's agency in this great matter, but all that is urged is that we obey the laws of the Spirit. (3) *Facts*. No instance can be shown where there has been *real* solicitude and opportunity on the part of the parents that their children should be godly, of such children having been permanently ungodly. There has not been permanent failure, though there may have been temporary. It would be horrible to believe that God had drawn forth the earnest yearning of the parent's heart for the salvation of their children—a yearning attested by all loving and consistent endeavour in the way of example, education, influence, direct and indirect—and yet, after all, such desire to be miserably and for ever disappointed. We will not believe it. And, on the other hand, there are innumerable instances which show that it is the rule that godly parents should have godly children. Nearly all the godly to-day are the children of the godly. Instead of the fathers have risen up the children. Such is God's blessed order, and we should be slow to believe that he ever sets it aside. It is well for every father and mother to take it to heart that if their children turn out ungodly the fault is, in all probability, theirs. But now note the opposite case—

II. THAT UNGODLY PARENTS SHOULD HAVE GODLY CHILDREN. We have referred above to such cases. And they frequently occur. The chaff nourishes the wheat in its bosom. The ungodly home nurtures godly children. How is this? 1. Sometimes it is because ungodly parents are more careful than even others about the companionships of their children. They try to gain a good for their children which they know they have not for themselves. Many a bad parent wishes his child to be good. 2. Sometimes the children, seeing how wretched sin makes their home, are led to seek "a more excellent way" for themselves. The ways of godliness seem like paradise to the victim of the ungodliness of many a home. How Sunday school children—many of them from terrible homes—love their school! 3. God willing to show them that there is nothing too hard for the Lord. Can a man bring forth a clean thing out of an unclean? Certainly not. But God can, and in these instances does. And the reasons for such gracious action may be: (1) Pity for the children. (2) Instruction to his Church. They are to despair of none. (3) The glory of his Name. Hence he snatches these, trophies as it were, from the very gates of hell; plucks them as brands from the burning. 4. *Conclusion.* Let us give God thanks that he does this. That Amons have Josiahs for children; Ahaz, Hezekiah; Henry VIII., Edward VI. That from such a court as that of the previous reigns our own beloved queen should have come. God be praised for this and every such instance!—C.

Ver. 29.—*The impassioned cry of God to man.* This cry, "O earth, earth, earth," etc., sounds out like the alarm of fire, or some bitter cry of distress. It startles by its earnestness, arrests and demands attention, and compels us to inquire into its cause. Note, therefore—

I. THE OCCASION OF IT. This will show us what word of the Lord's is meant. It was wrung out from the prophet's heart by the sight of the calamities now so swiftly coming upon his beloved land. To think of that land overrun by the cruel armies of Babylon, the holy city burnt with fire, the temple of the Lord desecrated and destroyed, and her kings, one after another, ending their days in misery; Josiah, the happiest of them, slain in battle; Shallum, his son, exiled in Egypt, and dying there; Jehoiakim carried off by Nebuchadnezzar, and perishing at a very early age, and in some miserable manner—"buried with the burial of an ass" (ver. 19); Jeconiah, with his mother, seized by the Chaldeans, torn from his home and taken to Babylon, and there living and dying in drear exile—he the last of the royal race, after whom none other filled the throne of David. It was the sight of all these calamities, and the shame and disgrace attached to them, and especially the remembrance of the cause of them all, that extorted this loud cry of pain, this impassioned appeal. (Cf. Stanley's 'Lectures on Jewish Church,' Lect. xl., for history of period.) Would we realize the prophet's distress, let us endeavour to imagine that the circumstances were our own; that it was our own land, people, temples, princes, thus threatened, thus exiled, thus miserably perishing. What should we think then? No wonder that Jeremiah was "the weeping prophet;" that he felt the woes of his country to be so great that he could appeal to all who witnessed them, "Is it nothing to you, all ye that pass by? behold, and see if," etc. (Lam. i. 12). And, like Dives in hell, who bethought himself of his five careless, godless brethren, and would have them warned; so the prophet of God, knowing how all the world was heedless of God, even as his own land had been, to its sore cost, now passionately cries, "O earth, earth, earth," etc. He would have sinners everywhere take heed, by Judah's awful fate, of how God will surely punish sin. The word he would have them hear was the word of warning. This is the lesson which the occasion of this appeal teaches us. There are many other words which God addresses to us—words of mercy, promise, instruction, and the like; but unless we take heed to this word and dread the sin which works such woe, all the others will be but lightly esteemed. And that which makes this word yet more emphatic is the position of privilege and honour and security which those now judged of God once occupied (cf. ver. 24). Coniah was as God's signet-ring, precious, honourable, and guarded with all care. But it made no difference: as a ring might be plucked off and cast away, so now God would root out and cast away these evil-doers, though once so dear to him. It matters not, then, what position of privilege, profession, reputation, service, and the like we fill, disobedience to God's commands will cast us down and work our ruin. "Let him that standeth take heed lest he fall;" "Be not high-minded, but fear;" "If God spared not the natural branches, take heed lest he also spare not thee."

II. THE MANNER OF IT. This will show how disregarded this word of the Lord too commonly is. There would have been no need of such impassioned appeal if men were eager to listen. But the cry has to be loud, repeated, and ever louder still. The world has but to whisper; the lowest accents of pleasure, self-interest, and often of sin, are caught in a moment and obeyed. But the word of the Lord finds no such reception ready. How different this from all other creatures of God!—from the holy angels that "excel in strength and do his commandments, hearkening unto the voice of his word," down to the meanest and humblest of all the works of his hands. Man alone stands out in disgraceful exception. One should have thought that the near approach of danger would quicken the sense of fear and lead to increased caution. As when the ship nears a perilous coast how frequent the soundings, how sharp the look out! But the ungodly, the nearer they come to the shore of the, for them, awful other world, the less concerned they seem to be, the more dull of hearing the word of the Lord. Like the cold, which benumbs and paralyzes the more intense it becomes. Hence, if man is to be awakened from his spiritual slumber, God must cry aloud, lift up his voice with strength, as here, " O earth, earth, earth," etc. Does not our own conscience bear witness to the truth of our backwardness to hear God's word which the manner of this appeal implies. How often God has called to us, by his Word, his Spirit, his providence, and we have not answered!

III. THOSE TO WHOM IT IS ADDRESSED. Thus we shall learn the importance and universality of this word. For by the earth which is appealed to we may understand : 1. *Inanimate nature.* As Isa. i., " Hear, O heavens, and give ear, O earth." As if the prophet would call on the very stones to cry out and attest the momentous importance of this word of the Lord; as if the earth might be trusted to hear though man would not. And is not this word important, in these days especially, when the sense of sin has become so feeble, and men trifle with it as a matter of indifference? It is every day ensnaring souls and hardening them more and more. And the time for awakening them is short. The crash of the gates shutting against them will arouse them, but then it will be too late. When the ship has struck, the shock of the blow is but the prelude to the cry of despair, which tells that there is no hope, for there is no time to escape. Yes, men need to be warned, need to hear this word of the Lord; and woe to them whose duty it is to declare it if they fail so to do. 2. But earth or land tells of the people who dwell thereon—*the inhabitants of the world.* The prophet appeals to them all, not to a mere section of them. Not to Palestine, still less Judah only, but to the whole earth. For it is a word which all need to give heed to : the believer, that his compassion for sinners may be aroused; the undecided, that his indecision may come to an end; and the ungodly, that they may tremble with a holy fear. Lastly—

IV. THE AUTHOR OF IT. This will show to us the heart of love that utters itself in it. The stern "threats of God do not lessen his love but enhance it. They are the crowning marks of mercy. A shepherd, foreseeing a snowstorm that will drift deep into the hollows of the hill, where the silly sheep, seeking refuge, would find a grave, prepares shelter in a safe spot and opens its door. Then he sends his dog after the wandering flock to frighten them into the fold. The bark of the dog behind them is a terror to the timid sheep; but it is at once the sure means of their safety and the mark of the shepherd's care. Without it the prepared fold and the open entrance might have proved of no avail. The terror which the shepherd sent into the flock gave the finishing touch to his tender care, and effect to all that had gone before it. Such precisely, in design and effect, are the terrible things of God's Word " (Arnot). It is because God is so intent on moving us from impending woe that he utters his impassioned appeals, and draws, in such terrible descriptions, the portraiture of his wrath. A mother seeking her child lost in the bush does not once whisper its name, but she repeats it again and again, with shrill, clear, loving, strong cry. And it is the like cry of God that is heard in all his warning words, awful as some of them are. God wants that we should be saved.

CONCLUSION. But by the earth which is bidden hear the word of the Lord, our thoughts have suggested to them the company of the dead. They are in the graves. They are gone "earth to earth;" and concerning them our Lord says, "Behold, the hour cometh when all that are in the graves shall hear the voice of the Son of man, and shall come forth " (John v. 25—28). What shall be the manner of that awakening, when the trumpet shall sound and the cry, " O earth, earth, earth," etc., is again heard? What? Shall it be unto life and immortality, or to shame and everlasting contempt? All depends on how we hear the Word of the Lord now. May he grant that we may both hear it and hear it aright!—C.

Vers. 1—9.—*A king addressed in mingled promise and warning.* Here is the announcement of what Jehovah requires from the king and his executive in particular; although it will be seen that exactly the same principles apply to the conduct of the king as to the meanest of his subjects. But inasmuch as the king was in circumstances of special power, responsibility, and temptation, it was just what might be expected from the Divine consideration for every man's position, that the king should receive special counsels. If he acted wrongly, his conduct would be quoted and his example followed by every one who wished to act in the same way. This warning message here, however, so timely and so plain, would take away all ground from those who thought they might do what a king did. Jeremiah, preaching righteousness to the meanest of the people, could insist on this, that he asked no more from them than he had been specially enjoined to ask from the very king himself. Note—

I. THOSE WHO WERE TO BE APPROACHED. This is a message for the king and for such people as live in palaces. Remarkable to notice how God's messengers have been brought into contact with the kings and grandees of the earth. Divinely guided, they have been able to find their way where others, even with large worldly influence, have been excluded. So Moses comes to deal with Pharaoh; Jeremiah with this king here; John the Baptist with Herod; Jesus with Pontius Pilate; Paul with Felix, Festus, and Agrippa. As God can make a way for his servants out of prisons, so he can also make a way for them into palaces. And once entered into the palace, the prophet was to address himself first and chiefly to the king. Kings have many counsellors, and their temptation is to say what may be agreeable to the royal ears. This king, maybe, had not one honest, disinterested man about him; if so, all the more need for Jeremiah's counsels. Further, the king is reminded of a former distinguished occupant of his throne. In pondering this expression, "the throne of David," there was much to fill the heart of a king, who was also a true man, with noble purpose and endeavour. David, even with all his transgressions and vicissitudes, was a fine example of the success and glory following on sensitiveness to God's commandments. If David had not been enabled to do so much that was good, his successors would not have found scope for the doing of so much that was evil. Then from the king there is a turning to those around them. Kings cannot help being a great deal influenced and even limited by those who stand next to them. God, who knows all conditions of life, sees the peculiar difficulties of kings and sympathizes with them. One of the greatest troublers of David's life was his headstrong servant Joab.

II. GOD'S DEMAND UPON THOSE WHO HOLD POSITIONS OF AUTHORITY. He sent his servant to show how a king's government may become stable, glorious, and happy. Nothing is said about victorious armies and increased territories. These were the things the Gentiles sought after, but God wished the powers and opportunities of the kings of his people to be used for far other ends. There was plenty of room for this king to make conquests, and conquests not easily made. He had his own selfish inclinations to repress, and the selfish proceedings of many of his people to undo. He is commanded to execute judgment and righteousness. He must not neglect the ever necessary functions of a judge; righteous principles must rule in all his decisions; and thirdly, he must see that the decisions are carried into effect. How can any human government be approved of God unless there are both righteous laws and a resolute execution of them? The king must also be the vigilant guardian of the weak and defenceless. From out of his palace his servants should go forth commissioned to champion those who are unable to protect themselves. Never should a strong man more exult in his strength than when it enables him to become sword and shield to the feeble. A righteous government will not wait until it is dinned with importunities. In many instances the king was the only one who could rescue from the hand of the oppressor. Every temporary occupant of the throne of David was in his turn a type of that abiding King and anointed One, of whom it is true in the highest sense that salvation is in no other (Acts iv. 12). And as the king was to deliver from the oppressor, so he was to be careful not to oppress. So subtle is selfishness in its influence upon us that we need to be peculiarly on our guard against taking advantage of the weak. Lastly, the king is not to be a shedder of innocent blood. He must not be weakly indulgent as to the blood of the guilty. If a man by the laws of the land has deserved to die the death, there must be no tampering with just deserts. And so, on the other hand, a king was not to allow his fury free course against some one who had offended him, and seek his death simply to gratify resentment. It is easy to see that the despotic character of Eastern kings in ancient times would make this injunction against the shedding of innocent blood to have an application such as it fails to have with the constitutional governments we are accustomed to.

III. The prophet has to point out that ACCORDING TO THE RECEPTION OF THESE COUNSELS THERE WILL BE CORRESPONDING RESULTS. The king is plainly told that it is for him to determine whether his reign shall be glorious and his palace continue and increase in splendour. The king who can rise above all temptations to mere outward show; who can be gloriously independent of selfish traditions and examples; who can show the spirit of a real king by living for his people, instead of expecting his people to drudge and sweat and groan for him;—this is the king whom God will reward. The reward will come in the very way such a man will desire. His throne will become more stable for his successors; the land more prosperous and better worth living in. On the other hand, if there is negligence of these counsels, the ruin of the negligent ruler will be correspondingly terrible. No man, however great his resources, can build up anything glorious and satisfactory on a foundation of disobedience to God. Against that tree of temporal prosperity which has been planted in selfishness and nurtured in selfishness, a consecrated axe is laid—laid at the root of the tree to cut it down altogether. The greatness of the prosperity measures the greatness of the ruin. We must delight in the Law of the Lord if we would be as trees of God's own planting; and then, assuredly, no weapon formed against us can prosper.—Y.

Vers. 10—12.—*The mistakes of the mourner.* Two persons are presented here as furnishing occasions for lamentation. One is Josiah, King of Judah, lately dead; the other is Shallum, his son, just succeeding him, and taken into captivity by Pharaoh-Nechoh, King of Egypt. The prophet, therefore, looks upon his countrymen as sorrowing both for the dead and the living. Moreover, he sees that, in accordance with all the natural tendencies of the human heart, a deeper sorrow is professed for the dead than for him who has been taken away into a foreign land. And yet this was not according to the necessities of the position. The captivity of Shallum, rightly considered, was a more distressing event than the death of his father. It may be truly said that we always exaggerate death as a calamity. In the instance of Josiah, his comparatively early death—for he seems to have been no more than forty when he perished in battle—produced peculiar feelings of pity. He seemed to be one whose "sun had gone down while it was yet day." But we must remember that this very death had been prophetically spoken of as a blessing (2 Kings xxii. 20): "Thine eyes shall not see all the evil that I will bring upon this place." For one who is faithfully trying to serve God, it can matter very little when he dies. His service goes on. A man may benefit the cause of God more by the faithful testimony of a Christian death than by fifty years of continued work. If a man has come to death by his own folly and recklessness, we do well to grieve over him; but death in itself is an event which we may only too easily come to look at in a distorted, exaggerated way. There are things far worse than death. Again and again it happens that people fall into severe illnesses, recover, and then return into the world, only to find that the years seemingly added in mercy to life have become a period of disaster and shame. In the midst of a world of misery, we cannot be too pitiful, too sympathetic, but we must be careful not to make erroneous estimates as to what most deserves our pity and sympathy. We can do nothing for the dead. When the last breath is breathed, there is straightway a great gulf fixed between us and them. But we may do much for the living, if only in a self-denying spirit we keep them in our recollection and strive to help them; seizing every opportunity, and economizing our energies so as to make the most of it.—Y.

Vers. 13—19.—*A right aim pursued by a wrong and cruel method.* I. A RIGHT AIM. What this aim was is indicated in ver. 15. Jehoiakim wanted to be a king. In one sense he was a king, without any effort of his own, for he had succeeded to the position and honours of his father. But very rightly he sought to be reckoned a king by virtue of something more than mere rank. He wished to do something which would mark off his reign as peculiar. He wished something more to be said of him than that he merely reigned so many years. His office would have made him to be remembered in a certain way, but he preferred that his office should be a mere vantage-ground to give him the chance of showing what he could do as a man. Bad as Jehoiakim was, he had individuality of character—a strong feeling that a king was bound to do something more than just sit on a throne, wear a crown, and hold a sceptre in his hand. There is nothing pleasing to God in our being mere colourless copies of those who have gone before us. Jehoiakim was right in so far as he wished to go in a way that was more than the mere beaten track of others.

II. A WRONG NOTION OF HOW THIS AIM WAS TO BE ATTAINED. Jehoiakim thought he could get great renown for himself individually by building a splendid palace. There would be such a contrast between it and the common houses in Jerusalem as to make people ask at once, "Whose abode is *that?*" and, in so acting, Jehoiakim showed that he understood pretty well the way in which popular opinion is most easily influenced. The way of the world is to estimate men by the visible splendours they can gather around them. One who lives in a wide house is looked at through the medium of his possessions, and thus becomes correspondingly magnified himself. But with all the worldly shrewdness of Jehoiakim, he was taking the wrong way to become really celebrated. Even supposing he had not been guilty of the peculiar wickedness rebuked in this passage, he would not have attained his end. The building of a big house sufficiently showed his ambition; but it did not of necessity show any of those peculiar powers by which men live lives that are remembered. Many of those whose fame will last as long as the world lasts, lived and died poor men. At least, they did not reside in wide houses. And thus the careers of such men, whenever they are considered, cast a permanent irony on the pursuit of mere external wealth.

III. THE PECULIAR WICKEDNESS CONSEQUENT ON THE TAKING OF THIS WRONG WAY. Jehoiakim's scheme was not only vain-glorious and delusive in itself, but very oppressive to his subjects in the carrying of it out. What we read of here makes us regard very dubiously many of the monuments of architectural power belonging to ancient civilizations. We may suspect that only too many of them were constructed by forced labour. How much of unrequited toil there must have been, not only in temples, palaces, Pyramids, but also in such plainly useful works as roads, bridges, and aqueducts! The results have been pleasing enough to the eye, and rich in giving resources to the lovers of art; but their beauty becomes only deformity, if we have reason to believe that force, fraud, and cruelty had a considerable share in the production of them. Even Christian cathedrals and churches may have been built in this way to a greater extent than we should like to think possible. There must always be a great temptation to the natural greed of man to get the largest amount of labour with the least remuneration. And this prophecy here shows that God has his eye on all such doings. His prophet sets forth principles which are the condemnation of slavery in all its forms, and by which every extortionate and greedy spirit will have to be judged.

IV. A CONTRAST WITH ONE WHO TOOK THE RIGHT WAY. Jehoiakim had been favoured with constant nearness to a good example of how a king should live and act, which made his wickedness the greater. Josiah, succeeding to a throne, had also wished to be more than a nominal king. But he had very different notions from his son as to how authority should be exerted. He was just and righteous, and paid special attention to the poor and humble, and the result was that all went well with him. Jehoiakim may have been feared, but he would be hated at the same time, or, if loved, loved only by those who found their chances in helping his pretentious schemes. Josiah was feared, but by the extortioners and knaves among his subjects. And he would be equally loved by all who, needing justice, knew that at his throne it was never sought in vain.

V. THE DISGRACEFUL END OF JEHOIAKIM'S PRIDE. He would die unregretted, and be buried like a beast. None of all who had been his associates while alive, would pay the slightest regard to him when dead. The prophecy here does not, of course, mean that God approves of such indecency to a corpse. He is simply pointing out how little selfish men may expect from their selfish associates. He who squeezes others like sponges, and throws them away when he can squeeze no more, only meets what may be expected when he comes to be thrown away in turn.—Y.

EXPOSITION.

CHAPTER XXIII.

The first eight verses form the necessary conclusion of the group of discourses sum- marized in ch. xxi., xxii. Like Isaiah, our prophet follows up denunciation with consolation, and will have the mind rest on the sure promises of God for the Messianic future. A part of the people has been already scattered abroad. In ch. xxiv. 8, "those who dwell in the land of Egypt" are a section no less important than "those who remain in this land;" and the Babylonian Captivity is an event only too certain to take place (comp. ver. 8). Unhappy Judah! for though not free from responsibility, it is the kings who are the prime authors of the calamity. Yet happy Judah! for "the days come" that an ideal king shall arise, even the promised Messiah. (Comp. Ezek. xxxiv., which seems like a development of this section.) Some have represented the promises of this chapter as fulfilled in the return from Babylon, with perhaps the Maccabean glories in addition. The fulfilment would in this case correspond but ill to the prediction; the context, too, is equally opposed to it. For, as Hengstenberg points out, the "gathering" and "bringing back" of Israel is in ver. 4 closely connected with the raising up of good shepherds; and, according to ver. 5, that promise is to find at any rate its culminating fulfilment in David's "righteous Branch," the Messiah. The mistake has been partly caused by a reluctance to increase the number of prophecies still awaiting their fulfilment, and partly by the false supposition that the events described must take place simultaneously (against this view, see vers. 7, 8). Hengstenberg himself thinks that the fulfilment lies in the conversion of Israel to the gospel. " Canaan had such a high value for Israel, not because it was its fatherland in the lower sense, but because it was the land of God, the place where his glory dwelt." To be in Christ is to be in the true Canaan.

Ver. 1.—**Woe be unto the pastors,** etc.! This "woe" is a pendant to the "woe" upon Jehoiakim in ch. xxii. 13. The original form of the verse shows the strong feeling with which the prophet both wrote and spoke: "Woe! shepherds who destroy," etc. By "shepherds" Jeremiah means rather the civil than the spiritual authorities, especially the kings—ποιμένες λαῶν, as Homer calls them. This is, in fact, the general Old Testament application of the term (see on ch. ii. 8). **That destroy.** If it is true of all sin that no one can calculate its issues, this is specially true of the sins of rulers. *Delirant reges, plectuntur Achivi;* or, as an inspired teacher puts it, " The leaders of

this people became false guides, and those whom they led were lost men " (Isa. ix. 16). How these evil shepherds "destroyed" the people we are not here told; but from ch. xxii. 3, 13, it is clear that sins of injustice, ranging from oppressive exaction to murder, are specially intended. **Scatter;** the captivities of the Jews being directly owing to the want of good government and teaching. How could the prophets stem the tide of popular corruption, when the ruling classes opposed their efforts? **The sheep of my pasture;** or, *the sheep of my pasturing*— the "pastors" are Jehovah's under-shepherds. The figure is a favourite one, especially with the psalmists of the school of Asaph (see Ps. lxxiv. 1; lxxvii. 20; lxxviii. 52 (comp. 70—72); lxxix. 13; lxxx. 1).

Ver. 2.—**The Lord God of Israel;** strictly, *Jehovah the God of Israel.* This national title of Jehovah suggests, in such a connection, that the crime of the kings is nothing short of sacrilege. **Ye have scattered,** etc.; *i.e.* been the cause of their scattering. **Have not visited them.** "To visit" often, by a natural association of ideas, means "to give attention to." By an equally natural association, it means "to fall upon, to punish." Hence, in the next clause, **I will visit upon you.** We have the same combination of meanings in Zech. x. 3.

Ver. 3.—Parallel passage, Ezek. xxxiv. 12—15. **I will gather the remnant.** For the ill usage of foreign oppressors has supplemented that of home tyrants, so that only a "remnant" is left. **And they shall be fruitful and increase.** The fertility of the Jewish race in modern times has been a frequent subject of observation, and supplies the best comment upon Jeremiah's prophecy.

Ver. 4.—**And I will set up shepherds;** *i.e.* rulers, not necessarily kings (see on next verse). **Which shall feed them.** For the evil shepherds "fed themselves, and fed not my flock" (Ezek. xxxiv. 8). **And they shall fear no more.** Ezekiel again contributes an essential feature to the description. The neglect of the shepherds left the flock exposed to the ravages of wild beasts (Ezek. xxxiv. 8). **Neither shall they be lacking.** A speaking phrase. Too many of the sheep had fallen down precipices or been carried off by lions. Yet the context rather favours a slight and palæographically natural emendation of Hitzig, "Neither shall they be terrified." The Septuagint omits the word altogether, which favours the supposition that they read as Hitzig would read, for they are apt to condense by omitting synonyms.

Vers. 5, 6.—(Comp. the parallel passage, ch. xxxiii. 15, 16.)

Ver. 5.—**Behold, the days come.** The use

of the analogous phrase, " And it shall come to pass in that day," would lead us to suppose that this verse describes a fresh stage in the progress of events, as if the faithful shepherds (ver. 4) were to precede the " righteous Branch " (ver. 5). Such a view, however, is not very plausible, for the Messiah, according to prophecy, is to appear in the darkest of times. The prophet simply means to impress upon us the greatness of the revelation which he is about to communicate. **I will raise unto David.** The promised Messiah, then, is certainly to be of the family of David (comp. Isa. ix. 7; xi. 1; Micah v. 2). **A righteous Branch** ; rather, *a righteous Plant .* the root means " to bud, or sprout." This is the first time in which the title " the Plant " is unmistakably applied to the Messianic King (possibly, but less probably, to the Messianic kings). It indicates that this great personage stands in connection with the divinely ordained and ancient royal family, but that he is in some way unique, and far surpasses his human ancestors. He " springs forth ; " therefore he is not a sort of meteoric appearance, without any natural home among men, but rather the blossom of the Jewish nation, the embodiment of its highest qualities. And yet there is something extraordinary about him, for it is needful that Jehovah himself should " raise " this Plant from the almost worn-out stock of David. Note that the word rendered here in the Authorized Version " Branch " is not the same as that in the parallel passage in Isaiah (xi. 1). It is, however, the word employed in Isa. iv. 2, which is taken by many, especially the older interpreters (but with very doubtful justice), to be a prophecy of the Messiah. It is also the word used by Zechariah (iii. 8 ; vi. 12), as a *proper name* of the Messiah, which is one strong reason for rejecting the view mentioned above that the word rendered " the Branch," or " the Plant," is to be taken collectively as equivalent to " branches," or rather " plants " (the article is not expressed in the Hebrew). In short, this passage and the prophecies referred to in Jeremiah are exceptions to the general Old Testament usage of the Hebrew word (*çemakh*), which is elsewhere a collective term equivalent to " plantation." It is true that in ver. 4 " shepherds," in the plural, are spoken of, but there is no reason why this title should be confined to kings—it may as fairly be extended to the chief rulers under a king as the term " king " itself (see on ch. xvii. 20); and true, further, that in ch. xxxiii. 17 a continuous succession is promised of Davidic heirs to the throne, but this is not decisive in favour of the collective meaning, any more than Isaiah's later prophecy that " the [reigning Davidic]

king shall reign in righteousness " disproves the strictly Messianic reference of his earlier promise in Isa. xi. 1. All prophecy is conditional; there may have been moral reasons why a continuance of the Davidic dynasty was held out by Jeremiah at one time as a possible prospect. (It is, however, extremely probable that ch. xxxiii. 14—26 is the work of some other inspired writer ; see *ad loc.*) The thirty-fourth chapter of Ezekiel, which is so closely parallel to this section, appears to interpret the prophecy of a single Messianic king (Ezek. xxxiv. 23). **And a King shall reign** ; rather, *and he shall reign as king ;* i.e. he shall be the realized ideal of an Israelitish king—a second David. **And prosper** ; or, *and deal wisely.* There is the same doubt as to the rendering of the verb in Isa. lii. 13 *a.* The radical idea is that of wisdom, and the analogy of Isa. xi. 2 favours the alternative rendering here. **Shall execute judgment** ; in contrast to the neglectful conduct of Jehoiakim (ch. xxii. 3).

Ver. 6.—**Israel shall dwell safely.** In the parallel passage (ch. xxxiii. 16) we read " Jerusalem," and there can hardly be a doubt that " Jerusalem " ought to be restored here. This is not the only instance in which, by mistake, the scribe has written " Israel " instead of " Jerusalem " (see ch. xxxii. 30, 32; li. 49; Zeph. iii. 14; Zech. xii. 1). In Zech. i. 19 the scribe discovered his mistake, and wrote the right word, " Jerusalem," after the wrong one, " Israel," but without cancelling the latter (Grätz, ' Monatsschrift,' 1880, pp. 97—101). **And this is his name whereby he shall be called.** There is a various reading, which may be rendered either, *whereby they shall call (him, or her),* or, *which they shall proclaim,* supported by the Peshito, Targum, Vulgate, and a few manuscripts (St. Jerome, too, mentions this reading). There is also a more important difference among the commentators as to the person who was to bear the name. The older Christian interpreters contended with all their might for the view that the name belonged to the Messiah, partly on real philological grounds, partly with the illegitimate theological object of obtaining a proof-text for the orthodox doctrine of the person of the Messiah and (in the case of Protestant writers) of justification. It is much to the credit of Hengstenberg that he sets this object aside, and while maintaining the Messianic reference of the pronoun, interprets the name with a single eye to the requirements of the context, " He by whom and under whom Jehovah will be our righteousness." The objection is, that in the parallel passage (ch. xxxiii. 16) Jeremiah assigns the name " Jehovah-Tsidkenu," not to the Messiah, but to Jerusalem. The prophet must be allowed to be his best interpreter, so that we must, it would seem, at any rate, reject the Messianic reference. But then how are we to explain the pronoun? It is right to refer the parallel pronoun in ch. xxxiii. 16 to "Jerusalem," because the pronoun there is feminine, and evidently refers to a city, but it is not natural in our passage to explain "his name" of "Israel," seeing that the subject of the noun in the parallel line is, not Israel, but the Messiah. But is the text here correct? A comparison of the parallel psalms xiv. and liii., and of the corresponding chapters in Samuel, Kings, and Chronicles, will show how easily errors made their way into duplicate copies of the same passage. Granting that we have such duplicate copies of this prophecy in Jeremiah, there can be no doubt which is the more original; the form of ch. xxiii. 6 has a difficulty from which ch. xxxiii. 16 is free—a difficulty of interpretation and a difficulty also of grammar. For, as Ewald has already pointed out ('Hebrew Grammar,' § 249 b), the contracted suffix is very rarely attached to the simple imperfect, and the clear style in which this section is written justifies us in regarding any unusual form with suspicion. "Israel" thus was probably written by mistake for "Jerusalem," and this error soon led to others—first, the omission of "her," and then the prefixing of "his name" for clearness, and (on the part of the authors of the points) the mispointing of the verb (so as to include in the form the pronoun "him"). It is some confirmation of this view that there are several other passages in which the words "Israel" and "Jerusalem" appear to have been confounded (see preceding note). Read, therefore, as in ch. xxxiii. 16, *And this is the name wherewith she shall be called.* **THE LORD OUR RIGHTEOUSNESS**; Hebrew, *Yahveh* (Jehovah) *Tsidkēnū*. The name is formed on the analogy of other symbolic names, such as El-elohe-Israel (Gen. xxxiii. 20), Jehovah-Nissi (Exod. xvii. 15), and especially Jehovah-Shammah (Ezek. xlviii. 35), also a name of Jerusalem. These names are, in fact, sentences; Jehovah-Shammah, for instance, means "The Lord (is) there;" and the name in the present verse, "The Lord (is) our Righteousness" (Hengstenberg's view mentioned above seems less natural). It is singular that Zedekiah's name should come so near to that announced by the prophet. But there is still a difference between them. Zedekiah must mean "The Lord (is) righteousness," *i.e.* is ever faithful to his revealed principles of action. But Jehovah-Tsidkēnū may be correctly paraphrased, "The Lord is the author of our prosperity," or, more strictly, "of the justification of our claims in the sight of our enemies" (comp. Isa. xlv. 24; l. 8; liv. 17; lviii. 8; lxii. 1, 2).

Similar applications of forensic language are familiar, *e.g.* "When they speak with their enemies in the gate" (Ps. cxxvii. 5).

Vers. 7, 8.—This is another of Jeremiah's repetitions (see ch. xvi. 14, 15). Either the Septuagint translator or the copyist of the Hebrew manuscript which he used appears to have thought that the passage might, therefore, be dispensed with. In the Septuagint it is placed at the end of the chapter (being possibly supplied from another Hebrew manuscript), and the form given in this version to the close of ver. 6 (Ἰωσεδὲκ ἐν τοῖς προφηταῖς, combining the opening words of ver. 9) shows that ver. 9 followed immediately upon ver. 6 in the Hebrew manuscript.

Vers. 9—40.—These verses form a complete prophecy, the title of which Jeremiah himself supplies in the words, "Concerning the (false) prophets" (see below); comp. ch. xlvi. 2; xlviii. 1; xlix. 1, 7, 23, 28. It is true the rendering of the Authorized Version (ver. 9), **Mine heart within me is broken because of the prophets,** is not purely arbitrary; it is favoured by the exegetical tradition represented by the Hebrew accents. But it is not probable that two entirely different causes should be given for the prophet's deep emotion (see the latter part of the verse). Besides, "breaking of the heart" is nowhere a sign of anger (as Authorized Version would suggest), but either of grief (see on ch. viii. 21), or, as the context implies here, physical disturbance at the solemn message of Jehovah (comp. ch. vi. 11; xx. 9). **All my bones shake.** It is a very uncommon verb, occurring only twice elsewhere (Gen. i. 2; Deut. xxxii. 11, in Piel). **The words of his holiness;** or, *his words of holiness;* i.e. his holy words, the words of the Holy One on the unholy doings of the false prophets.

Ver. 10.—**The land is full of adulterers.** The false prophets connive at flagrant immoralities, one of which is mentioned as a typical sin. As to the nature of the adultery, see note on ch. v. 7. **Because of swearing;** rather, *because of the curse;* the curse, namely, with which God punishes the guilty earth (comp. Zech. v. 3; Dan. ix. 11; and especially Isa. xxiv. 6, where in the original there is a paronomasia very similar to that here). **The land mourneth;** a figurative expression, suggested partly by the assonance of the word for "curse." Drought is what is meant (comp. ch. xii. 4; xiv. 1, 2). **The pleasant places of the wilderness;** rather, *the pastures of the prairie-land* ("wilderness" suggests ideas very alien to the context). **Their course;** literally, *their running* (comp. ch. viii. 6). The subject is "the inhabitants of the land." **Their force is not right;** rather, *their might* (or, *heroism*) *is untruth*. They are "mighty men" only in telling untruths (comp. ch. ix. 3; Isa. v. 22).

Ver. 11.—**Both prophet and priest are profane**; *i.e.* are unholy, disobeying the Divine commands (see on ch. v. 7). The same two important classes specified as in ch. vi. 13. **Yea, in my house**, etc. Evidently some sin specially incongruous with its locality is referred to, either idolatry (comp. ch. vii. 30) or the totemistic worship of figures of animals (Ezek. viii. 10, 11). Comp. note on ch. v. 7.

Ver. 12.—**Their way shall be unto them as slippery** ways, etc.; rather, *slippery places*. The passage has a manifest affinity with Ps. xxxv. 6 (in one of the Jeremianizing psalms; see on ch. xviii. 19, 20). **They shall be driven on**; or, as Ewald, taking over the last word of the preceding clause, *they shall be thrust into the darkness*. This involves a reminiscence, probable enough, of Isa. viii. 22 *b*. It is against the accentual tradition, but improves the rhythmical division of the verse. If we ask who "thrusts" them, Ps. xxxv. 5 supplies the answer—it is not merely external circumstances, but "the Angel of Jehovah," *i.e.* Jehovah himself. As Bishop Hall says, "God wounds us by many instruments, but with one hand." **I will bring evil upon them**, etc. Favourite expressions of Jeremiah (comp. ch. xi. 23).

Vers. 13, 14.—The prophets of Samaria were no doubt guilty enough, but their offences dwindled by the side of the "horrible" transgressions of those of the southern kingdom. The prophet apparently means, not only that the former, having fewer spiritual advantages, were less responsible than the latter, but also that they had not violated the moral code so conspicuously.

Ver. 13.—**I have seen folly**; rather, *absurdity* or *unseemliness*; literally, *that which is unsavoury* (comp. Job vi. 6). The word occurs with a similar reference to Jehovah in Job i. 22; xxiv. 12. To "prophesy by Baal" was absurd," "unseemly," because Baal was a "non-entity" (Isaiah's word for an idol). **In Baal**; rather, *by*, or *by means of, Baal* (see on ch. ii. 8).

Ver. 14.—**I have seen also**, etc.; rather, *But in the prophets of Jerusalem I have seen*. **Horrible**; as in ch. v. 30. **They commit adultery**, etc.; literally, *the committing adultery and the walking in lies*—a much more forcible way of putting it. **They are all of them**; rather, *They have become all of them;* viz. either the prophets or the people in general. **The inhabitants thereof**; viz. of Jerusalem.

Ver. 15.—On the punishment here threatened, see note on ch. ix. 15.

Vers. 16—22.—A warning addressed to the people against the false prophecies (comp. Ezek. xiii.).

Ver. 16.—**They make you vain**; *i.e.* fill you with vain imaginations. A similar phrase occurs in ch. ii. 5, on which see note. **A vision of their own heart**; the heart being the centre of the intellectual as well as of the moral life, according to the Hebrew conception.

Ver. 17.—**Unto them that despise me, The Lord hath said**. The Septuagint and the Syriac render the same text (the consonants are alone the text) with different vowels, thus: "Unto those who despise the word of the Lord." In favour of this it may be urged that the phrase, "The Lord hath said," is nowhere else used in this abrupt way to introduce a real or supposed revelation, and Hitzig and Graf accordingly accept it. **Ye shall have peace**; as ch. vi. 14. **After the imagination**; rather, *in the stubbornness* (see on ch. iii. 17).

Ver. 18.—**For who hath stood in the counsel of the Lord**; rather, *in the council*. This verse is connected with ver. 16; it gives the reason why the false prophets were not to be listened to. None of them had been admitted to the secret council of the Lord; the interrogation is here a form of denial. "To stand in the council" is not the same as "to sit" (Ps. i. 1); the latter phrase implies taking an active part in the consultations. It is specially applicable to the true prophets, according to ver. 22, and this, as we gather from other passages, in a twofold sense. Sometimes the prophets had visions, in which their inner eye was granted a sight of Jehovah in consultation with his trusted servants (Isa. vi. 1, comp. 8; 1 Kings xxii. 19); and the words of Eliphaz, "Wert thou listening in the council of God?" (Job xv. 8), appear to be descriptive of a similar experience. But the phrase may also be used in a wider sense of entirely unecstatic revelations. Amos says (iii. 7), "Surely the Lord Jehovah will do nothing, but he revealeth his secret counsel unto his servants the prophets;" and a psalmist extends the term "secret counsel" to the communion which God grants to the pious in general (Ps. xxv. 14; comp. Prov. iii. 32). Thus there is no hard-and-fast line between the experiences of the prophets and those of humbler believers. In so far as the latter are "disciples of Jehovah" (Isa. liv. 13), they too may be truly said to "stand," at least in the doorway, "in the council of Jehovah;" just as a well-known collect inherited from the Latin Church beseeches that "by God's holy inspiration we may think those things that be good." **Who hath marked his word?** A Jewish tradition, represented by the marginal notes in the Hebrew Bible, has taken offence at this variation in the expression, and would correct the reading to "my word." But such changes of person are of frequent occurrence, and we know that the prophets were thoroughly assured that the word which they spoke was not theirs, but that of him who sent them.

Vers. 19, 20.—These two verses seem to be connected with ver. 17. The false prophets say, "Ye shall have peace." How different the message of the true! (A duplicate of these verses occurs in ch. xxx. 23, 24.)

Ver. 19.—**A whirlwind of the Lord**, etc.; rather, *A storm of the Lord, even fury, is gone forth, and a whirling storm—upon the head of the wicked shall it whirl.* The hurricane has already broken out; it will soon reach Jerusalem. This seems to be the force of Jeremiah's expressive figure.

Ver. 20.—**The anger of the Lord.** The prophet's interpretation of the image. It is the judicial anger of Jehovah, personified as Divine manifestations so often are (hence "shall not return"). The form of the verse reminds us of Isa. lv. 11. **In the latter days**; rather, *in future days*, as Dr. Henderson rightly renders. It seems better to restrict the term "latter days" to the Messianic period ("the coming age," Matt. xii. 32), to which, in fact, it is often applied (*e.g.* Isa. ii. 2; Hos. iii. 5). The phrase in itself simply means "in the sequel of the days," *i.e.* in the future; its Messianic reference, when this exists, is inferred solely from the context. In the passage before us, and in Deut. iv. 30, xxx. 29, there can be no intention of pointing to the Messianic age. Precisely the same phrase occurs in an Assyrian inscription, where its meaning is clear from the context (*ana akhrat yumi irib*, "For a sequel of days—*i.e.* for a future time—I deposited"). In the present case it is no distant period to which the prophet refers, for he continues, **Ye shall consider it**, etc., or rather, *ye shall understand it clearly*, viz. that the calamities which will have come upon you are the Divine judgment upon your sins.

Vers. 21, 22.—In vers. 17—20 Jeremiah has shown that these cannot be true prophets, because their message is diametrically opposed to the true revelation. He now proves it from the absence of any moral effect from their preaching.

Vers. 23—32.—Jehovah has observed and will punish the false pretensions of the prophets.

Vers. 23, 24.—**Am I a God at hand**, etc.? ("At hand" equivalent to "near.") Eliphaz may again assist us with an illustration. "And thou sayest"—he is expostulating with Job—"What doth God know? can he judge through the dark cloud? thick clouds are a covering to him, that he seeth not; yea, he walketh upon the vault of heaven" (Job xxii. 13, 14). It might seem, from the

preponderance of the false prophets over the true, as if Jehovah were unaware of the mischief. Not so; Jehovah is omnipresent.

Ver. 25.—**I have dreamed.** Jeremiah mentions it as one of the marks of a false prophet that he appealed to his dreams (comp. ch. xxix. 8); true prophecy contented itself with less ambiguous media of communication with the unseen world. It may be objected that Abraham (Gen. xv. 12), at any rate, and Abimelech (Gen. xx. 3) received Divine revelations in dreams; but these were not officially prophets. Nathan and the contemporaries of the author of Job had messages from God by night, but these are called, not dreams, but visions (2 Sam. vii. 14, comp. 17; Job iv. 13). Deuteronomy (and this is one of its striking points of agreement with Jeremiah) expressly describes a false prophet as "a dreamer of dreams" (Deut. xiii. 1; comp. 1 Sam. xxviii. 6). Two passages in the Old Testament seem inconsistent with this discouragement of dreams as a medium of revelation—Numb. xii. 6, where the Lord is said to make himself known to prophets by visions and dreams, and Joel ii. 28, where the prophetic dreams of the old men are one of the features of a Messianic description; but it is noteworthy that the first of these refers to the primitive period of Israel's history, and the second to the distant Messianic age. In its classical period prophecy kept itself sedulously aloof from a field on which it had such compromising companionship (comp. Eccles. v. 7).

Ver. 26.—**How long shall this be in the heart**, etc.? *i.e.* how long shall this be their purpose, viz. to prophesy lies? But this rendering leaves out of account a second interrogative which in the Hebrew follows "how long." It is better to translate this difficult passage, with De Dieu and many moderns, thus: "How long (*quousque durabit hæc ipsorum impudentia*)? Is it in the heart of the prophets that prophesy lies, and the prophets of the deceit of their own heart; are they thinking (I say) to cause my people to forget," etc.? On this view, ver. 27 resumes the question interrupted in ver. 26.

Ver. 27.—**Every man to his neighbour.** Not merely one prophet to another prophet, for it is "my people" whom they cause to forget my Name (comp. ver. 32), but the prophet to his fellow-man. **Have forgotten my name for Baal**; or, *forgot my name through Baal.*

Ver. 28.—**Let him tell a dream**; rather, *let him tell it as a dream;* let him tell his dreams, if he will, but not intermix them with Divine revelations. Jeremiah, then, does not deny that there is a measure of truth in what these prophets say; he only demands a distinct declaration that their dreams are but dreams, and not equal in authority to the Divine word. For, as he continues, **What is the chaff to the wheat?** What right have you to mix the worthless chaff with the pure, winnowed grain? How, he implies, can such an adulterated message produce the designed effect of a prophetic revelation? (St. Paul has a somewhat similar figure, 1 Cor. iii. 10—13.) So Naegelsbach. Keil, however, denies that there is any thought of an adulteration of the Divine word by the "false prophets." According to him, the question in this verse is simply meant to emphasize the contrast between the false, dream-born prophecy of Jeremiah's opponents and the true revelations. How can the false prophecy pretend to be the true? They are as different as chaff and wheat. Both views are admissible. Naegelsbach introduces a new element by suggesting the intermixture of false and true in the utterances of the "false prophets;" but his view is not inconsistent with what the prophet has stated before, and it is favoured by ver. 30 and by the command, Let him speak my word faithfully; *i. e.* in its genuine form; comp. ch. ii. 21, "A faithful or trustworthy [*i.e.* a genuine] seed;" also, for the general sense, 2 Cor. ii. 17.

Ver. 29.—**Is not my word like as a fire?** As in vers. 19, 20, so here, the prophet contrasts the message of the false prophets with that of the true. The former flatter their hearers with promises of peace; the latter speak a stern but potent word, which burns like a fire, and crushes like a hammer. Observe, the prophet does not define the activity of the fire as he does that of the hammer; for the fire has a twofold effect—protection to God's friends and destruction to his enemies. On the figure of the hammer, comp. ch. l. 23; li. 20.

Vers. 30—32.—The punishment solemnly introduced by a three times repeated, Behold, I am against, etc., corresponding to three several features of the conduct of the false prophets. First we are told that the prophets steal my words every one from his neighbour. The latter part of the phrase reminds us of ver. 27, but the "neighbour" in this case must mean, at any rate primarily, a fellow-prophet, one who has really received a revelation at first-hand from Jehovah. The "false prophets," not trusting to their "dreams" alone, listen greedily to the discourses of men like Jeremiah, not with a view to spiritual profit, but to making their own utterances more effective. We must remember that they lived by their prophesying (Micah iii. 5).

Ver. 31.—**That use their tongues;** literally, *that take their tongue*, like a workman's tool —as if prophecy could be turned out to

order. **And say, He saith.** The word rendered "he saith" is one which the prophets habitually used to affirm the revealed character of their teaching. It is the participle of the verb rendered "say." Adopting a Miltonic verb, we might render, "and oracle oracles." The "false prophets" adopt the same forms as the true; but they are to them only forms.

Ver. 32.—**That prophesy false dreams** (see on ver. 25). **By their lightness.** The word is an uncommon one, and implies arrogance or boastfulness (comp. Zeph. iii. 4); the root means "to bubble over." **Therefore they shall not profit;** rather, *and they cannot profit.*

Vers. 33—40.—The abuse of a consecrated phrase. The prophets were accustomed to apply the term *massā* to their prophetic declarations in the sense of "oracle," or "utterance"—a sense derived from the use of the cognate verb for "to lift up the voice," *i.e.* to pronounce clearly and distinctly. But the word *massā* was also in common use for "load, burden," and hence the "false prophets" applied the term derisively to Jeremiah's discourses. "Rightly does he call his word a *massā;* it is not merely a solemn utterance, but a heavy burden;" as De Wette puts it, not merely a *Weissagung,* but a *Wehsagung.* The passage is important as indicating the sense in which the true prophets understood the term. It should be added that the term *massā* is prefixed to at least four Biblical passages which, not being of threatening import, do not admit of being entitled "burdens" (Zech. ix. 1; xii. 1; Prov. xxx. 1; xxxi. 1; comp. Lam. ii. 14). How remarkable is the line adopted by Jeremiah! He simply abandons the use of the term *massā,* consecrated as it was by the practice of inspired men! Better to adopt a new phrase, than to run the risk of misunderstanding or, even worse, profanity.

Ver. 33.—**What burden?** etc. The Hebrew text, as usually read, is extremely difficult; the Authorized Version is entirely unjustifiable. It is just possible to explain, with Ewald, "As to this question, What is the burden? the true meaning of the word is that," etc. But how harsh and artificial! By a change in the grouping of the consonants (which alone constitute the text), we may read, *Ye are the burden.* So the Septuagint, Vulgate, Hitzig, Graf, Payne Smith. We must in this case continue, *and I will cast you off,* as the same verb is to be rendered in ch. vii. 29; xii. 7. Instead of carrying you with the long-suffering of a father (Deut. i. 31; Isa. xlvi. 3, 4; lxiii. 9; Ps. xxviii. 9), I will cast you off as a troublesome load (Isa. i. 14).

Ver. 35.—**What hath the Lord answered?** *i.e.* a simpler phraseology is to be used,

Jehovah hath answered, saying, or, *Jehovah hath spoken,* according as a definite question had been put before the prophet or not.

Ver. 36.—**And the burden of the Lord,** etc.; *i.e.* ye shall no longer use the word *massā* at all. **Every man's word shall be his burden;** rather, *the burden to every man shall be his word;* i.e. his derisive use of the word *massā* shall be a burden which shall crush him to the ground. **Ye have perverted;** "*i.e.* have turned them round, and put them into a ridiculous light" (Payne Smith).

Ver. 38.—**But since ye say,** etc.; rather, *But if ye say,* etc. In case the false prophets disobey, and persist in using the old expression, the threatening already uttered shall come into operation.

Ver. 39.—**I, even I, will utterly forget you;** rather, *I will even take you up, and cast you off.* This involves a slight difference in the pronunciation of the text from that adopted by the Massoretes, but is adopted by the Septuagint, Peshito, Vulgate, a few manuscripts, and most critics; it is, in fact, almost required by the figure which fills the verse. And cast you **out of my presence.** "And cast you" is not in the Hebrew; nor is it necessary to supply the words, if the preceding clauses be rightly translated.

Ver. 40.—With this **verse,** comp. ch. xx. 11.

HOMILETICS.

Vers. 1—4.—*The character of leading men.* The character of its leading men is a matter of first importance to a people. Israel had been led astray by his kings; one of the first blessings promised to him on his return is the possession of good leaders. In the most free state there must always be leading men—men exercising influence by reason of their office, their rank and position, or their capacities. Observe this in regard to the various classes of leading men.

I. POLITICAL LEADERS. On their character depends the questions (1) whether laws shall be justly framed and justly executed, (2) whether the welfare of the subjects shall be honestly worked for, and (3) whether the dealings with foreign nations shall be just and peaceable.

II. SOCIAL LEADERS. The moral influence of the court is always great and widespread; how important that this should be pure! There are people whom rank or personal attractiveness, or powers of persuasion, endow with power to influence the customs of their age. These need be well advised that their influence may be on the side of truth, purity, and humanity.

III. INTELLECTUAL LEADERS. Shall the reformer be a Luther or a Voltaire? the poet a Wordsworth or a Byron? the historian an Arnold or a Gibbon? the philosopher a Butler or a Hume? Surely for the real welfare of a people the moral tendency of its literature is more important than the intellectual brilliancy.

IV. RELIGIOUS LEADERS. Are these men barren controversialists, or earnest practical guides to their flocks? Are they loyal to truth, or merely bigoted defenders of their own crotchets? Are they spiritual-minded servants of Christ, or ambitious priests? Are they true shepherds, or wolves in sheep's clothing? These questions touch the welfare of a people very closely. Note, the one essential is that the leading men should desire to serve the good of others and not simply to increase their own power and honour; to feed the flock, not to scatter it by reckless indifference, selfish ambition, or tyrannous cruelty. The power of leading men is a great and dangerous gift, only entrusted by Providence to those who possess it for the sake of the good it may be the means of conferring on the community at large. The state is in a healthy condition only when public characters are inspired by public spirit.

Ver. 5.—*The Branch of David.* The glorious prophecy of the Messianic future which here bursts forth from Jeremiah, after his denunciation of his nation's sin and lamentation over its approaching calamities, is necessarily clothed in the language of the age, and viewed in an especial relation to contemporary wants. The people are suffering from bad rulers and an unrighteous government. A good king, administering his kingdom happily and justly, is promised for the golden age of the future. Associated with this king is, no doubt, that succession of righteous sovereigns referred to in the fourth verse. It was not given to anticipatory visions to show how unique and solitary and eternal was to be the kingship of the Messiah. Yet even there he stands forth in marked prominence, and towers above his successors, who are only regarded as following his initiative. Regarding the prophecy with the fuller light of Christian times, we may see how it is a true foreshadowing of the nature and work of Christ, though, of course, only partial and limited, as the shadow can only indicate the general form of its object, and that in but one aspect.

I. THE ORIGIN OF THE MESSIAH. 1. He comes from a *human stock*. He is called a " Branch," or, rather, a " Sprout." Christ entered the world by birth; he was " made of a woman." Hence his oneness with us, his human sympathy, true example, and representative character as the High Priest of the race. 2. He comes of the *family of David*. This historical fact is significant. Christ is a born King, a rightful Sovereign. He realizes the ideal which the kings of the Jews had failed to attain, but which the best of them had aimed at. 3. He comes *quietly and gradually*. The sprout springs from a bud by slow growth. Christ began his life as an infant, and grew in physical, mental, and spiritual powers (Luke ii. 52). He did not astonish the world with a sudden apparition of majesty. His kingship is like his kingdom, a quiet and gradual growth as that of a tree from a seed (Matt. xiii. 31—32). 4. He comes with close relations to the *circumstances of the world*. The sprout is vitally connected with the earth and the atmosphere. It grows in the natural season of growth. Christ is associated with all human interests. The ages before his advent were preparing for him. He is the representative of their highest aspirations, the satisfaction of their deepest needs. He comes in the " fulness of time." 5. He comes from a *Divine origin*. God raises up the righteous Branch. The text tells us no more than that the coming of Christ is providential and through special Divine influences; but we know that God not only raised him, but was in him, as one with his very being.

II. THE OFFICE OF THE MESSIAH. He is to be a King. It was natural that the Jews should anticipate a temporal sovereign, and natural, therefore, that they should have been disappointed at the appearance and conduct of Jesus of Nazareth. Yet was he not, is he not, a King? He professed to be a King (John xviii. 37). The apostles claimed submission to him as to a King (Acts xvii. 7). His influence is kingly. The essence of kingship is not seen in the sitting on a material throne and wearing a visible crown, but in the exercise of power over men. Christ is the one true King, because he rules the thoughts and affections and wills of men. Human sovereigns can only command external obedience. While the slave cringes before the throne he may be cursing his master in his heart. Christ is satisfied with no such superficial loyalty. He seeks the allegiance of the heart, and he wins it from all his people. We must, therefore, recognize this great fact—Christ is a King as well as a Saviour. While he delivers us from ruin, he expects submission to his authority. He is a Saviour partly by being a King, for his royal influence is one means of his deliverance of mankind. Therefore the selfish Christianity which would accept escape from ruin, but would not accord loyal obedience, is a delusion. We cannot even be safe, cannot even escape from the ruin of our sin, except by bowing to the rule of Christ. We can only find rest unto our souls by taking on us his yoke. True faith, therefore, includes trust in the kingship as well as in the redemption of Christ, *i.e.* active fidelity in addition to passive confidence.

III. THE CHARACTER OF THE MESSIAH. 1. He is *righteous*. This was much in contrast to the unrighteousness of contemporary rulers. Taking the word "righteous" in the largest sense, we have assurance of the truth, justice, holiness, and goodness of Christ. If this righteousness of the Messiah is a ground of rejoicing to the prophet, how much more shall we Christians rejoice in witnessing his gentleness, compassion, and love? 2. He *rules righteously*. The character of the government is necessarily determined by that of the ruler. The great King comes to live not for himself, but for his people, and not to execute stern judgments upon them, but to secure their highest good. Christ reigns for the good of his people. If we submit to his rule we find our own blessedness secured thereby.

Ver. 6.—*The new name.* (See also ch. xxxiii. 16.) God's people are to have a new name. In the epistle to the Church at Pergamos, every one " that overcometh " is assured that he will receive " a white stone, and in the stone a new name written " (Rev. ii. 17). This is suggestive, not only of a change of character, but of a change of reputation. The redeemed will no longer be thought of in connection with the old associations of their sin and shame. These will be forgotten, and a new name given to them, describing their holier character and happier condition. Consider the significance of this new name—" The Lord our Righteousness."

I. GOD IS THE RIGHTEOUSNESS OF HIS PEOPLE. 1. He *justifies* his people in the face of their maligners by proving the rightness of their cause. For this, like David, they may appeal to him (Ps. xxxv. 23, 24). 2. God's righteousness is the *ideal* of righteousness for his people. True righteousness is that which is after God's mind. Men have their notions of right, which are often perverted by passion and prejudice. But the redeemed have a vision of a higher law and a purer type of goodness. God is righteousness to them. He is the Good, the only true Good (Mark x. 18). 3. God is the *Source* of righteousness to his people. None can make himself righteous; righteousness is an inspiration. This idea is suggested by Plato in the ' Meno,' where he represents Socrates as saying, " To sum up our inquiry—the result seems to be, if we are at all right in our view, that virtue is neither natural nor acquired, but an instinct given by God to the virtuous;" and again, " Then, Meno, the conclusion is that virtue comes to the virtuous by the gift of God." How singularly near is this to St. Paul's teaching about " the righteousness of God without the Law " (Rom. iii. 21—26)!

II. RIGHTEOUSNESS IS COEXTENSIVE WITH SALVATION. When the people are saved, they receive the new name. We are not delivered on account of our righteousness, but in our sin and need and ill desert. Nevertheless, salvation brings righteousness, includes the gift of righteousness—is, indeed, essentially a restoration of righteousness, a deliverance from sin to a state of holiness. The two ideas may be separated in thought; they cannot be separated in experience. It would be unjust and unholy for God to deliver a man from the penalties of his sin while he remained in the practice of it. But when deliverance comes, no part of it is more full of joy and blessedness to the redeemed, and none reflects more glory on the Redeemer than the salvation from the power of sin and the creation of a new nature of holiness.

III. THE DIVINE RIGHTEOUSNESS IS CONFERRED THROUGH CHRIST. The giving of the new name follows the advent of the Messiah and the exercise of his kingly rule. Here we are carried beyond the vague and apparently casual Platonic notion of the inspiration of virtue to the definite Christian doctrine of righteousness through Christ. 1. Christ secures redemption for us by his life-work and his sacrificial death, and with this comes righteousness. 2. Christ is the incarnation of the Divine righteousness, and breathes that into us by his vital contact with his people. 3. Christ rules in righteousness over a people whom he teaches to follow and obey him with righteousness. Therefore, if we crave the honour and the blessedness of the new name, let us yield our souls in trust and obedience to the claims and grace of Christ.

Ver. 16.—*Uninspired prophecy.* The Jews were warned not to listen to the prophets, because they were not inspired by God. This fact was considered to be a sufficient proof of their inefficiency, and necessarily so, since the prophets professed to be acting as the oracles of God, and not merely indulging in their own speculations and conjectures. Herein lay the danger of their position. They held official rank as religious teachers, their claims were backed by venerated tradition, they boldly professed to speak with Divine authority; yet they were not sent by God. The same danger accompanies the pretensions of men in our own day, who claim a right to be heard without question by reason of their high office in the Church, and yet have no Divine commission. The appearance of this uninspired prophecy in Jeremiah's age may, therefore, be a warning to modern times.

I. THE ORIGIN OF THIS PROPHECY WAS PRIVATE SPECULATION. The prophets spoke " a vision of their own heart." Such a vision could only be a revelation of themselves. This is what uninspired religious speculation amounts to. It is a revelation of man, not a revelation of God. Attempts are made to arrive at truth in three ways. 1. By *observation.* But observation cannot reveal (1) the future, (2) the Divine. 2. By *reasoning.* This must be based on experience, and can bear no more strain than its basis. It is not found that we have sufficient data in normal experience to warrant important predictions of history and conclusions on vexed theological questions. 3. By *intuition.* Intuition does reveal truth, but only the truth of our own nature. We have no reason for supposing that this is always a counterpart to the facts of the larger world.

II. PRIVATE SPECULATION WAS ESPECIALLY LIKELY TO IMPORT ERROR INTO THIS PROPHECY. It was always fallible, but in the present instance it was peculiarly likely to err. 1. It was attempting *too great a task.* The prophets were venturing to predict the future of their nation under the most difficult circumstances. 2. It was *biassed* by prejudice, passion, and interest. The prophets were swayed by their own inclination. In religious questions personal considerations blind men to pure truth.

III. NEVERTHELESS THIS PROPHECY WAS VERY POPULAR. 1. It was recommended by the *official* teachers. 2. It was recommended by the *majority* of the prophets. Jeremiah stood almost alone; his opponents were numerous. 3. It was *flattering* to the people; it represented them as less guilty, as deserving less punishment than was threatened by Jeremiah. 4. It was *pleasant.* The prophets spoke smooth words and promised comfortable things. Such teaching is only too popular.

IV. NO PROPHECY IS RELIABLE WHICH IS NOT INSPIRED BY GOD. The prophecy is condemned simply for want of this one fundamental condition. The history of religious speculation proves the helplessness of all attempts to solve the great problems of the future and of the spiritual by bare human intelligence. If, therefore, we believe that the Bible is inspired, weight should be given to its teaching as to an authority. In our own thought, and our meditation on the Scriptures, we need those lesser degrees of inspiration by which all Christians may be led into truth (John xvi. 13).

Vers. 23, 24.—*The omnipresence of God.* I. THE FACT. God must be thought of as fully present everywhere; not as a great Being who fills a great space with, however, only distinct parts in each section of space. The whole of God is present everywhere. He is as much present in every separate locality as if he existed nowhere else. All his infinite attributes of knowledge, power, and goodness are present, to be brought to bear on each individual of the infinite variety of things in the universe. God is as much present in the less seemly places as in those that are recognized as fitting temples for him to dwell in. He is in the earth as well as in heaven. Heaven is described as his throne, earth as his footstool. He is present with the godless as well as with the godly, in the heathen world as well as in Christendom. More particularly: 1. God is present with those who *do not recognize him.* The sunlight is not limited by man's vision; it shines as clearly about the blind man as about one with keen eyesight. So, though we may not think of God's presence, it is not the less near to us. 2. God is present with those who *refuse to obey him.* We cannot remove ourselves from the observation and control of God by forsaking all allegiance to him. Jonah could flee from his mission, but he could not flee from his God. God's eyes are on the evil as well as on the good. 3. God is present with those who are far *from enjoying the blessedness* of the full manifestation of his presence. God is present with the Christian all through his earthly pilgrimage. Though God appears to hide himself for a season, though thick clouds intervene between the soul and that beatific vision which is reserved for the future state, God is as truly with his people on earth as he will be in heaven.

II. PRACTICAL LESSONS. 1. *It is foolish to expect to escape from the judgment of God.* God never abdicates his right to be the Judge of all his creatures. There is no possibility of hiding from him. God searches us and knows our deepest heart-secret. Will it not, then, be best for us to be true and open and frank with him? 2. *We must not ascribe the confusion of the world to God's indifference.* If he knows all and does not set it right, this must be (1) partly because he gives large liberty to his creatures for the possibility of attaining higher good than would be reached by the exercise of any irresistible power, and (2) partly because he must have higher ultimate designs than any we can conceive of in the present imperfect condition of the world. 3. *No change of place will bring us nearer to God.* "He is not far from every one of us" (Acts xvii. 27). Therefore (1) it is needless to wait for some better time for approaching God. No time will be better than the present. He will never be nearer to us than he is now. He only waits that we should open our eyes. (2) It is a mistake to suppose that any outward event will lead us nearer to God. Death will not bring us more closely into his presence. No journey to a heavenly world will do this. We only need a change of heart to recognize and enjoy the eternal presence of God, which will make heaven wherever it is felt. 4. *Christians need fear no harm.* They must meet with troubles and temptations, but God is present to uphold them. They must go through the valley of the shadow of death, but God is there. They must enter the strange land of departed souls, but he is there also. And wherever God is it must be well with his faithful children.

Vers. 33, 34.—*The abuse of a word.* This is not a mere play upon a word, but a mocking abuse of the meaning of it, designed to convey a sinister insinuation. It illustrates what a dangerous and uncertain weapon language is. We are all inclined to attach too much importance to words, forgetting that they are not rigid landmarks of thought, but variable in meaning with the variations of the ideas we import into them.

I. THE WORDS OF TRUTH MAY BE USED IN THE SERVICE OF FALSEHOOD. The Jews repeated the phrase of Jeremiah, but with a new and false signification. The " burden " as an utterance, was entirely distinct from the " burden " as a weight to be borne. Of course, mendacity belongs to our thought and intention, not to our mere language. We may tell a lie by using true words in such a way as to infuse into them a false meaning. Such conduct is peculiarly mean and dishonourable. It is robbing the armoury of truth to turn its weapons against itself. No condemnation can be too strong for the treachery and dishonesty of those persons who appropriate the consecrated phrases of Christianity as a subterfuge under which to attack its spiritual truths. Let us be careful in using the Bible, not to read our own thoughts into the text, but to search simply for the original meaning of it.

II. CONTROVERSY BECOMES DISHONEST WHEN IT IS MAINTAINED BY THE CONFUSION OF WORDS. This is the essence of sophistry. A word is spoken with one meaning ; it is replied to with another. Often and often this is done unconsciously. Indeed, a large part of our contentions rest on nothing but " misunderstandings." Under such circumstances we may deplore the error, but we cannot severely condemn the moral conduct of the misguided disputants. But it may be done deliberately, to throw dust in the eyes of an opponent, to raise a laugh without justification, to gain a point by mere word-fencing. When this is the case it is untruthful and ungenerous. If we must dispute, let us be frank and fair, using every effort to understand our opponent, carefully guarding against misrepresenting him. So long as a word is used as the embodiment of a thought, it is a sacred thing to tamper with which may be to murder a truth.

III. NO VERBAL BULWARKS WILL PRESERVE THE INTEGRITY OF TRUTH. This is just a corollary on what precedes. But it is sufficiently important to claim distinct and emphatic notice. Truth must find its expression in words, and to be intelligible these should be clear and definite. Hence the need of formulæ. But nothing is more unreliable than a formula. Since it may be used against truth with all the force of its prestige if a new false meaning is foisted into it, we need to be constantly considering it afresh in the light of facts. Creeds may be useful as the expression of " views " of truth, but history proves that they are of little good as defenders of the faith.

IV. WHEN A WORD HAS GIVEN TROUBLE IN CONTROVERSY IT MAY BE WELL TO ABANDON IT. Jeremiah is bidden no longer to use the word " burden." We are too jealous of words. There is a superstition of phrases. It is foolish to fight for a word. Anxiety about words is generally a sign of the loss of hold upon truth. If we are sure of possessing the truth and feel the living reality of it, we can afford to abandon any form of language, and can soon find other words in which to clothe it. Truth will not suffer. If it loses the aid of old associations, it loses also the hindrance of misunderstandings and antagonisms, and it gains the freshness of new suggestions. Let us be careful not to be the slaves of a vocabulary. We shall often find it wise to melt down our theological phrases and cast them in a new form, or rather to bury the old ones and let new ones naturally spring up as the embodiment of fresh living thoughts. Remember, " the letter killeth."

Vers. 33—40.—*The " burden."* I. IT IS A MISTAKE TO REGARD THE REVELATION OF TRUTH AS A BURDEN. It comes to lighten our burdens. At first it may seem to increase them by making us conscious of them. It opens our eyes to our own condition. The very light may serve to reveal the existence of the deep mystery all around us, which was not felt while the soul slumbered in darkness. Yet the light does not make the darkness that fringes its radiance. Revelation does not create the burdens of which it makes us conscious. It has rather the opposite effect. 1. All truth clears away some of the *burden of superstition*. Men people the unknown with horrors. Midnight shadows shroud dread nightmares. Daylight dispels the shadows, and the evil dreams melt away. 2. Divine truth is expressly designed to liberate the soul from *spiritual burdens*. It is a light of blessing, not a message of death; an evangel promising consolation to the weary. Even the darker elements of truth have this object to attain, since the evil that they reveal is only made manifest that we may see how to escape it, or be prepared to endure it, or receive it so as to profit by it. On the whole and in the end the truth of God is revealed for the loosening of the weary weight of men's greatest burdens, the burden of unforgiven sin, the burden of impossible duty, the burden of unendurable sorrow, the burden of unintelligible mystery.

II. MEN WHO DO NOT RECEIVE THE REVELATION OF TRUTH MAY REGARD IT AS A BURDEN. Thus these Jews derided Jeremiah by mocking his language with words, however, which expressed their own sentiments if not their deeper convictions. To them his word was a weariness, a very burden. Is it not so regarded by many? We should note the causes of this sad mistake. 1. *Ignorance*. The word is heard, but it is not understood. On the outside it is harsh. This is the characteristic of much Divine truth. Far off it sounds like grating thunder, terrific and repellant. We must be near to hear its sweet but hidden music. 2. *Want of sympathy*. All truth is burdensome to those who have not sympathy with it. Spiritual truth is a weariness to the unspiritual. 3. *Partial faith*. Jeremiah's words produced enough conviction to rouse fear, but not enough to lead to confidence in the wisdom, righteousness, and goodness of God in his acts of discipline and chastisement. A weak faith always makes truth a burden. To be joyous and exultant we must be trustful.

III. THE REJECTION OF TRUTH WILL BRING A BURDEN. The revelation is not a burden, but the neglect of it will make one (ver. 36). Men turn from God's truth for the trouble they think it threatens. They will find that this very act will bring the greatest trouble upon their heads. 1. This involves the *loss of the blessing* that truth is designed to bestow upon us. If we reject the truth we must bear the inevitable which the acceptance of it would have lightened. We then go our own way to meet unaided the crosses and toils of life. 2. This involves the *addition of a new burden* of guilt for the sin of rejecting truth. A wilful rejection of light is, of course, wicked and most culpable in the sight of God. It must bring trouble.

HOMILIES BY VARIOUS AUTHORS.

Vers. 1—4.—*False shepherds and the true.* The reference here is to the kings of the house of David, as the leaders of a theocratic people; and secondarily, to the spiritual purpose of all true kingship.

I. THE MISCHIEF OF FALSE SHEPHERDING. This is twofold, viz. scattering and destroying. The false shepherd has no real interest in the sheep; being but a hireling, his chief consideration is a selfish one. The kings of Judah had sought to realize their own ambitions and to indulge their own lusts. The moral and spiritual advancement of the people—the foundation of all real material prosperity—was not sought. The royal example which ought to have been influential for righteousness was directly opposed to this, and all classes of the people were infected with the licentiousness of prince and noble. The results appeared in crime, idolatry, and banishment.

II. ITS JUDGMENT. The calamity was to come chiefly upon those who had been unfaithful stewards of great responsibilities. Office which is thus abused will soon be taken away. According to responsibility will be punishment. He who causes to offend is worse than the offender, and will meet with corresponding severity of judgment. The nation outlives the dynasty. Unfaithful shepherds of the theocracy sink in ignominy and ruin, but God preserves a seed to serve him, and a generation to call him blessed.

III. ITS CORRECTION. The deceived of God's people, being distinguished from the deceivers, will undergo a kindlier discipline. The shepherd's care, as the symbol of royal responsibility, is intended as an ideal corrective. It teaches the principle that the king exists for the people, and not *vice versâ*. It is under Christianity that popular liberties, national development, and social purity have become the aims of rulers. In modern times there have been many who have illustrated this ideal of royalty; but Christ alone is the Head of redeemed humanity—the good Shepherd that lays down his life for his flock. In him the throne of David is eternally restored. Not yet do we see all things put under him, but the time draws nigh when he shall reign from shore to shore, and from the river even unto the ends of the earth. Ancient Israel depended for its very existence upon spiritual obedience to God's Law. The Church of Christ in all its offices must respect his authority and be actuated by love to him. Its character and influence must be purely spiritual, or its message will be neutralized and soon perverted to unholy ends.—M.

Vers. 5, 6.—" *The Lord our Righteousness.*" I. THE RIGHTEOUSNESS OF GOD WOULD RULE IN THE MIDST OF HIS PEOPLE. The question of the singular or plural interpretation of the word "scion" need not trouble us. To the prophet it was enough to declare that the offspring of David would yet reign in righteousness. All lesser fulfilments of this prophecy are thrown into insignificance by the great Son of David, who so grandly fulfilled the essential conditions of the prediction. 1. *Righteousness would yet become the law of human life.* 2. *This would be achieved through a personal influence.* The King of men will wield a spiritual sceptre, but his influence will be the more real. Righteousness will be manifested as a life and vindicated in sacrificial death. 3. *The house of David would be restored in him as its offspring.*

II. THE RIGHTEOUSNESS OF GOD WOULD BE TRANSFERRED TO HIS PEOPLE. "The Lord our Righteousness," be it the title of Prince or people, is sufficiently significant to explain its own essential meaning. There would be a transfer of the righteous character of the Ruler to the ruled; their spirit and aims would be identical with his; and he would embody their ideal life and present it to God. Through him the Divine righteousness would be the possession of the least saint. This evidently could only be perfectly accomplished in Christ. Nothing less than a unity of spirit and life with Jesus Christ, through faith, could achieve such a result.

III. THE RIGHTEOUSNESS OF GOD THUS EMBODIED AND COMMUNICATED WILL SAVE HIS PEOPLE. 1. *The power of this righteousness.* 2. *Its desirability.* 3. *Its attainableness.* The ideal future of Israel and the Church.—M.

Vers. 16—18, 22.—" *Trying the spirits.*" In ver. 18 read, "For who hath stood in the counsel of Jehovah? Let him see and hear his word: who hath marked his word? Let him proclaim it."

I. HEARERS ARE TO DISCRIMINATE BETWEEN FALSE PROPHETS AND TRUE. A very serious permission. But not for an occasion only: to be exercised whenever the witnesses conflict. The essential principle of Protestantism. The prophet is one who speaks in God's Name and reveals his will. The question, therefore, is of interest for all time; is exceedingly important, but not morally difficult. 1. *The effect of false prophecy is disastrous.* 2. *Earnest and prayerful discrimination is the best safeguard against religious indifference.*

II. A DISTINGUISHING TEST IS FURNISHED. It is a moral one. By their relation to the Law of Moses were the different prophets to be judged of. 1. *The marks of the false prophet.* His influence is an unrighteous one. He encourages evil-doers, either by directly unrighteous teaching or through the indirect influence which he exercises. 2. *The marks of the true prophet.* He is as unmistakably in favour of morality and religion. He is distinguished: (1) By his reverence. "He who hath stood in the counsel of Jehovah." To *sit* in that counsel would be to pretend to be equal and advise; but the true prophet has no word from himself. His messages proceed from God, and in his Name he speaks. In every age the messenger of God is one who has communion with him, is conscious of a living Presence and a revealing Spirit. "That which I received of the Lord, delivered I unto you:" not "I think; I am of opinion," etc. No pretence of infallibility. (2) By diligent and devout attention to God's revelations.

In the first place the *written* Word, and in the next the *spoken*. Of the latter, only the prayerful and studious soul can be the vehicle. We have to be silent that God may speak. The Word of God already revealed will be respectfully and faithfully observed. Consecration and quietness are marks of waiting upon God. And the message delivered will be faithful to the original that was seen or heard, and agreeable to what is already known of the will of God. The careless arrogance of the false prophet is soon corrected by what God has already revealed of himself. It is the devout "hearer" who alone has right to speak in God's Name, and his testimony will be approved by the spiritual sense of believers and "signs following." The spiritual character of the messenger of God—how much of his message does it represent?—M.

Ver. 21.—*Unauthorized ministry.* The credentials of the ministers of God are ever a matter of consequence. Exceptional service in the Church demands exceptional qualifications, and amongst these a direct Divine call is imperative. The wickedness of those who usurp sacred office is that they ignore the necessity for such a call, and, adding deliberate falsehood to impiety, they speak in the Name of God without having heard his voice.

I. THE CONDITIONS OF LEGITIMATE SERVICE IN GOD'S NAME. 1. *Those who minister in his Name must be appointed by himself.* "I have not sent them." For the sake of order an outward and conventional human recognition of office may be requisite. But that is not the essential thing. The minister of God—prophet, priest, Christian minister—must be sent and set apart in the first instance by God. This is an immediate spiritual, Divine act. It may be performed variously, as we find in Scripture it actually was; but the original impulse and impression of obligation are from the Spirit of God. It may be impossible to define the mode, yet the fact and the nature of it cannot be mistaken. So as to the degree of intensity with which the "call" should be attended difference of opinion may exist; but the greatest ministers of God have been those who waited until the Divine ordination was certain and confirmed. A feeble impulse at the outset is less likely to result in a grand consecrated ministry. And yet there is a sense in which the "calling" cannot be made sure until after it has been acted upon. So little is it a mechanical act that sinks into historical background,—the individual must ever have it present to his consciousness and crescent through active fulfilment of it. And the "call" is ever a *differentiated one,* having regard to special service. It is not enough for one to assume the minister's office merely because he is fired with the general spirit of Christian enthusiasm. 2. *Only as he reveals it to men can they declare his truth.* "I have not spoken to them." The prophecies of the Old Testament were the outcome of special and particular inspirations, as a reference to the descriptions of prophets themselves will prove. With some the period of active inspired utterance was comparatively brief; others were visited by the inspirations of God all through life. But even the (generally) inspired prophet might be destitute of inspiration on particular occasions, or might outlive it. In such cases silence is highest duty and truest wisdom. "The Word of God" on special occasions, as generally, is a finely organized spiritual emanation, a delicate creation or outbirth of the infinite Spirit, and may be misrepresented by unsympathetic, unenthusiastic reception. He must first be a reverent, believing "hearer" who would worthily prophesy or preach (the modern phase of the same essential work). It is only as the Spirit takes the "things of Christ" and shows them to us that we can understand, appreciate, and livingly present them to others. This necessary experience is finely expressed in the old phrase, "It was laid upon me," or, as Jeremiah has it, "But his word was in my heart as a burning fire shut up in my bones" (ch. xxv. 9).

II. HE WHO USURPS THE SACRED OFFICE IS GUILTY OF THE GRAVEST SIN. It is instructive to observe that that which, when worthily fulfilled, is pleasing to God, is altogether otherwise if illegitimately performed. Because: 1. *True prophets are thereby discredited.* 2. *Divine truth is misrepresented.* By bald unsympathetic literalism, etc. 3. *Divine truth is actually contradicted.*

III. GOD WILL REPUDIATE AND DISCREDIT ALL SUCH. Through genuine revelations. In the event. By the results attendant upon faithful preaching. In the great day of account.—M.

Vers. 23, 24.—*The omnipresence of God.* I. A PERSONAL ATTRIBUTE. 1. *Infinitely near to all his creatures.* 2. *All-seeing.* 3. *Filling all in all.*

II. A MORAL INFLUENCE. The question is asked. Every conscience confesses it. The dispensation of the Spirit which convinces the world " of sin, of righteousness, and of judgment" is the latest expression of this. 1. *Deterrent.* 2. *Intensifying.* 3. *Encouraging.*—M.

Vers. 25—27.—*Dreams that make the Name of God to be forgotten.* This is a very difficult passage, but its general sense is plain. It seems to be this : The false prophets whom Jehovah had not sent imitated the form of inspired utterance—the dream as distinct from the vision—which could most easily and with least chance of detection be fabricated. This vehicle of communicating their false doctrines they strongly affected. "I have dreamed, I have dreamed." Although delivering these utterances in the Name of Jehovah, they thereby sought to alienate the people from him, and to cause his Name to be forgotten.

I. PERSONS MAY SPEAK IN GOD'S NAME WHO ARE REALLY HIS ENEMIES. These false prophets used the Name of God to commend their own deceitful doctrines and practices. The latter would have no permanent influence apart from this association. It is a favourite device of Satan to appear as an angel of light. There is nothing more diabolical, and the pretence should ever be regarded with critical suspicion, and exposed without hesitation when discovered. "Take heed that no man deceive you. For many shall come in my Name, saying, I am Christ; and shall deceive many" (Matt. xxiv. 5.

II. IT IS EASY TO IMPART A RELIGIOUS ASPECT TO THAT WHICH IS OPPOSED TO TRUE RELIGION. Here one of the chief vehicles of inspiration is employed for quite another purpose than the revelation of God's truth. Its mystery, vagueness, etc., imposed upon the people; and detection was rendered difficult, as no one could be sure whether the prophet dreamt or not. The real message they delivered was one of personal ambition, lust, etc. So men baptize their carnal dreams and desires with Christian names. It is very necessary to discriminate and to be sincere. Now it is a dream, anon an ordinance, at another time a doctrine.

III. FALSEHOOD IS MOST TO BE DREADED WHEN IT SIMULATES TRUTH. 1. *Because it is essentially unaltered.* By saying this is truth, it is really no more so than at first, but it gets the character of it. 2. *The association thus created greatly increases its power.* The sanctions of religion are given to ungodly and sinful practices. Delusion is most inveterate when it blends with superstition. 3. *It destroys those whom it professes to bless.* The mental habit is thereby corrupted, and the spiritual nature rendered unfit for real Divine communications. The danger is not discovered until it has made fearful advances and worked irrevocable mischief.

IV. IT SPECIALLY PROVOKES THE ANGER OF GOD. It is blasphemy ; mocks him; and arrogates his place and functions, becoming more daring with apparent impunity.—M.

Vers. 28, 29.—*The faithful utterance of Divine revelation.* If God in very deed reveals his will to men, it is essential that it be simply and truthfully conveyed.

I. HUMAN INTERMIXTURES WITH DIVINE TRUTH ARE HURTFUL AND WEAKENING IN THEIR INFLUENCE. The word of human origin is placed on the same level with the Divine. When the former is proved fallible or untrue, the latter is discredited. Efforts after novelty and strangeness generally ensue ; and these are condemned by the Word of God (vers. 30, 31).

II. THESE ARE WHOLLY UNNECESSARY, AS THE WORD OF GOD IS SUFFICIENT FOR ITS PURPOSE. "God's Word shall not return unto him void" (Isa. lv. 11). It is the truth, and must prevail.

III. THE SPURIOUS INTERMIXTURE WILL BE REVEALED BY THE DIFFERENCE OF ITS EFFECTS. "What has the straw to do with the grain?"—a question sure to arise in those who receive such messages. The connection of the one element with the other is evidently incongruous. The stalk sustains the ear which develops from it whilst growing; but when the field has been harvested the two are separated, and have to be used apart. To mix up the chopped straw with the grain would only be to spoil the latter. And so it is when human ideas are mixed with Divine revelations : the mixture fails to edify or satisfy. And in its effect upon the moral nature the true message distinguishes itself from the false. "Fire," in its scorching, consuming power, cannot well be counterfeited; but such is the effect of the Word of God. The "hammer that breaketh the rock in pieces" demonstrates its legitimacy as an instrument of grace by its power upon the hard and impenitent heart (Heb. iv. 12).—M.

Vers. 33—40.—*Despising prophesyings.* I. THE HONOUR OF GOD IS BOUND UP WITH HIS WORD. 1. *It expresses his character.* A careful, gradual unfolding of himself in his attributes and personal relations. 2. *It declares his will.* (1) His Law; (2) his gospel; both of which express his purpose. The prophecies of God with his promises and appeals. 3. *In its loftiest embodiment—Jesus Christ—it is identified with himself.* (John i. 1.)

II. HE WILL NOT SUFFER IT TO BE TREATED LIGHTLY. To do so would be to court contempt, if not to condone the offence. As a sign of his displeasure: 1. *He will give the false prophets another message to deliver.* This is said satirically (ver. 33); their circumstances will prove that the true message is not one of acceptance but of rejection. The whole nation will be thrust out of covenant relationship. 2. *Special penalties will be inflicted upon particular offenders.* (Ver. 34.) Handling the Word of God deceitfully will bring upon a man evident tokens of the Divine displeasure. 3. *The word "burden" itself will have a new and fearful significance.* It was a spiritual offence to talk about "burdens" so lightly. People to whom the true message of God had no awful impressiveness would be taught reverence and fear by that which he would inflict upon them. It would be a true "burden," not so readily got rid of (vers. 39, 40).—M.

Ver. 6.—"*The Lord our Righteousness.*" How pleasant it is, after a traveller has for long days of travel been occupied in passing through a dreary, monotonous country, to come to a region where Nature puts on her loveliest and most attractive aspect; where, instead of flat plains, unrelieved by hill or dale, or any object on which the wearied eye can fasten with delight, you find yourself in a land of noble rivers and rushing torrents, lofty mountains and exquisite valleys, flourishing cities and noble buildings! With what pleasure does the traveller enter such region after the far different and far less delightful scenes he has been fatigued with for so long! Now, akin to such pleasure is that of the persevering student of these prophecies of Jeremiah, when at length, quitting the monotonous and painful recitals of Israel's sins, and the distressing records of the dread judgments of God which were to come upon them in consequence, with which the foregoing chapters have been mainly filled, he enters, in these verses which belong to our text, on a portion of the prophet's writings which tells, not of sin, but of righteousness; not of the Lord the Avenger, but of the Lord the Redeemer and Saviour; the Restorer because the Righteousness of his people. It is like an oasis in the desert; like what Elim must have been to the Israelites after their weary journey to Marah, where burning heat and thirst and much distress had been their continued lot. And no doubt Jeremiah and the faithful few who adhered to him were wont to solace their saddened minds by turning their thoughts, as they do here, away from the dark and terrible present to the bright and happy future when Israel should dwell safely under the rule of the Lord their Righteousness. That was a bright onlook, by means of which the heavy burden of the days in which the prophet actually lived and laboured became more endurable, and their spirits were kept from being utterly overwhelmed. Now, concerning this glorious name of Jehovah, "the Lord our Righteousness," we will first show that—

I. THIS NAME BELONGS TO THE LORD JESUS CHRIST. It is impossible to conceive of any devout Jew ascribing the name of Jehovah to an ordinary earthly monarch, however great or famous he might be. Every Israelite would count it blasphemy so to speak of him. Moreover, the extravagance of the assertions here made, if regarded as descriptive of an earthly monarch, preclude the possibility of their having been so intended. How could any such be called the righteousness of his people? Zerubbabel was undoubtedly a noble prince, and in such measure as was possible to him answered to the prophetic description. He was a branch of the house of David, and nothing is known against him. But his power was very limited, and in no sense did he fill up the portraiture that is given here. Jew and Christian alike agree that neither he nor any of his obscure descendants could possibly answer to this name of "the Lord our Righteousness." Both alike affirm that the promised Messiah is meant, and to him along can it belong. And that our Lord Jesus was that Messiah the Scriptures constantly assert. He was "the Root and the Offspring of David," was born "of the house and lineage of David" according to the flesh. He was the tender Shoot, the Sprout that sprang from the original root when all the stock and branches of the stately tree that had once grown on that root had died down, decayed, and disappeared. But he was more than the Branch of Jesse: he was the Lord from heaven, the Son of God. Therefore to speak of him as Jehovah is consistent with all the Scripture representations of his Divine dignity. And although the day of his complete triumph has not yet come, nor is his kingdom fully set up, still we clearly see its beginnings, its advance, and its continual growth, so that it is not hard to believe in all those coming glories of his reign on which the ancient prophets, as Jeremiah here, loved to dwell. On all these grounds, therefore, we claim this high and sacred title for the Lord Jesus Christ. He the Church has held all along is "the Lord our Righteousness" whom the inspired prophet foretold. And—

II. This name is altogether appropriate to him. Not because of the righteousness of his character alone, nor either because of the happy condition to which he would one day bring the Jewish people. We believe that he will do for them all that is here said. We see no objection to the taking of the promises made concerning them in their literal meaning. But if this were all that is contained in this name, then St. Paul could not be justified in claiming, as he perpetually does, the righteousness of Christ to be to and upon *all* them that believe. This view is limited to no one age, no one country, no one people, but reaches out to all everywhere and of every age. But the true justification of this glorious title lies in such facts as these: 1. *The Lord Jesus makes us righteous in God's esteem.* God ever demands righteousness. It is his incessant appeal here in all these prophecies. But it is here that men have ever failed. They have evaded this Divine demand, and have endeavoured to substitute all manner of things in its place, and so to compensate for it. They have refused nothing so long as they might be let off this. Hence the word of the Lord, "There is none righteous, no, not one." It is in this emergency that "the Lord our Righteousness" comes forward, takes up our case, and causes us to be esteemed righteous before God—causes us to be looked upon as what we really are not; as righteous when there is much unrighteousness in us all, and scarce aught else in some. Of course this is objected to and cavilled at not a little, and many fail to see how it can righteously be. But all the while the like is occurring every day. Does not the government of a land continually do things which involve the whole people of the land, although many of them may entirely disapprove? Still it is the whole country that is regarded as acting by and through its government. And yet we assent to this arrangement, this principle of representation, as equitable, just, and necessary. And not merely in dealings between man and man, but in those between God and man, this same principle of representation may be seen perpetually at work. Assuredly the whole human race was represented in its first parents, and God held it to be so, so that the consequences of their actions have passed over to their posterity right down to the present day. And in each family the head of it involves all the members, so that there are many innocent victims of their fathers' sin, and more, we trust, who are recipients of favours won by their fathers' virtues and obedience to God's will rather than their own. It is the principle of representation again. Is it, then, a thing to wonder at that a good and gracious God should devise another system of representation to meet and counteract that which has wrought so much ill? That is, is it to be wondered at that the Lord Jesus Christ should be constituted as much the Head and Representative of his people as Adam was constituted the head and representative of all who have descended from him; that there should be a second Adam as well as a first, and that Christ should be that second Adam, as St. Paul declares he is? Surely there is nothing unreasonable in all this. It is in harmony with what we perpetually see. And if he who is our Representative *desired so to be,* as our Lord did—for he yearned to draw all men unto and into him—surely this, his own desire, makes his being constituted our Representative more reasonable still. And because *he qualified himself* for this office so perfectly. He came and was one of us, lived our life, bore our burdens, submitted to our sorrows, bore the penalty of our sins, "was in all points tempted like as we are, yet without sin." Now, if the principle of representation be just at all, surely it is still more so that the Lord Jesus should be that Representative. But if he be, then, because he is altogether righteous, acceptable, and well pleasing before God, we must be so too; yea, we are so, for he is "the Lord our Righteousness." God looks not upon us, but he beholds Christ, who is "our Shield;" he looks on "the face of his Anointed." "We are accepted in the Beloved." "Christ is made unto us righteousness." 2. *And he makes us to be as the righteous in our conditions.* So only can the paramount and predominant features of God's dealing with us now be accounted for. Man being what he is, why should he be dealt with so mercifully as he is? The answer is, because it is the Lord who is our Righteousness. If I see a number of poor destitute people taken, and clothed, and fed, and dealt with in all kind and beautiful ways, and I ask the explanation, I am at once pointed to some one who has secured all this favour for them, and by whose kindness it has become theirs. And when I see man, despising God, prayerless, sinning daringly day by day, ungrateful, evil, disobedient continually, destitute of all goodness, and yet treated with all kindness and love, must I not conclude that the righteousness of another is the secret of his mercies, and the real cause of the goodly portion he enjoys? 3. But Christ is "the Lord our Righteousness" *because he makes us righteous in ourselves.* If it were possible that God could for ever esteem and deal with as righteous, not only those who were not righteous, but who never could become so, we should find it difficult to maintain the truth taught us by this name. But God's counting us righteous in Christ is reasonable and right, because we are in the sure way to become so. For when any come to the Lord Jesus Christ in living faith, a new will is given them. They are, as our Lord says, "born again." It is as on a railway, where by one movement of the points the whole train is turned on to another line, and proceeds afterwards in quite a different direction. So by this coming to Christ the man is placed on another line, started in a new direction; a new will is his, and he is a new man. When the turbid stream of the Rhone falls into the Lake of Geneva it loses its old character, and its waters assimilate themselves to the exquisite clearness and colour of that lake, so that when they flow out at the other end they are as a new river altogether — "old things have passed away, and all things are become new." So is it in the great change when a man comes to Christ. And when we remember that whilst man looketh at the outward appearance, God looketh at the heart, it is easy to see that God may count a man to be righteous whom we should not think so at all. If the will, the heart, be Christ's, though it may be once and again overborne by the fierce rush of temptation, as David's was, yet, because the heart is right, God counts that man righteous still. And this new will, the new heart, ever tends to embody and express itself in act. It will be like a hidden fire, struggling and struggling on till it can find vent and work its good desire. And it shall do this in due time. Meanwhile God but anticipates; looks on to the harvest as the husbandman does even when the blade has not shown itself as yet above the ground. But he imputes the righteousness of the harvest to those fields though not a blade appears. The parent imputes the righteousness of the intelligent, loving youth to the little infant just born, not because it has it, but because he believes it will have it. And God counts us as righteous, not alone because Christ is our Representative, but because he will restore our souls. He will make us righteous in ourselves as well as before God. And he does this by setting before us in his own life the perfect example, and attracting us thereto by an ever-increasing attraction; and by imparting to us his own Spirit, who nourishes us in all goodness; and by bringing to bear upon us the mightiest motives which can ever control or influence the human heart—love, gratitude, holy fear, bright, blessed hope,—all these and yet others ; so day by day does he strengthen and confirm the good will which, when we first came to him, he gave us as his first gift. Thus does he make those righteous whom God for his sake now counts to be so. And now—

III. CAN WE SAY THAT THE LORD IS "OUR" RIGHTEOUSNESS? We may have correct views on this great doctrine, we may believe in a general and abstract way that the Lord is the Righteousness of his people, but all this is far short of being able to say that the Lord is *our* Righteousness. We can only say this as we daily and habitually trust him—as we "keep touch" with him, as it were, continually looking to him and relying upon him. For faith it is which vitalizes our connection with him. The wires of the electric cable may stretch all the way beneath the ocean, and each shore of the Atlantic be joined together by them; but there is no communication until the electric current is sent along that cable, and then the circuit is complete. And so the channel along which our faith may pass is provided; but until faith goes from our heart —that electric force of faith—the connecting bond may almost as well not be. Until then Christ is a Representative of man before God, but he is not *our* Representative. It is faith that vitalizes that connection, and he is not our Righteousness until we believe. Faith brings us into real union with him, reproduces in us the mind which was in him, lays hold on the grace which he holds out to us, leads us to repent, to love, to obey, to follow him in the daily walk and conversation. Remember, the Lord demands righteousness. We have it not in ourselves. In this our destitution the Lord comes to us and offers to be our Righteousness. We have but to appropriate and claim that which he offers. Shall we be so sinful, so mad, as to refuse? The great day when the banquet for God's saints shall be spread is hastening on, and we shall all of us be eager to crowd in and take our place there with the blessed. But what if, when the King comes in to view his guests, we have not on the wedding-garment, but are dressed in some robe of our own, which we think will answer as well? You know how he was dealt with who presumed so to do. Oh, then, that such may not be our doom, let us hasten unto Christ, and pray him now and for ever to be "the Lord our Righteousness."—C.

Ver. 28.—"*What is the chaff to*," etc.? One seems to see the flash of the prophet's eye, the tremulous emotion, the indignant scorn, with which he bursts out with this scathing question; one can almost hear his loud, vehement tones as he taunts with it the false prophets, against whose wickedness he had been protesting throughout the greater part of this chapter. What sternness, what biting severity, characterize it! As one has said, "It cuts like the edge of a razor. As a sabre flashing over one's head; a sword gleaming to the very point; a fire lurid with coals of juniper;—we are appalled as we glance at it. It strikes with implacable resentment. There is no word of mercy toward the chaff; not a thought of clemency or forbearance. He bloweth at it as though it were a worthless thing, not to be accounted of—a nothing, that vanishes with a puff." It reminds us, as so much in Jeremiah's character and experience does, of our Lord's indignation against the false teachers of his day. What terrible, burning words were those which *he* uttered against the "scribes, Pharisees, hypocrites," who swarmed around him! Where there is deep love of God and of man, there cannot but be such holy hatred of such as are what those were whom our Lord and the prophet denounced. Jeremiah in this chapter, from the ninth verse downwards, has been pouring out his soul against them. He declares himself broken-hearted because of them—by their conduct and the woes it was bringing upon his people. He laments the grievous wickedness of the nation, but charges it all upon these faithless prophets, who taught men to sin by their bad example, and encouraged them therein by their false teachings. And as he thinks of the worthless-ness of the men and of their prophesyings, his sacred anger and scorn mount up and burst forth in these terrible words, "What is the chaff to the wheat? saith the Lord. Is not *my* word like as a fire? saith the Lord; and like a hammer that breaketh the rock in pieces?" Yes, these are terrible words; but how applicable, how necessary they are to be insisted upon, even now! For, monstrous almost as it may appear, men are, as they have ever been, most prone to care more for the chaff than for the wheat; to spend themselves on securing that which is worthless, whilst that which is most precious they despise. And the danger is increased because those things which are as the chaff to the wheat are often, as the chaff and wheat themselves, closely associated together, have grown up together, are very difficult to separate, and are mutually dependent one upon another. It is easy enough, when we see the wind driving the chaff away, to discern the difference between it and the wheat, and the inferiority of the one to the other; but it is not so easy whilst the two are together, and seeming so much as if they were all of one nature and value. Now, apply all this in regard to sundry matters in which this discrimination needs sorely to be made. And—

1. To THE PROPHESYING OF THE PRESENT DAY. The occasion and connection of the

words we are considering at once suggest this application. And let us be grateful to God that, amid the much prophesying of our own day, we have much of that " sure Word" to which St. Peter bids us give heed, as to a light shining in a dark place. Yes, there are faithful ministries, blessed be God for them ; and that they are like the precious wheat, in contrast to the worthless chaff, has been proved over and over again by the testimony God himself has given to them. For, like the pure grain, they nourish the souls that are fed upon the Word they minister. The instruction that builds up, consolidates, and strengthens the spiritual frame is shown by that very fact to be not as chaff, but as wheat. And he would not only be ungrateful, but untruthful, who should deny that God has given and is maintaining many who minister to his people, whether young or old, in the congregation, the family, or the school, the pure Word of God. And the other striking characteristics of the true Word of God which are here spoken of are also found in their prophesyings. The Word of God which they minister is as *a fire*. How it enlightens, how it cheers, as on a cold wintry day! How it consumes the dross of the evil nature, burning on until all the evil in us be burnt out ! Ah, yes, the pure Word of God—which still, thank God, is preached—is as a fire consuming the miserable pretences of self-righteousness in which the souls whom it touches have hitherto been trusting, and compelling them to hasten for shelter to him who is "the Lord our Righteousness." And it is *a hammer*, which, smiting the obdurate heart, causes the tears of true repentance to flow forth and refresh those who long have been thirsting to see such living waters. As at Pentecost the hammer of that Word fell upon those hearts which had been hard enough to crucify the Lord, and it so smote them as to break them, rock-like though they were, and they cried out, " What *shall* we do ? " These are the signs of the Word of God, and they are not wanting still. *But yet there is much of instruction given that is far different from this*—as unlike it as chaff is unlike wheat. It may be the ministry of eloquence, or of ritual, or of philosophy, or of human learning, or of taste, or of fashion ; and not a little of such ministry there is in the present day. It is brilliant, attractive, followed by crowds, admired, applauded ; it is associated with all that art, culture, music, and ritual pomp can supply ; it is very fashionable ; for the sake of it humbler worship is abandoned, though that which is abandoned may be purer and more whole-some by far. But because in connection with all this ministry so pleasing to human likings there may be lacking that which alone nourishes the soul, and which has upon it the sure tokens of the Word of God, therefore, when there is this lack, God calls it chaff, and despises it accordingly. Do not think that all these things are in themselves to be despised. No; we would fain have the ministry of the Word of God surrounded with all that can serve to win attention, command reverence, and excite interest ; we should be alert to look out for such things, and to secure them so far as we may ; but let us see to it that they be but subordinate, that they all are used as aids to what is far higher and more important than themselves—that within this husk the pure grain of God's Word is enshrined and preserved. What is the good of any preaching or instruction, however pleasing or attractive it may be, that does not set the pure wheat of God's Word before hungry souls ? Souls must live, and they cannot live on chaff. Oh that all those who preach and teach may more and more hear ever sounding in their ears this startling word, " What is the chaff," etc.! Apply this word—

II. To OUR OWN INDIVIDUAL CHARACTER—what we, each one, are. If we are the children of God, believing in the Lord Jesus Christ, and humbly striving day by day to do his will and to be well pleasing to him, then there is much that is wheat-like in us. That repentance, that faith, that regenerating grace, that law of the Spirit of life in Christ Jesus, its meekness, patience, zeal, love,—all these things are as the wheat, and blessed be God they are to be found in some measure—would that it were larger—in us all. But *there is so much of a contrary nature*, so chaff-like, as well. Yes, verily, as chaff lying close by the side of our heart, wrapping it round, long associated with it, grown up with it, hard, hard indeed, to be parted from it ; so is the evil of our hearts, the fleshly nature, the carnal mind, which yet clings to us as the husk does to the grain. And often we are at a complete loss to tell whether there is more of wheat or chaff about us—whether our destiny is to be stored in the garner, or to be as the chaff which the wind driveth away. But do we think about the chaff and the wheat as God thinks about them ? Are we willing—yea, longing—to be utterly rid of the chaff? Are we content to bear "the bruising flails of God's corrections" until they have "threshed off from us our vain affections"? Do we desire that every portion of this chaff may be got rid of, and "that we, wholesome grain and pure may be," and that only? Perhaps God's flails are laid upon us now, or his winnowing work is stripping off much from us, and making "our very spirit poor." Oh, if it be but to rid us of this chaff, let us not complain. Death itself is but God's chief flail "to purge the husk of this our flesh away, and leave the soul uncovered." Complain not, for "what is the chaff," etc.? And not only the sin in us, but *much that looks and is reckoned as far other than sin*, may be, after all, only chaff. Much of that feeling and conduct which is associated with our religious life may be of itself of a very worthless sort. Those tears which flow so freely when the preacher is in a pathetic mood,—what are they all worth if they never lead to a genuine repentance, a real turning of the soul to Christ? And that open profession of religion, coming to the table of the Lord and partaking of the sacred bread and wine, what is that if it be not the index and outward sign of a heart that trusts, that loves, that is consecrated to Christ? And that correct and orthodox creed for which we are so ready to show fight, and the deniers or doubters of which we so eagerly condemn, what is the good of it if it be not the guardian of a God-fearing and righteous life? And that giving of money—for it is to the amount kept back after we have given, and to the motive which prompts the gift, that God looks to determine which is wheat and which is chaff. And that eager activity in many forms of Christian work which some show, unless it be the outcome of a heart aglow with love to Christ, counts for very little with him who here asks, "What is the chaff," etc.? Again we say we do not despise these things—we would that there were more of them ; but if at the heart of them there be not faith and love towards Christ, which alone are the wheat which these things are intended to serve and minister to, then they are but as the chaff which the wind driveth away. We are apt to think a great deal of them, and to rely upon them not a little for ourselves and for others. But they are not the wheat, only its husk, and "what . . . Lord." Apply this question—

III. TO THE FELLOWSHIP OF THE CHURCH. And without doubt it may be affirmed that if the pure wheat of God's garner be not to be found in the fellowship of the Church, it is to be found nowhere. What our Lord said of his Church at the beginning, "Ye are the salt of the earth . . . ye are the light of the world," is true still. Oh, how many, thank God, of meek, pure, devout, consecrated souls has the Church ever numbered in her fellowship, and does so even yet! But still, even on the best threshing-floors the chaff is mingled with the wheat. Even those Churches which claim to be most careful over admission to their fellowship, and demand valid evidence to be given that there has been a real change of heart, a true conversion to God—even those can no more keep out the chaff than others who throw the responsibility of religious profession entirely on those who make it. But the presence of the chaff along with the wheat could be better borne if the two were always estimated as they should be. But it is not so. Let an unspiritual, worldly minded, hard, and unloving man find his way into a Church—and many such do—and if he be rich, or hold a good position in the world, he will at once be allowed an influence and an authority which he ought not to have—no, not for an hour. And if a Church can get hold of a number of such people, if wealth, and social influence, and education, and fashion flock to their doors, there you have the Church of Laodicea reproduced in most exact form. They will count themselves, and others also will count them, to be "rich, and increased with goods, and to have need of nothing." But what will the Lord say when he cometh with his winnowing fan to throughly purge his floor? We are sorely tempted, all of us, to crave with a great craving the presence amongst us of persons of influence, wealth, and power. And all well and good if they be earnest, godly men at the same time. But we are in danger of welcoming them even if this great qualification be largely absent. And that we do too often find this sad intermixture of the worthless with God's wheat, is seen in the quick falling off of some of those who once were gathered with the Church of God. A little persecution, loss of worldly advantage, desire to stand well with those around,—these have all served as pretexts for not a few to break away altogether. Like "the nautilus, which is often seen sailing in tiny fleets in the Mediterranean Sea, upon the smooth surface of the water. It is a beautiful sight, but as soon as ever the tempest begins to blow, and the first ripple appears upon the surface of the sea, the little mariners draw in their sails and betake themselves to the bottom of the sea, and you see them no more. How many are like that! When all goes well with Christianity many go sailing along fairly in the summer tide, but no sooner does trouble, or affliction, or persecution arise, than where are they? Ah, where are they? They have gone." Let us see to it that we esteem the wheat, however poor its surroundings, above all chaff, however richly it may be endowed. And above all, let us by our own loyalty to God, our sympathy with Christ, our love to our brethren, our cheerful self-sacrifice, our daily obedience, show that *we* are of those whom the Lord will own at the last, and not as the chaff which he will despise and destroy.

IV. To GOD'S FINAL ESTIMATE OF US ALL. For the great question which concerns every man who reads or hears these words is—Which am I, chaff or wheat? And that question is to be decided, not according to man's estimate, but God's. It is what *he* will judge, not what we may. Here in this world we are all mingled together, in every Church, family, town, village, society, or community whatsoever. In all places, under all circumstances and in all ways in this world, this commingling of the evil and the good is found; the chaff is ever closely associated with the wheat. " Let both grow together until the harvest," is our Lord's command, and no endeavour of ours can sever the two completely. But the very word " until " which our Saviour employs shows that there shall be a separating time ; the two shall not for ever be conjoined as they are now. "Then two shall be in the field ; the one shall be taken, and the other left. Two men shall be in one bed; the one shall be taken, and the other shall be left." In the same church, sitting side by side in the same pew, there may be found both chaff and wheat. Anticipate that awful separating time. It will come upon us as it came upon those ten virgins, five of whom were wise and five were foolish, but which was which none knew until the cry was heard, " Behold, the bridegroom cometh!" And so, though now none of us can tell what those are who gather with us, and join in the same holy service, listen to the same gospel, and unite in the same prayers, praises, and confessions, though outwardly we are all as the wheat of God, yet whether we be so or no God alone can tell. But do any ask—How can I, though consciously worthless as the chaff, yet become as the wheat? Blessed be God, such a great change is possible. Go to the Lord Jesus Christ; tell him how poor, wretched, evil, you know yourself to be. Cast yourself down at his feet. Call upon him for his aid. Thou shalt become a new creature in Christ, old things shall pass away, all things shall become new. The chaff shall be changed into the wheat, death shall be exchanged for life, and now, worthless once, thou art in Christ precious for ever, and the garner of the Lord shall be thine everlasting home. Come unto Christ in faith and love, for the heart so yielded is alone God's wheat ; but if when the great separating day comes thou seekest to find safety in aught else, however precious you and others may deem it, he will spurn both it and you. For " what is . . . Lord."—C.

Vers. 5, 6.—*Jehovah-Tsidkenu.* It is in his kingly character that the uprising of the Messiah is here predicted. The shepherds that destroyed and scattered the flock of God were the corrupt rulers of the line of David. God was visiting upon them one after another " the evil of their doings ; " and after them he would raise up men of a nobler sort—men like Ezra, Nehemiah, and the Maccabees, who should be true leaders and commanders of the people (ver. 4). But these, again, would but prepare the way for One far greater. Beyond all these changes the eye of the prophet is fixed on the time when out of the seemingly withered root of David a sapling shall arise, "the righteous Branch ; " One who shall perfectly realize the Divine idea of " a ruler of men " (2 Sam. xxiii. 3, 4)—the King who shall "reign in righteousness," and of the " increase of whose government and peace there shall be no end " (Isa. ix. 6, 7 ; xi. 1—6; xxxii. 1; Zech. ix. 9). Towards him the hopes of loyal hearts through every previous age reached forth. In him the "desire of all nations" finds its glorious fulfilment. "And this is the name whereby he shall be called, The Lord our Righteousness." In unfolding the full significance of this name, consider (1) *the personal righteousness of Christ,* (2) *the way in which that righteousness becomes ours.*

I. HIS PERSONAL RIGHTEOUSNESS. He is emphatically " Jesus Christ *the Righteous,*" the one only absolutely righteous being ever born into the world. Our human nature, the beauty and harmony of which, in the person of Adam, the father of our race, the touch of moral evil had defaced and destroyed, appeared again in him, the "second Adam," in all its sinless, faultless perfection, absolutely free from the taint of evil. And this not as a development, but as a new Divine revelation; not as the consummate product of moral forces inherent in our nature, but as a supernatural phenomenon, a miracle, in the sphere of man's moral life. In him the "righteousness of God" appeared, embodied and illustrated in human form. Our faith in this historic fact rests on different grounds. 1. The angelic testimony (Luke i. 35). 2. The direct testimony of the Father (Matt. iii. 17; xvii. 5). 3. His declarations respecting himself (John viii. 29, 46; xiv. 30; xv. 10; xvii. 4). 4. The witness of his enemies (Judas, Herod, Pilate and his wife, the Roman centurion). 5. The apostolic testimony (Acts iii. 14; 2 Cor. v. 21; Heb. vii. 26; 1 Pet. ii. 22; 1 John ii. 1; iii. 5). 6. The profound impression left on our spirits by a careful study of the Gospel records. The absolute sinlessness of Jesus is one of the foundation-stones in the fabric of Christian doctrine, and to doubt or deny it is to undermine and destroy the whole. But his righteousness means more than faultless personal character. It includes the positive fulfilment of the Father's purposes and of the work the Father had given him to do. "I have glorified thee on the earth," etc. (John xvii. 4). "Wherefore when he cometh into the world, he saith, Sacrifice and offering," etc. (Heb. x. 5—10). His was a righteousness wrought out through all the patient obedience of a blameless life, consummated in the vicarious shame and sorrow of the cross. As the sunbeam receives no contamination from the foulest thing on which it may chance to fall, so did he pass triumphantly through all the evil of the world and go back to the bosom of the Father with a purity as unsullied as that in which he came. "Declared to be the Son of God with power, according to the spirit of holiness, by the resurrection from the dead" (Rom. i. 4).

II. How his righteousness becomes ours. 1. *As the ground of our forgiveness.* Faith in him as our righteous "Advocate with the Father" delivers us from condemnation. We believe in no "transference of a moral quality." As a man's sins are his own and not another's, so whatever of virtue there may be in him belongs to himself alone. But is it incredible that God should deal with sinful men in the way of mercy because of the perfect righteousness of "the man Christ Jesus"? "He was made sin for us, who knew no sin, that we might be made the righteousness of God in him" (2 Cor. v. 21). There is an instinctive witness in our souls to the fact that if "grace reigns" towards us it must be "through righteousness." This is God's answer to that instinct: "By the righteousness of One the free gift came upon all men unto justification of life" (Rom. v. 18). 2. *As the inspiring cause of our personal sanctification.* The gospel is God's method of making men righteous, not a scheme by virtue of which he reckons them to be so when they are not. Faith in Christ's mediatorial work as the ground of forgiveness draws the soul irresistibly into living sympathy with himself. It is impossible to dwell in fellowship with him without sharing his spirit and becoming "righteous even as he is righteous." Not more surely does the prepared surface receive the picture the sun's rays paint upon it, than does the reverent, trustful, loving soul reflect his image. "We all, with open face beholding as in a glass," etc. (2 Cor. iii. 18). Thus does his righteousness become ours. 3. *As the rectifying power in the general life of the world.* "A sceptre of righteousness is the sceptre of his kingdom," and wherever he reigns the discords of the world are resolved into a blessed harmony. He is the Creator of "the new heavens and the new earth, wherein dwelleth righteousness."—W.

Vers. 23, 24.—*The omnipresent God.* It is an essentially heathen conception of the Deity against which these grand words bear witness. There were two false tendencies of the heathen mind to which the Hebrew faith was a perpetual rebuke—one was that of thinking of the Deity as dwelling remote from the ways of men, "throned in sequestered sanctity," too lofty to take any interest in the affairs of earth; the other that of localizing and limiting the Deity, conceiving of him as exercising a partial jurisdiction, as belonging to a particular place and people. The God of the Jews was no mere distant abstraction, but an ever-present, ever-active power; not the God of one nation only, but of the "whole earth." Consider—

I. THE TRUTH ABOUT GOD HERE INDICATED. Two attributes—omnipresence and omniscience—are asserted. But they are so mutually dependent and so inseparable as to be virtually one. By the very necessity of his Being as the infinite Spirit, God is not more in one place or sphere of existence than another, but alike in all, "afar off" as well as "at hand," filling heaven and earth; and wherever he is, there he is in all the fulness of his perfect intelligence, not observant or cognizant of some things or beings more than others, but having infallible knowledge of all. Note respecting this divine attribute: 1. *Its mystery.* The being of One who is thus superior to the limitations of space and time and to all our finite conditions—to whom there is no nearness and no distance, neither past nor future, nothing new and nothing old, to whom "all things are naked and opened,"—must needs be inscrutable to us. Our boldest images are but the'veil of our ignorance, and even the sublimest representations of the inspired Word leave the problem as insoluble as ever. The celebrated dictum, "His centre is everywhere and his circumference nowhere," in no way helps us to any real comprehension of infinity; and such grand poetic utterances as those of the hundred and thirty-ninth psalm, however much they may find their echo in the depths of our spiritual consciousness, only call forth the confession, "Such knowledge is too wonderful for me; it is high, I cannot attain unto it." 2. *Its moral significance.* The moral conditions involved, the moral attributes associated with it, and their direct relation to ourselves, clothe it with profound interest and solemn importance. If God were at an impassable distance, it might little signify to us what his moral attributes were. But now that he is thus near—a presence from which we cannot escape, an eye that is always searching us through and through, a hand that is always laid upon us— the question as to what his dispositions towards us are is one of unspeakable moment. His absolute knowledge of us is connected with a present secret act of judgment, prophetic of the open judgment to come. And it is his perfection that is thus coming into perpetual contact with our imperfect thoughts and ways. His holy love is the light that searches into us, the fire that tries us. This attribute of omniscience derives tremendous importance from the fact that "our God is a consuming fire." 3. *The individuality of its application.* "Can any hide himself?" Like all other Divine truths, this is nothing to us until we bring it to bear on our own personal condition and doings. The fact itself is independent of all our thoughts about it, and even of our very existence. But for it to have any real influence over us we must reduce it from its vague generality to the narrow compass of our own being, and concentrate the force of it upon the single line of our own daily history—"Thou God seest *me.*" We apprehend the universal truth aright only so far as that cry of Hagar expresses our soul's deepest consciousness—as if the whole world of accountable beings around us were annihilated, and we stood, as in the solitudes of a desert, alone with God.

II. THE PRACTICAL EFFECT THAT TRUTH MAY BE EXPECTED TO PRODUCE. We cannot imagine one more fitted to have a salutary influence in every way upon us. Let God be to you only a distant object of contemplation, as he is to the mere theological disputant, and with whatever attributes you may clothe him, they touch no part of your being with any living power. Conceive of him, in a dreamy pantheistic way, as a mere impersonal, all-pervading force, and there is nothing in your belief to elevate your moral character and ennoble your life. But believe in the God of the Bible, whose voice is heard in the text, and you embrace the grandest and most influential truth the human soul is capable of entertaining. The truth, rather, will possess you, as no other truth can, moulding and governing your whole nature, and adapting itself in an infinite variety of ways to every aspect of your being and life. Chiefly two lessons are enforced: 1. *Self-scrutiny.* We shall be concerned to become acquainted with ourselves that we may know how far the spirit and tenor of our moral life is in harmony with the will and the life of God. Not that a mere curious and anxious habit of testing the quality of one's own feelings, and weighing and measuring one's motives, has necessarily any healthy moral effect. It may be the reverse. But the sense of God will naturally awaken a desire that the relation in which we stand towards him may be a right and happy one. "If our heart condemn us, God is greater than our heart," etc. (1 John iii. 23, 24). The loyalty of the heart to God is the essential principle of a religious life. The sin of these false prophets was the loosening of the bond of their spiritual allegiance to him. "They stood not in the counsel of the Lord." In the case of the Pharisees, their external proprieties were but the veil of internal hollowness and corruption and death; and Christ said to them, "Ye are they that approve yourselves unto men, but God knoweth your hearts." Let our hearts be right with God, let the main stream of our inner life be flowing heavenwards, and we need not tremble to know that " all things are naked and opened unto the eyes of him with whom we have to do." 2. *Earnest preparation for the future and final judgment.* "He hath appointed a day," etc. (Acts xvii. 31); "We must all appear," etc. (2 Cor. v. 10). Your personal alienation from God may give you little trouble now, but " what will you do when he riseth up? when he visiteth, what will you answer him?" (Job xxxi. 14). There is no way of preparation for the solemn judgment of the future but in that personal forgiveness and reconciliation, that moral cleansing and righteousness of life, that comes through fellowship with the Saviour (Phil. iii. 9).

> " Low at his cross we view the day
> When heaven and earth shall pass away,
> And thus prepare to meet him."

W.

Vers. 1—4.—*Shepherds, bad and good.* I. THE SENTENCE ON THE UNFAITHFUL SHEPHERDS. This is perhaps the most special and emphatic of all Jeremiah's references to the unfaithful shepherds. Nowhere does he go into such detail as Ezekiel does (ch. xxxiv.). But whatever may be lacking in illustrative detail, the essential facts are mentioned. Here are men upon whom is laid a charge such as is laid on a shepherd by the owner of the pasture and the flock. The business of such a man is to provide food for the flock, defend it from beasts of prey, prevent as far as he can any of the flock from wandering; and if any should wander do his best to restore them. This might be a task of no small difficulty to the literal shepherd of the literal sheep. It required courage, watchfulness, patience, promptitude, and above all, fidelity. And yet even a shepherd enriched by these virtues might have many losses and failures. God knew, indeed, that for kings and persons in authority to guide those under them was a task more arduous far than that of shepherding sheep; and it was not mere failure that he complained of. He complained because there had been no serious attempt to attain success. The very men who should have ruled firmly and righteously and with fidelity to Jehovah had been spoilers of the sheep, using them to serve their own ends, and leaving every one to do what was right in his own eyes. The rulers had thus rejected the authority and service of Jehovah and set up self in his place. Self was to rule, self was to be served. The sentence upon this traitorous conduct is given in very general terms, but was none the less real and effective. God did visit on these rulers the evil of their doings. It was necessary to give a hint of this in passing, to show that, while God delights in mercy, he must also always be just. The great matter to be spoken of here is the restoring and securing of the scattered flock, and if the judgment on those who have helped to make the mischief is simply mentioned in passing, it is enough. Besides, we must remember that the sheep also had their share of the shame. The rulers could not have done so much harm if under them there had been a people of a widely different spirit.

II. THE RESTORATION OF THE SCATTERED. The pastors are spoken of as those who have destroyed and scattered the sheep. The mischief they do is therefore not confined to a simple scattering. That which is destroyed cannot be restored. But the part that has been scattered, God has in his keeping; and in due time he will bring it together again. Note how Jehovah, who announces punishment to the unfaithful shepherds because they have scattered and dispersed his flock, goes on to say that his own hand has been concerned in this same dispersion. Here is a beautiful illustration of how God overrules calamities. Though it is the recklessness of evil men that has scattered Israel, yet the good hand of God is stronger than any hand of man; and the dispersion has been into such directions as God saw to be best. Though these remnants of the flock were far from their proper pasturage, they were nevertheless in safe places, where they would be exercised in a truly profitable discipline. They were perhaps but a very feeble remnant as man counts feebleness, and yet in God's hands a small part may be more effectual for his purposes than the incongruous whole from which it has been separated.

There may be in it a peculiar coherency and submissiveness, and a peculiar energy of growth; so that the promise of fruitfulness and increase will be amply fulfilled. The Divine course of action with this remnant seems to be much the same as that followed with Noah and his family in the repeopling of the world after the Deluge.

III. THE SUFFICIENCY OF PASTORAL OVERSIGHT PROMISED FOR THE FUTURE. Of bad shepherds there have been only too many, and of good shepherds none have been so good but what they might have been a great deal better. The cause of all these bitter experiences has, however, lain with the people themselves. Wanting to be like nations round about, they desired kings; and God gave them these desires to the full, to show what the end would be. Then when the folly of the sheep, in trying to choose shepherds of their own devising, has been illustrated sufficiently, God sends shepherds who shall be true shepherds. He alone is able, as he alone has right, to appoint such shepherds as will be equal to all the serious charge put into their hands. No pastors will be able to do anything for God's flock save those who are indubitably of God's appointment. Our wisdom is to allow God to provide out of his knowledge, rather than try ourselves to provide, seeing how ignorant we are. The acceptance of God's true teachers and guides has to come at the last, and many disappointments and vexations would be spared if this acceptance were allowed to come at the first.—Y.

Vers. 5, 6.—*The righteous Scion of David.* What is general in vers. 3 and 4 now becomes exceedingly definite. Attention is directed to one particular person in whom shall centre all the blessings that can come through a king worthy of the name. The days are coming in which he will rule in the midst of a kingdom worthy of him. Jehovah sees these days coming as a watchman might observe people approaching in the far distance and moving steadily in the right direction. These days are on the way, and the actual experience of them is only a matter of time. In these days will appear—

I. A SCION OF DAVID. "Branch" is a somewhat misleading word here, especially considering the use which is made of the branch in the New Testament. The branch is properly taken in relation to the trunk, both being parts of a living whole. "I am the Vine, ye are the branches." Instead of the Christ being spoken of as a Branch from David, David is rather to be spoken of, by virtue of his faith in the coming One, as a branch of the Christ. The real meaning, of course, is that, at some time in the future, one of the lineal descendants of David will fulfil these purposes of God and the consequent hopes of devout men. Hence the importance which belongs to the genealogies in Matthew and Luke. The more the Gospels are looked into, the more it will be seen how they are constructed on certain lines indicated in the prophecies. The two Gospel genealogies become additionally credible when we reflect what a motive there was to preserve the record of lineal succession from David. Considering how uncertain it is that any man will have lineal descendants centuries after his own times, it is a peculiarly noticeable miracle that he who appeared something like a thousand years after David to do such great works, should have been unquestionably David's descendant, born at Bethlehem and named as Son of David by the common people.

II. A RIGHTEOUS SCION OF DAVID. In a not unreasonable sense of the word, David was himself a righteous man. We cannot say anything for him, any more than for ourselves, if we contrast him with the righteous God. But we have also to look at him over against the vile men with whom he was so often in conflict, men who appear not to have had one generous feeling or upward aspiration. Especially we must contrast him with some of his own descendants. When we look down the line as far as history gives the opportunity, we see first good men and then bad men. And it is a great mystery in the Christ's human nature that he should have been a Scion of the bad as well as the good in this line. We are, therefore, obliged to recollect: 1. That David, who was righteous in a modified sense, was in due time followed by a descendant who was completely righteous. He who was ever reaching forward, trying to approximate more and more to the will of God, was followed by One who revealed that will in all the conduct of his life on earth. 2. That even as a bad father had a good son (or take, as a very striking illustration, the bad grandfather Manasseh and the good grandson Josiah), so all these bad kings had in due time a successor in Jesus of Nazareth, who was undefiled by any taint that might reasonably be supposed to have come down from them. As we think of the contrasts thus furnished, the use of all these deplorable records in the Books of Kings and Chronicles comes manifestly out. The mischief and misery which wicked kings can work must be seen in all their hideousness, so that all the more a disposition may be excited to attend to the blessings which Jesus will secure and multiply when he comes to reign as King.

III. THE PROSPERITY OF THIS RIGHTEOUS KING. It must be made clear in some great and everlastingly conspicuous instance that practical righteousness is followed by prosperity, and that nowhere is the connection more sure between a cause allowed fully to operate and its full effect. The most hurtful kind of wickedness, the men who commit it do not delight in for its own sake. Their aim is outward prosperity, to secure riches in the easiest and most rapid way ; and this may necessitate a degree of wickedness of which oftentimes they seem not in the least conscious. Then, of course, in the end the prosperity proves corrupt and ruins the man who risked everything for it. But now turn to the individual experience of Jesus. His course in this world had nothing in it of prosperity as some count prosperity. He lived in poverty; he did not live long; and he died as criminals die. All these experiences, however, only bring out the real prosperity. After the cross the manifestation of his glory and power began in the acceptance of him by hearts that he had completely subdued. There never has been such a king as Jesus of Nazareth ; never any one who has elicited such whole-hearted homage, such complete, faithful, self-denying service. He prospers and he makes his servants prosper. The more his glory shines, the more their lives are brightened. This surely is indeed a royal prosperity.

IV. THE PROSPERITY OF THE PEOPLE IS INDICATED : 1. By the king's own action in judgment and righteousness, or, as we might otherwise put it, in righteous judgment. As one in authority and power, he has to give decisions, and these decisions are always righteous. Human kings were arbitrary and capricious; their likes and dislikes, their political necessities, had much to do with the decisions they gave. But with this righteous Scion of David it is very different. He lays down great principles which, if men would only attend to them and take in the spirit of them, would stop all disputings and litigations. 2. By the security of the people. The subjects of Jesus have true safety. They are safe in themselves and safe in their spiritual possessions. He who enables them to acquire the true riches shows also how to hold them fast ; else the riches would not be true riches at all. And it is not the least boon that he gives them the power, if only they have faith to exercise it, of living without anxiety and distraction. It is very dishonouring to our great King not to believe that all our best interests are perfectly safe in his charge.—Y.

Ver. 14.—*Prophets strengthening the hands of evil-doers.* Jeremiah had much to say at different times on the unfaithfulness of the prophets—how flatly opposed they were in all their conduct to that required by the duties of their office, how utterly negligent they were of the great opportunities of rebuke which were peculiarly their own. And there stands in this verse an expression which gives a climax to their evil-doings. A prophet shows himself most of all an evil-doer when he upholds the hands of evil-doers.

I. THE PROPHET IS REQUIRED IN A SPECIAL MANNER TO DO WHAT HE CAN TO WEAKEN THE HANDS OF EVIL-DOERS. All who respect the will of God, and feel sympathy with what is right and true and Divine, are bound to hinder bad men in their actions; but he who held the office of a prophet among the people of God was looked to as speaking with an authority higher than that of a private person. Officialism, with all its drawbacks and perils, with all its risk of self-assertion, has been of great advantage to practical religion. It is true, on the one hand, that to put a bad man into a holy office is to bring that office into contempt, but surely it is also true, on the other hand, that a good man in a holy office has his power for good much increased. Here in Israel at this time there was a multitude of evil-doers, doing evil with both hands earnestly. At the same time, there were doubtless those who did evil with weak and uncertain hands. It is matter of thankfulness that evil-doers are so often practically restrained in this way. Disposition is willing, but resolution is weak. There is the desire to do very bad things, but the courage is lacking. We have an instance of this in those enemies of our Lord who were so often hindered in their designs because they feared the people. If all the evil could be done that is desired to be done, society would become intolerable. Now, the peculiar mischief that these prophets did was in strengthening the hands of wicked men who were also weak. They spoke encouragingly, and perhaps drew them on by example. Hence evil was done *openly* that otherwise might have been done *secretly*. Conspiracies and alliances became more practicable. Evil was made to put on the aspect of good, and men did energetically with perverted consciences what otherwise they might have done with much hesitation, and therefore with diminished force. There are certain men always to whom evil-doing becomes easy when it becomes respectable. Thus we see how great were the responsibilities and opportunities of the old Hebrew prophets.

II. Hence we see something of what A DUTY AND OPPORTUNITY BELONG TO ALL CHRISTIAN PEOPLE. Are not all the Lord's people prophets, if only they choose to regard their opportunities? With regard to evil men, it is especially laid on us to hinder *their action* by all wise and rightful means. The formation of their designs we cannot hinder; we cannot see beneath the surface, and prevent the germination of the poisonous growth; but when it appears above the surface, we may do our best to pluck it out. Under the specious guise of love for individual liberty we may tolerate the greatest evils till they grow beyond our control. The man who took a tiger's cub for a pet found it become perilous long before he expected. We should do all we can to strengthen those who are the modern equivalents to the Hebrew prophets. Such men appear from time to time, and we should pray for insight that we may discern their mission and claims. Such men are sent to weaken, and ultimately to paralyze, the strong hands of the wicked. They are the representatives of great causes; and if through cowardice, self-indulgence, and fear of being thought peculiar, we neglect them, then we may do much harm.

III. THE GREAT IMPORTANCE OF STRENGTHENING THE HANDS OF ALL WHO WANT TO BE GOOD. They are so often weak in action. "The spirit is willing, but the flesh is weak." They are hindered by strong temptations which come in their way, when they are striving to get nearer God's ideal for them. They are in need of sympathy. They have to be helped in reaching encouraging views of Divine truth. They need to be remembered in prayer, and generally to have more heart and spirit put into them; then, having abundant life within, they will not lack force, steadiness, and persistency of hand. If we are actively engaged in strengthening the hands of the good, we are to this extent weakening the hands of the evil. And, finally, it is very consoling to recollect that when those who profess to be good are found strengthening the hands of evil-doers, this is precisely the time when God's indignation is aroused and his opposition most effective. "If God be for us, who can be against us?"—Y.

Ver. 16.—*Speaking the vision of one's own heart.* Observe—

I. THERE IS THE PUTTING OF ONE'S OWN IMAGINATION IN THE PLACE OF GOD'S TRUTH. A prophet, divinely sent, expresses the words which God has put into his mouth, or reports the vision which God has made to rise before him. If, then, it was true that these prophets, as prophets, were speaking only the vision of their own hearts, it was quite enough to condemn them. It is very possible that they had brought themselves to believe that they were speaking the truth. In the days when prophetic vision was vouchsafed to man nothing was easier than for a heated imagination to see whatever it wanted to see; and then the subject of this vision would persuade himself that the vision was of God. How, then, was a prophet to know that what he had seen was truly of God? The answer is very largely to be found in considering the sense of burden and responsibility which evidently rested on true prophets. About a true prophet there was nothing egotistic, conceited, or impetuous. Generally, too, he had to say things which were painful for a sensitive man to speak, and humiliating for self-willed people to hear; whereas these prophets against whom Jeremiah warns the people managed to say things very agreeable. We read that they proclaimed peace and prosperity to the evil-doer. Now, whatever peculiarity there was in the visions given to the prophets, it is plain that there could be nothing contradictory to God's holiness and his laws, so clearly expressed, for human life. When prophets came with visions contradicting human self-will and human expectations, there was in this a presumption that they were sent of God. David desired to build a house for God in place of the old tabernacle, and doubtless the desire seemed to be one to which there could be no possible objection. Nathan, however, had a vision by which David was forbidden to build. It would have been pleasanter to go to the king with a message more accordant to his wishes, but he could only speak what God had shown him—a word requiring submission of the human will to a higher and a wiser one. So, turning to the New Testament, we find Ananias at Damascus and Peter at Joppa receiving visions which seemed to them full of incredibility, going right in the face of all their previous experiences and convictions. Furthermore, it must not be forgotten that some, at least, of these lying prophecies were purchased with money. People paid the diviners to hear pleasant things, and pleasant things must be told them even if they were false.

II. THERE WERE EFFECTIVE TESTS FOR THESE VAIN IMAGINATIONS FOR ANY WHO CARED TO EMPLOY THEM. Honest minds know how to receive a true prophet. There is a subtle sympathy between speakers of the right sort and hearers of the right sort. God, who sent so many prophets to Israel, was not likely to leave Israel without a sure way of testing them. So if the prophet or dreamer of dreams gave the people a sign or wonder, and then told them to go *after other gods*, they might thereby know that he was a deceiver. No sign, however specious and wonderful it be, can make that a truth to-day which yesterday was a lie. Every fresh prophet must be in harmony with the tried and approved prophets who have gone before him. There is, indeed, no greater peril than to turn away from any true messenger of God; and happily there is no need to do so, through uncertainty as to his credentials. Any one who points out a present wrong in our lives that needs to be put right immediately, is to that extent a prophet of God; and if, in addition, he ventures on certain predictions, then all we can do is to wait. Gamaliel's shrewd advice cannot be too constantly kept in mind. What we cannot be certain about while a thing is in the seed will be made clear when it comes to the fruit. The most important matters are ever those on which we have to decide at once; and God never fails to send forth his light and truth so as to make the decision right.—Y.

Vers. 23—32.—*The giving forth of the word of man as the word of God.* I. GOD'S UNFAILING OBSERVATION. All the reasonings within the minds of these false prophets are open to God. They themselves, audacious, and to some extent self-deluded, reckon on not being detected. They speak what the people wish to believe, and are thus pretty certain of finding acceptance from them. But they forget, or rather they have never properly understood, the omnipresence of God. If this attribute of God had been a reality to their minds, they would not have come so much under idolatrous influences. The possibility of lying or in any way distorting and manipulating the truth seems to depend on an utter forgetfulness of the fact that God is indeed everywhere, filling all space, so that his eye and ear are everywhere. When we read of God appearing to men in different places, we know that the men travelled from one place to another; but God, even when he appeared to them in the new place, was not a whit the less remaining in the old. That God is everywhere is a truth meant to have a most confirming and cheering influence upon the mind of man; but because this truth is not apprehended man both loses what he was meant to enjoy, and becomes presumptuous and reckless in his practical denial of God's authority. God, therefore, makes his assurance through the true prophet that his eye is upon every movement of the false ones. Those who assure themselves that God is ignorant would be far wiser in reckoning on the ignorance of the most vigilant and penetrating mind among their fellow-men.

II. God's observation being such, THE PROCEEDINGS OF THESE PROPHETS CAN BE EXACTLY KNOWN. What is here said of the false representations of these prophets is given forth, not as the result of human inquiry, but of a divinely perfect observation. Not all that God thus saw was here described, but only such things as the needs of the times demanded to be made known. Far more might have been told that was true, but there was no need to tell it. God does not publish the wickedness of these prophets for any delight that he has in exposing them, but that he may be justified in the sight of the people for the things that he is about to do. In their hearts, the prophets must have known that the thoughts of those hearts were discovered. How important it is to bear in mind that many of the indications as to the wickedness of wicked men in the Scriptures come from him who is the omnipresent and omniscient One, who sees everything exactly as it is, and who puts into the mouth of those speaking his Word just those expressions which will describe the things essential to be known! God published the deeds and character of these false prophets that those who were true to him might guard against them. So Jesus warned his disciples against the time-honoured, time-consecrated pretensions of the Pharisees. God puts into the hearts of those who keep near him a feeling which guards them against all who for their own selfish ends make a pretence of being interested in holy things.

III. There is in this passage a special charge against the prophets, to which the preliminary and more general accusations lead up. The prophets are charged with making a CONFUSION BETWEEN THE HUMAN AND THE DIVINE IN THEIR UTTERANCES. This charge is summed up in the question, "What is the chaff to the wheat?" or, as it is more nearly rendered, "What has the straw to do with the grain?" The straw and the grain, close together as they may be for a while, are separated at last; and one will by no means serve the purpose of the other. Grain is meant for man's support, and straw will not take its place. Straw has its own place, and may be very useful, so long as it is kept in it. But if straw and grain are to be all mixed up together, the result will be very unsatisfactory. We all need to bear in mind this illustration, for we may all have, to some extent, the duty and opportunity of being prophets of God. He is a rare man who can tell forth things exactly as they are. It is not for man, by a plausible eclecticism, to take something of human experience and something of Divine revelation and mix them up into what he trusts may somehow prove acceptable to men. Human experiences and conjectures have their part. When a man honestly tells us what *he* thinks and feels, we know how to estimate his statement; and when he comes professedly with a Divine message we have some notion how to test him. But what shall we do with him who claims to limit and modify Divine revelation, so that it may fit into what he is pleased to call the inexorable moulds of human reason? We must ever make the distinction between the straw and the grain in our search for truth. Some truth is discoverable by observation, experiment, deduction; other truth only by the spiritual intuitions of a devout and humble mind placing itself before the statements of Divine revelation. So with regard to human and Divine government. There is no possibility of acting so as to please both God and men. There is no possibility of building up a perfect society out of such elements as we have at present. On one hand, we have to bear in mind the limitations of society in the actual existence of it. What we make a law to ourselves, in our own individual relations to God, we cannot impose on others. On the other hand, we must not allow the low conceptions which others may have of God's claims to drag us down to their level. Let God's Law stand out distinct and authoritative before our minds to guide us in our individual life. That Law must not be in any way modified, under a notion that compliance with it is impossible of attainment. If we persevere in receiving God's Word and persevere in repeating it, we shall find that it will make its way mightily, not as by brute force, but because it is *the* Word of truth, the Word that has abiding fitness for the deepest needs of men.—Y.

EXPOSITION.

CHAPTER XXIV.

Again Jeremiah's ungrateful task is to take up an attitude of direct opposition to the king (comp. ch. xxii. 13—30), though, indeed, Zedekiah personally is so weak and dependent on others that he neither deserves nor receives a special rebuke. He and all the people that are left are likened to very bad figs, the good figs—the exiles—having been picked out and sent to Babylon, whence they will one day be restored. The vision is purely an interior process. This is indi-cated, not only by the phrase, "Jehovah showed me" (comp. Amos vii. 1, 4, 7; viii. 1), but by the contents of the vision.

Ver. 1.—**Two baskets of figs** were set be-fore, etc. (comp. Amos viii. 1—3). The description is apparently based on the law of firstfruits (comp. Deut. xxvi. 2), where the "basket" is mentioned, though not the word here used. The baskets were set down in readiness to be examined by the priests, who rigorously rejected all fruit that was not sound. **The princes of Judah.** A short phrase for all the leading men, whether members of the royal family or heads of the principal families (comp. ch. xxvii.

20). **The carpenters and smiths;** rather, *the craftsmen and smiths* ("craftsmen" includes workers in stone and metal as well as wood; the Hebrew word is rendered "smith" in 1 Sam. xiii. 19).

Ver. 2.—**Like the figs that are first ripe.** The early spring fig was considered a special delicacy (comp. Isa. xxvii. 4; Hos. ix. 10); "ficus præcox," Pliny calls it ('Hist. Nat.,' xv. 19, quoted by Trench). Tristram suggests that the "bad figs" were those of a sycamore tree.

Ver. 5.—**Acknowledge them;** or, *take knowledge (notice) of them* (as Ruth ii. 10, 19).

Ver. 6.—**I will build them,** etc. (comp. ch. i. 10; xii. 16). As the next verse shows, it is not merely outward prosperity that is meant, but spiritual regeneration.

Ver. 8.—**And as the evil figs.** (So ch. xxix. 16.) **That dwell in the land of Egypt.** Those who had fled thither during the war (comp. ch. xlii., xliii.); hardly those who had been carried captive to Egypt with Jehoahaz, who would presumably have been of the better sort, such as are symbolized by the good figs.

Ver. 9.—**And I will deliver them,** etc. (see on ch. xv. 4, and comp. ch. xxix.; Deut. xxviii. 37).

HOMILETICS.

Vers. 1—10.—*Two baskets of figs.* I. MORALLY MEN ARE DIVISIBLE INTO TWO DISTINCT CLASSES. The two baskets of figs represent two classes of Jews: the basket of good figs, Jeconiah and his followers; the basket of bad figs, Zedekiah and his party. The great distinction between these was moral. There were princes in both classes; yet the one stood far higher in the sight of God than the other. 1. The deepest line of cleavage which runs down through all sections of mankind is *moral;* all other separating marks are more superficial. 2. There are in the main *but two* classes—the good and the bad—though, of course, within each of these great varieties occur. 3. Both of these classes tend to grow *extreme.* The good figs are very good, the bad are very bad. Character is tendency. As character develops it moves further on along the lines on which it is founded. Good men incline to grow better and bad men worse. Like the rivers which flow down the two sides of a great watercourse, lives that begin in similar circumstances and are near together for a season, if they once diverge, are likely to separate more widely as the years pass.

II. THE BEST MEN MAY BE THE GREATEST SUFFERERS. The good figs represent the Jews who suffered most severely from the invasion of Nebuchadnezzar, who were torn from their homes, robbed of their property, driven into captivity; the bad figs represent the seemingly more fortunate Jews over whose head the tide of invasion passes, leaving them still in their homes and in quiet, and also those who escaped from it entirely by a flight into Egypt. We may often notice that very good people are not only not spared, but suffer the most severe calamities. The sinless One was a "man of sorrows, and acquainted with grief." No greater mistake can be made than that of the three friends of Job. Great misfortunes are certainly not indications of great guilt; often of the reverse. 1. High character may *directly invoke trouble.* It rouses the opposition of the wicked; it feels called to dangerous tasks and to a mission which excites enmity; it maintains a fidelity that excludes many avenues of escape which would be open to men of lower moral principles. 2. God *may bless and honour* his better children by sending to them the severer trials. "Whom the Lord loveth he chasteneth." Therefore chastisement is an evidence of God's love. Good men should understand this, and not be surprised at the advent of trouble, but expect it; not be dismayed at the incongruity of it, but recognize its fitness; not despair of themselves, and think that they must be hypocrites after all, nor doubt and distrust God, but submit to what is clearly foretold and wisely arranged.

III. GOD LOOKS FAVOURABLY ON THOSE WHO SUBMIT TO HIS CHASTISEMENTS. The good figs represent those Jews who obey the message of Jeremiah and submit to the invasion of the Chaldeans as to a Divine chastisement; the bad figs stand for those Jews who resist. It requires faith to recognize the wisdom and duty of submission. On the face of it such conduct would appear unpatriotic and cowardly, while resistance would seem noble and brave. It may take more courage, however, to submit than to resist. There is a yielding which is calm and reasonable and really brave, since it involves the curbing of instinctive combativeness and the pursuit of an unpopular course—one sure to be misunderstood and to provoke calumny. The sole guide must be sought in the question of what is right, what is God's will. We are not called to a fatalistic passiveness. There are circumstances in which self-defence or flight may be evidently right. What we are to submit to is not all opposition, all possible trouble, but God's will, the trouble which we know he has sanctioned. All the good fruit of chastisement will be lost if we rebel against it. No greater proof of faith in the goodness of God and loyalty to the majesty of God can be found than a quiet, unmurmuring acceptance of his harder requirements.

IV. THE HARDEST SUFFERING MAY LEAD TO THE HAPPIEST RESULTS. The captives are to be restored. Those Jews who remain in the land are ultimately to be driven forth as "a reproach and a proverb, a taunt and a curse." The short, sharp suffering will end in ultimate good. The temporary escape will be followed by final ruin. 1. God's chastisements are *temporary;* they will give place to lasting blessedness. The present affliction is light just because it endures "but for a moment" (2 Cor. iv. 17). Even if they outlast the present life, what is this brief span of earthly trial compared with the blessedness of an eternity? 2. God's chastisements *work our good.* They directly tend to produce the happier future. The tearful sowing is the cause of the joyful harvest. The spiritual improvement wrought in the soul by the discipline of sorrow is at once a source of future blessedness and a justification for it. "It is good for a man that he bear the yoke in his youth." 3. *A culpable avoidance* of Divine chastisement is *highly dangerous.* The escape from temporary trouble must incur greater future trouble; for (1) it prevents the chastisement from working the good in us which would have led to a happier future, and (2) it adds a new offence of direct rebellion against God which must invoke upon the head of the offender a terrible judgment.

Vers. 6, 7.—*Prosperity restored.* I. AFTER CHASTISEMENT HAS BEEN RIGHTLY RECEIVED, GOD LOOKS FAVOURABLY ON HIS CHILDREN. He sets his "eyes upon them for good." Men shrink from the eyes of God as from a keen and fatal scrutiny. But God is not always looking as the Judge. He beholds his children with love. There is a wonderful tenderness in this gaze, like that of a mother fondly watching over her suffering infant—a deep pity for sorrow, an earnest care to ward off harm, a kindly will to bestow all real good. It is blessed indeed to be so beheld by God. There are men possessed of such great power and influence that some consider a favourable look from them sufficient to make their fortune. What must be the effect of God setting eyes on a man for good?

II. WHEN GOD LOOKS FAVOURABLY ON HIS CHILDREN HE MAY SECURE THEIR TEMPORAL PROSPERITY. This will not always happen, for it will not always be for the real good of men. Still, it does often occur. We are too ready to confine the recognition of God's action in our lives to the sterner sides of it. God sends prosperity as well as adversity. If he banishes, he restores; if he pulls down, he builds up again. And the joy of the restoration and the glory of the latter building exceed those of earlier times. If earthly prosperity comes from God it is real and solid. God can maintain it after he has bestowed it. He will build so that none shall pull down. The man who is innocently enjoying a prosperity sent by God need have no superstitious fears of a jealous Nemesis. He is not secure from trouble; but he has no special ground for apprehending it simply because he is happy at present.

III. WHEN GOD LOOKS FAVOURABLY ON HIS CHILDREN HE WILL CERTAINLY SECURE THEIR SPIRITUAL PROSPERITY. This is seen in a restoration of a true knowledge of God. 1. It is *good for us* to know God. The knowledge of God is here represented not so much as a subject of duty as in the light of a form of spiritual blessedness. The loss of this knowledge leads to the darkness of a godless life. The enjoyment of this knowledge is eternal life (John xvii. 3). 2. A true knowledge of God is the recognition of God *as he is*—quite another thing from our common conception of his nature. Then we see and feel the grandeur, the mystery, the glory of "the eternal." 3. This knowledge of God depends on the condition of our *hearts.* The "heart" represents the whole inner life. When this is rightly disposed we can know God, and only then. What we need, therefore, is not a new revelation, but a change of heart. When our soul is in sympathy with God, when our spiritual vision is open, we can see indications of God's presence and character which would otherwise be obscure. 4. The right condition of heart for knowing God must be *produced by God*.   God promises to give them a heart to know him.   He only can create the heart anew.   The greatest blessing of redemption is that he will do this.

IV. THE WELFARE OF GOD'S CHILDREN IS RESTORED BY THE RESTORATION OF THE CLOSE RELATIONS BETWEEN HIM AND THEM.   "They shall be my people, and I will be their God."   This relation is twofold.   God exercises paternal influences, they engage in filial duties.   1. *God takes them under his care.*   They are his people, to be guarded and blessed by him.   So Christians are God's peculiar people (1 Pet. ii. 9).   2. *They take God for their portion.*   He is their God—theirs to worship, serve, love, rejoice in.

V. THE RESTORATION OF TRUE PROSPERITY DEPENDS ON THE GENUINE RETURN OF GOD'S PEOPLE TO THEIR FIDELITY TO HIM.   The restoration was not a mere compensation for the troubles of the exile.   Happiness does not necessarily follow trouble.   The father runs to meet the prodigal son when he returns, but cannot regard him favourably before this.   1. This return must be with *the heart*.   Repentance, of all acts, must be genuine and heartfelt.   A formal acknowledgment of God without a change of heart is a mockery and an insult to him, which can bring us no good.   2. This return must be with the *whole* heart.   A partial return to God is no true return.   He claims the whole heart or none of it.

Ver. 10.—*Sword, famine, and pestilence.*   I. TROUBLE BEGETS TROUBLE.   War devastating the fields, checking industry, robbing stores, etc., leads to famine; famine and war create horrible causes of pestilence.   Trouble does not tend to relieve itself, but the reverse.   The poor become poorer, the wretched more miserable.   Hence the need of a salvation outside ourselves.

II. TROUBLE IS CUMULATIVE.   The full force is not often felt at first.   One by one the blows fell upon Job.   Thus each is felt most acutely.   Though we can bear present calamities unaided, we still need a refuge for the future.

III. TROUBLE IS VARIOUS IN FORM—sword, famine, pestilence.   If we are not touched by one kind of trouble, we may fall under another.   Of what avail is it to escape the sword, only to perish of the pangs of hunger or to fall a victim to the ravages of pestilence?   Future punishment will probably be various in kind, yet so adapted to all varieties of character and condition that none of the impenitent will be able to escape.

IV. TROUBLE MUST BE CONQUERED BY REDEMPTION, NOT EVADED BY FLIGHT.   We may flee from some trouble, but cannot from all.   When this is judicial it is searching and penetrating, so that none can elude it.   It is vain to rest in the assurance that we have been able to devise means for resisting many troubles.   The army of them is so vast that no victory over scattered detachments can affect our ultimate condition. This fact should not induce despair, but urge us to turn to the full deliverance of Christ's redemption (Rom. viii. 1).

HOMILIES BY VARIOUS AUTHORS.

Vers. 1—10.—*The two baskets of figs; or, predetermining influences.*   These are not to be understood of the opposite development of character in two sets of persons in slightly differing circumstances, but rather of the primary influence of Divine faith as contrasted with the want of it amidst the trials of life.   The people left behind were disposed to felicitate themselves over their brethren who had been carried off into Chaldea, but this impression is corrected by Jeremiah.   The exiles were the true people of God, and were to be under his constant supervision and loving care; the others were to be cast off, to become a prey to inner corruption and the unchecked destructive influences of the world.

I. THE MYSTERY OF THE DIVINE ELECTION.   From comparatively similar circumstances to evolve distinct types of character and destiny.   Out of the same clay to mould the saint and the sinner.   It is the old lesson of the potter in another form.   There is nothing in a man himself to account for God's favour.   He chooseth whom he will and rejecteth whom he will.   Yet is it true that he willeth not the death of a sinner, but rather that all should come unto him and live.

II. THE MANNER IN WHICH ELECTIVE GRACE MANIFESTS ITSELF.   1. *Recalling.* (Ver.

6.) How unlikely under the circumstances! Yet rendered credible by the remarkable individuality of the Jewish people from age to age. *Reconstituting.* (Ver. 6.) The figure is twofold—building and life-growth (cf. Eph. ii. 21, 22). *Spiritually recreating.* (Ver. 7.) The aim of the previous discipline; but the beginning of great national glory and blessedness. For connection of these processes, cf. Rom. viii. 28—30. 2. *Circumstances are made to subserve a merciful purpose.* The immediate condition of the Chaldean exiles might appear a harder one than that of their compatriots at home; but in the end this would turn to their salvation. Not only will God overrule all things for the good of his people, but he will use them for their spiritual education. The influence of circumstances is thus shown to depend for the most part upon the spiritual state of those who are surrounded by them. 3. *Circumstances are appointed for the destruction of the obstinately impenitent.* Moral reprobation and political annihilation were to come upon these. There would be no swerving or slackening in the execution of their sentence. This is agreeable with the character of him who hates sin with an eternal hatred. The climax of misery here indicated is but a faint suggestion of that which will follow upon rejection of the gospel. And yet how simple are the elements of such a punishment! God has but to withdraw his grace, and the inner depravity of nature will work unchecked its fearful consequences, accelerating and directing the external circumstances of life. And all this has another aspect, which is full of comfort to those who are spiritually inclined. The faintest dawn of repentance is the opening of the "door of hope;" and when the heart is changed the tendency of untoward circumstance at once is altered, and the positive blessings of God again return.—M.

Vers. 1—10.—*Calamity with God and without him.* I. To THE CHILD OF GRACE. 1. *It is a chastening.* 2. *A restoration.*
II. To THE UNGODLY. 1. *An influence depreciating character.* 2. *A source of restlessness and fresh transgression.* 3. *An ever-increasing evil.* 4. *An ultimate destruction.*—M.

Vers. 1—10.—*Punished for salvation; left alone for destruction.* A general principle of God's moral government. The flower of Judah, about to be deported to Babylon, are followed by the prophet with wistful gaze. They are the seed of the true Israel; whereas those who are allowed to remain quietly at home are to be of no account in God's purpose.
I. How DIFFERENT OFTEN ARE THE EXTERNAL FROM THE SPIRITUAL PROSPECTS OF MEN! Jeconiah and his companions might have been pitied by their friends left behind. The outward position of any one is no index of his relations with God.
II. PRESENT TRIAL MAY BE A PROOF OF DIVINE LOVE, AND PRESENT IMMUNITY FROM MISFORTUNE IS NOT ALWAYS TO BE TAKEN AS AN EVIDENCE OF DIVINE FAVOUR. "Whom the Lord loveth he chasteneth, and scourgeth every son whom he receiveth." Punishment was needed to atone for the past and purify for the future. The exile in Babylon, with its deprivation of political and religious privilege, was a new point of view for the captives. It is a familiar experience to hear men who have done well in the world, or who have had a comparatively smooth life, say, "God has blessed us." This statement is often open to question. God may simply let alone those whom he has given up. The lethargy induced in many by good fortune is to be guarded against. Count them happy that "endure, as seeing him who is invisible." Inward depravity will soon work the destruction of those in whom it remains.
III. THE GLORY OF THE DIVINE IN MAN IS EVOLVED FROM THE HUMILIATION OF THE HUMAN. A mere remnant. How few of those who went forth would return! Children's children might be blessed, but not they themselves. And even then it would require not only reorganization, but rebirth in spirituality. It is ever so. A profound and radical change is needed ere any one can become a member of the true eternal Israel. Israel after the flesh is sentenced to death, that Israel after the Spirit may live for ever.—M.

Ver. 6.—"*I will set mine eyes upon them for good.*" The distressed and afflicted for his sake he ever regards with special attention and interest. "The captives are dearest to God." Banished from Palestine, they are still "*his* banished ones," and he will make them to return. Those who are undergoing severe trials, in circumstances, in faith, etc., but who are truly seeking after God, are to be comforted with this word. It is a promise that has been gloriously fulfilled. It pledges—

I. GOD'S CARE. 1. *Protection.* 2. *Provision,* temporal and spiritual. Although we see him not, he ever sees us and regards us with complacency and love.

II. GOD'S FAVOUR. This indicates interest, but because of something evoking it— the first germs of faith and repentance. When others see them not, he sees the longings of the soul and its efforts after better things ; and he will further them.

III. GOD'S GUIDANCE. Although they were led away into a strange land and amidst an alien people, he would never lose sight of them; but, directing their footsteps, would bring them back again to the land they had left and to himself. It was a strange way, but it was God's way, and his influence would be continually in them and upon them for good. It is the surest proof that God's eye is upon us for good when his Spirit is within us. As many as are led of the Spirit are the children of God.—M.

Ver. 7.—*The conditions and relations of salvation.* I. THE ABILITY TO KNOW GOD IS THE GIFT OF GOD. Not more facts, external, historical, etc., are required. Not a new Bible—the letter of the Bible is probably completed already. Nor even a new mode of spiritual demonstration. But a new heart. We cannot make a new heart. God will save us by renewing : 1. *The moral nature.* 2. *The whole life through it.*

II. THE BLESSINGS OF SALVATION CAN ONLY BE SECURED IN ABSOLUTE CONSECRATION. "They shall return unto me with their whole heart." Complete salvation is impossible without complete faith. To believe—to believe simply, to believe wholly,—this is the condition of perfect salvation.

III. THE IDEAL ISRAEL MUST EVER BE A THEOCRACY. In the obedience of faith they shall be God's people, and he will be their God. That upon which we depend in faith is that which we observe and respect in practice ; it is the law and inspiration of life. Christ leads us to the Father that he and we may be one in God ; not merged, confounded with Deity, but in eternal and ever-blessed subordination to him.—M.

Vers. 1—10.—*The two baskets of figs ; or, our character and destiny independent of our circumstances.* I. THE SYMBOLS EMPLOYED. The two baskets of figs—one very good, the other very evil. But : 1. *They had each the same advantages and disadvantages.* The same seed, soil, training, climate, sunshine, and other influences teeming on them. 2. *They were of directly opposite character.* (Ver. 2.)

II. THE PEOPLE REPRESENTED BY THEM. The men of Judah and Jerusalem. Now : 1. The circumstances of all these were the same. Parentage, religion, teachers, disciplines, privileges, opportunities. 2. But some of these people were symbolized by the good figs, and the other by the evil. Those who had been carried off to Babylon were the good ; those who remained still in Jerusalem were the evil. 3. The reverse results might have been looked for. For the good had been dealt with more sternly than the evil. How terrible and sad their lot appeared ! Torn away from all their wonted privileges ; made to endure a fate which others deserved far more than they ; surrounded with idolaters and blasphemers of God. But the evil continued in the possession of all those aids to religion and piety of which those others were deprived. So that the circumstances of the good were less favourable, and those of the evil far more so. Exile, which might have been thought to injure the captives, had done them good ; whilst exemption from it, which might have been thought to benefit the evil, had wrought them harm. "With the exiles were some of the choicest spirits of the nation. Ezekiel, second only to Jeremiah himself in the prophets of this epoch ; and, probably, the ancestor of Mordecai ; and Daniel, with his three companions." "The exiles became humble, repentant, reformed. The resident Jews became insolent, self-secure, defiant. The former became worthy of comparison with 'the first ripe figs ;' the latter as the 'naughty figs, which could not be eaten.'"

III. THE LESSONS TAUGHT THEREBY. *That character and destiny do not depend on circumstances.* We should have thought that either all would be alike, or else that the characters and destinies would have been the reverse of what they were. 1. Let the good who may be placed in adverse circumstances take encouragement from this fact. They can surmount and triumph over all the evil influences which surround and oppose them (cf. ver. 7.) 2. And the evil are to take warning. Prolonged privilege and opportunity have no necessary saving power. Such advantages *may* leave them worse than before. It was so here.

IV. OBSERVE THE GREAT ILLUSTRATION OF THE TRUTH TAUGHT HERE IN CHRIST AND HIS CHURCH. 1. Christ was "as a root out of a dry ground." How utterly opposed to all prospect of his becoming great, and his Name above every name, were the early circumstances in his history! And yet he has triumphed over all. 2. And so with the history of the Church. It was small as "a grain of mustard seed," feeble as "sheep amidst wolves," was as a thing of nought and despised. And yet what has it not become, what will it not become? And what is true of Christ and his Church shall be true likewise of all that are his. "Fear not, little flock," said our Lord; "it is the Father's good pleasure to give *you* the kingdom."—C.

Ver. 7.—*A heart to know the Lord.* It was "for good" that God sent the captive portion of his people "into the land of the Chaldeans" (ver. 5.) The germs of the better life of the future were preserved in them, and their very tribulations were the instruments of his gracious purpose and blessings in disguise. In the "evil figs"—the refuse left behind—there was nothing worth preserving (ver. 8). Of all the beneficent Divine purposes, this had in it the promise of highest good—"I will give them an heart to know me, that I am the Lord."

I. A TRUE KNOWLEDGE OF GOD HAS ITS SEAT IN THE HEART. Intellect cannot solve the mystery of his being. Reason alone cannot even demonstrate his existence. "Who by searching can find out God?" "The world by wisdom knew not God." It is a matter of pure spiritual sensibility. Moral sympathy is the true key to this knowledge. Reverence, humility, love, trust, submission, affections of the heart, are its conditions. Even right ideas of God depend very materially on the state of the heart towards him. The exhalations of a vain, frivolous, corrupt, or carnal heart pervert the soul's vision and obscure his glory. Only as our hearts are purged from every form of earthly defilement can we behold him as he is. "Blessed are the pure in heart: for they shall see God."

II. GOD HIMSELF CAN ALONE IMPART THIS KNOWLEDGE. "I will give them," etc. It is a matter of direct Divine revelation; a Divine science in which mere human teaching is of little avail. A secret, silent, gracious power above all natural influences can alone awaken in us those moral affections which lie at the root of it. A true knowledge, like a true Christian faith, must stand "not in the wisdom of men, but in the power of God." The blindness of the man of science to the deeper meaning of nature, and of the sceptical philosopher to the manifestation of God in Christ, and of the worldling to the Divine presence in his own life, does but indicate the lack of this power. God must unveil himself to us, by drawing our hearts into lowly and loving fellowship with himself, before we can truly know him.—W.

Vers. 1—10.—*The good and bad figs.* I. CONSIDER THE FIGS GENERALLY. We cannot, of course, say why figs should be chosen rather than another fruit, though the choice can hardly be a mere accident. Some reason probably appeared to the observant of that time which we are without sufficient information to discover. Possibly the goodness of good fruits was more obvious against the badness of bad ones, in the case of the fig than in the case of other fruits. It is to be noticed also that the figure chosen to set forth the difference between the good and the bad in Israel is *taken from fruit*. It was something presented as the result of growth and in connection with culture. The question was suggested how such a difference should come between the good and the bad. For if trees of the same sort grow in the same soil and have the same attention, and the same external influences, how comes some of the fruit to be very good and some very bad? Notice also *the sharpness of the distinction.* These fruits were either good or bad. To be excluded from one is to be included in the other. There is no third, no medium class. This exactly agrees with the way of speaking in the New Testament, especially by Jesus himself: *e.g.* the seed in the good and bad ground, the sheep and goats, the good kinds of fish and the bad ones, the five wise and the five foolish virgins. It is of the first importance to bear in mind that the imperceptible gradations, as we reckon them, count for nothing with God. There are only two kinds of hearts, the good and the bad.

II. CONSIDER THE BLESSINGS ON THAT CLASS IN ISRAEL SET FORTH BY THE GOOD FIGS. Painful external experiences cannot destroy the blessing coming from satisfactory internal character. These people represented by the good figs might say, "If we are indeed as good figs, why make us pass through such pains?" To this it might be answered, in the first place, that it was because of this very goodness that God thus treated them. They were being pruned and cleansed that they might bring forth more fruit. Secondly, when they looked on the fate of those represented by the bad figs, even captivity in a distant land would be seen as a blessing. God bends every word that he here speaks through his prophet so as to form a total of strong consolation and hope. 1. Though these people are called captives of Judah, yet this is only the conventional mode of description. In reality, Jehovah himself sends them into the land of the Chaldeans. So Joseph was made to feel that it was God who had brought him into Egypt. 2. God's eye is upon his people for good. That which God sees to be good he always regards for good. Whosoever has, to him is given more. Note, too, that the people were not merely remembered, as if God had stayed behind in the land of Israel. He was equally in Israel watching over it against the day of his people's return, and in the land of the Chaldeans watching over his faithful ones there. 3. There is to be in due time a restoration. He who sends away can also bring back. The external circumstances of his people are completely under his control. He was speaking to those in whose history was written down all the marvellous things of the Exodus from Egypt. 4. There is to be a Divine building and planting. What others had built God had pulled down, what others had planted he had uprooted. Every plant not of the heavenly Father's planting must be rooted up. All this was done, not for any delight God took in the ruin and the wilderness, but that a nation might be built up in righteousness, and bring forth only good fruit. 5. The giving of a true knowledge of God. God must give this knowledge, for it can only come to a renewed heart. The mere exhibition of God's name and person to the natural man is not enough. There may be very elaborate intellectual conceptions of Deity without the slightest profit or comfort. When the renewed heart begins to know, then God begins to be truly known. His love must not only be set before us, but must be shed abroad in our hearts by the Holy Spirit given to us.

III. THE CURSE ON THOSE SET FORTH BY THE BAD FIGS. There is the greatest possible contrast between the treatment of good fruit and bad fruit. And so there was the greatest possible contrast between the treatment of the people taken to Babylon and the treatment of those remaining at home and nearer home. Upon the surface and at the first aspect it might seem as if these latter had the best of it. And, indeed, there might be no immediate way of making clear the difference. But a difference there assuredly was, and every succeeding year would manifest and emphasize it the more. In the mean time here stood the contrast between the good and bad figs, which would be quite enough for the eye of faith. How the history of the Jewish people justifies the bitter words of vers. 9 and 10! Again and again the Gentile has treated the Jew according to the words of this prophecy, and found in them and similar words a justification of his treatment. Not, of course, that the prophecy did really justify the treatment, but God could speak beforehand of the way in which human passions would assuredly work.—Y.

EXPOSITION.

CHAPTER XXV.

This chapter may be illustrated by a comparison of it with ch. xlvi. There Jeremiah exults over the destruction of a nation (Egypt) which was one of the chief enemies of God's people, and on hearing or reading the inspired eloquence of the prophet the heart of a Jew could not but be moved with the liveliest sympathy. But it is another strain which meets us in this chapter, and one which to a Jew would certainly neutralize the favourable feelings which prophecies like that referred to must have awakened. Here Jeremiah announces that the last moment of grace for Judah is past, and the time for judgment come. The long-suffering of Jehovah has been exhausted; the fall of the commonwealth cannot any longer be delayed. Such was the strange destiny of the prophet; he was sent to "pull down" and "to build," but the destructive element (as ch. i. 10 suggests) was largely predominant. Specially predominant is it in this important chapter, in which the prophet begins to fulfil the mission to the heathen with which twenty-three years ago he had been entrusted. One by one, "all the nations" directly or indirectly connected with Israel are called up to hear their punishment. There is no indulgence, no respite ; only a gleam of hope in the promised final destruction of the tyrant-city Babylon (vers. 12—14). The prophecy falls naturally into three parts, vers. 15—29 forming the centre. The date assigned to this chapter in the first verse is remarkable : it is the fatal year of the battle of Carchemish, which brought Syria and Palestine within the grasp of Babylon.

Ver. 1.—**The first year of Nebuchadrezzar** (comp. 2 Kings xxiv. 12; xxv. 8; ch. lii. 12; xxxii. 1).

Ver. 3.—**From the thirteenth year**; etc. ; alluding to the chronological statement in ch. i. 2. **The three and twentieth year;** counting nineteen years under Josiah and four under Jehoiachin, and including the three months of Jehoahaz.

Vers. 4, 5.—(Comp. ch. vii. 25 ; xi. 7; xxxv. 15.) **They said**; literally, *saying*. The prophet mentally resumes the statement of ver. 4, "He hath sent his servants the prophets." **Turn ye**; rather, *return ye*, conversion being the return of the sinner to his natural home.

Ver. 9.—**The families of the north** (comp. ch. i. 15, note). **And Nebuchadrezzar the king of Babylon, my servant.** This is the rendering of the Targum, the Syriac, and the Vulgate, and corresponds with the reading of a few extant manuscripts. The received text, however, reads, "and unto Nebuchadrezzar," etc. Neither reading is satisfactory. The latter one is intolerably harsh ; the former makes Nebuchadrezzar a mere adjunct of the tribes of the north. In the other passages, moreover, where this king is solemnly entitled "my servant," the clause is the most prominent one in the sentence (see ch. xxvii. 6; xliii. 10). The words in question have a sort of family resemblance to the glosses which meet us occasionally both in the form of the Hebrew text represented by the Massoretic recension, and those by the principal ancient versions. The

words are omitted by the Septuagint. **My servant.** Generally to be a "servant" of Jehovah or of any supposed deity is to be a worshipper. Thus Daniel is called by Darius, "servant of the living God" (Dan. vi. 20), and thus Abdallah, "servant of Allah," has become a favourite surname of the followers of Mohammed. In the Book of Jeremiah itself (xxx. 10; xlvi. 27, 28), and in Ezekiel (xxxvii. 25), "my servant" is the form in which Jehovah addresses his chosen people ; and in the second part of Isaiah the suffering Messiah is so styled. Here, however, a foreign king is thus entitled. How is this to be explained? Cyrus, no doubt, in Isa. xliv. 28, xlv. 1, is called " my shepherd" and "my anointed one;" but then Cyrus, in the view of the prophet, was a genuine though unconscious worshipper of the true God (Isa. xli. 25), whereas Nebuchadrezzar was known to be a polytheist and an idolater. We must, therefore, take "servant" to be applied to Nebuchadrezzar in a lower sense than to the other bearers of the title. The Hebrew '*ebhed*, in fact, may be either "slave" in something approaching to the terrible modern sense, or in the sense in which Eliezer was one (*i.e.* little less than a son, and a possible heir, Gen. xxiv. 2 ; Gal. iv. 1), and which is still in full force in Arabia. **An astonishment** (see on ch. ii. 11). **An hissing** (comp. ch. xviii. 16; xix. 8).

Ver. 10.—**The sound of the millstones.** Modern travel enables us (so conservative is the East) to realize the full force of this image. The hand-mill is composed of two stones. As a rule, "two women (comp. Matt. xxiv. 41) sit at it facing each other; both have hold of the handle by which the upper is turned round on the ' nether' millstone. The one whose right hand is disengaged throws in the grain as occasion requires, through the hole in the upper stone" (Dr. Thomson). "The labour," remarks Dr. Robinson, "is evidently hard ; and the grating sound of the mill is heard at a distance, indicating (like our coffee-mills) the presence of a family and of household life" ('Biblical Researches,' ii. 181). Add to this **the light of** the **candle** (or rather, *lamp*), and we have two of the most universally characteristic signs of domestic life. No family could dispense with the hand-mill, and, as the sermon on the mount implies, the poorest household had its "lamp" (Matt. v. 15—the poverty of the family is indicated by the various uses to which the lamp-stand was applied). Comp. this verse with the imitation in Rev. xviii. 22, 23.

Ver. 11.—**Shall serve the king of Babylon seventy years.** Widely different opinions are held as to the meaning of this prophecy. The most probable view is that "seventy"

is an indefinite or round number (as in Isa.
xxiii. 17), equivalent to "a very long time."
This is supported by the analogy of ch. xxvii.
7, where the captivity is announced as lasting through the reigns of Nebuchadrezzar,
his son, and his grandson—a statement evidently vague and indefinite (see *ad loc.*),
and in any case not answering to a period of
seventy years. Besides, we find the " seventy
years " again in ch. xxix. 10, a passage
written probably eleven years later. Others
think the number is to be taken literally,
and it is certainly true that from B.C. 606,
the fourth year of Jehoiakim, to the fall of
Babylon, B.C. 539, sixty-seven years elapsed.
But is it desirable to press this against the
internal evidence that Jeremiah himself
took the number indefinitely ?

Vers. 12—29.—The judgment upon Judah
and the nations.

Ver. 12.—**Perpetual desolations.** Thus, too,
we read in Isa. xiii. 20, that Babylon "shall
never be inhabited." There is a dispute
between Dr. Keith and Dr. Kay on the one
side, and rationalistic commentators (*e.g.*
Kuenen) on the other, whether these prophecies have received a circumstantial fulfilment. The truth is that authorities are not
entirely agreed on the area covered by the
site of Babylon. General Chesney remarks
that, so far from being uninhabited, "A town
of considerable population, villages, date
groves, and gardens, are found still on the
very site of ancient Babylon " (extracts from
a private letter in B. W. Newton's ' Babylon : its Revival and Final Desolation,' pp.
38—42). Similarly M. Menant, a veteran
French Assyriologist, remarks that " Hillah,
according to M. Oppert, was a quarter of
Babylon, probably that which was inhabited
by the working population, without the precincts of the royal palaces. Numberless traces
of ancient habitations indicate this origin of
the modern town " (' Babylone,' p. 177). Mr.
George Smith, however, in his ' Assyrian
Discoveries,' simply states that, " A little
to the south rose the town of Hillah," apparently assuming (what is impossible to
prove, as the walls of Babylon have not
yet been discovered) that Hillah lay just
outside the city enclosure. But even he adds
that it was " built with the bricks found in
the old capital," which is, strictly speaking,
inconsistent with the absolute abandonment
of the site of Babylon implied in Isa. xiii.
20—22. The dispute is an unfortunate one,
as it tacitly implies that circumstantial fulfilments are necessary to the veracity of
prophecy. The truth seems to lie in the
mean between two opposing views. As a
rule, the details of a prophetic description
cannot be pressed ; they are mainly imaginative elaborations of a great central truth or
fact. Occasionally, however, regarding the

prophecies in the light of gospel times, it
is almost impossible not to observe that
"the Spirit of Christ which was in " the
prophets (1 Pet. i. 11) has overruled their
expressions, so that they correspond more
closely to facts than could have been reasonably anticipated. Such superabundant
favours to believers in inspiration occur repeatedly in the prophecies respecting Christ.
They may, of course, occur elsewhere for a
sufficient reason, but we have no right to be
surprised if we do not meet with them. The
general truth of the prophecy is that the
empire of Babylon shall fall for ever. As
Dr. Payne Smith remarks, it was practically
the work of one man (Nebuchadrezzar), and
after his death it only lasted for a few years,
during which its history is a series of murders and usurpations.

Ver. 13.—**And I will bring,** etc. Clearly
this verse cannot have formed part of the
original prophecy, but must have been added
whenever the collection of prophecies against
foreign nations finally assumed its present
form (see introduction on ch. l., li.). It
should be mentioned that the Septuagint
separates the last clause of the verse, "that
which Jeremiah prophesied," etc., and makes
it the heading of the group of prophecies
against the nations, which in the Hebrew
Bible stand at the end of Jeremiah's prophecies, but which, beginning with "Elam,"
the Alexandrian Version inserts at this
point.

Ver. 14.—**For many nations . . . shall
serve themselves of them also ;** *i.e.* put
forced labour upon them also. The same
phrase is used of the conduct of the
Egyptians to the Israelites (Exod. i. 14).
Of them also ; and "also" suggests that
the calamity of the Chaldeans is a retribution (comp. Isa. lxvi. 4), as the next
clause, in harmony with ch. l. 29, li. 24,
emphatically declares.

Ver. 15.—**For thus saith,** etc. Out of
this verse and the following, to the end of
the chapter, the Septuagint makes the
thirty-second chapter, ch. xxv. being completed by the prophecy against Elam (ch.
xlix. 34—39). The symbolic act which the
prophet is directed to perform is mentioned
in order to explain the word of threatening
just uttered. So, at least, we must understand it, if we accept the arrangement of
the Hebrew text. But the connection is
certainly improved if we follow Graf, and
omit vers. 11 *b*—14 ; ver. 15 thus becomes
an explanation of the threat against Judah
and the other nations in vers. 9—11 *a*.
The wine-cup of this fury ; or, *this wine-cup
of fury.* The wine with which the cup
is filled is the wrath of God. The figure
is not an unfrequent one with the prophets
and the psalmists (comp. ch. xlix. 12 ; li. 7 ;

Isa. li. 17, 22; Ezek. xxiii. 31—34; Hab. ii. 16; Ps. lx. 3; lxxv. 8).

Ver. 16.—**And be moved, and be mad;** rather, *and reel to and fro, and behave themselves madly.* The inspired writers do not scruple to ascribe all phenomena, the "bad" as well as the "good," to a Divine operation. "Shall there be evil in a city, and Jehovah hath not done it?" (Amos iii. 6). "An evil spirit from Elohim came upon Saul, and he became frenzied" (1 Sam. xviii. 10; see also Isa. xix. 14; xxix. 10; 1 Kings xxii. 19—23, and especially the very remarkable prologue of the Book of Job). To understand this form of expression, we must remember the strength of the reaction experienced by the prophets against the polytheism of the surrounding nations. It was not open to them to account for the existence of evil by ascribing it to the activity of various divinities; they knew Jehovah to be the sole cause in the universe. To us, "sicklied o'er with the pale cast of thought," such a doctrine occasions "great searchings of heart," and is sometimes a sore trial of our faith. But the prophets were not logicians, and their faith, compared to ours, was as an oak tree to a sapling; hence they can generally (see, however, Isa. lxiii. 17) express the truth of the universal causation of Jehovah with perfect tranquillity. **Because of the sword.** Here Jeremiah deserts the figure of the cup, and, as most commentators think, uses the language of fact. It is not, however, certain that "the sword" means that of God's human instruments; Jehovah himself has a sword (ch. xlvi. 10; xlvii. 6; l. 35—38; Isa. xxvii. 1; xxxiv. 5; and elsewhere), just as he has a hand (Isa. viii. 11; lix. 1) and an arm (Isa. xl. 10; liii. 1). All these belong to a group of childlike symbolic expressions for the manifestation of the Deity. Jehovah's "sword" is described more fully in Gen. iii. 24; it "turns hither and thither," like the lightning—a striking figure of the completeness with which God performs his work of vengeance (see also on ver. 27).

Ver. 17.—**Then took I the cup . . . and made all the nations to drink.** It is too prosaic to suppose either that Jeremiah made a journey to "all the nations," or that he actually went through the form of presenting the cup to the ambassadors who (it is conjectured, comp. ch. xxvii. 3 b) had come to Jerusalem to take measures against the common foe (so J. D. Michaelis). But the supposition arises (as Keil has well observed) out of an imperfect comprehension of the figure. It is not a cup with wine which the prophet receives from Jehovah, but a wine-cup filled with the wine of God's fury, which wine (one may add) is no more a literal wine than the "sword of Jehovah"

is a literal sword. The "making all the nations to drink" is simply a way of expressing the prophet's firm faith that the word of Jehovah will not "return unto him void"—that a prophecy once uttered must fulfil itself; and "sent me," in the last clause, merely means "entrusted me with a message" (comp. Prov. xxvi. 6). For the fulfilment of this detailed prediction, see on ch. xlvi.—li.

Ver. 18.—**The kings thereof** (see on ch. xix. 3). **As it is this day.** As to the meaning of this phrase, see on ch. xi. 5. The words evidently presuppose that the prediction has already been fulfilled (comp. ch. xliv. 6, 23); consequently, they cannot have stood here in the original draft of the prophecy. An early editor, or even Jeremiah himself, must have inserted them. They are omitted in the Septuagint.

Ver. 19.—**Pharaoh king of Egypt.** After leaving Judah and Jerusalem, the prophet turns to the far south—to Egypt; then he ascends to the south-east (Uz), and the south-west (the Philistines); thence he passes to the east (Edom, Moab, Ammon); and thence to, the west of the Holy Land (Phœnicia). This suggests the maritime lands "beyond the sea" (including especially Cyprus); a sudden transition brings the prophet to the Arabian tribes (Dedan, etc.), from whence he passes by the road of the north-east (Elam, Media) to the indefinitely distant north. Last of all, in solitary grandeur or infamy, Babylon is mentioned.

Ver. 20.—**The mingled people**; Septuagint, καὶ πάντας τοὺς συμμίκτους: Vulgate, *et universos generaliter.* The Hebrew 'erebh probably means, not "*mingled* [*i.e.* 'motley']" people," as the Authorized Version, but "foreign people," *i.e.* a body of men belonging to some particular nation *intermixed* or interspersed among those belonging to another. This explanation will account for the use of the word in all the passages in which it occurs (here and in ver. 24; also Exod. xii. 38; Neh. xiii. 3;[1] 1 Kings x. 15; ch. l. 37; Ezek. xxx. 5; and perhaps 2 Chron. ix. 14). The context here and in 1 Kings x. 15 seems to imply that the name was given especially to the tribes (probably Bedawin tribes) on the frontier of Judah towards the desert, though in Ezek. xxx. 5 it is evidently applied to a people which in some sense belonged to Egypt. In Exod. xii. 38 it may be doubted whether the phrase is used from the point of view of Egypt or of the Israelites; in ch. l. 37 it

---

[1] In Exodus and Nehemiah the word is pointed 'ērebh (with *çere* instead of *seghol*), but no one will think of denying that the word is the same as in Jeremiah, Ezekiel, and 1 Kings.

is used of the foreigners in Babylon in 2 Chron. ix. 14 the Massoretic critics have pointed the consonants of the text wrongly (*'arabh*, Arabia, instead of *'erebh*), but without injury to the sense; the Vulgate and Syriac have done the same in 1 Kings x. 15. The notion that the word means 'auxiliary troops" arises (as Thenius on 1 Kings x. 15 remarks) from the free rendering of the Targum at 1 Kings x. 15 and ch. l. 37. **Uz.** The land associated with the name of Job, and probably east or south-east of Palestine, and adjacent to the Edomites of Mount Seir (Lam. iv. 21). **Of the Philistines.** Observe, Gath is alone omitted of the five Philistine towns (Josh. xiii. 3; 1 Sam. vi. 17). It had been reduced to complete insignificance (Amos vi. 2), through Uzziah's having "broken down" its walls (2 Chron. xxvi. 6), and is equally passed over in Amos (i. 6—8), Zephaniah (ii. 4), and Zechariah (ix. 5, 6). **Azzah;** *i.e.* Gaza, the Septuagint form (the G representing the initial *ayin*), which is everywhere else adopted by the Authorized Version. **The remnant of Ashdod.** A significant phrase, which can be explained from Herodotus (ii. 157): For twenty-nine years Psamnutichus "pressed the siege of Azôtus without intermission." We can imagine that he would not be disposed to lenient dealings with the town upon its capture. (An earlier and shorter siege of Ashdod is mentioned in Isa. xx.)

Ver. 22.—**Kings of Tyrus . . . kings of Zidon.** Under the names of the two leading cities, the prophet includes the various dependent Phœnician commonwealths. Hence the plural "kings." **The isles.** The Hebrew has the singular, "the isle," or rather, "the coast-land" (more strictly, *the region*), *i.e.* perhaps either Tartessus in Spain, or Cyprus (which Esarhaddon describes as "lying in the midst of the sea," and as having two kings, 'Records of the Past,' iii. 108).

Ver. 23.—**Dedan, and Tema, and Buz.** Three tribes of North Arabia, bordering on Edom. The two former are mentioned as commercial peoples in Isa. xxi. 13, 14; Ezek. xxvii. 15, 20; xxxviii. 13; Job vi. 19. Elihu, Job's youngest friend, was of Buz (Job xxxii. 2). **All that are in the utmost corners;** rather, *all the corner-clipped* (see on ch. ix. 26).

Ver. 24.—**All the kings of Arabia.** Not "Arabia" in our sense (which is never found in the Old Testament), but the desert region to the east and south-east of Palestine, occupied by nomad or "Ishmaelitish" tribes. **The mingled people;** rather, *the intermingled people* (see on ver. 20); *i.e.* probably in this passage populations of a different race interspersed among the Aramaic tribes to which most of the inhabitants of the desert belonged.

Ver. 25.—**Zimri.** The Zimri were a people to the north-east of Assyria, against whom various Assyrian kings waged war (*Transactions of the Society of Biblical Archæology,* 1878, pp. 13, 15, 34; 'Records of the Past,' v. 41). Whether they are to be connected with the Zimran of Gen. xxv. 2 seems doubtful; their locality hardly suits. **Elam.** Elam, one of the most ancient monarchies in the world (comp. Gen. xiv.), is again coupled with Media in Isa. xxi. 2. It was a region on the east of the lower Tigris, bounded westward by Babylonia, northward by Assyria and Media, southward by the Persian Gulf. To say that it is put either here or anywhere else in the Old Testament for the whole of Persia seems a mistake, as the Persians were hardly known before the time of Cyrus.

Ver. 26.—**The kings of the north. The** distant, mysterious north. **Far and near, one with another.** The Hebrew has, "the near and the far, the one to the other;" *i.e.* whether near or far in relation to each other, for of course with regard to Judah they were all "the far north." **All the kingdoms of the world,** etc. This is far from being the only instance in which a special judgment upon a nation or nations is apparently identified with a great final judgment upon the world (see Isa. ii. 12; iii. 13; xiii. 9; xxiv. 1—12). The truth is that every great self-manifestation of the Divine Governor of the world is a fresh act in that great drama of which the universal judgment will be the close. Hence the prophets, whose perspective was necessarily limited, seeing the end but not all that was to precede it, speak as if the end were nearer at hand than it really was. **The king of Sheshach,** etc. This clause, however, is omitted in the Septuagint, and is too manifestly the insertion of an unwise copyist or editor. For, though perfectly true that Babylon was to suffer punishment afterwards, it is most inappropriate to mention it here at the end of a list of the nations which Babylon itself was to punish. "Sheshach," it should be explained, is the form assumed by the word "Babylon" in the cypher called Athbash (A = T, B = SH, etc.). It happens to convey a very appropriate meaning, viz. "humiliation" (comp. Isa. xlvii. 1). A similar instance of cypher allegory occurs in ch. li. 1. "Sheshach" occurs again in ch. li. 41, where, however, it is omitted by the Septuagint. [Dr. Lauth, of Munich, thinks that Sheshach is equivalent to Sisku, the name of a district in Babylonia; but the reading Sisku is uncertain. (See *Transactions of the Society of Biblical Archæology,* 1881, p. 48.)]

Ver. 27.—**Therefore thou shalt say,** etc.; rather, *And thou shalt say,* etc. This verse is probably a continuation of vers. 16, 17, vers.

18—26 being apparently inserted by an after-thought. The message given to Jeremiah to deliver is that the judgment is both over-poweringly complete and irreversible. If God's own people has not been spared, how should any other escape (comp. ch. xlix.12)?

Ver. 29.—**I will call for a sword.** It is probably that awful sword referred to in ver. 16 (see note).

Vers. 30—38.—The judgment upon the world.

Ver. 30.—**Therefore prophesy thou,** etc. Babylon, like the smaller kingdoms which it absorbed, has fallen, and nothing remains (for nothing had been revealed to the prophet concerning an interval to elapse previously) but to picture the great assize from which no flesh should be exempt. As the lion suddenly bursts, roaring, from his lair, so Jehovah, no longer the "good Shepherd," **shall roar from on high** (comp. Amos i. 2; Joel iii. 16) even **upon his habitation,** or rather, *against his pasture,* where his flock (ch. xxiii. 1) has been feeding so securely. **He shall give a shout.** It is the technical term used at once for the vintage-shout and for the battle-cry. In Isa. xvi. 9, 10, there is a beautiful allusion to this double meaning, and so perhaps there is here (comp. ch. li. 14).

Ver. 31.—**A noise.** The word is used elsewhere for the tumultuous sound of a marching army (see Isa. xiii. 4; xvii. 12). **He will plead;** rather, *he will hold judgment.* Jehovah's "contending" sometimes involves the notion of punishing, *e.g.* Ezek. xxxviii. 22; Isa. lxvi. 16. In 2 Chron. xxii. 8, the same verb in the same conjugation is forcibly rendered in the Authorized Version, "to execute judgment."

Ver. 32.—**A great whirlwind;** rather, *a great storm* (as ch. xxiii. 19). **The coasts of the earth;** rather, *the furthest parts of the earth.* The storm, as it appears on the horizon, comes as it were from the ends of the earth; perhaps, too, there is an allusion to the distant abode of the foe (comp. ch. vi. 22).

Ver. 33.—**The slain of the Lord;** *i.e.* those slain by the Lord, as Isa. lxvi. 16, where his sword is further spoken of as the agent (see on ver. 16). **They shall not be lamented,** etc.; parallel to ch. viii. 2; xvi. 4.

Ver. 34.—**Wallow yourselves** in the ashes. Supply rather, *in the dust* (comp. Micah i. 10), as more suitable to the figure (see on ch. vi. 26). The **shepherds,** and the **principal** (or, *noble ones*) **of the flock,** are, of course, merely different forms of expression for the rulers. **The days of your slaughter and of your dispersions are accomplished;** rather, *your days for being slaughtered are fulfilled; and I will scatter you* (or, *dash you in pieces*). This is the reading of an old and valuable manuscript at St. Petersburg, and is partly favoured by the pointing; it is adopted by most modern critics, the form in the text being ungrammatical. **Pleasant;** or, *precious* (comp. Dan. xi. 8, Authorized Version). Compare the figure in ch. xxii. 28.

Vers. 36, 37.—The prophet seems in his spirit to hear the lamentation to which in ver. 34 he summoned the "shepherds." **A voice of the cry** should be, *Hark! the cry* (omitting "shall be heard"); the clause is an exclamation. **Hath spoiled;** rather, *is spoiling* (or, *laying waste*). **The peaceable habitations;** rather, *the peaceful fields* (or, *pastures*). **Are cut down;** rather, *are destroyed;* literally, *are brought to silence* (comp. ch. ix. 10).

Ver. 38.—Close of the prophecy with a fuller enunciation of the thought with which the paragraph was introduced. **He hath forsaken;** comp. ver. 30, and notice the impressive non-mention of the subject (as ch. iv. 13, etc.). **Their land;** *i.e.* that of the shepherds. **The fierceness of the oppressor.** A various reading, supported by some manuscripts, the Septuagint and the Targum, and accepted by Ewald, Hitzig, and Graf, and is "the oppressing sword" (so ch. xlvi. 16; l. 16). The text reading is very difficult to defend, and the punctuation itself is really more in favour of the variant than of the received text.

HOMILETICS.

Vers. 1—7.—*A melancholy review of twenty-three years of work.* I. THE CHARACTER OF THE WORKER. A three and twenty years' experience furnishes a good test of character. So long a time is quite sufficient to eliminate the accidents of passion and temporary enthusiasm, and to bring to light the general principles of a man's conduct. These constitute his character; they reveal the true features of him. We should not judge a man by his latest action, perhaps a hasty and quite uncharacteristic one; to be fair, not to say charitable, we should consider the whole course of his life. To know ourselves we must look back on the years of our lives, and not pass a superficial judgment on our present mood. The character of Jeremiah, revealed by the test of twenty-three years of work under the most harassing circumstances, is worth our reverent study. Consider the salient points in it: 1. *Fidelity.* All this time he was working as God's servant, in opposition to the spirit of the age, provoking enmity, calumny, hatred. The bearer of a message which it must have been a pain for him to deliver, a message of denunciation and menace, Jeremiah boldly declared it and adhered to it, in spite of every inducement to follow the fashion of the prophets of flattery. We meet with men who are proud of representing the spirit of their age. Nothing is easier. Nothing is more simple than to be an echo, a reflection, a mouthpiece to the general voice. The difficulty is to utter a contrary voice, not out of stubbornness, or a spirit of wilful antagonism, but out of calm fidelity to duty. This is the task of the great. 2. *Perseverance.* For three and twenty years Jeremiah had persisted in his unpopular course. We know that he continued equally staunch for many more years. Here is the great test. It is possible to be an Elijah, and stand alone facing the howling multitude of priests and slaves of Baal in one supreme moment of conflict and speedy triumph, and yet after this to flee to the wilderness, and to feel unequal to the task of constant fidelity, in season and out of season, through long dreary years, without the excitement of a dramatic scene of heroism, worn and fretted by incessant, petty, spiteful enmity. Yet this was the experience of Jeremiah. 3. *Earnestness.* "I have spoken," he says, "rising early and speaking." The prophet is not a passive martyr, nor a mere confessor who dares to speak out his conviction when it is directly challenged. He goes forth on a mission urging his message upon men. He is a model preacher. He is no perfunctory official droning through a dreary task, no mere professional preacher, honestly discharging his work, but with little interest in it, like a hired pleader. His heart is with his work. He has an end in view, and he sets himself with all his might to accomplish it. In all this the prophet reveals to us the long-suffering and earnest desire of God to deliver his children. All this while God was inspiring Jeremiah, as he had inspired a succession of prophets, to rouse and urge the people to repentance.

II. THE RESULTS OF THE WORK. Apparent failure. "Ye have not hearkened, nor inclined your ear to hear." It would seem that all this labour, earnestness, persistence, and fidelity had been so much wasted work. 1. *The preacher must not be blamed for apparent fruitlessness.* No greater mistake can be made than that of judging a man by the manifest effect of his work. The most popular preacher is not necessarily the most faithful servant of God. The unpopularity and seeming failure of a preacher is not in itself a reason for condemning him. No fault can be found with the preaching of Jeremiah, yet it was not successful. Christ spake as never man spake, and "the Pharisees derided him." He was popular for a season, but ultimately "all men forsook him." The most important truths may be the least popular. 2. *The preacher must not be too confident in expecting time to reveal the fruits of his work.* Twenty-three years made no such revelation to Jeremiah. A faithful man may toil on through the long night of a whole lifetime of difficulty, and die without seeing the results of his labour. It is well to be prepared for this possibility. 3. *The responsibility of rightly receiving a Divine message rests with the hearers.* We are always lecturing the preachers. "Take heed how ye speak." These words are not in the Bible. Christ was more anxious about the hearers. "Take heed how ye hear." Of course the preacher has his high responsibilities, but so have the hearers. The poorest sermon of a good man who is trying to expound Divine truth may contain something of profit to a devout listener, who is more anxious to receive the good in it than to pass a barren criticism on its defects; for if the messenger is sadly wanting, and his language and thought as poor as possible, the message which he handles so badly is not the less God's truth. But if the preaching of a Jeremiah, of a Christ even, is unheeded, what qualities in the preacher can command success with an unsympathizing audience? 4. *Still no good work ultimately fails.* Jeremiah did not speak for nothing. His message bore good fruit with many of the captives—perhaps with Daniel. Preserved to our time, it has been a blessing to generations.

Vers. 5, 6.—*The chief purpose of prophecy.* Jeremiah here sums up the general purpose not only of his own mission—extending now over twenty-three years—but of that of the whole series of Hebrew prophets. We may thus see the one great aim towards which all their labours were directed.

I. PROPHECY IS PRACTICAL. Jeremiah's summary takes the form of an exhortation. The prophets were preachers, not philosophers. Their aim was not to satisfy curiosity but to affect conduct. In this they are an example to all preachers. The preacher's duty is to lead men, not merely to teach doctrines. Still the exposition of truth is necessary to effect this end. The prophets did not content themselves with simple exhortations to good conduct. These exhortations needed the enforcement of clear conviction. Their authority was not magisterial (a mere command of superior power) nor priestly (an influence of spiritual rank erected on unquestioning faith), but reasonable (the authority of truth seen and felt). Hence their revelations of God and of the future. Yet these were all given for a practical end. The preacher should make his most abstract expositions of truth point towards some course of conduct.

II. PROPHECY IS A CALL TO REPENTANCE. This urgent call rings through the messages of all the prophets. It was revived by John the Baptist (Matt. iii. 2), adopted by our Lord (Matt. iv. 17) and his apostles (e.g. St. Peter, Acts ii. 38; and St. Paul, Acts xvii. 30), and by all great reformers, such as Savonarola, John Knox, John Wesley, etc. 1. Men must be preached to about their own condition as well as about God's will. We want a Divine revelation that we may know ourselves just as much as that we may know God. A large part of the Bible is occupied with revelations of human nature. 2. Together with these revelations there comes the call to turn and change. The result of the exposure of mankind to itself is not satisfactory. This exposure alone is a call to turn from our evil ways. The mere exposure, however, is of little use. A Juvenal is not a Jeremiah. A satirist is not a prophet. There must be the call to a better life, and a declaration of the way to find it. 3. The prophets imply that men not only need to change but can change. The most fundamental change of heart must be through the influence of God. Yet this is only possible when men freely and willingly turn to him in repentance. 4. The special sin denounced was apostasy from God; the special repentance called for was a return to God. These are always the fundamental elements of sin and repentance.

III. PROPHECY IS A VOICE OF WARNING AND OF PROMISE. Evil is denounced to the impenitent; good is promised to the penitent. This is the simplest form in which the motives to repentance can be put. But the tracing out of it is not simple. It required an inspired prophet to detect the seeds of ruin in riotous prosperity and the dawning of a day of redemption in the stormy night of adversity. The prophets not only detect these facts, they discern the principles that govern them. Thus they speak for all ages. They show us how sin is ruinous; how God has a sure blessedness in store for his faithful children—a blessedness which is eternal.

Ver. 9.—" Nebuchadrezzar . . . my servant." A strange expression! It is not found in many manuscripts and versions. But it is more likely that dull officious scribes should erase such an " improper" phrase than that any should insert it in the manuscripts and Targum where it is preserved. We cannot suppose that Nebuchadrezzar is called God's servant in consideration of any characteristics of his later career, such as the repentant state following his insanity recorded in the Book of Daniel (iv. 33—37). The prophecy of Jeremiah belongs to a much earlier period. Nebuchadrezzar, a heathen, an idolater, entirely ignorant of the religion of the Jews, just appearing as the great conqueror and oppressor, and striking Syria dumb with terror by his victory at Carchemish—this man is called God's servant. The expression is significant.

I. GOD'S AUTHORITY EXTENDS TO ALL MANKIND. He is not the God of the Jews only, nor of the Christians only, nor of the religious only. He is the God of heaven and earth, the Sovereign and supreme Master of all creatures. We talk of the godless heathen. They may be living without the knowledge of God, but not without his knowledge of them, his care, his influence.

II. GOD CAN USE FOR HIS PURPOSES MEN WHO DO NOT KNOW HIM. Nebuchadrezzar did not know the true God. Yet he was an instrument in God's hands for the chastisement of the Jews. Many a man is unconsciously working out God's will even when he thinks he is fighting against it. God's purposes are deeper than our thoughts.

III. GOD CAN MAKE BAD MEN DO HIS WILL. Such men do not do God's will in themselves, but by doing their own evil will they produce results which fall in with God's larger designs. Of course this is no justification for their conduct, since our responsibility turns on our motives, not on the unexpected results of our conduct. It must not be supposed that God sanctions the wicked passions that drive a man to an action which God overrules for good. Nebuchadrezzar is to be punished for the very act in which God uses him as his servant (ver. 12). Yet the relation between God and his wicked servants is wholly mysterious.

IV. God exercises authority over the most irresponsible tyrants. Nebuchadrezzar is the greatest monarch of the world. He is just inflated with one of the grandest victories in all history. Naturally he is an autocratic tyrant who makes an idol of his own will. This man is really God's slave. God overrules all kings, shapes and moulds all history, and manifests his providence in the great onward march of humanity. This fact should give us confidence in the midst of the darkest events. It should humble the great to feel that they are as nothing before God.

V. The unconscious servants of God do not know the blessedness of his higher service. As they do not willingly serve, so they do not reap the spiritual joys of service. The service is nothing to them, though much to the world. The true servant of God knows his master's will and delights to do it, sacrifices his own will and submits obediently to the higher will. To fulfil such service is the highest privilege of mankind. In the accomplishment of it is peace and blessedness (Ps. xl. 6—8).

Ver. 15.—*The wine-cup of fury.* I. The wrath of God is like intoxicating wine. 1. It is *powerful.* The wine is strong drink. We are too ready to close our eyes to this aspect of the Divine nature. The love of God is so treated by some that it leaves no room for anger. But God is not weakly indulgent; if he were so, even his love would be found wanting, for there is no wrath more terrible than that of outraged love. 2. The anger of God *produces terrible effects.* The wine intoxicates. It cannot be a matter of no concern to us to know how God feels towards us. All affections tend to actions. The anger of a man is not likely to waste itself in aimless fury ; it will flow out in deeds. God is a King whose wrath will find expression in acts of sovereignty, a Father whose anger must necessarily affect his treatment of his children. If there are men at whose anger we may smile, there are others who cannot be safely despised. But who dare disregard the wrath of God ? Once it is outpoured it must be overwhelming, must take possession of men. 3. It will not only produce outward distress, but *inward confusion* and helplessness, so " that they shall reel to and fro, and behave themselves madly." Therefore the man who is smitten by Divine wrath has not those internal sources of comfort and strength with which we try to bear up under outward calamity.

II. There are times when the wine-cup of fury is poured out. It is not always flowing. Though "God is angry with the wicked every day," he is forbearing, and restrains his wrath till it cannot longer be justly withheld. Then we may suppose that the longer it has been accumulating the worse will be its outflow. Men have been treasuring up wrath against the day of wrath. Such seasons of the outpouring of the cup of fury may be noted in history ; *e.g.* in the invasions of Nebuchadrezzar, the destruction of Jerusalem by Titus, the sacking of Rome by Alaric. It is important to note that this happens in seasons. It is not always harvest. But the spring sowing prepares for the autumn reaping. We may be now preparing for an outburst of wrath. How foolish not to guard against it because it has not yet come ! Delay of judgment is no excuse for doubt about it, for this is part of the Divine method of action.

III. All the guilty must drink of the wine-cup of fury. Jeremiah summons the various nations to partake of it. The Jews are not spared though they are the " elect people." The heathen are not excluded though they do not recognize God truly. God is still the impartial Father of all, and must execute judgment upon all classes, while, of course, he has due regard to the light and opportunities of each. "Religious" people will have to drink of the dreadful cup, if they are morally corrupt. Worldly people will also have to receive it, though they may profess to have nothing to do with God and his laws. There is no escape in the day of judgment. Men may refuse to taste of God's love ; they cannot refuse to partake of his wrath (ver. 28).

IV. The bitter cup which Christ drank is an antidote to the wine-cup of fury. God could never have been angry with his beloved Son. He must have regarded him as he was in his pure goodness; could not have imputed to him sins of which he was not guilty, nor have looked wrathfully upon him when he was regarding him with nothing but love and approval. But Christ was so one with us, so took our place as our

High Priest, that he must have felt, as the most guilty man never felt, the horror of the wrath of God against the sinful world of which he stood forth as the Representative. He drank to the dregs the bitter cup of spiritual woe as well as that of his bodily passion. The gospel of his grace proclaims to us that they who are liable to the outpourings of a Divine judgment on their sins may find through Christ's sacrifice peace with God. By faith in Christ we are reconciled to God, and find that his anger is put away for ever in the free pardon of our sins.

Ver. 29.—*The ineffectual palladium of a great name.* Jerusalem was called by God's name; yet Jerusalem was not to be spared in the general outpouring of the wine-cup of fury. The Jews were vainly trusting in their name. We are all inclined to think too much of mere names. Certainly there is something in a name; it may command respect, influence, etc. Yet this applies only in regard to human considerations; it can have no weight with God. Even with men it is less potent than its possessors would fain believe. The influence of it is slowly won, easily lost, and only recovered with the utmost difficulty, if at all.

I. A NAME MAY BE GREAT BECAUSE IT REPRESENTS CONNECTION WITH THE GREAT. It may indicate relationship to a family, a clan, a nation. We are proud of the name of Englishmen. St. Paul, professing himself a Roman, was able to claim the rights of Roman citizenship (Acts xxii. 25). But the name is here useful only in so far as the privilege it implies extends. St. Paul had a right not to be scourged, but none to save him from being beheaded by the order of the emperor. We may claim undue privileges because we bear the name of Christian, because we were born in Christendom, are citizens of a Christian state, are members of a Christian Church. These associations count for nothing before God. We shall "*all* appear before the judgment-seat of Christ, that every one may receive the things done in his body" (2 Cor. v. 10). It will be vain then to say, "Lord, Lord, have we not prophesied in thy Name," etc.? if Christ must answer, "I never knew you: depart from me, ye that work iniquity" (Matt. vii. 23, 24).

II. A NAME MAY BE GREAT BECAUSE IT REPRESENTS HIGH RANK. Social distinctions cannot be ignored while they exist, and in them the favoured necessarily enjoy many amenities that are denied to the commonalty. But they are snares when they tempt their owners to expect peculiar privileges with Heaven. In spiritual matters we approach God, not as rich or poor, not as prince or beggar, but as man. Rank goes for nothing there; character is everything. This applies to ecclesiastical rank. They who hold high office in the Church are tempted to expect exceptional judgment. They will be judged, not as officials, not as popes, bishops, priests, but as men, and will find that their holy office will be no sanctuary when the awful sword of Divine judgment is unsheathed.

III. A NAME MAY BE GREAT BECAUSE IT REPRESENTS A GOOD REPUTATION. If the reputation is justly earned, the name is a real honour. "A good name," says the wise man, "is rather to be chosen than great riches" (Prov. xxii. 1). Shakespeare's Cassio exclaims, "Reputation, reputation, reputation! Oh, I have lost my reputation! I have lost the immortal part of myself, and what remains is bestial." Yet, if reputation is "got without merit," it is a poor refuge to flee to from before the all-seeing God. Even when it is solid and honest it stands only as a record of the past, and a presumption in our favour when our conduct is equivocal. But it does not mitigate the guilt of subsequent offences. We are judged by our conduct, not by our fame. It is vain to have a name to live if we are dead; the name will not galvanize us back into life.

IV. A NAME MAY BE GREAT BECAUSE IT REPRESENTS A GREAT PROFESSION. Men assume big names and flourish them before the world in pretended evidence of their own excellence, and the world, being too blind and too indolent to make very searching inquiries, commonly takes men much at their own reckoning. The advantage of such a deception can only be superficial and transitory. The foolish boast will soon be exploded. Before God it matters little what a man calls himself. The one question is as to what he is.

Vers. 34—38.—*Howling shepherds.* In the general calamity of the nation the shepherds are especially called upon to howl and cry and wallow in the dust. The shepherds are the leaders of the people. These leaders, therefore, are not to be exempt from the distresses of the common people ; on the contrary, trouble is to fall upon them in an aggravated degree.

I. HIGH RANK IS NO SECURITY AGAINST TROUBLE. It may free a man from many annoyances, it cannot defend him from all kinds of calamity. It is chiefly a safeguard against the smaller vexations of life ; the more serious troubles sweep over it unchecked. It is like a small breakwater that will keep back the little waves of a fresh sea, but is overwhelmed in the storm. When it is most needed it is of least use. Rank is no protection against disease and death, against general human calamities, such as the desolation of an earthquake, the ravages of a plague, the devastation of a war. Nevertheless men do trust to rank unreasonably, and find it a snare when their false confidence is exposed.

II. LEADERS OF MEN SUFFER FROM THE TROUBLES THAT FALL UPON THEIR FOLLOWERS. The shepherd suffers with his flock. The patron is dependent on his clients. The king is great with the greatness of his people, and brought into trouble by his nation's distress. This is more than sharing a general calamity. It is experiencing a trouble that is directly caused by the distress of dependants. History has proved the mistake of those tyrants who have thought to secure their own grandeur by the brutal degradation, the bondage and misery of their subjects. The truly prosperous sovereign is not the Pharaoh reigning in lonely magnificence over a nation of slaves, but the beloved ruler of a free and enlightened people.

III. PERSONS IN EXALTED POSITIONS ARE LIABLE TO PECULIAR TROUBLES FROM WHICH ORDINARY MEN ARE EXEMPT. Not only are they not free from the common distresses of mankind, not only are they directly affected by the distresses of those beneath them ; they are also subject to special dangers arising from their high and prominent position. 1. They are burdened with a *responsibility* that is proportionate to their elevation. If much has been given to them, much is expected of them. Every eye is upon them. Any mistake of theirs which might pass unnoticed in obscure men, is dragged into the full blaze of jealous criticism. If such men abuse a great trust they may expect to be visited with a great judgment. 2. They are liable to *special attacks of animosity*. Like officers in the field, they are picked out by opponents. Kings have dangers of assassination which obscure men need never fear. The highest tree catches the fiercest blast of the gale, while humble shrubs grow at peace in sheltered nooks. 3. They *feel the blow of trouble most acutely*. They who stand highest can fall lowest. Poverty is not the calamity to a born pauper that it proves itself to a bankrupt prince.

HOMILIES BY VARIOUS AUTHORS.

Vers. 1—7.—*Messages recapitulated.* I. CAREFUL REMINDER OF THE EXTENT OF HIS MINISTRY. (Vers. 1—3.) 1. *The moral value of this is great.* It is no vague indictment, but one made out with all accuracy and conscientiousness. We ought to take note of the extent of our privileges and opportunities, for we shall have to give an exact account of them all. 2. *Its evidential value is equally great.* The date of the prediction is thus fixed, and history becomes a long verification of his prophetic truth.

II. ASSERTION OF HIS OWN AND OF GOD'S DILIGENCE AND FAITHFULNESS. (Vers. 3—6.) 1. *God has been diligent.* He has " risen up early." The welfare of his people is of intense interest to him. The delays of his dispensations are only seeming. No earnestness on the part of the creature can ever anticipate or outrun his love or readiness to provide. 2. *His servant the prophet was so also.* It was God's Spirit in him that they heard. He was obedient to the heavenly Spirit, and announced its messages as they were received.

III. THE PERSISTENT UNBELIEF AND DISOBEDIENCE OF THE NATION DENOUNCED. (Vers. 3—7.) There is something very impressive in the repeated " Ye have not hearkened." It defines and characterizes the guilt of the apostate. There was not even the beginning of serious attention (vers. 5, 6) ; and their indifference had become systematic and habitual. What wonder that God should have been provoked to wrath ? And this is the sinner's position to-day. It would be impossible to fathom the depths of our depravity by nature, or to trace it to its ultimate issues.

IV. THE SPIRIT AND SUBSTANCE OF THE MESSAGE IS REPEATED. How great is the long-suffering of God! The unbelief of the people had been marvellous, considering the signs which had been given. Another opportunity, however, was afforded ere the catastrophe should take place. No details of the teaching are entered into, but great plainness of speech is used. The emphasis is upon essentials and permanent principles. The "spirit of prophecy" is intensely moral; and this is why the "testimony of Jesus" represents it. It is the grand resultant of all the forces working through ancient prophecy, and casts its revealing light backward upon the prophetic page. These repentances so often urged but never forthcoming, these "returns" and obediences which were to crown with blessing and surround with Divine favour, are only possible through his Spirit. The future of the world, as of every individual and nation, is inextricably associated with the cause of righteousness, and therefore with the gospel.—M.

Vers. 7—11.—*Judgment plainly declared.* The agents of the visitation are more precisely defined than hitherto, and the leader of the invasion is actually named. The extent also of the region to be devastated, and the time the captivity is to last, viz. seventy years, are set forth.
I. THIS TENDED TO HEIGHTEN THE MORAL CONSCIOUSNESS OF THE PEOPLE. A vague indefinite calamity or series of calamities would have failed to strike deeply enough into the conscience of the transgressors; whereas a precisely marked off and defined set of occurrences could not be misunderstood. 1. *The nearness and inevitable character of the judgment are thereby realized.* 2. *It is seen to be imposed by the moral government of God.* "My servant." God permits, nay, appoints, Nebuchadrezzar.
II. IT PRESENTED THE PERIOD OF CALAMITY AS PART OF AN ORDERED WHOLE, WITH A DEFINITE OUTCOME AND OBJECT. Great as the trial would be, it was nevertheless a measured and therefore a bearable one. There need be no wild abandonment to despair. The believer could possess his soul in patience. The allurements of heathenism would lose much of their power. A quiet, reverent, and repentant study of the meaning of the dispensation would be encouraged; and in this way it would act as discipline for the future. We can never be certain as to the limits of our trials; but we have the assurance that our Saviour, who has a fellow-feeling with his people, will not impose anything above what we are able to bear. And through the revelation of spirituality in the gospel, and the greater spiritualization of our hopes and aims through its teaching, we are able with greater calmness to contemplate our "light affliction, which is but for a moment."
III. THE PROPHECY WAS THEREBY PROVED TO BE GENUINE, AND THE PROVIDENCE OF GOD REVEALED BEYOND DISPUTE. As if conscious of this, Jeremiah for the first time calls himself "the prophet," when he has fairly committed himself to exact dates and personages. It would be open to the survivors of that predicted dispensation to denounce him an an impostor, and to discredit the practice of prophesying. But the seer was certain; and the verdict of history confirms his forecast, and demonstrates that it was no *ex post facto* fabrication, but real Divine foreknowledge of events yet future.—M.

Ver. 29.—*Judgment beginning at the house of God.* I. THE ORDER OF GOD'S JUDGMENT. 1. *It begins with his own people.* 2. *Reasons for this are:* (1) *The harmony of the Divine rule in the earth.* The Church is his own house. It ought, therefore, to be in perfect order first. His authority ought to be recognized among those whom he calls his own. He will therefore deal with them first, and then with better grace address the impenitent and unbelieving world. (2) *The purity of God's character.* He cannot endure wrong —cannot look upon sin. Yet he is to dwell in the Church, in individual believers. It is necessary, therefore, that they be made pure as he is pure. Their discipline must be immediate if they are to become vessels prepared unto honour. (3) *The justice of God.* Immediately the sin of the child is worse than that of the stranger, because it is done in the midst of light and privilege. Sharp and immediate chastisement is the only way in which he can show his sense of the wrong done (Amos iii. 2). (4) *The mercy of God.* If it begins with the children of God, it is that they may the sooner be saved. He embitters the breast of the world to wean them (Leighton). It is because he loves he rebukes and chastens. But the grief of sin begins first in the breast of God and in the person of his Son. It is of the nature of Divine love to suffer for the sinful, even to die, that he may be made a child of grace.

II. THE EXTENT OF IT. "All the inhabitants of the earth." Thus early—nay, from the first sin onwards—does he *begin* the judgment of the whole earth. The sin of one is but a symptom of the universal depravity of all. The oneness of the world in its fall and the evolution of its sin, is constantly declared in Scripture. 1. *This is demanded by the justice of God.* "Should ye be utterly unpunished?" It would be manifestly unfair that the child of God alone should suffer for that which is primarily a sin of all mankind. 2. *It is founded upon the solidarity of the race.* There is a universal kinship in sins. "In Adam (they) all die" (1 Cor. xv. 22).

III. THE MEASURE OF IT. "A sword" (cf. ver. 33). This signifies destruction, death. That which opposes itself to him will be utterly destroyed. He *begins* his judgment upon his own, but it passes from them and rests for ever upon his enemies. The picture painted by Jeremiah (vers. 30—38) is but one of many similar ones in the Bible. The utter holiness of God cannot endure the sinfulness of men; it must consume it and all that identify themselves with it. In the New Testament the horizon widens, and the spiritual world participates with the living upon earth in the sentence of the Judge. The first duty, therefore, of every awakened sinner is to flee from the "wrath to come." Whilst he remains unconverted he is a "child of wrath." Punishment has a different significance to him from what it would have if he were "in Christ." It is the same principle of solidarity which condemned us that now avails for our salvation. "For as in Adam all die, even so in Christ shall all be made alive" (1 Cor. xv. 22).—M.

Vers. 30—38.—*The vision of final judgment.* A sublime and terrible description; corresponding with many others throughout the Old and New Testaments.

I. IT SERVES A GREAT ETHICAL PURPOSE. The sense of wrong-doing is thereby intensified, and some idea is given of the awful consequences of sin and its hatefulness to the mind of God.

II. AN EVIDENCE OF THE HISTORIC SIGNIFICANCE OF SIN AND SALVATION. By such visions as these the ages of the world are linked together and shown to be convergent in one point. There are not to be so many judgments of isolated offences, but one judgment, towards which all the world has looked forward. Sin increases with the lapse of time, and develops into a more pronounced opposition to truth and goodness Only in final judgment can all its significance be comprehended and its issues be stayed.

III. AN EVIDENCE OF THE REALITY OF THE PROPHETIC GIFT AND ITS SPIRITUAL END. This vision is corroborated by the universal instincts of man, on the one hand, and by the endorsement of Christ on the other. The various minor judgments which have intervened between that time and this are so many proofs of the correctness of the prophet's intuition. And the manner in which he and other seers have laid chief emphasis upon this event exhibits the fundamental moral purpose of all prophecy. Its intention is to reveal the righteousness of God, and to lead men into its practice and love.—M.

Vers. 1—7.—*A twenty-three years' ministry.* Here we get a statement, brief but not at all uncertain, of what had been done in the prophetic way during twenty-three years. Three parties are concerned in this statement: (1) *God;* (2) *the prophet;* (3) *the people.*

I. GOD. Nebuchadrezzar, who is to act as the servant of God (ver. 9) in the great overthrowing work, has just come to his throne, and is unconsciously preparing for that to which God had appointed him. Hence it was fitting that, just at this crisis, God should point back over the past and show how very much he had done to bring about a different result. Not that this comprehensive view was likely at the eleventh hour to make any change in Israel itself; but it is well that it should stand recorded in the history. It is well that we who come after should be made to see clearly how continuously God protested against the wickedness of his people. Jeremiah himself, out of his own experience, speaks as a witness of what had been going on for twenty-three years; and he knew further that he was only one out of many agents by whom God had been doing the same kind of work.

II. THE PROPHET. Not Jeremiah peculiarly, but Jeremiah as representative of all the faithful prophets; those to whom he here refers as having been engaged in the same kind of service. He brings against the people a serious charge of persistent neglect; but it also involves a serious confession with respect to himself. A serious confession, but not a shameful one. Though his long ministry has not had the desired end, it is by no means a failure. For twenty-three years the work has been laid upon him of denouncing national apostasy and individual transgression, in all the varieties of it. The substance of this long ministry is written down and the spirit of the ministry made evident. We know the things he spoke of, and how he spoke of them; the enemies he made, the sufferings he endured, the pangs with which his heart was torn. In his ministry he gave himself, without stint. Nor does his work stand alone. He was not the first to exhort to repentance. He succeeded men who had been as faithful as himself, and engaged as long a time in the service of God. And yet, after so many remonstrances, the nation remains stubborn in its apostasy, infatuated as ever in its rapid descent to ruin. Hence we learn how chary we should be in talking of unsuccessful ministries. No ministry, whatever its other results may be, can be unsuccessful in the sight of God, if only there is unshaken fidelity to him. It is fidelity that he rewards, not obvious results. In spite of all the husbandman's care, digging about the tree and dunging it, it may yield no fruit; but the fidelity of the husbandman deserves a reward all the same. Industry cannot overcome the bad elements in what is given him to cultivate. All who have to engage in preaching and prophesying duties must learn the lesson, that more is needed for success than mere perseverance. Perseverance is like the dropping water which wears away the stone; but what is here required, is that the stone should be changed as to its nature, not worn away. If Jeremiah had been able to prophesy twenty-three centuries, instead of twenty-three years, the result would have been the same. All he could do was to reiterate, in the ears of the people, the necessity of repentance. It is in the light of a passage like this that we learn more of what Jesus meant when he came to fulfil the prophets. It was his not only to accomplish their predictions, but do what they could not possibly do by all their appeals—turn the hearts of the disobedient to God. Compare the barren ministry of Jeremiah, prophet of Jehovah, with the fruitful ministry of Paul, apostle of Jesus Christ. Yet Paul did not speak one whit more earnestly concerning righteousness and repentance and submission to God. The difference lay in this, that Paul was not only a preacher, but when he preached there was a subduing and renewing Spirit.

III. THE PEOPLE. This is a serious charge brought against them, that one man had been in their midst for all these years, with one message, never varying and never slackening, and yet that they had paid, as a nation, not the slightest heed to it. When Nebuchadrezzar did come, there was no chance for them to say that they had not received proper warning. They could not blame Jeremiah. Their very persecution of him was a witness against themselves. Thus there is a warning to those who are hearers of the gospel with all the voices with which it is addressed to them. It is not outside of themselves they must look for explanations of why the truths of the gospel have found no lodgment in their hearts. The cause is within. How many have been listening to the news of Jesus Christ for many more years even than twenty-three, and every year seems to bring a lessening probability that they will treat the message as having a practical concern for themselves!—Y.

Ver. 9.—*Nebuchadrezzar, the servant of God.* I. THE CONTRAST WITH OTHER SER-VANTS. Observe the mention, in ver. 4, of those very different servants of God, the prophets (so mentioned elsewhere). God had sent many of them and many times, and hardly any attention had been paid to them. Higher motives had been appealed to in vain. Considerations of duty and prudence were thrown to the winds. And now the mighty king Nebuchadrezzar comes, with a very different sort of force—not looking at all like a servant of God; and yet he is just as much the servant of God as is any of the prophets. Indeed, king of a great people though he was, his rank in the service of God was not so high as that of the prophets. He appears in this place as nothing more than the final executioner of justice.

II. NONE THE LESS EFFICIENT A SERVANT BECAUSE THE SERVICE WAS RENDERED

UNCONSCIOUSLY. Nebuchadrezzar, despot as he was, would have been very wrathful if he had known exactly how he appeared in the sight of God. He had certain purposes of his own, and he succeeded in effecting them; but the very energy with which he worked for himself only made him to render his service to God more complete. And may it not be happening in the world, a great deal more frequently than we think, that the very success of selfish and domineering men is being so handled by God as all the more to serve his purposes?

III. THE LIMITATIONS OF NEBUCHADREZZAR'S SERVICE. The service, with all its completeness, was only within certain limits. It does not require much intelligence to destroy what is destructible. But if there is to be a building-up work for God, then there must be a conscious, voluntary, and devoted service. Israel was meant to be a servant of God in the fullest and noblest sense of the word. It had been instructed in the will of God and borne with patiently in many failures to obey that will. Hence the description of Nebuchadrezzar as a servant is an implied rebuke of those who had refused to be servants. Note the great contrast found in the New Testament, where Christ's apostles, at the beginning of their Epistles, hasten to proclaim themselves as the servants of God.—Y.

Ver. 31.—*Jehovah's controversy with the nations.* This necessary controversy explains all the proceedings described from ver. 15 to the end of the chapter. Jeremiah is not a prophet to Israel only, but to all who are guilty of similar transgressions. The cup of God's holy wrath goes on filling wherever he beholds wrong-doing. It is easy to see, if we only ponder a little, that some such outburst as this must come in all true prophecy. As the Apostle Paul puts it, the nations that sinned without law perished without law. The peculiar light vouchsafed to Israel was not the only light for which men were responsible to God. Accordingly we find that it seems to have been one main ground of appeal taken by the apostle to the Gentiles that God had not left himself without witness amongst them. If, on the one hand, he could denounce Israel for being so indifferent to the Law he had formally given, so, on the other hand, he could denounce the Gentiles for their negligence of the light of nature. Idolatry, as we perceive, had produced the most fearful results in Israel; but everywhere else it must, of course, have produced results quite as bad, only they do not happen to occupy such a prominent position in history. And thus we have indicated to us here, as indeed in so many places elsewhere, the way in which to consider the decline and fall of great nations. It is not enough for the Christian to rest in the consideration of secondary causes. And if a nation's decadence be so gradual and imperceptible as to show no obvious sign of what secondary causes may be operating, then there is all the more need to rise to the height of a true faith in God and believe that his judgments are assuredly at work. Wherever there is unbridled self-indulgence, still spreading wider and wider, there we may be sure God is carrying on those judgments which cannot fail. But is there not also a brighter side suggested by one passage in this chapter? As we read of all these lands to which, in a kind of apocalyptic vision, Jeremiah presented the cup of Jehovah's fury, we cannot but think of that other list so graciously represented on the day of Pentecost. Nations, in the manifold wisdom of God, may rise, decline, and fall; but such a fate will trouble none save those who exaggerate patriotism into a cardinal virtue. The serious matter is when the individual will not show a timely wisdom, and in humble repentance put away his mistaken past, and in humble faith accept the redemption and guidance which God alone can provide.—Y.

EXPOSITION.

CHAPTER XXVI.

JEREMIAH'S TRIAL AND DELIVERANCE.

The prophecy in vers. 2—6 is a summary of that contained in ch. vii. 1—15; the narrative, which stands in no connection either with ch. xxiv. or ch. xxvii., relates the consequences of that bold declaration of the word of the Lord. The present position of the chapter is only surprising to those who assume that the works of the prophets were necessarily arranged chronologically. How many violations of chronological order meet us in other books. *e.g.* in Isaiah! It is only reasonable to expect similar phenomena in the Book of Jeremiah.

To estimate the circumstances of the prophecy aright, we must remember that in Jehoiakim's reign a Chaldean invasion was the danger by which all minds were constantly preoccupied.

Ver. 2.—Jeremiah is to take his stand in the court of the Lord's house; *i.e.* the outer court, where the people assembled (comp. ch. xix. 14), and preach unto all the cities of Judah; *i.e.* to the pilgrims who had come from the provincial towns (comp. ch. xi. 12). His discourse is not to be an eloquent appeal to the feelings, but a strict and peremptory announcement; he is to diminish (or, *subtract*) not a word (comp. Deut. iv. 2; xii. 32; Rev. xxii. 19).

Ver. 3.—That I may repent; literally, *and I will repent;* the idea or object is derived from the context. (On the Divine repentance, see note on ch. xviii. 8.)

Vers. 4—6.—The contents of the discourse (see especially on ch. vii. 12—15). The priests and the prophets interfere, arrest Jeremiah, and accuse him of a capital crime. It would appear that some at least of the "false prophets" were priests; thus Pashur, we are told, was a priest (ch. xx. 6).

Vers. 7—11.—To all devout Jews this prediction of the destruction of the temple must have been startling; but to those who placed their confidence in the mere existence of a consecrated building (ch. vii. 4), it was like a blow aimed at their very life. Besides, were not the majority of the prophets of Jehovah of entirely another way of thinking? Did they not promise peace? And what could justify Jeremiah in announcing not merely war, but the downfall of the Divine habitation itself? Hence no sooner had the prophet concluded his discourse, than he was arrested, accused, and condemned to death.

Ver. 8.—Had made an end of speaking. They allowed Jeremiah to finish his discourse (of which we have here only the briefest summary), either from a lingering reverence for his person and office, or to obtain fuller materials for an accusation (comp. the trial of Stephen, Acts vi. 12—14). All the people. The "people" appear to have been always under some constraint. As long as the priests and prophets were alone, they dominated the unofficial classes, but when the princes appeared (ver. 11), the new influence proved superior. In ver. 16 princes and people together go over to the side of Jeremiah. Thou shalt surely die. Death was the legal penalty both for blasphemy (Lev. xxiv. 16) and for presuming to prophesy without having received a prophetic revelation (Deut. xviii.

20). Jeremiah's declaration ran so entirely counter to the prejudices of his hearers that he may well have been accused of both these sins, or crimes. True, Isaiah and Amos had already predicted the destruction of Jerusalem (Isa. v. 5, 6; vi. 11; Amos ii. 4, 5; vi. 1, 2); but it may have been contended that the timely repentance of Judah under Hezekiah and Josiah had effectually cancelled the threatened doom, and though Isa. lxiv. 10, 11 evidently refers to a time later than Josiah, and represents the ruin of Jerusalem as practically certain, it would seem that the prophetic book (Isa. xl.—lxvi.) to which this belongs (to say the least) was not generally known.

Ver. 9.—Were gathered against; rather, *assembled themselves unto;* i.e. constituted themselves into a legal *qāhāl*, or assembly (see on ver. 17).

Ver. 10.—The princes. The term will include the members of the various branches of the royal family, who acted as judges (see on ch. xxi. 12), and the "elders," or heads of families (see ver. 17). Without the presence of the former, Jeremiah could only have had a mock-trial. Came up, etc. (see on ch. xxii. 1). Of the Lord's house; better simply, *of the Lord.* The gate is the same which is referred at ch. xx. 2.

Ver. 11.—This man is worthy to die; literally, a *sentence of death (belongs) to this man.*

Vers. 12—15.—Jeremiah's defence. He is conscious that he has not spoken uncommissioned, and leaves the result. He urges the people to amendment of life, while there is time, and warns them that his own unmerited death will bring a curse upon themselves.

Vers. 16—19.—The truth makes an impression upon the princes and the people, who declare Jeremiah to be a true prophet, and therefore innocent.

Ver. 17.—The elders of the land add their voice in favour of Jeremiah, not, however, without first of all consulting the people whose representatives they are. The whole verse is thoroughly technical in its phraseology. The word (*qāhāl*) rendered "assembly" is the traditional legal term for the "congregation of Israel" (Deut. xxxi. 30); comp. ver. 9, where the verb is the corresponding one to *qāhāl.* Thus, with all the faults of the government of Judah, which Jeremiah himself reveals to us, it was very far removed from the Oriental despotisms of our day. The "elders" are still an important element in the social system, and form a link with that earlier period in which the family was the leading power in the social organization. Originally the term denoted, strictly and in the full sense, heads of families; they have their analogue in the councils of the Aryan village communities. "References to their parliamentary status (if the phrase may be used) occur in Exod. iii. 16; 2 Sam. xix. 11; 1 Kings viii. 1; xx. 7. The institution lingered on during and after the Babylonian Exile (ch. xxix. 1; Ezek. xiv. 1; xx. 1; Ezra v. 5; vi. 7; x. 14; Matt. xxvi. 3, 47; Mark xiv. 43; Acts iv. 5, etc.)." We find another reference to their quasi-judicial authority in Deut. xxi. 2.

Vers. 18, 19.—**Micah the Morasthite**, etc. The "elders" appeal for a precedent to the case of Micah (called after his native place, Moresheth-Gath, to distinguish him from other Micahs), who had been equally explicit in his declarations of woe to Jerusalem, without incurring the charge of blasphemy. The prediction referred to is in Micah iii. 12, the form of which agrees verbally with our passage.

Ver. 19.—**Thus might we procure**, etc.; rather, *and we are about to commit a great evil against our souls* (not merely "against *ourselves*"). The blood of the slain would cry for vengeance against his murderers, who would come to an untimely end, their "souls" being sent down to lead a miserable parody of a life (βίος ἄβιος) in Sheol or Hades.

Vers. 20—23.—The murder of the prophet Urijah. At first sight, these four verses appear to belong to the speech of the elders, but the appearance is delusive, (1) because the issue of the affair of Urijah cannot possibly have taken place "in the beginning of the reign of Jehoiakim" (ver. 1); and (2) because the passage stands in no connection with what preceeds, whereas it is related, and that very closely, to ver. 24 (see below). The case is similar to that of certain passages in St. John's Gospel, where the reflections of the evangelist are put side by side with the sayings of our Lord. Jeremiah, writing down his experiences at a later time, introduces the story of Urijah to show the magnitude of the danger to which he had been exposed. The notice of Urijah has an additional importance, as it shows incidentally how isolated a spiritual prophet like Jeremiah was, and how completely the order of prophets had fallen below its high ideal. We have no further knowledge of the prophet Urijah.

Ver. 20.—**Kirjath-jearim**; a city in the territory of Judah, on the west frontier of Benjamin.

Ver. 21.—**His mighty men**. The "mighty men" (*gibbōrim*) are not mentioned again in Jeremiah, and the Septuagint omits the word. But it is clear from Isa. iii. 2 that the "mighty men" were recognized as an important part of the community. From 1 Chron x. 10 it appears that the term indicates a position of high command in the army, which is in accordance with the notice in 2 Kings xxiv. 16. **Went into Egypt**. Egypt was the natural refuge for a native of Palestine (comp. 1 Kings xi. 17, 40; Matt. ii. 14), just as Palestine was for a native of Egypt. The latter, however, proved to be not a safe asylum for Urijah, as Pharaoh was the liege lord of Jehoiakim (2 Kings xxiii. 34), and the extradition of Urijah as a criminal naturally followed.

Ver. 22.—**Elnathan**. The name occurs again in ch. xxxvi. 12, 25. Possibly this man was the "Elnathan of Jerusalem" mentioned in 2 Kings xxiv. 8 as the father-in-law of Jehoiakim.

Ver. 23.—**Into the graves of the common people**; literally, *of the sons of the people* (comp. ch. xvii. 19; 2 Kings xxiii. 6). "The graves" is equivalent to "the graveyard," as Job xvii. 1.

Ver. 24.—**Nevertheless the hand of Ahikam**, etc.; *i.e.* in spite of the prepossession against prophets like Jeremiah which this incident reveals, Ahikam threw all his influence into the scale of toleration. The same Ahikam is mentioned in circumstances which reflect credit on his religion in 2 Kings xxii. 12—14. One of his sons, Gemariah, lent Baruch his official room for the reading of the prophecies of Jeremiah (ch. xxxvi. 10); another was the well-known Gedaliah, who became governor of Judah after the fall of Jerusalem, and who was himself friendly to Jeremiah (ch. xxxix. 14; xl. 5).

HOMILETICS.

Ver. 2.—*The duty of declaring the whole truth.* I. THE DUTY. Jeremiah is commanded to "diminish not a word" from the Divine message. A similar obligation rests upon every man who is called to speak for God to his fellow-men. The duty is urgent for two reasons: 1. *Truth is a trust.* Thus Timothy is admonished by St. Paul to keep that which is committed to his trust (1 Tim. vi. 20); and the apostle speaks of the "gospel which was committed to my trust" (1 Tim. i. 11). 2. *Truth is needed by the world.* It is not a private monopoly; it belongs to mankind. The world is dying for lack of it. He who has possession of it and refuses to reveal it to others is like a man who has discovered a secret spring of abundant water and churlishly keeps his knowledge to himself though his companions are perishing of thirst. Divine truth is of practical moment. It is not a mere curiosity, to be exposed or hidden as its owner thinks fit, as though his treatment of it made little difference to other men. When the four lepers of Samaria found the Syrian camp deserted, their first impulse was to pillage it quietly and hide the treasures, keeping the great discovery secret; but wiser thoughts prevailed, and they hastened to acquaint the citizens with their unexpected deliverance (2 Kings vii. 3—11). So every one who has seen the redemption of Christ has no right to keep his knowledge to himself while the world is in sore need of it. The Church is entrusted with the gospel, not for her own enjoyment alone, but for the good of the world. The same duty applies also to the possession of darker truths. It is evident, indeed, that a certain liberty and discretion are left with us. It is for us to arrange and present truth as it seems best to us; to give relative prominence to its various parts according to our idea of their importance; to lead men up to the reception of it by degrees. It may be that there are truths which the teacher sees, but which the scholar is not yet fit to receive. If they were declared to him he would not understand them, and they would only injure him. A wise teacher will reserve these. We act in this way with children. It may be right sometimes to do the same with those who are babes in knowledge. But is not this a violation of the duty of the text? By no means. For: (1) If we are sure the truth will be misunderstood we cannot really teach it; for to teach a thing is to make another understand and know it, not merely to speak out unintelligible words about it. We are not to cast our pearls before swine, though we are to remember that no human beings are to be regarded as hopelessly and for ever swinish. (2) Truth may be withholden for a time with the object, not of suppressing it, but of the better leading them up to the ripe reception of it. (3) The vision of truth must be distinguished from the mission to declare it. No doubt the one directly leads to the other. But they may not be contemporaneous. Questions of method, order, seasonableness, come between. The duty is to diminish nothing of the prophet's message.

II. THE TEMPTATION TO FAIL IN THIS DUTY. 1. *Personal fear* may tempt a man to "diminish" part of the Divine message. Jeremiah knew that the full utterance of his message would provoke violent opposition. He was warned not to shrink from declaring it on that account. In Christian lands and quiet times we do not feel the same terrible temptation to unfaithfulness. But it comes to us in another form. There are ideas which we believe to be true, but we fear they are unpopular; they will excite controversy, they will provoke ridicule, they will lead to neglect of the preacher. He is tempted to shun these truths that he may swim with the tide of popularity. But he is guilty of gross unfaithfulness if he thus shuns to declare the whole counsel of God. 2. It may appear that *men will not receive the message.* Of course, as has been remarked, we must use wisdom and discretion, seeking rather to convince men than to provoke them. But it may even be a duty to declare a truth as a testimony against men. In any case the responsibility for rejecting it will lie with them, as it should. But who can tell whether or no his work will be fruitless? The most unsympathetic hearers have sometimes been reached and affected and subdued by the truth which they came to mock or oppose. When the bow is drawn at a venture it may hit the most unlikely marks. It is certain that more good has been missed by our faithlessness in not " sowing beside all waters" than harm done by our rashness in blurting out truths in unseemly circumstances. 3. Certain truths may seem to be of *no practical use.* We are inclined to neglect these for those that are plainly profitable. Now, there can be no doubt that some truths are of more practical importance than others, and these should naturally receive our more earnest attention. But it is a mistake to neglect any truth on this account. Truth should be loved and taught for its own sake. It is degraded when it is regarded solely from a utilitarian standpoint. It is well that men should be true philosophers—lovers of wisdom. Moreover, it is impossible to tell what will be the future practical influence of a truth. Some of the most abstruse scientific inventions have led to results of great, though unexpected, human advantage. If research were confined within the limits of the evidently practical, it is certain that many of the most important discoveries—discoveries of the greatest use to man—would never have been made. Thus, if electricity had not been studied for purely scientific purposes we should never have had the telegraph. We do not know all the effects of Divine truth. It may not affect others as it does us. It may have special effects in the future, not felt as yet. It is our duty to preserve and transmit it to the ages when it may bear most fruit. 4. Some truths may appear *difficult and mysterious*. Of course, if a truth is wholly unintelligible, it cannot be taught. We are only uttering words when we try to expound it. But without being unintelligible it may be mysterious, it may be inexplicable; it may come, so to speak, with trails of dark shadows. The temptation is to leave this and only touch what is clear throughout. But the very sense of mystery may be beneficial. So much of the truth as is clear may be useful. If we are convinced that a thing is true, we may accept it without explaining the whole rationale of it. The mystery may grow clearer as we practise what we know of the truth. In any case the Christian teacher is God's ambassador, commissioned to declare his Master's message entire, unmutilated, whatever opinions *he* may have of the utility of it.

Vers. 8—19.—*A scene in a Jewish court of law.* We have here a graphic picture of the procedure under the Hebrew criminal law, for it would appear that Jeremiah was indicted and tried in accordance with correct legal order. The details of such a trial are not unimportant to the student of constitutional history. But they are also full of human interest. The law-court is a strange mirror of character. Many as are the objections to the publication of police news in the daily papers, it does at least serve to open our eyes to the eccentricities as well as the enormities of our variegated human world. Let us see what light this trial of Jeremiah throws upon the various persons concerned.

I. THE ACCUSERS. The leading accusers are priests and prophets. The priests, also, were foremost in the accusation of our Lord. Jeremiah had threatened the temple; it is not wonderful that temple officials should be enraged with him. Religious persecution is generally instigated by the professional clerical class, whose vested interests have been attacked by the reformer. The prophets were directly opposed by the teaching of Jeremiah. If orthodoxy is to be decided by the vote of the majority, they were the orthodox of their day. They were annoyed by the contradiction of the greatest man of their order. Unable to answer him, they tried to suppress him. The conduct of these men may suggest some general lessons, viz. (1) fidelity to the ordinances of worship is no proof of fidelity to God; (2) professional religiousness may be far removed from religiousness of character; (3) they who claim to be regular teachers of religion may be the last to recognize fresh truth; (4) they who are interested in a controversy are bad judges of the merits of the case.

II. THE ACCUSED. 1. Jeremiah remains faithful to his message. He reiterates it with new emphatic warnings. His defence is that he is sent by God to speak as he has spoken. He rests on innocence, truth, Divine authority. With such a plea he dare not recant. The true servants of God will know that they ought to "obey God rather than men," and therefore, like St. Peter and St. John, that they "cannot but speak the things which they have seen and heard" (Acts iv. 20). 2. Jeremiah showed indifference to his own life (ver. 14). He was a brave man, though his enemies accused him of advocating a coward's policy. It is noble thus to have strength to act on the conviction that truth is more precious than life. 3. Jeremiah warned the people of the consequences of injustice (ver. 15). This he did more for their sakes than for his own. Nothing can be more fatal to a country than the corruption of justice.

III. THE JUDGES. The princes and elders seem to have the position of judges. They are cool and impartial. In the Jewish state the office of judge came with birth and rank. The most radical friend of the people may see that the superior culture and freedom from popular passions of these men may have fitted them in some measure for their work. Unhappily, Jeremiah has exposed another side of their character. It speaks well for them, however, after the severe castigation he had given "the shepherds" (*e.g.* ch. xxv. 34—38), that they had the magnanimity to lend the prophet an impartial hearing, in spite of the virulent opposition of the priests. But possibly these two classes of leading men were not on the friendliest of terms with one another. Even if this be the case it is well that, unlike Herod and Pontius Pilate, they did not come to an agreement through the sacrifice of an innocent victim. Some of the elders cited the precedent of Micah's case. We see here the value of such an illustration. It serves to detach the principle under consideration from the prejudice of the passions of the hour.

IV. THE JURY. The assembly of the people seems to have acted as a jury. The priests and prophets present their accusation to them and the princes. The people and the princes pronounce the opinion that Jeremiah is innocent. The elders address themselves exclusively to the assembly of the people. This assembly shows the weakness of a popular concourse. The people are swayed from side to side. First they side with the priests, then with the rulers. It also shows its advantages. The people are open to impression; they do not care for formal consistency to a previous conviction; they like to see fair play. When their broad human instincts are appealed to they respond rightly.

Vers. 20—23.—*The story of an obscure martyr.* I. UNORIGINAL MEN MAY DO GOOD SERVICE IF THEY FOLLOW GOOD LEADERS. Urijah had no new message; but he followed Jeremiah fully and firmly. Accordingly, though not especially inspired, he was able to prophesy " in the Name of the Lord." It is more important to be true than to be original. It is the duty of the Christian teacher to speak in the Name of God, but only according to the teaching of prophets and apostles, and above all, Jesus Christ. If we do this we can speak " with authority."

II. SMALL MEN MAY EXERT GREAT POWER WHEN THEY ARE ON THE SIDE OF RIGHT AND TRUTH. Urijah is an insignificant personage, yet all the court is in dismay at his preaching. There is irony in this fact, if not intended by the language with which it is described. We have " Jehoiakim the king, with all his mighty men, and all his princes," alarmed and enraged at the preaching of one obscure man. What a testimony to the power of truth! *Magna est veritas et prevalebit.*

III. OBSCURE MEN MAY SUFFER WHEN GREATER MEN ARE SPARED. Urijah is killed; Jeremiah is acquitted. The Jews were overawed by Jeremiah; Urijah was an enemy small enough to be made a victim without danger. There is something terribly humiliating to human nature in this. How often do we see the same meanness choosing the underling rather than the leader for spiteful but safe revenge!

IV. IT IS SOMETIMES SAFER TO FACE DANGER THAN TO FLEE FROM IT. Jeremiah held his ground, and his life was spared; Urijah fled to Egypt, and he was dragged back to Jerusalem and ignominiously slain. The dauntless courage of the one man overpowered opposition; the cowardice of the other tempted it. It is always better even for ourselves to be brave and faithful. After his previous recantations Archbishop Cranmer could feel little of the triumph of a Ridley and a Latimer in the flames of his martyrdom.

Ver. 24.—*A friend in need.* Ahikam proves himself to be a true friend to Jeremiah by standing by him in the hour of danger. He is not like Joseph of Arimathæa, who was unheard of till he came and begged the dead body of his Lord. When the danger was greatest, he first made himself known on the side of the prophet.

I. HE WAS JUST. Jeremiah had been maligned. But Ahikam knew him to be innocent. To have allowed him to perish would have involved complicity in the murder of the prophet. Yet how many would have washed their hands and contented themselves with taking no active part in a public crime! It is not enough to refrain from joining in an injustice; duty requires us to resist it.

II. HE WAS INDEPENDENT. Jeremiah was unpopular. Though the unanswerable truthfulness of his defence secured him a verdict of acquittal at the regular trial, there can be no doubt that his life was in imminent peril from unscrupulous conspirators, now that the general sentiment was against him. It is a proof of staunch fidelity to stand by a man when he is unpopular. There is little merit in showing friendship for men who are fawned upon by fashion.

III. HE WAS COURAGEOUS. He could only defend Jeremiah at the peril of his own life. By siding with the prophet he allowed his name to be associated with all that was disliked and feared in the persecuted man, and he must have known this. For a person in high station to come out in this way by himself and defend a solitary, persecuted man required no little boldness.

IV. HE WAS USEFUL. Ahikam could not prophesy; but he could save a prophet's life. Possibly but for him Jeremiah's mission would have been cut short. To him, therefore, we owe the possibility of all the remainder of the great prophet's work. It is noteworthy that Ahikam had shown respect for the prophetic order before this, when, with his father and others, he went on an important mission from King Josiah to consult the prophetess Huldah (2 Kings xxii. 12—14). Many a man who can do little directly may be the means of securing immense good by fostering and furthering the work of others. It would be happy for us to think less of our own prominence and more of the accomplishment of God's will, no matter who may be the honoured instrument. We may look beyond the human friend and see the hand of Providence in this deliverance of the prophet. God raises up helpers when we least look for them. Among all the blessings of life none should command more thankfulness to God than the gift of good friends.

HOMILIES BY VARIOUS AUTHORS.

Vers. 1—3.—*God's mercy shown in his messages.* I. IN THEIR BEING REPEATED. It was substantially the same message as had been delivered before and been rejected. The question was not finally closed. Jehoiakim might show a disposition to repent and alter the policy of his father's government. In any case a new chance is afforded him and his people. God is slow to anger (Rom. x. 21). The invitations of his love are still extended to us, notwithstanding the sins of the fathers and our own repeated violations of his Law (Heb. iv. 6—9). Even the backslider is addressed with frequent warnings and appeals—a proceeding which would have no meaning apart from God's reserved purpose of grace. II. IN THEIR TIMELINESS. It was not only at the middle or end of Jehoiakim's reign, when he might have thought himself involved too deeply to retrace his steps, but at the very beginning. With a new king a fresh opportunity is offered for the nation also to return to its allegiance. Similarly does he stand at the threshold of every life and the opening of every career. He has "risen up early" and anticipated the transgressor in his evil way, or guided his faithful child into the paths of peace (cf. John i. 9). III. IN THEIR FAITHFULNESS. "Stand in the court of the Lord's house, and speak unto all the cities of Judah; ... diminish not a word." To declare "all the words of this life" is the commission of Christ's servants, and to do this "in season and out of season." The exact situation of men, and the relation into which sin has brought them with respect to God, must be plainly stated; there is no room for flattery. It is absurd to suppose that such a policy is due to vindictiveness. It can only be explained on the hypothesis of an earnest and thorough-going scheme of salvation. Sinners require to be faithfully dealt with, in order to awaken their conscience and constrain them to take advantage of the means provided for their deliverance. IV. IN THEIR REVELATION OF HIS WILLINGNESS TO SAVE. It might almost appear weakness, yet is not Jehovah ashamed of this long-suffering. The attribute of mercy does not detract from the dignity or authority of Divine character; rather is it its glory. This forbearance and hesitation to inflict punishment can be attributed to no base motives. It is in harmony with his behaviour at all times. How important is it that the repentant sinner should know the merciful disposition of him with whom he has to do! It is essential in every preaching of the gospel that this impression should be produced. The failure of one generation, again, is no reason for another being condemned before probation. God is "not willing that any should perish" (2 Pet iii. 9).—M.

Vers. 1—17, 24.—*The prophet of God arraigned by the nation.* Jeremiah's position, as that of all prophets, was necessarily a public one; to every man is he sent with the message. It is inadmissible for him to soften or lessen what he has to speak, which is nothing else than an indictment of the entire people (vers. 4—6). In default of their repentance his arraignment by them is, therefore, all but inevitable. Indifference could not well be feigned; words like his were certain to produce an effect. I. HIS RECEPTION. It is tumultuous and threatening. He is treated as a criminal. The people, under the influence of his enemies, the priests and the prophets, said,

"Thou shalt surely die," and were "gathered together against "him (vers. 8, 9). It was to be expected that the priests and the prophets should have been his accusers (ver. 11), and they already anticipate an unfavourable verdict. It is the educated and influential amongst the laity who are his judges (ver. 10)—a fortunate thing for him, as the event showed. They seem to have been more open to conviction, as they were probably better acquainted with the moral condition of the court and the political situation. The opposition of men is to be expected by the follower and witness of truth, for "the carnal mind is enmity against God" (Rom. viii. 7). But some will ever be found, if not convinced by him, yet, through the work of the Spirit, open to conviction. There is nothing which true religion demands in these crises but a fair hearing and an impartial judgment.

II. HIS DEFENCE. He declares the reality of his mission—"the Lord sent me" (vers. 12, 15); his faithfulness to his instructions, and the merciful aim which he had in view (ver. 13); his helplessness and indifference to personal consequences (ver. 14); and his own innocence of any evil design against the nation. God's servants, when thus arraigned, ought to be gentle and yet faithful to their message; the issue is to be left to him. The fear of man is to be forgotten in the fear of God and the enthusiasm of salvation.

III. HIS DELIVERANCE. 1. The verdict is sensible and wise (ver. 16), and receives the adhesion of the people. It is the false prophets who are most obstinately opposed, who would probably have aroused the popular prejudices, had it not been for the interference of certain elders who recalled previous instances in point (vers. 17—23); and the strong personal influence of Ahikam, son of Shaphan. We are reminded of our Saviour's experience at the bar of Pilate (Matt. xxvii. 19—25). 2. The most prominent feature of the judgment is its consequence. God's children must frequently be disappointed in their appeals to men and their expectation of results from his Word. His ways are hidden, inscrutable, and hard to acquiesce in. A clear and intelligent verdict is not to be expected from those who are not prepared to yield themselves to God's authority. The clearest and most faithful expositions of truth will frequently appear to fail of immediate effect. The servant of God is to care chiefly to deliver his soul; his personal safety may be left to God. God can raise up influential friends for his people in critical times, but he will work out his schemes in his own way.—M.

Ver. 6.—*Spiritual prerogative not inalienable.* The utterance of these words is the chief charge against the prophet; only, as in the case of Stephen (Acts vi. 13), the statement is mutilated in the accusation, the condition of the prophecy being entirely ignored (vers. 9, 11). The principle of indestructible consecration is still clung to by many in the face of the plainest declarations of Scripture. It may be well, therefore, to discuss its bearings in the present instance.

I. THE CIRCUMSTANCES OF ITS BESTOWAL. It was Divine grace to which it was due; but for this Jerusalem would have been like other cities. This favour had to be continued from moment to moment, being indeed only secured by the continued indwelling of the Holy Spirit. What was due to grace could be freely withdrawn by its Donor. As a matter of history, the most sacred places of Israel were repeatedly ruined and profaned. This destruction is matter of ancient prophecy, as in the present instance (Dan. ix. 26; Mark xiii. 2).

II. THE TERMS OF ITS TENURE. The repeated warnings and injunctions given prove that the consecration of the sacred places depended upon their occupancy by God's Spirit, and this in turn upon the faithfulness of his people. Either these had no meaning or the grace could be taken away. Jeremiah said, "If ye will not hearken to me, then will I make this house like Shiloh." The testimony of 1 Kings ix. 6—8 is precisely similar (cf. Ps. lxxviii. 60; ch. vii. 12).

III. ITS OWN ESSENTIAL NATURE. Strictly speaking, all things made by God are good and holy, but they may be desecrated, in a secondary sense, by being misused, profaned, or defiled. Institutions, buildings, or material or mechanical structures of any sort, are at best but secondary receptacles of Divine grace. "God dwelleth not in temples made with hands." It is the person occupying these who is the true temple, and when he is defiled by sin or unfaithfulness there can be no virtue inherent in the places which he frequents. Consecration is alone transmissible through the operation and presence of the Holy Spirit, and ceases with the withdrawal of the same. It consists primarily in the personal character through which it is expressed, and only secondarily in places and things, through the uses and practices carried on by holy men in connection with them. To the unholy, therefore, every place and thing will be unholy, and *vice versâ* (Titus i. 15). Material edifices, organization, and official prerogative, are nothing apart from this personal consecration associated with them; and the loss of that involves the loss of usefulness, of peace, and of sacredness, even in connection with that with which they have been most identified.—M.

Vers. 8, 9.—*The perils of prophesying.* I. THE PROPHET OF GOD MEETS WITH UNIVERSAL OPPOSITION.

II. HE IS IN PERSONAL DANGER. 1. *The responsibility of the judgments predicted is attached to himself.* This is due to a false principle of association, having its root in human ignorance and depravity. Not even *God* is responsible. The sinner must blame himself (Gal. iv. 16). 2. *The worst consequences are threatened.* Hatred to God expresses itself in hatred to his servant. It is, therefore, violent and in defiance of all justice. Transgressors think to escape judgment by denying it and destroying its witnesses.

III. CHARACTER IS JEOPARDIZED. The verdict was but a half-hearted one, and did not meet with general assent. The worst charges are brought against Christian men who are faithful to their convictions; and it is not always the case that their groundlessness is made clear. This is part of the "reproach of Christ."—M.

Vers. 12—15.—*The defence of the witness for the truth.* I. AN APPEAL TO CONSCIENCE. The message repeated in its baldest form. Its genuineness insisted upon, and its reception earnestly urged upon men. A high moral standpoint is maintained, and there is no compromise or apology. He stands at the bar of human conscience.

II. OBEDIENCE TO LAWFUL AUTHORITY. He hands himself over to them to deal with him as they will; is careful to state his case as God gives him ability; and appeals to no unlawful means of deliverance.

III. REFERENCE OF THE WHOLE MATTER TO GOD. God sent him—that is sufficient. He has been faithful to his instructions; is really not to be judged by man, but leaves all with God.—M.

Ver. 24.—*Help raised up for God's servants in times of peril.* I. OF WHAT SORT IT IS. 1. *Unexpected.* 2. *Opportune.* 3. *Effective.* 4. *Not what man would choose.*

II. WHAT IT TEACHES US. 1. *The infinite resources of God.* 2. *The weakness of evil.* 3. *Those who will not willingly obey God are made to serve him unwillingly.* 4. *God chooses his own way of dealing with his servants and his truth.*—M.

Ver. 11.—*Jeremiah reckoned worthy of death.* I. WHO THEY WERE THAT PRONOUNCED THIS JUDGMENT. There is already a statement in ver. 8 that priests, prophets, and people had laid hold on Jeremiah with a threatening of death; but we must allow something for the feelings produced on the first reception of an exasperating and humiliating message. The case is worse when the priests and prophets, having had some time for consideration, however short, press upon the princes and people a demand for the death of Jeremiah. The lead the priests and prophets here take goes a long way in showing who were mostly responsible for the deplorable state of things in the land. If things were to be put right, these two classes of men must be conspicuous in repentance. Those who were so ready to sentence Jeremiah to death were really most of all deserving of death themselves. He had simply spoken words against the city and the temple, words which were not his own; those who condemned him had so lived that their life had been a sedulous undermining of all that constituted the prosperity and glory of their country.

II. WHAT IT WAS THAT PROVOKED THE JUDGMENT. Jeremiah had prophesied against the city. Observe, not simply that he had spoken blasphemous and contemptuous words against the city; but that he had *prophesied* against it. Thus did the priests and prophets show how little they understood the nature of true prophecy. They did not understand that when the Lord sends forth a man to speak, he puts a word in his mouth which shall commend itself to all who love truth and certainty. To the mind of these priests and prophets everything began with this postulate, that nothing must be said against Jerusalem and the temple. And to them it was no sort of answer that the sins of Jerusalem deserved and demanded that something should be said against it. The good name of Jerusalem, however lacking in any sort of correspondence with reality, had become a sort of point of honour. Thus we see how the pride of men goes before their destruction. A conventional sense of honour leads them into paths thickly strewn with stumbling-blocks. These men had become so stuffed with spurious patriotism that they could not bear to have Jerusalem spoken against. Hence they are logically compelled to imply that Jeremiah is a false prophet, and that God has not spoken at all. They were as those who shut their eyes, and then say there is nothing to be seen.

III. The doom they invoked. The man who speaks against Jerusalem is reckoned worthy of death. We must not, of course, measure this judgment by our notions of what may require the death-penalty. To speak against a parent was by the Law of Moses to incur the death-penalty. As the Apostle James uses many forcible expressions to illustrate, great is the power of the tongue; and a bad man may do mischief with his tongue worthy of the severest punishment men can inflict. If Jeremiah had gone about among the people stirring them up to rebellion and national discord, there would have been nothing very astonishing in an attempt to put him to death. But he gave no exhortation to the people save what each one could carry into effect without the slightest injury to any one; nay, rather the obedience of each would be to the real and abiding advantage of all. He spoke not of anything he himself intended to bring about, but of what was going to happen altogether irrespective of him. His death, supposing he were slain, would make no difference; nay, it would only help to proclaim his message louder and more abidingly. Those who feel themselves attacked by the truth, strike out recklessly with the first instrument they can get hold of; but though they may seem thus to destroy God's agencies, it is found in the end that they are efficiently promoting his work. They that were scattered abroad by the great persecution which arose at the time of Stephen's death, "went everywhere preaching the Word."—Y.

Ver. 16.—*Jeremiah reckoned not worthy of death.* The contrast is very decided between ver. 11 and ver. 16. In ver. 11 there is what appears an irresistible and deadly accusation, coming from men who hardly knew a check of any kind. In ver. 16 there is the answer of those to whom they speak, refusing to ratify their demand. What has happened between? Only the appeal of one who was strong in the consciousness that he had been a faithful servant of God. If we consider his words carefully, we shall see that underneath them there are three considerations, of which the first is more important than the second, and the second more important than the third.

I. We may say that, first of all, he is thinking of the God who had sent him. That which threatened him at the same time insulted and tried to thwart Jehovah. Not that Jeremiah was careless about his own safety, but the glory of his God was paramount in his thoughts. He had in him the true spirit of apostleship; the claims he had to make were not his own claims; he was a sent man, and sent of God. Just in proportion as a man feels that God has sent him, must be his distress to find that others do not recognize the credentials of the messenger and the importance of the message. On one side the prophet was dealing with God, on the other with men. Every day deepened on him the impression of God's intimate presence with him; and yet this same God who was so much to him was nothing to these people; the name that thrilled and subdued his susceptible heart, was perhaps the least potent of sounds in their ears. Hence the need of appealing to them again and again, if perchance there might be roused in them some sort of apprehension that they were dealing, not with a brother man, but with the almighty and holy God. While they were all absorbed in considerations of their own territorial dignity, God in his justice was coming ever nearer. Whatever happens to the people or to the prophet himself, that prophet will at all events exalt God before them to the latest hour of his existence. If he has to die, the message of God shall live more gloriously in his closing hours.

II. He is thinking of the interests of this apparently obdurate people.

Though at the present moment it is he who seems to be in danger, he well knows that his peril is but a surface trifle when compared with that attaching to the scowling enemies who are crowded around him. He can be rescued, if so it please God; but who is to rescue those who are striding onwards, ever more swiftly, to a righteous doom? God can deliver the prophet from his enemies, for the prophet himself interposes no obstacle to his deliverance; but these people of Judah and Jerusalem interpose insurmountable obstacles, in that they will not amend their ways and doings and obey the voice of God. More than that, it seems as if they were about to add a fresh obstacle by shedding the innocent blood of God's latest messenger. The persecutor is always in greater peril than the persecuted. Physical pain and physical death are transitory and unreturning ills, but the evil-doer has to face the worm that dieth not. Compare with the words of the prophet here the words of Jesus as he was being led to crucifixion : "Daughters of Jerusalem, weep not for me, but weep for yourselves, and for your children" (Luke xxiii. 28).

III. HE IS THINKING OF HIS OWN PRESENT POSITION. (See ver. 14.) This verse reveals a calm, intermediate position between the reckless fanaticism that even courts death and the spirit that turns back the moment threatening is heard. "I am in your hands," says the prophet. He admits their power to the fullest extent, and he does not in any way dare them to the exercise of it. He is neither anxious for life nor afraid of death. This surely is the spirit to be gained if one would be a true witness for God. Jeremiah seems to speak here as one who had gained, for the moment at least, something of the calm of eternity. And his very calmness must surely have been a considerable element in determining the rapid change of feeling among the multitude. Perfect presence of mind, when it comes from an all-sufficient Divine stay within, must have a wondrous power in checking those whose fury is roused by an attack on their base and selfish interests.—Y.

Vers. 17—23.—*An argument from history.* A prophet, a king, and a people belonging to a past generation are brought forward to justify the conclusion to which the princes and the people here had come. Here, then, is an eminent instance of what a practical study history may become. One must be so acquainted with the past as to seize just that completed event which will cast light on the duties and necessities of the present.

I. AN INSTANCE OF A PROPHET'S UNPALATABLE MESSAGE. No word could have been more provocative of resentment than this. It threatened those to whom it was spoken in the closest possible way. It meant that they were to be subjected to their enemies, driven from their homes, and deprived of their most substantial possessions. The message being such, what comfort Jeremiah might obtain from recollecting that his predecessors treading his thorny path before him were now remembered in such an honourable way! Micah had been faithful to his God, his message, and his audience; and the impression of his faithfulness is still deep when something like a century has elapsed. These people now listening to Jeremiah were thus made responsible for Micah's words as well as Jeremiah's. What harmony there is in true prophecy! False prophets, from their very position, cannot be got to agree; but here Jeremiah's words at once recall to mind Micah's similar words, and help to drive them with a deeper impression into some at least of this subsequent generation. Thus also, reciprocally, Micah's words help Jeremiah's. And not only was there harmony between the prophecies; there was harmony between the characters of the prophets as well. All the prophets would have understood one another perfectly if they had been gathered together in one assembly.

II. AN INSTANCE OF HOW A PROPHET SHOULD EVER BE RECEIVED. Jeremiah is able to look back on a man of like spirit with himself in the prophet Micah, but the present leaders of Israel have their thoughts turned to a very different king from Jehoiakim. We can guess how Hezekiah behaved toward Micah from the way in which he behaved toward Isaiah. The narrative here concerning the fate of Urijah seems to be introduced to show that, though Jeremiah escaped from peril at the hands of these priests and prophets, their nature and the nature of Jehoiakim remained the same. When Hezekiah heard the truth, bitter as it was, he humbled himself and averted doom. But Jehoiakim and his profligate and rapacious circle hated every one who spoke the truth. Hence it was not enough for them that Urijah fled; they followed him and brought him back to suffer their vengeance. Thus it is made evident how Jehoiakim was a man of very different spirit from Hezekiah.—Y.

Ver. 24.—*A friend in need.* I. THE EVIDENT PERIL OF JEREMIAH. A large body of the people had been somehow influenced to take his side, but how long their favourable mood of mind might continue, who could tell? There was no Hezekiah on the throne to encourage such a feeling and make it permanent. Moreover, there is an ebullition of fury which is fatal to one who, as far as the record enables us to judge, occupied a far less prominent position than Jeremiah. If Urijah was slain, how could Jeremiah hope to escape? We must try to get a distinct impression of all the peril in which Jeremiah was in order to appreciate the services rendered to him by Ahikam.

II. THE TIMELY HELP OF AHIKAM. Nothing is told us save the bare fact of protection. We must not assume that Ahikam was fully in sympathy with Jeremiah. We have no means of judging as to his character and his motives, as to the risks that he ran, and the ultimate results to him. The one clear thing is that at this time he was a man of power, and was for some reason disposed to shield the prophet. It may be that, if we could lay bare and analyze his motives, they would be found very mixed as to their kind. But, whatever the motives, the practical service was the same. Jehovah could, of course, have protected his servant by supernatural means, but it is his principle of working not to employ the supernatural when the natural would serve the purpose. Hezekiah could do more than Ahikam, seeing that he turned to God and kept back the dreadful visitations. But Ahikam did all that was necessary for the present occasion. Compare the position of Ahikam here with that of the Duke of Lancaster towards Wickliffe and the Lollards.—Y.

EXPOSITION.

CHAPTER XXVII.

This and the two following chapters are closely connected. They all relate to the early part of the reign of Zedekiah, and contain warnings arising out of the deepening gloom of the political horizon. It must, however, be noted that there is evidently some mistake in the first verse of ch. xxvii., and also that the contents of ch. xxix. point to a somewhat earlier time than ch. xxvii., xxviii. (viz. the first or second year of King Zedekiah). To understand the circumstances of ch. xxvii., we must remember that Zedekiah had accepted the throne as the vassal of Nebuchadnezzar (2 Kings xxiv. 17). The self-righteousness and formalism of the people, however, would not allow them to remain quiet under such a humiliation. Deuteronomy, it seemed to them, had promised success and prosperity to an obedient performance of the Law, and the priests and the prophets assured them that these conditions had been complied with. In the fourth year of Zedekiah (comp. ch. xxviii. 1) the popular discontent was still further stimulated by the presence of ambassadors from the neighbouring nations, who had come to organize a common movement against the common enemy. Jeremiah believed that he could not give more forcible expression to the Divine warnings of which he was the bearer than by a symbolic act akin to that related of Isaiah in Isa. xx. 2. He appeared in some public place, where the ambassadors would be sure to pass, with a yoke upon his neck, and in this strange guise delivered an impressive exhortation to the foreign visitors. It would appear as if Jeremiah's exertions on this occasion were successful, so far as Judah was concerned; for we are informed (ch. li. 59) that, in the fourth year of his reign, Zedekiah took a journey to Babylon, doubtless to renew his oath of fidelity to the King of Babylon.

It is instructive to compare this chapter as given in the Hebrew Bible with the form in which it appears in the Septuagint. We must not too hastily assume that the Greek is incorrect, but examine in each case which form gives most force and expressiveness to the prophecy.

Ver. 1.—**In the beginning of the reign**

of Jehoiakim. The Syriac substitutes for "Jehoiakim" "Zedekiah," to bring the passage into conformity with ch. xxviii. 1, where the fourth year of the reign of Zedekiah is expressly mentioned. But is this emendation sufficient? Can the fourth year be called "the beginning of the reign of Zedekiah," when that reign lasted altogether only eleven years? Is it not probable that the transcriber has inadvertently copied the heading of ch. xxvi., which corresponds verbally with ch. xxvii. 1, except that "unto Jeremiah" is wanting?

Ver. 2.—Make thee bonds and yokes; rather, *bands and poles;* i.e. the bands which secured the two pieces of wood placed respectively above and beneath the neck of the ox, so forming a yoke. Hence, in Lev. xxvi. 13, we find the phrase, "the poles [Authorized Version wrongly, 'the bands'] of your yoke." It is clear from ch. xxviii. 10 that this account is to be taken literally.

Ver. 3.—And send them, etc. The letter of the text certainly suggests that Jeremiah actually delivered a separate yoke to each of the five ambassadors. Some commentators, however, finding such an act almost incredible, suppose the statement to be allegorical, and the "sending of the yoke" to mean the declaration of the subjection of the nations to Nebuchadnezzar which follows, somewhat as in ch. xxv. 15 the "causing all the nations to drink" means the utterance of a prophecy of woe to the various peoples concerned. But we can hardly pronounce upon this passage by itself. We have to consider whether a whole group of similar statements is or is not to be taken literally. It may be enough to instance ch. xiii. 1—7. Which come; rather, *which are come.*

Vers. 5, 6.—Jehovah is the Creator and Proprietor of the earth and all that is therein. Therefore he can give any part of it to whomsoever he will. Therefore, Jeremiah being his trustworthy prophet, the kings are called upon to take notice that Jehovah has transferred their kingdoms to Nebuchadnezzar. Observe, in chs. xxvii.—xxix. the form employed is not "Nebuchad*r*ezzar," but "Nebuchad*n*ezzar" (so also ch. xxxiv. 1; xxxix. 5). (See on ch. xxi. 7.)

Ver. 6.—My servant (see on ch. xxv. 9). The beasts of the field; *i.e.* the wild beasts. This last feature indicates the unlimited character of Nebuchadnezzar's power.

Ver. 7.—Him, and his son, and his son's son. This is intelligible only if the seventy years predicted by Jeremiah in ch. xxv. 11, 12, xxix. 10, are a round number. Nebuchadnezzar died in B.C. 561, and was succeeded by his son Evil-Merodach, who, after two years, was put to death by Neriglissar. In B.C. 555 Laborosoarchod (?) became king, but after nine months a usurper

belonging to another family, Nabonedus or Nabunita, ascended the throne, which he occupied till B.C. 538, the year of the fall of Babylon. "Seventy years," taken literally, only brings us to B.C. 555, seventeen years short of the conquest of Babylon by Cyrus. Until the very time of his land come; rather, *until the time of his own land come.* Nebuchadnezzar cannot ensure his realm against captivity. Shall serve themselves of him. (For the meaning of the phrase, see on ch. xxv. 14.)

Ver. 9.—Your dreamers; rather, *your dreams.* So in ch. xxix. 8 the "dreams" of the people are expressly distinguished from the utterances of the prophets and soothsayers. In our passage the "dreamers" are appropriately mentioned between the "diviners" and the "enchanters," because the skill of the soothsayers partly lay in the interpretation of dreams (comp. Gen. xli. 8; Dan. ii. 2).

Ver. 10.—To remove you far; or, more distinctly, *that I may remove you far.* So Isa. vi. 12, "(Until) Jehovah have removed men afar off." The deportation policy of the Assyrians and Babylonians was overruled by God for his own deep purposes.

Ver. 11.—The nations that bring their neck, etc. The Hebrew has, "The nation that shall bring its neck," etc.

Vers. 12—15.—But the warnings of Jeremiah were not confined, far from it, to the neighbouring kings. Zedekiah had received a precisely similar message. Bring your necks. The plural is used, for Zedekiah was but an individual among a number of much more vigorous personalities (comp. on ch. xxii. 2).

Vers. 16—22.—The warning to the priests and to the rest of the people. The last four verses of this section appear in a much shortened form in the Septuagint, and it must be admitted that the description is singularly lengthy. It is, therefore, quite conceivable that this is one of the cases in which the Hebrew text has been disfigured by wilful interpolation. On the other hand, it is also possible that the description was filled out by an editor, *e.g.* by Baruch, conscientiously for the benefit of later readers.

Ver. 16.—The vessels of the Lord's house; *i.e.* the golden vessels which Solomon had made, and which Nebuchadnezzar had taken away (1 Kings vii. 48—50; 2 Kings xxiv. 13). Now shortly. These words are wanting in the Septuagint, and, considering that the Greek is also without the prediction in ver. 22, that the vessels of the temple and of the palace should be brought back in the day of visitation (which seems inconsistent with ch. lii. 17), the question arises whether the words "now shortly" here are not due to a hasty copyist.

Ver. 18.—**But if they be prophets**, etc. The "false prophets," so Jeremiah declares, have neglected one of the principal functions of a prophet, viz. intercessory prayer (comp. on ch. vii. 16). Seeing that a part of the sacred vessels had been carried to Babylon, all true prophets ought to intercede with Jehovah that those still left might be spared. The end was that the remaining vessels were carried off on the capture of Jerusalem (2 Kings xxv. 13).

Ver. 19.—This and the two following verses are thus given in the Septuagint: "For thus saith the Lord, . . . and the rest of the vessels which the king of Babylon took not, when he carried Jeconiah captive from Jerusalem; they shall come to Babylon, saith the Lord." This shortened form throws a light on the fact of the absence of "now shortly" in ver. 16 (see note). **The pillars**, etc.; *i.e.* the two bronze pillars called Jachin and Boaz (1 Kings vii. 21). **The sea**; *i.e.* the molten "sea," or basin (1 Kings vii. 23). **The bases** (1 Kings vii. 27).

HOMILETICS.

Ver. 5.—*The rights of the Creator.* This address on the rights of the Creator is made to heathen men because God has rights over all men, and because they who cannot yet understand his higher character may be able to recognize his natural rights.

I. THE FOUNDATION OF THE RIGHTS OF THE CREATOR. 1. They rest on the fact that all things that exist were *created*. It is a fundamental axiom of science that everything that has a beginning must have a cause. The universal testimony of experience is against the notion that existences could spring forth spontaneously from nothing, or that organisms could come of themselves from a lawless chaos. The theory of an endless chain of causation is illogical. If this is regarded as cyclic we have nothing to account for the motion of the whole cycle. The notion is parallel to that of a wheel revolving because the several parts of the circumference press on those which are before them—a mechanical absurdity. If, however, the chain is regarded as infinitely long, we have another absurdity. Since it is made up of finite links each of which is no perfect cause in itself, we have not solved the question, we have only driven it back to the infinite distance. It is the grand lesson of the first chapter of the Book of Genesis—whatever we may think of the details of that chapter—that it comes to our rescue with the assertion of a personal Creator, the only doctrine that will fit the requirements of the case. 2. The rights of the Creator rest on the fact that all things were created by *his energy.* We do not know what subordinate agencies God may employ. But in any case the fundamental power must be his. He cannot delegate powers of creation in the sense of investing any beings with them without any dependence on his power. The power must be God's, though the channel through which it flows may be some lower agency. The doctrine of evolution would not touch this fact. The important question is not as to the method of creation, but as to the originating power. This lies behind the question of design. It is the question of primitive causation. Whether with successive sudden emergencies or through gradual development, it is equally true that God has created the world by his great power and by his outstretched hand.

II. THE NATURE OF THE RIGHTS OF THE CREATOR. They are absolute. We know nothing like them among men. A man is supposed to have a right to dispose of the work of his own hands. But his work is not creation. If he has built a house he has not made the ground on which it stands, nor the stone and wood of which it is constructed. But by Divine creation we understand not merely building up the materials of the universe into new forms, but the original making of these materials and the determination of the laws of nature. From this fact comes the right of God to dispose of his creation as he thinks fit, to give the world and its contents to whomsoever he pleases. But in admitting this we are saying that he will do that which is best for the world itself. For God is just and good and merciful. He will please to do that which is right, and that which will bless his creatures. God exercises his rights through his will. If creation reveals the rights, Christ reveals the will. Through this higher revelation we see reasons for acquiescing in God's exercise of sovereignty, not with mere resignation to the inevitable, nor even only with dutiful yielding to recognized law and authority, but with thankful submission to the care of a merciful Father. Thus we see that the exercise of God's rights is limited by his character; limited by his justice, so that he can never dispose of things arbitrarily or cruelly; limited by his love, so that he will dispose of them so as to secure the welfare of his children. This is a consideration of the first importance. The neglect of it has led to the interpretation of such words as those of our text so as to represent God as an arbitrary, capricious Sovereign, who may be feared and must be submitted to, but cannot be loved or freely adored.

Vers. 6, 7.—*God's disposal of man's possessions.* I. GOD HAS A RIGHT TO DISPOSE OF MAN'S POSSESSIONS. He made them, and they are always his, only lent to be withdrawn or transferred when he wills. If the Lord gave, he has a right to take away (Job i. 21). If he takes much, we should be thankful for what he leaves—for this even we have no claim. Nations should feel that God has rights over them. Their liberties are subject to his government, their territory to his disposal.

II. GOD DOES DISPOSE OF MAN'S POSSESSIONS. He exercises his right. He is no *roi fainéant*. God does not reserve his interference for the last day of judgment. He is always working among the nations. In a national disaster we should recognize the hand of Providence; so should we in the advent of national glory. God does not only overthrow; he appoints, prospers, gladdens.

III. GOD DOES NOT ALWAYS GIVE THE GREATEST POWER TO THE BEST MEN. Nebuchadnezzar was a bad man; yet God gave him the largest dominion in the world. We may believe that he was best suited for the work that was required of him. His mission was to be a scourge of the nations. An angel would find himself ill at ease in such a work. In appointing a hangman we do not expect to get the most high-souled person in the kingdom for the post. God can overrule the evil nature of bad men and make it serve some good end, as we can employ the refuse of one factory as useful materials in another.

IV. GOD DOES NOT ALWAYS GIVE THE MOST ABUNDANT POSSESSIONS TO THE BEST MEN. We see bad men enriched, good men pauperized. Goodness seems on the whole to be favourable to temporal prosperity, but with innumerable exceptions. Therefore we must conclude that God does not value earthly prosperity so highly as we value it. He regards it as subordinate to higher interests.

V. GOD'S DISPOSAL OF MAN'S POSSESSIONS DOES NOT HINDER THE FREE EXERCISE OF MAN'S POWERS. God gave Nebuchadnezzar his powers, but the king put these forth of his own will. By his daring, his energy, the use of his resources, he won his brilliant victories and conquered his vast dominions. God works through our work. He gives to the diligent.

VI. GOD'S DISPOSAL OF MAN'S POSSESSIONS DOES NOT LIMIT MAN'S RESPONSIBILITY. It Nebuchadnezzar got his territory by violence and rapacity, he was not the less guilty because God assigned it to him. For he was responsible for his own actions and their motives, irrespective of any unknown design that God might work out through them. We cannot throw the blame of our misconduct on the providence of God. He overrules the issue of our actions, but he does not fetter or force the choice of our wills.

Ver. 11.—*The duty of non-resistance.* Again and again in various forms Jeremiah recurs to the advice of submission to Nebuchadnezzar. In the present instance he addresses it to representatives of foreign nations, and urges it as politic, while to the Jews he was more anxious to show that it was in accordance with God's will. Viewed from various standpoints there were several grounds for non-resistance.

I. THE WILL OF GOD. This was the highest reason. It could not be fully appreciated by the heathen; yet even they were reminded that the Creator was the supreme disposer of the destiny of nations. The condition of the Jews, however, was peculiar. They were living under a theocracy. The prophets were the ministry of the Divine King. Their utterances were revelations of law for the government of the people. To resist Nebuchadnezzar in opposition to these utterances was to rebel against the decree of the supreme Sovereign of the nation. We do not stand in the same outward circumstances. But we should learn that the first thought in public as well as in private affairs should be as to what is right, what is God's will; and all considerations of glory etc., should be subordinate to this. We cannot learn God's will from oracular teachers but we can ascertain it from a devout study of revelation, prayer, and honest thought

II. SOUND POLICY. Events proved that Jeremiah was politically as well as morally right. Religious duty lies nearer to useful policy than either fanatic dreamers or worldly statesmen are able to see. History shows that all resistance to the mighty flood of the Babylonian invasion was futile. Timely submission alone could secure a mitigation of its violence. It is foolish for a nation to flourish empty notions of glory above considerations for the welfare of the people. The loyal statesman will care less for the fame of a great name, or the splendour of brilliant achievements, than for the peaceful prosperity of his fellow-countrymen. The first interest of a nation is this peaceful prosperity. There may be times when to maintain it self-defence becomes a duty. But when self-defence cannot secure it, when it is rather hindered than helped by resistance, it is foolish to resist for the sake of mere pride.

III. Wholesome moral good. The Jews were taught that the invasion by Nebuchadnezzar was sent by God as a chastisement for sin. To submit to it was to submit to profitable correction. In the end the nation might hope to be the better for it. We have no right to complain of troubles which our own misconduct has brought upon us. We may " count it all joy " that we have fallen into tribulation if this works our higher and lasting good. Temporal distress should be patiently borne in the prospect of eternal blessedness, material adversity calmly endured when this is the means of securing inward spiritual good.

Ver. 18.—*Prophecy tested by prayer.* I. It is the duty of a prophet to pray. He should be spiritually what the priest can only be ceremonially, the mediator between man and God. Mediation has two sides. It implies the work of the intercessor as well as that of the prophet—the speaking to God for men as well the speaking to men for God. The former work, however, is in more danger of falling into neglect. It is more spiritual, it requires more humility, it gains less credit from men. But no prophet can even discharge his mission to men aright unless he is also a man of prayer. God reveals himself to those who seek him. Revelations from Heaven are vouchsafed to those who live in communion with Heaven.

II. Inspiration is requisite for prayer as well as for prophecy. The true prophet is the inspired man; he also has the first requisite for prayer. We need inspiration for prayer to bring us into sympathy with God. Prayer is more than asking for the satisfaction of our wants—it is communion with God; and communion implies sympathy. Like the bird which soars aloft because its wings rest on the surrounding air, we can only rise heavenwards as we bear ourselves up through an atmosphere of heavenly thought. Without the breath of God's Spirit in us we cannot withdraw from the world and attain to the vivid consciousness of spiritual things. For prayer involves the rising above our common, our ordinary life. Thus we may understand the mission of the Spirit as an intercessor. Christ intercedes for us with God. The Holy Spirit intercedes for God in us, helping our infirmities, teaching us what we should pray for, and how to pray, and breathing into us yearnings deep and unutterable (Rom. viii. 26).

III. Divinely inspired prayer will be reasonable and according to God's will. If the prophets were inspired they would not ask for the impossible; they would not pray for that which they knew was contrary to God's will; they would not utter prayers of greed and pride. Inspiration does not make a man irrational; on the contrary, it makes him see facts as they are. If these prophets were inspired they would see the folly of asking back the lost vessels. Inspiration is concerned with the present and the future. It is foolish to waste time in lamenting the irretrievable. Let us see that we preserve what still remains with us, and secure what is best for the future. It is absurd to be boasting of great things when we cannot secure small ones. If the prophets could not protect the vessels in Jerusalem, much less could they recover those which had been already removed to Babylon. They might be uttering great prayers about the lost treasure; but while they made no prevailing prayer to secure the treasure still in hand they only exposed their own incompetence.

IV. Prayer and its results are tests of a man's spiritual condition. If it can be said of a person, " Behold, he prayeth! " we may know much of him. Prayer is the barometer that rises or falls with the changing tone of the spiritual atmosphere. When we " restrain prayer " this is a sad sign that our better life is failing. It is useless to boast of spiritual attainments such as those of the professional prophets; these are nothing but delusions if the prayer-test reveals a condition of spiritual deadness,

The results of prayer are a further test.   We cannot say that a particular prayer is not acceptable to God because it does not bring us the particular thing we seek, since we are always making foolish requests, and God mercifully deals with us according to his wise and good will rather than according to the letter of our language.   Still, if no answer is ever received to prayer, something must be wrong.   Either all our prayers are mistaken, which shows we could not be receiving the help of God's inspiration; or our spiritual condition is one of separation from God, in which condition no prayer could be answered.   If not in every detail, yet in the main, religious experience may be tested by the facts of life.   The prophet must find his prediction confirmed by history. The man of prayer must show some fruits of his devotion.

HOMILIES BY VARIOUS AUTHORS.

Vers. 1—22.—*Divine judgments not to be resisted.*   A conference of ambassadors from neighbouring nations had been held at Zedekiah's court to consider plans of revolt against Nebuchadnezzar.   The king himself and a patriotic party were bent upon resistance.   This movement Jeremiah checked at its very outset by his symbolical warning.

I. GOD IS RULER OF ALL THE KINGDOMS OF THE EARTH.   He made them, and controls their destinies.   Of the earth he says, " I have given it unto whom it seemed meet unto me."   His control over human interests, possessions, and destinies is absolute and unlimited.

II. EVEN THE UNGODLY MAY BE INSTRUMENTS OF HIS PURPOSES.   " Nebuchadnezzar, my servant,"—a remarkable title when applied to a heathen prince.   The character of the authorities, the agents, and the instrumentalities by which we are opposed is not in itself a reason for resisting them if they are evidently of Divine appointment.   In such a case we should be fighting against God.   Moral evil is ever to be resisted and witnessed against, but that which God appoints must be acknowledged and submitted to.

III. IN SUCH CASES CIRCUMSTANCES WILL CLEARLY SHOW WHETHER THE APPOINTMENT IS OF GOD OR NOT, AND NOW WE MUST BE GUIDED IN OUR CONDUCT.   The advice of the prophet is not to be interpreted as an expression of mere political prudence.   It was the moral significance of Nebuchadnezzar's supremacy to which he appealed.   In default of revelation our own conscience and common sense must be our guides.   1. *In cases of unmistakable Divine dispensations the law of submission is clearly taught.*   Of this class is the rule of submission to the powers that be; of cheerful contentment with one's lot in life, so far as it seems beyond our own legitimate control or to be providentially arranged.   2. *The ordinary miscellaneous trials and difficulties of life are not to be regarded in this way.*   Where there is not witness of conscience enjoining submission, energetic effort must be made.   The Bible is no book of fatalism.   It inculcates self-help, manly fortitude, and believing, intelligent enterprise.

IV. GUIDANCE AND INSTRUCTION MAY BE GRANTED TO MEN EVEN WHILST UNDER DIVINE DISCIPLINE.   1. *Injunctions.*   To be punished does not mean to be cast off; quite the contrary.   And therefore, if there be any gracious purpose in the dispensation, it is well that it should be explained.   False prophets have foretold favourable turns of fortune with mischievous effect.   These must be contradicted, and their tendency exposed.   The Bible is full of instruction to the perplexed in all ages, and the Spirit of God still speaks to the hearts of his children.   2. *Signs.*   Sometimes these will be of one kind, sometimes of another.   Here a crucial test was proposed, viz. the challenge to the false prophets to bring back the vessels of the temple from Babylon.   If God heard their prayer, then it would appear that their advice was sound. Signs will never be wanting to those who earnestly seek to know God's will.   3. *These are to be sought through prayer and waiting upon God.*—M.

Ver. 18.—*Prophets tested by prayer.*   I. BY THIS THEIR DISPOSITION WAS DISCOVERED.   Prayer is one of the most vital indications of the presence of spiritual life. It is only by constant devotion and spiritual intercourse with God that any one can be truly acquainted with him or know his will.   The taunt of the prophet is to the effect that they are not over addicted to this practice, but prefer to indulge in political trifling and bombast. They had no pleasure in the exercises of true piety; and it might be were even afraid directly to invoke Jehovah. It was the neglect of the latter by themselves and their idolatrous followers which had entailed the present evils upon Judah. The prophet points out, therefore, the true method of discovering the will of God, and of restoring, not only the vessels to the temple, but the exiles to their land.

II. THEIR PRETENSIONS WOULD BE TESTED BY THE EFFICACY OF THEIR INTERCESSION. This is the most disinterested form of prayer. By betaking themselves to it, instead of prophesying lies, they would do real service to the nation. Because he who can effectually intercede : 1. *Is a source of blessing to all who are about him.* He has true sympathy and insight, and can bring down forgiveness even upon the undeserving. The grandest promises of Holy Scripture are encouragements to this practice. 2. *Is thereby acknowledged and accepted by God.* As Elijah provoked with a similar challenge the prophets of Baal, so Jeremiah taunts his enemies with their spiritual impotency. The restoration of the vessels under the circumstances would be nothing short of a miracle, and supernatural aid would be required. He alone is truly great who can prevail with God. And the greatest of the prophets is he who makes intercession for mankind according to the Divine will.—M.

Vers. 1—11.—*Jehovah's consideration towards some neighbours of Israel.* I. GOD FORESEES THE NATURAL PROBABILITY OF A STRUGGLE. Nebuchadnezzar and his hosts are not to drop from the clouds on the land of Jehovah's people whom Jehovah has now doomed. These hosts come from a distant land, and have many intervening lands to pass through; and how can they pass through in any but a destroying, impoverishing fashion ? If the King of Babylon is to reach Jerusalem, the lands here mentioned must assuredly suffer from him scarcely less than Judah itself. And naturally they will prepare to meet him. Alliances will be formed; resources will be accumulated; the greatest strain will be put on every one in order to make the defence successful. These attacked people cannot assume that, because Babylon is such a mighty power, it is folly to think of resisting it. Thus they seem to have sent to Zedekiah, hoping to make a confederation strong enough to drive the invader back.

II. NATURAL AS THE STRUGGLE MIGHT BE, IT WAS DOOMED TO CERTAIN FAILURE. Doomed, not because it was the strength of many against the weakness of few, but because God's great purposes required that any scheme of defence should be a failure. If the defenders had become as the invaders in point of strength, and the invaders as the defenders, this apparently decisive exchange of resources would have left the result unaffected.

III. The struggle, therefore, being vain beyond all doubt, THE TRUE WISDOM WAS NOT EVEN TO ATTEMPT IT. These nations, persevering in a vain struggle, were only committing self-slaughter. If the issue had been in any way uncertain, self-respect would have said " fight." But the issue was clear ; and to make it clear and impressive by some visible symbol, God commands his prophet to send these yokes to the kings of the nations by their messengers. When the yoke is seen on the neck of the ox labouring at the plough or drawing the waggon, that yoke signifies, not only submission, but a submission that is inevitable. The ox is made for the service of man, and although when young it may rebel and defy for a while, it must submit at last. The superior intelligence and the ordained master cannot but conquer. And what the ox is in the hands of man, that every nation, even the strongest and bravest, is in the hands of God. Babylon, conqueror and spoiler as it was, was no more free from God's yoke than any of the nations it defeated. It is quite compatible with the carrying out of God's great purpose that there should be the most striking disparities in the temporal conditions of both individuals and nations. That Babylon should be the victor and these other nations the vanquished, was in his eyes a matter of very secondary moment. He cannot recognize, as a state of things to obtain even a modified permanence, that any nation should have the right to any particular territory. Men count it a great matter that they can show a title, as they call it, to a piece of land. This simply means that for the purposes of present society it is better for one particular person to have the piece of land than any one else. But wars and revolutions make short work of these so-called rights of property. The Lord has given the earth in trust to the human race, and one division he puts here and another there, one man here and another there. From the throne where Jehovah sits in his righteousness, human patriotism and mere territorial pride are esteemed as nothing more than the feelings of ignorant children. We also, as taught of God, must become less interested in the traditions and rivalries of the kingdoms of earth, and more interested in that great procedure of God by which the whole earth will become a part of the kingdom of heaven.—Y.

EXPOSITION.

CHAPTER XXVIII.

Hananiah's false prophecy; his reprimand from Jeremiah; and his fate. The preciseness of the date in ver. 1 is to emphasize the supernatural character of Jeremiah's prediction. The latter was uttered in the fifth month of the fourth year of Zedekiah, and Hananiah died in the seventh month of the same year (ver. 17).

Ver. 1.—**In the beginning of the reign of Zedekiah.** It seems strange that the fourth year of a reign which only lasted eleven years in all should be called "the beginning. Is it not probable that the clause was interpolated here by a later copyist on account of ch. xxvii. 1, where at present a similar clause (see note) is found? Originally placed in the margin as a gloss upon the words "the same year," it would very easily find its way into the text. **Hananiah . . . the prophet** (see on ver. 15). **Gibeon.** This was a priestly city (Josh. xxi. 17), so that Hananiah was probably himself a priest like Jeremiah (ch. i. 1) and Pashur (ch. xx. 1). The modern El Jîb, on an isolated, rocky hill, doubtless represents the ancient Gibeon. **In the presence of the priests and of all the people.** Apparently the event took place on either a new moon or a sabbath, when the people would throng to the temple.

Ver. 2.—Hananiah opens his prophecy with the usual formula, claiming Divine inspiration in the fullest sense. His message is short and sweet: **I have broken—** i.e. I have decreed to break (the perfect of prophetic certitude)—**the yoke of the king of Babylon.** Had Hananiah stopped here, he might, perhaps, have escaped Jeremiah's indignant rebuke. But with light-hearted arrogance he ventures to fix a time close at hand for the event, which, no doubt, was destined to occur, but after a long interval. Dr. Payne Smith suggests that he probably cherished the belief that the confederacy then on foot (ch. xxvii. 3) would defeat Nebuchadnezzar.

Ver. 4.—**And I will bring again . . . Jeconiah.** Hananiah thus directly contradicts the assurance of Jeremiah (ch. xxii. 26, 27) that Jehoiachin would not return, but would die in a foreign land. Has he a political object in his favourable prognostication for the deposed king? Does he, in short, belong to a Jehoiachin party opposed to the friends of Zedekiah? The view is possible, and may seem to be confirmed by the emphatic repetition of the fall of Nebuchadnezzar, the liege lord of Zedekiah. Still there is evidence enough in modern history that the return of an exile is not necessarily tantamount to his reinstatement in his office.

Vers. 5—9.—Jeremiah's reply. He heartily wishes that Hananiah's prediction were capable of fulfilment, but it runs directly counter to the declarations of all the older prophets. "War, and evil, and pestilence" was their constant burden, for the people to whom they prophesied were unworthy of the golden age of felicity in which the prophets so firmly believed. Only by a terrible judgment could the people of Israel be purified for the Messianic age. This appears to be what Jeremiah means by ver. 8. True, he speaks of "countries" and "kingdoms" in the plural, but all the great prophets include the nations best known to them within the range of their preaching, and even of their Messianic preaching. Isaiah, for instance, threatens sore judgment upon Egypt and Assyria, and yet he holds out the cheering prospect that Egypt and Assyria will have a part in the Messianic felicity. Thus Hananiah's prediction has probabilities very strongly against it. He not only prophesies "peace," but attaches no condition to his promise, which, therefore, has double need of verification by the event (comp. Deut. xviii. 22).

Vers. 10, 11.—Instead of any rejoinder, Hananiah has recourse to violence, tears off and breaks the yoke on Jeremiah's neck, and repeats his declaration of the fall of Nebuchadnezzar within two years. Jeremiah meekly suffers.

Vers. 12—17.—No long time after this the prophet is commissioned to tell the bitter truth more fully than he had done before, and to warn Hananiah of his coming punishment.

Ver. 13.—**The yokes of wood;** rather, a yoke of wood. The word rendered in the Authorized Version "yokes" means properly "poles," two of which, with the "bands," composed a "yoke" (see on ch. xxvii. 2).

But thou shalt make; rather, *but thou hast made*. The sense in which Hananiah is said to have made "a yoke of iron" (we should render in the singular) comes out in ver. 14. The point is that there was a certain justification for Hananiah's violent act, but not that which he supposed. Jeremiah's wooden yoke was really an inadequate symbol; the prophet was too tender to his people. Thus God made the truth appear in still fuller brightness from the very perverseness of its enemy.

Ver. 14.—**The beasts of the field** (see on ch. xxvii. 6).

Ver. 15.—**The prophet Jeremiah unto Hananiah the prophet.** In one sense Hananiah was a prophet as much as Jeremiah. He claimed to have received the prophetic call, and God alone, who searcheth the heart, could pronounce upon the justice of his claim. Whatever training was regarded as necessary for the office he had probably gone through, and now for a number of years he had been universally recognized as a member of the prophetic class. Probably he had those natural gifts, including a real, though dim and not unerring, "second sight," which seems to have formed the substratum of Old Testament prophecy; but he certainly had not the moral backbone so conspicuous in Jeremiah, and he lacked that intimate communion with God (this became clear on the present occasion) which alone warranted the assurance that "Jehovah, the God of Israel, hath sent me."

Ver. 16.—**I will cast thee**; rather, *I send thee away*. Possibly, as Hitzig suggests, there is an allusion to the preceding verse, in which the same verb occurs. **Thou hast taught rebellion**; literally, *thou hast spoken turning aside*. To "speak turning aside (or, 'rebellion')" is a phrase of Deuteronomy (xiii. 6), where it is used, as here, of opposition, not to Jehovah, but to revealed truth.

HOMILETICS.

Vers. 1—17.—*The story of Hananiah the prophet.* Hananiah, priest and professional prophet, now presents himself as the rival and opponent of Jeremiah. A rude and shallow man, he probably thrusts himself forward unasked, as the representative of the popular prophets of smooth things whom it is the true prophet's painful duty to refute and rebuke. His own conduct and Jeremiah's behaviour to him are both clearly brought before us in this chapter.

I. THE CONDUCT OF HANANIAH. 1. He utters a *pleasing prophecy*. He promises a speedy overthrow of the tyranny of Nebuchadnezzar. Even Jeremiah heartily echoes the wish that the prediction could be true. It is always easiest to prophesy smooth things, to soothe and flatter rather than convince men of sin and persuade them to accept the darker truths. 2. Hananiah speaks with *great positiveness*. He boldly claims the authority of God for what he says (ver. 2). His assertions are definite, minute, inherently consistent. Daring assumptions such as those of Hananiah carry the unthinking as by storm. A brazen face, a loud voice, a positive assertion, are enough to convince many people without the slightest ground in reason. You have only to say a thing very strongly and to repeat it very often, and the mere force of utterance will make way for it where calm, measured reasoning quite fails. Hananiah is definite in detail. People have a tendency to believe what they can understand clearly and imagine vividly. We must be warned, therefore, (1) that they who make the loudest claims to speak for God may have least right to do so; (2) that the truth of a statement must be measured, not by the vehemence with which it is asserted, but by the strength of the grounds on which it rests; and (3) that the reality of things cannot be ascertained by reflection on the consistency, clearness, and fulness of our subjective ideas about them. 3. Hananiah manifests a *stupid insolence* under contradiction. He cannot reason with Jeremiah, he cannot refute the great prophet's words, he has no new thoughts to contribute; he can only repeat his former assertion with loud words and passionate actions. He is a poor, unintellectual creature, whose notion of controversy is like that of foolish people we sometimes meet with—people who imagine that to argue is just to repeat an assertion with dogged obstinacy. Hananiah loses his temper and behaves with rudeness to Jeremiah. The last refuge of the helpless controversialist is insolence and abuse.

II. THE BEHAVIOUR OF JEREMIAH TO HANANIAH. 1. He heartily assents to the false prophet's *desire for the happiness* of the nation. "Jeremiah said, Amen: the Lord do so," etc. (ver. 6). He had been accused of a traitorous wish to see his country humiliated. No charge could be more false. The preacher who feels it his duty to threaten Divine punishments to wicked men should not be accused of wishing them evil. He may speak with grief and regret, as God also punishes reluctantly (Ezek. xxxiii. 11). 2. Jeremiah appeals to the *example of the older prophets.* He is true to their teaching, while Hananiah contradicts it. This appeal should be unanswerable to one who, like Jeremiah's opponent, professes to be the successor of these men. Amongst men who believe in the Bible the appeal to Scripture should be a first resort. How can a Christian teacher maintain his ground if he is contradicting this highest authority? Jeremiah was fond of "the old paths," the traditions and examples of earlier prophets. There is a consistency in prophecy, a common spirit, common ideas and principles in the prophets, and in revelation generally. 3. Jeremiah appeals to the *confirmation of facts.* (Ver. 9.) He dares to await the verdict of history; he challenges Hananiah to do the same. We are too hasty in following the loud and pushing popular spirits of the hour. Wait and see the issue of their work when the first excitement has died away. 4. Jeremiah meets the insolence of Hananiah with *quiet courtesy.* He calmly reasons with him at first. When he finds his opponent proof against arguments which only rouse his temper, he quietly leaves him. There are times when men are too heated for argument, and there are men with whom it is always useless to argue. Under such circumstances the interest of truth, our own rightful dignity, and charity to our opponent, caution us to leave him in silence. 5. Jeremiah *reiterates his prediction* at a later time, with more stringent threats, and pronounces a solemn *sentence of death* on Hananiah. This he does after receiving fresh communications from Heaven and under the urgency of a Divine commission. It is always our duty to forgive our enemies; but if they are also the enemies of God, we may recognize the justice of God's judgment on them. It is to be noted that Jeremiah did not compass the death of Hananiah; he only foretold it, and this under a Divine impulse. The words of Jeremiah were verified. Hananiah died long before events proved the futility of his own prophecy. Perhaps this was best for him. His death is a solemn warning to people who may be tempted to sacrifice truth for popularity.

Ver. 8.—*An appeal to ancient prophecy.* I. THE PRINCIPLES OF THE APPEAL. Several important principles are here illustrated. 1. The value of a *precedent.* Novel circumstances demand novel actions. The spirit of progress should teach us to improve on the conduct of our forefathers. Yet the most radical progressionist must often see the use of a precedent. It is an appeal from the confusion and excitement of the moment to an example which can be studied more calmly. If the precedent is respected by both parties of a quarrel, there is in it a common meeting-place for a reconciliation. The Bible is useful to us in this way for its great examples. 2. The duty of *referring to Scripture.* Jeremiah did not simply refer to antiquity; he referred to ancient prophecy—to the authority of a series of inspired teachers. This is the justification of our appeals to the Bible. It is not that the Bible is an old book, but that it is the fountain of special Divine illumination. 3. *The unity of Scripture.* The most original thinkers have usually started on the foundation prepared by their predecessors. But such men as Kepler and Newton have left their teachers far behind, and exposed the error of much of their teaching. It is different with the Bible. Here, too, there is the progressive development of thought, the growing light of revelation. But while the outer husk of the earlier ideas of the Bible is cast aside, those ideas themselves are not discarded, but enlarged and glorified by a fuller evolution. Definite laws are changed, but vital principles remain. Thus there is a marvellous unity in the Bible.

II. THE RESULT OF THE APPEAL. This led to a confirmation of the darker view of the future. It was a sad result. It is only too true that the old prophets were preachers of repentance, threatening wrath and judgment. Their visions of the brighter future were few compared with their more stern predictions. The former, too, referred to distant times, the latter to circumstances of immediate interest. It is a terrible thought that an inspired view of human nature should lead so many great and good men to this gloomy conclusion. If these men rose from their graves and lifted up their voices in our own cities would they completely change their tone? Such a man as Thomas Carlyle seemed to realize something of the spirit of these old Hebrew prophets, and to him the condition of the modern world suggested the gloomiest forebodings. Happily, we do not look to the verdict of a prophet for our salvation. Christ has come. We listen to the teaching of apostles as well as to that of prophets. We have a New Testament. If the prophet exposes our sin and threatens our ruin, the gospel teacher points to the remedy in the redemption of the world by our Lord and Saviour Jesus Christ.

Vers. 13, 14.—*Yokes of iron.* Hananiah broke the wooden yoke which Jeremiah wore in token of the approaching servitude of the Jews. In return he was told that the real yoke of Babylon would be much more severe—a yoke of iron.

I. FACTS ARE MORE IMPORTANT THAN OPINIONS. If the rule of Babylon really would be as a yoke of iron, what was the use of circulating milder views of the future? We are too much inclined to judge of ideas by their fitness for our own previous notions, instead of testing them solely by their consistency with facts.

II. THE FUTURE MAY BE WORSE THAN WE EXPECT. There are dreadful events in past history. May there not also be dreadful events in future experience? Life is not a harmless plaything, nor the earth a thornless garden. There are terrors, judgments, agonies, in this strange world of ours. Who knows what may be in the next? This much we should all know: God is not the easy, indulgent Being of lax principles that shallow optimists fancy him to be, but wisely firm as well as infinitely merciful where mercy can be justly exercised.

III. NEGLECT OF TIMELY WARNING WILL INCREASE FUTURE SUFFERING. If the yoke of wood is broken, a yoke of iron shall be forged to take its place. The longer we delay hearkening to the warnings of God the worse must be our future punishment, because our sin is increasing while we remain impenitent; because to sin against light, against admonition, is to sin more plainly and wilfully; and also because the rejection of a warning sent in mercy is itself an act of resistance to the will of God.

Ver. 16.—"*This year thou shalt die.*" It is a great mercy that God has hidden from us the date of our death. If this were known all life would be deranged; some would grow reckless, some negligent of their highest duty till death was near, some despondent and unfit for all work, some overclouded with grief for the approaching separation from loved friends. We may be thankful, therefore, that God keeps the secret to himself. "Our times are in his hand." Still, it may be profitable for us to question ourselves how we should act if such a revelation were made—if an angel came to us with the message, "This year thou shalt die." What would be the effect of such a message?

I. IT WOULD URGE US TO PUT OUR TEMPORAL AFFAIRS IN READINESS FOR DEATH. We should wish to "put our house in order," to see that all was left right and straight for those who come after us, to do all in our power to provide for those who are dependent on us. But none of us knows but that he may die this year. We should not, therefore, delay in providing for those who will be left. It is foolish for a man not to make his will till he knows he is dying. Cruel injustice has often been done through the postponement of this duty until too late.

II. IT WOULD URGE US TO BE READY FOR ANOTHER WORLD. It would matter little what happened to us for the few months that remained of our earthly course. This life would then seem a poor shadow, its treasures not worth a thought. All anxiety would be fixed on "that undiscovered country." But we do not know but that we shall die this year; and we do know that life is fast fleeting. Should we not be ready in any case? Should we not feel as pilgrims and strangers, and seek for better treasures than those of earth, which all lie a prey to thief and moth and rust? Besides, spiritual preparation for death is not the simple, mechanical thing it appears to be in conventional language. Do we know we shall ever be able to fit ourselves for another world if we postpone all considerations of this momentous subject? It should be remembered, too, that he who is not fit to die is not fit to live; that spiritual condition which is real preparedness for heaven is just the condition for serving God here; if we are rightly living now we are fit to die—then and only then.

III. IT WOULD URGE US TO A DILIGENT COMPLETION OF OUR LIFE'S WORK. It would be a call to earnest effort to redeem the short remainder of our days. There would be much that we should desire to see finished. It would be sad to let the task fall from our hands unaccomplished. But the same appeal is made to all of us. Life is short, and the work of life is great. There is much for the longest life to do. In any case there is no time for idle postponement of service. Every day has its duty; neglect this, and you can never return to it without neglecting the duty of the morrow. Let us all "work while it is day," seeing that "the night cometh, when no man can work" (John ix. 4).

IV. IT SHOULD NOT TROUBLE THE CHRISTIAN WITH ANY FEAR. To him death has lost its sting. The natural human shrinking from it may remain, but this should be overwhelmed by the thought of the home beyond. For him to die is to end "the heart-ache, and the thousand natural shocks that flesh is heir to," and to enter the rest, the safety, the joy of heaven. But to the spiritual man it is more than this. All his better days he has been seeking to be nearer to God; for God he has been panting and yearn-ing. Death will be the fruition of this his heart's hunger; it will make him "for ever with the Lord." Earthly ties will still be strong, but he will feel that all is well that is God's will. If God's will be that he live, he will rejoice in the privilege of service; if it be that he die, he will feel this as "gain," so that, "whether he live or die, he is the Lord's."

> "Lord, it belongs not to my care
> Whether I die or live;
> To love and serve thee is my share,
> And this thy grace must give."

HOMILIES BY VARIOUS AUTHORS.

Vers. 1—17.—*How to answer those who oppose the truth.* Where the light is there will be the deepest shadow; the truth is ever sharply defined against falsehood. Just when it was most important that the will of God and the real position of Israel should be ascertained, there were many striving to deceive and misrepresent. The behaviour of Jeremiah on this occasion was twofold.

I. ACCORDING TO HUMAN KNOWLEDGE AND JUDGMENT. 1. *With moderation.* "Amen: the Lord do so." Under such trying circumstances the behaviour of the prophet is praiseworthy in the extreme. The contradiction and indignity to which he had been subjected might have excused a hot rejoinder. He is willing to have the dispute settled in a very effectual way. Meanwhile he is careful to make it clear that he too desired what his opponent had prophesied. This was the disposition of the Master, and should be copied by all his disciples. "A soft answer turneth away wrath;" "The servant of the Lord must not strive, but be gentle unto all men." 2. *By an appeal to the great principle that the event will determine the truth of their predictions or the wisdom of their conduct.* (Vers. 8, 9.) This was an appeal to the conscience of his opponent. 3. *Quiet submission to the will of God.* "And the prophet Jeremiah went his way." When there is no sign of reasonableness in our antagonists, or no prospect of immediate success, it is well to submit quietly and to wait God's time. This is the test of spiritual reality. True Christianity will show itself in earnest, unobtrusive actions and patient waiting for Christ. The most eloquent enforcement of the gospel is a quiet, consistent life.

II. AS INSPIRED. Whilst he had no direct message he was silent. But God, who will not leave his servants without a witness, and who resents the slightest dishonour to which they are subjected, came to his rescue. The whole attitude of the prophet is now changed. With certainty he recovers also his vivacity, energy, and fearless power of denunciation. He is now the minister of judgment. 1. *To the nation.* The yoke of wood gives place to one of iron. The complicity of the people in the guilt of the false prophet must be punished. Their resistance to the will of God and disbelief of his servant involves them in a heavier sentence. So it is with all impenitence and rejection of God's Word. The position of the transgressor cannot remain the same. With each step he plunges into deeper guilt and more fearful judgment. 2. *To the originator of the offence.* In this case the sentence is proportionately heavier and more immediate. Death is pronounced against the offending prophet with terrible brevity and clearness. There is ever a distinction between offenders and those who cause them to offend. Primacy in disobedience will ensure a special and unmistakable mark of God's anger. This announcement of doom, simple as it was in itself, must have been appalling to its hearer, whose inner sense of degradation and falseness would enhance its force. It is possible that the time and manner of this communication may have been intended to awaken repentance; failing which it was carried into effect. All around us such judgments are taking place, and it is well for men to examine what manner of spirit they are of ere they presume to occupy sacred offices or to set themselves against the laws of God's kingdom.—M.

Vers. 10, 11.—*Presumption increasing with impunity.* The meekness of Jeremiah's reply emboldened the false prophet, and he forthwith proceeded from words to actions. The symbol appointed by God was publicly removed from the shoulders of Jeremiah and destroyed. Opposition to the spirit and will of God could scarcely go further. The interpretation given to the action reveals how false and dangerous the position assumed.

I. THE SERVANTS OF GOD ARE FREQUENTLY AT APPARENT DISADVANTAGE AS COMPARED WITH THE SERVANTS OF SATAN. The action was so sudden and unexpected that Jeremiah had but little to say, and eventually went his way, sad but silent. Everything seemed to favour his opponent. The "patriotic party" was enthusiastic, and not to be restrained. The wisdom of this world is prompt and versatile because it is unprincipled; and it is bold because it is profane and unbelieving. Yet this is the condition under which the followers of the truth are to contend.

II. THE SERVANTS OF SATAN ARE THEREBY ENCOURAGED TO MORE PRONOUNCED BEHAVIOUR, AND COMMIT THEMSELVES BEYOND RECALL. Hananiah's case illustrates this in two ways, viz.: 1. *Sacrilegious action.* Touching the person of the prophet. Deliberately destroying the yoke which he must have known was of Divine appointment. 2. *Its definitive interpretation.* He not only rebelled against the Lord, but committed himself to a prediction with a fixed date, and one that must soon arrive. The necessity of the position he had assumed was upon him. Woe to the prophet of lies who ventures upon definite and verifiable prophecies! There is no halting-place to those who begin systematically to oppose God's truth. They must ere long be caught in their own snares. With the sense of reverence the fear of consequences is forgotten and caution is discarded.

III. BY SO DOING THEY HASTEN THEIR OWN JUDGMENT. The triumph is brilliant but short-lived, and purchased at terrible cost. Let sinners pause when their crimes are made easy for them and excess follows upon excess. The motion of the rapid may but precede the fall (Jude 8—13). When human resources and precautions are exhausted, it may be a sign that God will undertake his own cause. His servants are justified at such a time in looking for and invoking his help, which is likely to be of a very signal and determining kind.—M.

Vers. 1—17.—*A false prophet and his fate.* I. HANANIAH'S PRESUMPTION. Note *his direct challenge to the true prophet.* He seeks out Jeremiah in the house of Jehovah, "in the presence of the priests and of all the people." A prophet was, of course, bound to make his utterances in public, but Hananiah waited his chance until he found an opportunity of bearding the hated Jeremiah in as open a way as possible. He speaks *explicitly in the Name of Jehovah.* He is not afraid to take the great Name in vain. Let us be warned lest we heedlessly utter, under the pretended authority of God, what is nothing more than the daring imagination of our own hearts. The false prophet ventures on *the very figure which had been employed by the true prophet.* It would almost seem as if Jeremiah had habitually borne something in the shape of a yoke, and if so, it must have been a very irritating sight to the false prophets. Little wonder that, under the pretence of a prophetic mission, he ventured on the removal of this yoke. Above all things, there is *the confident assertion with respect to time.* Notwithstanding all the manifest difficulties of the achievement, Hananiah is not afraid to say that in two years Judah will again be firmly resting on its old foundations. Thus from all these indications of presumptuous action, we have an illustration of how confident heretics are in their error. Too often we are doubtful and partial in our statements of truth. We lack that faith and that thorough-going assertion of the truths God has revealed which are so necessary to make those truths full of operative and irresistible force. Hananiah here is as confident as he can be in all his deadly errors. He has not the least fear of plunging into the greatest responsibilities with regard to definite predictions. He passes from the ground of mere expostulations and remonstrances, and ventures on statements which in a very short time must either make him or ruin him. Let us learn from our enemies, and labour to be confident and determined in our assertion of truth, seeing there is no lack of determination on the part of those who have cast in their lot with error.

II. HANANIAH'S PERSISTENCE. It is very noticeable that Jeremiah does not meet him in anything of an angry or denouncing manner. It would have well pleased the true prophet to see the predictions of the false prophet brought about; for it is made abundantly evident that the sufferings of his country were an unspeakable grief to Jeremiah. An angry reply served no good purpose. The true prophet could manifest a dignified patience, and leave time to vindicate both the validity of his prophetic claim and his fidelity in speaking the truth. Meantime, he can only recommend Hananiah to consider well the lessons of history, and how the prophets of old had spoken of stern dealings with many wicked nations. Unfortunately, bad men are hardly ever discriminating students of history. Hananiah was here given an opportunity of repentance, if only he had chosen to avail himself of it. But so full was he of his own devices that gentle treatment only increased his audacity, and he drew public attention more than ever to himself by removing the symbolic yoke from Jeremiah's neck. That he was allowed to do all this should teach us a lesson of patience and trust when we see wicked men pursuing, undisturbed, their chosen path. They are only climbing higher that their ultimate ruin may become more widely manifest.

III. HANANIAH'S DOOM. The first result of his presumptuous conduct is to bring a more emphatic prophecy with regard to the captives. The second is to bring a sentence of death on the false prophet himself. He who has dealt rashly with the ordering of times and seasons is to know by a bitter experience that God has these times and seasons in his own hands. He is to die within the year. Notice the sin which he is charged with committing. He is doomed to death, not simply for the falsehood or the profanity, but for this, that he had taught rebellion against Jehovah. His words were an incitement to make a useless and premature attempt at liberation. God's prediction with regard to the captivity in Babylon had in it the nature of a command.

IV. HANANIAH'S DEATH. It came very quickly. Two months at the outside was the space between the utterance of a false rebellious statement and the confirming of a true one. The death came at such an interval as was very impressive. Compare the relations between Jeremiah and Hananiah here with those between Peter and Ananias. Both Hananiah and Ananias dealt presumptuously with the holiest of things.—Y.

EXPOSITION.

CHAPTER XXIX.

Despised and rejected at home, Jeremiah turned his thoughts to those distant brethren in captivity, whom he had already likened to "good figs, very good" (ch. xxiv. 3, 5). He had heard with sorrow that they could not readily submit to their altered circumstances. Judah, with its consecrated associations, was still too near to them in spirit. Probably a rumour of the expected confederacy (ch. xxvii. 3) had troubled their minds, and the discontent was increased by the pernicious discourses of prophets and soothsayers similar to that Hananiah of whom we have just heard. Two of these in particular are

mentioned, and a terrible fate is held out to them. The appendix (vers. 24—32) deals with another prophet of the same type, who had not, indeed, offended so deeply as his companions, but had stirred up those at home to persecute Jeremiah in revenge for the preceding letter.

The chapter is evidently, what it professes to be, a letter, at any rate in substance. From the looseness of its structure (see especially on vers. 16—20) it has been thought to have been dictated, like those Epistles of St. Paul, of which it may be regarded as a precursor (Ewald). The date seems to be a little earlier than that of the two preceding chapters (comp. ver. 2 with ch. xxiv. 1);

the messengers in ver. 3 are therefore not to be regarded as Zedekiah's companions in the journey mentioned in ch. li. 59.

Ver. 1.—**The residue of the elders;** i.e. the surviving elders. Some may, perhaps, have died from natural causes, some by violence, some from grief.

Ver. 2.—**The queen;** rather, the queen-mother (see on ch. xiii. 18). **The eunuchs, the princes of Judah and Jerusalem.** A marginal gloss appears to have intruded itself into the text, for there is no other passage in which the " eunuchs," or (as the word may equally well be rendered, with the margin), "chamberlains," are called "princes of Judah."

Ver. 7.—**Seek the peace of the city,** etc. Interest yourselves in the "peace" or welfare of the city, whether Babylon or any other place where ye may be in exile, and pray for its welfare, for your own well-being is inseparable from it.

Ver. 8.—**Let not your prophets and your diviners,** etc. It seems as if the Babylonian "Jewry" were a copy of that at home. It had not only its "princes" and its "elders," but its "prophets" and its "diviners," who encouraged the same false hopes as those in Judah (comp. ch. xxvii. 9; xxviii. 2). **Your dreams which ye caused to be dreamed;** or, which ye cause yourselves to dream (comp. ch. xxvii. 9).

Ver. 10.—**Seventy years** (see on ch. xxv. 11). **At Babylon;** rather, for Babylon. A long period, such as seventy years, is appointed for Babylon "to enjoy" the fruits of her ambition; when this is over (comp. Gen. xv. 13—16), God will pay heed to his people. **Visit you.** To "visit" frequently has the sense of "taking notice of," or "paying heed to" (e.g. ch. xxiii. 2). **My good word.** "Word," equivalent to "promise;" the allusion is to ch. xxiv. 6.

Ver. 11.—**For I know the thoughts,** etc.; i.e. though seventy years must pass over you in exile, yet do not apprehend that I have forgotten you, for I know full well what my purpose is towards you—a purpose of restoring to you "peace" and prosperity. **An expected end;** rather, a future and a hope; i.e. a hopeful future (comp. ch. xxxi. 17, "There is a hope for thy future"). That unexpectant apathy which is the terrible accompaniment of so much worldly sorrow was not to be an ingredient in the lot of the Jews.

Ver. 12.—**And ye shall go and pray unto me.** "Go," that is, to the places "where prayer is wont to be made." The clause seems to refer to common prayer for a common object. Comp. striking passages in Solomon's prayer (1 Kings viii. 48), and in Deuteronomy (iv. 29, 30).

Vers. 15—23.—Jeremiah's denunciation of two leading false prophets at Babylon, with a digression on the fate of Zedekiah and Jerusalem. Some eminent critics maintain that vers. 16—20 are an interpolation, and this view is certainly supported by the omission of these verses in the Septuagint. It must also in fairness be admitted that the natural connection of ver. 15 is with ver. 21, not with ver. 16. But it does not follow that vers. 16—20 are an arbitrary interpolation. They may be regarded either as a digression in the original letter, or as inserted by an after-thought when the substance of the letter was brought into its present form.

Ver. 16.—**Know that thus saith the Lord;** rather, Surely thus saith the Lord.

Ver. 17.—**I will send upon them,** etc.; alluding to ch. xxiv. 10. **Vile figs;** literally, figs exciting a shudder. The figure involves an allusion to ch. xxiv. 2, 3.

Ver. 19.—**But ye would not hear.** The prophet, by a very natural illusion, falls out of the style of letter-writer into that of the prophet. For the moment he fancies himself addressing an audience of his countrymen (comp. ch. xxv. 3, 4, 7, 8).

Ver. 21.—**Zedekiah.** The name is interesting; it shows that this prophet belonged to a family which took pleasure in the thought of Jehovah and his righteousness. Doubtless, too, he did so himself; but he under-estimated the demands of that righteousness, which extended to the heart as well as to the outward conduct.

Ver. 22.—**A curse;** i.e. a formula of cursing (comp. Isa. lxv. 15). There is here a play upon words, such as the Biblical writers delighted in, partly with the view of assisting the memory. "A curse" is in Hebrew kelālāh, and "to roast" is kālāh. **Roasted in the fire.** "Casting into the midst of a burning fiery furnace" was a common punishment both among the Assyrians and the Babylonians, see e.g. 'Records of the Past,' vol. ix. p. 56; and comp. Dan. iii.

Ver. 23.—An important and melancholy addition to our knowledge of these false prophets. They were not only misleading prophets, but immoral men in their private capacities. **Villany;** rather, folly, as the word is always rendered elsewhere. The phrase "to commit folly in Israel" is always (except Josh. vii. 15) used of sins of unchastity.

Vers. 24—32.—A threatening oracle against the false prophet Shemaiah. Great excitement had been caused among the so-called prophets in Babylon by the emphatic language of Jeremiah. Accordingly one of them, named Shemaiah, wrote letters to the Jews at home, and especially to a high official called Zephaniah (see on ver. 26) to put a stop to Jeremiah's bold agitation. Zephaniah, however, was not the man for whom Shemaiah took him, and read the letter to the intended victim. Upon this, Jeremiah received a special revelation, announcing dire punishment to Shemaiah and his family (according to the principle of the Divine government described in Exod. xx. 5).

Ver. 24.—**To Shemaiah**; or, *of, concerning* (as the same preposition is rendered in vers. 16, 21, 31). The oracle itself speaks of Shemaiah in the third person (vers. 31, 32). The Authorized Version, however, can be defended by its accordance with ver. 25. **The Nehelamite.** This is evidently a patronymic, but whether of the family or the locality of the bearer cannot be decided. The analogy of "Jeremiah of Anathoth" (ver. 27), however, favours the view that it is local.

Ver. 26.—**In the stead of Jehoiada the priest.** Some (Grotius, Hitzig, Graf) think that this Jehoiada was the famous high priest of that name, who is said to have "appointed *officers* over the house of the Lord" (2 Kings xi. 18; 2 Chron. xxiii. 18). It is true that Zephaniah was not literally the successor of Jehoiada, but he was so in the same metaphorical sense in which the scribes are said by our Lord to "sit in Moses' seat" (Matt. xxiii. 2). It is safer, however, to suppose that another Jehoiada is meant, of whom we have no further information. It is not said that either Jehoiada or Zephaniah was high priest, and as the special object of the elevation of the latter is said to be the supervision of the temple police, it is more probable that Jehoiada and he were successively "second priests," or, to use a phrase which seems to be synonymous, "deputy governors in the house of the Lord" (ch. xx. 1). The passage may thus without violence be harmonized with ch. lii. 24; 2 Kings xxv. 18, where Seraiah is called "the chief priest" and Zephaniah "the second priest." It is possible that Jehoiada had been favourable to the better class of prophets. In this case there will be a delicate hint to Zephaniah that God had his own purpose in promoting him to honour, viz. that unruly prophets like Jeremiah might be held in with a tighter hand (Ewald). **That ye should be officers**; rather, *that there should be officers.* Zephaniah himself was an "officer" or "deputy" (see above); but he was also "chief in the house of the Lord," and had the appointment of inferior "officers," whose duty it was to preserve order in the temple. To understand the

following words, we must remember that the outer court of the temple was a favourite place for prophetic teaching (comp. ch. vii. 2; xxvi. 2). **For every man that is mad, and maketh himself a prophet;** *i.e.* to keep an eye upon "madmen" and prophetizers. The term "mad" is used in a disparaging sense (as 2 Kings ix. 11; comp. Hos. ix. 7), with regard to the apparently senseless behaviour of those who were overpowered by the spirit of prophecy. In earlier times, no doubt, the phenomena of prophecy were more violently opposed to everyday life than in Jeremiah's time; but such symbolic acts as appearing in public with a yoke upon his neck would at least excuse the application of the epithet even to Jeremiah. It is more than probable, however, that it was not so much the abnormal actions as the contents of Jeremiah's prophecies which stirred up such vehement opposition; observe how in the next verse only the sound of these descriptive nouns is retained ("which maketh himself a prophet"). It was the making prophecy a reality which disturbed the men of routine, and Shemaiah well knew this when he made this appeal to Zephaniah. There was no harm in being nominally a "prophet," but to "make," or rather, "show one's self as a prophet," to be an energetic prophet, a prophetizer (if the word may be invented),—this was wormwood to those who cried, "Peace, peace," when there was no peace. **In prison, and in the stocks;** rather, *in the stocks* (see on ch. xx. 2) *and in the collar.* The meaning seems to be that Jeremiah was subjected to both forms of punishment at once.

Ver. 27.—**Reproved;** *i.e.* threatened with punishment.

Ver. 28.—**For therefore**, etc.; *i.e.* the consequence of Jeremiah's not having been kept within bounds by authority is that he has even ventured, in his fanatical zeal, to trouble the exiles in Babylon. **This captivity is long;** rather, *It* (*is*) *long;* a more forcible expression.

Ver. 29.—**And Zephaniah the priest**, etc. This should rather be printed as a parenthetical remark.

Vers. 30—32.—**Then came the word of the Lord**, etc. A fresh introduction of the Divine oracle was rendered necessary by the long description of Zephaniah's letters. The reason for Shemaiah's punishment, however, is stated here a little differently. Of course, it was equally contrary to the will of God to deliver a false prophecy and to stir up persecution against his true prophet. **Taught rebellion** (see on ch. xxviii. 16).

HOMILETICS.

Vers. 4—7.—*How to make the best of adversity.* Jeremiah advises the captives in Babylon to take a course that is eminently brave and wise. The first inclination would be to stir up a useless revolt, the second to sit down in sullen despondency. When trouble overcomes us we are tempted to follow one or other of these courses—to rebel or to despair. Jeremiah teaches us, as he taught the Jews of his day, that neither is right. He indicates a better way.

I. SUBMIT PATIENTLY TO INEVITABLE ADVERSITY. We are not required to court trouble, nor to yield weakly when we might successfully throw it off. But when it is plainly inevitable resistance is wrong as well as foolish. 1. It is *foolish.* Why dash our heads against the prison walls? The brain will suffer before the granite. The Jews could not successfully revolt against Babylon; to live on the eve of rebellion, as restless conspirators, would be dangerous and futile. The mistake of such misplaced patriotism was seen later in the wretched failure of the fanatic attempts of the Jews to throw off the yoke of Rome. The folly of the Jews would be the greater that the lengthy duration of the Captivity had been predicted and revealed as a Divine judgment. When we know the providential assignment of adversity, to resist this is to resist the power of Heaven. 2. This resistance is *wrong.* The Captivity was ordained by God (ver. 4). It was sent as a wholesome chastisement. To those who understood the teaching of the prophets on this point, rebellion was at once disobedience to God's will and the refusal of a useful corrective. We should remember this when we grow impatient under trouble, and learn to bow silently before the will of our King and our Father, to receive without complaining the discipline which is intended to cleanse and strengthen our spiritual life.

II. SEEK THE BRIGHTEST COURSE UNDER THE DARKEST CIRCUMSTANCES. The captives could not return home. They were not, therefore, to treat the land of their exile as a hopeless desert, but to build and plant and eat the fruit of it. 1. How often trouble is *worse in prospect* than in experience! The Captivity loomed in the distance as a very purgatory; when it came it was found to contain many of the fruits and flowers of quiet happiness. 2. Our lot in life will be very much *what we make* it for ourselves. If we treat it as a " waste, howling wilderness," it will be that to us. But the hardest lot will prove to have many alleviations for him who searches for its mercies rather than for its grievances. Surely it is best to do this. Mourners are inclined to nurse their sorrows with a melancholy satisfaction in aggravating the pain of them, or as though any abatement of grief were a sacrilege. But we should learn a more robust treatment of adversity. There is no virtue in distressing one's self beyond necessity.

III. CHERISH HOPES FOR THE FUTURE UNDER THE MOST TRYING PRESENT CIRCUMSTANCES. The Jews were to remember the promise of the restoration. They were not to allow their race to die out (ver. 6). A great future was still before them. History has confirmed the prediction of the prophets. The scattered and ruined people were recalled to their homes. From the stock of the despondent exiles there sprang not only all that was great and good in later Jewish history, but also Jesus Christ and Christianity. In our darkest moments we should not forget that, though not a ray of light has yet appeared on the horizon, the sun will surely rise and the day return. Christianity is peculiarly a religion of the future; it encourages us to press forward to the golden age which is yet to come.

IV. FIND OUR HAPPINESS BY SEEKING THE WELFARE OF OTHERS. " Seek the peace of the city . . . for in the peace thereof shall ye have peace." The alien was to act with the loyalty of a citizen. Though a nation may be under the unrighteous rule of a conqueror, it should still remember that it has duties to the government under which it lives, and claims of charity in regard to the people of the superior power. If it is our duty to seek the peace of a strange city, how much more are we bound to interest ourselves in public duties for the good of our own country? Private citizens will find their personal condition improved through the successful discharge of public duties. The citizens reap the fruits of the peace of the city. In ministering to others generally we shall discover the secret of our own blessedness.

Ver. 7.—*Civic duties.* From the duty of the Jews to the cities of their exile we may deduce the still more urgent duties of citizens to their own city.

I. ONE OF THE FIRST INTERESTS OF A PEOPLE IS PEACE. There are times when war is necessary and right—to defend the hearth and home, to save the weak from oppression, etc. But such war must only be the means for securing a better, more lasting peace. The glory of war is an empty dream. The people gain little and suffer much, though the kings may win fame and power.

II. PEACE IS TO BE SOUGHT BY THE ACTION OF CITIZENS. Individual men cannot wage a war or declare a truce. But the units constitute nations. If each is peaceable the nation is peaceable. Insignificant people have vast power for harm if they choose to execute it. It should be understood that seditious conduct is not only a political offence, it is a sin in the sight of God, a cruelty to the many people whom it disturbs and injures.

III. PRIVATE MEN HAVE PUBLIC DUTIES. We all reap benefits from the state. It is mean to accept them without taking our part in bearing the burdens of the state. There are people who deny the right of Christian men to take part in "worldly politics," yet these people are glad to avail themselves of the protection and other advantages which are provided for them by the secular government they affect to despise. The neglect of public duty evidences a narrow and selfish disposition.

IV. PRIVATE MEN ARE BENEFITED BY PUBLIC PROSPERITY. We are members one of another. There is a general harmony and health of the whole body, over and above the well-being of each member, when all work together for the mutual good. As individual men, we have great reason to be thankful for the general prosperity of the nation and for the maintenance of public peace.

V. WE SHOULD DISCHARGE OUR DUTIES TO THE STATE THOUGH WE MAY NOT APPROVE OF THE GOVERNMENT. To be in opposition is no excuse for being in sedition. Unless we can change the government it is foolish and wrong to revolt against it. The nation is larger than the government.

Ver. 10.—*Seventy years.* I. SEVENTY YEARS ARE A LIMITED TIME. Babylon was to tyrannize for a limited period only; the Jews were to suffer for a limited period. 1. God has set a limit to the triumph of evil. The storm rages; yet God says to it, "Hitherto shalt thou come, and no further." The lions roar, but they are chained. Wicked men fling the reins to their passions, break through all restraints of respect for the will of God and appear to be at liberty to work evil and revel in the fruits of sin *ad libitum;* but God has put bounds about their course. In due time he will lay his hand upon them and arrest them. 2. God has set a limit to the duration of trouble. The sorrow of God's people is temporal; their blessedness will be eternal. Every trouble is weighed and measured by God. "Our times are in his hand."

II. SEVENTY YEARS ARE A SHORT TIME IN THE HISTORY OF A NATION. The Captivity was to last for seventy years; prosperity had been enjoyed for hundreds of years before this, and would return and endure long after. The troublesome times are conspicuous, while the quiet times glide by unnoticed. Hence we are likely not to note how much more we have of the latter. History reads like a record of wars and commotions, because the happy but dull annals of prosperity do not contain many striking events. It is much the same in private life. For most of us the blessings greatly outnumber the troubles, the times of quiet far exceed those of distress. Yet it is difficult to recognize this, because what hurts us impresses our memory more than what pleases us.

III. SEVENTY YEARS ARE A LIFETIME. Few, if any, of the first captives would survive the exile. To the individual man it was as bad as if it were perpetual. Yet if they were true patriots the national hope must have been a great comfort in the darkness of personal suffering. And the patriotic hope of Israel was one of the grandest features in the Hebrew character. We are all too selfish in our hopes. Christians should consider the cause of Christ and the interest of humanity as of far more importance than their private prosperity. If in the end Christ will triumph, and the world will be lifted out of the sin and sorrow which have overwhelmed it, should not we rejoice, though our lot may not be to live till this is accomplished? Moses rejoiced in the Pisgah-view of the land he could never enter; Simeon was glad at seeing the infant Saviour, and could depart in peace with the assurance of a redemption not yet accomplished. Still, the Christian may have a great personal hope beyond this. Seventy years!—but a span compared with eternity! When these swift days have flown the door will be opened to the infinite ages of eternity. What if the little life be tempest-tossed? the voyage is short, the haven is near (2 Cor. iv. 17, 18).

Ver. 11.—*God's thoughts concerning us.* I. GOD THINKS. If God exists he must be a thinking being. To apply the name " God " to a stream of tendencies, a collection of laws, the totality of being, etc., is to misapply it. Either God is personal or there is no God, for the conception of personality is essential to that of divinity. If God is a person he may be "without parts or passions." The anthropomorphic ideas of repentance, wrath, etc., may be as much mere metaphorical images as those of the eyes and the hands of God; but thinking is essential to the nature of what we understand by a person, by a spiritual being. Unless God thinks, he is no spirit, no person.

II. GOD THINKS ABOUT US. As far as he is revealed to us in the Bible and in Christ, and as far as we may verify this revelation by experience, he is directly concerned with his works and his children. His thoughts are not to be imagined as only consisting of vast abstractions, infinite ideals. They may soar to lonely heights where no finite intellect can follow, but they can also stoop to humble concerns of human life. He is but an imperfect thinker who is so absorbed with philosophic speculation that he has no room in his mind to consider his family. The greatest thinker will be wide as well as lofty, able to take in small details in addition to grand abstractions, and, above all, wise to apply the highest thinking to the simplest practical necessity. It is a great comfort for us that God so thinks. With sublime ideas of eternity, and innumerable cares of the universe in his infinite mind, God has yet room for thoughts about us, and condescension to concern himself with them.

III. WHAT GOD THINKS ABOUT US IS OF GREAT IMPORTANCE TO US. 1. God thinks what is *true and wise and good.* If, therefore, we can know God's thoughts about anything we shall see the thing in its true light. Our thoughts are blinded by prejudice, coloured by passion, limited by ignorance, broken, fragmentary, perverted. God's only are clear and perfect as truth. 2. God's thoughts are the *prelude to his actions.* If we know what he thinks concerning us we know how he intends to act. God's thinking is not the contemplation of the philosopher, it is the consideration of the king. We forget this when we are so very anxious about what the world will think of us and so very indifferent about God's thoughts concerning us. A brave man will learn to dare the world's misjudgment, its scorn, its condemnation. But who can face God's thoughts if they mean evil to us?

IV. GOD THINKS THOUGHTS OF PEACE CONCERNING US. So Jeremiah saw in the case of the Jews; so we may see for all mankind how that Christ " has broken down the middle wall of partition between us." Even when God finds it necessary to punish his desire is to bless, and when he chastises it is in mercy, that he may reclaim. But this is not seen at the time. There are things which prevent us from seeing that God's thoughts are of peace. Thus—the peace is not yet enjoyed; when God chastises us it looks as though he meant evil to us, because we feel the blow before we see the good fruit of it; we cannot see God's thoughts, and must accept them in faith, waiting for a later confirmation of experience. Yet if God does think thoughts of peace concerning us, is it necessary for us to know the exact nature of them? They are known to him if they are not known to us, and he can carry them out without any previous understanding of them on our part.

V. GOD'S THOUGHTS OF PEACE WILL BE ULTIMATELY REALIZED. God promises that he will make " a future and a hope." God's best thoughts are not memories, but hopes, promises, intentions. The grandest page of revelation is prophecy. But though these thoughts refer to the future, we must not lose faith in their practical interest. 1. The realization is *delayed by our fault*, not by God's will. He thinks, intends peace. But he is hindered from carrying out his intention by our conduct. He waits to be gracious. If, therefore, we prepare ourselves for the accomplishment of God's thoughts, there is nothing further to prevent us from enjoying the peace they presage. 2. God is as *great in power* as he is wise and good in thought. He has bestowed upon us the noble but perilous faculty of free-will, and we cannot measure the limits of this faculty.

Yet we may rest assured that by some means the infinite God can and will ultimately accomplish all his great designs of peace for his children.

Ver. 13.—*Seeking God with the whole heart.* I. GOD MUST BE FOUND BEFORE HE CAN BE KNOWN AND ENJOYED. "He is not far from each one of us : for in him we live, and move, and have our being." Yet this natural nearness of God may be unrecognized by us, and may not be sufficient to bring us into the spiritual communion with him. The God of nature may be "the unknown God," or he may be recognized and yet not enjoyed as the "Portion" of the soul. 1. *Sin* hides the vision of God, and drives the soul into remote spiritual banishment from God, even though it cannot affect his physical presence. 2. Our *natural limitations* of thought and experience surround the idea of the Divine with mystery, and make us feel that though God is partly known there are still ways of God that are far beyond our ken, so that we exclaim in bewilderment and distress, "Verily, thou art a God that hidest thyself!" (Isa. xlv. 15). II. TO BE FOUND, GOD MUST BE SEARCHED FOR WITH THE WHOLE HEART. 1. He must be *searched for.* God does discover himself to men unexpectedly, as to Hagar in the desert and to Moses on Horeb, though we may rest assured that even such exceptional revelations were made to souls whose habit it was to seek after him. Nevertheless before such experience, God draws near to those who do not seek him, to urge them to search and find him (Isa. lxv. 1). He seeks us before we seek him. Our search is the response of our hearts to his invitation (Ps. xxvii. 8). But this search must be made. The promise of finding is attached to the condition of seeking (Matt. vii. 7). The prodigal must return to his father before he can receive the welcome home. Men are waiting for God to visit them, reveal himself to them, do something that will bring them back to him. They may wait for ever, and in vain. God is waiting for us. It is our part to arise and seek him. 2. This search must be with *all the heart.* The reason why we are disappointed of the answers of our prayers is often that our prayers are so insincere, so cold, so half-hearted. It is reasonable to expect God, the all-seeing, to answer our prayers, not according to the vigour of the language, but according to the fervency of our desires. If we value the knowledge and communion of God aright, we shall seek him with all the heart: (1) with the heart, *i.e.* sincerely, spiritually, inwardly, not with mere formal inquiries; and (2) with the whole heart, *i.e.* with singleness of purpose, intensity, earnestness. III. THE REWARD OF SEEKING GOD WITH ALL THE HEART WILL CONSIST IN FINDING HIM. 1. The search will be *successful.* God may not be found at first, or, being found, may not be recognized in the way expected. But Scripture and experience both testify to the utility and fruitfulness of the soul's search after God. If we have not yet found, that may be because (1) we have not sought with "all the heart;" or (2) have not sought in the right way as far as our light and knowledge have indicated it— *i.e.* humbly, penitently, and as Christians through Christ. 2. The success of the search will be *its own reward.* The finding of God is described as a blessing of the restoration. It will bring other and lower benefits in its train (ver. 14), but it is itself the greatest boon. "Blessed are they that seek God with all the heart, for they shall find him,"—that is enough for a perfect beatitude. To find God is to find our light, our rest, our home. To know him is life eternal; to commune with him is the joy of heaven.

Vers. 20—32.—*Shemaiah.* I. HIS ACTION. 1. He is *irritated* at the letter of Jeremiah. From Babylon he writes back in a rage. It is foolish to be thus angry with those who tell us unpleasant truths, but it is very common. 2. He describes Jeremiah as *mad.* People often depreciate the intelligence of those who differ from them. Weak men set down strong words to the excitement of the speaker because they have not the imagination or the nerve to receive them as true. 3. He urges the temple officials to *arrest and punish* Jeremiah. We have here another instance of the common effort to suppress those whom we are unable to answer. II. HIS MORAL CONDUCT. 1. He *usurps* the name of a prophet, though he is not sent by God. His pretence to speak in the Name of God is unwarranted. A prophet is one who acts as God's messenger, as an apostle is one who acts as the messenger of Christ. No man has a right to enter the ministry of Christ unless he is called to it, nor to speak as God's ambassador unless he is convinced in his conscience that he is sent by God. 2. He *deceives* the Jews into "trusting in a lie." It is not only that he falsely claims to be a prophet; his prophetic message is also false. Truth is sacred; to tamper with it is a sin, but to deceive others to their hurt increases the sin. 3. He instigates *revolt* against God. If it is wrong to utter a falsehood to serve a good end, it must be more wrong to do so with a bad intention. But all false religious teaching tends to induce disobedience to the will of God.

III. HIS DOOM. 1. He is to be *punished.* The evil that he discredits shall fall upon him. This is a severe but an appropriate punishment for a deceiving prophet. 2. His *children are to share* his doom. There is a great mystery in the hereditary character of punishment, and it is increased in some respects by the fact that tendencies to sin are also hereditary. But the fact is as clearly visible in nature as it is revealed in Scripture. 3. He is *not to see the joy of the restoration.* They who refuse wholesome chastisement cannot receive the happy fruits that follow it. It is natural and reasonable that the wilful rejection of Divine warnings should be followed by a severe judgment.

HOMILIES BY VARIOUS AUTHORS.

Vers. 1—14.—*Duties and consolations of God's captivity.* I. THEIR DUTIES. The imposition of definite lines of conduct and policy upon the exiled, was one proof that they were not cast off; the promise of deliverance was another. Although amongst the heathen, they were not to be as the heathen; neither were they to be wholly given over to despair. As children of God they were to exhibit the virtues of: 1. *Industry.* (Ver. 5.) Misanthropy and despair are the parents of idleness; Divine faith endues men with energy. The exiles had a testimony to bear before the heathen. It was a present duty to achieve an honest independence. 2. *Domestic attachment.* (Ver. 6.) The family, with all its joys and responsibilities, is still to be cared for. If the present be forfeited the future is still capable of being redeemed. The new generations would reap the advantages of which the fathers had been deprived. 3. *Public spirit.* (Ver. 7.) They were not to abstain from the duties of citizenship merely because they were amongst heathen conquerors. Even there they might exert an influence for good. The fundamental law of God's kingdom is to seek the good of all men. Work faithfully rendered to the commonwealth would not be vain or without its reward. Even the heathen and the men of this world can appreciate good citizenship. That a distinctive work and testimony still remained to the Church as a Church, is no reason for neglecting those less direct and more general duties which so powerfully commend the religious profession that inculcates them. 4. *Cheerfulness* This is not so much to be classified along with the preceding as to be understood as the spring and governing principle of them all. What more natura. than a spirit of resentment under the circumstances? How easy to hang the harp on the willows! But this would only be to misunderstand God and thwart his purposes. He seeks the happiness and prosperity of his people— even here and now, and notwithstanding the discipline to which he may be subjecting them. Not resignation merely, but cheerful acquiescence and co-operation, are, therefore, to be expected of his people. "I opened not my mouth, because thou didst it."

II. THEIR CONSOLATIONS. These were partly to consist in the natural results of the course of conduct enjoined, or the happiness inseparably associated with the observance of it; but chiefly in the anticipation of the future. 1. *A definite term was set to their captivity.* (Ver. 10.) It was one that could easily be verified, and was not too far distant to extinguish hope. Some of those who as children were taken to Babylon, might in their old age return to the land of promise. There is measure as well as meaning in all God's discipline. He never imposes upon his people a burden greater than they can bear. The darkest night is illumined by light beyond. When they sorrow, their sorrow is not without hope. 2. *The present was linked with the future.* They might be comforted in the fulfilment of their daily tasks by the knowledge that everything done in obedience to God and the spirit of true benevolence would have its influence upon the promised deliverance. At the very worst, what was done in this disposition would not retard that event or rob it of its fulness of blessing. In like manner the children of God are assured that this earthly life is but a "sojourning,"

and that " all things work together for good." This life will have an immense influence
upon the complexion of the next.   The duties of every day are therefore to be attended
to in the full conviction of their absolute worth and avail in the sight of God.   They
have the promise not only of the life which now is, but of that which is to come.   3.
Spiritual blessings were promised. (Vers. 11—14.)   The good will and faithfulness of
God ; the restoration of religious communion ; the gathering and reconstitution of the
theocracy.—M.

Vers. 12—14.—*Signs that God's favour is restored.*   I. WHAT HE DOES IN HIS
PEOPLE.   1. *In turning their hearts to himself.*   They had been worshipping Baal and
the gods of heathendom.   Only now and then did they offer a half-hearted worship to Jehovah.   The idolatries that pandered to their lusts were uppermost in
their thoughts, and it was only occasionally, in seasons of desperate need, they
bethought themselves of Jehovah.   Now he was to assume a higher place in their
regard.   Their views of life, its purposes and destinies, would be elevated, and he would
become their chief desire.   The new era of favour and happiness would be distinguished
by intense personal love for God.   In Nehemiah's day a measure of spiritual affection
like this showed itself, but it could only be fully developed through the personal manifestation of Christ, who was to draw all men unto him.   2. *In pouring forth the spirit
of true prayer.*   Where the heart's affections go forth towards God the spirit of true
prayer commences.   It is that which cries within us, " Abba, Father," which is the
spirit of prayer and supplications.   It has been supposed that the first clause of ver. 12
refers to private and the second to public prayer.   The habit and delight of devotion
were to be restored.   Where these are there is already the earnest of all substantial
and eternal good.   Pentecost was prefaced and penetrated with prayer.
   II. WHAT HE DOES FOR HIS PEOPLE.   1. *In revealing himself.*   They who seek for
him with their whole heart will find him.   The veil will be withdrawn, and calamity,
understood as fatherly chastisement, patiently borne.   In the subsequent history of
Israel this was largely experienced ; but the fulness of the spiritual meaning of the
promise was only realized in Christ and the outpourings of his Spirit.   2. *He will
hearken to their petitions.*   The sense of acceptance will come, even in the midst of
captivity.   Faithful hearts will fill with presage of coming deliverance, and prayer will
not only be effectual but be felt to be so.   It is in this exercise the true relationship of
God and his people becomes evident, and the blessings of a present and ultimate
redemption are secured.   There can be no more marked proof of God's favour towards
any one than answers to his prayers.   3. *He will bring back to the promised land and
the privilege of covenant relationship.*   That is a matter of course, seeing he already
hears them.   And yet none the less imposing will their redemption be.   How complete
the restoration ! how miraculous !   Its supernatural character is to be as evident as
that of their dispersion.   That which under anomalous circumstances has been a
difficult, unauthorized, or intermittent exercise will become easy, honourable, and
constant as they will return to their own land, where every man will sit under his own
vine and fig-tree, none daring to make him afraid.   In the case of the Christian this
promise will be fulfilled in either the gradual conquest of the world by the Church, or
entrance into heaven.   But there is a foretaste of this in the self-conquest and perfected
spiritual life of the regenerate soul.—M.

Vers. 20—32.—*The punishment of false prophets.*   The opposition between Jeremiah
and the false prophets is one of the most interesting phenomena of the period to which
these prophecies belong.   It is a real battle, albeit not with earthly weapons.   The
question between them could not be suffered to remain doubtful, as it involved
immense consequences.   A striking correspondence is discovered in the antagonism to
the labours of the apostles.   There is the same barefaced, fearless lying and dishonesty,
the same terrible denunciation of judgment.   (We are reminded of the sentence on
Simon Magus, " Thy silver perish with thee," etc., Acts viii. 20—24; and the reply to
Ananias, the high priest, " God shall smite thee, thou whited wall," Acts xxiii. 3.)
How is the latter to be regarded ?   Evidently as the word of God through his true
servants, and not as the expression of vindictive feeling.   In regard to this punishment
notice—

I. ITS NATURE. It had direct reference to that concerning which they spoke. From the future they had denied they were to be cut off. In the case of Ahab and Zedekiah the instrumentality of man is indirectly employed; in that of Shemaiah it is brought about by what we might regard as natural causes. In both instances the penalty was: 1. *Exceptionally severe.* The fate of the lying prophets, even apart from its associated consequences in the eternal sphere, was tragic in the extreme, and presents hardly an element of hope. Ahab and his companion are subjected to a fearful death and an eternity of shame in Israel. Shemaiah is consigned to effacement and deprived both as regards himself and his posterity, of the promised blessings. 2. *Exemplary.* Unmistakably these men were but the leaders of many of like mind, and it was intended they should be marked out for signal retribution. Their fate would appeal to the imagination and spiritual feeling of their people, and in either case it corresponded closely with the peculiarity of their conduct. In their heathen exile they were to be taught that God's hand could still reach them and that an exact justice waited upon their actions. Ahab and Zedekiah so lived that even a heathen monarch had to make them examples. 3. *Graduated according to heinousness of offence.*

II. ITS JUSTIFICATION. 1. *The opposition to God's truth was necessarily direct and malicious.* Nothing could well be more consciously wicked than their whole behaviour. It occurred at a critical period, when great destinies were determined. The prophet of God was thereby discredited and hindered, and the people prevented from receiving and acting upon his message. In every season of critical consequence and great spiritual activity such manifestations occur. Merely to overcome them is not sufficient. The victory must be signal and conspicuous. 2. *The offence was one to which God himself is ever most sensitive.* It affected his character and prerogatives, and was therefore nothing else than blasphemy (cf. Matt. xii. 32. "Even I know, and am a witness, saith the Lord," ver. 23). 3. *The interests of truth required the penalty.* The people had to be overawed by the presence of the supernatural; their obedience had to be won to the direction of the true prophet, and the spiritual ends of the Captivity were thus to be secured. A moral demonstration like this was requisite, and enables the human mind more completely to realize the Divine conceptions of righteousness and truth.—M.

Vers. 4—7.—*God's message to the captives.* There is an encouraging tone in this Divine message to the captives in Babylon that must have been strikingly fitted to call forth every better element of thought and feeling within them. They were not, indeed, to dream of deliverance. The appointed time must run its course. The generation then in their prime could not hope ever to see their own land again. But their children should. Their wisdom, therefore, lay in making the best of their condition, and nourishing, as far as possible, the resources and the strength of their family life. Let them build, and plant, and marry, and enjoy the good of that strange land as if it were their own. Let them sow, though it be with many tears, for the better and happier future. Let them so live as to commend themselves to the good will of their conquerors, that even "their enemies may be at peace with them," identifying themselves with the interests of the place of their captivity, seeking by their prayer to bring down blessings upon it from above, seeing that in its well-being and peace they would find their own. This is strictly in harmony with the general Divine purpose as to the relation in which the Jews should stand towards other nations. They were called to be a separate and peculiar people only that they might the better be instruments of blessing to the world. The Captivity was not merely a punishment for their sins, but a part of the method by which God taught them to fulfil their mission. Important lessons are suggested respecting the relation the people of God should always maintain towards the world in which he has placed them. Note—

I. THE FREE USE IT IS PERMITTED THEM TO HAVE OF THIS WORLD'S GOOD. "Build ye houses, and dwell in them," etc. In being carried beyond the bounds of Israel these captives were not passing beyond the domain of Israel's God. He is the "Lord of the whole earth." And whether in Jerusalem or in Babylon, all resources, all materials, all power to labour, and all products of labour, are his. Shall not the children of the heavenly Father make themselves "at home" in their Father's world, free to use and to enjoy whatever good he puts within their reach? Remember St. Paul's counsel to the Corinthians, "Whatsoever is sold in the shambles," etc. (1 Cor. x. 25, 26). All natural good has the stamp of God's ownership upon it. Whatever, therefore, comes to you in the honourable commerce of life do not shrink from it or refuse it. It is yours to enjoy because he made it; it is yours because it is his. The freedom of the earth is given to his true children. There is a sense in which it may be said of all outward good that they who know best how to use it aright have most right to its use. There is no "possession" of these things like that which springs from spiritual affinity and sympathy with him who gave them, and from the power to discern and appreciate their inner meaning. There is no "right" like that of Divine sonship. "All things are yours," etc. (1 Cor. iii. 21—23). We dishonour our Christian faith when we move about in the world timidly or gloomily, as if we had no right to live in it, or as if it were a mere "house of bondage;" hedged in on all sides with painful restrictions, bound with fetters of restraint; afraid to share with a free, hearty, childlike gladness any of its innocent delights. If this is "Emmanuel's land," have we not the range of all its delectable mountains? Is it a world that our Father's hand has made and filled with the tokens of his beneficence, and that has been trodden by the feet of the great Redeemer, and shall we throw over it the shadow of our discontent or fear (Neh. viii. 10; Eccles. ix. 7; 1 Tim. iv. 4, 5)?

II. THE IDENTITY OF INTEREST SUBSISTING BETWEEN THEM AND THE WORLD. "Seek the peace of the city," etc. Captives and bondmen as these Jews were, they were nevertheless involved in all that affected the welfare of the Babylonian state. The administration of its affairs for good or ill, for peace or war, must needs be a matter of great interest to them, since they would so largely share the consequences. (See illustrations in Joseph and his brethren, Daniel and the three Hebrew youths, Esther and Mordecai, etc.) The citizens of the heavenly Jerusalem have also an earthly citizenship to maintain, the bonds of which are not broken through their being raised spiritually to a higher level than that of the worldly life around them. Rather are those bonds correspondingly raised and made more sacred and binding. Their Christian faith elevates the character of their earthly citizenship, invests it with a new dignity, attaches to it higher and diviner sanctions. "In the peace thereof shall ye have peace." All parts of the social system are so linked together by a law of mutual dependence and influence that the well-being of one is, in a measure, the well-being of all. "The eye cannot say to the hand," etc.; "Whether one member suffer," etc. We are all personally affected for good or ill by the political order and the general tone of the moral life around us. There are deep rankling wounds in the body politic—ignorance, drunkenness, roving beggary, domestic vice and violence, the systematic training of the young in crime, the oppression of the hireling in his wages, etc.—which it is to the interest of us all most earnestly to seek to heal. No class of the community can escape the ill effect of these things, and religion does but bring us into the deeper sympathy with those who most suffer by such forms of wrong.

III. THEIR RESPONSIBILITY TO LIVE FOR THE WORLD'S HIGHEST BENEFIT. "Seek the peace of the city, . . . and pray to the Lord for it." Real peace is the fruit of righteousness. There can be none while the Divine order is violated and the Divine will set at nought. The gospel is in every way God's message of peace to the world. The Church is called to be the "light of the world" and the "salt of the earth," as a witness for God's truth and righteousness. The Christian philanthropist alone has in his hands a thorough cure for the diseases and wounds of our humanity; and of all the weapons he can wield in his conflict with them, none so mighty as prayer, inasmuch as that unseals the fount of all blessing, and brings down from heaven the healing, saving power. Well may a Christian apostle enlarge and emphasize the old prophetic message, saying, "I exhort therefore, first of all, that supplications, prayers, intercessions, thanksgivings, be made for all men," etc. (1 Tim. ii. 1—4).—W.

Ver. 11.—*Thoughts of peace.* Such is the consoling word that God sends to his "banished ones" in their affliction. He bids his servant "speak comfortably" to them, even now that their "warfare" is only beginning, and they are having their first taste of the bitterness of exile. Blending with the lamentations of the weeping captives as they "hung their harps on the willows by the waters of Babylon," we can imagine that this gracious word would have a more salutary effect upon them than the living voice of the prophet ever had. What message has it for us?

I. THE MIND OF GOD IS A PROFOUND MYSTERY TO US, BUT HE KNOWS HIS OWN COUNSELS. 1. *God has his "thoughts," even as we have ours.* We believe in a God who is no mere philosophic abstraction, but a living, personal being, of whose infinite intelligence ours is but the dim and distant reflection. 2. *His thoughts are immeasurably higher than ours.* "As the heavens are higher than the earth," etc. (Isa. lv. 9). We cannot solve the mystery or trace the course of our own mental processes, and how should we be able to comprehend his? Our minds, with all their utmost range and activity, move but upon the outskirts of the glorious realm of the infinite and eternal thought of God. 3. *His thoughts are all conformed to the eternal truth of things.* Indeed, they *are* themselves the eternal truth of things. For what are all created existences—material and spiritual, all laws, forces, etc., but embodiments and reflections of the "thoughts" of God? And whatever his purposes may be they are not variable ; they partake of the immutability of his essential nature. "The counsel of the Lord standeth for ever, the thoughts of his heart to all generations" (Ps. xxxiii. 11).

II. GOD'S WAYS OF DEALING WITH US ARE OFTEN PERPLEXING, BUT A GRACIOUS PURPOSE GOVERNS ALL. "Thoughts of peace and not of evil" lie concealed within his darkest providences. 1. *The constitution of the universe, in spite of all its discords, bears abundant witness to the benign spirit that inspires it.* We have no sympathy with that gloomy and morbid view of it according to which, for aught that appears, it might have been fashioned by some spirit of cruelty and hate. True as it may be that "the whole creation groaneth and travaileth in pain together," there is proof enough that "God's tender mercies are over all his works." 2. *The Bible has its anomalies, but it is the unfolding of a redemptive purpose.* The revelation of God's mercy towards a guilty, ruined world in the person of the Christ is the key to all its historic dispensations. As every chastisement inflicted on the Jewish people had some gracious design in it as regards themselves, so the whole course of their national life and ecclesiastical polity played its part in the development of that world-wide plan. And through all the changes and storms and conflicts that may yet be in store for the Church and the world, Scripture keeps alive the blessed hope of the future. The prophetic word is "as a light shining in a dark place, until the day dawn and the day-star arise in our hearts" (2 Pet. i. 19). 3. *The saddest experiences in our personal life have their beneficent Divine intent.* Every cloud has its "silver lining." Our keenest sorrows often prove to be "celestial benedictions in a dark disguise." God's "thought of peace" is at the heart of all our earthly tribulations (Heb. xii. 6—11).

III. THE ISSUE ALWAYS JUSTIFIES GOD'S THOUGHTS AND WAYS. The "expected end," when it comes, never fails to solve the mystery of the path that led to it. The gracious purpose, hidden in the secrecy of the Eternal Mind, veiled under many forms of dark disguise, is then made manifest. God is his own Interpreter, and the day of his glorious self-vindication will surely come.

> "His ways are love—though they transcend
> Our feeble range of sight,
> They wind through darkness to their end
> In everlasting light."

W.

Vers. 1—7.—*The letter to the captives.* Notice the mention of those who bore this letter. We may conclude they were not mere messengers having no interest in the message they conveyed, but those who themselves would have much to say over and above what was written.

I. GOD'S CONSIDERATION FOR HIS PEOPLE IN THEIR CAPTIVITY. He not only means to bring that captivity to an end in his own time, but while it lasts it is to be made as little like captivity as possible. It was not enough that he should leave the nation in Babylon till the time of his chastisement expired. While they remained there, they were to have the largest opportunities compatible with the circumstances in which he had found it necessary to place them. And so when the circumstances of any life are untoward, when perhaps we have made them so by our own folly, God shows his solicitude that we should nevertheless have peace in our own hearts, and such ample guidance as may turn even the untoward into the helpful. God will not banish circumstances merely because we find them hard; but this we may always be sure of, that he will enable us to make the very best of them.

II. God's assertion of his part in bringing this captivity about. He had caused his people to be carried away from Jerusalem to Babylon. The place of their present abode was by his arrangement. It was their own fault as a nation that they had had to leave Jerusalem; but it was in God's own wisdom that they were planted in Babylon rather than another place. Clearly to perceive that the omnipotent God was disposing their outward relations, would enable them to listen all the more attentively to what instructions he had to give them for making the best of their present circumstances.

III. God's plan for the profit and comfort of the present generation. The people are plainly told that they are to be there for seventy years. No energy of their own can get them away a year sooner; and no might of their captors can keep them a year later. Hence it is the true wisdom to accept the divinely settled position. No man among them was to neglect the possibilities of his brief temporal life by reason of a baseless expectation that he might soon return to his own land. He might indeed say, "If I show signs of settling down here, I shall be reckoned a very poor patriot." And so over against all temptations to restlessness and utter waste of existence there is this explicit direction from Jehovah. If any Israelite lives a wasted life in Babylon it will be his own fault. So to speak, God makes Babylon, for the time, a sort of substitute for the promised land. If the Israelite has only sufficient of the spirit of true faith and obedience in him, he may make even the land of captivity a place of blessing. For the nation Babylon was a mere place of sojourning, but for the individual it was to be his chief abode on earth. Hence the loving-kindness of God is manifest in telling him he might build a house and make a home and plant fields, thus settling down to a useful and cheerful life.

IV. God's will with regard to the relations between Israel and Babylon. Israel was to seek the peace of Babylon. It was to support everything that promoted peace and security. Naturally Israel would expect to find its chance in the difficulties of Babylon. If any formidable foe threatened the country, or the equal danger of civil war, it might only too easily seem to Israel that this would give the chance for liberty. But so far from this being really the case, God assures his people that Babylon's peace is their peace. This sets before us a principle of action which Christian people cannot too diligently observe. While it is true that we are not of this world, but must constantly rise superior to its habits and maxims, yet at the same time we cannot do too much to maintain the stability of governments and the public order of the land in which we live. While Christ would have us turn away from the cant of what is called patriotism, he would also have us to abhor everything that tends to anarchy. While the Spirit of God promotes the highest individuality, he also promotes the greatest order (1 Tim. ii. 1—4).—Y.

THE

BOOK OF THE PROPHET JEREMIAH

VOL. II

EXPOSITION.

CHAPTER XXX.

THIS and the three next chapters form a kind of book in themselves, which contrasts admirably with ch. xxvii.—xxix. In the latter Jeremiah aimed at casting down the delusive hope that the time of trial would soon be over and the captives restored; here he assumes that all are aware of the sad reality, and concentrates himself on the happier topics of comfort and encouragement. Ch. xxx. and xxxi. shine out among all Jeremiah's prophecies; there is a combination of softness and vigour which, even from a purely literary point of view, is most attractive. Strictly speaking, they ought to form but one chapter; they represent (as ver. 4 states) the revelation from Jehovah "concerning Israel and concerning Judah." It is, indeed, most touching, this yearning of the inspired prophet for the reunion of the two branches of the nation (comp. ch. iii. 1—iv. 2). A "union in spirit" was not enough for him; there must be a visible drawing together, to prove to all men that, as God is one, so his people is one. God's love is imperishable, and his election of Israel cannot be reversed. The very extent of Israel's misery is a pledge that her God will not leave her to herself too long. And how is the restoration of Israel to be conceived? Surely nothing less than a new covenant will satisfy the conditions of the problem—a new covenant written in the heart. Something akin to this encouraging prophecy may be traced here and there in earlier chapters (see ch. iii. 14—19; xvi. 14, 15; xxiii. 3—8; but here the prophet is entirely absorbed in that glorious future which could alone save him from utter despondency.

Ver. 2.—**Write thee all the words . . . in a book.** The form of expression leaves it doubtful whether a summary of all Jeremiah's previous discourses is intended, or merely of the promises concerning Israel and Judah which he had just received. There are, no doubt, numerous allusions to preceding chapters, but ver. 5 seems rather to favour the latter view. The word rendered "book" will equally suit a short discourse like the present (comp. ch. li. 60) and a large collection of prophecies as in ch. xxxvi. 2. Observe, the discourse was to be written down at once, without having been delivered orally; it was to be laid up as a pledge that God would interpose for his people (comp. Isa. xxx. 8; Hab. ii. 2, 3).

Vers. 5—11.—The great judgment of Israel's deliverance. It is nothing less than the "day of Jehovah" which the prophet sees in spirit—a day which is "great" (ver. 7; comp. Joel ii. 11; Zeph. i. 14) and terrible (vers. 5, 6; comp. Amos v. 18, 20; Isa. xiii. 6; Joel ii. 1, 11) for Israel, a day of "trouble" (ver. 7), but for his enemies of destruction.

Ver. 5.—**A voice of trembling**; rather, *a sound of trembling*, a sound causing men to tremble; doubtless it is "the sound of the trumpet, the alarm of war" (ch. iv. 19). **Of fear, and not of peace**; rather, *there is fear, and no peace.* "Peace," as usual, means the harmony of a well-ordered, secure, and peaceful community. Literally, it is *wholeness*; its opposite is "breaking," i.e. outward ruin and inward anguish.

Ver. 6.—**Whether a man doth travail with child.** Great, indeed, must be the terror when no adequate figure suggests itself but that of a woman in her pangs (comp. ch. vi. 24; xiii. 21; xxii. 23; Isa. xiii. 8). **All faces are turned into paleness.** So Joel (ii. 6) and Nahum (ii. 10), "All faces withdraw their colour." For "paleness" the Septuagint has "jaundice"—a possible meaning of the Hebrew; comp. χλωρὸς, "pale, bilious-looking" in medical writings, but properly "greenish-yellow," like the Hebrew noun.

Ver. 7.—**That day**; *i.e.* "the day of Jehovah," the day of the great judgment upon the world, of which the fall of Babylon is regarded as the opening scene. **It is even the time of Jacob's trouble**; rather, *and a time of distress shall it be (even) to Jacob.*

Ver. 8.—**His yoke.** Not that imposed by the enemy (as Isa. x. 22 and xiv. 25 might suggest), but that suffered by Jacob. This is clear from the last clause of the verse.

Ver. 9.—**David their king**; viz. the "righteous Branch" or "Plant" of ch. xxiii. 5.

Vers. 10, 11.—**Therefore fear thou not, O my servant Jacob**, etc. These two verses, omitted in the Septuagint, are among the passages which Hitzig (carrying out an idea of Movers) attributes to the editorial hand of the author (a pious Jew of the Captivity, according to him) of Isa. xl.—lxvi., and it cannot be denied that the tone and phraseology of ver. 10 is more akin to that of Isa. xl.—lxvi. than to those of the greater part of Jeremiah. Graf, in controverting Hitzig's view, points out, however, that the expressions referred to by Hitzig as "Deutero-Isaianic," are also found in other books besides the latter part of Isaiah, and that, on the other hand, "the expressions of ver. 11 are all as foreign to Isa. xl.—lxvi. as they are current in Jeremiah." As for the expression, "my servant Jacob" (which only occurs again in Jeremiah in the duplicate of this passage, ch. xlvi. 27, 28, and which is specially characteristic of the second part of Isaiah), it is worth noticing that it is found once in the Book of Ezekiel (xxxvii. 25), which, on Hitzig's theory, was written before the so-called Second Isaiah. It still remains for the student to consider whether these two verses are not an insertion by some later hand (without attempting to discover whose that hand was). That the prophetic writings have received additions from editors and scribes is a fact which cannot reasonably be gainsaid, supported as it is by the phenomena of the historical books. It would be very natural for a pious Jew in the Captivity, not wholly devoid himself of the spirit of prophecy, to encourage his people, in the Name of the Lord, with this glowing word of promise.

Ver. 11.—**In measure**; rather, *according to what is just*; i.e. not capriciously, to satisfy a feeling of revenge such as the untaught mind is apt to ascribe to God (see on ch. x. 24). **And will not**, etc.; rather, *for I cannot.*

Vers. 12—17.—Miserable indeed is the condition of Israel! No wonder; for its sins were great. And yet, just because it is so forlorn, Jehovah will interpose for its relief.

Ver. 12.—**For thus saith**, etc. If the two preceding verses are a later insertion, we must render, *But surely* (more strictly, *surely*, but particles of asseveration easily acquire an adversative force from the context). Bright, indeed, is the prospect for Judah, "but surely" his present condition is very much the reverse; comp. Isa. ix. 1 (Authorized Version, "nevertheless"). **Thy bruise is incurable,** etc. One of Jeremiah's characteristic repetitions (see ch. x. 19; xiv. 17; xv. 18). **That thou mayest be bound up.** This rendering follows the accents. But the mixture of figures is very incongruous. It is much better to connect the words a little differently and to render, *for thy sore thou hast no medicines (nor any) plaster.*

Ver. 14.—**All thy lovers**; *i.e.* the peoples confederate with thee (as ch. xxii. 20).

Ver. 16.—**Therefore**; *i.e.* because of the extremity of thy need. Comp. Isa. x. 23, 24, "The Lord Jehovah Sabaoth shall make a consumption. . . . Therefore be not afraid of Assyria;" and Isa. xxx. 17, 18, "At the rebuke of five shall ye flee. . . . And therefore will Jehovah wait, that he may be gracious unto you."

Ver. 17.—**Restore health**; rather, *apply a bandage.* **They called thee an Outcast.** Jehovah, speaking after the manner of men, cannot bear to hear his enemies, as they pass along, scornfully denominating the holy city an Outcast.

Vers. 18—22.—A picture of the regenerate commonwealth of Israel.

Ver. 18.—**Upon her own heap**; rather, *upon her own mound,* the *tell* or eminence on which an Eastern town was built (comp. Josh. xi. 13, where "in their strength" should rather be "on their own mound"). **Shall remain**; rather, *shall be inhabited.*

Ver. 19.—(Comp. this verse with ch. xxiii. 11.) **Out of them**; *i.e.* out of city and palace. **They shall not be few**; rather, *not be diminished.* **They shall not be small**; rather, *not be lightly regarded.*

Ver. 20.—**Their children**; rather, *his children*; i.e. the "children of Israel."

Ver. 21.—The future rulers of Israel shall be of the native stock, not foreign tyrants. **Their nobles**; rather, *his noble one,* a synonym for "his ruler," *i.e.* the (earthly) king of Israel. It is remarkable that no reference is made here to the Messiah, who, in fact, is not as conspicuous a figure in the prophecies of Jeremiah as in those of Isaiah. And yet even in Isaiah there is one striking prophecy in which the inspired seer uses language not (in the hands of a literalist) reconcilable with the prospect of the personal Messiah. The Messiah appears, as it were, in a lightning flash, and then disappears for a time. The prophecy of Isaiah referred to is Isa. xxxii. 1, 2 (comp. ch. xxxiii. 17), in which the prospect of a truly God-fearing king, with princes of the same high character, entirely occupies the mind of the writer. "Nothing indicates that the Messiah is intended; king and princes are placed quite on a level, in accordance with the actual state of things under the so-called monarchy." **And I will cause him to draw near.** It is doubtful whether Israel or Israel's ruler is referred to. A priestly relation (such as "drawing near" implies, see Numb. xvi. 5) might be predicated of either, at any rate in the regenerate form of the Israelitish commonwealth; but it is more natural to suppose the ruler to be here indicated, for it is scarcely descriptive enough to say that he shall belong to the chosen people. **Who is this that engaged his heart**; rather, *that pledgeth his heart* (or, *courage*); i.e. that ventureth. The rejection of the old line of Davidic kings might well raise the thought that the intimate relation between Jehovah and his earthly representative for Israel, promised of old to David (2 Sam. vii.), could no longer be hoped for. But with this renewed promise the kings of the new Davidic line may venture to "draw near ; " otherwise—who is he *that ventureth ?*

Ver. 22.—This verse is omitted in the Septuagint, and (unless the existence of later insertions is denied altogether) is all but certainly due to a later hand (comp. ch. vii. 23). Comp. on vers. 10, 11.

Vers. 23, 24.—These verses occur in a form evidently more original in ch. xxiii. 19, 20. In all probability they were first inserted from memory in the margin, and then incorporated into the text at a time subsequent (how long subsequent we cannot say) to Jeremiah.

HOMILETICS.

Ver. 2.—"*Scripture—the written Word of God.*" Jeremiah was required to write his prophecy in a book. Israel had received the Law first by a voice of thunder, but the voice was followed by the writing on the tables of stone (Exod. xxxiv. 1). St. John was commanded to write his vision in a book (Rev. i. 11). Without definite commands of this character, prophets and apostles, historians and evangelists, have committed to writing what they knew and taught. Thus we have a written revelation, a Bible. We may see the great value of this without becoming guilty of bibliolatry, or lowering our spiritual conceptions to slavish subservience to the " letter that killeth."

I. CONSIDER THE VALUE OF SCRIPTURE, AS CONTAINING THE WORD OF GOD IN WRITING. 1. *Accuracy.* Words may be spoken in haste, under excitement ; a book is presumably considered and reconsidered, its words weighed and measured. "Writing makes an exact man " (Bacon). 2. *Permanence.* The spoken word may soon be forgotten, or it may be recollected imperfectly with unconscious embellishments and deficiencies. The written word can be studied carefully and at leisure. 3. *Publicity.* The spoken word is heard only by one audience, present in one place, at one time. The written word is capable of being spread over a wider area. If but one copy is written, this can be sent about and frequently re-read to various hearers, like the circular letters of the New Testament. But the book can be copied, and thus the area of its influence enlarged. Since the invention of printing, and with the facilities for multiplying and cheapening the production of books, this extensive influence of literature beyond that of speech has been immensely increased. 4. *Transmission to the future.* The spoken word dies with the breath that utters it ; the written word can be treasured for ages, and transmitted to distant generations. The orator is peculiarly a man of his own age ; the literary genius belongs to all time. If the Divine Word had been handed down only by tradition we know how terribly it must have been corrupted. We in these later days can enjoy its fresh power because it is crystallized in literature, because prophecy has become Scripture.

II. CONSIDER THE WAY IN WHICH WE SHOULD DEAL WITH SCRIPTURE THAT CONTAINS THE WORD OF GOD. Several duties and wise courses of action are suggested by the fact that the Word of God is written in a book, viz. : 1. *Care to preserve the purity of the text.* Correct readings and accurate renderings of this are of first importance, since they guard the thoughts of God from perversion. 2. *Reverence for the authority of Scripture.* If we believe that it embodies the words and ideas of God, we shall feel that, even when it teaches spiritual principles which we cannot as yet see well established, it has a claim to be listened to with the reverence of the ignorant pupil for his wiser master. As far as it brings before us God's thoughts, it must be read and examined and estimated by quite a different standard from that by which we decide questions of purely human literature. 3. *Diligence in searching the Scriptures.* The Bible is to be used. It is not to be treated as many men treat the classics, "without which no gentleman's library can be complete," but as a text-book, a book of daily reference. It must also be inquired into. There are mines of spiritual wealth to dig, things new as well as things old that a well-furnished scribe can bring out of it. There is in it "milk for babes, and meat for strong men," and the latter needs to be "read, marked, learned, and inwardly digested," if we would profit by it. 4. *Care to extract the spiritual thought from the visible letter.* The letter is human, the form of speech is human. It is the spiritual idea that is Divine, and this is the most important thing to us. This is the real and eternal truth, the Word of life and power. We need an inspiration ourselves to help us to peel off the husk of speech, and find the precious kernel of Divine thought beneath.

Vers. 10, 11.—"*Fear not.*" I. WHY ISRAEL MIGHT FEAR. For various reasons, viz.: 1. *Present trouble.* Already some had been led into exile. What was thus experienced seemed to presage future and worse distress. Grief tends to despondency. In disappointment we are ready to think that all things must grow worse and worse. 2. *The anticipation of necessary punishment.* This is confirmed in the prophetic message— "for I cannot leave thee altogether unpunished." Guilt is the parent of fear. "Conscience makes cowards of us all." 3. *Incurable wretchedness.* (Ver. 12.) Left to themselves, the people were in a hopeless condition. (1) They could not cure their moral disease; Josiah's abortive reformation was a proof of this. (2) They could not cure their external distress; it was vain to attempt to break the yoke of great Babylon. 4. *Solitude.* "All thy lovers have forgotten thee" (ver. 14). In the hour of trial boon companions fall away and leave their wretched comrade forlorn and helpless. The soul must face its darkest trouble alone. While society dispels fear, the silence and desertion of loneliness provoke it. It is not surprising, therefore, that with so many concurrent incentives to fear Israel should be overwhelmed with it, nor is it surprising that similar causes should produce a similar effect among us. Yet it is not the less deplorable. Fear is an evil. It is distressing beyond measure. The vague and threatening spectres of horror that haunt the imagination of the soul when it is a slave to fear may be far more painful than the real evils of which they are the magnified shadows. But fear is injurious as well as painful. It paralyzes effort, dissuades from dangerous tasks of duty, drives to rash and foolish resorts for escape. It is important to see if so sad and injurious a condition can be avoided.

II. WHY ISRAEL SHOULD NOT FEAR. For various reasons, viz.: 1. *The security of God's service.* Israel was God's servant. It is reasonable to suppose that God will protect and save those whom he honours with his name and calls to his work. 2. *The promise of ultimate deliverance.* "Lo, I will save thee from afar," etc. Fear may threaten now, but rest and quietude will come in the future. Fear must be overcome by hope, the darkness of the near future triumphed over by the exceeding brightness of the greater future. We shall not fear what the world can do against us when we live in the hope of what eternity will do for us. Looking at ourselves, we see our wounds incurable, and we despair; looking at the good Physician, we see the promise of health, and we hope. 3. *The assurance of the presence of God.* "For I am with thee." Thus Abraham was not to fear because God was his "Shield, and exceeding great Reward" (Gen. xv. 1); and David could say, "Though I walk through the valley of the shadow of death, I will fear no evil: for thou art with me; thy rod and thy staff they comfort me" (Ps. xxiii. 4). When hope fails faith may yet be strong. Better than the vision of the future haven far over the waves are the strong hand and sure eye of the pilot with us in the storm. When the hope of heaven fails faith in God may still sustain us. 4. *A knowledge of the limitation and good purpose of suffering.* This is (1) given to correct, either as chastisement for sin, or as pruning to make the fruit-bearing branch more fruitful; and (2) given only in just measure, not beyond desert, requirement, or endurance. If we have these reasonable thoughts about our troubles they will not be able to conjure up the terrors of illimitable distress which they naturally inspire when we do not see that they are controlled by purposes of Divine goodness.

Ver. 17.—*Divine healing.* I. GOD IS THE GREAT HEALER OF HIS PEOPLE. 1. God is *not satisfied* to leave his people unhelped in sin and wretchedness. We may grow accustomed to the evil of the world till we pass it unheeded. But it is not so with the Father of us all. He cannot endure the perpetual continuance of the wretchedness we accept (for others) with so little concern. 2. God *designs to restore* his people. It would seem easier to destroy the old weary world and create a new world, than to redeem and restore that which is so abandoned. But it is the glory of the gospel that it seeks and saves the lost. 3. The restoration of God's people can only be effected through the *healing* of them. Israel cannot be restored to the Holy Land until the people are healed of their unholiness, and restored to God spiritually. Men are too ready to regard redemption externally as a change of state, a deliverance from distress and ruin, a gift of blessings, heaven, etc. It is all this, but not primarily. In the first and chief place redemption is healing, is not a change of circumstances, but a change in the soul itself. The richest possessions are of little use to the sick man. The sick body needs health, not wealth ; and the sick soul needs healing before all external changes of condition. 4. It is a great thing to see the *source* of this healing in God. No soul can cure itself. No man can heal his fellow. The disease is naturally incurable (ver. 12). It is healed only by God and through a miracle. The miracles of Christ are thus visible parables of his great work of redemption. The good Physician saves men's souls by working miracles of spiritual healing upon them.

II. THE GREATNESS OF HIS PEOPLE'S DISTRESS INCLINES GOD TO HEAL THEM. Because Israel is called " an Outcast," God interferes to save him. David prays that God will pardon his iniquity, " *for* it is great " (Ps. xxv. 11). We feel that our sin is so great that we dare not ask for forgiveness, our wretchedness so abject that it is useless to seek for deliverance. But we may reverse the argument. The greater the sin the more does it need forgiveness, the deeper the misery the more loudly does it call for help. As claims of merit we have nothing. But when we look for pleas for mercy we find that the very bitterness of distress creates them. As the Judge, God cannot be invoked to help the sinner ; as the Healer, he is most ready to come in the deepest need. The reasons for this are apparent. 1. The *love* of God. Love is moved by need rather than by desert. If God loves his children he will be most ready to help in their sorest distress. 2. The *honour* of God. The people who were called by the Name of God were also called " outcasts." Here was a reproach on the great Name of their God. For his Name's sake God saves. 3. The special *design of redemption*. The physician finds his vocation in the healing art. Sickness is a call for the exercise of special functions. The worse the patient is, the more may he expect of the physician's care and attention. " They that are whole need not the physician." He is the helper of the sick. Therefore the very greatness of a man's sin and wretchedness, instead of discouraging his faith, should encourage him to seek Christ. They who are in such circumstances may know that they are the very persons Christ chiefly seeks to help.

Vers. 18—21.—*Joys of redemption.* The joys of the restoration of Israel are suggestive of the joys of redemption which belong to those who have been healed of their sins and recovered to the favour of God. Let us consider some of the elements of these joys.

I. A RESTORATION TO LOST RIGHTS AND POSSESSIONS. The city is to be built again " upon her own mound." The people not only find the vines they grow in Chaldea fruitful; they are restored to their own land. The prodigal would not have been satisfied if his comrades had helped him to affluence and pleasure again; he must return to the old home. There is something imperfect in the return of prosperity to Job in the fact that though he has greater riches and as many sons and daughters as before his calamities, his dead children are not raised from the grave, and the loss of them cannot be really compensated by the gift of a new family. So is it with earthly losses. The greatest are irretrievable. But the glory of God's ultimate salvation is that it restores old lost blessings as well as gives new blessings, both comforting memory and satisfying hope.

II. AN ENJOYMENT OF INWARD GLADNESS AND THANKSGIVING. The true life is the inner life. Outward sunshine may find this black as midnight, and leave it so. It is much, therefore, to know that redemption from sin brings real gladness. We might have thought that it would have been haunted with dark memories. But God's deliverance is so complete that it dispels the gloom of a guilty conscience. The Christian should, therefore, be a man of inward joys and thankfulness.

III. AN EXTENSION OF POWER AND GLORY. The exiles were scattered and their wealth and influence lost; the return at first promised little satisfaction to the poor and feeble band of patriots that attempted to rebuild the ruins of the ancient nation. But great promises encouraged the faithful to believe that ultimately their numbers would be multiplied, that they should have glory, and not "be lightly regarded," and should be ruled by men of their own people of noble and royal orders. The Christian Church began, like restored Israel, in a small and humble sphere. But she has grown marvellously, and is destined to grow in numbers, in power, and in glory. Redemption is a work worthy of God; no meagre saving of a few as "by the skin of their teeth," but a work of right royal magnificence, calling multitudes to its blessings, and giving them liberty and honour for their old shame and bondage. The Christian receives more than salvation; he is an heir of glory.

HOMILIES BY VARIOUS AUTHORS.

Vers. 1—3.—*Written in a book; or, words held over.* The portion of these prophecies here referred to (probably ch. xxx., xxxi.) contains the most tender expressions of the Divine love. It is full of revelations of the deep unalterable affection and gracious purpose of God for his people, even when they were as yet unrepentant. They are regarded in it as sorrowing for their sin, and returning spiritually to him who restored them to their land. Now, many of these statements it would have been inexpedient for the exiles to hear, whilst as yet they showed no sign of contrition. The prophet is therefore bidden to write them in a book, that they may be read at the fitting season. The words of Christ, "I have yet many things to say unto you, but ye cannot bear them now," are strikingly parallel. This command impresses us with—

I. THE FULNESS OF THE DIVINE WORD. It is not one communication but many, and under circumstances of the utmost conceivable variety. Not in one book but many—a library, representing every stage of human history and spiritual progress. No age or exigency of human nature has found God silent. How great is the multitude of his messages! How many words have been spoken and acted that have not been recorded (cf. John xxi. 25)! The written book is like a vessel let down into the great ocean of the unwritten words and deeds of the Eternal.

II. GOD'S CARE AND ADAPTATION WITH RESPECT TO IT. This prophecy was to be preserved in a book, that no portion of it should be allowed to perish until its fitting time should arrive. The words it contained were all precious, and of pregnant significance in the future of the Church and the world. The adaptation of the prophecy is not less striking. It would not bear public announcement at the time of its communication to the prophet, and it might have imperilled his life; but it occurred then in the natural order of God's thought and purpose; by-and-by the people would be in a better mood and frame to consider it; therefore it was held over. It is written in a book that it may present a faithful transcript of the Divine thought. The progress of revelation has been slow; but that is not the fault of the Revealer, but the necessity imposed by the conditions of human progress. "In the *fulness of the time* God sent forth his Son" (Gal. iv. 4; cf. 1 Pet. i. 20).

III. THE REASONS THERE MAY BE FOR THE DARK DISPENSATIONS OF PROVIDENCE. Who in these stern times could tell the depth of the tenderness of God? It is necessary on such occasions to appeal to the fears of transgressors. The most awful calamities that befall the Church and the individual Christian are inflicted in love; but that love cannot express itself until the requirements of righteousness have been satisfied. The soul that is afflicted ought, therefore, to submit itself to the mighty hand of God, and wait patiently for light. The best wine is kept to the last; the gospel interprets all antecedent revelations.

IV. THE INFINITE RICHES OF REVELATION THAT AWAIT THE SPIRITUAL MATURITY OF THE SAINTS. There are educative, wayfaring truths; and there are truths at which we are to arrive in the end of our growth and pilgrimage. Truth is not only prospective but reflective; not only directive to the feet of the Christian, but revealing the mind and heart of God. How much is held over until these earthly days are ended (cf. 1 Cor. xiii. 12)?—M.

Ver. 16.—*The twofold wonder of Israel's salvation.* I. THE PUNISHMENT OF ITS ENEMIES. 1. *Because of their strength.* The enemies of Israel, especially Babylon, were very strong. But they contained within themselves the elements of their own destruction. It is a property of the *world*, in all its aspects, to appear strong and real and stable. This illusion must be dissipated in order to the free spiritual development of God's children; therefore Christ has said, "Be not afraid; I have overcome the world." How many and how great have been the foes of the Church, and the individual saint! yet has God reduced them to nothingness. 2. *Because of the manner of their punishment.* Evidently more than one nation is referred to here, and they are dealt with in sovereign authority. "The nations are but as a drop in a bucket." (1) Their guilt towards Israel determines the measure of their requital. The Church is the centre and pivot of the world's destiny. In it and for its sake the world is judged (cf. Matt. xxv. 40, 45). (2) The degrees of punishment will correspond to the guilt. Even in vast concerns and through long time God observes an exact and equitable rule of award.

II. ITS OWN RECOVERY. This was to be not only partial but complete, and was to be a terror to the onlooking nations. 1. *Nothing could be more unlikely at the time this was spoken.* This was a part of the wonder of God's saving power, and a vindication of his agency. 2. *That which men despised and neglected God raised up.* He thereby proved the freedom of his grace, and demonstrated the impossibility of salvation by works. The matchless condescension and infinite love of God were proved in this, that Zion deservedly rejected is nevertheless restored. The power was of God. Nothing is so abject as a spiritual organism without the Spirit of God; nothing is so glorious or sufficient when the Spirit of God is present. 3. *The historic accomplishment of this was to be outdone by the spiritual.* Evidently the reference is through the immediately impending event to the spiritual future of the Messiah. God's goodness has ever some higher possibility sheathed in its first expressions. The imperfect efforts of Nehemiah and his colleagues but shadow forth the achievements of the cross. The new Israel will be incomparably more holy, powerful, and blessed than the old. Daily are the miracles of his saving mercy being performed; "the chief of sinners," the fallen, the outcast, are being welcomed into the company of the redeemed and regenerate.—M.

Vers. 18—22.—*The multitude of God's mercies.* A rapid and brilliant enumeration of the characteristics of national glory and human happiness and well-being. Representative and suggestive, but not exhaustive.

I. SEVERALLY SPECIFIED. Set forth with great distinctness, as one might in a legal document; and yet a complete and comprehensive view of a nation's restoration. 1. *Return of the people to their own land.* (Ver. 18.) The representatives of those who had been exiled would be brought back. The shifty and uncertain character of their sojourning ("tents") in a strange land would be exchanged for a settled, civic life. As an outward symbol of this Jerusalem would be rebuilt upon its ruins. "He that made of the city a heap (Isa. xxv. 1) can when he pleaseth make of a heap a city again" (Henry). The habits and customs, the public order and life of God's people, are important as being sacred even as their specially religious observances, and are therefore cared for. True religion is not merely to sojourn in the world, but to dwell there, and influence permanently the conditions and usages of human life. Nothing less than the reconstitution of human society is herein sought (cf. John xvii. 15). 2. *Restoration of religious institutions.* (Vers. 18—20.) Of these the chief, centre, and condition of all the rest—the temple, or "palace"—is first referred to. From its conspicuous and characteristic position amongst the public buildings of the city, it is mentioned in connection with its rebuilding. Because of its presence therein the latter is also sacred ; and so it is said, "Out of *them* shall proceed," etc. The great festivals are to be restored. Worship, in its most imposing and joyous forms, will be celebrated ; and this supposes for its possibility the presence in Israel of a religious, self-governing community. The spiritual training of the people will be resumed (ver. 20). Much attention was always devoted by pious Jews to the upbringing of their children, who are here promised to be "as aforetime," *i.e.* as Jewish children were wont to be according to the covenant, strictly and piously brought up. In this a fresh security is afforded of the religious and social prosperity of God's people. The Church can never afford to ignore the upbringing of the children. As it is a positive injunction ("Feed my lambs "), so is it a gracious privilege and favour granted to his servants that they should discharge it. The sunniest and most hopeful department of religious effort is that which relates to the young. "How is it your flowers are so grandly developed ?" was asked of a gardener. "Chiefly," he replied, "because I take care of my seedlings." The sacred community of Israel will also thereby be increased and established. New, trained members will be supplied for the spiritual offices, and the ordinary membership of the congregation. It is observable that the chief increase of the Church is thus implied to be from within itself. And so it must be to-day. 3. *National prosperity.* This appears in the first place as social well-being. The family life will be greatly blessed, and the population multiplied. It is a result of moral order, etc., and also a means of securing and extending the influence of righteousness. In the next place is political freedom. Tyranny will be abolished (ver. 20) ; and their ruler shall be one of themselves, representing their aims and aspirations, and not imposed upon them by a foreign conqueror. Lastly, political influence will extend abroad (ver. 19). 4. *Covenant relations will be renewed.* (Ver. 22.) This is the culminating and all-comprehensive blessing. Whilst the preceding suppose this, they are really but as antecedents to its complete realization. God will then recognize his people, and regard them with complacency. Neither will be ashamed of the other.

II. MUTUALLY RELATED. How essential is it that human life, in its interests and activities, should be regarded as a whole, the secular with the religious, the duty with the right, the responsibility with the privilege! It is a distinct loss when one portion of it is taken apart from the others and concentrates attention upon itself. Here we have a grand ideal for the individual and the community : the life of man, to be complete and healthy in its development, must extend indefinitely outwards and upwards. The deepest reverence for truth, righteousness, and God is consistent with the truest liberty. The blessings and good things of life, to be truly enjoyed, must be received as sacramental ; as the outcome and expression of communion between man and God.—M.

Ver. 21.—*The ideal ruler.* The immediate reference is to Zerubbabel and the elders who returned from the Captivity ; but there is a larger significance than any merely human personage could exhaust or satisfactorily correspond to. There can be no doubt as to the Messianic character of this promise. But it is precisely the vagueness of the reference, the primary uncertainty as to who it was to be in whom all the hope of Israel was to be realized, that constituted the moral force of the prediction. In Israel was the secular government to be identified with and crowned by the moral and spiritual ; but to the very last was it kept in reserve as to whether or not the kingdom thus foretold was to be of this world. Jesus Christ had himself to declare the real essence and nature of his kingdom. He constituted the ideal Ruler of Israel—

I. IN HIS RELATION TO HIS SUBJECTS. 1. *He was to be of the same kindred.* A stronger guarantee of the Divine favour could not be given. No foreigner was to hold permanent sway over the Israel of God. In one of themselves the holy people would find a legitimate centre for loyal attachment and patriotic devotion. That from their own midst their Prince should spring was proof that their independence, liberty, and national individuality should be preserved. He would therefore represent its honour, and secure for himself the strongest personal attachment. The hopes of the race would be embodied in such a personage, who would vitally perpetuate its glory. 2. *He was to be allied to them in their experience and sympathies.* As their fellow-countryman he will understand their aims and aspirations. By the vicissitudes of their fortune his sympathies will be drawn forth, and he will share the enthusiasm of their future. In Jesus Christ these conditions were fulfilled.

II. In his mediatorial influence. "To draw near" is used in a priestly or mediatorial sense. Israel as a people, or as represented in its ruler, was to have this privilege conferred upon it. A Divine as well as a human qualification is therefore requisite for the perfect governor ; he must not only belong to the people but he must please God. 1. *The grace of God will rest upon him and work within him.* Of Zerubbabel in the first instance, but much more of Christ, is this statement true. He was "full of grace and truth." He is the great Temple-builder and Restorer of the kingdom ; and he is the Accepted of God : "Thou art my beloved Son ; in thee I am well pleased" (Luke iii. 22). 2. *His own nature will respond to the Divine influence.* He is to be one who "engages his heart to approach unto" God. Responsibility drives him to no rash or illegitimate expedients, but to a Divine trust and a desire to please his God. In all this there is evinced the utmost freedom (cf. Matt. iv. 1 ; xvi. 22 ; Luke xii. 50 ; John xii. 27 ; Matt. xxvii. 42). 3. *The admiration and delight of God are to be called forth by him.* "Who is this," etc.? is no inquiry for the sake of information, but an expression of complacency and satisfaction. This feeling finds frequent expression in the prophets, and is noticed in the Gospels. It is for the subjects of such a King to yield themselves to his rule, and identify themselves with his priestly intercession. It should be their great desire to be in him, "who of God is made unto us wisdom, and righteousness, and sanctification, and redemption" (1 Cor. ii. 30).—M.

EXPOSITION.

CHAPTER XXXI.

Vers. 1—6.—The promise of ch. xxx. 22 is expressly declared to apply to both sections of the nation. Jehovah thus solemnly declares his purpose of mercy, and dwells with special kindness on the happy future of Ephraim.

Ver. 2.—**The people** which were left of **the sword,** etc.; literally, *the people of those left of the sword.* The expression clearly implies that the Jews at the time spoken of had escaped, or were about to escape, in some great battle or some other kind of slaughter. Hence the "finding grace in the wilderness" cannot refer to the sequel of the passage through the Red Sea, and we must perforce explain it of the second great deliverance, viz. from the Babylonian exile. This view is strongly confirmed by ch. li. 50, where the Israelites who escape the predicted slaughter at Babylon are called "escaped ones from the sword," and exhorted to remember Jehovah and Jerusalem "afar off." The "wilderness" of the present passage, like the "afar off" of ch. li. (and of the next verse) seems to mean Babylon, which was, by comparison with the highly favoured Judah, a "barren and dry land" (comp. Ps. lxiii. 1), a spiritual Arabia. It may be objected that the tense here is the perfect ; but there is abundance of analogy for explaining it as the prophetic perfect. The restoration of the chosen people to favour is as certain in the Divine counsels as if it were already an event past. (It seems less appropriate to understand " the wilderness" of the country which separated Assyria from Palestine. It was in Babylon that

the covenant of Sinai was renewed to God's repentant people.) Even Israel, when I **went to cause him to rest**; rather, *when I went to cause Israel to rest* (literally, *to cause him—Israel—to rest* ; but the pleonastic pronoun need not be represented in the English). Another possible and perhaps preferable rendering is, *I will go to cause,* etc. "Rest" could only be had in the consciousness of God's favour. With all the outward prosperity of many of the Jews in Babylon, there was no true "rest." Comp. ch. vi. 16, "Ask for the old paths ... and walk therein, and ye shall find rest for your souls" (the same verbal root in the Hebrew for "rest" in both passages).

Ver. 3.—**The Lord hath appeared of old unto me.** The Church of the faithful Israel is the speaker. "From afar" (so we ought to render, rather than "of old") she sees Jehovah, with the eye of faith, approaching to redeem her ; comp. Isa. xl. 10 and lix. 20 (only that in these passages it is to Jerusalem, and not to Babylon, that Jehovah "comes" as the Redeemer) ; also the promise in ch. xxx. 10, "I will save thee from afar," and ch. li. 50, quoted above. (Septuagint reads "unto him ;" but an abrupt change of person is not uncommon in Hebrew.) Saying, **Yea, I have loved thee,** etc. "Saying" is inserted to make the connection plainer. The genius of Hebrew does not require such a distinct indication of a change of speakers as our Western languages. For other instances of this, see Gen. iv. 25 ; xxvi. 7 ; xxxii. 31 ; 1 Kings xx. 34. **With loving-kindness have I drawn thee**; rather, *do I continue loving-kindness unto thee.* "To continue" is literally, *to draw out at length.* The idea is the same as that in the great prophecy which follows that of the suffering Saviour, "With everlasting kindness will I have mercy on thee" (Isa. liv. 8; comp ver. 10).

Ver. 4.—**I will build thee.** A nation, like a family, is frequently compared to a building (so ch. xii. 16; xxiv. 6; comp. Eph. ii. 22). **O virgin of Israel.** The people of Israel is personified as a virgin (comp. ch. xiv. 7). **Adorned with thy tabrets,** The expression will not, of course, bear to be logically criticized, for it was not the whole people who went out with "tabrets" or "timbrels," but the "damsels," who, it is true, formed an important part of religious processions (Ps. lxviii. 25), and doubtless of secular ones also (comp. Judg. xi. 34). Joyousness is an essential part of the Biblical ideal both of religion and of a normal state of society: "The joy of the Lord is your strength."

Ver. 5.—**The mountains of Samaria.** "Samaria" is used, equally with Ephraim, for the northern kingdom. **Shall eat them as common things;** rather, *shall enjoy the fruit.* The word, however, literally means *shall profane them.* The more common phrase, "shall eat the fruit," occurs in Isa. lxv. 21, where the same promise is given. The law was that newly planted fruit trees should be left alone for three years; that in the fourth year their fruit should be consecrated to God; and that in the fifth year their fruit might be "profaned," *i.e.* devoted to ordinary uses (comp. Deut. xx. 6; xxviii. 30).

Ver. 6.—The termination of the schism between north and south will be shown by the anxiety of the Ephraimites (see on "Samaria," ver. 5) to take part with their brethren in the festival of the new moon. It was the custom, at any rate in later times, to station watchmen at elevated points to give notice of the first appearance of "the slender sickle, which shines so brightly in the clear Oriental heaven." **Let us go up.** Not with reference to the physical elevation of Jerusalem, for the phrase, "to go up," is used of an army withdrawing from Jerusalem (ch. xxi. 2; xxxiv. 21). This seems to indicate that the term was sometimes used in a weakened sense, to which parallels might easily be given. These words, "Arise ye, and let us go up," etc., were, at a later period, the formula with which the leader of the pilgrims from any particular district summoned the members of his caravan to fall into the procession.

Vers. 7—14.—The restoration of Israel; its blessedness and joyousness.

Ver. 7.—**Sing with gladness,** etc. It is not stated who are addressed; but we may doubtless understand, from Isa. lxvi. 10, "all ye who love him," whether Jews or Gentiles. The latter, too, are interested in the restoration of Israel, because Israel is as it were a "priest" or mediator for the other nations (Isa. lxi. 6). **Among the chief of the nations**; rather, *because of the chief of the nations.* Israel is called the "chief of the nations" (so, with a cognate word for "chief," in Amos vi. 1) because Jehovah has "chosen" it as his *peculium* (to use the language of the Vulgate), Deut. vii. 6, and because no other nation "hath God so nigh unto them," and "hath statutes and judgments so righteous," as Israel (Deut. iv. 7, 8).

Ver. 8.—The weakest among the Israelites will share the blessings with the strongest, even **the blind and the lame** (comp. Isa. xxxiii. 23, "The lame take the prey"). Elsewhere we are told that, in the Messianic age, "the eyes of the blind shall see," and "the lame man shall leap as an hart" (Isa. xxxv. 5, 6). **Shall return thither;** rather, *hither;* i.e. to Palestine, where Jeremiah writes this prophecy. The word for **company** is *kahal,* the proper word in the Pentateuch for the Israelitish national "congregation."

Ver. 9.—**With weeping**; *i.e.* with a joy dashed with sorrow at the thought of the sin which has rendered such an interposition necessary (comp. ch. xxxi. 18). **Cause them to walk by the rivers of waters.** The reference here is primarily to the homeward journey of the exiles, which shall be free from the trials of the first Exodus, but not exclusively (see on next verse). The question arises how this prediction is to be reconciled with facts. For, as Kimchi has remarked, we find no reference to miracles performed for the Jews who returned from Babylon. A twofold reply seems admissible. We may say either that to those who enjoy a vivid sense of the favour and protection of God no trial is grievous, no circumstances exclude an under-current of joy (comp. Ps. xxiii.); or that the prophecy is still waiting for its complete fulfilment, Israel having still a great future reserved for it upon its recognition of the true Messiah. **In a straight way**; or, *in an even way,* i.e. one free from hindrances. Comp. Ezra's prayer (Ezra viii. 21), and Ps. cvii. 7, in both of which passages "right" should probably be "even." **Ephraim is my firstborn.** It is doubted whether this simply means that Ephraim (*i.e.* North Israel) shall be in no respect inferior to Judah—a strong form of expression being chosen, on account of the longer continuance of Ephraim's captivity; or whether it implies a restoration to the tribes of Joseph of the prerogative conferred upon the sons of Joseph (1 Chron. v. 1, 2; comp. Gen. xlviii. 15). The former view seems hardly consistent with the dignity of a prophetic writer. "Forms of expression," *i.e.* rhetorical phrases, may be admitted in poetical passages, but hardly in solemn prophetic revelations. It was true that Judah had " prevailed above his brethren ; " but the original " gift of God " to Ephraim was " without repentance." With regard to the fulfilment of this prediction, we must remember that the remnant of the northern tribes whose faith was strong enough to induce them to profit by the edict of Cyrus, was smaller than that of the southern. Hence the outward signs of God's favour to Ephraim could not be so great as they would have been had the moral conditions of the fulfilment of the promise been more fully complied with.

Ver. 10.—**The isles ;** *i.e.* the distant countries of the West (see on ch. ii. 10). So great an event as the restoration of the chosen people would be of world-wide importance. **He that scattered Israel will gather him,** etc. " The Israelites were the flock of Jehovah (Ps. lxxvii. 20 ; lxxx. 1), but during the Captivity a scattered and miserable flock. Jeremiah says that his eye ' shall run down with tears, because the flock of Jehovah is carried away captive ' (ch. xiii. 17). The change in the fortunes of the Jews is compared by the prophets to a shepherd's seeking his lost sheep, and feeding them again in green pastures (ch. xxxi. 10 ; l. 19 ; Ezek. xxxiv. 11—16). The reference is not so much to the homeward journey of the exiles as to the state of temporal and spiritual happiness in which they would find themselves on their return. The same figures occur in a psalm, where a reference to the return from exile is excluded by the pre-exile date, ' . . . feed them also, and carry them for ever ' (Ps. xxviii. 9)" (from the writer's note on Isa. xl. 11).

Ver. 12.—**Shall flow together to the goodness of the Lord;** *i.e.* the Ephraimites, after praising God on the holy hill, shall spread themselves over their own territory like an overflowing stream, and enjoy the " goodness " or good gifts of Jehovah—the corn (not simply the wheat), the wine, the oil, etc. (comp. Deut. viii. 8). **Sorrow;** rather, *languish*. As Dr. Payne Smith well says, "It expresses the poverty and helplessness of exiles unable from home-sickness and want of confidence to do anything with spirit. Restored to their homes, they will be as full of vigour as a garden irrigated with water under a Southern sun."

Ver. 13.—Young and old, men and women, shall give themselves up to joy and merriment, the centre of the mirth being the maidens with the timbrels (ver. 4). **Both young men and old together;** rather, *and young men and old (shall rejoice) together.*

Ver. 14.—**And I will satiate ;** literally, *water* (same word as in Ps. xxxvi. 8). The " fatness " means the fat parts of the thank offerings, which were given to the priests (Lev. vii. 34). **Satisfied.** " Satiated " would be a happier rendering. The word is different from that rendered "satiate" just above.

Vers. 15—22.—From this glorious prospect Jeremiah's eye turns to the melancholy present. The land of Ephraim is orphaned and desolate. The prophet seems to hear Rachel weeping for her banished children, and comforts her with the assurance that they shall yet be restored. For Ephraim has come to repentance, and longs for reconciliation with his God, and God, who has overheard his soliloquy, relents, and comes to meet him with gracious promises. Then another voice is heard summoning Ephraim to prepare for his journey home. This verse is quoted by St. Matthew (ii. 17) with reference to the massacre of the innocents, with τότε ἐπληρώθη prefixed. The latter formula of itself suggests that there was a previous fulfilment of the prophecy, but that the analogy of the circumstances of the innocents justifies—nay, requires—the admission of a second fulfilment. In fact, the promise of the Messianic age seemed in as much danger of being rendered void when Herod wreaked his fury on the children of Bethlehem, as when the tribes of Israel were scattered in exile. Dean Stanley finds a geographical inconsistency in the two passages. " The context of ch. xxxi. 15 implies that the Ramah of the prophet was in the northern kingdom, probably Ramah of Benjamin. The context of Matt. ii. 18, on the other hand, implies that the Ramah of the evangelist was within sight of Bethlehem " ('Sinai and Palestine,' p. 225). But this remark involves the assumption that the quotation was not intended merely as an application.

Ver. 15.—**A voice was heard ;** rather, *is heard*. It is a participle, indicating the continuance of the action. **In Ramah.** In the neighbourhood of which town Rachel was buried, according to 1 Sam. x. 2 (" the city " where Samuel and Saul were—ix. 25—appears to have been Ramah). **Rachel weeping for her children.** Rachel ("Rahel" is only a Germanizing way of writing the name), being the ancestress of the three tribes, Ephraim, Manasseh, and Benjamin, is represented as feeling like a mother for all the tribes connected with those three. Her " weeping " is no mere figure of speech. Jeremiah believes that the patriarchs and holy men of old continue to feel an interest in the fortunes of their descendants (comp. Isa. lxiii. 16).

Ver. 16.—Rachel is admonished to cease from weeping, because her work has not

really been in vain ; her children shall be restored. **Thy work shall be rewarded.** Like
the Servant of the Lord, Rachel had said
(though with the voiceless language of
tears), "I have laboured in vain ; I have
spent my strength for nought and in vain ;"
and like the ocean-mother of Zidon, "I have
not travailed, nor brought forth children,
neither nourished up young men, nor brought
up virgins" (Isa. xxiii. 4). Rachel's work
had been that of rearing up the patriarchs,
"in whose loins" the tribes themselves
were, in a certain sense. **From the land
of the enemy;** *i.e.* from the countries of
Israel's dispersion. But in the spirit of St.
Matthew, we may fill the passage with a
higher meaning, of which the prophet (like
Shakespeare sometimes) was unconscious,
namely, "from death;" and the passage
thus becomes an undesigned prophecy of
the Resurrection.

Ver. 17.—**Hope in thine end ;** rather,
hope for thy future (comp. on ch. xxix. 11).
There is no occasion to render, with the Septuagint and Rosenmüller, "for thy posterity"
(comp. Ps. cxix. 13, Hebrew) ; for Rachel
identifies herself by sympathy with her
descendants.

Vers. 18, 19.—The ground of this hope,
viz. that Ephraim will humble himself
with deep contrition.

Ver. 18.—**As a bullock unaccustomed to
the yoke;** literally, *as an untaught calf*
(comp. Hos. x. 11). **Turn thou me,** etc.
Jeremiah has a peculiarly deep view of conversion. Isaiah (i. 16—20) simply calls
upon his hearers to change their course of
life; Jeremiah represents penitent Ephraim
as beseeching God so to prepare him that
he may indeed "turn."

Ver. 19.—**After that I was turned, I repented** ; rather, *after my turning away* (as
ch. viii. 4), *I have repented.* It is a different kind of "turning" which is here
meant, a turning away from God. **I was
instructed**; literally, *I was made to know;*
i.e. brought to my senses by punishment.
I smote upon my thigh; rather, *I have
smitten,* etc. Ephraim describes his present
state of mind, and the symbols by which
he translates it into act. Smiting upon the
thigh was a sign of mourning (comp. Ezek.
xxi. 17). **I did bear,** etc. ; rather, *I have
borne,* etc. The "reproach of Ephraim's
youth" is that which he brought upon himself in early times by his unfaithfulness to
Jehovah.

Ver. 20.—The Divine speaker asks, as it
were in surprise, whether Ephraim, who has
so flagrantly sinned against him, can really be
his **dear** (or, *precious*) **son,** his **pleasant child**
(literally, *child of caressing,* i.e. one caressed).
The latter expression occurs in a remarkable passage of Isaiah (v. 7). **Since I spake**

against him; rather, *as often as I spake
against him;* i.e. as often as I pronounced
sentence against Ephraim—such a sentence
as is recorded in Isa. ix. 8—21 (where the
future tenses should be perfects) and xxviii.
1—4. We must remember that, with God,
to speak is to perform. Often as Jehovah
punished Israel, he still remembered him
in love—a love which was the pledge of his
future restoration to favour upon his true
repentance. **I do earnestly remember**;
rather, *I verily remembered.* "To remember" is the Old Testament term for providential care (comp. Gen. viii. 1; xix. 29).
My bowels are troubled; literally, *sound,
moan* (so Isa. xvi. 11; lxiii. 15). Something
analogous to the thrilling sensation of deep
human grief is predicated of Jehovah. Such
is the "humility" of the God of revelation
(Ps. xviii. 35; comp. Hos. xi. 8).

Ver. 21.—**Set thee up waymarks.** The
"virgin of Israel" is addressed. She is
directed to mark out the road for the returning exiles. The command is obviously rhetorical in form ; the general sense is that the
Israelites are to call to mind the road so
familiar to their forefathers, though only
known to themselves by tradition. The
word rendered "waymarks" occurs again in
2 Kings xxiii. 17 and Ezek. xxxix. 15. It
apparently means a stone pillar, which
might be used either as a waymark or a
sepulchral monument. The **high heaps**
seem to mean much the same thing ; "sign-
posts" would be a better rendering. **Set
thine heart toward the highway** ; rather,
turn thy thoughts, etc., for the heart is here
evidently the symbol of the intellectual
rather than the moral life (comp. 1 Kings
x. 2, and many other passages). A passage
in the Psalms (lxxxiv. 6) will occur to
every one, in which a psalmist, longing at a
distance for the services of the temple, pronounces blessed the man "in whose heart
are the highways [to Zion];" here, it is
true, "heart" has the double meaning of
"mind" and "affections," but "highway"
has almost exactly the same sense as in the
passage before us. **To these thy cities.** The
unseen speaker is supposed to be in Palestine.

Ver. 22.—**How long wilt thou go about?**
We must suppose the Israelites to be hesitating whether to set out on their journey or
not. They are now admonished to put away
their rebellious reluctance, and a special
reason for this is added. **The Lord hath
created**—*i.e.* hath decreed to create—**a new
thing in the earth** (or, *in the land*) ; comp.
Isa. xliii. 19 which suggests that a complete
reversal of ordinary experience is indicated,
as indeed the word "create" of itself prepares us to expect. And what is this promise granted as a sign to reluctant Israel ?
A woman shall compass a man ; *i.e.* instead

of shyly keeping aloof, or worse (as hitherto), Israel, Jehovah's bride, shall, with eager affection, press around her Divine husband. The phrase, however, is extremely difficult. Of other explanations, the most plausible philologically is that of Schnurrer and Gesenius, "a woman shall protect a man" (comp. Deut. xxxii. 10). The part of a sentinel, pacing round and round his charge, seems most unfitted for a woman. When enemies are abroad, it is the men's natural duty to perform this part for the women. But in the coming age, the country shall be so free from danger that the places of men and women may safely be reversed. But would a paradox of this kind be likely to be uttered in this connection? Surely a clearer statement would be necessary to remove the reluctance of the Israelites. Vers. 19, 20 suggest that Ephraim needed reassurance as to the attitude of Jehovah towards him. The promise of ver. 22, as explained above, would give precisely the needed strength and comfort. The exposition of St. Jerome and other Fathers, that the birth of Christ from a virgin is referred to, is altogether inadmissible, (1) because the nouns which form the subject and the predicate respectively indicate sex, not age, and the first in particular cannot be tortured so as to mean "virgin;" and (2) there is no article to confine the reference to any particular persons.

Vers. 23—26.—But the prophet would not have Judah suppose that Ephraim has supplanted her; she too shall be restored, and shall enjoy a happy pastoral and agricultural life.

Ver. 23.—**As yet**; rather, *again* (as ver. 4). **Mountain of holiness.** Does this mean simply Mount Zion, or the whole highland country of Judah (comp. Isa. xi. 9)? The former view is the safer; it is by no means clear that "mountain" in Isaiah or anywhere else in the Old Testament means the Holy Land.

Ver. 24.—The ideal of outward life exhibited by the prophets is still the agricultural and pastoral. Jeremiah puts this more forcibly than the Authorized Version represents. Instead of, **And there shall dwell in Judah, etc.**, he says, *And there shall dwell therein* (viz. in the land) *Judah and all his cities together as husbandmen, and they shall go about with flocks*, i.e. they shall attend to their ancient pursuits without let or hindrance from invaders (comp. Isa. xxxii. 20). "Go about" (literally, *break up*) is the regular word for the periodical journeying of the nomad life.

Ver. 25.—For Jehovah will have fulfilled every unsatisfied craving. **I have satiated** (literally, *watered*) means "I have decreed to satiate;" it is the perfect of prophetic

certitude, which represents an event as already having taken place in the Divine counsels. **Sorrowful**; rather, *languishing* (see on ver. 12).

Ver. 26.—**Upon this I awaked**, etc. Who the speaker is here has been much debated. That Jehovah is meant is not an admissible view. A weak believer may say complainingly, "Why sleepest thou?" but God himself cannot be represented under the image of a sleeper. There seems, however, to be no reason why the prophet should not have used this language. The doubt is whether a real, physical sleep is meant, or merely an ecstatic condition resembling sleep. Hengstenberg decides for the latter. But there is no parallel for sleep in the sense of ecstasy, and, on the other hand, there is evidence enough for dreams as the channels of Divine revelation (Gen. xxxi. 10, 11; 1 Kings iii. 5; ix. 2; Joel ii. 28). As Naegelsbach points out, this is the only unqualifiedly comforting prophecy in the whole book, and may well have left a sweet savour in the prophet's memory. Stern, indeed, was the reality which the moment of his waking brought back to him.

Vers. 27—30.—The physical side of the Messianic blessing. Its effect upon the heart of the pardoned sinners will be such that they will fully recognize the justice of the Divine judgments. There will no longer be any room for a certain favourite proverb; the death of a sinner will be universally acknowledged to be the reward of his personal sin (Keil).

Ver. 27.—**I will sow**, etc. The passage may be illustrated by Isa. xxvi. 18, where the Church of the restored exiles is represented as complaining that the land (of Judah) has not been brought into a state of security, and that inhabitants (in sufficient numbers) have not been begotten. Similarly here, only the tone of complaint is wanting. The thought has suggested itself — Will the Israelites of the latter days be sufficient to fill up the land? Yes, is the answer of revelation: for Jehovah will perform a wonder, and make the people and their cattle so prolific that it will seem as if children and young cattle grew up like plants.

Ver. 28.—**As I have watched . . . so will I watch**, etc. The allusion is to the twofold commission given to the prophet (ch. i. 10), which was partly to pluck up and to destroy, partly to build and to plant. Jehovah has hitherto been "watchful" (another point of contact with ch. i.; see on ch. i. 12) over the fulfilment of the destructive prophecies; he will now be equally zealous for that of the promises of regeneration.

Ver. 29.—**Have eaten a sour grape**; rather, *sour grapes*. The prophet (like Ezekiel, ch. xviii.) condemns the use of this proverb, and declares that the sinner is the artificer of his own ruin. At first sight, it may seem as if Jeremiah opposes the second commandment, which describes how God "visits the iniquity of the fathers upon the children" (Exod. xx. 5). This, however, cannot really be, for he endorses this declaration later on (ch. xxxii. 18). The fact is that he is not so much condemning the proverb, as the blasphemous application of it made by the Jews of his time. It is an eternal truth that sin perpetuates itself (except by the miracles of grace) in the children of transgressors, and intensified sin leads to intensified punishment. But the children of transgressors do not cease to be responsible for their own share in the sin;—this was the truth which Jeremiah's contemporaries ignored. He does not deny the solidarity of the family or the race, but he superadds the neglected truth of the special responsibility of the individual. This is one among many evidences of the deepening sense of individual life in the later period of the Jewish monarchy. (A somewhat different view is offered by Delitzsch, 'Messianic Prophecies,' § 50. According to him, Jeremiah looks forward to a time when the individual shall be liberated from the consequences of his solidarity with his race, and when personality shall be "invested with its rights." But can the individual be thus liberated?)

Vers. 31—34.—The new covenant. A prophecy which stands out from the rest of Jeremiah by its evangelical character, in which it strongly reminds us of parts of the second half of Isaiah. The doctrine of the covenant is "the thread which binds together the hopes and the fears of the prophet, his certainty of coming woe, his certainty of ultimate blessing." A covenant was granted of old, but that covenant had on man's side been broken. Still "the gifts and calling of God are not to be retracted" (Rom. xi. 29); and Jeremiah felt that the very nature of God guaranteed the renewal of the covenant on a new basis. "Covenant" is, no doubt, an unfortunate rendering. The Hebrew word so rendered means, primarily, a decision or appointment, and there is a whole group of passages in the Old Testament which requires this meaning (see the present writer's note, in 'The Prophecies of Isaiah,' on Isa. xlii. 6). We retain it, however, as that with which the reader is familiar, and only remind him that God is everything, and man nothing, in fixing the terms of the transaction. The characteristics of the new covenant are three: (1) The relation between God and his people is protected from all risk by God himself making the people what he would have them be. (2) "Whereas, in the

case of the old, the law of duty was written on *tables of stone*, in the case of the new the law is to be written on the *heart*; whereas, under the old, owing to the ritual character of the worship, the knowledge of God and his will was a complicated affair, in which men generally were helplessly dependent on a professional class, under the new, the worship of God would be reduced to the simplest spiritual elements, and it would be in every man's power to know God at first hand, the sole requisite for such knowledge as would then be required being a pure heart." And (3) "whereas, under the old, the provisions for the cancelling of sin were very unsatisfactory, and utterly unfit to perfect the worshipper as to conscience, by dealing thoroughly with the problem of guilt, under the new God would grant to his people a real, absolute, and perennial forgiveness, so that the abiding relation between him and them should be as if sin had never existed" (Dr. A. B. Bruce, in *The Expositor*, January, 1880, pp. 70, 71). Comp. the abolition of the ark indicated in ch. iii. 16.—The inspired author of Hebrews tells us (viii. 6—13), speaking generally, that this promise delivered through Jeremiah was fulfilled in the gospel. But it must be remembered that the gospel has not yet taken form outwardly, except in a comparatively meagre sense. If the Jews as a nation (that is, the better part or kernel of Israel) should embrace the gospel, not necessarily in the logical expression familiar to the West, but in its essential facts and truths, we should see quite another embodiment of the promise, and feel the spiritual impulse in ourselves as we have not yet done. It seems appropriate, in conclusion, to quote a finely expressed passage from De Quincey's exposition of the New Testament term μετάνοια. Without pledging ourselves to the absolute correctness of his explanation of that word, his language may be well applied to Jeremiah's prophecy. "What would have been thought of any prophet, if he should have promised to transfigure the celestial mechanics; if he had said, 'I will create a new pole-star, a new zodiac, and new laws of gravitation;' briefly, 'I will make new earth and new heavens'? And yet a thousand times more awful it was to undertake the writing of new laws upon the spiritual conscience of man."

Ver. 32.—**Although I was an husband unto them.** The translation of the Septuagint κἀγὼ ἠμέλησα αὐτῶν, is undoubtedly wrong, though adopted for consistency's sake by the author of Hebrews (viii. 9). The phrase is the same as in ch. iii. 14, where even the Septuagint has ἐγὼ κατακυριεύσω ὑμῶν.

Ver. 33.—**After those days**; *i.e.* after they have fully come; not, after they are over.

I will put my law, etc. Of course, not the Pentateuch, but the principles of which the rules in the Pentateuch were the temporary application. It is not here denied that there were, or might be, some under the Old Testament dispensation who had the Divine Law in their heart (see some of the psalms), but speaking of the people as a whole, it must be said that the Law was an external dictator rather than a bosom friend, λόγος ἔμφυτος (Jas. i. 21).

Ver. 34.—On this verse, see note on the paragraph.

Vers. 35—37.—Guarantee of Israel's national continuance. A marvellous promise, in the face of the Babylonian Captivity.

Ver. 35.—**The ordinances of the moon ;** *i.e.* the moon in its appointed changes (comp. ch. xxxiii. 23). **Which divideth the sea when,** etc.; rather, *which stirreth up the sea, so that,* etc. This is one of the points of content in Jeremiah with the latter-part of Isaiah (see Isa. li. 17 ; and comp. Job xxvi. 12).

Ver. 37.—**Thus saith the Lord.** "It is not without meaning that the prophet so frequently repeats : 'Thus saith the Lord.' This formed the A and Ω; his word was the sole ground of hope for Israel. Apart from it, despair was as reasonable as now it was unreasonable " (Hengstenberg).

Vers. 38—40.—The connection is not very clear. The main point of these verses is that Jerusalem, when rebuilt, shall be altogether " the Lord's." Its circumference shall even be extended with the single object of including spots at present unclean, but then to become holy like the rest of the city. According to Hengstenberg and Keil, Jerusalem is here a figure of the kingdom of God in the latter days.

Ver. 38.—**The tower of Hananeel.** This lay at the north-east corner of the city (Neh. iii. 1; xii. 39). **The gate of the corner.** At the north-west corner (2 Kings xiv. 13 ; 2 Chron. xxvi. 9). Both this and the tower of Hananeel are mentioned together again in the prophecy of the glorification of Jerusalem, in Zech. xiv. 10.

Ver. 39.—**Over against it upon the hill Gareb ;** rather, *straight forward unto the hill Gareb.* The hill of Gareb is not mentioned elsewhere ; its meaning is probably " Leper's Hill." It must, of course, have been outside the city, and may be identified (after Schleussner and Hitzig) with " the fourth hill, which is called Bezetha " (Josephus, 'De Bell. Jud.,' v. 4, 2). **To Goath ;** rather, *to Goah.* But the reading of the Peshito, " to Gibeah," should probably be adopted.

Ver. 40.—The southern boundary of the city. **The whole valley of the dead bodies, and of the ashes ;** rather, . . . *even the dead bodies and the ashes.* It is assumed by most that Jeremiah means the valley of Hinnom, which, after its defilement by Josiah (2 Kings xxiii. 10), had become a receptacle of rubbish and offal. It is, however, against this view that the word for " valley " is not *gai* (elsewhere connected with Hinnom), but *'ēmek*, i.e. " deep-lying plain." The " dead bodies " are the corpses of men and animals, destroyed by the judgment of God, and lying unburied ; but where, seems uncertain. **Ashes.** Wood ashes are not here meant, but those of flesh and fat, which remained after the burning of a sacrificial victim (see Lev. i. 16 ; and comp. iv. 12). **The horse gate.** Mentioned in Neh. iii. 28. **Holy unto the Lord.** The unclean spots in the neighbourhood having been transformed. The expression reminds us of Exod. xxviii. 36 (the legend on the forefront of the high priest's mitre).

HOMILETICS.

Ver. 1.—*The close relations of God and his people.* I. THE OCCASION OF THE ESTABLISHMENT OF CLOSE RELATIONS BETWEEN GOD AND HIS PEOPLE. 1. After *chastisement.* This and the other blessings promised in " the book of consolation " are to follow the endurance of the Captivity. God often accords the choicest spiritual blessings to those of his children who are called to endure the bitterest trials. 2. After *repentance.* The people learned to grieve for their wickedness, and return to God in penitence and trust under the wholesome lessons of adversity. Then they were ready for reunion with God. Mere suffering will not lead to this. Suffering is useful just because it may be a means of leading us to humble ourselves and turn to God. 3. Accompanying a restoration of *temporal prosperity.* The glories of the restoration referred to in the last chapter are closely associated with the high spiritual privileges promised in the text. Earthly good things are of little use unless they are crowned by higher blessings. The difference between the prosperity of the wicked and that of true Christians is that the one is the highest good enjoyed, and thus tends to become an idol and a snare, while the other is subordinate to better things and purified by their pervading influence. Thus received, prosperity may be safely enjoyed. 4. Contemporaneously with the *punishment of the wicked.* "At the same time," etc. God is discriminating in his judgments because he is calm and just, though we cannot discern his course and aim. The highest spiritual good is received only when our spiritual foes are overthrown.

II. THE PERSONS WHO ENJOY THESE CLOSE RELATIONS. 1. *Israel.* The promise was to the favoured nation, to the exclusion of others. Elsewhere prophets foretold the spread of the blessings of redemption to all nations, but always on the understanding that those nations entered into the Jewish covenant and became spiritual Israelites. The highest blessings are offered to all men, but with the condition that they who would receive them become his true children. The invitation is to mankind; the promise is to the people of God. 2. The *families* of Israel. God gives distinct family gifts, blessing children through their parents. Religion sanctifies the family. Family life is the largest and highest form of natural human life. 3. *All* the families of Israel. The privileges are not confined to certain selected families—to those which had always remained faithful, to any spiritual aristocracy, to any priestly order; not Aaron's family alone, nor Levi's tribe, nor Judah to the exclusion of the ten tribes; but all are to be restored. All Christians are called to the free enjoyment of God's peculiar people; spiritual privileges are confined within no exclusive limitations. All Christians are kings and priests; all can now enter the holiest sanctuary, enjoy the closest communion with God.

III. THE CHARACTER OF THESE CLOSE RELATIONS. 1. It has a *human side*: "I will be the God of all the families of Israel." (1) Jehovah is acknowledged. The people had followed Baal. They return to the true God. Christians who acknowledge God and Christ should frankly confess their faith. (2) God is worshipped. If he is regarded by us as becomes his being and character, he must be honoured as well as acknowledged. (3) God is obeyed. If he is admitted to be our God, he must be submitted to as our sovereign Lord. (4) God is trusted. Our God is our supreme Helper. When we enter into right relations with God, we learn to confide in him. (5) God is enjoyed. He is *our* God as our Portion. 2. The character of this relation between God and his people has also a *Divine side*: "And they shall be my people." Religion is not only an exercise of human spiritual activities; it is also a sphere in which God works, influencing his people. Though his people are unworthy of God, he is not ashamed of them. He owns them. If God regards any men as his people, great consequences follow. (1) He will prize them as his treasures, showing to them love, bestowing upon them favours, guarding them from harm. (2) He will lay obligations upon them, call them to service, honour them with trusts. These two characteristics of the close relation of God and his people are nearly allied. God will not honour and protect us while we forget or disown him; but his great favours to us help us the better to own and serve him.

Ver. 3.—*The everlasting love of God.* God appeared "from afar" to Jeremiah. When he seems to have forsaken us he is not loving us the less. In these dark hours he may give to us, as to Jeremiah, the richest assurance of his everlasting love.

I. CONSIDER THE WONDER OF THE FACT THAT GOD'S LOVE IS EVERLASTING. There is a wonder about this fact, since there are so many things that might well be thought likely to limit and stay the love of God to such beings as we are, viz.: 1. Our *unworthiness.* God is holy, and must delight only in holiness; he is great, and can create innumerable beings of far higher powers than ours. Why, then, should he love such imperfect creatures as men?—why love those who are corrupt and sinful? 2. Our *indifference.* Love looks for a return of love; but men have treated God's love with neglect. Through the long ages during which God has been visiting his children with ceaseless loving-kindness they have been coldly turning aside to their own ways, deaf to the entreaties of an infinite condescension. 3. Our *unfaithfulness.* For love to remain unbroken it is expected that it should be honoured by fidelity. Unfaithfulness is naturally regarded as a reason for withdrawing the privileges of affection. But God's children have been untrue to him. They have forsaken his ways, abused his blessings, flung insult on his mercy. How, then, can he continue to love them? It is, indeed, a marvel that, through these long ages of the world's wild wanderings, God should still follow his unworthy children with ceaseless love, never refusing to bless them, always entreating them to return to him. And it must be a marvel to us that, through all the years of our unworthy lives, he has shown the same long-suffering, forbearing mercy to each of us. It is wonderful that God should ever love such unworthy creatures as we are, but it is " passing strange " that he should not cease to love us after all our provocations of his wrath, that he should love us with "an everlasting love," and should " have continued his loving-kindness unto " us.

II. INQUIRE INTO SOME OF THE REASONS WHY GOD'S LOVE IS EVERLASTING. We must not look for these in any hidden merits of our own, which our modesty has passed over while God's favour has been won by them. The secret of the love of God and of its eternal endurance is to be sought in his nature and in his relations to us. 1. *The nature of God.* " God is love." He loves because he cannot but love, because he delights to love, because his love must be ever flowing and is so vast that it must needs flow out eternally in all directions. It is not the attraction of the object, but the character of the love, that accounts for its perpetual endurance. The earth is bathed in summer sunlight without having any peculiar attractions for light—only because the vast stores of the sun must ever empty themselves by radiating out into space. The stream fertilizes the valley through no influence of the plants drawing it thither, but just because abundant springs pour forth their waters. And God radiates love, pours forth floods of blessing, because he is full of love, because love has its laws of diffusion. Such love is not destroyed by the unworthiness of the object. Closed shutters do not prevent the sunshine from playing about the house. Sandy deserts, in which the waters of the stream are lost, do not stay the torrents from flowing down the mountain-sides. It is the nature of true and perfect love to be eternal. " Charity endureth all things," and " never faileth." " Love is love for evermore." 2. God's *relations with us.* God is our Father. We are his children by nature, and can never cease to be so. The prodigal son was an unworthy child, yet in his degradation he could still think of his *father* (Luke xv. 17). A parent's love is not caused nor limited by the merits of his children. It has a deeper, a more unselfish source. It survives all the destruction of just claims. God's love is the perfect parent's love. A mother whose daughter had left the home years back always kept her door on the latch at night, that, if her poor child returned at any hour, she should never find it barred against her. Human nature is weak. A mother's love *may* fail, but God's never (Isa. xlix. 15).

III. NOTE THE PRACTICAL CONSEQUENCES THAT FLOW FROM THE EVERLASTING LOVE OF GOD. 1. God will *do all that is possible for our highest good.* We may believe with William Law "that no creature can suffer from any evil from which infinite goodness can deliver it." God has gone so far as to give his only begotten Son to die for us (John iii. 16). We may be sure that he will do all else that is ever possible for the salvation and blessing of his children. May we not, then, well hope that an everlasting love will outlast and wear down all opposition of the stubborn but finite natures even of the worst of us, though it take vast ages to accomplish the result? At all events, he is a rash man who would set limits to the future triumphs of the "ceaseless, unexhausted grace" of God. 2. *We should return to him with trust and love.* The worst man living, if he repent, need not dread a harsh reception, for God's love has outlived his sins. Here is infinite encouragement for penitence; here is hope for the lowest. God loves even him. Surely, therefore, God will welcome his unworthy child when he returns home. We have in this everlasting love of God inducements to urge us (1) to repent and no longer abuse his goodness; (2) to trust in him; (3) to love him in return for his love; (4) to find our rest and joy in him; (5) to devote ourselves to his service (with love "all tasks are sweet"); and (6) to love our brethren with God-like love for the sake of God's love (1 John iv. 11).

Vers. 15—17.—*Rachel weeping for her children.* I. RACHEL HAS NATURAL CAUSE FOR HER GRIEF. Sword, pestilence, and famine ravage the land. The invasion by Nebuchadnezzar desolates the old home of the family of Rachel, bringing death to those who cling to it and scattering the survivors in exile. Such a calamity was in itself most mournful; but the disappointment it brought to the cherished hopes of Israel in a golden future deepened the distress to despair. It looked as though it were the shipwreck of all the Messianic dreams of ancient prophecy. So also the " massacre of the innocents," with reference to which these words of Jeremiah are quoted in the New Testament, was more than an ordinary disaster. It threatened Christ and his redemption. If earthly trouble is great, how far greater would be the destruction of the higher spiritual hopes of God's people! We may be thankful that we have no such cause of distress as that of Rachel at Ramah and at Bethlehem. Though the Christian's earthly fortunes may be tempest-tossed, his highest hopes are founded on a Rock. No worldly trouble can touch these. It is noteworthy that Rachel, and not Jacob, is here represented as weeping for her children. It is the mother's heart that breaks first when her children are taken from her. Even the savage tigress knows this natural grief. It is so bitter that no earthly consolation can assuage it.

II. RACHEL GIVES NATURAL VENT TO HER GRIEF. She weeps. She may thank God for tears; they are nature's relief to a burdened heart. It is best not to hide a sorrow till it eats out the heart like a canker.

> " Give sorrow words; the grief that does not speak
> Whispers the o'erfraught heart and bids it break."

Christ does not inflict harsh and unnatural restraints upon mourners, like those of Stoicism. At the grave of Lazarus "Jesus wept." St. Paul invites sympathetic Christians to "weep with them that weep." Yet it is well to convert our tears into prayers. If the bruised spirit cannot speak, cannot think, can but moan, yet it may make its inarticulate cry an utterance to heaven that the all-pitiful God will hear. The mistake of the mourner is not that she "refuseth to be comforted"—" comfort scorned of devils" may be but a mockery—but that while she weeps she forgets to bring her burden to him who has promised to sustain. It is natural to express sorrow; it is Christian to carry the sorrow to Christ.

III. RACHEL HAS DIVINE CONSOLATIONS FOR HER GRIEF. Human comfort is vain in such anguish as hers. Our little platitudes with which we would quiet the mourner are plasters that only irritate the wound they cannot heal. But God has his higher consolations. He does not bid the tears to stay without good reason. Rachel is to refrain her voice from weeping because there is hope for her in time to come. Jesus bade the widow of Nain not to weep because he was about to restore her son. God will wipe away all tears from his children's eyes by giving them a real harvest of joy for their sowing in tears. The Christian is comforted by hope. He should not sorrow as those without hope. Israel was to be restored to Canaan. The Christian families shall be reunited in the home above.

Ver. 18.—*Ephraim's return.* I. THE MOST ABANDONED OF GOD'S CHILDREN MAY RETURN TO HIM. Ephraim was unfaithful before Judah, and fell into greater wickedness. The northern tribes were punished for their sins by a scattering that destroyed for ever their national existence as a separate kingdom. Yet even Ephraim is to return. No one of God's children—no one of the great human family, we of the New Testament revelation may say—is beyond God's love. God loved Ephraim as well as Judah. Ephraim is a dear son (ver. 20). God loves the whole world. Therefore all may return; therefore we may be sure God has a way by which all can return. Christ, lifted up, will draw *all* men unto himself.

II. GOD LEADS HIS CHILDREN TO DESIRE TO RETURN TO HIM BY MEANS OF CHASTISEMENT. Ephraim says, "Thou didst correct me, and I received correction." Herein is one of the chief ends of suffering; even when deserved for sin it is not to give penal deserts and only satisfy justice, but rather to urge the wrong-doer to see his fault and repent. Chastisement leads to reflection, humbles, makes us feel our need and helplessness, shows the want of God and his consolations, and so inclines us to return to him. To profit us, however, it must be rightly endured. We must *receive* correction, not harden our hearts against it.

III. BEFORE RETURNING TO GOD, MEN ARE BOTH FOOLISH AND OBSTINATE IN SIN. Ephraim is like "an untaught calf." Ephraim had worshipped calves; in course of time Ephraim degraded himself to the nature of his gods. We cannot rise higher than the object of our worship. Every man is made after the image of his God; but in all men this special quality of Ephraim is found so long as they remain away from God in sin. 1. They are *foolish* as the untaught calf. The wicked man may be worldly wise, but he is ignorant in spiritual matters—must become a little child, and learn as a child, if he would enter the kingdom of heaven. 2. They are *obstinate.* Pride and self-will rule the unrepentant heart. Herein is the great hindrance to the wholesome fruits of chastisement.

IV. THE DIVINE LIFE IN MAN BEGINS WITH THE TURNING ROUND OF THE SOUL TOWARDS GOD. This "conversion" is the first step. It may not be suddenly discernible. It may not be indicated by any one epoch in our history. But it must take place. We have been wandering further and further from God. The most momentous step is the first step back to him. We have to learn the necessity of this; to understand that while we remain in the old way, however pleasant it may be, it is leading us away from God, our mission, and our home; to see the importance of a change, a revolution, a regeneration, a new creation. Religion cannot begin with a sinful man in a mere improvement, much less in a natural development. He must turn round.

V. GOD ONLY CAN TURN HIS CHILDREN BACK TO HIMSELF. Ephraim prays, "Turn thou me, and I will return." We lack the desire to return until he "from whom all good desires proceed" implants the earnest wish in our hearts. We have not the strength to return. Old habits of sin are fetters that bind us down to the old life. The will is corrupt, and therefore we cannot will aright. But God does move us to return and give us power to return. The gospel is not only an invitation; it is the power of God. By his Spirit God gives us new birth and the free life of his children. Yet for this grace we must seek in faith and penitence. Ephraim prays that God will turn him. We cannot turn ourselves. God will not turn us against our will. If we seek his grace, he will turn us to himself.

Ver. 25.—*Divine satisfaction*. There are always the weary who need rest, the sorrowful who need consolation. 1. *Naturally* we all have restless longings, large desires that go out beyond the present and the attainable. The soul has its appetites, its hunger, its thirst. 2. *Sin and sorrow* have deepened our need. The Jews in their calamities were a type of mankind in its sin and weariness.

I. NO EARTHLY SATISFACTION WILL MEET THESE WANTS. Food for the body cannot satisfy the soul. Man is not able to live by bread alone. The life is more than meat. We are too large for the world and its gifts, rich and abundant as they may be.

> "We look before and after,
>   And pine for what is not;
> Our sincerest laughter
>   With some pain is fraught;
> Our sweetest songs are those that tell of saddest thought."
>
> (Shelley.)

Hence the restlessness and dissatisfaction we experience in the height of prosperity. Thank God for these feelings. They are indications of a heavenly birth, indications of immortality.

II. GOD OFFERS US FULL SATISFACTION. He will satisfy—satiate. 1. God gives *all* we need. God does not keep his children on half-rations. He has rich stores, and he offers freely. From our broken cisterns we turn to his ever-flowing fountains. 2. What God gives is of the *kind* we need—true light, not mocking speculations; Divine consolations of hope and peace, not barren philosophic maxims, but full and free forgiveness. What God does he does perfectly. He does not call us to a bare salvation, but to a full satisfaction, meeting the peculiar and deep wants of the soul with the special satisfaction they need, and bestowing this to satiation.

III. THE FULL ENJOYMENT OF DIVINE SATISFACTION BELONGS TO THE FUTURE. Much may be enjoyed now. Larger faith would open at once more abundant stores. God's hand is not shortened. It is we who limit our own enjoyment of his grace by unbelief and sinfulness. Still there can be no perfect satisfaction in this imperfect world. Heaven will be totally different from earth in the fact that here we are always reaching out to the beyond; there for the first time all needs will be satisfied. The hope of such a condition should lead to patience and a faithful following of the way of the cross now that leads to the home of rest hereafter.

Ver. 29.—*Heredity and individual responsibility*. The passage before us is interesting as indicating a great advance in freedom and justice of thought from the old orthodoxy that was satisfied with the punishment of children together with their parents to a new and wiser doctrine of individual reponsibility. But it is important to observe that it is more than a sign of advancing thought. It is a prophecy concerning facts, a prediction of a higher justice of the future. The old notion here condemned is not condemned because it is false; nay, it is treated as true for the present. The new idea is not substituted as a better interpretation of the facts of experience; it is a description of a higher order of facts not yet realized. The old doctrine applies with a considerable measure of truth to Judaism; the new is part of the larger justice of Christianity. For the Jewish religion was essentially a family religion; its advantages came to the individual through the nation, the tribe, the family; the first condition for receiving them was descent from Abraham, Isaac, and Jacob. But Christianity is fundamentally individualistic. It elevates the family, it creates the Church—one grand family of Christian brethren; but it begins with individual faith and ends with individual responsibility. Nevertheless, we have not yet perfect justice. Jeremiah's prophecy is still a prophecy to us. Let us examine the two conditions of life that are brought before us by the contrast of prediction with the present order of affairs.

I. THE PRESENT CONDITION OF HEREDITY. It is true now that if "the fathers have eaten some grapes the children's teeth are set on edge." Hereditary punishment and hereditary moral corruption are among the darkest mysteries of "all this unintelligible world." But they are facts that follow necessary social and physiological laws. 1. Children suffer the *punishment* of their parents' sins. Poverty, dishonour, disease, pass from parent to child. The child of a spendthrift becomes a beggar, the son of a thief is ostracized, the drunkard's child diseased, perhaps insane. 2. Children inherit *moral corruption* from their parents. Where this is the case it may be thought to lighten the mystery of hereditary punishment. However that may be, it is itself a deeper mystery, a more horrible injustice. It is remarked that if God visits "the iniquity of the fathers upon the children unto the third and fourth generation," it is to generations of "them that hate" him. But if the wickedness that seems to justify the long-lived punishment is also hereditary, is not the case the more hard? Now, Jeremiah teaches us that we are not to be satisfied with this as a final and equitable arrangement. It belongs to these present times that are out of joint, and it will be superseded by a better order.

II. THE FUTURE CONDITION OF INDIVIDUAL RESPONSIBILITY. (Ver. 30.) This was to come with the Messianic era. We have seen it beginning in the revelation of Christianity. It can only be perfected when Christ's work is perfected by his second advent for judgment. A right social order may do something in this direction. Jeremiah anticipated a wiser, more discriminating exercise of justice in the restored nation after the Captivity. But the full realization must be left for a future dispensation of Divine justice. At the last every man will be called upon alone to answer for his own sins, and judgment will be swift and appropriate. Present inequalities will then be rectified. Meanwhile the injustice of hereditary punishment can be compensated, not only by future alleviations but by turning the punishment into a wholesome discipline, while the injustice of moral corruption will be corrected ultimately by judging a man according to the free choice of his will—how he behaved when he was free to act, how far he took new steps downwards, with all due allowance for natural weakness and hereditary tendencies.

Vers. 31—34.—*The new covenant.* I. THE GRANTING OF A NEW COVENANT. Hitherto the Messianic era with all its glories has been regarded as the development and perfection of earlier ages. Here, for the first time, it is revealed as the realization of an entirely new order. This is the first clear indication of the difference between the Law and the gospel which grew more distinct as the latter was better understood, till St. Paul accomplished his great work of finally severing the two. In these verses we have the first justification for dividing religion into two dispensations and the Bible into two "Testaments." They constitute a great landmark in the history of religious thought. To us who live in the Christian age they are further most practically valuable for the description they give of our high and peculiar privileges and the promises they contain of greater blessing yet to be unfolded. Still, it is important to observe that these privileges and blessings were not always enjoyed. 1. Truth is eternal, but the *know-*

ledge of truth is progressive. Hence the religious ideas of the race change, widen, rise to higher visions. The Bible is a progressive revelation. Theology—the human interpretation of Scripture and speculation on Divine things—is also progressive. Christians must not be bound by the *ipsissima verba* of Old Testament texts. The Old Testament itself says that these shall be superseded. Christians of one age should not be fettered by the orthodoxy of an earlier age. 2. God is changeless, but his *modes of action vary* according to the varying conditions of men. The same principles of justice and love ever pervade his dealings with his creatures. But, like the parent who changes his domestic regulations as his family grows older, God has new dispensations for the later ages of the human family. He educates his children through different standards. There must ever be milk for babes and meat for strong men. Children need restraints and simple instruction, which gradually give place to more freedom and confidence and higher teaching. These changing requirements are met by the suitable adaptation of God's revelation from age to age.

II. THE CONTENTS OF THE NEW COVENANT. 1. The *Law written in the heart* takes the place of the Law written on the stone tables. Religion becomes more internal, spiritual, personal. (1) Real *knowlege* is enjoyed. The people might have the Law in writing, and never read it or fail to understand what might be to them mere words. The Law in the heart is understood, grasped, possessed in thought, not only in words. (2) *Principles* take the place of outward ordinances. For a multitude of petty details, for a complication of rules, for a set of narrow maxims, men are to have large principles in their hearts, such as truth, justice, purity, love to God, and love to man. This makes religion and morality more comprehensive, more deep, more real, and at the same time more free. (3) *Affection* becomes the ruling motive. The Law is in the heart as a treasure, loved rather than feared, obeyed from healthy impulse instead of compulsion. It becomes part of a man's very soul. Ultimately, from being a constraint to his will, it becomes identical with his will, transforming that to its own image. 2. The *spread of the knowledge of the true God is to be universal.* (1) It is vouchsafed to the *individual.* The distinctions of the priestly class and of the prophetic order are abolished. All Christians are priests ; all may enjoy a measure of prophetic inspiration (Joel ii. 28, 29 ; Rev. i. 4). This is partly a result of the first principle. An outward religion only can be corporate and representative. Thoughts are private ; spirituality is personal ; inward religiousness is individual. (2) It is promised to *all men.* All nations are to enjoy the new, larger privileges. Christ breaks down the middle wall of partition between Jew and Gentile. This great fact is also partly a result of the first principle. National distinctions are mostly external. Questions of birth and geographical boundary that have much to do with a visible organization and the administration of external laws do not apply to spiritual conditions. It is right that an inward spiritual law should be universal. But the promise goes beyond the character of the new dispensation to an assurance of its universal acceptance. "All men *shall* know the Lord, from the least unto the greatest"—young and old, simple and noble, foolish and wise, worthless and good, savage and civilized. Here is the great encouragement for Christian missions. They do not follow a mere desire of charity. They are realizing a promise of God. 3. These results follow *perfect forgiveness of sin.* This is the peculiarly Christian and evangelical element of the new covenant. The Law can only be written on the heart after the old sin has been washed out. The enjoyment of spiritual religious knowledge must follow a renewal of the spiritual nature. These privileges were impossible under the Law, because no outward ordinances, no " blood of bulls and goats," could take away sin. But when Christ came as the perfect Sacrifice, "the Lamb of God that taketh away the sin of the world," and brought in perfect forgiveness, he made it possible for us to enjoy the inward vision and brought the privilege within the reach of all men.

Vers. 35—37.—*Guarantees of perpetuity.* These words are a promise to the Jews, and plainly refer to the national existence of Israel ; but the breadth and spirituality of the covenant they confirm warrants us in seeing in them the pledges of God's faithfulness and the Church's stability for all who enjoy the privileges of the covenant. These pledges are to be seen in the symbolism of nature. The God of grace is the God of nature. Spiritual revelation throws light on the vague religion of nature ; but nature sends back confirmations for the truths of the higher revelation. Two are named here.

I. THE UNIFORMITY OF LAW. This great doctrine has come to the forefront of modern science. By some it is thought to be a difficulty in the way of religious belief. But Jeremiah shows us how to regard it as an encouragement for faith. It proves to us the unchangeableness of God. Events shift and vary, but laws remain. The seasons come and go, but the sun still shines and rules them. Though the sea rages and roars, its wild waves are curbed by invisible reins, linked to heavenly motions, obedient to unvarying laws. So we may learn that amid the changing circumstances of life and the varying actions of God in providence the same great principles are maintained and the promises of God work out their blessed results unceasingly. This is true of God's thoughts and will. It is true of our personal enjoyment of the privileges of his covenant. Israel is to endure. The Church is founded on a rock. The "final perseverance" of the Christian follows from his identification of his life with eternal laws of God. God will no more cast off his people than the sun cease to rule the seasons or the moon the tides; for in grace, as in nature, eternal laws and principles preserve eternal stability to the spiritual universe.

II. THE IMMEASURABLE GREATNESS OF THE UNIVERSE. As a mere figure of speech, ver. 37 is highly expressive. By appealing to an impossible feat God pledges his word the more clearly and the more forcibly. But we have here also an analogy based upon common principles of the material and spiritual worlds. 1. The Creator of heaven and earth is too great to be changeable. Change is a sign of weakness. Strength secures stability. 2. Our action is a small thing in the sight of God. It cannot shake the foundations of the universe, cannot even touch them. To us it appears to revolutionize all things; but God sees it in its true light and treats it with calm pity. It is not in the power of such beings as we are to overturn the counsels of God. 3. As nature is wrapped in mystery, so is the spiritual kingdom of God. There are in both hidden forces the action of which we cannot predict. Therefore it is rash and foolish for us to judge God's actions by our limited knowledge. He may appear to cast his people off. We may no longer see him. His actions may seem harsh and cruel. But we are not competent to judge. Out of the mystery of Nature and her dark depths of being, out of midnight and winter, there issue life and light; out of God's darkest dispensations of providence his eternal counsels of love proceed to their unerring beneficent results.

HOMILIES BY VARIOUS AUTHORS.

Ver. 2.—*Grace preparing for grace.* There is some doubt as to the time alluded to, whether that of the Exodus or that of the Exile. A careful examination would seem to make it clear that the former alone corresponds to the description. Pharaoh's cruel edict and the judgments and wars of the desert thinned the ranks of the Israelites. A remnant was left, with whom God entered into covenant relationship. Their survival under these circumstances was a sign of the Divine favour, at the time hard to be understood, but in the future abundantly confirmed. Their ultimate entrance into Canaan was the seal of their acceptance.

I. THE PRESENT TROUBLES OF SAINTS ARE NO PROOF OF THEIR REJECTION. The history of the Church shows this. Here is an instance; there have been many such. The best of God's servants have been most severely tried, and that just before attaining great rewards and satisfactions. The exiles of Babylon are, therefore, to be of good cheer. The afflictions of the present may not only be the punishment for past transgressions, but much more—a preparation for future blessedness and usefulness, a grace in germ if not in formation. In the case of the Church they may bring back to a study of the title-deeds of faith; in that of the individual they may promote humility, heart-searching, and efforts to amend. However hard to bear, they should be endured as a grace preparing for grace.

II. WHERE THE ESSENCE OF GOD'S GRACE IS PRESENT, THE FULNESS OF IT MAY BE WAITED FOR. 1. *What is the essential element in grace?* Is it not the consciousness of acceptance with God? The child of God knows that he is such, and that therefore he is the subject of gracious influences from the Holy Spirit, and heir of all that is truly good.   2. *It is in view of this that present circumstances are to be interpreted.*   The good as well as the evil.   Our true, eternal blessedness lies beyond our greatest present happiness, amongst the "things prepared."   Our anxiety should be, not for immediate possessions, but for meetness for the inheritance, and for entering in by the right way.—M.

Ver. 3.—*The character of the Divine love inferred from its history.*   I. ITS HISTORY 1. *It was self-declared.*   A free, spontaneous *promise* on God's part.   This revelation was itself a grace, as the actual sentiment of God toward Israel might have been concealed.   By the circumstances of its declaration all doubt was removed, and it became a fundamental article of Jewish faith, and a factor of Jewish life and national development.   2. *It existed from the very first.* (Cf. Deut. iv. 37 ; x. 15.)   The dealings of God with Abraham, and with the children of Israel in Egypt, proved this.   Anticipating the beginnings of spiritual life : "We love him, because he first loved us" (1 John iv. 19 ; cf. Rom. iv. 9—12).   3. *It was constant and unceasing.*   With this truth the Israelites were familiar.   Too often they had presumed upon it.   But the continued existence of such a little nation in the midst of its great neighbours was nothing less than a miracle of watchful, unceasing, Divine love.   4. *The same favour is extended to the Babylonian exiles.*   It comes to them freely as it came to their ancestors.   Through them the same purpose of love would work, and their misfortunes would be overruled for ultimate blessing.   II. ITS CHARACTER AS INFERRED FROM THIS.   A love like this was as remarkable as it was vast, and had to be accounted for.   A misunderstanding of its character had frequently involved the Jews in national crimes and disasters.   1. *It was gracious and undeserved.*   There was nothing in the fathers to create such an affection ; as little was there anything in themselves.   And even if there had, the constancy of it throughout so many ages of idolatry and wickedness demonstrated that it could not be the reward of human desert.   2. *It was merciful and righteous in its purpose.*   This it was which sanctified it and endued it with such moral power.   A love of delight and complacency, independently of the character of those upon whom it was bestowed, would have been weak and reprehensible.   But the enduring mercy of God, whilst it is a continual reproof to the impenitent, is full of encouragement and help to the weakest soul that truly seeks for righteousness.   The misfortunes of Israel were as much the proofs of that love as the prosperity ; the one consistent purpose of redemption stringing together the most diverse historic experiences.   Did he choose Israel ? it was that they "should be holy."—M.

Ver. 6.—*The unity of the Church.*   Ephraim represented the ten tribes of Israel, and Jerusalem the tribes of Judah and Benjamin, the sections of the divided kingdom.   In days to come this division was to be healed, as the "watchmen" or prophets of Israel would lead their people to the temple at Jerusalem.   I. THE IMPORTANCE OF UNITY AMONGST GOD'S PEOPLE IS SHOWN BY THE PROMINENCE GIVEN TO IT IN THIS PROPHECY.   Dissension and strife between the followers of truth is not only an unseemly spectacle, it is productive of misery and ruin.   Judah and the ten tribes were too jealous of one another to unite in works of defence or internal administration.   The rival temples of Gerizim and Jerusalem were mischievous in their influence, and, as time would accentuate differences, there would be danger of the common truth being forgotten.   The unity of the Church must ever be important to those whose hearts are filled with the love of God.   Christ's prayer (John xvii. 21) shows how dear the thought is to the purest and best.   The children of God should be bound together in the closest bonds of sympathy and love.   Only thus will their efforts to evangelize the world be successful, and the glory of the kingdom of God be realized on earth.   II. BY WHAT INFLUENCES WAS IT TO BE BROUGHT ABOUT ?   That there were various causes tending to this result is evident to every student of sacred history.   But chief amongst these were : 1. *The events of providence,* by which they discovered, amidst exile and misery, a common brotherhood and faith, and attained to : 2. *A more intense spiritual aim and life.*   The desire to meet with God overcame all prejudice and difference, and revealed the true unity of Israel.   The nearer they were to God the nearer they became to one another, and the more they delighted in assembling together (Ezra iii. 1; Isa. ii. 3; Micah iv. 2). 3. *God was to manifest himself in the person of his Son at Jerusalem.* To the temple, then, all eyes were increasingly turned as the appointed time drew on. 4. *Through Christ's connection with the temple, local holy places were abolished, and men sought God through him.* (John iv. 21.)—M.

Vers. 10—14.—*The redemption of Israel a great and notable event.* It is to be proclaimed as of universal import and consequence. The scattering of Israel may be alluded to in speaking of "the nations" and "the isles," or these may be addressed simply as onlookers of the mighty drama. What happens to God's people must concern the whole world.

I. As an exhibition of Divine grace and power. (Vers. 10, 11.) 1. *It betokened the restoration of God's favour.* (Ver. 10.) The term of punishment was to draw to a close, and the era of reconciliation to commence. Just as he had "scattered" the Israelites, now he was about to recall them to Canaan. In the one act, as in the other, the Divine intervention and its moral significance would be made manifest. The greatest judgments of God on earth have their limits. "He will not always chide, neither will he keep his anger for ever." How carefully should the times of Divine discipline and reconciliation be observed by those who are concerned in them! 2. *The power of God would be displayed in it.* (Vers. 10, 11; cf. ver. 8.) As Sovereign. The words used, "He that scattered Israel will gather him," would seem to mean—he that scattered Israel would alone know where to discover them again. The figure of a shepherd and his flock is also suggestive of skill and authority. As the restored unity and national life of Israel were to be a marvellous phenomenon, much more would the spiritual unity of God's people throughout the world, of which the former was but the prototype. "The Lord knoweth them that are his." Another proof of the Divine power was afforded in the fact that Israel was to be delivered from one "that was stronger than he." The power of Nebuchadnezzar was to be broken. So the world-power which prevents the true freedom and unity of the Church from being realized will be destroyed. Indeed, already Christ has declared himself as "him that overcometh the world;" and in view of this the "little flock" are not to be dismayed. The day is coming when all enemies will be put under the feet of Christ, the Lord of the Church.

II. As resulting in national and spiritual prosperity. (Vers. 12—14.) It was not only to be a restoration of the people to their own land. God does nothing by halves. The industry, social and national development, and the spiritual life of Israel would be abundantly blessed. 1. *The well-being of God's people is viewed as connected.* The spiritual with the material, and the material with the spiritual. There is no austerity in the religion of the restored, and yet their life is full of the spirit and practice of religion. The blessing of God upon the fruits of the earth is gratefully recognized, and as with a common thankfulness the people "flow together" to the great festivals of the temple. It is only as men exhibit this spirit—the spirit of righteousness and thankfulness—that the earth will yield the fulness of her increase. Other things being equal, the good man will succeed better than the wicked, even in secular pursuits. "Godliness is profitable unto all things," etc. (1 Tim. iv. 8). 2. *It is to be complete and glorious.* How spontaneous the piety of the redeemed! In the picture here sketched we seem to catch a glimpse of the fulness of the millennial joy. It is a state of overflowing, ecstatic blessedness. The religious and the secular pursuits of men are to be harmonized. Age is to forget its weakness, and the bereaved their grief. The Church is to share in the general prosperity, and, as a consequence of the efficiency and fervour of its ministrations, the people are to be "satisfied with my goodness." When shall this vision of human life in its wholeness and its glory be realized? Our own times exhibit few signs of such a golden age. Yet the Word of the Lord has spoken it, and we should with patience both labour and look for its fulfilment.—M.

Vers. 15—17.—"*Rahel weeping for her children.*" The great mother of Israel and Judah is represented by a figure as mourning over the desolation of the land. God comforts the sorrow thus occasioned by a promise greater than could be fulfilled in the return of the Babylonian captivity. Rahel was an ancestress of the Old Testament

Church, whose spirit she might be said to personify. The Church of Christ may still be said to weep for her children, and to be comforted by the promises of God. Matthew's reference to this passage is only accommodative—a spiritual and not a literal parallel. We may understand the passage, therefore, as representative of—

I. THE SORROW OF THE CHURCH. 1. *Its occasion.* The loss of her sons and daughters through sin, alienation, or death. Especially might this apply in times of spiritual sterility and worldly influence. The Church cannot look upon the indifference or hostility of her legitimate children without grief. 2. *Its intensity.* Loud and bitter, as of one not to be consoled. The blessing of which she is bereft promised to be so great; the consequences to the "banished ones" themselves may be so serious. Are Christ's people sufficiently alive to the losses which are continually inflicted upon his communion through worldliness or particular sins? 3. *Its character.* Ver. 16, "Thy *work.*" Energy has been put forth. All her resources have been exhausted in vain efforts for the recovery of the exiles. In the first instance our concern for the "banished ones" should lead us to persistent and manifold effort for their restoration; and when that fails, we must cast ourselves in lamentation and prayer before God. In this way our sorrow shall prove to be a "work," in a double sense.

II. HER CONSOLATION. 1. *The restoration of the lost ones is promised.* This would be the only adequate comfort for those who mourn over dear ones as spiritually dead. God's scheme of redemption is greater than our utmost hopes or preparations. 2. *This will in a sense be the reward of her work.* When direct and immediate efforts have failed, a further Divine grace will prove effectual. The children of the Church are beneath the eye of God, who will lead them back again from the captivity of sin, and even from the sepulchres of spiritual death. The labours and prayers of the faithful shall not be in vain in the Lord. The unity of spiritual labour in the past, present, and future (cf. John iv. 37, 38). 3. *God himself comforts her even now.* In his "exceeding great and precious promises." By the Spirit of hope. By the gradual realization of the fruits of salvation. The end is made very real and bright through faith.—M.

Vers. 18—21.—*Ephraim bemoaning himself; or, the penitent's restoration.* The exiled Israelites are represented as about to grieve over their apostasy, and to seek God in confession and prayer. The answer of God is full of mercy and encouragement. The Captivity is to be brought back, and the cities of Israel are to be again occupied.

I. THE STAGES AND PROCESSES OF TRUE REPENTANCE. (Vers. 18, 19.) 1. *Conviction and acknowledgment of sin.* The unbroken steer a forcible metaphor, but not stronger than the circumstances warrant. How stupid and heinous our offences seem when once we see them in God's light! It is *sin* that is bemoaned, not mere misfortune or pain; and the wrong done to the Divine character by our unbelief and misconception. 2. *Prayer for conversion.* The stubborn resister of God's commands is now consciously helpless to convert himself. He feels how necessary the power and grace of God to "turn" him. 3. *The complete work of repentance is now accomplished.* Sorrow for past sins and shame for inward depravity are felt as never before. With deeper knowledge of God's mercy and his own sin, the sinner attains to more intense sorrow and shame. "Smote upon my thigh" (cf. Ezek. xxi. 12; Homer, 'Iliad,' xv. 113 : xvi. 124).

II. GOD'S ANSWER TO THE PENITENT. (Vers. 20, 21.) He prophesies this experience from afar; he represents himself as overhearing it. The first beginnings of grace in the heart, although invisible to human eyes, are noted by our heavenly Father. 1. *Complacency, sympathy, and mercy are awakened in the Divine mind.* 2. *Encouragement is given.* By *promise of salvation,* and by *directions* as to the way by which sinners are to return (ver. 21). 3. *God declares his own readiness to receive us.* He will go forth like the father of the prodigal.—M.

Vers. 31—34.—*The new covenant.* Religion is only possible and of advantage as based upon an understanding between man and God. The perpetuation of the word "covenant," in the New as well as in the Old Testament, shows how essential this idea is. And God's infinite mercy and royal condescension is shown in instituting a new covenant when the old was "ready to vanish away."

I. AS RESULTING FROM THE OLD COVENANT. 1. *It was necessitated by past failure.*

The first covenant had been repeatedly and flagrantly broken. As a system of morals, it was perfect and without flaw ; but human nature, being corrupt, was unable to keep its conditions (Rom. vii. 12). Universal corruption witnessed to the hopelessness of salvation by such a method. And yet the transgressions of men were not thereby excused. The essential depravity of man was revealed in a stronger and more definite character ; but it already existed, and was an occasion of the Divine anger. As the author of the Epistle to the Hebrews phrases it, God, "finding fault with them" (Heb. viii. 8) reminds Judah and Israel of his delivering mercy ("I took them by the hand," etc.), and declares his constancy and uninterrupted tenderness ("I was an *husband*," etc.). 2. *It illustrated Divine mercy.* In strict justice the transgressors of the Law had no claim to any consideration. They had incurred the righteous displeasure of God. But his merciful purpose was not laid aside. Another opportunity of salvation was afforded, and when the first covenant failed, a second covenant was designed of grander conception and more universal adaptation. The love of God, affronted, does not withdraw itself, but busies itself with new schemes to supplement human frailty and diminish the occasions and possibilities of failure.

II. In its distinctive difference from it. It is evident from this description that the gospel dispensation is referred to. The characteristics of the new covenant are mentioned as differing from those of the old in : 1. *Inwardness.* A form of speech signifying that the Law would be rooted in the affections of men, and grow up within them as a second nature. Paul, whilst conscious of the condemnation of the Law, yet approved it as "holy, and just, and good." No longer will it be a limiting, restraining influence acting from·without, but an impulse and inspiration from within. It is much the same in effect as when God promises to give his Spirit to men. And, indeed, a work like this—the new birth—as it is beyond the power of man, must ·be effected by the power of God. He will reveal himself to them by an inward experience. 2. *Universality.* A revelation of this kind will naturally be more extensive than one which appeals first to the intellect. Being spiritual and experimental, it will anticipate and underlie intellectual apprehension. The child and the unlearned person will thereby be placed on an equality with the scholar and the wise man. Yet is not this light given to Israel, or Judah, or to any others, apart from their own voluntary acceptance of it. It is to be distinguished from the natural light of conscience as involving a voluntary submission of the will to the revealed will of God, and as originating in the recognition of a new filial relation between the soul and God. Thus it is said, "He will reveal himself to them as he does not unto the world." And because of the supernatural character of this revelation, "the least" are placed at an advantage relatively to "the greatest;" for "Not many wise men after the flesh, not many mighty, not many noble, are called" (1 Cor. i. 26). The possession of this Divine illumination will of itself constitute a man a citizen of the new Israel, of which it is an essential feature that all its constituents shall know God. 3. *Absoluteness and duration.* "I will forgive their iniquity, and I will remember their sin no more." Acceptance with God is, therefore, final and complete. Under the new covenant the sins of the redeemed are not only *forgiven*, but *forgotten* ; not only *cancelled*, but "*blotted out* as a morning cloud" (Isa. xliv. 22) ; not only *removed from before his face*, but "*cast behind his back into the depths of the sea*" (Micah vii. 19). Under the Levitical priesthood, offering for sins had frequently to be made, being in itself powerless to take them away ; but Christ's sacrifice, being of absolute avail with God, would only have to be once offered in order "to perfect for ever them that are sanctified" (Heb. x. 14).—M.

Ver. 34.—*Missions put an end to.* Many persons, at the outset of modern missionary enterprise, strongly objected to it upon various pleas, but chiefly as an interference with providential arrangements and an opposition to the will of God. Even now there are some who regard it as a quixotic and presumptuous folly. It may console such persons to know that even the Bible looks forward to the abolition of missions. But in a very different way from theirs !

I. The means by which this is to be accomplished. 1. *What it is.* Communication of the knowledge of God. Not by one act or word, but in a sustained and continuous way. By careful and intelligent explanation of God's character, laws, and purpose ; even more by realizing in one's own life and behaviour the love and grace of

God. Every life ought to be a revelation of God. 2. *Where it is to be applied.* The important thing to observe here is the point of departure. Our eyes are not to be in the ends of the earth. The persons upon whom our first efforts are to be put forth are close beside us—our "brother" and our "neighbour." This describes an immediate and direct responsibility. How many have fulfilled it? Some such work as this was done when the Jews returned from the Exile, without teachers numerous or learned enough for the instruction of the people in the Law. The scribes of the great synagogue gave themselves to the work, making itinerant journeys throughout Israel and Judah at stated intervals. But this was not sufficient, and so it had to be supplemented by popular and domestic efforts. Happily the people were enthusiastic and earnest, and, literally, every man taught his brother and his neighbour. This was but a prelude to the work which the Church of Christ has to take up. The missionaries and ministers of the cross are to "go everywhere" preaching the Word. But that will not suffice. Multitudes are hungering for the truth as it is in Christ—multitudes whom we person-ally may never hope to reach. What, then, can we do? We can tell our brother and our neighbour—in that way the tidings of salvation will spread; and others more at liberty and more enterprising may be encouraged by our zeal and liberality to go forth to heathen nations. In any case the first quarter to which the Church should look for increase is *within itself.* The language is explicit, and no man need waste his time in inquiring, "Who is my neighbour?" The parable of the good Samaritan has settled that matter for all time.

II. THE EVIDENCE THAT IT IS ACCOMPLISHED. 1. *Universal knowledge of God.* The gospel is intended for all men. Every man has a personal interest in its message. To keep back the truth from any one who has come within our reach is a sin; especially is this the case with regard to those who are our daily companions and closest friends. The words are not satirical, but a gracious promise. It is an end towards which we should hopefully and constantly aim. Some day it will be realized; "for the earth shall be full of the knowledge of the Lord, as the waters cover the sea" (Isa. xi. 9; Hab. ii. 14). *So long as one soul is ignorant of God, we are bound to continue the work.* 2. *Universal experience of the blessings of salvation.* It is no speculative abstraction we have to communicate, but a "word" which has in it the power to awaken, convert, and reconcile eternally to God. This knowledge of him is therefore experimental and prac-tical. It will not leave men as it finds them. It will purify and redeem, and introduce them to the blessedness of a complete and enduring salvation. God will seal the labours of his servants by "signs following"—by righteous and holy fruits, and by the assurance that the sins of them that believe through their teaching will be forgiven for ever.—M.

Vers. 38—40.—*The new Jerusalem.* The law or condition of the spiritual life of the future having been referred to, the organized embodiment or community to which they will give rise is next described. This will be—

I. THE ANTITYPE OF THE OLD JERUSALEM. 1. *An organized community.* With permanent constitution and laws, and subject to a central authority. Comprehending and unifying the manifold relations of human life. A true "city of God" on earth. 2. *With an earthly manifestation.* It would not be a mere idea, but would realize itself, in part at least, in sensible forms and external manifestations. It would be the incar-nation of spiritual principles and their practical realization. 3. *And a sacred character.* This would be its distinguishing characteristic, as it had been that of the former city. There would be a wall of consecration, and a special aim and direction given to the life, of which it would be the dwelling-place and home. It would be built "to the Lord," and would in its entirety be "holy to the Lord."

II. CONTRASTED WITH IT. 1. *More complete in its surroundings and defences.* Jeho-ash had destroyed the wall in the north and north-east, in the reign of Amaziah. On this side, therefore, the old city was most defenceless. A large portion of this was rebuilt by Nehemiah (iii. 1), but probably not the whole. The new city will be entirely rebuilt and thoroughly defended, "a city compact and built together." 2. *More comprehensive.* Outlying places would be included, and the bounds of the city vastly extended. The whole earth will be included in the city of salvation. 3. *More inclusively consecrated.* The hill Gareb (perhaps that of the lepers), and the hill Goath (possibly Golgotha), and the valley of Hinnom, the foul Gehenna—even these which had confronted the old city as a reproach, would be cleansed, transformed, and included. The sources of disease and the occasions of defilement would thus be entirely removed. 4. *More permanent in its duration.* It is to be preserved from all injury, and is to stand for ever.

III. WHOLLY DISTINCT FROM IT. At no time in the history of Israel were these predictions fulfilled with regard to the earthly Jerusalem. Portions of the description might appear to correspond with what took place in the time of Nehemiah and others, but in its entirety it is evident that the city here spoken of is utterly distinct from the geographical and historical Jerusalem. It is associated with it according to the law of Divine continuity, but in itself it is a new creation. The " wall great and high " is of no earthly material ; the extension is not one of yards or miles, but of nations and ages ; the consecration of the unclean places is but typical of the regenerative force of Christianity, which reclaims the moral wastes of the world, and purifies the carnal affections and sinful tendencies of human nature ; and no material city could ever " stand for aye." Only the kingdom and Church of Christ could satisfy the conditions of such a prophecy.—M.

Vers. 1—9.—*The restoration of Israel.* To cheer the hearts of the exiles, to lift up the despondent, and to vindicate the faithfulness of God, is the intent of this and the many other predictions concerning the restoration of Israel. In a limited sense they were fulfilled by the restoration at the close of the Captivity ; but the events of that period can hardly be said to have filled up the meaning of the emphatic language which the prophets were wont to employ. Hence it has been felt to be necessary to look further for the complete fulfilment of these many most glorious predictions. And in the yet future restoration of Israel, in the gathering home to their own land again in all their national entirety, not a few see the real meaning of the prophets' words. Others, whilst clearly seeing that the return of the exiles from Babylon could not satisfy the inspired Word, find that which more than meets the case in the restoration of humanity at large—in that which our Saviour called " the regeneration," and St. Peter " the restitution of all things," and St. Paul " the gathering of all things in one, even in Christ." And, as in a microcosm, we may see in the redemption of every individual soul the varied characteristics which shall be more broadly and conspicuously displayed when these prophetic utterances shall have their perfect fulfilment in the kingdom of God. In the above verses (1—9) some of these characteristics are indicated ; *e.g.*—

I. ITS AUTHOR. This is the Lord. See how in all these opening verses this fact is emphatically proclaimed. In ver. 1 it is the Lord who declareth that he " will be the God," etc ; in the second verse " the Lord " speaks, saying, " I caused him to rest ; " in the third the Lord it is who declares to his servant the unchanging love which is at the root of all this restoration ; and in ver. 4 it is again, " *I* will build thee," etc. Let these prophecies be understood as they may, the blessings of which they tell are every one of them due to the Lord alone, whether we apply them to the return from exile, the national restoration of Israel yet to come, the redemption of humanity, or to the individual soul. He is the gracious Author of every such restoration, and to him is the praise to be given.

II. THE BLESSINGS OF SUCH RESTORATION. There will be : 1. *Gladness and joy.* (Cf. vers. 4, 7.) Under the imagery of a festive dance the prophet declares this. The mournful monotone of humanity's sorrow, its ceaseless moan, shall be replaced by the song, the dance, the shout of joy. 2. *Peace.* For centuries the vine-clad hills of Samaria had been the object of the marauder's repeated attack ; invasion after invasion had fallen upon " the planters " that planted there. But now, undisturbed, unmolested, they shall not merely plant, but eat the fruit of their vines. It is an image of unruffled peace which arises from the perfect security in which God's people shall for ever dwell. In the turmoil of life, amid its tossings to and fro, and its painful agitations, there are not a few to whom the thought of this blessed peace is the chief charm of the hoped-for future. 3. *Unity.* (Ver. 6.) The watchmen of Ephraim, who were stationed on the high mountains to proclaim the advents of the feasts and festivals of God's people, shall cry, " Arise ye, and let us go up to *Zion.*" What a change here from the old sad past! Then Israel would not worship in Zion, but stood aloof in her own worship within her own borders. But now Israel and Judah shall go together to worship in Zion. Not discord now, but blessed unity. It can hardly be questioned that the spirit of strife, which is an all but universal feature in human character, and never has been wanting in vigorous expression, must have been designed for some good end. But who will not welcome the day when it can be done without, and the nations shall learn war no more? 4. *God shall be all and in all.* The going up to Zion shall be " to the Lord our God." This fact is the key-stone of the whole arch of promise and of blessing. Without it all would crumble away, could have no existence, still less permanence. III. ITS PROCESS. 1. The proclamation of God's grace is made. Faith to believe it is given. Then and thence " praise " to God for his goodness and " prayer " pleading with God to make good his word. " O Lord, save," etc. (ver. 7). 2. Then God actually proceeds to bring them away from the many lands where they are scattered. Distance is no obstacle (ver. 8). Their own infirmities shall not hinder (ver. 8). The dreadful desert, with its thirst, its pathless extent, its rough rock-strewn ways, shall not hinder ; for (ver. 9) God shall give them " rivers of waters," and "a straight way wherein they shall not stumble." 3. We see them approaching their own land : " They shall come with weeping," etc. (ver. 9). It is the sense of God's goodness that more than aught besides leads to that godly sorrow which is the sure guarantee of complete abandonment of those sins which in the past had brought such evil upon them, and which, until abandoned, would render restoration impossible.

IV. THE REASON AND MOTIVE OF IT. Ver. 9, " For I am Israel's Father," etc. It is this fact of the fatherhood of God that explains the darkest experiences of life, for such experiences are God's disciplines, the pruning of the vine, etc. And it enables us to sustain them and warrants the highest and most blessed hopes for those who are called upon to endure them. God's fatherhood is at the same time the most awful and the most blessed fact the soul can know. Let us see to it that, by loving obedience to his will, we know only the Father's smile and escape the Father's frown.—C.

Ver. 1.—*The steps of the kingdom of God.* " I will be the God of all the families of Israel, and they shall be my people." Day by day we pray, " Thy kingdom come," and what that means the next sentence of the prayer tells us. It is that God's will should be done on earth as it is done in heaven. All blessedness for man is contained in the fulfilment of this prayer, even as all man's misery is due to its non-fulfilment. But how do we expect the kingdom of God to come? By what means will the blessed condition of God's will being perfectly done on earth be brought about? The answer which is commonly given is that, by means of the preaching of the gospel and the consequent conversion of the ungodly world, the kingdom of God shall come. Hence the prayer is perpetually put up that God would send his Spirit, and make his Word powerful in men's conversion. Now, God forbid that any should disparage such work, or do aught other than desire most earnestly that the preaching of God's Word may be far, far more successful to this end than it commonly is. Would that the Church might win from the world far more numerous converts than have yet been given to her ! God speed the work of conversion ! But it is not by this means alone that the coming of God's kingdom is to be brought about. There is another, a more ancient, and we may also say a more scriptural and therefore more successful way, and that is *by the increase of godly families.* When God is the God of all the families in Israel, then the nation shall be his people. The family, the Church, the kingdom of God,—these are the successive steps by which, according to the Scriptures, it is the Divine intent to bring in the kingdom.

I. THE FAMILY. God has not taken means to secure the perpetuation of any special political, ecclesiastical, or social institutions, but he has determined that, whilst these may come and go, the institution of the family shall abide. Therefore from the beginning " God made man in his own image," " male and female created he them." The Divine ideal contained this twofold element. And he has also ordered it that the one should be in all respects the complement of the other, and as such should mutually seek and delight in the companionship of the other. And to their union he gave the blessed gift of children and the love that accompanies them, and so amid all the vicissitudes of nations and governments, the institution of the family has been perpetuated; that has not perished, whatever else may have. And there results from all this the formation of a certain spirit and type of character. There are family like-nesses, not in feature and form only, but in mental, moral, and physical characteristics as well. And these enlarge and become characteristics of whole tribes, races, nations. It is evident, therefore, that, in the institution of the family, there is present a propa-gating power for whatever moral and spiritual forces the heads of such family may be themselves possessed with. Abraham, God knew, would be sure to "order his house-hold" after him. And to this day the characteristics of the Jewish race are discernible everywhere. Moral and spiritual forces travel along this road rather than any other. It is God's great highway for those principles which, when fully embraced by men's hearts, shall bring in the kingdom of God itself. And it is by the natural increase of the family that God designs his truth should spread and his way come to be known upon earth, and his saving health amongst all nations. But ere this be accomplished the family will have developed into—

II. THE CHURCH. This will be the further step in the coming of the kingdom of God. When one and another household are possessed of a common spirit, share a common faith and hope, and render obedience to one Divine law, it is in accordance with all spiritual instincts that these should meet together for their mutual comfort, edification, and support. "Then they that feared the Lord spake often one to another." And so strong has been in all ages the force of this spiritual instinct, that no fear of persecution, no terror that their enemies could inflict, has been able to deter those who believed in God from thus meeting together. There need have been no martyrs, or scarce any, if the faithful would but have individually kept their opinions to them-selves. But spiritual force cannot be dammed in and held back. It will be sure ere long to burst through all restraints and barriers and go its own way. But this irre-pressible instinct has been the cause and creator of the Church. And such holy convocations have reacted on the family , and deepening the hold of those sacred principles which first drew the members of the Church together have made more firm the faith and hope which already existed. Thus by the Church the spirit of the family is not only preserved, but strengthened, and its perpetuation and reproduction made more certain in the future. And the process goes on. Divine principles, faith in God, fear and love of his Name, established in the family, expand and develop into the Church, and there slowly, with ever-accelerating force, surely and irresistibly, they make their way until at length it will be seen that the godly seed has the start of the seed of the wicked one, and is ever pushing it out of the way, driving it forth from its long-held but usurped dominion. In illustration of this see how the Christian races do even now inherit the earth. The Puritans of America, the colonies that are ever being founded by our own people. See, too, how the Jews have ever held their own—what tenacity of life, what spiritual force, are inherent in them. These are but illustrations, and but feeble ones, of how spiritual force, if it take possession of the family, will live and spread and grow until the mustard shall become the goodly tree. And thus—rather than by occasional conversions from the ranks of the worldly —does it seem God's mind and will that the coming of—

III. THE KINGDOM OF GOD should be brought about. "There is an established hereditary moral connection between parents and their offspring, and every known principle of reason, of justice, and of holiness suggests that this connection exists for purposes of good, and not exclusively for purposes of evil." "The character of the family lies at the very foundation of all permanent moral improvement in the human race generally, and in Christian Churches in particular; and until it be intelligently, and, under the influence of right principles, practically attended to, all the preaching and all the religious machinery with which we are furnished will fail, as they have hitherto failed, to improve materially the moral condition of the world." As Baxter says, "The preaching of the Word by public ministers is not the first ordinary means of grace to any but those that were graceless till they came to hear such preaching; that is, to those on whom the first appointed means—godly nurture in the family—hath been neglected or proved vain. I doubt not to affirm that a godly education is God's first and ordinary appointed means for the begetting of actual faith and other graces in the children of believers. Public preaching is appointed for the conversion of those only that have missed the blessing of the first appointed means." Yes; let God be the

God of our families, and he will soon become the God of our nation, the God of the whole human race, and his kingdom will have come, and his will be done on earth as it is done in heaven.—C.

Ver. 2.—*Troubles lessened by increase.* "The people which were . . . wilderness." The sword by which Israel had been decimated, her ranks thinned, her homes desolated —what a trouble was that! And now it is to be followed by "the wilderness"—that "waste howling wilderness" so vividly described by Moses (Deut. i. 19; viii. 15; xxxii. 10). This would seem another, a new, a sore trouble, but it was to be the means of healing the wound caused by the first. Cf. "I have given the valley of Achor for a door of hope" (Hos. ii. 15). I. THE MEANING OF THESE WORDS. It is not easy to say certainly what sword and what wilderness the prophet had in his mind when he thus wrote. Perhaps the sword of Pharaoh and the wilderness of Sinai. Yet more likely the sword of their Babylonian conquerors; and the wilderness, that great Syrian desert across which they must travel on their homeward way—a wilderness far more deserving of the dread epithets which Moses applied to the wilderness of Sinai. Or the wilderness may mean the whole condition of the Jews in their exile, the deep sorrow, shame, and distress which their captivity seemed to threaten them with. II. But, let it be understood how it may, THE PROPHETIC STATEMENT IS TRUE. In the wilderness of Sinai what grace God's people found there! Blessings in 'basket and in store, in guidance, governance, guardianship; in instruction, discipline, and development as a nation: how they were welded together, trained for duty, qualified for the high honour God designed for them! And in the wilderness which they had to cross on their return from their exile, infested, then as now, with robber tribes, to whom their comparatively scant numbers, their unwarlike character, and above all their treasures of gold and silver destined for the temple of God, would offer an irresistible temptation, how could the exiles have escaped this peril of the wilderness, to say nothing of many others, but for the grace of God? It was emphatically true that they "found grace in the wilderness." Those dreary leagues of burning sand, the awful dangers of the way, might well have daunted them, and no doubt did deter the majority of the people from all attempt at return; for it was but a remnant that came back. But all these perils were surmounted. Day after day for four months the caravan of the exiles crept along the wilderness way. "Unlike that of Sinai, it was diversified by no towering mountains, no delicious palm groves, no gushing springs. A hard gravel plain from the moment they left the banks of the Euphrates till they reached the northern extremity of Syria, with no solace except the occasional wells and walled stations. Ferocious hordes of Bedouin robbers then, as now, swept the whole trail." But like their great ancestor, "they went forth to go into the land of Canaan; and into the land of Canaan they came." "They," as he, "found grace in the wilderness." And so abundant was that grace that their perilous enterprise became a veritable march of triumph. "The redeemed of the Lord shall return, and come with singing unto Zion; and everlasting joy shall be upon their head: they shall obtain gladness and joy; and sorrow and mourning shall flee away." "As before some royal potentate, there would go before them an invisible Protector, who should remove the hard stones from the bare feet of those that ran beside the camels, and cast them up in piles on either side to mark the broad track seen for miles along the desert." (Cf. Isa. xl. 1—4, for description of this grace found in the wilderness.) And so what seemed so sore a trouble added on to the sword of the exile, was in reality the healing of the wound caused by that sword. But this is often the Divine plan. The second trouble heals the first, and so trouble is lessened by increase. Note— III. FURTHER ILLUSTRATIONS. The plague of London was followed by the fire, but that fire purged the city as nothing else could, and no such plague has visited it since. In medical science it is well known how often one disease is driven out by another. In the hot, close valleys of mountainous lands the wild storm is welcomed, notwithstanding its fierce might, overturning and destroying in ruthless manner, for it purges the whole atmosphere and drives away the seeds of disease and death. The heat was terrible, and the storm, but the second trouble lessened the first. To have to leave Paradise and to go out into a wilderness in which thorns and briars should abound was another trouble, but the labour the second demanded was to be the healing force whereby the first loss should be lessened and the curse turned into a blessing. What a tissue of troubles Jacob's life seems to have been made up of! and yet once and again the new trouble healed the old. The imprisonment of his sons in Egypt led to his recovery of his lost son Joseph. Death follows on disease. Ah! what a new trouble is death in instances not a few! but in that wilderness of the grave what grace the departed soul finds there! Take our Lord's illustration of the birth of children: how the last sorrows of the birth-throes, the dread hour of travail, because thereby a new life is born, are with all the pain that went before forgotten, "remembered no more"! And in things spiritual the law of our text is true. The prodigal's outward misery was followed by the inward pangs of shame, remorse, and sorrow. But they led to the "I will arise and go," etc. And to a renewed soul what misery there is in the return of temptation! and if it have overcome the soul, what yet greater misery haunts the soul then! "Out of the depths have I cried unto thee, O Lord." But that new distress is to render the recurrence of the first less and less possible, and by-and-by impossible. In God's providential ordering of our affairs, this same law is often shown. The straitened means that follow bereavement of the bread-winner of the household—that poverty often develops character, compels the mind to turn from perpetual brooding over its loss, which it is so apt to do, draws forth sympathy of friends, and in innumerable ways works good. "All things" do, as a fact, "work together for good to them that love God."

IV. The philosophy of this. (Cf. Rom. v. 3, 4.) The outward ills may not always be removed, but their power to do aught else than bless the believer is taken away. Instead of casting him down, they lead him into the full possession of that hope, having which the soul is independent of all that man or hell can do against it.

V. Its lesson. If "the wilderness" should follow "the sword," we need not fear; that is to say, if a second sorrow should come upon the steps of a former one, we may regard it as a probable means of lessening the former, and not increasing it. The long sorrow of no Isaac born to Abraham was followed by the awful command to slay him; but that led to an issue that swallowed up in glory and joy all the darkness and sorrow of all the past, and lit up all the future of the long ages to come with a light whose radiance is as bright to-day as ever. Then let our song be, "Father, I wait *thy* daily will," etc.—C.

Ver. 3.—*The love of God.* In these chapters, the thirtieth and the thirty-first, we have a delightful change from the prolonged accusations, warnings, and threatenings which form the staple of well-nigh all that has gone before. Here we have a series of good and comfortable words designed for the encouragement of God's people in the midst of the sorrows of their exile. This verse declares that the love of God was the real cause of all that had befallen his people. Now—

I. Without doubt there was much in their history that seemed to be very contrary to what love would do. "I have loved thee with an everlasting love," said God. "What!" we can imagine a perplexed soul exclaiming—"What! love, everlasting love, and Israel a scattered people, her throne overturned, her kings slain or in exile, her people perished by tens of thousands, her temple and city burnt with fire, her lot so exceeding hard, bitter, and hopeless! Where is the love in all this?" And so it is still. It is hard to persuade men to believe in the love of God; to understand how, under the omnipotent rule of a beneficent and loving God, these many things can be which we know by experience are—pain, loss, disappointment, death, and yet worse, moral evil, sin in all its forms; and the darkness in which we continue in regard to all these. Who can understand all this, or adequately explain the great mysteries of human life?

II. But nevertheless God's love is at the root of all things. "I have loved thee with an everlasting love" was true for Israel and is true for us. For note in regard to Israel: 1. *The purpose of God towards them was such as love only would cherish.* What of honour and glory and blessing did God not design for his people! The whole of the Scriptures teem with his promises and declarations as to this. They were to be his people and he would be their God, in all the fulness of blessed meaning that such an assurance intends. 2. *And there was no other way whereby his gracious ends could be secured*, less painful than that which he had been constrained to adopt. We may be sure of this; for the same love that first formed the gracious purpose would be certain to choose the most direct and happy means to secure it. For: 3. *It was in the power of Israel*—a power which they exercised with fatal effect for themselves— *to compel God to take circuitous routes to reach his designed end.* The heart of a people cannot be dealt with as God deals with mere matter. The power of choice, the free-will of man, can baffle for a long time the benevolence of God, and delay and thwart not a little the accomplishment of that on which his heart is set. They would try their own ways, and only when they had found how full of sorrow these were would they consent to God's way. And all this involved long weary years and much and manifold sorrow. 4. *And what was true of Israel is true of mankind at large.* God has purposes of grace for man. He so loved the world, and loves it still. But sin can for a while baffle God, and compel the use of the pains and penalties which we see associated with it, in order to eradicate the love of it from the heart of man.

III. No OTHER KEY SO UNLOCKS THE PROBLEM OF LIFE. If we find it hard at times even with this key, we shall find it much harder with any other. No malignant being would have implanted love in human hearts. The existence of that one blessed principle in man renders the word of the faithless servant, "I knew thee that thou wert a hard man," for ever glaringly untrue. A capricious being would not have established "the reign of love" which we find everywhere. The settled uniformity of the principles on which God's universe is governed disprove that. An indifferent being, such as the Epicureans taught that the gods were, would not have contrived so many means whereby the ease and comfort of his creatures are secured. Only a God of love would be to man what we perpetually see God is to us. The innumerable and palpable proofs of his beneficence affirm this, and when we regard the sorrows and ills of life as but love's sharp remedies, they will not disprove it.

IV. OUR WISDOM IS TO ASSUME, EVEN WHERE WE CANNOT PROVE IT, THAT THIS IS SO. For thus we shall surely come to find more and more "the soul of good" that there is in even the most evil things, and we shall be able to "both hope and quietly wait for the salvation of the Lord."—C.

Ver. 3.—*God's will done at last.* I. WHAT IS THAT WILL? To gather his children round him. God creates each individual soul only that he may have fresh objects on which to lavish his love. The "dower of blessed children" which God gives to us, he gives because he delights in the possession of children. And the Father of us all wants us to gather around him in the true home of our souls.

II. THE MOTIVE OF THAT WILL. Love. What else can it be?

III. THE FORM IT ASSUMES. Everlasting love. It wears not out, it "hopeth all things, beareth all things, endureth all things."

IV. ITS EXERCISE. Drawing men to himself. How perpetually and by what manifold agencies this is being accomplished! "I, if I be lifted up . . . will *draw* all men unto me," said he who came to do the will of God.

V. THE GREAT POWER WHICH THAT WILL EMPLOYS. Loving-kindness. "With loving-kindness have," etc. Seen most of all in the attraction of the cross of Christ.

VI. THE RESISTANCE IT IMPLIES. There is such resistance—sin.

VII. ITS ULTIMATE RESULT. "I *have* drawn thee." The Father will be able to say that of all his children when Christ's work is finished. "Then cometh the end, when he shall have delivered up the kingdom to his Father, that God may be all in all."—C.

Ver. 10.—*The Scatterer the Gatherer.* "He that scattered Israel," etc. It is possible that there should be *a scattering which has no gathering.* Not seldom we see men squandering every gift and blessing God has endowed them with—time, health, opportunities, friends, etc. And such scattering has often no gathering to follow it, save of the appropriate harvest of ruin whose seed has been so diligently sown. But there may be also a *gathering which has never been preceded by any scattering.* The Father's house may never have been forsaken, the children therein may have grown up in his love and service, without a thought or wish for the far country whither prodigals love to go. As the former fact, the scattering that has no gathering, is the saddest of all, so this latter, the gathering which has known no scattering, is the most blessed of all. It is that of those who have lived ever in the love of God; it is that of the holy angels. But there is a *scattering which is followed by a gathering.* Such is spoken of in this verse (10). God was the Author of both in regard to Israel. Let us take—

I. ILLUSTRATIONS OF SUCH PROCEDURE. There is that of the *sower.* He scatters his grain in the furrows, and throws it broadcast o'er the land. But by-and-by he gathers in the rich harvest. *The merchant.* He scatters his wealth in this venture and in that, in the confidence that he shall, in due time, gather large increase of wealth thereby. The *father of a family,* when disease has broken out in the home. The children are sent hither and thither, scattered, but with the intent that when the disease is banished they may all be gathered again without loss or harm. *And God* has scattered the children of men, and the fortunes of men oftentimes, but with the intent of gathering them again. Job. Jacob. Israel's exile. The sending forth and return of our Lord's apostles. The persecution of the Church about Stephen. The whole company of the children of God which are scattered abroad, all to be gathered in at last in the Father's house on high.

II. REASONS OF IT. In the case of such as the sower, etc., these are obvious. But the reasons that influence them in their conduct are akin to those which we may believe order the like Divine procedure. By scattering his people hither and thither broadcast o'er the world, God looks for a harvest from such seed; and how often he has gathered such harvest from such sowing! And the parent's reason—scattering his children to protect them from evil which would have befallen them had they remained together in one place, but purposing to gather them again when the fear of the evil is no more—how much of the painful scatterings which in this life we know and experience may be explained so! When the fire of the foe threatens the massed ranks of an army, the commander scatters his men, bids them take "open order," and so saves them. When the fire ceases, they close up once more. It was to save men from a great sin that God scattered them at Babel. Such divisions and separations are needful now. But he that scattereth will gather.

III. LESSONS. 1. *Submission.* There is wise and good reason for all that now is. What is, is best. 2. *Hope.* Yes; "let our eyes look right on, and our eyelids straight before us." "He that scattereth will gather." Meanwhile: 3. *Obedience.* If God have scattered me or mine, inquire why he has done so. Put yourself in line with God's purposes; for "he always wins who sides with thee."—C.

Ver. 11.—*Strong, stronger, strongest.* Israel, Babylon, God. Note—

I. THE STRONG. Was not Israel so? Regarding Israel as including Judah and Jerusalem, how strong, even materially, was Israel! In her numbers, wealth, fortresses —especially Jerusalem, which was one of the most impregnable of all the cities of the world! in her privileges, memories, promised help of God! in her past prestige and influence! in her long traditions of freedom and greatness! and in much beside! But Israel may be taken as a type of all humanity. Looking upon our first parents, the head of our race, surely we should have thought their position of happiness, holiness, and Divine favour, impregnable. What safeguard did they lack? what motive to withstand the tempter was wanting? And how many there are now who say of themselves, and others think it, that they shall never be moved? Their mountain seems to stand so strong. Lands where pure gospel ministry exists; children of godly homes; men who have long walked in God's ways. But facts all too often show that, "strong" as these may be, there is—

II. THE STRONGER one who overcomes them. The Chaldean armies were too strong for Israel. "The hand of" Babylon "was stronger than he." And the facts of human life all reveal how humanity has come under the cruel dominance of one who is stronger than man. Behold *the body,* a prey to feebleness, disease, pain, and death; *the mind,* to corrupt imagination, to delusion, and deceit; *the affections* clinging to things evil, debased, perverted; *the will* enslaved, made to do that which it would not; *the soul* earth-bound, unable to rise up to God and heaven, as it was made to do. Yes; the evidence is abundant and everywhere that a stronger than man has overcome him to his harm. But this verse tells of deliverance from the hand of this stronger one, by one who is—

III. THE STRONGEST of all. It came true of Israel, and shall come true again. It is true in regard to humanity and the individual soul. It may be thought, considering the comparatively small number of the exiles who returned to Jerusalem, that this prediction was scarcely verified. But in the increase of the Jewish race in the lands of their exile, in their preservation from the hatred of their enemies (cf. Book of Esther), in the deliverance of them from the snare of idolatry, in the implantation in their hearts of a deeper love and understanding of God's Word,—in all these and in other respects Israel *was* delivered. And humanity *is* redeemed, ransomed. When Christ said, " It is finished," then was virtually accomplished that deliverance for which, in its full realization, the world yet groans. But in every triumph of Divine grace, every conversion, every breaking away from evil, every tightening of the blessed bonds which bind us to Christ, every advance the gospel makes, every missionary triumph, every act of self-consecration, there is present proof of what by-and-by shall be perfectly proved. And the means by which all this is accomplished are suggested to us by the word " ransomed ; " it sends our thoughts to him who said of himself that he came to give his life a " ransom for many." Therefore : 1. Let us each look on beyond that mighty one, the prince of this world, who is stronger than we, to him, the Saviour of us all, the Mightiest, who is stronger than he. 2. And ask ourselves the question— Under whose rule and service do we ourselves live ? That is the all-important question. God help us to give it the right answer.—C.

Ver. 14.—*Satisfied.* I. THERE IS A SATISFACTION WHICH IS NOT TO BE DESIRED. 1. That of *the worldling,* which says, " Soul, take thine ease," etc. 2. That of *conventionalism.* This looks only to the ordinary standard of religious attainment, and so long as it can come up tolerably near to that standard, it desires no more. They are " at ease in Zion," and the " woe " denounced on such is theirs. 3. Of *Pharisaism,* which thanks God that it is not as other men are. 4. *Of the Stoic,* that has drilled itself not to feel the sorrows of men. 5. Of the *selfish,* which, because it swims, cares not who sinks.
II. BUT THERE IS A SATISFACTION WHICH IS GREATLY TO BE DESIRED. 1. That *of trust,* which prevents all murmuring at the dispensations of God, and which says, " I will trust, and not be afraid." 2. That of *meekness,* which says, " It is the Lord ; let him do what seemeth good in his sight." 3. *That of belief in God's promises in Christ.* " Being justified by faith, we have peace with God." 4. That of *experience*—the consciousness that God is carrying on his work within us, deepening the hold of that which is good, loosening more and more the power of that which is evil. Consciousness of growth in grace. But none of these, precious as they are, come up to what is meant here. For it tells us that—
III. THERE IS A SATISFACTION BETTER THAN ALL THESE. It is that of *the realization of the promises of God.* This, not now, but hereafter. In all the kingdom of nature where God has implanted any hunger, he has made provision for its supply. Is the soul of man to be the solitary exception ? The seeds obtain their full development ere they die ; but not one single soul that God has created ever does so. We cannot be satisfied with either what we know or attain to here. What satisfaction we have is all based on the conviction that we know not, see not, possess not, now ; we shall hereafter. See to it, that we be in the road that leadeth to that realization. " I am the Way," said Jesus.—C.

Vers. 15—17.—*Strong consolation.* In this touching passage let us note—
I. THE SCENE. The exiles, with bowed heads and many tears, are being hurried away from their beloved land. Fierce soldiery urge them on. The smoking ruins of their towns, cities, homes, and, above all, of the greatly beloved city of God, Jerusalem, are behind them. A wail of distress goes up from these broken-hearted captives as they stand on the frontier hills of their land, and have to say farewell to it for ever. The whole scene rose up vividly before the prophet, and he seems to see the spirit of Rachel, the genius of their nation, the mother of the tribes on whose border-land the exiles are now standing. She hovers over the sad-hearted company, her face wet with uncontrollable tears, and her lamentations for her poor lost children heard incessantly. She has arisen from her tomb, which was hard by Ramah, and is bewailing the misery of her children.

II. THE SORROW. It is that of parents for their children. How *intense* this sorrow is! Rachel refuses to be comforted, because her children are not. It is greater than the sorrow of the children. In God's blessed ordering of things, children rarely grieve deeply. They soon forget, as they ought to do. It is not they that grieve, but their parents for them. And if the parents' grief be greater than that of the children, it is greater still than that which the parents feel for themselves. It matters little what becomes of them: it is the children for whom they care. What a *holy* thing this love of parents is! It is by means of this, appealing to it, that "out of the mouths of babes," etc. And how *frequent*, in this weary world of ours! We know how the deep distress of those mothers whose little ones Herod slew recalled the sorrow told of here. The words of the prophet find plentiful application. Not on one ground alone, but on many, parents often have to mourn for their children. But for the people of God there is ever—

III. RICH CONSOLATION. 1. Is the sorrow, as here, *that which is caused by the sight of sore calamity coming upon our children which we cannot ward off*? Oh, how many a father, as he looks around the circle of his children, seems to see a black spectre of care hovering over every one of those curly heads! and the vision sends a chill into his very soul. Their mother is to die, the means of their support is failing, disease has already fastened on some of them; trouble manifold is appointed for them. Their foes are many, their friends few. Now, to all such parents this word of consolation is sent. It tells us how God will care for them if we cannot. His love will never fail, and there is hope for them. Life, after all, will not be to them what we think. O anxious fathers and mothers—and what a crowd of you there are!—trust the God of Israel for your children. 2. Or is it the sorrow *that comes from having prodigal children*? This is a sorrow worse still. But art thou, O parent, a believer in God? dost thou seek him evermore in fervent prayer? Then be assured that he who caused that the prodigal of whom our Saviour tells should "come to himself," will do the like for thine. Never believe that the seed of the godly, for whom earnest prayer is offered, can be ultimately lost. 3. Or is it that you *have been bereaved of your children*? So was it with the mothers at Bethlehem, to whose sorrow St. Matthew applies these words. The salvation of children is as certain as the existence of God himself. To think otherwise would be to render impossible all hope, trust, and love towards God. "Of such is the kingdom of heaven;" "Their angels do always behold the face of my Father which is in heaven;" "It is not the will of your Father in heaven that one of these little ones should perish." True, heartless because childless priests have taught that there is a *limbus infantum*—a children's hell. Good God! that any should believe it! And yet in many districts still the children who die unbaptized are refused Christian burial. But we turn from theologians to God's Word, and clasp the precious promise of these verses to our hearts, as, thank God, we are altogether warranted in doing. Let, then, all to whom God has given children trust him for them—for their bodies' and their souls' welfare, for their well-being in the life that now is and in that which is to come, whilst you continue to bow your knees to "the God and Father ... in whom *every* family in heaven and earth is named."—C.

Vers. 18, 19.—*Bemoaning one's self.* The very word suggests sorrow, weariness, distress. And all the more when the reason of such bemoaning is not something external to ourselves, as when Rachel wept for her children, but something in ourselves, when we are the cause of our own distress.

I. INQUIRE WHEREFORE THIS BEMOANING. 1. That he had called down upon himself the chastisements of God. 2. That these chastisements had been of no avail. 3. That now it was made evident there was no hope of amendment in himself.

II. COMFORTING THOUGHTS CONCERNING THIS BEMOANING. 1. The Lord surely heard it. Cf. "There is joy in the presence of the angels of God over one sinner that repenteth." 2. There is no attempt to excuse or palliate his sin. 3. That it had led him to despair of help in himself. 4. That in his misery he seeks the Lord. 5. That it was and is the forerunner of genuine conversion.

CONCLUSION. 1. Welcome the smart and pain of sorrow for sin. 2. Dread that apathy which is so common in the slaves of sin. 3. Remember that it is only as the Lord turns us that our conversion is genuine and real.—C.

Ver. 18.—*Our yokes.* I. That which is hard and yoke-like is appointed for us all.

II. The reason of this appointment is that thereby we may render service which otherwise we could not.

III. That to refuse or resist this yoke will bring down the chastisements of God.

IV. That until we are really turned to God by his grace we shall so resist.

V. We do not cease from such folly without great pain. "I have . . . heard Ephraim *bemoaning* himself."

VI. In that pain is our hope.—C.

Ver. 19.—*Conversion and repentance.* I. BOTH THESE ARE TOLD OF HERE. *Conversion* is. It is spoken of as "being turned" and "instructed." *Repentance* is. It is spoken of plainly, and again figuratively: "I smote upon my thigh." This is a common mode of expressing indignation and grief.

II. AND REPENTANCE IS SAID TO COME AFTER CONVERSION. And this is ever so. Not that there is no repentance prior to conversion. There is, and a genuine one. The "bemoaning" spoken of in the previous verse tells of that repentance which comes prior to conversion. But the true, deep, abiding repentance comes after. It consists, not so much in some passionate outburst of sorrow over sin, but in a settled hatred of it, and a remembrance ever with shame of the time when we allowed ourselves in it. In proportion as we see the love of God in Christ will this repentance deepen. It is in the light of that love that sin takes on its darkest hue. And if it be not so, then our conversion, our turning, our being instructed, has been apparent, not real. For—

III. THERE MAY BE REPENTANCE WITHOUT CONVERSION. We find many instances in Scripture of transgressors saying, "I have sinned," and their words were true, and felt to be true by themselves. They were the utterance of grief and real distress; but because such repentance never roused the energies of the will to resolve on the abandonment of the sin, therefore, though there was repentance, it led to no conversion. And even a true repentance in its initial stages, and until it has led the soul really to God, exists without conversion. It is a most solemn fact that there can be real distress about sin, and yet no forsaking of it. And if sin be not forsaken, then this distress, which is God's distinct call to turn unto him and live, grows fainter and fainter with every repetition of the sin.

IV. AND THERE MAY BE THE FRUITS OF CONVERSION WITHOUT REPENTANCE. There may be the hatred of sin, the love of goodness and of God, without the previous process of conversion. The gift of regeneration is essential to every soul, but some regenerate ones are kept by the grace of God from ever needing that deep repentance which is essential to conversion. It is possible to grow up in the kingdom of God, never to go away from the Father's house. That does not mean to be faultless, but to live, as the settled tenor of one's life, in love, obedience, and trust. These are the most blessed ones, who are "kept from the evil that it should not hurt them," to whom the Father will say, "Son, *thou* art ever with me, and all that I have is thine." But—

V. GENERALLY THERE HAS BEEN BOTH IN GOD'S SAVED ONES. Therefore it is safer for the most of us to conclude that we need both, and to seek both from him who is "exalted to give repentance and remission of sins." And let us not be content with repentance alone, unless it lead on to conversion, nor let us deem our conversion genuine unless it cause, as here in this verse, our repentance to deepen more and more.—C.

Vers. 31—34.—*The new covenant.* The consideration of this new covenant will enable us to understand how it is that, whilst many Christian men are at peace and content in regard to their justification before God and their acceptance with him, they are very far from content in regard to their attainment in Christian character and their practical sanctification. The reason is that, whilst they are content simply to look in faith to Christ for the former, they forget that this is precisely the condition of the latter also. Hence they are for ever struggling and making good resolves, labouring earnestly to conquer this sin and that and to win one and another as yet unwon grace. But the new covenant is a promise, is the assurance indeed, that God has taken the matter of our salvation into his own hands. It is all of grace; he gives everything; nothing is left to our own solitary effort. If we read over the words of the covenant as they are given here from first to last, there is not a single word about anything to be done by us. The whole covenant is not so much between man and his Maker as between Jehovah and man's Representative, the Lord Jesus Christ. The human side of the covenant has been already fulfilled by Jesus, and there remains nothing now but the covenant of giving, not the covenant of requirements. The whole covenant with regard to us, the people of God, now stands thus: "I will give this; I will bestow that; I will fulfil this promise; I will grant that favour." The old covenant said, "Do this, and thou shalt live." The new says, "I will do all." In considering this new covenant, note—

I. ITS RESEMBLANCES TO THE OLD. 1. *Both are based on the goodness of another.* The Jew in the old covenant knew that it was for Abraham's sake he had been chosen and called and privileged above all other nations. And that our privileges are all "for Christ's sake" is among the alphabet of the truths of the faith we hold. 2. *Both demand fitness and preparation for the enjoyment of the blessings they promise.* For the Jew, obedience to the Law of God was the condition of his entering into and living happily in the land God had promised to his fathers. Because they failed in this obedience, the carcases of a whole generation of them fell in the wilderness. And for the Christian, faith is the imperative condition. "He that believeth shall be saved, and he that believeth not shall be damned." 3. *Both gave help and direction for the fulfilment of these conditions.* To Israel was given an external Law; to the Christian, an indwelling Spirit. Hence most fitly was the gift of the Spirit on the day of Pentecost; for that day commemorated the giving of the Law on Mount Sinai. It was fitting, therefore, that the giving of the new law of the new life should be on the day that told of the giving of the law for the old life.

II. ITS CONTRASTS. 1. The old covenant related to *the possession of an earthly inheritance, the new to the attainment of a spiritual character.* The one was of earth, the other of heaven. The one held before Israel the winning and keeping of the promised land; the other, the possession of likeness to God. 2. The old covenant was chiefly characterized by *external law;* the new, by *the gift of the Spirit.* 3. The old *asked before it gave;* the new *gave before it asked.* True, there was the promise made to Abraham, but Israel could not enter into it unless they kept the commandments of God. But in the new covenant God does not ask for holiness till he has given the Holy Spirit, until he has put his Law in our inward parts, and written it upon our hearts. As when he bade the palsied rise and walk, he did not ask before he gave; for along with the command went the power to obey. And this power resides in the influence of the love of Christ upon the believing soul. It is at the cross of Christ that the writing of the Law upon the heart most of all takes place. Regeneration is in connection, inseparable connection, with the cross. Do any ask—

III. THE REASON OF THE OLD COVENANT, NOTWITHSTANDING IT SO PERPETUALLY FAILED? It was necessary to show the hopelessness of all covenants of works. Twice had the experiment been tried; with our first parents, Adam and Eve, in the garden of Eden; then under the most advantageous circumstances such covenant was tried and failed again with Israel.

IV. THE SUPERIORITY OF THE NEW. It is manifold and manifest—in its nobler aim, in its universality, in its nobler result in character, in its surer foundation, in its light and easy yoke, etc.

CONCLUSION. Do any say, "I have not yet experienced the blessings of this new covenant"? Remember the Law is not written *all at once,* and that we must seek the Lord's help. It is his work.—C.

Vers. 31—33.—*Great encouragements for those returning to God.* It is sad enough that there should be any going away from God so as to require a return. It is better never to have gone away from him than to return after such departure. Better be the son to whom the Father says, "Thou art ever with me, and all that I have is thine," than the one who came back in misery and shame, notwithstanding all the compassionate love wherewith he was welcomed. Let all young children, and they who have the training of them, remember this; and all young converts to Christ. The same grace that forgives the going away, when in penitence the wanderer comes back, is ready to prevent any such going away at all. And this preventive grace is what we should all desire and seek. But the sad fact is that vast numbers have wandered from God. How few can leave themselves out of the prophet's confession, "All we like sheep have gone astray, we have turned aside every one to his own way"! In this emergency the question arises as to what is to be done. If God were at once to inflict vengeance on the transgressor, or, which would amount to the same thing, if the wanderer were allowed to go on in his own way, none could complain or say that God did aught that was unjust. But instead of that, he mercifully causes that the way of the transgressor should be hard; he makes it grievous unto him, to the end that he may weary of it and long for the good ways he has left. And by-and-by he will and does, and it is here at this point the blessed promise of these verses meets him for his great encouragement. He has found out how bitter and evil a thing it is to sin against the Lord, how full of folly and madness his conduct has been, and in deep humility and contrition he is returning "with his whole heart." But such as thus return are full of self-distrust and deep fear lest they should wander off again and fall once more. They have been beguiled before and led to doubt God's Word. Now, these verses promise that the three great avenues by means of which unbelief, the fountain sin of all sin, enters the man, shall each one be securely guarded against such entrance for the future. The verse contains three distinct promises. Note how such safeguard is secured by—

I. THE FIRST PROMISE. "I will put my Law in their inward parts," etc. (ver. 33). Now, the avenue that this guarded was that of *the understanding*. The people to whom the prophet wrote had been sorely tempted to question whether, after all, God *was* the Lord—that is, was the supreme Ruler and Disposer of all events; for had they not seen how other nations who acknowledged him not had risen up and prospered, whilst his own faithful people had often been in sore straits? (Cf. homily on *Idolatry*, ch. x. 1—17, vol. i. p. 275.) There was very much to be said in favour of the gods of other nations, and very much was said. And when all this was encouraged and secretly seconded by the lurking likings of their lower nature, what wonder if their understandings in regard to this great question were sometimes bewildered? We can see how unbelief would find occasion to enter in in force through such bewildered and doubting minds. And perhaps never can the question be settled by the intellect alone. God does not reveal himself in all his infinitude to that part of our nature. It is *the heart* which must know "that he is the Lord." But this promise is for this very thing. Such a heart shall be given. The rational conclusions of the understanding shall be supported by the mighty force of the heart's intuitions, and the two combined will for ever render utterly impossible all doubt whether God be the Lord. The peace of God keeps the heart and mind in Christ Jesus (Phil. iv.). If we have not heart-knowledge of God, that of the intellect alone will be likely to fall away and leave us with no knowledge of God at all. How blessed, then, cannot but be this promise to all those who, because they have lacked such knowledge hitherto, have sinned and brought on themselves such distress, but who now are returning to God with their whole heart! It is a mighty encouragement indeed.

II. THE SECOND PROMISE. "And they shall be my people." The avenue that this guards is that of *man's circumstances*. Doubt does often enter by such way. If a man be surrounded with distress, almost worn out with "the slings and arrows of outrageous fortune," broken-hearted and bankrupt of all earthly good, let none condemn such, or only those who are themselves without sin though they have been in like manner tried, if doubt do haunt these troubled ones and faith in God dies down. Do we not admire Job just because he held so fast to his faith under such awful circumstances? Is not our very admiration of him proof of our conviction as to the sore difficulty of faith keeping its hold at such times? Did not even he than whom Christ said none of women born was greater—John the Baptist—find the drear dungeon into which Herod had flung him, and the cruel death which he knew awaited him, more than his spirit could bear? And so he sent to the Lord, saying, "*Art* thou he that should come, or," etc.? Oh, it is easy under sunny skies and amid happy surroundings and when all is well, to sing sweet hymns about trusting in God and the blessedness of faith. But let all that prosperity vanish, and be replaced by grim, gaunt poverty, in which and because of which you have to see your beloved wife or children, or both, hunger and perhaps die, because you have not enough to ward off from them the sufferings they have to endure. Ah! where would be the faith of myriads of those well-to-do Christians who love to sing "Sweet it is to trust in him"? Not a little of the sad unbelief of the poor is accounted for, and we cannot but think rendered far less guiltful, by the fact of the terrible privations that are so often their lot. (Cf. homily on *The moral disadvantages of the poor*, ch. v. 4, vol. i. p. 133.) But this promise, "They shall be my people," assures that such trial of faith shall not be permitted. For the promise means that God will bestow on them such signal favour; he will so graciously deal with them that it shall become evident to all that they are his people, the beloved of the Lord. They shall have that "blessing which maketh rich and addeth no sorrow thereto." They shall not any more have to eat the bread of affliction or drink the water of afflic- tion, but their circumstances shall be so happy and peaceful as to utterly prevent that unbelief to which adversity so often gives rise. The beggar Lazarus is carried by the angels into Abraham's bosom; not one word is said about his character; and this surely seems to teach that the poor, to whom belief in the love of God has been so difficult here, shall hereafter in happier circumstances see and enjoy that love of which here they are only told. Of course, happy circumstances, such as are involved in this promise, would be of little avail without the bestowment of the other promise, "a heart to know that I am the Lord;" but with that this gives a double defence, within which blessed are they who abide. And if it be said that God does not now, as he did in Old Testament days, make any promise to his servants that they shall be exempt from adversity, as in fact they are not, it is to be remembered that they have far clearer light than had the saints of the Old Testament concerning that blessed home of God's people, of whose inhabitants it is said, "They shall hunger no more, neither thirst any more, neither shall the sun light upon them, nor," etc. If not now, assuredly then, shall they be known as God's people by the happy external lot which will be theirs.

III. THE THIRD PROMISE. "I will be their God." The avenue which this guards is that of *the heart*. Man's understanding may be convinced, and his circumstances be all favourable and prosperous, but if he have not rest of his soul in God, unbelief will still assail and, not unlikely, overcome him. "Nostrum cor inquietum est donec requiescat in te." He must be able to say of the Lord, "He is *my* God" (Ps. xc. 2), ere ever he has rest in God. God must be his joy; he must "delight himself also in the Lord," and be happy in God, would he effectually bar out all unbelief. But this third promise ensures this. "I will be their God." It tells of this joy which they shall have in him, and of their happy rest in him.

CONCLUSION. Then let us "*return unto God with our whole heart*." Perhaps it is because we have not returned in this whole-hearted way that we yet have to wait for these promises to be fulfilled; and that we still find unbelief, though banished for a while, yet returning and haunting us once more. It is said of Joshua and Caleb that they served the Lord "fully." It is this thoroughness which is needed. Let but this be, and the understanding will be satisfied; the circumstances of our life will be pleasing to us, because they are those the Lord pleases; and our heart shall sing for gladness, because God is our "exceeding joy."—C.

Ver. 32.—*God the Husband of his people.* (Cf. homily on ch. iii. 14.)—C.

Ver. 3.—*The everlasting love of God.* I. IN CONTRAST TO OTHER LOVERS. Note ch. xxx. 14, "All thy lovers have forgotten thee," etc. Israel had had many lovers pro- fessing regard and offering service; but what had their regard and service come to? They were now cold, careless, perhaps even hostile. They had shown the appearance of love to Israel, not that they cared for Israel, but because they themselves were advantaged. Now, that is no true affection which changes when the thing loved ceases to gratify us. Yet this was all the affection of these other lovers amounted to— a mere name of love; a feeling which, in the course of time, was to evince their own instability and bring shame to them. But God is a contrast to all this. He loves with an everlasting love. He loves Israel, not only in the days of prosperity and wealth and beauty, but in the days of downfall and despair. His thought penetrates through to the abiding worth of humanity. We do not slander human affection, or in any way under-estimate it, when we say that man cannot love his fellow-man as God loves him. God it is who first of all shows man what love really is; then man, having the Spirit of the Divine Father breathed into him, learns to love also. We cannot attain to anything which will give us the right to say with respect to duration that ours is an everlasting love; but, as true Christians, we may have something of the quality of that affection.

II. IN SPITE OF UNRECIPROCATED AFFECTION. Israel had had other lovers, and she had loved them in return. They had bestowed gifts on her, and she had bestowed gifts on them, and so there was profession of mutual regard as long as it was profitable to make it. But there was no love to God. His holiness, his goodness, was not seen. Year by year his open hand was stretched forth, filled with the corn and the wine and the oil; and the people greedily laid hold of the gifts, and thought nothing of the Giver. Not but what there were individuals whose hearts went out gratefully and devotedly to God, as the Psalms show. But then these individuals would not find very many to respond to the invitation, "Oh, love the Lord, all ye his saints." And still the love of God goes on. Men need the manifestations of God's love all the more, just because of their unreciprocating attitude towards him. Love cannot prevent the headstrong prodigal from seeking his own desires, but it can keep things ready for the season of repentance and return. The manifestations of the Divine love are to constitute a great spectacle, breaking down the heart of the selfish man.

III. THE LOVE IS DECLARED WHEN MOST THE DECLARATION IS NEEDED. Love does not always look like love. The spurious puts on the appearance of the genuine, and the genuine gets hidden behind the necessary manifestations of righteousness and fidelity to law. They that break law must be punished and suffer. They that have false, unstable, misleading lovers cannot escape the consequence of their foolish connection with them in the day when the lovers are destroyed and go into captivity (ch. xxii. 20, 22). Israel itself must suffer loss and go into exile and sit with dust and ashes on its head. But in that very day comes the assurance of everlasting love. The lower skies are filled with cloud and storm and rain, but the abiding sun is still above, and its radiance will remain when the storm has passed away.—Y.

Ver. 5.—*Work yet to be found in the vineyard.* Here is to be an evidence of the everlasting love spoken of in ver. 3.

I. THE RESTORATION OF WHAT HAD BEEN LOST. This is not the first prophecy in the book concerning vineyards. It had been declared that the nation from afar should eat up the vines and the fig trees of Israel (ch. v. 17). "I will surely consume, saith the Lord. There shall be no grapes on the vine" (ch. viii. 13). The bright prophecy here could not have been made but for the dark prophecies going before. The literal fulfilment of the prophecy is, of course, the least part of it. The deepest meaning is that, whatever we may lose through God's chastisements, we shall get much more in a spiritual and truly abiding way.

II. THE FUTURE IS DESCRIBED IN TERMS OF THE PAST. One of the occupations of the past had been to plant vineyards in Samaria. What associations there must have been with the sunny slopes! It is the way of God to speak of future comforts and glories in terms drawn from the present and from things around us. The future will give opportunities for profitable work. We shall always have some place to work in which shall be as the mountains of Samaria, and some work to do which shall be as the planting of vines. Fruitless toil and crushed hopes are but a disciplining episode in the career of those who are the heirs of eternal life.

III. THE STABILITY IMPLIED IN THIS PROMISE. Five years, according to the Mosaic Law, had to pass from the planting to the time of fruitage. The prophecy was therefore a prophecy of peaceful settlement. The whole outlook gave a sense of security. Looked at in this light, one sees the reason of previous overthrowing and destruction. The aim is to get down to something solid and stable, to purify the heart from unworthy aims and love of the fleeting. The things that are shaken are removed, that the things which cannot be shaken may remain.

IV. THE INCLUSIVENESS OF THIS PROMISE. Vineyards are to be planted, but vineyards are not the first necessity of life. To promise the planting of vineyards implied the promise of other things. The corn and the oil went along with the wine. The vineyard is doubtless here mentioned as a symbol of joy. He who is able to plant a vineyard is able to plant all good things. Note the evidence we have of the temporal fulfilment of this promise. From vineyards our Lord drew some of his most suggestive teaching. We may be sure they had often been seen by him, and their spiritual significance apprehended. Vine-planting was a suitable industry, an industry to be expected in the land out of which the spies had brought the ponderous cluster of grapes.—Y.

Vers. 8, 9.—*God the Gatherer of his people.* I. WHENCE HE GATHERS THEM. The place is spoken of very indefinitely, not from any doubt as to its reality, but because it was largely a *terra incognita.* It was the land away in the northward direction, but what its extent or what its power for mischief there were but few who could guess. One thing, however, was possible to consider in the days of exile, when the north country had become a sad actual experience, namely, how Jeremiah had been sent to speak joyful tidings as well as mournful ones with respect to the power of this north country. True, he had spoken again and again concerning the evil and the great destruction coming out of the north; but here is a word from the same man and under the same authority to say that the power of the north country is not to continue. God uses even great nations for his own purposes. There is indication that these powers of the north were astonished at their own success. "The kings of the earth, and all the inhabitants of the world, would not have believed that the adversary and the enemy should have entered into the gates of Jerusalem" (Lam. iv. 12). They were only the agents of God, and God could take his people out of their midst again when once the Exile had done its work. Distance is no difficulty. God can hinder or facilitate in a journey just as seems him best. Once he kept his people forty years in a journey from one land to another that, if he had chosen, might have been accomplished in a very short time.

II. THOSE WHOM HE GATHERS. The Lord's compassions fail not. To the young, the strong, the healthy, those perfect in body, nothing was needed but to say, "The time is come for return. Make your start." But then all were not so placed. The weaklings have ever to be considered, and God considers them, as it were, first of all. There are the blind—God will keep them in the way; there are the lame—God will provide that they be conveyed and sufficiently helped; there are women, with all their peculiar anxieties, who need to be dealt with very tenderly, and all grounds for alarm taken out of their way as far as possible. Well, God specifies these cases as representative of the provision he makes for every sort of weakness. It is the mark of God's way for men that it is a way for the weak, a way in which provision is made for every sort of infirmity. There are ways in the world which are only for the strong; the weak soon get pushed aside. And God can bring all these weak people along, because the right spirit is in them. They come in weeping and in prayer. You can be eyes to a blind man, if he admits his blindness and is willing to be guided; but if he insists upon it that he can see, what are you to do with him? This is the only means by which God's true people can be gathered into one way, moving with one purpose towards one place, namely, that they be each one of them from the very heart submitted to the Divine will and control.

III. THE SPIRIT IN WHICH GOD GATHERS. The spirit of a father. Israel must needs go into exile and chastisement for a while; but the place left vacant is the child's place, and none but the child can fill it. It is the evidence of a father's tenderness that he cares for the blind and the lame and the weak. The house of Israel had said to a stock, "Thou art my father; and to a stone, Thou hast brought me forth." And their delusion had borne fruit in banishment and captivity. But the true Father remembered them all the time; and with the power of the true God and in the spirit of the true Father, he gathered them and guided them home.—Y.

Ver. 10.—*The Scatterer also the Gatherer.* I. GOD AS THE SCATTERER. Seeing that the Scatterer becomes the Gatherer, it is evident that scattering is used to describe his action by a sort of accommodation. Outwardly it looks like scattering; but there is a spirit and a purpose and a regulative principle in the action which makes it to be really only a stage in a more complete gathering worthy of the name. It is, perhaps, worthy of note that there is in the Hebrew word something of the idea of scattering even as seed is scattered. Now, when seed is scattered, it is with a perfect knowledge of the large gathering which will result. Seed is not flung at random, and then left for ever.

Beforehand there is preparation and afterwards there is expectation. And so we see that when God uses the same name for an action that we do, it by no means follows that he is doing just the same thing as we should indicate by the name. Note also that in this very prophecy here there is a reference to a very old intimation of the distresses that might come on Israel in the event of disobedience, " I will scatter you among the heathen " (Lev. xxvi. 33).

II. GOD AS THE GATHERER. What a difference here between man and God! Oftentimes it is easy for man to scatter; but how shall he gather again? One fool can undo in a few hours what wise and diligent men have taken years in building up. But since God scatters upon principle, he knows where every fragment is, and continues to superintend and guide it as part of the whole. We see only disjointed parts, and so there is something very nondescript and puzzling and ineffectual-looking about their operations. God, however, sees the whole. Hence the insistence in apostolic teaching upon unity. Christians could not be kept in one place. Persecution drove them apart; the needs of the gospel sent each apostle into his own field; and Christians sprang up in many far-separated places. But though scattered and separated in appearance, they were still one, because the one Spirit was in them. The gathering principle is, in Christians, a principle that rises dominant over all earthly distinctions. Men cannot be kept permanently together unless the Christian spirit is in them; and if the Christian spirit is in them, there is no power that can keep them permanently separated.

III. GOD AS HE WHO KEEPS HIS PEOPLE FROM A SECOND SCATTERING. We cannot put too much force into this thought of God keeping his people as a shepherd does his flock. What a significance it adds to the way in which Jesus speaks of himself as the good Shepherd! Who shall scatter when it is God's will to gather and to unite in an abiding company? Who shall scatter when he who gathers has in him not only the spirit of a shepherd, but also the power to keep his sheep from all danger? And what a warning to us against all needless separations! Men are betrayed into danger to themselves by pushing individual liberty to extremes. The shepherd will keep every member of the flock so long as it holds to the flock. God will only keep us so long as we are in his way, within his boundaries, subject to his directions.—Y.

Vers. 12—14.—*Praise waiting for God in Zion.* I. THE PLACE OF PRAISE. To speak of Zion was to speak of the dwelling-place of Jehovah. To sing in the height of Zion, therefore, was to sing, as it were, at the door of God's own house. While God ever visited idolatry with the severest punishments, he yet localized his presence by the sanctities connected with the ark. It was the holy of holies that made Zion a sacred place, and if the people were helped in praise and worship by assembling there, then there is every reason for mentioning Zion as the great place of national rejoicing. But we must take care not to consider any literal fulfilment of this prophecy as sufficient. The word is one taking our thoughts to that Mount Zion, which is part of the city of the living God, of the heavenly Jerusalem. The days of earthly localization are for ever past. The principle of assembly now is that, wherever two or three are gathered together in the Name of Christ, there he is in their midst.

II. THE CAUSE OF PRAISE. Praise and gladness always have some cause, but the question remains to be asked whether it be a cause which God will approve. If it be gladness rising out of some selfish triumph or gain, then the joy will assuredly be turned into mourning. But here the goodness of Jehovah is emphatically described as being the cause of the joy and singing. There is something substantial to sing about—corn, and wine, and oil, and cattle: the appropriate produce of the land, something that is at once the reward of righteous striving and the gift of an approving God. Everything is right externally and internally. The very life of the people is like a watered garden, which surely is a very suggestive expression to indicate that all is as it ought to be. A watered garden suggests a piece of land worth cultivating, well cultivated, and supplied with every factor contributing to fruitfulness. But what has been said of the *place* of praise must also be said of the *cause* of praise. Corn and wine and all the rest of the good things are only symbols of deeper blessings that have to do with the satisfaction of the heart. " Man liveth not by bread alone, but by every word that proceedeth out of the mouth of God." It is an easy thing for him, if needs be, to make up the defects of nature, which he showed at the feeding of the five thousand. Yet, in spite of this, famines are not always interfered with. God is not solicitous to go beyond what he has provided in nature for the support of natural life. But he is solicitous that we should apprehend the great spiritual abundance within our reach. The deepest meaning of this prophecy is that spiritual men only can really praise God, because they are praising him out of hearts that are being sustained by the richness of spiritual blessings in heavenly places in Christ Jesus.

III. THE CERTAINTY OF PRAISE. The satisfied heart must praise, else there is a proof that the heart is not really satisfied. Satisfaction can no more be concealed than dissatisfaction. When in the writings of the apostles we come across outbursts of doxology, it is just what we might expect as being in harmony with the greatness of the blessings received. And this is just what often makes the praise part of worship eminently unsatisfactory, that men are thanking God for what they have not received. All compositions having praise and thanksgiving for their elements, and being successful compositions, must, by the very nature of the case, owe their origin to some actual experience of God's goodness. Hence it is important in this passage to notice how three things are bound together in the one prediction. 1. There is the gift of God. 2. The consequent satisfaction. 3. The irrepressible joy. And what greater gift can we have from God than a heart filled with pure, abiding joy, free from reproach, free from apprehension?

IV. THE UNIVERSALITY OF THE PRAISE. Young and old, priests and people, are joined together in the common song. God's spiritual blessings are for all. There is much significance in that promise, "I will satiate the soul of the priests with fatness." That means that the people are right religiously, and that again means that the priests are attentive to their own proper duty. Liberality to all Christian institutions, to all that is truly evangelistic and charitable, to all that is in the way of the highest ministry to mankind, is a sign of spiritual prosperity.—Y.

Vers. 15—17.—*Sorrowing mothers and their consolation.* I. THE GRIEFS OF BEREAVED MOTHERS. There is an innumerable company of women who have seen the children die to whom they themselves had given birth, and Rachel is their great representative. She stands before us here as the mother of a nation; for surely it only spoils a grand poetical idea to attach her to some tribes rather than others. She sees the nation which sprang from her husband Jacob going from the land of promise into captivity, and straightway she reckons it as a dead nation. Bear in mind distinctly that the mourning is not over dead individuals, but over a dead nation. The individuals went on living, but the nation in its pride and privilege was gone. So one might think of some representative spirit bewailing dead Greece and dead Rome. The figure, moreover, derives its strength from what must have been very frequent in the land of Israel, as in every land before or since, namely, the sad sight presented by a mother weeping over her dead child. The mother's sorrow is unique; its elements can only be imperfectly apprehended by others. The object of so much hope, solicitude, and pleasure is gone. The proper order of things is reversed. The mother should see the child grow to manhood or womanhood, and then go first into the unseen world. Death, coming in this way, seems to furnish a plausible ground of complaint, and if anything can be said to lessen the mystery and the sorrow and make hope rise in the heart, it should be said.

II. CONSOLATION IN SUCH TIME OF GRIEF. The real Rachel needed no such consolation. But bereaved mothers both need it and can have it. They have worked for something else than death and the breaking off of their purposes, and their work shall not be in vain. Death is a great deceiver in making his power seem greater than it is. When children are taken from this world into the next, opportunities are not lost, they are only changed. God will assuredly not allow the highest joys belonging to human nature to suffer from a cause so purely external as the duration of temporal existence. When Herod slew the children at Bethlehem, this prophecy had a sort of fulfilment, and surely so far as it was fulfilled it was fulfilled altogether. To every one of those weeping mothers it might have been said, "Refrain thy voice from weeping and thine eyes from tears." The weeping and the tears are natural enough, but after all they have no sufficient ground in reason. As a general rule, life must be taken with all its risks and casualties, seeing that risk and casualty, as we call them, are after all, according to a law. Sometimes there are extraordinary preservations of infant life, and when some life so delivered has afterwards unfolded into eminence and usefulness, there is a talk of something specially providential in the preservation. Some such preserved lives, however, turn out a great curse, and then where is the providence? The great thing every mother should seek is such faithfulness, such wisdom, such right dealing in all ways as will enable her to be a true mother to her children, however long they live. Then, whatever happens, there is the certainty that her work will be rewarded. The work of individual obedience can never come to anything but reward in the end. The mischief is that very often we want the reward to come in our way and not in God's.—Y.

Ver. 26.—*Sweet sleep.* Assuming that Jeremiah is here the speaker, what a suggestion there is of restless, unrefreshing nights on other occasions! And little wonder. It may have been the case that many of his prophecies came to him at night, and if so, considering the elements of those prophecies, his nights must often have been very troubled ones. But if we look attentively at the contents of ch. xxx. and xxxi., we find very sufficient causes for the sweetness of the prophet's sleep. Jehovah makes one long announcement of favour, restoration, and comfort. Hitherto when the prophet has had to listen to Jehovah, if there have been consolatory utterances, they have been mingled with denunciation and words of the most melancholy import. But now there is one unbroken stream of good tidings, and the effect is shown even in sleep. And if in sleep, how much more in waking hours! The whole round of the day becomes different when God looks favourably on the life. Sweetness of sleeping hours must come from all being right in waking hours. Now, with Jeremiah, as to his own personal life, all was right in waking hours, but with his nation all was wrong; and so through the day he went about seeing sin and foreseeing suffering, and at night his vivid imagination must often have kept him awake or peopled what broken sleep he got with the most terrible dreams. Bad men may sleep better than good ones, so long as there is nothing to awaken their selfish fears and good men spend restless nights over the troubles of those in whom they are interested. Yet the restlessness must come from the failing to see the abiding goodness of God. Here, for a little, God drove every cloud from the sky of his servant, and showed him how heavenly brightness was a thing entirely above earthly confusions; and then his servant could get sweet sleep. And God will give to all that wait upon him that quiet calm of the heart which is to our higher life what sweet sleep is to the body. It is God's will that our present life, with all its varied needs, should have all the refreshment he can give.—Y.

Vers. 29, 30.—*Jehovah visiting the individual for his sins.* I. THE SIN OF SOME AND THE SUFFERING OF OTHERS. This is put before us in a very striking figure. Literally, the taste of a sour grape would be an instantaneous sensation; but here we are asked to imagine the possibility of a man getting whatever other advantage there might be in the grape, whatever nourishment, whatever refreshment, and then handing on the one bad element of sourness. And truly it often seems as if there were this kind of division. The wrong-doer goes on succeeding, enjoying himself, getting his full of life, and then his children come in to find that the father's wrong-doing is like a millstone round their necks, destroying every chance they might otherwise have. The figure here presents from the human side that fact of experience which from the Divine side is presented as a law. "I the Lord thy God am a jealous God, visiting the iniquity of the fathers upon the children" (Exod. xx. 5).

II. THE SIN OF SOME AND THEIR OWN SUFFERING. We need to look somewhat carefully at the point brought out in ver. 30. At first it seems as if daily experience were contradicted, for we leap to an inference that the children's teeth will not be set on edge by the sour grapes their fathers have eaten; whereas it is abundantly plain that children still suffer for the sins of their fathers. But observe that this is not at all denied. The great point insisted on is that the fathers will suffer themselves; and this is a point that needs to be insisted on, for the fallacy is continually arising that a man may, by some magic, some precaution, escape the consequences of his evil, and so he may escape from some consequences. But observe, again, the all-comprehending word here used, "he shall *die*," and this word has a retrospective force. There never has been any other law but that a man shall die for his own iniquity. Possibly we should take this passage as having some sort of reference to the old custom of making revenge an hereditary thing. If the doer of a wrong escaped vengeance and died peacefully in his bed, then his son stood in the father's place, and became an object of attack till the punishment due to the father was visited on him. It seems so plain to us that a man should die for his own iniquity, punishment falling on the head of him who does the wrong, that we find it hard to imagine a day when the ethical code was otherwise. Whereas it is tolerably clear that in Old Testament times and countries the feeling was that *somebody must be punished*; and if the real criminal escaped, why, then take his nearest blood relation. That the Christian looks on things so differently is the clearest proof that this prophecy has been fulfilled.

III. THE NEED THERE IS THAT EVERY ONE SHOULD CLASSIFY THE SUFFERINGS OF HIS LIFE. It is not enough that we seek deliverance from suffering. It is right for us to do so, and suffering, we may be sure, is not by the will of God. But as there is suffering which comes from causes within our control, so there is suffering coming from causes outside our control; and it is with the former only that we can deal. Besides, it is the worst suffering, seeing that it comes from trouble and unrest of conscience. God has so made us that the worst wounds from others are but as surface scratches compared with the wounds that in our folly we inflict on ourselves. Then we have to look, not only on the sufferings, but enjoyments. We may so live as to rise above the worst that men can do to us, and at the same time, we may be the better for whatever good man is disposed to do. If sometimes it is true that the fathers eat sour grapes and the children's teeth get set on edge, is it not also true that the fathers eat sweet grapes, yet little of the sweetness they seem to taste—it is a sweetness standing over for the children?—Y.

Vers. 31—34.—*The new covenant and the old.* I. THE LIGHT CAST ON THE OLD COVENANT. It would be a mistake to describe it as a covenant that failed. Paradoxical as the expression sounds, the very breaking of the covenant furnished the proof of its success. It made man's position clearer to him; it prepared the world for Christ. The old covenant had been broken in spite of all the teaching connected with it. "Know Jehovah" had been dinned into the ear, and doubtless many had a notion that they did know Jehovah, whereas all that they knew was a certain round of ritual observances. At all events, it was a knowledge that left iniquity unforgiven and sin still registered in the book of God's remembrance. It was such a knowledge as the wrong-doer has of his judge. It was the knowledge of a force that thwarted all selfishness, and came with overwhelming completeness to ruin the plans of man. It was not the knowledge coming from trust and leading to greater trust—knowledge of God as a Guide, Director, and Provider. Yet some indeed knew. The man who said to his neighbour and his brother, "Know Jehovah," must have been, in some instances at least, one who himself had some real knowledge. As there were men of the reforming spirit before the Reformation, so there were Christians in essence before Christianity. The breaking of the old covenant shows the thing that was needed, namely, a new power in the hearts of men. The knowledge of God is not to be gained by mere teaching. Teaching has its place, and within its own limits is indispensable; but who could teach a child to eat, to see, to hear? If faculties are not inborn, we cannot do anything with them.

II. THE CONFIDENT PREDICTIONS ON THE NEW COVENANT. The old covenant starts with law; the new one springs out of life. Ver. 33 gives one of the Old Testament ways of expressing the doctrine of regeneration. God writes the laws of spiritual life on the heart, just as he writes the laws of natural life on every natural germ; and then all the rest is a matter of unfolding, of growth, of encouragement, of culture. The old covenant was one long, exhaustive, thorough experiment by which the fact became clear that in the *natural man* there was nothing to unfold. The new covenant established within a very brief period that, given a new life-principle working within him, man is indeed a being of glorious capabilities. The first man of the new covenant, in point of quality, is of course the Man Christ Jesus himself. God's Law was written in the heart of his Son. Here is one way in which the Law and the prophets are completed. The ark with its inscriptions vanishes; we hear nothing of it later than ch. iii.

16. And in its place there comes the loving heart trusted to the utmost liberty. Well might there be confidence in speaking of the new covenant. When good seed and good soil and favourable circumstances meet, then there is certainty of perfect and abundant fruit. The new covenant is above all things a covenant with the individual. It is made to depend upon individual susceptibility and individual fidelity. Also it is a knowledge that comes in repentance, forgiveness, and favour. And all this teaches us that a special meaning must be put into the term, "people of God." The true people of God are constituted by the aggregation of individual believers. They do not begin their journey to the heavenly land of promise marching as one constrained company through a miraculous Red Sea passage; they rather go, one by one, through a straitened entrance, even through a needle's eye, some of them.—Y.

Vers. 35—37.—*The seed of Israel; signs of its everlasting duration.* I. THEY ARE SIGNS WITH MUCH REVELATION OF GOD IN THEM. The sun, the moon, the stars, the heavenly spaces with all their occupants, the terrestrial surface with the fathomless depths beneath it. We shall never know all that is to be known about these existences; but we may soon know enough to know through them something of their Maker. That they are the common work of one hand, the common expression of one wisdom and love, soon becomes plain. The unity of all we see is a truth becoming clearer in the light of scientific investigation. God drove Israel from the land they had polluted and forfeited by their idolatries; but their share in the common possessions of mankind remained. It is plain that man gets good from all these signs here mentioned, and the largeness of the good depends on the righteousness and understanding shown in the use.

II. THEY ARE SIGNS WITHIN THE COMPREHENSION OF ALL. Even a child can be made to understand the unfailing regularity that belongs to them. They are signs all over the world. It is not a sign drawn from Jerusalem or from anything comparatively stable in the Israelites' *peculiar* experience. Sun and moon and stars know nothing of national distinctions. Each nation doubtless can claim its territory to the very centre of the globe, but beyond a certain depth, that globe is defiant of them all. One man may know more than another of the constitution of these signs, by reason of peculiar opportunities, but all can know enough for the purpose here required.

III. THEY ARE SIGNS DRAWN FROM GOD'S INDEPENDENT OPERATION. Not from operations which as a general rule depend on our co-operation. God's operations in sun, moon, and stars are independent of us—unaffected by our disobedience, our negligence, unsteadiness; uplifted far above our interference. Indeed, what can show more clearly how God's operations on the earth's surface are interfered with by human ignorance and indolence than the contrast with heaven's regularity?

IV. THE THING SIGNIFIED WILL OUTLAST THE SIGNS. The thing signified is the everlasting duration of the seed of Israel. That seed will remain when the signs themselves, having done their work, are vanished. The things that are seen are temporal. As our body is but the earthly house of this tabernacle, so the visible universe itself is but as the tabernacle wherein God dwells with us. But all these visible things will come to their end when they have done their work, not through failure of Divine power. They will disappear into a more glorious transformation, and serve some purpose to God's true Israel, the very outlines of which we cannot yet comprehend.—Y.

EXPOSITION.

CHAPTER XXXII.

Jeremiah was far from wishing to depress his fellow-countrymen to the point of disbelieving in the inalienable promises of God to Israel. He fully recognized an element of truth in the preaching of the "false prophets," viz. that Jehovah was still the God of his people Israel, though for wise purposes he chose to hide his face for a time. His own faith was intense, to the pitch of an even Roman heroism (see Livy, xxvi. 11). The opportunity (or rather—see below—the right) of purchasing a piece of ground at Anathoth was the occasion which called forth the most striking proof of his sublime confidence in God. Not that he understood how it could be God's will that he, in the besieged city, should constitute himself a landed proprietor. He had his difficulties; but instead of brooding over them, he laid them before Jehovah in prayer. And the Divine revelation came that, though long-continued transgressions had brought upon Judah the sorest punishment, they should yet be restored to their land; and, though the first covenant had been broken, a second and an everlasting covenant should in future times be granted to God's people; and the sign that the first part of this promise should in very deed be realized is the purchase of the field by Jeremiah.

Vers. 1—5.—Time and circumstances of the following revelation. It took place in the tenth year of Zedekiah, the eighteenth of Nebuchadnezzar (comp. ch. xxv. 1; lii. 12). The siege of Jerusalem had begun in the preceding year (ch. xxxix. 1), but had been temporarily raised on the approach of an Egyptian army (ch. xxxvii. 5, 11). Jeremiah, who had declared resistance hopeless, had been accused of treason, and imprisoned (ch. xxxvii. 13), and in prison he remained till the close of the siege. Like St. Paul at Rome, however, he was allowed free communication with visitors, as appears from ver. 8 and ch. xxxviii. 1. Vers. 2—5 are parenthetical (see on ver. 6).

Ver. 2.—In the court of the prison; or, *the court of the guard*, which adjoined the royal palace (Neh. iii. 25).

Ver. 3.—Had shut him up. A brief and general account of the circumstances related more in full in ch. xxxvii. For the prophecies referred to, see ch. xxxiv. 3—5; xxxvii. 17; xxxviii. 17—23 (the following verse is almost identical with ch. xxxiv. 3).

Ver. 5.—Until I visit him; *i.e.* until I take notice of him. "To visit" is used in a good (ch. xxvii. 22; xxix. 10) as well as in a bad sense (ch. vi. 15; xlix. 8), so that no definite announcement is made respecting Zedekiah's future. There was no object to gain by extending the scope of the revelation beyond the immediate present, and Zedekiah's offences did not require such an anticipative punishment as the clear prediction of the details of his fate (ch. xxxix. 6, 7; lii. 11).

Vers. 6—15.—The purchase of the field. Ver. 6 resumes ver. 1, after the long parenthesis in vers. 2—5.

Ver. 7.—Hanameel. Another form of *Hananeel*; comp. Γεσέμ, in the Septuagint = Goshen, Μαδιάμ = Midian. In ch. xxxi. 38 the Authorized Version has *Hananeel*, and the Septuagint Ἀναμεήλ (of course, the persons referred to are different). The son of Shallum thine uncle. It is strange that Hanameel should be called at once Jeremiah's uncle's son and his uncle; and yet this is the case—the former in vers. 8, 9, the latter in ver. 12. There is, therefore, no reason why we should deviate (as most commentators do) from the ordinary Hebrew usage, and suppose "thine uncle" in this verse to refer to Shallum, and not rather to Hanameel. But how are we to explain this singular variation in phraseology? Either from the fact that the Hebrew for "uncle" is simply a word expressive of affection (it means "beloved," see *e.g.* Isa. v. 1), and might, therefore, just as well be applied to a cousin as to an uncle; or else, upon the supposition that the word for "son (of)" has fallen out of the text before "mine uncle," both in this verse and in ver. 12.

Ver. 8.—The right of inheritance (or rather, *of taking possession*) is thine. The right, however, was dependent on the previous right of redeeming the land. Hence the speaker continues: The redemption is thine; buy it for thyself. The Law directs, "If thy brother be waxen poor, and hath sold away some of his possession, and if any of his kin come to redeem it, then shall he redeem that which his brother sold" (Lev. xxv. 25). Jeremiah's kinsman, however, ascribes to him the right of pre-emption. This is not mentioned in Leviticus; but, of course, no one would care to purchase a property till he was sure that the next kinsman would not insist on redeeming it. No one, it may be remarked, could purchase land unconditionally—the usufruct of it till the year of jubilee was all that was legally transferable; and even the original occupant had only a life interest in his land, the ownership of which was, strictly speaking, vested in the commune. This seems to be the necessary inference from a comprehensive view of the passages relative to land in the Old Testament (see Mr. Fenton's 'Early Hebrew Life;' and an article in the *Church Quarterly Review*, July, 1880). Then I knew, etc. We may, perhaps, interpret this notice combined with that in ver. 6 thus: Jeremiah had had a presentiment, founded, perhaps, upon the distress to which his cousin had been reduced, that the latter would invite him to carry out the provisions of the Law; and his presentiments were generally so ordered by the Divine Spirit of prophecy as to be ratified by the event. Still, he had a measure of uncertainty till Hanameel actually came to him, and so demonstrated "that this had been the word of the Lord." In recording the circumstances, he not unnaturally reflects his later feeling of certitude in his description of the presentiment.

Ver. 9.—Seventeen shekels of silver; *i.e.* about £2 5s. 4d. (taking the shekel at 2s. 8d.). This has been thought a small price. Thirty shekels were paid for the potter's field (Matt. xxvii. 7); fifty by David, for Araunah's threshing-floor and oxen (2 Sam. xxiv. 4). The Hebrew has "seven shekels and ten of silver;" hence the Targum increases the price by supplying "minas" before "of silver," bringing up the sum to one hundred and seven shekels. This, however, seems too much. Even if Jeremiah wished to be liberal, he would hardly have been able to go so far (probably) in excess of the market price. Who would have purchased the land on speculation, if Jeremiah had refused? The famine made life, the siege, a continuance of personal liberty, terribly uncertain. And, putting this out of the question, there may have been but a short time to elapse before the year of jubilee, when the land would revert to its original occupant (see above). The singular form of expression in the Hebrew, at which the Targum stumbled, may, perhaps, be the usual style of legal documents.

Vers. 10—14.—The Authorized Version is here so far wrong, on technical terms, that it seems best to retranslate the whole passage: "And I wrote (the circumstances) in the deed, and sealed it, and took witnesses, and weighed the money in the balance. And I took the purchase deed, that which was sealed (containing the offer and the conditions), and that which was open; and I gave the purchase deed unto Baruch the son of Neriah, the son of Maaseiah (rather, Makhseiah), in the sight of Hanameel my uncle, and in the sight of the witnesses who subscribed the purchase deed, in the sight of all the Jews who were sitting in the court of the guard. And I charged Baruch before them, saying, Thus saith Jehovah Sabáoth, the God of Israel, Take these deeds, this sealed purchase deed, and this open deed; and put them into an earthen vessel, that they may continue many days." The deed was made in two copies, so that if the open one were lost, or suspected of having been tampered with, an appeal might always be made to the sealed copy. The latter was to be placed in an earthen vessel, to preserve it from injury by damp. It ought to be added that the words in ver. 11, rendered "containing the offer and the conditions," are difficult. "Containing" is not expressed in the Hebrew, and "offer" is not the ordinary meaning, though etymologically justifiable.

Ver. 15.—Shall be possessed; rather, *shall be bought.*

Vers. 16—25.—Jeremiah obeys the Divine command, but is so besieged by

misgivings that he applies for a further revelation of God's purposes.

Ver. 17.—Ah, Lord God! rather, *Alas! O Lord Jehovah* (as ch. i. 6). Too hard for thee. It is the word usually rendered "wonderful," but rather indicating that thing or person lies outside the common order (comp. Gen. xviii. 14).

Ver. 18.—Into the bosom, etc. The ample dress of an Eastern rendering a bag or basket unnecessary (comp. Ruth iii. 15).

Ver. 20.—Even unto this day. A loose expression. Jeremiah simply means that signs and wonders equal to those wrought in Egypt have continued to the present time. And in Israel; rather, *both in Israel.*

Ver. 21.—Almost identical with Deut. xxvi. 8. The great terror which the Israelites inspired is constantly referred to (see Deut. ii. 25; Exod. xxiii. 27; Josh. v. 1).

Ver. 24.—Behold the mounts (see as ch. vi. 6). Is given. Resistance being hopeless, Jerusalem was virtually in the hands of its besiegers.

Ver. 25.—For the city is given; rather, *whereas.* It is a reflection of the prophet's.

Vers. 26—44.—The Divine answer. This falls into two parts. First, Jehovah repeats the burden of so many prophecies, that Israel has only to blame himself for his punishment (vers. 26—35); and then a bright future is disclosed beyond the gloomy interval of conquest and captivity—a future when men shall buy fields, and comply with all the legal formalities, precisely as Jeremiah has done (vers. 36—44).

Ver. 28.—I will give; rather, *I am on the point of giving* (present participle).

Ver. 29.—And burn it. A still more significant prediction to Jewish hearers than to us, for it implies that Jerusalem had become utterly rebellious, and deserved the punishment of the old Canaanitish cities. It was to be made a *chérem* (Deut. iii. 6).

Ver. 30.—From their youth (see on ch. iii. 21, 25; xxii. 21). The children of Israel, in the first half of the verse, must have a narrower sense than in the second half. The fall of Jerusalem is the climax of the series of punishments which the two separated and yet (in God's sight) united portions of the people of Israel have had to undergo.

Ver. 31.—From the day that they built it. It is useless to tell an impassioned orator that his words are not strictly consistent with primitive history. The Israelites may not have built Jerusalem, but Jeremiah was not to be debarred from the strongest form of expression open to him for such a reason. He means "from the earliest times."

Vers. 34, 35.—Repeated, with slight variations, from ch. vii. 30, 31. "Baal" and "Molech" are identified as in ch. xix. 5 (= ch. vii. 31), and even more distinctly.

Ver. 36.—And now therefore. This introduces the strange and lovely contrast to the gloomy picture which has gone before. It will be observed that there is no direct reference to Jerusalem, but the capital was only emphasized before as the heart of the nation, and it would, of course, be no comfort to say that Jerusalem's inhabitants (alone) would be restored.

Ver. 39.—One heart, and one way. Unity is always given as the "note" of the ideal, Messianic period (comp. Zeph. iii. 9; Zech. xiv. 9; John x. 16). **That they may fear me for ever.** This reminds us of a phrase in the exhortation in Deut. iv. 10, as the next clause does of Deut. vi. 24.

Ver. 40.—An everlasting covenant. It is the "new covenant" of ch. xxxi. 31, etc., which is meant (for the phrase, comp. Isa. lv. 3; Ezek. xxxvii. 26). **That I will not turn . . . to do them good.** The comma in the Authorized Version impairs the sense. The prophet means, "That I will not

cease to show them favour" (comp. Isa. liv. 10).

Ver. 41.—Assuredly; literally, *with faithfulness*; i.e. with perfect sincerity, without an *arrière pensée*, as the next words explain it; comp. 1 Sam. xii. 24; Isa. xxxviii. 3 (Graf).

Ver. 42.—Like as I have brought, etc. The prophet still has in his mind the thought expressed in ch. xxxi. 28, that the brighter part of his revelations must as surely be accomplished as the darker.

Ver. 43.—Fields; rather, *land;* the Hebrew has "the field," *i.e.* the open country (as ch. iv. 17, etc.). We must then continue "in this country," and in ver. 44, "men shall buy lands."

Ver. 44.—Subscribe evidences; rather, *write* (particulars of their purchase) *in the deed* (as ver. 10). **In the land of Benjamin,** etc. The catalogue of the districts of the Jewish kingdom heightens the realistic effect (see on ch. xvii. 26). Everywhere the old social system will be reproduced in its entirety. The land of Benjamin is mentioned first, on account of the property of Jeremiah at Anathoth.

HOMILETICS.

Vers. 6—9.—*Faith tested by action.* Jerusalem is besieged; the fields are occupied by the invader; Jeremiah knows that the Jews will be driven from their country; he is a prisoner. Yet he buys of piece of land! The transaction is carried out calmly, carefully, with all legal exactitude, and every precaution against future mistakes as to ownership, just as if the prophet were at liberty to enter into possession and enjoy his purchase without fear of molestation. His conduct is striking; to those who heard his warnings of the approaching Captivity it would seem singularly inconsistent. But the secret of it is explained to us, and this shows it to be a sublime act of faith. It was right that Jeremiah should make the purchase under ordinary circumstances, to keep the land in the family. He was now urged by a Divine impulse, which made him feel without doubt that it was God's will that he should buy the land, and he did it without questioning. After he had made the purchase, however, he inquired of God for the meaning of it, and was assured that the land of Israel would revert to the Jews after the Captivity, and would be bought and sold again with confidence in security of possession. Jeremiah's purchase was to be an anticipation of that happy future. His conduct is thus an illustration of the influence of faith on outward actions.

I. FAITH WILL REVEAL ITSELF IN DEEDS. Faith is not a merely intellectual exercise. It is primarily that which connects thought with action, and it is invariably an active principle. "Faith without works is dead." Jeremiah showed his faith by his works. A man's faith may be measured by the influence it has upon his conduct. The trying time is when faith comes into conflict with present impressions. Then, if those impressions are vivid and faith is feeble, they may overcome it. It is useless to claim to have an unquestioning conviction in face of such a failure. The failure proves the deficiency of faith. We should all ask ourselves—How far does our faith mould our conduct? How different would our life be if our faith were to cease? Would the effect be but slight or would it be a very revolution? The answer to these questions will determine whether our faith is a solid reality or a dreamy sentiment.

II. THOUGH FAITH IS A SPIRITUAL GRACE, IT WILL INFLUENCE OUR CONDUCT IN SECULAR AFFAIRS. Jeremiah showed his faith by the very thorough way in which he carried through an elaborate piece of conveyancing business. He did not confine his faith to the temple and to his preaching. He showed it in the market-place and in business. The sharp line which we draw between the spiritual and the secular is false and irreligious. Religion will be satisfied with no limited sphere. It claims the whole domain of life. Faith cannot be confined to any section of our conduct. If it is real, it will be a broad fundamental principle influencing all we do. If our faith bears no fruit in our business, it is a vain and worthless thing.

III. FAITH IN GOD WILL LEAD TO IMPLICIT OBEDIENCE TO HIS WILL. Jeremiah believed that God wished him to buy the field, and he did so, though at first he could not discover the utility of the purchase. 1. Faith will lead *to obedience*. It has two sides—a passive side, that shows itself in trust, submission, resignation; and an active side, that expresses itself in obedience. There are those who seem to ignore the latter. To them faith is wholly receptive, simply a leaving of our case in the hands of God and accepting what he gives. But the obedience of faith is not less important than its submission. 2. This obedience must be *implicit*. From the nature of the case we cannot at first understand all the reasons of the command. If we could there would be no room for faith. But when we know that God is great and good, and know that a certain act is according to his will, faith will find her place in doing it in the darkness, resting assured that all is right.

IV. GOD'S PROMISES FULLY JUSTIFY HOPEFUL ACTION UNDER DARK CIRCUMSTANCES. Jeremiah's conduct looked inconsistent. It was justified by God's promise of the restoration. When all is dark in the present we are inclined to despair of the future. But the future is in God's hands, and he has promised deliverance and blessedness to his people. Faith in God, therefore, will be a parent of hope. Because we trust God, we know that he will fulfil his good promises, and therefore we can act as though we saw the accomplishment of them.

Vers. 16—25.—*The prayer of a perplexed soul.* I. THE GENERAL CHARACTER OF THE PRAYER. Jeremiah is sorely perplexed by God's command to him to buy a field when the Jews are about to be driven from the land and he is a prisoner at Jerusalem. He does not permit his perplexity to paralyze his obedience. But *after* he has done the thing commanded by God he naturally and rightly seeks an explanation of the strange Divine commission. It is right that we should bring our doubts and difficulties to God. Though we should not allow them to hinder our performance of duty, we cannot help feeling them, and if we have true confidence in God we shall frankly confess them to him. We often trouble ourselves sorely, without ground, because we keep our doubts to ourselves, and try to solve them in the twilight of our own confused thinking, when, if we had more faith or more courage, we should bring them to God to seek such a solution as may be vouchsafed to us in the light of his presence. The character of Jeremiah's prayer and the way in which he thus seeks relief from God are deeply significant. He does not begin by asking the meaning of the command that perplexes him. Most of his prayer contains no reference to this. It is devoted to a contemplation of God, of his nature, his grace, and the justice of his severe actions. Thus he prepares his own soul for a right view of God's dealings with him. It would be well if our prayers contained more of this contemplation of God. Let us understand that the deepest prayer is not petition, but communion. It is more important that we should be brought near to God and realize rightly his presence and nature than that we should ask certain definite things of him. Therefore that part of prayer which in words may consist of invocation and adoration, should not be treated as a mere introductory formula, such as that with which we address a person of title. It is neither a mere call like that of the priests of Baal to obtain a hearing (1 Kings xviii. 26), nor only an expression of praise and thankfulness as a fitting introduction to a request for further favours. It should be felt to be the most precious element in prayer, the means by which our souls are lifted into fellowship with heaven. If it secures this result, the chief end of our prayer is attained. Then, if ever, our difficulties will vanish and our wants be satisfied, even if there be no change in God's actions towards us.

II. THE LEADING DETAILS OF THE PRAYER. 1. A contemplation of the *greatness* of God (ver. 17). This is realized by a consideration of the stupendous works of God in nature. Thence we learn (1) that as God accomplishes such great works as are manifested in creation, no difficulty or failure can arise from his inability to bring about the very best condition of affairs ; and yet (2) that surrounding such great works there must be ineffable mysteries, so that we may be perplexed by much that comes from so wonderful a being as God. 2. A contemplation of the *goodness and wisdom* of God (vers. 18, 19). God is kind to multitudes, and yet necessarily searching in his justice. Therefore it is apparent that he will require no unreasonable sacrifice and no useless exertion. His commands may appear arbitrary and capricious. But his character teaches us to trust that the strangest of them are governed by his mercy, justice, and wisdom. 3. A contemplation of the *providential action* of God (vers. 20—22). A review of providence should confirm our faith even under the strangest trials. God had delivered Israel in the past, fulfilled his promises in the face of apparently insuperable difficulties, and given them a rich inheritance. Was there not good ground to trust him after that? 4. A contemplation of the justice of God's *severest actions* (vers. 23, 24). From this we see that the calamities of judgment are deserved. That fact should increase our faith in God, though by itself it may make hope more difficult, as it did in the case of Jeremiah. 5. A *confession of perplexity* at God's command (ver. 25). This is not made till after the contemplation of the character and works of God. The contemplation has not destroyed the difficulty, but it has prepared the prophet to receive an explanation. Thus it is well that we should confess our doubts distinctly to God and ask for light, and if we do this after prayer and spiritual communion with God, we may hope that light will open upon us as it did upon Jeremiah.

Ver. 27.—*The omnipotence of God.* I. THE SOURCE OF THE OMNIPOTENCE OF GOD. 1. His *essential being.* He is the Lord, Jehovah, the Self-Existent. God is not only greater than all other existences, he differs from them in his essential being. He is eternal ; they have come into being. He is self-contained ; they are created. 2. God's *relation to all other existences.* He is the God of all flesh. He is the First Cause, the Source of the first being of all things, and the ground of their continued being. But for him they could never have been and could not now endure. We human creatures, " flesh," may realize this especially in regard to ourselves. Therefore to us in particular God, who created us all, and in whom we all live and move and have our being, must be almighty.

II. APPARENT LIMITATIONS TO THE OMNIPOTENCE OF GOD. 1. The *character of God.* We say that God cannot do wrong. But this simply means that his character is such that he never will do wrong. He is physically as able to do the actions which are wrong as those which are right. If he were not, there would be no goodness in his refraining, for purity is not impotence to do evil, but a will not to do it in face of the power to do it. Omnipotence is a physical characteristic. Goodness, the moral characteristic, does not destroy this by controlling the action of it. The power of the steam-engine is not lessened because the driver turns the steam on and off at will. 2. The *free-will of man.* This introduces an unfathomable mystery, which no philosophy has solved or is ever likely to solve. But the mystery is more especially felt on our side. If God created us and gave to us free-will, and, being omnipotent, can at any time destroy us and withdraw it, this must not be regarded as any real limitation to his power.

III. HOW A CONSIDERATION OF THE OMNIPOTENCE OF GOD SHOULD AFFECT OUR CON-DUCT. We are not called to worship mere power. To do so would be to renounce the rights of conscience. We worship God, not because he is almighty, but because he is supremely good and morally great. But starting from this position, we have to take account also of the omnipotence of God. 1. It shows the utter *vanity of all resistance* to the will of God. This is a most obvious inference? The more strange, then, that it is so little acted on. We need to feel it as well as to believe it. 2. It should lead us to *trust* that God will overcome difficulties which to us appear insuperable. The restoration of Israel appeared impossible ; the salvation of the world seems too great and difficult to be realized ; there are special difficulties in special cases, but some with all, so that we may exclaim, " Who then can be saved ? " But if " with God all things are possible " (Matt. xix. 26), how can we fix *any* limit to the ultimate triumphs of redemption? "The mercy of the Lord endureth for ever ; " then God will always seek the recovery of his lost children. " Is anything too hard for me ? " Then, in spite of present unbelief, impenitence, wild wanderings further astray, may we not believe that he will find his children at last? 3. These considerations should lead us to seek the *help of God's strength* in our weakness. How foolish for the sailors to weary themselves toiling in vain at their oars against the tide, when if they would spread their sails the strong wind would carry them swiftly on ! How foolish of us to toil on only in our natural power and with mere earthly means, when there are heavenly influences of omnipotence ready to help us if we will seek them !

Ver. 39.—*Unity.* I. UNITY IS PROMISED AS A CHARACTERISTIC OF THE GOLDEN AGE OF THE FUTURE. This is unity of thought, " one heart," and unity of conduct, " one way." Men shall then see " eye to eye," discord and controversy cease, peace and amity prevail. There may still be diversity of ideas in the sense of personal difference, because individual characters, positions, and opportunities must still vary. But in a perfect condition there will be no discord. The variations will harmonize. So all will not do exactly the same thing in exactly the same manner. There will, doubtless, be various spheres of action and various personal styles of work. But these will not conflict. They will all tend the same way.

II. UNITY IS INVOLVED IN THE IDEA OF PERFECTION. 1. Unity of *thought*. Truth is one. It may be variously conceived ; at first broken lights caught up in opposite quarters may look very different. But the more we eliminate personal " views," the more we can get of the white light of facts, the nearer we approach to the central verity, the more unity shall we obtain. Absolute truth is an absolute unity. This is apparent in mathematics. Two and two cannot be both four and five at the same time—four to one man, five to his neighbour. 2. Unity of *action*. As there is but one absolute truth, so there is but one absolute right. Under all circumstances there can be but one thing which is absolutely the best to be done. That one thing is the right. Till we find this, we make blundering attempts to reach it from different directions. Hence the contradictions in the conduct even in good men. When the right is found and followed by all, there must be unity of conduct.

III. UNITY IS TO BE REALIZED THROUGH THE PERFECTED INFLUENCE OF CHRISTIANITY. It was promised as one of the great Messianic blessings. In Christianity we see the growing realization of those blessings. 1. This is accomplished by the *personal influence of Christ*. One powerful centre of attraction binds into unity all that comes under its influence. The sun makes one system of the several planets that revolve about it. The general of genius welds the scattered regiments of his army into one body through his common command over them and their common devotion to him. Christ exerts a similar influence. He is broad enough in his humanity and strong enough in his divinity to attract and influence all kinds of men. Thus " he is our Peace, who made both " (Jew and Gentile) " one, and broke down the middle wall of partition " (Eph. ii. 14). All may see a unity of truth in him who is " the Light of the world," and be led in one way as they follow his footsteps. 2. This unity is further realized in the *inwardness of Christianity*. The new covenant is written on the heart (ch. xxxi. 33). We differ most in externals ; under various clothes there beats the same human heart. When we come to the heart we come to unity. Thus the inward principles of truth and love in Christianity tend to bind Christians together. We are divided because these have not yet their perfect work. No external compulsion will accomplish the same end. On the contrary, this will only aggravate internal dissension. Persecution is the parent of heresy ; charity is the mother of unity.

Ver. 41.—*God rejoicing.* I. GOD HAS JOY. He is not indifferent, nor is he morose ; we are to think of him as the " blessed " God, *i.e.* as essentially happy. The brightness and beauty of the world are reflections from the blessedness of God. Because he is glad, nature is glad, flowers bloom, birds sing, young creatures bound with delight. Nothing is more sad in perversions of religion than the representations of God as a gloomy tyrant. Less terrible, but scarcely less false, are those monkish ideas which deny the tyranny but cherish the gloom of a sombre divinity more suited to chill, dark cloisters than to that glorious temple of nature in which the eternal presence dwells and manifests himself symbolically. These fragrant meadows, broad rolling seas of moorland heather, rich green forest-cities of busy insect life, flashing ocean waves, and the pure blue sky above, and all that is sweet and lovely in creation, swell one symphony of gladness, because the mighty Spirit that haunts them is himself over-flowing with joy. Our God is a *Sun*. And if divinity is sunny, so should religion be. The happy God will rejoice in the happiness of his children. Innocent mirth, though forbidden by Puritan sourness, can be no offence to such a God. The typical citizens of his kingdom are little children ; and what is so joyous as childhood ?

II. GOD FINDS JOY IN HIS CHILDREN. Here is the wonderful fact about the joy of God. He must have joy in his own purity and perfection. Then he has infinite resources at his command. The whole universe can be made to minister to his delight. All high and pure intelligences that form the choir of heaven aim at glorifying him. Yet he finds delight in such poor creatures as we are, in his fallen and erring children. How is this ? 1. Because God is *love*. He loves all his children. Love finds delight in the loved ; so God is compared to the bridegroom rejoicing over the bride (Isa. lxii. 5). 2. Because God is essentially *blessed*. The happy find sources of gladness in the most unlikely quarters, just as the cheeriest scenes cannot lift the load of sadness from those who are naturally mournful. God is so joyous that he finds joy even in us.

III. GOD FINDS JOY IN BLESSING HIS CHILDREN. He rejoices over them to do them good. God's joy is most unselfish. It is the greatest blessedness—the blessedness of giving rather than that of receiving. It is the joy of sacrifice. God, being good, can find joy only in good ; being merciful, can find none in harshness. He must punish the wicked, but he takes no delight in that. Like the shepherd who has recovered the lost sheep, like the woman who has found the lost money, like the father who has welcomed the wanderer home again safe and sound, God rejoices in the return of the penitent, till his joy overflows and is caught up by the angels about his throne. From this we may learn (1) confidence if we return as penitents; (2) assurance that all our life is safe in his hands; (3) care not to grieve his Spirit; (4) desire to live in communion with him.

IV. GOD WILL CALL HIS CHILDREN TO SHARE IN HIS JOY. All joy is sympathetic. We call our friends and our neighbours to rejoice with us. But if we have special joy in any person we naturally desire this joy to be reciprocal. Christ desired his disciples to share his joy (John xv. 11). Joy is contagious. If we are with the happy and in sympathy with them, we naturally receive a share of their gladness. Whence comes the joy we anticipate in heaven? Escape from the evils of this life when God shall wipe away the tears from all eyes? Deliverance from sin and temptation? Reunion with the lost but not forgotten blessed dead? Opportunities for happy service? All these things and more; but these are not the sources of chief joy. That is to share the joy of God, to be "for ever with the Lord."

HOMILIES BY VARIOUS AUTHORS.

Vers. 1—5.—*Silencing a prophet.* A short time before an attempt was made upon his life; now it is imagined that the prophet will yield to harsh treatment and intimidation. The natural heart of man is so foolish that it cannot but credit man with the authorship of Divine truth, and suppose that he can control and modify the inspired messages of God. Nay, the sinner is often so left to himself as to suppose that his own precautions will prevent the communications of God's Spirit, or at least the carrying of these into effect!

I. FAITHFUL WITNESSES OF THE TRUTH MAY SOMETIMES BE BROUGHT INTO GREAT STRAITS. God does not guarantee a smooth experience and an easy life to his servants. Quite the contrary. His Son prepares his disciples for suffering many things (Matt. x. 16—22). Jeremiah would seem to be alternately exposed to harshness and kindness—he was in the prison and yet in the palace. The bribe, or the deceitful promise, may be as great a trial as the cruelty. Seclusion for a prophet and patriot must have been very hard to endure at such a time, and full of spiritual perplexity. Great things were being done, and national destinies decided, whilst he was held fast, helpless, and with little reliable information of what was going on. So God often lays aside his servants just at a time when there would seem to be most occasion for their activity. "His thoughts are not as our thoughts."

II. THE WORD OF GOD IS NOT THEREBY HINDERED. 1. *It is not silenced.* (Ver. 1; cf. ch. xxxiii. 1.) The communion of the soul with God cannot be broken by external means. As well might one say, "Thus far, and no further," to the ocean or the day. Many of the grandest revelations of God date from prisons. 2. *Resistance only hastens its progress and fulfilment.* Persecution and martyrdom have done more for Christianity than a thousand direct agencies. How the voices multiply! 3. *Those who oppose it ensure its speedy visitation upon themselves.*

III. GOD WILL UPHOLD AND COMFORT HIS AFFLICTED SERVANTS. The greatest trial to Jeremiah would have been God's silence: at this season the "Word of the Lord" must have been his greatest consolation and reassurance. Earthly deprivation may be heavenly liberty. Sufferers for the truth know and feel that God is with them.—M.

Vers. 6—15.—*Purchasing by Divine command.* The passage a *locus classicus* for various questions and formalities connected with the Mosaic Law. Abraham bought a field for his dead; Jeremiah bought one for a nation yet unborn. If no other circumstance had been recorded concerning the latter, this alone would entitle him to be enrolled amongst the fathers of the faithful.

I. GOD'S SERVANTS ARE SOMETIMES CALLED TO PERFORM STRANGE AND SINGULAR ACTIONS. The prophet bidden to purchase a field when the land is overrun by the Chaldeans; a poor man to procure and expend money upon a speculation for which there was no earthly security; a prisoner to acquire land there seemed so little likelihood of his ever seeing. Much of Christian duty is summed up in that experience. We are not to stumble at earthly anomalies or anachronisms, but to live and labour and spend "as seeing him who is invisible."

II. THE WILL OF GOD IS A SUFFICIENT REASON FOR DOING SUCH THINGS. That is, the *revealed* will. Men who act by revelation have not to ask for reasons before acting. Obedience is their *rôle*; afterwards they may ask for light. Christians have to commit their way unto the Lord, and trust where they cannot trace. They are led by a higher reason, which cannot err.

III. WHAT GOD COMMANDS OUGHT TO BE DONE PROMPTLY, LOVINGLY, AND WITH EXACTITUDE. Jeremiah at once performs the duty. He hastens to relieve his kinsman from perplexity and loss. And the business part of the engagement is executed with the greatest care and all the formalities of law. No flaw is suffered to enter into the bargain. The importance and duty of Christians being model business men. What is done for God and under his supervision should be done thoroughly. Justice precedes and facilitates charity.

IV. TRANSACTIONS APPARENTLY SMALL AND TRIFLING MAY HAVE GREAT MEANINGS. How different the feelings of the parties to this transaction! The money absolutely of little amount; relatively it was worth much. We are reminded of the widow's mite. That document was the title deed to a kingdom. *This is the spirit in which Christians should do business.* We ought never to forget that we are heirs of the kingdom. The world has been sold under sin, but we are free. Let us strive to "lay up treasure in heaven." Let us make our title clear to its liberties and joys. In the meanest undertaking let us be guided by this spirit. In the confidence of Christ let us redeem the world. Let our motto be "Everything in the spirit of Christ!" Men cannot be just and honest unless they are inspired, even for the least things, as Jeremiah was. A large and general brotherliness, an implicit faith in God's Word, ought to govern us in all our affairs. Above all, our own relation to Christ, our personal transactions with him, should at once, with prayer and faith, be made sure!—M.

Vers. 16—25.—*The prayer of Jeremiah.* I. CLEAR AND UNMISTAKABLE DUTIES SHOULD BE FULFILLED ERE MEN ENTER UPON DIVINE EXERCISES. The deed had already been executed.

II. CIRCUMSTANCES OF TRIAL AND PERPLEXITY SHOULD LEAD MEN TO THE THRONE OF GRACE.

III. THE KNOWN CHARACTER AND PAST ACTION OF GOD SHOULD INFLUENCE MEN'S JUDGMENTS OF PRESENT EXPERIENCES AND STRENGTHEN THEIR FAITH. It is good to rehearse these even in private devotions.

IV. SINS SHOULD BE FREELY AND HONESTLY CONFESSED.

V. ONE SAINT MAY INTERCEDE FOR MANY SINNERS.

VI. The prayer of faith is answered.   (Vers. 26—44.)—M.

Vers. 37—40.—*The unities of the Divine kingdom.*   (Cf. John xvii.)   I. Unity in THE EXPERIENCE AND PRIVILEGES OF SAVING GRACE.   (Ver. 37.)
II. Unity with God.
III. Unity in spirit and labour with one another.   (Ver. 39.)
IV. Unity of destiny.   (Ver. 40.)—M.

Vers. 1—44.—*A story of God's sustaining grace.* This whole chapter may be summed up under some such heading as this. For it begins with showing us God's servant Jeremiah in a position in which he sorely needed sustaining grace, and then it proceeds to narrate the threefold process by which this grace was communicated to him. The manner in which God sustained Jeremiah is very much akin to that in which he will sustain all his servants who may be in similar need. If any be so now, let them give heed to this record. Note—
I. The need of God's servant. Ver. 2 tells us that Jeremiah was at this time shut up in prison. His confinement was not so severe as that which he had suffered in his former prison; but yet there was very much in his present circumstances to make him need the sustaining grace of God. The story of his imprisonments is full of interest, but it has to be gathered here a little and there a little from different parts of his prophecies. These have been compiled on a principle which it is impossible to discover. Events of early date are placed in later chapters, and those of later date in early chapters. The chronological confusion is complete. Hence it is the task of every student of these prophecies to disentangle this confusion so far as it may be done. In saying this, nothing is charged against the inspiration and authority of the book. That remains intact; but our reverence for what is so evidently of God in the book does not hinder that we should note and regret the disorderly way in which some human hands—whose we know not—have put together its various parts. Tracing out, however, the history of these imprisonments, it would seem that they were brought about somewhat as follows. Jeremiah had clearly foreseen and foretold that the ungodliness of the people would bring down the Divine chastisements. Moreover, he discerned and declared with equal clearness that the instrument of God's wrath would be the rapidly rising empire of Babylon. He saw how everything yielded to the might of her armies; that no power, not even that of Egypt, could withstand her assault. But all this was by no means so clearly seen by those to whom Jeremiah was sent. They did not believe in the nearness of God's judgments, and were not a little angry with the faithful prophet for denouncing them. But Jeremiah saw also that, certain as was the approach of these judgments, they probably would be mitigated if, instead of exasperating the armies of Babylon by useless resistance, they submitted themselves and acknowledged her supremacy (cf. ch. xxvii.). But the same spirit in the nobles and princes of Judah and in the people generally, which made them refuse to listen to him when he told of God's judgments coming upon them, made them impatient of his oft-repeated counsels to do now the best thing under the circumstances—bow to the Babylonian storm, and so, though they could not save all, yet save some of their cherished possessions. But at length it became evident that Babylon did mean to assail them. Instead, however, of adopting either of the two better methods—of humbling themselves before God and imploring his protection, or of conciliating the Babylonian king, they formed alliance with Egypt (ch. xxxvii.), notwithstanding Jeremiah's solemn assurance of the uselessness of such alliance. But in the ninth year of Zedekiah the Chaldean army besieged Jerusalem. Jeremiah (ch. xxxiv. 2) plainly tells the king how hopeless all resistance is. Under the alarm of this siege, the wealthy Jews released their poorer brethren, of whom, contrary to God's Law, they had made bond slaves (ch. xxxiv.). But the Egyptian army coming to their aid (ch. xxxvii. 5), the Chaldeans raised the siege. Thinking now that all cause for fear was gone, the Jewish leaders quickly went back to their old ways, and, though indignantly denounced by Jeremiah (ch. xxxiv.), enslaved their brethren again. But he had taken advantage of the withdrawal of the Babylonian forces to quit the city. It was no place for him. His purpose, however, was prevented. Foes not a few, to whom his fidelity had been hateful, now seized on him on the pretence that he was about to desert to the

Chaldeans (ch. xxxvii.). In the insolence begotten of their fancied deliverance, they thought they might do anything to God's servant. They therefore dragged him before the princes, procured his condemnation, smote him, and then cast him into deep dungeons, where, had he lingered long, death must soon have put an end to his misery. But the King Zedekiah, whose mind was ill at ease, and who could not help believing Jeremiah, whilst allowing himself to be overawed by the violence of those around him, sent for the prophet and caused him to be placed in less severe custody. But he was not to stay there long. His former enemies came round the king, and brought such accusations against him that the king, weakly yielding as his manner was, gave him up to their will; like as Pilate delivered Jesus. Speedily they flung him into a dungeon, which appears to have been a disused well, the bottom of which was still deep in mire. There they leave him miserably to perish. But again he is delivered. An eunuch of the court intercedes for him, and he is drawn up tenderly and carefully, as his half-dying state probably required, from the horrible pit into which he had been cast, and brought back again into that milder captivity which is indicated by "the court of the prison," and where we find him when this chapter (xxxii.) opens. Now, if we try and realize the prophet's condition, we can easily see how a despondency like to that of John the Baptist when he sent two of his disciples to Jesus to ask him, "Art thou he that should come," etc. ?—we can see how a like despondency might well have fallen upon the prophet's mind. He was no robust, stern Stoic, to whom rough treatment and the scorn and hate of his fellow-men were as nothing. His piteous pleading for his life (ch. xxxvii. 20), his ready yielding to the king's suggested subterfuge (ch. xxxviii. 27), his reiterated confessions of his distress, the long wail of his lamentations, all reveal a man who, though in the strength of God's grace he would not flinch in delivering the message God had entrusted to him, whatever it was, whoever might oppose, nevertheless felt keenly the perils of his position and the misery of his lot. Again and again had he been seemingly given over unto death, and even now there was nought but the poor protection of the word of the weakest of monarchs to save him from the rage that was ready to destroy him the first opportunity that should be given. His whole horizon was dark, unillumined by any cheering ray of hope. If the besieging armies did their worst—and it seemed certain that the obstinacy of the people would provoke them to do so—what prospect of deliverance and restoration could there be then? For himself and for his country the outlook was all dark.

II. But, next, see HOW GOD MET HIS NEED. He did this in a threefold manner. 1. *He led him to commit himself openly to the faith of the restoration of Israel.* He had proclaimed this restoration many times before. He was now by a public significant act to avow again his confidence in what God had promised. This is the meaning of the purchase of the land told of in vers. 6—15. In the most explicit formal manner he was to do this which his own predictions of the Babylonian conquest seemed to render absurd. It seemed like throwing money away. Why the vendor wanted to sell the ground we do not know. The conviction that all was lost for Judah may have led to it. But when the offer was made, as God told Jeremiah it would be, he saw that it was from the Lord, and that he was, by purchasing it, to testify to his faith that the land should be restored to them again. Hence he did all in the most formal manner : paid for it, took receipt, registered the purchase, and had duplicate made out, handed over the documents to Baruch in presence of many witnesses. Now, had Jeremiah refused to buy this property, it would be tantamount to his apostasy from faith, to his renouncing all his trust in God. His despondency would bid him do so. But the thought of throwing up all faith, renouncing it, and denying God, the very thought seems to have provoked a blessed reaction, and to have made him resolve that he would make it yet more difficult for himself to go back from his faith by committing himself to it in this open, deliberate, and formal way. *Thus God made him use what faith he had in order to his winning more.* "To him that hath," and uses what he has, "shall be given." It is ever so. Have you little of the spirit of prayer? Pray, and more will be yours. Little love to God? Do something especially and avowedly for him, and your love will deepen. As with the body and the mind, in trade and all departments of life, the use of what strength we have gains more. 2. *By leading him to lay all his difficulties before God.* This is the meaning of the prayer in vers. 17—25. After the prophet had committed himself by this purchase of the land, a purchase so irrational and absurd as it would seem in many eyes, and as it perhaps partly seemed even in his own eyes, he felt need still of more assurance and confidence than he yet possessed. And so in this prayer he pours out his perplexities before God. And if we analyze this prayer, we shall see that he begins by going over in devout confession and adoration the many reasons which ought to establish his faith. First he confesses the sure truth—nothing is too hard for the Lord. Then he proceeds from this general truth to several proofs of it in Israel's own history—how, in spite of all difficulty, God redeemed, preserved, and settled his people in the land he promised. Then he turns to the perplexing facts which, at the moment, were so staggering his own mind—the dreadful wickedness of the people and the actual presence of God's judgments. How, in the face of all this, could God's promises be fulfilled? It is as if he had said, "Lord, I believe, I ought to believe, but I am sore perplexed, I desire to believe yet more; help my unbelief." Such seems to have been the meaning of this prayer. It is prayer because this is its meaning, though there is not one word of petition in the whole of it. The prayer has to be read between the lines. And God does ever so read the desires of his servants, even when not expressed in words, or when words are used that are not formal prayers. Nor can we doubt that thus coming to the Lord with his perplexities was of great help to the prophet. It must have been so; it ever is so. 3. *God gives him fresh grasp of his promises, new assurance of the truth of his Word.* This is the third and last step in this sustaining grace, of which this whole chapter tells. The account of this answer to the prophet's prayer is given in vers. 26—44. He gave him to feel afresh the blessed truth that *nothing* was too hard for the Lord (ver. 27). Therefore it mattered not, even though he could not understand all God's ways, though the Chaldean armies were thundering at the gates of Jerusalem, though the people were so hopelessly wicked. "Therefore" (ver. 36) "saith the Lord," and then follows a whole series of "I wills" and "shall be's," in which God again bears in upon his servant's soul the certainty of the things he had already declared. And more than he had declared should be—a spiritual restoration as well as a literal one. And then (vers. 43, 44), referring to Jeremiah's own transaction, "fields shall be bought in this land," etc. That which now seemed so unreasonable and hopeless should be matter of everyday occurrence in the blessed times of restoration which God would surely bring about. The instruction, therefore, for every perplexed soul is—Use what faith thou hast; tell all thy perplexities to God; receive the new assurance of his faithfulness he will surely give.—C.

Ver. 5.—*O blessed death!* "Until I visit him." Zedekiah does not seem to have been a bad man, though he did evil. Weak rather than wicked. One like our own Charles I. or Louis XVI. of France. One of those men unhappily called to places of great responsibility and difficulty, without the moral strength requisite for so arduous a post. A sadder life than that of King Zedekiah, the last king of Judah and Jerusalem, cannot be conceived. It is a piteous tale. Bereaved, a captive, blinded, he was dragged to Babylon, and there died. And it is because the prophet of God recognizes that death to such an one could not but be a sweet messenger of relief, therefore he calls it " the Lord visiting him." True, the visit of the Lord often means the wrath of the Lord. He will " visit the sins of the fathers," etc. But it yet more often means the *goodness* of the Lord. "The Lord hath visited and redeemed his people." He visited Hannah. He visits his flock. And this gentler meaning it has here; for the sore punishment of his sins Zedekiah had already been visited. This visit, therefore, tells of God's merciful visitation.

I. DEATH NOT ALWAYS A VISIT OF MERCY. Not to those who die in their sins. It is represented often as the judgment of God. "It is a fearful thing to fall into the hands of the living God," as they who die impenitent and unbelieving fall.

II. BUT DEATH IS MORE OFTEN THE LORD'S VISIT OF MERCY. It is: 1. *To those whom God punishes in this life.* Zedekiah was an instance. Cf. those of whom St. Paul says (1 Cor. xi. 33) that they were judged now that they might not be condemned with the world. And probably there are many such. 2. To the sorrowful *and those whose lives are a prolonged pain.* We speak of death for such as being a merciful relief; and we are right. 3. *To all believers in the Lord Jesus Christ.* Death for them is the Lord's visiting them—Christ's coming again, as he said he would, and receiving them unto himself, that where he is they may be also, Which kind of visitation of the Lord shall death be to *us?*—C.

Vers. 6—15.—*A parable of redemption.* For the sake of variety and interest, it is lawful now and then to make the transactions of earth tell of the transactions of heaven; to make prosaic matters of fact—as the redeeming of this field—parables of spiritual realities. Let us so deal with this narrative. Here was—

I. A POSSESSION IN AN ENEMY'S POWER. The field, as the whole land virtually was so at that very moment. So man.

II. THE LORD PROMPTING REDEMPTION. Jeremiah knew that it was "of the Lord." God is the Author of redemption. "He so loved the world that," etc. "God was in Christ reconciling," etc.

III. THE REDEEMER VOLUNTARILY UNDERTAKING THE WORK. Jeremiah might have refused. So Christ thought not his equality with God a thing he should tenaciously retain, but emptied himself (Phil. iii.). "For our sakes, though he was rich, yet he became poor."

IV. THE SEEMING HOPELESSNESS OF SUCH REDEMPTION. What likelihood did there seem in Jeremiah's payment that he should ever possess the land? What could Christ's cross do to redeem man? "The offence of the cross."

V. REDEMPTION ACCOMPLISHED AND ATTESTED. The prophet paid the silver, and the transaction was attested in due form. Christ paid our ransom, and that that great purchase was valid was attested by the resurrection from the dead: that was the seal.

VI. WITNESSES ARE COMMISSIONED TO DECLARE THE TRUTH. (Vers. 12, 13.) So Christ commanded his apostles to testify of what he had done.

VII. THE TWOFOLD TESTIMONY. (Ver. 14.) There was that which was sealed and that which was open. So is it of the great redemption. There is a testimony that is sealed, hidden from the world, but revealed to the believer by the Spirit of God in his inward experience, the witness of God in his soul, the Spirit bearing witness with his spirit. And there is that which is open—the historic evidence of the resurrection of Christ and of the truth of Christianity.

VIII. THE DEPOSITARIES OF THIS TESTIMONY. The prophet put his in an earthen vessel. We, too, have this treasure in earthen vessels. Let the literal suggest the spiritual; Jeremiah, Paul.

IX. THE UNDERLYING AND EFFECTUATING WILL. (Ver. 15.) The Lord *would* have the land to be restored, the Captivity *should* return. So he "*will* have all men to be saved." Have we claimed our share in this redeeming work?—C.

Ver. 19.—*Nothing hid from God.* "Thine eyes are open upon all the ways of the sons of men." No truth more forgotten than this. Men assent to it, but it has no power over the vast mass of men, and far too little power even over religious men. How different it is with the presence or absence of our fellow-creatures! We have often much to conceal from them, and we would often make great efforts to prevent them knowing much of our lives. Hence it makes all the difference in the world to us whether they be with us or away from us. It regulates our conduct, our words, our looks, our very tone and movement. But how little of such effect does the thought of the Divine eye seeing all and always what we are and do, even to the understanding of our thoughts afar off! Therefore such forgetfulness of God's presence as that which we are all of us so liable to be guilty of requires that we should diligently consider the many proofs of the truth declared in this verse. Note some of them.

I. HE HAS LAID DOWN LAWS TO REGULATE AND GOVERN THE WAYS OF MEN. He has done this not only for those that are open and manifest, but those that are most secret as well. He is a "discerner of the thoughts and intents of the heart" (cf. Ps. cxxxix.). "God looketh at the heart." Now, he could not thus largely and minutely lay down these laws if he did not know completely the ways which they concern.

II. HE DISCOVERS THEM. If we have been engaged in some secret way, or such as we thought was secret, where no eye was upon us as we imagined; if afterwards some one meets us and tells us all that we did, we know that, unseen to us, he must by himself or by others have been present at that secret hour. Now, thus we know that God has been ever present. For: 1. *He tells us all about them.* What is memory? what, especially, is conscience, but God telling us that *he* is perfectly acquainted with all that we thought unknown? 2. *He tells others of them.* He told David (1 Sam. xxiii. 12) that the men of Keilah would deliver him up into the hand of Saul. He told Joseph of Herod's purpose to kill the infant Saviour. He warned the wise men from whom Herod hoped to have acquired the knowledge he needed. And again, he warned Joseph about Archelaus. And many such instances there are. Now, they all show that God knows all the ways of men.

III. HE TURNS THEM WHICH WAY HE WILL. Sometimes he gives men their heart's desire, satisfying the longing soul. Sometimes he overrules them for ends far other than the doers of them designed. As when they crucified our Lord (Acts ii. 23), God ordered which way their sin should issue, which was quite other than they thought (cf. history of Joseph). Sometimes he baffles and denies them altogether. If he did not, this world would be hell. What if all the sin men conceive of they were to commit! Hence (Gen. xx. 6) God says he withheld Abimelech from sinning against Abraham, and suffered him not to touch Sarah. And God is for ever graciously strangling sin in its very birth. But all this shows that "his eyes are open upon all the ways of the sons of men."

IV. HE RECOMPENSES THEM. 1. When our secret ways have been evil, cannot we tell in the darkening of the face of God that he knows all? And when they have been such as the Lord delighteth to see in secret, do not our hearts know when we come to him that there is the answering smile? 2. And he recompenses them in his present outward dealings with us. The sinner's most secret sin finds him out not seldom in this world. And the patient continuance in well-doing, however humble and obscure, rarely fails to meet with its reward. 3. And God will judge them in the last great day. Then the thoughts of all hearts shall be revealed. "God shall bring every work into judgment, with every secret thing, whether it be good or whether it be evil." Again is it made evident that he knows all. He is "the Father who seeth in secret."

CONCLUSION. Understand what is the right use of this great doctrine. Not that we should be trying every hour of the day to be thinking of the all-seeing eye of God. We cannot, and God does not intend that we should, be ever thus conscious of his presence. Children are not of the presence of their parents. They are utterly unconstrained. But should need arise for their parents' help, should they be tempted to do what they know their parents would forbid, then in a moment they become conscious of their presence, and the needed aid is asked for, and the tempting sin is resisted. Now, thus should we remember the continual presence of God. "The right state of mind plainly is to have the thought of God's presence so perpetually at hand that, as with Joseph in his great temptation, it shall always start before us whenever it is wanted." This is living with God and communion with Christ; and it is won by prayer and close walking with him, and blessed are they who win.—C.

Ver. 27.—*Truth confessed, but not realized.* "Is there anything too hard for the Lord?" In ver. 17 the prophet had confessed "nothing is too hard for thee," but it is evident that, though he thus confessed the blessed truth, he did not realize it so as to enjoy it and get the comfort of it (cf. homily on vers. 1—44). Now, there are many causes which hinder our realization of this truth which we nevertheless both confess and believe. But they may all be summed up under the three headings of trouble, guilt, and sin. It was the first of these, though not exclusively, which was clouding the prophet's mind, and making even this axiom of Divine truth seem doubtful for the time. Glance at these causes of this sad questioning whether some things be not too hard for the Lord, and their several cures.

I. GREAT TROUBLE. Cf. circumstances of the time and of prophet especially. Oh, what doubt and misgiving do the troubles of life, the terrible events, "the stings and arrows of outrageous fortune," cause to souls not a few! It was so here. Now, observe *the antidote to this doubt.* To strengthen his faith the prophet draws an argument from the creation. Then, with no resources from without, God formed the earth and the world. Then, when the material out of which the ordered universe should come had all to be brought into order, "the earth was without form and void, and darkness," etc. Then, when all was created, all had to be preserved and daily sustained. Let any one contemplate the proofs that these facts give of the existence, the power, the wisdom, and the beneficence of God, and the question, " Is anything too hard for thee ? " can meet with but one answer. How can any doubt the Divine resources in view of the creating and sustaining providence of God.

II. GUILT. If it be hard sometimes in the face of the calamities of life to realize the fulness of the Divine resources, it is harder still in the face of human guilt. Is there a God able and willing to supply my material and temporal need? is a question less difficult than that which asks whether there be a God able and willing to pardon my sin. For to minds not few nor feeble, the forgiveness of sin seems an insoluble problem. If the punishment of sin be righteous, and every witness affirms that it is, ought God to remit it ? And if it be inevitable, the sure reaping of the previous sowing, can God remit it ? Have we not something here that is too hard even for the Lord ? If in all departments of nature, we everywhere see effects surely following their appropriate causes, and if spiritual death be the appropriate effect of sin, how can this cause and effect be severed any more than any other ? True, the human will can step in and arrest or turn aside this or that effect; we see this perpetually. But here is a question, not of power, but of right, not in the sphere of the material, but of that which is moral. It is a case in which mere power goes for nothing. What, then, is to be done? *The atonement of our Lord Jesus Christ solves the problem.* He, in our humanity, offered to God for us that perfect sacrifice whereby all who claim their share in its benefits are pardoned, accepted, and saved. " God was in Christ, reconciling," etc. (2 Cor. v.). It is everywhere recognized that a true confession of wrong done, and an earnest entreaty for forgiveness, should suffice to remove all wrath on account of such wrong from the heart of the offended one. That law which God enjoins upon us he observes himself. " The sacrifices of God are a broken spirit," etc. But such confession of human sin and intercession for its forgiveness Christ offered in humanity to God for us, and *so* God can be just and yet the Justifier of him who believeth in Jesus. Thus is this hard problem solved ; the " Lamb of God taketh away the sin of the world." But there is—

III. SIN. Can God subdue that in the heart of a man ? When we see the outrages, the duration, the strength of hold, the universality, the attractiveness, the prestige, and the love of sin, it does seem as if the subjugation of this was too hard even for the Lord. To turn back the tides, to reverse the law of gravity, to alter any other law of the universe,—this were an easy task compared with the stupendous change which must be wrought in man before the love of sin can die out of him, and the love of God rule in its stead. What endeavours have been made ! what schemes devised ! what philosophies elaborated ! but all in vain. Hence, despair for ourselves and for others too often predominates in our souls. Evil we are, and evil we must be. Who can bring a clean thing out of an unclean ? *Can* a corrupt tree bring forth good fruit ? But " there is nothing too hard for the Lord." The history of the Church of God proves that there is, *in the regenerating, sanctifying Spirit of God,* that power which is needed here. He is the renewing, transforming, sanctifying Spirit. Baptized with the Spirit, " I walk not after the flesh, but after the Spirit." " The law of the Spirit of life in Christ Jesus has made me free from the law of sin and death." May we more and more, as we may and should, in our own experience, prove this true.—C.

Vers. 31—33.—*Love's labour apparently lost.* As we read this record (ver. 33) of the persevering and earnest, but nevertheless fruitless, labours of God's servants, and remember that they were sent by the Lord, we are almost led to ask, " To what purpose is this waste ? " We can understand loving, earnest labour persevered in, though nothing may come of it, when those who so toil are sustained by hope, even though it may be sometimes hoping against hope. But " love hopeth all things, believeth all things, endureth all things," and "never faileth." How many and how pathetic are the stories that might be told where such love has toiled to save some reprobate from the doom he would persist in bringing on himself!—the loving wife, sister, mother, striving to save those who won't be saved! How full this weary world is of such cases! But it is evident that these continue to labour and pray because they cannot *know* that they shall fail, and their hope is that they shall succeed. How David fasted and wept whilst his child was yet alive! but when the child was dead, David arose and ate, anointed himself, and put on his royal robes. And when his servants asked him wherefore he so altered his behaviour, he said, "Whilst he was alive I fasted and wept: for I said, Who can tell if God will be gracious to me, that the child may live? But now he is dead, wherefore should I fast? Can I bring him back again?" It was hope that sustained the sorrowing king; but when hope was gone, he gave over his fruitless toil. Now, all this we can understand and sympathize with. But in the long-continued ministry of Jeremiah and others like him, when all the while God knew what the end would be, how apparently wasted it would all be, when he could never have any hope of a different result from that which actually occurred, the inquiry is suggested—Wherefore did God commission, and wherefore does he still, such fruitless toil? "Known unto God are all his works from the beginning." There can be nothing contingent with him. Hope is a mental condition impossible to God; he cannot be said to hope for anything. It is entirely human; but to an omniscient and omnipotent Being who "ordereth all things after the counsel of his own will," hope, or doubt, or uncertainty of any kind cannot be. Therefore, knowingly, with full certainty that all his servant's severe labour would not bring the people to repentance, as in fact it did not, nevertheless God commissioned him and his fellow-servants to go and speak to them. How are we to explain this? Reasons suggest themselves in connection with—

I. THE PROPHET HIMSELF. 1. *That his trust in God might not fail.* Had the career of the guilty nation been cut short because God foresaw what the certain end would be, such certain foresight being impossible to any but God, the faith of his servants would have been severely strained. They had ever heard of God as the long-suffering God. They would have found it hard to believe that, if but more time had been given, and a longer ministry allowed, and the whole truth had been put before the people perseveringly and earnestly, they would after all have remained unrepentant. The miserable paralysis of doubt as to the Divine equity would have fastened on them, and their power as his prophets would have thenceforth ceased. 2. *That trust and love might be greatly increased.* This could not but be when the prophet saw that the long-suffering of God was no mere word, but a reality, a reality greater than could have been conceived. What human authority would endure to be despised and set at nought as God endured that his should be? "Who is a God like unto thee, that pardoneth iniquity," etc.? Such was once and again the adoring exclamation of those who witnessed and marvelled at the all but infinite patience of God. And this too when all the while God knew, as his prophet did not, that there was no hope. "We are saved by hope;" but *there is no such salvation for God.* He goes on blessing and doing good to those whom he knows will turn upon him in defiance and black ingratitude to the last day of their lives. It is wonderful. The Saviour went about doing good amongst a people whom he *knew* would crucify him. What an added conception of the Divine love does this fact give! Now that his servants the prophets might yet more know and rejoice in the God in whom they believed, God was and is long-suffering to those whom nevertheless he is compelled to condemn. 3. *The prophet's own spiritual improvement.* Such labour, severe though it be, is not lost on him who engages in it. Was not "the Captain of our salvation made perfect through sufferings," and those of a kindred kind? And for the discipline and development of the spiritual powers of his servants, to further in them that which is well pleasing in his sight, and for which process the unseen and eternal world will, in all probability, have constant though blessed employ, —for such reasons God keeps his servants in the world, and spares the world, guilty and ready for condemnation though it be.

II. THE WITNESSES AND ALL THEY WHO SHOULD AFTERWARDS HEAR OF HIS JUDGMENTS ON THE GUILTY NATION. 1. *The righteousness of God would be vindicated.* All would see that it was not without cause God dealt with them as he did. 2. *Sinners in all ages would be warned* not to presume on the long-suffering of God. St. Paul says of these ancient records, "All these things were written for our learning." 3. *Sin would be seen to be exceeding sinful.* Men are ready to attribute their sorrows to any and every cause but sin. But by thus branding sin with God's mark of sore displeasure, men would be better able to resist its attractions and overcome its power.

III. THE UNREPENTANT PEOPLE THEMSELVES. God having borne with them so long, now that at length his judgment had come, the remembrance of that long-suffering would: 1. *Silence them.* All would feel that God was just when he spoke against them, and clear when he condemned them. That Ps. li. and other penitential psalms bear many marks of having been adapted to, if not produced by, the sorrows of the Exile; cf. too Ezra's confession and prayer. 2. *Humble them.* Jeremiah declares once and again that it is their "pride" which was causing them to persist in their evil ways (cf. ch. xiii. 17). They had trusted in their national descent, on the possession of so many and so great privileges; cf. "The temple of the Lord, The temple of the Lord, . . . are these" (ch. vii.). As they realized their present misery they would see the worthlessness of all those lying words in which they had so fondly trusted, and they would be bowed down with shame, as they now knew what their pride had brought upon themselves and their children. "Humbled in the dust" would be the fitting description of them as they thought of the way in which they had despised the long-continued and loving warnings of God. 3. *Convert them.* For God intended that they should be restored; he would bring them again, give them a heart to know him (cf. vers. 36—44). And no means could be more adapted to subserve this end than those which God employed. Had they been cut off in their guilt, or had the Exile taken place much earlier, there could not have been the feeling which we know was aroused, and which was so salutary that they were without excuse. The wise physician knows that there are fit times and seasons for the successful administration of his medicines, and till such times all administration of those medicines would be of no avail. And so, until a right condition of mind was brought about in the exiled people, no real conversion could take place. They must be without excuse before they could be made to feel that they were so, and therefore a further reason why God bore with them so long, that this their utter inexcusableness and their undeniable guilt might be the more deeply felt and more contritely and sincerely confessed. 4. *Accomplish the number of his elect amongst them.* For it is not to be thought that the prophet's ministry was utterly lost. The better part of the people were called out, educated, and prepared for the purifying discipline which awaited them by means of it. And it was that which brought the exiles back sadder but yet wiser men. And during the Exile the souls of the people were nurtured by the prophet's words which, during this prolonged ministry, he had spoken to them. That ministry was one proof out of so many more that God's Word shall not return to him void, although, in regard to immediate and much-desired effect, it may seem as if all were apparently lost. Now, all these considerations which apply to Jeremiah and his ministry and the long-suffering of God with Judah, apply with equal force to like long-suffering of God now—for God often repeats his mercies and judgments both—and happy shall we be if the gracious purposes of God in his forbearance are realized by us.—C.

Vers. 36—41.—*The refiner's fire.* The better part of Judah were cast as precious metal into a crucible by their being sent into exile at Babylon. And the effect was as that which results from such purifying process. Note—

I. WITHOUT DOUBT THEIR EXILE TRIED THEM AS FIRE. Fire is often the symbol of pain; and that there was indeed pain and sore distress in the exiles' lot is certain. Degradation, slavery, loss of their land, their high privileges as the people of God, in short, of their worldly all, had to be submitted to by them; and they lived, where they were permitted to live, at the mere caprice of a powerful, despotic, and merciless monarch. What that caprice could do, and often actually inflicted in the way of cruel tyranny and oppression, the books of the Bible which belong to the times of the Captivity, and the sculptures brought from those lands and now in the museums of this and other countries, clearly reveal—the merciless slaughters and the horrible punishments, etc. And all this woe they had brought on others—as their children—who were entirely innocent of their parents' wrong. "The fathers had eaten sour grapes, and the children's teeth were set on edge." And to add to their distress was the bitter reflection that they were designed to have filled a position so entirely different and better; that they were intended to be the first in the favour of God, but now had become last; and all this by their own persistent, wilful wickedness, wickedness persisted in in spite of every kind of warning, protest, and entreaty that God could send them. Yes, it was as fire, as a furnace seven times heated.

II. BUT IT WAS NEVERTHELESS AS A REFINER'S FIRE. It was to issue in their good. For it did not destroy them. They were to be brought out of all this woe. "I will bring them again" (ver. 37). And it should work them good by separating them from:

1. *Their sins.* They were torn away from the scenes, the people, the places, the manifold circumstances, which were inseparable from that idolatry into which they had so often fallen. 2. *And from those who tempted them thereto.* For that loose, evil multitude which were dealt with apparently less sternly than themselves at the first, were the prompters and the persuaders to that wickedness which had wrought them so much harm. Those who were obnoxious and therefore, in ch. xxiv., compared to the figs which could not be eaten, were, though left awhile in the possession of their own land, at length destroyed. The corrupt and poisonous leaven was taken utterly away, so that that which was sound and healthful or capable of becoming so might be preserved. The pure ore was separated from the base alloy, the worthless dross, by the action of this refiner's fire.

III. In proof of this, note : 1. God brought them back to their own land. 2. They had given them "a heart to know" God. 3. And their after history proved this. For they were a noble people for generations afterwards. Of course, there were the less worthy amongst them ; but let their records be studied, their thrilling Maccabean history, for example, and it will be seen what a refining process that was through which they had been made—as was so necessary for them and for mankind at large, who were to be blessed by means of them—to pass. The absence of prophets and prophesyings, which is so marked a feature of the history written on that page which separates the Old Testament from the New, instead of being a reproach to them, is rather a proof that their general national health was such that the sharp surgery, the stern ministry, of the prophetic order was not then needed as it had been, so deplorably, in former days.

IV. What made the difference between them and the baser sort who were destroyed. It was the possession of the Spirit of God. The holy fire enkindled by him had been all but quenched, but not entirely ; the dying embers could be made to glow with radiant heat once again. But of that fire God has said, "It shall ever be burning on the altar, it shall never go out ; " and though they had all but smothered it beneath the heap of idolatrous superstitions and practices, and other evil compliances with wrong, it was burning still. And the exile across that wide desert to the plains of Babylon let in again the air from heaven, and the fire burnt up once more. And that this might be, God dealt with them as he did, and as he ever does, blessed be his Name ! in like circumstances.

Conclusion. Paul's question, therefore, comes to our mind as we study such history as this : "Have ye received the Holy Ghost ? " Seek him ; for he will baffle the power of the destroyer, and, better still, if we will but follow his leading, he will keep us from ever needing to be cast into the crucible as these were, and from needing the refiner's fire. That would have been best of all, but thank God there is a second best. "Covet earnestly the best gifts."—C.

Ver. 42.—*The ratio of sorrow and joy.* I. There is such ratio. Sorrow and joy are not flung down at hap-hazard into this world at the caprice of the Ruler of all, and irrespective one of the other, only that for the mass of men the sorrow is far greater and more pervading than the joy. But the relations between these two it is the glory of Scripture and of the gospel especially to reveal.

II. Scripture teaches it. Here in this verse ; cf. also Ps. xc., "Make us glad according to the days," etc. ; Job ii. 10, "Shall we receive good at the hand of God, and shall we not also receive evil ? " parable of Dives and Lazarus : "Thou in thy lifetime receivedst thy good things, and likewise Lazarus evil things ; but now he is comforted, and thou art tormented" (Luke xvi.).

III. Nature illustrates it. It is said that on the Scotch lakes the depth of the lake is almost always the same as the height of the surrounding hills. And is it not the same with the great depths of ocean and the lofty mountains of the world ? They have long, long winter in the Northern climes, but when the light does come back, the day so stretches out that you can read by the light of the midnight sun. And if we look into the faces of men, those indices of the soul within, it will be found that the looks of sorrow and of joy are about equally distributed. God is not a partial, unjust Father, petting one and neglecting others of his children. Sometimes we think so, but a larger survey will lead to truer thought.

IV. It is a truth full of comfort. For it teaches : 1. *That if sorrow be sent, joy is not far off.* "If I had been a little child among the Israelites, I think I should have known, when father set the bitter herbs upon the table, that the lamb was roasting somewhere, and would be set out too—'With bitter herbs shall ye eat it'—and so if there be bitter herbs, the dainty dish is near" (Spurgeon). 2. *That the two come from the same hand.* If there be a designed proportion then, not two independent minds are at work, but one only; ratio and proportion ever argue unity of mind. There is not an evil god who hurls sorrow upon men, and another a gracious God who sends only joy. That was the old Manichæan heresy, which is not dead yet. But the truth is that there is a likeness, a proportion between the good which God sends upon his people and the evil he has brought upon them. From one hand both come. But—

V. THE RATIO IS NOT EQUAL FOR THE CHILD OF GOD. "Our light affliction, which is but for a moment, worketh for us a far more exceeding and eternal weight of glory." The proportion of the evil we suffer to the good we shall enjoy is not that of equals, but that of the very little to the infinitely great.

VI. THE RELATIONSHIP ALSO IS THAT OF MOTHER AND CHILD. Sorrow is the mother of joy. Cf. our Lord's own metaphor: "A woman when she is in travail hath sorrow, because her hour is come: but as soon as she is delivered of the child she remembereth no more the anguish, for joy that a man is born into the world." "Weeping may endure for a night, but joy cometh in the morning." Cf. also above: "Our light afflic-tion . . . worketh for us," etc., so that joy is begotten of sorrow.

VII. BUT THIS CAN ONLY BE FOR THE CHILD OF GOD. Therefore—

> "Help, Lord, that we may come
> To thy saints' happy home,
> Where a thousand years
> As one day appears;
>   Nor go
> Where one day appears
> As a thousand years
>   For woe!"

C.

Vers. 6—15.—Jeremiah showing his faith by his works. Jeremiah, as a prophet of Jehovah, had not only to utter warnings and predictions, but to show, on needful occa-sion, that he himself believed in them. He who would have others obey the Lord, must keep on persuading them to obedience by being prominent in obedience himself. Observe—

I. HOW THE LORD PREPARES JEREMIAH AGAINST A DIFFICULTY. Hanameel, we may take it, was coming in any case with this proposition of purchase, and, but for the Divine warning, might have come on the prophet unexpectedly, so that he would hardly know what to do. There may have been many considerations to perplex Jeremiah. But all perplexities were removed by a plain commandment. Moreover, Jeremiah was helped to come into an obedient and restful mood of mind by the very fact that the visit of his relative was foretold. He was made to feel that God's eye was on him—on his ways, his needs, his difficulties. Things he himself could not prepare for, God prepared for. Instead of the prophet having to ask, "Shall I buy or shall I not?" his way was made clear by a plain commandment. And surely we have here an indication how God ever watches over his true servants. We make difficulties greater than they otherwise would be by neglecting to ascertain whether there be not some clear expression of God's will concerning them.

II. THE EXAMPLE HERE GIVEN TO US OF THE OBEDIENCE OF FAITH. Jeremiah, left to himself, might very well have said that this was no time either for buying or selling. The King of Babylon's army would soon have the whole country, and where then could be the worth of purchases and contracts? Let us for a moment suppose there had been no Divine commandment at all, and that Jeremiah had been left to his own judgment to decide on Hanameel's demand. If he had refused to buy, then there would not have been wanting those to exclaim that Jeremiah, so eloquent about the neglected duties of others, was shirking his own duties. On the other hand, if he had bought, then he would have been viewed with suspicion, as not really believing, after all, in the alienation of the land to Babylon. And of course, actually buying as he did, no doubt some sarcastic criticisms were made on his conduct. But then, through all, he was secure in the certainty that he was doing God's will. The transaction, however inconsistent or ridiculous it might look to others, was really one of the most prudent and well-based that ever man engaged in. Jeremiah himself could not well see how things were going to come right again, but he trusted in the foresight and omnipotence of Jehovah.—Y.

Ver. 33.—*Man's neglect of God's teaching.* I. GOD'S ATTITUDE AS A TEACHER TOWARDS MAN. God's complaint is that man turns to him the back and not the face. Hence we are to understand that God turns his face to us, full of meaning and very earnestly. Consider that expression, "I will guide thee with mine eye." Of course all such expressions are purely anthropomorphic, but behind them there is the truth that, when God speaks to us, it is in the same way as we do when we are most earnest and concerned in speaking. We speak then in every feature.

II. GOD'S ASSIDUITY AS A TEACHER. Rising early and teaching them. The effort to make the people understand truth and duty is continuous and unremitting. Nothing was left undone that could be done, so far as the *Teacher's side* was concerned. Laws and symbols, great providences, great deliverances, great punitive visitations on other peoples, punishments of men like Korah and Achan and Saul, chastisements like those of David,—thus Israelite-history abounded in lessons from God. Here is instruction from the great Teacher to all teachers. God was ready to seize on every opportunity to give a lesson, for opportunity is a great part of success. And seeing that God is thus declared among his people as a great Teacher, we should look on the Old Testament as a lesson-book, and study how far it may be useful to us. For though we have our own peculiar lesson-book in the New Testament, yet even the New Testament becomes clearer the better we understand the Old.

III. MAN'S ATTITUDE AS SCHOLAR TOWARDS GOD. His proper attitude is with the face, eyes looking on the Teacher, an expression of interest manifested, ready with the lip to ask further instruction and explanation.

IV. THE FACES OF THESE PEOPLE WERE TURNED TO OTHER TEACHERS. The fact is, man must ever be learning from somebody; and Israel, with the back to God, had its face towards the priests of idolatry, the ministers of cruelty, and was obedient to all their worst instructions. Let every one who has truth to teach and heavenly light to give remember that he is a rival of those who teach falsehood, error, cruelty, vice, superstition. If he is not successful in teaching the principles that liberate the spirit, then others will be successful in leading it into the worst of bondage.—Y.

Vers. 36—41.—*The bonds of abiding attachment to God.* Jeremiah has seen the war prospect, and it is one of siege, captivity, and destruction. He speaks as one who has the long-threatened hour before his eyes (ver. 24). But God, looking from a higher point, sees the enduring bright result beyond. Observe in this passage—

I. GOD'S THOROUGH GOOD WILL TOWARDS HIS PEOPLE. His will is ever to show favour and do good to mankind. That will is always in action, but it can only be in manifestation when men themselves, by their spirit of submission to God and obedience to his directions, make such a manifestation possible. As he is thorough in his anger against the rebellious and idolatrous, so he is thorough in his favour towards the repentant. It is well that we should ever remember this deep good will of God to men when things are going wrong with us. The fault of untoward experiences may be in us or it may be in others; it cannot be in God. We must not put down to arbitrariness in him the painful workings of that law which manifests itself in sequence to human ignorance and folly.

II. GOD'S SUFFICIENT OPPORTUNITY TO DO GOOD TO HIS PEOPLE. The confident tone that runs through this passage is most encouraging. Bad as the people have been, far as they have been driven, widely as they have been scattered, God can put all right again if only the people are willing to have it so. All God waits for is to hear the prodigal nation say, "I will arise and go to my Father." If only *we* give God the opportunity, he will make us to abound in supplies for our necessities and blessedness. We let many opportunities slip for doing good, and never do we use any such opportunity to the full. But God delights in the opportunities men give him, and here is an illustration of how he presses forward to use them. "I will plant them in this land assuredly with my whole heart and with my whole soul." Only be willing to be a plant of God's own planting, and there is no reason why you should not feel the whole heart and soul of God going out for your highest good.

III. GOD WORKING TOWARDS THE UNITY OF HIS PEOPLE. One is reminded of the unity proclaimed in Eph. iv. 3—6: one God, one people, one heart, one way, one covenant because an everlasting one, one character for the future. This unity stands out in contrast to the previous scattering. The previous scattering was only an outward symbol of the scattering within. If even the people had continued in Jerusalem, that would have given them no unity save the unity of place, which is the most precarious, mocking, and delusive of all unities. But the new unity is that of one heart. As one life flows through all the organs of the body, making the life of each the life of all and the life of all the life of each, so God will make it among his true people. God binds each to himself by the law written in the heart, and so all are bound to one another.

IV. THE EVERLASTING COVENANT THUS MADE POSSIBLE. God has now found something deep in the heart of his people whereby he can get an abiding hold. His covenant finds a firm anchorage in the regenerated inward man. With one heart and one way there is a starting-point for doing Divine good, not to one generation, but to many. How much good we may hinder by our spiritual blindness and indifference! And on the other hand, what copious showers of blessing may be the result of a timely turning to God!—Y.

Ver. 42.—*Evil the measure of good.* I. WITH REGARD TO CERTAINTY. Here is evil actually upon the city and country. Evil that has come, not in some inexplicable, unexpected way, but in correspondence with prophetic announcements, extending over a long time and frequently repeated. And now out of the very perceived certainty of this evil, God takes occasion to create ground of hope and encouragement for the people. He who without fail has sent chastisement for the disobedient will equally without fail keep all his promises to the obedient. It is the principle of sowing and reaping. The harvest will assuredly be according to the seed that is sown. We have the choice of alternatives, and only of alternatives. Either by our negligence we shall lay ourselves open to have God bring great evils upon us, or by our obedience and regard we shall receive all that great good which God promises to those who obey.

II. WITH REGARD TO AGENCY. The emphasis of the verse is especially upon the agent. Those who fail to see that it is God who has brought all this great evil will fail to get much comfort from his most comprehensive and gracious promises. Behind the unseen instruments we must see the unseen Director and Controller. We must try to trace out the wrath of God in manifestation against the unrighteousness of men. As we trace the miseries that come from human selfishness and self-indulgence, we must learn to see God in them—God as well as man; we must recognize righteous law as well as wicked folly. We are not to depend for the best things upon uncertain man, but upon God, with his unvarying love, his exhaustless power.

III. WITH REGARD TO EXTENT. One would not wish for its own sake to measure the height, and depth, the breadth, and length, of human misery, but we have to do it to estimate its cause and bring about its cure. And always the peril is to look upon it superficially and hastily. Now, by this very superficiality and haste we miss a great source of gladness. For our estimate of possible good must have for one of its elements our experience of actual evil. A man must sink low if he would rise high. We do not mean, of course, that he must sink low by an exceptionally depraved and vicious life; that would be to recommend what Paul denounces—sinning in order that grace may abound. We must sink low in our estimate of ourselves. We must see that, unless we also repent, a great evil will inevitably come upon us, whereas, if we are wisely obedient, we shall be the recipients of a splendid good—a good which ever has its forerunners in the gracious promises of God.—Y.

EXPOSITION.

CHAPTER XXXIII.

A chapter of promises, having reference, first, to the people and kingdom in general (vers. 4—13), and then to the royal and priestly offices in particular (vers. 14—26). The first part is but the expansion of passages in the preceding prophecy, to which this chapter is attached by the opening verse. The remaining portion is less closely connected; it is occupied by promises of the perpetual duration of the house of David and of the Levites. It should be noticed by the student that there are difficulties connected with the authorship of vers. 14, 26 (see below).

Ver. 1.—**In the court of the prison**; rather, *of the guard* (ch. xxxii. 2).

Ver. 2.—**Thus saith the Lord, the Maker thereof**, etc.; rather, *Thus saith Jehovah, who doeth it, Jehovah who frameth it that he may establish it, whose name is Jehovah.* It was needless to express the object of the verbs. Jehovah's great purpose is the regeneration of his people. To "frame" or "form" is synonymous with "purpose" (see on ch. xviii. 11). The meaning of the verse is that Jehovah's very Name is a pledge of his fidelity to his promises (comp. ch. xxxii. 18). To "establish" is synonymous with to carry out."

Ver. 3.—**Mighty things**; rather, *secret things* (literally, *inaccessible*). It must be admitted that this introduction hardly corresponds to the sequel, which does not contain any special secrets, as we should have thought. Either vers. 2, 3 have been inserted by a later (inspired) editor, whose mind was absorbed in high thoughts of the latter days—for this view may be urged the style and phraseology, which are hardly those of the surrounding chapters, hardly those of Jeremiah; or else we must adopt Hengstenberg's perhaps over-subtle suggestion, which, however, does not touch the question of the phraseology, "that throughout Scripture dead knowledge is not regarded as knowledge; that the hope of restoration had, in the natural man, in the prophet, as well as in all believers, an enemy who strove to darken and extinguish it; that therefore it was ever new," or, in the words of Jeremiah, "great and secret things, which thou knowest not."

Vers. 4—9.—The houses of Jerusalem, destroyed by the engines of the besiegers or filled with dead bodies, shall be restored; the captives shall be brought back; their sins shall be forgiven, and God be glorified.

Ver. 4.—**By the mounts, and by the sword**; rather, *because of the mounds* (see on ch. xxxii. 24) *and because of the weapons of war.* The latter are the warlike instruments used by the besiegers from their batteries or breastworks.

Ver. 5.—**They come to fight with the Chaldeans, but it is**, etc. The passage is obscure, so obscure that we cannot avoid inferring that it is corrupt. "They come" could only refer to the Jews, but these would rather be said to "go out;" the Hebrew writers are particular in distinguishing between to "come" and to "go out." Besides, there is no grammatical connection with the preceding verse. The Septuagint omits "they come," but the passage still remains enigmatical.

Ver. 6.—**I will bring it health and cure**, etc. "Health" is properly the fresh skin which grows over a healing wound (as ch. viii. 22; xxx. 17). First the city is spoken of, then its inhabitants. **Will reveal unto them**; or perhaps, *will roll unto them* (comp. ch. xi. 20; xx. 12). In this case the figure will be that of a mighty stream (comp. Amos v. 24; Isa. xlviii. 18; lxvi. 12). **Truth**; rather, *continuance* (comp. ch. xiv. 13).

Ver. 7.—**I will cause the captivity . . . to return** (see on ch. xxix. 14). **Will build them** (see on ch. xxxi. 14).

Ver. 8.—**I will cleanse them**, etc. Restored prosperity without spiritual purification would be of no avail; how could it give happiness (comp. ch. xxxi. 34)?

Ver. 9.—**And it shall be**; viz. Jerusalem. **A name of joy**; rather, on the analogy of Isa. lv. 13, etc., *a monument of joy;* i.e. joy-giving. **They shall fear and tremble.** As feeling the contrast between their "unprofitable" idol-gods and the faithful God of Israel.

Ver. 10.—**In this place**; *i.e.* "in this land," as in ch. vii. 7 and elsewhere. **Shall be desolate**; rather, *is desolate.*

Ver. 11.—**The sacrifice of praise** (see on ch. xvii. 26).

Ver. 12.—**An habitation**; rather, *a pasture* (including the idea of an encampment). The expression reminds us of ch. xxiii. 3, 4, but it is preferable to take the present passage in its literal sense rather than as metaphorical.

Ver. 13.—**In the cities**, etc. A parallel description to ch. xvii. 26; xxxii. 44. **The vale**; rather, *the lowland* (about the Mediterranean, on the south). **The south.** It is the Negeb, or south country, which is meant.

Under the hands; rather, *at the beck.* **Of him that telleth** them. Comp. Milton, ' L'Allegro '—

" And every shepherd tells his tale
Under the hawthorn in the dale."

Virgil, ' Ecl.,' iii. 31—

'· Bisque die numerant ambo pecus, alter et hædos."

Vers. 14—26.—These verses are omitted in the Septuagint, and some leading critics think that both the style and the contents point to a different author from our prophet. In particular it is urged that the promise of a multitude of Levites and of descendants of David is isolated among the prophecies of Jeremiah, who elsewhere speaks of a single great representative of David as the object of pious hope, and of the intercourse between Jehovah and his people as being closer and more immediate than under the old Law. A variation in the form of expressing the Messianic hope is, however, not of much importance. Isaiah, for instance, sometimes refers to a single ideal king (ix. 6, etc.); sometimes to a succession of noble, God-fearing kings (xxxii. 1 ; xxxiii. 17).

Ver. 14.—**That good thing which I have promised**; viz. in the parallel passage, ch. xxiii. 5, 6 (which see).

Ver. 15.—**The Branch of righteousness;** rather, *the Plant of righteousness* (see on ch. xxiii. 5).

Ver. 16.—**Wherewith she shall be called ;** viz. Jerusalem ; in ch. xxiii. 6, the parallel passage, the subject is " Israel," unless there is a corruption of the text. **The Lord our righteousness;** rather, *The Lord (is) our righteousness.*

Ver. 17.—**David shall never want a man,** etc. This is, in fact, a republication of the promise given by Nathan in 2 Sam. vii. 12—16. It agrees in form with the announcements in 1 Kings ii. 4; viii. 25; ix. 5.

Ver. 18.—**Neither shall the priests the Levites,** etc. It has been thought that this passage is inconsistent with the prophecies of a time when the ark should no more be remembered (ch. iii. 16), and when all should know Jehovah from the least to the greatest (ch. xxxi. 34). But though sin offerings would in this glorious time become things of the past, yet thank offerings are expressly excepted from abolition (ver. 11), and

in ch. xxxi. 14 a special latter-day promise is given to the priests. Moreover, Ezekiel, who repeats the prophecy of the new spiritual covenant (xi. 19; xxxvi. 26; xxxvii. 26), gives an elaborate sketch of a new temple with a sacrificial system (ch. xl., etc.); and, if there is any inconsistency, we find the same one in the latter part of Isaiah. In Isa. lxi. 6 the whole regenerate people of Israel is called " the priests of Jehovah ; " but in Isa. lxvi. 21 the prophet distinctly states that there will be, in some sense, a priestly class within the chosen people.

Vers. 20—22.—The constant, regular succession of day and night is an emblem of the equally regular supply of royal descendants of David and of Levitical priests, and the countless grains of sand are symbolic of the wonderful increase of their numbers. At first sight the latter part of the promise seems a little unlike a blessing. But we have seen already (on ch. xix. 3) that the members of the various branches of the royal family probably occupied the principal offices of the state, and the prophet imagines the future in forms borrowed from the present. A numerous sacerdotal class seemed equally necessary for the due magnificence of the ritual ; and we must remember that preternatural fertility of the soil was a standing element of Messianic descriptions. The expressions used are, no doubt, hyperbolical, but the meaning seems clear enough. (Hengstenberg's notion, that the prophet rather indicates the abolition of the royal and sacerdotal distinctions (comp. Exod. xix. 6), is surely very far-fetched.)

Vers. 23—26.—The permanence of Israel as the people of God, with rulers of the house of David.

Ver. 24.—**This people ;** *i.e.* not Egyptians or Babylonians (as some have supposed), but the people of Judah, regarded as alienated from Jehovah (hence the touch of disparagement), as elsewhere in Jeremiah (ch. iv. 10, 11; v. 14, 23; vi. 19; vii. 33, etc.). There were unworthy Jews, who, seeing their nation fallen from its high estate, despaired of its deliverance and regeneration. **That they should be no more,** etc.; rather, *so that they are no more a people*—no more an independent people. The " two families," of course, are the " two houses of Israel " (Isa. viii. 14), *i.e.* the two kingdoms of Israel and Judah.

HOMILETICS.

Vers. 1—3.—*An invitation to prayer.* I. THE CIRCUMSTANCES OF THE INVITATION. (Ver. 1.) 1. It was to Jeremiah; *i.e.* (1) to a *good man.* All men may pray, but it is " the supplication of a righteous man that availeth much in its working " (Jas. v. 16) ; and (2) a *prophet.* Therefore a prophet needs to pray. No man knows so much or is so far advanced spiritually as to be able to dispense with prayer. Christ prayed. 2. The invitation came to Jeremiah *in prison.* Stone walls cannot shut out God from us, nor prevent our souls from rising in prayer to him. The persecutor cannot rob his victim of his choicest jewel. God often visits the soul in scenes of earthly distress. 3. The invitation came a *second time.* God repeatedly visits his troubled children. The prayer of yesterday will not make that of to-day needless. 4. The invitation to prayer *did not bring deliverance from trouble.* Though God visited Jeremiah in prison once and again, the prophet still remained there. We have no right to think that when God visits us for good he will remove our earthly trouble; he may find it better to bless us in it. Therefore, on the other hand, the continuance of the trouble is no evidence that we are deserted by God—perhaps the reverse, because " whom the Lord loveth he chasteneth."

II. The grounds of the invitation. (Ver. 2.) God gives to Jeremiah good grounds for assurance in prayer before inviting him to pray. We cannot pray to an unknown God with intelligence and earnestness. To pray with faith we must have grounds of confidence. These are offered to the prophet in the manifestation of the nature of God in his works, and the revelation of his higher character in the sacred Name, Jehovah. 1. The manifestation of God in *his works.* (1) He is the Maker of all things; therefore he has power to make all right again. (2) He *established* the world; therefore there is a permanence in the law, and will, and procedure of God, which no passing accidents can set aside. 2. The revelation of *his higher Name,* " Jehovah; " " The Lord in his Name." This revelation not only suggests the self-existent and eternal supremacy of God, so infinitely superior to all those evil powers of life feared by us timid mortals ; it is also associated with the willingness of God to save, since it was revealed in connection with the deliverance from Egypt (Exod. iii. 14), it may well be quoted in anticipation of the deliverance from Babylon.

III. The character of the invitation. (Ver. 3.) 1. God *invites to prayer.* Therefore (1) we may have good assurance that he will hear prayer; and (2) nevertheless, we are reminded that, though he is favourably disposed to us, he waits to bless us until we " call unto " him. 2. God *promises a revelation in response to prayer.* Here is an encouragement that the prayer will not be fruitless. The Bible does not represent prayer as a mere subjective exercise; it treats it as a power prevailing with God, securing from him blessings asked. We have here a special encouragement for the perplexed to pray for light. Mysteries are not necessarily eternally hidden. Some once hidden have been revealed (*e.g.* Col. i. 26); others may yet be made more clear. The seeker after truth should be a man of prayer. The deepest spiritual truth is not discoverable by speculation; it is revealed in communion. It is seen through spiritual thought and sympathy with God, aided by his Spirit's inspiration.

Ver. 6.—(See on ch. xxx. 17.)

Ver. 8.—*Forgiveness and cleansing.* I. Forgiveness and cleansing must be closely associated. When God pardons he also cleanses. The first justification that treats as righteous by forgiveness is the seed of the second justification that makes righteous. It is often noted that it would be neither just in God nor wholesome for us that sin should be pardoned without the creation of a clean heart. But we should observe further that it would not even be possible for this to happen. For the essence of forgiveness is reconciliation, not a mere remission of penalties. Even if these are remitted, while personal enmity is cherished there can be no forgiving. To forgive is to effect a mutual reconciliation after alienation through wrong-doing on one side, by concession on the other. The very act of reconciliation implies such a change in the person forgiven as involves the cessation of all opposition on his side. Now, in the root of it sin is just departure from God, and its ripe fruit is enmity to God. Forgiveness must, therefore, by its very nature, imply a cleansing from this sin.

II. God promises perfect cleansing and forgiveness. 1. This is *given by God.* He only can forgive, since it is against him that we have sinned. He only can cleanse, since only the Creator can create anew. 2. This is given *through Christ.* Hints of the means only appear in the Old Testament. The gospel revelation brings it more clearly before us (1 Pet. ii. 24). In the sight of the cross we see the great assurance of deliverance from sin in the revelation of the means by which this is brought about. Since Christ has died for our sins we have good reason to ask for forgiveness and cleansing. 3. The promised cleansing and forgiveness are *perfect*; i.e. (1) from all sins—none can be too black for the "Lord of all flesh" to overcome, for "is there anything too hard for him"? and (2) a complete deliverance—a forgiveness that forgets and bears no grudge, a cleansing that leaves no stain and produces a regeneration of life.

III. PERFECT FORGIVENESS AND CLEANSING ARE TO BE RECEIVED THROUGH REPENTANCE AND FAITH. 1. As God accomplishes the perfect deliverance from sin, it is foolish for us to begin a small and imperfect and certainly futile cleansing on our own account. But we must desire the justification and the pardon, else it is unreasonable to expect God to bestow them. This desire, real and active, is *repentance*. 2. Then must follow *faith*. It is not necessary for us to understand the *rationale* of the atonement in order to profit by the fruits of it. But it is necessary to trust in the Saviour. Faith is a very different thing from an intellectual comprehension and conviction of a complex set of doctrines. It is a personal trust. This trust is an essential condition of cleansing and forgiveness. Till we yield ourselves to the influence of God's grace, and trust to his love, we cannot expect him to deliver us.

Ver. 9.—*The Church an honour to God.* What is here promised to the Jews finds its fulfilment, not in the Jews alone, nor in them at all until they submit to the Christian influences of the new covenant, but in all the spiritual Israel—in the Church of Christ. I. CONSIDER THE FACT THAT THE CHURCH IS AN HONOUR TO GOD. It is described as a "monument of joy" because God takes delight in it (ch. xxxii. 41), and as "a praise and an honour" because by means of it God's glory is manifested abroad. This, in turn, is an honour to the Church. Though God picks his fallen children up from the mire of sin he does not leave them in shame and degradation. The prodigal is stripped of his rags and clothed with the best robe. God regards his Church, even here, with the stains of war and toil and sin upon her, as capable of manifesting forth his glory. What greater mission could she have? II. INQUIRE INTO THE SOURCES OF THIS HONOUR. How comes it that the Church is an honour to God? Her own excellences can scarcely be considered as glorious in themselves. It is not in the inherent worth of these that we find the secret of the glory given by the Church to God. The Church is formed by God, redeemed by his mercy, delivered by his power, maintained by his help. Her very existence is a witness to God's forgiving and restoring grace. All that she does for good is not accomplished by her own might, but through the inspiration of his Spirit. The picture is an honour to the painter because it is the fruit of his well-directed labour. We do not admire it only for its simple beauty. If it is a representation of the humblest scene in nature, the reality must be infinitely more beautiful than the picture; yet we give great admiration to the work of art because it is a work and because it reveals art. So the Church is an honour to God as the fruit of his work and of Christ's sacrifice. III. NOTE THE EFFECTS OF THIS HONOUR. 1. It is to impress the world. The Jews were a standing witness of the power and goodness of God to the neighbouring nations. The Church of Christ is called to a similar mission on a world-wide scale. The very existence of the Church as the ark upon the waters preserved and blessed by God is one of the greatest means of making known the grace and glory of redemption. More eloquent than any words is the silent testimony of the good and peaceful lives of godly men. 2. Therefore a great responsibility rests upon all Christians. God entrusts his honour to his Church. If, therefore, she can glorify him, she has also the power to bring dishonour on his Name. The "good soldier of Jesus Christ" is an honour to his Captain; but the sluggard, the coward, and the traitor are a discredit to his high name, and their faithlessness does something to smirch the beauty of the banner of redemption.

Vers. 10—13.—*Town and country life.* In describing the happy future of Israel after the restoration Jeremiah draws a pair of idyllic pictures of town and country life. Both the city of Jerusalem and the outlying regions were so depopulated and wasted by the Chaldean invasion that it was difficult to believe the sun of prosperity would ever shine on them again. But under the providence of God there is a wonderful recuperative power in the human world as well as in the natural. It is remarkable how soon the battle-field with its hideous relics becomes a flowery meadow. The rapid revival of the French nation after the war of 1870 was an astonishment to Europe. This may be accounted for partly on natural principles, since war rarely touches the permanent resources of a country; if it drains the stream, it does not stanch the fountain-head. The capital of a country is always being consumed and remade in peaceful times, so that the destruction of it in war is not so great a calamity as might appear at first sight. But a true revival of prosperity depends on higher causes. A nation is only really prosperous when its people are advancing in moral tone, when there is a Divine root to their recovery. This is implied in the description of restored Israel. Let us consider the two pictures of the restoration.

I. TOWN LIFE. In the happy city described by Jeremiah there is a repopulation of the deserted streets. What a melancholy sight is a city in ruins, silent and solitary! The very suggestion of life and bustle increases the gloom of the unnatural stillness that haunts the place. The first step towards restoration is to bring back the inhabitants. The strength of a nation resides ultimately in its population. No empire has yet been ruined through over-population; many, from Rome downwards, by the decay of population. There was a great economic truth in the Hebrew estimate of the value of a thickly inhabited country. In the city we see this concentrated. That is a human world in itself. If man is a social being, if co-operation and sympathy are good things, there we may look for true advancing prosperity. But the congregation of human beings in a city aggravates the evils of life when these are not restrained. In the city disease, misery, vice, and crime find their victims. The saddest sight in modern civilization (?) is the wretched condition of the back slums of the greatest cities of Europe, and the moral state of too much of the remainder. Men do not find prosperity and happiness by merely crowding together. In Jeremiah's picture of the new Jerusalem there is no room for those ugly scenes that Victor Hugo and Dickens make familiar in their representations of Paris and London. There is joy. There is worship. There is sacrifice and devotion to God. When the temple is the true centre of the city, when religion presides over her commerce and her pleasure, then, and then only, can true happiness be enjoyed by the citizens.

II. COUNTRY LIFE. Jeremiah paints a companion picture of country life with skilful adaptation of parallels and contrasts. The scene is pastoral. Prosperity is witnessed in quiet industry and growing wealth of flocks and herds. Such a life is no more idle than that of the city—often less so, and it is more calm. The stimulus of competition and the aid of co-operation are lost, but the reflections of solitude are gained; communion with nature takes the place of communion with man. This may be an ideal state of happiness to him who knows how to enjoy it. Both forms of life will be blessed when rightly followed; neither when abused. Dr. Johnson showed his wisdom in appreciating the merits of town life, but Cowper had good reasons for preferring the country. Country life has its vices, its ignorance, narrowness, and brutality, its poverty and lonely distresses. This also needs a higher life to keep it pure and happy. The Christian may find good in whichever condition his lot is cast, since God can bless both to him.

Ver. 15.—"*The Branch of righteousness.*" If these words were intended by the prophet to refer to a succession of kings the promise they contain is nevertheless fulfilled in one, and one only, Jesus Christ. The glory of redeemed Israel is to find its consummation in the restoration of the throne of David with righteous government. The true glory of redemption is seen in the righteous rule of Christ. Much of what is taught here is similar to the suggestions of a former passage (ch. xxiii. 5). But the verse before us has also some lessons of its own, viz.—

I. CHRIST IS A BRANCH (OR SPROUT) OF RIGHTEOUSNESS. He is of the stock of David, preserving the tradition and inheriting the rights of the royal family. But he is far above the old kings in character as well as in nature. Jeremiah repeatedly insisted on a fact that is only too apparent in the historical books of the Old Testament —the fact that the ruin of Israel was largely due to the bad conduct of her kings. Christ is the one perfectly righteous King. This righteousness of Christ is of great significance. 1. It secures and justifies his position. There is no reason to depose him as there was to depose many of the ancient kings. 2. It gives him great claims for honour and obedience from his subjects. Such a king deserves loyal service. 3. It gives worth to his sacrifice. Christ is a Priest as well as a King—the Melchisedec of the New Testament. When he intercedes for the world, and so redeems to himself "a people of acquisition" (1 Pet. ii. 9), his righteousness affords weight to his pleading." 4. It makes his example to be of supreme authority. As the righteous King he is the type of what the righteous subject should be. A further inference, drawn by the prophet himself, is worth more extended notice.

II. CHRIST MAINTAINS A RIGHTEOUS GOVERNMENT. Under a personal rule the character of the administration is an exact reflex of the character of the monarch. We see in the history of the Jews how bad conduct in the kings meant iniquitous treatment of the subjects. Christ, the righteous King, will necessarily rule righteously. From this fact certain important consequences flow. 1. Negatively, Christ will abolish the injustice under which many of his people suffer. It may be necessary that the process shall be slow. But it must be accomplished in the golden future. Meanwhile it is a consolation for the wronged to feel that even now they are not unfairly dealt with by their great Master; and surely to the Christian Christ's behaviour should be far more important than anything the world may do. 2. Positively, Christ will maintain the right, and effectually rebuke the wrong within his kingdom; he is a King as well as a Saviour, and a righteous King executing judgment. Mild and gentle, he is yet holy and firm. The Christian who would enjoy the favour of his Master must win his approval by loyal obedience and pure living. Christ is no lax and careless Monarch. It would be ill for his Church if he were so. 3. Christ will lead his people into righteousness. He rules in righteousness, not only to execute justice, but to make his people righteous. This is the highest idea of righteous government. How do we stand in relation to this righteous kingship of Christ? Are we submitting to it for our own improvement and his glory? Are we ignoring, or resisting, or dishonouring it only to bring a judgment from the righteous God upon our heads? Let the careless remember that the Saviour is a King and a Judge.

Ver. 16.—(See on ch. xxiii. 6.)

Vers. 19—26.—*Nature's aids to faith.* We see faith and science flung into conflict. In the Bible they not only harmonize, but science is regarded as a stay to faith, and nature, instead of being treated as a hindrance to faith, is repeatedly called in to strengthen it. As science advances old formulæ are necessarily discarded. But may we not approach the difficulties of our age in the spirit of the Bible, and hope for some large synthesis which shall restore the old relation of science as the handmaid of religion? In the mean time the general correspondences suggested by Jeremiah are as true now as they were in his day.

I. THE PERMANENCE OF NATURE IS AN ASSURANCE OF THE PERMANENCE OF GRACE. The same God rules in the physical and spiritual spheres. In the one he is not capricious and uncertain. Why should we fear his being so in the other? Night, tempest, winter—things dark and wild—do not set aside the eternal ordinances of beneficent nature. The blue sky survives the black cloud that hides it for a season only to reveal it the more clearly after shedding itself in thunder-showers. Why, then, should we think that the heavenly grace of God's love should be less enduring? If the ordinances of nature fail we may expect the same of the covenant of grace, but not till then, since both depend on the same Divine endurance.

II. THE SUCCESSIONS OF NATURE ARE PLEDGES OF THE SUCCESSIONS OF GRACE. Nature is ever changing, though changing according to uniform laws. In spiritual experience we meet with change. Neither of God's kingdoms is a Chinese empire. Progress marks both; and progress means change. But the change, though it alters events, does not alter principles; it only develops them to fuller exercise. Do the changes of life make us fear the loss of God's blessing? Let us remember that the changes in nature do not upset its laws. Our experience varies, but God's love is changeless. He shows this love, however, rather by a succession of blessings than by maintaining present blessings unaltered. So is it in nature—day and night, summer and winter, alternate. To-day's grace will not last for to-morrow; but new grace will be bestowed then if we seek it. The succession does not fail in nature, nor will it in grace.

III. THE ABUNDANCE OF NATURE IS A PROMISE OF THE ABUNDANCE OF GRACE. We cannot count the stars. Can we count the contents of our own world? of one small section of it? The great and multitudinous variety of nature was a wonder to the ancient Hebrews. How much more wonderful is it to us! There we see no failing of resources, but an infinite abundance, an almost reckless prodigality that sometimes shocks our economic notions, founded as they are on the requirements of limited means, but not applicable to an infinite wealth. Why then should we fear that the fountains of grace that flow from the same God should ever run dry? God administers his grace with a royal bounty. There is enough for all; there is abundance for each.

HOMILIES BY VARIOUS AUTHORS.

Ver. 1.—(Cf. ch. xxxii. 1—5.)—M.

Vers. 1—3.—*Revelation of God's purpose to him who performs his will.* Jeremiah had resolutely witnessed to the truth, and now he was confined in the king's prison in order to his being silenced. But so far from the Divine communications being less frequent, they were more so, and, if possible, more weighty and important. The word of the Lord came to him the *second* time (ver. 1), and a gracious revelation of God's power and willingness to bless.

I. GOD IS WITH THOSE WHO SUFFER FOR HIS SAKE. It was a token of his love that Jeremiah should receive this assurance, and one which he was most certain to appreciate. Prisoners and martyrs for conscience' sake in all ages of the Church have been similarly consoled. There are special and peculiar consolations for persons so situated. God is nearer then than at other times. His promises are greater and brighter, and his presence more felt. Who would not suffer thus to be thus comforted?

II. GOD REQUESTS US TO ASK OF HIM THE THINGS WE MOST DESIRE. Not that there are not circumstances of such a character as to call forth spontaneous proofs of his favour and love. But seeking and asking are exercises of faith, which cannot long be dispensed with in our intercourse with our heavenly Father, even although "he knoweth what things we have need of before we ask him" (Matt. vi. 8). And this because: 1. *The exercises of the soul in prayer and faith are greater benefits in themselves than most things that are to be procured through them.* 2. *Such exercises are a preparation of the soul for heavenly gifts and communications, and keep it in readiness for them.* 3. *They are pleasing to God, and gratify his love.* The answer is certain, and, indeed, waiting; but he loves to be asked. There is no more endearing position in the sight of God than that of prayer.

III. THOSE WHO FAITHFULLY OBEY GOD'S WILL WILL LEARN SOMETHING OF HIS PURPOSE. Revelations of surpassing magnitude await the prophet in the darkness of his prison-house. He did not hesitate to proclaim God's will, and to submit to the consequences of so doing; he is to receive his reward in further disclosures. And these are of the most gracious and consolatory description. But apart from this, the mere communication of the Divine purpose to him was a sign of favour and honour; his truest satisfaction and peace were to be found in hearing God's voice, and being considered worthy to share the secrets of the Divine future. Man is steward of the present; God retains his hold upon the future, and only discloses it for the reward of faithful men, and for great and merciful ends. 1. *Great* things, in their scope, character, and influences as belonging to salvation. 2. *Secret things* (Authorized Version renders this word "mighty"). Not belonging to ordinary experience, but to God's counsel.—M.

Vers. 15, 16.—(*Vide* on ch. xxiii. 5, 6.)—M.

Vers. 17, 18.—*Perpetuation of the kingly and priestly stock.* I. THE SIGNIFICANCE OF THESE OFFICES. To single out these two offices from the others existing within the Jewish nation is to emphasize their importance. They are thereby recognized as the pillars of the theocratic constitution. 1. *The king.* The grandest unit of human society. Evidently no accidental office, but an ordained and significant one. The king, as representative of God, was the supreme authority of the state. As the chosen of God, or as legitimately descended from such a one, he ruled by Divine right. He was the centre of patriotic attachment, and the authoritative embodiment and enforcer of Divine righteousness—at least that was the ideal. How few of the princes of the Davidic succession realized this the history of Judah can witness. But it was ever held before the people as a sacred promise that a "king should reign in righteousness." 2. *The priest.* The covenant of priesthood was a covenant of *peace* (Numb. xxv. 12), of *life and peace* (Mal. ii. 5). It was the mediatorial or reconciling element in the constitution—that through which the nation in its individual citizens, and as a whole, was related acceptably with God, and made partaker of his righteousness. The consecration of the priesthood in a mediate sense sanctified the people; and in the continued existence of the priesthood a guarantee was afforded of the favour of God and the permanence of Israel's mission as the righteous servant of God.

II. How THE PROMISE WAS FULFILLED. What is actually predicted concerning the Davidic and Levitical succession is that it will never be quite cut off; it will never happen that there is wanting any one in whom the house may be perpetuated. In the Captivity such a gap took place: *Jeconiah was written childless.* But it was never to occur again. Now, how are we to understand this promise? In its literal sense it was only approximately fulfilled; spiritually and figuratively the fulfilment was complete: 1. *In our Lord Jesus Christ.* Of the house of David after the flesh, he is eternal King and Lord of the spiritual Israel. He is also "a Priest for ever after the order of Melchisedec." As the great High Priest of mankind, he appears before God "making continual intercession" (Heb. viii. 3). 2. *Christians, too, realize the ideal here presented.* Through the atoning work of Christ they are made "kings and priests," a "royal priesthood" (1 Pet. ii. 5—8). The identification of the Lord with his servant dignifies and ennobles the latter, making him a new centre of spiritual dominion and of intercessory and reconciling influence. "If we suffer [endure] we shall also reign with him" (2 Tim. ii. 12) is a promise which looks forward to the completion of the Messianic kingdom. The Levitical priesthood, too, is lost and absorbed in the priestly character of Christ and his people.—M.

Vers. 19—22.—*The covenant of God permanent as the laws of nature.* A curious inversion of Gen. viii. 22, but very instructive. There, what is considered by the secular mind as secured by the laws of matter operating mechanically, is declared as a promise, and consequently as dependent upon the good will and gracious purpose of God; here, what appears at first to be within the power of one or both parties to it, is stated to be as absolute and permanent as if it were not a moral engagement but a material law. Accepting, as in vers. 17 and 18, the Messianic as the true fulfilment of this prediction, what do we learn?

I. THE INTRINSIC POWER OF GOD'S WORD. The creative fiat was omnipotent; the promise is to be not less so. It is as if a power dwelt within it to bring to pass what it declares. Of course this is not so in the one case any more than in the other. God is in his Word, making it effectual even to its remotest end. We are reminded of Christ's utterance, "Heaven and earth shall pass away, but my words shall not pass away," which seems to make an even stronger assertion. Equally potent is the Word of God in the gospel, its warnings, invitations, and transforming energies.

II. THE ABSOLUTE, ETERNAL SIGNIFICANCE OF THE PERSON AND WORK OF CHRIST. The human element in the Divine covenant relation has ever been the variable and uncertain one. But through the unique personality of the God-Man, and of his atoning sacrifice, that element is strengthened and made secure. An incarnation like that of Emmanuel, an act like the death on the cross, once achieved is irreversible, and its consequences must affect the remotest eternity. The spiritual laws comprehended and illustrated in the transactions of the gospel are as irreversible as those of nature; and in the person and work of Christ there is an objective basis presented that can never be destroyed by the weaknesses or unbelief of men, any more than "my covenant of the day, and my covenant of the night."

III. THE SPIRITUAL INFLUENCE OF THE NEW COVENANT. (Ver. 22.) It is really a creative word, because it calls into existence the Church or community of believers, who are the true successors of the seed of David and the Levitical priesthood. In its constant triumphs and the ever-increasing nature of the Messianic kingdom, fresh

securities are given for the perpetuation of the kingly and priestly functions as developed through the grace of God in human nature. Where the gospel is faithfully
preached, and spiritual life truly energizes, believers will, as at Pentecost, be "added
daily" and "multiplied." It is like *leaven,* a *seed,* etc. As appealing to the deepest
needs and yearnings of human nature, it is bound to overcome the world and comprehend the whole race within the zone of its influence. "So shall my word be that goeth
forth out of my mouth ; it shall not return unto me void, but it shall accomplish that
which I please, and it shall prosper *in the thing* whereto I sent it " (Isa. lv. 11).—M.

Ver. 3.—*The reasonableness of prayer.* "Call *upon* me, and I will answer thee," etc.
This is one of the blessed promises of God given for the help of sorrowful and struggling
men. None but God knows how many have been helped by it and by the glorious
throng of Divine words which are like unto it, or how often, or how mightily. "Ah!
you think so," replies a voice not unfrequently nor too modestly heard in these days.
'Tis the voice of the disciples of science, which says, "Yes ; you religious people think
God answers your prayers and hears you when you call upon him ; but really it is no
such thing ; it is all a mistake, and, what is more, you ought to know and confess it,
and therefore give over what you are pleased to call your prayers. Prayer! how is
such a thing possible in a universe governed everywhere by fixed laws as ours is ?
Where in such an order is there room for what you call 'answers to prayer'? It is
scientifically impossible, not to say absurd, and the marvel is that people don't see
this." So speak, and some of them with far more of arrogance and scorn than now represented, not a few of the scientists of the day. The calling upon God in the day of
trouble is nothing more, so one of the most distinguished of modern philosophers has
said, than the piteous cry of the hare when she knows that the hounds are upon her.
A bitter cry of distress wrung out from the soul. It is thought by those who utter
it to go up to God, and that God will hear it and help; but that is all a vain imagination ;
it goes out into mere space ; nothing does come of it, and nothing can. This is what is
said, and it is based upon the observed uniformity and inflexibility of law. All science
is built up upon this faith of the unbroken order and regularity of law, and without it
there could be no science, and indeed no life at all. The reign of law is everywhere ;
how then can prayer be reasonable ? and where is there room for those Divine interpositions which prayer asks for and thinks it receives ? What is the use, then, of the
mother weeping her heart out in her prayers that God would give back the health of
her beloved child ? What the use of national fasts and days of prayer for rain, for
removal of pestilence, for restoration of the health of princes, and the like ? If these
things lie in the order of fixed law, they will come to pass without any prayer; if not,
they will not be in spite of all the prayers of all the Churches in all the world. Now,
this is what is so loudly and largely being said on all sides. What have we to reply ?
Has the Christian preacher nought to urge on the other side ? We think he has. He
has a right to ask the scientists such questions as these—

I. Has science discovered all God's fixed laws? Are you quite sure that
nowhere there may be some law which shall provide for these results which Christians
call "answers to prayer"? We are bound to be grateful for the magnificent discoveries
of the laws of the universe which science has already made. But has it discovered *all*
these laws? and if not, why amongst those as yet undiscovered ones may there not be
that which the Christian needs to justify his prayer? It is the same argument as
John Foster urges against the atheistic doctrine that there is no God! "What ages
and lights are requisite for this attainment, the *knowing* that there is no God! This
intelligence involves the very attributes of divinity, while a God is denied. For unless
this man is omnipresent, unless he is at this moment in every place in the universe, he
cannot know but that in some place there may be manifestations of a Deity by which
even *he* would be overpowered. . . . Unless he knows all things, that is, precludes
another deity by being one himself, he cannot *know* that the Being whose existence he
rejects does not exist." Now, in like manner, the Christian may meet the scientific
unbeliever by asking him whether he has traced every effect up to its cause. May
not, then, the cause you do not know be the one which meets the Christian's need and
secures answer to his legitimate prayers ?

II. What more right has science to reject the facts from which the Christian

DEDUCES HIS DOCTRINE THAT GOD ANSWERS PRAYER, THAN THE CHRISTIAN HAS TO REJECT THE FACTS UPON WHICH SCIENCE BASES HER DOCTRINE OF INVARIABLE LAW? Science marshals her facts. They are a goodly array, and drawn from all departments of creation, animate and inanimate; from all kinds of living organisms, whether animal or vegetable; and they have forced upon you, we readily admit, the conviction of the universality and invariability of natural law. Christians are bound to believe you. We are not going to question your facts, though we may some of your inferences from them. Let your facts once be proved to be facts, as so many of them have been, and we will candidly accept them. Yes, though they compel us to set aside some old and cherished interpretations of Scripture, and to confess that we have read our Bibles wrongly in more than one instance. We trust you in your statement of facts; we believe you to be good men and true. Now we turn and ask you to deal with us and our facts in like manner. For we, too, have facts from which we have drawn the conclusion that, let prayer be according to the will of God, he will assuredly answer it. Some of our facts which have much force with us you perhaps would not admit, since you would explain them on the ground of mere coincidence, and we could not prove that, apart from prayer, they could not have been. *E.g.* persons in distress have called upon God; relief has unexpectedly come and in very remarkable ways. The believer looks on such instances as answers to prayer; nothing can persuade him that they are not. Still, it cannot be denied that they *may* have occurred without such prayer. Other such instances are those in which life despaired of has been given back in answer to, or in connection with, fervent prayer for such restoration; as the Prince of Wales's recovery in 1872. Now, this recovery *might* have been—we cannot prove that it could not—apart from prayer, and therefore, whilst these instances are very convincing to the believer, they are not so to others. But there are facts concerning which we can say they are valid for our argument, because they never have occurred and never do occur, apart from prayer. *E.g.* in the coming away of any soul from its attachment to the world to surrender itself in trust and love to Christ—that which is called conversion; was this ever known apart from prayer? Did ever any find the Lord without seeking him—*i.e.* without prayer? Also in the ordinary conduct of the Christian life, who among us is able to keep his garments unspotted from the world, to overcome besetting sin, to confront and conquer temptation, to preserve the hands clean and the heart pure, without continual prayer? Again, who are they that have attained to a high degree of spiritual life and vigour, to whom it is their habit to walk with God; who "rejoice in the Lord always;" who are God's saints indeed, the very elect, about whose being born of God we have no doubt? Now, every one of these will tell you that they owed their all to the habit their Lord enabled them to maintain of constant prayer. Press on in thought to the realms of the blest, move up and down amid the throng of God's redeemed; is there one who has or could have attained that blessedness if on earth he had not sought God in prayer and called on the Name of the Lord? So with any really living Church, a Church that is a power for good, a blessing to the neighbourhood, a Church at peace, at work, and blessed with the prosperity of God, is the life of such a Church ever possible apart from this same power of prayer? Its life is nurtured, not by its wealth, numbers, rank, culture, intellect, eloquence, or any such gifts, but by its prayers. All the rest would let it starve; by prayer alone it lives. One other instance—the winning of our children for God. Does any parent or teacher ever secure this great joy without prayer? Never. Such are our facts; in them we are sure that God answers prayer; and hence we believe also that in the material world he does the same. And as we receive the facts of science, so we ask that our facts may be received likewise.

III. IS NOT GOD OUR FATHER? The scientific hypothesis denies his fatherhood, if not his very existence altogether. If he do exist, he is, according to the scientist, so enclosed in his own laws and in the visible adjustment of things that he has no room for freedom of choice, for exercise of will. Like the mainspring of a watch, he is shut up in his own works, and can only act in one given way. Or, like the locomotives on our railways, he must keep to the rigid appointed iron track, and not swerve therefrom in the least. But that is not our conception of God. We believe him to have a mind, a will, a heart; and hence we conclude that, like the best earthly parents, whilst keeping ever in view the true welfare of his children, he yet allows himself, *within those limits*, freedom of action as may seem to him wisest and best. Now, within these limits there is room for prayer and room for answers to prayer. We cannot believe him to be so tied down by his physical laws that, when it is consistent with the highest good of his children, and yet more when it is necessary for that good, he is unable to modify or alter them even though he would. A God so bound by physical law is really no God, and the creed of the atheist will alone harmonize with the assertions of science. If there be a God, he must be a personal God; but if he be a Person, then he must have will, the power of choice; but if he have will, he must be able to modify the action of his laws, as we can and do continually; and if he be our Father, as we believe, then we need not doubt that the fervent believing prayer of his children will avail much to induce him to modify his laws for our good. And hence we maintain that it is good to call upon him, and that he is nigh unto such and will save them. Prayer, then, is not unreasonable if there be a God; not unreasonable if we adopt the very methods of science itself, and deduce our doctrine from our facts; not unreasonable, unless it can be shown that science is aware of and has registered *every* fixed law of God.—C.

Ver. 6.—*The Divine treatment of sin.* "Behold, I will bring it health and cure, and I will cure them." Here, as in so many other Scriptures, the moral, political, social, and spiritual recovery of Israel is spoken of under the image of bodily healing. For all healings of the body are types and pledges of the better healing. If God so cares for the body, which to-day is and to-morrow is cast into the tomb, shall he not care for the soul, which is eternal? This ver. 6 is a promise that the Divine treatment of sin shall be effectual. The Lord is Jehovah-rophi. He heals them that have need of healing.

I. SIN IS AN AWFUL FACT. All nations have recognized this and mourned over it. But it has not been created by Christianity. True, the Christian faith brands it with the stigma of shame as none other does; for everywhere sin has cast its deep shadow and driven noble souls, not a few, to utter despair. But it was here before Christianity. Hence—

II. THE QUESTION OF QUESTIONS HAS BEEN—WHAT IS TO BE DONE WITH IT? And the answers have been very different. Note: 1. *The answer of the philosopher, which extenuates it*, on the ground: (1) Of the imperfection of our nature. If we knew more, it is said, had larger comprehension of truth, we should not sin. But is that true? Is increase of knowledge always increase of virtue? Are little children, who know so little, less virtuous than many an educated man? The names that are accursed for ever, Nero, Herod, Balaam, Philip II. of Spain, Alva, and many more, were all educated men. (2) Of the tyranny of the body. It is this cursed flesh, they say. Get rid of that, and the soul will be pure. Hence one reason wherefore St. Paul's doctrine of the resurrection was so opposed at Corinth, because they thought it was a bringing back of all that dread source of evil which it was hoped was done with for ever when death came. Now, no doubt, the flesh is the occasion of sins not a few. But there are many sins, and those which probably God will most sternly condemn, which are quite independent of the body. Malice, envy, hatred, and all uncharitableness need no "flesh" for their existence. And even in those sins which are especially of the flesh, myriads of victories over it, victories continually renewed, prove that it can, as it ought to, be kept under and brought into subjection. (3) Of its being a form of good. Without it, it is urged, virtue could not be attained; for it is in the conflict with sin that virtue is developed, disciplined, and strengthened. Virtue would lie dormant, lethargic, and be a miserable weakling, were it not that sin roused her up, exasperated her, and forced her to stand on her defence. But such argument confounds temptation with sin. What is urged is true of temptation, but never of sin. Nor is sin needed as the foil, the dark background on which virtue shall shine out with greater lustre than but for this foil had been possible to it. For sin is, some affirm, a necessary condition, almost an ingredient, of good. Moral evil cannot be so evil as it is thought. The devil is not so black as he is painted. But is sin necessary to manifest goodness? Where, then, is such background in God, or in the angels, or in the saints in glory? None, therefore, of these extenuations will stand. Reason, conscience, and God's Word alike condemn them. 2. *There is the answer of despair*, which regards it as inevitable and invincible. This answer does not make light of it, but regards it as that which can neither be helped nor overcome. They believe there is a kingdom of evil, independent of God, with its all but omnipotent, omnipresent, and omniscient head, like unto God. This was the creed of ancient Persia, against which, that his countrymen might not be carried away by it,

Isaiah protested with all his might; cf. Isa. xlv. 5—7, "I am the Lord, and there is none else, there is no God beside me . . . I form the light, and create darkness : I make peace, and create evil : I the Lord do all these things." And Manicheism was a like heresy. And the moral despair which regards sin as inevitable is practical Manicheism. But this is a terrible error; for he who has come to believe in the existence of a god of evil as well as a God of goodness will soon come to believe only in the former and not in the latter at all. Moreover, conscience in her deepest utterances gives no countenance to this invincibility of evil. "Father, I have sinned," is its confession. It never urges that it had no power to resist—that it was forced to sin. It is a dread snare of the devil to persuade men that sin is invincible. Believe him not. Myriads of holy souls give him the lie; and, through the might of Christ your Lord, you may give him the lie likewise. But note now—

III. CHRIST'S ANSWER TO THIS QUESTION. This verse is one of innumerable others which affirm the same truth. 1. *He does not make light of it or extenuate it.* His high and holy teaching, his blameless life, the doom he pronounced on sin, above all, the death he died, were one emphatic protest against and condemnation of sin. But : 2. *He did not regard it as invincible.* He distinctly promises deliverance from it, and : 3. *This he gives.* By blotting out the record of the past. By the present help of his Spirit. By the bright prospect of eternal life. Facts prove all this. He healed them that had need of healing. No disease baffled him. His resources did not run out, and the healing was a real one. *And so it is still.* Let us come to him and see.—C.

Ver. 9.—*Fruits of pardon.* Some of these are declared here; *e.g.*—
I. IN REGARD TO GOD. 1. *Joy.* God, not *Deus impassibilis*—a God who does not feel. 2. *Praise and honour.* The theme of the Church on earth, and especially in heaven, is this, "Unto him that loved us," etc. There is no glory equal to that which shall accrue to God by "Jesus Christ," for through him pardon comes to guilty men.
II. IN REGARD TO THE PARDONED THEMSELVES. They enjoy the goodness and prosperity which God procures them. Pardon is not mere acquittal, but acceptance and adoption, and hence the goodness and prosperity.
III. IN REGARD TO THE WORLD AT LARGE. "They shall fear and tremble." Why this? 1. Because of its *manifestation of power.* His people a feeble flock, but thus raised and exalted. 2. Because of its *exposure of idolatry.* It will be seen how foolish they have been to trust in their false gods. 3. Because of its *manifestation of grace.* The fear and trembling shall not be of dread so much as of repentance—repentance wrought by the evident grace of God in the rich pardon he has bestowed.—C.

Vers. 10—18.—*Paradise lost and regained.* I. THE PICTURE OF A PARADISE LOST. This is given in ver. 10. The land desolate; the flocks and herds all gone; no human being to be seen ; the cities laid waste. Now, this meagre outline would recall to the mind of the Jews the blessed days when the land teemed with inhabitants ; when the cities were numerous, wealthy, populous, and strong ; when the hills and dales of their country-side were covered over with flocks; and when, in the glad prosperity of all, the very fields were said "to shout for joy and also sing" (Ps. lxv.). But all that is past ; desolation reigns, the lands stripped, the cities burnt with fire, and the people slain or in exile; the whole land desolate of both man and beast.
II. PARADISE REGAINED. Such is the bright, joyous picture set forth in these verses (11—18). Its elements are : 1. *Righteousness.* Not mere innocence, as in Eden, but virtue tested and triumphant, and so issuing in a settled righteousness. This must be the basis of all truly blessed life. The people must be all righteous. This secured by him who is called "the righteous Branch," "the Lord our Righteousness." 2. *Love.* (See ver. 11.) The joyous picture of the gladness of the bridegroom and the bride. And that companionship which is the most blessed in the world, and that love which is deepest and purest of all, are fitly taken as the symbol of that love which shall constitute the home of God's redeemed more than a paradise regained. 3. *Worship.* (Ver. 11.) The picture of the temple service has risen up before the prophet's mind. He hears the glad chant, the loud response of the people, "Praise the Lord." He sees the altar fire and the priests and sacrifices, and by this representation he teaches us that *worship* is part of the blessedness that is to be. 4. *Healthful and universal employ.*

(Vers. 12, 13.)   It has often been said, " God made the country, man made the town ; " and the saying may be read truly or falsely, as each one wills.   For he who says there is nought of God in the city speaks as falsely as he who says there is only God in the country.   But there can be no doubt that the highest, purest, and most healthful forms of life are connected with the country.   " Four words, each of them full of meaning, comprise the conceptions which we attribute to the paradisaical state. They are these *innocence, love, rural life, piety* ; and it is towards these conditions of earthly happiness that the human mind reverts, as often as it turns, sickened and disappointed, from the pursuit of whatever else it may have ever laboured to acquire. The innocence we here think of is not virtue recovered, but it is moral perfectness, darkened by no thought or knowledge of the contrary.   This paradisaical love is conjugal fondness, free from sensuous taint.   This rural life is the constant flow of summer days, spent in garden and field, exempt from our exacted toil.   This piety of paradise is the grateful approach of the finite to the Infinite—a correspondence that is neither clouded nor apprehensive of a cloud" (Isaac Taylor).   Now, in these verses, when the prophet would set forth the blessed life that the restored people should enjoy, he draws a picture, not of city, but of country life; not of hard exacting toil, but of healthful, peaceful occupation—the pastoral life of a quiet, beautiful land.   It is a symbol of all healthful employ, and such employ shall be a further feature in the blessedness that is to be.   Therefore, "Sursum corda !" a righteous, loving, worshipful, and healthful life awaits the sons of men "for I will cause their captivity to return, and have mercy on them," saith the Lord.—C.

Ver. 11.—*The prophet's refrain.*   "For I will cause to return the captivity of the land."   This declaration is heard again and again.   We have it in substance times without number in this and in previous chapters.   We have a similar statement in ch. xxxii. 37.   But we have the exact words, the very same form of expression, in ch. xxxii. 44, and in vers. 7 and 26 of this chapter.   Hence we have called it the prophet's refrain.   And the like theme of God's purposes of grace towards mankind generally should be the refrain of all the prophets of the Lord in these our days.   For—

I. THE BLESSINGS ASSURED ARE SIMILAR.   In connection with each several repetition of this promise, " I will cause their captivity to return," is named some specific blessing which that return shall bring along with it.   In connection with its *first* mention (ch. xxxii. 44) God's purpose is given as the reason wherefore his now afflicted people should again possess their land.   And there is a life eternal, a true, real, blessed life for humanity ; a life compared with which this life is like the hard lot of the captive Israel compared with the glowing glad life promised in the days when their captivity should return.   Then in connection with its *second* mention (ver. 7 of this chapter) there is the promise of " health and cure," moral and spiritual health, when their iniquity should be cleansed and their sin forgiven.   And is not the promise of man's redemption like to this ?   In the eternal life there shall be health and cure indeed.   And with the *third* mention of this promise (ver. 11) there is associated gladness and joy.   " There shall be . . . the voice of joy and the voice of gladness," etc. (ver. 11).   And with the *fourth* there is (ver. 26 of this chapter) the promise of permanence for all that has been before, the permanency as of the covenant of day and night, and the perpetual sovereignty of their own royal house, the seed of David.   And so we look for a new order of things, which shall not be as this, troubled and transient, but characterized by a rest and joy that shall be eternal.   Thus analogous are the blessings promised to the return of Israel and the redemption of mankind.

II. THE MOTIVES OF SUCH PROCLAMATION OF GOD'S PURPOSES OF GRACE ARE ALIKE. The reason of the prophet's refrain were such as these.   1. *He so delighted in the truth he had to tell.*   Often and often he had been charged with a message of a far less welcome kind ; but this was blessed to his soul.   And so, would we effectually speak of God's purposes of grace, they must be the joy of our soul.   We must ourselves delight in them.   2. *He really believed it.*   The oft repetition of this word shows his confidence in it.   He speaks with no bated breath.   "I believed, therefore have I spoken."   And this must ever be the spiritual force with which our gospel must be charged if it is to have any effect on those who hear it.   3. *He knew it would so comfort the cast down.* Many already were mourning along with the prophet over the desolations so surely coming on the land, and many more when away in exile would mourn. But the prophet knew that their hearts would be cheered and sustained by the earnest and confident assurance that " their captivity should return." For their sake, therefore, he reiterated this word. And in order to our now earnestly proclaiming the message of God's love, we too must believe that it will do the people good, that it will be for their help and comfort. And we must have for them, as the prophet had for his people, a real love and concern. This has ever been an attendant of and is essential to a successful ministry. 4. *He knew that it would so vindicate God.* Questionings and perplexities not a few were being occasioned by the prophet's solemn declarations of the coming destruction. They contrasted his terrible word with the oft-repeated promises made by God " to David and to his seed for ever," and to Zion, concerning which he had said, " There will I dwell, for I have delighted in it." These and the many more like promises seemed for ever to forbid the possibility of that which the prophet, and now the actual course of events, declared to be close at hand. How were the two to be reconciled, and the truth and goodness of God to be vindicated? It was by the truth declared in this refrain of the prophet. That rendered both Divine words harmonious and true. Thus the enemies of the prophet would be silenced, and the company of them that feared God would be reassured. The house of God was dear to the prophet; and so must it be to us would we earnestly preach his Word. " The zeal of thine house hath eaten me up;" " Wist ye not that I must be about my Father's business?" So was it spoken of or by the Lord Jesus Christ; and so in like manner in our measure and degree must it be true of us if we are to be true witnesses for him and for his grace. The gospel is the vindication of God to-day, as the return of the Captivity was in the days of the prophet. And being jealous for God, he proclaimed incessantly that return, as we must the redemption of mankind.—C.

Ver. 16.—" *The Lord our Righteousness.*" (Cf. homily on ch. xxiii. 6.)—C.

Vers. 17, 18.—*Do the prophets prophesy falsely?* If the statements of these verses be taken literally, it would seem as if they did. The house of Israel never, since its exile, has had a throne at all, nor has any descendant of David been acknowledged as its prince. Yet these verses say, " David shall never want," etc. And, literally, it never can come to pass, for in the lapse and confusion of the ages their genealogical tables have been utterly lost, so that none can certainly say who is of the house of David or who of the house of Levi. The Asmonean princes who occupied the throne of Judah were of the tribe of Levi, and Herod was no Jew at all. Now, the promise of these verses is one that is perpetually repeated (cf. 2 Sam. vii. 16; 1 Kings ii. 4; Ps. lxxxix. 4, 29, 36; Numb. xxv. 12, etc.). How, then, are they to be understood, since events have most surely falsified them if understood in any literal way? And so the Prophet Hosea cheered the ten tribes of Israel—those of whom we speak now as the lost ten tribes—by promises of their restoration, and Jeremiah does the same (cf. Hos. vi. 2; ch. iii. 14, etc.; l. 17—20, etc.). But in spite of all these prophecies, the " ten tribes never were restored, and never, as a whole, received any favour from God after they went into captivity" (Pusey). Now, what shall we say to these things? Shall we say—

I. THE PROPHETS WERE BUT MEN, AND HENCE THEY WERE CERTAIN TO BE WRONG WHEN THEY VENTURED INTO THE DOMAIN OF THE FUTURE? This is the rationalist's reply. He attributes all these utterances to the wish to cheer their countrymen in their sorrow, and perhaps to maintain their own credit. Sanguine enthusiasm will account for all. Is, then, the estimate that our Lord and his apostles and the Church universal held concerning these " holy men of old, who spake as they were moved by the Holy Ghost," to be regarded as false? Are the prophets themselves to be convicted as liars, affirming, " Thus saith the Lord," when not the Lord, but only their own poor weak selves were speaking? And are all the manifest fulfilments of prophecy to go for nothing in establishing their authority? The rationalist's reply will not do.

II. THAT THE EXILES DID NOT FULFIL THE CONDITIONS OF THE PROMISED RESTORATION? (Cf. homily on *A never-to-be-forgotten principle of interpretation,* vol. i. p. 451.) But does this principle apply here? No; for the promise of restoration carries along with it the promise of the " new covenant," which included " the new heart "—the heart of stone taken away and the heart of flesh given instead. The conditions necessary for the restoration were the subjects of promise as much as the restoration itself. God took the whole matter into his own hand.

III. THAT THE PROPHETS, LIKE THE APOSTLES CONCERNING THE RETURN OF THE LORD, DID NOT KNOW CONCERNING THE RETURN OF THE CAPTIVITY? The apostles do undoubtedly speak of the Lord's return as a thing close at hand, to be looked for in their own day. But such language is to be regarded rather as the language of desire than of knowledge. For the Lord had distinctly told them that it was not for them to know the times and the seasons. Therefore we can only regard their words as those of desire, hope—permitted hope, indeed, but not of Divine assurance. May we do thus with the prophetic word on the return of the Captivity? No; because they so distinctly claim the Divine authority (cf. vers. 25 and 26 of this chapter and *passim*, for what they affirm). The apostles do not; 1 Thess. iv. 15, "By the word of the Lord," is an exception. The Lord's revelation referred only to such as should be alive and remain at his coming, not to that generation then living.

IV. THAT THE PROMISE IS BUT DELAYED? This is loudly maintained by many. They who believe that the Jews will be restored to their native land, expect it on the express ground that Canaan has never been actually and permanently theirs. A certain tract of country, three hundred miles in length by two hundred in breadth, must be given, or else they think the promise has been broken. "If there is nothing yet future for Israel, then the magnificence of the promise has been lost in the poverty of its accomplishment." This reply is not to be lightly dismissed. If the kingdom of God, for whose coming we daily pray, do mean that which all who heard our Lord so perpetually speak about it, understood it to mean—and he never, in the main substance of their belief, even hinted that they were wrong—if it mean *the reign of God upon earth*, as we believe it does, in which, under Christ, the Israel of God, the Church, shall be first in the kingdom of heaven, having been of those blessed ones who had part in "the first resurrection," then the literal fulfilment of the prophetic word may reasonably be looked for. This was "the hope of Israel," of which St. Paul spoke; "the restitution of all things," and "the times of refreshing," of which St. Peter spoke; and this belief has at least this vast advantage, that it enables those who hold it to read the Scriptures literally, and to understand by David, Jerusalem, Levi, Israel, etc., that which they seem to mean, and not whatsoever the too facile process of spiritualizing may say that they mean. Of course, if the kingdom is of this world, this age, as our Lord distinctly told Pilate it was not, then a literal fulfilment of these prophecies is out of the question; but regarded as the kingdom to be revealed in another age, after the resurrection and the Lord's return, then all is as possible as it will be blessed.

V. THAT IT IS FULFILLED ALREADY? This is what they affirm who regard our Lord as embodying in himself both the regal and priestly functions, and the Church as being the nation whom God has restored. The Jew's national life and his religion were the two things most dear to him. These, it is said, have been preserved to him in the Church, and in him who is the Church's Head. But surely these are the exigencies of exegesis, and but *preterœa nihil*.

VI. THAT SUCH PREDICTIONS ARE INSTANCES OF GOD'S LAW OF ILLUSION? (Cf. on this F. Robertson's sermons on the 'Illusions of Life,' vol. iii. p. 83.) We have illusions *in nature*. The sun, etc., seem to move round us whilst we are at rest. The hedges, fields, etc., fly along whilst the train in which we are seems to be stationary. The mirage. We have them in moral and mental life.

> "Hope springs eternal in the human breast,
> Which never is, but always to be, blest."

What pictures we draw in our youth of what life is going to be for us! Then see what life really turns out. We are all subjects of the law of illusion. Now, was it so in these Bible histories? Abraham was promised Canaan. But he never had a foot of it to call his own (cf. Acts vii. 5). All the patriarchs "died in the faith, *not* having received the promises, but were persuaded of them" (cf. Heb. xi.). The early Church was persuaded that "the Lord was at hand;" "the coming of the Lord draweth nigh." And yet he never came, and has not come to this day. Now, may not these predictions be further instances of this law of illusion? Ten thousand times "No," exclaim as many people; "it is to make God a liar." Is it so? Of course, then, we would rather not be deceived; we would have all our illusions done away. Would we? As for "Hope," let her be put an end to, seeing what an incurable liar she is. But distinguish between being subject to delusion and illusion. He who is subject to the former hopes for some good thing and gets *nothing*. He who is subject to the latter, hopes for some good thing and, if the illusion be of God's permission, gets something *better*. Our hopes lure us on. We acquire character, habits of patient industry, etc., better far than the mere material thing hoped for. The patriarchs hoped for an earthly Canaan; they won such faith in God that by it they all "obtained a good report." They never complained of God deceiving them (read Heb. xi.); for they knew that, if not the thing they hoped for was given, God had provided that which was better (Heb. xi. 8—10). Our own belief is that, in regard to this world, these promises were illusions, but in regard to the world to come, they shall in substance and reality be fulfilled there. Meanwhile let us all have faith in God, who, in ways better far than we think, will fulfil that which now it sometimes seems as if he never fulfilled at all.—C.

Ver. 6.—*The abundance of peace and truth.* I. THE NEED OF SUCH A REVELATION. There is already abundance of discord, mutual hostility, instability, deceit. What a picture of misery is at once suggested by contrast with the state presented in this promise! Instead of the welcome salutation of peace, there is too often threatening. And when the salutation does come, it is too often only a mere conventional expression, and in some instances even an elaborated hypocrisy put forward to carry on war behind it; and instead of the feeling that one is on a sure foundation, there are continual quakings that disturb what is underneath, and continual blasts that disturb what is above. And beside what attacks man from without, there is within a spirit of hostility and rivalry to others, a spirit striving to shake their position and triumph over them. So that peace and truth need to be revealed within us first of all. We need, not merely to have amicable feelings towards others, freedom from envy and malice, but we need positive cordiality. Loving, unselfish cohesion is the true way to escape bitter habitual contention. Moreover, this peace and truth are needed in abundance. It must be said of them, as is said in the New Testament of God's Spirit, that they are given without measure. The promise of the peace that passeth all understanding is assuredly a promise correspondent to our necessity.
II. THE FACT OF SUCH A REVELATION. Peace is revealed in Jesus Christ. In him there is the secret of a composure and a steadfastness unaffected by all the common causes of discord and instability. He had an unusual number of enemies, and this because he was so persistent in declaring righteousness; and yet all the time he had that peace within which showed how outside forces only affected the mere shell of life. In this life there was ever the joint manifestation of peace and steadfastness, and the steadfastness was explained by the fact that he came from God, continued in God, did the will of God, and so, ever having this hold on the Eternal, and being held by the Eternal, the shaking influences of time did ever more and more both to reveal his strength and their own weakness. All the exhortations of Jesus with respect to faith are meant to reveal to us the abundance of peace and truth. With what pity Jesus must look on the abortive, melancholy attempts of men to trust in the untrustworthy! and yet the unveiled magnificence of peace and truth is unseen. What we have to do is to look desiringly, hopefully, towards God's revelation; for surely the complete revelation includes not only something gracious to be seen, but full insight to see it. The apocalypse to John in Patmos came to one who "was in the Spirit on the Lord's day."—Y.

Vers. 10, 11.—*The mournful stillness of the present, and the gladsome voices of the future.* I. THE PRESENT STILLNESS. What makes it so painful? Not all stillness is painful; indeed, stillness is often very grateful, a thing to be sought, a timely refuge for those who are stunned and confused by the clamours of the world. The stillness of night is pleasant after the noise of day. The stillness of the mountain and the wilderness seems more still when one has come from the city's bustle. There is even something suggestive of escape into everlasting peace when one looks at the stillness of death as contrasted with all the power of sound in the previous life. But the stillness here is painful, because it does not come in any normal way; it is stillness where there ought to be sound—sounds of traffic, sounds of friendly intercourse, sounds of children playing, sounds of worship. To come into the individual life, it is the silence of the dumb, the silence of that which was made to speak, intended to speak, and can only be silent because of some inexplicable interference with natural constitution. Dumbness ought not to be, and so the state of things here represented, when in the houses and streets of Jerusalem there was sound neither of man nor beast, was one which ought not to have been. There was no occasion for it in the very constitution of things. It came by man's own bringing of it. The present silence had been preceded by many voices that ought never to have been heard—voices of threatening, voices of greedy demand, voices of revenge, voices of complaint and of indignant appeal against injustice.

II. THE VOICES OF THE FUTURE. The sounds of life are to flow back into the now desolate streets, but they are to be the sounds of a different kind of life. Sounds springing from righteousness within and from a principle of obedience to Jehovah. Sounds that come from a universally satisfied people. Not sounds of joy and gladness in palaces, and sounds of privation and despair in hovels; but sunshine falling everywhere, and everywhere the hearts of the people ready to break forth into song. In the eleventh verse there is first of all the general indication of gladness. Every one is full of healthy life, which, as a matter of course, breaks forth into joyful manifestation. Then, as a very significant illustration, there is the gladness of the bridegroom and the bride. This signifies a stable society, a hopeful prospect, the joys of home life. Probably there was no joy so demonstrative as that connected with wedding festivities. Then the joy of religion comes in to crown and conclude all. Praise to Jehovah for his goodness and his enduring mercy, and offerings of thanksgiving in his house. If joy of this kind had been absent, the other joy would not long have lasted. From what God sends down into our lives as causes of abiding joy, we must send back to him responses of intelligent and heart-felt praise.—Y.

Vers. 12, 13.—*Returning flocks.* In ch. xxxi. there has been mention of planting vineyards, and of God's goodness with respect to the corn, the wine, the oil. But agriculture was only one of the important industries of the land. To have set ploughmen and vine-dressers to work again, and left shepherds unprovided for, would have meant only a partial restoration. God has a remembrance of all classes of the community, and all varieties of the surface of the earth. Shepherds were not to go away into exile without a special promise to comfort them. By "causing the flocks to lie down" we may take to be meant that a sense of security and restfulness will be established; and that "the flocks will pass again under the hands of him that telleth them" suggests their numerousness. There seems to be also a distinct remembrance of the places most appropriate for flocks. Nor must we let slip the spiritual sense of this prophecy when we call to mind the references to pastoral life in the New Testament. It is the power of Christ, the Branch of righteousness growing up unto David, who makes spiritual flocks and spiritual pastors to abound. And instead of the selection from the literal flocks for sacrifices, there is the self-presentation of every one in the spiritual flock as a living sacrifice.—Y.

Ver. 15.—*The righteous Scion of David.* Here is a great leading prediction, which enables *us* to interpret as to the time and mode in which the rest of the glorious predictions connected with it were to be fulfilled. We know full well who this righteous Scion was, and when we look at his work, we can translate all the figurative language into spiritual realities. We no longer go looking for Israel and Jerusalem in any mere local way, and the vineyards and corn-lands and pastures of the restored people of God we understand to be only feeble indications of the spiritual satisfactions coming through Christ. Note—

I. THE ORIGIN OF THIS RIGHTEOUS SCION. He springs from David. According to the flesh, he is connected with a name suggestive of past days of prosperity and glory. David himself is emphatically to be reckoned as a righteous stock. That he fell into grievous backslidings is not to be denied; but we know his aspirations, his sighings and strugglings after conformity with the Law of God.

II. THE IMPLIED CONTRAST WITH OTHER SCIONS WHO WERE NOT RIGHTEOUS. Scions of unrighteousness had already sprung up, had their day, and done their mischief. Their position made their character and doings peculiarly pernicious. With a disposition to act unjustly and unrighteously, they had power to act over a very large area. So we should ever contrast Christ with the men of large powers who have widely influenced the world, and yet have influenced it for evil, because their powers have been directed by selfishness and error. There can be no doubt that a son of David means here one who will act as a king; and that reminds us how many kings have been tyrants, looking on those under them as merely so much convenient material, by which they might effect their plans. The exiled people, thinking of their restoration, would have to include the thought of king in the complete ideal; and surely this would bring very distinctly before them the evil some of their kings had wrought in the past.

III. THE COMING SCION IN HIS RIGHTEOUSNESS. Righteousness is emphasized as his great quality. It is needed in a king above all things that he should be just. He must not be an Ahab stealing Naboth's vineyard. Being in a fiercer light than other men, he must be unusually careful as to the aspect of his actions. Love is not mentioned here as a quality of this Scion, not because it is not needed, but because righteousness is the great quality that, for the comfort of Jeremiah's auditors, needed to be emphasized. Nevertheless, it is well for us to remember that this Scion of David secures righteousness, because he ever acts from a loving heart.—Y.

Vers. 17, 18.—*King and priest in perpetuity.* The declarations of these verses come by a natural association after the declaration of his advent who is the righteous Scion of David. Kingship and priesthood in perpetuity—that is the general assurance; but what a difference between the assurance looked at from the point of view given by Jeremiah's time and the point of view given by ours! We look back on the achievements of history, and then see how much more a prediction means than anything that could have been supposed possible at the time it was spoken. Observe—

I. THE NEEDFUL PERPETUITY OF THE OFFICES. Kingship and priesthood cannot perish out of God's true Israel. There must always be a king; there must always be a priest. These offices, properly discharged and honoured, are as needful to the prosperity of Israel as fruitful lands and pastures well occupied with flocks. All government has to come at last to some personal authority. That the authority of some single person rests on the choice and acceptance of the many does not make that authority less needful, less real. And so with priesthood. The priestly office is needed, however it may change its forms and channels. Mediation between God and man is a necessity, which more and more unfolds its depths as man reflects more on the possibilities of his being. Even priestcraft, with its marked repugnances to intelligence and liberty, has at least this much good about it, that it is a testimony to man's need of mediation.

II. THE WAY IN WHICH THE PERPETUITY IS MANIFESTED. The king is one; the priest is one. Looking back, we are made to see this clearly. "Of his reign there shall be no end," says Gabriel to Mary. Whatever wisdom, power, and beneficence are in Jesus, are in perpetual exercise. Death, which ends the authority of purely human kings, only enlarged and deepened the authority of Jesus. He not only claims perpetuity for his demands, but we have ample reason now to say that the claim is admitted. And as to priesthood, what more need be said than make a reference to the expositions of the priesthood of Jesus made in the Epistle to the Hebrews? It is the priesthood for ever according to the order of Melchisedec. What an abidingly helpful thought it should be that we look to a Mediator ever active in sympathy with human wants, ever understanding them, knowing them indeed far better than the subjects of them! All the externalities are gone—sacrifices of beasts, furnishings of the holy place, symbolic garments of the priests, symbolic ordinances of service; but the reality remains and must remain in the priesthood of Jesus Christ. The deepest evils of human life, the evils that cause all others, are swept away by the priesthood of Jesus. And so also the greatest goods of human life, those that are seminal and full of energy towards the production of other goods, come through the same priesthood. Compared with the possibilities of the future, the predictions of these verses are, indeed, only at the beginning of their fulfilment.—Y.

EXPOSITION.

CHAPTER XXXIV.

This chapter must be taken in connection with ch. xxxv. The whole section consists of three passages, introduced with a superscription in the same form, but otherwise unrelated. It serves to finish off the earlier prophetic portion of the book, ch. xxxvi. opening a series of narratives.

The first passage (ch. xxxiv. 1—7) is virtually a postscript to ch. xxxii., xxxiii.; it apparently contains the prophecy referred to in ch. xxxii. 3—5 as the cause of Jeremiah's imprisonment. The same prophecy recurs in a shorter form in ch. xxxvii. 17, and, by comparing the context of this passage with ch. xxxii. 1, etc., we are enabled to infer that the original prophecy was uttered at the renewal of the siege of Jerusalem by the Chaldeans, who had withdrawn for a time on the news of the approach of Pharaoh's army.

Ver. 1.—**All the kingdoms of the earth**; etc.; rather, *of the land.* The accumulation of phrases is to convey the composite character of the Chaldean army. **And against all the cities thereof**; *i.e.* the fortified cities which still held out—against Lachish and Azekah, if no more (ver. 7).

Vers. 2, 3.—(Comp. these verses with ch. xxxii. 3—5.)

Ver. 4.—**Yet hear the word of the Lord**, etc. Clearly this introduces a limitation of the foregoing threat. Zedekiah will, it is true, be carried to Babylon, but he will not suffer a violent death; he will "die in peace," and be buried with all customary royal honours. A difficulty, however, has been felt in admitting this view. How could Zedekiah be said to die in peace, when he was "in prison till the day of his death" (ch. lii. 11)? and how could the deposed king of a captive people be honoured with a public mourning? The reply is (1) that, as compared with a cruel death by flaying or impalement, it *was* "peace" to live in the obscure quiet of a prison; and (2) that, as the Jews appear to have been left very much to themselves (see Ezekiel, *passim*), it is credible enough that they were allowed to show the customary honours to a deceased representative of David. At any rate, the alternative view seems not in accordance with sound exegesis, viz. that the verse means this, "If thou obey the word of the Lord, and surrender thyself to Nebuchad-

nezzar, thou shalt live and die in peaceable possession of the throne." What parallel can be produced for this violent interpretation?

Ver. 5.—**With the burnings of thy fathers.** It was customary to burn spices at royal funerals (2 Chron. xvi. 14; xxi. 19). Saying, **Ah lord!** (see on ch. xxii. 18).

The second of the group of prophecies in ch. xxxiv., xxxv. is composed of vers. 8—22. It contains a denunciation of the Jews who, at the beginning of the siege, had emancipated their Hebrew slaves (according to Exod. xxi. 1—4; Deut. xv. 12), but after the withdrawal of the Chaldeans had resumed possession of them. Ver. 21 is couched in a form which indicates the precise date of the prophecy, viz. before the Chaldeans returned to renew the siege of Jerusalem.

Ver. 8.—**A covenant.** The scene of this "covenant" was the temple (vers. 15, 18). Solemn agreements of this kind were not uncommon (comp. 2 Chron. xv. 12; 2 Kings xi. 17; xxiii. 3; Neh. x.). **To proclaim liberty unto them.** The phrase, a very peculiar one, is taken from the law of jubilee (Lev. xxv. 10), though the prescription on which the covenant was based refers exclusively to the seventh year of the slave's servitude.

Ver. 9.—**Should serve himself of them**; literally, *should work through them;* i.e. "should employ them for forced labour;" as in ch. xxv. 13.

Ver. 10.—**Now when all the princes**, etc. This verse should rather be rendered thus: *Then all the princes, and all the people,* etc., *obeyed, every one letting his slave, and every one his handmaid, go free, not serving themselves of them any more; they even obeyed, and let them go.*

Ver. 13.—**Out of the house of bondmen.** Egypt had been a "house of bondmen" to their fathers (Exod. xiii. 3; Deut. vi. 12, and elsewhere); let them not make the holy city thus grievous to those who were equally with themselves children of Jehovah's redeemed ones.

Ver. 14.—**At the end of seven years**, etc. This is the literal rendering, but the sense, as is clear from the parallel passage in Deut. xv. 12, and indeed from the next clause of this very verse, is "in the seventh (*not*, the eighth) year."

Ver. 15.—**Ye were now turned**; or, *ye returned* (the primary meaning is simply "to turn;" hence (1) to turn away, as in ver. 16; (2) to return, as here; comp. ch. viii. 4).

Ver. 17.—**I proclaim a liberty for you.** Judah is henceforth to be "lord of himself—that heritage of woe;" or rather, he is to become the slave of Sword, Pestilence, and Famine. The "liberty" now proclaimed does not profit Judah, who so much desires it. **I will make you to be removed**; rather, *I will make you a shuddering* (as ch. xv. 4). Ver. 18.—**When they cut the calf in twain, etc.** This clause should be translated differently, and placed, for clearness, in a parenthesis *(the calf which they cut in twain, and between the parts of which they passed).* The division of the calf might, in fact, be called in Hebrew either "the covenant" or "the token of the covenant" (comp. Gen. xvii. 10, 11). It was a solemn assurance that he who should transgress God's Law should share the same fate as the victim. The same idea seems to have dictated the Hebrew phrase, "to *cut* a covenant," and the Greek and Latin equivalents (ὅρκια τέμνειν: *fœdus icere*); comp. the parallel narrative in Gen. xv. 10.

Ver. 20.—**And their dead bodies, etc.** One of Jeremiah's repetitions (see ch. vii. 33).

Ver. 21.—**And Zedekiah . . . and his princes.** Graf infers from the separate mention of the king and his princes that these had themselves been unfaithful to the covenant. But the threat in this verse seems merely intended to enforce the preceding one by specializing the most prominent sufferers. Parallel passage: ch. xxi. 7. **Which are gone up from you** (see ch. xxxvii. 5).

HOMILETICS.

Vers. 1—7.—*A king's doom.* Jeremiah reveals to King Zedekiah his approaching doom. The invader is already occupying the land and coming up before the walls of Jerusalem (ver. 7). It is now too late to escape, resistance is vain, the doom is certain. What a terrible scene is that in the royal palace when the mournful prophet stands up to deliver his message to the terror-stricken monarch! Such events are rare in history. Yet the general truths on which the message of Jeremiah depended are eternal and clear to all who will see them. We have no prophet to tell us of the exact nature and date of our future judgments. But we know the principles of God's government and can apply them to ourselves. We know that God is just and must punish sin; we know that "the wages of sin is death." Therefore, though no voice sounds in our ears, the sentence is virtually pronounced every day we sin, and hangs over us continually until our sin is forgiven.

I. THE DOOM. 1. *The city is to be destroyed.* She has shared the king's sin, therefore she must share his punishment. The destruction of Jerusalem was especially a blow to Zedekiah. They who have most can lose most. Jerusalem was a favoured city—the greater, therefore, was the guilt of her apostasy, and the heavier must be her doom. Past favours are no charms against future judgments. 2. *The king shall not escape.* (Ver. 3.) Rank is no safeguard against the judgment of Heaven. God will call kings to account. So all who have accepted responsible posts will have to answer for their conduct in them. Zedekiah would find his sufferings aggravated by being a witness to the triumph of Nebuchadnezzar. Shame, remorse, mental anguish, are to the sensitive worse penalties than bodily torture.

II. THE MITIGATION. The doom is not utter. "In wrath God remembers mercy." God never delights to punish, never gives one blow more than is absolutely necessary; does not hate, but pities and grieves for the victim. So Zedekiah's life is to be spared, and he is to receive a measure of honour in his captivity. There are degrees of punishment in the Divine execution of justice—some will be beaten with few stripes, some with many (Luke xii. 47, 48). In this fact we may see the hope of mercy to the penitent, for God does not wholly cast a soul off. The shadows fall thick, but the darkness is not that of midnight. When trouble comes we are too ready to complain if we do not fall into despair. We should look for mitigating circumstances, those rifts in the clouds that tell of the mercy not yet wholly gone, and give hopes of light after the storm is over. But it is foolish for any to take spiritual comfort to himself for the future life in such thoughts as these, for we may well fear that the lightest doom then will be unspeakably terrible. The refuge we are to seek is not in that poor mitigation, but in the full forgiveness and perfect salvation of Christ now offered to the worst men, even to those over whom hangs the heaviest threat of doom (Heb. vii. 25).

Vers. 8—11.—*Superficial repentance.* In liberating their slaves under the influence of terror, and reclaiming them when the cause of alarm had disappeared, the Jews afford a striking instance of superficial repentance. This must be distinguished from an insincere repentance referred to in an earlier prophecy (ch. iii. 10). That is nothing but a hollow mockery from the first, a mere pretence of conscious hypocrisy; but this is genuine so far as it goes—only it goes but a very little way.

I. THE CAUSE OF SUPERFICIAL REPENTANCE IS FEAR OF PAINFUL CONSEQUENCES. When the invader was at their gates Zedekiah and his people were so terrified that they were willing to do and promise anything that would mitigate the wrath of God who had permitted the calamity to visit them for their sins. Fear was the sole motive of their hasty covenant of emancipation. Now, this may be a useful initiative of a thorough repentance; but then it must lead to deeper feelings of hearty detestation of sin on its own account. Fear of penalties, without any abhorrence of the moral evil that merits them can only produce superficial results. Earnest repentance involves a turning from sin rather than a flight from its penalties. Hence the importance of seeking to lead men to repentance through influencing the conscience, rather than by means of mere appeals to selfish terror. Thus St. Paul reasoned with Felix "of righteousness and temperance" as well as of "judgment to come" (Acts xxiv. 25). Lurid pictures of the horrors of hell may work upon the feelings of people with visible effect, but if these take the place of the far more difficult rousing of the moral sense, the effect of them will be very superficial and not all spiritual. Such a sensational style of preaching is tempting because it is easy, and apparently very effective, but its fruits are disappointing, and come short of the less pretentious efforts that aim at awakening the conscience.

II. THE CHARACTERISTIC OF SUPERFICIAL REPENTANCE IS CHANGE OF CONDUCT WITHOUT CHANGE OF HEART. That was no genuine reformation which Zedekiah hurried through in the face of imminent danger. True, the slaves were freed and the Law was obeyed. But there was no indication of a revived respect for the Law, nor of a lessening of greed and cruelty, nor of a larger recognition of the rights of fellow-citizens. There was no change of heart, in fact. Such is the result of a repentance of fear without conviction of conscience. This reformation is worthless in the sight of God, who looks at the disposition of the heart.

III. THE EFFECT OF SUPERFICIAL REPENTANCE IS A TEMPORARY REFORMATION. As soon as Nebuchadnezzar withdrew his army, the Jews renounced their covenant and took back their slaves. The motive for the change was gone, and with it the change ceased. A repentance of terror is not likely to outlive the terror. The fears of the night are forgotten in the thoughtless confidence of the day. This is strikingly illustrated in the vacillation of Pharaoh—willing to let the Hebrews go while a plague was raging, but withdrawing his promise as soon as it was stayed. Therefore this superficial repentance is practically worthless. Nothing can be solid and enduring in life that does not spring from personal conviction and true feeling. We need a real desire to turn from sin, and a determination to seek a better life for its own sake, in order to secure a lasting change. For this we must seek Divine grace, in order that we may be "born from above."

Ver. 17.—*Liberal punishment for illiberal conduct.* The Jews will not set free their enslaved fellow-citizens; God therefore liberates sword, pestilence, and famine upon them. If they are illiberal in their conduct, God will not be stinted in his punishment of them.

I. THE EVILS OF LIFE ARE UNDER THE RESTRAINT OF GOD. They appear to be uncontrolled, but they are really God's slaves. He holds in the hounds of retribution with his leash. They would fain tear their victim. But they vent their rage in vain till their Master lets them loose. Men can only be tormented by Satan when they are delivered over to Satan (1 Cor. v. 5).

II. OUR CONDUCT DETERMINES OUR FATE. The terrible doom is no chance accident, nor is it a cruel act of despotism. It depends upon our behaviour whether or no God will liberate the powers of evil to do their fell work upon us.

III. ILLIBERAL CONDUCT WILL LEAD TO PERSONAL LOSS. The mean man overreaches himself. "There is that withholdeth more than is meet, but it tendeth to poverty" (Prov. xi. 24). History has proved that slavery is a commercial failure. Slave labour is most expensive. But beyond this it may bring upon itself justly earned calamities. Slavery was the curse of the ancient world—the scene of its blackest iniquity, and the root of its direst misery. Few things are more terrible in the history of Rome than the social wars rising out of slavery. The persistent clinging to slavery by the Southern States of America caused the evils of war to be set free amongst them.

HOMILIES BY VARIOUS AUTHORS.

Vers. 8—22.—*False obedience.* An incident of the siege of Jerusalem by the Chaldeans. At the first alarm the liberation of the Hebrew slaves was declared and solemnly ratified, according to the sabbatic law, which had long sunk into desuetude. The aim of this was a purely military one, viz. the advantage to be derived from the services of the freedmen in the army, and the removal of disabilities that might occasion disaffection within the walls. Yet an appearance of religion was given to it by the form it was made to assume as connected with the Law, and the solemn rites which were observed. That it was really only a time-serving expedient was shown by the restoration of the state of slavery directly it appeared as if the Chaldeans were going to desist from their purpose.

I. WHEREIN IT DIFFERS FROM TRUE OBEDIENCE. This will consist in the essence of the action, which, being moral, must have to do with *motives.* The form of the action was religious, but the real aim of it was one of selfish policy. Good people and bad are frequently found doing the same good and proper actions, but events frequently prove that they have acted from the most opposite motives. It was not to glorify God or to benefit the bondmen that the edict was put forth, but simply to advance their own interests and to "serve themselves" in a more effective way of their brethren. When righteousness is immediately and evidently advantageous, there are many who will become formally righteous; and when religion is fashionable, there are many who will be religious. When misdeeds are rectified it is so far a good thing; but that the reform may be real and permanent it must proceed from true repentance, and an earnest desire to serve God and the interests of our fellow-men.

II. CONSIDERATIONS DETERMINING THE REAL NATURE OF REPUTED OBEDIENCE. In discovering the true character of reputed obedience it is well to study : 1. *The circumstances.* Here there were immediate pressure and distress, the existence of a dangerous element in the state, and the possibility of advantages from the military service of the freedmen. The greatest care is requisite in judging of the professions of persons in straitened or perilous circumstances, and to whom religion presents pecuniary, social, or other advantages. The existence of such circumstances affords a presumption against the genuineness of their conversion; and yet it is not of itself conclusive. A better criterion is to be found in : 2. *Subsequent conduct.* The speedy consignment of the freedmen back again to a state of slavery showed that the observance of the Law was unreal. Actions are ever more eloquent than words. So, when ardent and apparently enthusiastic professions 'rapidly cool down, and give place to calculating and selfish conduct, we see that the religious movement *has had no deep root* or *has been unreal from its commencement.* Death-bed repentances are proverbially doubtful, because of the impossibility in most cases of applying this test; nevertheless we are justified in believing that in some cases these are genuine. Prisoners frequently belie their declarations when set at liberty. The subject of false repentance may deceive himself, the emotion being genuine, but the nature not being radically changed. Hence the necessity of insisting upon continued obedience from all who are under the influence of conviction, or who appear to be so.

III. THE PECULIAR OFFENSIVENESS OF FALSE OBEDIENCE. It is not a simple act of transgression, but complex and supremely self-conscious. As on this occasion the Jews were manifoldly sinful in (1) their breach of faith with God and their fellow-countrymen ; (2) in the dishonour they showed to God by lightly regarding the most solemn oath and ordinance; and (3) in the hypocrisy by which the whole proceeding was characterized; so the false saint is a sinner of the deepest dye. Nor is he at liberty to confine his transgression within definite and foreseen limits; once committed to the false attitude, a repetition and intricate complexity of sin is inevitable. It is, therefore, often a culminating sin.

IV. THE PUNISHMENT OF FALSE OBEDIENCE. (Vers. 17—22.) The penalty inflicted is very terrible and thorough; as if there were no hope for such men to be spiritually renewed again. 1. *Exemplary.* A curious and instructive parallelism between their crime and its punishment is to be observed: "Behold, I proclaim a liberty for you," and "Their dead bodies shall be for meat unto the fowls of the heaven, and to the beasts of the earth." This is in harmony with the didactic and symbolical character of the old dispensation. 2. *Thorough and unmitigated.* No word of hope or compassion is uttered. An end is to be made of such transgressions. 3. *An element of scorn and contempt is discoverable.* There is a terrible irony in the words, "I proclaim a liberty for you," etc., which reveal the depth and absoluteness of their curse. The gospel dispensation, as it offers greater privileges and blessings to the truly penitent, is also accompanied with more awful penalties (Heb. iv. 11, 12; vi. 4—8; x. 29; Prov. i. 26).—M.

Vers. 1—7.—*The Lord, the prophet, and the king.* It is a sad scene that these verses bring before us.

I. THE LORD SEEKING TO SAVE THE LOST. This was the intent of the prophet's being charged with his message to King Zedekiah. If it were possible to save him, the Lord would do so, and, therefore, sent his servant again and yet again. Not lightly will the Lord let any evil-doer go his own way.

II. THE PROPHET FAITHFULLY DISCHARGING A TERRIBLE DUTY. It was terrible every way. 1. *In itself.* To have to be the bearer of such evil tidings, and to one unprepared and unwilling to give heed to them. How much pleasanter to prophesy smooth things than these evil ones! 2. *To his influence as a prophet.* Men would desire to disbelieve him, and at length would—as they had done—persuade themselves that they might do so. A whole atmosphere of unbelief and dislike would surround him and shut up men's ears and hearts against him. 3. *To his personal safety.* Of course nothing but enmity was to be expected from such messages as these, and the prophet reaped the harvest to the full. They sought his life again and again, and wrought him all the ill they could (cf. subsequent chapters). And yet the prophet of God faithfully went through with his commission. Here is the test of fidelity, not in speaking that which men expect of you and will praise you for, but in speaking, when needful, that which men hate to hear. Can *we* lay claim to aught of such fidelity as this?

III. THE KING INFATUATED BY EVIL COUNSELS. There is reason to believe that, left to himself, he would have hearkened to the prophet. But those around him persuaded him to disregard all that the prophet said. Hence this opportunity of salvation for himself and for his people was put away. For had he obeyed, the threatening would not have been carried out (cf. ch. xviii. 8—12). But his heart was hardened by the deceitfulness of sin. In face of that, no fidelity, no evidence, no earnestness of appeal, no pleading, no voice of conscience, could prevail. He was joined to his idols. Because sentence against an evil work is not executed speedily, therefore the heart of man is set in him steadfastly to do evil. Pray that from all such hardness of heart and contempt of God's Word and commandment, the Lord would deliver us.—C.

Ver. 2.—*The woe of weakness.* "Zedekiah, King of Judah." The life of this unhappy monarch is a piteous but powerful illustration of the misery of instability of character, the sorrows that dog the footsteps of the infirm will. What men need, in order to be happier and better than they are, is not more knowledge of what is right—they are amply supplied with that; or the presence of plentiful good purpose and desire to do the right—hell itself is paved with good intentions; but what is needed is strength of will, firmness and stability of character. It is for lack of that that men go so wrong and make such a miserable confusion of their own life and that of others. The history of Zedekiah illustrates all this. Therefore note—

I. HIS CHARACTER AS SHOWN BY HIS HISTORY. He was son of the good King Josiah, and may have been one of the "princes" carried off to Babylon in the days of Jehoiakim. He appears to have attracted the favourable notice of Nebuchadnezzar, probably on the ground of the hope that Jeremiah the prophet cherished concerning him. That hope was expressed in the name given him—Zedekiah, "the Lord our Righteousness," a name fulfilled only in One, but telling of the hopes that gathered round this young king. At twenty-one years of age he was placed on the throne of Judah by Nebuchadnezzar, and then the extreme difficulties of his position became evident. In his own country and in those adjoining, a smouldering rebellion prevailed. This the great enemy of Babylon, Egypt, did not fail to fan and further to the utmost of her power. Only a leader was wanting, and the rebellion would at once break forth. The chief of Zedekiah's own people were eager for him to head the revolt. For a time he refused, and seems (cf. ch. li. 59) to have taken a solemn oath of allegiance to Nebuchadnezzar. But keeping this oath was not easy. It was a cruel position for him, and he had not the strength which so critical a time and emergency demanded. The influence of Jeremiah and his fear of the Baby-lonian power drew him one way; the clamour of his princes, priests, and people, and the promised aid of Egypt drew him another. And so at length he yielded, and treated his oath as so many idle words. Loud and stern were the protests of the prophet of God against such shameless and senseless falsehood (cf. Ezek. xvii. 14; ch. xxviii.). But the princes of his court, as he himself pathetically admits (ch. xxxviii.), had him com-pletely under their influence: "Against them," he complains, "it is not the king that can do anything." He was thus driven to disregard the counsels of the prophet, which, as the event proved, were perfectly sound; and "he who might have kept the fragments of the kingdom together, and maintained for some generations longer the worship of Jehovah, brought its final ruin on his country, destruction on the temple, death to his family, and a cruel torment and a miserable captivity on himself." And there are other recorded instances of his lack of moral strength. His allowing the rich men and all those who, contrary to the Law, had held their brethren as bondslaves, to enslave them once more, notwithstanding that in the most solemn way they had covenanted with God not to do so; then his treatment of the Prophet Jeremiah,—all showed, not so much that he was wicked, as that he was weak. Cruelly imprisoned by his enemies, the king sent for the prophet and placed him in gentler captivity in the court of his own palace. But there assailed by the angry accusations of the prophet's foes, the king yielded, and let them cast him into a horrible pit, where, had he been long left, he must have miserably perished. Conscience, stirred up by the remonstrance of a faithful servant, led the king to interpose again for his relief, and to have him remitted to his prison in the king's court. There Zedekiah treated him kindly; when the famine was raging in the city, he procured bread for him; he asked his prayers, and held long and frequent converse with him, but was all the while in abject fear lest the nobles should discover what their conversation had been about, and he prevailed upon the prophet to condescend to an evasion of the truth in order not to betray him, poor weak king that he was (ch. xxxviii.). Altogether wise was the counsel the prophet gave, but the king would and he would not. He did not know his own mind. But events moved on. The city was captured. The king and his household endeavoured to escape, were caught, carried before Nebuchadnezzar; his children were crucified in his presence; then his eyes were put out; and, loaded with fetters, he was dragged across the weary desert to Babylon, where he lived in misery until the Lord visited him (ch. xxxii. 5)—that is, until the Lord mercifully sent death to put an end to all his woe. It is a pitiful story, but one that teaches much concerning this instability of character which was this poor monarch's ruin.

II. WHAT THIS HISTORY SUGGESTS AS TO SUCH CHARACTER. It suggests: 1. *Its nature.* That it is a halting perpetually between two opinions—a condition of perpetual inde-cision! You never know where to find such men, or can be sure as to what they will do. They promise so well; they turn out so ill. Like a chip on a stream, driven, tossed, turned hither and thither, entangled, engulfed at last—so is such a man. In secular matters it is ruin, in spiritual it is more disastrous still. 2. *Its results.* What a miserable man this Zedekiah must have been! And so are all such. The debtor's pillow is proverbially a restless one, because of its wretchedness. Yet more so is that of the man who has no will of his own. And what sorrow he brings upon others! He drags them down into the same vortex in which he is himself swallowed up. What ruin is wrought by such men in all the circles to which they belong! 3. *Its cause.* Want of a guiding principle in life. Without this, having no fixed rules, secular life is ruined. But in things spiritual this endeavour to serve God and mammon, this divided heart, is absolutely fatal. In such men the surrender to Christ has never been thorough and complete. They are as the seed on the stony ground. 4. *Its cure.* Living under the abiding realization of the presence of Christ. In armies that have begun to waver, the approach, the word, the eye of their leader has rallied them again and won them victory. So if, when tempted to waver, we feel the eye of Christ on us, *we shall be firm*. Therefore let him be the Lord of your souls.—C.

Vers. 8—22.—*Playing fast and loose with God.* See the history. Under fear occasioned by the prophet's earnest appeals and the obvious fact that the judgment of God was drawing near—for the Chaldeans were at the gates—the king and his people solemnly vow to release their slaves. They had no right to retain them; they were sinning against God and them in so doing. Hence they let them go. But the fear departs, they think their danger has disappeared, and they enslave their brethren again. It was an abominable wickedness, and the prophet denounces awful doom upon them for it. Now, concerning such playing fast and loose with God, note that—

I. THIS IS A VERY FREQUENT SIN. Illustrations are Pharaoh, Balaam, Israel's whole career. And there are many such instances now. All insincere repentances are such. They may be: 1. *Very general.* This was so. All the people joined, high and low. Like the professed repentance of the people at John's baptism. 2. *Very solemnly entered upon.* How deeply moved these people seemed! What vows they uttered! 3. *And some fruits meet for repentance may be produced.* These people did for a while set free their slaves. There was a real reformation for the time. The evil spirit went out of the man. 4. *But yet it is all worthless,* for the evil spirit returns, and with increased power. The repentance was so short-lived that it was as if it had never been. Yea, worse: "The last end of that man was worse than the first."

II. ITS ORIGIN AND CAUSE ARE THE UNCHANGED HEART. Underneath the superficial soil there is, in spite of all the seeming repentance, the hard layer of rock. The motive was not the conviction of sin wrought by the Holy Spirit, but a craven fear and a desire, therefore, to buy off God's anger. And in this case it was a cheap way, for liberating their slaves was the best means of securing a strong addition to the forces by which they would defend their city and themselves. Hence, when danger ceased, as they thought, their repentance ceased along with it. What need we all have to be on our guard against the semblances of real religion which our evil hearts are so prone to take up with! And what need to pray that the Lord would show us if we be now self-deceived, and that he would perfectly renew our hearts within us!

III. ITS GUILT IS VERY GREAT. What an outrage it is to God! We would not bear the like conduct from our fellow-men. What awful presumption it manifests! what hardness of heart! And its guilt is the more aggravated because such conduct so plainly shows that we clearly know and understand God's will, though we only make pretence of obeying it.

IV. ITS DOOM IS VERY TERRIBLE. See the burning words of the prophet here (vers. 17—22). And we have portents of that future doom in the hardening of the heart, the searing of the conscience, the being "given over to a reprobate mind," the audacity in wickedness which such conduct produces. How hard to bring such men to repentance! or, if conviction of sin do come, into what depths of despair does it plunge the sinner! All these are indications of the holy displeasure of God which rests on such sin. May he keep us from it.—C.

Ver. 17.— *Slavery.* "Ye have not hearkened unto me," etc. The Jews had become shamefully guilty of this sin of enslaving their brethren. They who had once been slaves themselves, but redeemed by God; they whose whole Law was a protest against it in its real forms of permanence and cruelty; they who were on no higher level than those they enslaved, all being on the same equality with God, members of the same race, worshippers of the same God;—the slavery they were now practising was abhorrent indeed. Concerning slavery—the permanent and absolute possession of a fellow-man, to buy and sell and do with him as he please—this is ever a great sin.

I. NATURE CONDEMNS IT. 1. *We have a moral nature,* a conscience, and this plainly condemns the degradation of a human being to a mere chattel. 2. *Think of ourselves as slaves,* and then how prompt we are to condemn. But if one man may be so held, then every man may. 3. *All are on an equality before God,* and have equal rights and responsibilities. 4. And chiefly because *man is made in the image of God.* Dare we make a chattel of him who bears the image and superscription of Deity? At once our heart condemns.

II. THE WORD OF GOD CONDEMNS IT. 1. Not by *direct prohibition.* Enough is known in the circumstances of the ages of the Bible to show abundant reason wherefore the servants of God were not commissioned to go and everywhere denounce this practice. 2. Nor by *the absence of examples* of good men who kept slaves. It was the universal practice. 3. Nor by *absence of implied sanctions* of this relationship. These facts have been urged in its favour, but we may urge: (1) That if everything not distinctly prohibited in the Bible be right, then many very wrong things would be justified. For very few detailed rules for definite acts are given, but principles from which the mind of God may be easily inferred and his Law applied to all the minutiæ of daily life. (2) Paul no more sanctioned slavery than he did the vilest despotism, for if he told slaves to obey their masters, he bade all men be subject to the higher powers. Now, Nero was on the throne at that time. What the Word of God and experience alike teach is that the violent subversion of evil almost always inflicts greater evil than it removes. (3) And the sacred writers had faith in the sure, even if silent, spread of the great principles of Christ which taught " All things whatsoever ye would that men should do to you, do ye even so to them." (4) And as to the Old Testament slavery and the Mosaic laws in regard to it, it is to be noted that it was a far milder and more genial thing than aught that modern times have known; and next, that the laws of Moses were given on this matter " for the hardness of men's hearts," so that, as with the law of divorce, what could not wisely be at once put down should be so limited and controlled as to be divested of its greater evils. But no greater slander or falsehood can be maintained than to say that the Bible upholds slavery. Its tone and teaching and its universal influence have been to put an end everywhere to the accursed thing.

III. EXPERIENCE CONDEMNS IT. Its influence on the slave, on the master, on the nation, the Church; its moral, domestic, political influence,—all are disastrous and deadly. It is the prolific parent of the worst vices—selfishness, cruelty, licentiousness, tyranny. It has sealed the doom of all nations that have adhered to it, and must ever do so; whilst justice and freedom have ever had resting on them the manifest blessing of God. Christ came to preach liberty to the captives; his gospel is the Magna Charta of the human race.—C.

Vers. 8—22.—*A right act done in a wrong spirit.* I. CONSIDER THE ACT ITSELF. It was emphatically a right act in itself. It did not become right or necessary merely by becoming a covenanted thing. It was an act that meant the attainment of liberty to a very considerable number of people who were not their own masters. God is always on the side of liberty, for only to the free individual is full opportunity given of serving God. And yet this must be said with qualification. External liberty is only of use when it is accompanied with deliverance from inward bondage. Hence, in the New Testament, no great stress is laid upon civil liberty; that would come in due time, and, irresistibly, by the growth and conquering power of Christian principle. The stress in the New Testament is on the maintenance by the individual of liberty within himself. But in ancient Israel there was a God-governed nation as well as God-governed individuals, and civil liberty had to be sought as far as possible by Divine provisions and commands.

II. THE CAUSE OF THE LIBERATION, SO FAR AS IT WAS ACCOMPLISHED. There is some obscurity as to the origin of the covenant and act. Some unmentioned motive seems to have combined king and people to resolve on the liberation of all slaves; but it could only have been a motive of fear and worldly prudence. The same sort of forces must have been in operation as we observe in Pharaoh. A plague drags him a little in the direction of letting Israel go; then the plague ceases, and he draws back again. External force, then, or a shallow repentance, or perhaps something of both, led the people into making this covenant. It was not a deep pity for the oppressed that moved them. The covenant did not come from a deep and perfect insight into the golden rule. Thus there is a revelation of the moral attainments of the people. It is already shown to us how little the better they were for all their opportunities of knowing God's Law and will.

III. THE RESULT OF A RIGHT ACT DONE IN A WRONG SPIRIT. The result is just what might have been expected. Inconvenience, awkwardness, daily, almost hourly, irritation, must have come at once. Just try to estimate some of the results. Only when the slaves had become free would the masters understand how dependent they had been upon them. The work of the covenant was not done when the slave was liberated. Really, it was only begun. The master had then to set to work for himself. His former servant is now given opportunity to become his rival. Moreover, the liberated slave himself does not all at once get the spirit of a free man. When things have been going wrong for generations, they cannot be got right by some magical swiftness. Hence, many potent considerations tempted the masters in forcing a return to the former state of things. They had not counted the cost in beginning, and thus, it seems, they were able to take only a very few steps in the right course.

IV. THE PUNISHMENT. This is specially attached to the breaking of the covenant. The people had really no excuse to offer for breaking it, save the inconvenience and the temporal loss occasioned by keeping it. As far as we can see, this particular covenant was a voluntary one on their part. It recognized a law that had been made in the very coming out from the land of bondage, and it was a covenant to perform a certain outward act. The punishment was just enough; the real wonder would have been if something of the kind had failed to fall on those breaking such a covenant.—Y.

EXPOSITION.

CHAPTER XXXV.

The third member of this group of short prophecies. In it, Jeremiah points to the faithful obedience of the Rechabites, as putting to shame the infidelity of Judahites. It belongs obviously to the time before the arrival of Nebuchadnezzar, perhaps to the summer of B.C. 606. (See Dr. Plumptre's poem, " The House of the Rechabites," part ii., in ' Lazarus and other Poems.')

Ver. 2.—**The house of the Rechabites** ("house" equivalent to "family"). From a notice in 1 Chron. ii. 55 it appears that the Rechabites were a subdivision of the Kenites, the nomad tribe so closely connected with the Israelites (Judg. i. 16; iv. 18—22; comp. Numb. x. 29), especially with the tribe of Judah (1 Sam. xxvii. 10; xxx. 29). The names of Jonadab and of Jaazaniah and his progenitors (which include the sacred Name), together with the zeal of Jonadab for the worship of Jehovah (2 Kings x. 15, 23), seem to indicate that the religion of the Rechabites approximated closely to that of the Israelites. There seem, in fact, to have been two branches of the Kenites—one having Edomitish, the other Israelitish, affinities. Records of the former still exist in the Sinaitic inscriptions, and in the Arabian histories; indeed, there is still a tribe called Benu-l-Qain (often contracted into Belqein) in the Belqâ (the ancient land of Ammon); and it would seem that there is an Arab tribe in Arabia Petræa, eastward of Kerak, which traces itself to Heber the Kenite, and goes by the name of Yehūd Chebr, though it now denies any connection with Jews. There were also Jews of Khaibar, near Mecca, who played an important part in the early history of Islam (see further 'Zeitschr. der deutschen morgenländ. Gesellschaft,' viii. 706; xiv. 438; xxviii. 568, 571). **Into one of the chambers.** There were many "chambers" of different sizes attached to the temple, and employed partly for stores, partly for councils and assemblies, partly for guard-chambers, and other official purposes (comp. 1 Chron. xxviii. 12; Ezek. xl. 17). In ch. xxxvi. 10 we even find a private person occupying one of the "chambers." That into which Jeremiah conducted the Rechabites was, no doubt, one of the largest size; it was appropriated to the use of a single priestly family—the "sons of Hanan" (ver. 4).

Ver. 4.—**A man of God.** The title, according to Hebrew usage, belongs to Hanan, not to his father, and means "prophet" (see e.g. 1 Kings xii. 22); comp. Plumptre—

" There the chamber stands
　　Where Hanan's followers gather up the words
Their master speaks."

The chamber of the princes; i.e. the room " where the princes," i.e. the most distinguished laymen, especially the "elders of the people," assembled before the temple services. **Maaseiah the son of Shallum.** Probably the father of Zephaniah, "the second [or, ' deputy '] priest " (ch. lii. 24), himself a functionary of high rank, as he is called a **keeper of the door** (or rather, threshold). There were three of these "keepers," corresponding to the number of the gates of the temple, and they ranked immediately after the high priest and his deputy (ch. lii. 24); comp. " I had rather be a doorkeeper," etc., in one of the Korahite psalms (lxxxiv. 10).

Ver. 5.—**Pots full of wine ;** rather, *bowls*, large round vessels (*crateres*), out of which the drinking-cups were filled.

Ver. 6.—**Jonadab the son of Rechab our father.** Jonadab (the contemporary of King Jehu) is here called the "father" of the Rechabites (comp. vers. 14, 16), in the same sense in which the disciples of the prophets are called the "sons of the prophets;" he was a teacher, if not (in some sense) a prophet. This illustrates the uncompromising zeal of Jonadab in 2 Kings x. 23 ; the religion of Baal was probably at the opposite pole in the matter of luxury to that of Jehovah as practised by Jonadab.

> "Not for you the life
> Of sloth and ease within the city's gates,
> Where idol-feasts are held, and incense smokes
> To Baalim and Ashtaroth ; where man
> Loses his manhood, and the scoffers sit
> Perverting judgment, selfish, soft, impure."
> (Plumptre.)

Ye shall drink no wine, etc. The Rechabites were, in fact, typical Arabs. The Wahhabee movement, in our own century, may be taken as partly parallel, though, of course, a settled life is not one of the abominations of the neo-orthodox Islam. A still more complete parallel is given by Diodorus Siculus (xix. 94), who states it to be the law of the Nabatæans, "neither to sow corn, nor to plant any fruit-bearing herb, nor to drink wine, nor to prepare houses," and gives as the motive of this the preservation of their independence.

Ver. 11.—**And for fear of the army of the Syrians.** We are expressly told in 2 Kings xxiv. 2 that, after the rebellion of Jehoiakim, "bands of Syrians" made incursions into Judah.

Ver. 12.—**Then came the word of the Lord,** etc. The substance of the severe address which follows must have been delivered in one of the outer courts of the temple, when Jeremiah had left the Rechabites.

Ver. 16.—**Because,** etc. This rendering is against Hebrew usage, and any reader will see that the obedience of the Rechabites stands in no inner connection with the sentence pronounced upon Judah. Ver. 16 is rather an emphatic recapitulation of what has preceded. It runs literally, (*I say) that the sons of Jonadab have performed*, etc., *but (that) this people hath not hearkened unto me ;* or, in more English phraseology, "Yea, the sons of Jonadab," etc.

Vers. 18, 19.—A promise to the Rechabites (perhaps removed from its original connection). The form of the promise is remarkable ; it runs, **Jonadab the son of Rechab shall not want a man to stand before me for ever.** The phrase is, as Dr. Plumptre remarks, "all but essentially liturgical. It is used of the Levites (Deut. x. 8 ; xviii. 5, 7), of the worship of the patriarchs (Gen. xix. 27), of the priests (1 Kings viii. 11 ; 2 Chron. xxix. 11 ; Neh. vii. 65), of prophets (1 Kings xviii. 15), of priests and Levites together (Ps. cxxxiv. 1 ; cxxxv. 2)." It is, however, rash, perhaps, to maintain, with the same acute scholar, that the Rechabites were adopted into the tribe of Levi. The phrase may be simply chosen to indicate the singular favour with which Jehovah regarded the Rechabites—a favour only to be compared to that accorded to his most honoured servants among the Israelites—the patriarchs, the priests, and the prophets.

HOMILETICS.

Vers. 1—11.—*The Rechabites.* A curious interest attaches to these singular people, whose relation to the settled life of the Jews may be compared to that of the gipsies in modern Europe. They were nomads in the midst of cities, preserving the habits of the desert among all the scenes of civilization. But they were in some respects strikingly superior to their more civilized neighbours—a people whose simplicity and abstemiousness was a living rebuke to the debased luxury of the times. Three leading characteristics of the Rechabites are worthy of special note.

I. THEIR NOMADIC HABITS. It is refreshing to meet these quiet, simple people after wearying ourselves with sickening sights of the vice and hyprocrisy of the court and city life of Jerusalem. We are inclined to think too much of external civilization. Making allowance for exaggerations and eccentricities, we may find some much-needed lessons in the protest of Mr. Ruskin against the industrial ideal of the age. Inventions, commerce, wealth,—these are but means to an end. What is the use of the working of wonderful machinery if the outcome is poor and profitless ? Many a man's business is a Frankenstein which becomes a tyrant to him. By others the science and resources of the age are only used as ministers to selfish pleasures. Thus the men and women may be none the better for all the advance that is made in the material appliances of the most complex civilization. Yet the personal condition of these men and women, and not that of the machinery of life, is the one matter of final importance. The quieter, simpler life of the Rechabites had many points which it would be instructive for us to consider. It was out of all the rush and worry of town life. It was calm and comparatively free from care. With few wants, the Rechabites had few anxieties. Are we so much better off than they in this respect? Then, as a wandering life, it was a reminder of the truth, so often forgotten to our serious harm, that all men who live a life higher than the earthly must be pilgrims and strangers here, and must "seek" a better country, that is, a "heavenly." The man of the world is rooted to the earth; and is there not a danger lest many of us should be so absorbed in the busy pursuits of the world as to neglect greater interests, or so satisfied with earthly possessions as to forget that this is not our rest?

II. THEIR ABSTEMIOUSNESS. These Rechabites were the prototypes of the modern teetotalers. They were no ascetics. They made no pretence to the peculiar holiness of the "self-imposed worship" of "dealing hardly with the body" (Col. ii. 23). On the contrary, they were probably a cheerful and unpretentious people, finding more human happiness in a simple abstemious life than the citizens of Jerusalem could ever discover in the unwholesome luxuries of a corrupt civilization. They teach a lesson which our age greatly needs. We may differ as to the necessity or desirability of total abstinence from wine and such things. But all of us should feel the terrible danger that comes from the enervating influence of luxury. In the present day we see little of "plain living and high thinking." Life is both eager and materialistic. It would be well if we could deny ourselves more, that there should be less grossness about our habits, dragging us down from the calm heights of spirituality.

III. THEIR CHANGELESSNESS. The Rechabites are like the Arabs of the desert who were contemporaries of the Pharaohs, and who live now just as they lived in the days of Abraham. Where shall we find such staunch conservatives? Now, of course, we Western Christians believe in a principle of progress, and rightly set ourselves to realize it. But in the pursuit we may lose something that the Rechabites retained. Mere change is not progress, and a restless love of change endangers the fruitfulness of measures which take time to ripen. On the other hand, there is a true loyalty to the past, a just fidelity to our forefathers. At all events, it is grand to see a people independent of passing fashions, bold to resist the spirit of the age when they think that wrong for them, and firm in their own convictions and determinations. Such conduct is bracing to witness; unhappily it is not common.

Vers. 11—17.—*Filial obedience.* The filial obedience of the Rechabites is here adduced as a rebuke to the people of Israel for their disobedience to their Father in heaven.

I. WE OWE A DUTY OF FILIAL OBEDIENCE TO GOD. Obligation corresponds to privilege; peculiar relationship involves peculiar duties. If God is our Father, we owe special obedience to God on account of our relationship with him. The doctrine of the fatherhood of God is no excuse for the relaxation of the fidelity which we felt to be obligatory so long as he was regarded only as our supreme Ruler. Instead of making us more careless, this doctrine should increase the assiduity of our devotion. Strict religionists who dread the moral effects of the modern broad enunciation of this great truth, and lax self-indulgent people who fancy it will allow them to defy the Law of God at pleasure, both fall into a grievous mistake. The father has rights over his children possessed by no one else, and they owe obedience to him as to no other person. This was recognized and carried out much further in the ancient world than it is among us. 1. It is based on nature; the child naturally belongs to the parent. 2. It is increased by experience. For years the child is wholly dependent on his parents. Helpless, and needing constant attention, he finds in them sustenance, protection, and happiness. Parental anxiety, labour, and sacrifice should bind the children by ties of deepest gratitude. Repayment is impossible, nor is it expected; but the least that can be done is to offer obedience. 3. It is recognized by law. The old Roman law gave the father absolute power over the life of his child. Modern law, though it interferes more with the relations of the family, sanctions wide parental rights. Now, if God is our Father, similar obligations bind us to filial obedience to him over and above the obligation we may feel to his Law, his holiness, and his supremacy (Mal. i. 6).

II. THE NEGLECT OF FILIAL OBEDIENCE TO GOD IS REBUKED BY THE NEGLECT OF

FILIAL OBEDIENCE TO MEN. The Rechabites were a rebuke to the Israelites. Yet the Israelites had less excuse for disobeying their heavenly Father than the Rechabites would have had for neglecting the ordinances of their ancestor. Matthew Henry clearly indicates the points of contrast somewhat as follows. I give his thoughts with abridgment :—1. The Rechabites were obedient to one who was but a man; but the Jews were disobedient to an infinite and eternal God. 2. Jonadab was long since dead, and could neither take cognizance of their disobedience nor give correction for it; but God lives for ever to see how his laws are observed, and to punish disobedience. 3. The Rechabites were never put in mind of their obligations to their father; but God often sent his prophets to his people, "rising early and speaking," etc. 4. Jonadab never did that for his seed which God had done for his people; he left them a charge, but left them no estate to bear the charge; but God had given his people a good land, etc. 5. God did not tie up his people to so much hardship as Jonadab required of his descendants; and yet Jonadab's orders were obeyed, and God's were not.

HOMILIES BY VARIOUS AUTHORS.

Vers. 1—6.—*Temptation by Divine command.* I. SO FAR AS IT WENT IT WAS REAL. The scene and the circumstances of authority and religious sanction given to the invitation were calculated to influence the mind. The "pots full of wine" were also an appeal to the eye. God has tried his servants often, but with no intention of making them fall. He tried Job, Abraham, David, etc. He often does this by his providence, the withholding of his grace, etc.

II. IT WAS DONE WITH THE CERTAINTY THAT THE TEMPTATION WOULD BE RESISTED. The same wisdom that devised the incident knew what would be its issue. We are assured of God that he tempteth no man (Jas. i. 13), and that he will not suffer men to be tempted beyond their ability to resist (1 Cor. x. 13). Yet God is continually testing and trying his people, that they may discover their own weaknesses and apply to him for succour.

III. A GREAT END WAS TO BE SERVED. The scene is dramatic and carefully arranged, that it may be publicly impressive. The lesson to be learnt on this occasion is not that of temperance, but simply of filial obedience in one of its most singular and emphatic illustrations. To Israel the lesson was a comparative one. They were put to shame by the steadfastness of men who had no such exalted Person to obey in the matter of their peculiar customs, but who yet had unswervingly adhered to it. Israel, with all the reasons for a similar fidelity, had been weak and fickle, and finally apostate. Men are tried, not only for their own sakes, but for the sake of others. The patience of the saints is a potent reason for our patience and obedience. Christ himself is the Example and Inspiration for all mankind. He was faithful when he was tempted by circumstances infinitely more trying than any that can assail us; and his power is at our disposal when we ask for it.—M.

Vers. 6—10.—*The filial obedience of the Rechabites.* There is something very remarkable in this simple history. Originally aliens in race (1 Chron. ii. 55), they gained a place in the land of Israel (Judg. i. 16). Jonadab the son of Rechab, the ancestor of the race, was the true founder of the family. His character was so high that Jehu affected his company in order to gain esteem from the people (2 Kings x. 15, 16). From him their ascetic rule of life was received, and they had continued to observe it with unswerving strictness. We have here an illustration of—

I. AN EXAGGERATED VIRTUE. 1. *Their asceticism was a real virtue.* In its various elements of temperance, simplicity, and hardihood, it presents a most exemplary and attractive aspect. It must have tended to holiness and happiness. It would be well for the men of our own day were they to imitate this race in these respects. Most of our social evils are easily traceable to the influence of intemperance, luxury, etc. It was a noble ideal nobly realized; yet : 2. *It was exaggerated beyond natural limits.* This is the penalty of those who rigidly observe one mode of life. Excellent as that may be at the first, and, as a whole, may still continue to be, it gets out of joint with the advancing customs of the age, isolates its votaries from the general current of the national life, and stereotypes the degree of civilization or barbarism which gave it birth. In its rigid observance it leads to anachronisms, inconveniences, etc. Its accidental features become more noticeable than its essential ones. Unless grounded on sufficient reasons and continually referred to these, unless adapted in its accidental features to the changing circumstances of the world,—it tends to become unreal, and to produce unreal moral distinctions. There is something of weakness to be detected in the explanation of their presence in Jerusalem (ver. 11). They were out of place. 3. *The secret of this was that it was founded upon an exaggerated sentiment.* Asceticism is in itself neither good nor bad. It receives its real moral importance from the motives and aims that underlie it. In this instance the motive was excellent so far as it was legitimate, but it was clothed with a factitious sacredness and obligation. Consistently carried out, such a principle would stay all progress and sanction the most horrible crimes. That their ancestor had enjoined their mode of life was hardly a sufficient reason for it, and the motive of policy with which he had commanded it was not an exalted one. The true justification for a peculiar mode of life, especially when of this trying description, must be found in the great human and spiritual aims which religion —especially in its later evangelical phase—presents for our achievement. To guard the weakness of a brother, to further the moral and religious welfare of men, and to glorify God by holiness and unselfishness of conduct, are aims that may be ours if we will.

II. A MAGNIFIED PERSONAL INFLUENCE. The hold this man obtained over the conduct of his descendants through so many generations was most remarkable. A man of marked character, great reputation for sanctity, wisdom, and power of impressing others with his peculiar views, forms a conception of what life ought to be, especially for those who, like his own family, are strangers living on sufferance in the midst of another people. The Eastern feeling of respect for parents and reverence for ancestors and of the sacredness of tradition and custom associates itself with his teaching and example, and soon his rule of life becomes a fixed, ineradicable principle amongst his descendants far more potent than any law of the statute-book. This shows: 1. *The power of personal influence.* "Influence is the best kind of power." It belongs more or less to all of us; and we shall be held responsible for its legitimate increase and direction. The influence of any one of us is probably both greater and less than he suspects. It is a natural and proper instinct for man to seek this moral power, and the relations of life afford many opportunities for acquiring and exercising it. Parents. 2. *The importance of securing that our influence shall be of the right kind.* Ultimate results and effects must be left to God; but we have to do with our own character and aims, and with the known tendency of the means at our disposal. We should seek that our influence should be of the very highest kind. It is better to discover moral principles and communicate spiritual inspirations than merely to initiate a custom. Jonadab's influence was on the whole very salutary, but it was not of the highest kind, because he did not furnish his imitators with a morally sufficient motive. So fixed and mechanical, indeed, had their obedience become that they appeared to have more regard to his precept than for the direct command of God (ver. 5). In this respect Jesus Christ is immeasurably his superior. His precepts are self-evident, and commended by his own personal example. He did not appeal to mere self-preservation, but to the noblest moral instincts and principles of our nature. We are not coerced by the personality of Jesus, but persuaded by the sweet reasonableness of his doctrine and Spirit. Influence like this may be slower in making its way, but in the end it is sure to be more lasting and universal.—M.

Vers. 18, 19.—*The blessing of the Rechabites.* I. WHAT IT INCLUDED. It is very startling to find that their blessing is precisely that which is pronounced upon the spiritual Israel of the future. There are two factors in the blessing. 1. *Continuity of the family.* 2. *Perpetuation of its religious standing and moral character:* "To *stand before me* for ever." It is said that descendants of the Rechabites have been discovered in Youcan, and that they still observe the strict *regimen* of their forefathers.

II. WHY IT WAS BESTOWED. The reason given is simple enough, viz. their filial obedience; but it hardly seems to account for the character of the blessing. It is manifest that the bestowal of such a blessing is not to be taken as implying that their conduct had attained to the highest moral standard. But it is significant that the fifth commandment, enjoining this very duty, should be the first with promise. Why is emphasis laid upon filial obedience in the Old and New Testaments? Is it not because *the sentiment of filial affection and respect is a necessary antecedent and preparative for the love of God, which is the supreme and universal law of life?* Of the latter it is the shadow and type. Secondary occasions for the solemn utterance of the blessing on this occasion were probably found in (1) the fact that their conduct had furnished a signal reproof of the apostasy of the nation from its true, eternal Father; (2) that *they acted up to the light which they had;* and (3) that the principle of filial obedience, and the habits of temperance which in their case it had enjoined, were thereby more powerfully commended to the observance of men.—M.

Vers. 5, 6.—*Fathers of temperance.* "Intertwined with the history of Israel is that of a wild and independent tribe of Kenites. When the western Israelites abandoned the roving Arab life to settle in the cities of Canaan, the Kenites still retained their pastoral habits. One of the characteristics which we trace in their history was a fierce resentment against oppression and idolatry. It was a Kenite woman, Jael, who smote Sisera, even in her own tent. It was a Kenite sheik, Jonadab, the son of Rechab, who washed his fierce hands in the blood of Baal's worshippers and Ahab's house (1 Kings xvi.)." The free and eager air of the desert had passed into their lives, and they loved it dearly, and determined never to abandon it, especially when they saw the ruin wrought by the oppression and luxury which were overspreading the inhabitants of the cities they knew most of. Hence the Rechabite vow. But the triumphant march of the vast squadrons of Nebuchadnezzar swept the deserts as well as the cities which lay in his way. And for the time even the hardy Kenites were compelled to set up their tents within the walls of Jerusalem. To them God sent Jeremiah, that he might test and behold and then declare their fidelity to their ancient vow. Amid a population given to excess and gluttony, their total abstinence from wine and their temperate habits could not but excite attention, as much as the strange sight of their black tents pitched in the open spaces and squares of the city. Intimation was given to Jeremiah to teach from their obedience a lesson on the disobedience of the people amid whom they were sojourning. "Inviting these rude and faithful Bedouins into a chamber of the temple, he gave them the invitation which the revellers of Jerusalem would only have been too eager to accept, 'Drink ye wine.' But the Rechabites were not to be tempted. They had adopted their law of temperance at the bidding of a mighty ancestor, as a protection against the temptation of cities. They continued it because conscience approved and health rewarded a noble choice. Broken once—even to please a prophet of the Lord— it might be broken again, and soon the glory of their race would have fled. Therefore they at once replied, plainly, even bluntly, 'We will drink no wine; for,' etc." Now, learn from this—

I. GOD SANCTIONS THE TEMPERANCE VOW. (Cf. ver. 18.) How many and manifold are these sanctions! By the rewards of obedience thereto; by the doom which follows disobedience to the laws of temperance; by his providence and his Spirit speaking within; by the laws of health, of thrift, of social well-being, of conscience; by sanctions negative and positive alike; by the example of some of the foremost and best of men, and by his Word;—by all, he witnesses in favour of the temperance vow.

II. AND THERE IS SORE NEED FOR IT. "If I were to tell you," says one, "that there is in the British Isles a being into whose treasuries are annually poured in unproductive consumption more than one hundred and forty millions of our national wealth; whose actions crush year by year more victims than have been crushed for centuries together by the car of Juggernaut; whose unchecked power causes year by year horrors incomparably more multitudinous than those which the carnage of any battle-fields can present; if I were to say that the services wrought by this being were, if any at all, which is an open question, yet almost valueless in kind, infinitesimal in extent, while, on the other hand, the direct admitted indisputable miseries he inflicts were terrible in virulence and vast in ramification; if I were to say that at his right hand and at his left, as eager and ever active ministers, stood Idiocy and Pauperism, Degradation and Brutality; and at that point you were all to rise up at once and cry aloud, 'Tell us the name of this being, that we may drive him with execration from the midst of us, and that every one of us may strive to extirpate his power and expel his polluting footsteps from our soil;' and if I were to say that, far from doing this, we all as a nation, and nearly all of us as individuals, crown him with garlands, honour him with social customs, introduce him into gladdest gatherings, sing songs in his glory, build myriads of temples to his service, familiarize our very children with his fame and praise;—were I to say this, then sentence by sentence, clause by clause, word by word, it would be literally true, not of a man, but of a thing, and that thing *intoxicating drink*."

III. HOW MAY WE FURTHER THE TEMPERANCE CAUSE? Certainly there is no help equal to that of taking this vow ourselves. If, wherever we are, we will touch not, taste not, handle not, on the ground that we regard it as the curse of this land, that entire abstinence will speak more eloquently than aught beside. And besides this, train your children as Jonadab trained his; command them, saying, "Ye shall drink no wine." A generation so trained, what a difference they would make on the side of temperance and all that is good! Never allow a sneer at those who have taken the temperance vow. Strike at the aids and abettors of intemperance, such as badly drained, ill-lighted, comfortless, unventilated houses; lack of means of reasonable recreation and amusement; want of education and leisure, etc. Never treat drunkenness, however grotesque and absurd its forms, as a thing to be laughed at. We never really hate that at which we laugh. And let each one be sure that he does something in this great cause, that he comes "to the help of the Lord against the mighty."—C.

Ver. 14.—*The children put to shame by the stranger.* The men of Judah were the children, inmates of God's house, members especially of his family. These Rechabites, a wandering tribe of the desert, were the stranger. But their fidelity to the command laid upon them by their ancestor Jonadab is contrasted with and rebukes the shameful disregard of the laws of God, of which the men of Judah were so guilty. For near three hundred years the Rechabites had, out of regard for their father's ordinance, adhered to their self-denying customs, and were adhering to them still, whilst God's own people had set at nought all his counsel and would none of his Law.

I. OBSERVE THIS CONTRAST. 1. *In the motives for obedience which existed on either side.* The one was an earthly father, the other Divine; the one man, the other God. The one, long dead, and whose right to control the actions of his descendants had therefore lapsed; the other, the ever-living God, whose right is as eternal as himself. The one had given an arbitrary command against which much might have been urged; the other had given commands which reason, conscience, and experience alike consented to as wise and good. 2. *In the nature of the obedience rendered.* The one was full of self-denial—a hard, stern law; the other contemplated life in a land flowing with milk and honey, and its ways were ways of pleasantness, and all its paths peace. 3. *In the results of obedience.* In the one, obedience had kept together a small, hardy tribe of half-barbarian herdsmen, without home, friends, religion, wealth, or any marked earthly good. In the other, obedience had been crowned with every blessing, so that all men confessed, "Blessed is the man that feareth the Lord." And yet, notwithstanding the service of the Lord was every way better, that service was disregarded by his people, whilst the ill-requited obedience to a long-deceased ancestor had been so faithfully maintained.

II. AND SUCH CONTRAST STILL EXISTS. Look at the obedience rendered to the laws of the Korân by the followers of Mahomet; to the laws of honour, of trade, of human masters; everywhere we may see human law obeyed, whilst Divine are set at nought. The world can command the prompt, implicit obedience of her votaries; but God calls, and no man answers.

III. EXPLAIN SUCH CONTRASTS. It is because to those who faithfully obey human laws the transient and inferior are as if they were eternal and supreme, whilst to those who profess to be bound by Divine laws the eternal and supreme are as if they were transient and inferior.

IV. WHAT DO SUCH FACTS SAY TO US? Seek the purged vision, that we may clearly see the relative values of things, that our estimates may be corrected, and so we may come to regard as "first" the kingdom of God and his righteousness, and "all other things" as secondary thereto.—C.

Ver. 15.—(Cf. homily on *The Divine long-suffering worn out*, vol. i. p. 204.)—C.

Vers. 18, 19.—*Rewards of filial piety.* We have an instance here. Literally, the promise annexed to the commandment, "Honour thy father," etc., was fulfilled; for their "days were long in the land which the Lord their God gave them." Now—

I. THERE ARE SUCH REWARDS. 1. Promised in God's Word (cf. *passim*). 2. Visible in happy home life. 3. Perpetuated in prosperous communities, nations, etc. 4. Sanctioned by the laws of nature, of man, and of God.

II. THEY ARE THE PRODUCTS AND PROOFS OF THE LOVE OF GOD TO MAN. Hence: 1. The heart of the parent is filled with love to his children. 2. This love leads to desire earnestly the child's well-being. 3. To secure this, God has given (1) a responsive love in the heart of the child towards its parent; (2) the instinct of trust; (3) the direct sanctions of his Word, his Spirit, his providence, to strengthen and maintain that filial piety which so ministers to the good of all.

III. THE GREAT EXEMPLAR OF SUCH PIETY. Our Lord Jesus Christ. "I do always," he said, "those things which please my Father." As God is the realization of perfect fatherhood, so is the Lord Jesus Christ the embodiment of perfect sonship. That sonship was tested and tried as no human sonship ever can be, and it never failed, even under the pressure of the agony, the cross, the seeming abandonment. In him, therefore, we see our Model, and in his exaltation now our reward.—C.

Vers. 1—11.—*The power of a father's command.* The Rechabite habit is, of course, brought forward here to contrast obedience to an earthly and arbitrary demand with the disobedience of Israel to heavenly and essentially righteous laws. But it is worth while to look into this Rechabite habit altogether, in its origin, its causes, its results, its power.

I. THE ORIGIN OF THIS HABIT. The only information we have here is that the habit originated in a command of Jonadab. But, of course, Jonadab must have had some reason seeming weighty to him; and on looking at 2 Kings x. we can make a shrewd guess as to the ends he had in view. He sees the sanguinary and extirpating zeal of Jehu against the scions of Ahab and the worshippers of Baal, and is it not fair to presume that he wished to guard his kinsfolk and posterity against falling into idolatry such as would involve a like terrible fate? Then it occurs to him that he can best do this by separating his people from the dwellers in Israel. This can best be done by urging on them to live a wandering and pastoral life; and still again, the tent life is to be secured by separating the Rechabites from the Israelites in their pleasures. The Rechabite has his plain rule of conduct: "I drink no wine." "Very well," says the indulgent, idolatrous Israelite, "I care not for your company." Idolatry was always connected with debauchery, sensuality, and indulgence of animal passions, and to all these things wine might come to be a minister. Unquestionably Jonadab was a shrewd man, and something of what he aimed at he seems to have gained.

II. THE TEST OF THIS HABIT. No doubt the habit had often been tested, and presumably the same answer would ever be given: "Our father has commanded us to drink no wine." Was it a sufficient reason, one may ask? To which it may be replied that, generally speaking, a father's command would not be enough. We must always ask—What is the thing commanded? Here the question is simply one of positive precept. No one could say that drinking wine was a moral duty, or that the Rechabites injured any one by refusing to drink it. And, indeed, they might have enlarged on the advantages that had come to them through their strict compliance with Jonadab's command. But, in doing so, they entered on debatable ground, and might have been forced into argument. They did the best thing in their position—they fell back on a simple, unreasoning assertion of ancestral custom. Notice, too, *the circumstances in which this habit was tested.* They are divinely prepared circumstances. It is not a band of revellers in the house of feasting who ask them to drink wine. God commands it to be put before them in the house of the Lord, and in the chamber of a man of God. God wishes his people to see for themselves the power of a paternal request; for never before surely had the reasons seemed so great for departing from the rule.

III. THE DISADVANTAGES OF THIS HABIT. The habit did secure what Jonadab meant it to secure. The Rechabites had been kept apart from Israel. But now notice that an advantage gained from some purely external practice is very likely to have some accompanying disadvantage. The Rechabites become tent-dwellers, and then, on the approach of the Chaldeans, having no continuing city, no place of defence, they flee to Jerusalem.   After all, the principle of Rechabitism, the principle of separation and isolation, has its limits.   If we would fairly claim the advantages of human society in times of peril, we must not play the hermit and ascetic at other times.   To be in the world and yet not of it, that is both the problem and the possibility.—Y.

Vers. 12—17.—*Rechabites unconsciously reproving Israelites.*   I. How FAR THE MEN OF JUDAH WERE REALLY CONDEMNED ; *i.e.* How far were the cases really parallel? The first question to be asked is—Were the men of Judah as able to obey the commandments of Jehovah as the Rechabites were to obey the precept of Jonadab? and, of course, the answer is that for many reasons they were not.   But passing this over for the present, let us notice the one respect in which Israelites were *lamentably different* from Rechabites.   The Rechabites gloried in their attachment to the precept of their ancestor ; it was a sort of point of honour with them ; whereas the Israelites were in no way grieved, humiliated, or ashamed because of their disobedience.   If only it had been a continual and sore trouble of heart that there was not in them strength to obey God, why, this very trouble would have been a measure of obedience.   But they both disobeyed and disobeyed in the most heedless and audacious way.   Instead of receiving prophets with contrition and as messengers of God, they laughed them to scorn, abused them, and even put them to death.   And similarly the Rechabites reprove us.   In the midst of all our natural inability to give a true obedience to Divine requirements, we should be incessantly troubled by this ; then would the way be made open for revealing to us how obedience becomes possible.

II. How FAR THE RECHABITES WERE REALLY PRAISED.   After all, Rechabite and Israelite were really the same sort of beings.   If they had exchanged places, they would have exchanged conduct.   The Israelite was quite capable of sticking, with utmost tenacity, to some external rule.   And the Rechabite, we may be quite sure, was equally incapable, with the Israelite, of obeying the commandments of God.   But the Rechabite was to be praised in this that he recognized an authority outside of his own wishes.   The law under which he lived might not go very far; but it operated with certainty so far as it did go.   The Rechabite would have died rather than violate the ancestral prohibition.   God ever recognizes conformity to law as a good thing.   We must, therefore, not go seeking in these Rechabites more than God has appointed us to find.   The one good thing in them was singled out to point a most humiliating lesson and vindicate the need of a severe chastisement. Compared with the benefits of Jehovah toward Israel, what had Jonadab done for the Rechabites ?—Y.

Vers. 18, 19.—*God's recognition of the Rechabite obedience.*   This is just in accordance with what we might expect.   The Rechabites, when they have been used to put Israel to shame, are not allowed to go away without a sufficient stamp on their noble conduct.   The Divine estimate of that conduct is sufficiently shown by the words Jeremiah is authorized to speak.

I. GOD WILL ALWAYS RECOGNIZE A SPIRIT OF OBEDIENCE.   Here we lay emphasis, not so much on actual obedience, as on a *spirit* of obedience.   As to actual obedience, there may be dispute of claim and conflict as to authorities.   But the spirit of obedience is one running through the whole of life.   And God must have seen the spirit of obedience very strong in these Rechabites.   Perhaps it is not too much to say that, if they had been in the place of Israel, it would have been a sore grief to them that they were not able properly to obey the commandments of Jehovah.   Their obedience was tried, it must be remembered, not in the ordinary associations of life, but in extraordinary and difficult circumstances.   They showed the stuff that martyrs are made of, and if God specially recognized their obedience in what was only a matter of external conduct, how sure we may be that he will recognize all obedience that goes deeper !   The thing he would have us do is to find out the right Master, right Teacher, right Leader, and then follow him to the death.

II. THE PARTICULAR PROMISE WHICH GOD MAKES HERE.   Very likely, in a certain sense, it was literally fulfilled.   We must take "for ever" in the limited meaning so often found in the Scriptures, and then we shall have no difficulty in believing that the Rechabites for many generations had a special providence surrounding them.   But recollecting the spiritual significance of prophecy, we may take "for ever" in its largest sense. The essence of the promise is not fulfilled to sons of Jonadab according to the flesh. Promises to natural succession were only to serve a temporary purpose. As all who have a spirit of trust in them are reckoned children of Abraham, so all who have in them the spirit of obedience may be reckoned children of Jonadab. Where the spirit of obedience is, knowledge of God's will becomes easy. Where the spirit of obedience is, actual obedience becomes easier and easier and more a matter of satisfaction.—Y.

EXPOSITION.

CHAPTERS XXXVI.—XXXVIII.
Narrative of Events preceding the Siege of Jerusalem.

CHAPTER XXXVI.
The Roll of Prophecy destroyed by Jehoiakim.

In the fourth year of Jehoiakim (which, it is important to remember, was the first of Nebuchadnezzar) Jeremiah was directed to write down all his previous revelations, from the beginning of his ministry to the present day. Such, at least, is the literal meaning of vers. 1, 2; but it would seem that the literal meaning can hardly be the right one. First of all, a historically accurate reproduction of the prophecies would not have suited Jeremiah's object, which was not historical, but practical; he desired to give a salutary shock to the people by bringing before them the fatal consequences of their evil deeds. And next, it appears from ver. 29 that the purport of the roll which the king burned was that the King of Babylon should "come and destroy this land;" whereas it is clear that Jeremiah had uttered many other important declarations in the course of his already long ministry.

Now, it is remarkable, and points the way to a solution of the problem, that ch. xxv. is said (ver. 1) to have been written in the very same year to which the narrative before us refers, and that it is mainly concerned with the invasion of Nebuchadnezzar and its consequences (indeed, entirely so, if we admit that ch. xxv. 12, 26 have received interpolation).

Is not *this* the prophecy which Jeremiah dictated to Baruch ?[1] and is not ver. 2 a loose,

inaccurate statement due to a later editor? That the prophetic as well as the historical books have passed through various phases (without detriment to their religious value) is becoming more and more evident. The seventh and eighth chapters of Isaiah, and the thirty-seventh and thirty-eighth of the same book, have demonstrably been brought into their present shape by an editor (see Cheyne's 'Prophecies of Isaiah,' vol. i.); is it not highly reasonable to conjecture that these narrative chapters of Jeremiah have, to a greater or less extent, passed through a similar process (see below on ver. 6)? (The main point of this theory— that relative to ch. xxv.—has been brought forward by Dr. H. Grätz, in his 'Monatsschrift für Geschichte und Wissenschaft des Judenthums,' vol. xxiii. p. 298, etc.)

Ver. 4.—**Baruch.** Already mentioned as Jeremiah's attendant, in ch. xxxii. 12. He appears to have been of high rank (see on ver. 15), as Josephus, indeed, expressly states ('Ant.,' x. 9, 1). Maaseiah, his grandfather, was governor of the city (2 Chron. xxxiv. 8), and Seraiah his brother (ch. li. 59) held some equally honourable, though not so easily definable, position in the court.

Ver. 5.—**I am shut up.** Not so; Jeremiah was not detained by material force. Some strong reason he had (perhaps of a ceremonial kind), but as it was irrelevant to the narrative, it is not given. Render, *I am detained* (same verb as in 1 Sam. xxi. 7).

Ver. 6. — **Upon the fasting-day.** The mention of the fast-day suggests that ver. 9 is out of its place, which again confirms the view that the narrative before us has received its present form from an editor. **In the ears of all Judah** (see ver. 9).

Ver. 7.—**They will present their supplication**; literally, *their supplication will fall* (as margin). The phrase seems to be suggested by the gesture of a suppliant. Hence humility is one idea; but success is entirely another. That which lights down before one's eyes cannot be disregarded. Hence, in ch. xxxvii. 20 and xlii. 2, the Authorized Version renders, "be accepted." This is,

---

[1] There is a striking confirmation of this view in the relation of ch. vii. to ch. xxvi., the former containing the prophecy shortly summed up in the latter.

at any rate, a better rendering than that quoted above, which is both weak in itself and obscures the connection. **And will return**; rather, *so that they return*. "Returning,"*i.e.* repentance, is necessary, because their "evil ways" have provoked Jehovah to "great anger and fury;" but is only possible by the Divine help (comp. Acts v. 31, "To *give* repentance unto Israel"). Hence prayer is the first duty.

Ver. 9.—**In the fifth year of Jehoiakim.** It is remarkable that the Septuagint has here the *eighth* year; and Josephus, too, relates that Jehoiakim paid tribute to Nebuchadnezzar in his eighth year. This latter statement seems to tally with the notices in 2 Kings xxiv. The vassalage of Jehoiakim is there said to have lasted three years; this followed the rebellion; while the siege of Jerusalem was reserved for the short reign of Jehoiachin. Now, as this siege must have been the punishment of Jehoiakim's rebellion, and as the reign of the latter king lasted eleven years, we are brought to the same date as that given by Josephus for the commencement of the vassalage, viz. the eighth year. It is to this year, then, that 2 Kings xxiv. 1 refers when it says, "In his days Nebuchadnezzar King of Babylon came up, and Jehoiakim became his servant;" and also the narrative before us in the statement that "they proclaimed a fast before Jehovah to all the people in Jerusalem, and to all the people that came from the cities of Judah unto Jerusalem." What other event would have produced such a concourse of worshippers? The battle of Carchemish (which took place in the fourth year of Jehoiakim)? But it was by no means clear as yet that the consequences of this would be disastrous for Judah. Carchemish was too far off for the people of Judah to show such serious alarm (similarly Grätz, 'Monatsschrift,' etc., vol. xxiii. p. 300). If so, Jeremiah kept his prophecy by him for several years, till the right moment came. **The ninth month.** As this is a winter month (see ver. 22), Jeremiah evidently reckons by the Babylonian calendar, the ninth month of which, Kisiluv (Hebrew, Chisleu), began from the new moon of December.

Ver. 10.—**The chamber** (see on ch. xxxv. 4) **of Gemariah . . . the scribe.** Gemariah was favourably disposed to Jeremiah (ver. 25); he was probably the brother of Jeremiah's friend, Ahikam (ch. xxvi. 24). He was one of the royal secretaries, and reckoned among the "princes" (see ver. 12). **In the higher court.** "Higher" equivalent to "inner." **The new gate** (see on ch. xx. 2).

Ver. 12.—**He went down** (see on ch. xxvi. 10). **Sat there.** In deliberation on

the affairs of the state. **Elishama the scribe.** Gemariah, then, had a colleague. So in Solomon's cabinet (if the word may be used) there were two *sôferim*, or secretaries, one perhaps for the civil and one for the military business (1 Kings iv. 3; comp. ch. lii. 25). **Elnathan.** Mentioned already, ch. xxvi. 22.

Ver. 14.—**Jehudi . . . the son of Cushi.** A genealogy which contains a history. Jehudi is not a true proper name, any more than Gadi ("a Gadite"), the quasi-name of the father of Menahem (2 Kings xv. 14), or than Cushi, the quasi-name of Jehudi's great-grandfather. Cushi himself was, doubtless, an Ethiopian, and probably (like Ebed-melech, ch. xxxviii. 7) a eunuch, or at least chamberlain; his son and grandson were both worshippers of Jehovah (as their names indicate), but were not qualified to become Jewish citizens. The Egyptian was not, indeed, to be abhorred, but not until the third generation could his descendants be admitted into "the congregation" (Deut. xxiii. 8). Egypt and Ethiopia were historically connected (see Lenormant's 'Ancient History,' index to vol. i.). For the name of "Jehudi," comp. "Jehudith," daughter of Beeri the Hittite (Gen. xxvi. 34).

Ver. 15.—**Sit down now.** The princes evidently recognize Baruch as belonging to a family of distinction (see on ver. 4); and from vers. 19, 25 we may infer that they were favourably inclined both to Baruch and to his master (comp. ch. xxvi.).

Ver. 16.—**They were afraid both one and other**; rather, *they turned shudderingly one to another.* Such an announcement as Jeremiah's at such a serious crisis startled them by its boldness. We may infer that the prophet had for some time, by Divine command, kept his sombre anticipations in the background. **We will surely tell the king**; rather, *we have to tell the king.* Friendly feeling would have prompted them to hush up the affair (see ch. xxvii. 20, 21), but duty forbade.

Ver. 17.—**How didst thou write all these words at his mouth?** Two questions seem to be combined here—"How didst thou write all these words?" and "Didst thou write it all at his mouth?" Baruch's answer is good for both.

Ver. 18.—**He pronounced**, etc.; rather, *He kept dictating . . . while I wrote with ink*, etc. The addition of the last clause suggests (and was, perhaps, intended to do so) that Baruch's function was simply mechanical.

Ver. 20.—**Into the court**; *i.e.* into the inner court, in which the royal apartments were apparently situated (comp. 1 Kings vii. 8).

Ver. 21.—**Which stood beside the king**; literally, . . . *above the king.* The standing courtiers, of course, rose above the king; comp. Isa. vi. 2, "Seraphim stood *above* him."

Ver. 22.—**In the winter-house**; *i.e.* that part of the royal palace (*beth*, house, may also be rendered *apartment*) which was arranged for a winter habitation (comp. Amos iii. 15). According to Dr. Thomson ('The Land and the Book,' p. 309), the more airy part of a house is called "summer-house," and the more sheltered room "winter-house." The ninth month, in which the events now being related took place, corresponded approximately to our December. It was, therefore, the cold and rainy season; December is a stormy month in Palestine. A fire on the hearth; rather, *in the chafing-dish* (or, *brazier*). It was a vessel with live coals placed in the centre of the room, still used in the East in cold weather.

Ver. 23.—**Three or four leaves**; rather, *columns* or *compartments*. "Leaves" would imply that it was a book out of which Jehudi read, whereas it was a roll (*m'gillah* never has any other meaning). But "books" were not yet known, nor would a knife have been necessary to separate the pages. **He cut it.** The subject may be either the king or Jehudi (at the bidding of the king). The term implies that the action of cutting was repeated several times; but we are not to suppose that each successive portion was cut off as it was read. The indignation of the hearer translated itself into the repeated mutilation of the roll, until all the roll was (cast into the fire and) consumed. **With**

the penknife; literally, *with the scribe's knife*. **On the hearth**; rather, *in the chafing-dish* (or, *brazier*).

Ver. 24.—**Yet they were not afraid.** Unlike Josiah (2 Kings xxii. 11), and even Ahab (1 Kings, xxi. 27). **Nor any of his servants**; *i.e.* the courtiers, as opposed to the "princes."

Ver. 26.—**The son of Hammelech**; rather, *a royal prince* (we should render similarly in ch. xxxviii. 6; 1 Kings xxii. 26; 2 Kings xi. 1, 2; Zeph. i. 8). We have seen already that the number of such royal princes was very large (see on ch. xvii. 9); any one, in fact, who had a king among his ancestors was a "royal prince." **The Lord hid them**; *i.e.* saved them from discovery.

Vers. 27—32.—Punishment denounced against Jehoiakim, and second writing of the former prophecy.

Ver. 29.—**Thou shalt say to Jehoiakim**; rather, *concerning Jehoiakim*. Intercourse between Jehoiakim and the prophet was broken off by the preceding scene. The speech begins in the *oratio directa*, but soon passes into the *obliqua*. **Cause to cease** ... **man and beast.** A forcible description of the completeness of the devastation.

Ver. 30.—**He shall have none to sit**, etc. Substantially a repetition of the prophecy in ch. xxii. 18, 19 (comp. 30).

Ver. 31.—**I will bring upon them**, etc. (comp. ch. xxxv. 17; xix. 15).

Ver. 32.—**Many like words.** Thus Jehoiakim gained nothing by his sin (comp. Introduction).

HOMILETICS.

Vers. 1—4.—*The writing of the roll.* I. WHO WERE ENGAGED IN THE WRITING OF THE ROLL? 1. *God.* (1) The thoughts of the prophecies to be recorded were inspired by God. "Prophecy" means "inspired utterance." Jeremiah was to write "the words that I have spoken unto thee." We should seek in the Bible chiefly, not the scribe's letters (grammatical study), nor the prophet's words (historical theology), but God's thoughts (spiritual truth). (2) God commanded the writing of the roll (ver. 2). The Bible is given to us by God. It is his will that the sayings of ancient prophets and apostles should be the lamp for all ages. Therefore (*a*) he will bless the right reading of the Bible, and (*b*) he will call us to account for the use we make of it. 2. *Jeremiah.* God does not speak to mankind by a direct and audible voice as with the thunder-tones of Sinai. He speaks through an instrument—a man, a prophet. And this prophet is plainly not just a mechanical mouthpiece to the Divine voice. His personality counts for something. His style, mode of thought, experience, general knowledge, spiritual condition, etc., all mould his utterances of inspired truth. Jeremiah's prophecies are characteristic of Jeremiah. 3. *Baruch.* The scribe has neither the genius to conceive the thought, nor the oratorical and literary gifts to clothe it in language. He is a simple amanuensis. Yet his work is important. For some reason not expressed, possibly like St. Paul on account of bodily weakness, Jeremiah did not write out his prophecies with his own hand. Thus work was found for Baruch. God finds offices corresponding to all varieties of gifts. But the less gifted are too often ambitious to perform the more honoured tasks of greater men, or, failing in these, they are often reluctant to fulfil their more lowly calling.

II. WHY WAS THE ROLL WRITTEN? This roll was not to contain a new composition. It was to be only a writing of utterances which had already been made public. Why, then, was it written? 1. That the prophecies might be *preserved*. Truth is eternal. A truth once discovered should be cherished as a lasting possession. It may be lost, but it can never decay. "The Word of the Lord endureth for ever;" therefore the record of it should be preserved as of permanent value. 2. That the prophecies might reach a *larger audience*. The roll could be frequently perused and by various readers. Revelation is not for the few initiated; it is for all who need its light. 3. That the prophecies might be *reread* to those who had already heard them. The use of them was not expended when they were first spoken. We are too ready to be attracted by mere novelty. The latest books and the latest ideas are run after to the neglect of greater thoughts and greater works of older date. But truth is more important than novelty. And old truths need to be repeated, because (1) they may have been received with inattention at the first hearing; (2) they may be better understood or newly applicable under fresh circumstances, and after the hearer has gained larger powers of insight by his growing experience; (3) they may be so profound as to be practically inexhaustible, or so eternally fresh and inspiring as to be always useful; (4) they fail of their end till they affect our conduct, and must be repeated "line upon line" while men fail to do what they know. 4. That the prophecies might he *studied carefully and compared together*. So we should study the Bible, searching the Scriptures and comparing parts together, as we can only do when the whole lies written before us.

III. WHAT WAS THE SCOPE AND AIM OF THE ROLL? 1. It was a record of *God's wrath against sin and a denunciation of judgment*. The words so important that they needed to be thus recorded were spoken "against Israel, and against Judah, and against all the nations" (ver. 2). People like to forget disagreeable ideas and cherish only those that please them. Yet there are times when it is for our own profit to face them. Surely it is best to know our danger if by the knowledge of it we can find a means to escape it, or, at the worst, be prepared to meet it. But if the revelation of judgment, and of temporal judgment, contained in Jeremiah's prophecies was so precious as to be committed to writing under a solemn Divine commission, what value shall we set on the revelations of heavenly things and declarations of the glad tidings of salvation that are written in other parts of the Bible? 2. It aimed at *leading the people to repentance*. (Ver. 3.) The threats of future calamities were first uttered with this end, and they were to be repeated for the same object. Thus the darkest words of revelation are spoken in mercy. If they are repeated, it is because God is so forbearing and anxious to save that he will not give his people up. The aim of revelation is practical. It is a lamp to our feet (Ps. cxix. 105). The chief purpose of its warnings and its words of grace is to lead us back from sin to God. Thus the Bible, though the crowning work of all literature, should not be regarded chiefly from a literary point of view, but rather as containing messages from our Father to guide and help our conduct.

Vers. 5—21.—*The reading of the roll.* I. THE READER. Baruch, the secretary of Jeremiah, is sent to read the roll. We do not know what cause detains the prophet. He has often made bold utterances in public before this. But if he cannot go the truth must not be hidden. "The Word of God is not bound" (2 Tim. ii. 9). Truth is more important than the speaker. It matters little who is the messenger; all importance attaches to the message. Men forget this when they run after a Jeremiah and neglect a Baruch, though the scribe may be the bearer of the prophet's teachings. We should recollect how much more important the gospel preached is than the man who preaches it. If a Chrysostom, a Paul, or an angel from heaven preach any other gospel but the true gospel of Christ, "let him be anathema." But if Christ is proclaimed, we must be thankful for that, though the preacher and his conduct may not quite approve themselves to us (Phil. i. 18). Perhaps it was best that the prophet should not appear in person to repeat his message. His presence might rouse personal feelings to the neglect of his message. He desired the truth to carry its own fair weight. Baruch did his work bravely and modestly. In repeating the prophet's unpopular words, he would invite the odium that attached to them to pass on to himself. But *his* duty was to read the roll. *God* would see to the consequences. With this courage there was a remarkable modesty. The occasion was a tempting opportunity for Baruch to exercise his own powers by way of comment or addition. But he said nothing beyond what was written in the roll. He knew his place. The scribe is not a prophet. Why should not the great sermons of great preachers be sometimes read in our churches?

II. THE CIRCUMSTANCES OF THE READING. The roll was read to three audiences. 1. The *people* (vers. 9, 10). The Bible is a book for the people, not for the priests or the learned only. The occasion of that reading was "a fasting-day" (ver. 6). Then the people would be in the best mood for receiving the call to repentance. We should learn to speak "in season." The place of the reading was the temple (ver. 10). Instruction should be associated with worship. 2. The *princes* (vers. 11—19). Divine truth is of importance to all classes. They who are in responsible positions are especially called upon to study the signs of the times. 3. The *king* (vers. 20, 21). It was necessary that what concerned the fate of the kingdom should receive the most careful consideration of its monarch. Even kings must bow before the utterance of truth. A prophet can speak with authority to a king.

III. THE EFFECT OF READING. The effect on the people is not here indicated. Probably little moral good came of it; but there was evidently some impression made if the feelings of one man, Michaiah, may be taken in illustration. This man was so much stirred by what he heard that he immediately reported it to the princes at the court (vers. 11—13). From this report other consequences flowed. If but one man out of a great congregation is seriously impressed by a sermon, that sermon has not failed; possibly through the one man it may be instrumental in effecting vast and lasting good. When the roll was read to the princes they were first dismayed (ver. 16). How graphic is that picture of the great men of the kingdom as "they turned shuddering one to another," terrified and confounded by the prophet's words! Perhaps some of them had heard the same words before unmoved. The time may come when the most hardened will be roused. The terror of princes might be a wholesome beginning of a genuine repentance. But if no appropriate action followed, it would soon die away, leaving the conscience the more hardened and demoralized. We need to "bring forth *fruits* meet for repentance." The princes inquired as to the origin of the roll. Were its words true? On what authority were they written? Such inquiries are reasonable. We should have a reason for accepting what we believe to be a Divine message. Yet it is dangerous to divert attention from the moral weight of truth by too much intellectual criticism about literary curiosities. The princes reported the matter to the king with a warning to Baruch—patriotic and generous conduct. The king's reception of the book was very different. Unlike the princes, who neither accepted the message without question, nor rejected it for its unpleasant contents, but inquired calmly and carefully as to the authority of it, Jehoiakim flew into a rage and hastily destroyed it. What an act of supreme folly! The truth was not the less important because the record of it was burnt. "We can do nothing against the truth, but for the truth" (2 Cor. xiii. 8).

Vers. 22—26.—*The burning of the roll.* When the princes informed Jehoiakim of the circumstances connected with the reading of Jeremiah's prophecies, the king sent an attendant, Jehudi, to fetch the roll and read it to him. It has been said that he showed contempt for the Word of God by relegating the reading to a page instead of sending for Baruch. But Baruch had probably escaped to seclusion at the warning of the courtiers (ver. 19), and as he had left the roll in other hands, what was more natural than that Jehoiakim should send for it without a thought of Jeremiah's appointment of a reader? Indeed, it matters little who reads; the question is—How is the reading received?

I. CONSIDER THE ACTION OF THE KING. It was December—the cold and rainy month. A fire blazed on the brazier. As the roll was read, the king cut it up and flung the sections into the fire, till he had destroyed the whole of it. His action was one of rage and folly. He would have no more of the prophet's dreadful words for himself; he would prevent them from further influencing others; he would vent his rage upon the record, though he could not touch the truths contained in it. Are there not many who inwardly sympathize with this violence of Jehoiakim? They dare not say they wish the Bible to be destroyed. But there are things in it which testify against them so strongly that they would keep them for ever out of sight. The special features of Jehoiakim's action are significant. 1. It was *beyond his rights*. King as he was, the roll did not belong to him. Neither had he any authority over the inspired word of prophecy.

Earthly power confers no privilege and power in Divine things. 2. It was *brutally violent.* Jehoiakim cut up and burnt the roll—that was all he could do. To refute its contents was beyond his power. 3. It was *vain and futile.* The roll might be burnt, but the truth it contained could not be destroyed, nor could it even be suppressed. Another roll could be written, and the burning of the first would be an advertisement for the second. Violent opposition thus benefits the cause it would destroy. The burning of Tyndale's Bibles was one of the best means for securing the circulation of a larger number of English Bibles. 4. It was *suggested by a temptation.* The fire was at hand—an unusual thing, apparently, just suited to the occasion. There is an evil providence as well as a higher providence of good. It is not safe to follow the superficial indication of events. That is as likely to come from below as from above. 5. It was *deliberate.* Piece by piece the roll was cut up and burnt. Hasty passion might excuse the first burning, but not the whole process. 6. It was *complete.* All the roll was consumed. There was no discrimination. The act was symbolical. The rejection of one part of truth will lead to the rejection of the whole of it. 7. It was *really injurious only to the perpetrator.* The roll could not feel ; the truth could not be destroyed; another roll could be written. But the burning of the roll was to the king's own loss. That roll contained the only available prescription for the healing of the distresses of himself and his kingdom. The Bible is really sent for the good of the worst of men. Their rejection of it is only to their own loss.

II. CONSIDER THE CONDUCT OF THE COURTIERS. 1. *Some stood by and watched the burning.* They did not aid it ; but they did not hinder it. Therefore they shared the responsibility of the king. For we are resposible for the evil we will not restrain as well as for that we commit, so that in doing little harm we may yet be guilty of much. The courtiers had no valid excuse for their indifference. Royal authority cannot justify acquiescence in wrong. Personal fear is no excuse, since it is better to die for the right than desert it in sheer cowardice. These men showed no fear (ver. 24). They had been alarmed (ver. 16). But religious fears are transitory, and if not acted on leave the heart more hardened than they find it. 2. *Some expostulated.* These men had been more permanently affected by the reading of Baruch. They carried the impressions made in the temple to their conduct at the court. That is a proof of a real influence of the words of Jeremiah upon them. It is little that we feel the weight of religion in church. The test is how far this dwells with us in the world, and when it would urge to unpopular, difficult, or dangerous actions.

Vers. 27—32.—*The rewriting of the roll.* Under the inspiration of God Jeremiah requires Baruch to write another roll, containing all that was in the burnt roll and also some additional matter. We may take the following points connected with the rewriting of the roll—

I. THE FRUSTRATION OF ALL ATTEMPTS TO SUPPRESS DIVINE TRUTH. Jehoiakim is a king and a tyrant. But there is a limit to his power. It is vain for him to attempt to hinder the declaration of God's truth. If one roll is burnt another can be written. If one prophet were killed another could be raised up. Truth is eternal. It will survive all enmity, and it will find its way ultimately to the light. He who is against it plays a losing game.

II. THE PERSISTENCE OF GOD'S DESIGNS. They are not to be set aside by all the scheming and all the violence of men. God does not change because we oppose his will. There is something awful in the thought of that great, inflexible will, firm as granite against all the raging of man's foolish passions. By opposition we can only bring ourselves into collision with it to our hurt, as the waves dash themselves to spray on the rock they cannot break. We cannot stay its invincible progress—

> "Though the mills of God grind slowly,
>   Yet they grind exceeding small."

If we wish to find God's will working with us and for our good, we must submit to it. We cannot expect the great God to change his plans to suit our inclinations.

III. THE CONTINUANCE OF GOD'S MERCY. Why should the roll be rewritten ? The threats it contained could be executed without any reissue of them. If all fair warnings were disregarded, no more could be required. True, and no more were required.

Yet out of his great, long-suffering grace God issued his warnings afresh. This is the deeper truth that underlies the command to write out the prophecies once more. The same truth is illustrated in all the history of the Jews. God sent a succession of prophets, "rising up early and sending," to impress upon the people the same unheeded lessons. The continuance of revelation with us is a reminder of God's forbearing mercy.

Ver. 32 (last clause).—*The development of revelation.* "And there were added besides unto them many like words." The second roll was a transcript of the first, but with numerous additions, though these were all similar in character to the original prophecies. We have here, on a small scale, an instance of that development of revelation which is evolved on similar principles through the whole realm of knowledge.

I. REVELATION FOLLOWS A PROCESS OF GRADUAL DEVELOPMENT. There are those to whom the word "development" has an evil sound, because of the excuse Roman Catholics have found in it for perversions of New Testament doctrines; while others object to it on account of its use in the scientific world, where they think it is meant to take the place of the will and wisdom of God. But the abuse of a word should not hide us from the important idea that it naturally denotes. Nothing is more true and grand and wonderful in all God's works than the principle of development which his great power and wisdom has made to run through them. The dawn advances through twilight to full day; the seed grows slowly—"first the blade, then the ear, then the full corn in the ear;" man begins life as an infant, and toils up to his full stature through years of childhood and youth; the kingdom of heaven began as a grain of mustard seed, and is slowly spreading till, from the work of that little company in the upper room at Jerusalem, "the earth shall be full of the knowledge of the Lord as the waters cover the sea." Revelation is no exception to the same universal Divine process. God did not flash all his truth upon the world in one dazzling moment. The Bible is a slow growth of many centuries. Progress is observable in the Old Testament. Isaiah saw further than it was given to Abraham to see. Jeremiah's vision of the new covenant (ch. xxxi. 31—34) is in advance of the Levitical Law. The New Testament is a decided manifestation of broader knowledge and fuller light than the earlier revelation contained. Christ said to his disciples, "I have yet many things to say unto you, but ye cannot bear them now" (John xvi. 12). St. Paul's teachings go beyond the doctrines held in his day by the Church at Jerusalem. We cannot say that God has nothing further to reveal. The Christian believes that "holy Scripture containeth all things necessary to salvation." But all the analogy of God's past action would lead us to think that there may be much truth which men were not at first able to see in the Scripture, and yet which may be known in successive ages and found to be of great profit. 1. The *human occasion* of this development of revelation may be seen in the fact that the thoughts of men grow. God reveals his truth in human thinking. Men must seek him, and, feeling after the truth, are rewarded by God's revelation. But the revelation is proportionate to the progress of the search. 2. The *Divine purpose* of this development may be noted in such facts as these: God reveals truth as man is able to receive it, as he is spiritually educated to understand it, as he is in a moral condition to profit by it, as changing circumstances may bring need for new stages in the development of it.

II. THE DEVELOPMENT OF REVELATION IS CONSISTENT WITH ITSELF. 1. *It does not set aside old truth.* In the new roll all the contents of the old roll were rewritten, so that the fresh matter was not a substitute but an addition. Christ came to fulfil the Law and the prophets, not to destroy them (Matt. v. 17). The gospel exceeds but does not supersede the spiritual truth of the Old Testament. No new discovery can ever destroy what is once known to be real and true. 2. This development maintains *an essential likeness between its earliest and its latest stages.* The added words of Jeremiah's roll were "like unto" those which were first written. All truth must ultimately harmonize. One great test of a new doctrine is its agreement with previously established truth. All Christian truth must agree with the teachings of Christ and his apostles. That many so-called developments of truth are really perversions of truth may be proved by the application of this test. Thus to us Protestants it seems clear that many Roman Catholic dogmas which profess to be developments of Christianity are so utterly contrary to its spirit that they must be regarded either as pagan additions or as relapses towards Judaism. So there are "liberal" notions that are really negations of essential elements of the gospel. It is monstrous to call these developments. The oak is a development of the acorn; but the hollow, blasted stump, which is the last stage in the history of the tree, is surely not a further result of the same process. Decay is not development.

HOMILIES BY VARIOUS AUTHORS.

Vers. 1—4.—(*Vide* ch. xxx. 1—3.)—M.

Vers. 5—8.—*Vicarious ministry in holy things.* The "vicar," an ecclesiastical officer of mediæval times,—explain the origin and nature of his duties. Show how large this question of vicarious service, and how universal its necessity, in business, society, the state, the Church, etc. This incident illustrates—

I. ITS ESSENTIAL NATURE. Not merely that one should do, be, or suffer instead of another, but as representative of him. More or less consciously, sympathetically, adequately. That one man and not another should do a given duty, for instance, may be but the chance of fortune; but that he should do it *for* and *in place of* that other is for him to be that other's "vicar." This essential character of the transaction is not altered by the fact of the superiority, equality, or inferiority of the substitute.

II. ITS SUGGESTIVE INTEREST. An element of pathos and mystery. Perhaps the end better served in this than in the alternative way. Conceivable that the reading, the authoritative publication, and the supernatural interest, may have been enhanced rather than otherwise by the substitution. 1. *The community of true service.* How different in importance, etc., the function of the prophet in receiving the message and communicating it from that of the scribe! yet both are on this occasion indispensable. One man's service the condition of another's or its complement. All true service associated in relation to final ends and rewards (John iv. 37, 38; Heb. xi. 40). 2. *An impression of urgency produced.* This was the message it was absolutely important for Judah to hear at that time. God always speaks at the right time, even when that requires extraordinary efforts and unusual means. The latter on this occasion must have eloquently suggested that *now* was the "accepted time" and "the day of salvation." 3. *The earnestness of the prophet and his Inspirer.* Jeremiah was the true friend of the nation and the devoted servant of Jehovah, therefore he did not excuse himself from the task because of its difficulties. 4. *How inevitable the message!* It was not to be evaded or suppressed. From the prison or hiding-place the prophet will still be heard.

III. ITS ETHICS. Service of the kind here described was justifiable only on the supposition that the original or principal in responsibility is unable to do his own proper work, or that it can be better done by being delegated to another. Jeremiah is careful to explain why he does not do it himself. Would that the reasons for non-attendance in the sanctuary, or inoccupation in spiritual work, were as real and valid in the case of professing Christians! 1. *On the part of the person instead of whom the service was rendered.* He did not ask his substitute to do what he could do himself; and what he alone could do was done with the utmost care and diligence. It is calculated that the writing out of the roll from the prophet's dictation occupied nine months, and many delays and difficulties must have been experienced. His solicitude, too, on behalf of the proper delivery of the message by Baruch, is very instructive and inspiring. He sought (God's end in) the repentance of the people, and everything was to conspire to produce this. By example and moral influence he sought to fill Baruch with his own enthusiasm, and a sense of the importance of the task. The preacher is the vicar of the Church; so with the Sunday school teacher, etc. By prayer, sympathy, and loving co-operation Christians should encourage these. 2. *On the part of the substitute.* Baruch sought to do his part faithfully and with minute exactitude. His success in producing an impression proved how he exerted himself. A sense of responsibility should ever rest upon those who minister in the house of God. A certain measure of boldness was also required to do such a thing. The people or their princes might turn against him. Boldness is essential to the preaching of the gospel. But there cannot but occur to most readers the parallelism there is in all this to what Christ has under-taken for us. Another temple from whose service we are "shut up" by reason of personal unfitness, or that we remain in the flesh. Christ, our great Forerunner and Vicar, or Substitute, has entered into its holy of holies, with his own eternal sacrifice and intercession. Upon him all our hope must be placed; we must follow him in spirit; and we must imitate Jeremiah in the zeal and labour with which we execute our part of the great process of salvation.—M.

Vers. 9—16.—*Free course of the Word of God.* The progress made by the messages of Jeremiah when read aloud in the scribe's cell at the entrance of the higher court of the temple was very remarkable, and fully justified the great care and ingenuity with which it was effected.

I. A SANCTIFIED INGENUITY SHOULD BE SHOWN IN TAKING ADVANTAGE OF OR CREATING SUITABLE OCCASIONS FOR MAKING KNOWN GOD'S WORD.

II. THE WORD OF GOD IS COMMENDED BY ITS GENERAL AND SPECIAL HUMAN INTEREST.

III. WHEN ONE INSTRUMENTALITY FAILS, GOD WILL RAISE UP ANOTHER, UNTIL HIS MESSAGE ATTAINS ITS DESTINATION.—M.

Vers. 16—18.—*The mystery of inspiration.* I. THE NATURAL DESIRE TO SOLVE IT. 1. *This has its root in mere curiosity.* A desire to know for the sake of knowing—laudable enough in itself, but in danger of passing into irreverence and idle speculation. Religious movements and supernatural phenomena have excited this wonder in all ages. Religion interests many as a problem, where it is refused attention or respect as a law. 2. *This is increased by the attraction of the forbidden and unlawful.* An anticipation of the "profane and vain babblings, and oppositions of science [the knowledge] falsely so called," against which Timothy is warned (1 Tim. vi. 20; cf. Col. ii. 8, 18, 19). The sin of Simon Magus was analogous. 3. *It is also increased by the natural mind's intolerance of mystery.* There are multitudes who would willingly inquire *how* a miracle may be wrought, who have no desire to learn *why.* It is humiliating to our natural pride to realize that there are so many things in the universe we cannot explain. The authority which the supernatural lends to the doctrines and revelations of religion is resented.

II. HOW IT IS SATISFIED. 1. *The direction of their questioning.* They asked concerning the mechanical process—the manner, etc., of the prophet, apparently unconscious that the real problem lay behind all that. "Did the prophet stammer whilst the inspiration was upon him? Was his manner wild or strange?" Now, we know that the manner of the person receiving Divine inspiration may be perfectly indistinguishable from that of those who are under ordinary human conditions. But they fell into the error of supposing that, when that was determined, the solution of the problem would be advanced. 2. *Where it ended.* There is no further curiosity; they remain at arm's length from the kernel of the whole question. The moral conditions of it are of no concern to them. Theirs is the radical carelessness with respect to religion *as such* which characterizes the carnal mind. Their inquiries ended just where they ought to have begun; just as those of many nowadays—lingerers or loiterers in the porch, who never enter into the temple. Conscience could answer much that curiosity leaves untouched. The deep necessity of God-communion for every man and nation to which it witnesses, is what the whole process of revelation presupposes. God will not leave man alone. His supernatural workings continually witness to his presence and authority. And man cannot do without God and his Word.—M.

Vers. 20—26.—*"Jehoiakim's penknife."* This became a proverbial phrase for religious indifference of the most callous description. Not that Jehoiakim actually cut the roll himself; but Jehudi, who did it, was evidently under his orders. It is a little uncertain as to whether the whole of the manuscript, or a part only, was read; but as "had read" represents an imperfect tense, and the words "till all the roll was consumed" imply a gradual process, it seems more probable that the former was the case. There is here the same unconquerable spirit of curiosity to know what the prophet said, utterly separated from religious earnestness or obedience. It is a fearfully impressive tableau which is presented, suggestive of—

1. The enmity of the carnal mind to Divine truth. The king cannot leave the manuscript alone, but he strives to make up for that weakness by : 1. *Contempt*. A page or domestic scribe is employed to read, instead of the king reading for himself; whilst the chief officers sit with their royal master, ridiculing it. There are many who dare not part company with religion, who revenge themselves by making light of its warnings and ordinances. Their contempt is a little overdone, in proportion to the latent, unconfessed fear. 2. *Destruction*. Dislike of the truth itself transfers itself also to the vehicle by which it is conveyed. It is a sign of the indwelling of the evil one, who seeks to destroy the works of God. 3. *Persecution*. The servants of God who have communicated his Word are also hated, and they are sought out with a view to their hurt. This is a characteristic of the confirmed sinner, which repeats itself over and over again in history. The world hates the servants of Christ because it hates their Master.

II. The hardness of heart produced by continual sin. 1. *Deliberate profanity*. If the text is rightly interpreted, it describes a repeated action, performed with the greatest coolness and clearest intention. How different from that young king who rent his garments at the message from the book so mysteriously lost and found again! 2. *Resolute disobedience*. The treatment to which the roll was subjected showed how thoroughly the mind of the king was made up. And the remonstrances of his councillors were unheeded. Evidently the messages of God would be wasted upon such a king, and consequently his doom would be forthwith pronounced (vers. 30, 31).

III. The foolishness of those who fight against God. This is revealed in their methods. Here the burning of the book and the persecution of its authors are all that occurs to the infatuated king to do. But the prophet and his scribe are nowhere to be found, for " God hid them ; " and the burnt manuscript appears in a second and enlarged edition. Persecution and the *Index Expurgatorius* have been potent allies of the truth they have been used to suppress. It is an unequal warfare when God is on one side and man on the other. In such a case the truest wisdom is capitulation. God's indictment against us is unanswerable, and there is no escaping his judgments. When such devices occur to the sinner, he may well fear for himself. Truly understood, these warnings are but the efforts of Divine love to awaken to repentance, and thus afford opportunity for its free and uninterrupted exercise.—M.

Ver. 26.—" *The Lord hid them*." I. To what straits the cause of God is sometimes reduced! Those in high position are opposed to it, and its advocates and representatives have to seek concealment. No open ministry was, therefore, possible. Self-preservation had to be first attended to. There have been times when religion was tolerated, but as under apology ; *this* was an instance of utter exclusion. How good men must have despaired and bad men triumphed! All that God could do for his servants seemed to be to hide them. At the same time, how easy it would be to miscalculate the moral power of the Word! Is not persecution better than languid indifference?

II. How hopeless their efforts who contend with God! With seeming ease and yet mysterious skill, the secrets of nature are made to subserve his will. And even that which is, as it were, an extremity—a last resource—is so mysteriously effected as to convey the impression of infinite skill and endless resources. 1. *They are baffled at the very outset*. There seems to have been some interposition of the Divine in making the concealment of the prophet and his companion so inscrutable ; and it impressed men. All the means at their disposal were exhausted in their efforts to discover them, but in vain. It is: 2. *With an apparent ease*. It is but one move on the great chessboard, but it is effectual and sufficient. It is even conceivable that the pursued took no special pains to conceal themselves, but left it in the hand of him whom they served. 3. *And with significant gentleness*. Some grander deliverance he might have effected, but this is enough. And it simply prevents the wicked king and his court from adding further to their guilt. How thankful ought wicked men to be that they are not suffered to carry out all their evil designs! So God sometimes " prevents," that he may not have to pursue and destroy.

III. How secure God's servants are when he undertakes for them! It is merely said he "hid them," that their concealment was effectual and inviolate being understood without further words. Elijah (1 Kings xvii. 2) and his successor (2 Kings vi.) were so hidden. The Lord of the universe knows its every secret. 1. *In temporal things.* The children of God will not escape misfortune or sorrow. Persecutions are amongst the promises. But the true evil of evil will not reach them. They cannot know it. He hides them in his "secret place" until the storm and fury are overpast. Nay, in distress his tenderness will be the more conspicuous and manifest. "Hide me under the shadow of thy wings" (Ps. xvii. 8); "I flee unto thee to hide me" (Ps. cxliii. 9). There is an inward, inaccessible peace, which is the gift of every true disciple (John xiv. 27). 2. *In things spiritual.* Isaiah spoke of the day when "a man shall be as an hiding-place from the wind," etc. (xxxii. 2). And we know that our "life is hid with Christ in God" (Col. iii. 3). When the unpardoned shall call upon the rocks to fall on them, and the hills to cover them from his wrath, they that believe shall be safe in the keeping of their Lord. 3. *And this is so because the saints are precious in his sight.* He keeps them as the apple of his eye. Not a hair of their head shall fall to the ground without their Father. They are the firstfruits of his Son's agony and sacrifice, and bear his likeness. All the resources of his kingdom are held in readiness for their salvation.—M.

Vers. 27—32.—*The Word of God : wherein it can and wherein it cannot be destroyed.*
I. Wherein it can be destroyed. 1. *In its outward form and medium.* The roll; inspired records; religious institutions and means of grace; individual believers and Churches. 2. *As a vehicle of blessing to a man's own soul.* Jehoiakim deliberately cut off his own salvation, and, destroying the roll, he caused his name to be blotted out of the book of life. To him it brought no blessing. We can destroy the Word of God in this way *for ourselves*, by heedlessness, unbelief, disrespect, enmity.
II. Wherein it cannot be destroyed. Even over the material embodiment and vehicle of the Word shall we not believe that Providence watches? God restores, enlarges, multiplies his Word. But: 1. *The spiritual Word cannot be destroyed.* It is independent of stone, or parchment, or paper; is continually renewed by the Divine Spirit in its communications with the children of men. Even at the worst there is a "law written upon the heart." It cannot be too strongly impressed upon men's minds that, were all the Bibles and manuscripts in the world destroyed, God would restore his Word and continue to reveal himself; like that temple which, destroyed, would be raised in three days again. 2. *The consequences of God's Word,* whether these be *good* or *evil.* What he willeth will be, and his Word stands sure. "Heaven and earth shall pass away, but my word shall not pass away," etc.; *i.e.* what it foretells and declares will remain certain and will fulfil itself. It secures to the saint an indestructible life and inheritance, and to the sinner the reward of his transgression. The true escape from the threatenings of the Divine Word is not to destroy it, but to obey its teachings and yield ourselves to the discipline and grace of Christ.—M.

Vers. 1—32.—*Hearers of God's Word.* This chapter brings before us an instructive variety of these hearers.
I. Such as the prophet. To him and such as he the Word of God came, and was received with reverent submission and diligently obeyed at all costs. They could say, "Speak, Lord; for thy servant heareth."
II. Such as the people generally. (Ver. 10.) The mass seemed unaffected. We do not read of their being in any wise wrought upon by what they had heard. But there was an exception (ver. 11). Michaiah was really aroused, impressed, and alarmed. Often it is thus; the general congregation unmoved, but one here, one there, touched and led to God.
III. Such as Michaiah. We have seen how it affected him. He could not keep it to himself, but went to tell the princes of it (ver. 12). He unfeignedly believed. Now, he came of a godly house. It was his grandfather who, in King Josiah's day, had first received the book of the Law which had been found in the temple. Hilkiah the high priest gave it to him, knowing, no doubt, that it would be reverently dealt with. And so it was; for first he read it himself, and then read it aloud to the young king, and that led to the reformation which the king carried out. And the father of this Michaiah was a man of a like spirit. From the balcony of his house Baruch had read his book to the

people; Michaiah's father had lent him a pulpit. And it was this same man who, with two others, tried, but in vain, to stay the king's hand when about to burn the book (ver. 25). Hence Michaiah came of a godly stock. It is the training of such homes that more than aught else prepares and predisposes the heart to receive the Word of God.

IV. SUCH AS THE PRINCES. These are a very instructive group, (vers. 11—26). They listened patiently to the Word, and gave it much attention. They were much moved, and desired to hear it over again exactly as it had been given, and so they sent for Baruch, and listened in like manner to him. They seriously deliberate, and resolve to go and warn the king; for that in all probability was their motive. They show affection to God's servants, and desire to protect both them and the written Word. They go in to the king, notwithstanding they must have known the peril of so doing. And some of them endeavour to stay the king from his evil intent to destroy the book. But there they stop. The king's rage overpower them, and they keep silence when they ought to utter strong protest. They are an illustration of "the fear of man which bringeth a snare." How often the like cause leads to like unfaithfulness still !

V. SUCH AS THE KING. The words fix his attention, but they excite his rage and then they ensure his doom. He comes to hate both the Word and the writers of the Word, and he disregards the feeble remonstrances of its timid friends. Thus he seals his own destruction, as such ever do. *We* are hearers of the Word. To which class do we belong ?—C.

Ver. 2.—*The written Word.* "Take thee a roll of a book, and write therein all the words that I have spoken unto thee." "This is the first recorded instance of the formation of a canonical book, and of the special purpose of its formation." No doubt other prophets had committed to writing more or less of their teachings—the quotations of one prophet from another, the later from the earlier, prove this; but here is the first record of any such act, and hence it has especial interest. It is the forerunner of all those several Scriptures which together form now the depository of our religion, and justify the well-known saying of Chillingworth, "The Bible and the Bible only is the religion of Protestants." For note—

I. OUR RELIGION DEPENDS ON THE WRITTEN WORD. Great contempt has been poured on the idea of a "book revelation." As if there were something even ridiculous in the idea of God revealing himself by means of a book. A recent missionary traveller (Gilmour) among the Mongols states that they feel the force of this objection very strongly, and that when the missionary holds up his little Bible as the revelation of God, it seems to them very absurd. But these people can claim distinguished companionship amongst our own countrymen. And in addition to the rejection of a book revelation at all, this particular book, the Bible, is objected to exceedingly. All manner of ridicule is poured on it, and there is scarce a single ground on which fault could be found with it which some one has not occupied. But in reply note—

II. THE WRITTEN WORD IS, HOWEVER, NOT THE REVELATION BUT ONLY THE RECORD OF IT. It is not claimed for it to be more than this. God did not give to mankind a book, but he revealed himself to "holy men of old," and especially through the Lord Jesus Christ. And this book is the record of that revelation. Hence the only question that concerns us is—Is it a faithful record ?

III. BUT SUCH A RECORD WAS ABSOLUTELY NECESSARY. For if the existence of God be allowed, and that it is his desire to reclaim men from their sin and to bring them back to himself, it may be asked : 1. *How could this be done except by his revealing himself to men ?* They *must* be enabled to know him, and to know him in such manner as would be likely to move them in the direction desired. 2. But if it be granted that a revelation was a necessity, *how could that revelation be of use to mankind at large unless it were put on record ?* For all events are related to time and space; they must have happened—God's revelation of himself amongst others—somewhen and somewhere. But how, except by a record, could those who dwelt in other generations and in other parts of the world know of this revelation ? But for that it may as well not have been. 3. *And so long as the Divine ideas are conveyed to our mind, what does it matter about the means employed ?* All the magnificence of nature—the Alpine heights, the starry universe, etc.—serve us only as they convey true and worthy ideas, as they wake up in us fit and appropriate thoughts. If they fail in this, they might as well not be so far as we are concerned. But there are many who never have opportunities of beholding the magnificence of nature—their lives are one long round of sordid toil in scenes dark and squalid ; and others who have such opportunities are too little educated to learn from them what they assuredly have to tell. The road that leads from nature up to nature's God is a thinly travelled one ; few go that way. But now, if by the written Word, which can be carried everywhere, perpetuated, multiplied, and is everywhere and at all times accessible—if by this there can be conveyed to the mind fit, true, and heart-moving ideas about God, what an advantage this is! Instead of being a cause of scorn, it should awaken our gratitude. 4. *And those features in this record which seem to some unworthy of its great mission, these really are of great service.* No doubt there is much of homeliness and of trivial and seemingly insignificant detail in this record. It is a very plain, prosaic book in many parts. But is not this a great boon ? Had God's revelation of himself to us been accompanied by a blaze of splendour, with such manifestations of Divine power to the senses or to the intellect as some seem to desire, the revelation would have been lost in the record ; no one would look at the picture, their attention being so much occupied with the setting. Hence it is good for us that we live so long after the times of the Bible. It is expedient for us that Christ has gone away. For in proportion to men's nearness to those times " events having God in them took a more forcible hold upon their mind than God in the events." The atmosphere of time is needed in order to our right viewing of the marvellous facts of the Bible.

IV. OUR ONE QUESTION IS—IS THE RECORD FAITHFUL ? 1. *As to the facts themselves*—in their main substance and meaning. This question is quite apart from inspiration. Nothing but honesty and intelligence are asked for here. Of course, if any start with the assumption that the supernatural is not, and hence miracles are by their very nature impossible, and tne belief of them absurd, such a one will refuse all credence to this record. But first let his assumption be proved ere doubt be thrown on either the honesty or the intelligence of the writers of the Bible. 2. *As to the interpretation and meaning of the facts they record.* "Just as on gazing at a picture of Raphael's we should rejoice to have at hand a companion who had familiarized himself with the spirit of the great artist and acquired an insight into his genius, to furnish us with such brief notices as might assist us to a comprehension of the profounder ideas expressed by the painting, for want of which it would lose very much of its intellectual meaning ; so with the memoirs of Christ before us, as the spiritual revelation of God to our religious sense, we require, in order to adequate instruction and profit, the comments of . . . those who shall be qualified to point it out to our duller vision. What poets are to the natural exhibition of God in his works, these men will be to the moral exhibition of God in his Son." Now, that the sacred writers answer to this need is shown by the fact that they " commend the truth to every man's *conscience* in the sight of God." In this commendation to our conscience is the evidence that they have read aright the facts they record. And to this we may fearlessly appeal. We do not assert this of men's theologies and divinity schemes—too many of them outrage the conscience and trouble the moral sense ; but we do assert it of the great verities of the faith, as taught in the Scriptures, and of the doctrines which the Bible as a whole plainly teaches.

> " Within this ample volume lies
> The mystery of mysteries.
> Happiest they of human race
> To whom their God has given grace
> To read, to fear, to hope, to pray,
> To lift the latch and force the way ;
> And better had they ne'er been born
> Than read to doubt or read to scorn."

Cf. on this whole subject Miall's ' Bases of Belief.'—C.

Ver. 3.—" *It may be.*" We can understand the prophet thus speaking, but how can there be anything uncertain or contingent with God ? And yet it is he who here speaks and says, " It may be." We are accustomed to say, " God knows all the past, and all the present, and all the future " (cf. Isa. xlvi. 9—11). Reason and Scripture alike seem to say that there can be nothing probable with God. But yet this is *his* word. Why does he thus speak ? Perhaps—

I. BECAUSE THERE WAS NO LAW, NO DECREE, AGAINST THE PEOPLE'S REPENTANCE. He had made no such law, and man had not. There is no decree of reprobation.

II. IT MAY BE CONSISTENT, AFTER ALL, WITH THE TRUTH OF THINGS FOR GOD THUS TO SPEAK, THOUGH WE CANNOT SEE HOW. We infer certain conclusions from what we read and learn about God, and these conclusions seem to deny the possibility of there being any " it may be " with him. But we may be wrong after all, and the fact that he does thus speak lends to the suspicion that we are.

III. BECAUSE IT WOULD BE ILL FOR US WERE HE TO REVEAL THE CERTAINTIES OF THINGS. If they were to be such as we would desire, we should cease to labour for them. If otherwise, we should sit down in despair. But God desires us to labour and pray, and therefore hides the future from our eyes. Presumption and despair are both great evils ; therefore to prevent them, God speaks after the manner of men, if not after the manner of God.

IV. BECAUSE HE INTENDS HIS " MAY BE " TO BECOME " SHALL BE." He would have us fellow-workers with him, and therefore he encourages our efforts, but hides from us that which would lead us to think them unnecessary. And probably the " may be " will become " shall be," though not at the time nor in the manner we expect. Let us, therefore, be ever cheered forward when God says, " It may be."—C.

Ver. 23.—*The indestructible Word.* The king's knife and fire did what they could to destroy the prophet's word, but with what result this chapter shows. The king was Jehoiakim ; the prophet, Jeremiah ; the word, his written prophecies. It was necessary that these should be written down. The army of Babylon was already in the land, and drawing near to the doomed city of Jerusalem, if they had not already captured it for the first time. There was no hope of successful resistance. Therefore, for a testimony when all that had been foretold came to pass, and for a solace and warning to that and to all coming generations, it was necessary that the twenty-three years' witness which the prophet had borne against that guilty nation should be put on record. Jeremiah was " shut up," whether by his own will, or the word of the Lord, or for fear of his enemies, we cannot certainly say ; but Baruch, who seems to have been to Jeremiah as Timothy to Paul, was commanded to write these prophecies, and then, on the " fasting-day," to read them in the hearing of all the people. He did so. One of his hearers, alarmed and troubled, hastened away to the council of the princes, and told them what he had heard. Baruch was sent for, and declared again what he had before read to the people. The book was too terrible to show to the king ; they therefore commanded that it and its author should be concealed, whilst they went in to the king to announce its fearful contents. A third time these prophecies were recited, but the king demanded that the book itself should be read to him. But when brought and the reading had begun, the angry king had no patience to listen beyond the first three or four leaves, but snatching it from the hand of the reader, he vented his rage upon it by cutting and hacking it with his knife, and then, to make short work of it, cast it, in spite of the horror-stricken entreaties of his princes, into the burning coals before him, where it was utterly consumed. Then he commands, but in vain, for " the Lord hid them," that Baruch and Jeremiah be arrested ; but the Lord commands that these prophecies be written again, which was done, with the doom of the king added, and " beside them many like words." But this King Jehoiakim, in his dealing with the Word of God, and in its dealing with him, has had many successors. He is the type of—

I. THOSE WHO ARE IMPATIENT WITH THE WORD OF GOD. Jehoiakim only heard three or four leaves read, when he put a stop to the reading altogether in the foolish way we have seen. He would not hear the whole. Did any man ever destroy the Bible who knew it *wholly ?* Many have thrown it into the fire who have heard or read a part only. The difficulty is in the " three or four leaves." How many stumble because they won't read on !

II. THOSE WHO BECOME VERY ANGRY WITH THE BIBLE. To men of this king's stamp the Bible has not one word of comfort, commendation, or hope. It is all full of thunder and storm. It is a dreadful book to the impenitent. No wonder that he snatches it from the reader's hand, and hacks at it with his knife, and then flings it into the blazing fire. Yes ; be like this *king*, and you will do as he did, *and be done unto as he.*

III. THOSE WHO STRIVE TO DESTROY THE BIBLE. 1. *Some would only partly do this.* They admit a large amount of good in the book ; they only desire to cut out what they think is otherwise. *Theologians* use their penknives. They practically put out of the Bible what makes against their favourite ideas. *Science* seems to be for ever at this miserable cutting. *Philosophy* is equally guilty ; but *sin* is worst of all. It loves not the hard things the Bible will keep saying against it ; therefore it would cut them out —only it cannot. 2. *There are those who would destroy the book altogether.* What Bible-burnings there have been ! The histories of pagan and Romish persecutions are full of them. Are there none now ? What is the difference between such burning and utter disregard of the book as too many are guilty of ? If we trample it underfoot, in our hearts, our lips, our lives, how could burning it be any worse ?

IV. THOSE WHO FIND THE BIBLE TOO STRONG FOR THEM. " O Galilæan, thou hast conquered ! " said the Emperor Julian shortly before he died. And that has been the confession in regard to the Word of God on the part of all those who have tried to destroy it (ver. 30). The Word of God can neither be bound nor burned. It has been cut, cast into flames, proscribed, branded, corrupted, and treated with every conceivable form of opprobrium ; but here it is to-day, a living and mighty factor in the lives of the foremost men and nations throughout the whole world. And the ungodly who practically seek to destroy it for themselves, *they* will find they cannot do this. Its truths will come back, its teachings reassert themselves, and will add beside " many like words."—C.

Ver. 26.—*The Lord's hidden ones.* " But the Lord hid them." He has many such, and in all manner of unthought-of places. If we read the history of the world aright, how continually God is bringing forth his hidden ones to render service to their fellowmen ! " Oh how great is thy goodness, which thou hast *laid up* for them that fear thee ! " Think of some of these hidden ones.

I. SUCH AS THE PROPHET HERE TOLD OF. And how God has hidden his people from the rage of men ! " In the secret of his tabernacle shall he hide me." Let the records of the martyr Churches in Rome, Switzerland, and wherever God's saints have been persecuted—let all these tell how he has often hidden his servants. Moses was hidden three months when an infant ; then again with Jethro in Midian afterwards. How God hid David again and again from Saul !

II. THOSE DESTINED FOR GREAT SERVICE. How often, when a Church seems to have been brought to its lowest, God raises up some one who is the means of reviving it ! David amongst the sheepfolds. Gideon and the judges. Our Lord at Nazareth. In all unlikeliest places God has his hidden ones, whom in due time he will manifest to the surprise and joy of his Church.

III. SUCH AS ARE NOT YET IN THE VISIBLE CHURCH. Amongst those whom we deem outside the Church, God has his chosen, whom one day he will call. Who, looking on the murderers of St. Stephen, would have thought that amongst them God had one of his choicest servants ? This is the dispensation, not of universal conversion—that is to come—but of calling out those who shall be the instruments of the universal ingathering. God is blessing his Church that " his way may be known upon earth." etc. We are therefore to despair of no nation, community, class, family, or neighbourhood. In all God has his hidden ones.

" O grace, into unlikeliest hearts
It is thy wont to come."

IV. THE BLESSED DEAD. There is to be a manifestation of the sons of God. Meanwhile their " life is hid with Christ in God." " Wherefore comfort one another with these words."—C.

Ver. 28.—*Disaster not defeat.* What dismay must have filled the minds of those who saw the book destroyed, and of those who heard of it—Baruch, Jeremiah, and others !

I. IT WAS GREAT DISASTER. The book was most precious. See its gracious intent. See how it had already moved many for good. What might not be expected from it ?

II. AND IT SEEMED IRRETRIEVABLE. There was no copy of it kept. No human memory could reproduce it. The word had not sunk into the hearts of the people so as to render it no longer needed.

III. BUT THE DISASTER WAS NOT DEFEAT. God interposed, commanded the prophet to write again, enabled him to do so, supplied him with many more like words.

IV. BY MEANS OF IT MORE GOOD WAS WROUGHT. What endorsement of the Word did its remarkable reproduction supply! How it would show the vanity of all human rage against the Divine will! How the faith of the godly would be strengthened, whilst the daring of the wicked would be rebuked!

V. AND THIS INSTANCE IS BUT ONE OUT OF MYRIADS MORE. Read the history of the Church, and see how perpetually out of seeming disaster God has brought real good and increased good. And so in our own personal histories, providential and spiritual alike. "Trust thou in the Lord at all times."—C.

Ver. 3.—*God's eye to every possibility.* I. THE THING WHICH GOD GREATLY DESIRES. That man may repent, thus enabling him to forgive. He ever has his eyes on the ways of evil men, noticing the slightest sign of their weariness in them and disposition to leave them. This is always a thing to be suspected and prepared for. That any man should suddenly become uneasy and hesitating in the midst of evil courses is nothing wonderful when we consider that man was made for goodness and holiness. Thus what else should we look for than frequent expressions of desire on the part of God that man should again be found in the right way?

II. GOD LEAVES NOTHING UNDONE TO BRING THIS ABOUT. There is something even touching about this word, "it may be." As if it were allowed that probabilities all pointed in one unfavourable direction, but still not one of them was such a certainty that the contrary possibility should be excluded. As the common proverb says, "While there's life there's hope." Every instance of a rejected appeal and an abused prophet lessens the probability, but it does not destroy the possibility. God goes on sending his prophets. Each man comes with his own personality, his own peculiar emphasis, and thus with evermore the same message there is variety both in the messenger and the form of his message. And at last, when the messenger gets shut up, his words are written down and transmitted by another. We cannot get rid of the Word of God. There are a thousand channels to the heart of man, and the violent stoppage of some may only result in the enlargement and efficacy of others.

III. THERE IS AN EXAMPLE FOR US IN GOSPEL WORK. Scripture shows us God using many ways in trying to get at the human heart. Surely the great principle in this matter is that every way is right if it be not wrong in itself. We must not do evil that good may come; but we must be all things to all men that we may save some.

IV. THERE MAY BE ADDED GUILT TO THOSE REJECTING THE GOSPEL. It was one of the worst elements in the guilt of Israel that it had been indifferent to so many appeals and such various ones. God did not send these people into exile upon one refusal or even upon a few. There was sufficient intimation of his demands and his designs. And we may take it that there always is sufficient intimation. With the constant extension of gospel effort and the wider diffusion of Bibles, tracts, and all sorts of printed agencies, we may say that each generation gets more of light than the one before it. Indeed, we may lay it down as a general principle that when all the opportunities of every human being are summed up, it will be found that he is without any excuse for pleading ignorance or doubt as to God's demands.—Y.

Ver. 6.—"*Things new and old.*" I. THE OLD. The message itself was old. It had been proclaimed before in parts and on different occasions. There was not, indeed, opportunity for anything new. The audience also was to some extent old. But then let it always be understood that God speaks according to the necessities of the case, not according to the itching ear of man ever clamouring for novelty and relief from *ennui.* "If they hear not Moses and the prophets, neither will they be persuaded though one rose from the dead." There may come a time in every man's life, when it is not the new but the old and neglected or misunderstood that will prove the necessity of the soul.

II. THE NEW. 1. *The messenger.* Not Jeremiah, but Baruch; not a prophet, but a prophet's deputy; not a word spoken, but a word read; not a part of Jeremiah's utterances, but the whole, so that people might have it brought home to them how much they had neglected. Old truth appears in new framework and new relations, so that it may arrest people who have become indifferent to the old associations. There was a time when Jeremiah's face was fresh, and curiosity would make people stop to hear what this babbler might say. But after hearing him often, they ceased to heed him. Then Baruch comes forward, and words that were an exact repetition of words heard before got a flavour of novelty. 2. *The occasion.* The fasting-day. Read Isa. lviii. carefully to discover the avowed purpose and yet utter uselessness of the fasting-day in Israel. The people met together to acknowledge their sins, to punish their bodies, to please God, to avert his displeasure. It might, therefore, be assumed that then, if ever, they were in a state prepared to listen to the volume of one great prophet's utterance. If anything was to be got out of seizing the best available occasion, then surely it was to be got here. Thus we learn how occasion adds responsibility to utterance; responsibility both for him who speaks and those who hear. These people were not stopped in the street or the market; their homes were not invaded by prophetic messages; they had no pretence for saying they were interfered with. They put themselves in Baruch's way. His work, as reader of Jeremiah's prophecies, was in exact harmony with what ought to have been the feelings and desires of his audience. 3. *The audience.* That audience, as we have said above, was to some extent old, but to some extent also it would be new. A new message to some people in Jerusalem, and quite new doubtless to the bulk of those who came from the cities of Judah to Jerusalem. The whole proceeding helps us to see how valuable the public reading of the Scriptures may be. For old as they are, with so much in them that savours of vanished ages and customs, they have, nevertheless, to do with perennial wants, miseries, and possibilities.—Y.

Ver. 23.—*Burning the Word of the Lord.* I. THE KING'S MOTIVES IN THIS ACT. Perhaps he was not conscious of any distinct set of motives. He was but a despot, and despots are in many things like spoiled children; they act not from any clear reason, good or bad, so much as from the caprice of the moment. If this act had been a singularity of Jehoiakim's, there would have been less need to attend to it, but unhappily it only illustrates a whole series of acts by those occupying stations of power among men. Putting Jeremiah in prison, burning Baruch's roll, slaying the innocents at Bethlehem, putting apostles in prison, and all the long list of martyrdoms,—what are these but the same essential act all through? Jehoiakim would have been in full sympathy with Roman Catholic priests burning the Scriptures in translations understood of the common people. Jehoiakim was a man buttressed with privileges, pampered with privileges; and here he had a document forced upon his ears which contained assertions by no means compatible with the continuance of his privileges. And there was one thing he could do—he could get rid of the offensive document. He stands before us as a great example of those—and how many there are!—who, in their eagerness to get rid of an unpleasant subject, take the first means that comes to hand for getting rid of it.

II. LOOK AT THE ACT IN THE LIGHT OF HISTORY. Jehoiakim burnt Baruch's roll, but he did not destroy Jeremiah's prophecies; nor did he nullify the truth of Jeremiah's predictions; nor did he stop other prophetic utterances. If Jehoiakim can, he may burn, not only Baruch's roll, but Baruch and Jeremiah as well. Suppose this done; yet Ezekiel, Daniel, Haggai, Zechariah, Malachi, and probably many more, of whose words we know nothing, have to be reckoned with. This is the peculiar folly of men like Jehoiakim, that they perform acts monumental of their folly. Jehoiakim might have quietly said, "If these words are true, then we cannot make them false; and if they be false, time will show their falsity, and bring to shame both the dictator and the writer of them." Instead of acting thus with dignified endurance, Jehoiakim, in burning the roll, challenged the attention not only of his own people but of all ages. He did what there was no sort of need for him to do. It may be said—Why not apply the same line of remark to Luther burning the pope's bull? To this the answer is obvious, that Luther's act was a message of renunciation, a summons of the papacy's bondslaves to freedom, an act of sublime trust in God. Looked at from the point of view given in the present, it is seen to have been an inspiration. But what did Jehoiakim's act amount to? Only empty bravado. He had nothing to fear from men. Luther did something when he burnt the bull. Jehoiakim did nothing but proclaim his own shame, and advertise the glory of that God over against whose throne his paltry throne had been set up.—Y.

Ver. 26.—*Jehovah hiding his servants.* I. THE NEED OF SUCH INTERPOSITION. Baruch and Jeremiah had already been told by the princes to hide (ver. 19); but what was any effort purely of their own likely to avail? Indeed, it is only as we appreciate the uselessness of a purely human effort for this purpose that we shall see the need of a Divine intervention. God does not mean miracles and special providences to do the work of man's prudence. But when it is made evident that man can do little or nothing, then God's action appears manifest and admonitory. It may be too much to say that this action of God was intended as an answer to Jehoiakim's audacity in burning the roll; but it was an answer nevertheless.

II. THE MANNER OF THE INTERPOSITION. This is left untold. Either Jeremiah could not explain the manner of his hiding, or it was purposely left unexplained to heighten the impressiveness of the fact. It may have been through a marvellous combination of human kindness and sympathy, such as showed a Divine directing hand; or there may have been miracle. God is an effectual hider. How much there is hidden away in the very things we see, so that knowledge may be kept from all but the humble and obedient! God could not be the revealer that he is, unless he were also an effectual hider. The great end was gained if people of the right sort in Jerusalem were made to feel that this hiding was in no sort the work of man, and could only be explained by the intervention of a higher power.

III. THE RESULT OF THE INTERPOSITION. Jeremiah was hidden and preserved because his work was not yet done. His words had to be put down in writing; and it is interesting to notice that the second copy was an improvement on the first. All that was in the first was also in the second, and many like words were added. God never does wonders for the mere sake of doing wonders. When he hides his servants, or delivers them from prison, it is soon made manifest that he had a purpose in view. We have to remember this in reading such a book as the Acts of the Apostles. Stephen is left to be stoned to death, while Peter has an angel to take him out of prison. The fact was Stephen had the greatest work of his life to do in the hour of his death. " Man is immortal till his work is done." Whatsoever God has clearly given us to do, we must go on with it boldly, yet prudently, sure that he will take care of us who hid Jeremiah in the hour of his danger.—Y.

EXPOSITION.

CHAPTER XXXVII.

Nothing worthy of relation appears to have happened to Jeremiah till the latter period of the reign of Zedekiah. The first two verses of this chapter form the transition. The embassy to Jeremiah mentioned in ver. 3 took place after the temporary withdrawal of the Chaldeans from Jerusalem.

Ver. 1.—**Coniah**; *i.e.* Jehoiachin (see on ch. xxii. 24). **Whom Nebuchadrezzar . . . made king.** Zedekiah, not Jehoiachin, is referred to (see 2 Kings xxiv. 17).

Ver. 3.—**And Zedekiah the king sent.** This was Zedekiah's second embassy to Jeremiah. His request on the former

occasion had been for a prophecy; on the present it was for an " effectual fervent prayer," such as Hezekiah's embassy asked of Isaiah (Isa. xxxvii. 6). But the issue was to be very different from that in the case of Sennacherib's invasion! **Jehucal.** The same man appears in ch. xxxviii. 1, among those who brought about the imprisonment of Jeremiah. **Zephaniah.** The high priest's deputy, mentioned again in ch. xxi. 1; xxix. 25; lii. 24.

Ver. 4.—**Now Jeremiah came in and went out**, etc. Had he been a prisoner, an embassy of high officials could not, with propriety, have been sent to him (comp. ver. 17; ch. xxxviii. 14).

Ver. 5.—**Then Pharaoh's army**, etc.; rather, *And Pharaoh's army had*, etc.; as a further description of the circumstances under which the embassy was sent. The withdrawal of the Chaldeans seemed to offer a gleam of hope. The Pharaoh referred to was the Hophra of the Jews, the Apries of Herodotus, the Uah-ab-ra of the monuments. His interference was useless ; indeed, Hophra was one of the most unfortunate of the Egyptian kings (see ch. xliv. 30).

Ver. 10.—Even if the Jews had defeated the whole Chaldean army, and there remained but *a group of sorely wounded men*, these in their weakness would be enabled to carry out God's sure purpose. But **wounded men** hardly brings out the force of the Hebrew ; the word rendered "men" is emphatic, and expresses paucity of numbers, and that rendered "wounded" is, literally, *pierced through*.

Ver. 11.—**For fear of**, etc. ; rather, *because of*.

Ver. 12.—As soon as communication with the outside world was possible, Jeremiah took the opportunity of going to his native country, to obtain something or other which he could only obtain "thence." The Authorized Version says that his object was **to separate himself thence.** But (1) the rendering is linguistically untenable ; and (2) the assumed object is incongruous with the circumstances and character of Jeremiah, who was neither inclined to seek safety in isolation nor had any motive at present for doing so. The only safe rendering is, *to claim his share thence.* Whether there was just then a reallotment of communal lands must be left undecided ; this would, however, be the most plausible hypothesis, if we could be sure that the present was a sabbatical year. The additional words, **in the midst of the people**, would then acquire a special significance. The "people" would be the representatives of families who had an equal right to allotments with Jeremiah.

Ver. 13.—**The gate of Benjamin** ; *i.e.* the gate looking northwards towards Benjamin (comp. ch. xx. 2 ; xxxviii. 7 ; Zech. xiv. 10). It appears to be the same as the gate of Ephraim (2 Kings xiv. 13 ; Neh. viii. 16). **Thou fallest away**, etc. Perhaps an allusion to Jeremiah's declaration (ch. xxi. 9) that " he that falleth away to the Chaldeans . . . he shall live."

Ver. 15.—**The princes were wroth with Jeremiah.** As Graf has pointed out, the princes, who had evinced their respect for Jeremiah on former occasions (ch. xxvi., xxxvi.), had probably shared the captivity of Jehoiachin ; Zedekiah's "princes" would be of a lower origin and type, and ready (like the judges in the French "terror") to accept any charge against an unpopular person without proper examination. **The house of Jonathan the scribe.** "Scribe," *i.e.* one of the secretaries of state. The house of Jonathan seems to have been specially adapted for a prison, as the next verse shows. Chardin, the old traveller, remarks, "The Eastern prisons are not public buildings erected for that purpose, but a part of the house in which the criminal judges dwell. As the governor and provost of a town, or the captain of the watch, imprison such as are accused in their own houses, they set apart a canton of them for that purpose when they are put into these offices, and choose for the jailor the most proper person they can find of their domestics " (Chardin).

Ver. 16.—**Into the dungeon, and into the cabins.** The former word undoubtedly implies an underground excavation. The latter is of more uncertain signification. It most probably means " vaults ; " but it may mean " curved posts "—something analogous to stocks (see on ch. xx. 2).

Ver. 17.—Meantime the Chaldean army has returned, and reinvested the city. Zedekiah, in his anxiety, sends for Jeremiah privately to his palace. **Thou shalt be delivered**, etc. (comp. ch. xxxii. 3, 4 ; xxxiv. 2, 3).

Ver. 21.—**Court of the prison** ; rather, *court of the watch* (as ch. xxxii. 2). **A piece of bread** ; literally, *a circle* (i.e. round cake) *of bread.* This is mentioned elsewhere in descriptions of poverty (1 Sam. ii. 36 ; Prov. vi. 26) ; but as the ancient Oriental bread was not our delicate white bread, it was a real "staff of life." The Syrian peasants still eat cakes of coarse meal, of about the thickness of parchment, and equal in size to a large plate (Orelli's 'Travels'). **The bakers' street.** Probably the several trades were confined to special quarters and streets. In Cairo each trade has still its own bazaar (saddlers, carpets, hardware, goldsmiths, sweetmeats, etc.).

HOMILETICS.

Vers. 1—3.—*Prayer without obedience.* Though Zedekiah will give no heed to the message from God to him through Jeremiah, he is not the less anxious to secure the prophet's intercession with God for deliverance from approaching calamity. The king illustrates the too common case of those people who will fly to the protection of religion in trouble, though they neglect all its obligations of holiness and of service.

I. RELIGION REQUIRES OBEDIENCE TO GOD'S WILL. It is not all on one side. God speaks to us, and speaks words of command as well as words of consolation. It is, therefore, our duty to hear and obey. 1. *Ignorance* is no excuse, if we wilfully refuse to hear the truth. Zedekiah and his servants did not obey because they did not "hearken," *i.e. would* not hearken. We are not responsible for failing through not knowing our duty if we could not know it. But if we could, it was our duty to ascertain it. The soldier who puts aside the despatch of his commander unopened, and then acts contrary to the orders contained in it is, of course, as guilty as if he did so knowingly; for it was his duty to read the orders he received before going into action. 2. The *example* of those who have done wrong before is no excuse. Zedekiah followed the example of Jehoiakim. But he knew it was wrong. He had seen the miserable end of his predecessor's reign. He should have taken warning from this. But men are more inclined to imitate the crimes of the wicked than to learn the lesson of their fate. 3. *High position* does not mitigate guilt, but, on the contrary, it aggravates it. Zedekiah led the people with him in his rejection of God's message through Jeremiah. He knew what influence he exerted, and he ought to have been the more careful that it was not wrongly used.

II. PRAYER WITHOUT OBEDIENCE IS VAIN. Zedekiah seeks Jeremiah's prayers, but in vain. It is not necessary, indeed, that our obedience should be faultless before God will hearken to a single prayer. If this were the case, no prayer of man's could be heard. But it is requisite that we should repent of our past disobedience, and should be unfeignedly desirous of obeying God in the future. For otherwise our purely self-seeking religion is an insult to God. Besides, we cannot hope to change the essential principles of God's action by our prayer. If it is his will to chastise us for our sin, he cannot change his will so long as we remain unchanged in conduct. But when we turn from the sin which deserves the penalty, it may be possible for God to modify his treatment of us in answer to our prayer of submission. Therefore it is so necessary that we should pray through the intercession of Christ. Then, though our obedience is still most imperfect, if we desire to do better, Christ is our Representative and the promise of our future obedience, and therefore his good merits go to plead with God to answer our prayer offered in his Name.

Ver. 9.—*Self-deception.* "Deceive not yourselves."
I. THE CHARACTERISTICS OF SELF-DECEPTION. As fallible beings, surrounded with mystery, and often beset by illusions we are likely to fall into unavoidable mistakes for which we cannot be held responsible. There are other errors which we might avoid if we took the right means for ascertaining the facts; but from indifference, or from indolence, or from unwillingness to see an unpleasant truth that is already half suspected, we neglect these means, and thus land ourselves in a delusion. This is self-deception. 1. It may be *conscious and deliberate.* The very notion is paradoxical. But we are not logical machines; our belief is often most inconsistent. Our will and feelings have great influence over our convictions. We rarely contemplate things in the white light of truth. And in so far as we permit our vision to be blinded by passion or distorted by prejudice, we may deceive ourselves. 2. This self-deception may be *unconscious.* Yet it is culpable if we voluntarily neglect the means of seeing things as they are. We may not know that we are deceiving ourselves. But we must know that we are not doing all we can to avoid delusions.

II. THE OCCASIONS OF SELF-DECEPTION. 1. These may be found in the *superficial appearance* of events. The outward seeming does not correspond with the inward verity. The temptation is to rest satisfied with the mere appearance and assume that it is an index of the underlying fact. Thus when the Chaldean army retreated from before Jerusalem at the advance of Pharaoh-Hophra, Zedekiah was ready to believe that his revolt was successful. 2. Occasions may be found in *our own inclinations.* Zedekiah wished to see no more of the Chaldean army, and "the wish was father to the thought." 3. They may be found in *preconceived notions.* We expect the facts to verify our opinions, and we contrive to make them do so by ignoring what will not agree with them, and selecting for consideration only what is favourable. All this may be traced in the history of religious delusions. People blind themselves to the thought of future judgment because, on the surface of life and for the present, all goes well. They are too ready to form their creed according to their inclination, dropping out unpleasant ideas as though there were no dark truths in existence. They go to the

Bible for confirmation of their own " views " rather than for instruction, and, if need be, correction of them, and of course they have eyes only to see those texts which make for this confirmation. Note : Jeremiah tried to deliver the Jews from self-deception. A Divine revelation is necessary to save us from religious self-deception. The Bible aims at this result as well as at enlightening our ignorance.

III. THE EVIL OF SELF-DECEPTION. 1. It is *disloyal to truth.* It is our duty not to rest in a delusion. The obligation of truthfulness reaches to our thinking as well as to our speaking. 2. It is *dangerous to our own souls.* Facts remain unchanged whatever fanciful notions we may weave about them till they are quite unrecognizable, and when the time for action comes, they will act as they are, not as we think them. The careless, who decline to consider a future judgment, are not the less amenable to it. Those people who have sought refuge in the Roman Catholic Church from the torment of doubt have not done anything to settle the facts about which they were troubled ; like the ostrich, who hides his head in a bush, they have quieted their doubt by turning from it; but if it was well grounded originally, it must be ultimately confirmed to their undoing.

Ver. 10.—*The irresistible will of God.* I. THE FACT. The Jews were ready to believe that Egypt was a match for Babylon, and to hope that through the conflict of these two powers they might regain their liberty. Even if they were justified in thinking so from a calculation of the material resources of these great empires, Jeremiah reminded them that there were other considerations to be taken into account before the result could be predicted. It was the will of God that Babylon should conquer Jerusalem. Therefore, if the Chaldean army were reduced to a disorganized group of wounded men, Jerusalem would still succumb. The Jews had found that, while they were faithful to God, they were strong against hordes of enemies. They were to learn that when they had put themselves against God, the position was reversed, and the weakest foe could overthrow them. So it was true against them, as it had been on their side, that " a little one should chase a thousand." It has been the mistake of kings and of peoples to leave out of their calculations the chief factor of their history—to forget that God is ever working out his will through their cross purposes. Do we not make the same mistake in our private lives ? If God is almighty, it follows beyond question that he must accomplish what he purposes, though to us there seems no means of doing so, and though he neither reveals the means nor in most cases the end, working them out "deep in unfathomable mines." Still, we know some things concerning God's will and the way he works it out ; *e.g.* he always wills what is just and good ; material events are largely beyond our control and under the influence of providence ; moral influences count for much in history, and these are directly affected by the spiritual relations of God with the minds of men.

II. THE RELATION OF THIS FACT TO FATALISM AND TO NECESSARIANISM. 1. The relation of it to *fatalism.* It must be distinguished from materialistic fatalism, which denies all will in nature ; from pagan fatalism, which sets the decrees of the fates above the power of the gods; from Mohammedan fatalism, which ascribes every event to the will of God, but regards that will as the unfettered choice of an irresponsible despot. The irresistible power in providence as revealed in the Bible is a will, a Divine will, a holy will, that always works out purposes of justice, purity, and love. 2. The relation of this fact to *necessarianism.* If God's will is irresistible what room is there for our will ? Must not that be necessarily bound by his will ? This question arises from confusing two phases of the will of God. The phrase, " will of God," represents two things—(1) what God purposes to do himself, and (2) what he desires us to do. The first governs his actions, the second inspires his Law. Now, it is the first that is irresistible ; the second is plainly resistible. All sin is nothing but man's rebellion against God's will, *i.e.* God's will in the second sense—what he wishes us to do. This is really no contradiction to what we know of the first will of God—what he purposes to do himself—because in his almighty will of action he chooses to give us free-will containing the power of resisting his Law. Still, God's will to act must harmonize with his will in his Law for our conduct. If we resist the second will, we shall find ourselves in conflict with the first, against which all resistance is futile. Therefore true wisdom will lead us to do God's will where we are free in relation to it, that we may find ourselves in agreement with God's will where opposition means only failure and ruin.

Vers. 11—21.—*Jeremiah imprisoned as a traitor.* I. THE CIRCUMSTANCES LEADING TO THE IMPRISONMENT. Whatever interpretation we are to set on the ambiguous passage which gives the reason for Jeremiah's attempt to leave Jerusalem (ver. 12)— whether it were to escape from the city, or to abandon a work that appeared to be fruitless for work in the country districts, or to take a possession at a redistribution of land in the sabbatical year, or to claim his share as a priest,—it is difficult to acquit him of all blame for allowing personal considerations to move him from what he ought to have known was his post. At the best, his conduct was open to misinterpretation. Even when we mean no wrong it is our duty to avoid the appearance of evil. Still, we must not be harsh in condemning the prophet. A servant of God has his natural human rights and the civil rights which he shares with his fellow-citizens. People are very unjust in charging good men with worldliness for exercising those rights, and in assuming that religious people are to be blamed for self-interested conduct which in itself is irreproachable and is acknowledged to be so amongst men under ordinary circumstances. We are not surprised, however, to find the prophet accused of treason. He had frequently advised submission to Babylon. It was now hastily assumed that he and his friends were about to secure their own escape from the horrors of a siege by basely deserting their fellow-citizens. The best men are liable to the vilest accusations. The world holds no man above suspicion. Christ was accused of a great crime. Therefore we should learn patience under similar inflictions, remembering that God knows all, and that it is far better to suffer unjustly than to be unpunished but guilty. We should also learn to avoid the mistake of the Jews. People are too much inclined to put the worst construction on a doubtful action. "Charity thinketh no evil."

II. THE CIRCUMSTANCES FOLLOWING THE IMPRISONMENT. Jeremiah had been harshly treated—struck by the courtiers of Zedekiah and thrust into a dungeon. There God met him (ver. 17), as God repeatedly visited him, in prison. His life's work was not stayed by outward restraints. That must have been some consolation to the prophet. A devoted servant of God is more concerned about his mission than about his personal comfort. Apprehending a return of danger from the Chaldean army, the weak Zedekiah sent and consulted Jeremiah secretly. The prophet's reply was bold and clear (ver. 17). Never had he been more definite or more concise. What courage and fidelity to truth for a prisoner thus to address a king! Having delivered his message, Jeremiah proceeded to plead his own cause. How many of us reverse the order, putting self-interest first and crowding other interests into the background! Jeremiah was favourably heard by the king, and his condition considerably ameliorated. He did not suffer this time for his fidelity. It is fair to note that faithfulness does not always lead to martyrdom. In the *end* it is always safer to be brave and true than to play the coward's part.

HOMILIES BY VARIOUS AUTHORS.

Vers. 2, 3.—(*Vide* ch. xxi. 1, 2.)—M.

Vers. 5—10.—*Hopes that betray.* The king, continuing in his rebellion against God as well as against Nebuchadnezzar, invoked the aid of Pharaoh-Necho. At the tidings of his advance the Chaldeans raised the siege, but only that they might defeat the Egyptians, and return again in greater force and fury. I. THE NATURE OF THESE HOPES. 1. *They are based upon human means alone.* 2. *They arise from following the dictates of our own will and wisdom.* II. HOW THEY BETRAY. 1. *They are full of promise, and gain confidence.* 2. *They must fail,* (1) because they are inadequate to the real need, and (2) they are opposed to the will of God. 3. *They spiritually ruin.* They lead us first to ignore and then to resist the will of God. In this alone is our welfare secured. For although the first expression and demand of that will be gloomy and severe, the end of it to the obedient is peace and salvation (1 Pet. i. 3—9).—M.

Ver. 10.—*God's purpose independent of means.* The declaration of the certainty of the judgments upon Judah is absolute. They are not to be avoided by any human effort or apparent success. The soldiers of Chaldea, although they were to be wounded ("thrust through" equivalent to "dead"?), would still avail for the work they had to do, and would be raised again to do it.

I. THE LESSON. A twofold one, viz.: 1. *The inevitableness of the Divine will,* whether it be to destroy or to save. 2. *God's independence of human means.* He can save by "many or by few." He is declared able "of these stones to raise up children unto Abraham." It pleased him by "the foolishness of preaching" to save many, etc. (1) The sinner in rebellion against God, however great his outward success and however feeble the opposition to him, has reason to fear. It is an easy thing for his Maker to crush him. It will not require a *great* instrumentality. Herod was eaten of worms. (2) The Christian worker should rejoice and be encouraged. Every true word or work will have its effect. He must succeed, however insignificant his company or his means.

II. THE TYPE. The ghostly army that was to "burn the city with fire" represents the mighty power of God to create his agents, and symbolizes the *death and resurrection of Christ.* It is the dead Christ who is raised again to fulfil the will of God in judgment and salvation.—M.

Vers. 11—16.—*The servant of God accused of treason.* This attempt of Jeremiah's to go out of Jerusalem, whatever its special purpose may have been (as to this there is great diversity of view), was at once suspected of being treasonable, or, at any rate, it was made an occasion of accusing and punishing him. His asseverations were not listened to, but quickly and with much anger he was consigned to a loathsome prison, where he languished for many days. This teaches that—

I. THOSE WHO ARE FAITHFUL TO GOD WILL FREQUENTLY BE SUSPECTED OF THE WORST MOTIVES. The immediate purpose to be served by going out from Jerusalem was innocent enough, viz. mere resort to the country as safer than the city, or to take possession of his inheritance in Benjamin. No effort was made at concealment, it was done "in the midst of the people." Yet he was accused of being about to "fall away [desert] to the Chaldeans." It would appear as if the prophet's persistent declarations of the success of the Chaldean arms and the downfall of Judah were attributed to his sympathy with the enemy. Many of the greatest servants of God have had similar experiences. Christ himself was accused of the worst intentions against the Jewish nation.

II. HOW IS THIS? 1. *Because the natural mind fails to understand the things of God.* The motive power or central principle is so diverse, or the means employed are so peculiar, that the real benevolence of intention is not perceived. When Christians remember how hard it is for even themselves to justify God's ways, they ought to expect that others not expressly taught of him will fail thoroughly to apprehend their drift. The policy of the Divine life and service, even in its plainest duties and appointments, is surrounded with mystery; its wisdom is not of this world. It is often hard for those who are condemned by Christ's ministers to realize that the denunciations to which they are subjected do not spring from personal enmity. The greatest efforts ought, therefore, to be made to prove how good and loving the spirit is in which words of Christian rebuke are uttered. And the whole conduct of believers should be careful and blameless. "Be ye therefore wise as serpents, and harmless as doves" (Matt. x. 16). 2. *The natural mind is predisposed against truth and goodness.*—M.

Vers. 2—4.—" *Give us of your oil.*" Here we have King Zedekiah, his servants, and his people, asking the prayers of the prophet of God, whose word of counsel and warning they had all along despised. The verses remind us of the parable of the ten virgins; for, as there, the foolish say unto the wise, " Give us of your oil; for our lamps are gone out," so here the foolish king and people entreat the aid of the wise servant of God when, as the midnight cry came to those virgins, so the dread judgment of God came to them. " Pray now unto the Lord our God for us," say they who had refused to listen when he spoke to them from the Lord their God. Note—

I. HOW GRIEVOUSLY WICKED THE PEOPLE HAD BEEN. (Cf. ver. 2.) It was with them as with the family of the rich man told of in Luke xvi. He, being in torments, thought of his five brethren who were all of them living in sin. There, as here, there were none righteous. And so with Sodom and Gomorrah.

II. YET HOW VERY ANXIOUS THEY WERE FOR THE PROPHET'S PRAYERS. Ver. 3, " Pray now," etc. Reasons of this were: 1. They had waked up to the conviction that the prophet's message was true. 2. They were in sore peril, and knew not how to help themselves. 3. They knew that the prophet had power with God. 4. They felt they could not go to God in prayer themselves. How much of the asking for the prayers of God's ministers on the part of those who are on their death-bed is owing to like causes!

III. HOW USELESS SUCH PRAYERS ARE. Did the prayer of Dives do any good? or of the five foolish virgins? or those of the prophet, for we may suppose that he did pray? Now, the reasons of their uselessness are such as these: 1. To have granted them would have defeated God's purpose in regard to his people. That purpose was to purify them, to separate them from their sins. But they did not wish when they asked these prayers to be severed from sin, only to be relieved of trouble. But such desire could not be granted; therefore God held them down to the consequences of their sin. 2. Their request was an insult to God. Such men are well described in Mrs. H. W. B. Stowe's book, 'Uncle Tom's Cabin,' where one of them, Haley, is thus spoken to by a comrade: "After all, what's the odds between me and you? 'Tain't that you care one bit more or have a bit more feelin'; it's clean, sheer, dog meanness, wanting to cheat the devil and save your own skin. Don't I see through it? And your 'gettin' religion,' as you call it, arter all, is too p'isin mean for any crittur; run up a bill with the devil all your life, and then sneak out when pay-time comes! Boh!" Is there not a vast amount of this meanness? Its despicableness is only equalled by its uselessness. 3. It would make God the minister of sin.

CONCLUSION. Learn, unless there be true repentance, neither our own prayers nor those of other people, though they be the greatest saints of God, will avail us anything. Even coming to Christ apart from repentance will fail us. "The sacrifices of God are a broken spirit," etc.—C.

Ver. 5.—*Building on the sand.* Such was the conduct of the people who encouraged themselves to hope from the withdrawal of the armies of Babylon from around Jerusalem that now they were delivered for good and all, and had no further cause for fear. They misread facts, interpreting them according to their desires rather than according to the truth. It was true that the army of Egypt was advancing and that of Babylon retreating. But, as the onflux of the wave does not prove that the tide is coming in nor its reflux that the tide is going out, so this temporary advance and retreat told of no permanent results or of what the real issue should be. But yet they thought it did. It was a case of building on the sands of unwarranted hope rather than on the rock of the Word of God. Hope ever tells a flattering tale, but never so much so as when she promises peace to those to whom God has said there shall be no peace. Now, concerning such building on the sand, note—

I. THE FOUNDATION. There are many such; *e.g.*: 1. Reasonings from the observed prosperity of the wicked. 2. The assertions or suggestions of the sin-loving heart: that there is no God; if there be, he is too merciful to punish sin; repentance at last will do; the efficacy of sacraments, etc. These are all of them instances of 1. 3. The slow-footedness of God's judgments. "Because sentence against an evil work is not executed speedily, therefore the hearts of the sons of men are steadfastly set in them to do evil." And God *is* long-suffering, not willing that any should perish.

II. THE STRUCTURES RAISED THEREUPON. They are often characterized by much material comfort. Worldly prosperity is not too weighty for them. Great freedom from anxiety, "Not in trouble as other men are." They are very attractive, and seem to be the abodes of true happiness. Mirth, festivity, and song abound in them often far more than in those which are built upon the rock.

III. THE OVERTHROW. This always comes. It came in the instance given here. The armies of Babylon did come back. It may come in this life. There are warnings of it every day. But if not now, then in the great day of judgment. And this overthrow will make us full of sorrow according to the days wherein we have never been afflicted, and the years wherein, as we have thought, we have seen no evil.

CONCLUSION. Read the events of God's providence, not by the light of thy sin-loving heart, but by the light of God's sure Word, of God's Spirit within thee, and of God's not partial but complete dealing with men, taking in the whole of life, and, if needs be, eternity also. "Be not deceived."—C.

Ver. 9.—"*Be not deceived.*" There was ground for this exhortation, and there is still. Then as now—
I. VERY MANY WERE DECEIVED.
II. APPEARANCES WERE DECEPTIVE.
III. NONE COULD CLAIM EXEMPTION FROM THE POSSIBILITY OF BEING DECEIVED.
IV. THERE WAS A TRAITOR WITHIN THE CAMP. Their hearts wished that to be true which they therefore thought to be true.
V. To BE DECEIVED IS TO BE PLUNGED IN THE UTTERMOST OF SORROW.
VI. WE NEED NOT BE. There is One who says, "I will guide thee with my counsel."—C.

Ver. 13.—*Falsely accused.* Our Lord Jesus said, "It is sufficient for the servant that he be as his Master." Now, as he was falsely accused, so here we find his servant likewise. Note—
I. To BE FALSELY ACCUSED IS THE COMMON LOT OF GOD'S PEOPLE. How many instances we have!—Abel, Joseph, Moses, David, etc. Because of such slanders the psalmist said, "All men are liars." And here the Prophet Jeremiah, having no thought of deserting his countrymen, is nevertheless accused of so doing. And to-day the world is ever ready with its slander. It avows that all the godly are but hypocrites, knaves, or fools. With what eagerness does it fasten upon the faults of a good man! How ready to take up an accusation against him!
II. How IS IT TO BE ACCOUNTED FOR? We reply: 1. Men of the world do not understand the principles on which the godly act. Hence what they do not understand they misrepresent. 2. They know their own motives, and attribute the like to the godly. They act from purely worldly motives, and hence they conclude godly men do the same. 3. They hate religion, and therefore are always ready to revile it. 4. It is "a comfort to Sodom" to think that the godly are no better than themselves after all. But—
III. How IS IT TO BE DEALT WITH? 1. *Sometimes by silence.* Silence leaves opportunity for and suggests reflection. How often of our Lord is it said, "He answered not a word" (cf. John xiii.)! 2. *Sometimes by indignant denial.* Thus the prophet acted here; ver. 14, "It is false," etc. They might have known, and probably did know, how false their accusation was. Where there is great and true indignation felt at being thought capable of a given crime, that feeling may often be shown; often, indeed, it ought to be, as when (1) the honour of God is concerned; (2) the good of his Church; (3) what is shameful as well as sinful is charged against us. 3. *Sometimes by showing the necessary untruthfulness of the accusation.* This also our Lord did, as when they charged him with being in league with Beelzebub. 4. *Sometimes by committing it all to God.* Of our Lord it is said, "When he was reviled, he reviled not again, ... but committed himself to him that judgeth righteously." 5. *Sometimes by showing the motive of the false accusation.* As when our Lord likened those who found fault with him to petulant children playing in the market-place, who would be pleased with nothing. 6. *Always by remembering that we are in the fellowship of Christ herein, and seeking his Spirit's aid to rightly bear this trial.*—C.

Vers. 14, 15.—*Characteristics of injustice.* They may be traced in the incident recorded in these verses. Unjust judges as were these—
I. WILL NOT HEARKEN TO THE ACCUSED.
II. ARE BIASSED BY PASSION.
III. ARE NEEDLESSLY CRUEL.
IV. SEEK NOT RIGHT, BUT REVENGE.
LEARN. To be careful what manner of spirit we are of whenever we are called upon to judge one another. Let us be thankful that the Judge before whom we stand, and who surveys all our ways, is that gracious Lord to whom the Father has committed all judgment, and who judges not righteously only, but in all mercy as well.—C.

Ver. 20.—*"Out of weakness made strong."* This verse an utterance, not of a sturdy invincible soul, but one of a gentle, shrinking, and often timid nature. Note—

I. THE PROPHET JEREMIAH belonged to the company of those who, out of weakness, God has made strong. 1. By nature and temperament *he was the reverse of strong.* Proof in this verse. Suffering was ever terrible to him. Hence he piteously pleads for the king's help. And *passim* we have indications of the gentleness of his nature (cf. ch. i. 6, "Ah, Lord, I cannot;" and homily on ch. iv. 19—30, "*The fellowship of Christ's sufferings,*" vol. i. p. 100). But: 2. Notwithstanding this, *see how strong he became.* When it came to the test, how he endured (cf. ch. i. 10, 17, 18)! Nothing would induce him to alter his word towards the king, the prophets, and the people generally. He softened not one line of his message, although it would have been so much to his advantage to have done so. Now—

II. THIS IS THE GLORY OF GOD'S GRACE ALWAYS. There will be glory *by-and-by,* an outward glory on every child of God. "Eye hath not seen," etc. *But the present glory* of God's grace is this, that out of weakness it makes its recipients strong. See what it did for the apostles, and especially for St. Peter—they the recreants and the denier of the Lord, but afterwards his valiant and undaunted witnesses. And grace has done the same for not a few in prospect of suffering and trial from which beforehand they would have utterly shrunk away. Women and children were amongst the number of the martyrs; and in the moral martyrdoms of this softer age they are so still. God strengthens his servants "with might by his Spirit in the inner man." *And this is the glory of his grace.* Not the numbers of the Church, nor her wealth, rank, gifts, or aught of such sort, but the spiritual strength that characterizes her. "I can do all things," said St. Paul, "through Christ which strengtheneth me." *And it will be so yonder in the better world hereafter.* The glory of that day will not be the golden streets, the gates of pearl, the foundations of precious stones; not the vast throng of the redeemed, nor aught that belongs only to their circumstances, happy as they will be; but it will be *the character* of them all. And this will be *their security also.* The defences of that condition of the redeemed will not be outward, but inward. They, having been strengthened with might by the Spirit of God in the inner man, will have come to be rooted—like the giant oak, which no tempest can uproot from the ground—and grounded—like the deep-laid foundation of the temple, which naught can overthrow—in love, and so "Christ will dwell in" their "hearts." Yes, their glory will be their defence also.

CONCLUSION. Seek, therefore, this grace of Divine strength. Bow your "knees to the God and Father of our Lord Jesus Christ," that, "according to the riches of his glory," he would grant you this. Then, though weak and wavering by nature, steadiness and strength shall be given to your will, your heart, and so God will make you as he did his prophet—as "a defenced city, an iron pillar, a brazen wall" (ch. i. 18).—C.

Ver. 21.—*The rough wind stayed in the day of the east wind.* Very terrible to the prophet were the sufferings he had to bear. Hence he seeks for relief by petitioning the king for help, which the king is led to bestow (ver. 21). It is an illustration of how God stays his rough wind, etc. Note—

I. GOD OFTEN LETS SORE TROUBLE COME TO HIS SERVANTS.

II. BUT HE APPOINTS IT ACCORDING TO THEIR POWER OF ENDURANCE. He is not a hard master, gathering where he has not strawed, nor reaping where he has not sown. He fits the back for the burden it has to bear. If staying in the dread dungeon was too great a trial for his prophet, he will have him taken out. The wave that would have sunk the boat in which our Lord was with his disciples was never permitted to beat into it. A great many others came, but not that one. And so it ever is. "As thy day, so thy strength." God will be our "arm every morning."

III. THEREFORE "TAKE NO THOUGHT FOR THE MORROW," etc.—C.

Ver. 3.—*A request for intercession.* A request of this kind has always to be looked at through the character of the man who prefers it. It makes all the difference whether it be the utterance of grovelling superstition or of enlightened piety. It is a long way from this request of Zedekiah to the request of Paul: "Brethren, pray for us." Let us try to estimate—

I. THE NOTION ZEDEKIAH HAD OF GOD. A notion evidently altogether detached from any considerations of character; we are told in ver. 2 that Zedediah did not hearken to the words of the Lord through his prophet Jeremiah, and we could infer as much from the request here addressed to the prophet. Zedekiah looked upon Jehovah pretty much as he did upon the deities of surrounding nations. The notion was that the immense power of these deities could be turned in any direction desired, if only they were sufficiently propitiated. Now, if Zedekiah had cared to attend to the volume of prophecy, he would have seen very clearly that he who comes to God must believe that he is a God who will not pass over the misgovernment, the cruelty, the injustice, of human kings. And so when we come to God our prayers will have reality just in proportion as they show a distinct understanding of the character of God.

II. THE NOTION ZEDEKIAH HAD OF PRAYER. Had he indeed any notion at all? Did he mean anything more than that Jeremiah should go and do whatever he thought necessary and effectual? Intercessory prayer can be of little use to those who do not pray for themselves. Zedekiah wanted a certain end, namely, that by help of Egypt he should repel the Chaldeans. And he looked upon Jehovah as being a sort of heavenly Pharaoh. And just as he had sent, doubtless, one ambassador to ask for Pharaoh's help, so now he wants to make Jeremiah an ambassador to Jehovah. This was all very foolish, ignorant, and presumptuous on Zedekiah's part; but what better are we when we make up our prayers of petitions for things that we desire without stopping to consider that no petition is worth anything unless it not merely accords with the will of God, but even springs from that will? The use of prayer is that God may serve us according to his estimate of our needs, not according to our estimate.

III. THE NOTION ZEDEKIAH HAD OF THE PROPHET. He had a superstitious feeling that Jeremiah could do something for him he could not do for himself. We see here the secret of the power of priestcraft. We see how it was that false prophets got such a hold. We see how it is that priestcraft and spiritual dictation still prevail. The great bulk of men will not do the right thing towards God, they will not repent and crucify self, but a deep necessity impels them to do something, and so they seek to other men. Zedekiah was making an altogether wrong use of the prophet. His duty was to obey the prophet's messages, then he would not have needed to ask Jeremiah to pray for him. And let all people understand with respect to ministers of religion, that they exist to teach and help in a brotherly way; but that also they are frail and fallible, and possess no mystic virtue to make their prayers more efficacious than the prayers of other people. Intercessory prayer is the duty, the privilege, the power, of every Christian.—Y.

Vers. 9, 10.—*Israel's delusion as to its enemy.* I. THE DELUSION ENTERTAINED. That a great army is before Jerusalem is, of course, no delusion, and that it may effect a great deal of damage of a certain sort is no delusion. The delusion lies here, in supposing that the removal of the army would be the removal of the danger. And this delusion being strong in the minds of the people led them to seek the help of Egypt. A carnal foe was to be overcome by the help of a carnal friend. And similarly we are all led into most mistaken policies of life by seeing only our visible enemies. In our solicitude to guard against the seen enemy, and keep in safety our own visible possessions, we make too much of visible things altogether. It is very hard, of course, to admit this; it is very hard for the natural mind to see its delusions; but then it is the very mark of delusions that they put on the semblance of fundamental and important truths. Again and again appeal is made to what is called common sense to testify to the validity of delusions. The common belief of the multitude is cited to stop the mouth of any one who ventures to proclaim what he is sure is true. Those who have got to the heights and advanced places of spiritual experience know full well that the maxims and rules of the natural man are little but a mass of pernicious delusions. Thus men carefully preserve the shell of life, while the interior treasure for which the shell exists is utterly neglected.

II. THE DELUSION EXPOSED. God makes plain who the real enemy of Jerusalem is, an enemy whom a thousand Pharaohs and a thousand Egypts would vainly contend against. In one sense Jehovah himself is enemy, but what he says amounts to this, that Jerusalem itself is its own worst enemy. While it is rebellious against him, and full of all unrighteousness, he must work against it by all available instruments.   To destroy the Chaldean army is only as it were to break the warrior's sword; he can seize another and continue the conflict.   It is of the greatest possible consequence that we should know in any conflict whether we are fighting simply against man, or whether behind the man who is in front of us there be the purpose and the strength of God.   How much of human energy has been wasted, how many have had failure stamped on all their efforts, simply because it has not been known that God has been behind human conflicts!   God would have us make sure—and he gives us ample means for the attainment—that we are not fighting against him.

III. THE DELUSION MAINTAINED.   This is made plain to us as we read on in the narrative.   An example is given to us of how people often do not wake to the delusions of life till too late.   They walk contentedly in a vain show, and the realities flowing out of the ministry of Christ they reckon to be dreams.   We may depend upon it that delusions will be maintained, most ingeniously, most tenaciously, until by the power of God our eyes are opened to distinguish reality from appearance, and truth from falsehood.—Y.

Vers. 17—19.—*The secret question of a king and the bold answer of a prophet.*   I. THE SECRET QUESTION OF A KING.   1. *The secrecy.*   Why should a king with all his authority do a thing in secrecy?   Was it policy or fear that dictated this secret consultation with Jeremiah?   Fear, probably, was the largest element.   He was afraid of what the princes and courtiers around him would say.   Note other secret interviews sought by men of rank and authority.   Herod, a king, privily calls the wise men from the East.   Nicodemus, a ruler of the Jews, comes to Jesus by night.   What men of position do cannot be concealed easily.   The very effort to conceal is often only a more effective publication.   The lesson is that, however quietly and unobtrusively we may do a thing, we must do it so as not in the least fearing publicity.   The very difficulty of keeping secrets is a divinely ordained difficulty to help in keeping men in the paths of righteousness.   2. *The evident faith of the king in Jeremiah's office.*   The faith was superstitious and unpractical, but still, such as it was, it exerted a power over the king's conduct.   This increases the king's responsibility, for it shows that he was not able to get Jeremiah and his message out of his mind.   3. *The indication as to what sort of answer was expected.*   Not in words, of course, but we can guess what the tone of the inquiry was.   Jeremiah came from a prison to prophesy, and doubtless the king thought that the privations of the past and the hopes of liberty might draw some flattering word from the prophet.   Altogether, what a pitiable position this king was in—waiting eagerly, half in terror, half in threatening, upon the word of one of his humble subjects, and the same a prisoner!

II. THE BOLD ANSWER OF A PROPHET.   What great things are required from a prophet!   He must always be in close and living relation to truth.   He must always be ready to meet the manifold temptations which beset a man who is specially sent forth to speak the truth.   His first question must ever be, not—What is the safe path, or the easy path? but—What is God's path?   Here he was in close and private dealing with a king.   Perhaps, as he looked upon Zedekiah thus sending for him secretly, he compassionated him rather than feared him.   It was such a revelation of the hollowness of human grandeur.   Jeremiah here before Zedekiah is even somewhat of a type of Jesus before Pilate.   Jesus will go on testifying to the truth.   He will not make Pilate's task one whit easier by accommodating himself to Pilate's desires.   Truth, eternal realities, fundamental duties, fidelity to the clear voice of God within the heart,—these must prevail in every one who would follow in the path of Jesus or of prophets and apostles. There is neither real prudence nor real charity without these things.—Y.

EXPOSITION.

CHAPTER XXXVIII.

CONTINUATION.

The object of the princes being frustrated (for in the "court of the guard" Jeremiah had perfect freedom and opportunity of speech), the princes resolve upon a more effectual means of stopping the prophet's mouth.   He is thrown into a miry pit, with the object that he may die of starvation.

Ver. 1.—Two Pashurs appear to be mentioned here : one probably the same who put Jeremiah in the stocks (ch. xx. 1, 2); the other a member of the first of Zedekiah's two embassies to the prophet (ch. xxi. 1). On Jucal, see ch. xxxvii. 3. **Had spoken**; rather, *kept speaking*.

Vers. 2, 3.—**He that remaineth**, etc. Jeremiah repeats what he had said to Zedekiah's embassy in ch. xxi. 9, 10.

Ver. 4.—**For thus**; literally, *for therefore*; i.e. because he is left in impunity (comp. the use of the phrase in ch. xxix. 28). **He weakeneth the hands of the men of war**; i.e. he dispirits them. It is important to get this " outside view " of the preaching of Jeremiah. There is evidently some excuse for the opponents of Jeremiah. It was a matter of life and death to resist the Chaldeans, and Jeremiah was, according to the politicians, playing into the hands of the enemy (see further in general Introduction). The addition of the words, **that remain**, shows that the bitter end of the resistance was fast approaching.

Ver. 5.—**He is in your hand**. The growing power of the " princes " (see on ch. xxii. 4) seems to have confined the king to a merely secondary *rôle*.

Ver. 6.—**The dungeon**; more literally, *the cistern*. "Every house in Jerusalem was supplied with a subterranean cistern, so well constructed that we never read of the city suffering in a siege from want of water" (Dr. Payne Smith). A grotto bearing the name of Jeremiah has been shown at Jerusalem since the fifteenth century. Under its floor are vast cisterns, the deepest of which professes to be the prison into which the prophet was thrown. The objection is that the sacred narrative proves that the prison was in the city, whereas " the present grotto was not included within the walls until the time of Herod Agrippa" (Thomson, ' The Land and the Book,' 1881, p. 555). **The son of Hammelech**; rather, *a royal prince* (as ch. xxxvi. 26).

Ver. 7.—**Ebed-melech the Ethiopian**. The name means " the king's slave." Ebers remarks that the eunuchs employed in the modern East are nearly all negroes, on whom the shameful operation has been performed by Copts in Upper Egypt. Zedekiah's harem is referred to in vers. 22, 23.

Ver. 9.—**For there is no more bread in the city**. It would almost seem as if the little remaining bread had been brought together by command of the magistrates, and that it was given out in rations by them (comp. ch. xxxvii. 21).

Ver. 10.—**Thirty men**. Why so many were sent is not clear. Are we to suppose that the princes would resist Jeremiah's release ? But " the king is not he," etc. (ver. 5). Is it not a scribe's error for " three " (so Ewald, Hitzig, and Graf)?

Ver. 11.—**Under the treasury**; rather, *to (a room) under the treasury*. **Old cast clouts**, etc.; literally, *rags of torn garments and rags of worn-out garments*.

Ver. 14.—**The third entry**. What this means exactly is not clear; probably the " entry " led from the palace to the temple. It must have been a private place, else it would not have been chosen for this interview. **I will ask thee a thing**; rather, *I will ask of thee a word*; i.e. a revelation from Jehovah (comp. ch. xxxvii. 17).

Ver. 15.—**Wilt thou not hearken**; rather, *thou wilt not hearken*.

Ver. 16.—**That made us this soul**. A very unusual formula (comp. Isa. lvii. 16).

Ver. 17.—**The king of Babylon's princes**. Nebuchadnezzar himself was in Riblah (ch. xxxix. 5).

Ver. 22.—**All the women that are left**; i.e. probably the wives of Zedekiah's royal predecessors, who had passed into his own harem as concubines. Even Hezekiah, as Payne Smith well points out, had a numerous harem (' Records of the Past,' i. 39, where " daughters " is equivalent to " girls "). Zedekiah's own wives are spoken of in the next verse. **Thy friends have set thee on**, etc. The first half of this taunting song (*máshāl*) reminds of Obad. 7 (for other points of contact with Obadiah, see on ch. xlix. 7 —22). The meaning is that, after urging the weak-minded Zedekiah on to a conflict with the Chaldeans, they have left him involved in hopeless difficulties.

Ver. 23.—**So they**, etc.; rather, *and they*, etc. The women spoken of are different from those in ver. 22. **Thou shalt cause this city to be burned**. The literal rendering (see margin) is, *Thou shalt burn this city*; but the Septuagint, Peshito, and Targum have " As for this city it shall be burned," which suits the parallelism better.

Ver. 27.—**He told them according to all these words**. A controversy has arisen as to whether Jeremiah was justified in concealing the truth. But is a man bound to confess the truth to a murderer ?

Ver. 28.—**And he was there when**, etc. The words, of which this is an incorrect version, ought to begin the first verse of the next chapter. Render (with Coverdale), *And it came to pass when Jerusalem was taken (in the ninth year of Zedekiah came Nebuchadrezzar, etc.; in the eleventh year . . . the city was cleft open) that all the princes*, etc. The correctness of the reading is, however, open to some doubt (see introduction to next chapter).

HOMILETICS.

Vers. 1—13.—*Jeremiah in the pit.* I. JEREMIAH PREACHES FAITHFULLY. (Vers. 2, 5.) His conduct is wise, brave, and noble. On the surface it savours of pusillanimity. But so much the greater the wisdom and courage that inspire it. Personally Jeremiah is in greater danger from his fellow-citizens than from the invaders. To rouse the anger of the people amongst whom he is living by apparently favouring the plans of their enemies requires no little firmness of character. Moreover, strong moral courage is requisite for such a course as that of Jeremiah's. His patriotism is certain to be taken for treachery, his wisdom for cowardice. He stands alone with his unpopular advice, sure that it will not be followed, sure that his motives will be misunderstood and his character maligned. To a sensitive man the situation would be exquisitely painful. Fidelity under it reveals a noble courage. Thus we see how the bravest man may be he who appears to be most weak, while the rash and boastful daring that rushes heedlessly with the multitude but shrinks from a course of unpopularity, is really feeble and cowardly.

II. THE PRINCES ARE ALARMED. (Ver. 4.) They have some reason to dread the effect of Jeremiah's preaching upon the defence of Jerusalem. If they are certain of the wisdom of the course they are pursuing, it is difficult to see how they can regard the prophet with anything less than dismay. Every time his Cassandra notes are heard in the streets it seems as though disaffection were being urged upon the people. The mistake of the princes is in being so wedded to their policy as never to consider the advice of Jeremiah as of any weight and wisdom. Thus we judge and condemn men with absolute certainty to our own mind, but often only because we assume, without reason, the infallibility of our own position.

III. THE KING WEAKLY YIELDS. (Ver. 5.) Zedekiah is helpless in the hands of his courtiers. Like Pilate, he thinks to throw off all responsibility on the accusers whom he dare not oppose (John xviii. 31). But he cannot do this. His weakness is culpable. He is not like a constitutional monarch, legally fettered by a responsible ministry. He is by position a responsible ruler. If he cannot discharge the functions of his position, he should abdicate. In no case is he justified in lending the weight of his name to a deed of which he does not approve. We cannot free ourselves from responsibility by declining to act when it is our duty to interfere and prevent a wrong from being done.

IV. JEREMIAH IS CAST INTO THE PIT. (Ver. 6.) 1. The action of the courtiers is *cruel.* They treat the prophet with needless indignity and evidently design for him the slow torture of a death by starvation. 2. It is also *cowardly.* They dare not execute him openly. The horrible fate is assigned to him because it is less dangerous to themselves. 3. The prophet is now in the *lowest condition* of wretchedness, down in the pit, sunk in the mire, left in that cold, dark solitude to the horrors of approaching starvation. Those of us who are ready to murmur at slighter trouble should remember how much better men than we have had to endure far greater suffering and humiliation than ours. What shame and agony were heaped upon Christ the Son of God!

V. THE ETHIOPIAN INTERCEDES. (Vers. 7—9.) 1. This man was a *heathen* by nation, but a good man. Character, not profession, is the one thing of significance with all of us. 2. He was a man of an apparently *inferior race.* It is better to have a black skin and a humane heart than a white skin and a black heart. 3. He was regarded as an *effeminate creature.* True manliness belongs to our conduct, not to our appearance and manners. God raises up friends in the most unlikely quarters. One of the advantages of trouble is that it reveals unknown friends.

VI. JEREMIAH IS DELIVERED. The weak king only wants the encouragement of his chamberlain to do an act of justice which his own conscience must have urged him to all along. When the distress and danger of Jeremiah are vividly brought before him, he rouses himself. Many people are too weak to do their duty till their imagination and feelings are wrought upon. They live in comfortable indifference to the wretchedness of others simply because they have not been made to feel it. They are not to be excused on this account. But knowing the fact, we should do more to make the needs of the poor, the sick, and the heathen felt by the indifferent who ought to help them. A higher providence leads to the deliverance of Jeremiah. God watches over him in the dungeon, and God sees that he is saved from it. So God will save his people from all their troubles, though in some cases the minister of deliverance is that dark angel of death whose advent the miserable in Andrea Orcagna's picture at Pisa welcome with joy.

Ver. 6.—*The apparent misanthropy of revelation.* The political aspect of these words is evident; let us now consider their moral bearings. The inspired prophet of God is taken for an enemy of his neighbours. The experience of Jeremiah is not without parallel, nor is it wanting in certain reasonable grounds of justification.

I. THERE ARE THINGS IN REVELATION WHICH APPEAR TO INDICATE MISANTHROPY. When God utters his voice he does not always speak in dulcet notes. We may hear harsh, grating thunders of Sinai. The message is not always pleasant. It makes us feel uncomfortable, exposes our worst characteristics, and has no pity on our little contrivances for putting the best face on our conduct. It stays our hand in many a favourite occupation. It cries "vanity of vanities" to our pet schemes. It puts a veto on our proud ambition. It frowns at much of our pleasure. For the future it threatens judgment and bitter penalties. When we fancy we have found some neat plan of escape, it exposes the rottenness of our hope and plunges us for the moment into blank despair. Such is the work of certain parts of revelation, and being so, it is not unnaturally regarded by some as misanthropic. Bearing this fact in mind, we must not be surprised at the aversion that the irreligious feel to religion. Judging from this standpoint, they may regard their best friend as their enemy, and imagine that the angry voice of God indicates nothing but his settled wrath against them.

II. THIS MISANTHROPY IS ONLY APPARENT. Jeremiah was the best friend of Jerusalem, and the fanatical leaders of resistance her most fatal foes. His advice was really wise and patriotic. The Bible, which to some is a gloomy Book, darkening the aspect of human life, contains the secret of its true blessedness. The religion of the Bible may be sombre in the eyes of some when compared with the sunny religion of Greece. But the Hellenic faith could not save its followers from utter moral corruption and ruin. Through the sterner faith of the Jew and the Christian we are led to that one satisfying brightness of life which comes from the rising upon us of the Sun of righteousness. We must judge of words by their aim, not by their sound. The Bible contains threats of terrible doom, but as we discover the purpose of them we see that they are not curses but warnings. God often opposes us, stays our course, puts up the red signal, only to save us from rushing to some fatal calamity. Elijah, Jeremiah, John the Baptist, Savonarola, and John Knox were regarded by their contemporaries as misanthropic. Now we see that they were the salt of the earth, true saviours of society. Even Christ uttered words which might seem to indicate misanthropy, but all with the intention of leading men to escape from the evils he deplored and find salvation in his grace.

Ver. 11.—"*Old cast clouts and old rotten rags.*" I. THERE IS A USE FOR EVERYTHING. These rags were possibly thrown aside as useless. Yet they were found to serve a distinct purpose. Amongst the wonderful combinations of invention and economy in the present day, none are more remarkable than those which turn waste materials to serviceable ends. There is a mission for every life. No man is so low, so worn, so worthless, but that he may find some way in which to serve God and his fellows. If a rag has a mission, shall a soul find none?

II. IF WE CANNOT ATTAIN THE HIGHEST OBJECT AIMED AT, WE SHOULD NOT NEGLECT THAT WHICH IS WITHIN OUR REACH. The rags may once have been prince's robes. Now they are only fit for the lowest uses. Then let them be so used. There is an impractical idealism which paralyzes all effort. Because a thing cannot be turned to the highest account we will not use it at all. So there are those who refuse to do anything because they can do nothing very great, or who, being compelled to give up a work of honour, are too proud to undertake a more lowly task. We should remember Goethe's maxim, "Do the thing that lieth nearest thee." Thus a useful rag may be a rebuke to a useless man.

III. THE GREATEST MAN MAY HAVE NEED OF THE MOST COMMONPLACE APPLIANCES. A prophet finds comfort from a rag. We are none of us emancipated from relation to the lowest things. This should humble those who make the dignity of their nature a reason for despising the offices of lowly things and persons. It should encourage those who have but small means. They may be of material comfort to some far above them. Great and small, we are linked together for our mutual helpfulness.

IV. DEEDS OF KINDNESS SHOULD BE PERFORMED IN A KIND MANNER. Carelessness and roughness of demeanour may spoil half the effect of the most well-meant offices of charity. There are philanthropists who would lift the prisoner from the pit, but with hard, coarse ropes, without any consideration for his sore and weary body. The purpose is gracious, but the manner is brutal. Christians should not be mere patrons, wounding the feelings of those whom they help in other respects, but the brethren of the distressed, aiding them carefully, gently, courteously. This is the manner of God's great deliverance of mankind; it is by a Saviour who "shall not cry, nor lift up, nor cause his voice to be heard in the street. A bruised reed shall he not break, and the smoking flax shall he not quench" (Isa. xlii. 2, 3).

Vers. 19—23.—*The fear of ridicule.* I. THE FEAR OF RIDICULE IS A COMMON FAILING OF WEAK MEN. Zedekiah is a weak man. His first thought when he contemplates the possible effects of obedience to the Divine command is that it may result in his being delivered into the hands of the captives at Babylon to be mocked by them (ver. 17). This he dreads above all things. Many men who would stand up without flinching to be shot at cower before a laugh. Let them understand that their conduct is weak and foolish and wrong.

II. THE FEAR OF RIDICULE IS A FREQUENT CAUSE OF NEGLECT OF DUTY. This is one of the chief weapons of persecution and temptation exercised in our own day. The rack and the stake are out of fashion; the sneer and the gibe have taken their place. Milton's Satan has been superseded by Goethe's Mephistopheles. The young are specially sensitive to ridicule. They especially should seek grace from God to stand firm against it.

III. THE FEAR OF RIDICULE PROVOKES RIDICULE. Jeremiah showed the king that disobedience coming out of his dread of being mocked would result in worse mockery. Fearing the laughter of captive soldiers, he would be mocked by women; dreading the contempt of strangers, he should meet with that of his own house (ver. 22). Face a laugh, and you foil its spiteful intention; quail before it, and you give it the victory and furnish occasion for fresh contempt. The young man who sneaks away from his religious principles because his companions in business laugh at him for them is only despised for his contemptible weakness, while that young man who quietly holds his ground unmoved by senseless ridicule wins the secret respect of observers, and makes them inwardly ashamed of their folly.

IV. THE FEAR OF RIDICULE MAY END IN FATAL RESULTS. Jeremiah pointed this out to the king (ver. 23). The horrible charge of having brought about the burning of the city would be attached to his name, and the guilt of it to his soul. Here was a far greater cause of alarm than the danger of a laugh. Weak men who are moved by such contemptible motives as those that influenced Zedekiah should be roused by a rude shock, if that is necessary, for them to see the dread and solemn issues of life and the fearful evils they may evoke while trifling with duty in childish timidity.

V. IT IS OUR DUTY TO CONQUER THE FEAR OF RIDICULE BY FAITHFUL OBEDIENCE TO THE WILL OF GOD. Here lies the remedy (ver. 20). To some this fear is keen and almost irresistible. But it is wholly selfish. It is associated with morbid, self-regarding thoughts. If we realize the idea that God is speaking to us and watching us, all ideas of the thoughts of men about us should sink to the dust. With earnest convictions of duty and true efforts of obedience inspired by the grace of Christ, which is sufficient for us, we may brave this thorn in the flesh—the fear of man that bringeth a snare.

Ver. 20.—*The blessedness of obedience.* Jeremiah entreats Zedekiah to obey the voice of God urging him with promises of deliverance. Note here—

I. THE ENTREATY. Jeremiah says, "I beseech thee." This is characteristic of the kindliness and earnestness of the prophet. It is also indicative of the character of God who inspired him. With St. Paul he might have said, "We are ambassadors therefore on behalf of Christ, as though God were entreating you by us; we beseech you on behalf of Christ, . . . be ye reconciled to God" (2 Cor. v. 20). This Divine entreaty signifies (1) *earnestness*—God truly desires our good; (2) *kindliness and sympathy*; (3) *condescension*; and (4) the *greatness of the issues at stake*.

II. THE DUTY. 1. This is *obedience*, the cardinal duty of the Old Testament. The importance of this duty in the New Testament has been underrated. There, too, it takes a first place in the teaching of Christ (John xv. 14) and of his apostles—St. Paul (Rom. ii. 8), St. Peter (1 Pet. iii. 1), St. John (1 John iii. 24), and St. James (Jas. i. 22). Indeed, all religion consists in submission (passive faith) and obedience (active faith). 2. Such obedience must be *implicit*. Zedekiah did not understand the reason of the Divine command. To carry it out was unpalatable to him and his people. But once we know God's will, questions of mystery and of inclination should not affect us. In the gospel dispensation obedience is more intelligent. We have spiritual principles in place of formal precepts. Yet here also there is often mystery and fear as to the results of obedience, and then our duty is the soldier's duty of unquestioning obedience.

> "Theirs not to reason why;
> Theirs but to do and die."

III. THE CLAIM. 1. It rests on the *will of God*. The king is to obey the voice of God. The monkish duty of obedience stayed with the ecclesiastical superior. But the spiritual Christian must feel that he owes his supreme allegiance directly to God. Our King and Father commands. We must obey *his* will. 2. It is determined by the *revelation of the will of God*. The obedience is to be given to the voice as it is made known by the prophet. "Which I speak unto thee." We are only responsible for obedience to God's will as far as he has revealed it to us. But we cannot plead total ignorance of his will. That has been declared by prophets and apostles, manifested in Christ, confirmed by the Spirit of God in our conscience.

IV. THE PROMISE. 1. *Whatever happens*. "It shall be well"—a vague promise, but sufficient. We cannot tell what is well for us. The thing God sends may not seem good as it approaches. But in the result it shall be well. That is enough for faith. 2. *Life is secured*. "And thy soul shall live." What is the use of the preservation of our possessions if our life is taken? Men toil for earthly gain and forget that the one condition of enjoying it may go at any moment. Life in the highest sense, eternal life, is the full reward for obedience.

HOMILIES BY VARIOUS AUTHORS.

Vers. 4—13.—*Foreshadowings and analogies of the cross.* The pitiable fate of Jeremiah, so uncalled for and unexpected both in its inflictions and deliverances, the light and shade so strongly contrasted, become charged as we proceed with a certain suggestiveness of something unspeakably greater yet to come. In other words, Jeremiah is perceived to be not only a prophet, but a type of Christ. The charge of treason, the defiance of legal safeguards and requirements by the princes, the wavering and helplessness of the king, the living death in the miry dungeon, and the resurrection through the kind aid of Ebed-Melech, are types of the most unmistakable kind of the characteristic redemptive experiences of the Man of sorrows. And this is only one out of many proofs that *human history, especially sacred history, betrays a system of correspondence in its events with those which constituted the earthly experience of the Messiah*.

I. THEY CALL ATTENTION TO THE MANIFESTATION OF CHRIST AND HELP TO FIX AND IDENTIFY IT. All along the line of Old Testament revelation there were these fingerposts or indicators of the coming struggle between righteousness and sin. The cross is closely associated with the very first pages of revelation, and gives meaning and connection to the loftiest, deepest, and most anomalous utterances and occurrences of the Old Testament. With its many anticipations, echoes, and secondaries, the cross of Christ asserts itself as the central and most commanding principle of human history.

II. THEY REVEAL THE SAME LAW OPERATING THROUGHOUT THE WORLD'S HISTORY AND HUMAN EXPERIENCE. Prehistoric myths and heathen religions, although incapable of attaining to such a Divine conception, yet presuppose and grope after it. And in many an illustrious and obscure human consciousness had the cross made its impress ere the Redeemer of mankind was called upon to suffer. 1. *They proved the necessity of Christ's sufferings.* As the true character of the issue between good and evil declared itself more and more plainly, it became evident that some more decisive determination of it must take place. Each previous or subsequent experience of the conflict is indecisive and incomplete apart from the Messianic sufferings. Christ must needs suffer, if only to bring to a head and final settlement the long-pending question as to whether good or evil is the true law of human life and of the world. It was no accidental, abnormal series of occurrences that constituted our Saviour's experience, but the culmination of ages of mutual development in the forces of righteousness and sin, and the true exponent of their respective characters and tendencies. 2. *They helped to deepen and educate the spiritual sense of men, and to prepare them for a true appreciation of the mystery of the cross.* It is the cross in us that leads us to the cross without. The deep tribulation of the saints of the early Church led them to more profound conceptions of moral action and spiritual requirement. Jeremiah was here a type of Judah, the feet of whose king were " in the mire " (ver. 22). Each occasion like this of Jeremiah's condemnation and imprisonment was a loud warning of the possibilities of evil that were still in the womb of time, and showed the direction of the tendency of the world-spirit. It showed, too, how closely related was the life of men with the unseen and the eternal. A moral order behind the chain of events was continually declaring itself. Its very peculiarities and anomalies demonstrated the existence of a higher law. The awful depths and heights yet to be attained by the moral nature of man were suggested, and the certainty gradually induced that the kingdom of light would yet meet and overcome the force of the kingdom of darkness. The faith, obedience, and meekness of man would yet be vindicated by the invincible power and authority of God.—M.

Vers. 7—13.—*Ebed-Melech; or, unlooked-for sympathy and help.* I. Its CIRCUMSTANCES. These were such as to impress the mind of the prophet. He was deliberately consigned by the princes of the people to the dungeon, and the king consented, so that there would appear to be no appeal. His heart must have failed him as he felt himself sinking in the mire. In a prison like that he was in imminent danger of being forgotten and starved. Apparently it was intended as an effectual means of "putting out of the way." And all this was due to what? Doing his duty. The very persons whom he sought to benefit either turned against or ignored him. The whole situation was desperate. It appeared as if no human help could save. It is just at such times that faith receives its confirming, ultimate lessons.
II. Its CHARACTER. 1. *In itself.* It was: (1) *Thoughtful.* It has been suggested that, as the dungeon was in the palace, "he came to the knowledge of it by hearing Jeremiah's moans." This may or may not have been; but when he knew of the situation of the prophet he was concerned and full of sympathy. It is this spirit which true religion, and especially the gospel of Christ, ever fosters, and the world has need of it. (2) *Prompt.* In a question like that of a few hours at the utmost, no delay had to be made if the prisoner was to be saved. As the king was "then sitting in the gate of Benjamin," he went out immediately and sought an audience. And he urged expedition. One of the finest recommendations of help is that it is given when it is needed. The case is taken up as if it were his own. How many philanthropies miss fire because they are kept too long without being carried into effect? *Bis dat qui cito dat.* (3) *Courageous.* He went straight to the king, by whose order he must have known the thing had been done, and spoke with quick, nervous fearlessness and condemnation. There was not only feeling here, but principle. He was evidently careless as to the consequences to himself. (4) *Practical.* Ebed-Melech meant that the thing should be done, and so he took the requisite steps to carry it out. Everything is thought of and applied to the purpose. Even in the "old cast clouts" there is evidence of forethought and careful, if novel, application of means to ends. 2. *In its origin.* Ebed-Melech was: (1) An alien. A negro, and not a Jew, and one from his office disqualified from participating in the benefits of the covenant. It is the more remarkable that none of Jeremiah's countrymen interposed. (2) A servant of a vicious king. The establishments of such princes are usually stamped with the same character, and their

members are but the creatures of their masters. There is something doubly unlooked-for, therefore, in such an advocate and friend. It is like a salutation from one of "Cæsar's household." (3) It is also probable that he was one called out by the occasion. No mention of him is made either before or after.

III. WHAT IT TEACHES. 1. *True religion does not depend upon conventional forms.* Not that these are therefore without value, but they are not of the essence of religion. It is Divine faith, with its outflowing charities and works, that alone can save man and glorify God. Rahab the harlot and Naaman the Syrian are but instances of many formally outside of the kingdom of God, but really within it. Let each ask, "Am I, who have received so much privilege, really a child of grace?" 2. *The kingdom of God is always stronger than it seems.* As to Elijah the assurance, "Yet I have left me seven thousand in Israel," so to Jeremiah is this experience. We are never justified in despairing of human nature if God be in his world. 3. *Implicit trust in God as the only Saviour.* The raising up of such a deliverer was so unique and unexpected as to call attention to it as a work of God. It was supernatural and special, and spoke of gracious intervention. He would not abandon his servant, nor will he any who put their trust in him.—M.

Vers. 11, 12.—"*Old cast clouts.*" This incident is very vividly described; and "the touch of human kindliness in the good negro's direction to Jeremiah to put under his armpits the soft rags thrown down to him, to prevent the chafing of the cords which drew him up, is inimitably natural." The sharp cords would otherwise have cut him so severely as to render his elevation exceedingly painful, if not practically impossible. To how many conflicting thoughts and feelings do these rags, brought from the king's house under the treasury, not give rise? What vicissitudes must they have passed through! Now, after they have been cast aside as useless, a new, unthought-of use is suddenly discovered for them. Rags it may be of royal garments used in stately pageants; was not even this a kingly service to which they were put?

I. OF HOW EXQUISITE A SYMPATHY WERE THEY THE EXPRESSION! The whole situation of the prophet had been thoroughly entered into and grasped by his friend. He is not satisfied with merely drawing him up; he will do this in the gentlest and most considerate way. It is thinking of these little things that shows the depth of our sympathy for others. They are specially remembered and sought out, and are brought forward with as much care as the thirty men. 1. *Our good deeds should not be half conceived or badly executed.* "What is worth doing is worth doing well." 2. *Where there is a real desire to be kind and helpful, the means will be discovered.* We scarcely know whether to admire the most the kindliness or the ingenuity of Ebed-Melech. 3. *A true sentiment will dispose of false scruples.* Rags! Well, they were best fitted of anything at hand to effect the purpose in view. There was no time to settle the question of the niceties. Much loving and useful work is never done because of such scruples. The servants of God cannot often work in kid gloves. 4. *The dignity of a thing consists in the use to which it is put.* These rags served the best of purposes, and are worthy of all honour. There is nothing God has made but has some gracious use if we but seek for it.

II. THROUGH WHAT HUMILIATIONS ARE GOD'S SERVANTS DELIVERED! As if the mire and helplessness were not enough! To an unspiritual perception it would appear almost an uncalled-for indignity to inflict the rags upon the prophet of God. But they were necessary. And so is it with all the God-sent humiliations of life. They are intended to subdue pride, exercise faith, and reveal the hidden grace and power of God.

III. THERE ARE DIVINE USES FOR MEAN THINGS AND THINGS CAST ASIDE. God, who made all things, can see a thousand adaptations and utilities for that which man supposes has been used up. Are there not weapons in the King's armoury that have been allowed to rust when they might have done good service? talents that have been hid in a napkin when they should have been at usury? There need be no idle members in the King's household. He takes out of his treasury things new and old, and calls upon the blind, the halt, the maimed, the aged, the poor, the ignorant, to do him honour and service. "But I have no talents in that direction," etc. Yet God can use you if you will ask him. He will regenerate you by using you; purify you of all the moral dross and filth that adhere to you; and develop higher faculties and a diviner serviceableness, if you will but let him. There were kingly robes in Judah that day that had not a tithe of the honour of these "old rotten rags;" and there are great, wise, and noble who will have to give place in the day of judgment to the weak things, and things which have been despised (1 Cor. i. 26—31).—M.

Vers. 17—23.—*God's terms of salvation hard.* I. IN WHAT THEY ARE HARD. 1. *They attack our pride.* Zedekiah was afraid of the mockery of "the Jews that are fallen to the Chaldeans." He did not like to acknowledge himself in error. There was no glory in surrender. Pride is one of the first hindrances to salvation. We want to be our own saviours. 2. *They crush self-will.* "Not as I will, but as thou wilt"— the first and last prayer of the true child of God. It was not Zedekiah's plan, and contradicted all the policy of his rebellion. It should be sufficient to the sinner to know that God has appointed the way of escape. He has no right to choose. 3. *They require faith.* How was the king to be certain that yielding himself into the hands of the princes of the Chaldeans would secure the ends desired? He hardly realized that it could be so. And similarly it is asked, "How can Jesus save?" He is to the Jews a stumbling-block and to the Gentiles foolishness, but to them that believe the Power of God and the Wisdom of God. " *Only believe,*" that is the hardest thing the unregenerate soul can do. Yet it is necessary.

II. THEY DO NOT ADMIT OF COMPROMISE. 1. *See how relentless the alternative.* There is no middle way, no royal road to salvation. It was a step simple enough in itself, but it involved everything, and could not, therefore, be qualified. Christ and his salvation are our only hope: "And in none other is there salvation: for neither is there any other Name under heaven, that is given among men, wherein we must be saved" (Acts iv. 12; cf. Gal. i. 8). 2. *Nor is the messenger of God at liberty to alter them.* These are the terms for all, and they represent the infinite wisdom and love of God. It is not for man to attempt to improve upon them. To do so would be equivalent to creating a human gospel. Jeremiah, although he had reasons for ingratiating himself with the wicked king, yet presents an example of faithfulness to every minister of the truth. He might not suffer himself to corrupt the Word of God even for such considerations.

III. YET IS THEIR HARDNESS MORE APPARENT THAN REAL. 1. *Belief and obedience will remove every difficulty.* The troubles of Zedekiah were almost wholly imaginary. Had he not been assured that everything would be made sure by adopting the advice given? One act of faith on the part of the sinner will save him. Henceforth it will be infinitely easier to do the things that remain, and to pass from faith to faith. 2. *How mild are they compared with the consequences of disobedience!*—M.

Ver. 4.—*Counted an enemy for speaking the truth.* "Hast thou found me, O mine enemy?" said Ahab to Elijah. The Israelites were about to stone the two faithful spies. And here the prophet of God was, as in these other and in many more instances, counted an enemy for speaking the truth. And a like alienation of mind and heart often takes place now for the same reason—the telling of unwelcome truth. Now, note—

I. WHEREFORE DO MEN SO DISLIKE TRUTH? Some of the reasons are: 1. Because *truth must often say many things that are unpleasing.* No matter by what voice the message comes—Scripture, conscience, or our fellow-men,—truth at times will become *censure,* and that hurts our self-love. 2. *We are not really in earnest in our desire to be set right.* We profess to be so, but we are not. "I have been a great sinner," said a sick man to his minister, who was sitting by his bedside. "Yes," said the minister, "you have." "Who told you, I should like to know?" angrily exclaimed the sick man, indignant that anything more special and personal than vague general confession should be thought to be needed by him. He had no desire for cure, but only for comfort. 3. *Pride has much to do with this dislike of truth.* Our reprover becomes for the time being our superior, stands above and over us, and we do not like this. 4. There may be *real difference of opinion* on the point in dispute; hence the censured has the further offence of being condemned on what he deems partial evidence. 5. Because of our *suspicion of the motives* of him who speaks the unwelcome truth. We are slow to credit such with purity and unselfishness of motive. We think not only of what is said, but of who says it

II. HENCE IT IS VERY DIFFICULT TO TELL UNPLEASANT TRUTHS. Most men avoid it, will say nothing, will shirk the duty by every conceivable means. No one likes to act the part of the candid friend. None like to be the bearers of ill tidings. David's servants feared to tell him that his child was dead. How we admire, because of its rarity and difficulty, the fidelity of Nathan's " Thou art the man"!

III. BUT NEVERTHELESS SUCH TRUTH OUGHT TO BE SPOKEN WHEN NECESSARY. It is not always necessary. Often not wise. " The chapter of accidents is the Bible of the fool." To let hard facts speak is sometimes best. But not always. Hence when unwelcome truth has to be spoken, take care: 1. *To be very certain of your ground.* Do not go upon mere rumour. Let your proof be full, clear, and strong. 2. Let the *purity of your motive* in speaking, the unselfishness and the love for your brother which prompt you, be made manifest. 3. *Choose fit times, tones, and words.* Many reserve their telling of such truths for moments when they are in a passion; then they will blurt it out, and, of course, only do more harm than good. 4. *Be strengthened by the remembrance of the duty you owe your brother,* and the accusation he will have against you of blood-guiltiness, if you fail to tell him the truth, unwelcome though it be.

IV. SUCH TRUTH SO SPOKEN, IF REJECTED, IS FOLLOWED BY THE CONDEMNATION OF GOD ON THEM WHO REJECT IT. It is part of that condemnation that men take friends for foes, as Ahab did, and foes for friends. They love flattery and hate truth; the blind lead the blind, and with the inevitable result. Therefore let our feeling be that of the psalmist, who said, " Let the righteous smite me; it shall be kindness : and let him reprove me; it shall be an excellent oil, which shall not break my head."—C.

Ver. 5.—"*Put not your trust in princes.*" What a proof does this incident give of the wisdom of this counsel! Note—

I. ALL ARE TEMPTED TO PUT TRUST IN MEN. To very many man is the highest being they know or believe in. Then, our fellow-men are near at hand; we can understand them and they us; are of like nature—they can be touched with the feeling of our infirmities; and they in whom we trust appear to us to possess that which we need but have not.

II. STILL MORE ARE WE PRONE TO PUT OUR TRUST IN PRINCES. We do this because : 1 Of the *law of honour* which is supposed to bind them. The word of a king, where that is there is power. 2. *They have such vast capacity of help.* Unlimited resources seem at their command. 3. They are *independent* of and superior to the influences which govern inferior men. 4. And very often *they have rendered great help* to men in need thereof.

III. But there are many instances which show that THIS TRUST SHOULD BE VERY LIMITED. Here is a case in point. How miserable this king's conduct! Now, wherefore did Zedekiah, and do such as he, disappoint men's expectations (cf. Shakespeare, ' Henry VIII.,' Wolsey's dying speech)? It is because they are governed, not by principle, but by expediency. A tree standing on the summit of a lofty hill needs to be more firmly rooted than trees in the sheltered valley, for it is exposed to every wind that blows. But if it be not so rooted, it will soon fall. So with exalted personages; they are exposed to influences on all sides; all parties seek to gain them over to their views and to enlist them in their favour. Hence if a prince have not firm principles to guide him, he will sway from side to side and finally fall. So it was with this King Zedekiah. He was influenced now by one party and now by another (cf. homily on *The woe of weakness,* ch. xxxiv. 2). " Like a wave of the sea driven of the wind and tossed." And all this is true in measure and degree of all who fill high stations, and in whom men are apt to put great trust. But—

IV. UNLIMITED TRUST SHOULD BE IN GOD ALONE. The prophet of God was doubtless less surprised than grieved, but he had long learned to commit his way unto the Lord. Let us do likewise, and then we may rest assured that, let men above us favour or frown upon us, that which is best for us and for all will assuredly be done.

> " Ill that thou blessest turns to good,
>   And unblest good is ill,
> And all is right that seems most wrong,
>   If it be thy sweet will."

C.

Vers. 6—13.—" *Cast down, but not forsaken.*" As we look on the prophet as here portrayed, these words of St. Paul are brought to our mind. We have here, as there—

I. A SERVANT OF GOD CAST DOWN. See the prophet's allusions to his sad condition in Lam. iii. 52—57; and Ps. lxix. can hardly be other than descriptive of Jeremiah at this time. And such seasons of depression and distress seem to be the appointed lot of all God's servants. Not one, from our Lord downwards, has been exempted. Manifold are the reasons for such appointment. In this particular case of Jeremiah—

II. THE CAUSES OF HIS DISTRESS were: 1. The cruelty of his treatment acting on a nature such as his. 2. Its coming upon him after he had been led to hope that now he was secure from all such treatment. 3. His knowledge that he desired to be, and was, his foes' best friend, and yet they dealt with him thus. 4. The hopelessness of his condition. Such were the immediate causes of his being cast down.

III. WHEREFORE DOES GOD SUFFER HIS SERVANTS TO BE SUBJECTED TO SUCH DISTRESS? To deepen their hold upon God, as the storms cause the trees to take deeper root in the earth. To make them realize more than ever the help they have in God. To cultivate and foster those fruits of the Spirit, such as patience, humility, trust, etc., which will hardly grow in any other soil or by any other process. To make them mighty witnesses before men of the salvation of God and of the present help he is in trouble. To qualify them to sympathize with and succour others in their distress. How such thoughts are calculated to sustain the soul in distress! And they do, for—

IV. GOD'S SERVANTS ARE, THOUGH CAST DOWN, NOT FORSAKEN. Here was a stranger to the commonwealth of Israel and from the covenants of promise, one who least of all might have been expected to care for the prophet of God, and this stranger proves to be God's good angel of mercy. God raised up this helper in the hour of his servant's need. See what was done in connection with and by this noble-hearted Ethiopian. 1. God caused intelligence of the prophet's sufferings to reach him (ver. 7). 2. He touched his heart with compassion (vers. 7, 9, 11). 3. He led him to resolve to attempt the prophet's deliverance. 4. He gave him clearly to see the wickedness of the prophet's enemies, and the truth of the prophet himself. 5. He filled his heart with courage. For courage was needed. He was alone. The consequences of his interference might have been fatal to himself. He had to reprove and condemn both the king and the king's counsellors. 6. He gave him good success. The king at once yielded, went right over to his side (contrast ver. 5), took all precaution that the deliverance should not be hindered. And he did all this at once. Further, he took oath that Jeremiah should not be so dealt with in the future. Now, all this proves the blessed truth for God's servants that, though they may be cast down, yet they shall not be forsaken.

V. WHAT ARE WE TO LEARN FROM SUCH A RECORD? Much every way. 1. *Concerning God.* He is never at a loss for messengers of mercy and help to his servants. 2. *Concerning his tried and troubled servants.* Patiently wait. Trust at all times. Hope continually, till your eyes see his salvation, as they assuredly shall. 3. *Concerning the enemies of the Lord.* Their designs and purposes must fail, however certain of success they seem to be; for God is against them.—C.

Ver. 16.—*The value of an oath.* The prophet of God evidently attributed such value, or he would not have asked of the king to make oath unto him. On the general subject note—

I. THE TEMPTATIONS TO GO FROM ONE'S WORD ARE OFTEN VERY NUMEROUS AND VERY STRONG. They were so in this case. Jeremiah knew what strong influence there was against him in the court of the king. He had suffered from this already. And he knew how weak and unstable the king was. Hence there was needed that which would steady and strengthen the wavering will. And there is often the like need now.

II. BUT THE VALUE OF AN OATH LIES IN THE FACT THAT IT MEETS THIS NEED. It brings in the thought of *God* and of his displeasure. And does this in most solemn way. And it has around it human sanctions as well as Divine. And all this tends to strengthen conscience and to resist the temptation to untruth. As a fact, it is found that men who are careless about truth in an ordinary way hesitate much before they will disregard an oath. " An oath for confirmation is an end of all strife."

III. IT IS BEST, HOWEVER, NOT TO NEED SUCH AID. Our Saviour has said, "Let your communication be, Yea, yea; Nay, nay; for whatsoever is more than these cometh of evil." The taking of oaths is allowed, as other practices, "for the hardness of men's hearts." But for the Christian his word ought to be as sacred as his oath. He is no Christian if it be not.—C.

Vers. 17, 18.—*The path of obedience the path of safety.* The circumstances here recorded show that—

I. IT MAY BE MUCH ELSE. It may be (1) a *difficult* path; (2) *humiliating;* (3) *repellant* to our whole disposition and will; (4) seemingly *unlikely,* arguing after the manner of men.

II. BUT IT WILL BE SAFE. 1. *It would have been so in this case.* For the king, his misery, exile, and degradation would have been escaped. The city of Jerusalem would not have been destroyed; nor the temple. All that would have been needful was submission to the rule of Babylon, which would have been neither intolerably harsh nor of long duration. For the prophet knew the rapidly approaching doom of both Babylon and her king. Hence he gave the counsel here told of. Whilst, on the other hand, he knew that if the wrath of the King of Babylon was aroused, all that now might be saved would then be utterly lost. Nebuchadnezzar was now like a sated lion, not desiring to destroy or devour. But let him be angered, and then woe to the weakling that had dared his rage! Submission was, therefore, the prophet's perpetual and earnest counsel. It was a case in which arguments were not merely to be counted, but weighed. 2. *And it is so always.* The path of obedience to God may have much urged against it, and truly urged, but it will ever be found to be the right and best way after all.

III. AND THE REASON IS: the path God commands is the path which pleases him who knows and who controls all events. All other paths are the self-chosen ways of men, who know but little and can control less.

IV. THIS ESPECIALLY TRUE IN REGARD TO THE SINNER'S RECONCILIATION WITH GOD. That path is protested against by voices not a few from within and without. But it is the *right* way, cannot but be so. We, therefore, as ambassadors for God, beseech you "in Christ's stead, be ye reconciled to God."—C.

Ver. 24.—*Trying to serve two masters.* Zedekiah was seeking to do this. He wanted to be on the prophet's side, and yet not to break with the princes who were the prophet's foes. We see the shifts to which he was driven, and we know the miserable outcome of his impossible attempt. We learn from it—

I. HOW DESPICABLE SUCH ATTEMPTS MAKE A MAN IN HIS OWN EYES.

> " To thine own self be true,
> And it shall follow, as the night the day,
> Thou canst not then be false to any man."

But how far from this conscious rectitude he must be who seeks to serve two masters, who acts as Zedekiah did!

II. HOW OTHER MEN DESPISE THEM.

III. How GOD CONDEMNS THEM. How do the instances of Balaam, Pilate, Judas, and others shine out as warning beacons!

IV. How USELESS, AFTER ALL, SUCH ATTEMPTS ARE. No more miserable fate could have befallen a man than that which came upon King Zedekiah. And in the highest matter of all, what are they who say, " Lord, Lord," but do not the things the Lord commands—what are they but would-be servers of two masters? And to them the Lord will say, " I never knew you; depart," etc.

V. How MUCH FULL DECISION FOR GOD IS NEEDED. This alone will keep us from such sad endeavour; but this will. Therefore seek grace from God to make and abide by this choice; and bring yourselves under the blessed attraction of Christ; so shall you be drawn to him more and more, and made to abide in him.—C.

Ver. 27.—*A question of casuistry.* A deservedly esteemed commentator observes on this conduct of Jeremiah, " Though we must be so harmless as doves as never to tell a wilful lie, yet we must be so wise as serpents as not needlessly to expose ourselves to danger by telling all we know." But many are not satisfied with this defence, and they hesitate not to apply the terms "equivocation," "subterfuge," and other like censures to the prophet's reply to the princes. Note, therefore—

I. WHAT IS URGED AGAINST SUCH CONDUCT. One says, "The plain meaning of such words is that Jeremiah hoodwinked them. He did not lie to them, certainly; but he did not tell the truth, and left them with a false impression. It comes very near to deception; it was evasive, and certainly was not an honest act. It seems *an oblique lie.*" And this view of the case is supported on grounds such as these: 1. Had he not been afraid, he would have told the whole truth; *but fear does not justify falsehood,* though it often occasions it. 2. What must the king have thought of a prophet of God so complaisant as this? 3. What would the princes say of his vaunted righteousness when they learnt how he had dealt with them? 4. Our Saviour and his apostles never did the like. 5. It had all the effect of a lie, since it left a false impression on the minds of those to whom he spoke. 6. The very fact that it needs laboured argument to justify it against our instinctive condemnation of it shows that it does not belong to the noble family of truth, etc. But *audi alteram partem.* Therefore note—

II. WHAT MAY BE URGED IN DEFENCE. 1. *In reference to the foregoing arguments.* The first *assumes* that there was no motive but fear. The second and third are assumptions also. The fourth is, to say the least, doubtful (cf. John vii. 8, 9; Acts xx. 20—26). Concerning the fifth, it is not true that *all* the effect of a lie, nor its worst effect, is that stated. And as to the sixth, it may be said that instinctive condemnations may be unjust as well as just. 2. *Other replies* to the charge against the prophet are: (1) He spoke no untruth. (2) Expediency, if not unlawful, is obligatory. (3) It has been ever recognized as lawful, under certain circumstances, to mislead an enemy; cf. Rahab's conduct (Josh. ii. 1) and its commendation (Heb. xi. 31; Jas. ii. 25). The commonly supposed case of a murderer asking you which way your friend has gone, in order that he may overtake and murder him; in such case, not only might you mislead, but would you not be bound to do so? 3. *There are sacred principles on which such suppression of the truth as Jeremiah's is justified.* (1) The right to truth may be forfeited, as the right to liberty and life may be forfeited, by wrong-doing. In the vast majority of cases men have a right to the truth, but in all the cases cited above they had no such right. (2) Truth is not an end in itself, but only a means to an end, which is the honour of God and the well-being of man; and there are occasions, doubtless very rare, when the end can only be secured by the sacrifice of the ordinary means. Therefore let all who presume to condemn great saints of God as guilty of lying, because they had no mere superstitious idolatry of veracity, as some have, hesitate before they bring such charge. Who are we to sit in judgment on such? But, on the other hand, let none pervert these reasonings, as the Jesuits did and many yet do, into a justification for lying and departing from the truth whenever it may be found convenient. It needs a healthy conscience to decide when these reasonings are applicable—a conscience enlightened by God's Spirit and animated by his love, and then such a one, and only such a one, may be left to do as he wills in cases like those we have considered.—C.

Ver. 4.—*Prophecy and patriotism.* I. THE ETHICS OF PATRIOTISM. Here are four men who go to the king with a complaint against Jeremiah; and in doing so they do not take low ground. Indeed, there are many people interested in affairs of state who would say they took very high ground. What sounds more plausible than to say that a whole country should never be more united than when the common enemy attacks it? Should there not at such a time be mutual encouragement, the bold and brave men of a state striving to animate all the citizens with their own ardour and resolution? Thus the whole question is opened up with respect to a man's allegiance to his country. How far does the claim extend of a country upon those who live under its laws, having their person and their property protected by these laws? That national history, great national events, patriotic feelings, have their place in the machinery of government, every Christian would allow; but it may not be so easy to settle exactly what that place is. Everything turns on what should have the first place in a man's affection, duty, and service; and so we have the example of Jeremiah here to guide us. He, a Jewish prophet, teaches us—

II. THE FIRST DUTY OF A CHRISTIAN. From this world's point of view Jeremiah did an eminently unpatriotic thing. Instead of uniting the people into resistance, he, as it were, divided them into two classes. He made it a time for individual and not for common action. But, after all, in every conflict there comes a time for yielding; the attacking party must retire in failure, or the defending party submit in defeat. To Jeremiah it was given to see the certain result. He knew that not the Chaldeans but Jehovah himself had to be reckoned with. The first duty of a prophet was to Jehovah, and so for that matter was the first duty of every Israelite. Thus in the same way, the first duty of a Christian is to Christ. He who serves Christ most completely serves his country best. In such a service the Christian may be misrepresented, miscalled, stamped even as traitor, but that only means that he is called to pass through Jeremiah's experience here. Why, even a man of pagan Rome can teach us in this matter; for Cicero, in the fourth book of his 'De Officiis,' speaking of gradations of duty in the state, says that a citizen's first duty is to the immortal gods, and his second to his country. "Render unto Cæsar the things that are Cæsar's, and to God the things that are God's."—Y.

Vers. 7—13.—*A friend in need.* I. THE NATIONALITY OF EBED-MELECH. An Ethiopian. Jeremiah had asked in prophecy, "Can the Ethiopian change his skin'?" from which question we may assume that Ethiopians were well known in Israel. One cannot but feel that here we have a sort of counterpart to that other Ethiopian eunuch of whom we read in the New Testament. The Ethiopian Ebed-Melech helps Jeremiah in his temporal need; Philip helps the servant of Queen Candace in his spiritual need. What a rebuke there is here to bigoted and frenzied patriotism!—if, indeed, "patriotism" is the proper word to be used and not rather a spirit of blind nationality. Perhaps the very fact that Ebed-Melech was an *alien* helped him to see needs and duties, cruelty and injustice, which were hidden from the eyes of the natives. Even natives would be obliged to admit that Ebed-Melech could not be expected to look on the position with their traditional eyes. Even so it was reserved for a Gentile to say at the Crucifixion, "Truly this was the Son of God."
II. THE HUMANITY OF EBED-MELECH. That the eunuch should have pitied the prophet sunk in the dungeon mire may not seem at first a matter to be singled out for special notice. Why should a man be praised for humanity more than for honesty? We must, however, recollect the difference of times. Those who put Jeremiah in the dungeon thought it served him quite right. And yet if there is nothing extraordinary in the humanity of Ebed-Melech, there must be something exceptionally fiendish in the conduct of those who put the prophet in the dungeon; whereas, in point of fact, they were only doing a usual thing. What a long time it has taken to work the world up even to its present attainments in humanity and compassionate feeling! And still through all these centuries Ebed-Melech rebukes us for our too often thoughtlessness and forgetfulness with respect to human pain.
III. THE COURAGE OF EBED-MELECH. He could not do a thing of this sort without making enemies and running into peril. The humane man has often to be a brave man, going into elements of danger for the sake of humanity, as a lifeboat crew must do, or a band of explorers in a colliery accident. But there are also exercises of humanity which demand moral courage—courage that will stand alone in protesting against cruelties and brutalities that have been accepted through long custom. If we are resolved to be consistent and thorough in our humanity, we must be prepared for ridicule and scorn. There are only too many who will check us in humane endeavours by calling them mere sentimentality and weakness.
IV. THE INFLUENCE OF EBED-MELECH. His office tells us that he was a man about the court, and his action here tells us that he was a man who had influence with the king. What we see of his conduct here makes us feel that he had won his influence in a perfectly legitimate way. Thus at last the opportunity comes for making good use of it. Here is an example of how good a thing it is to cultivate influence with those in authority, if it can be done in a right way without flattery and servility. Men like kings need some one near them to speak the truth plainly and effectually.
V. THE THOUGHTFULNESS OF EBED-MELECH. Something more is needed than the king's permission to get Jeremiah out of the dungeon. Probably his stay in a miry,

pestilential hole had made him very feeble.   Ebed-Melech was evidently a man who could take in all that needed to be done in any difficulty.   Just the sort of man who could find usefulness in things that were cast away as worn out and useless.   "Useless" is only our ignorant way of naming things we cannot use.   The humane man must be thoughtful as well as courageous.—Y.

Ver. 20.—*Obeying the voice of the Lord.* I. GOD HAS A VOICE FOR THOSE IN DOUBT. Poor Zedekiah, king though he be, is in a state of great vacillation.   Counsellors speak one thing, and a prophet speaks another.   Counsellors proclaim continued and resolute resistance, though it is by no means plain that they believe in what they say, and from ver. 19 it is clear that there were very considerable divisions in the city.   Jeremiah, on the other hand, speaks like a man who is perfectly sure of his ground.   He was often-times wretched and depressed in his own heart, but never did he speak the message of Jehovah with a doubt as to whether it was a real message at all.   The world abounds in doubters, coming continually to a place where two ways meet, and standing long in uncertainty and fear which way to take.   And yet they are uncertain only because they do not see the direction which God has given.   For even as at cross-roads finger-posts are put up to direct strangers, so God has his finger-posts for every doubtful traveller in the ways of terrestrial life.   Zedekiah seems to have had a feeling that he was seeking in the right direction when he sent again to Jeremiah.   He seems to have made himself ready to listen, without hinting that he expected some particular answer. So to speak, it was Zedekiah's last chance, and he gave the prophet the opportunity of speaking with corresponding plainness.   And as God's Word is here, so it is everywhere, spoken with the utmost assurance and from the whole nature of the messenger.

II. THE VOICE CALLS TO IMMEDIATE OBEDIENCE.   There is always some duty that lies nearest us.   Part of the mischief of doubt is that, while we are doubting, some good thing is left undone, the opportunity for it passing away unused.   There was just one thing for Zedekiah to do at this moment—go forth and surrender himself to the generals of the King of Babylon.   Repentance and amendment of life—these were no longer available to avert the capture of Jerusalem.   *That* was a thing settled on.   But carnage and destruction might be averted by a timely surrender.   Every day there is some-thing made plain for us to do that day.   It may be difficult, painful, in all ways hard to the flesh; but if it is neglected, then we shall only meet something still more painful to-morrow.   "Obey the voice of the Lord, and it shall be well with thee," is a word to us all.   The voice of self or the voice of others may hint at procrastination or at some qualified obedience.   Our only safety is in attending to the clear and urgent voice from heaven.   Paradox as it seems, the most difficult way is really the easiest, and the easiest the most difficult.   Zedekiah did not attend to the prophet's imperative utter-ance, and the next chapter tells the dreadful things which happened.   The king really made things worse by going out of his way to seek for direction, and then, when he had got it, paying no attention to it.—Y.

Ver. 23.—*The end of Zedekiah's irresolution.*   Irresolution it may be called rather than disobedience.   There is nothing to show that he had definitely made up his mind not to obey the voice of the Lord.   In spite of the clear announcement made to him, he seems to have gone on, hoping against hope that some decisive disaster would over-take the Chaldeans.   Yet Jeremiah closes his address by this sentence, so well calcu-lated to bring even an irresolute man to decision: "Thou shalt cause this city to be burned with fire."

I. A DECLARATION OF PERSONAL RESPONSIBILITY.   Already in ver. 18 there is the declaration that the Chaldeans will burn the city with fire, and Zedekiah is well able to infer, if he likes, that this is a calamity he may prevent.   But he is not left to inference.   The prophet's exhortation goes on, maintaining its cogency and directness, and then in the last word he individually is made responsible.   The sting of the address is emphatically in the tail.   Zedekiah is now brought face to face with his obligations as a king.   Jeremiah could not have said to any one else, "*Thou* shalt cause this city to be burned with fire," because no one else could have set in train the course of events which would avert such a calamity.   Here is an example to teach those who are tempted to envy the grandeur of kings and the fame of such as are ruling men in a state. Zedekiah's decision affected not himself only, or a few people, but a whole city. The responsibility was further increased by his having sent for the prophet who said this very thing. It is not every ruler who at a critical moment has his way made so clear as was the way of Zedekiah here. How much in the way of preventing evil may depend on one single man !

II. MATTER IS FURNISHED TO EMBITTER THE REFLECTIONS OF THE FUTURE. Whether Zedekiah saw the blazing city we cannot be sure. If he did, what a pang for his heart to think that the city where he was king, in which he and his ancestors had taken such pride, was burning, through his want of decision at a critical time! He feared to do what looked unpatriotic, and in the end he virtually destroyed the city he might have saved.

III. THERE WAS A LIMIT TO ZEDEKIAH'S POWER OVER THE SITUATION. Truly it was a great deal for one man to be able to do—either to save a city from the flames or hand it over to them. But this power only looks great according to the standard given by temporal and superficial relations. An almost boundless area for human powers and opportunities lay altogether outside of Zedekiah's reach. As man is unable purely by his own effort to confer the highest benefits on his fellow-man, so he is also unable to inflict the worst evil. The worst evils are ever self-originated. Zedekiah did far more to hurt himself than any one else. Jeremiah had been charged to make it quite clear to every one that he who went forth to the Chaldeans should live.—Y.

Vers. 24—28.—*The unkingly position of a king.* I. THE PROFESSION OF A KINGLY ATTRIBUTE. The king holds the power of life and death. He can pardon without giving a reason. And Zedekiah maintains the name of this kingly right, even upon the very heels of Jeremiah's awful words. Such is the power of long-accepted habit and privilege. Did he really think that if Jeremiah published the conversation he had power to put him to death? Or did he think that such a suggestion would move the prophet in the least? Possibly he did ; or more likely he was talking at random ; or it may be that in these last decaying days of dignity he asserted, by a kind of instinct, all that was left him to assert. We know well that he had no real power over Jeremiah, for the Lord who had hidden his prophet before could hide him again (ch. xxxvi. 26). Pilate followed in the train of Zedekiah when he said to Jesus, " Knowest thou not that I have power to crucify thee, and have power to release thee ? " (John xix. 10). This, then, is the first element in the unkingly position, that Zedekiah is professing what he cannot perform.

II. HE IS AFRAID OF THE LEADING MEN IN THE STATE. He will not rise independent of them, neither will he consult them. Instead of fearing Jehovah and trembling at the thought of what he has just heard, his soul is filled with the fear of men who probably derived their places from his own appointment. He shrinks from being forced to tell any of them that he has had to contemplate as a possibility a voluntary surrender to the Chaldeans. Truly it was quite time for a new order of things to rise in Jerusalem, even if it meant the destruction of a city. A true king would not have feared that his interview with a prophet of God should be known anywhere. Kings among men, those who are kings by nature and by the grandeur of their acts, fear no one but God. They act in the darkness just as if they were in the light ; in private relations just as if they were in public. They never need to go begging and entreating people to conceal things.

III. HE IS A SUPPLIANT TO ONE OF HIS SUBJECTS. In the same breath he tells Jeremiah he shall not die and begs Jeremiah to grant him a favour. All at once he sets before this prophet, so straightforward and unreserved, a nice question of casuistry. With the suggestion of burning Jerusalem before him, he is thinking first on the present inconvenience to himself and providing a nice quibble to escape from it. Yet even here is a sign of God's bearing with him to the last. The request he makes, undignified as it is, is nevertheless one within the power of the prophet to grant. If Zedekiah feels it to be consistent with his regal dignity, Jeremiah feels it not inconsistent with his integrity. The impression we get from the whole conversation is that the torches of the Chaldeans did not come at all too soon.—Y.

EXPOSITION.

CHAPTER XXXIX.

This chapter is very confused as it stands. To restore order it is absolutely necessary to suppose that some passages (viz. vers. 1, 2, and vers. 4—13) have been inserted by after-thoughts. It is important to notice that the latter of these passages is omitted in the Septuagint. We need not go so far as to excise them altogether, but we must at any rate enclose them in parentheses. The chapter then becomes a narrative of the solemn session held by the Babylonian officers in the " middle gate," and the charge which they gave to Gedaliah to take Jeremiah under his protection. Vers. 1, 2 appear to be taken from 2 Kings xxv. 1—4 (= ch. lii. 4—7); vers. 4—10 to be shortened from 2 Kings xxv. 4—12 (= ch. lii. 7—16). It is difficult to believe that Jeremiah himself made these insertions, not merely because they interrupt the sense, but because they involve several historical difficulties. According to ch. xxxviii. 28, Jeremiah " abode in the court of the watch till the day that Jerusalem was taken;" but the *primâ facie* meaning of our vers. 13, 14 is that Nebuzar-adan sent to liberate Jeremiah, and yet, according to 2 Kings xxv. 8 (=ch. lii. 12), this officer did not arrive at Jerusalem till a month after its capture. Another difficulty is that, according to ver. 14, Jeremiah was set free by order of Nebuzar-adan, whereas ch. xl. 1—5 states distinctly that Jeremiah had been taken in fetters to Ramah, where he was liberated by Nebuzar-adan himself. Even if there should be some reasonable way of harmonizing these various statements (see especially below on ver. 14), yet is it likely that Jeremiah himself used such inconsistent language? Still, the notice in vers. 11, 12 is in itself not improbable, and the spelling " Nebuchadrezzar " separates it from the rest of the passage (vers. 4—13); it is possible, therefore, that, in spite of its omission in the Septuagint (which wrongly retains vers. 1, 2), they are the work of Jeremiah.

Ver. 3.—**And all the princes,** etc. ; rather, *That all the princes,* etc. (see on ch. xxxviii.

28). The fact mentioned in this verse is not recorded in 2 Kings xxv.; ch. lii.; and its preciseness is a considerable pledge of its accuracy. The princes are four in number, and two of them have official titles attached. **Nergal-sharezer** is the Hebraized form of Nirgal-sarra-ucur, *i.e.* " Nirgal (or Nergal), protect (or perhaps, has created) the king "—the name, as often, is a prayer. **Samgar-nebo** is probably a modification of Sumgir-nabu, " Be gracious, Nebo;" but it has not yet been found in the inscriptions. **Sarsechim** has the appearance of being corrupt; the first part, however, may, perhaps, be the Babylonian for "king" (" prince " in Hebrew). **Rab-saris** has a meaning in Hebrew—"chief of the eunuchs;" but the analogies of "Rab-mag " and "Rab-shakeh " suggest that it is merely the Hebraized form of some Assyrian title. In any case, it would be better to render " the Rab-saris," and to attach it closely to the preceding name, Sarsechim being himself the official called Rab-saris (see, however, ver. 13). **Rab-mag.** This was "one of the highest titles in the state" (G. Smith). The etymology of the latter half of the phrase is uncertain; for the connection of " mag " with " Magi " is a mistake which has been exposed by Dr. Schrader, in his work, ' Die Keilinschriften und das Alte Testament' (of which a translation is announced). The native form of the name may be *rubu emga* (Schrader) or *rubu mâkhê* (Friedr. Delitzsch), and the whole title will mean " high priest " or " chief of the sorcerers " (comp. Delitzsch, " The Hebrew Language viewed in the Light of Assyrian Research," Lond., 1883, p. 14). " *The* Rab-mag " would be more accurate, and the title ought to be attached to the preceding name, Nergal-sharezer. As a matter of fact, a Nirgal-sarra-uçur, who held the office of *rubu emga*, is mentioned in the cuneiform inscriptions, and we may plausibly conjecture that he is the person here mentioned among the "princes." He was afterwards raised to the throne by the conspirators who murdered Evil-merodach, the son of Nebuchadnezzar (he is better known as Neriglissar). It is singular that two Nergal-sharezers should be here mentioned; possibly the first mention is due to a mistake. The names are hardly recognizable in the Septuagint. The " princes " took up their station **in the middle gate.** The " breach " spoken of in ver. 2 enabled the Babylonians to occupy the whole of the lower city to the north-east of Zion. The " middle gate " probably separated these two parts of Jerusalem, and those who were posted there commanded the temple and the citadel.

Ver. 4.—Here begins the second parenthesis, to be read apart from the principal, though shorter, narrative (see introduction to chapter). Observe elsewhere in the Book of Jeremiah events known from other sources are only briefly referred to (comp. ch. xxix. 2; xxxii. 1—5; xxxiv. 1, 7; xxxv. 11; xxxvii. 5); see 2 Kings xxv. 4—12.

Ver. 9.—**Nebuzar-adan**; *i.e. Nabu-zira-iddina*, "Nebo gave a seed."

Ver. 13.—**Nebushasban**. The name occurs in a list of proper names, under the form *Nabu-sizibanni*, "Nebo, rescue me!" It is remarkable that a different name is given to the Rab-saris in ver. 3; and the conjecture is not unreasonable that Sarsechim is a corruption of the latter part of the name Nebushasban. In ver. 3 the Septuagint has *Nabusachar* instead of Sarsechim (other copies read Nabusarsechim).

Ver. 14.—Gedaliah, whose father had already befriended the prophet on a serious occasion (ch. xxvi. 24), and who, according to ch. xl. 5, had been appointed (though

himself a Jew) Babylonian "governor over the cities of Judah," is directed to **carry him** (Jeremiah) **home**, or rather, *into the house;* obviously some house close by is meant—either Gedaliah's temporary dwelling or the royal palace. This statement conflicts (see introduction) with that in ch. xl. 1—5, but only as to the time when Jeremiah was liberated. The latter narrative being more explicit, deserves the preference. Thus Jeremiah **dwelt among the people**; *i.e.* could go in and out at his pleasure.

Vers. 15—18.—A prophecy to Ebed-melech is here introduced, which, though uttered previously (see ch. xxxviii.), could not have been mentioned before without breaking the sequence of events. For **came**, we might render *had come*.

Ver. 16.—**Go and speak**. Ebed-melech must be supposed to come into the court of the watch, so that Jeremiah might communicate with him.

Ver. 18.—**For a prey unto thee.** The same remarkable phrase in ch. xxi. 9; xxxviii. 2.

HOMILETICS.

Vers. 1, 2.—(See homily on ch. lii. 4—7.)

Vers. 4—7.—(See homily on ch. lii. 8—11.)

Vers. 8—10.—(See homily on ch. lii. 8—16.)

Vers. 11, 12.—*A prophet befriended by a heathen king.* Rumours of Jeremiah's efforts to induce the Jews to submit to the Babylonian power must have reached the ears of Nebuchadnezzar, and have led him to regard the prophet with favour. If his fellow-countrymen considered Jeremiah to be a traitor, it was natural that the Chaldeans should think he was on their side. Both parties were ignorant of the motives and aims of the prophet, which were as patriotic as they were prudent. But, though perhaps from an undue opinion of his friendliness to them, the invaders did a real service to Jeremiah, and that was good on its own account.

I. GOD BRINGS DELIVERANCE TO HIS CHILDREN IN THEIR GREATEST DANGER. Jeremiah was a prisoner. Jerusalem was given over to the rapine of a lawless soldiery. Then came the prophet's escape.

II. GOD CAN USE THE MOST UNLIKELY MEANS AS INSTRUMENTS OF HIS GRACE. He does use means, delivering through the action of men overruled by his providence. Such is his wise and mighty control that fierce despots may be his angels and ministers of grace.

III. THE SCOURGE OF JUDGMENT FOR THE WICKED MAY BE THE ARM OF DELIVERANCE TO GOD'S PEOPLE. Nebuchadnezzar was the fearful foe whose approach had been foreshadowed as the advent of doom and ruin to the guilty city of Jerusalem. This man was the friend and deliverer of Jeremiah. So the awful judgment at the end of the world will be, to the Christian, the occasion of the " salvation ready to be révealed in the last time." The greatest evils in the world are overruled to work the good of God's children.

IV. A HEATHEN MAY BE AN EXAMPLE OF HUMANENESS TO MEN WHO PROFESS THE HIGHEST RELIGION. There is no cruelty so bitter as that of persons who call themselves enlightened and religious. This is the most refined and heartless cruelty. *Corruptio optimi pessima.* On the other hand, with all that is brutal and lawless, there may be a genuine unsophisticated kindliness among men who are in great moral and religious darkness. Let us thank God that he has not left himself without a witness in the conscience even of a Nebuchadnezzar.

V. IF A HEATHEN KING'S FAVOUR IS VALUABLE, HOW SHALL WE ESTIMATE THE BLESSEDNESS OF THE FAVOUR OF THE DIVINE KING? If Jeremiah profited by the patronage of Nebuchadnezzar, what shall the grace of Christ be to us? If the prophet found release and comfort at the approach of the Babylonian monarch, what greater good is in store for those who shall " behold the King in his beauty "? Jeremiah was protected by Nebuchadnezzar, but he did not put his trust in the human monarch. The one safe trust is in the one true Prince and Saviour.

Vers. 15—18.—*Spared on the ground of faith.* I. THE MAN. 1. He is an *Ethiopian.* " God is no respecter of persons." This man, with his heathen nationality, his negro countenance, and his humiliated state, is selected for deliverance in the general destruction, because in him is found the right spiritual condition, whilst men with the pure blood of Abraham in their veins perish. We have not to wait for St. Paul to teach us the breadth of God's grace and the spirituality of its requirements. 2. He is a *court servant.* There were Christians in Cæsar's household. A king's favour is no substitute for the grace of God. Ebed-Melech felt that he needed more than the protection of the royal guard, even when all was fair in the outside world. 3. He stands *alone.* He is alone in his faith. So much the more real and vital must his faith be. He is alone in his reward. A special message and a special promise are accorded to this man. God does not overlook any solitary servant of his. All religion is individual—individual faith, individual grace.

II. THE FAITH. Ebed-Melech had befriended Jeremiah. Yet it is remarkable that this fact is not mentioned here. His act of kindliness by itself would not have been enough to have secured him a Divine promise of special safety. But the act evinced faith. It is implied that Ebed-Melech befriended Jeremiah because he had faith in God, and therefore acknowledged the Divine message of the prophet and accepted the truth of it. We are saved on account of our faith. Faith must show itself in deeds or it is dead and worthless. But the personal trust in God and in Christ is the sole and universal condition through which God's mercy is bestowed.

III. THE REWARD. Ebed-Melech is to be spared in the general wreck of the Jewish state. His presence in the scene of destruction will enhance his sense of the providential character of his escape. We must all revolt from the heartless doctrine of Thomas Aquinas, that one of the elements of the joy of the redeemed in heaven will be the contemplation of the agonies of the lost. Nevertheless, to have escaped from a terrible fate that has been brought very near to us is a source of greater joy than never to have known danger. This is the Christian's condition. He can have only pain in witnessing the suffering of others. But he has large ground for thankfulness when he sees how near he was to ruin, and how God has plucked him as a brand from the burning.

HOMILIES BY VARIOUS AUTHORS.

Vers. 9, 10.—*The poor better off than the rich.* I. IN WHAT SENSE THEY WERE SO. 1. *They were spared because of their insignificance.* 2. *Pitied because of their helplessness and privations.* 3. *Their condition could hardly be altered otherwise than for the better.*

II. OF WHAT THESE WERE THE TYPE. 1. They represent the *meek* who inherit the earth, and the *poor in spirit* whose is the kingdom of heaven. Christ the Conqueror will enrich them. 2. *Their fortune represented the law of reversal in the kingdom of God.* The first shall be last, and the last first; but not universally. " *Many* that are first," etc. Christ's servants will be most numerous amongst the poor and the despised. They will be recognized and honoured by him, when others are put to shame. But it will not be their *poverty,* but the *virtues of their poverty,* which shall be rewarded. They who know themselves poor will receive all things at his hands (cf. Rev. iii. 17, 18).—M.

Vers. 11—14.—(cf. ch. xl. 1—6).—*God's servant delivered from the judgment of transgressors.* The whole proceedings in connection with Jeremiah's deliverance are striking and noteworthy. It is a heathen prince to whose care and respect he owes his liberation, when his own people have treated him so cruelly. Very evident is the hand of God " disposing the hearts of princes," and making "all things work together for good to them that love him."

I. JEREMIAH'S EXCEPTIONAL CASE SHOWED THAT, IN THE MIDST OF THE MOST TERRIBLE CALAMITIES, GOD IS FREE TO WORK OUT THE PEACEABLE ENDS AND GRACIOUS REWARDS OF HIS KINGDOM. He was but one out of the entire nation, and might easily have been overlooked. Indeed, his sympathetic brotherliness had all but destroyed the advantage so specially designed for him. An interposition like this, so marked and resolute, had an evidently supernatural origin, and bore a moral or spiritual character. If his welfare could be so thoroughly and carefully attended to in the midst of such heart-rending and widely disastrous circumstances, the whole of the political changes then taking place must have been a portion of the moral order of the world, and under the direct superintendence of God. In the midst of judgment he remembers and pursues his merciful schemes. The darkest hour of a nation's or an individual's history is charged with ministries of light, and the most awful judgments do not interfere with the persistent will of God to save and to bless mankind. And how nicely adjusted and delicately balanced are the deserts of saints and transgressors!

II. SOME OF THE PURPOSES TO BE SERVED BY THIS PROVIDENCE. 1. *It showed that the calamity did not arise from a mere necessity or accident of circumstances.* Even the heathen Nebuchadnezzar learnt that. 2. *Spiritual guidance and comfort were secured for those left behind.* 3. *Jeremiah learnt to perceive and obey the Divine will as respected his future.* His sallies from Jerusalem proved how needful the lesson. 4. *God commended his love to his servant in making good accrue to him in the general evil of the time.* 5. *The reverence to God and consideration towards his prophet shown by heathen princes put to shame the unbelief and disobedience of the chosen people.*—M.

Ver. 14.—" *So he dwelt among the people.*" In how many respects was Jeremiah a type of Christ! And just in these points was he an example to the spiritual worker and the Christian preacher.

I. THE POSITION OF THE TRUE PASTOR. 1. How miserably anomalous—a pastor without a flock, or living at a distance from them! There is something wrong with one or other when they remain apart. Only now and then, and for brief periods, can solitude be the place of duty. 2. The cure of souls can only be followed successfully by constant intercourse with them. The experience, sympathy, and moral influence acquired by the minister in the midst of his flock will stand him in good stead in directing him as to what to teach, and preparing for it a favourable reception.

II. THE SPIRIT OF THE TRUE PASTOR. 1. *Absence of ambition.* The promises of the Chaldeans were much more brilliant than the future that was likely to lie before him. in Palestine. It was not comfort, worldly emolument, or personal advancement that he sought. Like Moses, he chose " rather to suffer affliction with the people of God, than to enjoy the pleasures of sin for a season " (Heb. xi. 25). 2. *Sympathy with the miseries and spiritual needs of men.* The interests of the Divine kingdom would be better served by his remaining at home. Here was work ready to his hand, and he dare not leave it. The servant of God has " to preach as a dying man to dying men." 3. *True patriotism.* What intense affection he had for the land of his fathers! This was at the very core of the religion of the ancient Jew. All the promises of God and realizations of his kingdom on earth seemed to be associated with the Holy Land. This sentiment has been universalized and made more personal by the Spirit of Jesus. " Our kind " must have our constant care and prayers. " The enthusiasm for humanity " must support and inspire the spiritual worker.—M.

Vers. 15—18.—*Faith's reward.* I. IN BEING ACKNOWLEDGED. 1. *The character of its work recognized.* Jeremiah is to speak in the Name of " the God of *Israel*," as if to say that henceforth Ebed-Melech is to be regarded as a true Israelite, having his destiny bound up with God's people. That which he did is attributed to no merely passing compassion, but to *faith:* " Thou hast put thy trust in me, saith the Lord." So God perceives the secret motives of actions. 2. *In being further and specially exercised.*

Definite direction is given to the attention of Ebed-Melech, and he is encouraged to look forward to the fulfilment of the words spoken by Jeremiah. As a further confirmation of his share in the Divine events about to take place, he is assured of personal safety—an assurance as yet only a matter of faith and not of sight. One of the surest proofs of true faith being acknowledged by God, is its being thus tested and exercised. Men without faith may be let alone; but the believer, even if his faith be as a grain of mustard seed, will be taken hold of by the providence and grace of God, and led " from faith to faith." Those who trust in him he will reward with his confidence and the custody of his mysteries. " Lord, increase our faith."

II. In BEING VERIFIED. 1. *The believer will see the fulfilment of what he has believed.* He will be honoured by being made a witness of the truth of God. The moral tendencies and spiritual consummations that make up the kingdom of God in the world will be revealed. Experience will illustrate and confirm faith, and faith will interpret experience and render it spiritually profitable. 2. *He himself will be saved from the destiny of the wicked.* This is " the physical and palpable reward of faith ; " but it is also one which may open up the way to future spiritual blessedness. Ebed-Melech is obviously spared, not only from the suffering of the exile, but from the degrading influences of it, and the rejection from covenant blessings it, in so many instances, involved. Those who " receive a prophet shall receive a prophet's reward."—M.

Vers. 1—8.—*The retribution of God.* What an accumulation of woe do the eight verses with which this chapter opens present ! Let thought dwell on the several statements made here, and let imagination seek to realize what they must have meant to those upon whom the calamities they speak of came ; and it will be seen, in vivid lurid light, that the retribution of God upon sin and sinners has been in the past no mere empty threat, and it will lead to the salutary suggestion, so questioned now, that his like threatened retribution in the future is no empty threat either. How unreasonable, in the face of historic facts such as those told of here, and in the face of actual facts of to-day in which dread suffering and awful calamity are seen overtaking wicked doers, to doubt that God will do the like again should necessity arise ! But yet many do doubt and deny the teachings of God's Word on this matter. Note, therefore—

I. The GROUNDS ON WHICH THIS TRUTH IS QUESTIONED. They are such as these : 1. *Death ends all.* But who can prove this? Why is it less possible that we should live in another condition than that we should have been born into the one in which we now are ? Resurrection is not antecedently more incredible than creation. 2. *God too merciful.* But is he? Does he not do or suffer to be done fearful things now? 3. *Retribution comes in this world.* In part it does to some, but to others sin seems one long success. 4. *Christ's death atones for all.* Yes, but in what sense ? Certainly not in the sense of saving from suffering now. Why, then, if the conditions of salvation be not fulfilled, should the atonement avail hereafter more than now ?

II. The PROBABLE MOTIVES OF THIS DENIAL. Not irresistible conviction or any satisfactory knowledge of the falsity of what is denied, but such as these : 1. *The desire that the doctrine denied should not be true.* How often in questions like these the wish is father to the thought ! Our opinions follow the line of our interest. 2. *The belief that the doctrine renders impossible men's love and trust in God.* Without question there are and have been settings forth of this doctrine which to all thoughtful minds must have this effect. The conception that God has created—of course, knowingly—myriads of human souls to sin and suffer for ever is one that must darken the face of God to the thoughtful soul. Why, it will almost passionately be asked—" Why, if it were so much better that they should never have been born, were they born ? " It is " he, the Lord, that hath made us, and not we ourselves." But we are not shut up to such conception. God " will have all men to be saved ; " still through what fiery disciplines may he not have to compel the perverse and unruly wills of sinful men to pass ere they shall come to themselves and say, " I will arise," etc. ? 3. *Atheistic, agnostic, or materialistic.* They who come under such names alike will dislike such doctrine as this. They will not simply disbelieve, but protest against them.

III. The SUCCESS, SUCH AS IT IS, THAT THESE DENIALS HAVE HAD. 1. They have dulled and sometimes deadened the fear of the Lord in many souls. But : 2. They have never been able to convince any that there is no judgment to come. The dread of it haunts them still, the evidence for it being too strong and clear. Hamlet's soliloquy, "To be or not to be, that is the question," etc., still expresses men's fear of death. "For in that sleep of death what dreams may come!" 3. It is difficult to see aught of good that has been done—nothing but more or less ill. Therefore note—

IV. THE WARNING THAT COMES TO US FROM THESE DENIALS. Cherish a deep and holy fear of God. Judge each one ourselves, that we be not judged of the Lord.—C.

Vers. 4—7.—*Too late.* These verses tell of the flight of Zedekiah and his miserable capture by the Chaldean army. *Picture the scene.* The breach made in the wall. The dead hour of night. The rush upon the temple. The slaughter there. The alarm spreading to the palace. The attempted escape, before dawn, of the king, his wives, and his children. See them muffled, disguised, laden with such precious things as they could snatch up in the hurry of that awful moment, stealthily making their way along the narrow alley between the walls, speeding down the ravine, up over the slopes of Olivet, then down again to the plains of Jericho, where they were overtaken and made prisoners. Many an opportunity of escape had been given to Zedekiah during these last months and previously, but he had neglected them all. For a while his present attempt seemed successful, but he was soon in the cruel grasp of the Chaldeans, and then worse than all he had feared came upon him. He tried to escape, but *too late.* This history, unutterably sad as it is, has many parallels and much instruction. Consider—

I. INSTANCES IN WHICH THIS VERDICT OF "TOO LATE" IS APPLICABLE. There are many. 1. *Scriptural.* No doubt that not a few, when the Lord had shut Noah in the ark, and they saw the lowering clouds, the overwhelming rain, and the rising waters, repented and sought safety in the ark. But then, because they had been "sometime disobedient" (cf. 1 Pet. iii. 19), they were now too late. "Remember Lot's wife." The Israelites after their repulse at Ai; after their disbelief of the faithful spies (Numb. xiv. 44). Our Lord's words to Jerusalem, "But now they are hid from thine eyes." The foolish virgins (Matt. xxv.). Cf. also "When once the master of the house has risen up and shut to the door," etc. 2. *Historic.* Archias, magistrate of Greece, revelling and feasting. Plot formed to assassinate. A friend sends intelligence. Arrives as feast is going on. "Serious things to-morrow," said the senseless man. That night he was slain. The massacre of Glencoe would never have occurred but for the tardiness of the chief of the clan in giving in his submission to the government. A snowstorm hindered him when at last he did set out for this purpose, and the last day of grace came and ended, and the chief's submission had not been made. The massacre followed (cf. Macaulay). 3. And in *less notable events* in common everyday life, how perpetually are we seeing like instances! School life wasted, no making it up again. Opportunities in business, in the home, in the Church, missed; above all, in regard to the life eternal,—and not recoverable. The tide in the affairs of men not taken at the flood; instead of fortune, the few ships which men have launched lie wrecked or stranded on the shore. "Too late!" With what disappointment and despair is this often said, and will it be said hereafter, and with what truth as well! Therefore note—

II. THE MISERY OF HIM WHO IS TOO LATE. This arises from: 1. *Shame before men.* They will not pity, but despise and blame. 2. *Sting of conscience.* We know it might have been otherwise; we might have secured what we have let go. 3. *Sight of the consequences* brought on ourselves and others through our neglect. 4. The *irrecoverability* of what is lost. It can never be all the same to any soul, no matter what theory of the future we may hold, if he has thrown away opportunities of grace and squandered the days of salvation with which he was blessed. This thought, that he was "too late," was the "torment" of the rich man in the hell into which God sent his soul after death.

III. HOW COME MEN TO BE TOO LATE? Sometimes it is: 1. *The opportunity passes away.* The tide which should have been taken at the flood has begun to ebb. 2. Yet more often, *the power of the law of habit.* Opportunities may be plentiful, but the habit of resisting the call to use them has become fixed, and therefore it it really "too late" for the man, even when he might if he would seize upon them for his good. We sing—

"And while the lamp holds out to burn,
The vilest sinner may return."

Yes, no doubt; but will he? If he has got so into the habit of saying "No" to God will he—is it likely?—at the last turn and say, "Yes"? Death-bed repentances!—are there any such things? That which determines a soul's destiny is not death, but this law of habit. Long before death it may have been settled whether that soul shall be saved or lost. And death may come, as it does to the young, and the matter be not settled, the law of habit not having had time to declare itself whilst life in the body lasted. The law of habit, not the hour of death, is that from which we have most to hope and most to fear. 3. *The gambling spirit that is in all men.* The trusting to chance, the hope in good luck, in regard to things secular; the hope for a more convenient season in regard to the things of the soul. There is this spirit in us all. It has its uses, for there are "ventures of faith" as well as all too many ventures of a very different kind. Read this history of King Zedekiah, and see how he gambled away his crown, his kingdom, his life, his all.

IV. SAFEGUARDS AGAINST THIS EVIL. Under God, this same law of habit of which we have spoken. Resolve, and strengthen your resolve by prayer, that you will not put off till to-morrow what you should do to-day. Act on it, and to-morrow you shall act on it again, and the next day, and so the blessed habit shall be formed of practically remembering that "*now* is the accepted time," and for you or by you the miserable verdict of "too late" shall never have to be pronounced.—C.

Ver. 10.—"*Blessed are ye poor.*" The Chaldean invasion, which wrought such ruin on princes, nobles, and all the great in Judah and Jerusalem, had far other and happier effect on the poor. The storm which tore down the lofty tree left the lowly flowers that nestled amid the herbage untouched. This verse recalls—

I. OUR LORD'S WORDS, "BLESSED ARE YE POOR." The poor do not excite the wrath of the great. They are least affected by outward change. They are dealt kindly by when the rich and great are cast down. "He hath put down the mighty from their seat, and hath exalted," etc. But, chief of all, because they are "rich in faith." So said our Lord; and it can only be that the poor have an undying conviction of the love of God, an unquenchable faith therein, that they so patiently endure the ills of their present lot. Let that faith die out, as it has in some places and generations, and murderous revolution and anarchy burst forth. Our Lord distinctly encouraged this belief in the love of God towards the poor. He said his mission was "to preach the gospel to the poor." In the parable of the rich man, Lazarus, for no other reason than that he was poor, receiving here, as is the lot of the poor so often, only "evil things," was "carried by the angels into Abraham's bosom." And we may well believe that they who here have been unable by reason of the misery of their condition to see that God is love—as Israel in Egypt could not believe in it by reason of the bitterness of spirit which their bondage caused them—shall in some blessed Abraham's bosom hereafter see it clearly, and then shall their hearts go out towards God in that faith and love which are the conditions of the kingdom of heaven, but which have been scarce possible to them here. Therefore are the poor blessed. But this verse teaches also the sure truth—

II. "HE THAT IS DOWN NEED FEAR NO FALL." Here it was lowliness of position which saved the poor of the land. But the proverb is yet more true where the lowliness is of the heart and mind—that yoke of Christ which, if we take, then rest, the undisturbed peace of the soul, is our reward.

III. THE COMMON PROVERB, "IT IS AN ILL WIND THAT BLOWS NO ONE ANY GOOD." The prince's ruin was the poor man's riches; the noble's downfall his uprising. Therefore in our own troubles let us remember that we are never as a target at which the arrows of God's judgments are aimed, and in the hitting of which their purpose is fulfilled; but rather are we the channels of blessing, which by and through us shall flow on to do good to others, perhaps many others. Cf. Paul's allegory, the casting out of the natural branch, the Jew, and the ingrafting of the wild branch, the Gentile. And illustrations are innumerable.

IV. GOD'S LAW OF COMPENSATIONS. If he takes away on the one side, he gives on the other. These poor people were favoured.

V. THE FIRST BEATITUDE, "BLESSED ARE THE POOR IN SPIRIT: FOR," etc. These poor had lands in Judæa; the poor Christ speaks of shall receive "the kingdom of heaven."

It is not always true that the literal poor are dealt with in the way told of here, but the recompense of the poor in spirit never fails. They have an earnest of it in the rest and peace of soul it is theirs to enjoy now amid all the cares and distractions of this life. But no man makes himself poor; he must be made so. God's providence sends the literal poverty, God's Spirit that spiritual condition to which is promised the kingdom of heaven. But if we place ourselves in the hands of Christ, surrendering ourselves to be dealt with as he sees fit, he will, by his Spirit, bring us to that blessed mind without which none enter the kingdom, but with which we assuredly shall.—C.

Vers. 11—14.—*Churchwardens.* 1. These are *generally chosen from the friends of the Church*, as they who are to defend and guard the Church's interests should be. Who should care for the Church if not her friends? 2. But sometimes *men who are no friends of the Church have charge of her interests.* 3. And not seldom *they are amongst her best servants*, and do their work diligently and well. 4. In these verses *we have a signal instance* of this. Here is the fierce, heathen, Israel-destroying Nebuchadnezzar, busying himself seriously about the safety of God's prophet Jeremiah. It is not simply a case of God shutting the lions' mouths, but constituting the lions his servant's sure though strange defence (cf. ver. 12). "Is Saul also among the prophets?"—that was thought to be a marvel. But that the Chaldean monarch should be the faith's defender and the prophet's guard is no less strange. 5. And there have been *other such instances* before and since this. See what Egypt was to Joseph and Moses, the Philistines to David, the Persians to Daniel, Greece to Jews in Alexandria, Rome to Paul; see also history of the Lollards, Reformers, etc. And how often in the straits of God's people have they had to confess that he has raised up for them from most unlikely sources the helpers they have needed! "The barbarous people showed us no little kindness" (Acts xxviii. 2),—as we have seen sometimes a weak, defenceless creature dwelling in the same cage with strong, cruel beasts, and not only unharmed, but protected by them. 6. *How is all this to be explained?* In this instance of Jeremiah the motives of Nebuchadnezzar are clear and comprehensible. Jeremiah had done his best to persuade his countrymen to submit to Babylon. His influence would be strong with the captives in Babylon and serviceable to her monarch. The king would show that, whilst he punished his foes, he did not forget his friends. The reverence and awe which Jeremiah, so evidently God's prophet, aroused in the monarch's mind. But: 7. *He was guarded of God.* Jeremiah was no partisan of Babylon. The most terrible prophecies against her are his (cf. ch. l.). No other explanation than that the care of God was over him can account for their favour to one who spoke so plainly and so evil concerning them. And their forbearance is the more remarkable when we remember the proud, cruel, and arrogant character of the monarch whom Jeremiah thus, as it were, defied. 8. *Many and most helpful are the lessons of such facts as these.* Enemies God can make our friends, perils our protectors; and because "the Lord's portion is his people," his will is ever to do them good. Such deliverances as these are designed to foreshadow our final and perfect deliverance, and to deepen our confidence in regard thereto.—C.

Vers. 15—18.—"*In that ye ministered to the saints.*" "God," says the writer of the Epistle to the Hebrews, "is not unrighteous to forget" such ministry. It is a strong expression, and seems to imply that God would be unrighteous if he did forget. Here, in the story of Ebed-Melech, we have an instance of God's rewarding ministry to his saints. For what Ebed-Melech did, cf. ch. xxxviii. 7, etc. For his recompense, see these verses (15—18). Consider—

I. THESE RECOMPENSES. They are: 1. *A fact.* How many instances there are!—the widow of Sarepta; the Shunammite woman; Dorcas; Paul's friends, Onesiphorus, etc.; Jonathan; Mary of Bethany; Cyrus and the Persian nation, for their goodness to Israel; the people of Malta (Acts xxviii.); our own country, for offering asylum to persecuted Hollanders and Huguenots. And, besides such instances, there are repeated declarations to the same effect: "I will bless them that bless thee;" "They shall prosper that love thee." The cup of cold water given in the name of a disciple "shall in no wise lose its reward." "Whoso shall receive one such little child in my Name receiveth me." 2. *Very great.* (Cf. illustrations given.) How comparatively slight was the ministry! how cup of cold water-like! yet how great the reward! How much this country owes, in her commerce, her character, her fame, to her ministry to God's saints! Many people denounce Cromwell for most things he did, but all applaud his interference with the bloody papists on behalf of the persecuted Waldenses. Milton's grand lines, "Avenge, O Lord, thy slaughtered saints," etc., have immortalized that deed as it deserved. No, indeed; "God is not unrighteous to forget," rather is he most gracious to remember, all such ministries. 3. *Varied.* Sometimes the recompense is given at the time, in tangible, material blessing. Sometimes such recompense is delayed, but comes afterwards in full measure. Sometimes it comes not here at all in outward recompense, but in spiritual joy and peace—sunshine in the soul, approval of conscience, gladness of heart, confirmation in good. But for all, and most of all, in eternity. "That is the great harvest-season of holy and benignant deeds." "They shall be recompensed at the resurrection of the just." But: 4. *Ever sure.* They *shall* be recompensed. None of that good seed shall fall on other than good ground, or yield other than bountiful and beneficent fruit. The little gift "shall *by no means*," saith our Saviour, "lose its reward." And his many present recompenses all confirm our faith in the truth of that blessed Word.

II. THEIR REASONS. Some of them are probably such as these: 1. *For the Lord's own sake.* Such ministries demonstrate the presence in the heart of that which he most of all prizes—love. They show "some good thing toward the Lord God." They delight the Father's heart, and his smile cannot be concealed nor his hand held back from blessing. 2. *For the sake of those who thus minister*, as Ebed-Melech did. God recompenses them because they have thus committed themselves on the side of righteousness, and he would encourage them. 3. *For the sake of those ministered to.* God blessing their friends tends to raise up friends for them, as they often need. "We will go with you, for we see that the Lord is with you." 4. *For the sake of truth and righteousness generally.* God, by such recompenses, makes it evident on which side he is. Thus he cheers his people, dismays his adversaries, decides the waverer, and so advances the good cause in the world.

III. THEIR ADMONITION. Follow the Lord's example; do not *you* forget those who have stood up for truth and right. Sympathize with, applaud, defend such. *Be such yourselves.* Would you have done as Ebed-Melech did? Do you when the Christian lad or girl is jeered at by godless comrades, in the school, the counting-house, the shop, the kitchen? "Stand up, stand up, for Jesus!"—C.

Vers. 1—8.—*Siege and savagery.* I. THE MANNER IN WHICH THE CAPTURE OF JERUSALEM IS RELATED. Just enough is told to certify to us the complete and exact fulfilment of prophecy. There is a long siege, a great destruction, and great humiliation and suffering for the captured king. It is no part of the province of Scripture writers to dwell on war, battle, siege, and pillage for the sake of making striking narratives. But behind this very brevity what room there is for imagination! What suffering, gradually mounting to the climax of famine and thirst, during those eighteen months of siege! The very natural advantages of Jerusalem, enabling the people to resist longer, added to their calamities. Indeed, we may say that when a man employs his natural strength wrongly, his suffering in the end is not unlikely to be proportioned somewhat to his strength. A weaker man would not suffer so much or suffer so long.

II. THE SAVAGERY CONNECTED WITH THE CAPTURE. This savagery is a point to be studied as throwing a light on the ancient civilizations. Nobody thought, we may safely say, not even prophets themselves, that there was anything out of the way in all this destruction. Savagery was the accepted consequence of a successful siege. Jehovah used these Chaldean soldiers as instruments, but they had to act according to their individuality. A Roman army would have behaved no better. Indeed, humanity in war is a Christian idea. Paradox as it seems, God was working through the very savagery of this war to destroy all war. Men will fight; they will foment discord and accumulate large armies; but it is the glory of God to bring good out of all the conflicts. When the reign of the Prince of peace is fully come, then we shall see, as we cannot see now, the good that men have worked, *unconsciously*, by war. We are deceived now because we cannot get away from our thoughts physical destruction and suffering.

III. THE FATE OF ZEDEKIAH. Brought on him by his own indecision as much as by the savage hands of Chaldeans. If these verses stood by themselves, we should not know this; but we do know it from the record going before, of Jeremiah's dealings with him.—Y.

Ver. 10.—"*The poor of the people.*" I. How THEY HAD COME INTO THIS POSITION. Poverty is, of course, a mischief, having many causes, and no fallacy is greater than that of singling out one cause for some particular reason, and then treating it as if it were the only cause. Still, there is need that in this place the injustice of the rich towards the poor should be remembered. The fact that there are proverbs bearing on this point shows that such oppression was not at all unfrequent. "He that oppresseth the poor to increase his riches, and he that giveth to the rich, shall surely come to want" (Prov. xxii. 16; xxviii. 15). And now these oppressors had attracted to themselves the desiring eye of Babylon. Why were the rich men carried away and the poor left? The chief reason was that they heightened the triumph, for when despoiled they were just as poor as the poorest, and the contrast between their former and present state spoke for itself. Then, too, there is something in considering the rich men as themselves part of their riches. Thus the rich and poor are brought together in one great judicial act, and the rich are made to feel that in the end the poor are really better off than they are.

II. THE ADVANTAGES OF POVERTY. Poverty usually presents such disadvantages on the surface, and so demands sympathy and help, that it almost seems like irony ever to talk of its advantages. And yet, if there be such advantages, it is very necessary to consider them, in order to do something for the prevention of envy, repining, and perplexity. As with the advantages of external wealth, so with the disadvantages of external poverty; neither goes very deep. In the time of spoliation the poor man can look on with a light heart, so far as personal loss is concerned. Probably the poor people of Israel were now better off than they had been for years. Amid all the burning and pillage here is one good effect already perceptible in the benefit that is being worked for the poor. Without contradiction, it may be affirmed that the Jehovah of the Old Testament and the Father of Jesus Christ in the New are alike on the side of the poor. All oppression of the poor, all unfair treatment of them, all selfish employment of them, will show in the end that the poor need lose nothing of what is best.

III. THE EMPLOYMENT OF THE POOR. They were employed in that which was of greatest moment to them. Vineyards and fields were given to them—things they could all make use of; things which would repay their toil, and give them the chance of building up a really honourable wealth. If Nebuzar-Adan had given them something of the plunder, it would not have been near so useful as what he actually did give. Man is nearest to the pure, untainted fulness of nature when he is cultivating the soil.—Y.

Vers. 11—14.—*The safety of God's prophet.* I. THE MANNER IN WHICH IT IS ASSURED. There is no working of miracle, though miracle was available if it had been needed. But natural forces were carrying out Divine intentions in working the safety of the man who had been faithful to his duty. We have no exact information as to why Nebuchadnezzar was so interested in the prophet's safety, but we may well suppose that he had a sort of respect for a man who served his God so faithfully. The news of fidelity, courage, and endurance goes far, when only one here and there shows the qualities. Moreover, the King of Babylon was very likely to have heard of Jeremiah's predictions; the very knowledge that such predictions existed would nerve him in his attack; and when the attack succeeded, the very fulfilment of the predictions would produce in him a superstitious fear lest the utterer of them should come to any harm. Thus we see how the course of human affairs, without any special intervention, works out good for the brave maintainers of right.

II. SAFETY IN SUCH CIRCUMSTANCES. This is of great importance to notice. Jehovah was not concerned to preserve the life of every prophet from a violent end. His prophets, at times, had to trust him even to death, and prophesy even when the prophecy was sure to be followed by a mortal blow. Jeremiah was preserved in safety at this time, not so much for his own sake, as for the effect his preservation would have on the minds of others. His safety was specially provided for *at the time when unrestrained destruction was going on.* Thus his very preservation was itself a prophecy.

And it is all the more noticeable because Jeremiah himself had, in due course, to make predictions against Babylon. Why some of God's servants live long lives and some short ones is not a fortuitous matter; there is always a reason, could we but see it, and sometimes, as in this instance, there is a glimmer of light upon the reason.

III. THE PROPHET'S DESTINATION. Nebuchadnezzar's order was that he should be treated as he desired. We read that in the end "he dwelt among the people." Hence we may conclude that this was his desire. And where could a prophet better be? Especially if he went among the poor of the people, toiling away in their vineyards and fields, and tried to inspire them with the promises of better times. "Dwelling among the people" is a very suggestive expression when applied to a man like Jeremiah, his office, his character, his experience, being such as they were. The people knew that he lived among them by his own free choice, preferring to share their hardship and poverty. As far as we can see, he might have enjoyed the luxuries of Babylon; but what were these to a man like him?—Y.

Vers. 15—18.—*Ebed-Melech's safety, and the secret of it.* I. EBED-MELECH'S DANGER. He was a court official, and like all others connected with the court, in more danger than if he had been merely one of the multitude. He appears to have been in favour with the king, and all such would be put down by enemies as exciting the king to continued resistance. That is, it would seem to Ebed-Melech so; for why should he suppose that any one should be so specially interested in him as to describe his deeds exactly to the Chaldeans?

II. EBED-MELECH'S SAFETY. 1. *The usefulness of Jeremiah even as a prisoner.* Jeremiah cannot get out among the people, but there is sufficient mitigation of his imprisonment to make him useful to one man. Even in prisons God's servants find opportunities of doing good work for him—so Bunyan writes his 'Pilgrim's Progress.' With peculiar joy Jeremiah must have delivered such a message to one who had been so kind to him. In this, too, we can trace a Divine arrangement. Surely God's delight is to give peculiar joys to such as are diligent in doing his will. 2. *Words of hope are always possible to individuals.* There is no longer any chance for the nation; as a nation it must be scattered and spoiled; but every individual is treated according to his deserts. There is no reason to suppose that Jeremiah and Ebed-Melech were the only individuals to whom God was specially gracious,—it was necessary to mention them; but in all ages there have been many special providences not mentioned.

III. THE SECRET OF EBED-MELECH'S SAFETY. He had put his trust in Jehovah. What does this mean, seeing he is also described as being afraid? We take it that the reference is to his deliverance of the prophet from the dungeon. He really was exercising a faith in God more than he was aware of at the time. In stretching out his hand to rescue the prophet he had got upon the rock of his own safety. In other words, he had shown his faith by his works. A voice from the unseen had spoken and told him to get Jeremiah out of the dungeon, and his consequent action had in it the essence of faith; for he obeyed this voice from the unseen. God sees faith where we, with our prepossessions, would only too often be unable to discern it.—Y.

EXPOSITION.

CHAPTER XL.

The first of a series of chapters (xl.—xlv.) describing Jeremiah's fortunes and ministry after the fall of Jerusalem.

Vers. 1—6.—The liberation of Jeremiah. Ver. 1.—**The word that came to Jeremiah.** The formula seems to announce a prophecy; but no prophecy follows. It is not allowable to suppose, with Keil and others, that "the word" describes the entire body of prophetic utterance in ch. xl.—xlv. (in spite of the fact that ch. xliv. and xlv. have special

headings). The use would be unexampled; and a prologue of forty verses (see ch. xlii. 7) is equally contrary to prophetic analogy. Apparently the "word," or prophecy, which originally followed the heading has been lost or removed to some other place. **Had let him go from Ramah.** Here is an apparent discrepancy with the account in ch. xxxix. 14. The brevity of the latter seems to account for it. No doubt the more precise statement in our passage is to be followed. After the capture of the city, a number of captives, including Jeremiah, were probably conducted to Ramah (see on ch. xxxi. 15), where they had to wait for the royal decision as to their fate. Jeremiah, however, had already been in custody in the "court of the watch," and the writer of ch. xxix. 14 simply omits the second stage of his captivity (Keil). **In chains.** See ver. 4, "The chains which were upon thine hand."

Ver. 3. **The Lord hath brought it**, etc. The colouring of the speech is that of a Jewish prophet (comp. Isa. xxxvi. 10).

Ver. 5.—**Now while he was not yet**, etc. This rendering, however, seems against the Hebrew usage. Two renderings are open to us. 1. "But since one returneth not from Babylon, then go back to Gedaliah," etc.; so Hitzig. 2. Taking ver. 5 as a continuation of "but if it seemeth ill to thee," etc., "forbear" (in ver. 4), and, supplying, "I have spoken the word," continue, "and it shall not be reversed; yea, go back;" so Graf, regarding the passage as an explanation of the permission to "forbear." **A reward**; rather, *a present.*

Ver. 6.—**To Mizpah.** A place in the tribe of Benjamin, where Samuel judged, and where Saul was elected king (1 Sam. vii. 15, 16; x. 17).

Vers. 7—12.—The Jewish fugitives resort to Gedaliah, who promises them protection as long as they are loyal to Babylon.

Ver. 7.—**In the fields**; rather, *in the field*; i.e. in the open country, as opposed to the towns. **Men, and women, and children.** Old and worn-out men, helpless widows, and fatherless children. Royal princesses were among them (ch. xli. 10).

Ver. 8.—**Jonathan.** This name is omitted in the parallel passage (2 Kings xxv. 23), and by the Septuagint here. It may, of course, be a corruption of Johanan, as Ewald supposes. If so, we must read "son" for "sons," with Septuagint. **The Netophathite.** Netophah was in the neighbourhood of Benjamin. **The son of a Maachathite**; rather, *the Maachathite.* Maachah was a Syrian district in the neighbourhood of Hermon (Deut. iii. 14; Josh. xii. 5). Jezaniah was, therefore, a naturalized foreigner, like Doeg the Edomite (Hitzig).

Ver. 10.—**To serve the Chaldeans**; rather, *to stand before the Chaldeans* (so literally); *i.e.* to mediate between you and them (comp. ch. xv. 1). **Gather ye wine**, etc. It was the fifth or sixth month (comp. ch. xli. 1; 2 Kings xxv. 8), the end of July or the beginning of August, when grapes, figs, and olives become ripe. Observe, "wine" is here the wine in the grape; the Hebrew *yayin* seems originally to have meant a cluster of grapes, like the corresponding word (*wain*) in Arabic (comp. on ch. xlviii. 33). **That ye have taken**; rather, *that ye shall have taken.* (The "captains" had up to this time been in the open country, ver. 7.)

Vers. 13—16.—Gedaliah receives a warning of a plot against his life.

Ver. 14.—**Baalis the king of the Ammonites.** Perhaps the same king referred to in ch. xxvii. 3 as seeking alliance with Zedekiah. He was naturally opposed to the Babylonian official, Gedaliah. **Hath sent Ishmael.** Ishmael was connected with the royal family (ch. xli. 1), and was probably jealous of Gedaliah.

HOMILETICS.

Vers. 1—5.—*Jeremiah's release.* I. THE INNOCENT OFTEN SUFFER WITH THE GUILTY. It would seem that orders had been given in Jerusalem for the liberation of the prophet (ch. xxxix. 11—14), but that, in the confusion of the sack of the city, inferior officers had led off Jeremiah in chains with the rest of the captives. Thus he shared the indignities and hardships of companions who deserved a fate from which his innocence should have saved him. It is part of the discipline of life that we should suffer one with another. Amongst men justice is irregular; ignorance and mistakes often result in unintentional cruelty. Men are dealt with in masses, and the individual must suffer with the multitude.

II. JUSTICE WILL BE ULTIMATELY EFFECTED. Jeremiah is discovered at Ramah, and the mistake rectified. This does not always happen so soon. It is sad to think that, even with our enlightened system of justice, there may be innocent men suffering long years of penal servitude in convict establishments, without a chance of clearing their character this side the grave. How much more often must such mistakes occur in more barbarous countries! But it is a consolation for all who are unjustly treated to know that this is but one of the trials of life, overruled to work wholesome discipline, and is but transitory. Ultimately God will visit each man individually with strict fairness and no possibility of error. There were mistakes made in the sack of Jerusalem; there will be none in the judgment of all men at the end of the world. All will be judged, but in the vast crowd of cases there can then be no error, for "shall not the Judge of all the earth do right?"

III. A RECOGNITION OF THE JUSTICE OF GOD TENDS TO MAKE MEN MORE JUST. The captain of the guard had given sufficient attention to the teaching of Jeremiah to see that the destruction of Jerusalem was predicted by him as a punishment for the sins of the Jews. It may appear hypocritical for one of the soldiers, who had been engaged in the cruel carnage, to reflect piously on the Divine justice of the fate of his victims. But is it not quite possible that the impressive words of an inspired prophet— of which his own are evidently a literal repetition—may have led to his sincere adoption of this view? Alaric seemed to have honestly believed in his mission as a scourge of God. Might not some such idea have taken possesssion of Nebuchadnezzar and his soldiers, if only as an after-thought? Then it would raise their minds to the sense of the obligations of justice.

IV. LIBERTY IS ONE OF THE FIRST OF EARTHLY BLESSINGS. This is now accorded to Jeremiah. Like health and wealth, it is not appreciated till it is lost. We who enjoy it, however, should remember to be more grateful, and to fulfil our noble mission of carrying it to others who are yet languishing under tyranny or in slavery. One of the first promises of the gospel is the gift of liberty to captives (Isa. lxi. 1). Physical freedom is but the smaller half of the liberty we need. We may have this and yet be slaves. Jeremiah could enjoy it to the full, because he was also possessed of that higher, glorious liberty of the sons of God.

Ver. 6.—*The choice of a residence.* The captain of the guard gave to Jeremiah the choice between an honourable asylum in Babylon and a return to his own land. The prophet selected the latter course. Why did he do so? Although the circumstances of the case were peculiar, the answer to this question may throw light on some of the considerations which should guide men generally in the selection of their places of abode. Several characteristics may be noted in Jeremiah's decision, viz. :—

I. PATRIOTISM. Jeremiah had been accused of a treasonable friendship for Babylon. His conduct in deciding to remain in his native land, wrecked and deserted as it was after the war, in preference to enjoying the position of a privileged guest at Babylon, is an ample refutation of all such charges. Patriotism is more than a sense of duty, it is an affection. It does not speak much for the depth of a man's nature that he can leave his native country without a sigh of regret. If we find it necessary to emigrate, genuine patriotism will certainly incline us to settle in one of the colonies of the British Empire rather than in a foreign country. This point should be insisted on as a duty, not merely treated as a question of sentiment.

II. CONSIDERATION FOR RELIGIOUS ASSOCIATIONS. Babylon was a heathen city. Jeremiah preferred to remain in the Holy Land. Surely the religious advantages of a neighbourhood should be taken into account as of first importance. Yet many people seem to be strangely blind to all such considerations. The soil, the scenery, the society, the convenience of the house, are duly considered; but the Church accommodation is scarcely thought of. A gravel soil is most essential; healthy religious influences are regarded as of very secondary interest. A beautiful view must be got, though the enjoyment of it means banishment from all healthy Church life. How strange that heads of families professing to be Christian should act like pagans in this matter, and care so little for the spiritual atmosphere in which their children are to be brought up!

III. THE SACRIFICE OF PERSONAL CONVENIENCE TO THE GOOD OF OTHERS. Ezekiel could minister to the captives in Babylon. Jeremiah had his work in comforting the remnant in the land of Israel. If he had consulted his own convenience, he might have accepted the offer of a safe and probably honourable position in the land of exile. But he had his work to do at home, and he stayed to do it. Such conduct is a fine example to those of us who, in choosing a place of residence, think of our own plea- sure and profit rather than of the good we may do. More especially does this apply to Christian ministers. If the choice lay between easy work in a beautiful place in Devonshire, and the toil of service amid all the squalor and ugliness and wretchedness of a densely populated district in the east end of London, should we be willing to choose the harder but more useful life?

IV. CONTENTMENT AND SIMPLICITY. These are minor characteristics of the choice of Jeremiah, but they are not without their significance. Jeremiah was satisfied to stay in the old land with the poor, after the wealthy and great had been banished. To the luxuries of court life at Babylon he preferred the homely ways of the peasants of Israel. In abandoning simplicity for display and excitement, the fashion of our age drives men and women to a life that is neither healthy nor happy. Even if the outward surroundings of a quieter life are not so attractive, its true experience will give a restfulness and a satisfaction that cannot be found in the race of worldly pleasures.

Vers. 7—12.—*The duties of adversity and their reward.* I. THE DUTIES. 1. *Submission.* We are not required to yield before avoidable troubles; but finding some to be irresistible, we are to learn the wisdom and obligation of bending to them without further demur. The captains were no cowards; they had fought and had lost. Their resistance against the inevitable was a mistake; continued resistance after defeat would have been nothing but folly. Submission is much easier when we remember that the trouble is in accordance with the will of a God who is always wise, fair, and merciful. 2. *Industry.* Gedaliah advised the people to set to work at their regular avocations. "But ye, gather ye wine, and summer fruits, and oil, and put them in your vessels," etc. (ver. 10). It is difficult for a dispirited, humiliated, poverty-striken people to settle down to quiet, earnest work. Nevertheless, their duty and their happiness lie in their doing so: (1) their *duty*, for adversity is no excuse for indolence; and (2) their *happiness*, because (*a*) the fruits of their labour would be a beginning of a return to prosperity and wealth, and (*b*) in the very exercise of work they would find a solace and a refreshment. There is nothing so weak or so injurious as an idle brooding over trouble. Be up and doing! And though the work is irksome at first, it will prove itself a great healer of distress.

II. THE REWARD. 1. *A healthy influence over others.* The example of the quiet condition of the remnant of Jews in their native country attracted fugitives to return from the neighbouring countries (ver. 11). Their action was a confirmation of the wisdom of their brethren. A man's behaviour under great trial is keenly observed. If he do well then, he may be the means of influencing others as he can never influence them under ordinary circumstances. Thus he may find consolation for his sorrow in the enlargement of his service to his fellow-men. 2. The *successful issue of industry.* The Jews reaped an unusually abundant grape and fruit harvest (ver. 12). "They that sow in tears shall reap in joy." If we complain and despair under distress, we have no right to expect a happy issue out of it. But patient endurance and diligent attention to duty may make us reasonably expect brighter days in the future. Borne with these accompaniments, trouble often reveals itself as less terrible than our fears. When distress comes, we imagine that it has blighted every tree in the orchard and every grape in the vineyard, and so we neglect what consolation we might have in those fruits of patient industry which might still be given to us. Let us remember that during the sad seventy years, and even just after the horrors of the Chaldean invasion, the Jews could gather "wine and summer fruits *very much.*"

HOMILIES BY VARIOUS AUTHORS.

Ver. 13—ch. xli. 4.—*The murder of Gedaliah; or, noble credulity.* No sooner was the new government in a fair way of being settled and prosperous, than untoward circumstances occurred. Ishmael, son of Nethaniah, son of Elishama, a connection of the royal house, inspired, perhaps, with a jealous feeling towards Gedaliah, began to plot with the King of Ammon against him. Under cover of paying his respects to the new governor, he visited him at Mizpah, and partook of his hospitality. Although warned by Johanan the son of Kareah that Ishmael entertained hostile designs against him, Gedaliah refused to credit the information, and indignantly forbade his informant carrying out his proposal to assassinate Ishmael. The latter, finding thus a clear way for his schemes, took advantage of the trustfulness of Gedaliah to accomplish his murderous purpose and to deceive his leading supporters. This done, crime followed upon crime with startling rapidity, until Johanan overtook the miscreant at the "great waters that are in Gibeon," and delivered the prisoners whom he was carrying off. In this tragic incident we see—

I. HOW THE VIRTUE OF ONE POSITION MAY BE THE VICE OF ANOTHER. A trusting, ingenuous man like Gedaliah was out of place in more senses than one as governor of such a people. In any circumstances it is necessary that the utmost precaution should be taken with respect to the person of a ruler, as there are always evil-disposed persons who may take advantage of an opportunity, and accidents and misfortunes are continually possible. The off-hand openness, therefore, which is so admirable in the private citizen, upon whose life so little depends, is highly reprehensible in one occupying so responsible a position. When it is remembered that the people over whom Gedaliah ruled were wholly undisciplined, and had but recently been exposed to the most demoralizing influences, his rashness will be even more apparent. It is well when a ruler can combine the trustful ingenuousness of the private citizen with the sagacity and watchfulness his responsibilities impose upon him. Life is full of such misplaced virtues. The poor man open-handed and lavish as when he was wealthy; the rich man meanly careful as when he had everything to acquire, etc.

II. How much is required to justify a wrong action. It was a case, apparently, on Johanan's showing, of self-protection. Ishmael contemplated murder and treachery; what more natural than that he should be killed? Yet this consideration had no weight with Gedaliah. His informant might be mistaken, and was, perhaps, interested. It was foreign to his disposition to be suspicious: and he could not brook the idea of assassination. If the governor was wrong in neglecting the most ordinary precautions, he was certainly right in this. The instinct of the true man is ever averse to underhand actions, even although their object be to avert contingent or certain evils. It is *never* right to do evil that good may come or evil may be averted. The weapons which God's children have to wield are ever those of truth and honour; and these are sufficient if they be sagaciously handled.

III. How great a crime and calamity may be divinely permitted. 1. Jeremiah, for the most part, resided with Gedaliah, and yet no warning appears to have been given him of the catastrophe. How was this? Had it not as profound a bearing on the future of God's people as the march of Nebuchadnezzar's armies? It is a great mystery, and there are many like it. How appalling the wickedness of our Saviour's crucifixion! Yet are the fruits of it a world's salvation. 2. The dictates of common sense and worldly experience, had they been attended to, might have proved sufficient. God's interpositions are not always to wait upon human folly. It is our duty to make the best of the means and information at our disposal. This is especially incumbent with regard to the warnings and instructions of the gospel. The rich man, eager for an evangel from Hades to his careless, sinful brethren, is assured, "If they hear not Moses and the prophets, neither will they be persuaded, though one rose from the dead" (Luke xvi. 31). We may wait long if we expect to be converted by a miracle. The commandment is binding now: "Believe on the Lord Jesus Christ, and thou shalt be saved."—M.

Vers. 2, 3.—*The blind seeing, the seeing blind.* This heathen captain, who could not be expected to know the truth, who was, as it were, born blind as to the truth of God, sees clearly that truth, and declares it; whilst the people of Judah and Jerusalem, their kings, their priests, their nobles, all of whom regarded themselves as knowing the truth, who, as in John ix. 41, said, "We see," are found to be completely blind as to that truth. Note herein—

I. How clear was the recognition of God. He ascribes all to "the Lord thy God." He recognizes the prophet as sent of God (ver. 3), "According as he hath said." He traces their calamities to their true cause—sin against God. He recognizes that Babylon and her troops are but ministers of God to do his will.

II. The probable sources of his knowledge. Perhaps: 1. The general belief that each nation had its own deity. 2. Yet more, the prophecies of Jeremiah. 3. Also the strength of Jerusalem. Never, apart from the people's sin, has such a fortress been overthrown. 4. The madness of the people. *Quem deus vult perdere prius dementat.* Only a God-forsaken people could have thrown away their well-being as these had done. 5. The judgments that came upon them.

III. What such facts as these—the blind seeing, etc.—reveal. 1. How clear the light of truth which God has given! Were it not so clear, such as this heathen would not see it. 2. How dense the darkness which persistent sin spreads over the soul!

Hence the "seeing blind." 3. How awful the doom of those who seeing, see not! Cf. Matt. xi., "Woe unto thee, Chorazin," etc. !—C.

Vers. 4, 5.—"*A strait betwixt two.*" St. Paul tells how he was in such strait. He was willing to stay, but ready to depart home to his eternal rest, which would be far better. And oftentimes we are in perplexities as to choice in the common events and circumstances of our lives. It is so difficult to see what we ought to do, what it would be best to do. Here we have an instance. The patriotic prophet had a perplexing choice put before him. Consider—

I. THE ALTERNATIVES PROPOSED. 1. He *might go to Babylon*, where, no doubt, the same favour that had shown him such consideration thus far would bring him to honour there. 2. He *might stay amongst his own people*. Amid their poverty, their displeasure, their disgrace. 3. Or he *might go anywhere he pleased*—to Tarshish, as Jonah tried, if so he pleased.

II. THE ARGUMENTS FOR AND AGAINST EACH. 1. *For Babylon.* Safety, wealth, honour, help to his countrymen there. 2. *For staying in Israel.* There he had been called; there he was yet needed; Ezekiel and Daniel were in Babylon. Against this, he had no command of God; the peril in which he would be placed.

III. THE DECISION. He resolved to stay. This come to, not because the captain (ver. 5), who saw him lingering, bade him go back, but because the hardness of the duty seemed to declare it was his duty. In such cases *choose what you like least.*—C.

Vers. 7—12.—"*That we may be godly and quietly governed.*" These verses are an illustration of men's desire for such government. In the disorder and confusion of the times, men were looking out for some settled rule. Companies of armed men were camping about, only waiting for some sign to indicate to whose standard they should repair. That which they wanted seemed to be found in Gedaliah. Hence they go to him (ver. 8). The incident here recorded suggests, in regard to government generally—

I. THE COMMON CONSENT OF MEN AS TO ITS NECESSITY. It was not merely one company of the scattered Jews that were on the look out for a leader, but *all* the companies, and not the men only, but their officers also. And in every collection of human beings, however they group themselves, however casually they may have been thrown together, if they have to dwell and to work together the choosing of a leader, one who shall rule them, is a never disregarded need.

II. THE PRINCIPLES ON WHICH THIS CONSENT RESTS. They are such as these: 1. There can be no well-being—strength, peace, happiness—without order. 2. No order without law. 3. No law without a lawgiver, and a law-upholder, *i.e.* a government. It may be monarchical, an oligarchy, a republic, a democracy, only in some way law must be expressed and upheld. Because men feel that this last is necessary to the first, men will ever seek after government, good, if possible, but any is felt to be better than none. Anarchy is so much misery. Thus do men reason in regard to their temporal affairs.

III. THE EXCEPTION WHICH MEN MAKE TO THIS CONSENT. It is strange that there should be exception, but there is. We find it when we look at men's spiritual affairs. Government there is as necessary as in that which is temporal—indeed, far more so, considering the far greater value of the interests at stake. And yet men will not have it. Each seeks to do that which is right in his own eyes. What would be ruin in regard to their secular affairs they deem to be no great harm in things that are spiritual. We see this anarchy at times in *the things of the Church.* If the Church of Christ is to do her work and glorify her Lord, there must be unity, cohesion, subordination, obedience. But these words, and yet more the things they represent, are hateful to not a few. And so the paralysis that has come over large sections of the Church. The prince of this world knows the force and value of the maxim, *Divide et impera*, and he has sought all too successfully to do the one that he may attain to the other. And so in the *individual sphere of the soul.* The one rightful ruler is God, speaking by his vicegerent conscience. All our sin and misery is owing to our disregard of this rule. The world is so mournful a world because it is so sinful a world. Loyal obedience is our life and health and peace. And because we refuse this, we are weak and sad, as well as sinful.

IV. THE DIVINE METHODS OF BRINGING THIS EXCEPTION TO AN END. For he will bring it to an end, glory be to his Name. He *must* reign till he hath put all things under his feet. And he thus works to this end: 1. *By powerful instructors.* Conscience. His providence, shown now in blessing, now in stern judgment. His Word, in which his law is laid down. 2. By *bringing to bear the most mighty of motives.* Love, which rises at the cross of Christ. Hope of his acceptance and reward. Fear of his awful displeasure and doom. 3. *By his Spirit striving ever with men.*—C.

Ver. 13—ch. xli. 11.—*Misplaced charity.* "Charity," says St. Paul, "thinketh no evil." But without question, there are times when it ought to think evil, and not to think so is evil. For else charity will be misplaced, thrown away, productive of hurt and harm and not of good. Now—

I. THERE HAVE BEEN AND ARE MANY INSTANCES OF SUCH MISPLACED CHARITY. 1. The miserable way by which Gedaliah came by his death, as told in the above section, is an illustration. He ought to have been on his guard. He was warned. He would not believe, but blamed severely the friend who warned him. And all because of his over-confidence in Ishmael, who murdered him. 2. And there have been many other such instances. Perhaps the king who said, concerning the wicked husbandmen, "They will reverence my son." And Paul, who, though warned again and again, would go to Jerusalem. He thought that the loving gifts he bore from the Gentile Churches to the mother Church in Jerusalem would soften their hard hearts. But it was not so. The elder son—though he was quite wrong—thought that his father's treatment of his prodigal younger brother was as unwise as it was kind. We have known those who would never let themselves speak anything but good of others, and the result was that they often misled those who trusted to their over-lenient judgments. How often, after the most atrocious crimes, there will be found some who would try to prevent the criminal receiving the due reward of his deeds! What is it but charity in the wrong place? 3. But most of all are we guilty of this *toward ourselves.* We so little like to think harshly of ourselves, and hence we make all manner of excuse for our faults. We tamper with temptation; we spare ourselves when we ought to be most stern.

II. AND MUCH SORROW AND TROUBLE ARISE THEREFROM. Cf. above history; the massacres that followed; the ruin of the nation. Never did a seeming virtue work such ill. Charity to the evil is cruelty to the good. Choosing Barabbas means crucifying Christ. It discourages all virtue. Wherefore should I strive after excellence if the worthless are to be dealt with even as I? This was the elder son's complaint (Luke xv.). And there seemed to be a good deal in it; hence the father took care to point out to him how much preferable was his own lot: "Son, *thou* art ever with me," etc. Thy lot is ever so much the best, as the lot of him who never leaves the father's house is far better than that of him who comes back after a wretched leaving of it for the far country. But most of all the evil results are seen in our misplaced charity to ourselves. Temptation tampered with triumphs, and we who would not be stern with ourselves perish. Hiding from ourselves the truth as to our real condition, we never go to him who alone can make us what we need to be, and so souls are lost.

III. HOW EXCELLENT THE EXAMPLE AND TEACHING OF OUR LORD ON THIS SUBJECT! Full of charity as he was, tender and gentle as a mother to the weak and sinful, to the poor outcasts who came to him, yet he was never guilty of any spurious charity. He did not, nor does he, warm vipers in his bosom who should sting him at the last. Cf. John ii. at end, "Jesus did not commit himself unto them." "But"—so the Gospel goes on; the word is unfortunately rendered "and" in our Authorized Version—"there was a man of the Pharisees," etc. (John iii. 1). 1. It means that our Lord did commit himself to this man—as we see he did—since he was very different from those whom our Lord could not and would not trust. His treatment of Judas was no exception to his rule. He *knew* him from the beginning. Nor is his treatment of ourselves, poor, sad recompense as we make him. He has taken us in hand, and he will not put us out of his hand until he has wrought in us all that he designs. He exemplified his own word about being, whilst harmless as doves, wise as serpents also. He says (Matt. vii. 1), "Judge not." But almost the next verse bids us *not* cast pearls before swine! The intent is that, whilst we should not be censorious, we are not to be blind fools, who will imagine in their false charity that pearls will be appreciated by pigs. Charity *is* to think evil when evil is palpably there.

IV. WHAT LEADS TO THIS ERROR. Cf. the history. 1. Perhaps Gedaliah's conscious integrity; his freedom from all intent of evil. 2. Or over-elation at the loyalty and trust that were being displayed on all sides. 3. The accused man had himself (ver. 8) come to Gedaliah. 4. Or dislike to Johanan and his proposals. 5. Or reliance on his own capacity of taking all due care. And when we are wrongly charitable to what is evil, our motives are akin to these. We intend no evil; that which is said to be evil has wrought no harm in others. We intend to be on our guard, and deem ourselves to be quite able to take care of ourselves. We dislike the safeguards proposed. We do not believe in the peril against which we are warned. We are disposed to think well of and to like the evil.

V. OUR SAFEGUARDS. 1. Seek the knowledge of man. 2. Seek the Spirit of Christ.—C.

Vers. 2—6.—*Jeremiah a free agent.* We have here an expansion of vers. 13 and 14 of the previous chapter.

I. ONE OF THE BEST THINGS A MAN CAN HAVE IS FULL INDIVIDUAL LIBERTY. The royal master of the captain of the guard was anxious to do the best he could for the prophet; and he seems to have understood fully that only the prophet could decide on this best. The captain of the guard, in all he says, is but the mouthpiece of the king. Very likely the captain, if he had been left to decide, would have said, "What better thing can happen to this man than go to Babylon with me?" and so, meaning well enough, he might have done ill. Good intentions are not enough in providing for others. We go rather by our notion of what they want than by what they really want; and thus we are disappointed in our efforts. There never can be anything wrong in giving a man the largest scope to settle his path for himself. We may easily become cramped as a result of the ignorant kindness of others.

II. THERE WAS AN INCREASED RESPONSIBILITY FOR JEREMIAH. For a long time he had been in prison, and all he had to do was to endure captivity in a patient, trustful way. But now comes liberty, and in his case a peculiar responsibility. Few men, perhaps not even a single one, had the liberty enjoyed by him at this moment. Others had not been asked whether they would go to Babylon or stay. The conquerors settled all that. But Jeremiah has free choice, and he has to decide in very altered conditions of the land. Freedom brings human judgment into full strength and exercise.

III. JEREMIAH WAS SURE TO DECIDE RIGHTLY. Why? Because the first thing he would look to was the will of Jehovah. What lesson had he been learning all through his prophetic life but this, that negligence of the will of Jehovah brought incalculable mischief? Here is the necessity for us to keep in a state of discernment with respect to the will of God. As a general rule, we do not need special intimations of the Divine will; right is seen to be right and wrong to be wrong. But there are also times when, as we need such special intimations, they are sure to be given.—Y.

Vers. 7—12.—*The difficulties of a governor.* To govern a country is never an easy task; but how difficult it must be when the work is that of reconstruction! Gedaliah has to begin, as it were, at the beginning. One of his first difficulties is to know exactly what he has to deal with. There are turbulent as well as peaceful elements, bands of free-lances, who, now that the Chaldean has gone, make their appearance before the governor to see what the prospect may be. Another difficulty is that of inspiring confidence. Those who have just been plundered may be excused for apprehensions lest they should soon be plundered again. On the other hand, Gedaliah was better off than the king who had just been dethroned. The latter vainly held on to a tottering building, whose very foundations were going, while the former was free from the pernicious elements which so long had made all government in the land an abomination. With all his difficulties, Gedaliah had some encouragements. There appears to have been a general gathering to him as a centre. Most men generally tend to the point where there are the greatest prospects of social order, security, and stability.—Y.

Ver. 16.—*Trusting a traitor.* I. IN SPITE OF CAUTIONS. Gedaliah was told that Ishmael meditated his death. Told, not by one man, but by all who had opportunity of knowing the traitor's designs. Was it, then, blameworthy in him to neglect the information? We cannot tell. It may have been that he knew of jealousies which made him think that the rest of the captains were slandering Ishmael. Slanderers, be it remembered, are quite as numerous as traitors. The fault of Gedaliah, if fault it was, was that of a generous heart. It is one of the weapons of a traitor to put on the semblance of a true man. Then probably Gedaliah was further influenced by the proposition to kill Ishmael. If the informers had merely urged him to guard himself, they might have been better attended to. But those were days when, if people wanted to get rid of a troublesome man, they had little scruple in taking the most effectual way.

II. AN INSTANCE OF RASH JUDGMENT. Gedaliah in one breath judged the traitor to be a true man and the speaker of truth to be a slanderer. In this world of uncertainties there is no need to refuse any accusation. Only let the accusation be accompanied with evidence. Trumped-up evidence soon shows its faults and contradictions. If Gedaliah had bid Ishmael meet the accusation, he might have prevented the serious migration spoken of at the end of the next chapter. He had to take care of himself not only for his own sake, but as the representative of Babylon.—Y.

EXPOSITION.

CHAPTER XLI.

Vers. 1—10.—Assassination of Gedaliah and other Jews.

Ver. 1.—**In the seventh month**; *i.e.* two months after the destruction of Jerusalem and the appointment of Gedaliah. It seems strange, however, that the occurrences related in ch. xl. and xli. should have taken so short a time. Grätz calls in question the accuracy of the chronological statement. He quotes Ezek. xxxiii. 24—29, which shows that at least six months (according to his calculation) after the fall of Jerusalem Jewish fugitives still lingered on, and hoped to obtain possession of their fatherland, and points out that time was necessary for Gedaliah to erect a temple at Mizpah (see on ver. 5), for cities to arise out of their ruins, and for cultivation of the soil to be resumed (ch. xl. 10).[1] Besides, according to ch. lii. 30, a third deportation of Jews is mentioned. How can this be accounted for, if, only two months after the fall of Jerusalem, the remnant of the Jewish population emigrated under Johanan ben Kareah to Egypt? Grätz shows reason for thinking that this last deportation stands in close connection with Gedaliah's death, and that consequently the interval between this latter event and the fall of Jerusalem lasted, not two months, but five years. **The son of Elishama.** Perhaps the Elishama mentioned in ch. xxxvi. 12 as a secretary of state; or perhaps a son of David of that

[1] 'Monatsschrift für Geschichte und Wissenschaft des Judenthums,' 1870, pp. 268—275.

name (see 2 Sam. v. 16; 1 Chron. iii. 8; xiv. 7; "son" being taken here in a wider sense). **And the princes of the king;** rather, *and (one of) the princes of the king.* **Even ten men;** rather, *and ten men.* Eleven determined bravoes overpower a crowd of unprepared men. **Did eat bread together.** Gedaliah, then, had invited them to a friendly banquet.

Ver. 2.—**Smote Gedaliah.** The day of the murder of Gedaliah (the third day of the seventh month) was kept as a fast-day by the post-Captivity Jews (see Zech. vii. 5; viii. 19). It was the day on which the hope of living a separate life in the promised land, for a time at least, vanished; and the murder was avenged by a new captivity (see above).

Ver. 3.—**The Chaldeans.** Gedaliah's Chaldean body-guard. **And the men of war;** rather, *even the men of war.* Jewish as well as Chaldean warriors are meant; the non-military Jews, including the prophet, were carried away captive (see vers. 10, 16).

Vers. 4—7.—The news of the deed of violence had not yet been spread, and Ishmael seized the opportunity of imbruing his hands in fresh blood. He could have had no personal motive; but his employer, Baalis, desired that "the remnant in Judah might perish" (ch. xl. 15).

Ver. 5.—**There came certain from Shechem,** etc. A number of pious pilgrims, descendants of the old ten tribes, passed by on their way to the holy site of the temple at Jerusalem (?) (comp. 2 Chron. xxxiv. 9; xxx. 11). **From Shiloh.** The Vatican Codex of the Septuagint has a plausible reading, "from Salem," which is apparently supported by Gen. xxxiii. 18, "And Jacob came to Shalem, a city of Shechem," and by its improvement thus introduced into the geographical order (Shiloh is, in fact, nearer to Mizpah than Shechem, and ought to be mentioned first). But though there is now a village called Sâlim, to the east of Nablûs (Shechem), we have no sufficient ground for assuming a city of that name in the Old Testament. The rendering of Genesis, *l.c.* needs correction ("came in peace to the city," etc.) **Their beards shaven,** etc. They had, then, all the outward signs of mourning (for the public calamities); comp. ch. xvi. 6; xlviii. 37. **To bring them to the house of the Lord.** Yet the temple at Jerusalem was destroyed. Hence Thenius and Grätz have conjectured that Gedaliah had erected a provisional temple at Mizpah, which was already hallowed by its association with the Prophet Samuel. This is confirmed by 1 Macc. iii. 46, where it is said of the pious Jews in the Maccabean rising, that they "assembled themselves . . . and came to Maspha, over against Jerusalem; for in Maspha was the place where they prayed aforetime in Israel."

Ver. 6.—**Weeping all along as he went.** To testify his sympathy with their grief. But the reading of the Septuagint is more natural, "As they were going along and weeping."

Ver. 7.—**The pit** (see on ver. 9).

Ver. 8.—**Slay us not,** etc. Bishop Callaway refers to this passage in his 'Zulu Nursery Tales' (i. 242), in illustration of a Zulu form of deprecating death on the ground of having some important work in hand which absolutely requires the life of the person in danger. But the "ten men" do not, as the bishop supposes, beg their lives on the ground that they had not yet harvested, but rather offer a bribe. **We have treasures** (literally, *hidden things*) **in the field.** The allusion is to the "wells or cisterns for grain," in which "the farmers store their crops of all kinds after the grain is threshed and winnowed. These cisterns are cool, perfectly dry, and tight. The top is hermetically sealed with plaster, and covered with a deep bed of earth; and thus they keep out rats, mice, and even ants, the latter by no means a contemptible enemy. . . .

These ten men had doubtless thus hid their treasures to avoid being plundered in that time of utter lawlessness" (Thomson, 'The Land and the Book,' p. 509). **Honey.** Probably that obtained from wild bees.

Ver. 9.—**Now the pit . . . which Asa the king had made,** etc. Nothing is said of this "pit" in the historical books, but only (1 Kings xv. 22 = 2 Chron. xvi. 6) that Asa used the material with which Baasha had fortified Ramah to build Geba and Mizpah. It would seem that this "pit" formed part of Asa's defensive works; probably it was a cistern to supply the town with water during the siege. **Because of Gedaliah,** was it. The rendering "because of" must be abandoned. The Septuagint has, in this part of the verse, the very natural words, "was a great pit," and this reading is adopted by Movers, Hitzig, and Graf.

Ver. 10.—**The king's daughters;** rather, *the royal princesses* (see on ch. xxxvi. 26).

Vers. 11—18.—Rescue of the captives from Ishmael, and plan for taking flight to Egypt.

Ver. 12.—**The great waters . . . in Gibeon;** *i.e.* the pool mentioned in 2 Sam. ii. 13. Dr. Thomson (p. 670) speaks of a "pond or small lake" near El-Jîb. Ishmael seems to be lingering over his journey to Ammon, in order to find the subterranean stores spoken of in ver. 8.

Ver. 14.—**Cast about;** *i.e.* turned about (an archaism).

Ver. 17.—**And dwelt in the habitation of Chimham.** Chimham was the son of the rich Gileadite Barzillai (2 Sam. xix. 37—40), who probably founded this "habitation," or rather "hospice" ("khan," "caravanserai"), for the accommodation of travellers—a characteristic mark of public-spirited liberality. Josephus and Aquila, however, appear to have read "by the hurdles of Chimham"—a very possible name for a locality in such a pastoral country.

Ver. 18.—**Because of the Chaldeans.** They were afraid of being held responsible for the crime of Ishmael. And they had good reason for their alarm, as the Chaldeans would naturally look upon Ishmael as the representative of the Davidic dynasty, and the heir of that dynasty's claims to the loyalty of the Jews.

HOMILETICS.

Vers. 1—3.—*The assassination of Gedaliah.* I. HIGH POSITION BRINGS GREAT DANGER. Kings are little to be envied. The world sees their state and majesty. It does not see the apprehensions which would make some of them willingly exchange places with the humblest peasant. Nevertheless, it is as cowardly and selfish to refuse to occupy a high position when duty calls to it as it is to fail in fulfilling one's mission in any of the lower walks of life.

II. A GOOD MAN WILL PREFER TO SUFFER DEATH RATHER THAN TO DEFEND HIMSELF BY UNRIGHTEOUS MEANS. Gedaliah had been warned of his danger, but he had refused to accept the warning (ch. xl. 13—16). It is better for one's character, if not for one's earthly fate, to be over-generous than to be over-suspicious. Though we may think Gedaliah wanting in discernment, we must commend his justice in refusing to consent to the assassination of Ishmael. When we are in doubt about the guilt of any one, it is our plain duty to give him the benefit of that doubt. In no case have we a right to defend ourselves against a future wrong by anticipating the blow with an act of unlawful violence.

III. POLITICAL CRIMES ARE THE GREATEST CRIMES. Much vagueness exists as to the character of these crimes. If the assassin is successful, the world condones his offence, while, if he fails, his memory is execrated and he is condemned as a murderer. Many political acts are viewed as crimes by one party and as heroic deeds by another. But the moral character of a deed is not determined by such accidents as these. If it be really a crime, an offence against the eternal laws of right, its relation to public and national affairs aggravates its wickedness, inasmuch as it immensely enlarges the arena of its mischievous results (ver. 3).

IV. PUBLIC INTEREST IS NO EXCUSE FOR POLITICAL CRIMES. Ishmael might have contended that he was a patriot helping his people to throw off the yoke of Babylon. If he were acting that noble part, his method of carrying it out would still have been odious and unpardonable. Patriotism is no excuse for private treachery. Moreover, public interest is never truly advanced by crime. Ishmael's crime resulted in serious trouble to the Jews. It destroyed the hope of a quiet life in the land of Israel for the returned fugitives and the poor remnant of the nation. It probably led to a third deportation of exiles to Babylon.

Vers. 4—8.—*The slaughter of the pilgrims.* I. A NEEDLESS CRIME. Of course no crime is necessary, but some crimes have their plausible excuses. This had none. Ishmael had tasted blood, and murderous passions urge him to wanton violence. His only object in slaughtering quiet, inoffensive pilgrims must have been to please his master by the further depopulation of the land. So great a crime with so poor a motive evidences bloodthirsty tyranny. The worst crime is crime held cheap till it is pursued for no reason. All wickedness makes future wickedness more tempting. Done at first for some ulterior object, it becomes at length a passion and a delight in itself. This is the very devilry of crime.

II. A TREACHEROUS CRIME. Ishmael led the pilgrims to trust themselves in his hands, and then abused the sacred relations of hospitality. Such an act shows as much meanness as villainy. But all wickedness is essentially false, degrading, treacherous.

III. A SACRILEGIOUS CRIME. These men were pilgrims of religion, bearing incense in their hands. To us it may seem no more wicked to murder a pilgrim than to murder an innocent man. In itself the acts are equally wicked. But guilt depends on the criminal's idea of his crime, as well as on the inherent character of the act. Now, wherever sacred places are venerated and visited by pilgrims, the pilgrimage is regarded as a sacred work, a religious service. To slay a pilgrim is, therefore, held as a distinct insult to the service of God. This must have been the way in which Ishmael's act would have been regarded, and he must have known it. Therefore, judging him by the ideas and manners of the time, as it is only fair to judge him, we must acknowledge that he was guilty of a wilful affront against the religion of his nation. In all sin we sin against Heaven as well as against man. In some offences the offence to Heaven is more palpable than in others. Then the sin is the more horrible in its guilt on the conscience of the criminal.

IV. A COLD-BLOODED CRIME. The thing was done deliberately. The richer pilgrims were allowed to buy their lives for a ransom. The ten men who had treasure in the field purchased their escape (ver. 8). The rest, poorer men, were slain. Such a transaction reveals the cool calculator as well as the hardened murderer. The passionate man is responsible for the evil done in his rage, because he ought to restrain himself; but the calmer man, who can and does restrain himself in certain respects with regard to his own interest, is far more guilty for the wickedness he commits in clear self-possession.

HOMILIES BY VARIOUS AUTHORS.

Vers. 1—10.—*Devils incarnate.* 1. If ever there was such a one, this Ishmael was of whom these verses tell. His atrocities remind us of the Indian Mutiny, its leader, and the well at Cawnpore (cf. ver. 9). Treachery, ingratitude, murder, massacre, greed, cowardice,—all are gathered in this detestable character (cf. Mr. Grove's article "Ishmael," Smith's 'Dictionary of the Bible'). 2. And such men are permitted to be. So clearly seen is this, that every drama has its villain; they are recognized as having definite place and function in this poor life of ours. History is full of them. But for them one might almost say there would be no history. 3. Can we explain this permission? Wherefore are such men created and preserved? It is a part of the great question of moral evil, for the full solution of which we must wait. Like as was said to a lad of one of our public schools, who had heard his master say in a sermon in the school chapel that in mathematics there were lines in the same plane ever converging but which never met. The lad heard this, and as he knew something of mathematics himself, he believed and said to a senior in the school that the master was wrong. The senior defended the master, and told the lad of the lines that mathematicians call asymptotes. "But explain," said the astonished lad. "No, I can't," said the other. "*You must wait till you get there.*" The lad had not read on so far in the science as that, and hence there was nothing for it but to believe that, though it was at present incomprehensible to him how such lines as those spoken of could be, nevertheless, when he had read on further, he would see it clearly enough. And so we have to hear and see things which, to fully reconcile with the existence and superintendence of an all-loving and all-powerful God, is beyond our power, and there is nothing for it but that we must "wait till we get there"—there where the reading of these problems will be ready and clear. But the existence of such men as this Ishmael is but one out of the many terrible facts in God's providence, such as plague, famine, earthquake, etc. In regard to such men, we can see some purposes that they subserve.

I. They make evident the hideous capacities of evil which are in our nature, and the need, therefore, for God's restraining grace.

II. They are warnings to increased watchfulness on the part of those in whom the tendencies to like evil exist.

III. They are God's scourges for men's sin (cf. Attila, the Scourge of God).

IV. They weld together the people they oppress in one common league against them, and thus out of scattered tribes a nation is formed.

V. They clear out much that is evil (cf. French Revolution; Napoleon). But sometimes, as here, we cannot see what good they do; and then we can only wait.

CONCLUSION. But we can get above these and all such afflictors of our lives. The fear of God will lift us up above their power.

> "Fear him, ye saints, and you will then
> Have nothing else to fear."

On the wings of the fear and love of God let us mount up; and like as the little birds escape the hawk by keeping above it, so shall we escape all fear of fiercest human evils if we are upborne by the fear and love of God.—C.

Ver. 8.—*Sin hindered by sin.* "So he forbare," etc. This was a case of bloodthirsty cruelty *versus* greed. Ishmael would have killed these men but for his greed of the wealth they had. It is satisfactory to think he never gained possession of it. Nevertheless, his greed made him guilty of one sin less. This story suggests that—

I. GOD HAS MANY WAYS OF HINDERING SIN. There is: 1. The best way of all. By granting a true repentance and his Holy Spirit, creating the clean heart and renewing the right spirit. 2. But there are other ways. By keeping the opportunity and the will apart. How much of our freedom from sin do we owe to this blessed providential severance! By fear of present evil consequences of our sin. 3. And sometimes, as here, by one sin getting in the way of another. Thus *pride* holds back not a few; not love of God, gratitude to Christ, love of holiness, but pride. And *coveteousness* checks the sinner in many sins he would be guilty of but for this. *Anger*, breaking up the alliances of transgressors; as when, in the days of Jehoshaphat, the Ammonites who were coming against him fell out one with the other (2 Chron. xx. 22). The old saying is, "When thieves fall out, honest men come by their rights." *Sensual self-indulgence.* The vilest Roman emperors were those who least persecuted the Church—Tiberius, Commodus, etc. They were too absorbed in their own indulgences to trouble about the Christians.

II. BUT THESE OTHER WAYS LEAVE MEN AS GREAT SINNERS AS BEFORE. The question is not as to your freedom from transgression so much, but—What kept you free? Only the first and best way is accepted of God.

III. NEVERTHELESS, LET US BE THANKFUL THAT SIN IS SELF-DESTRUCTIVE IN ITS VERY NATURE. It is a blessed anarchy, for it protects many who would otherwise suffer.

IV. BUT FOR OURSELVES LET US SEEK THAT SIN MAY BE DESTROYED BY CHRIST.—C.

Vers. 11—15.—*The devil a bad paymaster.* These verses record the pursuit and overthrow of Ishmael. He had sold himself to work all manner of wickedness. What had he not been guilty of? And now we hear the last of him. He is seen in flight to Ammon, whence he came out, escaping with his life, but stripped of all his captives and his plunder. He had taken a world of trouble, incurred a load of guilt, filled his soul with evil, dishonoured his name for ever. And this was what came of it all. Every one of his purposes, plans, hopes, all his toil and villainy, all his apparent success, utterly lost and gone. He is one out of many more proofs of the miserable wages of sin. Now—

I. IT IS EVER SO. Men may go on in sin for a long time, and be undisturbed save by conscience; may find their sin very pleasant and very gainful, and they may seem to escape with utter impunity; but the visitation of God comes upon them, sometimes here in this life, certainly, if not here, hereafter. The Bible history, the world, are full of proofs of this.

II. BUT MEN CANNOT BE GOT TO BELIEVE THIS. Else why do they persist in evil ways?

III. WHY IS IT THAT THEY WILL NOT BELIEVE? They do not wish to believe. Sentence against evil work is not executed speedily, sometimes not at all here in this world in any visible way.

IV. WHY, THEN, DOES NOT GOD DEAL DIFFERENTLY WITH SIN? Because his purpose is to foster trust and love, neither of which could find place in a system of prompt and visible punishments such as some would desire.

V. DOES GOD, THEN, DO NOTHING TO CHECK THE SINNER AND TO ENCOURAGE THE OBEDIENT? Yes; much. 1. He causes the way of transgressors to be hard. Loss of peace, of hope, of Divine favour, of purity, of strength, of sympathy with and from the good, often of present and visible good; conscience is deadened, and the soul perishes. Besides this, there are frequent direct judgments sent. 2. On the other hand, he orders that in keeping of his commandments there is great reward. "His ways are ways of pleasantness, and all his paths are peace." It is related how an aged couple in the vicinity of London, who in the early part of life were poor, but who by the blessing of God upon their industry enjoyed a comfortable independency in their old age, were called upon by a Christian minister, who solicited their contributions to a charity. The old lady was disposed to make out some excuse, and to answer in the negative, both for her husband and for herself, and therefore replied, "Why, sir, we have lost a deal by religion since we began; my husband knows that very well." And being wishful to obtain her husband's consent to the assertion, she said, "Have we not, Thomas?" Thomas, after a long and solemn pause, replied, "Yes, Mary, we *have* lost a deal by our religion! I have lost a deal by my religion. Before I got religion, Mary, I had got a water-pail in which I carried water; and *that,* you know, I lost many years ago. And then I had an old slouched hat, a patched old coat, and mended shoes and stockings; but I have lost them also long ago. And, Mary, you know that, poor as I was, I had a habit of getting drunk and quarrelling with you; and that, you know, I have lost. And then I had a burdened conscience and a wicked heart, and then I had ten thousand guilty feelings and fears; but all are lost, completely lost, and like a millstone cast into the deep sea. Before we got religion, Mary, you had a washing-tray, in which you washed for hire, and God Almighty blessed your industry; but since we got religion you have lost your washing-tray. And you had a gown and bonnet much the worse for wear, though they were all you had to wear; but you have lost them long ago. And you had many an aching heart concerning me at times; but those you happily have lost. And I could even wish that you had lost as much as I have lost, and even more; for what we lose by our religion will be our eternal gain." We need not add that the preacher did not go away without substantial proof of the sincerity of what had been said in his hearing. And to all those who like the rich man in the parable (Luke xvi.), who asked that one from the dead might be sent to warn his five brethren, the same answer may be given, "They have Moses and the prophets," and we may add, in our day, far more than these; "if they hear not them, neither will they be persuaded, though one rose from the dead."—C.

Ver. 17.—*Too near the edge.* This is one of the reflections that come to us as we read of the place whither Johanan led his followers, and as we see the events that happened immediately after. This chapter is a record of disappointments. First the hopeful prospects of Gedaliah's governorship, which seemed starting so fairly and happily for all, these are shattered and overthrown by the villainous conduct of Ishmael. Then it is a grievous disappointment that we do not hear of Ishmael's death, only of his escape. That such a wretch should escape with his life seems a reflection upon that justice which generally follows on the track of wrong-doers such as he was, and metes out to them their due. Escape seems too lenient a dealing with him. And now here is another disappointment that Johanan, instead of seeking to follow in Gedaliah's footsteps, should be for leading the people down into Egypt. "At the caravanserai of Chimham, in Bethlehem—the natural halting-place on the way to Egypt—Johanan held a council of war, and then, against the prophet's advice, finally determined to abandon their homes, and to make for the refuge, to which the worldly Israelite always had recourse, across the Egyptian border." It was a bad place to halt at; it was too near that beguiling land, the witchery of which not a few of them had long been feeling and would now feel more than ever. Whenever Israel went thither, it was always a "going *down* into Egypt." This was more true morally and spiritually than even geographically, to which the word "down," of course, refers. And the present was no exception. Looking at them there at Chimham, we note—

I. THE RESEMBLANCE THEY OFFER. Are they not like all those who *tamper with temptation?* They know, as Israel knew, that they are in a forbidden path, and yet they do not keep clear of it. Like moths fluttering around the flame, so men will dally with sin. They know that to yield would be both most wrong and ruinous, and yet they go close to the border.

II. THE REASONS WHICH GOVERNED THEM. The Jews came to Chimham because their will had already consented to go further—on and down into Egypt. For like reasons men come to such places. There has been already the secret yielding of the will. There was no need of the Jews being at Chimham. It was not the way back from Gibeon. It was a deliberate going into temptation. So those who act like them have, as they, already consented in heart. And the causes of that consent are akin. They falsely feared what the Chaldeans might do, though there was no ground for such fear; and they falsely hoped for good—freedom from war and want—which they never realized. And such persons will ever magnify both the difficulties of the right path and the looked-for pleasures and advantages of the wrong. Thus would they persuade themselves that the right is wrong and the wrong is right.

III. THE RESISTANCE THEY SEEMED TO MAKE. The Jews did not yield all at once. They appeal to the prophet. They ask his prayers. They make repeated and loud —much too loud: "Methinks he doth protest too much"—professions. They wait patiently the prophet's message. And yet all the while (ver. 20) they were dissembling in their hearts, "regarding iniquity" there (cf. history of Balaam). They would have God on their side, not themselves on God's side. All this is most melancholy matter of fact with those who, of their own accord, go too near the edge.

IV. THE RESULTS THAT FOLLOWED. Of course they went over the edge; such people always do. They showed the insincerity of their prayers by their anger when they were denied (cf. ch. xliii. 2, etc.). They escaped none of the evil they dreaded; they gained none of the good they expected. "So disastrous did this step appear to the next and to all subsequent generations of Israel, that the day of Gedaliah's murder, which led to it, has been from that time forth and to this day observed as a national fast. It seemed to be the final revocation of the advantages of the Exodus. By this breach in their local-continuity a chasm was made in the history, which for good or evil was never filled up." Yes; they who will go so near temptation will go into it, and be borne down by it to their sore hurt and harm.

V. THE REMEDY RECOMMENDED. Jeremiah urged them to return to their own land and stay there (ch. xlii. 8, etc.), promising them the blessing of God if they obeyed, and threatening his sore anger if they did not. This counsel ever wise. Get away from the border-land back into safety. Think of what will follow on your conduct—the blessing or the curse. "Stay not in all the plain, but escape for thy life." As "the angels hastened Lot," so would we hasten all those who have foolishly and wrongly chosen to go too near temptation's edge.—C.

Vers. 1—18.—*A great crime and its consequence.* I. A GREAT CRIME. The slaying of Gedaliah was accompanied by circumstances making it peculiarly atrocious. 1. *The breach of good fellowship.* There had been professions of amity before. Gedaliah shows by deed his confidence in Ishmael, sitting down with him at a common meal. 2. *The subsequent slaughter.* The slaying of Gedaliah was not enough to serve the purpose. A man, once entered on the ways of crime, cannot say, "So far I will go, and no further." Ishmael had to go on killing to secure his own safety and mastery.

II. THE CONSEQUENCE. The chief consequence was the departure to a point nearer to Egypt, to escape if possible the vengeance of the Chaldeans. One man sins and other people suffer. The great lesson is to stop crime in its beginnings. Ishmael gained none of the ends he seems to have had in view, and was this much the worse, that he had deep stains of murder on him.—Y.

EXPOSITION.

CHAPTER XLII.

Jeremiah receives a request to inquire of God concerning the proposed emigration, and a "word of the Lord" follows.

Ver. 1.—**Jezaniah the son of Hoshaiah.** For "Jezaniah," the Septuagint has "Azariah," the name given in the Hebrew text of ch. xliii. 2.

Ver. 2.—**Said unto Jeremiah the prophet.** Jeremiah, we have been already told, was one of the refugees at Mizpah (ch. xl. 6), and consequently was forced into the train of Ishmael (ch. xli. 16). **Pray for us.** This petition has been accused of hypocrisy, but the prophecy of Jeremiah assumes throughout that it was made in earnest (ver. 20 proves nothing to the contrary). The "captains" never supposed it possible that Jeremiah could direct them to stay in Judah; the only question with them was as to the best direction for flight.

Ver. 5.—**A true and faithful witness between us;** rather, *against us.* If they broke their promise, Jehovah was to "witness against" them by punishing them.

Ver. 7.—**After ten days.** Why this delay? Keil thinks it was for the sake of the people, who needed time to collect themselves and listen calmly to the revelation. Ezekiel once waited seven days (iii. 16); but this was owing to his own disturbed

state of mind. The answer of the Lord extends to ver. 18, the last four verses being an epilogue enforcing the Divine declaration. It consists of the promise (vers. 9—12) that, if the people will remain quietly in the land, they will be protected; and of the threat (vers. 13—18) that, if they presume to migrate into Egypt, they will perish there by sword, famine, and pestilence.

Ver. 10.—**Build you, and not pull you down,** etc. Some of Jeremiah's favourite phrases (see on ch. xxiv. 6). **I repent me.** And yet in 1 Sam. xv. 29 we read that "Israel's Trust . . . is not a man that he should repent." The key to the discrepancy may be found in Ps. xviii. 25, 26, "With the pious thou showest thyself pious, . . and with the froward thou showest thyself froward." There is no change in the nature or purpose of God, but only in his conduct towards man. The term "repent" is, therefore, only used analogically.

Ver. 12.—**I will show mercies unto you;** rather, *I will procure you mercy.* **And cause you to return to.** As if the journey to Bethlehem were a virtual Exodus. But it is far more natural to read the consonants of the text in a slightly different manner, rendering, "and cause you to dwell in." So the Syriac, the Vulgate, and Aquila.

Ver. 15.—**And now therefore.** Omit "and;" the *vau* simply marks the apodosis of the two previous verses.

Ver. 16.—**The sword, which ye feared**; rather, *which ye fear*. The calamities mentioned were precisely those of which the Jews were apprehensive in their own country. So afterwards, "whereof ye are afraid." **Shall overtake you there.** For a further explanation, see ch. xliii. 8—13.

Ver. 20.—**For ye dissembled in your hearts**; rather, *for ye have gone astray (from the right path) at the risk of your lives*; or, another possible rendering, *for ye have led yourselves astray*. Hypocrisy is certainly not the accusation which Jeremiah brings against the people.

HOMILETICS.

Vers. 1—6.—*Taking counsel with God.* I. TROUBLE DRIVES MEN TO PRAYER. In their trouble "all the people, from the least even unto the greatest," sought help from God through the prayers of Jeremiah. In deep distress there are common wants of humanity, which touch alike the prince and the peasant. Then one common cry will burst from all lips to the God of all flesh. The beggar and the king in their agony utter the same moan, "My God!" There was but "a remnant" of the Jews left in the land. All these united to seek counsel of God. United prayer is prevailing prayer. If we are few, the more reason we should be united, and the more reason that each of us should come forward and do his part. If a congregation is small, it can the less afford that any one member should be prayerless or idle.

II. IN PERPLEXITY WE SHOULD SEEK LIGHT FROM GOD. His Spirit is a Spirit of light. We have a right to expect guidance because we have Divine assurances of this (Ps. xxxii. 8). God will guide us, however, through our own thinking, and not by audible voices, nor should we look for the direction in mystic inward impressions, the origin and character of which we cannot test. God has given us eyes, and he expects us to use them. His guidance is the purging of our vision, that we may see the better with our own organs of sight; the rectifying and strengthening of our intelligence and conscience, that we may use these as right instruments for discerning truth.

III. CHRISTIAN MEN SHOULD PRAY FOR OTHERS. Every Christian has now the privilege of being a prophet (Joel ii. 28) and a priest (Rev. i. 6). Every Christian, therefore, has the responsibility which accompanies his privilege, and is required to act as the intercessor for others. Are we not too selfish in our prayers? Nevertheless it must be remembered that men gain little good from the prayers of others unless they will also pray for themselves. The worst man is not left dependent on the intercession of good men. Through Christ he may approach the heavenly throne with his own cry for mercy.

IV. IT IS THE DUTY OF THOSE WHO ARE CONSULTED TO GIVE PAINFUL AS WELL AS PLEASANT ADVICE. Jeremiah warned the people that he would "keep nothing back." The seeming kindliness that restrains the utterance of unpleasant but important home-truths is really only a cloak for selfishness. The preacher must not shun to declare the whole counsel of God—the hard sayings of Scripture, the unpopular doctrines of Christianity, the unflattering truths of human nature.

V. IF WE TAKE COUNSEL WITH GOD, WE MUST CONSENT TO OBEY HIM. Otherwise our prayer is a mockery; for God is not an Oracle, but an Authority. What he reveals is not merely hidden mystery, but obligations of duty. He guides us to his will. It is our place to follow the guidance and do what is thus not only declared, but commanded.

Ver. 3.—*Divine guidance.* I. THE NEED OF DIVINE GUIDANCE. 1. It arises out of our *obligation to do the will of God.* We are not left to carve out a career for ourselves, but to fulfil a Divine vocation. With this definite end before us, our life must fail unless we are directly making for it. A harmless life, following its own whims and fancies, is a wasted life. But only God knows his own will. Therefore we need that he shall reveal this to us, to show us, not only the path of safety, but the way he wills us to go. The most clear-sighted need this guidance. As servants, we wait for our Master's orders; as soldiers, we are to follow our Captain's commands. Without these, how can we do the one thing needful? 2. It arises out of our own *ignorance and blindness.* We do not know all the circumstances which surround us; we cannot predict the exigencies of the future; the ultimate issue of our actions is beyond our reckoning; the limits of our powers are not known to us; our future requirements and capacities cannot now be gauged. Yet we must decide and act at once in relation to all these unknown quantities. Therefore only a higher wisdom and a larger knowledge can secure us from fatal blunders.

II. THE METHOD OF DIVINE GUIDANCE. The Jews appealed to a prophet. We have no Jeremiah. Yet we have essentially the same means of guidance, now broken into two parts, for the higher education of our spiritual nature. 1. *The revelation of God's will and truth in Scripture.* There we have God's guidance in the words of the prophets, and in addition to that in the higher thought of the apostles of the New Testament and of Christianity. Above all, we have the great example, the speaking lessons, of the life and character of Christ, who is the "Light of the World." In all this we have larger, clearer views of God's will and of man's duty than were given to the Jews under the earlier dispensation. 2. *The light of the Spirit of God in our mind and conscience.* It may be urged that, while the instructions of the prophets for the guidance of Israel were definite and particular, the lessons which we may gather from revelation are general; and that, though the ideas of conduct thus communicated to us are higher and larger than those of the Jewish economy, they are nevertheless so abstract that we may make great mistakes in the practical application of them. This is true; and therefore, with the less particular revelation, God gives to us more light for the interpretation of it. We live under that dispensation of the Spirit wherein all Christians are, in a measure, prophets, and God's Spirit is poured out upon all flesh (Acts ii. 17). By God's light in our souls, interpreting God's revelation in Christ, we may know God's will concerning our lives; and, no longer slaves to the letter of unintelligible precepts, we may carry out the broad principles of the spiritual life by a thoughtful and conscientious application of them to the details of daily life.

III. THE USE OF DIVINE GUIDANCE. God reveals the way; we must walk therein. The direction may be so clear that he who reads may run, yet he must run. The sign-post is not a carriage to convey the indolent traveller to his journey's end. God reveals his will; he leaves it to our free choice and effort to obey it. He does not guide us, like the horse or mule, with bit and bridle. We are not forced to follow the revelation, but we are bound in moral obligation to do so. The main object of the revelation of truth is to guide us in practice. God enlightens our darkness that we may gird up our loins and walk in his ways.

Vers. 5, 6.—*Implicit obedience.* The people swear to obey the voice of God before they know what injunctions it will lay upon them. They contemplate the possibility of receiving unpleasant commands; but they leave the decision in the hands of God, undertaking to follow it, whatever form it may take. Thus they bind themselves to implicit obedience. Let us consider the obligation and the limitation of implicit obedience.

I. THE OBLIGATION OF IMPLICIT OBEDIENCE. This requires us to obey the voice of God when it calls us to do anything within the range of right and possibility; *i.e.* anything which a wise and good God would ever command. It implies a possible conflict with our inclination, our opinion, or our worldly interest. Otherwise the obedience becomes a mere form. If we only obey when we like to do the thing required, we are not really obeying a higher will, but simply following out our own will in accidental coincidence with the will above us. True obedience only begins when it leads us to do what our own wisdom or desire would not have prompted. It must, therefore, be prepared to run counter to these private tendencies. It must be the submission of our will and opinion to God's will and wisdom. Now, not only is this implicit obedience obligatory, but it is a certain fact that God will put it to the test. His higher will and larger wisdom must often conflict with our foolishness and self-will. Moreover, amid the trials of life, God will certainly sometimes require us to do what seems evil to us, *i.e.* what is painful and contrary to our wish. Therefore faith is essential to obedience. In so far as we can trust God, we shall be able to obey his darker counsels.

II. THE LIMITATION OF IMPLICIT OBEDIENCE. The highest obligation is to do right. If, therefore, we could be required by a supreme being to do what we knew was wrong, it would be our plain duty to disobey his will. The being who laid such a mandate upon us could not be God. He would be an almighty demon. Were such a monster to exist, it would be the duty of all creatures to resist him, though they became martyrs for their fidelity to righteousness. Our obligation to obey God rests on the fact that he is supremely good, and not merely on his infinite power and greatness. Let us suppose that we received a seemingly Divine mandate requiring what we felt to be wrong —what should we do? Three courses would then be open to us. We might believe that it emanated from a supreme being who was wicked, and should therefore be disobeyed; we might conclude that we were mistaken in supposing it to come from a supreme being—that we were suffering from a hallucination; or we might feel convinced that it was sent by the holy God, and that we were wrong in our impression of its unrighteous character. To Christians who believe in a perfectly good God, only the two latter alternatives could present themselves. But here the choice lies between the inward and the outward voice. If, then, the inward voice is clear and unmistakable, we are bound to give the preference to this. The outward voice claims to come from God; but so does the inward voice. If the two conflict, we must choose between them, and then we should feel that it is more likely we are suffering from a delusion in our external perceptions than that what we firmly believe in our conscience to be wrong is yet right. Loyalty to God will lead us to obey God's voice in the conscience above all things. At all events, so long as we believe—though even erroneously—that a thing is wrong to us, it is wrong, and no prophet's or angel's words should lead us to perform it without first convincing us that it is right.

Ver. 7.—*The answer to prayer delayed.* I. THE FACT. Ten days elapsed before Jeremiah was able to give an answer to the people. When Christ was asked to give his aid at the wedding feast where the wine ran short, he refused to do anything immediately (John ii. 4); and when summoned to the sick-bed of Lazarus, "he abode at that time two days in the place where he was" (John xi. 6). We must, therefore, expect that a similar delay may sometimes attend the answer of our prayers. Perhaps the interval will be much longer. We have cast our bread upon the waters, and it will not appear till after many days. We should learn, therefore, that prayer does not fail because the response is not immediate. Whatever be the delay, we may be sure that to a true prayer in Christ's Name the right answer will come at the right time. God is not dilatory. He will never wait beyond the very best season for acting.

II. THE CAUSE. Much of this is mysterious, and we must learn to accept the mysteries of Providence with faith in the unfailing love of God. But some grounds for the delay of God's answers to our prayers may be discerned and should be considered to check our impatience. 1. There is a *season* for everything. God will watch for the fitting opportunity, and send his blessing when it will be most profitable. 2. The fitness of God's answer to prayer depends on *our condition.* There are things which would injure us as we are. God waits to be gracious, waits till we are in a fit state to receive his grace. 3. Some things given as the answer to prayer *require time for development.* At the beginning of Daniel's prayer the angel was sent, but some time elapsed before the prophet received his message (Dan. ix. 23). God may set in train the actions which are in answer to our prayer immediately the prayer is made, and we may only be waiting for that result which could not come quicker. 4. Meanwhile God *tests our faith* by delaying the answer to our prayer. The time is not lost. It is profitably spent in the trial and culture of our own souls. So it is with the greatest blessing of the heavenly reward and with many lesser good things; God withholds them for a time that we may learn to walk by faith.

Vers. 9—12.—*The blessedness of patient endurance.* In answer to the appeal of the people for guidance, Jeremiah has to tell them that good will attend them so long as they stay in their land, but curses if they flee to Egypt. Hardships crowd upon them at present, and dangers threaten for the future. But if they will but endure these patiently, God will save and prosper them.

I. WHY THE PEOPLE WERE REQUIRED TO REMAIN IN THEIR LAND. 1. It was the *will of God.* When we know his will, if we know nothing more, that alone should be a final answer to all questions. Because he is our King we are bound to obey, and because he is our Father his will must be for our good. 2. It was the *course of faith.* Flight to Egypt was always regarded as a sign of distrust in God and reliance upon the arm of flesh. Repeatedly had the people been warned not to trust "upon the staff of this bruised reed, even upon Egypt, on which if a man lean, it will go into his hand, and pierce it : so is Pharaoh King of Egypt unto all that trust on him" (2 Kings xviii. 21). When Pharaoh takes the place of Jehovah, when any earthly judge is trusted rather than God, it will surely betray us. 3. It was a *safeguard for purity*. Egypt was a heathen power. An asylum in Egypt would bring temptations to immorality and unfaithfulness to the God of Israel. It is always unwise and wrong to run into temptation in order to escape from trouble. 4. It was a *sign of contentment*. It is happiest for a man to do his duty in that state of life into which it has pleased God to call him, though if God calls him out of one state to a more prosperous one, he may enjoy the greater comfort thus gained.

II. WHAT PROMISES WERE GIVEN TO THOSE WHO REMAINED IN THEIR LAND. 1. *Prosperity would be restored*. The troubles of God's people are transitory. Patient endurance will see the end of all of them. Then God will bring, not bare deliverance, but happiness and prosperity. The Jew looked for this in temporal concerns; the Christian expects it in eternal things. 2. *The people would be delivered from danger*. God would save them from the King of Babylon. And if this salvation was possible, shall we not believe that all other deliverances are possible, and rest calmly assured that to those who patiently and obediently submit to God no real harm can come ? Nebuchadnezzar may triumph insolently ; but God can cast him down to the level of the brutes. The lions may roar, but they are chained, or God will send an angel to shut their mouths.

III. WHAT ASSURANCES THE PEOPLE HAD THAT IT WOULD BE THUS WELL WITH THEM IF THEY REMAINED IN THEIR LAND. 1. They were assured of the *presence of God*. "I am with you" (ver. 11). If God is with us, we can dispense with the patronage of a Pharaoh, even though a Nebuchadnezzar is thundering at our gates. 2. They were assured of the *active help of God*. "I am with you—to save you." The very object of God's presence is his people's good. When present he does not only observe ; he acts, saves, delivers. 3. They were assured of the *continued mercy of God*. "I will procure you mercy" (ver. 12). 4. They were assured that *God would overrule their enemy and convert him into their friend*. Nebuchadnezzar should be made to have mercy upon the people. Thus what we most fear is led by God to work our good when we are obedient and submissive.

Ver. 19.—*Contradictory requirements*. The Jews were here required not to flee into Egypt. Joseph was warned by an angel in a dream to "arise, and take the young child and his mother, and flee into Egypt" (Matt. ii. 13). The Scriptures represent both commands as coming from God. Yet they are contradictory. This is but one instance of a discrepancy often to be met with. Let us consider the meaning of it.

I. DIVINE REQUIREMENTS MAY BE OUTWARDLY CONTRADICTORY AND YET CONSISTENT IN PRINCIPLE. In general principle what is right once is right eternally ; what is right for one man is right for all men ; what is right in one place is right everywhere. The moral laws of God are eternal, immutable, universal. They are as true in Sirius as on the earth, to angels and to demons as to men. But the application of these principles necessarily varies. 1. *The same act has a different character under different circumstances*. Egypt was an imposing heathen power in the days of Jeremiah ; it was but a Roman province in the time of our Lord. Flight to Egypt at the earlier time meant distrust in God and reliance on the arm of flesh ; no such alternatives accompanied the decision of Joseph. Thus it often happens that consistency to principle will permit and require great variations of conduct according to the changing necessities and dangers of life. 2. *The same act may have a different character with different persons*. Identical general moral obligations apply to all of us equally. But men have different duties in the carrying out of those principles, according to their constitutional differences of capacity and disposition. One man can stand on the verge of a precipice without a tremor, another turns giddy as he approaches it. For the one to be there is harmless, but it is most dangerous for the other. The first man may do what is no risk to him, but the second will be foolish and wrong if he follow his example. So there are scenes which afford temptation to some temperaments and none to others. The duty to avoid them must vary with this variation of danger. 3. *The same act may have a different character according as it is performed with a different motive.* Flight may denote cowardice or prudent caution. Passive endurance may be determined by weakness and indolence, or it may result from submissive trustfulness. II. THE OUTWARD CONTRADICTION OF DIVINE REQUIREMENTS WARNS US TO ESTIMATE ACTIONS SOLELY BY THEIR INNER CHARACTER. 1. We should be *careful not to condemn others* because their behaviour strikes us as superficially opposed to what is right from our own point of view. Their circumstances, character, and motives may be quite different from what we suspect. The man who is condemned as a miser may be wisely thrifty. He who is regarded as a meddlesome busybody may be conscientiously discharging what to him is a public duty. The seeming devotee of pleasure may be generously laying himself out to brighten the sad world with ministries of happiness to others. The apparently ambitious despot may be an enthusiast for the regeneration of humanity. 2. We must beware of the *slavish imitation* of the best examples. What was wise and right in them may be positively wrong in us. Even our imitation of Christ must be spiritual rather than external. Surely in calling us to follow him, he does not require us, like St. Francis, to become homeless wanderers, because the Son of man had not where to lay his head. Because he drove out the desecrators of the temple with violence, it may not be right for us to use similar violence, when what was done by him from pure zeal might only be followed by us with angry passions.

HOMILIES BY VARIOUS AUTHORS.

Vers. 1—6.—*Inquiring of God in great crises.* I. THE RIGHT AND DUTY OF IT. 1. *Because of his claim to respect and obedience.* It was a traditional custom in Israel. Jehovah was their national God. He had delivered them, created them into a nation, and laid them under eternal obligations. (1) There is a general obligation upon all so to do. Even those who do not recognize any special relation existing between God and themselves have reason for drawing nigh to him. There are moments when the things of life assert their sacredness and awful mystery, when God besets them behind and before. His providence is a continual appeal. And the sense of sin, of helplessness, and of indefinite hope leads them to his footstool. (2) It is specially incumbent upon those who are related to him through grace. Judah represented ancient Israel, and, although now but a remnant, was still privileged with the presence of a true prophet of God. Christians should be eager and ready to call upon him, as they have the promises reaffirmed in Christ, and the witness of his Spirit in their hearts that they shall not ask in vain. Their whole position is due to his grace, and it is but right that this should be acknowledged. 2. *Because of helplessness and danger.* The petitioners were "left but a few of many." They knew that it was through their own folly for the most part that they had been brought to such a pass. We know that in the great crises of life we are unable to guide ourselves. The future is dark and full of trouble. 3. *Because of God's wisdom, power, and love.* He knows all things, and is able to deliver from all evil; and he has assured us of his willingness to guide and protect. The larger, grander policy of life is only possible with his inspiration. II. THE SPIRIT IN WHICH IT SHOULD BE ENTERED UPON. 1. *Humility.* In external attitude and language they left little to criticize (ver. 2). Consciousness of our own need and weakness. 2. *Confidence.* We must believe that he is, and that he is a rewarder of all them that diligently seek him. Their requesting Jeremiah to pray to the Lord his God, and their expression of willingness to do as he should advise, showed a measure of faith. 3. *Obedience.* This they professed (ver. 6). 4. *Sincerity.* (Ver. 6.) III. THE DANGERS TO WHICH IT IS EXPOSED. Notwithstanding all their profession, we can detect: 1. *Signs of systematic neglect of God and religious ordinances.* The expression "came near" suggests a previous habitual distance from Jehovah. They appear more anxious to conciliate the prophet than him whom he served. There is no confession of sin. Probably Jeremiah had been all but ignored up to that time. What a strange phrase, "the Lord *thy* God"! The prophet seeks gently to lead them to a better standing—"the Lord *your* God;" which they seem to adopt. "*To whom we send thee*" still betrays the absence of filial love and intimacy. Their subsequent behaviour showed that: 2. *They were unreal and hypocritical in their whole attitude.*

They had made up their mind as to what was best for them to do, as the resort to the "habitation of Chimham" already proved. With one foot in Canaan, as it were, and another out of it, they pretended to inquire of God. This is a very common practice, but it is one which not only robs prayer of its meaning and efficacy, but also brings upon the head of those who are guilty of it a grievous curse, as in this instance. A portion of their prayer *was* answered, but in a way they little expected: "The Lord be a true and faithful witness between us."—M.

Vers. 19—22.—*Carnal predispositions.* I. THEY ARE THE GREAT SOURCES OF UNREALITY IN RELIGION. In sending Jeremiah to God they did not mean what they said. There was no honest willingness to do as the prophet might reveal. The only hope for them in their forlorn condition is thus tampered with and destroyed. It is possible that at first they may have meant well, but as they proceeded with their inquiry through the prophet they must have known that they had only one intention, which they had not laid aside or even held in abeyance. Yet such is the subtlety of the hypocritical heart that it continues in its hypocrisy until it deceives itself. "They inquire not to learn what is right, but only to receive encouragement to do what they wish."

II. THOSE WHO INDULGE THEM ARE THEIR OWN WORST ENEMIES. 1. *They deceive and injure themselves.* "Ye dissembled in your hearts" (ver. 20); literally, *deceived yourselves;* "used deceit against your souls" (margin). Thinking they were taking counsel of God, they were really obeying their fears and lusts. Can a greater wrong be done to one's self than this—to think one's self religious and obedient to the heavenly will when one is only selfish and sinful? Safety and happiness lay in following simply the Divine guidance; but this they could not do, for they knew not God's message when it came. "Thinking themselves wise, they became fools." Their spiritual nature is henceforth unreliable, and their greatest perils will be encountered in their most religious hours, and when they think themselves most in agreement with God's will. 2. *The curse of God is denounced against them.* What they choose will be their destruction. The very things they sought to avoid by going to Egypt are met there. And there is no mitigation; the position is one wholly wrong, and consequently the wrath of God is unceasing until they cease to occupy it. To remain in Egypt, with its idolatries and abominations, was virtually to annul the covenant. Soon every trace of true religion would disappear, and they would become like their neighbours, and be absorbed into the nations in whom God had no pleasure. He cannot tolerate falsehood, pretension, the form of godliness without the reality. And this severity is true mercy. Many a one "plucked as a brand from the burning" has had reason to thank his Saviour that "the way of transgressors is hard." "Let a man examine himself." "Be not deceived: God is not mocked."—M.

Ver. 1—ch. xliii. 7.—*Dissembling in prayer.* This section may teach us much on this very serious matter.

I. WHAT IT IS TO DISSEMBLE IN PRAYER. It is: 1. *To pray in a deliberately continued unregeneracy of heart.* The hearts of not a few of those Jews who now sought Jeremiah's prayers were deliberately held in a condition of disobedience. They had never really repented. How many such pray, but their prayer is a dissembling! 2. *When allowing ourselves in forbidden paths.* The Jews had no business on that border-land. It was a yielding to temptation to go there. So when we come from sin to the throne of grace, and go thence to sin again, this is, etc. 3. *When we are not setting ourselves to mortify our evil affections.* The Jews here showed no real, sincere intention to give up their own will and to obey God's. They would not have been on that border-land had such been the case. And so where there is no real striving against sin, this is, etc. 4. *When whilst we pray we regard iniquity in our heart.* That is to purpose and intend it; or to look upon it complacently and desiringly. The Jews, whilst praying to know God's will, were all the while looking with strong desire after what they knew was wrong. Like as when Balaam offered his many sacrifices, his heart was all the while going after its covetousness.

II. WHAT CAN LEAD MEN TO BE GUILTY OF SUCH DISSEMBLING? We should imagine they never could be; that the thing would be too outrageous, wicked, and absurd for any one to be guilty of. And yet there have been and are many such prayers. They may be partly explained by : 1. *The force of habit.* The locomotive, if left to itself, will run along the rails for considerable time and distance, slowing and stopping only very gradually, though the steam has been shut off the whole while. So those who have been wont to offer prayers will keep up the form and habit, though the heart be wanting. 2. *They may be themselves deceived.* Their strong desire for God's sanction might lead them to imagine they would gain it by their prayers. 3. *They would not break with God altogether*, and they deem that they can keep up their communications by such methods as these.

III. How PRAYERS ARE PROVED TO HAVE BEEN OF THIS EVIL CHARACTER. 1. *By anger at their refusal.* See how angry these Jews were. The state of mind with which we come away from our prayers will show much the true nature of those prayers. 2. *When we make them only through others.* The Jews left it to Jeremiah. So now men leave to their ministers or friends the prayers they profess to value. 3. *When they are followed by open and defiant disobedience.* So was it here (ch. xliii. 1—7). Nothing could more plainly have shown how hollow and insincere were their prayers. And so now, when men pray, and rise up and go and do worse than before, what can their prayers have been ?

IV. WHAT ARE THE RESULTS OF SUCH PRAYERS? They grieve the Spirit of God. They harden the heart, and tend to make men of a reprobate mind. Cf. our Lord's words to the Pharisees—the pattern dissemblers of his day. They pave the way to " the damnation of hell." Therefore—thus let us conclude—be our prayer, " Search me, O God, and try my heart," etc.—C.

Vers. 7—18.—*Man's utter dependence upon God.* These verses plainly show this much-forgotten but never-failing truth. They tell how the land of Judah, desolate, unprotected, and oppressed, could be and should be made a happy land for them. Whilst Egypt, the land they hoped so much from, should bring on them all the sorrows which they thought by going there to escape. Thus we are taught that it is according to God's favour our lives are blessed or unblessed, bright or dark. Mere circumstances are unable to ensure either the one or the other, but the presence or absence of God's favour alone. Now—

I. MEN DO NOT THINK THIS. See their frantic endeavours to make their circumstances pleasant. And how they struggle against adversity, as if all evil were contained in that! Their opinion is very clear.

II. BUT YET IT MUST BE. For : 1. Our happiness or unhappiness depends entirely *on the way in which we regard these circumstances.* That is to say, it depends upon our mind, upon that which is within us rather than that which is without. Hence what gives great pleasure to one yields none or even the reverse of pleasure to others. The merry laugh of children, *e.g.*, to one in deep sadness, or irritable, or discontented. And *vice versâ.* But : 2. *God has constant access to the minds of us all*, and he has made their satisfaction to depend upon him. " Nostrum cor inquietum est donec requiescat in te " (Augustine). He can flood them with joy in the darkest hour—Paul and Silas in the dungeon at Philippi ; and he can make the most favourable circumstances powerless to render a man happy—Haman because of Mordecai ; the conscience-stricken, those from whom for any cause he hides his face, are illustrations. And abundant facts prove the powerlessness of mere circumstance over the minds of men.

III. THE INFLUENCE THAT THESE CONSIDERATIONS OUGHT TO HAVE UPON US. 1. *Not to lead us to despise circumstances*, and so to be careless as to the outward lot of either ourselves or others. For though they have not all power over the mind, God has given them very much power—a power that they lose only when he pleases. 2. But *to estimate them rightly.* This we can only do as we bring into view the unseen and the eternal, which can only be as we live in view of it by the habit of prayer, thought, and practical regard to God's will as expressed in conscience and his Word. So shall our balances be adjusted, and we shall rightly judge. There is a machine employed at the Mint of such perfect accuracy and finish that, when a number of sovereigns are tested by it, it will automatically and instantly and infallibly reject every one that fails in the least degree to come up to the proper standard of weight. So if we thus bring into view the unseen and eternal, all the crowd of facts and events that come before us day by day will each one spontaneously, promptly, and infallibly be judged, and we shall neither under nor over estimate them but as we ought. 3. To seek above all things the favour of God; for "in his favour is life, and his loving-kindness is better than life itself."—C.

Vers. 1—6.—*Waiting on the Divine ordinance.* I. THE REQUEST OF THE PEOPLE. 1. *The apparent unanimity of it.* All the people come, from the least to the greatest. Certainly there were not very many of them. They were but a remnant to begin with, and now still further reduced. But such as they were, an outward unity obtained among them. Outward unity is often obtained with comparative ease, but it must not be forgotten that it may cloak indifference, discord, opposition, and may be followed by contradictory conduct, even on the part of those who make the largest professions of submission. 2. *The profession of submission to Jehovah.* The request described a real want, whether the people meant all they said or not. And there is no reason to suppose that they did not mean it at the present time of asking. Men ask sincerely enough for Divine guidance, not being able to see at the time how hard it will be to follow it up. They want to be shown a way in which to walk, and then, when the way is shown, it looks too hard and perplexed to be God's way. They want to be shown the thing to do, and, when it is shown, there appears to be no use in it, no obvious relation of means to ends. Here is a result of prophetic teaching. The people had learnt from many prophetic utterances what they ought to ask for. 3. *Their dependence on the prophet.* Here is man showing his need of mediation. The people had come to know at last that Jeremiah was the faithful and accepted servant of God. This is the best way of recognizing a good man—to ask him to help those in need. And they wished also to commend their desires to the prophet. They wished him to pray a prayer that should be his as well as theirs.
II. THE PROPHET'S ANSWER. That he complies with the request is little to say. The prayer was one he could pray with all his heart. Well would it have been if he had been asked to offer it years before. That which taxed him was to tell them that he would faithfully report the answer. For he knew that God's message would go deep into the necessities of the case; that God's answer could not be comprehended by the limits of man's desires. This is the temptation of messengers, to keep something back through fear, or expediency, or mistaken kindness. Now, Jeremiah was well assured from a long experience that Jehovah never said a word too many or too few. The genuine promptings of the Spirit of God are the very best guide as to what we should tell men in the hour of their need.
III. THE PROMISE OF THE PEOPLE. They seem to hint that they are ready for difficult and painful requirements. History is not lost upon them so far as their professions are concerned. They hint how they have learnt that disobedience to God brings the worst of evils. One thing, however, they had not yet learnt, and that was the difference between knowledge and power. When men are in great straits they will make large promises in the hope of deliverance; not at all insincerely, but meaning all they say. It was with the people here as it is with people in dangerous illnesses—the way of restored health is to be the way of obedience and piety. That people make such promises shows that the promises are right; the wrong thing is that they lack in strength, persistency, and inward purpose to keep them. God has to make this lack plain before men will humble themselves to have it supplied.—Y.

Vers. 7—12.—*Divine comforts for those in doubt and fear.* I. THE MEANING OF THE INTERVAL. There are ten days to wait between the prayer of Jeremiah and the answer of Jehovah. Why this waiting? It must have been in some way for the sake of the people. They had said very emphatically they would be obedient; would they be obedient to begin with, to the extent of waiting ten days for God's answer? It had also to be seen whether they would continue in the spirit of obedience at all; and would they *all* continue in the same spirit?
II. EVERYTHING DEPENDS ON THE DISPOSITION OF THE PEOPLE. God will do great things for them if only they do not destroy the effect of his actions by their self-will and instability. They were to show their trust in God by abiding in the land. Nothing could be done without this. God uses, to indicate his work for them, two words

which imply fixity—building and planting. Let *us* also recollect the greatness of God's power to them that believe. If we take no trouble to furnish the occasion, we must not complain.

III. The great work God is disposed to do. It is indicated by these two not infrequent figures of building and planting. God was willing to make these people his husbandry, his building (1 Cor. iii. 9). He had been lately engaged in a great pulling down and rooting up; and why? Because his people had been putting up the wrong buildings, planting the wrong plant. Every plant not planted by God must be rooted up. God is the Builder, not a mere helper in building. We may be said to be fellow-workers with God, but it can never describe him rightly to call him fellow-worker with us. The work and the glory are his of building up the holy character, the perfect manhood, the everlasting home. He it is who makes his people fruitful in every good word and work. And the way for all this building and planting was now clear so far as God himself was concerned. All the pulling down and rooting up was done. Only let the people give the needed opportunity and all else would prosper.

IV. Caution against needless fear. The temptation here, as so often, was to fear man too much and God too little or even none at all. "The fear of man bringeth a snare." The people feared the King of Babylon, forgetting the limits of his power and the way in which he was controlled by Jehovah.—Y.

Vers. 13—18.—*A land to be avoided.* How solemn and urgent this warning! Let us ask why it was needed, why God seemed thus to cast doubt on the power of the people to obey him.

I. The perilous land was near. They were right in the way to Egypt, having, indeed, moved Egyptwards rather than in any other direction (ch. xli. 17).

II. It had obvious attractions. 1. *It seemed to be a land of peace.* Egypt had been looked to as a friend and ally. The desolation of Jerusalem had come from the north. When people have been going through a time of war and siege, peace is naturally the blessing put in front of their thoughts. And is not this a good thing, it may be asked? Yes, surely, if peace be desired on high grounds, and from a horror of discord among men. But men may seek it simply to escape from disturbance and from loss of life and property. Their seeking of peace may be a sign of cowardice and altogether grovelling aims. Danger may be escaped by the outer man, only to be concentrated more effectually on the man within. 2. *It would be a land of bread.* Another recommendation of a land which it was unquestionably right for men to attend to. Egypt was one of the great granaries of the ancient world. But it did not therefore follow that it was a land to live in. Israelites, in particular, needed to recollect how their fathers, beginning by going to Egypt for bread, ended by sinking into most oppressive bondage. Besides, even the land of bread was at times a land of famine. 3. *It consequently looked a land to dwell in.* God is the God of his people only when they are in their proper place. He was God of the exiles in Babylon, because their going into Babylon was of his operation. But those who went to Egypt in search of mere immunity from toil and inglorious ease could not expect to have the Divine favour. They wanted to get the great ends of life without discipline, sacrifice, and endurance.

III. The vain purpose to escape from evil. God tries to make the people understand that they take the germs and principles of evil with them. What we find in any place depends on what we bring; and what we bring we must, in process of time, inevitably find. What had there been to hinder the land of Israel from being a land of peace and a land of bread? Nothing but the faithlessness and general wickedness of the people. We cannot sow wickedness in one place, and then hope to go and reap only good things in some other place. God can turn any place, however fruitful, into a wilderness; and, on the other hand, we know how Jesus made a wilderness a place to feed five thousand men. Jehovah spoke with all this severity to these people to make them understand how hard a thing real obedience was.—Y.

Vers. 19—22.—*Searching the heart.* There is here a very sudden and striking turn away from the tone of the previous part of the message. God looks into the future, and, seeing what actually will happen, seeing that Egypt will maintain its attraction, he warns the people they are going towards a certain doom.   Their present state was one of undue, overweening self-confidence; and God will not allow people to remain under deception as to their own weakness, if a startling and abrupt message will serve to arouse them from it.   Perhaps we shall not be far wrong in assuming that the changing tone of the prophecy is occasioned by the changing mood of the audience.   While the prophet is speaking of the dangers of Egypt, their deep desire after Egypt is half revealed.   The one gate into which they wished to enter is peremptorily closed against them.   All at once there may have been a sort of awakening to the fact that God knew their hearts better than they did themselves.   We must recollect, too, that Jeremiah spoke out of no short or imperfect experience.   He saw that the people were disappointed; that, instead of a word pointing them towards Egypt, there was sentence upon sentence warning them against it.   How hard it is to be sure of knowing the will of God! How easy to mistake for it the impulses of indulgent human prudence! God tells the people plainly they are going to seek for things they will never find.   Instead of living in peace, they are to die by the sword.   Instead of getting abundance of bread, they are to die by famine and by the pestilence that accompanies lack of bread.   Here altogether is an example of the need of that prayer in Ps. cxxxix. 23, 24.—Y.

EXPOSITION.

CHAPTER XLIII.

The flight to Egypt; Jeremiah's prediction of Nebuchadnezzar's conquest of Egypt.

Ver. 2.—**All the proud men.** It would seem as if the "proud men" were distinguished from others.   Jeremiah had called the whole people together (ch. xlii. 8); but a few domineering men assumed to represent the rest.

Ver. 3.—**Baruch the son of Neriah setteth thee on.** A singular supposition—Jeremiah leaving the initiative to his secretary!   It may be conjectured that Baruch had somehow made himself specially unpopular; he may have been a more practical man (comp. ch. xlv. 5) than Jeremiah.

Ver. 5.—**All the remnant of Judah, that were returned from all nations.** The specification is peculiar, as it seems to leave out of sight the most important part of the gathering at Mizpah, viz. the "men, and women, and children, and those of the poor of the land" (ch. xl. 7)—the very persons who are mentioned just afterwards.   Possibly there is some confusion in the text. "All nations" doubtless means especially Moab, Ammon, and Edom.

Ver. 7.—**Tahpanhes.** An Egyptian frontier city (see Ezek. xxx. 18 and note on ch. ii. 16), where the fugitives had to wait till the views of the Egyptian government respecting them were made known.   The supposed site of the Pelusiac Daphnæ has not yet been explored; a single inscribed fragment would reveal the Egyptian name, and probably ratify the identity of Daphnæ with the Tahpanhes of the prophets (R. S. Poole, 'The Cities of Egypt,' p. 177).

Ver. 9.—**Take great stones,** etc. A strange symbolic act of Jeremiah's is here described. "We must not suppose, arguing from our Western and precise notions, that he would be at all necessarily interfered with.   In fact, he would have a twofold security, as a prophet of God to those who acknowledged him as such, and in the opinion of others as insane, and, according to Eastern ideas, thus especially under Divine promptings in his acts" (Streane).   He is directed to take great stones and embed them in the mortar (not "clay") in the brick pavement at the entry of the palace.   When the events predicted came to pass, these stones would testify that Jeremiah had predicted them.   The word rendered "brick pavement" is of doubtful meaning.   In Nah. iii. 14 it signifies "brick-kiln."

Ver. 10.—**And will set his throne,** etc.; viz. for the victorious king to hold judgment (comp. ch. i. 15, 16; xlix. 38).   **He shall spread his royal pavilion**; rather, *his tapestry* (the root means "brilliance"); *i.e.* the bright-coloured covering of the throne.

Ver. 11.—**He shall smite the land of Egypt.** On the invasion of Egypt by Nebuchadnezzar, wrongly controverted by some, see note on ch. xlvi. 13.   **Such as are for death.** Such as are destined for death (*i.e.* pestilence, as ch. xv. 2; xviii. 21).   The words, "and deliver," prefixed in the Authorized Version, are unnecessary; "land" is equivalent to "population."

Ver. 12.—**Burn them**; viz. the temples.   Egypt was full of gorgeous and imposing temples, which could not, however, always be burned, nor were the conquerors of Egypt anxious to display hostility to Egyptian religion.   **Carry them away captives**; viz. the idol-gods (comp. ch. xlviii. 7, "Chemosh shall go forth into captivity;" and Isa. xlvi. 2, "Their soul [or, ' personality '] hath gone into captivity"). The prophet speaks from the point of view of a believer in the idol-gods. **He shall array himself with the land of Egypt**, etc. (For "array himself with" and "putteth on," read *wrap himself in* and *wrappeth himself in*.) Ewald well explains this figure. "As easily as the shepherd in the open field wraps himself in the cool night in his mantle, will he be able to grasp Egypt with his hand and fling it round him like an easily managed garment, in order then to leave the land as an absolute conqueror, clothed in this attire of booty, in peace, without an enemy."

Ver. 13.—The images of Beth-shemesh;

rather, *the pillars of Beth-shemesh;* i.e. the obelisks of the temple of Ra, the sun-god, from which Heliopolis derived its sacred name "Pe-Ra" "the abode of Ra." It was the custom to place obelisks in pairs at the entrance of their temples. Only one of those of Heliopolis is still standing, though that, indeed, is the oldest in Egypt, for it was "set up at least four thousand years ago" (R. S. Poole, ' The Cities of Egypt,' p. 131). **That is in the land of Egypt.** To distinguish it from the Beth-shemesh in Palestine. But we may also render "which are," etc.; comp. "the gods of Egypt" in the second verse-half. The Septuagint reads, "which are in On."

HOMILETICS.

Ver. 2.—*Moral causes of unbelief.* The causes of unbelief may be either intellectual or moral. It is not just to assume that they are of the latter character. There is an honest doubt, and many a brave soul has been forced to fight its way over a wild desert of difficulties before seeing the light of Divine revelation. Nevertheless, it is necessary for our own warning and in controversy with others to remember that there are moral causes for unbelief, and that in some cases these may be much more operative than any purely intellectual consideration. Azariah and his friends have discovered no good ground for doubting the Divine authority of Jeremiah's message. They have seen nothing to detract from the claims of the prophet and nothing to contradict what he says. Yet they reject his message and charge him with falsehood. The palpable explanation of their conduct may serve to explain the ground of much unbelief in our own day. In the main this consists in two things.

I. THE UNPOPULARITY OF THE DOCTRINE. Jeremiah had run counter to the determination of the leaders of the people. Instead of modifying their conduct in obedience to the Divine message, they preferred to reject the message and deny its authority. This was most irrational. Yet it is a sample of the commonest conduct. People test their creed by their will instead of their reason and conscience and its own evidences. They say they do not *like* certain ideas, as though truth were a matter of taste. But truth is the statement of facts, and facts are not altered by sentiments. In the present instance the question was as to God's will. Was it not possible from the first that this might contradict the opinions of the people? Otherwise what was the use of the prayer for direction, that these very men had asked Jeremiah to offer, and the reply to which was his unpopular message? If God's will and truth always agreed with our private notions, what would be the good of revelation and commandment? It is in the conflict of the two that the chief value of the Divine message is to be found.

II. THE PRIDE OF MAN. We are expressly told that they were "proud men" who rejected the prophet's message. The rest of the people seem to have been willing to acquiesce in it. There is nothing so blinding as pride. Your proud man is an inevitable bigot. By undue assurance of knowledge he closes the avenues of fresh knowledge and limits his own possession of it. Thus pride cuts away the ground beneath its own feet.

Ver. 3.—*The credulity of unbelief.* I. UNBELIEF INVOLVES CREDULITY. Johanan and his companions here bring before us a striking instance of the credulity of unbelief. Refusing to admit that Jeremiah was divinely inspired, they asserted that he was instigated by Baruch the scribe. Now, we have seen Baruch acting solely as the amanuensis and spokesman of the prophet—indeed, effacing himself with genuine humility and wisdom to serve the prophet the more faithfully; could this man be the inspirer of his master's most decided utterances? The idea is preposterous. It is an evidence of gross credulity—the credulity that believes in one's own inventions, though they are infinitely less reasonable than the opposite ideas they are set up to oppose. All unbelief is belief —it is belief in the negation of a proposition, and it requires as much evidence as the proposition it denies. It also has its consequences in reason which should be followed out remorselessly. Defenders of the faith have been too apologetic. They would often have been wiser if they had turned the flank of opponents and exposed the weakness of their position. It might often be shown that, in accepting this position, the opponents were standing on less firm ground than that which they dispute. For something must be true. If we came down to absolute nihilism, and discovered that nothing existed, even that discovery would be a truth. The absolute rejection of one proposition involves the acceptance of its opposite. But this opposite may be beset with heavier difficulties or favoured with weaker evidences than those which accompany the rejected proposition. If so, to accept the opposite proposition is really a mark of greater credulity than to admit that which presented the first claims.

II. THE CREDULITY OF UNBELIEF MAY BE ILLUSTRATED IN THE CONTROVERSIES OF THE AGE. Consider it in relation to the main topics of these controversies, viz.: 1. *The being of God*. If there be no God, then the world must be eternal or self-created —conclusions which may be shown to leave more difficulties than the hypothesis of a Creator—and all the best thoughts of the highest orders of minds must be misconceptions—a strange result for those who would regard the mind of man as the highest existence in the universe. 2. *The immortality of the soul*. Difficulties beset the theory of immortality. But what greater difficulties they have to face who, first believing in God (and we now have a right to start from that position), hold that the deepest appetite of man is destined never to be satisfied, that his highest aspirations are directed to an impossibility, and that his greatest powers are doomed to be blighted before they have grown to their full development? What credulity is required to make us believe that a good God could create a Tantalus! 3. *The inspiration of the Bible*. If the Bible be not inspired of God, the first literature of the world, containing by far its deepest, wisest, purest thoughts, and exercising unbounded influence for good, is founded on a delusion or a lie; for the writers of the Bible plainly claim to be inspired. 4. *The Divine origin of Christianity*. Christianity is the greatest fact in history; it revolutionized the decaying life of the old world, and gave a fresh upward movement to humanity; it is now the leading factor in the highest life of the foremost races of mankind; and it claims to be Divine. It seems to some of us that to say this claim is false, and thus to force upon us the inevitable alternative that its founders were deluded, and that it is a mere growth of human thought and effort, requires a faith which is so irrational as to be justly characterized as credulity.

Vers. 8—13.—*Prophetic stones*. Jeremiah planting stones at the entrance of Pharaoh's palace was prophesying by act. The stones were mute prophecies interpreted by the verbal prophecies which in turn they were to confirm in the future. These prophetic stones have their lessons for us.

I. DIVINE PURPOSES ARE FIRM AND PERMANENT. They are like the great stones. Words are but air-waves; to the incredulous the strongest words may be mere sound and fury, signifying nothing; they melt as they fall. But in the stone we have weight, massiveness, persistence, something that cannot be blown aside with a breath, which will not fade with time, which may be handled, and which remains after it is forgotten, and can be exhumed after being buried. Such is a Divine purpose—thus solid and thus enduring.

II. DIVINE PURPOSES MAY BE HIDDEN UNTIL THE TIME FOR THE EXECUTION OF THEM. Jeremiah hides the stones. There are prophecies which have been uttered once, and the method of executing them kept secret from us until they are fulfilled. But many Divine purposes are never known till they are accomplished.

III. EARTHLY THRONES ARE SET UP ON FOUNDATIONS OF DIVINE APPOINTMENT. Jeremiah lays the foundation of a throne (ver. 10), and he does this as a servant of God executing his will. All earthly power rests ultimately upon a Divine sanction. Yet this fact does not diminish the human responsibility of those who exercise it. The prophet planted the stones; he did not erect the throne. Nebuchadnezzar would be responsible for the throne he set up, the way he established it, and the use he made of it.

IV. GOD EMPLOYS HUMAN INSTRUMENTS IN THE EXECUTION OF HIS JUDGMENTS. Nebuchadnezzar is God's servant. There is a Divine economy in this. If evil cannot be stayed without the withdrawal of those liberties that God sees it to be right to leave intact, the harm of it may be mitigated by making it self-counteractive, the wickedness of one hindering or punishing that of another.

V. FLIGHT FROM THE JUDGMENT OF GOD IS IMPOSSIBLE. The Babylonian yoke was a Divine chastisement upon the Jews. They were urged by inspired prophets to submit to it as appointed by God. Some refused and fled to Egypt. But in Egypt they were neither out of the reach of God nor beyond the power of his instrument Nebuchadnezzar. There is no escape from God but by fleeing to God, no deliverance from the doom of sin but in submission to him against whom we have sinned.

VI. COMPANIONS IN GUILT WILL BE COMPANIONS IN DOOM. The Jews who fled to Egypt were to share the punishment of that nation. The Egyptians who harboured the Jews were to bring upon themselves the fate that followed the refugees.

HOMILIES BY VARIOUS AUTHORS.

Vers. 8—13.—*The stones of Tahpanhes.* Great uncertainty as to the fulfilment of this prophetic parable. Are we bound to assume that it was actually carried out? It is possible, according to some critics (but see Exposition on ch. xlvi. 13), that the accomplishment of the prediction, as of many others, was only contingent. It is very vivid and definite, but that is quite consistent with the intermediate occurrence of circumstances in the spiritual state of the Jewish sojourners that enabled God to cancel it. Just as at this time their disposition may have been alarmingly idolatrous and worldly, so at a later stage it may have changed.

I. WHAT THE PARABLE MAY HAVE SUGGESTED. 1. *The contingent certainty of Divine judgment.* The action may have represented, not only the sequence of events, but that of principles. If, then, the events did not occur, it would still remain true that, in the kingdom of God, such a dependence of principles is eternal; sin is ever nigh to cursing. So much is this the case, that it may be said to contain the elements of its own punishment, like the stones hidden in the clay. (1) The stones are hidden in the clay with which, although heterogeneous, they stand in a divinely appointed relation. (2) The interpretation given by the prophet further strengthened this impression in the minds of the spectators. It was the same power, viz. the Chaldean, which had already scourged Judah, that was to follow the remnant into distant Egypt. The continuity of the judgment with those which preceded it is thus forcibly set forth. Nebuchadnezzar, if or when he came, could not be mistaken for other than a divinely ordained instrument of vengeance. The advantage of such an understanding of the prophecy is obvious—it ceases to have a particular and transitory significance, and becomes at once necessary and universal. We need that lesson graven upon our hearts to-day: "The soul that sinneth it shall die;" "He that soweth to the flesh," etc. 2. *That dependence upon any earthly power is utterly vain.* Egypt is dreamt of as a refuge from their woes. Its power, typified by the clay of the kiln or brick-field, only overlies the power of God, typified by the stones. They would be in his hands still, although they knew it not. Through the clay of worldly dependence they must needs fall upon the stones of Divine judgment. Man cannot flee from his Maker. There is no earthly security from the consequences of sin. If the remnant of Judah, pursuing its tendency towards worldly mindedness and idolatry to the bitter end, should persist in putting its trust in the Egyptian power, to whose religion and life it was in such imminent danger of assimilating itself, woe to it! Through Pharaoh even will they be confronted with Nebuchadnezzar yet again. God is the only true Helper and Saviour, and in the practice of holiness and the precepts of true religion is security alone to be found. What assurance company can shield the sinner from the consequences of his misdeeds? And if God be for any man, who can be against him?

II. WHAT THE PARABLE MAY HAVE EFFECTED. It has been conjectured (by Naegelsbach and others) that the symbolic action of Jeremiah and its interpretation so forcibly appealed to the imagination and conscience of the Jews as to change their hearts. That some such consequence as this was intended seems very probable. If it resulted

as they suppose, then the judgment was averted which depended upon their misconduct and worldliness. "God repented him of the evil." This is one of the great
aims of such teaching—so to affect the heart through the imagination as to subdue
its evil tendencies and lead it to the pursuit of righteousness and truth. The
crowded Jewish colony of Alexandria may then be taken, not as a refutation of the
words of Jeremiah, but as a proof that these words produced their legitimate impression, and brought about a deep and lasting reformation. The lesson of all which is
that the relation between sin and its punishment, and the futility of earthly securities
and screens from Divine vengeance, cannot be too forcibly represented. God will
bless the faithful preaching of his Word, and is infinitely more willing to have mercy
than to prove his predictions by allowing men to harden their hearts.—M.

Vers. 1—13.—*Hearts set to do evil.* Such were the hearts of these Jews. They
show concerning such—
I. THAT AFFLICTION WILL NOT ALTER THEM. It is not always true that affliction
will make the heart better. It serves this blessed end with some—cf. "Before I was
afflicted I went," etc.—but not with all. Did not in this case, but though "often
reproved," they only "hardened their neck."
II. PRAYERS AND PROFESSION OF RELIGION DO NOT CONTROL THEM. They can go
together. Alas! that it should be so; but they will not rule. They are but so many
cobwebs, which the heart set to do evil will break through as easily as a man
breaks through the gossamer filaments which stretch across the path on which he is
walking.
III. PRETEXTS AND PRETENCES ARE ALWAYS READY TO EXCUSE THEM. "Thou
speakest falsely," they said to God's prophet. "Baruch . . . hath set thee on." *So,*
so pitifully, they try to justify themselves.
IV. GOD DOES NOT INTERFERE TO PREVENT THEM. We often wish he would, depriving us of our liberty when it would only do us ill. But his method is to let us go
our own ways, and if, as is so wretchedly often the case, they be evil ways, then,
when we are filled with the fruit of them, we may come to a better mind, and so
more firmly choose the good which we should have chosen at the first. How much
happier a man for ever that younger son would have been if he had never previously
left his father's home for that far country!
V. TERRIBLE JUDGMENTS ARE SURE TO FOLLOW THEM. They did in this case; they
always do sooner or later. For the will *must* bend to God.
VI. GOD'S FAITHFUL SERVANTS WILL NOT BE DISMAYED BY THEM. See how bold as
a lion is the prophet of God; how fearlessly he denounces his people's sin. Oh, for
fidelity such as that in all the prophets of the Lord!—C.

Vers. 8—13.—*Building on the sand.* The Jews trusted in the strength of Pharaoh.
They had done this before, but to no purpose. The prophets of God always protested
against such trust (cf. Isa. xxxi.). Here, in spite of all warning, they are resolving
upon such reliance again. But they were building on sand. The destruction came;
the very destruction they thought, by their acting as they had done, they had
certainly escaped. Thus do and shall be done by all who are like them. Such are—
I. They that think to establish themselves by wicked ways.
II. Those that rely upon men and not on God.
III. Those that trust to uncertain riches.
IV. Those that think saying "Lord, Lord," whilst living ungodly lives, will save
them.—C.

Ver. 1.—*The view of a prophet's complete work.* I. A PROPHET IS ONE WHO HAS
TO SPEAK THE WORDS OF JEHOVAH. Not his own words, not the words of other
men. This applies to the substance of the message; for it is plain that each prophet
has his own style. The chief thing to be remembered is that a prophet never goes
forth on his own impulse. Men in their zeal for right may go out to protest against
wrong and fight against it, but this does not make them prophets. The prophet's
strength and claim and responsibility lie in this, that he can ever preface his announcements by "Thus saith the Lord." And all preachers and teachers will approach the

prophet's position just in proportion to the extent in which they can fill their addresses with Divine declarations. The essential elements of prophecy can never be out of place.

II. HE HAS TO SPEAK ALL THE WORDS OF JEHOVAH. The prophet is not to be an eclectic, picking out some of God's words as suitable and others as unsuitable. God's omniscience can alone judge what is suitable. If to him it seems suitable a word should be spoken, then it is suitable. God speaks not to apparent needs, but to real ones. God, always saying something for the present, makes his weightiest words to bear upon the future. The responsibility of the prophet is simply that of being a brave and faithful messenger.

III. HE IS SENT TO SPEAK THESE WORDS. He does not merely take up words of Jehovah which he thinks suitable for the emergency. This is his work to act as a special messenger from Heaven. Others have to expound the Word already spoken, already written; but the prophet hears a voice directly from the excellent glory, "Go and make known my will to men." And in all prophecy there is evidence, to one who will look for it, that the prophet is a sent man.

IV. HE HAS TO SPEAK WORDS TO THOSE ON WHOM GOD HAS A CLAIM. Jehovah is not only the God of Jeremiah, he is the God of all the people. This was an historical fact of which they could not get rid. It was the glory, security, and blessing of the people, if only they could see it. And is not Jehovah also our God?—God coming for a while more closely in contact with one nation, that ultimately he may be in contact with all. If we admit the claim of Jesus, we admit the claim of Jehovah also. He speaks through ancient prophets to us, because the essentials of their message have to do with the permanent life of men.

V. HE SPEAKS TO ALL THE PEOPLE. In this particular instance the request came from all the people, so the message was correspondingly to all. Prophets, of course, had often messages for particular men, but even these messages are so founded upon general principles as to become worthy the attention of all. Prophecy concerns man as man; it meets the young with dawning consciousness, and grasps the old till their latest hour.

VI. THE PROPHET MUST TAKE CARE TO MAKE AN END OF HIS PROPHECY. He does not simply cease speaking; he has to make people feel he has said all he has to say, and that the time has come for them to have their say, or rather for them to enter with promptitude and devotion upon corresponding deeds. They may not hear all they would like to know, and thus it must be made clear they have been told all that it is good for them to know. With God all things are for edifying, not to inform curiosity or comply with every actual desire.—Y.

Vers. 8—13.—*The visitation upon Egypt.* Here again is one of the symbolic acts which the prophets were commanded at times to perform. So the hiding of the girdle by Euphrates (ch. xiii.), the commanded celibacy of the prophet (ch. xvi.), the dashing of the potter's bottle to pieces (ch. xix.). But while these symbolic acts are described in terms which make them perfectly clear, the hiding of the great stones mentioned here needs more full explanation than we can reach to get the significance it. Still, this much of the drift of the action we perceive that Jehovah will make quite manifest, that Nebuchadnezzar's conquest of Egypt is one divinely ordained and sustained. Not, of course, that Egypt is to suffer simply because these men have gone there; its idolatries are the deepest ground of its calamities. But the delusion of the men of Judah must be looked at in the light of the sufferings of Egypt. In all this experience of death and captivity and slaughter, of temple-burning and image-breaking; in all this entire appropriation of Egypt by the Babylonian king, these men of Judah must not expect to escape. There is no second land of Goshen for them—a place of immunity and peace. If only they had stayed where they thought there would be no safety, then they would have been safe; and going where they made sure of safety, they found the worst of ruin. It reads as if Egypt was to come under Babylon more even than Jerusalem had done.—Y.

EXPOSITION.

CHAPTER XLIV.

Jeremiah's debate with the Jewish fugitives in Pathros; his last prophecy.

Vers. 1—14.—Accusation brought against the obstinately idolatrous people.

Ver. 1.—**Which dwell**; rather, *which dwelt*. It appears from this verse that the Jewish fugitives had separated in Egypt, some going to the two northern frontier cities, Migdol (on which see R. S. Poole, 'The Cities of Egypt,' ch. viii.) and Tahpanhes or Daphnæ, others further south to Noph, *i.e.* Memphis, or, less probably, Napata (see on ch. ii. 16), and Pathros (*i.e.* Upper Egypt; comp. Isa. xi. 11).

Ver. 6.—**Was kindled in**; rather, *burned up*.

Ver. 7.—**Against your souls**; *i.e.* against yourselves. The "soul" is the personality.

Ver. 8.—**That ye might cut yourselves off**; rather, *that ye might cut (them) off from you*. Who are meant is clear from ver. 7.

Ver. 9.—**Have ye forgotten**, etc.? The prophet wonderingly asks if they have forgotten the sins of their forefathers and the consequent calamities. No other explanation of this present idolatry seems possible; and yet how passing strange is it! **Their wives.** The Hebrew has "his wives," *i.e.* according to Kimchi and Hitzig, the wives of each of the kings (sometimes great patrons of idolatry). But it is better to adopt, with Ewald, Graf, and Dr. Payne Smith, the reading of the Septuagint, "his princes."

Ver. 10.—**They are not humbled**; rather, *not made contrite* (literally, *not crushed*, viz. by repentance).

Ver. 11.—**To cut off all Judah**; *i.e.* the Judah in Egypt, not that in Babylon. Notice the qualification of this too absolute statement in vers. 14, 28.

Ver. 14.—**They have a desire**; literally, *they lift up their soul* (comp. ch. xxii. 27).

Vers. 15—19.—The reply of the people. The special mention of the women suggests that the occasion of the gathering was a festival in honour of the Queen of Heaven.

Ver. 15.—**Had burned incense**; rather, *were burning incense*. The practice was still going on.

Ver. 17.—**Whatsoever thing goeth forth**; rather, *the whole word which hath gone forth*. A particular vow to the divinity is meant. **The queen of heaven** (see on ch. vii. 18). **Then had we plenty of victuals,** etc. An extremely important passage, as revealing the view taken of their misfortunes by Jews of the average type. Jeremiah regarded the misfortunes of his country as proofs of the displeasure of Jehovah; these Jews, on the other hand, of his impotence.

Ver. 19.—This part of the reply belongs to the women, who declare that, their husbands' consent having been given to their vow, Jeremiah has no right to interfere (see Numb. xxx. 6, 7). **Burned ... poured,** etc.; rather, *burn ... pour*. **Did we,** etc.; rather, *do we*, etc. **To worship her.** The sense of the Hebrew is doubtful; but the best reading seems that of Rashi, Graf, and Dr. Payne Smith, "to make her image." **Without our men**; rather, *without our husbands*.

Vers. 20—30.—Jeremiah's rejoinder.

Ver. 21.—**Remember them**; *i.e.* the repeated acts of idolatry.

Ver. 25.—**With your hand**; rather, *with your hands*. **Ye will surely accomplish,** etc.; rather, *ye shall*, etc., *by all means perform your vows, and take the consequence*. The irony of the passage is lost by the "will" of the Authorized Version.

Ver. 26.—**My Name shall no more be named.** Because no Jews will be left alive in Egypt.

Ver. 28.—**Yet a small number,** etc. Isaiah's doctrine of the remnant. In the midst of judgment, God remembers mercy, and his ancient covenant. A remnant is saved as the nucleus of a regenerate people.

Ver. 29.—**A sign**; rather, *the sign*.

Ver. 30.—**I will give Pharaoh-hophra,** etc. The sign consists in the capture of Hophra by his deadly enemies. Henceforth he will live in constant alarm, for he is in the hands of those "that seek his life." All that we know of the fate of Hophra (Apries) is derived from Herodotus (ii. 169), who states that Amasis "gave Apries over into the hands of his former subjects, to deal with as they chose. Then the Egyptians took him and strangled him" (see further on ch. xlvi. 13).

HOMILETICS.

Vers. 1—10.—*Warnings from the past.* History has its moral lessons. We who are heirs of the ages should learn wisdom from the mistakes as well as from the good examples of the past. Let us consider how this may be done.

I. WARNINGS FROM THE SIN OF THE PAST. Jeremiah calls upon the Jews in Egypt to reflect on the wicked conduct of their nation, tracing it back from the present through successive generations of iniquitous court and private life. It is a gloomy task, but a wholesome one. Tacitus was, perhaps, the greatest moralist of his age, because he saw into the moral side of history, and ruthlessly exposed the vice and cruelty and treachery which underlay the splendour of Roman imperialism. Because we can read history with some measure of detachment from the passions and prejudices of the hour, we may learn to see therein the character of actions which are closely parallel to others nearer home. Thus the past may become a mirror of the present, and one that rectifies the images from the confusion which accompanies the direct vision of what is very closely connected with our own person.

II. WARNINGS FROM THE DIVINE VOICE IN THE PAST. God had instructed and urged his people to forsake their sins. He had not left them in the dark or unchecked— "Howbeit I sent unto you all my servants the prophets." This had been done with earnestness and emphasis—"rising early and sending them." It was a revelation of the evil character of their deeds—"this abominable thing;" an appeal to them to cease from such wickedness—"Oh, do not this abominable thing!" and a declaration of the Divine abhorrence of their conduct—"that I hate." All this has been said concerning the wickedness of the past; but it is to be reflected upon for its application to the present. We also may find profit in considering the ancient voices of heaven. The warnings of the Bible may be re-read and re-applied in our own day. If we see no new Jeremiah, we have the inspired words of the old Hebrew prophet, and they are as true now as ever. What God hates he hates eternally. What he forbids is always wrong. The object of his urgent appeal should command submission at all times.

III. WARNINGS FROM THE PUNISHMENTS OF THE PAST. The object of punishment is twofold. First, it concerns the guilty; secondly, it has lessons for witnesses. It is chastisement to the offender, it is warning to others. No punishment would be just if it were simply given as a deterrent. But being deserved and needful on account of the conduct of the victim, it is then utilized in perfect justice for the general benefit of the community. We should be thankful for the fact that the fate of others is not altogether obscure, so that we may profit by the sad lessons of their experience.

Ver. 16.—*Open rebellion.* I. GOD LEAVES US FREE TO ACCEPT OR REJECT HIS AUTHORITY. Whatever may be urged from the standpoints of abstract philosophy and of speculative theology, in practice, as Butler says, we all act as though we were free. In the Bible, too, this practical freedom of the will is constantly implied and appealed to. Though we have no moral right to renounce the Law of God, though we shall suffer if we do so, the terrible power of rebellion is entrusted to us that our loyalty may be proved and our service may remain free and willing.

II. ALL EVIL CENTRES IN THE WILL. The idolatrous Jews *will* not hearken to the word of Jeremiah. Herein lies the sum and substance of their offence. Depraved appetites and wicked passions are temptations to the evil will or products of its deeds. In themselves they are no more wicked than the external temptations which appeal to the purest elements of our common human nature. Guilt consists in yielding to them —in the act of the will that consents, indulges, or urges.

III. WILFUL REJECTION OF TRUTH IS REBELLION AGAINST GOD. Not to hearken is to revolt. We must be careful to distinguish pure intellectual doubt and unbelief from this revolt of the will against truth. The latter may not deny the correctness of what it rejects; it simply refuses to follow it. If it does fail to believe the truth, but through only wilfully closing all avenues of evidence, the blame of an evil will must be attached to it.

IV. SELF-WILL IS AN EVIL WILL. In rejecting the Divine message the idolatrous Jews insolently add, "We will certainly do the whole word which hath gone forth out of our own mouth" (see ver. 17). 1. Self-will even in regard to *things innocent* in themselves is nevertheless an evil will. For we are not our own masters. The servant is wrong if he disobey his master, though to do a harmless act. The soldier is guilty in disobeying orders, whatever other course he may take. We are "under authority." If our Captain says, "Go," we are not free to stand for the most innocent reason. 2. Self-will is too often directed to *evil things.* Those Jews who deliberately rejected the Divine message chose to perform acts of idolatry of their own will. Our will is corrupt.

Left to itself it chooses much that is evil. To keep it pure we must lift it up to union with a higher will. When it breaks loose and defiantly chooses its own private course, its evil nature will incline it to a bad course.

V. COMPANIONSHIP IN SIN BECOMES CONSPIRACY IN GREATER SIN. The husbands support their wives in the evil practices of the women, and together they declare that for the future they will pursue these practices openly and deliberately. But the closest relationship and the warmest affection are no reasons for defending wicked conduct, much less for encouraging and sharing it. When the love of husband and wife conflicts with the love of God, even that most near and sacred tie should yield to the highest of all obligations. Otherwise the marriage relation, which is instituted for the blessings of mutual comfort and happiness, becomes a curse.

Ver. 18.—*Chastisement misinterpreted.* I. IT IS POSSIBLE TO MISTAKE THE CAUSE AND PURPOSE OF GOD'S PROVIDENCE IN CHASTISEMENT. Instead of accepting their calamities as punishments for their sins against Jehovah, the Jews in Upper Egypt argue from them to conclusions of unbelief in the power and goodness of the God of their fathers. They are not alone in their error. The problem of suffering and its source and aim is profoundly difficult. The glib repetition of old platitudes only mocks at the mystery it can never solve. Job's friends were good men, and two of them able men; but "miserable comforters" were they all, because their explanation of the cause of the tragic agony before them was so utterly inadequate. Two reasons for error in the interpretation of chastisement may be detected in the case of Jeremiah's contemporaries. 1. *An evil disposition.* These men had no desire to recognize the hand of the true God in their experience. They had followed their wives in favouring the immoral rites of a heathenish cult. Jeremiah's teaching was rejected with insult; the idolatrous religion was grasped with obstinate self-will. Behaving in this way, the Jews in Upper Egypt were not in a fit state to judge fairly of the meaning of God's dealings with them. Our "views" of truth depend materially on our attitude towards it. Bad passions and a corrupt will prevent men at all times from profiting by chastisement. 2. *The delay of chastisement.* This was not contemporaneous with the sin. It would seem that the corruption which followed the reformation of Josiah was not so bad as that which preceded it. Yet it was after this that the blow fell. Now, a similar experience may often be noted. Charles II. was a worse king than James II., and Louis XV. than Louis XVI. The revolutions did not occur when things were at their worst. They took time to ripen. The chief causes of them were not their immediate antecedents. The same may be expected in private lives. Therefore it may require searching thought to trace the trouble down to its real root.

II. IT IS POSSIBLE TO FALL INTO RELIGIOUS ERROR THROUGH MISINTERPRETING GOD'S PROVIDENCE IN CHASTISEMENT. By a false inference drawn from the experience of trouble, the idolatrous Jews were led to fling off the last relic of their ancient faith, and to renew their allegiance to the heathen religion they had partially renounced in outward act, though not, as it now appears, in the inclinations of their hearts. Consider the process by which this result was reached. 1. *A delusion as to the nature of repentance and its effects.* The Jewish refugees had imagined that their abandonment of open idolatry would have warded off the impending doom. They were enraged at discovering their mistake, and they took the result as a reason for daring scepticism. Important lessons may be derived from their mistake, *e.g.* (1) that outward reformation is useless before God without heartfelt repentance; (2) that there are necessary consequences of sin which no repentance can obviate—improvidence leading to poverty, intemperance to disease, crime to secular punishment, in spite of all the genuine tears of a Magdalene; (3) that when God accepts repentance and forgives the penitent, it may still be necessary to chastise him for the good of his own soul. 2. *The mistake of judging of the truth of a religion by the worldly advantages that accrue from it.* Godliness has "promise of the life that now is" (1 Tim. iv. 8). Under the Old Testament economy this promise was emphasized. Nevertheless, even in the Jewish religion it was often recognized that suffering might fall upon the people of God (*e.g.* Ps. xxii.). With our fuller light, we know that the temporal advantages of religion are but a small part of its blessings; that under certain circumstances it may bring more worldly loss than gain (*e.g.* to the martyrs, etc.); that there are Christians who reckon that if in this life only they have hoped in Christ, they are of all men most pitiable (1 Cor. xv. 19). Therefore we should settle it well in our minds that, as worldly injustice and calamities of all kinds may fall upon the devoted servants of Christ, the experience of these things should not shake our faith. This fact needs to be well considered and realized, because there is no more frequent cause of sudden and violent scepticism than a series of great and inexplicable troubles. 3. *The sin of pursuing religion for its worldly profit.* Even if godliness is profitable for all things, it cannot be truly followed for the sake of gain. To choose our religion according to the advantages it may give us, is to subordinate truth to convenience, and to degrade to the position of a servant that which claims to rule as a master, or will have nothing to do with us.

Ver. 22.—*The limit of God's forbearance.* I. GOD'S FORBEARANCE IS LIMITED. There is no limit to his love. His mercy "endureth for ever." There is no limit to his patience, his endurance of the most provoking wickedness. But there is a limit to God's forbearance. Consider what determines this. 1. *Justice.* There is a point where necessary justice must interfere to prevent further wrong and punish what is already done. 2. *The good of the community.* Mercy to the criminal may involve injustice to the victim. There are abandoned wretches whom the world would find inestimable advantage in caging up out of the power of doing further mischief. There must be a point where their rights cease and the rights of others step in. In the Divine government this must be noted and acted on. 3. *The advantage of the offender.* It is a curse to a man to leave him for ever unchecked and unpunished. He may be left for a season to give all necessary scope for the operation of milder measures and for his own free repentance. But when the gentleness has failed, the only chance lies in some drastic treatment.

II. IT IS POSSIBLE TO REACH THE LIMIT OF GOD'S FORBEARANCE. It was reached by the antediluvians, by the cities of the plain, by the Jews at the time of the Captivity, by the Jews when Jerusalem was destroyed by Titus, by many a nation and many a man since. It may be reached by us. This subject, therefore, is not a question of abstract theology, touching only the ideal relations of Divine attributes. It is tremendously practical. 1. The limit may be reached in *our lifetime.* Men presume on their prosperity till God providentially strikes them down in desolation, and they learn in their anguish the folly of their long abuse of God's long-suffering mercy. 2. It will come to the impenitent in *the next life.* Death will bring it if it has been stayed during all the earthly life. The longer it is delayed the more fearful will be its consequences to those who "treasure up to themselves wrath in the day of wrath."

III. IT MUST BE UNSPEAKABLY TERRIBLE TO REACH THE LIMIT OF GOD'S FORBEARANCE. Then all the vials of wrath will be outpoured. The horror of the judgment ensuing can only be measured by the greatness of the forbearance which restrains it. If that were not very fearful, why should God hesitate so long in letting it loose? Why should he use all other possible means to prevent the necessity of resorting to it? Why should he urge and plead with us to hear his voice to-day and harden not our hearts?

Ver. 25. *Sinful vows.* I. SINFUL VOWS ARE AMONG THE MOST WICKED OF SINS. Some sins are committed hastily and in passion, these with more deliberation; some without strong desire, these most earnestly.

II. IT IS A SIN TO PERFORM SINFUL VOWS. If we were not at liberty to make the vows, we are not at liberty to perform them. We cannot be bound to do that which we have no right to do. If we have promised to do an unlawful act, we should not consider that promise binding upon us, since our word cannot abrogate the law that forbids the act.

III. GOD LEAVES MEN FREE TO EXECUTE THEIR EVIL INTENTIONS. The Jews in Upper Egypt were to be left to the performance of their vows to the queen of heaven. This implied no sanction; it was only the withholding of forcible restraints. What a solemn responsibility lies in the fact that we have this large liberty after we have chosen an evil way, and before we are called to judgment for it!

IV. GOD SOMETIMES CEASES TO WARN MEN OF THE DANGER OF THEIR WICKED COURSES. They are then left to themselves till their sin ripens. It is a terrible fate, but consistent with the goodness of God, as we may be sure that, if God deliberately ceases to warn a man, it is because warnings are lost on him or simply harden him. We may so sin as to become "seared in our own conscience with a hot iron" (1 Tim. iv. 2).

V. THE FRUIT OF THE WICKED COURSES WHICH MEN HAVE CHOSEN FOR THEMSELVES WILL BE THE WORST PUNISHMENT OF THEM. They need no external penalties performed by executioners of justice. Sin is its own executioner, the natural effect of sin its own punishment. In the natural results that followed the performance of their wicked vows the idolatrous Jews will reap the bitterest harvest of retribution. "The sin, when it is full-grown, *bringeth forth* death" (Jas. i. 15).

Ver. 28.—*The remnant of the remnant.* Of the Jews who escaped the sword of Nebuchadnezzar in the invasion of their land, "a remnant" fled to Egypt; of this body of refugees "a remnant" was to survive the dangers that would destroy the greater part. Thus but a small number would return to Jerusalem in safety. For their folly in fleeing to Egypt the fugitives would suffer a second desolation, while the captives in Babylon and the patient poor people who remained in the land of their fathers would be spared. Yet even out of this further calamity some few would be brought in safety.

I. JUDGMENT IS TEMPERED WITH MERCY. Many are spared at the first blow. Some of these are only hardened in wickedness. A second blow falls. Still some are spared. God is reluctant to give his people up. If he can find room for any mercy in the midst of the severest judgment, he will exercise it.

II. GOD'S JUDGMENT IS DISCRIMINATING. Even now it must be so; for "shall not the Judge of all the earth do right?" But we do not yet know its purposes and its methods, and therefore to us it looks as though it could not take note of individual deserts. Ultimately we shall see how God has overlooked no exceptional case. Noah is picked out of the drowning world. Lot is remembered in Sodom. Elijah is provided for in the general drought. We can look for no such evidences of an interfering Providence in earthly things now, perhaps, but the truth they illustrate holds good, and must work its blessed results in the day of final account. Natural selection does not always result in the survival of the morally fittest on earth. On the contrary, the good may become martyrs, the bad triumphant tyrants. But we see only the opening acts of the drama. The final catastrophe will reveal the justice that regulates.

III. LEFT TO THEMSELVES, NO MEN COULD ESCAPE THE DOOM OF SIN. In the eternal judgment there could not even, be a remnant of a remnant. "All have sinned, and come short of the glory of God." All would, therefore, receive the wages of sin.

IV. BY THE REDEMPTION OF CHRIST ALL WHO HAVE SINNED MAY BE SAVED. This is large enough to deliver, not merely a remnant of a remnant, but every man who has fallen, however low he lies in the mire.

V. AT FIRST BUT A REMNANT OF A REMNANT ARE SAVED BY CHRIST. The question whether few were to be saved was not to be answered for the satisfaction of idle curiosity (Luke xiii. 23). But that only a few sought the grace of Christ at first is a historical fact. The number has grown wonderfully, and yet how large a part of the world must be accounted still dark and dead in sin! But the few are saved that they may win the many. The first disciples became apostles. The small remnant laid the foundation of a great nation. The Church is called to evangelize the world.

HOMILIES BY VARIOUS AUTHORS.

Vers. 1—14 (*vide* ch. xliii. 8—13).—*The condition of hardened sinners desperate.* I. WHY IS IT SO? 1. *Because repeated warnings have been rejected.* (Vers. 4, 5.) These have been inspired and infallible. Had they believed ever so little they might have trusted implicitly what was spoken, accompanied as it was with such miraculous credentials. We, in these last times, have had the Lord himself. He has revealed the *heart* of the Father. (2) They were sufficiently numerous and seasonable. God "rose up early and sent them." He sent them *all.* No opportunity or peculiarity of individual influence was omitted. Christ is greater than all the prophets put together, and his gospel is universally declared and universally authoritative over the consciences of men. God cannot send another messenger, nor would it avail if he could. 2. *Because the lessons of experience have been ignored.* (Vers. 9, 10.) How terribly severe had not these been! It was scarcely possible for greater temporal punishments to be inflicted. Yet it was in the discipline of these judgments they were to have been saved. The path of transgressions, as the sinner looks back upon it, is marked by ruin and death. Yet will he not repent. 3. *Their persistent disobedience is an intolerable offence to God.* (Ver. 8.) God's judgments are not exhausted, but his patience may be. The history of offence and punishment will not repeat itself indefinitely. There are abysses of wrath. There is an eternal fire. Let them beware lest they be utterly consumed.

II. WHAT ARE THE SIGNS THAT IT IS SO? 1. *The Word of God is wholly against them.* The indictment has no redeeming feature. 2. *The pathos and pitifulness of God's entreaty.* (Vers. 4, 7.) There is compassion in the Divine mind because of the consequences that impend. Who so able to understand the sinner's circumstances as his Father? He who can see before and after, and who can fathom the mystery of iniquity, fears for his erring child.

III. WHAT ELEMENT OF HOPE, IF ANY, IS STILL LEFT FOR THEM? 1. *God still pleads.* Silence would mean hopelessness. Whilst his servant is authorized to speak, there may remain a way of escape. 2. *The fatherly compassion his voice betrays.* There are tears in the entreaty: "Oh, do not this abominable thing that I hate!" It is the birth-cry of an evangel; a prophecy of Jesus. Mercy may move and melt where judgment has failed. "For the love of Christ constraineth us," etc. (2 Cor. v. 14); "But God commendeth his own love toward us, in that, while we were yet sinners, Christ died for us" (Rom. v. 8).—M.

Vers. 15—23.—*Credentials of religion.* Very important to know why we prefer one religious system to another, and also why we ought to prefer it. A man is continually in need of having to give a reason for the hope that is in him. The higher religions find the field already occupied by many great systems, and have to vindicate themselves. The arguments employed here are those most commonly adduced, because most superficial. As appealing to the sensuous and material side of human nature, they are very influential.

I. WORLDLY ARGUMENTS FOR A RELIGION. Here they are employed on behalf of a false religion, an idolatry; but they are often made use of in recommending true religion. They are generally of two classes, viz. pertaining: 1. *To authority.* The idolatry here defended was (1) general and fashionable; (2) ancient; (3) patronized by royalty; (4) practised in the mother city of God's people. 2. *To tendency.* It was alleged to have promoted prosperity and peace.

II. THEIR INCONCLUSIVENESS. 1. *Authority is only valuable as it helps to establish truth.* Sin in its most flagrant forms, ignorance and inhumanity, have been more and longer prevalent than the greatest religions the world has seen. The most cruel and debasing religions are the most ancient in most countries. The only authority which can be admitted in such a connection is that of the best, *i.e.* the wisest and purest. 2. *The tendency argument is open to similar objections.* It is a great deal to say in favour of a religion that it has promoted the welfare and happiness of its supporters; but it is not so easy to prove it. Here the prophet alleges that it was their idolatry which lay at the root of all the misery of the people of Judah. It requires a very wide, varied, and lengthened induction of a people's circumstances ere such a statement is legitimate either way. And even if it were made out to one's satisfaction that a religious system had a beneficial effect upon the material condition of a people, it must still be remembered that man is a spiritual being, and that his moral and spiritual nature will sooner or later enter an imperious claim to attention and satisfaction. Only that which is right and true can meet the wants of the human spirit under all circumstances. And God is the one Being who can satisfy the spiritual aspirations and needs of his creatures. If the best and the holiest of men cannot be content with material advantages and comfort, but are ever yearning for something beyond, it is evident that utilitarianism must be interpreted in a very spiritual sense indeed ere it can pass muster as a tolerable criterion of any religion. It is chiefly because Christianity has revealed a Divine communion and a universal moral basis that it is destined to supplant all other creeds. But at the same time, it is also enforced by the test of utility in its more material aspect. No religion has so advanced the comfort, civilization, and peace of this world.—M.

Vers. 26—28.—*The danger of corrupting true religion.* God has from the beginning been solicitous for the purity of his revelation and worship. He would never suffer his ordinances to be tampered with, or share his honour with other gods. "Thou shalt worship the Lord thy God, and him only shalt thou serve" (Deut. vi. 13; Luke iv. 8).

I. It has been guarded by awful sanctions. Frequently in Old Testament history the death-penalty was inflicted upon spiritual pretenders, false prophets, and idolatrous worshippers of Jehovah. The warning of the text is very significant; a time was to come when no Jew would any more swear by Jehovah in Egypt, for the very good reason that there would be none there. "In the form of asseveration the Name of Jehovah would be still retained, although they had long since been devoted to the service of other gods. But Jehovah, who is a jealous God, rejects honour and acknowledgment which he must share with others; and so his Name shall no longer be heard from the mouth of any Jews in Egypt" (Hitzig). In the New Testament men are warned of making the Word of God "a cloke for lasciviousness;" of "perishing in the gainsaying of Core;" of tasting of the powers of the world to come, and falling back; of making gain of godliness; of handling the Word of God deceitfully, and wresting it to their own destruction; or of adding aught to the revealed truth (Rev. xxii. 18, 19).

II. Reasons for this severity. 1. *Objective.* (1) The slow advance of truth. (2) The costliness of the Divine relation. 2. *Subjective.* (1) Partly in the very nature of the case—moral simplicity being sacrificed in the self-consciousness of a corrupt worship. (2) The necessity of inspiration by the truth in order to the spiritual welfare and true immortality of man.—M.

Vers. 1—30.—*Jeremiah's last sermon.* There are other prophecies of Jeremiah recorded in this book in the chapters that remain, but this discourse is the last that we know of his delivering. And with it the curtain falls upon this great prophet of God; upon Baruch, his beloved companion and helper; and upon the wretched Jews for whose good he had laboured, but in vain. A long interval separates it from that in the previous chapter; for we see the people not now at Tahpanhes, at the border of Egypt, but gathering from all parts of the land to Pathros, to a great heathen festival there. And a very awful discourse it is. There is not one word of gospel in it, but the boom of the heavy bell of doom is heard resounding all through it—not one solitary chime of grace, or mercy, or hope anywhere. It is like the words of the Son of man when he comes to judge the world, and all nations are brought before him, to those on his left hand. They are told their sin and their doom. They make such defence as they can, which is rather a defiance than a defence; they are answered, and their sentence is pronounced again. There is throughout both these discourses nought but "a fearful looking for of judgment and of fiery indignation." "There remaineth no more sacrifice for sin." Such sermons might well have suggested these apostolic words. In this one note—

I. Its commencement—the indictment of the condemned. The prophet reminds them that they had seen God's judgments upon their brethren and fathers, and they knew the cause, that it was their sin against God. They had heard warning after warning addressed to themselves against the same sin. And not only had these warnings been repeated, but many messengers had been sent, and these had given their message with all earnestness and zeal, in season and out of season, and God himself had deigned to entreat with them and plead with them, saying, "Oh, do not this abominable thing that I hate!" But they had disregarded, despised, disobeyed all, and they were not humbled (ver. 10) even now. Therefore was their judgment pronounced against them and their doom was fixed.

II. The answer of the people. They would not believe in their doom. They resolved to persist in their sin. They declared they were every way better off in serving idols than in serving God.

III. THE PROPHET'S REPLY AND REITERATION OF GOD'S JUDGMENT AGAINST THEM.

CONCLUSION. As we read and ponder this terrible chapter, and remember that as its declarations concerning the past were true, so also were those that related to the future; for the judgment came upon them to the uttermost, far more than fell on those in Babylon. What can our hearts say to this? " Who would not fear thee, O Lord? " " Keep back thy servant . . . from presumptuous sins."—C.

Vers. 1—30.—*The end of Jeremiah; or, going down in clouds.* With this chapter Jeremiah disappears from view. The sadness which surrounded his first ministry accompanies it to the last and deepens at its close; like a sunset in clouds, going down in darkness and storm. The path along which he had been led had been a *via crucis,* a *via dolorosa* indeed ; a lifelong tragedy, an unceasing pain. We can only hope that death came soon to him after his recorded history closes. We have seen him torn from his native land and carried down to Egypt. We see him in the forty-third chapter at the border of the land; in this, in the heart of Egypt, at Pathros, probably forced to witness the degrading idolatry of his people, and unable to do aught to prevent it. An idol festival, accompanied, doubtless, with all the wonted pollutions of such worship, is proceeding, and he lifts up his voice once more in stern protest. But in vain, as heretofore. He vanishes from our view at an hour when his country-men, so far from being less addicted to idols, were now open in their sin, vaunting it and declaring their determination to adhere to it, and their regret that they had ever done otherwise. What a farewell between a minister of God and the people of his charge ! There never was but one other like it—the farewell of him who said, as he wept over another doomed Jerusalem and a future Jewish people, " Behold, your house is left unto you desolate." What became of Jeremiah from this date we know not. " No man knoweth of his sepulchre unto this day." " There is the Christian tradition rest-ing doubtless on some earlier belief, that the long tragedy of his life ended in actual martyrdom, and that the Jews at Tahpanhes, enraged by his rebukes, at last stoned him to death." The testimony to the martyrs at the close of the eleventh chapter of the Epistle to the Hebrews is thought to contain allusion to him : " They were stoned "— so we read. There is a Jewish tradition, however, which says that he made his escape to Babylon, but Josephus, like the Bible, is utterly silent as to the prophet's end. And it has been suggested that the tradition of the Jew and the silence of the historian are alike owing to a desire to gloss over some great crime. The suggestion is a probable one. " But he did not need a death by violence to make him a true martyr. To die with none to record the time or manner of his death was the right end for one who had spoken all along, not to win the praise of men, but because the Word of the Lord was in him as ' a burning fire.' The darkness and doubt that brood over the last days of the prophet's life are more significant than either of the issues which present them-selves to men's imaginations as the winding up of his career." " But a careful examina-tion of his writings show that, whilst the earlier ones are calmer, loftier, more uniform in tone, the latter show marks of age and weariness and sorrow, and are more strongly imbued with the language of individual suffering." How glad we would have been had the clouds lifted ere he died, and a gleam of sunshine had irradiated the hitherto almost unbroken gloom ! Some of the prophets were permitted to have a blessed onlook into the better days that were coming. He who wrote the closing portion of Isaiah's prophecies did so ; like Moses from Mount Pisgah. But it was not so to be with this prophet of God. His sun was to go down in clouds, and, though he had faithfully kept God's commandments, there was not for him in this life any " great reward." Though out of love for his countrymen he had refused the offer of a peaceful and honoured home in Babylon, like Moses, " choosing rather to suffer affliction with the people of God," he yet failed to win their affection or obedience ; and they remained in the same evil mind to the last. He had walked in the fear of the Lord. But those ways had not been for him " ways of pleasantness," nor its paths " paths of peace." The broken-hearted old man appeals to God and man, " Behold, and see if there be any sorrow like unto my sorrow." The twenty-second psalm—that which seems to tell so clearly of the sufferings of our Lord—is thought by many to have been written by him, and to tell of his own deep distress. Priest, patriot, prophet, martyr, hero of the faith indeed, what a life was thine from beginning to end, from thy first call by God to thy last rejection by men! These lines, translated for our day, and sung by our comfortable congregations—with what consistency they who sing them best know—

> " If I find him, if I follow,
>   What his guerdon here?
>   Many a sorrow, many a labour,
>   Many a tear;"

—are applicable enough to one like that great prophet of God, whose career began, continued, and, most of all, ended, in sorrow, labour, and tears. But the review of such a ministry must assuredly have its lessons. As we think of it are we not reminded—

I. OF " THE MAN OF SORROWS," OUR LORD JESUS CHRIST? (Cf. homily on *Jeremiah's ministry*, vol. i. p. 9.) No doubt other great servants of God, whose ministry and especially whose end have been like that of Jeremiah, come into the mind. John the Baptist in Bible history, and Savonarola in later days. The parallel between this great Florentine preacher and our prophet has often been noticed. The insistance upon spiritual religion, the sad and terrible close of his career,—these have led many to look upon Savonarola as the Jeremiah of the Middle Ages. But these resemblances are incidental and undesigned. That, however, between our Lord and his honoured servant who, in so many ways, preceded him, is not incidental, nor can it be called undesigned. But whilst the prophet is like our Lord in so many respects, yet, great as were his sorrows, those of the Man of sorrows were greater still. For our Lord knew more of the evil of sin and hated it more intensely. He sacrificed more and endured more. And so the experience of the prophets, like that of all God's servants, only goes to show that Christ has sounded deeper depths of sorrow than any that his servants can ever know.

> " Christ leads us through no darker room
>   Than he's been through before."

Hence always " underneath," however deep the depths out of which we cry, " are the everlasting arms " of his sympathy and love and help.

II. OF THE LIGHTNESS OF OUR BURDENS COMPARED WITH THOSE OF MANY OF THE SERVANTS OF GOD? How it shames us to think of the things we murmur about, when we contrast them with what such men as Jeremiah continually endured! Surely as we think of the severity of his cross, and especially that of our Saviour, we shall cease to complain of what ours may be.

III. OF WHAT THE GRACE OF GOD CAN DO? Did the prophet of God endure and contend so nobly, and was he faithful unto death? But is not " Jesus Christ the same yesterday," etc.? Then he who so strengthened his servants in days gone by will do the same still. Let us, therefore, go forward without fear.

IV. OF THE NECESSITY OF COUNTING THE COST ERE WE ENTER UPON THE SERVICE OF GOD? We see in the career of Jeremiah what may be required of us. Our Lord said to one candidate for discipleship, " The foxes have holes, and," etc. He would have the man consider if he were prepared to bear a life like that. And as we read what has been demanded of the Lord's servants, and may be of us, it is well that we, too, should count the cost. But do not count it so as to decline it; no, but that you may hasten to the treasure store of Christ, to the riches of his grace who will make his strength perfect in our weakness.

V. OF THE GREAT ARGUMENT FOR A FUTURE LIFE WHICH SUCH A CAREER AS THAT OF JEREMIAH FURNISHES? We have seen how uninterruptedly sad his life was, and how darkly it ended. Now, can any say that there is nothing more for such a man as that; that he and all they " who have fallen asleep in Christ have perished "—that is, the noblest, the purest, the best; those whose lives were beautiful, brave, God-like, —that *these* have *perished?* And yet, if death ends all, they have. It is incredible.

VI. IF SUCH MEN DEEMED IT WELL TO SACRIFICE ALL THEIR PRESENT FOR THE FAVOUR OF GOD, ARE WE WISE WHO REFUSE TO SACRIFICE ANYTHING, who love the world and cling to it and make it our good?—C.

Ver. 4.—*The mind of God towards sin and sinners.* "Oh, do not this abominable thing that I hate!" Idolatry is the sin specially referred to here. And it was indeed an "abominable thing." Pollution, cruelty, degradation, were inseparably associated with it. But the words may be applied *to all sin*—should be so applied. For *what is sin?* It is the acting out of that evil corrupt nature which we know to our cost lurks within us all. It is the stream that naturally flows from an evil fountain, the fruit that is sure to grow on a corrupt tree. Now, this view declares the mind of God—

I. TOWARDS SIN. 1. *He calls it "this abominable thing."* Thus he brands it. See how justly. For what do we call abominable? *Is wrong done to a benefactor abominable?* Is not every sin such a wrong? God does not command more than he deserves when he says, " Thou shalt love the Lord thy God with all thy heart," etc. What do we not owe to him? and how do we requite him? *Is wrong done to one who has entrusted his goods to us* that we may employ them for him, who has made us his stewards that we may employ rightly that which he has committed to our care,—is faithlessness to such abominable? But is not sin precisely such a wrong? Our mind, affections, will, our body with all its faculties and passions,—what are they aught else but our Maker's goods with which, as stewards, he has entrusted us? Let conscience declare the use we have made of them—that sin makes of them. *Is wrong done to the defenceless and innocent abominable?* Do we not cry out loudly against such a one? But is not sin such a wrong? We sin not to ourselves. We entail the consequences of our actions on those who cannot defend themselves, who are utterly innocent, and who will surely suffer by what we do. No man dieth to himself. He drags down in the vortex in which he himself is engulfed children, friends, neighbours, companions, all whom he has influenced and helped to make sinful like himself. *Is wrong done to vast numbers abominable,* so that when we hear of how one has brought ruin upon multitudes our anger against him grows the more? Surely it is so. But where do the ever-widening circles of sin's deadly influence stop? How wide an area do they enfold? " Jeroboam the son of Nebat ... made Israel to sin." *Is that which pollutes and defiles,* which is sensual and unclean, abominable? But sin is guilty of all this. For all these reasons and others sin is an abominable thing. 2. *He hates it.* " Do not ... *that I hate!* " God hates nothing that he has made. To us some creatures are hateful and some persons. But not so to God. He does not hate even the sinner, but only his sin. It is not alone that it is abominable in its own nature that he hates it, but it *works such ruin,* spreads sorrow and desolation far and wide. *It has opened and peoples the abodes of the lost.* And *it does despite and dishonour to the Son of God.* How, then, can God do otherwise than hate it?

II. TOWARDS THE SINNER. Note the pleading tone of this verse, " Oh, do not," etc.! What pity, what compassion, what yearning love, are all discernible in this beseeching entreaty which God addresses to the sinner! " Hear, then, God say to you, 'Do it not!' Now, what are you going to do? Do you mean to tell me that you will persist in it? *Do you really mean that?* Now, think! Do you really mean to go on sinning in the face of such a message as this?—with conscience smarting, and saying in its guilty smart, *Do not that abominable thing!* with memory weighted with the recollection of past transgressions, and saying by the leaden burden which it carries, *Do not that abominable thing!* With all this, and much more, do you mean to say that you will continue in sin? With remorse, like spiritual tempest, already springing up within your soul, and threatening to destroy all your joy and peace; with a fearful looking for of judgment and future indignation; with your miserable convictions, and with your bitter fears; with your gloomy forebodings, and with your knowledge of the results and consequences of sin;—do you mean to tell me that you are determined to continue? Well, if you be determined to continue, when the offended Father comes down to you in his marvellous condescension, and cries, 'Oh, do not this abominable thing that I hate!' then, we fear, there is but little hope; and certainly, if this state of heart continue, we cannot have much hope concerning you. It is probable that if some of you pass by many more seasons of conviction, God will say, 'He is joined to his idols; let him alone;' and you will be, in this world, left alone. You will come here, perhaps, according to your custom, but you will be left alone. I shall never have a message to you; I shall never have a prayer for you; no warning from these lips will ever reach you; you will be insensible as the very pews in which you sit, and nothing shall seem, in these ordinances, to be a voice from Heaven to your guilty and needy soul. Thus will you live until, with a seared conscience, you lie down on the bed of death, and there, perhaps, when it is too late, all your old fears will be awakened. You may send to your minister upon that bed of death, and he may come, but by your bedside he may be speechless, his very power to pray may depart from him, and in trying to ask mercy for you all his utterances may be choked; and you may go from that wretched dying bed to *hell*. And as you sink down into the pit, the millstone about your neck will be *the abominable thing which God hates*" (Rev. S. Martin).—C.

Vers. 17, 18.—*The apparent profitableness of sin.* This was what they asserted. And there seemed something in the assertion. All the great nations around them, and of which they knew anything, were idolaters—Assyria, Tyre, Babylon, Egypt, and the powerful Philistine, desert and other tribes. But Israel was in great trouble and humiliation. But the argument would have been valid if at the time of their fidelity they had always suffered, and if in their disobedience they had always prospered. They knew, if they would speak the truth, that the very reverse was the fact. When faithful, a thousand fell at their side, etc., but it came not nigh them. But when disobedient— though God bore with them for a while, and this forbearance they perverted into an argument for their sin, as so many do still—then it was their troubles came. But, no doubt, ungodliness did and does at times seem to be the most profitable course. This is so because—

I. If it were not so, then there could be no such thing as faith.

II. Nor could there be holiness—no love of goodness and God for their own sake.

III. The ungodly are held back by no scruples as the godly are.

IV. And they have the advantage of concentration of energy. They care only for one world; the believer cares for two, and most not for this but for the next.

V. The long-suffering of God may lead them to repentance.

VI. Therefore, let us not grudge the wicked their prosperity, nor deem their ways better than the ways of God.—C.

Ver. 17.—*Wretched reasons for a wrong resolve.* When we come to a good reso- lution there can always be found good reasons for it. But when we come to a bad resolve the reasons for it do not always appear so bad as they are. They can be plausibly urged and maintained, and appear very valid until they are more closely examined and the light of God's Word is brought to bear upon them. Then they appear what they really are. That Word is the Ithuriel's spear, which detects and declares what seemed to be something altogether different. Thus is it with the reasons urged here by the miserable exiles in Egypt for their persistence in their idolatry. Note—

I. THEIR RESOLVE. It was (1) that they would not hearken to the prophet of God; and (2) they would go on paying their vows, and burning their incense "unto the queen of heaven." Now, (3) this was a resolve proved to be wrong by the plain Word of God, the example of the noblest men of their race, the experience of their forefathers, and by the sorrows that had come and were yet to come upon themselves. But they urged—

II. THEIR REASONS. These were: 1. *Their vows.* As if a sinful vow could be made less sinful by keeping it; cf. Herod's vow to Herodias's daughter. Bad promises are ever better broken than kept. 2. *Custom,* which they said had in its favour: (1) *Antiquity.* Their fathers did so. Yes; some of them had; but not all, nor the best. (2) *Authority.* Their kings, princes, etc. But this, also, largely false. (3) *Unity.* They all did it. But there were a faithful few still. (4) *Universality.* It was done everywhere. Not everywhere, but, no doubt, extensively and very much, it was true, in Jerusalem, the metropolis of their land. All this was but a portion of the truth. 3. They pleaded *advantage.* They were better off when they acted thus; only trouble came when they worshipped God. No doubt sentence against their evil work was not executed speedily, and for a while their prosperity was not interrupted. Hence they perverted this forbearance of God—as men do still—into a pretext for going on in their evil way. Then when the judgments did come, and under the lash of them they gave up their idols, it was only an outward abandonment, not a genuine repentance, and such con- duct did not bring back the forfeited favour of God. Hence, they said, it had been better not to have forsaken their idols at all.

III. AND THESE WRETCHED REASONS ARE IN FORCE STILL. How many excuse and defend their idolatry of the world and self and sin on the ground of custom, of gain thereby, and of loss if they act otherwise! And the force of these so-called reasonings is great indeed with " men of this world." Where, then, can be found that reasoning which will beat back and beat down their fatal force? In this alone—the Divine Spirit acting through a consistent, believing, happy Church.—C.

Ver. 19.—*The husband's responsibility.* " Did we make her cakes to worship her . . . *without our men?* " These women pleaded that they had their husbands' sanction for what they did. It could not have been otherwise considering the subordinate position women occupied in Oriental nations. No doubt, therefore, the husbands and the male heads of families generally not only permitted, but even prompted these things. Hence it was some sort of excuse and defence for these women thus engaged in idolatrous worship. Such defence is allowed in human law. For the husband, by Christ's law as well as man's, is the head of the wife. If so, then the chief responsibility and the chief guiltiness on account of the sin of the household rest on the man at the head of it. The especial blessing of God was pronounced on Abraham because, says God, " I know him, that he will command his household after him." The anger of God came on Eli because he failed to do this. To escape such guilt, let husbands: 1. *Be in the Lord themselves.* 2. *Marry only in the Lord.* 3. *Be careful to maintain family religion.* 4. *Set themselves to seek the grace of God's regenerating Spirit for all their households.*—C.

Vers. 1—10.—*A severe lesson unlearned.* I. OPPORTUNITY TO LEARN THE LESSON. The suffering had not happened a long way off and to a people of strangers. Those who were to be taught had seen for themselves. The suffering was the very cause that prompted them to seek a home in Egypt, and even at this moment it was no great distance that separated them from the land of desolation. And so also have we opportunities, only too many, to learn from the sufferings of others. All suffering teaches something, if only we are willing to learn, and the suffering that comes through sin should have a peculiarly instructing power. Opportunity is also given, not only to learn ourselves, but to teach others. The daily newspaper, with its records of crime, folly, violent death, and lifelong disgrace, puts all who read it under a great responsibility for ordering their lives aright.

II. THE FULL EXPLANATION OF THE SUFFERING. The cause of it all is clearly stated. The unfaithfulness of a nation to their God. Even to have begun a departure from God was great wickedness, but persistency still further intensified the guilt. Other nations were faithful to their gods, though they were really no gods and had rendered no service, whereas Israel owed its growth, its position, its prosperity, its fame, to Jehovah. We do not know the origin and moulding of any other people as we do those of the people of God. We cannot think of the great suffering connected with the desolated cities of Judah without thinking also of Jehovah's long-suffering, and of the continuous prophetic means he employed to set before his people their wickedness and peril. On the other hand, we have a lesson with respect to what seems unpunished iniquity. Suffering is surely being gathered up for it. Time is being given for repentance and amendment.

III. THE LESSON IS ALTOGETHER UNLEARNED. We say " unlearned," because it effected no change. Suffering by itself cannot change. Suffering, indeed, appears to have different effects with different people, but the suffering is not really a cause. It but gives occasion to see whether men will yield to the new life and energy which comes from God. There had been a great upheaval in Judah, but so far as concerned the Jews dwelling in the land of Egypt the only change was one in the scene of their idolatries. They were the same men in Egypt as at Jerusalem.—Y.

Vers. 11—14.—*The doom on those making sure of safety in Egypt.* I. A FIXED RESOLUTION. The obstinate self-will of man brings into relief the inflexibility of the righteous judgments of God. The remnant of Judah *set their faces* to go into the land of Egypt to sojourn there. What, then, is to be expected but that Jehovah should *set his face* against them? The more self-will becomes a power in the life, the more nearly does it move in direct opposition to him who is the true Sovereign and Disposer of every human life.   We can guess something of the thoughts of these Egypt-seekers.   They say to themselves, " Henceforth we shall consult for our own safety."   They speak as if the peculiar perils hitherto besetting them were the perils of one place rather than another.   Perhaps even they reckoned that outside the land of Israel they were beyond Jehovah's reach.   Here there is a lesson for us in our selfish aims and pursuits.   All selfishness is bad, but even in selfishness a lesser badness is a degree of goodness, and it is well for a man if he gets frequently shaken in his selfishness; for then, his face not being steadily against God, he will find God looking on him encouragingly, to draw him out of his selfishness altogether.

II. A COMPLETE DESTRUCTION.   Complete, that is, in the sense of general and final. There was but a remnant to begin with, and of that a very small remnant might escape.   The very smallness of the remnant, however, would but magnify the completeness of the destruction.   No place is secure against the visitations of God's righteous wrath.   Indeed, the greater the appearance of natural security, the more manifest will be the breaking in on this security of the Divine justice.   Men must be taught, even by terrible lessons, that, as there is the best kind of safety under the shadow of God's wings, so there is the worst kind of danger the further we go from God.   To multiply our own defences is really to multiply our own perils.

III. A NULLIFIED PURPOSE.   This remnant, not finding in Egypt the expected safety, thinks there is nothing easier than to go back again to the land of Judah.   Whereas they find too late that, while departure from their own proper place is easy enough, return to it may be impossible.   Opening the door to get out was one thing; opening it to get in again quite another.   Seventy years was to pass before they of the Captivity should return from Babylon—indeed, it would really be another generation altogether; and should those who sought Egypt in contumacy and rebellion expect to fare better? We must be wise in time.   To be wise too late gives suffering its keenest edge.   So Judas brought back in vain the thirty pieces of silver, and Esau found no place of repentance though he sought it carefully with tears.   This is why God is so earnest in promising wisdom and light to those who seek for them, that we may seek for them at the right time, at the beginning of the great opportunity of life, and at the beginning of every smaller opportunity.—Y.

Vers. 15—19.—*Supposed and real reasons for calamity.*   I. A SUPPOSED REASON. What is the calamity?   Sword and famine.   Certainly a calamity to be removed and as far as possible averted for the future.   And casting about to discover a reason for the calamity, the men of Judah, or rather the women, for it is they who appear most prominently in this declaration, discover that the reason is to be found in the discontinuance of their offerings to the queen of heaven.   What a family matter this offering was is shown by ch. vii. 18.   The women kneaded dough to make cakes to the queen of heaven.   These offerings must have been very generally given up when the migration into Egypt took place, and then, on the coming of the sword and famine, what was more natural than for these women to connect the calamity with the discontinued offerings?   In one thing they were quite right; there was a supernatural reason for the calamity.   Wrong as they were, it was well they did not rest in any mere natural reason.   They were sure that a Divine Being of some sort or other had to do with their troubles.   The direction of thought is different now.   When calamity comes upon people, if they connect it with God at all, they very often do so in an arbitrary kind of way, as if nothing but a mere superior will, without reason or purpose of any sort, had sent calamity to them.   It is easy to pity what we call the ignorance and superstition of this crowd of women, but always we can see the errors of other times far more easily than those of our own.   The causes of suffering need to be inquired for very carefully, very patiently; for wrong conclusions only bring more suffering than ever.

II. THE REAL REASON.   They had forsaken Jehovah.   Not that there is any necessary connection between the forsaking of Jehovah and the sword and famine.   Nothing but our faith in the reality of a prophet's predictions can enable us to see this connection. There is oftentimes an utter forsaking of God, yet neither sword nor famine follow. The true and necessary result of going after something else than God is found in the consequent misery and emptiness of the life.   Continually we suffer from our inability to see things in their right proportions. Bad as sword and famine may be, there are things infinitely worse. The fact that this multitude was debasing itself by worshipping the queen of heaven pointed to a state of things far worse than any physical suffering could be. Physical suffering may at any time be removed, if desirable, by a miracle. But that darkness of the heart producing essential idolatry, a darkness so loved and cherished, who is to remove that? Nay, the very fulness of temporal comforts may become a veil between God and the soul. The very thing which helped to deceive the people here as to the real causes of things lay in this, that at the time when they were worshipping the queen of heaven they had plenty of victuals, and were well, and saw no evil.—Y.

Ver. 27.—*Watching over men for evil.* I. THIS WATCHING IS NEVER IRRESPECTIVE OF CONDUCT. If God ever watches over any man for evil it is because the man's conduct deserves it. It is not so necessarily with our watching. We may watch over a man for evil either from intensity of malice or intensity of selfishness. We may wish to do him ill from revenge or because his prosperity seems to mean our adversity. A word announcing watch over men for evil is a very serious word to fall even from Divine lips; and while God may speak it, perhaps we ought never to speak it. But at the same time, we cannot help watching over men for evil, and what we need especially to guard ourselves against is the doing of this from wrong motives. We must follow in the footsteps of God himself. When we censure others, or oppose them, or make them suffer in any way, let it be clear to ourselves and as far as possible clear to the world that their conduct has demanded it.

II. EVIL CONDUCT IS NEVER SEPARATED FROM SUCH WATCHING. God says that he is watching in this particular instance, but we know that he watches for evil against all evil-doers. We speak of evil-doing as being invariably followed by suffering, but this is only one way of putting the matter. We may also say that when suffering follows our wickedness it is the proof that God is watching for evil over the evil-doer. And in this matter we need zealously and boldly to do as God does, though, of course, we must do it according to the measure of human limits and infirmity. When any one is engaged with determination in any evil pursuit, it must be ours to show that we are by no means indifferent. God's watching over wicked men for evil is often done through the eyes of his own people; for if we have the Spirit of God in us there will be something of Divine discernment.

III. A CONNECTED TRUTH THAT NEEDS TO BE CONSIDERED AT THE SAME TIME. If God watches over the wicked for evil and not for good, it is equally true that he watches over the righteous for good and not for evil. Not one life, going on patiently and bravely in uprightness, is unobserved by him. Whatever the appearances may be, the abiding realities of life are against the wicked and for the righteous.—Y.

Ver. 28.—*Human and Divine confidence.* I. IN WHAT THEY ARE ALIKE. 1. *In the assurance with which they are expressed.* Here are men, in their worldly wisdom, perfectly certain that the course they have adopted will turn out right. It is always important to notice the assured unquestioning spirit in which men will set out on their enterprises. They do not seem to see the failures, disgraces, and humiliations of others; such overwhelming troubles are not to come nigh them. And all this is great testimony to the use of faith to men. God means men to be confident. The confidence which he ever expresses himself is meant to find a correspondent confidence in us. We need never be dubious in matters of a spiritual kind, however dubious we have to be as to certain external results. If we only act in the right, divinely ordained way, then we can continually be confident that all will come right. 2. *In the time of waiting needful to justify the confidence.* God speaks words, the truth and profound significance of which it may take not merely generations but even millenniums to make manifest to the whole world. Everything immediately apparent to the outward eye may contradict what he says. And something of his own wisdom and insight into the future he gives to men of the right spirit, so that they may work for results which are to be developed through long periods. He makes it possible for men to go on believing, hopeful and patient through all discouragements, and even to die in the faith that what they have sown others will reap. Thus faith which God makes to stand in the beginning he strengthens and establishes even to the end. And that faith which makes men themselves to utter confident dogmatic words will not be shaken all at once. Time is to try all things—the wisdom of the wise and the folly of the fools, the result of that which is sown to the Spirit and that which is sown to the flesh.

II. IN WHAT THEY DIFFER. In respect of real and deep insight into the future. The man who is confident in worldly wisdom is simply confident in the doctrine of chances. His chance of stability and success is equally good with that of others. Some must fail, but some must succeed. But God would have us ever to understand that success of this sort is only a deferred failure. If men could only see far enough, success and honour and safety would be utterly transmuted into failure, disgrace, and ruin. But God's confidence is based on certain and complete knowledge. The end of all unsettlement and change must be something stable and continuous, and when God sees men reckoning themselves on a true foundation, which after all is miserably brief and frail, he can only assert the truth. If men will not believe, the only thing remaining is to wait. The utter downfall of the Jewish nation from such a height to such a depth was predicted even in the days of their outward glory. The Word of God stands because he can discern the certain exhaustion of purely human resources even when those resources show themselves in exuberant exercise and impressive achievement.—Y.

EXPOSITION.

CHAPTER XLV.
PROMISE TO BARUCH.

Ver. 1.—**These words**; *i.e.* the revelations which Baruch had committed (or was committing) to writing.

Ver. 3.—**Hath added grief to my sorrow.** Baruch felt "sorrow" or "pain" at the sinfulness of the people; "grief" or "anxiety" was added by Jeremiah's announcement of the judgment. **I fainted in my sighing**; rather, *I am weary with my sighing;* comp. Ps. vi. 7 (Authorized Version, 6).

Ver. 4.—**That which I have built**(comp. ch. i. 10 and parallel passages). **Even this whole land**; rather, *and that is the whole earth.*

Ver. 5.—**Seekest thou great things,** etc.? All around is passing through a sore crisis, and canst thou expect a better lot? It is no time for personal ambition, when the very foundations of the state are crumbling. **In all places whither thou goest.** This seems to indicate that Baruch's time of exile would be a restless one; it would nowhere be safe for him to take up a settled habitation.

HOMILETICS.

Vers. 1—5.—*The grief of one soul, and its consolation.* This chapter is devoted to one man. Among the large prophecies concerning whole nations, room is found for a prophecy to a single individual. The Bible is at once universal and individualistic in character. Its narratives alternate history with biography. God cares for the whole world, and truth is large as the universe; yet God does not forget one soul in its private distress, and truth has special applications to special cases.

I. THE GRIEF. Baruch had a double distress—grief added to sorrow. 1. *The first sorrow.* Probably this arose from a consideration of the wretched condition of the nation in its vice and decay. It is right and natural that good men should feel deep concern at the state of their country. The Christian should have the spirit of him who "when he beheld the city, wept over it." Moreover, if we see much of the wickedness of the world, we should not be satisfied with steadily condemning it, nor with congratulating ourselves on our own superior goodness. The sight should fill us with sorrow. They who go thus astray are our own brethren. And is not there much of the same sin in all of us? Often the wickedness which shocks us in others is only the full development of the very sin that lurks in our own hearts. 2. *The added grief.* (1) This came from the *prophecy.* Baruch was commissioned to write and read. His privileged position, so near to the fountain of inspiration, only deepened his distress. High spiritual privilege may bring only sadness in this world's experience. Increase of knowledge may be increase of sorrow. Revelation is sometimes a cause of distress. In the present case the prophecy was a declaration of the approaching doom of Jerusalem. We should contemplate the punishment of the impenitent with profound grief. Revengeful, triumphant, or self-complacent feelings in regard to this terrible subject are quite unchristian. (2) Baruch had *personal grounds* for his distress. In the approaching overthrow of his nation all his cherished hopes of personal ambition were shattered. The most sanguine too often suffer the bitterest disappointments. (3) *Jeremiah's grief* would add to that of Baruch. Sorrow is contagious. He who is much with " the Man of sorrows " will be likely to feel strange grief in contemplating the evil of the world. Baruch could find no rest in his grief. The greatest weariness is not the result of hard work ; it comes from distress of heart. It is trouble, not work, that breaks down the strong life to premature old age. The blessedness of the heavenly rest is that it is rest from sorrow as well as from toil.

II. THE CONSOLATION. Jeremiah has a prophecy for Baruch. God speaks to individual souls. The preacher must be preached to. Has not he who would save others a soul of his own to be saved? How sad that any preacher should declare the Divine message to the people, but hear no voice speaking peace to his own troubled soul! If he were as faithful as Baruch, he might expect, like Baruch, to receive a Divine consolation. Note the characteristics of this consolation. It did not deny the cause of grief. Much comfort is unreal and false in trying to do this. The consolation for Baruch consisted chiefly in furnishing him with advice regarding his views of God's action and his own aims in life. 1. *A lesson of acquiescence in the Divine will.* God is acting within his rights. It is vain to rebel. Peace is found in submission. 2. *A rebuke to ambition.* Self-seeking brings distress. As we live out of self we gain Divine peace. 3. *A promise of safety.* After the lessons intended to lead Baruch into a right mood, God promises him his life—only this, but this is much for a humble man who knows he does not deserve it, and a good man who will devote it to God's service.

Ver. 4.—*Divine destruction.* I. GOD CAN DESTROY HIS OWN WORK. What he made he can unmake. People dogmatize about the indestructibility of matter, of atoms, of souls. How do we know they are indestructible? Is God's omnipotence limited by the properties of his own works? But apart from all metaphysics, the complex world, being *constructed*, is plainly subject to *destruction.* It is monstrous to think the universe is a huge Frankenstein, able to escape from the power of its Maker.

II. GOD HAS A RIGHT TO DESTROY HIS OWN WORK. There is no property so clearly belonging to a person as the work of his own hands. All things that exist were made by God, and all belong to him. What he gave us he has a right to withdraw. His gifts are loans, talents to be used for a season and then returned. No creature has a right to its own life before God. He freely gave it ; he may withdraw it. Much less have we sinful creatures any such right.

III. GOD WILL NOT DESTROY HIS OWN WORK WITHOUT GOOD REASON. A power is not necessarily always put forth nor a right in perpetual exercise. God does not act capriciously nor cruelly. He is the Creator rather than the Destroyer. He delights in creating because he loves his creatures. He takes no pleasure in destroying, but will only do it under urgent necessity.

IV. NEVERTHELESS THERE ARE CIRCUMSTANCES UNDER WHICH GOD WILL DESTROY HIS OWN WORK. All things were good when they came from their Maker's hands. But some have been corrupted. When a thing is hopelessly corrupt there is no reason for preserving it and much for destroying it. See this in earthly experience—the Flood, the destruction of Jerusalem, and in greater judgments—the wages of sin, death, and the final destruction of the world. Therefore let us not presume that any work or institution is eternal because it was established by the eternal God, that any possession of ours must be permanent because it came from him, or that our own life is safe because God breathed it into us.

Ver. 5.—*Self-seeking.* Self-seeking is treated in the Bible, especially in the New Testament, as both wrong and not really profitable to the self-seeker, although it seems to be prompted by natural instincts and supported by good reasons. Let us consider the grounds of these representations.

I. WHY SELF-SEEKING IS WRONG. God does not require absolute altruism ; we are only commanded to love our neighbours *as* ourselves. Natural self-regarding instincts created by God can surely be innocently exercised. It cannot be necessary for all efforts of men to rise in social position, etc., to be condemned. What, then is the self-seeking which is blameworthy? 1. That which offends against *justice* by seeking selfish gain at the expense of others. What frightful injustice ambition must answer for, in liberty destroyed, lives sacrificed, confusion and misery sown broadcast! 2. That which offends against *charity* by disregarding the good of others. In the spirit of Cain it cries, "Am I my brother's keeper?" So long as it attains its own ends, it will not lift a finger to move another man's burden. But Christ teaches us that it is not enough that we do not injure others, we must also actively help them; it is not enough that we do not steal, we must go further and "give to him that asketh." 3. That which offends against *duty* by sacrificing the vocation of life to private gain. We are not free to live to ourselves, because we are not our own masters. We are called to God's service. Our duty is to serve God, not self, so that whatsoever we do may be done "unto the Lord." Self-seeking is rebellion against our Lord and Master. In times of *public distress* self-seeking is peculiarly odious. Such were the times in which Baruch lived. Then there are loud calls of duty and noble tasks to be done. The general grief makes the thought of one's own pleasure and profit out of place. To use that distress as a ladder by which to rise to greatness is indeed despicable.

II. WHY SELF-SEEKING IS NOT PROFITABLE. In a worldly sense and for a time it may be, but not really and ultimately. Even in the lower human relations, how often do the seeds of ambition bring a harvest of anxiety! The self-seeker reaches the climax of his endeavours, his most brilliant dream is realized, he is a king—and he wears a hidden coat of mail, hides himself in a fortress-castle, has not the liberty of his meanest subject, is driven near to madness by the fear of assassination.

> "He who ascends to mountain-tops shall find
> The loftiest peaks most wrapped in clouds and snow;
> He who surpasses or subdues mankind
> Must look down on the hate of those below."

When extreme greatness and extreme disappointment are neither realized, lesser self-seeking brings its corresponding trouble. It narrows the heart and destroys the purest and best delights—the joys of human sympathy. Christ shows to us deeper grounds for regarding it as a vain pursuit. "The first shall be last, and the last first." The reason he gives is that "Whosoever would save his life shall lose it: and whosoever shall lose his life for my sake shall save it." Only in proportion as we live out of self can we enjoy a life worth living; only then, indeed, do we truly live at all. By trying to make ourselves great, though we may reach a high external position, we fall to a low internal condition—we become mean and small; while in forgetting self and sacrificing self for God and for mankind we become unconsciously great.

HOMILIES BY VARIOUS AUTHORS.

Vers. 1—5.—*Baruch's message; or, God's consideration for his servant.* It is not always well to know more than others. Future things are for the most part mercifully hidden from us. The prophecies of God's kingdom in the world, as they awaken new hopes, also occasion new anxieties; and the latter will be the greater in proportion to our failure to comprehend and sympathize with the Divine purpose. Baruch was not in the same relation of spiritual sympathy and self-effacement with relation to the Word as Jeremiah was; he did not share the same moral elevation, and therefore his perplexities. In reward of his faithful, self-denying work as amanuensis to the prophet, a special communication is made to him with reference to his state of mind on hearing the threatenings of God against Israel and the nations.

I. TO RECEIVE SUCH A COMMUNICATION WAS A DISTINGUISHED HONOUR. In identifying his name with the book he wrote it immortalized him. His work was a comparatively humble one, but it required its own virtues, and these are recognized. Nothing done for God in a right spirit is forgotten by him. Amidst imperial and world-wide changes the interests of his servants are ever watched over with special care. When we see the

Sovereign Disposer of events, when empires are as small dust in his balance, arranging for the welfare of a single individual, merely because of help given to one of his prophets, shall we not acknowledge how precious in his eyes is even the least of his servants? They are children of the great King.

II. IT MINISTERED TO HIS PERSONAL COMFORT AND PEACE OF MIND. The anxiety and fear which weighed upon Baruch are thereby dissipated. God loves to see his children cheerful and in sympathy with his will. It is just from the "sorrow of the world that worketh death," he seeks to deliver us. The work of Baruch would be easier and less oppressive when he was assured that his own safety would be secured. But how poor is this promise compared with the "life and immortality brought to light in the gospel"! The children of promise are not only delivered from the sorrows and disappointments of this present evil world, but made sharers in the final triumphs of redemptive love.

III. IT CORRECTED A SPIRITUAL FAULT. 1. *The caution.* "And seekest thou great things for thyself? seek them not." Earthly ambition has often crept into the heart of God's servants. It is not consistent with faithful, single-eyed service. They that would further the kingdom of God in the world must seek it first. Baruch was reminded that this is not our rest. And when the powers of the world were being shaken was no time for self-advancement. His sighs were not pure. He mourned over opportunities lost, not of laying up treasure in heaven, but of accumulating it on earth. 2. *The promise.* "Thy life will I give unto thee for a prey." It seems poor, compared with his hopes. He perhaps anticipated a slight rebuke and chastisement of Israel, a few changes and adjustments, and the carrying on of the Divine purposes to a speedy issue. This illusion is gently but firmly checked. The world has a severer ordeal to pass through ere the ancient offence can be expiated, and the arena cleared for the Divine future. His hopes are, therefore, not wholly destroyed, but transferred. He will be spared to see the things beyond, and meanwhile it will be his privilege to help on that better time. Happy for him if, thus corrected, he attains to a diviner calm of spirit and a more thorough acceptance of the Divine terms and conditions. He too was but a sinner, whose deliverance was in itself a great and undeserved mercy (cf. Matt. xxiv.).—M.

Vers. 1—5.—*Baruch; or, the young recruit reheartened.* Baruch reminds of Mark (Acts xiii. 13). Both were good and faithful men; both became discouraged; both were reheartened; both found profitable to the ministry and true to the end. Now, as we look on this Divine reheartening of Baruch, we are taught much—

I. CONCERNING GOD. 1. We see *his grace.* He does not overlook or forget his servants. He notes their distresses and devises means for their relief. "Like as a father pitieth," etc. 2. We see *his methods* with those who are as Baruch was. (1) Though animated by love, they were severe rather than soothing; stern rather than gentle and consolatory. We have many parallels to this. Cf. ch. xii., "If thou hast run with the footmen," etc. How stern the dealing of God with Moses! No entreaty could procure the alteration of the sentence of exclusion from Canaan that had gone out against him. See also our Lord's message to John the Baptist in prison: "Go, tell John," etc. No gentle message of sympathy, but rather of rebuke for his failure of faith. So with Paul's thorn in the flesh, the Lord would not remove it. In all these cases there is rather the sharp, bracing, rousing summons to duty than words of soothing pity and tenderness. Far more like Paul's dealing with the recreant Mark— he virtually cashiered him—than that of Barnabas, who, Son of Consolation that he was, was all for comforting him and dealing gently with him. (2) God tells him that he has heard his complainings. When we talk to ourselves, we often forget that every word is audible to God. The people about our Lord were often talking to themselves concerning him, and, though they said nothing out loud, we constantly read how "Jesus *answered* and said," showing that he had heard all they said. (3) He gives him to understand that his purpose is not to be set aside because of his complainings. "The Lord saith thus." If we cannot bring our circumstances to our mind, our wisdom is to bring our mind to our circumstances. Baruch was shown that he must do this. (4) He implies that a seeking after "high things" for himself had much to do with his complaining. He was of great ability, of noble lineage (ch. li. 59; Josephus, 'Ant.,' x. vi. 2; ix. 1), the grandson of Maasiah (2 Chron. xxxiv. 8), and this may well have animated him with hopes of high office in the state, such as his brother had held; or his nearness to Jeremiah may have led him to believe that he should be the prophet's successor. (5) He promises him that his life shall be spared, though with much difficulty—" given to him as a prey." We cannot tell what afterwards became of him. Tradition varies. There was not much comfort in all this, but rather a " What doest thou here, Elijah ? " (1 Kings xix.). 3. *His motives.* The leaders of an army must not be weaklings. Those who have stern work to do must themselves be stern. Luther, not Erasmus, must head the Reformation movement. Hence God disciplines his most trusted servants by very severe methods. Even our Lord, " He learned obedience by the things that he suffered ; " " He was made perfect through sufferings." 4. *His success.* That which he purposes is ever done. Baruch here, as Mark afterwards, was reheartened and did good service again.

II. Concerning the prophetic work. Demands self-denial, involves much suffering, and has much sorrow in it. No wonder that in ancient days men shrank from the pastoral office. " Nolo episcopari " meant something then. Are any thinking of it ? Count the cost. Are any in it ? Let them, as they need, seek daily strength from God.

> " Chief Shepherd of thy chosen sheep,
> From sin and death set free,
> May every under-shepherd keep
> His eye intent on thee."

Let those not so charged of the Lord pray for those that are.

III. Concerning young soldiers of Jesus Christ. 1. There is much that is delightful in them. Their ardour, their zeal, their affection. Elisha to Elijah, Timotheus to Paul, so here Baruch to Jeremiah. 2. But they are apt to be discouraged and desponding. They need enduring power. Melancthon thought he should soon convert men to the truth. But Luther tells how the old Adam was soon found to be too hard for the young Melancthon. 3. Let them submit cheerfully to the methods of discipline God has appointed for them, and be on their guard against all self-seeking ambition. 4. And they are to remember that, though their life be given to them, it shall be " as a prey." They will have to watch, to toil, to contend, to struggle, even for that.

> " The Son of God goes forth to war . . .
> Who follows in his train ? "

C.

Ver. 5.—*Ambition prohibited.* " Seekest thou great things," etc. ? God searches the heart, and probably discovered that, lurking secretly there, there was somewhat of an unhallowed ambition. Had he been other than one of God's chosen messengers, such ambition would have been natural and reasonable (cf. former homily). God does not directly charge him with this, but sets him on self-examination. This ever the Divine method. Are we seeking great things for ourselves ? If we are, God says to us, " Seek them not." And the reasons are many. Some of them are such as these—

I. We cannot tell whether they are designed for us. If they are not, they will bring us only misery ; cf. David in Saul's armour. If they are, they will come without our seeking.

II. To make *ourselves* our supreme object is ever wrong, despicable, and in the end ruinous. The corn of wheat must fall into the ground and *die*, give up its own life. If it do not, it abideth alone; if it do, it bringeth forth fruit. " He that loveth his life shall lose it, but he," etc. (John xii.).

III. Great things mean great responsibilities and terrible possibilities of great guilt and harm done to others and ourselves.

IV. Whilst seeking them, we let go what is more precious than them all. " Whilst I was busy here and there, lo, he was gone."

V. They tend to tie us down to earth and to fill our hearts with that love of the world which is death. " Ah ! Davie, Davie," said Johnson to Garrick, as they wandered through the beautiful demesne of a great nobleman, " these are the things that make it so hard for a man to die." A similar story is told of Cardinal Richelieu, who caused himself, when near death, to be borne into his magnificent picture-gallery, and there is reported to have made, to one near him, a like remark.—C.

Vers. 1—5.—*Counsel and comfort for the man overcome with bad tidings.* I. Consider the effect on Baruch's own mind of what he had had to write. Baruch came in simply to be a scribe and transmitter. Seemingly a friend of Jeremiah, he must have been in considerable sympathy with the prophet in his purposes and predictions. Doubtless he had made himself acquainted with each prophetic utterance as it came forth from Jehovah. But he had never had them all before his mind at one time, as now became necessary, through his having to write them down. Hence we have here an illustration of how more is required than the *mere utterance* of a word of God in order to produce a deep effect from it. A man may think he understands and receives it, and yet the understanding and reception may be far from what they ought to be. Not till Jeremiah's prophecies stand before Baruch in one mass does he fully discern the trouble coming on his people. Jehovah has spoken many times, and always in the same way, against the wicked and their wickedness. And so we see how important it is to get the impression, not only of successive parts of God's words, but of that Word as a whole. Moreover, if Baruch was oppressed by the consistent mass of threatening, it is equally possible for us to be uplifted and strengthened by a consistent mass of promises and encouragements. We shall ever find in the Scriptures that which we look for and prepare ourselves to find.

II. Some indication of Baruch's own character. Baruch seems to have been, not exactly what we should call an ambitious man, but still one who wanted to get on in the world. Perhaps he had a position which made it reasonable for him to expect influence and authority. But what can a man of this sort look for in a state rapidly declining to its fall? Baruch had to learn all at once that he must seek for such things as God would have him seek for. Thus we see God combining a lesson for the individual with the message for the nation. Baruch could hardly have been the only man competent to act as a scribe, but God, in taking him, took one who needed correction, needed to have his purposes turned into a more submissive way and a less self-seeking one.

III. Temporal blessings must depend upon circumstances. There had been times in the Jewish state when Baruch might have been a very useful man in some high position. But every man must accept the conditions of the time in which he lives. At one time the great temporal blessings may be those of attainment, at another those of escape. And so, to some extent, it is in spiritual things. There are times when what Christ does for us puts on the aspect of salvation; we are glad because of the great evils from which we are delivered. There are other times when we are not contented with merely thinking of deliverance; we want something positive—growth, fruitfulness, perfection. Then we are seeking great things spiritually—things which are always to be sought. And we may add they are always to be found, however adverse temporal conditions may be.—Y.

EXPOSITION.

CHAPTER XLVI.

This chapter, the first of a series, consists of two prophecies united, though it is probable enough that the latter was intended to supplement the former, for vers. 2—12 are clearly incomplete (from the point of view of this group of prophecies) without a distinct and unmistakable prediction of the conquest of Egypt. The earlier prophecy is, in fact, not itself a prediction, but a triumphal ode, analogous to such as we find in the Books of Isaiah and Ezekiel. It falls into three stanzas: (1) vers. 3—6; (2) vers. 7—9; (3) vers. 10—12. In the first two the great event is described with poetical imagery; in the third, its cause is declared, and the irremediable completeness of its effects. The point of time assumed is immediately before the battle of Carchemish. The Egyptian army has taken up its position by the Euphrates, and Jeremiah, from his prophetic watch-tower, recognizes the importance of the step. He knows that a collision of the two great powers is inevitable, and that the fortunes of *his* world will be decided by the result. It is, in short, a "day of Jehovah" which he sees before him. As a prophet, he cannot doubt what the issue will be. He falls into a lyrically descriptive mood, and portrays the picture which unrolls itself before his imagination.

Ver. 1.—**Against the Gentiles**; rather, *concerning the nations* (as distinguished from Israel). This heading relates to all the seven prophecies in ch. xlvi.—xlix. 33.

Ver. 2.—**Against Egypt, against the army**; rather, *concerning Egypt, concerning the army*. **Pharaoh-necho.** Necho II., a member of the twenty-sixth Egyptian dynasty, son of Psametik I. (Psammetichus), who had for a time revived the declining power of Egypt. Herodotus (ii. 158) credits him with being the first to construct a canal to the Red Sea, which seems an exaggeration (see Sir Gardner Wilkinson's note *ap.* Rawlinson), also (iv. 42) with having caused the circumnavigation of Africa, after which the Phœnician seamen brought back the startling news that they had had the sun upon their right hand. This energetic monarch noticed the decline of Assyria, and, at the battle of Megiddo (Herodotus, ii. 159, wrongly says Magdolus or Migdol), reattached Judah to the Egyptian empire. Four years later, at the battle of Carchemish, he himself sustained a crushing defeat at the hands of the Babylonian king Nebuchadnezzar (2 Chron. xxxv. 20). **Carchemish.** This was the great emporium of Mesopotamia, Syria, and Palestine. Its true site was discovered by Mr. George Smith, in his last fatal journey, to be at Jerâbis or Jirbâs, on the right bank of the Euphrates. It was anciently a city of the Kheta (equivalent to Khittim, "Hittites"), but passed to the Assyrians, under Sargon, under whom it attained the highest commercial prosperity, especially after the overthrow of Tyre by Sennacherib. The "mana," or *mina,* "of Gargamis" is constantly referred to as a standard weight in the commercial cuneiform inscriptions. **In the fourth year,** etc. Marcus Niebuhr wishes to put a stop before these words, so as to make them a definition of the date of the prophecy. He thinks the date of the battle of Carchemish was the third and not the fourth year of Jehoiakim. This view, however, is very uncertain (see Keil), and it is exegetically very unnatural to detach the closing words of ver. 2 from those which precede. The obvious inference, moreover, from the prophecy (vers. 2—12) is that it was written at or about the time of the battle; a special date for the prophecy did not require to be given. Should Niebuhr's chronological combinations, however, turn out to be correct, the mistake would probably not be that of Jeremiah, nor of his scribe, but of his editor, who may easily have fallen into error in the mere minutiæ of chronology.

Ver. 3.—**Order ye,** etc. The leaders of the Egyptians are heard summoning their men to make ready their armour, and set themselves in array (comp. ver. 9). The **buckler** (Hebrew, *māgēn*) is the small shield; the **shield** (Hebrew, *çinnāh*) is the large one (*scutum*), which covered the whole body (comp. 2 Chron. ix. 15, 16).

Ver. 4.—**Harness the horses**; viz. to the war-chariots, for which Egypt was famous (comp. Exod. xiv. 6, 9; 1 Kings x. 28, 29; Isa. xxxi. 1). **Get up, ye horsemen.** An equally possible rendering, and one which better suits the parallelism, is, "mount the chargers." **Put on the brigandines.** "Brigandine" is an archaic word (Hakluyt's 'Voyages'), meaning the armour of a "brigand" or member of a "brigade," or "troop" (comp. Italian, *brigata*). The Hebrew word means "coats of mail."

Ver. 5.—That so well-equipped an army should flee seems incredible. Hence the astonished question, **Wherefore have I seen,** etc.? literally, *Why do I see (that) they (are) dismayed, turning back?* **And look not back.** With the object of rallying the scattered forces. **For fear was round about.** It is a pity that the Authorized Version has not kept one uniform rendering for this favourite expression of Jeremiah. In ch. vi. 25 (see note) it is translated, "fear is on every side" (Hebrew, *māgōr missābīb*).

Ver. 6.—**Let not the swift flee away.** A strong way of expressing that even the swiftest *cannot* expect to flee, just as, in Isa. ii. 9, "forgive them not" means "thou canst not forgive them." Nothing seems to have struck the Jews so much as the unparalleled swiftness of the Chaldean warriors (Hab. i. 6, 8; ch. iv. 13). **They shall stumble**; literally, *they have stumbled;* it is most probably the prophetic perfect ("they shall certainly fall"), though Ewald denies this, and consequently maintains that the prophecy was written *after* the battle of Carchemish. **Toward the north**; *i.e.* "in the northern region," or, more loosely, "in the north" (comp. ver. 10). Carchemish was, of course, far to the north of Jerusalem.

Ver. 7.—**Who is this,** etc.? "Once more surprise at the [same] phenomenon recurs, and in a stronger form; a monstrous, devastating river appears to roll itself wildly along, overwhelming all countries: who is it? It is Egypt, which is now threatening to overrun the earth and to lay everything waste, whose various nationalities are advancing fully equipped" (Ewald). **As a flood**; rather, *as the Nile* (*y'ōr*), a word of Egyptian affinities, and only once used of another river than the Nile, Dan. xii. 5, 6, 7).

The naturalness of the figure in this context needs no exhibiting. It reminds us of Isa. viii. 7, 8, where the Assyrian army is compared to the Euphrates. **Are moved as the rivers**; rather, *toss themselves as the rivers.* By the "rivers" the prophet means the branches of the Nile, which are described by the same word in Isa. xix. 8; Exod. vii. 19.

Ver. 8.—**Egypt riseth up,** etc. The answer to the question in ver. 7. **The city.** The article is not expressed; and there can be no doubt that the word is used collectively of cities in general (comp. ch. xlvii. 2).

Ver. 9.—A call to the army, particularizing its two grand divisions, viz. the warriors in chariots, and the light and heavy armed infantry. M. Pierret, of the Egyptian Museum at the Louvre, writes thus: "The army was composed (1) of infantry equipped with a cuirass, a buckler, a pike or an axe, and a sword; they manœuvred to the sound of the drum and the trumpet; (2) of light troops (archers, slingers, and other soldiers carrying the axe or the tomahawk); (3) warriors in chariots. Cavalry, properly so called, was not employed. . . . The Egyptians also enlisted auxiliaries, such as Mashawash, a tribe of Libyans, who, after the defeat of a confederation of northern peoples hostile to Menephtah, into which they had entered, refused to leave Egypt, and entered the Egyptian army; the Kahakas, another Libyan tribe; the Shardanas (Sardinians); the Madjaiu, who, after having been in war with the Egyptians under the twelfth dynasty, enrolled themselves under the standard of their conquerors, and constituted a sort of gendarmerie," etc. ('Dictionnaire d'Archéologie Égyptienne,' pp. 64, 65). Among the mercenaries mentioned by Jeremiah, the Ludim deserve special mention. They are generally supposed to be a North African people (and so Ezek. xxx. 5). Professor Sayce, however, thinks they may be the Lydian soldiers by whose help Psammetichus made Egypt independent of Assyria, and his successors maintained their power (Cheyne's 'Prophecies of Isaiah,' ii. 287). **Come up, ye horses;** rather, *bound* (or, *prance*), *ye horses.* The verb is literally *go up,* and seems to be used in the same sense, only in the Hiphil or causative conjugation, in Nah. iii. 3 (which should begin, "Horsemen making (their horses) to rear"). Ewald and others render, "Mount the horses," the phrase being substantially the same as in ver. 4 (see above). But the parallelism here is opposed to this; and the prophet has evidently been a reader of the prophecy of Nahum, as the very next clause shows. **Rage, ye chariots;** rather, *rush madly, ye chariots* (alluding to Nah. ii. 5). **The Ethiopians;** Hebrew, *Cush;* often mentioned in connection with Egypt. The whole Nile valley, as far as Abyssinia, had been reduced to an Egyptian province. At last Cush had its turn of revenge, and an Ethiopian dynasty reigned in the palaces of Thebes (B.C. 725—665). **The Libyans;** Hebrew, *Put* (which occurs in combination with Lud, as here with Ludim, in Ezek. xxvii. 10; xxx. 5). This appears to be the Egyptian Put (nasalized into Punt), *i.e.* the Somali country on the east coast of Africa, opposite to Arabia (Brugsch).

Ver. 10.—The contrast. *And yet that day is (the day) of the Lord, Jehovah Sabáoth* (the rendering of the Authorized Version, **For this is the day,** etc., is clearly a mistake). The " day of Jehovah" is an expression so familiar to us that we are in danger of losing a part of its sublime meaning. It is, in brief, " that crisis in the history of the world when Jehovah will interpose to rectify the evils of the present, bringing joy and glory to the humble believer, and misery and shame to the proud and 'disobedient. . . . This great crisis is called a day, in antithesis to the ages of the Divine long-suffering: it is *Jehovah's* day, because, without a special Divine interposition, there would be no issue out of the perplexities and miseries of human life." We may say, with equal truth, that there are many " days of the Lord," and that there is only one. Every great revolution is a fresh stage in the great judgment-day; " *die Weltgeschichte ist das Weltgericht*" (Schiller). The *loci classici* for the expression in the prophets are Amos v. 18, 20; Zeph. i. 7, 14; Joel ii. 1, 11; Isa. ii. 12; xiii. 6, 9 (in Isa. ii. 12, the phraseology closely resembles that of our passage—" for there is a day unto Jehovah Sabáoth;" Jehovah, that is, hath it in readiness in the supersensible world, where there is no time, and where all God's purposes have an ideal, but no less real existence. We might, in fact, render our passage, " but that day (is the day that belongeth) unto the Lord," etc.). **The Lord** here, as generally elsewhere, is that expressive form which intimates the universal lordship of the God who has revealed himself to Israel. **The sword.** A comparison with Isa. xxxiv. 6 suggests that it is " the sword of the Lord " which is meant—a symbolic phrase for the Divine vengeance, which meets us again in ch. xii. 12; xlvii. 6; Deut. xxxii. 41, 42; Judg. vii. 20 (comp. Josh. v. 13); Isa. xxvii. 1; xxxi. 8; xxxiv. 5, 6; lxvi. 16; Zech. xiii. 7. If Jehovah can be spoken of as having an Arm, a Hand, and a Bow, why not also as having a sword? Both expressions represent the self-revealing side of the Divine nature, and are not merely poetical ornaments, but correspond to awful objective realities. Divine vengeance exists, and must exercise itself on all who oppose the Divine will. **Hath a sacrifice.** The same figurative expression occurs in Isa. xxxiv. 6, and, developed at considerable length, in Ezek. xxxix. 17—20, where the slaughtered foes are described as fatted beasts, rams, lambs, he-goats, bullocks —animals employed in the Jewish sacrifices. This, then, is the purpose for which this immense host "rolls up from Africa"—it is that it may fall by the Euphrates, at once as a proof of God's justice, and as a warning to transgressors.

Ver. 11.—**Go up into Gilead** (see on ch. viii. 22). **In vain shalt thou use**, etc.; rather, *in vain hast thou used*, etc.; a much more vigorous, pictorial expression. **Thou shalt not be cured.** The literal rendering is more forcible, *there is no plaster for thee;* i.e. no bandage will avail to heal the wound (comp. ch. xxx. 13).

Ver. 12.—**Hath filled the land**; rather, *the earth*, corresponding to "the nations."

Ver. 13.—**The word**, etc. This verse is the heading of a new prophecy, which, however, for the reason already mentioned (see introduction to this chapter), is not to be regarded as entirely independent of the preceding prophecy, but rather as a supplement (just as Isa. xviii., though not in strict sequence to xvii. 12—14, is yet a supplement to it). The heading does not expressly state when the prophecy was written, but from the mention of Nebuchadnezzar, both in the heading and in the prophecy itself, we may assume a date subsequent to the battle of Carchemish, for the earlier prophecies contain no reference to that redoubtable name. An important question now arises—When did Nebuchadnezzar invade and conquer Egypt? and what would be the consequences of admitting that a Babylonian subjugation of that country is historically not proven? There can be no doubt that Jeremiah did hold out such a prospect; for he not only says so here, but also in ch. xliii. 8—13 and xliv. 30. In the latter prophecy it is not Necho, but Hophra, in whose reign the blow is to fall. But no monumental evidence has as yet been found [see, however, postscript to this note] of anything approaching to an invasion of Egypt by Nebuchadnezzar; nor do the accounts of Herodotus (ii. 159, etc.) at all supply the deficiency (on this, however, see further at end of note). It is true that Josephus quotes passages from Berosus, the Babylonian historian, to the effect that Nabopolassar had set a Chaldean governor over Egypt, but that this governor had revolted, and that Nabopolassar's son, Nebuchadnezzar, crushed the rebellion and incorporated Egypt into his empire. But these events happened, according to

the quotation from Berosus, partly before, partly immediately after, the death of Nabopolassar, and was consequently earlier than the prophecy in this chapter. Another fact of importance must be mentioned in this connection, viz. that Ezekiel repeats the announcement of the Babylonian conquest of Egypt, of which he speaks as if it were to happen at the close of the thirteen years of Nebuchadnezzar's siege of Tyre (Ezek. xxix. 17—21). Thus there is a gradual increase in the definiteness of the announcement. Looking at our chapter by itself, we might suppose that the conquest was to take place soon after the decisive battle at Carchemish. After the murder of Gedaliah, when Jeremiah had removed to Egypt, we find him foretelling the sore punishment of Egypt in greater detail, and the name of Hophra (instead of Necho) is introduced as that of the deposed king. Finally, Ezekiel (as we have seen) specifies a definite time. Now, it is true that our knowledge of this period is somewhat incomplete. We have not the direct historical proof that could be wished as to the result of Nebuchadnezzar's siege of Tyre, though it would be fastidious to scruple at the evidence which satisfied so cool a judgment as that of George Grote. The great historian denies, however, that Tyre at this time suffered such a terrific desolation as is suggested by a literal interpretation of Ezek. xxvi., and continues in these remarkable terms : "Still less can it be believed that that king conquered Egypt and Libya, as Megasthenes, and even Berosus so far as Egypt is concerned, would have us believe —the argument of Larcher, 'Ad Herodot.,' ii. 168, is anything but satisfactory. The defeat of the Egyptian king at Carchemish, and the stripping him of his foreign possessions in Judæa and Syria, have been exaggerated into a conquest of Egypt itself" ('Hist. of Greece,' vol. iii. p. 445, note 1). Supposing Mr. Grote's view of the facts of the siege of Tyre to be correct, it is clear that the prophet's reproduction of the Divine revelation made to him was defective ; that it presents traces of a stronger human element than we are accustomed to admit. Tyre had to suffer a fall; but the fall was not as yet to be so complete a one as Ezekiel, reasoning upon his revelation, supposed. It is equally possible that Jeremiah and Ezekiel, reasoning upon the revelation of the inevitable fall of Egypt, mistook the time when, in its fulness, the Divine judgment was to take place. The case may, perhaps, turn out to be analogous to that of an apparently but not really unfulfilled prophecy in Isa. xliii. 3. A literal interpretation of that passage would give the conquest of Egypt to Cyrus; as a matter of fact, we know that it was Cambyses, and not Cyrus, who fulfilled the prophecy. It would not be surprising if we should have to admit that it was Cambyses, and not any earlier monarch, who fulfilled the prophecy of Jeremiah. Certain great principles of God's moral government had to be affirmed; it was of no moment whatever whether Nebuchadnezzar, Cyrus, or Cambyses was the instrument of their affirmation. A parallel from Isaiah may again be adduced. The shameful captivity of Egypt, and perhaps Ethiopia, which Isaiah foresaw in the time of Sargon (Isa. xx. 3), was not realized in fact until Esar-haddon despoiled Tirhakah, King of Egypt and Ethiopia, of the whole of Upper Egypt. There are cases in which a literal fulfilment of prophecy may be abandoned without detriment to Divine revelation, and this seems to be one of them. And yet we must always remember that even the letter of the prophecy may some day turn out to be more nearly in harmony with facts than we have supposed, our knowledge of this period being in several respects so very imperfect. It has been acutely pointed out that the oracle given to Necho (Herod., ii. 158), " that he was labouring for the barbarian," seems to imply a current expectation of an invasion of Egypt by Nebuchadnezzar, and that the gradual conquest by that king of one neighbouring country after another suggests that the invasion of Egypt was at any rate the object at which he aimed. The silence of Herodotus as to a Chaldean invasion is, perhaps, not very important. He does not mention Necho's defeat by Nebuchadnezzar at Carchemish, nor does he ever refer to the victories over Egypt of any King of Assyria.

POSTSCRIPT.—The above note is left precisely as it was written, February, 1881, in ignorance of Wiedemann's then recent discovery of a contemporary hieroglyphic inscription which, as the report of the German Oriental Society expresses it, " ratifies the *hitherto universally doubted* fact of an invasion of Egypt by Nebuchadnezzar." The hieroglyphic narrative is supplemented and confirmed by two cuneiform records, and the combined results are as follows. In the thirty-seventh year of his reign, Hophra or Apries being King of Egypt, Nebuchadnezzar undertook an expedition against Egypt, and penetrated as far as the island of Elephantine, and damaged the temple of Chnum, which stood there. His army could not, however, pass the cataracts. At Syene the Egyptian troops, under Neshor, met and repelled the invaders. Two years later, however, the Babylonians came again, were victorious over the Egyptian host under Amasis, and compelled the whole

land to pay tribute. Thus we have a remarkable confirmation of Ezekiel's prophecy that Egypt should be " waste and desolate from Migdol unto Syene, even unto the border of Ethiopia " (Ezek. xxix. 10). It should be mentioned that the Babylonians are not described in the hieroglyphics by their proper name, but as " the Syrians (?), the peoples of the north, the Asiatics ; " it is from a terra-cotta cuneiform tablet that we learn that, in Nebuchadnezzar's thirty-seventh year (B.C. 568-7), a war arose between him and the King of Egypt, which ended with the payment of tribute to the former (Wiedemann, in ' Ægyptische Zeitschrift,' 1878, pp. 2—6 and 87—89 ; ' Geschichte Ægyptens,' 1880, pp. 168—170). The value of prophecy does not, happily, depend on the minuteness of its correspondence with history, and the evidential value of the argument from such a correspondence is but secondary. Still, as long as such a correspondence can be proved, even in part, by facts such as Wiedemann has discovered, the apologist is perfectly justified in using it in confirmation of the authority of Scripture.

The second prophecy falls into two parts —vers. 14—19 and 20—26 respectively.

Vers. 14—19.—The cities of Egypt are called upon to prepare to meet the foe. But it is in vain ; for all that is great and mighty in the land—Apis, the mercenary soldiers, and the Pharaoh—bows down before that terrible one who is comparable only to the most imposing objects in the inanimate world. Pharaoh's time is over ; and Egypt must go into captivity.

Ver. 14.—**Declare ye** ; viz. the approach of the foe (comp. ch. iv. 5). The news is to be told in the frontier towns Migdol and Tahpanhes, and in the northern capital Noph or Memphis (see on ch. ii. 16 ; xliv. 1). **The sword shall devour**, etc. ; rather, *the sword hath devoured those round about thee.* The neighbouring nations (the same phrase occurs in ch. xlviii. 17, 39) have one after another succumbed ; no ally is left there.

Ver. 15.—**Why are thy valiant** men, etc. ? The literal rendering of the received text is, *Why is thy strong ones* (plural) *swept away* (or, *cast down*) ? *He stood not, because Jehovah thrust him!* It is true that the first half of the verse might, consistently with grammar, be rendered, " Why are thy strong ones swept away ? " But the following singulars prove that the subject of the verb in the first verse-half must itself be a singular. We must, therefore, follow the reading of the Septuagint, Vulgate, Aquila, Symmachus, and Theodotion, and many of the extant Hebrew manuscripts, and change the plural " strong ones " into the singular "strong one." The word so rendered is elsewhere in Jeremiah one used (in the plural) of strong horses (ch. viii. 16; xlvii. 3; l. 11); but there is no necessity to bind ourselves to this acceptation. Other possible meanings are (1) strong man, e.g. Judg. v. 22 and Lam. i. 15; (2) steer, bull, e.g. Ps. xxii. 13 and l. 13, and (metaphorically of princes) lxviii. 31. It is a tenable view that "thy strong one" is to be understood distributively as equivalent to "every strong one of thine." But it is certainly more plausible to regard the phrase as a synonym for Apis, the sacred bull in which the supreme god Osiris was believed by the Egyptians to be incarnate. This was a superstition (strange, no doubt, but not so ignoble as some have thought) as deeply ingrained in the Egyptian mind as any in their complicated religion. "In fact, they believed that the supreme God was with them when they possessed a bull bearing certain hieratic marks, the signs of the incarnation of the divinity" (Pierret). His death was the signal for a mourning as general as for a Pharaoh, and the funeral ceremonies (accounts of which are given in the inscriptions) were equally splendid. M. Mariette has discovered, in the neighbourhood of Memphis, a necropolis in which the Apis-bulls were successively interred from the eighteenth dynasty to the close of the period of the Ptolemies. For the Apis to be "swept away" like ordinary plunder, or "cast down" in the slaughtering-trough (comp. Isa. xxxiv. 7), was indeed a token that the glory of Egypt had departed. It is a singular coincidence that the very word here employed by Jeremiah for "bull" (abbîr) was adopted (like many other words) into the Egyptian language—it received the slightly modified form aber. The Septuagint, it should be added, is in favour of the general view of the verse thus obtained, and the authority of the Egyptian-Jewish version in a prophecy relative to Egypt is not slight. Its rendering of the first half is, "Why hath Apis, thy chosen calf, fled?" But the probability is that it read the Hebrew differently, "Why hath Khaph (= Apis), thy chosen one, fled?" This merely involves grouping some letters otherwise, and reading one word a little differently.

Ver. 16.—**To fall**; rather, *to stumble*. The fugitives are in such a wild confusion that they stumble over each other. The parallel passage in the earlier prophecy (ver. 12) suggests that the Egyptian warriors are here referred to, the most trustworthy portion of which, since the time of Psammetichus, was composed of mercenaries, the native troops having lost that military ardour for which they had

been anciently renowned (see Herod., ii. 152, and Sir Gardner Wilkinson's note *ap*. Rawlinson). Being devoid of patriotic feeling, it was natural that these hired soldiers should hasten from the doomed country, exclaiming, as the prophet puts it, **Arise, and let us go again** to our own people. Greeks were probably among the speakers, at any rate, Ionians and Carians formed the mercenary troops of Psammetichus, according to Herodotus (ii. 152).

Ver. 17.—**They did cry there**, etc.; rather, *they cry there*, viz. the following words. But why should attention be called to the place where the cry is made? and why should the mercenaries (the subject of the preceding verb, and therefore presumably of this verb) have their exclamation recorded? Alter the vowel-points (which merely represent an early but not infallible exegetical tradition), and all becomes clear. We then get a renewal of the summons in ver. 14 to make a proclamation respecting the war. The persons addressed are, not foreigners, but the children of the soil, and the summons runs thus: "Call ye the name of Pharaoh, King of Egypt, Desolation." No longer "Pharaoh," honoured by titles indicating that he, like Apis, is a Divine incarnation (*neb*, i.e. lord, and *nuter*, i.e. god), but *Shāōn*, the Hebrew for Desolation, is the fittest name for the fallen monarch. The custom of changing names with a symbolic meaning is no strange one to readers of the prophecies. We have met with it in this very book (see ch. xx. 3); and Isaiah contains a parallel as exact as could be desired, in the famous passage in which the prophetic name (itself symbolic) of Egypt (**Rahab**, *i.e.* boisterousness, arrogance) is changed into "Rahab-hem-shebheth" (*i.e.* "Rahab! they are utter indolence"). In behalf of this view we may claim the authority of a tradition still older than that preserved in the vowel-points, for the Septuagint (followed substantially by the Peshito and the Vulgate) has, Καλέσατε τὸ ὄνομα Φαραὼ Νεχαὼ βασιλέως Αἰγύπτου, Σαών. **He hath passed the time appointed.** A difficult clause, and variously interpreted. One thing is clear, that "passed" cannot be correct, as the verb is in the Hifil or causative conjugation. We must, at any rate, render, "He hath let the time appointed pass by." This is, in fact, the simplest and most natural explanation. There was a time within which repentance might have averted the judgment of God; but this "accepted time" has been foolishly let slip.

Ver. 18.—The threat implied in ver. 17 is set forth more fully; he who speaks is a very different "king" from the fallen Pharaoh. **As Tabor is among the mountains.**

The sense is deformed by the insertion of "is." The King of Babylon is compared to "Tabor among the mountains and Carmel by the sea." Mount Tabor is a most prominent object, owing to the wide extent of the plain of Esdraelon, in which it is situated; and a similar remark applies to Mount Carmel. The view of Tabor differs considerably according to the point from which it is taken; but "its true figure is an elongated oval" (Thomson). Carmel, so called from the rich orchards and vineyards with which it was anciently adorned, is not lofty (being only about six hundred feet above the sea), but the form in which it breaks off towards the sea has a beauty of its own. It is now deprived of its rich forest and garden culture, but is still described as "a glorious mountain."

Ver. 19.—**0 thou daughter dwelling in Egypt**; literally, *O inhabitress-daughter of Egypt.* The phrase is exactly parallel to "virgin daughter of Zion." The "daughter of Egypt" means the population of Egypt, the land being regarded as the mother of its people. **Furnish thyself to go into captivity.** The rendering of the margin is, however, more exact. The "vessels of captivity [or, 'exile']" are a pilgrim's staff and wallet, with the provisions and utensils necessary for a journey (so in Ezek. xii. 4).

Vers. 20—26.—A figurative description of the dark future of Egypt.

Ver. 20.—**Like a very fair heifer.** (The insertion of "like" weakens the passage.) The well-nourished heifer reminds of the prosperity of the fruitful Nile valley. But **destruction cometh; it cometh out of the north**; rather, *a gadfly from the north hath come upon her* (not, "hath come, hath come," as the received text has—a very slight change in one letter is required, supported by the versions). The figure is precisely analogous to that of the "bee in the land of Assyria" (Isa. vii. 18). St. Chrysostom renders "a gadfly" (see Field, 'Origen's Hexapla,' ii. 708); and so virtually Aquila and Symmachus.

Ver. 21.—**Also her hired men are in the midst of her**, etc.; rather, *also her hirelings in the midst of her are like*, etc. These seem to be distinguished from the mercenaries mentioned in ver. 9, the Ethiopians, Libyans, and Arabs, who were never adopted into the midst of the Egyptian people. On the other hand, the description will exactly apply to the Carians and Ionians in the service of Psammetichus and Apries (Herod., ii. 152, 163), who were "for many years" settled "a little below the city of Bubastis, on the Pelusiac mouth of the Nile." In this fertile country, itself comparable to "a very fair heifer" (ver. 20), these pampered and privileged mercenaries became "like calves

of the stall." **They did not stand**, etc.; rather, *they have not stood (firm), for the day of their destruction is come upon them.*

Ver. 22.—**The voice thereof shall go like a serpent**; rather, *her voice is like (the sound of) a serpent gliding away.* Egypt (like Jerusalem, in Isa. xxix. 4) is imagined as a maiden (comp. ver. 19) seated on the ground, and faintly sighing; and her feeble voice is likened to the rustling sound of a serpent in motion. **Come against her with axes.** A sudden change of figure. Egypt, or, more strictly, Egypt's grandeur—its rich and complex national life, its splendid cities, its powerful army, all combined in one, is now compared to a forest (comp. ch. xxi. 14; xxii. 6, 7; Isa. ii. 13; x. 18, 19, 33, 34). It seems far-fetched to suppose, with Graf and Dr. Payne Smith, that the comparison of the Chaldean warriors to wood-cutters arose from their being armed with axes. It is probably true that the Israelites did not use the battle-axe, but the axe is merely an accident of the description. It is the forest which suggests the mention of the axe, not the axe that of the forest, and forests were familiar enough to the Israelites.

Ver. 23.—**They shall cut down**; better, *they cut down.* The prophet is describing a picture which passes before his inner eye. **Though it cannot be searched**; rather, *for it cannot be searched out.* The subject of the verb is uncertain. De Dieu's explanation is, "Because the forest is so dense, so intricate, it is necessary to clear a path by cutting down the trees." But this does not seem to suit the context. Surely no other reason was required for the destruction of the "forest" than the will of the wood-cutters. "Searching out" occurs in Job (v. 9; ix. 10; xxxvi. 26; comp. also 1 Kings vii. 47) in connection with numbering, and the second half of the verse expressly describes the foe as innumerable. The singular alternates with the plural, as in Isa. v. 28, a host being regarded sometimes as a whole, and sometimes as an aggregate of individuals. **Than the grasshoppers**; rather, *the locust.* The name is one of nine which we find given to the various species of locusts in the Old Testament, and means "multitudinous."

Ver. 24.—**Shall be confounded**; rather, *is brought to shame;* the next verb too should rather be in the past tense.

Ver. 25.—**The multitude of No**; rather, *Amon of No.* Amon-Ra, or rather Amen-Ra, was the name adopted at Thebes (Homer's Thebes "of the hundred gateways," 'Iliad,' ix. 383, called here "No," and in Nah. iii. 8 "No [of] Amon") from the time of the eleventh dynasty, for the sun-god Ra.. Amon (Amen) signifies "hidden," for it is the mysterious, invisible deity who manifests himself in bodily form in the sun. From this name comes the classic designation, Jupiter-Ammon. **Their gods . . . their kings** ; rather, *her gods . . . her kings* (viz. Egypt's). The "kings" are probably the high officials of the state, not a few of whom were either by birth or marriage members of the royal family. **Even Pharaoh, and all them that trust in him.** With a suggestive allusion to the many in Judah who "trusted" in that "broken reed" (Isa. xxxvi. 6).

Ver. 26.—**Afterward it shall be inhabited,** etc. After all these gloomy vaticinations, Jeremiah (as elsewhere in this group of prophecies ; see ch. xlviii. 47 ; xlix. 6, 39) opens up a brighter prospect. "In the days of old," patriarchal and unmilitary, the fertile valley of the Nile offered a peaceful and a happy home to its teeming inhabitants ; those times shall yet come again. To understand this, we must assume that during its period of depression Egypt has been but sparsely peopled, owing to the large numbers of its inhabitants carried away captive. Another explanation, "afterwards Egypt shall stay at home [*i.e.* 'be quiet']," though equally justifiable from the point of view of the lexicon (comp. Judg. v. 17 ; Ps. lv. 7), seems less natural. Possibly Ezek. xxix. 13—16 is a development of our passage ; it contains a promise of future remission of punishment, though a promise qualified in such a way as to be akin to a threat. The words, "And it shall no more be the confidence of the house of Israel" (Ezek. xxix. 16), seem like a comment on Jeremiah's threat to "Pharaoh, and them that trust in him," in the preceding verse.

Vers. 27, 28.—A word of comfort to Israel, obviously not written at the same time as the preceding prophecy. The prophet is suddenly transported in imagination into the period of the Babylonian exile. Egypt and its fortunes are far away ; the troubles of Israel entirely absorb his attention. After thinking sadly of the reverses of his people, he bursts out with an encouraging exhortation not to fear, though, humanly speaking, there was everything to fear. Did Jeremiah write these verses here ? There is strong reason to doubt it ; for they occur, with insignificant variations, in ch. xxx. 10, 11, where they cohere far better with the context than here.

HOMILETICS.

Vers. 1—26.—*The judgment of Egypt.* This is twofold, first in the defeat at Carchemish (vers. 1—12), and then in a complete overthrow of the kingdom (vers. 13—26), which Jeremiah seems to have anticipated immediately after, just as the early Christians connected the destruction of Jerusalem with the expected end of the world. Though this anticipation was not chronologically correct, the essence of the prophecy was ultimately fulfilled. The kingdom of the Pharaohs has passed away.

I. EGYPT WAS A HEATHEN COUNTRY. The two prophecies about Egypt occur first in a series of predictions concerning the Gentile nations. God is the God of the Gentile as well as the Jew, of the heathen as well as the Christian, of the godless as well as the godly. In him all men live and move and have their being ; from him they receive every blessing of life ; to him they will have to give account of their deeds. Therefore God notes the conduct of heathen nations, and chastises them when needful ; so he does with individual men who renounce his authority over them or are brought up in ignorance of it. The heathen will be judged by their heathenish light, and not by the high standards of Christian principles ; but there is enough in that light to allow of a genuine judgment and a just sentence (Rom. ii. 14, 15). The 'Book of the Dead' contains a high and noble system of morality. With this in his possession, the Egyptian was without excuse in his vice and cruelty.

II. EGYPT WAS AN ANCIENT NATION. Her history dates back long before the time of Abraham. But she found no immunity in age. If judgment is long delayed, it will come in God's appointed time. The mere continuance of peaceful circumstances hitherto is not the slightest ground for crediting them with a special charm to ward off the sentence of Divine justice. The hoary sinner will not be spared out of regard to his years. Age is not venerable in itself. It is only odious when it is the ripening and rotting of a long life of sin.

III. EGYPT WAS A LAND OF WEALTH AND SPLENDOUR. (For this point, see homily on ver. 20.)

IV. EGYPT WAS A HOME OF SCIENCE AND PHILOSOPHY. There philosophy arose, and the knowledge of nature was first systematically pursued. There strange mystic religions had their birth. If knowledge could save a people, Egypt of all lands should be safe. But though knowledge is power, there are foes against which it is impotent. The science of the encyclopædists was no protection against the horrors of the French Revolution. Modern science cannot find an antidote to sin, nor can modern inventiveness devise any armour that shall resist the piercing darts of Divine justice. Our religious speculation will not redeem our souls.

V. EGYPT WAS THE ALLY OF ISRAEL. The alliance of the Church is no safeguard when the Church herself is erring. Companionship in sin with men who have been accounted Christians will do nothing to lighten the weight of guilt. They will have to suffer for their share in the wickedness, and if their previous reputation cannot shield them, it can have no protection to extend to others.

VI. EGYPT MADE A BRAVE RESISTANCE. Jeremiah describes the battle array in stirring words. The army was imposing. Yet was defeated. It is vain to resist the decree of Divine judgment. He who fights against this is striking at Heaven. The blow can only recoil on his own head.

VII. EGYPT WAS TO BE INHABITED AGAIN. God mingles mercy with judgment. He has pity on the heathen. He seeks the ultimate recovery of those whom he first punishes. In later years Egypt became the home and centre of the most brilliant Christian life and thought.

Ver. 11.—*Incurable diseases.* I. WHAT DISEASES ARE NATURALLY INCURABLE ? 1. *Sin.* No man can root out his own evil nature. The wicked man, left to himself, will never grow into righteousness. Sin does not burn out; it continually finds fresh fuel and kindles a greater fire. 2. *The judgment of sin.* This cannot be resisted, for it comes from the hand of the Almighty. It cannot be bought off by compensating merits, for the most we can do is not to deserve more punishment in the future by new sin. When we have done our best we are " unprofitable servants; we have done that which was our duty to do."

II. HOW GOD CURES THE NATURALLY INCURABLE DISEASE. Christ is the good Physician, the great Healer. Where medicine fails miracle triumphs. She who "had suffered many things of many physicians, and had spent all that she had, and was nothing bettered, but rather grew worse," was made whole by a touch of the hem of the Saviour's garment. The cure may be impossible with man, but with God all things are possible. 1. *The cure for sin.* This is in the new birth which makes the Christian a " new creation " in Christ Jesus, and the constant aid of the Spirit of God to cleanse and purify the soul. 2. *The cure for the judgment of sin.* This is in the free pardon offered to the penitent who trust to Christ, and it is secured through his mediation, his one sacrifice for sin, and his perpetual intercession for sinners.

Ver. 20.—*The heifer and the gadfly.* " Egypt is a very fair heifer, but a gadfly cometh."

I. WORLDLY ADVANTAGES ARE NO SAFEGUARDS AGAINST TROUBLE. The heifer is very fair, yet the gadfly attacks her. Egypt, rich in her fertile Nile valley, the granary of the East; splendid with vast and gorgeous temples, whose ruins are now the wonder of the world; in the forefront of speculation and science; hoary with antiquity, and proud of her æons of history even in Jeremiah's age—twenty-five dynasties had already passed away;—this great Egypt is to suffer humiliation at the hand of the upstart Babylon. Her very magnificence attracts the greedy invader. Wealth and rank may ward off some distresses, but they will invite others which never condescend to attack the poor and obscure.

II. WORLDLY ADVANTAGES AFFORD LITTLE CONSOLATION IN TROUBLE. If the heifer is very fair, her beauty is no antidote to the pain she feels when the probe of the gadfly is in her back. Egypt may have every advantage of wealth and science, and yet she finds no comfort in these things when her life-blood is flowing beneath the sword of the rude invader. The death of her firstborn is as heavy a blow to the queen as to the meanest slave in the land. The rich man feels his gout at least as acutely as the poor man. Mental distress, anxiety, and care are not to be bought off with money.

III. A SMALL OCCASION MAY PRODUCE GREAT TROUBLE. The gadfly is but half an inch long. Yet it can so irritate the heifer that she will rush madly about, with head thrust forward and tail stuck out, in the vain hope of escaping from her tormentor. Many a man has just one cause of trouble, looking to others quite insignificant, yet which is to him the fly spoiling the most precious ointment. How much of the distress of life comes from the fret and worry of little things! It is a comfort that we are not only invited to cast our burden upon the Lord, but to cast all our " care upon him, for he careth for us."

IV. WE MAY BE UNABLE TO PREVENT THE ATTACK OF THE SMALLEST OCCASION OF TROUBLE. The horns, which would be good weapons for attacking a large animal, are useless against the gadfly. Many troubles come like this fly. We cannot touch them; they are swift to attack, and once they are upon us no defence is possible. In our own strength we cannot throw off the smallest sin. Perhaps we are strong to resist great temptations, and fall victims to miserable little failings. The devil is not always a roaring lion; sometimes he is more like a gadfly. We can drive off the lion; we cannot resist the gadfly. Lying, theft, murder, etc., may be kept out, and yet our souls may lose all peace and Divine communion by yielding to hasty temper, discontent, cowardice, etc. But Christ comes as the Saviour from all evil and all sin, including those meaner sins which may ruin our spiritual life even when greater sins are avoided.

Vers. 27, 28.—(See homily on ch. xxx. 10, 11.)

HOMILIES BY VARIOUS AUTHORS.

Ver. 1.—*The judgment of the nations.* I. UTTERED BY THE PROPHET OF THE THEOCRACY. 1. *Because they are related to the theocracy.* Even in antagonism; but sometimes in conscious or undesigned co-operation. The future of the kingdom of God is not, therefore, to evolve itself independently of these, but in close connection with them. It is this, and this alone, which gives them their importance. They are associated with the destinies of God's people. What mysterious necessity is it that ever blends God's kingdom with the main stream of history? It is the dominant influence even when it seems to be temporarily overthrown. 2. *The kingdom of God is to be fulfilled in the whole earth.* Not only in Israel is it to come, but in the "uttermost parts of the earth." The kingdoms of this world are to "become the kingdoms of our Lord, and of his Christ" (Rev. xi. 15). For this reason their history, too, is sacred, and is to be read in the light of revelation if it is to be understood. The true history of every nation and individual is determined by relation to the truth of God. 3. *For the instruction and comfort of God's people.* It is manifest that Divine providence can be explained worthily only upon such a scale. And the subjects of the Divine kingdom have to be taught the real character and destiny of the powers into relation with which they are brought. God is seen as ruling, not only in a little corner, but in the whole earth. II. UTTERED TOGETHER AT ONE TIME. There is a question as to which order ought to be observed in mentioning them. 1. But the selection is made upon an evident principle, viz. that of (nearly) contemporaneous relation to Israel. And whatever their relations amongst themselves or toward Israel at any given time, *in general they are opposed to the kingdom of God,* and represent the influences with which it has to do in its progress amongst men. They are "the world-powers" as opposed to the "powers of the world to come." 2. It is part of the scheme of Divine revelation to arraign from time to time the spirit of this world in its varying forms and phases. The world's life and history thus cease to be complex and involved, and are seen to resolve themselves into the principles of good and evil, darkness and light. The turmoil and movement are really those of a great duel—that of the kingdom of God against the kingdom of this world. III. UTTERED FINALLY AND ABSOLUTELY. It is destruction that is predicted, and as real historic powers we do not hear of them again. There is something very grand and solemn in this arraying and dismissal of the nations. Their political influence, military power, or commercial supremacy avails not against this imperative Word of the Most High. What is it but an anticipation of the judgment of the earth by the Son of man

(Matt. xxv. 31)? Has not our Saviour already ground for his claim, "I have overcome the world"? The gospel of the kingdom of God is, therefore, no little thing done in a corner, but the economy of a world, and the law of life and death throughout all ages.—M.

Vers. 27, 28.—(*Vide* on ch. xxx. 10, 11.)—M.

Vers. 1—28.—"*Judgment*" *going on* "*from the house of God.*" The former chapters have shown judgment beginning at the house of God. This and the following chapters show that judgment going on.

I. JUDGMENT BEGINS AT THE HOUSE OF GOD. This whole life here is more or less a time of trial. God never suffers his Church to be long at ease. But there are especial times of trial, as in persecutions, bereavements, uprisings of the power of sin. And sometimes, as in the former chapters is told, God sends his actual judgments and chastisements upon his people. Now, concerning this, note : 1. *It is just that judgment should begin at*, etc. For God has a right to the reverence and obedience of his own people. If a father be not obeyed in his own house, where else should he be ? More of light, privilege, and grace are given to his Church, and more of ill follows from their sin ; and hence no wonder that judgment begins, etc. 2. *And it is fit and suitable.* Who cares for the household as the father ? I hear a child in the streets use profane or foul language, and I am shocked that any child should use language like that. But if it were *my* child, with what horror and indignation should I be filled ! All the father's affection clusters round and centres in his home, and hence he will spare no pains nor refuse any methods—even judgments when they are needed, as once and again they are—whereby the highest well-being of his children may be secured. 3. *And it is merciful likewise.* It was not judgment, but mercy also, that "drove out the man" from Paradise. Some discipline sterner than Paradise afforded was needed now for the subdual of that evil nature which had become dominant in man. And that nature must be subdued and the better nature formed in us, or the high and holy purpose of God cannot be fulfilled in us.

II. BUT IT DOES NOT STOP THERE. To show this is the purport of this and the following chapters. 1. *And how true this is generally !* There is the sorrow of the world as well as that of the believer; and who would not rather have that of the believer than that of the world? 2. *And how much greater is the sorrow of the world !* "If they do these things in the green tree, what," etc.? said our Saviour. "If the righteous scarcely be saved, where," etc.? said St. Peter. And that "their sorrows shall be multiplied" is inevitable. For they have *no inward spring of consolation* beneath them. There is so *much more to be done* in order to rescue them from their ways. The processes of agriculture are sometimes severe; but what are they compared to the stern work needed for bringing the land into cultivation. The police of a well-ordered town cause some burden to the inhabitants; but what is that to martial law ? *They touch the all of the world, only the lesser good of the believer. And they stay so much longer time.* There was no such restoration for the Gentile people told of here as there was and especially will be for the Jewish race. The Church of Christ has often been judged, but she has ever been restored, and will be yet more. But during her history, Rome, Venice, and political states within Christendom have risen, decayed, and disappeared. 3. *How admonitory all this is !* (1) *To the child of the house of God.* It bids him be thankful because he knows the motive, the measure, and the sure end of what he has to bear. Submission that he may at once escape the heavy hand of God and shelter in his heart. (2) *To those not in the house of God.* It says, "Come in, that judgment may be turned into chastisement, wrath into fatherly correction, and that the gates of death when they close upon you may shut out the further approach of sorrow, and not, as if there be no repentance they will, shut you in with it and with innumerable other sorrows more than the first. 'Verily I say unto you,' saith our Lord, 'ye shall not come out thence until ye have paid the uttermost farthing.'"—C.

Ver. 8.—*Premature glorying.* In this verse and in others we have the vain vauntings of Egypt. Thus far the judgments of God have been declared against his people. Now, having begun at the house of God, judgment goes on to the Gentile nations, one

after another of whom are told of in the chapters that succeed this, and ending with
the judgment on Babylon.   Egypt and Babylon were the two great empires between
which unhappy Judæa was "like a nut between the forceps," so that when these two
drew together it went ill with the little kingdom that lay between.   Now, in these
chapters Egypt takes the lead and Babylon closes, the lesser nations occupying the
central position.   The invasion and conquest of Egypt is the subject of this forty-sixth
chapter from the thirteenth verse.   Its decisive defeat at Carchemish is told of in the
previous portion.   It was in anticipation of that disastrous battle that Egypt, persuading herself that it would issue so differently, is heard uttering the proud boastings
of this eighth verse.   At first it seemed as if these boastings were not vain, for at
Megiddo, where King Josiah was slain, the Egyptian army did obtain a victory; but,
three years after, when they had pushed on to the banks of the Euphrates, Nebuchadnezzar fell upon them there and completely vanquished them.   Crestfallen and crushed,
they had to make their weary way back to their own land; and shortly after we read
(2 Kings xxiv. 7), "the King of Egypt came not again any more out of his land: for
the King of Babylon had taken from the river of Egypt unto the river Euphrates all
that pertained to the King of Egypt."   That was what came of all their vauntings, and
the history is a noticeable one on many grounds.   Now, it recalls to our mind the wise
exhortation, "Let not him that girdeth on his harness boast himself as he that putteth
it off" (1 Kings xx. 11).   Let us note—

I. SOME MANIFESTATIONS OF THIS SPIRIT of over-confidence.   The Bible is full of facts
which illustrate this spirit.   Pharaoh, in the days of Moses, asking, "Who is the Lord,
that I should obey him?"   Goliath of Gath striding down the valley in furious pride
to meet the stripling David.   He swore by all his gods he would give those young
limbs as a prey for the vultures to feed upon.   Rabshakeh, again, general of the host
of the King of Assyria, terrifying and dismaying the devout Hezekiah with his fearful
threatenings.   And we know how the distress lasted until Hezekiah took the letter of
the haughty heathen and laid it before the Lord.   Then, serene and strong, his spirit
rose up, and he was able to make fit answer.   And we know how Jehovah avenged
Judah, her king, and her people upon the vast multitude of their foes who in battle
array lay around them.   For—

> "Like the leaves of the forest when autumn hath blown,
>   That host on the morrow lay withered and strewn;
>   For the angel of death spread his wings on the blast,
>   And breathed in the face of the foe as he passed.
>
> "And the tents were all silent, the banners alone;
>   The lances unlifted, the trumpet unblown;
>   And the might of the Gentile, unsmote by the sword,
>   Had melted like snow in the glance of the Lord."

And we think, too, of Haman in his rage at Mordecai, vowing vengeance, and surely
reckoning on wreaking it to the full.   And Samson, imagining that nothing could
deprive him of his great strength, so confident that at any moment he could break
through every barrier, but at length enticed, betrayed, overcome, and ruined.   And,
passing to the region of spiritual things, we think of Israel pledging themselves, as
they stood at the foot of Mount Sinai, to perfect obedience.   Of that rich "fool" of
whom our Lord tells, and who made so sure of many years to enjoy his "much goods"
laid up in store.   And of the many who were candidates for discipleship, avowing
themselves ready to follow him everywhere.   And of Peter, boasting that, though all
men should forsake the Lord, yet would not he.   And Judas, who trembled not to
take the office of apostleship though so incapable of sustaining it.   And *in common
life* how often we see this same spirit!   Our Afghan disasters in 1879 were largely
owing to it.   But *in spiritual life* there is the same peril.   There may not be the
uttered words of vain vaunting, but the spirit may be there notwithstanding.   For
how little there is of the trembling, the watchful, the prayerful spirit lest we should
be overcome!   How far too much tampering with temptation!   How few "pass the
time of their sojourning here in fear" lest they should "seem to come short" of eternal
life!   How many are like the foolish virgins, who, all careless as to the unsupplied

condition of their oil-vessels, nevertheless contentedly lay down to sleep! How many are at ease in Zion, allowing themselves in a carnal security which too often is but the herald of a fearful awakening!

II. INQUIRE—WHAT LEADS TO THIS SPIRIT? Some are of a boastful disposition. These Egyptians evidently were. He concerning whom the cautionary words already quoted were used, "Let not him that girdeth on his harness," etc., was another such habitual boaster. And this is human nature. Our pride dies hard, but is puffed up with wonderful ease. Then: 2. *False estimates* have a great deal to do with it. *Underestimating* our adversaries', *over-estimating* our own, resources and strength. Hence Benhadad, who thought such scorn of Israel, on the very eve of battle was, we are told, drinking himself drunk in his tent. Hence many are found dallying with danger, fluttering, mothlike, round the flame by which they are sure soon to perish miserably. The jocular way in which the devil is so generally spoken of proves that we do but little believe in him; for what men seriously believe they never joke about. And this false estimate is rendered more credible to us if we have obtained aught of success heretofore. Egypt had at Megiddo; Benhadad had. Hence their estimates. 3. *Perversion of God's truth.* We encourage ourselves in this spirit of over-confidence by dwelling too exclusively on promises of protection to the neglect of those which command all watchfulness and prayer. Men will read *parts* of the Bible only—those which please them most; and without doubt many have dwelt so much on the promises of God's upholding grace and his perfecting that which he begins, that they have laid ide their armour—that indispensable armour of God. But any reading of God's Word which leads us thus practically to disobey his command is thereby proved to be a wrong reading. For, just as the chemist's litmus paper, plunged into a solution containing acid, at once reveals by its turning red the presence of that acid, however invisible and imperceptible it may have been before, so any interpretation of the Scriptures which leads to false security, premature and presumptuous confidence, which makes us red with this sad sin, proves that that interpretation contains the acid of falsehood. It is a sure test. God help us to heed it as we should.

III. NOTE WHAT MISCHIEF IT WORKS. These are seen strewn over every pathway along which this spirit hath been; like the bleached bones in the desert show the track of the caravan.

IV. Consider, therefore, SOME SAFEGUARDS AGAINST IT. God himself at times undertakes its cure. He did so with Peter. He let him go his way and fall, and in that crash the spirit of boastfulness was for ever crushed. But we shall be aided by remembering the words of Christ and his apostles and of all his most faithful servants. They all warn against this spirit, and urge the spirit of watchfulness and prayer. Remember, too, that better men than ourselves have fallen. The very fact that armour is provided shows that we need it. And note that there are chinks in your armour; and that some armour is of very worthless sort.

CONCLUSION. Whilst bidding you boast not, with equal emphasis we say, "Despond not." "The gist of all this is, confide in God, but distrust yourselves. Have done with every glorying except glorying in the Lord. . . . There is nothing like full assurance for excellence, and nothing like presumption for worthlessness. Never mistake the one for the other. You cannot trust God too much nor yourself too little. I read a book one day called 'Self-Made Men,' and in its own sphere it was excellent; but spiritually I should not like to be a self-made man. I should think he would be an awful specimen of humanity. At any rate, a self-made Christian is one of a sort the devil very soon takes, as I have seen a child so take a bran doll and shake it all out. He likes to shake out self-made Christians till there is nothing left of them. But God-made men,—these are they that do exploits; and God-made Christians, who fall back upon the eternal strength at all times and confide there,—these are the men to hold on their way and to wax stronger and stronger" (Spurgeon).—C.

Ver. 10.—*The terror of sacrifice without its blessing.* The ancient sacrifices had much about them that was very repulsive. The slaughtering and dismemberment of the vast herds of animals that were year by year brought to the altar must have involved in it very much that was of a revolting nature. No doubt their sensitiveness to such scenes of blood was far less than ours; but at the best it must have been a most painful spectacle. Hence scoffers have called it the religion of the shambles. But the salvation and blessing that came through the sacrifices divested them of all that was painful or repulsive to the offerer. But there may be all that is terrible about sacrifice—agony, blood, death, carnage—without any corresponding blessing. Such is the meaning here. Slaughter, but no salvation. The same word for "sacrifice" is used as in those which were offered according to the Law on the altar in the temple. And so in the parallel passages in Isa. xxxiv. 6 and Ezek. xxxix. 17, which should be compared with this, and which are alluded to by St. John in the Revelation. In all these there is the terror of sacrifice, but none of its blessing. And there is that which corresponds to this now. Even Christ's sacrifice may be a terror and not a salvation. It is so to: 1. *Those who refuse it.* 2. *Those who apostatize from it,* who count the blood of the covenant an unholy thing, trampling underfoot the Son of God (Heb. x.). 3. *Those who make it the minister of sin.* Who "turn the grace of God into lasciviousness." There is, then, a twofold aspect of the Lord's sacrifice. Either it must be that by it we rise or fall. "This child is set for the fall and rising again." The gospel is "a savour of life unto life, or," etc. Christ is a Rock on which we may build, or which, falling on the impenitent, crushes him to powder. Which for *ourselves?*—C.

Ver. 15.—*The real cause of the decline of empires.* "Because the Lord did drive them." If we read ordinary histories, the overthrow of any monarchy is traced to such an invasion or to the loss of such a battle, or to some other ordinary and well-known cause. And no doubt it is true that, through and by these things, the said results have been brought about. But there is ever a moral cause which lies behind, and it is to that must be traced up the series of events which have followed. The history of most ancient empires, in their origin, progress, decline, and fall, has been very much the same. A hardy, temperate, courageous people, driven by necessity or attracted by the hope of gain, fall upon some decrepit power, destroy it, and on its ruins build their own fortunes. For a while the same courage and virtue which enabled them to gain possession of their prize are manifested in consolidating their power and in building up their rule. But after the lapse of years, they have gained secure foothold and are able to live less on their guard against enemies. Wealth and luxury increase and exert their enervating power. In this soil the vices, whatever they may be, to which as a people they are predisposed, grow rapidly and affect the national habit and character. Then their decay has begun. It hastens rapidly on until, in their turn, this once victorious people are vanquished, overthrown by a nation more bold and righteous and therefore more powerful than themselves. This law can be readily traced in the histories of Egypt, Assyria, Babylon, Persia, Greece, Rome, and in more modern instances as well. Were there no moral causes at work in the overthrow of the French empire under Napoleon I.? In all cases it will be seen that, in one form or another, God's love of righteousness has been outraged, and vengeance has speedily, or surely if not speedily, come. What was the Reformation but the revolt of men's consciences against the abominable sins of the Catholic Church? But how came that Church—once so fair, so beautiful, so glorious—to have sunk so low as to become hateful in men's eyes? It was this same enervating influence of wealth, power, and other forms of earthly prosperity which sapped her spiritual strength until she became utterly unworthy of men's confidence, and she was punished, and is so to this day, by the loss of well-nigh all Northern Europe, the noblest half of her ancient domain. Therefore learn—

I. WHAT ARE NOT A COUNTRY'S SAFEGUARDS, THOUGH OFTEN THOUGHT TO BE. Not *commerce,* or Tyre would not have fallen. Not *art,* or Greece would never have perished. Not *strong political organization,* or Rome would have continued. Not *religious profession,* or Jerusalem and Catholic Rome would not have suffered the disasters that befell them. Not *ancient renown,* or Egypt would have stood fast. All these things have been relied on, and especially *vast armies,* but they have one and all been tested and have proved ropes of sand, battlements taken away because they are not the Lord's. Therefore note—

II. WHAT IS A COUNTRY'S SAFEGUARD? There is but one answer, and that is *righteousness.* It, and it alone, exalteth a nation. The form of government, whether monarchical or republican, matters not, whether political power be in the hands of the many or the few, but the character of the people—their possession or not possession of the "fear of the Lord." Whilst Israel possessed this she was impregnable. "A thousand fell at her side, and," etc.

III. WHAT, THEREFORE, IS TRUE PATRIOTISM? Not alone adding to the material wealth or the intellectual force of the nation, not alone philanthropy or political energy,—none of these things are to be held in light esteem; but the truest patriotism, and it is one which all can exhibit, is the cultivation of godly character, that fear of God which lies at the basis of all moral excellence whatsoever. Yes, not for our own salvation's sake alone, but for our country's sake, even as for Christ's sake, let us seek to resemble him, breathe his Spirit, manifest his character, copy his example, and spread abroad those true principles of national well-being which, by his life and death, he taught us.—C.

Ver. 26.—*Punishment not destruction but purification and preservation.* In ver. 28, in ch. xlviii. 21, and in ch. xlix. 6, 39, we have similar assurances that "afterwards," when God's judgments have done their work, the chastised and afflicted nations shall be restored. Such promise is here made to Egypt. It is repeated in Ezek. xxix. 8—14. And from this reiterated word concerning, not one people only, but so many, we gather the intent and purpose of God in regard to all his punishments which he sends upon men—that they are not for men's destruction, but for their purification and preservation. Note—

I. SOME OF THE BASES OF THIS BELIEF. 1. *Such Scriptures* as these now referred to. 2. The *salutary results* that have followed so much of human suffering. That suffering has shamed indolence, roused energy, stimulated invention, and the results have been safeguards to life and health and general well-being, which would never have been thought of or sought after if suffering had not goaded men on. Hence we conclude that such results were intended and ever are by like causes. 3. The fact that *God created man.* It is incredible that he should create beings whose destiny is an eternity of sin and suffering. If it had been really better for any men that they had never been born, as in this case it undoubtedly would, and as for far less and altogether inadequate reasons we sometimes say it would concerning ourselves or others, then they never would have been born. Our Lord's word concerning Judas is not to be literally pressed. It was a proverbial expression used concerning especially unhappy or ungodly men. 4. The very *name of "Saviour."* Christ either is or is not the Saviour of the world. If he be not, but only fain would be, then the name of "Saviour" cannot be truly his. We do not give the names of "deliverer," "saviour," "benefactor," to those who only desire to be such but are not such. We are forced to believe—and with what thankfulness we would do so!—that he who is called "the Lamb of God" does not merely in wish, but in fact, "take away the sins of the world." 5. The *value of the great sacrifice.* If it do not reconcile the world unto God, as St. Paul affirms it does, then it is less precious than men have thought. But it is inconceivable that such a sacrifice should fail to accomplish that for which it was especially designed. 6. The *express declaration* that the Son of God was manifested to destroy the works of the devil. But are not sin and suffering his work? If, then, they be eternal, how can they have been destroyed? 7. The *necessity involved in the first and great command,* "Thou shalt love the Lord thy God," etc. Now, it is not in the power of the human heart to love any being that it does not conceive as lovable or worthy of love. But a God who created men, knowing that they would eternally sin and suffer, is not lovable by the human heart. What do we say of men who do deeds which they know can only issue in misery and wrong? But is that righteous in God which we should denounce in men? *Abhorrendum sit.*

II. CONCLUSION. 1. *Not that there is no such thing* as God's punishment for sin. 2. *Nor that that punishment is but a little thing.* Ah, no! "It is a fearful thing" for an impenitent unbelieving man " to fall into the hands of the living God." He is a consuming fire to such, and the fire will burn on until all the dross and evil be burnt out. Wellington said, "There is only one thing worse than a great victory, and that is a great defeat." He knew at what cost victory is won. And so there may be only one thing worse than some men's salvation, and that is that they should be eternally lost. 3. *But that we should learn to "love and dread" God.* Love him for his gracious purpose towards men, but dread lest we should compel him by our rejection of his gospel to lead us by sterner ways. For he *will* have all men to be saved and to come to the knowledge of the truth.—C.

Ver. 28.—*Correction, but in measure.* (Cf. homily on *God's reserve of mercy,* vol. i. p. 95.)—C.

Ver. 15.—*Why the valiant are swept away.* I. THEY ARE SWEPT AWAY. Notice the host described in previous verses of the chapter—horsemen and chariots and archers; the Ethiopian, the Libyan, the Lydian; an imposing host, whose magnificence could not but strike the eye. It was meant that they should produce a feeling of being irresistible. And thus in due time, when they were scattered and broken up, there came a complete contrast. The magnificence, the order, the force, were all somehow utterly vanished. The present overthrow became all the more noticeable because of the magnitude of what had been overthrown. And so God will ever make plain the sweeping away of all his foes. Their defeat is not left a doubtful thing. It may be very difficult to account for, but it cannot be questioned.

II. THE NEED FOR ASKING WHY THEY ARE SWEPT AWAY. 1. Because of *their magnificent appearance.* They look strong, and according to a certain standard they are strong. This Egyptian army had been gathered together to do a certain work. It was known that they had to meet no common and easily conquered foe. Therefore there were strong men on strong horses, with powerful weapons and well defended. Yet after all this preparation there came, not merely defeat, but what is called a sweeping away. Assuredly this wants explaining. 2. Because of *past victories.* We cannot suppose they were an untried host. If they had won battles and campaigns before, why did they lose this? And why were they so utterly and lastingly defeated? 3. Because there is no *obvious explanation.* It is not to be looked for in the strength of their human opponents. It is not to be found in some difference between what they were in the hour of confusion and what they had been in previous hours of victory. There is no ground to say they were less brave, less disciplined, worse commanded. The reason for this sweeping away, whatever it be, passes ordinary human search.

III. THE SUFFICIENT REASON IS FOUND IN THE ACTION OF JEHOVAH. Jehovah drove them. All forces that find expression in matter are completely at God's disposal. He can paralyze the mightiest army in a moment. The mighty man is not to glory in his might (ch. ix. 23). True it is that God lets the strong man do generally all his strength permits him to do. The success military men look for is on the side of the strongest battalions. But then all strength of this sort fails against spiritual strength. Not all the armies of Rome and not all the wild beasts of the amphitheatre could persuade a single true Christian to forsake Christ. The strength of this world achieves great things in its own field, but directly it goes beyond and tries to interfere with conscience and spiritual aspirations, its weakness is made manifest.—Y.

Vers. 27, 28.—*God's care of his own.* I. THE NEED OF THE FULLEST POSSIBLE ASSURANCE. Jehovah, who has visited Israel with many and great sufferings, will also visit other peoples. Egypt is spoken of in this chapter; and Philistia, Moab Ammon, and Babylon in following chapters. Hence the need of Divine words such as would keep the believing element in Israel calm and confident through all these disturbances, and so it ever is meant to be with the true Israel of God. God is ready with comforting words amid the necessary turmoil of external conditions.

II. THE SOLID GROUNDS OF THIS ASSURANCE. They lie in Jehovah's continued connection with Israel, and his purposes for its safety, peace, and prosperity. We have no assurance in ourselves or our circumstances, but the moment we can feel that we are in God's hands, that he has plans with respect to us, and a future preparing for us, then assurance is possible. God never tells man to take courage and put away fear without giving good reason for the exhortation, and showing that fear is rather the unreasonable feeling to allow. The moment we can take in the full force of that wonderful word, "I am with thee," then we are freed from alarms and from dependence on the shifting phenomena of this present life.

III. THE DIFFERENCE GOD WILL MAKE BETWEEN ISRAEL AND OTHER NATIONS. A full end is to be made of them. And a full end has been made of them. Here, of course, the distinction must be borne in mind between nations and the individuals composing them. A nation is but a certain arrangement of human beings, and this arrangement may be productive of such wrong feelings and such danger to the world as to make it fitting that the nation should cease. But the people composing the nation remain, and their descendants pass into new and better combinations. So with regard to Israel; the people who are to return and be in rest and without fear, the people who are not to be made a full end of, are those of whom literal Israel is but the type. There are really but two nations in the world—those who believe in God and in his Son, and show their faith by their works; and those who trust in themselves, in their power and their purposes. Of all these latter God must make a full end, if in no other way by bringing them to see their folly, so that they may turn to the ways of faith.

IV. JEHOVAH'S CHASTISEMENT OF HIS OWN EVEN WHILE HE PROTECTS THEM. There is a purpose in all suffering, a real need for it. Men seem to be mixed up indiscriminately, and suffering looks as if it often fell irrespective of character, but this is only a seeming. The suffering of Israel, though it may look the same outwardly, is really as different as possible from the suffering of Egypt. There is a fire which ends in the destruction of what passes through it. It must be so, for the thing is destructible and shows its nature when the fire tries it. The same fire attacking indestructible things only separates destructible accretions from them, and consumes these accretions away. God's intention is that the believer may be able to say, " I cannot be destroyed in this furnace of trials; I cannot go to pieces as others do. But still I must remain in it for a while; I must submit to God's wise ordinances so that at last I may return to my true rest and fear no more for ever."—Y.

EXPOSITION.

CHAPTER XLVII.

PROPHECY ON THE PHILISTINES.

It is clear from the contents of the prophecy (and the inference is thoroughly confirmed by its position) that it was written after the battle of Carchemish, with reference to the dreaded northern foe—Nebuchadnezzar, King of Babylon. The prophecy against Egypt precedes, because Egypt was by far the most important of the nations threatened by the advance of Nebuchadnezzar. But chronologically and geographically, it ought rather to have been placed at the end of the series, for Palestine had to be conquered before a design upon Egypt could have a reasonable chance of success. The commentators have given themselves much unnecessary trouble with the heading in ver. 1, which assigns the date of the prophecy to a period prior (as it would seem) to the battle of Carchemish. They forget that the headings are not to be received without criticism as historical evidence for the date of the prophecies. Knowing, as we do, that the prophecies were edited, not only by the disciples of the prophets, but by students of the Scriptures long after their time, it is

gratuitously embarrassing one's self to give as much historical weight to the statement of a heading as to a clear inference from the contents of a prophecy. No doubt Providence watched over the movements of the editors; they must even be credited with a degree of inspiration, so far as moral and religious truths are concerned; but they were not exempt from being dependent on the ordinary sources of information in matters of history. It would seem, then, that, out of the various sieges of Gaza in the last century of the Jewish state, one in particular had fixed itself in the memory of the Jews; and it was not a siege by the Babylonians, but by the Egyptians. Seeing a reference to Gaza in ver. 5, a late editor of Jeremiah appended to the heading already in existence the words, "before that Pharaoh smote Gaza." He was wrong in so doing, but he only carried out, like many favourite modern preachers, what has been called the atomistic method of exegesis, by which a single verse is isolated from its context, and interpreted with total disregard of the rest of the passage.

But which Pharaoh did this editor mean? and when did he lay siege to Gaza? The general view is that he means Pharaoh-necho, who, according to Herodotus (ii. 159), first defeated "the Syrians at Magdolus," and then "made himself master of Cadytis, a large city of Syria." It is assumed that Magdolus is a mistake for Megiddo, and that Cadytis means Gaza; and the former supposition is probable enough (a similar confusion has been made by certain manuscripts at Matt. xv. 39; comp. the Authorized and Revised Versions); but the latter is rather doubtful. It is true that in iii. 5 Herodotus speaks of "the country from Phœnicia to the borders of the city Cadytis" as belonging to "the Palestine Syrians;" but is it not more probable that Herodotus mistook the position of *Jerusalem* (*Cadushta*, "the holy (city)," in Aramaic) than that he called Gaza "a city almost as large as Sardis"? Gaza was never called "the holy city;" Jerusalem was. Sir Gardner Wilkinson (*ap*. Rawlinson's 'Herodotus') takes a different view. According to him (and to Rashi long before) it was Pharaoh-hophra or Apries who captured Gaza. We know from Herodotus (ii. 161) that this king waged war with Phœnicia, which is, perhaps, to be taken in connection with the notice in ch. xxxvii. 5, 11, of the diversion created by an Egyptian army during the siege of Jerusalem. This hypothesis is to a certain extent confirmed by the mention of "Tyrus and Zidon" in ver. 4, but stands in much need of some direct historical confirmation.

Ver. 1.—**Against the Philistines**; rather, *concerning* (as usual in similar cases). **Before that Pharaoh**, etc. (see introduction to chapter).

Vers. 2—4.—Hostile bands advance from the north; horror seizes the Philistines.

Ver. 2.—**Waters rise up**. The prophets think in figures, and no figure is so familiar to them (alas for the unstable condition of those times!) as that of an overflowing torrent for an invading army (see on ch. xlvi. 8, and add to the parallel passages Isa. xxviii. 18; Ezek. xxvi. 19; Dan. xi. 10). **Out of the north**. To suppose that this refers to Pharaoh-necho returning from Carchemish seems forced and unnatural. If Necho conquered Gaza at the period supposed, it would be on his way to Carchemish, and not on his return. Besides, "the north" is the standing symbol for the home of the dreaded Assyrian and Babylonian foes (see on ch. i. 14). Isaiah had uttered a very similar prediction when the Assyrian hosts were sweeping

through Palestine (xiv. 31). **An overflowing flood**; rather, *torrent*. The same phrase occurs in Isa. xxx. 28, where the "breath" of the angry God is described with this figurative expression. It is in autumn-time that the torrents of Palestine become dangerous, and water-courses, dry or almost dry in summer (comp. ch. xv. 18), become filled with a furiously rushing stream.

Ver. 3.—A fine specimen of Hebrew word-painting. **The rushing of his chariots**. "Rushing" has the sense of the German *rauschen*, to make a rustling, murmuring sound. It is used (but as the equivalent of a different Hebrew word) in the Authorized Version of Isa. xviii. 12, 13 of the confused sound made by an army in motion. In the present passage, the Hebrew word means something more definite than that in Isaiah, *l.c.*; it is the "crashing" of an earthquake, or (as here) the "rattling" of chariots. **The rumbling of his wheels**. "Rumbling" is a happy equivalent. The Hebrew (*hămōn*) is the word referred to in the preceding note as meaning an indefinite confused sound. **The fathers shall not look back to their children**, etc. An awful picture, and still more effective in the concise language of the original. The Hebrew Scriptures excel (as still more strikingly, but with too great a want of moderation, does the Korân) in the sublime of terror. So overpowering shall the panic be that fathers will not even turn an eye to their helpless children. Observe, it is said "the fathers," not "the mothers." The picture is poetically finer than that in Deut. xxviii. 56, 57, because the shade of colouring is a degree softer. **Feebleness of hands**. A common expression for the enervation produced by extreme terror (see ch. vi. 24; Isa. xiii. 7; Ezek. vii. 17; Nah. ii. 11).

Ver. 4.—**The day that cometh**; rather, *the day that hath come* (i.e. shall have come). It is "the day of the Lord" that is meant, that revolutionary "shaking of all things" (to use Haggai's expression, ii. 21), as to which see further in note on ch. xlvi. 10. **To cut off . . . every helper that remaineth**; *i.e.* every ally on whom they could still reckon. This passage favours the view that the judgment upon the Philistines took place at the same time as that upon Tyre. Nebuchadnezzar's object was to isolate Tyre and Sidon as completely as possible. **The remnant**. The Philistines had suffered so much from repeated invasions as to be only a "remnant" of the once powerful nation which oppressed Israel (see on ch. xxv. 20). **The country of Caphtor**. Some would render "the coast-land of Caphtor," but the idea of "coast" seems to be a secondary one, derived in certain passages from the context. Properly speaking, it is a poetic synonym for "land,"

and is generally applied to distant and (accidentally) maritime countries. "Caphtor" was understood by the old versions to be Cappadocia. But as the remains of the Cappadocian language point to a Persian origin of the population which spoke it, and as the Caphtorim originally came from Egypt, it is more plausible to suppose, with Ebers, that Caphtor was a coast district of North Egypt. Crete has also been thought of (comp. Amos ix. 7; Gen. x. 14; Deut. ii. 23).

Vers. 5—7.—The prophet changes his style. In ecstasy or imagination, he sees the calamity which he has foretold already come to pass. Philistia is not, indeed, altogether annihilated; it was not the will of God to make a full end as yet with any of the nations round about. But it is reduced to extremities, and fears the worst.

Ver. 5.—**Baldness.** A sign of the deepest sorrow (comp. on ch. xvi. 6). **Ashkelon is cut off.** Ruins of Ashkelon are still visible. "It is evident that the walls of the old city were built on a semicircular range of rocky hills, which ended in perpendicular cliffs of various heights on the seashore. Wherever nature failed, the weak places were strengthened by the help of earthworks or masonry. On the southern and south-eastern sides, the sand has penetrated the city by means of breaches in the walls, and every day it covers the old fortifications more and more, both within and without. The ancient towns alone rise distinctly, like rocky islands, out of the sea of sand. The ruins on the north are bordered by plantations of trees. They lie in such wild confusion that one might suppose that they were thrown down by an earthquake. There is no secure landing-place; the strip of sand at the foot of the western wall is covered at high tide, when the waves beat against the cliffs. Still J. G. Kinnear, in 1841, found some remains of a mole, and this discovery is confirmed by Schick [the able German architect now at Jerusalem]." Thus writes Dr. Guthe, in the Journal of the German Palestine Exploration Society (1880), remarking further that, in a few generations, the ruins of Ashkelon will be buried under the drifting sand. It is partly the sand-hills, partly the singular fragmentariness of the ruins of Ashkelon, which gives such an air of desolation to the scene, though, where the deluge of sand has not invaded, the gardens and orchards are luxuriant. Dr. W. M. Thomson, in the enlarged edition of 'The

Land and the Book' (London, 1881, p. 173), observes that "the walls and towers must have been blown to pieces by powder, for not even earthquakes could throw these gigantic masses of masonry into such extraordinary attitudes. No site in this country has so deeply impressed my mind with sadness." With **the remnant of their valley.** "With" should rather be "even." "Their valley" means primarily the valley of Ashkelon; but this was not different from the valley or low-lying plain (more commonly called the *Shefêlah*) of the other Philistian towns; and the whole phrase is an enigmatical, poetic way of saying "the still surviving population of Philistia." But this addition certainly weakens the passage, and leaves the second half of the verse abnormally short. It is far better to violate the Massoretic tradition, and attach "the remnant," etc., to the second verse-half. But "their valley" is still a rather feeble expression; a proper name is what we look for to make this clause correspond to those which have gone before. The Septuagint reads differently, for it renders καὶ τὰ κατάλοιπα Ἐνακείμ. We know from Josh. xi. 22 that some of the Anakim were left "in Gaza, in Gath, and in Ashdod;" and in David's time the Philistines could still point to giants in their midst (1 Sam. xvii. 4; 2 Sam. xxi. 16—22), who, like the Anakim (Deut. ii. 20), are called in the Hebrew, Rephaim. It may be objected, indeed (as it is by Keil), that the Anakim would not be traceable so late as Jeremiah's time; but Jeremiah was presumably a learned man, and was as likely to call the Philistines Anakim, as an English poet to call his countrymen Britons. No one who has given special attention to the phenomena of the Hebrew text elsewhere can doubt that "their valley" is a corruption; the choice lies between the "Anakim" of the Septuagint and the plausible correction of a Jewish scholar (A. Krochmal), "Ekron." **How long wilt thou cut thyself?** Shall thy lamentation never cease? (comp. on ch. xvi. 6). The question is in appearance addressed to "the remnant" (personified as a woman), but in reality the judicial Providence who sends the calamity.

Ver. 6.—**O thou sword,** etc.; rather, *alas! thou sword of the Lord.* It is the mystic sword of which we have heard already (see on ch. xii. 10; xlvi. 10).

Ver. 7.—**The seashore.** So Ezekiel speaks of "the remnant of the seashore" (xxv. 16), referring to Philistia.

HOMILETICS.

Vers. 1—7.—*The judgment of the Philistines.* I. A JUDGMENT ON THE ANCIENT ENEMIES OF THE PEOPLE OF GOD. They have long ceased to be a power; now they shall cease to have any national existence. They are but **a** remnant; even this is to be cut off. Gradually the spiritual foes of the Christian are reduced in power and number. Old sins and old temptations are slowly subdued. Some linger on till the end of life. But all shall be overthrown, even the last enemy, death.

II. AN OVERWHELMING JUDGMENT. It comes up like a flood; *i.e.* it is swift, and it spreads far and wide. Such is a characteristic of Divine judgments. 1. They may be long delayed, but when they appear they rush down as a flood. 2. They penetrate to secret hiding-places and flow to the most remote quarters, reaching those who would fain separate themselves from their companions in sin when they are forced to be also companions in suffering.

III. A DISTRESSING JUDGMENT. The Philistines suffer grief—they cry and howl; these people are also smitten with the paralysis of fear—" the fathers shall not look back to their children for feebleness of hands" (ver. 3). Some troubles can be endured and lived down by fortitude, by patient submission, or by the comforting resources of the inner life. But this is not possible with the judgments of Heaven. They are too terrific to be calmly endured. The inner sources of consolation are withheld. The soul is punished as well as the body. There is the bitterest drop in the cup of anguish. The soul will be tortured with shame, with remorse, with horror. That is hell.

IV. A DESTRUCTIVE JUDGMENT. "Baldness is come upon Gaza; Ashkelon is cut off." Great cities are overthrown, the ruins of them testifying to this day to the violence they have undergone. The end of the broad way is *destruction*. "The wages of sin is *death.*" Whatever be the exact character of the destruction and death, the analogy of national judgment and the known deadening effects of sin upon the spiritual, the intellectual, and even the physical powers lead us to expect that the fearful fate of sin continued, unchecked, and unrepented of through all stages of chastisement will be some destroying process.

V. AN ENDURING JUDGMENT. "Alas! thou sword of the Lord, how long will it be ere thou be quiet?" (ver. 6). Philistia has never been restored. Some judgments appear to be irretrievable. All punishment must be sufficiently enduring to effect its end. The punishment of the next world is always referred to as terribly enduring, as partaking of the awful duration of æons. How long such vague, vast ages will last none can say. May it not be the fate of any of us to make the experiment!

Vers. 6, 7.—*The sword of the Lord.* I. THE TERROR OF MAN BEFORE THE SWORD OF THE LORD. (Ver. 6.) 1. *God wields a sword.* There are terrors in some of the doings of the God of love. "Our God is a consuming fire." It is foolish and wrong to blind ourselves to the stern side of God's government, and to represent him as almost soft and weak in his indulgence of his children. 2. God's sword may be seen in *earthly calamities.* It does not flash before us as when it was held by cherubim at the gates of Eden. It works in the form of natural calamities. It also makes use of human actions, wars, etc. Above the sword of man there glitters this terrible, irresistible sword. Thus calamities in this world are sent by God or overruled by God. 3. God's sword may be *restlessly active.* It is not displayed for one fearful moment and then sheathed. Often there comes blow upon blow. Thus Job cries out beneath the wearying strokes, "How long wilt thou not depart from me, nor let me alone till I swallow down my spittle?" (Job vii. 19). 4. We *cannot see the reason* for the terrible work of the sword of the Lord. We cry out in dismay before it. From a human point of view it may appear cruel and relentless. 5. We may naturally *feel pity* for those who suffer from this terrible sword. It is right, too, that we should intercede for them if it be possible for the judgment of Heaven to be stayed.

II. THE DIVINE MISSION OF THE SWORD OF THE LORD. (Ver. 7.) 1. The wielding of the sword is *necessary.* "How *can* it be quiet?" There are moral necessities which even the Almighty God freely accepts. Justice must be done. Right must be established. Evil must be suppressed. The process may be painful, and such as God would not choose on its own account and can take no delight in. Yet for these high requirements, though his children suffer and his own heart is wrung with commiseration, he cannot sheathe the sword till its work is done. 2. The wielding of the sword is for a *good purpose.* The necessity is not blind and objectless. The sword has its mission. To us who are in the thick of the battle this may not be discernible. The dust and heat, the rush and noise and confusion, the mingled cries of triumph and pain, are all we can observe; the plan of the commander cannot be read through all the turmoil of the field. But he has a plan, and the whole battle is converging to it. 3. *The sword cannot be sheathed till its mission is accomplished.* The mission is more important than the temporary comfort arising out of the immediate quieting of the sword. If this were to be done before the end were obtained, where would be the use of all that was already suffered? If the sword is stayed before victory is won, every drop of blood spilt is wasted, every pang suffered is suffered in vain. If the discipline of life were to cease before its great purpose were accomplished, its earlier stages would be stultified. 4. *When the mission of the sword is accomplished the sword will be sheathed.* It is drawn for a definite object. "The Lord is a man of war" for a season and for a purpose, not by delight nor perpetually. He is essentially the God of peace. No one is more anxious to see the sword laid aside than he who wields it. His joy is in peace and in benediction. Judgment is temporary. The victory and rest that follow will be eternal.

HOMILIES BY VARIOUS AUTHORS.

Ver. 5.—*The sorrow of the ungodly.* The allusion is to a fashion common to the Philistines and other idolatrous nations in appealing to their gods. We perceive a similar tendency in the natural mind in its first moral concerns and spiritual troubles. It is the sorrow of the world to which, as to the Philippian jailor, the injunction has to be addressed, "Do thyself no harm." Notice—

I. THE PRINCIPLE IN HUMAN NATURE. It is that self-inflicted suffering or deprivation will be of spiritual advantage and secure Divine favour. This is the secret of penance, pilgrimages, monastic life, and asceticism in general. The saying, often uttered of losses or pains over which one has no control, "Ah, well! it will be set down to our credit!" witnesses to the same idea. Remorse is largely explained on the same principle.

II. THAT IT IS FOUNDED ON A MISCONCEPTION OF THE DIVINE NATURE. Baal was a cruel god—a huge abortion and monstrosity. Not less cruel are the ideas of God's character entertained by many reputedly religious persons. 1. *The gospel declares that "God is love."* Such self-inflictions are but folly, and have no religious value in view of this great truth. "Sacrifice and offering thou wouldest not . . . Lo, I come . . . I delight to do thy will, O my God" (Ps. xl. 6—8; Heb. x. 5—7); "I will have mercy, and not sacrifice" (Matt. ix. 13; cf. Hos. vi. 6); and "Wherewithal shall I come before the Lord, . . . he hath showed thee, O man, what is good; and what doth the Lord require of thee, but to do justly, and to love mercy, and to walk humbly with thy God?" (Micah vi. 6—8),—are the expressions of the spirit of true religion, which alone harmonizes with the doctrine of a loving God. 2. *God himself in the person of his Son has "borne our griefs and carried our sorrows."* The worship which is alone acceptable to the Father must begin with the recognition of this. There is a "godly sorrow," but its advantage consists in its moral influence on ourselves, making us hate sin and follow after righteousness, etc. 3. *Everything which ignores the merit of Christ's sufferings and God's revelation of himself must needs be hateful to him, and bring upon its authors his wrath and curse.*—M.

Vers. 6, 7.—*The sword of Jehovah.* I. A PERSONIFICATION OF DIVINE WRATH. "Sword of Jehovah" is an expression that seems to suggest the Philistines as the speakers; "for, though not bad Hebrew, it has a foreign sound, and makes the impression that the speakers attribute the sword raging against them only unwillingly and hesitatingly to Jehovah" (Naegelsbach). God in his true character is still unknown, but conscience witnesses to him as a dimly realized agent of moral recompense. Such language tells: 1. *How ceaseless and terrible is the judgment of the heathen world.* Ezekiel uses the same figure in relation to the Amorites (xxi. 30). "There is no peace, saith my God, to the wicked;" "Surely thou wilt slay the wicked, O God" (Ps. cxxxix. 19); "When they shall say, Peace and safety; then sudden destruction cometh upon them," etc. (1 Thess. v. 3). 2. *Of ignorance and moral distance from God.* He is only conceived of as a God of vengeance—an all but impersonal fate. 3.

Of the helplessness and superstitious dread of sinners. An imperfect knowledge is eked out and distorted by a diseased imagination. All moral strength seems to have gone out of them.

II. EXPLAINED AND JUSTIFIED AS A DIVINE APPOINTMENT. At first the answer of the prophet appears little other than a repetition of the Philistines' thought; but it is far more. 1. *This is not blind fate, but judgment strictly meted out and determined.* 2. *It declares, in effect, that the wicked cannot be suffered to remain on the earth.* They must be subjects of continual and exterminating judgment. There is no escape. Is this so? Yes, so long as they remain impenitent and at a distance from him. Is it contradictory, then, for Zechariah to prophecy the *conversion* of the Philistines? The rightful end of judgment is mercy. The sinner is driven into the arms of the Divine love. Our helplessness prepares for the reception of his salvation.—M.

Ver. 7.—*The sword that cannot be quiet.* This chapter tells of another of the Gentile nations on whom the judgment of God was to come. These nations all lay in the march of the Babylonian armies, and were one after another overthrown. Philistia is represented as asking of the sword of the Lord, when it will be quiet, and the answer is, "How can it be quiet, when," etc.? (ver. 7). It reminds—

I. OF THE SWORD OF CONSCIENCE. The Lord hath given it a charge, and, though we may blunt it, we cannot perfectly quiet it (cf. Macbeth, Judas, and other conscience-haunted men).

II. OF THE SWORD OF SCRIPTURE. "The Word of the Lord is not bound. How men have sought to sheathe it in the scabbard, to hide and hold it there, so that they may go on unchecked in their own ways! But it has leapt forth in spite of them; and, in spite of pagan, Roman, and other persecutions, has asserted its supreme might."

III. OF THE SWORD OF THE DIVINE JUDGMENT AGAINST SIN. Sin and sorrow are eternally married, and can never be put asunder. Where one is the other is never far off, and never will be in this world or the next. But for every believer *Christ* has offered his own heart as a sheath for it. For such that sword is sheathed therein, and will be quiet there for ever.

> "When Christ gave up the ghost
>   The Law was satisfied;
> And now to its most rigorous claims
>   I answer, 'Jesus died.'"

                                                                              C.

Vers. 6, 7.—*Apostrophe to the sword.* I. WHAT IS MEANT BY THE SWORD OF JEHOVAH. Any man, or army of men, or any inanimate thing even, may be as a sword in the hand of God. Men are restricted in their agents to injure and destroy, and well it is so, though in old and superstitious times some of them were believed to control the powers of nature so that they could raise winds and tempests. But God, with his real and complete control over all natural forces, can turn them against rebellious man whenever and to whatever extent it may be necessary. It is not a case of a strong arm and a weak weapon, or a weak arm and a strong weapon beyond what the arm can wield. God smites, and not imperfectly; nor does he need to smite twice.

II. WHAT IS SUGGESTED BY THE APOSTROPHE. 1. *The thought of God's enemies.* Here the Philistines are mentioned, so long the troublesome and jealous neighbours of Israel. But they are only types. There are still enemies numerous enough and active enough to keep the sword of God from lying quiet in its scabbard. Why were these Philistines reckoned enemies? Simply because of their wickedness. God is hostile to nothing but wickedness in man, and to that he is always hostile. There are Philistines still against whom a charge has to be given to the sword of God. And such must ever be destroyed, that is, not the men themselves must be destroyed, but that in them which selfishly upholds evil and profits by it. And even they themselves, if they continue the foolish war against God, must perish in the end. 2. *The thought of God's opposing activity to his enemies.* Wherever there is enmity to God, Divine opposition to it becomes manifest. Hard as it may be to fight for God, it is harder still to fight against him. In being on God's side against evil all the difficulties are at the beginning; in being on the evil side against God the difficulties, though they may look as nothing to start with, soon multiply and increase to the end. A charge is given to all God's servants to be resolute and uncompromising in their opposition to all wickedness. 3. *The thought of ultimate cessation of the sword's activity.* Surely the time is to come when the sword will lie quietly in the scabbard. He who came not to bring peace but a sword has peace for his ultimate aim. He will not say, " Peace, peace," when there is no peace ; and when at last he will say, " Peace," we may be sure of the reality corresponding with the word.—Y.

EXPOSITION.

CHAPTER XLVIII.

This prophecy is so full of repetitions that the question has naturally arisen whether the most prominent of these may not be due to interpolation. For instance : 1. Vers. 29—38 recur in Isa. xvi. 6—10 ; xv. 4, 5, 6 ; xvi. 12, 11 ; xv. 2, 3 ; not, indeed, without many peculiarities, and those peculiarities are so striking, and so little in harmony with Jeremiah's usual mode of using his predecessor's writings, that some have held that vers. 29—38 were inserted by one of Jeremiah's readers. 2. Vers. 43, 44 so closely resemble Isa. xxiv. 17, 18, and cohere so loosely with the context, that interpolation is a not unreasonable hypothesis. 3. Vers. 45, 46, which are omitted in the Septuagint, are evidently based on Numb. xxi. 28, 29. 4. Vers. 40, 41 closely resemble ch. xlix. 22 ; the portion corresponding to that passage is omitted in the Septuagint.

Vers. 1—8.—The prophet foresees the calamity of Moab, and the attendant confusion and dismay. Yes ; flee, save your lives, if ye can ; for your confidences have proved untrustworthy ; there is no hope left. Ver. 1.—**Against Moab** ; rather, *concerning Moab*. **Nebo** ! Not, of course, the mountain range referred to in Deut. xxxii. 49 and xxxiv. 1 as that from which Moses viewed the land destined for Israel, but a town in the neighbourhood, deriving its name, not from the mountain, but from the same old Semitic (and not merely Babylonian) deity. **Kiriathaim.** " The double city." A place of uncertain situation, but probably in the same district as Nebo ; mentioned in Gen. xiv. 5, as the abode of the " terrible " aboriginal tribe called the Emim. **Is confounded** ; rather, *is brought to shame* (as ch. xlvi. 24). **Misgab** ; rather, *the fortress*. The connection shows that some definite fortress is intended, but it is difficult to say which. Graf thinks of Kir-heres (vers. 31, 36) or Kir-hareseth (another form of the same name ; comp. Isa. xvi. 7 ; 2 Kings iii. 25),

generally identified with Kir-Moab, the chief fortified town of the Moabites. Ver. 2.—There shall be **no more praise of Moab** ; rather, *Moab's glory* (or, *glorying*) *is no more* (comp. ver. 29). **In Heshbon they have devised evil,** etc. There is a word-play in the Hebrew, which may be reproduced thus : " In Plot-house they plot evil against it" (so J. F. Smith's Ewald). **Against it** (literally, *her*) means "against Moab." Heshbon was at the time an Ammonitish town (it had in days gone by been Amoritish, Numb. xxi. 26) ; see ch. xlix. 3 ; but was on the border of Moab. **O Madmen.** There seems to be again a word-play, which has been to some extent reproduced thus : " Thou shalt become still, O Still-house." The name Madmen does not occur again, though an allusion to it has been fancied in Isa. xxv. 10, where the Hebrew for " dunghill " is *madménah*.

Ver. 3.—**Horonaim.** This Moabite town was probably on the borders of Edom ; hence, perhaps, " Sanballat the Horonite."

Ver. 4.—**Moab is destroyed.** The mention of Moab in the midst of towns is certainly surprising. We should expect Ar-Moab. **Her little ones.** The received text, as it stands, is untranslatable, and our choice lies between the correction suggested by the vowel-points, and the reading of the Septuagint and a few of the extant Hebrew manuscripts, " unto Zoar." In favour of the latter, which is adopted by Ewald and Graf, it may be urged that Zoar and Horonaim are mentioned together, not only in ver. 34, but also in Isa. xv. 5, which has evidently been imitated in the following verse. It is not quite clear what " her little ones " in the first-mentioned correction mean. Some think, the children ; others, the poor ; Hitzig prefers the small towns of Moab. On the site of " Zoar," see Smith's ' Dictionary of the Bible,' but compare Canon Tristram in ' The Land of Moab.'

Ver. 5.—**For in the going up of Luhith,** etc. The verse is substantially taken from Isaiah (xv. 5), but with variations peculiar to this chapter. The most peculiar of these is that in the first verse-half, which is literally, *weeping goeth up* (not, *shall go up*) *with weeping*, which is explained by Dr. Payne Smith to mean "one set of weeping fugitives pressing close upon another." To the present commentator (as also to Delitzsch —see his note on Isa. xv. 5) there seems no reasonable doubt that *b'ki*, the word rendered "weeping," should rather be *bō*, "upon it," so that the passage will run, as in Isaiah, "for the going up of Luhith with weeping doth one go up it." Hitzig (whom for once we find agreeing with Delitzsch) remarks that the miswriting *b'ki* for *bō* may be easily accounted for by the fact that *ki*, "for," is the word which follows next. We have no right to ascribe to Jeremiah such an artificial and un-Hebraic an expression as that of the received text. Small as the matter may be in itself, it is not unimportant as suggesting to the *Old* Testament student a caution against the too unreserved adoption of the canon *Lectioni faciliori præstat ardua*. **In the going down of Horonaim.** An interesting variation from Isaiah. The older poet, less attentive to minutiæ, had said vaguely, "in the road to Horonaim;" by a slight change of expression, the younger and more reflective writer produces a striking antithesis between the ascent to the hill-town, and the descent to the hollow in which Horonaim ("double cavern") appears to have been situated. It is possible, however, that Jeremiah has preserved the original reading, and that "the road" in Isaiah, *l.c.*, is due to the carelessness of a scribe. **The enemies have heard a cry of destruction.** But why this reference to the enemies? The rendering, however, is ungrammatical. The text is, literally, *the enemies of the cry of destruction have they heard.* The prophecy in Isaiah omits "the enemies of," and has a different verb for "have they heard." Can the inserted words be an intrusion from the margin? The later scribes were accustomed to insert glosses in the margin on occasions where we should have thought them entirely unnecessary for the purpose of explanation. But then why "the enemies of"? It is an insoluble enigma.

Ver. 6.—**Flee, save your lives**; literally, *your souls.* The prophet's human feeling prompts him to this counsel; but he knows full well that a life of abject misery is the utmost that can be hoped for. **And be like the heath in the wilderness**; literally, *and (your souls) shall be like destitute ones in the wilderness.* Imagine the case of one who has been robbed of everything, and left alone in the desert; not less miserable is that of the Moabite fugitives. The word rendered "the heath" (*'arŏ'ēr*) is either miswritten for *'ar'ar*, which occurs in the sense of "destitute" in ch. xvii. 6 (see note), or also a rare plural form of the same

word. The sense remains the same. It is tempting to see an allusion to one of the towns called Aroer (as in Isa. xvii. 2). But the only Aroer the prophet could be thinking of is that on the Arnon (Deut. ii. 36), which could not be described as "in the wilderness."

Ver. 7.—**In thy works**; *i.e.* either "in thy evil deeds" (comp. Isa. xxviii. 15) or "in thy idols" (frequently called "the work of men's hands," *e.g.* Deut. iv. 28, and sometimes simply "works," *e.g.* Isa. xli. 29; lvii. 12; comp. Isa. i. 31). **Chemosh.** In Numb. xxi. 29 Moab is called "people of Chĕmósh," the patron-god being the king and lord of his people. In accordance with the strictly localizing theory of the nature of deity, current among primitive nations, Chemósh is said to go into captivity together with his worshippers (comp. ch. xlix. 3; Amos i. 15). This helps us to understand the idolatry into which the Jews fell during the Exile (Isa. xlii. 17); they imagined that Jehovah himself was "in captivity," and restrained from putting forth his power on behalf of his worshippers. The textreading is not Chemósh, but Chemísh; the latter form does not occur elsewhere, but has been thought to illustrate the name of the Hittite city Carchemish (the Hittites or their predecessors may have been worshippers of this deity), *i.e.* "castle of Chemósh."

Ver. 8.—**The valley . . . the plain.** The latter (Hebrew, *mïshōr*) is the upland region which extends from the Jordan eastward of Jericho into the Arabian desert; in Numb. xxi. 20 it is called the "field" (*i.e.* "open country") of Moab. The former means that part of the Jordan valley which borders on this upland "plain" towards the west.

Vers. 9—16.—So sudden is the blow that Moab stands in need of wings to make good his escape. Were the human instrument to delay, the curse meant for Moab would come upon himself. Is a reason demanded? It is that Moab has long been in a state of morally perilous security, and requires to be thoroughly shaken and aroused, in order that he may discover the inability of Chemósh to help his worshippers.

Ver. 9.—**Give wings**, etc. Comp. ver. 28; also Isa. xvi. 2, where the fugitive Moabites are likened to "wandering birds."

Ver. 10.—**Deceitfully**; rather, *slackly, negligently.*

Ver. 11.—**Moab hath been at ease from his youth.** The "youth" of Moab dates from its subjugation of the aboriginal Emim (Deut. ii. 10). Since that event, though often at war, sometimes tributary and sometimes expelled from a part of the territory claimed by them (see the inscription on the Moabite Stone), yet they had never been disturbed in their ancestral homes to the south of the river Arnon. **He hath settled on his lees.** It was the custom to leave wine for a time on its lees or sediment, in order to heighten its strength and flavour (comp. Isa. xxv. 6). **Emptied from vessel to vessel.** Thevenot, an old traveller in Persia, remarks of the Shiraz wine that, after it is separated from the lees, it is apt to grow sour. "The wine is put into large earthen jars, each holding from ten or twelve to fourteen *carabas*; but when a jar has been opened, it must be emptied as soon as possible, and the wine put into bottles or *carabas*, otherwise it spoils and becomes sour" ('Voyages,' ii. 245, quoted by Lowth on Isa. xxv. 6). In the application of the figure, the "taste" of Moab means obviously the national character.

Ver. 12.—**Wanderers, that shall cause him to wander**; rather, *tilters, and they shall tilt him.* The earthen jars of which Thevenot speaks were doubtless similar to those of the Israelites. They would be tilted on one side, that the wine might run off clear from the dregs. **Their bottles;** rather, *flagons* or *pitchers* (of earthenware). The confusion of numbers and pronouns is remarkable. First, Moab collectively is spoken of as a wine-jar; then the Moabites individually as Moab's jars; last of all, the Moabites are spoken of as possessing "jars" (*i.e.* all the institutions, public and private, of the state and of society).

Ver. 13.—**Ashamed of Bethel;** *i.e.* of the golden calf or bull at Bethel, set up by Jeroboam I. as a symbol of the strong God, Jehovah. This idolatry was odious to the prophetic teachers of a nobler and more spiritual form of religion. They saw that the deity and the symbol were too much confounded, and that such a religion would not save its adherents from captivity and ruin (comp. Hos. x. 15; Amos iii. 14; v. 5, 6).

Ver. 14.—**We are mighty;** rather, *we are heroes.* The Hebrew is *gibbōrim*, the name of David's select warriors (2 Sam. xxiii. 8). The exclamation is designed to represent vividly to the mind the sinful vain-glory specially characteristic of Moab.

Ver. 15.—**Moab is spoiled, and gone up out of her cities.** The latter part of this clause in the Hebrew is extremely difficult; the Authorized Version is indefensible. It is even doubtful whether it can be translated at all consistently with grammar, though Hitzig, a good grammarian, has adopted the suggestion of Grotius, rendering, "and her cities have gone up," viz. in smoke, *i.e.* they have been burnt; comp. Judg. xx. 40, the end of which verse ought to run thus: "The whole city went up to heaven." But even if the verb in third masc. sing.

be allowable after the plural noun, it is very harsh to give it such an interpretation, when the context says nothing about fire or smoke. J. D. Michaelis and Ewald, therefore, propose to change the vowel-points of the first word, rendering, "The spoiler of Moab and of her cities is gone up;" and Dr. Payne Smith inclines to follow them. We thus obtain a striking antithesis; the enemy has "gone up," and Moab's young men **are gone down,** *i.e.* are felled by murderous hands (comp. Isa. xxxiv. 7).

Ver. 16.—**The calamity of Moab,** etc. The form of the verse reminds us of Deut. xxxii. 35; Isa. xiii. 22.

Vers. 17—25.—How lamentable that such a glorious sceptre should be broken! But there is no remedy. Even Dibon, that highly honoured town, is disgraced. There is no hiding the sad fate of the Moabites; the crowds of fugitives sufficiently proclaim it. Judgment has been passed upon all the cities of Moab, a long roll of whose names is recited.

Ver. 17.—**All ye that are about him;** *i.e.* the neighbouring nations (comp. on ch. xlvi. 14). The invitation to condolence is not ironical, but in the deepest spirit of human sympathy, as in the parallel prophecy in Isaiah (see on Isa. xv. 5). **The strong staff;** *i.e.* the sceptre as an image of royal authority (comp. Ezek. xix. 11—14). **Rod;** as in Ps. cx. 2.

Ver. 18.—**Dibon;** now *Dibán,* one of the chief towns of Moab, on two adjacent hills, now covered with ruins (Tristram), in the plain of Medeba (Josh. xiii. 9), north of Aroer and the Arnon. Here the famous Moabite Stone (on which see Dr. Ginsburg's exhaustive monograph), with the inscription of King Mesha (2 Kings iii. 4), was found, which, after having been broken up and pieced together, has now found a resting-place in the Louvre. It is difficult to say to which Israelitish tribe Dibon was, strictly speaking, attached; for while in Josh. xiii. 17 it is given to Reuben, in Numb. xxxii. 34 and in the Moabite Stone (line 10) it is assigned to Gad. Apparently the Israelitish population fluctuated. Sometimes Gad was the most adventurous in occupying Moabitish territory, sometimes Reuben. On the phrase, **the daughter,** etc., see note on ch. xlvi. 19. The form of the first verse-half is modelled on Isa. xlvii. 1. **Sit in thirst.** The expression is unexampled, and it is possible that we should alter one of the vowel-points (which constitute no part of the Massoretic text), rendering, "sit in thirsty (ground)," *i.e.* the dust (comp. the parallel passage, Isa. xlvii. 1). Or there may be a less-used collateral form of the Hebrew for "thirsty" (*çāmē*). Canon Tristram speaks of the "waterless plain" of Dîbân ('Land of Moab,' p. 132). **Thy strong holds.** It appears from the Moabite Stone that Dibon was the centre of a district which was reckoned as belonging to it; so at least we may account for the phrase, "*all* Dibon was submissive" (line 28). Compare the phrase in Numb. xxi. 25, "Heshbon, and all the villages thereof" (comp. on ch. xlix. 2).

Ver. 19.—The inhabitants of **Aroer** will come out in eager expectation to meet the fugitives, and ask, **What hath happened?** (so the question should be rendered). There were several Aroers (one belonged to the Ammonites, Josh. xiii. 25), but as the enemy is driving the Moabites southward, the Aroer here intended can only be the town by the Arnon, which separated Moab proper first of all from the kingdom of the Amorites (Deut. iv. 48; Josh. xii. 2), and afterwards from the territory of the Israelites (Deut. ii. 36; iii. 12). The picture drawn in this verse is singularly appropriate to the site of Arnon, "just by the edge of the arterial highway of Moab," and commanding a complete view of the pass of the Arnon (Tristram, 'Land of Moab,' p. 132). There is the same variety of statement as to the Israelitish tribe to which Aroer belonged as in the case of Dibon (see ver. 18). Josh. xiii. 16 speaks in favour of Reuben; Numb. xxxii. 34 in favour of Gad.

Ver. 20.—The answer of the fugitives begins in the latter part of this verse, and, continues to ver. 24. **Confounded** ought, as usual, to be *brought to shame*. The address, **howl and cry,** which is in the feminine, refers to Moab, which has just before been spoken of in the feminine ("It is broken down," or rather, "she is dismayed," refers to Moab, not to Dibon). **In Arnon**; *i.e.* in the region of the Arnon; better, *beside Arnon* (comp. ch. xiii. 5, "by Euphrates").

Ver. 21.—**The plain country.** The *mishōr* (see on ver. 8). **Holon** is not known from other sources. **Jahazah** (called Jahaz in ver. 34), according to Eusebius, still existed in his days, and lay between Medeba and Dibon. Like Heshbon and Dibon, it was claimed by the Reubenites (Josh. xiii. 18), and Mesha, in the famous inscription, states that the then King of Israel (Jehoram) "fortified Jahaz and dwelt in it, when he fought against me" (lines 18, 19). This was a great but only a temporary success, for Mesha adds that "Chemósh drove him out before me" (line 19). **Mephaath** was apparently near Jahaz, since it is always mentioned with that town (Josh. xiii. 18; xxi. 37; 1 Chron. vi. 79).

Ver. 22.—**Dibon** (see on ver. 18). **Nebo** (see on ver. 1). **Beth-diblathaim.** Mentioned here only. There is an Almon-diblathaim in Numb. xxxiii. 46, mentioned in connection with Dibon.

Ver. 23.—**Kiriathaim** (see on ver. 1). **Beth-gamul.** Nowhere else mentioned. **Beth-meon.** Called Baal-meon, Numb. xxxii. 38; Beth-baal-meon, Josh. xiii. 17. The extensive ruins of Ma'in are a short distance south of Heshbon.

Ver. 24.—**Kerioth.** Perhaps a synonym of Ar, the old capital of Moab (Isa. xv. 1). Hence in Amos ii. 2, "I will send a fire upon Moab, and it shall devour the palaces of Kerioth." **Bozrah.** The capital at one time of the Edomites (see ch. xlix. 13). The ownership of particular cities varied from time to time in this contested region. **Far or near**; *i.e.* towards the frontier or inland.

Vers. 26—35.—And what is Moab's crime? At an earlier point the prophet said that it was the callousness produced by long prosperity (ver. 11); but here another sin is mentioned—Moab's haughty contempt of Jehovah. "For this it deserves that its contempt should be thrown back upon itself, by its being made, like a drunken man, the scorn of all" (Ewald). The figure is, no doubt, a coarse one, but not unnatural in the oratory (we must put aside inspiration, which leaves the forms of speech untouched) of a rude people like the Jews. It occurs not unfrequently elsewhere; see especially Isa. xix. 14; Hab. ii. 15, 16; and, for milder examples of the figure, ch. xiii. 13 and xxv.

Ver. 26.—**Make ye him drunken.** The command is issued to the agents of the Divine wrath (comp. vers. 10, 21). **He magnified** himself **against the Lord.** Offences against Israel being also offences against Israel's God (see Jephthah's striking words in Judg. xi. 23, 24). **Shall wallow**; rather, *shall fall heavily* (literally, *shall clap*—a pregnant expression).

Ver. 27.—**Was he found among thieves? for,** etc.; rather, *. . . that, as often as thou speakest of him, thou waggest thy head.* What giveth thee the right to show such scorn and insolent triumph towards Israel, as if he were one who had been arrested in the very act of robbery (comp. ch. ii. 26)?

Ver. 28.—**Dwell in the rock.** Jeremiah probably thinks of the rocky defiles of the Arnon, so splendidly adapted for fugitives (see Consul Wetzstein's excursus to the third edition of Delitzsch's 'Jesaja;' he speaks of perpendicular walls of rock). **Like the dove** (*i.e.* the wild dove); comp. 'Iliad,' xxi. 493; 'Æneid,' v. 213.

Vers. 29, 30.—These verses are an expansion of Isa. xvi. 6. The boastfulness of

Moab seems to have much impressed its Israelitish neighbours (comp. vers. 14, 27). It has been thought to be illustrated by the inscription on the Moabite Stone; but we must remember that all national monuments of this sort have a tendency to exaggeration.

Ver. 29.—**We have heard ;** viz. the prophet and his countrymen.

Ver. 30.—**But it shall not be so,** etc. This is a case in which the accentuation must most decidedly be deviated from; it implies a faulty view of the word rendered in the Authorized Version, "his lies." But the rendering of our version is neither in itself tenable nor is it that intended by the accentuation. The rendering suggested by the latter is "his praters" (*i.e.* soothsayers), as the word, no doubt, must be taken in ch. l. 36; Isa. xliv. 25. But it is much more natural to render thus : "And the untruth of his pratings [*i.e.* of his boastings]; the untruth that they have wrought." In his words and in his works (and a word is equal to a work before the Divine Judge) Moab was essentially "untrue." Truth, in the Biblical sense, is to know and serve the true God.

Ver. 31.—Based upon Isa. xvi. 7. **Therefore.** Moab cannot escape the catastrophe, for his moral basis is utterly insecure. "Therefore," etc. **Will I howl.** It is at first sight strange that the prophet should speak thus sympathetically after the strong language in ver. 26. But the fact is that an inspired prophet has, as it were, a double personality. Sometimes his human feelings seem quite lost in the consciousness of his message; sometimes (and especially in Jeremiah) the natural, emotional life refuses to be thus restrained, and will have itself expressed. **All Moab ;** *i.e.* Moab in all its districts, both north and south of the Arnon, or, at any rate, the fugitive populations. **Mine heart shall mourn.** The Authorized Version effaces one of the points of difference between Jeremiah and his original. The former leaves the subject indefinite—*one shall mourn.* **For the men of Kir-heres.** Isa. xvi. 7 has "for the raisin-cakes of Kir-heres" (*i.e.* for the cakes of pressed grapes, for which Kir-heres was specially famous)—a much more expressive phrase. Jeremiah, *or his scribe,* has changed *ăshishē* into *ānshē,* and the Targum and Septuagint have adopted this weak reading in Isaiah, *l.c.*

Ver. 32.—Shortened from Isa. xvi. 8, 9. **With the weeping of Jazer ;** rather, *more than the weeping of Jazer.* This may mean either "more than I weep for Jazer" (which is favoured by the insertion of "for thee ") or "more than Jazer weeps" (for the devastated vineyards of Sibmah); comp. Isaiah, *l.c.* The site of Jazer is placed by Seetzen between Ramoth (Salt) and Heshbon, where

some ruins called Sîr are now found. "Sibmah," according to St. Jerome, was not more than half a mile from Heshbon. King Mesha is thought to refer to it under the form Seran, miswritten for Seban (Sebam—so the form should be read—is an Old Testament version of the name ; see Numb. xxxii. 3) ; see inscription on Moabite Stone, line 13. It appears to have been famous for its vineyards ; and Seetzen tells us that grapes and raisins of specially good quality are still carried from the neighbouring Salt to Jerusalem. **Thy plants are gone over the sea ;** rather, *thy shoots passed over the sea.* The prophet here describes the extensive range of these vines. The northern limit of their culture was Jazer, its southern or western the further shore of "the sea," *i.e.* the Dead Sea. By a touch of poetic hyperbole the prophet traces the excellence of vines such as those of En-gedi (on the western bank of the Dead Sea) to a Moabitish origin. The reference to the **sea of Jazer** throws the whole passage into confusion. There is no lake or large pool at present to be found at Jazer, and the simplest explanation is that a scribe repeated the word "sea" by mistake. The true text will then be simply, "they reached unto Jazer." **The spoiler.** Isa. xvi. 9 has the more picturesque expression, "the shouting," *i.e.* the wild battle-cry.

Ver. 33.—Nearly identical with Isa. xvi. 10. **The plentiful field ;** rather, *the garden-land ;* i.e. land planted with "noble" plants, especially vines and olives. **Wine.** Here clearly sweet and unfermented wine (comp. Amos ix. 13, 14). **None shall tread with shouting.** This involves a very harsh construction of the Hebrew, and it is better (considering the numerous other errors of the same kind in the received text) to correct in accordance with Isa. xvi. 10, "the treader shall not tread." **Their shouting** shall be **no shouting.** "Shouting" (Hebrew, *hēdād*) may be taken in two senses : (1) the cheerful, musical cry with which "the treaders" pressed out the juice of the grapes (comp. ch. xxv. 30); (2) the wild cry (ch. li. 14) with which the enemy "fell upon the summer fruits and upon the vintage" (ver. 32), reducing the inhabitants to abject misery. In Isa. xvi. 9, 10 an allusion is made to this double meaning, and so, perhaps, it may be here ("There shall be shouting, but not that of the peaceful vintagers at their work"). Or, as others, we may explain "no shouting" as equivalent to "the opposite of shouting," *i.e.* either silence or lamentation (comp. Isa. x. 15, "not-wood" equivalent to "that which is specifically different from wood ;" and xxxi. 3, "not God," equivalent to "the very opposite of Divine ").

Ver. 34.—Based on Isa. xv. 4—6. The cry of one town echoes to another, and is taken up afresh by its terrified inhabitants. Heshbon and Elealeh lay on eminences but a short distance apart, so that the shrill cry of lamentation would be heard far away in the south-east at Jahaz. Zoar and Horonaim both lay in the southern half of Moab (see on vers. 3, 4). **An heifer of three years old.** If this is the right rendering, the phrase is descriptive of Horonaim, which may, in the time of Jeremiah, have been a " virgin fortress." But the phrase, thus understood, comes in very oddly, and in the parallel passage in Isaiah it stands, not after Horonaim, but after Zoar; it hardly seems likely that there were two Gibraltars in Moab. Another rendering (Ewald, Keil) is, " (to) the third Eglath." This involves an allusion to the fact that there were other places in Moab called Eglath or Eglah, which has been rendered highly probable by Gesenius. **The waters also of Nimrim.** Canon Tristram speaks of the " plenteous brooks gushing from the lofty hills into the Ghor-en-Numeira." Consul Wetzstein, however, says that nature appears there under so unspeakably gloomy an aspect, that the identification is impossible. He proposes a site in the Wâdy So'êb, about fourteen miles east of the Jordan, which with its luxuriant meadows, covered with the flocks of the Bedouin, is probably suitable to the passages in Isaiah and Jeremiah (Excursus ii. in Delitzsch's 'Jesaja,' 4th edit., pp. 572, 573). So also Seetzen, who remarks that the lower part of this wâdy is still called Nahr Nimrin. In Josh. xiii. 27 a place called Beth-nimrah is mentioned as situated in the valley (i.e. the Jordan valley); no doubt this was in the wâdy referred to by the prophets. " The valley " seems to have been sometimes used in a wider signification, so as to include lateral valleys like that of Nimrim. The antiquity of the name is shown by its occurrence in the Annals of Thothmes III., who penetrated into the heart of Palestine, and, in the temple of Karnak, enumerates the cities which he conquered. From before B.C. 1600 to nearly A.D. 1900 this secluded valley has borne precisely the same name!

Ver. 35.—**Him that offereth in the high places**; rather, *him that goeth up to a high place.* Apparently a reminiscence of Isa. xv. 2 and xvi. 12. As Dr. Payne Smith well remarks, "The last stage of natural ruin is reached, when thus the rites of religion entirely cease."

Vers. 36—42.—The description of Moab's lamentations continued.

Ver. 36.—Based on Isa. xvi. 11; xv. 7. **Like pipes.** Isaiah has, "like the harp [or, 'lute ']." The pipe, or flute, was specially used at funeral ceremonies (Matt. ix. 23;

Luke vii. 32), and therefore, perhaps, seemed to Jeremiah more appropriate. **Because the riches**, etc. This is, no doubt, what we should have expected, but this is not what Jeremiah wrote; "because" should rather be *therefore.* Jeremiah simply transferred a clause (substantially at least) from his original, Isa. xv. 7, but into a context where it stands rather less naturally. The meaning of the words in Isaiah is that, the desolation being so great, the Moabites shall carry away as much of their goods as they can. In this new context, however, we can only explain this unexpected " therefore " by referring to a habit of the Israelitish mind by which that which contributed to a result was regarded as worked purposely for that result. Good instances of this habit are Gen. xviii. 5; Ps. xlv. 3; li. 6; comp. Winer's 'New Testament Grammar' (Clark), pp. 573, 574, especially note 1 on p. 574, though the idiom also occurs in Old Testament passages in which the religious view of life is hardly traceable.

Vers. 37, 38 (first part).—Based on Isa. xv. 2 (latter part), 3 (first part). On the primitive Arabic, Egyptian, and Hebrew custom of cutting off the hair, see on ch. xvi. 6, and comp. Herod., ii. 36. **Clipped.** The difference from the word in Isaiah is so slight that it may easily have arisen from a copyist. The meaning is virtually the same. **Cuttings.** So of Philistia (ch. xlvii. 5); see on ch. xvi. 6.

Ver. 38.—**Lamentation generally**; literally, *all of it is lamentation;* i.e. nothing else is to be heard. **Like a vessel**, etc. For this figure, see on ch. xxii. 28 (Jeremiah repeats himself).

Ver. 39.—**They shall howl**, saying, etc.; rather, *How is it dismayed! (how) they wail! How hath Moab turned the back ashamed! Yea, Moab becometh*, etc.

Vers. 40, 41.—The Septuagint has a shorter form (see introduction to chapter).

Ver. 40.—**He shall fly as an eagle**; rather, *he shall swoop* (same word and figure in Deut. xxviii. 49). The subject is not named, but (as in ch. xlvi. 18) is Nebuchadnezzar.

Ver. 41.—**Kerioth is taken.** Kerioth has been already mentioned in ver. 24 (see note). Another possible rendering is, *The cities are taken*, and this certainly agrees better with the parallel line. But a plural of *kiryāh*, a city, does not occur elsewhere. If the identification of Kerioth with Ar-moab, the capital of Moab, be accepted (see on ver. 24), the equalization of Kerioth and " the strong holds " seems to be a stumbling-block. **Strong holds**; or, *mountain fastnesses* (ch. li. 30).

Vers. 43—47.—Hence, as the final result, escape is absolutely impossible, for one danger succeeds another in an endless series.

The last and greatest danger besets those who seek refuge behind the strong fortifications of Heshbon. It is from this very city that the hottest fire of the enemy breaks forth. Chemósh has not saved his people; and yet there is hope for Moab in the future.

Ver. 43.—**Fear, and the pit, and the snare.** An alliteration in the Hebrew, which occurs again in Isa. xxiv. 17. In German it can be represented better than in English—*e.g.* by Hitzig's "grauen, graben, garn." All primitive poetry delights in such alliterations.

Ver. 45.—Apparently quoted from memory from Numb. xxi. 28; xxiv. 17, except the first clause; the application, however, is peculiar to this passage. **They that fled,** etc.; rather, *The fugitives stand without strength in the shadow of Heshbon.* There is a difficulty here, for, according to ver. 2, the hostile raid into Moab started from Heshbon. Surely the fugitives would not think of escaping northwards, much less would they be able to elude the vigilance of the foe and reach Heshbon. But it is not surprising that the author of so long a poem should now and then make a slip; the author of the Book of Job is sometimes inconsistent with

the Prologue, and ver. 2 is as far away from the passage before us as the Prologue of Job is from Job xix. 18. Nor can we be absolutely certain that our prophecy is exactly as Jere-miah wrote it. **Shall come forth;** rather, *hath come forth* (or, *cometh forth*), **From the midst of Sihon.** Sihon being, perhaps, regarded as the leader and representative of his warriors. **The corner of Moab;** rather, *the sides* (literally, *side,* used collectively) *of Moab.* **The tumultuous ones;** literally, *sons of tumult,* a poetical phrase for warriors. The prophet has substituted the more common word *shāōn* for its synonym *shēth.*

Ver. 46.—Based on Numb. xxi. 29. The chief difference is in the second half of the verse, in which the bold expression of Che-mósh "giving his sons and his daughters into captivity" is changed for a mere ordinary and prosaic phrase.

Ver. 47.—On the phraseology of this verse (omitted in the Septuagint), see on ch. xxix. 14; xxiii. 20, and on the brighter prospect held out for Moab, see the analogies given in note on ch. xlvi. 26. **Thus far is the judgment of Moab** is clearly an editor's note (comp. ch. li. 64). "Judgment" as in ver. 21.

HOMILETICS.

Vers. 1—47.—*The judgment of Moab.* As the prophet's "eye in a fine frenzy rolling" sees the flood of the Chaldean invasion sweeping over one after another of the nations, his words flash out in pictures full of energy and fire. If this world's calamities are thus terrible, how shall the awful realities of eternity be contemplated? Why should some of us be so shocked at the strong language of preachers? Strange and fanatical as it may appear, the fury of a Knox is more consonant with much of life and revelation than the complacent mildness of an Addison. Visions of judgment are no topics for graceful moral essays. Nevertheless, however hot the language may be, it must not descend to mere wild, whirling words; it must be characteristic and truthful. The succession of pictures of approaching judgment which Jeremiah draws are not monotonous repetitions of the same description. They are definite and distinctively applicable to the respective subjects of them. Let us observe the special features of the judgment of Moab.

I. THE CHARACTER OF THE PEOPLE. The grounds of the judgment are given in the revelation of the sins of Moab. The head and front of her offence is *pride* (*e.g.* ver. 29). Other characteristics are closely related, viz.: (1) *trust in wealth and material resources* (ver. 7); (2) *self-indulgent ease* (ver. 11); (3) *boastfulness* (ver. 14); (4) *scorn* (ver. 27); (5) *defiance of Heaven* (ver. 26). Such a catalogue of offences is peculiarly hateful to God. Sins of appetite and passion are partly the result of weakness. The culpability of them is less than that of the intellectual and spiritual sins by all the weight of temptations which arise out of the natural constitution of man. For such sins as those of Moab there is no excuse. They are nearest to the most diabolical wickedness. Adam fell by a sin of appetite; Satan by a sin of spiritual pride.

II. THE NATURE OF THEIR DOOM. 1. *Destruction.* (Ver. 4.) The general doom of all the nations. This is the leading form of the evil fruits of sin. 2. *Shame and humiliation.* (Ver. 13.) "Moab also shall wallow in his vomit" (ver. 26). What a terrible anti-climax from the pride and haughtiness which are the chief characteristics of this people! 3. *Derision.* Moab had mocked at Israel, now "he also shall be in derision" (ver. 26). Thus scorn is rebuked with scorn, and the mocker is mocked. 4. *Gloom and grief.* (Ver. 33.) The ease and self-complacency which had characterized Moab are exchanged for their opposites. 5. *Poverty.* "The riches that he hath gotten are perished" (ver. 36). Moab had trusted in wealth. His punishment will consist in part in the loss of this. Finally, to Moab, as to other nations, there is promised an ultimate restoration. "Yet will I restore the prosperity of Moab in the latter days, saith the Lord" (ver. 47). Most beautifully does this one verse close the terrible vision of judgment, like one ray of light breaking through the dense black thunder-clouds and promising the dawn of a new day of life and gladness. Even to a heathen people the promise is made, and by the mouth of a Hebrew prophet. Who, then, shall dare to set limits to the future restoring power of the grace of God?

Ver. 7.—*The dangers of riches.* Riches are not evil things in themselves. The gifts of God in nature, or the fruits of man's industry, they are valuable just because they have in them some serviceableness for human wants. Money is not the root of all evil, but the love of it (1 Tim. vi. 10). It is they who trust in riches who find it impossible to enter into the kingdom of God (Mark x. 24). But riches are snares, and the possessor of them had need beware of the dangers they necessarily bring. When the servant becomes a god the degraded worshipper is on the road to ruin. Let us consider some of the dangers of riches.

I. A DANGER OF DELUSIVE TRUST. The wealthy man is likely to think his riches will do more for him than it is in their power to do. He finds that money brings a number and variety of comforts and helps him out of many a difficulty. He is in danger of looking upon it as omnipotent. But money will not buy the choicest blessings. It will not purchase friends, nor peace of mind, nor spiritual blessedness here, nor the heavenly inheritance hereafter. To trust to riches for these things is to miss them. Yet they are the truest treasures. The poor man who seeks them aright, not being allured by the rich man's peculiar temptations, may step in first; and so Dives may come to envy Lazarus.

II. A DANGER OF WORLDLINESS. Rich Moab lives at her ease (ver. 11). A wealthy man is tempted to be satisfied with his possessions. The earth is very fair to him. Possibly he is in the land of the lotus-eaters, "where it is always afternoon." He is thus in danger of caring only for this world, and making no provision for the better world. For he may value his earthly jewels so much as not to care to search after the pearl of great price, or to be unwilling to make any sacrifice in order to purchase it. He tends to become so engrossed with material things as to lose all appetite for and all perception of spiritual things. His treasure is on earth, and his heart is there also. Thus he loses the solid, lasting possessions of eternity while grasping at the shadowy treasures of time.

III. A DANGER OF PRIDE. Rich Moab is proud. The wealthy man is tempted to transfer his high estimation of his possessions to himself. Because he has much he is induced to think that he is much, and the world too often urges him to this mistake by its despicable sycophancy to mere money. When will people learn to value men by their characters and not by their purses? If pride has any valid excuse for existence, this must be found in the true nature of a man and his own personal excellences. Before God we are judged solely by what we are. Our possessions will only aggravate our guilt if they have been abused, for they will be regarded as talents to be accounted for, never as merits to secure us any reward. Therefore the pride of the rich man may be his ruin.

Ver. 10.—*Slack service.* "Cursed be he that doeth the work of the Lord *slackly.*" These words refer immediately to the terrible work of destruction. We shudder at hearing so fearful a curse; but we should remember that, if the slaughter were believed to be in accordance with God's will, and therefore also believed to be right and necessary, there could be no excuse for neglecting it. We may derive from this extreme instance a most forcible argument against slack service. If such slackness could appear cursed to the Jew under the most trying circumstances, when pity and all humane instincts cried out against the work, how much more guilty is it in the Christian work of love!

I. INDICATIONS OF SLACK SERVICE. 1. *Negative goodness.* Great care to avoid all forms of impurity may be found together with a reluctance to make any sacrifice or put forth any exertion. 2. *Conventionalism.* A man follows in the rut of his predecessors, evinces no originality, has no device with which to meet an emergency, never inquires into the suitability of his work to its end, never thinks of improving it, sticks to old ways when the old objects of them are obsolete, cannot break up new ground though new requirements call him to it. 3. *Working at half-power.* What service is rendered does not come up to the level of requirement nor to the measure of ability. It is done in a slow, dreamy style. 4. *Failure before difficulty.* The molehill is magnified into a mountain. The opposition, which is the spur to enthusiasm, puts a complete stop to slack service.

II. CAUSES OF SLACK SERVICE. 1. *Worldliness.* The clay of selfishness is mingled with the strong metal of devotion. A man would serve God and mammon. He tries to do the work of God with one hand, while he advances his own interest with the other. But no work for God is acceptable which is not done with both hands. 2. *Unbelief.* This paralyzes much of our work—more, I am persuaded, than we are ready to admit. The God served is a shadowy Being, and no wonder the service is faint and feeble. 3. *Want of devotion.* The service of the hands is given without the love of the heart. This mechanical work is a poor, spiritless thing. It is love and love only that can inspire a service of unwearying energy. 4. *Cowardice.* There is a fear to do difficult and dangerous work. We pity this for its weakness. We should condemn it as wicked. Should not the servant of Christ be willing to suffer all torments and die for his Lord who suffered and died for him? "Be thou faithful unto *death*." 5. *Mere indolence.* Indolence may be partly constitutional, as in persons of lethargic temperament. Some men are habitually tardy and dilatory. They should learn to resist these tendencies as temptations to fatal unfaithfulness.

III. EVILS OF SLACK SERVICE. It is no slight failure to be gently rebuked. The curse of God lies upon it. "*Cursed* be he," etc. 1. It is very *wicked*. We are God's servants, and bound by ties of nature and of gratitude. 2. It is likely to be *fruitless*. Negligence in work may imperil the whole results of it. If the ship is carelessly steered it may be wrecked. 3. It *injures the man* who works negligently. Our manner of work reacts upon ourselves. Indifferent service produces a low tone of life, coldness, lethargy, unspirituality.

IV. CALLS TO BETTER SERVICE. 1. From the *curse of slack service.* This curse is a solemn warning. The evils that necessitate it should terrify us from incurring it. 2. From the *obligations of duty.* "We are not our own; we are bought with a price." When we do our best we are unprofitable servants. Solemn voices of time and eternity bid us "work while it is day." "Whatsoever thy hand findeth to do, do it with thy might." 3. From the *need of the world.* Our Christian service is no profitless treadmill drudgery. It is for the good of mankind. The call in the text was to execute wrath; ours is to do deeds of mercy. The world in its darkness, its misery, its sin, cries loud for the Christian mission of consolation and redemption. Can we sleep while such calls pierce our ears? 4. From the *constraining love of Christ.* He died for us; he only asks that we shall live for him. But the least we can do is to live faithfully, earnestly, and devotedly, serving the Saviour with all earnest zeal. 5. From the *heavenly reward* (Heb. xii. 1, 2).

Ver. 11.—"*Wine on the lees.*" This is a figure of a people left for ages in a condition of ease. They are like wine settled on its lees, unchanged and unpurified.

I. IT IS BAD FOR A PEOPLE TO REMAIN LONG IN A CONDITION OF EASE. 1. *Evil is not purged out.* The wine is still on its lees. In times of quiet we settle down contented with ourselves as well as with our surroundings. We say—Why disturb the air with cries for change while all is still and calm and dreamy as a summer noon? The old ruin stands unshaken in the fair weather. But presently the tempest rises, the wind howls, and the broken walls tremble to their foundations. Then we see that repairs must be executed or a new building erected. 2. *Progress in good is stayed.* Wine should improve with keeping. But of this wine it is said, "His taste remained in him, and his scent is not changed." Progress needs the stimulus of conflict. Trouble promotes reflection and urges to improved action in the future. "Woe unto you when all men shall speak well of you!" (Luke vi. 26). 3. *Corruption and decay are induced.* Ease means stagnation, and stagnation decomposition. If the vital functions are arrested, the body will not remain like a marble statue. Very soon other actions are set up, and the quiet of death gives place to a horrible scene of rapid corruption. The stagnant soul becomes the dead soul, and this a mass of moral rottenness.

II. THE EVILS OF A CONDITION OF EASE BELONG TO ALL CLASSES OF LIFE. 1. The *nation*. Moab had lived for ages amongst her hills and fertile fields beyond the surging tide of the world's restless changes which swept along the western side of the Jordan between Egypt and the northern nations. She was not the better for this isolation. Wars, invasions, revolutions, turn out to be ultimately serviceable to the cause of human progress. 2. The *Church*. The Middle Ages, when the Church was all-powerful and at ease, were the dark ages of Christendom. The disturbance of the Reformation was a new birth to the Church, in the good of which even the Roman Catholics shared by the stimulus it brought to zeal and the check it put on the paganizing spirit prevalent in Italy in the fifteenth century. 3. The *individual Christian*. In times of ease we tend to become worldly, and our devotion cools. Trouble drives us to prayer and wakens the deeper instincts of the soul (Heb. xii. 11).

Ver. 29.—*Pride.* With accumulated phrases emphasis is laid upon this leading sin of Moab, a sin which is condemned throughout Scripture as one of great wickedness.

I. THE NATURE OF PRIDE. Pride is a passion rising out of an inordinate opinion of our own worthiness. It is to be distinguished from vanity. Vanity is eager for the admiration of others, though, perhaps, in its own heart conscious of possessing but little to deserve it. But pride is inwardly elated with the feeling of self-importance, and may be quite indifferent to the opinion of the world. Indeed, the height of pride is to scorn the admiration as much as the hatred of other men, to look down upon the "dim multitude" as in all respects beneath contempt. Vanity craves social position; pride is essentially lonely. (Nevertheless we must beware of the common injustice of mistaking all reserve for pride; this may arise from constitutional habit, from sensitiveness, even from extreme humility.) Vanity smiles with the desire of pleasing; pride frowns in haughty independence. It is possible, however, for a man to have a very high opinion of his own powers, importance, etc., without much pride. For pride is not a mere conviction of the great worth of one's self, it is an emotion, a passion, a disposition to dwell on one's own merits and make idols of them.

II. THE SINFULNESS OF PRIDE. Why is this so strongly condemned in Scripture? so hateful to God? Consider how it must appear in his sight. We are all his helpless children; "we have erred and strayed from his ways like lost sheep;" before him we are foul with sin, humiliated with failure; our best works are poor and imperfect; in free grace he spares, endures, pardons. Where, then, is there ground for pride? Pride is the denial of guilt, the assumption that the good we receive from God is deserved; it is, therefore, a gross presumption, an evidence of base ingratitude, a proof of self-will that refuses to humble itself before the good and holy Father.

III. THE INJURIOUS EFFECTS OF PRIDE. 1. *It blinds us to our own danger.* It assumes that all must be well. But the assumption does not alter facts. It only aggravates the danger by preventing us from taking precautions against it. Moab was not saved in the general overthrow of the nations for all her pride. Humility sees the stumbling-block in the path, but pride holds its head so high as never to observe it, and so falls over it (Prov. xvi. 18). 2. *It prevents us from securing our own highest good.* This can only be given by the mercy of God, and he can only bestow it on the humble, the contrite, the submissive. The proud man bars his own heart against the incoming of the grace of God. 3. *It hinders the good work of life.* It is directly opposed to charity; it is incongruous with that spirit of mutual concession and co-operation which is required in the service of life. Thus pride often wastes those very powers on the existence of which it stands. To conquer pride let us look at our lives in the light of the life of the meek and humble Jesus of Nazareth.

HOMILIES BY VARIOUS AUTHORS.

Vers. 11—13.—*The ease of Moab.* A figure: wine-casks long undisturbed, whose contents improve and mellow in their taste, at length tilted by the coopers so that the wine is spilled.

I. Worldly prosperity is often very great and uninterrupted. 1. *Frequently remarked.* Heathen nations, whose very backwardness and barbarism have isolated them from the disturbing stream of the world's life ; and empires that seem to be based upon irreligion and wrong, and that are nevertheless in the van of civilization. The men who make the colossal fortunes of modern times are not, as a rule, distinguished for their religious virtues. Sins that immediately destroy some are committed with impunity by others. Many of the most ancient and lucrative vested interests of the world are owned by persons without moral character, and are prostituted to the basest purposes. 2. *The moral perplexity of this.* When wealth and influence almost phenomenally great are thus acquired and used, they cannot fail to trouble the minds of good men. The difficulties of a moral and religious life are so great that such a spectacle tempts and saddens. Israel had been afflicted from her youth (Ps. cxxix. 1—3), whilst Moab was at ease. David was envious when he saw the prosperity of the wicked (Ps. lxxiii. 3).

II. Sinners are thereby confirmed in their evil habits and beliefs. The material wealth and secular position of Moab were doubtless greatly advanced by this long security, and a kind of prestige attached to him amongst neighbouring nations. His customs gradually acquired a fixed and immovable authority. The national character, with all its inherent vices, developed a strong individuality : "His taste remained in him, and his scent is not changed." One trait of this character, for which Moab was notorious and intolerable, was his pride (ver. 29). His attachment to idolatry was also intense ; his inhabitants were the "people of Chemosh" (ver. 46). To add to the cup of his transgression, he "magnified himself against the Lord" (ver. 42). All this is in strict analogy with what may be observed anywhere under similar circumstances. National pride grows with impunity and conquest; and prejudice strengthens itself in the apparent success of its policy of life and the blessing that seems to attach to its religious observances. Israel was a derision to Moab (ver. 27).

III. But their position is insecure, and destruction, though delayed, will be the more certain and complete. The uncertainty of worldly prosperity is represented frequently and under many figures in Holy Writ. It is "that which moth and rust corrupt, and thieves steal ;" it "takes to itself wings and flies away ;" the whole life of which it is the material embodiment, is "even as a vapour, which appeareth for a little time, and then vanisheth away" (Jas. iv. 14). Here the metaphor is that of a tilted vessel. There will come a day when the cup of a nation's or individual's iniquity will be full ; then will they be as Sodom and Gomorrah, whose cry was great and their sin very grievous (Gen. xix. 20). It is just this confidence, born of long impunity, that becomes intolerable to God and provokes his wrath. The rich fool (Luke xii. 16—21).—M.

Ver. 13.—*Betrayed by their gods.* This statement, as it is more especially from the religious standpoint, is a generalization of the cause of Moab's ruin, full of spiritual insight and sagacity. It is in such directions as these we are to seek for the reasons of human success or failure; everything else is but superficial.

The true causes of human success or failure, happiness or misery, are of a moral or spiritual kind. We do not know the exact nature of the Chemosh-worship of Moab, but it is evident that, like other idolatries, it favoured materialism and the gratification of passion (ver. 7). The idol was the centre and representative of the whole life of the people. 1. *Material circumstances are in themselves indifferent towards the achievement of national or individual greatness, but trust in material circumstances is an invariable precursor of ruin.* It is the virtues that are the true bulwarks of a people. "If all the historians who record the ultimate extinction of nations were inspired of God to give the true reasons of their fall, we should often meet this testimony : 'Perished of national pride, producing contempt of God and of fundamental morality'" (Cowles) ; Prov. xiv. 34. 2. *The chief object of desire to any one is his ruler and destiny.* The god is the embodiment of all the sentiments and passions associated with its worship; the leading desire attracts towards itself and assimilates all others. It gradually but inevitably becomes his god. His whole life will henceforth take its complexion and direction from it. He conceives it to be the best and to be able to secure for him all that is desirable. From this we see : (1) *The peril of idolatry.* Pandering to the worst and most selfish passions, it blinds and infatuates its votaries and leads them eventually to their ruin.   (2) *The importance of a true worship.*   It cultures the nature according to its essential principles, and secures the supremacy of the moral and spiritual.   And all true guidance, help, and comfort are afforded in answer to believing prayer.—M.

Ver. 6.—" *The heath in the wilderness.*"   Such will the sinner be; for, like it, he will be : 1. *Barren.*   No rich, strength-sustaining fruit does the heath bear.   A mere hard berry.   The camel and the ass may browse thereupon, but it is no food for man. " Can men gather grapes of thorns, or figs of thistles ? "   And thus barren of good is the sinner.   2. *Unlovely.*   There is no form nor beauty about the heath; a stunted, misshapen shrub.   Its wood can be used for no manufacture.   It is fit only to be burned.   And when our eyes are opened to see things as they are, sin and the sinner will appear in all moral unloveliness ; all present outward charm gone, and only their evil deformity seen.   3. *Alone.*   Surrounded by drear expanse of sand ; no companion trees to form it into a grove or a verdant mass of plant-life.   And so will the sinner be one day.   Christ goes with the believer down the dark valley, but the sinner goes forth alone.   He stands at the bar of God with no advocate.   None of all his old companions can redeem his soul or give to God a ransom for him.   Alone ; helpless. 4. *The gracious influences of Heaven do him no good.*   The dew and the rain, the sun's warmth, come upon it ; but it remains the unlovely, solitary, barren thing it ever was. So the impenitent man is visited by the influences of Heaven, the pleading of the Spirit, the varied means of grace ; but they avail him not.   5. *Soon to perish.*   The driving sand, the scorching heat, the browsing camel, the encampment fire, all threaten its life, and by one or other of them it soon perishes.   And they who are like to it are never safe.   " How are they destroyed as in a moment ! "   *Conclusion.*   But the godly are not so.   " He shall be like a tree planted by," etc. (Ps. i.).—C.

Ver. 10.—*Doing the work of the Lord deceitfully.*   We observe—
I. THE WORK OF THE LORD IS OF VARIED KINDS.   Here it has reference to the vengeance to be taken on Moab, and denounces a curse on that soldier who failed to do his duty in the most thorough and terrible manner.   No pity, no motive of any kind, was to lead them to spare the doomed nation.   But whilst such dread work may be at times the work of the Lord, the expression more commonly points to that which is spiritual, and tends to man's highest good.   In the apostolic Epistles we have constant reference to the work of the Lord in this happier sense.
II. BUT THERE IS PERIL, WHATEVER THE WORK BE, OF DOING IT DECEITFULLY. Now, the work of the Lord is done deceitfully : 1. *When it is not done thoroughly.* When we shirk our work ; do no more than we can help; get away from it as fast as we can.   And how much of the " work " is thus done!   Alas that it should be so! Evidently counted a drudgery rather than a delight.   Do we not all know that there is danger of our thus working ?   2. *When it is not done sincerely.*   How varied and how questionable often the motive which leads men to engage in the work of the Lord !— custom, ostentation, fear of reproach, sting of conscience, hope of gain, fashion, etc. These and such as these may crowd out the only right and sincere motive—the love of Christ.   All others make us more or less hypocrites, and can find no acceptance of the Lord in the great day.   But is there no peril from such motives ?   We know there is.   3. *When it is not done earnestly.*   When our heart is not in our work.   When it is laid hold of not, as it should be, " with both hands earnestly," but, as it were, with one of the fingers.   Some thus work ; others as with one hand ; others, indeed, with both hands, but slowly, loosely, not earnestly.   " Whatsoever thy hand findeth to do, do it with thy might."   Only such as obey that Word are sincere workers.   4. *When it is done hypocritically.*   In the days of sore persecution there was but little peril of this ; but when and where religion goes, as it is. said, in silver slippers, there is real peril of men taking up with the Lord's work in order to further, not the work of the Lord, but their own poor worldly well-being.   What they do is all a pretence, a kind of deception.   God keep us all therefrom !   For note—
III. THE SEVERITY WITH WHICH THE LORD LOOKS UPON HIS WORK DONE DECEIT- FULLY.   " Cursed be he," etc. (ver. 10).   Now, wherefore this severity ?   1. *It is an insult to God.*   It is as good as saying to him that his work does not deserve true

labour; that it is of so little importance that anything will do for it—the parings of your time, your energy, your thought, your means, your strength. What could be a greater affront to God? 2. *The work is so great and urgent* that it is traitorous thus to engage in it. What do we say of the watchman sleeping at his post (cf. Ezek. xxxiii.)? of all who betray their trust or neglect it? 3. *Such deceitfulness is contagious.* How many a young servant of Christ is checked and chilled by the evil influence of professed servants of Christ like himself, but older, less fervent, and who are guilty of that which is here denounced! Such demoralize many in the army of the Lord. 4. *It renders the work itself far more difficult.* For the world sees clearly and judges keenly those who say they do the work of the Lord. They know what that work is, what it professes to aim at, what the interests involved in it. But they who do that work deceitfully cause men to laugh at all such work, to disbelieve all its claims, and to decline more stoutly than ever to surrender their hearts to it. 5. *Such deceivers harden their own hearts,* and steep themselves in a fatal slumber, from which there is no waking. Never has Satan a firmer hold on a man than when he can get him to do the work of the Lord deceitfully. The man is fully persuaded that he is all right, and dies with a lie in his right hand, and is not undeceived till, to his awful amazement, he hears the Lord say to him and to all such, "I never knew *you;* depart from me." That thus it may not be with us, note—

IV. OUR SAFEGUARDS AGAINST SUCH SIN. 1. Solemn recollection and pondering of God's severe anger against it. 2. And chiefly by continually seeking and cherishing in your hearts that love of Christ which the Holy Spirit creates and maintains there, and which alone, but ever, makes all our work sincere, acceptable, effectual, and true.—C.

Ver. 11.—*Much ease, much peril.* "There is a reference here to wine, or to the process by which it is prepared and finished. It is first expressed from the grape, when it is a thick discoloured fluid or juice. It is then fermented, passing through a process that separates the impurities and settles them as lees at the bottom. Standing thus upon its lees or dregs in some large tun or vat, it is not further improved. A gross and coarse flavour remains, and the scent of the feculent matter stays by and becomes fastened, as it were, in the body of the wine itself. To separate this and so to soften or refine the quality, it is now decantered or drawn off into separate jars or skins. After a while this is done again and then again; and so, being emptied from vessel to vessel, the last remains of the lees or sediment are finally cleared, the crude flavours are reduced, the scent itself is refined by ventilation, and the perfect character is attained." Now, the prophet affirms here that Moab had been at ease from his youth. It is difficult in the face of the somewhat checkered history of Moab to see the exact meaning of this. Probably he refers to the long lapse of time since their great and awful defeat told of in 2 Kings iii. 21. Some two centuries and a half had rolled away since that dread day, and in that interval Moab regained all, and more than all, of its former prosperity. For the land was beautiful and rich in the extreme. Its pastures were covered over with sheep and its valleys with corn. The very name "Moab" is thought to mean the land of desire, that is, the desirable land. Now, during these long periods, the description here given is applicable. They had enjoyed much ease, and the natural evils engendered by their cruel idolatrous system had become more fixed and settled; "their scent had not changed." The truth, therefore, which is here taught is that prolonged and abundant ease, however coveted by men, is full of peril to their higher nature, and tends continually to the deterioration of character and the hardening of the habit of evil. Now, we note that—

I. GOD IS EVER TEACHING US THIS TRUTH. 1. *In his Word.* Cf. Ps. lv. 19, "Because they have no changes," etc. Cf. also Heb. xii., where the writer urges the acceptance of the Divine chastisements on the ground that no child of God is without them. "For what son is he whom the father chasteneth not?" And as we go over the roll of names of patriarchs, prophets, apostles, saints, and above all *the* Son of God—not one was without chastisement. Of Christ it is said, "The chastisement of our peace was upon him" (Isa. liii.). And so in the history of the chosen people. How they were moved from vessel to vessel! What changes and adversities, what agitation and tossing about by wars, rebellions, invasions, captivities, etc., they had to endure! And so of the history of the Church! What a checkered and often tumultuous and much-tried career was allotted to her! All these illustrations from God's Word, showing the determination of God that his people should not suffer the peril of overmuch ease and become as Moab, and as they who because they have no changes, therefore, etc. 2. 2. *By analogy.* God suffers nothing to be without change. Even the rocks and hills, the solid globe, all have experienced, and do and will experience, change. The seasons alternate in their orderly change. Storm and tempest cleanse the air which, as in the Swiss valleys, would otherwise become stagnant. The great sea one prophet describes as " the troubled sea," because it can never be quiet. And yet more is this refusal of ease and quiet, this law of change, seen in all forms of life. (1) In *vegetable life.* " Except a corn of wheat fall into the ground and die," etc. And it springs up, " First the blade, then the ear, then," etc. All the varied and ever-acting processes of change in the whole plant-world are in proof. (2) In *animal life.* Change is ever proceeding there. Even when we are asleep the work still goes on. For it to be otherwise is dissolution and death. (3) In *mental life.* Not to have that aroused, stirred by the study of fresh truth and the readjustment of old, would be to condemn to feebleness and semi-idiocy. (4) In *social life.*

" The old order changeth, giving place to new. . . .
Lest one good custom should corrupt the world."

(5) In *ecclesiastical life.* What was the Reformation but the tempest-storm that rushed through the valleys of the Church life of that day, where the air had become stagnant and so corrupt and poisonous that men could not breathe it and live? But the wild storm came and the air was made pure, not in the reformed lands alone, though there chiefly, but in those also that cling to the old faith. Such corruption and abominableness as characterized the ante-Reformation Church were not again possible. (6) In *political life.* Where that is healthy, overmuch ease is not possible. It has not been so with us. It has in the empires of the East, China, etc., and see the result. (7) In *moral life.* Virtue must be tried, there must be conflict and struggle if it is to continue and grow more truly itself. Hence, as in all other forms of life, we should conclude that the moral law would hold good in the spiritual life. And that this is so we learn also : 3. *By experience.* We do not glide into heaven. We are not translated, whilst in a trance, out of the kingdom of darkness into the kingdom of God. But the often severe spiritual conflicts of repentance and confession and striving against sin. " Yea, we must fight if we would win." And God's providence without us as well as his Spirit within is ever forbidding our being at ease continually. Sorrows and losses, temptations and trials, changes and adversities,—they are ever " moving us from vessel to vessel." God forces on us " changes," lest we fear not his Name.

II. BUT WHY IS ALL THIS ? Because in our nature there are rooted evils which can only be got rid of by the action of this law of change. Such evils are : 1. *Self-will.* You have seen a mountain stream come brawling along over its stony bed. But on it goes, heeding not until, right in mid-stream, there is a huge rock. Down comes the stream full tilt against it, as if it were saying, " Just you get out of my way." But that is precisely the thing the rock does not do, and so the stream comes right against it. And then what a fuss, and a froth, and a foam there arises! but the rock does not move, and after a moment you will see the stream gliding softly, smoothly, quietly round the rock, and going more gently on its way. That is one of the ten thousand natural parables with which the world is full. That stream of our self-will, determined to go its own way, rushes on its course. The rock of God's law of change and adversity and trial stands in its way and will not move, and the stream of self-will is broken against it, as God intended it should be. Only by this law can this evil be cured. 2. *Pride.* Trial forces men to call on God. 3. *Unbelief.* This law of trouble and change shatters the materialism and atheism of the present day. They break down, and the soul in the day of its trouble calls upon God. 4. *Selfishness.* Ease fosters this, as it fosters all those other evils named. But trial, adversity, teach men to be " touched with the feeling" of their brethren's infirmities. 5. *Love of the world* ; and 6. *Indolence.* These which ease fosters, God's law of change does much to cure.

III. HOW, THEN, SHOULD WE BEAR OURSELVES TOWARDS THIS LAW OF CHASTENING CHANGE? Cf. Heb. xii., which teaches : 1. *That we do not despise it.* By denying it, or by defying it. Some do this and persevere in the sins which it was designed to amend. 2. *That we do not "faint" under it.* We are not to give up in despair, letting the hands hang down and the knees totter and become feeble. But we are to take this law as a spur and lash and ask, " Wherefore dost thou contend with me ? " and see to it that we amend. But: 3. *Submit ourselves unto God.* " Shall we not much rather be in subjection unto the Father," etc. ? Let his will be ours; let his way our way.

> " He always wins who sides with thee;
> No chance by him is lost;
> Thy will is sweetest to him when
> It triumphs at his cost."

(Faber.)

Then let us welcome whatever God sends, trying though it be, remembering the peril of ease and the sure profit of trial.—C.

Ver. 27.—*Touching the apple of God's eye.* A father may chasten his son, but will be very wroth if he sees another man so dealing with him. No one may punish the child but the child's father. Now, thus is it with the Lord and his people. He will, he does, punish them himself, but he allows none other to do so ; or, if they presume to touch them, as Moab had done to Israel, then sure, if not swift, vengeance follows. Then is fulfilled the saying, " He that toucheth you toucheth the apple of mine eye " (Deut. xxxii. 10; Zech. ii. 8). Now, why is this ? The case supposed of the father who, though he chastens his own son, is yet angry if another touch him, may help us to answer this question. 1. *The child is under no obligation to the stranger.* The father has right to claim all obedience from his child ; not so another. 2. *The child is not beloved by a stranger.* Anger and revenge can alone impel the stranger to do the child harm. But these are the last motives, are never the motives, of the chastisements the father inflicts. 3. *The child is unknown to the stranger* or but little known. Such a one, therefore, even if he be not actuated by evil motives, cannot possibly deal wisely with one of whom and whose character, circumstances, and needs he is ignorant. 4. *The child will get no good from chastisement by a stranger.* A father's chastisement, because of the father's love, cannot but have a mighty moral influence upon the child for his good. " What son is he whom the father chasteneth not ? " But what good could come, or ever did come, to Israel and Judah from the cruelties inflicted upon them by such people as the Moabites, and of which the prophet here tells ? 5. *The child will very likely be dealt cruelly and injuriously with by a stranger.* A father will chasten for his child's profit; wisdom and love will guide him. True, the writer of the Epistle to the Hebrews says, " We have had fathers of our flesh who *verily* chastened us *after their own pleasure.*" But we trust that his experience was a limited one, and that there were, and yet more that there are, but few fathers who " for *their own* pleasure " would chastise their children. 6. And *the child, with all its guilt*—in the case of the Lord's children—*deserves to suffer less than they who have presumed to punish him.* Israel and Judah were guilty without doubt ; but were Moab and Ammon, Babylon and the rest, less guilty ? Had they nothing to answer for ? Had they not far more ? And so, whilst the sin of a child of God is sin indeed, yet it does not make him so heinous, so black, so repulsive, as the persistent, high-handed, never-repented-of sin of the godless, the profane, and the unbeliever. To see one who is chargeable with great sin punishing one whose sin is comparatively trivial; the man who had incurred the debt of ten thousand talents taking by the throat him whose debt was but a hundred pence ;—that is evidently a monstrous thing. 7. But chief of all, because *God's people are God's children in Christ.* We are identified with the well-beloved Son. " Members of his body, his flesh and his bones, one with him." It is so, but it is not so with those who have never yielded themselves to God. Such surrender, which is faith, vitalizes the connection between us and God, and he becomes our Father, in a sense that he never was before. *Conclusion.* All history demonstrates the truth now insisted on, that " he that toucheth you," etc. Let us thank God that he will suffer none to chasten us but himself. Seek that such chastisement may be no longer necessary. Strive to do good to all, " especially to them that are of the household of faith," and tremble to do them harm. " Whosoever offendeth one of these little ones," said our Lord, " it were better for him that a millstone," etc.—C.

Ver. 29.—*Concerning pride.* The graces of God's Spirit are like choice flowers and fruits. They will not grow just anywhere, nor without cultivation and careful tending, and they are easily destroyed. Not so with moral evils like pride. They are as the ill weeds which grow apace. They will grow anywhere, and require no cultivation; the more you let them alone the more they will increase, and, do what you will, you can hardly destroy them. Now, concerning this ill weed, pride, note—

I. THAT IT IS VERY HATEFUL IN THE SIGHT OF GOD. See here, in this verse, with what varied names it is branded. Evil names, all of them. And turn to the many utterances in Scripture concerning this same sin, and the condemnation of God upon it will be yet more clearly seen. "There never was a saint yet that grew proud of his fine feathers, but what the Lord plucked them out by-and-by ; there never yet was an angel that had pride in his heart, but he lost his wings, and fell into Gehenna, as Satan and those fallen angels did ; and there shall never be a saint who indulges self-conceit and pride and self-confidence, but the Lord will spoil his glories, and trample his honours in the mire, and make him cry out yet again, 'Lord, have mercy upon me !' less than the least of all saints, and the ' very chief of sinners.' The first Adam was for self-exaltation, and to be as gods ; the second bids us be as he was, ' meek and lowly in heart.'"

II. ITS SIGNS AND TOKENS. Sometimes it is so *concealed and masked that only* a very intimate acquaintance with the man enables you to detect it; and sometimes the man himself may be unaware how proud he is, and may deem himself a very Moses for meekness, when he is just the reverse. But at other times it may be discerned *in the countenance.* There is " a proud look." The face is the dial-plate of the character, "the expression" of what lies silent in the mind. *Conduct* yet more betrays it. Note how a man acts towards those whom he deems superior or inferior to himself; he will fawn upon the former, and be disdainful towards the latter. He will "mind high things," but will not "condescend to them that are of low estate." Who does not know pride's hateful ways, and has not had to suffer from them; and also, alas! has made others suffer from them at one time or another? But note—

III. SOME OF ITS OCCASIONS AND EXCITEMENTS. 1. *Birth* is one of them ; as if a man chose his own father and mother. Men pride themselves that they come of a certain family, that they are "well born." "We are Abraham's children;" what a multitude of sorrows did that notion originate ! They who pride themselves on those who were their ancestors in generations gone by are, as one has quaintly said, "like those useful vegetables of which we are wont to eat—the best part of them is underground." 2. *Physical strength.* "It always seems to me to be a very insane thing for a man to glory in his animal force, for there can be no merit in it. In the strength of those brawny limbs of theirs and those powerful muscles, some vaunt themselves abundantly. Though ' the Lord taketh not pleasure in the legs of a man,' yet some count it a very wonderful thing that they can outrun or outleap their fellows. O athlete, though thou be strong as Samson or swift as Asahel, what hast thou that thou hast not received ? Hadst thou been born with a tendency to consumption, or with some other hereditary weakness, couldst thou have prevented it? And now that thou art strong, art thou to be praised for that, any more than a horse or a steam-engine ?" (Spurgeon). 3. *Beauty.* What a fount of pride this is ! 4. And *talent*—of intellect, power of application, artistic taste, and the like. 5. *Acquirements.* "I have noticed of self-made men," says one, "that they generally have great respect for their Maker." And he who has acquired wealth is in sore peril of the pride which it is apt to beget. Position, influence, high office, and the like,—these, too, are acquirements won, it may be, by diligent toil, yet, when won, may do a man much harm by generating an unhallowed pride. And even God's grace to a man in giving him a name and a place amongst sincerely religious men, even this may be an occasion of pride. Our best works may be made fuel to the fire of pride. "The demon of pride was born with us, and it will not die one hour before us. It is so woven into the very warp and woof of our nature that, till we are wrapt in our winding-sheet, we shall never be completely rid of it."

IV. SOME OF ITS MANY EVILS. They are such as these: 1. *It leads to the forgetting of God.* " What hast thou that thou hast not received?" (1 Cor. ix. 7). " Is not this great Babylon that I have built?" so spake the God-forgetting and therefore the God-forsaken Nebuchadnezzar " (Dan. iv. 30). 2. *It sets but little value upon God.* God dwindles in the proud man's esteem, whilst to himself he himself ever grows greater. The reverse of John the Baptist's thought is his. John said, " He must increase, but I must decrease." The proud man changes the place of the " he " and the " I." 3. *It makes a man despise his fellows.* He looks down upon them, and therefore is unjust to them. 4. *It leads him to make bad use of what gifts he has.* He is so taken up with admiration of the machinery that he fails to apply it to those ends which it was designed to serve. 5. *It is the prelude not seldom to some great fall.* " Pride goeth before destruction, and a haughty spirit before a fall." 6. *It makes a man content with the inferior,* when, instead of so admiring what he has, he should be aspiring after what is higher and better still. It is said of an artist that, when he had painted a picture which satisfied himself, he threw away his brushes ; for now, he said, " I never shall go beyond this." And so he who is self-satisfied will never rise to a higher degree. 7. *It dishonours Christ and his cause.* A proud Christian helps the devil, for he makes men hate Christianity and all belonging to it.

V. SALUTARY SUGGESTIONS FOR ITS CURE. 1. How entirely all our gifts *are* gifts! Much as we may think of ourselves on account of them, we are excelled by very many. If we have many gifts, that does but mean much and solemn responsibility. How ill it would fare with us were we to be called now to account for the use we have made of our gifts in the past! How but for the mercy of God in Christ, the most gifted is but a poor lost sinner, cast out from the presence of God for ever!—C.

Ver. 2.—*The departed praise of Moab.* I. NOT FOR WANT OF DISPOSITION TO PRAISE. If the things had still remained which people had been in the habit of praising, they would have gone on praising. But the God of righteousness takes them away, and then there is necessary silence. Instead of praise there is humiliation, astonishment at a change so complete, but no insight into the hollowness and instability of that which had been praised. If it had all come back again, it would have been praised as much as ever. Thus we see—

II. A THING MAY BE PRAISED WITHOUT BEING PRAISEWORTHY. This can easily be understood from the experience of many who once praised things to which they are now indifferent, which they may even utterly condemn. Why this change? It may be to some extent from change in the things, but it more frequently comes from growth and increase of light and the reception of higher principles. We have ever to be on our guard against what is merely popular. Not in a cynical way, as if we grudged any one success, but recollecting what power belongs to fashion and to the love of pleasure. Let our effort be to discern, measure, and profit by intrinsic excellence.

III. THINGS NOT PRAISEWORTHY MAY GET THE HIGHEST PRAISE. Mere cleverness and astuteness, the exercise of power irrespective of ends, visible and material success on a large scale,—these attract the laudations of inconsiderate men. This is just what we may expect. If things the most praiseworthy, fullest of virtue and blessing, are yet neglected by the eyes of those who have opportunity to see them, then it is little wonder that the things most approved by the common multitude are those which God has branded as utterly bad. What changes need to be effected in human judgments, that we may be willing to burn what we adored and adore what we would have burned!

IV. GOD GIVES FRESH TOPICS OF PRAISE IF THERE BE A DISPOSITION TO CONSIDER THEM. Those whose tongues had been full of the praises of Moab needed not to be silent. The very overthrow of Moab would be a signal for praise and congratulation among the good. When the unhallowed praises of men are silenced by destruction of the things they praised, then angels begin to sing. And they who praise low, earthly things may have their thoughts introduced to heavenly ones, and then they will discover what man was made to praise. How the words that are exaggerated and altogether disproportioned when applied to the works of men, have in them an exquisite fitness when we speak of the works of God or of Christ, or of men properly engaged in Christian service!—Y.

Ver. 7.—*The consequence of a wrong confidence.* I. THE CAPTURE WAS THEIR OWN FAULT. Not all capture is so. There may be a going into durance for conscience' sake ;

there may be the necessary surrender to superior strength; the captured one may be the victim for a time to the unscrupulous selfishness of others. We must be careful not to draw rash conclusions from suffering to sin; for therein we may be adding suffering to suffering. As a rule, when suffering comes from sin, the sufferer is not left without a witness in his own heart. But inasmuch as it is a whole people that is here suffering nationally, there needs to be a distinct mention of why they are suffering. We are also reminded how important it is to make the distinction between what comes through our own fault and what comes through other causes.

II. WRONG OBJECTS OF TRUST ALWAYS INVOLVE SOME DISASTER. It is but the form that differs; the real, essential mischief is always there. God mentions here the best things a man can have outside of God himself. There is his own worth, that into which he puts his energy, skill, and experience; where also he profits by the work of those who have gone before him. There are also the pleasures of life, all that a man, in his best judgment, reckons to be best. Moab would reckon among its pleasures its men of war, its chosen young men, its accumulation of wealth. But all these things, solid and extensive as they look, give no guarantee of abiding security and prosperity. They may, by the very falsehood of appearances, become the ministers of ruin. The case is as if a plant should seek root in its own substance, as if a man should try to maintain physical life from his own body. And to trust other people is an even more precarious ground of support than we find in ourselves. For in ourselves there is at all events the element of self-interest to help us. No doubt, by the work and the pleasures here mentioned, there is a reference to the idol worshipped in Moab, which indeed is mentioned in the same verse. We can hardly understand the feeling ourselves, but great must have been the confidence of Moab in its god; and this, of course, amounted to nothing else than its own imagination of deity. So we may be trusting in an apparent connection with God, in forms of religion, in works that look as if they were meant for God's glory and for our good. But nothing is of any use as a ground of confidence unless it has a living connection with the Infinite and the Eternal.—Y.

Ver. 10.—*Doing the work of Jehovah deceitfully.* I. THE ENTRUSTING OF JEHOVAH'S WORK TO THE HANDS OF MEN. Here is a great work of judgment, and Jehovah effects such works either through operations of his own or through agents to whom he makes the awful duty evident. What he has done himself is sufficiently illustrated in many terrible visitations recorded in the Old Testament; nor is there entire absence of such a record in the New. But men have also been called to visit upon others their iniquity in a solemn and thorough way. That men have made the command of God a pretext for the greatest cruelties, and for indiscriminate slaughter on an extensive scale, does not in the least alter the fact that such commands have been given—given out of the greatest wisdom and with the best results. Every nation reckons that the temporal life of its subjects is at its disposal; they must be ready to serve with life or in death, as may be required. And shall not the God of all the earth dispose of temporal life according as his all-comprehending wisdom sees may be best for the whole world and for all ages?

II. THE TEMPTATIONS TO DO THIS WORK DECEITFULLY. Not, perhaps, with an intention to deceive, but with sophistical evasions, with attempts to make something less than completeness seem complete. Such an act was that of Saul when he went out with a stern command ringing in his ears—the command of one proved to be a prophet, that he should utterly slay the Amalekites. He seemed to have reason in the pleas he urged for the imperfect execution of the command. And so it may often be. There looks to be needless severity, needless waste. Oftentimes there is an amount of suffering, suffering even of the innocent, which takes all will and vigour out of the arm that should strike God's blow. Besides, it needs to be always borne in mind that the Word of God requiring severity and suffering is only a part of God's work. We shrink from it through mere sensitiveness to pain. But there is another large sphere of work where there is plain benefit, where we have to make no one suffer, where we are contributors to something positive. The husbandman is not for ever plucking up weeds; his main work is to sow good seed and reap it. "Cursed be he that doeth the work of the Lord deceitfully" is a word that has its correspondence in Paul's ejaculation, "Woe is me if I preach not the gospel." Jesus put his servants through an exacting discipline, a self-revealing one, in order that they might do his work thoroughly, uprooting all evil, getting down to proper foundations, making no compromises, ready for all persecutions. They who, after preparation and warning and putting their hands to the work, yet do that work with slack hands, cannot wonder if God should in due time make manifest his anger with them for their heedlessness.—Y.

Vers. 11, 12.—*Moab settled on the lees.* Here we find a not uncommon difficulty in the Old Testament, namely, that of an illustration which *to us* is by no means so clear as the thing to be illustrated. The words are spoken with regard to a wine country. This will be seen on looking at the references in vers. 32, 33 to the wine of Sibmah, the spoiled vintage, the wine that has failed from the wine-presses, the silence where once was shouting of those who trod the grapes. An illustration drawn from the process of making wine perfect was, therefore, most appropriate. It would be understood and convey its lesson at once to those of the right disposition. We, however, must go to the underlying truth at once, without pretending to see the propriety of the illustration in all its parts. Moreover, we must look on Moab itself as representative of individuals. We have to look at individuals, at the possibilities of their life, at the experiences they ought to pass through, and the results which come from missing those experiences.

I. THE POSSIBILITIES OF LIFE. "Moab hath settled on his lees." Moab is, therefore, compared to wine. There are sour grapes with which nothing can be done; but there are also grapes of splendid natural quality, that have had the best culture of the vineyard and have come to all due ripeness. That which is to become perfect wine starts from a fruit of which much is expected. The wine-producer knows that his wine will be according to his grapes. Now, from Moab much was expected; this truth being involved in the very comparison to wine. There was something that had in it the making of an exquisite taste and an exquisite scent.

II. HOW THE POSSIBILITIES ARE MISSED. There is the chance of ease, enjoyment, and self-indulgence, and this chance is ignobly accepted. Of some men the character is tried by difficulties and repeated discouragements; the strength and worth that lie deep in them are manifested by their perseverance. Other men are tried by the absence of difficulties. They are born to a competency. As children they have whatever money can provide for in the way of instruction and pleasure. Everything external to them is made as easy as it can be made. Many voices, near to them every day and all day long, say, "Soul, thou hast much goods laid up for many years: take thine ease, eat, drink, and be merry." Everything depends on the way the young man, placed in such circumstances, looks.

III. THE RESULT OF NEGLECTED DISCIPLINE. Possessions give opportunities of service, opportunities denied to many, who see the needs of others, have the will to meet them, and lack the power. Is it not a righteous thing that God should deal severely with those whose circumstances give them the means and the time for doing great good, and yet who fill their lives with selfish pleasure? Such lives will come out at last in pitiable contrast with what they might have been. To change the figure: "If the salt have lost its savour, wherewith shall it be salted? henceforth it is good for nothing but to be cast out and trodden under foot of men." Note how the vessels that should have been used toward the perfection of the wine, and the bottles that should have held them, become at last useless. If we will not use our opportunities for God's purpose, God will secure, in due time, that we should not use them for our own.—Y.

Vers. 26, 27.—*Moab exulting over fallen Israel.* Here is another allusion to a wine country. Moab knew well what it was to drink to excess. The drunkard with his silly talk and behaviour is a common object of ridicule everywhere. And Moab shall become to other nations abject and degraded as the drunkard. This is the end of its wrong excitement over the fall of Israel. Moab has seen Israel in its days of power and glory and pride, and, seeing, has feared. Could the days of Balak and the prophecies of Balaam be forgotten? Nor is it likely that Israel would be without unseemly exultations and reciprocal jealousies. And now at last Israel falls. And all that Moab can take knowledge of is the fact of the fall. That it has been caused by disobedience and rebellion, that Jehovah is the real Author of it and not the King of Babylon, who is but as Jehovah's sword, Moab cannot well have means for knowing. All it can see is a rival fallen, and as it seems permanently fallen. Therefore Moab must be taught a lesson. In exulting over Israel it is exulting against Jehovah. Indeed, there is no reason why we should reject the notion of some open and bold comparison between the weakness of Jehovah, God of Israel, and the strength of Chemosh, god of Moab. As if the people said, "See how strong Chemosh is; for we are still here, though Babylonian armies have not been far from us! and see how weak Jehovah is; for the nation to whom he was God is gone into a distant captivity!" To exult over the fall of those who have been avowedly the servants of God is a dangerous thing to do. The man who is tempted and falls should be an object of pity, one to be helped up and reinstated, even though the work needed for this be one with some loss and risk to ourselves. And surely we should be especially careful not to rejoice over the calamities of those whose calamity seems to give us a better chance. Moab had now to drink to the dregs a cup of shame, because it had failed to comprehend the duty of rejoicing with those who rejoiced and weeping with those who wept.—Y.

Ver. 38.—*The broken vessel.* I. NOT BROKEN BY ACCIDENT. A vessel broken by accident would not have furnished the proper figure. Lives that are as real serviceable vessels in the hand of God never do get broken by accident. Earthen vessels though they often be, there is a providence and a watchfulness which preserves them till their work is done. They are kept through days of persecution; they are restored from sickness; they live on into a good old age, while men apparently stronger and of greater physical resource are stricken down. And when there seems sometimes a premature and unaccountable breaking, yet it is really to be regarded in another light, namely, as a change to higher and fuller service.

II. NOT BROKEN BY CAPRICE. That which is not broken accidentally must have been broken purposely. And if purposely, either with a reason or through mere recklessness. Men too often destroy things in a reckless, thoughtless way, from the first unconsidered impulse that comes into the mind. It is an action in which is expressed, by a sort of bravado, the sentiment that a man may do what he likes with his own. But God would ever have us feel that, though he has made the world and all that therein is, his disposition of these works is regulated by fixed laws, and our disposition of things under our control should be regulated in the same way. Never let it be said of us that we have destroyed or injured anything without sufficient reason. We should not even pull a flower to pieces through mere thoughtlessness, mere vacuity of mind.

III. BROKEN FOR A SUFFICIENT REASON. Moab is a vessel in which there is no pleasure. It is of no real use to God. Whether we shall be vessels of use to God or not depends upon whether we put ourselves as clay into his hands as Potter. Moab was a nation which had loved to shape its own life, to hew its own designs. And just in proportion as it persevered in this path did it become useless to God. Appearance is only a small thing. The first consideration is use. The commonest earthenware pitcher, if without a flaw, is worth more than a cracked golden pitcher that will hold no water— worth more, that is, as a pitcher. Gold is a rare, glittering, fascinating thing compared with common earth, but after all it is the common earth out of which vessels are made for daily use. The real value of a human life depends upon what God gets out of it.—Y.

Vers. 43, 44.—*No ultimate escape.* I. THERE ARE TEMPORARY EVASIONS OF DOOM. As there are great varieties of wickedness, so there is also great variety in the consequences of it. Sometimes the visitation is sudden, quick, and terrible, as in the case of Ananias and Sapphira. But oftener men go on sinning with no bad consequences to themselves, so far as appearance goes. They do not lose health; they do not seem to lose reputation; there are no checks in their success; and perhaps they even furnish an example whereby worldly wisdom hangs its maxim that it is not well to be too particular. The frequent prosperity of the wicked is indeed a fact not at all concealed or qualified in the Scriptures. A man of the world takes his own worldly way to keep peril at a distance, and he seems to fall into no pit, no snare. Let all this be allowed. Nothing is gained by trying to make out that the wicked have no advantages. It was an old-world legend that some men sold themselves to the devil, and that his protection secured to them their wonderful immunities and prosperity.

II. THERE IS NO WAY OF ESCAPE FROM DANGER SAVE GOD'S WAY. All that is gained is in the way of postponement. Wicked men travel in a narrowing path, and at last are shut up to face the judgments of God. The moment of what seems to them complete success is quickly followed by the moment of complete collapse. We have the crowning illustration of this in the death of Jesus. His enemies seemed to have succeeded. All their efforts to bring his death about had been wonderfully favoured. And what could they do but be jubilant when he was actually dead? The death of Jesus, however, was really a condition for the utter downfall of these enemies. The grave of Jesus, so to speak, was the snare in which spiritual evil was finally taken and overcome. It is one of the triumphs of faith to be well assured in our own hearts that there is no ultimate escape for wickedness. God has his own wise reasons in tolerating wicked men for a long time, and the evil they do to others is not so great in reality as it is in appearance. They cannot inflict more than outward suffering and inconvenience on God's people. Indeed, the mischief they mean to do can be wonderfully transmuted to good.—Y.

EXPOSITION.

CHAPTER XLIX.

On Ammon, Edom, Damascus, Kedar and Hazor, and Elam.

Vers. 1—3.—The violence of the Ammonites shall be severely punished.

Ver. 1.—**Hath Israel no sons?** The violent seizure, perpetrated before his eyes, of parts of the sacred territory, forces the indignant question from the prophet, "How can these things be?" It was so on a former occasion (see ch. ii. 14), and it is so again, now that the Ammonites are occupying the land of the Gadites. True, the present generation has lost its property, but the next is the heir to all its rights and privileges. **Their king**; rather, *their King—* their Mélech or Molech; it is the heavenly, not the earthly king who is referred to (so in Amos i. 15; Zeph. i. 5). The Septuagint, the Syriac, and the Vulgate, however, read *Milcom,* which was the name of the Ammonite deity; this is only a different vocalizing of the consonants of the text. The actual vowel-points give "malcam." This reading *may,* of course, be interpreted of the *earthly* king of the Ammonites. But this view ignores the obvious parallelism of ch. xlviii. 7, " Chěmósh shall go forth into captivity." **Inherit.** The primary meaning of the word is " to take possession of, especially by force, 1 Kings xxi. 6" (Gesenius, *ad voc.*), and this is the sense evidently required here (comp. ch. viii. 10).

Ver. 2.—The punishment of Ammon. Its capital, Rabbah (see 2 Sam. xii. 26, 27), and the "daughter" cities (comp. Numb. xxi. 25, margin; Josh. xv. 45 and xvii. 11 in the Hebrew), shall be laid waste. **The alarm of war** ("alarm" equivalent to "shout"), as in ch. iv. 19. **A desolate heap.** Fortified towns were built on "heaps," or slight elevations (comp. on ch. xxx. 18), the Hebrew name for which (in the singular) is *tel.* The "heap" and the ruins of the town together are aptly

called a " heap of desolation." **Then shall Israel be heir,** etc. ; rather, *then shall Israel dispossess those who dispossessed him* (comp. ver. 1). The form of the phrase reminds us of Isa. xiv. 2.

Ver. 3.—**Heshbon.** Here mentioned as *de jure* a Gadite, but *de facto* an Ammonitish, town; in Numb. xxi. 26 it appears as "the city of Sihon" the Amorite. In Isa. xv. 4 and xvi. 9 it is reckoned to the Moabites. There was a continual warfare between the neighbouring tribes of Reuben and Gad on the one hand, and the Moabites and Ammonites on the other. Let Heshbon lament, because **Ai is spoiled.** The introduction of Ai, which is only known to us as a Canaanitish town, near Bethel, on the wrong side of the Jordan for Moab, is startling. It is replied that we have no list of the Ammonitish cities, and that there may have been another town named Ai. The reply is valid; but leaves a second difficulty untouched, viz. that the mention of a third place destroys the continuity of thought. First, we are made acquainted with the fall of Rabbah; then Heshbon (probably the second place in the country) is called upon to wail because *x* has been taken by storm; then the populations of the "daughter" cities are summoned to join in the lamentation over Rabbah;—is it not reasonable to conclude that the subject of the mourning is one and the same? Now, it is well known that the received text abounds in small errors arising from the confusion of similar Hebrew letters, and that among the letters most easily confounded are *yod* and *resh.* Is it not an obvious conclusion that for *Ai* we should rather read *Ar* (" the city "), a name as suitable for the capital of Ammon as for that of Moab? It is true that we have no example elsewhere of Rabbah being called by the name of Ar; but in 2 Sam. x. 3, 14 it is described as " the city," and we have to be on our guard against the argument *a silentio* —that favourite weapon of destructive criticism! Since a conjecture must be made, it is more respectful to the prophet to choose the one which is most suitable to the context. **Daughters of Rabbah** ; *i.e.* unwalled towns (as in ver. 2). **Run to and fro by the hedges** ; rather, *by the enclosures* ; i.e. wander about in the open country, seeking a lodging-place in the enclosures of the sheepfolds (so Numb. xxxii. 24, Hebrew) or the vineyards (so Numb. xxii. 24, Hebrew). **Their king** ; or, *Milcom* (see on ver. 1).

Ver. 4.—**The valleys** ; *i.e.* long-extended plains, such as were suitable for corn-fields (Isa. xvii. 5 ; Ps. lxv. 14), and such as characterized the territory of the Ammonites. **Thy flowing valley.** "Flowing ; " that is, abounding with rich crops. The meaning of the phrase, however, is only probable.

Ver. 5.—The Ammonitish community dissolved ; every one caring for himself. **Every man right forth** ; *i.e.* straight before him, in a wild panic which expels every thought but that of self-preservation. **Him that wandereth.** Collectively for "the wanderers," *i.e.* the fugitives. So it is said of the Babylonians, that they are "like sheep with none to gather them."

Ver. 6.—Revival of the Ammonites (see on ch. xlviii. 47).

Vers. 7—10.—A startling picture of the judgment impending over Edom, the severity of which is to be inferred from the behaviour of the sufferers. Observe, no allusion is made by Jeremiah to any special bitter feeling of the Edomites towards the Israelites, such as is implied in Isa. xxxiv. ; Ezek. xxxv., and other passages. With regard to the fulfilment of the prophecy, we may fairly quote in the first place Mal. i. 2—4. The agents in the desolation there referred to (still fresh in Malachi's recollection) are probably the Nabathæans (an Arab race, though writing Aramaic), who, after occupying Edom, dropped their nomad habits, devoted themselves to commerce, and founded the kingdom of Arabia Petræa. Meantime the Edomites maintained an independent existence in the midst of the Jewish colonists, till John Hyrcanus compelled them to accept circumcision about B.C. 130. In spite of this enforced religious and political union, the Edomites remained perfectly conscious of their nationality, and we find them mentioned as a distinct factor in the community in Josephus's account of the great Jewish war. They pass away from history after the destruction of Jerusalem, A.D. 70.

Ver. 7.—**Teman** was celebrated for its "wisdom," *i.e.* for a practical moral philosophy, similar to that which we find in the less distinctly religious portions of the Book of Proverbs. It was this "wisdom" which formed the common element in the higher culture of the Semitic peoples, and of which

the sacred narrator speaks when he says that "Solomon's wisdom excelled the wisdom of all the children of the east country " (1 Kings iv. 30). One of Job's friends, Eliphaz, was a Temanite (Job ii. 11). From ver. 20, however, it appears that Teman is here used for Edom in general, of which it formed a part. "Wisdom" was doubtless cultivated throughout Idumæa (Obad. 8), the "land of Uz," in which Job dwelt, was probably in the east of Edom (see on ch. xxv. 20). **Is their wisdom vanished ?** The Hebrew, with its characteristic love for material symbols, has, "Is their wisdom poured out ? " So in ch. xix. 7, "I will pour out [a different word, however, is used] the counsel of Judah." The body being regarded as a vessel, it was natural to represent the principle of life, both physical (Isa. liii. 12) and intellectual (as here), under the symbol of a liquid.

Ver. 8.—**Turn back.** The grammatical form is peculiar (literally, *be made to turn back*). If the punctuation is not an oversight, the object is to suggest the compulsiveness of the change of route of the Dedanites. **Dwell deep** ; *i.e.* tarry in the deepest recesses ye can find, so as to avoid the calamities of the Edomites. The Dedanites, it will be remembered, were a tribe devoted to commerce (see on ch. xxv. 23). Isaiah had already, on an earlier occasion, given the same advice as Jeremiah, viz. to leave the beaten track and take refuge in a less exposed part of the desert, where shrubs and thorn-bushes ("the forest," or rather, "the thickets ") would secure them to some extent from observation (Isa. xxi. 13). See, however, ver. 10.

Ver. 9.—**If grape-gatherers**, etc. Jeremiah modifies his original in Obad. 5 ; the interrogative clauses here become affirmative. Render, *If vintagers come to thee, they will not leave any gleanings : if thieves by night, they destroy what is sufficient for them.*

Ver. 10.—**But**, etc.; rather, *for.* The verse gives the reason why the destruction is so complete. "It is I, Jehovah, who made Esau bare," etc. "Esau," *i.e.* Edom (Gen. xxv. 30). **His seed** ; *i.e.* the Edomites. **His brethren**, or kinsmen ; *i.e.* the Amalekites (Gen. xxxvi. 12). **His neighbours** ; *i.e.* the tribes of Dedan, Tema, and Buz (ch. xxv. 23).

Vers. 11—13.—A merciful mitigation of the prophet's stern threat. The true God will provide for the widows and orphans, if Edom will but commit them to him. And let not Edom think it strange that he is punished ; for even Israel, the chosen people, has drunk of the bitter cup. Yea, Jehovah has sworn "by himself" that all Edom's cities shall be laid waste.

Ver. 11.—**Leave thy fatherless children**,

etc. The invitation means more than might be supposed. It is equivalent to a promise of the revival of the Edomitish people (comp. on ch. xlvi. 26; xlviii. 47).

Ver. 12.—**Whose judgment was not, etc.**; rather, *to whom it was not due,* etc. Jehovah condescends to speak from a human point of view. So, in Isa. xxviii. 21, the punishment of Jerusalem is called his "strange work." **Have assuredly drunken**; rather, *shall surely drink.*

Ver. 13.—**Bozrah.** This seems to have been at one time the capital of Edom (see Amos i. 12; Isa. xxxiv. 6; lxiii. 1). It was a hill city (comp. on ver. 16); a village called Busaira (*i.e.* little Bozrah) now stands among its ruins. **Perpetual wastes.** A phrase characteristic of Jeremiah (see also ch. xxv. 9) and of the second part of Isaiah (lviii. 12 ; lxi. 4).

Vers. 14—18.—Based at first on the older prophecy (see Obad. 1—4); then follow two verses in Jeremiah's peculiar manner. As yet Edom feels himself secure in his rocky home. But a Divine impulse already stirs the nation, through whom Jehovah wills to humble the proud. Edom shall become a second Sodom.

Ver. 14.—**I have heard a rumour.** In Obadiah it is "*we* have heard," *i.e.* the company of prophets (comp. Isa. liii. 1, "Who hath believed *our* report?" according to one interpretation). Jeremiah, to justify his adoption of the outward form of his prophecy, declares that he is personally responsible for its substance. "Rumour," or as the word is elsewhere rendered, "report," is a technical term for a prophetic revelation (Obad. 1; Isa. xxviii. 9, 19; liii. 1 ; comp. Isa. xxi. 10; xxviii. 22); and it is from this Old Testament usage that ἀκοή acquires its special meaning in Rom. x. 16, 17. In fact, ἀκοή, or bearing, is a more exact equivalent of the original. A prophet is one who has "listened in the council of God" (Job xv. 8, corrected version; comp. Amos iii. 7), and "when the Lord Jehovah hath spoken, who can but prophesy?" (Amos iii. 8). Prophetic perception of Divine truth is so exceptional a thing that it can only be expressed approximately in terms of everyday life. One while it may be called a "hearing," a "report," another while a "vision," or "intuition." He who makes to hear or see is, of course, Jehovah, through the objective influence of his Spirit. It is important to study the Biblical phraseology, which has a depth of meaning too often overlooked, owing to the blunter edge which time has given to our modern speech. **An ambassador**; rather, *a herald.* **Unto the heathen**; rather, *unto the nations.* There is no religious idea involved; the word *goyim* literally means "nations," and there is no

reason for deviating from the primary sense. In the next verse it is even more necessary to make this correction.

Ver. 16.—**Thy terribleness.** This is certainly the best rendering of this ἅπαξ λεγόμενον. The "terribleness" of Edom consisted in the fact that the other nations shrank from disturbing her in her rocky fastness. **In the clefts of the rock.** Probably with an allusion to the rock-city Sela, or Petra ("rock"); as perhaps in "the height of the hill" to the situation of Bozrah; see on ver. 13 (Graf). **As the eagle.** Not any eagle is meant, but the griffon (*Gyps fulvus*), or great vulture (Tristram).

Ver. 17.—**A desolation**; rather, *an astonishment.* The word is from the same root as the following verb. The phrase is characteristic of Jeremiah, who has no scruple in repeating a forcible expression, and so enforcing an important truth (comp. ch. xxv. 11, 38; l. 23; li. 43). What so "astonishing" as the reverses of once flourishing kingdoms! For the Bible knows nothing of the "necessity" of the decay and death of nations. The "covenant" which Jehovah offers contains the pledge of indestructibility. **Every one that goeth by it**, etc. Another self-reminiscence (see ch. xix. 8).

Ver. 18.—**As in the overthrow**, etc.; comp. Deut. xxix. 2, which explains the reference in "the neighbour cities" (Admah and Zeboim). The verse is repeated in ch. l. 40. It does not, of course, mean that fire and brimstone should be the agents of destruction (nor is even Isa. xxxiv. 9 to be understood literally), but that the desolate appearance of Edom should remind of that of the neighbourhood of the Dead Sea (comp. Isa. xiii. 19 ; Amos iv. 11).

Vers. 19—22.—Figures descriptive of the unique physical qualities of the destined conqueror of Edom. Both figures have been used before (see ch. iv. 7 ; xlviii. 40).

Ver. 19.—**He shall come.** The subject is withheld, as in ch. xlvi. 18 (see note); xlviii. 40. **The swelling of Jordan**; rather, *the pride of Jordan;* i.e. the luxuriant thickets on its banks. See on ch. xii. 5, where the phrase first occurs. **Against the habitation of the strong**; rather, *to the evergreen pasture.* The word rendered "evergreen" is one of those which are the despair of interpreters, from their fulness of meaning. The root-meaning is simply "continuance," whether it be continuance of strength (comp. Micah vi. 2, Hebrew) or of the flow of a stream (Deut. xxi. 4; Amos v. 24), or, as here, of the perennial verdure of a well-watered pasturage. **But I will suddenly make him run away from her.** Make whom? The lion? Such is the natural inference from the Authorized Version, but the context absolutely forbids it. It seems useless to mention the crowd of explanations which have been offered of this "obscure and much-vexed passage," as old Matthew Poole calls it, since in ch. l. 44 we have precisely the same phrase, but with another suffix, which clears up the meaning. We may, therefore, either *read* (with the Septuagint and the Syriac Version), "For I will suddenly make them run away from it" (viz. the pasture), or keep the old reading "him" for "them," and explain "him" as meaning the Edomites. The expression used for "suddenly" is very forcible; we might render, with Ewald, "in the twinkling of an eye." **And who is a chosen** man, etc.? A still more difficult clause. If the text is correct, which cannot be assumed as certain, we should probably render, with Ewald, "and will appoint over it [*i.e.* the land of Edom] him who is chosen," viz. Nebuchadnezzar. **Who will appoint me the time?** The same phrase is rendered in Job ix. 19, "Who shall set me a time to plead?" (comp. the Latin phrase *dicur dicere*). To drag a defendant before the tribunal implies equality of rank. One might venture to do this with Nebuchadnezzar, if he were not the representative of One still mightier. Finally, **Who is that shepherd that will stand before me?** The land of Edom has been likened to a pasture; it is natural that the ruler should be now described as a shepherd (comp. ch. xxix. 34).

Ver. 20.—**The counsel of the Lord.** At first sight this appears to detract from the perfection of Jehovah. But another prophet declares that the Divine "counsels" are "framed" from eternity (Isa. xxii. 11; xxxvii. 26). **Surely the least**, etc.; rather, *Surely they shall drag them along, the weak ones of the flock; surely their pasture shall be appalled at them.* Such is the sad fate of the sheep, now that the resistance of their shepherd has been overpowered. "The weak ones of the flock" is a phrase quite in Jeremiah's manner; its opposite is "the noble ones of the flock" (ch. xxv. 34).

Ver. 21.—**Is moved**; rather, *quaketh* (as ch. viii. 16). It is a pity that the Authorized Version has not preserved the present tense throughout the verse. The prophet seems to see his prediction realized before him. **In the Red Sea**; rather, *beside the Red Sea;* comp. 1 Kings ix. 26, "Eloth, on the shore of the Red Sea, in the land of Edom."

Ver. 22.—**Behold, he shall come up . . . Bozrah.** Repeated from ch. xlviii. 40, with the substitution of "Bozrah" for "Moab," and the addition of "and he shall come up" from ver. 19. For "Bozrah," see on ver. 13. **And at that day.** Repeated from ch. xlviii.

41 (latter half), with the exception that "Edom" stands for "Moab."

Vers. 23—27.—The heading **Concerning Damascus** is too limited (like that of the partly parallel prophecy in Isa. xvii. 1—11); for the prophecy relates, not only to Damascus, the capital of the kingdom of south-eastern Aram (or Syria), but to Hamath, the capital of the northern kingdom. (The third of the Aramæan kingdoms, that of Zobah, had ceased to exist.) Damascus had already been threatened by Amos (i. 3 —5), and by Isaiah (xvii. 1—11). We may infer from the prophecy that Damascus had provoked the hostility of Nebuchadnezzar, but we have as yet no monumental evidence as to the facts.

Ver. 23.—**Hamath.** Still an important city under the name of Hamah, situated to the north of Hums (Emesa), on the Orontes. It formed nominally the boundary of the kingdom of Israel (Numb. xxxiv. 8; Josh. xiii. 5), was actually a part of the empire of Solomon (2 Chron. viii. 4), and was conquered for a short time by Jeroboam II. (2 Kings xiv. 25). Under Sargon it was fully incorporated into the Assyrian empire (comp. Isa. x. 9); rebellious populations were repeatedly transplanted into the territory of Hamath. **Arpad.** Always mentioned together with Hamath, whose fate it appears to have shared (Isa. x. 9). A tell, or hill, with ruins, about three (German) miles from Aleppo, still bears the name Erfâd (*Zeitschrift* of the German Oriental Society, xxv. 655). There is **sorrow on the sea**, etc.; *i.e.* even the sea participates in the agitation of that troublous time: somewhat as in Hab. iii. 10 the sea is represented as sympathizing in the terror produced by a Divine manifestation. But by the slightest possible emendation (viz. of *caph* into *beth*) we obtain a more natural sense—"with an unrest *as of* the sea, which cannot be quiet." In Isa. lvii. 20 we read, "For the ungodly are like the troubled sea, for it cannot be quiet;" and it can hardly be doubted that Jeremiah is alluding to this passage. If he altered it at all, it would be in the direction of greater smoothness rather than the reverse. Not a few manuscripts of Jeremiah actually have this corrected reading, which should probably be adopted.

Ver. 25.—**How is the city of praise not left**, etc.! A difficult passage. The construction, indeed, is plain. "How is not," etc.! can only mean "How is it that the city of praise is not," etc.? (comp. 2 Sam. i. 14). The difficulty lies in the word rendered "left." The ordinary meaning of the verb, when applied to cities, is certainly "to leave without inhabitants;" *e.g.* ch. iv. 29; Isa. vii. 16; xxxii. 14. This, however, does not suit the context, which shows that "the daughter of Damascus" personified is the speaker, so that ver. 25 ought rather to mean, "How is it that the city of praise *is* [not, ' *is not* '] forsaken ?" Either, then, we must suppose that "not" has been inserted by mistake—a too arbitrary step, seeing that there is no negative in the context to account for the insertion (the case is different, therefore, from Job xxi. 30 ; xxvii. 15, where such an insertion is at any rate justifiable) ; or else we must give '*ǔzzěbhāh* the sense of "let go free" (comp. Exod. xxiii. 5 ; Deut. xxxii. 36 ; Job x. 1). It is the obstinate incredulity of love which refuses to admit the possibility of the destruction of the loved object. *The city of praise.* The city which is my " praise," or boast. Few cities, in fact, have had so long and brilliant an existence as Damascus.

Ver. 27.—**And I will kindly**, etc. A combination of clauses from Amos i. 14 and i. 4. Three several kings of Damascus bore the name of Ben-hadad : one the contemporary of King Baasha of Samaria ; another, of Ahab ; a third, of Joash. (Ben-hadad, however, should rather be Ben-hadar, agreeably to the Assyrian inscriptions and the Septuagint.)

Vers. 28—33.—Against the nomad and partly settled Arabs—the former described under the name **Kedar** (see on ch. ii. 10), the latter under that of **Hazor** (connected with *hāzēr*, an unwalled village ; comp. Lev. xxv. 31). This use of Hazor is remarkable ; elsewhere the name denotes towns in Palestine (Josh. xi. 1 ; xv. 23 ; Neh. xi. 33). There are two plainly marked strophes, vers. 28—30 and 31—33, both beginning with a summons to the foe to take the field.

Ver. 28.—**Hazor** (*i.e.* the settled Arabs) is said to have **kingdoms**. " King " is used in Hebrew in a wider sense than we are accustomed to (comp. ch. xxv. 24, " All the kings of Arabia "). The " kings " of Hazor would be mere sheikhs or emirs. **Shall smite** ; rather, *smote*. There is no justification whatever for the future. The statement is obviously a later addition, to show that the prophecy was fulfilled. On the form "Nebuchadrezzar," see on ch. xxi. 2. **The men of the east.** A general designation of the inhabitants of all the countries in the east of Palestine (Gen. xxix. 1 ; Judg. vi. 3 ; Job i. 3).

Ver. 29.—All the possessions of the nomad are here mentioned—first his tents and his flocks ; then the hangings of which the tent is composed (ch. iv. 20 ; x. 20), and the vessels which it contains ; and finally the camels which the Arab rides, not to mention their other uses. All this shall be ruthlessly appropriated by the Chaldean invaders. **Fear is on every side.** Again Jere-

miah's motto recurs (see on ch. vi. 25). It expresses here, not the war-cry itself, but the result produced by it.

Ver. 30.—The prophet turns to the Arabs in villages who have still more to tempt the cupidity of plunderers, and urges them to flee while there is still time. **Dwell deep** (see on ver. 8). **Against you.** This is the reading of the Septuagint (Alex. MS.), the Targum, the Vulgate, and many extant Hebrew manuscripts. The received text, however, has "against them." Such alternations of person have met us again and again, and there is no occasion to doubt the ordinary reading.

Ver. 31.—**How easy is the expedition** to which the Chaldean army is invited !—it is a mere holiday march. Resistance is impossible, for an enemy has never been dreamed of. The tribes of Hazor are *not*, indeed, a **wealthy nation**, for they have but little wealth to tempt either the conqueror or the merchant ; they " live alone ; " they are an uncommercial and unwarlike, but a profoundly " tranquil, nation, that dwelleth securely [or, ' confidently ']"—a description reminding us of Judg. viii. 7 ; Ezek. xxxviii. 11. In their idyllic, patriarchal state they feel no need of walls with their accompanying double gates (the gates of ancient cities were so large that they were divided) and bars. Like Israel in the prophetic vision (Numb. xxiii. 9), " they dwell alone."

Ver. 32.—**Them** that are **in the utmost corners.** Another of Jeremiah's characteristic phrases, which should rather be rendered, *the corner-clipped* (i.e. having the hair cut off about the ears and temples ; see on ch. ix. 26). **From all sides.** " Nebuchadnezzar will so arrange his troops that the Bedaween [but the people of Hazor were not Bedaween, *i.e.* desert-Arabs] will be surrounded on all sides, and, being thus unable to escape in a body, will be scattered to ' all the winds,' to the four quarters of the earth " (Dr. Payne Smith).

Ver. 33.—The same fate predicted for Hazor as for Edom (ver. 18). **Dragons** ; rather, *jackals* (see on ch. x. 22).

Vers. 34—39.—Concerning Elam. The title places this prophecy later than those in ch. xlviii. 1—xlix. 33 ; viz. at the beginning of the reign of Zedekiah. From this fact, and from the absence of any reference to Nebuchadnezzar as the instrument of Elam's humiliation, Ewald conjectures that the Elamites had been concerned in the events which led to the dethronement and captivity of Jehoiachin. Dr. Payne Smith is inclined to accept this hypothesis, remarking that the Elamites " appear perpetually as the allies of Merodach-baladan and his sons in their struggles for independence." We are not yet, however, in possession of information as to the relations of Elam to the great Babylonian empire which rose upon the ruins of the Assyrian. Ewald's conjecture is a possibility, and no more. And what was Elam? One of the most ancient kingdoms in the world (see Gen. xiv.). Geographically it was the tract of country, partly mountainous, partly lowland, lying south of Assyria and east of Persia proper, to which Herodotus gives the name of Cissia, and the classical geographers that of Tusis or Tusiana. This is clear, says Schrader, from the Persian text of the Behistun inscription of Darius. It is frequently mentioned under the name "Ilam," or "Ilamti," in the Assyrian inscriptions, especially in those of Sargon, Sennacherib, and Assurbanipal. In B.C 721 Sargon states that he annexed a district or province of Elam (and hence, perhaps, we must explain the mention of the Elamites in the Assyrian army in Isa. xxii. 6), which was, doubtless, one cause of the embittered feeling towards Assyria of the portion which remained independent. The annals of the heroic struggle of Merodach-baladan contain repeated reference to the King of Elam. Assurbanipal made no less than three invasions of Elam, and the singular pretext for the third is, curiously enough, associated with the remarkable fourteenth chapter of Genesis. It was this—that the Elamite king had refused to deliver up an image of the goddess Nana, which Kudur-nankhundi, an ancient Elamite monarch, had carried off, and which had remained 1635 or (perhaps) 1535 years in Elam.[1] This king has been plausibly conjectured to be a member of the same dynasty as "Chedorlaomer [= Kudur-Lagamar] King of Elam." This time it was all over with Elam; Shushan itself was plundered and destroyed, and far and wide the country was laid waste. That so restless and courageous a people should have become famous among the surrounding nations was only to be expected; and it is a striking proof of this that Ezekiel, in describing the companions whom fallen Egypt would meet with in Hades, mentions "Elam and all her multitude" (Ezek. xxxii. 24). The fact that the Septuagint has the heading twice over—first very briefly (in ch.

[1] George Smith, 'History of Assurbanipal,' pp. 222—254.

xxv. 14, where it is followed by this prophecy), and then at full length (in ch. xxvi. 1, at the end of the prophecy of Elam)—has been variously explained. It is, at any rate, clear that there is some confusion in the present text of this translation. In connection with this prediction it is interesting to notice one of the results of a new cuneiform discovery among some tablets acquired in 1878 by the British Museum. At the very time when Nebuchadnezzar was taking an oath of allegiance from Zedekiah, he was also engaged in hostilities against Elam. "We do not know," says Mr. Pinches, "what brought the Babylonians into hostilities with the Elamites, but the result of the expedition was to bring the whole kingdom of Elam within the boundaries of the Babylonian monarchy" (*Transactions of the Society of Biblical Archæology*, vii. 214).

Ver. 35.—**The bow of Elam.** So Isaiah in prophetic vision, "And Elam bare the quiver" (xxii. 6).

Ver. 36.—An emblem of the utter hopelessness of escape. **The four winds** (figuratively spoken of by Zechariah (vi. 5) as "presenting themselves" before God, to receive his commissions) shall combine their forces to scatter the doomed nation. **The outcasts of Elam.** This is the marginal reading in the Hebrew Bible; the text has, "the perpetual outcasts." No philological eye can doubt that the correction should be admitted (a *yod* for a *vav*).

Ver. 38.—**I will set my throne;** *i.e.* my tribunal (as ch. xliii. 10). **The king and the princes;** rather, *king and princes.* The threat is not merely that the reigning king shall be dethroned, but that Elam shall lose its native rulers altogether.

Ver. 39.—**But . . . in the latter days;** *i.e.* presumably in the Messianic age. Into the fulfilment of this promise we need not inquire in too prosaic a spirit. It is true that "Elamites" are mentioned among the persons present on the great "day of Pentecost" (Acts ii. 9). But this would be a meagre fulfilment indeed. The fact is that, both in the narrative in the Acts and in this prophecy, the Elamites are chiefly mentioned as representatives of the distant and less civilized Gentile nations, and the fulfilment is granted whenever a similar people to the Elamites is brought to the knowledge of the true religion.

HOMILETICS.

Ver. 1.—*Israel's heirs.* "Hath he no heir?" Most wonderful is the preservation of the Jews as a distinct race amid the strangest vicissitudes of fortune and through centuries of exile—surviving the devastating deluge of the successive Oriental monarchies, the captivity in Babylon, the cruelties of Antiochus Epiphanes, the sweep of Roman conquest, the persecution of the Middle Ages, and the cosmopolitan citizenship of our own day. Yet, much as Israel has contributed to the philosophy and trade of the modern world, and great as her future mission may yet be, we cannot blind ourselves to the fact that her lonely glory of religious pre-eminence has passed away. Others have entered into this proud inheritance.

I. THE INHERITANCE. 1. *The knowledge of the true God.* This, and not the land flowing with milk and honey, was the chief treasure of Israel's inheritance. When all neighbouring nations were following polytheism, idol-worship, and immoral rites, Israel was led by prophetic voices to look to one God—a spiritual presence who could only be worshipped " in the beauty of holiness." That people, therefore, which has the highest knowledge of God, and the purest religious life and worship, will be the true heir of this part of the ancient possession of the Jews. 2. *The mission to enlighten the heathen.* The Jew was not called to his privileged position wholly for his own sake. He was an elect people that he might be an apostle to the world; that in him there might be developed the revelation of truth which was for the healing of all the nations; that he might cultivate, preserve, transmit, and disseminate this abroad. His was the proud mission of the torch-bearer to the nations that sat in darkness, that through his light they might see their light and life. This mission was often ignored, and it was never perfectly developed in Old Testament times; but the work of Jonah and Daniel, and the prophecies of Isaiah and Jeremiah concerning the heathen, are partial accomplishments of it. It waited till Christ came for its full exercise. Then the Jew became the missionary of the gospel. The faith of the new age was given to the world by Jew-apostles.

II. THE HEIRS. If the Jew has lost his proud religious pre-eminence, who has become his heir? 1. *The Christian is the heir of the Jew's knowledge of the true God.* He and he alone, whether he be of the stock of Shem, of Ham, or of Japheth, is the true Israelite, the "royal priesthood," etc. For Christianity is the fulfilment and perfection of the Jewish faith (Matt. v. 17—20). In the New Testament we see a higher knowledge of God, a more spiritual worship, a more devoted service. If this be true, to reject it and rest contented with the lower faith of the Old Testament must be to give way in the race. 2. *The most Christian missionary is the truest heir to Israel's mission to evangelize the world.* If there be any one race upon whom the mantle of Israel has fallen, may we not think that this is the great English-speaking peoples of Britain and America? Such an inheritance is not to be made out by ingenious arguments about the fate of the lost ten tribes. If we were the descendants of those apostate Israelites, we should be none the better for the fact, nor are we under any disadvantage because the hypothesis of an Israelite origin proves to be groundless. To make much of such a point is to go back to the lower conceptions of Judaism, and to disregard the higher spiritual conditions of Christianity. The true heir of Israel is the possessor of Israel's faith in its full development. It is not our birth and descent, but our personal religion, that can secure the inheritance to us.

Ver. 7.—*The failure of wisdom.* Edom, the country of Job, the haunt of ancient lore, is to find that her learning and science will prove no safeguard against the deluge of destruction that is about to burst over the nations. The disaster which fell upon ancient " wise men " of the East may be a warning to the higher intelligences of all ages. The failure of wisdom is twofold—negative and positive.

I. NEGATIVE : THERE ARE EVILS WITH WHICH WISDOM CANNOT COPE. 1. *Physical.* Science can do much to avoid troubles into which ignorance falls, to mitigate inevitable disasters, and to devise means of escape from those which are already present. Sanitary science will help to prevent disease, and medical science to cure it. Military science will put a country in a certain state of security ; economical science will check dangers of poverty. But how many of the worst things in life are beyond the power of science ! The philosopher cannot arrest the hand of the invader. The most terrible diseases are the most fatal. Men have long since given up the vain search for the elixir of life. Science is powerless before death. 2. *Moral.* Still less can science " minister to the mind diseased." What consolation is a knowledge of the processes of a malady to the mourner, the light of whose eyes is darkened for ever by its fatal work ? What comfort can science whisper to the widow and the orphan ? The great burden of the world's sorrow, and the weariness of the unceasing cares of life, it does not so much as touch. The deeper evil of sin flows in a foul, black stream, unchecked by science. The mission of science is great and glorious, and we should be profoundly thankful that we live in an age when its bright torch confers many a boon and relieves many a trouble. But we must not ignore the fact that the greatest ills that flesh is heir to are just those which it cannot cure.

II. POSITIVE : THERE ARE EVILS WHICH WISDOM INVOKES UPON ITS OWN HEAD. Knowledge is good and Divine, and in itself a blessing of the first order. Yet it brings a snare, and the abuse of it terrible disasters. 1. The *knowledge of inevitable evil only increases distress.* "Where ignorance is bliss," etc. 2. Superior wisdom may engender *pride.* Hence arises a false sense of security which only increases danger. The wise man is slow to tread those lowly paths which lead to true rest. It is difficult for him to become as a little child, that he may enter into the kingdom of heaven. 3. *Wisdom may come to be trusted to for help that it cannot afford.* Men make an idol of science, as though it were a new evangel. The ultimate disappointment must correspond to the grossness of the delusion. We must learn, therefore, while avoiding a foolish depreciation of science and philosophy, to look still for our safety and blessedness to that higher wisdom of God, that gospel of the Crucified, which is still to some as foolishness.

Ver. 11.—*A promise for orphans and widows.* I. GOD BRINGS SOME MITIGATION TO THE SEVEREST CALAMITY. The merciful assurance of care for the helpless sufferers occurs in the midst of a stern denunciation of doom upon Edom, as a strange and startling relief to the terrible words that follow and precede. Here is a rift in the cloud through which a sunbeam of Divine love falls upon the dark scene of judgment. The thunderstorm of God's wrath never so covers the whole heavens that no ray of mercy can penetrate to the wretched sufferers. Behind the stern frown there is always the melting heart of Divine pity. God's anger is the anger of love, not that of hatred. Wherever it is possible to give relief he will do so.

II. WHEN GOD SENDS TROUBLE HE ALSO SENDS A DELIVERANCE. Possibly the trouble is beyond escape; for a season it must be endured; but in the end there is a Divine salvation for those who will seek it aright. Repeatedly denunciations of woe against some guilty nation are followed by the promise that " in the latter day " God " will bring again the captivity " of it (*e.g.* ch. xlvi. 26 ; xlviii. 47; ver. 39). The promise to Edom of the preservation of the children implies a future for the race. The widows and children are helpless sufferers, and it is for these alone that the deliverance is promised. God has peculiar pity on the most needy.

III. ORPHANS AND WIDOWS HAVE SPECIAL ENCOURAGEMENTS TO LOOK FOR HELP FROM GOD. If such a merciful promise as that of our text is made to a heathen nation, how much more assurance may the people of God feel! and if it is given to the families of the wicked and in the midst of the sentence of punishment, how much more must it apply to the families of true Christians ! God is " a Father of the fatherless, and a Judge of widows " (Ps. lxviii. 5) ; " He relieveth the fatherless and widows " (Ps. cxlvi. 9); " He will establish the border of the widow " (Prov. xv. 25). If God numbers the hairs of our head, will he neglect our children ? If they who are desolate indeed cry unto him, can the All-merciful neglect *their* prayer ?

IV. GOD'S PROMISES FOR ORPHANS AND WIDOWS SHOULD ENCOURAGE FAITH IN HIM. 1. *The father should trust his children to God.* That is a terrible moment when the strong man feels the sentence of death within him, and bows his head, knowing that he must leave his helpless ones behind. Yes, *must* leave them. Then let him leave them to God. Here is a call to resignation and to trust. The promise is in a measure conditioned by it. If the dying man would have his little ones cared for when they are set adrift on the cold, homeless world, let him entrust them to God. Such a trust will never be broken. But if he refuse to do this, *he* cannot complain should they suffer harm after he has gone. 2. *The widow must trust for herself.* "Let thy widows trust in me." The children may be too young to seek refuge in God. Their father must do this for them. But the widow must exercise her own faith. Her husband's faith will not avail for her. Let her trust, and then, but not till then, she shall find her consolation in the great Comforter.

Ver. 16.—*A people deceived by its own terribleness.* I. THEY WHO ARE A TERROR TO ALL HUMAN FOES MUST ULTIMATELY TREMBLE BEFORE SPIRITUAL FOES. Edom was to fall before Babylon, in spite of her terrible aspect. Much more must the fierce, proud sinner succumb to the unseen angel of Divine judgment. The rocks that keep back an army cannot retard the onrush of the heavenly host.

II. THEY WHO NOW STAND HIGHEST IN PRIDE AND POWER WILL FALL LOWEST AT THE FINAL JUDGMENT. Rank, social position, honour, influence, will then count for nothing. Pride may have sat high as the eagle in its eyrie, but "every one that exalteth himself shall be abased;" "The first shall be last."

III. THEY WHO POSSESS EARTHLY GREATNESS ARE IN DANGER OF DELUDING THEM-SELVES WITH AN UNWARRANTABLE TRUST IN IT. Such cities as the rock-hewn Petra, and Bozrah seated on her lofty hill, would seem by natural position impregnable. Consequently their inhabitants would grow insolent and proud, and thus deserve the more that fate which their natural resources could not avert, and their self-confidence would prevent them from mitigating. Worldly resources are dangers when they lead us to forsake the true Refuge in order to trust in them. The rich and great are not the more secure for their privileges, and they will be the less safe if they lean upon them when without them they would seek help in God.

Ver. 29.—*"Fear on every side."* This is a sadly familiar phrase of Jeremiah's. It is frequently applicable. The causes of alarm are numerous; so are the sufferers.

I. FEAR IS AN EVIL. It is not only the shadow of future calamity; it is evil itself—evil even if it is not justified by the event. 1. It is *distressing.* 2. It is *degrading*—debasing the mind, crushing out all that is noble and unselfish. 3. It is *paralyzing.* Under the influence of fear we are confused and helpless; all energy is gone.

II. THERE ARE MANY OCCASIONS OF FEAR. Jeremiah frequently exclaims, "Fear on *every* side!" We know not how many dangers surround us—political, social, domestic, personal; dangers to property, family, health, and life. The wonder is that they who have no refuge above themselves are so complacent. Such unwarrantable calmness must be traced to moral dulness rather than to true courage. For how truly terrible is the condition of the sinner! The laws of the universe are against him. If he flees from this life new horrors await him in the dread unknown land.

III. THE DEEPEST SOURCE OF FEAR IS OUR OWN SIN. 1. This brings the greatest *danger* upon us—the penalty of outraged justice and broken law. 2. This awakens the *feeling* of terror. Conscience makes cowards of us all.

IV. IN GOD IS THE REFUGE FROM FEAR. Men fear God in their guilt. Yet it is he who alone can deliver them from fear, (1) by *removing the evil* feared; (2) or by *strengthening them* to endure it; and also (3) by *calming the troubled soul* as one whom his mother comforteth. It is well that we should feel fear on every side if it leads us to cry, "What must we do to be saved?" and then to hear and follow the gospel answer, "Trust to the Lord Jesus Christ, and thou shalt be saved."

HOMILIES BY VARIOUS AUTHORS.

Vers. 1, 2.—*The paradox of Israel's inheritance.* The fittingness of this prediction is very striking. It is Ammon, the appropriator of Gad, who is the special subject of it.

I. ITS UNLIKELIHOOD. At the time the prediction was uttered appearances were completely against it. The original promise seemed doomed to failure. The flower and hope of Israel was in exile, and the land lay desolate. Interlopers reaped the benefit of their misfortunes, and seized upon portions of the unoccupied land. In the history of Christianity there may be perceived remarkable correspondences. Vast spaces of the civilized world have lost the spiritual traditions of the gospel in which once they gloried, and vaster regions still amongst the heathen are occupied by ancient faiths that offer a steady and powerful opposition to the missionary efforts of the Church. Yet the whole earth has been promised to the Church of Christ. The utmost zeal, devotion, and watchfulness are needed in order to prevent the inroads of worldliness and unbelief. At times the despairing cry may be heard, "Where is the hope of his coming?

II. THE METHOD OF ITS REALIZATION. It is well to ponder these facts in the light of God's Word, for it suggests an escape from the perplexity they occasion. Where the induction of the natural reason fails to render a hopeful explanation, the Spirit of God sheds an unthought-of light. Jeremiah's interpretation, viz. *that present dispossession need not mean utter disinheritance*, is full of spiritual light and comfort. This impression is deepened and confirmed when he seals it with prophetic certainty and declares that *Israel shall be heir to his heirs*. But still remains the mystery to be solved: 1. *How this will take place.* Israel seems all but annihilated, or in danger of absorption into heathen nations, and his land is unoccupied. But according to promise (1) a seed shall be preserved and shall be restored; and (2) through the " seed of David," viz. Christ, a new Israel will be created, in spiritual succession to the ancient people of God, and destined to redeem from heathenism not only Palestine but the whole earth. 2. *What will this involve?* It will involve (1) the judgment and overthrow of Israel's neighbours, especially such as Ammon, the traditional " land-thief" of his border; (2) the purification and discipline of Israel as the heir of the kingdom of God; and (3) the conversion of many " out of every kindred, and tongue, and people, and nation " (Rev. v. 9). In this sense also will God "bring again the captivity" of Moab, of Elam, and even of Ammon. 3. The following *lessons* are clearly taught by this prophecy, viz.:—(1) *A unity of purpose pervades the vicissitudes of Israel's and the world's history:* (2) *human affairs are governed by a strict and never-failing justice;* and (3) *a happy future awaits the children of faith—the spiritual Israel —even on earth.*—M.

Ver. 7 (cf. Obad. 8; Isa. xix. 11; xxxiii. 18).—" *Where is the wise?* " Edom, celebrated for its wisdom from of old (Obad. 8; Job xi. 11; Baruch iii. 22, 23), had secured itself in inaccessible fastnesses of the mountains, dwelling in rock-hewn cities. Eliphaz was a Temanite. It was chiefly in international relations that the skill or subtlety of the Idumæans displayed itself. Their diplomacy was full of craft and falsehood, and could not be relied upon. Their wisdom was essentially of this world— cold, calculating, and unscrupulous. Of this it is predicted by Jeremiah that it shall be brought to nought. How did his prophecy fulfil itself? In relation to the kingdom of God.

I. IT FAILED TO OVERTURN IT. The Edomites watched the signs of the times, and sided with what promised to be the strongest power, and in the last resort trusted to their own inaccessible position. Their ambassadors were amongst those of neighbouring nations who came to Zedekiah to advise united resistance to Nebuchadnezzar (ch. xxvii. 3); yet they triumphed over the prostrate city when it was captured by the Chaldeans (Lam. iv. 2; Ezek. xxxv. 15; xxxvi. 5; Ps. cxxxvii. 7). Their country had been tributary to Israel under David, but, taking advantage of the Chaldean invasion, they appropriated much of the territory of Israel proper, and extended their territory to the Mediterranean. The same spirit seems to have actuated its remote descendants, the Idumæan princes of the Herodian line. Herod the Great " slaughtered the innocents " in hope of destroying the Christ, but was circumvented by the providence of God; and his son Antipas was the Herod before whom Christ appeared by arrangement with Pilate (Luke xxiii. 12). In the later years of Christ's ministry the Herodians were constantly opposed to him, and plotted with the Pharisees against him. So God has defeated the continual antagonism of worldly men, guarding the residue of his Church, and evolving new generations of faith and fresh conquests of truth from the apparent failures and ruins of the past.

II. IT FAILED TO SECURE PERMANENT ADVANTAGE TO ITSELF. The prophet declares that it was to drink of the same cup as Israel, but it is not certain as to whether Nebuchadnezzar, or Alexander the Great, or other conquerors are alluded to. 1. The movement westward of the Idumæan power, during the Babylonian exile, was the occasion of its overthrow. The Nabathæan Arabs, ruling a large part of Arabia, seized upon Petræa, and settled down as its occupants. These were in turn conquered by the Romans. In time the country fell under Mohammedan misrule; and lapsed into permanent desolation early in the Christian era. The rock-cities of Petræa are amongst the most striking monuments of fulfilled prophecy. 2. The same fate has overtaken all the empires that set themselves against the kingdom of God. Their history is a series of dissolving views. Failing to overthrow it, they have themselves been overthrown. And the wisdom which could not subvert has equally shown itself unable to assimilate the " wisdom that cometh from above." The reason for all this is contained in the crowning proof of its folly, viz. that—

III. IT HAS FAILED TO UNDERSTAND IT. Had the Idumæans known the might of a spiritual religion, they would not have leagued against Israel. Had the Herodians known the wisdom of God, "they would not have crucified the Lord of glory " (1 Cor. ii. 8; Acts iii. 17; vii. 51). Had Rome known the power of the truth, it would never have corrupted the religion of the cross, and thus prepared for its own disintegration and decay in the Middle Ages, and the manifold complications of worldly religion in modern times. The whole conception of God's kingdom—its spirituality, other-world-liness, and purity—is still a strange thing to the wise men of the world. But it continues to grow and to realize itself amongst men; and it is destined to fill the whole earth, absorbing and assimilating its ancient antagonists; for " he must reign until he hath put all enemies under his feet " (1 Cor. xv. 25).—M.

Ver. 12 (cf. ch. xxv. 29; Prov. xi. 31; 1 Pet. iv. 18; and, for original, Obad. 16).— *Israel's judgment an argument for Edom's.* I. AN ILLUSTRATION OF THE CHARACTER OF GOD. 1. *Proving his strict righteousness.* There is no respect of persons. His love for righteousness and hatred of wrong are such that even his chosen people do not escape punishment. Salvation will not, therefore, be by favour or independent of character. The least sin will be judged. Individual saints shared in the general calamity. 2. *His unfailing faithfulness.* It was predicted particularly concerning Israel, and was declared as the law of his kingdom. Its fulfilment, therefore, vindicates the Divine veracity.

II. AN ARGUMENT BASED UPON IT. If such a God reigns amongst men, can any transgressor escape? To such sinners, then, as the Edomites, the heathen or worldly enemies of godliness and the truth : 1. *Punishment would be certain.* Their present immunity was only as the lull before the storm. Conscience gathers no comfort from apparent prosperity. Israel's punishment is a certain guarantee of Edom's. 2. *Punish-ment will be proportional to the sin.* In such cases as that of Edom—an open, flagrant, and conscious foe to the kingdom of God—it would be far more severe. There is no promise of " bringing again their captivity." It was to be " as if it had not been." Where the heathen, on the other hand, have not sinned so clearly against light, there will be condoning circumstances which will be taken into account.—M.

Ver. 23.—*The unrest of the wicked.* Isaiah (xvii. 12, 13; cf. lvii. 20, 21) uses the same figure of Damascus, and Jeremiah must, therefore, have either borrowed it from him or from some common source. It is possible that the figure was a common expression amongst the Jews of the time. The neighbourhood of Damascus and its associated cities was always a populous one, with a varied nationality and conflicting interests and affinities. From its character there was no religious unity, and its position exposed it to dangers on every hand, especially from Babylon and Egypt. It was a motley people, with vast commercial relations and strong tendency to pleasure, but no religious earnestness or capacity of moral influence or initiation. This is another of those phases of the world-spirit which Jeremiah paints in his panorama of the nations' judgment.

I. THE UNREST OF WORLD-LIFE IS LIKENED TO THAT OF THE SEA. 1. *Continual.* 2. *Vast and tumultuous.* 3. *Not to be stilled.* 4. *Sad and ruinous in its effects.*

II. BECAUSE THE WORLDLY THEMSELVES ARE LIKE THE SEA. 1. *Unstable.* How easily ruffled! Uncertain, irresolute (Jas. i. 6), subject to sudden panics. This is moral and spiritual. 2. *With no central controlling power.* The very constitution of the sea renders storms sudden and terrible. So it is with the sinner's character. There is no central controlling influence; no moral principle or spiritual power. True calm comes from within. He of the Galilean sea can alone tranquillize the troubled nation or the alarmed sinner.—M.

Ver. 1.—*Might not right.* Ammon had taken possession of the territory of Israel (cf. chapter). Had done so as if it were his right, as if they were the lawful heirs of the land. Because of this judgment is denounced against them. They are to learn that might is not right.

I. THERE MAY BE RIGHT WITHOUT MIGHT. It was so with Israel at this time. Is so with the true Church of God. "All things are yours"—so we are told, but it is only *de jure*, not *de facto*. But—

II. THERE MAY BE MIGHT WITHOUT RIGHT. In the case here given. And it is common enough. Perfect justice is not attainable in this life. Even in the little world of the home, the school, the Church, injustices will occur. And, painful as they are to witness and to bear, they have to be borne. It is hard sometimes to see the justice of the Divine ways; how much more, then, of human ways! Nevertheless—

III. MIGHT MAY BE RIGHT. "La carrière aux talents," said Napoleon—that was to be the law of his empire. "The tools to him who can use them"—such is our common maxim. The "king," the ruler, the lord paramount of the state, what is he but—if the etymology be correct—the "can"-ning man, the man who can, the able man? And so not seldom when we see might, we see right too. In the colonization of lands inhabited by savages who are letting the capabilities of glorious territories lie unimproved or running to waste, such colonization is not wrong. Might is right. "The tools," etc. It is a stern law to the incapable, but a just and beneficent one for the human race. "Take therefore the talent from him, and give it unto him that hath ten talents" (Matt. xxv. 28); what is this but the sanction of this combination? "To him that hath shall be given." There we have it once more. But—

IV. GOD'S WILL IS, AND OURS SHOULD BE, TO GIVE MIGHT TO RIGHT. Right one day shall be might as well as right. 1. *This is the burden of the promises of God* in his Word. "Thy kingdom come; thy will be done"—the will that is ever-righteous—"on earth," etc. 2. *The constitution of human nature* is in favour of it (cf. Butler's ' Analogy '). 3. *Conscience ever takes the side* of right, whatever our conduct may do or be. 4. And *God's providence is slowly working to this end.* 5. "*Faith*" is simply the giving ourselves up to the righteous One, to be " his faithful servant and soldier, and to fight manfully under his banner until our lives shall end."

CONCLUSION. Let us seek to be on the side of *right* always, let the cost be what it may.—C.

Ver. 8.—*Desirable habitations: a new year's sermon.* "Dwell deep, O inhabitants of Dedan." The prophet is foretelling the calamities that are to come on the different heathen nations who dwelt around the land of God's people, and from whom they, at various times, had received sore wrong and harm. The Edomites—the descendants of Esau—were the traditional foes of Israel, and it is they who in all probability are referred to. The country they inhabited was full of rocks, cliffs, deep gorges in the sides of which were many all but inaccessible caves. The rocky dwellings of Edom have been often told of—how they served as an almost impenetrable fortress for the robber bands which mostly inhabited them. But now vengeance was to come on these people, and the prophet is bidding them betake themselves in flight to the far-off desert, or to hide themselves in the deep recesses of their rocky caves, and there, if possible, safely dwell. "Dwell deep . . . Dedan" (cf. also ver. 30). For disaster was threatening Hazor also. The ruthless King of Babylon would fall on them in his march westwards to Egypt, and well would it be for them if the forests and caverns, the lofty rocks and the deep valleys of their rugged land should provide them with secure retreat. It was in such hidden caves that David, during much of his fugitive life when hunted by Saul "like a partridge upon the mountains," so often found refuge. And this fact he is for ever commemorating in his psalms by calling God his Rock, his Refuge, his Hiding-place, his Fortress, his Secret Place. And the history of these lands tells once and again of the devices of military commanders to dislodge the inhabitants of these almost inaccessible retreats. Herod, so Josephus tells, caused a number of huge timber boxes to be made, in which stood armed soldiers, and these were lowered down the precipitous sides of the cliffs in which the robber caverns were until they reached the cavern mouths. Then, rushing in, they would massacre the inhabitants, or else by huge hooks drag them forth and then hurl them down to the dread depths beneath. But generally these hidden habitations proved secure refuges for those who dwelt in them, and it is to this fact that the prophet refers. He is bidding them betake themselves thither, for danger was at hand—a relentless foe was threatening them. Now, the like exhortation may be addressed to us; for for us there are provided strong habitations unto which we may continually resort, sure refuges in which we may safely hide, Divine retreats in the deep recesses of which we may securely dwell. Therefore we would say—

I. DWELL DEEP IN THE LOVE OF GOD. For the firm faith of the love that God hath toward us will be found to be a shelter, a solace, and a strength, such as nought else can render. St. John says concerning that love, "We know and have believed the love that God hath towards us." Yes; sometimes we can clearly see it, we know and feel it. God's providence, God's grace, God's Word, are all filled and flooded with it. But there are other times when we cannot say we know, but only that we *believe* the love that, etc.—when providence seems adverse, when our path is rough and beset with thorns, when those you trusted prove treacherous and your own friends turn against you, when your home is left desolate and dark clouds of anxiety gather heavy and thick over you. But those times are made far less fearful for us if we will but dwell, dwell deep, in the love of God. It was through this ever-cherished home of his soul that our Lord was able to endure so calmly and to meet with such meek majesty and Divine dignity the unspeakable sorrow of his earthly lot. Often did the tempter seek to drag him forth from that secure retreat by his mocking suggestion, "If thou *be* the Son of God," etc. But he tried in vain. Dwelling deep in the love of God, that inaccessible refuge, that sure retreat, he looked forth upon the path he had to tread and the cross he had to bear, and he could endure the one and despise the other in the might of that love in which he ever abode. And it is well that we should dwell where he dwelt, and so be blest as he was blest. And not a few of his people have done so—Abraham, David, Daniel, Paul, and myriads more, as God grant we may likewise.

II. DWELL DEEP IN THE KNOWLEDGE OF HOLY SCRIPTURE. For no surer aid to our obeying the former exhortation can be given than our obedience to this. And yet there are few books of importance that are neglected as the Scriptures are, notwithstanding the invaluable help which such knowledge has imparted and must ever impart. What is the hundred and nineteenth psalm but one long panegyric on the blessedness of this knowledge of the Word of God? And he who knows what the Word of God can do for his soul will deem no praise too extravagant, no admiration and love too enthusiastic. Oh to be mighty in the Scriptures! for that is to be mighty through them, capable and ready for all God's will. The dark problems of life cease to dismay; the mysteries which meet us on every side cannot shake our faith; we become open-eyed to signs and tokens of God's love which otherwise we should not see. Integrity and uprightness preserve us, and we run the way of God's commandments, because God, by means of them, hath enlarged our heart. It is this prayerful habitual study of God's Word which is dwelling deep therein, and which is so fruitful of good to all that will so dwell.

III. DWELL DEEP IN THE FELLOWSHIP OF CHRIST. Cherish and guard with a holy care that communion with him which is the joy and strength of our souls. A sure test of the value of any spiritual aid is given us in the intensity of the opposition which Satan offers to our use of such aid. Now, measured by this standard it is difficult to over-estimate the value of this communion with Christ in which we say, "Dwell deep." This is not easy to do. For persistent indeed are the endeavours which Satan makes to destroy this communion. Who that kneels in prayer is ignorant of these endeavours?—thoughts wandering; desires earth-bound; faith feeble; love cold. Hence many neglect prayer, or they become formal in it. But there can be no real communion with Christ without this. Therefore we must rouse ourselves to earnestness. Pray that we may pray. Kneel down again and pray once more our as yet unprayed prayer. Let us resolve we will not be conquered. Encourage ourselves by remembering that the very difficulties we meet are evidences of the truth of true prayer. And that such difficulties can be overcome; for they have been. And not only by prayer, but by walking with Christ in obedience and sympathy and love.—C.

Ver. 11.—*Consolation for a father's dying bed.* Perhaps there is no greater sorrow than is suggested here—the husband and father leaving widow and helpless children apparently without a friend to support or aid them. If it were not for the beatific vision of God, the perfect persuasion of his wisdom and power and love, which the blessed dead enjoy, they would be entreating God piteously to allow them to return hither once more, and to shelter their loved ones from the cruel hardships of this pitiless world. We wonder, sometimes, how it is possible for a loving mother who was wont to lavish her heart's deepest, tenderest affection upon her children, to find joy and to be happy in heaven, whither she has been suddenly translated, leaving her husband and children heart-broken at losing her. Here she could never be happy without her children. How can she be happy there and they yet here? Because she is at the fountain of all love, from which all her love was but a rill; she is with God, who *is* Love, and who she knows will deal only in the best of ways—ways far better than she herself could have devised, for those who are now weeping over her grave, and missing and mourning her every hour of the day. Now, of those told of in this verse we note—

I. THAT TO LEAVE THEM TO GOD IS ALL WE CAN DO. We may and we ought to make provision for them to the best of our power. That is but a spurious and miserable travesty of faith in God which would neglect all such aids as life insurance and the like, on the ground that making such provision shows distrust and unbelief in God. Some speak thus, but they speak foolishly. Might we not as well refuse to work for our daily bread, on the ground that it is written, " My God shall supply all your need "? But who does not know that God's way of supplying our need is by giving us strength to work and minds to think, enduing us with the means of gaining our bread? And is it not so in this case also? Would not a man be most wrong who, because of what is here said, neglected to make all due provision in his power? But having done this, like Jacob and Joseph, we may safely leave our children, as they did, to the care of God, confident that he will care for them according to his word.

II. AND GOD HONOURS SUCH TRUST. As a fact, and a very interesting one it is, how wonderfully such bereaved children and widows are cared for! How God raises up one friend here and another there, and probably, if a comparison could be made, it would be found that such children have been as well cared for as any others; life has been as bright to them as for those whose earlier years were clouded over by no such sore bereavement. There may be exceptions, but the rule is surely for God to honour such trust. Can he who has said, "Ask, and ye shall receive," refuse the prayer of a believing man at such a time?

III. AND IT IS A REASONABLE TRUST. What would we desire more for our children than that they should be cared for by such a one who, so far as man can be, is like God?—having the power and the will, the knowledge and wisdom, and, above all, the love, which are in God. Who would not crave for our dear ones a guardian like that?

IV. THE CONDITIONS OF THE TRUST are that he who is about to leave behind widow and children should be himself one who trusts in God; that he have trained his children in the ways of the Lord, and sought to make his home a godly home. Verily such shall have their reward, yonder in heaven and here on earth, and especially at that supreme moment when he has to leave his loved ones and to lie down and die. Then for him shall the faith of this promise be precious indeed.—C.

Ver. 16.—*Vain confidences.* "Thy terribleness hath deceived thee," etc. Taking the different expressions in this verse, we can see how such confidences are begotten in men's minds.

I. THEIR FELLOW-MEN HELP TO DECEIVE THEM. " Thy terribleness," etc. All around them held them in terror, were afraid of them, deemed them too mighty to be overcome. And the consciousness of this kept in them a confidence which now was to be shown to be but vain.

II. MEN'S OWN PRIDE. "The pride of thine heart." What myriads has not pride slain! what woe hath it not brought upon mankind! "Pride goeth before destruction," etc. (Cf. homily on *Pride*, ch. xlviii. 29.) See Sennacherib's army (Isa. xxxvii.), Pharaoh's overthrow (Exod. xiv.); and "all the ages all along" pride has done the like and does so still.

III. MEN'S CIRCUMSTANCES. No dwellings could seem more secure than were theirs; their fortress seemed impregnable. Hence they " said in their hearts," " We shall never be moved." (Cf. on these dwellings, introduction to homily on *Desirable habitations, supra,* ver. 8.) Cf. the rich fool (Luke xii. 20). Prosperity and security do tend to beget these vain confidences.

IV. PAST SUCCESS. Not only did these Edomites dwell in the clefts of the rock, but they had *held them fast* hitherto against all invaders. A career of success, opponents vanquished, difficulties surmounted, wealth and honour won; who can persuade such a man to call himself a poor, lost sinner, dependent utterly on the mercy of God? It is much easier to say, "Have mercy on us miserable sinners," than to feel and believe we are so.

CONCLUSION. There are two ways in which this spirit of false confidence may be got rid of or kept under. 1. *By surrender of the soul to Christ.* He makes us like himself, forms his Spirit in us, so that the truer the surrender the more we become "meek and lowly in heart" as he was. This the best way, the easy yoke, the light burden. 2. *By the crushing force of God's judgments.* Edom was to be humbled thus. And there are many who will only be humbled so. They will have their own way, and they have it for their woe, and then, after a weary while, they come to themselves. They "made their bed in hell," and as they made it so they had to lie upon it, until even there God's hand shall find them, and they shall humble themselves beneath the mighty hand they had heretofore dared to defy. 3. *And in some way this humility must be wrought in us.* For God *will* have all men to be saved; but without this lowly mind, this rejection of all vain confidences, we cannot be. Which way, then, shall it be—through Christ or through the fire of hell?—C.

Ver. 23.—*Lessons from the sea.* "There is sorrow on the sea; it cannot be quiet." We must remember that the sea to the Jew of old time was an object of almost unmixed terror. Nearly all the allusions in the Bible tell of its power and peril, never of its preciousness and value to man. The Jews were a non-seafaring people; they dreaded it. In Deut. xxviii. 68 the being taken back to Egypt in ships is held out as a great threatening. They had no seaport worth mentioning. For centuries their seaboard was held by the Philistines. All their conceptions of it relate to its hurtful and destructive power (cf. Ps. cvii., "They that go down to the sea in ships," etc.; cf. also histories of the Deluge, Exodus, Jonah). The epithets applied to it are never pleasing, but all more or less terrible. It is "raging," "roaring," "troubled," "breaking ships of Tarshish." Hezekiah failed to construct a navy. And hence St. John (Rev. xxi. 1), when telling of the beauty, the glory, and the joy of the new heavens and the new earth, is careful to add, "And there was no more sea." Now, this ver. 23 is an illustration of this common Jewish feeling. But this Jewish feeling was a false one, though not so to them. For the sea is one of God's most blessed gifts to man. Life would be impossible without it. It has been justly called, "the life-blood of the land, as the blood is the life of the body. It is the vital fluid that animates our earth, and, should it disappear altogether, our fair green planet would become a heap of brown volcanic rocks and deserts, lifeless and worthless as the slag cast out from a furnace." We remember, too, how God said of the sea that it was "very good," and no mistaken Jewish ideas must be allowed to reverse that verdict. Think of: Its *vapours.* Each recurring harvest is really the harvest of the sea as much as of the land. For from the sea ascend those vapours which form the clouds and which descend in the fertilizing indispensable rain. Its *currents,* bearing along the sun-heated waters of sub-tropical climes, far away northward and southward, and giving to regions like our own that mild and on the whole beautiful climate which we enjoy, whereas but for these warm waters of the sea our shores would be bleak, inhospitable, barren, and all but uninhabitable, like the shores of Labrador. Its *breezes,* so health-giving, imparting fresh life to the sick and feeble. Its *beauty,* ever presenting some fresh form of loveliness in colour, movements, outline, brilliancy. Its *tides,* sweeping up the mouths of our great rivers and estuaries, and all along our shores, washing clean what else would be foul, stagnant, poisonous. Its *saltness,* ministering to the life of its inhabitants, retaining the warmth of the sun, and so aiding in the transmission of those currents spoken of above, preserving from corruption, etc. But these thoughts were not those of the Jew. To him the sea was a type of manifold ills, and he rejoiced to believe that in his eternal home there should be "no more sea." For it told of unrest, instability, painful mystery, afflictions, separation, and hence impossibility of intercourse and death. For all these the sea serves in the Scriptures as a symbol, as reference to the passages which speak of the sea will show. But it has its brighter teachings also. Note—

I. ITS WAVES. See them in their blithe merry-heartedness, their buoyant spring and rush, coming in landwards from out the far distance, gleaming and sparkling as they roll along, "clapping their hands" as David would say, praising God as they leap and bound in their joy. How often we have seen them coming in such fashion, long lines of them!—nearer and nearer they approach, the sea-breeze filling them with vigour, and the sunshine gleaming on them and adorning them with the most exquisite colouring, until at length the shelving shore stops them, and they fall over, and in masses of snow-white foam, with merry rush and roar, they dash up the beach, brightening everything they touch; and then, their strength all gone, they glide down the sands and hie away back to their ocean-home, to begin the same joyous career all over again. Now, surely this perpetual process suggests the *joyful vigour* of the sea. True, its waves lie broken on the beach, their spray scattered far and wide, and it would seem as if that were but a poor ending for such a career. But not heeding that at all, the waves just gather up their strength again, and, never knowing when they are beaten, return again and again to the charge. And does not this teach us *how we should meet rebuff and disappointment?* Not lie down and moan, but hie back again to the source of our strength once more, and then again to the work God has given us to do. They seem to say to us, "Never be discouraged; see us as we begin again after each rebuff, how we sparkle all the more that we are scattered and broken, and then go back to come on again. So do you. Hope continually, and praise God more and more."

II. Its MISTS AND VAPOURS—its clouds and exhalations—they also have their lessons. How common these mists are all who know the sea know well. But in and by them the sea renders up her strength, pays her tribute to the heavens. But *how bountifully she is recompensed!* How comes it that the sea abides wholesome, that it is not the source of malaria, a deadly mass of waters, in which no plant or fish can live? And part of the reply is in the fact that those mists and vapours which ascend from the sea descend to the earth in rain and showers, and fill the springs and fountains, which are the sources of the rivers, which are the carriers into the sea-depths of those varied salts and other products which serve as ministers of health to the innumerable forms of life with which the sea abounds. Thus is the sea repaid for the tribute she renders to the heavens. And so these sea-mists teach the blessedness of rendering up to God all he asks for. Thy God commandeth thy strength. The recompense of the sea assures us how abundantly God will recompense all who obey this command. And they suggest *the sure way of deliverance from all inward evil.* They ascend from the sea, but they leave all its saltness behind; from the pools and lakes and from stagnant marsh, but they leave all their unhealthful, corrupting properties behind; and when they come back again in form of rain, they are sweet and wholesome and precious, to quench the thirst of man and beast, and to gladden the whole face of the earth. And so with ourselves. In ascending to God, in spiritual drawing near to him, we leave all our evil behind. God says to the waters, "Come up hither," and *they are cleansed in the coming.* And so he says to us, "Come up hither," and we, too, are cleansed in the coming. And when we come back our hearts and lives, our whole influence, will be healthful and salutary, a blessing to all with whom we have to do.

III. Its TIDES. They teach *the power of the unseen.* Their mighty movements are all governed by a force imperceptible to our senses. And it is the unseen, the intangible, that which the senses cannot perceive—*thought*, which governs the world. They teach also the *gradualness of the religious life.* It is often hard to say, on looking at the sea, whether the tide ebbs or flows. You must compare it after a while with its present position, and then you shall know. And so it is with the religious life. There are no leaps and bounds, no great starts and strides, but gradual, slow, step by step—such is the Divine ordering. Now, hence a lesson : 1. *Of consolation.* We are not to write bitter things against ourselves because our advance is slow. 2. *Thankfulness.* No man can leap into hell any more than he can into fitness for heaven. God holds us very fast, and only very slowly will he let us go. 3. *Caution.* Judge not that all is well because of no sudden great change in you. There may be the gradual ebbing away. Are there now large portions of your life which the fear of God does not govern, though once it controlled them all? If so the tide *has* ebbed.

IV. THE DEPTHS of the sea tell of that complete putting away of our sin which God promises to us (cf. Micah vii. 19). God will utterly put them away, casting them, not near the shore, in the shallows, or in the tide-way, but in the depths, where they will be sunk out of sight and out of reach for ever.

V. ITS SANDS. (Cf. ch. v. 22.) They teach how *God makes our weakness strong*. What more feeble than the sand? And yet by it the mighty sea is held in. "To them who have no might God increaseth strength." But what are we and the surroundings of our lives but weak, shifting, unstable as the sand? But God can so fill them with strength that they shall beat back the fierce waves which would overwhelm us. Then let us fear not. He who makes the weak sand a sure bar against the ocean's rage can and will make our weakness strong to triumph over all that would harm us. Such are some of the lessons of the sea.—C.

Ver. 24.—*The fall of Damascus; or, the lovely and the lovable lost.* Here and in Isaiah and Amos we have predictions of the overthrow of Damascus. "The burden of Damascus," says Isaiah. "Behold! Damascus is taken away from being a city, and it shall be a ruinous heap." Jeremiah likens the agitated minds of the multitude of her inhabitants to the unquiet sea—still not for one moment. And the cause of that unquietness is their sorrow at the desolations coming on them. *And yet she was no mean city.* No; she was distinguished indeed. The hearts of men, in all ages of the world, have been drawn to her, and are so still. For she was and is surpassingly lovely. Beautiful for situation, the joy of the whole land around, compared to the Paradise in which our first father was placed by God, and celebrated by every writer, sacred and secular, that has had occasion to speak of her or her history. "It is the oldest city in the world. Its fame begins with the earliest patriarchs and continues to modern times. While other cities of the East have risen and decayed, Damascus is still where and what it was. While Babylon is a heap in the desert, Nineveh buried beneath her mounds, and Tyre a ruin on the seashore, it remains what it is called in the prophecies of Isaiah, 'the head of Syria.' And ever since, down to our own days, its praise is celebrated. It was 'a predestinated capital.' Nor is it difficult to explain why its freshness has never faded through all its series of vicissitudes and wars." Men have ever loved it and love it still. As the traveller from the west climbs up and up the steep passes of the great Lebanon range, and at length nears their eastern side, there, on the summit of a cliff, high up above the plain beneath, he looks down on the city of Damascus. "At the foot of the cliff on which the beholder stands, a river bursts forth from the mountain in which it has had birth. That river, as if in a moment, scatters over the plain, through a circle of thirty miles, the verdure which had hitherto been confined to its single channel. It is like the bursting of a shell, the eruption of a volcano—but an eruption, not of death, but of life. Far and wide extends in front the level plain, its horizon bare, its lines of surrounding hills bare, all bare, far away on the road to Palmyra and Bagdad. In the midst of this plain lies at your feet the vast island of deep verdure, walnuts and apricots hanging above, corn and grass below." The river is its life. It is drawn out in watercourses and spread in all directions. For miles around it is a wilderness of gardens—gardens with roses among the tangled shrubberies, and with fruit on the branches overhead. Everywhere among the trees the murmur of unseen rivulets is heard. Even in the city, which is in the midst of the garden, the clear rushing of the current is a perpetual refreshment. Every dwelling has its fountain; and at night, when the sun has set behind Mount Lebanon, the lights of the city are seen flashing on the water. All travellers in all ages have paused to feast their eyes on the loveliness of the city as they first behold it from the cliffs of Lebanon. Abana and Pharpar still flash and gleam as they flow along amid her fragrant gardens and by her dark olive groves. Snow-capped Hermon and the rugged range of Lebanon still keep over her their wonted watch and ward. Hence she may well be taken as the symbol of all that is lovely and fair in outward life, all that is bright and beautiful in the moral nature of man. *But yet she fell,* and she has lost her place amongst the nations for ever. Thus she suggests to the thoughtful reader the heart-searching truth that *the lovely and the lovable may yet be lost*—those on whom Jesus, looking, loves them, because they are so lovable, may yet miss of the life that is eternal; and he may say, as he did to one of them, "One thing thou lackest." Observe, then—

I. THERE HAVE BEEN SOULS CHARACTERIZED BY MUCH THAT IS LOVELY AND LOVABLE, AND YET HAVE NOT ENTERED INTO THE KINGDOM OF GOD. Read the history of Orpah. Then there was *that young ruler* to whom reference has already been made. And the many who flocked around our Saviour when he was here on earth, and *whom he likened to the stony-ground hearers.* They all had much that was excellent and good about them, but they failed to bring forth fruit unto life eternal.

II. AND THERE ARE MANY SUCH NOW. Were our Lord amongst us now, he would love them as he did him of whom the Gospel tells. They may be young in years; in the morning of life, fair and comely to look upon, vigorous and strong, well educated, intelligent, bright and clever, cultured themselves and loving refinement and culture in others; they may be possessed of very attractive moral qualities, amiable and kindly, ready to do a kind action and scorning to do a mean one, possessed of and deserving an honourable reputation, of unquestioned veracity, of high honour, modest and pure in word and deed, gentle and courteous in manner, unassuming, thoughtful of the feelings and wishes of others; parents and friends, family and neighbours, all speak well of them, and those who know them best honour and love them most. Now, there are thousands of such as these. They are loved and lovable; they must be so. And as we picture them to ourselves we almost shrink from saying that such may nevertheless miss of the kingdom of God; like Damascus in all that is externally beautiful, and yet, like her, come under the condemnation of God. It seems scarce believable, and yet in the face of God's Word what can we say? Nicodemus was one such, and yet our Lord told *him*, "Except a man be born again," etc. We would be as charitable as the Word of God—and if we were that would make us far more charitable than the most of us are—but we would not be more so, for that would be to be uncharitable and unfaithful both to God and to the souls of men. And therefore we say that a man may be all that is externally fair and lovable, and yet, like bright beautiful Damascus, come under the condemnation of God; lovely and lovable like him whom Jesus loved, and yet, because lacking the *one* thing, shut out—self shut out—from the kingdom of God. And observe—

III. THIS RULE OF GOD IS NOT ARBITRARY, BUT JUST AND INDISPENSABLE. For all that we have said may coexist along with the will alien from the will of God, the heart not yet truly surrendered to him. It was so in that typical instance of this character to whom we have so often referred. For when brought to the test he refused the will of God. For the proof of our loyalty to God is seen, *not* in the many things that we are and do which are in keeping with our own inclinations, but in those that we are ready to do when they involve a real taking up of the cross and contradict those inclinations. A cultured, refined disposition may lead us, out of regard to our own self-interest, to do and be that which wins for us the applause and favour of our fellow-men. It would be a pain and grief to us to be otherwise. All the commands of the moral law we may have kept from our youth up, and hence conclude, and others —even Christ's disciples—may think also, that we lack nothing. And in fact we may lack nothing but that one thing without which all else is vain and useless for our admission into the kingdom of God. *But in that kingdom the will of God must be paramount*, or it ceases to be the kingdom of God. Suppose one of the heavenly bodies could choose, and did so, to swerve at times from its appointed orbit, and to take a course of its own; the whole universe would be thrown out of order, and confusion and destruction must ensue. Suppose one string of harp, one pipe of organ, instead of giving its proper note, were to resolve to utter a sound different from that which was appointed for it; what jarring discord must result! no true music could such harp or organ give. And so in God's kingdom, if there be one discordant will, how can the harmony and peace and blessedness of heaven any longer exist? If in our homes the law of the house be violated by any one of its members, how little would such a household deserve the sweet name of home! *For the good of all*, therefore, and not for any arbitrary reason, one law, one will, must be paramount. It is so in our earthly homes; it must yet more be so in the home of God, the kingdom of heaven. The heart, the will, *must* be surrendered to God if we are to be at last numbered amongst the inhabitants of God's eternal home.

IV. WHAT, THEN, SHALL WE SAY TO SUCH? Shall we bid you set light store by those varied qualities which draw forth the affection and esteem of your fellow-men? Shall we say—Care nothing for that which, when Jesus looked upon, even he could not but love? Still less shall we say that all these things are of the nature of sin. On the contrary, we would say—*Give God thanks for these things.* For, indeed, it is of his great mercy that you have been led to approve of them, and to turn away with disgust and abhorrence from that which is contrary thereto. Why were you made to hear God's voice?—for it was his voice which called you, and his hand which led you to this good choice. Without doubt the parents of that young ruler gave God thanks again and again when they saw the character of their son unfolding and developing in all such high-minded, pure, and amiable ways. And when we see the like in our children, do we not, ought we not to, give thanks likewise? What, then, do we say to you but this?—(1) *Render thanks to God* that he has thus inclined your heart; and then (2) go on to ask him who has been so good to you thus far that he will be more gracious still, and *give you that one thing which yet you lack*—the new heart, the perfectly surrendered will, the faith in God of which such surrender is the chief expression. Remember that the merchantman who became the happy owner of the pearl of great price was not content with the many goodly pearls after which he had been seeking and which he had already attained. No; but when he saw that pure, all-precious, lustrous pearl, he resolved that that should be his, and hence all was surrendered that he might make it his own. Now, you resemble him in two out of the three great facts of his history. Like him, you have sought and found many goodly pearls. The goodly pearls of moral excellence, virtue, amiability, many things lovely and of good report. You prize these things, as you ought to do. You have sought after them and have found them. And now, again, like that merchantman, there is shown and offered to you that pearl which is more precious than all—even the gift of God, which is Jesus Christ, the eternal salvation which comes to us alone through him. Yes, that *is* offered to you—that gift of the regenerated nature, that new heart and right spirit, which they who come to Christ receive. But now, in *the third and chief point of all*, would that you resembled that merchantman. He was willing to part with all he had for the sake of the pearl of great price. Are you? To persuade hereto we add two words. 1. The first by way of *encouragement*. That merchant had to part with his goodly pearls for the sake of the one all-precious one. You not only will not have to do this, but they will become more goodly and more indisputably yours than ever if the all-precious one be yours. You will have to renounce none of them, nothing lovely and of good report, nothing wherein there is any virtue or any praise. On the contrary, they shall gain an added lustre from their association with that chief excellence which we would have you win. Like as there is so great difference between a fair landscape on a bright summer's morn, and that same scene looked upon amid the mists of winter, so shall all that is virtuous and good in us attain to a higher beauty, a more perfect loveliness, by the bright shining of the Sun of righteousness upon them. Apart from him they are cold, dim, vague, uncertain; but in him and through him they become radiant and more beautiful than ever. And not only so, but they are more securely yours; they are far less likely to be lost. 2. *By way of warning,* let me remind you that on the wedding garment in which we must all be clothed if we would enter in and share in the festivities of the marriage supper of the Lamb—on that garment there shines resplendent but *one* jewel; it is this pearl of great price. If we have not that, no bedizening of ourselves with such goodly pearls as we may possess, or think we possess, will serve instead. Many will seek, do seek, so to adorn themselves. But all such righteousness is rejected, all such trust refused. Oh, then, to your virtues and other lovely and lovable qualities add this—trust in the blessed Saviour's Name, which will include in it the heart perfectly surrendered, the will yielded up to him!—C.

Vers. 1, 2.—*A usurper in the inheritance.* I. ACTUAL POSSESSION IS NOT THE ONLY THING TO BE CONSIDERED. Ammon is the actual present possessor of the territory of Gad. But every possessor must be ready upon occasion to show his title. With respect to the most trifling article the possessor must be able to make clear that it is his own, that he bought it, or inherited it, or had it given to him; in short, that it came to him in some entirely lawful way. Ammon had taken Gad by force, probably a very easy thing to do in the depressed condition of Israel's fortunes. And if it be said in reply that Israel had originally taken this very territory of Gad by force, such a statement is, of course, quite correct. But then we have to keep in mind the typical character of Israel. Everything depends on the point of view from which we look. Certain rules of legal ownership are an indispensable necessity of present social order, but at intervals in the course of the world revolutions come more or less extensive, and existing legal ownerships get utterly swept away. The Maker of the world, who is also the Bringer-forth of the abundance of the soil, is to be looked to as the real Disposer of what he has made. And therefore, with respect to every actual possession of man, we have the question to ask—Is it as the possession of Ammon, or as the possession of Israel? And chiefly we should ask the question with respect to ourselves. Whatever it be, external goods, or office, or reputation, have we got it, proceeding on the very highest principles of action, those which God himself would have us to employ?

II. Abiding possession, and how it is to be gained. Ammon now holds Gad, as it seems, very firmly. What can Israel now do to get the territory back? That question Jehovah will answer in his own time, and Ammon will have to suffer for violently laying hold of what was not its own. And yet, bear in mind that this very action came through Ammon's alienation from the true Lord and Guide of men. That alienation may manifest itself in different ways, but all sin and all chastisement of sin are traceable back to the alienation. Ammon was really trying to gratify a right desire in a wrong way. The desire for possession and for increase of possession, continuous and ever-expanding, is a right desire. But it must be a possession assimilated to all that is best, all that is most enduring in our nature. Legal ownership is often in inverse proportion to actual enjoyment. The spiritual Israelite, the genuine, devout, habitual believer in Jesus Christ, is to be heir of all things. The things unseen and eternal are his, and they are his because a correspondence has been divinely produced between him and them (1 Cor. vi. 9—11; xv. 53). Inheritances gained after the natural fashion very soon turn out delusive.—Y.

Ver. 16.—*The pride of apparent security.* I. The real extent of the security. Not without some cause did Edom pride itself on its position. Security is a relative word. Mountain fastnesses are a sufficient defence against such attacks as Edom can measure and understand. Mountain fastnesses have done much for the cause of national liberty and independence. They ought not to be the shelter and home of brigands; but it is right to notice their glorious place in history as the shelter and home of struggling freemen. God would not have us undervalue any security so far as it is a real security. The mistake is when we live as if *all* precious things could be preserved by securities which Providence has only given for the preservation of certain outward things. So far from our overvaluing securities coming from our own strength and external resources, it may truly be said that we rather undervalue them. If we could only use them in the right way, with insight and without prejudice, we should find many dangers of the present life greatly diminished.

II. The way in which a security may become a peril. Edom lives as it likes among its great natural strongholds. Long experience has taught it exactly how to deal with every attacking force, and it sees no danger with which it cannot effectually deal. Thus the dangers and deliverances which come out of the unseen alike escape attention. Men are protected outwardly; they have all that heart can wish; but mean-while the heart is left exposed to every temptation. The fewer dangers there are outwardly, the more dangers there are inwardly; and the more dangers there are outwardly, the fewer there may be inwardly. For when men live amid dangers and inconveniences to the outward life, then their eyes are open to the comparative super-ficiality of such dangers. They see how the deepest treasures of life, the most abiding ones, may remain perfectly safe while outward things are going to pieces. Better would it have been for Edom to live in the exposed plain, if thereby it had been brought to trust and know that God who is the only true Refuge.

III. The fallacy of seeking security in a higher degree of the essentially insecure. The eagle dwells in inaccessible heights, and thus it may be reckoned a symbol of the greatest security attainable here below. But after all, the word "inaccessible" is only a synonym for what is exceedingly difficult of attainment. Courage, patience, and perseverance may do much to blot out the word "inaccessible." And if this be so from the human point of view, how much plainer is it that all human securities, however high the degree they attain in our estimate, are in the sight of God as nothing! The great thing that sends us wrong in trying to make life really secure is that, instead of fixing our thoughts on an entirely different *kind* of danger, we allow ourselves to act as if the only thing needful was to guard against a higher degree of the danger already perceived. To God dealing with the ungodly and the unrighteous, mountain and plain are alike.—Y.

Ver. 23.—*The perils of the sea.* I. THE FEELING PRODUCED BY MARITIME DANGER. Sorrow is far too vague a word for the feeling here referred to. Fear, anxiety, constant watchfulness against close and sudden and increasing danger, a sense that utter destruction may come at any moment,—these are the feelings going to make up the complex state of mind with which Damascus is so profoundly disturbed. No discomposing effect produced by a land danger was enough to serve the prophet's purpose. Not but what land perils taken in the sum of them are greater than sea ones; but they do not produce the same effect on the mind. Away out at sea one is so completely at the mercy of the waters. There is no chance to say, "Run for your life." There is nothing left for it but patience, submission, and hope trying to rise above opposed emotions. Those who have been in such circumstances will be best able to realize the force and peculiarity of the figure here employed. The Old Testament furnishes one illustration in Jonah's disobedient voyage, and the New Testament another in the experiences connected with the shipwreck of Paul.

II. THE WAY TO PREPARE FOR SUCH AN HOUR. The hour in which human strength and wisdom can do nothing may come on us unawares, may come fated with terrible appearances beyond all previous imaginations, but it by no means follows that such an hour is to come unprepared for. More preparation is needed than simply that of counting on the chances of escaping such an hour altogether. The hour may be escaped, but all who go down to the sea in ships cannot escape it; and therefore they do wisely to prepare for it, especially as the preparation arises from a state of mind which brings the greatest positive blessings. The peace that passeth all understanding is a peace that comprehends and subdues every possible disturbing cause. The attainment of this peace and the benefits consequent upon it have been wonderfully proved in terrible cases of shipwreck. The true wisdom for us all in this world so full of perils, whether we have to face the dangers of sea or of land, is to have the real treasures of life in heaven. Then when we have done all that human resources can compass, we are sure that the most precious things remain safe beyond the reach of harm.—Y.

Vers. 34—39.—*The fate of Elam.* I. THE ELEMENTS OF DOOM. 1. *Loss of active strength.* The breaking of the bow ought, perhaps, to be taken somewhat literally. Elam may have been a people where skill in archery reckoned for much of its strength. Whatever our peculiar natural strength may be, God can break it to pieces. We should never pride ourselves on what is peculiar to us, for the really best things are those which may become common to all men. 2. *The loss of all union.* The two ways in which nations perish. (1) They retain their corporate existence, remain in their country, but lose their independence and enter into servitude. (2) They are scattered, and lose all the outward signs of a nation. Thus in this scattering we have a symbol of the way in which men who have been joined together for evil purposes may be disunited. Union itself is strength so long as it lasts, even if no actual step be taken. God can destroy the schemes of men and at the same time throw them into new relations as individuals, so that they may be forced each one into a new scheme and plan for himself. When God scatters and humbles nations, there is pain to the individual for the time in his feeling of nationality, but for all that the scattering is a good thing for the individual and for the world. 3. *The destruction of the ruling men in Elam.* God will set up his throne. The visible power and glory of those who represented Elam is to pass away. In a monarchy the king and his nobles give a centre, around which the whole nation gathers. When this centre is taken away there is nothing to act as a sufficient point of union for the scattered ones if they are so disposed. What God does he does completely.

II. NOTE THAT THE REASON OF ALL THIS IS NOWHERE DISTINCTLY EXPRESSED IN THE PROPHECY. And yet we know there is nothing capricious and arbitrary in all this severity. Elam must have done much wickedness in the sight of Jehovah. Wherever there is suffering there is sin; and, more than that, when God indicates his own special interference we know that he has a sufficient reason for it in the wrong-doing of those with whom he thus deals.

III. The element of hope. The captivity of Elam, as it is called, is not to endure for ever. A brighter future is coming, spoken of very indefinitely, but not therefore uncertainly. Not, of course, that Elam was to be re-established literally in its old possessions and glory. Such verses as this must be taken spiritually. It is God's way of setting before us the truth that, whatever may be lost by a particular community or a particular generation, only vanishes to reappear in a far greater gain to every individual, spiritually considered.—Y.

EXPOSITION.

CHAPTERS L. AND LI.

On Babylon.

CHAPTER L.

We have now reached a point at which some reference is necessary to the controversies of the so-called " higher criticism." An attempt must be made to put the reader in possession of the data which are so variously estimated by critics of different schools. Theological considerations need not, and therefore ought not, to be admitted ; like every other critical question, that which we are now approaching can be argued out on purely literary grounds. At first sight, indeed, it would appear not to require a long debate, seeing that in ch. l. 1 and li. 60 the prophecy is expressly attributed to Jeremiah. But, on the other hand, it must be observed that the authorship of the heading in ch. l. 1 is altogether obscure ; very possibly, like those of so many of the psalms, the heading may be incorrect. And as to ch. li. 60, can we be absolutely certain that the expression, " all these words," was intended to refer to the prophecy which now precedes ch. li. 59—64 ? No doubt Jeremiah did write a prophecy against Babylon, and give it to Seraiah with the charge described in ch. li. 61—64. But how do we know that this prophecy has come down to us in the form in which it was written ?

This attitude of reserve is not assumed without substantial grounds, derived from two sources—the epilogue (ch. li. 59—64) and the prophecy itself. First, as to the epilogue. It is clear that the words, " and they shall be weary," are out of place in ver. 64, and that they are wrongly repeated from ver. 58. But how came they to be repeated ? Because, originally, the declara-

tion, " Thus far are the words of Jeremiah," stood at the end of ver. 58. When the short narrative in vers. 59—64 (ending at " I will bring upon her ") was combined with ch. l. 1—li. 58, the declaration in question was removed from ver. 58 to ver. 64, and, by accident, the preceding word (in the Hebrew) was removed with it. This leaves it open to us to doubt whether the present prophecy on Babylon is really the one referred to in ver. 60, supposing, that is, there are other reasons, derived from the prophecy itself, for questioning its Jeremianic authorship.

The reasons which have been adduced for doing so are analogous to those which lead so many students to doubt the Isaianic authorship of Isa. xl.—xlvi.[1]

1. The author of the latter prophecy (or the greater part thereof) writes as if he were living at the close of the Babylonian exile. So does the author of ch. l. and li. " Yet a little while," he says (ch. li. 33), " and the time of her harvest shall come "— the time, that is, of that judicial interposition which (comp. Isa. xvii. 5, 11 ; Matt. xiii. 39) is the heavenly antitype of harvest. He urges his fellow-countrymen to flee, while there is still time, from the doomed city (ch. li. 6, 45). He mentions, as the instruments of the Divine vengeance, the Medes (ch. li. 11, 28), and, as it would seem, refers, though obscurely, to Cyrus (ch. li. 20—23).

2. Although the above statement is literally true of most of Isa. xl.—lxvi., yet there are some passages which are much more suggestive of a Palestinian origin than of a Babylonian (see Cheyne's 'Prophecies of Isaiah,' ii. 202). Precisely so in ch. l. and li., at least according to one

[1] 'Encyclopædia Britannica,' ninth edition article " Jeremiah."

prevalent interpretation of ch. l. 5; li. 50 (which are thought to imply a residence in Jerusalem); l. 28; li. 11, 35, 51 (suggestive, perhaps, of the continuance of Jerusalem and the temple); l. 17; li. 34 (implying, as some think, that Nebuchadnezzar was still alive). Still, there is so much doubt respecting the soundness of the inferences, that it is hardly safe to rely too confidently upon them. The case of ch. l. and li. is, therefore, in so far rather less favourable to Jeremiah's authorship than that of Isa. xl.—lxvi. is to that of Isaiah.

3. Amongst much that is new and strange in the style of phraseology of Isa. xl.—lxvi., there is not a little that reminds one forcibly of the old Isaiah. Similarly with ch. l. and li., as compared with Jeremiah, "Every impartial judge," says Kuenen (who will not be suspected of a prejudice for tradition), "must admit that the number of parallel passages is very large, and that the author of ch. l. and li. agrees with no one more than with Jeremiah." For instance, the formula, "Thus saith Jehovah Sabáoth, the God of Israel" (ch. l. 18; li. 33), also occurs in ch. vii. 3; ix. 15, and some twenty-six other passages; comp. also ch. l. 3 with ix. 9; l. 5 with xxxii. 40; l. 7 with ii. 3, xiv. 18, xvii. 13; and see other passages referred to in the Exposition.

The probability would, therefore, appear to be that, whatever solution we adopt for the literary problems of Isa. xl.—lxvi., an analogous solution must be adopted for ch. l. and li. The whole question is so large, and connects itself with so many other problems, that the present writer declines to pronounce upon it here. Only it should be observed (1) that both subject and tone remind us of Isa. xl.—lxvi. and the kindred prophecies scattered about in the first part of the Book of Isaiah, and more especially of Isa. xiii. and the closely related prophecy, Isa. xxxiv.; (2) that these two chapters, ch. l. and li., present some striking points of contact with Ezekiel, who, though contemporary with Jeremiah, was still a *later* contemporary, and allusions to whom (since Ezekiel was a literary rather than an oratorical prophet) imply that his prophetic book was already in circulation—in other words, suggest a date well on in the Exile for the prophet who alludes to him; (3) that,

though there are many Jeremianic allusions in ch. l. and li., there are also several passages copied almost verbally from prophecies of Jeremiah, and applied to Babylon and its assailants (it seems difficult to believe that Jeremiah should have been such a good economizer of his literary work). It deserves to be added (4) that, though Jeremiah is a great student of the earlier prophetic writings, and makes numerous allusions to them (see especially ch. xlvi.—xlix.), nothing approaching to the mosaic-work in ch. l. and li. can be pointed to in the undoubted prophecies of Jeremiah. In fact, the Exposition will show that the author of these two chapters has borrowed almost the whole of their contents from other prophets—his own property, so to speak, being too insignificant to be worth mentioning.

Here, in justification of (1), is a list of points of contact between ch. l. and li. and Isa. xiii.:—

(a) "To consecrate [or, 'sanctify.'],'' used of persons, ch. li. 27; Isa. xiii. 3. *Here only* (elsewhere with "war" following).

(b) "Lift ye up a banner," ch. l. 2; li. 27; also Isa. xiii. 2.

(c) Comp. ch. l. 16 with Isa. xiii. 14; close phraseological agreement.

(d) Comp. ch. l. 6, 17 with first part of Isa. xiii. 14; agreement as to sense.

(e) "Behold, I will stir up against Babylon," ch. li. 1 (comp. l. 9); so Isa. xiii. 17. Comp. also, however, Isa. xli. 25; Joel iii. (Hebrew, iv.) 7—9.

(f) Comp. ch. li. 3 (ch. l. 14, 29) with Isa. xiii. 18; agreement as to sense.

(g) Comp. ch. li. 11, 28 with Isa. xiii. 17 (mention of the Medes).

(h) Comp. ch. l. 39, 40 with Isa. xiii. 19—22.

This last parallel may, perhaps, be questioned. At first sight it may appear tha' both ch. l. 40 and Isa. xiii. 19 are based upon ch. xlix. 18 (which see), but when we inspect Isa. xiii. 19 *b* more closely in the Hebrew, we shall find reason to conclude that the original, both of this passage and of ch. l. 40, is Amos iv. 11. We must, therefore, put ch. xlix. 18 out of the question, and learn to be on our guard against plausible inferences. The only point which remains to be decided is the relation between ch. l.

40 and Isa. xiii. 19; which passage is the original? One important element in our decision will be the naturalness in the mode of reference to Sodom and Gomorrah; to the present writer this seems to determine the question against ch. l. and li. and in favour of Isa. xiii. (The imitation is limited to Isa. xiii. because Isa. xiv. passes on to another though a related subject.)

And here, in justification of (2), are points of contact between ch. l. and li. and the Prophet Ezekiel.

(*a*) *Ideas and "motives."* (α) Figure of scattered flock, ch. l. 6, 7 (Ezek. xxxiv.). (β) Effects of the avenging Sword of Jehovah, ch. l. 35—38 (Ezek. xxi. 30; xxxiii. 1—6).

(*b*) *Words and phrases.* (α) No word is more distinctly peculiar to Ezekiel than *gillūlīm*, idol-blocks, which occurs no less than thirty-nine times in his book, and elsewhere only once in Leviticus, once in Deuteronomy, six times in Kings, and once in Jeremiah (l. 2). (β) *'Ānaq*, to groan, occurs thrice in Ezekiel, once in Jeremiah (li. 52), and nowhere else. It is remarkable that in the latter passage we find not only a word but a phrase of Ezekiel's (see Ezek. xxvi. 13). (γ) Pekod, the name of a Chaldean district, occurs in ch. l. 21; also Ezek. xxiii. 23. (δ) The striking combination, *pakhōth ūsĕghānīm*, occurs in ch. li. 28, 57; also Ezek. xxiii. 6, 12, 23. (ε) *Kasdīm* for "Chaldea" (properly the Chaldeans), ch. l. 10; li. 24, 35; also Ezek. xvi. 29; xxiii. 16. (ζ) Ch. li. 25, 26 seems to allude to Ezek. xxxv. 3—5, 9 (see the Hebrew, and verify the statement by the Hebrew concordance).

(*c*) *General characteristics of style.* Granting that the style of ch. l. and li. approaches nearest on the whole to that of Jeremiah, it must be admitted, in the words of the latest German critic, Budde, that it "frequently enough declines from the simple, plain, and rather loose style of Jeremiah, to the flowery and turgid manner of speech of Ezekiel;" also that the points of contact are such as imply the originality of Ezekiel and the dependence upon him of ch. l. and li.

Ver. 1.—**Against**; rather, *concerning.*

Vers. 2—10.—Babylon's fall and Israel's deliverance.

Vers. 2, 3.—The prophet, with the eye of faith, sees his revelation accomplished.

Babylon (like Moab) *is* taken; her idols *are* destroyed. In his exuberant joy, he calls on the bystanders to proclaim the good news to the sympathetic nations, and to **set up** (or rather, *lift up*) **a standard** (as ch. iv. 6), to call the attention of those who might not be within hearing of the proclamation. The idols have been convicted of false pretensions; they are *ashamed* and *dismayed* (so we should render rather than **confounded and broken in pieces**) at the terrible result to their worshippers. **Bel and Merodach** are not different deities, but merely different names of one of the two principal gods of the later Babylonian empire. Bel, it is true, was originally distinct from Merodach, but ultimately identified with him. Merodach was the tutelary god of Babylon, and Nebuchadnezzar seems to have been specially addicted to his worship, though, indeed, he mentions Nebo also with hardly less honour. This is the beginning of an inscription of this king's, preserved at the India House:—"Nebuchadnezzar, King of Babylon, glorious prince, worshipper of Marduk, adorer of the lofty one, glorifier of Nabu, the exalted, the possessor of intelligence" (Mr. Rodwell's translation, 'Records of the Past,' v. 113). Elsewhere Nebuchadnezzar speaks of Marduk as "the god my maker," "the chief of the gods," and of himself as "his (Marduk's) eldest son, the chosen of his heart." **Her images.** It is a very pecular word (*gillūlīm*), specially frequent in Ezekiel, and also found in a chapter of Leviticus with which Ezekiel has affinities (Lev. xxvi. 30). It evidently involves a sore disparagement of idol-worship. The etymological meaning is "things rolled," which may be variously interpreted as "idol-blocks" (Gesenius), or "doll-images" (Ewald).

Ver. 3.—**Out of the north.** There was a peculiar mystery attaching to the north in the Hebrew mind, as, in fact, the word very for "north" in Hebrew (literally, *the hidden*) indicates. The burnt offering was to be sacrificed on the north side of the altar (Lev. i. 11), and the four cherubim, in the vision of Ezekiel, are described as coming from the north (Ezek. i. 4). The horror with which Babylon was regarded was intensified, apparently, by its northern position (ch. i. 14), and now the "hidden" north again pours forth its swarms of warriors against Babylon herself. **They shall remove, they shall depart**; rather, *they are fled, they are gone*; almost the same clause occurs in ch. ix. 10. The prediction is realized as past.

Ver. 4.—**In those days**, etc. The destruction of Babylon is immediately followed by the deliverance of Israel. But the description of the latter is a remarkable one. We are by no means to regard it as an idealized picture of the return of the Jews under Zerubbabel, any more than we can suppose the glowing promises in the second part of Isaiah to have their sole fulfilment in that disappointing event. No; it is the characteristic of Messianic prophecy that, with "foreshortened perspective," the prophets represent as equally near events which are really separated by ages. In the Book of Isaiah, for instance, preliminary judgments are repeatedly described in terms which, properly speaking, only apply to the great final judgment. In fact, each great political revolution is a stage in the Divine drama of judgment, which will reach its close in the final cataclysm. And so too here (as well as in Isa. xl.—lxvi.) the promise of mercy to Israel, which began to be fulfilled in the edict of Cyrus, is represented as if the still future conversion of the people of Israel were actually accomplished. The description reminds us of ch. iii. 18—21. Notice the penitence of the returning exiles, and the reunion of Israel and Judah (see on ch. iii. 18). **Going and weeping ; they shall go ;** rather, *they shall go, weeping as they go.*

Ver. 5.—**Thitherward ;** rather, *hitherward.* The prophet is evidently writing from Jerusalem (comp. ch. li. 50). **Let us join ourselves.** A conjectural emendation (*nilveh* for *nilvu*, a difficult reading, meaning, perhaps, "join yourselves "). **A perpetual covenant.** The same phrase occurs in ch. xxxii. 40. The addition, " that shall not be forgotten," reminds us of " the ark of the covenant," which was "not to be remembered " (ch. iii. 16).

Ver. 6.—**Lost sheep.** Not merely with reference to the scattering of the Captivity (as in Isa. xxvii. 13, where the Authorized Version has " ready to perish "), but to the transgressions of the Law of God, of which the Jews had been constantly guilty (comp. Ps. cxix. 176 ; Isa. liii. 6). **Their shepherds . . . mountains.** This is the marginal correction in the Hebrew Bible ; the text has, " Their shepherds have caused them to go astray upon the seducing mountains "—a strange expression, which is, however, defended by Naegelsbach on the ground of ch. ii. 20 ; iii, 2, 23 ; xvii. 2. **Their resting-place ;** literally, *their couching-place ;* i.e. their pasture, Jehovah, at once their Pasture (ver. 7) and their true Shepherd (Ps. xxiii. 1).

Ver. 7.—**We offend not ;** rather, *we incur no guilt.* As long as Israel lived a life consecrated to Jehovah, "all that devoured him incurred guilt " (ch. ii. 3). But now that he had wandered from Jehovah, and so forfeited his protection, his adversaries denied that they could be brought to account. **Habitation of justice ;** strictly, *pasture of righteousness.* The same title is

applied in ch. xxxi. 23 to Jerusalem. But Jerusalem's spiritual efficacy is only derivative ; rest and life flow from Jehovah alone, who is, therefore, the true Pasture of his people. In the Hebrew, " Jehovah " is placed emphatically at the end of the verse. **The hope of their fathers** (comp. Ps. xxii. 4). To forsake Jehovah was an act of treason to the former generations.

Ver. 8.—The prophet returns to the fate of Babylon. He exhorts the captive Israelites to flee in time, before the hostile army reaches the city (comp. Isa. xlviii. 20). **Be as the he-goats before the flocks ;** rather, *as the rams,* whose example is followed unhesitatingly by the flock. The "flocks " in this case are the strangers in Babylon (ver. 16).

Ver. 9.—**I will raise ;** literally, *I will stir up* (or, *awaken*) ; comp. ch. vi. 22 ; Isa. xiii. 17. **An assembly of great nations.** So in a parallel prophecy, " the kingdoms of nations gathered together " (Isa. xiii. 4). Callias in Ebers' learned story, ' The Egyptian Princess,' speaks of " an empire so casually heaped together, and consisting of seventy populations of different tongues and customs, as that of Persia." **From thence ;** i.e. from the head-quarters of the array of nations. **As of a mighty expert man ;** rather, *as of an expert warrior* (or, *mighty man*). The marginal rendering of the Authorized Version represents a various reading of the Hebrew found in three old editions, and presupposed in the Targum and Vulgate, " one making childless," i.e. " a destroyer." The received reading, however, is self-evidently right. **None shall return in vain.** It seems doubtful whether this refers to the arrow or to the mighty man. The arrow may be said to "return [or, turn '] in vain " when it misses its aim or strikes the mark without piercing it (comp. 2 Sam. i. 22, where, however, it is the sword which is thus spoken of) ; the mighty man when he retires from the field defeated. This wider use of the phrase is sanctioned by Isa. lv. 11.

Vers. 11—20.—*Babylon's desolation and Israel's glorification.*

Vers. 11, 12.—**Because ye were glad,** etc. ; rather, *Truly ye may be glad ; truly ye may rejoice, ye spoilers of mine heritage ; truly ye may leap as a heifer at grass, and neigh as steeds ; yet your mother,* etc. Your triumph shall be of short duration ; disgrace follows closely upon its heels. " Your mother " is a term for the nation regarded as a whole (comp. Isa. l. 1 ; Hos. ii. 2 ; iv. 5). " At grass " is the reading adopted by the Septuagint and Vulgate ; the pointed text has (the vowels alone are different), " (a heifer) that thresheth," i.e. allowed to eat its fill of corn, agreeably to the direction in Deut. **xxv. 4.**

It is not clear why the Authorized Version deserted the received pointing. **Behold, the hindermost of the nations** shall be a **wilderness**; rather, *Behold, the hindermost of the nations! a wilderness*, etc. The subject understood in the first part is obviously the people, in the second the land, of Babylon.

Ver. 13.—All but the first clause of this verse is taken from ch. xix. 8; xlix. 17.

Ver. 14.—**Put yourselves in array**, etc. The Authorized Version, guided, perhaps, by considerations of rhythm, has misplaced the first stop, which ought to be after "bow." The Medes are referred to in a parallel prophecy as great archers (Isa. xiii. 18).

Ver. 15.—**Shout against her**; *i.e.* raise the battle-cry (comp. Josh. vi. 16; Isa. xlii. 13). **She hath given her hand.** This action is generally mentioned as a pledge of friendship or a ratification of a promise (2 Kings x. 15; Ezek. xvii. 18; Ezra x. 19); but the notion of surrender or submission would naturally follow (so in 1 Chron. xxix. 24; 2 Chron. xxx. 8). Dr. Payne Smith well quotes the words of Turnus, when begging his life of Æneas, "Vicisti, et victum tendere palmas Ausonii videre" ('Æneid,' xii. 936). **Her foundations.** The word is difficult, but a comparison with the Syriac suggests the rendering, *her walls*. "Foundations" is obviously wrong.

Ver. 16.—**Cut off the sower**, etc. "Babylon" here probably means Babylonia, for it is clear from ver. 12 that the curse belongs to the country as well as the city of Babylon; indeed, "Babylon" in ver. 13 seems to be used in the wider sense. Others think of the open spaces within the walls of Babylon, in which it is said that crops were raised to provision the city in case of a siege (see Rawlinson, 'Ancient Monarchies,' ii. 513); but this is less natural. **They shall turn**, etc. The subject is, not the husband-men, but the strangers in Babylonia; comp. the parallel passage, Isa. xiii. 14, on which this passage is based. Æschylus ('Pers.,' 53) speaks of the πάμμικτος ὄχλος in Babylon. Whether brought by force from their homes, like the Jews, or voluntary residents for the sake of commerce, all should hurry from the doomed city.

Ver. 17.—**Israel is a scattered sheep**, etc. Here a pause in the discourse occurs. The prophet returns to the present condition of Israel, who is likened to a sheep scared away from its fold by lions. The ruin wrought by the lions is described first as "devouring" and then as "breaking the bones" of Israel—in either case it is complete destruction, but the completeness is more emphasized by the second figure. In fact, when the "ten tribes" were carried captive, the elements of the theocracy still remained in the southern kingdom.

Ver. 19.—**The flock restored. His habitation** is an unfortunate rendering, which obscures the beautiful figure; read, *his pasture* (as in ver. 7). The places mentioned were all famous for their rich pasturage (comp. ch. xxii. 6; Isa. xxxiii. 9; Micah vii. 14 (especially); Ezek. xxxiv. 13, 14; Cant. iv. 1).

Ver. 20.—**In those days**, etc. An evangelical promise, reminding us of ch. xxxi. 34 and xxxiii. 8, and of the combination of spiritual with temporal blessings in the latter part of Isaiah.

Vers. 21—28.—The punishment of Babylon, corresponding to her crimes.

Ver. 21.—**The land of Merathaim**; *i.e.* of double rebellion. Probably enough an actual geographical name may lie at the root of this singular expression; but we are not able at present to say what it was. The prophet has, at any rate, modified it in such a way as to convey a definite meaning, symbolic of the character of Babylon (comp. on ver. 31). What was this meaning? According to Gesenius, there is an allusion to the two great blows inflicted on Israel and Judah by Assyria and Babylon respectively; but as these two powers were but the instruments of a higher Hand, this explanation would seem to be inconsistent with the prophetic teaching. Dahler, De Wette, and Keil take the two rebellions to be the spiritual ones of idolatry and pride; and there is no obvious objection to this. But the dual may be simply intended to express intensity; comp. ch. xvii. 18, "Destroy them with double destruction" (see note). **The inhabitants of Pekod**; *i.e.* of punishment. But here too a geographical name very probably lies underneath. The Taylor cylinder-inscription of Sennacherib mentions a Pukudu (= Pekod), together with Havrann (Hauran) and Nabatu (Nabathæans); but this was the name of a tribe. In Ezek. xxiii. 23 we read, "The Babylonians, and all the Chaldeans, Pekod, and Shoa, and Koa," etc.; and in 'Records of the Past,' xi. 92, we find a town Pikudu mentioned, lying to the south of Babylon, which may, perhaps, have given its name to a district, and to this district the prophet not improbably alludes. M. Halévy conjectures that the event which corresponds to the prophecy is the decisive battle which virtually terminated the Babylonian empire. According to the newly discovered Cyrus-inscription, this battle was fought near a place called Rutu, which appears to have been situated in the neighbourhood of Pukudu ('Records,' *l.c.*). About the symbolic meaning there can be no doubt: Pekod is a worthy pendant to Merathaim. Sin and punishment are so closely connected in the prophetic mind that one word sometimes covers both notions. It is doubtful, for instance, whether the better rendering of Isa. v. 18 is "draw sin as with a cart-rope" or "draw punishment."

Ver. 23.—**The hammer of the whole earth.** So in Isaiah (xiv. 5), "Jehovah hath broken the staff of the wicked, the rod of the rulers; which smote peoples in passion with an unceasing stroke." In the next chapter a similar title is conferred upon Israel, with the right to retaliate upon Babylon all the evil which Babylon had done to Zion (ch. li. 20—24). Compare the epithet *Martel*, "The Hammer," given to Charles, Duke of the Franks, on account of his great victory over the Saracens at Tours; it is tempting to add "Makkābi," the epithet of Judas (Maccabæus), but the *k* is not the same letter as that in *maqqab*, hammer.

Ver. 24.—**I have laid a snare for thee.** It was very natural, as long as Cyrus's own account of the capture of Babylon was unknown, to refer for a fulfilment to the stratagem which, as Herodotus relates, that king employed, viz. diverting the waters of the Euphrates into an already existing reservoir, and entering the city unexpectedly by the river-channel (Herod., i. 191). But the cylinder-inscription, translated by Sir H. Rawlinson in 1880, shows that Babylon opened its gates of its own accord, on hearing the defeat and capture of Nabonidus. There is no occasion to look for any further fulfilment of the prophecy than the surprise which must ever come upon the bystander when he sees a mighty empire suddenly pass into the hands of its enemies. The tenses in this verse are not very happily rendered. It would be better to translate, *I laid a snare for thee, and thou wast taken, O Babylon, unawares; thou wast found,* etc., *because thou hadst striven against the Lord.*

Ver. 25.—**Hath opened his armoury.** A truly grand figure. The north country (the "hidden" part of the earth, as it was called in Hebrew) is regarded by the prophet as a storehouse of young and "inexhaustible" nations, from which Jehovah can at any time "bring forth weapons of his indignation." The latter phrase occurs again in the parallel prophecy (Isa. xiii. 5), where it is evidently applied to the army of Medo-Persian invaders. **For this is the work,** etc.; rather, *For the Lord, Jehovah of hosts, hath a work.*

Ver. 26.—**Come against her;** rather, *Come to her.* Dr. Payne Smith infers that Babylon has already fallen, and that the persons addressed are not warriors only, but plunderers of every kind. This is almost too subtle. The prepositions "to" and "against" (literally, *upon*) are so frequently interchanged (comp. ch. xlvi. 22; xlix. 9).

From the utmost border; rather, *all together;* it is an idiom expressing universality. Those who are spoken of are regarded as a totality, "from the utmost end" of which its members come. **Cast her up as heaps;** rather, *Cast it up as sheaves;* i.e. ransack the repositories of Babylon's wealth, and heap it up like corn; last of all, **destroy** her (rather, *it*) **utterly.** The verb is a very emphatic one. Its primary meaning is "to cut off, or shut off." Hence *khérem,* a devoted thing, is applied in the Law to that which is "tabooed," as it were, cut off from any but sacred uses. In Lev. xxvii. 21 it is used of a field wholly appropriated to the sanctuary, and in 1 Sam. xv. 21 and 1 Kings xx. 42 to living beings doomed to destruction. Destruction is generally a part of the meaning; but it is not merely destruction, but an act of homage to the Divine justice.

Ver. 27.—In this verse we are told that the *khérem,* i.e. the Divine ban, falls upon the entire male population, as in the holy wars of Joshua (Josh. vi. 21; xi. 11, 20). **All her bullocks.** As in ch. li. 40 and Isa. xxxiv. 6, the doomed people is likened to sacrificial victims (comp. ch. xlvi. 10). The same fact is described without figure in ch. xlviii. 15. **Go down to the slaughter;** *i.e.* be forced down to the slaughtering-trough.

Ver. 28.—**The voice of them that flee,** etc.; rather, *Hark! those that flee,* etc. A confused murmur indicates the approach of the fugitives with their great tidings. **The vengeance of his temple;** *i.e.* the punishment due to Babylon for burning the temple; comp. next verse, also ver. 15, "The vengeance of the Lord," and ch. li. 11.

Vers. 29—40.—The completeness of Babylon's destruction.

Ver. 29.—**Call together the archers,** etc. A dramatic way of indicating that the siege is about to begin.

Ver. 30.—With the exception of "her" in the second clause, a repetition of ch. xlix. 26.

Ver. 31.—O thou **most proud;** rather, *O Pride!* Just as in ver. 21 Babylon is called Merathaim, and as Egypt is, in Hebrew poetry, called Rahab, *i.e.* "boisterousness" or "arrogance" (Isa. xxx. 7; li. 9; Job xxvi. 12; Ps. lxxxvii. 4; lxxxix. 10).

Ver. 32.—**The most proud;** rather, *Pride.* **Raise him up.** For the sake of uniformity, "her" would be better; for it is Babylon who is spoken of. There is an inconsistency in the use of the persons in the original. Elsewhere in this description Babylon is feminine; here it is masculine, to agree with "Pride."

Ver. 33.—At the end of ver. 32 a pause occurs in the discourse. Then the prophet takes up the theme again with renewed emphasis. Were **oppressed**; rather, *are oppressed*. Because the oppression of Israel and Judah still continues, whereas Israel has by this time been amply punished (" received double," Isa. xl. 2) for her transgressions, Jehovah will himself interpose. He is, in fact, Israel's *Goel* (" Redeemer "), i.e. charged, like the next of kin, with the duty of recovering thy rights and avenging thy wrongs (comp. Isa. xli. 14; xlvii. 4). On the *Goel*, see Lev. xxv. 25; Ruth iv. 6; Numb. xxx. 19.

Ver. 34.—**That he may give rest to the land**; rather, *to the earth*. Babylon was one of the great world-empires; we can hardly dispense with this convenient Germanism. It was the wont of the Chaldeans, as Habakkuk puts it (i. 6), "to walk through the breadth of the earth, to possess dwelling-places that were not theirs." Observe the striking contrast—"rest" to the world which has been too long deprived of it, and "disquiet" to those who have hitherto spread it far and wide (comp. Isa. xiv. 2, 3).

Vers. 35—38.—No human aid avails against so terrible a foe; therefore Jehovah calls upon his Sword (see on ch. xlvii. 6) to avenge the cause of his people.

Ver. 35.—**A sword is**, etc., should rather be, *Sword upon the Chaldeans*; it is an exclamation equivalent to "Let the Sword come upon the Chaldeans"—that sword which never "returns empty." **The wise men** are, partly the astronomers and astrologers at the various observatories in Babylonia, whose duty it was to send in monthly reports of the appearances in the sky, which were regarded as having an occult political significance (comp. Isa. xlvii. 13). In the next verse they are called **liars**, or *praters*. In Isa. xliv. 25 this word stands parallel to "diviners." Possibly "liars" may be a wider term than "wise men," and in-

cludes an inferior grade of pretenders to " wisdom."

Ver. 37.—**The mingled people**; rather, *the foreign peoples*. Even if in ch. xxv. 20 the Hebrew *'erebh* is an ethnographical term reminding us of the Assyrian *Urbi* used of Bedouin tribes,[1] it is clear that no such explanation will suit here (see on ch. xxv. 20).

Ver. 38.—**A drought**. The Massoretic critics, in their prosaic realism, were unable to see how a "sword" could be "upon the waters;" hence they altered *khéreb* into *khōreb*. But the sword is merely a symbol of the Divine vengeance, and may be interpreted differently according to the exigencies of the context. Render, *Sword upon the waters*. **They are mad upon their idols**; rather, *through Terrors they befool themselves*. "Terrors" is a synonym for the gods of the heathen, which inspired a feeling of awe rather than affection, unlike Jehovah as he revealed himself through the authors of the psalms and prophecies.

Ver. 39.—Parallel passages: Isa. xxxiv. 14; xiii. 20—22. **The wild beasts of the desert**; rather, *wild cats* (so Bochart, 'Hierozoicon,' p. 862). **Wild beasts of the islands**; rather, *jackals*. **Owls**; rather, *ostriches*.

Ver. 40.—A verbal copy of ch. xlix. 18.

Ver. 41—ch. li. 4.—The instruments of the judgment. The section is partly a cento from other prophecies. Thus vers. 41—43 are a repetition of ch. vi. 22—24, except that what is there said of Jerusalem is here applied to Babylon; and vers. 44—46 of ch. xlix. 19—21, the reference, however, being in the latter passage to Edom. In ver. 46 **At the noise of the taking of Babylon** would be more literally rendered, *At the cry, Babylon is taken*.

---

[1] Friedr. Delitzsch, 'Wo lag das Paradies?' (Leipz., 1881), p. 306.

HOMILETICS.

Ver. 2.—*The judgment of Babylon*. The position and history of Babylon give a peculiar significance to the judgment against her.

I. BABYLON HAD BEEN THE GREATEST POWER OF HER TIME. 1. Earthly greatness is *transitory*. The supremacy of the world is an insecure position. Rivalries and hatreds inevitably spring up about it. 2. No might nor dignity can secure a people from the *judgment of Heaven*. The more talents are entrusted to a nation the heavier must its responsibility be. England will have to answer to God for her use of the vast resources on which she foolishly prides itself. The wealth and population of London are no defence against Divine judgments.

II. BABYLON HAD BEEN THE MOST VICTORIOUS KINGDOM OF HER TIME. She had conquered in her wars with neighbouring nations. While they failed she had succeeded; fortune, frowning on them, had smiled upon her. Yet Babylon's time came. No ground of confidence is more delusive than previous success. If success induces carelessness and self-indulgence, it is sure to prepare the way for future failure. The

" fortunate man " has not the slightest reason for presuming that his good fortune will help him in the future life. If he can argue anything from it, he may conclude that, since he has had his good things in this life, the evils that fall to his share must await him in the next.

III. BABYLON HAD TRIUMPHED OVER THE PEOPLE OF GOD. Some might have thought that this was a victory of her patron god over the Jehovah of the Jews. But now " Bel is confounded, Merodach is broken in pieces." For a season the evil powers of the world may triumph over the Church of Christ. But ultimately they must succumb. Persecution cannot finally crush the truth. Unbelief, proud and insolent as it may be for a while, must ultimately bow before the power of faith. For truth is great and eternal, and God is fighting on its side.

IV. BABYLON HAD BEEN AN INSTRUMENT IN THE HANDS OF GOD. Jehovah speaks of Nebuchadnezzar as " my servant " (ch. xxvii. 6). Yet he must suffer. For he was not a deliberate, willing servant. If God overrules the action of a man for good, this result is no justification of his conduct. For he is judged by his aims and motives, and not at all by the unintentional and unforeseen results of his actions. The only service of God which renders the servant acceptable in his sight is conscious, willing, obedient service. We may be used by God for other service, and then be cast off and suffer for our sinful deeds as much as if no Divine ends had been fulfilled in them. Thus the scourge is scourged.

Vers. 4, 5.—*Returning penitents.* This picture of the restoration of Israel is interesting for the prominence given to the spiritual reformation of the people. It would be vain for them to return to their land unless they also returned to their God. The spiritual recovery that thus forms the centre of the Messianic restoration is typical of the recovery of God's wandering children as returning penitents. Consider the leading points of it.

I. REPENTANCE FOR THE PAST. The two elements of repentance are here indicated. 1. *Sorrow for sin.* The children of Israel are depicted as " weeping as they go." A due sense of sin will produce sorrow. The penitent will feel himself a " miserable sinner." But to be genuine the sorrow of penitence must rise directly out of the conviction of sin. If it were induced by sympathy, by sensational influences, etc., it would be a vain and useless thing. Moreover, grief arising out of the fear of the painful consequences of sin is not the grief of repentance. This must be a sorrow of conscience directly produced by regret for the sin itself. 2. *Change of conduct.* The penitents are to " come " and " go," etc. The prodigal arises and goes to his father. Mere idle tears are not repentance. Real repentance is the turning round of the soul from darkness to light, the active desire to amend one's ways. It is true that repentance is not regeneration. It is not a renewal of nature nor is it the realization of a better life. But it is the first step towards this, and it must grow out of an honest desire to attain it.

II. AWAKENED RELIGIOUS DEVOTION IN THE PRESENT. 1. *Inquiry.* They " seek the Lord ; " they " ask the way." The penitent becomes the seeker after light. Truth, which was once a matter of indifference, or a subject of abstract questions, is now felt to be of great practical importance. 2. *A return to God.* The sinner had feared the visitation of God, but the penitent now voluntarily seeks to enter his presence. There is awakened a desire to be reconciled to God and to enjoy close communion with him. 3. *A revival of interest in public worship.* The penitents are described with their faces turned Zionward. Love to God induces interest in the worship at his house, no doubt a far less important thing than the spiritual return to God, yet noteworthy as an evidence of this. One of the leading signs of a change of heart is a renewed interest in the ordinances of religion. 4. *Brotherly companionship.* The children of Israel and the children of Judah come together. The tears of repentance melt away the old barriers of jealousy and contention. When on our knees before God we are all brethren. The forgiveness of our sin by God is conditional on our mutual forgiveness of one another (Matt. vi. 14, 15). Through union with the common Saviour all the redeemed become one family.

III. A NEW COVENANT FOR THE FUTURE. Repentance is but a beginning. The wicket-gate is entered ; now the pilgrimage must be followed. The soldier is enlisted ;

the warfare lies before him. The Christian must live in the future, not wasting his remaining days in idle grief for the misspent past, but "forgetting those things which are behind, and reaching forth unto those which are before." It is dangerous to depend upon the new-born fervour of the hour of penitence. We need a solid conviction, a firm resolution, a covenant. He who becomes a Christian enters a covenant. He receives blessings from Christ, but he binds himself to the service of Christ. In the course of years he may be tempted to forget it. He therefore needs constant prayer and watchfulness. God will not be satisfied with the fact that some one "great transaction" is "done." The transaction is the forming of a perpetual covenant. It brings the obligation of lifelong fidelity—faithfulness "unto death."

Ver. 6.—*Lost sheep.* I. MEN ARE LIKE GOD'S SHEEP. In the Old Testament the Jews appear as the only flock, but Christ teaches us that all mankind is so regarded by God. 1. We are like *sheep*, because (1) we are *foolish* and prone to err; (2) we are *weak and defenceless*; and yet (3) of some *value* in the sight of God. 2. We are like *God's* sheep, because (1) we are not our own masters, we belong to God; (2) he watches over us, guides, feeds, protects, and blesses us.

II. SIN IS LIKE THE STRAYING OF LOST SHEEP. 1. It is straying from *God*. The shepherd goes first; the way he chooses may be narrow, steep, rugged; it may seem to lead to pastureless deserts or to dangerous forests; but it is the duty of the flock simply to follow the shepherd wherever he goes. It is our one duty to follow God in Christ. To sin is to follow the devices and desires of our own heart instead of following his will. 2. It is straying from our own *vocation*. There is a path for the sheep. There is a path for every man—a way of life into which he is called to walk. When he knows this, if he turn from his duty to any other way, no matter how pleasant and profitable it may be, he is failing in his mission, wandering from the right way.

III. MEN ARE LED ASTRAY BY BAD SHEPHERDS. It is terrible to think of the fatal work of men of great talents who have spent them in deluding or debasing their fellows. What vast harm has been done by the evil genius of great men! Intellectual leaders, philosophers, religious teachers, poets, directly turn men astray when their teaching is false and corrupt. Political leaders bring nations into great criminal wars. Court influence is potent for evil when the court is corrupt. Nevertheless men cannot throw off their own guilt upon their leaders. For they act with their free-will.

IV. THE RESULT OF STRAYING IS HOMELESS WANDERING. 1. It is to be *homeless*. The sheep are lost on the mountains. God is the Home of his sheep. To be far from God is to be on the wild mountains, open to the tempest, at the mercy of the fiercest foes. 2. It is to be *restless*. The sheep "have forgotten their resting-place." The fascination of liberty to roam over the mountains tempts the sheep to wander from their shepherd. They soon find that this very liberty becomes a curse, and the wandering a doom of wretchedness. What the soul wants is *rest*, and it can find no rest but in God.

V. CHRIST RECOVERS THE WANDERING SHEEP. The sheep could not find their way back to the fold, neither could men find their way back to God. Christ came to *seek* as well as to save. As the good Shepherd, he gave his life for the sheep. They who have wandered furthest are not beyond recovery by Christ. If but one sheep be still straying, he will not be satisfied till that one is brought back. If, then, we have wandered, our safety will be found in hearkening to the voice of the good Shepherd and following him back to our home in God.

Ver. 20.—*Perfect forgiveness.* I. IN WHAT IT CONSISTS. When God forgives a man he pardons him completely, as Christ thoroughly cured all the sick persons whom he healed in any way. There is no middle course here. Either the forgiveness is total or it is not accorded at all. 1. This is *more than the remission of penalties.* Some consequences of sin must still remain, though these are no longer indications of God's anger, but converted into merciful chastisements. But the essence of forgiveness lies deeper than any manipulation of external experience. It is inward, in the relation of God to the soul. 2. This spiritual forgiveness consists in the *removal of all estrangement* between God and the sinner. It is perfect reconciliation with no shadow cast upon it by old offences. Many men profess to forgive and yet bear a grudge, or say they will forgive but cannot forget, or forgive partially but retain a certain suspicion and coolness. God's forgiveness goes further. He is said to remove our sin from us "as far as the east is from the west," to "cast it into the sea," to "remember it no more." He treats his guilty but penitent child as if the sin had never been committed. No record of guilt is preserved, none can be found, even if an enemy search for it. The prodigal is not made a hired servant; he is welcomed with joy. The Christian is not grudgingly received into the outer courts of God's house; he is called to the presence of his Father and blessed with full privileges of sonship. If he is justified he is also glorified. Hence we may learn (1) that, after genuine repentance and faith, a man need not remain in a state of fear and sadness; he may rejoice with confidence. His sin is not to be found; then he need think no more of it. If God has forgotten it he also may forget it. The typical Christian is not a weeping Magdalene, but a happy, hopeful servant of Christ. We may also learn (2) to extend more charity and confidence to other men in their penitence. If God has forgiven them, who are we that we should treat them with contempt or anger?

II. How it is obtained. 1. Often *after chastisement.* The promise to Judah and Israel is forgiveness after the sufferings of the Captivity. This is not invariably the case; for (1) chastisement may fail in its work upon the soul, and then the forgiveness will not follow; or (2) God may bring the sinner to penitence by milder means. But it is the design of chastisement to lead us to the blessedness of reconciliation. 2. *After repentance.* The people are first depicted as "going, weeping as they go." Forgiveness is offered to the worst man who repents, but not to the mildest offender who remains impenitent. 3. *Through the mercy of God.* This forgiveness is part of the blessedness of the restoration which God promises to effect for his children. It is not earned by future good conduct nor by any sacrifice or penance. We now know that it is not cheap. The price is no less than the life of the Son of God. But to us it is a free gift of God's love.

Ver. 34.—*The strong Redeemer.* I. The character and power of the Redeemer. 1. *God is the Redeemer.* He is the *Goêl*, the Friend, Advocate, Avenger, and Saviour of his children. (1) The *goêl* was the next of kin (Lev. xxv. 25). No man is so nearly related to us as God is. (2) The *goêl* was bound by law to redeem or avenge the sufferer. Human laws, in so far as they are just and good, are shadows of the Divine laws, *i.e.* of the ways of God's procedure. If the Jewish law of redemption was inspired by God, it was made after the pattern of God's manner of acting. In the New Testament we see this side of God's work brought into leading prominence. Jesus Christ is the manifestation of God in the flesh, and Jesus Christ is pre-eminently "the Redeemer" (Eph. i. 7). 2. *The almightiness of God is our assurance of redemption.* The massive strength of the rock makes it painful for us to fall upon it, and fearful and fatal for it to fall upon us; but this very characteristic renders it a blessing if we rest under its shadow, build on its foundation, or cling to it for support in the driving tempest. Men may well shrink from the might of God when they are opposed to it, and tremble and despair when it rises up, awful and irresistible, to crush them; but if they can turn to it with trust and know it is working their good, they will find in it a ground for solid assurance. How disastrous would it be for us to have a weak God, though he might have all other Divine perfections! His love might be infinite; but if he could only pity, and not effectually save us, his grace would be of little use. But our Redeemer is the Lord of hosts. If a host encamp against us, the Lord of hosts is on our side. The strength of the Redeemer is of importance, because (1) our foes are great—earthly trouble, sin, death; (2) our evil state is disastrous—we have fallen far into sin, some of us, perhaps, into deep wretchedness, only a strong hand can pull us out of so horrible a pit; (3) our own strength is slight. We are not able to cope with the dangers that beset us. In face of the great forces of evil we are like withered leaves before the autumn blast. Hence to us weaklings amid the strange and awful powers of time and eternity, what grand comfort lies in the thought that "our Redeemer is strong"!

II. The method and fruits of his redemption. 1. *The method.* "He shall throughly plead their cause." The case is intricate, many cross issues arise. The honour of God, justice, the maintenance of respect for law, the government of the universe, the highest good of all creatures, are concerned in the sin of man and its effects, and they must all be considered and fairly treated before redemption is possible. But we have no weak Advocate. God has gone through the whole labour and sacrifice. He has paid the price—even the gift of his Son to die for us. 2. *The fruits.* (1) *Rest.* "That he may give rest to the land." This was the greatest blessing to people who had been harried by invasions and wearied with exile. Rest is what the world most wants in its war and confusion, its toil and its sorrow. "Peace on earth" is the gospel benediction. Rest is what the soul most needs—rest from sin, from self, from fear and doubt and wearing grief. Rest is the blessing Christ offers to those who will "come unto" him. Heaven is rest. (2) *The overthrow of foes.* Babylon, the troubler of the nations, will be disquieted. Christ, the Rock of salvation, is to his enemies "a stone of stumbling and a rock of offence." In the spiritual redemption of Christians the spiritual foes are vanquished; sin and death, the last enemies, are slain. We can only have rest to our souls in proportion as our sins are conquered. So the Redeemer who brings balm for our soul's wounds brings a sword for its sins.

HOMILIES BY VARIOUS AUTHORS.

Vers. 2—5.—*Israel's deliverance.* This is described as twofold—the historical circumstances and the correlative spiritual experience. Apart from its verification in the case of ancient Israel, it is true to the actual process of many an individual conversion. I. A PROVIDENTIAL EVENT. The outward circumstances of life are altered. External tyrannies are brought suddenly to an end, and the children of God are set free to serve God or not as they please. In every life there are some such occurrences. The spell of evil is broken and moral freedom rendered possible. And this is often brought about impressively, with the stamp of the supernatural upon it. Especially was it so with Israel's escape from Babylon, because of the permanent influence that event was to have on the spiritual history of mankind. 1. *It was of world-wide import.* Babylon was the central world-power, holding in iron subjection many nations. As a universal empire it is to be broken in pieces, and its sentence is not only announced, but published abroad as an evangel to the nations. 2. *Of evidently Divine authorship.* The clear prophecies; the moral recompense involved in its fall, and so wonderfully corresponding to its deserts, and the vast spiritual consequences accruing therefrom, make this indubitable. And equally, we may be sure, was the hand of God visible to those who were the subjects of the deliverance (see Ps. cxxiv.). II. A SPIRITUAL EXPERIENCE. This corresponds to the external circumstances and gives them their real significance and effect. 1. *Sorrow for past offences.* "Weeping" —tears of grief and shame. The marvellous grace of God has broken their hearts. Tears, too, of joy and gratitude. 2. *Return to the true God.* Idolatry was henceforth and for ever forsaken. The sublimity and spirituality of God have taken possession of imagination and heart. Each step of the way to Palestine is a further removal from the sin which took them away. And it is not the carnal delights of the promised land which constitute its attraction. It is Zion they seek, the house of the Lord, that they may rebuild her ruins and restore her worship. This proves repentance real. 3. *Renewal of the covenant.* In this is repentance perfected. It is to be a new covenant—more spiritual, vital, and therefore eternal. The awful years of visitation have left an undying memory; but the interposition and grace of God have written his covenant upon their heart.—M.

Vers. 4, 5.—" *To Zion, with their faces thitherward.*" A picture of genuine repentance. The action and attitude suit the profession. The point of attraction is Zion, not Carmel or Bashan. Repentance is— I. UNREAL. When the outward behaviour contradicts the profession, or the conduct exhibited is only conventional or intended to deceive. It is either: 1. *Half-hearted,* not having its root in deep conviction of sin, and unaccompanied by thorough separation from carnal interests. The looks of the heart are alternately attracted towards Zion and towards the world, whilst the feet go to and fro or stand still. Or: 2. *Hypocritical.* When there is no conviction and the behaviour is a pretence. When worldly aims are cloaked by religious profession.

II. REAL. "Their faces thitherward." The attitude and movement correspond with the profession. Every preparation is made to go away from "Babylon," and the journey is commenced at once. Grief and heavenly longing are the grand motives. 1. *Genuine sorrow.* "Weeping" as they go. 2. *Pure aspiration.* They seek Zion. "Seek ye first the kingdom of God and his righteousness," etc. 3. *Resolute endeavour.* The return is at once made, notwithstanding its difficulties and dangers. Only in Palestine can the perfect theocracy, the spiritual future, be realized, *i.e.* in a true Church fellowship, which they hasten to realize. 4. *Inward and eternal fidelity.* Covenant relationship is renewed. A new spiritual covenant, whose provisions are written on their hearts, is entered into. They are no longer their own, but the servants of God, "bought with a price." 5. *Perfect unanimity.* Both Israel and Judah. A guarantee this of success and thoroughness. The lesson has been learnt by all, and united Israel is "holiness to the Lord."—M.

Vers. 6, 7, 17—20.—*Israel as lost sheep.* This is a favourite theocratic title of Israel—the sheep of God's pasture. In itself an appeal to the traditional pastoral character of the nation, and to the marvellous guidance of their forefathers by Jehovah through the wilderness. He was the Shepherd of Israel. *The extent of their apostasy* is here described.
I. IT WAS COMPLETE. 1. *They had wandered.* The allurements of idolatry had led them on and on, and they had at length yielded to them. They had sought other pastures and acquired preferences for other worship. It is an evil sign when men lose taste for the simple services of a spiritual religion. God should be sought alone and for his own sake. 2. *They became alienated.* A natural consequence. Step by step they went so far that they could not find their way back. Spiritual unfaithfulness produces confusion and spiritual darkness. They forgot their own fold. 3. *They became degraded and morally odious.* They bore the sign of their spiritual fall upon them. Their history, too, was the record of their shame to the neighbouring peoples. The backslider can never erase the past. He will bear his Cain-mark to the end, and even the heathen and unbeliever will despise him. Their oppressors are so struck with the justice of their sentence that they justify themselves in even greater cruelties than were warranted. There is no corner of the world where the backslider can escape God's curse or hide his shame. Do what he may, he will not be as other men.
II. YET IT DID NOT BAFFLE THE SHEPHERDING OF GOD. 1. *To avenge.* The overdone punishment is not lost sight of; it will be duly recompensed. And the sacred character of the exiles will add to the guilt of those who used it as an excuse for their cruelties. God is the Judge of his lost ones even to the end. He commits his authority to no other. He who causes a child of God to go further astray, and delights in his degradation and ruin, will have to account terribly for this to his Father and Saviour. 2. *To bring back.* God's arm is *strong* to destroy the detaining influences, and outstretched far enough to reach his wanderers, even to the extremities of transgression and ruin. And he can detect them in every hiding-place and covert. He is the good Shepherd. No wilderness too wide, no mountain too high or rocky, for him to traverse. He will bring them back to righteousness and then to happiness and peace.—M.

Ver. 20.—*Divine forgiveness an absolute oblivion.* The attribute of completeness characterizes God's work of *destruction* (vers. 14—16); equally does it pertain to his work of *salvation* (vers. 19, 20). In both is manifested his righteousness in its elements of wrath and mercy. His forgiveness acts in perfect harmony with his severity.
I. How IT MANIFESTS ITSELF. 1. *Retrospectively.* Sins that are past are to be blotted out. A complete severance is to be effected between the era of apostasy and the new one upon which they are to enter. The strictest justice, the most jealous hostility, will fail to make out a valid indictment. 2. *Prospectively.* (1) In the character. It will be purified and confirmed in the righteousness of God. (2) In the conduct. There will be no more lapses or infidelities. Israel will be "a peculiar people, zealous of good works." It is for the sake of this new future that the guilty past has been cancelled; and it is the legitimate fruit of the experience of God's pardoning grace that the "reserved" ones shall give themselves "with a glad heart and free" to his service and glory.

II. TO WHAT IT IS DUE. Not to Divine goodness in conflict with Divine righteousness, but to the *satisfaction of Divine righteousness*. 1. *In atonement*. The sacrifice of Christ was anticipated, and for its sake the national tribulation through which Israel had passed was accounted a satisfaction for guilt incurred. In itself that tribulation could never effect such an end, nor in any sense as supplementary of the sufferings of Christ, but only symbolically and representatively, such as the lamb slain on the temple altar. The sinner is identified with the Saviour. 2. *In making righteous*. "*Justice* looking at the sinner, not simply as the fit subject of punishment, but as existing in a moral condition of unrighteousness, and so its own opposite, must desire that the sinner should cease to be in that condition; should cease to be unrighteous—should become righteous; righteousness in God craving for righteousness in man, with a craving which the realization of righteousness in man alone can satisfy. So of holiness." (Macleod Campbell.)—M.

Vers. 21—23.—*The hammer broken*. Babylon was to be crushed by Persia—one hammer by another. As universal world-powers, the rise and fall of these had immense importance, and they illustrate the duties and responsibilities of power.

I. ALL POWER IS A STEWARDSHIP FROM GOD. The vast extent and influence of those empires, and the special mission divinely appointed them, cannot but impress one with a sense of special responsibility. There seems something supernatural in their very origin and continuance. And yet it is equally true that the humblest power is a responsibility. It might be said that a great deal of the influence of great nations arises unconsciously, mechanically, and as it were as the result of their own momentum; and also that the distribution of official duties divides, if it does not quite dissipate, individual responsibility. Yet each contributes his quota to the general result, and in the end each will have to account for his own influence. The nation as a whole will be judged, and in that judgment each will be apportioned his due share. How much more, therefore, may the individual be held responsible for the use of those powers belonging to his own nature and person, and which are under his own control or have been in great part created by his own cultivation. We are doubly responsible, viz. (1) *for the acquisition*, and (2) *for the use* of power.

II. IT IS POSSIBLE TO BE THE INSTRUMENT OF DIVINE JUSTICE AND YET BE GUILTY. Babylon was clearly and definitely "commanded" to perform its work of conquest and destruction. But it overdid its task through arrogance and unbelief. It was the land of "Double-defiance" (Merathaim), inasmuch as it had first illegitimately acquired its position by revolt against Assyria, and secondly it had triumphed in a cruel and unseemly manner over Israel (Naegelsbach). For this it was brought to account, and, therefore, is again named "Visitation." This self-sufficiency and unbelief rendered it guilty ("Against Jehovah hast thou striven," ver. 24), and yet the work it did, even in excess, was turned to account by God. We are responsible, not only for doing what God commands, but for doing it in the right spirit and manner. That God should overrule our evil for the good of others does not alter its character, which depends upon motives and dispositions. Especially in judging or punishing others ought we to keep watch over ourselves and examine our own hearts. National and official action will entail moral responsibility as much as personal, although, it may be, not so directly.

III. THE ABUSE OF POWER WILL BE TERRIBLY AVENGED. In the case of Babylon it involved it in complete destruction. The influence which had in part been a Divine creation rapidly degenerated into a merely human and sinful one. 1. *Because the consciousness of power tempts to greater arrogance and depravity*; and: 2. *Because all power has involved in it corresponding moral capacity*. 3. *It is the perversion and abuse of a gracious privilege*.—M.

Vers. 4, 5.—*Godly sorrow*. In these verses we have given us not a few of the characteristics of real repentance—that repentance which never needs to be repented of. Note some of these as seen in Israel and Judah.

I. THEY ACTUALLY SET OUT TO SEEK THE LORD. The time of thinking about it and talking of it was over. All indecision on the matter had ceased, and we see them arising and going on this blessed journey.

II. TEARS. Had there not been the actual setting out, these tears might not have counted for much. But it is said they were "*going* and weeping." Too many are quite capable of the weeping, but the other and the far more important part they fail in altogether. But when the fruits go along with the signs of godly sorrow, then those signs are of real worth, telling as they do of the broken and contrite spirit with which God is ever well pleased.

III. SINKING OF ALL DIFFERENCES AND OLD RIVALRIES. Unity taking the place of strife. The old rivals, Israel and Judah, were united now. And the giving up of former grudges and grievances is a real sign of a genuine work of grace in the soul.

IV. INQUIRY. This was an open and practical acknowledgment of their former wrong, a real confession like the "Father, I have sinned," of the returning prodigal.

V. THE ZIONWARD FACE. Ver. 5: "With their faces *thitherward*," it is said. There are many who talk about religion, but with their faces all the while world-ward. What does our common talk, our every-day life, our ordinary spirit and conduct, declare? They show which way our face really is, no matter what our tears or inquiries have been.

VI. STIRRING ONE ANOTHER UP TOWARDS THE GOOD WAY. "Come, and let us," etc. (ver. 5). When we see men trying to win others for God, to lead men not away from him, as heretofore, but to him, we conclude that that man's repentance is real.

VII. SOLEMN COVENANTING WITH GOD. The value of such vows and covenants is that they render going back from God more difficult. They help to steady the will and confirm the wavering purpose. They commit us to the right side. It is a kind of breaking down the bridges behind us, a burning of the boats, so that the soldiers started on the enterprise may not be able to recross the river. Hence we urge such open and solemn avowal, consecration and covenanting with God. It tends to make your adhesion to God "perpetual," and your holy purpose to serve him far less likely to "be forgotten." Thus was it with Israel and Judah—never since have they fallen into idolatry, and though yet "the veil is before their faces," they are far other than what they were. And in our own Churches such consecration has again and again been greatly blessed.—C.

Ver. 6.—*Forgetting our Resting-place.* This chapter was written for the comfort of exiles in Babylon. They were told that their oppression was not to be for ever. "God giveth songs in the night." He will not utterly cast down. But before he gives comfort he clearly shows the people their sin. And one chief part of that sin was that they had forgotten their resting-places. So many generations had lived and died in the neglect of God, their Resting-place, that he had become forgotten by them. The habit of resorting to him was broken; other gods had been chosen instead. And now, in the sorrow of their exile, they knew not where to turn. Treating the subject generally, we note—

I. A PRECIOUS TRUTH IMPLIED. There is a Resting-place provided for us. Weary we often are, by reason of conscience and temptation and earthly trouble and fear. But there is a resting-place for us. "We who have believed" in the Lord Jesus Christ "do enter into rest." His one sacrifice gives rest as to the past, his intercession ensures grace sufficient for all the present and the future too, and his resurrection is the pledge that "he will redeem" *my* "life from destruction, and crown" me "with loving-kindness and tender mercy."

II. A SAD ACCUSATION MADE. That we "have forgotten," etc. Now, this is very grievous; for: 1. *It involves deep ingratitude.* Think at what a cost our rest was purchased for us. Our pardon, peace, sanctification, and life eternal were not the result of a mere wish on the part of God, but they cost the life and death of the Son of God. Ponder that vast price paid for redemption, and think what must that heart be that forgets all this—what Christ has done for us, is doing, and will do. "The ox knoweth his owner, and the ass," etc. (Isa. i. 3). 2. *And it is such folly.* For no more surely do we need the bread that perisheth for our bodily life than we do "the Bread of life," which is Christ, for the sustenance of our spiritual life. And this not mere theory, but all who have ever known him as our Rest, know what a Rest—how gracious, how perfect, how constant and sure!—he is. And to neglect, abandon, forget that!—"Can the force of folly further go?" It is an exchange of Eden for the wilderness, of the father's house for the swine-feeding and the husks, light for darkness, life for death. 3. *It causes such misery.* See the picture in the verse. It is that of a hunted, worried sheep. If that were the condition of such sheep, instead of being led by the shepherd by green pastures and lying down there by the still waters, what would its life be worth? And so with our souls; their misery betrays itself in the haggard look or the flippant laugh, or the hideous attempt to stifle all thought and memory in the wild pursuit of pleasure, of business, or—worst of all—of sin. Conscience will rebuke; memory will recall bitter times and moan, "Oh that it were with me as in times past!" Prayer and the means of grace seem unable to help; we are powerless for good; and the scorn of men of the world. Yes; thus to forget is misery indeed. 4. *And the danger is very great.* For if we do not return, we are lost. The terrible words of the writer of the Epistle to the Hebrews (vi. 4—6) will be fulfilled in us, and then all hope is gone. " O ye children of God, ye have a Resting-place; how is it that ye can forget it? Touch upon the things of nature, how they chide you! Bring to your remembrance the birds of the air, the beasts of the forest, the dumb driven cattle accustomed to the yoke, and let them chide you; for they forget not their resting-place. Carried away to the city the other day, the dove was taken from its cage, and they let it loose, fastening to it the message that was to be sent. It mounted aloft, it whirled around awhile, that it might see where it was. It was far, far away from the dove-cote; it was found hundreds of miles away; but whither did it fly? Swift as an arrow from the bow, it sought its resting-place with the infallibility of affection; it found its nearest way to the cote where it had been reared, and brought its message safely there. And even the dog which thou despisest, taken away from its master, carried many miles away, in darkness too, so that it might not know its way, has been known to swim rivers, cross byways it could not have known, and then is found barking for admission at its master's door; oh, so happy when it hears its master's voice again. It could not rest elsewhere. O my heart, wilt thou let the pigeon outstrip thee in affection? art thou more doggish than a dog? Dost thou forget thy Lord, when dogs remember well their masters? Let us learn from them and forget our Resting-place nevermore " (Spurgeon).

III. EARNEST INQUIRY SUGGESTED. 1. *As to the source* of such forgetfulness. Sometimes it arises from mere *thoughtlessness.* Cf. the seed that fell by the wayside (Matt. xiii.). Or from the *unsubdued heart,* which likes not to retain the memory of God. Or from *the cares of this world.* The children of Israel when in Egypt could not listen to Moses by reason of the bitterness of their bondage. And yet more often from *wicked worldliness.* The hurry and drive, the everlasting rush of business, and the setting aside of everything that stands in its way, the determination to be rich at all hazards. *Unbelief* is also another cause, the materialistic doubts, the questioning that arises as to the truth of there being any such resting-place at all. And the *bewilderment caused* by sin. The soul is stunned, dazed, and has lost its powers. 2. *As to its cure.* "Let the wicked forsake," etc. (Isa. lv. 7).—C.

Vers. 19, 20.—*The forgiveness of God.* These words are a beautiful setting forth of God's abundant pardon. Concerning it note how—

I. IT BRINGS UNSPEAKABLE JOY. In the former part of this chapter (cf. ver. 6) the prophet has pictured Israel and Judah like to a driven, hunted flock of sheep, never allowed to rest in peace, worried by fierce dogs, and hence in perpetual distress. But here there is a complete contrast. The flock feeds on Carmel and Bashan, the richest pastures. The most perfect rest is theirs. The lot of the flock told of in Ps. xxiii. 2 is theirs. So full of peace and joy are they. And the forgiveness of God does bring deep joy to the soul. *The sense of such forgiveness* is very delightful—the realization that God doth no more remember our sin. And *the manifestations of that forgiveness* are also very blessed. For very generally God causes his providence to be gracious and kindly to that man whom he has pardoned. And *the fruits of it* are also blessed, in the character, the peace, the energy, the strength, it imparts. But—

II. IT IS CHALLENGED. " The iniquity of Israel shall be sought for " (ver. 20). There are those who question very much the Divine forgiveness, who maintain that the sin is still where it was. Often *the forgiven man himself* does this. He cannot "read his title clear; " he trembles at the future and cannot be persuaded that God has put away his sin. He is filled with doubts and fears. But often the seeking after the iniquity of God's people is *done malignantly.* The enemies of God rejoice when they can find a solitary blot or blemish in the character of God's children. What a yell of triumph they raise when they light on such a discovery! Satan is "the accuser of the brethren." He is ever on the search for their iniquity. And they who are of him are ready with the charge of cant, hypocrisy, etc.; refusing to believe that there can be any such person as a real saint of God. And *pharisaically* also Israel's iniquity is frequently "sought for." See that elder son in the parable (Luke xv.). How slow he was to believe in anything but the hardened iniquity of his younger brother! A great deal may be urged in favour of his view of things. Such kindly treatment did seem unjust, putting bad and good on one level. He would not have objected—as such men, and there have been and are myriads of them, do not object—to show some little favour to a repentant sinner, after a long course of testing him and proving whether he was worthy of any further forgiveness; but to give him all at once such complete pardon, such elder sons never believe in that. And by some the iniquity of those whom God has pardoned is sought for *philosophically.* "Plato, Plato," said Socrates, "I do not see how God can forgive sins." And when we see, as we do see, how in the whole realm of nature every force goes on until it has produced its full effect—there is no loss of force anywhere—how can sin be made an exception? how can it be prevented from having its due and full effect, sad and terrible as that is? Philosophically speaking, there can be no forgiveness. What a man soweth, that *must* he also reap, in nature and measure, in kind and degree. Thus is God's forgiveness challenged. But—

III. It is VINDICATED. Ver. 20, "The iniquity . . . shall be sought for, and there shall be *none;* and the sins . . . and they shall not be found." The *sacrifice and the Spirit of Christ* are the vindication of God's forgiveness. *The former* by vindicating the Divine righteousness in such forgiveness. For there are two ways of accomplishing this. One is the way of condign punishment. But God desires atonement, reconciliation, as well as vindication, and therefore this way will not serve. The other the way of repentance, the accepting the contrite confession of sin, and prayer for its forgiveness. And this is the way God has chosen. Cf. "I said I will confess . . . and thou forgavest," etc.; "The sacrifices of God are a broken spirit," etc. Now, this way of dealing with sinners vindicates God's righteousness. For, though we cannot offer an adequate confession, repentance, and intercession, yet, in Christ, this has been done; and when, in sympathy with him, in "the fellowship of his sufferings," and "made conformable to his death," we make our confessions and prayers, they are accepted for the sake of him who has offered perfectly the spiritual sacrifice which we can offer only imperfectly. Now, this way of dealing with sinners vindicates God's righteousness; yea, it causes sinners to be made "*the* righteousness of God in him," that is, Christ (2 Cor. v. 21). God's righteousness is thus made illustrious, conspicuous, as by no other means whatsoever. For when it is clearly seen, as in the kingdom of God it will be clearly seen, (1) the depths whence the sinner has been drawn, and (2) the glorious height of purity and excellence to which he has been by this grace of God upraised, that spectacle will silence all objections, and will prove that that way must have been a righteous way which has had such righteous results. And *the Spirit of Christ*, producing sanctity in the hearts and lives of believers, is the vindication of this way of grace to all elder sons, and, indeed, to all else who challenge what God has done.

CONCLUSION. 1. Rejoice in such forgiveness, that you have it to proclaim, to think of, to rest your soul upon. 2. Adore. What else can we do but sing our "Magnificats" to such a redeeming God?

> "Who is a pardoning God like thee?
> And who hath grace so rich and free?"

3. Come away from all self-trust, all reliance on your own deeds for justification and forgiveness. 4. Tremble, O unsaved one, to be found amongst those who have despised such grace. "How *can* we escape if we neglect so great salvation?"—C.

Ver. 23.—*Hammer versus hammer.* Babylon was "the hammer of the whole earth" in the days in which and of which Jeremiah wrote. Nineveh had striven to resist, as had Tyre, Syria, and Egypt, but one by one they had been crushed beneath Babylon's ponderous blow. And now Judah and Jerusalem were crushed likewise. But God's

Word was that other hammer, against which even the force of the hammer of the whole earth should be put forth in vain. "Is not my Word . . . as a hammer, saith the Lord, which breaketh the rock in pieces?" (ch. xxiii. 29). And it did thus break the power of Babylon, and made her "a desolation among the nations." Now, all this is a parable of what is and long has been in the spiritual world. Note—

I. THERE IS A HAMMER-LIKE FORCE WORKING AGAINST GOOD IN THE WORLD. See how it crushes joy, innocency, purposes of good, noble endeavours, life itself. It is the kingdom of Satan; such crushing of so much that is good is of those "works of the devil" to destroy which the Son of God was manifested.

II. BUT THERE IS A GOD-LIKE FORCE WHICH SHALL PROVE A MIGHTIER HAMMER STILL. The strong one shall be driven out by the stronger. For proof of this, see: 1. *The progress of humanity.* Surely he must be blind who will deny the improvement in the general condition, conduct, and character of men since Christ lived and died on this earth. Most admit it, but ascribe it to merely secular, natural, and subordinate causes. 2. *The laws of civilized nations.* How much more just, humane, and righteous they are than they once were! 3. *The philanthropic instinct* amongst men. What abundance of objects there now are on which this instinct flings itself and toils for their good! Now, these things are, at least, "aids to faith," in a fuller and more complete deliverance of man from all evil, which it is the glory of the gospel both to promise and to promote. But see this Divine power at work in *the individual soul.* The fear which hath torment is taken away. The sin which tyrannizes is broken and subdued. The good which was weak is made strong, the evil which was strong is made weak. The sorrow which killed all joy is hushed. Death which destroyed is itself destroyed by the resurrection of Christ from the dead. These are some of the present trophies of the grace of God, and they are but an earnest of more and far better things to come. But in virtue of them we believe in the Son of God, who shall subdue all things unto himself. God's Word, God's providence, God's Spirit, all unite to testify to the existence and by-and-by the exercise of that triumphant power by which all the might of evil shall be crushed, shattered, and broken for ever. On which side, then, are we taking *our* place?—C.

Ver. 34.—*A strong Redeemer.* "Their Redeemer is strong."

I. IT WAS NECESSARY THAT HE SHOULD BE SO. 1. *This is true of Israel's Redeemer.* See the power ranged against them. *Physical*, in the might of Babylon and the many hostile nations. *Spiritual*, in the justice of the sentence under which they were suffering. *Moral*, in the enfeebling effects of their disobedience, causing despondency, despair, timidity, giving power to evil habits, and making very difficult the acquirement of such as were good. But: 2. *It is true of our Redeemer.* The powers by which humanity is held in captivity are more terrible and unconquerable than were those by which Israel was held. These powers are commonly classified under the threefold division—a trinity of hell—of the world, the flesh, and the devil. Consider the power: (1) *Of the world*, in enslaving the soul of man. The seductiveness of its smile, the terror of its frown, the overpowering force of its rewards, the awfulness of its punishments. And yet all this might is against God and against the soul. (2) *Of the flesh.* Yes; it does beat against the spirit, it warreth against the soul. If it once have gained dominion, is that dominion ever entirely destroyed while this life lasts? And in some, yea, many, its dominion is allowed as something that cannot be broken. A moral despair comes over many in regard to it, and they cease to contend against a tyranny which they affirm they are powerless to escape from. (3) *Of the devil.* He is no mere imagination, or myth, or invention of a credulous and superstitious age, but a living reality, against whom our Saviour, who knew his strength and terror as none other did—for he had just come away from his encounter with him—bade us in our daily prayer say, "Deliver us from the evil one." Who but he is it that is ever plying us with unhallowed thought and suggestion, causing the will and opportunity to sin so fatally to combine? But who of us is or can be ignorant of his devices? And when the force of all these terrible foes is augmented, as it is by the force of habit, of example, of inherited tendency, of enfeebled power of resistance the result of past defeats,—oh, what need, indeed, is there that our Redeemer should be strong! But—

II. BLESSED BE GOD, HE IS SO. In regard to *Israel*, he did redeem them in part, and their more complete redemption is yet to come. In regard to *humanity at large*, he is strong likewise. See in proof of this : 1. *His mighty power when here on earth.* All those signs and wonders, those glorious miracles, were designed to confirm our faith in our Redeemer as One " *mighty to save.*" Hence diseases fled, devils were cast out, nature obeyed, Death gave up her dead, at his word. All these things were, as St. John calls them, "signs." 2. *His might displayed in his Church.* "I *will* build my Church," he said; and in spite of the feebleness in numbers, in influence, in intellectual or social power, in adaptation of methods, in selection of men ; in spite of all the force that numbers, wealth, power, rank, cruelty, hate, could bring to bear ;— still his word was accomplished and is yet being accomplished. Must we not confess, in view of facts like these, that our Redeemer is strong? 3. *His power over the individual soul.* How he gives strength against the terror of a violated law, the might of an indwelling sin, the crushing power of earthly sorrow, the king of terrors, death itself! "Conversion is the standing miracle of the Church"—the transformations of character, condition, and conduct, which are perpetually being wrought by the power of Christ. All these compel the glad confession that Christ is "mighty to save." Now, note—

III. THAT HIS STRENGTH BECOMES OURS BY MEANS OF OUR FAITH. For faith in him brings to bear the power of : 1. *The unseen.* 2. *Gratitude.* 3. *The new life.* And so these marvels are wrought.

> " Mighty Redeemer, set me free
> From my old state of sin."
>
> C.

Ver. 36.—*The liars' sword.* I. IT IS ONE WHICH THEY WIELD. It cuts asunder : 1. *The ties which bind man to man.* 2. Those which bind *the soul to truth and virtue.* 3. Those which bind *the heart to God.* 4. Those which would lead *the man to eternal life.*

II. IT IS ONE WHICH THEY FEEL. It pierces the soul with *shame*, with *anguish*, with a *deadly wound.*

III. IT IS ONE BY WHICH THEY WILL SOONER OR LATER BE DESTROYED. 1. It is often so *in this life.* Men will league themselves together against a liar as against a wild beast or serpent, to destroy it. In the hearts of all men there is a protest against lies. That protest cannot be stifled universally, or for long, or over wide reaches of the world. It will break forth. It did break forth, and down went the paganism of the Roman empire, the priestly lies of the Church of Rome in the days of the Reformation, the political lies of despots as in the French Revolution, the Jesuitical lies by which that order has been disgraced and on account of which it has once and again been driven forth in shame. And the like of all this is seen in the condemnation and punishment of the convicted liars even now. 2. But yet more will it be so *hereafter.* See the awful doom that is pronounced against liars in the Word of God : " All liars shall have their part in the lake of fire, which is the second death."

CONCLUSION. 1. Dread this sword. 2. Love and cherish truth, in thought, word, and deed. 3. Give yourself to him who is *the* Truth.—C.

Ver. 46.—*The fall of hell.* Babylon is continually taken in Scripture as the type of the kingdom of evil, that which our Saviour termed "the gates of hell." Her antiquity, her vast power, her wickedness and cruelty, her utter overthrow, all justify the similitude which St. John especially so frequently employs. But the kingdom of evil is to be destroyed. For this purpose "the Son of God was manifested, that he might destroy the works of the devil." And as when the literal Babylon fell there was a "cry," so shall it be when that yet more dread power of which she was the type shall, in its turn, fall and perish. But that cry will be of a varied nature. On the part of all those who have trusted in and served it there will be—

I. A CRY OF TERROR. Their confidence, their pride, will be shattered, and they will quail at "the wrath of the Lamb" which they have provoked. But there will be many who will behold that overthrow and from them—

II. A CRY OF WONDER will be heard. That kingdom of evil so widespread, so ancient, so established, so seemingly undisputed in its possession during all the long ages hitherto, now completely overthrown. How many valiant soldiers of the cross and faithful servants of God have in past ages hurled themselves against her ramparts and tried to storm her citadel, and have, apparently, but thrown their lives away! Therefore, when at length it is proclaimed, "Babylon is fallen!" what wonder and astonishment will fill the minds of all beholders! But it will be also—

III. A CRY OF JOY. It will be the day of jubilee, the setting free of the oppressed, the opening of the prison doors, the giving of liberty to the captives. Hence the psalms perpetually bid us sing unto the Lord—sing a new song; "for he cometh, he cometh to judge the earth." We are accustomed to speak of the judgment day as one of terror only; we forget that it will be a day of unspeakable joy to the multitudes of the oppressed, like as, when Israel saw the Egyptians dead on the seashore, they sang their song of triumph. And it will be also—

IV. A CRY OF THANKSGIVING, of adoration and praise. How can it be otherwise? "The whole creation groaneth and travaileth in pain together" beneath hell's dread oppression. Shall there not be unspeakable gratitude felt when the Lord crushes this awful tyranny and destroys it for evermore?

CONCLUSION. 1. Remember that this overthrow *will* take place. They who believe in this kingdom of evil say, "We shall never be moved." But they are deceived and will, one day, be terribly awakened. 2. Which cry shall be ours?—C.

Vers. 4, 5.—*Reunited Israel seeking Jehovah.* I. THE VOLUNTARINESS OF THIS QUEST. How it is exactly that Israel becomes master of its own choice is not indicated here. Nor need we stop to notice the indications elsewhere. The great thing to note is that Israel, being free to choose, chooses the right thing. Israel might have chosen to stop in Babylon. Thus a great difference is indicated between the circumstances in which the first covenant with Israel was made, and these circumstances of the second covenant. We search the Book of Exodus in vain for any evidence of such a free and profoundly penitent spirit as we find here. God has shown by the history of Israel that a covenant made in constraint may be necessary, but also it can only be preparatory. All the elements here are of strong voluntary action. The people come; they are not driven. They weep with the noble emotion of penitence. All the waste of past centuries stands before them, seen as it might have been seen before if only they had had eyes to see. Then there is the seeking, hoping spirit to be considered. The people are *willing* now to go to God, whom so long they had forsaken in idolatry and unrighteousness.

II. THE UNION OF THOSE WHO HAD BEEN UNNATURALLY SEPARATED. Why this distinction between the children of Israel and the children of Judah? The very names indicate something wrong, something having its basis in self-will and jealousy. For the children of Judah were also children of Israel. Thus the common Christianity underlies all sectarian names. These names originate in certain historical necessities, and the sects keep them because they are thinking of the different starting-points whence they have come rather than of the common goal whither they tend. In uniting thus together, Israel and Judah were doing things meet for repentance. They were doing all they could do while they remained in exile. Past alienations and antipathies were submerged in the rise of a strong feeling of desire after their God. When men *want* to be brothers and companions, most difficulties in the way can be easily pushed aside.

III. A SUBORDINATE ELEMENT IN THE QUEST OF JEHOVAH. The people know they must turn their footsteps toward a certain place, even Zion. God is always to be sought in a certain appointed way. Seeking Zion, the people are doing a great deal towards finding God. The people knew the way to look toward Zion, even from afar; we have illustration of this in the praying attitude of Daniel, who bowed his knees three times a day, his windows being open in his chamber toward Jerusalem. Whether we shall find God depends upon where we are disposed to seek him. We shall certainly never find him apart from Jesus Christ, nor anywhere else than as connected with the heavenly Zion, the city of the living God. The vague aspirations of natural human sentiment promise a great deal, but they perform nothing. They follow an *ignis fatuus,* and not the star that goes on till it stands over Bethlehem. God is to be found by those who will accept the guidance of his Spirit, making known to them the riches which are in Christ.—Y.

Vers. 6, 7.—*The wolf excusing himself.* These verses remind us of the well-known fable of the wolf and the lamb. The wolf, acting according to its wolfish nature, devours the lamb, but first of all it makes a pretence of having some show of reason to go upon. So here the cruel spoilers of Israel try to make out that all their cruelty and rapacity were perfectly right, because Israel had done so much wrong. We have here—

I. A TRUE ACCUSATION. Israel's wrong-doing is not at all overstated. They have sinned against Jehovah. Nor is this accusation left in all its wide generality. Note the rendering of Naegelsbach: "Jehovah the true Pasturage and their fathers' Hope." Thus the figure begun in the previous verse is continued. For the sheep a true, ample, rich pasturage is provided and protected. The shepherd makes that pasturage with all its needs his peculiar charge. If the sheep will not have faith in their shepherd, submission to his ordinances, satisfaction with his provisions, and general content in all their appointed lot; if they prefer an erratic, self-providing, self-protecting lot;—then they must take the consequences. There was nothing wonderful in Israel having becoming a lost and miserable flock. The wrong-doing of a man does not excuse bad treatment of him by others, but it explains how bad treatment often becomes possible. If, overleaping the bounds and laws of Divine wisdom, we go of our own choice into the way of the adversary, we must not complain of consequent spoliation and suffering.

II. A BAD REASON. The adversaries of Israel made Israel's wickedness a plea for their own wickedness. We must distinguish between the conquerors of Israel as made use of by Jehovah and the purposes and feelings of the conquerors themselves. It is evidently God's principle to make use of what already exists: these people were bent on attacking the land of Israel, and, when Israel had so utterly apostatized in heart from Jehovah, there was no reason why he should defend them. The wickedness of man often wonderfully serves a Divine purpose, but that does not make it wickedness any the less. Wicked men are not necessary to God, however useful they may be in the present conditions of things. Vain will it be for any man to plead that, in the event, his wickedness has brought some good thing to light. The purposes of his heart were evil and only evil, and by those purposes he must be judged.

III. INDICATION OF THE PROPER TREATMENT. The proper treatment of the sheep that have forgotten their resting-place is fully revealed in the Gospels. There the true Shepherd is set before us, no self-indulgent one, no self-seeker, no hireling; but he who came to seek out the lost sheep, and who dies for his own. We must never forget, in all comparisons between straying men and straying sheep, that God means us thereby to be deeply impressed with the need of his provisions and protections. He who remembers that we are dust, remembers also that at the best we are as sheep, needing for the present to be watched very closely, and kept within a place of safety by all sorts of checks and constraints.—Y.

Ver. 11.—*The punishment of those who rejoice wrongly.* I. THE SPIRIT IN WHICH BABYLON SHOULD HAVE DONE ITS DESTROYING WORK. Jehovah meant Babylon for the chastisement and the humiliation of his own people, that they might be enlightened and purified through the losses they thus sustained. They lost many things they loved, but at the same time they lost things which tempted and ensnared. The description here, "Destroyers of mine heritage," indicates sufficiently the spirit in which Babylon acted. What God wanted was the thorough purification of his heritage, not at all its destruction. Babylon cared nothing as to whether Israel was better or worse for its afflictions. It could only rejoice over another nation conquered, another territory acquired, and a fresh degree of brightness added to its military glory. It is surely a terrible thing when men do good work unconsciously and not meaning it to be good work at all. When we have to engage in any work that inflicts suffering, shame, and loss on others, it ought to be under the sternest pressure of necessity and as the sorrowing ministers of violated law. There are times when we cannot escape being the agents of suffering to wicked and foolish men; but if we only act in the right spirit, keeping our hearts free from all that is vengeful and exulting, we may even have some share in turning them from their wickedness. Everything that savours of our personal satisfaction and gain must be kept away when we have to make others suffer.

II. THE CERTAIN RETRIBUTION ON THOSE WHO REJOICE IN THE SUFFERINGS OF

OTHERS. A disposition to rejoice in this way indicates, of course, a general iniquity of life which is sure to bring retribution. But retribution will take special forms according to the sin, and those who have gloated over the humiliations of others are taking a sure way to have others gloat over them in the day of their humiliation. Israel itself, which had been rejoiced over by Babylon, had first of all been rejoicing where it ought not to have rejoiced. If we exult and insult where we ought to pity, then nothing is more certain than that we shall meet with insult in turn.

III. A DIRECTION SUGGESTED IN WHICH THERE MAY BE GREAT REJOICING. Man was made to rejoice; the pity is that so often his rejoicing comes from individual and selfish considerations. When the right spirit is in our hearts, we too shall rejoice that so many are cast down, but it will be because of the opportunities given to lift them up. There should be the greatest of gladness in serving the lowly and the needy. Thus, while there never can be joy at suffering for its own sake, there can be much joy because of the opportunities given for glorifying Christ.—Y.

Vers. 19, 20.—*The feeding-places of the flock.* Consider—

I. WHAT JEHOVAH HAD PROVIDED AND THE PEOPLE HAD LOST. Carmel and Bashan, Ephraim and Gilead, were not something altogether new. They were memories of the past as well as hopes of the future. Israel had been a scattered sheep. Out of Christ not only are we ourselves lost, but we have lost the use of the appropriate possessions of humanity. Really what God does in restoring his people is to bring them to something a great deal better than the places mentioned; but these places represent an actual, experienced good. And it is well that God should give us, as one aspect of the future, a restoration of all that was satisfying in the past.

II. JEHOVAH IS ABOUT TO RESTORE: HOW WILL THE PEOPLE USE WHAT IS TO BE RESTORED? Restoration by itself will do nothing. If the man comes back to his possessions as he went away, then he can only misuse and squander as of old. The house swept and garnished only presented to the evil spirits a chance for greater riot and defilement than before. To the old land there comes back a new people. After tasting the bitterness of wanderings, they have tasted also the powers of the world to come— old carnal temptations no longer charm, new spiritual considerations stand full in view. Formerly, even on Carmel and Bashan, Mount Ephraim and Gilead, there had been discontent, because, with all the goodness in these places, there was not enough for the carnal heart. But now, when things are used spiritually, there is enough and more than enough. If only we follow where God leads there will be ample provision and ample blessedness.—Y.

Ver. 20.—*A vain quest.* I. IN CONTRAST WITH PREVIOUS QUESTS OF THE SAME KIND. Then hardly anything but iniquity and sin were to be found. The few righteous and godly men only called attention more emphatically to the general wickedness. God is ever seeking in the earth for all that is true and good, and whatever there be of it he is sure to find. He misses nothing, searching into every man according to the fundamental thoughts of his heart. In former days sin and iniquity had been the great burden of prophetic deliverances, and the mention of them a continual exasperation to the people.

II. THE REASON WHY THE QUEST HAS BECOME VAIN. All is pardoned. There has been deep and adequate repentance, adequate atonement, and consequently there is full forgiveness. Iniquity and sin cannot be found, because they have vanished as disturbing elements in human consciousness. What an intensely evangelical verse this is, full as it can be of one of the great results of the gospel! God, who sends prophets into the midst of sinful men, calling attention to the universal presence of evil, works to remove that evil, so that it shall no longer be possible to find it. This inability to find evil is not the report of man merely; if so, we might suspect the worth of the report as being nothing more than shallow optimism. When *God* says that evil cannot be found he means that it has ceased to exist.

III. THIS VAIN QUEST IMPLIES OTHER QUESTS EQUALLY VAIN. No consequences of sin shall be left. When the roots are gone, clean extirpated, vain will it be to seek for the fruits. There can be no pain where there is no sin. There can be no death. Fulness of life and health will succeed. There will be no seed but good seed, no ground but good ground. And hence there will only be good fruit springing forth abundantly.

IV. ANOTHER QUEST THAT WILL BE SUCCESSFUL. The matter must be looked at positively as well as negatively. Iniquity is not to be found, *i.e.* complete conformity to Law is found everywhere; sin is not found, *i.e.* every man in his own nature is fully glorifying his Maker and his Redeemer. More and more we must seek to see the depth and reality of present iniquity and sin; so shall we better understand the work whereby God will slowly remove—slowly, that is, to our apprehension—all these evil things away—and cause harmony, holiness, and happiness to rise enduringly in their place.—Y.

Vers. 35—37.—*The sword everywhere.* I. THE DESTROYING AGENT. Not a deluge, not fire from heaven, but an ordinary human agent, working with energy and thoroughness. The weapon which Babylon in its greed of conquest had used against Jerusalem is turned against itself. First of all, Babylon looks covetously on the land of Israel, and spoils it of its people and their possessions. And then, enriched, Babylon becomes in turn an object of desire. God has only to leave covetousness and grasping alone, whether in nations or individuals. There will generally come in some human agency to dissipate ill-gotten gains. As Babylon became richer in external goods, it became weaker in manly resources. There was more to invite attack, more need of the best defences, and yet at the same time less ability to defend. The sword stands here as the great symbol of human physical force. We must not infer that God approves it: he simply points out how it must have free scope upon the surface of things. Babylon took the sword, and she in turn must perish by the sword; and that same sword, successful against Babylon, points to the destruction of those who wielded it. Nothing abiding, nothing permanently satisfying, is to be achieved by the sword.

II. THE EXTENT OF THE DESTRUCTION. Physical force can make short work of all man's natural treasures; all that is wanted is a sufficient amount of it. Skill compensates for force only up to a certain point. Vain was it for Babylon to count up its mighty men and parade its horses and chariots. If we would arrive at right conclusions in the matter of security we must know the strength of our enemies as well as our own. As to one element in its strength in particular, Babylon would be dreadfully deceived. It could not realize how, as the agent of a punishing Jehovah, there had been more than its wonted strength bestowed on it against sinning Israel. It plumed itself too much on conquered Israel, and thought itself stronger than it really was.—Y.

Ver. 46.—*Capital events in history.* Capital events in history are of two kinds. 1. Those which by the magnitude of them arrest attention and deeply impress the imagination of the world. Such was the taking of Babylon. It was like the fall of a mighty building; when the fall came, it could not but shake the earth. The effects were of necessity far-reaching. The political centre of gravity got shifted. The fall of Babylon meant a new kind of government for a great many people. It meant a total change in temporal circumstances. Then the whole thing was to a large extent unexpected. Many such events have happened in history. Great struggles between nations and confederated nations, lasting for years, come to their consummation in some battle, and then for a while there is comparative equilibrium. 2. Those which excite little or no attention at the time. The death of Christ is the crowning instance of events of this kind. Locally and for a short time it did make a deep impression, but certainly the earth was not moved, nor was there a cry heard among the nations. The movement was in spiritual regions; heaven it was that got moved; and the cry was heard among the principalities and powers in the invisible world, whether they were good ones or bad ones. We need a divinely chosen standpoint from which to measure the magnitude of terrestrial events. We enlarge where we should diminish, and diminish where we should enlarge. It has truly been said that history is too full of wars and conquerors. These have been recorded, while other events dropped into oblivion, which now we should give a great deal to understand. We must guard against letting the deepest impression on us be produced by mere noise and bulk. As history is commonly written, critical, seminal events are to be looked for in the quiet corners of it, and often they are treated in a very hasty way. If we would discover the fountains of what is really momentous in human affairs, we must be obedient to the guidance of

God's Spirit. We must be delivered from the snares of mere national prosperity and glory. Then, conversely, in our own actions we must not be troubled if little attention is paid to them by others. A man may be sowing the seeds of immense, world-wide benefits, all unconsciously, knowing only this, that he is doing the thing, the evidently appointed work for him—lying nearest to his hand.—Y.

EXPOSITION.

CHAPTER LI.

Ver. 1.—**Against them that dwell in the midst of them that rise up against me.** The Hebrew has *lēb-kāmai*, which is *Kasdim*, or *Chaldea*, written in the cypher called Athbash (see on ch. xxv. 26); just as *Shēshach* in ver. 41 is equivalent to Babel. The question arises whether the prophet himself is responsible for this covert way of writing, or a scribe in later times (so Ewald). In favour of the former view it may be urged that Babylon and Chaldea receive symbolic names (though not in Athbash) in the connected chapter (l. 21, 31, 32); in favour of the latter, that the Septuagint has Χαλδαίους in ver. 1, and does not express Sheshach in ver. 41, also that the clause to which Sheshach belongs in ch. xxv. 26 is of very dubious genuineness. **A destroying wind;** rather, *the spirit (rūakh) of a destroyer* (or perhaps, *of destruction*). The verb rendered in this verse "raise up," when used in connection with *rūakh*, always means "to excite the spirit of any one" (ver. 11; Hag. i. 14; 1 Chron. v. 26).

Ver. 2.—**Fanners.** This is supported by the Septuagint, Peshito, Targum, Vulgate, according to the Massoretic pointing, however, we should render "enemies." Possibly the prophet intended to suggest both meanings, *ā* and *ō* being so nearly related. **Shall empty her land.** The original has a much more striking word, "shall pour out" (for the figures, comp. ch. xlviii. 12), which occurs again in similar contexts in Isa. xxiv. 1; Nah. ii. 3 (Hebrew, 2).

Ver. 3.—**Against him that bendeth,** etc. There are two readings in the Hebrew Bible—one that given by the Authorized Version; the other, "Against him that bendeth (let) him that bendeth his bow (come)." The difficulty, however, is in the first two words of the clause, which are the same in either reading. It would be much simpler to alter a single point, and render, "Let not the archer bend his bow; and let him not lift himself up in his coat of mail" (for the old word "brigandine," see on ch. xlvi. 4); which might be explained of the Babylonians, on the analogy of ch. xlvi. 6, "Let him not bend his bow, for it will be useless;" but then the second half of the verse hardly suits the first—the prohibitions seem clearly intended to run on in a con-

nected order. On the other hand, the descriptions, "him that bendeth," and "him that lifteth himself up in his brigandine," seem hardly a natural way of putting "the Chaldean army."

Ver. 4.—**In her streets;** *i.e.* in the streets of Babylon.

Vers. 5—14.—The covenant between Jehovah and Israel is one reason why Babylon must fall; and Babylon's own guilt is another. Hence pity is out of place.

"Here liveth piety where pity ends ;
Can any man be guilty more than he
Whose bias with the doom of God contends ?"
     (Dante, 'Inferno,' xx. 28, Cayley.)

Flee, therefore, lest ye be involved in Babylon's ruin. For Jehovah's purpose of vengeance cannot be reversed.

Ver. 5.—**Hath not been forsaken.** The Hebrew is much more forcible, "is not widowed"—alluding to the fundamental Old Testament idea of a mystic marriage between God and his people (comp. Isa. l. 1; liv. 4—6; Hos. ii.). **Was filled with sin;** rather, *with guilt* (Hebrew, *āshām*).

Ver. 7.—Babylon, as the instrument used by God for his judicial purposes, is likened to a wine-cup, which "made all the earth drunken" (comp. ch. xxv. 15, 16); and, more than this, to a golden cup, such was the impression made upon the Jewish prophets, by Babylon's unexampled splendour. (Golden cups were not unknown in Palestine; Jehu sent some to Shalmaneser; Smith, 'Assyrian Canon,' p. 114.) So, in Nebuchadnezzar's vision of the image, the head of the image is of gold (Dan. ii. 32, 38). But neither her splendour nor her honourable position as God's minister could save her from merited destruction.

Ver. 8.—**Destroyed.** The Hebrew, more forcibly, has "is broken." The Authorized Version wished, perhaps, to avoid the objection that a golden cup could not, properly speaking, be broken. But if we once begin to harmonize the language of Hebrew poetry, we shall have no end. It is not the cup which falls, but the state, considered as a house (the "breach" of God's people is constantly referred to; *e.g.* Ps. lx. 2; Isa. xxx. 26). **Howl for her.** Sympathetic bystanders are dramatically appealed to. From the next verse it would seem that they are the various foreigners who, whether by choice or force, have been resident in Babylon, and who have acquired an interest in her fate. Hitzig thinks the foreign mercenaries (ch. l. 37) or allies are specially referred to. **Take balm for her pain** (comp. ch. viii. 22; xlvi. 11). The images of fracture and wound are combined, as in Isa. xxx. 26.

Ver. 9.—**We would have healed Babylon.** Experience shows that it is useless to attempt to correct such inveterate evils. **Every one into his own country** (as ch. l. 16). **Her judgment**; *i.e.* her punishment. Perhaps there is an allusion to the fate of Sodom and Gomorrah, burned by fire from heaven. But we might also render "her crime" (comp. Deut. xix. 6, where "worthy of death" is more strictly "a capital crime").

Ver. 10.—**Our righteousness**; literally, *our righteousnesses*; not in the sense of "righteous deeds" (as in Isa. lxiv. 6; Judg. v. 11), but "those things which prove us to be righteous; *i.e.* by punishing Babylon he hath justified us" (Payne Smith).

Ver. 11.—**Make bright**; rather, *polish*, so that the arrows may penetrate easily (comp. Isa. xlix. 2, "a polished shaft"). **Gather the shields**; rather, *fill the shields* (viz. with your arms); *i.e.* take hold of them. Comp. the phrase, "to fill the hand with the bow" (2 Kings ix. 24). The rendering "quivers" is wanting in philological authority, and seems to have been inferred from this passage, where, however, it is unnecessary. **The kings of the Medes.** The prophet speaks of the Medes and not the Persians (comp. Isa. xiii. 17). "The reason, probably, is twofold: (1) that the name *Mādai* became known to the Jews at an earlier period than *Pārās*, 'Persia;' and (2) that the generals of Cyrus were apparently Medes (*e.g.* Mazares and Harpagus, Herod., i. 157, 162)" (Cheyne's 'Prophecies of Isaiah,' ii. 275, 276). The new Cyrus-inscription throws light on the latter circumstance.

Ver. 12.—**Upon the walls of Babylon**; rather, *toward the walls* (as ch. iv. 6). The "standard" was carried before the army, to show the direction of the march. **Make the watch strong.** Not merely for the safety of the invaders, but to blockade the city. Comp. the phrase, "Watchers [a synonymous Hebrew word is used] came from a far country" (ch. iv. 16); *i.e.* besiegers. **Prepare the ambushes.** To press into the city when the besieged have made a sally (as Josh. viii. 14—19; Judg. xx. 33, 37).

Ver. 13.—Babylon is addressed as **thou that dwellest upon many waters**, with reference, not only to the Euphrates, but to the canals, dykes, and marshes which surrounded the city. **The measure of thy covetousness.** A strange expression, even

when we have supplied (and have we a right to do so?) a suitable verb, such as "is full." "Measure" is, literally, *ell*, "covetousness" should rather be *gain*, or *spoil*. Another possible rendering is, "The ell-measure of thy cutting off." In fact, the root-meaning of the word rendered "gain," or "covetousness," is "to cut off;" and the figure of cutting off a man's half-finished life, like a web from the loom, is familiar to us from the psalm of Hezekiah (Isa. xxxviii. 12; comp. Job vi. 9).

Ver. 14.—**Surely I will fill thee**, etc. This is the rendering of Hitzig and Graf; the enemies are compared to locusts, as in ch. xlvi. 23. But the expression, "to fill a city with men," is more naturally taken of the increase of the population of the city; and it is better to render, with Ewald and Keil, "Even though [or, 'Surely even though'] I have filled thee with men, as with locusts, they shall raise over thee the cheer of the vintage;" *i.e.* the millions of Babylon's population will not save her from the most utter ruin. For the vintage cheer, see on ch. xxv. 30; and for the figures, see especially, Isa. lxiii. 1—6.

Vers. 15—19.—Probably interpolated from ch. x. 12—16 (the only verbal difference is in ver. 19, where "Israel" is left out before "the rod of his inheritance"). But may not Jeremiah have quoted himself? Conceivably, yes; but he would surely not have quoted such a passage here, where it spoils the context. For granting that a point of contact with ver. 14 may be found for vers. 15, 16 (Jehovah who has sworn has also the power to accomplish), yet the passage on the idols stands quite by itself, and distracts the attention of the reader.

Vers. 20—26.—Israel is now to be Jehovah's hammer, striking down everything, even the Chaldean colossus. But though Babylon may be as great and as destructive as a volcanic mountain, it shall soon be quite burnt out.

Ver. 20.—**My battle-axe**; or, *my mace*. The mace (for a picture of which, see Rawlinson, 'Ancient Monarchies,' i. 459) was a weapon constantly employed by the Assyrians and presumably by the Babylonian kings. The battle-axe was much less frequently used. But who is addressed by this terrible title? The commentators are divided, some inclining to Babylon, (1) because Babylon was the last person addressed (see ver. 14), and (2) because a similar title was given to Babylon in ch. l. 23: others to Israel, on the ground that tenses are the same throughout the passage (vers. 20—24). The latter view is probably the best. How could Babylon be said to shatter her own "governors" and "viceroys" (for the prophet deliberately chooses the

Babylonian official names)? The argument from the context is not very weighty; for it is clear that the connection of the parts of this prophecy is very loose. We may assume, then, that ver. 20 begins a fresh paragraph, standing quite apart from that which precedes. The objection of Graf and Keil, is that Israel could not himself be styled a "mace," it being Israel's destiny to be delivered by others. But is not a very similar statement made of Israel in Isa. xli. 15; Ps. cxlix. 7—9? (Kuenen offers a third explanation—Cyrus.) **The nations . . . kingdoms.** First the great social organisms are mentioned; next comes the military power; next the population, according to sex, age, and class.

Ver. 23.—**Captains**; rather, *governors*. It is the Hebraized form (*pekhāh*) of the official name of an Assyrian or Babylonian governor (*pakhat*). **Rulers**; rather, *viceroys*; Hebrew, *segāmin* (plural). The singular, *sāgān*, is Hebraized from the Assyrian *sakun*, Babylonian *saqun*.

Vers. 25, 26.—Another image for the destruction of Babylon.

Ver. 25.—**O destroying mountain.** The description evidently points to a volcano. (1) Jehovah says that he will roll the mountain down from the rocks, which can only be understood of the stones and lava hurled down from the crater; (2) that he will make it a "mountain of burning," *i.e.* either to a burning, or, more forcibly, a burnt-out mountain; and (3) that, as a consequence of this, its stones shall be unsuitable for the purposes of the builder. Now, Palestine, it has been clearly made out, "lies almost in the centre of one great volcanic region of the earth's surface, that, namely, which includes the basin of the Mediterranean and the provinces of Western or Central Asia. Traces of that volcanic action are found in every direction. The black basaltic rock of the Haurân, the hot springs of Tiberius and Emmaus and Gadara, the naphtha-fountains near the Dead Sea, the dykes of porphyry and other volcanic rocks that force their way through the limestone, the many caves in the limestone rocks themselves,—all these show that we are treading on ground where the forces of the hidden fires of earth have been in times past in active operation. We are, that is, in a zone of earthquakes" (Plumptre, 'Biblical Studies,' p. 136; comp. Pusey's note on Amos iv. 11). There is a striking parallel to this prophetic description in Rev. viii. 8, where the destruction of a great empire is likened to the submersion in the sea of a great burning mountain. (Vitringa has noticed the parallel.)

Ver. 26.—**And they shall not take of thee,** etc. "Of thee," *i.e.* "of the Babylonian power" personified—not "of Babylon," which was built of brick, not of stone. The figure of the mountain is still preserved.

Vers. 27—37.—A more detailed sketch of the conquest of Babylon; followed (somewhat out of the natural order) by a complaint on the part of Israel, and a promise of championship on that of Jehovah.

Ver. 27.—**Prepare the nations**; literally, *consecrate the nations*; viz. by religious rites. It is in an especial sense a religious war to which they are summoned (see on ch. vi. 4, and comp. Isa. xiii. 3). **Ararat.** Ararat appears in the cuneiform inscriptions under the form "Urartu." In Isa. xxxvii. 38 the Authorized Version renders correctly by "Armenia." The Assyrian kings, since Shalmaneser, were constantly at war with the Armenians; Assurbanipal reduced them to pay tribute. **Minni.** The Mannai of the cuneiform inscriptions. The locality of this tribe has been hitherto wrongly given as the mountain country about Lake Vau. But Professor Sayce has shown that they are rather to be looked for to the south-west of Lake Urumiyeh. **A captain.** The word (*tifsar*) is singular, but is probably to be understood collectively as equivalent to "captains," like the word (*sūs*, "horse," equivalent to "horses") to which it is parallel. It is here used loosely of certain officials of the Armenians; but properly it is an Assyrian word (adopted from the Accadian or proto-Babylonian), meaning "tablet-writer," and derived, according to Friedrich Delitzsch, from *dip* or *dup*, a tablet, and *sar*, to write (Accadian words). **As the rough caterpillars.** This is the third of the four kinds of locusts mentioned in Joel i. 4; or, to speak more precisely, it is the locust in its penultimate stage, when its wings are already visible, but enveloped in horn-like sheaths, which stand up upon its back. Hence the epithet "rough," or "bristling." Keil's rendering, "as the dreadful (horrifying) locust," implies a faulty interpretation of Joel i. 4. It would be strange indeed if Joel had accumulated four synonymous terms for locust in such a peculiar context.

Ver. 28.—**The captains . . . the rulers**; rather, *the governors . . . the viceroys* (as ver. 23). **Thereof** refers to the land of Medea; **his dominion** to the King of Medea, as the suzerain of the inferior chiefs.

Ver. 29.—**Shall tremble and sorrow.** The Hebrew has "trembled and sorrowed" (or, "quaked and writhed for pain"); and in the sequel, "have stood" (*i.e.* been ratified by the event, as ch. xliv. 28). The prophet here, as so often, regards what is still future as past from the point of view of eternity.

Ver. 30.—Despair of the Babylonian warriors. **Have forborne to fight** should rather be *have ceased to fight*. In their holds. The word is used of hill or mountain fastnesses (comp. 1 Sam. xxiii. 14, 19; Judg. vi. 2; 1 Chron. xi. 7), and such presumably are referred to here. **Their might**; rather, *their courage*. **They have burned**, etc. The subject is "the enemies." **Her bars**; viz. those with which the city gates were secured (comp. Isa. xlv. 2; Amos i. 5).

Ver. 31.—**One post shall run to meet another**, etc. The wall being broken through at various points, couriers would meet each other on their way to the royal palace. This was itself a fortress in the centre of the city, on the Euphrates. The newly discovered cylinder-inscription, however, shows that Nabonidus, the last King of Babylon, was not actually in the city at the time of the capture. **At** one **end**; rather, *from end to end* (see on ch. l. 26).

Ver. 32.—**And that the passages are stopped**; rather, *are seized* (as ch. xlviii. 41). Babylon, it should be remembered, was divided nearly in half by the Euphrates. It was guarded, says Professor Rawlinson, "by two walls of brick, which skirted them along their whole length. In each of these walls were twenty-five gates, corresponding to the number of the streets which gave upon the river; and outside each gate was a sloped landing-place, by which you could descend to the water's edge, if you had occasion to cross the river. Boats were kept ready at these landing-places to convey passengers from side to side; while for those who disliked this method of conveyance, a bridge was provided of a somewhat peculiar construction" ('Ancient Monarchies,' ii. 514). **The reeds they have burned with fire.** This rendering is no doubt tenable, though it gives an unusual meaning to the first noun. The "reeds" would be those of the marshes in the neighbourhood of Babylon; and Kimchi suggests that these would be cut down to facilitate the entrance of the army into the city. Surely a very forced explanation. The natural meaning of the first noun is "pools" or "lakes," and, considering that Herodotus (i. 185) speaks of a lake in connection with the defences of Babylon, it has been thought (e.g. by Vitringa) that the prophet may refer to something which was to happen to this and similar lakes; "burned with fire" is then regarded as a hyperbolical expression equivalent to "dried up" (comp. ver. 36). This, however, is hardly less forced than the first interpretation; and we seem almost compelled to assume a corruption of the text, and to read (for *'agammim*) *'armōnim*, palaces. If "palaces" (i.e. lofty houses, for such is the etymological meaning) were not uncommon at Jerusalem (Isa. xxxii. 14), much more frequent must they have been at Babylon. Or perhaps the prophet refers to the two magnificent royal palaces, which, together with the temple of Bel, constituted the wonders of Babylon. They were on opposite sides of the river, and were guarded with triple enclosures, the circumference in the one case amounting to sixty stadia (nearly seven miles), and in the other to thirty (Rawlinson, 'Ancient Monarchies,' ii. 514, etc.).

Ver. 33.—**It is time to thresh her**; rather, *at the time when it is trodden* (i.e. made level by treading or trampling); comp. Isa. xxi. 10; Micah iv. 13.

Ver. 34.—The Jewish captives are introduced, describing the offences of Babylon. **Hath devoured me**; rather, *hath devoured us*, and so on. "My delicates" (delights), however, is correct. **He hath made me**; rather, *he hath set us (down) as*. **Swallowed me up like a dragon**; or, literally, *like the dragon*. Comparing this with **ver. 44**, it is difficult not to see an allusion to the Babylonian myth of the Serpent, who in the fight with Marduk (Merodach) devoured the tempest, which rent asunder her belly. The cuneiform text is given in *Transactions of Society of Biblical Archæology*, vol. iv. part 2, appendix plate 6. Part of it runs thus—

25. *ip-te-va   pi-i-sa   Ti-amtu   a-na*
Opened also her mouth   Tiamtu   to
la-h-a-h-sa
swallow it.

26. *rukhu   limnu   yus-te-ri-ba   a-na*
The evil wind he caused to enter into
la   ca-par   sap-ti-sa
the uncovering of her lips [= into her lips before she could close them]

27. *iz-zu-ti   rukhi*
violent (were)   the winds (which)
car-sa-sa   i-tsa-mi-va
her belly   filled; and

28. *in-ni-kud   lib-ba-sa   va-*
she was pierced in her heart and
pa-a-sa   yus-pal-ki (?)
her mouth   it caused to divide.[1]

Readers of Smith's 'Chaldean Genesis' will remember Tiamtu the dragon, and the representations thereof given from the gems. In line 27 the word rendered "her belly" contains the Babylonian analogue of the word rendered in this verse "his belly" (*k'rēs*). **With my delicates, he hath cast me out**; rather, . . . *cast us out*; or, *from my delights he hath cast us out*. For the variation of person, comp. Judg. xi. 19, "Let us pass, we pray thee, through thy land into my place;" and on the whole phrase, Micah ii. 9, " . . . ye have cast out from their pleasant homes."

---

[1] From a private letter of Professor Sayce's.

Ver. 35.—**And to my flesh**; rather, *and my (eaten) flesh* (comp. Micah iii. 3). **Inhabitant**; rather, *inhabitress;* i.e. virgin inhabiting.

Ver. 36.—**Her sea**; *i.e.* the Euphrates (comp. Isa. xxi. 1), or perhaps the lake dug by Nitocris to receive the waters of the Euphrates, Herod., i. 185 (Payne Smith). Comp. on "the reeds," ver. 32. **Her springs**; rather, *her reservoirs.* There are no "springs," remarks Dr. Payne Smith, in the flat alluvial soil of Babylonia. The Hebrew word *mākōr* is used here collectively for the whole system of canals and reservoirs for the storing of the water.

Ver. 37.—**Heaps.** "Vast 'heaps,' or mounds, shapeless and unsightly, are scattered at intervals over the entire region where it is certain that Babylon anciently stood" (Rawlinson, 'Ancient Monarchies,' ii. 521). **Dragons**; rather, *jackals.*

Vers. 38—49.—Fall of Babylon; joy of the whole world.

Vers. 38, 39.—**They shall roar. . . . In their heat**; rather, *They may roar . . . (yet) when they wax warm (with lust) I will prepare.* The banquet which Jehovah will prepare is the "cup of bewilderment" spoken of in Ps. lx. 3; comp. Isa. li. 17 (*i.e.* a calamitous judgment).

Ver. 40.—**I will bring them down**, etc. (comp. Isa. xxxiv. 6; Ezek. xxxix. 18).

Ver. 41.—**How is Sheshach taken!** The Septuagint omits "Sheshach" (see, on the name, ch. xxv. 26), and very possibly rightly.

Ver. 42.—**The sea is come up**, etc. It is not clear whether this is to be taken literally or metaphorically (of the sea of nations, comp. ver. 55). Probably it is meant literally. It is said that the annual inundations of the Euphrates at present render many parts of the ruins of Babylon inaccessible.

Ver. 44.—**Bel**; *i.e.* Merodach, the patron deity of Babylon (see on ch. l. 2). **Swallowed up.** An allusion to the myth mentioned above (see ver. 34). That which Bel, *i.e.* Babylon, has "swallowed up" is not only the spoil of the conquered nations, but those nations themselves. **Yea, the wall of Babylon shall fall**; literally, *is fallen* (is as good as fallen). The famous wall of Babylon (comp. ver. 58) is described by Herodotus (i. 179, 181). From this clause down to the first half of ver. 49 is omitted in the Septuagint.

Ver. 46.—**And lest your heart faint**, etc.; rather, *and (beware) lest,* etc. **A rumour shall both come**; rather, *for a rumour shall come.* The war, then, will last some time, and all kinds of rumours will be in the air. Keil compares Matt. xxiv. 6.

Ver. 48.—**From the north.** The same statement as in ch. l. 3, 9, 41.

Ver. 49.—**As Babylon hath caused**, etc.

The verse is very difficult. Ewald and others render thus: "Not only must Babylon fall, O ye slain ones of Israel, but slain ones of the whole earth have fallen because of Babylon." But why this address to the slain ones of Israel? Besides, the antithesis indicated in the Hebrew is thereby destroyed. Keil explains the antithesis thus: "Just as Babylon was intent on the fall of slain ones in Israel, so also there fall because of Babylon slain ones of all the earth," viz. because there are to be found, in the capital of the empire, people from all quarters of the world, who are slain when Babylon is conquered. A better antithesis seems to be gained if we follow the Peshito, and read, at the end of the verse, "*in* the whole earth." It will then be asserted by the prophet that, just as Babylon was the cause of the slaying of Israelites, so (as a punishment) the Babylonian fugitives shall be slain wherever they may wander.

Vers. 50—58.—Conclusion of the prophecy.

Ver. 50.—**Ye that have escaped the sword.** Evidently Jews are the persons addressed. It is not, however, perfectly clear whether the escape is from the sword of Babylon or from that of Divine vengeance. The parallel of Isa. xxiv. 14 would suggest the latter; but in the following verses the fall of Babylon is described as still to come. **Stand not still.** Lest ye be overtaken by the judgment.

Ver. 51.—**We are confounded.** A reflection of the exiles, expressing their deep shame at the ignominy which has been their lot. **Are come**; or, *came.*

Ver. 53.—**The height of her strength**; *i.e.* her lofty walls and towers.

Ver. 55.—**The great voice**; rather, *the loud sound;* i.e. the tumult of the city. **When her waves**; rather, *and her waves;* i.e. the conquering hosts (comp. ch. xlvi. 7).

Ver. 56.—**The Lord God of recompenses shall**, etc.; rather, *The Lord is a God of recompense; he will,* etc.

Ver. 57.—**Her captains, and her rulers** (see on ver. 23).

Ver. 58.—**The broad walls of Babylon . . . and her high gates.** See Herod., i. 179, 181, and the parallel accounts from other authors, cited by Duncker ('Hist. of Antiquity,' iii. 373, etc.), who taxes Herodotus with exaggeration, but admits as probable that the walls were not less than forty feet broad. **Utterly broken**; rather, *destroyed even to the ground* (literally, *made bare*). **The people**; rather, *peoples.*

Vers. 59—64.—*Epilogue.* **The word**, etc. (see ver. 61). **Seraiah.** Apparently the brother of Baruch. **With Zedekiah.** The Septuagint has "from Zedekiah," which is referred by Bleek and Grätz. It would thus be an embassy, of which Seraiah was the head. According to the ordinary reading, Zedekiah went himself. **A quiet prince.** Not so. The Hebrew means probably, "in command over the resting-place," *i.e.* he took charge of the royal caravan, and arranged the halting-places. But the Targum and the Septuagint have a more probable reading (not, however, one involving a change in the consonants of the text, "in command over the gifts," *i.e.* the functionary who took charge of the presents made to the king. M. Lenormant speaks of an official called "magister largitionum" (*bel tabti*) in the Assyrian court ('Syllabaires Cunéiformes,' par. 1877, p. 171).

Ver. 61.—(Comp. l. 3; li. 26.) **And shalt see, and shalt read;** rather, *See that thou read.*

Ver. 64.—**And they shall be weary.** Accidentally repeated from ver. 59 (see introduction to ch. l.). **Thus far,** etc. Proving that the Book of Jeremiah once ended with ch. li.

HOMILETICS.

Ver. 5.—"*Suffering, but not forsaken.*" Israel is not forsaken because she is driven from her home. Babylon is not more favoured because she flourishes for a season as a "golden cup in the Lord's hand." For the land of the Chaldeans is filled with sin against the Holy One of Israel. Thus the truth is quite contrary to appearances.

I. WHEN GOD CHASTISES HIS PEOPLE HE MUST NOT BE THOUGHT TO HAVE FORSAKEN THEM. The chastisement is for their own good. It is, therefore, a proof that God has not neglected them. Instead of being an indication of hatred or indifference, chastisement is a sign of God's love. Moreover, when his people suffer God is peculiarly near to them. Those captives who hung their harps on the willows by the rivers of Babylon found God more present than he had been to the careless sinful Jews who assembled in the courts of his temple. It is to be remembered that God is near to us when we do not perceive him, and often nearest in those dark hours when bitterness of soul prevents us from having any comforting hope in him.

II. THOUGH GOD WILL CHASTISE HIS PEOPLE HE WILL NEVER FORSAKE THEM. This is a further step. Not only is the chastisement no proof of God's having forsaken his people, but in no case will he forsake them; no such proof can ever be found. True, they may be separated from God and may become "castaways;" but this is only because they forsake him. He is ever true to his side of the covenant. Let us, therefore, be prepared to expect the chastisement, but also be well settled in faith that the far worse trouble, the neglect of our souls by God, can never come.

III. OUTWARD CIRCUMSTANCES ARE NO INDICATIONS OF OUR RELATIONS WITH GOD. The great contrast between Israel and Babylon furnishes a striking instance of this truth. It is strange. For one would have thought that the outward and inward life would harmonize. So they will ultimately. Then the "golden cup" will be broken and the suffering child of God exalted to honour. But now the world is in confusion, evil is allowed a certain liberty for the consequent discipline of good, and thus the sufferers may be near to God while the fortunate and happy are far away in sin.

Ver. 10.—*Public thanksgiving.* In the destruction of Babylon and the restoration of Israel the devout sufferers of the Captivity see the justification of their conduct which had lain under a shadow while they shared in the punishment of their guilty brethren. So happy an issue from their troubles calls for devout gratitude, and this finds its expression in hymns of praise and public thanksgiving.

I. PRAISE IS ONE OF THE MOST IMPORTANT ELEMENTS OF WORSHIP. Two faults may be observed in much of our worship—both arising from our centring it in ourselves. 1. It is *too selfish.* We are more earnest in prayer than in praise. In sore need we cry out with terrible anxiety; but when the need is satisfied we return thanks in poor and faint tones. We are eager to obtain blessings for ourselves, but little desirous of glorifying God. Yet the essence of worship is self-surrender. We degrade it and contradict its spirit when we make it serve the ends of self-seeking. 2. It is *too subjective.* We dwell much on our own feelings instead of going out of self in the contemplation of God. Consequently our worship is pitched too much in the minor key. We wail out "Misereres" when we should be shouting "Magnificats." We have much to say about our low estate, but little concerning the way in which God has regarded it. But the highest worship is adoration—the going out of self in wonder, love, and praise towards the glory of God. It would be well if we made less mention of our own feelings and were more ready to "declare the work of the Lord our God."

II. PRAISE MUST BE DEFINITE IF IT IS TO BE EARNEST. Much of our worship is vapid and senseless because it is expressed in big vague phrases which carry little thought to our minds. 1. We should praise God by *declaring his works*. It is his character that we adore. But we see and realize this as it is reflected in his works. We see the glory of the sun, not by gazing with eagle vision into its dazzling centre, but by looking abroad on the many hues that it casts on land and sea and sky. We cannot see the glory of God by abstract speculations on divinity; we must study his works in nature, providence, and redemption. 2. We should praise God by noting *those particular works which affect our experience*. This is the secret of earnest praise. The Jews declare the works they have witnessed; *i.e.* the special blessings of the restoration. Each man can call to mind some of the blessings he has personally enjoyed, and in the consideration of these see good ground for glorifying God.

III. THE EXPRESSION OF PRAISE SHOULD BE PUBLIC. The people come together; they assemble at Zion, the place of public worship; they declare—make public—the works of God. This is fitting for many reasons. 1. It *glorifies God*. This is the only way in which we can glorify him. We cannot add to his glory, but we may reflect it. 2. It *increases our own thankfulness*. Joy is sympathetic. By sharing it we increase it. 3. It *leads others to see the same glory and goodness of God*. A song of praise is the most effectual sermon on the grace of God; for it is (1) the language of experience, (2) an expression of feeling, and (3) a vivid representation of "the works of the Lord our God."

Ver. 19.—(See homily on ch. x. 16.)

Ver. 20.—*God's battle-axe.* I. GOD SOMETIMES WORKS DESTRUCTION. He does not delight in destruction. It is not his chief work. But he has performed it and he may again. When a thing is absolutely evil it is best that it should cease to be. For the prevention of further evil it must be destroyed. The Creator then becomes the destroyer.

II. GOD USES HUMAN INSTRUMENTS. He might have sent death, as he created life, with a word. But he chose to use a weapon, "a battle-axe," *i.e.* a human instrument. Thus (1) he honours good men by making them his servants, and (2) he counteracts the evil influence of bad men by overruling it for ends of Divine judgment.

III. THEY WHO CANNOT SERVE GOD IN THE HIGHER WORK MAY YET SERVE HIM IN SOME NEEDFUL MISSION. The man who cannot become a prophet may act as "God's battle-axe." In God's great kingdom there is work for all classes and kinds of men. Rough and rude natures may find some mission. Still the highest mission is not that of destruction. The most worthy servant of God is he who follows Jesus Christ and "goes about doing good."

Ver. 45.—*Flight from the city of Destruction.* As Christ advised his disciples to flee from Jerusalem when the judgment of heaven was about to fall, Jeremiah here calls upon the Hebrew residents in Babylon to escape from the doomed city. The parallel suggests that similar circumstances may render similar conduct again desirable.

I. THE SINFUL WORLD IS A CITY OF DESTRUCTION. The world as God created it is good and safe. But man has made the world a dangerous place by his abuse of its lower properties. Thus the worldly spirit is an evil spirit, and the prince of this world is the supreme power of wickedness. Jesus Christ blended together his picture of the destruction of Jerusalem with a larger vision of the end of the world. In what way the wider and more distant fulfilment of his prophecy will come about we cannot tell; the day of it is known to no man, not even to the "Son of man" (Matt. xxiv. 36). Meanwhile the world lies under a certain doom. It has been so corrupted and abused that to yield to its spirit, to follow its ways, to live mainly for its advantages, is to court ruin.

II. THE CHRISTIAN IS URGED TO FLEE FROM THIS CITY OF DESTRUCTION. (2 Cor. vi. 16—vii. 1.) It would seem that the sharp line of separation between the world and the Church is melting away. Perhaps it was somewhat stiff and arbitrary. Many innocent things were once put under the ban which most of us would not now think of condemning, and an unhealthy sanctimoniousness was fostered by the idea that strictness was holiness. We are growing more free and more reasonable in some respects, learning that "every creature of God is good, and nothing is to be rejected, if it be received with thanksgiving: for it is sanctified through the Word of God and prayer." Moreover, we may hope that the Spirit of Christ has penetrated into the world beyond the boundaries of the Church, so that the very atmosphere of worldly society is more or less permeated by purifying Christian ideas. Nevertheless the approach of the world and the Church is mutual. If the world is coming nearer to the Church, the Church is in some respects approaching the world. A worldly spirit in business, in pleasure, even in religion, is too apparent. We forget that we are pilgrims and strangers here and seek another city. We live too much as if worldly prosperity were the goal of life. We need to be reminded that "this is not our rest," that in so far as we yield to the spirit of worldliness we court the doom of the city of Destruction.

III. THE CHRISTIAN'S FLIGHT FROM THE CITY OF DESTRUCTION MUST BE SPIRITUAL. Jews were to flee bodily from Babylon and Christians from Jerusalem. But the flight we need is wholly different in character. Monks and hermits thought to flee from the world by hiding within still cloisters or far away among desert solitudes. But they made a double mistake. They neglected their duty to the world and yet they did not escape from the evil of it. We may carry the world into the wilderness, for it is in our hearts. While we have bodies and live on the earth no change of place will be an escape from the world. Then we have a mission to fulfil, and no pretence of care for our own souls can excuse us for shirking the work of life; certain views of salvation are often put forth according to which Christianity is supreme selfishness—the saving of one's own soul even though others suffer. These are false. The great duty of the Christian is to live for the good of his fellow-men. To do this he must be in the world. Intercourse with the world for such a purpose is right. It is foolish to visit an infected locality for pleasure, but divinely charitable to do so to minister to the sick. The flight from the world must be escape from its spirit, its evil influence, its sinful delights. Christ prays, not that we shall be taken out of the world, but that we shall be saved from the evil of it. Through him we may have this deliverance, because he has "overcome the world."

Ver. 50.—*The duty and encouragement of the saved.* I. THE DUTY. "Stand not still." 1. *Why the duty is requisite.* Past deliverance is no security for the future. The first arrow missed the mark, but the second may strike. The tide advances; though the waves have not yet reached us, they will overwhelm us if we remain where we are. (1) It is possible to avoid one earthly trouble and succumb to another—to escape the sword and fall a prey to the pestilence. (2) It is possible to escape much distress in this world and then to fall under a terrible doom in the next world. (3) It is possible to be safe now from the terrible effects of sin and to yield to future temptation and so bring upon our heads ruin in the future. 2. *How the duty is to be performed.* (1) We must be prayerful. As the danger is ever renewed so must the grace be. Therefore we need to be always seeking aid from heaven. (2) We must be watchful. New dangers may arise at any moment. (3) We must be anxious to flee from evil. Our whole course must be with the back to the city of Destruction. (4) We must be diligent. The attainments of the past will not suffice. Forgetting those things which are behind, we must press forward. The Christian's safety is not in indolent reliance upon Christ, but in trustful obedience.

II. THE ENCOURAGEMENT. "Remember the Lord from afar, and let Jerusalem come into your mind." 1. God's grace in the past is an encouragement for the future. Past deliverances will not secure us against future danger, but they will furnish reasons for seeking safety again in God. 2. The chief reason for pressing diligently and hopefully forward is to be found in the contemplation of God. His holiness should make us fear sin; his love should make us trust in his helping grace. That we may not stand still, we should "remember the Lord." 3. Our very remoteness from God should urge us not to stand still. We may have wandered far from God in sin, or have forgotten him among the crowd of worldly distractions. But when we realize our condition, when we come to ourselves, we shall see that our only safety will be in arising and going to our Father. We can never be too far to return by Christ "the Way." The further we are from God the greater is our danger, the nearer we approach him the more of his grace and help shall we enjoy. 4. Thoughts of our mission and destiny should induce us not to stand still. The Jews are to remember Jerusalem, their ancient home, the seat of their future destinies. If there were no such city they might despair in their exile. The thought of Jerusalem suggests a centre of union and an aim for the future. If a man loses all hope, he loses himself. When we think of our possible future and of our mission, we are roused to take up the tangled threads and weave our life's work with patience according to the pattern of God's will.

Vers. 52—64.—*The book cast into the river.* I. MEN DO NOT SUFFER FOR THEIR SINS WITHOUT WARNING FROM GOD. Seraiah was to go to Babylon and see that he read there the words of the prophecy concerning the city. God has warned us of the doom of sin, and he has sent the warning to us. We have not to search for it. It sounds in our ears. It is written large in the Bible. It is repeated in the lessons of providence.

II. IF A DIVINE WARNING IS DISREGARDED IT IS USELESS TO THE DOOMED. The prophecy seems to have had little or no effect on the people of Babylon. No doubt it was sent in mercy like Jonah's preaching against Nineveh, to lead the people to repentance. But if they failed to repent, the Divine message could afford no protection. Unless we are influenced by the Bible, it will be useless for us to hold it in our hands. It can be then only a witness against us. Neither the mere possessor of Scripture, nor the reader, nor the student of it finds a way of safety in its teachings, but only he who follows its truths in practice. He who hears Christ's sayings and *does* them builds on the rock.

III. WHEN A DIVINE WARNING IS PROVED TO BE INEFFECTUAL, IT MAY BE WITHHELD. The book, no longer of use, is to be cast into the river and sunk with a stone attached to it. The voice of conscience grows silent from being long unheeded. While men neglect to obey the teachings of Scripture, they harden themselves against the reception of them. If there is no more warning, they may grow careless as though there were no more danger. They should rather take this silence as ominous of the approaching destruction which the warning has been ineffectual in urging them to escape.

HOMILIES BY VARIOUS AUTHORS.

Ver. 5.—*Divine love not to be severed from its object.* A marvellous statement. A down-trodden, sinful remnant of his people, who had broken every engagement of his covenant, is still owned and cared for.

I. A PROOF OF THE FAITHFULNESS AND LONG-SUFFERING MERCY OF GOD. 1. Having entered into covenant relations with Israel, he will not withdraw from them, even although their portion of the agreement has not been kept. He remains faithful, notwithstanding human unfaithfulness. The awful guilt of the elect nation cannot invalidate the obligations God has imposed upon himself. He is ready, therefore, at any moment to fulfil these when the conditions are complied with. 2. But it is rather to be taken as illustrating Divine mercy. The purposes of his love are never laid aside. He devises schemes of salvation when we are yet sinners. 3. Though hidden from human eyes, Divine love works continually and through all things. It was hard for mere men to see the favour of God in such times. Many of the Israelites themselves, doubtless, imagined themselves forsaken. Yet was redemption nearer to them in Babylon than when at Jerusalem they insulted and disobeyed him. "*All things* work together for good to them that love God," etc.; "Though he slay me, yet will I trust in him" (Job xiii. 15).

II. A REVELATION FULL OF WARNING AND ENCOURAGEMENT. 1. *The enemies of the Church are not to presume upon her misfortunes.* 2. *The Church itself, although cast down and feeble, is to be of good courage, for it is not cast off.* Adversity is not forsakenness. "Lo, I am with you alway." There is no room for presumption, for the chastisements of love have greater severities in store for aggravated guilt. But, relying on the grace of God, it may arise and recommence the mission it has forsaken.—M.

Vers. 6, 50.—*The duty of separating from the world.* I. IN WHAT SENSE OBLIGATORY UPON THE CHILDREN OF GOD. 1. *Spiritual detachment is always the duty of saints.* In heart and life they are to be separate unto the Lord. Their motives, ulterior aims, and dispositions are to be such as the Holy Spirit creates and fosters. They obey the law of the resurrection-life, and "seek those things which are above, where Christ sitteth on the right hand of God, setting their affection on things above, not on things on the earth" (Col. iii. 1, 2). 2. *Physical removal may be requisite* when (1) all hope of saving or benefiting sinful men is at end; or (2) there is danger that we shall yield to the temptations of their society, or encourage them in their evil courses, and thus share their curse. The Jews were to seek the peace of Babylon so long as that was possible; to share in civic life, business pursuits, and social intercourse, until this prophecy came to their knowledge.

II. THE MOTIVES AND AIMS THAT ARE TO INFLUENCE US IN DOING THIS. They are not selfish. It is only when spiritual interests are at stake. There must be no idleness or lingering when the call of duty comes. The Jew was to arise and seek his long-forsaken land at once. His motives were: 1. *Allegiance to God.* He was to "remember the Lord afar off." God was indeed near to him, even there in Babylon. He is to seek more closely to serve and honour him. And this ought ever to be the aim of Christians: "a closer walk with God." And if he be spiritually minded, he will feel the attraction of the Divine presence and the blessedness of the Divine communion, which far more than make up for temporal loss or sorrow incurred for conscience' sake. It is the special duty of Christians to call upon God and obey him when amongst those who do not know his Name. 2. *The interests of the kingdom of God on earth.* God sought to separate and sanctify to himself a peculiar people in olden time, that it might witness to his truth. He still seeks to gather a spiritual Church, whose communion consists of those who are redeemed by the blood of his Son. Through its manifold ministries he is carrying out the salvation of the world. Every Christian is bound to connect himself with it in some form or other, and to take his part in its worship and work. The language of the ancient exile might well be adopted by every member of the new Israel—Ps. cxxii.; cxxxvii. 5, 6.—M.

Ver. 10.—*Praise the outcome of saintly experience.* These are the words of Jeremiah, but there can be little doubt he is but instinctively interpreting the emotion that must fill the breasts of his countrymen when his predictions were accomplished. As a representative Israelite, he expresses the deep-seated impulse that is felt when the greater providences and special spiritual deliverances of life are realized.

I. EXPERIENCES OF SAVING GRACE AN OCCASION OF THANKSGIVING AND PRAISE. We owe thankful recognition to God for our creation, preservation, and the recurring mercies of our temporal life; but there are stronger emotions awakened by the experiences of grace in the spiritual nature. 1. *Notice some of these.* This deliverance from Babylon. Conversion, or the rescue of the soul from the spiritual Babylon. The triumphs of the gospel; faithfulness of saints; increase of spiritual power and influence; preservation of Christian institutions in times of spiritual apathy or persecution; evangelization of heathen lands, etc. Special answers to prayer, or peace and comfort in private fellowship with our heavenly Father. 2. *Their general character.* "The Lord hath brought forth our righteousness" ("righteousnesses"). This deliverance was a great act of *judgment.* The cause of God's people was vindicated, and the guilt of Babylon avenged (cf. Ps. xxxvii. 6). The whole world was witness of the character and meaning of the event. And this is the element in all the experiences of grace that awakens special thanksgiving—they are manifestations of Divine righteousness in the life of men; triumphs of truth and holiness and love.

II. THE SPECIAL DUTY TO WHICH THEY CALL US. 1. *Declaring and interpreting God's work to men,* (1) by word; (2) by work. 2. *Public celebration in God's house.* Zion was the most fitting and representative place for such a duty. Public worship should be linked with the experiences of private devotion and the spiritual life. Public and common praise is the privilege and delight of Christians.—M.

Ver. 6.—*" Escape for thy life!"* "Flee out of the midst of Babylon," etc. This word was addressed to those who should be found in Babylon when the day of vengeance came upon her (cf. Gen. xix. 15). And it seems to anticipate what was afterwards the fact—that many of the Jews would not care to go away from Babylon. Note—

I. WHO ARE TO ESCAPE. This word was not addressed to all. Many of God's people did " let Jerusalem come into their mind," and, as soon as ever opportunity was given them, they returned to their own land. But there were many who chose to stay. They had long dwelt in Babylon. They had got to like her rule, for they had prospered in this world's wealth. The surrounding idolatries did not " vex " their souls. They felt secure in her; they had become morally and spiritually enslaved. Hence they would not return with their brethren when the opportunity came. And how like is the position of men now! They are in bondage and spiritual captivity under the power of " the prince of this world." Some have heard the word and have escaped, but others care not to flee. They are content to be where and as they are.

II. WHENCE THEY ARE TO ESCAPE. Babylon stands for the kingdom of evil, which is ruled over by the spirit of evil. Now, that kingdom is fitly represented by Babylon. The power, the attractiveness, the fascination, the deceptiveness, the widespread and long-continued rule of the one find their type and likeness in the other. And the unwillingness which was felt by the great majority of Jews to quit Babylon is paralleled by the more sad unwillingness to abandon that kingdom of evil which God is ever bidding us escape and flee from.

III. WHY WE ARE TO ESCAPE. It is " for our life." This cannot be taken literally of the Jews in Babylon. For, so far as this life was concerned, they prospered greatly under the Persian rule (cf. Book of Esther in proof). And their descendants lived on right down to the times of the apostles, and were those " of the dispersion " of whom we read in the New Testament. But for the most their national and spiritual life was lost by their disobedience to this command. They ceased to be Jews, and were absorbed in the heathen nations around. And, of course, their religious life perished at the same time (see histories of the Captivity). And so in regard to the spiritual analogies of these events. Men will not, do not, literally lose this life by refusing to come away from the kingdom of evil into the kingdom of God. On the contrary, they seem to flourish greatly. The prosperity of the ungodly has been a notorious and perplexing fact in all ages of the world. And it is a sore temptation and trial to those who feel the drawings of the kingdom of God. And the temptation can only be overcome by remembering that the *life of the soul* depends upon our obedience to this word. It is when the unseen and the eternal are seen by faith that the gloss and glamour of the world are seen at their real and poor value, and the solid worth of the kingdom of God is confessed and yielded to. The angels had to " hasten " even " just Lot," though the fire of the Lord was on the point of descending on " the cities of the plain." And how we need hastening now! How slow to believe that judgment is nigh! For with the advent of death that judgment begins to every soul that enters into eternity unforgiven and unsaved.

IV. HOW WE SHALL ESCAPE. The one all-essential question is—Do you really wish to? For if there be the genuine desire, the path of escape will be soon revealed. No directions are of any use until this desire be awakened in the soul. But where it exists, it will express itself in what the Bible calls " seeking the Lord." And, as this is continued, there will be deepened in the soul that hatred of sin and aspiration after holiness which lie at the root of all true religious life. Repentance will thus be formed within the soul, and will be fostered by careful obedience to the will of God as declared in his Word. But—

V. WHITHER SHALL WE ESCAPE? There is but one answer to this. To the Lord Jesus Christ. It is as we look up to him in lowly, earnest trust, renouncing all self-reliance, that the new life is begotten in us, and we are grafted in him, and so become "new creatures," as St. Paul tells, and so are we *in* the kingdom of God, and clean escaped from the kingdom of the evil one. We are pardoned, accepted, made possessors of the Holy Ghost and of eternal life.—C.

Ver. 10.—*The response of the redeemed.* "The Lord hath . . . come, and let *us*," etc.
I. WHAT THE LORD HATH DONE. "Brought forth our righteousness." Now, by this we may understand: 1. *The Lord hath brought forth*, made known, revealed, *him who is our Righteousness* (cf. homily on " *The Lord our Righteousness*," vol. i. p. 527). By

his representative character, what is done by him is as done by us. "We thus judge, that if one died for all, then were all dead" (2 Cor. v. 14). There is nothing unreasonable in this. We are perpetually *imputing* to others what is not in them or but very faintly in them. We do so when we treat strangers with all kindness for the sake of those—some honoured and beloved ones—who commend them to us. We cause to flow over on them the worth and goodness of those by whom they are commended. They may not merely be strangers, but unworthy and evil, and yet, for the sake of others, we deal with them, not as they are, but as those are from whom they come. So is the Lord Jesus our Righteousness, blessed be his Name! 2. *The Lord hath brought forth righteousness in us.* But for him there would have been no righteousness at all. Some speak of "natural goodness." There is no such thing. *All* goodness, like all light, has but one source. Divines tell of ruined arches, stately pillars, etc., relics of the noble fabric that once was. But Scripture rather teaches that sin wrought death. If, then, there be aught that is beautiful and good, fair and righteous—and there is, and much—it is not a relic, but a new creation. It comes from him who is "the Light that lighteth every man that cometh into the world" (John i. ; cf. Jas. i. 16). And when a man yields up his soul to Christ, then—vitally grafted into him, the true Vine, and having become a living branch—he will more and more yield the fruit of righteousness, as he never did or could before. 3. *The Lord hath brought forth his covenant.* That is to say, he hath brought forth in his own mind, so as to remember, his covenant that he made (cf. Ps. cv. 8—15 ; cxi., etc.). It is ever declared to be on the ground of this covenant that God dealt well with his people. Now, that covenant had been, as it were, put out of the Divine mind by the multitude of their sins. But now he brings it forth again. 4. *The Lord hath vindicated us.* The enemies of the Lord blasphemed his people. Counted them as having no worth or goodness at all ; as far inferior to all others. But, despised as his people were and condemned, now, by God's redemption of them, he was to bring forth their righteousness, vindicate them, on and before all (cf. Ps. xxxvii. 5—7). This, which he did for Israel, he will do for all his people—"will bring forth their righteousness as the light, and their judgment as the noonday."

II. WHAT, THEREFORE, SHOULD WE DO? "Come, and let us declare in Zion the work of the Lord our God." This is what we are to do. 1. *Why should we do this?* For the honour of God. It is his due. For our own soul's sake ; to keep silence on what he has done for us is not only dishonouring to him, but disastrous to our own souls. For the encouragement of others, that they may be led to trust in him. 2. *How should we do this?* Openly : "Let us *declare* in Zion," etc. Not concealing our obligation, not refusing to confess him. Unitedly : "Come, and let *us*," etc. Join with them of a like mind. Heartily : calling on others to do the like, "Come," etc. In his Church : "In Zion." There taking our place, falling into rank in the army of the Lord. In the heavenly Zion the redeemed of the Lord never tire of thus declaring the work of the Lord.—C.

Ver. 19.—"*The Portion of Jacob*" (cf. homily, vol. i. p. 277).—C.

Ver. 20.—*The Church God's battle-axe.* God ever employs instruments to accomplish his purposes. He is a God that "hideth" himself. Hence many see nothing but instruments, and forget, or deny, the hand that uses them. "That does not seem much of a sword," said one, as he looked upon the treasured weapon of a great national hero and valiant soldier. "Ah! but you do not see the hand that wielded it," was the just reply. So as we look on the agencies God employs, how feeble they seem to be ! But think of the force behind them, and then the works they accomplished are explained. Now, this is true of all God's works. Especially is it true in all the great spiritual achievements which we have heard of or seen. This verse refers to Israel, in reference to the idolatrous nations around them, and to Babylon especially. Israel was the unseen cause that led to the overthrow and destruction of one nation after another. For the Church's sake God governs the world. "All things are yours." Now, note—

I. THE WITNESS OF HISTORY to the truth that God's people are his "battle-axe and weapons of war." "I came not to send peace upon earth, but a sword," said Jesus, and in the same sense as this verse declares that word is true. "Magna est veritas, et prevalebit," is another rendering of the same fact. 1. *Before the birth of Christ* the pure monotheistic faith of Israel had, after their captivity, begun its iconoclastic work. Over large portions of the then civilized world that faith began to permeate and cleave its way. So that the old idolatries were in many places stricken with a mortal blow before even he was proclaimed who was to draw all men unto him. 2. *The downfall of paganism.* Notwithstanding the many accretions of error and superstition with which the pure faith of Christ so soon became encumbered, there yet remained inherent in it and inseparable from it such vital and mighty energy that it smote as with a " battle-axe " one falsehood after another, until they were well-nigh all slain. The forces against her in that ancient world were simply tremendous, but the Church went forth conquering and to conquer. In vain the scorn of the great, the fires of awful persecution, the power of venerable superstition ; in vain the hindrances which she herself put in her own way ; the Church was still God's destroying power against the false religions of that age, until at length the last emperor of Rome who endeavoured to revive paganism, Julian—whom a corrupt hierarchy malignantly branded as " the apostate," though, in fact, he was less apostate than themselves—confessed with his dying breath, " O Galilæan, thou hast conquered ! " In all that long and heart-stirring conflict this declaration of the prophet was illustrated again and again. 3. *In the Reformation.* Not alone in those nations in which the Reformation principles took root, but in the Church of Rome herself, was the error and evil destroying power of the truth that dwelt in the hearts of God's people made manifest. See in such a book as Ranke's ' History of the Popes ' what vast difference and improvements were brought about in the Catholic Church itself by the awful discipline through which she had then to pass. Whatever stern censures may have to be passed on that Church since the days of the Reformation—and they are neither few nor light—yet candour must admit that they are far fewer and far lighter than those which the outraged conscience of Christendom heaped upon her in the generations before. 4. *In all missionary and evangelistic triumphs over heathendom.*

II. THE WITNESS OF INDIVIDUAL CHRISTIAN EXPERIENCE. We are wont to speak of the truth of God as "mighty to the pulling down of the strongholds of sin and Satan." This is a Christian commonplace. And is it not true ? What but this battle-axe slew the giant sins that ruled and oppressed in each soul ?

III. THE SECRET OF THIS FORCE. What makes the Church God's battle-axe ? We answer : 1. *The truth that sustains her.* The truth concerning God and our relations to him—he our Father and we all his children. 2. *The spirit that animates her ;* not one of hate or disregard to man, as was common before Christ came, but love—love even towards the vilest for Christ's sake. 3. *The rule that regulates her.* The heathen looked on with amazement at the blamelessness of life and the sanctity of character which the faith of the Church produced, and they felt and owned its power. 4. *The love that constrains her.* She ever "bore about in the body the dying of the Lord Jesus," and, mindful of that, she shrank from no suffering and refused no service. 5. *The hope that cheers her.* She wrought, not for a corruptible crown, but an incorruptible ; and the hope, "that blessed hope," of her Lord's appearing to receive and reward his people, cheered them on amid the awful sufferings which they were called on to bear. And still it is in proportion as these mighty motives animate the Church in the individual soul that faithful and effectual service is done for Christ against the many and mighty adversaries of God with which the world abounds.—C.

Ver. 25.—*A fatal fact.* " Behold, I am against thee."
I. ITS TRUTH CONFESSED. When Jerusalem was taken the captain of Nebuchadnezzar's army avowed that what had happened was of God (cf. ch. xl. 2). So afterwards when, by the Roman army, Jerusalem was again captured, as our Lord foretold it would be, then too we have it on record that a like avowal was made by the leader of the Roman armies. And so here in regard to Babylon, no other conclusion could be come to. So vast was the power of Babylon that only the Divine opposition could explain the calamities that came upon her. And so when we see nations, Churches, men, that have every worldly advantage nevertheless brought low, as Rome was by the Goths, we can account for it only by this fact—" I am against thee."
II. ITS FATALITY SHOWN. If empires like Babylon cannot stand when God is against them, who else can stand ? " If these things be done in the green tree, what shall be

done in the dry?" If the mightiest fall beneath the Divine opposition, who of lesser power can hope to endure? "Let him that thinketh he standeth take heed lest he fall." He is sure to if these do.

III. Its conclusion evident. Send an embassage and seek conditions of peace (Luke xiv. 31). "Be ye reconciled unto God." "Acquaint thyself with God, and be at peace."—C.

Ver. 33.—*Harvests of horror and threshings of wrath.* The Bible continually makes use of the similitude of the harvest and its labours, but it is only by its qualifying words that we can know what kind of harvest is meant. Here we have the frequent metaphor, but it tells of no joy, of sorrow only. *Similar language has been used of Israel* as is here used of Babylon (cf. Isa. xxi. 10; xli. 15). Israel's sins had been the seed of that harvest, and it was a terrible one. All the sorrows of the invasion and destruction of their beloved land and city, their holy city, Jerusalem, and all those which were associated with and sprang out of their bitter exile in Babylon, were but parts of that harvest and strokes of "the bruising flails of God's corrections." *But here it is Babylon that is spoken of* (cf. Isa. xxi. for a yet earlier prediction of Babylon's fall). She had sown the seed; the cup of her iniquity was full ere the harvests and threshings told of here came upon her. "Dissolute and luxurious in their habits, the Babylonians hid under their soft luxurious exterior a fierceness, an insatiable lust for blood, such as marked many Eastern tribes—such, for instance, as we ourselves have found in 'the mild Hindoo.' The Hebrew prophets describe them as 'a bitter and hasty,' a 'terrible and dreadful' people, 'fiercer than the evening wolves,' a people who 'made the earth tremble and did shake kingdoms.'" They conquered well-nigh all the kingdoms of the then known world; they pillaged every country they conquered, and often went far to depopulate the countries they pillaged. In Judæa, for instance, the land became a mere haunt of wild beasts after the Babylonians had subdued it, and from Jerusalem they pillaged even the sacred vessels of the temple. Hence to Isaiah they appeared as "the spoiler spoiling, and the destroyer destroying." And besides all this, there seems to have been an inherent and ineradicable wickedness in the nation itself, or it could hardly have been selected, as it is, as the type of all that is abominable and hateful in the sight of God. For many a generation and century she had been spared. From the beginning to the end of the Bible we read of her. In her decayed greatness there was a little Christian Church there, of which St. Peter tells (1 Pet. v. 19). But up to the time of the Exile, and during far the greater portion of it, Babylon seemed only to advance in splendour, in wealth, and power. But at length the time of her harvest—an awful time, indeed—came, and in the sorrows connected with her capture and overthrow, and in the hard and hated rule of her Persian lords, there was the "threshing" of which both Isaiah and Jeremiah tell. The contemplation of it filled the Prophet Isaiah with an unspeakable horror: "My loins are filled with pain: pangs have taken hold on me" (Isa. xxi. 3, 4). Jew as he was, he could not behold the dread vision of what was to come on Babylon without deep anguish. She "must have filled in his thoughts much the place which Rome held in the mind of a cultivated Spaniard or Carthaginian of the early Christian centuries. To him the Medes and Persians, plunging down from their unknown, mysterious mountain fastnesses upon the wealthy Babylonian plain, must have seemed much as the Goths and Vandals seemed to the more civilized races of Europe, when they came pouring down the Alps, to carry sword and fire through the storied plains of Italy. The whole Christian world shuddered when Rome fell; and as her fall to the modern so was the fall of Babylon to the ancient world." Harvest and threshing: these images of the barn commonly suggest that which is peaceful and joyous; but here they tell of the reverse of that—of horror and woe unspeakable. Learn, therefore—

I. Sins are seeds which may have a late, but shall surely have a large and terrible, harvest.

II. Reluctant as God may be to afflict the children of men, he will not spare a single stroke so long as they cling to the evils which degrade and destroy them.

III. The judgments and punishments of God are not vindictive and final, but the "threshings of the corn of his floor" (Isa. xxi. 10). The separation, that is, of the evil from the good, the worthless from that which is precious and shall be preserved for evermore.—C.

Ver. 48.—*Joy over judgment.* I. THE SINNER WILL WEEP AND WAIL. This is the constant declaration of the Word of God. "There shall be weeping and gnashing of teeth." Would that the sinner would look steadily on to the end, and so consider his ways!

II. HUMAN NATURE, IN SYMPATHY WITH THE SINNER'S WOES, WILL SORROW. (Cf. Isa. xxi. 10.) We have need to be on our guard against this. In the present day our sympathy with the suffering leads us to forget the causes and the blessed results that come from the judgment of God. No criminal is ever condemned to die but at once there are those who strive to get his punishment remitted. It is a false sympathy and needs to be resisted.

III. BUT HEAVEN AND EARTH REJOICE. Cf. the many psalms in which we are called on to rejoice because the Lord " cometh to judge the earth." The grounds of this joy are: 1. Righteousness is vindicated. 2. The oppressed are delivered. 3. Men will learn righteousness. 4. They that are judged will be brought to a better mind.' 5. The kingdom of God will more speedily come.—C.

Ver. 50.—*The charge to them that are spared.* This charge, addressed to Israelites spared from Babylon, may be applied to all in Christ. For—

I. ALL IN CHRIST ARE SPARED ONES. Spared from: 1. The condemnation due to sin. 2. The abiding tyranny of sin. 3. The crushing power of sorrow. 4. The misery of alienation from God. 5. The might of death.

II. TO SUCH THIS THREEFOLD CHARGE IS ADDRESSED. 1. *They are to "go away, stand not still."* As Israel from Babylon that had enslaved them, so these from the sins which God has forgiven them. "Let him that nameth the name of Christ depart from iniquity." Many Jews despised this charge, and stayed on in Babylon. Some not merely stayed in Babylon as Jews, but probably far more of them were "mingled with the heathen, and learned their ways." "Evil communications corrupt good manners." Even those who disobeyed only the letter of the command suffered, whilst those who disobeyed both the letter and the spirit were simply lost, cut off from the house of Israel. *And they who have received Christ,* if they do not break away from their old sins and from all that would hold them in bondage to such sins, will lose their religion and are in sore peril of apostatizing from Christ. Therefore let such put further and further distance between themselves and their former life, lest again they be entangled and overcome. 2. *To "remember the Lord afar off."* In their sin and misery God seemed afar off to Israel. "My way is hid from the Lord, and my judgment is passed over from my God"—such was their grievous lament. But they were to remember him, turn their thoughts and prayers toward him, and believingly wait his promised answer. And to the believer now "it doth not yet appear what we shall be;" we are far off from that; but we are to remember the Lord, though we be yet in condition and character so far off from him. Remember him in our meditations, prayers, purposes, and aims; *wait* on him, and so renew our strength. 3. *"Let Jerusalem come into your mind."* How blessed to be there! how she demands our earnest service!—her joys, her sanctity, her children, her employ; our place there prepared for us, and our preparation for the place. So remember her, and so be delivered from being wearied and faint in our minds.—C.

Ver. 58.—*"The broad walls."* I. THE EMPIRE OF SIN HAS SUCH WALLS. Those referred to here may be taken as a type of them. They were: 1. *To separate.* Have we not proof of this in the wide distance, the invincible barriers, which keep the ungodly from sympathizing, associating, or in any way uniting, with the people of God? The kingdom of evil remains shut up from the kingdom of God. Mansoul cannot be entered by way of the gates; the messengers of the King seek admission, but cannot obtain it. And hereafter the separation will continue (cf. Luke xvi., "Between us and you there is a great gulf fixed"). Separation, which is voluntary now, becomes involuntary then. 2. *For security.* A terrible security it is. In vain do the ambassadors of God endeavour to penetrate within those walls. In vain do his soldiers seek to scale them and his weapons of war to destroy them. The strong man armed keepeth his goods in peace. What minister of Christ has not again and again retired baffled from before these broad walls, so high, so strong, so impregnable? 3. *For enjoyment.* The broad walls of cities such as Babylon were places for pleasant walking for recreation and enjoyment. So does the sinner's fancied security lull his soul to rest, make him cry, "Peace, peace!" when there is no peace. But—

II. THE KINGDOM OF GOD HAS ITS BROAD WALLS. (Cf. Neh. iii. 8, where we read of the broad walls of Jerusalem.) Let us see to it that we maintain and preserve those walls. 1. *For separation.* Let us not seek to come close to the world, in its habits, maxims, spirit, behaviour. Keep the wall broad, strong, high. We cannot serve God *and* mammon. Let there be no attempt at compromise. And these walls are also 2. *For security.* If we do not maintain them we run great risk for ourselves. Tampering with sin is perilous work. And let us not think that we are more likely to win the world by such breaking down of the broad walls. The result is all the other way. See how broad a wall Christ maintained between himself and the world. God has built these walls. His power, his wisdom, his love, his promise, are all portions of these walls by which his Church is guarded and against which the gates of hell shall not prevail. 3. *For enjoyment.* What comfort there is in the thought of them, of the sure defence, the wall of fire, which God will be to his people! And on these walls, as we "walk about Zion, and go round her, and tell the towers thereof," what rest, what communion one with another, and what bright prospects are ours! The broad walls of Babylon shall be "broken down;" but these are eternal. Are we within them?—C.

Ver. 64.—*The weariness of sin.* "They shall be weary." With these sad words the Prophet Jeremiah closes his book. The shadows are over it all, nor are they in the least lifted where we most love to see them lifted—at the end. They are spoken of the inhabitants of Babylon, and repeat what was said in ver. 58. They suggest the theme—*The weariness of sin.*

I. WEARINESS IS ALWAYS PAIN. It may be of *the body,* and then exhaustion and fatigue render exertion any longer only so much torture. Or of *the mind.* The brain becomes dazed, bewildered, incapable of effort. Or of *the heart*—that which is caused by disappointment, ingratitude, unfulfilled desire, hopelessness. Or that *of the soul,* which is the weariness told of here. But in all cases it is full of pain.

II. WEARINESS IS A UNIVERSAL EXPERIENCE. The child of God is often weary. Such are exhorted not to be "weary in well-doing," the exhortation implying the more than possibility of such weariness being experienced. And our Saviour knew this weariness—never of, but often in, his work. In a world like this there are causes enough for such weariness to lay hold on the servants of God. But if they know weariness, yet more do the children of this world; for—

III. THE WORST WEARINESS IS THAT OF SIN. For a while the enjoyment which springs from sin may so intoxicate and dazzle the wrong-doer that he will laugh at the idea of weariness, and declare that his is the alone path of pleasure and good. But after a while that ceases, and then comes satiety and weariness. 1. *The causes of this are:* (1) *Negative.* In serving sin we have not those great aids to endurance and restoration of strength which are ever present to the child of God. The servant of sin has no high and noble motive, no worthy motive at all, in what he does. The motives of affection, of duty, of gratitude, of love, which sustain so mightily the mind of the Christian,—these are all lacking in the servant of sin. *Good hope* also cheers the child of God; but what harvest can the sinner expect to reap? It is such as he dares not, and therefore will not, contemplate. *The communion of the Spirit of God*—that Spirit who "giveth songs in the night," is present to the Christian, and in the deepest distress enables him to rejoice. But nought of this can the ungodly know in their hard work and service. *Drawing near to God* is another aid of the child of God. For—

> "We may kneel and cast our load,
> E'en while we pray, upon our God,
> Then rise with lightened cheer;
> Sure that the Father, who is nigh
> To hear the famished ravens cry,
> Will hear in that we fear."

This most real help the ungodly never know. (2) *But there are positive causes of weariness* in the service of sin. Jesus said, "Weep not for me, but weep for yourselves and for your children." His cup of woe was bitter, but theirs would be more bitter still. Now, the positive causes of the weariness of sin are such as these. The powerlessness of sin to minister pleasure continually. The goadings of conscience, which will not be silent. God's judgments—so full of pain, so inevitable, so irremediable, as these on Babylon. The hopelessness of sin's outlook—nothing but a fearful looking for of judgment. 2. *The effects* of this weariness are seen in such as Saul and Judas, and in the myriad others who have sought, in self-destruction or by wild plunging into yet deeper sins, to escape that weariness which tracks their footsteps continually. Well might Paul ask, "What profit had ye in those things whereof ye are now ashamed?" Who would begin a career that ends in such a way? What an argument such facts furnish for seeking, if haply we may find it: 3. *The cure* of all such weariness! The child of God knows it well. The ungodly may know it too if they will. It consists in submission to that Lord who says to all such, "Come unto me all ye that are weary and heavy laden," etc. There alone is the cure.—C.

Ver. 5.—*Unforsaken Israel.* I. AN APPARENT FORSAKING. Israel looked forsaken. It was in exile, in captivity, and under the asserted judgment of Jehovah. We have always, to a certain extent, to accept the appearances of things. God's presence had been manifested in outward favour and prosperity, and what was more plausible than to say that the withdrawing of the favour and prosperity meant the withdrawing of God himself? But then it is forgotten that God's presence may be manifested in many ways. Outward prosperity is not essential to signify God's satisfaction with us. Nor must we infer that, because a backsliding Christian has fallen into trouble and misery, therefore God has forsaken him. The signs of man forsaking God are made very clear, so that there may be all possible incentives to repentance; but if God ever does forsake a man, leaving him utterly to his own folly and recklessness, no sign of it is given to us. There is quite enough already in our own wild fancies to make us desponding and despairing.

II. A PLAUSIBLE CAUSE FOR FORSAKING. The land of Israel was filled with sin against the Holy One of Israel. Men think of God as they do of themselves. The patience of the human master soon gets exhausted with the servant who disobeys many commandments and obeys others in the most perfunctory way.

III. A REAL CAUSE FOR CLOSE ADHERENCE. That Israel, chosen and beloved of God, fills his land with sin, so far from being a reason for forsaking, is a reason for closer adherence than ever. The shepherd leaves the ninety-nine sheep in safety and goes into the wilderness after the lost one. If only men, brought at last to a sense of their wickedness and recklessness, could see how near God is to them, how ready and able to help, they would be filled with hope. "God is love," and therefore the greater our need the greater his nearness. The real difficulty is that we flee to the succours and solaces of self, and so the nearness of God, with all his suitable and ample supplies, is only too easily obscured.

IV. A FRESH MANIFESTATION OF THE HOLY ONE OF ISRAEL. Never does God's holiness so appear as when he is dealing with sinners in the way of long-suffering, if perchance they will surrender at last and permit him to restore them to righteousness and peace. Surely God's holiness shines most in his greatest attribute, and that is love. God is marked off from all created things by his power and his righteousness, but most of all by his transcendent love. Here is the most glorious aspect of his holiness, that, no matter how much men may sin against him, neglect his will, and abuse his world, yet, when they are ready to turn, he is close at hand with everything prepared to receive them.—Y.

Ver. 6.—*Individual escape.* Two whole chapters are taken up in enforcing the inevitable doom on Babylon. The city as a whole cannot possibly escape; therefore so much the more necessary is it to point out escape for the individual and put hope into his heart. Observe—

I. HOW THIS EXHORTATION TO THE INDIVIDUAL SETS BEFORE US CLEARLY THE GENERAL DOOM. All who stay in heedlessness and unbelief must perish. Particular inhabitants of Babylon have not to sin some special sin in order to bring destruction on themselves. All they have to do is just to go on in their buying, selling, and getting gain. So the natural man everywhere has just to go on within the common worldly limits and according to the common worldly traditions. Going on quietly accepting the position of the unregenerate, he will assuredly come to the end of such. "Out of Christ we *may* perish" is not the word to be said, but "Out of Christ we must perish."

II. GOD'S CONSTANT CONSIDERATION FOR THE INDIVIDUAL. Masses of men have to suffer because the great bulk of them will ever be heedless of the signs of danger. But every wise, foreseeing individual, in whose heart there are steady inclinings to the right, may escape. Certainly we cannot escape always involvement in temporal calamities. It might even be cowardly and selfish to run away from them. To run away from a temporal calamity might be the very way to bring on ourselves the severest spiritual calamity. But with respect to spiritual perils, in comparison with which temporal perils are mere trifles, every individual has his chance. He must have individuality of character in this matter, ability to see danger when others see none, and courage to flee when others stand still and laugh at him. Recollect that there may be flight in one sense, while in another sense things remain unchanged. We may remain in a community, and yet flee from all danger by avoiding its follies and its disobedience to God.

III. THE NEED OF PROMPTITUDE AND DECISION. Not specified, promptitude is yet evidently implied. Flee at once; for if you wait until you can see danger, it may be too late.—Y.

Ver. 10.—*Declaring in Zion the work of the Lord.* I. THAT WHICH HAS TO BE DECLARED. The work of Jehovah, the God of Israel, that work being the bringing forth of what is described as " our righteousness." What, then, was this righteousness? We can only conjecture, but probably it was that righteousness, ever well-pleasing to God, shown by those who believe in his promises and obey his directions. There was ample field for righteousness of this kind on the part of the Israelites in captivity; for had not God told them expressly, however unlikely the event might appear, that they would yet return to their former dwelling-place? In due time there was to be a vindication of their faith. But out of that faith there is to be kept every element of self-glorification. It is man's blessedness, but not his praise, that he recognizes the certainty of what a promise-keeping, omnipotent One will do for him. Declaring the work of God is always a satisfactory thing, for the work of God itself is always satisfactory. Well-begun, thorough, completed, necessary work it is.

II. THOSE WHO DECLARE IT. Those who are the materials of the work and for whom the work is done. They are not mere bystanders and spectators. The sign that real Divine work is being done in a human heart comes when praise and acknowledgment of the great Worker is expressed. We are God's workmanship. It is he who extricates us from our confusions, nullifies the vain doings of the merely natural man, and makes us capable of actions that will abide and glorify him. It is part of God's very work to put into us the spirit of declaration, so that we perceive the change wrought in us, the Worker of it, the continuity of it, in short, all the good connected with it. And perceiving all this, how should we do other than declare in one mingled utterance the glory of God and our gratitude to him?

III. THE PLACE OF DECLARATION. In Zion, with its memories of Jehovah's presence in the past. Zion was a name to humble Israel, in the thought of former apostasy and idolatry; but Zion was nothing but glorious so far as Jehovah was concerned. Zion had been too long neglected, not indeed so far as a certain outward worship was concerned, but the worship of the heart was lacking. Now Zion would appear in an altogether new aspect. Instead of mere words, mere ritual routine, there was an acknowledgment of deeply felt benefit at the hands of God. The place of worship was the same, yet not the same, for the old scene had new associations. We may acknowledge God anywhere; we must acknowledge him everywhere; but yet there is a suitability in making certain acknowledgments in certain places. What could be more appropriate than to utter forth words of true spiritual recognition on that sacred spot where God had been so long misunderstood and defied?—Y.

Ver. 13.—*The dweller on many waters.* I. THE RECOGNITION OF NATURAL RESOURCES.

The great natural advantages of Babylon are allowed to the fullest extent. She stands on "the great river Euphrates." A great river for navigable purposes means prosperity to a city. There is also to be considered the facility of getting water for all the other purposes of life. The abundance of Babylon's treasures was in part a result of her dwelling on many waters. The waters helped to set off the magnificence and splendour of her buildings. Nothing is gained by minimizing the treasures of this world. Let them be displayed and acknowledged to their fullest extent (see Rev. xviii.).

II. These resources cannot avert doom. The fact is that the abundance of these resources can only manifest itself in certain directions. There is abundance of that which ministers to carnal ambition and lust, abundance of that which feeds the pride of individuals and nations, abundance of that which gives merely human security against merely human attack. But when we come to consider the highest satisfactions and the greatest dangers, then we find scantiness instead of abundance. The many waters dry up into a shallow pool here and there. The characteristic of the abundance given by Christ is that it avails for all possible needs. Never can it be said to the Christian, livingly connected as he is with his heavenly treasures, that his end is come. Of his treasure, his blessedness, and his security, there shall be no end.

III. An indication of what made these resources so deceitful. They were, largely at least, the accumulations of covetousness. We must not look too closely at the magnificent houses of a great city, with their contents, or else we shall be speedily undeceived as to their real glory. We shall see how much greed and unjust gain and the grinding of the poor had to do with such buildings. Grand buildings for some men to live in can have no charm to the Christian eye, if a necessary condition for their existence is that many others should live in ruinous hovels. The just and loving God must look on splendid cities with a very different eye from the human one. And doing so, he must of necessity fix a limit to covetousness. Covetousness goes on adding to its treasures, until at last it excites the covetousness of others. And even apart from this, outward treasures, unduly esteemed, must in time corrupt the inward man.—Y.

Ver. 15.—*The resources of Jehovah.* Here are the resources of Jehovah as over against the resources of Babylon. Note the differences between them.

I. They are resources in Jehovah himself. It is from the very being of Jehovah that his works flow forth, whether those works be considered as illustrating his power, his wisdom, or his understanding. When a prophet of Jehovah has to speak of human resources, he speaks of things outside the man. Apart from the soil on which he stands, the world in which he lives, what can man do? His very body is derived from the soil, and to the soil returns. His chosen treasures, the things on which he leans, are treasures upon earth. But when a prophet comes to speak of Jehovah, he can think of him separated from all the visible and tangible. He does not depend on these things, for they would have had no existence but for him. We may, in a certain qualified sense, speak of human power, wisdom, and understanding; we must indeed use such terms, for some men are so weak that others must be spoken of as powerful, some so foolish that others must be spoken of as wise, some so shallow and ignorant that others must be spoken of as men of understanding. But the very power of a man reveals in time his essential weakness, his very wisdom his essential folly, his very understanding his essential ignorance. God alone is power, and in him is no weakness at all; God alone is wisdom, and in him no folly at all; God alone is understanding, and in him nothing of the limited and erroneous knowledge which is so often a humiliation to human pride.

II. They are resources united in one Being. Judged according to human standards, some men are powerful, some men wise, and some are men of understanding; but very seldom, even according to the human standard, are all three qualities united in one man; and it is not very often that even two of them are found. Man may have power, mere muscular strength, the power of the athlete, the power of the ox, without anything worthy the name of wisdom. So there may be wisdom without power; and there may be a very high degree of wisdom apart from large knowledge or a powerful understanding. Men are made so that what is defective in one may be supplied by another. The greatest human works are done when the power of one is joined with the wisdom of a second and the understanding of a third. But with Jehovah all these qualities, in their highest degree, are found united in One. The only account after all that man can give of the making of matter is that it has been made by a God. And then his wisdom has reduced everything to order, arranged the world in all its grades, organisms, and mutual connections. The natural man comes nearest to God when he can combine the power of one, the wisdom of another, and the understanding of yet a third, to make as it were one new man for the doing of special work; and the spiritual man comes nearest to God when, still preserving his individuality of action, he exchanges for his natural weakness the spiritual power of Christ, for his natural folly the spiritual wisdom of Christ, and for his often useless and deluding knowledge of the things of this world that knowledge which comes in the revelation of the glory of God in the face of Jesus Christ.—Y.

Ver. 19.—*The Portion of Jacob contrasted with the confidences of Babylon.* I. THE NAME BY WHICH JEHOVAH IS HERE INDICATED. The Portion of Jacob. So the psalmist says, "My flesh and my heart faileth . . . but God is my Portion for ever" (Ps. lxxiii. 26; see also Ps. xvi. 5). Men had their appointed portions, and no doubt they varied in value. But few were those who could rise above mere external things and look on the invisible God as their real Portion. And yet these were the only ones who had a portion and inheritance in the fullest sense of the words. For only so were they lifted above all temptation to envy, and above all the consequences of terrestrial impairments and losses. True, we have an inheritance of invisible and everlasting things, of which the present visible possessions give the preparatory conditions; but to possess these things we must possess God, must be sure of his interest, his spiritual providence, his sufficiency, for only in him can even spiritual possessions have their beginning and continuance. Nor must we fail to note what may be called the mutual character of this portion and inheritance. Jehovah being the Portion of Jacob, it is equally true that Jehovah's portion is his people (Deut. xxxii. 9). Even the best possessions of a natural man are not mere legal property, not mere intellectual knowledge, but those human beings whom he can call friends. Such a one is rich according to the quality of his friends, those on whom he has claims and who have claims on him. He is rich according to the opportunities he has of getting service from them; richer still according to his opportunities for rendering service, on the principle that it is more blessed to give than to receive. And so God will be our Inheritance just in proportion as we are God's inheritance. We cannot get satisfaction out of God unless he is getting satisfaction out of us. Our faith, our obedience, our devotion, are the conditions of his peculiar and richest bounty.   II. THE CONTRAST OF JACOB'S PORTION WITH THE PORTION OF OTHERS. They inherit a barren land. It may look promising; it may yield the appearance of fruit; but real and abiding fruit there is none. Babylon has taken Bel for its portion, and now the portion and the possessors are alike turned to confusion. Indeed, the portion has vanished into nothingness; for never was it anything but a name, an imposing fiction, a proof both of man's need of a portion and how incompetent he is to make such a portion for himself. But Jehovah always remains a Portion. The typical Jacob, the typical people of God that is, were unable to keep Jehovah as their Portion; they never had any real grasp of him, never more than the merest external acquaintance. But for those who can lay hold of him he is surely a Portion still.—Y.

Vers. 25, 26.—*The destroying mountain destroyed.* I. THE DESTROYING MOUNTAIN. The mountain is a very fitting symbol of a people eminent among the nations and seeming easily to dominate over them. In such a symbol there is involved the undisputed assertion of superiority. The mountain looks down on the plains, and the plains accept the position. But whereas, in nature, the mountain looks down upon the plains with a mingling of benefits and injuries, of which even the injuries are seen to be benefits when looked at more closely, here we have a destroying mountain spoken of— a mountain that destroys the whole earth. God is against Babylon, not merely for the hurt it has inflicted on his own people, but because destruction is the very element in which it lives. Wheresoever Babylon came it brought spoliation, enslavement, and misery. Men and nations are made eminent that, like the mountains in the natural world, they may communicate good everywhere. But if they form destroying purposes then their very eminence increases their destroying power. The mountain that by its very elevation helps to distribute pleasant and profitable waters over the face of the earth, when turned to a volcano is just as well placed for sending down the lava-torrents.

II. ITS UTTER DESTRUCTION. That which must be considered first of all is the safety of the whole earth. It is God's way to uproot all that menaces the security and peace of his universe. To impair and enfeeble is not enough; the evil thing must be destroyed. And this is possible because it is God who is against it. He can destroy and obliterate where men would not for a moment dream of such a possibility. Did not Jesus tell his disciples that great mountains could be plucked up and cast into the sea, great obstacles and great menaces to Christian progress be utterly removed? And here the prophet signifies the completeness of the destruction by asserting that Babylon shall become as a mountain reduced as it were to mere ashes. To that mountain men have been in the habit of resorting to find corner-stones and foundation-stones, but such is their resort no longer. There is complete destruction of the enemies of God's people, and of course this implies complete safety of God's people themselves. (For a corresponding metaphor, see Isa. xxx. 14.)—Y.

Ver. 30.—*Effeminacy.* Doubtless in this utterance there is something of the then customary scorn with respect to women. But this must not make us forget that one of the worst things to be said of a man is that he has become as a woman, just as one of the worst things to be said of a woman is that she has become as a man.

I. THIS UTTERANCE DOES NOT REPROACH THE WOMAN, BUT THE MAN. Woman has her natural limitations. Her usual place is not in the battle-field or on the walls of the attacked city. An army of women against an army of men would be an unnatural, a revolting spectacle. But this very difference between the proper place of women and the proper place of men intensifies the reproach against a man when it can truly be said of him that he has become as a woman. Those qualities which in a woman are womanly in a man are only effeminate.

II. THE CORRESPONDING POSSIBLE REPROACH UPON WOMEN. A woman must not allow it to be said of her that she has become as a man. She must never forget the limitations and duties of her sex. Yet on the other hand, she must not be too ready to accept common opinion in interpreting those limitations and duties.

III. THERE ARE TIMES WHEN IT MAY BE THE GREATEST HONOUR TO A MAN TO BECOME AS A WOMAN. There are times when the strength of the man, without being lost, becomes unnoticed because of the presence of a woman-like tenderness. And of course there is the corresponding truth that woman may be honoured in becoming as the man, else where would be the fame of Joan of Arc and the Maid of Saragossa? Both men and women alike must have the courage to face mere external reproaches. Nothing is easier than to taunt a man with being unmanly and a woman with being unwomanly, but if only men and women alike persevere in what they feel to be right, they will in due time escape from the region of baseless taunts. After all, the humanity common to men and women alike is greater than peculiarities of sex. In Jesus Christ there is neither male nor female.—Y.

Ver. 36.—*Making the springs dry.* I. MAN'S EFFORT TO SUPPLY HIS NEED. There are the springs breaking forth among the hills and inviting men freely to use them. But there are also the wells men dig for themselves. Men must have water, yet they cannot always go and live by the natural springs, and so where they have to live they dig wells, and wonderfully do they succeed oftentimes in getting what they want. Water comes apparently in exhaustless abundance. Thus it is with the natural resources which man strives to obtain for himself. They open out before him far larger than any present wants. And thus when man sees all this within his reach, he naturally devises great undertakings on the strength of such great resources.

II. THE SELFISH USE OF HIS SUCCESS. It not unfrequently happens that the man who digs a well for himself does it at the expense of others, making their wells to run dry. The thing may be done unintentionally, or almost on a commonly accepted principle of every one looking out for himself; still it is to be looked on as pure selfishness. The resources of Babylon were increased by diminishing the resources of other peoples.

This is a point to be always looked at in estimating men of large resources, namely, how far those resources have been gained by leaving others without resource at all or with but a scanty one.

III. GOD'S REMOVAL OF HIS RESOURCES. "I will make her springs dry." God can dry up all humanly provided wells. We must not boast ourselves of their number, their depth, or the ease with which they keep to a certain level in spite of all drains upon them. Powerful nations, proud of their history and their achievements, need to remember this Divine interference. Men, looking back on a long course of individual success, need to remember the same. One can imagine a city in a time of siege, thoroughly provisioned, knowing exactly how much it had for food, and not troubling itself at all about drink, seeing that it had a deep well, the waters of which showed hardly any difference even in the driest summer. Yet all at once that well may fail, and, however large the other supplies, thirst will compel surrender. God dries up all wells that have been dug in covetousness and injustice.

IV. THE IMPLICATION OF OTHER ENDURING RESOURCES. "With thee is the fountain of life," says the psalmist (Ps. xxxvi. 9). We must look, not to the wells of our own digging, but to the springs from the everlasting hills. Especially we must catch the spirit of Ps. lxxxvii. There the psalmist praises Zion, and finishes up by saying, "All my springs are in thee." Let our springs be in the holy and abiding mount of God (Heb. xii. 22).—Y.

Ver. 50.—*A timely recollection and its practical effect.* Jehovah is making his severest judgments to fall on Babylon. How severe they are is indicated by the fact that two long chapters are occupied with denunciations upon her. But all the time Israel is in her midst. Israelites are domiciled and settled down. How far they lived by themselves and how far they mingled with their captors we cannot tell. One thing, however, we are sure of, that in the midst of so much destruction to Babylon they, or at least the bulk of them, were preserved. It must have been a very discomposing time for them, even though they had tolerable confidence that all would turn out right. There may be real safety where as yet there is not clear perception of it, and therefore no possibility of untroubled peace. But at last the danger is over, and what will the Israelite do then? He may elect, for reasons personal to himself, to stay in Babylon. He may be tempted to forget his duty as a part in a greater whole. Not for himself, however, not to further any aims of his own, was he thus preserved. He has escaped the sword only that he may the better serve God. Present ease, pleasant associations, may rise attractively in his mind. Not, of course, that these could be found in desolated Babylon, but they might surely be found somewhere else than in Jerusalem so far away. Against natural thoughts of this kind the prophet's word comes in here as a guard. It is a word for those Israelites living in Babylon at the time of Babylon's downfall. The things near to them, which their eyes see and their hands handle, are the least important. The really important considerations are those which may most easily be forgotten. Thus, so to speak, they must be pushed before the mind. Every right-hearted Israelite would keep the God and the city of his fathers in his heart. And so we should keep Jehovah and Jerusalem in mind. The greatest duties and hopes of our life come from our connection with such recollections.—Y.

Ver. 60.—*Evil written in a book.* I. THE FACT THAT EVIL IS WRITTEN AS WELL AS SPOKEN. The evils that Jehovah denounced against Babylon were such as could be written in a book, because the denunciations were not those of selfish and hasty passion, but expressed the calm wrath of a righteous God. The judgment on Babylon arose from the necessity of the position. A righteous God could not have acted otherwise. What a difference between his words in anger and our words! If all our angry, hasty, petulant words were perforce written in a book, what a record of shame there would be! Such a consequence of their utterance might make us a little more cautious, but still the words would come at times. If we are to understand what it is to be really angry and sin not, we must look at the deliberate records of Jehovah's wrath in the Scriptures. We are glad that *our* angry words should be forgotten; God, so to speak, takes trouble that his words should be remembered.

II. THE NECESSITY THAT THESE WORDS SHOULD BE WRITTEN. It is not enough that the words might be written—there had to be a reason for the writing. This is found in the necessity for doing all that could be done by way of warning and preparation. What was written could be shown first to one and then another. There was a necessity that even people of Babylon themselves should have ample opportunity to profit by the words spoken against their city. A necessity too in history. The fall of Babylon is a remarkable event in history, altogether outside of Scripture records, but the real secret of its fall is only to be known when we read such solemn and sustained predictions as are found in these two chapters.

III. GOD'S DENUNCIATIONS ARE NOT HIS ONLY WRITTEN WORDS. God has to write down his threatenings, but we are bound to remember that they are only a part—and how small a part they are!—of the total that he has caused to be written. How different he is in this respect from men! Their threatenings and angry words would sometimes fill a goodly volume, but their words of kindness and long-suffering, oh, how few are they! God's delight is to cause words of grace and promises of reward to be written.—Y.

Vers. 63, 64.—*A symbol of irretrievable loss.* It was fitting that the exhibition and record of a symbol such as this should close the long denunciation of Babylon. Where God determines to destroy no man can either avert or recover. This stone, perhaps, still lies at the bottom of Euphrates, and possibly even there may be something to signify the book once attached to it. We know not what relics of Old Testament times might yet be disentombed, what confirmations and revelations are still in actual existence.

I. GOD'S POWER OF UTTER DESTRUCTION. The impossibility of discovering this stone has to be considered relatively. Strictly speaking, it might perhaps have been recovered if it had been worth while. But for all practical purposes it was finally lost. Here is the difference between human destructions and the Divine destruction. Babylon is a wilderness still. Where God has chosen to make special marks of his wrath with the unrighteousness of men there rests a blight which no human effort can overcome; and generally speaking there is no disposition to overcome it. But where destruction comes simply through human passion and power there may be comparatively speedy recovery. This is a side of war on which we do well to reflect. Wars, with all their terrible accompaniments, may do something to get rid of some evils, and may thus be the condition of great good. Man cannot destroy where God wills to preserve. But where God destroys he destroys finally, and it is just this dreadful possibility of final ruin that should make men cautious in their estimate of the future, and prompt to turn from all evil and selfish paths.

II. THE CHEERING SIDE OF GOD'S UTTER DESTRUCTIONS. With God destruction always means salvation. Destruction is never for its own sake, never an arbitrary, aimless thing. All Divine destruction must be looked on as part of the process of salvation. Nations are scattered, human institutions overthrown, the temporal life of individuals ended, but the individual man in his abiding relations to God remains. This stone lost in one sense was not lost in another. Nay, it was serving a higher purpose than any it could have served simply as a stone. It became a teacher, and it is a teacher still. Abel, being dead, yet speaketh. And this stone from the bottom of Euphrates speaks still, warning all ambitious men and all neglecters of the commandments and predictions of Jehovah.—Y.

EXPOSITION.

CHAPTER LII.

The contents of this chapter prove that it is not an independent narrative, but the concluding part of a history of the kings of Judah. It agrees almost word for word with 2 Kings xxiv. 18—xxv. 30, from which we are justified in inferring that it is taken from the historical work which the editor of the Books of Kings closely followed. It is most improbable that Jeremiah was the author. Would the prophet have contented himself with the meagre statement that Zedekiah "did that which was evil in the eyes of the Lord" (ver. 2), or with such a summary description of the siege of Jerusalem? Apparently the editor who attached ch. lii. as an appendix to the

Book of Jeremiah omitted the account of Gedaliah (preserved in 2 Kings xxv. 22—26) because a fuller narrative had been already given in ch. xl.—xlii. Apparently, too, either the same or some later editor inserted vers. 28—30 (not found in the Septuagint) from another source ; the passage differs in several respects from 2 Kings xxiv. The text of ch. lii. seems to be a nearer approach to the original document than that of 2 Kings xxiv. 18—xxv. 30 (see Graf's commentary). Compare ch. xxxix.

Ver. 3.—**It came to pass.** The implied subject of the verb is Zedekiah's evil-doing. **That Zedekiah rebelled.** There ought to be a full stop before these words, and "that" should rather be "And."

Ver. 6.—**The famine was sore** (see the pathetic descriptions in Lam. i. 19, 20 ; ii. 11, 12, 20 ; iv. 9, 10).

Ver. 7.—**Broken up**; rather, *broken into.* **The plain.** The Hebrew has, "the Arábah," the name constantly given to the chalky depression in the midst of which the Jordan ran.

Ver. 9.—**Gave judgment** (see on ch. i. 16).

Ver. 11.—**In prison** ; literally, *in the house of custody.*

Ver. 22.—**All of brass,** etc. ; rather, *all of brass: and like unto these had the second pillar, and pomegranates.*

Ver. 23.—**On a side** ; rather, *towards the outside.*

Ver. 28.—**In the seventh year.** As Ewald and Keil agree, we should correct "seventh" into "seventeenth" (just as in 2 Chron. xxxvi. 9, for "eight" we should read "eighteen"). On the small number of Jews deported Ewald remarks, " Nothing so clearly shows the extent to which the best men from the upper classes had been already despatched by the Chaldeans across the Euphrates, as the fact that in all the years of the second, and, if it be insisted on, of the third revolt, put together, they found only 4600 men more whom they thought worth the trouble of transporting" ('History of Israel,' iv. 265). As to the third deportation, see on ch. xli. 1.

Ver. 31.—**Lifted up the head of Jehoiachin.** Ewald thinks that Jehoiachin was regarded by the Jews in exile as the legitimate king, and compares Lam. iv. 20 ; ii. 9.

HOMILETICS.

Vers. 4—7.—*The siege and capture of Jerusalem.* I. GENERAL LESSONS OF THE SIEGE. 1. *God will perform his threats.* The capture of Jerusalem had been long and frequently predicted. The accumulated prophecies were now fulfilled. 2. *Delay of judgment is no reason for expecting it to be permanently withheld.* The fate of Jerusalem seemed to be long postponed. But at length it came. 3. *Previous immunity is no security for the future.* The Jews fondly idolized Jerusalem as a charmed city. It seemed impossible that she should fall into the hands of her foes. We grow careless and confident through a series of fortunate escapes. But our confidence is irrational unless it has any deeper ground. 4. *The favour of God is no protection against the punishment of sin.* The Jews regarded themselves as Divine favourites. They had received many peculiar privileges. But these made the duty of fidelity only the more obligatory. For the most favoured people to be faithless was a great and terrible wickedness. Indeed, the favour of God, instead of mitigating punishment, makes a heavier penalty to be fitting for those who are so ungrateful as to sin against it.

II. SPECIAL FEATURES OF THE SIEGE. 1. *It was thorough.* The great king Nebuchadnezzar came in person and "all" his army, and pitched a camp and built forts. Every effort was made to secure the city. The instruments of Divine vengeance are terrible, earnest, and vigorous. 2. *It was protracted.* It lasted for eighteen months How wearily those days and weeks and months must have dragged themselves along, every hour increasing the agony! But what is this period to the vast, dim reaches of the "punishment of the ages," which awaits lost souls? 3. *It produced horrible sufferings.* In the madness of famine, women devoured their own children. Thus God punished (1) "satiation and disgust towards his holy Word and soul-food; (2) the terrible offering up of children to Moloch; (3) the loose discipline of children" (Cramer, quoted by Naegelsbach). From a merely selfish position, who that knew and realized the frightful consequences of his sins would bring these upon his head for the sake of the poor pleasures of an hour? 4. *It was successful.* The siege ended in the capture of Jerusalem. The force of Nebuchadnezzar was great and terrible, but behind it was the judicial will of Heaven. To withstand this was certainly futile. All resistance to the decrees of Divine judgment must be vain. Our one hope is not in opposition, but in penitent cries for God's mercy and unresisting submission to his will.

Vers. 8—11.—*The fate of Zedekiah.* I. THE CAUSES WHICH LED TO THE FATE OF ZEDEKIAH. 1. *The general calamity of his nation.* The king suffers with his people. Unfortunately it too often happens that an innocent people is punished for the fault of its sovereign. We must not be surprised if the converse is sometimes true. We are all members one of another. Not only kings, but in a less degree private individuals, must expect to share the troubles of the community, apart from the exact measure of private desert. In this life the execution of Divine justice is general; in the next life it will be particular—then the judgment will be individualistic. 2. *His own sin.* Zedekiah did "evil in the eyes of the Lord" (ver. 2). Others may have done worse and escaped. But if we have no more severe a fate than we deserve, we can find no ground for complaint in the fact that more wicked men receive (at present) a milder treatment. 3. *His weakness.* Zedekiah was more weak than wicked. It is often observable in history that the weak king suffers calamities which the bad king escapes. But weakness is a culpable defect in a sovereign. If he is not strong enough for his duties he should resign the reins of power. No one has a right to retain a post which he cannot efficiently fulfil. Moral weakness is always wrong—to be blamed as much as to be pitied—for it can be overcome (Isa. xl. 29—31). 4. *His erroneous policy.* Zedekiah was set on the throne by Nebuchadnezzar; he plotted with Pharaoh against his suzerain; and when his rebellion roused the vengeance of Babylon, he found Egypt to be only "a broken reed." In his case the vanity of trust in princes was illustrated. 5. *The will of God.* The fate of Zedekiah had been predicted by Jeremiah (xxxiv. 1—7). The prophecy implied a Divine decree. God has no hard, cruel decrees irrespective of our conduct and will. But following our wrong-doing, God's fixed counsels of judgment make flight hopeless. II. THE LEADING FEATURES OF THE FATE OF ZEDEKIAH. 1. *He was captured in the agonies of flight.* According to Josephus, this was not till he had reached the banks of the Jordan. How terrible to be so nearly saved, and yet to fall a prey to vengeance at last! To be only almost saved is worse than never to have had a hope of deliverance. They who have been near to the kingdom of heaven and have not entered it will feel the more bitterly the doom that they will share with the city of Destruction. "Remember Lot's wife." 2. *He was carried to Babylon and tried before King Nebuchadnezzar.* The triumph of the great monarch was the shame of his vassal. 3. *His children were slain before his eyes.* Parents suffer in the sufferings of their children more than in the pain of their own bodies. The action of Nebuchadnezzar was cruel, brutal, devilish. There are no such spiteful elements in God's punishment of the wicked. His is given in sorrow and with reluctance. 4. *His eyes were put out.* Here was the greatest refinement of cruelty. Zedekiah's sight was preserved till he had witnessed the death-agonies of his children. Then he was blinded, so that the last vision to dwell in his memory was the harrowing spectacle of his children's massacre. But after so terrible a sight would the wretched man care to look on the light of day? 5. *He was detained in prison till his death*—a punishment worse than death. Dethroned, humiliated, in chains, in a dungeon, bereaved of his children, the poor blind king is left to the agony of his own bitter thoughts. May God deliver us from a similar fate in the future world!

Ver. 13.—*The destruction of the temple.* I. THE GREATEST EARTHLY SPLENDOUR IS DESTRUCTIBLE. Solomon's temple was the pride of the Jews. For centuries it had stood mellowing with age. But when the brutal Chaldeans flung their torches at it the magnificent pile of buildings was soon reduced to a mass of smouldering ruins. *Sic transit gloria mundi.* An invasion, a revolution, a conflagration, may destroy the work of years in a night. Splendid possessions are poor refuges. A palace is not necessarily a castle. II. THERE IS NO SAFETY IN HOLY PLACES AND CONSECRATED THINGS. The temple was burnt, and its treasures and sacred vessels were carried to Babylon. The flames that leaped up on the private houses of Jerusalem found no charmed circle to keep them off from the temple. The building was holy only in so far as it was put to holy uses. But when it was desecrated by sin no magical influence could prevent it from complete destruction. And if the temple could not preserve itself, much less could it protect its superstitious devotees. It was vain indeed for them to cry, " The temple of the Lord," as though the words were a spell to ward off trouble. Thus all who trust in holy sites, ceremonial services, etc., apart from spiritual devotion, will find their faith wrecked, even if the idol of their superstition is not destroyed.

III. WHEN THE SPIRIT OF DEVOTION HAS FORSAKEN A TEMPLE THE DESTRUCTION OF THE BUILDING MAY BE A GOOD RATHER THAN AN EVIL. The temple is then worse than useless; it is a snare, tempting men to believe that all is well so long as it stands. So the ordinances of religion delude men into false confidence. While these are duly administered with imposing solemnity, it is difficult to believe that the spirit of religion has fled. Let these go too and men have their eyes open to their true condition. The temple without true worship is a mockery to God. When the soul has gone the body had better be put away as soon as possible. If the Christian has ceased to offer spiritual sacrifices in his body as in a temple of the Holy Ghost, his life is no longer of any true value. When this temple is destroyed the fate is striking and alarming, yet it is but little after its sad desecration through sin.

IV. THE ONLY DURABLE WORK IS SPIRITUAL AND HOLY WORK. " Each man's work shall be made manifest: for the day shall declare it, because it is revealed in fire" (1 Cor. iii. 13). There will be a test to the work of life. This may be splendid as a temple, but if it is unholy and earthly in character it must pass away ultimately. How many temples, and cities, and kingdoms, " cloud-capped towers, and gorgeous palaces " have left " not a rack behind "! It is the spiritual work of a man that endures. Even this fails, fruitless, unless it is good in character.

Ver. 16.—*Sparing the poor.* I. THE FACT. Whilst the king, the nobles, the wealthy, and many others were carried into exile, certain of the poor were still left in the land. We are accustomed to speak of the hardships of poverty, but there are compensating advantages not a few. Many evils of the worst character only visit the rich. In times of public trouble the houses of the rich are attacked and the persons of the great are threatened, while the poor are left in happy neglect. Great men are beset with anxieties such as are unknown to the simpler lives of the poor. Who would be a king now that kings are all marks for the assassin? In those countries where the sovereign is compelled to take elaborate precautions for his safety, the poor citizen can move about the streets without fear. The one is a prisoner in his own palace, the other a free man with liberty to roam over the whole kingdom. Ambition aims at distinction, but that is a poor crown to win. Distinguished men have peculiar vexations and dangers of their own. There is more happiness in obscurity. The wise man will say, " Give me neither poverty nor riches;" and the Christian will add, " Not my will, but thine, be done," knowing well that for him that lot is best which his heavenly Father assigns to him.

II. THE EXPLANATION. What was there in the condition of the poor to induce the Chaldeans to spare them? 1. *Their innocence.* The peasants had not been plotting against Nebuchadnezzar, and the vengeance that the Babylonian monarch vented on the king and the seat of his government was naturally averted from the quiet country-folk. These men were also more innocent in the sight of God. The leading people had shown their faithlessness in turning from Jehovah to Egypt; they, too, had probably descended the lowest in the vices of the age, which brought upon the nation the wrath of God. Poor men may be bad men. But there are sins to which they are less liable than great men. 2. *Their weakness.* While the great men were removed to Babylon, there would appear to be little danger of an insurrection among the poor people scattered over the farms, who had enough to do to earn their daily bread. There is a protection in weakness. A little strength often courts danger. They who are weak in themselves may be strong in the protection of God's providence. 3. *Their usefulness.* These poor people were left to work as " vine-dressers and husbandmen." Nebuchadnezzar had no wish to see his newly acquired territory converted into a desert. It was for his advantage that some of the people should be spared. There is no protection like usefulness. Be serviceable and you will be safe. He who lives for the real good of his fellow-men and the glory of his great Master may be sure that no harm can touch him so long as he is faithful to his task.

Vers. 31—34.—*The deliverance of Jehoiachin.* The new king signalized his accession to power by an act of clemency. Possibly he saw no reason to continue the cruelty of his predecessor now that the Jews were quieted; possibly he was influenced by Daniel. Whatever the cause of it may have been, it is pleasant to see how mercy " becomes the throned monarch better than his crown."

I. DELIVERANCE MAY COME AT LENGTH AFTER PROLONGED SUFFERING. Jehoiachin had endured thirty-seven years of imprisonment. He must have lost hope long before his liberation. Yet the longest night has its end. If trouble outlast life, there is the blessed liberator, death, that ultimately frees the most wretched from his distresses. Then what will thirty-seven years of suffering be to the ages of eternity? It is a weary time to endure, but, compared with the life beyond, it will seem both light and brief.

II. THE PROLONGED ENDURANCE OF SUFFERING MUST MAKE THE RETURN OF THE COMMON MERCIES OF LIFE A WONDERFUL BLESSING. What a meaning there is in the word "liberty" in the ears of the captive! Only the sufferers from thirst know the sweetness of water. The sick, when restored, enjoy health as the strong never can. Jehoiachin would find his change of circumstances wonderful beyond all expression.

III. NO EARTHLY DELIVERANCE IS PERFECT. The old man had endured captivity so long that he must have been bewildered and distracted by his release. For him, once a proud tyrant, now an aged, humiliated captive, crushed with the imprisonment of more than a third of a century, the thoughtless merriment of a court would seem like the life of another world or like a dream of childhood. His sufferings must have been too severe and too protracted for him to enter at once into the liberty and honour that were offered to him. One can scarcely think that he could ever feel at home with them. We know not what will be the first impressions of a new world when the soul escapes from its earthly captivity and enters the court of heaven. But there is an essential difference between Jehoiachin's condition and this. Jehoiachin remained an old man, worn with suffering as well as with years. The Christian has the gift of eternal life. To him the liberation by death is more than a change of external circumstances. He looks for the renewal of the fresh vigour of youth. Jehoiachin was never restored to his kingdom; at best he was an honoured subject of Babylon. But the Christian is restored to more than the primitive rights of man—to glory and kingship. Finally, there is no indication that Jehoiachin was changed in character. His long, lonely sufferings and the many reflections of thirty-seven years of imprisonment may have humbled him to penitence. But the historian does not appear to know of any such change. Yet a man's greatest enemy is himself. Deliverance of the body from a dungeon is a small boon if the soul is still captive to sin. The salvation in Christ effects this complete deliverance.

HOMILIES BY VARIOUS AUTHORS.

Ver. 1.—*Zedekiah.* (Cf. former homily, ch. xxxvii. 1.)—C.

Ver. 3.—*The Lord creating evil.* This is one of the passages of Scripture the meaning of which does not lie on the surface. It seems to represent God as instigating sin. For "through the anger of the Lord" it is said "that Zedekiah rebelled." But it was for that very rebellion he was so sorely punished, and yet it is said it was "through the Lord." Note—

I. THERE ARE OTHER PASSAGES LIKE THIS. Cf. "the Lord hardening Pharaoh's heart." The history of Judas. "None of them is lost, but the son of perdition; that the Scripture might be fulfilled" (John xvii. 12). Again, "Is there evil in the city and I have not done it?" (Amos iii. 6; Isa. xlv. 7). And St. Peter's word to the Jews on the day of Pentecost (Acts ii. 23). They wickedly did what nevertheless God had determined before to be done. And there are yet other Scriptures besides these.

II. THEY GIVE RISE TO GREAT DIFFICULTY. It is not difficult to understand that men should do wrong, or even the particular wrong which is charged against them and for which they are punished; but the difficulty is that the sin should be seemingly ascribed to God. And the Jews seem to have believed that God did prompt men to sin; cf. John ix. 1, "Who did sin, this man or his parents *in order that* (*ἵνα*) he should be born blind?"

The effect, the man's blindness, they looked on as designed and intended by God, and hence the cause producing that effect must have been designed also. As we read over Scriptures like these, the question of Abram starts immediately to our lips, "Shall not the Judge of all the earth do right?" (cf. Rom. iii. 5—8). God "may and must transcend our understanding. He will by the very nature of the case dazzle and confound our imagination by the unsuspected riches and glory of his many mansions; but he must not trouble our *sense of right* if he would retain our homage and our love." But it is this sense of right that *is* troubled by what seems to be the teaching of Scriptures like these. They seem to teach that God prompts men to sin and then punishes them for it. Some who reasoned with St. Paul appear to have suggested (cf. Rom. iii.) that in such cases God was "unrighteous" who took "vengeance." The apostle does not attempt to argue the matter, but treats the suggestion with a sort of "Get thee behind me, Satan," which is what his μὴ γένοιτο really amounts to. And where the suggestion is made from mere captious motives, or with the intent only to support a foregone conclusion and determination to disregard God, then such a reply is the proper one to make. But it can never be other than right to endeavour to meet the honest difficulties which some of the utterances of God's Word and some of the actings of his providence do unquestionably give rise to. If the suggestion were true that God made men to sin and then damned them for it, nothing could be more horrible, and no possible force could make men trust, love, or sincerely worship a God who would act so. But the suggestion is not true; for—

III. THE DIFFICULTY IS APPARENT, NOT REAL. God is never the author of sin. "The Lord is holy in all his ways, and righteous in all his works." "Let no man say when he is tempted," etc. (cf. Jas. i. 13). But when sin has been begotten in a man's soul by his own evil desires, then *the special form* in which that sin shall manifest itself *is* very often ordered by God. This is how we understand all these passages. That very Babylon in connection with which this ver. 3 is written may supply an apt illustration. Isaiah calls Babylon "the desert of the sea," for when, by reason of the melting of the snows which fed the Euphrates and her many tributaries, the great river overflowed its banks, the great plain on which Babylon stood became like a vast sea. But the great Assyrian lords cut their canals and constructed their massive dams and reservoirs so that the superabundant and otherwise destructive waters were directed into safe channels, and could do no further harm. Those monarchs were not the authors of the floods, but by their skill and wisdom they directed which way those floods should flow. On one of our great railways a little while ago, a signalman saw to his horror that an engine had somehow got away without its driver, and was rushing on with ever-increasing speed to its own destruction and that of the first unhappy passenger train—and one was nearly due—that it should meet. Quick as thought the signalman seized his levers and turned the runaway into a siding where it could harm no one but itself. In every large fire the firemen act in a similar way. *And so God.* When sin has broken out by no will of his, but altogether contrary to his will, he does not let it run riot, as it might, but he *orders the way it shall take.* Thence it came to pass "through the Lord" that "Zedekiah rebelled against the King of Babylon" (ver. 3).

IV. THIS ORDERING OF SIN'S WAY ON THE PART OF GOD IS A THING MUCH TO BE REMEMBERED. 1. *For our consolation and comfort.* Mad and monstrous as sin is, it is yet under God's control. Like as to the raging sea, he can say and does say to it, "Thus far shalt thou go, and no further," etc., and cf. ch. v. 22. 2. *For the warning of the sinner.* The flames of the eternal fire are lit within our own soul. Sin is ever twisting and knotting its own scourge. What a man soweth that shall he also reap. The seed of all our punishments was sown by our own hand, though we never intended the harvest. The way sin shall take is utterly out of our power. If it does somewhat that we did intend, it does for men that we never dreamt of nor desired. 3. *For instruction to all thoughtful readers of God's Word and beholders of his providence.* God "does" the evil that is in the city (Isa. xlv.), but he does not originate it, and that which he does is but *the ordering of its way.*—C.

Vers. 4—34.—*The march of doom.* These verses tell of the awful progress of the judgment of God on the doomed city of Jerusalem, her king, and people. To all who imagine that God is too full of love and graciousness to sternly judge and punish men, the contemplation of the events told of here may be painful, but assuredly they will be salutary also.   We are shown the Babylonian armies gathering round the city; the long and dreadful siege; the gaunt famine that fastens upon the besieged; the walls broken at last and the inrush of the infuriated foe; the flight, capture, and tragedy of the king; the burning of the city and temple; and the carrying off into exile or slaughter of all but the poorest of the people.   Ten weary years are covered by these events, and they were years full of lamentation, affliction, and woe.   Now, all this teaches plainly—

I. THAT THE JUDGMENTS OF GOD ARE SLOW TO BEGIN.   He is slow to anger.   How long he bore with Judah and Jerusalem ere these tribulations came!

II. BUT WHEN BEGUN THEY GO ON.   What a procession of one calamity after another it is!

III. THEY CANNOT BE ARRESTED OR TURNED ASIDE.   All that endurance, courage, and skill could do was done in that memorable siege.   Cf. Ezek. vii. 6, " An evil, an only evil, behold, it is come," etc.

IV. THE DISTRESS AND ANGUISH DEEPEN.   (Cf. Ezek. vii.; viii.; xi.; Lam. ii. 11, 12, 19; iv. 4, etc.)

V. THEY ARE RELENTLESS AND KNOW NO PITY.   Prayers and entreaties are in vain (cf. Prov. i. 24—31).

VI. THEY CEASE NOT TILL THEIR WORK IS DONE.   See this history.   The heart of the deceived evil-doer protests that God cannot deal so.   But he has dealt so with ungodly men, not once nor twice alone; and when he declares that he will again, of what avail is man's mere protest that he will not?   Cf. the whole Book of the Revelation. How loudly, therefore, do facts like these cry out to the sinner, "Flee from the wrath to come"!—C.

Vers. 4, 6, 12.—*Days whose duties are indelible.*   Note the particularity of the dates given in each of these verses.   Not the year only, but the month; and not the month only, but the day; and sometimes not the day only, but the hour, whether morning or evening, during the light or dark.   Now—

I. THERE ARE SUCH DAYS.   In the record of the Flood we have such exactness of date.   And in the later history of Jerusalem, the story of its decline and fall under its last kings, we again and again, as in this chapter, meet with such careful giving of exact dates.   And in our own experience, looking back over the record of our lives, how vividly some dates stand out!   We know the year, the month, the day, and hour, and it seems likely that we shall never forget them nor the events connected with them.

II. BUT THESE DAYS ARE NEARLY ALWAYS DAYS OF PAIN AND DISTRESS.   It was so in the instances given in these verses.   There are anniversaries which we keep, but these are for the most part joyous days, the memory of which we will not willingly let die.   But the fact of our keeping them shows that there is probability that such memory would die if we did not carefully keep it up.   But the days whose dates are indelible need no anniversaries to remind us of them.   We cannot forget them, though, perhaps, we would fain do so.   They are burnt in upon our souls so deeply that they are written as on a rock for ever.   And they are days, not of joy, but of sore distress; as when first the fierce Babylonian forces beleagured the holy city, and as when after weary months of obstinate defence the awful famine at length broke them down; and as when the proud conqueror in his rage burned down the sanctuary of God.   Days of judgment were they, never to be forgotten by Israel any more.   And there were many such days. We read of the " fasts " of the different months, many of which commemorated these sad events.

III. AND THEIR DATES ARE INDELIBLY WRITTEN IN OUR SOULS.   1. *Because of the contrast* which they offer to well-nigh all other days.   If any mark stands out conspicuous—like the black marks on a white page, or white on black—it proves that the ground upon which such mark stands out so conspicuously is of an entirely opposite colour, a complete contrast.   And so the very blackness of these indelible days proves that the days against which they stand out so conspicuously have been of a far other and happier kind.   Our very trials, by the vividness with which we remember them, prove the general goodness of our God, because they are such exception to his rule.   2. *Because of their intensity.*   The mark is not merely dark, but deep.   The sword pierces through the soul.   It is the intensity of the pain that makes it so memorable.   3. *Because of the shadow they cast.*   All our after life may be darkened—it often is so—by the effect of some awful blow, and the shadow ever starts from and guides our thoughts up to the terrible fact which has caused it.

IV. BUT THESE DATES ARE NOT INDELIBLE FOR EVER. Cf. our Lord's illustration: "A woman when she is in travail hath sorrow, . . . but as soon as she is delivered . . . she remembereth no more the anguish, for joy." So it is oftentimes even in this world. Life would not be bearable were all sorrows indelible. But they are not. The lapse of time, the pressure of necessary work, the awakening of other interests, and, above all, the bestowment of new joys—all tend to scatter the gloom of the soul and to thrust into oblivion memories that could only give pain. And none of them shall follow us into our eternal home. We shall not—it does not appear possible—forget facts that have occurred, but we shall see them in such new lights and irradiated by such love of God that all the pain that belonged to them will depart and be seen no more.

> "Help, Lord, that we may come
> To thy saints' happy home,
> Where a thousand years
> As one day appears;
> Nor go
> Where one day appears
> As a thousand years
> For woe!"

C.

Ver. 6.—*Famine.* One of the most frightful that ever befell any city is told of here. Its ghastly details may be traced out from this verse and different parts of the writings of Jeremiah and Ezekiel. This verse tells how the store of bread gradually failed; ch. xxxvii. 21 and xxxviii. 29 with what difficulty ever so little was gained (also Ezek. v. 16; v. 16; xii. 19). Then Lam. iv. 7 and v. 10 tell of the sufferings of the nobles; Lam. iv. 5 and Ezek. iv. 12—15 of the degradation of the high-born ladies of Jerusalem, snatching morsels of bread from the dunghills. The cries of the poor little children (Lam. ii. 11, 12, 19; iv. 4); the hard-heartedness of their parents (Lam. iv. 3). Fathers ate the flesh of their own sons (Ezek. v. 10); mothers that of their new-born babes (Lam. ii. 20; iv. 10). Thus frightful was this famine. And it is ever a fearful thing, let the cause be what it may. Note—

I. WHEREFORE THEY ARE SENT. 1. *As punishment:* (1) *For violation of natural law.* When men will crowd together in space too limited or on lands that will not yield sufficient, or will out of greed or selfishness refuse to cultivate aright the land they have, then sooner or later famine will come. (2) *For violation of Divine laws.* So in the case of famine told of here. But: 2. *They are sent as prompters and promoters of repentance and amendment.* In case of violated natural laws they have again and again performed this needed office. Men have spread themselves abroad, communications between one district and another have been opened up, improved methods of cultivation have been adopted, wiser and juster laws have been enacted, and men's energies and thoughts have been roused to devise remedies and safeguards against the recurrence of the evil. And when it is the Divine laws that have been violated, the Divine laws against sin—for natural laws are also Divine—famine has brought many a prodigal to himself, and led him to say, "I will arise and go to my Father, and will say unto him, Father, I have sinned." It did so in the case of the Jews.

II. BUT FAMINE IS AN UNNECESSARY AND UNNATURAL THING. For in our Father's house there is bread enough and to spare, and none need perish with hunger. The world contains ample store; the resources of nature are in no degree exhausted, and therefore it can only be by negligence of God's laws in nature that famine can in ordinary cases occur. And why need any go away into the far country of sin, and so compel the righteous and loving Father to send such sore judgment after them in order to bring them back? "O Israel, thou hast destroyed thyself!" It is not according to God's will in any case.

III. AND WHAT IS TRUE OF THE LITERAL IS TRUE ALSO OF THE SPIRITUAL FAMINE. 1. *It is caused by man's disobedience.* So it was at the first. Sin thrust him forth from the Father's house, the happy home where he never knew what want was. And so it is still. Had those who knew of Christ and his redemption but obeyed the word, "Let him that heareth say, Come," long ere this the whole world would have been evangelized. And if the same command were obeyed now, the like result would speedily follow. Christ has given a self-propagating power to his Church, which it has failed to use, and therefore spiritual famines are and will be until the Church obeys her Lord's commands. But : 2. *Such famine need not be.* Christ is the "Bread of life" for all, and there is enough and to spare for all.

CONCLUSION. Let not thy brother hunger if thou canst give him of this bread. Think of what famine means, and let thy charity be aroused. Take care that thou eatest—not merely talkest—of the Bread of life thyself.—C.

Vers. 8—11.—*The irony of a name.* These verses tell of King Zedekiah—of the tragedy of Zedekiah, we might say, for never was there a tragedy more terrible than that in which he bore the chief part. But think of his name—"Jehovah our Righteousness." "As the last note of Jeremiah's dirge over Jehoiachin died away, he had burst forth into one of those strains of hope, in which he had represented the future ruler of Israel as the righteousness or justice of Jehovah (cf. ch. xxiii. 5—7). It may be that, in allusion to this, the new king assumed that name Zedek-Jah on his accession to the throne. He was a mere youth, but not without noble feelings which, in a less critical moment, might have saved the state." And his very name attested the hope which was cherished concerning him. But read the history of his career and his awful fate, and see if ever there could be sadder irony than in the name he bore. It was a glorious name, but how miserably belied! Defeated, dethroned, disgraced, bereaved, tortured, blind, an exile, a slave,—so he dragged out the last weary years of his life. We know not how many they were, we can only hope they were but few.

I. SUCH IRONY OF NAMES IS FREQUENT. The degenerate bearers of noble and hallowed names are many. The children of Abraham were told by our Lord that they were children of the devil. A good name should be an inspiration; it often is ; *noblesse oblige.* That it may be so is often the motive wherewith it is given by parents to their children. But, as with Zedekiah, their character and their names are in sad contrast.

II. NOTE THE CAUSE OF THIS SAD IRONY IN THIS CASE. It was *not lack of right knowledge.* For a while he was under the teaching and influence of God's prophet Jeremiah. And men rarely go wrong from lack of knowledge. *Video meliora proboque, deteriora sequor.* Nor for *lack of right feeling.* He had again and again good purposes and aspirations. So with men like him. Nor were there wanting *sundry endeavours to act according as God prompted him.* He made one and another attempt. But the secret of his sad failure was his *lack of strength,* infirmity of will, weakness of resolve. And thus it perpetually is with men who turn out failures in life. There is no more pitiful sight in this world than the spectacle of these ruined men. Jeremiah lamented bitterly over Zedekiah, as he well might.

III. LET THIS ILL-APPLIED NAME LEAD US TO THINK OF HIM WHOSE NAME WAS NOTHING BUT BLESSED TRUTH—JESUS. He was called Jesus because "he should save his people from their sins." For in him is the remedy for all such as Zedekiah was. Give up our will to him, come to be in him by a living faith, and his strength shall be reproduced in us, and out of weakness we shall be made strong.—C.

Vers. 1—3.—*Zedekiah as king.* I. THE POSITION OF A YOUNG MAN. He was twenty-one years old when he began to reign. Out of boyhood, looking round him at a time when he had become responsible for the conduct of his life. In England the age of twenty-one is full of significance to many young men, for then they become free from legal disabilities and restrictions. Any young man about the age of Zedekiah becomes thereby an object of special interest.

II. AN UNEXPECTED POSITION. At least we may fairly assume this from 2 Kings xxiv. 17. Zedekiah was not in the succession. Of course it is just possible there may have been aims and intrigues by which Zedekiah gained the crown. But that does not make less noticeable the fact that young men often do find themselves in unexpected positions. They have been making ready for one course, when all in a moment they are turned into a new course where they have to act without much time for consideration.

III. A RESPONSIBLE POSITION. Responsible in any case as that of a young man ;

peculiarly responsible as being called to a throne. To be called to a position of peculiar responsibility may sober a man if he is inclined to be reckless, may rouse him if inclined to be easy-going and self-indulgent. This point may be illustrated by the traditional belief in the change that came over Henry V. on his accession to the throne, especially as this view is brought out in Shakespeare.

IV. A POSITION UNUSUALLY DIFFICULT. A king appointed by a foreign conqueror would be regarded with dislike by many. In such circumstances the best of personal qualities were needed, decision of character combined with the utmost circumspection.

V. A POSITION IN WHICH ZEDEKIAH HAD A COMPETENT ADVISER. Not any of his own courtiers, though there may have been men among them marked by prudence and insight. He has a prophet of Jehovah, a man with a keen sense of right and wrong, a man with revelations from on high, to help him. Moreover, it is on record that he actually sought Jeremiah out. Note the many references in the course of the book to the dealings between the king and the prophet. By the plain speaking of such a man many doubts might be cleared and many errors corrected. It is the censure on Zedekiah (2 Chron. xxxvi. 12) that "he humbled not himself before Jeremiah the prophet speaking from the mouth of the Lord."—Y.

Ver. 8.—*Zedekiah's army scattered.* Zedekiah's aim was to keep his army together, for as long as he could do that there was a chance of averting the evil day, and perhaps in the end escaping it altogether. But without his army he was utterly helpless. He could not bring himself to heed Jeremiah's counsels, doing the right and putting his trust in Jehovah. And so when the army was gone everything was gone. Nothing remained but random, desperate attempts at flight, and the certainty of ultimate capture. We have to ask ourselves what we shall do when our army is scattered from us, when the resources of our own making are vanished. The chief battles of our life are not to be fought with external resources at all. In every warfare where the weapons are carnal the weapons must fail at last. Only when we are engaged in truly spiritual warfare, and have the hosts of heaven on our side, can we be sure that our army will not be scattered from us.—Y.

Ver. 11.—*Zedekiah's fate.* Here is a triple bondage—the bondage of blindness, fetters, and imprisonment. Truly a dreadful doom! Look—

I. AT THE CAUSE OF IT. 1. *The cause so far as it lies in his own conduct.* There was no need for him to accept a throne as viceroy for Babylon, but, having done so, he had entered into an implied covenant. No wonder that the King of Babylon took special care to stamp such conduct in a peculiar way. 2. *The cause so far as it lies in the notions of the time.* Zedekiah was treated, not only vindictively, but savagely. The meaning must have been to humiliate him, to make the iron enter into his very soul. What a difference Christianity has made in the treatment of conquered foes! The change has come very slowly, but it is real and stable. One cannot imagine the time returning when a captured enemy would be deprived of his eyesight.

II. AT A CONTRAST IMMEDIATELY SUGGESTED. One cannot but think of Samson, whose external condition was exactly that of Zedekiah, blinded, fettered, and imprisoned. Reduced to this state the Philistines reckoned he was impotent. Zedekiah really was impotent; he seems to have gone on to the day of his death in monotonous submission to what he felt necessity. But it was only necessity because he made it so. The worst limitations our fellow-men can put on us may become in certain conditions like an easily snapped thread. Zedekiah might have risen above all these insults and pains. Perhaps he did rise. It is well for us to recollect how God has placed the essential liberty of every individual in his own hands.—Y.

Vers. 12, 13.—*A great burning.* I. THE BURNING IN GENERAL. The sum of the details amounts to a statement that the city was reduced to ashes. For this not Babylon is to be blamed, but Zedekiah and his predecessors, together with their advisers. Babylon was only acting according to the fashion of the times. The hand of Jehovah was withdrawn, the hand that might have averted the torch; and it was withdrawn because the destruction of Jerusalem had become a better thing for the world than its preservation. Still, it is not to be said in the fullest sense of the word that *Jehovah* destroyed Jerusalem say as he destroyed *Babylon*. In the course of a few generations Jerusalem rose from its ashes, temple included. The mere destruction of buildings, terrible as it is at the time, may soon be got over, as witness the rebuilding of London, and Chicago. The decay of national spirit and national resources is the thing to be feared.

II. THE BURNING OF THE TEMPLE IN PARTICULAR. Babylon had no fear in destroying the house of the Lord. Doubtless it was quite a common thing in war to destroy the temples of gods, for they were looked upon merely as part of the resources of nations. We must distinguish between what is essentially sacred and what is sacred only by association and to serve a purpose. When the purpose is accomplished the sacred sinks back into the common. God dwelleth not in temples made with hands. He was none the poorer for all this burning. Babylon learned hereafter that, though his house had been burned, his power was not at all diminished. The chief value of the temple lay in this, that it had been an expression of the piety and devotion of David and Solomon. Kings and people alike had proved themselves unworthy of their great ancestors.—Y.

HOMILETICAL INDEX

TO

THE BOOK OF THE PROPHET JEREMIAH.

VOLUME I.

HOMILETICAL INDEX

TO

THE BOOK OF THE PROPHET JEREMIAH

—◆—

VOLUME II.